Merriam Webster's VISUAL Dictionary

SECOND EDITION

Under the direction of
Jean-Claude **Corbeil**

Merriam-Webster, Incorporated

Springfield, Massachusetts
USA

Merriam-Webster Inc.

Published by Merriam-Webster Inc. 2012

© 2012 QA International.
All rights reserved.

ISBN: 978-0-87779-151-5

Merriam-Webster's Visual Dictionary, Second Edition,
was created and produced by:

 Québec Amérique International
329 de la Commune Street West, 3rd Floor
Montréal (Québec) H2Y 2E1 Canada

Phone: +1 514.499.3000
FAX: +1 514.499.3010
ikonet.com
qa-international.com
québec-amérique.com

Original French terminology developed by
Jean-Claude Corbeil and Ariane Archambault.

Printed and bound in Malaysia. First printing 2012.
8 7 6 5 4   20 19 18 17 16
642 version 4.0.1

ACKNOWLEDGEMENTS

Our deepest gratitude to the individuals, institutions, companies,
and businesses that have provided us with the latest technical
documentation for use in preparing this edition of the
Visual Dictionary.

Canadian Space Agency (Réjean Lemieux, Danièle Laroque, Antoinette
Cickello); Claude Arsenault (president, Association des moulins du Québec);
Michel Ballarin (soccer pioneer); Pierre Boulé (president, Confort Expert);
Centre de formation professionnelle de Sorel-Tracy (Alain Boucher,
Jacques Doyon, Andrée-Anne Martin); Pierre Chastenay (Montréal
Planetarium); Ève Christian (meteorologist); Luc Cockenpot (Institut du
tourisme et de l'hôtellerie de Montréal); Jacques Dancosse (Montréal
Biodome); Patrice Desbiens (nuclear engineer); Laval Dupuis (École des
métiers de l'équipement motorisé de Montréal); Entreprise Garant
(Julie Nolet, Stéphanie Lacroix); Fédération de basketball de France
(Julien Guérineau); Fédération de basketball du Québec (Daniel Grimard,
Isabelle Watier); Fédération d'haltérophilie du Québec (Augustin Brassard);
Caroline Gagné (Studio du Verre); Jacqueline Goy (Institut océanographique
de Paris); Christian Guibourt (technical director, Badminton Québec);
Michel J. Houle (Hewitt); Hydro-Québec (terminology); Robert Lacerte
(sports commentator, Radio-Canada); Robert Lamontagne (Université
de Montréal); Lozeau (Alexandre Gagné, Frédéric Montpetit); Olivier-Louis
Robert (science journalist); Iris Sautier (silk screen printing); Société
Radio-Canada, Service linguistique et Direction générale des
communications et images de marque (Annie Nociti Dubois, assistant,
internal and institutional communications); Gilles Taillon (executive
director, Baseball Québec); Pierre Turcotte (agronomist-plant breeder).

PUBLISHER

QA International, a division of
Les Éditions Québec Amérique Inc.
President and CEO: Jacques Fortin
Publisher: Caroline Fortin

Editorial Director: Martine Podesto
Artistic Director: Johanne Plante

EDITORIAL STAFF

Editor-in-Chief: Anne Rouleau
Editorial Assistants:
  Myriam Caron Belzile
  Jeanne Dompierre
  Catherine Gendreau

TERMINOLOGICAL RESEARCH

Terminology Advisor: Jean-Claude Corbeil
Sophie Ballarin
Carole Brunet
Hélène Mainville
Kathe Roth

ENGLISH DEFINITIONS

Nancy Butchart
Rita Cloghesy
Tom Donovan
Diana Halfpenny
Kate Morris
Kathe Roth
Donna Vekteris
John Woolfrey
Locordia Communications

PRODUCTION

Production Coordinator: Véronique Loranger
Print Production: Salvatore Parisi

LAYOUT

Senior Graphic Artist: Pascal Goyette
Edgar Abarquez
Karine Lévesque
Fernando Salvador Marroquín
Julie Villemaire

ILLUSTRATION

Senior Illustrator: Anouk Noël
Manuela Bertoni
Marthe Boisjoly
Érica Charest
Jocelyn Gardner
Guillaume Grégoire
Anik Lafrenière
Alain Lemire
Raymond Martin
Jordi Vinals

PROGRAMMING

Senior Programmer: Gabriel Trudeau-St-Hilaire
Marc-André Benjamin
Alex Gagnon
Ronald Santiago

LINGUISTIC REVISION

Veronica Schami Editorial Services

PREPRESS

Benjamin Dubé
François Hénault

MERRIAM-WEBSTER EDITORS

Susan L. Brady
Rebecca R. Bryer-Charette
Daniel B. Brandon
Christopher C. Connor
Joanne M. Despres
Daniel J. Hopkins
Benjamin T. Korzec
John M. Morse
Joan I. Narmontas
Madeline L. Novak
Maria A. Sansalone
Adrienne M. Scholz
Neil S. Serven
Kory L. Stamper
Mark A. Stevens
Linda Picard Wood

COVER DESIGN

Lynn Stowe Tomb, Merriam-Webster Art Director

CONTRIBUTIONS

QA International would like to extend a special thank you to the following people for their contribution to this work:

Jean-Yves Ahern, Danielle Bader, Stéphane Batigne, Jean Beaumont, Sylvain Bélanger, Pascal Bilodeau, Yan Bohler,
Mélanie Boivin, Guy Bonin, Catherine Briand, Julie Cailliau, Jessie Daigle, Serge D'Amico, François Fortin, Éric Gagnon,
Hélène Gauthier, Mélanie Giguère-Gilbert, Benoît Grégoire, Nathalie Guillo, Claude Laporte, Martin Lemieux,
Rielle Lévesque, Émilie McMahon, Philippe Mendes Campeau, Patrick Mercure, Tony O'Riley, Carl Pelletier,
Sylvain Robichaud, Michel Rouleau, Claude Thivierge, François Turcotte-Goulet, Gilles Vézina, Kathleen Wynd.

QA International would also like to acknowledge the contribution of Jean-Claude Corbeil and Ariane Archambault, authors of
the original French terminology of the *Visual,* who were also instrumental in defining the table of contents and overseeing the
development and evolution of the three first editions of the publication.

Introduction

The *Visual Dictionary,* more than 25 years of history

Merriam-Webster's Visual Dictionary, Second Edition, is designed to advise and assist users who are seeking information about the world around them and the words used to describe that world. As such, it will support an wide range of personal and professional needs: finding an unknown term, checking the meaning of a word, and being a handy resource for writers, teachers, and translators. In addition, the dictionary can serve as a vocabulary-building resource, as users will find here the vocabulary they need to master in regard to many aspects of life, such as food, clothing, transportation, science, and sports.

The aim of this dictionary has been to bring together in one volume the technical and everyday terms required to understand the contemporary world and the specialized fields that shape our daily experience. In effect, it provides an inventory of our physical environment for users who need to know and understand general and specialized terms in a wide variety of fields.

The history of the *Visual Dictionary*

Merriam-Webster's Visual Dictionary, Second Edition, is based on the new fourth edition of QA International's *Visual Dictionary,* published on the 25th anniversary of the publication of the first edition of this reference work in 1986. The idea for this dictionary was the product of a meeting between editor Jacques Fortin and linguist Jean-Claude Corbeil in 1982 in Paris. The meeting led to the development of an original project that brought together a team of linguists, researchers, translators, illustrators, and experts in terminology, and culminated in the release of the first *Visual Thematic Dictionary.*

As stated in the introduction to the 1986 edition, the goal was to fill a void that existed among reference works by becoming "the first basic dictionary to focus on terminology and bring together in one volume thousands of technical and nontechnical terms used by a society in which science, technology, and their products have become a part of everyday life."

From the beginning, illustration was chosen over photography because of its ability to "bring out the most significant details of an object, purging the image of everything that is ancillary or accidental. … The image appears simpler and more stripped down, gaining conceptual clarity for a better definition."

The growth of knowledge and technology over the past 25 years has led to changes to the dictionary's contents. For this new edition, all existing subjects were examined to assess their relevance and accuracy, and as a result, thousands of changes were made throughout the book. For example, the section on photography was entirely redesigned to take into account the growth of digital photography, and the section on the solar system was updated to present the new classification of celestial bodies.

Many subjects have also been expanded, often by illustrating previously little-known or nonexistent objects (the touch screen smartphone, the tablet computer, etc.), or by introducing diagrams that explain phenomena or processes. And new subjects, such as the global positioning system (GPS), alternative fuels, and modern medical equipment, have also made an appearance.

To accomplish this, the number of

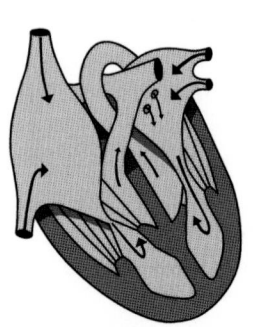

1986

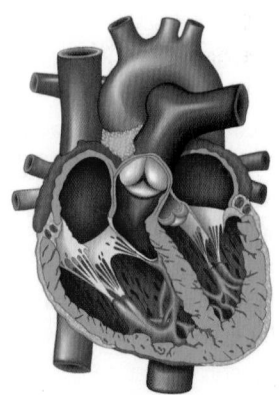

1992

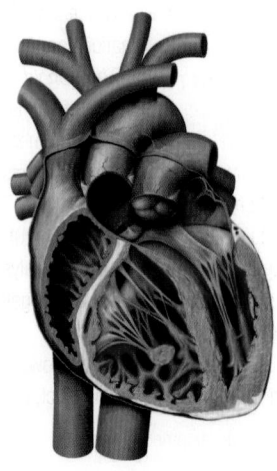

2011

illustrations has been increased, bringing the total number to more than 8,000. Many other illustrations have been entirely redrawn or retouched. Another indication of the expanding coverage in the dictionary is the growth in the number of terms covered, with more than 4,000 new entries, bringing the total to nearly 25,000 in each language.

Structure of the *Visual Dictionary*

This book has three sections: the front-matter pages, including the table of contents and the list of themes; the body of the text, that is, the detailed treatment of each theme; and the alphabetical index. Information is presented in hierarchical form, moving from the most abstract to the most concrete: theme, subtheme, title, subtitle, illustration, terminology.

The content of this book is divided into 18 THEMES, which are then divided into SUBTHEMES. For example, the theme Astronomy is divided into three subthemes: Celestial bodies, Astronomical observation and Astronautics. The TITLE has a variety of functions: to name the illustration of a unique object, of which the principal parts are identified (e.g., *exterior door*); and to bring together under one designation illustrations that belong to the same conceptual sphere but that represent a variety of elements, each with its own designations and terminology (e.g., the title *household appliances* brings together illustrations of a refrigerator, freezer, etc.). At times, the chief members of a class of objects are brought together under the same SUBTITLE, each with its own name but without a detailed terminological analysis (e.g., the subtitle *armchair* brings together various types of armchairs).

Finally, the ILLUSTRATION shows realistically and precisely an object, a process, or a phenomenon, and the most significant details from which it is constructed. It serves as a visual definition of the term.

Terminology

Each word in the dictionary has been carefully selected after consulting authoritative sources that reflect the appropriate level of specialization. There may be cases where documented usage indicates that different terms are used to name the same item. In such instances, the word most frequently used by the most highly regarded authors has been chosen.

The INDEX lists all significant words in the dictionary in alphabetical order. Many terms have been grouped to make it easy to search for precise illustrations or words. For example, the terms *morphology of a bird* and *skeleton of a bird* have been grouped under *bird,* with a referral back to the corresponding pages in the book.

Methods of consultation

One may gain access to the contents of the *Visual Dictionary* in a variety of ways:

- Users can start from the list of THEMES at the end of the front-matter pages, or by using the detailed TABLE OF CONTENTS in the front matter and at the start of each theme.

- With the INDEX, users can find a word, so as to see what it corresponds to, or to examine the illustration that depicts it.

- Users can take advantage of the illustrations and hierarchical structure to enable them to find a word even if they have only a vague idea of what it is—a valuable feature when you don't know what word you are looking for.

2011

1992

1986

Explanatory Chart

Title

The title is featured at the top of the page, and its definition is found below. If the title refers to information that continues over several pages, it is shown in a shaded tone with no definition on the following pages.

Color reference

The color reference also appears on the spine and back of the book. It identifies and accompanies each theme to facilitate quick access to the corresponding section in the book.

Theme

The name of the theme is shown with its definition on the double-page spread at the beginning of the section. It is then repeated on each page of the section, but without the definition.

Definition

The definition explains the inherent qualities, function, or characteristics of the element depicted in the illustration.

Dotted lines

Dotted lines link the word and definition to the item indicated. Where too many lines would make reading difficult, they have been replaced by color codes with captions or, in rare cases, by numbers.

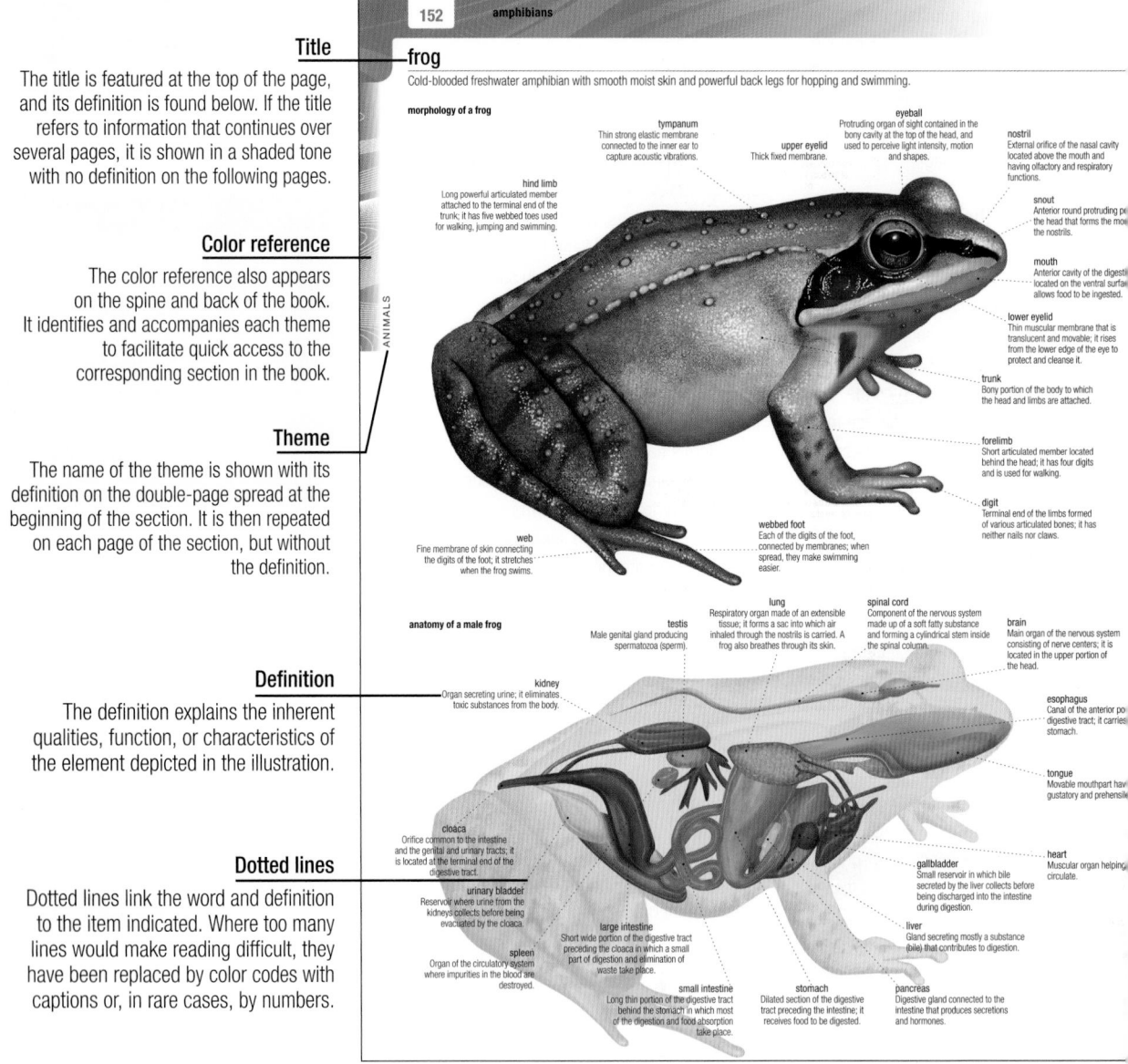

152   amphibians

frog

Cold-blooded freshwater amphibian with smooth moist skin and powerful back legs for hopping and swimming.

ANIMALS

morphology of a frog

tympanum
Thin strong elastic membrane connected to the inner ear to capture acoustic vibrations.

upper eyelid
Thick fixed membrane.

eyeball
Protruding organ of sight contained in the bony cavity at the top of the head, and used to perceive light intensity, motion and shapes.

nostril
External orifice of the nasal cavity located above the mouth and having olfactory and respiratory functions.

hind limb
Long powerful articulated member attached to the terminal end of the trunk; it has five webbed toes used for walking, jumping and swimming.

snout
Anterior round protruding part of the head that forms the mouth and the nostrils.

mouth
Anterior cavity of the digestive tract located on the ventral surface; it allows food to be ingested.

lower eyelid
Thin muscular membrane that is translucent and movable; it rises from the lower edge of the eye to protect and cleanse it.

trunk
Bony portion of the body to which the head and limbs are attached.

forelimb
Short articulated member located behind the head; it has four digits and is used for walking.

digit
Terminal end of the limbs formed of various articulated bones; it has neither nails nor claws.

web
Fine membrane of skin connecting the digits of the foot; it stretches when the frog swims.

webbed foot
Each of the digits of the foot, connected by membranes; when spread, they make swimming easier.

anatomy of a male frog

testis
Male genital gland producing spermatozoa (sperm).

lung
Respiratory organ made of an extensible tissue; it forms a sac into which air inhaled through the nostrils is carried. A frog also breathes through its skin.

spinal cord
Component of the nervous system made up of a soft fatty substance and forming a cylindrical stem inside the spinal column.

brain
Main organ of the nervous system consisting of nerve centers; it is located in the upper portion of the head.

kidney
Organ secreting urine; it eliminates toxic substances from the body.

esophagus
Canal of the anterior portion of the digestive tract; it carries to the stomach.

tongue
Movable mouthpart having gustatory and prehensile functions.

cloaca
Orifice common to the intestine and the genital and urinary tracts; it is located at the terminal end of the digestive tract.

urinary bladder
Reservoir where urine from the kidneys collects before being evacuated by the cloaca.

spleen
Organ of the circulatory system where impurities in the blood are destroyed.

large intestine
Short wide portion of the digestive tract preceding the cloaca in which a small part of digestion and elimination of waste take place.

small intestine
Long thin portion of the digestive tract behind the stomach in which most of the digestion and food absorption take place.

stomach
Dilated section of the digestive tract preceding the intestine; it receives food to be digested.

pancreas
Digestive gland connected to the intestine that produces secretions and hormones.

heart
Muscular organ helping circulate.

gallbladder
Small reservoir in which bile secreted by the liver collects before being discharged into the intestine during digestion.

liver
Gland secreting mostly a substance (bile) that contributes to digestion.

Subtheme

Themes are divided into subthemes. These are shown on the introductory page of a theme along with their definitions.

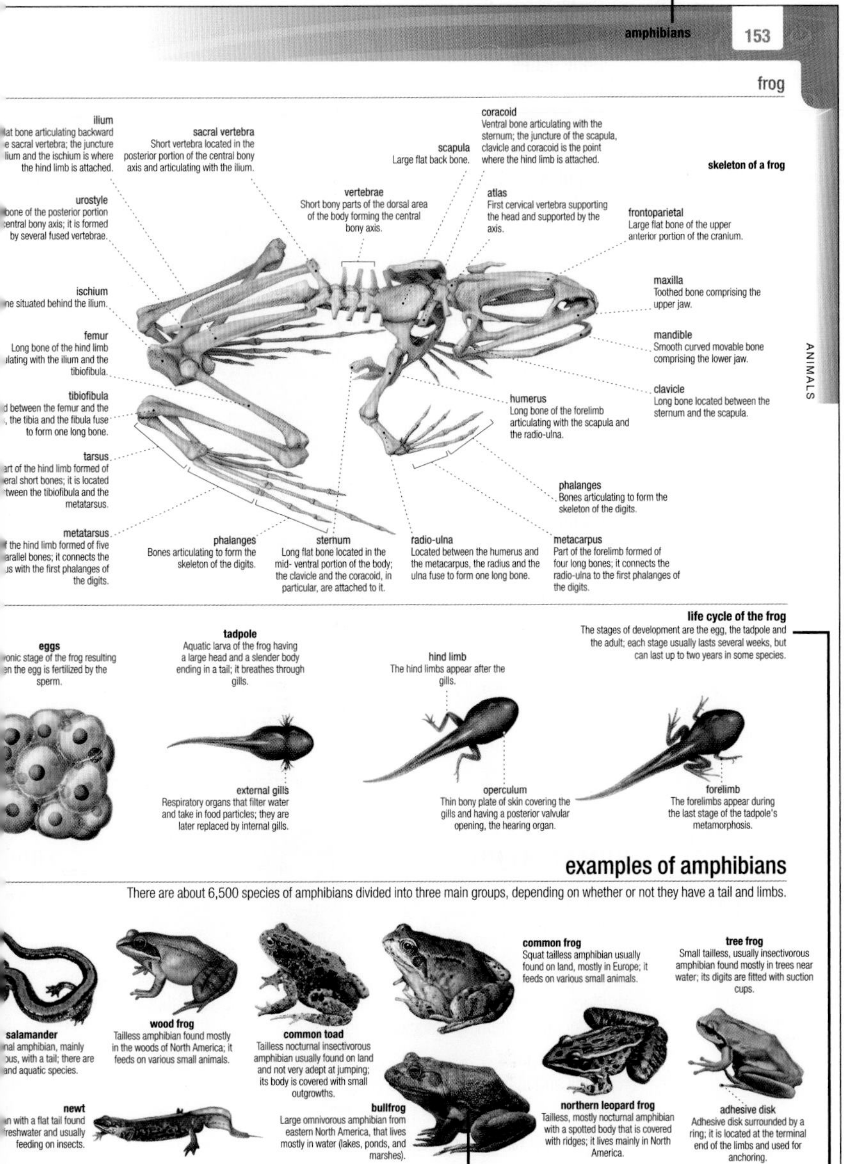

amphibians 153

frog

skeleton of a frog

ilium
Flat bone articulating backward to the sacral vertebra; the juncture of the ilium and the ischium is where the hind limb is attached.

sacral vertebra
Short vertebra located in the posterior portion of the central bony axis and articulating with the ilium.

scapula
Large flat back bone.

coracoid
Ventral bone articulating with the sternum; the juncture of the scapula, clavicle and coracoid is the point where the hind limb is attached.

urostyle
Bone of the posterior portion of central bony axis; it is formed by several fused vertebrae.

vertebrae
Short bony parts of the dorsal area of the body forming the central bony axis.

atlas
First cervical vertebra supporting the head and supported by the axis.

frontoparietal
Large flat bone of the upper anterior portion of the cranium.

ischium
Bone situated behind the ilium.

maxilla
Toothed bone comprising the upper jaw.

femur
Long bone of the hind limb articulating with the ilium and the tibiofibula.

mandible
Smooth curved movable bone comprising the lower jaw.

tibiofibula
Located between the femur and the tarsus, the tibia and the fibula fuse to form one long bone.

humerus
Long bone of the forelimb articulating with the scapula and the radio-ulna.

clavicle
Long bone located between the sternum and the scapula.

tarsus
Part of the hind limb formed of several short bones; it is located between the tibiofibula and the metatarsus.

phalanges
Bones articulating to form the skeleton of the digits.

metatarsus
Part of the hind limb formed of five parallel bones; it connects the tarsus with the first phalanges of the digits.

phalanges
Bones articulating to form the skeleton of the digits.

sternum
Long flat bone located in the mid-ventral portion of the body; the clavicle and the coracoid, in particular, are attached to it.

radio-ulna
Located between the humerus and the metacarpus, the radius and the ulna fuse to form one long bone.

metacarpus
Part of the forelimb formed of four long bones; it connects the radio-ulna to the first phalanges of the digits.

ANIMALS

life cycle of the frog
The stages of development are the egg, the tadpole and the adult; each stage usually lasts several weeks, but can last up to two years in some species.

eggs
Embryonic stage of the frog resulting when the egg is fertilized by the sperm.

tadpole
Aquatic larva of the frog having a large head and a slender body ending in a tail; it breathes through gills.

external gills
Respiratory organs that filter water and take in food particles; they are later replaced by internal gills.

hind limb
The hind limbs appear after the gills.

operculum
Thin bony plate of skin covering the gills and having a posterior valvular opening, the hearing organ.

forelimb
The forelimbs appear during the last stage of the tadpole's metamorphosis.

examples of amphibians
There are about 6,500 species of amphibians divided into three main groups, depending on whether or not they have a tail and limbs.

salamander
Terminal amphibian, mainly ... ous, with a tail; there are ... and aquatic species.

wood frog
Tailless amphibian found mostly in the woods of North America; it feeds on various small animals.

common toad
Tailless nocturnal insectivorous amphibian usually found on land and not very adept at jumping; its body is covered with small outgrowths.

common frog
Squat tailless amphibian usually found on land, mostly in Europe; it feeds on various small animals.

tree frog
Small tailless, usually insectivorous amphibian found mostly in trees near water; its digits are fitted with suction cups.

newt
... with a flat tail found ... freshwater and usually ... feeding on insects.

bullfrog
Large omnivorous amphibian from eastern North America, that lives mostly in water (lakes, ponds, marshes).

northern leopard frog
Tailless, mostly nocturnal amphibian with a spotted body that is covered with ridges; it lives mainly in North America.

adhesive disk
Adhesive disk surrounded by a ring; it is located at the terminal end of the limbs and used for anchoring.

Illustration

The illustration serves as the visual identification of the terms associated with it.

Subtitle

The subtitle groups together illustrations representing members of the same class of objects.

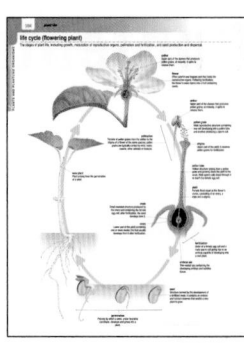

Diagram

More abstract natural phenomena or processes are represented by descriptive diagrams. Colored arrows indicate links between the various elements of the diagram.

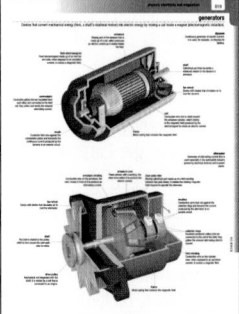

Section

In certain cases, where the inner parts of the illustrated object are being highlighted, blue lines have been traced over the cut lines to avoid any confusion about the true appearance of the object.

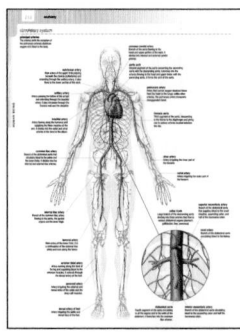

Magnifier or zoom

The magnifier or zoom enlarges certain areas of a complex illustration to facilitate viewing of the major parts.

Contents

ASTRONOMY

Science whose aim is the observation and knowledge of celestial bodies: position, movement, structure, evolution and so forth.

solar system

Region of our galaxy under the influence of the Sun; includes eight planets and their natural satellites as well as dwarf planets, asteroids and comets.

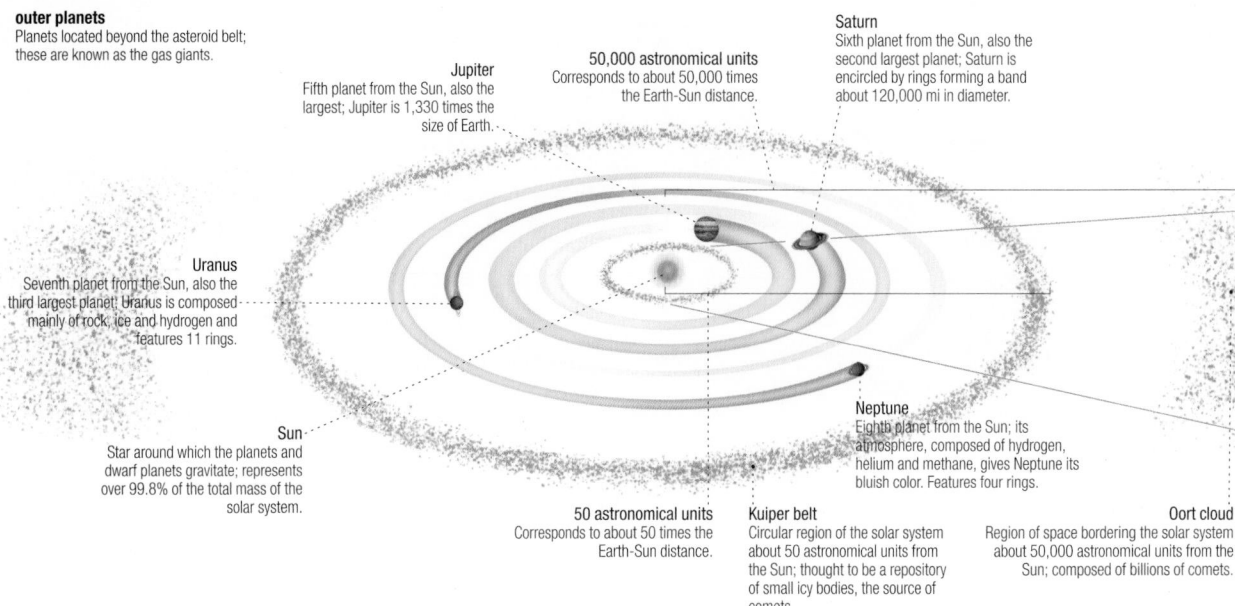

outer planets
Planets located beyond the asteroid belt; these are known as the gas giants.

Jupiter
Fifth planet from the Sun, also the largest; Jupiter is 1,330 times the size of Earth.

50,000 astronomical units
Corresponds to about 50,000 times the Earth-Sun distance.

Saturn
Sixth planet from the Sun, also the second largest planet; Saturn is encircled by rings forming a band about 120,000 mi in diameter.

Uranus
Seventh planet from the Sun, also the third largest planet; Uranus is composed mainly of rock, ice and hydrogen and features 11 rings.

Sun
Star around which the planets and dwarf planets gravitate; represents over 99.8% of the total mass of the solar system.

50 astronomical units
Corresponds to about 50 times the Earth-Sun distance.

Neptune
Eighth planet from the Sun; its atmosphere, composed of hydrogen, helium and methane, gives Neptune its bluish color. Features four rings.

Kuiper belt
Circular region of the solar system about 50 astronomical units from the Sun; thought to be a repository of small icy bodies, the source of comets.

Oort cloud
Region of space bordering the solar system about 50,000 astronomical units from the Sun; composed of billions of comets.

planets, satellites and dwarf planets

Planets and dwarf planets orbit the Sun; satellites orbit the planets and dwarf planets. They are represented from left to right in order of their distance from the Sun, with their relative sizes reflected by the size of their pictures.

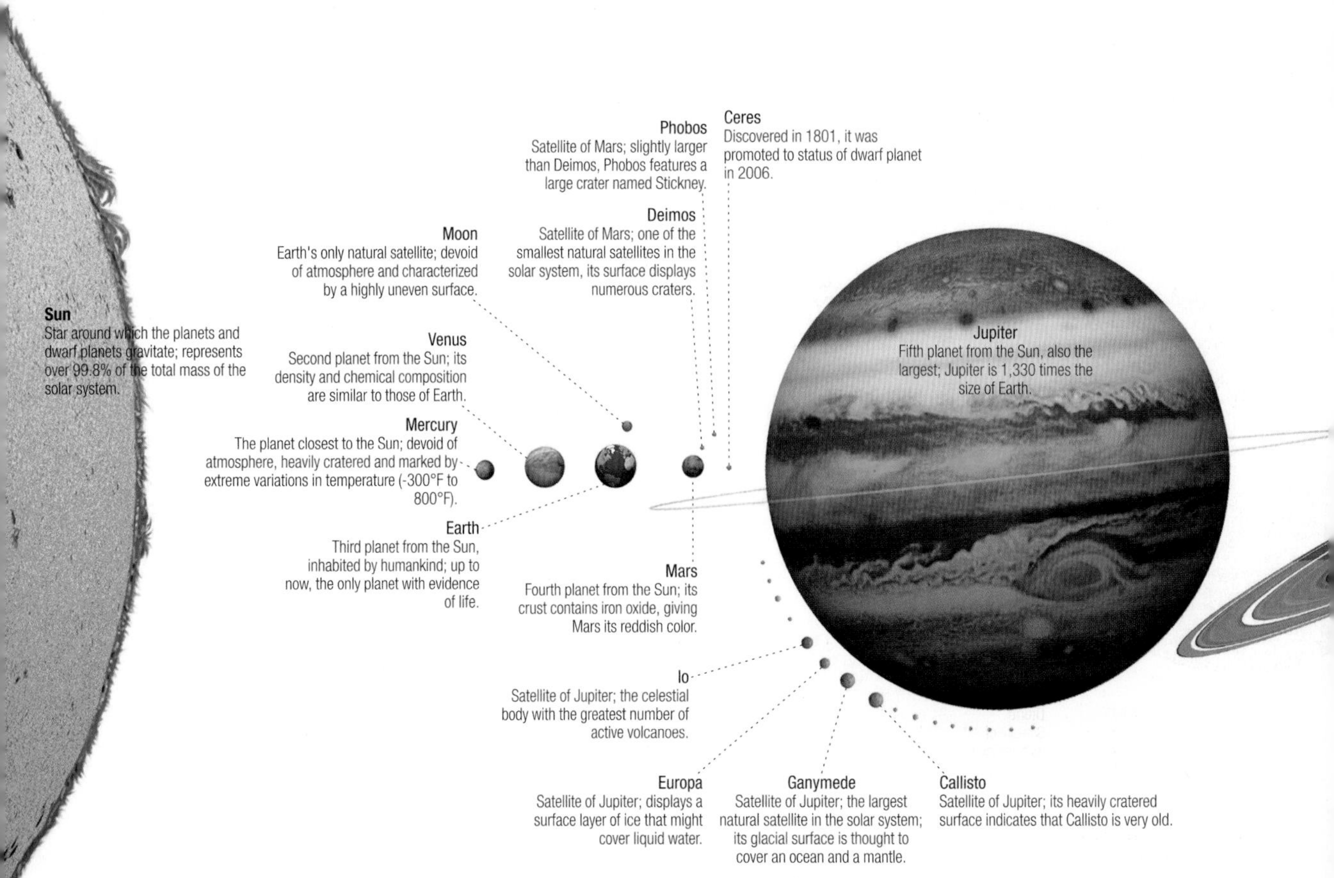

Sun
Star around which the planets and dwarf planets gravitate; represents over 99.8% of the total mass of the solar system.

Moon
Earth's only natural satellite; devoid of atmosphere and characterized by a highly uneven surface.

Venus
Second planet from the Sun; its density and chemical composition are similar to those of Earth.

Mercury
The planet closest to the Sun; devoid of atmosphere, heavily cratered and marked by extreme variations in temperature (-300°F to 800°F).

Earth
Third planet from the Sun, inhabited by humankind; up to now, the only planet with evidence of life.

Phobos
Satellite of Mars; slightly larger than Deimos, Phobos features a large crater named Stickney.

Deimos
Satellite of Mars; one of the smallest natural satellites in the solar system, its surface displays numerous craters.

Ceres
Discovered in 1801, it was promoted to status of dwarf planet in 2006.

Jupiter
Fifth planet from the Sun, also the largest; Jupiter is 1,330 times the size of Earth.

Mars
Fourth planet from the Sun; its crust contains iron oxide, giving Mars its reddish color.

Io
Satellite of Jupiter; the celestial body with the greatest number of active volcanoes.

Europa
Satellite of Jupiter; displays a surface layer of ice that might cover liquid water.

Ganymede
Satellite of Jupiter; the largest natural satellite in the solar system; its glacial surface is thought to cover an ocean and a mantle.

Callisto
Satellite of Jupiter; its heavily cratered surface indicates that Callisto is very old.

solar system

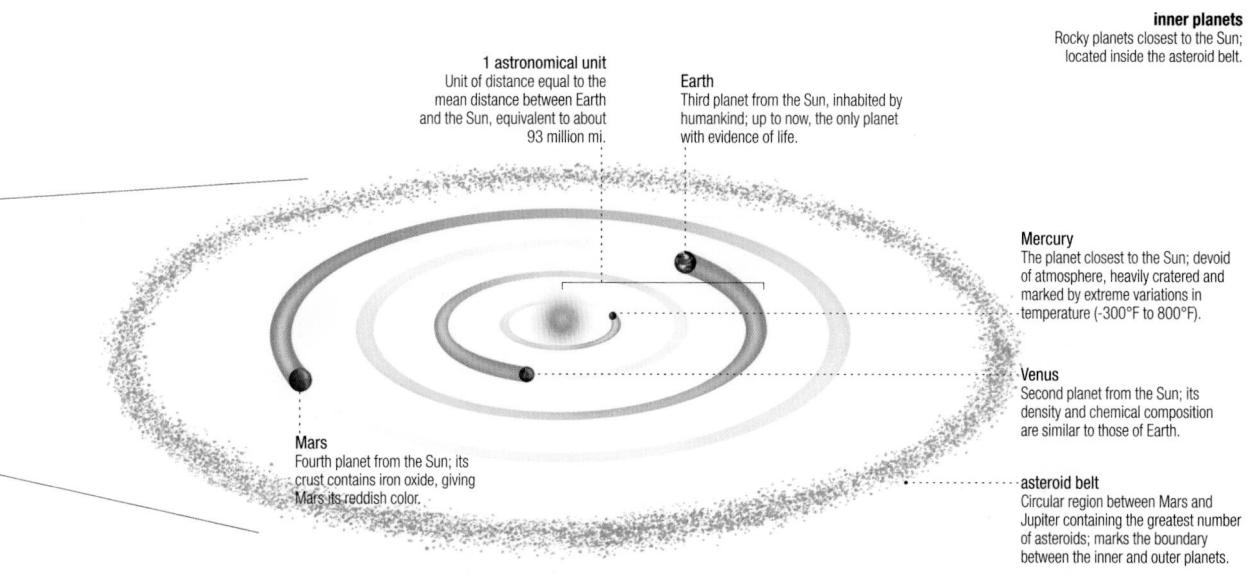

inner planets
Rocky planets closest to the Sun; located inside the asteroid belt.

1 astronomical unit
Unit of distance equal to the mean distance between Earth and the Sun, equivalent to about 93 million mi.

Earth
Third planet from the Sun, inhabited by humankind; up to now, the only planet with evidence of life.

Mercury
The planet closest to the Sun; devoid of atmosphere, heavily cratered and marked by extreme variations in temperature (-300°F to 800°F).

Venus
Second planet from the Sun; its density and chemical composition are similar to those of Earth.

Mars
Fourth planet from the Sun; its crust contains iron oxide, giving Mars its reddish color.

asteroid belt
Circular region between Mars and Jupiter containing the greatest number of asteroids; marks the boundary between the inner and outer planets.

planets, satellites and dwarf planets

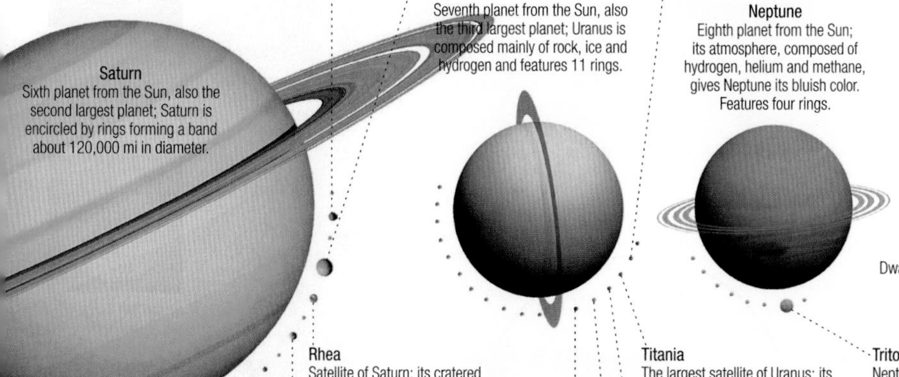

Charon
Pluto's only satellite; almost equal in size and mass to Pluto itself.

Pluto
Discovered in 1930, it was long considered the ninth planet of the solar system. Since 2006, it has been classified as a dwarf planet.

Nāmaka
The smaller of Haumea's two satellites.

Iapetus
Satellite of Saturn featuring a bright side composed of ice and a dark side composed of unknown matter.

Titan
Saturn's largest satellite, 1.5 times the diameter of the Moon.

Oberon
The most distant satellite of Uranus; its craters are often surrounded by light rays.

Hi'iaka
The larger of Haumea's two satellites.

Uranus
Seventh planet from the Sun, also the third largest planet; Uranus is composed mainly of rock, ice and hydrogen and features 11 rings.

Neptune
Eighth planet from the Sun; its atmosphere, composed of hydrogen, helium and methane, gives Neptune its bluish color. Features four rings.

Makemake
Dwarf planet, discovered in 2005, with no satellites.

Eris
Dwarf planet discovered in 2005, with a diameter bigger than Pluto's. It has a satellite, Dysnomia.

Saturn
Sixth planet from the Sun, also the second largest planet; Saturn is encircled by rings forming a band about 120,000 mi in diameter.

Haumea
Dwarf planet, discovered in 2005, with two natural satellites.

Dysnomia
Natural satellite of the dwarf planet Eris.

Rhea
Satellite of Saturn; its cratered surface is covered with ice as hard as rock.

Titania
The largest satellite of Uranus; its surface displays numerous valleys and faults.

Triton
Neptune's largest satellite; together with Pluto, Triton is the coldest object in the solar system.

Mimas
Satellite of Saturn; features a crater named Herschel spanning one-third of its surface.

Dione
Satellite of Saturn; its cratered surface features ice deposits.

Umbriel
Satellite of Uranus; its heavily cratered surface is very dark.

Tethys
Satellite of Saturn thought to be composed of ice; visible on its surface is an immense impact crater named Odysseus.

Miranda
Satellite of Uranus whose surface is cratered in places; displays vast expanses of arêtes and furrows.

Ariel
Satellite of Uranus; its cratered surface is composed of numerous long valleys and extremely high escarpments.

Sun

Star composed of 92.1% hydrogen atoms and 7.8% helium atoms, around which the planets gravitate; represents more than 99.8% of the solar system's total mass.

structure of the Sun
From the center to the periphery are the core, the radiation and convection zones, the photosphere, the chromosphere and the corona.

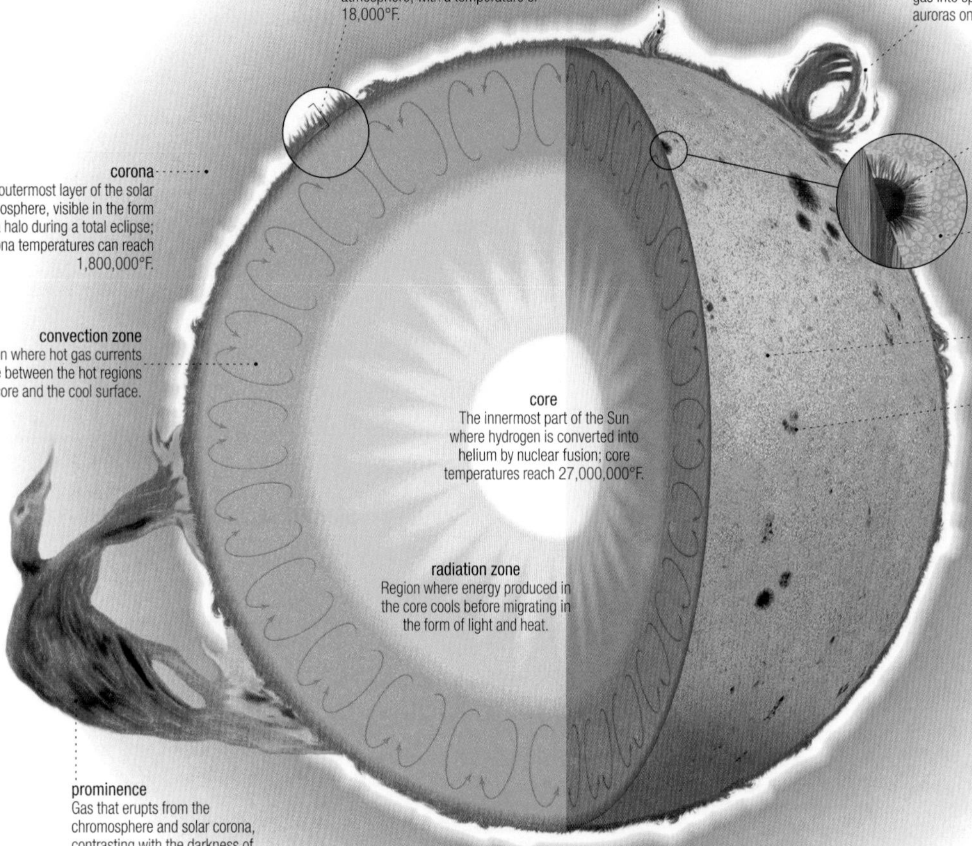

chromosphere
The lowest level of the solar atmosphere, with a temperature of 18,000°F.

spicule
A narrow jet of gas in the form of a plume observed in the solar chromosphere.

flare
Violent projection of extremely hot gas into space, provoking polar auroras on Earth a few days later.

sunspot
A dark, slightly cooler zone of the photosphere where the magnetic field is more intense.

corona
The outermost layer of the solar atmosphere, visible in the form of a halo during a total eclipse; corona temperatures can reach 1,800,000°F.

granulation
Network of cells on the photosphere brought about by the convective movement of hot gas from the Sun's interior.

convection zone
Region where hot gas currents circulate between the hot regions of the core and the cool surface.

photosphere
Visible surface of the Sun, with a temperature of 10,000°F.

core
The innermost part of the Sun where hydrogen is converted into helium by nuclear fusion; core temperatures reach 27,000,000°F.

facula
Luminous region of the photosphere.

radiation zone
Region where energy produced in the core cools before migrating in the form of light and heat.

prominence
Gas that erupts from the chromosphere and solar corona, contrasting with the darkness of space.

types of eclipse
There are three types of solar eclipse, bas[ed]
on the degree of obscuration.

annular eclipse
Occurs when the Moon comes between Earth and the Sun, reducing the latter to luminous ring.

partial eclipse
Observed by anyone within the penumbr[a] zone during an eclipse.

total eclipse
Occurs when the lunar disk completely covers the solar disk and only the Sun's corona remains visible.

solar eclipse
Obscuration of the Sun brought about by the passage of the Moon between Earth and the Sun.

umbra shadow
On Earth, the observer in this region will see a total or annular eclipse.

Earth's orbit
Elliptical path of Earth revolving around the Sun under the effect of gravitation.

Moon
Natural satellite of Earth.

Sun
Light source eclipsed by the Moon.

penumbra shadow
On Earth, the observer in this region will see a partial eclipse.

Earth
Third planet from the Sun, Earth takes a full day to rotate once on itself, one year to revolve once around the Sun.

Moon's orbit
Elliptical path of the Moon revolving around Earth under the effect of gravitation.

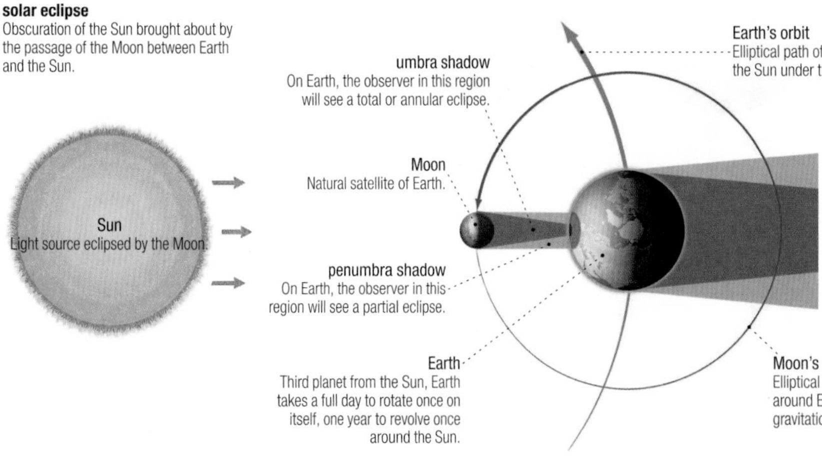

Moon

Earth's only natural satellite; devoid of atmosphere, it displays a highly uneven surface.

types of eclipse

[There] are two types of eclipse based on the [de]gree of obscuration: partial or total.

partial eclipse
When the Moon enters the umbra shadow, its bright side diminishes little by little.

total eclipse
Occurs when the Moon is completely within the umbra shadow and takes on a reddish appearance.

cliff
Steep rock face shaped by a sea.

bay
Small plain of hardened lava located along the edges of a sea.

crater
Circular basin dug out by the impact of a meteorite.

ocean
A very large sea.

cirque
Vast crater characterized by remarkable relief; varies between 12 and 120 mi in diameter.

crater ray
Band that radiates from a young crater, the result of matter ejected during a meteorite impact.

lunar features

Aspect of the Moon determined by past volcanic activity, meteorite impact and soil fractures.

lake
Small isolated plain of hardened lava.

highland
Designates bright regions riddled with craters; these oldest regions cover 85% of the surface.

sea
Designates the vast plains of hardened lava forming the dark regions; younger than the highlands, these cover 15% of the surface.

mountain range
Vestiges of the walls of a once-large crater; semicircular in shape, it can span hundreds of miles.

wall
Mountain usually surrounding a cirque.

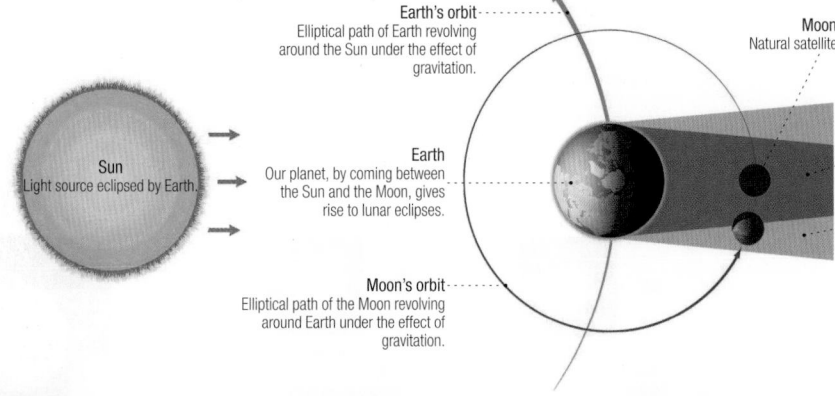

Earth's orbit
Elliptical path of Earth revolving around the Sun under the effect of gravitation.

Moon
Natural satellite of Earth.

Sun
Light source eclipsed by Earth.

Earth
Our planet, by coming between the Sun and the Moon, gives rise to lunar eclipses.

Moon's orbit
Elliptical path of the Moon revolving around Earth under the effect of gravitation.

lunar eclipse
Eclipse during which the Moon enters Earth's umbra shadow in part or in full.

umbra shadow
When the Moon is completely in this region, the Sun's light no longer reaches it; the eclipse is therefore total.

penumbra shadow
When the Moon enters this region, it slowly ceases to be illuminated by the Sun.

phases of the Moon

Changes in the Moon's appearance over the course of a month; result from the movement of the Moon in relation to the Sun, as seen from Earth.

new moon
[The] Moon lies between the Earth and the [Su]n; it is not visible, as the Sun's light is too brilliant.

new crescent
The Moon is visible in the early evening in the shape of a thin crescent.

first quarter
The visible face of the Moon grows increasingly bright; the lunar crescent gradually changes until it forms a semi-circle after one week.

waxing gibbous
As the Moon moves away from the Sun, its shadow gradually recedes.

full moon
[The] visible face of the Moon is completely illuminated by the Sun's rays.

waning gibbous
As the Moon moves closer to the Sun, its shadow begins to obscure the Sun's disk.

last quarter
The bright side gradually recedes until it becomes a half-moon.

old crescent
The Moon lies to the right of the Sun and appears in the sky at dawn in the form of a thin crescent.

meteorite

Fragment of rock, iron or another mineral that crashes into Earth instead of completely burning up as it crosses the atmosphere.

iron meteorite
Meteorite consisting mainly of iron and nickel, marked by small faults.

stony-iron meteorite
The rarest class of meteorites, characterized by the presence of almost equal quantities of rocky matter and metals.

stony meteorites
Meteorites composed mainly of rocky matter. Divided into two groups: chondrites and achondrites.

chondrite
The most common meteorite, characterized by the presence of rock or sulfurous matter in the form of minuscule spheres (chondrules).

achondrite
Meteorite whose composition is similar to that of certain terrestrial rocks; believed to come from the Moon or from Mars.

comet

Small icy body that partially evaporates as it approaches the Sun; made up of a head with a solid core and tails composed of gas and dust.

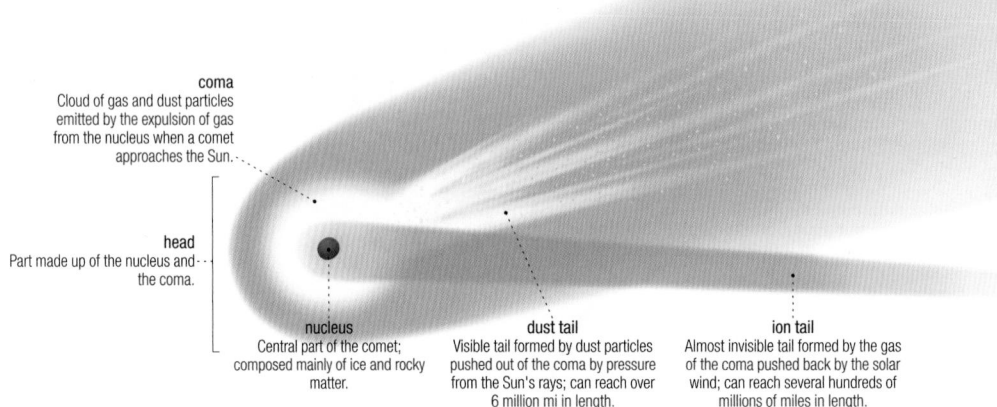

coma
Cloud of gas and dust particles emitted by the expulsion of gas from the nucleus when a comet approaches the Sun.

head
Part made up of the nucleus and the coma.

nucleus
Central part of the comet; composed mainly of ice and rocky matter.

dust tail
Visible tail formed by dust particles pushed out of the coma by pressure from the Sun's rays; can reach over 6 million mi in length.

ion tail
Almost invisible tail formed by the gas of the coma pushed back by the solar wind; can reach several hundreds of millions of miles in length.

star

A sphere of gas massive enough to generate light and heat through nuclear reactions that transform hydrogen into helium in its core.

low-mass stars
Stars whose mass is less than 1.5 times that of the Sun.

massive stars
Stars whose mass is more than 1.5 times that of the Sun; can be up to 50 times the mass of the Sun.

supernova
A supergiant that collapses onto itself and explodes with such force that it releases more energy than millions of suns.

black hole
Results when the core of a massive star collapses; the gravitational force is so strong that not even light can escape.

red giant
An old star whose hydrogen reserve has been exhausted; its luminosity can be 100 times that of the Sun.

brown dwarf
Star whose mass is not sufficient to generate a nuclear reaction.

black dwarf
Dead star, likely the residue of a dwarf that has totally exhausted its energy resources.

white dwarf
An old, extremely dense star of faint luminosity, formed by the nucleus of a red giant contracting until it reaches the size of Earth.

pulsar
A neutron star that rotates rapidly on itself, thereby emitting regular radio waves.

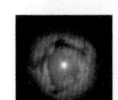

planetary nebula
Expanding gaseous envelope that corresponds to the external layer of a red giant that is gradually fading away.

nova
A white dwarf that assimilates gaseous matter from a neighboring star, suddenly becoming extremely bright before it returns to its initial brightness.

main-sequence star
Star whose mass is sufficient to generate a nuclear reaction.

neutron star
Star formed of compressed neutrons, believed to be the residue of a supernova explosion.

supergiant
An old, extremely luminous star of considerable mass; its diameter can be as much as 100 times that of the Sun.

galaxy

Grouping of stars and interstellar matter linked together by gravitation; each galaxy comprises an average of 100 billion stars.

Hubble's classification

Classification of galaxies according to their form, devised by astronomer Edwin Hubble in the 1920s; it is still used today.

elliptical galaxy
Spherical or oval galaxy with no spiral arms.

lenticular galaxy
Flat, lens-shaped galaxy with a large bulge but no arms.

normal spiral galaxy
Galaxy composed of a large nucleus from which spiral arms emerge.

  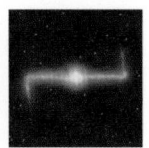

barred spiral galaxy
Galaxy crossed by a bar of stars and interstellar matter; the spiral arms emerge from the ends of the bar.

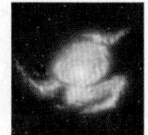 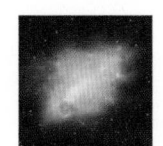

type I irregular galaxy
re type of galaxy that seems to possess
iral arms without displaying a specific
symmetry.

type II irregular galaxy
Rare type of galaxy whose structure
obeys no specific symmetry.

Milky Way

Spiral galaxy composed of 200 to 300 billion stars, including the Sun; thought to be 10 billion years old.

Milky Way: seen from above

From above, the Milky Way appears as a spiral that rotates on itself around a nucleus.

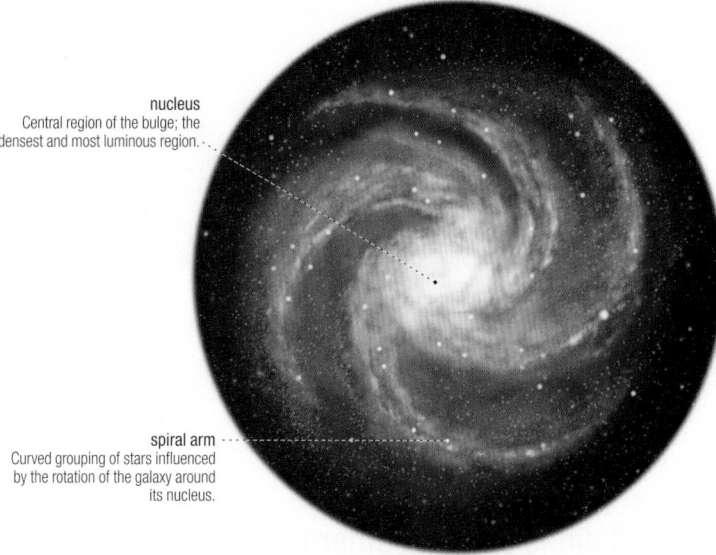

nucleus
Central region of the bulge; the densest and most luminous region.

spiral arm
Curved grouping of stars influenced by the rotation of the galaxy around its nucleus.

Milky Way: side view

From the side, the Milky Way appears as a disk because its spiral arms are seen from the same angle.

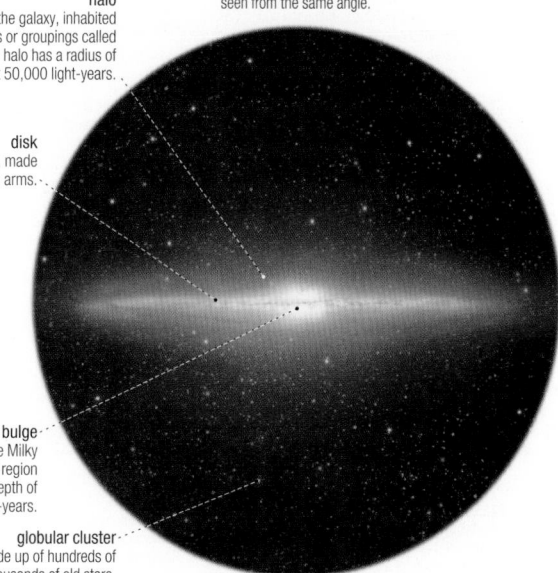

halo
Region surrounding the galaxy, inhabited by isolated stars or groupings called globular clusters; the halo has a radius of about 50,000 light-years.

disk
The main part of the galaxy, made up of a bulge and attaching arms.

bulge
The central bulge of the Milky Way's disk; the densest region of the Milky Way, with a depth of 15,000 light-years.

globular cluster
Cluster made up of hundreds of thousands of old stars.

planetarium

Structure where a projector is used to simulate the movement of the celestial bodies on a dome representing half of the celestial sphere.

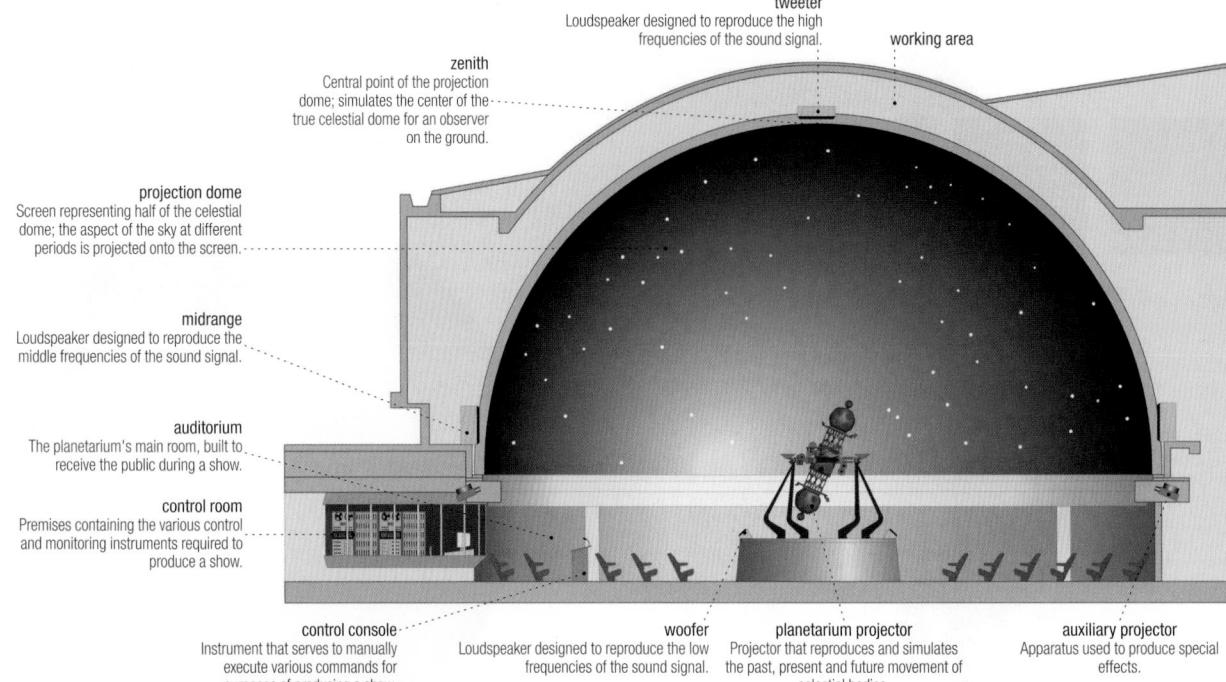

tweeter
Loudspeaker designed to reproduce the high frequencies of the sound signal.

working area

zenith
Central point of the projection dome; simulates the center of the true celestial dome for an observer on the ground.

projection dome
Screen representing half of the celestial dome; the aspect of the sky at different periods is projected onto the screen.

midrange
Loudspeaker designed to reproduce the middle frequencies of the sound signal.

auditorium
The planetarium's main room, built to receive the public during a show.

control room
Premises containing the various control and monitoring instruments required to produce a show.

control console
Instrument that serves to manually execute various commands for purposes of producing a show.

woofer
Loudspeaker designed to reproduce the low frequencies of the sound signal.

planetarium projector
Projector that reproduces and simulates the past, present and future movement of celestial bodies.

auxiliary projector
Apparatus used to produce special effects.

constellations of the Southern Hemisphere

Groupings of stars whose position on the celestial dome of the Southern hemisphere, as seen from Earth, forms figures; this makes them easier to locate and has often inspired names.

1   Cetus
Large, mostly southern constellation containing a remarkable star, Mira Ceti; in the 16th century, Mira Ceti became the first star of varying luminosity (variable star) to be discovered.

2   Aquarius
Zodiac constellation between Capricorn and Pisces; contains several faint stars.

3   Aquila
Mostly northern constellation containing Altair, 12th brightest star in the sky.

4   Capricornus
Zodiac constellation marking the beginning of winter in the Gregorian calendar.

5   Microscopium
Small constellation recorded in the 18th century; originally formed part of the Southern Fish.

6   Pisces Austrinus
Constellation composed of seven stars; the brightest is named Fomalhaut, meaning "mouth of a large fish".

7   Grus
Constellation discovered in the 17th century whose shape recalls that of a bird in flight.

8   Sculptor
Constellation composed of faint stars recorded in the 18th century.

9   Eridanus
Large constellation containing Achernar, ninth brightest star in the sky.

10   Fornax
Small faint constellation discovered in the 18th century.

11   Horologium
Faint constellation discovered in the 18th century.

12   Phoenix
Faint constellation recorded in the 17th century.

13   Tucana
Constellation harboring the third closest galaxy to Earth, the Small Magellanic Cloud, an irregular galaxy located about 200,000 light-years away.

14   Pavo
Constellation recorded in the 17th century; contains only one bright star, Alpha Pavonis.

15   Indus
Small faint constellation discovered in the 17th century.

16   Telescopium
Constellation composed of faint stars discovered in the 18th century; shares stars with neighboring constellations.

17   Corona Australis
Small faint constellation recorded in the 2nd century.

18   Sagittarius
The last zodiac constellation of the fall; features, in particular, the greatest number of variable stars (stars of varying luminosity).

19   Scutum
Small constellation composed of five faint stars recorded in the 17th century.

20   Scorpius
Zodiac constellation between Libra and Sagittarius; contains Antares, 16th brightest star in the sky.

21   Norma
A faint constellation recorded in the 18th century.

22   Ara
Small faint constellation recorded in the 2nd century.

23   Triangulum Australe
Small constellation discovered in the 17th century whose three brightest stars form a triangle.

24   Apus
Constellation composed of faint stars recorded in the 17th century.

25   Octans
A faint constellation recorded in the 18th century; includes the South celestial pole.

26   Hydrus
Constellation containing only about 20 stars, most often barely visible to the naked eye; discovered in the 17th century.

27   Mensa
Faint constellation recorded in the 18th century; includes part of the Large Magellanic Cloud.

28   Reticulum
Small constellation recorded in the 18th century.

constellations of the Southern Hemisphere

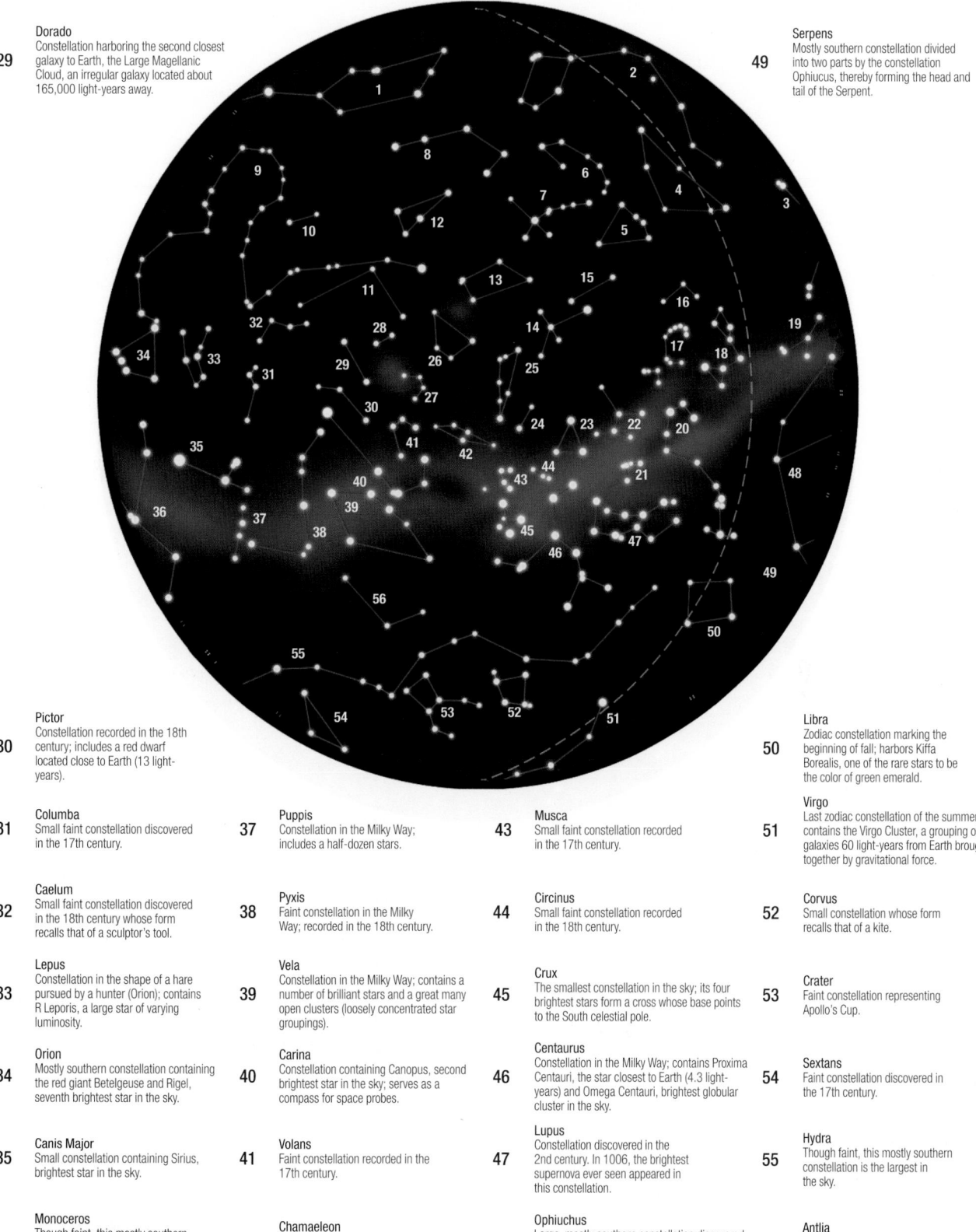

29 Dorado
Constellation harboring the second closest galaxy to Earth, the Large Magellanic Cloud, an irregular galaxy located about 165,000 light-years away.

49 Serpens
Mostly southern constellation divided into two parts by the constellation Ophiucus, thereby forming the head and tail of the Serpent.

30 Pictor
Constellation recorded in the 18th century; includes a red dwarf located close to Earth (13 light-years).

50 Libra
Zodiac constellation marking the beginning of fall; harbors Kiffa Borealis, one of the rare stars to be the color of green emerald.

31 Columba
Small faint constellation discovered in the 17th century.

37 Puppis
Constellation in the Milky Way; includes a half-dozen stars.

43 Musca
Small faint constellation recorded in the 17th century.

51 Virgo
Last zodiac constellation of the summer; contains the Virgo Cluster, a grouping of galaxies 60 light-years from Earth brought together by gravitational force.

32 Caelum
Small faint constellation discovered in the 18th century whose form recalls that of a sculptor's tool.

38 Pyxis
Faint constellation in the Milky Way; recorded in the 18th century.

44 Circinus
Small faint constellation recorded in the 18th century.

52 Corvus
Small constellation whose form recalls that of a kite.

33 Lepus
Constellation in the shape of a hare pursued by a hunter (Orion); contains R Leporis, a large star of varying luminosity.

39 Vela
Constellation in the Milky Way; contains a number of brilliant stars and a great many open clusters (loosely concentrated star groupings).

45 Crux
The smallest constellation in the sky; its four brightest stars form a cross whose base points to the South celestial pole.

53 Crater
Faint constellation representing Apollo's Cup.

34 Orion
Mostly southern constellation containing the red giant Betelgeuse and Rigel, seventh brightest star in the sky.

40 Carina
Constellation containing Canopus, second brightest star in the sky; serves as a compass for space probes.

46 Centaurus
Constellation in the Milky Way; contains Proxima Centauri, the star closest to Earth (4.3 light-years) and Omega Centauri, brightest globular cluster in the sky.

54 Sextans
Faint constellation discovered in the 17th century.

35 Canis Major
Small constellation containing Sirius, brightest star in the sky.

41 Volans
Faint constellation recorded in the 17th century.

47 Lupus
Constellation discovered in the 2nd century. In 1006, the brightest supernova ever seen appeared in this constellation.

55 Hydra
Though faint, this mostly southern constellation is the largest in the sky.

36 Monoceros
Though faint, this mostly southern constellation contains a great number of stars and nebulae.

42 Chamaeleon
Faint constellation discovered in the 17th century.

48 Ophiuchus
Large, mostly southern constellation discovered in the 2nd century; includes Barnard's Star, second closest star to Earth (6 light-years).

56 Antlia
A faint constellation recorded in the 18th century.

constellations of the Northern Hemisphere

Groupings of stars whose position on the celestial dome of the Northern hemisphere, as seen from Earth, forms figures; this makes them easier to locate and has often inspired names.

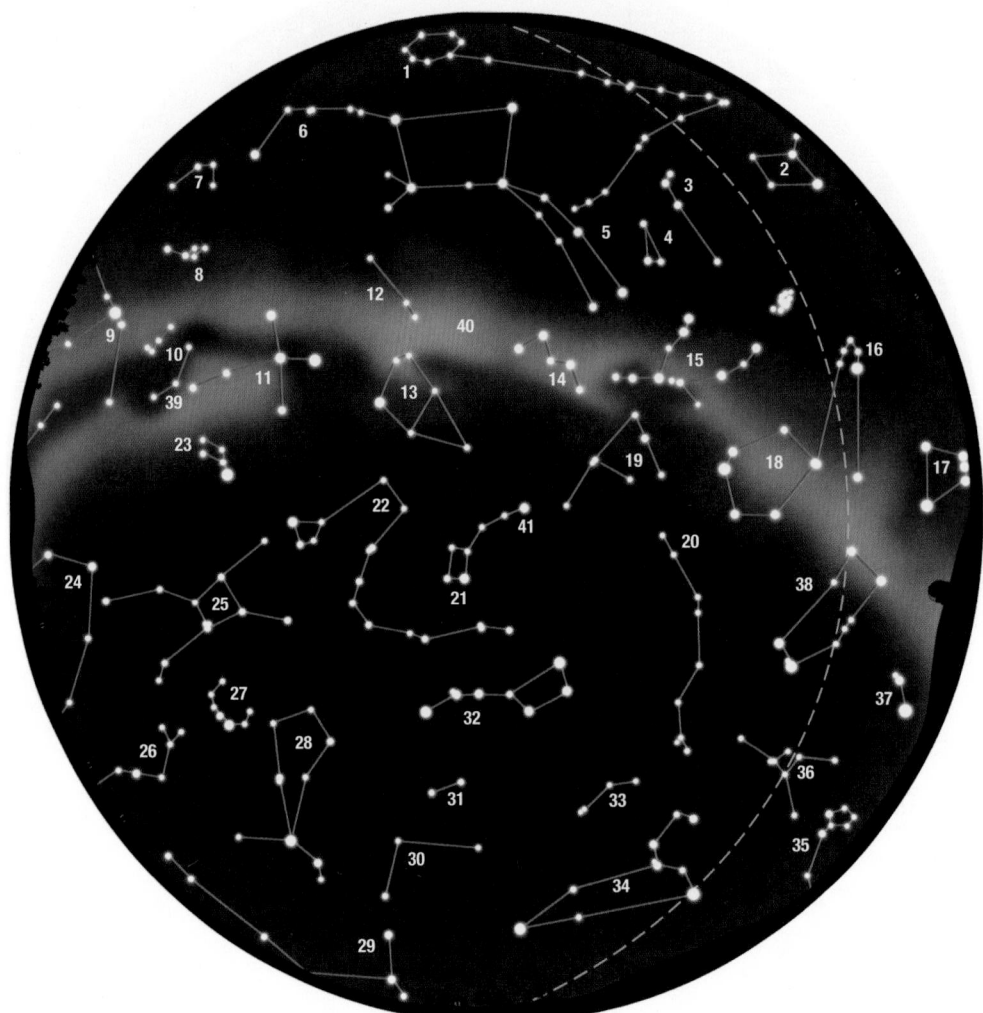

Pisces

1   Last zodiac constellation of the winter; while extremely far-reaching, it harbors only faint stars.

Cetus

2   Large, mostly southern constellation containing a remarkable star, Mira Ceti; in the 16th century, Mira Ceti became the first star of varying luminosity (variable star) to be discovered.

Aries

3   Zodiac constellation marking the beginning of spring in the Gregorian calendar.

Triangulum

4   Constellation harboring M33 (third largest galaxy close to Earth), located about 2.7 million light-years away.

Andromeda

5   Constellation harboring the Andromeda nebula (second largest galaxy close to Earth), located about 2.25 million light-years away.

Pegasus

6   Vast constellation easily located thanks to the quadrangle that three of its brilliant stars form with Sirrah (Andromeda); this asterism known as the "Great Square of Pegasus".

Equuleus

7   Small constellation composed of faint stars recorded in the 2nd century.

Delphinus

8   Small constellation harboring faint stars discovered in the 2nd century.

Aquila

9   Mostly northern constellation containing Altair, 12th brightest star in the sky.

Sagitta

10   Small constellation containing only a few stars visible to the naked eye; contains a fairly bright globular cluster.

Cygnus

11   Constellation whose shape recalls that of a swan in flight; contains Deneb, 20th brightest star in the sky.

Lacerta

12   Constellation formed of faint stars recorded in the 17th century.

Cepheus

13   Constellation harboring Delta Cephei, a prototype of stars of varying luminosity, named Cepheid variables for this reason.

Cassiopeia

14   Constellation easily identified thanks to the "W" formed by its five principal stars; contains a number of stars of varying luminosity (variable stars).

Perseus

15   Constellation harboring a great number of stars of varying luminosity and two large star clusters, h and Chi Persei.

Taurus

16   Zodiac constellation located between Aries and Gemini; contains the star Aldebaran (14th brightest star) as well as two clusters, the Hyades and Pleiades.

Orion

17   Mostly southern constellation containing the red giant Betelgeuse and Rigel, seventh brightest star in the sky.

Auriga

18   Constellation containing Capella, sixth brightest star in the sky.

Camelopardalis

19   Faint constellation discovered in the 17th century.

Lynx

20   Constellation composed of faint stars recorded in the 17th century.

Ursa Minor

21   Constellation containing the North Star, 47th brightest star in the sky; also called "Little Dipper" owing to its size in relation to the "Big Dipper".

constellations of the Northern Hemisphere

22 Draco
Vast constellation composed of a great many faint stars.

23 Lyra
Constellation containing Vega, fifth brightest star in the sky.

24 Ophiuchus
Large, mostly southern constellation discovered in the 2nd century; includes Barnard's Star, second closest star to Earth (6 light-years).

25 Hercules
Large constellation containing Rasalgethi, a red giant about 830 times brighter than the Sun and more than 680 times its diameter.

26 Serpens
Mostly southern constellation divided into two parts by the constellation Ophiucus, thereby forming the head and tail of the Serpent.

27 Corona Borealis
Small constellation whose principal stars form an incomplete circle; recorded in the 2nd century.

28 Boötes
Constellation containing the red giant Arcturus, fourth brightest star in the sky.

29 Virgo
Last zodiac constellation of the summer; contains the Virgo Cluster, a grouping of galaxies 60 light-years from Earth brought together by gravitational force.

30 Coma Berenices
Constellation containing the Coma Cluster of galaxies, located 260 light-years from Earth.

31 Canes Venatici
Faint constellation harboring numerous galaxies, among them the spiral galaxy M51, located 37 million light-years from Earth.

32 Ursa Major
Constellation whose seven principal stars draw the outline of a giant saucepan; these seven stars are also called "the Big Dipper". Contains several spiral galaxies.

33 Leo Minor
Small faint constellation discovered in the 17th century.

34 Leo
Zodiac constellation between Cancer and Virgo; its brightest stars form the silhouette of a lion. Harbors numerous galaxies.

35 Hydra
Though faint, this mostly southern constellation is the largest in the sky.

36 Cancer
Zodiac constellation marking the beginning of summer in the Gregorian calendar.

37 Canis Minor
Constellation containing Procyon, eighth brightest star in the sky.

38 Gemini
Last zodiac constellation of the spring; contains Castor and Pollux, 18th brightest star in the sky.

39 Vulpecula
Small constellation composed of faint stars recorded in the 17th century.

40 Milky Way
Faint milky band that is our galaxy, as seen from our spiral arm.

41 North Star
Star located at the end of the Little Dipper handle; nowadays serves to indicate the direction of the North celestial pole.

celestial coordinate system

Imaginary horizontal and vertical lines used to describe the position of an object on the celestial sphere.

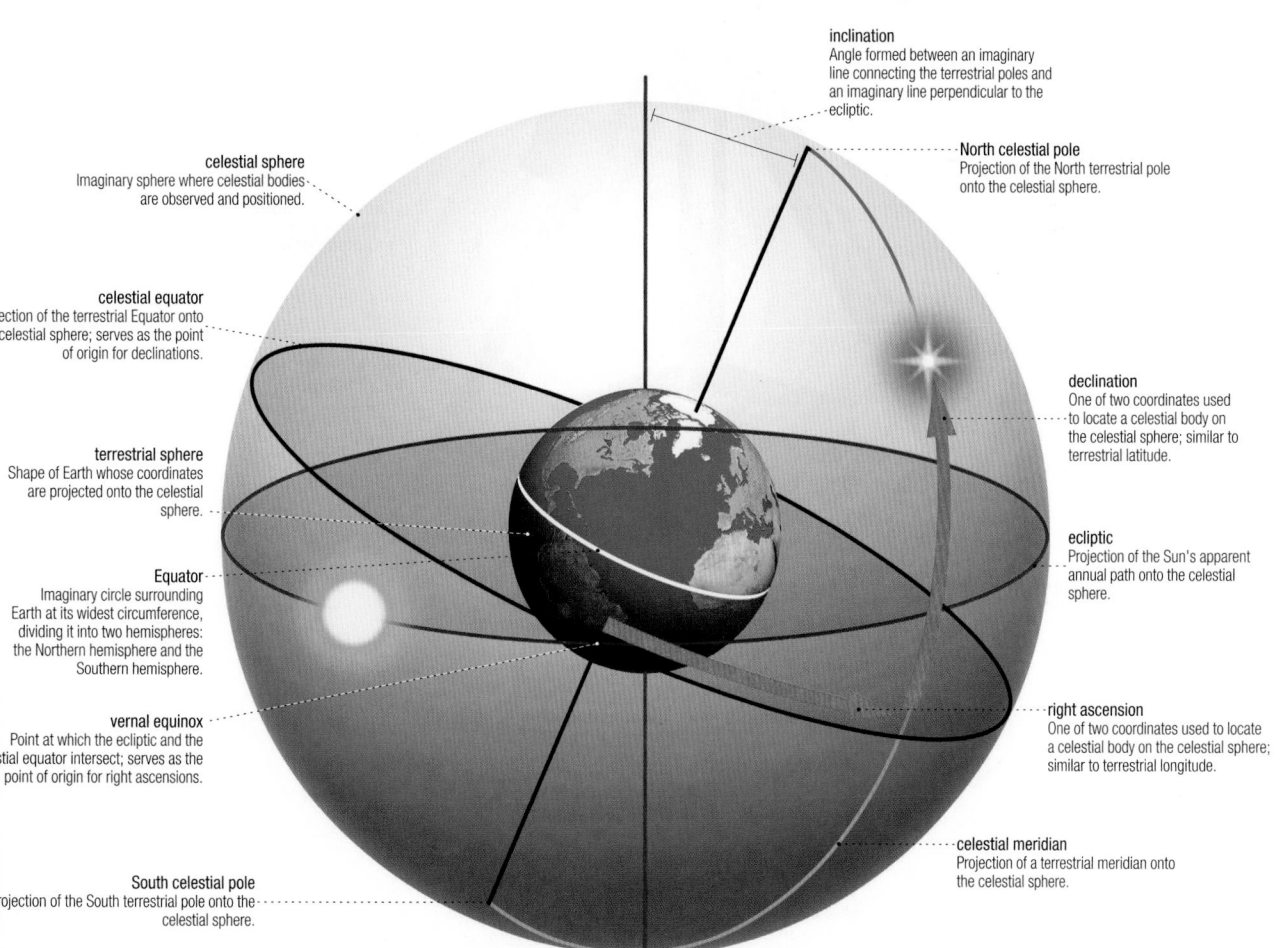

inclination
Angle formed between an imaginary line connecting the terrestrial poles and an imaginary line perpendicular to the ecliptic.

celestial sphere
Imaginary sphere where celestial bodies are observed and positioned.

North celestial pole
Projection of the North terrestrial pole onto the celestial sphere.

celestial equator
ection of the terrestrial Equator onto celestial sphere; serves as the point of origin for declinations.

declination
One of two coordinates used to locate a celestial body on the celestial sphere; similar to terrestrial latitude.

terrestrial sphere
Shape of Earth whose coordinates are projected onto the celestial sphere.

ecliptic
Projection of the Sun's apparent annual path onto the celestial sphere.

Equator
Imaginary circle surrounding Earth at its widest circumference, dividing it into two hemispheres: the Northern hemisphere and the Southern hemisphere.

right ascension
One of two coordinates used to locate a celestial body on the celestial sphere; similar to terrestrial longitude.

vernal equinox
Point at which the ecliptic and the stial equator intersect; serves as the point of origin for right ascensions.

celestial meridian
Projection of a terrestrial meridian onto the celestial sphere.

South celestial pole
rojection of the South terrestrial pole onto the celestial sphere.

ASTRONOMY

refracting telescope

Optical instrument that uses an objective lens to observe celestial bodies.

general view

finderscope
Small low-magnification telescope with a wide field of view; serves to locate celestial bodies.

cradle
Part that tightens around the main tube to secure it to the base.

main tube
The barrel of a telescope housing the optical system; light rays travel through the main tube.

dew shield
Device placed in front of the objective to limit stray light and condensation.

eyepiece
Lens or system of lenses meant to magnify the image when placed before the eye.

eyepiece holder

star diagonal
Part serving to deflect the light toward the eyepiece, thereby providing a comfortable observation position.

focusing knob
Adjusting device that makes it possible to obtain a clear image of the object.

declination setting scale
Graduated disk indicating the declination of the celestial body observed.

azimuth clamp
Clamp serving to lock the telescope along its horizontal axis.

altitude clamp
Clamp serving to lock the telescope along its vertical axis.

azimuth fine adjustment
Fine-tuning device serving to position the telescope horizontally.

altitude fine adjustment
Fine-tuning device serving to position the telescope vertically.

right ascension setting scale
Graduated disk indicating the right ascension of the observed celestial body.

fork
Mount with dual forks used to secure the telescope to the tripod.

counterweight
Weight serving to balance the components of the telescope, making it easier to pivot and adjust smoothly.

tripod accessories shelf

tripod
Stable three-legged stand of variable height.

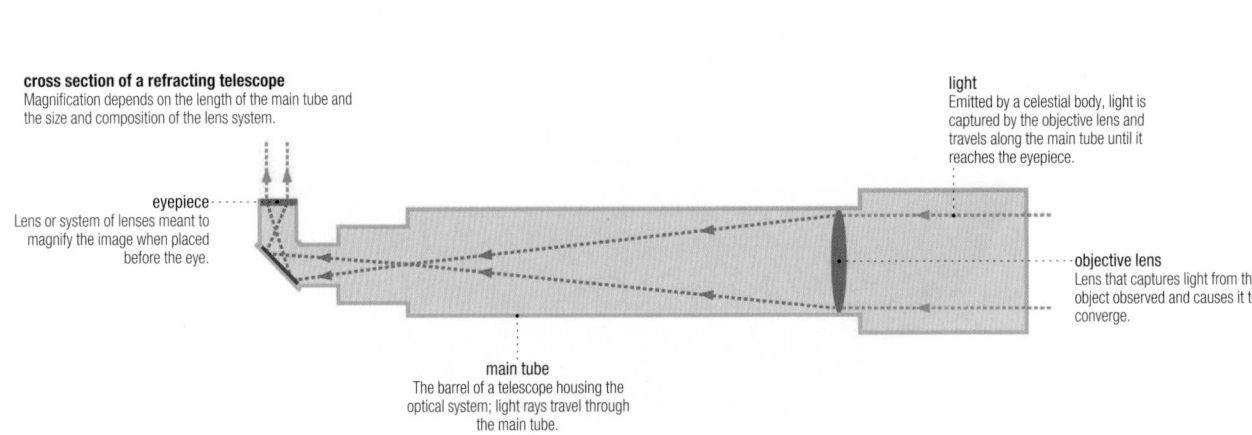

cross section of a refracting telescope
Magnification depends on the length of the main tube and the size and composition of the lens system.

light
Emitted by a celestial body, light is captured by the objective lens and travels along the main tube until it reaches the eyepiece.

eyepiece
Lens or system of lenses meant to magnify the image when placed before the eye.

objective lens
Lens that captures light from the object observed and causes it to converge.

main tube
The barrel of a telescope housing the optical system; light rays travel through the main tube.

reflecting telescope

Optical instrument that uses an objective mirror to observe celestial bodies.

general view

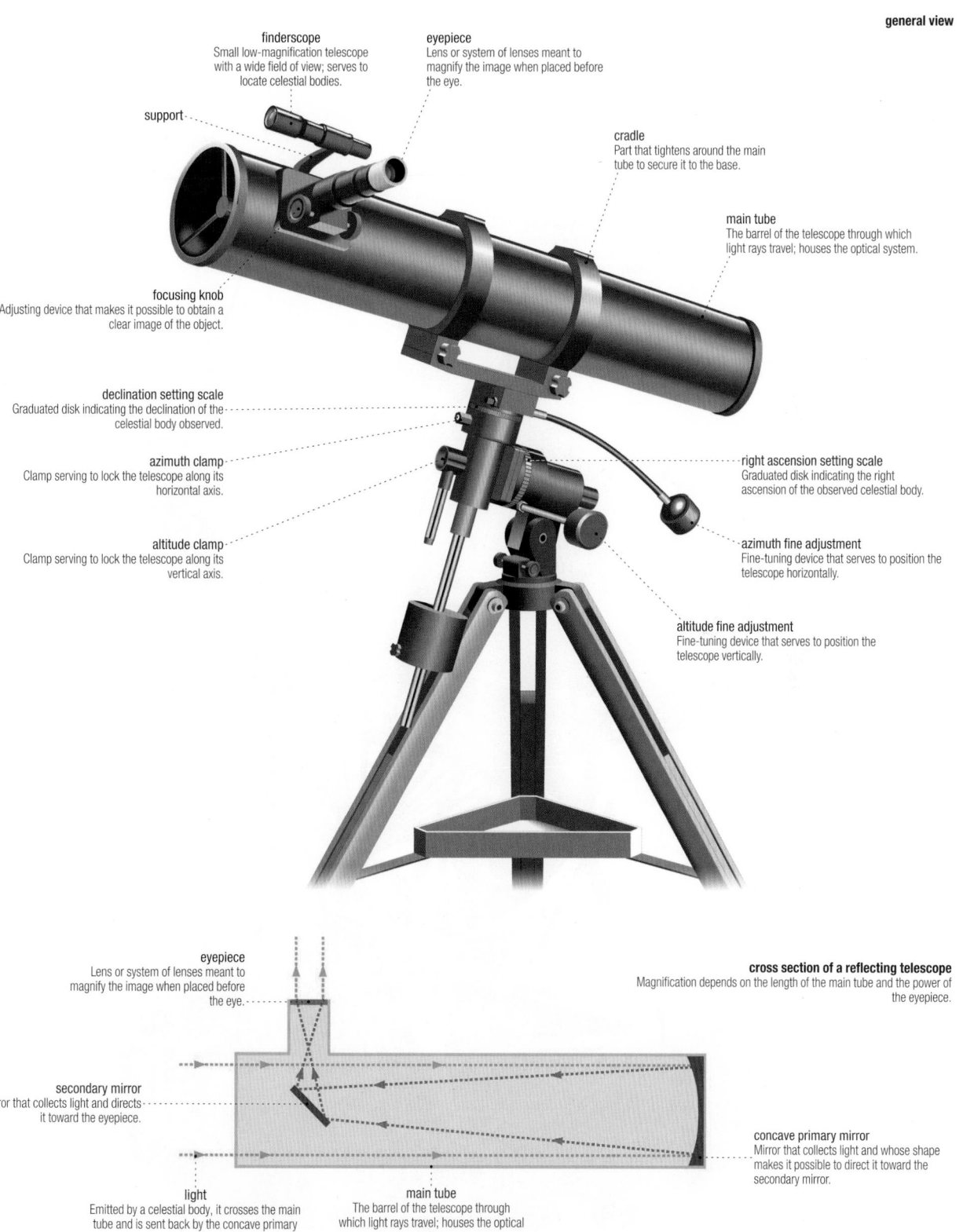

finderscope
Small low-magnification telescope with a wide field of view; serves to locate celestial bodies.

eyepiece
Lens or system of lenses meant to magnify the image when placed before the eye.

support

cradle
Part that tightens around the main tube to secure it to the base.

main tube
The barrel of the telescope through which light rays travel; houses the optical system.

focusing knob
Adjusting device that makes it possible to obtain a clear image of the object.

declination setting scale
Graduated disk indicating the declination of the celestial body observed.

azimuth clamp
Clamp serving to lock the telescope along its horizontal axis.

altitude clamp
Clamp serving to lock the telescope along its vertical axis.

right ascension setting scale
Graduated disk indicating the right ascension of the observed celestial body.

azimuth fine adjustment
Fine-tuning device that serves to position the telescope horizontally.

altitude fine adjustment
Fine-tuning device that serves to position the telescope vertically.

eyepiece
Lens or system of lenses meant to magnify the image when placed before the eye.

cross section of a reflecting telescope
Magnification depends on the length of the main tube and the power of the eyepiece.

secondary mirror
Mirror that collects light and directs it toward the eyepiece.

concave primary mirror
Mirror that collects light and whose shape makes it possible to direct it toward the secondary mirror.

light
Emitted by a celestial body, it crosses the main tube and is sent back by the concave primary mirror; the secondary mirror intercepts it and directs it toward the eyepiece.

main tube
The barrel of the telescope through which light rays travel; houses the optical system.

radio telescope

Instrument used to capture, concentrate and analyze radio waves emanating from a celestial body or a region of the celestial sphere.

steerable parabolic reflector
Type of adjustable radio telescope in the shape of a saucer; its power depends on its diameter.

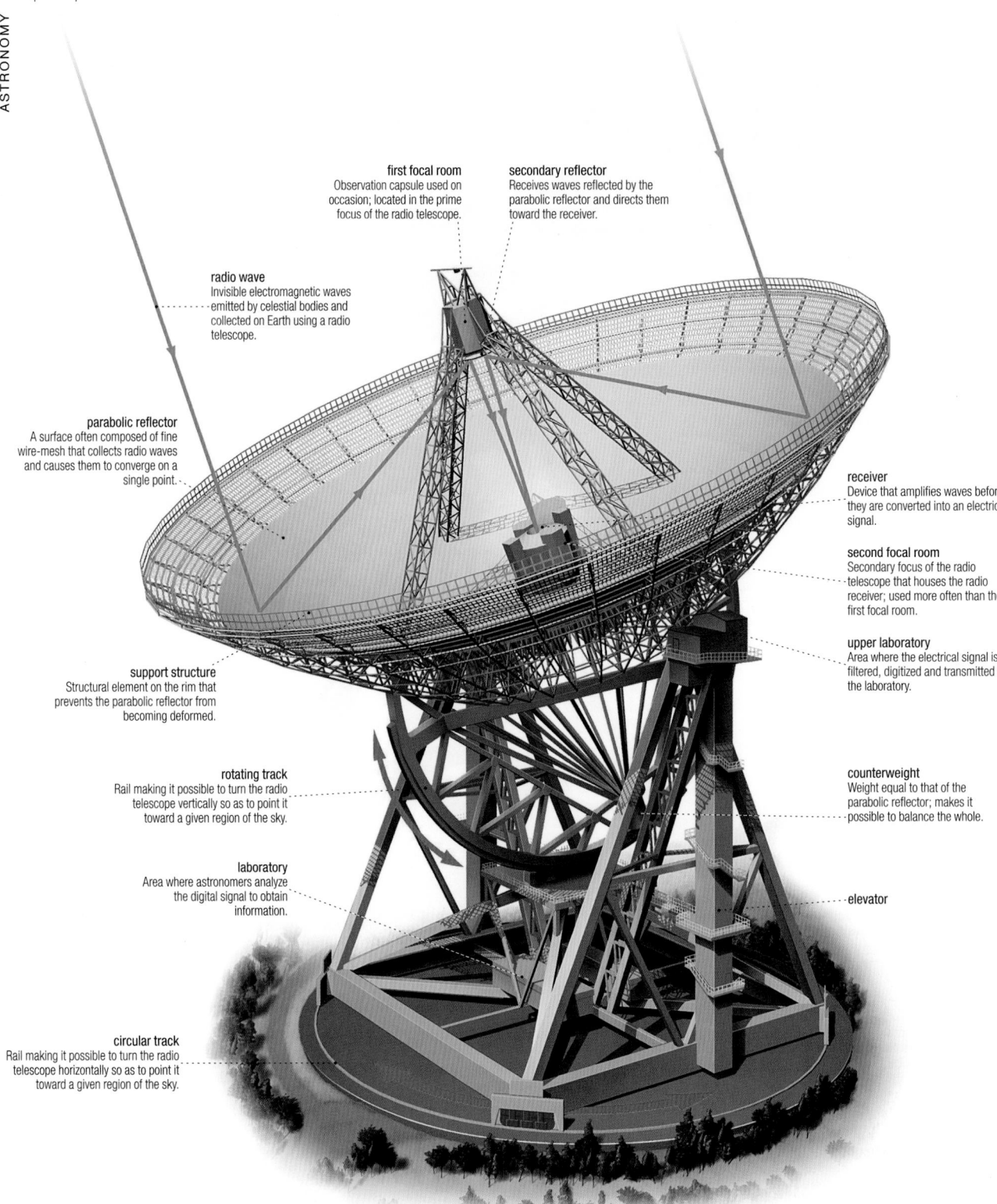

first focal room
Observation capsule used on occasion; located in the prime focus of the radio telescope.

secondary reflector
Receives waves reflected by the parabolic reflector and directs them toward the receiver.

radio wave
Invisible electromagnetic waves emitted by celestial bodies and collected on Earth using a radio telescope.

parabolic reflector
A surface often composed of fine wire-mesh that collects radio waves and causes them to converge on a single point.

receiver
Device that amplifies waves before they are converted into an electrical signal.

second focal room
Secondary focus of the radio telescope that houses the radio receiver; used more often than the first focal room.

upper laboratory
Area where the electrical signal is filtered, digitized and transmitted to the laboratory.

support structure
Structural element on the rim that prevents the parabolic reflector from becoming deformed.

rotating track
Rail making it possible to turn the radio telescope vertically so as to point it toward a given region of the sky.

counterweight
Weight equal to that of the parabolic reflector; makes it possible to balance the whole.

laboratory
Area where astronomers analyze the digital signal to obtain information.

elevator

circular track
Rail making it possible to turn the radio telescope horizontally so as to point it toward a given region of the sky.

space telescope

Telescope placed in orbit above Earth's atmosphere, making it possible to observe the universe without the interference of the atmosphere.

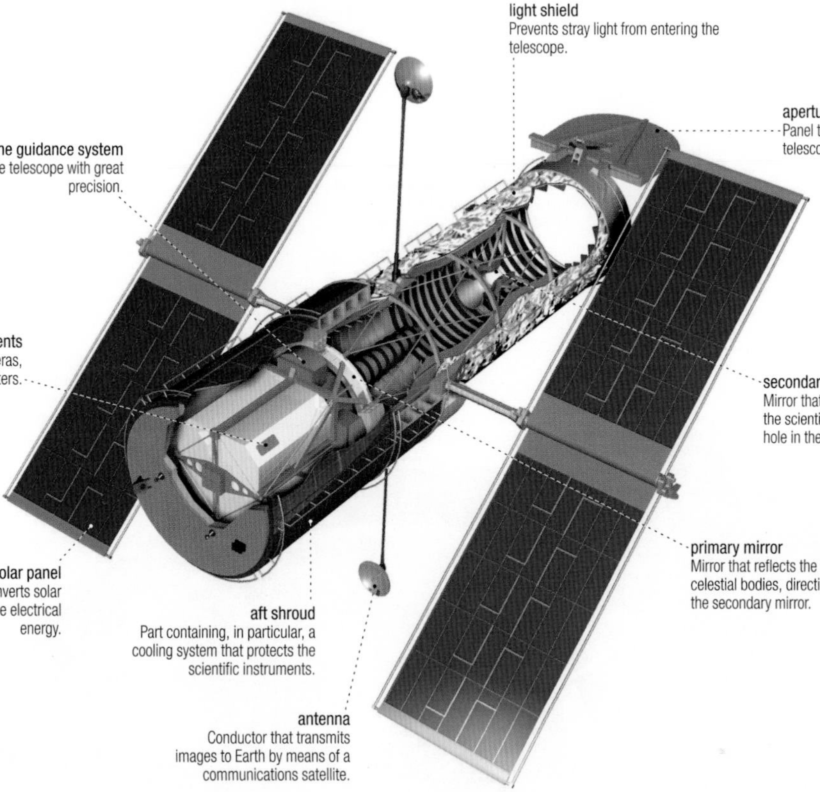

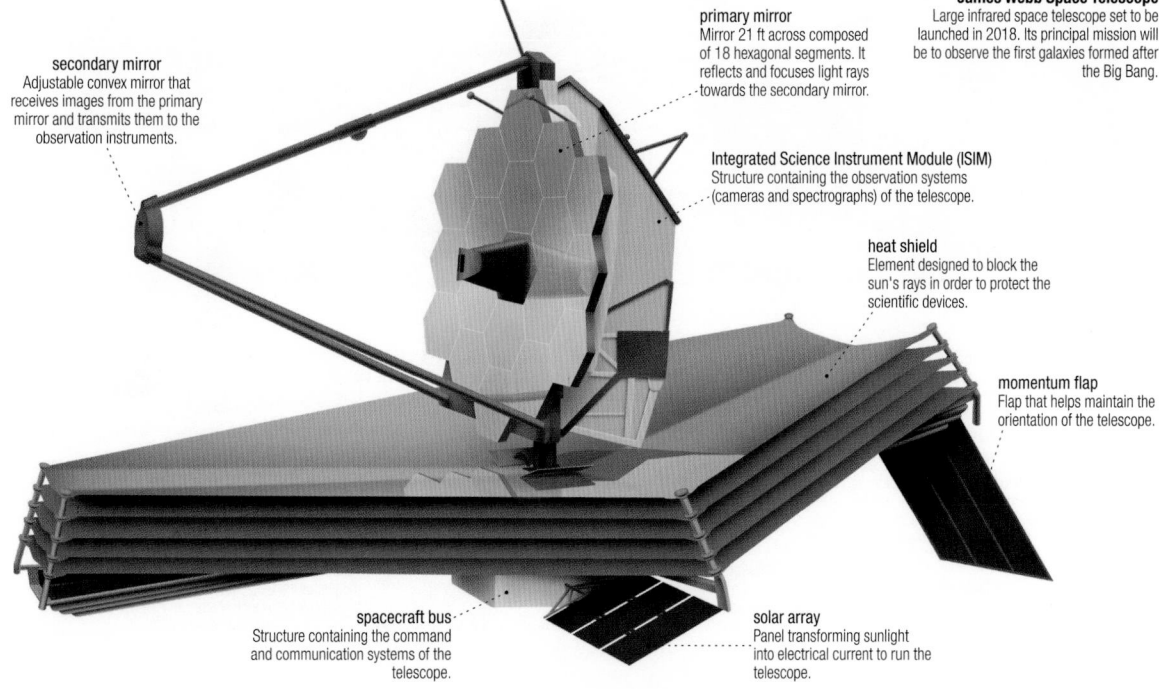

Hubble Space Telescope
Space telescope with two mirrors, covering the entire spectrum of light. It was launched into orbit in 1990.

light shield
Prevents stray light from entering the telescope.

aperture door
Panel that opens and closes over the telescope's optical system.

fine guidance system
Makes it possible to point and control the telescope with great precision.

scientific instruments
These include cameras, spectrographs and photometers.

secondary mirror
Mirror that sends light back toward the scientific instruments through a hole in the primary mirror.

solar panel
Power supply device that converts solar energy into immediately usable electrical energy.

primary mirror
Mirror that reflects the light of celestial bodies, directing it toward the secondary mirror.

aft shroud
Part containing, in particular, a cooling system that protects the scientific instruments.

antenna
Conductor that transmits images to Earth by means of a communications satellite.

James Webb Space Telescope
Large infrared space telescope set to be launched in 2018. Its principal mission will be to observe the first galaxies formed after the Big Bang.

secondary mirror
Adjustable convex mirror that receives images from the primary mirror and transmits them to the observation instruments.

primary mirror
Mirror 21 ft across composed of 18 hexagonal segments. It reflects and focuses light rays towards the secondary mirror.

Integrated Science Instrument Module (ISIM)
Structure containing the observation systems (cameras and spectrographs) of the telescope.

heat shield
Element designed to block the sun's rays in order to protect the scientific devices.

momentum flap
Flap that helps maintain the orientation of the telescope.

spacecraft bus
Structure containing the command and communication systems of the telescope.

solar array
Panel transforming sunlight into electrical current to run the telescope.

ASTRONOMY

astronomical observatory

Building specially designed to house a large telescope.

cross section of an astronomical observatory

external view

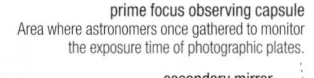

dome shutter
Upper part of the dome that opens so that light can enter the telescope.

rotating dome
Roof of the observatory that pivots on itself so that all parts of the sky can be observed.

prime focus observing capsule
Area where astronomers once gathered to monitor the exposure time of photographic plates.

telescope
Optical instrument that uses an objective mirror to observe celestial bodies.

secondary mirror
Mirror that intercepts light and redirects it toward the Cassegrain focus through a hole in the center of the primary mirror.

horseshoe mount
Mount used to support a large telescope and point it toward the celestial pole.

hour angle gear
Drive mechanism allowing the telescope to follow the polar axis.

prime focus
Focal point of the primary mirror where the light rays concentrate.

light
Emitted by the celestial body, light is sent back toward the Cassegrain focus by the primary and secondary mirrors.

exterior dome shell
Protects against foul weather.

telescope base
Pedestal on which the telescope mount rests.

flat mirror
Adjustable mirror making it possible to choose the location of the focus.

polar axis
Axis parallel to Earth's axis of rotation; its rotation is opposite to that of Earth, making it possible to capture fixed images of an observed celestial body.

primary mirror
Mirror that reflects the light of celestial bodies, directing it toward the prime focus.

coudé focus
Focal point located at a distance from the telescope, obtained using a series of mirrors; stationary, it is used to conduct complex analyses and experiments.

laboratory
Area where the chemical composition of obse celestial bodies is studied using spectrosco

observation post
Area where most observations are carried out.

Cassegrain focus
Focal point where the image forms; located behind the primary mirror.

interior dome shell
Regulates the temperature of the telescope so as to avoid air turbulence and prevent the mirror from becoming deformed.

astronomical observatory

binocular telescope
Telescope composed of two mirrors mounted on a shared base.

Mount Graham binocular telescope
Telescope composed of two mirrors 27.5 ft in diameter located on Mount Graham, in Arizona, at over 10,500 ft altitude.

external view

sliding shutter
Structural element that slides in order to shutter a door.

binocular telescope
Telescope composed of two mirrors mounted on a shared base.

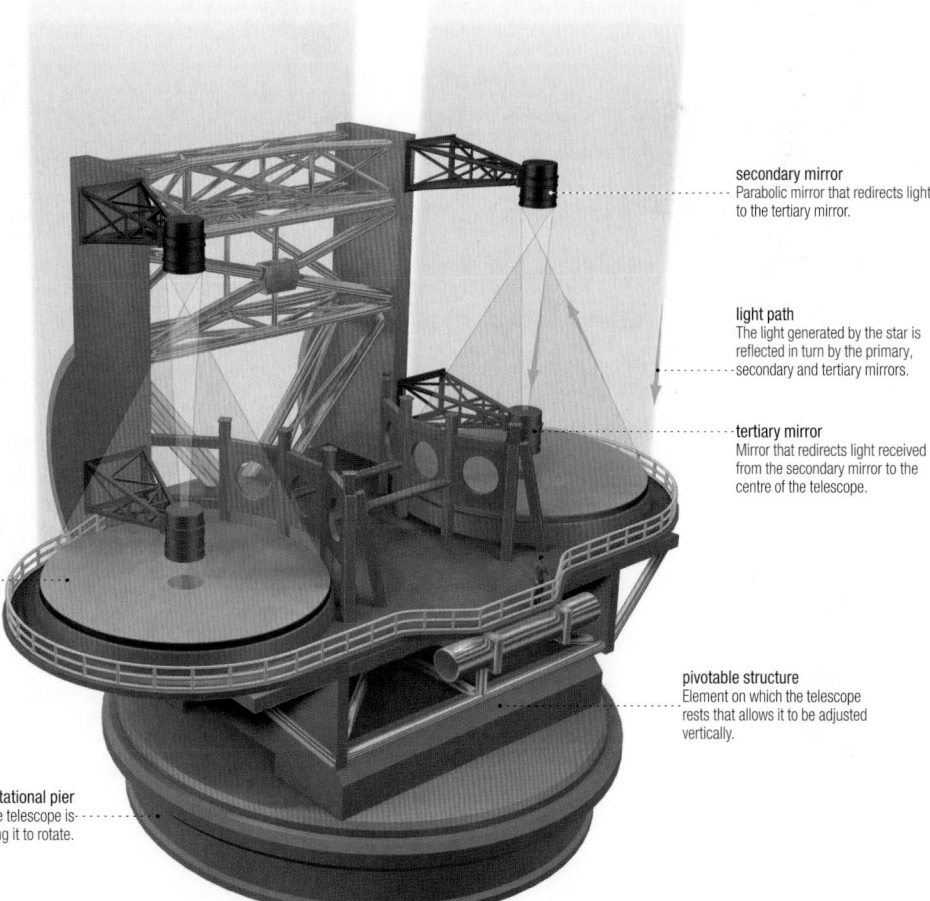

secondary mirror
Parabolic mirror that redirects light to the tertiary mirror.

light path
The light generated by the star is reflected in turn by the primary, secondary and tertiary mirrors.

tertiary mirror
Mirror that redirects light received from the secondary mirror to the centre of the telescope.

primary mirror
Mirror that reflects and focuses light towards the secondary mirror.

pivotable structure
Element on which the telescope rests that allows it to be adjusted vertically.

rotational pier
Base on which the telescope is mounted, allowing it to rotate.

space probe

Unmanned craft launched in the direction of a celestial body in the solar system for purposes of studying it.

examples of space probes

Since the end of the 1950s, over 125 space probes have been launched to study the planets and satellites of the solar system.

Pioneer 10 (Jupiter, 1972–2003)
In 1973, Pioneer-10, en route to Jupiter, became the first probe to cross the asteroid belt.

Mariner 10 (Mercury, 1973–1975)
Mariner 10 photographed the surface of the planet Mercury three times in the mid-1970s, revealing a world quite similar to that of our Moon.

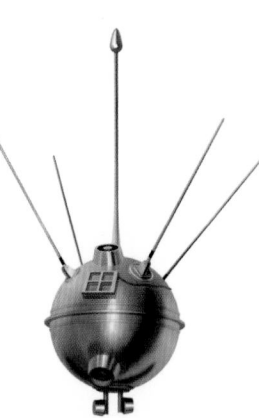

Luna 1 (Moon, 1959)
Soviet probe launched in 1959, the first spacecraft to pass close to the moon.

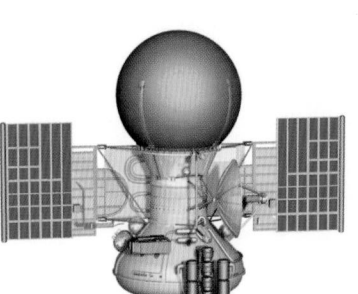

Venera 9 (Venus, 1975)
In 1975, Venera-9 transmitted the first photograph of the Venusian soil before it was crushed by the planet's atmospheric pressure.

Voyager (gas planets, 1977–)
Voyager 1 and 2 transformed our knowledge of giant planets; over 30 years after they were launched in 1977, they continue to explore the heliosheath, the outermost region of the solar system.

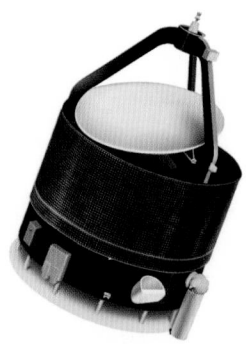

Giotto (Halley's Comet, 1985–1992)
European probe launched in 1985, which approached to within 370 mi of Halley's Comet.

Magellan (Venus, 1989–1994)
While in orbit around Venus from 1990 to 1994, Magellan mapped 98% of its surface.

Galileo (Jupiter, 1989–2003)
The first probe to thrust into orbit around Jupiter (1995), Galileo also explored the planet's four largest satellites.

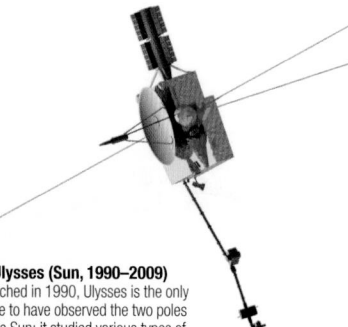
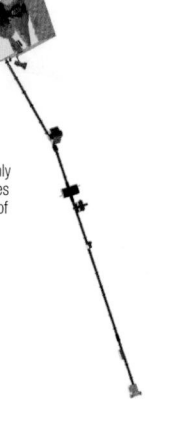

Ulysses (Sun, 1990–2009)
Launched in 1990, Ulysses is the only probe to have observed the two poles of the Sun; it studied various types of solar rays.

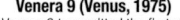

space probe

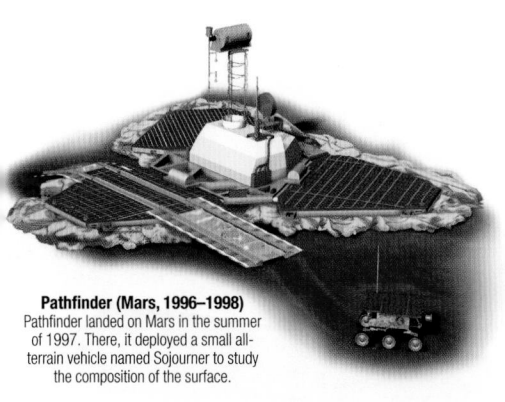

Pathfinder (Mars, 1996–1998)
Pathfinder landed on Mars in the summer of 1997. There, it deployed a small all-terrain vehicle named Sojourner to study the composition of the surface.

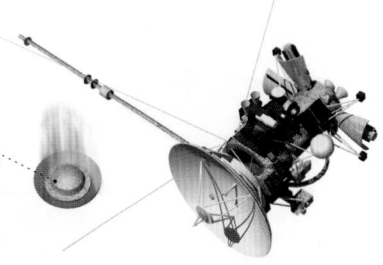

Huygens (Titan, 1997–2005)
The Huygens probe was released by Cassini after it reached orbit around Saturn; Huygens landed on Titan early in 2005.

Cassini (Saturn, 1997–)
The probe, launched in 1997, has been in orbit around Saturn since 2004.

Mars Reconnaissance Orbiter (Mars, 2005–)
American probe launched in 2005; placed in orbit around Mars, its mission is to study the planet's surface, atmosphere, and climate.

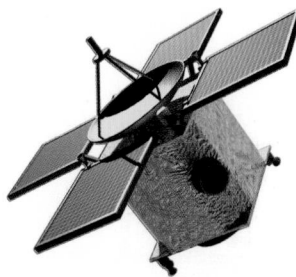

NEAR Shoemaker (Eros asteroid, 1996–2001)
This probe thrust into orbit around the asteroid Eros in 2000 and landed on it in 2001.

Stardust (Wild-2 comet, 1999–2006)
Stardust's mission was to collect fragments of interstellar dust, hence its name; it returned to Earth in 2006.

2001 Mars Odyssey (Mars, 2001–)
Mars Odyssey was put into orbit around Mars in 2001 to study its geology and environment; it has detected large amounts of frozen water just below the surface.

impactor
Projectile sent from the probe to strike the surface of the comet in order to dislodge debris for analysis.

Phoenix (Mars, 2007–2008)
American probe launched in August 2007, which landed on Mars in May 2008; it studied the soil in the planet's arctic region.

Deep Impact (Tempel 1 comet, 2005)
American probe launched in January 2005; it studied the composition of Comet Tempel 1 by causing a collision between the comet and an impactor.

New Horizons (Pluto, 2006–)
This American probe, launched in 2006, will be the first to reach Pluto and its satellite, Charon, in 2015; it will then study the Kuiper belt.

space probe

orbiter (Viking, 1976–1980)
Part of the Viking mission that flew over
Mars before placing itself in orbit in order
to study the planet.

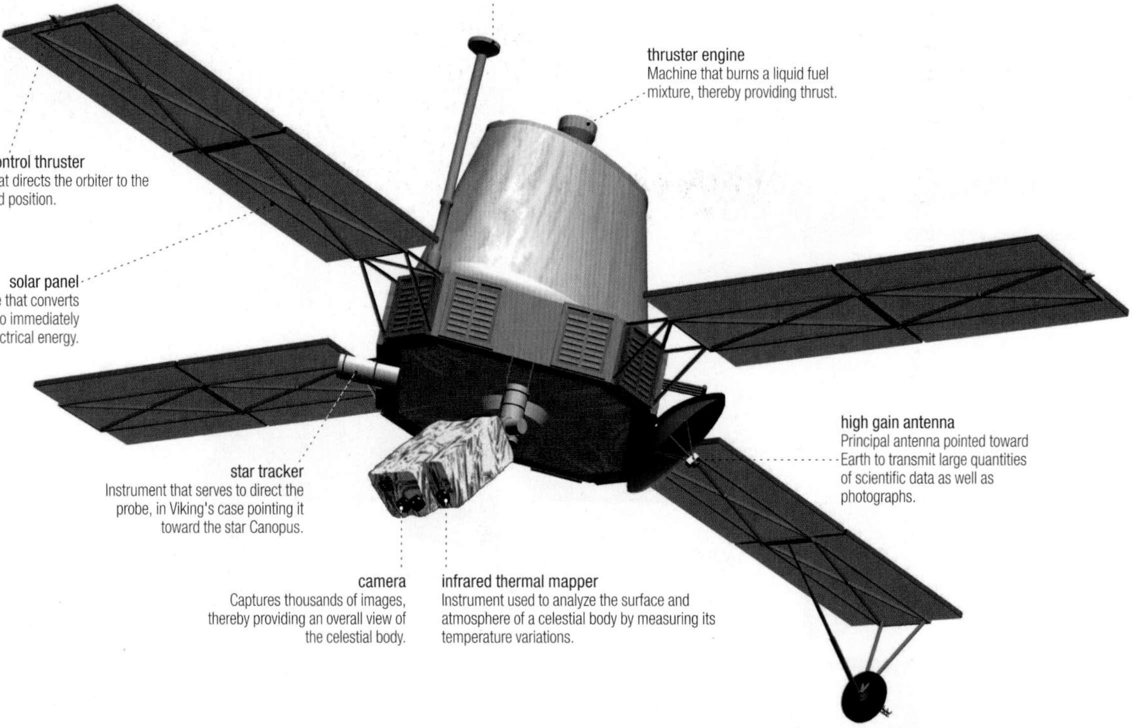

low gain antenna
Secondary antenna used to
communicate with Earth when the
high gain antenna cannot be used.

thruster engine
Machine that burns a liquid fuel
mixture, thereby providing thrust.

attitude control thruster
Small rocket engine that directs the orbiter to the
desired position.

solar panel
Power supply device that converts
solar energy into immediately
usable electrical energy.

star tracker
Instrument that serves to direct the
probe, in Viking's case pointing it
toward the star Canopus.

camera
Captures thousands of images,
thereby providing an overall view of
the celestial body.

infrared thermal mapper
Instrument used to analyze the surface and
atmosphere of a celestial body by measuring its
temperature variations.

high gain antenna
Principal antenna pointed toward
Earth to transmit large quantities
of scientific data as well as
photographs.

lander (Viking)
Spacecraft designed to touch down on
the surface of Mars so as to study it.

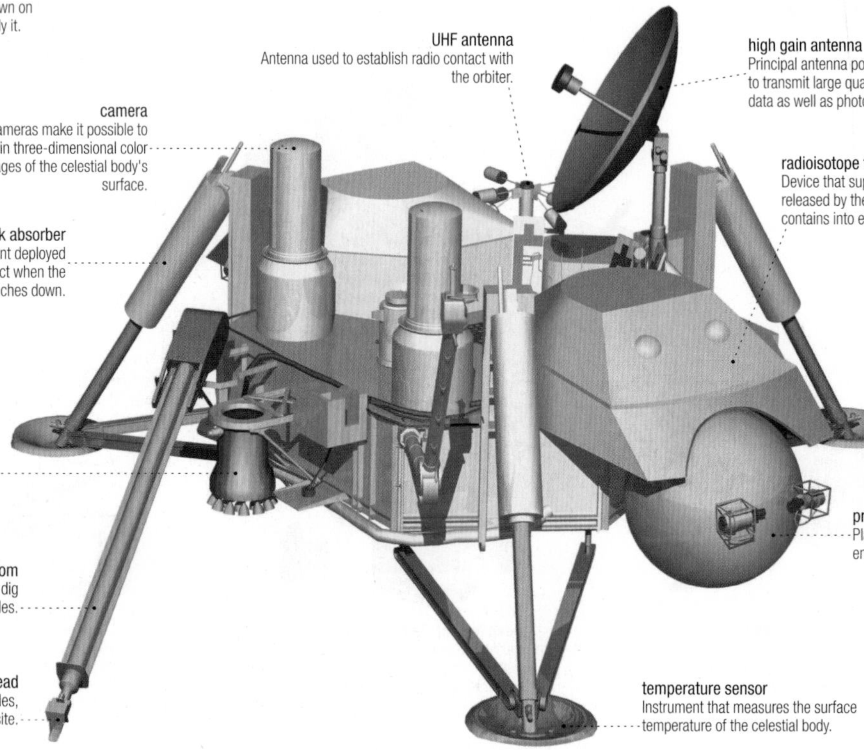

UHF antenna
Antenna used to establish radio contact with
the orbiter.

camera
Two cameras make it possible to
obtain three-dimensional color
images of the celestial body's
surface.

high gain antenna
Principal antenna pointed toward Earth
to transmit large quantities of scientific
data as well as photographs.

shock absorber
Piece of equipment deployed
to cushion the impact when the
lander touches down.

radioisotope thermoelectric generator
Device that supplies electrical power; converts the
released by the radioactive decay of a substance
contains into electricity.

terminal descent engine
Rocket engine that allows the
lander to slow down before it
touches the ground.

furlable boom
Mobile extension arm serving to dig
into the soil and collect samples.

collector head
Shovel used to collect soil samples,
which are analyzed on-site.

propellant tank
Place where fuel for the descent
engines is stored.

temperature sensor
Instrument that measures the surface
temperature of the celestial body.

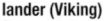

spacesuit

A pressurized watertight suit that provides the astronaut with oxygen and protects against solar rays and meteorites during space walks.

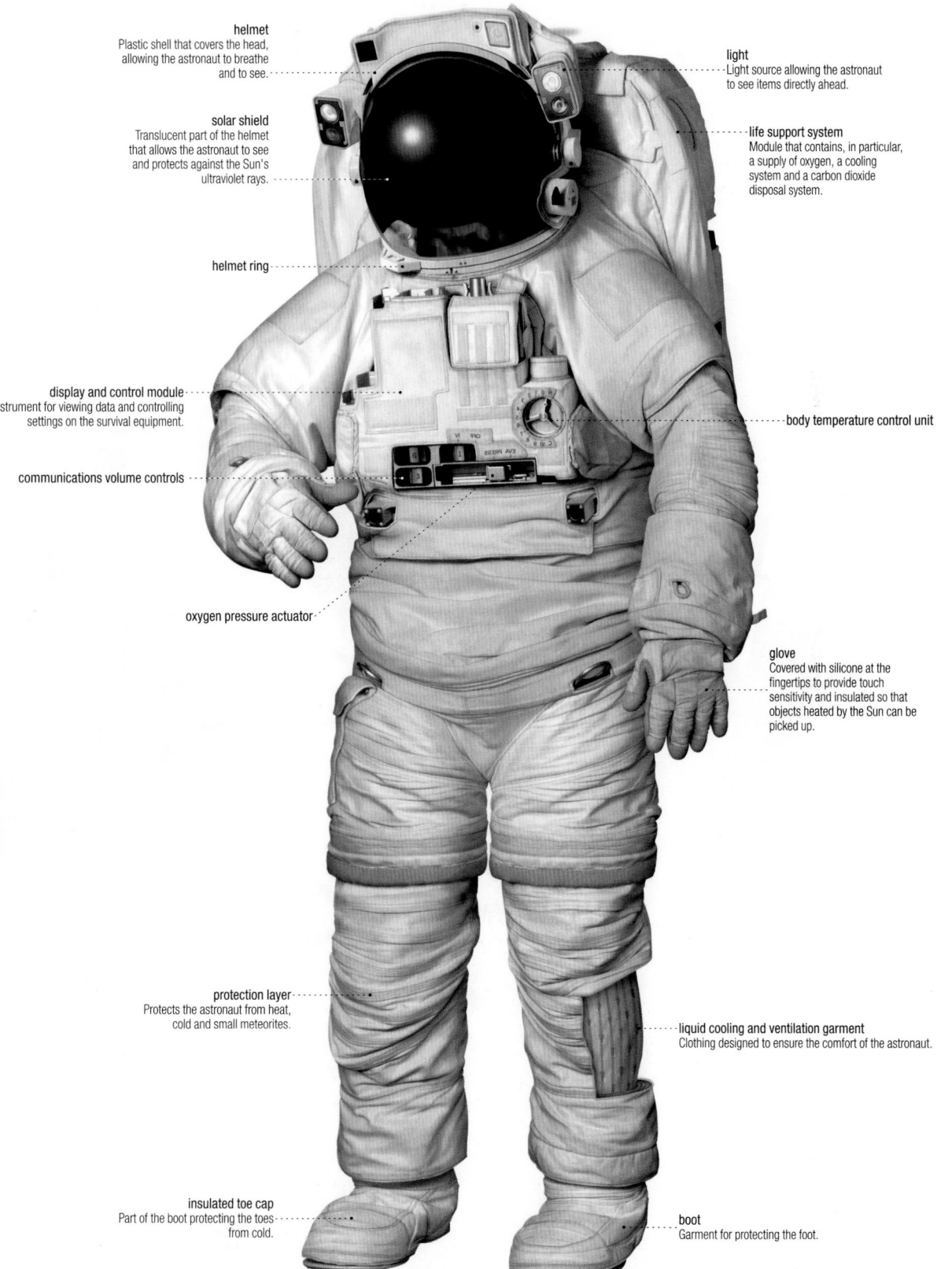

helmet
Plastic shell that covers the head, allowing the astronaut to breathe and to see.

solar shield
Translucent part of the helmet that allows the astronaut to see and protects against the Sun's ultraviolet rays.

helmet ring

display and control module
Instrument for viewing data and controlling settings on the survival equipment.

communications volume controls

oxygen pressure actuator

protection layer
Protects the astronaut from heat, cold and small meteorites.

insulated toe cap
Part of the boot protecting the toes from cold.

light
Light source allowing the astronaut to see items directly ahead.

life support system
Module that contains, in particular, a supply of oxygen, a cooling system and a carbon dioxide disposal system.

body temperature control unit

glove
Covered with silicone at the fingertips to provide touch sensitivity and insulated so that objects heated by the Sun can be picked up.

liquid cooling and ventilation garment
Clothing designed to ensure the comfort of the astronaut.

boot
Garment for protecting the foot.

international space station

Complex made up of some 10 modules in orbit around Earth; built and assembled by 15 countries, it is used to conduct scientific and technological research in a nearly weightless environment.

general view

mating adaptor
Connector on which the space shuttle orbiter docks during most of the station's supply and assembly missions.

U.S. experiment module
Designed to carry out scientific activities, particularly in the life sciences and in physics.

European experiment module
Designed to conduct research in the life and materials sciences, in physics and in numerous other technologies.

truss structure
Truss frame attached to the U.S. laboratory.

U.S. habitation module
Designed to provide living space as well as supplemental power and data storage.

Russian module
Generates the station's electrical energy using photovoltaic cells.

Automated Transfer Vehicle (ATV)
Vehicle for resupplying the Space Station.

Soyuz crew return vehicle
Space vehicle used to return the crew to earth in case of emergency.

international space station

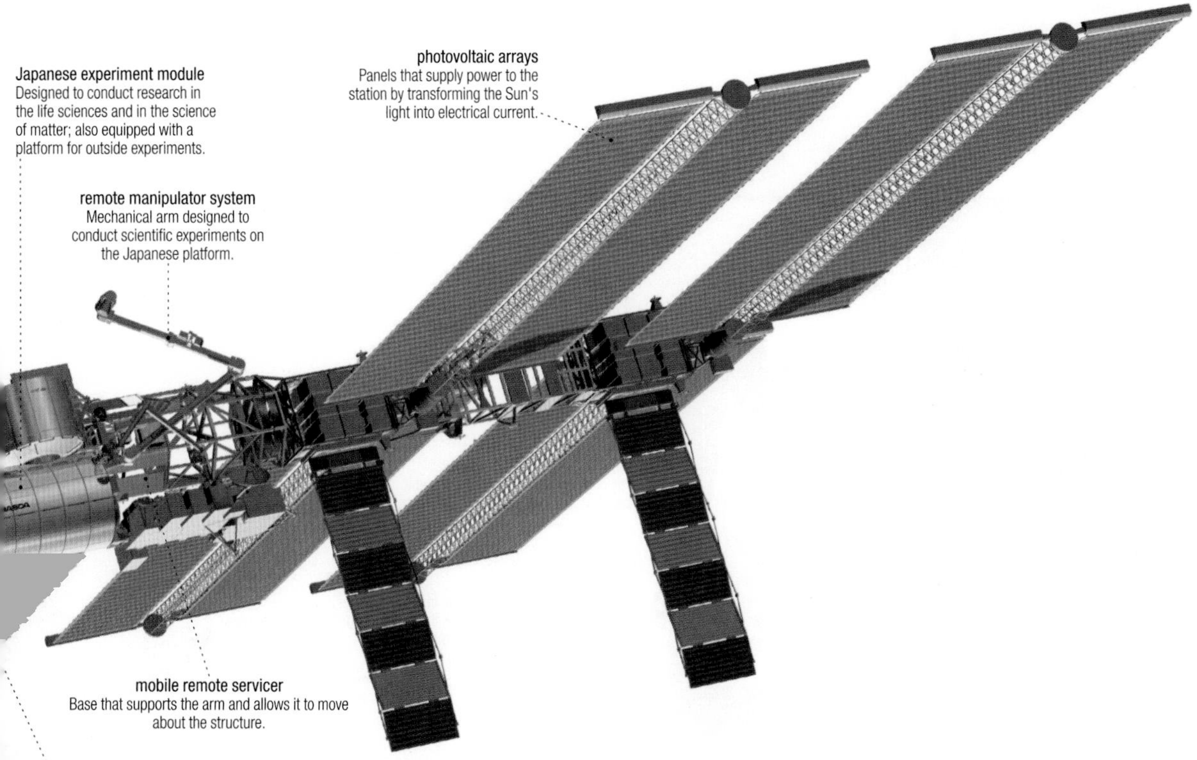

Japanese experiment module
Designed to conduct research in
the life sciences and in the science
of matter; also equipped with a
platform for outside experiments.

remote manipulator system
Mechanical arm designed to
conduct scientific experiments on
the Japanese platform.

photovoltaic arrays
Panels that supply power to the
station by transforming the Sun's
light into electrical current.

mobile remote servicer
Base that supports the arm and allows it to move
about the structure.

radiators
Corrugated panels ensuring heat
evacuation from the station.

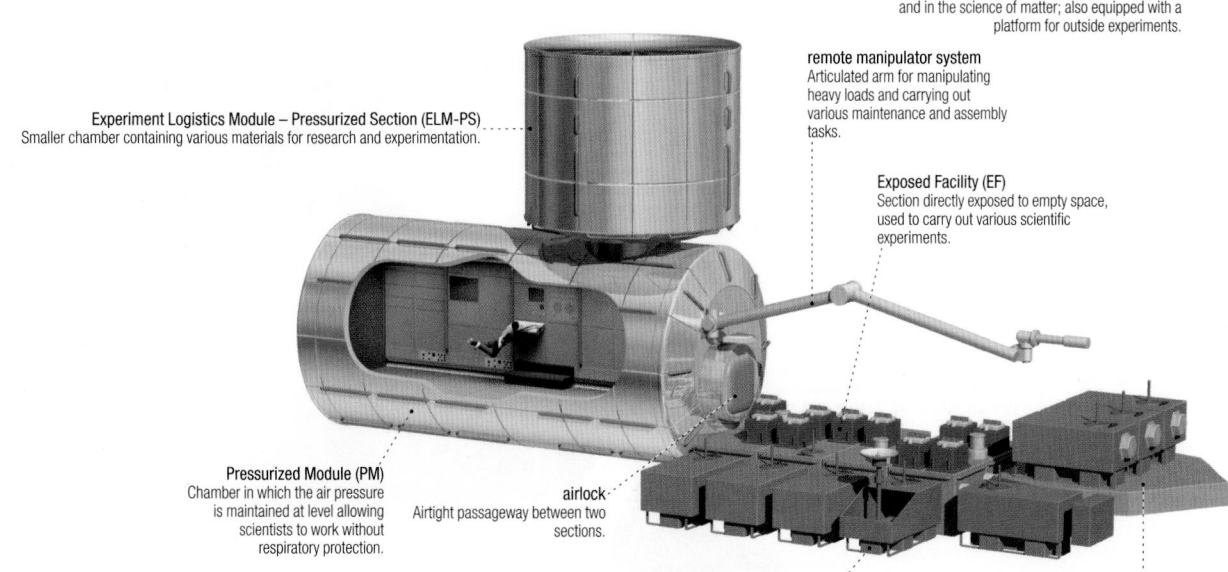

**cross section of the Japanese
experimental module**
Designed to conduct research in the life sciences
and in the science of matter; also equipped with a
platform for outside experiments.

remote manipulator system
Articulated arm for manipulating
heavy loads and carrying out
various maintenance and assembly
tasks.

Exposed Facility (EF)
Section directly exposed to empty space,
used to carry out various scientific
experiments.

Experiment Logistics Module – Pressurized Section (ELM-PS)
Smaller chamber containing various materials for research and experimentation.

Pressurized Module (PM)
Chamber in which the air pressure
is maintained at level allowing
scientists to work without
respiratory protection.

airlock
Airtight passageway between two
sections.

Inter-Orbit Communication System (ICS)
Instruments allowing for communication between the
Space Station and Earth.

**Experiment Logistics Module – Exposed
Facility (ELM-EF)**
Installation for the storage of scientific material,
maintenance equipment and various reserves.

spaceship

Crewed space vehicle, reusable or not, used to transport humans into space. It is also equipped with instruments relaying data and images.

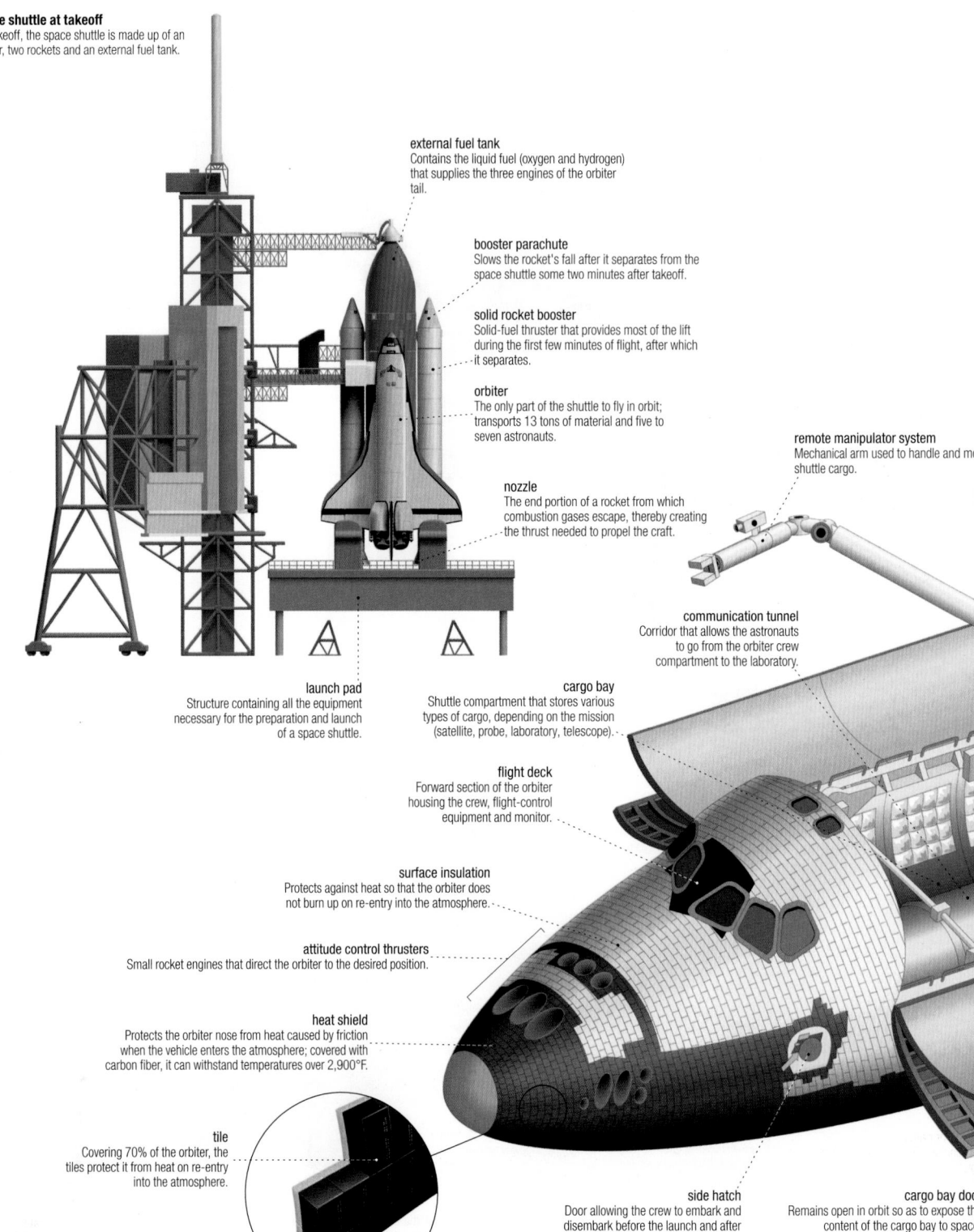

space shuttle at takeoff
On takeoff, the space shuttle is made up of an orbiter, two rockets and an external fuel tank.

external fuel tank
Contains the liquid fuel (oxygen and hydrogen) that supplies the three engines of the orbiter tail.

booster parachute
Slows the rocket's fall after it separates from the space shuttle some two minutes after takeoff.

solid rocket booster
Solid-fuel thruster that provides most of the lift during the first few minutes of flight, after which it separates.

orbiter
The only part of the shuttle to fly in orbit; transports 13 tons of material and five to seven astronauts.

remote manipulator system
Mechanical arm used to handle and move shuttle cargo.

nozzle
The end portion of a rocket from which combustion gases escape, thereby creating the thrust needed to propel the craft.

communication tunnel
Corridor that allows the astronauts to go from the orbiter crew compartment to the laboratory.

launch pad
Structure containing all the equipment necessary for the preparation and launch of a space shuttle.

cargo bay
Shuttle compartment that stores various types of cargo, depending on the mission (satellite, probe, laboratory, telescope).

flight deck
Forward section of the orbiter housing the crew, flight-control equipment and monitor.

surface insulation
Protects against heat so that the orbiter does not burn up on re-entry into the atmosphere.

attitude control thrusters
Small rocket engines that direct the orbiter to the desired position.

heat shield
Protects the orbiter nose from heat caused by friction when the vehicle enters the atmosphere; covered with carbon fiber, it can withstand temperatures over 2,900°F.

tile
Covering 70% of the orbiter, the tiles protect it from heat on re-entry into the atmosphere.

side hatch
Door allowing the crew to embark and disembark before the launch and after the return to Earth.

cargo bay door
Remains open in orbit so as to expose the content of the cargo bay to space.

spaceship

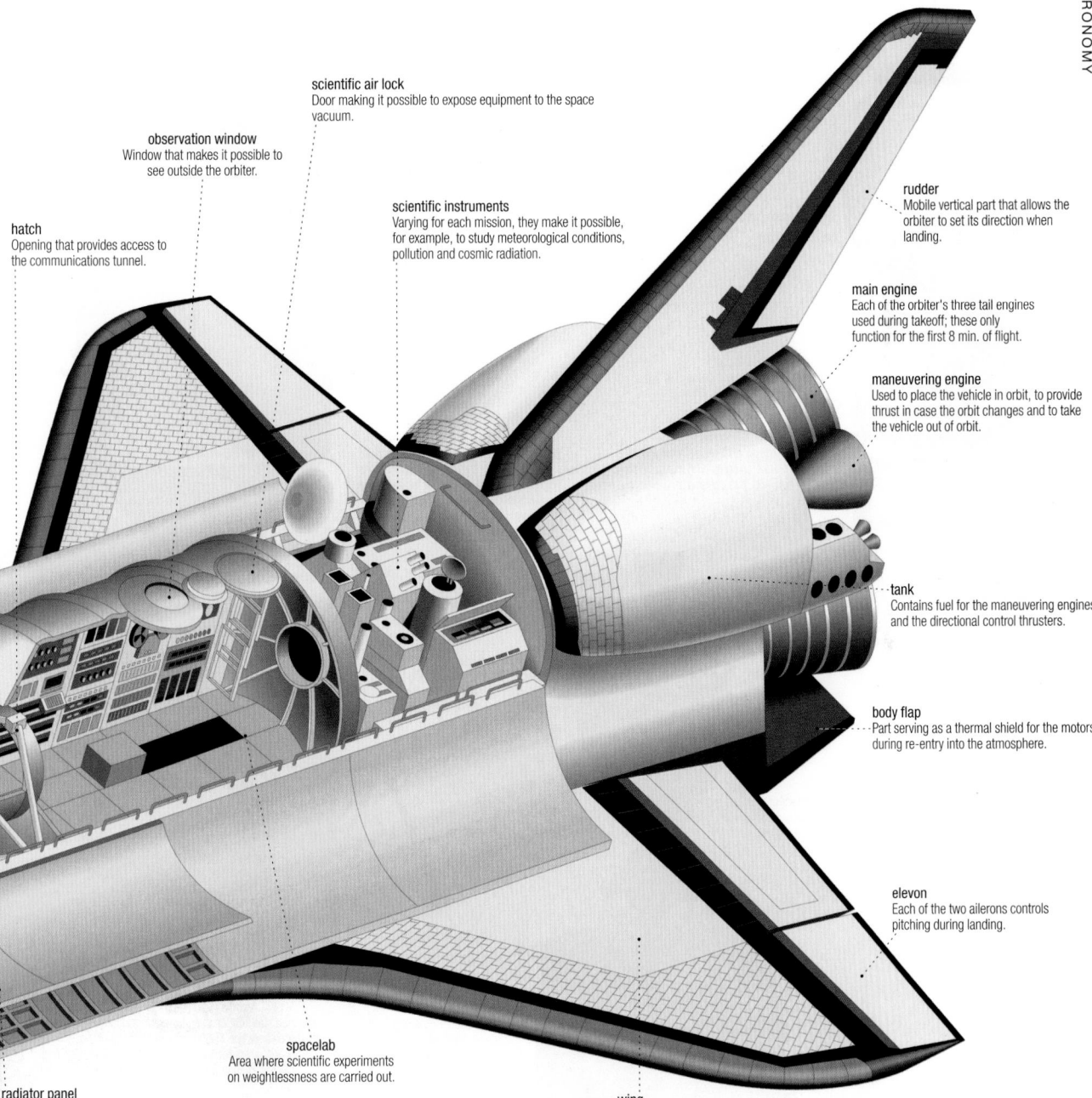

orbiter
The only part of the shuttle to fly in orbit; can transport 13 tons of material and five to seven astronauts.

scientific air lock
Door making it possible to expose equipment to the space vacuum.

observation window
Window that makes it possible to see outside the orbiter.

scientific instruments
Varying for each mission, they make it possible, for example, to study meteorological conditions, pollution and cosmic radiation.

hatch
Opening that provides access to the communications tunnel.

rudder
Mobile vertical part that allows the orbiter to set its direction when landing.

main engine
Each of the orbiter's three tail engines used during takeoff; these only function for the first 8 min. of flight.

maneuvering engine
Used to place the vehicle in orbit, to provide thrust in case the orbit changes and to take the vehicle out of orbit.

tank
Contains fuel for the maneuvering engines and the directional control thrusters.

body flap
Part serving as a thermal shield for the motors during re-entry into the atmosphere.

elevon
Each of the two ailerons controls pitching during landing.

spacelab
Area where scientific experiments on weightlessness are carried out.

radiator panel
Discharges into space the heat produced by the functioning of onboard equipment.

wing
Horizontal surface acted on by aerodynamic forces that keep the orbiter aloft in the atmosphere.

spaceship

examples of spaceships

docking assembly
Electronic device that guides ships as it docks with the Space Station.

orbital module
Section of the ship used as living quarters by the cosmonauts during space travel.

periscope
Optical instrument used for observing objects outside of one's field of vision.

descent module
Section of the ship carrying the crew on its return to Earth.

instrumentation and propulsion module
Section of the ship containing navigation and guidance instruments and ship controls as well as the main batteries.

service module
Houses the main propulsion system and supplies energy, electricity, water and other provisions.

command module
Section of the craft where the crew resided during the mission; one astronaut stayed on board during the Moon landing. It was the only section of the Apollo craft to return to Earth.

lunar module
Inhabited section of the craft; enabled two men to walk on the Moon and spend a few days there before returning to dock with the Apollo capsule.

service module
Section of the ship housing the propulsion system and used for storing various provisions, including water.

Soyuz (1967–)
Crewed Russian spaceship, used since the 1960s to carry cosmonauts into orbit, in particular now to the International Space Station.

Orion spacecraft
Section in which the crew will live. This is the only section that will return to Earth.

lunar lander
Vehicle used for landing on the surface of the Moon.

Apollo (1961–1975)
Manned craft that enabled six crews to land on the Moon between 1969 and 1972. On July 20, 1969, Neil Armstrong and Buzz Aldrin became the first men to explore another world.

Orion (2015)
American space exploration vessel in development since 2006. It is meant to replace the space shuttle in resupplying the International Space Station.

space launcher

Rocket that serves to place satellites in Earth's orbit or to send probes into the solar system.

examples of space launchers

Ariane IV (1988–2003)
Rocket of the European Space Agency, replaced in 2003 by riane V, which can handle greater loads.

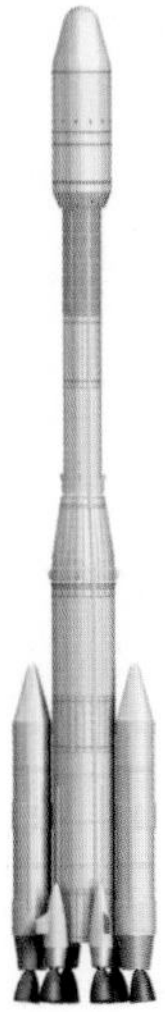

Soyuz (1966–)
Family of Soviet/Russian rockets used since the 1960s to put commercial and military satellites as well as crewed spaceships into orbit.

Saturn V (1967–1973)
The most powerful rocket ever built served to launch the Apollo missions; the only launcher never to have failed.

Titan IV (1989–2005)
auncher used in particular to unch large military satellites.

Delta II (1989–)
In service since 1989, this launcher places meteorological and communications satellites in orbit.

cross section of a space launcher (Ariane V)
In service since 1996, this European launcher transports heavy payloads, including the most powerful communications satellites.

fairing
The tip of the launcher that houses and protects the payload.

satellite
A spacecraft transported by the launcher and placed in orbit around Earth.

payload
Space probe or satellite carried by the launcher.

lower section
Composed of the main cryogenic stage and the solid booster stage.

main cryogenic stage
Central body that ensures propulsion after the solid booster stage separates.

solid booster stage
Provides the main thrust during takeoff before separating from the main cryogenic stage.

upper section
Composed of the storable propellant upper stage and the payload.

payload adaptor
Ensures satellite/launcher interface and is compatible with all satellite platforms.

dual launch structure
Module used to insert two independent payloads into orbit.

vehicle equipment bay
Houses most of the onboard electronic equipment and flight-control systems.

storable propellant upper stage
Upper stage used to propel the payload toward its final orbit.

liquid oxygen tank
Oxygen, burned on contact with liquid hydrogen, serves as engine fuel.

liquid hydrogen tank
Hydrogen, burned on contact with liquid oxygen, serves as engine fuel.

solid rocket booster
Solid-fuel thruster that provides most of the lift during the first few minutes of flight, after which it separates.

rocket engine
Ensures launcher propulsion by means of liquid hydrogen combustion in contact with liquid oxygen.

nozzle
The end portion of a rocket from which combustion gases escape, thereby creating the thrust needed to propel the craft.

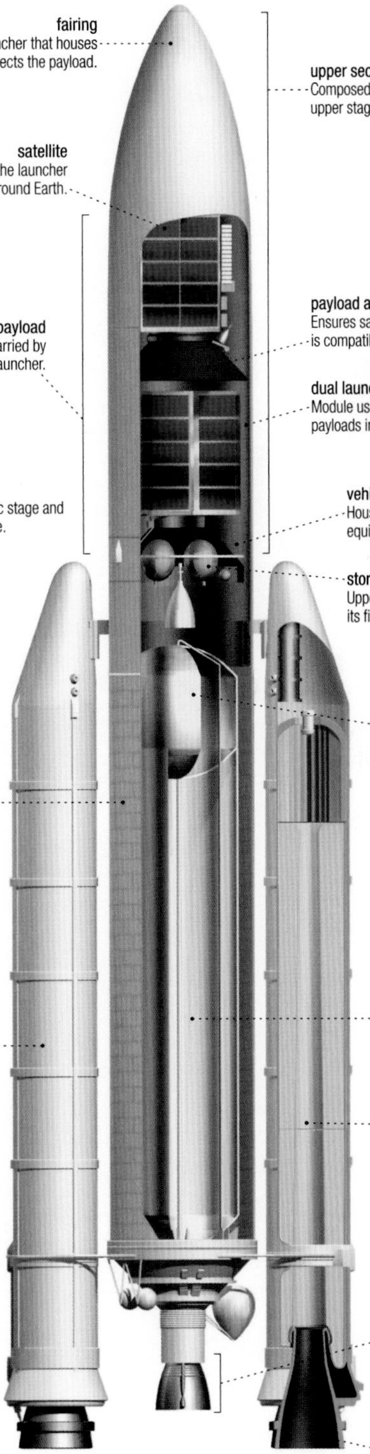

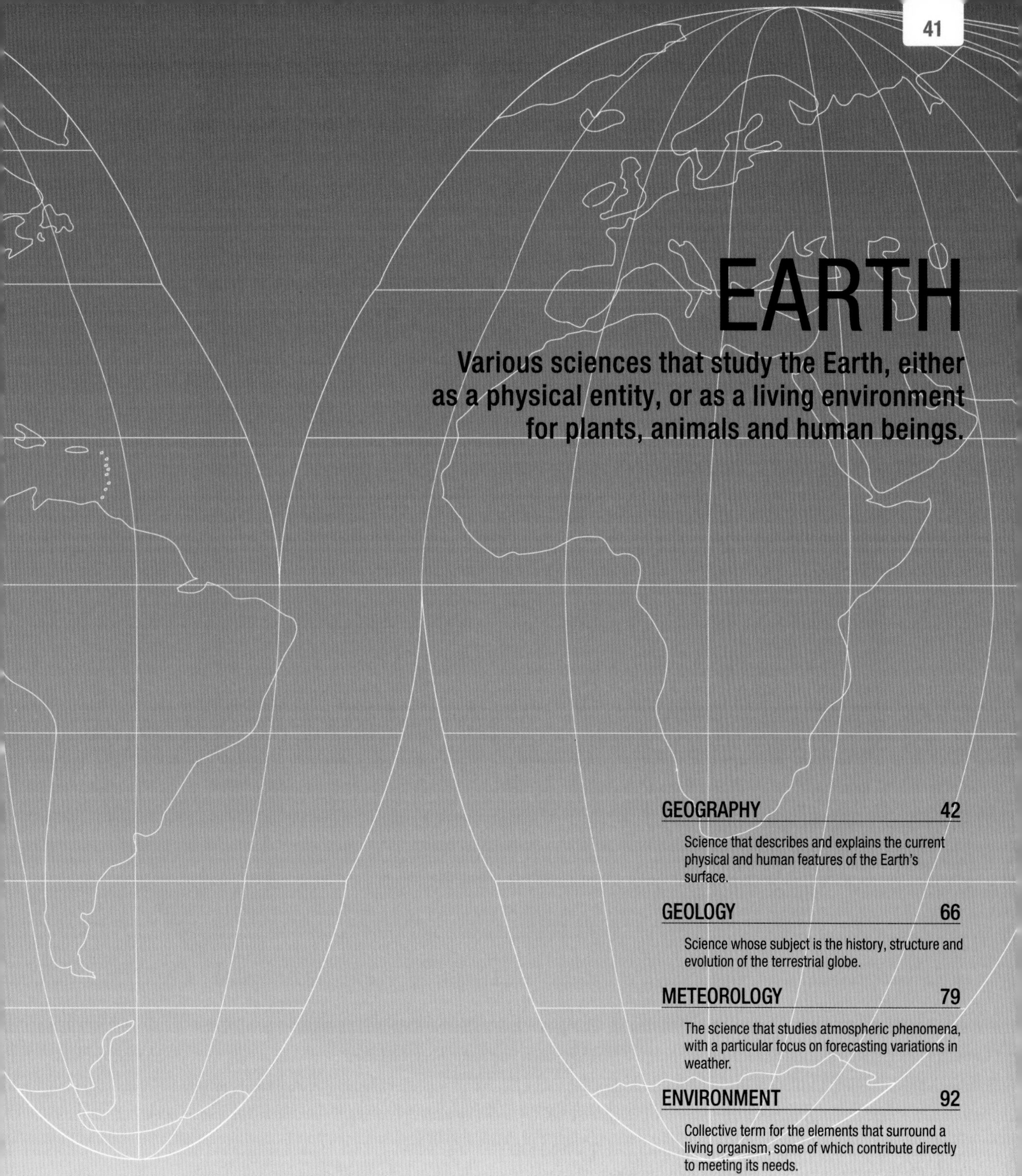

EARTH

Various sciences that study the Earth, either as a physical entity, or as a living environment for plants, animals and human beings.

EARTH

Earth coordinate system

The intersection of two imaginary lines, longitude and latitude, makes it possible to locate a precise point on the Earth's surface.

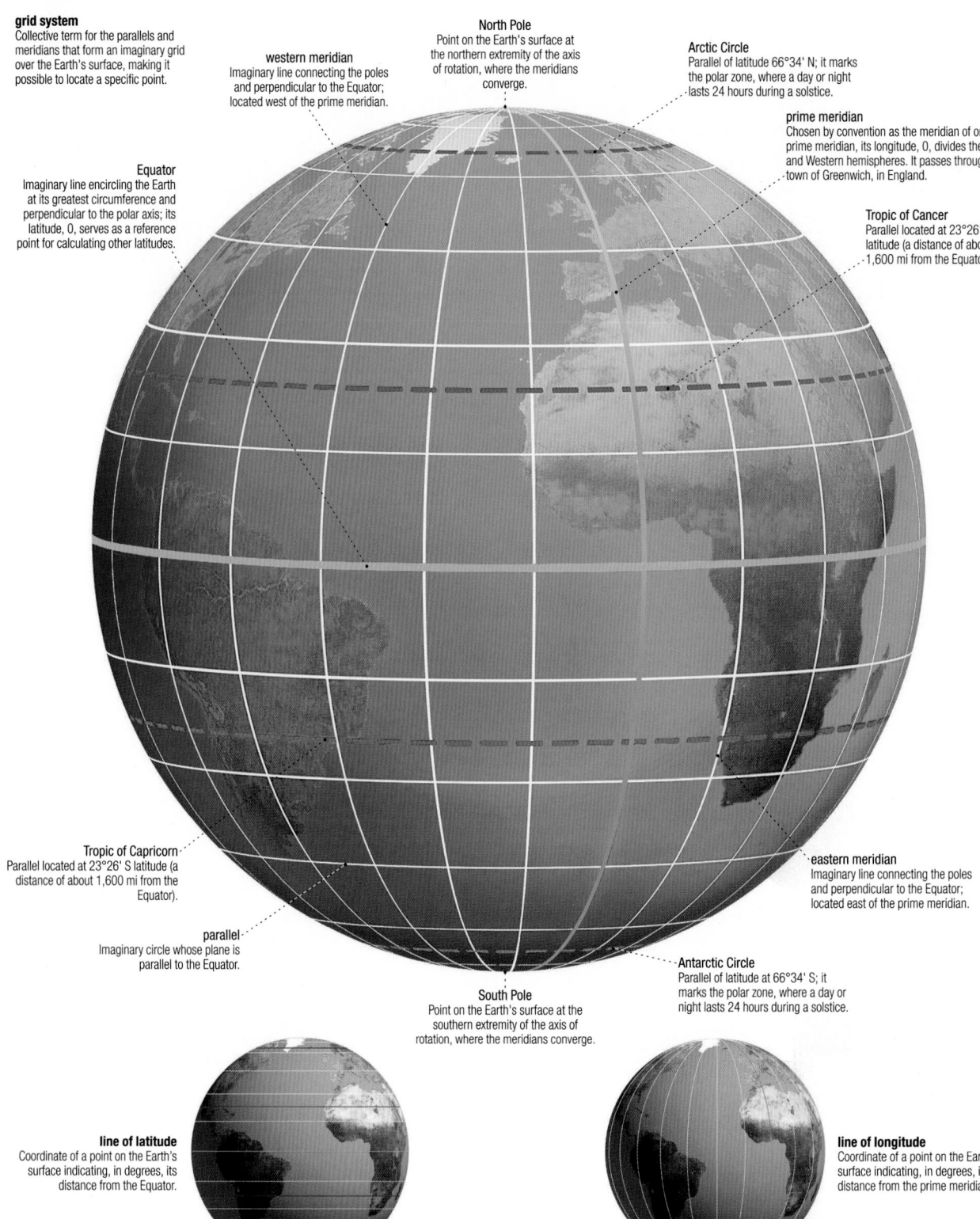

grid system
Collective term for the parallels and meridians that form an imaginary grid over the Earth's surface, making it possible to locate a specific point.

western meridian
Imaginary line connecting the poles and perpendicular to the Equator; located west of the prime meridian.

North Pole
Point on the Earth's surface at the northern extremity of the axis of rotation, where the meridians converge.

Arctic Circle
Parallel of latitude 66°34' N; it marks the polar zone, where a day or night lasts 24 hours during a solstice.

prime meridian
Chosen by convention as the meridian of origin c prime meridian, its longitude, 0, divides the East and Western hemispheres. It passes through the town of Greenwich, in England.

Equator
Imaginary line encircling the Earth at its greatest circumference and perpendicular to the polar axis; its latitude, 0, serves as a reference point for calculating other latitudes.

Tropic of Cancer
Parallel located at 23°26' latitude (a distance of about 1,600 mi from the Equator).

Tropic of Capricorn
Parallel located at 23°26' S latitude (a distance of about 1,600 mi from the Equator).

parallel
Imaginary circle whose plane is parallel to the Equator.

South Pole
Point on the Earth's surface at the southern extremity of the axis of rotation, where the meridians converge.

eastern meridian
Imaginary line connecting the poles and perpendicular to the Equator; located east of the prime meridian.

Antarctic Circle
Parallel of latitude at 66°34' S; it marks the polar zone, where a day or night lasts 24 hours during a solstice.

line of latitude
Coordinate of a point on the Earth's surface indicating, in degrees, its distance from the Equator.

line of longitude
Coordinate of a point on the Earth's surface indicating, in degrees, its distance from the prime meridian.

Earth coordinate system

hemispheres

The globe is divided by convention into four half spheres, using the prime meridian or the Equator as a reference point.

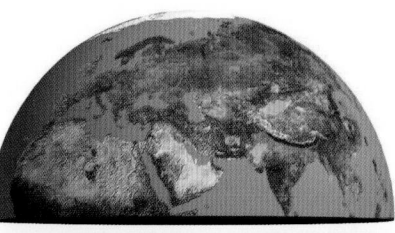

Northern Hemisphere
Northern half of the globe in relation to the Equator.

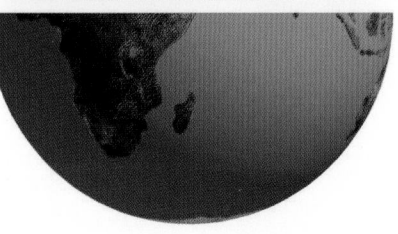

Southern Hemisphere
Southern half of the globe in relation to the Equator.

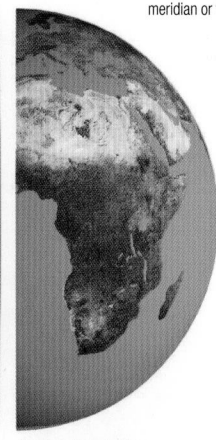

Western Hemisphere
Western half of the globe in relation to the prime meridian.

Eastern Hemisphere
Eastern half of the globe in relation to the prime meridian.

EARTH

azimuthal projection

Representations of the Earth's surface on a plane.

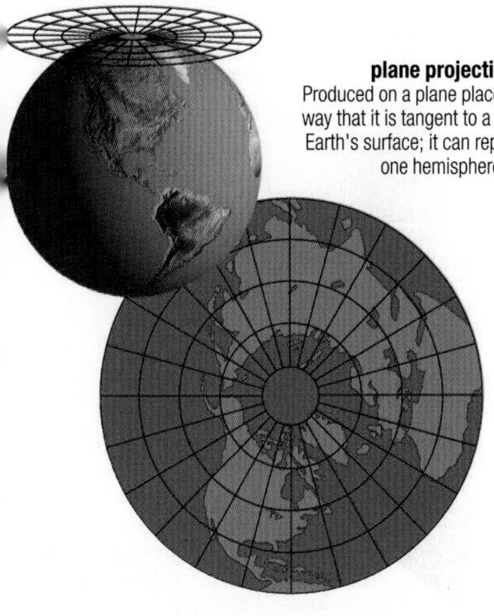

plane projection
Produced on a plane placed in such a way that it is tangent to a point on the Earth's surface; it can represent only one hemisphere.

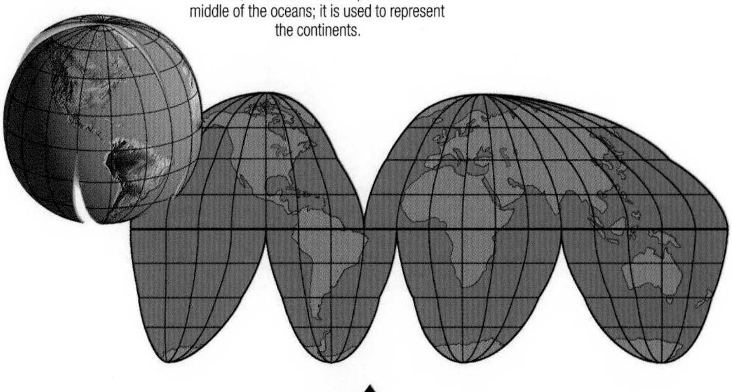

interrupted projection
Results in a map that is not continuous but cut off, the divisions often placed in the middle of the oceans; it is used to represent the continents.

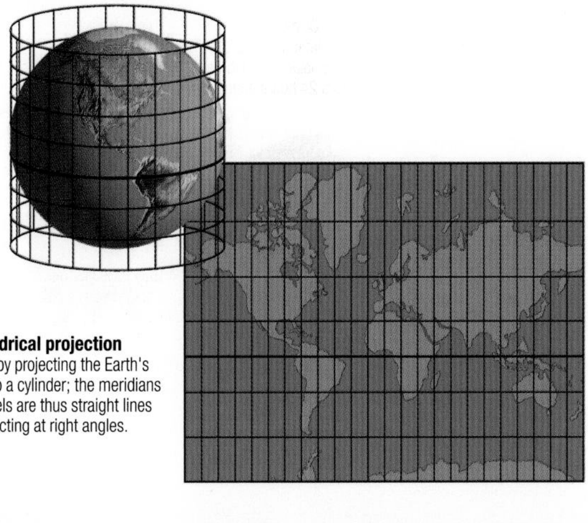

cylindrical projection
Obtained by projecting the Earth's surface onto a cylinder; the meridians and parallels are thus straight lines intersecting at right angles.

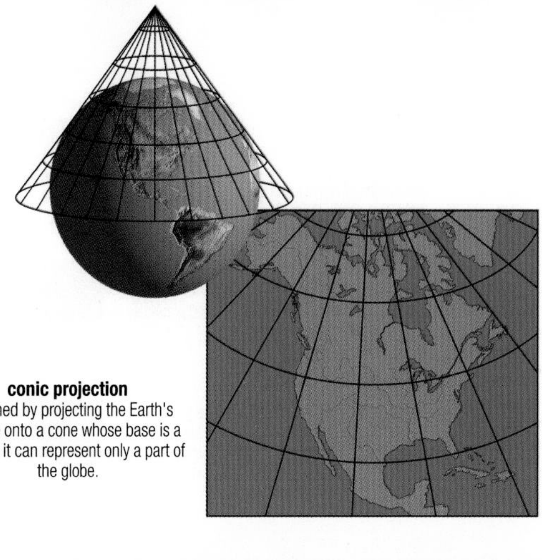

conic projection
Obtained by projecting the Earth's surface onto a cone whose base is a parallel; it can represent only a part of the globe.

EARTH

configuration of the continents

The continents are vast tracts of land surrounded by water; they cover about 30% of the Earth's surface.

planisphere
Map depicting the Earth's two hemispheres.

Norwegian Sea
Section of the Atlantic between Norway and Iceland.

Mediterranean Sea
One of the largest inland seas in the world (965,000 mi^2); it lies between Europe, Africa and Asia and connects to the Atlantic Ocean through the Strait of Gibraltar.

Black Sea
Inland sea (162,000 mi^2) between Eastern Europe and Asia; it opens into the Mediterranean through two straits, the Dardanelles and the Bosporus.

Arctic Ocean
The smallest of the oceans (5.8 million mi^2), bordered by the northern coasts of Asia, America and Europe; it is largely covered with pack ice.

North Sea
Relatively shallow sea (220,000 mi^2) in the North Atlantic and bordered by the coasts of Europe; some major European ports are located along its estuaries.

Arctic
Vast region inside the north polar circle; it includes the Arctic Ocean and the lands bordering it.

Caspian Sea
The world's largest lake (140,000 mi^2), located between Europe and Asia; it has no link to an ocean and is diminishing in size.

Bering Sea
Northern part of the Pacific between Kamchatka (in Asia and Alaska; it is deepest in its southern portion.

Atlantic Ocean
The world's second largest ocean (36 million mi^2); it covers 20% of the Earth's surface.

South China Sea
Part of the Pacific Ocean bordering the entire southeast coast of Asia as well as Borneo, the Philippines and Taiwan.

Pacific Ocean
The world's largest ocean (69 million mi^2), the Pacific covers 30% of the Earth's surface, more than all of the continents put together.

Central America
Extends from the Isthmus of Tehuantepec in Mexico to the Isthmus of Panama.

Indian Ocean
Relatively small ocean (29 million mi^2) located between Africa, Asia and Australia; it has high water temperatures and is dotted with numerous islands.

Caribbean Sea
Body of water (1.1 million mi^2) located between Central America and the northern portion of South America.

Red Sea
Sea (165,000 mi^2) located between Africa and the Arabian Peninsula; it connects to the Mediterranean through the Suez Canal.

Antarctica
The only uninhabited continent (5 million mi^2), located inside the south polar circle; 98% of its surface is covered with an ice cap. Antarctica holds 90% of the Earth's freshwater reserves.

North America
Its area (9.3 million mi^2) represents about 16% of the world's land; the Central American isthmus is an extension of North America.

Europe
Western extremity of the vast Eurasian continent that, by convention, is separated from Asia by the Ural Mountains; it covers a relatively small area.

Eurasia
Composed of Europe and Asia, Eurasia represents about 39% of the world's land; it forms a true continent that geographers have distinguished for historical and ethnographic reasons.

South America
Represents 12% of the world's land; linked to North America by Central America; it includes the Andes in the west and plains and plateaus in east and central regions.

Asia
The largest and most populous continent, Asia represents 32% of the world's land; it is dominated by imposing mountain ranges.

Oceania
Section of the planet that features a great many islands in the Pacific Ocean (Micronesia, Melanesia, Polynesia), as well as Australia. This section represents 6% of the world's land.

Africa
Continent that represents about 20% of the world's land; two-thirds of its surface lies north of the Equator. Characterized by very hot climates, Mediterranean in the north and south, tropical and arid elsewhere.

physical cartography

Group of techniques used in producing maps representing the Earth's surface.

physical map
Type of map representing the Earth's surface (topography, watercourses, aquatic areas) using various techniques (contour lines, colors).

sea
Vast body of saltwater at some distance inland; it is not as deep as an ocean.

bay
Indentation in a shoreline that reaches far inland and is delimited by two capes.

strait
Natural arm of a sea between two coasts; it connects two bodies of water.

mountain range
A row of connected mountains characterized by high summits and deep valleys.

island
Expanse of land completely surrounded by water.

prairie
Vast expanse of relatively flat land that is characterized by grasses and is naturally devoid of trees.

estuary
Mouth of a river that is influenced by the tides; it forms an indentation in the coastline that varies in width and depth.

mountain mass
Group of closely spaced mountains.

lake
Body of water completely surrounded by land; it varies in size and depth.

river
Natural watercourse of minor or intermediate size that empties into another watercourse.

peninsula
A piece of land connected to a larger body and extending into water.

altitude (feet)
The colors represent the elevation of the regions of the world in relation to sea level.

archipelago
Group of islands.

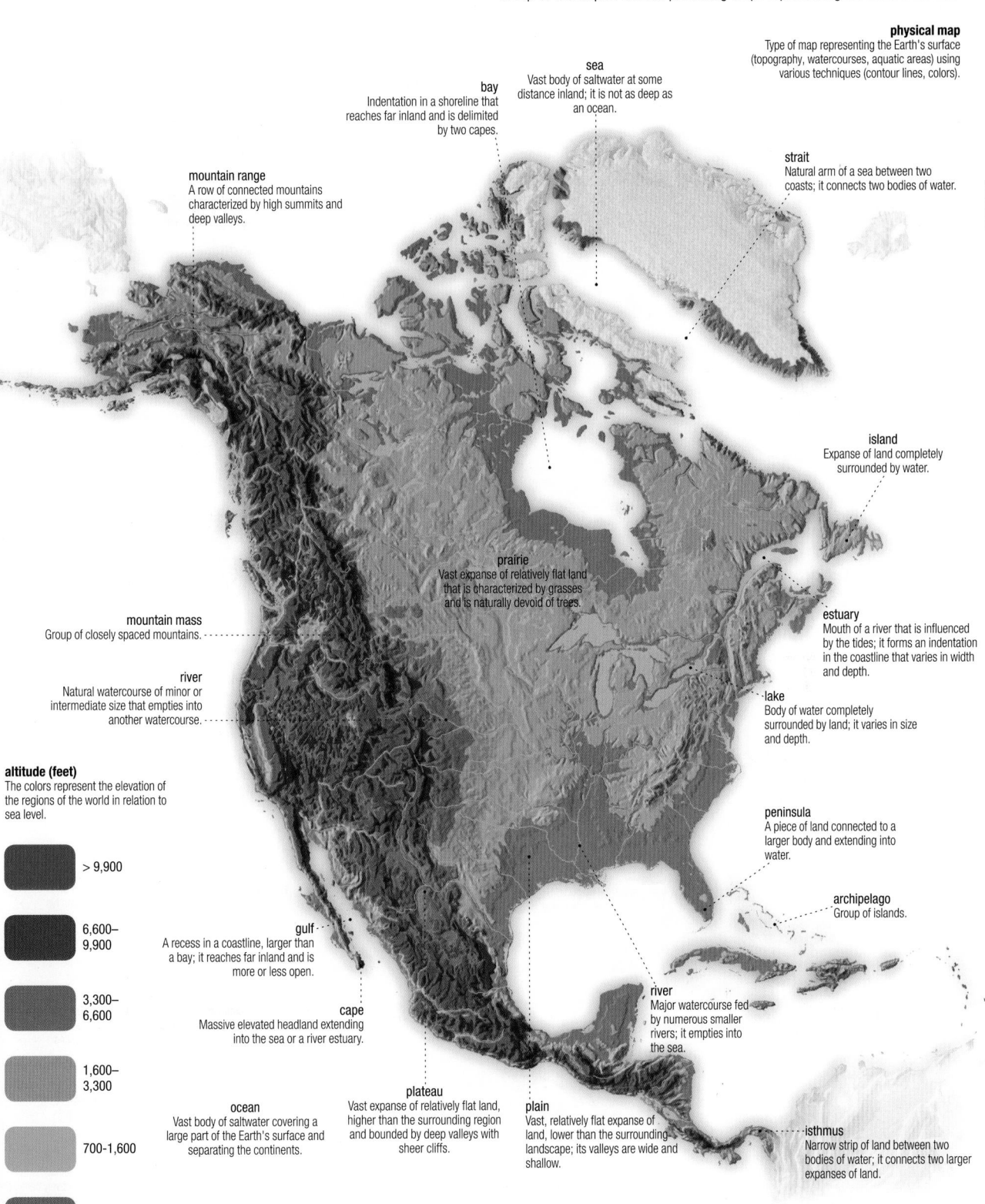

	> 9,900
	6,600– 9,900
	3,300– 6,600
	1,600– 3,300
	700-1,600
	0–700

gulf
A recess in a coastline, larger than a bay; it reaches far inland and is more or less open.

cape
Massive elevated headland extending into the sea or a river estuary.

river
Major watercourse fed by numerous smaller rivers; it empties into the sea.

ocean
Vast body of saltwater covering a large part of the Earth's surface and separating the continents.

plateau
Vast expanse of relatively flat land, higher than the surrounding region and bounded by deep valleys with sheer cliffs.

plain
Vast, relatively flat expanse of land, lower than the surrounding landscape; its valleys are wide and shallow.

isthmus
Narrow strip of land between two bodies of water; it connects two larger expanses of land.

physical cartography

Arctic
Vast region located inside the Arctic Circle, including the Arctic Ocean and the land bordering it.

Alaska
Vast territory comprising a state of the United States, separated from Russia by the Bering Strait.

Bering Strait
Some 62 mi wide, it connects the Pacific and Arctic Oceans and separates Asia from North America.

Chukchi Sea
Sea separating the northeast of the Asian continent from Alaska, connected to the Pacific by the Bering Strait.

East Siberian Sea
Part of the Arctic Ocean between the shores of Russian Siberia, the Chukchi Sea to the east and the Laptev Sea to the west.

Laptev Sea
Part of the Arctic Ocean bordered to the west by the shores of the Siberian Taimyr Peninsula and to the east by the East Siberian Sea.

Beaufort Sea
Part of the Arctic Ocean between Alaska and the Arctic Archipelago.

Canada
Second largest country in the world by area, it occupies the northern part of North America.

Russia
The largest country in the world, stretching from the Baltic Sea to the Pacific Ocean, and north to the Arctic Ocean.

Arctic Circle
Parallel of latitude 66°34' N; it marks the polar zone, where a day or night lasts 24 hours during a solstice.

Kara Sea
Part of the Arctic Ocean located to the east of Novaya Zemlya.

Arctic Ocean
The smallest of the oceans (5.8 million mi²) is bordered by the north shores of Asia, America and Europe and is covered in large part by ice floes.

Novaya Zemlya
Russian archipelago in the Arctic Ocean, composed of two main islands and some smaller ones, having mountainous landscapes.

Baffin Bay
Mass of deep water between Greenland and Baffin Island, connected on the north with the Arctic Ocean and on the south with the Labrador Sea.

Barents Sea
Area of the Arctic Ocean lying north of the Scandinavian Peninsula and Russia; it is partially ice-covered.

Greenland
The largest island in the world after Australia, stretching over 836,000 mi², 95% of which is ice-covered. It belongs to Denmark.

Finland
Scandinavian country in the northeast of Europe, bordered to the south and west by the Baltic Sea.

Labrador Sea
Part of the Atlantic Ocean between Labrador and Greenland.

Sweden
Scandinavian country in the northwest of Europe, bordered by the Baltic Sea to the southeast and the North Sea to the southwest.

Denmark Strait
About 155 mi wide, it separates Greenland and Iceland.

Iceland
Volcanic island subject to regular earthquakes; it has over 3,100 mi of coastline.

Greenland Sea
Sea (465,000 mi²) in the North Atlantic; it is bordered by the coast of Greenland.

Norwegian Sea
Section of the Atlantic between Norway and Iceland.

Norway
Scandinavian country in the northwest of Europe, bordering the Norwegian Sea.

Antarctica
The only uninhabited continent (5 million mi²), located inside the Antarctic Circle; 98% of its surface is covered with an ice cap. Antarctica holds 90% of the Earth's freshwater reserves.

Antarctic Circle
Parallel of latitude at 66°34' S that marks the polar zone, where a day or night lasts 24 hours during a solstice.

Atlantic Ocean
The southern parts of the Atlantic, Indian, and Pacific oceans are collectively called the Southern Ocean or the Antarctic Ocean.

Queen Maud Land
Oldest and largest part of Antarctica, Queen Maud Land also forms its continental shelf.

Drake Passage
Almost 560 mi wide, it separates Tierra del Fuego from Antarctica and connects the Atlantic to the Pacific; its currents are very powerful.

Weddell Sea
Sea northwest of Antarctica, partly delimited by the Antarctic Peninsula; more than half of its surface is covered with pack ice.

South Pole
Point of the terrestrial surface at the southern extremity of the Earth's axis of rotation; the Norwegian Amundsen and his expedition first reached it in 1911.

Antarctic Peninsula
Extends far beyond the polar circle and includes several mountain systems; parts that crumble away from its tip form small islands.

Amery Ice Shelf
Its immense size makes it one of the world's most remarkable ice shelves.

Filchner Ice Shelf
Fed by adjacent continental ice sheets and by local precipitation; it borders the Weddell Sea.

Wilkes Land
Region of the Antarctic continent that takes its name from a 19th-century American mariner and explorer.

Marie Byrd Land
Region at an altitude of over 6,500 feet.

Pacific Ocean
The southern parts of the Atlantic, Indian, and Pacific oceans are collectively called the Southern Ocean or the Antarctic Ocean.

Ross Ice Shelf
Mobile ice shelf beginning at the edge of the continent's southern slope and ending in the Ross Sea.

Transantarctic Mountains
Mountain chain that is an extension of the Andes Cordillera in South America; its peaks reach heights of more than 13,000 feet.

Indian Ocean
The southern parts of the Atlantic, Indian, and Pacific oceans are collectively called the Southern Ocean or the Antarctic Ocean.

physical cartography

North America
Its area (9.3 million mi²) represents about 16% of the world's land; the Central American isthmus is an extension of North America.

Baffin Island
Largest island in the Arctic Archipelago; Baffin Bay separates it from Greenland.

Hudson Bay
Inland sea that opens onto the Atlantic Ocean through Hudson Strait; the bay is frozen during winter months.

Mackenzie River
Canada's longest river (2,635 mi).

Greenland
The second largest island in the world (after Australia), Greenland has an area of over 836,000 mi², with 95% covered in ice. It belongs to Denmark.

Bering Strait
ome 62 mi wide, it connects the cific Ocean to the Arctic Ocean.

Beaufort Sea
Part of the Arctic Ocean between Alaska and the Arctic Archipelago.

Arctic Circle
Parallel of latitude 66°34' N; it marks the polar zone, where a day lasts 24 hours during the summer solstice and a night lasts 24 hours during the winter solstice.

EARTH

Gulf of Alaska
Northeast part of the Pacific Ocean, bordering Alaska.

Great Lakes
These five lakes constitute the world's largest reserve of fresh surface water (95,000 mi²).

Aleutian Islands
Archipelago that is an extension of Alaska; it is composed of 150 islands and islets stretching over more than 1,000 mi.

Newfoundland Island
Island separated from Labrador by the Strait of Belle-Isle. Labrador and Newfoundland comprise one of the Canadian provinces.

Rocky Mountains
Eastern margin of the western cordilleras, extending from Alaska to Mexico.

Saint Lawrence River
River (over 680 mi) that drains southeastern Canada and empties into the Atlantic Ocean.

Grand Canyon
The longest gorge in the world (220 mi); the Colorado River flows through it.

Appalachian Mountains
Old massif extending over 1,200 mi from the Canadian border to Alabama; its highest peak is Mount Mitchell (6,684 feet).

Mississippi River
The Mississippi (2,350 mi) drainage basin covers the entire area between the Rocky Mountains and the Appalachians.

Gulf of California
Separates the Baja California peninsula from the continent.

Tropic of Cancer
Parallel located at 23°26' N latitude (a distance of about 1,600 mi from the Equator).

Gulf of Mexico
Part of the Atlantic located between the U.S., Mexico and Cuba.

West Indies
Archipelago that includes more than 700 islands, including the Greater Antilles in the north (Cuba, Haiti, Jamaica, Puerto Rico) and the Lesser Antilles in the east.

Yucatan Peninsula
Vast plateau characterized by aridity in the northwest and abundant precipitation in the south, where a dense forest grows.

Central America
Extends from the Isthmus of Tehuantepec in Mexico to the Isthmus of Panama.

Caribbean Sea
Body of water (1.1 million mi²) located between Central America and the northern portion of South America.

Isthmus of Panama
Land that connects North America and South America; it is cut by the Panama Canal which opened in 1914 allowing maritime traffic to travel between the Caribbean Sea and the Pacific Ocean.

physical cartography

South America
Represents 12% of the world's land; linked to North America by Central America; it includes the Andes in the west and plains and plateaus in east and central regions.

Orinoco River
River in Venezuela (1,340 mi) that empties into the Atlantic through a vast delta; the volume of its flow is considerable.

Amazon River
The largest river in the world in volume of flow; it rises in the Andes and flows for 4,090 mi through more than 80% of Brazil's territory.

Gulf of Panama
Bounded in the north by the Isthmus of Panama, its coast is uneven and dotted with islands.

Equator
Imaginary circle surrounding Earth at its widest circumference, dividing it into two hemispheres: the Northern hemisphere and the Southern hemisphere.

Andes Cordillera
Longest mountain chain in the world (5,000 mi) and the second highest, it follows the western coast of South America; its highest peak is Aconcagua (22,834 feet).

Lake Titicaca
Located in the Andes Cordillera between Peru and Bolivia; at an elevation of 12,500 feet, it is the highest navigable lake in the world.

Tropic of Capricorn
Parallel located at 23°26' S latitude (a distance of about 1,600 mi from the Equator).

Atacama Desert
Among the driest deserts on the planet, receiving only a few inches of rain per year.

Paraná River
River (1,860 mi) with most of its course in Brazil; it marks part of the boundary between Brazil and Paraguay and between Paraguay and Argentina.

Patagonia
Plateau in Chile and Argentina; it is divided into Andean Patagonia with a humid climate and abundant vegetation, and the Patagonian plateau, which is dry and sparse.

Falkland Islands
Archipelago composed of two main islands separated by the Falkland Strait, as well as some 100 islets.

Tierra del Fuego
Archipelago separated from the continent by the Magellan Strait; its cold damp climate results in perpetual snows from as low as 2,300 feet.

South Georgia
Overseas U.K. territory. The largest city is Grytviken.

Cape Horn
Southernmost point of South America, only 620 mi from Antarctica; famous for its storms and dangerous reefs and shoals.

Drake Passage
Almost 560 mi wide, it separates Tierra del Fuego from Antarctica and connects the Atlantic to the Pacific; its currents are very powerful.

physical cartography

Europe
Western extremity of the vast Eurasian continent that, by convention, is separated from Asia by the Ural Mountains; it covers a relatively small area.

Lake Ladoga
Europe's largest lake (6,800 mi²) is located in Russia; it empties into the Baltic Sea.

Barents Sea
Area of the Arctic Ocean lying north of the Scandinavian Peninsula and Russia; it is partially ice-covered.

Gulf of Bothnia
Relatively shallow Gulf between Sweden and Finland; it is often icebound.

Kola Peninsula
Mostly mountainous peninsula located in Russia, above the Arctic polar circle.

Arctic Circle
Parallel of latitude 66°34' N; it marks the polar zone, where a day lasts 24 hours during the summer solstice and a night lasts 24 hours during the winter solstice.

Ural Mountains
Mountain range extending 1,500 mi from the Caspian Sea to the Arctic; it is traditionally considered the boundary between Europe and Asia.

Volga River
The longest river in Europe (2,300 mi) is ice-covered during winter months; its spring flood is substantial.

Norwegian Sea
Open sea west of Norway and east of Iceland.

Baltic Sea
Generally shallow inland sea that is low in salt content and devoid of major tides; it freezes along its coasts.

Iceland
Volcanic island subject to regular earthquakes; it has over 3,100 mi of coastline.

Scandinavian Peninsula
Vast Nordic peninsula that includes Norway, Sweden and part of Finland.

Dnieper River
River in Russia (1,350 mi) whose flow is slow but abundant; it is a major communications artery.

North Sea
Relatively shallow sea (220,000 mi²) in the North Atlantic and bordered by the coasts of Europe; some major European ports are located along its estuaries.

Irish Sea
Section of the Atlantic that separates Great Britain from Ireland.

Vistula River
Poland's principal river (680 mi) has its source in the Carpathians and joins the Baltic Sea at the Gulf of Gdansk.

English Channel
Relatively shallow sea between France and England; its extreme tides cause strong currents, making navigation difficult.

Alps
Largest mountain mass in Europe, extending 750 mi; Mont Blanc (15,771 feet) is its highest peak.

Black Sea
Inland sea (162,000 mi²) between Eastern Europe and Asia; it opens into the Mediterranean through two straits, the Dardanelles and the Bosporus.

Atlantic Ocean
World's second largest ocean; covers 20% of the Earth's surface.

Iberian Peninsula
Peninsula comprising Spain and Portugal; it extends from the Pyrenees to the Strait of Gibraltar.

Pyrenees
Mountain range whose northern slope is in France and whose southern slope is in Spain; Pico de Aneto (11,169 feet) is its highest peak.

Danube River
Second longest river in Europe (1,770 mi); it flows into the Black Sea through a vast delta with three branches.

Balkan Peninsula
Mountainous, easternmost peninsula of Europe whose crumbling coastline features peninsulas and scattered islands.

Carpathian Mountains
Mountain range in central Europe, lower than the Alps; its highest point is at an elevation of 8,711 feet.

Strait of Gibraltar
Channel (9 mi wide) between Spain and Morocco; it connects the Mediterranean to the Atlantic and is an important shipping route.

Mediterranean Sea
One of the world's largest inland seas, bordered by Europe, Africa and Asia; it connects to the Atlantic Ocean through the Strait of Gibraltar.

Adriatic Sea
Gulf of the Mediterranean, 520 mi long and 110 mi wide, located between Italy and the Balkan Peninsula.

Aegean Sea
Area of the Mediterranean Sea between Turkey and Greece; it contains numerous islands, the largest of which is Crete.

physical cartography

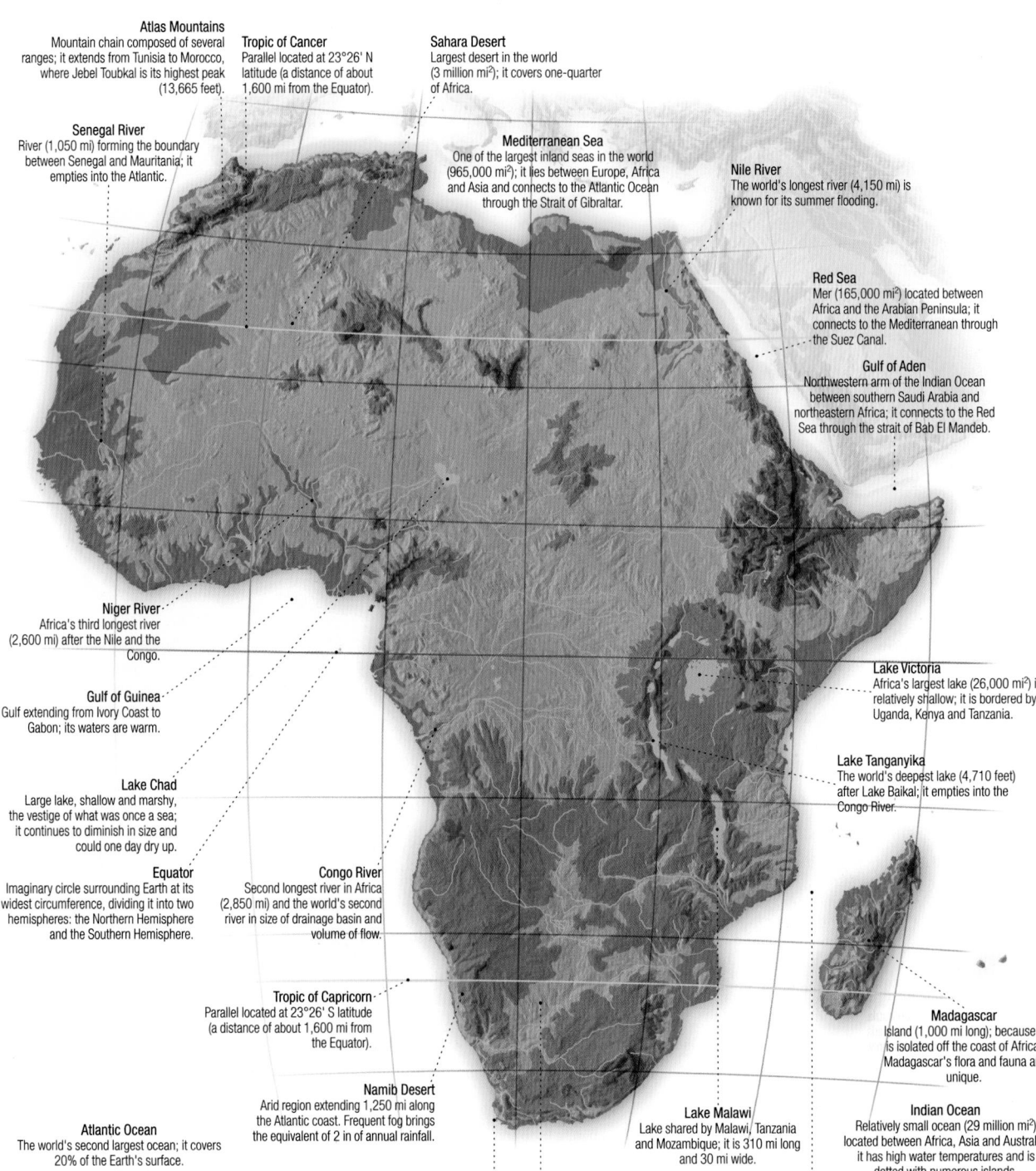

Africa
Continent that represents about 20% of the world's land; two-thirds of its surface lies north of the Equator. Characterized by very hot climates, Mediterranean in the north and south, tropical and arid elsewhere.

Atlas Mountains
Mountain chain composed of several ranges; it extends from Tunisia to Morocco, where Jebel Toubkal is its highest peak (13,665 feet).

Tropic of Cancer
Parallel located at 23°26' N latitude (a distance of about 1,600 mi from the Equator).

Sahara Desert
Largest desert in the world (3 million mi²); it covers one-quarter of Africa.

Senegal River
River (1,050 mi) forming the boundary between Senegal and Mauritania; it empties into the Atlantic.

Mediterranean Sea
One of the largest inland seas in the world (965,000 mi²); it lies between Europe, Africa and Asia and connects to the Atlantic Ocean through the Strait of Gibraltar.

Nile River
The world's longest river (4,150 mi) is known for its summer flooding.

Red Sea
Mer (165,000 mi²) located between Africa and the Arabian Peninsula; it connects to the Mediterranean through the Suez Canal.

Gulf of Aden
Northwestern arm of the Indian Ocean between southern Saudi Arabia and northeastern Africa; it connects to the Red Sea through the strait of Bab El Mandeb.

Niger River
Africa's third longest river (2,600 mi) after the Nile and the Congo.

Lake Victoria
Africa's largest lake (26,000 mi²) is relatively shallow; it is bordered by Uganda, Kenya and Tanzania.

Gulf of Guinea
Gulf extending from Ivory Coast to Gabon; its waters are warm.

Lake Tanganyika
The world's deepest lake (4,710 feet) after Lake Baikal; it empties into the Congo River.

Lake Chad
Large lake, shallow and marshy, the vestige of what was once a sea; it continues to diminish in size and could one day dry up.

Equator
Imaginary circle surrounding Earth at its widest circumference, dividing it into two hemispheres: the Northern Hemisphere and the Southern Hemisphere.

Congo River
Second longest river in Africa (2,850 mi) and the world's second river in size of drainage basin and volume of flow.

Madagascar
Island (1,000 mi long); because it is isolated off the coast of Africa, Madagascar's flora and fauna are unique.

Tropic of Capricorn
Parallel located at 23°26' S latitude (a distance of about 1,600 mi from the Equator).

Namib Desert
Arid region extending 1,250 mi along the Atlantic coast. Frequent fog brings the equivalent of 2 in of annual rainfall.

Lake Malawi
Lake shared by Malawi, Tanzania and Mozambique; it is 310 mi long and 30 mi wide.

Indian Ocean
Relatively small ocean (29 million mi²) located between Africa, Asia and Australia; it has high water temperatures and is dotted with numerous islands.

Atlantic Ocean
The world's second largest ocean; it covers 20% of the Earth's surface.

Cape of Good Hope
Former island now connected to the continent by a ridge of sand; located only 90 mi to the west of Africa's southernmost point.

Kalahari Desert
Semiarid region bordering the Namib Desert; the north is marshy while the south is characterized by very sparse vegetation.

Mozambique Channel
Large strait in the Indian Ocean between the African continent and the island of Madagascar.

EARTH

Asia
The largest and most populous continent, Asia represents 32% of the world's land; it is dominated by imposing mountain ranges.

Lake Baikal
The world's oldest (25 million years) and deepest (5,315 feet) lake; Lake Baikal is 370 mi long and 40 to 50 mi wide and is frozen six months of the year.

Gobi Desert
One of the largest deserts in the world (400,000 mi²), shared by China and Mongolia; the Gobi is a plateau situated at an elevation of about 3,300 feet.

Aral Sea
Sea once connected to the Caspian Sea; it is now an immense salt lake.

Arctic Circle
Parallel of latitude 66°34' N; it marks the polar zone, where a day lasts 24 hours during the summer solstice and a night lasts 24 hours during the winter solstice.

Caspian Sea
The world's largest lake (140,000 mi²), located between Europe and Asia; it has no link to an ocean and is diminishing in size.

Kamchatka Peninsula
Peninsula (12,000 mi²) on the Bering Sea; it is characterized by intense volcanic activity.

Black Sea
Inland sea (162,000 mi²) between ern Europe and Asia; it opens into Mediterranean through two straits, he Dardanelles and the Bosporus.

Sea of Japan (East Sea)
Area of the Pacific Ocean that separates Japan from the Asian mainland; it is divided into a warm region and a cold region.

Red Sea
65,000 mi²) located between a and the Arabian Peninsula; nnects to the Mediterranean through the Suez Canal.

Pacific Ocean
The world's largest ocean (69 million mi²), the Pacific covers 30% of the Earth's surface, more than all of the continents put together.

Japan
Archipelago made up of 1,000 islands, including four main islands that represent 95% of its territory; it is characterized by intense volcanic activity and frequent earthquakes.

Korean Peninsula
Peninsula that delimits the Sea of Japan (East Sea); its climate is marked by monsoons in summer and typhoons in the fall.

East China Sea
Area of the Pacific Ocean between Korea, the Ryukyu Islands (south of Japan) and Taiwan.

Philippines
Archipelago with more than 7,000 islands and islets; two principal islands (Luzon and Mindanao) make up 70% of its territory.

Gulf of Aden
western arm of the Indian Ocean veen southern Saudi Arabia and stern Africa; it connects to the Red rough the strait of Bab El Mandeb.

Himalayas
The world's highest mountain range; it contains some ten peaks above 26,000 feet, including Everest (29,035 feet).

Arabian Peninsula
Vast semiarid peninsula; it holds 50% of the world's oil supply.

Gulf of Oman
The narrowest part of the Arabian Sea; it connects to the Persian Gulf through the Strait of Hormuz.

Equator
Imaginary circle surrounding Earth at its widest circumference, dividing it into two hemispheres: the Northern hemisphere and the Southern hemisphere.

South China Sea
Southern part of the China Sea bordering the entire southeast coast of Asia as well as Borneo, the Philippines and Taiwan.

Indian Ocean
Relatively small ocean (29 million mi²) located between Africa, Asia and Australia; it has high water temperatures and is dotted with numerous islands.

Arabian Sea
Area of the Indian Ocean between India and the Arabian Peninsula; the Gulf of Oman is an arm of the Arabian Sea.

Bay of Bengal
Area of the Indian Ocean between India and the Indochinese Peninsula; the Ganges River empties into this bay through the world's largest delta.

Indonesia
Archipelago with almost 14,000 islands extending 3,100 mi from west to east; it is the world's most active volcanic zone.

Persian Gulf
Gulf (500 mi long) bordered by Saudi Arabia, Iran and Iraq; it is also called the Arabian Gulf and is an important maritime trade route.

EARTH

physical cartography

Oceania
Section of the planet that features a great many islands in the Pacific Ocean (Micronesia, Melanesia, Polynesia), as well as Australia. This section represents 6% of the world's land.

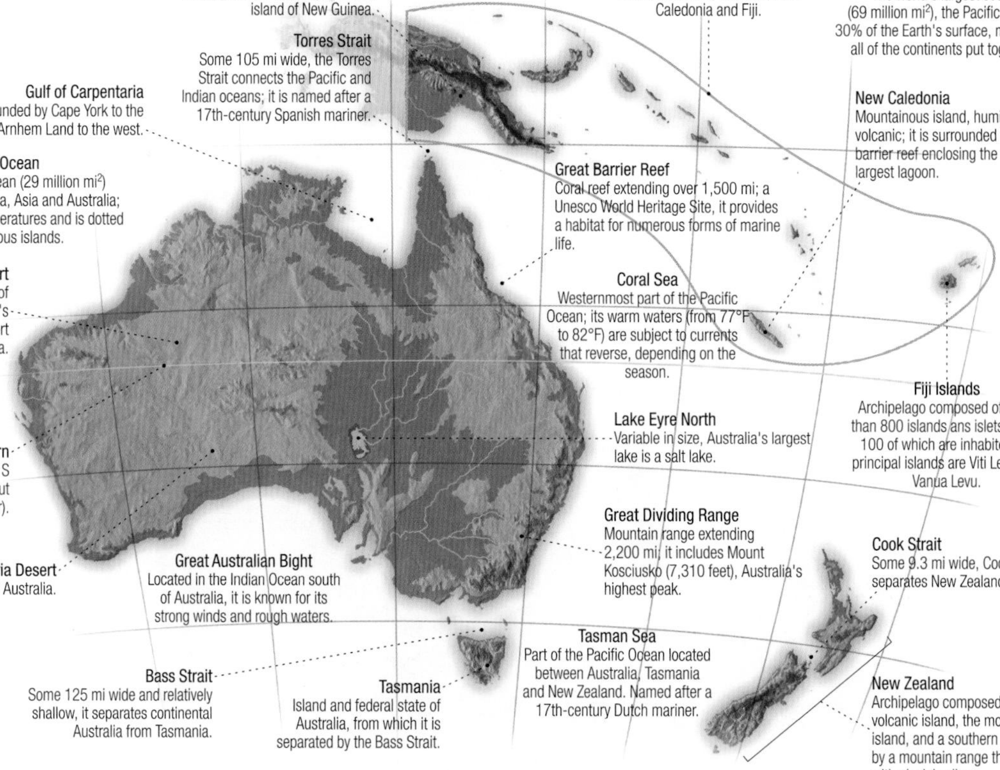

Papua New Guinea
Country on the eastern part of the island of New Guinea.

Melanesia
Part of Oceania (370,000 mi²) that includes Papua New Guinea, the Solomon Islands, Vanuatu, New Caledonia and Fiji.

Pacific Ocean
The world's largest ocean (69 million mi²), the Pacific covers 30% of the Earth's surface, more than all of the continents put together.

Torres Strait
Some 105 mi wide, the Torres Strait connects the Pacific and Indian oceans; it is named after a 17th-century Spanish mariner.

Gulf of Carpentaria
Gulf bounded by Cape York to the east and Arnhem Land to the west.

New Caledonia
Mountainous island, humid and volcanic; it is surrounded by a barrier reef enclosing the world's largest lagoon.

Indian Ocean
Relatively small ocean (29 million mi²) located between Africa, Asia and Australia; it has high water temperatures and is dotted with numerous islands.

Great Barrier Reef
Coral reef extending over 1,500 mi; a Unesco World Heritage Site, it provides a habitat for numerous forms of marine life.

Great Sandy Desert
The northernmost desert of Australia is also the world's second largest desert (730,000 mi²) after the Sahara.

Coral Sea
Westernmost part of the Pacific Ocean; its warm waters (from 77°F to 82°F) are subject to currents that reverse, depending on the season.

Fiji Islands
Archipelago composed of more than 800 islands ans islets, some 100 of which are inhabited; its principal islands are Viti Levu and Vanua Levu.

Tropic of Capricorn
Parallel located at 23°26' S latitude (a distance of about 1,600 mi from the Equator).

Lake Eyre North
Variable in size, Australia's largest lake is a salt lake.

Great Dividing Range
Mountain range extending 2,200 mi; it includes Mount Kosciusko (7,310 feet), Australia's highest peak.

Cook Strait
Some 9.3 mi wide, Cook Strait separates New Zealand's two islands.

Great Victoria Desert
Southernmost desert of Australia.

Great Australian Bight
Located in the Indian Ocean south of Australia, it is known for its strong winds and rough waters.

Tasman Sea
Part of the Pacific Ocean located between Australia, Tasmania and New Zealand. Named after a 17th-century Dutch mariner.

New Zealand
Archipelago composed of a northern volcanic island, the most populated island, and a southern island crossed by a mountain range that is deeply cu with glacial valleys.

Bass Strait
Some 125 mi wide and relatively shallow, it separates continental Australia from Tasmania.

Tasmania
Island and federal state of Australia, from which it is separated by the Bass Strait.

urban map
Precise and detailed representation of an area of a city, usually on a large scale.

railroad line
Communications route composed of two parallel rails along which trains travel.

railroad
Collective term for the network of rails and the structures needed to transport travelers and goods by train.

bridge
Structure allowing a communications route to span a natural obstacle or another communications route.

park
Area of a city set aside for leisure or recreational use.

suburb
A smaller community adjacent to or within commuting distance of a city.

cemetery
Place where the dead are buried.

river
Major watercourse fed by numerous smaller rivers; it empties into the sea.

monument
Structure that commemorates a historic event or holds aesthetic, religious or symbolic value.

woods
Small tract of land covered with trees.

street
Thoroughfare built inside a city and usually lined with buildings.

circular route
High-speed road that circles the downtown area, making it possible to divert traffic away from downtown or connect two outlying communities.

highway
Large thoroughfare with separate one-way lanes and no crossing streets; reserved for high-speed traffic.

traffic circle
Junction where several roads converge on a roadway that circles a round, central island; traffic moves in one direction only.

district
Area of a city having a distinguishing character.

avenue
Thoroughfare usually larger than a street; it services a district or an area of a city.

public building
Large building that houses public services.

boulevard
Very large, high-volume thoroughfare connecting various parts of a city.

physical cartography

road map
Map that uses lines to indicate a network of roads; it often features information for tourists.

highway
Large thoroughfare with separate one-way lanes and no crossing streets; reserved for high-speed traffic.

road
Communications route connecting two distant geographic points, usually urban centers.

route number

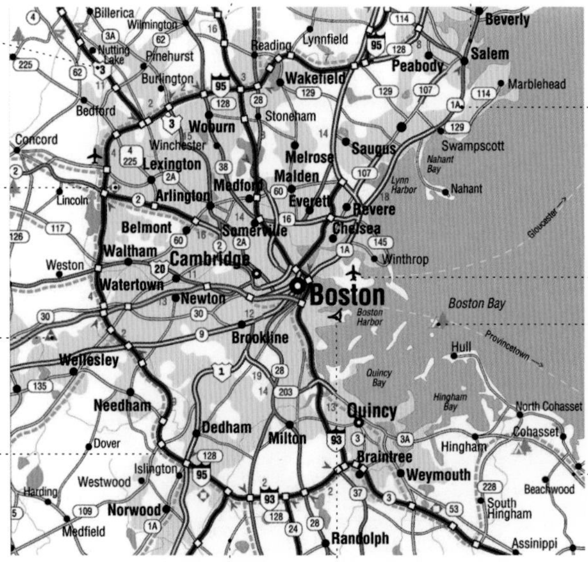

route number

rest area
An area developed for rest along a road or highway, usually equipped with restrooms and a picnic area.

airport
Location that contains all the technical and commercial facilities needed to support air traffic.

national park
Zone that the government designates with a view to protecting its natural, historic or scientific resources; access is granted under certain conditions.

service area
Area built alongside a highway providing services such as a gas station, restaurant, lodging and tourist information.

beltway
Branch of a highway built around an urban center to facilitate inbound and outbound access and to absorb through traffic.

scenic route
Road offering particularly scenic landscapes for travelers.

secondary road
A road connecting major roads or regional urban centers and usually supporting a lower volume of traffic.

point of interest
A unique or attractive feature.

political cartography

Collection of techniques used in the production of maps representing states, territories and administrative regions.

political map
Map that represents the boundaries and in some cases the subdivisions of political units (as countries or states)

province
Territorial division run by a government elected by the population (in Canada) or appointed by a central authority (China).

internal boundary
Boundary marking the territorial limits of a province or state within a federated state.

city
Major urban center, characterized by a concentrated settlement whose activities revolve around industry, commerce, services and administration.

international boundary
Boundary marking a country's territorial limits.

capital
City where the government is located.

state
Each of the territories constituting a federation; the United States is divided into 50 states.

country
Territory inhabited by a citizenry and administered by a government; its borders are clearly established.

political cartography

North America
Region stretching from close to the North Pole down
to the Isthmus of Panama, including the Antilles. It
represents 16% of dry land on Earth.

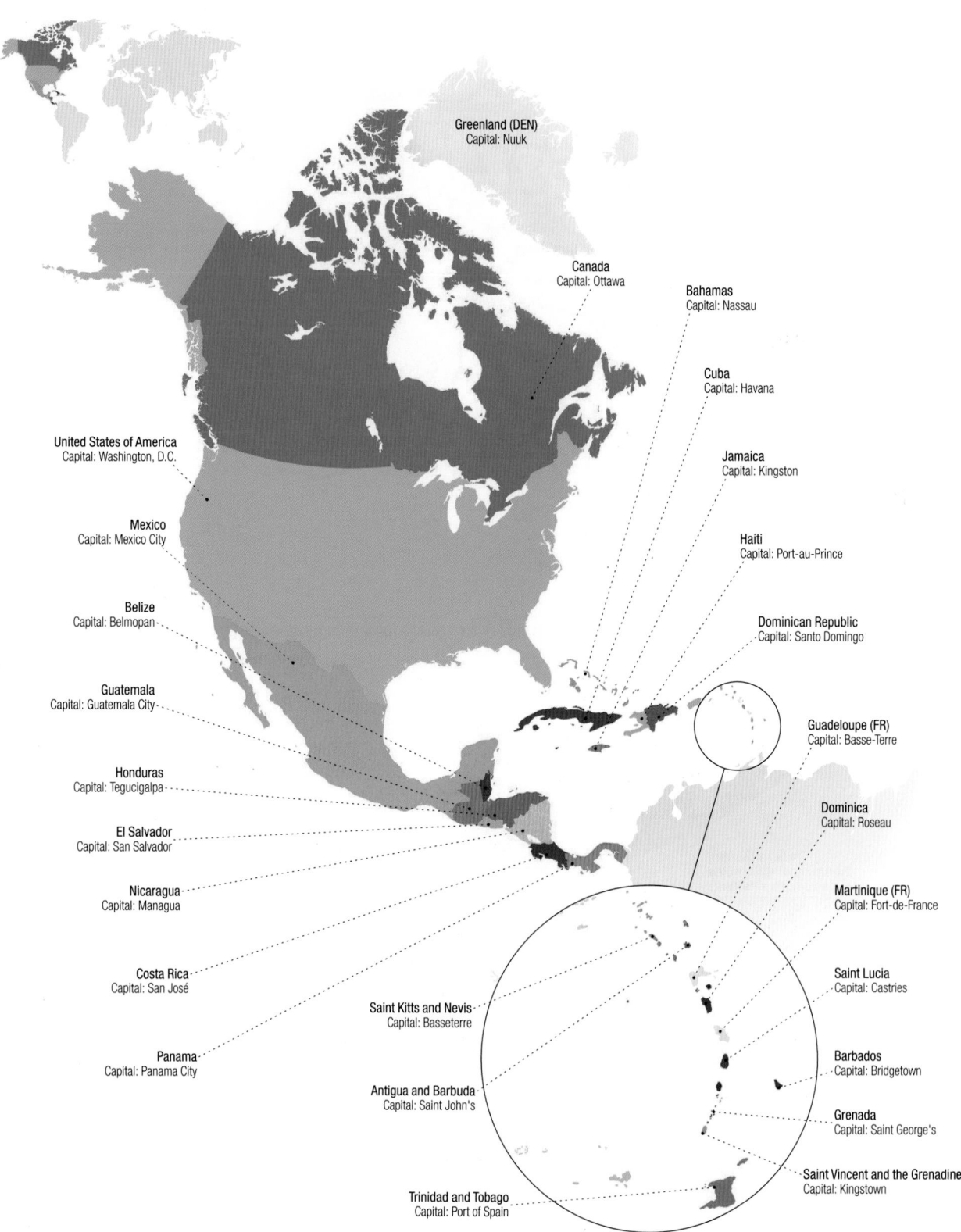

Greenland (DEN)
Capital: Nuuk

Canada
Capital: Ottawa

Bahamas
Capital: Nassau

Cuba
Capital: Havana

Jamaica
Capital: Kingston

United States of America
Capital: Washington, D.C.

Haiti
Capital: Port-au-Prince

Mexico
Capital: Mexico City

Dominican Republic
Capital: Santo Domingo

Belize
Capital: Belmopan

Guadeloupe (FR)
Capital: Basse-Terre

Guatemala
Capital: Guatemala City

Dominica
Capital: Roseau

Honduras
Capital: Tegucigalpa

El Salvador
Capital: San Salvador

Martinique (FR)
Capital: Fort-de-France

Nicaragua
Capital: Managua

Saint Lucia
Capital: Castries

Costa Rica
Capital: San José

Saint Kitts and Nevis
Capital: Basseterre

Barbados
Capital: Bridgetown

Panama
Capital: Panama City

Antigua and Barbuda
Capital: Saint John's

Grenada
Capital: Saint George's

Saint Vincent and the Grenadines
Capital: Kingstown

Trinidad and Tobago
Capital: Port of Spain

political cartography

South America
Continent located primarily in the southern
hemisphere, between Central America and
Cape Horn. It Represents 12% of dry land
on Earth.

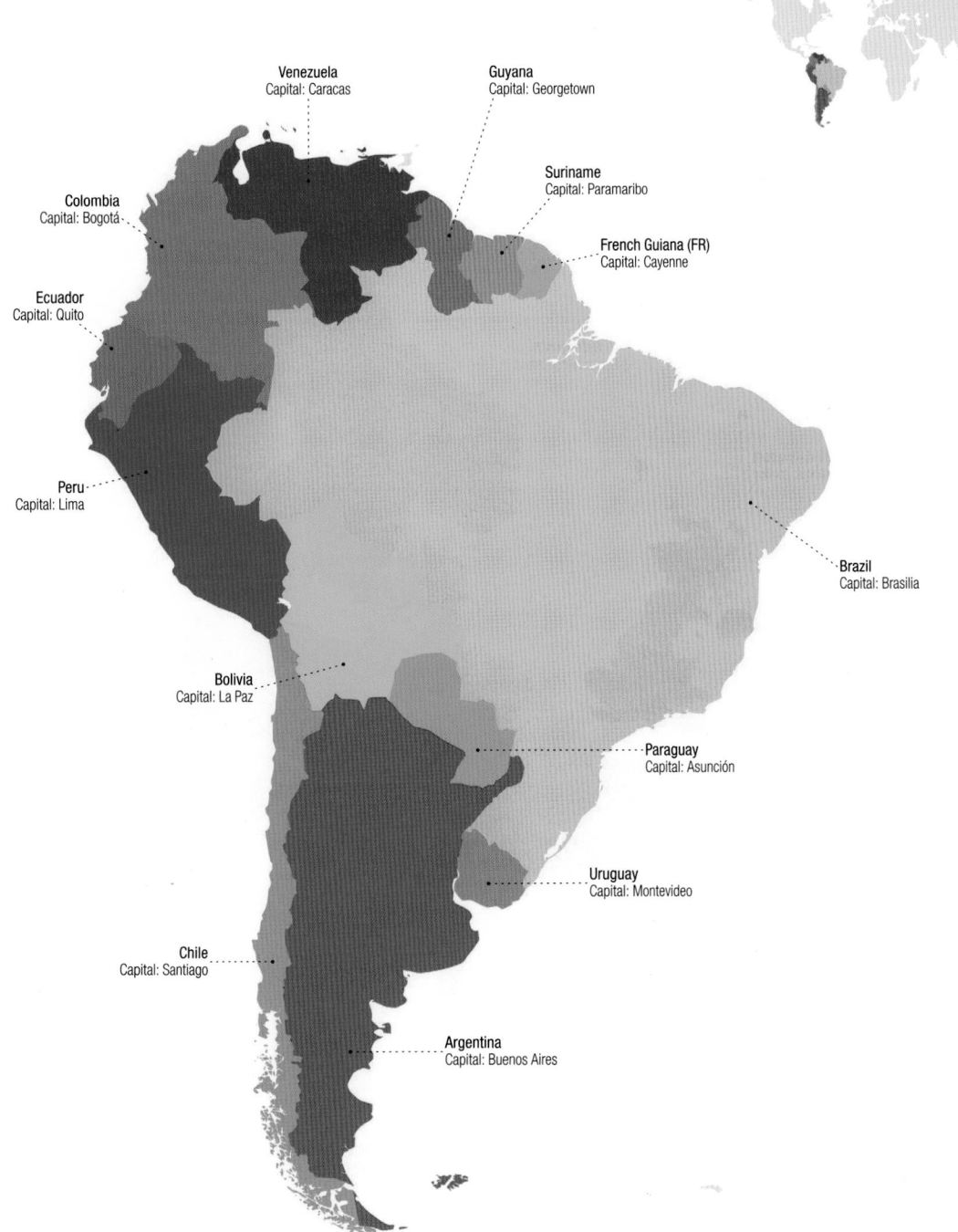

Venezuela
Capital: Caracas

Guyana
Capital: Georgetown

Suriname
Capital: Paramaribo

Colombia
Capital: Bogotá

French Guiana (FR)
Capital: Cayenne

Ecuador
Capital: Quito

Peru
Capital: Lima

Brazil
Capital: Brasilia

Bolivia
Capital: La Paz

Paraguay
Capital: Asunción

Uruguay
Capital: Montevideo

Chile
Capital: Santiago

Argentina
Capital: Buenos Aires

EARTH

political cartography

Europe
Western end of the vast Eurasian supercontinent,
separated from Asia, according to convention, by
the Ural Mountains. It represents 7% of dry land
on Earth.

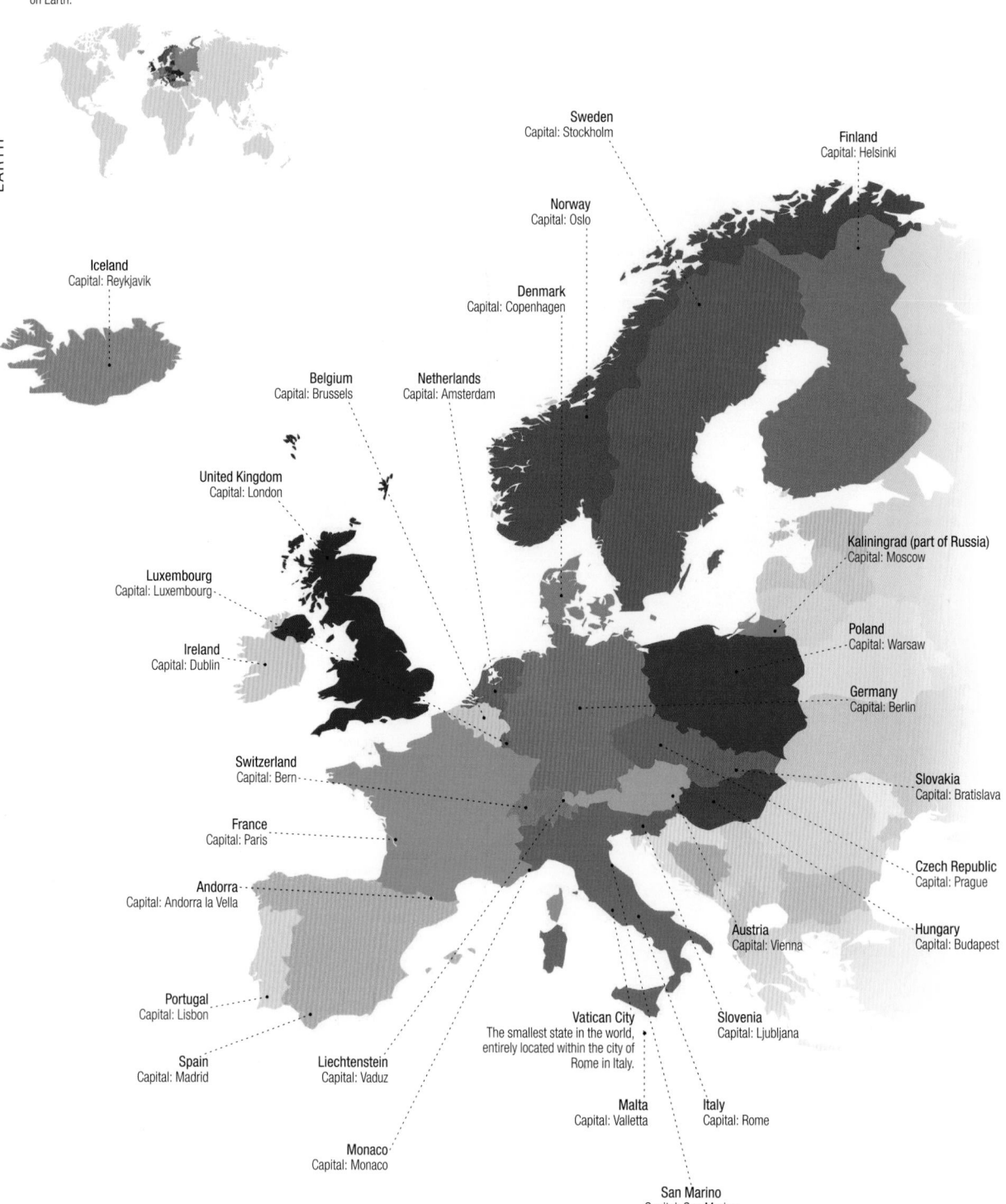

Sweden
Capital: Stockholm

Finland
Capital: Helsinki

Norway
Capital: Oslo

Iceland
Capital: Reykjavik

Denmark
Capital: Copenhagen

Belgium
Capital: Brussels

Netherlands
Capital: Amsterdam

United Kingdom
Capital: London

Kaliningrad (part of Russia)
Capital: Moscow

Luxembourg
Capital: Luxembourg

Poland
Capital: Warsaw

Ireland
Capital: Dublin

Germany
Capital: Berlin

Switzerland
Capital: Bern

Slovakia
Capital: Bratislava

France
Capital: Paris

Czech Republic
Capital: Prague

Andorra
Capital: Andorra la Vella

Hungary
Capital: Budapest

Austria
Capital: Vienna

Portugal
Capital: Lisbon

Slovenia
Capital: Ljubljana

Vatican City
The smallest state in the world,
entirely located within the city of
Rome in Italy.

Spain
Capital: Madrid

Liechtenstein
Capital: Vaduz

Malta
Capital: Valletta

Italy
Capital: Rome

Monaco
Capital: Monaco

San Marino
Capital: San Marino

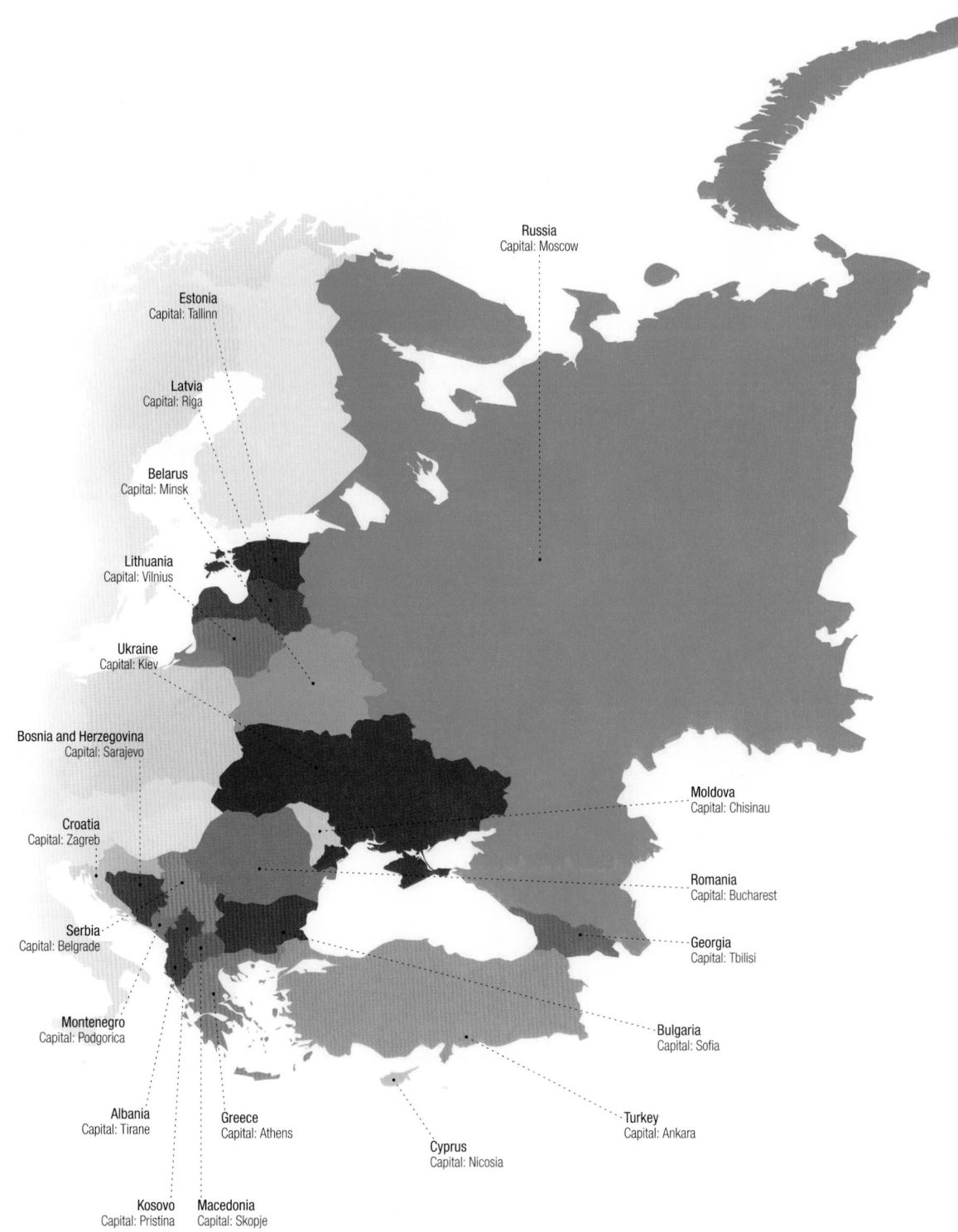

Russia
Capital: Moscow

Estonia
Capital: Tallinn

Latvia
Capital: Riga

Belarus
Capital: Minsk

Lithuania
Capital: Vilnius

Ukraine
Capital: Kiev

Bosnia and Herzegovina
Capital: Sarajevo

Moldova
Capital: Chisinau

Croatia
Capital: Zagreb

Romania
Capital: Bucharest

Serbia
Capital: Belgrade

Georgia
Capital: Tbilisi

Montenegro
Capital: Podgorica

Bulgaria
Capital: Sofia

Albania
Capital: Tirane

Greece
Capital: Athens

Turkey
Capital: Ankara

Cyprus
Capital: Nicosia

Kosovo
Capital: Pristina

Macedonia
Capital: Skopje

political cartography

Asia
Largest continent by area and population, representing 32% of dry land on Earth.

EARTH

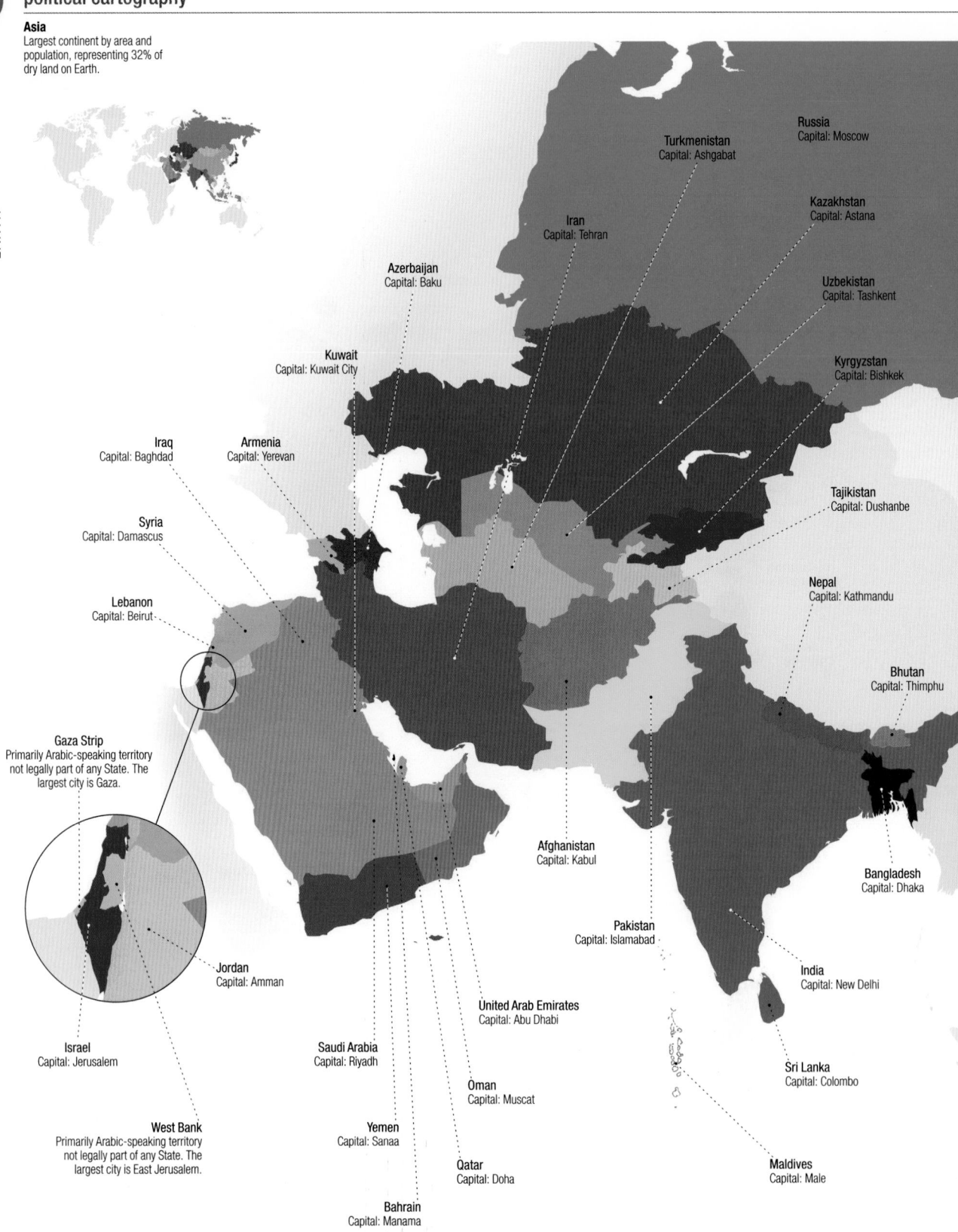

Russia
Capital: Moscow

Turkmenistan
Capital: Ashgabat

Kazakhstan
Capital: Astana

Iran
Capital: Tehran

Uzbekistan
Capital: Tashkent

Azerbaijan
Capital: Baku

Kyrgyzstan
Capital: Bishkek

Kuwait
Capital: Kuwait City

Iraq
Capital: Baghdad

Armenia
Capital: Yerevan

Tajikistan
Capital: Dushanbe

Syria
Capital: Damascus

Nepal
Capital: Kathmandu

Lebanon
Capital: Beirut

Bhutan
Capital: Thimphu

Gaza Strip
Primarily Arabic-speaking territory not legally part of any State. The largest city is Gaza.

Afghanistan
Capital: Kabul

Bangladesh
Capital: Dhaka

Pakistan
Capital: Islamabad

India
Capital: New Delhi

Jordan
Capital: Amman

United Arab Emirates
Capital: Abu Dhabi

Israel
Capital: Jerusalem

Saudi Arabia
Capital: Riyadh

Sri Lanka
Capital: Colombo

Oman
Capital: Muscat

West Bank
Primarily Arabic-speaking territory not legally part of any State. The largest city is East Jerusalem.

Yemen
Capital: Sanaa

Qatar
Capital: Doha

Maldives
Capital: Male

Bahrain
Capital: Manama

EARTH

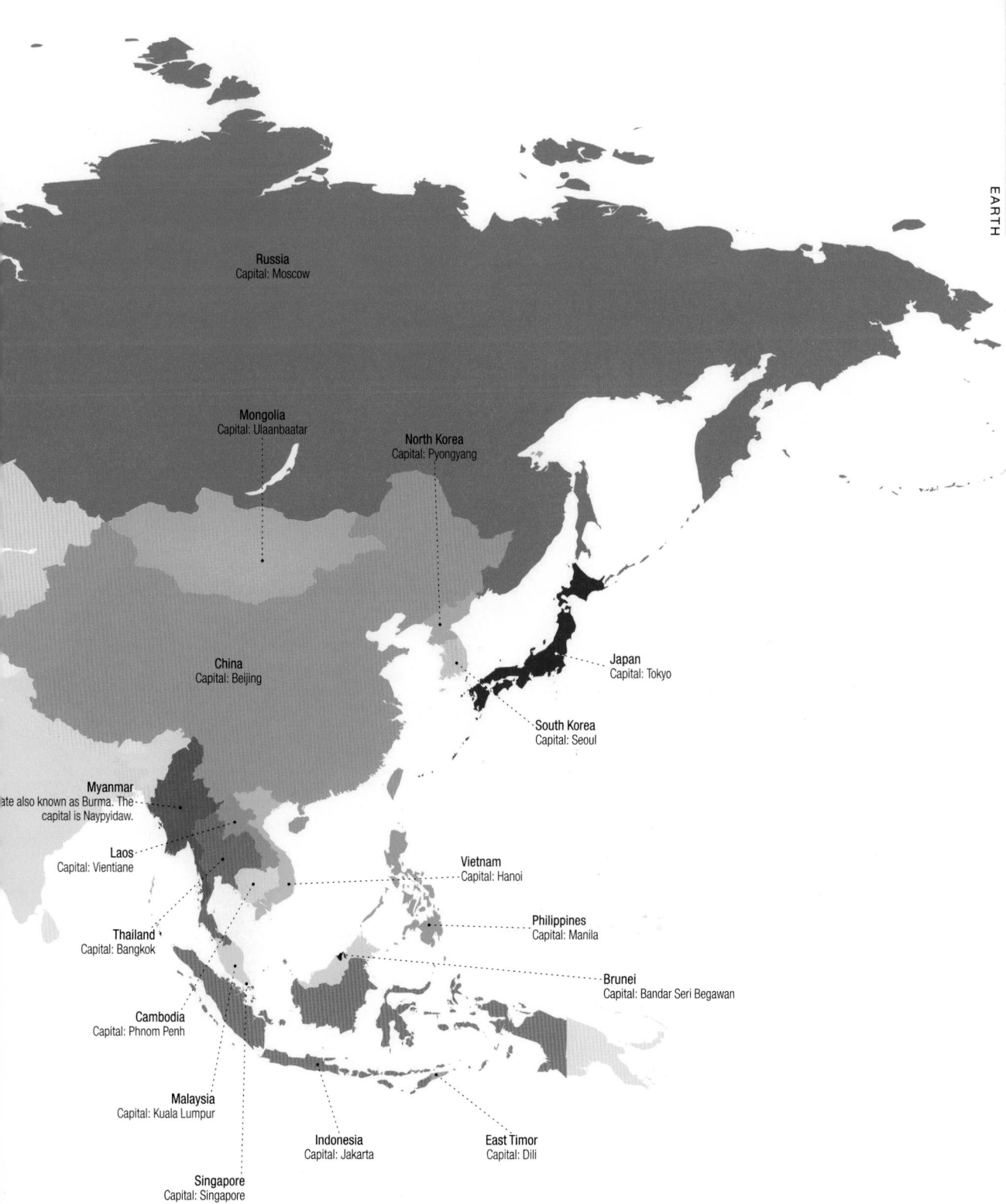

Russia
Capital: Moscow

Mongolia
Capital: Ulaanbaatar

North Korea
Capital: Pyongyang

China
Capital: Beijing

Japan
Capital: Tokyo

South Korea
Capital: Seoul

Myanmar
ate also known as Burma. The
capital is Naypyidaw.

Laos
Capital: Vientiane

Vietnam
Capital: Hanoi

Thailand
Capital: Bangkok

Philippines
Capital: Manila

Brunei
Capital: Bandar Seri Begawan

Cambodia
Capital: Phnom Penh

Malaysia
Capital: Kuala Lumpur

Indonesia
Capital: Jakarta

East Timor
Capital: Dili

Singapore
Capital: Singapore

political cartography

Africa
Continent representing 20% of dry
land on Earth, two thirds of which
are located north of the equator.

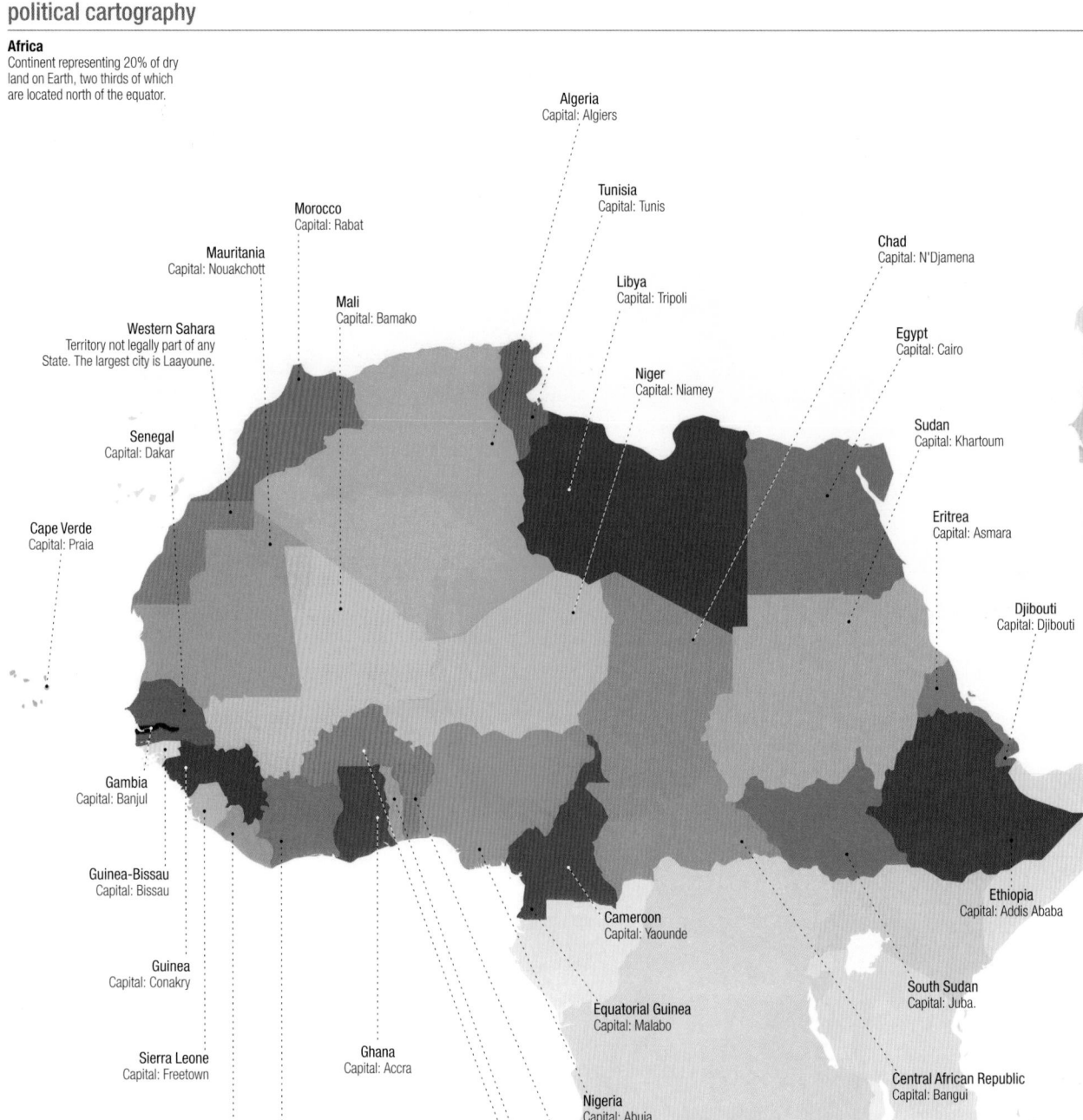

Algeria
Capital: Algiers

Tunisia
Capital: Tunis

Chad
Capital: N'Djamena

Morocco
Capital: Rabat

Libya
Capital: Tripoli

Egypt
Capital: Cairo

Mauritania
Capital: Nouakchott

Mali
Capital: Bamako

Niger
Capital: Niamey

Sudan
Capital: Khartoum

Western Sahara
Territory not legally part of any
State. The largest city is Laayoune.

Eritrea
Capital: Asmara

Senegal
Capital: Dakar

Djibouti
Capital: Djibouti

Cape Verde
Capital: Praia

Gambia
Capital: Banjul

Cameroon
Capital: Yaounde

Ethiopia
Capital: Addis Ababa

Guinea-Bissau
Capital: Bissau

Guinea
Capital: Conakry

South Sudan
Capital: Juba.

Equatorial Guinea
Capital: Malabo

Sierra Leone
Capital: Freetown

Ghana
Capital: Accra

Central African Republic
Capital: Bangui

Nigeria
Capital: Abuja

Liberia
Capital: Monrovia

Burkina Faso
Capital: Ougadougou

Benin
Capital: Porto-Novo

Ivory Coast
Capital: Yamoussoukro

Togo
Capital: Lome

EARTH

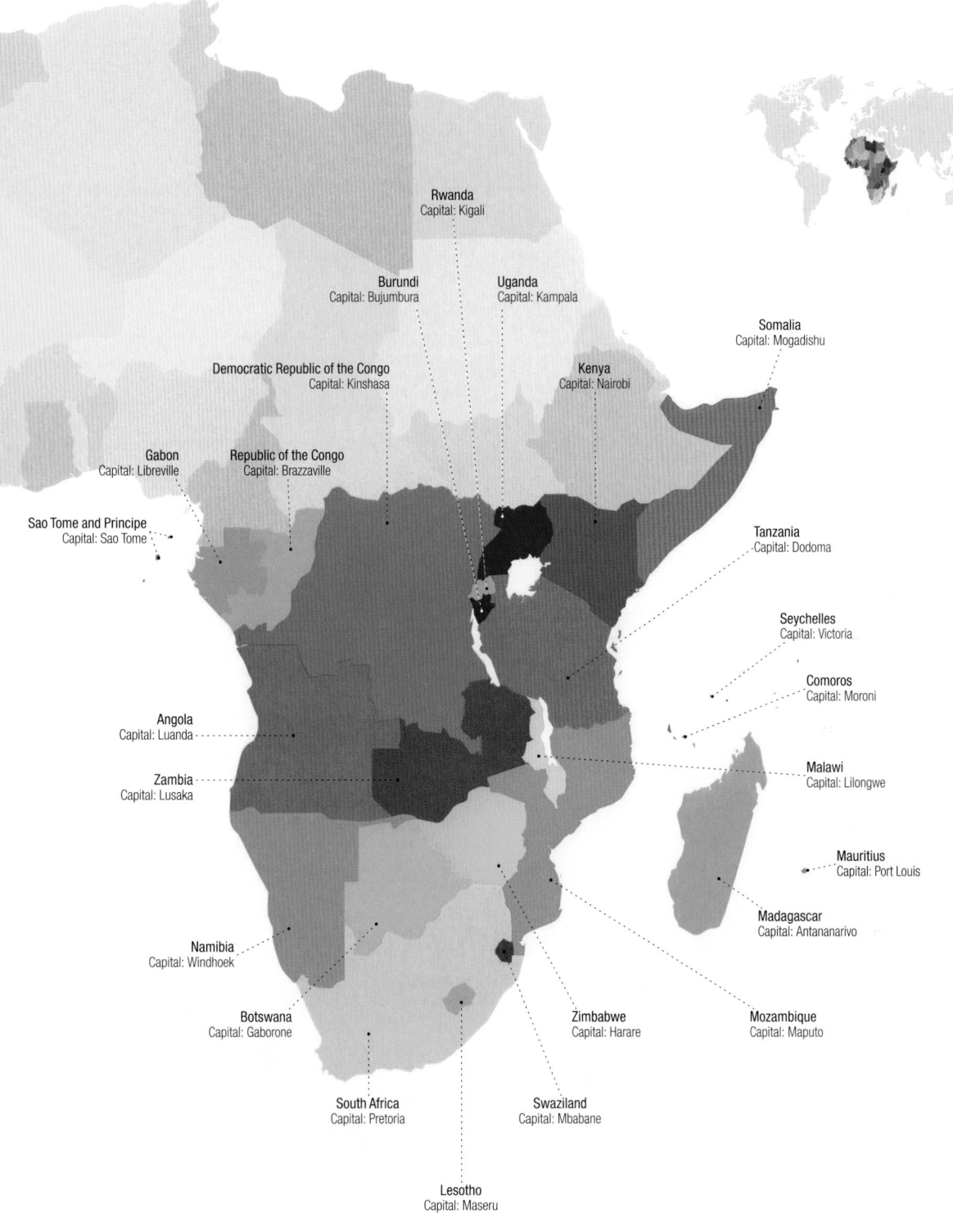

Rwanda
Capital: Kigali

Burundi
Capital: Bujumbura

Uganda
Capital: Kampala

Somalia
Capital: Mogadishu

Democratic Republic of the Congo
Capital: Kinshasa

Kenya
Capital: Nairobi

Gabon
Capital: Libreville

Republic of the Congo
Capital: Brazzaville

Tanzania
Capital: Dodoma

Sao Tome and Principe
Capital: Sao Tome

Seychelles
Capital: Victoria

Comoros
Capital: Moroni

Angola
Capital: Luanda

Malawi
Capital: Lilongwe

Zambia
Capital: Lusaka

Mauritius
Capital: Port Louis

Madagascar
Capital: Antananarivo

Namibia
Capital: Windhoek

Botswana
Capital: Gaborone

Zimbabwe
Capital: Harare

Mozambique
Capital: Maputo

South Africa
Capital: Pretoria

Swaziland
Capital: Mbabane

Lesotho
Capital: Maseru

political cartography

Oceania
Continent representing about 6% of dry land on
Earth, and composed of a profusion of islands
scattered about the Pacific Ocean, the largest
being Australia.

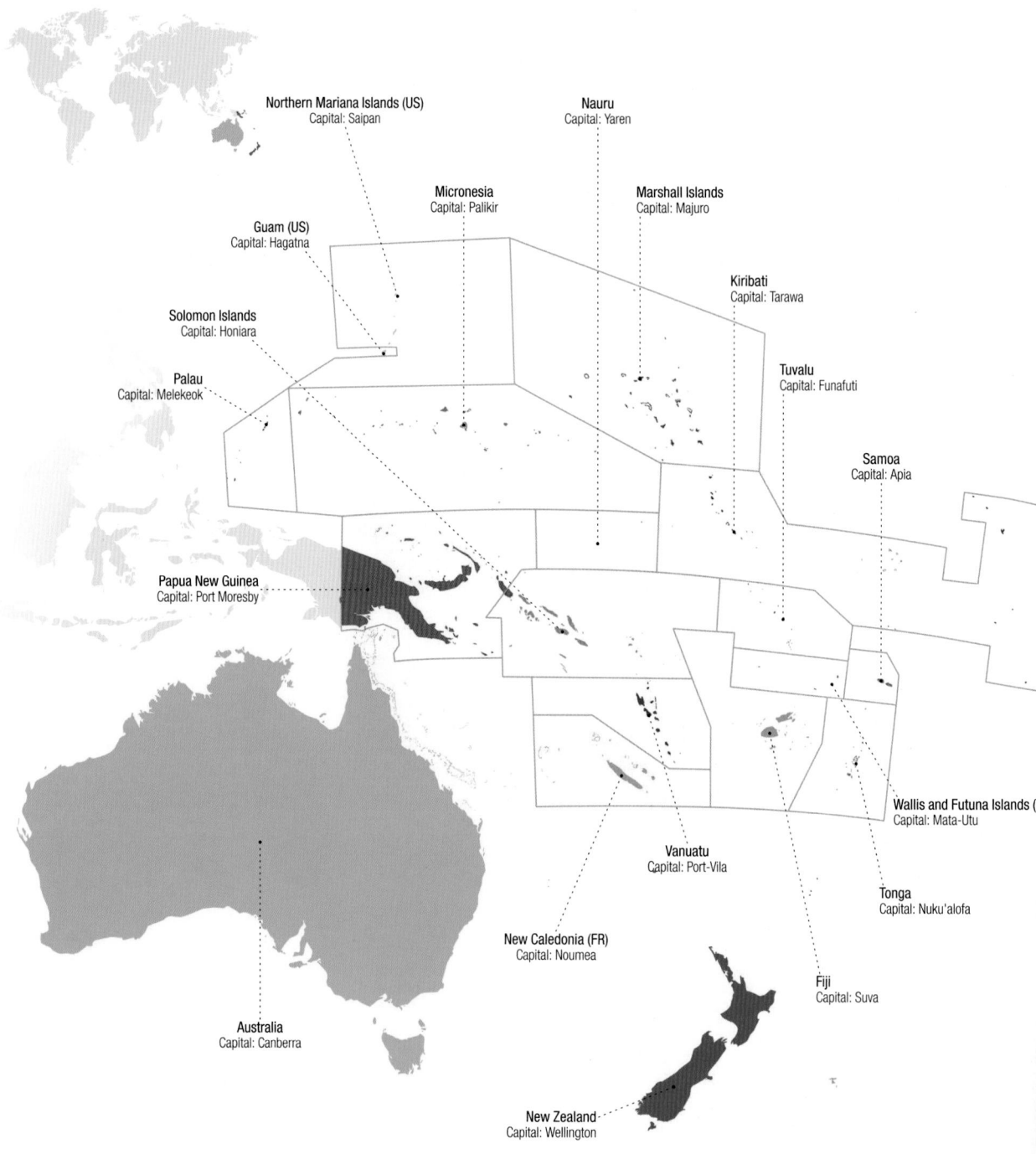

Northern Mariana Islands (US)
Capital: Saipan

Nauru
Capital: Yaren

Micronesia
Capital: Palikir

Marshall Islands
Capital: Majuro

Guam (US)
Capital: Hagatna

Kiribati
Capital: Tarawa

Solomon Islands
Capital: Honiara

Tuvalu
Capital: Funafuti

Palau
Capital: Melekeok

Samoa
Capital: Apia

Papua New Guinea
Capital: Port Moresby

Wallis and Futuna Islands (F
Capital: Mata-Utu

Vanuatu
Capital: Port-Vila

Tonga
Capital: Nuku'alofa

New Caledonia (FR)
Capital: Noumea

Fiji
Capital: Suva

Australia
Capital: Canberra

New Zealand
Capital: Wellington

remote sensing

Technique that uses electromagnetic waves to obtain information about the Earth's surface and atmosphere from a distance.

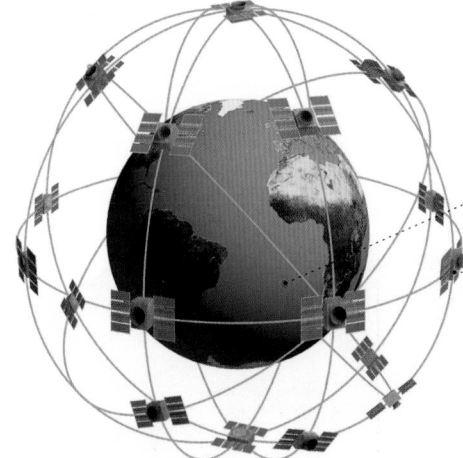

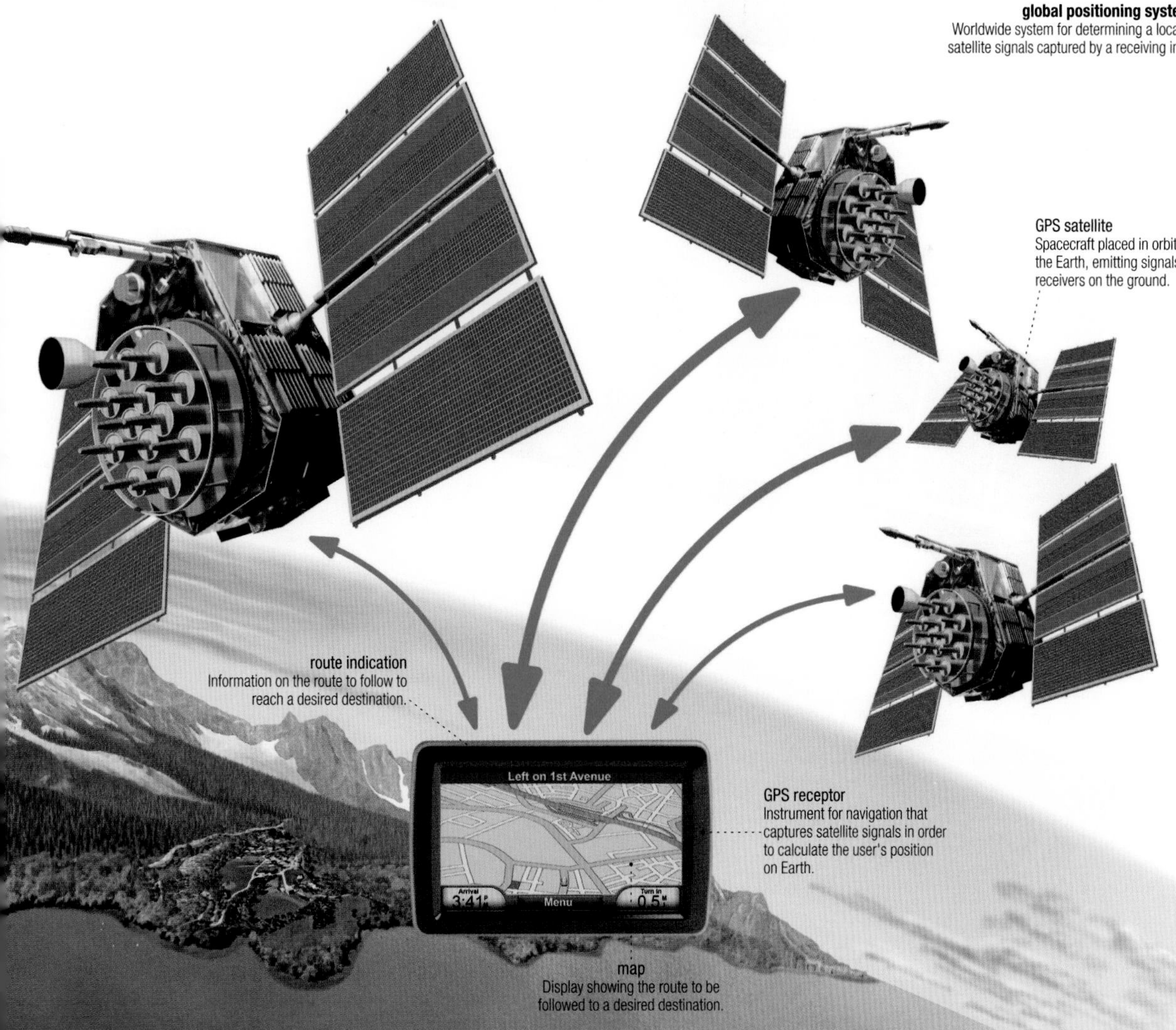

GPS navigation satellite network
All the satellites and ground control stations that make up the global positioning system (GPS).

ground control station
Ground installation from which satellite orbits are calculated and the satellites are checked to ensure they are functioning properly.

GPS satellite
Spacecraft placed in orbit around the Earth, emitting signals to receivers on the ground.

global positioning system (GPS)
Worldwide system for determining a location using satellite signals captured by a receiving instrument.

GPS satellite
Spacecraft placed in orbit around the Earth, emitting signals to receivers on the ground.

route indication
Information on the route to follow to reach a desired destination.

Left on 1st Avenue

Arrival
3:41
Menu
Turn in
0.5

GPS receptor
Instrument for navigation that captures satellite signals in order to calculate the user's position on Earth.

map
Display showing the route to be followed to a desired destination.

EARTH

remote sensing

radar
Detection device that emits
electromagnetic waves and
receives their echoes.

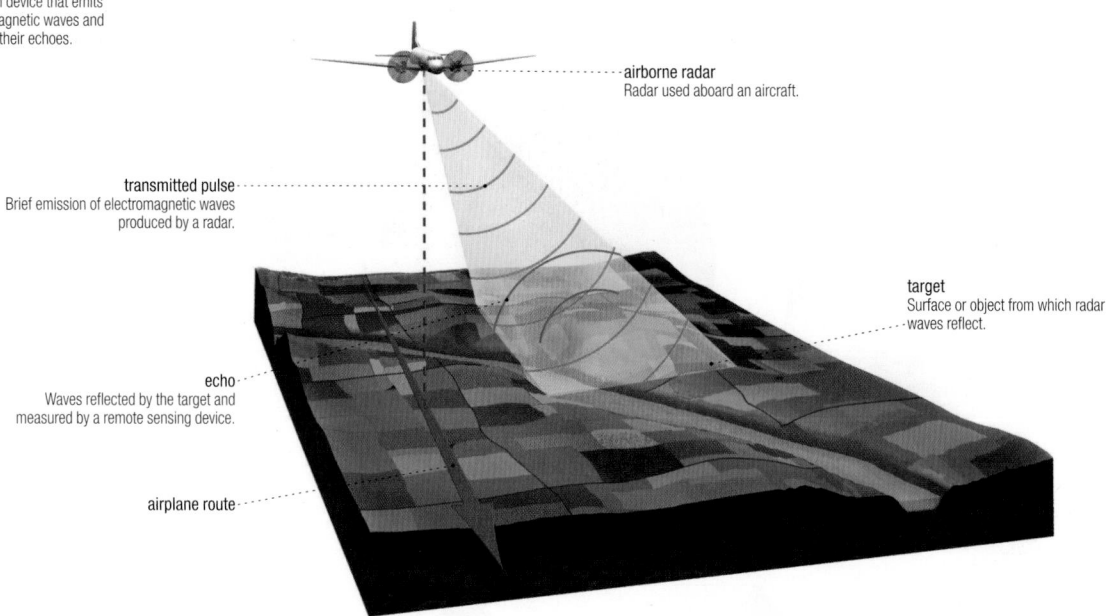

airborne radar
Radar used aboard an aircraft.

transmitted pulse
Brief emission of electromagnetic waves
produced by a radar.

target
Surface or object from which radar
waves reflect.

echo
Waves reflected by the target and
measured by a remote sensing device.

airplane route

Radarsat satellite
Canadian-built Earth observation
satellite used to monitor
environmental changes and natural
resource use.

bus module
Section of the satellite connected to the
payload and equipped with the resources
needed to make it function.

thruster
Piece of equipment that generates
the impetus required to move the
satellite.

Earth sensor
Instrument that locates the Earth's horizon
so that the radar antenna can be positioned
correctly.

Sun sensor
Instrument that positions the solar
panels in the direction of the Sun to
capture its energy.

solar array
Power supply device that converts
solar energy into immediately
usable electrical energy.

payload module
Section of the satellite that
houses detection materials and
maintenance equipment.

remote command antenna
Type of antenna that allows the ground operat
center to transmit commands to the satellite.

support structure

radar antenna
Antenna designed to emit
electromagnetic wave beams and
to capture the echo reflected by the
Earth's surface.

X-band antenna
Type of antenna that emits and
receives extremely high-frequency
waves.

radar beam
Collective term for the fan-shaped
trajectories of electromagnetic
waves emitted in a given direction
by a radar.

sensor swath
Width of the Earth's surface
observed during the passage of a
satellite.

remote sensing

sonar
Detection system emitting
ultrasound; it is used for detection
mainly in a marine environment.

ship

ultrasound waves emission
Production of very high-frequency
sound vibrations whose echo is
captured and analyzed.

target
Surface or object from which sonar
waves reflect.

echo
Waves reflected by the target and
measured by a remote sensing device.

energy source
The origin of the remote sensing
process is an energy source,
for example the Sun, used to
illuminate the target.

satellite remote sensing
Observation of the Earth's surface
and atmosphere by a satellite
equipped with a sensor.

passive sensor
Instrument that receives the waves
produced when the target reflects
the Sun's natural rays.

data recording
If the satellite is unable to
communicate with the terrestrial
station, data is registered on board and
transmitted later.

active sensor
Instrument that itself emits the
energy required to illuminate the
target and receives the waves it
reflects.

data recording
If the satellite is unable to communicate
with the terrestrial station, data is registered
on board and transmitted later.

data processing
Raw data is interpreted and
analyzed to extract information
about the target.

natural radiation
When the sky is clear, the satellite
captures the reflection of the Sun's
rays from the Earth's surface.

data reception
Raw data reaches the terrestrial
station in digital form.

reflection
Phenomenon by which natural
or artificial waves bounce off the
target and toward the satellite.

artificial radiation
When atmospheric conditions hide
the Sun's rays, the active sensor itself
emits radiation waves.

target
Surface or object that reflects the
Sun's rays.

target
Surface or object that reflects the
artificial radiation.

data transmission
The sensor transmits raw data, if
possible immediately, to a terrestrial
station for processing.

structure of the Earth

The Earth is formed of three concentric layers: the core, the mantle and the crust; these are separated by transition zones called discontinuities.

cross section of the Earth

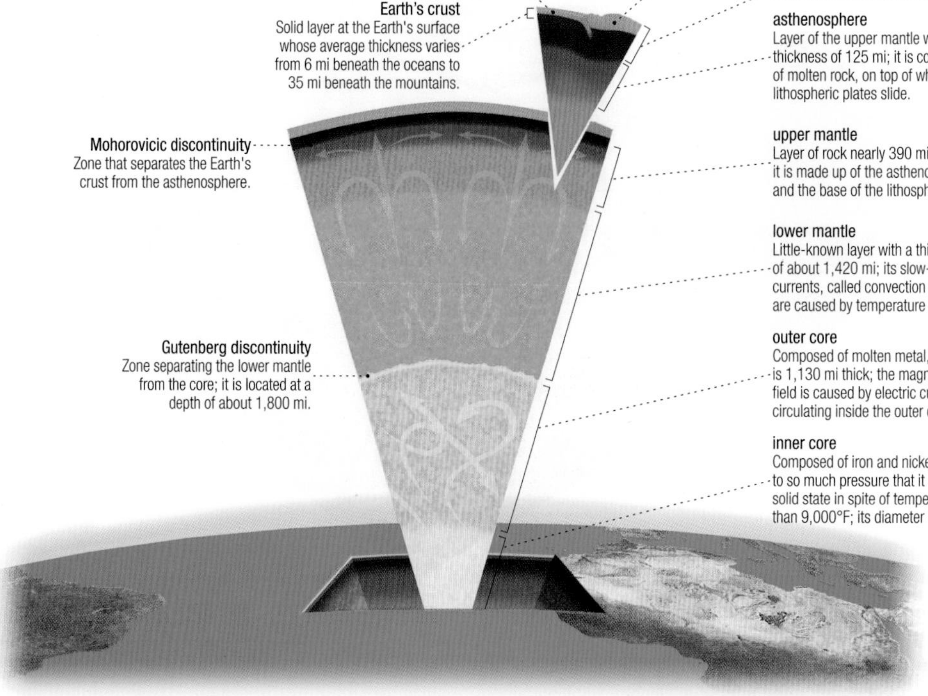

oceanic crust
Layer forming the ocean floor; it is thinner, denser and younger than the continental crust.

continental crust
Layer varying in thickness from 20 to 45 mi and composed mainly of granite. It forms a number of distinct landforms: the continents.

lithosphere
Layer from 30 to 60 mi thick that comprises the Earth's crust and the solid part of the upper mantle; it is divided into tectonic plates.

Earth's crust
Solid layer at the Earth's surface whose average thickness varies from 6 mi beneath the oceans to 35 mi beneath the mountains.

asthenosphere
Layer of the upper mantle with a thickness of 125 mi; it is composed of molten rock, on top of which the lithospheric plates slide.

Mohorovicic discontinuity
Zone that separates the Earth's crust from the asthenosphere.

upper mantle
Layer of rock nearly 390 mi thick; it is made up of the asthenosphere and the base of the lithosphere.

lower mantle
Little-known layer with a thickness of about 1,420 mi; its slow-moving currents, called convection currents, are caused by temperature variations.

Gutenberg discontinuity
Zone separating the lower mantle from the core; it is located at a depth of about 1,800 mi.

outer core
Composed of molten metal, it is 1,130 mi thick; the magnetic field is caused by electric currents circulating inside the outer core.

inner core
Composed of iron and nickel, it is subject to so much pressure that it remains in a solid state in spite of temperatures higher than 9,000°F; its diameter is 1,000 mi.

section of the Earth's crust
The Earth's crust, continental and oceanic, is composed mainly of sedimentary, metamorphic and igneous rock.

sea level
Average height of seawater observed for a given time (day, month, year); it is used as a reference point to define coastal features and measure land elevations.

intrusive rocks
Igneous rocks that have risen close to the Earth's surface.

volcano
Landform built up as lava and ash are ejected from the upper mantle during successive eruptions, accumulating and solidifying on the surface.

sedimentary rocks
Rocks formed by the accumulation, compaction and cementation of fragments of eroded rock and debris left by living organisms.

mountain range
A row of elevated connected landforms characterized by high summits and deep valleys.

deep-sea floor
Part of the Earth's surface beneath the seas and the oceans; its topography is highly variable.

basaltic layer
Layer of basalt, a rock denser than granite, that forms the deep-sea floor and is covered with various types of debris.

granitic layer
Layer of granite that gives the continents their essential form.

metamorphic rocks
Rocks made from igneous or sedimentary rocks that have been subjected to high pressure and very high temperatures.

igneous rocks
Rocks formed from molten magma that has cooled and solidified inside the Earth; also called magmatic rocks.

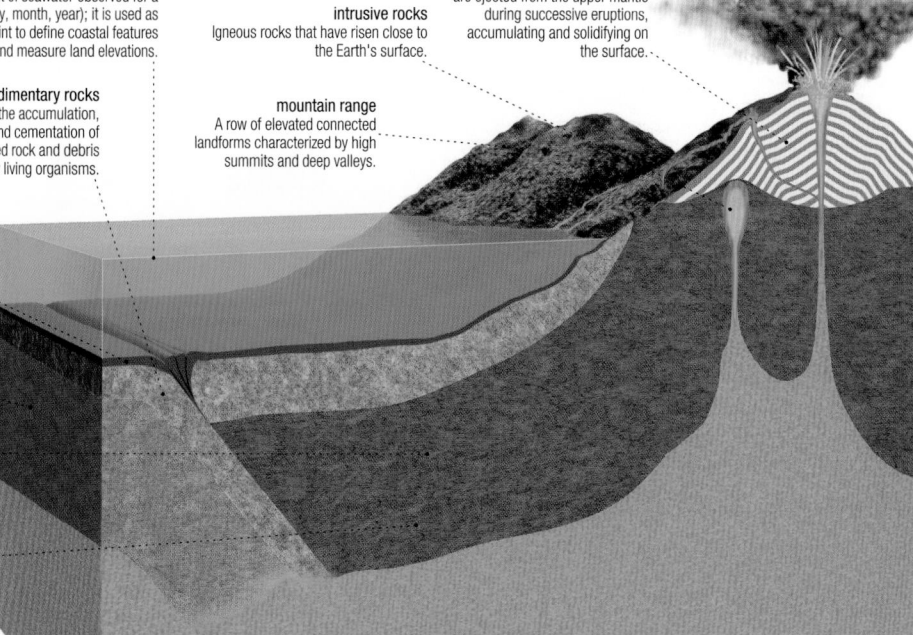

EARTH

ocean floor
Part of the Earth's surface beneath the seas and the oceans; its topography is highly variable.

continental slope
Slope of a few degrees that extends from the continental shelf; it is 660 to 6,600 feet deep.

submarine canyon
Deep valley that is frequently the extension of a river; it ends in a sediment buildup.

continental rise
Gently sloping section of the continental margin; it connects the continental slope to the abyssal plain.

abyssal plain
Zone located at a depth of 6,600 to 20,000 feet; it covers most of the ocean floor.

continent
ay of the vast landmasses and their submerged margins.

mid-ocean ridge
Group of underwater mountain chains criss-crossing the oceans; it is formed by an outpouring of magma.

sea level
Mean water level observed for a given duration (day, month, year); it is used as a reference to define coastal features and calculate the elevation of topographical elements.

abyssal hill
Rounded underwater rise of low elevation.

continental margin
Underwater extension of the continent; it comprises the ontinental shelf, the continental slope and the continental rise.

continental shelf
Section of the continental margin extending from the coast of the continent to the continental rise; its depth is no more than 660 feet.

guyot
Ancient volcano whose summit has been cut off by erosion and then submerged.

seamount
Isolated mountain of volcanic origin featuring a pointed summit.

island arc
String of volcanic islands formed when two tectonic plates meet.

magma
Molten rock and gas under very high pressure that can reach extremely high temperatures.

trench
Extremely deep elongated depression bordering a continent or island arc; it occurs when one tectonic plate moves under another.

volcanic island
Volcano whose summit rises above sea level.

cave
Natural underground cavity that results from the slow dissolution and erosion of rock by water.

column
Crystalline rock formation that results when a stalactite meets a stalagmite.

stalactite
Crystalline rock formation caused by the partial evaporation of water droplets from the vault of the cave.

sinkhole
Basin formed by continuous water infiltration into calcareous rock, causing the dissolution of the rock.

karren
Calcareous rock surface with crests separated by grooves that are often deep; it is shaped by the water.

gorge
Deep narrow ravine along which a permanent or intermittent river flows.

pothole
Natural well connecting a sinkhole to an underground swallow hole.

swallow hole
Deep hole connecting the ground surface to an underground gallery; it is caused by the collapse of the cave's vault.

waterfall
Almost vertical flow of a watercourse, caused by a sudden change in the level of its bed.

dry gallery
Underground corridor that forms when the water table drops.

rimstone
A deposit formed around the edge of a small basin hollowed out by water.

water table
Vast expanse of underground water fed by rainwater filtering through the earth; it supplies springs and can be collected in wells.

subterranean stream
Watercourse that flows through underground cavities.

stalagmite
Crystalline rock formation caused by the evaporation of water droplets that fall on the floor of the cave.

resurgence
The surface reappearance of a watercourse after having disappeared underground.

structure of the Earth

tectonic plates

Immense portions of the lithosphere that slide over the asthenosphere; this shifting movement shapes the Earth's topography.

Cocos Plate
Plate along the coast of Mexico and Central America; it is sinking beneath the North American Plate and the Caribbean Plate.

Arabian Plate
Secondary plate that travels 2 in to the northeast annually along the Dead Sea Fault, resulting in strong seismic activity along that corridor.

Pacific Plate
The only entirely oceanic plate, it is also among the most rapidly shifting plates (4 in per year).

Caribbean Plate
Plate subducting under the American plates; the Caribbean Plate created the islands of the Lesser Antilles.

North American Plate
Together with the Pacific Plate, this plate creates the San Andreas Fault (750 mi), which extends from the Gulf of California to San Francisco.

Eurasian Plate
Plate converging with the Australian-Indian Plate; it created the Himalayas.

Philippine Plate
Plate that forms the Philippines archipelago by means of subduction with the Eurasian Pla

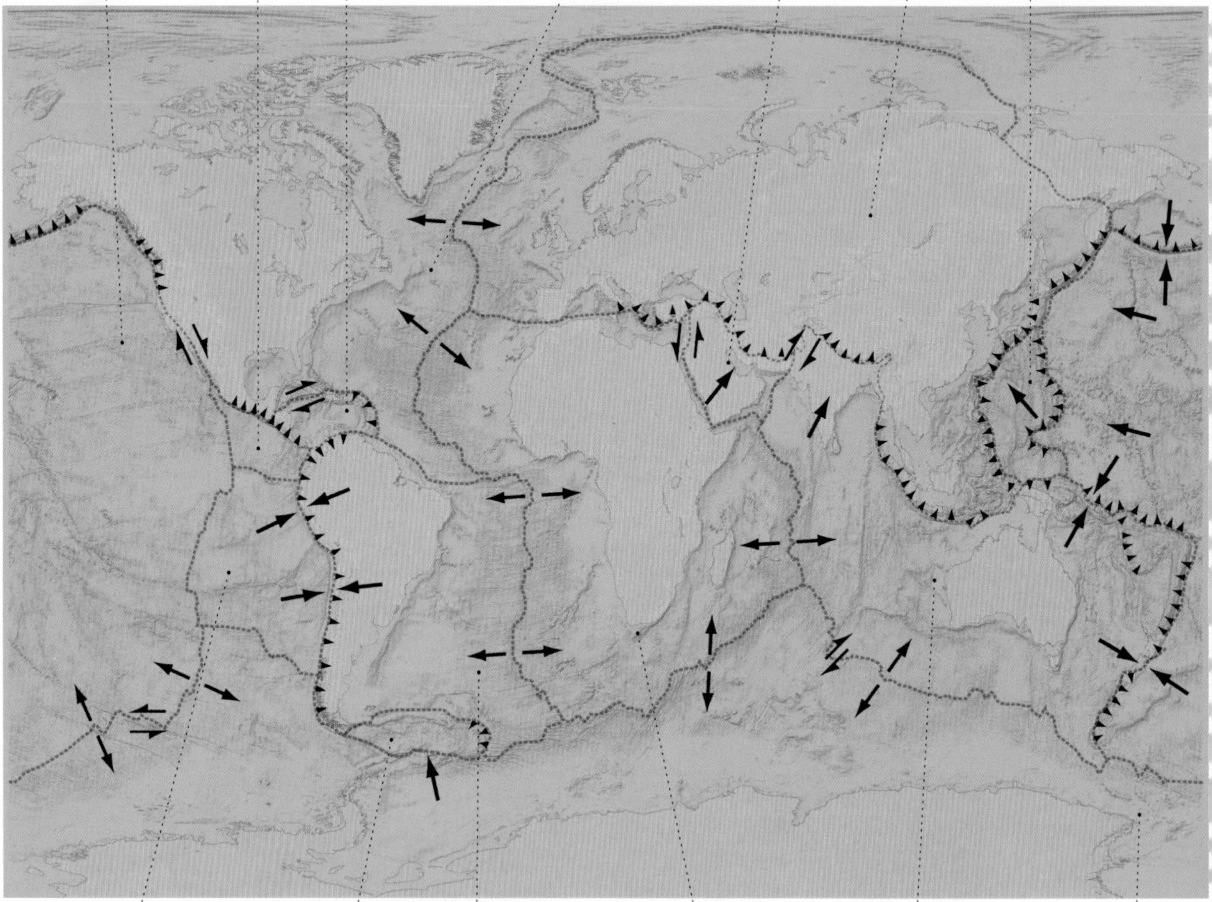

Nazca Plate
One of the most rapidly shifting plates, moving 3 in per year.

Scotia Plate
Small plate under which the Antarctic Plate and part of the South American Plate are sliding.

South American Plate
Plate that forms the Andes cordillera by means of subduction with the Nazca Plate.

African Plate
Plate that, diverging from the South American Plate, forms an underwater mountain chain.

Australian-Indian Plate
Plate that is moving north 3 in per year; it forms the Red Sea by means of divergence from the African Plate.

Antarctic Plate
The largest plate; it is station

subduction
Phenomenon by which an oceanic plate slides under a continental plate or under another oceanic plate, resulting in a trench.

transform plate boundaries
Plates that slide against each other, triggering earthquakes along faults of the same name.

convergent plate boundaries
Plates that collide, triggering either subduction or folding, which results in the creation of mountains.

divergent plate boundaries
Plates that are moving apart, causing magma to appear, which solidifies to generate a new crust.

structure of the Earth

ocean trenches and ridges
Trench: very deep, elongated cavity bordering a continent or an island arc; it forms when one tectonic plate slides beneath another.
Ridge: underwater mountain range that criss-crosses the oceans and is formed by rising magma in a zone where two plates are moving apart.

Puerto Rico Trench
Trench located off the coast of Puerto Rico, on the boundary between the South American and Caribbean plates; it features the deepest point in the Atlantic Ocean (28,374 ft).

Mariana Trench
Cavity located near the Mariana Islands, where the Pacific Plate and the Philippine Plate converge; it is the world's deepest trench (about 36,000 feet).

Aleutian Trench
rench (25,600 feet) extending from ska to the Kamchatka Peninsula; sults from the Pacific Plate sliding neath the North American Plate.

Europe
Western extremity of the vast Eurasian continent that, by convention, is separated from Asia by the Ural Mountains; it covers a relatively small area.

Ryukyu Trench
Trench (24,629 feet) located near the Ryukyu Islands; it marks the boundary between the Philippine Plate and the Eurasian Plate.

Japan Trench
Trench (27,929 feet) located east of Japan, on the boundary between the Pacific Plate and the Eurasian Plate; this zone is marked by intense seismic activity.

North America
Its area (9.3 million mi²) represents about 16% of the world's land; the Central American isthmus is an extension of North America.

Mid-Atlantic Ridge
Ridge about 7,000 mi long, located in the middle of the Atlantic Ocean; some of its mountains reach the surface, forming islands such as Iceland.

Asia
The largest and most populous continent, Asia represents 32% of the world's land; it is dominated by imposing mountain ranges.

Kuril Trench
Trench (34,587 feet) located northeast of Japan; it results from the Pacific Plate sliding beneath the Eurasian Plate.

EARTH

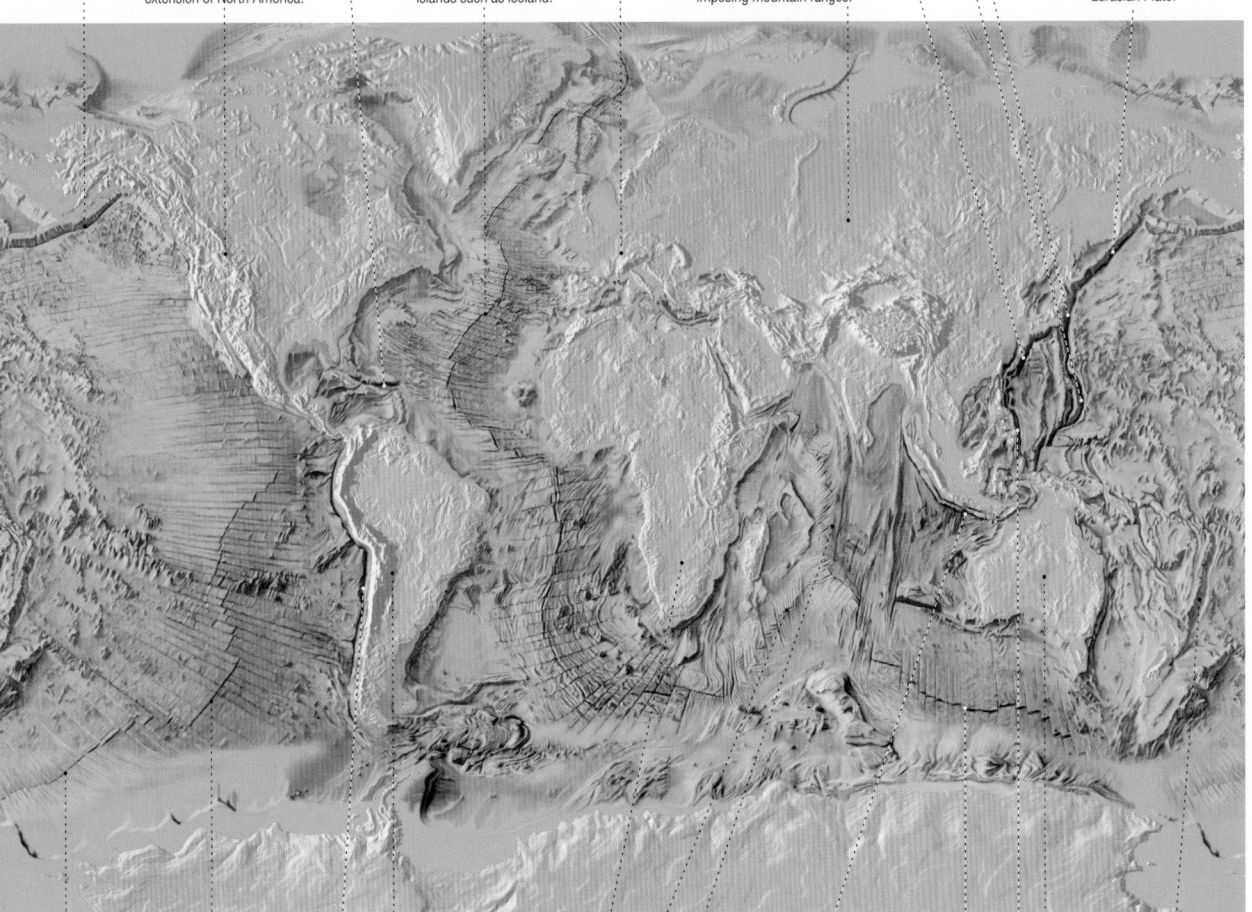

East Pacific Rise
Ridge that marks the boundary between the Pacific and Cocos Islands plates to the north, and the Pacific and Nazca plates to the south.

Africa
Continent that represents about 20% of the world's land; two-thirds of its surface lies north of the Equator. Characterized by very hot climates, Mediterranean in the north and south, tropical and arid elsewhere.

Java Trench
Trench located south of Indonesia, between the Australian-Indian and the Eurasian Plates; it is the deepest point in the Indian Ocean (25,344 ft).

Kermadec-Tonga Trench
Cavity located north of New Zealand, where the Pacific Plate meets the Australian-Indian Plate; it reaches depths of 35,702 feet.

Pacific-Antarctic Ridge
Mountain range separating the Pacific and Antarctic plates; it joins the eastern Pacific Ridge off the coast of South America.

Southwest Indian Ridge
Ridge separating the African and Antarctic plates; it joins the Mid-Indian and Southeast Indian ridges off the coast of Madagascar.

Southeast Indian Ridge
Ridge separating the Antarctic Plate from the Australian-Indian Plate; its topography is more regular than the topography of the Southwest Indian and Mid-Indian ridges.

Australia
The world's largest island (3 million mi²) is sparsely inhabited in spite of its size; because of its isolation, Australia's wildlife is unique.

Peru-Chile Trench
Trench (26,460 feet) bordering South America; the world's longest trench (3,700 mi), it is located on the boundary between the Nazca Plate and the South American Plate.

Mid-Indian Ridge
Mountain range in the middle of the Indian Ocean that separates the African and Australian-Indian plates.

Philippine Trench
Trench bordering the eastern Philippines, reaching depths of 34,578 feet; it results from the Philippine Plate sinking beneath the Eurasian Plate.

South America
Represents about 12% of the world's land and is linked to North America by Central America; its features include the Andes in the west and plains and plateaus in east and central regions.

Earth features

The surface configuration of the Earth's land and ocean floor.

EARTH

common coastal features
Area where the land meets the sea; its features vary depending on climate, wind, sea and the type of rocks of which it is composed.

stack
Needle-shaped column resulting from the collapse of an arch.

estuary
Mouth of a river that is influenced by the tides; it forms an indentation in the coastline that varies in width and depth.

dune
Accumulation of sand shaped by the wind.

lagoon
Shallow expanse of seawater separated from the sea by a rid of sand or a barrier island.

cave
Natural underground cavity that results from the slow dissolution and erosion of rock by water.

natural arch
Arch hollowed out of a headland by the sea.

barrier island
Long broad sandy island parallel to and protective shore.

beach
Accumulation of sand or pebbles along a coast.

sand island
Exposed summit of a sand de formed near or occasionally fa a shoreline.

tombolo
Ridge of sand joining an island to the shoreline.

rocky islet
Small island made of rock.

cliff
Steep rock face shaped by the sea.

spit
Elongated ridge of sand or pebbles extending into the water.

skerry
Rock tip just above the surface of the water.

headland
Tapering strip of land jutting into the sea.

examples of shorelines
Shoreline: strip of land where the sea meets the land.

barrier beach
Usually narrow ridge of sand or pebbles bordering the shoreline.

fjords
Deep glacial valleys filled with seawater and cutting into the shoreline.

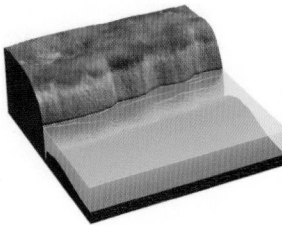

shore cliff
Steep rock face shaped by the sea.

delta
Section of the coastline where sediment builds up at the mouth of a river, divided into several arms.

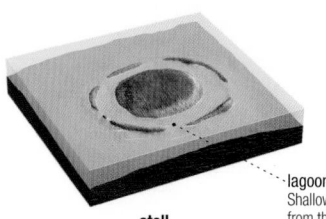

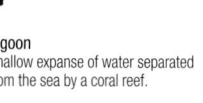
lagoon
Shallow expanse of water separated from the sea by a coral reef.

atoll
Ring-shaped coral-reef island enclosing a lagoon and often a central island.

rias
Coastal valleys that are filled by the sea and get shallower inland.

Earth features

mountain
Elevated landform characterized by steep slopes; it is usually part of a chain.

summit
The highest point on the mountain.

pass
Depression in a mountain landscape that creates a passage.

perpetual snows
Accumulations of snow on the highest reaches of a mountain that never melt.

spur
A lower mountain chain bordering a principal chain.

cliff
A steep and fairly smooth slope.

crest
Line intersecting two mountain slopes; a crest can run all the way into the valley.

peak
Mountain whose summit forms a cone or point.

ridge
Long narrow section at the highest point on a mountain.

mountain slope
A mountain face that reaches down into the valley.

mountain torrent
Watercourse flowing steeply with irregular flow; it is subject to violent floods when the snow melts.

hill
Moderately high landform whose slopes follow a gentle incline.

valley
Elongated depression shaped by a watercourse or glacier and bounded by the slopes of the surrounding land.

forest
Vast expanse of land covered with trees.

drumlin
Low hill sculpted by a moving glacier and formed of glacial drift; drumlins are usually found in parallel groupings.

kettle
Cavity formed as a mass of melting ice detaches from the tongue of a receding glacier; some kettles fill with water to form a lake.

plateau
Vast expanse of relatively flat land, higher than the surrounding region and bounded by deep valleys with sheer cliffs.

lake
Body of water completely surrounded by land; it varies in size and depth.

Earth features

glacier
Mass of ice resulting from the accumulation and compression of snow; it moves under its own weight.

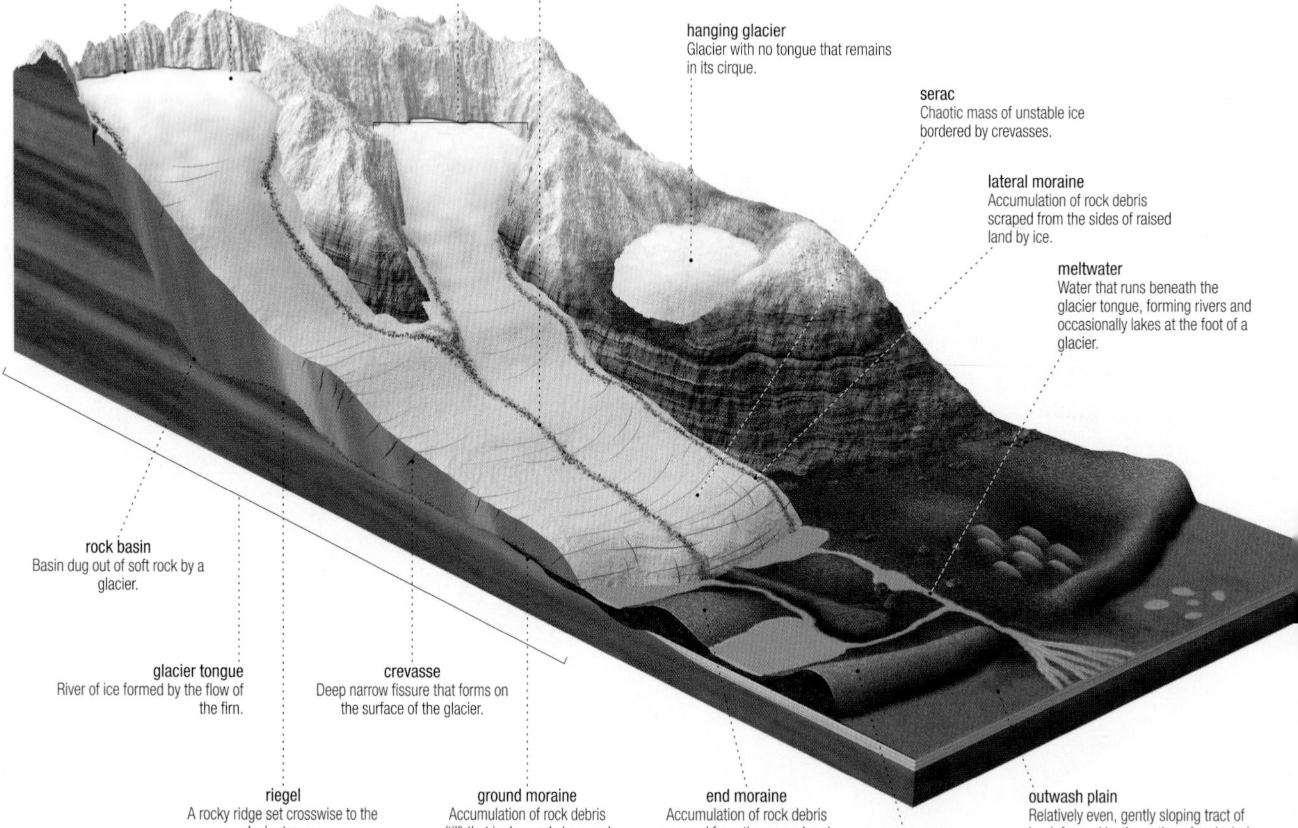

bergschrund
Crevasse between the firn and the rock face; it appears when the glacier breaks away from the rock face.

glacial cirque
Semicircular cavity with steep sides, carved out by ice.

firn
Accumulation of snow inside a cirque; compressed by its own weight, it is converted into ice and feeds the glacier.

medial moraine
Accumulation of rock debris that forms where the lateral moraines of two parallel glacier tongues come together.

hanging glacier
Glacier with no tongue that remains in its cirque.

serac
Chaotic mass of unstable ice bordered by crevasses.

lateral moraine
Accumulation of rock debris scraped from the sides of raised land by ice.

meltwater
Water that runs beneath the glacier tongue, forming rivers and occasionally lakes at the foot of a glacier.

rock basin
Basin dug out of soft rock by a glacier.

glacier tongue
River of ice formed by the flow of the firn.

crevasse
Deep narrow fissure that forms on the surface of the glacier.

riegel
A rocky ridge set crosswise to the glacier tongue.

ground moraine
Accumulation of rock debris (till) that is dragged along and deposited under the advancing glacier.

end moraine
Accumulation of rock debris scraped from the ground and pushed to the front of the glacier.

outwash plain
Relatively even, gently sloping tract of land, formed by the action of a glacier's meltwater.

terminal moraine
Accumulation of rock debris marking the glacier's most advanced position before it recedes.

Earth features

EARTH

watercourse
Natural flow of water that varies in size, depending on the ground slope and the number of tributaries.

brook
ll watercourse that is a tributary of a river or a lake.

glacier
Mass of ice resulting from the accumulation and compression of snow; it moves under its own weight.

spring
oint where underground water es to the surface; it may be the source of a watercourse.

upper course of river
Part of the river closest to its source.

gorge
Deep narrow valley bounded by steep or very sheer slopes, carved out by a watercourse.

river
Natural watercourse fed by numerous smaller streams; it empties into a larger river or the sea.

alluvial deposits
Sediment (mud, sand, gravel, pebbles) transported and then deposited by a watercourse.

valley
Elongated depression shaped by a watercourse or glacier and bounded by the slopes of the surrounding land.

oxbow lake
Crescent-shaped lake formed when a river changes course by flowing across the neck of an oxbow.

delta distributary
Channel that a river or stream follows near its mouth; several arms, separated by alluvial deposits, form a delta.

plain
Vast, relatively flat expanse of land, lower than the surrounding landscape; its valleys are wide and shallow.

floodplain
Level surface bordering a watercourse; it is subject to periodic flooding.

waterfall
Almost vertical flow of a atercourse, caused by a sudden change in the level of its bed.

sea
Vast body of saltwater at some distance inland; it is not as deep as an ocean.

lake
Body of water completely surrounded by land; it varies in size and depth.

affluent
Watercourse that flows into a larger watercourse or a lake.

effluent
Watercourse from a lake or glacier.

confluence
Point where two or more watercourses meet.

oxbow
Meander in which only a narrow neck of land remains between the two parts of the watercourse.

delta
Section of the coastline where sediment builds up at the mouth of a river, divided into several arms.

---

examples of lakes
Lake: body of water completely surrounded by land; it varies in size and depth.

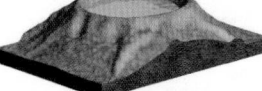

glacial lake
Lake that fills a basin dug out by a glacier, whose meltwater then forms the lake.

volcanic lake
Lake that fills the crater of an extinct volcano.

tectonic lake
Lake that occupies a natural basin resulting from a collapse of the Earth's crust.

oxbow lake
Crescent-shaped lake formed when a river changes course by flowing across the neck of an oxbow.

oasis
Desert zone made fertile by the presence of underground or surface water.

artificial lake
Lake created when a dam is built on a watercourse.

Earth features

desert
A region, usually characterized by heat, where aridity (less than 4 in of annual rainfall) is such that plant and animal life is scarce.

butte
Rocky hill shaped by erosion, with steep sides and a flat summit; it is smaller in area than a mesa.

mesa
Isolated plateau with a flat summit and very steep sides; it features a layer of rock that is resistant to erosion.

sandy desert
Desert where minuscule grains of rock (sand) form dunes by wind action.

needle
Tapering pointed column of rock shaped by the wind.

rocky desert
Most common type of desert, where rock fragments fracture due to temperature variations between night and day.

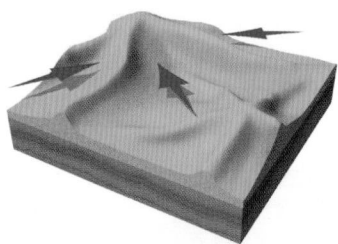
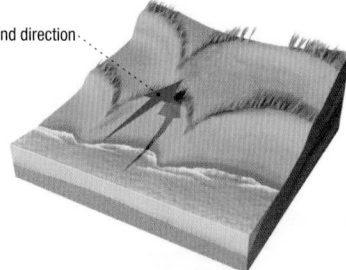

wadi
Often dry watercourse that is subject to sudden flooding in the event of rain.

palm grove
Zone where palm trees are planted.

saline lake
Lake characterized by high salt content due to considerable water evaporation and the concentration of dissolved mineral salts.

oasis
Desert zone made fertile by the presence of underground or surface water.

dune
Accumulation of sand transported by the wind, found in deserts and along coasts.

examples of dunes
Dune: accumulation of sand transported by the wind, found in deserts and along coasts.

wind direction

crescentic dune
Moving crescent-shaped dune whose arms extend in the same direction as the wind.

star dune
Star-shaped dune that forms where winds blowing in various directions meet.

parabolic dune
Crescent-shaped coastal dune whose arms point into the wind; vegetation often keeps it in place.

longitudinal dunes
Narrow elongated dunes that form when the wind blows in two convergent directions.

transverse dunes
Dunes that form perpendicular to the direction of the wind.

chain of dunes
Dunes aligned in the same direction, parallel to the wind.

geological phenomena

Events linked to the movement of tectonic plates or sections of the Earth's surface.

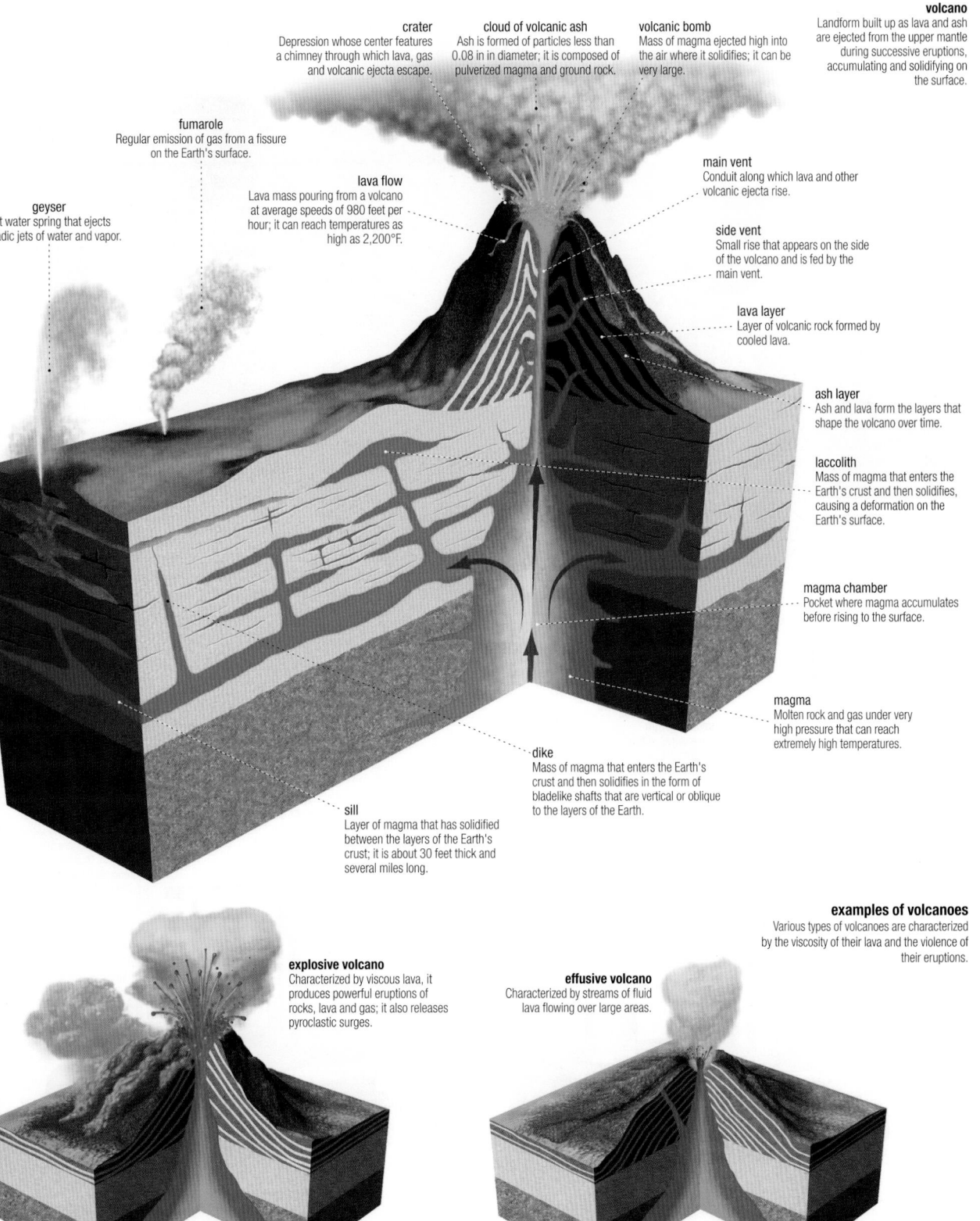

volcano
Landform built up as lava and ash are ejected from the upper mantle during successive eruptions, accumulating and solidifying on the surface.

crater
Depression whose center features a chimney through which lava, gas and volcanic ejecta escape.

cloud of volcanic ash
Ash is formed of particles less than 0.08 in in diameter; it is composed of pulverized magma and ground rock.

volcanic bomb
Mass of magma ejected high into the air where it solidifies; it can be very large.

fumarole
Regular emission of gas from a fissure on the Earth's surface.

main vent
Conduit along which lava and other volcanic ejecta rise.

lava flow
Lava mass pouring from a volcano at average speeds of 980 feet per hour; it can reach temperatures as high as 2,200°F.

side vent
Small rise that appears on the side of the volcano and is fed by the main vent.

geyser
...ot water spring that ejects ...adic jets of water and vapor.

lava layer
Layer of volcanic rock formed by cooled lava.

ash layer
Ash and lava form the layers that shape the volcano over time.

laccolith
Mass of magma that enters the Earth's crust and then solidifies, causing a deformation on the Earth's surface.

magma chamber
Pocket where magma accumulates before rising to the surface.

magma
Molten rock and gas under very high pressure that can reach extremely high temperatures.

dike
Mass of magma that enters the Earth's crust and then solidifies in the form of bladelike shafts that are vertical or oblique to the layers of the Earth.

sill
Layer of magma that has solidified between the layers of the Earth's crust; it is about 30 feet thick and several miles long.

examples of volcanoes
Various types of volcanoes are characterized by the viscosity of their lava and the violence of their eruptions.

explosive volcano
Characterized by viscous lava, it produces powerful eruptions of rocks, lava and gas; it also releases pyroclastic surges.

effusive volcano
Characterized by streams of fluid lava flowing over large areas.

EARTH

geological phenomena

earthquake
Sudden tremor in a region of the Earth's crust caused by one rock mass sliding against another.

fault
Fracture in the Earth's crust separating two blocks that slide against one another during an earthquake.

depth of focus
Distance between the focus and the epicenter; it can reach 430 mi.

epicenter
Point on the Earth's surface located directly over the focus, where the most violent tremors are felt.

isoseismal line
Curved line connecting the points on the Earth's surface that have been subject to tremors of the same intensity.

seismic wave propagation

Earth's crust
Solid layer at the Earth's sur whose thickness varies from beneath the oceans to 35 beneath the mountains.

seismic wave
Series of vibrations generated at the focus that disperse in all directions, causing shaking of the Earth's surface.

focus
Point in the Earth's crust where an earthquake is triggered. Also called the hypocenter.

energy release
It travels in all directions in the form of seismic waves.

seismographs
Instruments that record seismic wave amplitude at a given point on the Earth's surface.

vertical seismograph
Instrument that measures vertical ground movement.

horizontal seismograph
Instrument that measures horizontal ground movement.

mass
Independent of ground movement, it remains stationary during an earthquake, thus serving as a reference for measuring the amplitude of tremors.

spring
It keeps the mass from moving.

pen
Writing instrument that converts ground movement into a line.

rotating drum
Secured to the ground, it rotates under the pen, recording ground movements on paper.

seismogram
Graphic representation produced by a seismograph; the stronger the tremors, the greater the oscillations on the paper.

pillar
Very solid vertical support.

stand
Horizontal support that is secured to the ground.

bedrock
Extremely hard rock mass joined with the subsoil.

vertical ground movement

seismogram
Graphic representation produced by a seismograph; the stronger the tremors, the greater the oscillations on the paper.

mass
Independent of ground movement, it remains stationary during an earthquake, thus serving as a reference for measuring the amplitude of tremors.

pen
Writing instrument that converts ground movement into a line.

horizontal ground movement

rotating drum
Secured to the ground, it rotates under the pen, recording ground movements on paper.

geological phenomena

EARTH

tsunami
Gigantic wave produced by an underwater geological event (earthquake, volcanic eruption, landslide) that breaks along the coast.

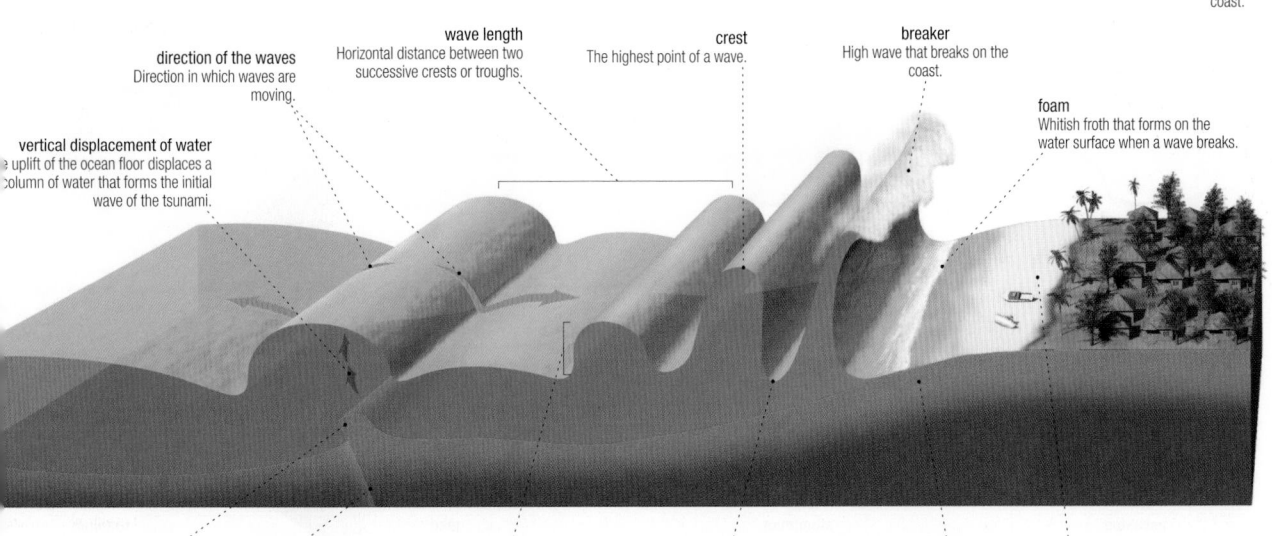

direction of the waves
Direction in which waves are moving.

wave length
Horizontal distance between two successive crests or troughs.

crest
The highest point of a wave.

breaker
High wave that breaks on the coast.

foam
Whitish froth that forms on the water surface when a wave breaks.

vertical displacement of water
e uplift of the ocean floor displaces a column of water that forms the initial wave of the tsunami.

uplift
ard movement of a part of the n floor, creating a shock wave moves through the water and results in surface waves.

fault
Fracture in the Earth's crust between two tectonic plates.

wave height
Vertical distance between the crest and the trough.

trough
The lowest point of the wave.

sand bar
Accumulation of sediment at the bottom of the sea, close to the shoreline; it is sometimes exposed at low tide.

shore
Strip of land where the sea meets the land.

landslides
Ground movements that vary in speed, depending on the slope's gradient, the nature of the soil and what triggers it.

rockslide
Rock mass that suddenly detaches and falls from the top of a steep slope; it is caused by freeze-thaw action or by gravity.

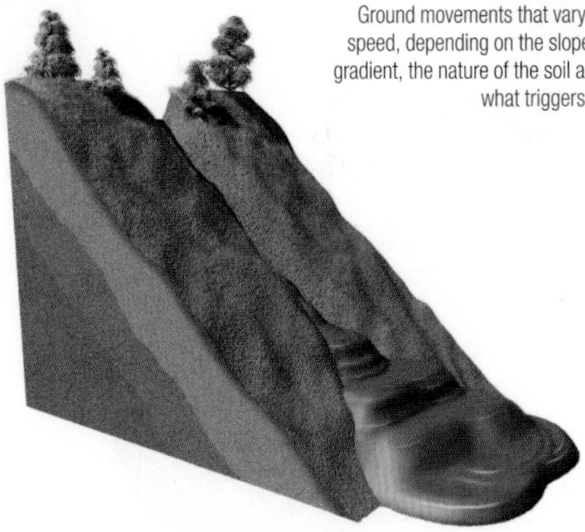

mudflow
Sudden flow of mud along a slope; it occurs when torrential rains quickly saturate the soil.

creep
Very slow, imperceptible movement of earth along a slope, caused mainly by alternating wet and dry periods.

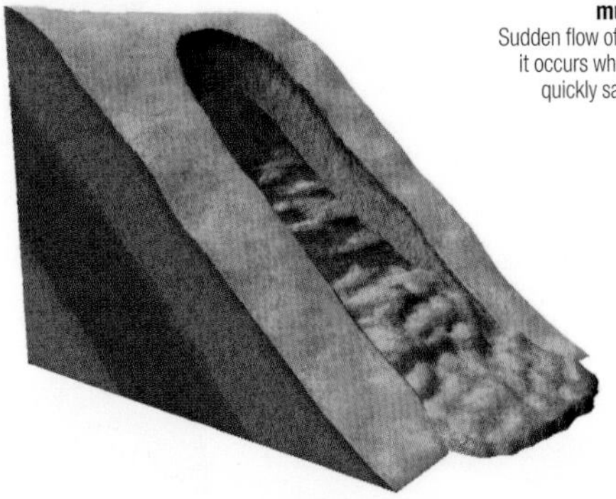

earthflow
The upper section of a sloping water-soaked terrain that collapses, forming a tongue of land the length of the slope.

minerals

Naturally occurring solid inorganic bodies having characteristic chemical compositions.

examples of common metals and minerals

Pure mineral: naturally occurring solid inorganic body having a characteristic chemical composition.

mercury
Liquid metal formerly used in some batteries.

chromium
Hard and non-oxidizing metal used as an anti-corrosive coating, as a catalyst, and in glass and paint colorings.

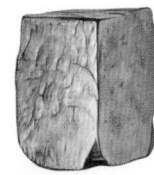

platinum
Precious metal, quite hard and resistant to corrosion. Used in jewelry and in the making of laboratory equipment and certain electrical contacts.

silver
Precious metal, malleable and non oxidizing. Used in jewelry, silver smith and photography, as well as in the ma of coins and medals.

asbestos
Fibrous mineral used to make fireproof materials.

aluminum
Light and malleable metal, oxidizes little in contact with air, and conducts electricity and heat well. Used in the making of vehicles and electronic appliances.

lead
Very dense, soft, and malleable metal used in batteries, glass, and to protect against radiation.

uranium
Slightly radioactive metal used as a raw material in the nuclear industry. It is found in the earth in the form of its ore (uranium dioxide).

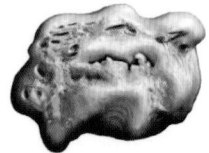

gold
Precious metal, unalterable by air and water, primarily used in jewelry. Its value previously served as a worldwide monetary standard.

nickel
Malleable metal, non-oxidizing and very resistant, used in many metal alloys. It is notably included in the making of coins.

iron
Malleable grey metal, magnetic, frequently used in manufacturing and technology, generally as part of an alloy (the best-known being steel).

copper
Very malleable metal, conducts heat and electricity well. Used for making utensils and electric wires.

tin
Soft and malleable metal, water resistant, but susceptible to acid. Used in soldering.

zinc
Bluish white metal, resistant to deterioration, with a dull finish. It is primarily used in galvanization (galvanized steel).

titanium
Metal, light and resistant to corrosion. Titanium dioxide is a pigment used in paint, paper and drugs.

examples of metal alloys

Metal alloy: substance resulting from the mixing of a metal with one or more other metals or chemical elements.

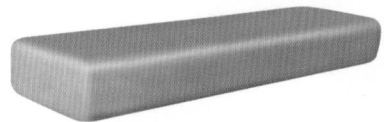

steel = iron + carbon
Steel is a very tough alloy often used in the construction of buildings, bridges and other structures.

bronze = copper + tin
Bronze is an alloy that is quite resistant to wear and corrosion, and is a good conductor of electricity. It is used for making statues, musical instruments and various electrical parts.

brass = copper + zinc
Brass is a malleable alloy notably used in the making of precision instruments, utensils and plumbing fixtures.

profile of the Earth's atmosphere

Atmosphere: layer of air that surrounds the Earth and is composed mainly of nitrogen (78%) and oxygen (21%); its density decreases with altitude.

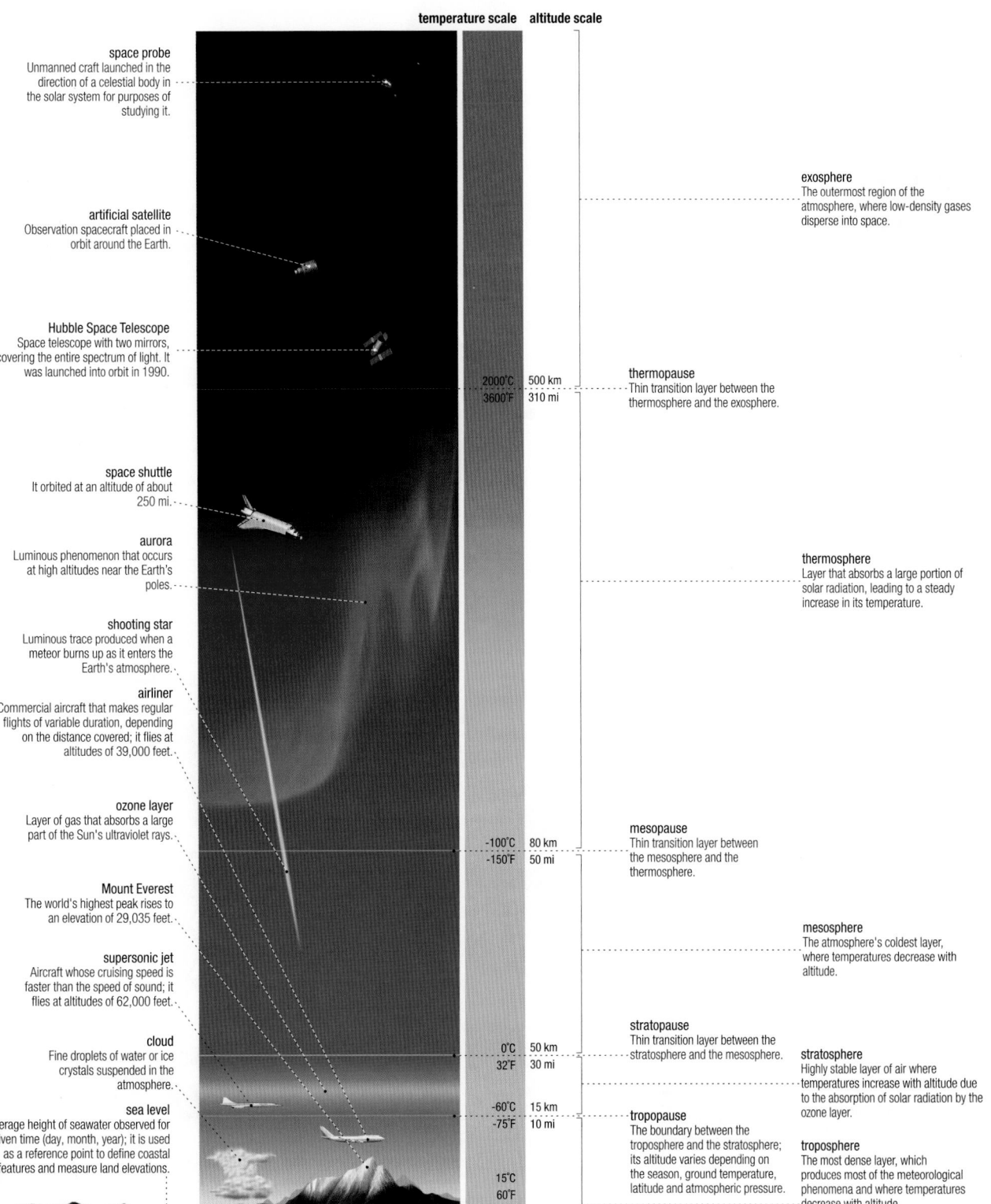

temperature scale   altitude scale

space probe
Unmanned craft launched in the direction of a celestial body in the solar system for purposes of studying it.

artificial satellite
Observation spacecraft placed in orbit around the Earth.

Hubble Space Telescope
Space telescope with two mirrors, covering the entire spectrum of light. It was launched into orbit in 1990.

space shuttle
It orbited at an altitude of about 250 mi.

aurora
Luminous phenomenon that occurs at high altitudes near the Earth's poles.

shooting star
Luminous trace produced when a meteor burns up as it enters the Earth's atmosphere.

airliner
Commercial aircraft that makes regular flights of variable duration, depending on the distance covered; it flies at altitudes of 39,000 feet.

ozone layer
Layer of gas that absorbs a large part of the Sun's ultraviolet rays.

Mount Everest
The world's highest peak rises to an elevation of 29,035 feet.

supersonic jet
Aircraft whose cruising speed is faster than the speed of sound; it flies at altitudes of 62,000 feet.

cloud
Fine droplets of water or ice crystals suspended in the atmosphere.

sea level
Average height of seawater observed for a given time (day, month, year); it is used as a reference point to define coastal features and measure land elevations.

exosphere
The outermost region of the atmosphere, where low-density gases disperse into space.

2000°C   500 km
3600°F   310 mi

thermopause
Thin transition layer between the thermosphere and the exosphere.

thermosphere
Layer that absorbs a large portion of solar radiation, leading to a steady increase in its temperature.

-100°C   80 km
-150°F   50 mi

mesopause
Thin transition layer between the mesosphere and the thermosphere.

mesosphere
The atmosphere's coldest layer, where temperatures decrease with altitude.

stratopause
Thin transition layer between the stratosphere and the mesosphere.

0°C   50 km
32°F   30 mi

stratosphere
Highly stable layer of air where temperatures increase with altitude due to the absorption of solar radiation by the ozone layer.

-60°C   15 km
-75°F   10 mi

tropopause
The boundary between the troposphere and the stratosphere; its altitude varies depending on the season, ground temperature, latitude and atmospheric pressure.

troposphere
The most dense layer, which produces most of the meteorological phenomena and where temperatures decrease with altitude.

15°C
60°F

EARTH

seasons of the year

Periodic climate changes over the course of a year; they are a function of the Earth's inclination toward the Sun and its rotation around it.

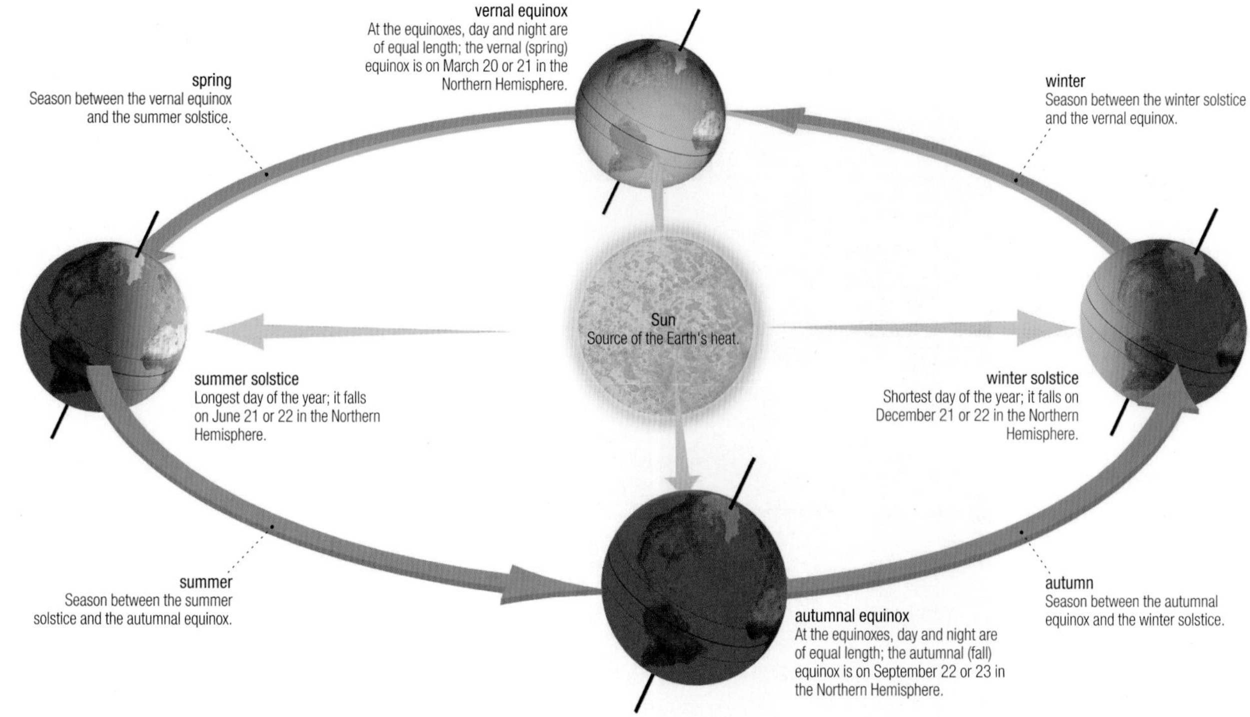

vernal equinox
At the equinoxes, day and night are of equal length; the vernal (spring) equinox is on March 20 or 21 in the Northern Hemisphere.

spring
Season between the vernal equinox and the summer solstice.

winter
Season between the winter solstice and the vernal equinox.

Sun
Source of the Earth's heat.

summer solstice
Longest day of the year; it falls on June 21 or 22 in the Northern Hemisphere.

winter solstice
Shortest day of the year; it falls on December 21 or 22 in the Northern Hemisphere.

summer
Season between the summer solstice and the autumnal equinox.

autumn
Season between the autumnal equinox and the winter solstice.

autumnal equinox
At the equinoxes, day and night are of equal length; the autumnal (fall) equinox is on September 22 or 23 in the Northern Hemisphere.

meteorological forecast

Scientific method that makes it possible to forecast atmospheric conditions in a particular region for a given period.

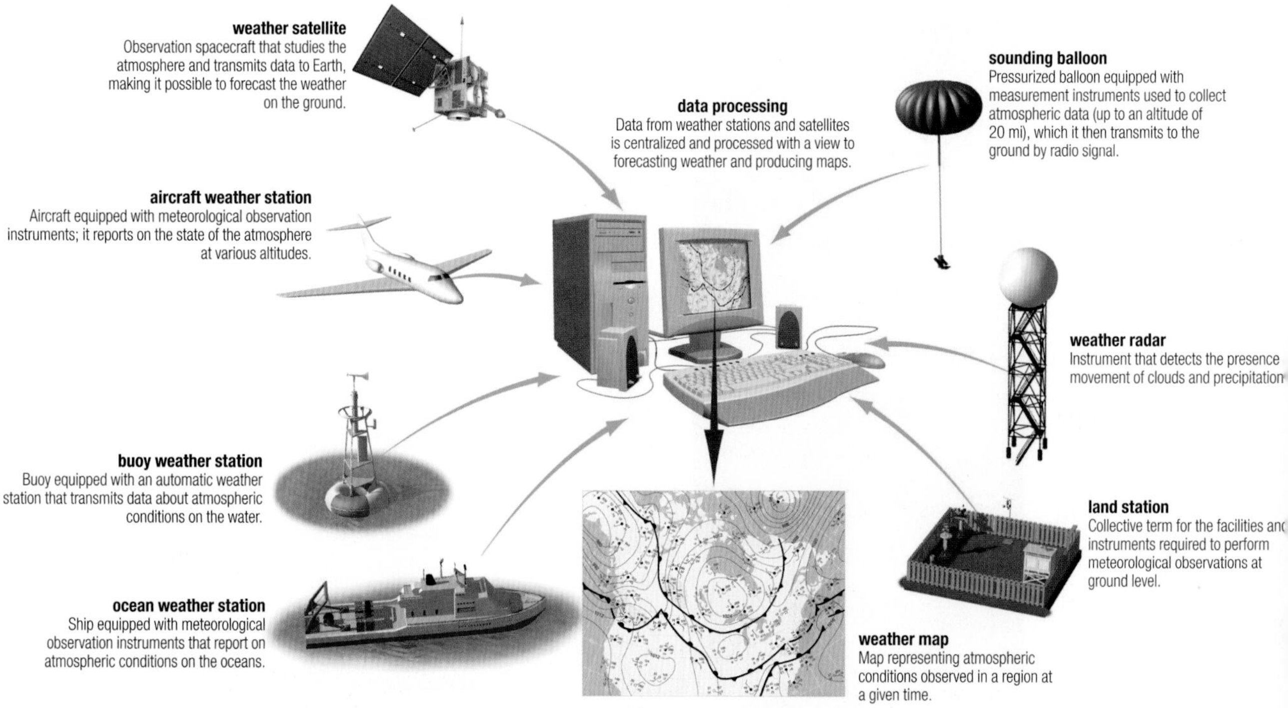

weather satellite
Observation spacecraft that studies the atmosphere and transmits data to Earth, making it possible to forecast the weather on the ground.

data processing
Data from weather stations and satellites is centralized and processed with a view to forecasting weather and producing maps.

sounding balloon
Pressurized balloon equipped with measurement instruments used to collect atmospheric data (up to an altitude of 20 mi), which it then transmits to the ground by radio signal.

aircraft weather station
Aircraft equipped with meteorological observation instruments; it reports on the state of the atmosphere at various altitudes.

weather radar
Instrument that detects the presence movement of clouds and precipitation

buoy weather station
Buoy equipped with an automatic weather station that transmits data about atmospheric conditions on the water.

land station
Collective term for the facilities and instruments required to perform meteorological observations at ground level.

ocean weather station
Ship equipped with meteorological observation instruments that report on atmospheric conditions on the oceans.

weather map
Map representing atmospheric conditions observed in a region at a given time.

EARTH

weather map

Map representing atmospheric conditions observed in a region at a given time.

barometric pressure
Measurement of the force that air exerts at a given point on the Earth's surface; it is expressed in millibars.

isobar
Curve connecting the points on the Earth's surface that have the same atmospheric pressure.

wind direction and speed

low-pressure center
Zone characterized by relatively low pressure that increases as a function of distance from its center.

precipitation area
Zone in which atmospheric water content condenses and falls from the clouds in liquid or solid form.

trough
Elongated zone in which atmospheric pressure is relatively low.

type of air mass
Air mass: a vast moving body of air; it takes on the climatic characteristics of the region lying below it.

high-pressure center
Zone characterized by relatively high pressure that decreases as a function of the distance from its center.

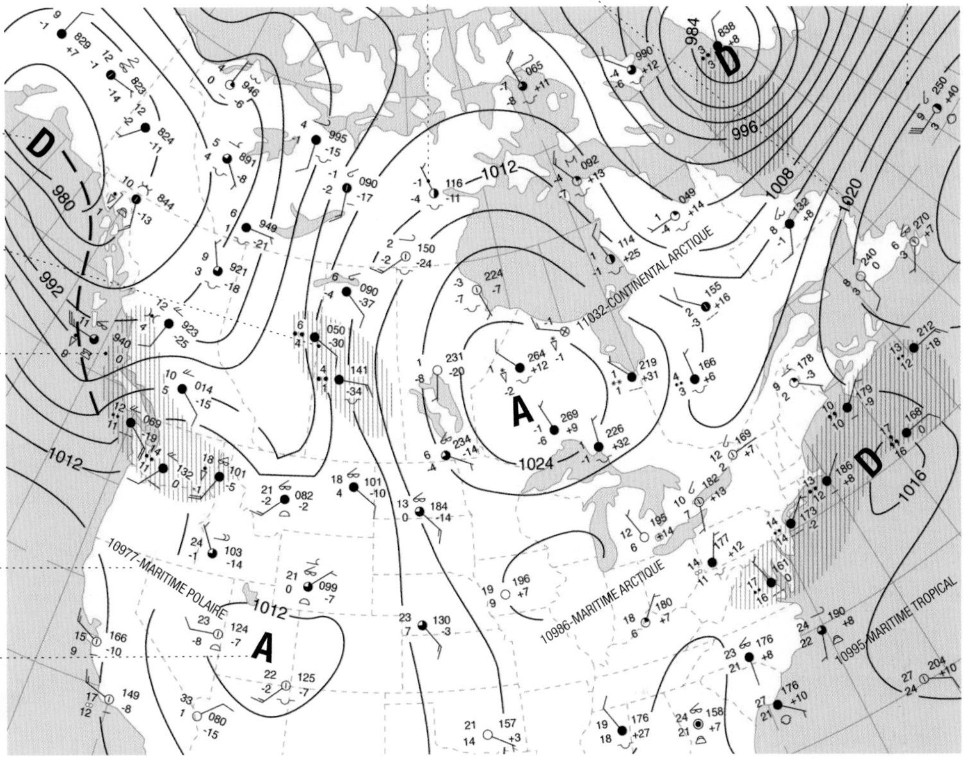

station model

Method of representing information collected by an observation station on a weather map using symbols and numbers.

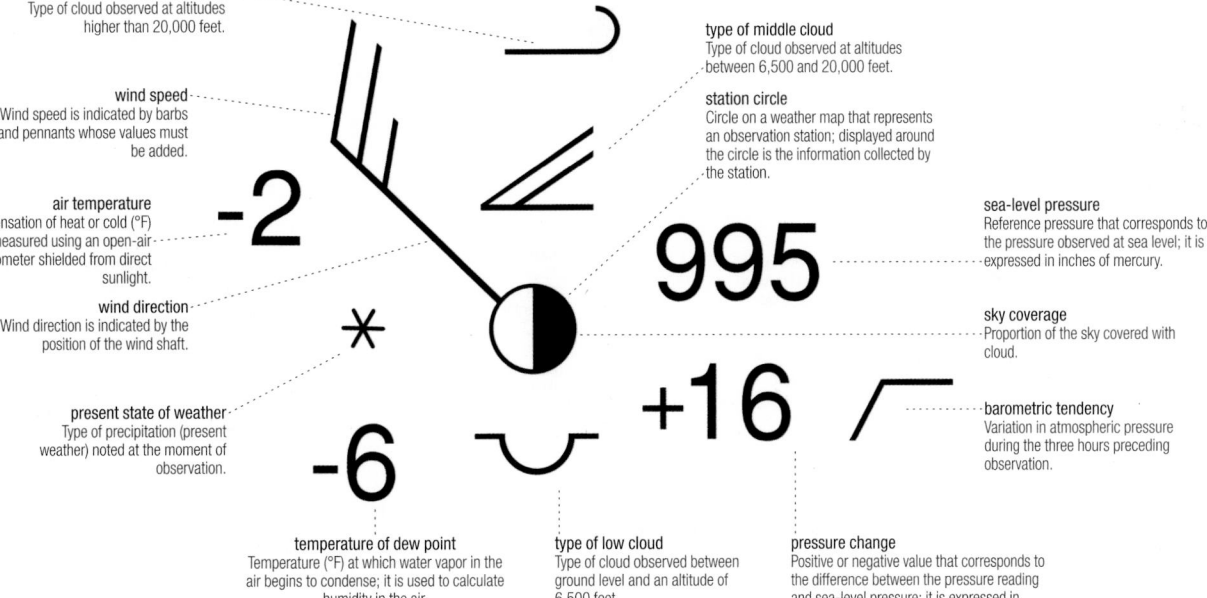

type of high cloud
Type of cloud observed at altitudes higher than 20,000 feet.

type of middle cloud
Type of cloud observed at altitudes between 6,500 and 20,000 feet.

wind speed
Wind speed is indicated by barbs and pennants whose values must be added.

station circle
Circle on a weather map that represents an observation station; displayed around the circle is the information collected by the station.

air temperature
Sensation of heat or cold (°F) measured using an open-air thermometer shielded from direct sunlight.

sea-level pressure
Reference pressure that corresponds to the pressure observed at sea level; it is expressed in inches of mercury.

wind direction
Wind direction is indicated by the position of the wind shaft.

sky coverage
Proportion of the sky covered with cloud.

present state of weather
Type of precipitation (present weather) noted at the moment of observation.

barometric tendency
Variation in atmospheric pressure during the three hours preceding observation.

temperature of dew point
Temperature (°F) at which water vapor in the air begins to condense; it is used to calculate humidity in the air.

type of low cloud
Type of cloud observed between ground level and an altitude of 6,500 feet.

pressure change
Positive or negative value that corresponds to the difference between the pressure reading and sea-level pressure; it is expressed in inches of mercury.

EARTH

international weather symbols

Standardized map symbols used to record observations from meteorological stations all over the world.

wind
Displacement of air caused by variations in pressure between two regions of the atmosphere.

calm
Symbol indicating the absence of wind.

shaft
Symbol of a wind blowing at a speed lower than 3 mph.

barb
Symbol of a wind blowing between 9 and 14 mph.

wind arrow
Symbol that uses the position of the shaft to indicate wind direction and the number of barbs and pennants to indicate wind speed.

half barb
Symbol of a wind blowing between 3 and 8 mph.

pennant
Symbol of a wind blowing between 55 and 60 mph.

fronts
Contact surface between two air masses with different temperatures and pressure.

surface cold front
Front consisting of a cold air mass that touches the ground and displaces a warm air mass.

surface warm front
Front consisting of a warm air mass that touches the ground and displaces a cold air mass.

occluded front
A composite front that forms when a cold front overtakes a warm front, which it pushes to a higher altitude before joining another cold front.

upper cold front
Front of a cold air mass that does not touch the Earth's surface and slides over a colder air mass.

upper warm front
Front consisting of a warm air mass that does not touch the ground and slides over a colder air mass.

stationary front
Front that moves very slowly owing to the parallel movement of hot and cold air masses.

sky coverage
Proportion of the sky covered with cloud.

very cloudy sky

cloudless sky

slightly covered sky

overcast sky

clear sky

cloudy sky

obscured sky

clouds
Fine droplets of water or ice crystal suspended in the atmosphere; the World Meteorological Organization classifies them according to 10 types.

stratus
Gray cloud forming a continuous veil that is similar to fog, though it never touches the ground; it can trigger light precipitation.

altostratus
Gray sheet that can completely cover the sky but allows the Sun to be seen without a halo phenomenon; it can trigger heavy precipitation.

cirrus
Cloud in the form of wisps or separate strips; it usually appears in advance of a depression.

cumulonimbus
Very imposing cloud that can reach a thickness of 6 mi and whose base is very dark; it can trigger violent precipitation.

nimbostratus
Cloud in the form of a dark layer sufficiently thick to block out the Sun; it triggers continuous precipitation.

cirrostratus
Whitish layer that can completely cover the sky and that creates a halo around the Sun.

cumulus
Fair-weather cloud with very clear contours; it has a gray, flat base and a white top with rounded protuberances.

altocumulus
Cloud composed of large white or gray flecks that sometimes form parallel layers; it foreshadows the arrival of a depression.

cirrocumulus
Cloud formed of white or gray flecks or strips, often arranged in rows.

stratocumulus
Gray and white cloud arranged in more or less continuous rolled layers; it does not usually trigger precipitation.

international weather symbols

present weather
All atmospheric phenomena observed, with the exception of clouds; this includes forms of precipitation as well as optical and electrical phenomena.

sandstorm or dust storm
Phenomenon of wind lifting sand or dust.

smoke
Solid or liquid particles suspended in the air; they are produced by various forms of combustion.

thunderstorm
Meteorological phenomenon manifested by lightning, thunder and gusts of wind, usually accompanied by rain showers or hail.

heavy thunderstorm
Storm with winds higher than 57 mph, hail or heavy rain.

lightning
Brief but intense luminous phenomenon caused by an electrical discharge between two clouds or between a cloud and the ground.

tropical storm
Low-pressure zone accompanied by precipitation and winds between 37 and 74 mph.

hurricane
Tropical cyclone comprised of a low-pressure zone accompanied by violent precipitation and winds between 74 and 185 mph.

tornado
Swirling column of air that extends from the ground to the base of a cumulonimbus; it produces violent winds that can reach 300 mph.

light intermittent rain
Rain: precipitation of water droplets produced when the air temperature is higher than 32°F.

light intermittent drizzle
Drizzle: uniform continuous precipitation of water droplets that fall very slowly and are less than 0.02 in in diameter.

light intermittent snow
Snow: precipitation of ice crystals produced when the air temperature is lower than 32°F.

moderate intermittent rain

moderate intermittent drizzle

moderate intermittent snow

heavy intermittent rain

heavy intermittent drizzle

heavy intermittent snow

light continuous rain

light continuous drizzle

light continuous snow

moderate continuous rain

moderate continuous drizzle

moderate continuous snow

heavy continuous rain

heavy continuous drizzle

heavy continuous snow

sleet
Precipitation in the form of water droplets or wet snow that freezes before it touches the ground.

mist
Light fog that does not limit visibility to 0.6 mi.

snow shower
Sudden abundant and short-lived precipitation of ice crystals produced when the air temperature is lower than 32°F.

drifting snow low
Snow that the wind blows into drifts no higher than 6 feet.

fog
Condensation of water vapor resulting in the suspension of microscopic droplets that reduce visibility to less than 0.6 mi.

rain shower
Sudden abundant and short-lived precipitation of water droplets produced when the air temperature is higher than 32°F.

drifting snow high
Snow that the wind blows into drifts higher than 6 feet.

haze
Mist composed of minuscule particles of dust, smoke, sand and other impurities; it gives the air a murky quality.

hail shower
Sudden abundant and short-lived precipitation of solid ice, usually in the form of pellets that vary from 0.2 to 2 in in diameter.

freezing rain
Precipitation in the form of raindrops that freeze on impact with the ground or with objects, forming a layer of ice.

freezing drizzle
Precipitation in the form of droplets that freeze on impact with the ground or with objects, forming a layer of ice.

squall
Sudden and short-lived increase in wind speed often accompanied by showers and thunderstorms.

EARTH

meteorological station

The installations and instruments required to conduct meteorological observations on the ground.

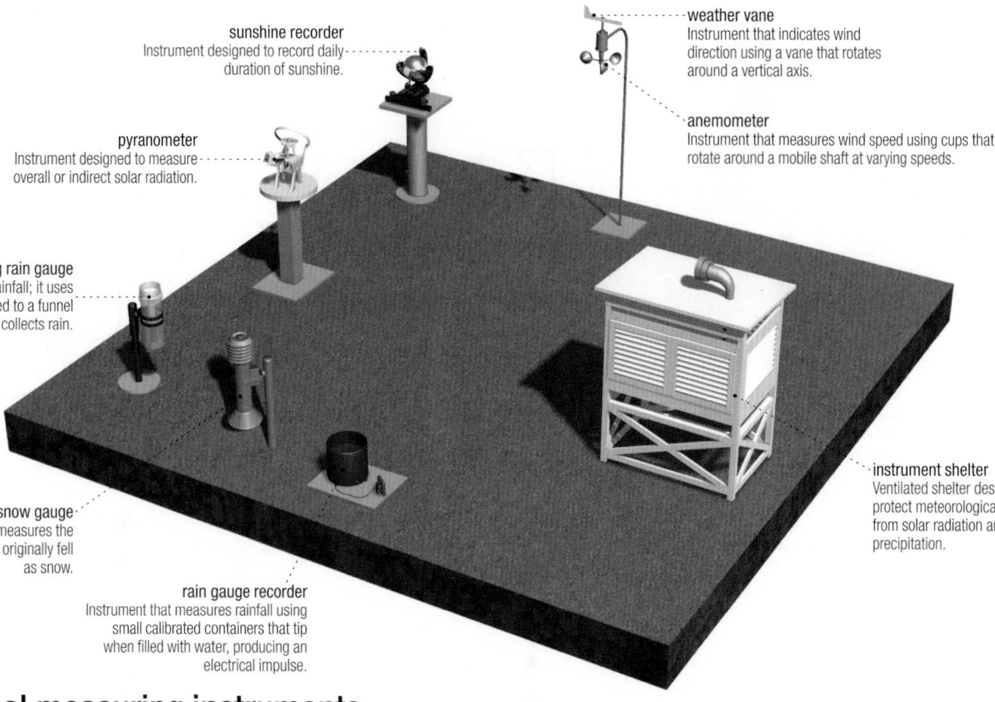

sunshine recorder
Instrument designed to record daily duration of sunshine.

weather vane
Instrument that indicates wind direction using a vane that rotates around a vertical axis.

pyranometer
Instrument designed to measure overall or indirect solar radiation.

anemometer
Instrument that measures wind speed using cups that rotate around a mobile shaft at varying speeds.

direct-reading rain gauge
Instrument that measures rainfall; it uses a measuring tube connected to a funnel that collects rain.

instrument shelter
Ventilated shelter designed to protect meteorological instrumer from solar radiation and precipitation.

snow gauge
Instrument that measures the depth of water that originally fell as snow.

rain gauge recorder
Instrument that measures rainfall using small calibrated containers that tip when filled with water, producing an electrical impulse.

meteorological measuring instruments

Instruments designed to measure air temperature and humidity, sunshine, atmospheric pressure, precipitation and wind.

measure of sunshine
Sunshine: direct sunlight to which a given area is exposed.

measure of sky radiation
Sky radiation: indirect solar radiation that passes through cloud and diffuses on the Earth's surface.

sunshine recorder
Instrument designed to record daily duration of sunshine.

lower sphere clamp
Two clamps secure the glass sphere into the position required to obtain an exact measure of sunshine; this position is based on the coordinates of the meteorological station.

sphere support

glass sphere
In the manner of a magnifying glass, it concentrates the Sun's rays on the sunshine card.

card support
Circular support for the sunshine card.

lower support screw

check nut

sunshine card
Strip of paper, calibrated in hours, that is burned by the Sun's rays; it registers the duration of sunshine.

leveling screw
Screw making it possible to level the instrument along its two axes, north-south and east-west.

lock nut
The nut of the leveling screw, which tightens to secure the base plate in a given position.

base plate
Stationary metal support in the form of a triangle; it is comprised of three coupling sleeves, each having a leveling screw.

sub-base
Adjustable metal support that makes it possible to level the instrument by means of leveling screws.

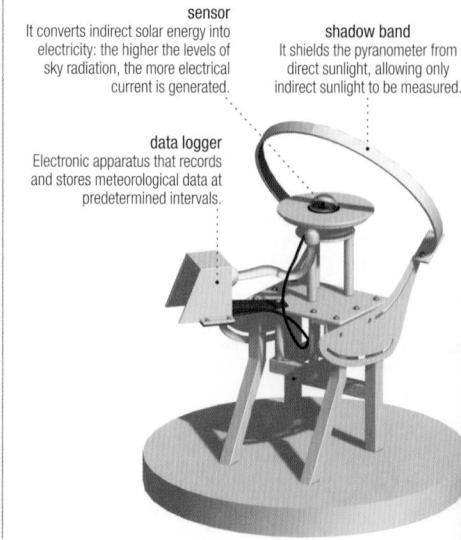

pyranometer
Instrument designed to measure overall or indirect solar radiation.

sensor
It converts indirect solar energy into electricity: the higher the levels of sky radiation, the more electrical current is generated.

shadow band
It shields the pyranometer from direct sunlight, allowing only indirect sunlight to be measured.

data logger
Electronic apparatus that records and stores meteorological data at predetermined intervals.

meteorological measuring instruments

direct-reading rain gauge
Instrument that measures rainfall; it uses a measuring tube connected to a funnel that collects rain.

collecting funnel
Cone-shaped vessel that gathers water and directs it into the measuring tube.

tightening band

measuring tube
Calibrated in inches or millimeters, it provides a direct reading of the quantity of water in precipitation.

container

support

rain gauge recorder
Instrument that measures rainfall using small calibrated containers that tip when filled with water, producing an electrical impulse.

measure of rainfall
Rainfall: quantity of water that falls to the ground during a given period.

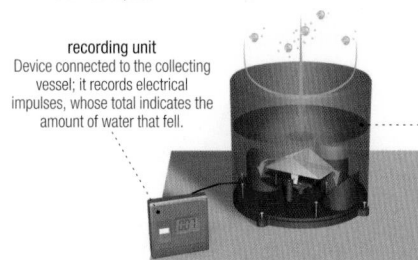

recording unit
Device connected to the collecting vessel; it records electrical impulses, whose total indicates the amount of water that fell.

collecting vessel
Container that gathers precipitation.

upper-air sounding
Technique used to measure the pressure, temperature and humidity of air as well as wind speed and wind direction at various altitudes.

sounding balloon
Pressurized balloon equipped with measurement instruments used to collect atmospheric data (up to an altitude of 20 mi), which it then transmits to the ground by radio signal.

radiosonde
Instrument composed of sensors that measure the pressure, temperature and humidity of air; it then relays the data to ground level using a radio transmitter.

measure of air pressure
Air pressure: force exerted by an atmospheric air column on a given surface; it is expressed in inches of mercury.

barograph
Instrument that measures variations in air pressure for a given interval.

mercury barometer
Instrument that measures atmospheric pressure using a mercury column that rises and falls with variations in air pressure.

measure of snowfall
Measurement of the depth of snow accumulation.

snow gauge
Instrument that measures the depth of water that originally fell as snow.

measure of humidity
Humidity refers to the amount of water vapor in the air.

hygrograph
Instrument that registers variations in the moisture content of the air by measuring the deformation of an object that is affected by humidity.

psychrometer
Instrument comprised of wet and dry thermometers that register air humidity.

measure of temperature
Measurement of heat or cold, carried out with a thermometer exposed to the air and shielded from direct sunlight.

maximum and minimum thermometer
Thermometer that marks the minimum and maximum temperature for a given period of time.

measure of wind direction
Wind direction: the point on the horizon from which the wind is blowing.

weather vane
Instrument that indicates wind direction using a vane that rotates around a vertical axis.

measure of cloud ceiling
Cloud ceiling: altitude of the base of the clouds, expressed in feet.

measure of wind strength
Wind speed: it is usually expressed in miles per hour.

anemometer
Instrument that measures wind speed using cups that rotate around a mobile shaft at varying speeds.

theodolite
Instrument used to measure angles whose intervals indicate the height of a given point in relation to another.

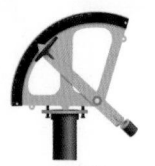

alidade
Instrument whose sighting axis, by moving along a calibrated circle, measures a cloud's angle in relation to the horizon, and thus its height.

ceiling projector
Spotlight whose point of luminous impact on a cloud serves as a reference for an alidade or theodolite sighting.

EARTH

weather satellites

Observation spacecraft that study the atmosphere and transmit data to Earth, making it possible to forecast the weather on the ground.

polar-orbiting satellite
Satellite that travels in a polar orbit around the globe 14 times per day; this allows it to cover the entire surface of the globe, due to the Earth's rotation.

Sun sensor
Instrument that locates the Sun so that the solar array can be positioned most efficiently.

radiometer
Instrument designed to measure electromagnetic radiation energy at a given frequency.

search-and-rescue antenna
Device that picks up distress signals emitted by ships or aircraft and makes it possible to determine their location.

reaction engine assembly
Micromotor that makes it possible to direct a satellite to the desired position.

instrument platform
Case in which the satellite's various measuring instruments are kept.

thermal louver
Adjustable mechanical component designed to modify thermal flux.

battery modules
Set of batteries that store electricity generated by the solar panels.

infrared sounder
Instrument that measures thermal energy in clouds and on the Earth's surface with a view to capturing nighttime images of weather systems and cloud cover.

solar array drive
System that controls the position of the solar array.

Earth sensor
Instrument that locates the Earth's horizon so that the antenna can be positioned correctly.

S-band antenna
Antenna that enables a satellite to transmit the data it collects to the terrestrial station.

antenna
Device that emits and receives radio waves.

Earth radiation scanner
Radiometer that analyzes a region of the globe by means of repeated scans.

ultraviolet spectrometer
Instrument that monitors ozone levels in the Earth's atmosphere.

solar array
Power supply device that converts solar energy into immediately usable electrical energy.

microwave scanner
Instrument that produces an image of an observed area even in cloudy conditions since microwave frequencies pass through clouds.

Earth radiation sensor
Radiometer that measures solar radiation and reflection in the Earth's atmosphere.

geostationary satellite
A satellite that travels in a geostationary orbit, allowing it to observe a considerable area of the Earth's surface on a continuous basis.

Earth sensor
Instrument that locates the Earth's horizon so that the antenna can be positioned correctly.

orbit of the satellites
Trajectory of a meteorological satellite around the Earth.

telemetry and command antenna
It allows terrestrial stations to monitor satellite operations and transmit commands to the satellite.

S-band high gain antenna
Main antenna pointed toward the Earth to transmit large quantities of scientific data.

sounder
Radiometer designed to measure temperature and humidity at different altitudes in the atmosphere.

imager
Radiometer that generates images of clouds and of the surface of the Earth and the oceans.

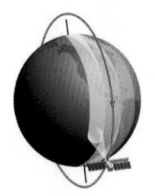

polar orbit
Orbit in which the satellite circles the Earth at an altitude of 530 mi, passing over both poles.

trim tab
Adjustable mechanical component that makes it possible to modify the satellite's position.

solar array
Power supply device that converts solar energy into immediately usable electrical energy.

magnetometer
Instrument designed to measure the Earth's magnetic field.

UHF antenna
Antenna that provides a radio link with terrestrial stations.

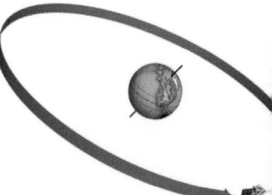

geostationary orbit
Orbit in which the satellite is synchronized with the Earth's rotation, making it appear stationary at an altitude of 22,200 mi above the Equator.

climates of the world

Climate is a collective term for the atmospheric conditions (temperature, humidity, air pressure, wind, precipitation) that characterize a given region.

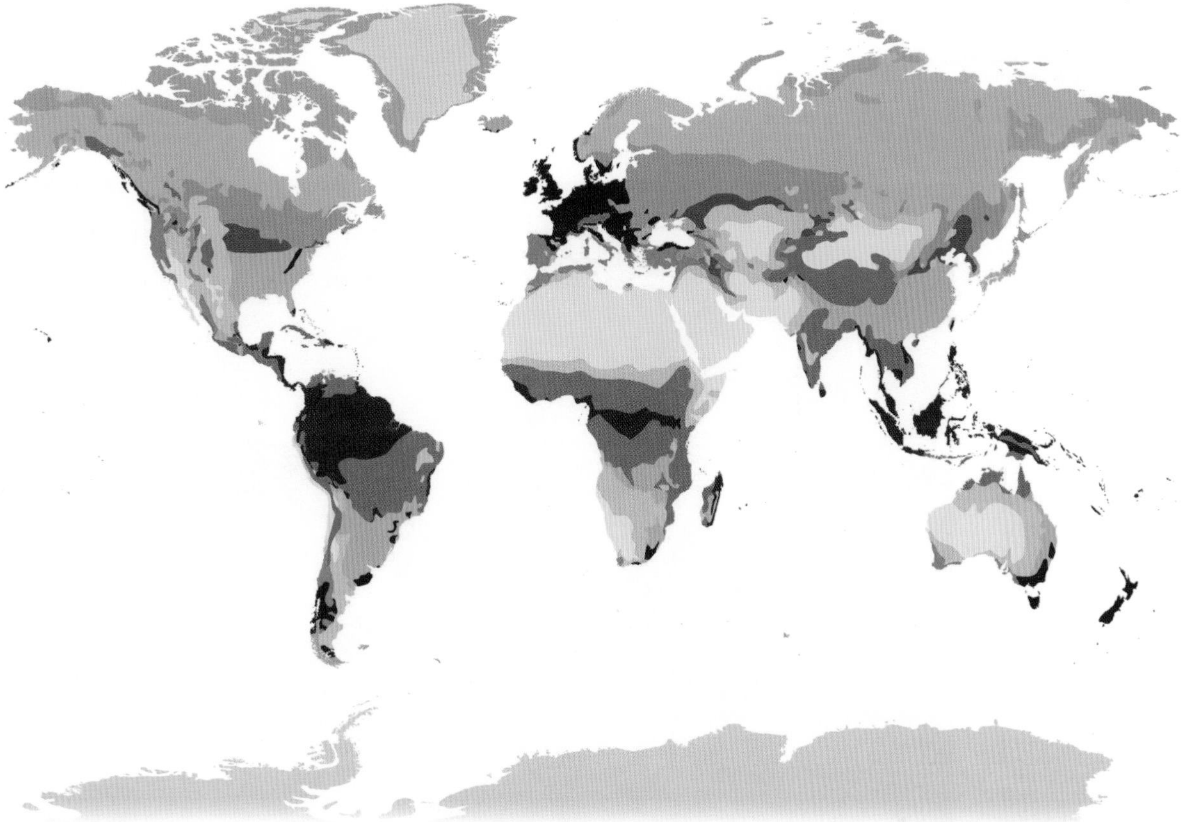

EARTH

tropical climates
Climates that are hot year-round and are characterized by alternating dry and rainy seasons.

tropical rain forest
Tropical, typically humid climate that fosters luxuriant vegetation and dense forests.

tropical wet-and-dry (savanna)
Tropical continental climate, with an extended dry season and vegetation composed of tall grasses and scattered trees.

cold temperate climates
Climates with four clearly defined seasons, including a cold winter and a hot or cool summer.

humid continental-hot summer
Climate characterized by a large annual range of temperature and relatively low rainfall. Summers are quite hot in these regions.

humid continental-warm summer
Climate characterized by a large annual range of temperature and relatively low annual rainfall. Summers are quite cool in these regions.

subarctic
Climate characterized by long, very cold winters and short cool summers; precipitation falls mainly in the summer.

warm temperate climates
Climates with four clearly defined seasons, including a mild winter and a hot or cool summer.

humid subtropical
Climate characterized by hot summers and mild winters, with precipitation distributed evenly throughout the year.

Mediterranean subtropical
Climate characterized by hot dry summers, intermediary seasons and mild rainy winters.

marine
Climate characterized by a limited annual range of temperature and by precipitation distributed throughout the year.

dry climates
Climates characterized by very low precipitation.

steppe
Region with hot summers and very cold winters; it is devoid of trees and covered with herbaceous plants adapted to arid climates.

desert
A region, usually characterized by heat, where aridity (less than 10 in of annual rainfall) is such that plant and animal life is rare.

polar climates
Extremely cold dry climates.

polar tundra
Region where the thaw lasts only four or five months and where only mosses, lichen and a few shrubs survive the cold.

polar ice cap
The Earth's coldest region (as cold as -130°F), where the temperature, always below 32°F, creates a permanent ice cover.

highland climates
Climates where temperatures decrease and precipitation increases with altitude.

highland

clouds

Fine droplets of water or ice crystal suspended in the atmosphere; the World Meteorological Organization classifies them according to 10 types.

EARTH

high clouds
Clouds at an altitude higher than 20,000 feet and composed of ice crystals; these clouds do not generate precipitation.

cirrostratus
Whitish layer that can completely cover the sky and that creates a halo around the Sun.

cirrocumulus
Cloud formed of white or gray flecks or strips, often arranged in rows.

cirrus
Cloud in the form of wisps or separate strips; it usually appears in advance of a depression.

middle clouds
Clouds at an altitude of 6,500 to 20,000 feet and composed of water droplets and ice crystals.

altostratus
Gray sheet that can completely cover the sky but allows the Sun to be seen without a halo phenomenon; it can trigger heavy precipitation.

altocumulus
Cloud composed of large white or gray flecks that sometimes form parallel layers; it foreshadows the arrival of a depression.

low clouds
Clouds that do not exceed 6,500 feet in altitude and are composed of water droplets occasionally mixed with ice crystals; they sometimes generate continuous precipitation.

stratocumulus
Gray and white cloud arranged in more or less continuous rolled layers; it does not usually trigger precipitation.

nimbostratus
Cloud in the form of a dark layer sufficiently thick to block out the Sun; it triggers continuous precipitation.

stratus
Gray cloud forming a continuous veil that is similar to fog, though it never touches the ground; it can trigger light precipitation.

clouds of vertical development
Clouds whose base is at low altitude but extend very high; the two types are cumulus and cumulonimbus.

cumulus
Fair-weather cloud with very clear contours; it has a gray, flat base and a white top with rounded protuberances.

cumulonimbus
Very imposing cloud that can reach a thickness of 6 mi and whose base is very dark; it can trigger violent precipitation.

tornado and waterspout

Column of swirling air going from ground or water to the base of a cumulonimbus.

wall cloud
Ring-shaped cloud mass, usually the first sign that a tornado is imminent.

funnel cloud
Cloud that extends from another cloud's base and reaches the ground; extremely high winds whirl around it.

debris
Cloud of dust and debris swept up from the ground.

waterspout
Tornado that occurs over the sea and is not as violent as a tornado on land.

tornado
Swirling column of air that extends from the ground to the base of a cumulonimbus; it produces violent winds that can reach 300 mph.

tropical cyclone

Low-pressure zone that forms over open water in the intertropical region and is marked by violent precipitation and swirling winds of 74 to 185 mph.

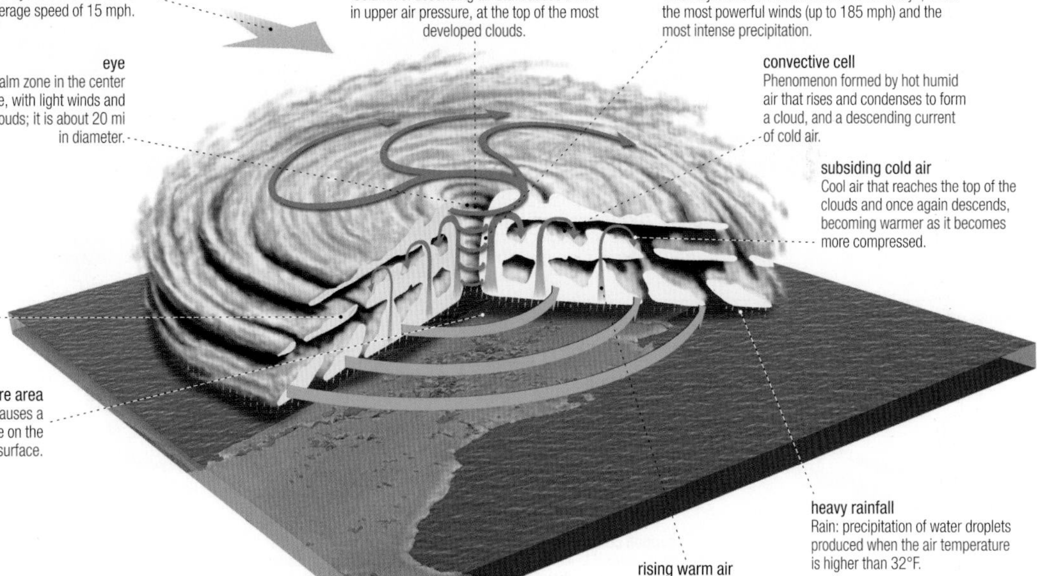

prevailing wind
It moves the cyclone forward at an average speed of 15 mph.

high-pressure area
Column of ascending air that causes a rise in upper air pressure, at the top of the most developed clouds.

eye wall
Thick layer of cloud that swirls around the eye; it has the most powerful winds (up to 185 mph) and the most intense precipitation.

eye
Relatively calm zone in the center of the cyclone, with light winds and very few clouds; it is about 20 mi in diameter.

convective cell
Phenomenon formed by hot humid air that rises and condenses to form a cloud, and a descending current of cold air.

subsiding cold air
Cool air that reaches the top of the clouds and once again descends, becoming warmer as it becomes more compressed.

spiral cloud band

low-pressure area
A rising column of air causes a decrease in air pressure on the ocean's surface.

heavy rainfall
Rain: precipitation of water droplets produced when the air temperature is higher than 32°F.

rising warm air
A hot air column forms when the ocean's surface is warmed by the Sun.

tropical cyclone names
From one region of the world to another, the same meteorological phenomenon is given different names.

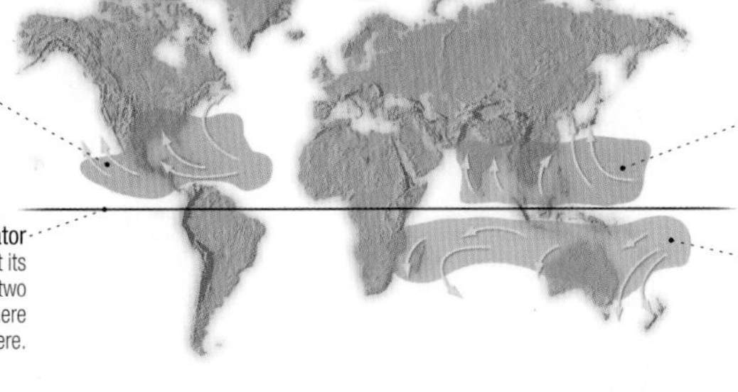

hurricane
Tropical cyclone in the Caribbean, the North Atlantic and the eastern Pacific.

typhoon
Tropical cyclone in the northwest Pacific and in the northern Indian Ocean.

Equator
Imaginary circle surrounding Earth at its widest circumference, dividing it into two hemispheres: the Northern hemisphere and the Southern hemisphere.

cyclone
Tropical cyclone in the Indian Ocean and in the southwest Pacific.

EARTH

precipitation

Collective term for water particles in the atmosphere that fall or are deposited on the ground in solid or liquid form.

rain forms

By international convention, precipitation in the form of rain is classified according to the quantity that falls.

drizzle
Uniform continuous precipitation of slow-falling water droplets less than 0.02 in diameter.

light rain
Precipitation of water drops over 0.02 in in diameter; it results in accumulations of 0.1 in per hour.

moderate rain
Precipitation that results in 0.1 to 0.3 in accumulation per hour.

heavy rain
Precipitation that results in over 0.3 in accumulation per hour.

winter precipitation forms

During the winter, water can fall in various forms, depending on the air temperature.

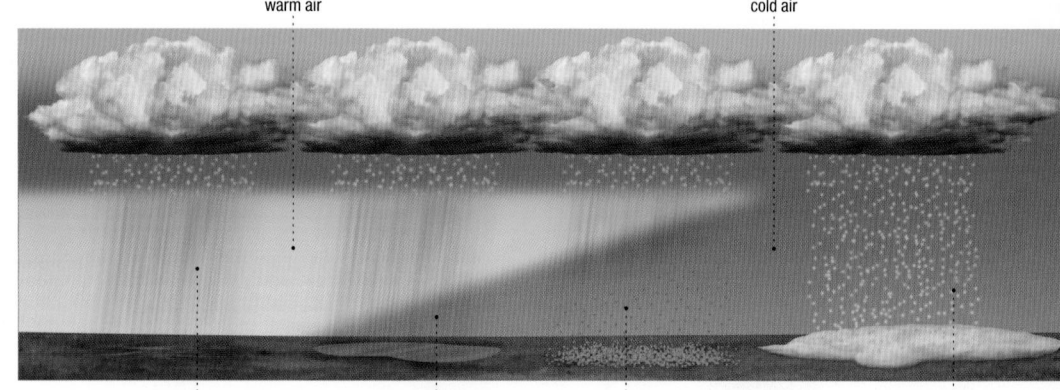

warm air   cold air

rain
Precipitation of water droplets produced when the air temperature is higher than 32°F.

freezing rain
Precipitation in the form of raindrops that freeze on impact with the ground or with objects, forming a layer of ice.

sleet
Precipitation in the form of water droplets or wet snow that freezes before it touches the ground.

snow
Precipitation of ice crystals produced when the air temperature is below 32°F.

snow crystals

Ice crystals whose form depends on temperature and humidity; they fall separately or in agglomerations of flakes.

needle
Translucent prism-shaped ice crystal; it is long and narrow and has pointed ends.

capped column
Ice crystal that is identical to the column, except for the thin hexagon-shaped cap at each extremity.

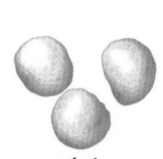

sleet
Ice crystal less than 0.2 in diameter that results from rain drops or snow flakes freezing before they touch the ground.

snow pellet
Opaque ice crystal less than 0.2 in in diameter that froze inside a cloud.

hail
Hard, usually spherical ice crystal that varies between 0.2 and 2 in diameter; it is formed of concentric layers of clear opaque ice.

column
Short translucent ice crystal with flat extremities; it is prism-shaped and occasionally hollow.

plate crystal
Ice crystal in the form of a thin hexagonal plate that is occasionally hollow.

spatial dendrite
Ice crystal characterized by complex branches similar to those of a tree.

irregular crystal
Ice crystal with no defined shape resulting from the agglomeration of several crystals.

stellar crystal
Star-shaped crystal with six branches.

precipitation

EARTH

stormy sky
A thunderstorm is characterized by lightning, thunder and gusts of wind, usually accompanied by rain showers or hail.

cloud
The very imposing cloud that generates thunderstorms is the cumulonimbus; it can reach a thickness of 6 mi and its base is very dark.

lightning
Brief but intense luminous phenomenon caused by an electrical discharge between two clouds or between a cloud and the ground.

rainbow
Luminous arc formed of bands of color; during a shower, it is visible in the opposite direction to the Sun.

rain
Precipitation of water droplets produced when the air temperature is higher than 32°F.

dew
Condensation of water vapor in the air that settles on cold surfaces in droplet form.

rime
Deposit of ice crystals on surfaces whose temperature is close to 32°F; it is caused by the condensation of water vapor in the air.

mist
Light fog that does not limit visibility to 0.6 mi.

fog
Condensation of water vapor resulting in the suspension of microscopic droplets that reduce visibility to less than 0.6 mi.

frost
Layer of ice on the ground or on an object; it is caused by the condensation of fine rain when the temperature is hovering around 32°F.

EARTH

vegetation regions

Vegetation: all plants growing on the surface of the Earth, varying according to the climate and the characteristics of the soil.

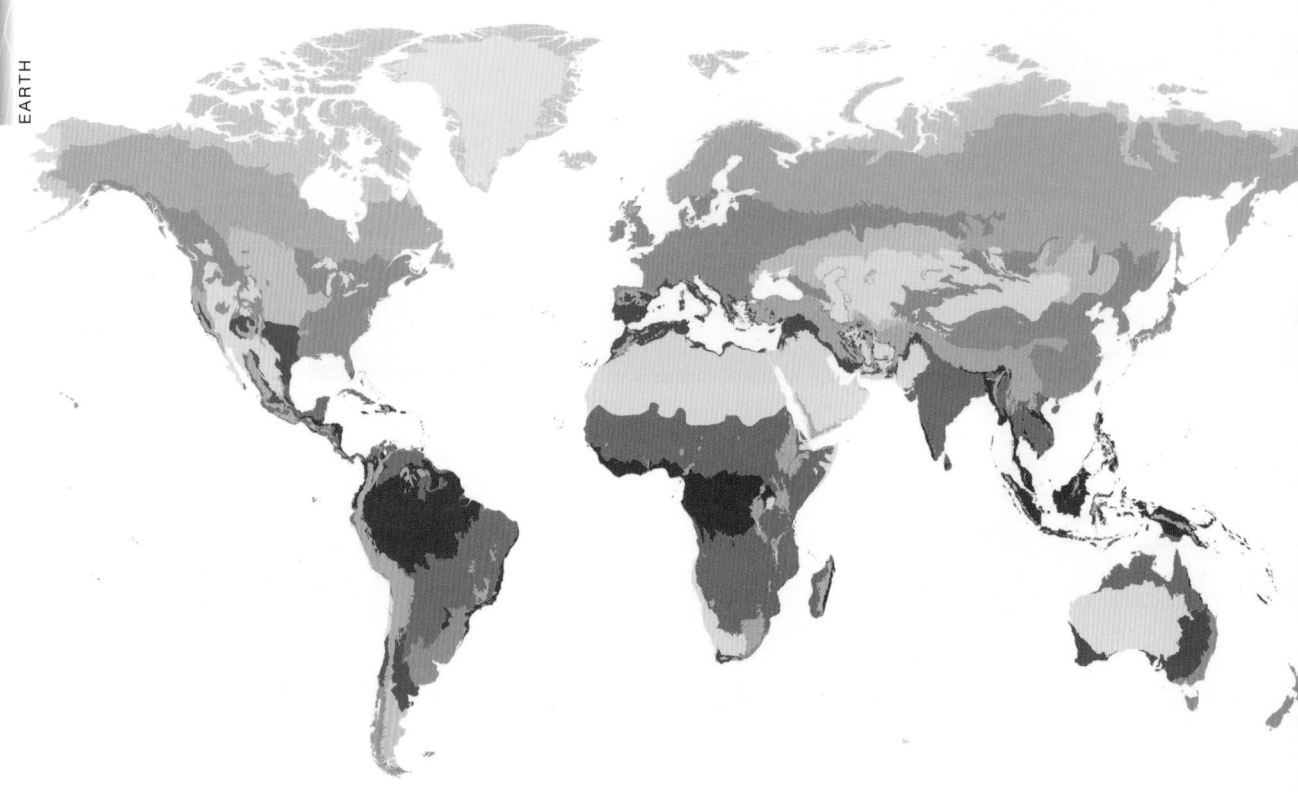

tundra
Plant formation that grows in relatively arid regions; it includes mosses, lichens, grasses, bushes and dwarf trees.

tropical rain forest
Dense forest whose biodiversity is among the richest; its growth is fostered by abundant and regular precipitation.

scrub
Vast expanse of vegetation composed of shrubs with evergreen leaves; it is adapted to summer drought.

boreal forest
Vast expanse of forest composed mainly of conifers, although certain deciduous trees also grow here.

temperate grassland
Vast expanse of herbaceous plants, mostly grasses; virtually devoid of trees, these regions are characterized by relatively cold, dry winters.

desert
Arid region (less than 10 in of annual rainfall), usually characterized by heat, where vegetation is sparse; plants are adapted to tolerate prolonged drought.

temperate forest
Forest composed mainly of deciduous trees, including oak, ash and beech.

savanna
Vast expanse of herbaceous plants, dominated by tall grasses and shrubs; it is typical of hot regions that have a rainy season.

rock and ice
Region where vegetation is rare or absent.

types of vegetation

Vegetation: all plants growing on the surface of the Earth, varying according to the climate and the characteristics of the soil.

boreal forest
Vast expanse of forest composed mainly of conifers, although certain deciduous trees also grow here.

temperate forest
Forest composed mainly of deciduous trees, including oak, ash and beech.

tropical rain forest
Dense forest whose biodiversity is among the richest; its growth is fostered by abundant and regular precipitation.

savanna
Vast expanse of herbaceous plants, dominated by tall grasses and shrubs; it is typical of hot regions that have a rainy season.

scrub
Vast expanse of vegetation composed of shrubs with evergreen leaves; it is adapted to summer drought.

temperate grassland
Vast expanse of herbaceous plants, mostly grasses; virtually devoid of trees, these regions are characterized by relatively cold, dry winters.

desert
Arid region (less than 10 in of annual rainfall), usually characterized by heat, where vegetation is sparse; plants are adapted to tolerate prolonged drought.

tundra
Plant formation that grows in relatively arid regions; it includes mosses, lichens, grasses, bushes and dwarf trees.

EARTH

food chain

Order of the relationships of predation and dependence among living organisms.

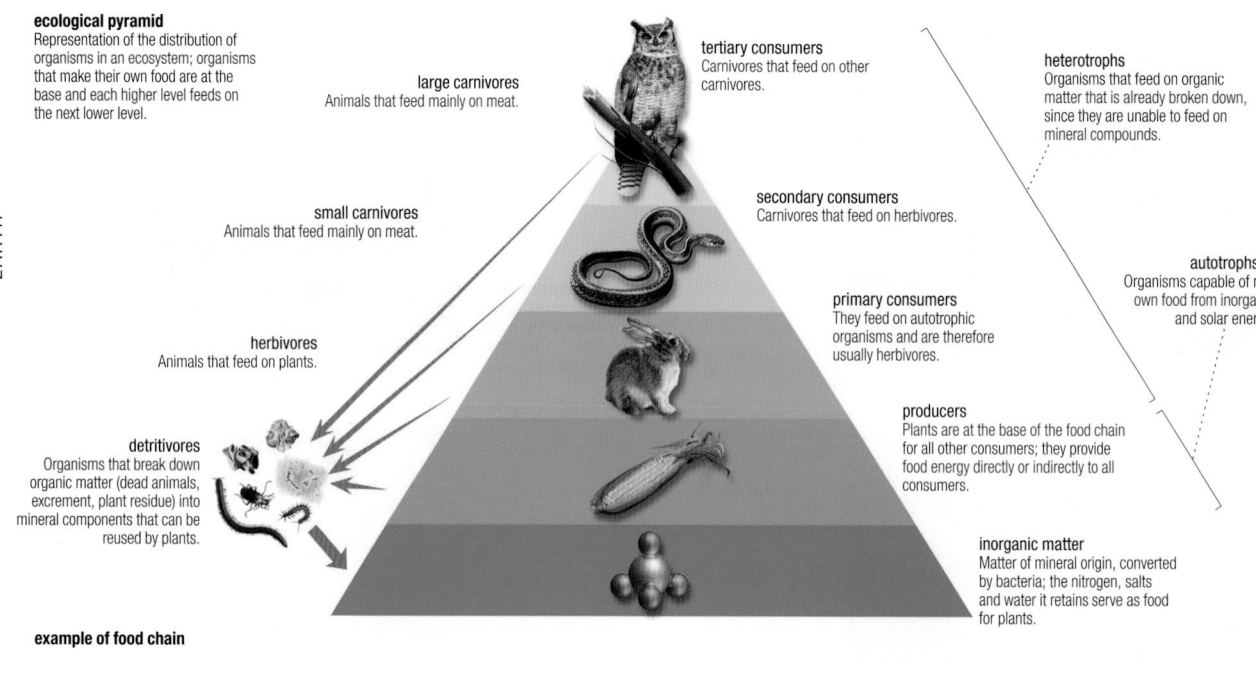

ecological pyramid
Representation of the distribution of organisms in an ecosystem; organisms that make their own food are at the base and each higher level feeds on the next lower level.

large carnivores
Animals that feed mainly on meat.

tertiary consumers
Carnivores that feed on other carnivores.

heterotrophs
Organisms that feed on organic matter that is already broken down, since they are unable to feed on mineral compounds.

small carnivores
Animals that feed mainly on meat.

secondary consumers
Carnivores that feed on herbivores.

autotrophs
Organisms capable of ma own food from inorgani and solar energy

herbivores
Animals that feed on plants.

primary consumers
They feed on autotrophic organisms and are therefore usually herbivores.

detritivores
Organisms that break down organic matter (dead animals, excrement, plant residue) into mineral components that can be reused by plants.

producers
Plants are at the base of the food chain for all other consumers; they provide food energy directly or indirectly to all consumers.

inorganic matter
Matter of mineral origin, converted by bacteria; the nitrogen, salts and water it retains serve as food for plants.

example of food chain

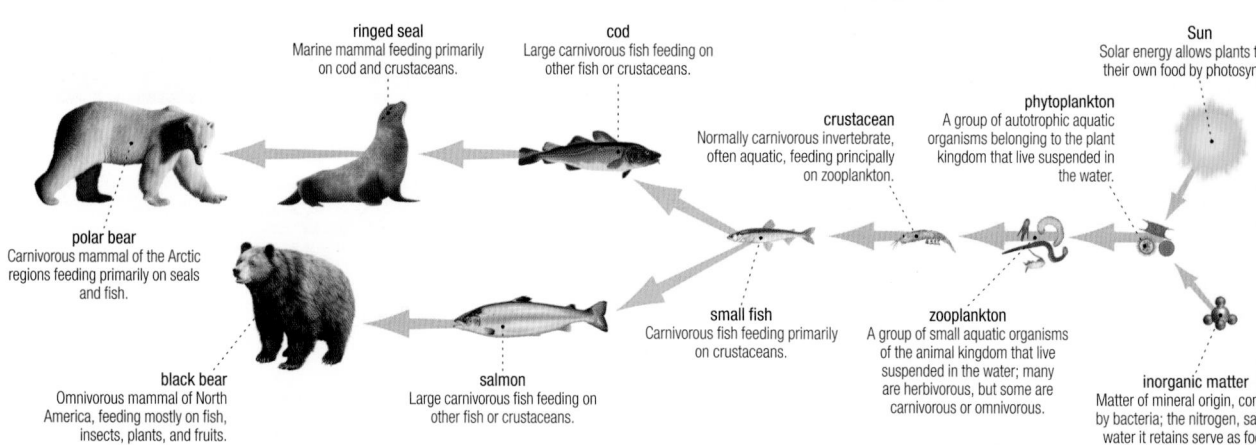

ringed seal
Marine mammal feeding primarily on cod and crustaceans.

cod
Large carnivorous fish feeding on other fish or crustaceans.

Sun
Solar energy allows plants t their own food by photosyr

crustacean
Normally carnivorous invertebrate, often aquatic, feeding principally on zooplankton.

phytoplankton
A group of autotrophic aquatic organisms belonging to the plant kingdom that live suspended in the water.

polar bear
Carnivorous mammal of the Arctic regions feeding primarily on seals and fish.

small fish
Carnivorous fish feeding primarily on crustaceans.

zooplankton
A group of small aquatic organisms of the animal kingdom that live suspended in the water; many are herbivorous, but some are carnivorous or omnivorous.

inorganic matter
Matter of mineral origin, con by bacteria; the nitrogen, sa water it retains serve as foo plants.

black bear
Omnivorous mammal of North America, feeding mostly on fish, insects, plants, and fruits.

salmon
Large carnivorous fish feeding on other fish or crustaceans.

structure of the biosphere

Biosphere: the part of the Earth where life is possible; it extends from the floor of the oceans to the summit of the highest mountains (about 12 mi).

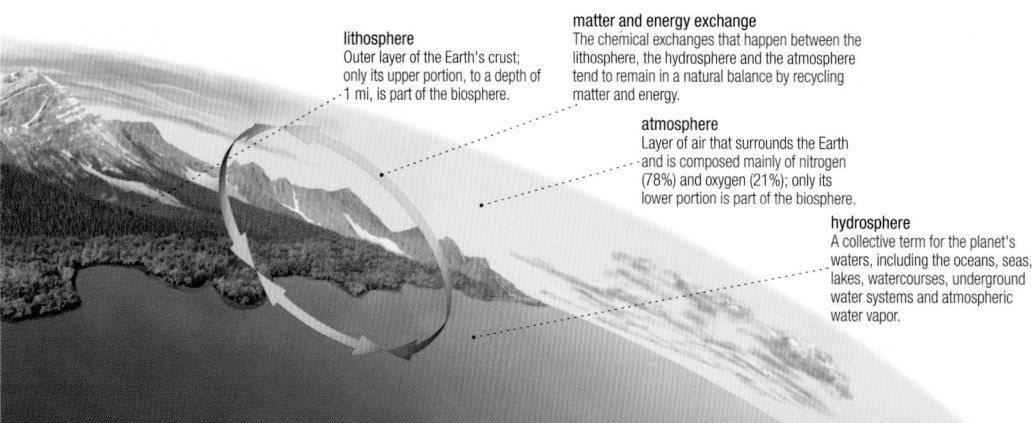

lithosphere
Outer layer of the Earth's crust; only its upper portion, to a depth of 1 mi, is part of the biosphere.

matter and energy exchange
The chemical exchanges that happen between the lithosphere, the hydrosphere and the atmosphere tend to remain in a natural balance by recycling matter and energy.

atmosphere
Layer of air that surrounds the Earth and is composed mainly of nitrogen (78%) and oxygen (21%); only its lower portion is part of the biosphere.

hydrosphere
A collective term for the planet's waters, including the oceans, seas, lakes, watercourses, underground water systems and atmospheric water vapor.

hydrologic cycle

Continuous circulation of water in its different states (liquid, solid and gaseous) between the oceans, the atmosphere and the Earth's surface.

action of wind
Driven by winds, clouds fly over the land.

precipitation
Various forms of water that fall from the atmosphere.

surface runoff
Flow of rainwater or melting snow on the surface of the ground; it produces watercourses.

precipitation
Various forms of water that fall from the atmosphere.

ice
Water that accumulates high in the mountains in solid form.

condensation
The process by which water vapor is converted, by means of cooling, into liquid or solid water in the form of clouds.

evaporation
Conversion, without boiling, of liquid water into water vapor at the surface of the liquid.

solar radiation
...ides heat that encourages water to evaporate.

evaporation
Conversion, without boiling, of water into water vapor at the surface of the liquid.

infiltration
Water penetrating into the soil through permeable rock.

ocean
Vast body of saltwater covering a large part of the Earth's surface and separating the continents.

underground flow
Movement of infiltrated water that joins a watercourse on the surface or flows directly into lakes or the ocean.

transpiration
Phenomenon by which plants discharge water vapor into the atmosphere.

carbon-oxygen cycle

A number of interactions that cause oxygen and carbon, two elements essential to life, to circulate through the biosphere.

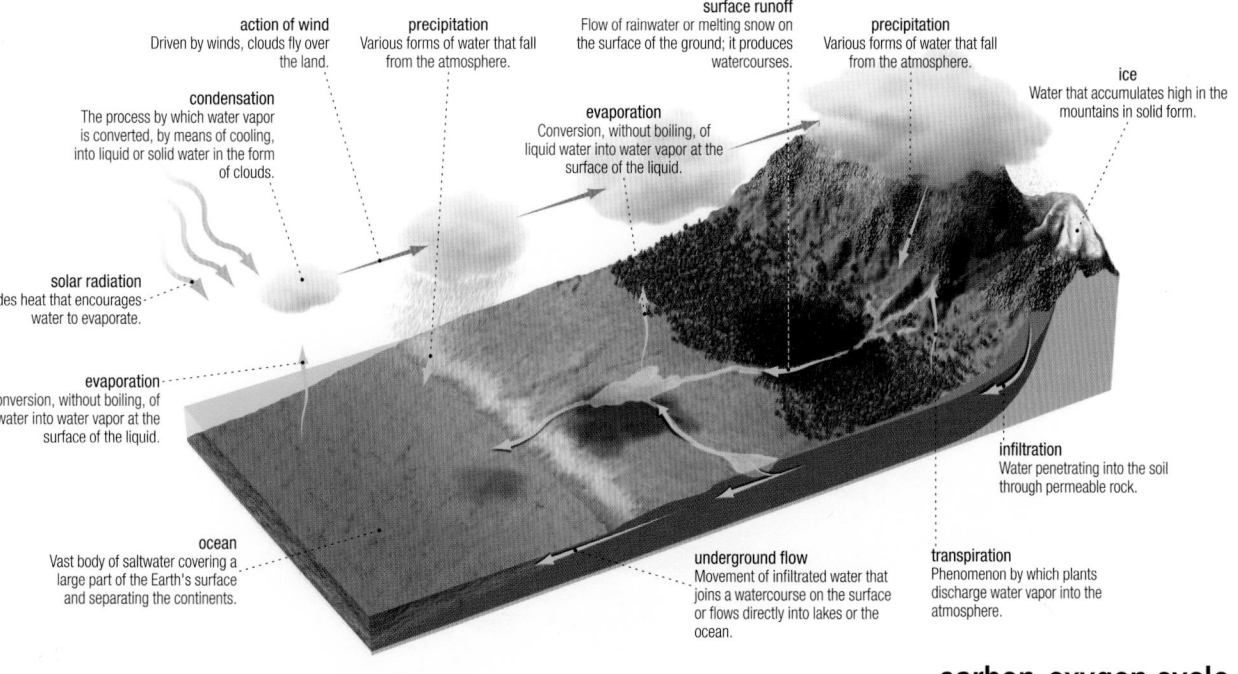

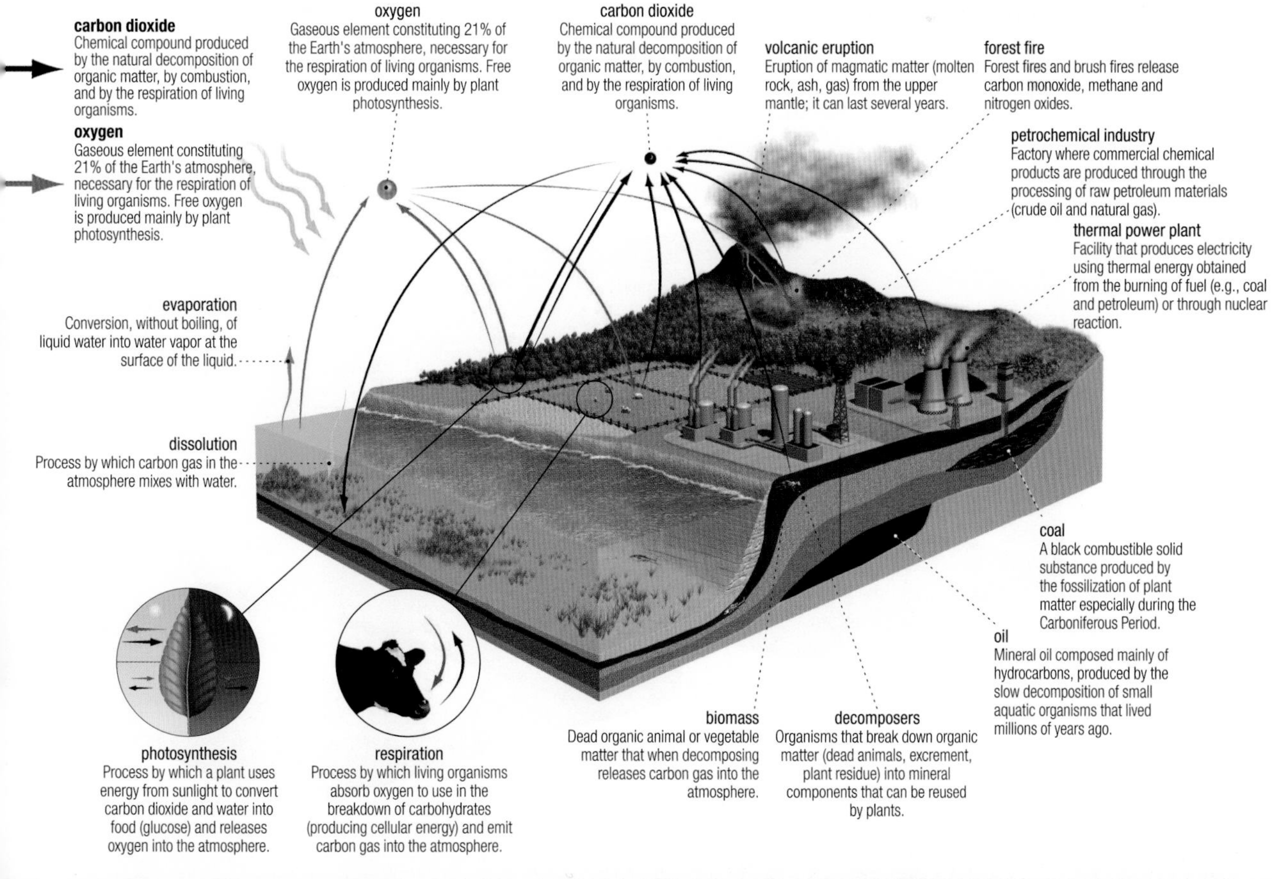

carbon dioxide
Chemical compound produced by the natural decomposition of organic matter, by combustion, and by the respiration of living organisms.

oxygen
Gaseous element constituting 21% of the Earth's atmosphere, necessary for the respiration of living organisms. Free oxygen is produced mainly by plant photosynthesis.

oxygen
Gaseous element constituting 21% of the Earth's atmosphere, necessary for the respiration of living organisms. Free oxygen is produced mainly by plant photosynthesis.

carbon dioxide
Chemical compound produced by the natural decomposition of organic matter, by combustion, and by the respiration of living organisms.

volcanic eruption
Eruption of magmatic matter (molten rock, ash, gas) from the upper mantle; it can last several years.

forest fire
Forest fires and brush fires release carbon monoxide, methane and nitrogen oxides.

petrochemical industry
Factory where commercial chemical products are produced through the processing of raw petroleum materials (crude oil and natural gas).

thermal power plant
Facility that produces electricity using thermal energy obtained from the burning of fuel (e.g., coal and petroleum) or through nuclear reaction.

evaporation
Conversion, without boiling, of liquid water into water vapor at the surface of the liquid.

dissolution
Process by which carbon gas in the atmosphere mixes with water.

coal
A black combustible solid substance produced by the fossilization of plant matter especially during the Carboniferous Period.

oil
Mineral oil composed mainly of hydrocarbons, produced by the slow decomposition of small aquatic organisms that lived millions of years ago.

photosynthesis
Process by which a plant uses energy from sunlight to convert carbon dioxide and water into food (glucose) and releases oxygen into the atmosphere.

respiration
Process by which living organisms absorb oxygen to use in the breakdown of carbohydrates (producing cellular energy) and emit carbon gas into the atmosphere.

biomass
Dead organic animal or vegetable matter that when decomposing releases carbon gas into the atmosphere.

decomposers
Organisms that break down organic matter (dead animals, excrement, plant residue) into mineral components that can be reused by plants.

EARTH

natural greenhouse effect

The greenhouse effect is an indispensable natural phenomenon; without it, the average temperature, currently 59°F, would be no higher than 0°F.

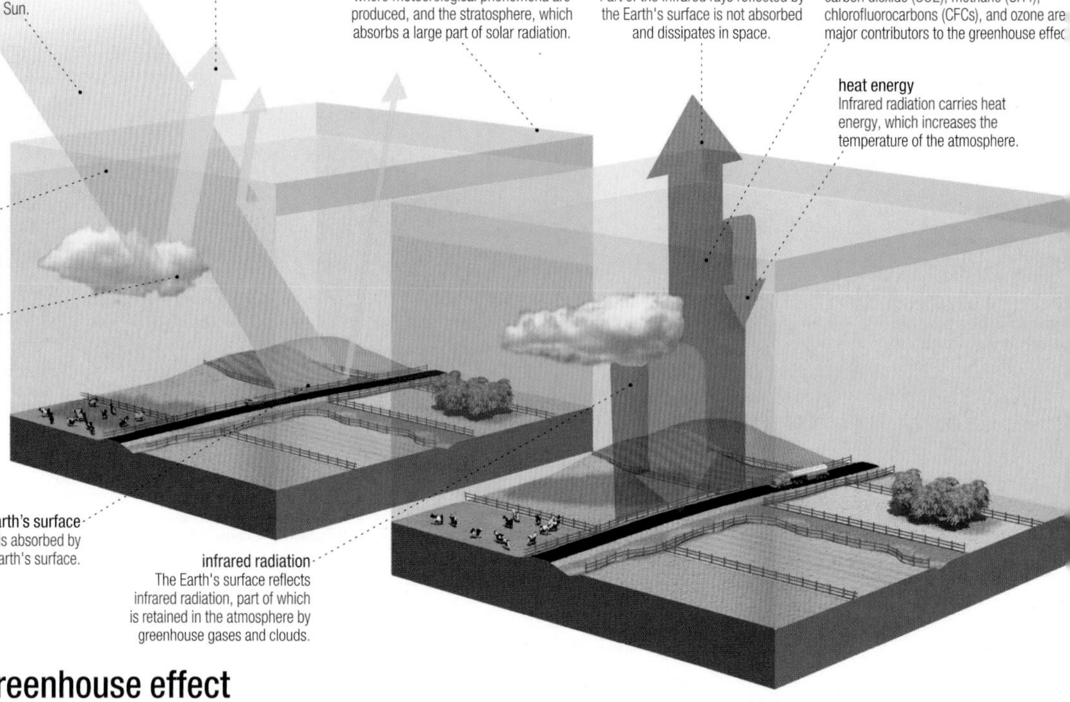

reflected solar radiation
Thirty percent of solar radiation is sent back into space by clouds, by particles suspended in the atmosphere and by the Earth's surface.

solar radiation
All the electromagnetic waves emitted by the Sun.

tropopause
Boundary between the troposphere, where meteorological phenomena are produced, and the stratosphere, which absorbs a large part of solar radiation.

heat loss
Part of the infrared rays reflected by the Earth's surface is not absorbed and dissipates in space.

greenhouse gas
Gas that traps heat in the atmosphere; carbon dioxide (CO_2), methane (CH_4), chlorofluorocarbons (CFCs), and ozone are major contributors to the greenhouse effect.

heat energy
Infrared radiation carries heat energy, which increases the temperature of the atmosphere.

absorbed solar radiation
A portion of solar radiation is converted into thermal energy by gaseous constituents in the atmosphere, in the clouds and on the Earth's surface.

absorption by clouds
A small amount of solar radiation is absorbed by clouds.

absorption by the Earth's surface
About 50% of solar radiation is absorbed by the Earth's surface.

infrared radiation
The Earth's surface reflects infrared radiation, part of which is retained in the atmosphere by greenhouse gases and clouds.

enhanced greenhouse effect

Human activity constantly emits greenhouse gases, which trap ever more heat in the atmosphere.

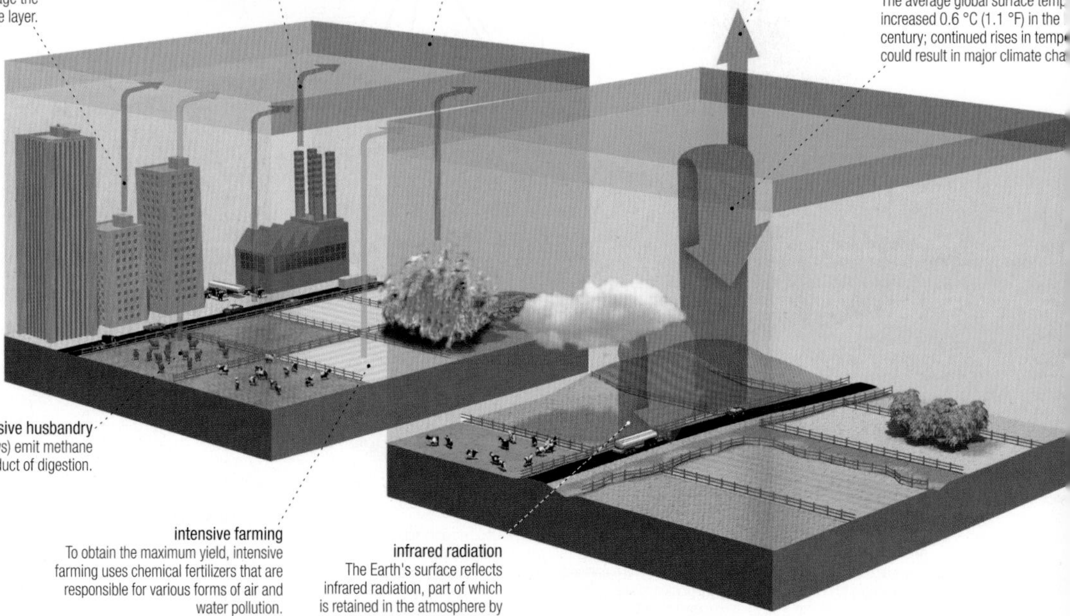

air conditioning system
Air conditioning systems use chlorofluorocarbons (CFCs) that absorb infrared rays and damage the ozone layer.

fossil fuel
The combustion of wood and fossil fuels (coal, oil, natural gas) emits carbon dioxide and methane into the atmosphere.

greenhouse gas concentration
Increasingly abundant greenhouse gases reflect more and more infrared rays toward the Earth's surface, accelerating global warming.

heat loss
Part of the infrared rays reflected by the Earth's surface is not absorbed and dissipates into space.

global warming
The average global surface temp increased 0.6 °C (1.1 °F) in the century; continued rises in temp could result in major climate cha

intensive husbandry
Ruminants (such as cows) emit methane into the air as a by-product of digestion.

intensive farming
To obtain the maximum yield, intensive farming uses chemical fertilizers that are responsible for various forms of air and water pollution.

infrared radiation
The Earth's surface reflects infrared radiation, part of which is retained in the atmosphere by greenhouse gases and clouds.

air pollution

The presence in the atmosphere of large quantities of particles or gases produced by human activity; these are harmful to both animal and plant life.

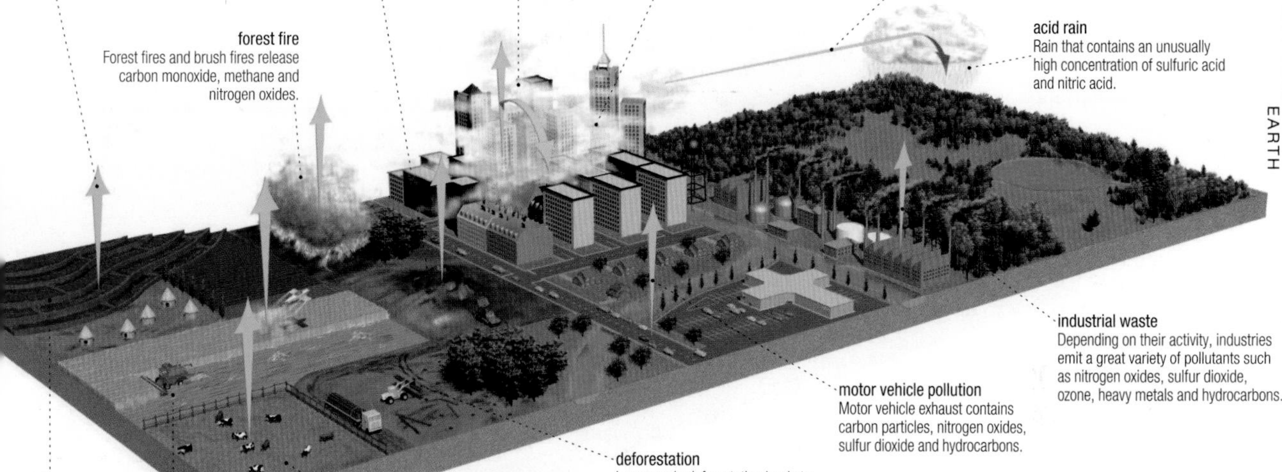

olluting gas emission
olluting gases are present
atmosphere in minuscule
ties, but human activity
ses their concentration.

authorized landfill site
In waste landfill sites, decomposing
organic matter produces methane.

air pollutants
The principal air pollutants are
sulfur dioxide, nitrogen oxides,
hydrocarbons, methane and carbon
dioxide.

smog
Harmful haze resulting from the
presence of polluting gases; it
forms over cities under specific
meteorological conditions.

wind
Polluted clouds are carried by
the wind, sometimes traveling
thousands of miles; their pollutants
then fall in the form of acid rain.

acid rain
Rain that contains an unusually
high concentration of sulfuric acid
and nitric acid.

forest fire
Forest fires and brush fires release
carbon monoxide, methane and
nitrogen oxides.

industrial waste
Depending on their activity, industries
emit a great variety of pollutants such
as nitrogen oxides, sulfur dioxide,
ozone, heavy metals and hydrocarbons.

motor vehicle pollution
Motor vehicle exhaust contains
carbon particles, nitrogen oxides,
sulfur dioxide and hydrocarbons.

deforestation
Large-scale deforestation leads to
increased carbon dioxide levels in
the atmosphere since plants alone
absorb and retain this gas.

paddy field
lds release considerable
antities of methane.

soil fertilization
Nitrogen fertilizers used to fertilize
the soil also release nitrogen
oxides.

intensive husbandry
Ruminants (such as cows)
emit methane into the air as a
by-product of digestion.

land pollution

Numerous factors contribute to soil pollution (e.g., household and industrial waste, fertilizers, pesticides).

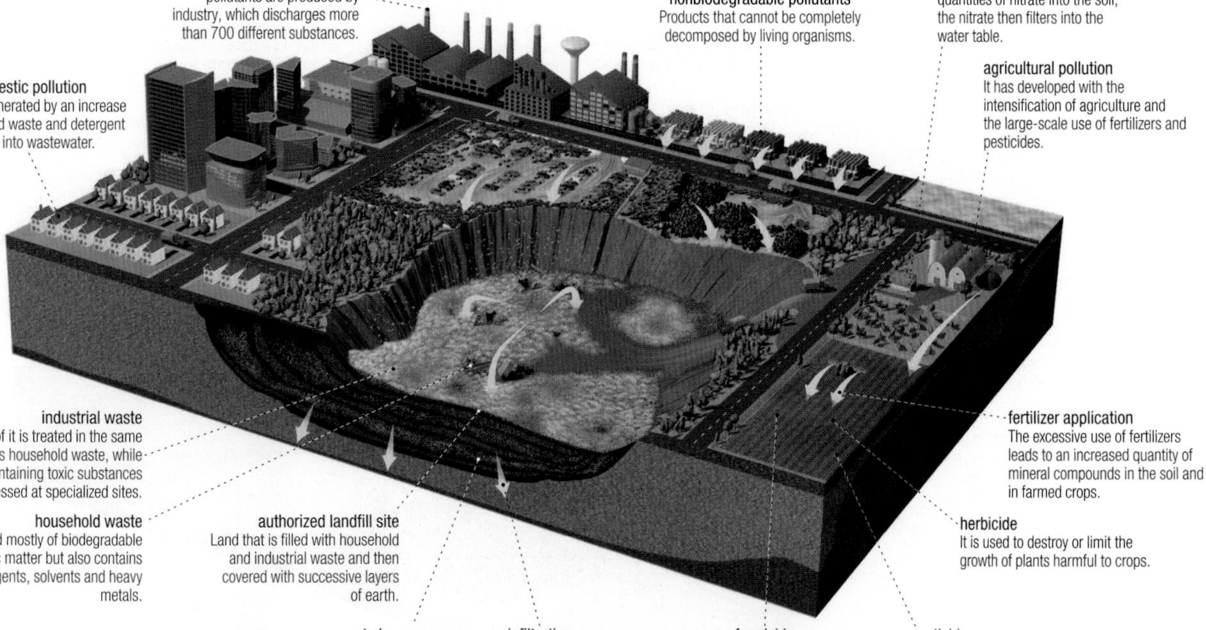

industrial pollution
Most nonbiodegradable soil
pollutants are produced by
industry, which discharges more
than 700 different substances.

nonbiodegradable pollutants
Products that cannot be completely
decomposed by living organisms.

intensive husbandry
Animal dung introduces large
quantities of nitrate into the soil;
the nitrate then filters into the
water table.

agricultural pollution
It has developed with the
intensification of agriculture and
the large-scale use of fertilizers and
pesticides.

domestic pollution
ollution generated by an increase
household waste and detergent
spilled into wastewater.

industrial waste
Some of it is treated in the same
manner as household waste, while
r forms containing toxic substances
are processed at specialized sites.

household waste
composed mostly of biodegradable
organic matter but also contains
tics, detergents, solvents and heavy
metals.

authorized landfill site
Land that is filled with household
and industrial waste and then
covered with successive layers
of earth.

fertilizer application
The excessive use of fertilizers
leads to an increased quantity of
mineral compounds in the soil and
in farmed crops.

herbicide
It is used to destroy or limit the
growth of plants harmful to crops.

waste layers
Each waste layer is sealed using a
plastic film or a base layer of clay.

infiltration
In spite of the sealing of waste
layers, rainwater runoff can allow
certain pollutants to seep into the
subsoil.

fungicide
It is used to destroy parasitic fungi
on crops.

pesticide
Product (insecticide, herbicide or
fungicide) that destroys harmful
organisms. It sometimes enters the food
chain and affects flora and fauna.

EARTH

water pollution

The cycle of the Earth's waters is continuous, carrying and spreading pollutants introduced by human activity all around the planet.

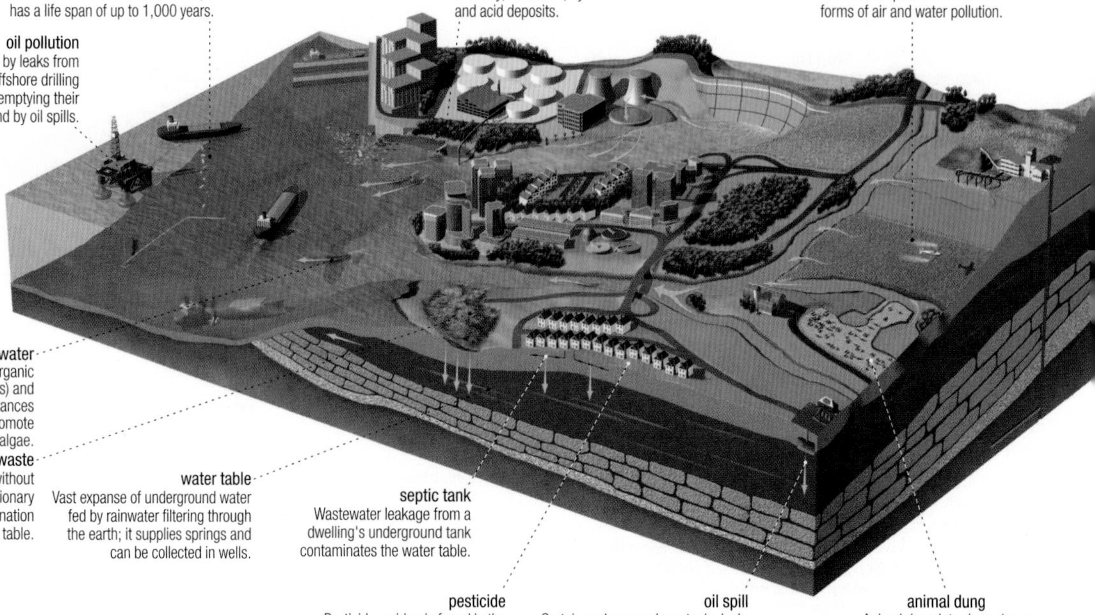

nuclear waste
Radioactive nuclear waste was once immersed at the bottom of the ocean; it has a life span of up to 1,000 years.

industrial waste
Industrial waste is highly variable; its principal components are lead, mercury, cadmium, hydrocarbons and acid deposits.

intensive farming
To achieve maximum production, intensive farming uses chemical fertilizers responsible for various forms of air and water pollution.

oil pollution
Pollution caused by leaks from refineries and offshore drilling platforms, by ships emptying their fuel tanks at sea and by oil spills.

wastewater
Untreated, it contains organic matter (e.g., bacteria, viruses) and potentially pathogenic substances that cause infection and promote the growth of algae.

household waste
Burying household waste without taking any particular precautionary measures leads to contamination of the water table.

water table
Vast expanse of underground water fed by rainwater filtering through the earth; it supplies springs and can be collected in wells.

septic tank
Wastewater leakage from a dwelling's underground tank contaminates the water table.

pesticide
Pesticide residue is found in the water table and in watercourses; it makes water unfit for consumption.

oil spill
Certain underground gas tanks leak, discharging hydrocarbons into the water table.

animal dung
Animal dung introduces large quantities of nitrate into the soil; the nitrate then filters into the water table.

acid rain

Rain that contains abnormally high concentrations of sulfuric acid and nitric acid.

cloud water
Nitric acid and sulfuric acid dissolve in cloud water.

nitric acid emission
Nitric acid forms when nitrogen oxides combine with cloud water.

atmosphere
Layer of air that surrounds the Earth and is composed mainly of nitrogen (78%) and oxygen (21%); only its lower portion is part of the biosphere.

wind
Polluted clouds are carried by the wind, sometimes traveling thousands of miles; their pollutants then fall in the form of acid rain.

acid rain
Rain that contains abnormally high concentrations of sulfuric acid and nitric acid.

sulfuric acid emission
Sulfuric acid forms when sulfur dioxide combines with cloud water.

acid snow
Acid rain can take the form of snowflakes and fog.

nitrogen oxide emission
Nitrogen oxide is discharged by motor vehicles and thermal power plants that burn fossil fuels.

sulfur dioxide emission
Sulfur dioxide is produced mainly by coal-fired thermal power plants and smelters that refine ores with high sulfur content.

fossil fuel
The use of fossil fuels by motor vehicles and industry triggers emissions of sulfur dioxide and nitrogen oxides.

watercourse
Natural flow of water that varies in volume, depending on the ground slope and the number of tributaries.

leaching
Acid rain robs the soil of nut that are indispensable to pla such as magnesium, calciu potassium.

soil
Surface layer of the Earth's crust; it results from the alteration of bedrock and the decomposition of organic matter.

water table
Vast expanse of underground water fed by rainwater filtering through the earth; it supplies springs and can be collected in wells.

lake acidification
It causes plankton depletion and creates an imbalance in the food chain, sometimes leading to the total disappearance of plant and animal life.

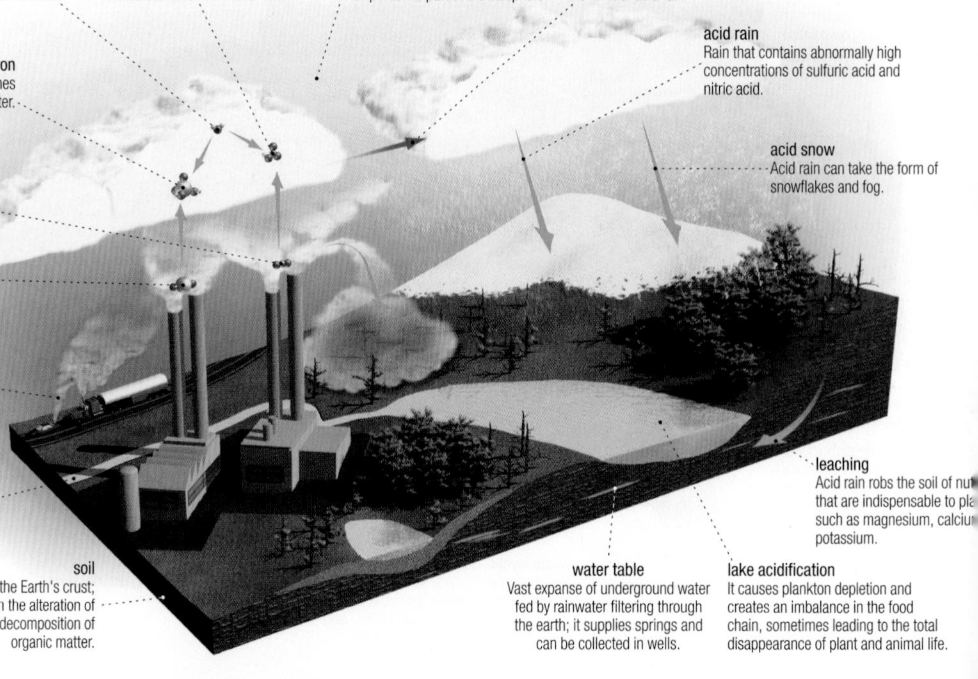

EARTH

selective sorting of waste

Its goal is to extract recyclable material from trash.

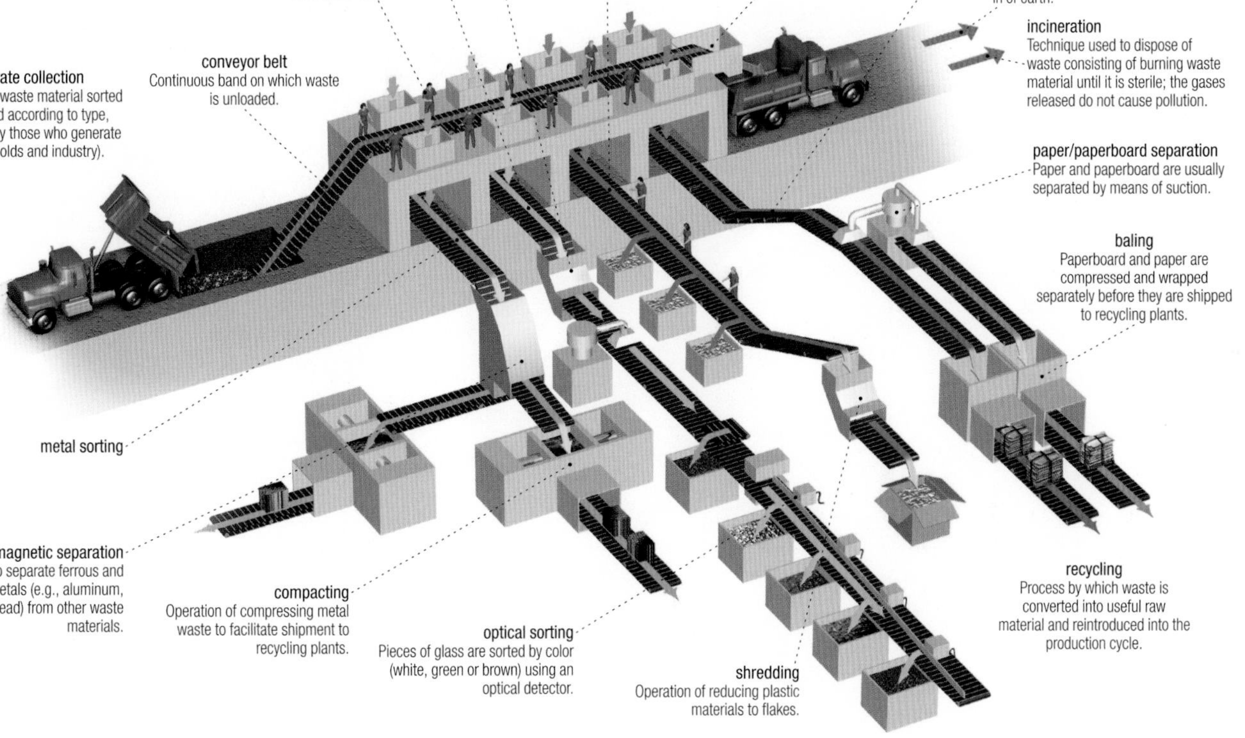

sorting plant
Facility that receives and sorts recyclable material and then delivers it to a recycling center.

crusher
Apparatus for crushing and tearing materials.

nonreusable residue waste
Waste that cannot be converted into useful matter for reintroduction into the production cycle.

glass sorting

plastics sorting

paper/paperboard sorting

burial
Operation of compressing waste into layers 7 to 10 feet thick, and then covering them with at least 6 in of earth.

manual sorting

incineration
Technique used to dispose of waste consisting of burning waste material until it is sterile; the gases released do not cause pollution.

separate collection
tion of waste material sorted orehand according to type, d out by those who generate households and industry).

conveyor belt
Continuous band on which waste is unloaded.

paper/paperboard separation
Paper and paperboard are usually separated by means of suction.

baling
Paperboard and paper are compressed and wrapped separately before they are shipped to recycling plants.

metal sorting

magnetic separation
used to separate ferrous and rous metals (e.g., aluminum, opper, lead) from other waste materials.

compacting
Operation of compressing metal waste to facilitate shipment to recycling plants.

optical sorting
Pieces of glass are sorted by color (white, green or brown) using an optical detector.

shredding
Operation of reducing plastic materials to flakes.

recycling
Process by which waste is converted into useful raw material and reintroduced into the production cycle.

recycling containers
Containers used to collect specific types of recyclable waste material such as glass, plastic, metal and waste oil.

per recycling container
volume container used by the of a building to dispose of paper ., newspapers, packaging).

glass recycling container
High-volume container used by the tenants of a building to dispose of glass.

aluminum recycling container
High-volume container used by the tenants of a building to dispose of metal containers.

paper collection unit
High-volume public container used by the citizens of a community to dispose of paper (e.g., newspapers, packaging).

recycling bin
Small-volume household container used to collect recyclable household waste.

glass collection unit
High-volume public container used by the citizens of a community to dispose of glass containers.

PLANTS AND PLANTLIKE ORGANISMS

Living things deriving their nourishment primarily or solely from photosynthesis and lacking locomotive movement.

plant cell

Smallest living structure and the constituent element of all plants; it varies in size and shape depending on its function.

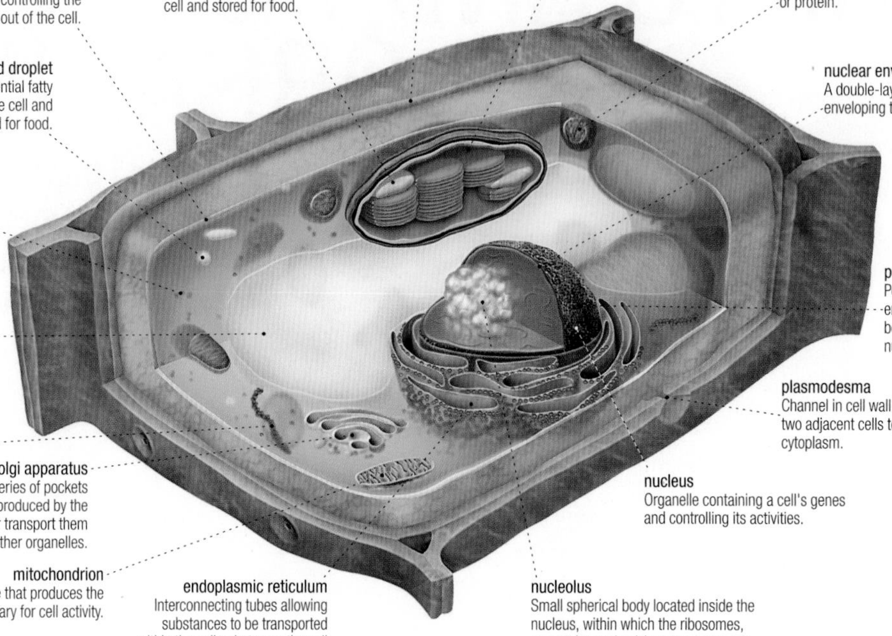

cell membrane
Flexible layer that encloses the cell's cytoplasm; it acts as a filter, controlling the passage of substances in and out of the cell.

starch granule
Concentric layers of complex sugars (starch) produced by the cell and stored for food.

cell wall
Stiff exterior layer that surrounds the cell membrane and gives the cell its shape.

chloroplast
Small structure, containing a green pigment called chlorophyll, which absorbs solar energy and uses it to produce glucose, the plant's food.

leucoplast
Small colorless structure that is specialized to store starch, lipid, or protein.

lipid droplet
Small sac filled with essential fatty acids that are produced by the cell and stored for food.

nuclear envelope
A double-layered membrane enveloping the nucleus.

cytoplasm
Clear gelatinous substance surrounding the various cellular structures.

vacuole
Spherical cavity containing water, waste and various substances required by the cell.

pore
Perforations in the nuclear envelope allowing for excha between the cytoplasm and nucleus.

ribosome
Small structure, occasionally attached to the endoplasmic reticulum; it generates proteins essential to the formation and functioning of living things.

plasmodesma
Channel in cell wall allowing two adjacent cells to exchange cytoplasm.

Golgi apparatus
Organelle composed of a series of pockets that receive proteins produced by the ribosomes and either transport them outside the cell or to other organelles.

nucleus
Organelle containing a cell's genes and controlling its activities.

mitochondrion
Ovoid organelle that produces the energy necessary for cell activity.

endoplasmic reticulum
Interconnecting tubes allowing substances to be transported within the cell or between the cell and its exterior environment.

nucleolus
Small spherical body located inside the nucleus, within which the ribosomes, or protein-synthesizing structures, are produced.

photosynthesis

Process by which a plant uses energy from sunlight to convert carbon dioxide and water into food (glucose) and releases oxygen into the atmosphere.

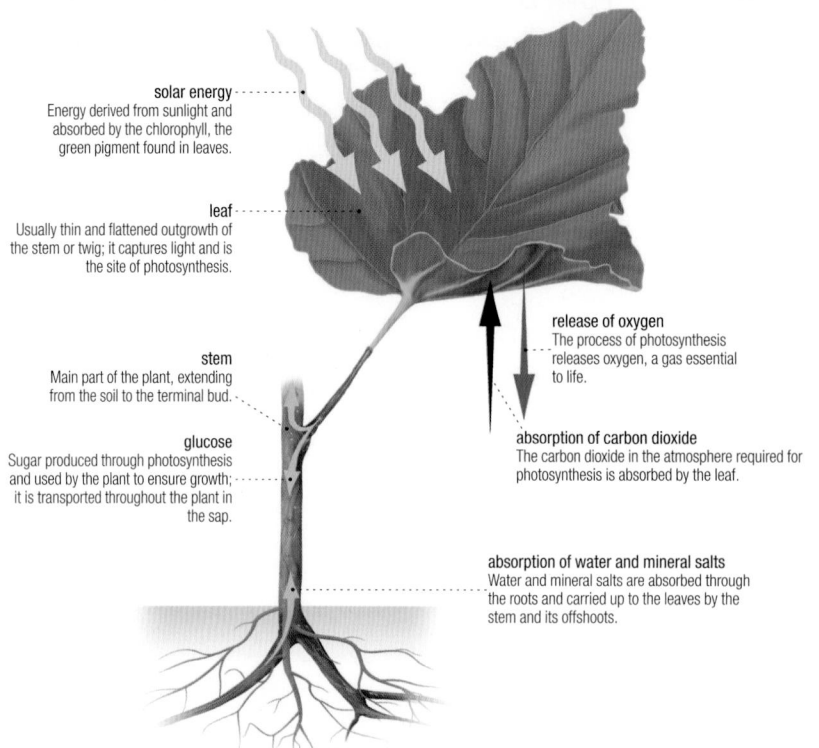

solar energy
Energy derived from sunlight and absorbed by the chlorophyll, the green pigment found in leaves.

leaf
Usually thin and flattened outgrowth of the stem or twig; it captures light and is the site of photosynthesis.

release of oxygen
The process of photosynthesis releases oxygen, a gas essential to life.

stem
Main part of the plant, extending from the soil to the terminal bud.

glucose
Sugar produced through photosynthesis and used by the plant to ensure growth; it is transported throughout the plant in the sap.

absorption of carbon dioxide
The carbon dioxide in the atmosphere required for photosynthesis is absorbed by the leaf.

absorption of water and mineral salts
Water and mineral salts are absorbed through the roots and carried up to the leaves by the stem and its offshoots.

unusual plants

Plants deriving water and nutrients from other living things; photosynthesis is usually limited or absent.

examples of parasitic plants

Parasitic plant: plant living on another plant and taking water and nutrients from it.

mistletoe
Parasitic plant growing on trees and inserting its sinkers (haustoria) into the host's xylem.

berry
Fruit in which the seed is surrounded by two visible layers: an outer exocarp and an inner fleshy layer of mesocarp and endocarp in direct contact with one or more seeds.

leaf
Usually thin and flattened outgrowth of the stem; it captures light and is the site of photosynthesis.

dodder
Parasitic herbaceous plant that twines itself around the stem of a host plant and inserts its sinkers (haustoria) into the host's xylem.

stem of the dodder
Main part of the dodder.

dodder's flowers
Colored and scented structure of the dodder, containing its reproductive organs.

host plant
Plant on which a parasitic plant lives.

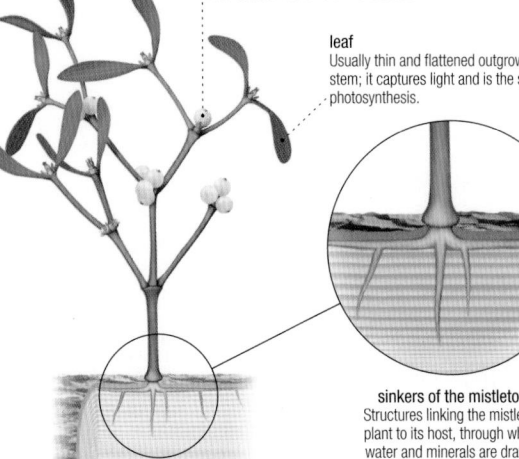

sinkers of the mistletoe
Structures linking the mistletoe plant to its host, through which water and minerals are drawn.

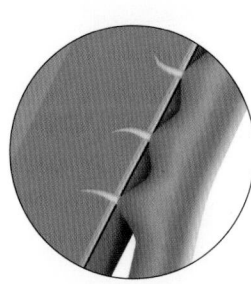

sinkers of the dodder
Structures linking the dodder plant to its host, through which water, minerals and food are drawn.

host tree
Tree on which a parasitic plant lives.

examples of carnivorous plants

Carnivorous plant: plant that traps and feeds on insects.

Venus flytrap
Plant whose lobe-shaped leaves capture flies attracted to its sweet sap.

petiole
Narrow stalk connecting the leaf to the stem.

fly
One of a large group of winged insects.

operculum
Part of the pitcher that works as a lid to prevent the leaf from filling with water.

pitcher plant
Plant with pitcher-shaped leaves filled with fluid in which insects become trapped.

leaf
Usually thin and flattened outgrowth of the stem; it captures light and is the site of photosynthesis.

sensitive hair
Hairlike outgrowth that signals the lobes to quickly close when it is touched by an insect.

digestive gland
Organ secreting a liquid containing enzymes used to digest insects.

pitcher
Pitcher-shaped leaf with a slippery interior and special hairs that prevent an insect's escape.

insect
One of a very large group of small invertebrate animals; it becomes trapped in the digestive liquid inside the pitcher.

tooth
All of the rigid outgrowths located on the edge of the lobe, which interlace when the two lobes are closed.

peristome
Thick, brightly-colored rim around the opening of the pitcher, with dentate outgrowths and covered in a sweet substance.

lobe
Each of the two halves of the leaf bordered by teeth and connected by a midrib.

digestive liquid
Substance containing enzymes secreted by the inner wall of the pitcher, allowing it to digest captured insects.

life cycle (flowering plant)

The stages of plant life, including growth, maturation of reproductive organs, pollination and fertilization, and seed production and dispersal.

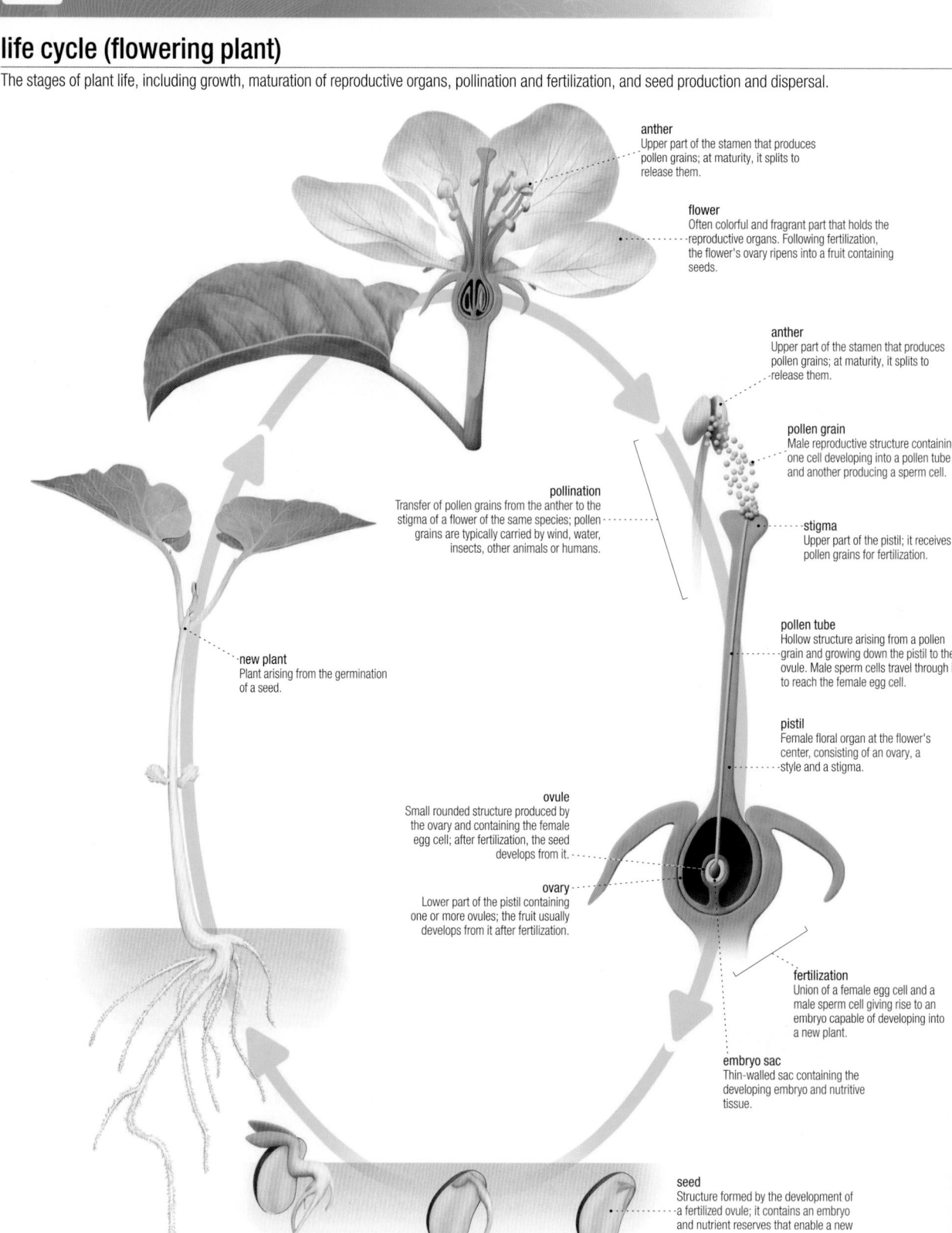

anther
Upper part of the stamen that produces pollen grains; at maturity, it splits to release them.

flower
Often colorful and fragrant part that holds the reproductive organs. Following fertilization, the flower's ovary ripens into a fruit containing seeds.

anther
Upper part of the stamen that produces pollen grains; at maturity, it splits to release them.

pollen grain
Male reproductive structure containing one cell developing into a pollen tube and another producing a sperm cell.

pollination
Transfer of pollen grains from the anther to the stigma of a flower of the same species; pollen grains are typically carried by wind, water, insects, other animals or humans.

stigma
Upper part of the pistil; it receives pollen grains for fertilization.

pollen tube
Hollow structure arising from a pollen grain and growing down the pistil to the ovule. Male sperm cells travel through it to reach the female egg cell.

new plant
Plant arising from the germination of a seed.

pistil
Female floral organ at the flower's center, consisting of an ovary, a style and a stigma.

ovule
Small rounded structure produced by the ovary and containing the female egg cell; after fertilization, the seed develops from it.

ovary
Lower part of the pistil containing one or more ovules; the fruit usually develops from it after fertilization.

fertilization
Union of a female egg cell and a male sperm cell giving rise to an embryo capable of developing into a new plant.

embryo sac
Thin-walled sac containing the developing embryo and nutritive tissue.

seed
Structure formed by the development of a fertilized ovule; it contains an embryo and nutrient reserves that enable a new plant to grow.

germination
Process by which a seed, under favorable conditions, develops and grows into a plant.

plant growth

Processes by which plants develop, grow and mature.

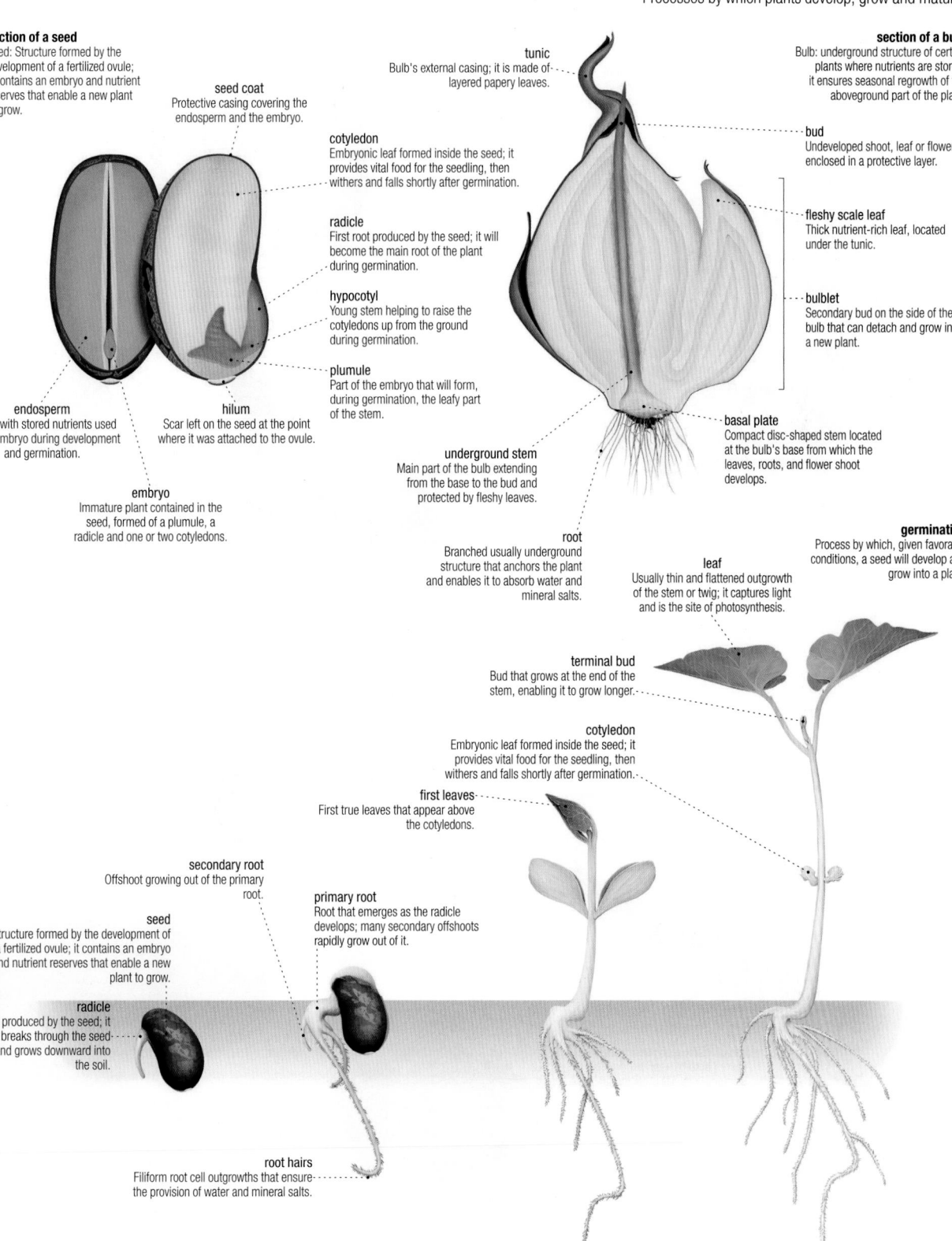

section of a seed
Seed: Structure formed by the development of a fertilized ovule; it contains an embryo and nutrient reserves that enable a new plant to grow.

seed coat
Protective casing covering the endosperm and the embryo.

cotyledon
Embryonic leaf formed inside the seed; it provides vital food for the seedling, then withers and falls shortly after germination.

radicle
First root produced by the seed; it will become the main root of the plant during germination.

hypocotyl
Young stem helping to raise the cotyledons up from the ground during germination.

plumule
Part of the embryo that will form, during germination, the leafy part of the stem.

endosperm
Tissue with stored nutrients used by the embryo during development and germination.

hilum
Scar left on the seed at the point where it was attached to the ovule.

embryo
Immature plant contained in the seed, formed of a plumule, a radicle and one or two cotyledons.

tunic
Bulb's external casing; it is made of layered papery leaves.

section of a bulb
Bulb: underground structure of certain plants where nutrients are stored; it ensures seasonal regrowth of the aboveground part of the plant.

bud
Undeveloped shoot, leaf or flower enclosed in a protective layer.

fleshy scale leaf
Thick nutrient-rich leaf, located under the tunic.

bulblet
Secondary bud on the side of the bulb that can detach and grow into a new plant.

basal plate
Compact disc-shaped stem located at the bulb's base from which the leaves, roots, and flower shoot develops.

underground stem
Main part of the bulb extending from the base to the bud and protected by fleshy leaves.

root
Branched usually underground structure that anchors the plant and enables it to absorb water and mineral salts.

leaf
Usually thin and flattened outgrowth of the stem or twig; it captures light and is the site of photosynthesis.

germination
Process by which, given favorable conditions, a seed will develop and grow into a plant.

terminal bud
Bud that grows at the end of the stem, enabling it to grow longer.

cotyledon
Embryonic leaf formed inside the seed; it provides vital food for the seedling, then withers and falls shortly after germination.

first leaves
First true leaves that appear above the cotyledons.

secondary root
Offshoot growing out of the primary root.

primary root
Root that emerges as the radicle develops; many secondary offshoots rapidly grow out of it.

seed
Structure formed by the development of a fertilized ovule; it contains an embryo and nutrient reserves that enable a new plant to grow.

radicle
First root produced by the seed; it quickly breaks through the seed coat and grows downward into the soil.

root hairs
Filiform root cell outgrowths that ensure the provision of water and mineral salts.

lichen

Organism formed from the symbiotic association of an alga and a fungus.

structure of a lichen

apothecium
Reproductive spore-bearing structure of the fungus.

thallus
Lichen's main structure formed by fungal filaments entwined with algal cells.

examples of lichens
There are more than 20,000 species of lichen, found growing on various substrates (tree trunks, rocks, surface of soil); they grow in all climatic zones.

crustose lichen
Lichen whose thallus forms a crust that is firmly attached to its substrate.

foliose lichen
Lichen whose thallus resembles leaves or lobes that are loosely attached to their substrate by rootlike filaments.

fruticose lichen
Lichen whose branching thallus resembles a small shrub; it is attached to its substrate at a single point.

moss

Flowerless plant, usually small in size, that grows in large tightly packed tufts to create a veritable soft carpet.

structure of a moss

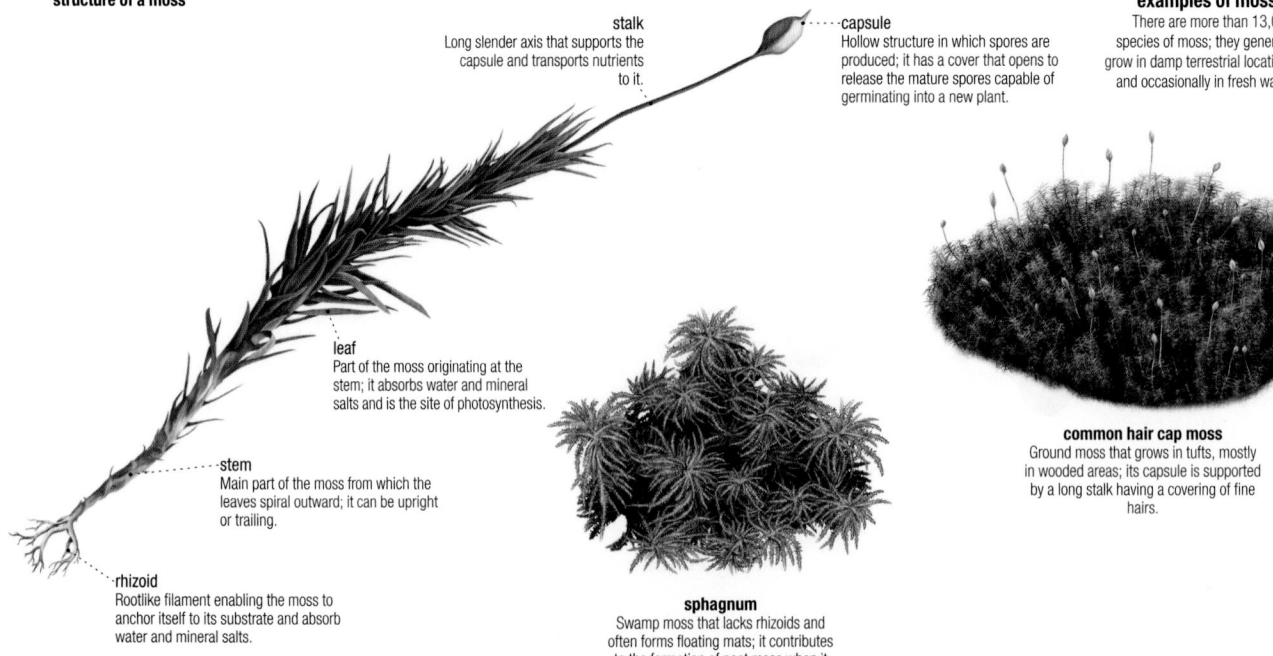

stalk
Long slender axis that supports the capsule and transports nutrients to it.

capsule
Hollow structure in which spores are produced; it has a cover that opens to release the mature spores capable of germinating into a new plant.

examples of mosses
There are more than 13,000 species of moss; they generally grow in damp terrestrial locations and occasionally in fresh water.

leaf
Part of the moss originating at the stem; it absorbs water and mineral salts and is the site of photosynthesis.

stem
Main part of the moss from which the leaves spiral outward; it can be upright or trailing.

rhizoid
Rootlike filament enabling the moss to anchor itself to its substrate and absorb water and mineral salts.

sphagnum
Swamp moss that lacks rhizoids and often forms floating mats; it contributes to the formation of peat moss when it decomposes and becomes compacted.

common hair cap moss
Ground moss that grows in tufts, mostly in wooded areas; its capsule is supported by a long stalk having a covering of fine hairs.

alga

Flowerless plant or plantlike organism that usually grows in aquatic environments; it lacks true roots, stems or leaves.

structure of an alga

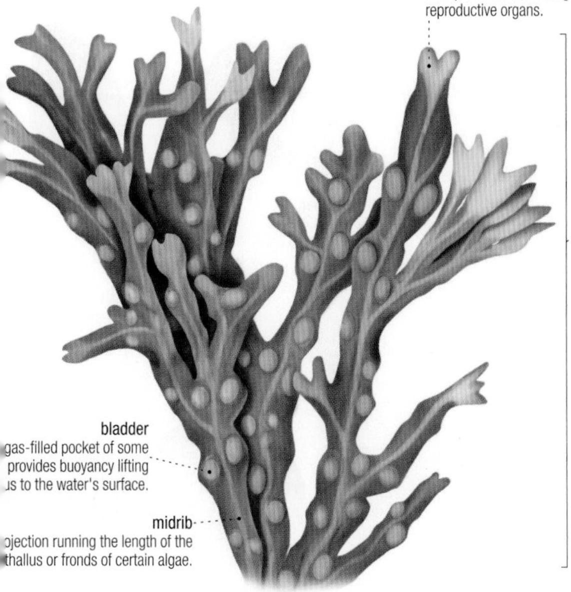

receptacle
Enlarged part, generally located at the tip of a frond, holding the alga's reproductive organs.

thallus
Alga's main structure, with undifferentiated stem and leaves.

bladder
gas-filled pocket of some provides buoyancy lifting us to the water's surface.

midrib
ojection running the length of the thallus or fronds of certain algae.

examples of algae
More than 25,000 species of algae live in aquatic environments or in some regions with damp soil; they vary in size from microscopic to over 100 ft in length.

lamina
Part of the thallus that is shaped like a blade; it is quite wide and looks like a leaf.

hapteron
Small, occasionally branched disk, located at the base of certain thalli; it serves as a holdfast enabling attachment of the alga to a substrate.

red alga
Red-pigmented alga that generally lives in salt water and at greater depths than other algae; there are more than 4,000 species of red algae.

brown alga
Brown-pigmented alga that usually lives in the sea, often in cold water; there are more than 1,500 species of brown algae.

green alga
Alga often found in freshwater, but also in seas and some nonaquatic environments; there are more than 6,000 species of green algae.

fern

Flowerless plant that reproduces by spores; ferns are found especially in the tropics and in rich damp soil in temperate climates.

structure of a fern

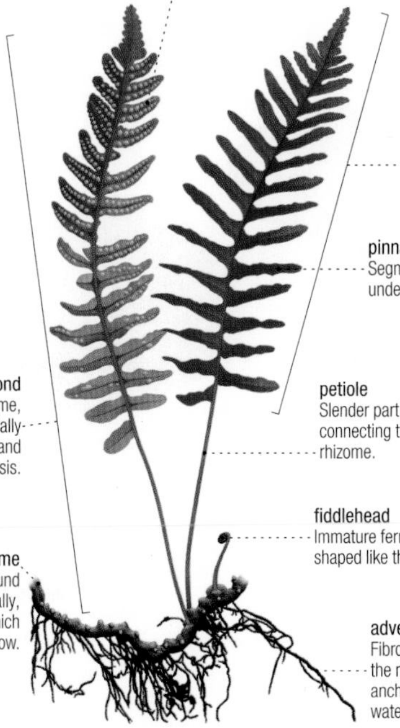

sorus
Cluster of small spore-producing structures covering the underside of a pinna.

blade
Main part of the frond; it is the site of photosynthesis.

pinna
Segment of the frond's blade, the underside of which bears sori.

petiole
Slender part of the frond connecting the blade to the rhizome.

fiddlehead
Immature fern frond; its coiled tip is shaped like the head of a fiddle.

frond
originating at the rhizome, ears sori and is especially dapted to capture light and perform photosynthesis.

rhizome
usually found underground that grows horizontally, ally vertically, out of which fronds and roots grow.

adventitious roots
Fibrous roots that grow out of the rhizome, enabling the fern to anchor itself to the soil and absorb water and mineral salts from it.

examples of ferns
There are more than 10,000 species of fern; they vary in size and grow from either a horizontal or vertical stem.

tree fern
Large fern that resembles a tree and can reach heights of up to 65 ft; it grows mainly in the tropics.

trunk
Main part of the fern, composed of a treelike stem covered with the stubs of old fronds and, often, with aboveground roots.

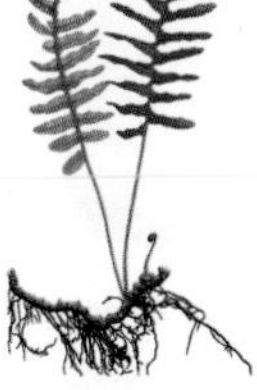

common polypody
Fern with fronds up to a foot long; it is usually found in damp overgrown soil, on rocks or tree trunks.

bird's nest fern
Fern that usually grows on another plant without deriving nourishment from it; its fronds grow in a rosette around a central rhizome, hence its name.

mushroom

Fleshy fungus that exists parasitically or symbiotically with other living things or grows on dead organic matter.

structure of a mushroom
The mushroom is composed of an underground part (mycelium) and an aboveground, often edible part that is also the reproductive organ.

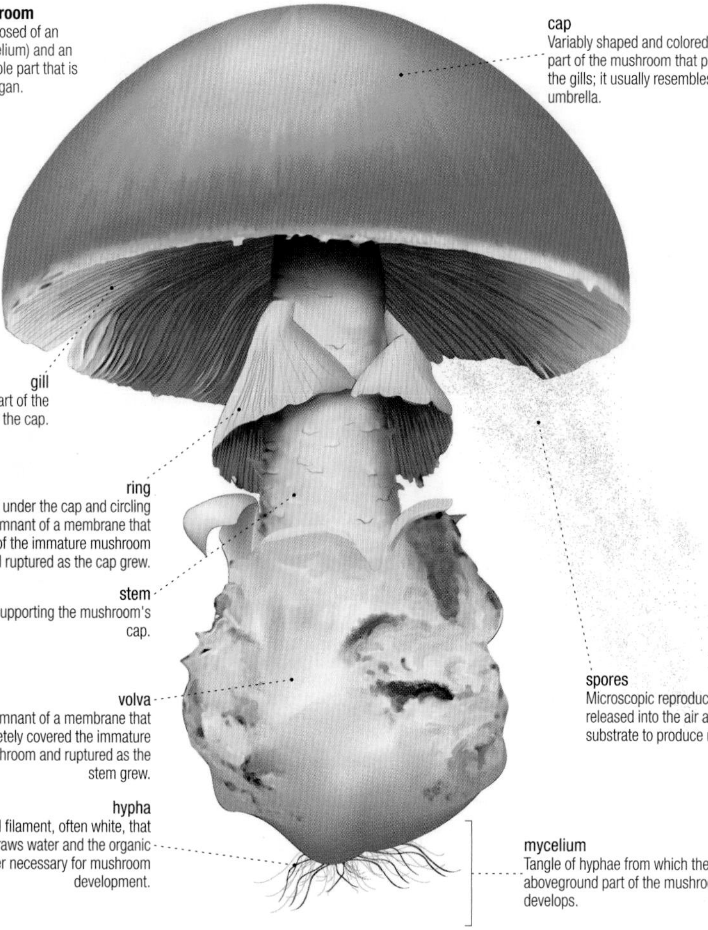

cap
Variably shaped and colored upper part of the mushroom that protects the gills; it usually resembles an umbrella.

gill
Spore-producing part of the mushroom, located under the cap.

ring
Membrane located under the cap and circling the stem; remnant of a membrane that covered the gills of the immature mushroom and ruptured as the cap grew.

stem
Axis supporting the mushroom's cap.

volva
Remnant of a membrane that completely covered the immature mushroom and ruptured as the stem grew.

hypha
Small filament, often white, that draws water and the organic matter necessary for mushroom development.

spores
Microscopic reproductive bodies usually released into the air and falling on a substrate to produce new mushrooms.

mycelium
Tangle of hyphae from which the aboveground part of the mushroom develops.

examples of edible mushrooms
Eaten raw or cooked as a vegetable, there are hundreds of edible mushrooms. About 20 species are cultivated commercially with the rest growing wild.

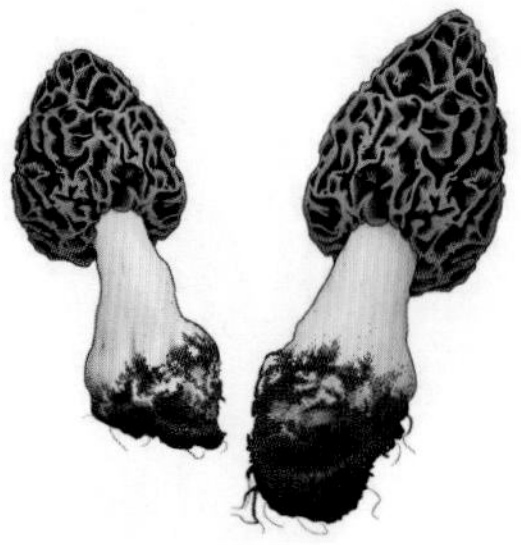

common morel
Edible mushroom having thin and scented flesh.

king boletus
Thick edible mushroom having white, firm flesh; it is also known as porcini or cèpe.

examples of poisonous mushrooms
Mushrooms containing a poison which produces various, generally non-fatal symptoms upon ingestion. There are about 100 species.

examples of deadly poisonous mushrooms
Mushrooms containing a poison which produces harmful and usually fatal effects upon ingestion. There are over 25 species.

Satan's boletus
Poisonous thick-stemmed mushroom; it has an unpleasant odor when mature.

fly agaric
Toxic mushroom with a red or orange cap; it was formerly used as an insecticide.

deadly lepiota
Highly poisonous mushroom having a cap with brown scales; it is found in woods and meadows.

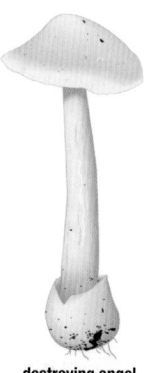

destroying angel
White mushroom of wooded areas with an unpleasant smell; the effects of its often deadly toxin act in a delayed manner, mainly attacking the liver and kidneys.

parts of a plant

Plants have one or more stems ending in roots and bearing leaves, offshoots and reproductive structures.

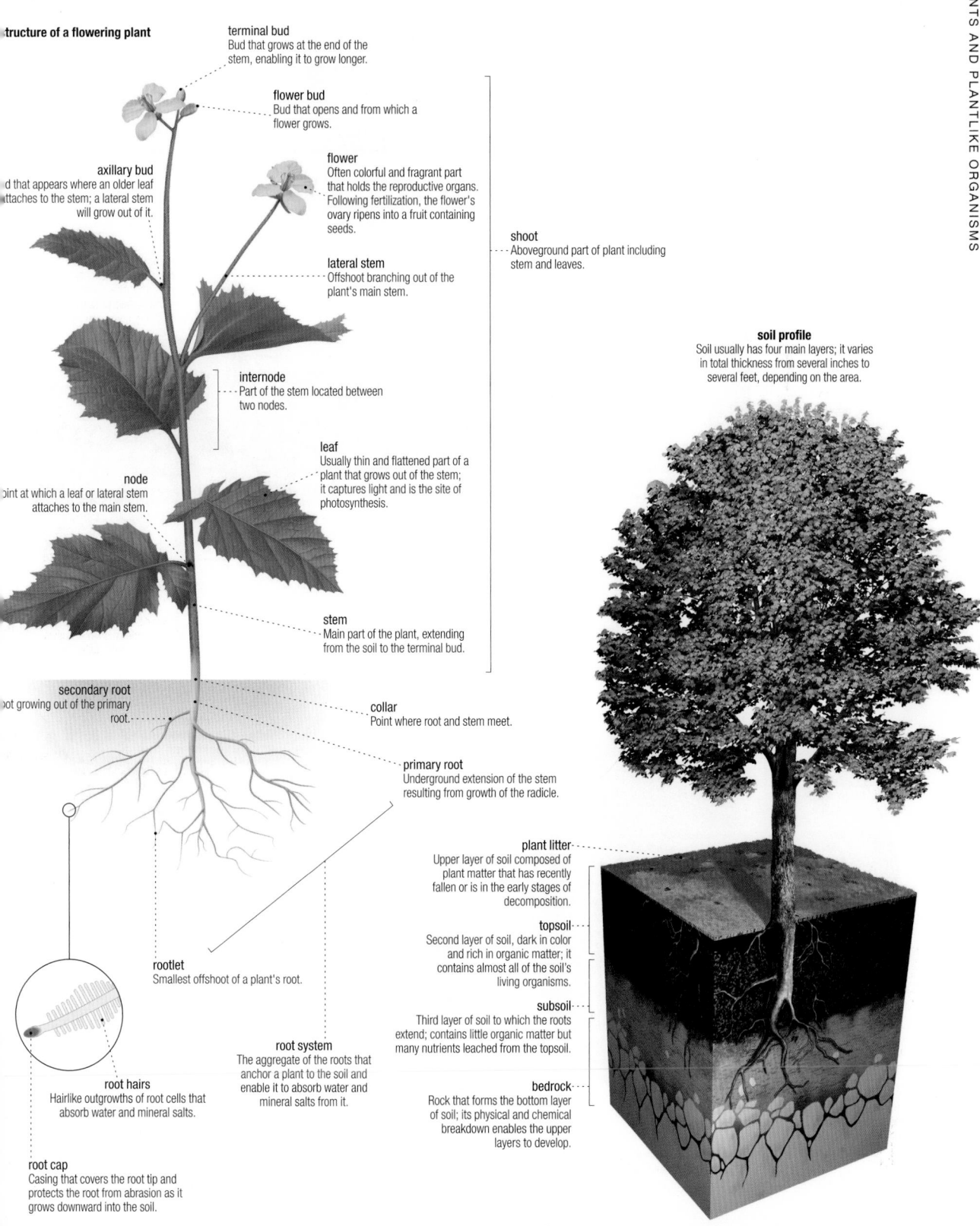

Structure of a flowering plant

terminal bud
Bud that grows at the end of the stem, enabling it to grow longer.

flower bud
Bud that opens and from which a flower grows.

axillary bud
Bud that appears where an older leaf attaches to the stem; a lateral stem will grow out of it.

flower
Often colorful and fragrant part that holds the reproductive organs. Following fertilization, the flower's ovary ripens into a fruit containing seeds.

shoot
Aboveground part of plant including stem and leaves.

lateral stem
Offshoot branching out of the plant's main stem.

internode
Part of the stem located between two nodes.

leaf
Usually thin and flattened part of a plant that grows out of the stem; it captures light and is the site of photosynthesis.

node
Point at which a leaf or lateral stem attaches to the main stem.

stem
Main part of the plant, extending from the soil to the terminal bud.

secondary root
Root growing out of the primary root.

collar
Point where root and stem meet.

primary root
Underground extension of the stem resulting from growth of the radicle.

rootlet
Smallest offshoot of a plant's root.

root hairs
Hairlike outgrowths of root cells that absorb water and mineral salts.

root system
The aggregate of the roots that anchor a plant to the soil and enable it to absorb water and mineral salts from it.

root cap
Casing that covers the root tip and protects the root from abrasion as it grows downward into the soil.

soil profile
Soil usually has four main layers; it varies in total thickness from several inches to several feet, depending on the area.

plant litter
Upper layer of soil composed of plant matter that has recently fallen or is in the early stages of decomposition.

topsoil
Second layer of soil, dark in color and rich in organic matter; it contains almost all of the soil's living organisms.

subsoil
Third layer of soil to which the roots extend; contains little organic matter but many nutrients leached from the topsoil.

bedrock
Rock that forms the bottom layer of soil; its physical and chemical breakdown enables the upper layers to develop.

root

Branched structure, underground or aerial, that anchors the plant and enables it to absorb water and mineral salts.

structure of a root

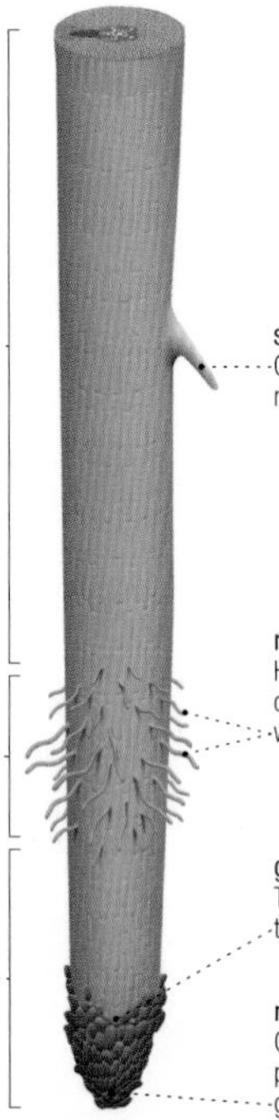

examples of roots

ramification zone
Part of the root that produces secondary roots.

secondary root
Offshoot growing out of the primary root.

claspers
Small aerial roots that enable the stem to attach itself to a support.

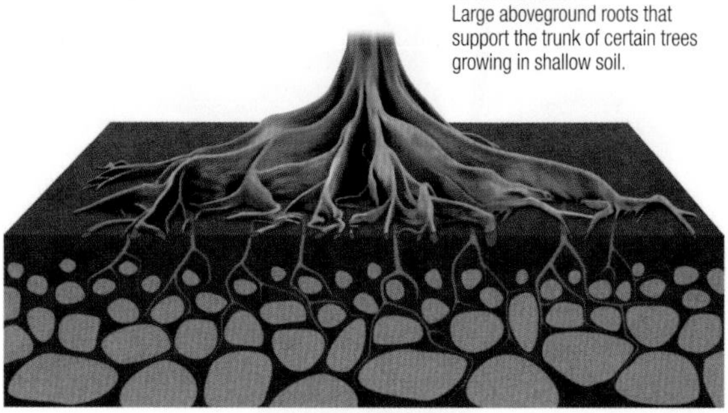

feeder root zone
Part of the root covered with absorbent hairs. It is always the same length, since the upper hairs degenerate as others form near the tip.

root hairs
Hairlike outgrowths from the cells of the roots, serving to replenish water and mineral salts.

buttress roots
Large aboveground roots that support the trunk of certain trees growing in shallow soil.

growth zone
Part of the root where the new cells produced by the growing point extend and differentiate into specialized tissues.

growing point
Tip of the root, composed of cells that are actively dividing.

root cap
Casing that covers the root tip and protects the root from abrasion as it grows downward into the soil.

stem

Main part of the plant, extending from the soil to the terminal bud.

section of a stem

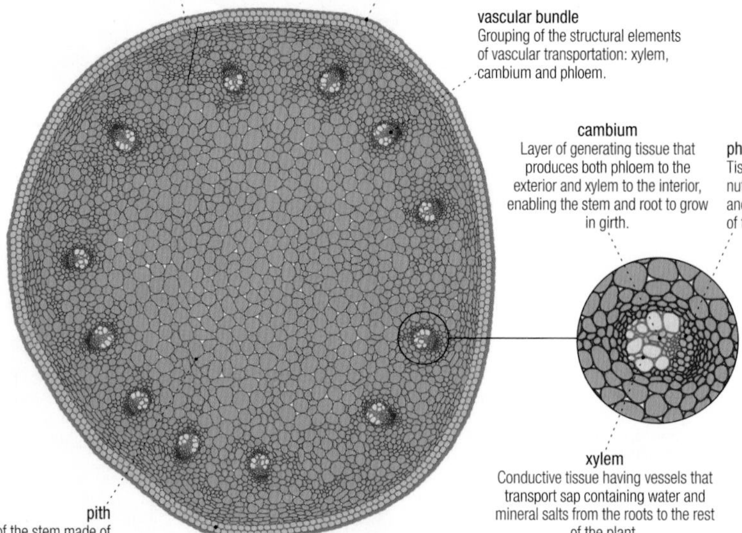

examples of atypical stems

cortex
Living tissue of the outer layer consisting mainly of thin-walled cells containing food reserves.

cuticle
Impermeable layer covering the epidermis and preventing water loss from inner tissue.

vascular bundle
Grouping of the structural elements of vascular transportation: xylem, cambium and phloem.

rhizome
Underground stem, thick and fleshy with stored food reserves.

cambium
Layer of generating tissue that produces both phloem and xylem to the interior, enabling the stem and root to grow in girth.

phloem
Tissue whose vessels carry the nutrients produced by the leaves and contained in the sap to the rest of the plant.

stolon
Thin horizontal stem; it sends out roots at the nodes, enabling a new plant to develop.

pith
Central part of the stem made of tissue rich in nutrient reserves essential to the growth of the young plant.

xylem
Conductive tissue having vessels that transport sap containing water and mineral salts from the roots to the rest of the plant.

epidermis
Outer covering of the stem made up of cells with thickened walls.

leaf

Usually thin and flattened part of a plant that grows out of the stem; it captures light and is the site of photosynthesis.

simple leaves

Leaves with an undivided blade; there are many types, grouped according to shape.

cordate
Simple leaf with a heart-shaped blade.

reniform
Simple leaf with a kidney-shaped blade.

orbiculate
Simple leaf with a somewhat rounded blade.

spatulate
Simple leaf in which the blade widens, taking the shape of a spatula.

linear
Simple leaf with a long and very narrow blade and almost parallel margins.

hastate
Simple leaf with a spear-shaped blade having bottom lobes that are turned outward.

ovate
Simple leaf with an egg-shaped blade.

lanceolate
Simple leaf with a narrow blade that is longer than it is wide, ending in a point.

peltate
Simple leaf with a petiole attached perpendicularly to the center of the blade's underside.

structure of a leaf

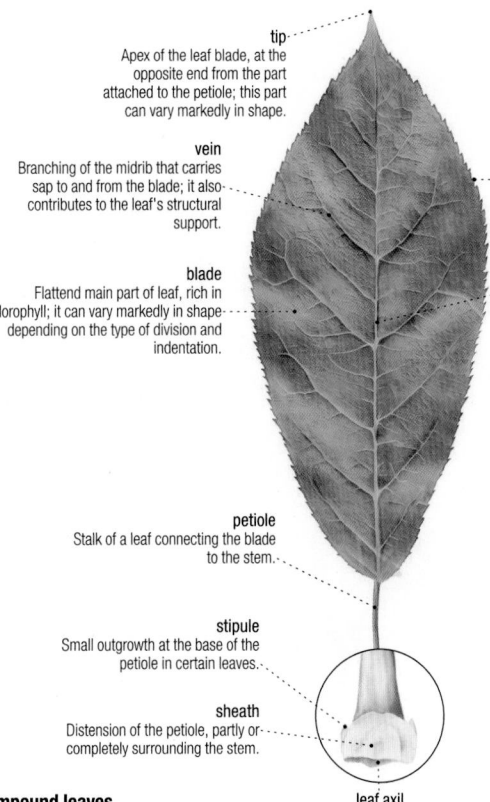

tip
Apex of the leaf blade, at the opposite end from the part attached to the petiole; this part can vary markedly in shape.

vein
Branching of the midrib that carries sap to and from the blade; it also contributes to the leaf's structural support.

blade
Flattend main part of leaf, rich in chlorophyll; it can vary markedly in shape depending on the type of division and indentation.

margin
Part that forms the outline of the leaf blade.

midrib
Hollow projection that extends the petiole into the blade and carries sap; it provides structural support to the leaf.

petiole
Stalk of a leaf connecting the blade to the stem.

stipule
Small outgrowth at the base of the petiole in certain leaves.

sheath
Distension of the petiole, partly or completely surrounding the stem.

leaf axil
Point at which the petiole attaches to the stem node.

compound leaves

Leaves with blades divided into several distinct sections, called leaflets, the arrangement of which determines the leaf type.

trifoliolate
Leaf having three distinct leaflets.

palmate
Compound leaf with all its leaflets attached at the same point, at the apex of the petiole.

pinnatifid
Compound leaf with partly connected leaflets on both sides of a common axis.

abruptly pinnate
Compound leaf with leaflets arranged on opposite sides of a common axis and ending in a pair of terminal leaflets.

odd pinnate
Compound leaf with leaflets arranged on opposite sides of a common axis and ending in a single terminal leaflet.

leaf margins

Parts forming the outline of the leaf blade. They can differ greatly in appearance, according to the shape and depth of the indentations.

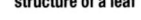

serrate
Leaf edged with pointy teeth of similar size.

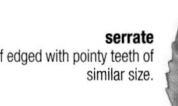

doubly serrate
Leaf edged with teeth of different sizes, the main tooth often having smaller teeth.

crenate
Leaf edge with rounded teeth.

ciliate
Leaf edge surrounded by short thin hairs called cilia.

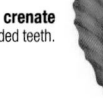

entire
Leaf edge with no indentations.

lobate
Leaf edge indented with deep notches.

flower

Often colorful and fragrant part that holds the reproductive organs. Following fertilization, the flower's ovary ripens into a fruit containing seeds.

structure of a flower

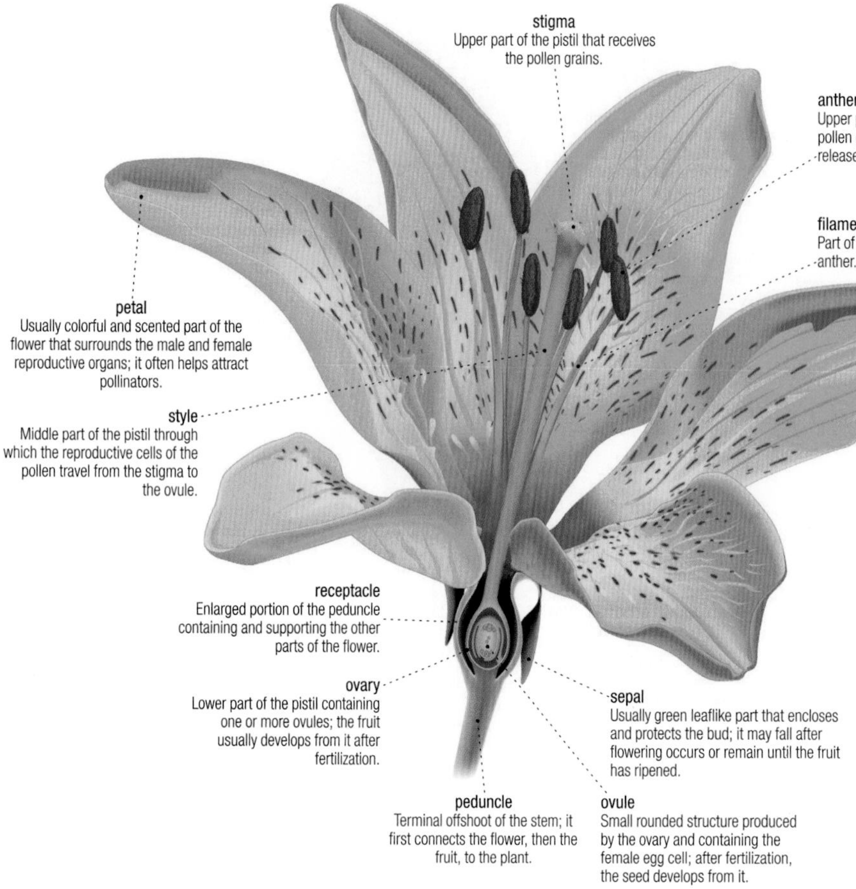

stigma
Upper part of the pistil that receives the pollen grains.

anther
Upper part of the stamen that produces pollen grains; at maturity, it splits to release them.

filament
Part of the stamen that bears the anther.

pistil
Female floral organ at the flower center, consisting of an ovary, style and a stigma.

petal
Usually colorful and scented part of the flower that surrounds the male and female reproductive organs; it often helps attract pollinators.

corolla
Part of the flower composed of its petals.

style
Middle part of the pistil through which the reproductive cells of the pollen travel from the stigma to the ovule.

receptacle
Enlarged portion of the peduncle containing and supporting the other parts of the flower.

ovary
Lower part of the pistil containing one or more ovules; the fruit usually develops from it after fertilization.

sepal
Usually green leaflike part that encloses and protects the bud; it may fall after flowering occurs or remain until the fruit has ripened.

stamen
Male floral organ, consisting of a filament and an anther.

calyx
Part of the flower composed of its sepals.

peduncle
Terminal offshoot of the stem; it first connects the flower, then the fruit, to the plant.

ovule
Small rounded structure produced by the ovary and containing the female egg cell; after fertilization, the seed develops from it.

types of inflorescences
Inflorescence: the arrangement of flowers on the stem of a plant.

raceme
Inflorescence composed of a main axis and laterally borne flowers with short stalks, pedicels, of equal length.

monochasial cyme
Inflorescence whose main axis ends in a flower under which a single lateral branch develops; the process is repeated under each terminal flower.

umbel
Flat- or round-topped inflorescence having flowers with pedicels of equal length, all orginating at the same point.

capitulum
Inflorescence composed of flowers with no pedicel, all borne on the top of a flattened receptacle.

spike
Inflorescence composed of a main axis and laterally borne flowers with no pedicel.

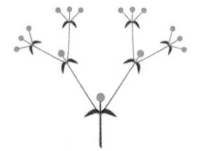

dichasial cyme
Inflorescence whose main axis ends in a flower under which two lateral branches develop; the process is repeated under each terminal flower.

corymb
Flat- or round-topped inflorescence composed of a main axis and laterally borne flowers with pedicels of unequal length, all ending at about the same height.

spadix
Infloresence composed of a main fleshy axis and numerous laterally borne small flowers with no pedicel.

flower

examples of flowers
There are thousands of different flowers prized for their great range of shapes, colors and scents.

tulip
Flower whose petals grow in the shape of a rounded vase; there are approximately 100 differently colored species.

lily of the valley
Small strongly scented bell-shaped white flower that grows in clusters.

carnation
Multi-petaled flower of various colors often used in floral bouquets.

rose
Flower cultivated for its beauty, scent and range of colors; it is used in floral arrangements.

orchid
Flower prized for the variety of its delicate shapes and colors; there are more than 20,000 species.

begonia
Ornamental flower that is native to South America and prized for its vibrant colors.

lily
Large usually strong-scented flower of various colors, prized for its beauty; the white lily is the symbol of French royalty.

violet
Small flower with four petals pointed upwards and one pointing downwards; it is often used for perfume production.

crocus
Small cup-shaped flower that blooms with the first warm rays of spring sunshine.

daffodil
Usually bright yellow trumpet-shaped flower that blooms in the spring.

poppy
Colorful wildflower usually having four to six petals and including some grown ornamentally.

thistle
Wildflower whose receptacle is covered with modified leaves covered with spines.

pansy
Brightly colored garden flower; it is a hybrid of several species of violet.

buttercup
Small bright yellow flower common in meadows and pastures.

daisy
Wildflower with white petals arranged around a yellow head.

primrose
Early blooming flower with numerous cultivars in a multitude of colors.

geranium
Showy usually red, pink or white flower widely cultivated for ornamentation.

dandelion
Common yellow wildflower composed of many small, tightly bunched florets; it is often considered a weed.

sunflower
Tall flower whose seeds provide a high-quality cooking oil. The head usually turns toward the Sun, hence its name.

fruit

Structure of flowering plants resulting from the development of one or several ovaries that, once mature, contains seeds; it is often edible.

fleshy berry fruit

Fruit in which the seed is surrounded by two visible layers: an outer exocarp and an inner fleshy layer of mesocarp and endocarp in direct contact with one or more seeds.

section of a grape

technical terms

pedicel
Part of the fruit that once connected it to the cluster's peduncle.

exocarp
Fruit's outer layer, covering the mesocarp.

funiculus
Slender strand that connects the seed to the ovary wall; it is used to transport food to the developing seed.

seed
Structure formed by the development of a fertilized ovule; it contains an embryo and nutrient reserves that enable a new plant to grow.

mesocarp
Plump part of the fruit, usually sweet and juicy. The inner endocarp does not form a layer distinguishable from the mesocarp.

style
Visible remnant of the flower's style, now withered, that once connected the stigma to the ovary.

usual terms

stalk
Part of the fruit that once connected it to the cluster's peduncle.

skin
Fruit's outer layer, covering the flesh.

seed/pip
Structure formed by the development of a fertilized ovule; it contains an embryo and nutrient reserves that enable a new plant to grow.

flesh
Plump part of the fruit, usually sweet and juicy.

section of a raspberry

The raspberry is an aggregate fruit; it consists of a number of small fleshy fruits attached to a common receptacle.

peduncle
Terminal offshoot of the stem; it attaches the flower, then the fruit, to the plant.

receptacle
Enlarged portion of the peduncle; it holds the raspberry's drupelets.

sepal
Leaflike part enclosing the fl bud; it remains until the frui ripens.

seed
Structure formed by the dev of a fertilized ovule; it conta embryo and nutrient reserve enable a new plant to grow.

drupelet
Small fleshy fruit attached to t receptacle; each one contains and develops from a separate within a single flower.

section of a strawberry

The strawberry is a complex fruit, with achenes borne by the fleshy receptacle of the flower.

peduncle
Terminal offshoot of the stem; it attaches the flower, then the fruit, to the plant.

epicalyx
All the small green leaves under the calyx.

receptacle
Enlarged portion of the flower's peduncle; in the strawberry, it becomes fleshy and bears the achenes.

calyx
All the flower's sepals, wi remain until the strawber

achene
Small dry fruit embedded receptacle's surface; eacl contains a seed.

flesh
Pulpy portion of the straw formed as the flower's re develops.

fleshy citrus fruit

Atypical berry with a segmented endocarp.

section of an orange

technical terms

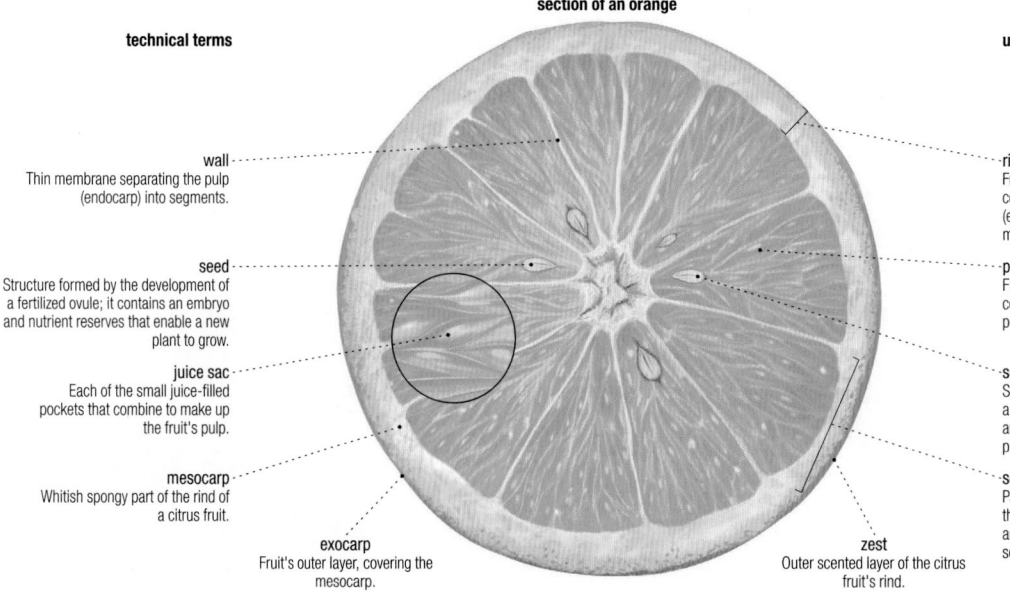

usual terms

wall
Thin membrane separating the pulp (endocarp) into segments.

seed
Structure formed by the development of a fertilized ovule; it contains an embryo and nutrient reserves that enable a new plant to grow.

juice sac
Each of the small juice-filled pockets that combine to make up the fruit's pulp.

mesocarp
Whitish spongy part of the rind of a citrus fruit.

exocarp
Fruit's outer layer, covering the mesocarp.

rind
Fruit's outer layer covering the pulp, composed of an outer colored part (exocarp) and an inner part (mesocarp) made of whitish tissue.

pulp
Fleshy portion of the citrus fruit, composed of small juice-filled pockets in every segment.

seed/pip
Structure formed by the development of a fertilized ovule; it contains an embryo and nutrient reserves that enable a new plant to grow.

segment
Part of a citrus fruit surrounded by a thin membrane containing the pulp and seeds; each segment derives from separate ovaries within a single flower.

zest
Outer scented layer of the citrus fruit's rind.

fleshy pome fruit

Fruit with a seed, or pip, surrounded by three distinct layers: an exocarp, a fleshy mesocarp and a stiff endocarp containing loculi.

section of an apple

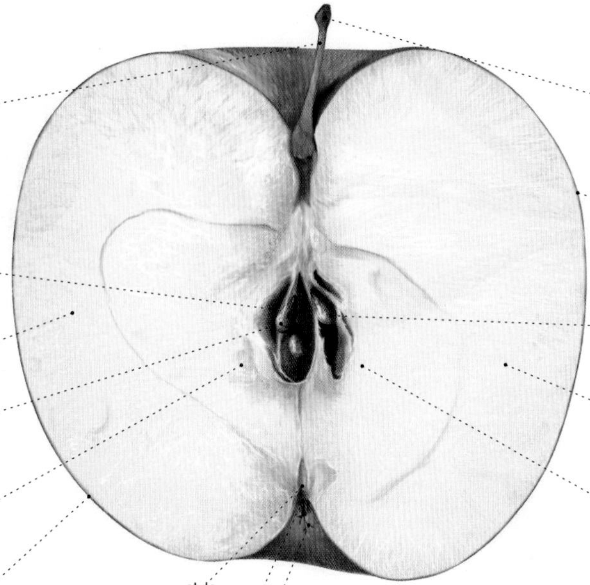

technical terms

peduncle
Terminal offshoot of the stem which attaches the flower, then the fruit, to the plant.

locule
Small cavity located under the endocarp, usually containing two seeds.

mesocarp
Spongy part of the fruit, usually sweet and juicy.

seed
Structure formed by the development of a fertilized ovule; it contains an embryo and nutrient reserves that enable a new plant to grow.

endocarp
The stiff inner layer of the fruit, surrounding and protecting the seed and covering the loculi.

exocarp
Fruit's outer layer, covering the mesocarp.

style
Visible remnant of the flower's style, now withered, that once connected the stigma to the ovary.

stamen
Remnant of the flower's stamens, visible as small hairs in the center of the depression on the bottom of the fruit.

sepal
Usually green, leaflike part that encloses and protects the flower bud; it may fall after flowering or persist until the fruit reaches ripeness.

usual terms

stalk
Part of the fruit that once attached it to the terminal offshoot of the stem.

skin
Fruit's outer layer, covering the flesh.

seed/pip
Structure formed by the development of a fertilized ovule; it contains an embryo and nutrient reserves that enable a new plant to grow.

flesh
Plump part of the fruit, usually sweet and juicy.

core
Central inedible part of the apple, comprising the endocarp, the loculi and the seeds within the loculi.

fleshy stone fruit

Fruit whose seed is surrounded by three distinct layers: an exocarp, a fleshy mesocarp and a hard stone, or endocarp.

section of a peach

technical terms

peduncle
Terminal offshoot of the stem which attaches the flower, then the fruit, to the plant.

exocarp
Fruit's outer layer, covering the mesocarp.

mesocarp
Spongy part of the fruit, usually sweet and juicy.

seed coat
Protective casing covering the embryo and the nutrients stored in the seed.

seed
Structure formed by the development of a fertilized ovule; it contains an embryo and nutrient reserves that enable a new plant to grow.

endocarp
Fruit's interior layer that surrounds and protects the seed; it is rough and extremely hard.

style
Visible remnant of the flower's style, now withered, that once connected the stigma to the ovary.

usual terms

stalk
Part of the fruit that once attached it to the terminal offshoot of the twig or branch.

skin
Fruit's outer layer, covering the flesh.

flesh
Plump part of the fruit, usually sweet and juicy.

seed/kernel
Structure formed by the development of a fertilized ovule; it contains an embryo and nutrient reserves that enable a new plant to grow.

stone/pit
Fruit's interior layer that surrounds and protects the seed; it is rough and extremely hard.

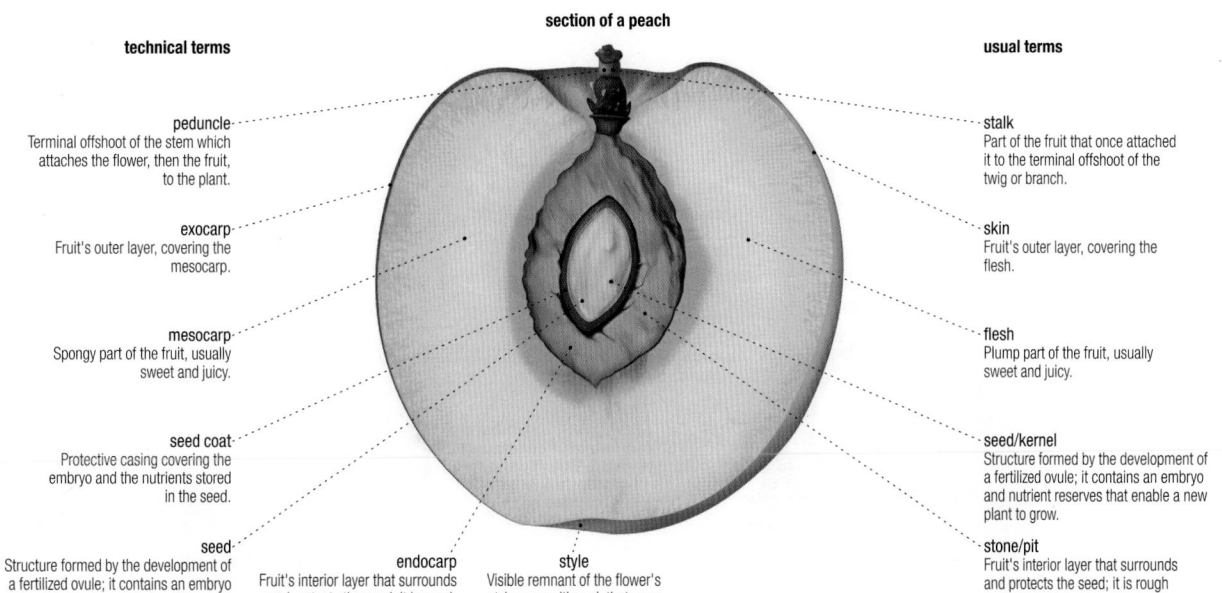

fruit

examples of dry fruits

Dry fruit: fruit whose seed, normally edible, is surrounded by one dry, more or less rigid layer.

section of a silique (mustard)

Silique: dry fruit with two valves that, when the fruit is ripe, split to release seeds.

valve
The two parts of the fruit's casing that, when it is ripe, separate to release the seeds.

seed
Structure formed by the development of a fertilized ovule; it contains an embryo and nutrient reserves that enable a new plant to grow.

septum
Thin partition, bearing seeds on each side that drop when the valves open.

style
Beak-shaped remnant of the flower's style; it once connected the stigma to the ovary.

section of a capsule (poppy)

Capsule: dry usually many-chambered fruit that opens laterally or at the apex when ripe; it contains a great many seeds.

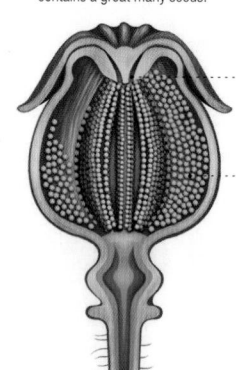

pore
Small opening through which see are released when mature.

seed
Structure formed by the develop of a fertilized ovule; it contains a embryo and nutrient reserves th. enable a new plant to grow.

section of a legume (pea)

Legume: dry single-chambered fruit that splits in two places when ripe: along the suture and along the midrib of its casing.

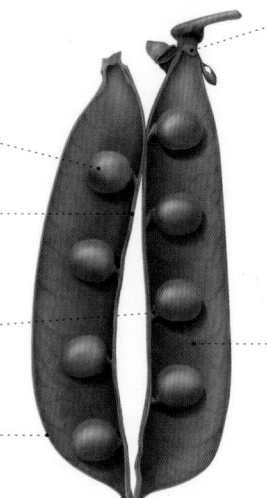

calyx
Whorl of the flower's sepals, which remain until the pod ripens.

pea
Round green seed of varying size; it is edible.

midrib
Hollow ridge that is an extension of the petiole; when ripe, the fruit splits along it to release its seeds.

funiculus
Slender strand that transports food to the developing seed.

suture
Visible seam on the surface of the fruit's casing, along which the fruit splits to release its seeds.

pod/hull
Ripened ovary wall (pericarp), which bears the seeds; when the fruit is ripe, it splits in two distinct places to release the seeds.

style
Visible remnant of the flower's style, now withered, that once connected the stigma to the ovary.

section of a follicle (star anise)

Follicle: dry single-chambered fruit that, when ripe, splits along the suture of its casing.

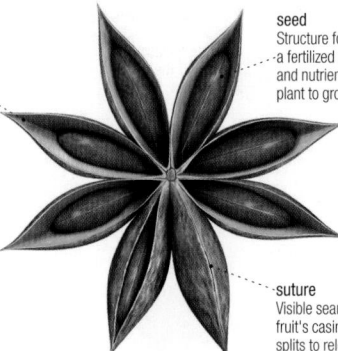

seed
Structure formed by the developme a fertilized ovule; it contains an emb and nutrient reserves that enable a plant to grow.

follicle
Each of the eight dry fruits that make up the star anise.

suture
Visible seam on the surface of the fruit's casing, along which the fruit splits to release its seeds.

section of a nut (hazelnut)

Hazelnut: fruit of the hazelnut tree; dry hard-shelled fruit usually enclosed in a dry or membranous covering and containing a single seed.

cupule
Thin scaly or prickly casing made of fused bracts; it partially or completely covers the hazelnut.

bract
Little leaf, smaller than the plant's other leaves, attached to the peduncle of the flower or fruit.

seed
Structure formed by the development of a fertilized ovule; it contains an embryo and nutrient reserves that enable a new plant to grow.

shell
Ripened woody ovary wall (pericarp); it does not split apart to release the seed.

stigma
Visible remnant of the flower's stigma, now withered, forming a point at the fruit's base.

section of a nut (walnut)

Walnut: fruit of the walnut tree, which has an edible seed; its shell is surrounded by a fleshy husk.

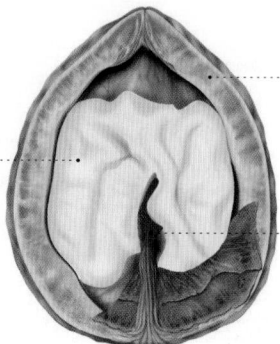

shell
Ripened woody ovary wall (pericarp); it does not split apa release the seed.

seed/kernel
Structure formed by the development of a fertilized ovule; it contains an embryo and nutrient reserves that enable a new plant to grow.

partition
Membranous layer that se the seed's two cotyledons

grape

Woody vine cultivated for its sweet fruit used in wine making or for the table.

bunch of grapes
A main axis bearing grapes that develop from a flower cluster on a fruiting shoot.

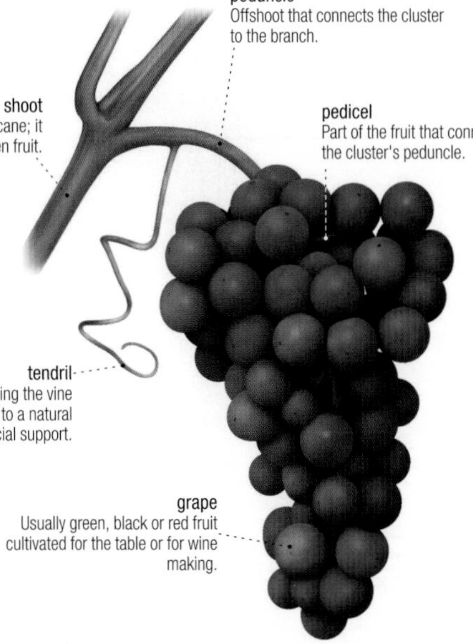

peduncle
Offshoot that connects the cluster to the branch.

fruiting shoot
Secondary offshoot of a cane; it first bears flowers, then fruit.

grape vine
Shoots of one grape variety are often grafted onto a disease- and pest-resistant rootsock of another variety.

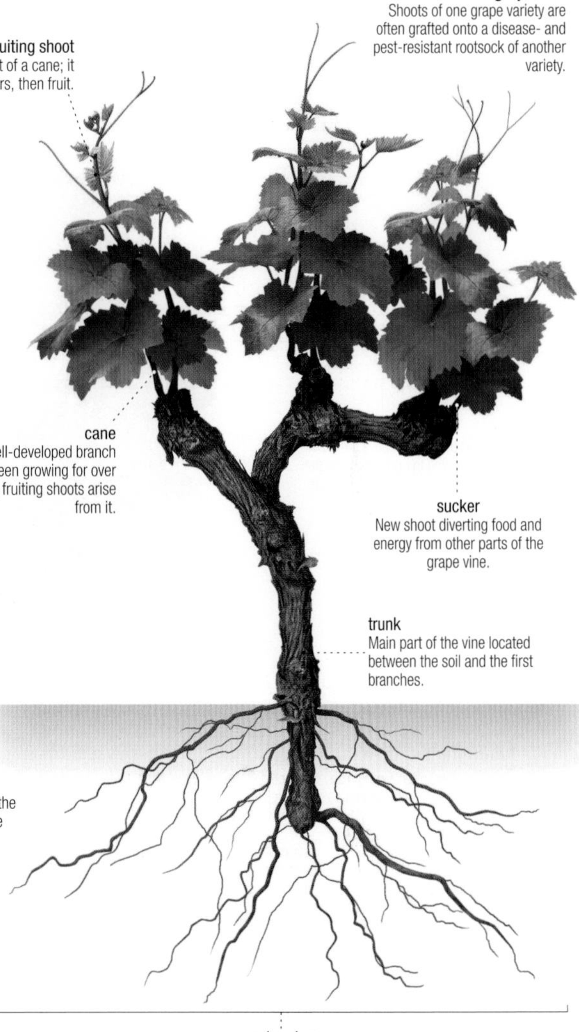

fruiting shoot
Secondary offshoot of a cane; it first bears flowers, then fruit.

pedicel
Part of the fruit that connects it to the cluster's peduncle.

tendril
Spiral strand enabling the vine branch to attach itself to a natural or artificial support.

cane
Young well-developed branch that has been growing for over one season; fruiting shoots arise from it.

sucker
New shoot diverting food and energy from other parts of the grape vine.

grape
Usually green, black or red fruit cultivated for the table or for wine making.

trunk
Main part of the vine located between the soil and the first branches.

grape leaf
Thin and flattened outgrowth of the grapevine stem; it captures light and is the site of photosynthesis.

terminal lobe
Somewhat rounded section of the blade comprising the apex of the leaf.

upper lateral sinus
Indentation of the leaf's main part, separating the terminal lobe from the upper lateral lobe.

upper lateral lobe
Somewhat rounded section of the blade located on the side of the leaf, in its upper quadrant.

petiolar sinus
Indentation of the leaf's main part, where it attaches to the petiole.

lower lateral sinus
Indentation of the leaf's main part, separating the upper lateral lobe from the lower lateral lobe.

lower lateral lobe
Somewhat rounded section of the blade located on the side of the leaf, in its lower quadrant.

root system
The aggregate of the roots that anchor a plant to the soil and enable it to absorb water and mineral salts from it.

fruit development and maturation
All the stages that occur from the initial appearance of flowers to harvesting of ripened grapes.

flowering
Flowers appear on fruiting shoots that arise from buds developed during the previous growing season.

fruit set
Small hard green berries (immature grapes) are formed following pollination and fertilization.

ripening
Final stage in growth when the grape changes color, softens and increases in size.

ripeness
Complete maturation of the grape when it is at optimum flavor, aroma, sugar content and acidity.

tree

Tall plant usually with a single woody main stem (trunk) with many branches and extensive root system; it produces oxygen and provides wood.

structure of a tree
The tree is composed of an underground part, the roots, and two aboveground parts, the trunk and the crown.

foliage
The aggregate of the leaves on a tree; the leaves capture light and are the site of photosynthesis.

branches
The aggregate of larger and smaller woody offshoots that provide support for the tree's leaves, flowers and fruit.

top
Apex of the tree's crown.

branch
Offshoot of one of the tree's limbs.

twig
The most slender offshoot of a tree branch.

crown
Part of the tree above the trunk, including the branches and the foliage.

limb
Offshoot growing directly out of a tree trunk, subsequently dividing into branches and twigs.

bole
Lower portion of the trunk; it has no offshoots and is usually of a wide girth suitable for lumber.

trunk
Main woody stem of the tree extending between the soil and the smaller branches.

shallow root
Root, often having many offshoots, growing somewhat horizontally into the rich moist topsoil.

taproot
First root growing out of the seed that grows vertically into the soil; it usually has few offshoots, its main function being to anchor the tree in the ground.

rootlet
Smallest offshoot of a plant's root.

root-hair zone
Part of the rootlet covered in slender absorbent hairs that ensure the tree is supplied with mineral salts and water.

cross section of a trunk
Moving from the center to the periphery there are six parts: the pith, the heartwood, the sapwood, the cambium, the phloem and the bark.

wood ray
Conduit connecting the cambium to the core and circulating nutrients and water horizontally within the trunk.

annual ring
Each of the concentric circles representing the layer of wood produced in one year; the age of the tree can be determined by the number of rings.

cambium
Growth tissue that simultaneously produces the external phloem and the internal sapwood, thereby enabling the tree to increase in diameter.

phloem
Tissue located immediately below the bark, whose main function is to transport nutrient-containing sap from the leaves throughout the rest of the tree.

sapwood
Relatively young outer layer of wood; it is composed of tissue (xylem) that conducts water and dissolved minerals in sap from the roots to the rest of the tree.

pith
Central part of the trunk, composed of soft tissue that contains nutrients essential for sapling growth.

heartwood
Hard dark-colored wood layer made of dead sapwood; it encircles the pith and supports the trunk and branches.

bark
Tree's external protective layer; its texture, color and thickness vary depending on the species.

stump
Lower part of the trunk that remains in place, with its roots when the tree is cut down.

shoot
New growth that sprouts out of the tree stump.

PLANTS AND PLANTLIKE ORGANISMS

examples of broadleaved trees
Broadleaved trees have mainly large flat leaves; in temperate zones, these usually fall as winter approaches.

oak
Large tree with deeply indented leaves, bearing acorns as fruit; it is prized for its hard and extremely resistant wood.

birch
Tree with smooth light-colored bark interspersed with dark markings; the outer layer of the bark usually peels readily off the trunk.

weeping willow
Tree with long flexible hanging branches; it is often used for ornamental purposes and generally grows near water.

poplar
Tall slender fast-growing tree; its soft wood is used to produce inexpensive lumber as well as pulp for papermaking.

palm tree
Tree native to tropical regions; among its various species are date- and coconut-bearing kinds.

maple
Tree producing the samara, a small dry winged fruit; its wood is prized by cabinetmakers. The sap of the sugar maple is used to make a sweet syrup.

beech
Smooth-barked tree, widely cultivated as a shade tree; its wood is used especially in woodworking and for heating.

walnut
Large tree that produces an edible fruit, the walnut; its hard compact wood is prized especially by carpenters for its use in making furniture.

tree

examples of broadleaved trees

ash
Tree with large leaves made up of many leaflets; its strong lightweight wood is used to make baseball bats.

linden
Tree with heart-shaped leaves and yellow scented flowers; it is commonly planted for shade or ornament.

elm
Large ornamental tree su to a destructive fungal in disease-resistant cultiva being developed.

olive
Tree found in Mediterranean climates, cultivated for its fruit, the olive, which contains an edible oil.

baobab
Large softwood tree of tropica regions; it is able to store larg quantities of water in the broa trunk to survive the dry seasor

conifer

Tree that usually retains its needle- or scalelike leaves all winter long; it bears cones, hence its name, and produces a sticky sap known as resin.

reproductive structures
Male or female plant parts involved in producing new plants of the same species.

seed
Structure formed by the development of a fertilized ovule; it contains an embryo and nutrient reserves that enable a new plant to grow.

cone
Reproductive structure consisting of scales arranged in a conical shape; seeds develop in ovules borne by the scales of female cones.

branch
Woody offshoot of a tree along which cones develop.

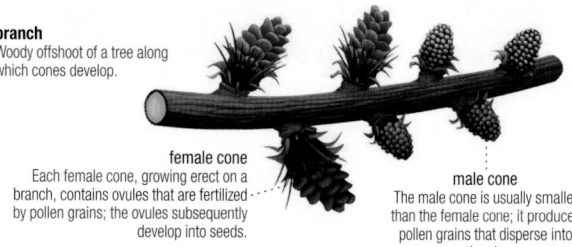

female cone
Each female cone, growing erect on a branch, contains ovules that are fertilized by pollen grains; the ovules subsequently develop into seeds.

male cone
The male cone is usually smaller than the female cone; it produces pollen grains that disperse into the air.

examples of leaves
Conifer leaves consist of scales or needles, varying in length and width.

pine needles
Pine leaves consist of long slender pointed needles; they mostly grow in groups of two, three or five out of the branch.

spruce needles
The leaves of the spruce consist of rigid needles th pointed and flat or 4-sided.

fir needles
Fir leaves consist of short stiff flattened needles; each needle grows directly out of the branch.

cypress leaves
The cypress has scales or small stiff leaves that grow directly out of small terminal branches.

conifer

examples of conifers

There are more than 550 conifer species; because they are well adapted to harsh climates, they often form the tree line on mountains and in subpolar regions.

umbrella pine
Conifer native to the Mediterranean area whose branches form a flattened crown, hence its name; it produces an edible seed, the pine nut.

cedar of Lebanon
Conifer of Middle Eastern origin with a large, flattened top; now rare, former civilizations made abundant use of its wood.

cypress
Conifer of temperate climates, with overlapping scalelike leaves; it is often cultivated for ornamental purposes.

giant sequoia
Massive conifer of the western United States; it has reddish wood and sometimes exceeds 270 ft in height.

spruce
Conifer with small flattened or 4-sided needles encircling the branch; it has reddish-brown bark and some species can grow to 200 ft.

larch
One of the few conifers that sheds its needles in the fall; it has aromatic rot-resistant wood used in construction and carpentry.

balsam fir
Aromatic conifer with flat needles arranged on each side of the branch; it has grayish bark, flecked with resin, and is commonly used as a Christmas tree.

eastern white pine
Conifer with needles growing in groups of five; its soft wood is used in woodworking and cabinetmaking.

PLANTS AND PLANTLIKE ORGANISMS

grain industry

All activities involved in the production and processing of cereal grain, primarily for human and animal consumption.

grain plants

Plants producing small dry one-seeded fruits (grains) and often subject to large-scale cultivation. Grains have for centuries been a staple in the diet of humans.

buckwheat
Cereal cultivated for its grain, mainly ground into flour; it is also used to feed livestock and poultry.

buckwheat: raceme
The raceme is composed of a main axis and grains that have a pedicel, clustered at the stem's apex.

wheat
Cereal widely cultivated for its grain, mainly ground into flour to produce bread, baked goods and pasta.

wheat: spike
The spike is composed of a main axis bearing grains without a pedicel; the grains are clustered at the stem's apex.

section of a grain of wheat

A grain of wheat is a small dry fruit whose single seed is fused to its casing; the varieties differ in size, shape and color.

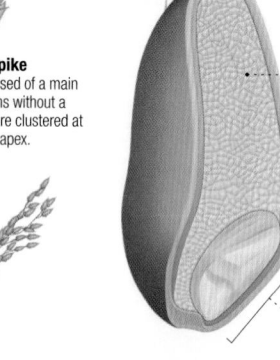
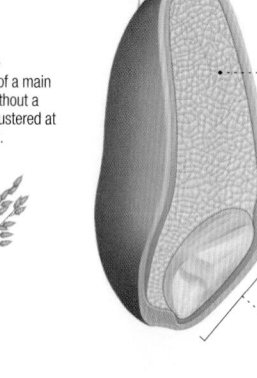

brush
Remnant of the flower's stigma; they resemble a tuft of hair at the grain.

starch
Part of the grain where the nutrients required for germ growth are stored; the starch can be ground into flour.

seed coat
Protective many-layered casing covering the starch and the germ; once separated from the grain, it is known as bran.

germ
The plant's embryo, located in the lower part of the grain; at germination, it develops into a new plant.

barley
Cereal cultivated for its grain; it is used mainly as livestock feed and to produce malt for brewing beer.

barley: spike
The spike is composed of a main axis bearing grains without a pedicel; the grains are clustered at the stem's apex.

rice
Cereal whose grain is a major food staple in many parts of the world; rice is generally grown in flooded fields.

rice: panicle
The panicle is composed of a main axis with offshoots, each stem bearing grains that have a pedicel.

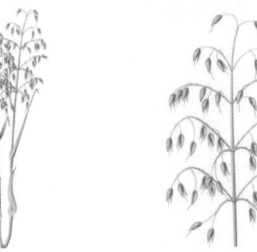

oats
Cereal cultivated for its grain; although it is mainly used to feed livestock, humans also eat it, mostly in the form of flakes (rolled oats).

oats: panicle
The panicle is composed of main axis with offshoots, each bearing grains that have a pedicel.

grain sorghum
Cereal cultivated for its grain used mainly as livestock feed, to make unleavened bread and to produce malt for brewing certain kinds of beer.

sorghum: panicle
The panicle is composed of a main axis with offshoots; at its apex, each stem bears a cluster of grains that have a pedicel.

rye
Cereal cultivated as forage or for its grain; the grain is used as livestock feed and to produce flour mixed with wheat flour to make bread.

rye: spike
The spike is composed of a main axis bearing grains without a pedicel; the grains are clustered at the stem's apex.

silk
Tuft of long silky filaments; they are remnants of the flower's stigmas and styles once connected to the ovaries.

cob
The cob is composed of a wide main axis with rows of tightly packed kernels; each cob grows in the axil of a leaf along the stem.

husk
Cob casing that protects the kernels and keeps them moist.

kernel
Each of the small dry fruits whose single seed is fused to its casing; a cob of corn holds several hundred kernels.

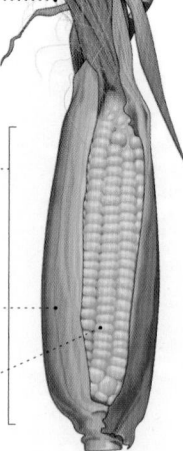

corn: ear
Fruiting structure on which hard grains (kernels) develop in rows around an axis and are protected by a husk.

millet
Cereal cultivated as forage or for its grain; the grain is used mainly to make unleavened bread and to feed domesticated birds.

millet: spikelike panicle
The spikelike panicle is composed of a main axis with offshoots bearing grains with a very short pedicel.

corn
Also known as maize, cereal cultivated for its starchy grains used whole or ground; it is also used to produce a sweet syrup and a cooking oil.

grain industry

examples of products
Cereal grains are consumed as is or in a multitude of processed forms.

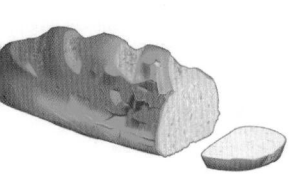

bread
Food made from flour and water; it often contains a leavening agent (yeast, baking soda) that makes it rise.

pasta
Made from hard wheat semolina and water, shaped into various forms and typically dried.

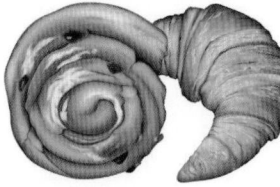

pastries
Sweet baked goods made with a leavened dough containing fat and usually eggs.

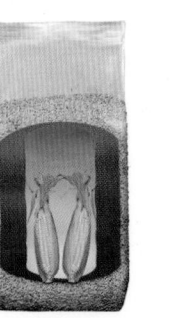

cornmeal
coarsely ground kernels of corn breads, hot cereal, polenta and tortillas.

breakfast cereal
Breakfast food made from cereal grains, water and often salt and sweeteners; it is flaked, puffed, shaped or shredded.

flour
Finely milled cereal grain, especially wheat; it is used mainly in making bread, pasta and baked goods.

couscous
Made from hard wheat semolina and water that is formed into grains and steamed; it is used similarly to rice.

vegetable oil
Fatty substance produced by pressing seeds (peanuts, soy beans, corn) or fruits (olive) and used in cooking, seasoning and preserving foods.

textile industry

All activities involving the extraction and processing of plant fibers to manufacture various goods.

fiber plants
Plants producing long fibers suitable for spinning and weaving.

examples of products
Textile fibers are used to produce various consumer products, including clothing, cordage and netting.

clothing
Object that covers the body to protect, conceal or adorn it.

flax
Plant whose seeds are used to make oil and as a nutritional supplement. The fibers of its stem are mainly used to make fabric.

hemp
Plant cultivated for its strong flexible fibers, used mostly to make rope, twine and heavy canvas.

rope
Large strong cord made of twisted strands of fiber.

cotton plant
Small tropical shrub whose fruit consists of a capsule containing seeds surrounded by fibrous hairs that are used to make fabric, stuffing and absorbent material.

cotton swab
Stick having ends covered with cotton wadding; it is typically used to clean and disinfect wounds.

rubber industry

All activities using latex to manufacture rubber objects.

natural rubber source
Latex, a milky white sap, is produced by a tropical tree known as the rubber tree.

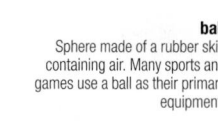

ball
Sphere made of a rubber skin containing air. Many sports and games use a ball as their primary equipment.

examples of products
Rubber is used in manufacturing to make many products, including tires, gloves, boots and balloons.

tire
Circular deformable unit made of rubber, mounted on the wheel of a vehicle and inflated with air.

rubber tree
Tropical tree from which latex, produced by specialized vessels in the bark, is harvested to make rubber.

latex harvest
Latex flows from an incision made in the bark of the rubber tree; it flows for several hours until it coagulates and seals the incision.

boot
High waterproof shoe made of rubber.

paper industry

All activities using wood to manufacture paper, newsprint, and cardboard.

pulp fiber sources
The fibers used to make paper pulp come primarily from the wood of trees, but also from recycled paper and rags.

stationery
Medium quality writing paper for everyday use.

examples of products
Paper pulp can be turned into different types of paper and cardboard.

black spruce
Tall conifer of North America having soft wood with long fibers commonly used to make paper pulp.

newsprint
Thin porous paper used to print newspapers; it is usually off-white and tends to yellow over time.

rags
Scraps of cloth (cotton, linen) used for their fibers in the making of high quality paper.

corrugated cardboard
Stiff durable paper consisting of an inner crimped layer glued between two flat outer layers; it is used mostly in cartons.

paper industry

papermaking
Paper is made from plant fibers, primarily from wood, which are first made into pulp, then into various paper products.

sawmill
Specialized site for mechanically transforming logs of wood into products usable in manufacturing.

wood chips
Small bits of wood made directly from harvested trees or generated as sawmill byproducts; they are used to make pulp.

pulp mill
Site whose primary function is to turn wood chips into a fibrous pulp used as raw material in making paper.

bleaching
Chemical procedure used to dissolve or eliminate more lignin in order to increase the whiteness of the pulp.

deinking
Process that consists of eliminating inks or finishes from old paper to produce recycled pulp.

debarking
Procedure that consists of removing the bark from the trunk using a machine called a debarker.

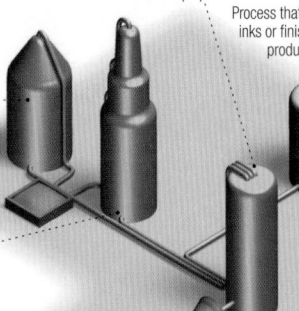

mechanical pulping
Physical breakdown of wood chips into fibers or bundles of fibers, usually by grinding. The pulp is often used for newsprint.

chemical pulping
Cooking of wood chips in a chemical solution to dissolve the lignin. The pulp is used for high quality white paper and packaging.

log
Trunk of a felled tree, still covered in bark but stripped of its branches.

refiner
Machine for mechanically treating pulp in order to increase fiber flexibility and strength.

recycled papers
Paper already used by the consumer that has been collected to be reused to make newsprint and lower quality papers.

mixing
Action of adding various products to the pulp (colorants, for example) depending on the type of paper wanted.

dehydration
Procedure consisting of withdrawing most of the water from the pulp in order to make easily transportable blocks.

paper mill
Site primarily used to manufacture paper.

headbox
First part of the paper machine. The paper pulp, which is 99% water, is sprayed onto a porous metallic sheet, allowing it to drain.

dilution
Adding of water to the block dehydrated pulp to obtain a homogeneous slurry.

forming pulp sheet
Porous rotating screen that dewaters the pulp.

cutting
Division of the paper web into smaller rolls, then into sheets of different formats.

web
Roll of paper.

paper machine
Machine designed to make a sheet of paper from a fibrous suspension by dewatering, pressing, and drying.

pressing
Step of thinning and drying the pulp by pressing it between two cylinders covered with absorbent felt, after which the pulp is 60% water.

coating
Step in which the paper is coated with a pigmented solution that improves its printing qualities.

ream
Block of 500 sheets of the same format, ready to be shipped.

drying
Step in which the pulp is dried between hollow heated cylinders and emerges in a thin sheet that is only 5% water.

calendering
Step in which the paper is smoothed by heavy rollers ensuring a uniform thickness.

ANIMALS

Grouping of all living things with more or less complex organs with which they move about and feed on plants and other animals.

ANIMALS

origin and evolution of species

Since its formation some 4.6 billion years ago, the Earth has witnessed the genesis of continents and oceans and the appearance of animals and vegetation.

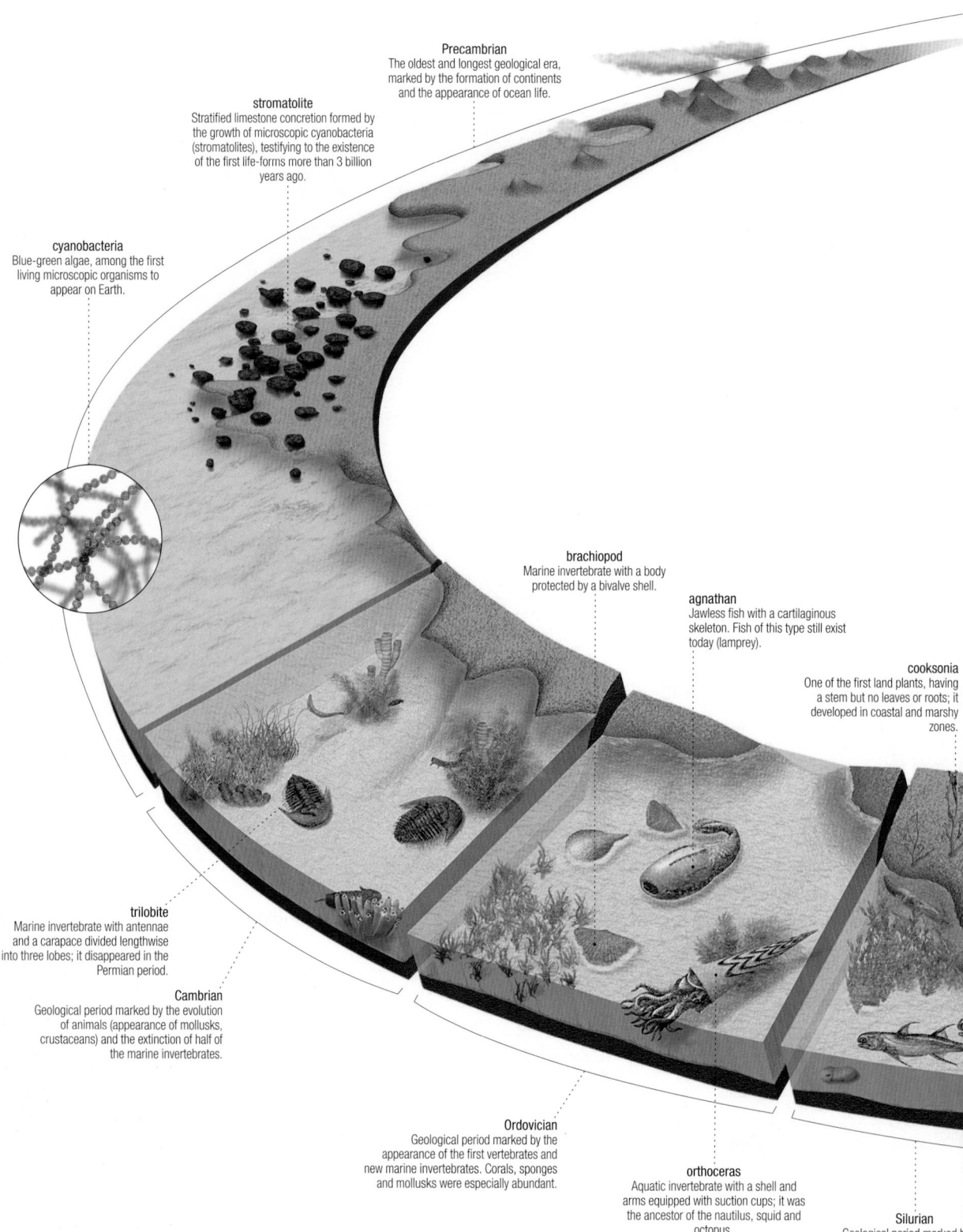

Precambrian
The oldest and longest geological era, marked by the formation of continents and the appearance of ocean life.

stromatolite
Stratified limestone concretion formed by the growth of microscopic cyanobacteria (stromatolites), testifying to the existence of the first life-forms more than 3 billion years ago.

cyanobacteria
Blue-green algae, among the first living microscopic organisms to appear on Earth.

brachiopod
Marine invertebrate with a body protected by a bivalve shell.

agnathan
Jawless fish with a cartilaginous skeleton. Fish of this type still exist today (lamprey).

cooksonia
One of the first land plants, having a stem but no leaves or roots; it developed in coastal and marshy zones.

trilobite
Marine invertebrate with antennae and a carapace divided lengthwise into three lobes; it disappeared in the Permian period.

Cambrian
Geological period marked by the evolution of animals (appearance of mollusks, crustaceans) and the extinction of half of the marine invertebrates.

Ordovician
Geological period marked by the appearance of the first vertebrates and new marine invertebrates. Corals, sponges and mollusks were especially abundant.

orthoceras
Aquatic invertebrate with a shell and arms equipped with suction cups; it was the ancestor of the nautilus, squid and octopus.

Silurian
Geological period marked by appearance of fish with jaw the first land plants.

archaeognatha
The oldest known insect fossil; it was wingless and had long antennae.

ichthyostega
Four-limbed vertebrate descended from ; the ancestor of today's amphibians and e of the first vertebrates to adapt to land.

ferns
These plants developed by the water's edge. Consisting of roots, a stem and leaves, they could reach the height of present-day trees.

acanthodian
First fish with a jaw; most of its fins were supported by a spine. It disappeared in the Permian period.

meganeura
Winged insect; no other insect has ever reached its size (28 in long).

arthropleura
Invertebrate with a multi-segmented body. Found in damp forests, it measured almost 7 ft in length.

Devonian
Geological period marked by the appearance of amphibians, insects and the first land animals. This period saw the proliferation of fish and plants.

Carboniferous
Geological period marked by the appearance of reptiles and winged insects. Plants of forests and swamps from this period formed extensive coal beds.

falcatus
Shark with sharp teeth. The male had a swordlike dorsal fin pointing forward.

origin and evolution of species

coelophysis
Two-legged carnivorous dinosaur having light hollow limb bones; it was extremely agile with sharp claws and teeth.

archaeopteryx
Animal capable of flight; it had certain characteristics of a reptile (claws, teeth, long bony tail) and others of a bird (wings, feathers).

plateosaur
One of the largest dinosaurs of t Jurassic period. This long-neck herbivore stood upright on its hind to reach the leaves of trees.

megazostrodon
About the size of a mouse, one of the first mammals to appear on Earth was a mainly nocturnal insectivore.

dimetrodon
Large carnivorous reptile with dorsal spines connected by a membrane to regulate its internal temperature; dominant in the Permian period.

mesosaur
First aquatic reptile with long sharp teeth and a powerful tail allowing it to propel itself in shallow water.

ichthyosaur
Swift carnivorous marine repti certain dolphin characteristic reached 33 feet in length. It dis during the Cretaceous per

nothosaur
Carnivorous dinosaur with short finlike limbs adapted to move on land and in the water.

Triassic
Geological period marked by the breaking apart of the supercontinent into two separate landmasses and the appearance of mammals.

Permian
Geological period marked by the predominance of reptiles and amphibians. The continental mass now formed into a supercontinent: Pangaea.

origin and evolution of species

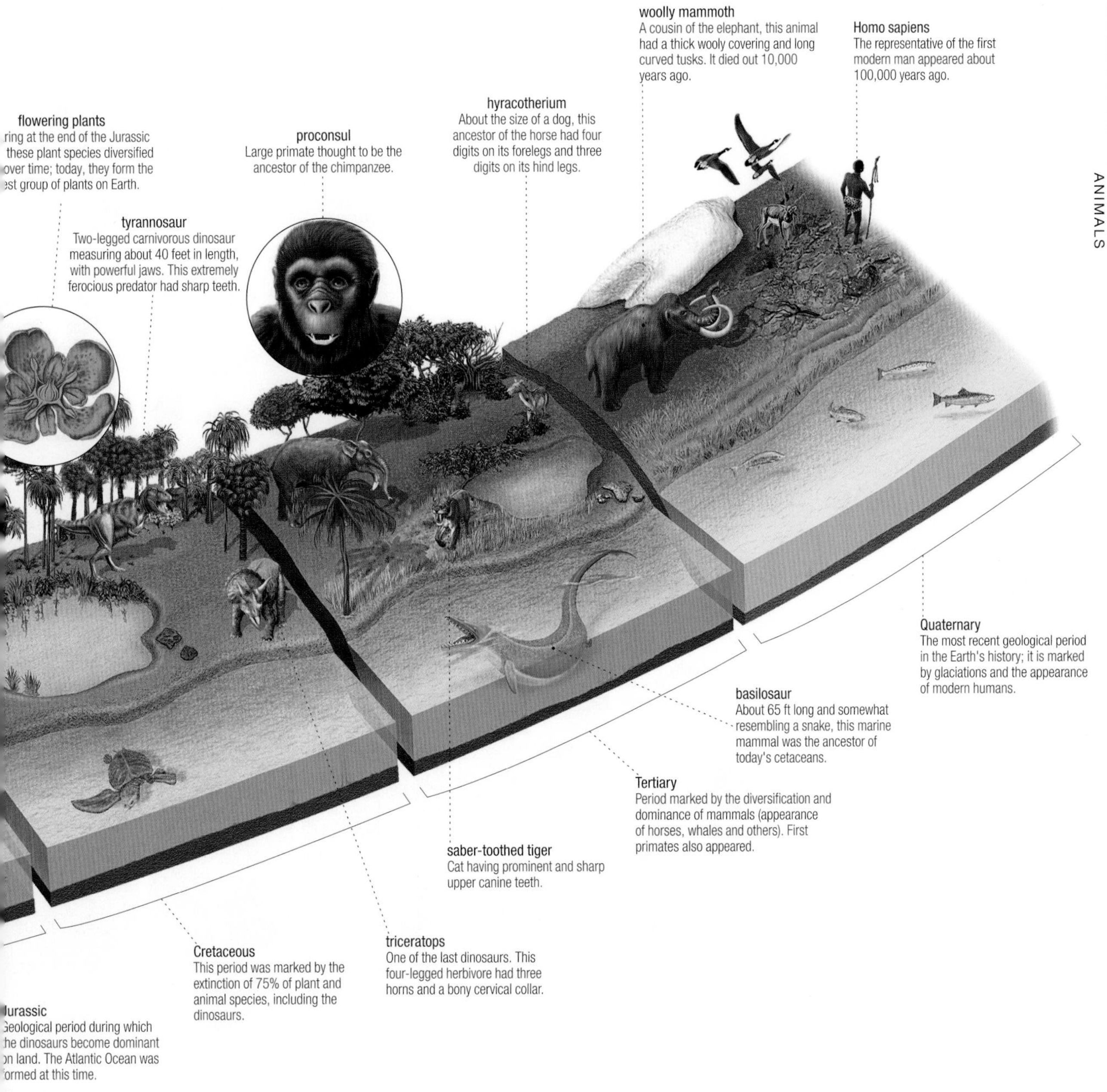

flowering plants
...ring at the end of the Jurassic
...these plant species diversified
...over time; today, they form the
...est group of plants on Earth.

tyrannosaur
Two-legged carnivorous dinosaur
measuring about 40 feet in length,
with powerful jaws. This extremely
ferocious predator had sharp teeth.

proconsul
Large primate thought to be the
ancestor of the chimpanzee.

hyracotherium
About the size of a dog, this
ancestor of the horse had four
digits on its forelegs and three
digits on its hind legs.

woolly mammoth
A cousin of the elephant, this animal
had a thick wooly covering and long
curved tusks. It died out 10,000
years ago.

Homo sapiens
The representative of the first
modern man appeared about
100,000 years ago.

Quaternary
The most recent geological period
in the Earth's history; it is marked
by glaciations and the appearance
of modern humans.

basilosaur
About 65 ft long and somewhat
resembling a snake, this marine
mammal was the ancestor of
today's cetaceans.

Tertiary
Period marked by the diversification and
dominance of mammals (appearance
of horses, whales and others). First
primates also appeared.

saber-toothed tiger
Cat having prominent and sharp
upper canine teeth.

Cretaceous
This period was marked by the
extinction of 75% of plant and
animal species, including the
dinosaurs.

triceratops
One of the last dinosaurs. This
four-legged herbivore had three
horns and a bony cervical collar.

Jurassic
Geological period during which
the dinosaurs become dominant
on land. The Atlantic Ocean was
formed at this time.

ANIMALS

biological taxonomy

System for classifying living organisms in relation to one another and defining their biological descent and common origins.

example of classification: cat

kingdom
Largest and most inclusive category typically consisting of five kingdoms (Fungi, Prokaryotae, Protista, Plantae and Animalia). The cat belongs to the kingdom Animalia.

phylum
Category made up of classes having a common distant ancestor. The cat belongs to the phylum Chordata that includes vertebrates, animals with a spinal column.

class
Category made up of related orders. The cat belongs to the class Mammalia, vertebrates who nourish their young with milk secreted by mammary glands.

order
Category made up of families having a common ancestor. The cat belongs to the order Carnivora, meat-eating mammals (carnivores).

family
Category made up of genera having a recent common ancestor. The cat, along with the lion, tiger and leopard, belongs to the family Felidae.

genus
Category made up of related species sharing distinctive physical characteristics. The cat, along with several wild relatives, belongs to the genus *Felis*.

species
Category made up of related individuals that can potentially reproduce with each other. All domesticated cats belong to the species *Felis catus*.

animal cell

Smallest living structure and constituent unit of all animals, including human beings; its size and shape vary according to function.

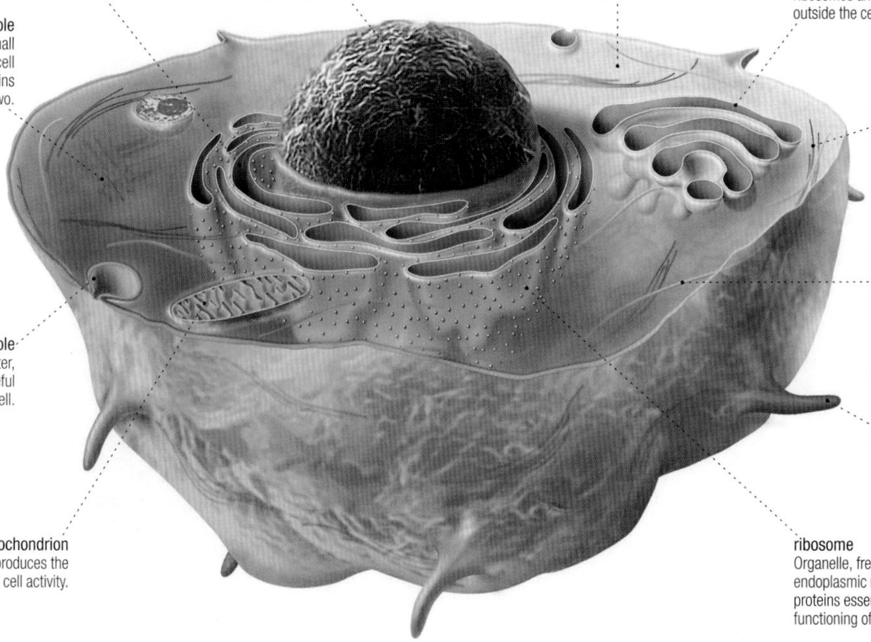

endoplasmic reticulum
Organelle formed of walls to which the ribosomes are attached.

centriole
Structure consisting of small rods that play a major role in cell division. Each cell usually contains two.

cell nucleus
Central membrane-enclosed organelle of the cell, containing the cell's genes and controlling its essential activities.

cytoplasm
Clear gelatinous substance surrounding the various cellular structures.

Golgi apparatus
Organelle composed of a series of pockets that receive proteins produced by the ribosomes and either transport them outside the cell or to other organelles.

microfilament
Rod-shaped structure supporting the cell and giving it its shape.

microtubule
Cylindrical structure supporting the cell and allowing organelles and substances inside the cell to move about.

vacuole
Spheroid cavity for storing water, waste or various substances useful to the cell.

cilium
Extension of the cytoplasm of some cells, used primarily for locomotion.

mitochondrion
Ovoid organelle that produces the energy necessary for cell activity.

ribosome
Organelle, free or attached to the endoplasmic reticulum, producing proteins essential to the constitution and functioning of living beings.

ANIMALS

unicellular organisms

Living organisms consisting of a single cell.

amoeba
Variably shaped single-celled organism, found in freshwater or salt water, in humid soil or, sometimes, as a parasite of animals. It moves about and feeds with the help of pseudopodia.

paramecium
Ovoid-shaped single-celled organism generally found in freshwater and covered with cilia, which allow it to move about and to feed, mainly on bacteria.

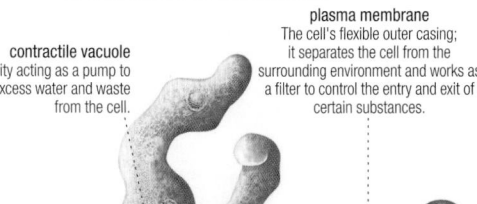
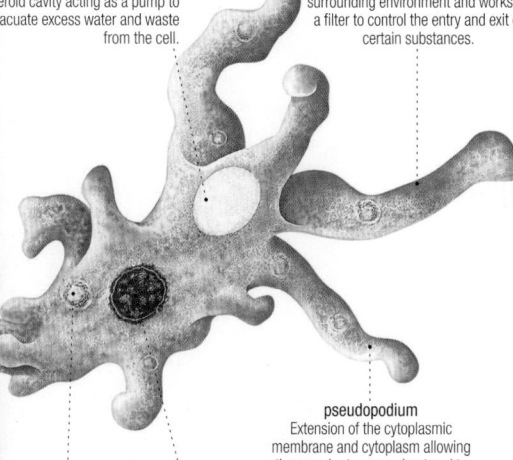

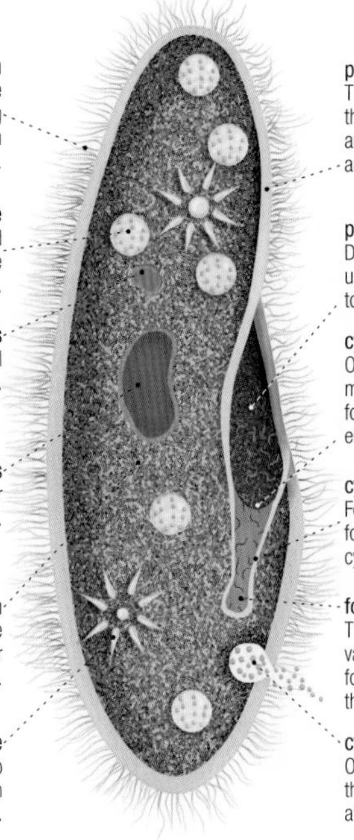

contractile vacuole
Spheroid cavity acting as a pump to evacuate excess water and waste from the cell.

plasma membrane
The cell's flexible outer casing; it separates the cell from the surrounding environment and works as a filter to control the entry and exit of certain substances.

cilium
Filament-like extension of the cytoplasmic membrane allowing the cell and certain substances on its surface to move about.

food vacuole
Spheroid cavity in which food particles from the cytopharynx are digested.

micronucleus
Small nucleus ensuring cell reproduction.

macronucleus
Large nucleus controlling cellular activities.

cytoplasm
Clear gelatinous substance surrounding the various cellular structures.

pseudopodium
Extension of the cytoplasmic membrane and cytoplasm allowing the amoeba to move about and to trap its prey.

food vacuole
Spheroid cavity in which the amoeba traps its prey to digest it.

nucleus
Central membrane-enclosed organelle of the cell, containing the cell's genes and controlling its essential activities.

contractile vacuole
Spheroid cavity acting as a pump to evacuate excess water and waste from the cell.

plasma membrane
The cell's flexible outer casing; it separates the cell from the surrounding environment and works as a filter to control the entry and exit of certain substances.

peristome
Depression lined with cilia, which undulate to direct food particles toward the cytostome.

cytostome
Opening corresponding to the mouth and allowing ingestion of food and rejection of undesirable elements.

cytopharynx
Fold of the plasma membrane; food particles originating in the cytostome are directed toward it.

forming food vacuole
The paramecium continually produces food vacuoles out of cytoplasmic membrane. Each food vacuole traps food particles accumulated in the bottom of the cytopharynx.

cytoproct
Orifice corresponding to the anus; the food vacuole opens into it, allowing waste to be eliminated.

ANIMALS

sponge

Porous multicellular organism, mostly marine (currently about 5,000 species); it anchors itself to a support and filters water to take in food particles.

morphology of a sponge

anatomy of a sponge

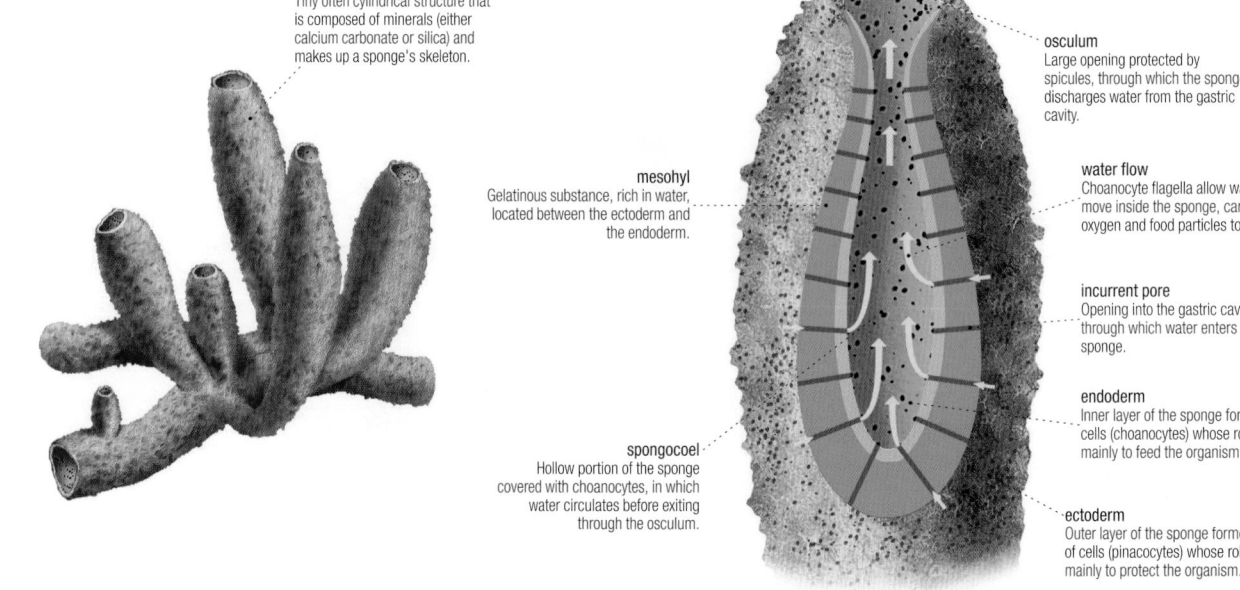

spicule
Tiny often cylindrical structure that is composed of minerals (either calcium carbonate or silica) and makes up a sponge's skeleton.

mesohyl
Gelatinous substance, rich in water, located between the ectoderm and the endoderm.

spongocoel
Hollow portion of the sponge covered with choanocytes, in which water circulates before exiting through the osculum.

osculum
Large opening protected by spicules, through which the sponge discharges water from the gastric cavity.

water flow
Choanocyte flagella allow water move inside the sponge, carryin oxygen and food particles to it.

incurrent pore
Opening into the gastric cavity, through which water enters the sponge.

endoderm
Inner layer of the sponge forme cells (choanocytes) whose role mainly to feed the organism.

ectoderm
Outer layer of the sponge formed of cells (pinacocytes) whose role is mainly to protect the organism.

jellyfish

Marine invertebrate with a swimming umbrella and appendages that are stinging; certain species are dangerously venomous and their sting may be fatal to humans.

morphology of a jellyfish

anatomy of a jellyfish

umbrella
Main structural part of the jellyfish, the muscles of which the jellyfish can contract in order to move about.

mouth
Anterior cavity of the digestive tube located on the ventral face, allowing the ingestion of food.

tentacle
Long appendage ending in an enlarged section or knob with stinging properties.

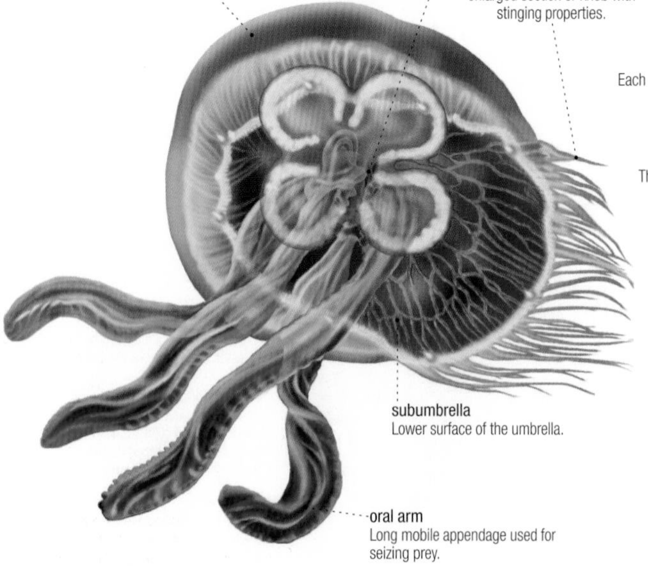

gonad
Each of four reproductive glands located in each gastric pouch and producing gametes.

stomach
Section of the digestive tube that receives food in order to digest it.

radial canal
Conduit located in the ur connecting a gastric pouc ring canal.

gastric pouch
Each of the four stomach cavities in which food is digested.

gastric filaments
Threadlike appendages that line the stomach and quicken the digestive process.

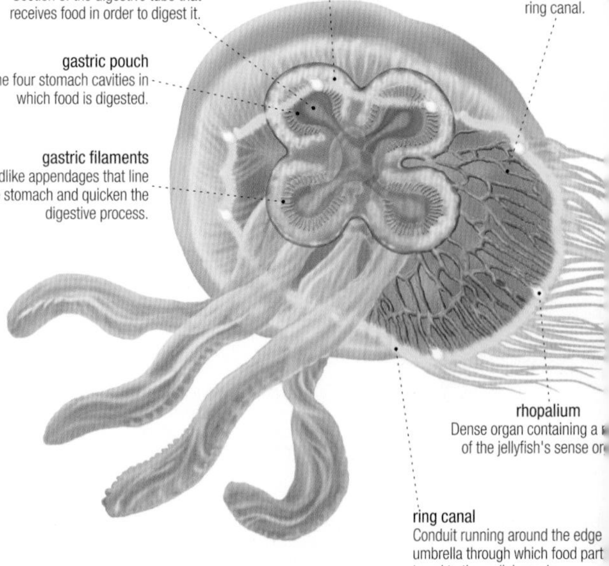

subumbrella
Lower surface of the umbrella.

oral arm
Long mobile appendage used for seizing prey.

rhopalium
Dense organ containing a r of the jellyfish's sense or

ring canal
Conduit running around the edge umbrella through which food part travel to the radial canals.

starfish

Carnivorous echinoderm found in the ocean depths; it generally has five arms, which allow it to crawl slowly along surfaces.

morphology of a starfish

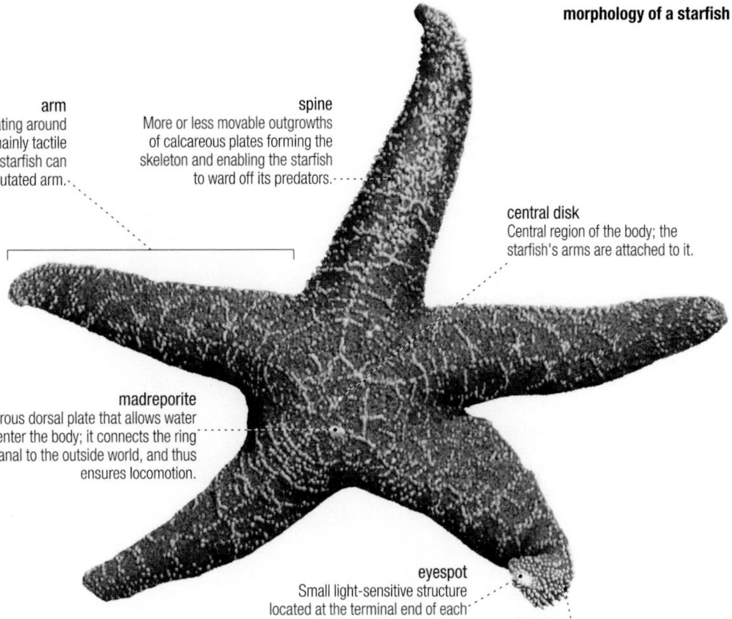

arm
Movable appendage radiating around the central disk; it has a mainly tactile and olfactory function. The starfish can regenerate an amputated arm.

spine
More or less movable outgrowths of calcareous plates forming the skeleton and enabling the starfish to ward off its predators.

central disk
Central region of the body; the starfish's arms are attached to it.

anatomy of a starfish

madreporite
Porous dorsal plate that allows water to enter the body; it connects the ring canal to the outside world, and thus ensures locomotion.

gonopore
Dorsal opening through which gametes (spermatozoa and ova) are expelled into the water to be fertilized.

anus
Terminal orifice of the digestive tract allowing waste to be ejected; most of the undigested food is regurgitated rather than expelled through the anus.

intestine
The digestive tract between the and the anus where absorption ents is carried out and waste is transformed into fecal matter.

ring canal
Circular canal in which filtered water enters through the reporite and branches out into the radial canals.

radial canal
canal running the length of the t receives water from the ring nal, which is then passed into the tube feet.

eyespot
Small light-sensitive structure located at the terminal end of each arm, allowing it to locate surfaces and prey.

tube foot
Small flexible tube extending and retracting with the action of the ampulla; it mainly allows the organism to move about, anchor itself to a support and capture its prey.

pyloric cecum
Radiated duct of the digestive tract producing digestive enzymes and also allowing digested food to be stored.

gonad
Each of the two glands located in each arm, producing gametes (spermatozoa or ova) depending on the sex of the starfish.

rectal cecum
Lateral duct of the terminal part of the digestive tract, where waste is stored before being expelled through the anus.

ampulla
at contracts to let water enter the oot, allowing it to extend; when it dilates, the foot retracts.

esophagus
Muscular membranous channel of the anterior section of the digestive tract; it allows food to reach the stomach.

mouth
Anterior cavity of the digestive tract located on the ventral surface that allows food to be ingested.

stomach
Dilated section of the digestive tract preceding the intestine; it receives food to be digested.

examples of simple organisms

There are several thousand species of simple organisms, found all over the planet.

earthworm
Worm with a body divided into ringlike segments that tunnels underground, eating bacteria and aerating the soil.

centipede
Terrestrial invertebrate with a flattened body divided into ringlike segments each having one pair of legs.

sea anemone
Carnivorous invertebrate with a gelatinous ody attached to a foot with a sucker allowing to anchor itself to rocks. Its many tentacles capture food.

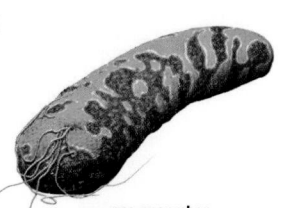

sea cucumber
Marine echinoderm with a soft body and rough skin, having suckers on its ventral side. It ejects toxins when it feels threatened.

sea urchin
Echinoderm found in the ocean depths and usually covered with movable spines; it has teeth that help it to graze on (rake) algae.

ANIMALS

univalve shell

Land or aquatic mollusk having a foot and head, which retract into a spiral shell made of a single piece.

morphology of a univalve shell

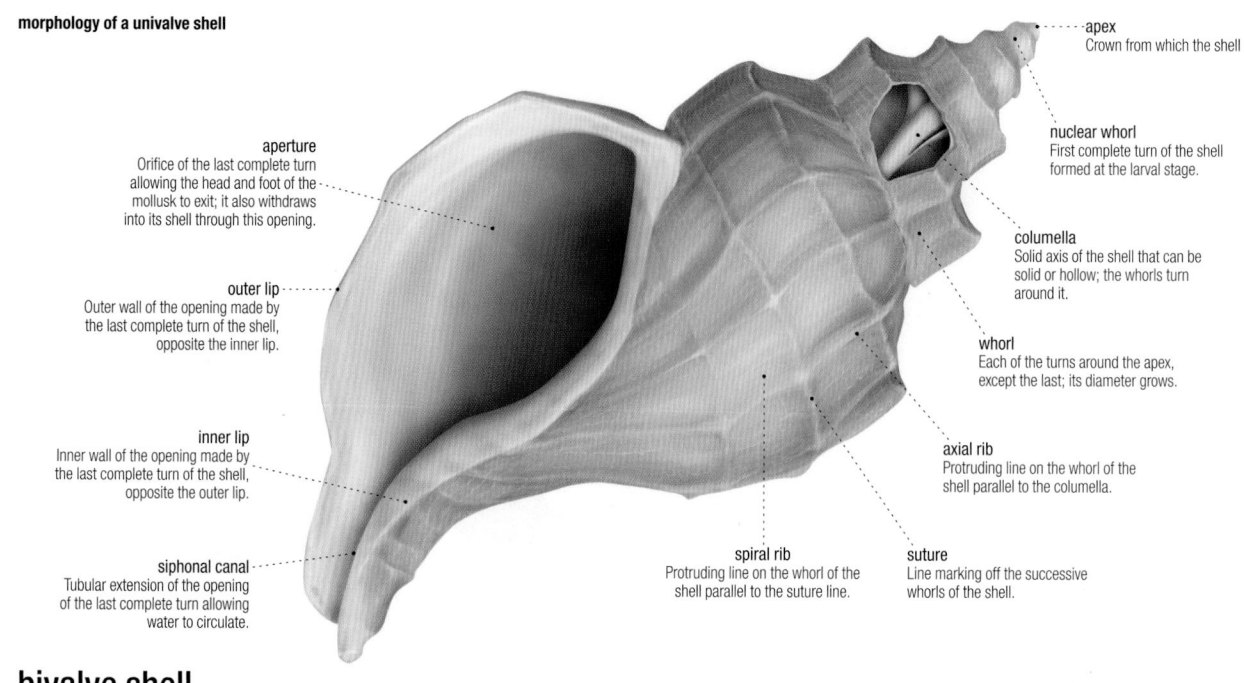

apex
Crown from which the shell gr

aperture
Orifice of the last complete turn allowing the head and foot of the mollusk to exit; it also withdraws into its shell through this opening.

nuclear whorl
First complete turn of the shell formed at the larval stage.

columella
Solid axis of the shell that can be solid or hollow; the whorls turn around it.

outer lip
Outer wall of the opening made by the last complete turn of the shell, opposite the inner lip.

whorl
Each of the turns around the apex, except the last; its diameter grows.

inner lip
Inner wall of the opening made by the last complete turn of the shell, opposite the outer lip.

axial rib
Protruding line on the whorl of the shell parallel to the columella.

siphonal canal
Tubular extension of the opening of the last complete turn allowing water to circulate.

spiral rib
Protruding line on the whorl of the shell parallel to the suture line.

suture
Line marking off the successive whorls of the shell.

bivalve shell

Aquatic mollusk without a defined head but having a foot, which retracts into a shell formed of two hinged parts.

anatomy of a bivalve shell

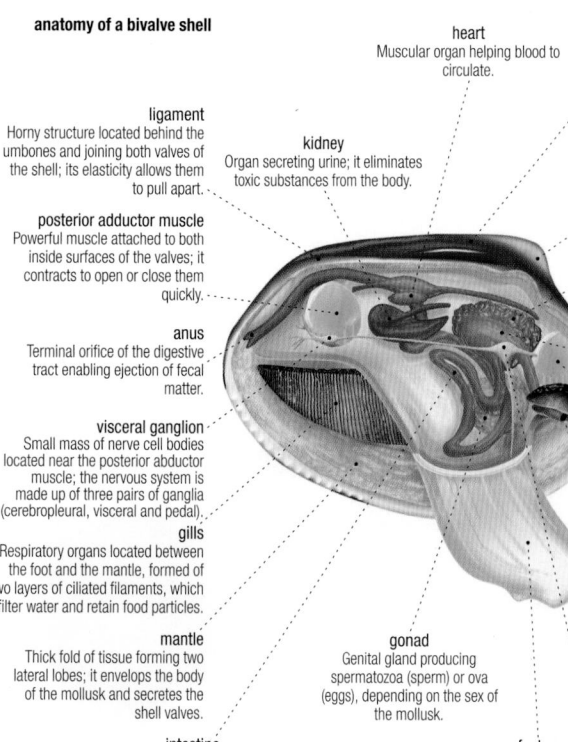

heart
Muscular organ helping blood to circulate.

shell
Calcareous casing produced by the mantle; it has three layers and protects the main organs of the mollusk.

morphology of a bivalve shel

ligament
Horny structure located behind the umbones and joining both valves of the shell; its elasticity allows them to pull apart.

kidney
Organ secreting urine; it eliminates toxic substances from the body.

umbo
Protuberance at the terminal end of the valve, from which the shell grows.

anterior end
Front terminal end of the shell located opposite the posterior lip; it allows the foot to exit.

posterior adductor muscle
Powerful muscle attached to both inside surfaces of the valves; it contracts to open or close them quickly.

digestive gland
Organ producing a secretion that contributes to digestion.

growth line
Small irregular protuberance or the valves of the shell indicating the stages of growth.

anus
Terminal orifice of the digestive tract enabling ejection of fecal matter.

stomach
Dilated section of the digestive tract preceding the intestine; it receives food to be digested.

lunule
Dorsal depression of the two va in front of the umbones; its surf smooth, unlike the rest of the st

visceral ganglion
Small mass of nerve cell bodies located near the posterior abductor muscle; the nervous system is made up of three pairs of ganglia (cerebropleural, visceral and pedal).

anterior adductor muscle
Muscle attached to both inside surfaces of the valves that contracts to open or close them quickly; it is less powerful than the posterior abductor muscle.

umbo
Protuberance at the termin end of the valve, from whic shell grows.

gills
Respiratory organs located between the foot and the mantle, formed of two layers of ciliated filaments, which filter water and retain food particles.

labial palp
Mouthpart that grasps food particles deposited on the gills and carries them to the mouth.

ligament
Horny structure located be the umbones and joining b valves of the shell; its elas allows them to pull apart.

mantle
Thick fold of tissue forming two lateral lobes; it envelops the body of the mollusk and secretes the shell valves.

gonad
Genital gland producing spermatozoa (sperm) or ova (eggs), depending on the sex of the mollusk.

mouth
Anterior cavity of the digestive tract surrounded by four labial palps, which enable food particles to enter.

escutcheon
Dorsal depression of the two va behind the umbones, through w the ligament extends; its surfac smooth, unlike the rest of the s

intestine
Section of the digestive tract between the stomach and the anus where absorption of nutrients is carried out and waste is transformed into fecal matter.

foot
Short flat movable muscular organ located on the ventral surface; it allows the snail to move or to attach itself to a support using elastic filaments.

cerebropleural ganglion
Small mass of nerve cell bodies located near the anterior abductor muscle; the nervous system is made up of three pairs of ganglia (cerebropleural, visceral and pedal).

valve
Each of the two parts of a bivalve shell, joined by a ligament.

posterior end
Rear terminal end of the shell, opposite the anterior lip, through which water enters and exits.

snail

Hermaphroditic herbivorous land mollusk having a spiral shell; some species of snails are edible.

morphology of a snail

whorl
Each of the swirls around the apex; they increase in diameter and form the shell.

shell
Calcareous spiral casing formed of three successive layers that protect the organs; the snail can withdraw into its shell.

growth line
Thin irregular protuberance of the whorl of the shell, corresponding to its successive growths.

apex
from which the shell grows.

eye
Organ of vision located at the terminal end of the eyestalk; the snail has poor eyesight.

head
Anterior portion of the foot of the snail containing the main sensory organs.

tentacle
Small muscular appendage, long and retractable, having a tactile role.

foot
Large elongated muscular organ forming the lower portion of the snail and containing the head; it allows the snail to crawl.

mouth
Anterior cavity of the digestive tract having a jaw and a rough tongue (radula) to graze on plants.

eyestalk
Large muscular appendage, elongated and retractable, bearing an eye at its terminal end.

anatomy of a snail

albumin gland
Organ opening into the hermaphroditic duct and secreting a viscous substance, which surrounds the fertilized ovum and contributes to the development of the egg.

ovotestis
Genital gland located at the apex of the shell ensuring production of sperm and eggs; the snail has both male and female organs.

kidney
Organ secreting urine; it eliminates toxic substances from the body.

heart
Muscular organ helping blood to circulate.

hermaphroditic duct
nel into which the ovotestis and en gland open; it separates into erm duct and an egg duct that emain, nonetheless, conjoined.

digestive gland
Organ producing a secretion that contributes to digestion.

lung
Pouch formed of a network of blood vessels inside the shell; it ensures respiration and communicates with the outside through an orifice.

intestine
Section of the digestive tract between the stomach and the anus where absorption of nutrients is carried out and waste is transformed into fecal matter.

copulatory bursa
Sac where sperm accumulate fore entering the spermatheca.

crop
Large sac located beyond the esophagus, where food is held before being digested in the stomach.

salivary gland
Organ located in the buccal cavity; it secretes saliva and enables especially the digestion of food.

spermatheca
uch discharging into the vagina and housing the sperm used to fertilize the eggs.

esophagus
Canal in the anterior part of the digestive tract; it carries food to the crop.

ureter
g canal originating in the kidney d carrying urine to the excretory pore.

radula
Tongue bearing numerous small horny teeth allowing the snail to grasp and tear up food before ingesting it.

stomach
Dilated section of the digestive tract preceding the intestine; it receives food to be digested.

mouth
Anterior cavity of the digestive tract having a jaw and a rough tongue (radula) to graze on plants.

spermoviduct
ale genital duct carrying sperm toward the penis.

pedal gland
Organ of the foot located near the mouth; it secretes an adhesive substance that allows the snail to crawl.

excretory pore
Terminal opening of the ureter allowing urine to be evacuated.

anus
Terminal orifice of the digestive tract enabling ejection of fecal matter.

penis
Male organ of copulation, internal when at rest; it is located on the ventral face of the foot, lateral to the vagina.

flagellum
Movable filament appended to the penis allowing sperm to move about during copulation.

vagina
Female organ of copulation located on the ventral surface of the foot, lateral to the penis.

dart sac
Calcareous part located inside the vagina containing the dart with which snails sting one another to achieve arousal before copulation.

gonopore
Opening common to the penis and the vagina and located at the side of the head; it allows copulation and entry of the sperm into the copulatory bursa.

octopus

Carnivorous marine mollusk with a head bearing eight powerful arms (tentacles) covered with suckers; the octopus can change color to camouflage itself. Certain species are edible.

morphology of an octopus

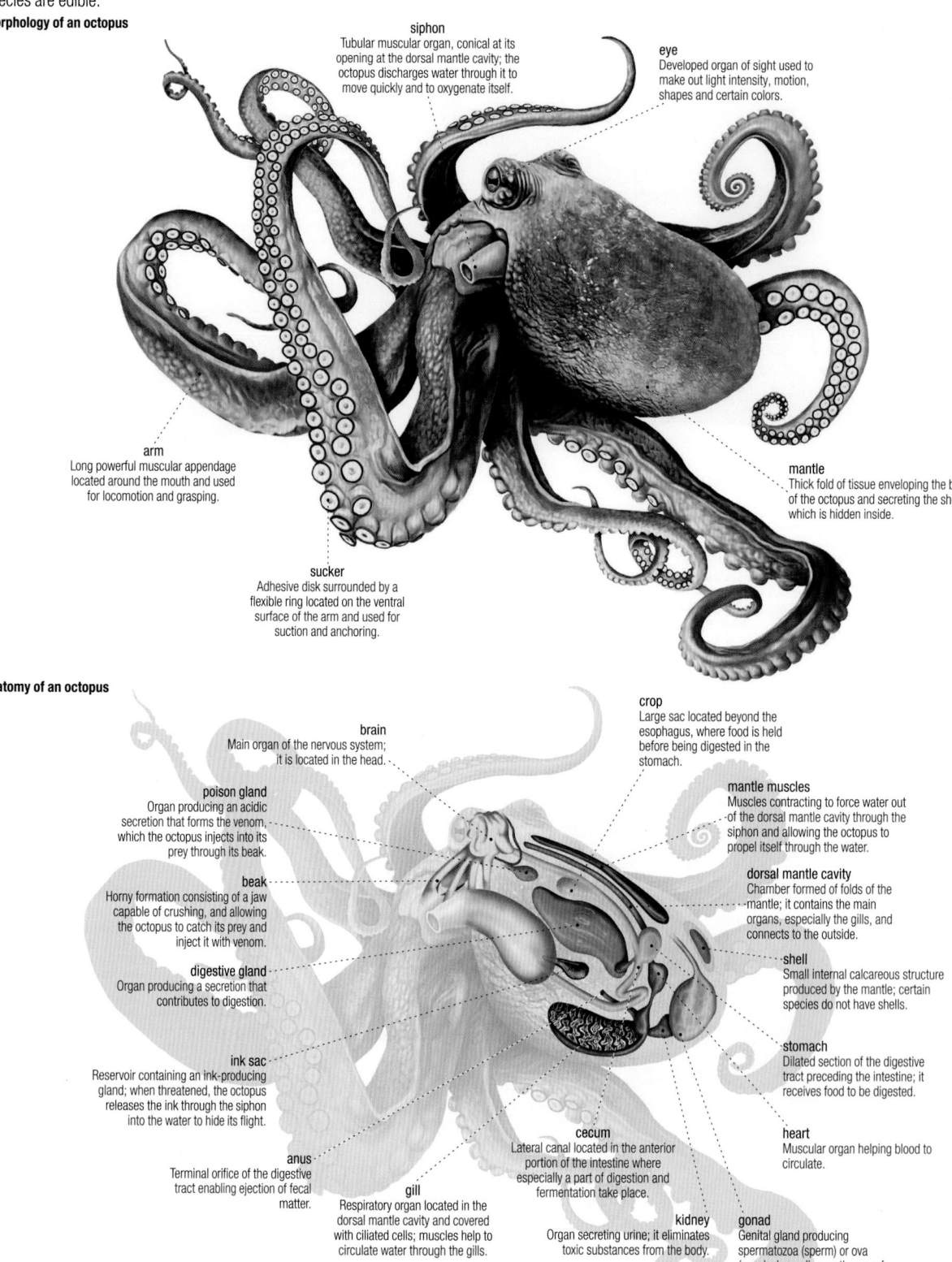

siphon
Tubular muscular organ, conical at its opening at the dorsal mantle cavity; the octopus discharges water through it to move quickly and to oxygenate itself.

eye
Developed organ of sight used to make out light intensity, motion, shapes and certain colors.

arm
Long powerful muscular appendage located around the mouth and used for locomotion and grasping.

mantle
Thick fold of tissue enveloping the body of the octopus and secreting the shell, which is hidden inside.

sucker
Adhesive disk surrounded by a flexible ring located on the ventral surface of the arm and used for suction and anchoring.

anatomy of an octopus

brain
Main organ of the nervous system; it is located in the head.

crop
Large sac located beyond the esophagus, where food is held before being digested in the stomach.

poison gland
Organ producing an acidic secretion that forms the venom, which the octopus injects into its prey through its beak.

mantle muscles
Muscles contracting to force water out of the dorsal mantle cavity through the siphon and allowing the octopus to propel itself through the water.

beak
Horny formation consisting of a jaw capable of crushing, and allowing the octopus to catch its prey and inject it with venom.

dorsal mantle cavity
Chamber formed of folds of the mantle; it contains the main organs, especially the gills, and connects to the outside.

digestive gland
Organ producing a secretion that contributes to digestion.

shell
Small internal calcareous structure produced by the mantle; certain species do not have shells.

stomach
Dilated section of the digestive tract preceding the intestine; it receives food to be digested.

ink sac
Reservoir containing an ink-producing gland; when threatened, the octopus releases the ink through the siphon into the water to hide its flight.

cecum
Lateral canal located in the anterior portion of the intestine where especially a part of digestion and fermentation take place.

heart
Muscular organ helping blood to circulate.

anus
Terminal orifice of the digestive tract enabling ejection of fecal matter.

gill
Respiratory organ located in the dorsal mantle cavity and covered with ciliated cells; muscles help to circulate water through the gills.

kidney
Organ secreting urine; it eliminates toxic substances from the body.

gonad
Genital gland producing spermatozoa (sperm) or ova (eggs), depending on the sex of the mollusk.

lobster

Large marine crustacean having a carapace and five large pairs of legs, the first of which bears powerful claws; its meat is highly prized.

morphology of a lobster

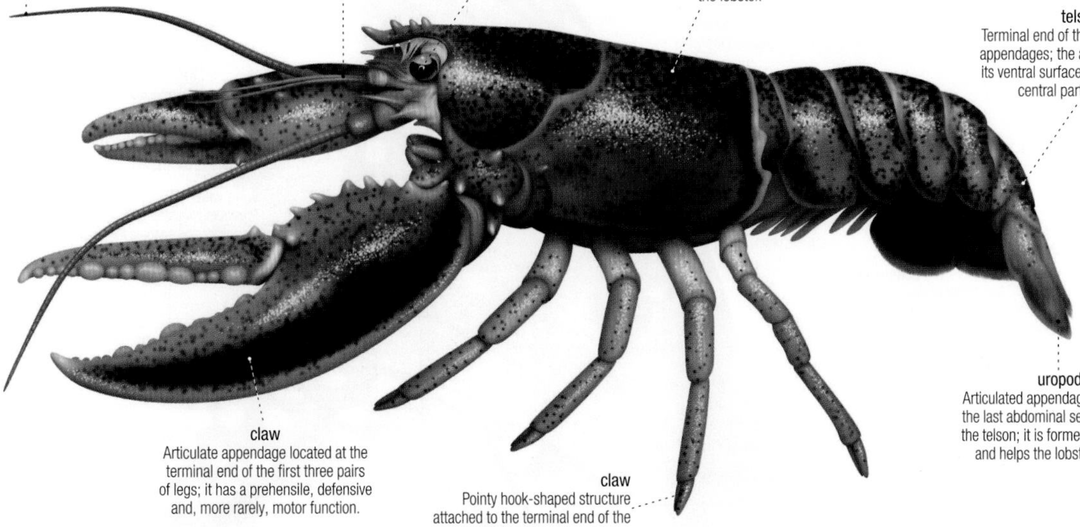

antenna
Long sensory organ having a tactile function.

antennule
Very short sensory organ covered with fine hairs and located in front of the head; it has an olfactory function.

eye
Organ of sight made up of several individual eyes positioned on a movable axis; adapted to low light conditions, it serves mainly to detect motion.

carapace
Hard covering produced by folds of tissue from the back segments of the head; it protects the body of the lobster.

telson
Terminal end of the body having no appendages; the anus is located on its ventral surface. It comprises the central part of the tail.

claw
Articulate appendage located at the terminal end of the first three pairs of legs; it has a prehensile, defensive and, more rarely, motor function.

claw
Pointy hook-shaped structure attached to the terminal end of the two last pairs of thoracic legs.

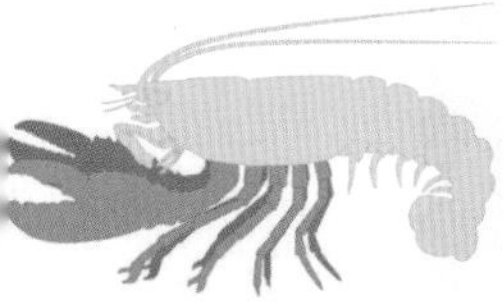

uropod
Articulated appendage attached to the last abdominal segment before the telson; it is formed of two lobes and helps the lobster to swim.

thoracic legs
Articulated limbs attached to the cephalothorax and having a prehensile and motor function; the first three legs bear pincer claws while the last two bear claws.

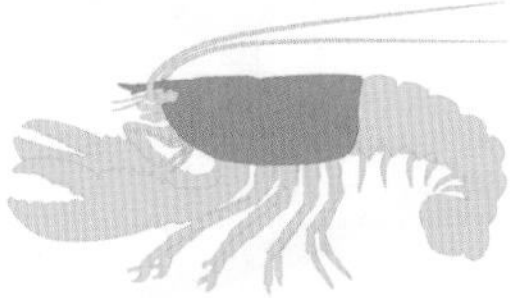

cephalothorax
Meeting of the head and the thorax that forms the anterior portion of the body of the lobster.

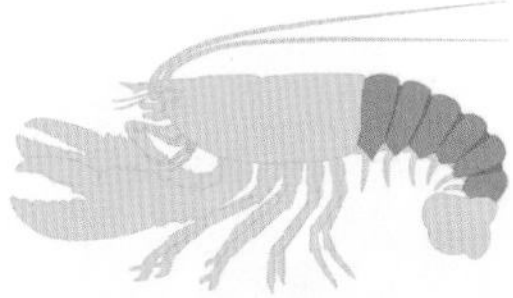

abdomen
Posterior portion of the body formed of six segments and bearing the pleopods, articulated appendages used for swimming, circulating water over the gills and holding the eggs.

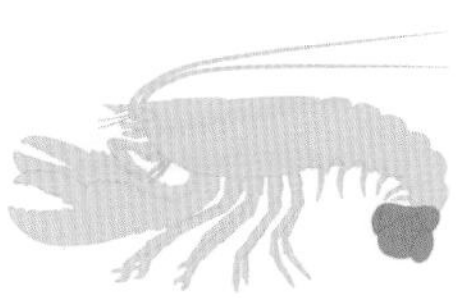

tail
Swimming organ formed of the telson and the two uropods.

cardiac stomach
Anterior chamber of the stomach; its calcareous parts grind food into fine particles so they can be digested in the pyloric stomach.

pyloric stomach
Posterior chamber of the stomach; food particles from the cardiac stomach are digested here.

heart
Muscular organ helping blood to circulate.

anatomy of a lobster

brain
Main organ of the nervous system; it is located in the cephalothorax.

testis
Male genital glands producing spermatozoa (sperm).

dorsal abdominal artery
Canal circulating blood from the heart through the posterior dorsal portion of the lobster.

green gland
Organ producing a secretion that allows toxic substances to be eliminated from the body; its opening is located at the base of the antennae.

mouth
Anterior cavity of the digestive tract located on the lower surface of the cephalothorax; it lets food enter.

intestine
Section of the digestive tract from the pyloric stomach to the anus.

ventral nerve cord
Main element of the nervous system extending over the entire ventral portion of the body.

digestive gland
Organ producing a secretion that contributes to digestion.

sternal artery
Canal circulating blood from the heart to the ventral artery of the lobster.

ventral abdominal artery
Canal circulating blood from the heart through the posterior ventral portion of the lobster.

anus
Terminal orifice of the digestive tract enabling ejection of fecal matter.

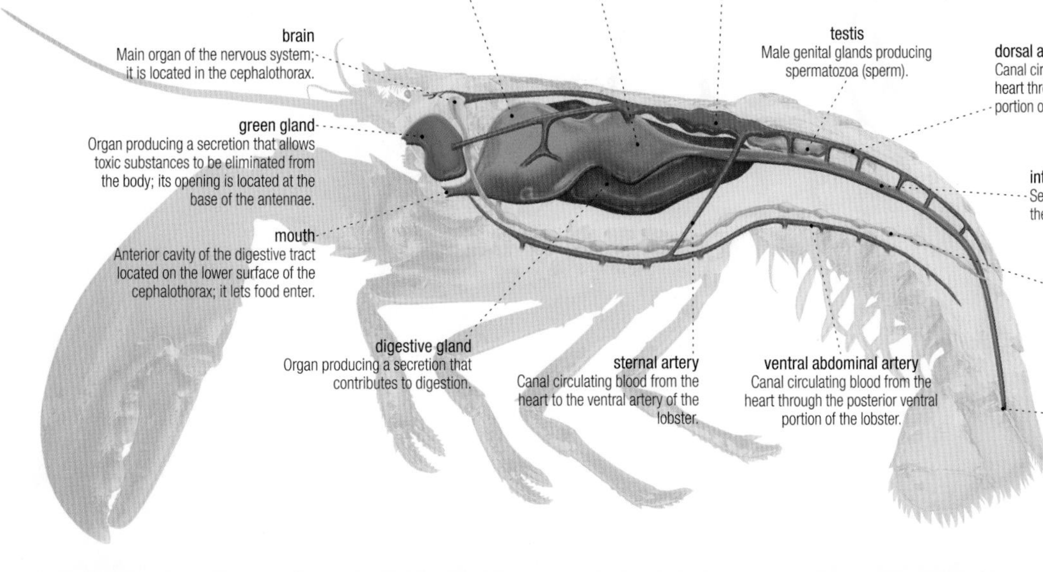

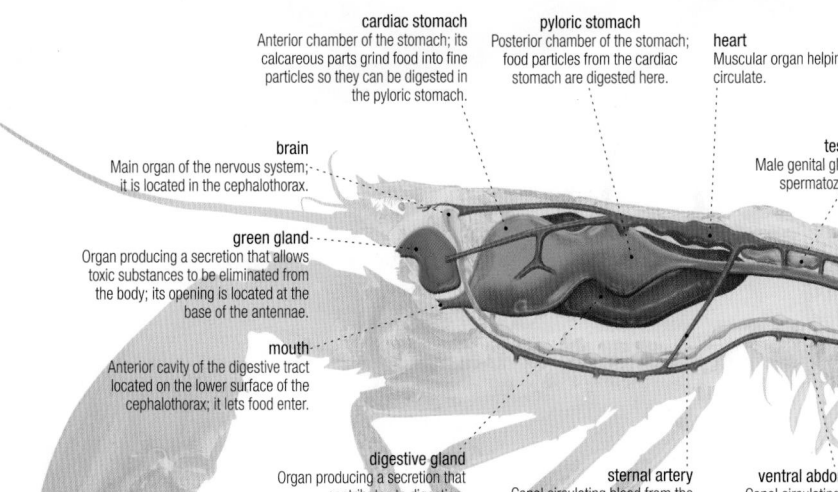
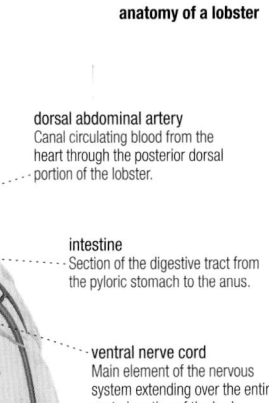

ANIMALS

butterfly

Adult insect having two pairs of wings and three pairs of legs; it emerges after the first three stages of metamorphosis: the egg, the caterpillar and the chrysalis.

morphology of a butterfly

cell
Constituent element of a butterfly's wing contained between the wing veins.

forewing
Appendage of flight attached to the central segment of the thorax.

head
Anterior portion of the butterfly's body containing the sensory organs and the brain.

wing vein
Protruding line that gives the wing its rigidity and enables the blood to circulate.

compound eye
Organ of vision made up of thousands of facets that perceive shapes, colors, motion and distance.

hind wing
Appendage of flight attached to the terminal segment of the thorax.

labial palpus
Sensory organ of the mouth having mainly olfactory and gustatory functions.

antenna
Sensory organ made up of several segments and having mainly tactile and olfactory functions.

proboscis
Mouthlike part allowing the butterfly to feed through aspiration; the proboscis folds back onto itself to avoid interfering with flight.

hind leg
Large articulated member attached to the terminal segment of the thorax and having powerful sensory organs.

thorax
Portion of the butterfly's body divided into three segments; it contains the motor appendages, such as the legs and wings.

coxa
Anterior segment of the leg articulating with the thorax and the trochanter.

foreleg
Articulated member attached to the first segment of the thorax and having powerful sensory organs.

trochanter
Segment of the leg between the coxa and the femur.

femur
Segment of the leg between the trochanter and the tibia.

middle leg
Large articulated member attached to the central segment of the thorax and having powerful sensory organs.

hind leg
Large articulated member attached to the terminal segment of the thorax and having powerful sensory organs.

abdomen
Posterior portion of the butterfly's body made up of 10 segments and containing the major vital organs, such as the heart, the intestines and the genital organs.

spiracle
Respiratory orifice located on the lateral portion of the thorax and abdomen; the butterfly has some 10 pairs.

tibia
Segment of the leg between the femur and the tarsus.

tarsus
Terminal segment of the leg, divided into five parts and having two claws.

claw
Pointy fang-shaped structure attached to the tarsus and enabling the butterfly to cling to things and feed itself.

butterfly

anatomy of a female butterfly

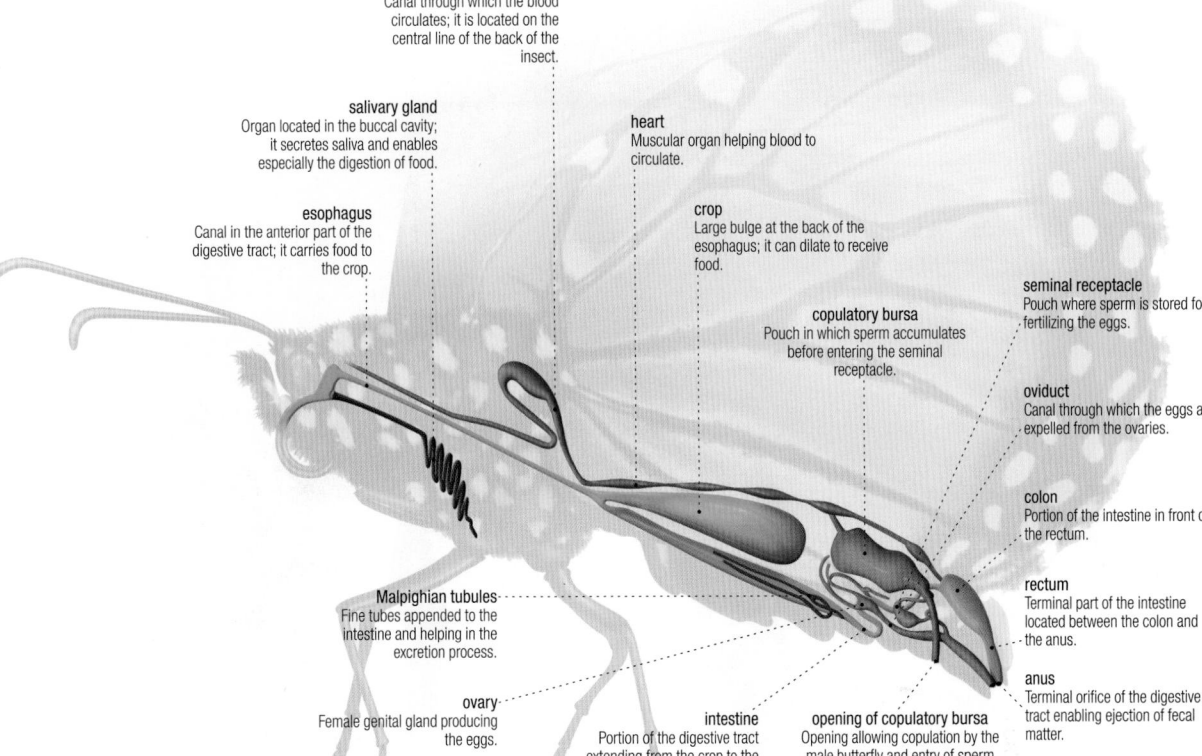

dorsal blood vessel
Canal through which the blood circulates; it is located on the central line of the back of the insect.

salivary gland
Organ located in the buccal cavity; it secretes saliva and enables especially the digestion of food.

esophagus
Canal in the anterior part of the digestive tract; it carries food to the crop.

heart
Muscular organ helping blood to circulate.

crop
Large bulge at the back of the esophagus; it can dilate to receive food.

copulatory bursa
Pouch in which sperm accumulates before entering the seminal receptacle.

seminal receptacle
Pouch where sperm is stored for fertilizing the eggs.

oviduct
Canal through which the eggs are expelled from the ovaries.

colon
Portion of the intestine in front of the rectum.

rectum
Terminal part of the intestine located between the colon and the anus.

anus
Terminal orifice of the digestive tract enabling ejection of fecal matter.

Malpighian tubules
Fine tubes appended to the intestine and helping in the excretion process.

ovary
Female genital gland producing the eggs.

intestine
Portion of the digestive tract extending from the crop to the anus.

opening of copulatory bursa
Opening allowing copulation by the male butterfly and entry of sperm into the copulatory bursa.

caterpillar
Butterfly larva having a long body and five pairs of grasping prolegs; the intermediary stage between the egg and the chrysalis.

simple eye
Organ of vision formed of a single facet that captures variations in luminosity and allows the caterpillar to orient itself.

head
Anterior portion of the body of the caterpillar containing the main sensory organs.

thorax
Part of the caterpillar's body divided into three segments; the walking legs are attached to it.

abdominal segment
Ring forming the caterpillar's abdomen.

spiracle
Respiratory orifice located on the lateral portion of the thorax and the abdomen.

abdomen
Posterior portion of the chrysalis's body.

metathorax
Embryo that will become the terminal segment of the thorax; the legs and rear wings are attached to it.

chrysalis
Intermediary stage between the caterpillar and the butterfly; the limbs and internal organs develop during this stage.

cremaster
Affixing element having one or more hooks; it is located at the posterior terminal end of the chrysalis's body.

wing
Embryo that will become the organ of flight; it is attached to the thorax.

antenna
Embryo that will become the sensory organ; it has several segments and its functions are mainly tactile and olfactory.

prothorax
Embryo that will become the first segment of the thorax; the front legs are attached to it, but not the wings.

mandible
like part enabling the insect grasp and grind its food.

walking leg
Articulated member having a motor function; it remains in the adult stage. The caterpillar has three pairs.

proleg
Adhesive disk located below the abdomen that disappears in the adult stage; the caterpillar usually has five pairs, including the anal claspers.

anal clasper
Last of five pairs of prolegs; it is located at the terminal part of the caterpillar's body.

mesothorax
Embryo that will become the central segment of the thorax; the middle legs and front wings are attached to it.

honeybee

Insect living in a highly complex social order; it instinctively produces honey as a food reserve.

morphology of a honeybee: worker

wing
Organ of flight attached to the thorax. In the bee, the front and rear wings on each side are attached and beat together.

thorax
Portion of a bee's body divided into three segments housing the motor appendages, such as the legs and wings.

compound eye
Organ of vision made up of thousands of facets that perceive shapes, colors, motion and distance.

antenna
Sensory organ made up of s[...] segments and having mainly [...] and olfactory functions

stinger
Pointed retractable organ located at the terminal end of the abdomen; venom flows through it from the venom sac.

abdomen
Segmented posterior portion of a bee's body containing the major vital organs.

hind leg
Highly specialized articulated member attached to the terminal segment of the thorax; it has a motor function and is used to collect and transport pollen.

pollen basket
Hollow bordered by long curved hairs and located on the outer side of the tibia; it is used to transport pollen.

middle leg
Unspecialized articulated member attached to the central segment of the thorax; it has a motor function and is used to clean the thorax and the wings.

foreleg
Articulated member attached to the first segment of the thorax; it has a motor function and is used to clean the eyes and the antennae.

mouthparts
Appendages used for graspin[...] ingesting food and adapted t[...] collection of nectar.

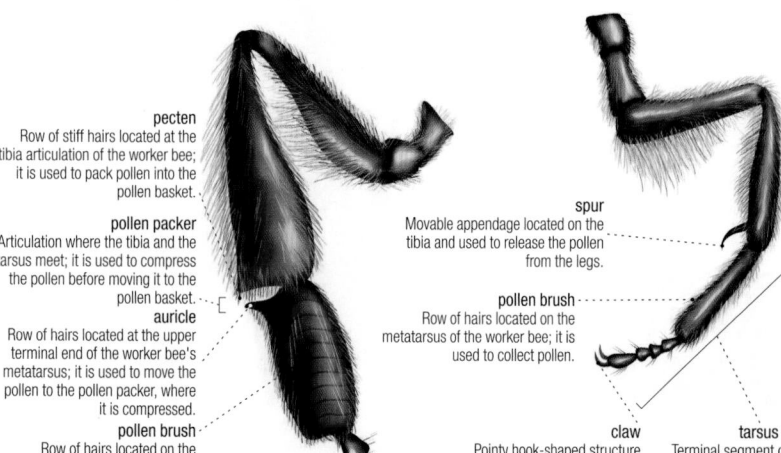

hind leg (inner surface)
Highly specialized articulated member attached to the terminal segment of the thorax; it has a motor function and is used to collect and transport pollen.

pecten
Row of stiff hairs located at the tibia articulation of the worker bee; it is used to pack pollen into the pollen basket.

pollen packer
Articulation where the tibia and the tarsus meet; it is used to compress the pollen before moving it to the pollen basket.

auricle
Row of hairs located at the upper terminal end of the worker bee's metatarsus; it is used to move the pollen to the pollen packer, where it is compressed.

pollen brush
Row of hairs located on the metatarsus of the worker bee; it is used to collect pollen.

middle leg (outer surface)
Unspecialized articulated member attached to the central segment of the thorax; it has a motor function and is used to clean the thorax and the wings.

spur
Movable appendage located on the tibia and used to release the pollen from the legs.

pollen brush
Row of hairs located on the metatarsus of the worker bee; it is used to collect pollen.

claw
Pointy hook-shaped structure attached to the tarsus and allowing the bee to grab hold of things.

tarsus
Terminal segment of the leg; it is divided into five parts and has two claws.

foreleg (outer surface)
Articulated member attached to the first segment of the thorax; it has a motor function and is used to clean the eyes and the antennae.

coxa
Anterior segment of the leg articulating with the thorax ar[...] trochanter.

trochanter
Segment of the leg between the coxa and the femur.

femur
Segment of the leg between the trochanter and the tibia.

tibia
Segment of the leg located between the femur and the metatarsus.

velum
Movable appendage located at the base of the tibia; it is used to clean the antennae.

metatarsus
First segment of the tarsus attached to the tibia; it is much larger than the other segments.

antennae cleaner
Notch covered with rigid hairs; v[...] the velum, its function is to cle[...] the antennae.

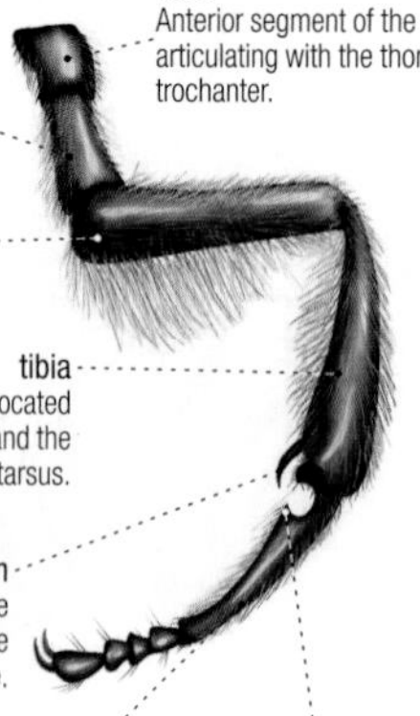

honeybee

anatomy of a honeybee

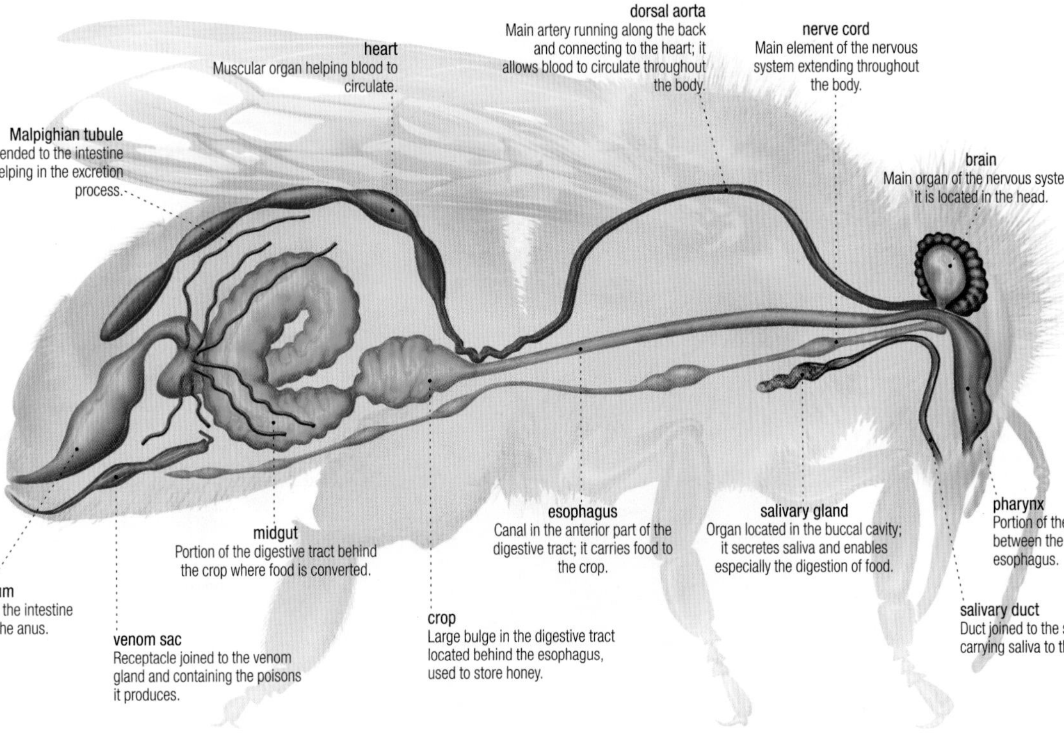

heart
Muscular organ helping blood to circulate.

dorsal aorta
Main artery running along the back and connecting to the heart; it allows blood to circulate throughout the body.

nerve cord
Main element of the nervous system extending throughout the body.

brain
Main organ of the nervous system; it is located in the head.

Malpighian tubule
ne tube appended to the intestine and helping in the excretion process.

rectum
minal end of the intestine preceding the anus.

venom sac
Receptacle joined to the venom gland and containing the poisons it produces.

midgut
Portion of the digestive tract behind the crop where food is converted.

crop
Large bulge in the digestive tract located behind the esophagus, used to store honey.

esophagus
Canal in the anterior part of the digestive tract; it carries food to the crop.

salivary gland
Organ located in the buccal cavity; it secretes saliva and enables especially the digestion of food.

salivary duct
Duct joined to the salivary gland carrying saliva to the mouth.

pharynx
Portion of the digestive tract between the mouth and the esophagus.

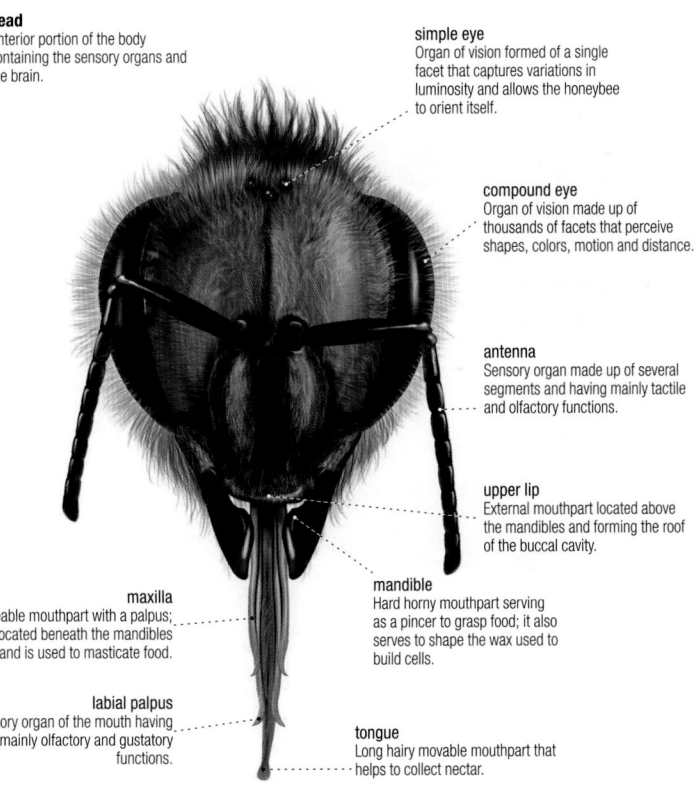

head
Anterior portion of the body containing the sensory organs and the brain.

simple eye
Organ of vision formed of a single facet that captures variations in luminosity and allows the honeybee to orient itself.

compound eye
Organ of vision made up of thousands of facets that perceive shapes, colors, motion and distance.

antenna
Sensory organ made up of several segments and having mainly tactile and olfactory functions.

upper lip
External mouthpart located above the mandibles and forming the roof of the buccal cavity.

maxilla
eable mouthpart with a palpus; located beneath the mandibles and is used to masticate food.

mandible
Hard horny mouthpart serving as a pincer to grasp food; it also serves to shape the wax used to build cells.

labial palpus
sory organ of the mouth having mainly olfactory and gustatory functions.

tongue
Long hairy movable mouthpart that helps to collect nectar.

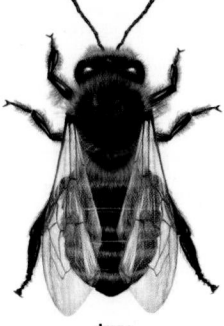

castes
The three types of bees in a hive are classified according to their function: the queen, the drones and the workers.

queen
The only reproductive female in the colony, whose sole function is to lay eggs; it is fertilized by five to 10 drones.

worker
Sterile female who does various tasks, such as searching for food, building cells and defending the colony.

drone
Stingless male bee; its only function is to reproduce.

ANIMALS

honeybee

hive
Shelter constructed to house a bee colony that produces honey and pollinates fruit trees.

exit cone
Opening through which bees exit the hive, but never enter it.

outer cover
Movable outer covering of the hive, forming its roof and frame.

super
Removable container used to collect the surplus honey reserves.

frame
Wax-coated removable wooden frame; it is used as a foundation for building combs.

alighting board
Edge of the hive allowing the bees to land and take off.

entrance
Opening of the hive allowing the bees to enter and exit.

roof
Top of the hive providing protection.

honeycomb
Cake of wax made by bees in the hive made up of cells placed side by side and filled with honey or used as brood chambers for embryos.

cell
Hexagonal cavity contained within walls of wax, the constituent unit of honeycombs.

queen excluder
Wire frame separating the brood chamber from the super; it prevents the queen from entering while allowing the worker bees to pass through.

brood chamber
Part of the hive formed of combs; its cells house the queen, eggs, larvae, pupae and reserves of pollen and honey.

hive body
Main portion of the hive enclosing the brood chamber.

entrance slide
Movable wooden slat for decreasing or enlarging the size of the entrance, mainly to prevent small animals from entering the hive.

section of a honeycomb

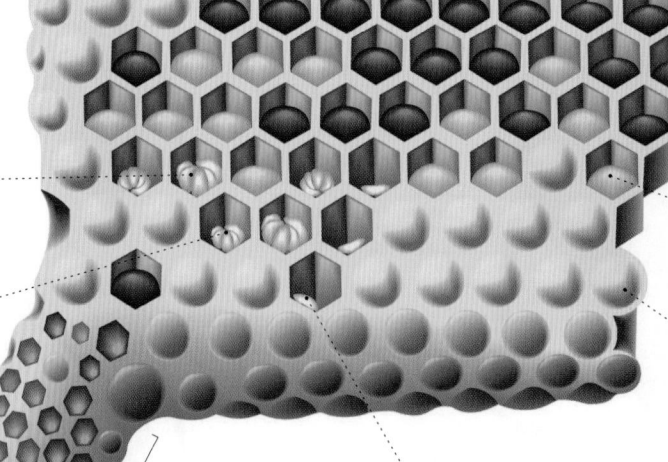

pupa
Intermediary stage between the larva and the adult bee, lasting between four and 10 days.

larva
Intermediary stage between the egg and the pupa.

honey cell
Cell in which workers store the honey they produced as larva food and winter reserves.

pollen cell
Cell in which workers store the pollen used to feed the colony.

sealed cell
Sealed with a wax cover, it might contain a pupa, honey or pollen.

queen cell
Large cell for the egg that will become the new queen.

egg
Reproductive method of certain animals: living cell with a casing and a food reserve, laid by the queen bee.

spider

Articulated arachnid with fangs and silk-producing glands; its body ranges in size from less than an inch to 3.5 in.

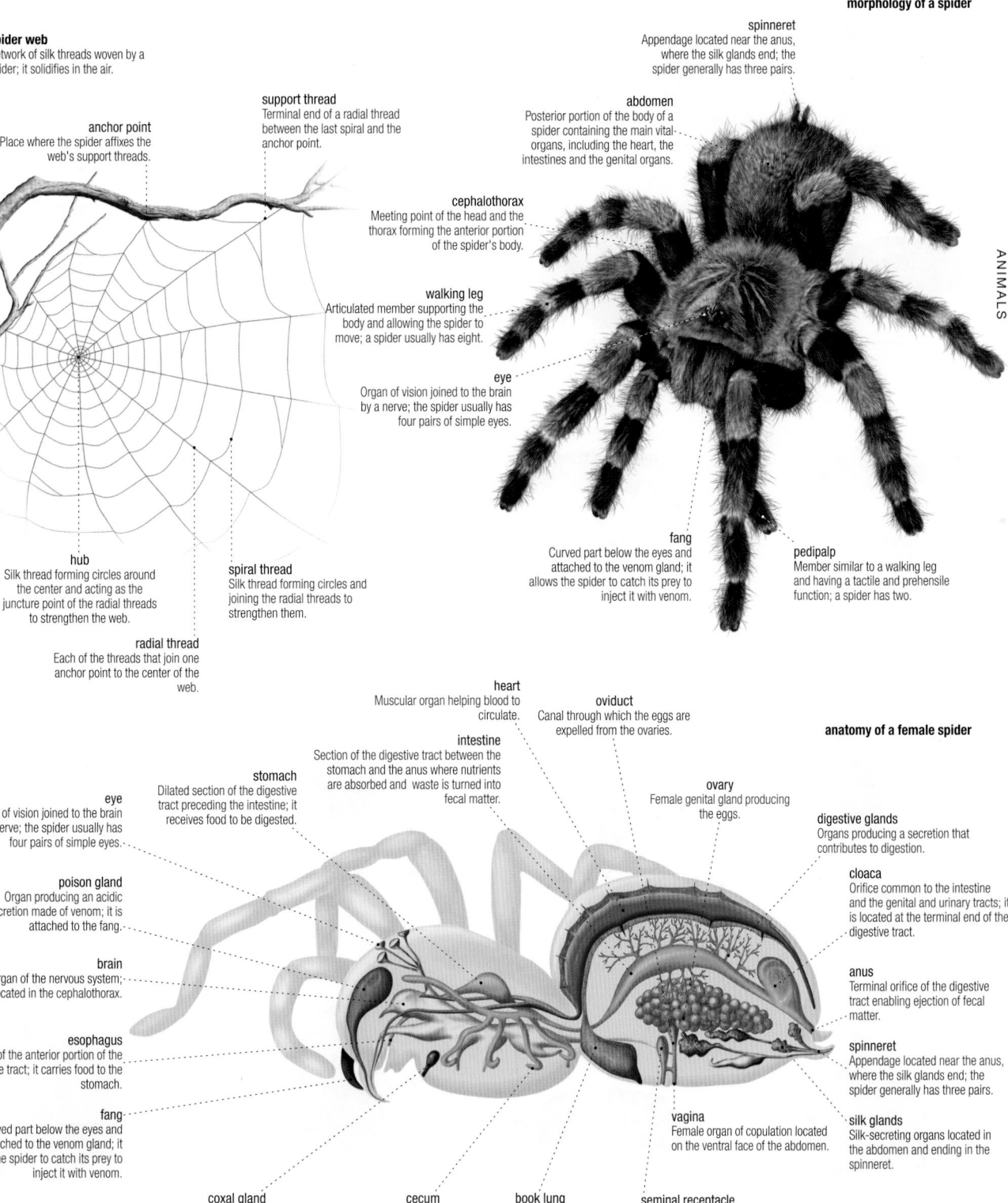

morphology of a spider

spider web
Network of silk threads woven by a spider; it solidifies in the air.

support thread
Terminal end of a radial thread between the last spiral and the anchor point.

anchor point
Place where the spider affixes the web's support threads.

spinneret
Appendage located near the anus, where the silk glands end; the spider generally has three pairs.

abdomen
Posterior portion of the body of a spider containing the main vital organs, including the heart, the intestines and the genital organs.

cephalothorax
Meeting point of the head and the thorax forming the anterior portion of the spider's body.

walking leg
Articulated member supporting the body and allowing the spider to move; a spider usually has eight.

eye
Organ of vision joined to the brain by a nerve; the spider usually has four pairs of simple eyes.

hub
Silk thread forming circles around the center and acting as the juncture point of the radial threads to strengthen the web.

spiral thread
Silk thread forming circles and joining the radial threads to strengthen them.

fang
Curved part below the eyes and attached to the venom gland; it allows the spider to catch its prey to inject it with venom.

pedipalp
Member similar to a walking leg and having a tactile and prehensile function; a spider has two.

radial thread
Each of the threads that join one anchor point to the center of the web.

heart
Muscular organ helping blood to circulate.

oviduct
Canal through which the eggs are expelled from the ovaries.

intestine
Section of the digestive tract between the stomach and the anus where nutrients are absorbed and waste is turned into fecal matter.

ovary
Female genital gland producing the eggs.

anatomy of a female spider

stomach
Dilated section of the digestive tract preceding the intestine; it receives food to be digested.

eye
Organ of vision joined to the brain by a nerve; the spider usually has four pairs of simple eyes.

digestive glands
Organs producing a secretion that contributes to digestion.

poison gland
Organ producing an acidic secretion made of venom; it is attached to the fang.

cloaca
Orifice common to the intestine and the genital and urinary tracts; it is located at the terminal end of the digestive tract.

brain
Organ of the nervous system; located in the cephalothorax.

anus
Terminal orifice of the digestive tract enabling ejection of fecal matter.

esophagus
Part of the anterior portion of the digestive tract; it carries food to the stomach.

spinneret
Appendage located near the anus, where the silk glands end; the spider generally has three pairs.

fang
Curved part below the eyes and attached to the venom gland; it allows the spider to catch its prey to inject it with venom.

silk glands
Silk-secreting organs located in the abdomen and ending in the spinneret.

vagina
Female organ of copulation located on the ventral face of the abdomen.

coxal gland
Organ appended to the hip and producing a secretion that contributes to excretion.

cecum
Lateral canal located in the anterior portion of the intestine where especially a part of digestion and fermentation take place.

book lung
Respiratory organ that helps to oxygenate the blood; the respiratory system has one or two pairs, depending on the type of spider.

seminal receptacle
Pouch where sperm is stored for fertilizing the eggs.

examples of insects

Insects: invertebrates with bodies divided into three parts; they usually have three pairs of legs, two pairs of wings and antennae.

ANIMALS

flea
Extremely small, wingless leaping insect, a parasite of certain mammals, birds and humans; it stings them to feed off their blood.

louse
Small wingless insect, a parasite of humans, mammals, birds and certain plants.

termite
Social insect that lives in hill colonies; it eats away at wood with its crushing mouthparts.

mosquito
Insect with two wings and long antennae; the female stings humans and animals to feed off their blood.

tsetse fly
Stinging African insect, a parasite of mammals, birds and humans; it is best known for transmitting sleeping sickness.

furniture beetle
Small insect whose larva feeds on lumber and dead wood.

ladybug
Brightly colored round-bodied insect that preys on aphids and mealybugs.

fly
Stocky insect of drab or metallic coloring and having a proboscis, two wings and short antennae; there are numerous species.

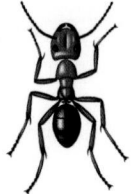

ant
Small social insect living in a highly complex colony; it has developed jaws and includes wingless and winged species. It consumes mainly insect pests.

burying beetle
Insect that lays its eggs on dead animals or decomposing matter, which it buries; the egg cache gives off a strong musky smell.

yellow jacket
Social insect; the female has a venomous sting that is painful.

hornet
Large wasp with a painful and dangerous sting; it feeds mainly on insects and fruit.

horsefly
Large swift-moving fly that is widely dispersed; the female stings animals and occasionally humans to feed off their blood.

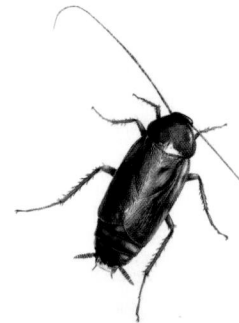

cockroach
Scurrying flat-bodied nocturnal insect that is widely dispersed; some species live in human dwellings, feeding on waste matter. It emits an unpleasant odor.

earwig
Long, flat insect whose abdomen ends at the rear in two pincers. It usually lives in cool and dark places.

stinkbug
Small flat-bodied land insect that stings and sucks and is a parasite of humans, animals and plants; it releases an unpleasant odor as a defense.

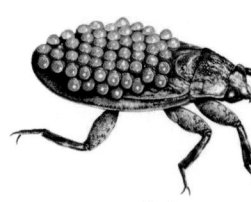

water bug
Large carnivorous insect with a lean flat body; it is widely dispersed and lives in aquatic environments.

clothes moth
Small whitish moth whose larvae eat linens and furs.

cockchafer
Common garden insect with fringed antennae; it eats leaves and tree roots. Infestations of this pest can cause serious damage.

bumblebee
Plump hairy insect related to the bee; it lives in colonies and produces honey.

scarab beetle
Insect with unusual antennae that end in segment made up of flattened plates which give it a club-shaped appearance. The offspring of some species feed on excrement.

examples of insects

ANIMALS

atlas moth
Large nocturnal butterfly with colored wings and a wingspan that can reach more than 1 foot; it is found mainly in Southeast Asia.

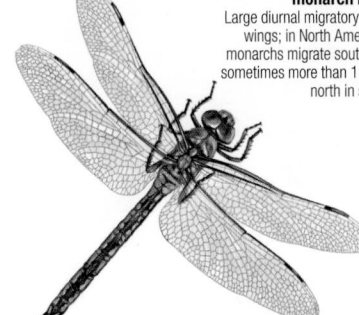

monarch butterfly
Large diurnal migratory butterfly with spotted wings; in North America, thousands of monarchs migrate southward in the autumn, sometimes more than 1,800 miles, and return north in spring.

cicada
Large sap-sucking insect; the male produces a shrill monotone sound in hot weather.

mantis
Long-bodied carnivorous insect found in tropical regions and blending in with its surroundings; its pincer-shaped front legs have spines.

dragonfly
Long-bodied carnivorous insect found near water, having four rigid wings and the largest compound eyes of any insect.

peppered moth
Large butterfly with delicate wings, active at night or at dawn; its caterpillar lives in birch trees, causing major damage.

bow-winged grasshopper
Hopping insect with short antennae and powerful hind legs; it lives especially in hot climates and emits an intense lively song.

water strider
Widespread carnivorous insect with a long thin body and six legs, of which the four longest help it to move across water.

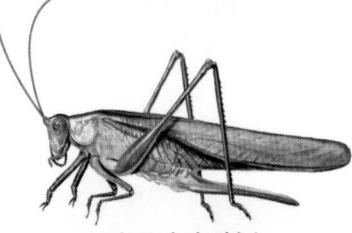

great green bush-cricket
Omnivorous leaping insect with long antennae, growing to 1 to 2 inches in length; the male produces a shrill sound.

examples of arachnids

Arachnids: invertebrates usually with four pairs of legs and two pairs of appendages attached to their heads.

crab spider
Widespread small arachnid that moves sideways and has powerful front legs; it changes color to catch its prey.

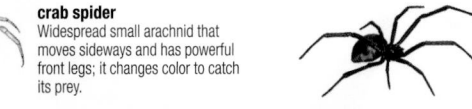

black widow
Carnivorous arachnid. The bite of the female injects a toxic venom.

scorpion
Relatively large carnivorous arachnid with spines, usually found on land; it has pincers and its abdomen ends in a tail with a venomous stinger.

garden spider
Arachnid with a bulging stomach that weaves large webs and is commonly found in fields and gardens; its various species can be found around the world.

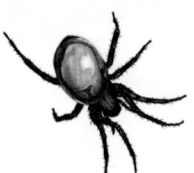

tick
Extremely small arachnid, parasite of animals and occasionally humans; it can transmit infectious diseases.

water spider
Aquatic arachnid found in Eurasia; to live in the water, it weaves a kind of bell that it fills with air and carries along on the hairs of its abdomen.

Mexican red-kneed tarantula
Large hairy arachnid found in Mexico, having a painful but usually innocuous bite; it lives underground in a closed compartment or cocoon.

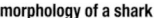

ANIMALS

shark

Large cartilaginous carnivorous fish with a tapered body and extremely powerful toothed jaws; it rarely attacks humans.

morphology of a shark

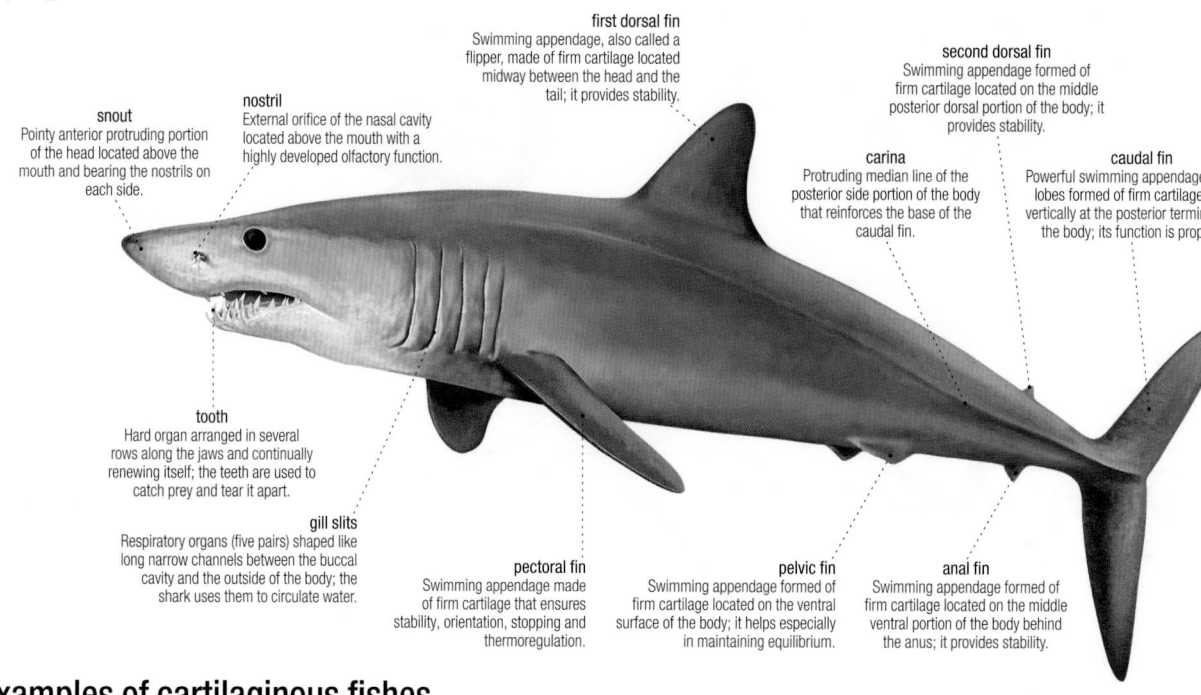

first dorsal fin
Swimming appendage, also called a flipper, made of firm cartilage located midway between the head and the tail; it provides stability.

second dorsal fin
Swimming appendage formed of firm cartilage located on the middle posterior dorsal portion of the body; it provides stability.

snout
Pointy anterior protruding portion of the head located above the mouth and bearing the nostrils on each side.

nostril
External orifice of the nasal cavity located above the mouth with a highly developed olfactory function.

carina
Protruding median line of the posterior side portion of the body that reinforces the base of the caudal fin.

caudal fin
Powerful swimming appendage w lobes formed of firm cartilage lo vertically at the posterior termina the body; its function is propu

tooth
Hard organ arranged in several rows along the jaws and continually renewing itself; the teeth are used to catch prey and tear it apart.

gill slits
Respiratory organs (five pairs) shaped like long narrow channels between the buccal cavity and the outside of the body; the shark uses them to circulate water.

pectoral fin
Swimming appendage made of firm cartilage that ensures stability, orientation, stopping and thermoregulation.

pelvic fin
Swimming appendage formed of firm cartilage located on the ventral surface of the body; it helps especially in maintaining equilibrium.

anal fin
Swimming appendage formed of firm cartilage located on the middle ventral portion of the body behind the anus; it provides stability.

examples of cartilaginous fishes

There are over 1,000 species of cartilaginous fish.

skate
Flat-bodied cartilaginous fish that feeds on crustaceans and mollusks.

spiny dogfish
Small edible shark, measuring less than 6 ft in length. Each of its two dorsal fins contains a sharp and venomous spine.

sawfish
Warm water cartilaginous fish with a long snout that can reach up to 7 ft in length.

tiger shark
Large predatory cartilaginous fish, usually between 10 and 13 ft long and found in tropical and temperate seas.

great white shark
Large cartilaginous fish, solitary predator, usually between 13 and 20 ft long. It has 4 to 6 rows of cutting teeth and highly developed hearing and smell.

perch

Bony carnivorous freshwater fish with an oval body and a spiny dorsal fin; its flesh is highly prized.

anatomy of a perch

otolith
Small calcareous structure of the inner ear ensuring the fish's equilibrium in the water.

brain
Main organ of the nervous system that is made up of nerve centers; it is located in the upper portion of the head and is protected by the skull.

olfactory nerve
...anial cord connecting the brain to the olfactory bulb.

olfactory bulb
...argement of the anterior ...al end of the olfactory nerve ...e its roots come together.

spinal cord
Component of the nervous system made up of a soft fatty substance and forming a cylindrical stem inside the spinal column.

skull
Bony structure enclosing and protecting the brain.

kidney
Organ that eliminates metabolic waste and maintains the pressure of internal fluids.

air bladder
Flexible air-filled sac located above the viscera; it allows the fish to remain buoyant at a specific depth.

urinary bladder
Reservoir in which urine from the kidneys collects before being evacuated through the urogenital aperture.

neural spine
Bony stem of the nervous system connected to the spinal column and forming the skeleton.

spinal column
Movable bony axis made up of various parts articulating with each other (vertebrae); it supports the skeleton and contains the spinal cord.

muscle segment
Muscular segment of the posterior portion of the body; its zigzag arrangement contributes to efficient motion.

urogenital aperture
Opening common to the genital and urinary tracts allowing the evacuation of gametes and urine.

anus
Terminal orifice of the digestive tract enabling ejection of fecal matter.

tongue
...gated movable mouthpart ...ng a gustatory function; it ...s the fish to swallow its food.

ventral aorta
...Canal circulating the blood from the heart to the gills, then on through the head and the rest of the body.

gills
...Respiratory and excretory organs (four pairs) each formed of two layers of filaments; they enable water to exchange oxygen and ammonium as it circulates over the gills.

heart
Muscular organ helping blood to circulate.

esophagus
Canal of the anterior portion of the digestive tract; it carries food to the stomach.

stomach
Dilated section of the digestive tract preceding the intestine; it receives food to be digested.

intestine
Section of the digestive tract between the stomach and the anus where absorption of nutrients is carried out and waste is transformed into fecal matter.

spleen
Organ of the circulatory system where impurities in the blood are destroyed.

pyloric cecum
Lateral canal of the digestive tract where a part of digestion mainly occurs, as well as fermentation.

eggs
In fish, the female produces eggs in the ovaries and the male produces soft roe in the testicles; the eggs and roe are expelled into the water, where fertilization occurs.

liver
Viscera that secretes bile, among other substances; bile helps digestion.

first dorsal fin
Swimming appendage formed of a membrane and usually prickly rays located on the middle anterior dorsal portion of the body; it provides stability.

second dorsal fin
Swimming appendage formed of a membrane and rays located on the middle posterior dorsal portion of the body; it provides stability.

ANIMALS

perch

morphology of a perch
Perch: bony carnivorous freshwater fish with an oval body and a spiny dorsal fin; its flesh is highly prized.

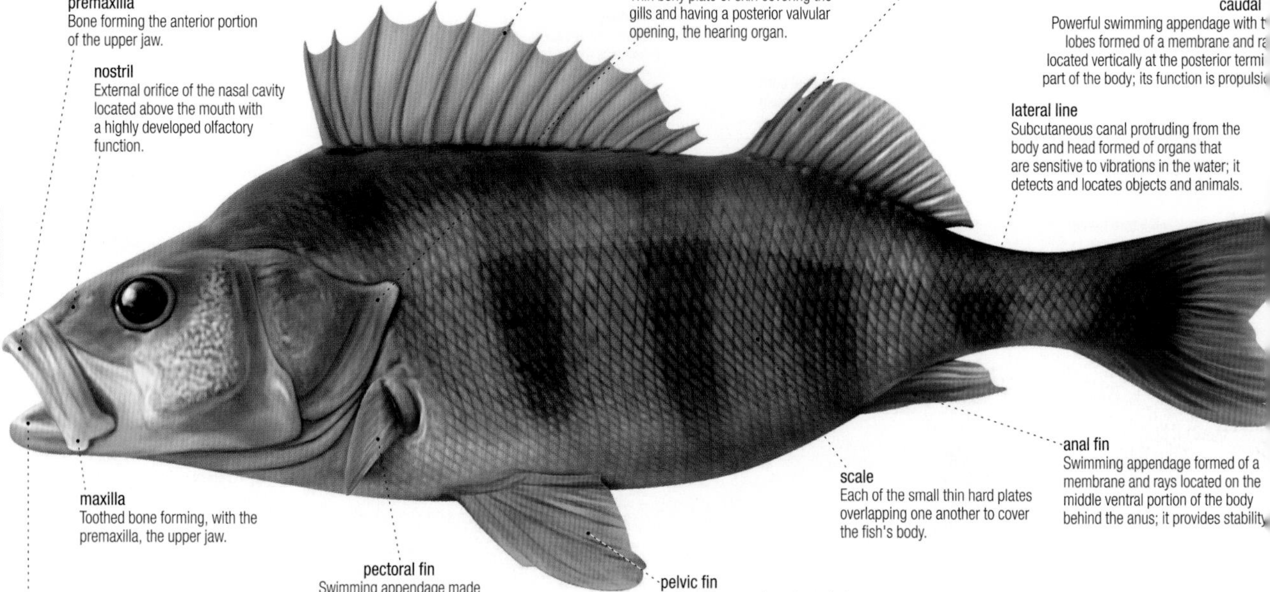

spiny ray
Hard sharp part supporting the membrane of the first dorsal fin.

operculum
Thin bony plate of skin covering the gills and having a posterior valvular opening, the hearing organ.

soft ray
Long Y-shaped flexible part supporting the membrane of the second dorsal fin.

caudal
Powerful swimming appendage with t[...] lobes formed of a membrane and ra[...] located vertically at the posterior termi[...] part of the body; its function is propulsio[...]

premaxilla
Bone forming the anterior portion of the upper jaw.

nostril
External orifice of the nasal cavity located above the mouth with a highly developed olfactory function.

lateral line
Subcutaneous canal protruding from the body and head formed of organs that are sensitive to vibrations in the water; it detects and locates objects and animals.

maxilla
Toothed bone forming, with the premaxilla, the upper jaw.

anal fin
Swimming appendage formed of a membrane and rays located on the middle ventral portion of the body behind the anus; it provides stability[...]

scale
Each of the small thin hard plates overlapping one another to cover the fish's body.

mandible
Toothed bone forming the lower jaw.

pectoral fin
Swimming appendage made of bone that ensures stability, orientation, stopping and thermoregulation.

pelvic fin
Swimming appendage formed of a membrane and rays located on the ventral surface of the body; it helps especially in maintaining equilibrium.

examples of bony fishes

With over 20,000 known species, bony fish are the largest group of fish.

goldfish
Small freshwater fish originally from Asia, often kept in aquariums.

piranha
Small carnivorous fish with powerful jaws armed with pointed teeth. Found in the rivers of South America and especially in the Amazon river.

clown fish
Small brightly colored fish found on Indian coral reefs. Lives in symbiosis with sea anemones.

sunfish
Large ocean fish than can weigh up to 2,200 lbs, inhabiting tropical and temperate waters.

blue marlin
Large bony fish found in warm and temperate seas, living near the surface of the water.

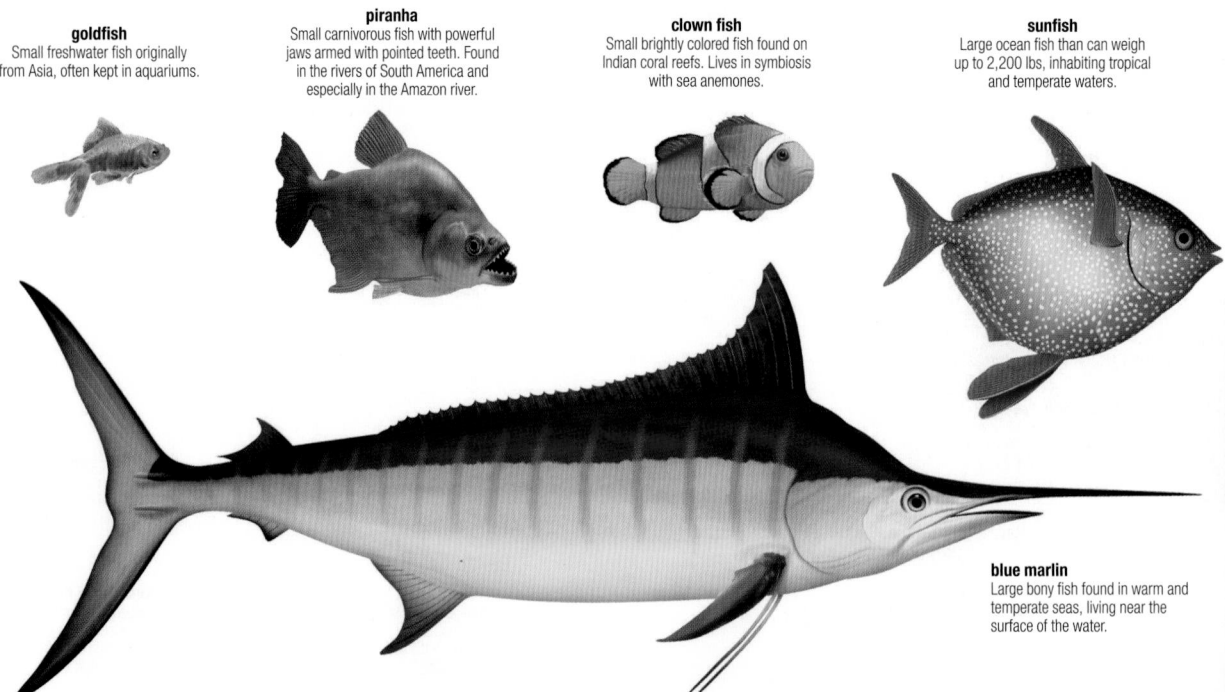

examples of bony fishes

flying fish
Fish found in warm oceans able to leap and glide out of the water with the aid of its large pectoral fins.

discus
Amazonian freshwater fish, whose sides are marbled with patterns that change color. It is popular as an aquarium fish.

deep sea anglerfish
Bony fish inhabiting deep seas, having a dorsal fin modified into a stem on the tip of which is a luminescent lure for attracting prey.

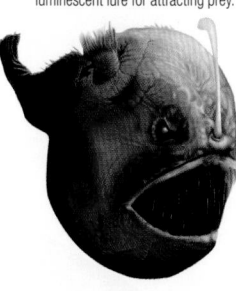

porcupine fish
Carnivorous fish living in warm seas. It is covered in spiny scales and can inflate itself to become much larger.

lungfish
Primitive bony fish with a lung allowing it to breathe air and even to crawl on mud.

catfish
Omnivorous scaleless bony fish with barbels resembling a cat's whiskers. It generally lives and feeds at the bottom of freshwater or coastal salt water.

sea horse
Small fish that swims in a vertical position and anchors itself to sea grasses with its tail. The male incubates the eggs in a ventral pocket.

lantern fish
Small marine fish able to emit light by chemical reaction. Lives in deep water.

bluestreak cleaner wrasse
Edible fish living in sea grasses and rocky bottoms, having thick lips it uses to clean parasites off of larger fish.

parrot fish
Brightly colored tropical marine fish with a large jaw able to grind up shells and coral rock.

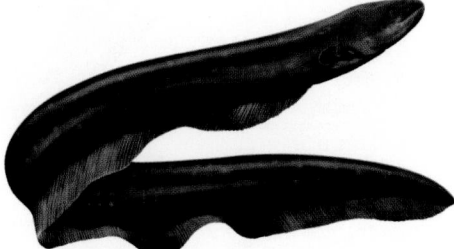
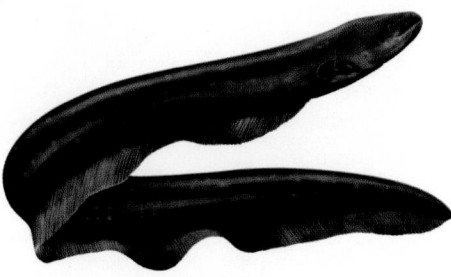

electric eel
Freshwater fish with no dorsal fin; it has organs capable of producing electric charges meant to paralyze its prey.

frog

Cold-blooded freshwater amphibian with smooth moist skin and powerful back legs for hopping and swimming.

ANIMALS

morphology of a frog

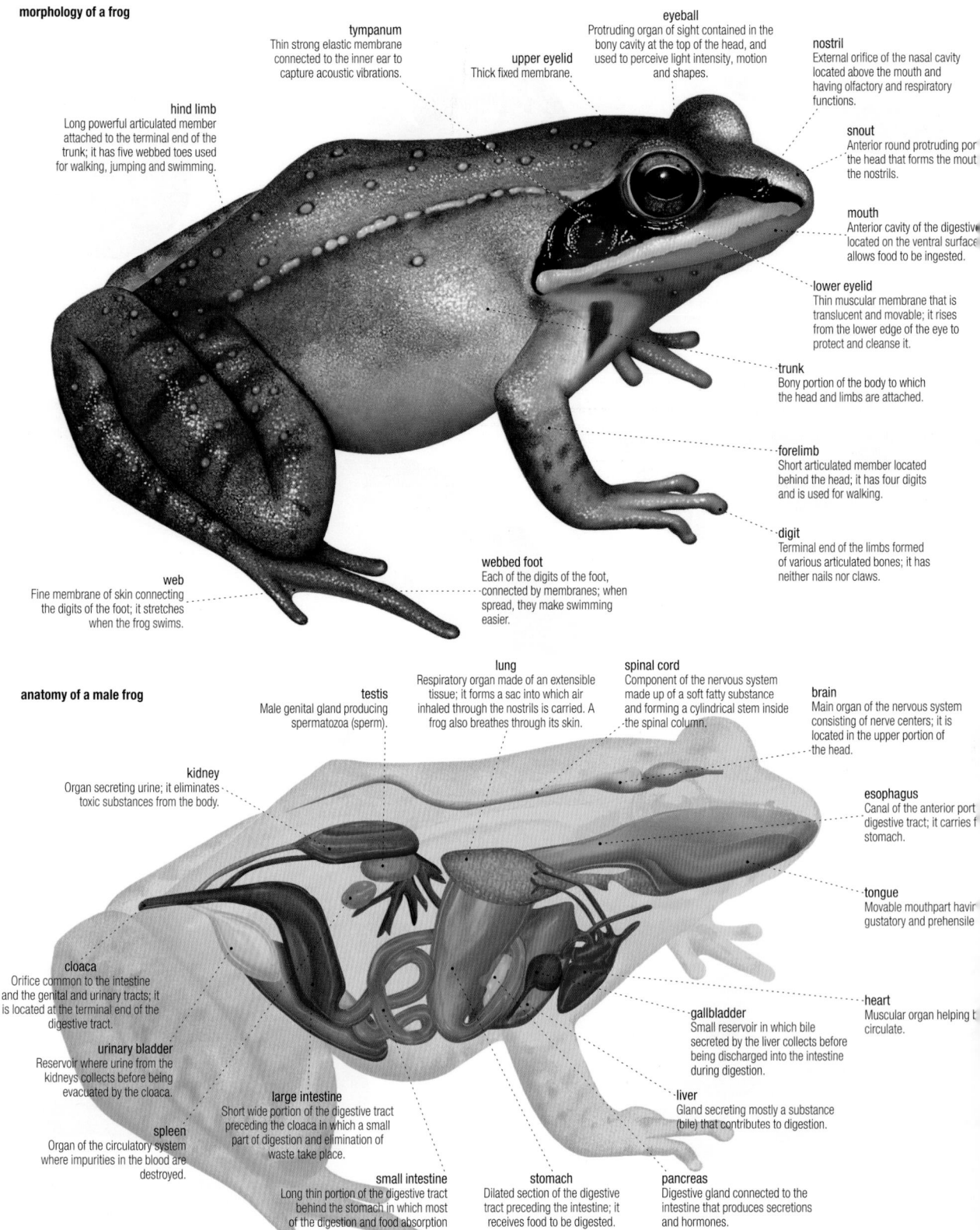

tympanum
Thin strong elastic membrane connected to the inner ear to capture acoustic vibrations.

eyeball
Protruding organ of sight contained in the bony cavity at the top of the head, and used to perceive light intensity, motion and shapes.

upper eyelid
Thick fixed membrane.

nostril
External orifice of the nasal cavity located above the mouth and having olfactory and respiratory functions.

hind limb
Long powerful articulated member attached to the terminal end of the trunk; it has five webbed toes used for walking, jumping and swimming.

snout
Anterior round protruding por the head that forms the mout the nostrils.

mouth
Anterior cavity of the digestiv located on the ventral surface allows food to be ingested.

lower eyelid
Thin muscular membrane that is translucent and movable; it rises from the lower edge of the eye to protect and cleanse it.

trunk
Bony portion of the body to which the head and limbs are attached.

forelimb
Short articulated member located behind the head; it has four digits and is used for walking.

digit
Terminal end of the limbs formed of various articulated bones; it has neither nails nor claws.

web
Fine membrane of skin connecting the digits of the foot; it stretches when the frog swims.

webbed foot
Each of the digits of the foot, connected by membranes; when spread, they make swimming easier.

anatomy of a male frog

testis
Male genital gland producing spermatozoa (sperm).

lung
Respiratory organ made of an extensible tissue; it forms a sac into which air inhaled through the nostrils is carried. A frog also breathes through its skin.

spinal cord
Component of the nervous system made up of a soft fatty substance and forming a cylindrical stem inside the spinal column.

brain
Main organ of the nervous system consisting of nerve centers; it is located in the upper portion of the head.

kidney
Organ secreting urine; it eliminates toxic substances from the body.

esophagus
Canal of the anterior port digestive tract; it carries f stomach.

tongue
Movable mouthpart havir gustatory and prehensile

cloaca
Orifice common to the intestine and the genital and urinary tracts; it is located at the terminal end of the digestive tract.

gallbladder
Small reservoir in which bile secreted by the liver collects before being discharged into the intestine during digestion.

heart
Muscular organ helping b circulate.

urinary bladder
Reservoir where urine from the kidneys collects before being evacuated by the cloaca.

liver
Gland secreting mostly a substance (bile) that contributes to digestion.

spleen
Organ of the circulatory system where impurities in the blood are destroyed.

large intestine
Short wide portion of the digestive tract preceding the cloaca in which a small part of digestion and elimination of waste take place.

small intestine
Long thin portion of the digestive tract behind the stomach in which most of the digestion and food absorption take place.

stomach
Dilated section of the digestive tract preceding the intestine; it receives food to be digested.

pancreas
Digestive gland connected to the intestine that produces secretions and hormones.

frog

ilium
flat bone articulating backward the sacral vertebra; the juncture e ilium and the ischium is where the hind limb is attached.

sacral vertebra
Short vertebra located in the posterior portion of the central bony axis and articulating with the ilium.

coracoid
Ventral bone articulating with the sternum; the juncture of the scapula, clavicle and coracoid is the point where the hind limb is attached.

scapula
Large flat back bone.

vertebrae
Short bony parts of the dorsal area of the body forming the central bony axis.

atlas
First cervical vertebra supporting the head and supported by the axis.

urostyle
g bone of the posterior portion e central bony axis; it is formed by several fused vertebrae.

frontoparietal
Large flat bone of the upper anterior portion of the cranium.

ischium
Bone situated behind the ilium.

maxilla
Toothed bone comprising the upper jaw.

femur
Long bone of the hind limb iculating with the ilium and the tibiofibula.

mandible
Smooth curved movable bone comprising the lower jaw.

tibiofibula
ted between the femur and the us, the tibia and the fibula fuse to form one long bone.

humerus
Long bone of the forelimb articulating with the scapula and the radio-ulna.

clavicle
Long bone located between the sternum and the scapula.

tarsus
Part of the hind limb formed of everal short bones; it is located between the tibiofibula and the metatarsus.

phalanges
Bones articulating to form the skeleton of the digits.

metatarsus
t of the hind limb formed of five g parallel bones; it connects the arsus with the first phalanges of the digits.

phalanges
Bones articulating to form the skeleton of the digits.

sternum
Long flat bone located in the mid- ventral portion of the body; the clavicle and the coracoid, in particular, are attached to it.

radio-ulna
Located between the humerus and the metacarpus, the radius and the ulna fuse to form one long bone.

metacarpus
Part of the forelimb formed of four long bones; it connects the radio-ulna to the first phalanges of the digits.

---

life cycle of the frog
The stages of development are the egg, the tadpole and the adult; each stage usually lasts several weeks, but can last up to two years in some species.

eggs
bryonic stage of the frog resulting when the egg is fertilized by the sperm.

tadpole
Aquatic larva of the frog having a large head and a slender body ending in a tail; it breathes through gills.

hind limb
The hind limbs appear after the gills.

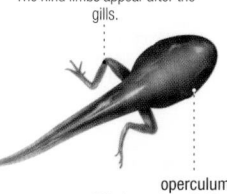

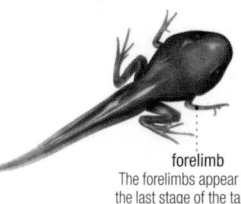

external gills
Respiratory organs that filter water and take in food particles; they are later replaced by internal gills.

operculum
Thin bony plate of skin covering the gills and having a posterior valvular opening, the hearing organ.

forelimb
The forelimbs appear during the last stage of the tadpole's metamorphosis.

---

examples of amphibians

There are about 6,500 species of amphibians divided into three main groups, depending on whether or not they have a tail and limbs.

common frog
Squat tailless amphibian usually found on land, mostly in Europe; it feeds on various small animals.

tree frog
Small tailless, usually insectivorous amphibian found mostly in trees near water; its digits are fitted with suction cups.

salamander
urnal amphibian, mainly orous, with a tail; there are d and aquatic species.

wood frog
Tailless amphibian found mostly in the woods of North America; it feeds on various small animals.

common toad
Tailless nocturnal insectivorous amphibian usually found on land and not very adept at jumping; its body is covered with small outgrowths.

newt
bian with a flat tail found n freshwater and usually feeding on insects.

bullfrog
Large omnivorous amphibian from eastern North America, that lives mostly in water (lakes, ponds, and marshes).

northern leopard frog
Tailless, mostly nocturnal amphibian with a spotted body that is covered with ridges; it lives mainly in North America.

adhesive disk
Adhesive disk surrounded by a ring; it is located at the terminal end of the limbs and used for anchoring.

snake

Legless reptile with a very long cylindrical body and tail, moving by undulation; there are about 2,700 species.

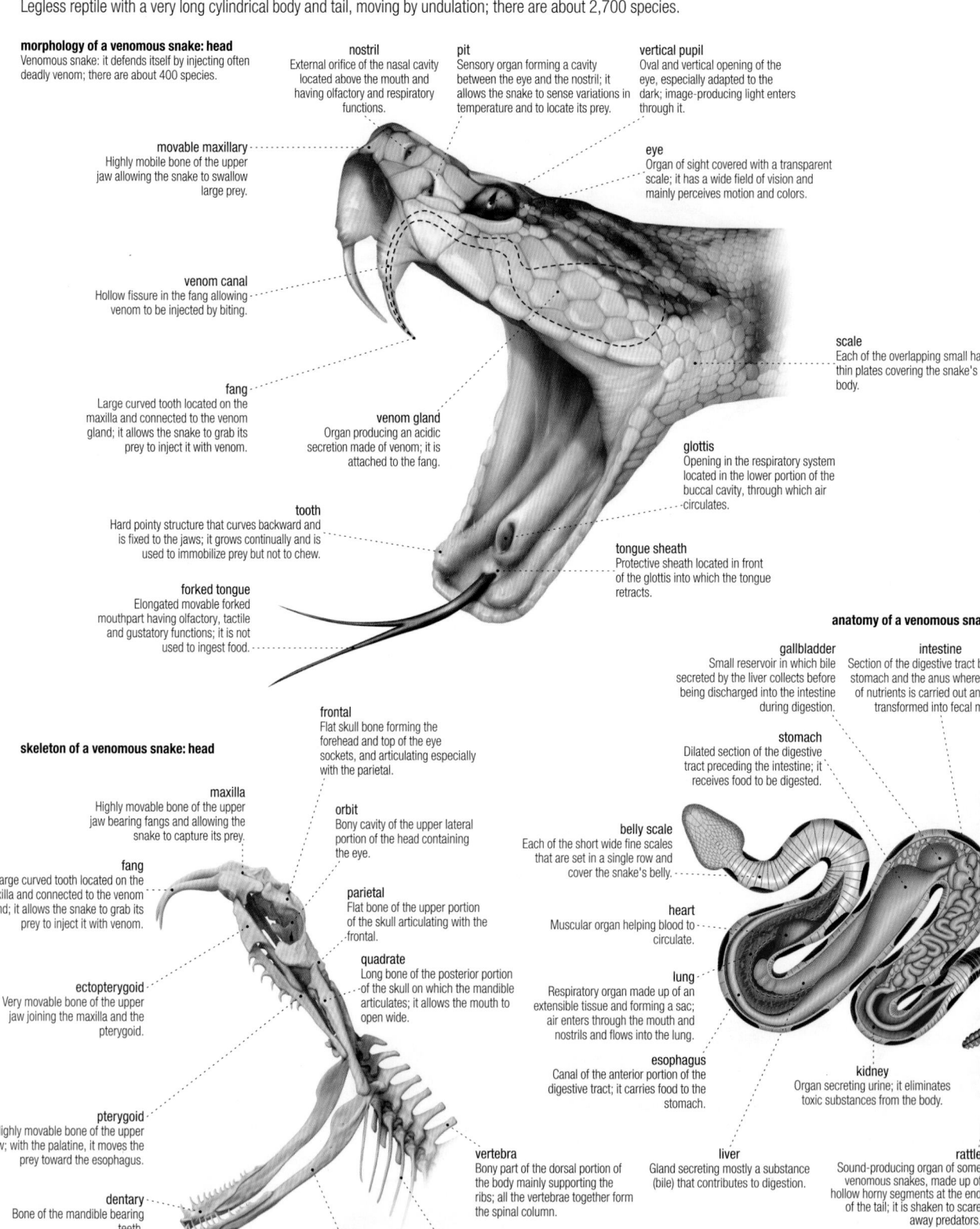

morphology of a venomous snake: head
Venomous snake: it defends itself by injecting often deadly venom; there are about 400 species.

nostril
External orifice of the nasal cavity located above the mouth and having olfactory and respiratory functions.

pit
Sensory organ forming a cavity between the eye and the nostril; it allows the snake to sense variations in temperature and to locate its prey.

vertical pupil
Oval and vertical opening of the eye, especially adapted to the dark; image-producing light enters through it.

movable maxillary
Highly mobile bone of the upper jaw allowing the snake to swallow large prey.

eye
Organ of sight covered with a transparent scale; it has a wide field of vision and mainly perceives motion and colors.

venom canal
Hollow fissure in the fang allowing venom to be injected by biting.

scale
Each of the overlapping small hard thin plates covering the snake's body.

fang
Large curved tooth located on the maxilla and connected to the venom gland; it allows the snake to grab its prey to inject it with venom.

venom gland
Organ producing an acidic secretion made of venom; it is attached to the fang.

glottis
Opening in the respiratory system located in the lower portion of the buccal cavity, through which air circulates.

tooth
Hard pointy structure that curves backward and is fixed to the jaws; it grows continually and is used to immobilize prey but not to chew.

tongue sheath
Protective sheath located in front of the glottis into which the tongue retracts.

forked tongue
Elongated movable forked mouthpart having olfactory, tactile and gustatory functions; it is not used to ingest food.

anatomy of a venomous snake

gallbladder
Small reservoir in which bile secreted by the liver collects before being discharged into the intestine during digestion.

intestine
Section of the digestive tract between stomach and the anus where absorption of nutrients is carried out and waste transformed into fecal matter.

frontal
Flat skull bone forming the forehead and top of the eye sockets, and articulating especially with the parietal.

stomach
Dilated section of the digestive tract preceding the intestine; it receives food to be digested.

skeleton of a venomous snake: head

maxilla
Highly movable bone of the upper jaw bearing fangs and allowing the snake to capture its prey.

orbit
Bony cavity of the upper lateral portion of the head containing the eye.

belly scale
Each of the short wide fine scales that are set in a single row and cover the snake's belly.

fang
Large curved tooth located on the maxilla and connected to the venom gland; it allows the snake to grab its prey to inject it with venom.

parietal
Flat bone of the upper portion of the skull articulating with the frontal.

heart
Muscular organ helping blood to circulate.

ectopterygoid
Very movable bone of the upper jaw joining the maxilla and the pterygoid.

quadrate
Long bone of the posterior portion of the skull on which the mandible articulates; it allows the mouth to open wide.

lung
Respiratory organ made up of an extensible tissue and forming a sac; air enters through the mouth and nostrils and flows into the lung.

kidney
Organ secreting urine; it eliminates toxic substances from the body.

esophagus
Canal of the anterior portion of the digestive tract; it carries food to the stomach.

pterygoid
Highly movable bone of the upper jaw; with the palatine, it moves the prey toward the esophagus.

liver
Gland secreting mostly a substance (bile) that contributes to digestion.

rattle
Sound-producing organ of some venomous snakes, made up of hollow horny segments at the end of the tail; it is shaken to scare away predators.

dentary
Bone of the mandible bearing teeth.

vertebra
Bony part of the dorsal portion of the body mainly supporting the ribs; all the vertebrae together form the spinal column.

tail
Thin elongated terminal end of the body.

mandible
Toothed bone forming the lower jaw.

rib
Highly movable curved bone articulating on the vertebrae; it plays a role in locomotion by providing support on the ground.

turtle

Squat land or aquatic reptile with short legs and bearing a carapace into which it retracts; there are about 250 species.

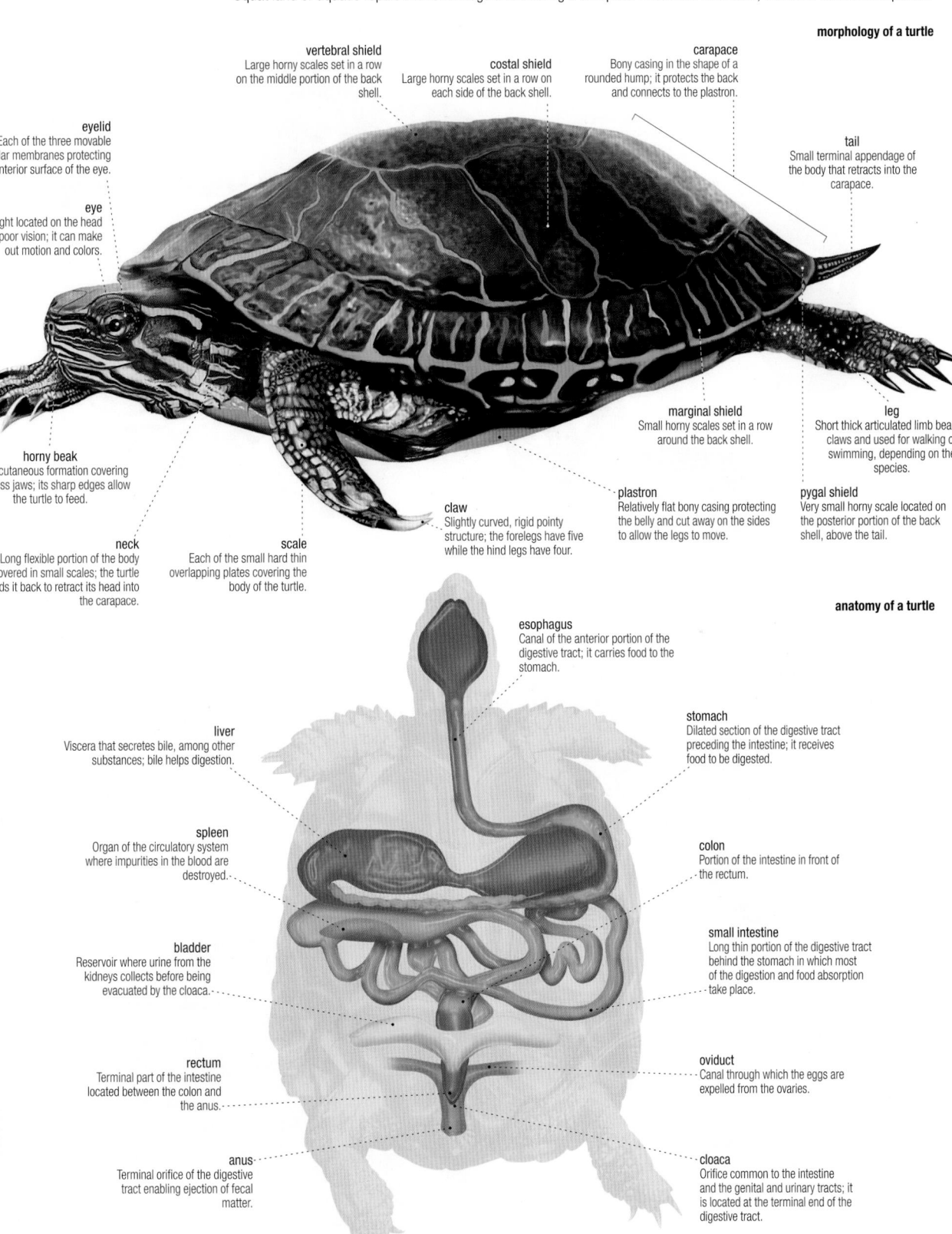

morphology of a turtle

vertebral shield
Large horny scales set in a row on the middle portion of the back shell.

costal shield
Large horny scales set in a row on each side of the back shell.

carapace
Bony casing in the shape of a rounded hump; it protects the back and connects to the plastron.

tail
Small terminal appendage of the body that retracts into the carapace.

eyelid
Each of the three movable ular membranes protecting anterior surface of the eye.

eye
sight located on the head poor vision; it can make out motion and colors.

horny beak
cutaneous formation covering ess jaws; its sharp edges allow the turtle to feed.

neck
Long flexible portion of the body covered in small scales; the turtle olds it back to retract its head into the carapace.

scale
Each of the small hard thin overlapping plates covering the body of the turtle.

claw
Slightly curved, rigid pointy structure; the forelegs have five while the hind legs have four.

marginal shield
Small horny scales set in a row around the back shell.

plastron
Relatively flat bony casing protecting the belly and cut away on the sides to allow the legs to move.

leg
Short thick articulated limb bearing claws and used for walking or swimming, depending on the species.

pygal shield
Very small horny scale located on the posterior portion of the back shell, above the tail.

ANIMALS

anatomy of a turtle

esophagus
Canal of the anterior portion of the digestive tract; it carries food to the stomach.

liver
Viscera that secretes bile, among other substances; bile helps digestion.

stomach
Dilated section of the digestive tract preceding the intestine; it receives food to be digested.

spleen
Organ of the circulatory system where impurities in the blood are destroyed.

colon
Portion of the intestine in front of the rectum.

small intestine
Long thin portion of the digestive tract behind the stomach in which most of the digestion and food absorption take place.

bladder
Reservoir where urine from the kidneys collects before being evacuated by the cloaca.

rectum
Terminal part of the intestine located between the colon and the anus.

oviduct
Canal through which the eggs are expelled from the ovaries.

anus
Terminal orifice of the digestive tract enabling ejection of fecal matter.

cloaca
Orifice common to the intestine and the genital and urinary tracts; it is located at the terminal end of the digestive tract.

examples of reptiles

Reptiles: cold-blooded vertebrates covered in scales (more than 8,000 species) having limbs that are sometimes atrophied or absent.

cobra
Venomous snake found in tropical regions of Asia and Africa; it inflates its neck when threatened.

viper
Venomous snake found in hot arid regions of Eurasia and Africa with a flat triangular head and short tail; its bite can be fatal.

coral snake
Slender venomous snake of the Americas living under rocks or hidden in the ground; its bite can be fatal.

garter snake
Widespread nonvenomous snake with a slightly flat oval head; its tail is longer than that of the viper.

boa constrictor
Medium-sized nonvenomous snake found in hot regions of the Americas; it lives mainly in trees or in the water and kills its prey by strangulation.

rattlesnake
Venomous land snake of the Americas; it rattles its scaly tail to warn off enemies.

python
Large nocturnal nonvenomous snake found in hot regions of Asia, Africa and Australia; it often lives in trees and kills its prey by strangulation.

anaconda
Large nonvenomous snake found in tropical regions of South America and living mainly in the water; it may sometimes reach up to 30 ft in length.

ANIMALS

gecko
nocturnal tree-dwelling lizard
found mainly in warm climates; its
digits often have adhesive pads
modified for climbing.

green lizard
Widespread diurnal and mainly
insectivorous land reptile with a
long brittle tail.

chameleon
Insectivorous lizard of Africa and
India with a prehensile tail; it lives
in trees and can change color to
hide itself.

monitor lizard
Large diurnal carnivorous lizard with an
elongated head found in hot regions of
Africa, Asia and Australia; there are land
and aquatic species.

iguana
Giant lizard found in tropical
regions of the Americas and the
Pacific islands and having a spiny
dorsal crest; it lives mainly in trees.

caiman
Medium-sized aquatic and land
reptile found in Central and South
America; it is less aggressive than
the crocodile and the alligator.

alligator
Short-legged aquatic and land reptile
found in North America and China; its
head is shorter and wider than that of
the crocodile.

crocodile
Aquatic and land reptile found in hot
regions; it has an elongated head,
strong jaws, short legs and a powerful
tail.

ANIMALS

bird

Vertebrate with a feather-covered body and a toothless bill; its forelimbs (wings) are usually adapted for flight.

morphology of a bird

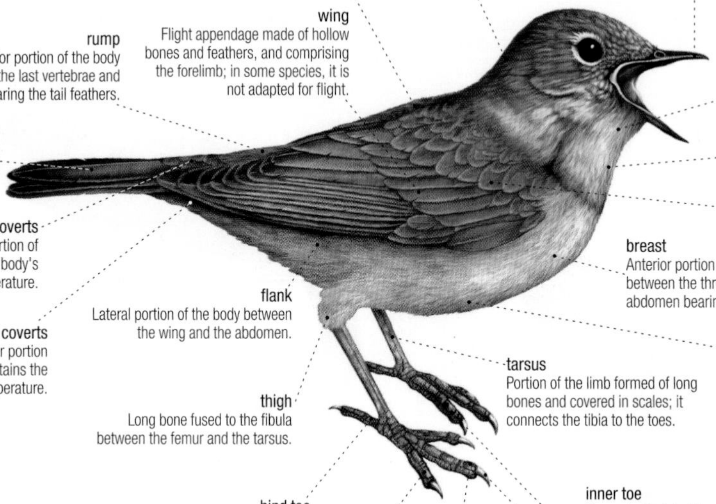

mantle
Upper posterior portion of the body between the head and the tail.

nape
Posterior portion of the neck below the head.

bill
Horny formation covering toothless jaws; the bird uses it to feed.

wing
Flight appendage made of hollow bones and feathers, and comprising the forelimb; in some species, it is not adapted for flight.

rump
Posterior portion of the body formed by the last vertebrae and bearing the tail feathers.

chin
Portion of the head below the mandible.

tail feather
Long stiff tail feather carried on the rump; it controls direction during flight.

throat
Anterior lateral portion of the neck between the chin and the breast.

wing covert
Short feather covering the upper portion of the base of the wing; it maintains internal body temperature.

upper tail coverts
Short feather covering the upper portion of the base of the tail; it maintains the body's internal temperature.

breast
Anterior portion of the body between the throat and the abdomen bearing the wings.

under tail coverts
Short feather covering the lower portion of the base of the tail; it maintains the body's internal temperature.

flank
Lateral portion of the body between the wing and the abdomen.

belly
Ventral portion of the body between the breast and the tail.

tarsus
Portion of the limb formed of long bones and covered in scales; it connects the tibia to the toes.

thigh
Long bone fused to the fibula between the femur and the tarsus.

hind toe
First articulated toe of the foot, usually made of a single phalange and pointing toward the back; it is also called the thumb.

inner toe
Second articulated toe of the foot, usually consisting of two phalanges.

claw
Pointy hook-shaped structure attached to the terminal end of the toes; it allows the bird to anchor itself.

outer toe
Fourth articulated bone of the foot, usually consisting of four phalanges.

middle toe
Third articulated toe of the foot; it is long and usually consists of three phalanges.

hea
Anterior portion of the bo containing the main sensory orga and the bra

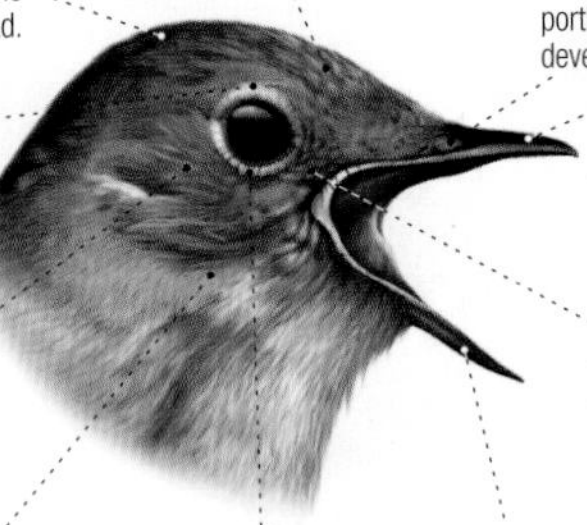

contour feather
Large rigid feather of the wings and tail enabling flight.

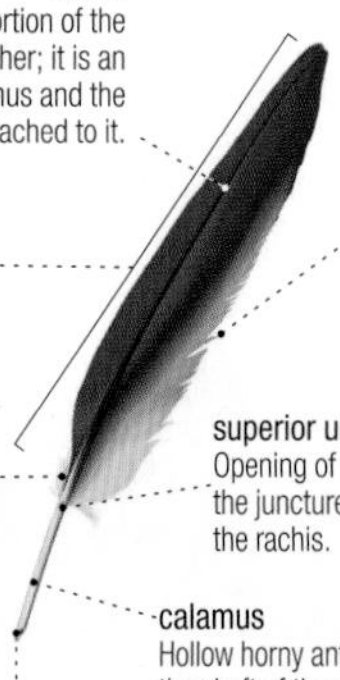

rachis
Solid horny upper portion of the shaft of the contour feather; it is an extension of the calamus and the barbs are attached to it.

barb
Each of the self-adhering filaments implanted on each side of the rachis.

crown
Top part of the skull, behind the forehead.

forehead
Upper front part of the head, between the bill and the crown.

nostril
External orifice of the nasal cavity located at the base of the upper portion of the bill having a poorly developed olfactory function.

vane
All the interconnected barbs on the same side of the rachis forming a waterproof surface.

supercilium
Band of small feathers above the eye.

upper mandible
Bone forming the upper port the bill.

afterfeather
Small soft light feathers usually located at the base of the main feathers on the abdomen; they help to insulate the body.

superior umbilicus
Opening of the shaft located at the juncture of the calamus and the rachis.

auriculars
Lateral portion of the head in back of the malar region at the level of the eye.

lore
Space between the base of t and the eye.

calamus
Hollow horny anterior portion of the shaft of the contour feather extending through the rachis.

inferior umbilicus
Opening of the shaft located at the lower portion of the calamus; it is implanted in the skin.

malar region
Lateral portion of the head below the eye extending from the base of the bill to the auriculars.

eye ring
Ring of tiny feathers surrounding the eye.

lower mandible
Bone forming the lower portion of the bill.

wing
Flight appendage formed of hollow bones and feathers, and comprising the forelimb; in certain species, the wing is not adapted for flight.

primary covert
Short feather covering the base of the primaries; it maintains the body's internal temperature and allows air to glide over the wing.

alula
All the short wing feathers inserted into the thumb; they provide stability during slow flight.

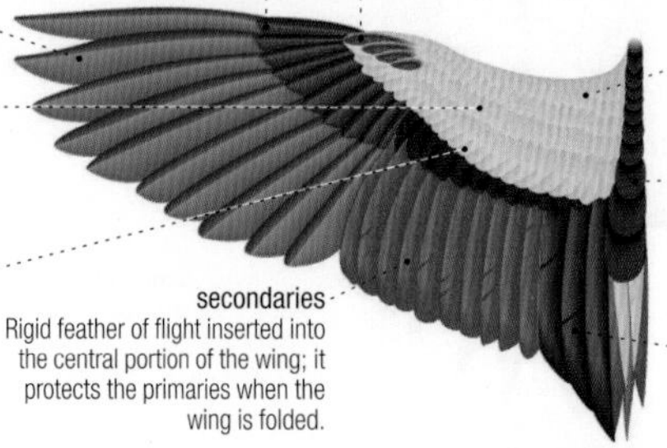

primaries
Rigid feather of flight inserted into the outer portion of the wing; it provides propulsion.

lesser covert
Covert feather at the base of the wing arranged in rows and highly exposed to wind action.

median covert
Covert feather at the base of the wing; it is protected by the lesser coverts when the wing is folded back.

scapular
Shoulder feather inserted into the edge of the back.

greater covert
Covert feather at the base of the wing protected by the median coverts when the wing is folded.

secondaries
Rigid feather of flight inserted into the central portion of the wing; it protects the primaries when the wing is folded.

tertial
Rigid feather of flight inserted into the inner portion of the wing; it helps to decrease air turbulence.

bird

skeleton of a bird

carpus
Portion of the wing formed of two short bones; it is located between the radius, the ulna and the metacarpus.

metacarpus
Portion of the wing formed of three long bones; it connects the carpus to the first phalanges of the digits.

phalanges
Portion of the wing formed of articulated bones bearing the primaries.

skull
Bony structure enclosing and protecting the brain.

ulna
Long sturdy bone located between the humerus and the carpus bearing the secondaries.

radius
Long wing bone located between the humerus and the carpus.

orbit
Bony cavity of the upper lateral potion of the head containing the eye.

humerus
Long wing bone articulating especially with the radius and the ulna and bearing the tertials.

maxilla
Bone forming the upper portion of the bill.

mandible
Bone forming the lower portion of the bill.

cervical vertebrae
s of the neck comprising erminal end of the spinal column.

synsacrum
Long bone resulting from the fusion of numerous vertebrae of the spinal column, preceding the pygostyle.

pygostyle
Bone of the terminal end of the spinal column resulting from the fusion of several vertebrae.

scapula
Large flat back bone serving as an attachment site for shoulder muscles.

ilium
Large flat back bone fused mainly to the synsacrum.

clavicle
g bone located in the anterior al portion of the body; the two icles fuse to form the furcula.

ischium
Bone behind the ilium; the ilium, ischium and pubis fuse together to form a single bone to which the leg is attached.

furcula
Bone resulting from the fusion of the lower portion of the two clavicles enabling the wings to spread.

pubis
Ventral bone posterior to the ilium.

keel
Bony ridge of the ventral surface of the sternum providing a solid support for the flight muscles.

rib
Thin curved bone articulating with the spinal column and the sternum.

femur
Long bone articulating especially with the tibiotarsus.

coracoid
Ventral bone connecting the scapula to the sternum.

sternum
Bone located at the ventral portion of the body and bearing the keel; the ribs are attached to it.

digits
Each of the four terminal ends of the legs formed of different articulated bones called phalanges; most birds have four digits.

tarsometatarsus
Bone formed by the fusion of the anterior portion of the tarsus and the metatarsus; the digits articulate with it. It is also called the tarsus.

tibiotarsus
Separate at the crown, the tibia and fibula fuse into a single bone to form the tibiotarsus.

anatomy of a bird

lung
Respiratory organ made up of an extensible tissue and forming a sac; air from the buccal cavity flows into it.

gizzard
Muscular pouch behind the proventriculus in which food is ground with the help of stones swallowed by the bird before being digested.

buccal cavity
Anterior portion of the digestive tract containing the tongue and the salivary glands.

kidney
Organ secreting urine; it eliminates toxic substances from the body.

esophagus
Canal in the anterior part of the digestive tract; it carries food to the crop.

pancreas
Digestive gland connected to the duodenum and producing digestive enzymes and hormones.

ureter
Long canal originating in the kidney and carrying urine to the cloaca.

trachea
Muscular cartilaginous canal carrying air from the buccal cavity to the lungs.

small intestine
Long narrow portion of the digestive tract behind the duodenum where part of digestion and food absorption takes place.

heart
Muscular organ helping blood to circulate.

rectum
Terminal end of the intestine before the cloaca.

crop
Large bulge at the back of the esophagus; it can dilate to receive food.

cloaca
Orifice common to the intestine and the genital and urinary tracts; it is located at the terminal end of the digestive tract.

proventriculus
Portion of the digestive tract opening out into the gizzard and secreting substances that help digestion.

liver
Gland secreting mostly a substance (bile) that contributes to digestion.

duodenum
Anterior portion of the small intestine into which secretions from the liver and pancreas empty.

cecum
Lateral canal located in the anterior portion of the intestine where especially a part of digestion and fermentation take place.

bird

egg
Reproductive method of certain animal species: a living cell with a casing and a food reserve, produced by the female.

vitelline membrane
Thin flexible transparent tissue enveloping the yolk.

blastodisc
Evidence of fertilization of the egg on the surface of the vitelline membrane; the embryo grows from it.

chalaza
Spiral filament of albumen maintaining the yolk in the center of the egg.

albumen
Viscous liquid substance, popularly known as egg white, surrounding the yolk and containing water and the proteins the embryo requires.

shell
Hard porous calcareous casing of the egg; it provides protection, fights bacteria and helps respiration.

shell membrane
Flexible porous tissue made of two superimposed layers covering the inside of the shell; it contributes to respiration and fights bacteria.

air space
Pocket of air contained between the two layers of the shell membrane at the base of the egg; it forms once the egg has cooled after being laid.

yolk
The embryo's food reserve located in the center of the egg.

examples of bills
A bill's shape is characteristic of the lifestyle of the bird species. Its main function is to allow the bird to feed, to construct its nest and to defend itself.

insectivorous bird
The long thin pointed bill allows the bird to glean small insects from vegetation.

aquatic bird
The large flat bill, with horny lateral plates, filters water and mud to extract food.

bird of prey
The short sturdy hooked bill tears apart large prey.

granivorous bird
The short sturdy conical bill is used to hull seeds: the sharp lower mandible cracks the seed, which the tongue holds in place on the upper maxilla.

wading bird
The long curved bill allows the bird to extract small animals and plants buried deep in the ground, in mud and in marshes.

examples of feet
The feet of birds are adapted to their lifestyle. They usually have four toes: one posterior (the hind toe) and three anterior.

bird of prey
Poorly adapted to locomotion, these sturdy powerful legs have talons to grip prey, immobilizing and killing it.

perching bird
The four toes end in a nail, which wraps around a support when the bird is resting; the hind toe provides equilibrium.

aquatic bird
Bird with webbed feet for ease of swimming.

aquatic bird
Bird with lobed toes for ease of swimming.

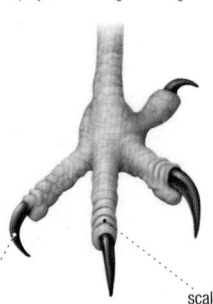

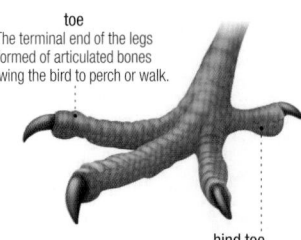

toe
The terminal end of the legs formed of articulated bones allowing the bird to perch or walk.

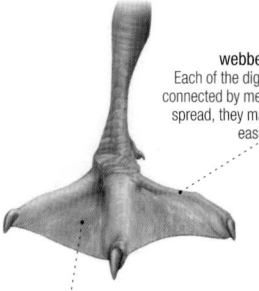

webbed toe
Each of the digits of the foot, connected by membranes; when spread, they make swimming easier.

lobe
Each of the round cutaneous divisions encircling the toe allow the bird to swim.

hind toe
First toe of the foot, facing backward and providing equilibrium.

talon
Very curved and pointy horny structure allowing the bird to seize its prey.

scale
Each of the small hard thin plates covering the toes in layers.

web
Fine membrane of skin connecting the digits of the foot; it stretches when the bird swims.

lobed toe
Each of the flat toes surrounding the lobes; they provide propulsion in the water and prevent slipping out of the water.

examples of aquatic birds and shorebirds

Aquatic birds and shorebirds live totally or partially on or around bodies of water.

tern
Widespread web-footed aquatic bird with long wings and usually a forked tail; it dives for the fish it feeds on.

duck
Web-footed aquatic bird spending most of its time on water; the domestic duck is raised especially for its meat and eggs.

auk
Web-footed bird of northern arctic and subarctic waters that has short wings which also serve as flippers.

gull
Web-footed omnivorous aquatic bird, usually nesting on the ground near freshwater or salt water.

kingfisher
Colorful fish-eating bird that spends most of its time perched by the water's edge.

oystercatcher
Swift long-billed bird found in Eurasia; it feeds mainly on shellfish.

pelican
Web-footed bird with a lower jaw featuring an extensible pouch for catching fish.

albatross
Web-footed aquatic bird of the South Seas; its wingspan can reach 10 ft, allowing it to glide for hours.

swan
Large web-footed bird found on bays, ponds and rivers in temperate and cold regions. The male and female mate for life.

heron
d found in shallow waters and feeding mostly on fishes and h a neck that folds into an S en in flight or at rest.

penguin
Flightless fish-eating marine bird living in colonies in the southern hemisphere; it has webbed feet and wings that have evolved into flippers.

stork
Wading bird found in marshes and fields; two species are threatened with extinction.

flamingo
Bird with webbed feet and usually pink plumage living in colonies in brackish or salt water; it feeds by filtering water through its bill.

examples of land birds

Land birds usually nest and feed on the ground (forests, fields, mountains, urban environments, etc.).

ANIMALS

bullfinch
Red-breasted bird found in the woods and parks of Eurasia; it feeds mainly on seeds and insects.

goldfinch
Brightly plumed songbird feeding mainly on the seeds of the thistle.

swift
Widespread and very swift insectivore; it is usually airborne since its toes make perching difficult.

hummingbird
Tiny brightly colored bird with a long thin bill found on the North American continent; it can hover and fly backward.

sparrow
Bird that feeds mainly on seeds and insects; it is widespread in cities and in the countryside.

jay
Usually noisy, often brightly colored bird found in forests; it feeds mainly on fruits, nuts, and seeds.

nightingale
Bird with a melodious song that feeds on insects and fruit; it is found in the bushes of forests and parks.

lapwing
Mainly insectivorous bird found in the wetlands and marshes of Eurasia and Africa; it has a tuft of upright feathers on its head.

European robin
European perching bird found in woods and gardens and emitting a fairly loud, lively, melodious song.

chaffinch
Small bird with a melodious s that is commonly found in woods and parks of Europe; i a conical bill adapted to brea the hulls of seeds.

toucan
Large yet gentle bird found in the forests of tropical America; its dentate bill allows it to feed especially on fruits and insects.

swallow
Widespread in the northern hemisphere and found in highly diverse habitats; it usually feeds on insects caught in flight.

turkey
Bird originating in the Americas with a bald head and neck covered with outgrowths; it is raised in captivity for its meat.

cardinal
Brightly colored bird with a crest o its head; it is found mostly in Nort American woods and gardens.

ostrich
Flightless bird of Africa reaching ov 7 ft in height, with powerful two-toe legs; it is raised for its feathers and meat.

guinea fowl
Wild terrestrial bird with a bald head and horned comb originally from Africa and domesticated in Europe for its meat.

peacock
Omnivorous bird originally from Asia; during the mating season, the male lifts and spreads its colorful tail feathers to attract females.

examples of land birds

quail
Bird found in fields and meadows and much prized as game; certain species are domesticated.

starling
Straight-billed omnivorous bird with dark plumage.

pigeon
Generally grain-eating bird with powerful flight muscles, including one (carrier pigeon) prized for its sense of direction.

shrike
Hook-billed bird found in fairly open countryside; it feeds on insects and small animals and may cache its prey by impaling it on a thorn.

macaw
Noisy brightly colored perching bird found in the tropical forests of the Americas; it feeds mainly on seeds and fruit.

northern saw-whet owl
Nocturnal bird of prey found in the forests of North America.

woodpecker
Stiff-tailed bird that uses its bill to proclaim its territory by drumming and to dig holes in tree trunks to search for insects and excavate nesting sites.

cockatoo
Noisy perching bird with drab plumage and a tuft of upright feathers on its head, found mainly in Australia; it can mimic human speech.

falcon
Diurnal bird of prey with piercing eyes and powerful talons and beak; it captures its prey in flight and is sometimes trained to hunt.

vulture
Diurnal bird of prey of the Americas and Eurasia, mainly a scavenger, with a bald head and neck, powerful beak and weak talons.

pheasant
Bird originally from Asia and characterized by its long tail; its meat is highly prized. Certain pheasants are raised solely for hunting.

raven
Strong-billed scavenger with usually black plumage.

partridge
Land-based bird that flies with difficulty.

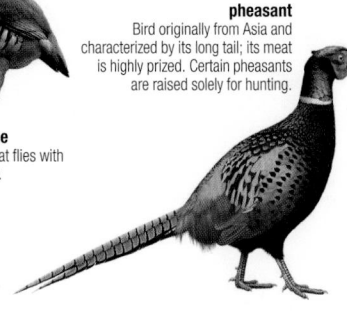

great horned owl
Nocturnal bird of prey found in the forests of North America, with a protruding tuft of feathers on each side of its head.

condor
Diurnal scavenger of the Americas, with a bald head and neck; one California species is facing extinction.

eagle
Widely prevalent bird of prey with piercing eyes, a hooked beak and sharp talons allowing it to catch live prey.

domestic goose
Booted bird of the northern are better adapted to land water; the domestic goose ed for its meat, eggs, and feathers.

chick
Newly hatched bird covered in down.

hen
Domestic fowl (female of the rooster) with a small serrated comb raised in captivity for its eggs and meat.

rooster
Domestic bird (male of the hen) with a large serrated comb and a long-plumed tail.

mole

Insectivorous mammal (about 40 species) found in Eurasia and the Americas; it digs underground tunnels with its front limbs to reach its food.

morphology of a mole

fur
Hair covering the entire body, except the nose; its main function is to maintain body temperature.

eye
Organ of sight covered with hairs t can perceive variations in light inte some moles are almost blind.

snout
Elongated front portion of the head covered with many sensory hairs, which have a highly developed tactile and olfactory function.

tail
Terminal appendage of the body having tactile hairs that detect obstacles.

forelimb
Wide powerful articulated limb ending in a scoop-shaped paw allowing the mole to dig in the earth.

hind limb
Articulated limb with sharp claws that supports the mole while it digs in the earth.

palm
Portion of the hand facing outward to make digging easier and to push the earth aside more efficiently.

claw
Somewhat curved, sharp pointy structure at the terminal end of the digits for digging in the earth.

skeleton of a mole

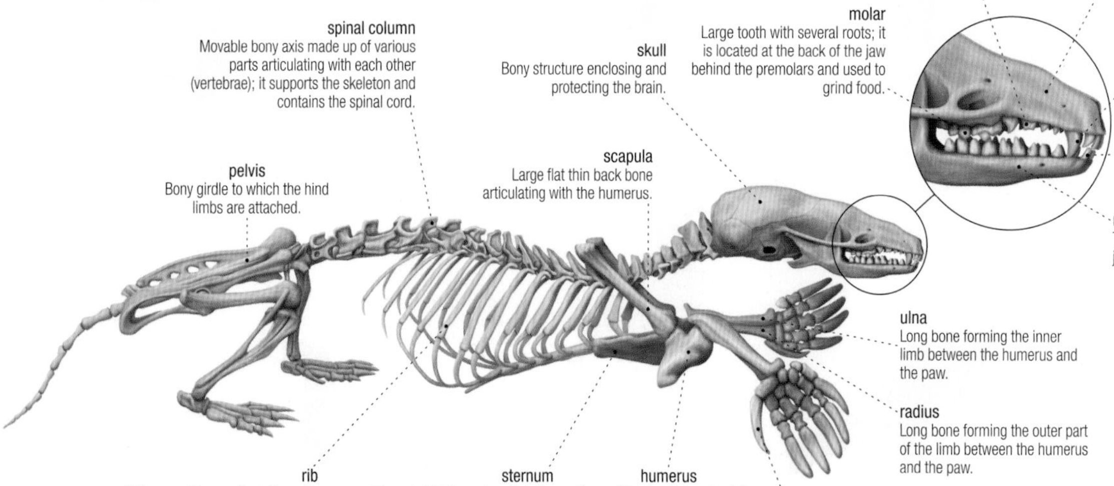

premolar
Tooth with usually a single root; it is located between the canines and the molars, and used to grind food.

maxilla
Toothed bone comprising the upper jaw.

molar
Large tooth with several roots; it is located at the back of the jaw behind the premolars and used to grind food.

canine
Pointed tooth with a sing it is located between the and the premolars, and gripping food and tearin

incisor
Flat tooth with a single r located at the front of th used for gripping food a it apart.

spinal column
Movable bony axis made up of various parts articulating with each other (vertebrae); it supports the skeleton and contains the spinal cord.

skull
Bony structure enclosing and protecting the brain.

scapula
Large flat thin back bone articulating with the humerus.

mandible
Toothed bone forming the jaw.

pelvis
Bony girdle to which the hind limbs are attached.

ulna
Long bone forming the inner limb between the humerus and the paw.

radius
Long bone forming the outer part of the limb between the humerus and the paw.

rib
Thin curved bone articulating with the spine and the sternum.

sternum
Elongated flat bone to which the ribs in particular are attached and bearing a crest on its ventral surface.

humerus
Bone of the forelimb articulating with the scapula, as well as with the radius and the ulna; it provides a large base for the muscles.

falciform sesamoid bone
Small curved bone located near the thumb reinforcing the paw and forming a cutting inner edge.

examples of insectivorous mammals

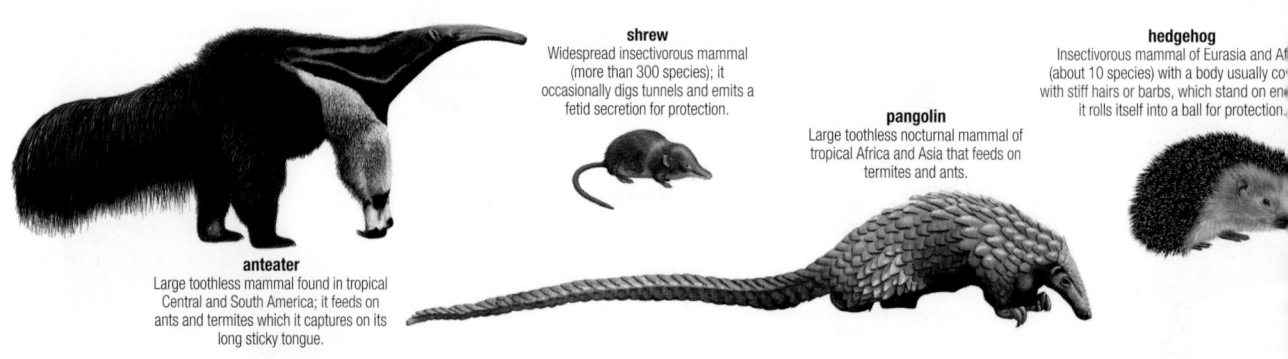

shrew
Widespread insectivorous mammal (more than 300 species); it occasionally digs tunnels and emits a fetid secretion for protection.

hedgehog
Insectivorous mammal of Eurasia and Af (about 10 species) with a body usually co with stiff hairs or barbs, which stand on en it rolls itself into a ball for protection.

pangolin
Large toothless nocturnal mammal of tropical Africa and Asia that feeds on termites and ants.

anteater
Large toothless mammal found in tropical Central and South America; it feeds on ants and termites which it captures on its long sticky tongue.

rat

mnivorous rodent characterized by its intelligence and voracious appetite; it frequents areas of human habitation and can transmit certain viruses and bacteria to humans.

morphology of a rat

pinna
External part of the ear made of cartilaginous lobes that capture sounds.

vibrissa
Long tactile hair located around the nose and mouth used to detect obstacles during nocturnal forays.

nose
Middle protuberance of the head with two orifices located above the mouth and having an olfactory and respiratory function.

digit
Terminal end of the limbs formed of various articulated bones bearing a claw and used mainly to feed and move about.

claw
Somewhat curved, sharp pointy structure used especially for digging and defense.

fur
Hair covering the entire body, except the nose; its main function is to maintain body temperature.

tail
Terminal appendage of the body covered with scales and containing blood vessels; it is used mainly for equilibrium.

skeleton of a rat

axis
Second cervical vertebra supporting the atlas; it allows the head to rotate.

scapula
Large thin flat shoulder bone articulating with the humerus.

lumbar vertebrae
Bony parts of the back located between the thoracic and sacral vertebrae.

ilium
Large flat back bone articulating with the sacral vertebrae.

cervical vertebrae
Bony parts of the neck comprising the upper terminal end of the spinal column.

thoracic vertebrae
Bony parts supporting the ribs between the cervical and lumbar vertebrae.

rib
Thin curved bone articulating with the spinal column and the sternum.

femur
Long bone of the hind limb articulating especially with the patella.

costal cartilage
Strong elastic tissue extending the front portion of the ribs to connect them to the sternum.

sacral vertebrae
Partly fused bony parts between the lumbar and caudal vertebrae.

parietal
bone of the upper portion of the skull.

pubis
Ventral bone posterior to the ilium.

ischium
Bone behind the ilium; the ilium, ischium and pubis fuse together to form a single bone to which the leg is attached.

atlas
rvical vertebra supporting ead and supported by the axis.

clavicle
ong bone located in the front ventral portion of the body articulating with the sternum.

humerus
the forelimb articulating with la, as well as with the radius ulna; it provides a large base for the muscles.

sternum
ngated flat bone to which the ibs in particular are attached bearing a crest on its ventral surface.

phalanges
ones articulating to form the skeleton of the digits.

metacarpus
Portion of the forelimb formed of veral long bones; it connects the carpus to the first phalanges of the digits.

carpus
Portion of the forelimb formed of short bones between the radius, the ulna and the metacarpus.

ulna
Long bone partly fused with the radius and forming the inner limb between the humerus and the carpus.

radius
Long bone partly fused with the ulna and forming the outer limb between the humerus and the carpus.

patella
Small flat slightly bulging triangular bone located on the inner limb and articulating especially with the femur.

phalanges
Bones articulating to form the skeleton of the digits.

tibia
Long bone partly fused to the fibula and forming the inner limb between the femur and the tarsus.

caudal vertebrae
Bony parts comprising the skeleton of the tail located at the terminal end of the spinal column.

fibula
Long bone partly fused to the tibia and forming the outer limb between the femur and the tarsus.

tarsus
Part of the hind limb formed of several small bones at the juncture of the tibia and the metatarsus.

metatarsus
Part of the hind limb formed of several long bones; it connects the tarsus to the first phalanges of the digits.

rat

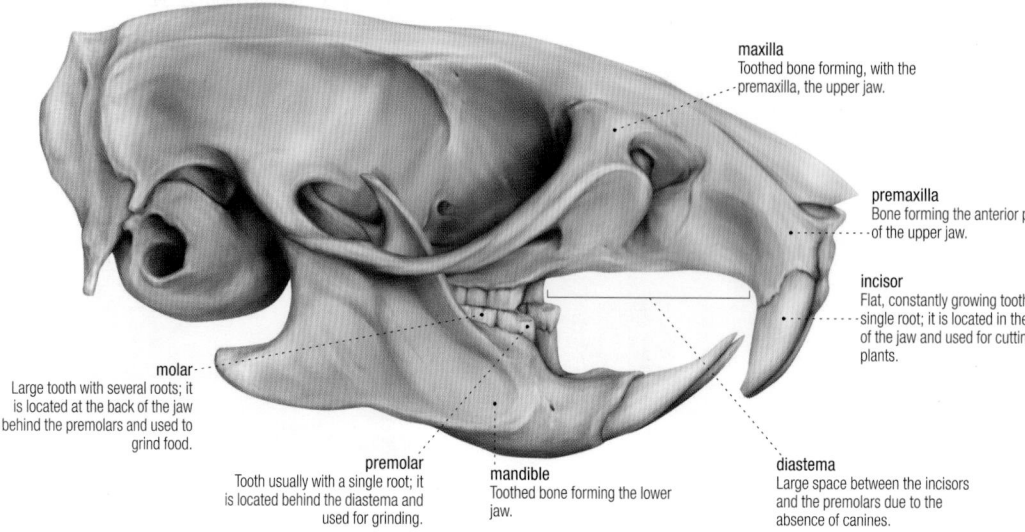

jaw of a rat
Each of the two bony structures carrying teeth, that form the mouth.

maxilla
Toothed bone forming, with the premaxilla, the upper jaw.

premaxilla
Bone forming the anterior portic of the upper jaw.

incisor
Flat, constantly growing tooth wit single root; it is located in the fror of the jaw and used for cutting up plants.

molar
Large tooth with several roots; it is located at the back of the jaw behind the premolars and used to grind food.

premolar
Tooth usually with a single root; it is located behind the diastema and used for grinding.

mandible
Toothed bone forming the lower jaw.

diastema
Large space between the incisors and the premolars due to the absence of canines.

examples of rodents

Rodents: four-legged herbivorous or omnivorous vertebrates (over 2,000 species) with a pair of sharp incisors that grow continuously.

field mouse
Rodent found in woods and fields; it moves about by hopping and can cause serious crop damage.

chipmunk
Small, mostly herbivorous rodent found mainly in North American forests and bushes.

hamster
Rodent found in dry regions of Eurasia that stores its food in cheek pouches; it is sometimes kept as a pet and used for laboratory experiments.

woodchuck
Rodent of North America, called groundhog; it hiberr five to six months a year and a high-pitched whistle whe danger.

rat
Omnivorous rodent characterized by its intelligence and voracious appetite; it frequents areas of human habitation and can transmit certain viruses and bacteria to humans. Some species are kept as pets and used for laboratory experiments.

jerboa
Rodent found in the deserts of Asia and Africa adapted for hopping and able to survive without drinking water.

squirrel
Mostly herbivorous rodent found in woods and forests around the world, except in Australia; some species of squirrels move about by gliding from tree to tree.

beaver
Semiaquatic rodent found in Eurasia and North America and prized for its fur; it uses branches to build lodges and dams in streams.

guinea pig
Rodent originating in South America, sometimes kept as pet but mainly used in laboratory experiments.

porcupine
Rodent found on land and in trees in warm and temperate regions; its body is covered with long sharp quills, which it raises to defend itself.

ANIMALS

rabbit

Widespread and extremely prolific lagomorph living in the wild in burrows; it is also raised for its meat and fur.

morphology of a rabbit

ear
Auditory organ, very mobile, also governing balance. The rabbit has a highly developed sense of hearing.

eye
Organ of sight used to perceive intensity of light and movements. Its night vision is eight times superior to that of a human.

nose
Middle protuberance of the head with two orifices located above the mouth and having an olfactory and respiratory function.

fur
Hair covering the entire body, except the nose; its main function is to maintain body temperature.

vibrissa
Long tactile hair located around the nose and mouth used to detect obstacles during nocturnal forays.

leg
Long and powerful articulated limb with toes at the end, used for walking and jumping.

jaw of a rabbit
Each of the two bony structures carrying teeth, that form the mouth.

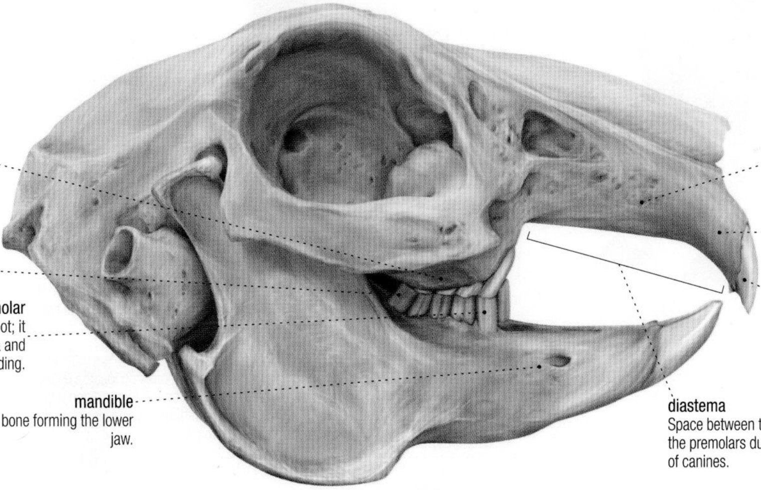

palatine
Fine bone of the maxilla; the horizontal portion forms the roof of the mouth.

molar
Large tooth with several roots; it is located at the back of the jaw behind the premolars and used to grind food.

premolar
Tooth usually with a single root; it is located behind the diastema and used for grinding.

mandible
Toothed bone forming the lower jaw.

maxilla
Toothed bone forming, with the premaxilla, the upper jaw.

premaxilla
Bone forming the anterior portion of the upper jaw.

incisor
Flat, constantly growing tooth with a single root; it is located in the front of the jaw and used for cutting up plants.

diastema
Space between the incisors and the premolars due to the absence of canines.

examples of lagomorphs

lagomorphs: small, four-legged, herbivorous vertebrates (about 60 species) with dense fur, a short or absent tail and two pairs of incisors that grow continuously.

hare
Widespread lagomorph with strong hind limbs adapted for swift running; it lives in the wild and is valued especially for its meat.

rabbit
Widespread and extremely prolific lagomorph living in the wild in burrows; it is also raised for its meat and fur.

pika
Tailless lagomorph living in the wild in the mountains of Central Asia and western North America.

horse

Maned ungulate (hoofed) mammal domesticated for riding and for use as a draft animal.

morphology of a horse

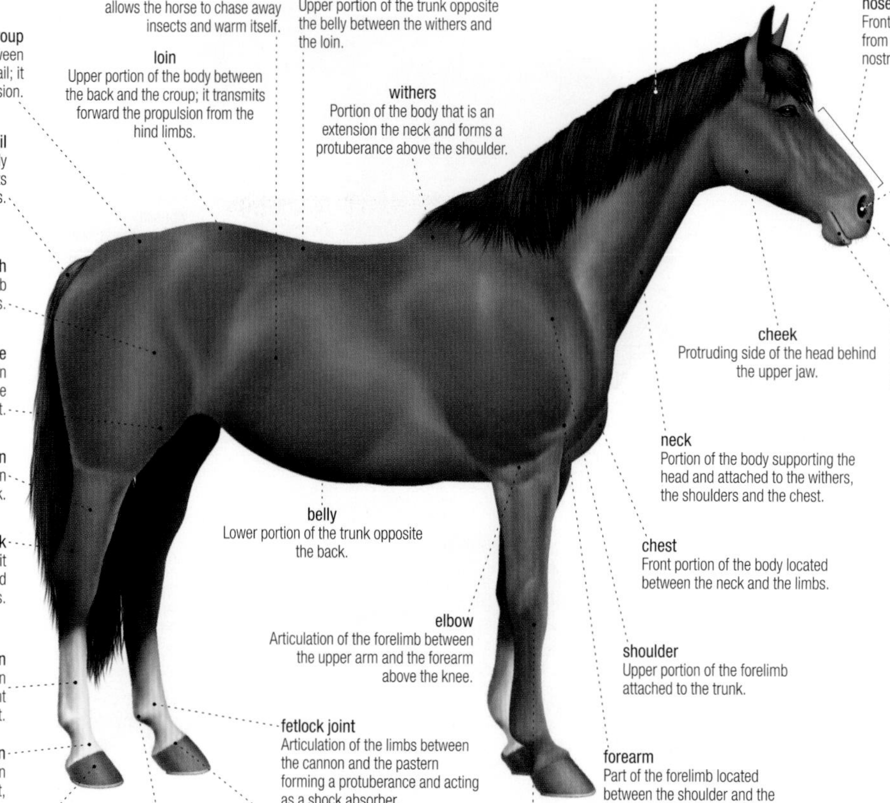

ANIMALS

mane
Long stiff hairs (horsehair) covering the neck used mainly to chase away insects.

forelock
Tuft of long stiff hairs (horsehair) on the upper terminal end of the mane and falling onto the forehead between the ears.

flank
Lateral portion of the body that ripples with the action of the muscles, which allows the horse to chase away insects and warm itself.

back
Upper portion of the trunk opposite the belly between the withers and the loin.

nose
Front portion of the head exten from the base of the eyes to th nostrils.

croup
Rear portion of the body between the loin and the base of the tail; it provides propulsion.

loin
Upper portion of the body between the back and the croup; it transmits forward the propulsion from the hind limbs.

withers
Portion of the body that is an extension the neck and forms a protuberance above the shoulder.

nostril
Each of the orifices of th having a respiratory and function.

tail
Terminal appendage of the body with long hairs; the horse whips its tail to chase away insects.

muzzle
Terminal end of the uppe having a tactile and pre function.

thigh
Upper portion of the hind limb having large powerful muscles.

cheek
Protruding side of the head behind the upper jaw.

lip
Each of two movable mus forming the contour of the having a tactile function.

stifle
Articulation of the hind limb between the thigh and the leg formed of the patella and the skin that covers it.

neck
Portion of the body supporting the head and attached to the withers, the shoulders and the chest.

gaskin
Portion of the hind limb between the stifle and hock.

belly
Lower portion of the trunk opposite the back.

chest
Front portion of the body located between the neck and the limbs.

hock
Articulation of the hind limb; it contributes to movement and absorbs shocks.

elbow
Articulation of the forelimb between the upper arm and the forearm above the knee.

shoulder
Upper portion of the forelimb attached to the trunk.

cannon
Portion of the hind limb between the hock and the fetlock joint supporting the horse's weight.

fetlock joint
Articulation of the limbs between the cannon and the pastern forming a protuberance and acting as a shock absorber.

forearm
Part of the forelimb located between the shoulder and the elbow corresponding to the humerus.

pastern
Portion of the limbs between the fetlock joint and the coronet, corresponding to the first phalange of the finger.

hoof
Thick horny casing covering and protecting the terminal end of the limb; it rests on the ground while the horse is walking and absorbs shocks.

fetlock
Tuft of hair located behind the fetlock joint.

coronet
Part of the limbs covering the upper edge of the hoof and corresponding to the second phalange of the finger.

knee
Articulation of the forelimb located below the elbow between the forearm and the cannon; it contributes to movement and acts as a shock absorber.

gaits
Natural or acquired means of locomotion used by a horse, based on limb movements. There are four principal gaits.

walk
Natural walking gait in four equal movements: each leg lifts and touches down diagonally in succession. This is a horse's slowest gait.

trot
Natural jumping gait between a walk and a gallop in two movements: both pairs of diagonal legs alternate in touching down, with a pause in between.

ANIMALS

anatomy of a horse

lung
Respiratory organ made up of an extensible tissue and forming a sac; air from the buccal cavity flows into it.

kidney
Organ secreting urine; it eliminates toxic substances from the body.

cecum
Lateral canal located in the anterior portion of the intestine where especially a part of digestion and fermentation take place.

rectum
erminal portion of the intestine, behind the colon allowing fecal matter to be ejected.

esophagus
Canal of the anterior portion of the digestive tract; it carries food to the stomach.

trachea
Muscular cartilaginous canal carrying air from the nasal cavity to the lungs.

colon
stinal part of the body between small intestine and the rectum ch waste collects before being elled in the form of excrement.

spleen
Organ of the circulatory system where impurities in the blood are destroyed.

heart
Muscular organ helping blood to circulate.

small intestine
ong thin portion of the digestive t behind the stomach in which most of the digestion and food absorption take place.

stomach
Dilated section of the digestive tract preceding the intestine; it receives food to be digested.

liver
Viscera that secretes bile, among other substances; bile helps digestion.

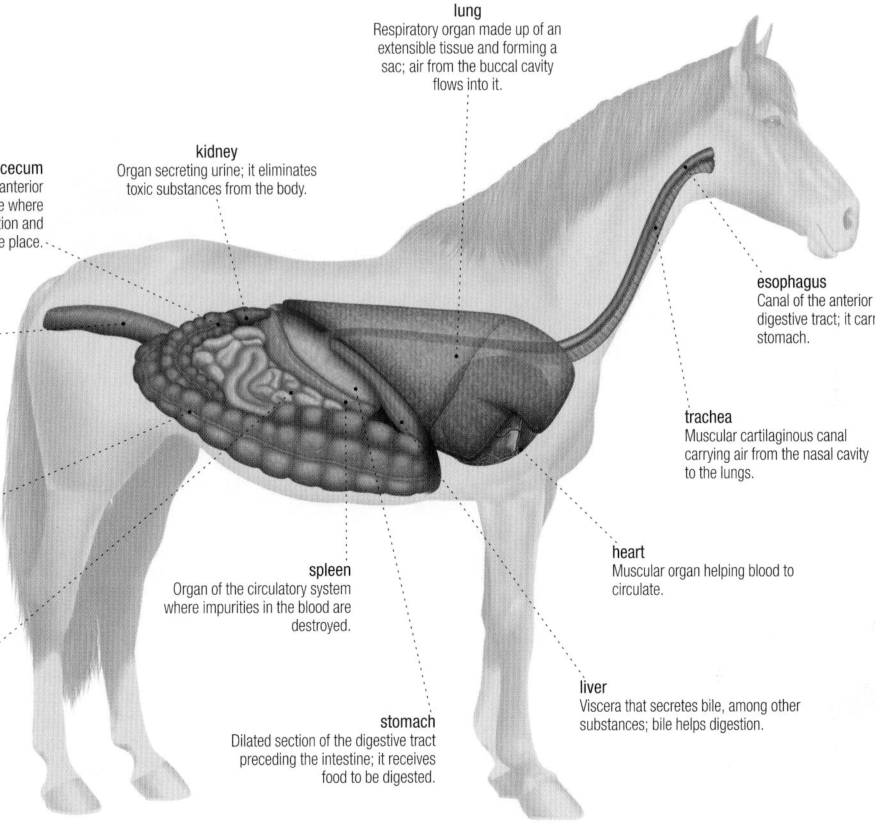

gaits

pace
Acquired jumping gait in two movements, extremely comfortable and faster than the trot; both pairs of lateral legs alternate in lifting.

canter
Natural gait performed in three unequal movements: both diagonal legs work together, while the other two work separately, with a pause in between.

horse

skeleton of a horse

ANIMALS

skull
Bony structure enclosing and protecting the brain.

atlas
First cervical vertebra supporting the head.

femur
Long bone of the hind limb articulating with the pelvis, the tibia and the fibula.

scapula
Large thin flat bone connected to the trunk by numerous muscles and ligaments; it has a wide range of motion.

rib
Thin curved bone articulating with the spinal column and the sternum.

fibula
Bone fused to the tibia the outer limb betwee and the tars

pelvis
Bony girdle transmitting propulsion forward.

mandible
Toothed bone forming the lower jaw.

humerus
Long bone of the forelimb whose articulation with the scapula allows shocks to be absorbed when the horse runs.

olecranon
Upper terminal part of the ulna articulating with the humerus; it forms the protuberance of the elbow.

radius
Long bone fused to the ulna and forming the outer portion of the limb between the humerus and the carpus.

carpus
Portion of the foreleg formed of short bones between the radius and the metacarpus.

metacarpus
Part of the forelimb formed of several long bones; it connects the carpus to the first phalange.

proximal sesamoid
One of two bones between the carpus (forelimb) or the tarsus (hind limb) and the first phalange forming the fetlock joint.

distal sesamoid
Small elongated bone of the third phalange of the digit allowing the lower part of the limb to move.

sternum
Long flat bone to which the ribs, in particular, are attached.

ulna
Bone fused to the radius and forming the inner limb between the humerus and the carpus.

patella
Slightly bulging, small flat triangular bone located on the front surface of the stifle and articulating especially with the femur.

tibia
Long bone fused to the fibula and forming the inner limb between the femur and the tarsus.

calcaneus
Posterior bone of the tarsus articulating with the tibia and forming the protuberance of the hock.

tarsus
Part of the hind limb formed of short bones located between the tibia, the fibula and the metatarsus; it acts as a shock absorber.

proximal phalanx
First bone of the digit corresponding to the pastern.

middle phalanx
Second bone of the digit corresponding to the coronet.

metatarsus
Part of the hind limb form several long bones; it conr the tarsus to the first phala the digit.

distal phalanx
Last phalange of the digit having a thick horny covering upon which the horse rests.

cervical vertebrae
Bony parts of the neck comprising the upper terminal end of the spinal column.

thoracic vertebrae
Bony parts supporting the ribs between the cervical and lumbar vertebrae.

lumbar vertebrae
Bony parts of the back located between the thoracic and sacral vertebrae.

sacral vertebrae
Bony parts that are fused together between the lumbar and caudal vertebrae; the pelvis articulates with them.

caudal vertebrae
Bony parts comprising the skele the tail located at the terminal en spinal column.

horse

ANIMALS

bulb
Horny eminence ending at the frog and joining with the heel.

heel
Rear portion of the wall of the hoof between the quarters and opposite the toe.

hoof: plantar surface
Horny lower surface of the hoof in contact with the ground.

median groove
Deep natural groove through the center of the frog.

bar
Terminal part of the wall of the hoof running along the edge of the frog.

frog
Part of the hoof made of soft but strong horny material located in the notch of the sole; it is used to absorb shocks and sense the terrain.

lateral groove
Natural groove separating the frog from the bars and the sole.

sole
Strong thin horny plate comprising the lower portion of the hoof and resting on the ground.

quarter
Side part of the wall of the hoof between the heel and the side wall.

wall
Horny material making up the perimeter of the hoof; it is produced by the coronet and grows from 0.3 to 1.0 inch per month.

side wall
Side part of the wall of the hoof between the toe and the quarter.

white line
Line of dense compact horny material bringing together the sole and the inner edge of the wall of the hoof.

toe
Front part of the wall of the hoof between the side walls and opposite the heel.

hoof
Thick horny casing covering and protecting the terminal end of the limb; it rests on the ground while the horse is walking and absorbs shocks.

horseshoe
Curved metal band nailed under the wall of the hoof to protect it against wear, to absorb shocks and to provide better traction on the ground.

heel
Terminal end of each branch of a horseshoe; it is rounded and beveled to prevent injury.

quarter
Part of the horseshoe under the quarter of the hoof.

nail
Pointy metal pin; its head lodges in the nail hole to attach the horseshoe to the hoof.

branch
Each of the two parts of the horseshoe starting at the toe and ending at the heel.

toe
Front part of the wall of the hoof between the side walls and opposite the heel.

toe clip
Triangular iron clip mounted on the toe of the hoof to protect the horny material and to hold the horseshoe in place.

coronet
Bulge from which the wall of the hoof grows; it secretes a varnish to protect the hoof from humidity and dryness.

bulb
Horny eminence ending at the frog and joining with the heel.

side wall
Part of the horseshoe under the side wall of the hoof.

outer edge
Outer contour of the horseshoe.

horseshoe
Curved metal band nailed under the wall of the hoof to protect it against wear, to absorb shocks and to provide better traction on the ground.

heel
Rear portion of the wall of the hoof between the quarters and opposite the toe.

inner edge
Inner contour of the horseshoe.

toe
Part of the horseshoe under the toe of the hoof.

nail hole
Rectangular opening made in the iron to hold the head of a nail; there are usually six to eight nail holes.

side wall
Side part of the wall of the hoof between the toe and the quarter.

quarter
Side part of the wall of the hoof between the heel and the side wall.

examples of hooves

Ungulate mammals can have an odd or even number of toes (from one to five); the number can vary for the forelimbs and the hind limbs.

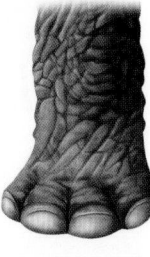

two-toed hoof
The deer, giraffe, bison, sheep and camel are the principal animals with this kind of hoof.

three-toed hoof
The rhinoceros, for example, has this kind of hoof.

one-toed hoof
The horse, zebra and ass, for example, have one-toed hooves.

four-toed hoof
The pig, wild boar, hippopotamus and elephant are the principal animals with this kind of hoof.

examples of ungulate mammals

There are many species of ungulate mammals; some are wild, some are domesticated and some are both.

peccary
Wild ungulate found in the forests of the Americas having a dorsal gland that emits a nauseous secretion; it is hunted for its hide.

wild boar
Wild ungulate found in forests and marshes with sharp canines that it uses to defend itself; it is hunted for its hide.

pig
Domestic omnivororous ungulate raised mainly for its meat and its hide.

sheep
Ungulate ruminant covered with a thick woolly coat domesticated for its milk, meat and wool.

okapi
Ungulate ruminant of Africa with an extensible and prehensile tongue; only the male has small horns.

antelope
Ungulate ruminant with hollow horns found throughout Africa and Asia; it runs very fast and is prized for its meat and hide.

goat
Ungulate ruminant with hollow horns able to jump and climb; it is domesticated for its milk, meat and wool.

white-tailed deer
Wild ungulate ruminant of North America; it runs very fast and is highly prized as game.

llama
Ungulate ruminant found in the mountains of South America; it can be wild or domesticated and is highly prized for its wool.

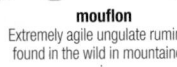

moose
Ruminant ungulate found in the cold regions of the northern hemisphere with wide hooves that allow it to wade through marshes and ponds.

mouflon
Extremely agile ungulate ruminant found in the wild in mountainous regions.

caribou
Ungulate ruminant found in cold regions of the northern hemisphere; it is domesticated by some peoples for its meat, hide and milk, and as a draft animal.

elk
Wild ungulate ruminant of cold regions; a good swimmer and runner, it is prized for its meat and antler and is sometimes raised in captivity.

ass
Wild maned ungulate originally from Africa domesticated as a pack animal.

mule
Sterile male, a cross between an ass and a mare (female of the horse); it is very hardy and can carry heavy loads.

horse
Maned ungulate mammal domesticated for riding and for use as a draft animal.

zebra
Maned ungulate that runs very fast; it is found in herds in the forests and steppes of Africa.

ANIMALS

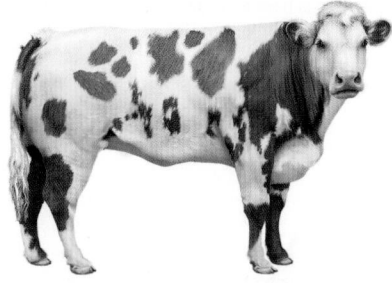

calf
Baby cow, male or female, up to the age of one year raised for its meat.

cow
Ungulate ruminant with horns (female of the bull); it is raised for its milk and meat, and for reproduction.

ox
Castrated bovine (male of the cow) domesticated for its meat and sometimes used as a draft animal.

rhinoceros
Ungulate found in the savannas and marshy areas of Africa and Asia with a one-horned or two-horned muzzle; it is threatened with extinction.

hippopotamus
Semiaquatic ungulate of Africa that can weigh up to 5 tons; it defends itself with its canine teeth, which grow constantly.

yak
Ruminant ungulate of Central Asia domesticated in Tibet for its milk and its hide, and as a pack animal.

dromedary camel
Single-humped ruminant ungulate of Africa adapted to arid climates; it is used especially as a pack animal and for riding.

Bactrian camel
Two-humped ruminant ungulate of Asia adapted to arid climates; it is domesticated especially for its meat, milk and hide, and as a pack animal.

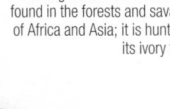

giraffe
Ruminant ungulate found in African savannas that is the tallest land animal today and can reach 19 feet in height; it has a prehensile tongue and small horns.

Cape buffalo
Ungulate ruminant with thick horns found mainly in the grasslands of sub-Saharan Africa; it is a powerful and deadly fighter.

elephant
The largest land mammal today, found in the forests and savannas of Africa and Asia; it is hunted for its ivory tusks.

bison
Ungulate ruminant of North America and Europe, usually wild, sometimes raised for its meat.

dog

Carnivorous mammal with an excellent sense of smell; it has been domesticated since prehistoric times and trained to perform a number of tasks: guarding and protecting, detecting, carrying and hunting.

morphology of a dog

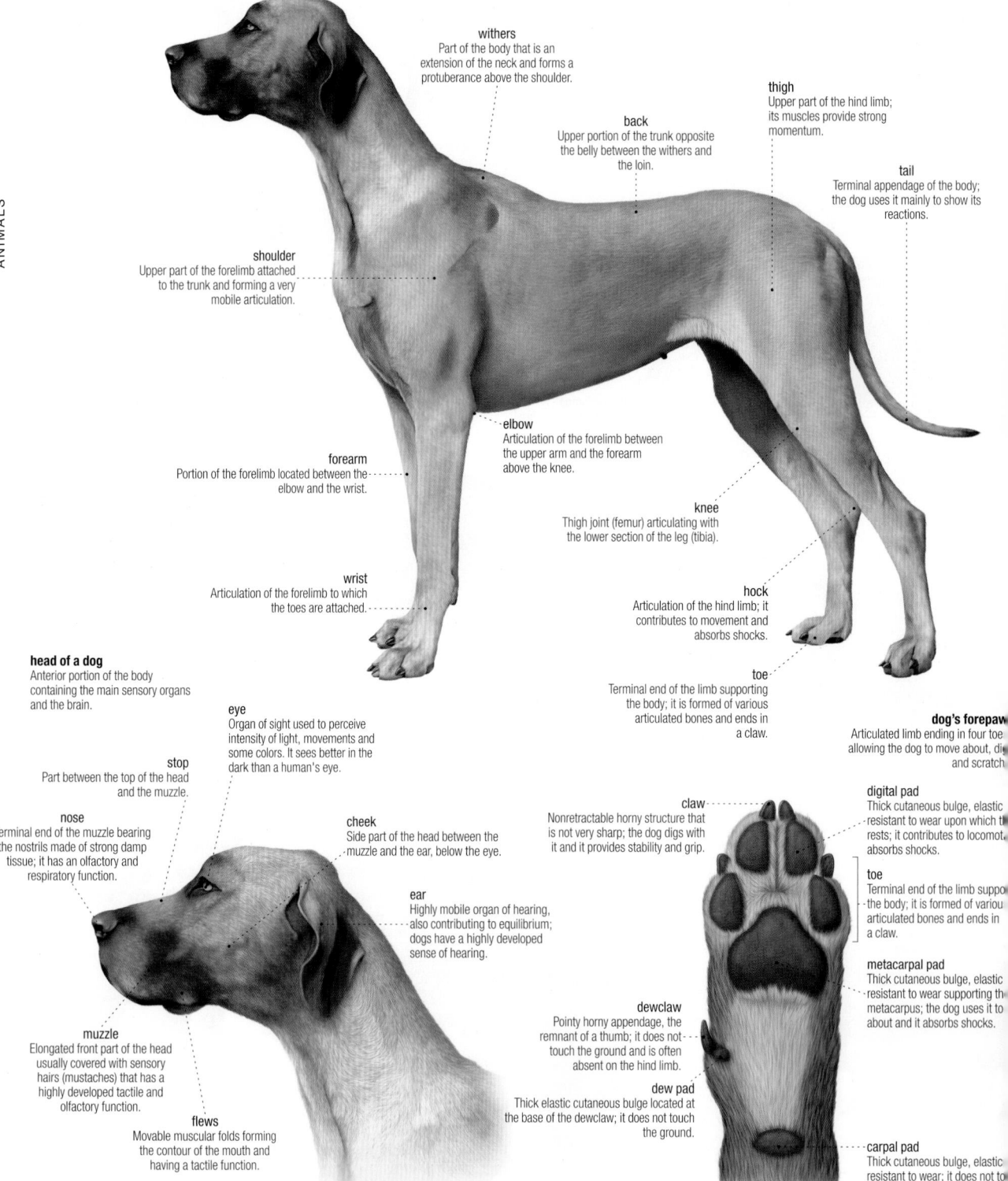

withers
Part of the body that is an extension of the neck and forms a protuberance above the shoulder.

thigh
Upper part of the hind limb; its muscles provide strong momentum.

back
Upper portion of the trunk opposite the belly between the withers and the loin.

tail
Terminal appendage of the body; the dog uses it mainly to show its reactions.

shoulder
Upper part of the forelimb attached to the trunk and forming a very mobile articulation.

elbow
Articulation of the forelimb between the upper arm and the forearm above the knee.

forearm
Portion of the forelimb located between the elbow and the wrist.

knee
Thigh joint (femur) articulating with the lower section of the leg (tibia).

wrist
Articulation of the forelimb to which the toes are attached.

hock
Articulation of the hind limb; it contributes to movement and absorbs shocks.

toe
Terminal end of the limb supporting the body; it is formed of various articulated bones and ends in a claw.

head of a dog
Anterior portion of the body containing the main sensory organs and the brain.

eye
Organ of sight used to perceive intensity of light, movements and some colors. It sees better in the dark than a human's eye.

stop
Part between the top of the head and the muzzle.

nose
Terminal end of the muzzle bearing the nostrils made of strong damp tissue; it has an olfactory and respiratory function.

cheek
Side part of the head between the muzzle and the ear, below the eye.

ear
Highly mobile organ of hearing, also contributing to equilibrium; dogs have a highly developed sense of hearing.

muzzle
Elongated front part of the head usually covered with sensory hairs (mustaches) that has a highly developed tactile and olfactory function.

flews
Movable muscular folds forming the contour of the mouth and having a tactile function.

claw
Nonretractable horny structure that is not very sharp; the dog digs with it and it provides stability and grip.

dewclaw
Pointy horny appendage, the remnant of a thumb; it does not touch the ground and is often absent on the hind limb.

dew pad
Thick elastic cutaneous bulge located at the base of the dewclaw; it does not touch the ground.

dog's forepaw
Articulated limb ending in four toes allowing the dog to move about, dig and scratch.

digital pad
Thick cutaneous bulge, elastic resistant to wear upon which the rests; it contributes to locomotion, absorbs shocks.

toe
Terminal end of the limb supporting the body; it is formed of various articulated bones and ends in a claw.

metacarpal pad
Thick cutaneous bulge, elastic resistant to wear supporting the metacarpus; the dog uses it to about and it absorbs shocks.

carpal pad
Thick cutaneous bulge, elastic resistant to wear; it does not touch the ground but prevents the dog sliding as it lands after a jump.

skeleton of a dog

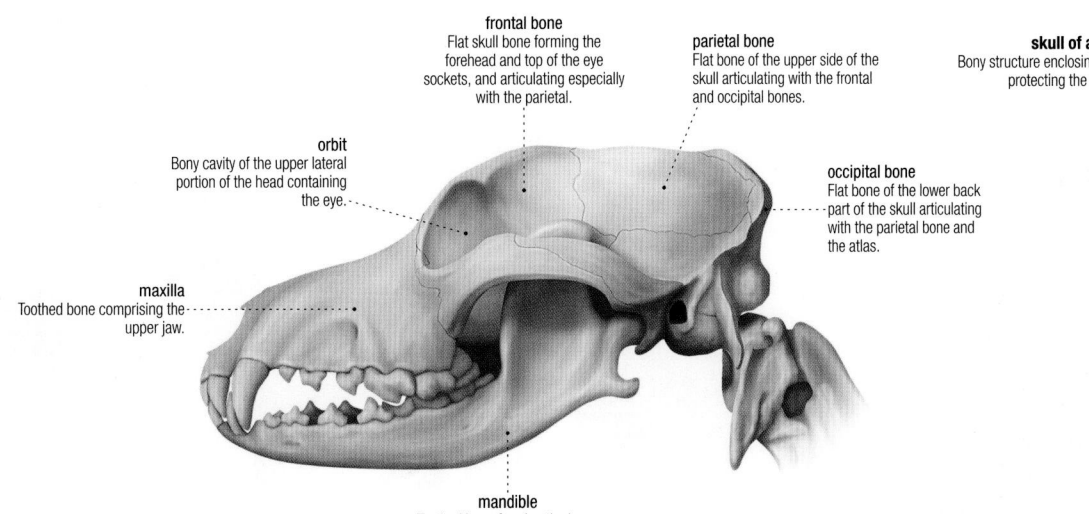

cervical vertebrae
Bony parts of the neck comprising the upper terminal end of the spinal column.

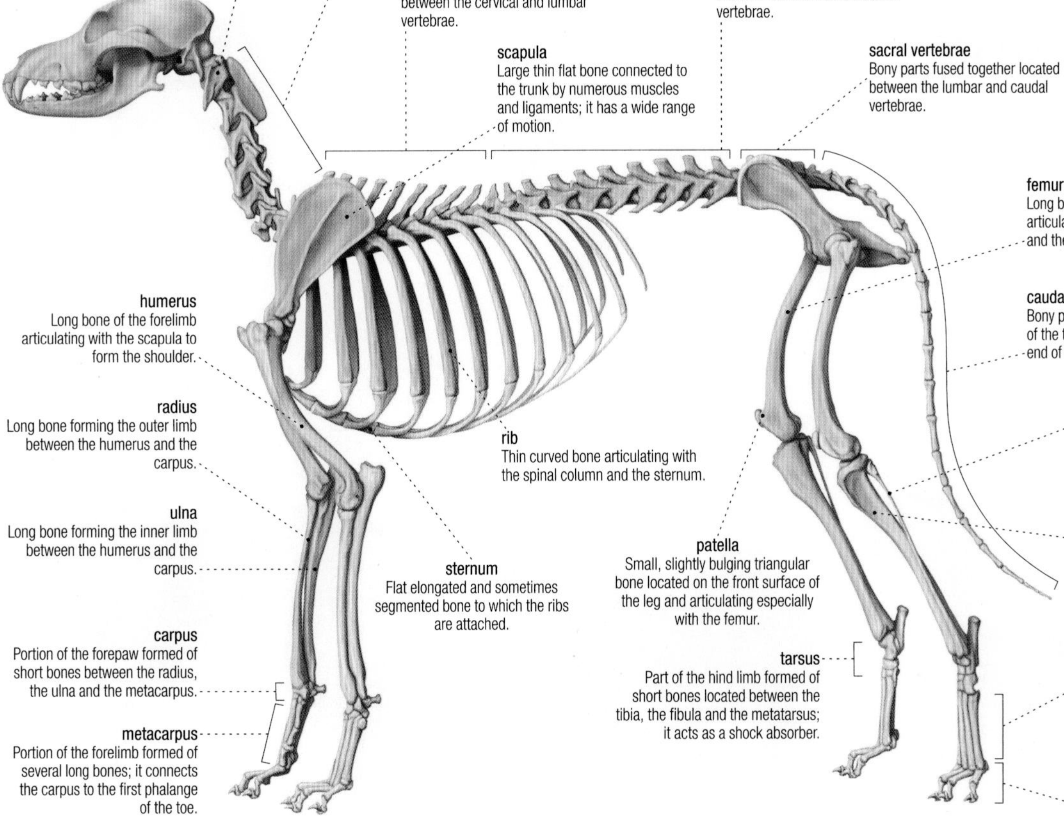

atlas
First cervical vertebra supporting the head and supported by the axis.

thoracic vertebrae
Bony parts supporting the ribs between the cervical and lumbar vertebrae.

lumbar vertebrae
Bony parts of the back located between the thoracic and sacral vertebrae.

scapula
Large thin flat bone connected to the trunk by numerous muscles and ligaments; it has a wide range of motion.

sacral vertebrae
Bony parts fused together located between the lumbar and caudal vertebrae.

femur
Long bone of the hind limb articulating with the pelvis, the tibia and the fibula.

humerus
Long bone of the forelimb articulating with the scapula to form the shoulder.

caudal vertebrae
Bony parts comprising the skeleton of the tail located at the terminal end of the spinal column.

radius
Long bone forming the outer limb between the humerus and the carpus.

rib
Thin curved bone articulating with the spinal column and the sternum.

fibula
Long bone forming the outer limb between the femur and the tarsus.

ulna
Long bone forming the inner limb between the humerus and the carpus.

patella
Small, slightly bulging triangular bone located on the front surface of the leg and articulating especially with the femur.

tibia
Long bone forming the inner limb between the femur and the tarsus.

sternum
Flat elongated and sometimes segmented bone to which the ribs are attached.

metatarsus
Part of the hind limb formed of several long bones; it connects the tarsus to the first phalange of the toe.

carpus
Portion of the forepaw formed of short bones between the radius, the ulna and the metacarpus.

tarsus
Part of the hind limb formed of short bones located between the tibia, the fibula and the metatarsus; it acts as a shock absorber.

metacarpus
Portion of the forelimb formed of several long bones; it connects the carpus to the first phalange of the toe.

phalanges
Articulated bones forming the skeleton of the toes.

frontal bone
Flat skull bone forming the forehead and top of the eye sockets, and articulating especially with the parietal.

parietal bone
Flat bone of the upper side of the skull articulating with the frontal and occipital bones.

skull of a dog
Bony structure enclosing and protecting the brain.

orbit
Bony cavity of the upper lateral portion of the head containing the eye.

occipital bone
Flat bone of the lower back part of the skull articulating with the parietal bone and the atlas.

maxilla
Toothed bone comprising the upper jaw.

mandible
Toothed bone forming the lower jaw.

examples of dog breeds

There are about 400 breeds of dog, classified into 7 groups according to their morphology and use.

ANIMALS

spaniel
Dog of various sizes often trained to be both hunting dog and pet.

poodle
Widely regarded as the most intelligent of domestic dog breeds; the poodle is bred in three varieties: standard, miniature, and toy.

fox terrier
Dog of English origin, with stiff or soft hair and a lively and energetic temperament.

schnauzer
Strong energetic dog originally from Germany, used as a guard dog and also as a pet.

chowchow
Pet originally from China, independent and reserved, it is also used as a guard dog.

collie
Scottish sheepdog and an affectionate and highly valued pet; the long-haired variety is more common than the short-haired variety.

dalmatian
Energetic and quite independent pet valued for its elegance; it also makes a good guard dog.

Yorkshire terrier
Small pet dog of English origin, originally used in hunting small game.

Pomeranian
Small pet dog originally from the Prussian province of Pomerania, in Germany. It has an alert and energetic temperament and makes a good watchdog.

bulldog
Extremely affectionate and playful pet with a muscular body; it becomes aggressive when its owner is attacked.

ANIMALS

greyhound
Muscular streamlined dog; it is very
swift and is used mainly for hunting
and sports competitions.

German shepherd
The most common multipurpose dog in
the world: sheepdog, guard dog, police
dog (detection and search), guide dog
for the blind and pet.

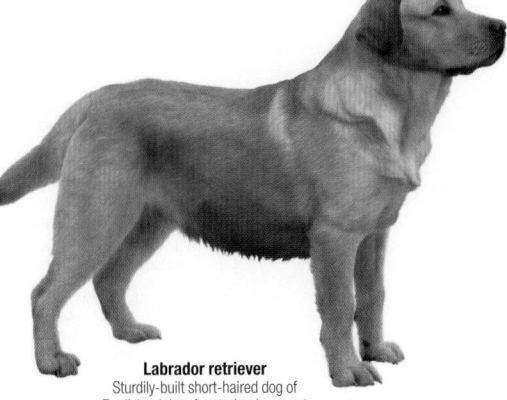

Labrador retriever
Sturdily-built short-haired dog of
English origin, often trained as a pet
or an assistance dog.

golden retriever
Hunting dog of English origin that
retrieves shot down prey. Affectionate
and docile, it is often used as an
assistance dog for handicapped
persons.

Saint Bernard
Large, very muscular dog used as
a rescue dog in the Alps.

Great Dane
Very tall pet and guard dog, originally
from Germany; it is affectionate and
well behaved.

cat

Carnivorous mammal with a supple muscular body and paws ending in retractable claws; it is a very common pet.

head of a cat
Anterior portion of the body containing the sensory organs and the brain.

whiskers
Highly sensitive long stiff hairs located above the eyes and having a tactile function.

upper eyelid
Thin muscular membrane lowering from the upper edge of the eye to protect and clean it.

lower eyelid
Thin muscular membrane that is translucent and movable; it rises from the lower edge of the eye to protect and cleanse it.

nictitating membrane
Thin muscular membrane extending sideways from the inside corner of the eye to protect and moisten it.

whiskers
Extremely sensitive long stiff hairs (vibrissae) located on the muzzle having a tactile function.

eyelashes
Hairs implanted on the free edge of the eyelid preventing dust and other particles from landing on the eye.

pupil
Central opening of the eye where light enters; it is particularly well adapted to the dark.

nose leather
Terminal end of the muzzle bearing the nostrils made of strong damp tissue; it has an olfactory and respiratory function.

muzzle
Short round front part of the head with whiskers; it has a highly developed tactile and olfactory function.

lip
Movable muscular part forming the contour of the mouth; a cat has two upper lips lined with whiskers.

retracted claw
When a cat walks, its claws retract into a cutaneous fold (sheath) and it moves on its pad.

claw
Curved pointy retractable horny structure allowing the cat to climb, catch its prey and defend itself.

metacarpus
Portion of the forelimb formed of several long bones; it connects the carpus to the first phalanx of the toe.

distal phalanx
Bone of the lower terminal end of the toe bearing the claw.

middle phalanx
Bone of the central part of the toe between the proximal and distal phalanges.

proximal phalanx
Bone of the upper terminal end of the toe connected to the metacarpus.

tendon
Fibrous tissue connecting the muscle to the bone; relaxing the tendon causes the claw to retract.

morphology of a cat

ear
Highly mobile organ of hearing, also contributing to equilibrium; cats have a highly developed sense of hearing.

eye
Organ of sight especially adapted to darkness; it mainly perceives light intensity, motion and certain colors.

tail
Terminal appendage of the body providing equilibrium when the cat jumps.

fur
Hair covering the entire body, except the nose; its main function is to maintain body temperature.

extended claw
A cat uses its claws only when necessary, mainly for climbing or killing its prey.

elastic ligament
Strong and elastic fibrous tissue located on the back of the distal and middle phalanges allowing the claw to retract into the sheath.

digital pad
Thick cutaneous bulge, elastic and resistant to wear upon which the toe rests; it contributes to locomotion and absorbs shocks.

plantar pad
Thick cutaneous bulge, elastic and resistant to wear, supporting the metacarpus; the cat uses it to move about and it absorbs shocks.

tendon
Fibrous tissue connecting the muscle to the bone; the traction causes the claws to extend.

examples of cat breeds

There are about 40 officially recognized breeds of domestic cat, classified into three groups according to the length of their hair (short, medium-long or long).

sphynx
Cat, originally from Canada, with very fine, downy fur and a very affectionate temperament.

Abyssinian
Svelte cat originally from Egypt or Ethiopia, docile and energetic; it has a melodious meow.

Siamese
Slender cat originally from Thailand, playful and affectionate; it has a loud raucous meow.

ANIMALS

Norwegian forest cat
Large cat of Norwegian origin having an energetic temperament.

Russian blue
Short-haired cat with green eyes, of Eurasian origin. It is calm and intelligent.

Manx
Tailless cat with hind limbs longer than its forelimbs.

Persian
Highly prized cat with silky fur, calm and affectionate; there are many varieties differentiated by the color of the fur and the eyes.

American shorthair
Energetic and resilient cat that is in great demand in the U.S. and Japan.

Maine coon
Sturdy cat, calm and affectionate, with a melodious meow; very popular in the U.S. but less common in Europe.

Bengal
Large cat developed originally in the U.S. by crossing a domesticated cat with a wild Asian leopard cat. Very affectionate, it also loves water.

ANIMALS

examples of carnivorous mammals

Carnivorous mammals (about 270 species) that have strong canines (fangs) and sharp molars (carnassials) adapted for eating flesh.

weasel
Very agile carnivorous mammal found mainly in the northern hemisphere; it is capable of attacking large prey (rats, voles, rabbits) in spite of its size.

stone marten
Mostly nocturnal carnivorous mammal of Eurasia; it is a good swimmer and climber and often catches birds, domestic rabbits and rats.

mink
Carnivorous semiaquatic and mostly nocturnal mammal with webbed feet found in Eurasia and the Americas; it is hunted and raised in captivity for its highly prized fur.

mongoose
Very agile carnivorous mammal of Africa and Eurasia; it is easily tamed and is used to destroy harmful pests (snakes, rats).

ferret
Small mammal formerly used in rabbit hunting, and today kept as a pet.

skunk
Carnivorous mammal of the Americas, whose fur is prized; when threatened, it releases a nauseous and irritating secretion from its anal glands.

marten
Mostly nocturnal agile carnivorous mammal of Eurasia and North America prized for its silky fur; it is a good climber.

river otter
Widespread carnivorous semiaquatic and usually nocturnal mammal with webbed feet feeding mainly on fish and prized for its fur.

badger
Mostly nocturnal, carnivorous mammal of the northern hemisphere digging complex tunnels; its hairs are used to make hairbrushes and paintbrushes.

fennec
Nocturnal carnivorous mammal found in the deserts of Arabia and North Africa; it is easily tamed and capable of going without water for long periods.

hyena
Carnivorous scavenger of Africa and Asia; hyenas live alone or in packs and will attack live prey.

fox
Very common carnivorous mammal living in a den and hunting at night (mostly rodents); its fur is highly prized.

raccoon
Mostly nocturnal carnivorous mammal of the Americas.

cougar
Carnivorous mammal of the Americas living in various habitats (mountains, forests); it hunts only at night and is famed for its ability to leap.

lynx
Very agile and powerful carnivorous mammal found in the forests of the northern hemisphere; it is a night hunter with piercing eyes and its fur is highly prized.

wolverine
Heavy and bulky mammal found in the tundra and coniferous forests of the northern hemisphere.

ANIMALS

leopard
Carnivorous mammal of Africa
and Asia with yellow fur and black
spots; it mostly lives in trees and
usually hunts at night.

tiger
Large and very powerful carnivorous
mammal of Asia; it hunts at night.

jaguar
Carnivorous mammal of Central
and South America with spotted
fur; it is an excellent swimmer and
hunts at night.

wolf
Nocturnal carnivorous mammal of
Eurasia and North America; it lives
in packs and hunts large mammals
(deer).

cheetah
Carnivorous mammal of Africa and the
Middle East with nonretractable claws;
it is the fastest of the land mammals,
reaching speeds of 62 mph.

lion
Large carnivorous mammal
common mainly in Africa that lives
in groups called prides; only the
male has a mane.

black bear
Mostly nocturnal carnivorous mammal
of North America; it is a good swimmer,
is an excellent climber and feeds
mainly on fruit and nuts.

polar bear
Carnivorous mammal of arctic regions; a good
swimmer, it feeds mainly on seals and fish, and is
the largest carnivorous land mammal.

dolphin

Marine mammal without hind limbs; it uses echoes of the sounds it emits (sonar) to orient itself and detect its prey.

morphology of a dolphin

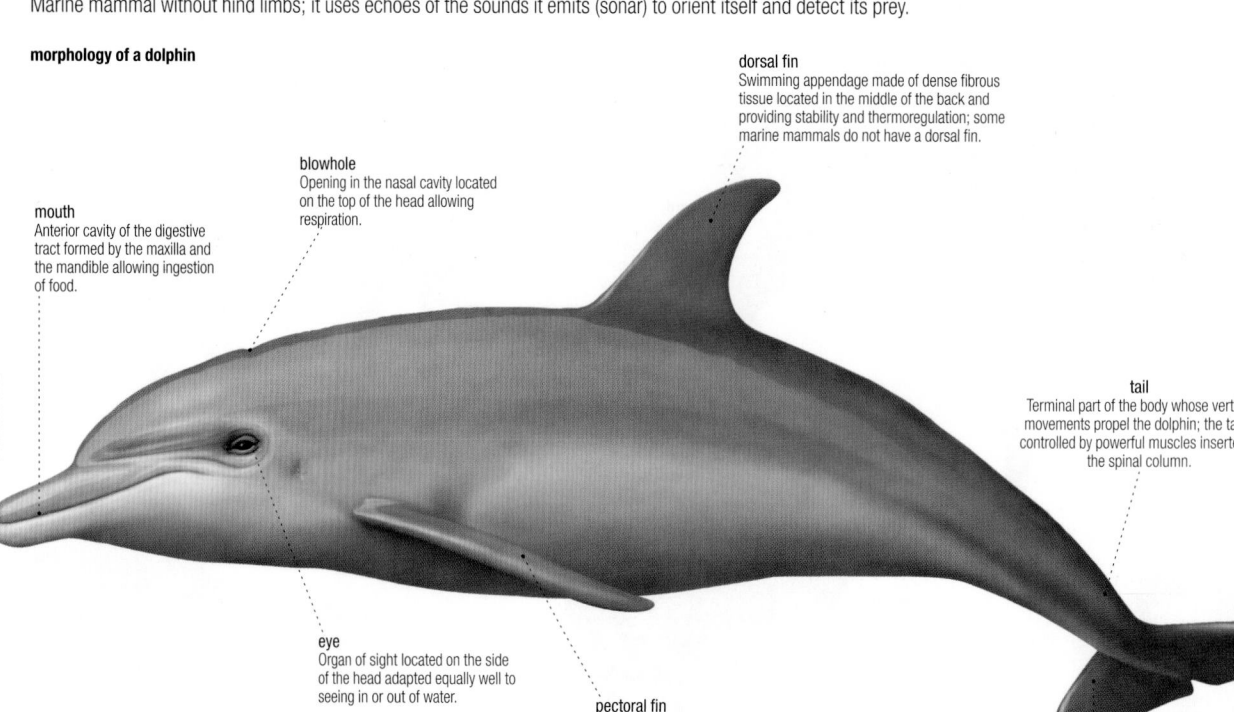

dorsal fin
Swimming appendage made of dense fibrous tissue located in the middle of the back and providing stability and thermoregulation; some marine mammals do not have a dorsal fin.

blowhole
Opening in the nasal cavity located on the top of the head allowing respiration.

mouth
Anterior cavity of the digestive tract formed by the maxilla and the mandible allowing ingestion of food.

tail
Terminal part of the body whose vertical movements propel the dolphin; the tail is controlled by powerful muscles inserted i the spinal column.

eye
Organ of sight located on the side of the head adapted equally well to seeing in or out of water.

pectoral fin
Swimming appendage made of bone that ensures stability, orientation, stopping and thermoregulation.

caudal fin
Powerful swimming appendage with two lobes formed of dense fibrous tissue located vertically at the posterior terminal part of the body; its function is propulsion.

skeleton of a dolphin

maxilla
Toothed bone comprising the upper jaw.

skull
Bony structure enclosing and protecting the brain.

orbit
Bony cavity of the upper lateral portion of the head containing the eye.

scapula
Large thin flat bone connected to the spinal column and allowing the pectoral fin to move.

vertebra
Bony part of the dorsal portion of the body mainly supporting the ribs; all the vertebrae together form the spinal column.

mandible
Toothed bone forming the lower jaw.

floating rib
Thin curved bone whose terminal end articulates with the vertebrae, while the other end remains free.

vestigial pelvis
Rudimentary bone resulting from the reduction of the pelvis and posterior limbs located in the muscle mass.

humerus
Short bone of the pectoral fin articulating with the scapula, the radius and the ulna.

phalanges
Fixed bones forming the skeleton of the digits.

metacarpus
Part of the pectoral fin formed of several long bones; it connects the carpus to the first phalange.

radius
Short bone of the pectoral fin between the humerus and the carpus.

ulna
Short bone of the pectoral fin between the humerus and the carpus.

carpus
Portion of the forelimb formed of short bones between the radius, the ulna and the metacarpus.

examples of marine mammals

Marine mammals: many actively hunted species (more than 110 out of 116) are protected or are subject to hunting restrictions.

walrus
Semiaquatic marine mammal of arctic regions; it is hunted for its hide, blubber and ivory tusks.

sea lion
Short-haired semiaquatic marine mammal with external ear flaps that moves about on land with the help of its four limbs; it is hunted mainly for its fur.

seal
Short-haired semiaquatic marine mammal lacking external ear flaps that moves about on land by dragging its body; it is hunted for its meat, blubber and fur.

narwhal
Mammal of arctic waters; the male, whose spiraled tusk can reach 10 feet in length, is hunted for its ivory.

dolphin
Mammal of warm and temperate waters famed for its intelligence; it is a swift swimmer (about 28 mph).

porpoise
Mammal found in cold and temperate waters whose flesh is highly prized; it is a protected species.

beluga whale
Marine mammal of arctic and subarctic waters emitting various whistles to communicate, hence its nickname "sea canary".

killer whale
Widespread swift aggressive marine mammal reaching up to 30 feet in length; it attacks mainly young whales and dolphins.

humpback whale
Widespread marine mammal with a mouth lined with horny plates (baleen) and numerous longitudinal grooves on its throat.

northern right whale
Marine mammal that can reach 60 ft in length and has a mouth lined with horny plates (baleen); it is a protected species.

sperm whale
Widespread deep-diving marine mammal reaching up to 65 ft in length; hunted mainly for its meat and blubber, it is now a protected species.

gorilla

Mainly terrestrial herbivorous primate of the equatorial forests of Africa; the largest of the primates, it can reach 6 ft in height.

skeleton of a gorilla

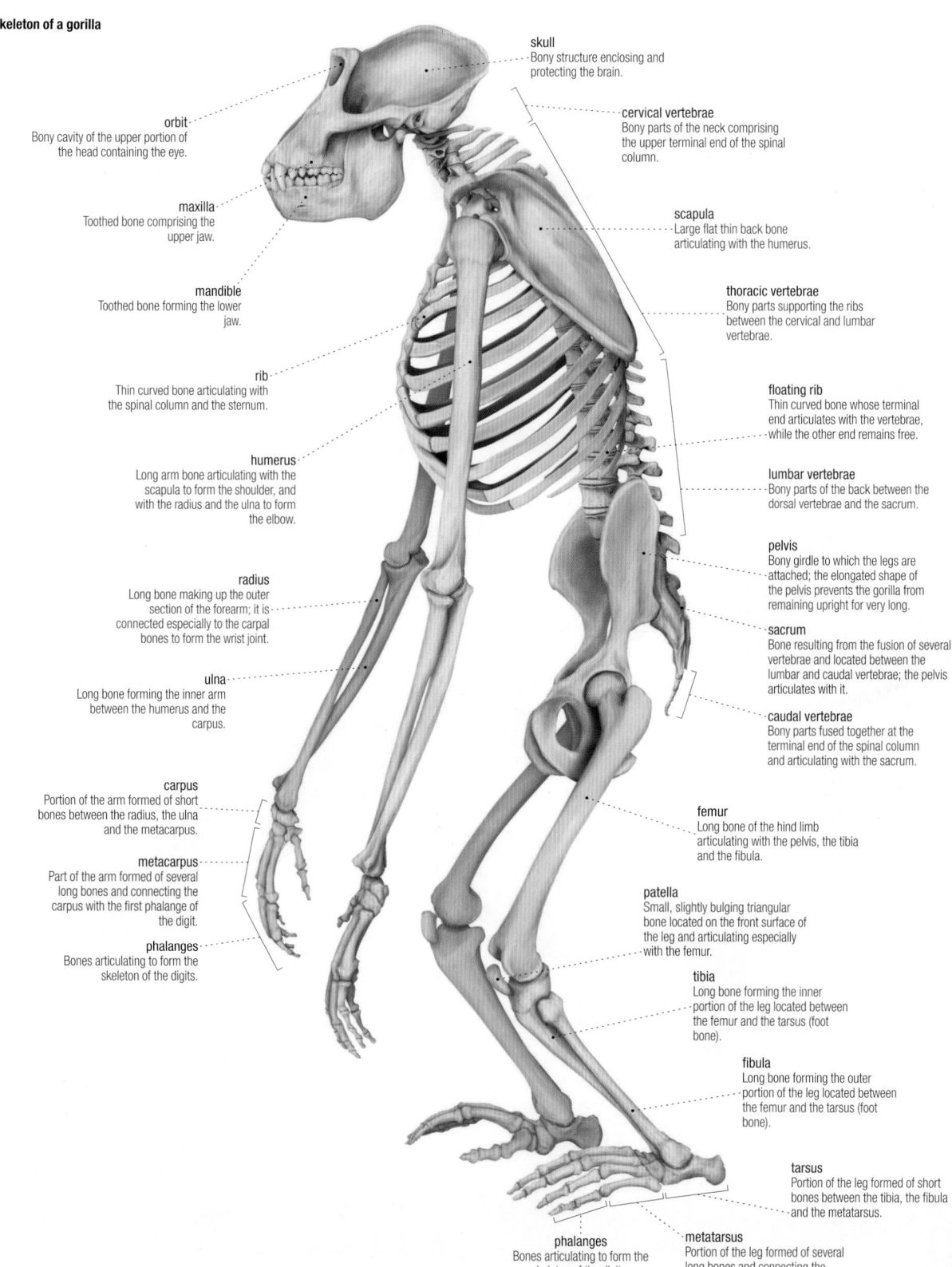

skull
Bony structure enclosing and protecting the brain.

orbit
Bony cavity of the upper portion of the head containing the eye.

cervical vertebrae
Bony parts of the neck comprising the upper terminal end of the spinal column.

maxilla
Toothed bone comprising the upper jaw.

scapula
Large flat thin back bone articulating with the humerus.

mandible
Toothed bone forming the lower jaw.

thoracic vertebrae
Bony parts supporting the ribs between the cervical and lumbar vertebrae.

rib
Thin curved bone articulating with the spinal column and the sternum.

floating rib
Thin curved bone whose terminal end articulates with the vertebrae, while the other end remains free.

humerus
Long arm bone articulating with the scapula to form the shoulder, and with the radius and the ulna to form the elbow.

lumbar vertebrae
Bony parts of the back between the dorsal vertebrae and the sacrum.

pelvis
Bony girdle to which the legs are attached; the elongated shape of the pelvis prevents the gorilla from remaining upright for very long.

radius
Long bone making up the outer section of the forearm; it is connected especially to the carpal bones to form the wrist joint.

sacrum
Bone resulting from the fusion of several vertebrae and located between the lumbar and caudal vertebrae; the pelvis articulates with it.

ulna
Long bone forming the inner arm between the humerus and the carpus.

caudal vertebrae
Bony parts fused together at the terminal end of the spinal column and articulating with the sacrum.

carpus
Portion of the arm formed of short bones between the radius, the ulna and the metacarpus.

femur
Long bone of the hind limb articulating with the pelvis, the tibia and the fibula.

metacarpus
Part of the arm formed of several long bones and connecting the carpus with the first phalange of the digit.

patella
Small, slightly bulging triangular bone located on the front surface of the leg and articulating especially with the femur.

phalanges
Bones articulating to form the skeleton of the digits.

tibia
Long bone forming the inner portion of the leg located between the femur and the tarsus (foot bone).

fibula
Long bone forming the outer portion of the leg located between the femur and the tarsus (foot bone).

tarsus
Portion of the leg formed of short bones between the tibia, the fibula and the metatarsus.

phalanges
Bones articulating to form the skeleton of the digits.

metatarsus
Portion of the leg formed of several long bones and connecting the tarsus with the first phalange of the digit.

gorilla

morphology of a gorilla

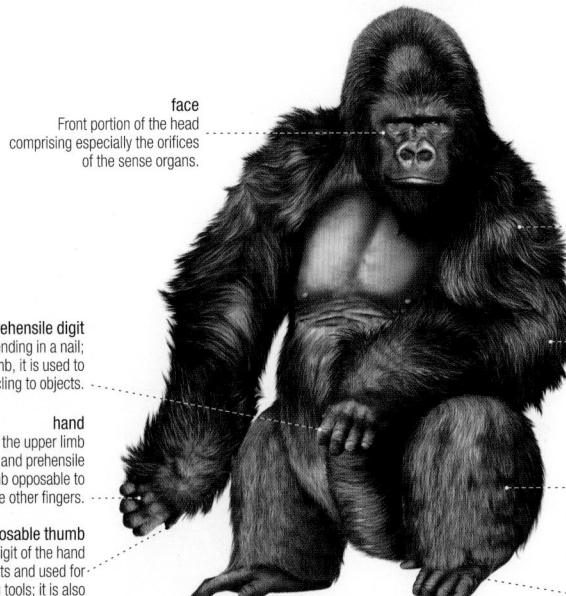

face
Front portion of the head comprising especially the orifices of the sense organs.

fur
Hair covering the body, with the main exceptions of the face, palms of the hands and soles of the feet; it maintains body temperature.

arm
Powerful muscular upper limb mainly supporting the body while walking.

prehensile digit
Articulated limb ending in a nail; along with the thumb, it is used to grasp food and to cling to objects.

hand
Terminal part of the upper limb having a tactile and prehensile function, with a thumb opposable to the other fingers.

opposable thumb
Short sturdy first digit of the hand facing the other digits and used for grasping and using tools; it is also used to hang from objects.

leg
Powerful muscular lower limb supporting the body in an upright position.

foot
Terminal end of the leg bearing five digits; it rests on the ground and has a prehensile and motor function.

examples of primates

Many species are protected, especially because of deforestation (destruction of their habitat) and hunting.

chimpanzee
Primate of equatorial Africa whose genetic makeup is very close to that of humans; it is used sometimes in medical research.

tamarin
Small hopping tree-dwelling primate of South America with elongated claws instead of nails that allow it to move about and to feed.

gibbon
Tailless tree-dwelling primate of Asia; it swings from branch to branch with agility, using its hands as hooks.

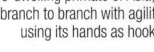

marmoset
Small South American primate with strong claws instead of nails that it uses to cling to the trees it lives in.

capuchin
Small tree-dwelling monkey of Central and South America with fur around its head resembling a hood.

orangutan
Primate found in Sumatra and Borneo with long powerful arms; it moves slowly and carefully between the trees in which it lives.

lemur
Tree-dwelling agile primate of Madagascar with a long tail; it is mainly nocturnal and feeds on insects and fruit.

baboon
Mainly terrestrial primate found mainly in Africa with colored callosities on the buttocks and large cheek pouches in which it stores food.

macaque
Common primate of Asia and North Africa including some short-tailed or tailless forms living on the ground and in trees; some species are used in laboratory experiments.

ANIMALS

bat

Usually insectivorous nocturnal flying mammal using echoes of the sounds it produces (echolocation) to orient itself and to find its prey.

morphology of a bat

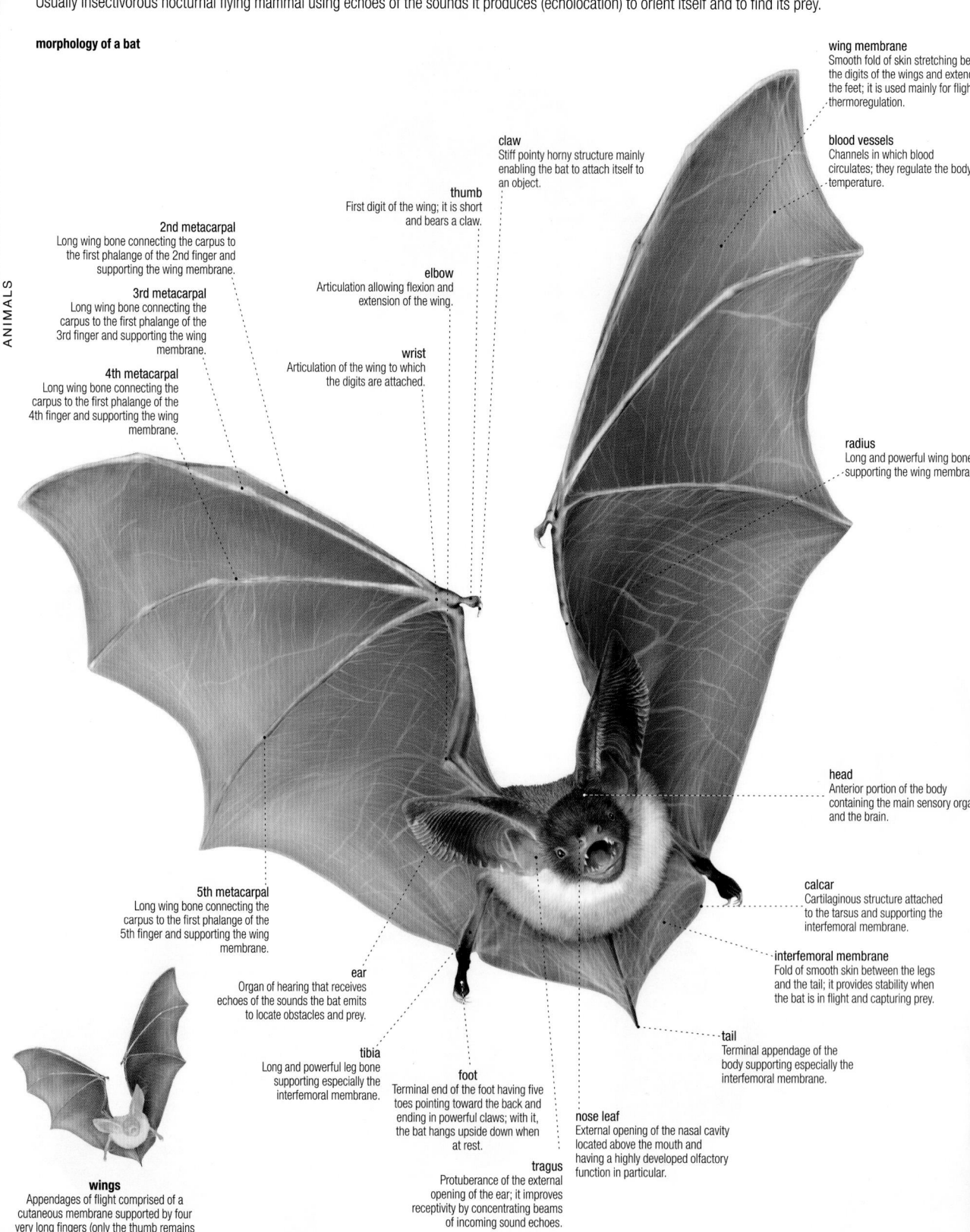

wing membrane
Smooth fold of skin stretching be the digits of the wings and extend the feet; it is used mainly for fligh thermoregulation.

blood vessels
Channels in which blood circulates; they regulate the body temperature.

claw
Stiff pointy horny structure mainly enabling the bat to attach itself to an object.

thumb
First digit of the wing; it is short and bears a claw.

2nd metacarpal
Long wing bone connecting the carpus to the first phalange of the 2nd finger and supporting the wing membrane.

elbow
Articulation allowing flexion and extension of the wing.

3rd metacarpal
Long wing bone connecting the carpus to the first phalange of the 3rd finger and supporting the wing membrane.

wrist
Articulation of the wing to which the digits are attached.

4th metacarpal
Long wing bone connecting the carpus to the first phalange of the 4th finger and supporting the wing membrane.

radius
Long and powerful wing bone supporting the wing membra.

head
Anterior portion of the body containing the main sensory orga and the brain.

5th metacarpal
Long wing bone connecting the carpus to the first phalange of the 5th finger and supporting the wing membrane.

calcar
Cartilaginous structure attached to the tarsus and supporting the interfemoral membrane.

interfemoral membrane
Fold of smooth skin between the legs and the tail; it provides stability when the bat is in flight and capturing prey.

ear
Organ of hearing that receives echoes of the sounds the bat emits to locate obstacles and prey.

tibia
Long and powerful leg bone supporting especially the interfemoral membrane.

foot
Terminal end of the foot having five toes pointing toward the back and ending in powerful claws; with it, the bat hangs upside down when at rest.

tail
Terminal appendage of the body supporting especially the interfemoral membrane.

nose leaf
External opening of the nasal cavity located above the mouth and having a highly developed olfactory function in particular.

tragus
Protuberance of the external opening of the ear; it improves receptivity by concentrating beams of incoming sound echoes.

wings
Appendages of flight comprised of a cutaneous membrane supported by four very long fingers (only the thumb remains free); the bat folds its wings when resting.

bat

scapula
Large thin flat bone; with the
vicle, it serves as an attachment
point for the wing.

mandible
Toothed bone forming the lower
jaw.

skull
Bony structure enclosing and
protecting the brain.

cervical vertebrae
Bony parts of the neck comprising
the upper terminal end of the spinal
column.

skeleton of a bat

humerus
Long wing bone articulating with
the scapula to form the shoulder.

clavicle
Long bone located between the
sternum and the scapula.

thumb
First digit of the wing; it is short
and bears a claw.

carpus
Portion of the wing formed of two
short bones; it is located between
the radius, the ulna and the
metacarpus.

rib
hin curved bone articulating with
spinal column and the sternum.

radius
g and powerful wing bone
rting the wing membrane.

lumbar vertebrae
Bony parts of the back located
between the thoracic and sacral
vertebrae.

sacrum
Bone resulting from the fusion of
several vertebrae and located between
the lumbar and caudal vertebrae; the
pelvis articulates with it.

ulna
one between the humerus
and the carpus.

femur
Long bone of the hind limb
articulating with the pelvis, the tibia
and the fibula.

sternum
Long flat bone to which certain
ribs are attached; powerful flight
muscles are inserted into its crest.

phalanx
Articulated bone forming the
skeleton of the fingers and
supporting the wing membrane.

ANIMALS

tarsus
Portion of the foot formed of short
bones between the tibia, the fibula
and the metatarsus.

tibia
Long bone forming the inner limb
between the femur and the tarsus.

metatarsus
Portion of the foot formed of
several long bones and connecting
the tarsus to the first phalange of
the digit.

caudal vertebrae
Bony parts comprising the skeleton of
the tail located at the terminal end of
the spinal column.

phalanx
Articulated bone forming the
skeleton of the toes and supporting
the interfemoral membrane.

calcar
Cartilaginous structure attached
to the tarsus and supporting the
interfemoral membrane.

pelvis
Bony girdle serving as an
attachment point for the legs.

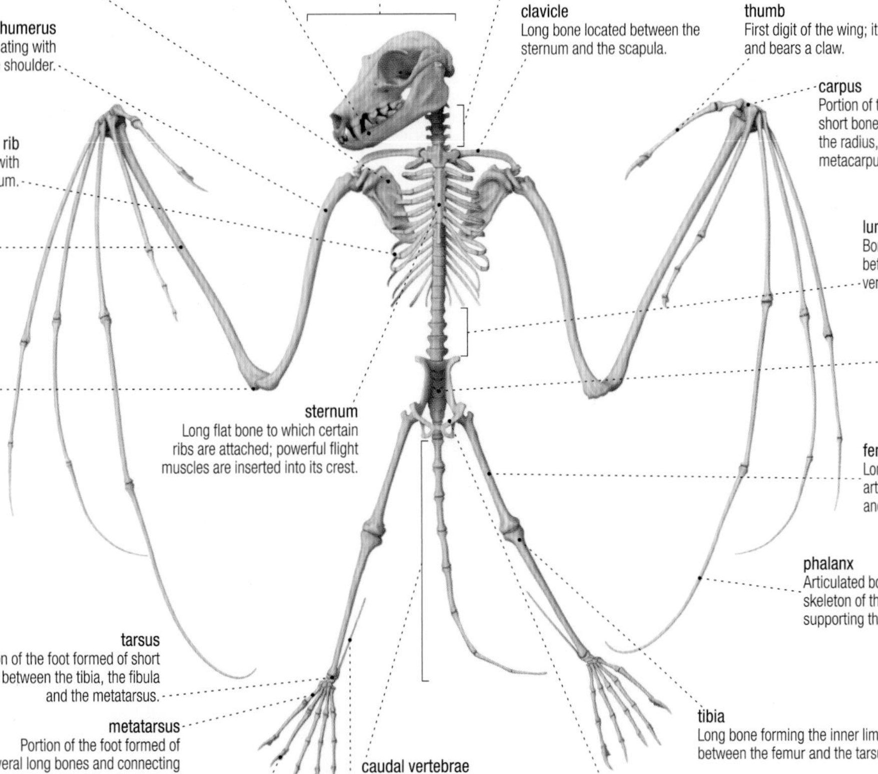

examples of flying mammals

Very widespread, some 900 species of bats live mainly in colonies, in trees or in caves.

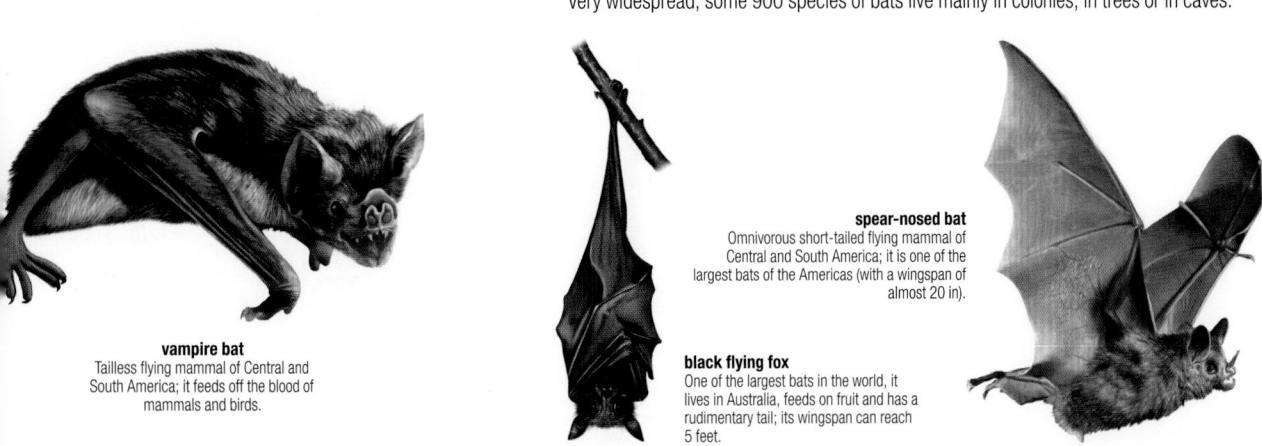

spear-nosed bat
Omnivorous short-tailed flying mammal of
Central and South America; it is one of the
largest bats of the Americas (with a wingspan of
almost 20 in).

vampire bat
Tailless flying mammal of Central and
South America; it feeds off the blood of
mammals and birds.

black flying fox
One of the largest bats in the world, it
lives in Australia, feeds on fruit and has a
rudimentary tail; its wingspan can reach
5 feet.

ANIMALS

kangaroo

Herbivorous marsupial with a highly developed tail; it lives in groups in Australia and Tasmania and moves rapidly by leaping.

skeleton of a kangaroo

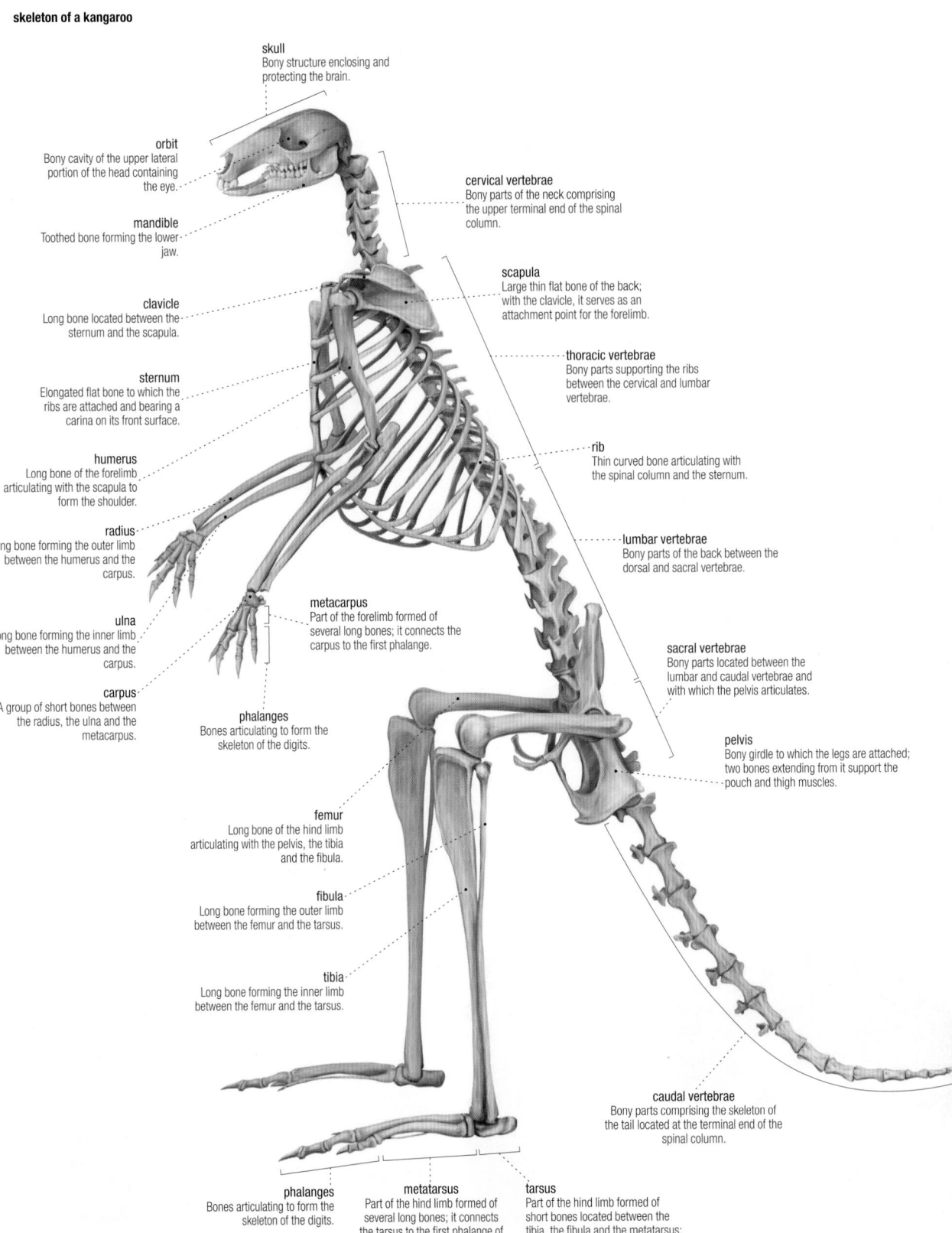

skull
Bony structure enclosing and protecting the brain.

orbit
Bony cavity of the upper lateral portion of the head containing the eye.

mandible
Toothed bone forming the lower jaw.

clavicle
Long bone located between the sternum and the scapula.

sternum
Elongated flat bone to which the ribs are attached and bearing a carina on its front surface.

humerus
Long bone of the forelimb articulating with the scapula to form the shoulder.

radius
Long bone forming the outer limb between the humerus and the carpus.

ulna
Long bone forming the inner limb between the humerus and the carpus.

carpus
A group of short bones between the radius, the ulna and the metacarpus.

cervical vertebrae
Bony parts of the neck comprising the upper terminal end of the spinal column.

scapula
Large thin flat bone of the back; with the clavicle, it serves as an attachment point for the forelimb.

thoracic vertebrae
Bony parts supporting the ribs between the cervical and lumbar vertebrae.

rib
Thin curved bone articulating with the spinal column and the sternum.

lumbar vertebrae
Bony parts of the back between the dorsal and sacral vertebrae.

metacarpus
Part of the forelimb formed of several long bones; it connects the carpus to the first phalange.

sacral vertebrae
Bony parts located between the lumbar and caudal vertebrae and with which the pelvis articulates.

phalanges
Bones articulating to form the skeleton of the digits.

pelvis
Bony girdle to which the legs are attached; two bones extending from it support the pouch and thigh muscles.

femur
Long bone of the hind limb articulating with the pelvis, the tibia and the fibula.

fibula
Long bone forming the outer limb between the femur and the tarsus.

tibia
Long bone forming the inner limb between the femur and the tarsus.

caudal vertebrae
Bony parts comprising the skeleton of the tail located at the terminal end of the spinal column.

phalanges
Bones articulating to form the skeleton of the digits.

metatarsus
Part of the hind limb formed of several long bones; it connects the tarsus to the first phalange of the digit.

tarsus
Part of the hind limb formed of short bones located between the tibia, the fibula and the metatarsus; it acts as a shock absorber.

ANIMALS

kangaroo

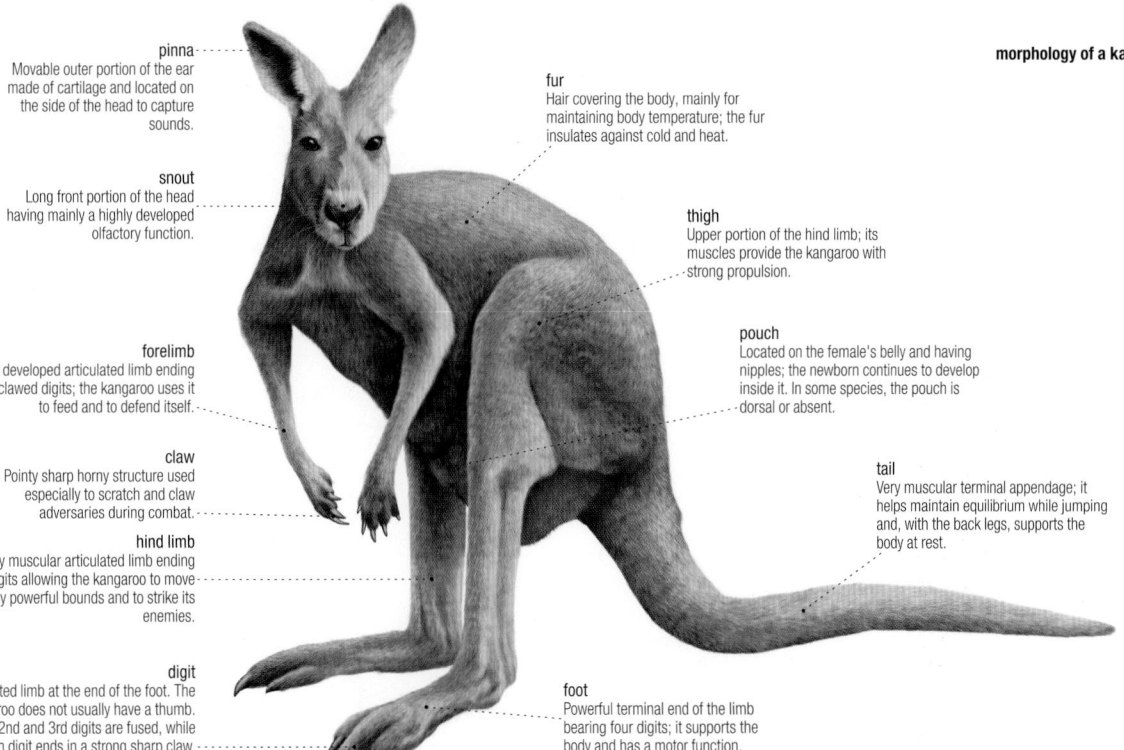

morphology of a kangaroo

pinna
Movable outer portion of the ear made of cartilage and located on the side of the head to capture sounds.

snout
Long front portion of the head having mainly a highly developed olfactory function.

forelimb
Poorly developed articulated limb ending in five clawed digits; the kangaroo uses it to feed and to defend itself.

claw
Pointy sharp horny structure used especially to scratch and claw adversaries during combat.

hind limb
Extremely muscular articulated limb ending in four digits allowing the kangaroo to move swiftly by powerful bounds and to strike its enemies.

digit
Articulated limb at the end of the foot. The kangaroo does not usually have a thumb. The 2nd and 3rd digits are fused, while the 4th digit ends in a strong sharp claw.

fur
Hair covering the body, mainly for maintaining body temperature; the fur insulates against cold and heat.

thigh
Upper portion of the hind limb; its muscles provide the kangaroo with strong propulsion.

pouch
Located on the female's belly and having nipples; the newborn continues to develop inside it. In some species, the pouch is dorsal or absent.

tail
Very muscular terminal appendage; it helps maintain equilibrium while jumping and, with the back legs, supports the body at rest.

foot
Powerful terminal end of the limb bearing four digits; it supports the body and has a motor function.

examples of marsupials

The 260 or so species live on land or in trees in Oceania and the Americas.

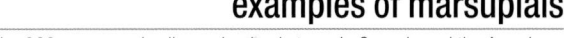
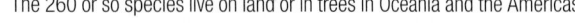

opossum
Nocturnal omnivorous marsupial of the Americas that has a prehensile tail and mostly lives in trees; certain species do not have a pouch.

Tasmanian devil
Carnivorous scavenging nocturnal marsupial with powerful jaws that allow it to devour its prey whole (flesh, bones, fur, feathers).

wallaby
Marsupial closely related to the kangaroo and living in Australia, Tasmania and New Guinea; certain species are prized for their fur.

koala
Tailless nocturnal marsupial of Australia; this solitary tree-dweller lives in eucalyptus forests and feeds on the tree's leaves.

kangaroo
Herbivorous marsupial with a highly developed tail; it lives in groups in Australia and Tasmania and moves rapidly by leaping.

HUMAN BEING

Living being representing the most evolved species on Earth, characterized especially by upright stance, spoken language and a large brain.

man

Male human being producing reproductive cells (sperm) able to fertilize eggs; the male's skeleton is generally larger and heavier than that of the female.

anterior view

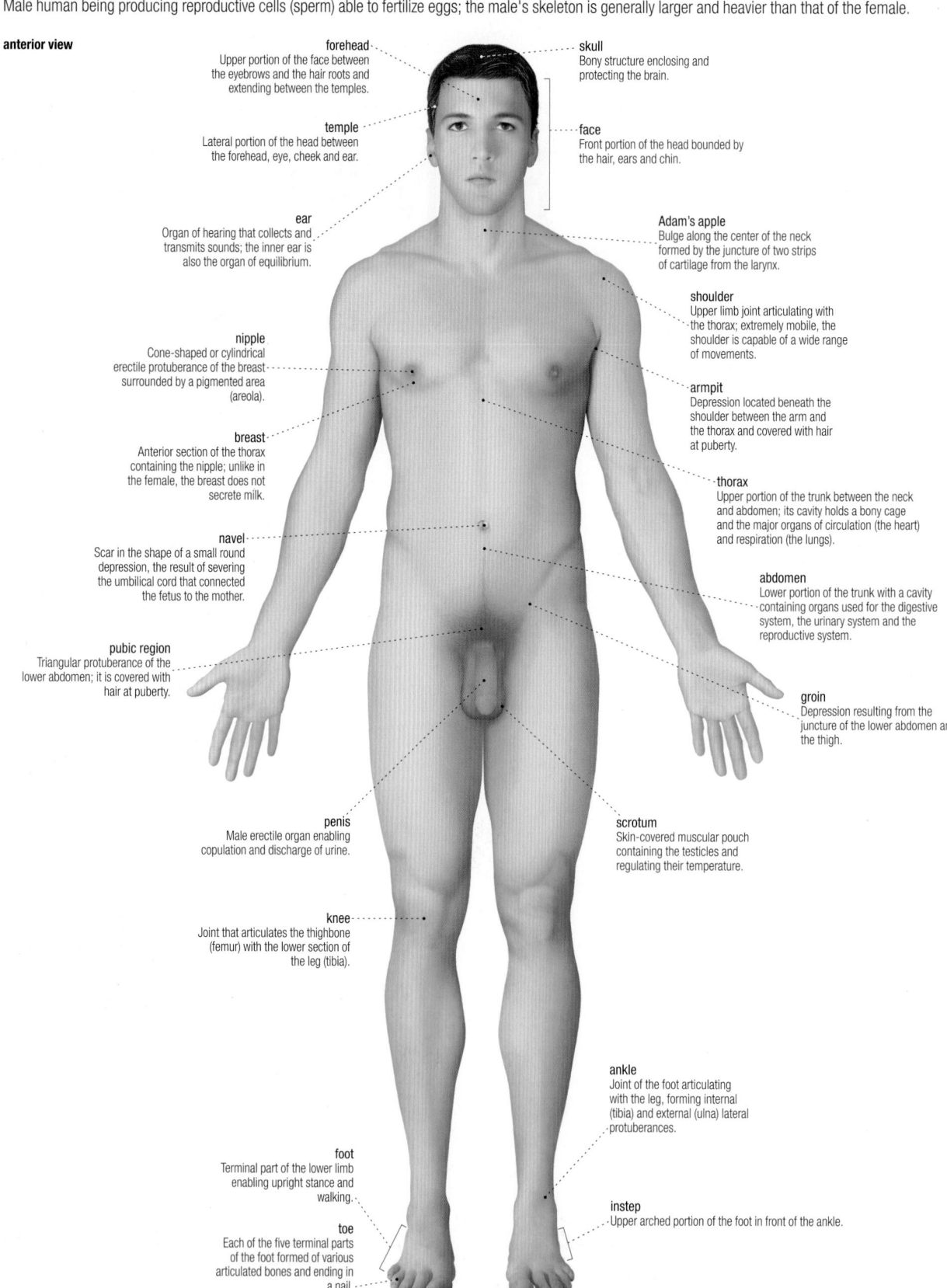

forehead
Upper portion of the face between the eyebrows and the hair roots and extending between the temples.

skull
Bony structure enclosing and protecting the brain.

temple
Lateral portion of the head between the forehead, eye, cheek and ear.

face
Front portion of the head bounded by the hair, ears and chin.

ear
Organ of hearing that collects and transmits sounds; the inner ear is also the organ of equilibrium.

Adam's apple
Bulge along the center of the neck formed by the juncture of two strips of cartilage from the larynx.

shoulder
Upper limb joint articulating with the thorax; extremely mobile, the shoulder is capable of a wide range of movements.

nipple
Cone-shaped or cylindrical erectile protuberance of the breast surrounded by a pigmented area (areola).

armpit
Depression located beneath the shoulder between the arm and the thorax and covered with hair at puberty.

breast
Anterior section of the thorax containing the nipple; unlike in the female, the breast does not secrete milk.

thorax
Upper portion of the trunk between the neck and abdomen; its cavity holds a bony cage and the major organs of circulation (the heart) and respiration (the lungs).

navel
Scar in the shape of a small round depression, the result of severing the umbilical cord that connected the fetus to the mother.

abdomen
Lower portion of the trunk with a cavity containing organs used for the digestive system, the urinary system and the reproductive system.

pubic region
Triangular protuberance of the lower abdomen; it is covered with hair at puberty.

groin
Depression resulting from the juncture of the lower abdomen and the thigh.

penis
Male erectile organ enabling copulation and discharge of urine.

scrotum
Skin-covered muscular pouch containing the testicles and regulating their temperature.

knee
Joint that articulates the thighbone (femur) with the lower section of the leg (tibia).

ankle
Joint of the foot articulating with the leg, forming internal (tibia) and external (ulna) lateral protuberances.

foot
Terminal part of the lower limb enabling upright stance and walking.

instep
Upper arched portion of the foot in front of the ankle.

toe
Each of the five terminal parts of the foot formed of various articulated bones and ending in a nail.

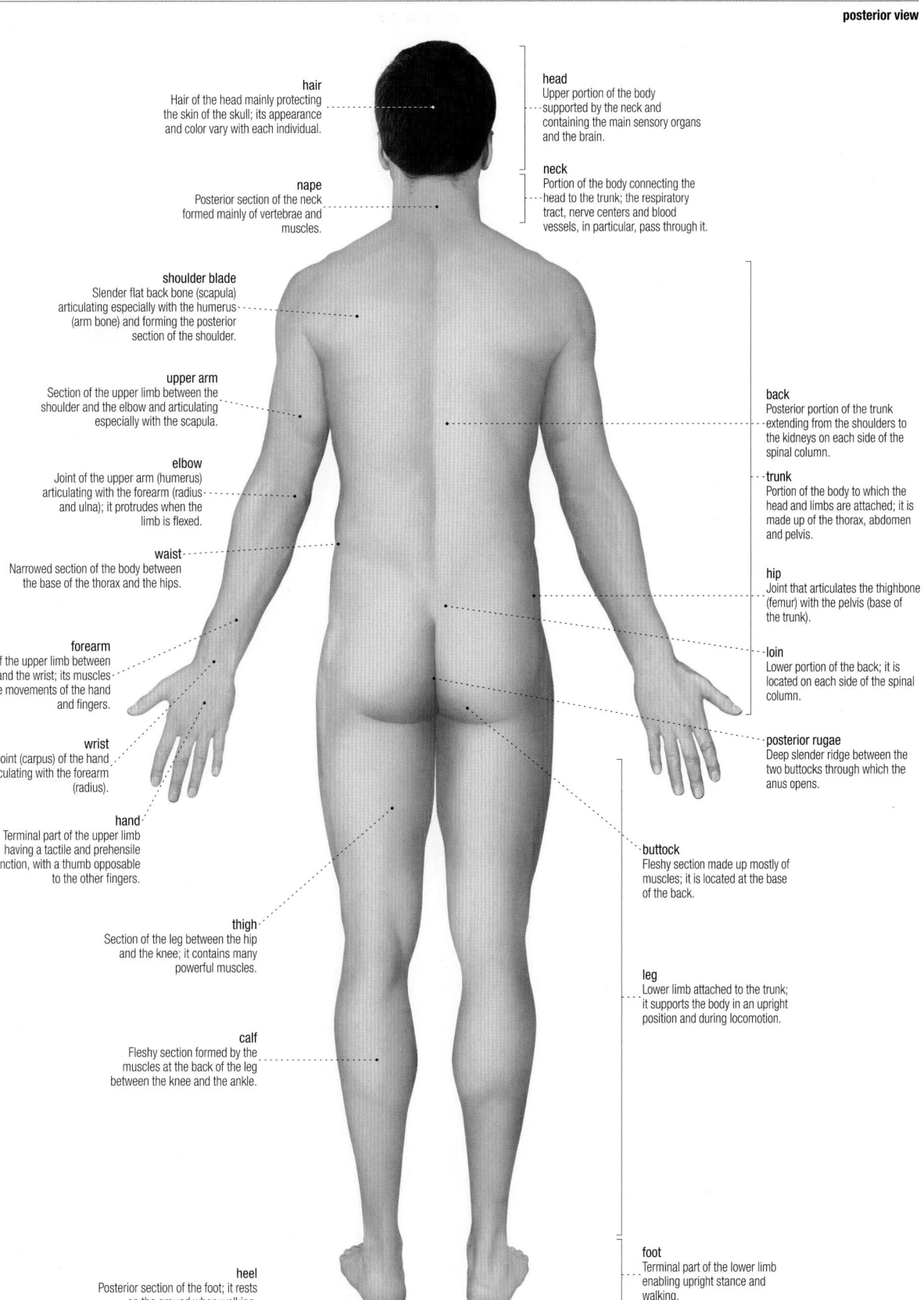

man

hair
Hair of the head mainly protecting the skin of the skull; its appearance and color vary with each individual.

nape
Posterior section of the neck formed mainly of vertebrae and muscles.

shoulder blade
Slender flat back bone (scapula) articulating especially with the humerus (arm bone) and forming the posterior section of the shoulder.

upper arm
Section of the upper limb between the shoulder and the elbow and articulating especially with the scapula.

elbow
Joint of the upper arm (humerus) articulating with the forearm (radius and ulna); it protrudes when the limb is flexed.

waist
Narrowed section of the body between the base of the thorax and the hips.

forearm
...ction of the upper limb between ...elbow and the wrist; its muscles ...ntrol the movements of the hand and fingers.

wrist
Joint (carpus) of the hand articulating with the forearm (radius).

hand
Terminal part of the upper limb having a tactile and prehensile function, with a thumb opposable to the other fingers.

thigh
Section of the leg between the hip and the knee; it contains many powerful muscles.

calf
Fleshy section formed by the muscles at the back of the leg between the knee and the ankle.

heel
Posterior section of the foot; it rests on the ground when walking.

head
Upper portion of the body supported by the neck and containing the main sensory organs and the brain.

neck
Portion of the body connecting the head to the trunk; the respiratory tract, nerve centers and blood vessels, in particular, pass through it.

back
Posterior portion of the trunk extending from the shoulders to the kidneys on each side of the spinal column.

trunk
Portion of the body to which the head and limbs are attached; it is made up of the thorax, abdomen and pelvis.

hip
Joint that articulates the thighbone (femur) with the pelvis (base of the trunk).

loin
Lower portion of the back; it is located on each side of the spinal column.

posterior rugae
Deep slender ridge between the two buttocks through which the anus opens.

buttock
Fleshy section made up mostly of muscles; it is located at the base of the back.

leg
Lower limb attached to the trunk; it supports the body in an upright position and during locomotion.

foot
Terminal part of the lower limb enabling upright stance and walking.

woman

Female human being capable of conceiving children from a reproductive cell (egg) fertilized by sperm.

anterior view

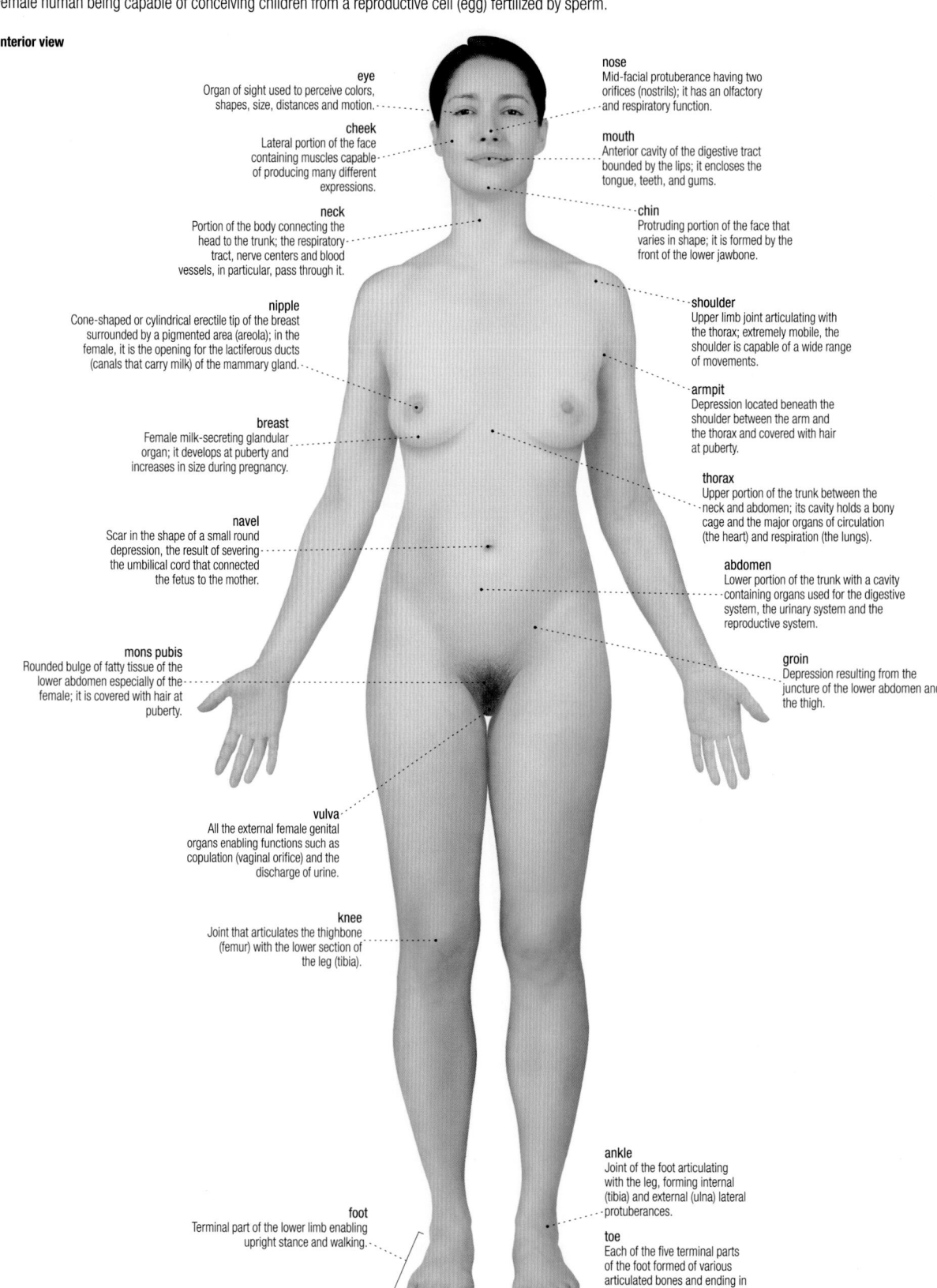

eye
Organ of sight used to perceive colors, shapes, size, distances and motion.

cheek
Lateral portion of the face containing muscles capable of producing many different expressions.

neck
Portion of the body connecting the head to the trunk; the respiratory tract, nerve centers and blood vessels, in particular, pass through it.

nipple
Cone-shaped or cylindrical erectile tip of the breast surrounded by a pigmented area (areola); in the female, it is the opening for the lactiferous ducts (canals that carry milk) of the mammary gland.

breast
Female milk-secreting glandular organ; it develops at puberty and increases in size during pregnancy.

navel
Scar in the shape of a small round depression, the result of severing the umbilical cord that connected the fetus to the mother.

mons pubis
Rounded bulge of fatty tissue of the lower abdomen especially of the female; it is covered with hair at puberty.

vulva
All the external female genital organs enabling functions such as copulation (vaginal orifice) and the discharge of urine.

knee
Joint that articulates the thighbone (femur) with the lower section of the leg (tibia).

foot
Terminal part of the lower limb enabling upright stance and walking.

nose
Mid-facial protuberance having two orifices (nostrils); it has an olfactory and respiratory function.

mouth
Anterior cavity of the digestive tract bounded by the lips; it encloses the tongue, teeth, and gums.

chin
Protruding portion of the face that varies in shape; it is formed by the front of the lower jawbone.

shoulder
Upper limb joint articulating with the thorax; extremely mobile, the shoulder is capable of a wide range of movements.

armpit
Depression located beneath the shoulder between the arm and the thorax and covered with hair at puberty.

thorax
Upper portion of the trunk between the neck and abdomen; its cavity holds a bony cage and the major organs of circulation (the heart) and respiration (the lungs).

abdomen
Lower portion of the trunk with a cavity containing organs used for the digestive system, the urinary system and the reproductive system.

groin
Depression resulting from the juncture of the lower abdomen and the thigh.

ankle
Joint of the foot articulating with the leg, forming internal (tibia) and external (ulna) lateral protuberances.

toe
Each of the five terminal parts of the foot formed of various articulated bones and ending in a nail.

woman

posterior view

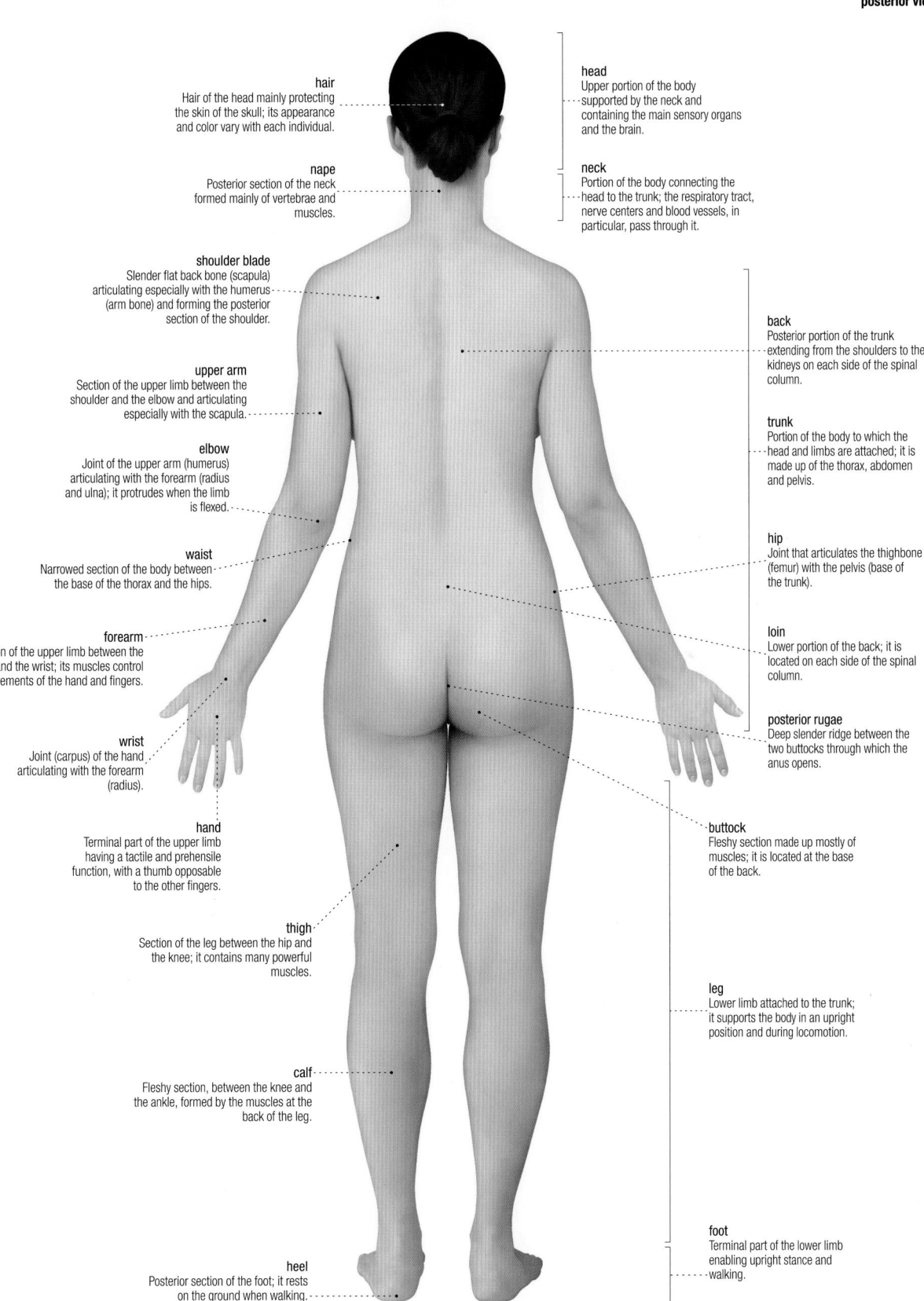

hair
Hair of the head mainly protecting the skin of the skull; its appearance and color vary with each individual.

nape
Posterior section of the neck formed mainly of vertebrae and muscles.

shoulder blade
Slender flat back bone (scapula) articulating especially with the humerus (arm bone) and forming the posterior section of the shoulder.

upper arm
Section of the upper limb between the shoulder and the elbow and articulating especially with the scapula.

elbow
Joint of the upper arm (humerus) articulating with the forearm (radius and ulna); it protrudes when the limb is flexed.

waist
Narrowed section of the body between the base of the thorax and the hips.

forearm
Section of the upper limb between the bow and the wrist; its muscles control e movements of the hand and fingers.

wrist
Joint (carpus) of the hand articulating with the forearm (radius).

hand
Terminal part of the upper limb having a tactile and prehensile function, with a thumb opposable to the other fingers.

thigh
Section of the leg between the hip and the knee; it contains many powerful muscles.

calf
Fleshy section, between the knee and the ankle, formed by the muscles at the back of the leg.

heel
Posterior section of the foot; it rests on the ground when walking.

head
Upper portion of the body supported by the neck and containing the main sensory organs and the brain.

neck
Portion of the body connecting the head to the trunk; the respiratory tract, nerve centers and blood vessels, in particular, pass through it.

back
Posterior portion of the trunk extending from the shoulders to the kidneys on each side of the spinal column.

trunk
Portion of the body to which the head and limbs are attached; it is made up of the thorax, abdomen and pelvis.

hip
Joint that articulates the thighbone (femur) with the pelvis (base of the trunk).

loin
Lower portion of the back; it is located on each side of the spinal column.

posterior rugae
Deep slender ridge between the two buttocks through which the anus opens.

buttock
Fleshy section made up mostly of muscles; it is located at the base of the back.

leg
Lower limb attached to the trunk; it supports the body in an upright position and during locomotion.

foot
Terminal part of the lower limb enabling upright stance and walking.

muscles

Contractile organs made of fibers allowing the body to move and maintain its posture; the human body has over 600 muscles.

anterior view

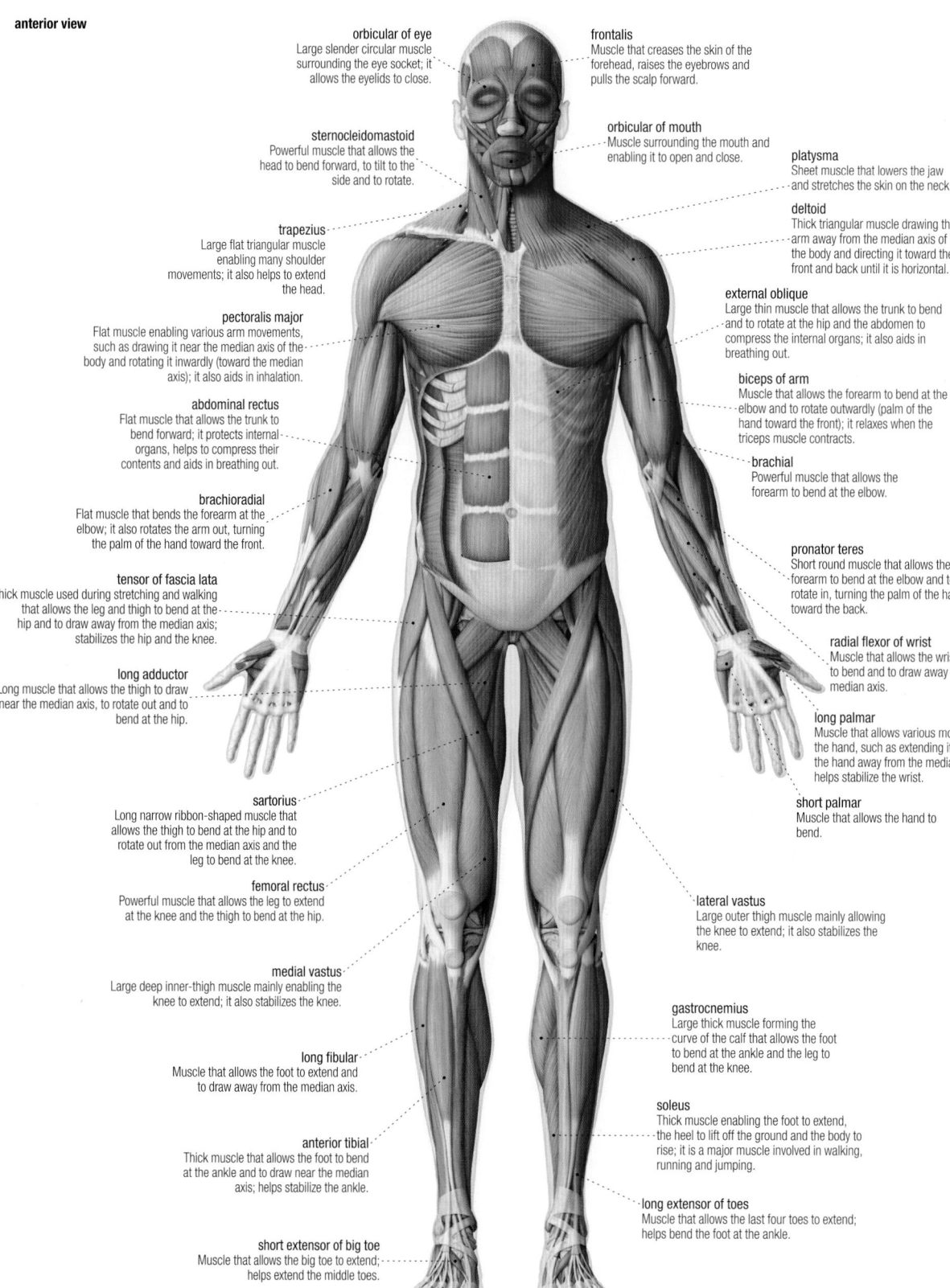

orbicular of eye
Large slender circular muscle surrounding the eye socket; it allows the eyelids to close.

frontalis
Muscle that creases the skin of the forehead, raises the eyebrows and pulls the scalp forward.

sternocleidomastoid
Powerful muscle that allows the head to bend forward, to tilt to the side and to rotate.

orbicular of mouth
Muscle surrounding the mouth and enabling it to open and close.

platysma
Sheet muscle that lowers the jaw and stretches the skin on the neck.

deltoid
Thick triangular muscle drawing the arm away from the median axis of the body and directing it toward the front and back until it is horizontal.

trapezius
Large flat triangular muscle enabling many shoulder movements; it also helps to extend the head.

external oblique
Large thin muscle that allows the trunk to bend and to rotate at the hip and the abdomen to compress the internal organs; it also aids in breathing out.

pectoralis major
Flat muscle enabling various arm movements, such as drawing it near the median axis of the body and rotating it inwardly (toward the median axis); it also aids in inhalation.

biceps of arm
Muscle that allows the forearm to bend at the elbow and to rotate outwardly (palm of the hand toward the front); it relaxes when the triceps muscle contracts.

abdominal rectus
Flat muscle that allows the trunk to bend forward; it protects internal organs, helps to compress their contents and aids in breathing out.

brachial
Powerful muscle that allows the forearm to bend at the elbow.

brachioradial
Flat muscle that bends the forearm at the elbow; it also rotates the arm out, turning the palm of the hand toward the front.

pronator teres
Short round muscle that allows the forearm to bend at the elbow and to rotate in, turning the palm of the hand toward the back.

tensor of fascia lata
Thick muscle used during stretching and walking that allows the leg and thigh to bend at the hip and to draw away from the median axis; stabilizes the hip and the knee.

radial flexor of wrist
Muscle that allows the wrist and elbow to bend and to draw away from the median axis.

long adductor
Long muscle that allows the thigh to draw near the median axis, to rotate out and to bend at the hip.

long palmar
Muscle that allows various movements of the hand, such as extending it or drawing the hand away from the median axis; it helps stabilize the wrist.

sartorius
Long narrow ribbon-shaped muscle that allows the thigh to bend at the hip and to rotate out from the median axis and the leg to bend at the knee.

short palmar
Muscle that allows the hand to bend.

femoral rectus
Powerful muscle that allows the leg to extend at the knee and the thigh to bend at the hip.

lateral vastus
Large outer thigh muscle mainly allowing the knee to extend; it also stabilizes the knee.

medial vastus
Large deep inner-thigh muscle mainly enabling the knee to extend; it also stabilizes the knee.

gastrocnemius
Large thick muscle forming the curve of the calf that allows the foot to bend at the ankle and the leg to bend at the knee.

long fibular
Muscle that allows the foot to extend and to draw away from the median axis.

soleus
Thick muscle enabling the foot to extend, the heel to lift off the ground and the body to rise; it is a major muscle involved in walking, running and jumping.

anterior tibial
Thick muscle that allows the foot to bend at the ankle and to draw near the median axis; helps stabilize the ankle.

long extensor of toes
Muscle that allows the last four toes to extend; helps bend the foot at the ankle.

short extensor of big toe
Muscle that allows the big toe to extend; helps extend the middle toes.

muscles

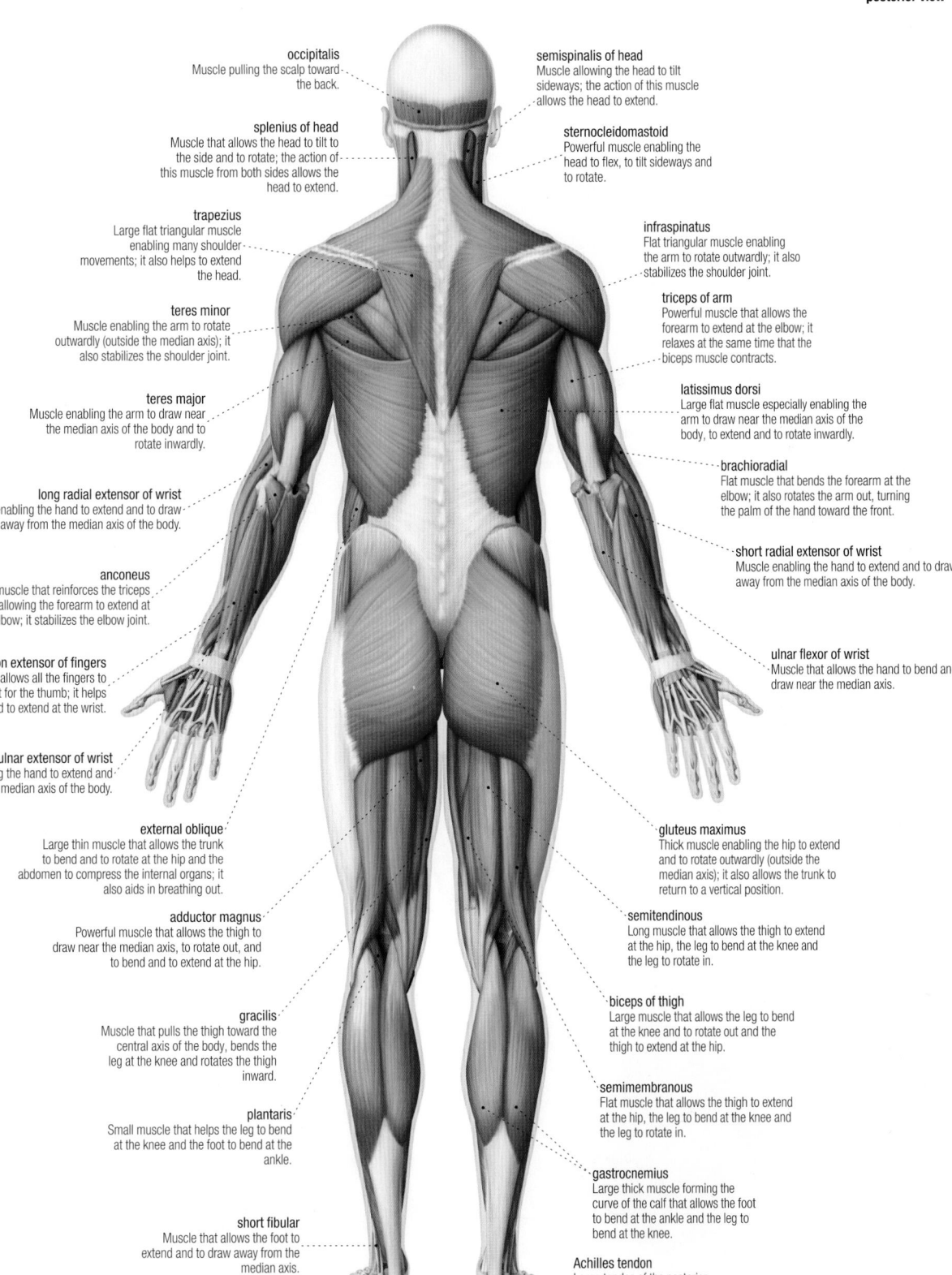

occipitalis
Muscle pulling the scalp toward the back.

semispinalis of head
Muscle allowing the head to tilt sideways; the action of this muscle allows the head to extend.

splenius of head
Muscle that allows the head to tilt to the side and to rotate; the action of this muscle from both sides allows the head to extend.

sternocleidomastoid
Powerful muscle enabling the head to flex, to tilt sideways and to rotate.

trapezius
Large flat triangular muscle enabling many shoulder movements; it also helps to extend the head.

infraspinatus
Flat triangular muscle enabling the arm to rotate outwardly; it also stabilizes the shoulder joint.

teres minor
Muscle enabling the arm to rotate outwardly (outside the median axis); it also stabilizes the shoulder joint.

triceps of arm
Powerful muscle that allows the forearm to extend at the elbow; it relaxes at the same time that the biceps muscle contracts.

teres major
Muscle enabling the arm to draw near the median axis of the body and to rotate inwardly.

latissimus dorsi
Large flat muscle especially enabling the arm to draw near the median axis of the body, to extend and to rotate inwardly.

long radial extensor of wrist
Muscle enabling the hand to extend and to draw away from the median axis of the body.

brachioradial
Flat muscle that bends the forearm at the elbow; it also rotates the arm out, turning the palm of the hand toward the front.

anconeus
Short muscle that reinforces the triceps muscle by allowing the forearm to extend at the elbow; it stabilizes the elbow joint.

short radial extensor of wrist
Muscle enabling the hand to extend and to draw away from the median axis of the body.

common extensor of fingers
Muscle that allows all the fingers to bend, except for the thumb; it helps the hand to extend at the wrist.

ulnar flexor of wrist
Muscle that allows the hand to bend and to draw near the median axis.

ulnar extensor of wrist
Muscle enabling the hand to extend and to draw near the median axis of the body.

external oblique
Large thin muscle that allows the trunk to bend and to rotate at the hip and the abdomen to compress the internal organs; it also aids in breathing out.

gluteus maximus
Thick muscle enabling the hip to extend and to rotate outwardly (outside the median axis); it also allows the trunk to return to a vertical position.

adductor magnus
Powerful muscle that allows the thigh to draw near the median axis, to rotate out, and to bend and to extend at the hip.

semitendinous
Long muscle that allows the thigh to extend at the hip, the leg to bend at the knee and the leg to rotate in.

gracilis
Muscle that pulls the thigh toward the central axis of the body, bends the leg at the knee and rotates the thigh inward.

biceps of thigh
Large muscle that allows the leg to bend at the knee and to rotate out and the thigh to extend at the hip.

semimembranous
Flat muscle that allows the thigh to extend at the hip, the leg to bend at the knee and the leg to rotate in.

plantaris
Small muscle that helps the leg to bend at the knee and the foot to bend at the ankle.

gastrocnemius
Large thick muscle forming the curve of the calf that allows the foot to bend at the ankle and the leg to bend at the knee.

short fibular
Muscle that allows the foot to extend and to draw away from the median axis.

Achilles tendon
Large tendon of the posterior face of the ankle, connecting the gastrocnemius and soleus muscles to the bone of the heel.

HUMAN BEING

HUMAN BEING

muscles

muscle tissue
Tissue made up of cells (myocytes) arranged into muscle fibers. There are three types of muscle fiber: skeletal, cardiac and smooth.

striated muscle (sartorius)
Voluntary muscle composed of cylindrical cells with multiple nuclei, having obvious striations.

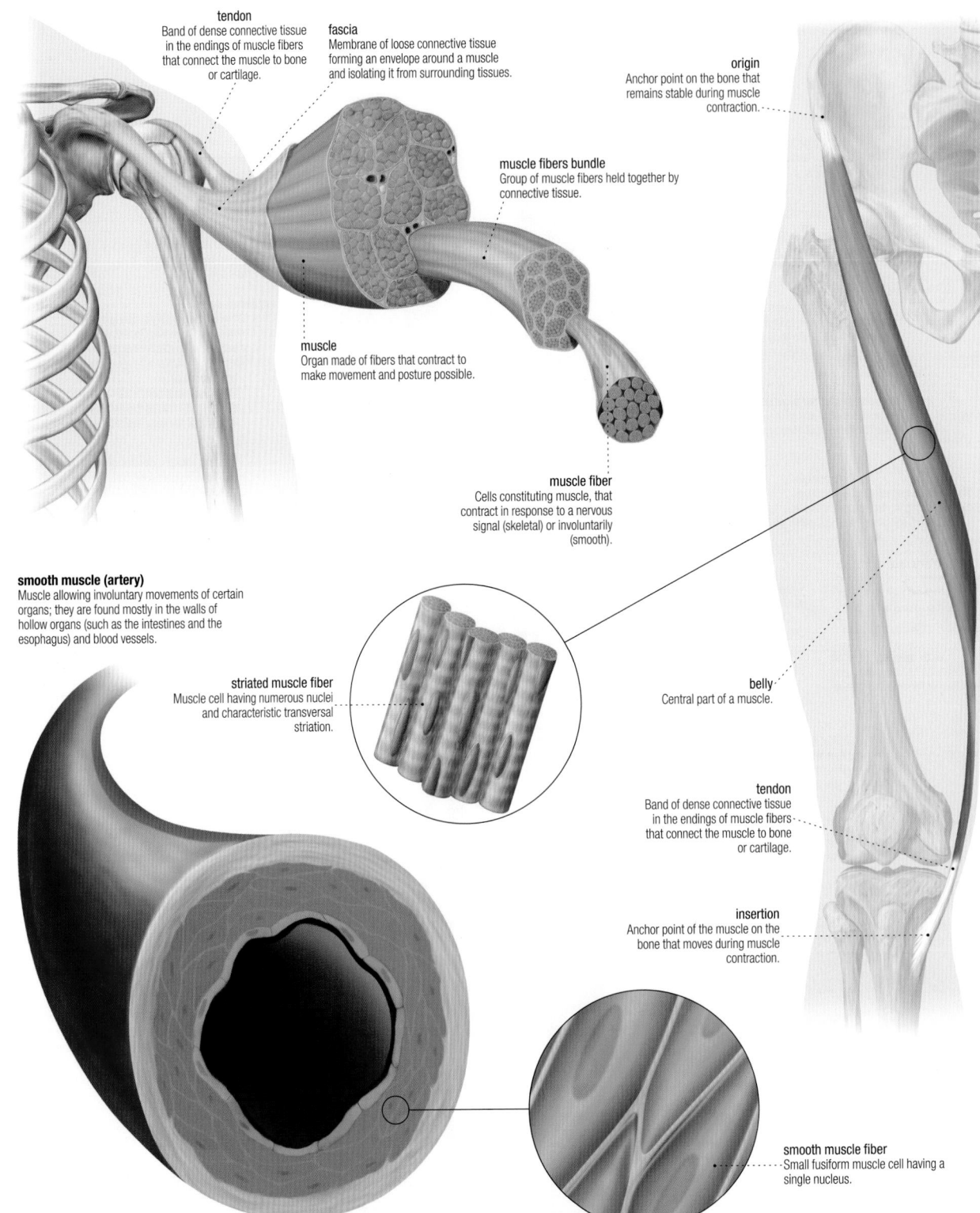

tendon
Band of dense connective tissue in the endings of muscle fibers that connect the muscle to bone or cartilage.

fascia
Membrane of loose connective tissue forming an envelope around a muscle and isolating it from surrounding tissues.

origin
Anchor point on the bone that remains stable during muscle contraction.

muscle fibers bundle
Group of muscle fibers held together by connective tissue.

muscle
Organ made of fibers that contract to make movement and posture possible.

muscle fiber
Cells constituting muscle, that contract in response to a nervous signal (skeletal) or involuntarily (smooth).

smooth muscle (artery)
Muscle allowing involuntary movements of certain organs; they are found mostly in the walls of hollow organs (such as the intestines and the esophagus) and blood vessels.

striated muscle fiber
Muscle cell having numerous nuclei and characteristic transversal striation.

belly
Central part of a muscle.

tendon
Band of dense connective tissue in the endings of muscle fibers that connect the muscle to bone or cartilage.

insertion
Anchor point of the muscle on the bone that moves during muscle contraction.

smooth muscle fiber
Small fusiform muscle cell having a single nucleus.

skeleton

All the articulated bones (about 200), of varying sizes and shapes, forming the frame of the body, supporting the muscles and protecting the vital organs.

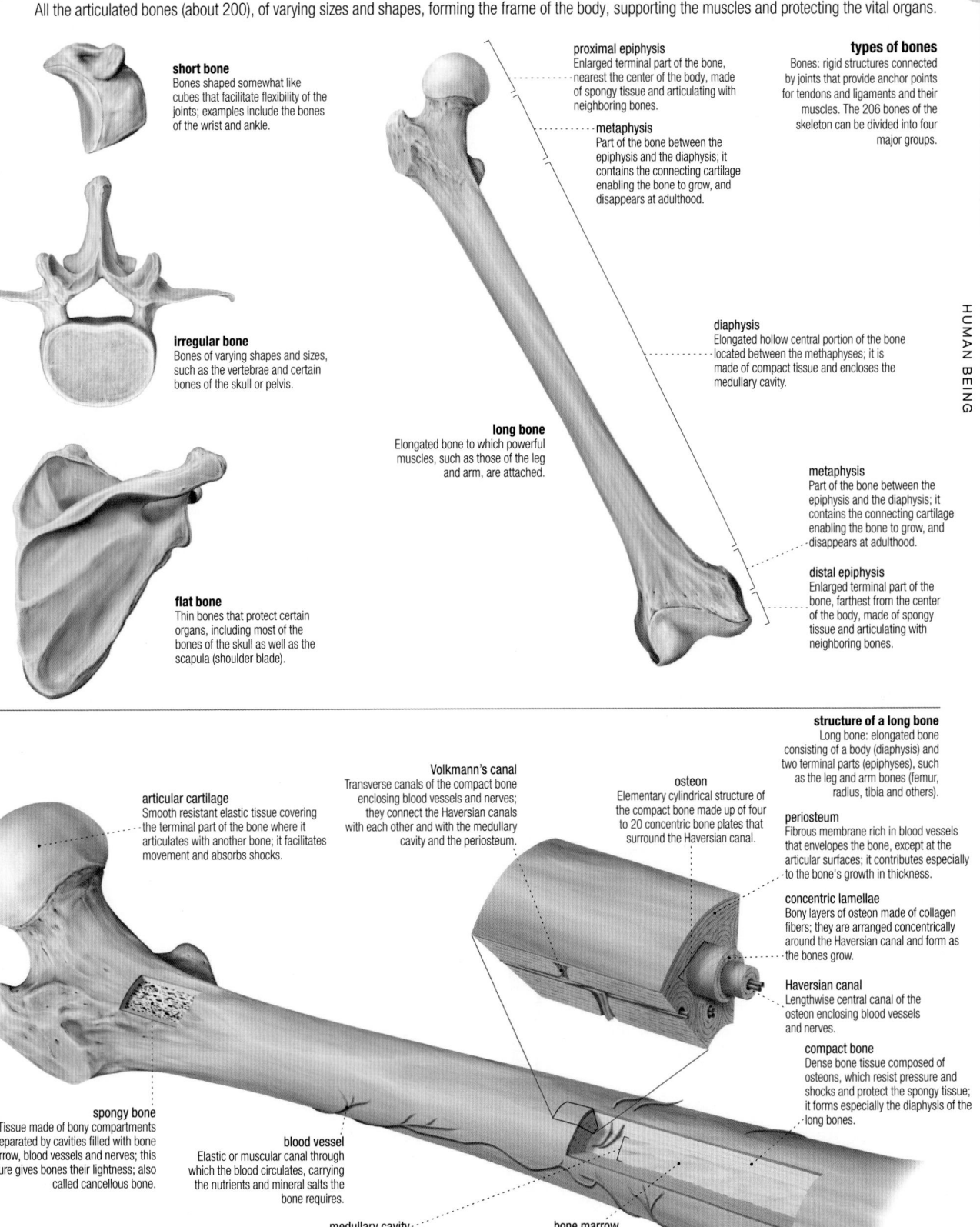

short bone
Bones shaped somewhat like cubes that facilitate flexibility of the joints; examples include the bones of the wrist and ankle.

irregular bone
Bones of varying shapes and sizes, such as the vertebrae and certain bones of the skull or pelvis.

flat bone
Thin bones that protect certain organs, including most of the bones of the skull as well as the scapula (shoulder blade).

proximal epiphysis
Enlarged terminal part of the bone, nearest the center of the body, made of spongy tissue and articulating with neighboring bones.

metaphysis
Part of the bone between the epiphysis and the diaphysis; it contains the connecting cartilage enabling the bone to grow, and disappears at adulthood.

long bone
Elongated bone to which powerful muscles, such as those of the leg and arm, are attached.

types of bones
Bones: rigid structures connected by joints that provide anchor points for tendons and ligaments and their muscles. The 206 bones of the skeleton can be divided into four major groups.

diaphysis
Elongated hollow central portion of the bone located between the methaphyses; it is made of compact tissue and encloses the medullary cavity.

metaphysis
Part of the bone between the epiphysis and the diaphysis; it contains the connecting cartilage enabling the bone to grow, and disappears at adulthood.

distal epiphysis
Enlarged terminal part of the bone, farthest from the center of the body, made of spongy tissue and articulating with neighboring bones.

articular cartilage
Smooth resistant elastic tissue covering the terminal part of the bone where it articulates with another bone; it facilitates movement and absorbs shocks.

Volkmann's canal
Transverse canals of the compact bone enclosing blood vessels and nerves; they connect the Haversian canals with each other and with the medullary cavity and the periosteum.

osteon
Elementary cylindrical structure of the compact bone made up of four to 20 concentric bone plates that surround the Haversian canal.

structure of a long bone
Long bone: elongated bone consisting of a body (diaphysis) and two terminal parts (epiphyses), such as the leg and arm bones (femur, radius, tibia and others).

periosteum
Fibrous membrane rich in blood vessels that envelopes the bone, except at the articular surfaces; it contributes especially to the bone's growth in thickness.

concentric lamellae
Bony layers of osteon made of collagen fibers; they are arranged concentrically around the Haversian canal and form as the bones grow.

Haversian canal
Lengthwise central canal of the osteon enclosing blood vessels and nerves.

compact bone
Dense bone tissue composed of osteons, which resist pressure and shocks and protect the spongy tissue; it forms especially the diaphysis of the long bones.

spongy bone
Tissue made of bony compartments separated by cavities filled with bone marrow, blood vessels and nerves; this structure gives bones their lightness; also called cancellous bone.

blood vessel
Elastic or muscular canal through which the blood circulates, carrying the nutrients and mineral salts the bone requires.

medullary cavity
Cylindrical central cavity of the bone containing the bone marrow; this canal encloses lipid-rich yellow bone marrow.

bone marrow
Soft substance contained in bone cavities, producing blood cells; marrow is red in children, yellow in the long bones of adults.

skeleton

anterior view

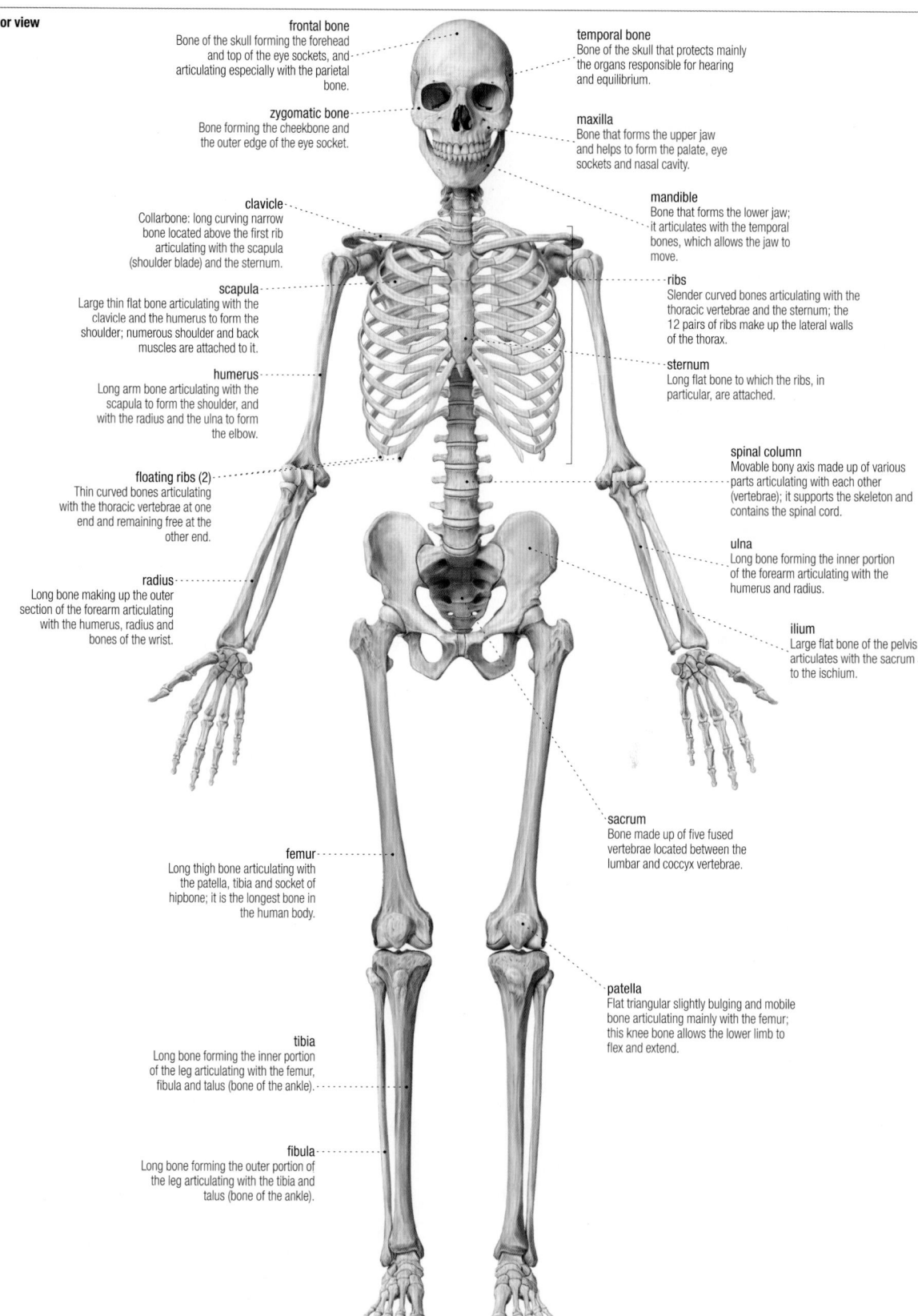

frontal bone
Bone of the skull forming the forehead and top of the eye sockets, and articulating especially with the parietal bone.

temporal bone
Bone of the skull that protects mainly the organs responsible for hearing and equilibrium.

zygomatic bone
Bone forming the cheekbone and the outer edge of the eye socket.

maxilla
Bone that forms the upper jaw and helps to form the palate, eye sockets and nasal cavity.

clavicle
Collarbone: long curving narrow bone located above the first rib articulating with the scapula (shoulder blade) and the sternum.

mandible
Bone that forms the lower jaw; it articulates with the temporal bones, which allows the jaw to move.

ribs
Slender curved bones articulating with the thoracic vertebrae and the sternum; the 12 pairs of ribs make up the lateral walls of the thorax.

scapula
Large thin flat bone articulating with the clavicle and the humerus to form the shoulder; numerous shoulder and back muscles are attached to it.

sternum
Long flat bone to which the ribs, in particular, are attached.

humerus
Long arm bone articulating with the scapula to form the shoulder, and with the radius and the ulna to form the elbow.

spinal column
Movable bony axis made up of various parts articulating with each other (vertebrae); it supports the skeleton and contains the spinal cord.

floating ribs (2)
Thin curved bones articulating with the thoracic vertebrae at one end and remaining free at the other end.

ulna
Long bone forming the inner portion of the forearm articulating with the humerus and radius.

radius
Long bone making up the outer section of the forearm articulating with the humerus, radius and bones of the wrist.

ilium
Large flat bone of the pelvis that articulates with the sacrum and is to the ischium.

sacrum
Bone made up of five fused vertebrae located between the lumbar and coccyx vertebrae.

femur
Long thigh bone articulating with the patella, tibia and socket of hipbone; it is the longest bone in the human body.

patella
Flat triangular slightly bulging and mobile bone articulating mainly with the femur; this knee bone allows the lower limb to flex and extend.

tibia
Long bone forming the inner portion of the leg articulating with the femur, fibula and talus (bone of the ankle).

fibula
Long bone forming the outer portion of the leg articulating with the tibia and talus (bone of the ankle).

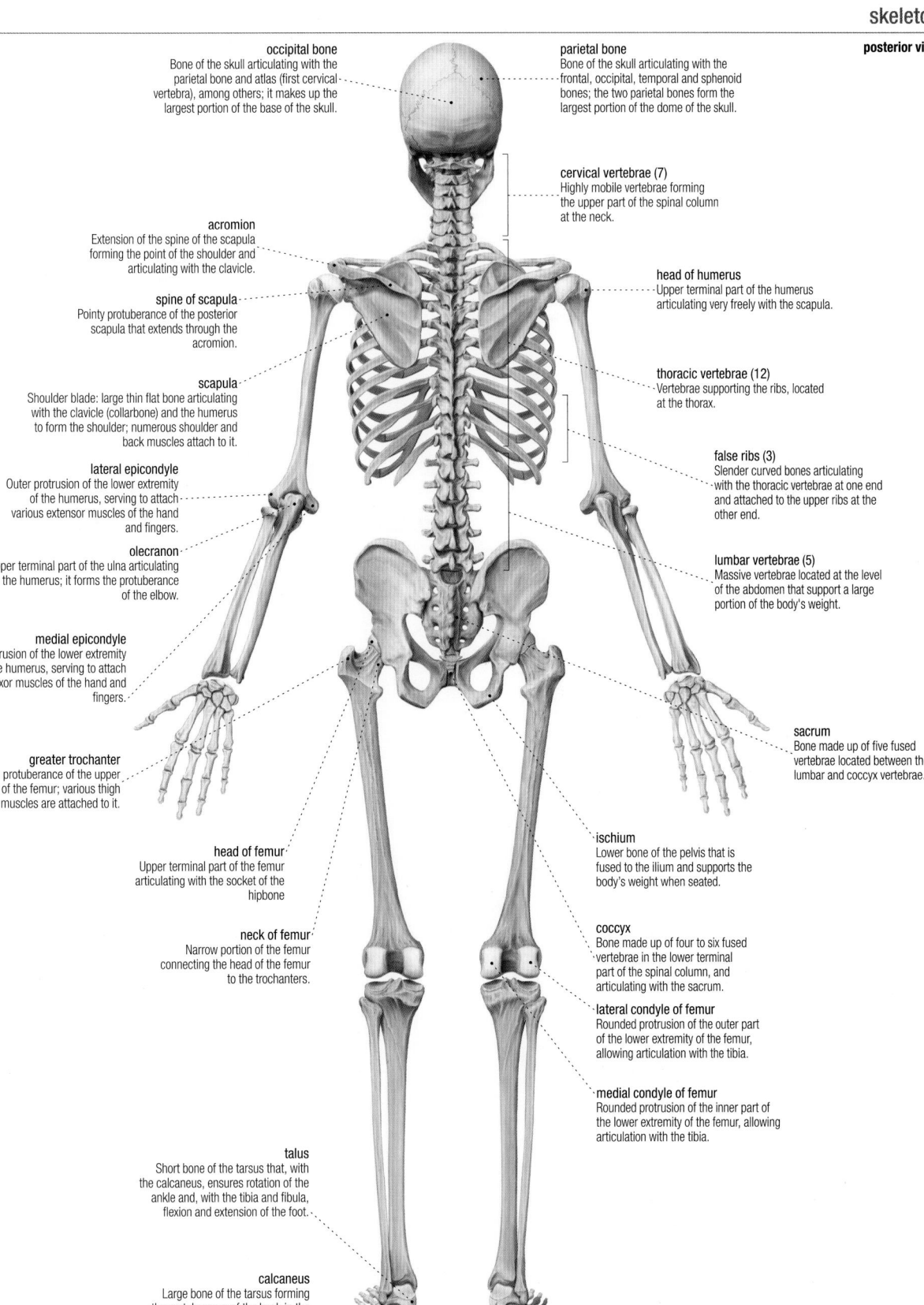

occipital bone
Bone of the skull articulating with the parietal bone and atlas (first cervical vertebra), among others; it makes up the largest portion of the base of the skull.

parietal bone
Bone of the skull articulating with the frontal, occipital, temporal and sphenoid bones; the two parietal bones form the largest portion of the dome of the skull.

cervical vertebrae (7)
Highly mobile vertebrae forming the upper part of the spinal column at the neck.

acromion
Extension of the spine of the scapula forming the point of the shoulder and articulating with the clavicle.

head of humerus
Upper terminal part of the humerus articulating very freely with the scapula.

spine of scapula
Pointy protuberance of the posterior scapula that extends through the acromion.

scapula
Shoulder blade: large thin flat bone articulating with the clavicle (collarbone) and the humerus to form the shoulder; numerous shoulder and back muscles attach to it.

thoracic vertebrae (12)
Vertebrae supporting the ribs, located at the thorax.

false ribs (3)
Slender curved bones articulating with the thoracic vertebrae at one end and attached to the upper ribs at the other end.

lateral epicondyle
Outer protrusion of the lower extremity of the humerus, serving to attach various extensor muscles of the hand and fingers.

olecranon
Upper terminal part of the ulna articulating with the humerus; it forms the protuberance of the elbow.

lumbar vertebrae (5)
Massive vertebrae located at the level of the abdomen that support a large portion of the body's weight.

medial epicondyle
r protrusion of the lower extremity of the humerus, serving to attach us flexor muscles of the hand and fingers.

greater trochanter
Large protuberance of the upper l part of the femur; various thigh ttock muscles are attached to it.

sacrum
Bone made up of five fused vertebrae located between the lumbar and coccyx vertebrae.

ischium
Lower bone of the pelvis that is fused to the ilium and supports the body's weight when seated.

head of femur
Upper terminal part of the femur articulating with the socket of the hipbone

coccyx
Bone made up of four to six fused vertebrae in the lower terminal part of the spinal column, and articulating with the sacrum.

neck of femur
Narrow portion of the femur connecting the head of the femur to the trochanters.

lateral condyle of femur
Rounded protrusion of the outer part of the lower extremity of the femur, allowing articulation with the tibia.

medial condyle of femur
Rounded protrusion of the inner part of the lower extremity of the femur, allowing articulation with the tibia.

talus
Short bone of the tarsus that, with the calcaneus, ensures rotation of the ankle and, with the tibia and fibula, flexion and extension of the foot.

calcaneus
Large bone of the tarsus forming the protuberance of the heel; in the upright position, it is the posterior contact point of the plantar arch.

HUMAN BEING

skeleton

hand
Terminal part of the forearm with a tactile and prehensile function and a thumb opposable to the other fingers. The skeleton of the hand has 27 bones.

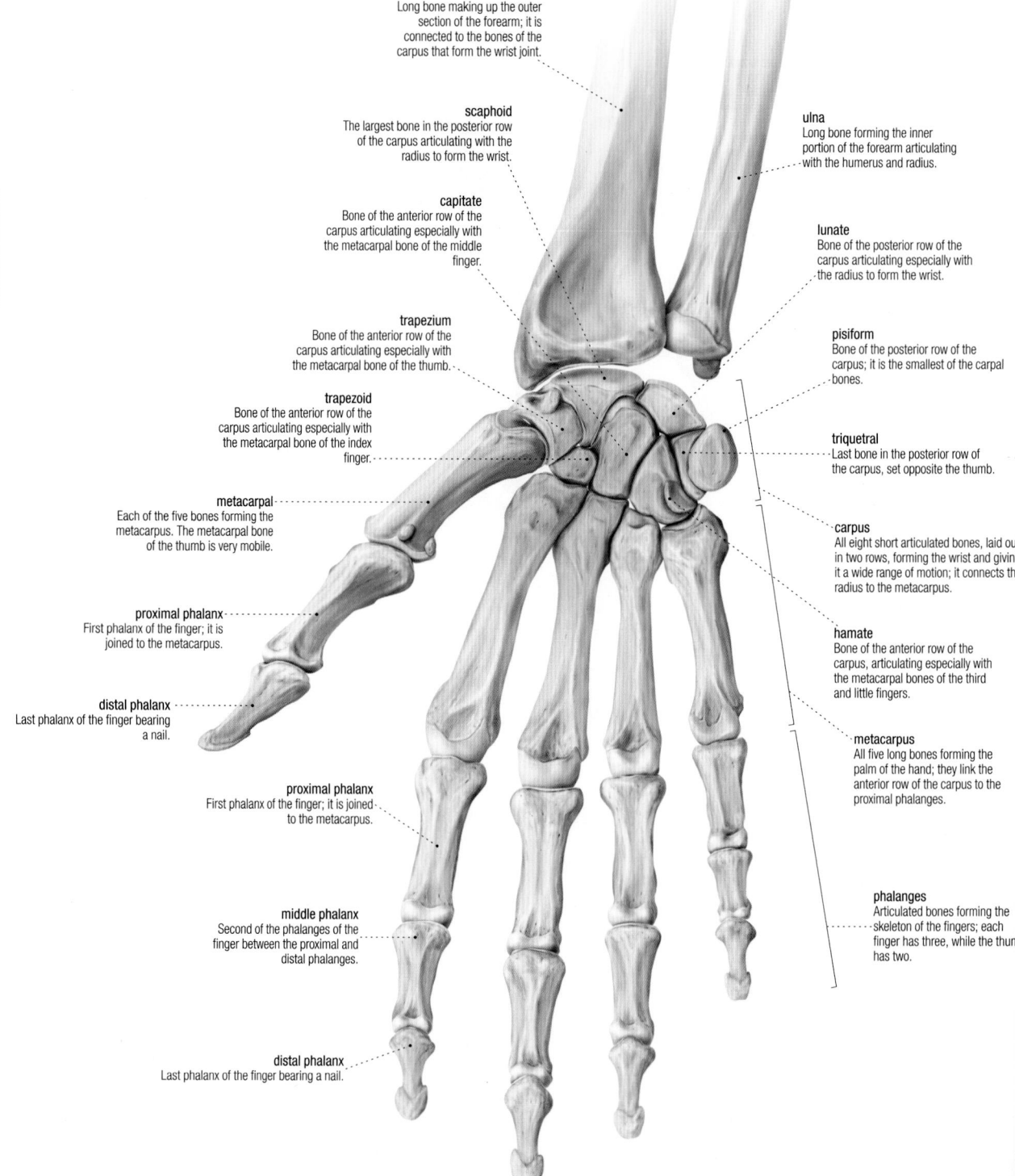

radius
Long bone making up the outer section of the forearm; it is connected to the bones of the carpus that form the wrist joint.

scaphoid
The largest bone in the posterior row of the carpus articulating with the radius to form the wrist.

capitate
Bone of the anterior row of the carpus articulating especially with the metacarpal bone of the middle finger.

trapezium
Bone of the anterior row of the carpus articulating especially with the metacarpal bone of the thumb.

trapezoid
Bone of the anterior row of the carpus articulating especially with the metacarpal bone of the index finger.

metacarpal
Each of the five bones forming the metacarpus. The metacarpal bone of the thumb is very mobile.

proximal phalanx
First phalanx of the finger; it is joined to the metacarpus.

distal phalanx
Last phalanx of the finger bearing a nail.

proximal phalanx
First phalanx of the finger; it is joined to the metacarpus.

middle phalanx
Second of the phalanges of the finger between the proximal and distal phalanges.

distal phalanx
Last phalanx of the finger bearing a nail.

ulna
Long bone forming the inner portion of the forearm articulating with the humerus and radius.

lunate
Bone of the posterior row of the carpus articulating especially with the radius to form the wrist.

pisiform
Bone of the posterior row of the carpus; it is the smallest of the carpal bones.

triquetral
Last bone in the posterior row of the carpus, set opposite the thumb.

carpus
All eight short articulated bones, laid out in two rows, forming the wrist and giving it a wide range of motion; it connects the radius to the metacarpus.

hamate
Bone of the anterior row of the carpus, articulating especially with the metacarpal bones of the third and little fingers.

metacarpus
All five long bones forming the palm of the hand; they link the anterior row of the carpus to the proximal phalanges.

phalanges
Articulated bones forming the skeleton of the fingers; each finger has three, while the thumb has two.

skeleton

foot: anterior view
Foot: terminal part of the leg enabling upright stance and walking. The skeleton of the foot is made up of 26 bones.

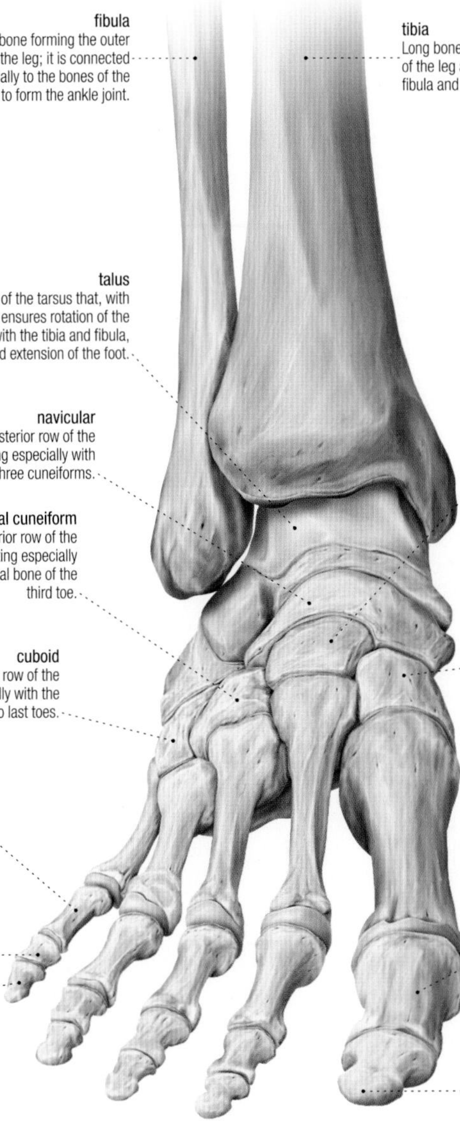

fibula
Long bone forming the outer portion of the leg; it is connected especially to the bones of the tarsus to form the ankle joint.

tibia
Long bone forming the inner portion of the leg articulating with the femur, fibula and talus.

talus
Short bone of the tarsus that, with the calcaneus, ensures rotation of the ankle and, with the tibia and fibula, flexion and extension of the foot.

intermediate cuneiform
Bone of the anterior row of the tarsus articulating especially with the metatarsal bone of the second toe and the scaphoid bone.

navicular
Bone of the posterior row of the tarsus articulating especially with the talus and the three cuneiforms.

tarsus
All seven short articulated bones, laid out in two rows, making up the heel and the ankle; it connects the tibia and the fibula to the metatarsus.

lateral cuneiform
Bone of the anterior row of the tarsus articulating especially with the metatarsal bone of the third toe.

medial cuneiform
Bone of the anterior row of the tarsus articulating especially with the metatarsal bone of the big toe and the scaphoid bone.

cuboid
Bone of the anterior row of the tarsus articulating especially with the metatarsal bones of the two last toes.

metatarsus
All five long bones that make up the sole of the foot; it connects the anterior row of the tarsus to the proximal phalanges.

proximal phalanx
First phalanx of the toe; it is joined to the metatarsus.

proximal phalanx
First phalanx of the toe; it is joined to the metatarsus.

middle phalanx
Second of the phalanges of the foot between the proximal and distal phalanges.

phalanges
Articulated bones forming the skeleton of the toes. Each toe has three, while the big toe has only two.

distal phalanx
Last phalanx of the toe bearing a nail.

distal phalanx
Last phalanx of the toe bearing a nail.

foot: lateral view
Foot: terminal part of the leg enabling upright stance and walking. The skeleton of the foot is made up of 26 bones.

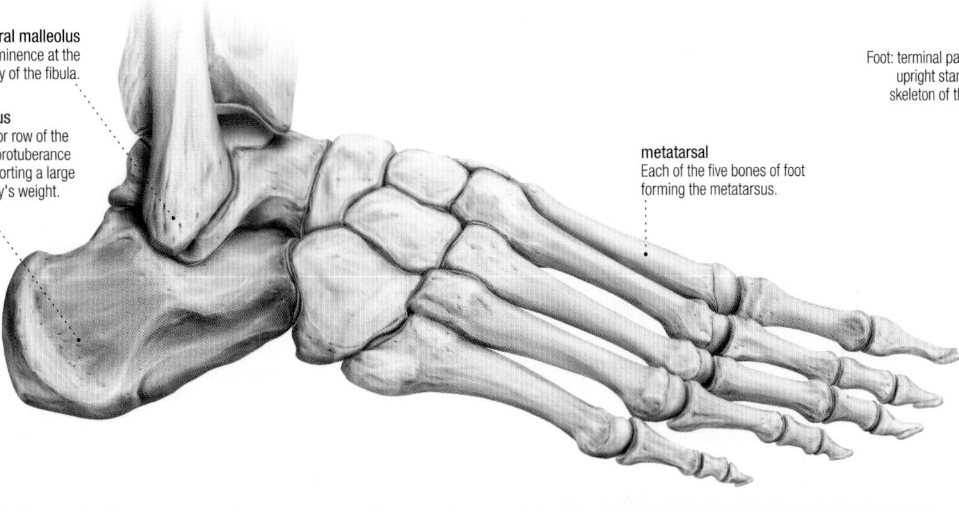

lateral malleolus
Round, bony prominence at the lower extremity of the fibula.

calcaneus
Bone of the posterior row of the tarsus forming the protuberance of the heel and supporting a large portion of the body's weight.

metatarsal
Each of the five bones of foot forming the metatarsus.

skeleton

spinal column

Movable bony axis made up of various parts articulating with each other (vertebrae); it supports the skeleton and contains the spinal cord.

lateral view

anterior view

cervical vertebrae (7)
Highly mobile vertebrae forming the upper part of the spinal column at the neck.

cervical vertebrae
Normal concave curvature of the spinal column at the cervical vertebrae.

thoracic vertebrae
Normal convex curvature of the spinal column at the thoracic vertebrae.

lumbar vertebrae
Normal concave curvature of the spinal column at the lumbar vertebrae.

thoracic vertebrae (12)
Vertebrae supporting the ribs, located at the thorax.

lumbar vertebrae (5)
Massive vertebrae located at the level of the abdomen that support a large portion of the body's weight.

sacrum
Bone made up of five fused vertebrae located between the lumbar and coccyx vertebrae.

coccyx
Bone made up of four to six fused vertebrae in the lower terminal part of the spinal column, and articulating with the sacrum.

atlas
First cervical vertebra supp[orting] the head and supported by [the] axis.

axis
Second cervical vertebra supporting the atlas; it allow[s] head to rotate.

vertebra prominens
Last cervical vertebra, havi[ng] protruding spiny apophysis serving as a transition betw[een] cervical and thoracic verteb[rae].

transverse process
Bony protuberance extendi[ng] laterally from each side of t[he] vertebra where muscles for spine attach.

intervertebral disk
Flat rounded cartilaginous structure separating two vertebrae; its elasticity allow[s] the spinal column to move.

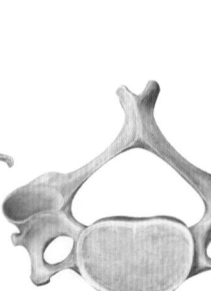

thoracic vertebra
Each of 12 vertebrae supporting the ribs, located at the thorax.

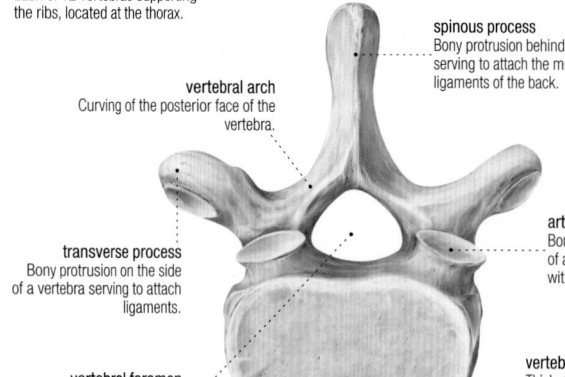

spinous process
Bony protrusion behind a vertebra serving to attach the muscles and ligaments of the back.

vertebral arch
Curving of the posterior face of the vertebra.

transverse process
Bony protrusion on the side of a vertebra serving to attach ligaments.

articular process
Bony outgrowth on the neural arch of a vertebra allowing it to articulate with adjacent vertebrae.

vertebral foramen
Aperture bordered by the vertebral body and neural arch of a vertebra, housing the spinal cord.

vertebral body
Thick disk-shaped bony element comprising the anterior part of a vertebra.

lumbar vertebra
Each of five massive vertebrae located beneath the thoracic vertebrae at the abdomen.

cervical vertebra
Each of seven highly mobile vertebrae forming the upper part o[f] the spinal column at the neck.

skeleton

coronal suture
Joint connecting the frontal bone to the two parietal bones; it begins to ossify during childhood and is not completely hardened until adulthood.

temporal bone
Bone of the skull that protects mainly the organs responsible for hearing and equilibrium.

frontal bone
Bone of the skull forming the forehead and top of the eye sockets, and articulating especially with the parietal.

squamous suture
Immovable joint made of fibrous tissue connecting the parietal and temporal bones.

sphenoid bone
Bone located behind the nasal cavity; it articulates with all the cranial bones.

parietal bone
Bone of the skull articulating with the frontal, occipital, temporal and sphenoid bones; the two parietal bones form the largest portion of the dome of the skull.

zygomatic bone
Bone forming the cheekbone and the outer edge of the eye socket.

lambdoid suture
Immovable joint made of fibrous tissue connecting the occipital and the two parietal bones.

nasal bone
Small flat bone making up the skeleton of the nose; the two nasal bones are joined along the bridge of the nose.

occipital bone
Bone of the skull articulating with the parietal bone and atlas (first cervical vertebra), among others; it makes up the largest portion of the base of the skull.

anterior nasal spine
Bony middle protuberance of the jawbone beneath the nasal cavity; it supports the cartilage of the dividing wall of the nose.

external auditory meatus
Canal in the temporal bone through which sounds captured by the pinna of the ear reach the eardrum. It is also called the auditory canal.

maxilla
Bone that forms the upper jaw and helps to form the palate, eye sockets and nasal cavity.

mandible
Bone that forms the lower jaw; it articulates with the temporal bones, which allows the jaw to move.

styloid process
Elongated protuberance of the temporal bone; several tongue muscles are attached to it.

mastoid process
Protruding cone-shaped part of the temporal bone located behind the outer ear. Certain neck muscles, such as the sternocleidomastoid, attach to it.

anterior fontanelle
Membranous space between the frontal and two parietal bones; it closes usually at the age of two or three years. This is the largest of the fontanelles.

coronal suture
Joint connecting the frontal bone to the two parietal bones; it begins to ossify during childhood and is not completely hardened until adulthood.

posterior fontanelle
Membranous space between the occipital and two parietal bones; it closes at about the age of two or three months. This fontanelle is smaller than the anterior fontanelle.

parietal bone
Bone of the skull articulating with the frontal and occipital bones during the growth years.

frontal bone
Bone of the skull forming the forehead and top of the eye sockets, and articulating especially with the parietal.

occipital bone
Bone of the skull articulating with the parietal bone and atlas (first cervical vertebra) during the growth years.

sphenoidal fontanelle
Membranous space between the frontal, parietal, temporal and sphenoid bones; it closes at about the age of two or three months.

mastoid fontanelle
Membranous space between the parietal, occipital and temporal bones; it closes at about the age of 18 months. This fontanelle is smaller than the sphenoidal fontanelle.

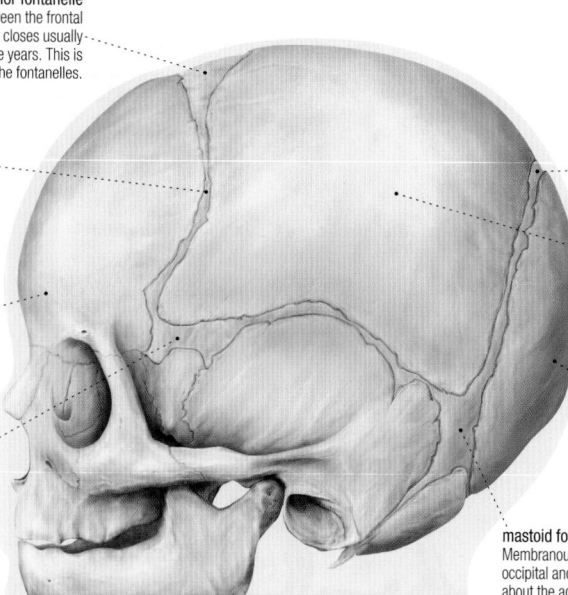

HUMAN BEING

teeth

Hard structures occupying individual sockets in the upper and lower jaws that are used for chewing food; full dentition in an adult consists of 32 teeth.

dentition, adult
The set of adult teeth placed in the upper and lower jaw; upper and lower teeth are identical in number and arrangement: four incisors, two canines, four premolars and six molars.

incisors
Flat teeth (8) located at the front of the upper and lower jaw, having a cutting edge that allows them to bite into food.

canine
Pointy tooth between the incisors and the premolars having only one root and used to tear apart food.

central incisor
Incisor located in the front section of teeth.

lateral incisor
Incisor located between the central incisor and the canine.

premolars
Each of four teeth between the canines and the molars; they have several roots and are used to grind food.

first premolar

first molar

second premolar

molars
Teeth (12) located at the back of the upper and lower jaw; large in size with several roots, they have a flat crown that allows them to grind food.

second molar

wisdom tooth
Last molar of the dental arch, appearing generally between the ages of 18 and 30 but missing in some people.

HUMAN BEING

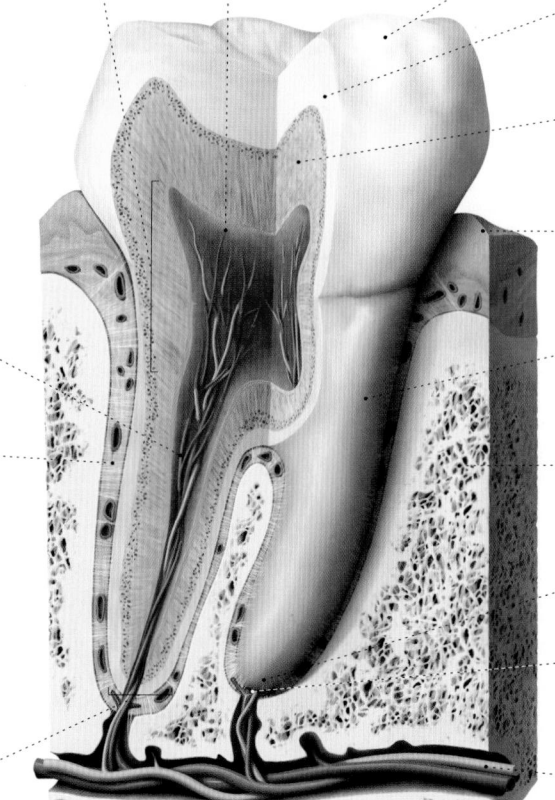

section of a molar
Teeth are formed of two main parts: the crown (the visible protruding part) and several roots (the part inserted into the upper or lower jaw).

pulp chamber
Central chamber of the crown enclosing the dental pulp and extending through the root canal.

dental pulp
Soft connective tissue rich in blood vessels and nerves; it gives the tooth its sensitivity and supplies it with essential nutrients.

cusp
Point formed by the enamel on the upper side of premolars and molars, allowing them to grind food.

enamel
Highly mineralized tissue covering and protecting the dentin of the crown; it is the hardest tissue in the body.

crown
Part of the tooth covered with enamel and protruding outside the gum.

dentin
Very hard calcified tissue forming the largest part of the tooth.

neck
Narrow part of the tooth surrounded by the gum separating the crown from the root.

gum
Thick section of the mucous membrane of the mouth that is rich in blood vessels and nerves; it covers the edge of the dental alveolus and adheres to the necks of the teeth.

root canal
Extension of the pulp chamber containing the dental pulp and opening at the apex of the root.

cementum
Hard mineralized tissue comparable to bone covering and protecting the dentin of the root.

periodontal ligament
Fibrous connective tissue joining the cementum to the bone, thus fixing the tooth into its dental alveolus.

alveolar bone
Bone of the upper and lower jaw containing tooth sockets and anchoring the teeth.

apex
Terminal part of the dental root whose opening (apical foramen) allows blood vessels and nerves to pass through.

root
Part of the tooth covered with cementum, and implanted into the dental alveolus of the upper and lower jaw; certain teeth, such as the molars, have several roots.

apical foramen
Narrow opening located at the terminal part of the apex allowing blood vessels and nerves to pass into the tooth.

dental alveolus
Tooth socket: bony cavity of the upper and lower jaw in which the root of the tooth is implanted.

dental plexus
Grouping of nerve fibers located around the roots of the upper teeth.

joints

More or less mobile structures linking bones in order to provide stability and mobility to the skeleton.

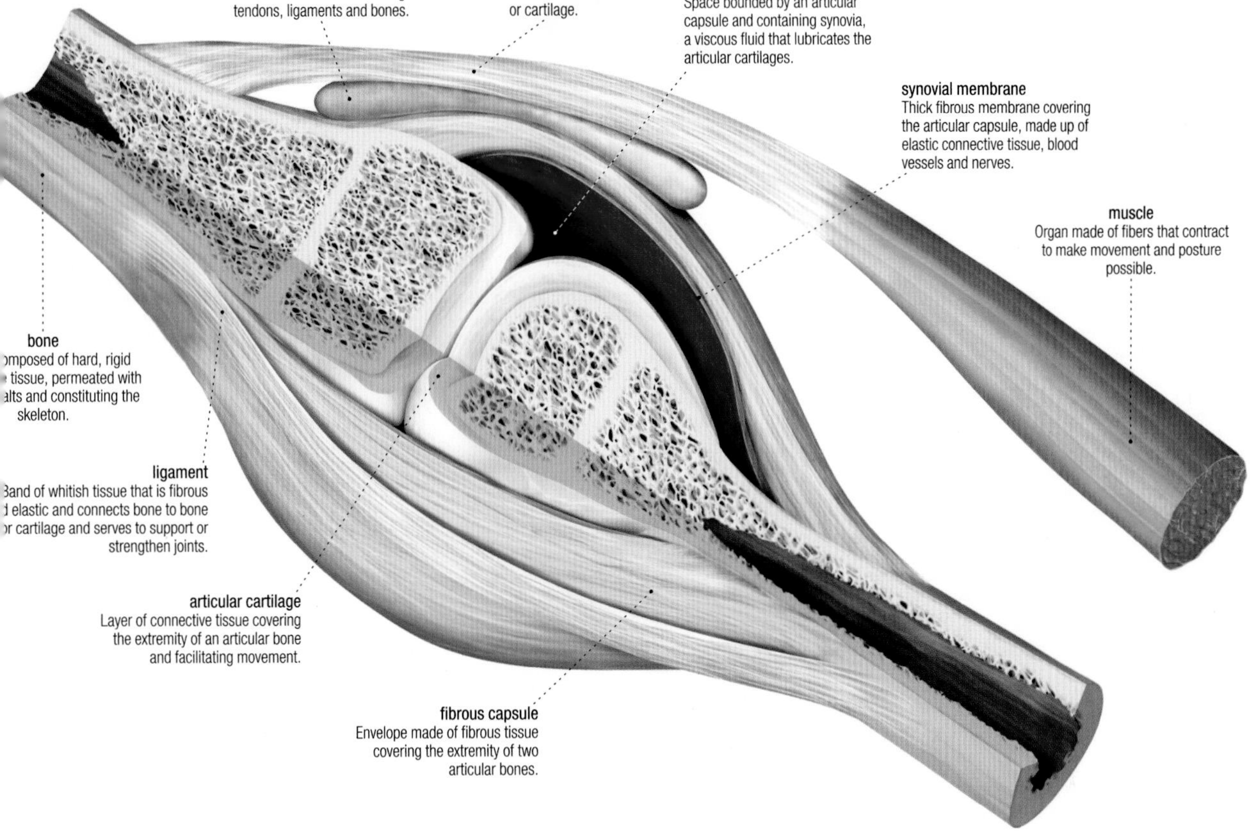

bursa
Small sac filled with synovia, located near a bone extremity or articular joint; it facilitates movement of the surrounding tendons, ligaments and bones.

tendon
Band of dense connective tissue in the endings of muscle fibers that connect the muscle to bone or cartilage.

synovial cavity
Space bounded by an articular capsule and containing synovia, a viscous fluid that lubricates the articular cartilages.

section of a synovial joint
Synovial joint: joint characterized by the presence of an articular capsule filled with a viscous liquid (synovial fluid). This is the most common type of joint.

synovial membrane
Thick fibrous membrane covering the articular capsule, made up of elastic connective tissue, blood vessels and nerves.

muscle
Organ made of fibers that contract to make movement and posture possible.

bone
Composed of hard, rigid tissue, permeated with salts and constituting the skeleton.

ligament
Band of whitish tissue that is fibrous and elastic and connects bone to bone or cartilage and serves to support or strengthen joints.

articular cartilage
Layer of connective tissue covering the extremity of an articular bone and facilitating movement.

fibrous capsule
Envelope made of fibrous tissue covering the extremity of two articular bones.

examples of synovial joints

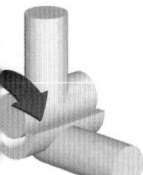

hinge joint
Enables flexion and extension along a single axis. The elbow is a particularly good example: the round terminal part of the humerus turns in the hollow of the ulna.

ball-and-socket joint
Allows movement in many directions; the ball-and-socket joint of the shoulder enables the humerus to flex and extend, to rotate, and to draw near and draw away from the trunk.

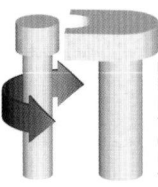

pivot joint
Enables rotation around a lengthwise axis: the cylindrical terminal part of a bone is encased in a hollow cylinder. Examples include the tibia and the fibula.

elbow
Example of a hinged joint; between the humerus and ulna.

shoulder
Example of a ball-and-socket joint; between the humerus and the scapula.

leg
Example of a pivot joint; between the fibula and the tibia.

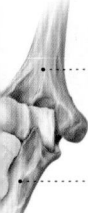

humerus
Long arm bone articulating with the scapula to form the shoulder, and with the radius and the ulna to form the elbow.

ulna
Long bone forming the inner portion of the forearm articulating with the humerus and radius.

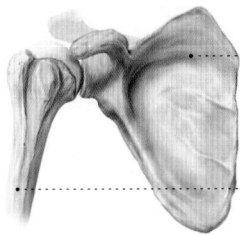

scapula
Shoulder blade: large thin flat bone articulating with the clavicle (collarbone) and the humerus to form the shoulder; numerous shoulder and back muscles attach to it.

humerus
Long arm bone articulating with the scapula to form the shoulder, and with the radius and the ulna to form the elbow.

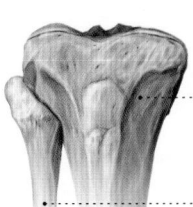

tibia
Long bone forming the inner portion of the leg articulating with the femur, fibula and talus (bone of the ankle).

fibula
Long bone forming the outer portion of the leg articulating with the tibia and talus (bone of the ankle).

joints

examples of synovial joints

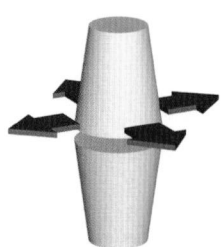

gliding joint
Surfaces of these joints are relatively flat and not very mobile; they allow only a narrow gliding range. Examples include certain bones of the wrist and foot.

saddle joint
Resembles the condyloid joint but allows a wider range of motion; this type of joint is rare.

condyloid joint
Allows movement in two directions. The wrist is a condyloid joint enabling the hand to flex and extend and be tilted sideways toward and away from the body.

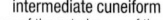

intermediate cuneiform
Bone of the anterior row of the tarsus articulating especially with the metatarsal bone of the second toe and the scaphoid bone.

navicular
Bone of the posterior row of the tarsus articulating especially with the talus and the three cuneiforms.

medial cuneiform
Bone of the anterior row of the tarsus articulating especially with the metatarsal bone of the big toe and the scaphoid bone.

metacarpal
Each of the five bones forming the metacarpus. The metacarpal bone of the thumb is very mobile.

trapezium
Bone of the anterior row of the carpus articulating especially with the metacarpal bone of the thumb.

radius
Long bone making up the outer section of the forearm articulating with the humerus, radius and bones of the wrist.

scaphoid
Bone of the posterior row of the carpus articulating especially with the radius to form the wrist.

lunate
Bone of the posterior row of the carpus articulating especially with the radius to form the wrist.

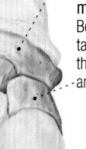

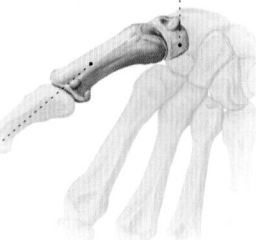

tarsus
Gliding joints allow certain bones of the foot to displace.

thumb
The thumb is an example of a saddle joint.

wrist
Example of a condyloid joint; between the radius and carpal bones.

example of fibrous joint
Fibrous joint: immoveable joint characterized by the presence of fibrocartilage connecting the bones.

examples of cartilaginous joints
Cartilaginous joint: joint having a cartilage plate fused with the articular surfaces; it allows only limited movement.

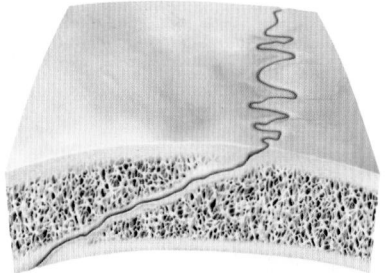

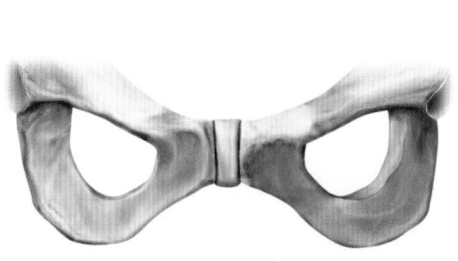

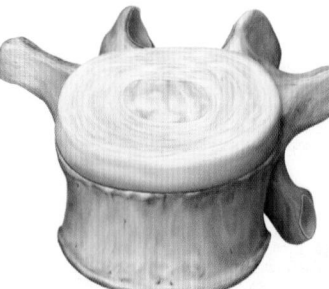

cranial suture
Fibrous joint connecting two bones of the skull and forming an irregular line; the sutures fuse with age, preventing all movement of the bones.

pubic symphysis
Slightly movable fibrocartilaginous joint connecting the two pubes.

intervertebral disk
Flat rounded cartilaginous structure separating two vertebrae; its elasticity allows the spinal column to move.

circulatory system

System formed by the heart, blood, blood vessels and lymph structures; blood is pumped by the heart through the body, bringing oxygen and nutrients and removing waste, carbon dioxide and extra fluids.

composition of the blood
Blood is made up of a watery liquid (plasma) in which solids (blood cells, platelets) are suspended. It accounts for 7% to 8% of the body's weight.

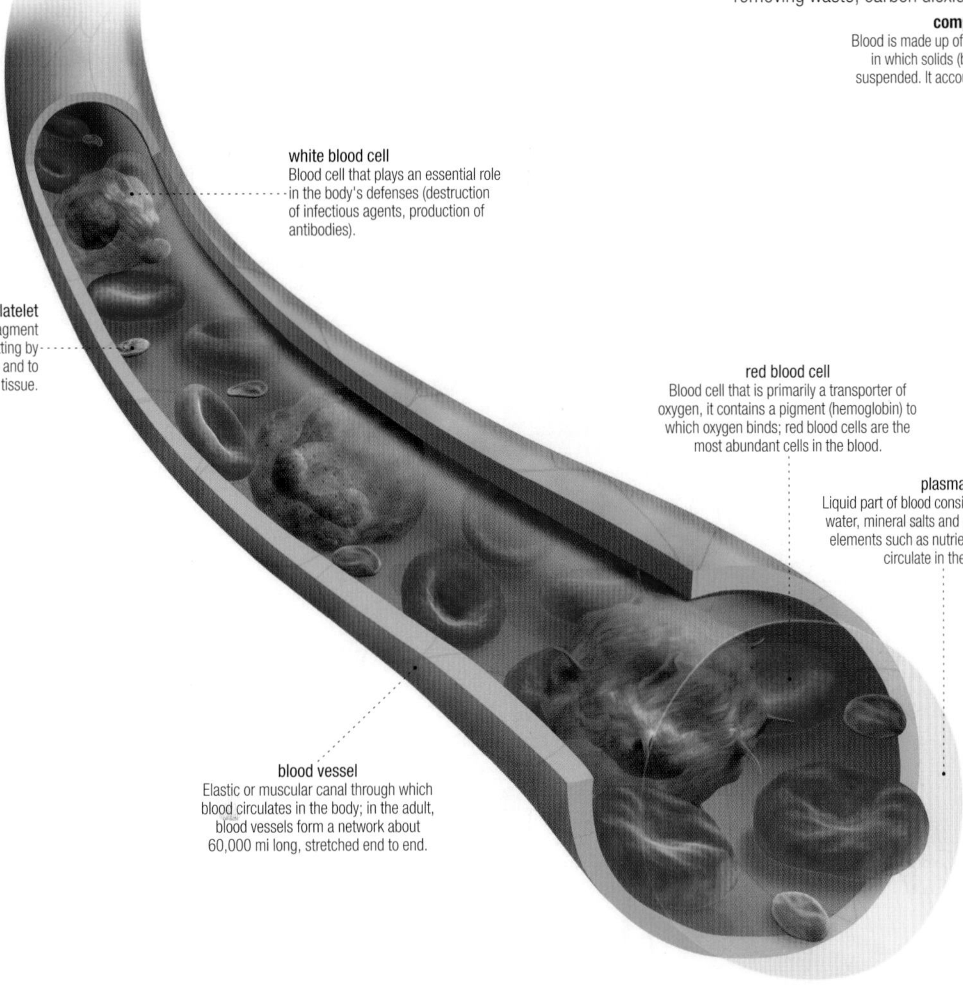

white blood cell
Blood cell that plays an essential role in the body's defenses (destruction of infectious agents, production of antibodies).

platelet
[Irre]gularly shaped cell fragment [th]at assists in blood clotting by [stic]king to other platelets and to tissue.

red blood cell
Blood cell that is primarily a transporter of oxygen, it contains a pigment (hemoglobin) to which oxygen binds; red blood cells are the most abundant cells in the blood.

plasma
Liquid part of blood consisting especially of water, mineral salts and proteins; it allows elements such as nutrients and waste to circulate in the blood.

blood vessel
Elastic or muscular canal through which blood circulates in the body; in the adult, blood vessels form a network about 60,000 mi long, stretched end to end.

[se]ction of a vein
[Vei]n: blood vessel carrying oxygen-[de]pleted blood from the organs [bac]k to the heart.

valve
Membranous fold inside a vein, preventing reverse blood flow.

section of an artery
Artery: blood vessel carrying oxygen-rich blood from the heart to all parts of the body.

endothelium
Epithelial tissue lining the interior surface of the blood vessel.

endothelium
Epithelial tissue lining the interior surface of the blood vessel.

lumen
Central opening of a hollow organ.

basal lamina
Membrane ensuring the adherence of epithelial cells to adjacent tissue.

smooth muscle
Muscle allowing involuntary movements of certain organs; they are found mostly in the walls of hollow organs (such as the intestines and the esophagus) and blood vessels.

external elastic lamina
Fibers mostly made of elastin, a protein capable of stretching and then returning to its original shape.

basal lamina
Membrane ensuring the adherence of epithelial cells to adjacent tissue.

tunica adventitia
Outer layer of the wall of the arteries and veins, rich in collagen fibers.

tunica adventitia
[O]uter layer of the wall of the arteries and veins, rich in collagen fibers.

smooth muscle
Muscle allowing involuntary movements of certain organs; they are found mostly in the walls of hollow organs (such as the intestines and the esophagus) and blood vessels.

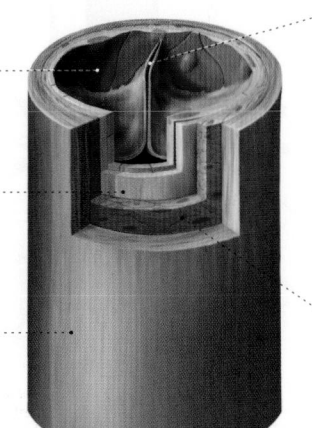

circulatory system

HUMAN BEING

principal arteries
The arteries (with the exception of the pulmonary arteries) distribute oxygen-rich blood to the body.

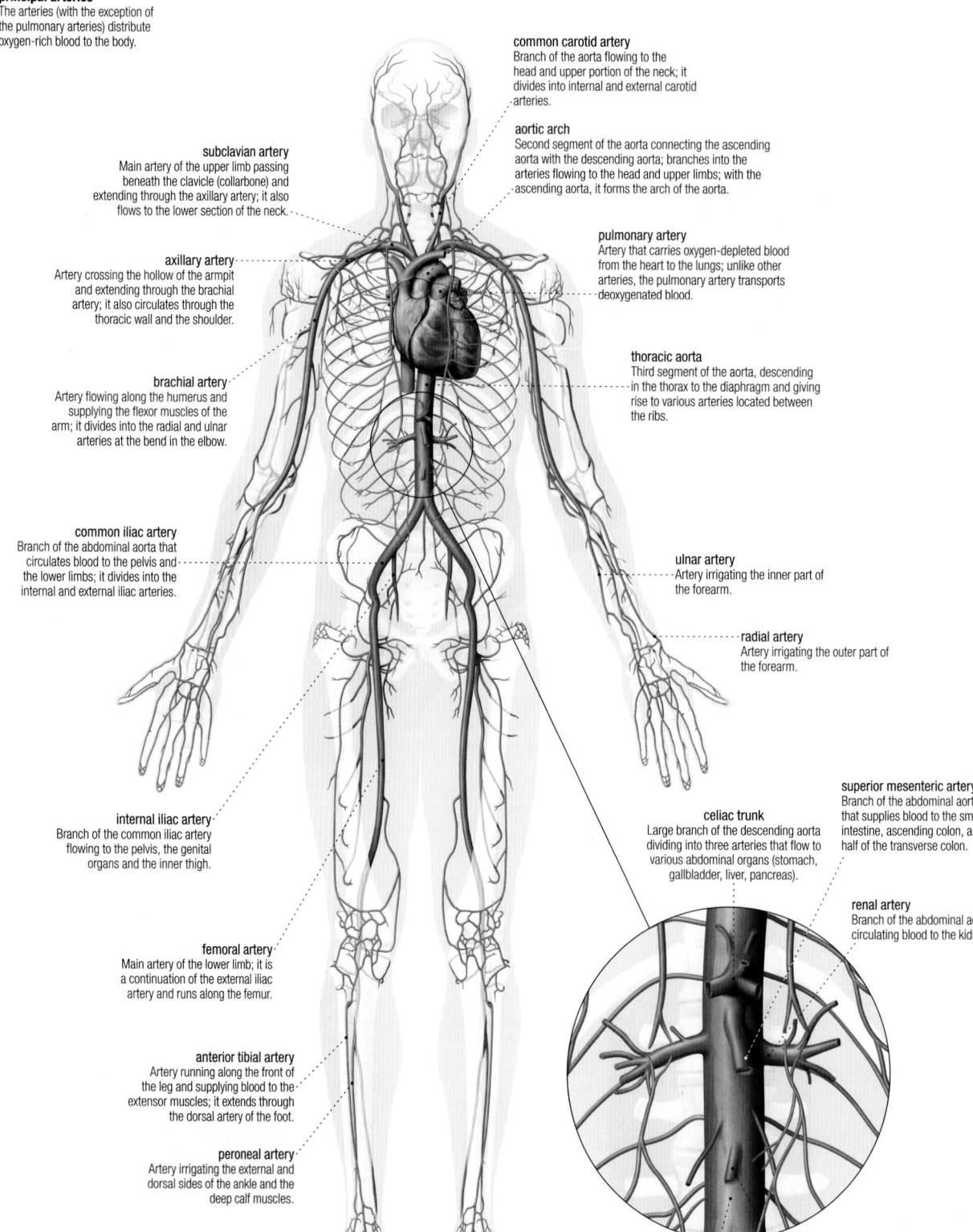

common carotid artery
Branch of the aorta flowing to the head and upper portion of the neck; it divides into internal and external carotid arteries.

aortic arch
Second segment of the aorta connecting the ascending aorta with the descending aorta; branches into the arteries flowing to the head and upper limbs; with the ascending aorta, it forms the arch of the aorta.

pulmonary artery
Artery that carries oxygen-depleted blood from the heart to the lungs; unlike other arteries, the pulmonary artery transports deoxygenated blood.

thoracic aorta
Third segment of the aorta, descending in the thorax to the diaphragm and giving rise to various arteries located between the ribs.

subclavian artery
Main artery of the upper limb passing beneath the clavicle (collarbone) and extending through the axillary artery; it also flows to the lower section of the neck.

axillary artery
Artery crossing the hollow of the armpit and extending through the brachial artery; it also circulates through the thoracic wall and the shoulder.

brachial artery
Artery flowing along the humerus and supplying the flexor muscles of the arm; it divides into the radial and ulnar arteries at the bend in the elbow.

common iliac artery
Branch of the abdominal aorta that circulates blood to the pelvis and the lower limbs; it divides into the internal and external iliac arteries.

ulnar artery
Artery irrigating the inner part of the forearm.

radial artery
Artery irrigating the outer part of the forearm.

internal iliac artery
Branch of the common iliac artery flowing to the pelvis, the genital organs and the inner thigh.

femoral artery
Main artery of the lower limb; it is a continuation of the external iliac artery and runs along the femur.

anterior tibial artery
Artery running along the front of the leg and supplying blood to the extensor muscles; it extends through the dorsal artery of the foot.

peroneal artery
Artery irrigating the external and dorsal sides of the ankle and the deep calf muscles.

dorsal artery of foot
Artery irrigating the ankle and dorsal face of the foot.

celiac trunk
Large branch of the descending aorta dividing into three arteries that flow to various abdominal organs (stomach, gallbladder, liver, pancreas).

superior mesenteric artery
Branch of the abdominal aorta that supplies blood to the small intestine, ascending colon, and half of the transverse colon.

renal artery
Branch of the abdominal aorta circulating blood to the kidney.

abdominal aorta
Fourth segment of the aorta circulating to all the organs and to the walls of the abdomen; it branches into the common iliac arteries.

inferior mesenteric artery
Branch of the abdominal aorta circulating blood to the ascending colon and half the transverse colon.

circulatory system

principal veins
The veins (with the exception of the pulmonary veins) carry oxygen-depleted blood towards the heart.

pulmonary vein
that carries oxygen-rich blood the lungs to the heart; unlike er veins, the pulmonary veins ansport oxygenated blood.

internal jugular vein
Vein collecting blood from the brain and from one portion of the face and neck; it is the largest vein in the neck.

superior vena cava
Vein carrying oxygen-depleted blood from the upper body (above the diaphragm) back to the right atrium.

subclavian vein
Vein collecting blood from the arm and part of the neck and face; it passes beneath the clavicle (collarbone) and receives the flow of the external jugular vein, among others.

external jugular vein
Vein carrying blood from the exterior walls of the skull, deep regions of the face and outer neck to the subclavian vein.

cephalic vein
Superficial vein of the outer arm emptying into the axillary vein; it also receives blood from the superficial veins of the shoulder.

basilic vein
Large superficial vein of the inner surface of the arm collecting blood from the hand and forearm; it empties into the axillary vein.

renal vein
Large vein collecting blood from the kidney; it flows into the inferior vena cava.

inferior vena cava
n that returns oxygen-depleted d from the lower portion of the y (below the diaphragm) to the t atrium; it is the largest vein in the body.

axillary vein
Deep vein running through the hollow of the armpit and ending at the subclavian vein; it receives the flow of the shoulder and thorax veins, among others.

superior mesenteric vein
Vein collecting blood from a section of the intestine (small intestine, right colon); it is one of the veins that flows into the portal vein.

common iliac vein
Vein carrying blood from the lower limb back to the inferior vena cava.

femoral vein
Vein collecting blood from the deep structures of the thighs and receives blood from the great saphenous vein, among others.

popliteal vein
Vein running the length of the dorsal side of the thigh and extending towards the femoral vein.

great saphenous vein
Superficial vein collecting blood from the inner leg and thigh and receiving blood from certain veins of the foot; it is the longest vein in the body.

small saphenous vein
Vein originating in the lateral part of the foot and rejoining the popliteal vein at the knee.

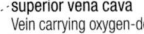

circulatory system

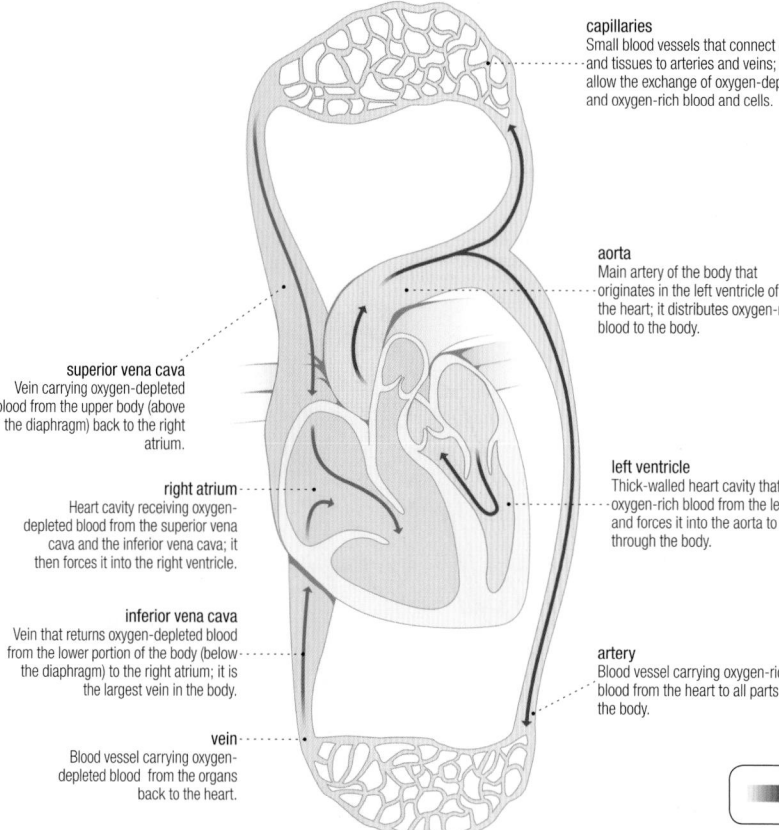

systemic circulation
All the blood vessels ensuring blood irrigation of tissues and organs.

capillaries
Small blood vessels that connect organs and tissues to arteries and veins; they allow the exchange of oxygen-depleted and oxygen-rich blood and cells.

aorta
Main artery of the body that originates in the left ventricle of the heart; it distributes oxygen-rich blood to the body.

superior vena cava
Vein carrying oxygen-depleted blood from the upper body (above the diaphragm) back to the right atrium.

left ventricle
Thick-walled heart cavity that receives oxygen-rich blood from the left atrium and forces it into the aorta to circulate through the body.

right atrium
Heart cavity receiving oxygen-depleted blood from the superior vena cava and the inferior vena cava; it then forces it into the right ventricle.

inferior vena cava
Vein that returns oxygen-depleted blood from the lower portion of the body (below the diaphragm) to the right atrium; it is the largest vein in the body.

artery
Blood vessel carrying oxygen-rich blood from the heart to all parts of the body.

vein
Blood vessel carrying oxygen-depleted blood from the organs back to the heart.

arterial blood
Blood rich in oxygen; it circulates from the lungs to the body through the pulmonary veins, left cav of the heart and the arter

venous blood
Blood depleted of oxygen and full of carbon dioxide returns from the body to lungs through the veins, cavities of the heart and pulmonary arteries.

pulmonary circulation
All the blood vessels that ensure the exchange of gases (as carbon dioxide and oxygen) between blood and air in lung tissue.

lung
Respiratory organ formed of expandable tissue, to which air from the nasal and oral cavities is carried and where blood is cleansed of carbon dioxide and enriched with oxygen.

pulmonary arteries
Arteries that carry oxygen-depleted blood and carbon dioxide from the heart to the lungs.

left atrium
Heart cavity receiving oxygen-rich blood from the lungs via four pulmonary veins; it then forces it into the left ventricle.

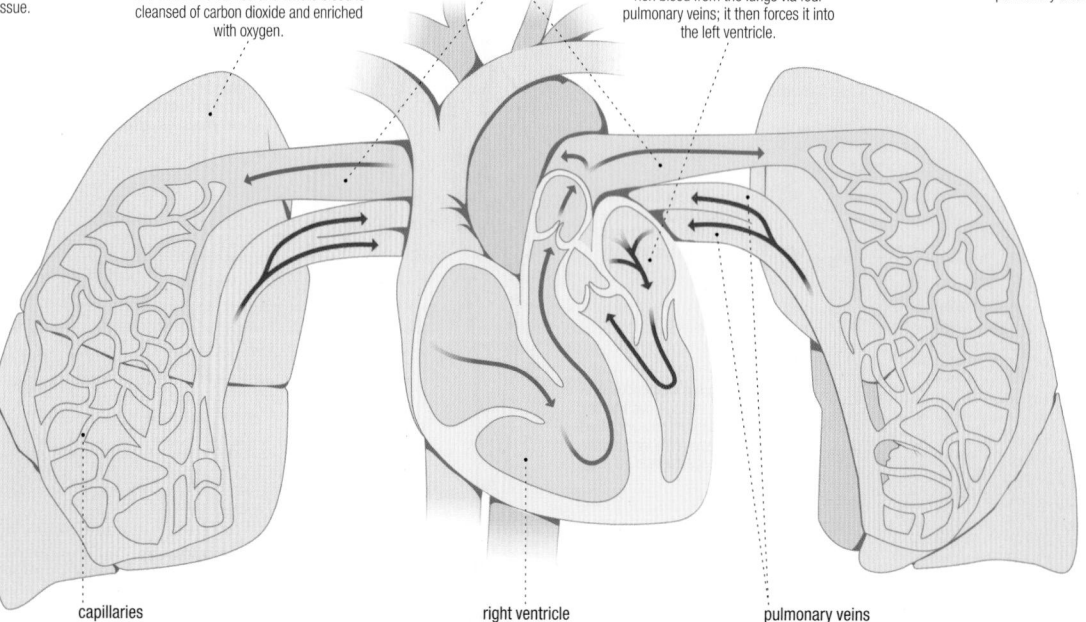

capillaries
Small blood vessels that connect organs and tissues to arteries and veins; they allow the exchange of oxygen-depleted and oxygen-rich blood and cells.

right ventricle
Thin-walled heart cavity that receives oxygen-depleted blood from the right atrium and forces it into the pulmonary artery leading to the lungs.

pulmonary veins
Veins carrying oxygen-rich blood from the lungs to the left atrium of the heart.

circulatory system

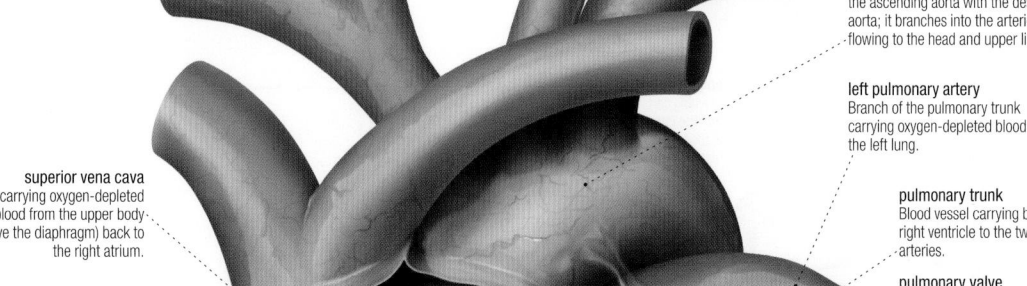

heart
Muscular organ made up of four chambers; its regular rhythmic contractions pump and circulate blood.

aortic arch
Second segment of the aorta connecting the ascending aorta with the descending aorta; it branches into the arteries flowing to the head and upper limbs.

left pulmonary artery
Branch of the pulmonary trunk carrying oxygen-depleted blood to the left lung.

pulmonary trunk
Blood vessel carrying blood from the right ventricle to the two pulmonary arteries.

pulmonary valve
Membranous fold made up of three walls; it carries blood from the right ventricle to the pulmonary artery and prevents its reflux.

left pulmonary veins
Veins carrying oxygen-rich blood from the left lung to the left atrium of the heart.

left atrium
Heart cavity receiving oxygen-rich blood from the lungs via four pulmonary veins; it then forces it into the left ventricle.

mitral valve
Membranous fold made up of two walls; it carries blood from the left atrium to the left ventricle and prevents its reflux.

left ventricle
Thick-walled heart cavity that receives oxygen-rich blood from the left atrium and forces it into the aorta to circulate through the body.

superior vena cava
carrying oxygen-depleted blood from the upper body (above the diaphragm) back to the right atrium.

right pulmonary artery
Branch of the pulmonary trunk carrying oxygen-depleted blood to the right lung.

right pulmonary veins
Veins carrying oxygen-rich blood from the right lung to the left atrium of the heart.

right atrium
Heart cavity receiving oxygen-depleted blood from the superior and inferior vena cava; it then forces it into the right ventricle.

aortic valve
Membranous fold made up of three walls; it carries blood from the left ventricle to the aorta and prevents its reflux.

tricuspid valve
Membranous fold made up of three walls; it carries blood from the right atrium to the right ventricle and prevents its reflux.

endocardium
Thin smooth membrane that lines the myocardium and makes up the inner layer of the heart.

inferior vena cava
Vein that returns oxygen-depleted blood from the lower portion of the body (below the diaphragm) to the right atrium; it is the largest vein in the body.

interventricular septum
Mostly muscular partition separating the right and left ventricles of the heart.

papillary muscle
Internal ventricular muscle limiting movement of the mitral or tricuspid valve and preventing it from being pushed back into the atrium during contraction of the ventricle.

right ventricle
Thin-walled heart cavity that receives oxygen-depleted blood from the right atrium and forces it into the pulmonary artery leading to the lungs.

myocardium
Thick muscle that forms the heart walls; its involuntary contraction, directed by autonomic nerves, pumps oxygen-rich blood to the body and oxygen-depleted blood back to the lungs.

respiratory system

System comprising the upper respiratory passages, trachea and the lungs that allows gas exchange, enriching blood with oxygen on inhalation and expelling carbon dioxide on exhalation.

main organs
The respiratory apparatus is comprised of the upper respiratory passages (nose, mouth, pharynx and larynx), the trachea and the lungs.

nasal cavity
Chamber where air inhaled through the nostrils is filtered and humidified; it also plays an olfactory role.

oral cavity
Secondary point of entry for inhaled air, used especially when the nasal cavity is obstructed or during physical exertion; it is also part of the digestive system.

epiglottis
Movable cartilaginous plate ensuring that the larynx closes during ingestion of food so that food cannot enter the respiratory tract.

pharynx
Muscular membranous channel connecting the nasal cavity to the larynx and the oral cavity to the esophagus; it enables breathing, ingestion of food and speech.

larynx
Muscular cartilaginous duct at the upper terminal part of the trachea; it contains the vocal cords and plays a role in speech and respiration.

vocal cord
Muscular fold aiding speech; the vocal cords close and vibrate when air is expelled from the lungs, thereby producing sound.

trachea
Muscular cartilaginous tract that is a continuation of the larynx; it divides into two main bronchi, each of which ends in a lung, and allows air to pass.

right lung
Respiratory organ divided into three lobes in which blood from the pulmonary artery is cleansed of carbon dioxide and enriched with oxygen.

left lung
Respiratory organ divided into two lobes where blood from the pulmonary artery is cleansed of carbon dioxide and enriched with oxygen.

upper lobe
Section of the right lung separated from the middle lobe by a horizontal fissure and from the lower lobe by an oblique fissure.

upper lobe
Section of the left lung separated from the lower lobe by an oblique fissure.

middle lobe
Section of the right lung separated from the upper lobe by a horizontal fissure and from the lower lobe by an oblique fissure.

lower lobe
Section of the right lung separated from the middle and upper lobes by an oblique fissure.

lower lobe
Section of the left lung separated from the upper lobe by the oblique fissure.

diaphragm
Main muscle of inhalation separating the cavities of the thorax and abdomen; its contraction increases the size of the thoracic cavity, causing the lungs to expand and take in air.

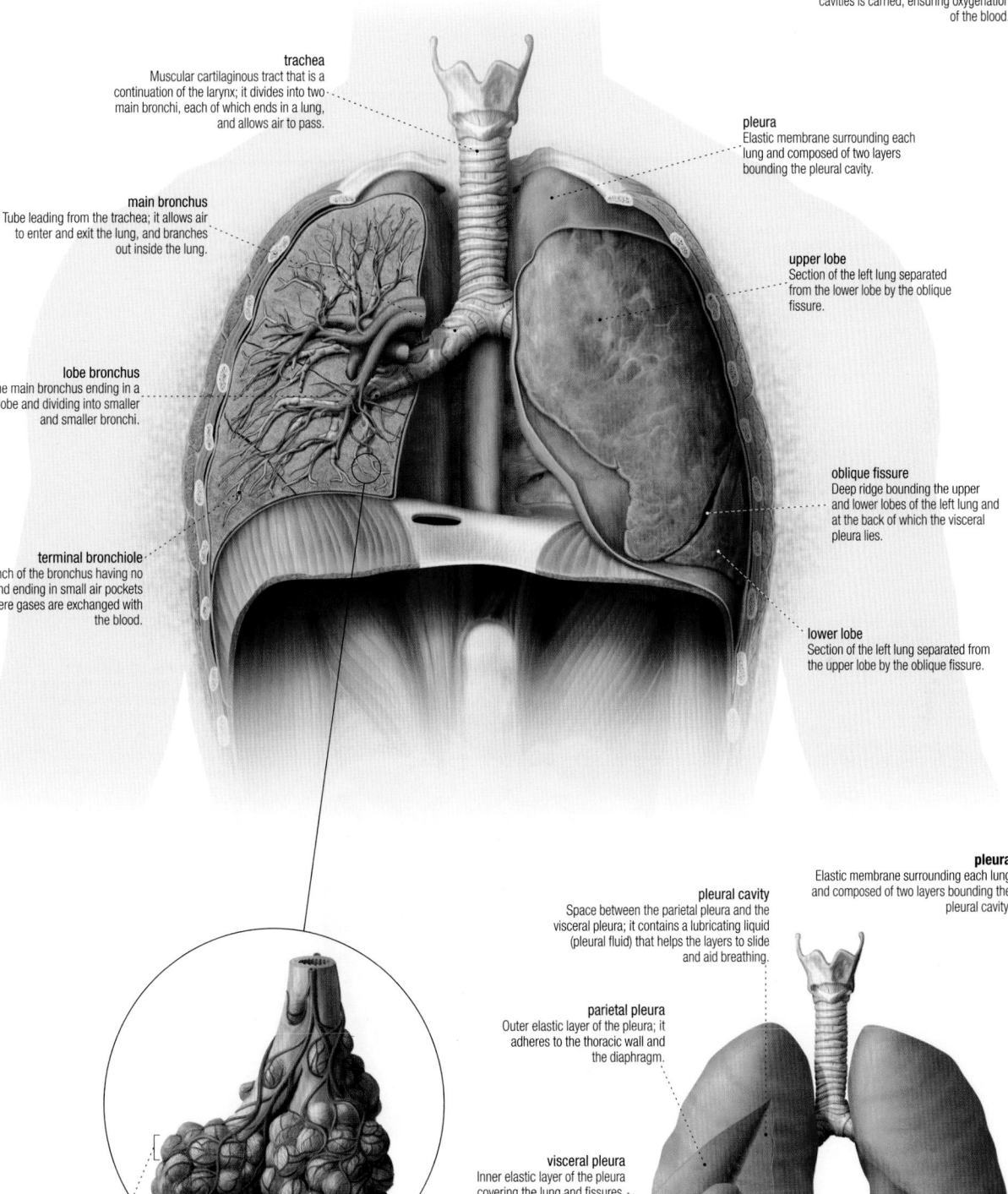

lungs
Respiratory organs formed of extensible tissue, in which air from the nasal and oral cavities is carried, ensuring oxygenation of the blood.

trachea
Muscular cartilaginous tract that is a continuation of the larynx; it divides into two main bronchi, each of which ends in a lung, and allows air to pass.

pleura
Elastic membrane surrounding each lung and composed of two layers bounding the pleural cavity.

main bronchus
Tube leading from the trachea; it allows air to enter and exit the lung, and branches out inside the lung.

upper lobe
Section of the left lung separated from the lower lobe by the oblique fissure.

lobe bronchus
h of the main bronchus ending in a nary lobe and dividing into smaller and smaller bronchi.

oblique fissure
Deep ridge bounding the upper and lower lobes of the left lung and at the back of which the visceral pleura lies.

terminal bronchiole
al branch of the bronchus having no age and ending in small air pockets e) where gases are exchanged with the blood.

lower lobe
Section of the left lung separated from the upper lobe by the oblique fissure.

pleura
Elastic membrane surrounding each lung and composed of two layers bounding the pleural cavity.

pleural cavity
Space between the parietal pleura and the visceral pleura; it contains a lubricating liquid (pleural fluid) that helps the layers to slide and aid breathing.

parietal pleura
Outer elastic layer of the pleura; it adheres to the thoracic wall and the diaphragm.

visceral pleura
Inner elastic layer of the pleura covering the lung and fissures.

lung
Respiratory organ divided into two or three lobes, managing exchanges of gas between the air and the blood.

alveolus of the lung
e of about 300 million air sacs (alveoli) grouped in clusters at end of bronchioles; thin walls veen the alveoli and capillaries allow the exchange of gases (carbon dioxide and oxygen).

digestive system

System formed by the mouth, the digestive tract and its glands that uses mechanical action, enzymes or secretions to break down food, absorb nutrients and expel waste.

main organs
The digestive apparatus is made up of three parts: the mouth, the digestive tract (esophagus, stomach, intestines) and the adjoining glands (salivary glands, liver, pancreas).

oral cavity
Cavity at the start of the digestive tract, used for ingesting liquids and food; it is also part of the respiratory system.

salivary glands
Each of the three pairs of organs secreting a liquid (saliva) that contains a digestive enzyme; it is used to moisten food to facilitate its ingestion.

pharynx
Muscular membranous channel connecting the nasal cavity to the larynx and the oral cavity to the esophagus; it enables breathing, ingestion of food and speech.

tongue
Flexible muscular structure of the oral cavity that aids in tasting, chewing and ingesting food; it also facilitates speech.

esophagus
Muscular membranous channel of the anterior section of the digestive tract; it allows food to reach the stomach.

liver
Organ secreting substances, including bile, that help digestion and break up certain toxins contained in the blood.

stomach
Dilated section of the digestive tract; it stores, stirs and mixes food with the gastric juices it secretes before emptying it into the duodenum.

gallbladder
Small muscular sac where bile secreted by the liver is stored before passing into the duodenum. Bile helps in the digestion of fatty substances.

pancreas
Digestive gland connected to the duodenum; produces secretions and hormones (especially insulin).

large intestine
Last segment of the digestive tract, where final digestion and elimination of waste matter take place.

small intestine
Channel of the digestive tract joining the stomach to the large intestine, where a part of digestion and most food absorption occurs.

vermiform appendix
Tubular extension of the cecum; this appendage is occasionally the site of appendicitis, a severe inflammation.

anus
Terminal opening of the digestive tract controlled by an involuntary inner muscle and a voluntary outer muscle enabling the release of waste.

digestive system

transverse colon
Second segment of the colon (middle section of the large intestine). The right colon (the ascending colon plus half the transverse colon) mainly enables absorption of water.

large intestine
Last wide section of the digestive tract, about 5 ft long, where the final stage of digestion and elimination of waste occurs; it includes the colon and the rectum.

ascending colon
First segment of the colon; it absorbs water from food residue before it is eliminated.

descending colon
Third segment of the colon; it stores waste before it is eliminated.

cecum
Anterior part of the large intestine; it receives food particles from the ileum.

rectum
Terminal section of the large intestine preceding the anus.

sigmoid colon
Fourth segment of the colon; it carries waste to the rectum.

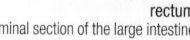
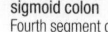

small intestine
Narrow section of the digestive tract, about 20 ft long, between the stomach and cecum, where a part of digestion and most food absorption occurs.

duodenum
Anterior section of the small intestine; secretions from the liver and pancreas, as well as food partially digested in the stomach, empty into it.

jejunum
Middle section of the small intestine between the duodenum and the ileum; the majority of nutrients are absorbed here.

ileum
Terminal part of the small intestine between the jejunum and cecum.

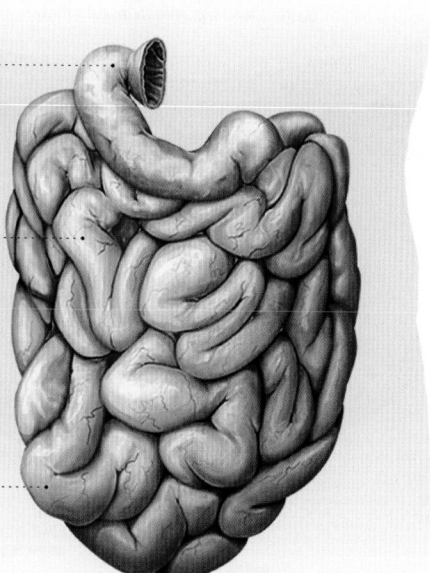

urinary system

System formed by the ureters, kidneys, bladder and urethra that produces and discharges urine, removing waste and adjusting levels of salt and water in the body.

main organs
The upper section of the urinary apparatus is composed of the ureters and kidneys, while the lower section is composed of the bladder and the urethra.

right kidney
Organ located beneath the liver; it filters the blood and secretes urine to eliminate toxic substances and waste from the body.

renal hilum
Opening of the inner edge of the kidney allowing the passage of blood vessels, nerves and the ureter.

urinary bladder
Muscular reservoir where urine from the kidneys collects before being discharged through the urethra.

adrenal gland
Endocrine gland located above the kidney; it secretes various hormones including steroids.

left kidney
Organ located beneath the spleen; it filters the blood and secretes urine to eliminate toxic substances and waste from the body.

ureter
Long muscular membranous canal extending from the renal pelvis; it carries urine from the kidney to the urinary bladder.

urethra
Membranous canal enabling the discharge of urine. In the male, it also allows sperm to pass.

urinary bladder: frontal section
Urinary bladder: muscular reservoir where urine from the kidneys collects before being evacuated through the urethra.

mucous membrane
Mucous membrane lining the inner side of the bladder; it forms folds when the bladder is empty.

trigone
Triangular-shaped region of the mucous membrane of the urinary bladder, bordered by the two ureteral orifices and the neck of the urinary bladder.

internal urethral sphincter
Muscle forming a ring around the neck of the urinary bladder; its involuntary release allows urination.

ureter
Long muscular membranous canal extending from the renal pelvis; it carries urine from the kidney to the urinary bladder.

detrusor muscle
Smooth muscle forming the essential part of the bladder wall.

ureteral orifice
Opening through which the ureter connects with the bladder.

neck
Lower extremity of the bladder connecting with the ureter.

urethra
Membranous canal enabling the discharge of urine. In the male, it also allows sperm to pass.

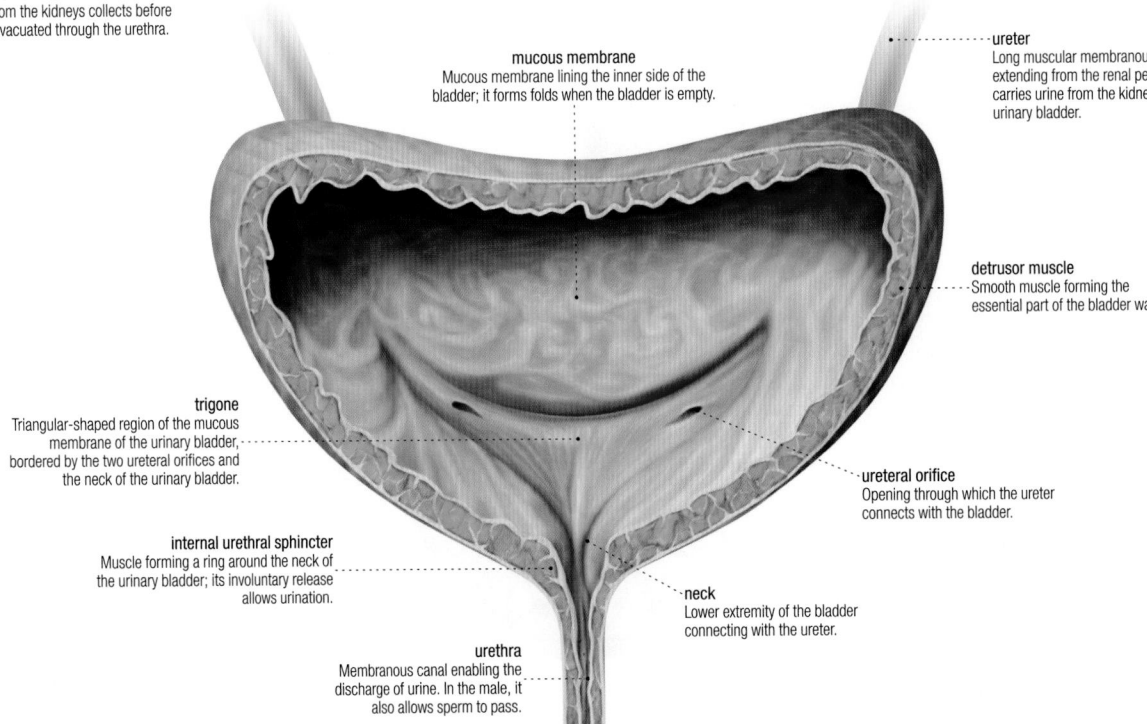

urinary system

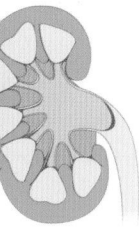

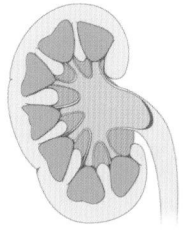

renal cortex
f the kidney covering the
renal pyramids.

renal medulla
Middle part of the kidney, made up
of renal pyramids.

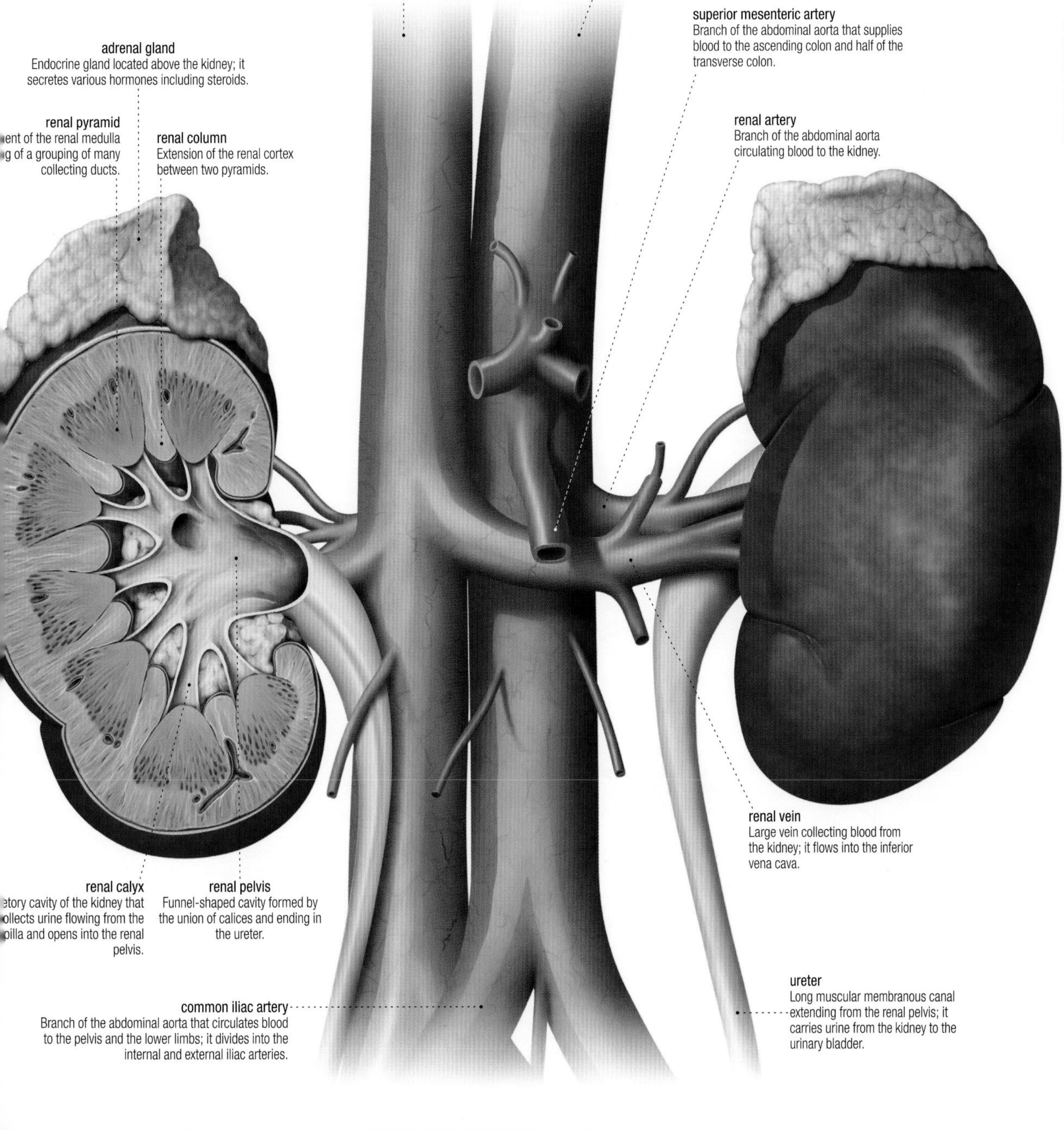

kidneys
Organs located below the liver that filter
blood and secrete urine to eliminate
toxins and waste from the body.

inferior vena cava
Vein that returns oxygen-depleted
blood from the lower portion of the
body (below the diaphragm) to the
right atrium; it is the largest vein in
the body.

abdominal aorta
Fourth segment of the aorta circulating
to all the organs and to the walls of the
abdomen; it branches into the common
iliac arteries.

superior mesenteric artery
Branch of the abdominal aorta that supplies
blood to the ascending colon and half of the
transverse colon.

adrenal gland
Endocrine gland located above the kidney; it
secretes various hormones including steroids.

renal artery
Branch of the abdominal aorta
circulating blood to the kidney.

renal pyramid
ent of the renal medulla
g of a grouping of many
collecting ducts.

renal column
Extension of the renal cortex
between two pyramids.

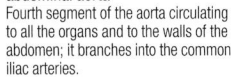

renal vein
Large vein collecting blood from
the kidney; it flows into the inferior
vena cava.

renal calyx
etory cavity of the kidney that
ollects urine flowing from the
pilla and opens into the renal
pelvis.

renal pelvis
Funnel-shaped cavity formed by
the union of calices and ending in
the ureter.

ureter
Long muscular membranous canal
extending from the renal pelvis; it
carries urine from the kidney to the
urinary bladder.

common iliac artery
Branch of the abdominal aorta that circulates blood
to the pelvis and the lower limbs; it divides into the
internal and external iliac arteries.

HUMAN BEING

nervous system

All the nerves of the body, formed by the brain and the spinal cord and the nerves that connect the brain and the spinal cord with other parts of the body.

structure of nervous system
The nervous system is made up of two distinct entities with defined roles: the central nervous system and the peripheral nervous system.

brain
Part of the central nervous system enclosed in the skull that consists of the cerebrum, the cerebellum and the brain stem.

cranial nerves
Group of 12 pairs of nerves that origina... from the lower surface of the brain, pro... sensation and stimulation (innervation) the head and neck, and serve a broader motor or sensory function for the body.

central nervous system
Brain and spinal cord, the control center for all bodily functions and activities. It receives, processes and responds to information from the peripheral nervous system.

peripheral nervous system
Nerves that transmit messages to and receive commands from the central nervous system. Some relay voluntary commands to sense organs, muscles and glands. Its autonomic nerves relay involuntary commands to internal organs, like the heart and lungs.

spinal cord
Part of the central nervous system located in the spinal column; it conducts sensory impulses to and motor impulses away from the brain and controls many reflex responses.

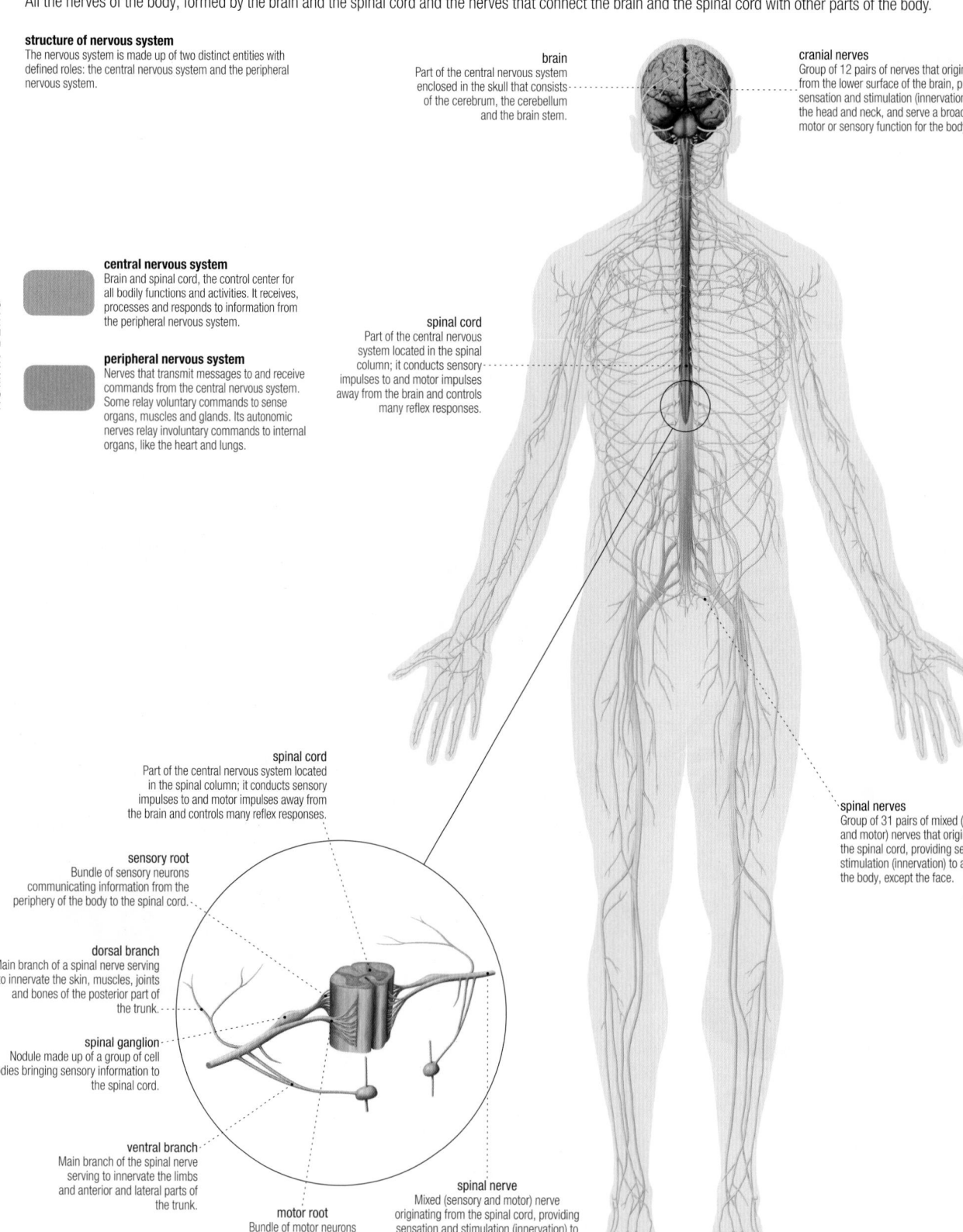

spinal cord
Part of the central nervous system located in the spinal column; it conducts sensory impulses to and motor impulses away from the brain and controls many reflex responses.

sensory root
Bundle of sensory neurons communicating information from the periphery of the body to the spinal cord.

dorsal branch
Main branch of a spinal nerve serving to innervate the skin, muscles, joints and bones of the posterior part of the trunk.

spinal ganglion
Nodule made up of a group of cell bodies bringing sensory information to the spinal cord.

ventral branch
Main branch of the spinal nerve serving to innervate the limbs and anterior and lateral parts of the trunk.

motor root
Bundle of motor neurons communicating information from the spinal cord to the periphery of the body, especially the muscles.

spinal nerve
Mixed (sensory and motor) nerve originating from the spinal cord, providing sensation and stimulation (innervation) to all parts of the body, except the face.

spinal nerves
Group of 31 pairs of mixed (se... and motor) nerves that origina... the spinal cord, providing sens... stimulation (innervation) to all the body, except the face.

nervous system

neuron
Cell of the nervous system allowing information to be carried in the form of electrical and chemical signals.

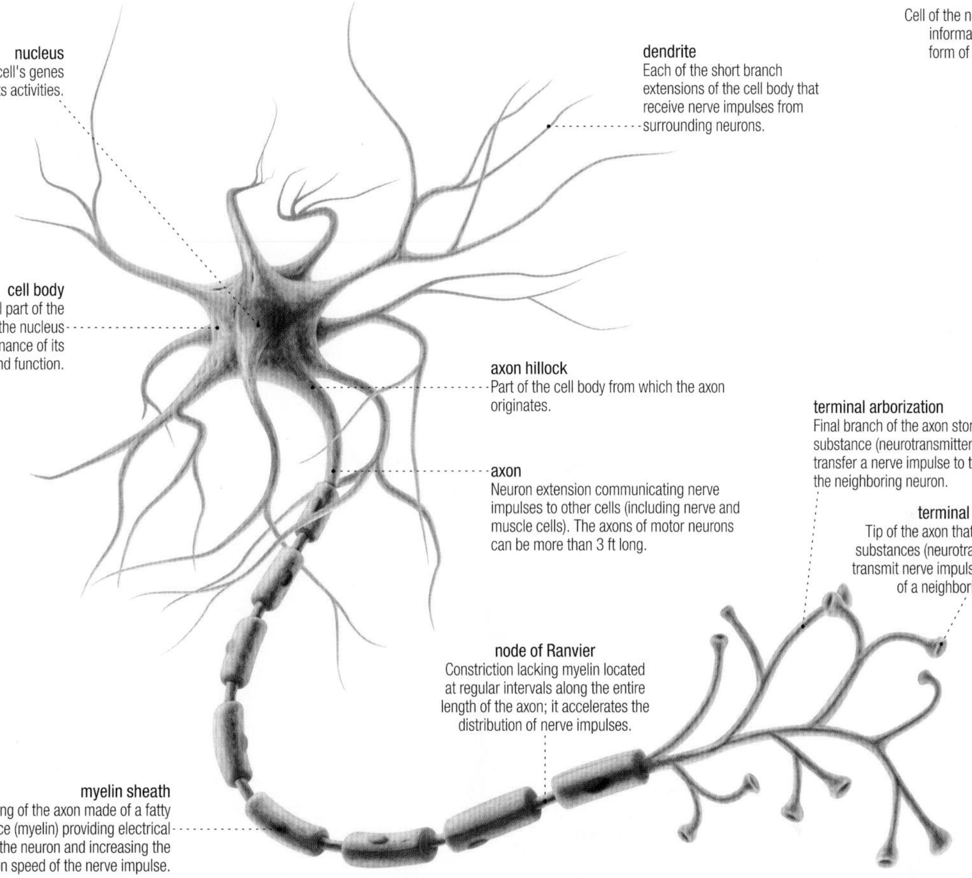

nucleus
anelle containing a cell's genes and controlling its activities.

dendrite
Each of the short branch extensions of the cell body that receive nerve impulses from surrounding neurons.

cell body
Bulging central part of the neuron containing the nucleus and ensuring maintenance of its structure and function.

axon hillock
Part of the cell body from which the axon originates.

terminal arborization
Final branch of the axon storing a chemical substance (neurotransmitter) used to transfer a nerve impulse to the dendrites of the neighboring neuron.

terminal button
Tip of the axon that stores chemical substances (neurotransmitters) used to transmit nerve impulses to the dendrites of a neighboring neuron.

axon
Neuron extension communicating nerve impulses to other cells (including nerve and muscle cells). The axons of motor neurons can be more than 3 ft long.

node of Ranvier
Constriction lacking myelin located at regular intervals along the entire length of the axon; it accelerates the distribution of nerve impulses.

myelin sheath
Casing of the axon made of a fatty substance (myelin) providing electrical insulation for the neuron and increasing the conduction speed of the nerve impulse.

HUMAN BEING

reflex arc
Pathway that transmits and receives electrical impulses between nerve cells (neurons) and the spinal cord without involving the brain; the knee-jerk response to a tap on the knee is a reflex action.

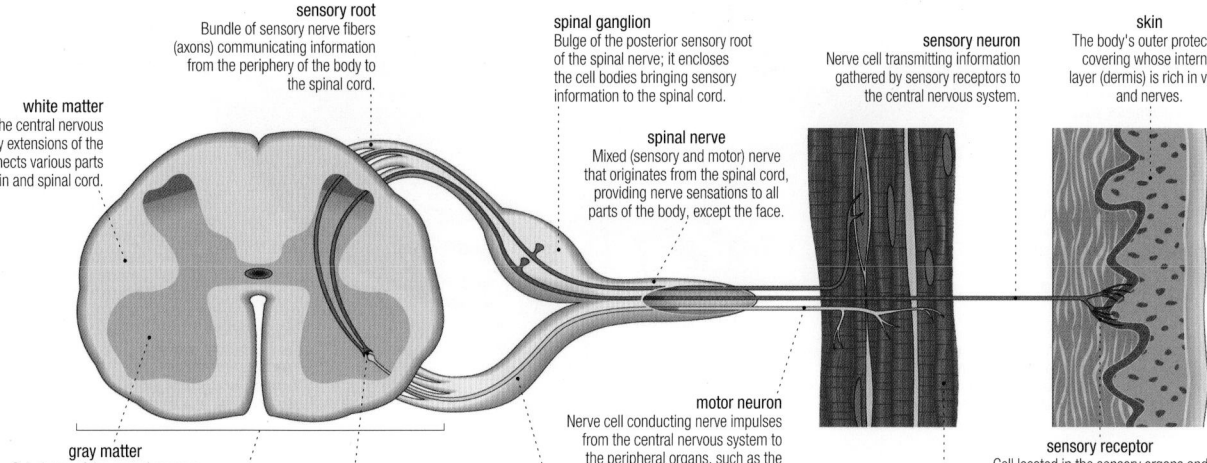

sensory root
Bundle of sensory nerve fibers (axons) communicating information from the periphery of the body to the spinal cord.

spinal ganglion
Bulge of the posterior sensory root of the spinal nerve; it encloses the cell bodies bringing sensory information to the spinal cord.

sensory neuron
Nerve cell transmitting information gathered by sensory receptors to the central nervous system.

skin
The body's outer protective covering whose internal layer (dermis) is rich in veins and nerves.

white matter
f the central nervous by extensions of the onnects various parts rain and spinal cord.

spinal nerve
Mixed (sensory and motor) nerve that originates from the spinal cord, providing nerve sensations to all parts of the body, except the face.

gray matter
Substance of the central nervous system formed by the cell bodies of neurons; it ensures the processing of nerve impulses.

motor neuron
Nerve cell conducting nerve impulses from the central nervous system to the peripheral organs, such as the muscles.

sensory receptor
Cell located in the sensory organs and capable of generating a nerve message when submitted to a physical or chemical stimulus.

spinal cord
Part of the central nervous system located in the spinal column; it receives and transmits nerve information and initiates reflex actions.

synapse
Contact zone between two neurons through which nerve impulses are transmitted.

motor root
Bundle of motor nerve cells (neurons) communicating information from the spinal cord to the periphery of the body, especially the muscles.

muscle fiber
Component tissue of the muscle; it contracts in response to a nerve impulse from the central nervous system.

nervous system

brain
Part of the central nervous system enclosed in the skull, consisting of the cerebrum, cerebellum and brain stem; it is responsible for sensory perception, most movements, memory, language, reflexes and vital functions.

frontal section

cerebrum
Largest and most complex part of the brain, it contains the centers for higher brain functions (including movement, language and memory).

lateral ventricle
Each of the two cavities located on either side of the third ventricle of the cerebrum, assisting in the production of brain and spinal cord (cerebrospinal) fluid.

corpus callosum
Connecting band of white nerve fibers enabling the two cerebral hemispheres to communicate.

third ventricle
Cavity of the brain assisting in the production of brain and spinal cord (cerebrospinal) fluid..

cerebral cortex
Superficial layer of the cerebrum, made up of gray matter, assuring the most advanced nerve functions.

white matter
Substance of the central nervous system formed by extensions of the neurons; connects various parts of the brain and spinal cord.

gray matter
Substance of the central nervous system formed by the cell bodies of neurons; it ensures the processing of nerve impulses.

cerebellum
Part of the brain controlling balance and coordination, muscle tone and posture.

hypothalamus
Small structure that plays a role in such processes as th action of autonomic nerves temperature, eating, sleep a the release of hormones fro pituitary gland.

optic chiasm
X-shaped intersection (chiasm) of nerve fibers that joins the brain to the two optic nerves; signals from the eyes cross to both sides of the brain.

pituitary gland
Gland secreting numerous hormones influencing growth, excretion, reproduction and other key functions.

pons
Mass of nerve fibers that connects the cerebellum to the lower brain stem and where four pairs of cranial nerves originate. Its nerves coordinate eye and facial movements, facial sensation, hearing and balance.

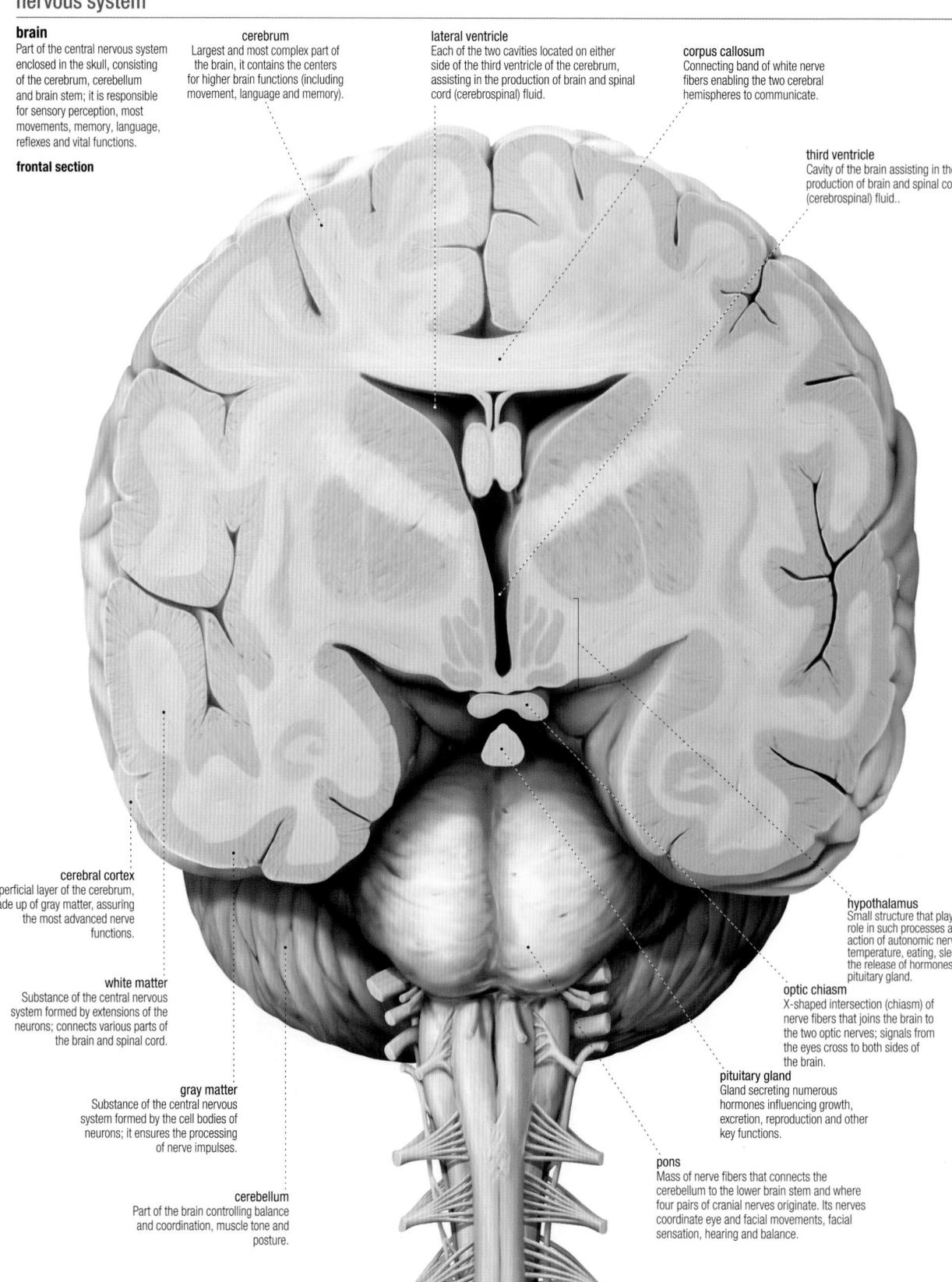

nervous system

cerebrum: superior view
Cerebrum: largest part of the brain, it contains the control centers for complex functions (including movement, language and memory).

left cerebral hemisphere
Left part of the cerebrum, controlling the movements of the right side of the body; it also specializes in analysis and logical thinking.

right cerebral hemisphere
Right part of the cerebrum, controlling the movements of the left side of the body; it is involved in artistic activities.

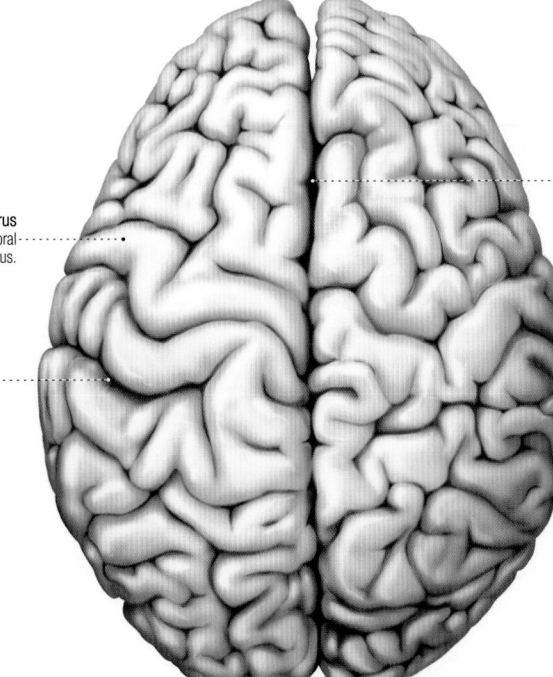

longitudinal fissure
Deep ridge separating the two cerebral hemispheres.

gyrus
Portion of the surface of a cerebral hemisphere bounded by a sulcus.

sulcus
Depression surrounding two convolutions of the cerebrum.

cerebrum: lateral view
Cerebrum: largest part of the brain, it contains the control centers for complex functions (including movement, language and memory).

parietal lobe
Lobe located in the middle part of the cerebrum, involved in taste, touch, pain and language comprehension.

frontal lobe
Lobe located in the anterior part of the cerebrum, behind the forehead, responsible for reasoning, planning, voluntary movements, emotions and spoken language.

occipital lobe
Lobe located at the back of the cerebrum, playing a role in vision.

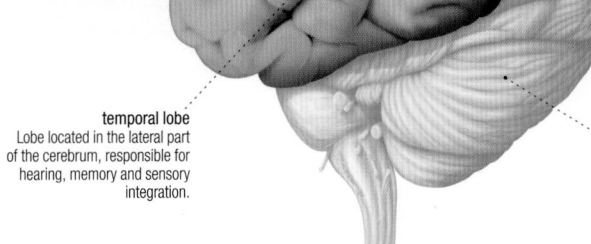

temporal lobe
Lobe located in the lateral part of the cerebrum, responsible for hearing, memory and sensory integration.

cerebellum
Part of the brain controlling balance and coordination, muscle tone and posture.

HUMAN BEING

nervous system

spinal cord
Part of the central nervous system located in the spinal column; it receives and transmits nerve information and releases the reflexes.

lateral view
The spinal cord is surrounded and protected by several membranes (meninges) and a clear fluid (cerebrospinal fluid); all 31 pairs of spinal nerves originate here.

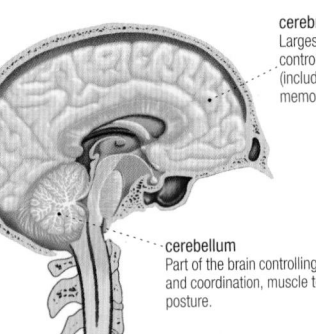

cerebrum
Largest part of the brain, it contains the control centers for complex functions (including movement, language and memory).

cerebellum
Part of the brain controlling balance and coordination, muscle tone and posture.

spinal column
Movable bony axis made up of various parts articulating with each other (vertebrae); it supports the skeleton and contains the spinal cord.

spinal cord
Part of the central nervous system located in the spinal column; it receives and transmits nerve information and releases the reflexes.

internal filum terminale
Final segment of fibrous filament arising from the base of the spinal cord; it is attached by the dura mater to the coccyx, helping to anchor the spinal cord.

external filum terminale
Fibrous filament mainly of the pia mater arising from the base of the spinal cord and extending to the second sacral vertebra.

spinal column: cross section
Spinal column: movable bony axis made up of various parts articulating with each other (vertebrae); it supports the skeleton and contains the spinal cord.

spinous process
Posterior middle protuberance of the vertebra; the attachment point of the neck muscles.

epidural space
Space filled with blood vessels and fatty tissue; separates the dura mater from the vertebra and has a protective function.

transverse process
Bony protuberance extending late from each side of the vertebra; muscles are attached to it.

sensory root
Bundle of sensory neurons communicating information from the periphery of the body to the spinal cord.

spinal cord
Part of the central nervous system located in the spinal column; it receives and transmits nerve information and initiates reflex actions.

spinal nerve
Mixed (sensory and motor) nerve that originates from the spinal cord, providing nerve sensations to all parts of the body, except the face.

motor root
Bundle of motor neurons communicating information from the spinal cord to the periphery of the body, especially the muscles.

vertebral body
Anterior bony cylinder of a vertebra surrounded by two transverse processes.

white matter
Substance of the central nervous system formed by extensions of the neurons; connects various parts of the brain and spinal cord.

gray matter
Substance of the central nervous system formed by the cell bodies of neurons; it ensures the processing of nerve impulses.

pia mater
Thin membrane (meninx) protectin the brain, the spinal cord and its nerve roots, the innermost of three layers (meninges), adhering to the spinal cord and containing numerous blood vessels.

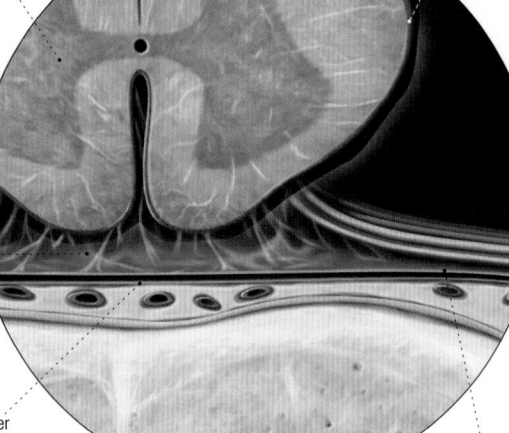

cerebrospinal fluid
Fluid contained between the arachnoid and the pia mater around the spinal cord and serving mainly as a shock absorber; it protects the entire central nervous system.

dura mater
Thick tough membrane (meninx) protecting the brain, the spinal cord and its nerve roots, outer of three layers (meninges); it is separated from vertebral bodies by the epidural space.

arachnoid
Delicate transparent memb (meninx) protecting the brain spinal cord and its nerve roots, of three layers (meninges) be the dura mater and the pia m

nervous system

main nerves
Nerve: bundle of nerve cells that carry sensory and motor signals (innervation) between the central nervous system and the rest of the body.

brachial plexus
Network formed of the last four cervical nerves and the first thoracic nerve whose branches provide innervation to the muscles of the upper limb.

cranial nerves
12 pairs of nerves that originate from the brain stem, provide innervation to the head and neck, and serve a broader motor or sensory function for the body.

median nerve
Branch of the brachial plexus providing innervation to various muscles of the forearm and part of the hand, where it divides into five branches.

axillary nerve
Branch of the brachial plexus that provides innervation to the deltoid muscle, the teres minor muscle and the shoulder.

ulnar nerve
Branch of the brachial plexus providing innervation, with the median nerve, especially to the flexor muscles of the forearm and hand.

iliohypogastric nerve
Branch of the lumbar plexus providing innervation to the muscles of one section of the abdominal wall and to the pubic region.

intercostal nerve
Nerve of the thoracic region providing innervation to muscles between the ribs, as well as to a portion of the diaphragm and the abdominal wall.

ilioinguinal nerve
Branch of the lumbar plexus providing innervation to the muscles of one section of the abdominal wall, external genital organs and inner thigh.

lumbar plexus
Network formed of the first four lumbar nerves whose six branches ensure movement and sensation in the lower limb.

lateral cutaneous femoral nerve
Branch of the lumbar plexus providing innervation mainly to the outer thigh.

sacral plexus
Network formed of several nerves whose branches ensure movement and sensation in the buttock and part of the thigh.

femoral nerve
large branch of the lumbar plexus providing innervation to the flexor muscles of the thigh and the extensor muscles of the leg.

radial nerve
Branch of the brachial plexus providing innervation especially to the extensor muscles of the arm and hand.

digital nerve
Nerve originating in the brachial plexus that provides innervation to the muscles of the fingers.

obturator nerve
Branch of the lumbar plexus providing innervation especially to the muscles of the inner thigh that draw away from the trunk.

saphenous nerve
Branch of the femoral nerve providing innervation to the inner leg and knee.

sciatic nerve
The largest nerve in the body, originating from the sacral plexus; it provides innervation to a large portion of the leg.

tibial nerve
Branch of the sciatic nerve providing innervation to muscles of the leg, sole of the foot and toes.

common peroneal nerve
Branch of the sciatic nerve that provides innervation to the muscles of parts of the lower leg and foot.

superficial peroneal nerve
Branch of the tibial nerve providing innervation mainly to the muscles of the side of the leg and top of the foot.

deep peroneal nerve
Branch of the tibial nerve that provides innervation to the muscles of the front of the leg and top of the foot.

HUMAN BEING

reproductive system

System formed by the organs of female or male reproduction that function to produce children.

female reproductive system
Mainly internal reproductive organs; they produce eggs capable of being fertilized by sperm and enable development of the embryo and fetus.

sagittal section
Front-to-back vertical section on the median line of the body.

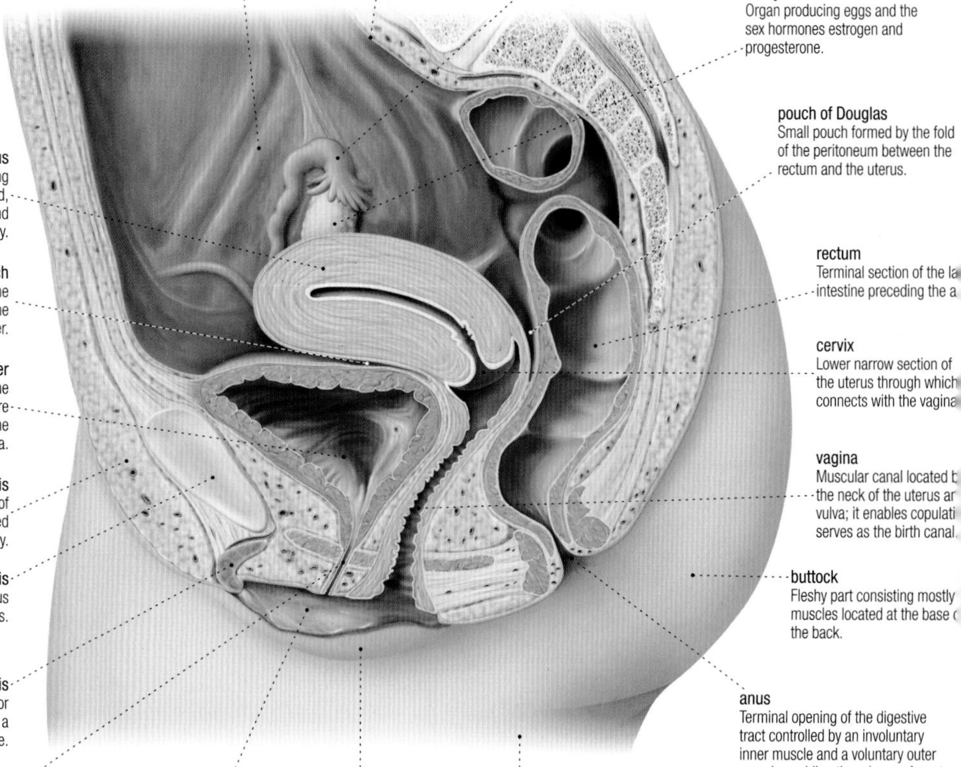

abdominal cavity
Lower portion of the trunk containing the majority of the organs of the digestive, urinary and reproductive systems.

peritoneum
Resistant membrane covering the internal walls and organs of the abdominal cavity and maintaining its shape.

fallopian tube
Canal through which the egg travels from the ovary to the uterus. Fertilization of the egg by the sperm normally takes place in the upper section of the tube.

ovary
Organ producing eggs and the sex hormones estrogen and progesterone.

uterus
Hollow muscular organ receiving the egg and, once fertilized, enabling its development and expulsion at the end of pregnancy.

pouch of Douglas
Small pouch formed by the fold of the peritoneum between the rectum and the uterus.

uterovesical pouch
Small pouch formed by the fold of the peritoneum between the uterus and the bladder.

rectum
Terminal section of the la[ ] intestine preceding the a[ ]

urinary bladder
Muscular reservoir where urine from the kidneys collects before being evacuated through the urethra.

cervix
Lower narrow section of the uterus through which connects with the vagina[ ]

mons pubis
Rounded bulge of fatty tissue of the female lower abdomen covered with hair at puberty.

vagina
Muscular canal located b[ ] the neck of the uterus ar[ ] vulva; it enables copulati[ ] serves as the birth canal[ ]

pubic symphysis
Slightly movable fibrocartilaginous joint connecting the two pubes.

buttock
Fleshy part consisting mostly [ ] muscles located at the base [ ] the back.

clitoris
Small erectile organ at the anterior section of the vulva constituting a major erogenous zone.

anus
Terminal opening of the digestive tract controlled by an involuntary inner muscle and a voluntary outer muscle enabling the release of waste.

urethra
Membranous canal enabling discharge of urine from the bladder.

labia minora
Mucous folds of the vulva located between the labia majora.

labia majora
Thick cutaneous folds of the vulva protecting the vaginal opening, often covered with hair at puberty.

thigh
Section of the leg between the hip and the knee; it contains many powerful muscles.

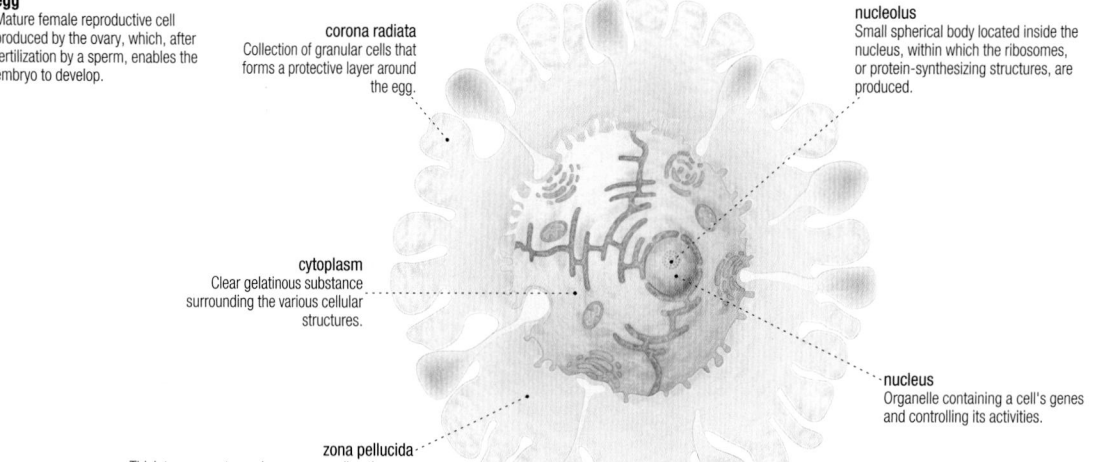

egg
Mature female reproductive cell produced by the ovary, which, after fertilization by a sperm, enables the embryo to develop.

corona radiata
Collection of granular cells that forms a protective layer around the egg.

nucleolus
Small spherical body located inside the nucleus, within which the ribosomes, or protein-synthesizing structures, are produced.

cytoplasm
Clear gelatinous substance surrounding the various cellular structures.

nucleus
Organelle containing a cell's genes and controlling its activities.

zona pellucida
Thick transparent membrane surrounding the egg; it allows a single sperm to penetrate and reach the egg before becoming impenetrable to other sperm.

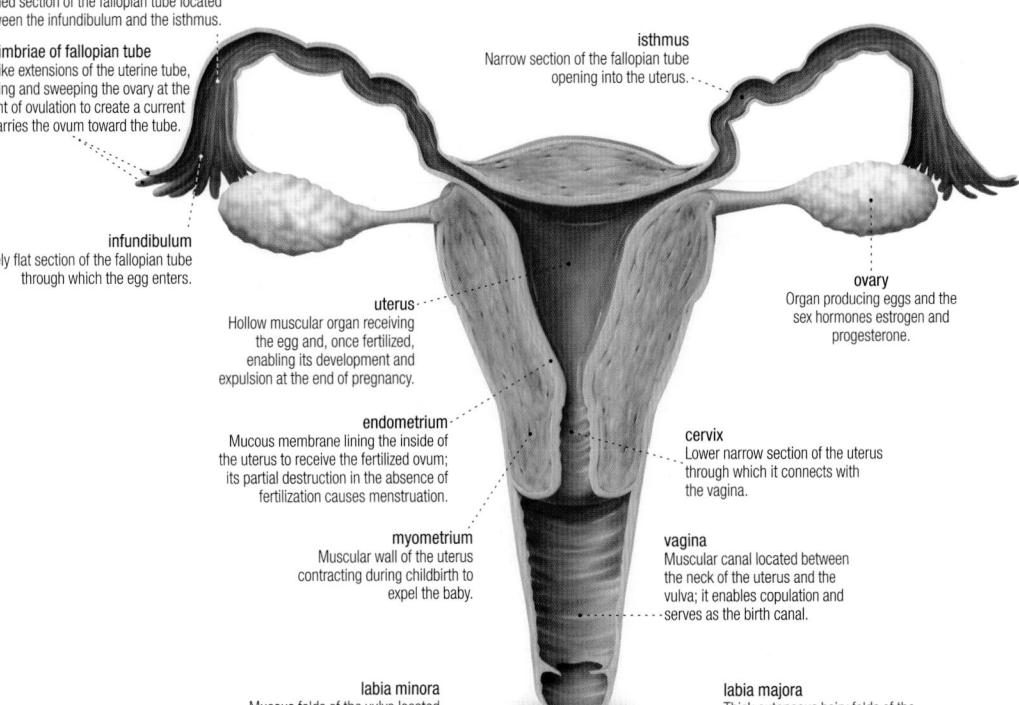

ampulla
Widened section of the fallopian tube located between the infundibulum and the isthmus.

fimbriae of fallopian tube
fringe-like extensions of the uterine tube, undulating and sweeping the ovary at the moment of ovulation to create a current that carries the ovum toward the tube.

infundibulum
Largely flat section of the fallopian tube through which the egg enters.

isthmus
Narrow section of the fallopian tube opening into the uterus.

uterus
Hollow muscular organ receiving the egg and, once fertilized, enabling its development and expulsion at the end of pregnancy.

endometrium
Mucous membrane lining the inside of the uterus to receive the fertilized ovum; its partial destruction in the absence of fertilization causes menstruation.

myometrium
Muscular wall of the uterus contracting during childbirth to expel the baby.

ovary
Organ producing eggs and the sex hormones estrogen and progesterone.

cervix
Lower narrow section of the uterus through which it connects with the vagina.

vagina
Muscular canal located between the neck of the uterus and the vulva; it enables copulation and serves as the birth canal.

labia minora
Mucous folds of the vulva located between the labia majora.

labia majora
Thick cutaneous hairy folds of the vulva protecting the vaginal orifice.

breast
Female milk-secreting glandular organ; it develops at puberty and increases in size during pregnancy.

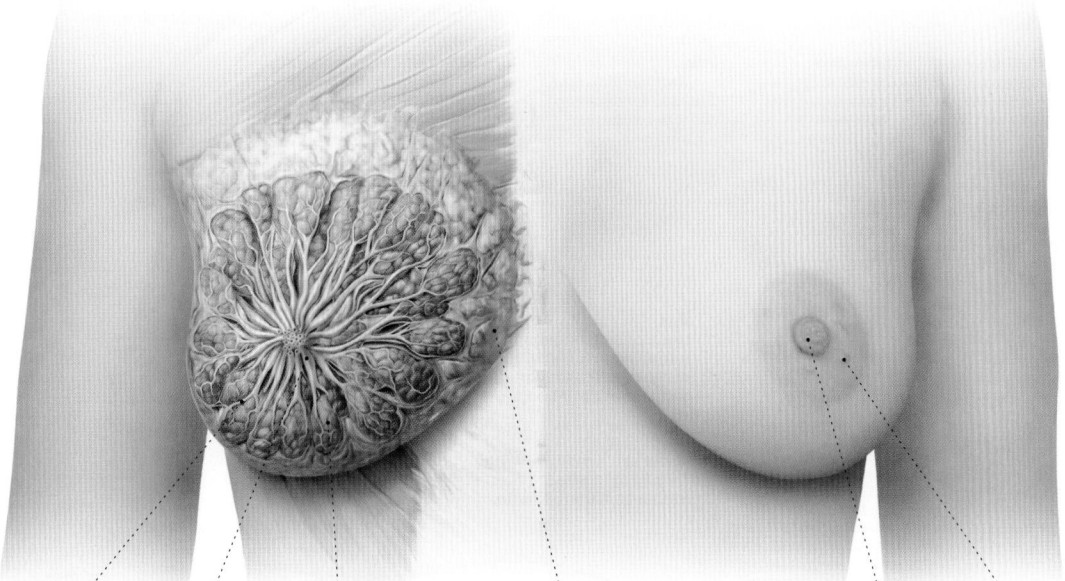

lactiferous duct
Canal carrying milk secreted by the mammary gland to the nipple.

lactiferous sinus
Enlargement of the lactiferous duct in which mother's milk accumulates between two feedings.

mammary gland
Organ consisting of usually 15 to 20 glands (lobes) ensuring secretion of milk.

adipose tissue
Fatty tissue surrounding the mammary gland and covering the pectoral muscles that support the breast.

nipple
Cone-shaped or cylindrical erectile tip of the breast surrounded by the areola that in the female is the opening for the lactiferous ducts of the mammary gland.

areola
Pigmented surface surrounding the nipple.

reproductive system

male reproductive system

External genitalia and internal reproductive
organs; they produce and deposit sperm into the
female genital tract during copulation.

sagittal section
Front-to-back vertical section on
the median line of the body.

peritoneum
Resistant membrane covering the
internal walls and organs of the
abdominal cavity and maintaining
its shape.

abdominal cavity
Lower portion of the trunk
containing the majority of the
organs of the digestive, urinary and
reproductive systems.

urinary bladder
Muscular reservoir where urine
from the kidneys collects before
being evacuated through the
urethra.

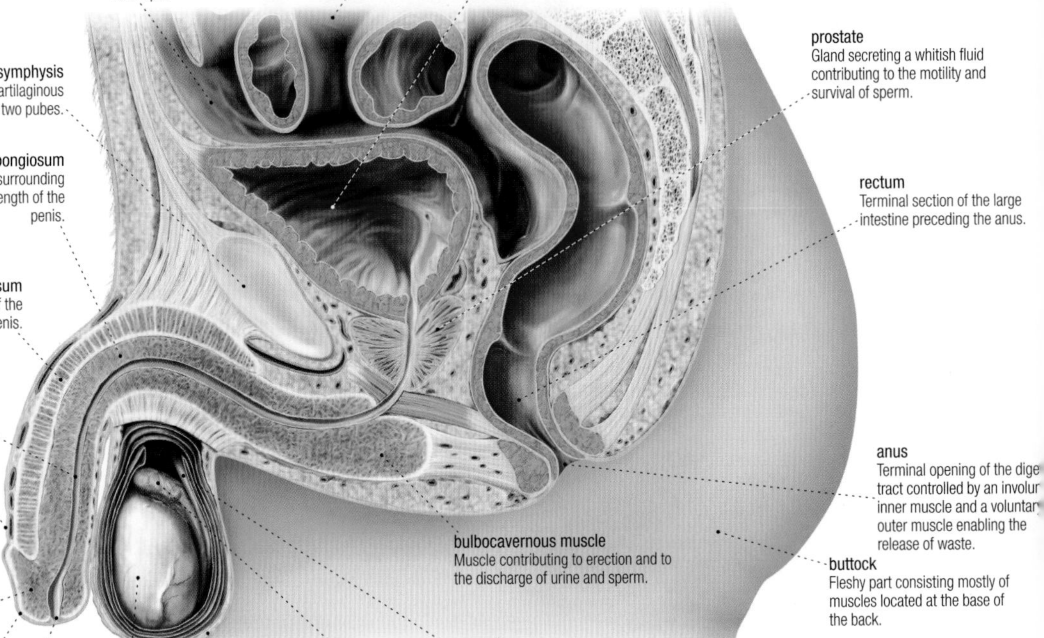

prostate
Gland secreting a whitish fluid
contributing to the motility and
survival of sperm.

pubic symphysis
Slightly movable fibrocartilaginous
joint connecting the two pubes.

corpus spongiosum
Cylinder of erectile tissue surrounding
the ureter along the length of the
penis.

rectum
Terminal section of the large
intestine preceding the anus.

corpus cavernosum
Erectile tissue of the back of the
penis extending to the glans penis.

urethra
Membranous canal
enabling the discharge of
urine. In the male, it also
allows sperm to pass.

penis
Male erectile organ allowing
for copulation as well as the
discharge of urine and sperm.

anus
Terminal opening of the dige
tract controlled by an involur
inner muscle and a voluntar
outer muscle enabling the
release of waste.

glans penis
Bulging anterior terminal portion
of the penis consisting of spongy
tissue; it is surrounded by the
foreskin and is where the meatus
of the urethra opens.

bulbocavernous muscle
Muscle contributing to erection and to
the discharge of urine and sperm.

buttock
Fleshy part consisting mostly of
muscles located at the base of
the back.

foreskin
Fold of skin covering the glans
penis.

vas deferens
Duct that channels sperm away
from the epididymis.

thigh
Section of the leg between the hip
and the knee; it contains many
powerful muscles.

urethral orifice
Terminal part of the ureter allowing
the discharge of urine and
ejaculation of sperm.

testicle/testis
Male genital gland that produces
sperm and the sex hormone
testosterone.

scrotum
Skin-covered muscular pouch
containing the testicles and
regulating their temperature.

epididymis
Long, tightly coiled tube in which sperm
produced by the testicles is stored and
undergoes maturation; it is connected to
the vas deferens.

sperm
Mature and mobile male reproductive
cell produced by the testicle; it
is discharged from the body in
ejaculatory fluid (semen).

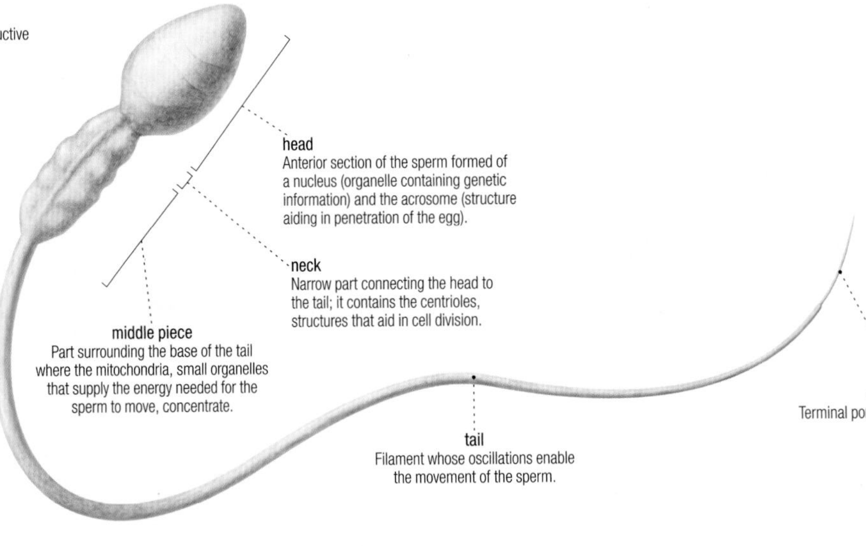

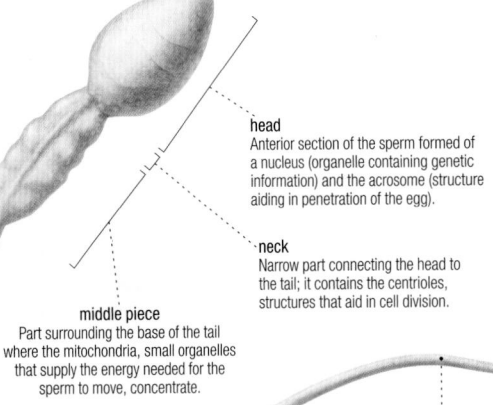

head
Anterior section of the sperm formed of
a nucleus (organelle containing genetic
information) and the acrosome (structure
aiding in penetration of the egg).

neck
Narrow part connecting the head to
the tail; it contains the centrioles,
structures that aid in cell division.

middle piece
Part surrounding the base of the tail
where the mitochondria, small organelles
that supply the energy needed for the
sperm to move, concentrate.

end piece
Terminal portion of the sperm's tail.

tail
Filament whose oscillations enable
the movement of the sperm.

HUMAN BEING

endocrine system

System of glands that release hormones which act on organs to maintain or stimulate vital processes or activity, such as metabolism, growth and reproduction.

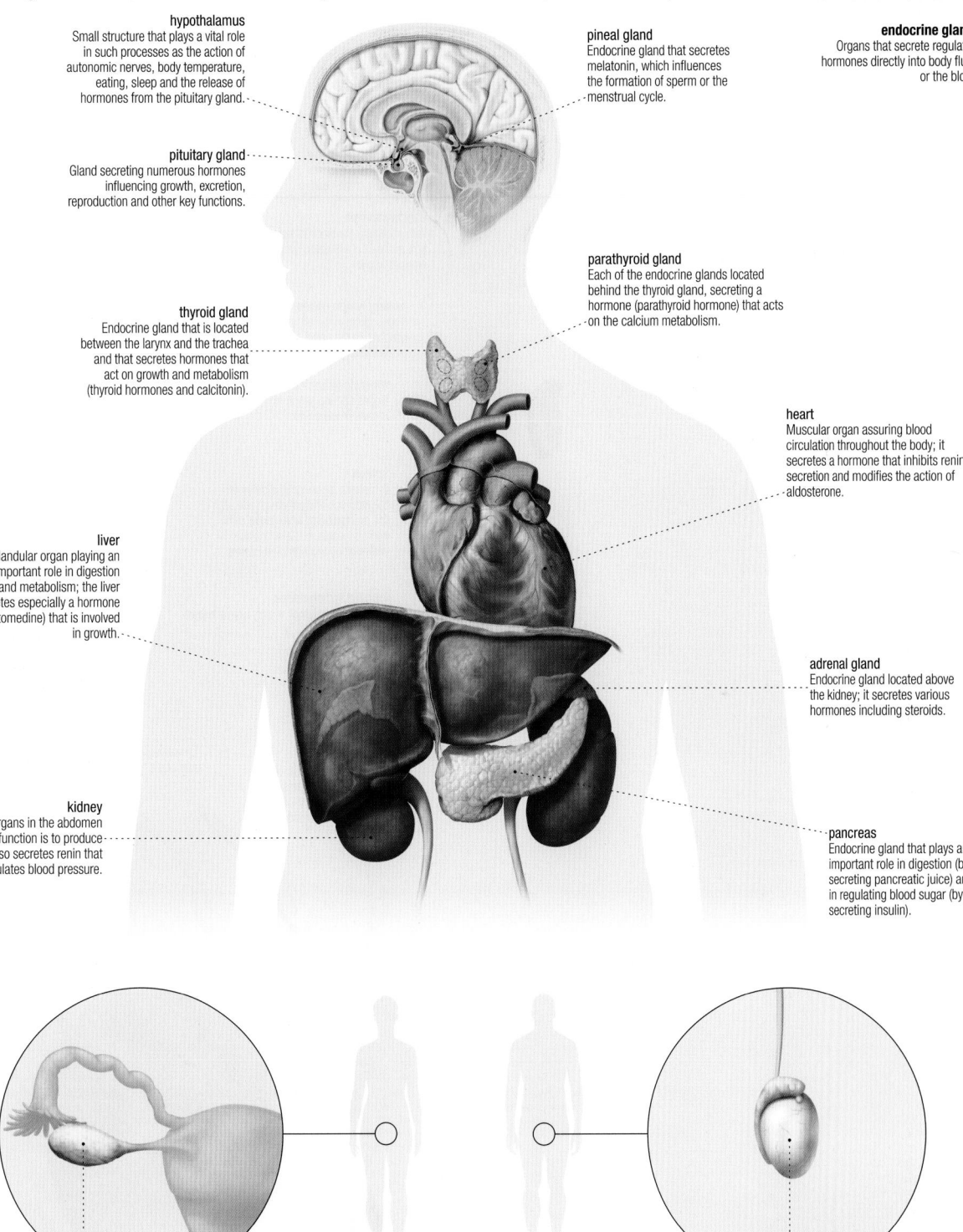

hypothalamus
Small structure that plays a vital role in such processes as the action of autonomic nerves, body temperature, eating, sleep and the release of hormones from the pituitary gland.

pituitary gland
Gland secreting numerous hormones influencing growth, excretion, reproduction and other key functions.

thyroid gland
Endocrine gland that is located between the larynx and the trachea and that secretes hormones that act on growth and metabolism (thyroid hormones and calcitonin).

liver
Glandular organ playing an important role in digestion and metabolism; the liver secretes especially a hormone (somatomedine) that is involved in growth.

kidney
of two organs in the abdomen se main function is to produce rine; it also secretes renin that regulates blood pressure.

pineal gland
Endocrine gland that secretes melatonin, which influences the formation of sperm or the menstrual cycle.

endocrine glands
Organs that secrete regulating hormones directly into body fluids or the blood.

parathyroid gland
Each of the endocrine glands located behind the thyroid gland, secreting a hormone (parathyroid hormone) that acts on the calcium metabolism.

heart
Muscular organ assuring blood circulation throughout the body; it secretes a hormone that inhibits renin secretion and modifies the action of aldosterone.

adrenal gland
Endocrine gland located above the kidney; it secretes various hormones including steroids.

pancreas
Endocrine gland that plays an important role in digestion (by secreting pancreatic juice) and in regulating blood sugar (by secreting insulin).

ovary
Female genital gland that produces eggs and the sex hormones estrogen and progesterone.

testicle/testis
Male genital gland that produces sperm and the sex hormone testosterone.

HUMAN BEING

lymphatic system

Group of organs and structures that collect extra fluid (lymph), break down cell waste and produce white blood cells and antibodies in an immune response.

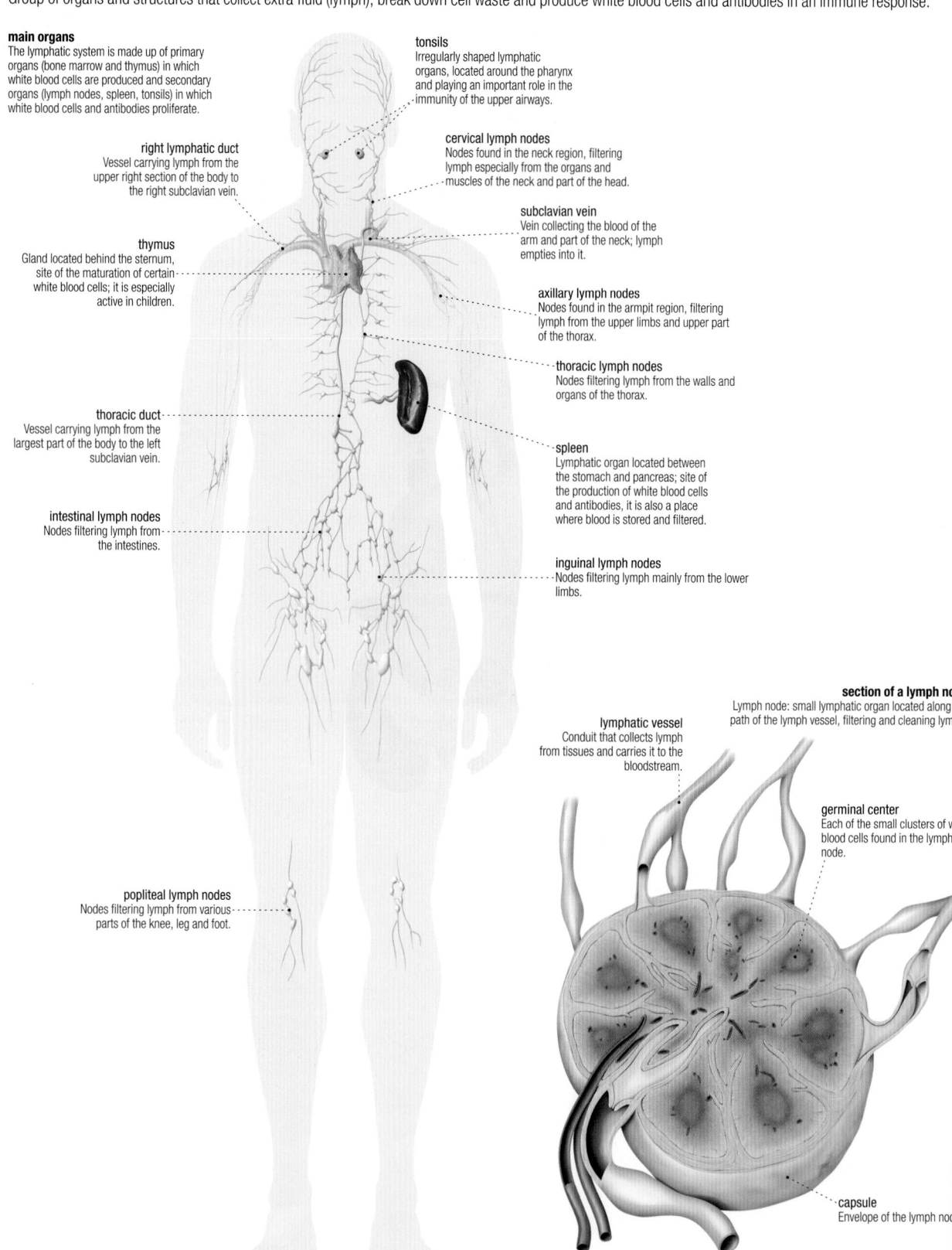

main organs
The lymphatic system is made up of primary organs (bone marrow and thymus) in which white blood cells are produced and secondary organs (lymph nodes, spleen, tonsils) in which white blood cells and antibodies proliferate.

right lymphatic duct
Vessel carrying lymph from the upper right section of the body to the right subclavian vein.

thymus
Gland located behind the sternum, site of the maturation of certain white blood cells; it is especially active in children.

thoracic duct
Vessel carrying lymph from the largest part of the body to the left subclavian vein.

intestinal lymph nodes
Nodes filtering lymph from the intestines.

popliteal lymph nodes
Nodes filtering lymph from various parts of the knee, leg and foot.

tonsils
Irregularly shaped lymphatic organs, located around the pharynx and playing an important role in the immunity of the upper airways.

cervical lymph nodes
Nodes found in the neck region, filtering lymph especially from the organs and muscles of the neck and part of the head.

subclavian vein
Vein collecting the blood of the arm and part of the neck; lymph empties into it.

axillary lymph nodes
Nodes found in the armpit region, filtering lymph from the upper limbs and upper part of the thorax.

thoracic lymph nodes
Nodes filtering lymph from the walls and organs of the thorax.

spleen
Lymphatic organ located between the stomach and pancreas; site of the production of white blood cells and antibodies, it is also a place where blood is stored and filtered.

inguinal lymph nodes
Nodes filtering lymph mainly from the lower limbs.

section of a lymph node
Lymph node: small lymphatic organ located along the path of the lymph vessel, filtering and cleaning lymph.

lymphatic vessel
Conduit that collects lymph from tissues and carries it to the bloodstream.

germinal center
Each of the small clusters of white blood cells found in the lymph node.

capsule
Envelope of the lymph node.

smell and taste

The nasal cavity and the oral cavity are connected, so the body's sense of smell (olfaction) affects its sense of taste. Humans can distinguish four basic flavors and almost 10,000 odors.

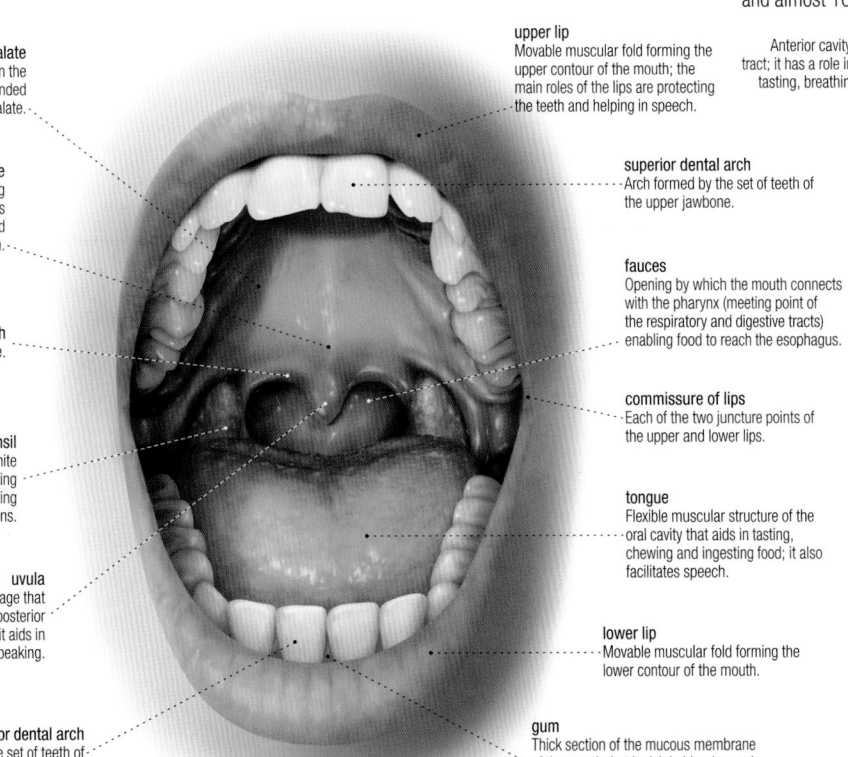

hard palate
Bony separation between the buccal and nasal cavities, extended by the soft palate.

soft palate
Muscular membranous wall separating the pharynx and buccal cavity; it assists especially in ingestion of food and vocalization.

palatoglossal arch
Muscular fold at the back of the soft palate.

palatine tonsil
Lymphoid structure (rich in white blood cells) involved in protecting the respiratory tract by fighting bacterial infections.

uvula
Fleshy movable appendage that is an extension of the posterior edge of the soft palate; it aids in ingesting food and speaking.

inferior dental arch
Arch formed by the set of teeth of the lower jawbone.

upper lip
Movable muscular fold forming the upper contour of the mouth; the main roles of the lips are protecting the teeth and helping in speech.

mouth
Anterior cavity of the digestive tract; it has a role in ingesting food, tasting, breathing and speaking.

superior dental arch
Arch formed by the set of teeth of the upper jawbone.

fauces
Opening by which the mouth connects with the pharynx (meeting point of the respiratory and digestive tracts) enabling food to reach the esophagus.

commissure of lips
Each of the two juncture points of the upper and lower lips.

tongue
Flexible muscular structure of the oral cavity that aids in tasting, chewing and ingesting food; it also facilitates speech.

lower lip
Movable muscular fold forming the lower contour of the mouth.

gum
Thick section of the mucous membrane of the mouth that is rich in blood vessels and nerves; it covers the edge of the dental alveolus and adheres to the neck.

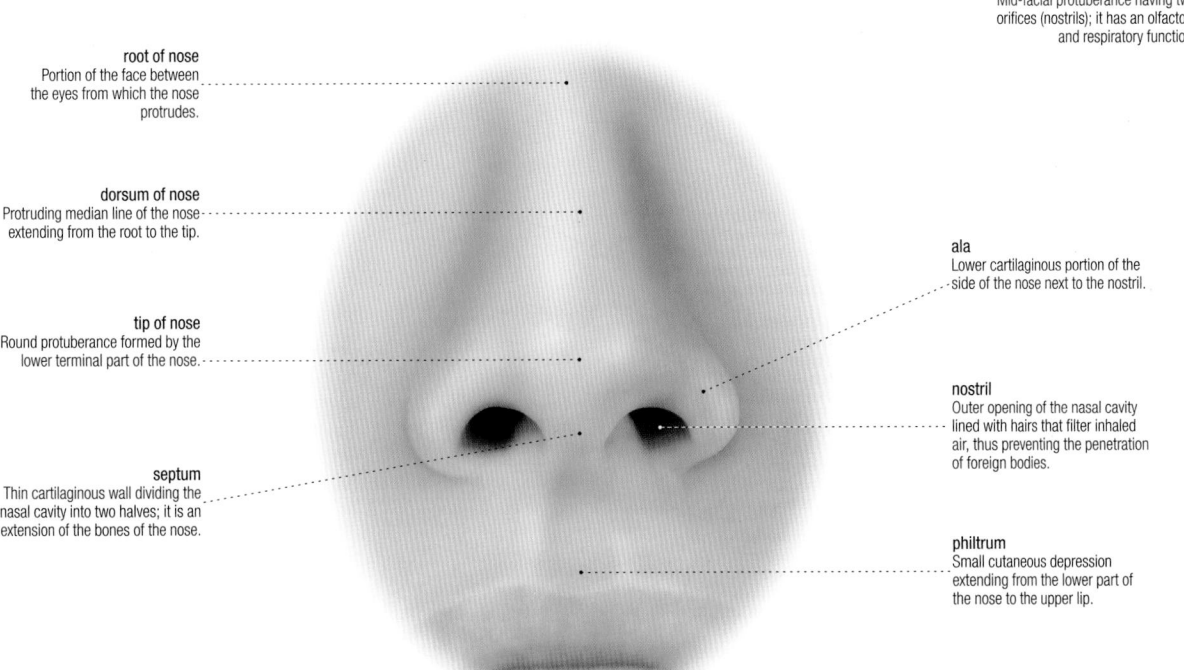

nose
Mid-facial protuberance having two orifices (nostrils); it has an olfactory and respiratory function.

root of nose
Portion of the face between the eyes from which the nose protrudes.

dorsum of nose
Protruding median line of the nose extending from the root to the tip.

tip of nose
Round protuberance formed by the lower terminal part of the nose.

septum
Thin cartilaginous wall dividing the nasal cavity into two halves; it is an extension of the bones of the nose.

ala
Lower cartilaginous portion of the side of the nose next to the nostril.

nostril
Outer opening of the nasal cavity lined with hairs that filter inhaled air, thus preventing the penetration of foreign bodies.

philtrum
Small cutaneous depression extending from the lower part of the nose to the upper lip.

smell and taste

nasal cavity
Chamber divided by a medial partition (the septum); it contributes to olfaction, breathing and vocalization.

frontal sinus
Cavity hollowed out of the frontal bone of the skull; it connects with the nasal cavity and warms inhaled air.

nasal bone
Small flat bone forming the skeleton of the root of the nose; the two nasal bones join along the bridge of the nose.

inferior nasal concha
Curved bony plate attached to the lateral wall of the nasal cavity.

cartilage
Smooth, strong and elastic tissue covering the ends of a bone at the place where it articulates with another bone. It facilitates movement and absorbs shocks.

maxilla
Bone that forms the upper jaw and helps to form the palate, eye sockets and nasal cavity.

middle nasal concha
Curved bony plate resting on the ethmoid. Among its functions, the nasal chamber warms inhaled air by increasing the mucous surface.

olfactory mucosa
Tissue lining a portion of the nasal cavity and containing olfactory cells, which detect odors and release nerve impulses.

sphenoid sinus
Cavity hollowed out of the sphenoid bone of the skull; it connects with the nasal cavity and warms inhaled air.

superior nasal concha
Curved bony plate resting on the ethmoid and contributing to olfaction by bringing inhaled air into contact with the mucous membrane.

eustachian tube
Tube connecting the middle ear to the nasopharynx; it allows outside air to pass through, thus equalizing air pressure on both sides of the eardrum.

nasopharynx
Upper part of the pharynx connecting with the nasal cavity.

soft palate
Muscular membranous wall separating the pharynx and buccal cavity; it assists especially in ingestion of food and vocalization.

uvula
Fleshy movable appendage that is an extension of the posterior edge of the soft palate; it aids in ingesting food and speaking.

hard palate
Bony separation between the buccal and nasal cavities, extended by the soft palate.

tongue
Flexible muscular structure of the oral cavity that aids in tasting, chewing and ingesting food; it also facilitates speech.

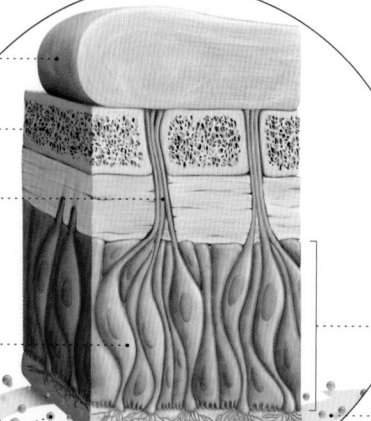

olfactory bulb
Nerve structure where fibers of the olfactory nerve end; it receives nerve impulses from the mucous membrane and transmits them to the olfactory tract.

cribriform plate of ethmoid
Curved bony plate forming the arch of the nasal cavity; its orifices allow the olfactory nerve fibers to pass between the mucous membrane and the bulb.

olfactory nerve fiber
Bundle of nerve cells formed by the axons of the mucous membrane's olfactory cells, which transmit nerve impulses to the brain.

olfactory sensory neuron
Each of the sensory neurons constituting olfactory receptors; their axons come together to form olfactory nerves.

odorous molecule
Volatile chemical substance transported in the air and causing odors.

olfactory epithelium
Sensory organ of smell lining the roof of nasal cavity; it consists of millions of olfactory cells whose stimulation by odorous molecules generates a nerve signal.

inhaled air

smell and taste

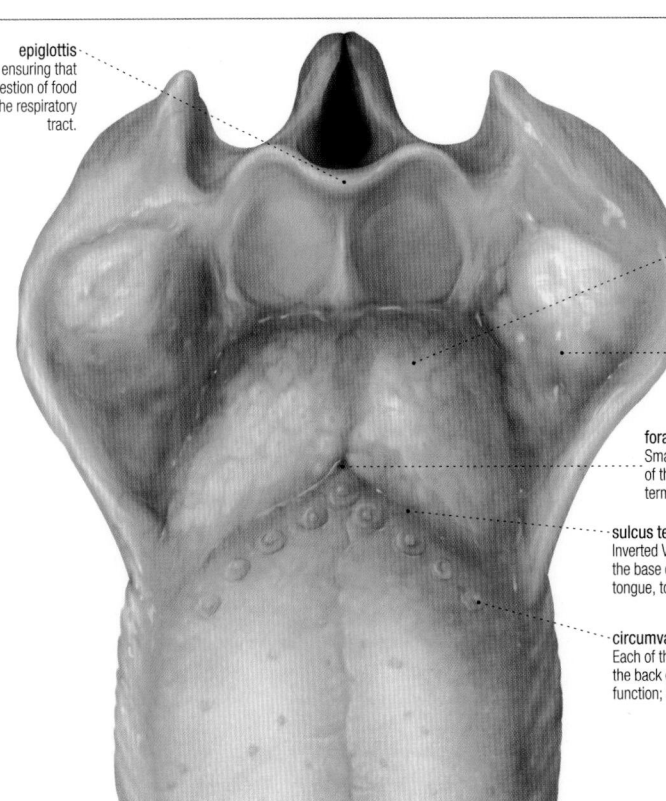

tongue: superior view
Tongue: flexible muscular structure of the oral cavity that aids in tasting, chewing and ingesting food; it also facilitates speech.

epiglottis
Movable cartilaginous plate ensuring that the larynx closes during ingestion of food so that food cannot enter the respiratory tract.

lingual tonsil
Lymphoid structure (rich in white blood cells) located at the base of the tongue; it assists in immune defense.

palatine tonsil
Lymphoid structure (rich in white blood cells) located on each side of the base of the tongue; it protects the respiratory tract by fighting bacteria.

root
t that fixes the tongue to the lower nd the hyoid bone of the skull; it is oined on each side to the walls of the pharynx.

foramen cecum
Small depression located at the base of the tongue, at the top of the sulcus terminalis.

sulcus terminalis
Inverted V-shaped depression separating the base of the body from the root of the tongue, topped by the foramen cecum.

circumvallate papilla
Each of the large taste buds (about 12) forming a V at the back of the body of the tongue, ensuring the taste function; they mostly perceive bitter flavors.

body
Free mobile portion of the tongue nposed mostly of mucous-covered uscles and bearing the taste buds.

median lingual sulcus
Depression extending over the entire length of the body of the tongue and separating it into two symmetrical halves.

apex
Mobile terminal end of the tongue; it mostly perceives sweet flavors.

taste receptors
The mucous membrane of the tongue is composed of small protuberances, lingual taste buds, distinguished by their particular sensitivity to one of the basic flavors: sweet, salty, sour, bitter.

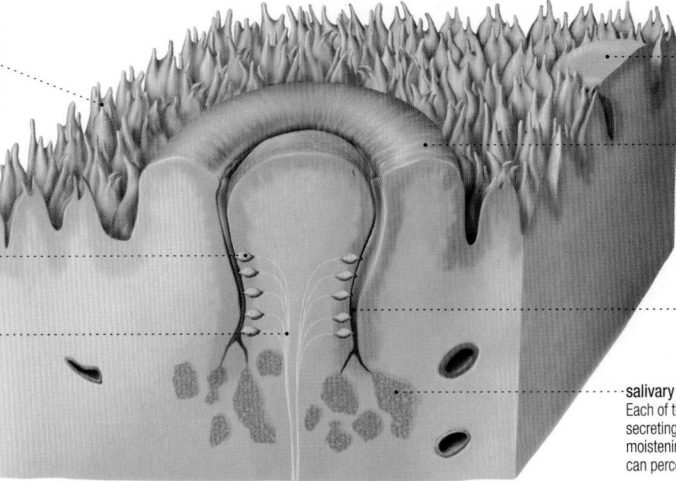

filiform papilla
Cone-shaped taste bud covering the rear of the tongue; its function is solely tactile. These taste buds give the tongue its velvety appearance.

fungiform papilla
Mushroom-shaped taste bud occurring in large numbers at the apex and on the sides of the tongue and having a taste function; it reacts mainly to sweet and salty flavors.

circumvallate papilla
Each of the large taste buds (about 12) forming a V at the back of the body of the tongue, ensuring the taste function; they mostly perceive bitter flavors.

taste bud
rgan of taste formed of sensory cells that, in contact with saliva, detect flavors and transmit them to the brain in the form of nerve impulses.

nerve fiber
Structure composed of the myelin sheath and the axon, along which sensory signals are carried.

sulcus
Saliva-filled depression containing taste buds that protrude through its walls.

salivary gland
Each of the three pairs of saliva-secreting organs responsible for moistening food so that the taste buds can perceive its taste.

HUMAN BEING

hearing

Sense that perceives sounds; the human ear is capable of distinguishing almost 400,000 sounds; it also maintains balance.

pinna
Soft cartilaginous outer portion of the ear located at the side of the head; it allows sounds to be collected. It is also called the auricle.

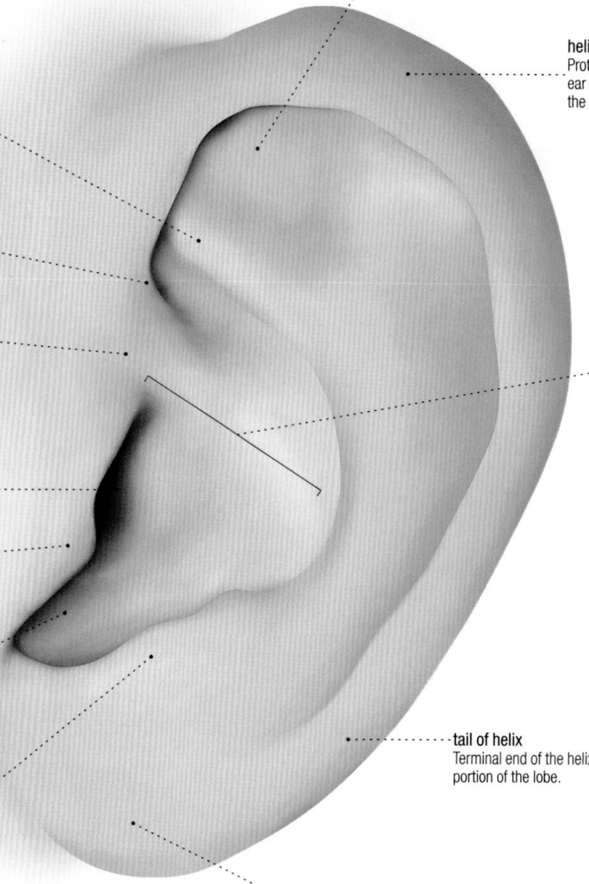

triangular fossa
Small depression located in the upper portion of the helix between its two branches.

antihelix
Protuberance parallel to and inside the helix dividing into two branches in its upper section.

helix
Protruding fold of the pinna of the ear extending from the concha to the lobe.

crus of helix
Front portion of the helix beginning at the base of the concha.

anterior notch
Deep depression separating the helix from the tragus.

concha
Deep cavity of the pinna of the ear above the antitragus; the external auditory meatus opens into it.

external auditory meatus
Canal through which sounds captured by the pinna of the ear travel to the eardrum cavity, located in the temporal bone. It is also called the auditory canal.

tragus
Flat triangular protuberance located in front of the external auditory meatus, protecting especially the concha.

intertragic notch
Deep depression at the base of the external auditory meatus between the antitragus and the tragus.

tail of helix
Terminal end of the helix extending to the upper portion of the lobe.

antitragus
Small triangular protuberance at the terminal end of the antihelix.

earlobe
Fleshy extension of the lower section of the pinna; it plays no role in hearing.

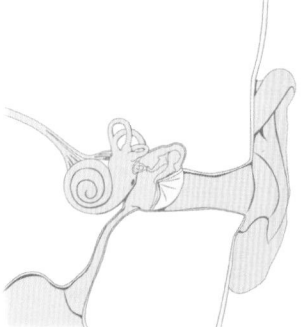

external ear
Visible portion of the ear enabling sounds to be collected and directed to the middle ear through the external auditory meatus.

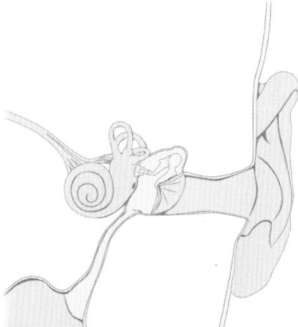

middle ear
Air-filled cavity hollowed out of the temporal bone; it receives sounds from the external ear, amplifies them through the ossicles and transmits them to the inner ear.

inner ear
Liquid-filled cavity hollowed out of the temporal bone that transforms sound vibrations into nerve impulses to be interpreted by the brain.

hearing

structure of the ear
The ear is made up of three distinct parts; hearing is controlled by the inner ear, which contains the sensory organs.

superior semicircular canal
Vertical canal perpendicular to the temporal bone; it monitors head movements to ensure that equilibrium is maintained.

posterior semicircular canal
Vertical canal parallel to the temporal bone; it monitors head movements to ensure that equilibrium is maintained.

lateral semicircular canal
Horizontal canal; it monitors head movements to ensure that equilibrium is maintained.

vestibular nerve
Nerve transmitting messages related to equilibrium to the brain; it emanates from the vestibule and the semicircular canals.

cochlear nerve
...smitting auditory messages ...d in the cochlea to the brain. ...ar and vestibular nerves join to form the auditory nerve.

vestibule
...tructure into which the three ...micircular canals open; with ...e canals, it is responsible for equilibrium.

cochlea
...y structure intended for hearing; it ...s vibrations from the ossicles and ...nsforms them into nerve impulses ...re transmitting them to the brain.

eustachian tube
Tube connecting the middle ear to the nasopharynx; it allows outside air to pass through, thus equalizing air pressure on both sides of the eardrum.

pinna
Soft cartilaginous outer portion of the ear located at the side of the head; it allows sounds to be collected.

eardrum
Slender resistant elastic membrane; it vibrates when sound waves are received from the external auditory meatus, then transmits the waves to the ossicles. The eardrum is also called the tympanic membrane.

external auditory meatus
Canal through which sounds captured by the pinna of the ear travel to the eardrum cavity, located in the temporal bone. It is also called the auditory canal.

HUMAN BEING

incus
Ossicle of the middle ear articulating with the malleus and the stapes.

malleus
Ossicle of the middle ear transmitting vibrations to the incus from the eardrum (to which it is attached).

stapes
Ossicle of the middle ear transmitting vibrations from the incus to the inner ear; at about 0.1 inch long, the stapes is the smallest bone in the body.

auditory ossicles
Each of the three small articulated bones of the middle ear that amplify the vibrations of the eardrum and transmit them to the inner ear.

mechanism of hearing
The pinna captures sound vibrations and directs them to the external auditory meatus where they make the tympanic membrane vibrate; the three ossicles amplify them and transmit them to the cochlea that then transforms them into a nerve impulse.

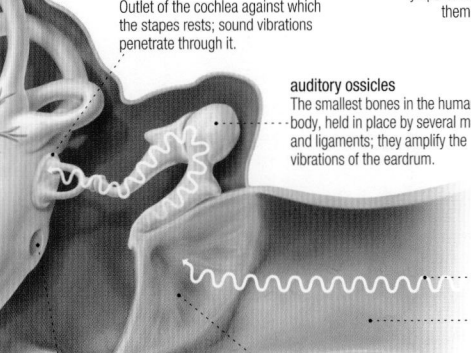

oval window
Outlet of the cochlea against which the stapes rests; sound vibrations penetrate through it.

cochlear nerve
Nerve that transmits auditory signals ...llected in the cochlea to the brain. The ...ochlear and vestibular nerves together compose the auditory nerve.

cochlea
Sensory organ of hearing, formed of a spiral tube filled with various fluids; it ...eives the vibrations of the ossicles and transforms them into nerve impulses.

auditory ossicles
The smallest bones in the human body, held in place by several muscles and ligaments; they amplify the vibrations of the eardrum.

sound waves
Vibration produced by sounds in the environment and felt by the ossicles of the ear.

external auditory meatus
Canal through which sounds captured by the pinna of the ear travel to the eardrum cavity, located in the temporal bone. It is also called the auditory canal.

round window
Outlet through which sound vibrations leave the cochlea after stimulating the organ of Corti.

eardrum
Slender resistant elastic membrane; it vibrates when sound waves are received from the external auditory meatus, then transmits the waves to the ossicles.

touch

Sense enabling the skin to detect sensations (contact, heat, pain and others) due to specialized receptors spread widely over the surface of the body.

skin
External protective envelope of the body, made up of three main layers: the epidermis, the dermis, and the hypodermis or subcutaneous tissue.

cuticle
Fold of skin covering the sides and root of the nail.

hair shaft
External part of hair at the slender end.

stratum corneum
Layer of the epidermis consisting of dead cells rich in keratin (the protein that protects the skin); it is shed as a new layer is formed.

stratum granulosum
Layer of the epidermis whose cells help to form keratin, which renders the skin impermeable.

stratum spinosum
Layer of the epidermis made up of cells migrating from the basal layer that continue to divide to form the granular layer.

stratum basale
Layer of the epidermis whose cells divide and migrate toward the surface to form the upper layers, thus ensuring renewal of the epidermis.

sebum
Fatty yellowish substance produced by the sebaceous glands, lubricating the skin and protecting it.

sebaceous gland
Gland found in the dermis and often near a hair follicle that excretes sebum to the surface of the skin.

Ruffini's corpuscle
Tactile receptor located in the dermis of hairy regions and articular capsules, sensitive to stretching of the skin and heat.

hair root
Part of the hair contained in the skin.

hair bulb
Enlarged end of the follicle from which the hair develops.

squama
Small fragment of the epidermis made up of dead cells, detaching from the layer.

epidermis
Surface layer of the skin covering and protecting the dermis; it contains protein make the skin impermeab block ultraviolet rays.

Meissner's corpuscle
Tactile receptor located in the upper part of the derm of sensitive areas (hands, feet, lips and genital organ stimulated by specific touc

dermis
Layer of skin enclosing tac receptors ensuring nutritio support of the epidermis.

Krause's end bulb
Tactile receptor located in dermis, sensitive to specif and cold.

subcutaneous tissue
Fatty tissue at the base of dermis rich in blood vesse nerves and acting especia as a shock absorber; it is a called the hypodermis.

connective tissue
Tissue rich in blood vessel and nerves made up especially of collagen and elastin fibers that give the its elasticity and resistance

arrector pili muscle
Muscle attached to a hair follicle and whose contract raises the hair on end as a result of cold or fear.

adipose tissue
Tissue enclosing numerous fat cells, thermally insulating the body and providing an energy reserve.

hair follicle
Envelope inside the dermis, within which the hair develops.

Pacinian corpuscle
Tactile receptor located in the deep dermis, sensitive to strong continuous vibrations and pressure.

nerve fiber
Structure composed of the myelin sheath and the axon of the neuron, along which sensory signals are carried.

HUMAN BEING

touch

hand
Terminal part of the upper limb having a tactile and prehensile function, with a thumb opposable to the other fingers.

palm
Inner portion of the hand corresponding to the metacarpus and located between the wrist and the proximal phalanges of the fingers.

middle finger
Third and longest digit of the hand.

ring finger
Fourth digit of the hand. Rings are worn on this finger, hence it is also called the ring finger.

lunula
Whitish section between the root and the body of the nail corresponding to the visible front portion of the matrix.

back
Outer part of the hand corresponding to the metacarpus and located between the wrist and the proximal phalanges of the fingers.

finger
Each of the five extremities of the hand, used for grasping objects.

index finger
Second digit of the hand used to point, hence its name.

little finger
Last and smallest of the fingers of the hand.

thumb
First digit of the hand formed of two phalanges; short and strong, it moves in such a way that it is opposable to the other digits, thereby enabling grasping.

fingernail
Hard horny plate covering and protecting the back of the distal phalanx; it also has a prehensile function and is continually growing.

wrist
Joint of the hand (carpus) articulating with the forearm (radius); it mainly enables the hand to flex and extend.

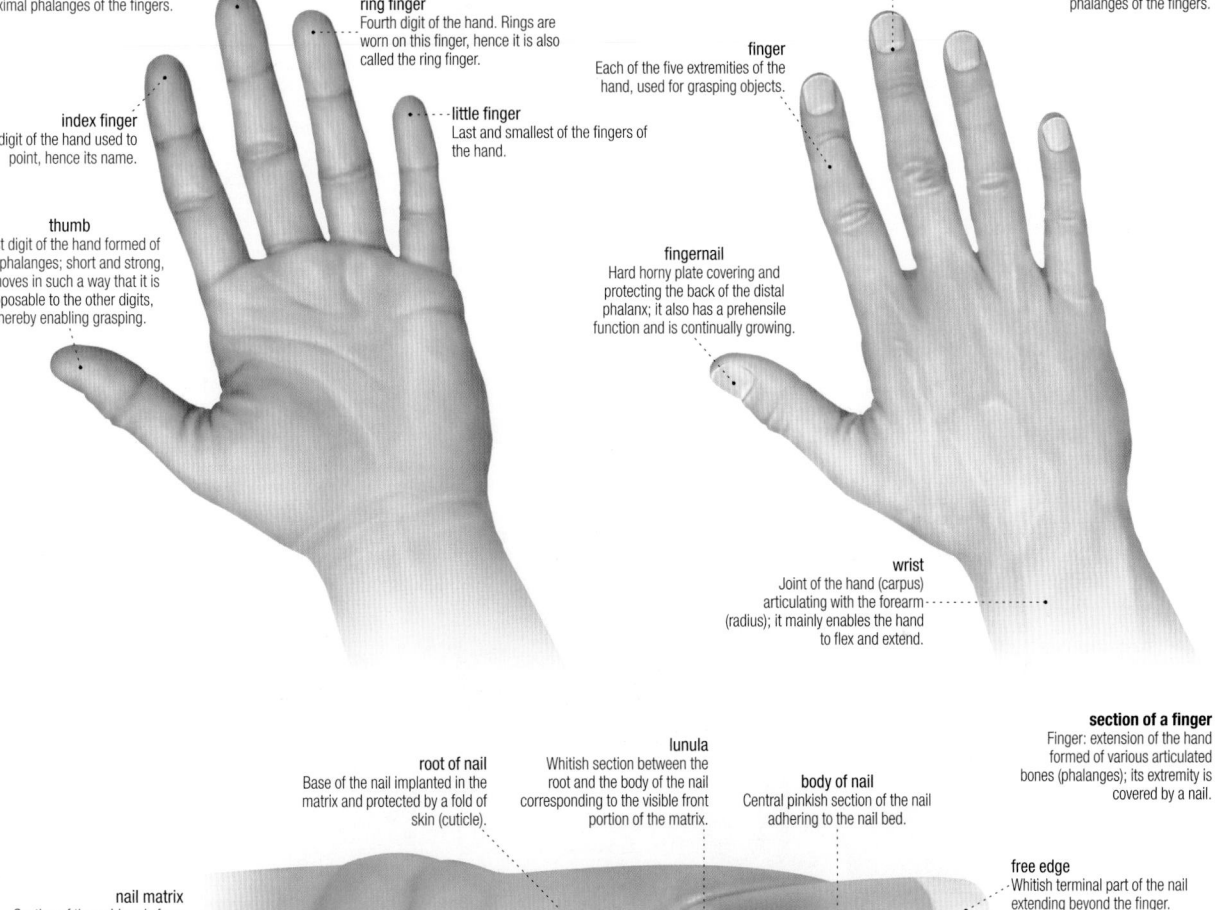

section of a finger
Finger: extension of the hand formed of various articulated bones (phalanges); its extremity is covered by a nail.

root of nail
Base of the nail implanted in the matrix and protected by a fold of skin (cuticle).

lunula
Whitish section between the root and the body of the nail corresponding to the visible front portion of the matrix.

body of nail
Central pinkish section of the nail adhering to the nail bed.

free edge
Whitish terminal part of the nail extending beyond the finger.

nail matrix
Section of the epidermis from which the nail grows.

nail bed
Portion of the finger upon which the nail sits containing numerous blood vessels, thus nourishing the nail.

distal phalanx
Last of the phalanges of the finger bearing a nail.

subcutaneous tissue
Fatty tissue at the base of the dermis rich in blood vessels and nerves and acting especially as a shock absorber; it is also called the hypodermis.

dermis
Layer of skin enclosing tactile receptors ensuring nutrition and support of the epidermis.

epidermis
Surface layer of the skin covering and protecting the dermis; it contains proteins that make the skin impermeable and block ultraviolet rays.

digital pulp
Fleshy terminal part of the inner finger.

HUMAN BEING

sight

Vision: the ability to see. Sight, considered the most highly developed of the human senses, enables a person to perceive colors, shapes, size, distances and motion.

eye
Organ of vision that allows a person to see.

upper eyelid
Thin movable muscular membrane descending from the upper edge of the eye. The eyelids protect the eye, emit tears and discharge waste. Batting of the eyelashes is very frequent.

eyelash
Each of the hairs lining the free edge of the eyelid; they prevent dust and other particles from entering the eye.

pupil
Central orifice of the eye whose opening varies to regulate the amount of light entering the eye; light causes the pupil to contract.

lacrimal caruncle
Small reddish mass located at the inner corner of the eye formed by the fold of the conjunctiva.

iris
Colored central portion of the eyeball composed of muscles whose dilation or contraction controls the opening of the pupil.

lower eyelid
Thin muscular membrane that is translucent and movable; it rises from the lower edge of the eye to protect and cleanse it.

sclera
Strong fibrous opaque membrane covered by the conjunctiva; it surrounds the eyeball and protects the inner structures.

eyeball
Enclosed in a bony cavity (orbit) and moved by six muscles, this complex organ collects light signals and transmits them to the brain to form images.

superior rectus muscle
Muscle allowing the eyeball to move upward.

choroid
Richly veined membrane located between the sclera and the retina, to which it carries nutrients and oxygen.

posterior chamber
Cavity of the eye surrounding the lens and containing the aqueous humor.

sclera
Strong fibrous opaque membrane covered by the conjunctiva; it surrounds the eyeball and protects the inner structures.

anterior chamber
Cavity of the eye between the cornea, the iris and the lens, containing the aqueous humor.

macula lutea
Small area located at the centre of the retina, near the optic disk, where visual acuity is best.

cornea
Transparent fibrous membrane extending the sclera and whose curved shape makes light rays converge toward the inside of the eye.

optic nerve
Nerve formed by the juncture of the nerve fibers of the retina; it carries visual information to the brain, where it is interpreted.

lens
Transparent flexible fibrous disk located behind the iris, acting as a variable lens refracting light rays.

blind spot
Region of the retina with no photoreceptors, where blood vessels and nerve fibers gather to form the optic nerve. It is also called the optic disk.

pupil
Central orifice of the eye whose opening varies to regulate the amount of light entering the eye; light causes the pupil to contract.

vitreous body
Transparent gelatinous mass (almost 90% of the eye); it maintains constant intraocular pressure so the eye keeps its shape.

aqueous humor
Transparent liquid contained in the anterior and posterior chambers; it nourishes the iris and maintains the pressure and shape of the eye.

retina
Inner membrane at the back of the eye covered in light-sensitive nerve cells (photoreceptors); these transform light into an electrical impulse that is carried to the optic nerve.

iris
Colored central portion of the eyeball composed of muscles whose dilation or contraction controls the opening of the pupil.

suspensory ligament
Fibrous tissue connecting the ciliary body to the lens, holding it in place inside the eyeball.

conjunctiva
Fine transparent mucous covering the sclera and inner surface of the eyelid; it facilitates sliding thus giving the eyeball its wide range of movement.

ciliary body
Muscle tissue secreting the aqueous humor; its muscles enable the lens to change shape to adapt vision for near or distant objects.

rod
Photoreceptor active in dim light and responsible for night vision (in black and white).

cone
Photoreceptor active in full light and responsible for perception of specific colors. There are three types: red-yellow, green and blue-violet.

sight

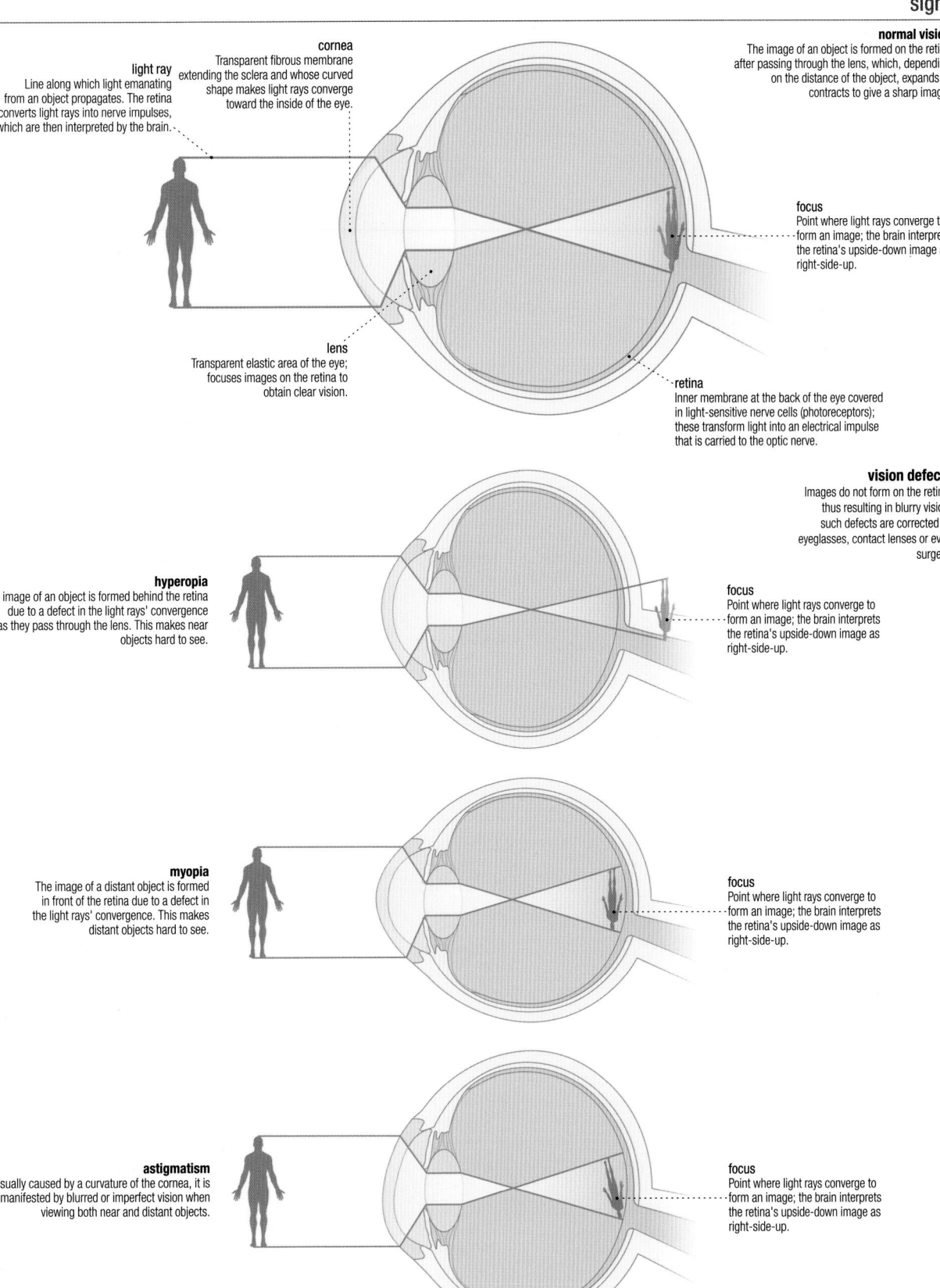

normal vision
The image of an object is formed on the retina after passing through the lens, which, depending on the distance of the object, expands or contracts to give a sharp image.

light ray
Line along which light emanating from an object propagates. The retina converts light rays into nerve impulses, which are then interpreted by the brain.

cornea
Transparent fibrous membrane extending the sclera and whose curved shape makes light rays converge toward the inside of the eye.

focus
Point where light rays converge to form an image; the brain interprets the retina's upside-down image as right-side-up.

lens
Transparent elastic area of the eye; focuses images on the retina to obtain clear vision.

retina
Inner membrane at the back of the eye covered in light-sensitive nerve cells (photoreceptors); these transform light into an electrical impulse that is carried to the optic nerve.

vision defects
Images do not form on the retina, thus resulting in blurry vision; such defects are corrected by eyeglasses, contact lenses or even surgery.

hyperopia
e image of an object is formed behind the retina due to a defect in the light rays' convergence as they pass through the lens. This makes near objects hard to see.

focus
Point where light rays converge to form an image; the brain interprets the retina's upside-down image as right-side-up.

myopia
The image of a distant object is formed in front of the retina due to a defect in the light rays' convergence. This makes distant objects hard to see.

focus
Point where light rays converge to form an image; the brain interprets the retina's upside-down image as right-side-up.

astigmatism
Usually caused by a curvature of the cornea, it is manifested by blurred or imperfect vision when viewing both near and distant objects.

focus
Point where light rays converge to form an image; the brain interprets the retina's upside-down image as right-side-up.

HUMAN BEING

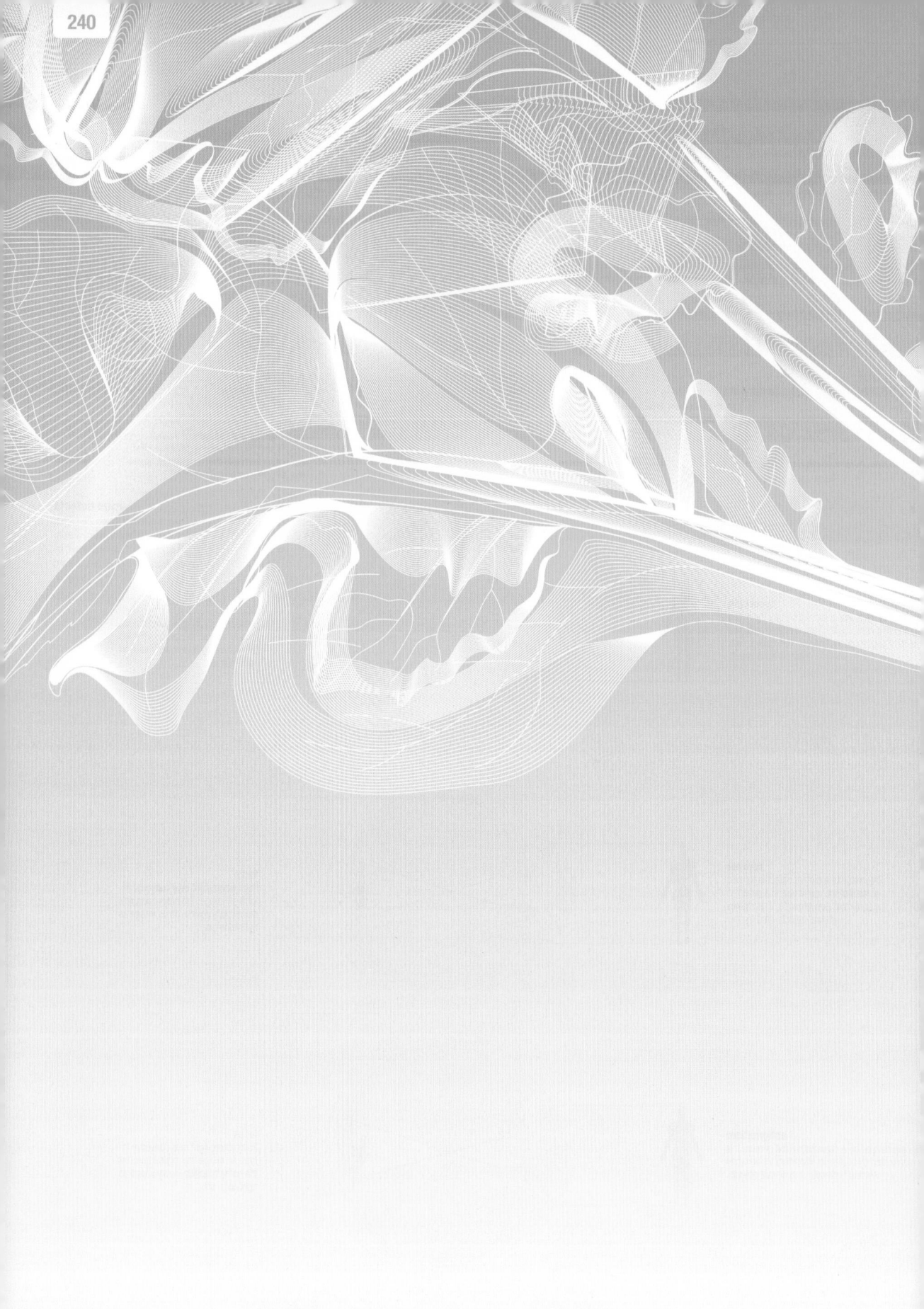

FOOD AND KITCHEN

FOOD AND KITCHEN

origin of food

Food can be harvested as-is from nature, hunted, or fished. It may also come from home gardens, local farms, or large-scale agriculture or livestock.

animal husbandry
The practice of keeping and feeding animals for slaughter or for their milk, eggs, or other products.

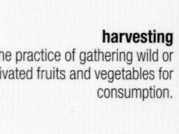

harvesting
The practice of gathering wild or cultivated fruits and vegetables for consumption.

hunting
The practice of killing wild animals in order to consume their meat.

cultivation
The practice of planting and growing forage crops, garden vegetables, and fruit for consumption.

fishing
The practice of catching sea animals (mainly fish, mollusks, and crustaceans) by line, net, or trap in order to eat them.

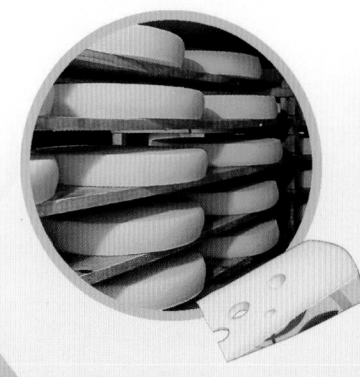

food industry
All the businesses that produce, process and market diverse food products.

supermarket
A large store that sells food and various everyday household goods.

farmstead

All the structures belonging to an agricultural concern (such as a farm) and used as dwellings or in its operation.

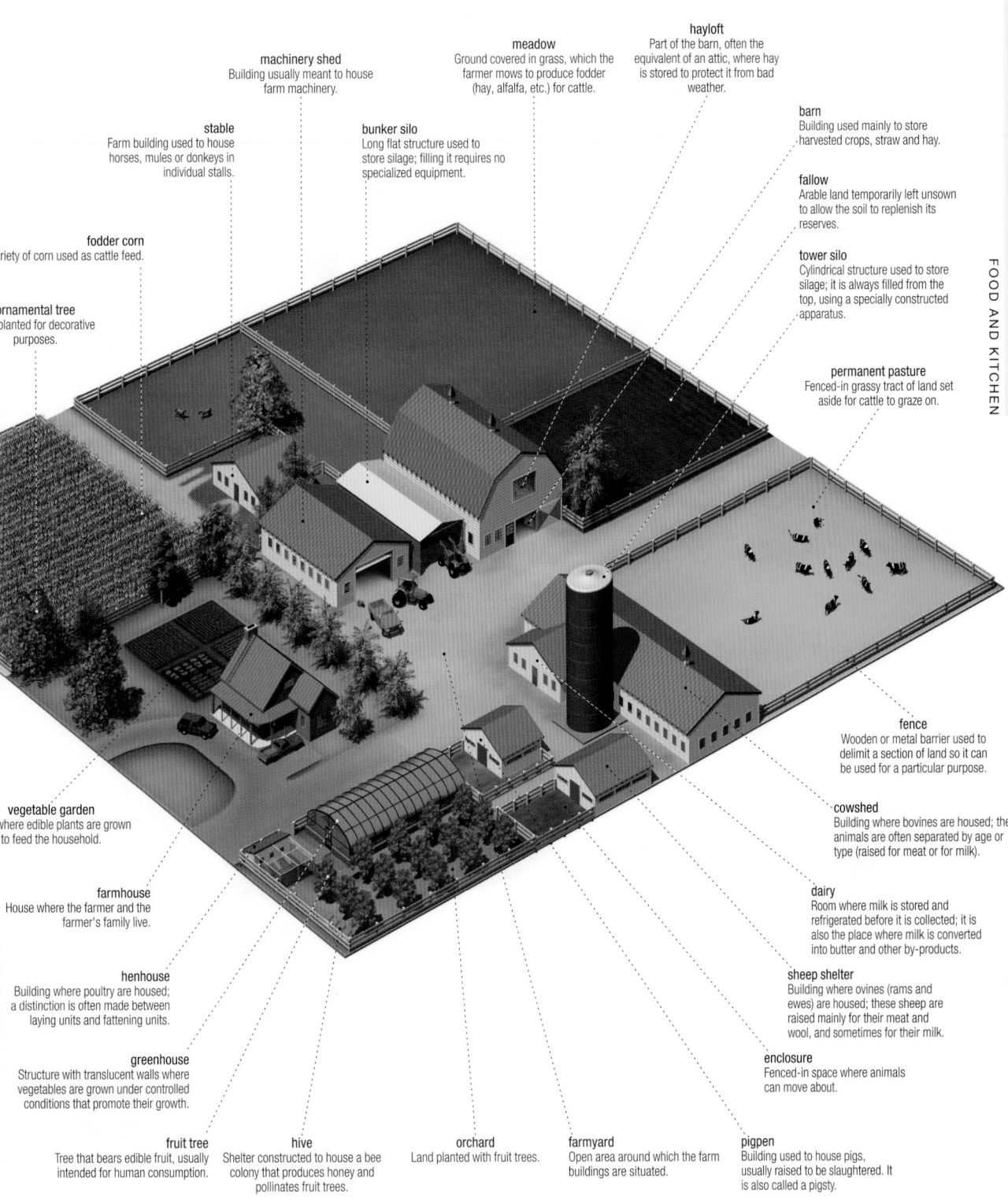

machinery shed
Building usually meant to house farm machinery.

stable
Farm building used to house horses, mules or donkeys in individual stalls.

fodder corn
Variety of corn used as cattle feed.

ornamental tree
planted for decorative purposes.

meadow
Ground covered in grass, which the farmer mows to produce fodder (hay, alfalfa, etc.) for cattle.

bunker silo
Long flat structure used to store silage; filling it requires no specialized equipment.

hayloft
Part of the barn, often the equivalent of an attic, where hay is stored to protect it from bad weather.

barn
Building used mainly to store harvested crops, straw and hay.

fallow
Arable land temporarily left unsown to allow the soil to replenish its reserves.

tower silo
Cylindrical structure used to store silage; it is always filled from the top, using a specially constructed apparatus.

permanent pasture
Fenced-in grassy tract of land set aside for cattle to graze on.

fence
Wooden or metal barrier used to delimit a section of land so it can be used for a particular purpose.

cowshed
Building where bovines are housed; the animals are often separated by age or type (raised for meat or for milk).

dairy
Room where milk is stored and refrigerated before it is collected; it is also the place where milk is converted into butter and other by-products.

sheep shelter
Building where ovines (rams and ewes) are housed; these sheep are raised mainly for their meat and wool, and sometimes for their milk.

enclosure
Fenced-in space where animals can move about.

vegetable garden
where edible plants are grown to feed the household.

farmhouse
House where the farmer and the farmer's family live.

henhouse
Building where poultry are housed; a distinction is often made between laying units and fattening units.

greenhouse
Structure with translucent walls where vegetables are grown under controlled conditions that promote their growth.

fruit tree
Tree that bears edible fruit, usually intended for human consumption.

hive
Shelter constructed to house a bee colony that produces honey and pollinates fruit trees.

orchard
Land planted with fruit trees.

farmyard
Open area around which the farm buildings are situated.

pigpen
Building used to house pigs, usually raised to be slaughtered. It is also called a pigsty.

mushrooms

Fleshy reproductive structure of a fungus; edible varieties are used raw or cooked as vegetables.

truffle
Underground mushroom hard to find and perceived as a luxury food; it is usually associated with game and poultry.

wood ear
Mushroom with a delicate flavor and jelly-like texture, eaten in soups or with vegetables in Asian cuisine.

Caesar's mushroom
Eaten raw or cooked, it has been prized since ancient times; it is not to be confused with the poisonous fly agaric, which it resembles.

saffron milk cap
Mushroom from which flows an orange milk when it is broken. It is used mainly in spicy sauce, mostly in Spain and southern France.

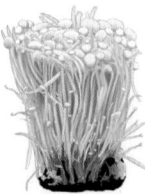

enoki mushroom
Long-stemmed, soft-fleshed mild-tasting mushroom. Can be eaten raw, in salads, or cooked, in soups and Asian dishes.

oyster mushroom
Grows on trees or on dead wood; its soft white flesh is a valued ingredient in sauces, where it can substitute for the button mushroom.

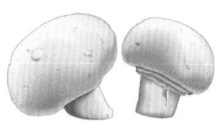

button mushroom
The most widely cultivated and consumed mushroom; it is eaten raw, in salads or with dips, or cooked, primarily in sauces and on pizza.

green russula
Its white brittle flesh has an aroma of hazelnut; it can be eaten raw or cooked, preferably grilled.

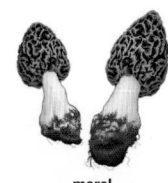

morel
The darker the specimen, the more flavorful its thin fragrant flesh; it should be thoroughly cooked to eliminate toxic substances.

porcini
Squat, it can grow up to 10 in height and diameter; it has a nutty flavor and is eaten raw or cooked often as an ingredient of soups and stews.

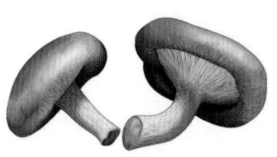

shiitake
Mushroom widely cultivated in Japan, where it is used in cooking (Asian dishes and sauces) and for therapeutic purposes.

chanterelle
Pleasantly fragrant and valued by gourmets; it is served most often with meat or omelettes.

portobello
Large mushroom marketed for its firm, meaty-flavored flesh. It is served stuffed as an appetizer or in sauces and stews.

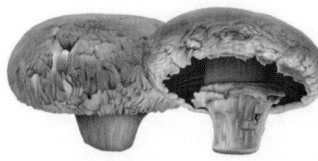

cremini
Mushroom with firm flesh and more taste than the button mushroom. It is eaten raw, grilled or in stews.

seaweed

Usually marine algae used in cooking as vegetables or as dietary supplements; they are primarily eaten in Japan, China and Korea.

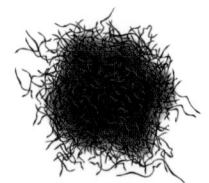

arame
Milder and less crunchy than hijiki, it is used mainly in salads and soups or served fried as a side vegetable.

wakame
Marine algae rich in calcium which has a delicate texture and flavor; often served with noodles or used in salads or soups.

kombu
Eaten since ancient times, it is sold in large blackish strips; it is used primarily as an ingredient in broth or to make a kind of tea.

spirulina
Freshwater cyanobacterium sometimes considered an alga; it is rich in nutrients and is used mainly as a dietary supplement.

Irish moss
Plentiful in the North Atlantic, it can only eaten cooked; also produces carrageen a substance used to thicken certain dis

hijiki
These dried twigs expand when soaked, resembling black, somewhat crunchy noodles; they are often served as a vegetable.

sea lettuce
Resembles lettuce leaves in taste and appearance; its soft leaves are eaten raw in salads or cooked in soups.

agar
Translucent strips derived from red algae, which is melted to produce a jelly that can replace gelatin in numerous recipes.

nori
Purplish alga that turns black when dried; usually sold in thin dried sheets, it is used mainly to make sushi.

dulse
Iron-rich, it has long been eaten by people living along Europe's coasts, used especially in soups and salads, has a soft texture and strong flavor.

bulb vegetables

The main edible part of these vegetables is their bulb, the underground structure where the plant's nutrient reserves are stored.

water chestnut
The aquatic bulb of a Chinese ant; its white crunchy flesh is an portant ingredient in many Asian dishes.

shallot
It has a more subtle flavor than the onion or the chive; it is eaten raw or cooked and often used as a flavoring ingredient in sauces.

garlic
The bulb is composed of bulblets called cloves; it has a pungent flavor and is widely used to season cooked dishes.

scallion
Its bulb is less developed than that of the green onion; the white part is used like the onion and the green is used to season a variety of dishes.

green onion
Mild onion picked before fully ripe; it is usually sold with the stem, in bunches. It is often eaten raw in salads or cooked in sautéed dishes.

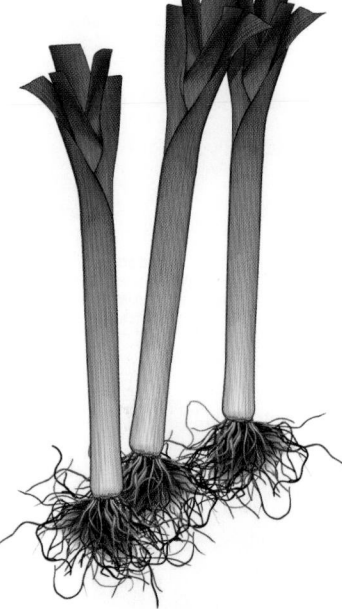

leek
The white part is the most popular, but the green part adds flavor to puréed soups and stews; it is often combined with potatoes in a cold soup called vichyssoise.

chive
allest member of the onion family; stem is used primarily to season various hot and cold dishes.

pearl onion
all white onion picked before fully it is primarily used to make pickles ts called acras; its an ingredient in stews such as beef bourguignon.

white onion
Mild and sweet, this onion is widely used as a flavoring ingredient; it is often eaten raw or deep-fried in rings.

red onion
The sweetest of the onions, it is often eaten raw, in salads or sandwiches.

yellow onion
The most common onion, widely used as a flavoring ingredient, either raw or cooked; it is also the essential ingredient in onion soup.

tuber vegetables

Tubers that are eaten like vegetables; they consist of underground growths containing the plant's nutrient reserves.

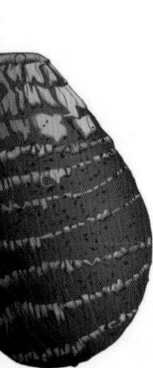

jicama
Its flesh is sweet, crunchy and juicy; it is eaten raw in salads, as an hors d'oeuvre or with dips; it adds a crunchy element to cooked dishes.

taro
Its starchy, sweet flesh is a staple in several tropical countries; it is poisonous when raw and must be cooked before being eaten.

crosne
Native to Asia, where it is very popular although little known elsewhere; it has a slightly sweet flavor and is used and prepared like the potato.

cassava
The sweet variety is eaten like the potato; the bitter one is used to make tapioca.

yautia
ble in the West Indies, where rated and used to make fried ts called acras; its strong taste hints of hazelnuts.

potato
A very common tuber in many parts of the world, it is often baked, cut up and fried, or boiled and mashed and eaten as a vegetable side dish.

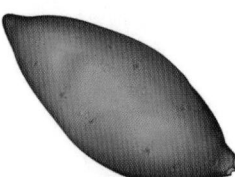

sweet potato
Sweeter than the potato but botanically unrelated; it is widely grown in tropical regions and is usually boiled, baked or candied.

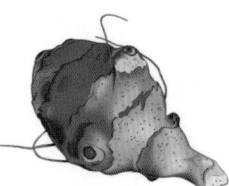

Jerusalem artichoke
Eaten raw, cooked or marinated; it has sweet, crunchy, juicy flesh.

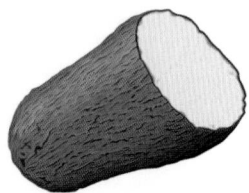

yam
A staple food in many countries, especially in South America and the West Indies, where it is eaten cooked, prepared like the potato.

leaf vegetables

Leaves of edible plants consumed as vegetables.

curled endive
The very frilly, somewhat bitter leaves are primarily eaten raw, in salads.

celtuce
A celerylike vegetable that is a variety of lettuce popular in China; it combines the flavors of celery and lettuce.

radicchio
Red-leaved chicory variety native to northern Italy and having a somewhat bitter taste. It is often served with other types of greens.

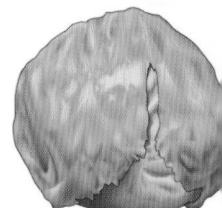

iceberg lettuce
The most widely sold lettuce in North America, it was initially covered with ice during transport hence its name.

romaine lettuce
Lettuce with firm crisp leaves used especially to make Caesar salad.

escarole
Its leaves are less bitter than those of the curled endive, to which it is related; it is usually eaten raw, in salads.

butter lettuce
Formed in a loosely compacted ball, its large soft leaves break off easily; Boston lettuce is a well-known variety of this species.

leaf lettuce
Lettuce having soft wavy leaves with curly edges; like most types of lettuce, it is usually eaten raw, in salads or sandwiches.

collards
It has thick, strongly flavored leaves and tough central ribs; it is eaten like spinach, either raw or cooked.

curled kale
Its very curly, stringy tough leaves have a strong flavor; it is almost always eaten cooked.

bok choy
A type of Chinese cabbage with thick crunchy stems; it is served in many Chinese and Japanese soups and dishes.

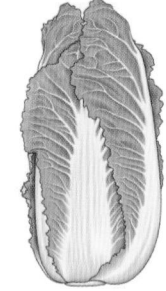

Chinese cabbage
A crunchy vegetable of Asian origin; it is served raw, cooked or pickled.

Brussels sprout
The smallest of the cabbages is usually eaten cooked and whole, as a vegetable side dish.

sea kale
Widely used in Europe, its leaves and wide fleshy stems are prepared like asparagus.

ornamental kale
Related to the curled kale; its differently colored leaves are added to salads, soups and rice, or used to garnish serving platters.

savoy cabbage
Cabbage with somewhat flexible leaves, making it well suited to preparing cabbage rolls.

green cabbage
When finely chopped, it is the main ingredient in coleslaw; it is also added to soups and stews.

red cabbage
Milder-tasting than other cabbages, it is usually eaten raw and finely chopped in salads.

white cabbage
After fermentation, it is used to make sauerkraut; it is also used as an ingredient in stews.

spinach
The vegetable used to make dishes à la Florentine. It is also eaten raw, in salads, and cooked, as a side dish or a stuffing ingredient.

arugula
Especially popular in southern France and Italy. Whether raw or cooked, it has a very strong flavor.

corn salad
Also called lamb's lettuce; its soft, mild-tasting leaves are primarily eaten raw, in salads.

dandelion
The leaves of this common plant can be eaten raw, in a salad; when cooked, they can be prepared like spinach.

garden cress
Picked while very young and sold in bunches; its tiny leaves add a hint of spice especially to salads, sandwiches and sauces.

nettle
Cooking or drying deactivates the stinging hairs of the leaves; it has a somewhat spicy flavor and can be prepared more or less like spinach.

watercress
Tender and juicy, it is mostly eaten raw, in salads; the delicate leaves have a slight mustard-like flavor.

purslane
Both the stems and the tender fleshy leaves are eaten; it has a slightly acidic, spicy flavor.

garden sorrel
Its slightly lemon-flavored leaves are traditionally served with fish and veal; it is used in soups, purées and sauces.

grape leaf
Associated with Mediterranean cooking, it is used to prepare dolmades (stuffed grape leaves) and as a garnish for fruit and salad platters.

Belgian endive
Its crunchy, slightly bitter leaves are much in demand for salads (used raw) or for such classic recipes as endive and ham au gratin.

fruit vegetables

Fruits of edible plants consumed as vegetables.

cherry tomato
Small firm tomato measuring about 1 in. Yellow, orange or red, it is usually eaten fresh especially in salads.

olive
Inedible when raw, the olive is treated to reduce its bitter taste, then cured in brine or sometimes in oil.

hot pepper
Cutting it or removing the seeds moderates its spicy burning taste.

okra
Vegetable containing a substance used to thicken soups and ragouts; it is used in many Creole dishes.

tomatillo
Picked when green, this berry is used to make sauces and is an essential ingredient in many Mexican dishes.

plum tomato
Small, oblong tomato. Firmer and less juicy than the common tomato, it is used primarily in sauces.

tomato
Originating in South America, this fruit is now widely cultivated and an essential component of many cuisines; it has a soft, juicy flesh.

grape tomato
Very flavorful juicy tomato characterized by its sweetness and small size.

avocado
Fruit of the avocado tree; its smooth greenish flesh is eaten raw, in salads or mashed.

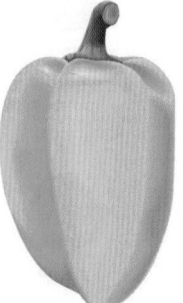

yellow pepper
Mild pepper picked when ripe; it is strongly scented and has a sweet taste; it is often used in salads.

red pepper
Mild pepper picked when ripe; it is very sweet and has a higher vitamin C content than the green pepper.

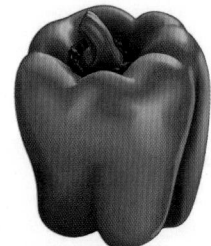

green pepper
Mild pepper picked before fully ripe; it is used raw especially in salads and cooked in sauces and main dishes.

cucumber
Related to squash and melons, it has edible seeds and skin and is usually eaten raw.

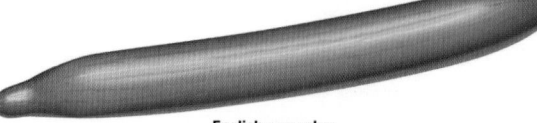

English cucumber
Thin-skinned European variety that is seedless or contains only a few small seeds; it is grown exclusively in greenhouses.

gherkin
Picked when not yet ripe, it is often pickled in vinegar and eaten as a condiment; it is also served raw in salads.

bitter melon
Too bitter to be eaten raw, it is an ingredient in various kinds of Asian cooking, such as soups or steamed dishes.

wax gourd
Its firm flavorful flesh is often used in Asian soups or spicy dishes. Also known as winter melon.

eggplant
Yellowish and spongy-fleshed vegetable that is sometimes sweated with salt to alleviate its bitter taste.

fruit vegetables

summer squashes
Squashes picked earlier in the season, having a relatively tender flesh. Their skin and seeds are edible.

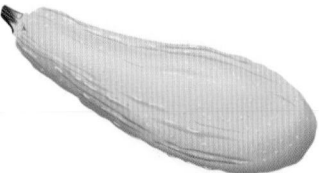

straightneck squash
Mild-flavored squash with tender skin; it is eaten raw or cooked. Also known as yellow summer squash.

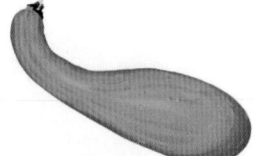

crookneck squash
The tender skin becomes warty and tough when ripe; it can be eaten raw or cooked when picked early.

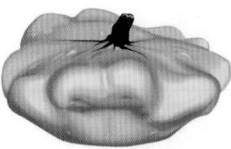

pattypan squash
Usually squat squash picked early when small; its flesh has a flavor similar to the artichoke.

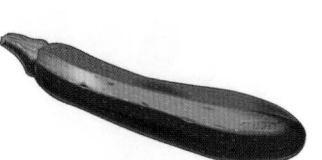

zucchini
Small white-fleshed squash picked before fully ripe; it is an essential ingredient in ratatouille.

vegetable marrow
Large squash (approximately 1 ft) that can be stuffed, baked, cooked au gratin or used in jams or chutneys.

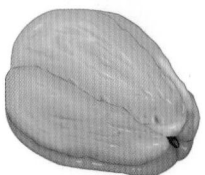

chayote
This squash, grown mainly in tropical countries, can be eaten raw or cooked; it has a large flattened edible pit with a nutlike flavor.

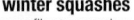

winter squashes
Sweeter and more fibrous squashes than the summer squashes, with inedible skin. Harvested when mature; they may be stored for several months.

pumpkin
Used primarily in North America, it can be recognized by its woody stem; its flesh is widely used in soups and desserts and its edible seeds are dried.

spaghetti squash
Derives its name from its cooked flesh, resembling spaghetti, which it can replace in most recipes.

acorn squash
Its smooth hard skin turns orange when fully ripe; the delicate, slightly fibrous flesh tastes of pepper and hazelnuts.

buttercup squash
Squat round heavy squash; its sweet and nutty-flavored flesh is used in soups, side dishes, and desserts.

stalk vegetables

Edible plants whose stems are consumed like vegetables; the leaves of some varieties are also edible.

asparagus
A member of the lily family, it is harvested early when tender; whether served hot or cold, it is always cooked.

tip
Top end of the spear; the most valued part of the asparagus for cooking.

leaf
Thin flattened part of the chard that grows out of the rib; it is eaten cooked or raw, mainly in salads.

spear
Young asparagus shoot that constitutes the plant's edible part and grows out of an underground stem; its hard end is usually removed before cooking.

bundle
A number of asparagus spears tied together; asparagus is usually sold in this way.

Swiss chard
A member of the beet family, grown for its ribs, prepared like celery or asparagus, and for its leaves, often said to resemble spinach.

kohlrabi
Very popular in Central and Eastern Europe, where its bulbous stem is eaten raw or cooked like turnip; its cabbage-flavored leaves can also be eaten.

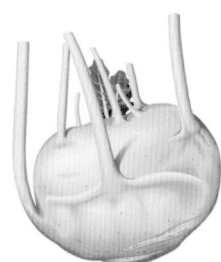

rib
The chard's long fleshy petiole, whitish or red depending on the variety, is both soft and crunchy.

fennel
Also known as Florence fennel; it is a variety of fennel with a bulblike stem base used raw or cooked especially in Italian dishes.

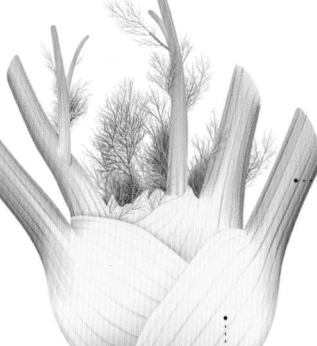

bamboo shoot
Very young stem of a bamboo plant; popular in Asian cuisine, it must be peeled and cooked before eating.

stalk
Part of the fennel growing out of the stem base and bearing small feathery dark-green leaves; it is traditionally used to flavor fish dishes.

cardoon
Resembles celery but has a flavor similar to the closely related artichoke; the stem must be cooked thoroughly to become tender.

celery
One of the best-known and most popular stalk vegetables, it is often served raw with dips; the leaves and seeds are used to season a variety of dishes.

stem base
Fleshy edible part of the fennel; it has a flavor similar to licorice or aniseed.

branch
Fleshy grooved stem with leaf-bearing offshoots; the main edible part of the celery is eaten raw or cooked.

fiddlehead fern
When coiled, this young shoot is ready to eat; it is especially popular in salads, pasta dishes and omelettes.

rhubarb
The stems are often cooked and used in jams, compotes, and pies; the leaves are poisonous.

head
Group of leafy branches joined at the base; the branches easily break off from the base and can then be cut to the desired length.

root vegetables

The fleshy roots of edible plants consumed as vegetables.

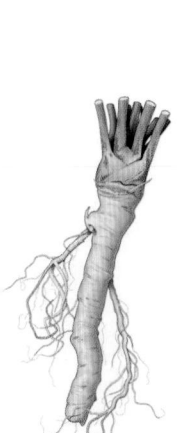

black radish
Popular in Eastern Europe, although less juicy than the red radish; it can be cooked or sweated with salt to alleviate its bitter taste.

radish
Juicy and crunchy, it is eaten raw, as an hors d'oeuvre or in salads; it is also popular served cooked or pickled, especially in Asia.

salsify
Its sweet mild flavor is often said to resemble the oyster's; its young leaves are also edible.

carrot
Eaten in a variety of ways: plain, in salads, in desserts, as a vegetable side dish or a juice.

black salsify
Closely related to salsify, its cream-colored flesh is less stringy and more flavorful; it is an ingredient in dishes such as soups and ragouts.

horseradish
...en used as a flavoring ingredient, ...ecially in sauces; its strong flavor ...comes milder when mixed with cream or mayonnaise.

daikon
White radish with mild-tasting flesh; it is used raw, cooked or pickled in many Japanese dishes.

burdock
Root of a plant harvested before the floral stem develops; it is used as a vegetable or as a flavoring ingredient.

parsnip
The yellowish flesh of this vegetable has a slightly nutty taste and a texture similar to the turnip; it can be eaten raw or cooked.

beet
...usually red flesh contains a juice that ...ins readily; it is eaten raw, pickled or ...ed, most famously in borscht, a hearty soup from Eastern Europe.

turnip
Often confused with the rutabaga, this white-fleshed vegetable is usually eaten whole, mashed, or in soups and stews.

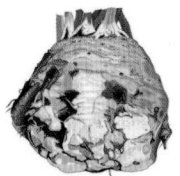

celeriac
A slightly spicy kind of celery; the raw vegetable, combined with mustard mayonnaise, becomes the classic celeriac remoulade.

rutabaga
Larger and stronger-tasting than the turnip, it can be recognized by its usually yellow flesh and by the bump on its top.

inflorescence vegetables

The flowers or flower buds of edible plants eaten as vegetables.

cauliflower
The head, composed of immature buds, is either white or purple; it is eaten raw or cooked.

broccoli
Native to Italy, it is often green and occasionally white or purple; it is chosen primarily for its flower buds but the stem and leaves are also eaten.

gai lan
Vegetable whose delicately flavored leaves, stems and flowers are eaten raw, or cooked like broccoli. Also known as Chinese broccoli.

broccoli rabe
Its slightly bitter stems, leaves and flowers can all be eaten, prepared like broccoli.

artichoke
Especially valued for its soft fleshy heart, it is often served with a dipping sauce; the leaves surrounding the heart can also be eaten.

legumes

The main edible part of these pod-shaped fruits is their seeds, consumed fresh, dried or sprouted; if dried, they often require soaking before they can be cooked.

miscellaneous legumes

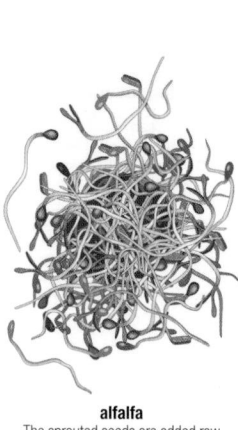

alfalfa
The sprouted seeds are added raw to sandwiches or used in various cooked dishes.

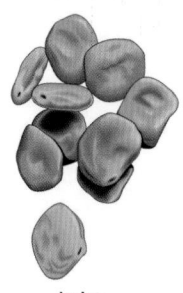

lupine
Protein-rich seed, prepared and served plain or sprinkled with lemon juice. Also known as lupini bean.

lentil
A main ingredient of hearty soups, it can also be puréed and made into croquettes; in India, it is often paired with rice.

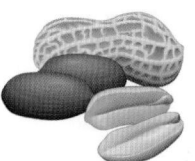

peanut
Often served as a snack, it is also made into a butter and a vegetable oil and, in some countries, into a spicy sauce served with a variety of dishes.

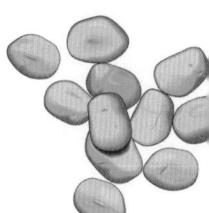

broad bean
Starchy and strong-tasting, it is typically puréed; it is also eaten wh[...] and added to soups and stews.

peas

The rounded smooth or wrinkled seeds of a vining plant; also used for related seeds having a similar appearance.

beans

Edible seeds of various bushy or climbing plants; they are usually oval or kidney-shaped and some may be eaten with their pods before they are fully ripe.

chickpea
Basic ingredient of hummus and falafel and found in couscous; it is also used in many Indian dishes. Also known as garbanzo bean.

split pea
Pea that has been dried and split in two, usually cooked down to a puree; it is used in soups and stews.

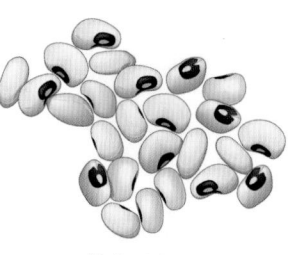

black-eyed pea
This flavorful seed has a black spot that resembles an eye, hence its name; it is typical especially of southern American cooking.

hyacinth bean
Characterized by a white ridge; its dried seeds must be cooked thoroughly to remove poisons.

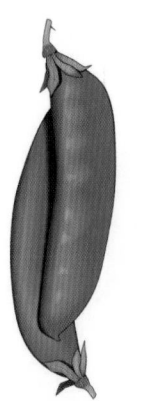

green pea
Starchy seed with a sweet flavor; it is eaten fresh, frozen or canned especially as a side dish.

snow pea
Eaten fresh or cooked along with the sweet and crunchy pod; it is often used in Chinese-style dishes.

yard-long bean
Although mostly eaten fresh and whole, like the green bean, it is less juicy and sweet; its pods measure up to 3 ft in length.

legumes

beans

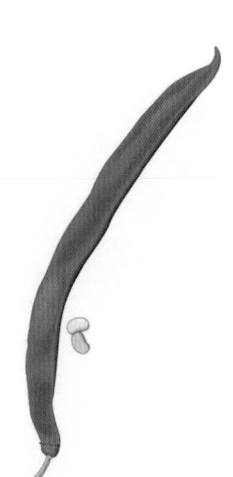

green bean
The young green pod is usually served as a vegetable side dish, sometimes with sauce or butter.

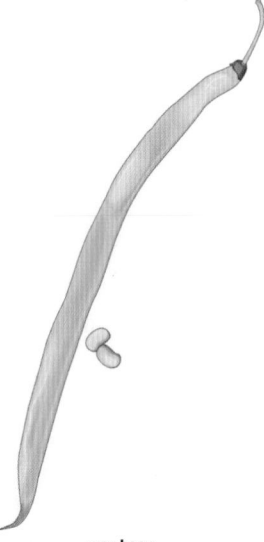

wax bean
Somewhat juicier than the green bean, it is sometimes eaten raw but mostly cooked, as a vegetable side dish.

roman bean
A staple of Italian cooking, it resembles the pinto bean, although often larger and darker; it absorbs the flavor of the foods it is cooked with.

pinto bean
When cooked, they turn pink; they are eaten pureed or mashed, or used whole in soups, stews, and salads.

scarlet runner bean
Flavorful bean usually eaten in salads or as a vegetable side dish.

adzuki bean
Has a delicate flavor and is often served with rice; in Asian countries, these beans are often made into a sweet paste that is used in many dishes.

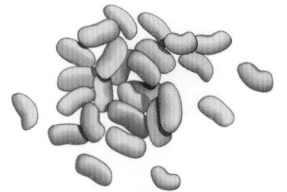

flageolet
Small pale green kidney bean with a creamy texture; it is a favorite in France, where it is traditionally served with leg of lamb.

mung bean
Native to Asia where it is often made into a puree or ground into flour; in the West it is mainly known as a source of bean sprouts.

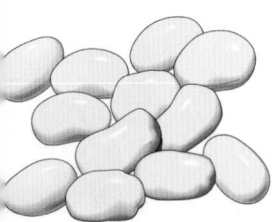

lima bean
Has a mild flavor and a starchy texture and is generally green- or cream-colored; when puréed, it can replace the potato.

black bean
Commonly used in Latin-American cuisine, it is a staple of Mexican cooking.

urd
Eaten whole or split, it is popular in India often mixed with rice to make pancakes and a spicy purée. Also known as black gram.

red kidney bean
One of the best-known beans, it is used to make the Mexican dish called chili con carne; it retains its shape when cooked so is often canned.

fruits

Edible plant parts serving as reproductive bodies of seed plants; may be eaten as part of a meal, as a snack or for dessert. Plants may be bred to produce seedless fruits.

berries

Small fleshy fruits containing one or several usually edible seeds.

currant
Small red or white berry primarily eaten cooked due to its sour taste; its juice can replace vinegar in salad dressing.

black currant
Black berry primarily used to make coulis, jellies, wine and liqueurs such as crème de cassis, an ingredient in kir.

gooseberry
Larger than the clustered berries, it is especially popular in Europe; the British use it to make a chutney that is served with mackerel.

grape
This variously colored fruit of the vine is enjoyed worldwide, either plain, cooked, dried or in juice; it is also the main ingredient in wine.

blueberry
Little known outside its native North America, it is primarily eaten plain or in desserts; the lowbush variety is the sweetest.

bilberry
Although not related to it, this berry of Europe and Asia resembles the blueberry and is used like it.

lingonberry
Closely related to the cranberry, this small tart berry is somewhat bitter and rarely eaten raw; it is used instead to make sauces, jams and desserts.

goji
Mildly tart berry originally from Asia, usually eaten dried or as juice.

Cape gooseberry
Slightly acidic and mildly sweet berry covered with a papery husk; it is eaten raw and used in jams, pies and sauces.

cranberry
Too tart to be eaten raw, it is primarily used for making desserts, sauces or juice; a traditional accompaniment to turkey in North America.

raspberry
Generally red, there are also different-colored varieties; slightly tart and very fragrant, it is often used in jams, sauces, and desserts.

blackberry
Grows on canes as does the raspberry, and is used like that fruit; the several trailing species are commonly called dewberries.

strawberry
Cultivated or wild, it can be eaten raw, cooked, in jam, desserts or fruit salad

stone fruits

Fruits whose somewhat juicy flesh surrounds a hard, usually inedible stone.

apricot
Often eaten dried or candied, its orange flesh can be very hard if picked before fully ripe; the kernel inside the stone contains a toxic substance.

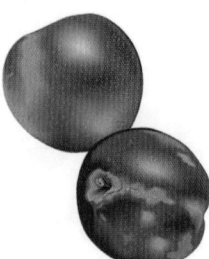

plum
Of various colors and sizes, it is eaten either raw or cooked and is used especially to make chutneys and jams; the dried plum is called a prune.

peach
A velvety skin covers its juicy fragrant flesh; it is especially enjoyed plain, in juice and in various desserts, such as the classic peach melba.

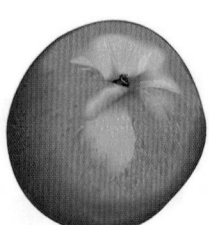

nectarine
Differentiated from the peach by its smooth, more colorful skin and by its more flavorful flesh; like the peach, it is eaten raw or used in certain desserts.

cherry
Often cooked or candied and used in pies and cakes or to garnish cocktails and desserts, some varieties are also eaten raw.

date
Has a high sugar content and is o... sold dried; in North America, it i... primarily associated with baked go... such as squares, muffins and cak...

fruits

dry fruits

Often called nuts, these fruits usually have a hard dry covering called the shell that encloses one or more edible seeds.

macadamia nut
...ular candy ingredient, it can also ...ded to mixed vegetables, curries, salads and desserts.

ginkgo nut
Extensively used in Japanese cooking but little known in the West, this nut is either eaten as is or is used in Asian dishes.

pistachio
Its greenish seed is covered with a brown skin; it is extensively used in Mediterranean and Asian cooking, as well as in pastry and candy-making.

pine nut
Edible seed inside the cone of certain species of pine that is often used in cooking and baking.

kola nut
Used in drink preparations such as Coca-Cola™; it contains stimulants that are slightly less potent than those in coffee.

pecan
...ive to North America, it is used ...make certain savory dishes and ...umerous desserts, such as the traditional pecan pie.

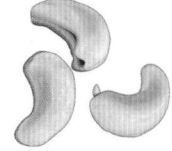

cashew
This fruit of the cashew tree is always sold shelled; its shell is covered by a juicy fleshy edible layer known as the cashew apple.

almond
It is used raw, blanched, or roasted in a variety of sweet and savory dishes, and is especially common in baked goods (often as almond paste) and candies. Almond essence flavors Amaretto and a variety of foodstuffs.

hazelnut
Often eaten raw or roasted, they are also ground and used to make pastes and butters. In candy-making they are often combined with chocolate.

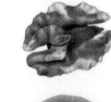

walnut
Eaten roasted or raw, the walnut is often used as a snack or appetizer, or added to a variety of baked goods, desserts, salads, sauces, and main dishes.

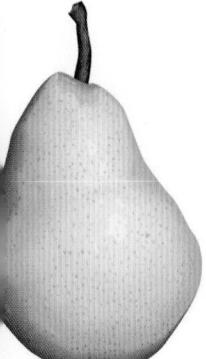
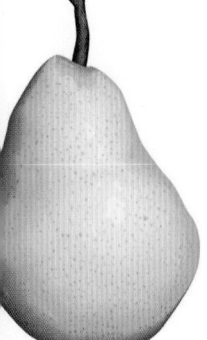

coconut
The whitish meat, known as copra, surrounds a cavity containing a refreshing liquid, not to be confused with coconut milk, which is derived from the grated flesh.

chestnut
Sturdy fruit of the chestnut tree; Europeans often serve it with game and poultry. When puréed, it is the main ingredient in the dessert known as Mont Blanc.

beechnut
Fruit of the common beech tree, its flavor resembles the hazelnut's; more flavorful toasted than raw, it also yields a cooking oil.

Brazil nut
Often served as an appetizer; it is also made into candy, such as when chocolate-coated. It replaces coconut in some recipes.

pome fruits

Fruits where the flesh covers an inedible central part, the core, comprising a certain number of seeds called pips.

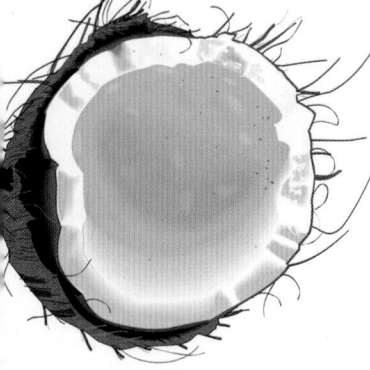

pear
...g its many and varied uses, it forms ...asis for a fruit brandy; it is picked ...e fully ripe to prevent the flesh from acquiring a granular texture.

quince
Fruit of the quince tree, native to warm climates; inedible raw, it is traditionally made into jams and jellies.

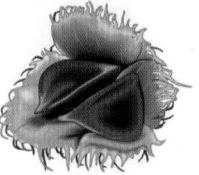

apple
There are 7,500 known varieties; it is used to make cider and is also eaten raw or made into juice, jelly, compote or desserts, such as pie or strudel.

loquat
Has thin skin enveloping a juicy, somewhat sour flesh and may be eaten raw or cooked; it is used especially for preserves.

fruits

citrus fruits

Somewhat acidic fruits with a high vitamin C content comprising numerous sections and covered with a rind that has an external layer called zest.

clementine
Citrus fruit produced by crossing mandarin and bitter oranges. The juicy and acidic flesh is slightly less fragrant than that of the mandarin orange.

kumquat
Small grape-sized citrus fruit with a sweet edible rind; it can be eaten raw and is often used candied, pickled or made into jam.

lime
Intensely fragrant and used like the lemon; it is an essential ingredient in ceviche, a raw marinated fish dish.

tangerine
Citrus fruit produced by crossing mandarin and bitter oranges; it is often eaten as-is.

lemon
Highly acidic, it is especia flavor various recipes and the flavor of certain foods main ingredient in leme

orange
Widely available, it is often eaten plain or in juice, and is also used to make sauces and orange marmalade. It yields a flavor essence and an essential oil.

blood orange
Orange variety with almost red flesh, usually seedless. It is sweet, juicy and fragrant.

mandarin
Similar to a small, slightly flattened orange, it is less acidic than most citrus fruits and is often eaten as is; it peels easily.

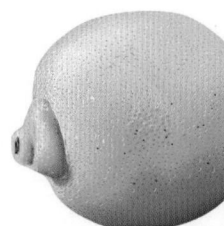

bergamot
Because its greenish flesh is inedit it is primarily used for the zest an essential oil derived from its rind especially in Earl Grey tea.

grapefruit
The pink grapefruit is sweeter and less bitter than the white one that has yellow flesh; it is often cut in half and eaten plain, with a spoon.

pomelo
Extremely popular in many Asian countries, it has only recently become available in the West; less juicy than the grapefruit, it is often eaten plain and its peel may be cooked or candied.

citron
Extensively grown in Corsica and Israel, this somewhat dry fragrant fruit is rarely found fresh and is mostly sold candied.

melons

Related to squash and cucumbers, these tender fruits are juicy sweet and refreshing; they are primarily consumed raw.

charentais
This orange-fleshed melon is characterized by its patterned textured ribs; it is widely consumed in France.

casaba melon
The flavor of its creamy white flesh, often less fragrant than that of other melons, can be enhanced with lemon or lime juice.

honeydew melon
Owes its name to its very sweet, green flesh; its smooth firm rind turns creamy-yellow as it ripens.

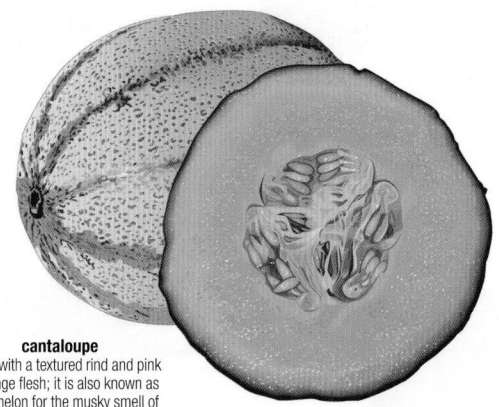

cantaloupe
Melon with a textured rind and pink to orange flesh; it is also known as muskmelon for the musky smell of its flesh.

Canary melon
Melon with sweet whitish flesh, tinted with pink near the central cavity. Very fragrant when ripe.

watermelon
This thirst-quenching fruit, named for its high water content, is primarily eaten plain, in slices.

Ogen melon
Small round melon originating in Israel; it has juicy, very sweet and usually pale green flesh.

fruits

tropical fruits

A variety of fruits, usually of exotic origin, more or less available in the West.

plantain
Nicknamed the "cooking banana", this staple of African and West Indian cooking is inedible when raw; it is primarily eaten as a vegetable, either steamed, roasted or fried.

banana
Eaten as is, sautéed, fried or flambéed with rum; it is a classic garnish for ice-cream dishes and is also used in muffins and cakes.

longan
Related to the lychee, its whitish translucent flesh is sweet and juicy; the peeled fruit is used raw, dried or canned.

tamarillo
Within the inedible skin there is a firm, slightly acidic flesh. If very ripe, it can be eaten raw; otherwise, it is often cooked like a vegetable.

passion fruit
Within its inedible skin that wrinkles when ripe, there is a highly aromatic gelatinous pulp. Often served plain, it is also used to flavor fruit punches and cocktails.

horned melon
Its green flesh contains soft edible seeds, similar to those of the cucumber; it is often peeled and then made into juice.

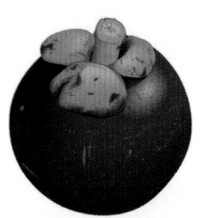

mangosteen
Within the inedible skin that hardens as the fruit ages, there is a sweet juicy white flesh that is divided into sections; it is eaten as is, like an orange.

kiwi
Its juicy, slightly acidic green flesh a high vitamin C content; delicio plain, its downy skin is generall discarded, although it can be eate

pomegranate
A large berry with a tough skin enclosing numerous seeds each with a juicy covering; it is used to make grenadine syrup, an ingredient in drinks and desserts.

cherimoya
The skin and the seeds inside the slightly granular flesh are inedible; the creamy flesh is eaten fresh with a spoon, sometimes sprinkled with orange juice.

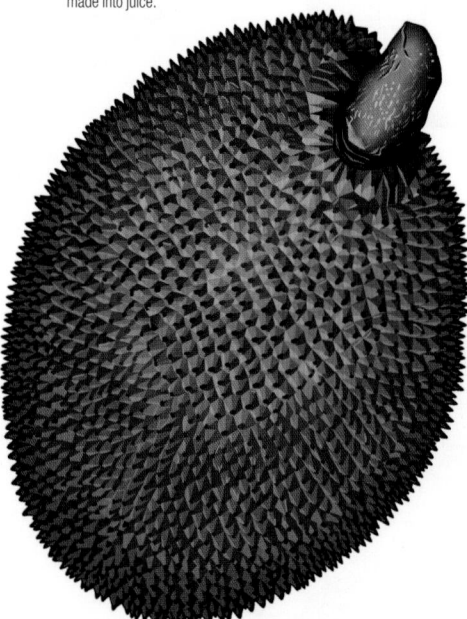

jackfruit
This very large fruit has edible seeds than can be boiled or roasted; the starchy flesh is eaten as a fruit or vegetable, either raw or cooked.

pineapple
Once the inedible rind has been removed, it is eaten raw, cooked or in juice; in North America, it is traditionally served with ham.

fruits

jaboticaba
Little known outside Brazil, it is eaten as is, like grapes, or made into jelly, jam, juice or wine; its translucent flesh is either white or pink.

lychee
Its juicy crunchy translucent flesh is more fragrant than the longan's; the fruit is eaten fresh, canned, or dried.

fig
Among its many varieties are the black, the green and the purple fig; whether fresh or dried, it is mostly eaten raw, but can also be cooked.

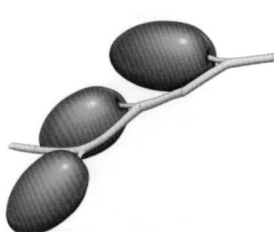

jujube
Somewhat dry stone fruit, eaten fresh or dried, raw or cooked, like the date; its juice is used in making candies of the same name.

sapodilla
Its flesh is sweet and juicy, fragrant and slightly granular; it can be eaten raw or cooked.

guava
Very popular in South America, its fragrant, slightly acidic flesh is eaten raw or cooked, with or without the skin and seeds.

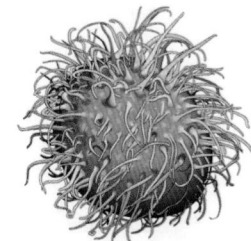

rambutan
The shell, covered in soft spikes, splits easily to reveal flesh like the lychee's but less fragrant; it is eaten fresh or canned, or made into jam.

Japanese persimmon
This national fruit of Japan is often eaten plain, with a spoon; the fuyu variety is eaten like an apple.

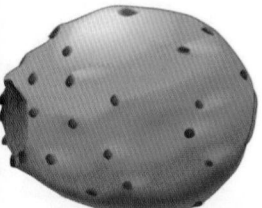

prickly pear
Fruit of a member of the cactus family; the spines and skin should be removed before eating the flesh, plain or sprinkled with lemon or lime juice.

carambola
Within the delicate edible skin is a juicy, slightly acidic flesh that can be eaten raw or cooked; it is also known as star fruit.

Asian pear
Most popular Asian fruit, primarily eaten plain; its flesh is sweet and juicy, like the pear's, and crunchy, like the apple's.

mango
Fruit with a flattened stone and a skin that should be discarded, as it irritates the mouth; it is mostly eaten ripe, but sometimes used green, as a vegetable.

durian
Large fruit that emits a disagreeable odor when ripe; its sweet creamy flesh is often eaten plain while the seeds are used like nuts.

papaya
Its usually orange, juicy flesh is eaten like the melon and contains spicy, edible seeds; when green, it is eaten like winter squash.

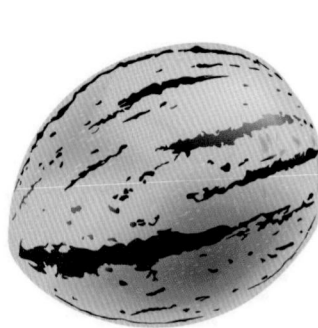

pepino
The orange or yellow flesh is slightly starchy. Before fully ripe, it is often cooked and prepared like a squash; once ripe, it is eaten like a melon.

feijoa
Has sweet fragrant, slightly granular flesh; after peeling, it is eaten raw or cooked, plain or in various desserts.

spices

Plant substances, often of exotic origin, used primarily for their flavor and pungency to enhance the taste of various recipes.

juniper berry
Fruit of the juniper tree with a resinous smell and slightly bitter flavor; it is the basis for gin and also flavors marinades, sauerkraut, meat and pâtés.

clove
The dried floral bud of the clove tree. Whole, it is often used with ham or simmered onion dishes; when ground, it flavors items such as gingerbread.

allspice
Also called Jamaican spice; it is used to flavor savory or sweet dishes and certain liqueurs.

white mustard
Its seeds are larger and less pungent than the black mustard's and are used especially to make American yellow mustard.

black mustard
The flavorful pungent seeds have a [high] concentration of essential oil; they a[re] used whole, ground or as a flavori[ng] agent.

black pepper
The most pungent and aromatic of the peppers, it comes from small berries that are picked while still green, then dried.

white pepper
Small berries picked when very ripe, then dried and skinned of black husk; this spice is less pungent than black pepper.

pink pepper
These dried berries, with a delicate fragrant and mildly pungent flavor, do not grow on the pepper plant but on another shrub; it is used like pepper.

green pepper
Small berries picked while still green an[d] usually dried or preserved in brine or vineg[ar] this pepper is mild but very fragrant.

nutmeg
Its spicy sweet flavor complements milk products but quickly deteriorates once the nut is ground; its red membrane, known as mace, is also used as a spice.

caraway
Its sharp bitter flavor enhances the flavor of breads and stewed dishes; it is used primarily in Eastern Europe, India and Middle Eastern countries.

cardamom
The pod is green, brown or white, depending on whether it was sun- or oven-dried, or bleached; its delicate peppery flavor characterizes Indian curry.

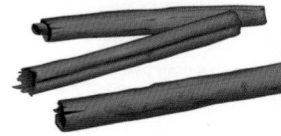

cinnamon
Dried bark of the cinnamon tree, sold in sti[cks,] ground or as an essential oil; it is often assoc[iated] with candy, sweet dishes and hot drinks[.]

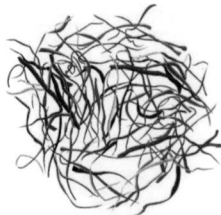

saffron
The most expensive spice, actually derived from the handpicked and dried stigmata of the crocus flower; it is an essential ingredient in paella and bouillabaisse.

cumin
Extensively used in traditional Middle Eastern, Indian and Mexican dishes; it has a strong smell and a warm, slightly bitter flavor.

curry powder
A staple of Indian cooking, the pungency of this blend of spices varies, depending on how much pepper or chile is used.

turmeric
Similar to ginger, it is cooked and ground into powder; among other uses, it is added to Indian curries and chutneys and provides the color for American yellow mustard.

fenugreek
Once roasted, the seeds [have a] bittersweet aftertaste; they [are used] in Indian cooking or, when [roasted,] added to salads.

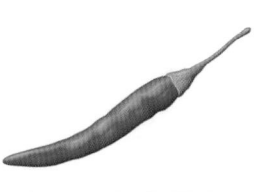

jalapeño
...ild to hot chile, native to Mexico ...sold fresh, dried or marinated; it turns red when ripe.

bird's eye chile
Small, intensely hot chile; removing the seeds and interior membranes alleviates the fiery taste.

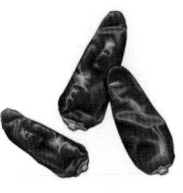

crushed chile
Dried crushed chiles that contribute flavor and spiciness to a variety of recipes; they are commonly used in pasta dishes.

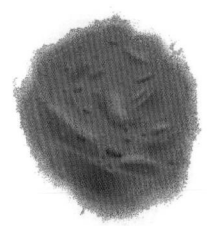

dried chile
The smaller dried chiles are generally stronger than the large ones, which can be dry-roasted before use to bring out their flavor.

cayenne pepper
Dried red chile powder also called red pepper in recipes; it is so hot that one pinch is enough to season an entire dish.

ground pepper
Obtained by grinding the black ...ppercorn, it is one of the most widely ...d cooking spices; although pungent, it ...es its flavor faster than peppercorns.

ajowan
Highly fragrant, it tastes like thyme; among other uses, it is added to starchy foods, legumes and Indian wafers.

asafetida
The dried gum derived from two species of giant fennel, its unpleasant smell dissipates with cooking; it adds flavor to vegetables, fish and Indian sauces.

garam masala
Indian spice blend of which there are countless varieties, some numbering up to 12 ingredients; it is used to season pilafs and meat dishes.

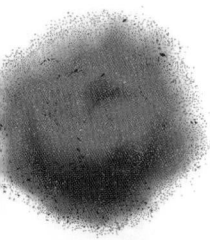

cajun spice seasoning
...y mix of salt, cayenne, garlic and onion ...r, and paprika; it is used to enhance the ...flavor of ragouts and Cajun dishes.

marinade spice seasoning
A mixture of spices added to fruit and vegetable preserves, chutney and vinegar; its composition varies.

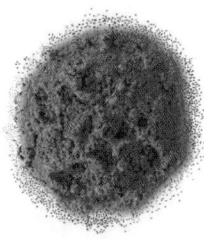

five spice powder
A blend of five ground spices used in Chinese cuisine; it includes star anise, cloves, fennel seeds, Chinese cinnamon and Szechuan pepper.

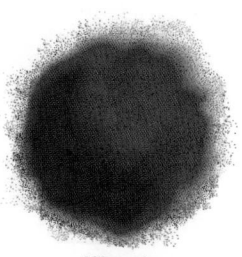

chili powder
Spice blend composed mainly of dried ground chiles, whose strength varies depending on the chiles used; it is widely used to flavor and color rice, pasta and stews.

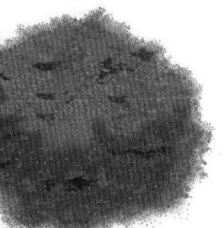

paprika
...ively used in Hungarian cooking, this ...t hot powder combines dried sweet red ...d red chiles; it is used to flavor and color ...ous foods, such as eggs and potatoes.

ras el hanout
Very fragrant Moroccan spice blend with dried flowers among its up to 50 ingredients; it is used to flavor game, couscous, rice and stews called tajines.

sumac
Dried berries, sometimes ground, with a slightly acidic, lemony taste; it is very popular in the Middle East, especially in salads and fish dishes.

poppy seed
Their nutty flavor, which intensifies with cooking, works especially well in bread, cakes and pastries; it also yields a cooking oil.

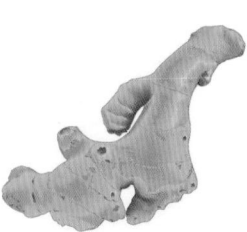

ginger
A staple of Asian cooking and a classic garnish for sushi; it is also used ground, especially in breads and cookies.

herbs

Aromatic fresh or dried plants used separately or mixed to bring out the flavor of recipes; they may be steeped in water, oil or vinegar to make infusions.

dill
Used primarily for its leaves and seeds, it imparts flavor to vinegar and pickles as well as to salmon and herring.

anise
Its seeds (aniseed) impart a licorice-like flavor to candies, breads, desserts and liqueurs; it is also used to flavor meat and vegetable dishes.

sweet bay
The leaves are usually used dried to flavor soups, stews and meat dishes; they are typically removed before serving.

oregano
Also known as wild marjoram, its pungent leaves are used fresh or dried; it is commonly used to flavor Mediterranean cooking.

tarragon
Has a slightly bitter, peppery anise fla that complements bland foods; it is c used with chicken and is always use béarnaise sauce.

basil
A popular choice for seasoning tomato and pasta dishes; it is also one of the main ingredients in French pistou and Italian pesto.

sage
Its pungent flavor complements a variety of dishes; it is often used with pork, duck and goose, as well as in Italian veal dishes.

thyme
Used with parsley and sweet bay to make bouquets garnis, a French herb mixture; because it withstands lengthy cooking, it is a popular choice for flavoring soups and stews.

mint
Gives a refreshing taste to numerous sweet and savory dishes, such as lamb; its aromatic essential oil is used to flavor candy, liqueurs and many other types of food.

parsley
The smooth flat-leafed parsley is less bitter and more fragrant than curly-leafed parsley; it is used to flavor numerous recipes, such as tabbouleh.

chervil
Has a subtle delicate taste and is used like parsley; it is often included with tarragon, parsley and chives in a French herb blend known as fines herbes.

coriander
Its leaves are used like parsley and it has edible musk- and lemon-scented seeds; the roots can be substituted for garlic. The leaves are also known as cilantro.

rosemary
Its fairly pungent, aromatic flavor is very popular in southern France and in Italy, where it is used especially in sauces and marinades, and with roast meat.

hyssop
The highly aromatic leaves are mostly used in salads, soups, ragouts and fruit platters, as well as in some liqueurs, such as Chartreuse and Benedictine.

borage
The cucumber-scented leaves are used fresh, dried or cooked; its edible flowers are used plain or candied as garnishes or decorations.

lovage
Resembles celery but with a stronger flavor. It is often served with potatoes and also goes well with ragouts, sauces and salads.

savory
Reminiscent of thyme, its flavor enhances legumes, meat and stuffing; it is also used to flavor vinegar and goat's milk cheeses.

lemon balm
Its lemon-scented leaves are comm used in teas and salads and as a gai it goes well with bitter foods.

cereals

Plants that are often cultivated on a large scale; their grains have been a major food staple for humans and certain domestic animals for centuries.

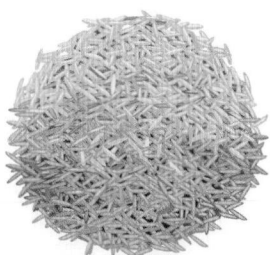

rice
A universal staple, used as a side dish, in sweet and savory dishes such as risotto and paella; it is the main ingredient in sake.

wild rice
Seeds from a North American aquatic plant; it is richer and higher in protein than rice and has a strong nutty flavor. It is sometimes mixed with other kinds of rice.

spelt
Wheat variety with small brown grains that, once hulled, can be used like rice.

wheat
Cereal cultivated for its grain, of great significance in human food production; it is used to produce foodstuffs such as flour, bread and semolina.

oats
Often eaten as porridge, it is also an ingredient in date squares, fruit crisp toppings, muffins, cookies and pancakes.

rye
Yields a flour that can be combined with wheat flour to make bread; it is also used in brewing (beer) and distilling (whisky).

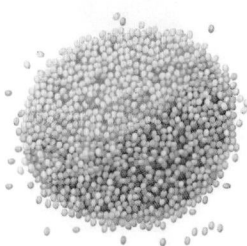

millet
With its strong flavor, it is mostly used for making pancakes and porridge; when sprouted and ground, millet is an ingredient in breads and muffins.

corn
Native to America, it is eaten as a vegetable, made into popcorn or ground into flour; it also yields a starch, a syrup and a cooking oil.

barley
Barley can be either hulled or pearled to remove its outer husk; it is often added to soups and ragouts and is also made into malt for brewing beer.

buckwheat
Eaten in soups and as porridge, it is also ground into a flour traditionally used to make crepes and pancakes.

quinoa
Grains should be thoroughly rinsed before cooking; it can be cooked like rice or ground into flour and is rich in protein.

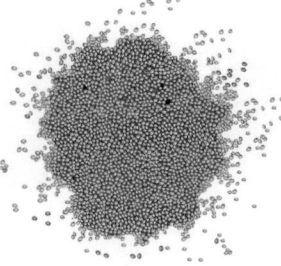

amaranth
These highly nutritious, slightly peppery grains can be eaten as is after cooking, sprouted or ground into flour.

triticale
A wheat and rye hybrid, its flour is used to make crepes and pasta; it must be combined with wheat flour to make bread.

coffee and infusions

Aromatic beverages derived from ground beans (coffee) or dried plants (tea, herbal tea) that are combined with boiling water.

herbal teas

Infusions made with aromatic dried leaves, flowers or fruits, often considered to have calming, digestive, tonic or curative properties.

linden
Tree whose dried leaves and flowers can be made into herbal teas, considered to have calming, sedative and soothing properties.

chamomile
Herbal teas made from the flowers and leaves of this plant are considered to have digestive and calming properties.

verbena
Herbal teas made from this lemon-scented plant are believed to have digestive and sedative properties.

mint
Herbal teas are made from one or more types of mint (peppermint, spearmint); it is considered to have digestive and calming properties.

coffee

The seeds of the coffee tree can be used to prepare an extremely popular beverage, drunk hot or cold (iced coffee), and well known for its stimulant properties.

green coffee beans
Processed and dried beans prior to roasting; they have a long shelf life, remaining flavorful for several years.

roasted coffee beans
Roasting darkens the beans and brings out the flavor and aroma. Roasting time and temperature affects the acidity and flavor.

ground coffee
Roasted and ground coffee beans. Unrefrigerated ground beans lose their aroma in less than a week.

tea

Infusion made from the dried leaves of the tea tree; drunk hot or iced, it is the world's most popular beverage after water; it is sold in bags or loose.

green tea
Made from tea leaves that are not oxidized before drying; it has a more bitter taste than black tea.

black tea
Made from tea leaves that are completely oxidized before drying; it represents more than 98% of the total worldwide production of tea.

oolong tea
Made from tea leaves that are partially oxidized before drying; it is more delicate-tasting than black tea.

mollusks

Usually marine-dwelling, soft-bodied invertebrates; some have shells and are sold live.

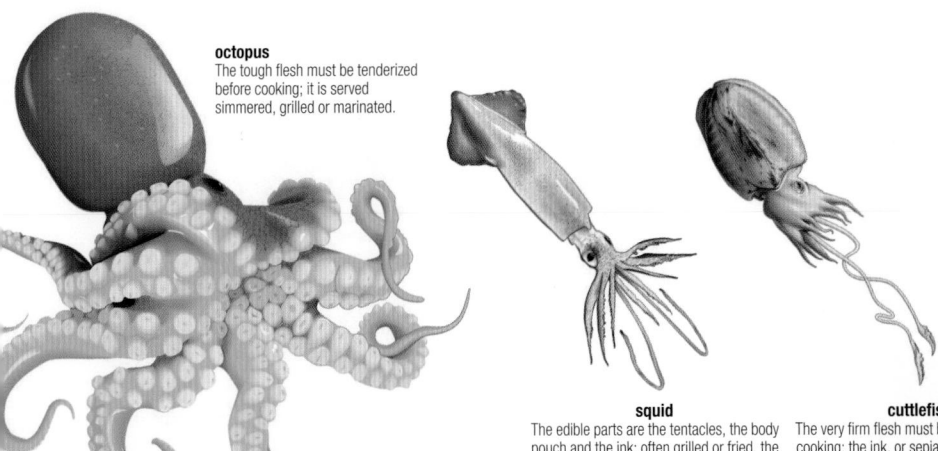

octopus
The tough flesh must be tenderized before cooking; it is served simmered, grilled or marinated.

squid
The edible parts are the tentacles, the body pouch and the ink; often grilled or fried, the lean flesh can occasionally be rubbery.

cuttlefish
The very firm flesh must be pounded before cooking; the ink, or sepia, can also be used to color certain recipes.

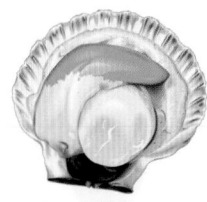

scallop
The main edible part is the nut (the muscle that opens and shuts the shells) and sometimes the coral (the orange part); excellent raw or cooked, it can be prepared in numerous ways.

hard-shell clam
Mollusk with a very hard shell whose flesh can be eaten raw or cooked; they are used to make chowder, a popular New England recipe.

soft-shell clam
Large, thin-shelled bivalve mollusk, mainly harvested in the Atlantic; related to the hard-shell clam, it can be used to replace it in recipes.

abalone
The muscle, also called the "foot", is served raw or cooked; it must be pounded before cooking.

great scallop
Related to the scallop, the delicately flavored flesh is prized by Europeans; the shells are resistant to heat and are often used as cooking and serving dishes.

snail
Snails are often sold canned, frozen or ready-cooked; served with garlic butter, they constitute a classic appetizer.

limpet
It has a single shell and is eaten raw with lemon juice or vinegar, or grilled, with butter.

common periwinkle
Its flesh resembles the snail's, which it can replace in most recipes; whether eaten hot or cold, it is always cooked first.

Venus clam
Related to the hard-shell clam, it is as tasty raw (with or without lemon juice) as it is cooked (in soups, or stuffed, like the blue mussel).

cockle
Generally designates the European variety, although others exist; it has a firmer texture and a more pronounced flavor than oysters and mussels.

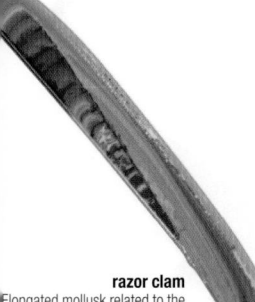

razor clam
Elongated mollusk related to the clams, with a shell sharp enough to cut skin, hence its name.

flat oyster
Less common than the cupped oyster, with a completely flat lower shell; the belon variety is particularly prized.

cupped Pacific oyster
Juicy and meaty, with a well-developed lower shell; like all oysters, it is often eaten raw, either plain or with lemon juice.

blue mussel
Fresh mussels are usually poached in broth or steamed until they open; those that fail to open should be discarded.

whelk
Resembles a large periwinkle; the flesh will toughen if it is cooked too long and it is often eaten sprinkled with lemon juice.

crustaceans

Aquatic invertebrates having a carapace over their bodies; they are sold live, frozen (raw or cooked) or canned.

spiny lobster
Spiny-shelled crustacean whose fles[h]
slightly less flavorful than the lobster[.]
tail is the part most commonly found
either raw or cooked.

crayfish
Small freshwater crustacean usually
prepared like lobster; only the tail is eaten
and its pinkish-white flesh is lean and
delicate.

lobster
To ensure maximum freshness, the
lobster should be cooked live, by
plunging it into boiling liquid.

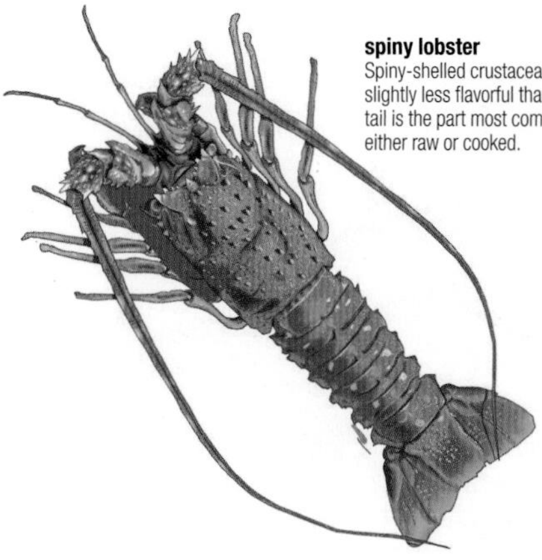

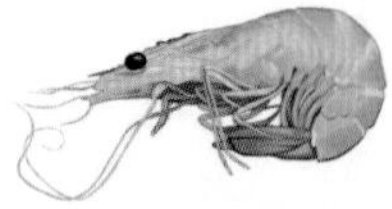

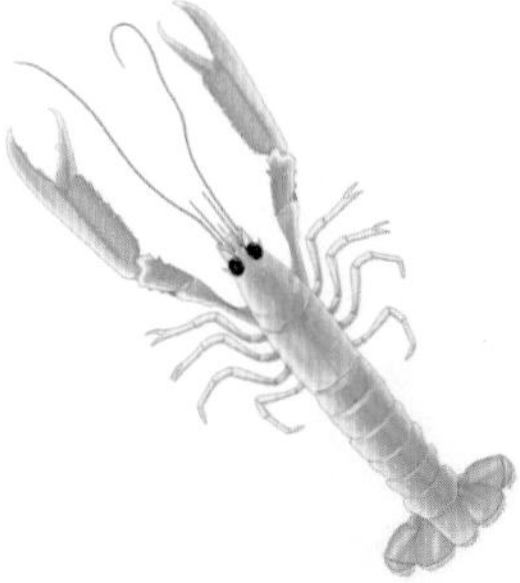

shrimp
Served hot or cold; although many prefer
them deveined, the intestine (the dark
vein running along the back) is edible.

langoustine
Rarely sold live, it resembles a small
lobster but has somewhat less flavorful
flesh; usually served with garlic butter.

crab
Sometimes sold live and cooked like the
lobster, its lean stringy flesh, its liver and
the creamy substance under the shell
can all be eaten.

marine fishes

Fish that normally live in saltwater.

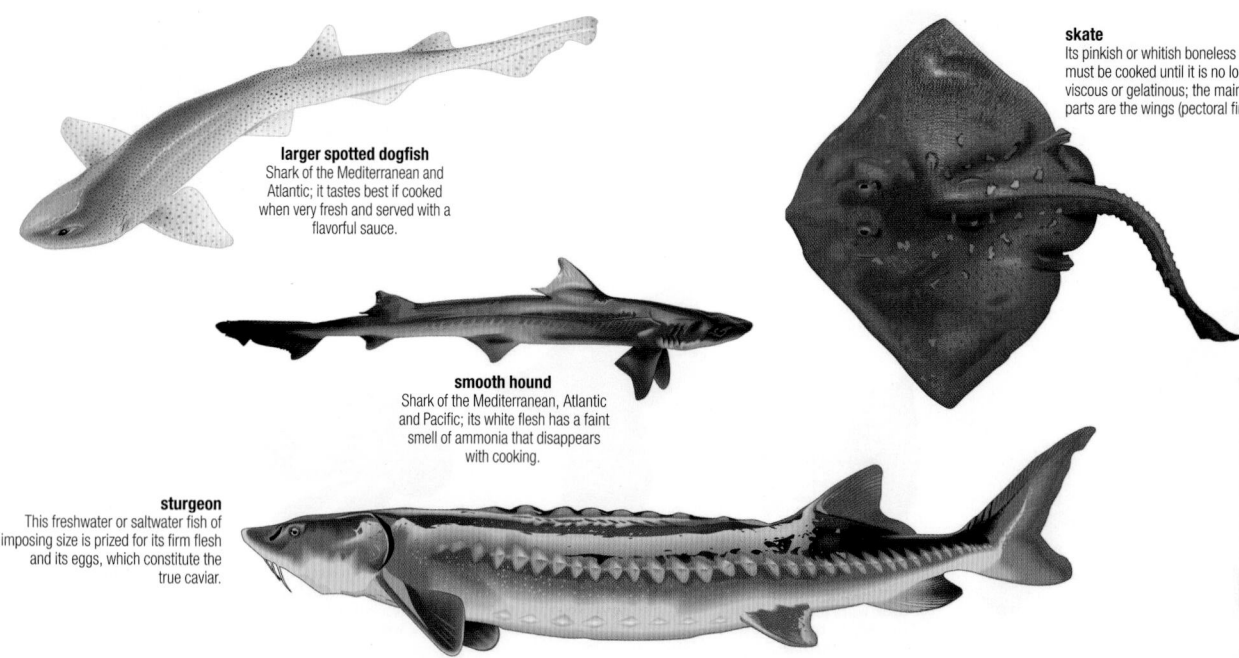

skate
Its pinkish or whitish boneless f[lesh]
must be cooked until it is no lon[ger]
viscous or gelatinous; the main
parts are the wings (pectoral fin[s])

larger spotted dogfish
Shark of the Mediterranean and
Atlantic; it tastes best if cooked
when very fresh and served with a
flavorful sauce.

smooth hound
Shark of the Mediterranean, Atlantic
and Pacific; its white flesh has a faint
smell of ammonia that disappears
with cooking.

sturgeon
This freshwater or saltwater fish of
imposing size is prized for its firm flesh
and its eggs, which constitute the
true caviar.

FOOD AND KITCHEN

anchovy
Very popular in Mediterranean countries, this highly perishable fish is often preserved in brine, oil or salt and sold in cans or jars.

sardine
Related to the herring, it is often canned (in oil, tomato sauce or white wine) and is eaten with bread, as is or with lemon juice.

herring
One of the world's most harvested species, it is sold fresh as well as canned, marinated, salted and smoked; it can replace mackerel in most recipes.

smelt
The somewhat oily cucumber-scented flesh is the main part eaten, but the head, bones, tail and eggs are also considered edible; it is most often simply gutted and fried.

sea bream
Its delicate lean white flesh can be prepared in many ways; it is served smoked, in sashimi or in ceviche.

goatfish
In spite of its many bones, it is highly prized, especially in southern France, for its particularly delicate flavor.

shad
Its somewhat tender, oily flesh has many small bones; acidic ingredients such as sorrel and rhubarb are often used in its preparation to aid in dissolving the bones.

mackerel
Traditionally served with gooseberry chutney, its somewhat oily flesh spoils rapidly if not eaten promptly.

monkfish
Also called anglerfish, only its tail is eaten and the taste is said to be similar to lobster; it is often served cold, with a dressing.

gurnard
Somewhat lean, it is often used in soups such as bouillabaisse and in fish stews; it is also served baked, poached, fried or smoked.

bluefish
Very popular in the U.S., this lean fish is often grilled, braised or poached; it is prepared like mackerel.

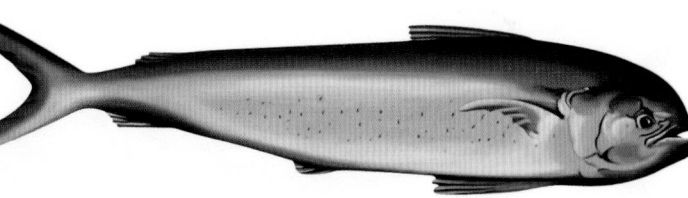

mahimahi
Tropical fish with thin and firm flesh, which is eaten pan-fried, poached, oven or steam baked.

swordfish
The highly prized flesh becomes easier to digest if it is poached before being prepared; the tail and fins are also edible.

marine fishes

sole
Often confused with plaice, it is mainly found in waters off the European coast; the most highly prized variety is the common or Dover sole.

John Dory
Usually prepared like sole or turbot, its medium-firm flesh contains gelatinous bones that make a unique fish stock.

common plaice
Because it has so many bones, it is often sold filleted and is one of the varieties used in fish-and-chips; it is found primarily off the European coast.

whiting
Its delicate flaky flesh is similar to cod's and is easy to digest; it is often wrapped in tinfoil or cooked in a flavored broth.

redfish
It is served raw, cooked or smoked; if cooked in broth or grilled, it is best to leave the skin on to prevent its flaky flesh from falling apart.

haddock
Related to cod but with flesh that is sweeter and more delicate; it is often smoked.

sea bass
Its firm lean flesh has few bones and withstands cooking well; it is best cooked simply, to avoid overpowering the delicate taste.

Atlantic salmon
The only species of salmon inhabiting the Atlantic; it is prized for its pink, somewhat oily and fragrant flesh and is sold fresh, frozen and smoked.

pollock
Especially popular in England, it is also used to make surimi, a paste from which imitation seafood is made.

Pacific salmon
King salmon (or chinook) has the oiliest flesh and is greatly prized; the leaner and less oily varieties are often canned.

tuna
Often canned in oil or water, it is one of the main ingredients in the Italian dish vitello tonnato; it is also used to make salads, sushi and sashimi.

Atlantic
It is often dried or salted and its yields an oil that is rich in vitam and D; it is fished extensively c Canadian and American co

halibut
The largest of the flatfish family, it is commonly cooked in wine or served with anchovy butter; its lean flaky flesh has few bones.

turbot
One of the tenderest saltwate with lean white flavorful flesh; whole or filleted, it is usually p or grilled.

freshwater fishes

Fish normally living in water (lakes, rivers, ponds, etc.) that is not salty.

black bass
Rarely found for sale, this sport fishing species has lean flaky flesh that is well suited to all cooking methods.

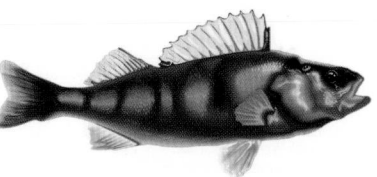

perch
Related to the pike perch, it is often poached, steamed or floured and fried in butter; its bony flesh has a delicate flavor.

American eel
Prized in Europe and Asia for its delicate firm oily flesh; its excess fat is removed when it is skinned.

trout
Mainly freshwater fish with medium-oily delicate and fragrant flesh; rainbow trout is the species most often raised in captivity.

carp
Soaking in vinegar water will make the sometimes muddy taste of the wild varieties disappear; it is especially prized for its tongue and lips.

pike perch
Its lean firm delicate flesh can be cooked in many ways; whole and filleted, it is prepared like perch or pike.

tilapia
Often raised in captivity, its somewhat fatty, firm pink flesh has a mild and lightly sweet flavor; usually eaten pan-fried.

brook trout
Native to North America, it resembles the trout and is greatly prized for its delicate flesh, which is best when simply prepared.

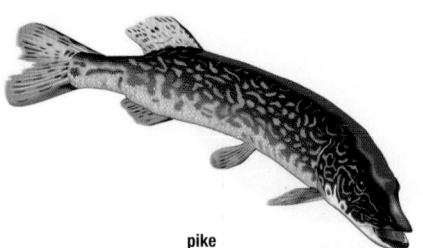

pike
The flesh sometimes has a slightly muddy taste that disappears with soaking; because it has many bones, it is often made into pâtés or quenelles.

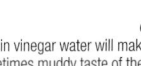

fish presentation

The fishmonger cuts or prepares the fish in sections for use in cooking.

salted fish
Fish that has been dried and covered in salt to preserve it. Eaten prepared as an appetizer or in dishes of many world cuisines.

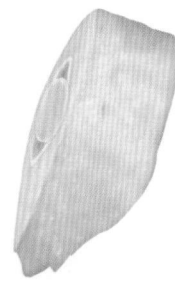

chunk
Thick cross section of a large fish.

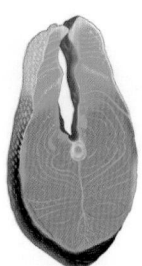

fish steak
Crosswise slice of fish, approximately one inch thick.

fillet
Round or flat piece of fish, taken from each side of the spine.

smoked fish
Fish preserved by smoking in a smoker or smokehouse. It can th be refrigerated, frozen, or canne

marinated fish
Raw fish covered in citrus juice or other acidic liquid or seasoned oil before being cooked or eaten as-is.

seafood platter
Dish made up of fish, crustaceans and edible mollusks.

canned fish
Marine fish usually salted and preserved in oil or water. Eaten prepared as an appetizer in salads or in sandwiches.

eggs

Foodstuff that female fowl, especially hens, produce by laying; there are many ways of preparing them: e.g., soft-boiled, scrambled and in omelettes.

ostrich egg
The largest of all eggs, it can weigh up to 5 lbs; one ostrich egg makes an omelette large enough to feed 10 people.

goose egg
These relatively large eggs weigh on average 1/3 lbs.; they are rarely found for sale.

quail egg
Very popular in China and Japan, it is usually eaten hard-boiled, often as an appetizer; it also has decorative uses.

duck egg
Used in Asian cuisine, it has a higher protein and fat content and sometimes a stronger taste than a chicken's egg.

pheasant egg
Rounder and smaller than a chick egg, it is not readily available; it mostly eaten hard-boiled, in sala or aspics.

hen egg
By far the most commonly eaten, is cooked as is or added to recipe used alone, the word "egg" refers hen's egg.

meat

Flesh of slaughter animals, consumed as food; a distinction is usually made between red meat, such as beef and lamb, and white meat, such as veal and pork.

Rock Cornish hen
chicken with thin and delicate
produced by crossing white
uth Rock and Cornish hens.

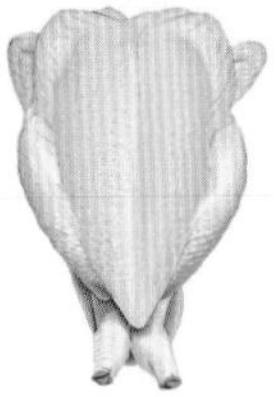

chicken
The offspring of a hen, from 4 to 12 months old; it is cheap, tasty and can be prepared in numerous ways, thus it is the most popular type of poultry.

duck
The magret, or breast meat, can be roasted, fried or smoked; they are force-fed to produce foie gras.

poultry
Term that refers to barnyard fowl, most of which have been domesticated for centuries and are now mass-produced.

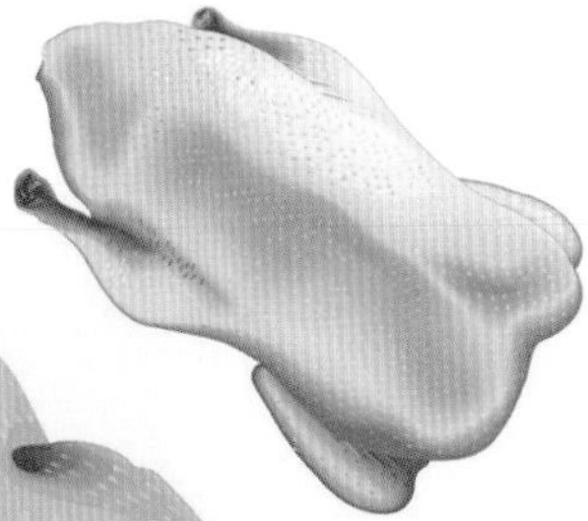

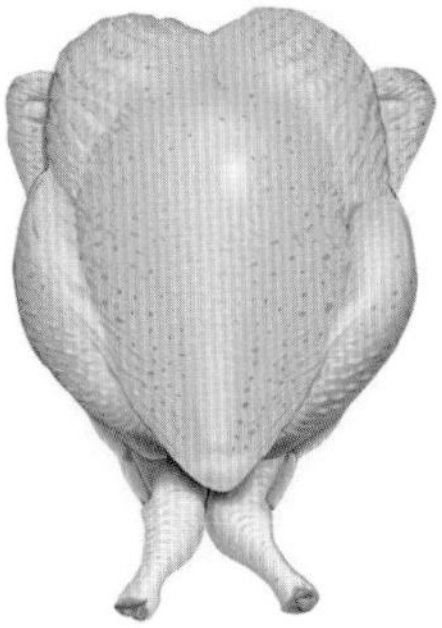

capon
Young rooster, castrated and fattened for slaughter; it grows to twice the size of a chicken yet has tender juicy meat.

turkey
Prepared like chicken although its meat is drier; in North America, turkey with stuffing is the traditional Thanksgiving and Christmas meal.

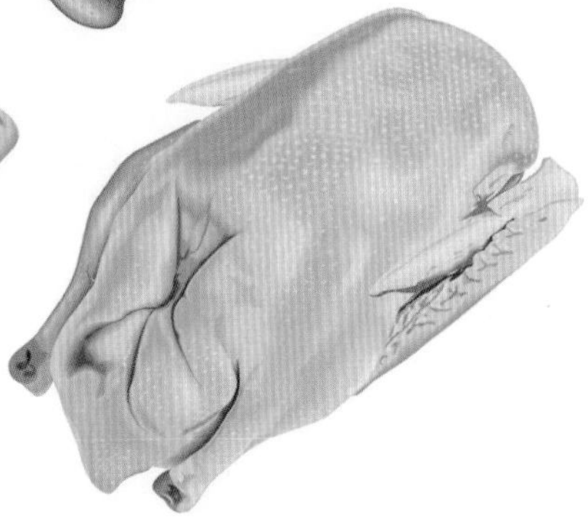

goose
Geese are often force-fed to produce foie gras. Roasted goose is often stuffed and served with a fruit sauce; goose stuffed with chestnuts is a classic European dish.

hare
e dark meat has a stronger flavor than
bit meat. Young hares can be roasted
autéed; older ones are marinated, then
ugged or made into terrine or pâté.

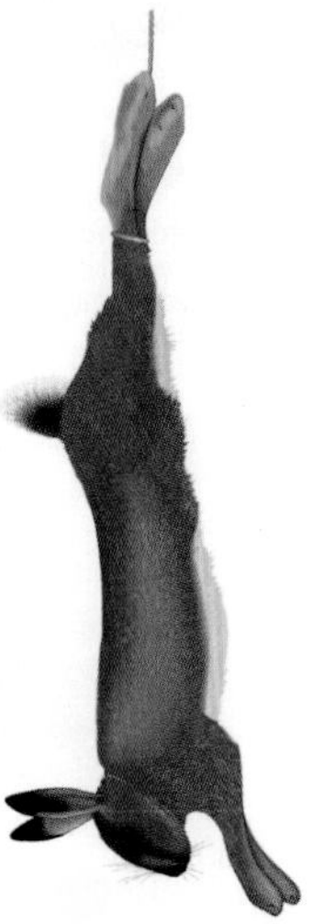

rabbit
Wild rabbit has a more pronounced flavor than domesticated rabbit, which tastes like chicken; it is often prepared with a mustard sauce.

game
Wild animals that can legally be hunted and eaten as food; includes large and small game animals and game birds.

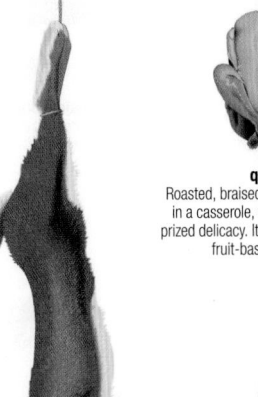

quail
Roasted, braised, broiled or cooked in a casserole, this small bird is a prized delicacy. It is often served with fruit-based sauces.

partridge
Partridge meat is low in fat and dries out quickly when cooked. The meat of the young partridge is more tender than that of the adult.

pigeon
Eaten since ancient times, pigeon is broiled, sautéed or roasted, or braised when the bird is mature; it is traditionally served with green peas.

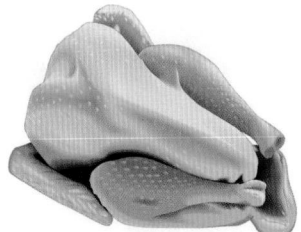

guinea fowl
The same size as a small chicken, it is more flavorful when young and weighs less than 2 lbs; its flesh is slightly gamy.

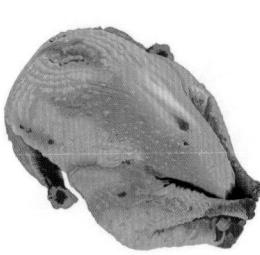

pheasant
Young pheasant are often broiled and served with a moist stuffing; as they age, they become dry and less tender and so are usually made into terrine or pâté.

meat

cuts of beef
Carcass of a large bovine, quartered and cut into ready-to-cook pieces.

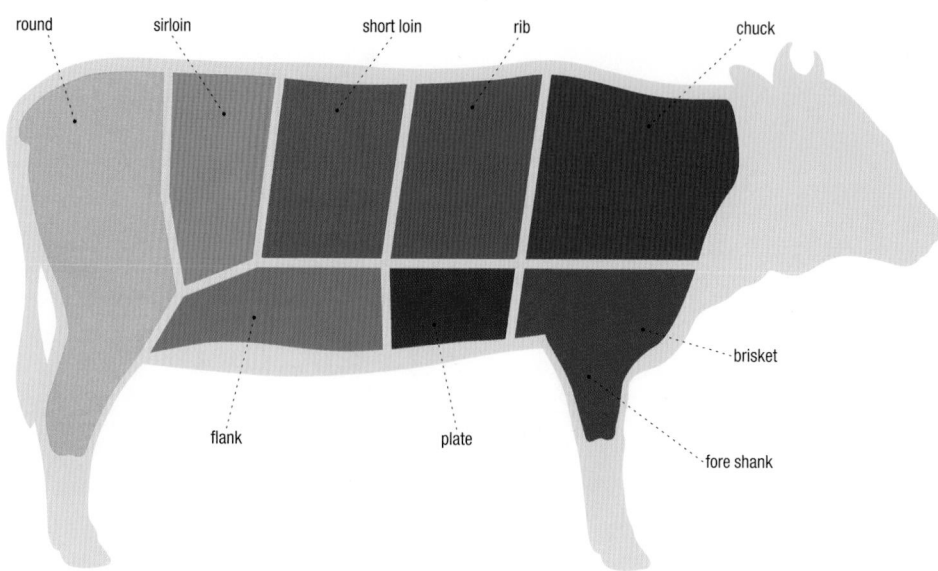

round   sirloin   short loin   rib   chuck

brisket

flank   plate   fore shank

examples of pieces
The flavor and tenderness of beef
varies greatly depending on the
origin of the piece.

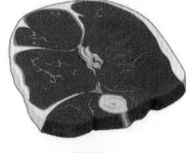

round steak
Thin slice from the hindquarter,
usually grilled or pan fried.

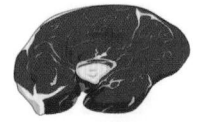

sirloin steak
Thin slice from the loin, usually
grilled.

T-bone steak
Relatively thick and tender slice
from the loin, prepared grilled
or fried.

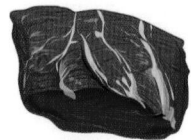

Chateaubriand
Slice of beef fillet cut from the
heart of the fillet.

tenderloin roast
Piece taken from along the spinal
column, prized for its tenderness.

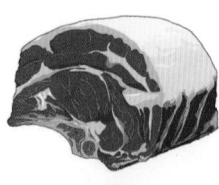

rib roast
Piece of meat intended for roasting,
taken from the animal's rib section;
this tender and tasty cut is one of the
most popular kinds of roast beef.

back ribs
They comprise sections of rib taken
from the back and the attached
muscles; they are often served with
a sweet-and-sour sauce.

cross rib roast
Piece of shoulder meat, usually
made as pot roast.

flank steak
Flavorful piece from the abdominal
section (flank), with a stringy
texture. Usually prepared grilled
or fried.

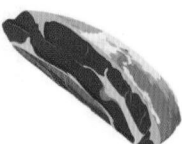

skirt steak
Slice taken from the plate, usually
grilled.

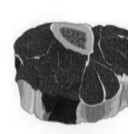

shank
Comes from a section of th
or hind leg of a steer; som
tough, it is primarily used in

meat

cuts of veal
Carcass of a calf of typically four months or younger, quartered and cut into ready-to-cook pieces.

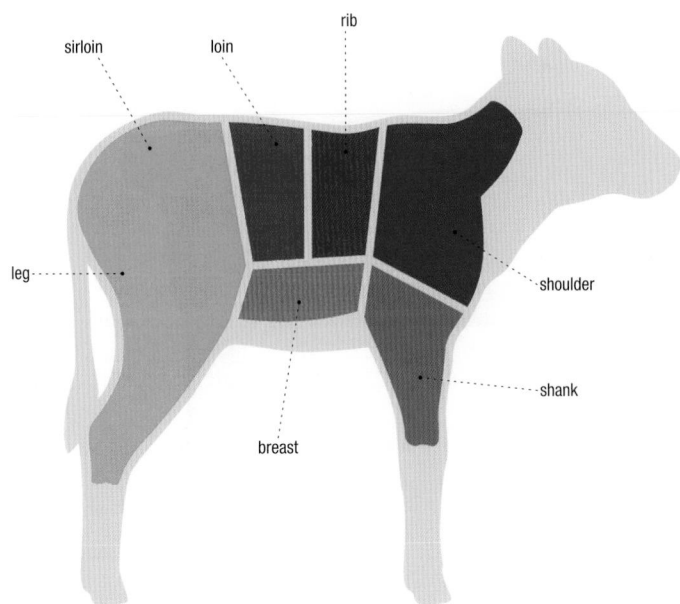

sirloin

loin

rib

leg

shoulder

shank

breast

examples of pieces
Veal is a tender and delicate meat ranging from pink to almost white in color.

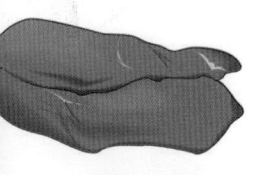

cutlet
Thin slice of very lean, boneless meat.

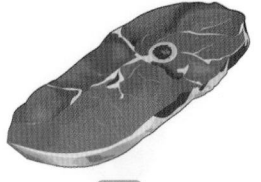

round steak
Sliced from the upper part of the leg, for grilling or frying.

loin chop
Sliced from the lower ribs for grilling.

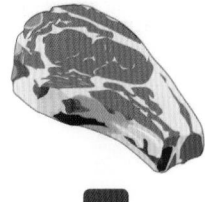

rib chop
Sliced from the upper ribs for grilling.

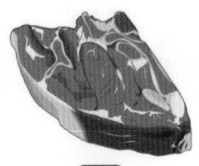

blade roast
Piece of meat for roasting, taken from the shoulder and left on the bone.

boneless shoulder roast
Piece of meat for roasting, taken from the shoulder and separated from the bone.

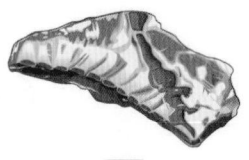

breast
Piece of meat for roasting that includes the lower end of the ribs.

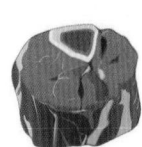

shank
Comes from a section of the front or hind leg of a calf; when sliced, it is primarily used to make the Italian dish called osso bucco.

meat

cuts of lamb
Carcass of a lamb of less than one year, quartered and cut into ready-to-cook pieces.

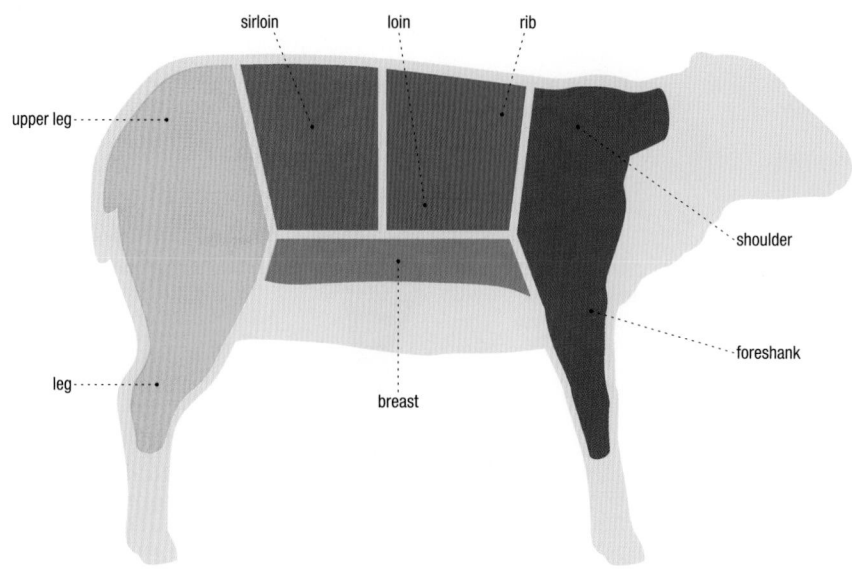

sirloin

loin

rib

upper leg

shoulder

foreshank

leg

breast

examples of pieces
Lamb is a lean red meat with a distinctive flavor, and is widely eaten especially in parts of Europe and the Middle East.

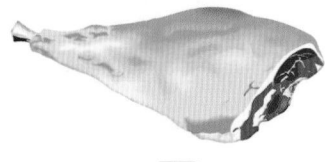

leg roast
Piece of meat for roasting taken from the thigh. It is a traditional Easter dish in some countries.

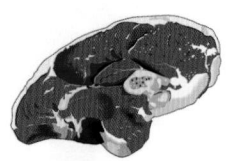

arm chop
Slice of lamb meat from the upper arm on the bone, usually grilled.

rib chop
Piece composed of a rib bone and the attached muscles, usually eaten grilled.

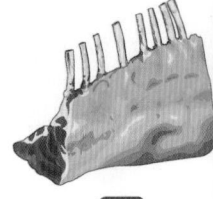

rib roast
Also known as rack of lamb, this piece from the rib section is meant for roasting.

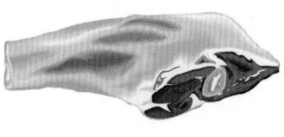

shank
Section of the front or hind leg of a lamb, often served braised.

boneless shoulder roast
Deboned piece from the shoulder, meant for roasting.

lamb belly
Fatty piece from the belly that is usually braised.

meat

cuts of pork
Carcass of a pig, quartered and cut into ready-to-cook pieces.

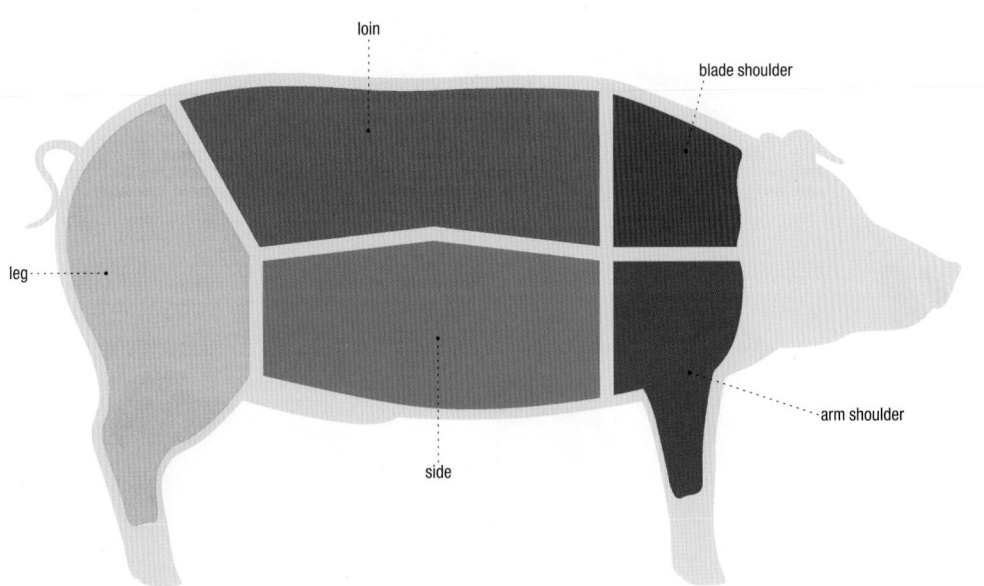

loin

blade shoulder

leg

arm shoulder

side

examples of pieces
The most tender cuts come from the loin. Cuts from the side, leg, and shoulder are less tender.

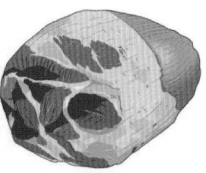

smoked ham
Taken from the pig's legs, this cut is preserved by smoking; it is sold as is, boned or sliced and can be prepared in numerous ways.

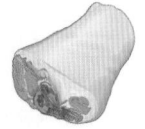

hock
Also called "shank end", it comes from the lower section of the pig's front or hind leg; it is used to make the traditional pork hock stew.

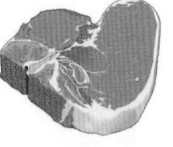

pork chop
Piece composed of a bone from the rib section and the attached muscles; some, like the butterfly chop, are sold boned.

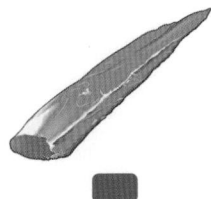

tenderloin
Piece from the back of the pig, usually roasted or stuffed and grilled.

blade roast
Piece taken from the shoulder of the pig, usually oven roasted.

spareribs
They comprise sections of rib taken from the back and the attached muscles; North American-style Chinese cooking usually serves them with sweet-and-sour sauce.

smoked picnic roast
Piece taken from the shoulder of the pig, smoked by the butcher. Usually grilled or eaten in sandwiches.

meat

meat presentation
The butcher cuts or prepares the meat in sections for use in cooking.

ground meat
Piece of meat passed through a grinder to be cut into soft bits.

meatballs
Small balls of spiced ground meat, used mainly in sauces and stews.

medaillon
Round or oval slices of meat, of varying thickness.

tournedos
Slice of beef cut from the fillet, often wrapped in pork fat or bacon.

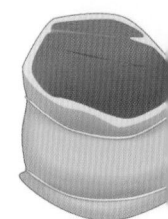

noisette
A small round slice of veal, la beef cut usually cut from the

aiguillette
Long and thin slice of beef or poultry.

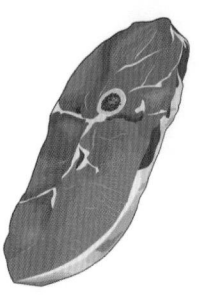

round steak
A steak cut from the round of beef, including the bone.

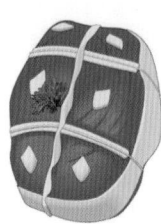

paupiette
Thin slice of meat rolled around stuffing (diced herbs, vegetables and meat) poached, steam-cooked, or oven roasted.

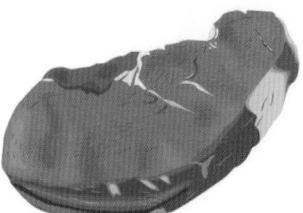

steak
Rather thin piece of meat of no specific shape.

cubes
Pieces of meat cut into sm squares, used in preparing ka or in stews.

variety meat
Edible parts of slaughter animals, apart from the meat.

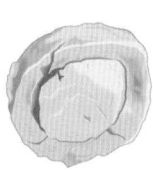

marrow
Soft fatty tissue found in the centre of bones; it is served mainly with roast beef and cardons and can also be used to add flavor to soups.

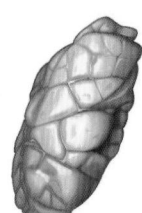

sweetbread
Designates the tender, delicately flavored thymus gland of calves, lambs and kids; veal sweetbreads are especially prized.

heart
Cooked in ragouts and casseroles, it can also be sautéed, roasted, braised or simmered; veal, lamb and chicken heart are the most popular.

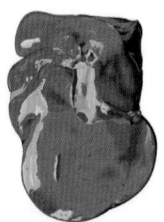

liver
People eat the liver of slaughter animals, poultry, game and some fish (cod); it has a high iron content.

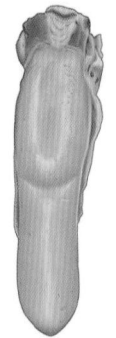

tongue
Covered with a thick skin that lifts off easily once cooked; calf tongue is the most tender.

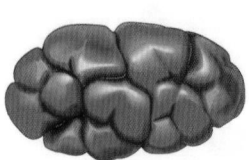

kidney
Young slaughter animals such as calves tend to have more tender kidneys; there is an unpleasant aftertaste if they are not prepared carefully.

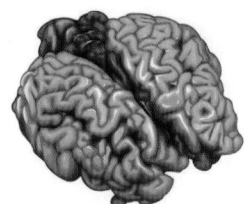

brain
Lamb, sheep and veal brains are the most prized, served in salads, au gratin, in croquettes, stuffings and sauces.

tripe
Ruminants' stomach lining, made ready for cooking; the main ingredient in many regional dishes, the best known being tripes à la mode de Caen.

delicatessen

Foodstuff made from the meat (usually pork) or offal of various animals; among the many different varieties, some are ready to eat; some need to be cooked.

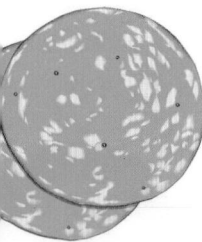

mortadella
Italian sausage made with
meat and fat and flavored with
ppercorns and often pistachios.

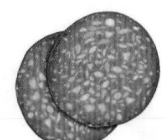

kielbasa
Native to Poland, it is made with
coarsely ground pork and beef,
seasoned with garlic and spices.

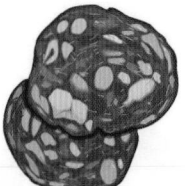

Genoa salami
Dry Italian sausage made with a
mixture of pork, veal and fat; the thin
slices are often served as an hors
d'oeuvre.

foie gras
Goose or duck liver, abnormally
enlarged by force-feeding; considered
a gourmet item, it is sold raw or ready
to eat.

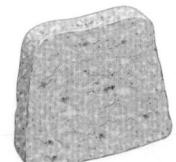

rillettes
Often made with pork or goose meat
and cooked in fat until the meat
disintegrates; they are always served
cold.

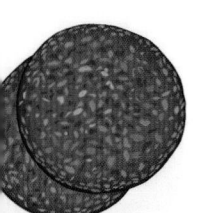

German salami
with finely ground beef and pork,
usually served sliced, as an hors
vre, but also on pizza and canapés
and in sandwiches.

blood sausage
Cooked sausage made from blood and
suet (usually from pigs) bound with crumbs
or a grain and seasoned with onions and
spices.

Boudin blanc
A light-colored sausage made usually
from cooked pork and various organ
meats, often milk, and seasoned with
onions and spices. In Louisiana, it often
includes rice.

pepperoni
This dry, somewhat spicy Italian
sausage is a favorite pizza topping;
diced, it is added to certain dishes to
give them more flavor.

chorizo
Semidry Spanish sausage seasoned
with red chiles, available in several
versions that vary in spiciness; it is
often added to paella.

Toulouse sausage
aw sausage, native to France,
ade with coarsely ground pork
and pepper; often added to
cassoulet.

merguez
Small, highly spiced sausage made with lamb,
beef or mutton; popular in North Africa and
Spain, it is usually eaten fried or grilled.

andouillette
Cooked sausage made from pig or
calf intestines; it can be grilled or
fried and served with mustard.

chipolata
Raw pork, or pork and beef, sausage
characteristically flavored with cloves;
it is often grilled or fried.

frankfurter
Smoked precooked sausage that is native
to Germany and made from a pastelike
pork mixture; among its many versions is
the American hot dog.

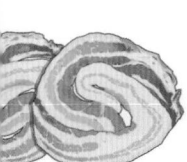

pancetta
ed Italian bacon, sometimes
it is an essential ingredient in
alla carbonara and also flavors
es, soups and meat dishes.

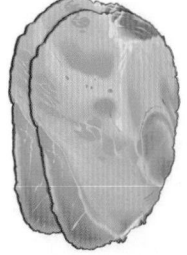

cooked ham
Salt-cured and cooked pork meat, usually
served thinly sliced; it is eaten hot or cold,
especially in sandwiches, and on croque-
monsieurs and canapés.

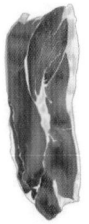

prosciutto
Raw dried ham native to the Parma
region of Italy; it is mostly eaten thinly
sliced and served with melon or fresh
figs.

Canadian bacon
Piece of salted, usually smoked, meat
from the pork loin; often consumed with
eggs, added to dishes such as quiches
and omelettes.

bacon
Salted and smoked side pork, cut
into thin slices; in North America,
it is traditionally served with eggs,
for breakfast.

FOOD AND KITCHEN

cereal products

Cereals that have been processed in various ways to make ground (flour, semolina), unground (rice) or manufactured products (bread, pasta, noodles).

flour and semolina
Products obtained by grinding grains and cereals; semolina is usually coarser and more granular than flour. Without a modifier, these words generally refer to wheat.

semolina
Refers to the granular flour derived from hard wheat, used to make pasta; fine semolina can also be eaten as a cereal (cream of wheat).

all-purpose flour
This blend of ground hard and soft wheat has many uses, but is primarily used to thicken sauces or to make bread and pastry.

whole-wheat flour
Because it is produced by grinding the entire grain, none of the nutrients is lost; the grain's outer layer, known as bran, gives it a brownish color.

unbleached flour
Like white flour, it comes from grinding wheat grains from which the bran and germ have been removed, but it is not artificially whitened.

corn flour
Primarily added to crepe, cake, m[...] and bread mixes; it must be comb[...] with wheat flour if the mixture [...] intended to rise.

wheat germ
Embryo of the wheat kernel, rich in fats, vitamins and proteins. Used to make oil or added to cereal, bread, muffins and pastries.

couscous
Hard wheat semolina that is formed into grains and used to prepare an eponymous dish of the Maghreb; it is traditionally steamed over broth.

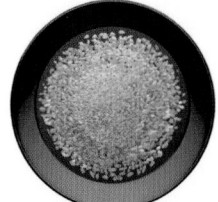

bulgur
Whole wheat grain that has been soaked, cooked, dried, and cracked into small pieces. Some of the bran is removed after drying. It has a nutty taste and is commonly used in tabbouleh.

buckwheat flour
Ground from the seed of an herb and not from wheat, it is gluten-free and does not rise when cooked. It is used mainly in noodles, biscuits, cookies, pancakes and blinis.

oat flour
Since it does not rise during cook[...] it must be combined with wheat [...] to make bread and other leaven[...] products; it makes these produ[...] heavier.

bread
Food made from flour, water and salt, often containing an agent (leaven or yeast) that makes it rise.

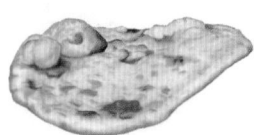

naan
The yogurt often used in this soft light sweetish bread helps it rise. Traditionally baked in a tandoor oven, it is eaten plain or stuffed.

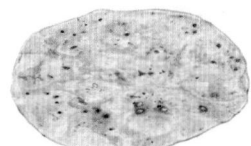

chapati
Flat crusty unleavened bread usually made of whole wheat flour. It is eaten warm and often broken into pieces to be used as a scoop for food.

tortilla
Disk of unleavened bread made with cornmeal or wheat flour that is the basis for many Latin-American dishes; it can be eaten plain or with a filling or topping.

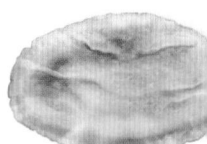

pita bread
Flat bread originally from the Middle East; its crust forms a [...] pocket that can be filled with hot [...] cold kinds of stuffing.

matzo
Light and crusty unleavened bread, eaten mainly during Jewish Passover; it has a long shelf life.

Danish rye bread
This bread is usually sweeter and lighter than German rye bread; it often contains molasses.

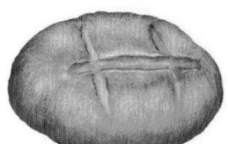

sourdough bread
Its thick, often floury crust and slightly acidic-tasting interior can last a long time without becoming stale; it can be used in a variety of ways.

Russian black bread
Made with a mixture of wheat and [...] flour, it has a thin but resilient cru[...] goes well with soups and ragou[...]

French bread
ong crusty loaf resembling an
ersized baguette; it stays fresh
mewhat longer than the typical
baguette.

baguette
This light crusty, typically French bread is
often served with a meal and also goes
well with cheese and pâté; it must be
eaten fresh.

epi bread
Baguette made so it can be easily
broken into pieces by hand.

bagel
Ring-shaped roll that is cooked by first
boiling then baking. It is commonly topped
with sesame or poppy seeds and served
warm often with cream cheese.

pumpernickel
Made from rye flour, this dense strong-
tasting bread goes particularly well with
seafood and smoked foods.

challah
Light soft sweetish bread traditionally
served on the Sabbath and other
Jewish festivals; it is usually braided.

croissant
A small roll of layered or puffed dough,
frequently eaten as a plain or stuffed
pastry; it is also used to make hors
d'oeuvres and sandwiches.

corn bread
ornmeal-based bread that is
den on the inside. A particular
orite in the south of the United
States.

whole wheat bread
Because it is made with whole
wheat flour, it is highly nutritious
and contains more minerals and
protein than white bread.

multigrain bread
Usually contains 80% white flour,
whole wheat flour or a mixture of the
two, to which other cereals (oats, rye,
etc.) are added.

German rye bread
Dark dense bread with a strong, slightly
acidic taste, made with rye and wheat
flour; it has a long shelf life.

brioche
Rich sweet bread made with eggs,
butter and milk.

bread loaf
Bread with a thin crust and chewy,
very white inside. Mostly eaten sliced,
in sandwiches.

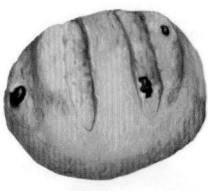

soda bread
The crust of this bread is marked with
a cross; it is made with baking powder,
which gives it a cakelike consistency.

Greek bread
Round loaf with a golden crust,
sometimes sprinkled with sesame
seeds; olive bread is one of its
many variants.

bread crumbs
Culinary product made mainly of fresh
or dried and crumbled bread, used
for breading, thickening sauces, or
topping au gratin dishes.

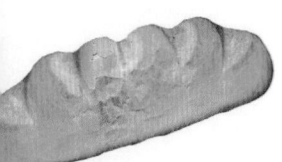

white bread
read made with white flour that comes in a
riety of shapes, thickness and textures; it is
less nutritious than whole wheat bread.

rye cracker
Thin crusty flat bread made
with rye flour, usually eaten with
cheese.

cracker
Thin crusty flat bread usually eaten with cheese.

phyllo
Flexible wafer-thin dough of
Greek origin, used to prepare hors
d'oeuvres and pastries, such as
baklava.

dairy products

Foods produced by processing fresh milk; they are used daily in Western countries, where they are known for their high calcium content.

yogurt
Semisolid substance produced by milk fermentation and the action of bacterial cultures; it can be eaten as is or cooked.

ghee
Clarified butter originating in Asia and traditionally made from buffalo milk; it is very popular in India and in Arab countries.

butter
Fatty rich substance produced by churning cream; it is used in cooking or is added to various recipes for sauces, pastries and creams.

cream
This product is obtained by skimming milk and is classified according to its milk fat content; it is used extensively in cooking, as is or whipped.

whipping cream
With a minimum 30% milk fat content, this is the richest cream; it is often whipped and used to make and decorate various desserts, such as cream puffs.

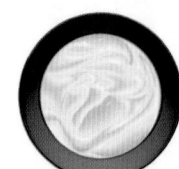

sour cream
Has a thick and creamy consiste and is obtained by fermentation bacterial action; it can be used to or garnish recipes.

milk
Highly nutritious white liquid secreted by some domesticated female mammals and consumed as food; used alone, the word refers to cow's milk.

cow's milk
The most commonly consumed milk, usually marketed pasteurized. Used as a drink or in the kitchen in soups, sauces, desserts, etc.

goat's milk
Whiter and stronger-tasting than cow's milk, it is also easier to digest.

milk forms
Milk comes in different forms for consumption.

homogenized milk
Milk processed so the fat partic remain suspended instead of ris to the surface; varieties includ whole, partially skimmed or ski

buttermilk
Tangy liquid that separates from cream during churning; today, commercial buttermilk is made by adding bacterial culture to milk.

evaporated milk
Milk from which a significant percentage of the water has been evaporated; it has a high milk fat content and is used primarily for making desserts.

powdered milk
Dehydrated milk that can be sto for one year without refrigeratio the container remains unopene

goat's-milk cheeses
Cheeses made from goat's milk, which is sometimes mixed with cow's milk; these medium-strong cheeses have a smooth texture and a high water content.

fresh goat cheese
Fresh rindless cheese that has a tangy, mild taste; it is sometimes flavored with herbs.

Crottin de Chavignol
Soft French cheese with a rind that is covered in mold; it is eaten fresh or dried and, as it dries, its flavor becomes more pronounced.

feta
Soft white cheese ripened in brine, made from sheep's, goat's or cow's milk.

fresh cheeses
Nonripened cheeses that contain up to 80% water; they are smooth and mild or slightly tangy; they spoil quickly.

cottage cheese
Low in fat and grainy in texture; it works well as a spread or can be added to salads, desserts and sauces.

mozzarella
This native Italian cheese has a rubbery texture and is firmer than other cheeses; it is the garnish of choice for pizza.

ricotta
Granular cheese with a smooth moist rind; it is used in Italian cooking, primarily for stuffed foods and desserts.

cream cheese
Made with cream, which is sometimes mixed with milk; it is smooth and spreads easily, and is used as a spread or as a dessert ingredient (e.g., in cheesecake).

dairy products

pressed cheeses
Ripened cheeses that are also cooked and pressed and contain less than 35% moisture; they usually have a firm compact texture and a hard rind.

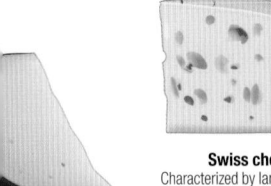

Swiss cheese
Characterized by large holes, this mild Swiss cheese is very popular in fondues and au gratin dishes.

Edam
cheese originally from
and, usually coated in
d paraffin wax.

Romano
Native to Rome, this dry granular cheese is made from cow, ewe or goat's milk or a mixture of all three; it is mostly used in grated form.

raclette
Cheese specifically made to be used in a traditional eponymous dish that originated in the Valais region of Switzerland.

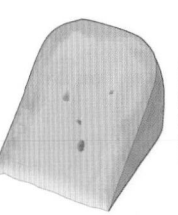

Gouda
Fatty cow's milk cheese from Gouda, Holland, usually coated in yellow or red paraffin wax. Its rather firm flesh contains scattered holes.

Gruyère
Swiss cheese with small holes called "eyes" and a medium-sweet taste; extensively used in cooking, either as is, grated or melted.

cheddar
tty cheese made from
lk. It has a mild flavor
omes sharper with age.

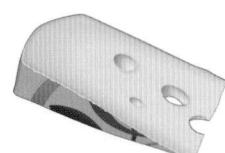

Jarlsberg
Norwegian cheese with large holes that has a characteristic nutty taste.

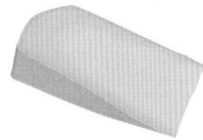

Oka
Firm cow's milk cheese with a strong odor and orange rind, made by the Trappist monks of Oka, Quebec.

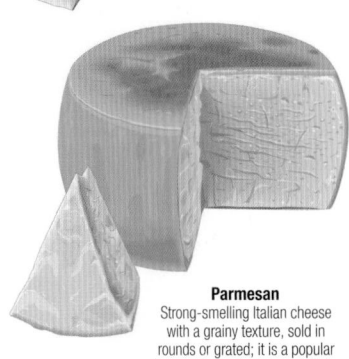

Parmesan
Strong-smelling Italian cheese with a grainy texture, sold in rounds or grated; it is a popular flavoring ingredient, especially for pasta dishes.

blue cheeses
Also called "blue cheese", it usually has a crumbly texture, is veined with mold and has a pungent peppery taste.

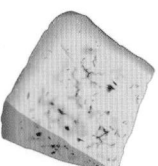

Roquefort
The best-known blue cheese, originally from Roquefort, France; it is made from ewe's milk and goes well with pears, cream and butter.

Stilton
English cheese with a firm but creamy texture; it is often served with crackers and port.

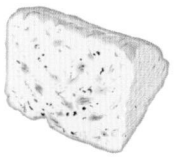

Danish blue
Native to Denmark, it has a pungent flavor, a creamy texture and a milk fat content of up to 60%.

Gorgonzola
Native to Italy and recognizable by its textured gray rind, spotted with red.

soft cheeses
Ripened but neither pressed nor cooked, these cheeses have a soft, creamy texture and a somewhat velvety rind, which is often edible.

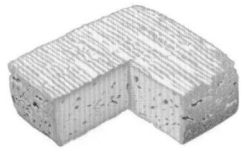

Pont-l'Évêque
Somewhat soft cheese with a pronounced odor; its name derives from the town in Normandy where it is made.

Coulommiers
Native to the area around Paris, it is similar to Brie but smaller; it contains from 45% to 50% milk fat.

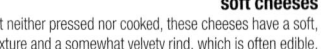

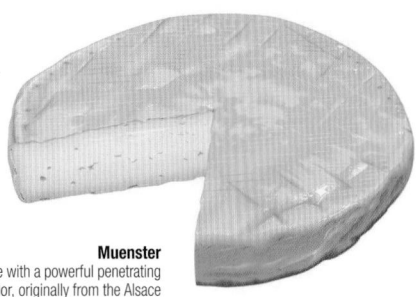

Muenster
Cheese with a powerful penetrating odor, originally from the Alsace region; it has a creamy texture and a smooth moist rind.

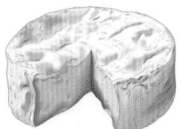

Camembert
Soft and easy to spread, France's most famous cheese is smaller and slightly firmer than Brie.

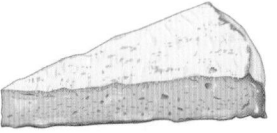

Brie
Native to Brie, near Paris, it is one of the best-known French cheeses; among its many varieties is the one from Meaux.

pasta

Made from hard wheat semolina and water, shaped into various forms and usually dried; they are bought ready-made.

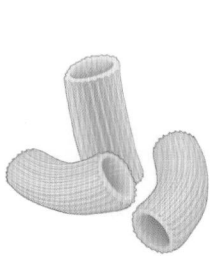

rigatoni
This fairly large tubular pasta is suitable for serving with all kinds of sauces because they cling to it readily.

ravioli
Pasta stuffed with meat, cheese or vegetables; a classic way to serve it is with tomato sauce, sprinkled with grated Parmesan.

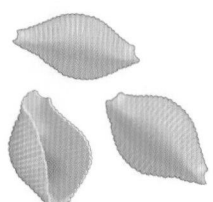

conchiglie
Small shell-shaped pasta that can be served with a sauce or added to soup or pasta salads.

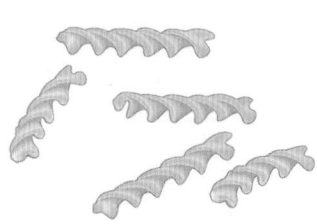

fusilli
This spiral-shaped pasta is thinner and longer than rotini, but can replace it in most recipes.

spaghetti
One of the best-known forms pasta and the most extensive used; it is traditionally served w tomato or meat sauce.

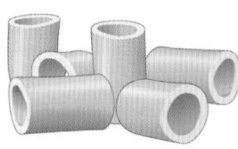

ditali
Short tube-shaped pasta that resemble fat macaroni, used especially in broth and vegetable soups.

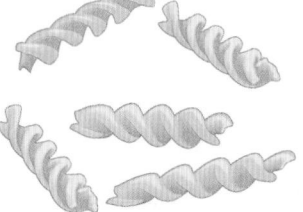

rotini
Because of its spiral grooves, it readily holds meat, cheese and vegetable sauces; it is also ideal for salads.

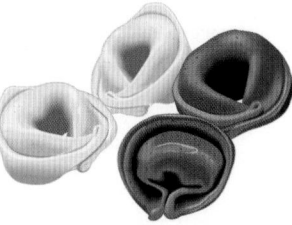

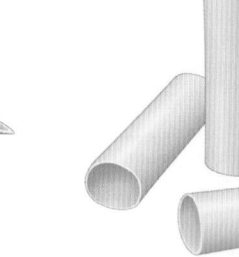

tortellini
Pasta stuffed with meat or cheese and sometimes colored with tomato or spinach; often served with tomato or cream sauce.

spaghettini
Thinner than spaghetti but thicke angel hair pasta or vermicelli no often served with delicate sau

elbow macaroni
Sometimes used in a salad, this type of macaroni is also served with tomato or cheese sauce.

penne
Tube-shaped pasta with diagonally cut ends, often served with a spicy tomato sauce in a dish called penne all'arrabiata.

cannelloni
This fairly large tubular pasta is usually stuffed with meat or cheese, covered with tomato sauce and baked au gratin.

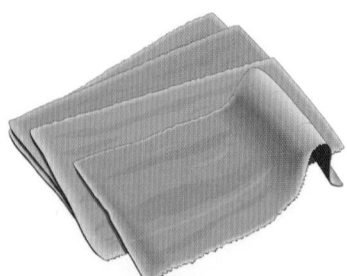

lasagna
These wide strips, green if spinach-flavored, are combined with a filling in alternate layers to create the eponymous dish.

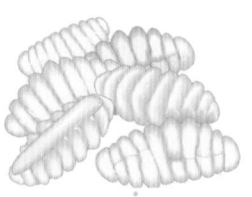

gnocchi
Often made from a potato or semolina dough with eggs and cheese; it is usually served au gratin, as an appetizer.

spinach tagliatelle
Flat ribbonlike pasta made with spinach and eggs, often served with meat sauce or cream sauce.

fettucine
Thicker but not as wide a tagliatelle, this pasta is oft served with Alfredo sauc

Asian noodles

This pasta is a staple of Asian cooking; generally classified according to its main ingredient: wheat, rice, buckwheat or mung beans.

soba
es made from buckwheat
ery popular in Japan, where
re often served cold, with
soy sauce.

somen
Fine whitish Japanese wheat
noodles that are often used in
salads and soups.

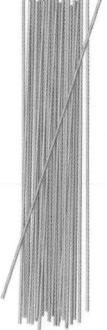

udon
These Japanese wheat noodles are
thicker than somen noodles; among their
various uses, they can be added to soup,
salads and sautéed dishes.

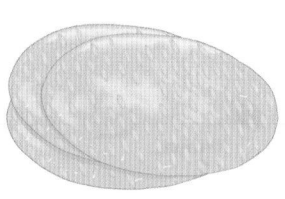

rice papers
Thin semitransparent sheets made
with rice flour, used in Asia to
prepare spring and imperial rolls.

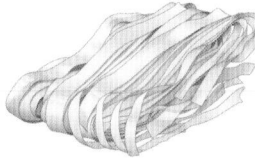

rice noodles
Wide ribbons made with rice flour
and water; they are often added
to soup.

bean threads
parent noodles made with
bean flour; before adding
to a recipe, they must be
d in hot or warm water. The
dles can also be deep fried
and added to salads.

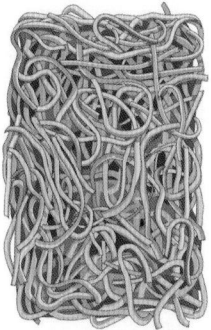

chow mein noodles
Wheat noodles made with eggs;
they are boiled in water, then fried
and used to make chow mein.

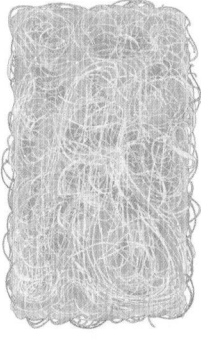

rice vermicelli
Fine rice noodles that are fried in oil
and shaped into a nest that is filled
with various kinds of Asian food.

wonton skins
Delicate sheets of wheat pasta that
are stuffed with meat, seafood or
vegetables; an essential ingredient in
wonton soup.

ramen
Thick egg noodle, straight or wavy.
It is quick to cook and served in
broth with meat and vegetables.

rice

Rice is commercially classified by the shape of the grain and the processing it has undergone before being packaged.

white rice
Milled rice from which the bran
and germ have been removed; it is
often enriched to compensate for
the loss of nutrients.

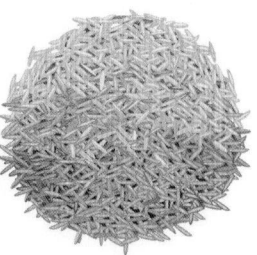

brown rice
Because it is not hulled, the grains
retain the bran and germ; it is highly
nutritious and has a stronger flavor
than white rice.

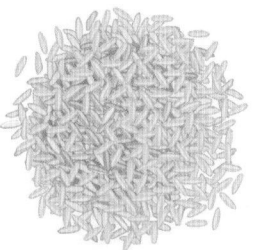

parboiled rice
More nutritious than white rice, it has
undergone a steam pressure process
prior to milling, to preserve the
grains' vitamin and mineral content.

basmati rice
Variety of fine-grained rice native to
India, it is known and prized for its
aroma and light texture.

soybean products

Food products made from soy.

soybean oil
Light and smooth yellowish oil extracted from soybeans. Widely used in processed foods. Used for cooking as well as unheated as a seasoning.

soybeans
Used mainly for their oil. High in protein, the beans are made into a variety of products, and produce a kind of milk mainly used to make tofu. When fermented, they are the main ingredient in soy sauce.

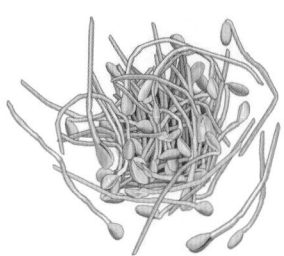

soybean sprouts
After sprouting for a few days they are ready to be eaten, either raw or lightly cooked; they are characteristic of Chinese cooking.

soy milk
Liquid obtained by grinding soybeans that have been soaked in water. Consumed plain or with added flavoring.

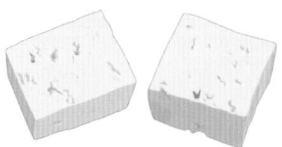

tofu
Protein-rich Asian food product, made from soy milk. It absorbs the flavor of the other ingredients in dishes.

fats and oils

Animal or vegetable fatty acids in solid or liquid form generally used to cook, flavor, thicken or preserve foods.

corn oil
Has relatively little flavor or odor; one of the most ubiquitous oils, used for cooking, frying and seasoning foods.

olive oil
This extract derived from olive pulp is essential to Mediterranean cooking, both for preparing and seasoning recipes.

sunflower oil
This delicately flavored oil is the main ingredient in margarine and dressings; it is also used for frying sweet foods.

peanut oil
Heat-resistant, mild-tasting oil equally well suited to frying and to dressing salads.

sesame oil
Very popular in Asian cooking and characterized by its rich delicate toasted-nut flavor; it is not well suited to high temperatures.

shortening
Substance produced by rendering pork fat; it is used for the lengthy cooking of certain ragouts, and for frying and for making pastry.

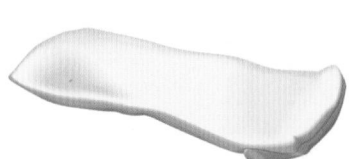

lard
Pork fat; fatback is rendered into shortening whereas side pork (fat streaked with lean) provides lardons and bacon.

margarine
Soft food product usually made from emulsified vegetable oil and skim milk and used as a substitute for butter.

sugar

Sweet-tasting foodstuff derived from certain plants; the most common varieties of sugar come from sugarcane and sugar beets.

granulated sugar
e most commonly used sugar
cooking and baking; it is white,
refined and composed of small
crystals.

powdered sugar
White sugar in powdered form,
containing about 3% corn or wheat
starch, added to prevent caking; it is
used mainly for icing and decorating.

superfine sugar
Sugar obtained by grinding and
sieving crystallized white sugar.

molasses
Thick liquid residue from the process
of converting sugarcane into sugar;
it is used to make rum, candy, soft
cookies and pies.

corn syrup
Thick sweet syrup used extensively
in making candy and pastry.

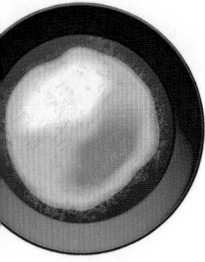

vanilla sugar
gar to which vanilla beans have
en added for flavor. Mainly used
in pastries and cakes.

brown sugar
Fine, only slightly refined sugar crystals
that still contain molasses; it has a
stronger taste than white sugar.

honey
Substance made by bees from
flower nectar; its color and flavor
vary depending on the nectar's
origin.

maple syrup
Produced by reducing sugar maple sap;
it is used to make various desserts and
to accompany pancakes, poach eggs
and glaze ham.

rock candy
White or brown sugar in very large
crystal form; it is used especially to
sweeten fruits in brandy.

chocolate

Smooth paste made with cocoa and sugar, extensively used in making candy and pastry and often eaten plain, as bars or squares.

dark chocolate
ncludes semisweet and bitter chocolate,
which contain from 35% to 70% chocolate
quor; it is often used in cooking and is also
eaten plain.

milk chocolate
Made with chocolate liquor and cocoa
butter mixed with powdered milk; it
cannot be used in cooking because the
milk solids it contains burn when heated.

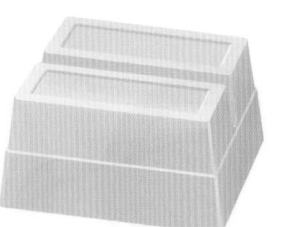

white chocolate
Made from cocoa butter, sugar and condensed or
powdered milk; it does not contain cocoa and is
often not considered a true chocolate.

cocoa
The key ingredient in chocolate; grinding
the beans of the cacao tree produces
chocolate liquor, which yields cocoa butter
and cocoa powder.

condiments

Natural or artificial substances used in cooking to bring out the flavor in a dish or to complement it.

Tabasco® sauce
Native to Louisiana, this sauce is made from crushed red chile peppers and is so pungent that a few drops are enough to season a whole dish.

miso
Salty, fermented paste made of soybeans or grain (rice or barley) mainly used to season various dishes.

Worcestershire sauce
British sauce made chiefly of vinegar, molasses, tamarind, garlic and anchovies; its robust flavor goes well in cocktails, sauces, soups and many other dishes.

caper
Bud of the caper bush, preserved in vinegar, brine, salt, or wine. Often used in mayonnaise or to garnish salads and other dishes.

vanilla extract
Aromatic substance extensively used in baking; it is often made of artificial ingredients that are less tasty than real vanilla, which is more expensive.

tamarind paste
Made from the fruit of the tamar... tree, this slightly acidic paste is u... as a foodstuff and as a condime... Asian cooking.

tomato paste
Tomato coulis reduced until it turns into a paste; it is used to make ragouts and sauces.

tomato coulis
Tomato purée of medium thickness that is served either hot or cold, as a sauce.

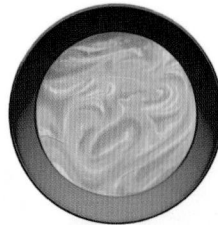

hummus
Lebanese condiment made from puréed chickpeas and sesame oil, commonly served as an hors d'oeuvre or with crudités.

tahini
Thick creamy nutty-tasting paste, made o... ground sesame seeds; it is added to sauce... and served with brochettes, bread, fruit an... vegetables.

hoisin sauce
Thick spicy sauce made from soybeans, spices, and garlic; it enhances braised foods, is served with Peking duck and is used as a marinade.

soy sauce
A key condiment in Asian cooking, this extremely salty sauce is made from soybeans and is used as a flavoring ingredient, dip or marinade.

relish
Condiment made of finely chopped vegetables (such as cucumbers, onions, tomatoes, and peppers) and sometimes fruit and mixed with vinegar, sugar, and spices.

mustard powder
Can be used as a seasoning or mixed with water to make a paste that resembles prepared mustard.

Dijon mustard
This strong mustard comes from Dijon, France; it is served with meat and is used in making sauces, salad dressings and various kinds of mayonnaise.

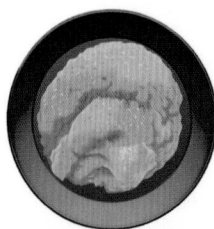

German mustard
Medium strong and slightly sweet mustard that goes well with sausages and deli meats.

English mustard
Very strong mustard, sold either prepared or powdered, traditionally served with roast beef and ham.

American mustard
Very mild, the traditional North American accompaniment to hot dogs and hamburgers; its bright yellow color comes from turmeric.

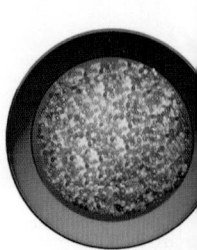

wholegrain mustard
Native to Meaux, France, this mild mustard is made from partly crus... seeds, giving it a grainy texture...

condiments

ketchup
um spicy tomato purée made from
erous different recipes; it is widely
e as a condiment or seasoning in
eat Britain and the United States.

plum sauce
Sweet-and-sour Chinese sauce
primarily served with deep-fried or
roasted dishes, such as pork and
roast duck.

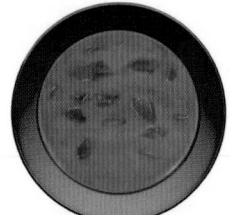

mango chutney
Thick sweet-and-sour relish,
originating in India and made with
mangoes, sugar and vinegar; it can be
served with a variety of dishes.

harissa
This chile-based purée is very popular
in the Middle East and North Africa; it is
used as is or mixed with broth and is a
key ingredient in couscous.

sambal oelek
Very spicy Indonesian sauce made from
chiles; it is used as a flavoring ingredient,
condiment or hors d'oeuvre sauce.

chili sauce
Sauce made from seasoned
matoes, often used to brush onto
eats and poultry, as an ingredient
in recipes, and as a condiment.

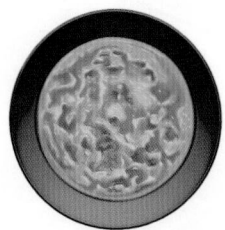

wasabi
Prepared from the root of an Asian
plant, the very pungent taste of this
condiment enhances Japanese
meat and fish dishes (sushi,
sashimi).

table salt
A standard table condiment and
also commonly used in cooking, it
is always refined.

coarse salt
This somewhat refined version is
sometimes used in cooking or to sweat
vegetables and preserve foods.

sea salt
Unlike rock salt, which is whiter and
comes from the subsoil, this usually
grayish salt is derived from seawater
through evaporation.

white balsamic vinegar
Made from white wine vinegar and aged
grape must, used as a condiment on
salads or seafood.

malt vinegar
Made from sprouted barley juice, it is
much too strong for salad dressings; it is
used instead to make mixed pickles and
chutneys.

rice vinegar
It is made from fermented rice wine
and is very popular in Asian cooking;
the Japanese version is sweet while the
Chinese one is spicier.

balsamic vinegar
nown condiment made from
t white grapes and aged in
casks; its low acidity makes it
r use in salads or in hot foods.

apple cider vinegar
Cider-based product whose strong taste
makes it unsuitable for salads; it is used
primarily for deglazing or as an ingredient
in fish and seafood dishes.

wine vinegar
White wine vinegar is less fragrant than
the red; the former goes well with fish
and seafood while the latter brings out the
flavor of blander foods.

white vinegar
Usually made from grain, it is used in
condiments (vinaigrette, mayonnaise,
mustard) or for making preserves
(marinades, pickles).

supermarket

A large self-service store that sells food and various everyday household goods; the part accessible to shoppers is surrounded by service areas reserved for storage and for preparing and preserving merchandise.

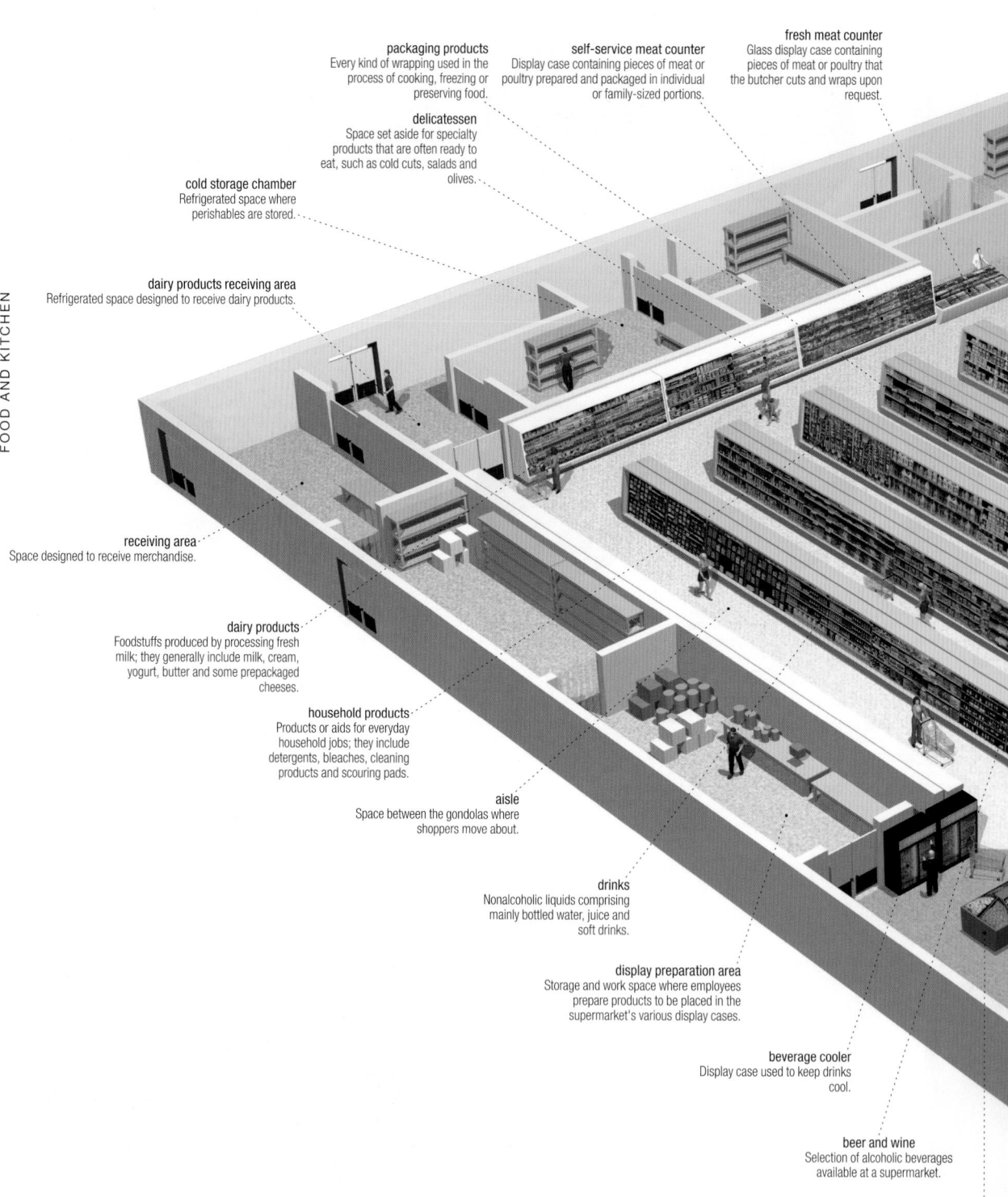

packaging products
Every kind of wrapping used in the process of cooking, freezing or preserving food.

self-service meat counter
Display case containing pieces of meat or poultry prepared and packaged in individual or family-sized portions.

fresh meat counter
Glass display case containing pieces of meat or poultry that the butcher cuts and wraps upon request.

delicatessen
Space set aside for specialty products that are often ready to eat, such as cold cuts, salads and olives.

cold storage chamber
Refrigerated space where perishables are stored.

dairy products receiving area
Refrigerated space designed to receive dairy products.

receiving area
Space designed to receive merchandise.

dairy products
Foodstuffs produced by processing fresh milk; they generally include milk, cream, yogurt, butter and some prepackaged cheeses.

household products
Products or aids for everyday household jobs; they include detergents, bleaches, cleaning products and scouring pads.

aisle
Space between the gondolas where shoppers move about.

drinks
Nonalcoholic liquids comprising mainly bottled water, juice and soft drinks.

display preparation area
Storage and work space where employees prepare products to be placed in the supermarket's various display cases.

beverage cooler
Display case used to keep drinks cool.

beer and wine
Selection of alcoholic beverages available at a supermarket.

fruits and vegeta
Plant products sold as foo in bulk or prepacka

storage chamber
Refrigerated space where
perishables are stored.

seafood
Section where fish and shellfish
are offered for sale at a self-service
counter or prepared to order.

gondola
Long unit with shelves; it is used to
display self-service products.

convenience food
Food prepared and presented in
such a way that it can be served
quickly and easily.

cheese counter
Glass display case holding a
variety of whole cheeses that the
employee cuts and wraps upon
request.

frozen food storage
Refrigerated space where frozen food is stored.

frozen foods
Various foodstuffs stored at very low
temperatures to preserve their quality
and nutritional content for as long as
possible.

prepared foods
Various foodstuffs, sometimes in individual
portions, prepared on-site or by a specialty
supplier; they are often ready to eat.

bakery
Section where bread, pastries and other
baked goods are sold, whether baked on the
premises or not.

pet food and supplies
Products used to feed and care for pets.

health and beauty care
Range of nonprescription drugs, and nonmedicated
personal hygiene, health and beauty products.

checkout
Counters with a cash register located
at the exit where shoppers pay for
their purchases.

checkout
Shoppers ready to pay for their
purchases check out at a counter
with a cash register where they are
assisted by cashiers and baggers.

cash register
Device that records the details of each
article and calculates the total amount
due. The collected sum is then placed in
the cash register drawer.

cashier
Employee who records the
purchases, receives payment and,
when necessary, gives change.

electronic payment terminal
Apparatus where shoppers can use a debit or credit
card to pay for their purchases.

shopping carts
Wheeled basket used to transport
shoppers' selected items to the
checkout and to the parking lot.

grocery bags
Paper or flexible plastic containers
in which the shoppers' purchases
are packed and carried.

endcap display
End of a gondola; it is used to
highlight certain items that are on
sale or whose sales need to be
increased.

optical scanner
Apparatus that reads the bar codes
of items and automatically displays
the price on the cash register
screen.

bagger
Employee whose main duty is to
bag the shopper's purchases and,
sometimes, to carry them out to
the shopper's car.

canned goods
Assorted foodstuffs, preserved in airtight
cans or jars using a process that allows them
to be kept for long periods of time.

restaurant

Business establishment where people pay to eat a meal prepared on the premises and served at their table; a restaurant's quality and prices vary depending on the menu.

general view

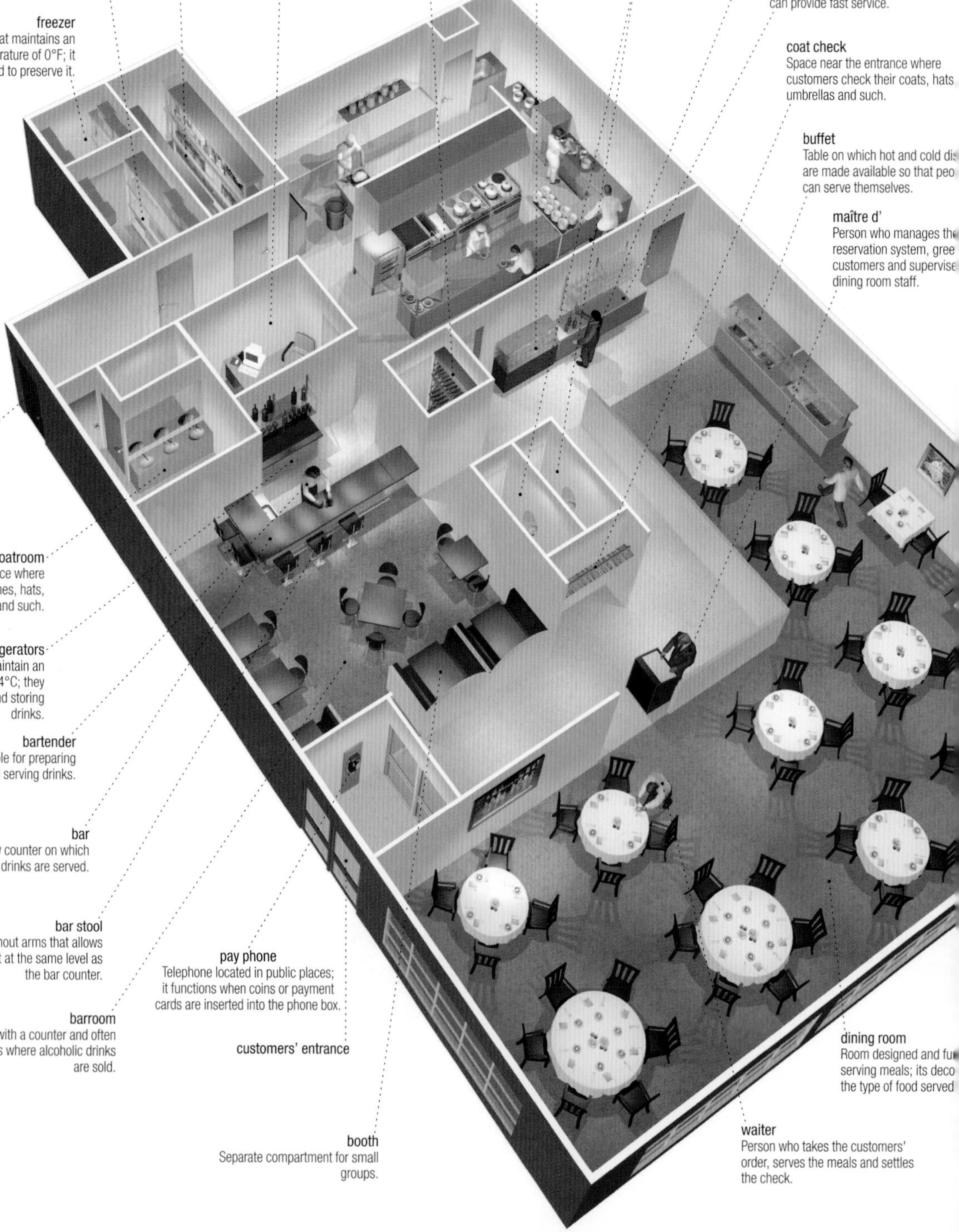

store room
Room for storing nonperishable items.

office
Workplace for administrative personnel.

refrigerated display case
Refrigerated unit for storing cold dishes that are prepared in advance.

wine steward
Person in charge of the wine cellar; the wine steward helps customers choose a wine and sometimes serves it as well.

refrigerator
Appliance that maintains an average temperature of 38°F; it is used for storing and chilling food.

wine cellar
Cabinet for keeping wine at constant temperature and humidity.

restrooms
Rooms equipped with toilets and sinks for customers' use.

service table
Furniture used for making extra utensils available to staff so they can provide fast service.

freezer
Appliance that maintains an average temperature of 0°F; it freezes food to preserve it.

coat check
Space near the entrance where customers check their coats, hats umbrellas and such.

buffet
Table on which hot and cold dis are made available so that peo can serve themselves.

maître d'
Person who manages the reservation system, gree customers and supervise dining room staff.

staff entrance

staff coatroom
Room near the entrance where employees store their clothes, hats, umbrellas and such.

refrigerators
Appliances that maintain an average temperature of 4°C; they are used for chilling and storing drinks.

bartender
Person responsible for preparing and serving drinks.

bar
Raised narrow counter on which drinks are served.

bar stool
Chair without arms that allows people to sit at the same level as the bar counter.

pay phone
Telephone located in public places; it functions when coins or payment cards are inserted into the phone box.

barroom
Area with a counter and often tables where alcoholic drinks are sold.

customers' entrance

dining room
Room designed and fur serving meals; its deco the type of food served

waiter
Person who takes the customers' order, serves the meals and settles the check.

booth
Separate compartment for small groups.

kitchen
Room where meals are prepared under the direction of a chef who is assisted by a kitchen staff.

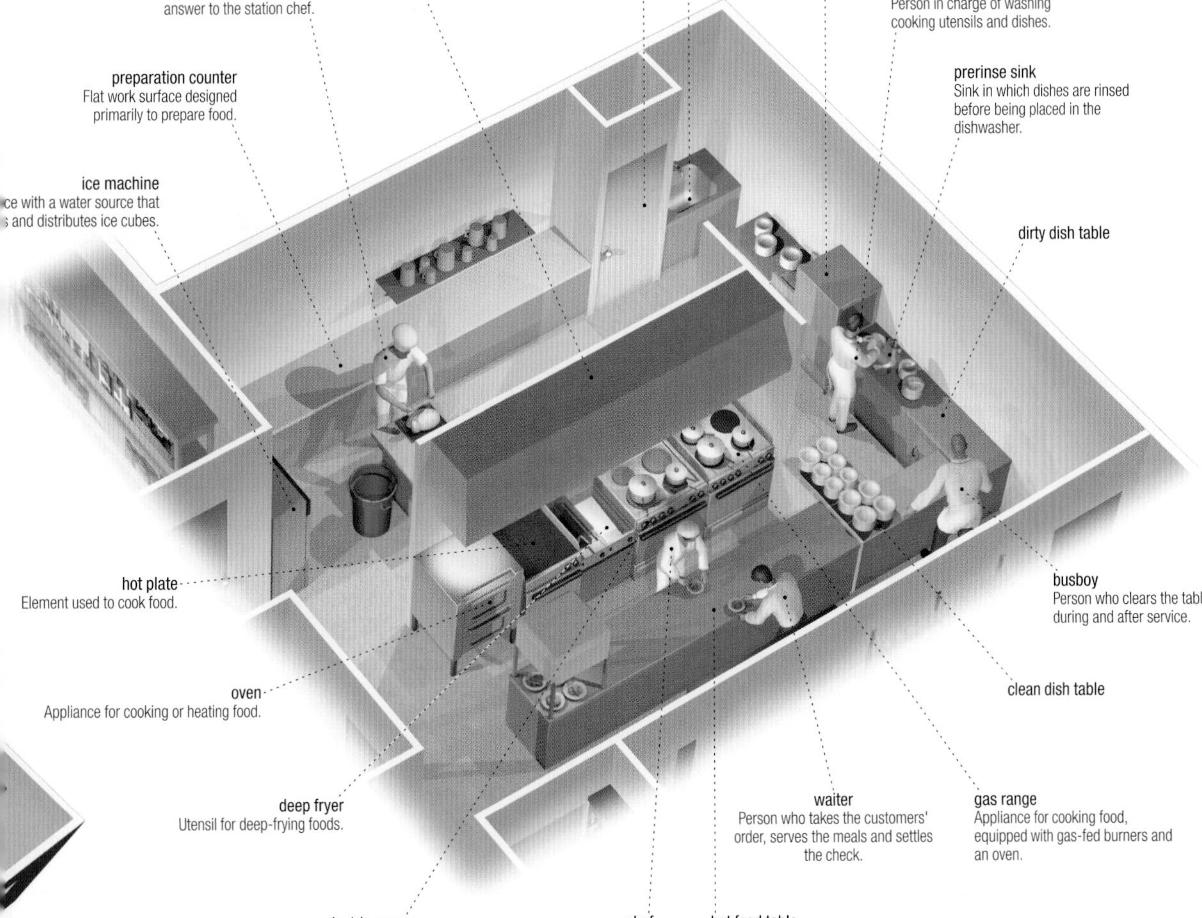

hood
Ventilation appliance expelling or recycling air that contains cooking fumes and odors.

pot-and-pan sink
Sink in which pots and pans and related cooking utensils are washed.

dishwasher
Appliance designed to automatically wash and dry dishes.

line cook
Person in charge of preparing the various dishes on the menu; specialized staff such as the sauce cook, roast cook and pastry chef answer to the station chef.

cleaning supplies
Cupboard for storing cleaning products.

dishwasher
Person in charge of washing cooking utensils and dishes.

preparation counter
Flat work surface designed primarily to prepare food.

prerinse sink
Sink in which dishes are rinsed before being placed in the dishwasher.

ice machine
ice with a water source that s and distributes ice cubes.

dirty dish table

hot plate
Element used to cook food.

busboy
Person who clears the tables during and after service.

oven
Appliance for cooking or heating food.

clean dish table

deep fryer
Utensil for deep-frying foods.

waiter
Person who takes the customers' order, serves the meals and settles the check.

gas range
Appliance for cooking food, equipped with gas-fed burners and an oven.

electric range
Electric appliance for cooking food, equipped with surface elements or griddles and an oven.

chef
Person whose main duties are to manage the kitchen staff, purchase supplies and plan menus.

hot food table
Counter for keeping dishes warm.

menu
Itemized list of dishes served in a restaurant.

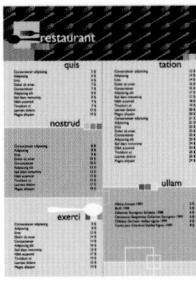

wine list
Itemized list of wines and spirits served in a restaurant.

check
Bill indicating the total amount to be paid by the customer.

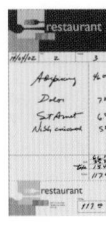

self-service restaurant

Restaurant with numerous food counters where customers can put together a meal of their choosing.

general view

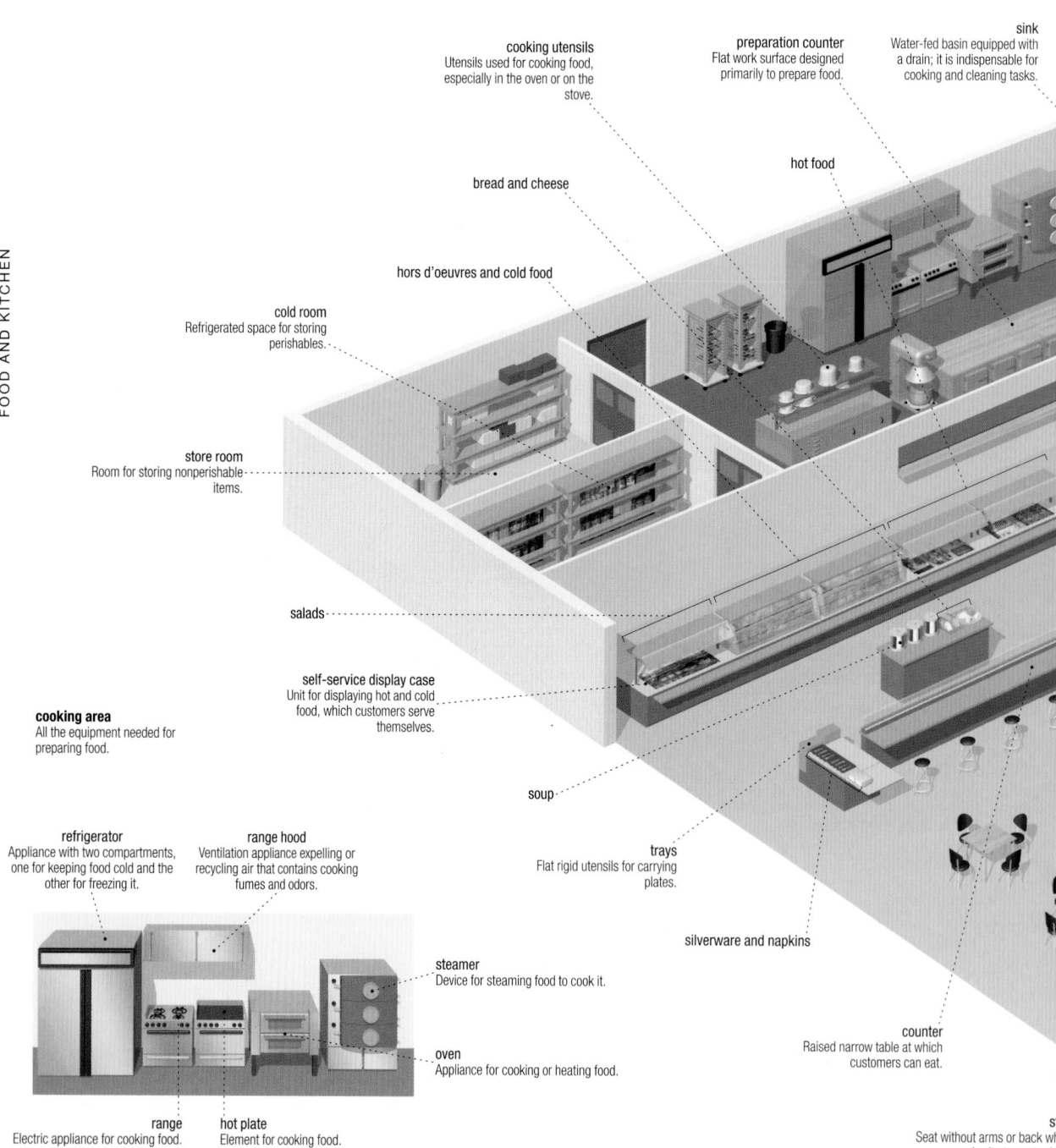

cooking utensils
Utensils used for cooking food, especially in the oven or on the stove.

preparation counter
Flat work surface designed primarily to prepare food.

sink
Water-fed basin equipped with a drain; it is indispensable for cooking and cleaning tasks.

hot food

bread and cheese

hors d'oeuvres and cold food

cold room
Refrigerated space for storing perishables.

store room
Room for storing nonperishable items.

salads

self-service display case
Unit for displaying hot and cold food, which customers serve themselves.

cooking area
All the equipment needed for preparing food.

soup

refrigerator
Appliance with two compartments, one for keeping food cold and the other for freezing it.

range hood
Ventilation appliance expelling or recycling air that contains cooking fumes and odors.

trays
Flat rigid utensils for carrying plates.

silverware and napkins

steamer
Device for steaming food to cook it.

oven
Appliance for cooking or heating food.

counter
Raised narrow table at which customers can eat.

range
Electric appliance for cooking food.

hot plate
Element for cooking food.

sto
Seat without arms or back whe people sit at counter lev

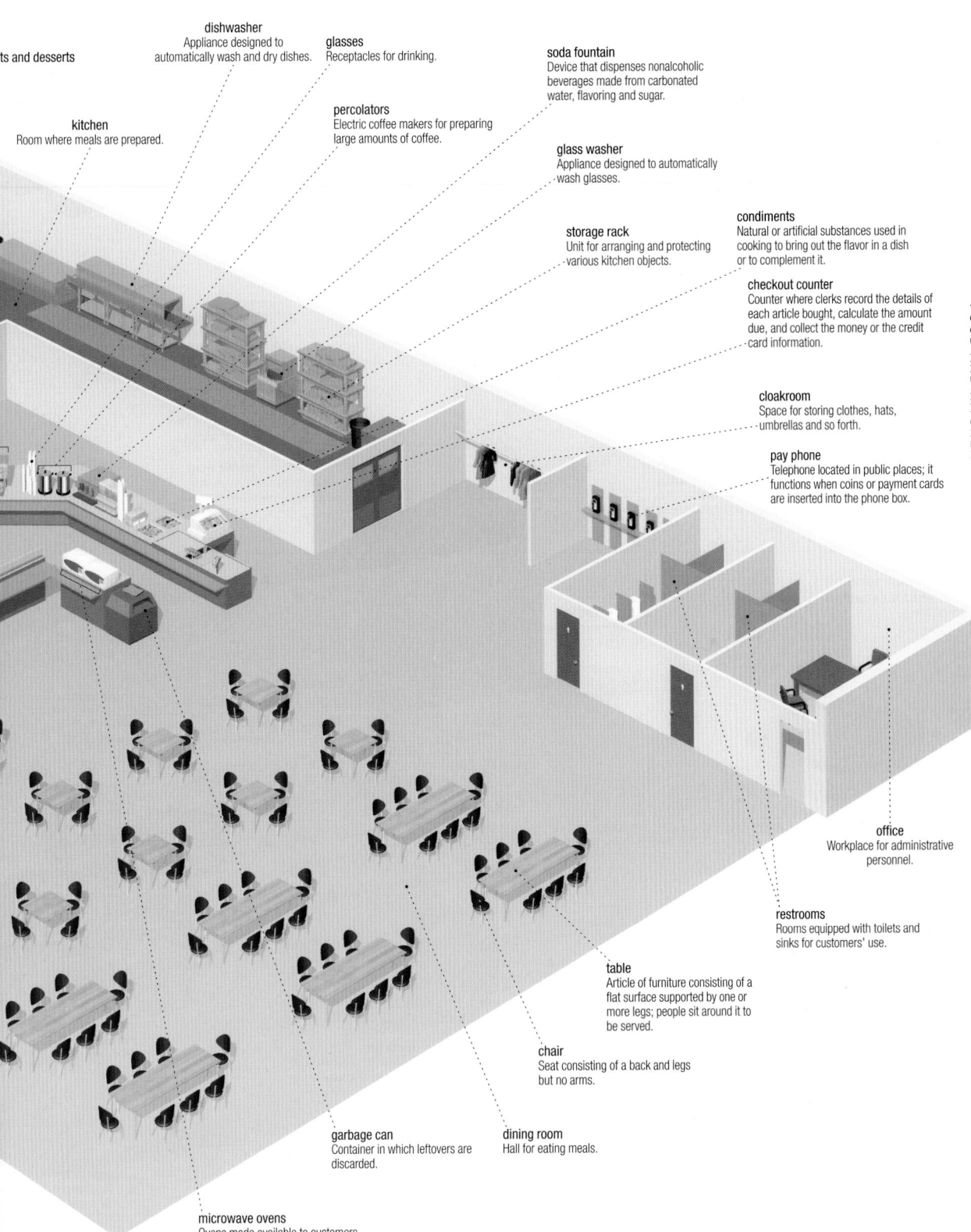

its and desserts

dishwasher
Appliance designed to automatically wash and dry dishes.

glasses
Receptacles for drinking.

soda fountain
Device that dispenses nonalcoholic beverages made from carbonated water, flavoring and sugar.

kitchen
Room where meals are prepared.

percolators
Electric coffee makers for preparing large amounts of coffee.

glass washer
Appliance designed to automatically wash glasses.

storage rack
Unit for arranging and protecting various kitchen objects.

condiments
Natural or artificial substances used in cooking to bring out the flavor in a dish or to complement it.

checkout counter
Counter where clerks record the details of each article bought, calculate the amount due, and collect the money or the credit card information.

cloakroom
Space for storing clothes, hats, umbrellas and so forth.

pay phone
Telephone located in public places; it functions when coins or payment cards are inserted into the phone box.

office
Workplace for administrative personnel.

restrooms
Rooms equipped with toilets and sinks for customers' use.

table
Article of furniture consisting of a flat surface supported by one or more legs; people sit around it to be served.

chair
Seat consisting of a back and legs but no arms.

garbage can
Container in which leftovers are discarded.

dining room
Hall for eating meals.

microwave ovens
Ovens made available to customers to warm up their meals.

food packaging

Methods of packaging used to contain food while insuring its freshness.

wraps and linings
Materials in thin sheets used mainly for wrapping, cooking, or preserving foods.

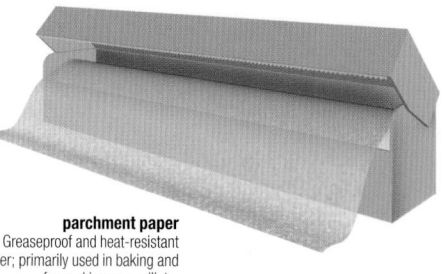

parchment paper
Greaseproof and heat-resistant paper; primarily used in baking and for cooking en papillote.

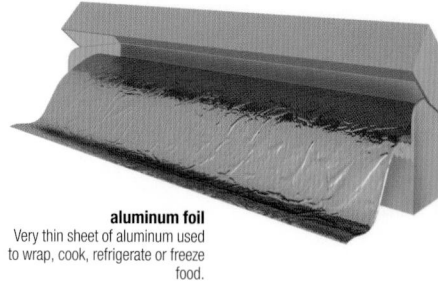

aluminum foil
Very thin sheet of aluminum used to wrap, cook, refrigerate or freeze food.

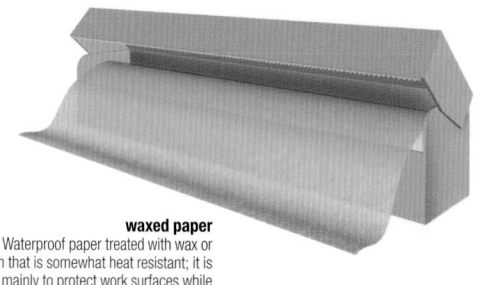

waxed paper
Waterproof paper treated with wax or paraffin that is somewhat heat resistant; it is used mainly to protect work surfaces while cooking.

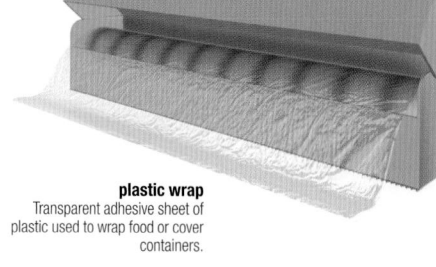

plastic wrap
Transparent adhesive sheet of plastic used to wrap food or cover containers.

containers
Receptacles in which food is presented, transported or preserved.

heat-sealed film
Sheet that can be sealed by heat, making a container airtight.

pouch
A small bag.

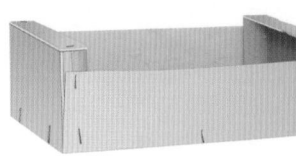

small crate
Small wooden or cardboard case usually designed for shipping and handling fruit.

plastic food storage container
Container in which foods are kept for carrying or preserving.

cup
Vessel of various sizes used for selling prepared foodstuffs.

mesh bag
Bag made of netting that allows fruit and vegetables to breathe.

canisters
Airtight containers designed to contain dry goods.

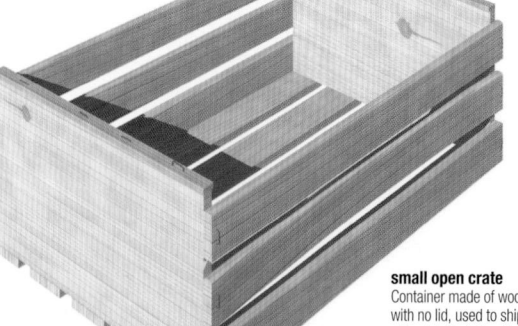

small open crate
Container made of wooden slats with no lid, used to ship a variety of foodstuffs (primarily fruit and vegetables).

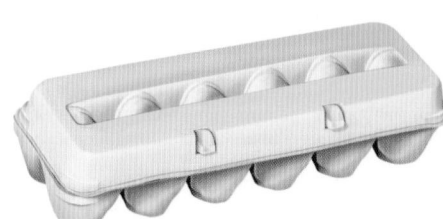

egg carton
Rigid receptacle, usually m
cardboard or plastic, comp
or 12 cavities designed to

food packaging

snack bag
Thin plastic bag, transparent and resealable, used to hold a small amount of various foods (raw vegetables, nuts, etc.).

sandwich bag
Thin plastic bag, transparent and resealable, used to hold a sandwich.

gallon bag
Thin plastic bag, transparent and resealable, used to hold a larger amount of food than the snack bag (vegetables, fruits, etc.).

freezer bag
Airtight bag used to freeze food.

can
Airtight metal container that holds cooked food.

glass bottle
Narrow-necked, elongated receptacle holding drinks (mineral water, wine, etc.) and liquid foodstuffs such as sauces.

screw cap
Threaded stopper that can be screwed on the top of a bottle.

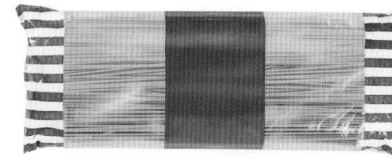

package
A unit formed of foodstuffs or objects of a similar nature that are packaged together.

tube
Flexible cylinder-shaped packaging with a flattened base containing a paste that is squeezed out by finger pressure.

multipack
Multiple products packaged together to facilitate shipping and handling.

pull tab
Small metal strip that can be lifted with a fingernail and fingertip to open a can.

mason jar
Glass jar with a lid in two sections, used especially in home canning.

beverage can
Small cylindrical aluminum container filled with products such as beer and soft drinks.

drink box
Small single-serving box in which juice can be kept for a long time.

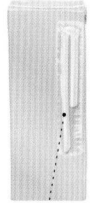

straw
A hollow tube used for sucking up a liquid.

gable top
Top part of a carton closed by flaps, one end of which can turn into a pouring spout.

butter cup
Single-serving portions served with bread in restaurants.

tea bag
Small filter bag filled with ground tea leaves, used for infusion in a tea kettle or directly in a mug.

cheese box
Small cylindrical container, generally made of wood or cardboard, containing a round of cheese wrapped in paper.

carton
Airtight container for the sale of liquid foodstuffs such as milk and juice; it comes in one- or two-quart sizes.

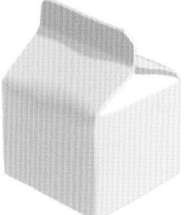

small carton
Small watertight container, usually filled with milk or cream; it comes in pint and half pint sizes.

milk/cream cup
Single-serving portion served with coffee.

food tray
Small molded receptacle, light and rigid, used to sell, freeze or reheat food.

brick carton
Container in which milk, juice and other drinks can be kept for a long time.

kitchen: general view

Room where meals are prepared and often eaten.

ice cube dispenser
Appliance with a water source that
makes and distributes ice cubes.

freezer
Appliance used to freeze and
preserve food.

range hood
Ventilation appliance expelling or
recycling air that contains cooking
fumes and odors.

drawer
Sliding compartment encased in a
piece of furniture.

refrigerator
Appliance for storing food at low
temperatures.

countertop
Flat work surface designed
primarily to prepare food.

wall cabinet
Storage cupboard, usually with
shelves, located above the
countertop.

pantry
Storage place for food not needing
refrigeration.

sink
Basin with a water source and a
drain, essential for cooking tasks.

cooktop
Top surface of the oven on which
heating elements are located.

patio door
Window at ground level whose
sliding panel serves as a door.

oven
Closed part of the range, equipped with
an upper heating element (broiler) and a
lower heating element, in which food is
cooked or heated.

dinette
Part of a kitchen reserved for
eating meals.

microwave oven
Appliance that generates high-
frequency waves to quickly heat or
cook food.

dishwasher
Appliance designed to
automatically wash and dry dishes.

base cabinet
Storage cupboard, usually with
shelves, located below the
countertop.

island
Extra work surface used to prepare
food.

stool
Seat with legs, having neither arms
nor back, of various heights.

glassware

Drinking receptacles; some are used to measure volume for cooking.

liqueur glass
Very small stemmed glass used for drinking liqueurs with a high alcohol content.

port glass
Small rounded stemmed glass used to serve port and dessert wines.

champagne glass
Stemmed glass, wider than it is tall, used to serve champagne and sparkling wines.

brandy snifter
Short-stemmed glass whose pear shape allows the cognac to warm up, and whose narrow lip concentrates the aroma.

Hock glass
...s with a long stem, usually green, used to serve Alsatian white wines.

burgundy glass
Stemmed glass whose wide mouth ensures maximum oxygenation of the wine; it is used mainly for Burgundies.

bordeaux glass
Tulip-shaped stemmed glass, mainly used for Bordeaux; tapering slightly at the top, it concentrates the aroma.

white wine glass
Somewhat narrow stemmed glass usually used for white wines.

water goblet
Large stemmed glass used to serve water at the table; taller and wider than wine glasses.

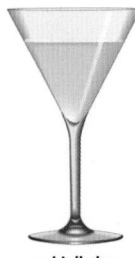

cocktail glass
Conical stemmed glass used to serve certain cocktails; before serving, the rim of the glass can be frosted or decorated with fruit.

highball glass
Tall narrow straight glass used for serving liquor such as gin, often over ice or sometimes mixed with water, soda, etc.

old-fashioned glass
Wide short straight glass with a thick bottom primarily used for serving whiskey.

champagne flute
...all and very thin stemmed glass used for ...hampagne and sparkling wines; because ...the air bubbles break more slowly, the wine retains its effervescence longer.

beer mug
Large cylindrical vessel with a handle used to serve beer; it is usually made of thick glass, ceramic or stoneware.

small decanter
Small carafe used in restaurants to serve wine.

decanter
Glass or crystal carafe with a wide base and a narrow neck used to serve water or wine.

knife

Piece of silverware consisting of a handle and a sharp blade used to cut food into bite-sized pieces.

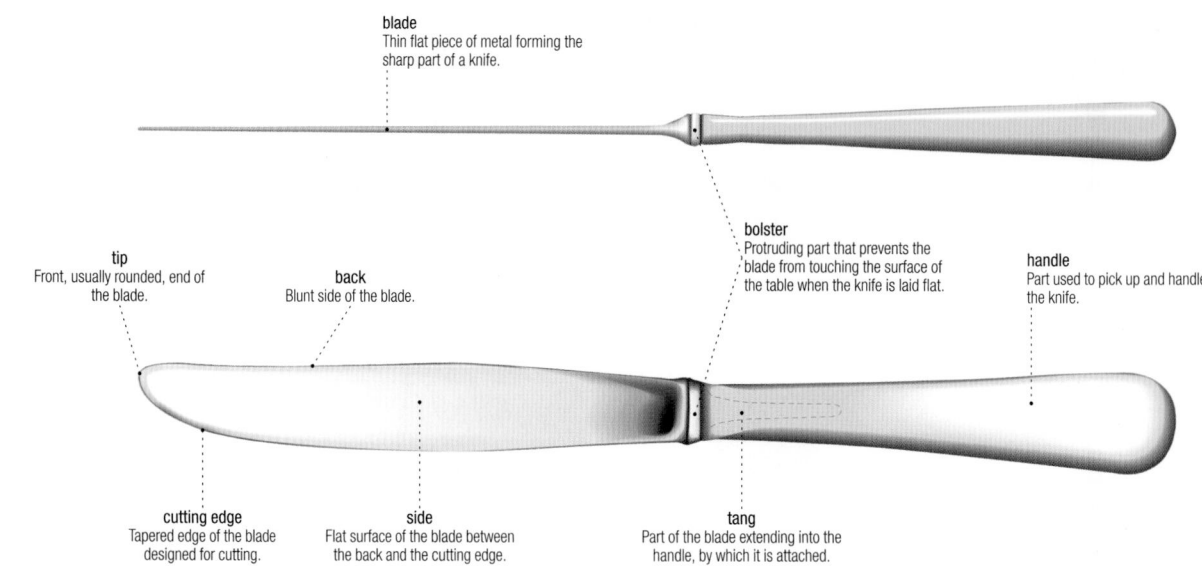

blade
Thin flat piece of metal forming the sharp part of a knife.

bolster
Protruding part that prevents the blade from touching the surface of the table when the knife is laid flat.

handle
Part used to pick up and handle the knife.

tip
Front, usually rounded, end of the blade.

back
Blunt side of the blade.

cutting edge
Tapered edge of the blade designed for cutting.

side
Flat surface of the blade between the back and the cutting edge.

tang
Part of the blade extending into the handle, by which it is attached.

examples of knives

There are many different kinds of knives, each with a specific use.

butter knife
Blunt knife set out when bread is served and used for buttering it.

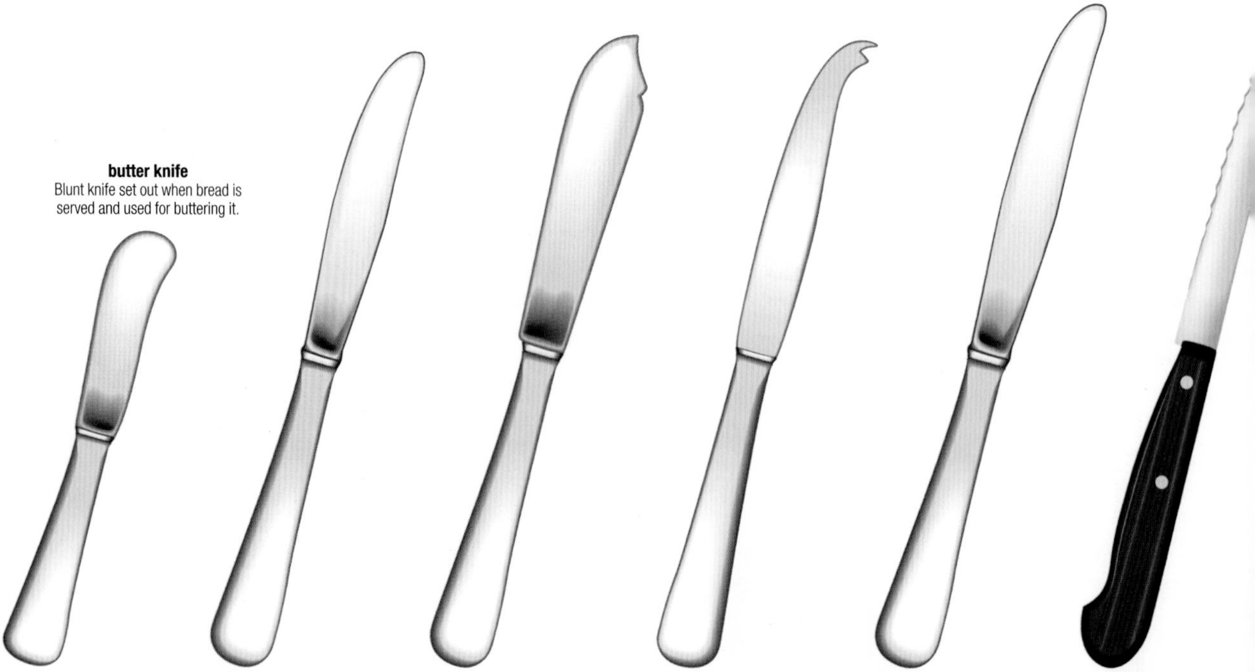

dessert knife
Small knife used to cut desserts into bite-sized pieces.

fish knife
Wide-bladed knife used to remove bones from a fish served whole.

cheese knife
Its curved, double-pointed tip makes it easier to spear individual pieces of cheese.

dinner knife
Large all-purpose knife that is part of a basic place setting.

steak knife
Very sharp knife, often serrated, used to cut firm pieces of meat.

spoon

Utensil consisting of a handle and a hollow part used to eat liquid or semisolid foods.

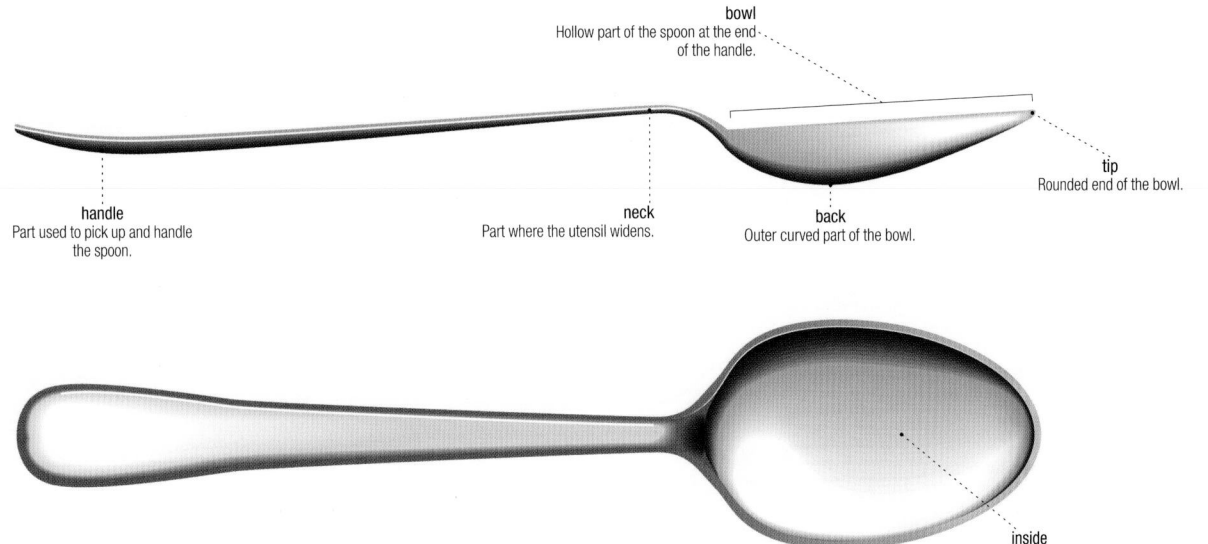

bowl
Hollow part of the spoon at the end of the handle.

tip
Rounded end of the bowl.

handle
Part used to pick up and handle the spoon.

neck
Part where the utensil widens.

back
Outer curved part of the bowl.

inside
Concave part of the bowl.

examples of spoons

There are many different kinds of spoons, each with a specific use.

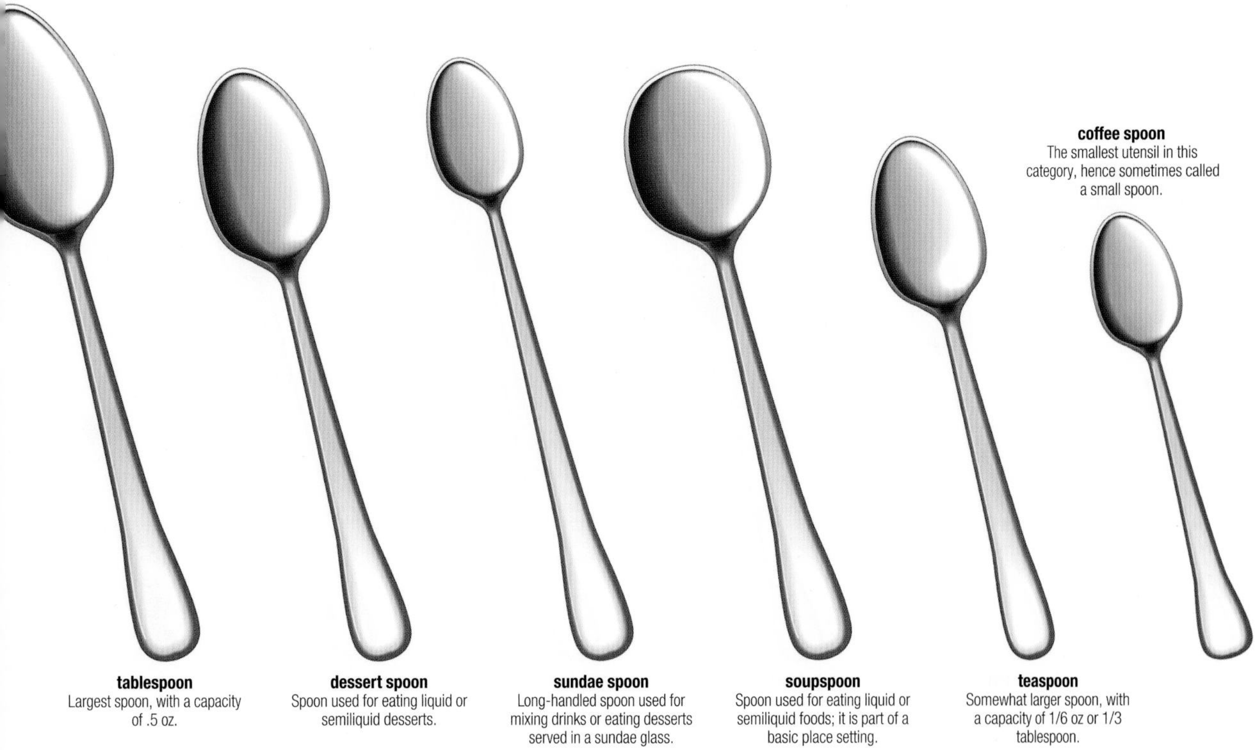

coffee spoon
The smallest utensil in this category, hence sometimes called a small spoon.

tablespoon
Largest spoon, with a capacity of .5 oz.

dessert spoon
Spoon used for eating liquid or semiliquid desserts.

sundae spoon
Long-handled spoon used for mixing drinks or eating desserts served in a sundae glass.

soupspoon
Spoon used for eating liquid or semiliquid foods; it is part of a basic place setting.

teaspoon
Somewhat larger spoon, with a capacity of 1/6 oz or 1/3 tablespoon.

FOOD AND KITCHEN

fork

Utensil with tines used to spear food and carry it to the mouth.

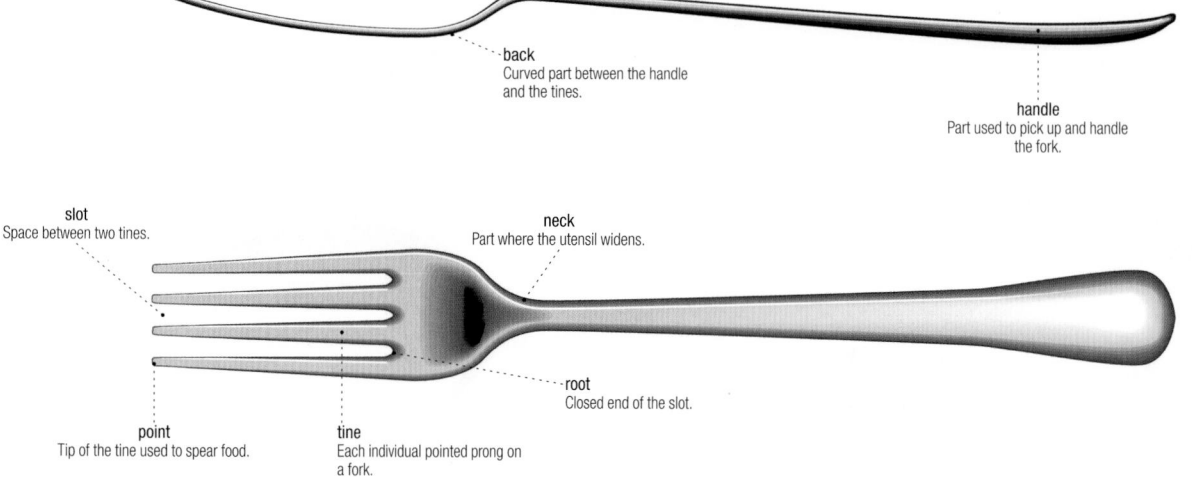

back
Curved part between the handle and the tines.

handle
Part used to pick up and handle the fork.

slot
Space between two tines.

neck
Part where the utensil widens.

point
Tip of the tine used to spear food.

tine
Each individual pointed prong on a fork.

root
Closed end of the slot.

examples of forks
There are many different kinds of forks, each one intended for eating a specific kind of food.

oyster fork
Fork used mainly to separate the flesh of a mollusk from its shell.

dessert fork
Fork used to cut desserts into bite-sized pieces.

salad fork
Fork used mainly for eating salad.

fish fork
Large fork, usually used for eating fish dishes.

dinner fork
Large all-purpose fork that is part of a basic place setting.

fondue fork
Fork used to spear the foods served with fondue.

FOOD AND KITCHEN

tableware accessories

Various pieces additional to the basic table setting.

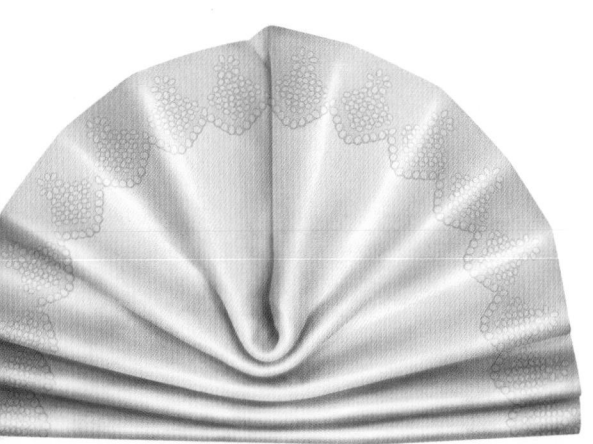

table napkin
Piece of cloth or paper used to wipe the lips or fingers and to protect clothing when it is laid across the lap.

napkin ring
Ring in which a napkin is placed for a table setting.

knife rest
Small support on which the knife can be rested during a meal.

dinnerware

Receptacles of various sizes, shapes and materials used to present food and for eating it.

coffee mug
Large cup used to serve café au lait.

teacup
Cup, larger than the demitasse, used to serve tea.

demitasse
Small cup for serving coffee.

water pitcher
Receptacle with a handle and a spout used mainly to serve juice and water.

teapot
Receptacle used for steeping and serving tea.

creamer
Small jug used to serve cream at the table.

sugar bowl
Small pot used to serve sugar at the table.

dinnerware

salt shaker
Small receptacle used to serve salt at the table, often paired with the pepper shaker.

pepper shaker
Small receptacle used to serve pepper at the table, often paired with the salt shaker.

ramekin
Small containers, suitable for oven and table, used to cook and serve individual portions.

gravy boat
Receptacle used to serve sauces at the table.

butter dish
Flat covered receptacle from which guests serve themselves butter.

soup bowl
Deep round container used to serve individual portions of soup.

bread and butter plate
Small flat plate used to hold a diner's bread and butter or desserts.

saucer
Small shallow dish in which a cup is placed.

salad plate
Flat plate commonly used to serve salads, appetizers, or desserts.

dinner plate
Large piece of flat or shallow dinnerware, usually containing individual portions of solid food.

rim soup bowl
Shallower round container used to serve individual portions of soup.

dinnerware

vegetable bowl
Large receptacle used to bring side vegetables to the table.

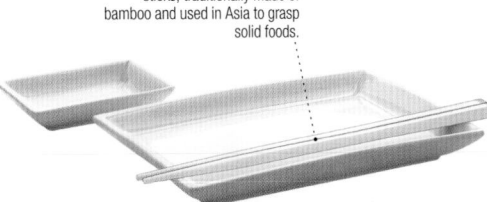

chopsticks
Utensils in the shape of tapered sticks, traditionally made of bamboo and used in Asia to grasp solid foods.

sushi set
Set including chopsticks and two trays on which pieces of sushi and various condiments are served.

rice bowl
Small receptacle in which rice is served as an accompaniment to a main dish.

soup tureen
Large bowl with a removable lid used for bringing soup to the table and serving it.

hors d'oeuvre dish
Serving platter divided into sections used to serve several complementary foods.

snail dish
Has several indentations for holding snails when they are served.

salad dish
Small container used to serve individual portions of salad.

salad bowl
Container of medium depth used to toss and serve salad.

platter
Large oval plate used to present and serve various solid foods, such as cuts of meat, roasts, grilled meat and omelettes.

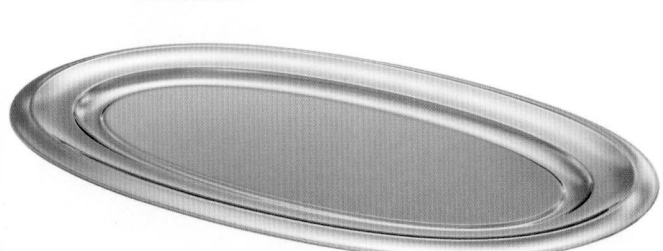

fish platter
Large oval plate used to serve a whole cooked fish.

cheese plate
Plate on which pieces of cheese are arranged to be served.

FOOD AND KITCHEN

place setting

Arrangement of the dishes, utensils, glasses and accessories on a table during a meal. It varies according to region and culture.

in the French style

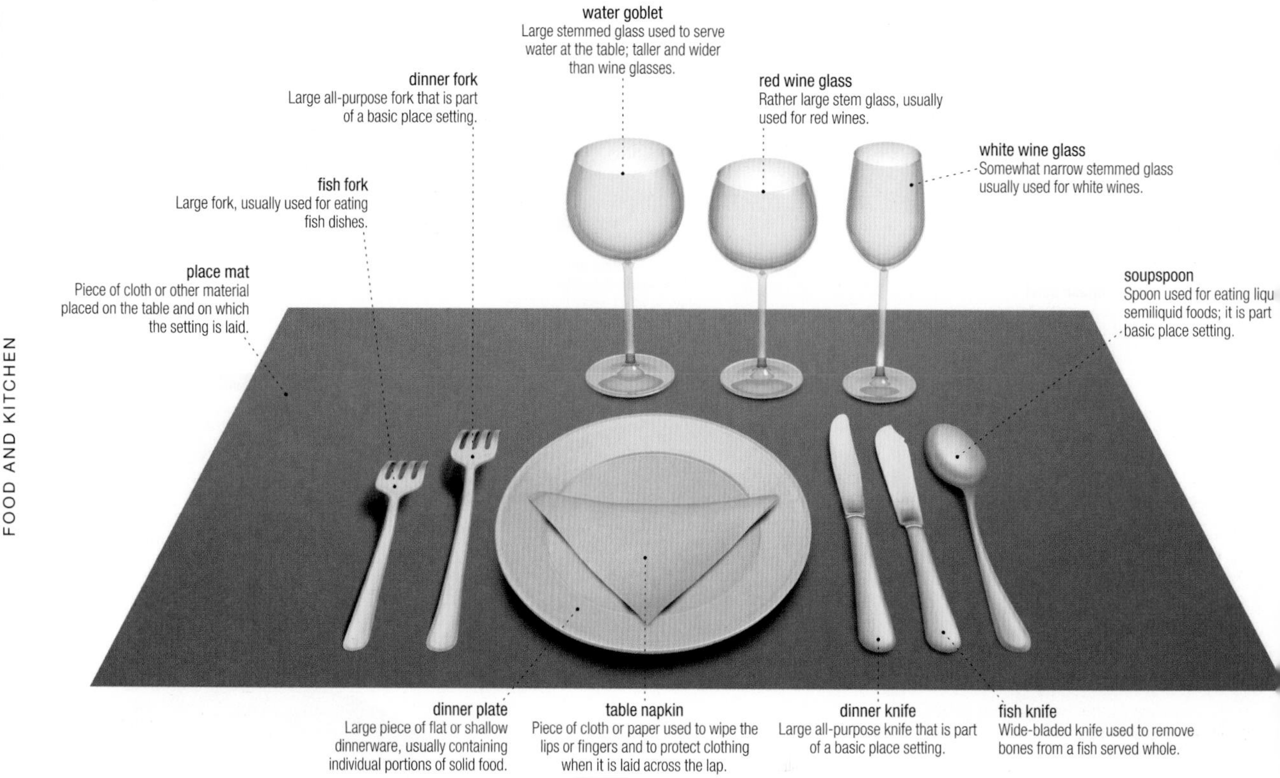

water goblet
Large stemmed glass used to serve water at the table; taller and wider than wine glasses.

dinner fork
Large all-purpose fork that is part of a basic place setting.

red wine glass
Rather large stem glass, usually used for red wines.

fish fork
Large fork, usually used for eating fish dishes.

white wine glass
Somewhat narrow stemmed glass usually used for white wines.

place mat
Piece of cloth or other material placed on the table and on which the setting is laid.

soupspoon
Spoon used for eating liqu semiliquid foods; it is part basic place setting.

dinner plate
Large piece of flat or shallow dinnerware, usually containing individual portions of solid food.

table napkin
Piece of cloth or paper used to wipe the lips or fingers and to protect clothing when it is laid across the lap.

dinner knife
Large all-purpose knife that is part of a basic place setting.

fish knife
Wide-bladed knife used to remove bones from a fish served whole.

in the English style

dessert fork
Fork used for eating dessert.

water goblet
Large stemmed glass used to serve water at the table; taller and wider than wine glasses.

red wine glass
Rather large stem glass, usually used for red wines.

dinner fork
Large all-purpose fork that is part of a basic place setting.

white wine glass
Somewhat narrow stemmed glass usually used for white wines.

place mat
Piece of cloth or other material placed on the table and on which the setting is laid.

soupspoon
Spoon used for eating liquid semiliquid foods; it is part o basic place setting.

table napkin
Piece of cloth or paper used to wipe the lips or fingers and to protect clothing when it is laid across the lap.

bread and butter plate
Small shallow dish on which bread is served as an accompaniment to a meal.

dinner plate
Large piece of flat or shallow dinnerware, usually containing individual portions of solid food.

dessert knife
Small knife used to cut desserts into bite-sized pieces.

dinner knife
Large all-purpose knife that is part of a basic place setting.

place setting

in the American style

red wine glass
Rather large stem glass, usually used for red wines.

water goblet
Large stemmed glass used to serve water at the table; taller and wider than wine glasses.

white wine glass
Somewhat narrow stemmed glass usually used for white wines.

bread and butter plate
Small shallow dish on which bread is served as an accompaniment to a meal.

place mat
Piece of cloth or other material placed on the table and on which the setting is laid.

table napkin
h or paper used to wipe or fingers and to protect when it is laid across the lap.

soupspoon
Spoon used for eating liquid or semiliquid foods; it is part of a basic place setting.

dinner fork
Large all-purpose fork that is part of a basic place setting.

dessert fork
Fork used for eating dessert.

dinner plate
Large piece of flat or shallow dinnerware, usually containing individual portions of solid food.

dessert knife
Small knife used to cut desserts into bite-sized pieces.

dinner knife
Large all-purpose knife that is part of a basic place setting.

in the Chinese style

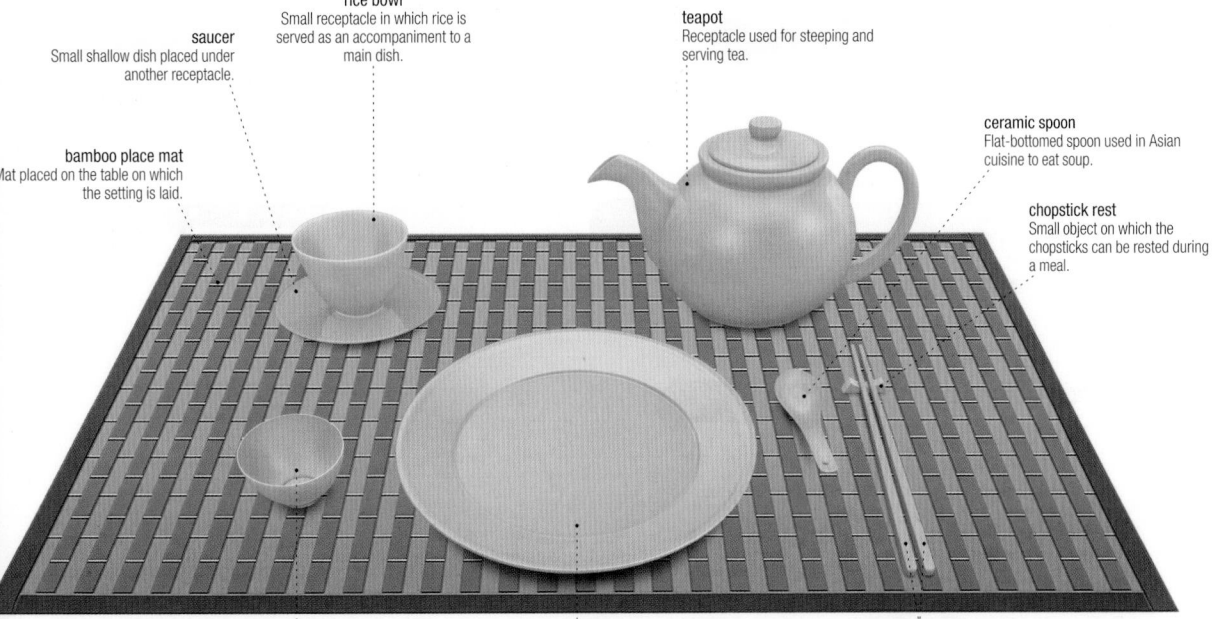

rice bowl
Small receptacle in which rice is served as an accompaniment to a main dish.

teapot
Receptacle used for steeping and serving tea.

saucer
Small shallow dish placed under another receptacle.

ceramic spoon
Flat-bottomed spoon used in Asian cuisine to eat soup.

bamboo place mat
Mat placed on the table on which the setting is laid.

chopstick rest
Small object on which the chopsticks can be rested during a meal.

teacup
Small cup used to serve tea.

dinner plate
Large piece of flat or shallow dinnerware, usually containing individual portions of solid food.

chopsticks
Utensils in the shape of tapered sticks, traditionally made of bamboo and used in Asia to grasp solid foods.

kitchen utensils

Accessories or simple mechanical devices used for preparing food.

kitchen knife
Kitchen knives are used to prepare (cut, slice, bone, trim) food.

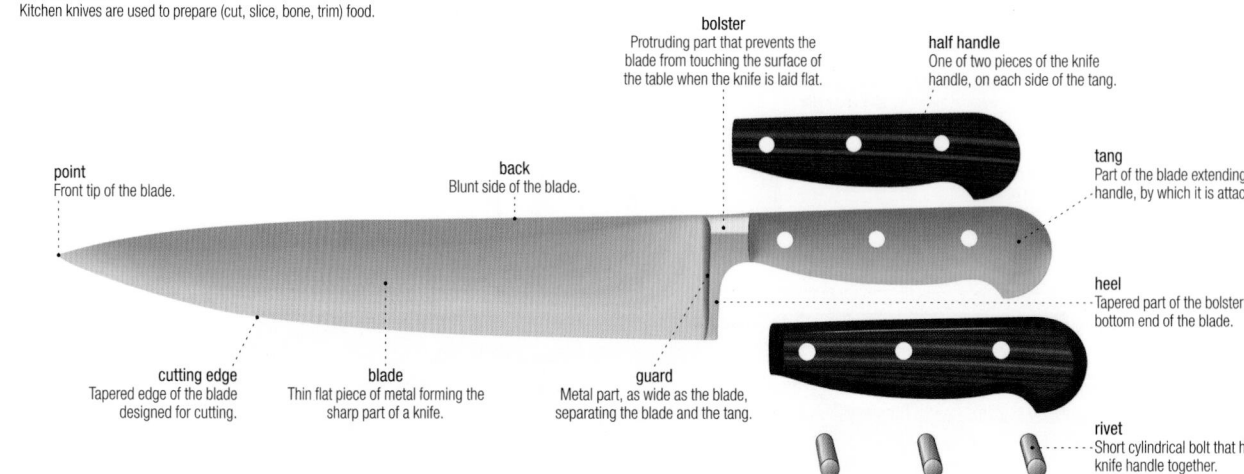

bolster
Protruding part that prevents the blade from touching the surface of the table when the knife is laid flat.

half handle
One of two pieces of the knife handle, on each side of the tang.

point
Front tip of the blade.

back
Blunt side of the blade.

tang
Part of the blade extending handle, by which it is attac

heel
Tapered part of the bolster bottom end of the blade.

cutting edge
Tapered edge of the blade designed for cutting.

blade
Thin flat piece of metal forming the sharp part of a knife.

guard
Metal part, as wide as the blade, separating the blade and the tang.

rivet
Short cylindrical bolt that h knife handle together.

cutting and peeling utensils

The shape and size of kitchen knives vary depending on their use and the type of food for which they are intended.

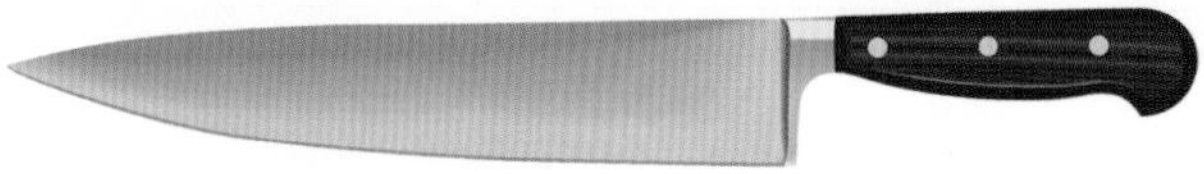

chef's knife
Knife with a wide range of uses, from cutting large pieces of meat to chopping fresh herbs.

cleaver
Knife with a wide rigid blade heavy enough to break bones.

bread knife
Serrated knife used for cutting fresh bread.

carving knife
Knife with a narrow blade used to slice pieces of cooked meat into portions.

ham knife
Knife with a ridged blade used to cut whole cooked ham.

paring knife
Miniature version of the cook's knife, it is used to clean, scrape and slice small pieces of food.

filleting knife
Knife with a long pointed blade used for separating fish into fillets.

boning knife
Small pointed knife with a tapered blade used to separate the meat from the bones.

grapefruit knife
Knife used to detach citrus fruit pulp.

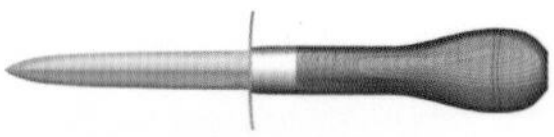

oyster knife
Double-edged knife with a guard used to open oyster shells by severing the muscle that holds them closed.

zester
Knife whose blade curves at the end and has five small cutting holes; it is used to remove thin strips of rind from citrus fruits.

FOOD AND KITCHEN

kitchen utensils

for opening
Instruments that remove lids, caps or corks from containers in order to provide access to their contents.

lever corkscrew
strument with a screw and two wings hat rise as the screw penetrates the ork; they then act as levers to open the bottle.

wine waiter corkscrew
Instrument with a screw and a lever that open wine bottles by leverage, a blade for cutting the hood around the top, and a bottle opener.

bottle opener
Instrument used to remove caps from bottles.

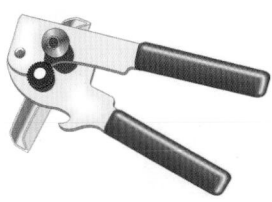

can opener
Tool used to open cans by cutting along the inside edge of the lid.

FOOD AND KITCHEN

for grinding and grating
Instruments that can reduce food to fine particles, shavings, powder, purées, etc.

nutcracker
sed to break nutshells and release the kernel inside.

mortar
Hemispheric receptacle made of marble, porcelain or hardwood in which certain foods can be ground with a pestle.

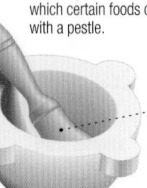

pestle
Usually heavy instrument whose short handle extends into a head; it is used mainly to grind seeds, dry ingredients and garlic.

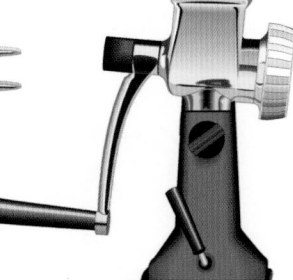

meat grinder
Instrument with a knife and interchangeable disks used to grind meat; the perforations in the disks determine the size of the grind.

garlic press
Utensil used to finely crush garlic cloves.

manual coffee grinder
Device with a rotating blade or burrs propelled by a hand crank, used to grind coffee beans or other ingredients, such as spices.

nutmeg grater
Small conical grater used to reduce nutmeg seeds to a powder.

citrus juicer
Instrument used to extract juice from citrus fruits, usually lemons or oranges.

rotary cheese grater
Instrument used to grate cheese by scraping it against the teeth of a rotating drum.

pusher
Bent part of the handle that presses the piece of cheese against the drum.

grater
Instrument used to reduce food such as vegetables, cheese and nuts into fine particles or a powder.

pepper mill
Device used for grinding peppercorns.

crank
Angled lever that makes the drum rotate.

drum
Cylindrical part of the utensil that grates the cheese.

handle
Part enabling the user to hold the grater and exert pressure on the pusher.

pasta maker
ment that can roll out and cut pasta dough into fferent shapes with its removable blades.

food mill
Instrument used to reduce cooked fruit and vegetables to a purée, the consistency of which depends on the disk used.

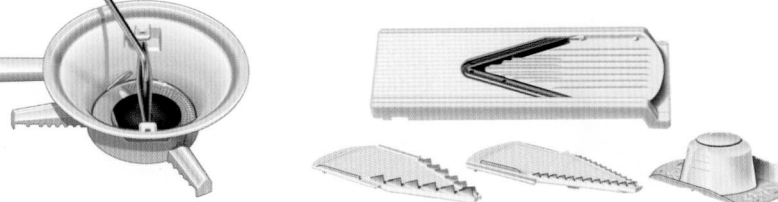

mandoline
Instrument comprising interchangeable cutting blades inserted in a frame; it slices vegetables in different ways, depending on the blade used.

FOOD AND KITCHEN

kitchen utensils

for measuring
Instruments designed to measure the volume or weight of ingredients, food
temperature, and cooking or preparation time.

meat thermometer
Thermometer inserted into a roast
to check its degree of doneness.

measuring cup
Graduated container with a pouring
spout used for measuring liquids.

instant-read thermometer
Digital thermometer that, when inserted into a
instantly indicates the meat's internal tempera

candy thermometer
Thermometer that is placed in hot
liquid sugar mixtures to measure their
exact temperature.

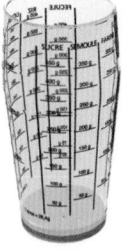

measuring beaker
Graduated container used to
measure dry and liquid ingredients.

measuring spoons
The bowls on these spoons
correspond to an exact quantity
of an ingredient, and are used to
measure it.

egg timer
Device with two glass vials, one of which is
filled with sand; the flow of the sand between
the vials measures a precise time period.

measuring cups
Receptacles used to measure the
exact quantity of an ingredient.

kitchen timer
Device used to measure a period of time;
once that time has elapsed, the timer rings.

oven thermometer
Thermometer that is placed
inside an oven to check the exact
temperature.

kitchen scale
Instruments used to weigh dry
ingredients (e.g., flour, sugar, rice

for straining and draining
Instruments used to filter dry or liquid foods, or to remove the liquid
used to wash, blanch, cook or fry certain foods.

funnel
Cone-shaped instrument ending
in a tube used to pour liquid into a
narrow-necked container.

mesh strainer
Instrument used to sift dry
ingredients or filter liquid ones.

chinois
Finely meshed cone-shaped
strainer used to filter broth and
sauces, and to reduce food to a
purée.

muslin
Cloth woven into a fine loose mesh
and used to strain creamed soups
and sauces so they become finer
and smoother.

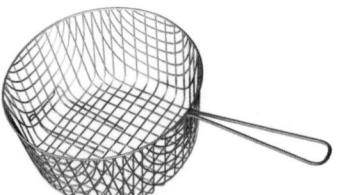

colander
Instrument used to drain food.

frying basket
Metal mesh receptacle designed to
hold foods during frying and drain
them afterward.

sieve
Strainer made of woven nylon, metal or
silk strands and attached to a wooden
frame; it is used to strain dry and liquid
ingredients.

salad spinner
Apparatus that uses centrifugal
force to remove water from freshly
washed lettuce leaves.

kitchen utensils

miscellaneous utensils

stoner
Tonglike device used to remove
bones from olives and cherries
without damaging the flesh.

larding needle
Tool used to insert strips of lard,
ham or truffles into cuts of meat.

apple corer
Utensil used to remove the core
from apples and pears.

melon baller
Spoon used to cut small round
pieces from the flesh of fruits or
vegetables.

trussing needle
Tool used to thread pieces of string
through poultry or to tie a roast.

poultry shears
Utensil used to cut poultry into
pieces.

kitchen shears
Multipurpose utensil used for
cutting fresh herbs, trimming meat
and vegetables.

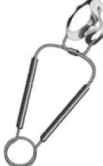

snail tongs
Utensil used to hold snail shells so
the snail can be extracted.

ice cream scoop
Spoon used to remove a serving of ice milk or ice
cream from a container.

tea ball
Hollow sphere that holds dried tea
leaves during steeping.

vegetable brush
Utensil used to clean certain
vegetables, such as potatoes.

egg slicer
Device that uses taut steel wires to
slice a hard-boiled egg.

tasting spoon
Wooden spoon consisting of two
bowls joined by a shallow groove
used to take and taste liquids.

spaghetti tongs
Two-armed utensil with teeth at
the end that facilitate serving long
strips of pasta.

baster
Utensil with a graduated tube and a rubber
bulb; it is used to suck up cooking liquid
and drizzle it over the meat.

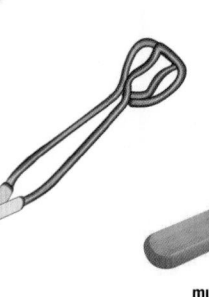

carving fork
Fork used to hold a piece of meat
in place when it is being cut into
portions.

mushroom brush
Utensil used to clean mushrooms.

tongs
Used for holding, turning
and serving food.

sharpening steel
Cylindrical steel rod with narrow
grooves used for honing a knife
edge.

pizza cutter
Utensil consisting of a sharp
beveled wheel on a handle, used
for slicing pizza.

sharpening stone
Abrasive stone used to sharpen
knife edges.

cutting board
Made of plastic or wood and used
for cutting up foods.

peeler
Its pivoting blade follows the
contours of the fruits and
vegetables it is used to peel.

butter curler
Utensil with a serrated hook that
creates butter curls when scraped
across cold butter.

groove
Furrow where cooking juices
collect.

kitchen utensils

baking utensils
Baking: refers to the production of cakes, cookies and other usually sweet comestibles made from cooked dough, pastry or batter.

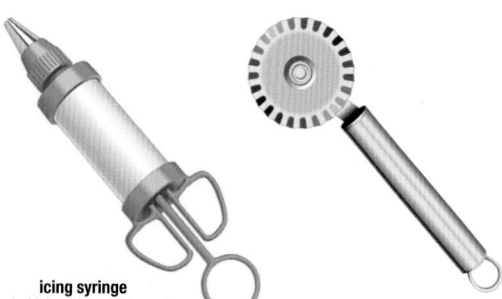

icing syringe
Fitted with interchangeable nozzles that are filled with icing, it is used to decorate baked goods and molded desserts.

pastry cutting wheel
Device used for cutting dough; the indented wheel gives it a fluted edge.

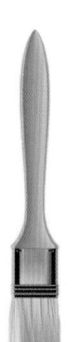

pastry brush
Device with silk or nylon bristles at one end, used to coat, brush or glaze pastries, or to grease baking pans.

egg beater
Mechanical device with two whisks activated by a crank handle; it is used to beat liquid and semiliquid ingredients.

whisk
Utensil made of several curved intersecting steel wires used to be beat or whip liquid and semiliq ingredients.

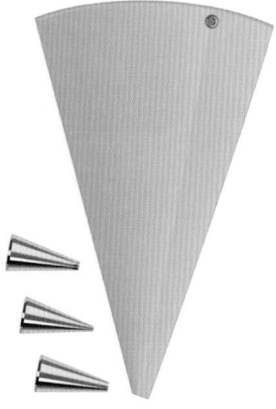

pastry bag and nozzles
Leakproof bag into which interchangeable nozzles are inserted; it is used to decorate dishes, baked goods and molded desserts, or to make pastries.

shaker
Container with a perforated lid used for sprinkling food with flour, sugar or grated cheese.

sifter
Device used to sift flour. It has a spring-loaded or crank handle that moves the flour about and makes it lighter before passing it though a sieve.

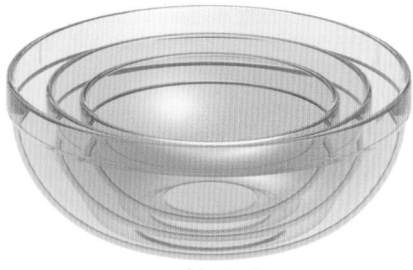

mixing bowls
Round containers of various sizes used to prepare or mix food and ingredients.

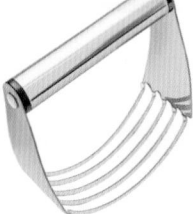

pastry blender
Utensil used to blend fatty ingredients with flour.

cookie cutters
Hollow metal molds used to cut dough into soft shapes that will be retained after baking.

baking sheet
Rectangular pan with low sides, usually made of aluminum, used for baking cookies, cakes and oth pastries that do not require molding.

rolling pin
Wooden cylinder that rolls freely between two lateral handles; it is used to roll out pastry.

soufflé dish
Deep porcelain dish that prevents the rising soufflé from overflowing as it cooks.

kitchen utensils

cake pan
Relatively deep metal baking pan
with enough room to allow the
cake to rise.

pie plate
Pan used to make a pie crust and
to bake a pie in the oven.

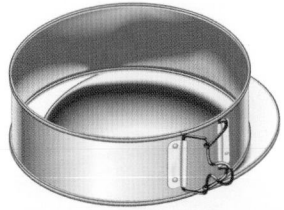

springform pan
Metal baking pan whose bottom, and sometimes its
side, come apart so the contents can be removed
more easily.

tart pan
Metal baking pan with a scalloped
edge that makes the crust of the
tart or quiche more attractive.

loaf pan
Metal container, usually
rectangular, deep enough to
allow bread to rise in it without
overflowing.

charlotte mold
Deep metal pan shaped like a pail
and used to cook a cream-based
sweet dessert surrounded by
biscuits.

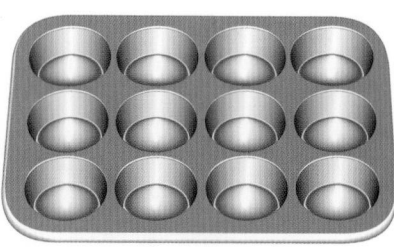

muffin pan
Baking pan with indentations used
to give muffins their distinctive
shape.

set of kitchen utensils
Main kitchen utensils, often matching, stored in a stand.

skimmer
d slightly concave spoon
ations; it is used to skim
auce, or to remove food
its cooking liquid.

draining spoon
Large elongated slightly concave
spoon with perforations; it is used
to remove small pieces of food
from their cooking liquid.

icing spatula
Long blade of variable width used
to turn food over during cooking.

spatula
Utensil used to handle cooked food
without breaking it.

ladle
Spoon with a deep bowl and a long
handle; it is used to decant liquid or
semiliquid food.

potato masher
Utensil used to manually purée
cooked fruits and vegetables.

FOOD AND KITCHEN

cooking utensils

Utensils used for cooking food, especially in the oven or on the stove.

wok set
Cooking utensil native to Asia used for rapidly cooking food in very little fat.

lid
Removable part that covers the wok during cooking.

rack
Half-moon-shaped grating used to drain or set aside food.

wok
Large cone-shaped frying pan; food collects at the center of the rounded bottom, where the heat is most intense.

burner ring
Metal base used to balance the wok over the burner or hot plate.

tajine
Varnished earthenware dish with a cone-shaped airtight lid used in northwestern Africa to cook an eponymous dish.

fondue set
Utensil designed to prepare and serve various kinds of fondue, such as meat, cheese or chocolate.

fondue pot
Container with one or two side handles used for cooking fondue.

stand
Metal base designed to hold the fondue pot and the burner.

burner
Compartment containin flammable liquid that k fondue pot warm throu meal.

fish poacher
Oblong receptacle that has a rack and a cover; it is used to cook whole fish.

rack
Perforated sheet; the hooks allow it to be lifted so that, once cooked, the fish can be drained and removed.

lid
Removable part that covers the fish poacher during cooking.

drip pan
Slightly concave rectangular pan used to roast meat or to catch the meat's cooking juices.

terrine
Container with a perforated lid that allows steam to escape; it is designed for cooking recipes with or without jelly.

pressure cooker
Stock pot with a screw-on, airtight lid designed to cook food rapidly using pressurized steam.

roasting pans
Somewhat deep large-capacity utensils used to roast meat in the oven.

pressure regulator
Device maintaining the pressure at a constant level.

safety valve
Device that regulates escaping steam when the stock pot is under pressure.

Dutch oven
Somewhat deep stock pot used for cooking food in a liquid.

stock pot
Container used for cooking large quantities of food in a liquid.

couscous steamer
Double container in which steam from the broth in which the food in the bottom part is simmering cooks and flavors the semolina in the top part.

frying pan
Utensil used to fry, sauté or brown food.

cast iron casserole
Oval or round receptacle most often used to cook foods on low heat.

steamer
Utensil comprising two saucepans; the steam from the boiling water in the bottom one cooks the food in the top one.

sauté pan
Similar to a frying pan but with a straight edge, used to cook food in fat, over high heat.

egg poacher
Device used to poach eggs by placing them in indentations in a tray suspended over a hot liquid.

pancake pan
Round thick-bottomed skillet with a shallow edge that allows a spatula to loosen and flip the pancake.

skillet
Deeper than a frying pan, this utensil is used to simmer or braise dishes.

clay cooker
Utensil composed of two skillets of porous clay that fit tightly together; it is used for braising food.

steamer basket
rated receptacle that is placed in a saucepan he water level and filled with food to be steam-cooked.

double boiler
Utensil comprising two saucepans; the bottom one contains boiling water, which cooks or heats the food in the top one.

saucepan
Low-sided receptacle commonly used to heat liquids or cook food in a liquid.

pizza pan
Large shallow round metal pan used for baking pizza in an oven.

small domestic appliances

Electric appliances used in the preparation of foods and dishes.

for mixing and blending

Appliances used for stirring, for blending several ingredients together or for changing the appearance of an ingredient.

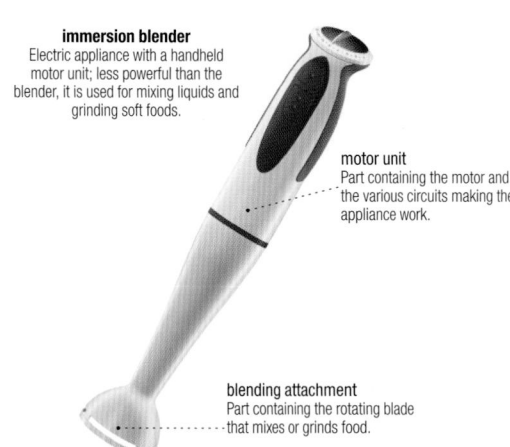

immersion blender
Electric appliance with a handheld motor unit; less powerful than the blender, it is used for mixing liquids and grinding soft foods.

motor unit
Part containing the motor and the various circuits making the appliance work.

blending attachment
Part containing the rotating blade that mixes or grinds food.

beater ejector
Button pressed to remove the beaters.

hand mixer
Electric appliance comprising two beaters and a motor unit used to beat or mix liquid or semiliquid food.

speed selector
Device for selecting the speed at which the beaters rotate.

handle
Part used to pick up and handle the mixer.

heel rest
Part on which the mixer rests when it is not in use.

beater
Device used to beat or mix food; the beaters are inserted into cogwheels that turn in opposite directions.

blender
Electric appliance comprising a motor unit with a container on top, in which raw or cooked food is mixed, crushed or puréed.

cap
Part that gives the container an airtight seal.

container
Glass jug in which food or ingredients are placed.

cutting blade
Propeller blade that mixes or grinds food as it turns.

control buttons
Buttons for selecting different functions, including the speed of the blade.

motor unit
Part containing the motor and the various circuits making the appliance work.

tilt-back head
The motor unit rotates on an axis so the beaters can be lowered into the bowl and lifted out of it.

stand mixer
Electric appliance comprising a powerful motor unit, two beaters and a stand used to beat or mix liquid or semiliquid foods.

beater ejector
Button pressed to remove the beaters.

beater
Device used to beat or mix food; the beaters are inserted into cogwheels that turn in opposite directions.

speed control
Device for selecting the s which the beaters rotate

mixing bowl
Round container of various sizes used to mix food in.

turntable
Enables the mixing bowl to be rotated so the contents will be beaten or mixed uniformly.

stand
Base that holds the mixing bow and the tilt-back head.

beaters

Instruments used to mix, beat or knead liquid or semiliquid foods.

four blade beater
All-purpose beater used to mix, beat or whisk various ingredients.

spiral beater
Beater used primarily to mix and knead light dough.

whisk attachment
Beater used to mix, emulsify or beat many different ingredients or to incorporate air into a mixture.

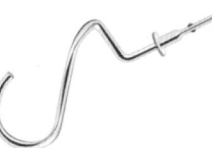

dough hook
Beater used to mix and knead dough.

small domestic appliances

for cutting
Appliances used primarily for separating elements into small parts or portions.

processor
ric appliance comprising a motor unit,
de and a set of disks used for cutting,
ping, slicing, grating, mixing, kneading, etc.

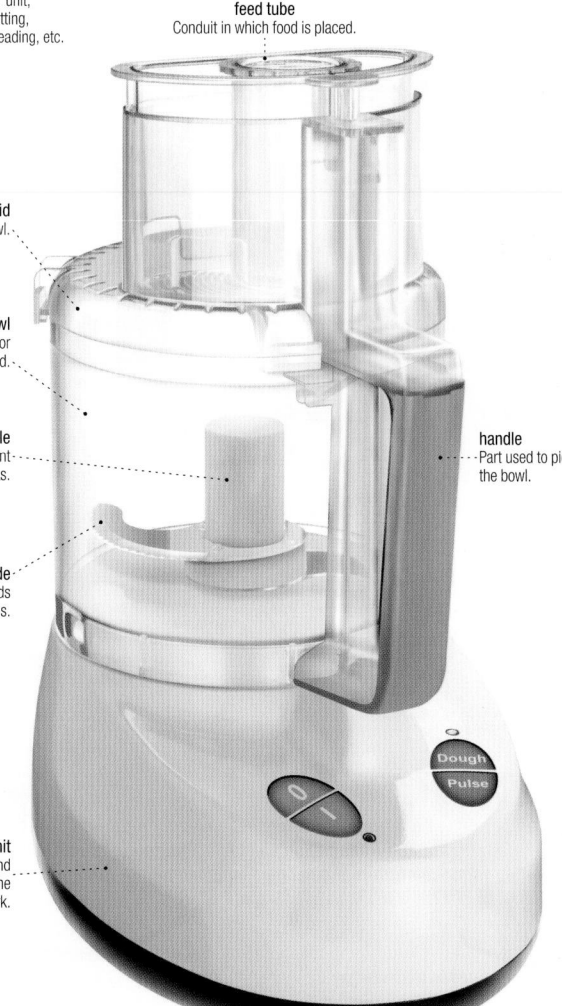

feed tube
Conduit in which food is placed.

lid
Removable part covering the bowl.

bowl
Container in which food or ingredients are placed.

spindle
t transmits the motor's movement to the blade or disks.

blade
Propeller blade that mixes or grinds food as it turns.

handle
Part used to pick up and move the bowl.

motor unit
Part containing the motor and the various circuits making the appliance work.

disks
Blades that can replace the cutting mechanism to grate or mince food.

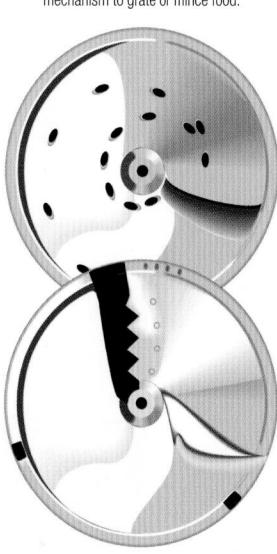

for juicing
Device designed to extract juice from fruit, especially citrus fruit, when pressure is exerted upon it.

electric knife
Electric appliance with a blade that has a back-and-forth motion used to facilitate cutting a piece of meat.

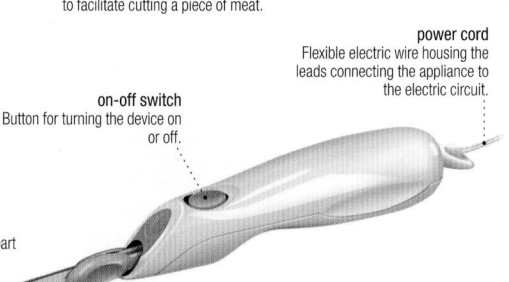

power cord
Flexible electric wire housing the leads connecting the appliance to the electric circuit.

on-off switch
Button for turning the device on or off.

blade
serrated removable part cutting mechanism.

citrus juicer
Electric appliance designed to extract the juice from citrus fruit.

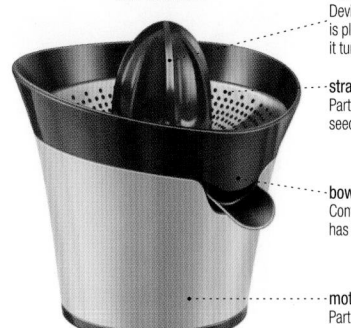

reamer
Device upon which the fruit half is placed and which reams it as it turns.

strainer
Part of the juicer that catches the seeds and the pulp.

bowl with serving spout
Container that collects the juice; it has a pouring spout.

motor unit
Part containing the motor and the various circuits making the appliance work.

FOOD AND KITCHEN

small domestic appliances

for cooking
Appliances that bring raw food into contact with a heat source in order to cook them.

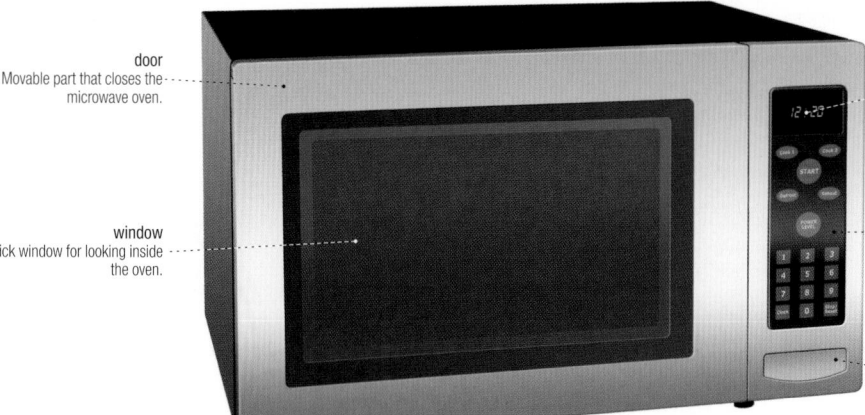

microwave oven
Appliance that generates high-frequency waves to quickly heat or cook food.

door
Movable part that closes the microwave oven.

window
Thick window for looking inside the oven.

clock timer
Displays either real time or the programmed cooking time.

control panel
Panel containing the programming keys.

latch
Device that opens the door when pushed.

waffle iron
Appliance comprising two indented plates, each one covering a heating element; it is used to cook waffles or grill food.

handle
Part used to raise and lower the lid.

lid
Movable part that closes the waffle iron.

plate
Indented cooking surface that, because it is attached to the inside of the lid, can be raised and lowered.

hinge
Jointed part that makes it possible to raise and lower the lid.

plate
Indented cooking surface designed to receive waffle batter or food intended for grilling.

temperature selector
Device used to regulate plate temperature.

bread guide
Metal grating for holding bread slices in place.

toas
Appliance with heating eleme that toast slices of bre

slot
Opening in which the b is placed.

lever
Spring-loaded device th the carriage holding th slices.

temperature control
Device used to regulate cooking temperature.

deep fryer
Container with a heating element that raises the temperature of fat high enough to deep-fry food.

lid
Removable part that covers the deep fryer during cooking.

handle
Device used to raise or lower the basket.

thermostat
Device used to regulate fat temperature.

timer
Device used to monitor cooking time.

indicator light
Light indicating when the desired temperature has been reached.

temperature control
Device used to regulate cooking temperature.

toaster ov
Small appliance used for bak heating or toasting various foc

timer
Adjustable device used to automatically turn off the appliance after a set period of time.

small domestic appliances

slow cooker
Appliance consisting of a removable pot placed inside a heating base, used to cook food slowly, on low heat.

lid
Removable section used to cover the pot.

ovable ceramic pot
n the food is cooked.

handle
ping when lifting the slow cooker.

control panel
n which the temperature
nd cook time can be set.

heating base
Base unit containing the heating elements for cooking food inside the removable pot.

electric steamer
Electric device comprising one or more covered trays resting on a water-filled base; the food in each tray is steamed separately.

lid
Removable section used to cover the steamer during cooking.

fish tray
Tray containing holes on which the fish is placed to be cooked.

cooking dishes
Containers that have a perforated base so the food they contain can be steamed.

drip tray
Tray containing holes that receives the liquid from the food cooking above it.

base
Base unit containing a heating element used to bring water to a boil.

indicator light
Light indicating that the heating element has been turned on.

water level indicator
Device that indicates the water level in the appliance's reservoir.

timer
Device used to monitor cooking time.

window
Thick glass through which the bread dough can be seen inside the mold.

bread machine
Electric appliance used to raise and bake bread dough.

lid
ble part that closes the bread machine.

loaf pan
r for the bread dough,
e baked, will become bread.

control panel
Panel containing the programming keys.

raclette grill
Appliance with covered heating elements used to melt cheese or grill meat and side vegetables.

cooking plate
Ribbed cooking surface covering the heating elements; it is used for grilling food.

dish
Small shallow nonstick container used for cooking individual servings of food.

base
Stand supporting the raclette with grill; it contains the heating elements that cook the food.

griddle
Electric appliance comprising a cooking surface and used for grilling food.

handle
d to pick up and move the griddle.

detachable control
used to regulate grill temperature
t can be detached from the unit.

cooking surface
Often nonstick cooking plate on which food is placed.

grease well
Hole through which cooking juices drain.

indoor electric grill
Electric appliance comprising a metal grill and a heating element used to cook food.

insulated handle
Part used to pick up and move the grill without burning oneself.

cooking surface
Metal grill on which the food is cooked.

drip pan
Container into which the cooking juices drain.

temperature control
Device used to regulate grilling temperature.

small domestic appliances

miscellaneous appliances

kettle
Container with a heating element used to boil water.

spout
Small tapered projection used to pour the boiling liquid.

body
Part of the kettle that holds the water to be boiled.

base
Stand supporting the kettle; it contains the heating element that boils the water.

handle
Part used to pick up and move the kettle.

on-off switch
Button for turning the device on or off.

indicator light
Light showing that the appliance is on.

juicer
Appliance that uses centrifugal force to extract the juice from vegetables and fruit, except citrus fruits, which must be reamed.

pusher
Device that pushes the fruits or vegetables into the appliance.

feed tube
Conduit into which fruit or vegetables are placed to their juice.

lid
Movable part that covers when it is in operation.

strainer
Device that allows only the fruit or vegetable juice to pass through.

bowl
Container into which the juice drains.

motor unit
Part containing the motor various circuits making the work.

can opener
Tool used to open cans by cutting along the inside edge of the lid.

pierce lever
Device connected to the blade that the user presses down so it pierces the can lid.

cutting blade
Knife that separates the lid from the can.

magnetic lid holder
Part that holds the lid once it has been removed from the can.

drive wheel
Cogwheel that helps rotate the can so the lid can be removed.

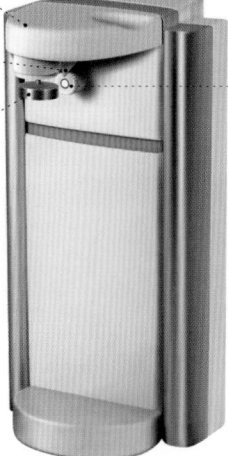

electric coffee grinder
Device with an automatic rotating blade or burrs, used to grind coffee beans or other ingredients, such as spices.

lid
Removable part that covers the coffee mill when it is in use.

hopper
Container into which the coffee beans are placed for grinding.

blade
Instrument used to grind coffee beans or other items.

grinding control
Device on which the type and duration of grinding can be set.

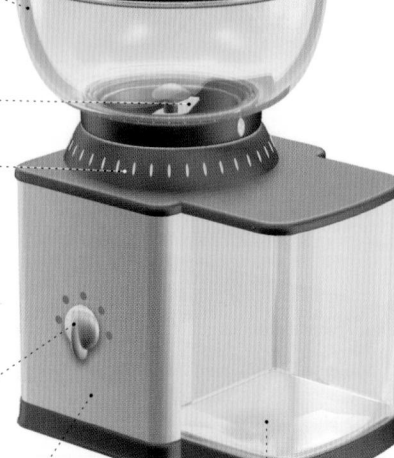

ice cream maker
Device composed of an insulated bucket with rotating paddles on the inside, used to make sorbets, ices, and ice cream.

motor unit
Part containing the motor and the various circuits making the appliance work.

cover
Movable part that covers the freezer bucket during food preparation.

timer
Adjustable device used to automatically turn off the appliance after a set period of time.

freezer bucket
Container designed to keep its contents cold.

handle
Part used to pick up and move the ice cream freezer.

motor unit
Part containing the motor and the various circuits making the appliance work.

ground coffee container
Container into which the coffee grounds fall.

FOOD AND KITCHEN

small domestic appliances

coffee makers
Appliances used to brew coffee. Different kinds are used to make different types of coffee.

automatic drip coffee maker
Electric coffee maker that allows hot water to drain into a paper filter containing the ground beans, and coffee to drip into the carafe below.

reservoir
er holding the water to be heated.

water level
how many cups of coffee can be made.

indicator light
nowing that the appliance is on.

on-off switch
on for turning the device on or off.

lid
Removable part covering the reservoir and under which the basket is located.

basket
Removable container that holds the filter with the ground beans.

carafe
Container with a spout into which the coffee drips and that is used to pour it.

warming plate
Surface used to keep the coffee warm.

Neapolitan coffee maker
Coffee maker that is placed on a heat source to boil the water; it is then turned over so the boiling water filters through the ground beans into the serving compartment.

FOOD AND KITCHEN

vacuum coffee maker
Coffee maker that brews coffee by causing the water to pass through the ground beans twice.

upper bowl
Compartment into which the brewed coffee rises and from which it drains into the lower bowl as the heat source cools.

stem
Conduit through which the hot water rises.

lower bowl
Compartment from which boiling water rises under pressure into the upper bowl, passing through the ground beans; the brewed coffee drains into it for serving.

espresso machine
Electric coffee maker that allows hot water to be forced under pressure through the ground beans.

on-off switch
turning the device on or off.

tamper
back the ground beans into the filter.

drip tray
nent into which excess liquid drains.

steam control knob
Device used to regulate the steam coming out of the nozzle.

filter holder
Removable part with a handle into which the metal filter containing the ground beans is inserted.

water tank
Reservoir where the water is kept before it is required for heating.

steam nozzle
Device that emits steam used to foam milk.

percolator
Electric coffee maker that allows the hot water to rise several times through a tube to percolate through ground beans.

coffee press
offee maker that allows hot water to be ed over ground beans; once the grounds ve steeped, the plunger is depressed to the grounds to the bottom of the carafe.

stovetop espresso maker
Coffee maker in which steam from the lower pot is forced through a filter filled with ground coffee, filling the upper pot with brewed coffee.

spout
Tube-shaped part through which the coffee is poured.

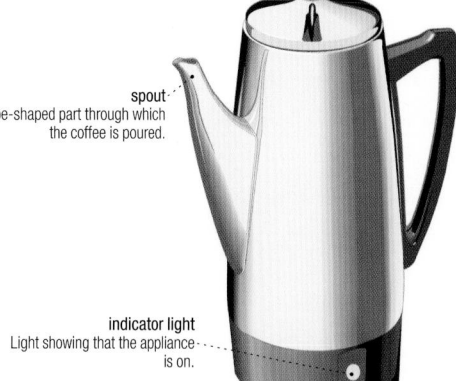

indicator light
Light showing that the appliance is on.

HOUSE

Structure built as a dwelling and equipped to provide a comfortable and secure life for people.

exterior of a house

View of a house on its site with the components of its exterior structure.

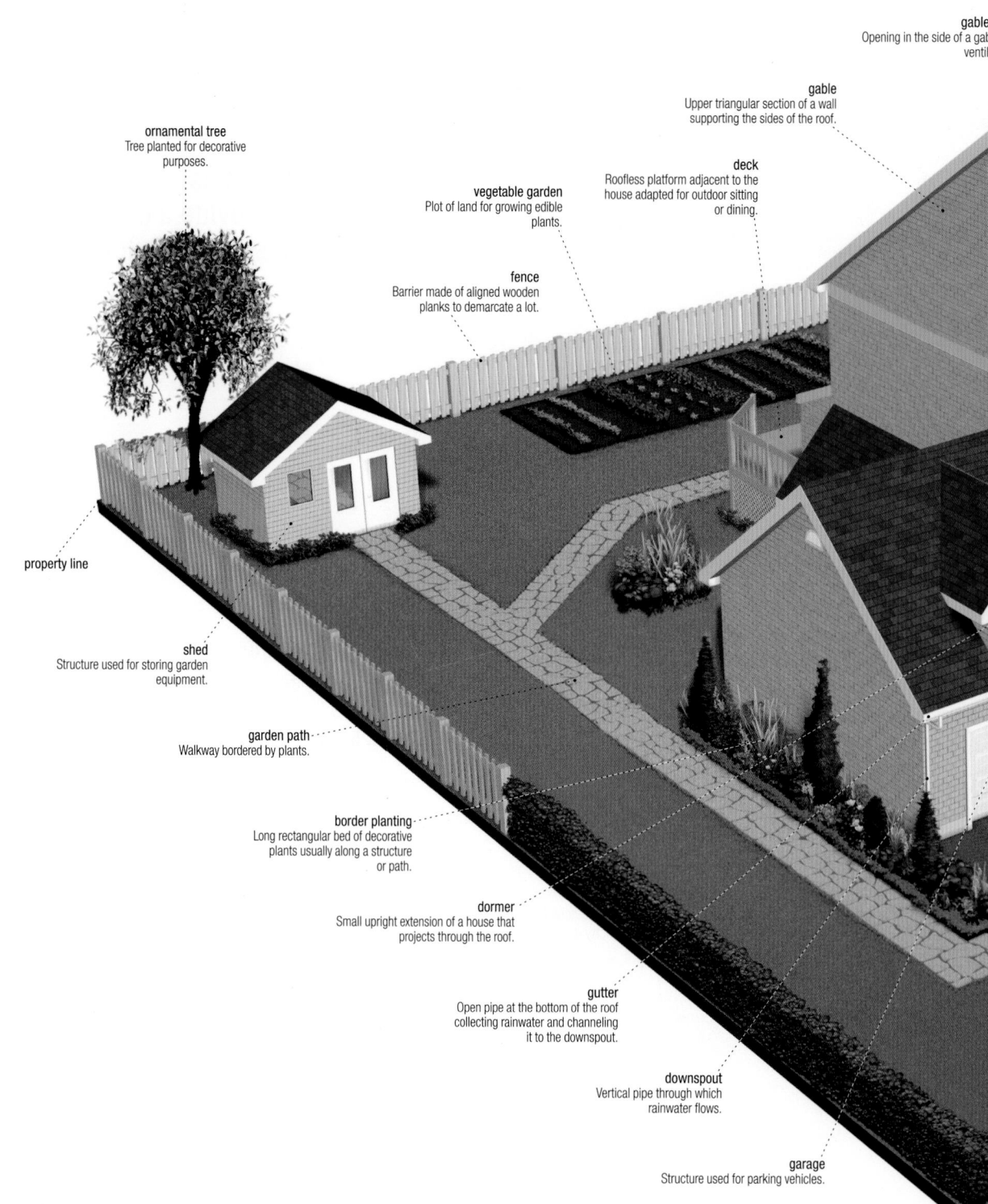

gable
Opening in the side of a gable
ventila...

gable
Upper triangular section of a wall
supporting the sides of the roof.

deck
Roofless platform adjacent to the
house adapted for outdoor sitting
or dining.

ornamental tree
Tree planted for decorative
purposes.

vegetable garden
Plot of land for growing edible
plants.

fence
Barrier made of aligned wooden
planks to demarcate a lot.

property line

shed
Structure used for storing garden
equipment.

garden path
Walkway bordered by plants.

border planting
Long rectangular bed of decorative
plants usually along a structure
or path.

dormer
Small upright extension of a house that
projects through the roof.

gutter
Open pipe at the bottom of the roof
collecting rainwater and channeling
it to the downspout.

downspout
Vertical pipe through which
rainwater flows.

garage
Structure used for parking vehicles.

exterior of a house

lightning rod
Metal spike attached to the roof; it protects the house by conducting lightning to the ground.

chimney cap
Protective cover above the top of a chimney flue; it helps to keep rain and animals out.

chimney
Part of the heating system that protrudes from the roof, and from where smoke escapes.

roof
House covering that protects it from the elements; it rests on the frame.

cornice
Extended section of a roof protecting the wall from rain.

protruding through the ...entilate and illuminate the ...low.

steps
Outdoor staircase ending in a landing that leads to the house entrance.

basement window
Opening in the wall of the bottom floor to let in light and air.

hedge
Bushes planted in a row to demarcate a lot.

lawn
Land covered by short thick grass requiring regular mowing.

foundation planting
Grouping of flowers and decorative shrubs.

sidewalk
Pedestrian walkway bordering a street.

porch
Covered part of a house entrance protecting the door and people from the elements.

driveway
Usually paved section of ground used as a path or parking space for vehicles.

pool

Man-made basin designed for swimming.

hot tub
Heated tub equipped with air jets;
the water it contains is kept at a
high temperature.

aboveground swimming pool
Pool whose structure is built above ground.

pool cover reel
Cylindrical piece with a hand wheel
used to roll up the pool cover.

deck
Elevated platform providing access
to the pool.

filter
Device removing and absorbing
impurities from the water.

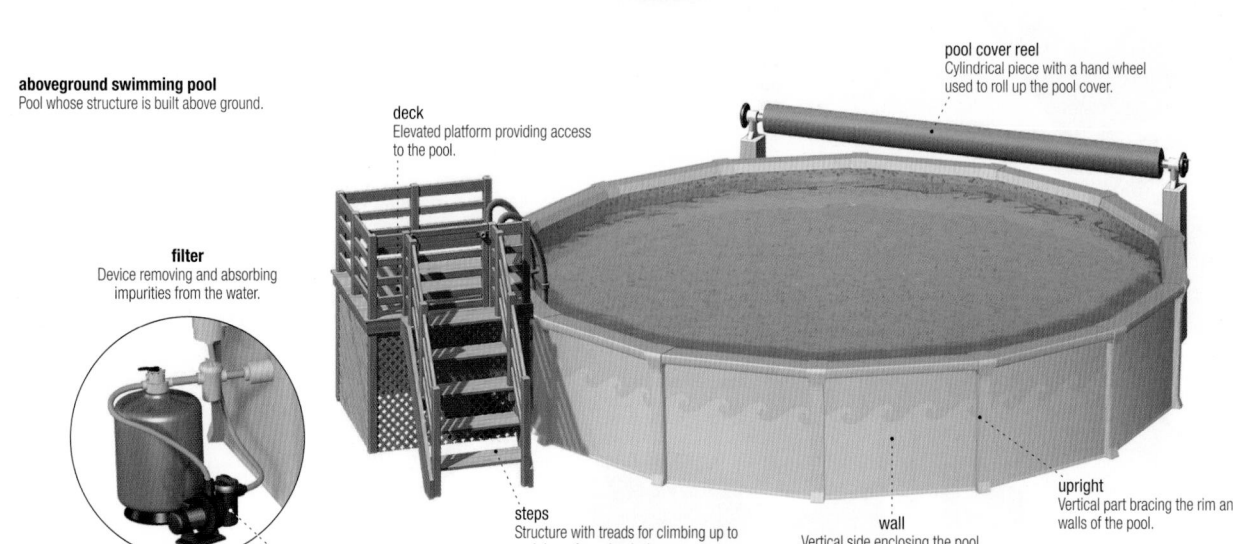

upright
Vertical part bracing the rim and
walls of the pool.

steps
Structure with treads for climbing up to
and down from the deck.

wall
Vertical side enclosing the pool.

pump
Device circulating the water
through the skimmer to the filter
before returning it to the pool.

inground swimming pool
Pool whose structure is mostly below ground level.

main drain
Covered opening used to channel
water to the filter or to drain the
pool.

diving board
Spring-held board providing
momentum for jumping or diving.

ladder
Used by swimmers to get into
out of the diving well.

underwater light
Light embedded in the wall; it
illuminates the pool underwater.

discharge outlet
Device returning filtered water to
the pool.

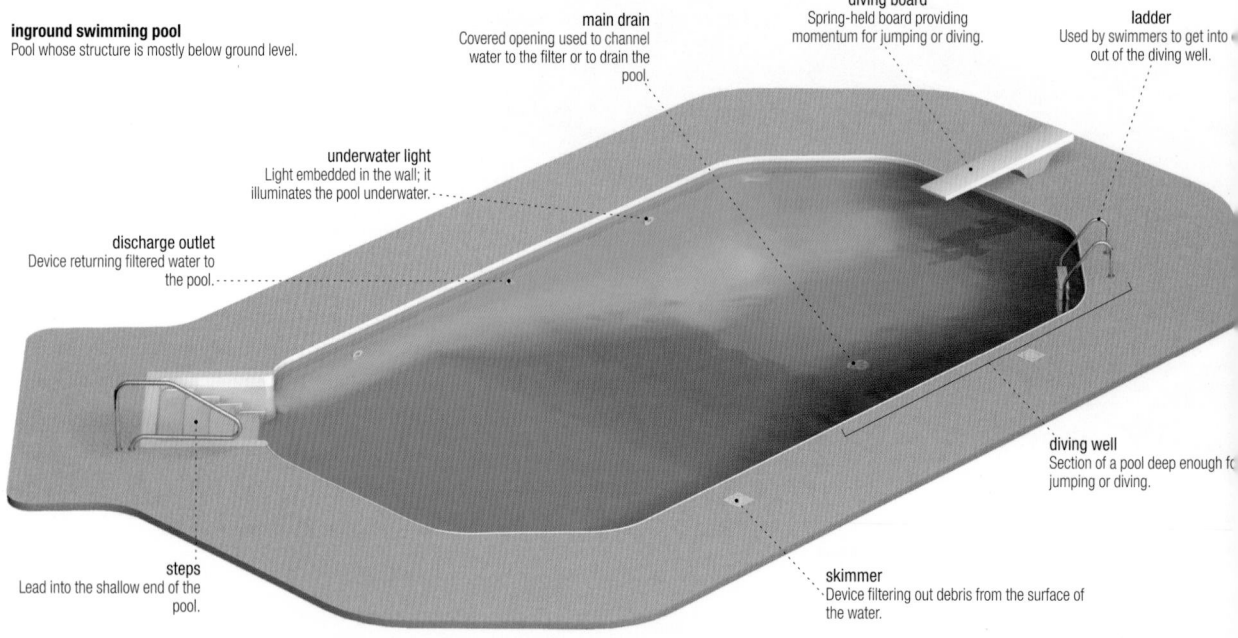

diving well
Section of a pool deep enough fo
jumping or diving.

steps
Lead into the shallow end of the
pool.

skimmer
Device filtering out debris from the surface of
the water.

exterior door

An exterior door comprises a leaf, or flat moving part, and a frame which often has both structural and decorative components. It provides access to and egress from the house.

cornice
Protruding decorative molding at the top of the entablature, protecting the parts beneath it from the rain.

entablature
Decorative grouping of horizontal pieces above the door.

head casing
Level frame part enclosing the upper part of a door's opening.

top rail
Level piece of wood at the top of the door.

side casing
Piece of the frame that forms one side of the door opening.

panel
Flat surface bordered by molding; it is often recessed.

mullion
Vertical piece of wood joining the top and lock rails.

shutting stile
Vertical part of the door on which the lock and doorknob are mounted.

lock rail
Level piece of wood in the middle of the door.

lock
Device mounted on the door allowing it to lock by using a key.

middle panel
Long narrow panel placed horizontally.

door handle
Device mounted on the door allowing it to open.

hanging stile
Vertical part of the door to which the hinges are attached.

hinge
Cylindrical metal part bent at an angle; it supports the door and allows it to swing.

weather strip
Sloped strip of wood allowing water to flow away from the door.

bottom rail
Level piece of wood at the bottom of the door.

threshold
Surface forming the bottom part of the door opening.

lock

Device mounted on the door allowing it to be locked by a key.

general view

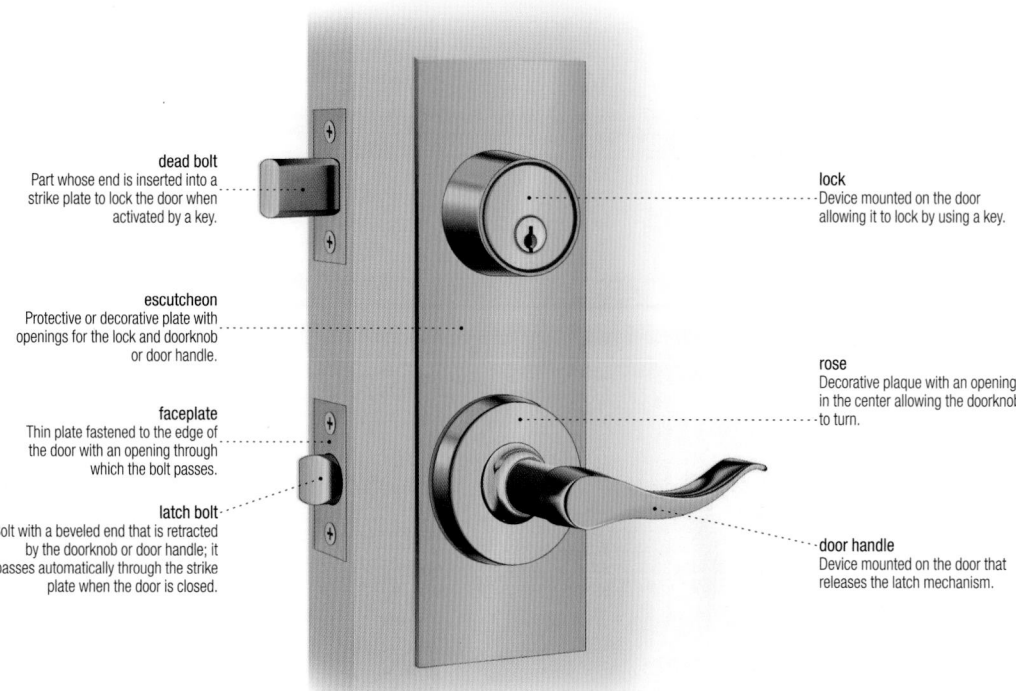

dead bolt
Part whose end is inserted into a strike plate to lock the door when activated by a key.

lock
Device mounted on the door allowing it to lock by using a key.

escutcheon
Protective or decorative plate with openings for the lock and doorknob or door handle.

rose
Decorative plaque with an opening in the center allowing the doorknob to turn.

faceplate
Thin plate fastened to the edge of the door with an opening through which the bolt passes.

latch bolt
Bolt with a beveled end that is retracted by the doorknob or door handle; it passes automatically through the strike plate when the door is closed.

door handle
Device mounted on the door that releases the latch mechanism.

tubular lock
Lock whose knobs activate a latch bolt and is locked by pushing a button; it is used for interior doors.

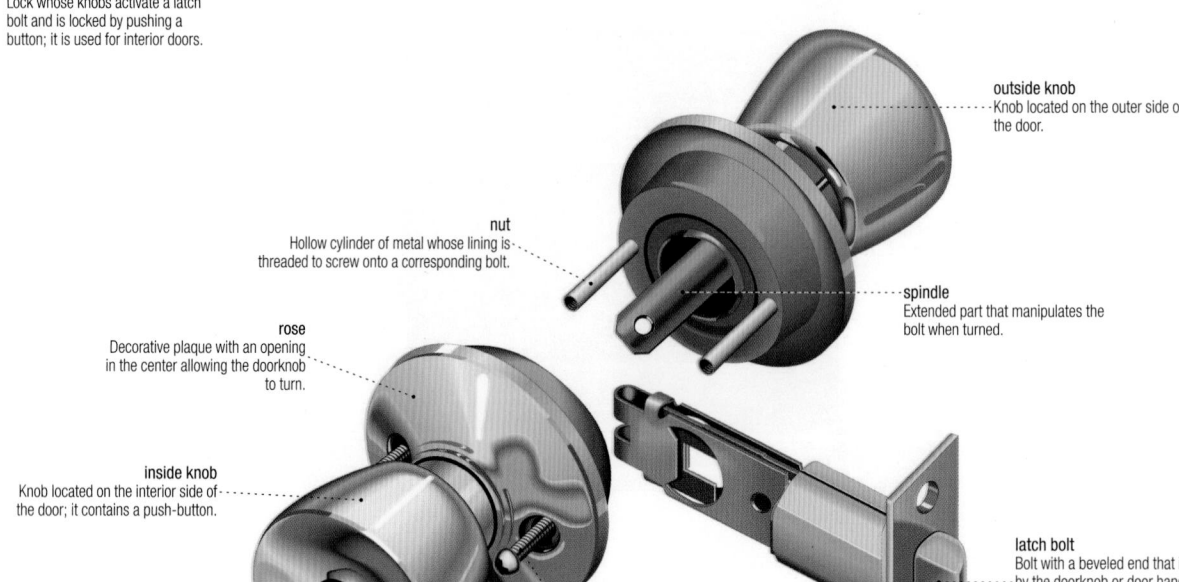

outside knob
Knob located on the outer side of the door.

nut
Hollow cylinder of metal whose lining is threaded to screw onto a corresponding bolt.

spindle
Extended part that manipulates the bolt when turned.

rose
Decorative plaque with an opening in the center allowing the doorknob to turn.

inside knob
Knob located on the interior side of the door; it contains a push-button.

push button
Button that activates the locking mechanism when pushed.

bolt
Metal threaded peg ending in a head; it screws into a nut.

latch bolt
Bolt with a beveled end that is retracted by the doorknob or door handle; it passes automatically through the strike plate when the door is closed.

faceplate
Thin plate fastened to the edge of the door with an opening through which the bolt passes.

HOUSE

lock

spring
Elastic piece of metal that, by pressing against the cotter pin, prevents the rotor from turning if the key's grooves do not match.

cylinder
Part that contains the lock mechanism.

stator
Fixed part of the lock mechanism interacting with the grooves in the key to make the rotor turn.

mortise lock
Lock fitted into a door whose dead bolt provides greater security; it is used especially on exterior doors.

key
Metal part whose unique grooves activate the lock.

cotter pin
Piece of metal that, by aligning itself to the key's grooves under pressure from the spring, enables the rotor to turn.

rotor
Rotating part of a lock mechanism that a unique key can turn in order to draw the bolt.

cylinder case
Hollow part of a lock into which the locking mechanism is fitted.

keyway
Channel complementing the shape of the key through which it is inserted into the rotor.

strike plate
Metal part fixed to the door frame and fitted with an opening to a cavity into which the bolt is inserted.

ring
Protruding cylindrical part on the door into which the key is inserted.

dead bolt
Part whose end is inserted into a strike plate to lock the door when activated by a key.

faceplate
Thin plate fastened to the edge of the door with an opening through which the bolt passes.

HOUSE

window

Opening in a wall fitted with glass to let in light and air.

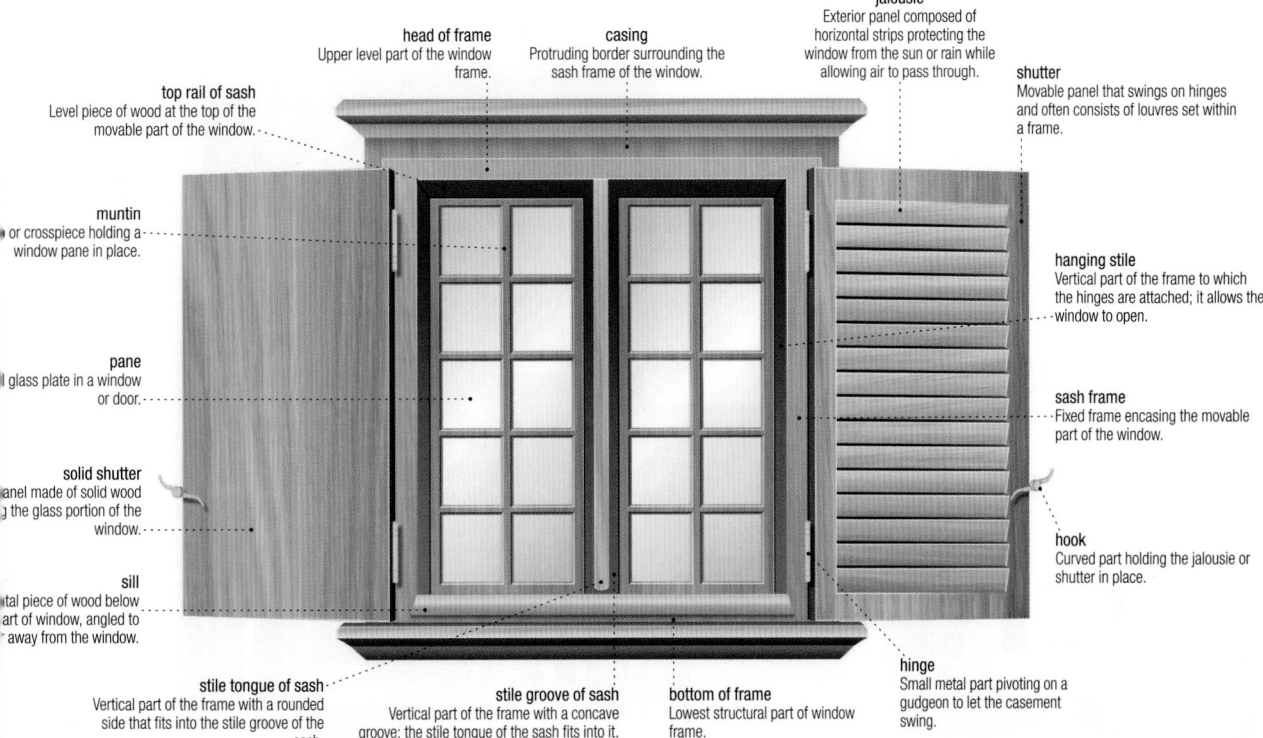

jalousie
Exterior panel composed of horizontal strips protecting the window from the sun or rain while allowing air to pass through.

head of frame
Upper level part of the window frame.

casing
Protruding border surrounding the sash frame of the window.

shutter
Movable panel that swings on hinges and often consists of louvres set within a frame.

top rail of sash
Level piece of wood at the top of the movable part of the window.

muntin
or crosspiece holding a window pane in place.

hanging stile
Vertical part of the frame to which the hinges are attached; it allows the window to open.

pane
glass plate in a window or door.

sash frame
Fixed frame encasing the movable part of the window.

solid shutter
anel made of solid wood g the glass portion of the window.

hook
Curved part holding the jalousie or shutter in place.

sill
tal piece of wood below art of window, angled to away from the window.

stile tongue of sash
Vertical part of the frame with a rounded side that fits into the stile groove of the sash.

stile groove of sash
Vertical part of the frame with a concave groove; the stile tongue of the sash fits into it.

bottom of frame
Lowest structural part of window frame.

hinge
Small metal part pivoting on a gudgeon to let the casement swing.

HOUSE

site plan

Graphical representation of the horizontal projection of a lot.

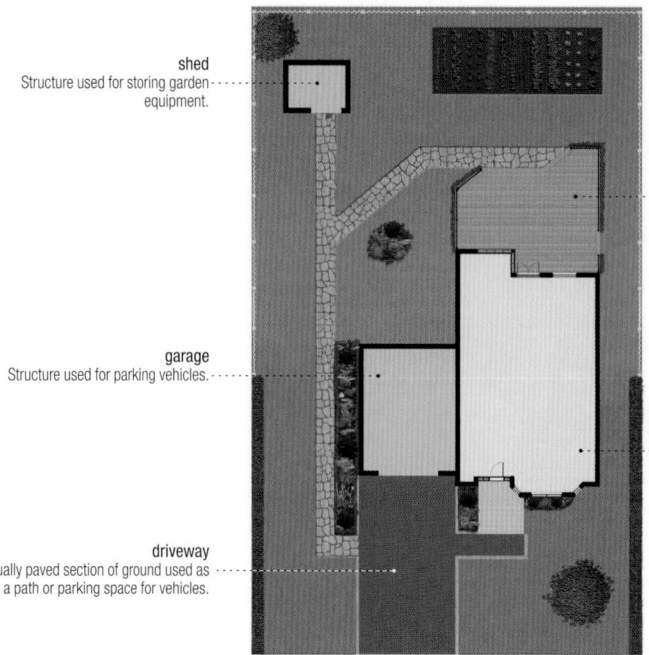

shed
Structure used for storing garden equipment.

patio
Outdoor area adjacent to the house that is often paved and adapted for ourdoor dining.

garage
Structure used for parking vehicles.

house
Structure built as a dwelling and equipped to provide a comfortable and secure life for people.

driveway
Usually paved section of ground used as a path or parking space for vehicles.

main rooms

elevation
Architectural drawing that shows one side of the house without using linear perspective.

lawn
Grass-covered land around a house.

shed
Structure used for storing garden equipment.

garage
Structure used for parking vehicles.

finished attic
Floor immediately below containing rooms or an part of the house.

second floor
Part of the house define and a ceiling; it is locate the first floor.

first floor
Part of the house close level.

basement
Part of the house that is underground or partiall under the ground floor.

main rooms

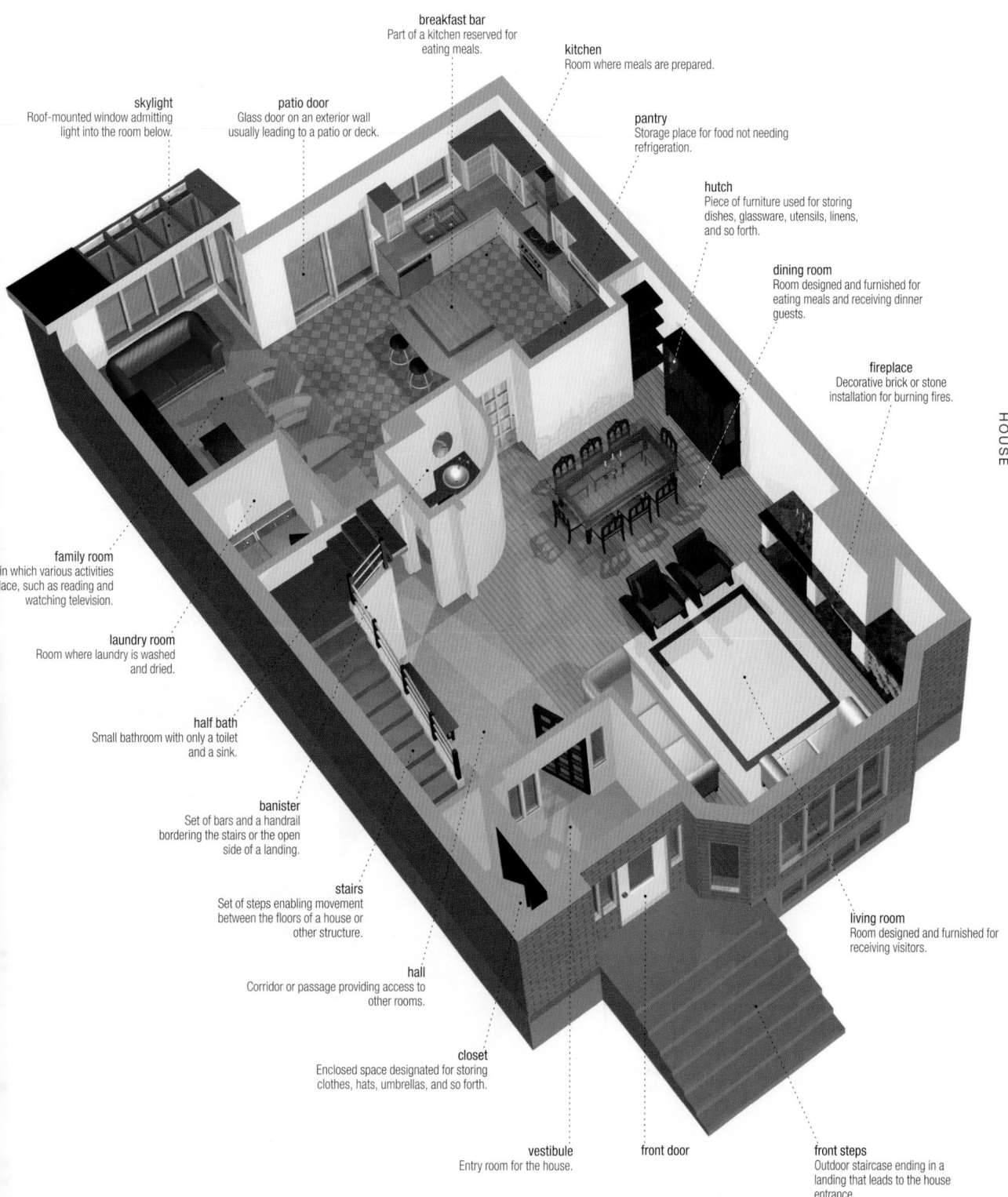

first floor
Part of the house closest to ground level.

breakfast bar
Part of a kitchen reserved for eating meals.

kitchen
Room where meals are prepared.

skylight
Roof-mounted window admitting light into the room below.

patio door
Glass door on an exterior wall usually leading to a patio or deck.

pantry
Storage place for food not needing refrigeration.

hutch
Piece of furniture used for storing dishes, glassware, utensils, linens, and so forth.

dining room
Room designed and furnished for eating meals and receiving dinner guests.

fireplace
Decorative brick or stone installation for burning fires.

family room
Room in which various activities take place, such as reading and watching television.

laundry room
Room where laundry is washed and dried.

half bath
Small bathroom with only a toilet and a sink.

banister
Set of bars and a handrail bordering the stairs or the open side of a landing.

stairs
Set of steps enabling movement between the floors of a house or other structure.

hall
Corridor or passage providing access to other rooms.

closet
Enclosed space designated for storing clothes, hats, umbrellas, and so forth.

living room
Room designed and furnished for receiving visitors.

vestibule
Entry room for the house.

front door

front steps
Outdoor staircase ending in a landing that leads to the house entrance.

HOUSE

HOUSE

main rooms

second floor
Part of the house defined by a floor and a ceiling; it is located above the first floor.

bathtub
Sanitary fixture for taking baths; it is shaped like a deep, elongated basin.

closet
Enclosed area for storing clothes.

landing
Platform at the top of a set of stairs providing access to rooms on that floor.

bedroom
Room for sleeping.

bathroom
Room designed for personal hygiene; it is equipped with running water and sanitary fixtures.

bedroom
Room for sleeping.

toilet
Sanitary fixture for disposing of bodily waste; it comprises a toilet bowl and a tank.

walk-in closet
Closet for storing clothes that is big enough to enter.

stairs
Set of steps enabling movement between the floors of a house or other structure.

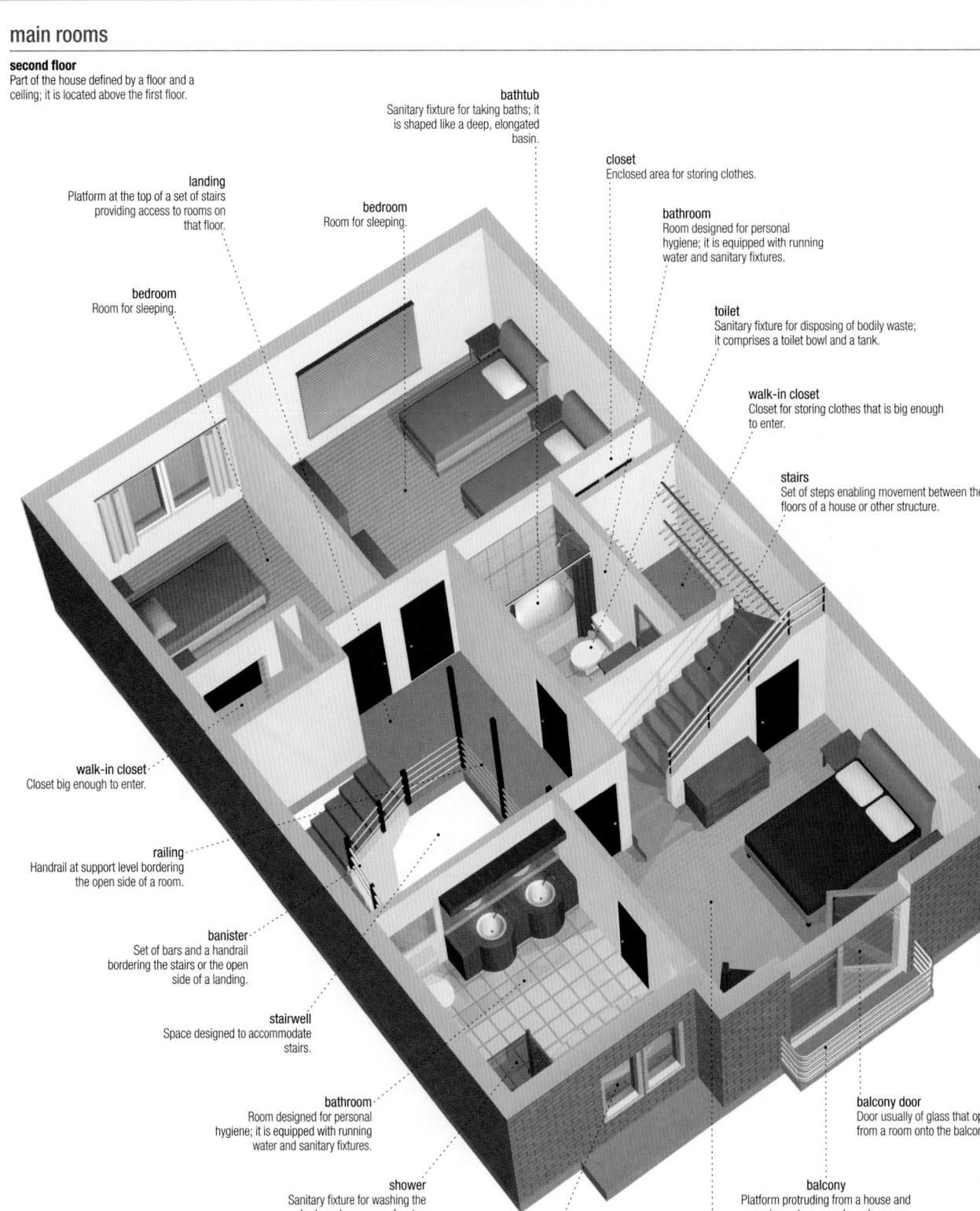

walk-in closet
Closet big enough to enter.

railing
Handrail at support level bordering the open side of a room.

banister
Set of bars and a handrail bordering the stairs or the open side of a landing.

stairwell
Space designed to accommodate stairs.

bathroom
Room designed for personal hygiene; it is equipped with running water and sanitary fixtures.

shower
Sanitary fixture for washing the body under a spray of water.

window
Opening in a wall fitted with glass to let in light and air.

master bedroom
The largest room for sleeping.

balcony
Platform protruding from a house and opening onto a room by a door or a balcony window; it is bordered by a handrail.

balcony door
Door usually of glass that op from a room onto the balcon

main rooms

finished attic
An upper room or space immediately
below the roof.

rug
Piece of thick heavy fabric usually
having a nap and covering a
section of the floor; it is removable.

armchair
Chair with armrests.

bookcase
Piece of furniture having shelves on
which to store books.

desk
Table designed to facilitate writing
or computer work.

study
Room intended for intellectual
work; it usually contains a
worktable.

HOUSE

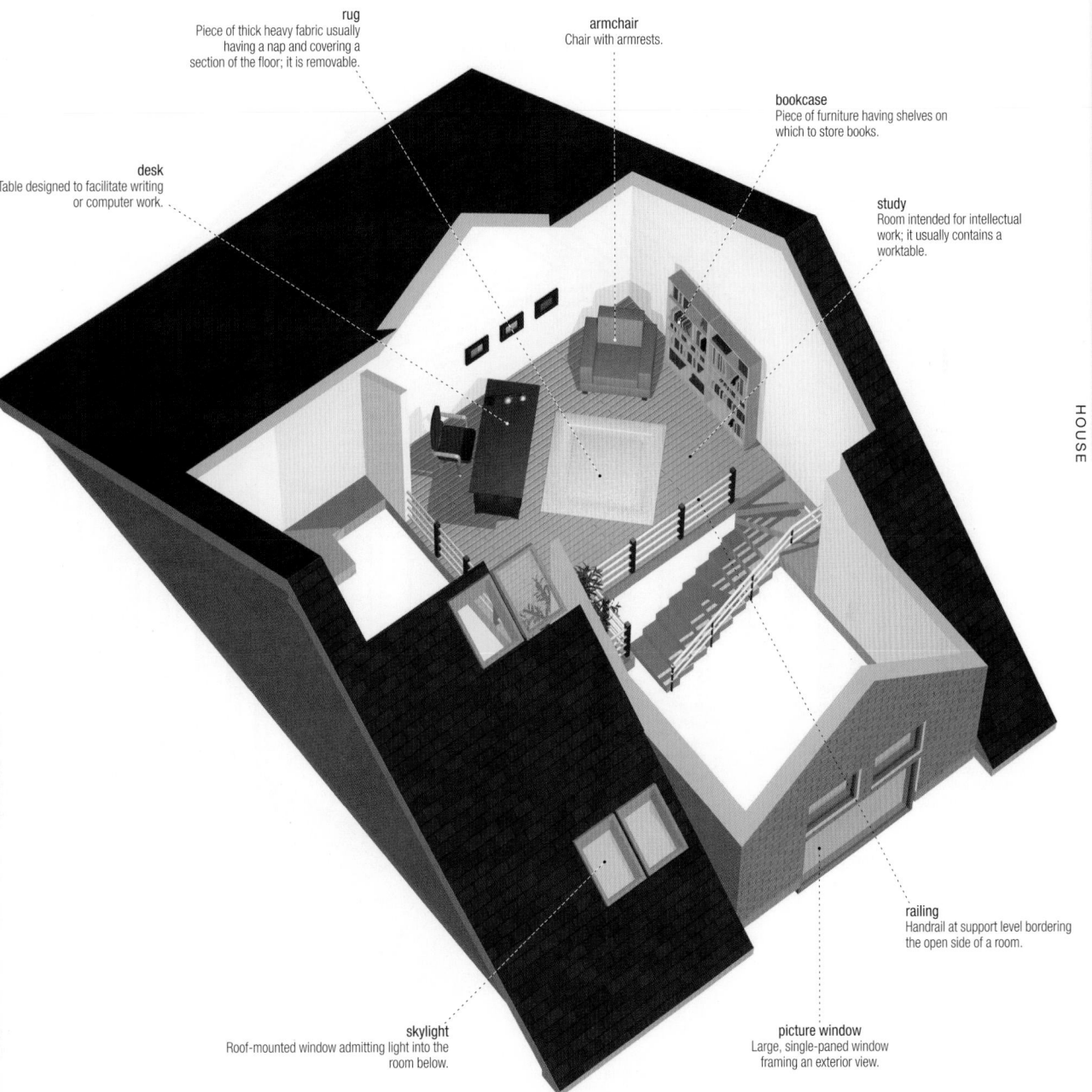

railing
Handrail at support level bordering
the open side of a room.

skylight
Roof-mounted window admitting light into the
room below.

picture window
Large, single-paned window
framing an exterior view.

HOUSE

frame

Assembly of members that consists of the load-bearing structure of a building and that provides stability to it.

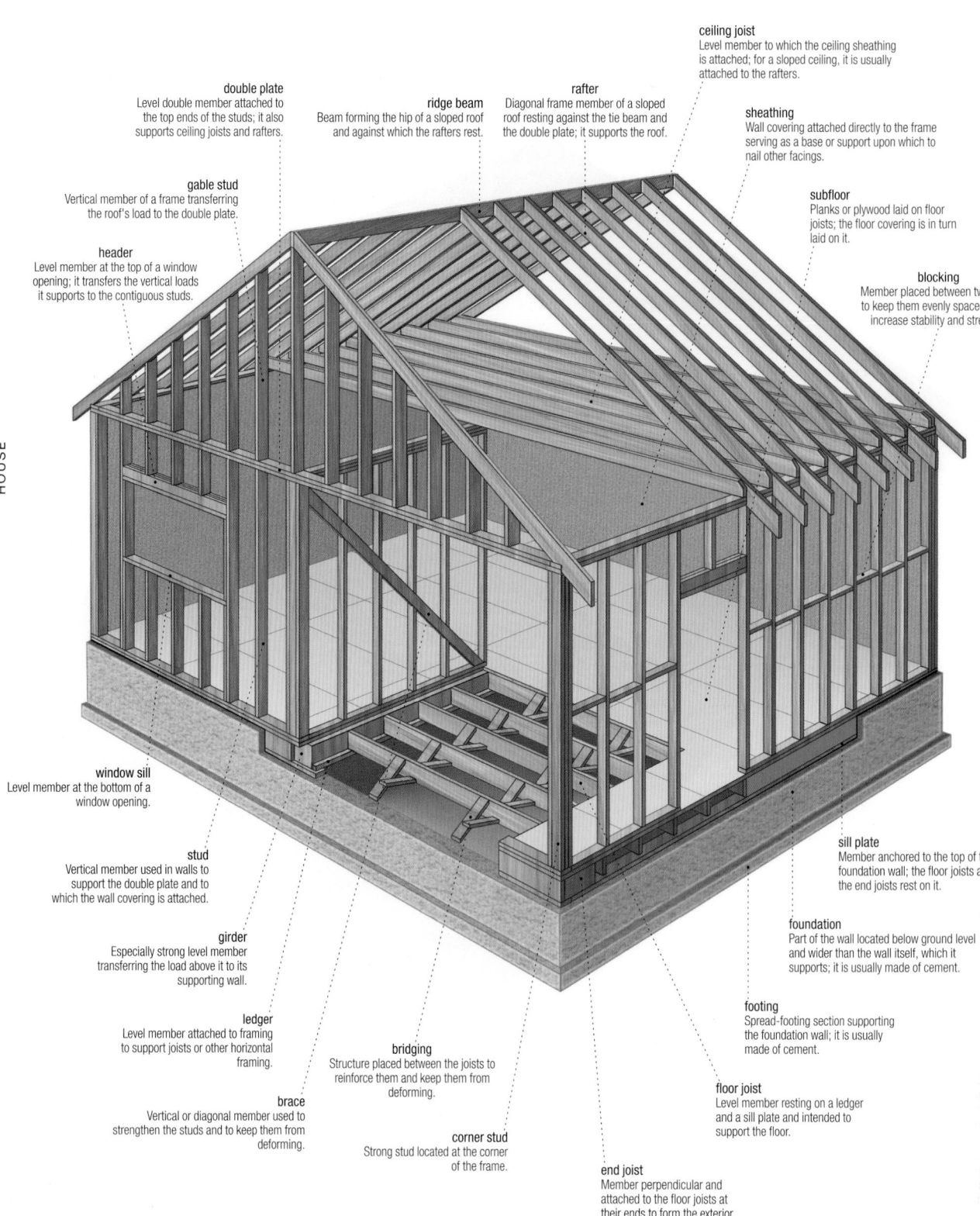

ceiling joist
Level member to which the ceiling sheathing is attached; for a sloped ceiling, it is usually attached to the rafters.

double plate
Level double member attached to the top ends of the studs; it also supports ceiling joists and rafters.

ridge beam
Beam forming the hip of a sloped roof and against which the rafters rest.

rafter
Diagonal frame member of a sloped roof resting against the tie beam and the double plate; it supports the roof.

sheathing
Wall covering attached directly to the frame serving as a base or support upon which to nail other facings.

gable stud
Vertical member of a frame transferring the roof's load to the double plate.

subfloor
Planks or plywood laid on floor joists; the floor covering is in turn laid on it.

header
Level member at the top of a window opening; it transfers the vertical loads it supports to the contiguous studs.

blocking
Member placed between tw to keep them evenly spaced increase stability and stre

window sill
Level member at the bottom of a window opening.

stud
Vertical member used in walls to support the double plate and to which the wall covering is attached.

sill plate
Member anchored to the top of t foundation wall; the floor joists a the end joists rest on it.

girder
Especially strong level member transferring the load above it to its supporting wall.

foundation
Part of the wall located below ground level and wider than the wall itself, which it supports; it is usually made of cement.

ledger
Level member attached to framing to support joists or other horizontal framing.

footing
Spread-footing section supporting the foundation wall; it is usually made of cement.

bridging
Structure placed between the joists to reinforce them and keep them from deforming.

brace
Vertical or diagonal member used to strengthen the studs and to keep them from deforming.

corner stud
Strong stud located at the corner of the frame.

floor joist
Level member resting on a ledger and a sill plate and intended to support the floor.

end joist
Member perpendicular and attached to the floor joists at their ends to form the exterior framework.

roof truss

Assembly of members composed of a triangular substructure to form the frame of a sloped roof; it supports the roof.

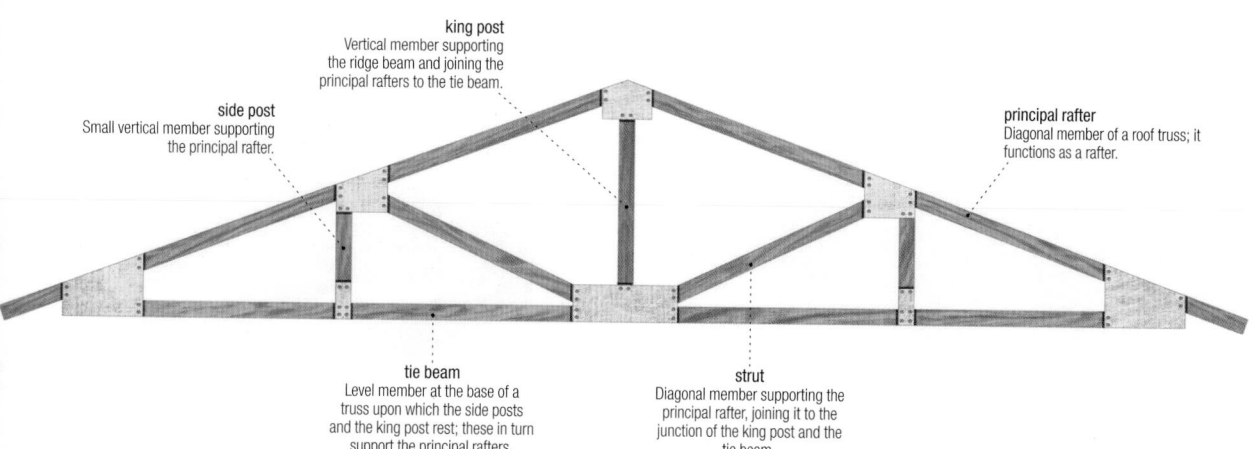

king post
Vertical member supporting the ridge beam and joining the principal rafters to the tie beam.

side post
Small vertical member supporting the principal rafter.

principal rafter
Diagonal member of a roof truss; it functions as a rafter.

tie beam
Level member at the base of a truss upon which the side posts and the king post rest; these in turn support the principal rafters.

strut
Diagonal member supporting the principal rafter, joining it to the junction of the king post and the tie beam.

foundation

Work done on-site in cement or masonry; it supports a structure's load and transfers it to the ground, thus providing stability.

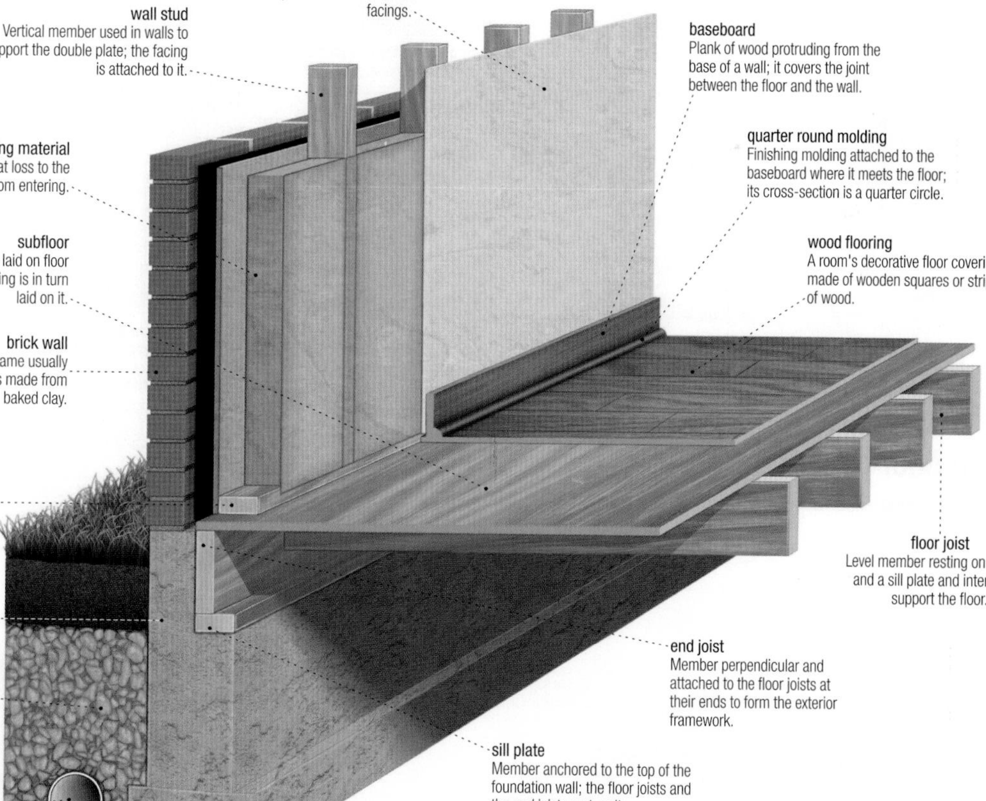

HOUSE

sheathing
Wall covering attached directly to the frame serving as a base or support upon which to nail other facings.

wall stud
Vertical member used in walls to support the double plate; the facing is attached to it.

baseboard
Plank of wood protruding from the base of a wall; it covers the joint between the floor and the wall.

insulating material
Material impeding heat loss to the outdoors or the cold from entering.

quarter round molding
Finishing molding attached to the baseboard where it meets the floor; its cross-section is a quarter circle.

subfloor
Planks or plywood laid on floor joists; the floor covering is in turn laid on it.

wood flooring
A room's decorative floor covering made of wooden squares or strips of wood.

brick wall
Exterior facing of a frame usually composed of blocks made from baked clay.

sill
el member to which the bottom ends of the studs are attached.

floor joist
Level member resting on a ledger and a sill plate and intended to support the floor.

foundation
t of the wall located below d level and wider than the self, which it supports; it is usually made of cement.

end joist
Member perpendicular and attached to the floor joists at their ends to form the exterior framework.

gravel bed
of small stones absorbing particles found in water to m from blocking the drain; b keeps the drain in place.

sill plate
Member anchored to the top of the foundation wall; the floor joists and the end joists rest on it.

drain tile
d pipe draining water from so protects the foundation st and pressure caused by wet soil.

footing
Spread-footing section supporting the foundation wall; it is usually made of cement.

HOUSE

wood flooring

A room's decorative floor covering made of wooden squares or strips of wood.

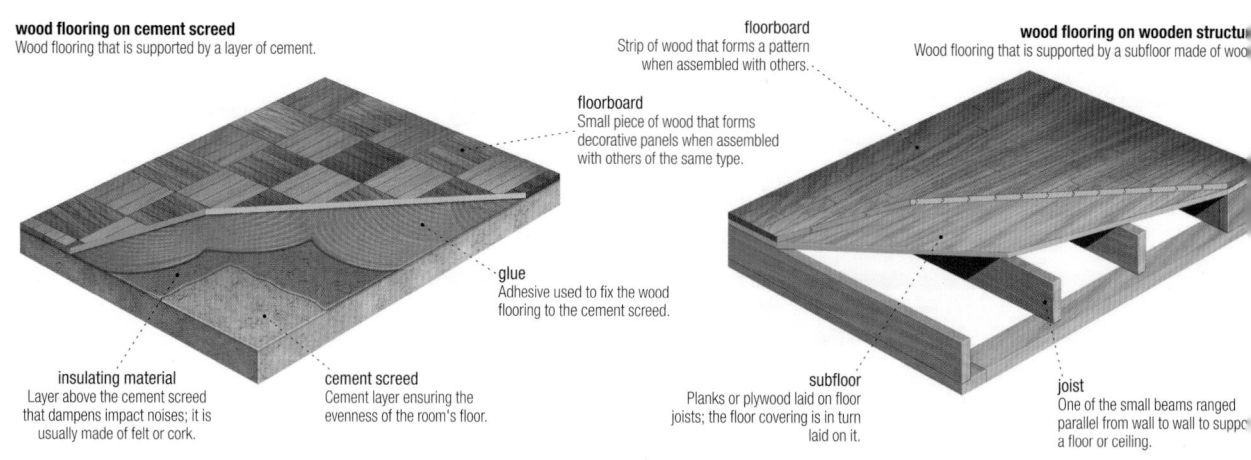

wood flooring on cement screed
Wood flooring that is supported by a layer of cement.

floorboard
Strip of wood that forms a pattern when assembled with others.

floorboard
Small piece of wood that forms decorative panels when assembled with others of the same type.

wood flooring on wooden structu
Wood flooring that is supported by a subfloor made of woo

glue
Adhesive used to fix the wood flooring to the cement screed.

insulating material
Layer above the cement screed that dampens impact noises; it is usually made of felt or cork.

cement screed
Cement layer ensuring the evenness of the room's floor.

subfloor
Planks or plywood laid on floor joists; the floor covering is in turn laid on it.

joist
One of the small beams ranged parallel from wall to wall to suppo
a floor or ceiling.

wood flooring arrangements
Strip flooring and parquetry are vehicles for creating various artistic patterns.

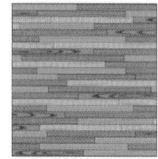

overlay flooring
Wood flooring with floorboards of different lengths laid parallel; its joints are distributed randomly.

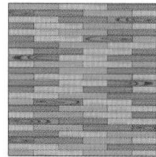

strip flooring with alternate joints
Wood flooring with floorboards of identical lengths laid parallel; its joints are offset by half a length from one row to the next.

herringbone parquet
Wood flooring of rectangular wood strips of equal lengths laid one against the other to form an angle of 45°.

herringbone pattern
Wood flooring of equal length
whose joints meet at 45° to 6(
cuts.

inlaid parquet
Wood flooring of parquetry assembled in a checkerboard pattern.

basket weave pattern
Wood flooring of parquetry creating a woven effect.

Arenberg parquet
Wood flooring composed of a border and of different geometric figures. Inspired by the Château d'Arenberg in Belgium.

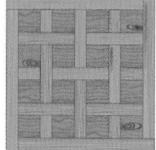

Chantilly parquet
Wood flooring composed of a border and of compartments positioned at right angles to it. Inspired by the Château de Chantilly in France.

Versailles parquet
Wood flooring composed of a bord
of compartments positioned diagor
relation to it. Inspired by the Châte
Versailles in France.

textile floor coverings

Textile floor coverings, such as rugs and pile carpets, are comfortable and attractive, and dampen impact noise.

rug
Piece of thick heavy fabric usually having a nap and covering a section of the floor; it is removable.

pile carpe
Piece of thick heavy fabric attache
to and covering the entire floor
a roor

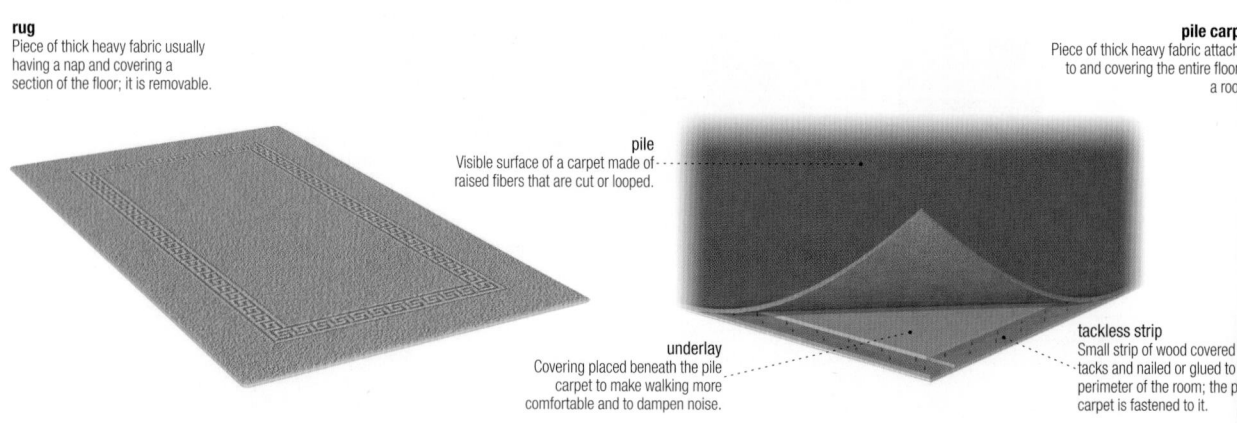

pile
Visible surface of a carpet made of raised fibers that are cut or looped.

underlay
Covering placed beneath the pile carpet to make walking more comfortable and to dampen noise.

tackless strip
Small strip of wood covered
tacks and nailed or glued to t
perimeter of the room; the pil
carpet is fastened to it.

stairs

Structure enabling movement from one level to another.

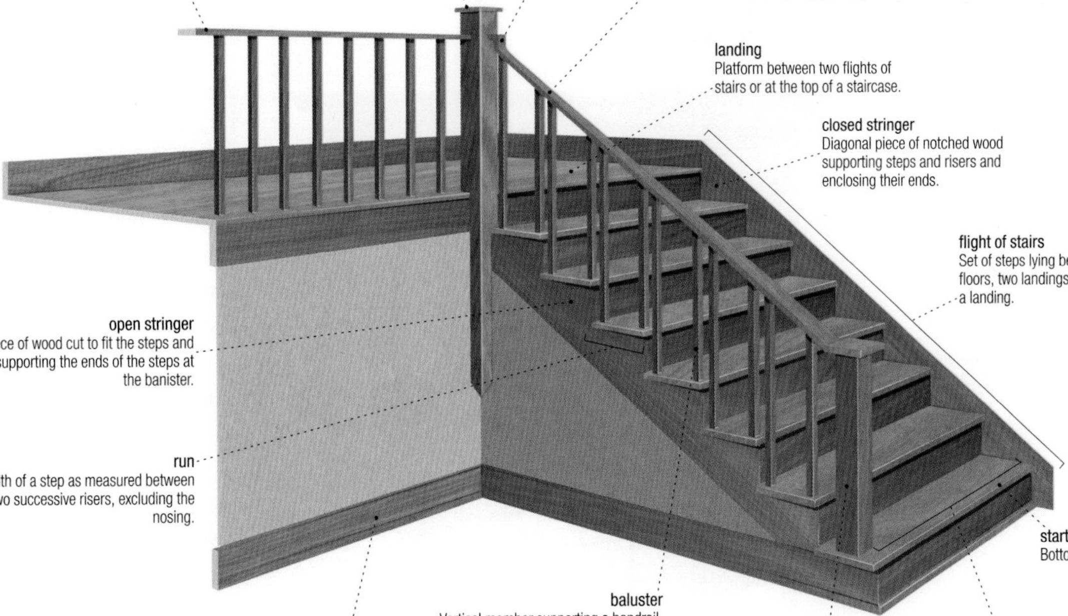

goose-neck
Decorative detail at the end of a handrail.

banister
Set of bars and a handrail bordering the stairs or the open side of a landing.

cap
Adornment for the top of a newel post.

handrail
Top part of a banister for gripping when climbing or descending a staircase.

landing
Platform between two flights of stairs or at the top of a staircase.

closed stringer
Diagonal piece of notched wood supporting steps and risers and enclosing their ends.

flight of stairs
Set of steps lying between two floors, two landings or a floor and a landing.

open stringer
...nal piece of wood cut to fit the steps and ...s and supporting the ends of the steps at the banister.

run
Width of a step as measured between two successive risers, excluding the nosing.

baseboard
Plank of wood protruding from the base of a wall; it hides the joint between the floor and the wall.

baluster
Vertical member supporting a handrail.

newel post
Strong post at the top or bottom of a staircase supporting the handrail.

starting step
Bottom step in a flight of stairs.

step groove
Width of the staircase.

HOUSE

step
Part of a staircase composed of a tread and a riser.

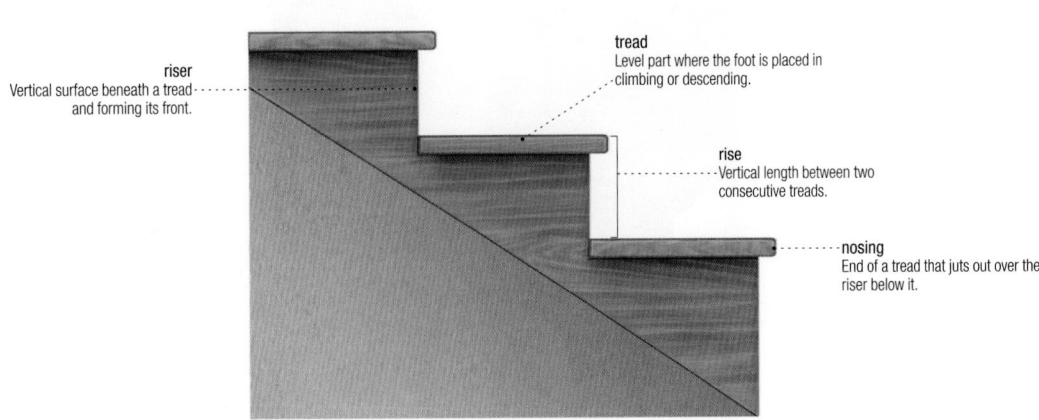

riser
Vertical surface beneath a tread and forming its front.

tread
Level part where the foot is placed in climbing or descending.

rise
Vertical length between two consecutive treads.

nosing
End of a tread that juts out over the riser below it.

wood firing

Creates heat by burning wood; nowadays, heating with wood is usually reserved as a backup.

fireplace
Masonry structure topped with a chimney and open in front; burning wood emits heat that is reflected from the inner hearth.

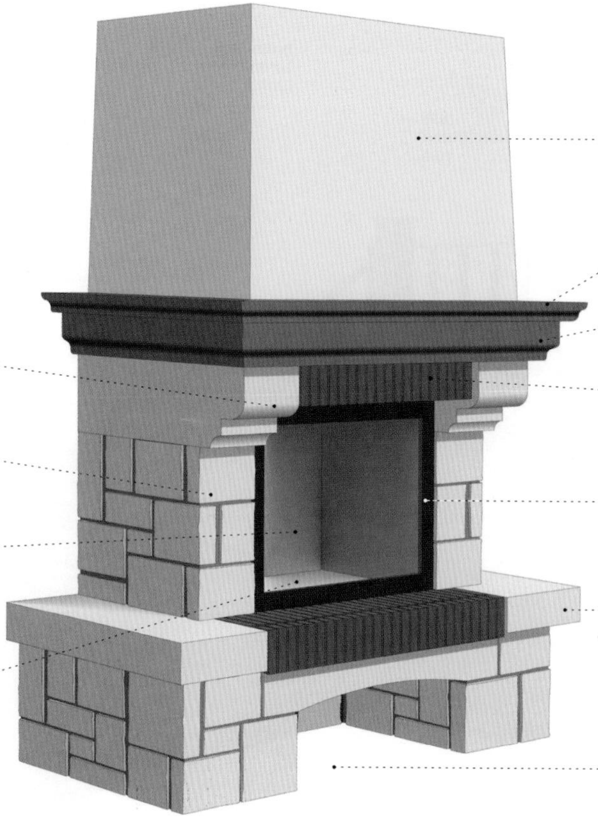

hood
Part of a fireplace located above the mantel; it hides the chimney and allows the smoke to escape to the outdoors.

mantel shelf
Level top part of a fireplace's mantel.

corbel
Piece protruding from a jamb or wall; it supports the mantel of a fireplace.

mantel
Part of the fireplace protruding over the hearth.

lintel
Horizontal crosspiece above the hearth and supporting the mantel.

jamb
Vertical facing making up the side of the hearth and supporting the upper parts of the fireplace.

frame
Metal piece around the edge of the fireplace opening.

firebrick back
Vertical facing making up the back of the hearth.

base
Pedestal protecting a room's floor from the heat produced by the fireplace.

inner hearth
Part of a fireplace where combustion takes place.

woodbox
Part of the fireplace where wood is stored.

wood stove
Closed heating device; the amount of air entering the fire box is controlled to slow down combustion.

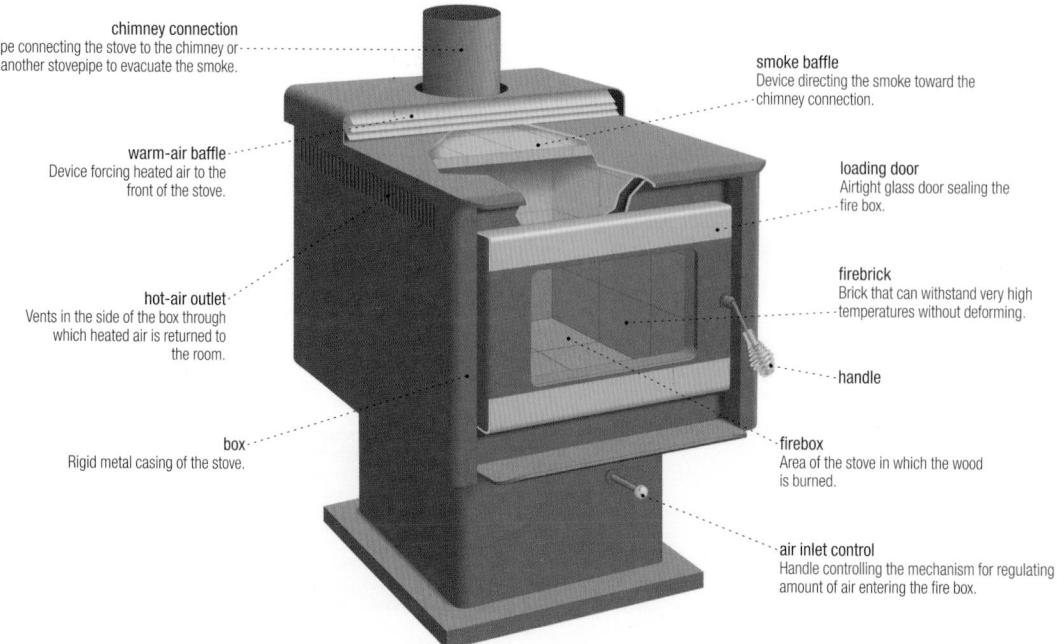

chimney connection
Pipe connecting the stove to the chimney or to another stovepipe to evacuate the smoke.

smoke baffle
Device directing the smoke toward the chimney connection.

warm-air baffle
Device forcing heated air to the front of the stove.

loading door
Airtight glass door sealing the fire box.

firebrick
Brick that can withstand very high temperatures without deforming.

hot-air outlet
Vents in the side of the box through which heated air is returned to the room.

handle

box
Rigid metal casing of the stove.

firebox
Area of the stove in which the wood is burned.

air inlet control
Handle controlling the mechanism for regulating the amount of air entering the fire box.

HOUSE

chimney

Channel through which smoke and combustion gases from a heating device are evacuated while ensuring the free flow of air.

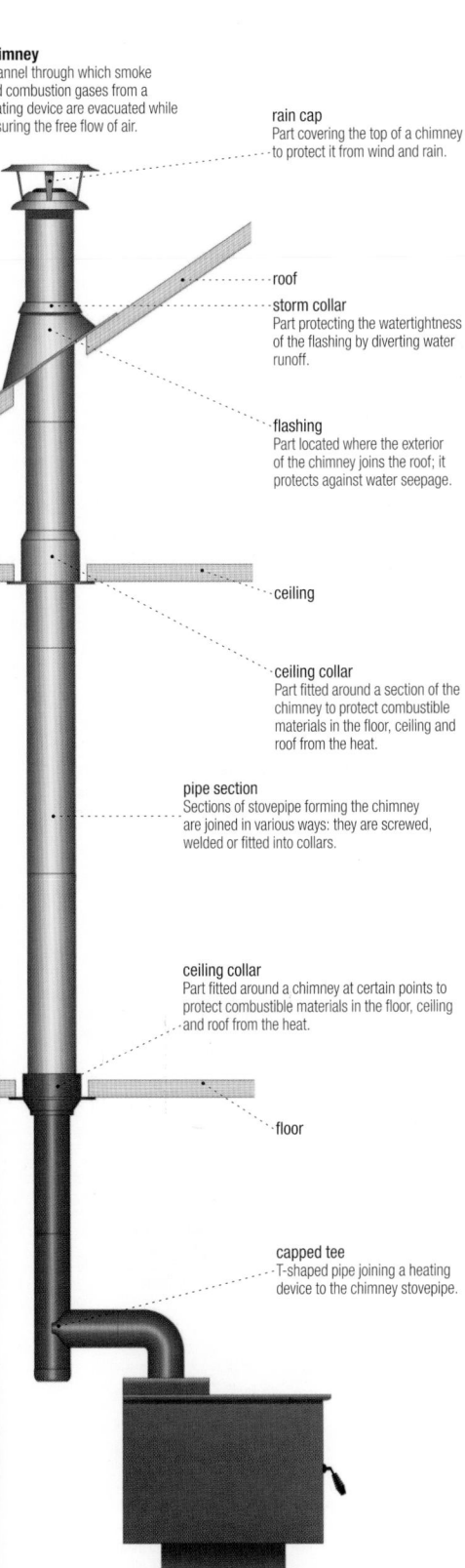

rain cap
Part covering the top of a chimney to protect it from wind and rain.

roof

storm collar
Part protecting the watertightness of the flashing by diverting water runoff.

flashing
Part located where the exterior of the chimney joins the roof; it protects against water seepage.

ceiling

ceiling collar
Part fitted around a section of the chimney to protect combustible materials in the floor, ceiling and roof from the heat.

pipe section
Sections of stovepipe forming the chimney are joined in various ways: they are screwed, welded or fitted into collars.

ceiling collar
Part fitted around a chimney at certain points to protect combustible materials in the floor, ceiling and roof from the heat.

floor

capped tee
T-shaped pipe joining a heating device to the chimney stovepipe.

fire irons

Tools used to grasp and move burning wood, revive the fire and collect the ashes.

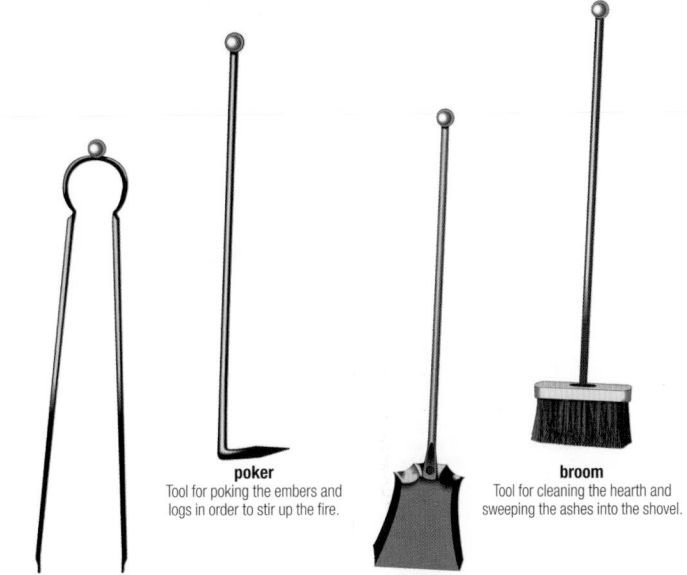

poker
Tool for poking the embers and logs in order to stir up the fire.

broom
Tool for cleaning the hearth and sweeping the ashes into the shovel.

fireplace tongs
Tool for grasping and moving logs and embers.

shovel
Tool for collecting the ashes.

andirons
Metal supports placed in the hearth for cradling the logs; they allow air to circulate during combustion.

log carrier
Basket for carrying firewood and storing it near the fireplace.

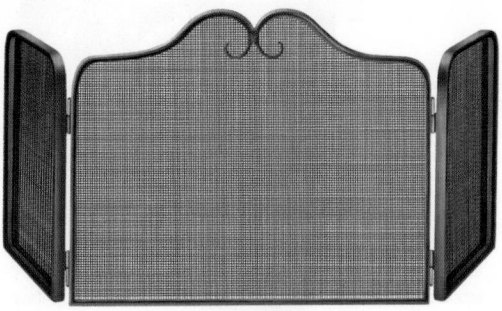

fireplace screen
Device placed in front of the fireplace opening to protect the floor from sparks.

forced warm-air system

In this type of system, air is heated in a furnace and blown by a fan through a network of ducts to the rooms of a dwelling.

plan of a system

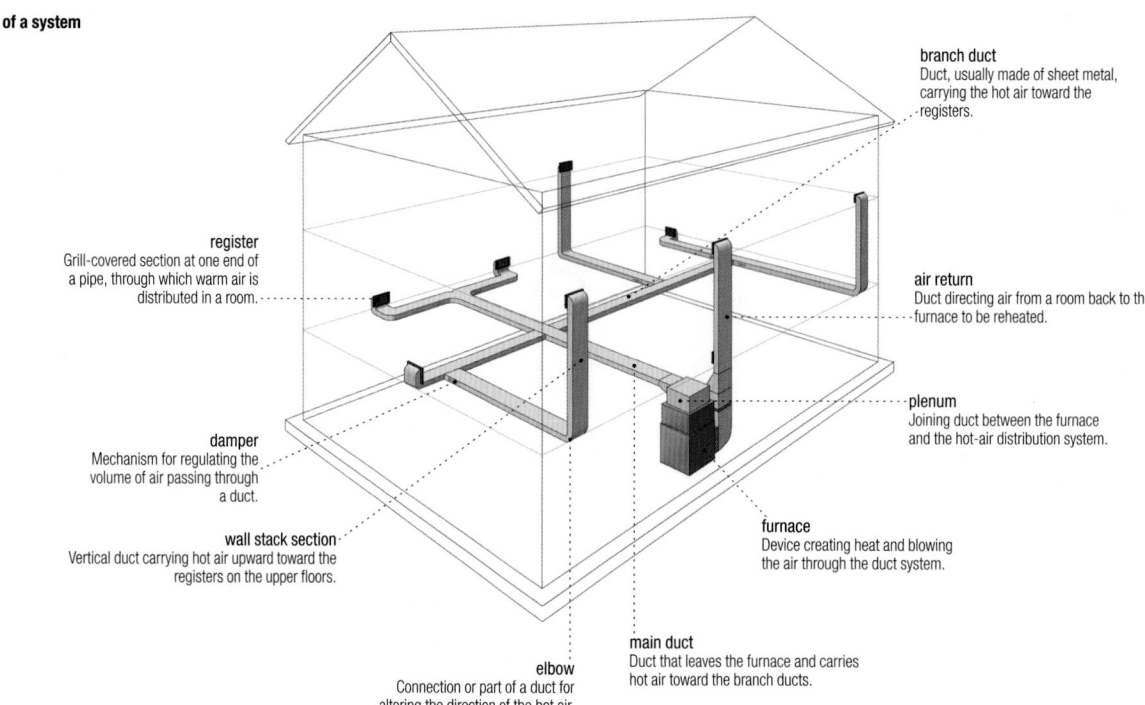

branch duct
Duct, usually made of sheet metal, carrying the hot air toward the registers.

register
Grill-covered section at one end of a pipe, through which warm air is distributed in a room.

air return
Duct directing air from a room back to the furnace to be reheated.

plenum
Joining duct between the furnace and the hot-air distribution system.

damper
Mechanism for regulating the volume of air passing through a duct.

furnace
Device creating heat and blowing the air through the duct system.

wall stack section
Vertical duct carrying hot air upward toward the registers on the upper floors.

elbow
Connection or part of a duct for altering the direction of the hot air.

main duct
Duct that leaves the furnace and carries hot air toward the branch ducts.

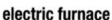

electric furnace
Device using electricity for creating heat and blowing it through the duct system.

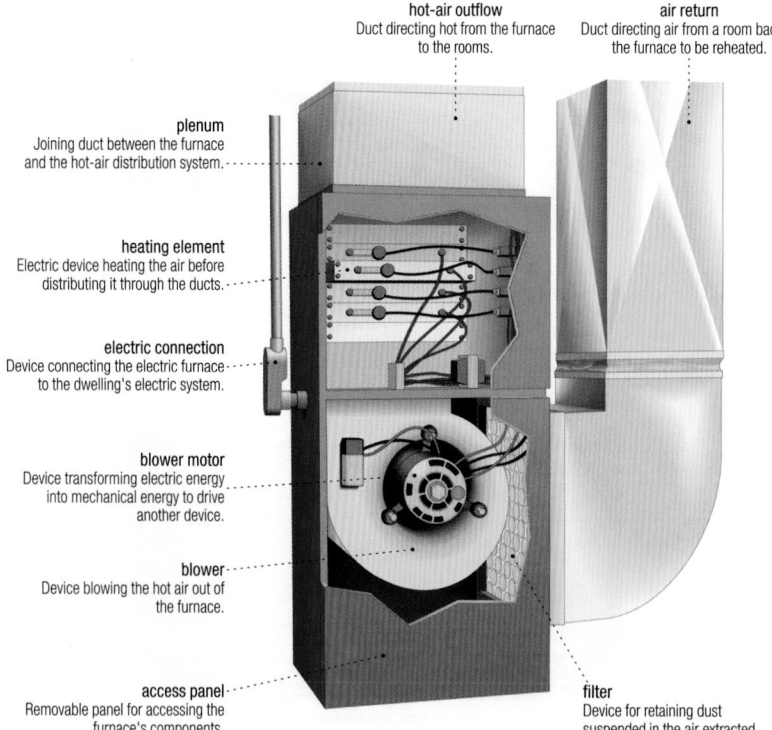

hot-air outflow
Duct directing hot from the furnace to the rooms.

air return
Duct directing air from a room back to the furnace to be reheated.

plenum
Joining duct between the furnace and the hot-air distribution system.

heating element
Electric device heating the air before distributing it through the ducts.

electric connection
Device connecting the electric furnace to the dwelling's electric system.

blower motor
Device transforming electric energy into mechanical energy to drive another device.

blower
Device blowing the hot air out of the furnace.

access panel
Removable panel for accessing the furnace's components.

filter
Device for retaining dust suspended in the air extracted from the dwelling.

types of registers
Registers are located at the ends of the ducts and are fitted at the bottom of a wall, in a floor or near the ceiling.

baseboard register
Adjustable grill located at the end of a duct through which hot air is distributed throughout a room.

wall register
Grill at the end of an air-return duct, which returns a room's air to the furnace.

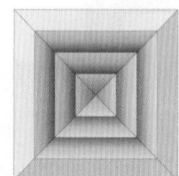

ceiling register
Grill at the end of a duct through which a room's air is drawn to mix it with the forced hot air.

forced hot-water system

Water heated in a boiler flows up to the radiators, where it releases its heat to the ambient air; the water then returns to the boiler to be reheated.

plan of a system

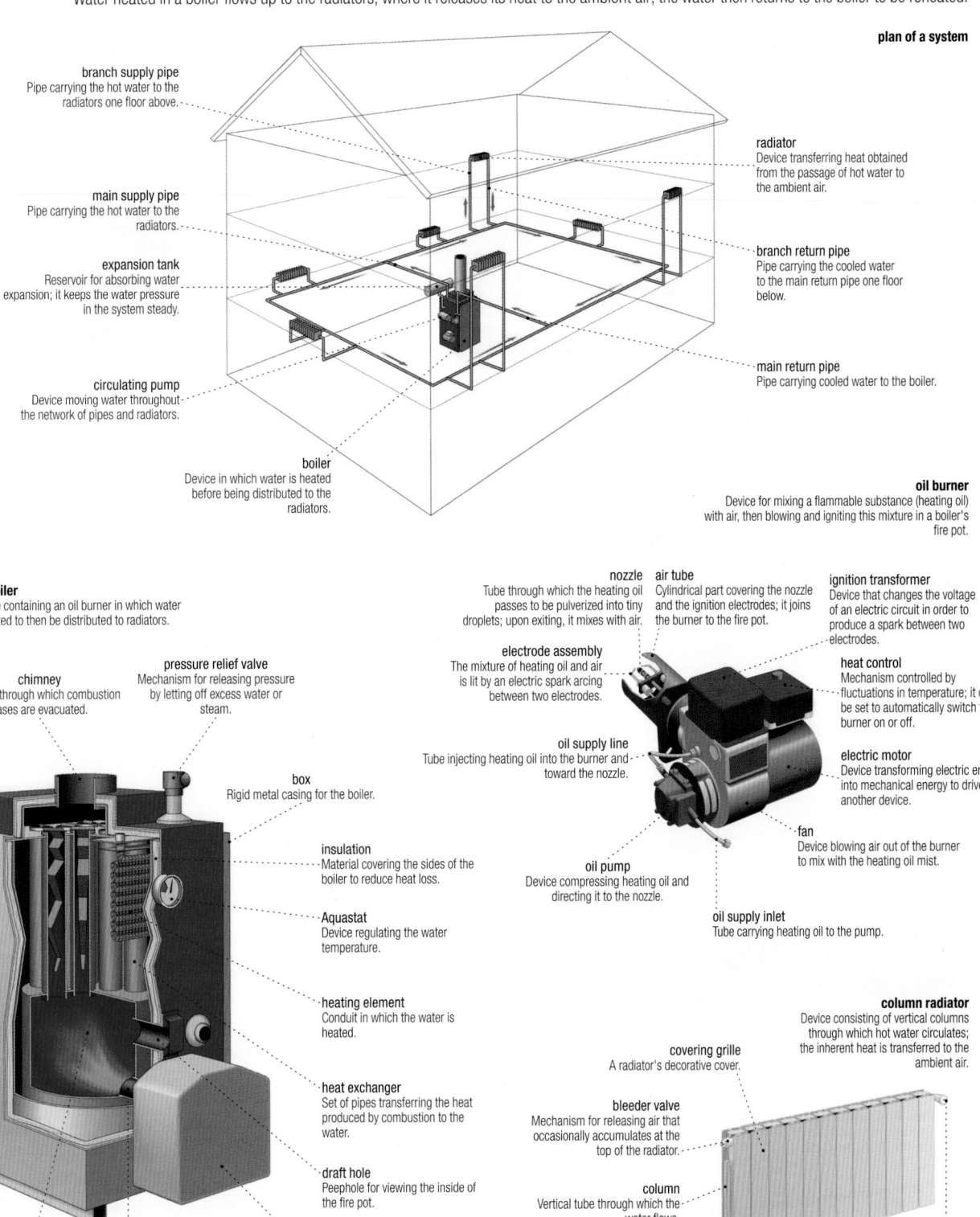

branch supply pipe
Pipe carrying the hot water to the radiators one floor above.

main supply pipe
Pipe carrying the hot water to the radiators.

expansion tank
Reservoir for absorbing water expansion; it keeps the water pressure in the system steady.

circulating pump
Device moving water throughout the network of pipes and radiators.

boiler
Device in which water is heated before being distributed to the radiators.

radiator
Device transferring heat obtained from the passage of hot water to the ambient air.

branch return pipe
Pipe carrying the cooled water to the main return pipe one floor below.

main return pipe
Pipe carrying cooled water to the boiler.

oil burner
Device for mixing a flammable substance (heating oil) with air, then blowing and igniting this mixture in a boiler's fire pot.

HOUSE

boiler
ice containing an oil burner in which water eated to then be distributed to radiators.

chimney
el through which combustion gases are evacuated.

pressure relief valve
Mechanism for releasing pressure by letting off excess water or steam.

box
Rigid metal casing for the boiler.

insulation
Material covering the sides of the boiler to reduce heat loss.

Aquastat
Device regulating the water temperature.

heating element
Conduit in which the water is heated.

heat exchanger
Set of pipes transferring the heat produced by combustion to the water.

draft hole
Peephole for viewing the inside of the fire pot.

fire pot
of the boiler where the stion of air and heating oil ace after they pass through the burner.

air tube
Cylindrical part covering the nozzle and the ignition electrodes; it joins the burner to the fire pot.

burner
Device for mixing a flammable substance with air, and fanning and igniting this mixture in a boiler's fire pot.

nozzle
Tube through which the heating oil passes to be pulverized into tiny droplets; upon exiting, it mixes with air.

air tube
Cylindrical part covering the nozzle and the ignition electrodes; it joins the burner to the fire pot.

electrode assembly
The mixture of heating oil and air is lit by an electric spark arcing between two electrodes.

oil supply line
Tube injecting heating oil into the burner and toward the nozzle.

oil pump
Device compressing heating oil and directing it to the nozzle.

oil supply inlet
Tube carrying heating oil to the pump.

ignition transformer
Device that changes the voltage of an electric circuit in order to produce a spark between two electrodes.

heat control
Mechanism controlled by fluctuations in temperature; it can be set to automatically switch the burner on or off.

electric motor
Device transforming electric energy into mechanical energy to drive another device.

fan
Device blowing air out of the burner to mix with the heating oil mist.

covering grille
A radiator's decorative cover.

bleeder valve
Mechanism for releasing air that occasionally accumulates at the top of the radiator.

column
Vertical tube through which the water flows.

hot-water outlet
Valve for draining the water from the radiator.

column radiator
Device consisting of vertical columns through which hot water circulates; the inherent heat is transferred to the ambient air.

regulating valve
Device for regulating the volume of water circulating through a radiator.

forced hot-water system

gas-fired boiler
Device containing an oil burner in which water is heated to then be distributed to radiators.

exhaust duct
Pipe through which the products of gas combustion are expelled into the air.

burner
Device that mixes air and natural gas to allow combustion.

gas burner
Device that mixes air and natural gas to allow combustion.

expansion tank
Reservoir for absorbing water expansion; it keeps the water pressure in the system steady.

heat exchanger
Set of pipes transferring the heat produced by combustion to the water.

combustion fan
Device that pushes air through the boiler.

circulating pump
Electric motor that pumps water around the heating system.

plate-type heat exchanger
Group of corrugated metal plates designed to raise the temperature of the water.

gas and water connections
Pipes through which gas and water enter the boiler.

digital boiler control unit
Controls of the boiler.

auxiliary heating

convector
Device that, by convection, draws air through its base, heats it inside, then diffuses it through a grille on the top.

outlet grille
Grille through which the heated air is diffused in the room.

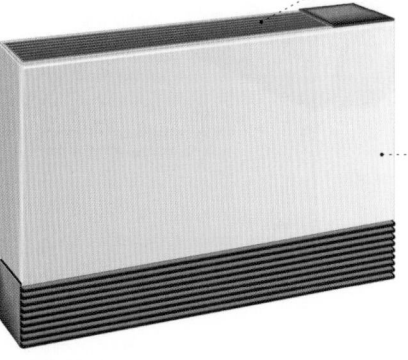

casing
Rigid metal box protecting the heater.

radiant heater
Device producing heat from a heating element and diffusing it in the form of light waves.

electric baseboard radiator
Device using electricity to heat air by drawing it in at its base and releasing it at the top by convection.

fan heater
Device in which the air is heated by electric elements and diffused by a fan.

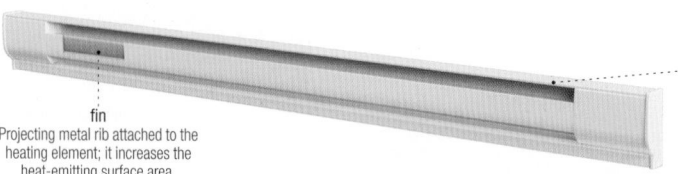

deflector
Part directing the heated air toward the room.

fin
Projecting metal rib attached to the heating element; it increases the heat-emitting surface area.

oil-filled heater
Device made of tubes that circulate oil heated by electric elements.

heat pump

Device exchanging heat between two environments of different temperatures; it can either heat or cool a house, depending on how the circuit is set.

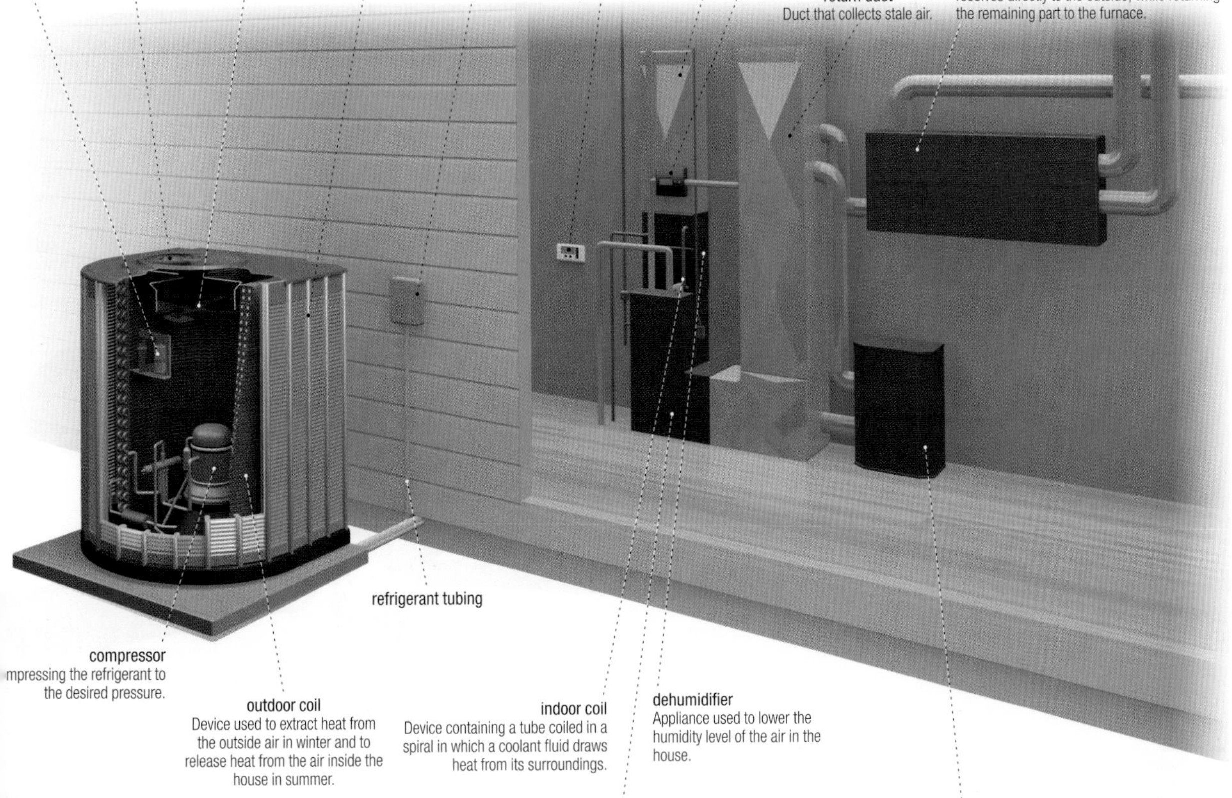

operations monitor
ic device that controls the
np.

fan
Device with rotating blades that
suck air in from the outside
(heating cycle) or expel air from the
inside (cooling cycle).

circuit breaker
Mechanism automatically cutting
off the power supply in the event
of overload.

supply duct
Duct carrying forced hot air
(heating mode) or cool air (cooling
mode) into the house.

fan grille
Perforated panel through which air
enters and exits.

steel cabinet
Metal cabinet containing the
components of the exterior module.

thermostat
Device that detects variations
in temperature and works as an
automatic on-off controller for the
appliance.

humidifier
Appliance used to raise the
humidity level of the air in the
house.

energy recovery ventilator
Appliance that expels a portion of the stale air it
receives directly to the outside, while returning
the remaining part to the furnace.

return duct
Duct that collects stale air.

HOUSE

compressor
mpressing the refrigerant to
the desired pressure.

refrigerant tubing

outdoor coil
Device used to extract heat from
the outside air in winter and to
release heat from the air inside the
house in summer.

indoor coil
Device containing a tube coiled in a
spiral in which a coolant fluid draws
heat from its surroundings.

dehumidifier
Appliance used to lower the
humidity level of the air in the
house.

tdoor unit
rt of the pump in which, depending
the setting, the outside air is
ped (heating mode) or the indoor
is cooled (cooling mode).

furnace
Appliance for heating or air-
conditioning and blowing air into
the distribution ducts in the house.

filtration system
System that collects dust particles
suspended in the air.

indoor unit
Part of the pump that, depending on the
setting, either transfers outdoor heat into
the house (heating mode) or transfers heat
from the indoors to the outdoors (cooling
mode).

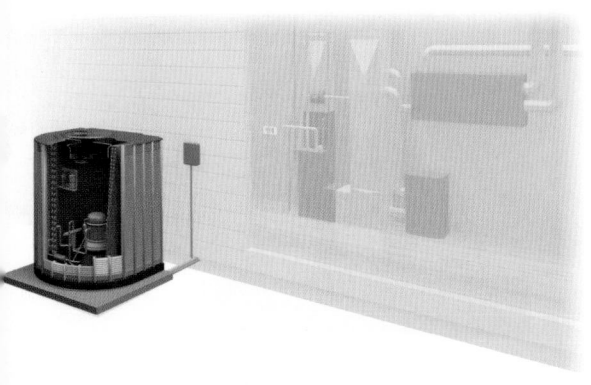

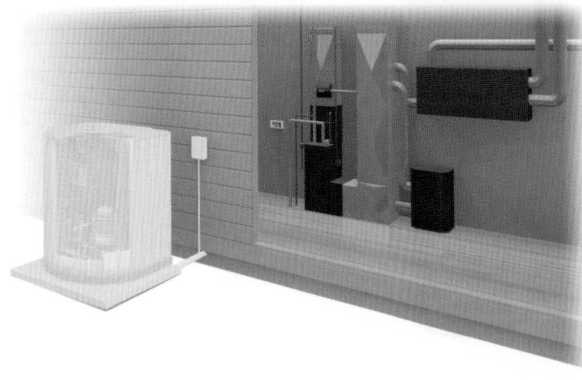

control devices

Devices used to regulate the ambient temperature.

programmable thermostat
Electronic device for keeping a house or
a room at a certain temperature; it can be
programmed to follow a schedule.

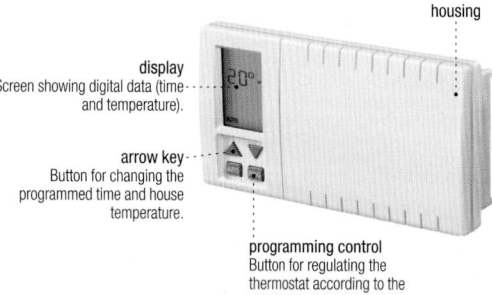

housing

display
Screen showing digital data (time
and temperature).

arrow key
Button for changing the
programmed time and house
temperature.

programming control
Button for regulating the
thermostat according to the
schedule chosen.

room thermos
Mechanism that, by sensing chan
in temperature, can be set to sw
the heating or air-conditioning on o
automatically in a room or hou

cover

temperature control
Knob for selecting the desired
temperature.

desired temperature
Desired temperature of the
ambient air.

actual temperature
A built-in thermometer shows the
current temperature of the room in
which it is located.

pointer
Metal needle attached to the
thermometer showing the ambie
temperature.

air-conditioning appliances

These appliances help make a house comfortable by cooling, filtering and humidifying or dehumidifying the ambient air.

dehumidifier
Device that lowers the humidity level
in a room's air by cooling it.

humidistat
Mechanism that, by sensing
changes in humidity, can be set to
automatically switch the humidifier
on or off.

front grille
Perforated panel through which the
air enters a room.

bucket
Tank collecting the water droplets
formed from the cooled air.

water level

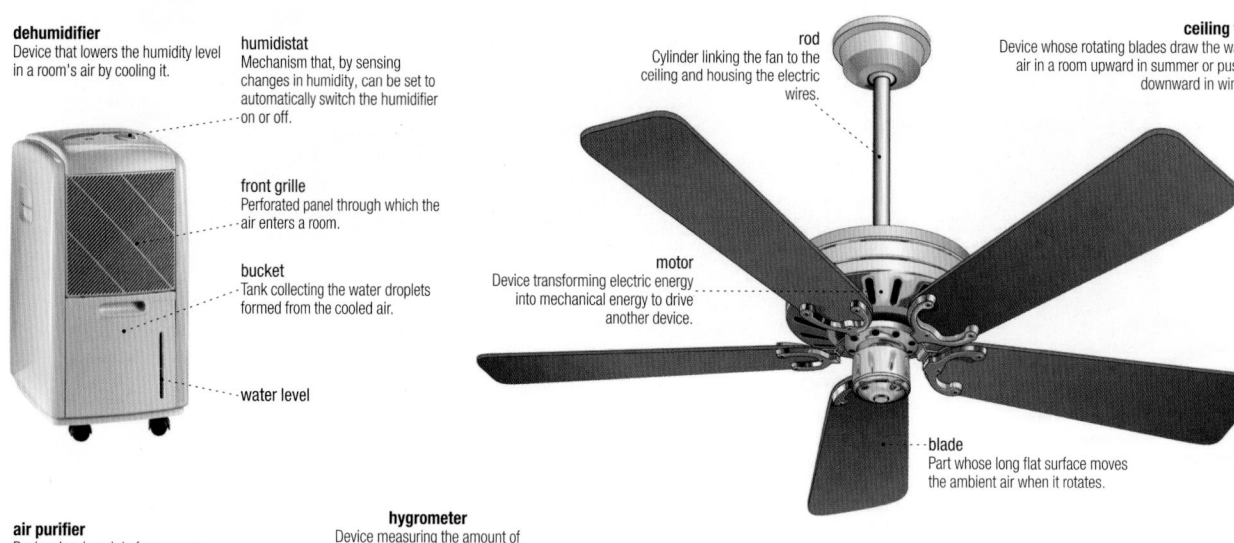

rod
Cylinder linking the fan to the
ceiling and housing the electric
wires.

ceiling
Device whose rotating blades draw the w
air in a room upward in summer or pus
downward in wir

motor
Device transforming electric energy
into mechanical energy to drive
another device.

blade
Part whose long flat surface moves
the ambient air when it rotates.

air purifier
Device drawing air in from a room
to filter it by removing its pollutants
before returning it.

hygrometer
Device measuring the amount of
humidity in a room's air.

temperature

humidity

portable humidi
Device that increases the humidity le
in the air of a ro

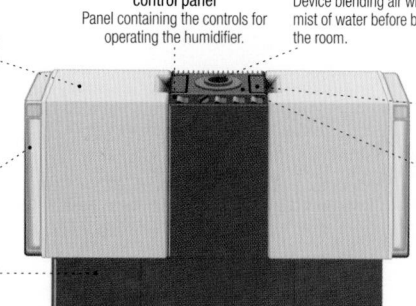

control panel
Panel containing the controls for
operating the humidifier.

vaporizer
Device blending air with a fine
mist of water before blowing it into
the room.

water tank
Reservoir containing the water to
be vaporized in the room.

air filter
Device that absorbs dust
suspended in the air.

water level

vaporizing grille
Perforated panel dispers
humidified air.

tray

air-conditioning appliances

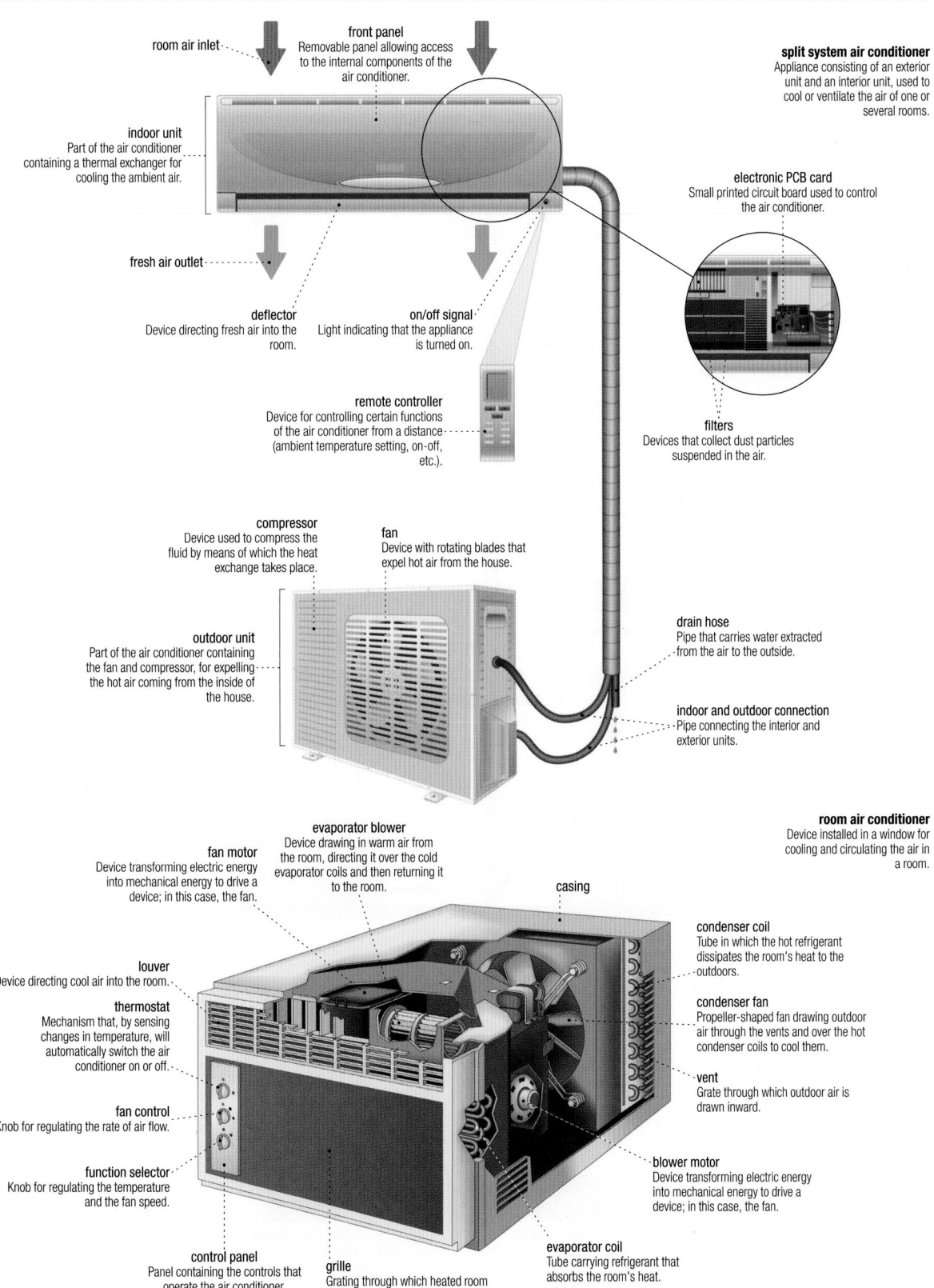

room air inlet

front panel
Removable panel allowing access to the internal components of the air conditioner.

split system air conditioner
Appliance consisting of an exterior unit and an interior unit, used to cool or ventilate the air of one or several rooms.

indoor unit
Part of the air conditioner containing a thermal exchanger for cooling the ambient air.

electronic PCB card
Small printed circuit board used to control the air conditioner.

fresh air outlet

deflector
Device directing fresh air into the room.

on/off signal
Light indicating that the appliance is turned on.

remote controller
Device for controlling certain functions of the air conditioner from a distance (ambient temperature setting, on-off, etc.).

filters
Devices that collect dust particles suspended in the air.

compressor
Device used to compress the fluid by means of which the heat exchange takes place.

fan
Device with rotating blades that expel hot air from the house.

outdoor unit
Part of the air conditioner containing the fan and compressor, for expelling the hot air coming from the inside of the house.

drain hose
Pipe that carries water extracted from the air to the outside.

indoor and outdoor connection
Pipe connecting the interior and exterior units.

HOUSE

room air conditioner
Device installed in a window for cooling and circulating the air in a room.

evaporator blower
Device drawing in warm air from the room, directing it over the cold evaporator coils and then returning it to the room.

fan motor
Device transforming electric energy into mechanical energy to drive a device; in this case, the fan.

casing

condenser coil
Tube in which the hot refrigerant dissipates the room's heat to the outdoors.

louver
Device directing cool air into the room.

condenser fan
Propeller-shaped fan drawing outdoor air through the vents and over the hot condenser coils to cool them.

thermostat
Mechanism that, by sensing changes in temperature, will automatically switch the air conditioner on or off.

vent
Grate through which outdoor air is drawn inward.

fan control
Knob for regulating the rate of air flow.

function selector
Knob for regulating the temperature and the fan speed.

blower motor
Device transforming electric energy into mechanical energy to drive a device; in this case, the fan.

control panel
Panel containing the controls that operate the air conditioner.

grille
Grating through which heated room air passes into the air conditioner.

evaporator coil
Tube carrying refrigerant that absorbs the room's heat.

HOUSE

plumbing system

In a house, there are four plumbing systems enabling water to circulate: hot and cold water distribution, pipe ventilation and wastewater evacuation.

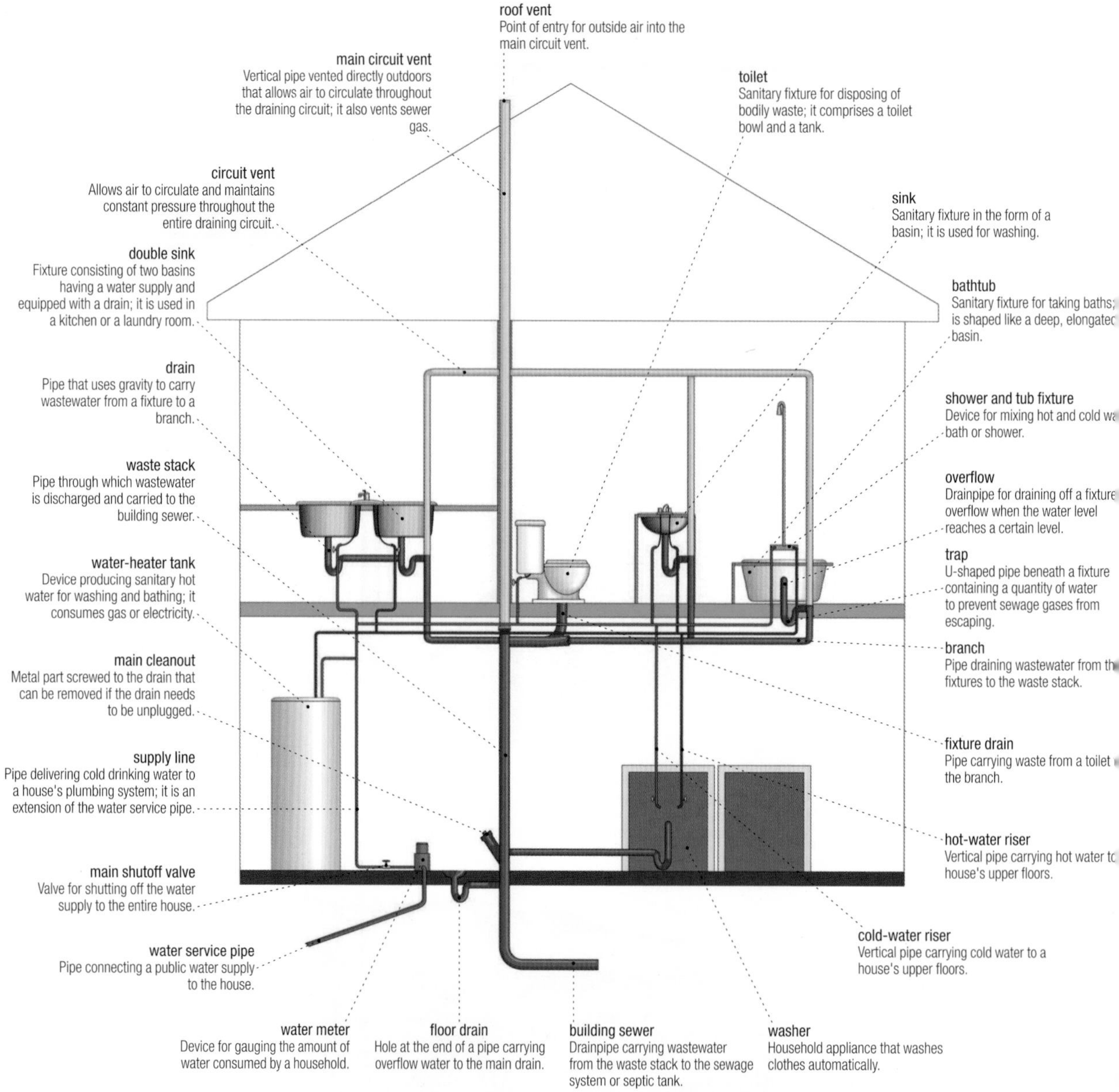

roof vent
Point of entry for outside air into the main circuit vent.

main circuit vent
Vertical pipe vented directly outdoors that allows air to circulate throughout the draining circuit; it also vents sewer gas.

toilet
Sanitary fixture for disposing of bodily waste; it comprises a toilet bowl and a tank.

circuit vent
Allows air to circulate and maintains constant pressure throughout the entire draining circuit.

sink
Sanitary fixture in the form of a basin; it is used for washing.

double sink
Fixture consisting of two basins having a water supply and equipped with a drain; it is used in a kitchen or a laundry room.

bathtub
Sanitary fixture for taking baths; is shaped like a deep, elongated basin.

drain
Pipe that uses gravity to carry wastewater from a fixture to a branch.

shower and tub fixture
Device for mixing hot and cold wa bath or shower.

waste stack
Pipe through which wastewater is discharged and carried to the building sewer.

overflow
Drainpipe for draining off a fixture overflow when the water level reaches a certain level.

water-heater tank
Device producing sanitary hot water for washing and bathing; it consumes gas or electricity.

trap
U-shaped pipe beneath a fixture containing a quantity of water to prevent sewage gases from escaping.

main cleanout
Metal part screwed to the drain that can be removed if the drain needs to be unplugged.

branch
Pipe draining wastewater from th fixtures to the waste stack.

supply line
Pipe delivering cold drinking water to a house's plumbing system; it is an extension of the water service pipe.

fixture drain
Pipe carrying waste from a toilet the branch.

hot-water riser
Vertical pipe carrying hot water to house's upper floors.

main shutoff valve
Valve for shutting off the water supply to the entire house.

cold-water riser
Vertical pipe carrying cold water to a house's upper floors.

water service pipe
Pipe connecting a public water supply to the house.

water meter
Device for gauging the amount of water consumed by a household.

floor drain
Hole at the end of a pipe carrying overflow water to the main drain.

building sewer
Drainpipe carrying wastewater from the waste stack to the sewage system or septic tank.

washer
Household appliance that washes clothes automatically.

ventilating circuit
Set of interconnected pipes allowing air to circulate in the circuit.

draining circuit
Set of interconnected pipes allowing wastewater to drain into the building sewer.

cold-water circuit
Set of interconnected pipes distributing cold drinking water throughout a house.

hot-water circuit
Set of interconnected pipes distributing h water from a hot-water heater.

pedestal-type sump pump

Device removing water from a pit dug in the ground in order to evacuate it to a sewer or septic tank.

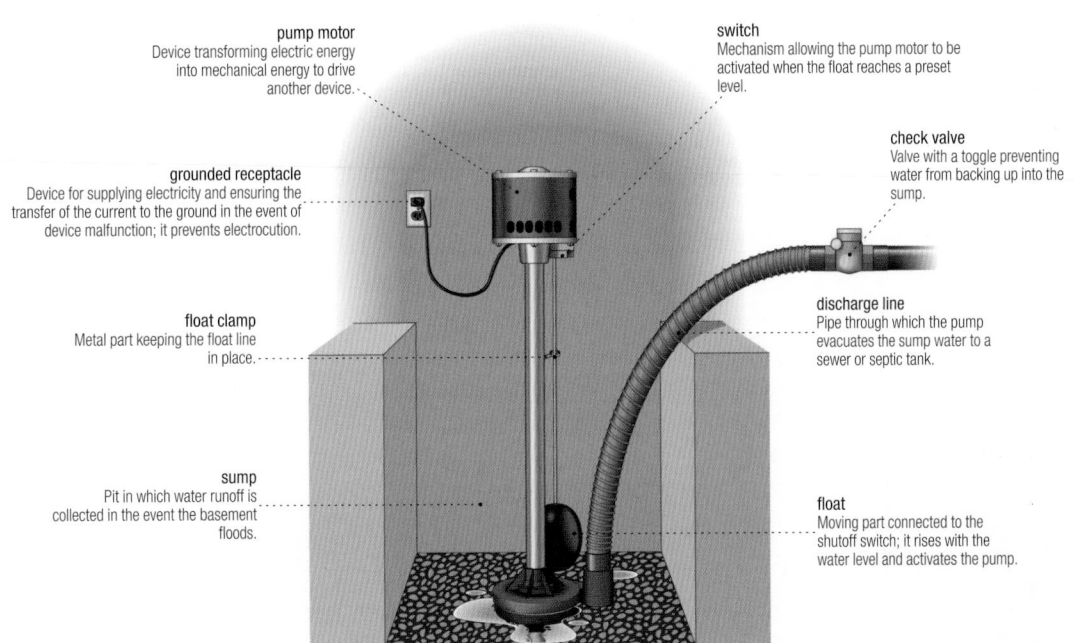

pump motor
Device transforming electric energy into mechanical energy to drive another device.

switch
Mechanism allowing the pump motor to be activated when the float reaches a preset level.

check valve
Valve with a toggle preventing water from backing up into the sump.

grounded receptacle
Device for supplying electricity and ensuring the transfer of the current to the ground in the event of device malfunction; it prevents electrocution.

discharge line
Pipe through which the pump evacuates the sump water to a sewer or septic tank.

float clamp
Metal part keeping the float line in place.

sump
Pit in which water runoff is collected in the event the basement floods.

float
Moving part connected to the shutoff switch; it rises with the water level and activates the pump.

septic tank

Underground system in which sewage is treated and dispersed.

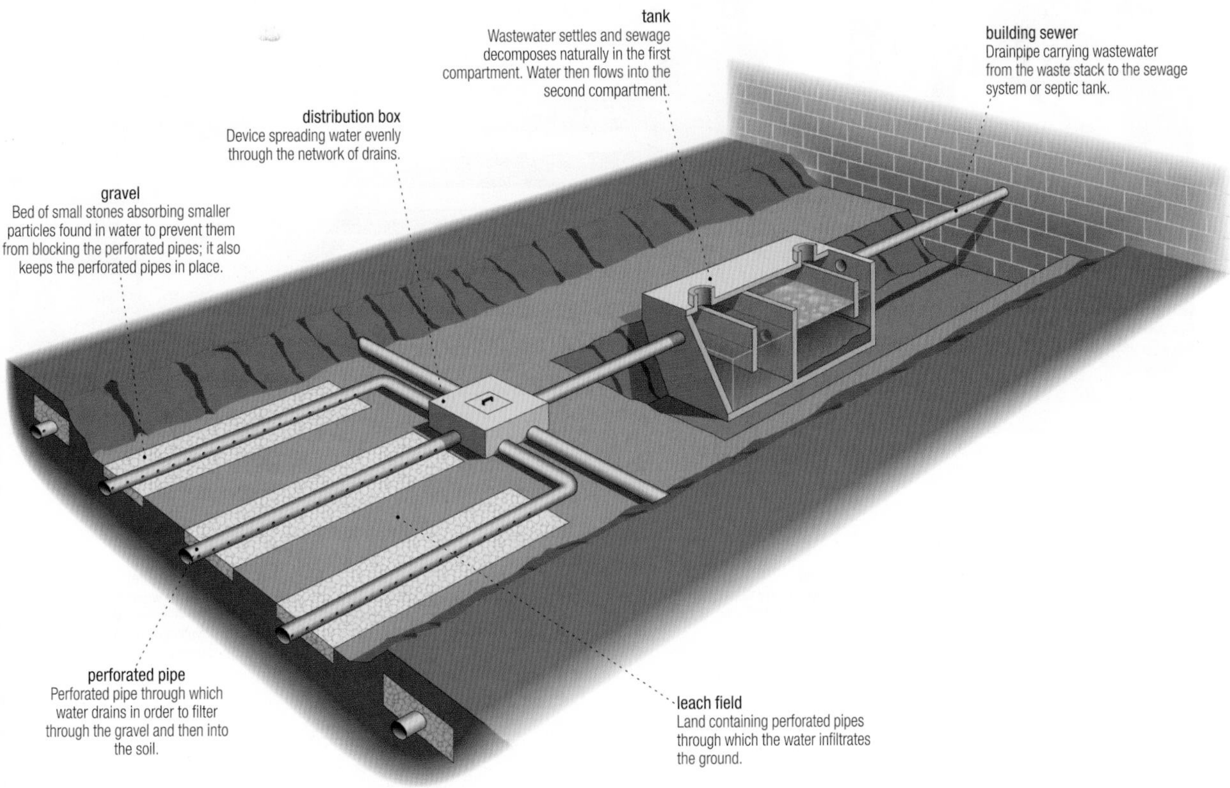

tank
Wastewater settles and sewage decomposes naturally in the first compartment. Water then flows into the second compartment.

building sewer
Drainpipe carrying wastewater from the waste stack to the sewage system or septic tank.

distribution box
Device spreading water evenly through the network of drains.

gravel
Bed of small stones absorbing smaller particles found in water to prevent them from blocking the perforated pipes; it also keeps the perforated pipes in place.

perforated pipe
Perforated pipe through which water drains in order to filter through the gravel and then into the soil.

leach field
Land containing perforated pipes through which the water infiltrates the ground.

HOUSE

bathroom

Room designed for personal hygiene; it is equipped with running water and sanitary fixtures.

spray hose
Flexible pipe allowing the shower head to be moved.

shower head
Perforated device through which water flows under pressure.

portable shower head
Movable handle equipped with a perforated shower head; it is used especially for rinsing hair.

overflow drain
Drainpipe for draining off a fixture's overflow when the water level reaches a certain level.

sliding door
Panel or panels of a door sliding horizontally along a set of tracks.

shower stall
Enclosed space in which a sanitary facility allows one to wash one's body under a spray of water.

faucet
Device stopping or starting the flow of hot or cold water, as well as regulating its flow rate.

mirror
Polished glass surface refl light and returning images

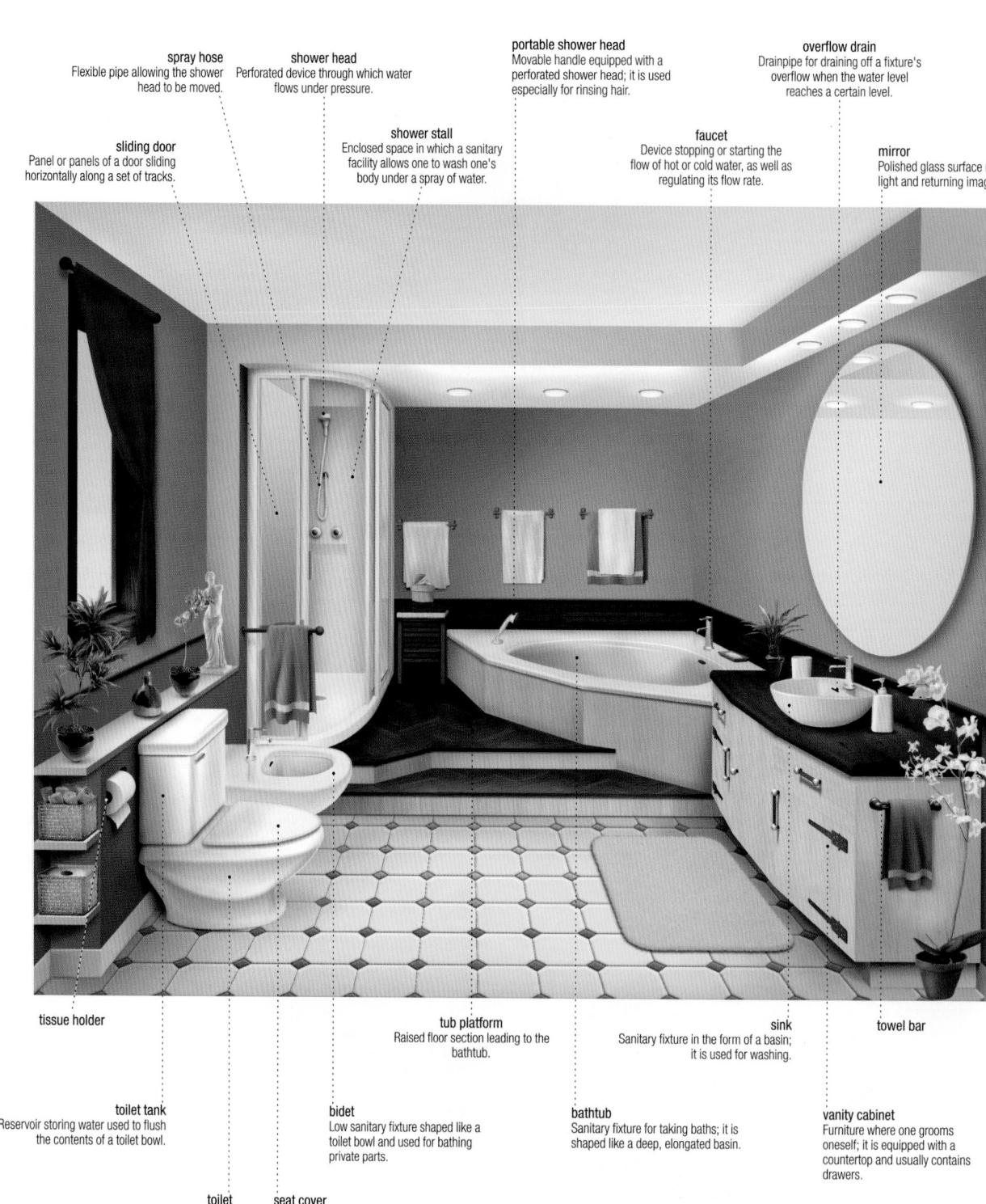

tissue holder

tub platform
Raised floor section leading to the bathtub.

sink
Sanitary fixture in the form of a basin; it is used for washing.

towel bar

toilet tank
Reservoir storing water used to flush the contents of a toilet bowl.

bidet
Low sanitary fixture shaped like a toilet bowl and used for bathing private parts.

bathtub
Sanitary fixture for taking baths; it is shaped like a deep, elongated basin.

vanity cabinet
Furniture where one grooms oneself; it is equipped with a countertop and usually contains drawers.

toilet
Sanitary fixture for disposing of bodily waste; it comprises a toilet bowl and a tank.

seat cover
Part covering the toilet-bowl seat and opening.

toilet

Sanitary fixture for disposing of bodily waste; it comprises a toilet bowl and a tank.

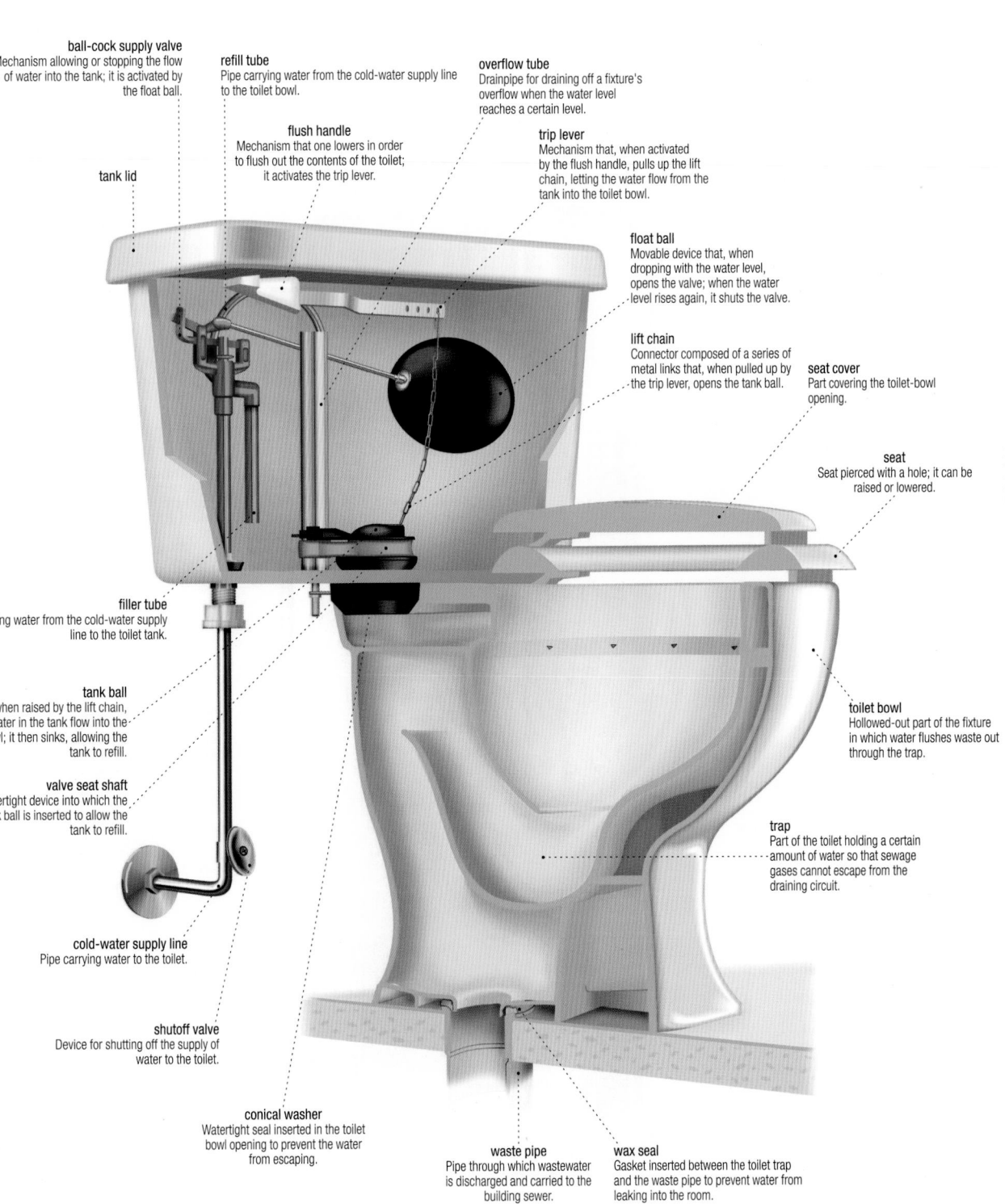

ball-cock supply valve
Mechanism allowing or stopping the flow of water into the tank; it is activated by the float ball.

refill tube
Pipe carrying water from the cold-water supply line to the toilet bowl.

overflow tube
Drainpipe for draining off a fixture's overflow when the water level reaches a certain level.

flush handle
Mechanism that one lowers in order to flush out the contents of the toilet; it activates the trip lever.

trip lever
Mechanism that, when activated by the flush handle, pulls up the lift chain, letting the water flow from the tank into the toilet bowl.

tank lid

float ball
Movable device that, when dropping with the water level, opens the valve; when the water level rises again, it shuts the valve.

lift chain
Connector composed of a series of metal links that, when pulled up by the trip lever, opens the tank ball.

seat cover
Part covering the toilet-bowl opening.

seat
Seat pierced with a hole; it can be raised or lowered.

filler tube
...ying water from the cold-water supply line to the toilet tank.

tank ball
...when raised by the lift chain, ...water in the tank flow into the ...wl; it then sinks, allowing the tank to refill.

valve seat shaft
...tertight device into which the ...nk ball is inserted to allow the tank to refill.

cold-water supply line
Pipe carrying water to the toilet.

shutoff valve
Device for shutting off the supply of water to the toilet.

conical washer
Watertight seal inserted in the toilet bowl opening to prevent the water from escaping.

waste pipe
Pipe through which wastewater is discharged and carried to the building sewer.

wax seal
Gasket inserted between the toilet trap and the waste pipe to prevent water from leaking into the room.

toilet bowl
Hollowed-out part of the fixture in which water flushes waste out through the trap.

trap
Part of the toilet holding a certain amount of water so that sewage gases cannot escape from the draining circuit.

HOUSE

water-heater tank

Device producing sanitary hot water for washing and bathing; it consumes gas or electricity.

electric water-heater tank

cold-water supply line
Inlet pipe for cold water to the tank.

hot-water outlet
Outlet pipe for hot water flowing into the hot-water circuit.

anode rod
Magnesium-coated electrode protecting the tank from the corrosive effects of the water.

pressure-relief valve
Device for lowering the pressure inside the tank by releasing excess hot water.

high-temperature cutoff
Mechanism cutting off the flow of electric current when the temperature of the water exceeds a set value.

upper thermostat
Device that senses changes in temperature and automatically switches the upper heating element on or off.

upper heating element
Coated electric resistor immersed in the upper part of the tank to heat the water.

access panel

tank
Insulated reservoir in which hot water is stored; it is usually cylindrical and enameled or glazed.

insulation
Material placed between the tank and the outer walls of the hot-water tank in order to reduce heat loss.

electric supply
Point where the hot-water tank connects with the household circuit.

overflow pipe
Pipe through which water escapes when maximum pressure is exceeded.

lower thermostat
Device that senses changes in temperature and automatically switches the lower heating element on or off.

lower heating element
Coated electric resistor immersed in the lower part of the tank to heat the water.

drain valve
Device for emptying water from the tank.

water-heater tank

gas water-heater tank

hot-water outlet
Outlet pipe for hot water flowing into the hot-water circuit.

flue hat
Device reducing the amount of air withdrawn by convection.

outer jacket
Metal casing protecting the tank.

pressure-relief valve
Device for lowering the pressure inside the tank by releasing excess hot water.

overflow pipe
Pipe through which water escapes when maximum pressure is exceeded.

insulation
Material placed between the tank and the outer walls of the hot-water tank in order to reduce heat loss.

cold-water supply line
Inlet pipe for cold water to the tank.

flue
Channel through which combustion gases are evacuated.

glass-lined tank
Insulated reservoir protected against corrosion by an enamel or glaze coating.

reset button
Mechanism allowing the burner to be manually restarted.

gas cock
Mechanism cutting off the gas supply when the water reaches the desired temperature.

control box
Box containing the set of controls that measure temperature and operate the burner.

temperature control
Device for setting the temperature.

drain valve
Device for emptying the water from the tank.

thermostat
Mechanism controlled by fluctuations in temperature; it can be set to automatically switch the burner on or off.

gas burner
Combustion device for an air-gas mixture.

HOUSE

faucets

The double-handle faucet controls the flow of hot and cold water; the single-lever faucet mixes the hot and cold water and controls their flow.

stem faucet
Device stopping or starting the flow of hot or cold water, as well as regulating its flow rate.

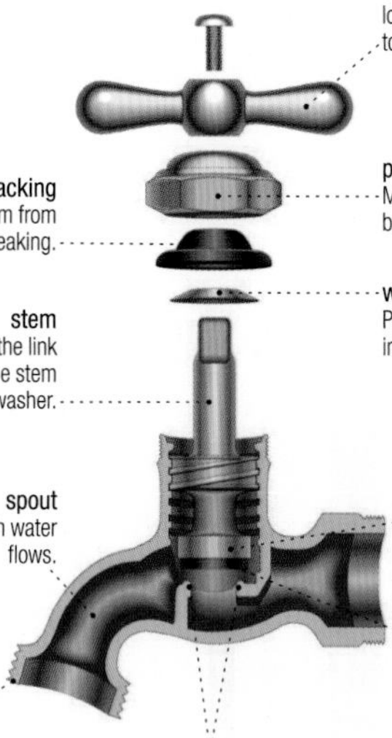

handle
Device turned by hand that raises or lowers the stem, allowing the water to be turned off or on.

packing
Gasket preventing the stem from leaking.

packing nut
Metal part allowing the packing to be tightened against the washer.

stem
Metal unit that provides the link between the handle and the stem washer.

washer
Part inserted over the stem that fits into the body of the faucet.

spout
Curved end out of which water flows.

stem holder
Bracket for the stem washer.

stem washer
Stopper attached to the bottom of the stem. When inserted into the valve seat, it blocks the inflow of water; when raised, it allows the water to flow.

thread
Helical grooves at the end of the spout to which an accessory, such as an aerator, can be attached.

valve seat
Part against which the stem washer presses to prevent leakage.

disc fau
Type of faucet fitted with two perforated discs regulate the water's flow and its tempera

handle
Lever for controlling water flow and the mixture of hot and cold water.

bonnet
Decorative part covering the body of the faucet; the handle turns on it.

cylinder
Part fitted with two discs: or activated by the handle, the stationary.

spout
Curved end out of which water flows.

seal
Washer protecting a water i from leaking.

water inlet
Tubular section through whi water enters the faucet.

aerator
Device fitted with a screen and attached to the spout; it aerates the water and prevents splashing.

escutcheon
Plate for covering and protecting water-intake pipes.

ball-type faucet
Type of faucet fitted with a perforated ball that regulates both the flow of water and its temperature.

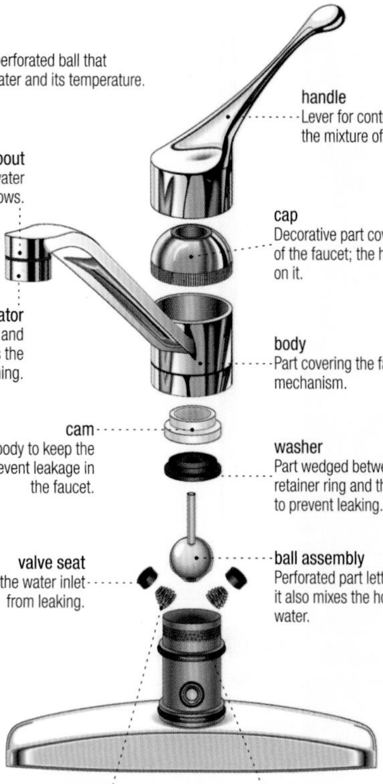

handle
Lever for controlling water flow and the mixture of hot and cold water.

spout
Curved end out of which water flows.

cap
Decorative part covering the body of the faucet; the handle turns on it.

aerator
Device fitted with a screen and attached to the spout; it aerates the water and prevents splashing.

body
Part covering the faucet's mechanism.

cam
Plastic part inserted into the body to keep the washer on the ball and to prevent leakage in the faucet.

washer
Part wedged between the packing retainer ring and the ball assembly to prevent leaking.

valve seat
Gasket preventing the water inlet from leaking.

ball assembly
Perforated part letting water enter; it also mixes the hot and cold water.

cartridge fau
Type of faucet fitted with a perforated cartridge regulates both the flow of water and its temperat

cover
Decorative part capping the top of the handle.

handle
Lever for controlling water flo the mixture of hot and cold w

cartridge
When its stem is raised by the handle, its lower end is lifted out of the seat to let water flow.

cartridge stem
Unit activated by the handle t drives the rotating movement cartridge.

spout
Curved end out of which water flows.

retaining ring
Plastic part inside the faucet t keeping the washer in place.

aerator
Device fitted with a screen and attached to the spout; it aerates the water and prevents splashing.

body
Part attached to the faucet's and serving to hide the cartric

spring
Elastic metal part that is kept under pressure to hold the valve seat in place.

O-ring
Circular gasket, usually made of rubber, preventing water from leaking from the base of the faucet.

O-ring
Circular gasket, usually made of rubber, preventing water from leaking from the base of the faucet.

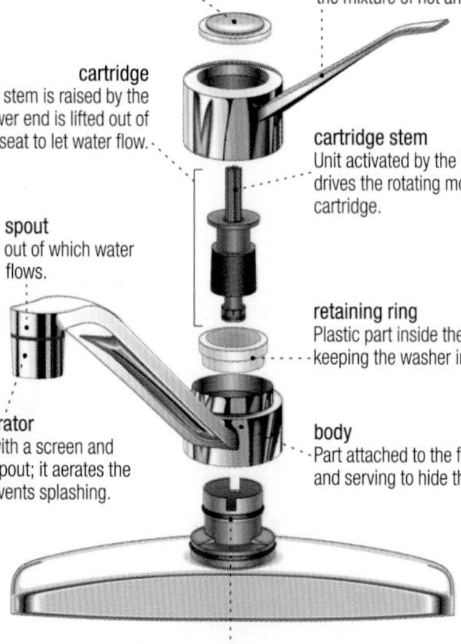

fittings

Transition fittings are used for joining components made of different materials, whereas fittings are used to join components of the same material.

plastic to steel
The tubes are joined by a threaded tube for the steel end, and by compression coupling or, for a plastic end, by gluing.

copper to plastic
The tubes are joined by union or compression coupling.

copper to steel
The tubes are joined by a threaded tube on the steel end, and by union or compression coupling on the copper end.

examples of transition fittings
Transition fittings allow tubes of different materials to be joined.

examples of fittings
Fittings are used to join two or more pipes, a pipe to a device, or a pipe to a cap or plug.

offset
...ing joining two pipes so that the ...ipe can bypass an obstacle.

tee
Fitting joining three pipes, one of which is perpendicular to the other two.

Y-branch
Fitting joining three pipes, one of which is oblique to the other two.

trap
U-shaped pipe beneath a fixture containing a quantity of water to prevent sewage gases from escaping.

cap
Plug inserted into the end of a pipe to close it off.

U-bend
...ing joining two pipes in order to ...hange their direction by 180°.

threaded cap
Plug screwed onto the end of a male threaded pipe to close it off.

90° elbow
Fitting for joining two pipes in order to change their direction.

45° elbow
Fitting for joining two pipes in order to change their direction by 45°.

pipe coupling
Threaded fitting with two female ends; it is used to join two pipes of the same diameter.

hexagon bushing
...n a hexagonal head. It joins two pipes of ...iameters: one pipe is screwed onto the ...d, and the other into the female end.

flush bushing
Fitting joining two pipes of different diameters. The larger pipe screws onto the male end and the smaller pipe screws into the female end.

nipple
Threaded fitting having two male ends; it is used to join two pipes of the same diameter.

reducing coupling
Fitting joining two pipes of different diameters in order to reduce the diameter of a pipe run.

square head plug
Cap screwed into the end of a threaded female pipe to close it off.

HOUSE

mechanical connectors
Pipes joined using nuts and threaded metal parts; a gasket is inserted to tighten them, thus preventing leakage.

union
Formed by using a nut to tighten a male union nut in a female union nut; leakage is prevented by placing a gasket where the two tubes meet.

ring nut
Part that enables a male union nut to be screwed into a female union nut.

union nut
Threaded on the inside so that a male union nut can be screwed into it.

pipe A

pipe B

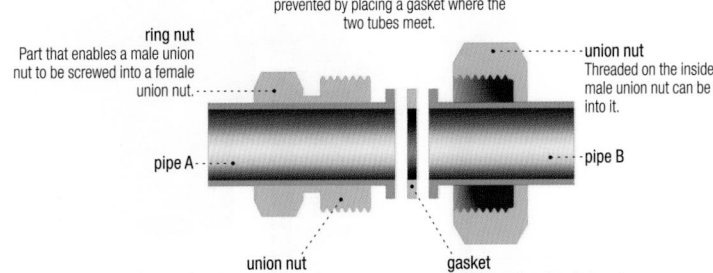

union nut
Threaded on the outside so it can be inserted into the female union nut.

gasket
Flexible washer placed where two tubes meet to prevent leakage.

...mpression fitting
...eaded part into which two tubes can be inserted; ...y are made watertight by a gasket tightened ...n a nut.

flare joint
Threaded part over which two tubes having bell-shaped ends can be tightened by a nut.

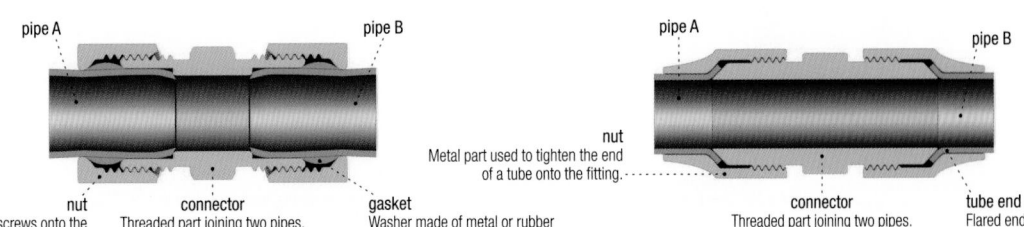

pipe A

pipe B

nut
...al part that screws onto the ...g so that the gasket can be tightened on the tube.

connector
Threaded part joining two pipes.

gasket
Washer made of metal or rubber compressed against the pipe to prevent leakage in the fitting.

nut
Metal part used to tighten the end of a tube onto the fitting.

pipe A

pipe B

connector
Threaded part joining two pipes.

tube end
Flared end of a pipe.

examples of branching

Branching: the way in which an appliance is hooked up to a house's plumbing system.

garbage disposal sink
Appliance used in a kitchen, sometimes with two basins, that is fed by water and equipped with a drain and a garbage disposal unit.

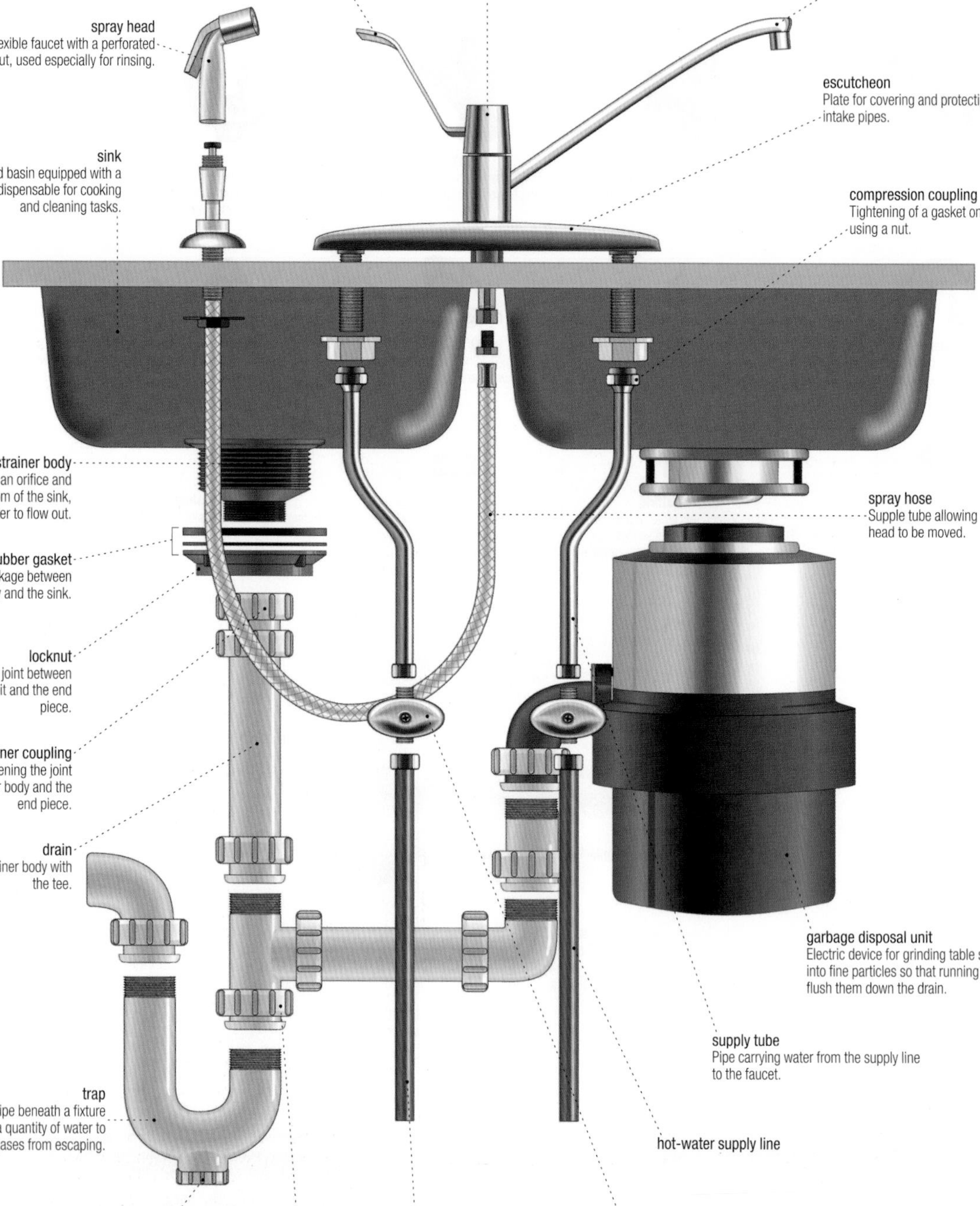

handle
Lever controlling the flow and mixture of hot and cold water.

single-handle kitchen faucet
Device acting as both faucet and hot and cold water mixer.

spout assembly
Curved end out of which wa flows.

spray head
Flexible faucet with a perforated spout, used especially for rinsing.

escutcheon
Plate for covering and protecting wa intake pipes.

sink
Water-fed basin equipped with a drain; it is indispensable for cooking and cleaning tasks.

compression coupling
Tightening of a gasket on a tub using a nut.

strainer body
Part equipped with an orifice and located at the bottom of the sink, allowing water to flow out.

spray hose
Supple tube allowing the sp head to be moved.

rubber gasket
Gasket preventing leakage between the strainer body and the sink.

locknut
Part for tightening the joint between the draining circuit and the end piece.

strainer coupling
Part for tightening the joint between the strainer body and the end piece.

drain
Pipe joining the strainer body with the tee.

garbage disposal unit
Electric device for grinding table scraps into fine particles so that running water flush them down the drain.

supply tube
Pipe carrying water from the supply line to the faucet.

trap
U-shaped pipe beneath a fixture containing a quantity of water to prevent sewage gases from escaping.

hot-water supply line

cleanout
Part screwed into the trap that can be removed in case it needs to be unblocked.

trap coupling
Movable part joining the trap with the tee.

cold-water supply line

shutoff valve
Device allowing the flow of water to the sink to be shut off.

HOUSE

examples of branching

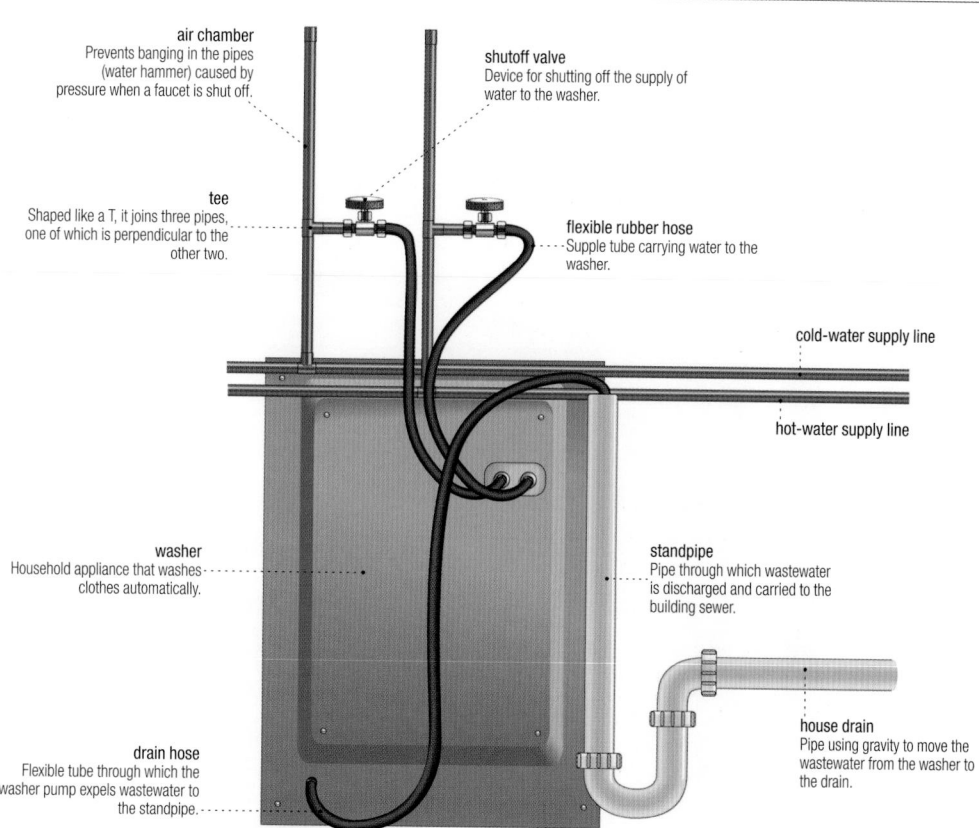

air chamber
Prevents banging in the pipes (water hammer) caused by pressure when a faucet is shut off.

shutoff valve
Device for shutting off the supply of water to the washer.

washer
Household appliance that washes clothes automatically.

tee
Shaped like a T, it joins three pipes, one of which is perpendicular to the other two.

flexible rubber hose
Supple tube carrying water to the washer.

cold-water supply line

hot-water supply line

washer
Household appliance that washes clothes automatically.

standpipe
Pipe through which wastewater is discharged and carried to the building sewer.

house drain
Pipe using gravity to move the wastewater from the washer to the drain.

drain hose
Flexible tube through which the washer pump expels wastewater to the standpipe.

HOUSE

dishwasher
Appliance designed to automatically wash and dry dishes.

drain hose
Pipe collecting wastewater from the dishwasher and carrying it to the drain.

dishwasher
Appliance designed to automatically wash and dry dishes.

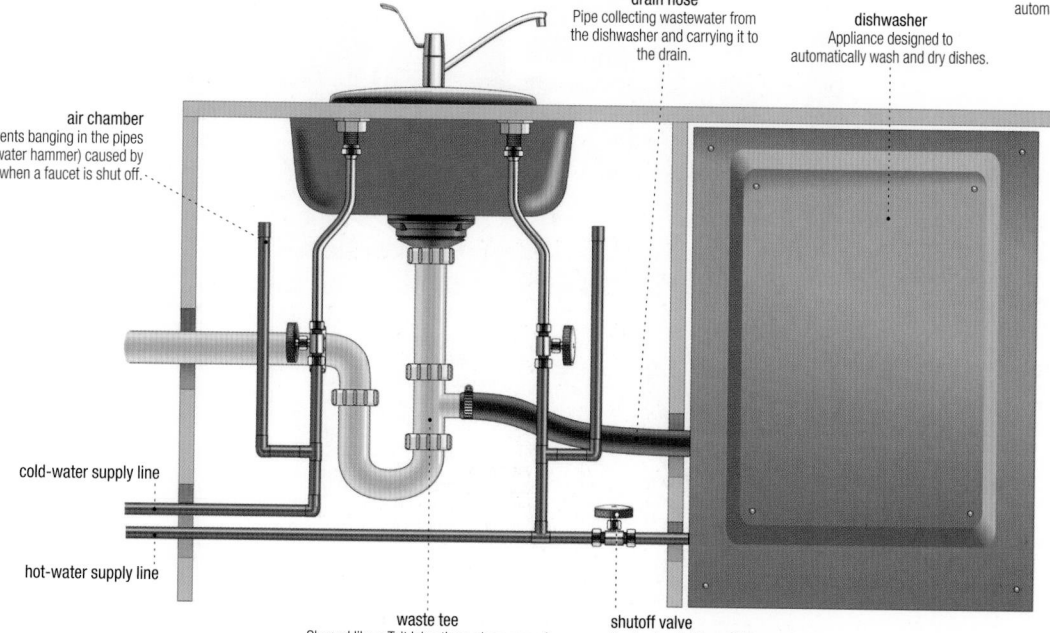

air chamber
Prevents banging in the pipes (water hammer) caused by pressure when a faucet is shut off.

cold-water supply line

hot-water supply line

waste tee
Shaped like a T, it joins three pipes, one of which is perpendicular to the other two.

shutoff valve
Device for shutting off the supply of water to the dishwasher.

distribution panel

Set of devices forming the junction of the public electricity grid and the electric circuits of a dwelling.

knockout
Partially cut-out metal part that can be removed if needed in order to attach a supplementary cable to the panel.

bonding jumper
Screw inserted into the metal box of the panel allowing it to be connected to the neutral hot bus bar.

240-volt feeder cable
Cable consisting of three wires, one neutral and two live, conducting an electric current from the grid to the distribution panel.

connector
Device for screwing the electric-connection conduit to the panel box.

main breaker
Mechanism controlling the supply of electricity to the hot bus bars; it allows the current to all the dwelling's circuits to be cut.

main power cable
Live wire conducting the electric current.

double circuit breaker
Protection device for a 240-volt circuit that, in the event of overload, is released and thus cuts off electricity to the circuits.

ground bond
Links the bonding jumper to the neutral hot bus bar.

single circuit breaker
Protection device for a 120-volt circuit that, in the event of overload, is released and thus cuts off electricity to the circuits.

240-volt circuit
Composed of two lives wire, neutral wire and one ground; this allows electricity to rea requiring a lot of power.

120-volt circuit
Composed of one live wire, one neutral wire and one grounded wire; it allows electricity to reach small appliance or a light.

neutral service wire
Wire having no electric charge that, via neutral hot bus bar, returns the current domestic circuits to the grid.

ground fault circuit interrupter
Device reducing the risk of electric shock in a humid place in the event of an accidental leak of current to the ground.

neutral wire
Wire having no electric charge that allows the current to return to the distribution panel and the grid.

hot bus bar
Conductive part of the panel into which the breakers for each circuit are plugge

ground/neutral bus bar
Receives the current from the neutral grounded wires of the various circuits and conducts them to the neutral service wire and the ground connection.

ground
Part connecting the neutral hot bus bar that allows the current from the circuit neutral wires to be transferred to the neutral service wire.

terminal
Part of the ground/neutral bus bar to which a neutral wire and the ground wire of a circuit are attached.

plastic insulator
Plate made of nonconductive material preventing the hot bus bars from coming in contact with the back of the panel.

ground wire
Wire conducting the current from the ground/neutral bus bar to the ground connection in the event of a short circuit.

ground connection
Metal conductor attached to the ground wire in order to ground the entire circuit.

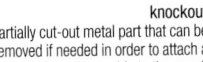

distribution panel

examples of fuses

Fuses: electric connection devices devised for
interrupting the current in the event of electric
overload by melting one of its components.

cartridge fuse
Having a maximum capacity of 60
amperes, it protects a circuit of 240 volts.

plug fuse
Having a maximum capacity of 30
amperes, it screws in like a lightbulb
and protects a circuit of 120 volts.

knife-blade cartridge fuse
Having a capacity of 60 to 600 amperes, it protects the
main electric circuit.

electricity meter

Device measuring the consumption of electricity by a dwelling.

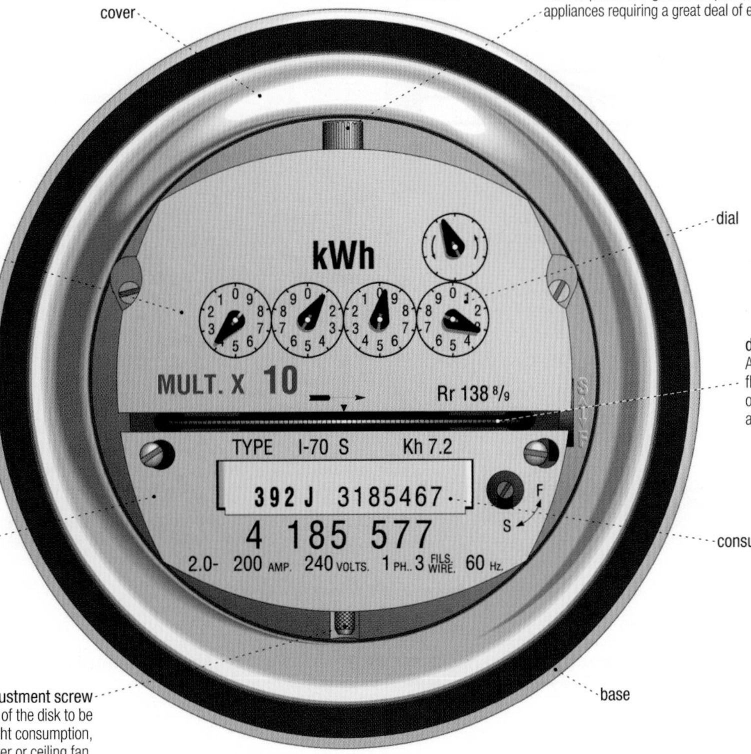

HOUSE

full-load adjustment screw
Screw adjusting the rotation speed of the disk so that
it corresponds to high consumption, such as in large
appliances requiring a great deal of electricity.

cover

register
Metering system measuring a dwelling's
electricity consumption expressed in
kilowatt hours (kWh).

dial

disk
Aluminum plate that turns as the current
flows through the meter; the number
of times it rotates is proportional to the
amount of electricity consumed.

nameplate
Plate bearing the various features
of an electric meter.

consumer number

light-load adjustment screw
Screw allowing the rotation speed of the disk to be
adjusted so that it corresponds to light consumption,
such as from a lamp, toaster or ceiling fan.

base

kWh

MULT. X **10** ___ ▸   Rr 138 8/9

TYPE I-70 S   Kh 7.2

392 J 3185467

4 185 577

2.0- 200 AMP. 240 VOLTS. 1 PH. 3 FILS. WIRE. 60 Hz.

network connection

Set of equipment and conductors allowing a customer's electric installation to be connected to the public grid.

overhead distribution system
All of the above-ground components of the electrical distribution system.

HOUSE

connection point
Place where the customer's electric hookup is connected to the electric grid.

customer's service entrance
The customer's portion of the electric hookup: from the service box to the connection point.

medium-tension distribution line
Overhead electricity-distribution lines with tension between 750 and 50,000 volts; its conductors are located at the top of the poles.

transformer
Device that alters electric voltage; voltage is decreased before being distributed by low-tension lines to areas of consumption.

phase cond
Live wire conducting the el
CL

neutral conductor
Conductor of a distribution line that, connected to a neutral point of the grid, returns the current.

supply point
Place where the customer's service entrance is connected to the low-tension distribution line.

distributor service loop
Set of conductors extending the distribution line to the customer's connection point.

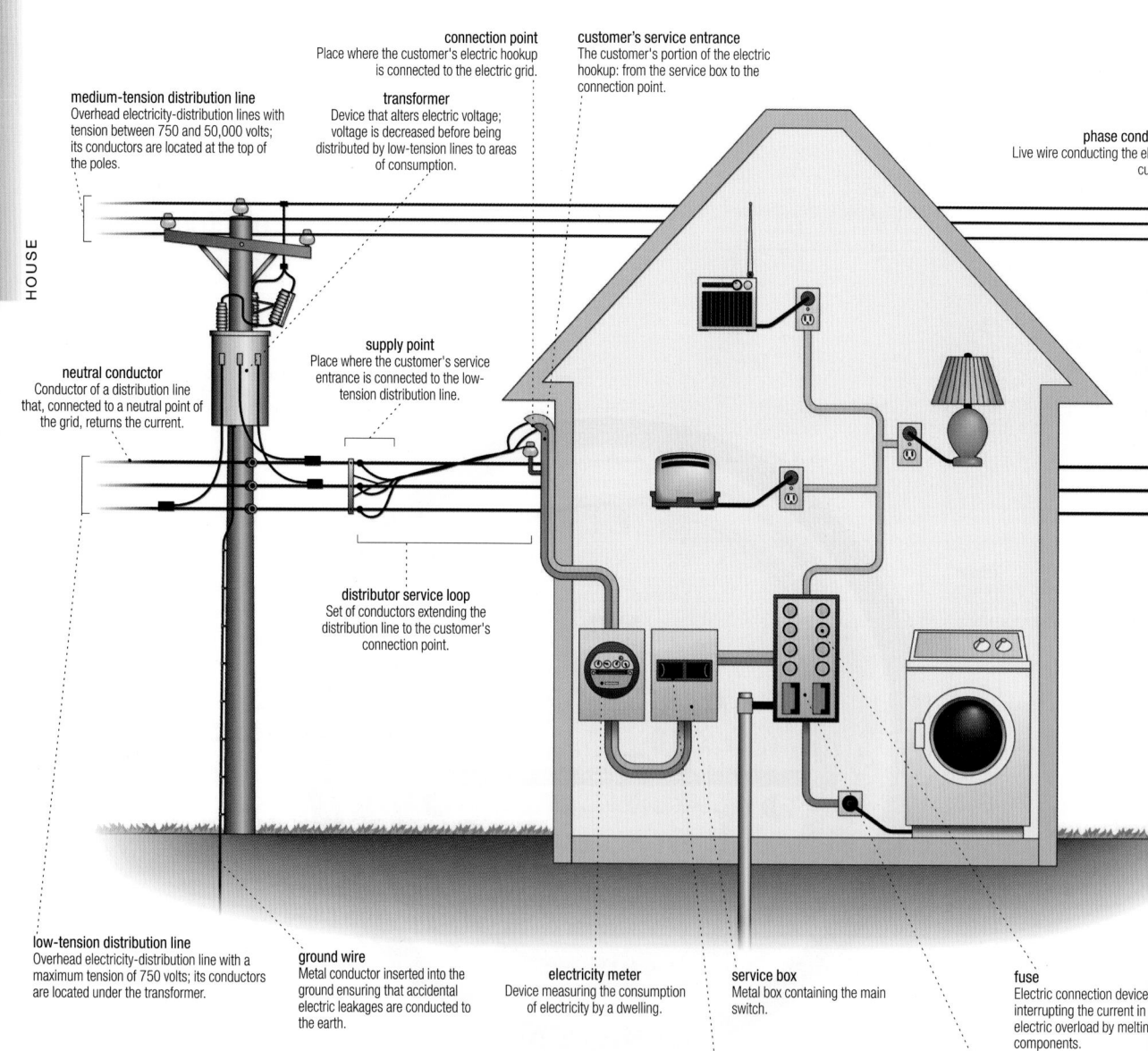

low-tension distribution line
Overhead electricity-distribution line with a maximum tension of 750 volts; its conductors are located under the transformer.

ground wire
Metal conductor inserted into the ground ensuring that accidental electric leakages are conducted to the earth.

electricity meter
Device measuring the consumption of electricity by a dwelling.

service box
Metal box containing the main switch.

fuse
Electric connection device interrupting the current in electric overload by meltin components.

main switch
Mechanism allowing a dwelling's current to be cut off.

distribution panel
Set of devices forming the junction of the public electricity grid and the electric circuits of a dwelling.

underground distribution system
All of the underground components of the electrical
distribution system.

disconnect cabinet
Appliance mounted on a base and containing various
devices for protecting the network or splitting it
isolating one section or appliance from the rest of the
network).

enclosure
Structure used for linking the low-voltage
conductors that transport electricity to the
client. It occasionally will have a lamppost
mounted on it.

pad-mounted transformer
Appliance for lowering the voltage of
the electricity in order to distribute it to
the consumption points.

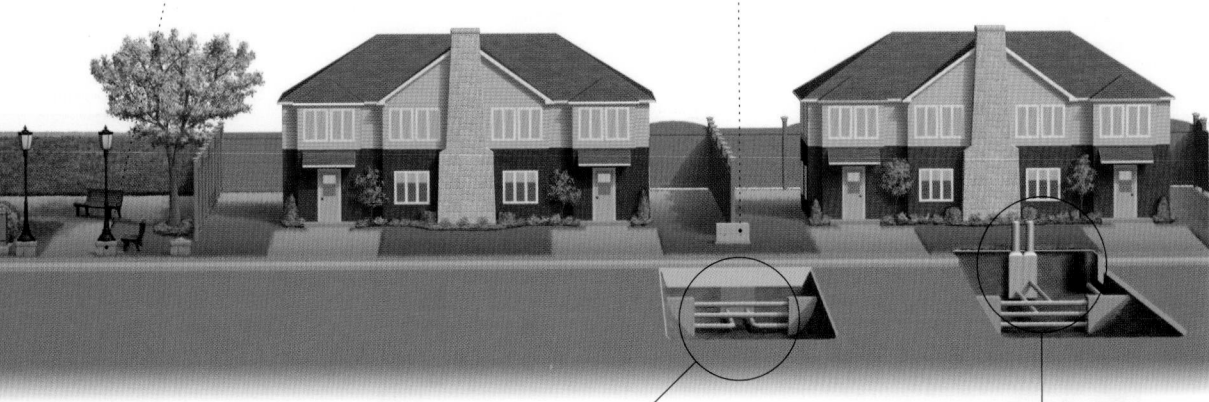

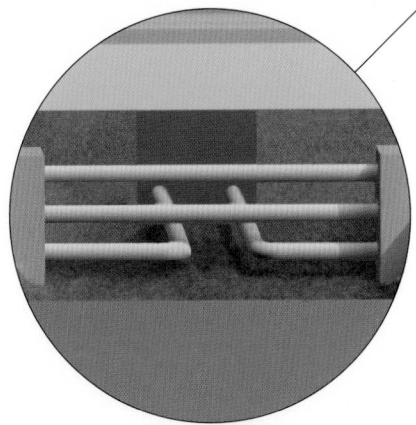

electrical pedestal
Structure that gives access to the
telecommunication companies'
distribution equipment.

underground conduits
Group of conduits in which are the
cables that transport the electricity.

manhole
Underground well of concrete with a
removable cover, that allows the linking
of the subscriber to the underground
equipment.

contact devices

Examples of components that connect a device to an electric circuit.

European plug
End part of an electric wire equipped with pins that are inserted into the socket contacts of an outlet to establish contact.

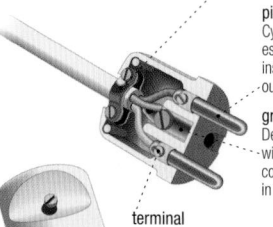

clamp
Metal part used for fastening a device's wire to the plug.

pin
Cylindrical metal part that establishes electric contact when inserted into the corresponding outlet.

grounding socket
Device connecting a circuit's ground wire, which allows the current to be conducted to the ground connection in the event of a short circuit.

terminal
Part to which an electric wire's conductors are attached.

cover
Part covering the internal components of a plug.

European outlet
Device fitted with sockets connecting an electric circuit to an electric device when the plug is inserted into it.

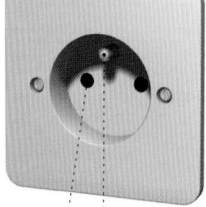

socket-contact
Hole intended to receive a plug's pin and establish electric contact.

grounding prong
Device connecting a circuit's ground wire, which allows the current to be conducted to the ground connection in the event of a short circuit.

American outlet
Device fitted with slots connecting an electric circuit to an electric device when the plug is inserted into it.

American plug
End part of an electric wire equipped with blades that are inserted into an outlet to establish contact.

blade
Flat metal part inserted into the slot of an outlet to establish electric contact.

grounding prong
Device connecting a circuit's ground wire, which allows the current to be conducted to the ground connection in the event of a short circuit.

parts of a lamp socket

cap
Component fitting onto the outer shell and covering the upper end of a lamp's socket.

socket
Device into which a lamp's base is inserted in order to connect it to the electric-supply circuit and to keep it in place.

insulating sleeve
Component protecting the outer shell from the heat.

outer shell
Decorative component covering the socket and the insulating sleeve.

plug adapter
Electric accessory adapting a plug to an outlet of a different configuration.

screw base
Base fitted with a screw pitch so it can be inserted into the corresponding socket.

bayonet base
Base fitted with two short metal pins so that it can be placed in the corresponding socket.

switch
Mechanism allowing the current in an electric circuit to be established or interrupted.

lamp socket
Device composed of a socket, its protective components and a switch.

switch plate
Protective plate covering an outlet or, in this case, a switch.

dimmer switch
Switch for varying the brightness of a lighting installation.

electrical box
Box housing the electric connections in order to protect the part of the dwelling's frame upon which it's mounted.

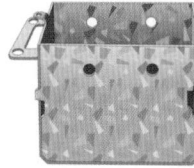

lighting

Set of devices allowing light to be diffused in a dwelling.

tungsten-halogen lamp
Lamp that is brighter and lasts longer than a traditional incandescent lamp, but that lets off more heat.

tungsten filament
Thin metal wire emitting light rays when an electric current passes though it.

inert gas
Gas inserted in the bulb to slow down evaporation of the filament; iodine or bromine are added as they combine with the tungsten at high temperatures.

base
Metal end of a lightbulb inserted into a socket to connect it to the electric circuit.

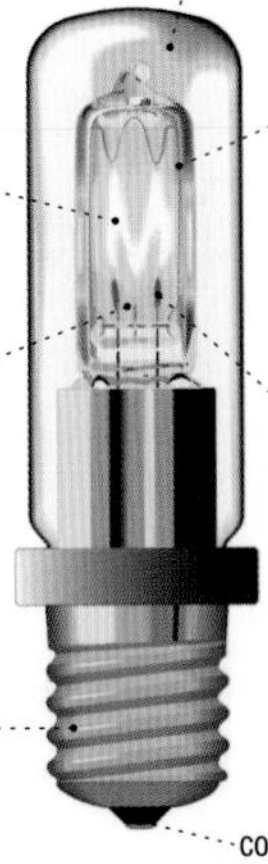

bulb
Gas sealed in a glass envelope into which the luminous body of a lamp is inserted.

filament support
Metal wire holding the filament.

electric circuit
Lamp component allowing the electric current to circulate through the tungsten filament.

contact
Metal part that establishes electric contact between the base of a lightbulb and the socket.

incandescent lamp
Lamp in which a filament heated by an electric current produces light rays.

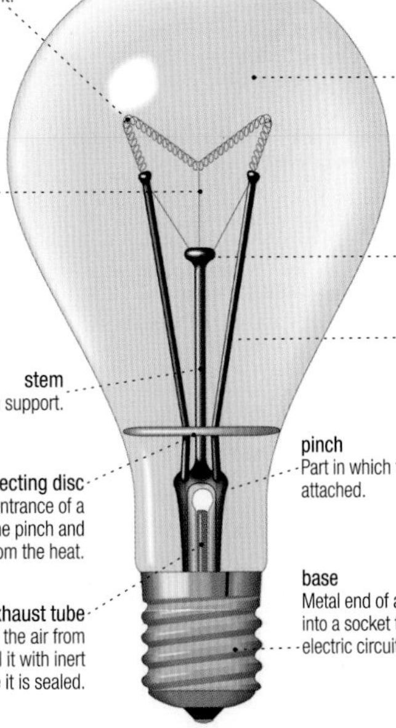

filament
Very thin metal wire, usually made of tungsten, emitting light rays when an electric current passes through it.

inert gas
Gas inserted in the bulb to slow down evaporation of the filament.

support
Metal wire holding the filament.

button
End of the stem; the filament supports are attached to it.

lead-in wire
Electric conductor carrying the current to the filament.

stem
Button support.

pinch
Part in which the lead-in wires are attached.

heat deflecting disc
Metal disc placed at the entrance of a lamp's neck to protect the pinch and the base from the heat.

exhaust tube
Glass tube used to empty the air from the bulb and then to fill it with inert gas before it is sealed.

base
Metal end of a lightbulb inserted into a socket to connect it to the electric circuit.

fluorescent tube
Tube in which the electric current produces ultraviolet radiation converted into visible light by a layer of a fluorescent substance.

lead-in wire
Electric conductor carrying the current to the filament.

exhaust tube
Glass tube used to empty the air from the bulb and then to fill it with inert gas before it is sealed.

pinch
Part in which the lead-in wires are attached.

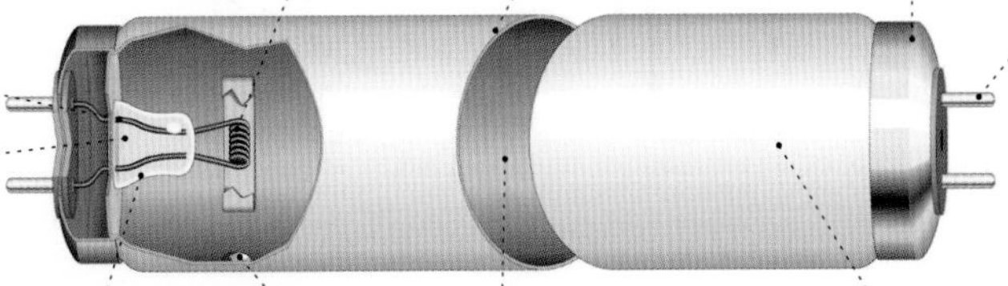

electrode
A device placed at each end of the tube; an electric discharge arcs between the two of them.

mercury
A small amount of vaporized mercury, added to the gas, emits ultraviolet radiation during the electric discharge.

phosphorescent coating
The tube's internal coating; it is composed of phosphate particles that convert ultraviolet rays into visible light.

gas
The tube is filled with an inert gas under low pressure, with mercury added.

pin base
End of the tube equipped with two pins that, when inserted into the socket, connect the tube with the electric circuit.

pin
Cylindrical metal part that establishes electric contact when inserted into the corresponding outlet.

bulb
Long glass cylinder enclosing the components of this type of tube and diffusing light.

mini halogen lamp
Small halogen lamp the base of which is replaced by prongs.

pin
Cylindrical metal part that establishes electric contact when inserted into the corresponding outlet.

compact fluorescent lamp
Fluorescent bulb with a miniaturized tube. It consumes less electricity than an incandescent lamp.

light-emitting diode (LED) lamp
Lamp that contains an electroluminescent diode. Its light is usually white and it consumes little electricity.

base
Metal end of a lightbulb inserted into a socket to connect it to the electric circuit.

light-emitting diode (LED)
Tube emitting light due an electric current circulating in one direction only.

bulb
Airtight glass envelope into which the electroluminescent diode is inserted.

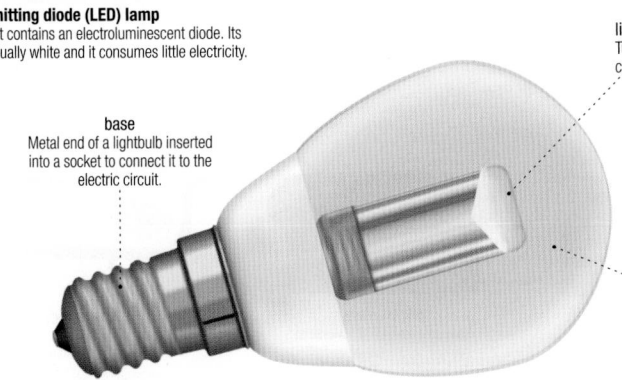

HOUSE

armchair

Chair with arms, a back and legs; its parts may or may not be decorative or upholstered.

parts of an armchair

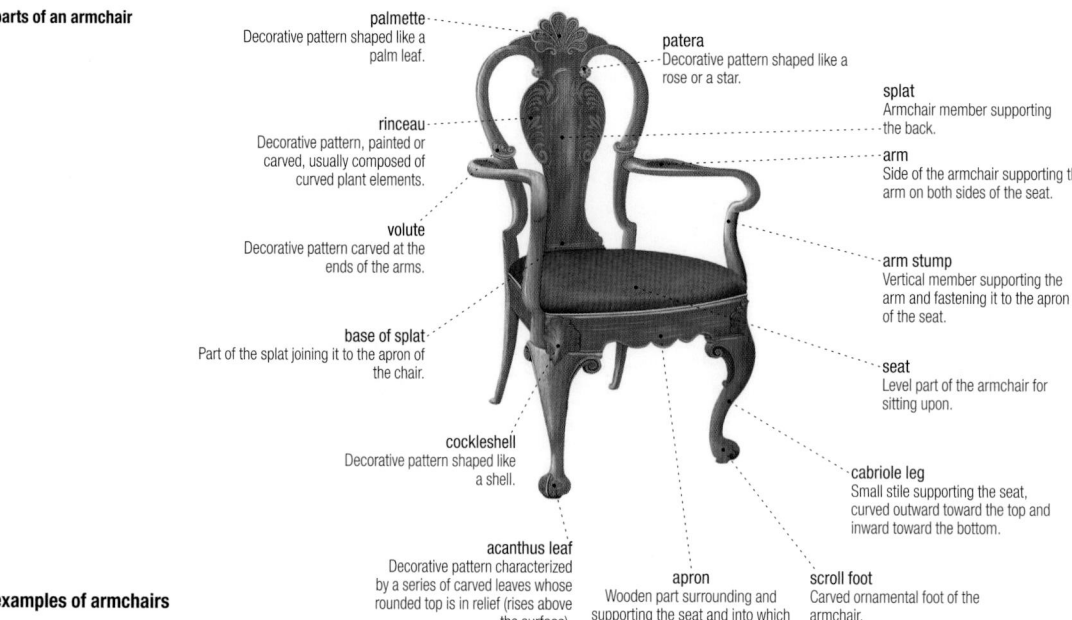

palmette
Decorative pattern shaped like a palm leaf.

patera
Decorative pattern shaped like a rose or a star.

splat
Armchair member supporting the back.

rinceau
Decorative pattern, painted or carved, usually composed of curved plant elements.

arm
Side of the armchair supporting the arm on both sides of the seat.

volute
Decorative pattern carved at the ends of the arms.

arm stump
Vertical member supporting the arm and fastening it to the apron of the seat.

base of splat
Part of the splat joining it to the apron of the chair.

seat
Level part of the armchair for sitting upon.

cockleshell
Decorative pattern shaped like a shell.

cabriole leg
Small stile supporting the seat, curved outward toward the top and inward toward the bottom.

acanthus leaf
Decorative pattern characterized by a series of carved leaves whose rounded top is in relief (rises above the surface).

apron
Wooden part surrounding and supporting the seat and into which the legs are fitted.

scroll foot
Carved ornamental foot of the armchair.

examples of armchairs

Wassily chair
Armchair with a tubular metal frame and whose back and seat are made of leather.

director's chair
Wooden armchair with a canvas back and seat that folds up in the middle.

cabriolet
Wooden 18th-century armchair with a curved back and armrests that curve outward.

rocking chair
Armchair with curved runners to rock on.

chair bed
Upholstered armchair with varic connected cushions that can b unfolded to form a bed.

club chair
Large deep upholstered armchair, usually made of leather.

bergère
Upholstered armchair with a cushioned seat.

Voltaire chair
Upholstered armchair with feet and a high and slightly inclined back.

tub chair
Low upholstered armchair with sides that flare out.

méridienne
Sofa with an irregular back joini two arms of different heights.

love seat
Sofa that seats two people.

sofa
Long upholstered armchair that seats several people.

chesterfield
Sofa upholstered with a quilted pattern; its arms are the same height as its back.

récamier
Long upholstered chair for reclinin with a headrest and back; the bac extends only part of the length of t chair.

side chair

Chair with a back and legs but no arms; its parts can be decorative or upholstered.

parts of a side chair

ear
Top end of a chair's stile.

top rail
Horizontal member located at the top of the back.

cross rail
Horizontal member located in the center of the back.

back
Part of the chair supporting the back.

stile
Part of a chair supporting both the back and the rear of the apron.

seat
Level part of the chair for sitting upon.

apron
Wooden part surrounding and supporting the seat and into which the legs are fitted.

support
Grouping that supports the seat, composed of the legs, spindle and apron.

rear leg
Bottom end of the stile completing the chair's support.

front leg
Bottom end of the front part the support.

spindle
Horizontal member joining two of the chair's legs.

examples of chairs

Windsor chair
oden chair with a rounded back having vertical bars.

rocking chair
Chair equipped with curved runners to rock on.

chaise longue
Folding chair upon which one can recline.

stacking chairs
Chairs designed to be placed one atop the other for storing.

folding chair
Chair whose seat and legs fold up for ease of storage and carrying.

seats

Furniture used for sitting with special features.

stool
Seat with legs but no arms or back; of various heights.

barstool
Seat with legs but no arms and often no back; high enough for a person to sit at a bar or a counter.

beanbag chair
Soft seat in the form of a bag filled with pellets which allow the outer material to curve to the form of the person sitting on it.

ottoman
Low upholstered seat having neither arms nor back.

storage bench
g and narrow unupholstered seat, under which there is a storage container.

bench
Long narrow unupholstered seat with or without a back, seating several people.

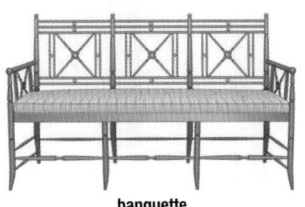

banquette
Bench with an upholstered seat.

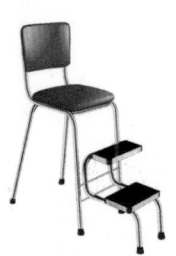

step chair
Chair whose foldaway lower part can be pulled out to form a step.

table

Piece of furniture consisting of a level top supported by one or several legs.

gateleg table
Table with a drop leaf and a pivoting leg to support it.

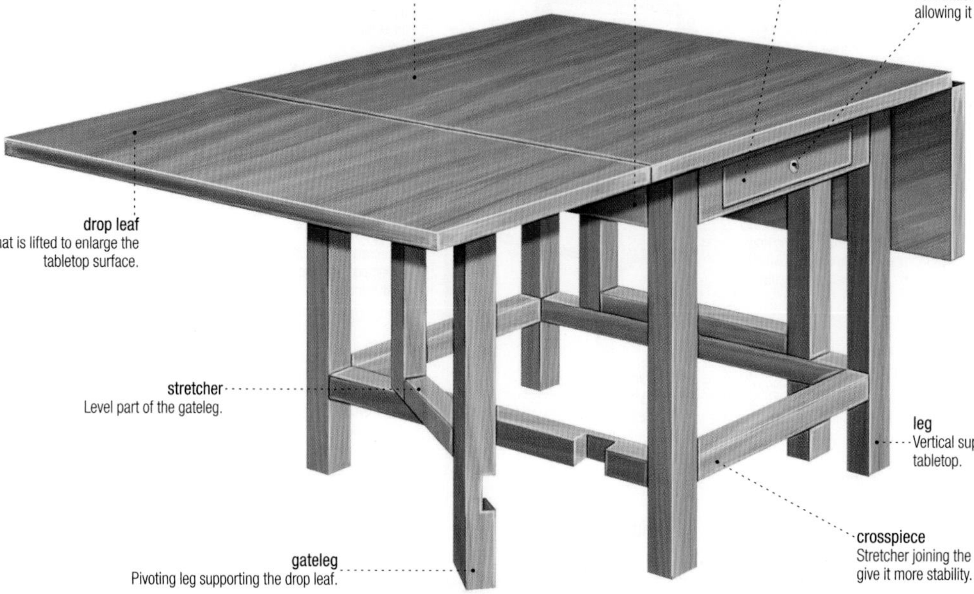

tabletop
Level panel made from any of a wide range of materials and forming the top of a table.

apron
Member forming the frame and supporting the top, and in which the legs are fitted.

drawer
Compartment for storage that slides open.

knob
Part attached to the drawer allowing it to open.

drop leaf
Panel that is lifted to enlarge the tabletop surface.

stretcher
Level part of the gateleg.

gateleg
Pivoting leg supporting the drop leaf.

crosspiece
Stretcher joining the legs of a table to give it more stability.

leg
Vertical support that holds up the tabletop.

examples of tables

tabletop
Level panel made from any of a wide range of materials and forming the top of a table.

nest of tables
Set of tables of various heights designed to stack one atop the other.

serving cart
Piece of furniture on which to place the dishes when the table is cleared.

extension
Panel inserted at the end of the tabletop or between the two halves to enlarge the surface.

extension table
Table to which one or more extensions can be added to enlarge the tabletop surface.

coffee table
Table with a low top.

bed

Piece of furniture to stretch out on for resting or sleeping.

parts of a bed

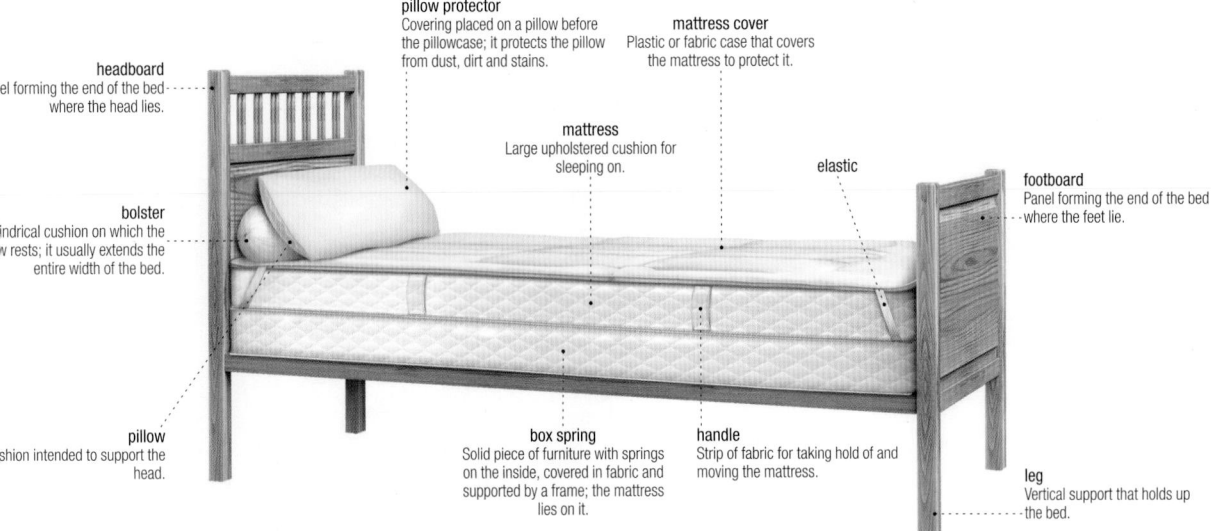

pillow protector
Covering placed on a pillow before the pillowcase; it protects the pillow from dust, dirt and stains.

mattress cover
Plastic or fabric case that covers the mattress to protect it.

headboard
el forming the end of the bed where the head lies.

mattress
Large upholstered cushion for sleeping on.

elastic

footboard
Panel forming the end of the bed where the feet lie.

bolster
indrical cushion on which the w rests; it usually extends the entire width of the bed.

pillow
shion intended to support the head.

box spring
Solid piece of furniture with springs on the inside, covered in fabric and supported by a frame; the mattress lies on it.

handle
Strip of fabric for taking hold of and moving the mattress.

leg
Vertical support that holds up the bed.

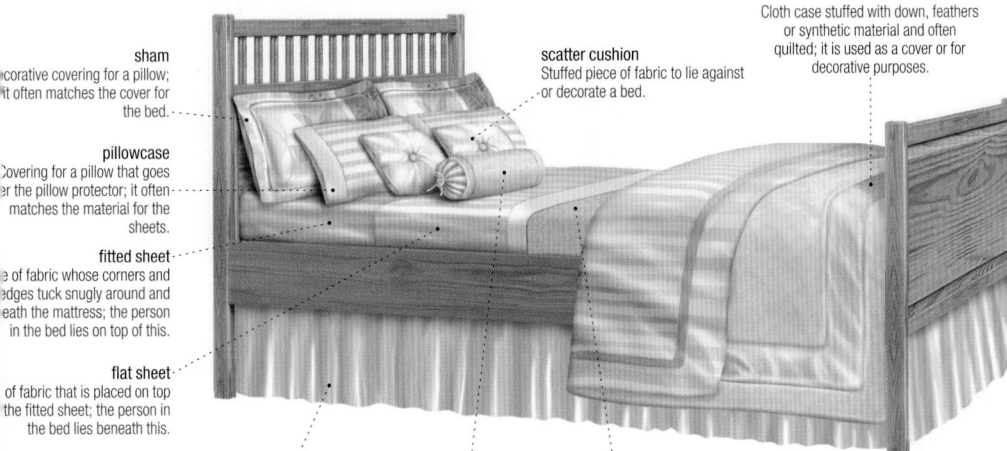

sham
corative covering for a pillow; it often matches the cover for the bed.

scatter cushion
Stuffed piece of fabric to lie against or decorate a bed.

comforter
Cloth case stuffed with down, feathers or synthetic material and often quilted; it is used as a cover or for decorative purposes.

linen
Set of fabrics, blankets and pillows covering a bed.

pillowcase
Covering for a pillow that goes er the pillow protector; it often matches the material for the sheets.

fitted sheet
e of fabric whose corners and edges tuck snugly around and eath the mattress; the person in the bed lies on top of this.

flat sheet
of fabric that is placed on top the fitted sheet; the person in the bed lies beneath this.

valance
Strip of fabric, usually pleated, trimming the base of the bed.

neckroll
Decorative cylindrical cushion.

blanket
Covering placed on top of the flat sheet and made of a warm fabric.

futon
Sofa that can be converted into a bed.

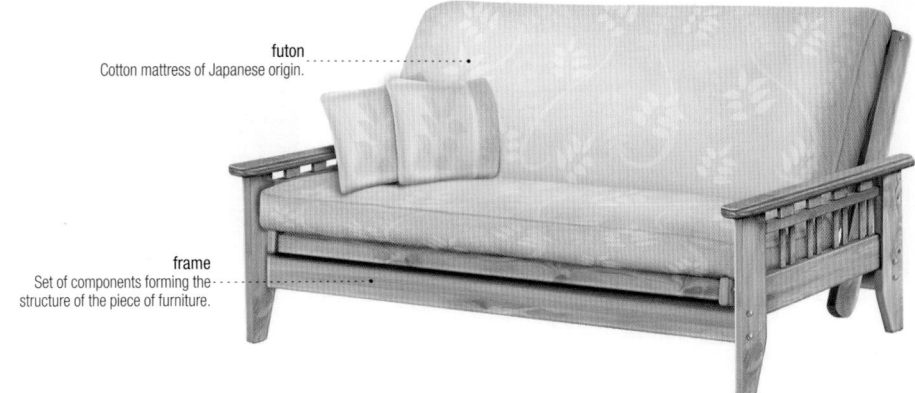

futon
Cotton mattress of Japanese origin.

frame
Set of components forming the structure of the piece of furniture.

storage furniture

Furniture used to store items in a place that is protected but accessible.

HOUSE

armoire
Tall piece of furniture enclosed by panels and equipped with shelves to store items such as linens, clothing and supplies.

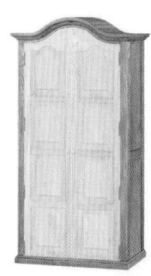

frame
Set of stiles and rails comprising an armoire's structure.

door
Each of an armoire's moving parts, acting as doors.

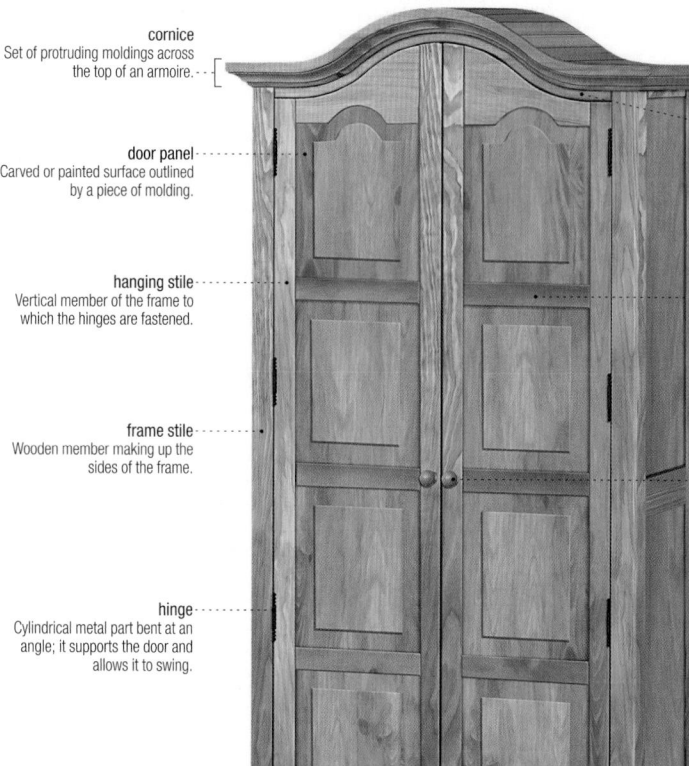

cornice
Set of protruding moldings across the top of an armoire.

door panel
Carved or painted surface outlined by a piece of molding.

hanging stile
Vertical member of the frame to which the hinges are fastened.

frame stile
Wooden member making up the sides of the frame.

hinge
Cylindrical metal part bent at an angle; it supports the door and allows it to swing.

frieze
Decorative molding abo cornice.

top rail
Horizontal wooden mem at the top of the frame.

rail
Flat section of the panel two raised decorative su

handle
Piece attached to the do used to open and close i

bracket base
Lower part of the frame.

bottom rail
Horizontal wooden member located at the bottom of the frame.

compartment
Compartment for storing various objects.

fall front
Panel closing the upper part of the secretary; it is lowered to form a writing table.

secretary
Piece of furniture for storing office supplies and stationery; it includes a drop panel serving as a writing table.

linen chest
Low piece of furniture shaped like a chest and closed by a lid.

dresser
Piece of furniture for the bedroom equipped with drawers, used for storing clothes; it often has a mirror mounted on top.

dressing table
Small table with a mirror often placed in a bedroom; used for grooming (brushing hair, applying makeup).

bedside table
Small table placed at the head of a bed; it might contain one or more drawers.

cellar
Piece designed for keeping wines, having an adjustable internal temperature.

closet
Part of an armoire equipped with a rod for hanging clothes.

shelf
Level board on which clothes are stored.

wardrobe
Piece of furniture in which one part is equipped with shelves and drawers for storing clothes and the other with a rod for hanging them.

corner cupboard
Piece of furniture designed to be placed in the angle formed by two walls.

drawer
Compartment for storage that slides open.

chiffonier
Tall narrow piece of furniture equipped with stacked drawers for storing accessories and clothes.

display cabinet
Glass cabinet for displaying collectibles and knickknacks.

liquor cabinet
Piece of furniture for storing liquor and the accessories used for making drinks.

buffet
Dining room or kitchen furniture for storing dishes, silverware and table linens.

glass-fronted display cabinet
Piece of furniture consisting of a buffet in the lower part and shelves for displaying dishes in the upper part.

children's furniture

Furniture designed and adapted for young children.

playpen
Bed that closes up, usually used when traveling.

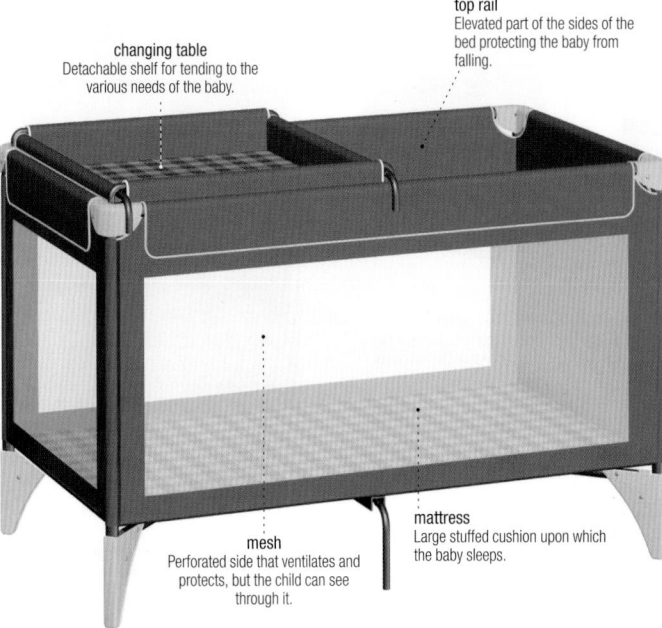

changing table
Detachable shelf for tending to the various needs of the baby.

top rail
Elevated part of the sides of the bed protecting the baby from falling.

mesh
Perforated side that ventilates and protects, but the child can see through it.

mattress
Large stuffed cushion upon which the baby sleeps.

booster seat
Seat that, when set upon a chair, raises the child so that he or she can sit at table level.

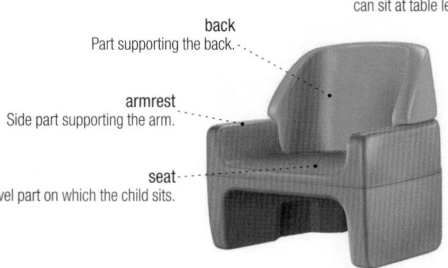

back
Part supporting the back.

armrest
Side part supporting the arm.

seat
Level part on which the child sits.

changing table
Piece of furniture equipped with storage space and a changing area.

contour changing pad
Upholstered cushion on which the baby is placed to have its diaper changed.

high chair
Elevated seat, closed in front by a removable tray, in which a baby sits for feeding.

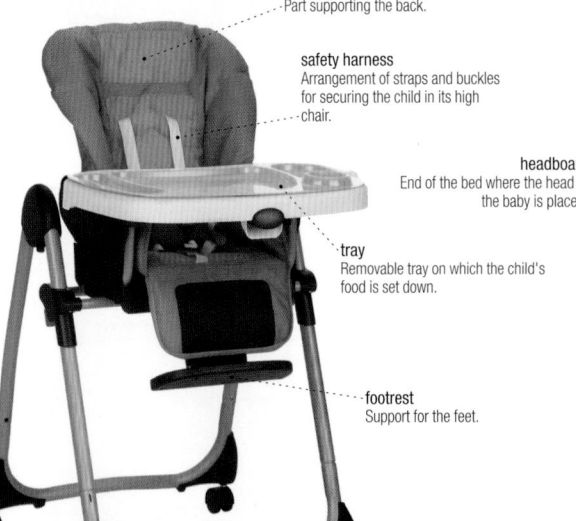

back
Part supporting the back.

safety harness
Arrangement of straps and buckles for securing the child in its high chair.

tray
Removable tray on which the child's food is set down.

footrest
Support for the feet.

leg
Part supporting and stabilizing the chair.

crib
Deep bed for a baby surrounded by bars, one side of which can be lowered; is equipped with a mattress whose height can be changed.

barrier
Assembly of bars enclosing the side of the bed.

slat
Vertical part of the barrier forming the sides of the bed.

headboard
End of the bed where the head of the baby is placed.

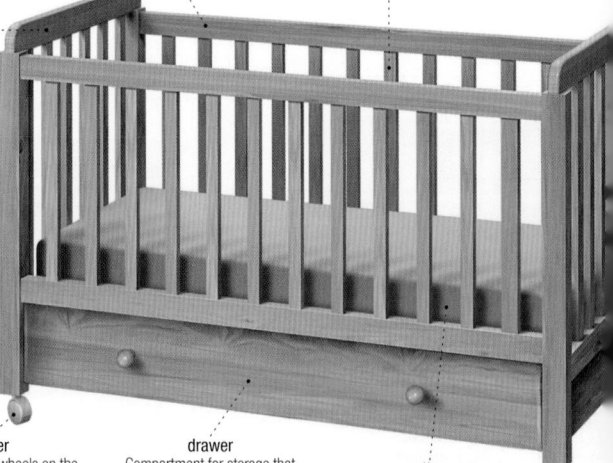

caster
One of the small wheels on the bottom of the crib that allow it to be moved with ease.

drawer
Compartment for storage that slides open.

mattress
Large stuffed cushion upon which the baby sleeps.

window accessories

Set of elements decorating a window.

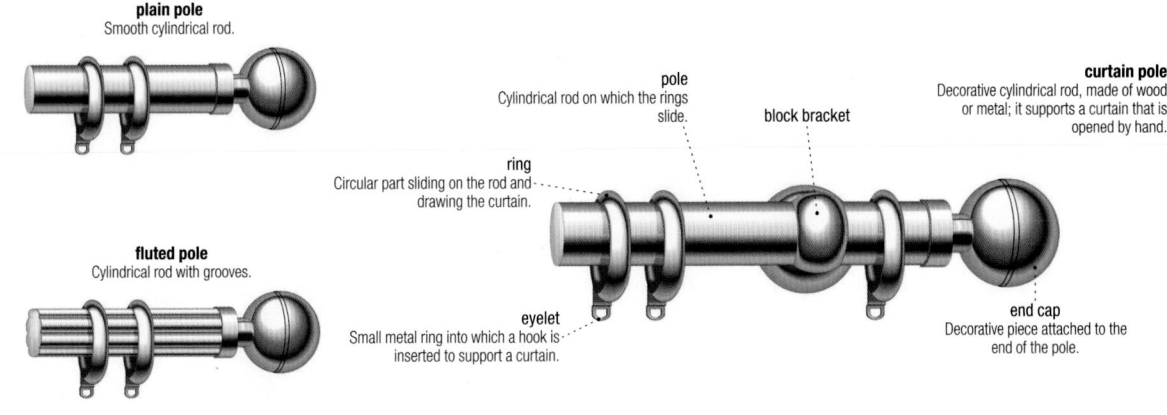

poles
Rods of various shapes and materials from which a curtain hangs.

plain pole
Smooth cylindrical rod.

pole
Cylindrical rod on which the rings slide.

block bracket

curtain pole
Decorative cylindrical rod, made of wood or metal; it supports a curtain that is opened by hand.

ring
Circular part sliding on the rod and drawing the curtain.

fluted pole
Cylindrical rod with grooves.

eyelet
Small metal ring into which a hook is inserted to support a curtain.

end cap
Decorative piece attached to the end of the pole.

single curtain rod
Rectangular metal bar composed of two parts: one is inserted into the other in order to adjust the length.

double curtain rod
Rod composed of two single rods, used to hang two curtains in front of the same window.

HOUSE

curtain track
Rectangular metal rod equipped with a track; the gliders that support the curtain move along it.

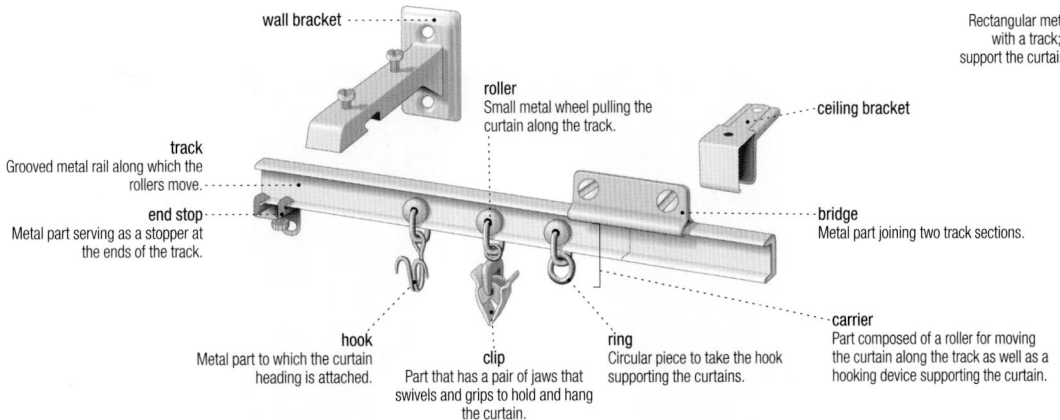

wall bracket

roller
Small metal wheel pulling the curtain along the track.

ceiling bracket

track
Grooved metal rail along which the rollers move.

end stop
Metal part serving as a stopper at the ends of the track.

bridge
Metal part joining two track sections.

carrier
Part composed of a roller for moving the curtain along the track as well as a hooking device supporting the curtain.

hook
Metal part to which the curtain heading is attached.

clip
Part that has a pair of jaws that swivels and grips to hold and hang the curtain.

ring
Circular piece to take the hook supporting the curtains.

traverse rod
Rectangular metal rod that adjusts to the exact width of a window and along which the carriers move, activated by an operating cord.

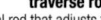

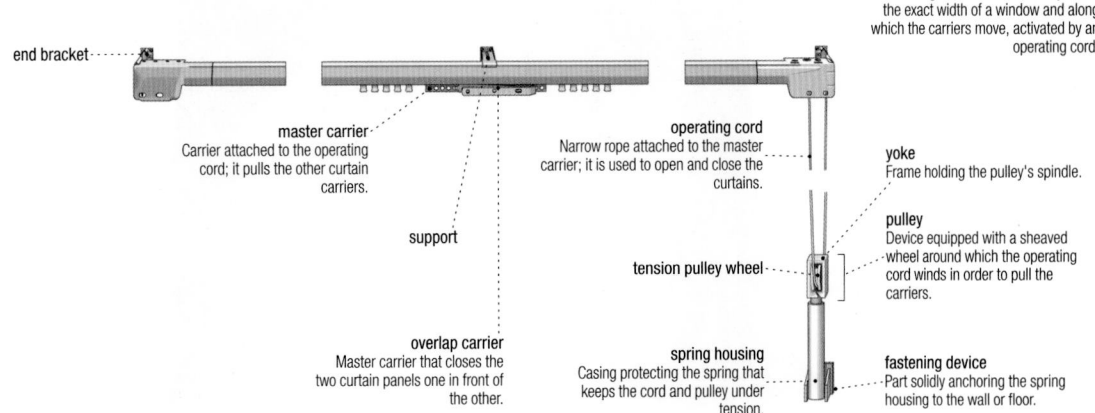

end bracket

master carrier
Carrier attached to the operating cord; it pulls the other curtain carriers.

operating cord
Narrow rope attached to the master carrier; it is used to open and close the curtains.

yoke
Frame holding the pulley's spindle.

pulley
Device equipped with a sheaved wheel around which the operating cord winds in order to pull the carriers.

support

tension pulley wheel

overlap carrier
Master carrier that closes the two curtain panels one in front of the other.

spring housing
Casing protecting the spring that keeps the cord and pulley under tension.

fastening device
Part solidly anchoring the spring housing to the wall or floor.

window accessories

curtain
Covering placed in front of a window for decoration, privacy, or to filter light; it is attached in various ways, hung separately or in layers.

valance
Pleated or gathered strip of fabric hiding the curtain rod.

cottage curtain
Curtain held to the side by a tieback, usually trimmed with a ruffle.

tieback
Strip of fabric or rope holding back and supporting a curtain.

café curtain
Curtain whose rod is located halfway up the window; it lets in light while providing privacy.

ruffle
Pleated or gathered strip of fabric trimming the curtain border.

drapery
Formal curtains that are long and heavy and often composed of several layers.

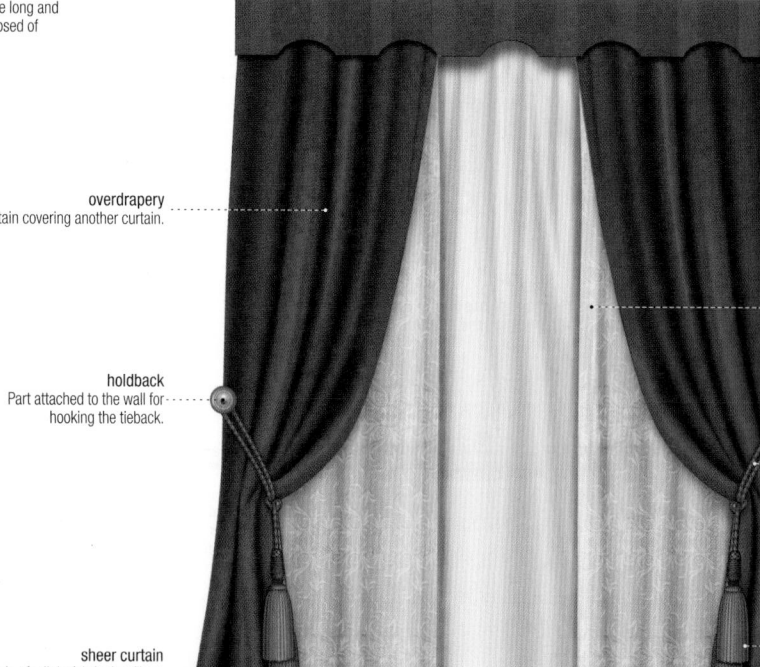

cornice
Strip of fabric affixed to rigid canvas or cardboard; it covers and hides the curtain rod.

overdrapery
Curtain covering another curtain.

draw drapery
Piece of decorative fabric sliding in front of a window to filter or block the light and provide privacy.

holdback
Part attached to the wall for hooking the tieback.

cord tieback
Plaited rope serving as a tieback.

sheer curtain
Curtain made of a light fabric that filters the light entering a room.

tassel
Decorative end of a cord tieback.

HOUSE

window accessories

examples of curtains
Types of curtains showing styles that add beauty and
create the mood or feeling in a room.

crisscross curtains
Curtains whose held-back sides
form an overlap.

attached curtain
Curtain on two curtain rods; it has
pleated sleeves at the top and
bottom of the fabric.

loose curtain
Curtain hung from a single curtain
rod and falling in soft pleats.

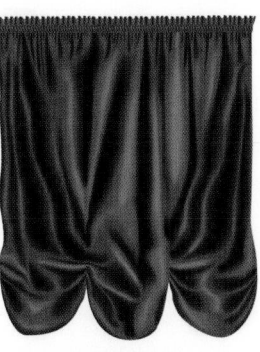

balloon curtain
Curtain that is raised like a blind and
whose pleats are gathered to make
them puffy.

examples of headings
Headings: decorative pleated, shirred or draped parts at the top
of the curtains.

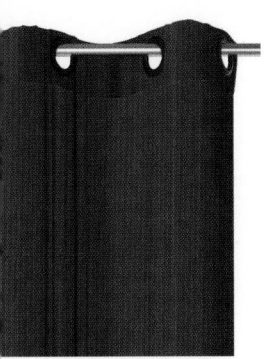

grommet curtain
Curtain with holes at the top,
through which a curtain rod is
inserted.

tab top heading
Heading with loops of fabric at the
top, through which a curtain rod
is inserted.

draped swag
Strip of fabric placed in front of the
curtain to hide the rod; it is arranged
to form loose pleats.

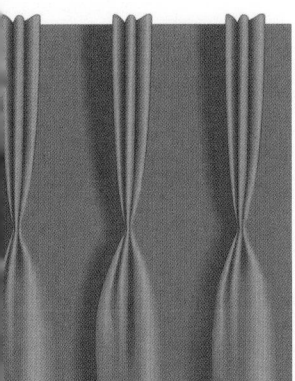

pleated heading
Heading made of pleats spaced at
regular intervals.

pencil pleat heading
Heading whose small vertical pleats
are shaped like tubes; they are made
by pulling on two threads sewn
through the fabric.

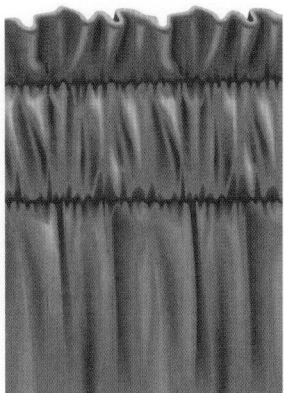

shirred heading
Heading made of pleats created by
pulling on strings inserted through
a ribbon.

window accessories

examples of pleats

Pleats: creases in fabric giving volume to
a curtain.

box pleat
Pleat formed by two folds that meet
in front and touch on the outside of
the fabric, thus forming a hollow in
the fabric.

inverted pleat
Pleat formed from two pleats that
meet on the reverse of the fabric.

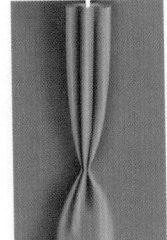

pinch pleat
Pleat formed from three pleats
stitched together at the bottom to
keep them together.

indoor shutters

Decorative wood panels placed in front
of a window composed of adjustable
horizontal louvers for controlling the
amount of light entering a room.

panel
Flat surface to which are attached
swiveling laths that can be closed
to cover the window.

lath
Each long, flat and thin strip that
can be adjusted to control the
amount of light passing through.

examples of blinds and shades

Devices that roll or fold up, serving to filter or
block light and provide privacy.

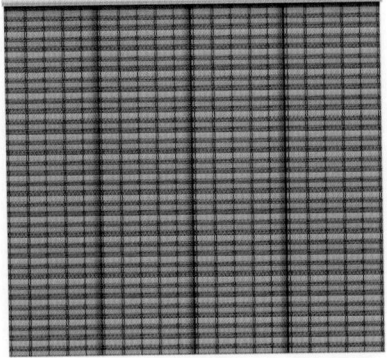

Japanese blind
Blind made up of sliding panels
traditionally made of bamboo.

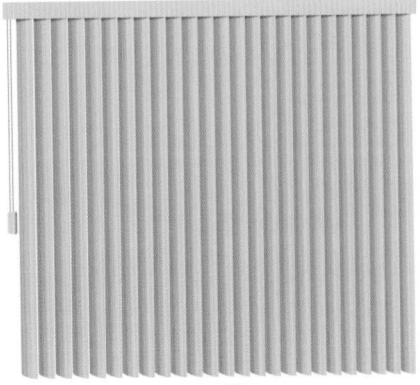

vertical blind
Blind with swiveling laths hung
vertically.

HOUSE

window accessories

roller shade
Shade with a roller containing a spring that
causes the shade cloth to roll up.

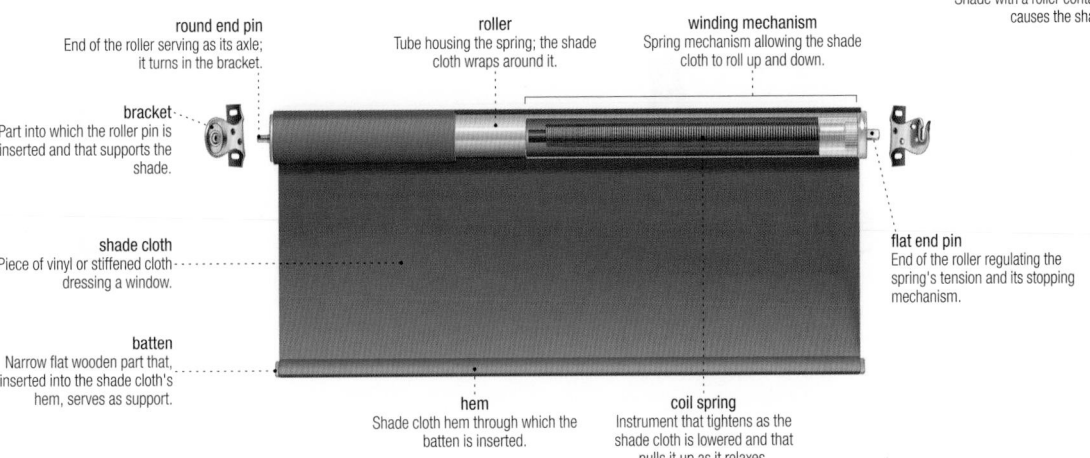

round end pin
End of the roller serving as its axle;
it turns in the bracket.

roller
Tube housing the spring; the shade
cloth wraps around it.

winding mechanism
Spring mechanism allowing the shade
cloth to roll up and down.

bracket
Part into which the roller pin is
inserted and that supports the
shade.

shade cloth
Piece of vinyl or stiffened cloth
dressing a window.

flat end pin
End of the roller regulating the
spring's tension and its stopping
mechanism.

batten
Narrow flat wooden part that,
inserted into the shade cloth's
hem, serves as support.

hem
Shade cloth hem through which the
batten is inserted.

coil spring
Instrument that tightens as the
shade cloth is lowered and that
pulls it up as it relaxes.

venetian blind
Blind made of adjustable horizontal slats
containing a mechanism for controlling its
height and orientation.

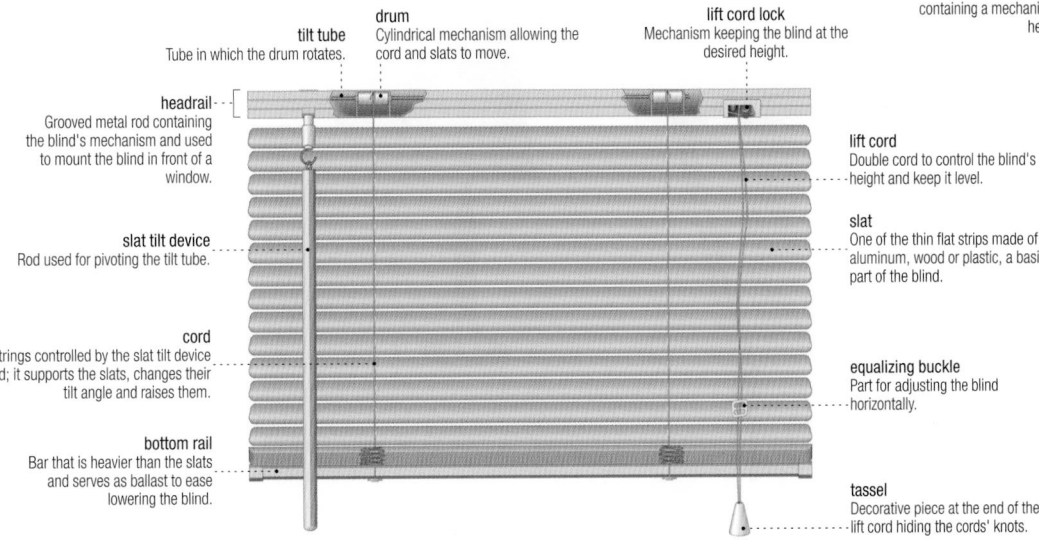

tilt tube
Tube in which the drum rotates.

drum
Cylindrical mechanism allowing the
cord and slats to move.

lift cord lock
Mechanism keeping the blind at the
desired height.

headrail
Grooved metal rod containing
the blind's mechanism and used
to mount the blind in front of a
window.

lift cord
Double cord to control the blind's
height and keep it level.

slat tilt device
Rod used for pivoting the tilt tube.

slat
One of the thin flat strips made of
aluminum, wood or plastic, a basic
part of the blind.

cord
System of strings controlled by the slat tilt device
and the lift cord; it supports the slats, changes their
tilt angle and raises them.

equalizing buckle
Part for adjusting the blind
horizontally.

bottom rail
Bar that is heavier than the slats
and serves as ballast to ease
lowering the blind.

tassel
Decorative piece at the end of the
lift cord hiding the cords' knots.

roll-up shade
Shade made of nonadjustable laths rolled up by
a system of cords and pulleys.

roman shade
Shade that forms layered pleats as it is raised
by means of cords sliding through rings on the
back of the cloth.

lights

Fixed or portable devices designed and used to diffuse electric light.

clamp spotlight
Small portable spotlight with a concentrated beam; it can be mounted on furniture with a clamp.

bed lamp
Small reading light that can be mounted on the back of a book or the headboard of a bed.

ceiling fitting
Light mounted directly on the ceiling.

hanging pendant
Light designed to be hung from the ceiling.

adjustable lamp
Multidirectional light usually mounted on a worktable by an adjustable clamp.

on-off switch
Button for turning the device on or off.

arm
Moving bar that folds and adjusts the position of the lamp shade.

spring
Elastic metal coil for changing and maintaining the position for the two sections of the arm.

adjustable clamp
Mechanism in the form of a vise for mounting the lamp to the edge of the worktable.

table lamp
Movable light with a short stand; it is placed on furniture.

shade
Translucent screen directing the lamp's light while decreasing its glare.

stand
Decorative base of a lamp of various materials and shapes; it supports the socket while concealing the electric wires.

halogen desk lamp
Desk lamp of greater luminous intensity and longer duration than a traditional lamp but that emits more heat.

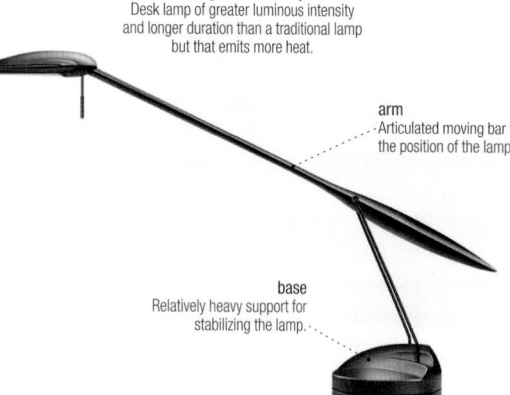

arm
Articulated moving bar for adjusting the position of the lamp shade.

base
Relatively heavy support for stabilizing the lamp.

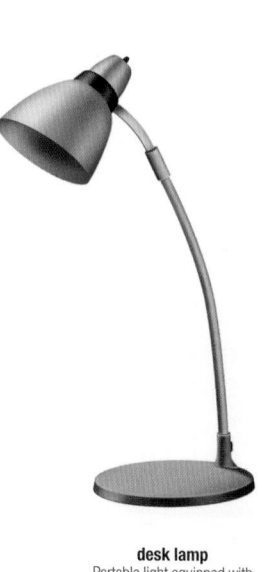

desk lamp
Portable light equipped with an opaque shield that directs and diffuses the light onto the worktable.

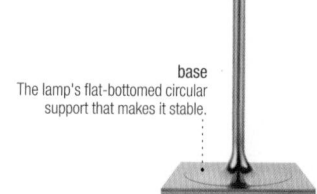

base
The lamp's flat-bottomed circular support that makes it stable.

floor lamp
Portable lamp having a high stand that is placed on the floor.

HOUSE

post lantern
Exterior light having a high stand that is fixed to the ground; it consists of a translucent or transparent cage containing a light source.

chandelier
Light suspended from the ceiling and consisting of several lamps.

bobeche
Small plate with a cupped shape placed at the base of the socket.

crystal drop
Decorative piece made of crystal hanging from a bobeche.

column
Mounting that supports the chandelier's branches.

crystal button
One of a set of crystal drops arranged in a garland.

track lighting
Device mounted to the ceiling to support spots and supply electricity to them.

bar frame
Part of the track fitted with two metal strips; the electric current passes through it.

transformer
Device adapting the electric current from the track to the spot's voltage.

spot
Small adjustable spotlight with a concentrated beam.

wall lantern
Exterior light mounted on a wall, consisting of a translucent or transparent cage containing a light source.

sconce
Interior light mounted on a wall.

swivel wall lamp
Interior light equipped with a movable and often folding arm mounted on a wall.

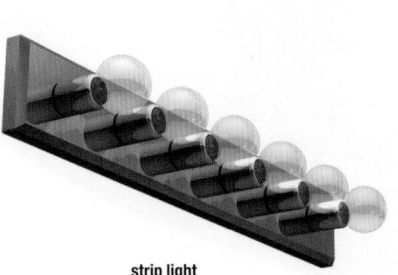

strip light
Device composed of a set of lights that are mounted on the same base.

home appliances

Domestic appliances operating on electricity.

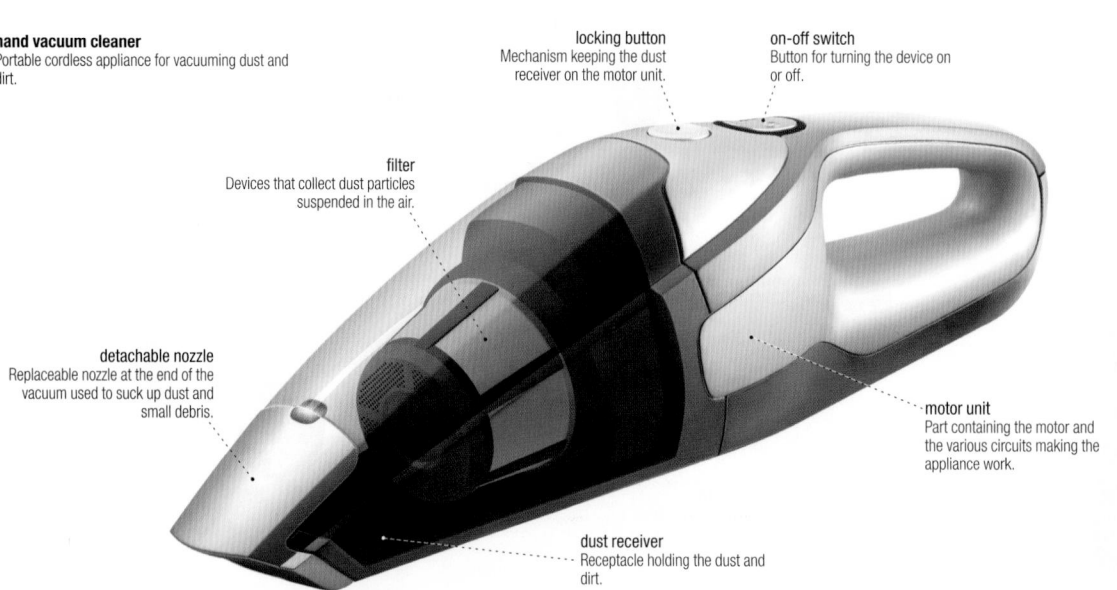

steam iron
Electric appliance producing steam and used to iron fabric.

temperature control
Device for regulating the iron's temperature.

handle
Part that is gripped in order to hold the iron.

cord
Flexible electric wire housing t leads connecting the applianc electric circuit.

power steam button
Device for turning water into mist to dampen the fabric.

spray button
Button for switching between steam and dry ironing.

variable steam control
Device regulating the flow of steam.

fill opening
Where water enters to fill the chamber.

spray
Device for turning water into mist to dampen the fabric.

vertical cord lift
Part keeping a section of the cor in an upright position in order to free up the ironing surface.

heel rest
Part upon which the iron rests while not in use.

indicator light
Light showing that the appliance is on.

front tip

soleplate
Flat metal part that usually heats to press a fabric; steam escapes from its holes.

water-level tube

body
Rigid casing covering and protecting the various working elements of the appliance.

hand vacuum cleaner
Portable cordless appliance for vacuuming dust and dirt.

locking button
Mechanism keeping the dust receiver on the motor unit.

on-off switch
Button for turning the device on or off.

filter
Devices that collect dust particles suspended in the air.

detachable nozzle
Replaceable nozzle at the end of the vacuum used to suck up dust and small debris.

motor unit
Part containing the motor and the various circuits making the appliance work.

dust receiver
Receptacle holding the dust and dirt.

home appliances

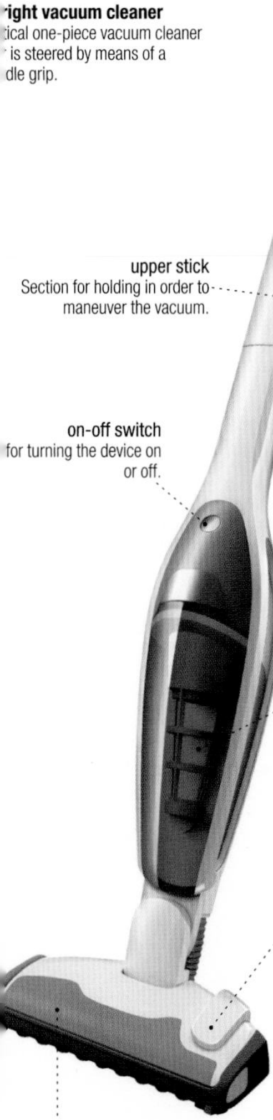

upright vacuum cleaner
...tical one-piece vacuum cleaner ...is steered by means of a ...dle grip.

power regulation
Switch for controlling the suction power.

locking device
Mechanism for locking the flexible hose onto the pipe.

canister vacuum cleaner
Electric appliance for vacuuming dust and dirt; it is equipped with wheels and a flexible hose.

cable holder
Piece designed to hold the electric cable in place.

upper stick
Section for holding in order to maneuver the vacuum.

flexible hose
Supple tube to which the pipe and cleaning tools are connected; it makes the appliance more manageable.

pipe
Cylindrical rigid tube that moves the rug and floor brushes and other cleaning tools.

on-off switch
...for turning the device on or off.

extension pipe
Cylindrical tube inserted into the end of the pipe to lengthen it.

bumper
Trim protecting the furniture if the vacuum cleaner collides with it.

bag compartment
Space for housing the bag that collects the dust and dirt.

hood
Rigid casing covering and protecting the various working elements of the appliance.

suction control
Switch for controlling the suction power.

cleaner height adjustment knob
Mechanism for controlling brush height depending on the thickness of the rug or pile carpet to be cleaned.

ventilating grille
Perforated panel through which aspirated air, cleansed of dust and dirt, is expelled.

carpet/hard floor nozzle
Accessory devised to vacuum dust and dirt from a rug, pile carpet or floor.

rug and floor brush
Accessory devised to vacuum dust and dirt from a rug, pile carpet or floor.

handle

on-off switch
Button for turning the device on or off.

wheel

HOUSE

vacuum cleaner accessories
Tools that can be attached to the pipe or hose of a canister vacuum cleaner.

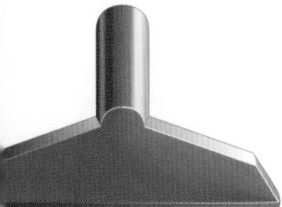

upholstery nozzle
...ccessory for vacuuming dust and dirt from fabric.

dusting brush
Accessory for vacuuming dust from various surfaces.

crevice tool
Accessory for vacuuming dust and dirt from narrow parts of furniture or hard-to-reach places in the home.

floor brush
Accessory equipped with bristles to avoid scratching the floor while vacuuming.

home appliances

range hood
Ventilation appliance expelling or recycling air that contains cooking fumes and odors.

filter
Device catching the cooking grease.

cooking unit
Heating element on which cookware is placed.

clock timer
Multifunction timekeeping mechanism; it shows the time, tracks cooking duration, starts the oven at a preset time, etc.

cooktop
Surface of the range on which the cooking units are arranged.

electric range
Electric appliance for cooking or heating food, equipped with surface elements or griddles and an oven.

control panel
Panel containing the programming keys.

cooktop edge
Protruding edge along the sides of the cooking surface.

control knob
Instrument for turning the cooking units on and off and for regulating the intensity of the units' heat.

oven
Closed part of the range, equipped with an upper heating element (broiler) and a lower heating element, in which food is cooked or heated.

handle
Part for opening and closing the oven door.

window
Thick window for looking inside the oven.

rack
Metal grille for supporting cookware; its height is adjustable.

drawer
Compartment that slides open for storing cookware.

gas range
Gas appliance for cooking or heating food, equipped with flame burners and an oven.

burner
Device producing a flame in order to cook food.

grate
Metal grille supporting the cookware over the burners.

burner control knobs
Instrument for starting and stopping the supply of gas and for controlling its flow.

cooktop
Surface of the range on which the burners are arranged.

control panel
Panel containing the programming keys for the burners and the oven.

oven
Closed part of the range, equipped with an upper heating element (broiler) and a lower heating element, in which food is cooked or heated.

handle
Part for opening and closing the oven door.

rack
Metal grille for supporting cookware; its height is adjustable.

window
Thick window for looking inside the oven.

door

home appliances

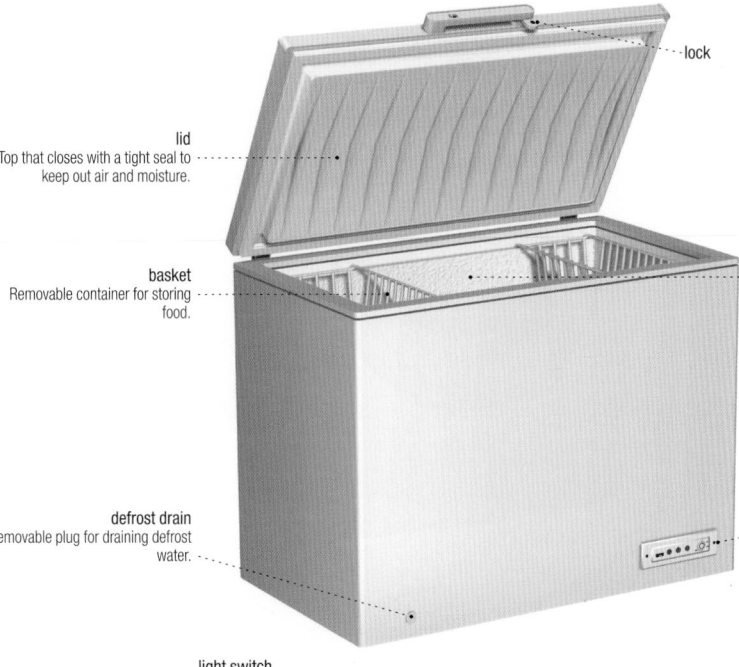

chest freezer
Large horizontal appliance for
conserving food at a very low
temperature (0°F).

lock

lid
Top that closes with a tight seal to
keep out air and moisture.

cabinet
Large insulated compartment for
storing food.

basket
Removable container for storing
food.

defrost drain
Removable plug for draining defrost
water.

temperature control
Device for selecting and
maintaining the degree of coldness
in the appliance.

HOUSE

refrigerator
Appliance with two compartments,
one for keeping food cold and the
other for freezing it.

light switch
Mechanism switching on the
refrigerator light when the door is
opened.

doorstop
Part that stops the door from
opening too far.

magnetic gasket
Rubber seal that closes the door
tightly using a magnetic strip to
keep out air and moisture.

shelf
Removable support whose height
is adjustable.

butter compartment
Compartment with a pull-down door for
storing butter.

handle
Part for opening and closing the
refrigerator door.

water dispenser
Apparatus that automatically
supplies water or ice cubes.

shelf channel
Notched part to which the shelves
attach.

freezer compartment
Refrigerator compartment for freezing
food.

refrigerator compartment
Compartment keeping food cold.

storage door
Door with rows of shelves and
compartments.

meat keeper
Compartment for storing meat.

guardrail
Part keeping food in place when
the door is opened or closed.

crisper
Compartment maintaining optimal
temperature for conserving fruits and
vegetables.

dairy compartment
Compartment for storing milk cartons.

home appliances

front-loading washer
Home appliance for washing laundry; access to the tub is via a door on the front of the appliance.

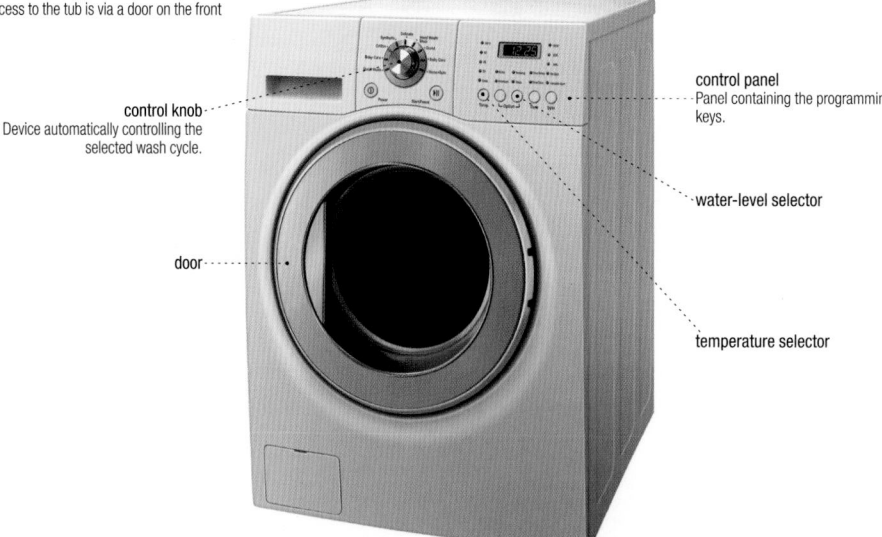

control knob
Device automatically controlling the selected wash cycle.

control panel
Panel containing the programming keys.

water-level selector

door

temperature selector

top-loading washer mechanism
Home appliance for washing laundry; access to the tub is via a lid on the top of the appliance.

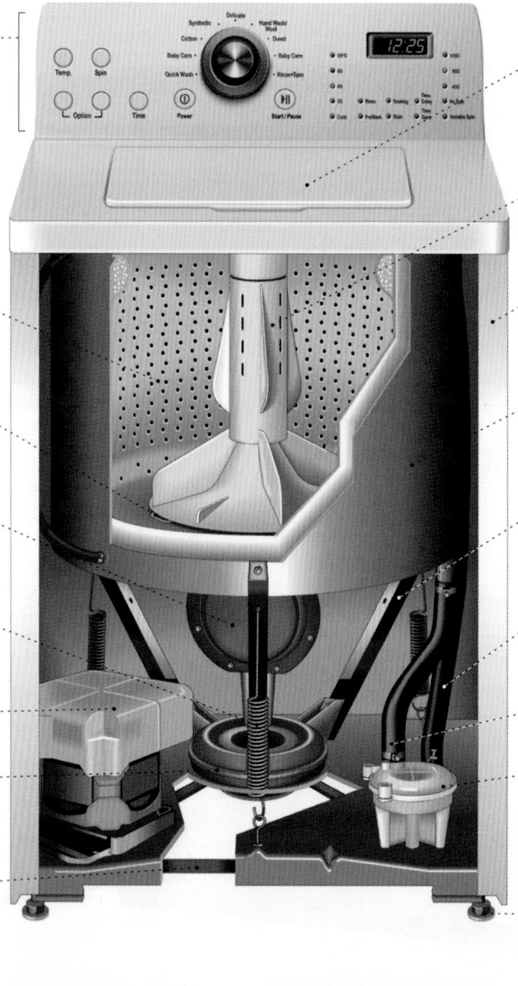

backguard
Vertical part across the back of the washer on which the appliance's various controls are found.

lid
Moving part for closing the washer's tub.

agitator
Device stirring the laundry.

cabinet
Enameled sheet-metal case covering and protecting the appliance's various components.

basket
Perforated drum into which the laundry is placed.

tub
Durable container into which the water flows.

lint filter
Device collecting fiber residue from fabric.

transmission
Mechanism allowing the agitator and basket to turn at various speeds.

suspension arm
Metal struts supporting the tub.

spring
Metal elastic piece attached to the suspension arm to reduce tub vibrations.

drain hose
Flexible pipe through which the washer's pump expels the wastewater to the dwelling's drain circuit.

motor
Device transforming electric energy into mechanical energy to drive another device.

emptying hose
Pipe through which the washer's pump empties the water from the tub.

torque converter
Mechanism controlling and adjusting the agitator and basket action.

pump
Device that evacuates wastewater from the tub and drives it into the drain hose.

drive belt
Device using a system of pulleys to transfer the motor's mechanical energy to the washer's transmission.

leveling foot
Adjustable part for supporting the appliance and making it level.

home appliances

dryer
Appliance for automatically drying laundry.

control knob
Device automatically controlling the selected drying cycle.

start switch

door

control panel
Panel containing the programming keys.

temperature selector

dryer mechanism

heating duct
Conduit in which air is heated and directed toward the drum.

vane
Part causing the laundry to tumble while drying.

drum
Cylinder whose rotation tumbles the laundry to dry it.

lint trap
Device collecting fiber residue from fabric.

safety thermostat
Device interrupting the current if the heating element temperature is too high.

fan
Device circulating the hot air in the drum.

motor
Device transforming electric energy into mechanical energy to drive another device.

leveling foot
Adjustable part for supporting the appliance and making it level.

backguard
Vertical part across the back of the dryer on which the appliance's various controls are found.

door switch
Mechanism stopping the drum's rotation when the door is opened.

cabinet
Enameled sheet-metal case covering and protecting the appliance's various components.

heating element
Electric resistor heating the air before it enters the drum.

home appliances

dishwasher: control panel
Dishwasher: appliance designed to automatically wash and dry dishes.

control buttons
Buttons for selecting the wash cycle.

indicator light
Light showing that the appliance is on.

air vent
Conduit for evacuating the steam during drying.

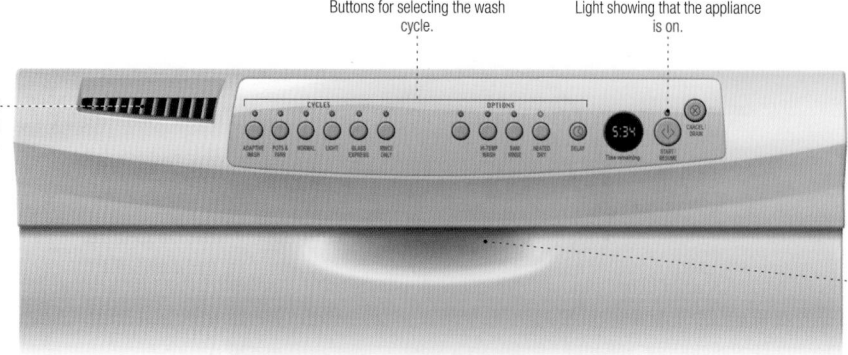

handle
Part for opening and closin door.

dishwasher mechanism

rack
Grillelike shelf in which the dishes are arranged.

wash tower
Mechanism spraying the dishes with hot water from the center of the appliance.

insulating material
Material lining the dishwashe walls in order to reduce heat and noise.

spray arm
Rotating perforated arm spraying the dishes with hot pressurized water to clean them.

tub
Durable container in which th are washed and dried.

overflow protection switch
Mechanism halting the water feed if the water level exceeds the tub's capacity.

slide
Mechanism supporting the b and enabling it to slide.

hinge
Fastener that folds; it allows the door to be raised and lowered.

water hose
Hot-water feed pipe to the dis connected to the dwelling's p circuit.

detergent dispenser
Device that is activated by the control knob and dispenses the detergent into the tub.

heating element
Submerged electric resistor t heats the water and dries the dishes.

drain hose
Flexible pipe through which the dishwasher pump expels wastewater into the dwelling's drain circuit.

pump
Device routing the water under pressure to the spray arms and evacuating the tub's wastewater into the drain hose.

gasket
Rubber seal keeping the door watertight.

leveling foot
Adjustable part for supporting the appliance and making it level.

rinse-aid dispenser
Device that is activated by the control knob and dispenses a rinsing agent into the tub.

cutlery basket
Grillelike container in which the cutlery is placed.

motor
Device transforming electric energy into mechanical energy to drive another device.

household equipment

Objects used for cleaning a dwelling.

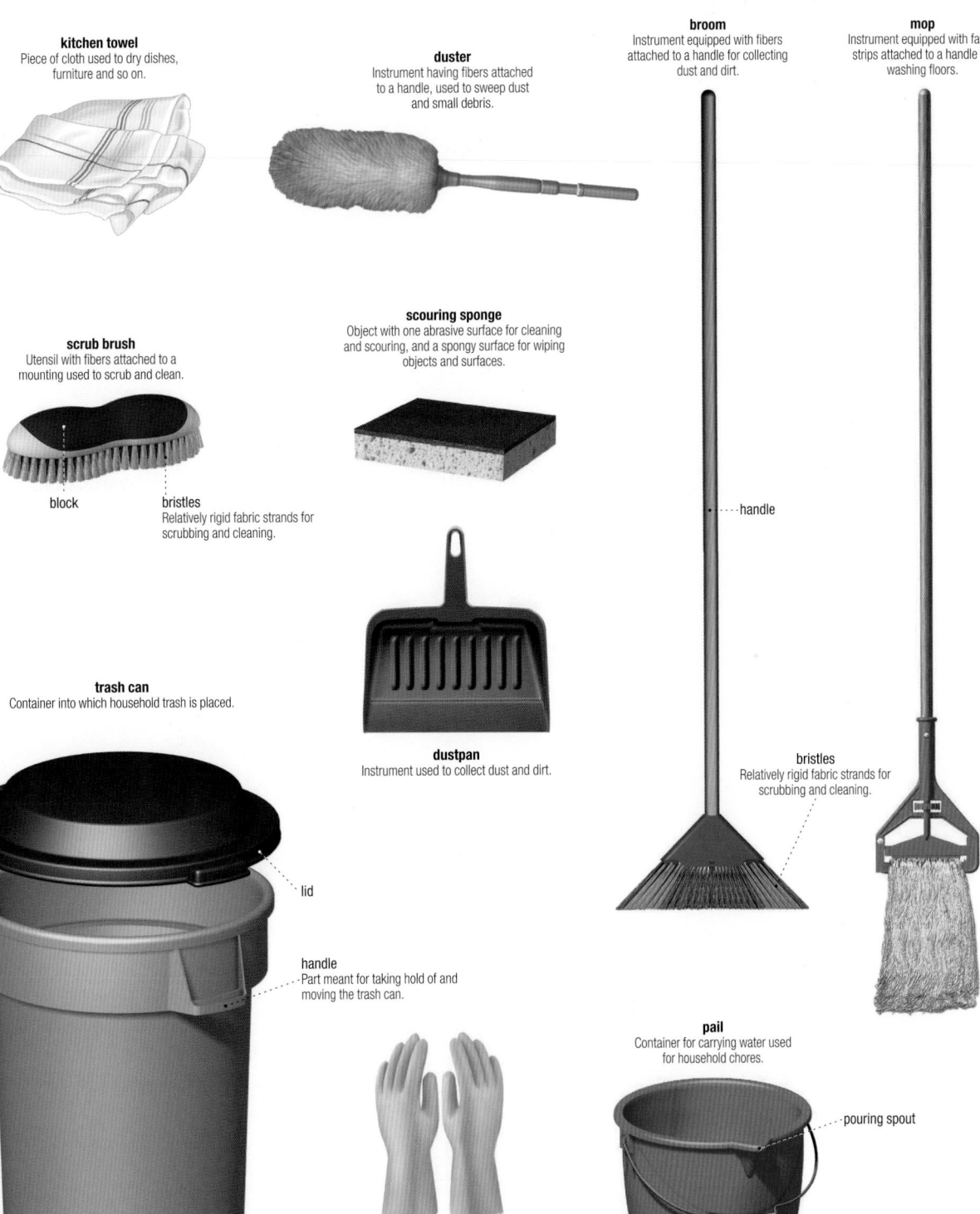

kitchen towel
Piece of cloth used to dry dishes, furniture and so on.

duster
Instrument having fibers attached to a handle, used to sweep dust and small debris.

broom
Instrument equipped with fibers attached to a handle for collecting dust and dirt.

mop
Instrument equipped with fabric strips attached to a handle for washing floors.

scrub brush
Utensil with fibers attached to a mounting used to scrub and clean.

block

bristles
Relatively rigid fabric strands for scrubbing and cleaning.

scouring sponge
Object with one abrasive surface for cleaning and scouring, and a spongy surface for wiping objects and surfaces.

handle

bristles
Relatively rigid fabric strands for scrubbing and cleaning.

trash can
Container into which household trash is placed.

lid

handle
Part meant for taking hold of and moving the trash can.

dustpan
Instrument used to collect dust and dirt.

HOUSE

rubber gloves
Heavy gloves that protect the hands from liquids and chemical products.

pail
Container for carrying water used for household chores.

pouring spout

handle
Part shaped like a semicircle for gripping the pail.

DO-IT-YOURSELF AND GARDENING

basic building materials

Components that, when assembled, form the structure of a building.

brick

Block of compressed baked clay, laid in rows with the help of mortar to form various masonry work, such as walls, partitions and chimneys.

solid brick
Small brick, not perforated, used especially in building or covering various types of walls.

perforated brick
Small brick with vertical holes, whose dimensions are usually no greater than 40% of the brick.

hollow brick
Large brick, over 40% of which is composed of horizontal cells.

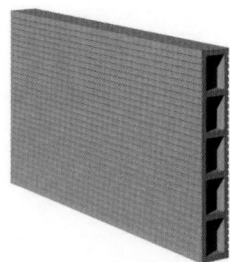

partition tile
Hollow brick, usually worked with the help of plaster, used to build or line partitions.

brick wall

mortar
Mixture of fine aggregates (pebbles, gravel, sand), water and a binder (cement or lime), used to join masonry components or to coat masonry after it is completed.

mortar
Mixture of fine aggregates (pebbles, gravel, sand), water and a binder (cement or lime), used to join masonry components or to coat masonry after it is completed.

firebrick
Brick that can withstand very high temperatures without deforming.

stone

Block of mineral matter, of irregular shape, used for masonry or as a facing.

flagstone
Flat stone of irregular shape, used to cover floors and walls and to pave walkways and patios.

rubble
Small block of rough or crudely carved stone, usually assembled with the help of mortar to build a wall.

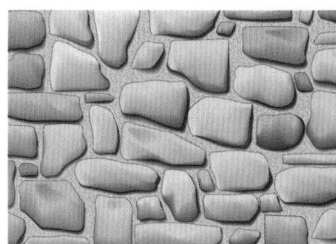

cut stone
Stone cut in regular shapes so that it can be fitted without a joint or with very thin joints.

stone wall

concrete and steel

Concrete is a material composed of aggregates, cement and water that, after hardening in a mold, forms a substance that is resistant to compression; steel is an iron- and carbon-based metal.

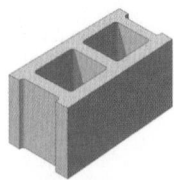

concrete block
Concrete component, solid or hollow, used mainly in the construction of masonry as a substitute for brick.

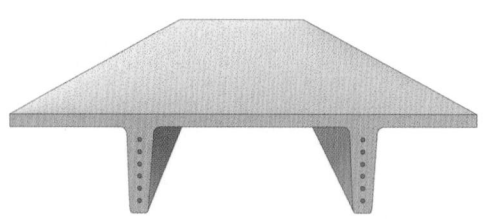

prestressed concrete
Concrete whose steel bars are stretched before cooling, creating a highly resistant and durable material; it is used to manufacture beams with long spans.

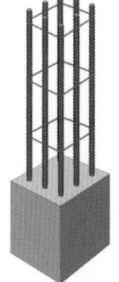

reinforced concrete
Concrete reinforced by steel bars, often used in the manufacture of load-bearing units in a building.

steel
Iron- and carbon-based metal, durable, frequently used in struct

covering materials

Materials covering a surface, usually for the purpose of protecting or decorating it.

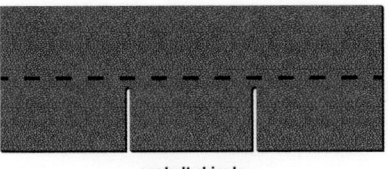

asphalt shingle
Roof-covering material, made with a framework (fiberglass, felt) coated with bitumen and covered with fine aggregate.

wooden shingle
Small wooden plank used to cover roofs and walls that are especially exposed to inclement weather.

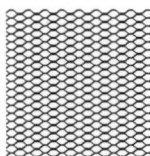

diamond mesh metal lath
Metal grid used as a framework or support for plaster and other coatings.

tar paper
Paper usually stapled directly to the roof or exterior walls, under the covering, in order to enhance impermeability.

roof tile
Hard surface, usually made of baked molded clay, used as a covering for roofs.

gypsum tile
Small molded-plaster component, solid or hollow, with holes on the sides; it is used to construct and repair walls.

tile
Small flat component of regular shape, made from various materials and used for covering floors and walls.

drywall
Large panel made of a layer of plaster covered with paperboard, usually used as a finishing material on a dwelling's interior walls.

insulating materials

Materials impeding the transfer of heat to the outside, or cold to the inside, of a building or a duct.

pipe-wrapping insulation
Flexible strips of thermal insulating material that can be rolled around a pipe.

pipe sleeve
Hollow cylinder of molded foam insulation used around a pipe.

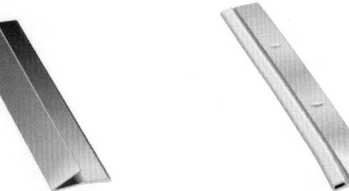

spring-metal weather stripping
V-shaped metal or vinyl strip used for blocking air leaks on exterior doors and windows.

vinyl weather stripping
Vinyl strip that compresses against a door or window to block air leaks.

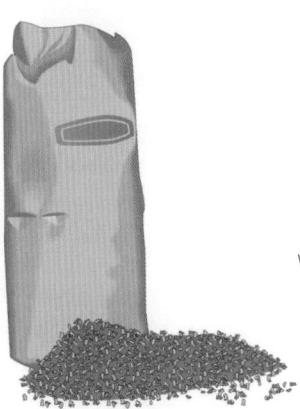

loose-fill insulation
Thermal insulation material in the form of particles used in the walls and roof space of some houses.

foam weather stripping
Adhesive-backed strip of foam insulation used around windows and doors.

blanket insulation
Continuous band of fiberglass or mineral wool insulating material used especially for wall cavities and attic spaces.

board insulation
Rigid panel made of fiberglass or plastic foam used as an insulating material for walls or doors in houses.

spray foam insulation
A usually polyurethane foam insulation that is sprayed into enclosed spaces in liquid form and expands and hardens quickly.

wood

Relatively hard, dense substance forming the trunks, branches and roots of trees. The wood of each species has distinct characteristics.

section of a log

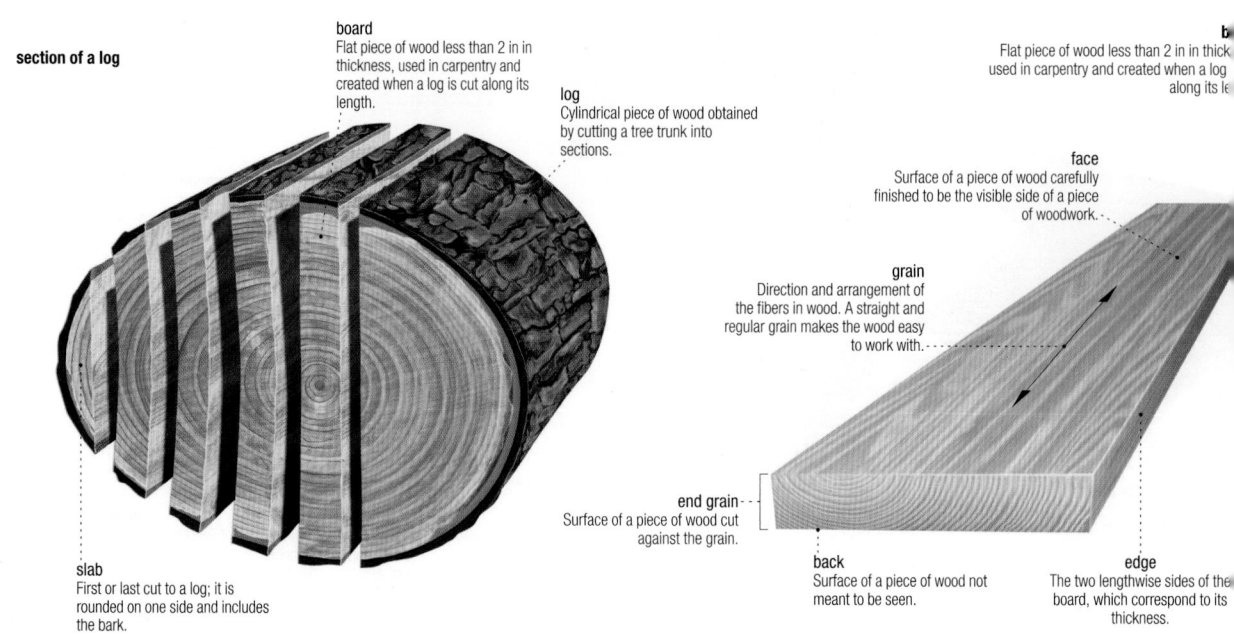

board
Flat piece of wood less than 2 in in thickness, used in carpentry and created when a log is cut along its length.

log
Cylindrical piece of wood obtained by cutting a tree trunk into sections.

b
Flat piece of wood less than 2 in in thick used in carpentry and created when a log along its le

face
Surface of a piece of wood carefully finished to be the visible side of a piece of woodwork.

grain
Direction and arrangement of the fibers in wood. A straight and regular grain makes the wood easy to work with.

end grain
Surface of a piece of wood cut against the grain.

slab
First or last cut to a log; it is rounded on one side and includes the bark.

back
Surface of a piece of wood not meant to be seen.

edge
The two lengthwise sides of the board, which correspond to its thickness.

wood-based materials
Materials obtained when a log is converted; also when various wood elements are assembled or agglomerated.

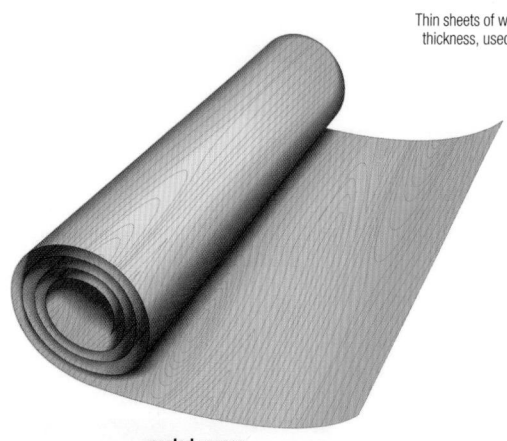

ply
Thin sheets of wood (veneer) of equal thickness, used for the manufacture of plywood.

plywood
Panel made from at least five layers, each glued to the other with their respective grains running perpendicular to the adjacent layer.

blockboard
Plywood panel made of two layers sandwich a central part (core), which is made up of wi slats glued side by side.

peeled veneer
Thin sheet obtained from rotating a log on a peeling machine and applying a blade (lathe) to it.

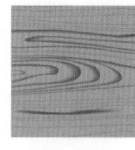

laminboard
Panel made of two layers sandwiching a central part (core), which is made up of narrow strips, or laminations, glued side by side.

waferboard
Panel made from wood chips mixed with glu then pressed at a high temperature to bond th

hardboard
Smooth and homogeneous board made when minuscule wood fibers are soaked in resin and pressed at a high temperature.

perforated hardboard
Smooth board punctured with holes created through high-temperature pressing of tiny fibers of resin-impregnated wood.

particleboard
Board made from wood particles mixed with resin, then pressed at a high temperature to bond them.

plastic-laminated particleboard
Particle board with a melamine surface layer that is ha and easy to wash.

accessories

Objects used for the transport or storage of tools and instruments.

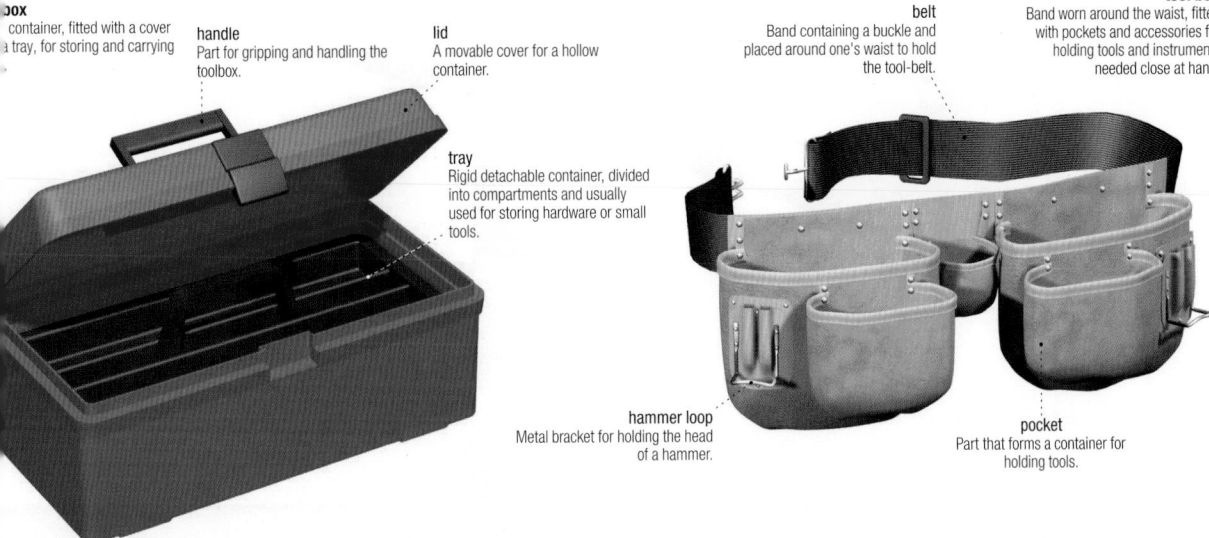

box
container, fitted with a cover a tray, for storing and carrying

handle
Part for gripping and handling the toolbox.

lid
A movable cover for a hollow container.

tray
Rigid detachable container, divided into compartments and usually used for storing hardware or small tools.

belt
Band containing a buckle and placed around one's waist to hold the tool-belt.

tool belt
Band worn around the waist, fitted with pockets and accessories for holding tools and instruments needed close at hand.

hammer loop
Metal bracket for holding the head of a hammer.

pocket
Part that forms a container for holding tools.

measuring and marking tools

Tools for tracing various lines or measuring lengths.

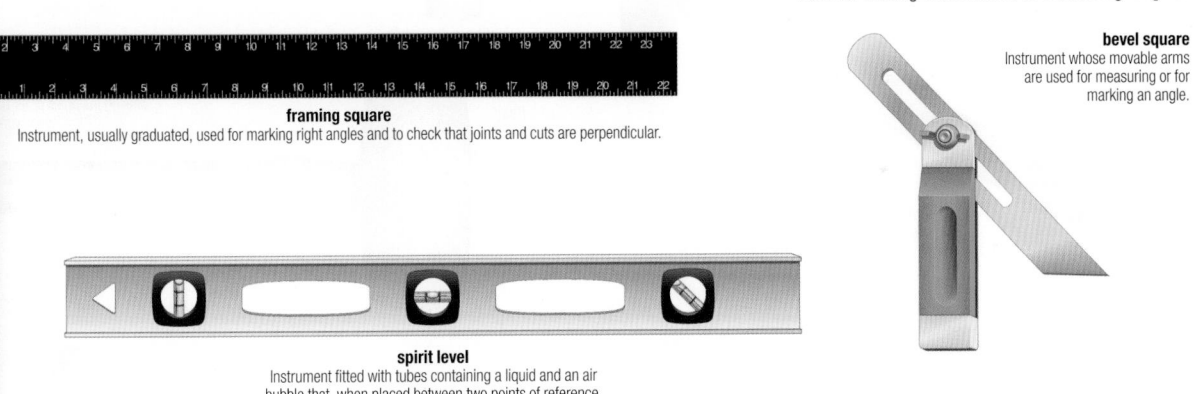

framing square
Instrument, usually graduated, used for marking right angles and to check that joints and cuts are perpendicular.

bevel square
Instrument whose movable arms are used for measuring or for marking an angle.

spirit level
Instrument fitted with tubes containing a liquid and an air bubble that, when placed between two points of reference, shows whether a surface is level, vertical or at 45°.

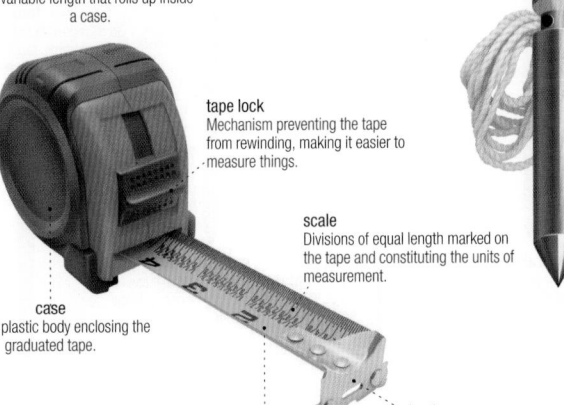

tape measure
Instrument for determining length made up of a graduated, flexible tape of variable length that rolls up inside a case.

tape lock
Mechanism preventing the tape from rewinding, making it easier to measure things.

scale
Divisions of equal length marked on the tape and constituting the units of measurement.

case
Metal or plastic body enclosing the graduated tape.

tape
Thin metal graduated band; it is narrow and flexible for measuring lengths.

hook
Bent metal end of the tape that is hooked onto an object; it also makes it easier to unroll the tape.

plumb line
Device composed of a piece of metal suspended by a string, used when adjusting pieces vertically.

chalk line
Instrument consisting of a cord that rewinds into a case filled with chalk powder; it is used for marking straight lines.

case
Metal or plastic body housing the chalk powder and the line.

crank handle
Device for rewinding the line into the case containing the chalk powder.

line
Chalk-covered cord that is pulled between two points to mark a straight line.

hook
Curved metal end of the cord that can be attached to an object; it also makes unwinding easier.

nailing tools

Tools used in attaching or assembling by means of nails.

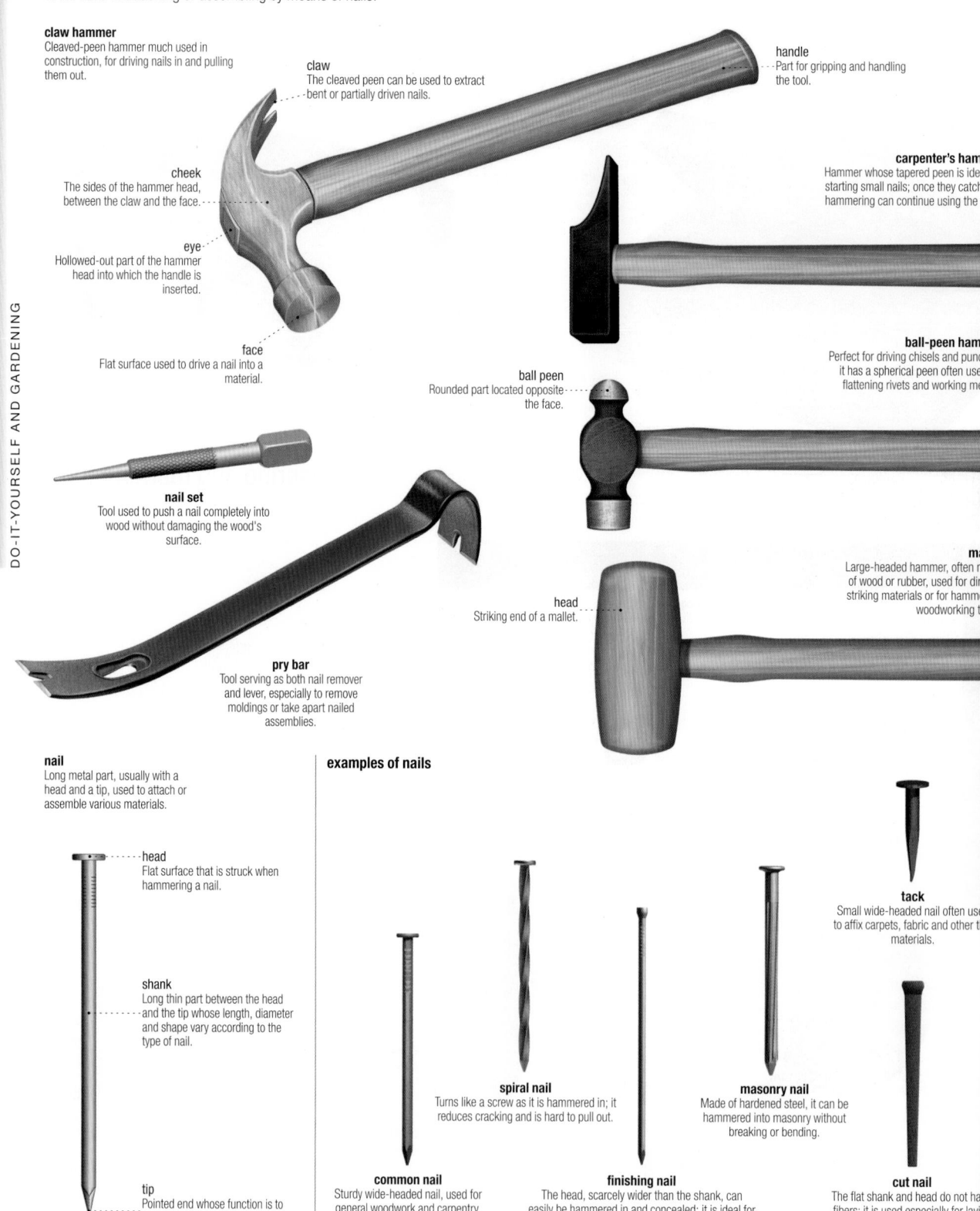

claw hammer
Cleaved-peen hammer much used in construction, for driving nails in and pulling them out.

claw
The cleaved peen can be used to extract bent or partially driven nails.

handle
Part for gripping and handling the tool.

cheek
The sides of the hammer head, between the claw and the face.

carpenter's ham
Hammer whose tapered peen is ide starting small nails; once they catch hammering can continue using the

eye
Hollowed-out part of the hammer head into which the handle is inserted.

face
Flat surface used to drive a nail into a material.

ball peen
Rounded part located opposite the face.

ball-peen ham
Perfect for driving chisels and punc it has a spherical peen often use flattening rivets and working me

nail set
Tool used to push a nail completely into wood without damaging the wood's surface.

ma
Large-headed hammer, often r of wood or rubber, used for dir striking materials or for hamme woodworking t

head
Striking end of a mallet.

pry bar
Tool serving as both nail remover and lever, especially to remove moldings or take apart nailed assemblies.

nail
Long metal part, usually with a head and a tip, used to attach or assemble various materials.

examples of nails

head
Flat surface that is struck when hammering a nail.

shank
Long thin part between the head and the tip whose length, diameter and shape vary according to the type of nail.

tack
Small wide-headed nail often use to affix carpets, fabric and other th materials.

spiral nail
Turns like a screw as it is hammered in; it reduces cracking and is hard to pull out.

masonry nail
Made of hardened steel, it can be hammered into masonry without breaking or bending.

tip
Pointed end whose function is to make it easier to drive the nail into the wood or other material.

common nail
Sturdy wide-headed nail, used for general woodwork and carpentry.

finishing nail
The head, scarcely wider than the shank, can easily be hammered in and concealed; it is ideal for finishing work and moldings.

cut nail
The flat shank and head do not ha fibers; it is used especially for layi wood flooring.

nailing tools

nailgun
Portable electric tool that will automatically drive nails into a surface.

motor
Device transforming electric energy into mechanical energy to drive another device.

jam-clearing latch
Device allowing the magazine to be recharged.

contact trip
Device that controls the nail's exit.

trigger switch
Connection mechanism for starting or stopping the tool by squeezing with the finger.

magazine
Part containing the nails.

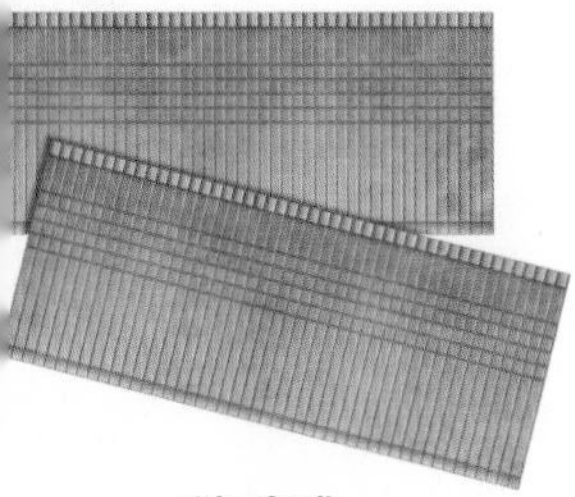

strip of nails
Set of nails for loading into a nail gun.

battery pack
Device that stores chemical energy while charging, then converts it to electric energy.

electric stapler
Portable electric tool used to automatically drive staples into a surface.

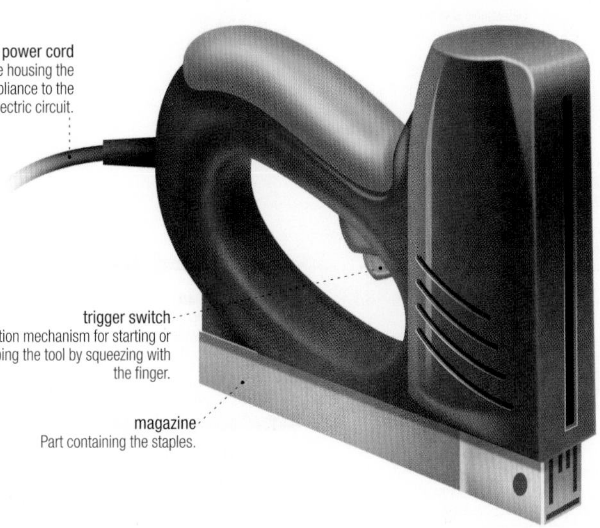

power cord
Flexible electric wire housing the leads connecting the appliance to the electric circuit.

trigger switch
Connection mechanism for starting or stopping the tool by squeezing with the finger.

strip of staples
Strip of metal pieces used in a stapler, to attach various materials.

magazine
Part containing the staples.

screwdriving tools

Tools used to attach or assemble pieces or materials using screws.

screwdriver
Hand tool used for tightening or loosening screws and bolts by applying a rotating motion.

shank
Metal part inserted into the screwdriver handle.

blade
Thin flat part forming the end of the shank.

tip
End of the blade or bit that fits into the groove of the screw or bolt.

handle
Part for gripping and handling the tool.

examples of tips
Tip: end part of the blade or bit; it adapts to screw or bolt's groove.

square-headed tip
Tip whose end cut fits into a socket-head screw.

Phillips-headed tip
Tip whose crisscross end fits into a crisscross-headed screw.

flat tip
Tip that fits into a screw's slot.

spiral screwdriver
Screwdriver with interchangeable bits fitted into a mechanism for screwing or unscrewing by simply pushing the handle.

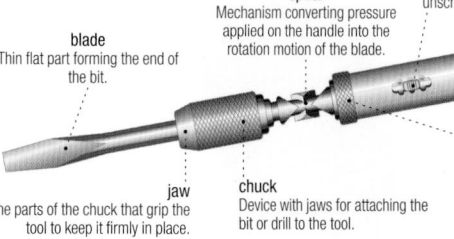

ratchet
Mechanical instrument for setting the direction of rotation of the spiral and the blade (screwing or unscrewing).

spiral
Mechanism converting pressure applied on the handle into the rotation motion of the blade.

blade
Thin flat part forming the end of the bit.

handle
Part for gripping and handling the tool.

jaw
The parts of the chuck that grip the tool to keep it firmly in place.

chuck
Device with jaws for attaching the bit or drill to the tool.

locking ring
Blocks the spiral's rotation allowing the tool to be used as an ordinary screwdriver.

spring wing
The spring under the wing keeps it folded along the bolt as it passes through a hole made in the wall; it then opens and acts like a nut.

cordless screwdriver
Battery-driven screwdriver with interchangeable bits, used for tightening and loosening screws and bolts.

reversing switch
Switch for selecting the bit's direction of rotation (screwing or unscrewing).

handle
Part for gripping and handling the tool.

battery
Device that stores chemical energy while charging, then converts it to electric energy.

tip
End of the blade or bit that fits into the groove of the screw or bolt.

toggle bolt
Part composed of a bolt with wings that deploy inside the wall to ensure a solid fastening.

bit
Detachable shank rotated by the motor to screw or unscrew a part.

wall anchor
Part composed of a bolt in a sheath that bends when the bolt is inserted, then flattens out against the inside of the wall.

screw
Metal part, composed of a head and a partially or completely threaded shank, used to secure fastenings and assemblies.

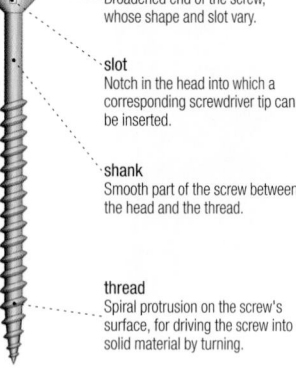

head
Broadened end of the screw, whose shape and slot vary.

slot
Notch in the head into which a corresponding screwdriver tip can be inserted.

shank
Smooth part of the screw between the head and the thread.

thread
Spiral protrusion on the screw's surface, for driving the screw into a solid material by turning.

examples of heads
Head: broadened end of the screw, whose shape and slot vary.

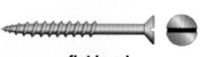

flat head
Slotted head becoming flush with the surface of the wood when completely embedded.

round head
Slotted rounded head whose base is flat so that it presses against the wood or metal surface.

one-way head
Slotted head having two opposing quarters removed so that the screw can be turned one way only, making it very difficult to unscrew.

Phillips head
Head whose crisscross indentation keeps the screwdriver in the middle of the head, providing a very firm grip.

socket head
Head with a square socket that varies in size.

oval head
Slotted head topped with an ornamental spherical part that is not driven beneath the wood's surface.

sawing tools

Tools used for cutting various materials.

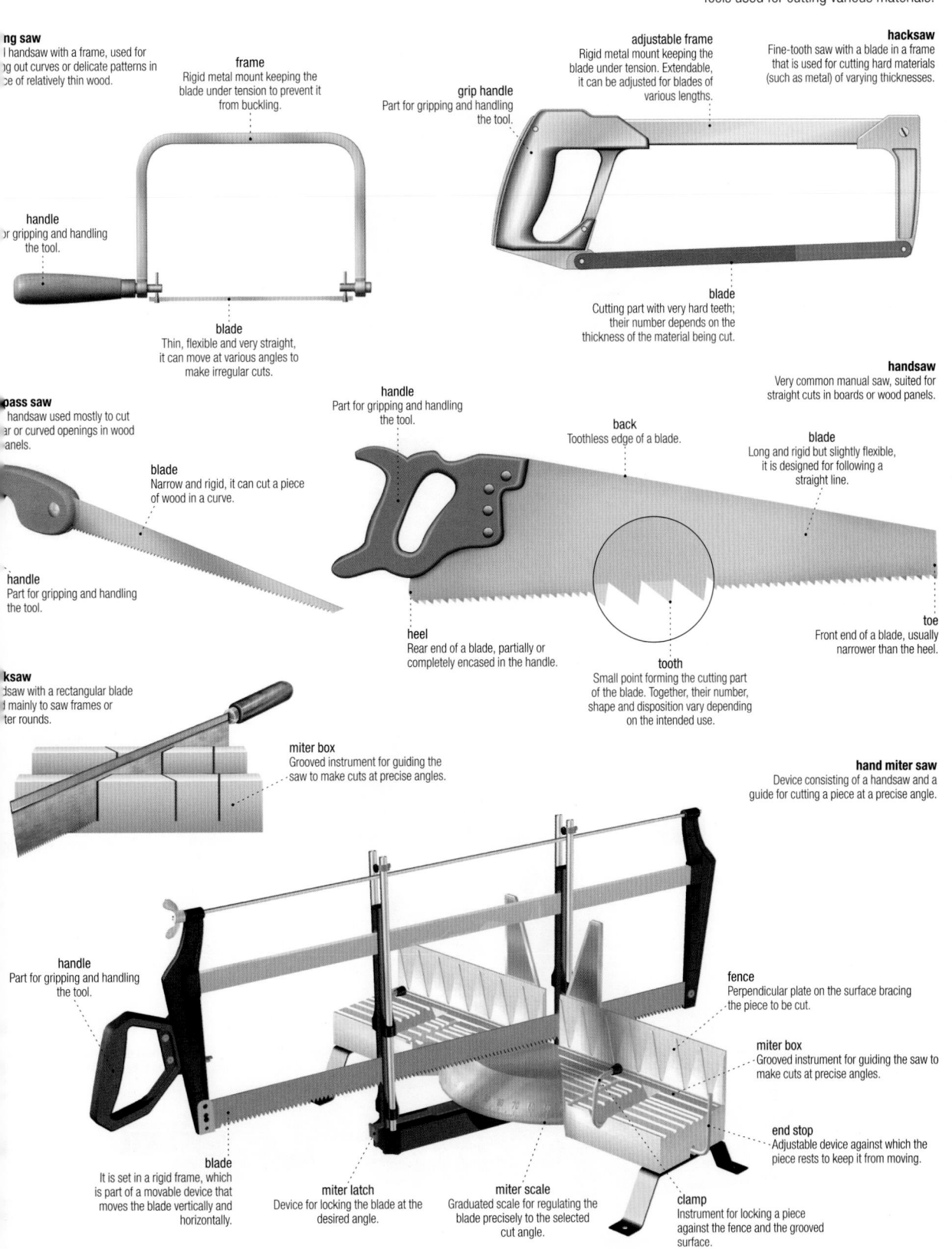

ng saw
handsaw with a frame, used for
g out curves or delicate patterns in
ce of relatively thin wood.

frame
Rigid metal mount keeping the
blade under tension to prevent it
from buckling.

adjustable frame
Rigid metal mount keeping the
blade under tension. Extendable,
it can be adjusted for blades of
various lengths.

hacksaw
Fine-tooth saw with a blade in a frame
that is used for cutting hard materials
(such as metal) of varying thicknesses.

grip handle
Part for gripping and handling
the tool.

handle
or gripping and handling
the tool.

blade
Thin, flexible and very straight,
it can move at various angles to
make irregular cuts.

blade
Cutting part with very hard teeth;
their number depends on the
thickness of the material being cut.

handle
Part for gripping and handling
the tool.

back
Toothless edge of a blade.

handsaw
Very common manual saw, suited for
straight cuts in boards or wood panels.

blade
Long and rigid but slightly flexible,
it is designed for following a
straight line.

pass saw
handsaw used mostly to cut
ar or curved openings in wood
anels.

blade
Narrow and rigid, it can cut a piece
of wood in a curve.

handle
Part for gripping and handling
the tool.

heel
Rear end of a blade, partially or
completely encased in the handle.

toe
Front end of a blade, usually
narrower than the heel.

tooth
Small point forming the cutting part
of the blade. Together, their number,
shape and disposition vary depending
on the intended use.

ksaw
dsaw with a rectangular blade
mainly to saw frames or
er rounds.

miter box
Grooved instrument for guiding the
saw to make cuts at precise angles.

hand miter saw
Device consisting of a handsaw and a
guide for cutting a piece at a precise angle.

handle
Part for gripping and handling
the tool.

fence
Perpendicular plate on the surface bracing
the piece to be cut.

miter box
Grooved instrument for guiding the saw to
make cuts at precise angles.

end stop
Adjustable device against which the
piece rests to keep it from moving.

blade
It is set in a rigid frame, which
is part of a movable device that
moves the blade vertically and
horizontally.

miter latch
Device for locking the blade at the
desired angle.

miter scale
Graduated scale for regulating the
blade precisely to the selected
cut angle.

clamp
Instrument for locking a piece
against the fence and the grooved
surface.

sawing tools

DO-IT-YOURSELF AND GARDENING

circular saw
Portable electric saw with a circular blade; it is used for making straight cuts in various materials.

handle
For optimal control of the tool, it is advisable to place one hand on the handle and the other on the knob handle.

trigger switch
Connection mechanism for starting or stopping the tool by squeezing with the finger.

upper blade guard
Fixed sheath covering the upper part of the blade to protect the user's hands and prevent sawdust from escaping.

height adjustment scale
Regulates the blade's height under the base plate, to control the depth of the cut.

blade
Thin metal disk with teeth; it rotates to cut pieces of metal or wood.

motor
Device transforming electric energy into mechanical energy to drive another device.

lower guard retracting lever
For manually raising the lower blade guard.

blade tilting mechanism
Device controlling the base plate's degree of inclination to the blade so that straight or beveled cuts can be made.

lower blade guard
Retractable sheath covering the lower part of the blade, which lifts as the cut advances.

knob handle
Handle for ease of guiding the tool while sawing.

blade locking bolt
Part attaching the blade to its rotation axle.

rip fence
Movable part, perpendicular to the surface, controlling the width of the cut in the lengthwise direction.

blade tilting lock
Mechanism for locking the blade at the degree of inclination selected, between 45° and 90°.

base plate
Support plate for the tool, which rests on the surface of the piece to be cut.

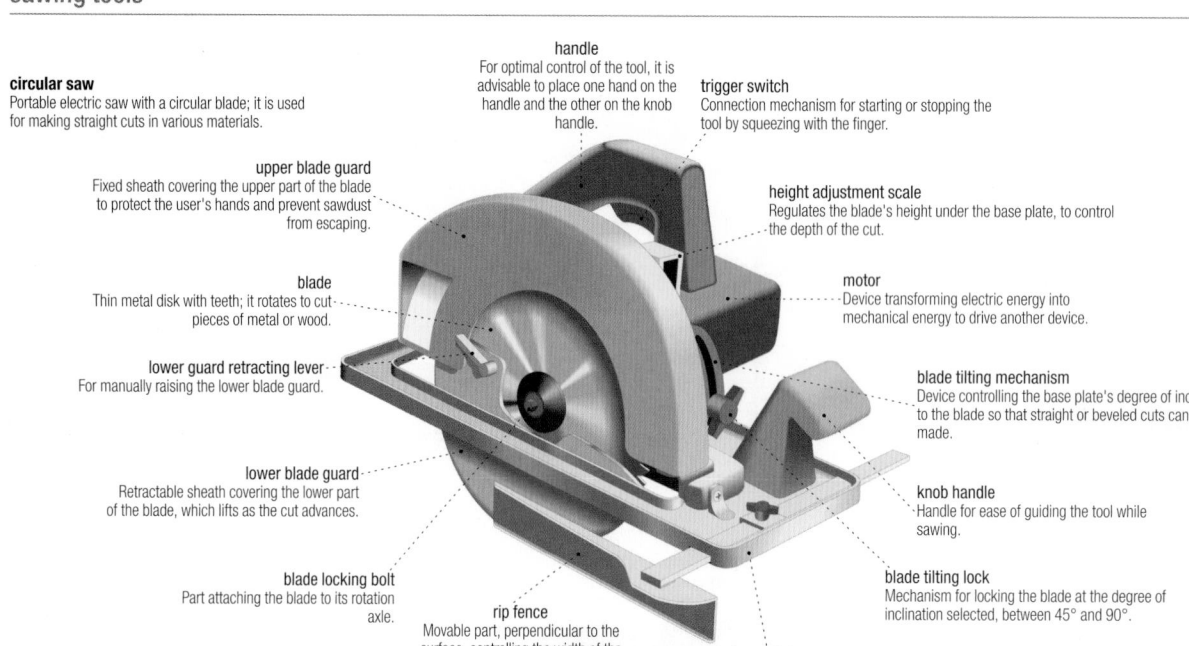

circular saw blade
Thin metal detachable disk, adaptable various types of circular saws.

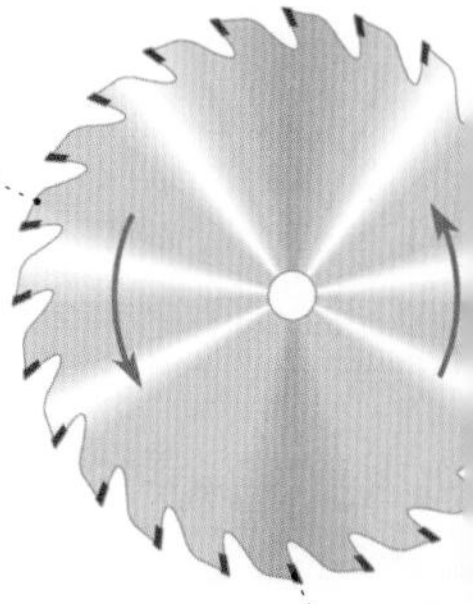

electric miter saw
System composed of a circular saw and guiding device for cutting at a precise angle.

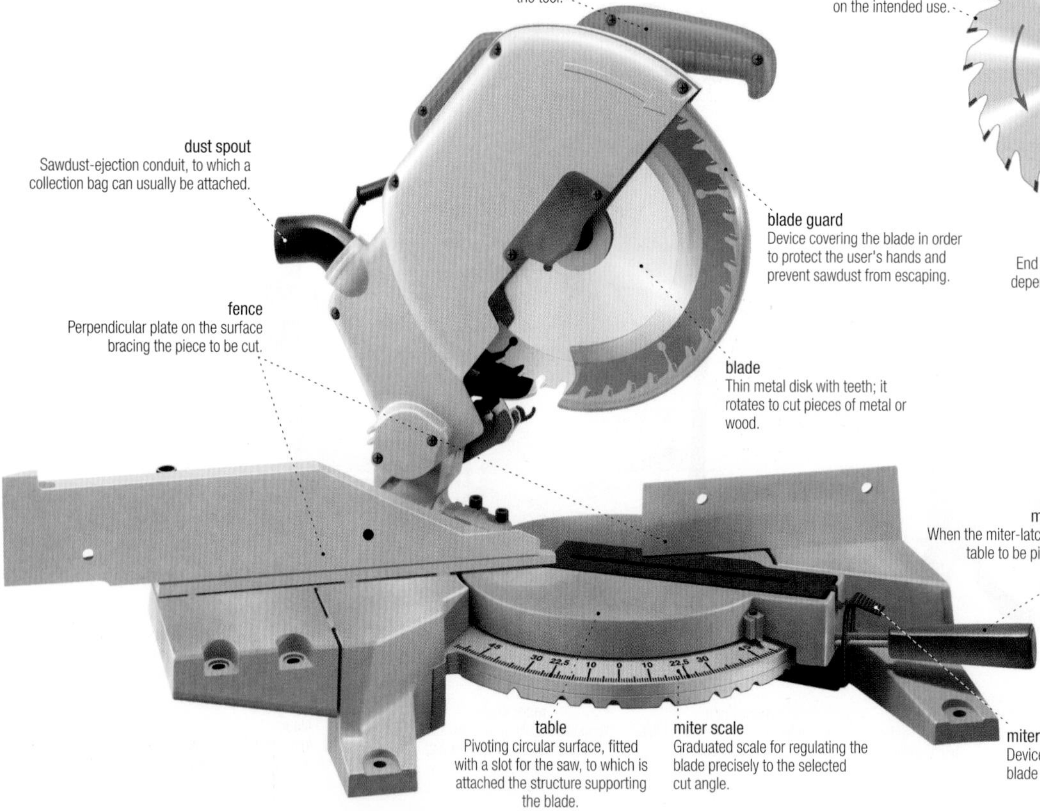

handle
Part for gripping and handling the tool.

tooth
Small point forming the cutting part of the blade. Together, their number, shape and disposition vary depending on the intended use.

dust spout
Sawdust-ejection conduit, to which a collection bag can usually be attached.

blade guard
Device covering the blade in order to protect the user's hands and prevent sawdust from escaping.

tip
End of the tooth whose compo depends on the nature of the m to be cut.

fence
Perpendicular plate on the surface bracing the piece to be cut.

blade
Thin metal disk with teeth; it rotates to cut pieces of metal or wood.

miter lock handle
When the miter-latch screw is disengaged, it table to be pivoted to select the cut ang

table
Pivoting circular surface, fitted with a slot for the saw, to which is attached the structure supporting the blade.

miter scale
Graduated scale for regulating the blade precisely to the selected cut angle.

miter latch
Device for locking the table and blade in the desired position.

sawing tools

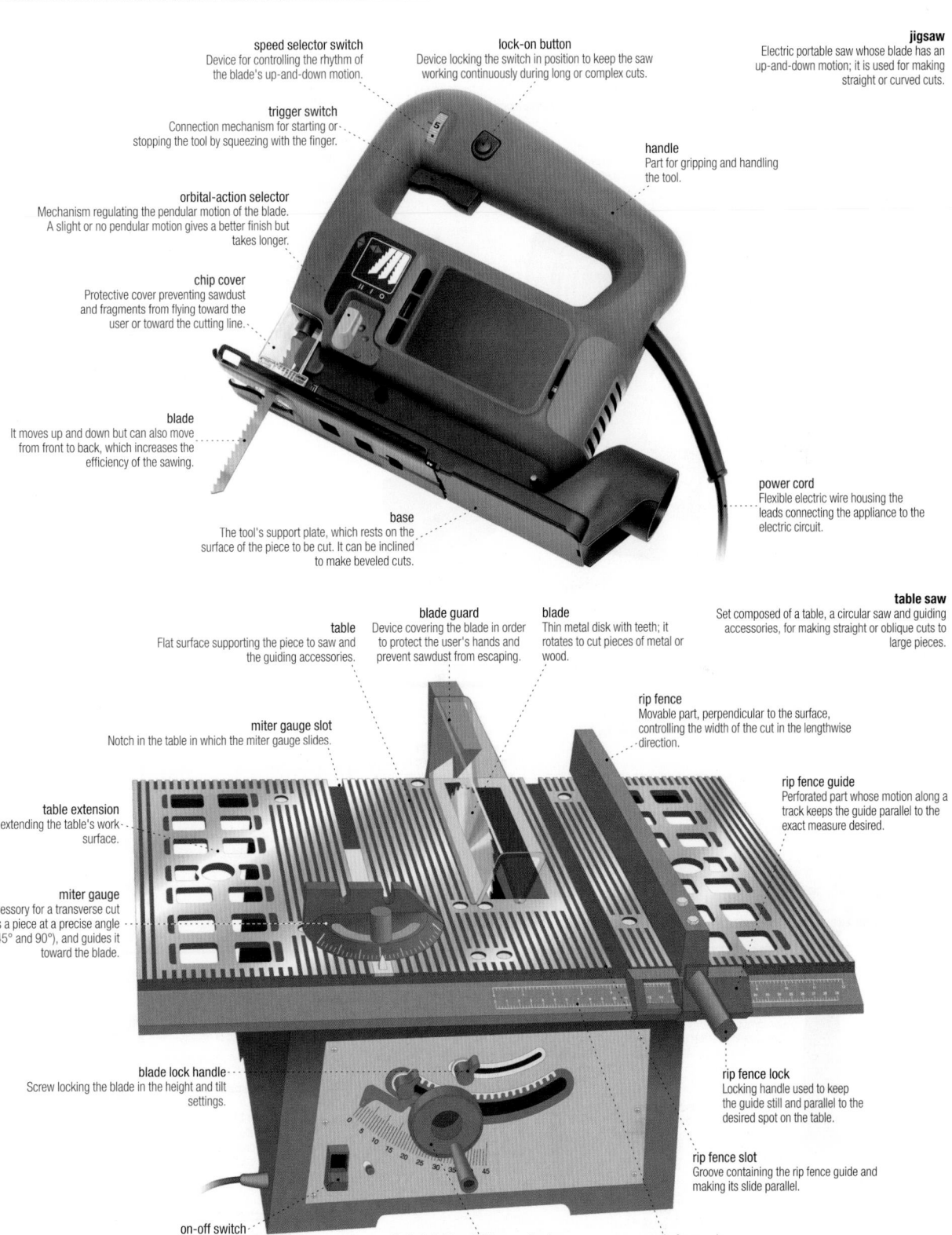

speed selector switch
Device for controlling the rhythm of the blade's up-and-down motion.

lock-on button
Device locking the switch in position to keep the saw working continuously during long or complex cuts.

jigsaw
Electric portable saw whose blade has an up-and-down motion; it is used for making straight or curved cuts.

trigger switch
Connection mechanism for starting or stopping the tool by squeezing with the finger.

handle
Part for gripping and handling the tool.

orbital-action selector
Mechanism regulating the pendular motion of the blade. A slight or no pendular motion gives a better finish but takes longer.

chip cover
Protective cover preventing sawdust and fragments from flying toward the user or toward the cutting line.

blade
It moves up and down but can also move from front to back, which increases the efficiency of the sawing.

base
The tool's support plate, which rests on the surface of the piece to be cut. It can be inclined to make beveled cuts.

power cord
Flexible electric wire housing the leads connecting the appliance to the electric circuit.

table saw
Set composed of a table, a circular saw and guiding accessories, for making straight or oblique cuts to large pieces.

blade guard
Device covering the blade in order to protect the user's hands and prevent sawdust from escaping.

blade
Thin metal disk with teeth; it rotates to cut pieces of metal or wood.

table
Flat surface supporting the piece to saw and the guiding accessories.

rip fence
Movable part, perpendicular to the surface, controlling the width of the cut in the lengthwise direction.

miter gauge slot
Notch in the table in which the miter gauge slides.

rip fence guide
Perforated part whose motion along a track keeps the guide parallel to the exact measure desired.

table extension
Part extending the table's work surface.

miter gauge
Accessory for a transverse cut, positions a piece at a precise angle (between 45° and 90°), and guides it toward the blade.

blade lock handle
Screw locking the blade in the height and tilt settings.

rip fence lock
Locking handle used to keep the guide still and parallel to the desired spot on the table.

rip fence slot
Groove containing the rip fence guide and making its slide parallel.

on-off switch
Button for turning the device on or off.

blade height and tilting mechanism
Wheel that moves along an angle indicator (between 0° and 45°) and regulates the blade's height and inclination.

rip fence rule
Scale showing the distance between the parallel guide and the blade, and, therefore, the width of the cut.

drilling tools

Tools used for making holes in various materials.

cordless drill/driver
Battery-powered portable electric tool used to drill holes and to screw and unscrew.

speed selector switch
Device for regulating the chuck's rotation speed.

screwdriver bit
Detachable tool inserted into the chuck and used for screwing and unscrewing.

torque adjustment collar
Ringlike part controlling the tool's torsion power. Screwing needs lower torque than drilling.

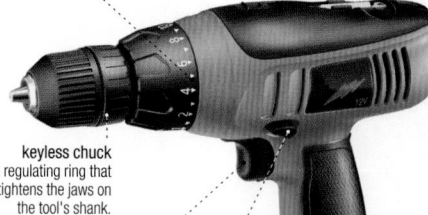

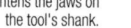

keyless chuck
Chuck with a regulating ring that automatically tightens the jaws on the tool's shank.

trigger switch
Connection mechanism for starting or stopping the tool by squeezing with the finger.

reversing switch
Switch for selecting the bit's or drill's direction of rotation (screwing or unscrewing).

battery pack
Device that stores chemical energy while charging, then converts it to electric energy.

battery pack
Device that stores chemical energy while charging, then converts it to electric energy.

charger
Electrical device for recharging the tool's battery.

electric drill
Portable electric tool using variable-speed rotation to pierce holes and to drive drills and bits.

jaw
The parts of the chuck that grip the tool to keep it firmly in place.

housing
Box enclosing and protecting the motor.

chuck
Device with jaws for attaching the bit or drill to the tool.

depth stop
Device used to gauge the depth that the drill or bit has reached.

chuck key
Part for tightening and loosening the chuck's jaws.

warning plate
Plate providing certain safety precautions to avoid injuries caused by misuse of the tool.

pistol grip handle
Part shaped like a pistol grip so the wrist remains straight while holding the tool.

trigger switch
Connection mechanism for starting or stopping the tool by squeezing with the finger.

switch lock
Device locking the switch in position to keep the drill working for a prolonged period.

auxiliary handle
Tubular handle providing a firm grip and stabilizing the tool while drilling.

cord sleeve
Protective casing around the cable to lessen twisting and prevent wear.

power cord
Flexible electric wire housing the leads connecting the appliance to the electric circuit.

examples of bits and drills
While both are intended for drilling holes in various materials, the bit has a center point while the drill ends in a cutting-edge cone.

twist bit
Bit with a spiral drill flute; it drills straight uniform holes and is very practical for inserting dowels.

shank
Upper part of the bit, on which pressure from the chuck's jaws is exerted.

flute
Groove in the body of the b[...] that removes debris from th[...] hole while drilling.

body
Part between the shank and the lead screw.

land
Flat surface between the flo[...]

fluted land
Cutting edge forming the edge of the land.

lead screw
Threaded pointed end for centering the bit in the middle of the hole at the start of drilling.

solid center auger bit
Bit made up of a central shank encircled by a twist; it is very durable and especially designed for making deep holes.

shank
Upper part of the bit, on w[...] pressure from the chuck's[...] is exerted.

twist
Spiral protrusion around the bit's shank; it removes debris from the hole being drilled.

spur
Lip that covers the outline[...] hole and removes debris, is then pushed to the twist[...] disposed of.

lead screw
Threaded pointed end for centering the bit in the middle of the hole at the start of drilling.

spade bit
Bit designed for shallow holes of wide diameter; it has a long lead screw for positioning on the center of the hole.

double-twist auger bit
Bit made up of two opposing twists; i[...] debris quickly as the hole is dri[...]

masonry drill
The carbide and tungsten tip, hard and durable, is designed to drill through material such as brick, concrete and stone.

twist drill
Usually used to drill holes in met[...] or wood, it is the most commo[...] type of drill.

drilling tools

turning handle
Handle whose rotation turns the drive wheel, which in turn transmits the motion to the pinion and the chuck.

hand drill
Gear-driven hand tool, used mainly to drill holes in wood, soft metal and plastic.

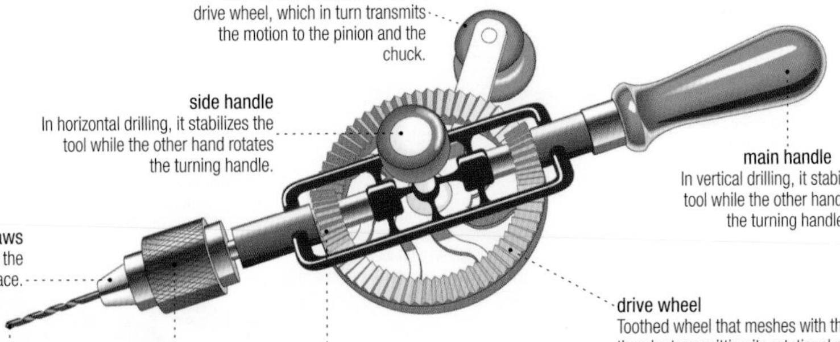

side handle
In horizontal drilling, it stabilizes the tool while the other hand rotates the turning handle.

main handle
In vertical drilling, it stabilizes the tool while the other hand rotates the turning handle.

jaws
The parts of the chuck that grip the tool to keep it firmly in place.

drive wheel
Toothed wheel that meshes with the pinion, thereby transmitting its rotational motion.

bit
Detachable shank that is inserted into the chuck, whose rotating motion drills holes in various materials.

chuck
Device with jaws for attaching the bit to the tool.

pinion
Small toothed wheel downshifting the turning handle's motion: each turn of the handle translates into at least three rotations of the chuck.

handle
Movable part for turning the crank.

cam ring
Metal cylinder covering the crank above the pawl.

brace
Hand tool, made up of an angled crank and a pawl and ratchet mechanism, for drilling holes.

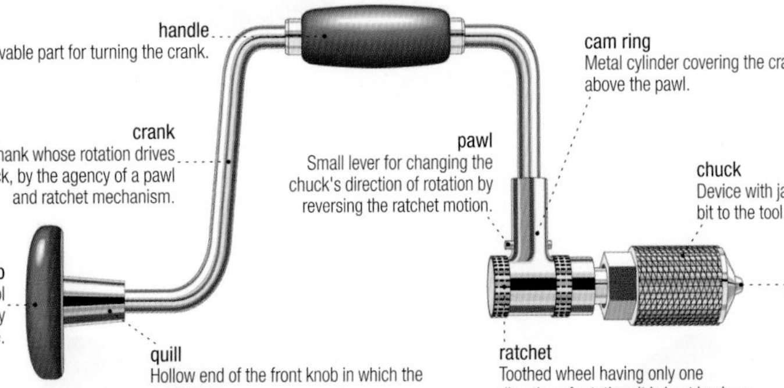

crank
Angled shank whose rotation drives the chuck, by the agency of a pawl and ratchet mechanism.

pawl
Small lever for changing the chuck's direction of rotation by reversing the ratchet motion.

chuck
Device with jaws for attaching the bit to the tool.

front knob
Knob for holding and stabilizing the tool while the other hand turns the crank by using the handle.

jaws
The parts of the chuck that grip the tool to keep it firmly in place.

quill
Hollow end of the front knob in which the crank turns.

ratchet
Toothed wheel having only one direction of rotation; it is kept in place by the pawl.

drill press
Set made up of an electric drill and a table mounted on a column, for drilling holes of a given depth in succession.

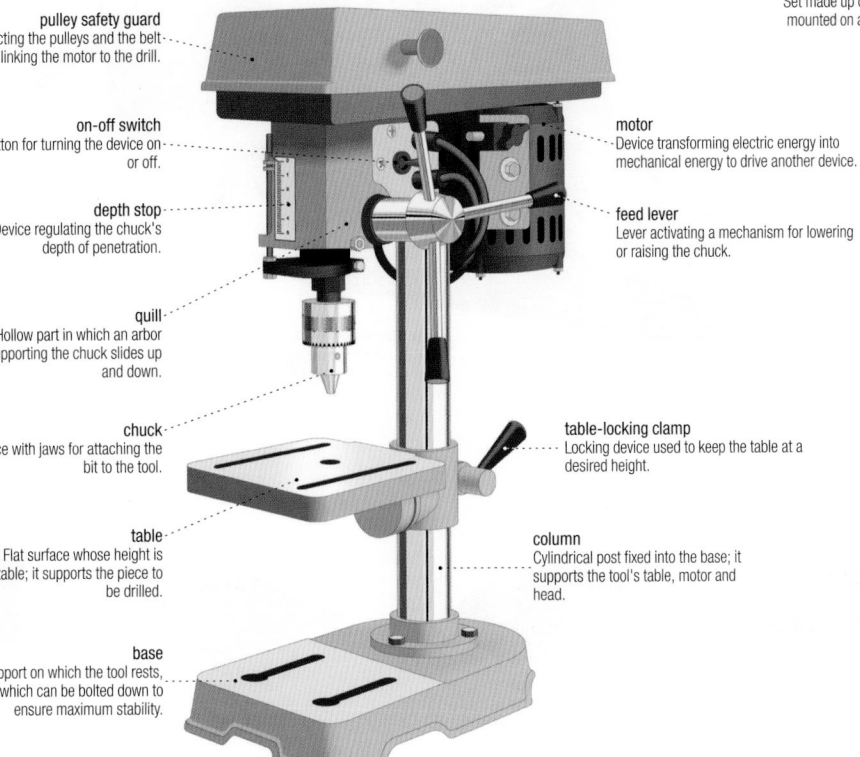

pulley safety guard
Case protecting the pulleys and the belt linking the motor to the drill.

on-off switch
Button for turning the device on or off.

motor
Device transforming electric energy into mechanical energy to drive another device.

depth stop
Device regulating the chuck's depth of penetration.

feed lever
Lever activating a mechanism for lowering or raising the chuck.

quill
Hollow part in which an arbor supporting the chuck slides up and down.

chuck
Device with jaws for attaching the bit to the tool.

table-locking clamp
Locking device used to keep the table at a desired height.

table
Flat surface whose height is adjustable; it supports the piece to be drilled.

column
Cylindrical post fixed into the base; it supports the tool's table, motor and head.

base
Support on which the tool rests, which can be bolted down to ensure maximum stability.

shaping tools

Tools used to sharpen, polish, sand, or plane a surface.

random orbit sander
Portable electric tool whose abrasive disk moves two ways (rotating and eccentric) to sand various types of surface.

lock-on button
Device locking the switch in position to keep the saw working for a prolonged period.

angle grinder
Portable electric tool used grinding, polishing, shaping, m

housing
Box enclosing and protecting the motor.

handle
Part for gripping and handling the tool.

grinding wheel
Somewhat rigid abrasive disk mounted on a grinder's spindle, whose roughness varies with the task (e.g., grinding, polishing, shaping).

spindle lock button
Device preventing the spindle from rotating while the grinding wheel is replaced.

on-off switch
Button for turning the device on or off.

trigger switch
Connection mechanism for starting or stopping the tool by squeezing with the finger.

dust canister
Receptacle collecting the dust drawn through the sander's openings and the corresponding perforations in the sanding disk.

wheel guard
Metal shield partially covering the grinding wheel to prevent any accidental contact or, in case of breakage, to protect the user from flying pieces.

side handle
Handle intended mainly for guiding the tool while ensuring maximum stability.

sanding pad
Cushion to which the sanding disk is attached. Usually made of flexible material, it is used for sanding flat and curved surfaces.

sanding disk
Paper, usually perforated and self-adhesive, that fits the sander's sanding pad.

belt sander
Portable electric tool with an abrasive belt used to smooth various surfaces or to remove finishing coatings.

trigger switch
Connection mechanism for starting or stopping the tool by squeezing with the finger.

rear handle
Part for gripping and handling the tool.

dust collection bag
Receptacle in which sanding debris collects.

front handle
Part for gripping and handling the tool.

cord sleeve
Protective casing around the cable to lessen twisting and prevent wear.

power cord
Flexible electric wire housing the leads connecting the appliance the electric circuit.

small pulley
Wheel around which is the strap holding the abrasive belt.

large pulley
Wheel around which is the strap holding the abrasive belt.

abrasive belt
Sandpaper placed the belt of a sander.

timing belt
Drive mechanism of the abrasive belt.

tension release lever
Device used to lessen the tension on the abrasive band in order to replace it.

abrasive material

grinding wheel
Somewhat rigid abrasive disk mounted on a grinder's spindle, whose roughness varies with the task (e.g., grinding, polishing, shaping).

sanding disk
Paper, usually perforated and self-adhesive, that fits the sander's sanding pad.

sandpaper
Paper usually coated with glass powder, used by itself or mounted on a tool for smoothing.

abrasive belt
Sandpaper placed the strap of a sander.

jointer plane
The longest in the plane family, it is used for planing large pieces of wood and is not thrown off by bumps or indentations.

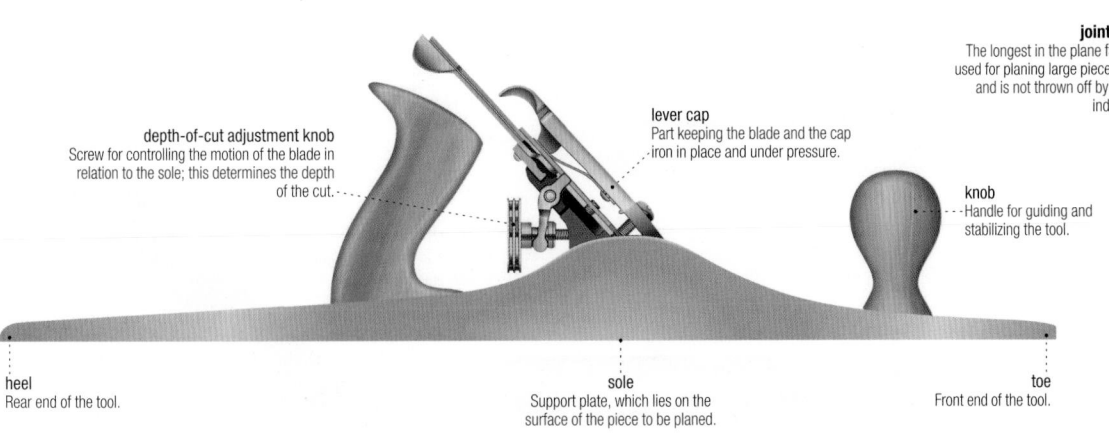

depth-of-cut adjustment knob
Screw for controlling the motion of the blade in relation to the sole; this determines the depth of the cut.

lever cap
Part keeping the blade and the cap iron in place and under pressure.

knob
Handle for guiding and stabilizing the tool.

heel
Rear end of the tool.

sole
Support plate, which lies on the surface of the piece to be planed.

toe
Front end of the tool.

cross-section of a plane
Hand tool with a cutting blade, intended mainly for planing a wood surface or to give it a shape (e.g., beveled, chamfered).

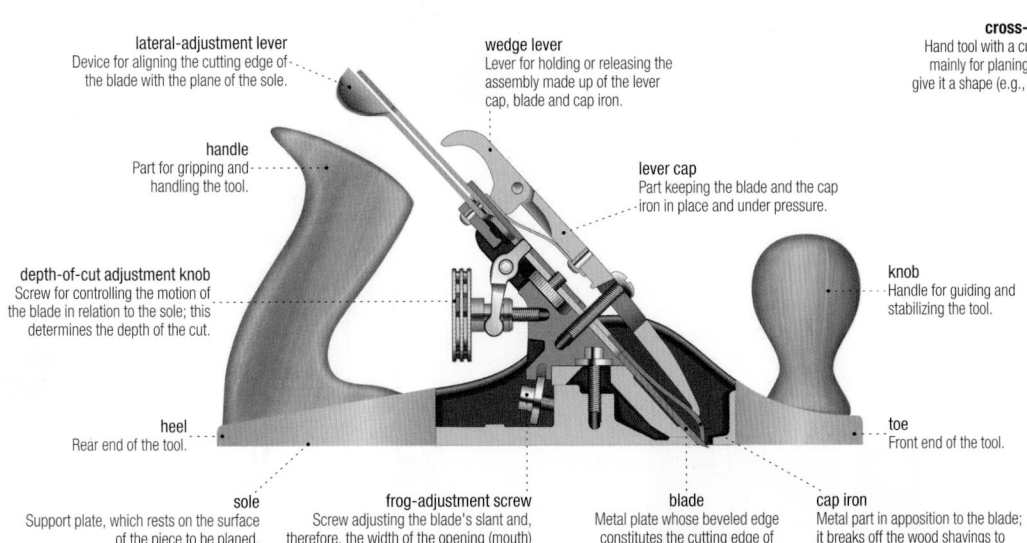

lateral-adjustment lever
Device for aligning the cutting edge of the blade with the plane of the sole.

wedge lever
Lever for holding or releasing the assembly made up of the lever cap, blade and cap iron.

handle
Part for gripping and handling the tool.

lever cap
Part keeping the blade and the cap iron in place and under pressure.

depth-of-cut adjustment knob
Screw for controlling the motion of the blade in relation to the sole; this determines the depth of the cut.

knob
Handle for guiding and stabilizing the tool.

heel
Rear end of the tool.

toe
Front end of the tool.

sole
Support plate, which rests on the surface of the piece to be planed.

frog-adjustment screw
Screw adjusting the blade's slant and, therefore, the width of the opening (mouth) that removes the shavings.

blade
Metal plate whose beveled edge constitutes the cutting edge of the plane.

cap iron
Metal part in apposition to the blade; it breaks off the wood shavings to facilitate their removal.

electric plane
Electric tool with a cutting blade, used on wooden surfaces mainly to flatten or to give them shape (beveled, for example).

trigger switch
Connection mechanism for starting or stopping the tool by squeezing with the finger.

dust outlet
Hole through which the wood debris is collected.

guide handle
Part for gripping and handling the tool.

toothed belt cover
Piece covering the drive mechanism of the blade.

sole
Support plate, which rests on the surface of the piece to be planed.

shaping tools

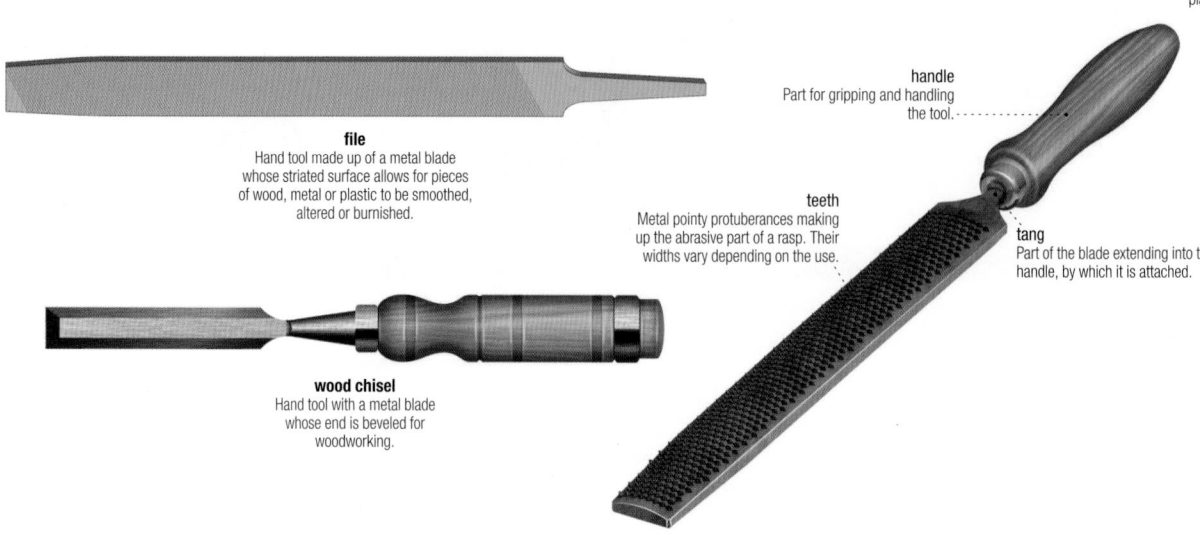

ra...
Hand tool made up of a metal bla...
whose tooth-covered surface (...
quickly rough out wood, meta...
plas...

file
Hand tool made up of a metal blade
whose striated surface allows for pieces
of wood, metal or plastic to be smoothed,
altered or burnished.

handle
Part for gripping and handling
the tool.

teeth
Metal pointy protuberances making
up the abrasive part of a rasp. Their
widths vary depending on the use.

tang
Part of the blade extending into the
handle, by which it is attached.

wood chisel
Hand tool with a metal blade
whose end is beveled for
woodworking.

router
Portable electric tool using rotating bits to
mill moldings, grooves and wood joints.

motor
Device transforming electric energy into
mechanical energy to drive another device.

depth adjustment
Device that regulates the depth of
the bit, thus controlling the depth of
the milling.

on-off switch
Button for turning the device on
or off.

power cord
Flexible electric wire housing the
leads connecting the appliance to
the electric circuit.

guide handle
Used to hold and guide
the tool.

collet
Ring-shaped part for tightening
or loosening the tool holder.

chuck
Device fitted with jaws for attaching
the bit to the router.

base
Support plate for the tool, which rests on
the surface of the piece to be worked on.

examples of bits

Bits: detachable tools fitted with edges or abrasive
parts; a router applies a rotating motion on them to
mill a piece of work.

rounding-over bit
Bit that, depending upon its position,
rounds the edge of a piece of wood or
makes a convex molding with a shoulder.

rabbet bit
Bit for cutting an edge at right
angles, used especially for
making frames and for various
cabinetmaking joints.

core box bit
Bit usually used to mill grooves in
wood in the shape of semicircles.

dovetail bit
Bit for making cuts shaped like a dov...
often used in joining drawers.

cove bit
Bit used especially for concave moldings
or for cutting articulating joints for a gateleg table.

chamfer bit
Bit for beveling edges at a 45°
angle to create decorative edge...
and joints.

gripping and tightening tools

Tools used to hold, turn or compress various objects.

ove joint pliers
rs with straight jaws, adjustable to
eral gap positions.

pliers
Hand tools with two movable jaws of fixed
or variable gaps, intended for gripping or
clamping objects.

straight jaw
Jaw whose interior side is
rectilinear for grasping or clamping
a flat, square or many-sided object.

bolt
Metal plug ending in a head and
threaded for screwing into a nut; it
forms the pliers' axle of articulation.

adjustable channel
Set of notches that receive the bolt to
change the jaws' gap.

slip joint pliers
Pliers with curved jaws and ending in a straight part,
adjustable to two widths of opening.

slip joint
Pliers' articulating axle, which slides
between two positions to change the
jaws' gap.

nut
Hollow cylinder of metal whose
lining is threaded to screw onto a
corresponding bolt.

handle
Long part that, in concert with its
exerts pressure to open or close
the jaws.

handle
Long part that, in concert with its
twin, exerts pressure to open or close
the jaws.

curved jaw
Jaw whose internal side is rounded
for gripping or clamping a round
object.

locking pliers
Tool used as a pliers, wrench and vise;
it has variable-gap jaws for gripping and
clamping objects.

spring
Tight when the handles are closed to
lock the pliers, it resumes its shape when
unlocked and the handles return to their
initial position.

lever
The pressure of the adjusting screw
raises or lowers it, thereby controlling
the jaws' gap.

adjusting screw
Screw regulating the jaws' gap.

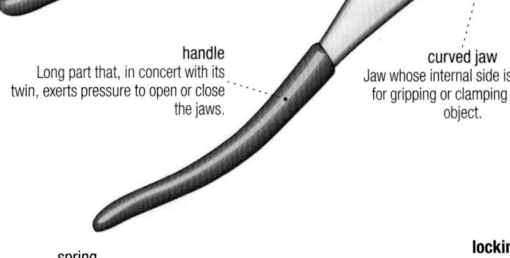

toothed jaw
Striated straight or curved part
that, with its twin, grasps or clamps
an object.

release lever
Lever for unlocking the pliers and
releasing the grip.

rivet
Riveted assembly part that is the axle
of articulation for the release lever.

washers
Ringlike parts placed between a nut or
a bolt and a part to be tightened; they
distribute the stress.

internal tooth lock washer
having protuberances on the inside so that a
w tightens securely and will not loosen.

external tooth lock washer
Washer having protuberances on the outside so that a
screw tightens securely and will not loosen.

lock washer
Slightly spiral-shaped washer,
which acts as a spring to prevent
screws from loosening.

flat washer
Placed underneath a screw or the head
of a bolt, it distributes the pressure
while protecting the work surface.

DO-IT-YOURSELF AND GARDENING

gripping and tightening tools

wrenches

Hand tools with fixed or variable openings, used for tightening and loosening nuts and bolts, and for assembling and disassembling objects.

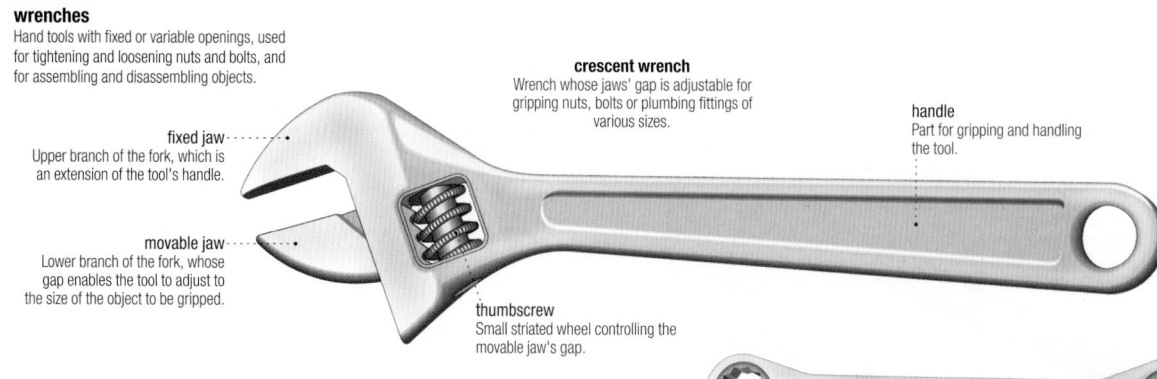

crescent wrench
Wrench whose jaws' gap is adjustable for gripping nuts, bolts or plumbing fittings of various sizes.

fixed jaw
Upper branch of the fork, which is an extension of the tool's handle.

movable jaw
Lower branch of the fork, whose gap enables the tool to adjust to the size of the object to be gripped.

thumbscrew
Small striated wheel controlling the movable jaw's gap.

handle
Part for gripping and handling the tool.

ratchet box end wrench
Wrench whose rings are fitted with a pawl, which limits the part's rotation in one direction, and a ratchet, which can be rotated in the opposite direction without loosening the grip.

flare nut wrench
Wrench with two many-sided heads, designed mainly to tighten plumbing joints.

open end wrench
Wrench with two openings of different sizes, each having parallel jaws.

box end wrench
Wrench that is usually bent and has two many-sided rings of different sizes; it grips the nut more firmly than the open end wrench.

combination box and open end wrench
Wrench with one forked end and one many-sided head, both ends are the same size.

ratchet socket wrench

Wrench fitted with a pawl and a ratchet: the pawl sets the direction of rotation, while the ratchet lets the handle turn in the opposite direction over the socket.

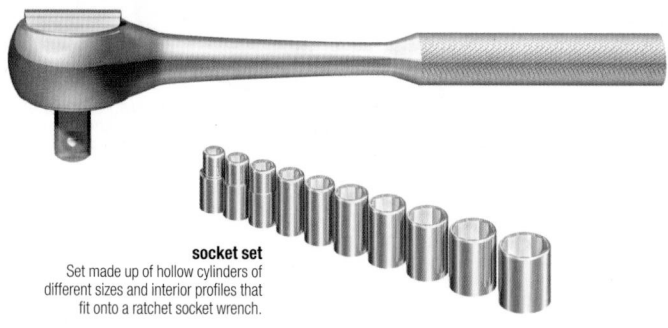

socket set
Set made up of hollow cylinders of different sizes and interior profiles that fit onto a ratchet socket wrench.

nuts

Metal parts with holes whose surfaces are threaded for screwing onto the corresponding bolts.

hex nut
Most common nut; it has six sides for tightening with a wrench.

acorn nut
Nut capped with a hollow dome that covers and protects the threaded end of the bolt.

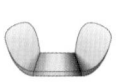

wing nut
Nut comprised of two protruding ends for tightening or loosening by hand.

bolts

Metal plugs ending in a head and threaded so they can be tightly screwed into nuts to secure fastenings and assemblies.

bolt
Metal threaded plug ending in a head; it is tightly screwed into a nut to secure fastenings and assemblies.

nut
Hollow cylinder of metal whose lining is threaded to screw onto a corresponding bolt.

head
Widened end of the bolt, of va[...] shapes and sizes.

shoulder bolt
Bolt whose head comprises a section of smaller diameter for concentrating the tightening pressure.

threaded rod
Elongated part whose surface has a spiral protrusion for screwing into a corresponding nut.

shoulder
Cylindrical nonthreaded protrusio[...] used as a bracket as the bolt is[...] being tightened.

gripping and tightening tools

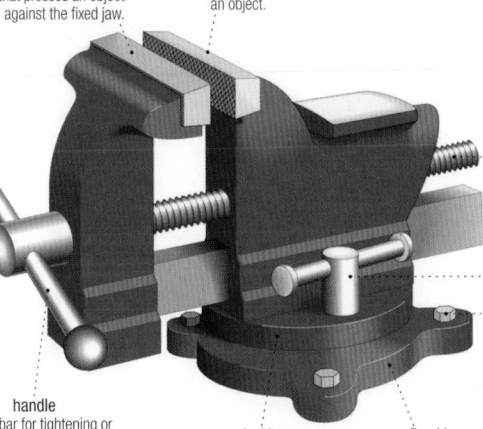

...s with two jaws; it is attached ...worktable and used for ...ping objects.

movable jaw
Smooth or striated jaw that presses an object against the fixed jaw.

fixed jaw
Smooth or striated part against which the movable jaw presses an object.

adjusting screw
Threaded shank whose rotation is controlled by the handle; it moves the jaw toward or away from the piece to be clamped.

swivel lock
Sliding bar clamping down the swivel base by locking it into the desired position.

bolt
Threaded metal plug with a head that is tightly screwed into a nut to secure the vise to a work bench.

handle
...ing bar for tightening or ...ening the adjusting screw, ...by spreading or closing the jaws.

swivel base
Rotating surface surmounting the fixed base, which allows the vise to turn 360°.

fixed base
The tool's supporting block, usually bolted onto a work bench.

C-clamp
Portable tool with a C-shaped frame, used for keeping objects from moving while working on them.

fixed jaw
Smooth or striated part against which the movable jaw presses an object.

movable jaw
Smooth or striated jaw that presses an object against the fixed jaw.

swivel head
End of the tightening screw; it pivots to adjust to irregularly shaped objects.

throat
Opening made by the frame.

adjusting screw
Threaded shank whose rotation is controlled by the handle; it moves the jaw toward or away from the piece to be clamped.

frame
Rigid metal support in the shape of a C, having the fixed jaw on one end, while the other end contains a hole for the adjusting screw.

handle
Sliding bar for tightening or loosening the adjusting screw, thereby spreading or closing the jaws.

...e clamp
...e press comprising a ...al pipe supporting a ...and a tail stop.

handle
Sliding bar that adjusts the screw to slide the tail stop's jaw up or down the pipe.

clamping screw
Threaded shank whose rotation, controlled by the clamping lever, causes the jaw to slide along the pipe to or from the object to be clamped.

jaw
Movable part for pressing more objects against the tail stop.

pipe
Hollow cylinder of varying length, along which the jaw and the tail stop slide.

tail stop
Movable jaw whose motion along the pipe quickly adjusts the tool to the length of the object to be clamped.

locking lever
Handle that fixes the tail stop at the desired position on the pipe.

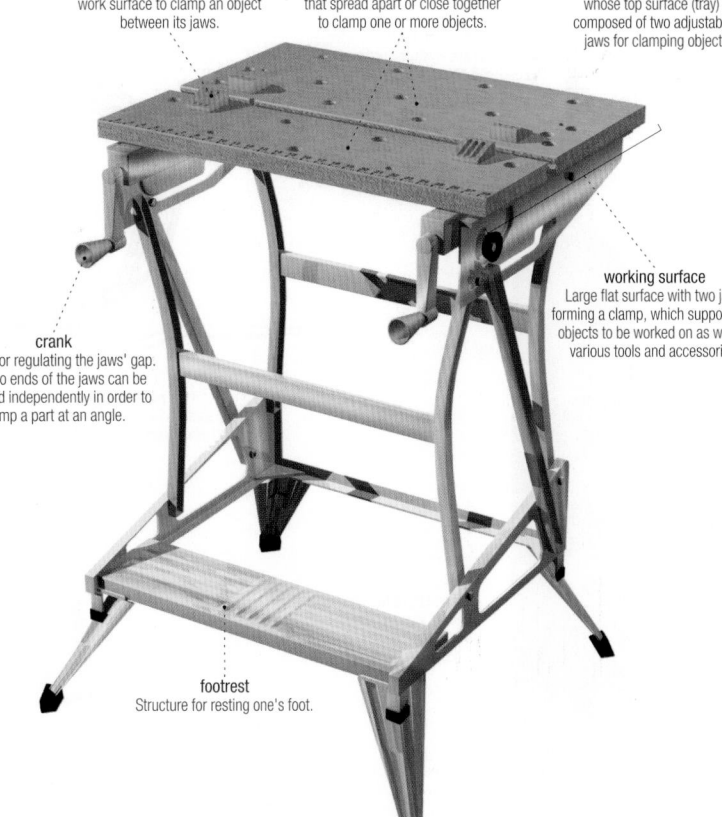

peg
Detachable part inserted into one of the openings on the work surface to clamp an object between its jaws.

jaws
The parts of the working surface that spread apart or close together to clamp one or more objects.

workbench and vise
Small, usually folding, worktable whose top surface (tray) is composed of two adjustable jaws for clamping objects.

crank
Handle for regulating the jaws' gap. The two ends of the jaws can be adjusted independently in order to clamp a part at an angle.

working surface
Large flat surface with two jaws forming a clamp, which supports the objects to be worked on as well as various tools and accessories.

footrest
Structure for resting one's foot.

plumbing tools

Tools used to install, maintain or repair the pipes and sanitary facilities in a dwelling.

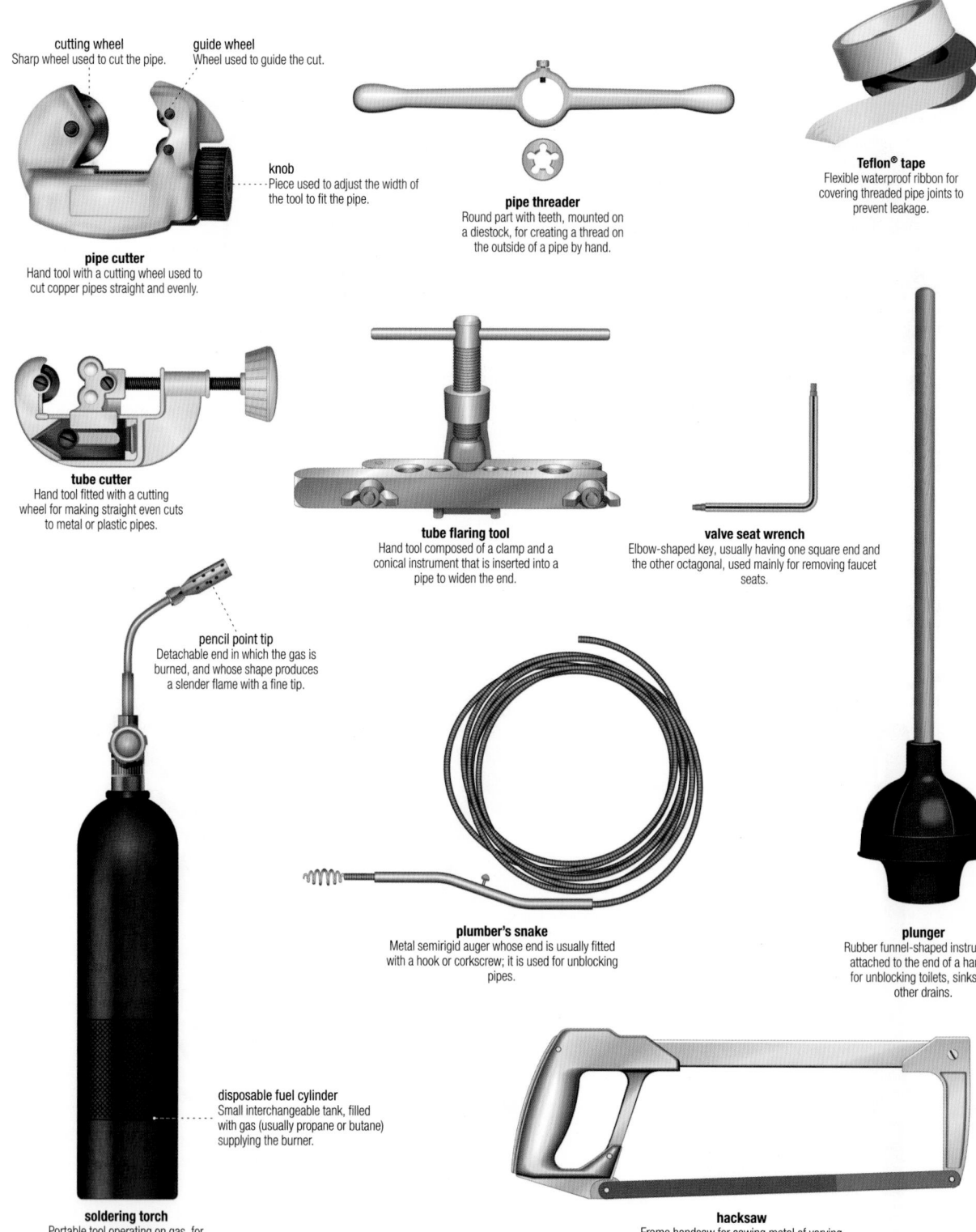

cutting wheel
Sharp wheel used to cut the pipe.

guide wheel
Wheel used to guide the cut.

knob
Piece used to adjust the width of
the tool to fit the pipe.

pipe cutter
Hand tool with a cutting wheel used to
cut copper pipes straight and evenly.

pipe threader
Round part with teeth, mounted on
a diestock, for creating a thread on
the outside of a pipe by hand.

Teflon® tape
Flexible waterproof ribbon for
covering threaded pipe joints to
prevent leakage.

tube cutter
Hand tool fitted with a cutting
wheel for making straight even cuts
to metal or plastic pipes.

tube flaring tool
Hand tool composed of a clamp and a
conical instrument that is inserted into a
pipe to widen the end.

valve seat wrench
Elbow-shaped key, usually having one square end and
the other octagonal, used mainly for removing faucet
seats.

pencil point tip
Detachable end in which the gas is
burned, and whose shape produces
a slender flame with a fine tip.

plumber's snake
Metal semirigid auger whose end is usually fitted
with a hook or corkscrew; it is used for unblocking
pipes.

plunger
Rubber funnel-shaped instrum
attached to the end of a hand
for unblocking toilets, sinks a
other drains.

disposable fuel cylinder
Small interchangeable tank, filled
with gas (usually propane or butane)
supplying the burner.

soldering torch
Portable tool operating on gas, for
fastening parts using a finishing metal
with a low melting point, such as lead.

hacksaw
Frame handsaw for sawing metal of varying
thicknesses.

plumbing tools

wrenches
Hand tools with fixed or variable openings, used for tightening and loosening nuts and bolts, and for assembling and disassembling objects.

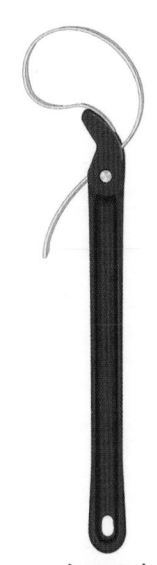

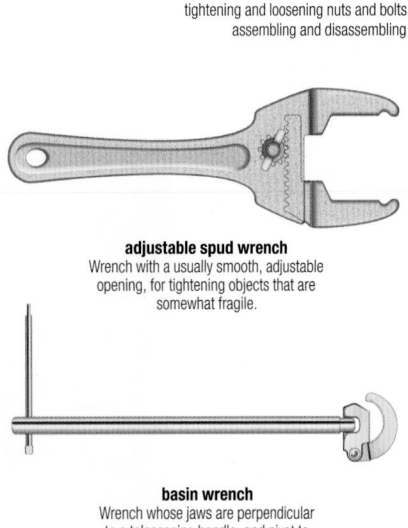

adjustable spud wrench
Wrench with a usually smooth, adjustable opening, for tightening objects that are somewhat fragile.

basin wrench
Wrench whose jaws are perpendicular to a telescoping handle, and pivot to open at variable positions; it is used for working in cramped spaces.

pipe wrench
Wrench with notched jaws and adjustable opening for firmly gripping nuts, couplings and thick-walled pipes.

strap wrench
Wrench whose strap acts as a jaw to grip objects that are difficult to access or whose surfaces must not be damaged.

chain pipe wrench
Wrench whose chain acts as a jaw for gripping large pipes and irregularly shaped objects.

DO-IT-YOURSELF AND GARDENING

masonry tools
Tools used in repairing or building with bricks, stones or concrete blocks.

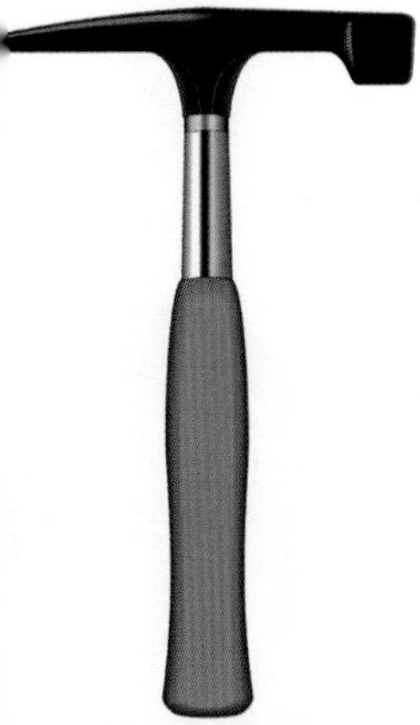

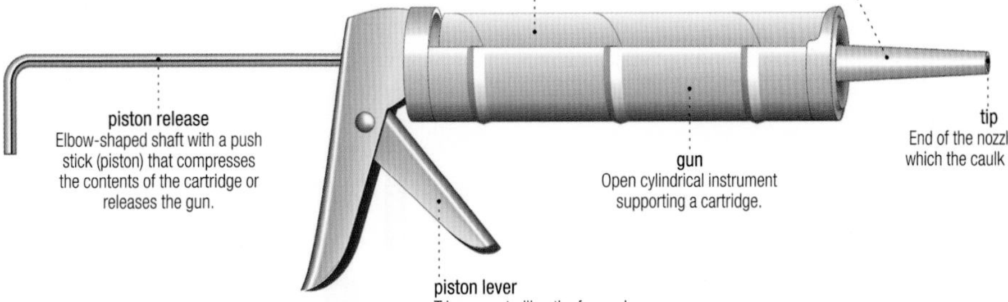

caulking gun
Instrument using a piston mechanism for applying caulking to seal joints and openings.

cartridge
Small replaceable reservoir, fitted with a nozzle and containing a malleable, adhesive caulking.

nozzle
Conical nozzle forming the end of the cartridge.

piston release
Elbow-shaped shaft with a push stick (piston) that compresses the contents of the cartridge or releases the gun.

gun
Open cylindrical instrument supporting a cartridge.

tip
End of the nozzle through which the caulk is applied.

piston lever
Trigger controlling the forward motion of the cartridge.

bricklayer's hammer
Hammer with a long, pointed peen, used for finishing brick and stone and for removing a damaged covering.

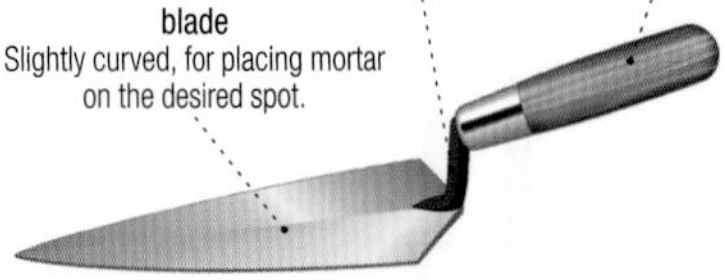

tang
Part of the blade extending into the handle, by which it is attached.

handle
Part for gripping and handling the tool.

blade
Slightly curved, for placing mortar on the desired spot.

hawk
Plate with a short handle, used mainly to hold mortar, plaster and coatings when applying them to a facing.

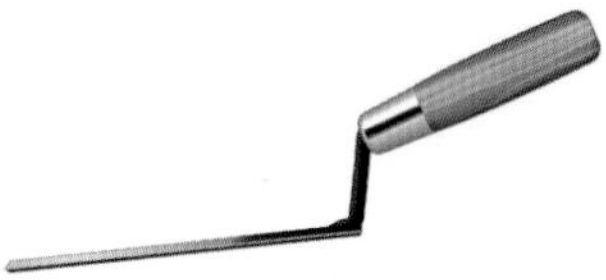

tuck pointer
Tool whose fine blade is used to smooth noticeable joints in a facing.

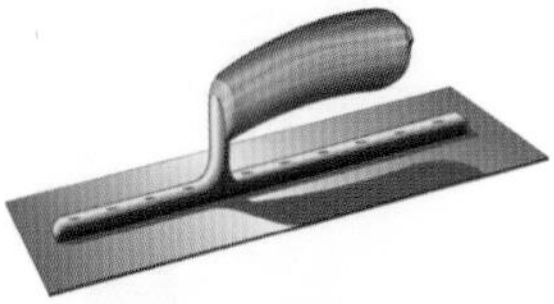

square trowel
Tool with a rectangular blade, usually used for smoothing plaster and small concrete surfaces.

mason's trowel
Tool with a trapezoidal blade, used mainly for spreading and smoothing mortar and concrete.

DO-IT-YOURSELF AND GARDENING

electrical tools

The purpose of the electrical trade is to install, maintain and repair electrical wiring and devices in a place or building.

multimeter
Device for measuring, among other things, a conductor's resistance, the voltage between two points and the strength of the current.

probe
Metal tip connecting the multimeter to the circuit being tested.

voltage tes
Screwdriver used for detecting an elec current in appliances, devices and lo voltage circl

display
Screen showing the reading taken by the device.

insulated blade
Metallic tip that connects the voltage tester to the circuit to be tested.

data hold
Function for keeping certain readings in memory.

auto/manual range
Button for choosing between the automatic and manual gauge for each function.

cord
Flexible electric wire housing the leads connecting the appliance to the electric circuit.

selector switch
Device for selecting the desired function and the appropriate gauge for the measurement.

insulated handle
Part for gripping the tool, made from a material that prevents an electric current from passing through it.

input terminal
Socket for receiving a probe's cord.

neon lamp
Small tube that lights up when the blade is in contact with a live conductor.

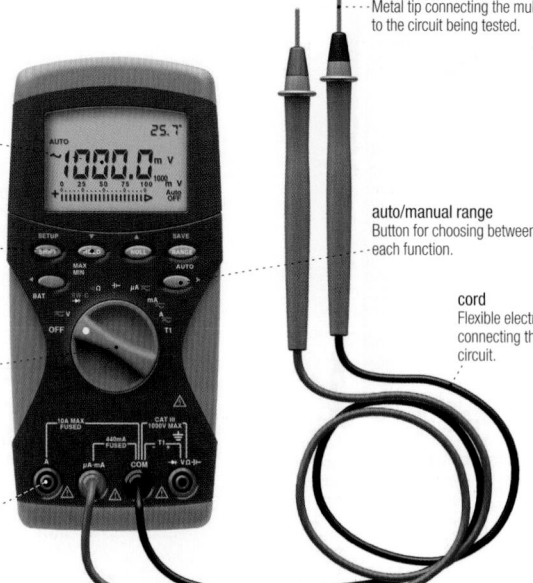

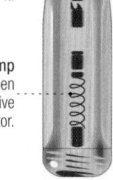

droplig
Portable electric lamp protected a guard and fitted with a long c allowing it to be mov

continuity tester
Instrument for detecting short circuits and open circuits and for testing fuses.

hook
Rounded metallic end by which the droplight can be hung.

reflector
Metal half sphere concentrating and directing the light from a lightbulb.

bulb
Glass envelope filled with gas, in which a luminous body is inserted.

guard
Metal mesh protecting the lightbulb while the drop light is being handled.

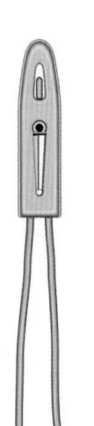

receptacle analyzer
Instrument for detecting any faults in the receptacle, such as grounding problems and crossed or unconnected wires.

convenience outlet
Device connected to an electric circuit; it transmits the current to an electrical appliance when its plug is inserted into the outlet.

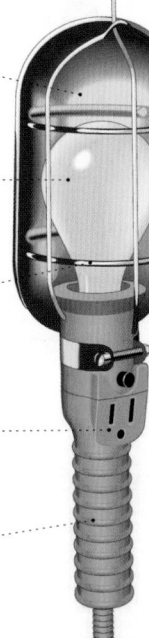

handle
Part for gripping and handling the tool.

neon tester
Instrument used for detecting the presence of an electric current in low-voltage appliances, devices and circuits.

high-voltage tester
Instrument used for detecting an electric current in high-voltage appliances, devices and circuits.

power cord
Flexible electric wire housing the leads connecting the appliance to the electric circuit.

fuse puller
Insulated pliers designed for handling cartridge fuses.

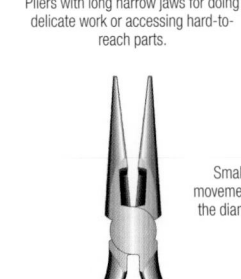

needle-nose pliers
Pliers with long narrow jaws for doing delicate work or accessing hard-to-reach parts.

adjustment wheel
Small striated wheel controlling the movement of the jaws so they adapt to the diameter of the electric wire being stripped.

wire stripper
Pliers with adjustable cutting jaws for removing the insulating sheathing from an electric cable or wire.

lineman's pliers
Pliers fitted with straight jaws that provide a powerful grip; they also include a wire cutter and jaws for pulling fish wire.

jaw
Straight striated part that, with its twin, opens and closes to grip, twist or cut an electric cable, wire or other object.

wire cutter
Part fitted with two cutting edges for cropping an electric wire.

pivot
Pliers' axle of articulation, which allows the jaws to open and close.

insulated handle
Long part of the pliers, covered with a material preventing the flow of electricity.

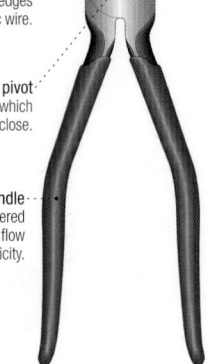

cutter
Knife with a curved blade used mainly for making incisions in the sheathing of a nonmetal electric cable or wire.

cable ripper
Tool with openings of various diameters for stripping a nonmetal electric cable or wire.

wire nut
Hollow part inside which electric wires are connected.

multipurpose tool
Pliers fitted with straight jaws, used especially for gripping, cutting and stripping electric wires.

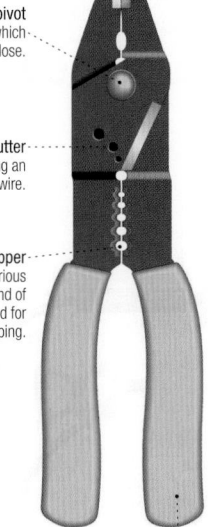

pivot
Pliers' axle of articulation, which allows the jaws to open and close.

wire cutter
Cutting edge for cropping an electric wire.

wire stripper
Pliers' cutting notch, of various diameters, in which the end of an electric cable is clamped for stripping.

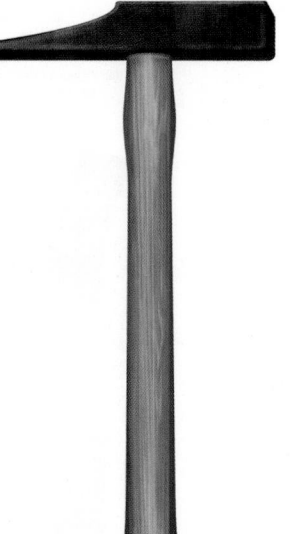

hammer
Hammer with an elongated head and a tapered peen, for attaching small parts and nailing in cramped spaces.

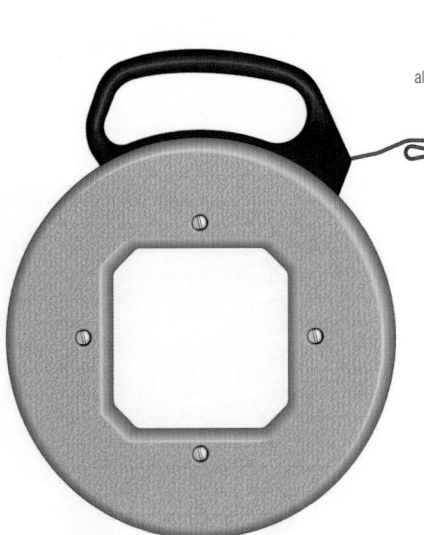

fish wire
Metal wire ending in a hook, used mainly for running electric cables through walls.

insulated handle
Long part of the pliers, covered with a material preventing the flow of electricity.

soldering and welding tools

Tools used to join to pieces by fusing their edges or by melting an alloy between them.

soldering gun
Electric tool that is more powerful than a soldering iron; it uses finishing metal with a low melting point, such as lead, to join parts.

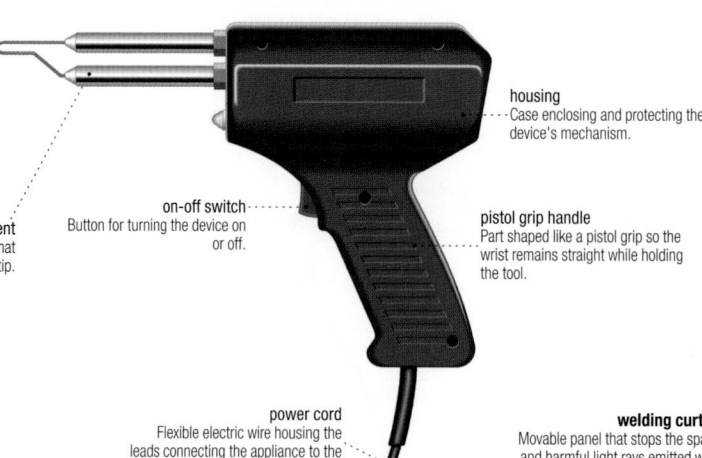

tip
Metal part forming the end of the gun, used to heat a solder.

heating element
Electrical resistor that quickly heats the tip.

on-off switch
Button for turning the device on or off.

housing
Case enclosing and protecting the device's mechanism.

pistol grip handle
Part shaped like a pistol grip so the wrist remains straight while holding the tool.

soldering iron
Electric tool with a tip for heating a solder, used to join parts that can take only weak mechanical pressure.

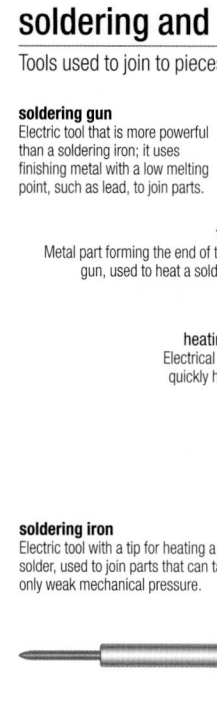

power cord
Flexible electric wire housing the leads connecting the appliance to the electric circuit.

welding curtain
Movable panel that stops the sparks and harmful light rays emitted while welding.

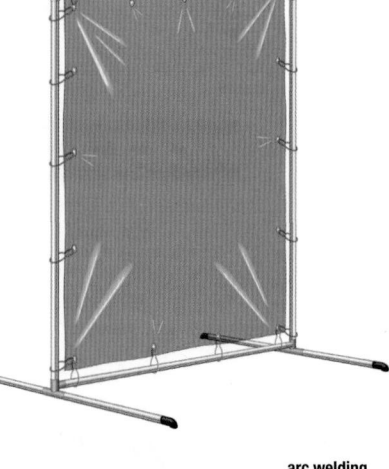

solder
Metal wire that, by fusing over a joint, joins two parts.

tip cleaners
Fine metal needles of various sizes used for clearing the inside of a nozzle, head or burner.

striker
Instrument producing a spark for lighting the gas emitted by a nozzle, head or burner.

friction strip
Abrasive surface on which a flint is struck to produce a spark.

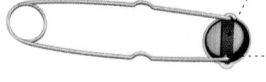

flint
Small stone that is scraped against an abrasive surface to produce a spark.

arc welding
Welding process in which the heat needed for fusing is provided by an electric arc between the electrode and the part to be welded.

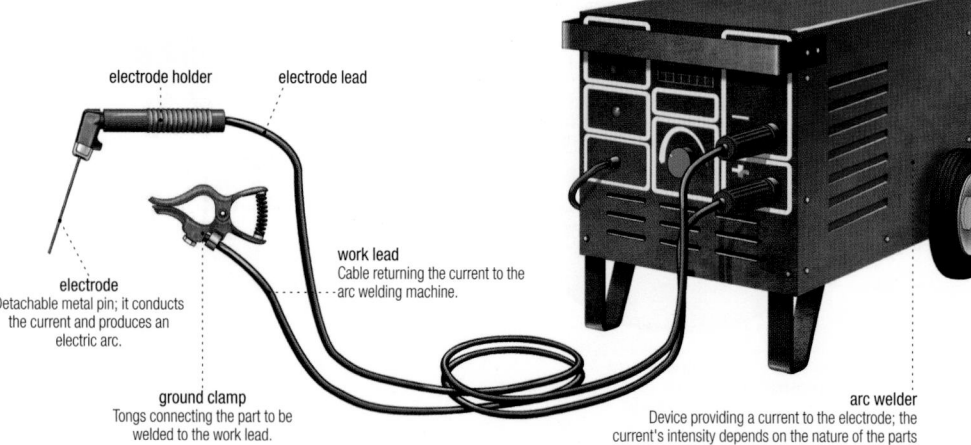

electrode holder   **electrode lead**

work lead
Cable returning the current to the arc welding machine.

electrode
Detachable metal pin; it conducts the current and produces an electric arc.

ground clamp
Tongs connecting the part to be welded to the work lead.

arc welder
Device providing a current to the electrode; the current's intensity depends on the nature of the parts to be welded and the electrode's characteristics.

protective clothing

goggles

face shield
Rigid protective face mask held in a harness behind the head that in glass window to see throug

hand shield
Rigid protective face mask held in a handle that includes a glass wi see through.

welding gloves
Fireproof gloves that cover the har and part of the forearm.

mitten
Fireproof covering that protects th wrist and part of the forearm ar has a separate section for the thu sometimes the first finger.

soldering and welding tools

handle
Rigid tube containing the conduits for the welding gas; it also makes the torch easy to handle.

welding torch
Torch for joining metal parts using a flame produced by burning gas.

pressure regulator (oxygen)
Device located at the opening of the canister of oxygen, that lowers and stabilizes the pressure of the gas flowing to the torch.

acetylene valve
Valve controlling the volume of acetylene entering the torch.

tip
End of the head tube; combustion takes place where it opens.

high-pressure gauge
Dial-operated device whose needle shows the oxygen pressure in the cylinder.

oxygen valve
Valve controlling the volume of oxygen introduced into the welding torch.

low-pressure gauge
Dial-operated device whose needle shows the oxygen pressure at the outlet port of the pressure regulator.

mixing chamber
Part of the torch where acetylene and oxygen are mixed. The proportion and flow of the gases, regulated by the valves, determine the flame's properties.

head tube
Detachable part conducting the gaseous mixture to the nozzle.

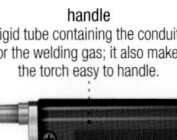
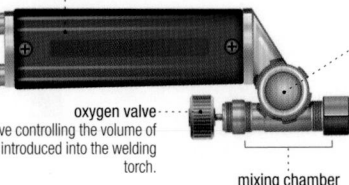
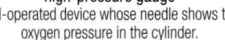
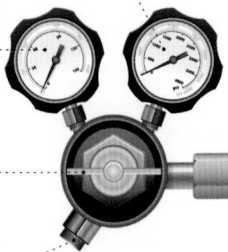

adjusting screw
Screw for controlling the oxygen pressure at the regulator outlet port, which corresponds to the oxygen pressure at the inlet of the torch.

cutting torch
Tool utilizing a concentrated acetylene flame hot enough to cut through metals such as steel.

hose connection fitting
Piece linking a tube to the pressure regulator.

inlet connection nut
Threaded piece attached to the outside of two tubes in order to join them.

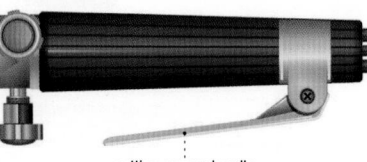

cutting oxygen handle
Device directing the oxygen to the cutting tip, where combustion takes place.

cutting tip
End of the torch, whose opening produces a flame concentrated on the surface to be cut.

oxyacetylene welding and cutting
Procedure in which the heat necessary for fusion or cutting is provided by the combustion of a mixture of acetylene and oxygen at the tip of a torch.

soldering torch
Portable tool operating on gas, for fastening parts using a finishing metal with a low melting point, such as lead.

cylinder cart
Wheeled cart for transporting oxygen and and acetylene cylinders.

pencil point tip
Detachable end in which the gas is burned, and whose shape produces a slender flame with a fine tip.

pressure regulators
Devices placed at the outlet port of each cylinder; they lower and stabilize the gas pressure reaching the torch.

hose
Flexible tube bringing gas from the cylinder to the torch.

flame spreader tip
Detachable end producing a wide flame for covering a larger surface.

acetylene cylinder
As acetylene burns at very high temperatures (6,000°F), it is used in steel and metal work, where a high temperature must be attained quickly.

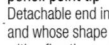

oxygen cylinder
Oxygen is the gas used to make the acetylene burn.

disposable fuel cylinder
Small interchangeable tank, filled with gas (usually propane or butane) supplying the burner.

cutting torch
Tool utilizing a concentrated acetylene flame hot enough to cut through metals such as steel.

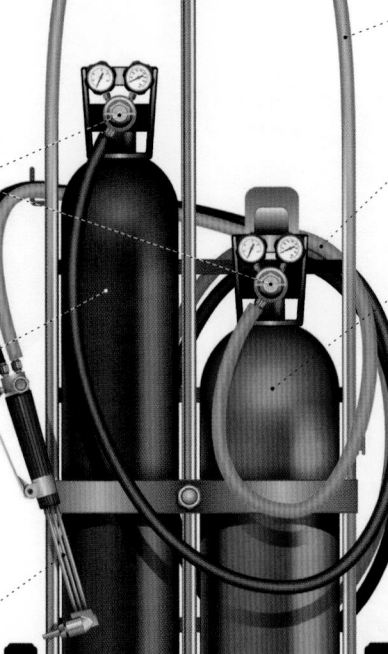

DO-IT-YOURSELF AND GARDENING

painting tools

Tools used in applying paint, stain or varnish to surfaces.

spray paint gun
Pneumatic device atomizing paint onto a surface, giving it a smooth uniform finish.

nozzle
Opening through which the paint flows; its size depends on the position of a conical part (pointer).

air cap
Part directing the compressed air toward the nozzle; here the air comes in contact with the paint jet, which is atomized.

trigger
Device that controls the supply of both air and paint.

vent hole
Opening through which the air enters the container to maintain the atmospheric pressure.

spreader adjustment screw
Movable part whose opening is controlled by a screw that adjusts the volume of air pushed into the air cap, thereby defining the size and shape of the paint jet.

fluid adjustment screw
Screw for controlling the maximum size of a pointer, thereby determining the amount of paint emitted by the nozzle.

air valve
Movable part whose opening is regulated by the trigger; it lets compressed air into the gun.

gun body

air hose connection
Threaded part receiving a flexible tube; it is connected to a compressor that allows the compressed air into the body of the gun.

container
Reservoir for the paint, which is connected to the gun by a tube; here a low-pressure zone is created causing the liquid to be sucked in.

brush
Natural or synthetic bristles att to a handle, used for spreading varnish or stain on a base

handle
Part for gripping and handling the tool.

ferrule
Metal part clamped around the end of the handle to keep the bristles firmly in place.

bristles
Stiff hairs made from natural or synthetic materials; they are filled with paint, varnish or stain to apply them.

air compressor
Machine compressing and storing the air that supplies a spray paint gun or other pneumatic tool.

pump
Machine drawing in ambient air and forcing it under pressure into the tank.

motor
Device converting the energy produced by fuel combustion into mechanical energy.

handle
Part for gripping and handling the tool.

air tank
Container storing compressed air.

scraper
Instrument with a blade used remove paint or varnish from surface.

knurled bolt
Bolt fastening the blade on the handle.

blade
Thin flat metal part that forms the cutting part of the scraper.

handle
Part for gripping and handling the tool.

heat gun
Electric device blowing very hot used mainly to soften paint and v to ease scraping them.

nozzle
End of the tool through which a jet of hot air is forced by a fan. It is usually possible to attach various accessories to it.

wheel
Circular instrument rotating around an axle so that the device can be moved.

on-off switch
Button for turning the device on or off.

paint roller
Instrument fitted with a detachable roller cover for spreading the paint evenly on a large surface.

tray
Container used with a roller; it has a deep area to hold the paint and a ribbed area for coating the roller cover with the amount of paint required.

handle
Part for gripping and handling the tool.

roller frame
Metal pivoting structure inserted into the roller cover as support.

roller cover
Detachable cylindrical pa covered with natural or s fibers adapted to the nat product being applied.

DO-IT-YOURSELF AND GARDENING

ladders

Structures for climbing up or down, composed of vertical rails supporting rungs or steps, used to reach relatively high areas.

foldaway ladder
...culating ladder that can be folded up into a trap door.

straight ladder
Ladder that leans against a wall, comprised of two parallel side rails joined by rungs.

hook ladder
Straight ladder with one end having fixed or detachable hooks to keep the ladder in place on a structure.

extension ladder
Straight ladder of adjustable height, made up of two superimposed planes that slide one on the other.

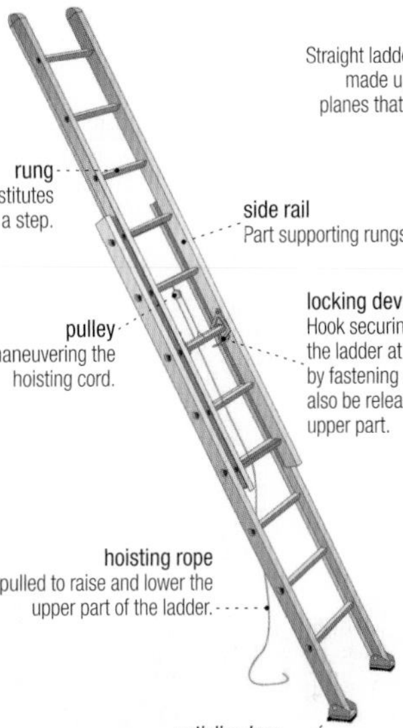

rung
Bar on a ladder that constitutes a step.

side rail
Part supporting rungs or steps.

pulley
Small wheel for maneuvering the hoisting cord.

locking device
Hook securing the upper part of the ladder at the desired height by fastening onto a rung; it can also be released to lower the upper part.

hoisting rope
Rope that is pulled to raise and lower the upper part of the ladder.

antislip shoe
Part attached to the bottom end of the side rail to prevent slipping.

rolling ladder
...le ladder fitted with a platform and ...ty rail; it can be moved on wheels ...uipped with blocking devices.

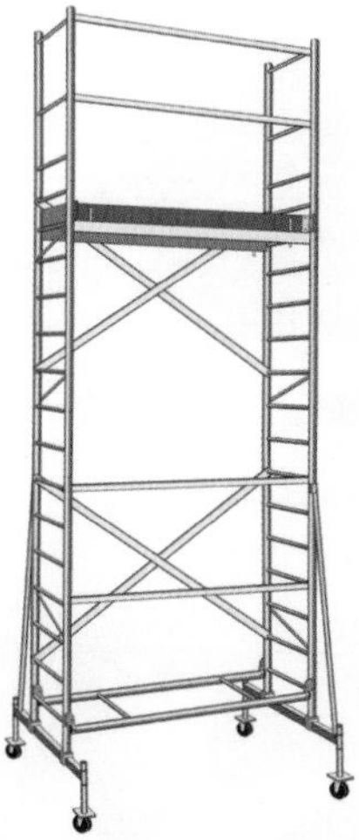

ladder scaffold
Movable structure made up of two vertical ladders and a work platform as well as wheels fitted with blocking devices.

fruit-picking ladder
Double ladder specially designed for picking fruit and for pruning and maintaining trees.

multipurpose ladder
Ladder with several folds, which can be locked in a number of positions.

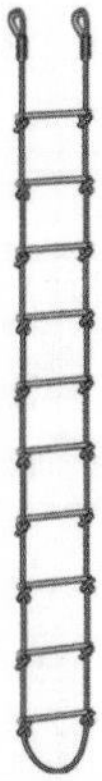

rope ladder
Suspension ladder whose side rails and rungs are made of cord.

stepladders

Free-standing ladders with at least four legs and broad steps used to reach relatively low areas.

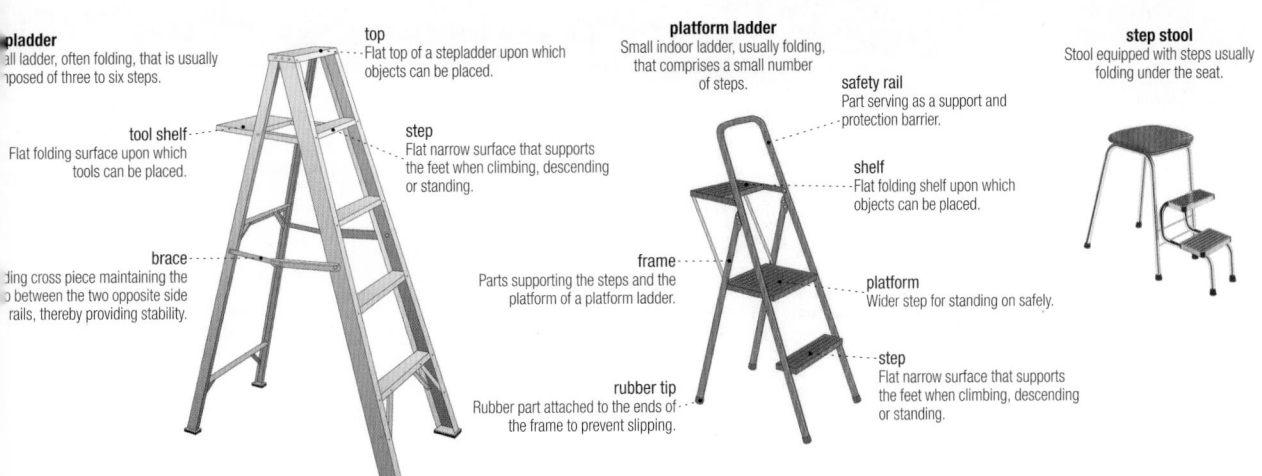

...pladder
...all ladder, often folding, that is usually ...posed of three to six steps.

top
Flat top of a stepladder upon which objects can be placed.

tool shelf
Flat folding surface upon which tools can be placed.

step
Flat narrow surface that supports the feet when climbing, descending or standing.

brace
...ding cross piece maintaining the ...o between the two opposite side rails, thereby providing stability.

platform ladder
Small indoor ladder, usually folding, that comprises a small number of steps.

safety rail
Part serving as a support and protection barrier.

shelf
Flat folding shelf upon which objects can be placed.

frame
Parts supporting the steps and the platform of a platform ladder.

platform
Wider step for standing on safely.

step
Flat narrow surface that supports the feet when climbing, descending or standing.

rubber tip
Rubber part attached to the ends of the frame to prevent slipping.

step stool
Stool equipped with steps usually folding under the seat.

garden

Plot reserved for cultivating ornamental plants where one strolls and relaxes.

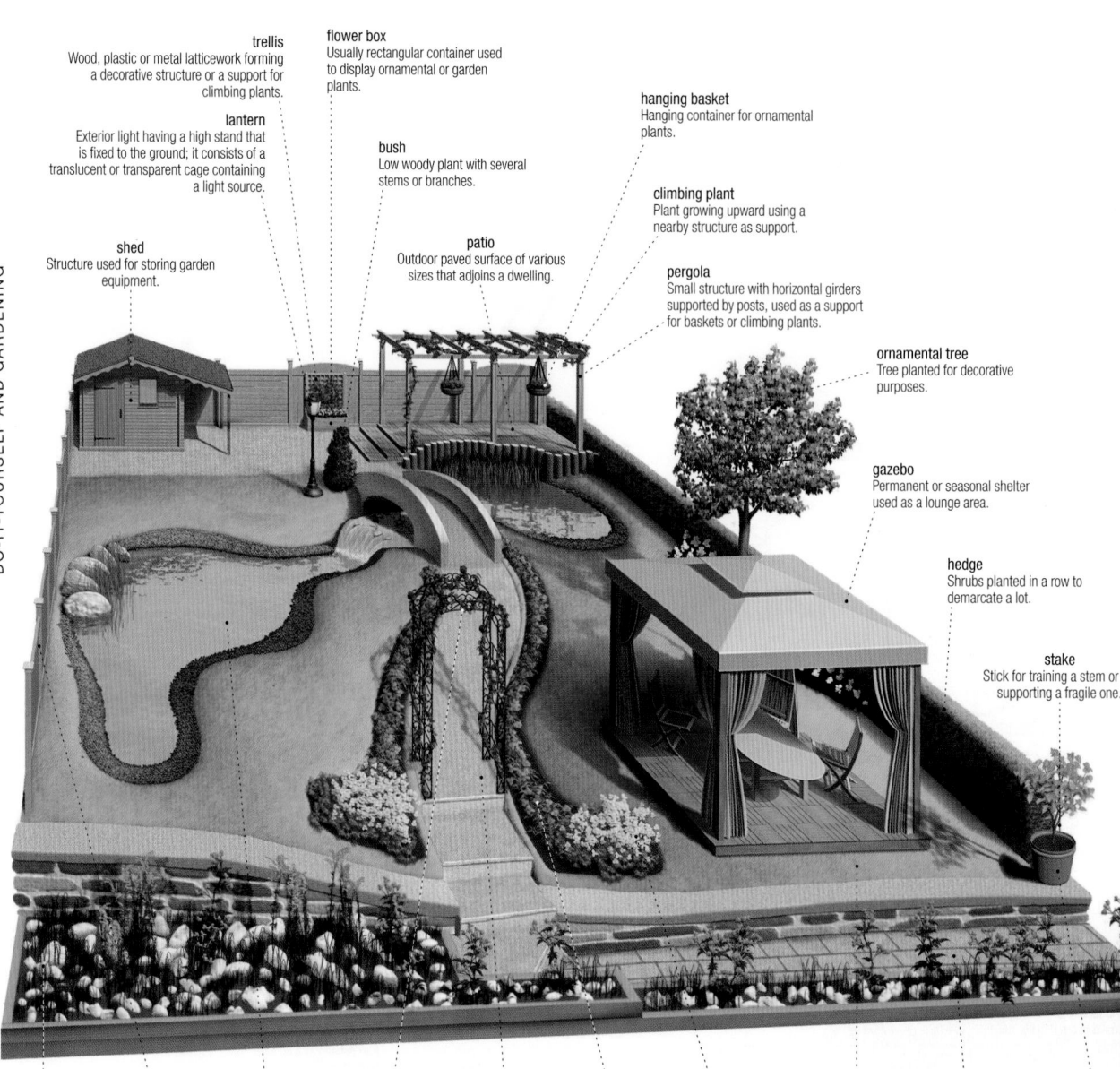

trellis
Wood, plastic or metal latticework forming a decorative structure or a support for climbing plants.

flower box
Usually rectangular container used to display ornamental or garden plants.

hanging basket
Hanging container for ornamental plants.

lantern
Exterior light having a high stand that is fixed to the ground; it consists of a translucent or transparent cage containing a light source.

bush
Low woody plant with several stems or branches.

climbing plant
Plant growing upward using a nearby structure as support.

shed
Structure used for storing garden equipment.

patio
Outdoor paved surface of various sizes that adjoins a dwelling.

pergola
Small structure with horizontal girders supported by posts, used as a support for baskets or climbing plants.

ornamental tree
Tree planted for decorative purposes.

gazebo
Permanent or seasonal shelter used as a lounge area.

hedge
Shrubs planted in a row to demarcate a lot.

stake
Stick for training a stem or f supporting a fragile one.

fence
Barrier made of wooden planks in a row, used to mark the border of a yard or part of a yard.

arbor
Decorative doorway with rounded apex.

flower bed
Small plot of land adorned with plants, usually flowers.

lawn
Short thick grass requiring regular mowing.

planter
Usually cylindrical con ornamental or garden

rock garden
Area of land scattered with ornamental rocks, among which plants grow.

ornamental pool
Small body of water, usually artificial, built for ornamental purposes.

path
Walkway bordered by plants.

clump of flowers
Grouping of flowers planted in a decorative manner.

paver
Flat piece of stone, brick, mart cement tile for covering a surfa

miscellaneous equipment

blower
...e that shoots out a jet of air, used
...oving leaves and other debris.

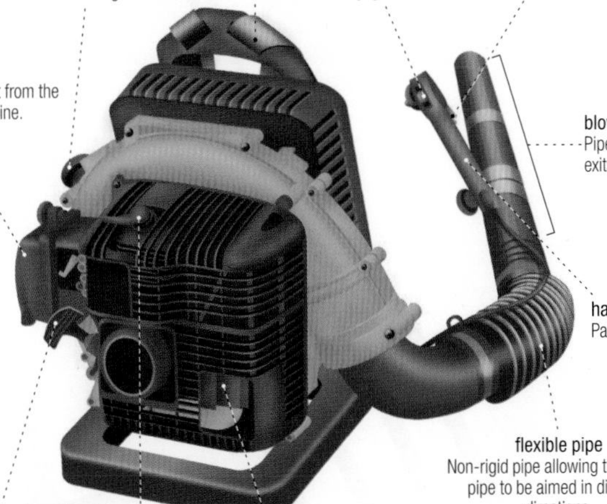

harness
Arrangement of straps allowing the
blower to be carried on one's back.

fuel tank cap
Cylindrical piece used to cover the opening on
the tank containing the fuel.

throttle position and stop button
Button for setting engine speed
and turning ignition on or off.

throttle trigger
Mechanical piece used to set the
speed of the blower by applying
pressure from the fingers.

air cleaner
...e that removes dust from the
...air entering the engine.

blower pipes
Pipes through which the air jet
exits.

handle
Part for directing air flow from tool.

recoil starter handle
Handle connected to a cable that is
pulled to start the engine.

spark arrestor/muffler
Piece used to muffle the sound of
the motor and block sparks from
shooting out.

flexible pipe
Non-rigid pipe allowing the blower
pipe to be aimed in different
directions.

spark plug
Electrical device that provides
the spark necessary to ignite
the mixture of air and gas in the
engine's cylinder.

motorized earth auger
Machine using a rotating bit to quickly dig holes of
various sizes in the ground.

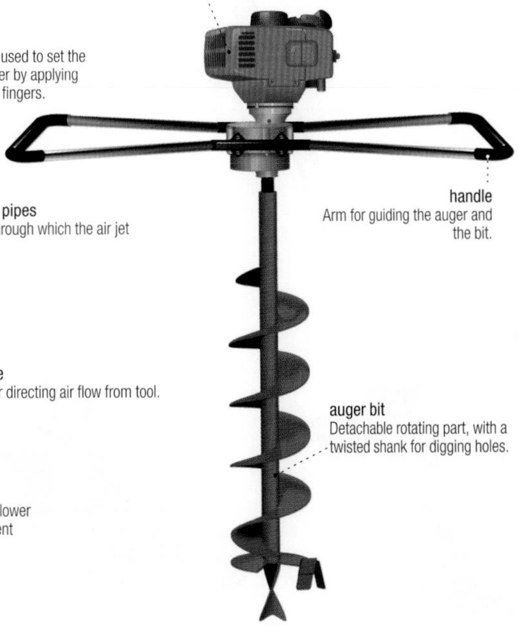

motor
Device converting the combustion of
fuel and air into mechanical energy.

handle
Arm for guiding the auger and
the bit.

auger bit
Detachable rotating part, with a
twisted shank for digging holes.

wheelbarrow
Small one-wheeled handcart for
transporting material such as
supplies, tools, soil and debris.

tray
Container designed to hold a load.

handle
Arm for lifting and moving the
wheelbarrow.

leg
Part supporting the wheelbarrow
when at rest.

wheel
Circular object rotating around an axle so
that the wheelbarrow can be moved.

...post bin
...ainer for decomposing organic waste from
...garden and kitchen to produce fertilizer
...post).

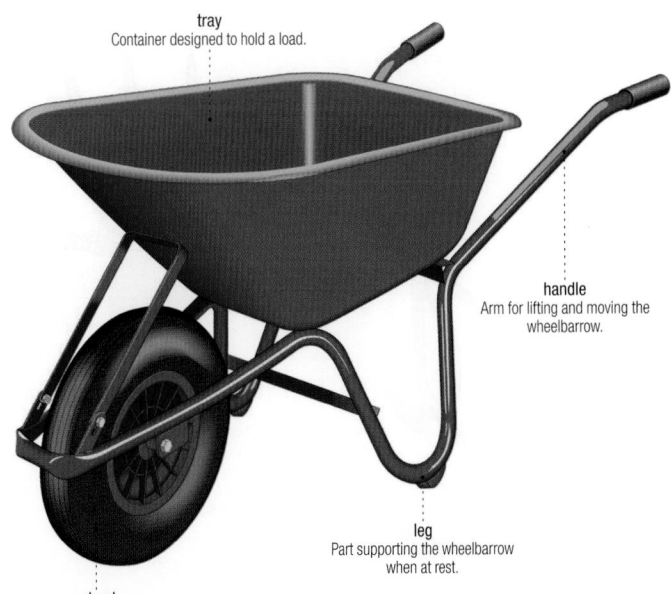

tools for loosening the earth

shovel
Tool used for digging holes
and manipulating various
materials, such as soil, sand
and compost.

spade
Tool with a flat or slightly concave
blade, used mainly for turning
over soil.

spading fork
Tool with metal tines, which make it
easier to loosen soil that is hard or
contains many stones or roots.

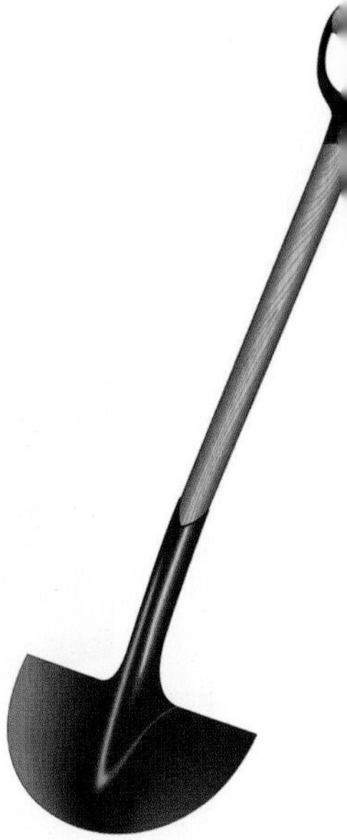

lawn edger
Tool with a semicircular blade for
trimming the edge of the lawn, usually
along a driveway, a patio or flower bed.

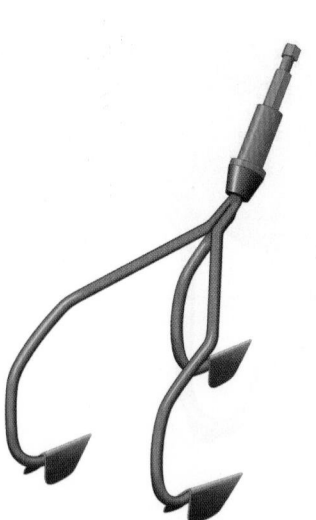

weeding hoe
Tool with claws designed mainly for
loosening and weeding soil.

hoe-fork
Tool with a blade, which serves
as a hoe, and tines; it is used
especially for making furrows.

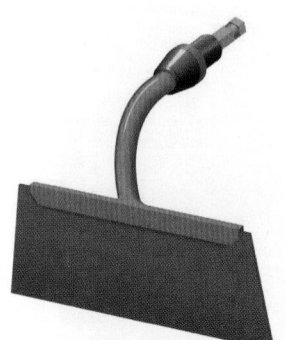

draw hoe
Tool whose blade loosens, weeds
and aerates the soil; it is also used
to groom the soil around a plant.

collinear hoe
Tool whose blade, more slanted th
that of the draw hoe, loosens, wee
and aerates the soil; it is also used
harvesting root vegetables.

tools for loosening the earth

pick
Tool whose head is pointed on one end and has a cutting edge on the other; it is used to break up hard or rocky soil.

hoe
Tool with a thick sturdy blade attached directly to the handle; it is used especially for loosening and weeding dense soil.

rake
Tool with tines perpendicular to the handle, for leveling the soil, removing pebbles and gathering debris.

hook
Tool with curved tines, used to handle fertilizer and compost, pull up root vegetables and loosen or weed the soil.

tiller
Motorized machine that uses its rotating tines to turn over and loosen the soil and mix fertilizer into it.

handlebar
Arm for steering the tiller.

clutch lever
Lever controlling the tiller's motion and the tines' rotation.

frame
Metal structure of the tiller.

forward/reverse
Mechanism for selecting the direction in which the tiller moves.

starter
activated device pulling a cable to start the motor.

motor
Device converting the combustion of fuel and air into mechanical energy.

tine
Cutting blade connected to a rotating axle; it digs into the soil to loosen it.

watering tools

hose reel cart
Reel mounted on a cart, for transporting and storing a garden hose.

garden hose
Circular pipe, flexible or semirigid, conducting water from a tap to a watering device such as a nozzle, gun or sprinkler.

hand crank
Handle for rolling up the garden hose on the reel.

reel
Spool for quickly rolling and unrolling a garden hose.

tap connector
Threaded part receiving a hose connected to a tap.

hose nozzle
Detachable instrument attached to the end of a garden hose, for adjusting the shape and flow of the water spray.

sprinkler h
Hose with small openings thr which water flows; placed o ground, it deeply waters a

bottle sprayer
Small atomizer used mainly for spraying plant foliage and seedlings.

tank sprayer
Device with a tank and a wand that sprays fine droplets of water or treatment products on plants and soil.

watering can
Container fitted with a long neck, usually with a rose at its end, used for sprinkling plants with water or treatment products.

handle
Part shaped like a semicircle for gripping the can.

rose
Detachable perforated part causing water or a liquid to pour in a shower.

watering tools

pistol nozzle
Watering nozzle activated by
means of a trigger flow switch.

watering wand
Long watering nozzle used mainly to
sprinkle water on hard to reach plants,
such as hanging plants.

spray nozzle
Watering gun with a wide head that
contains small holes, used for watering
flowers and delicate plants with a fine
shower.

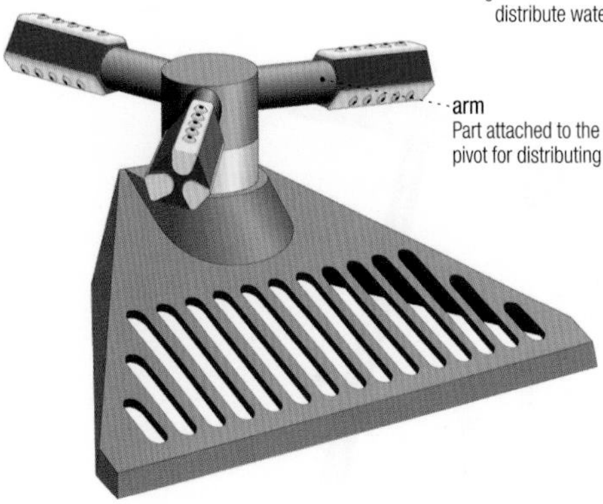

revolving sprinkler
Watering device with rotating arms that
distribute water in a full circle.

arm
Part attached to the sprinkler's
pivot for distributing water.

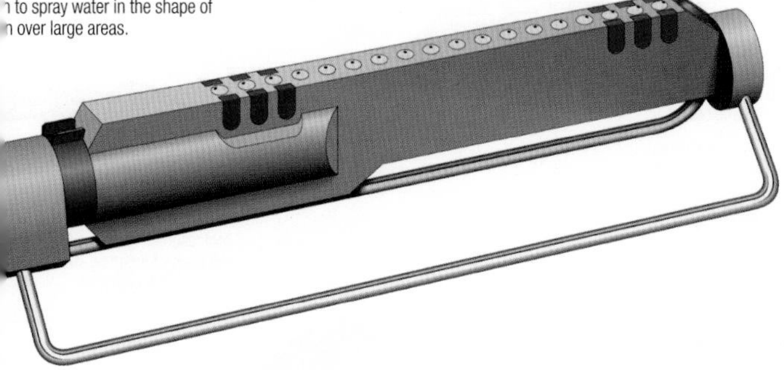

illating sprinkler
ice with a bar containing
tiple nozzles; it moves back and
n to spray water in the shape of
n over large areas.

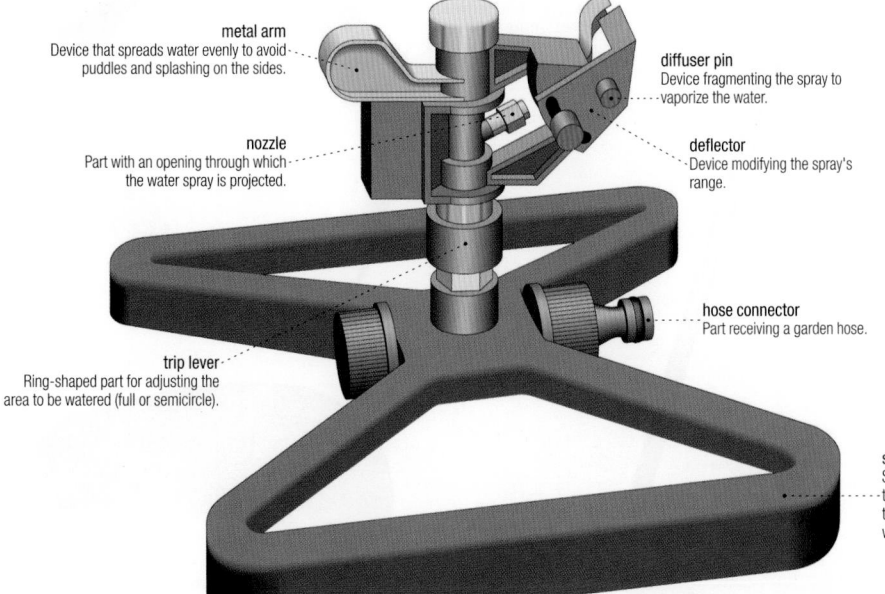

metal arm
Device that spreads water evenly to avoid
puddles and splashing on the sides.

diffuser pin
Device fragmenting the spray to
vaporize the water.

impulse sprinkler
Watering device whose single nozzle is
mounted on a pivot that rotates in jerks,
emitting a powerful spray to distribute
water in a circle or arc.

nozzle
Part with an opening through which
the water spray is projected.

deflector
Device modifying the spray's
range.

hose connector
Part receiving a garden hose.

trip lever
Ring-shaped part for adjusting the
area to be watered (full or semicircle).

sled
Support for the sprinkler; it allows
the device to be moved by pulling on
the hose, which avoids treading on
watered areas.

pruning and cutting tools

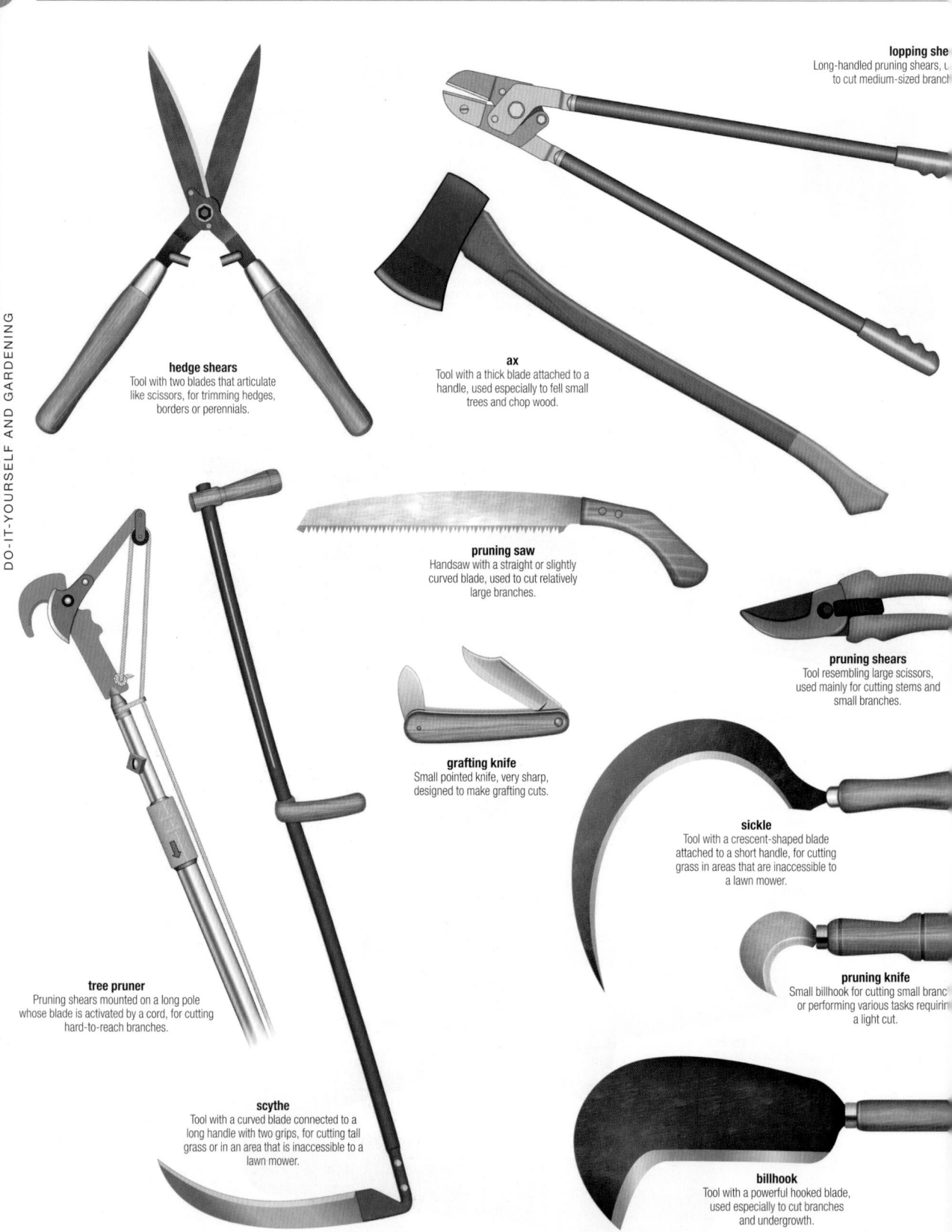

lopping she
Long-handled pruning shears, u
to cut medium-sized branch

hedge shears
Tool with two blades that articulate
like scissors, for trimming hedges,
borders or perennials.

ax
Tool with a thick blade attached to a
handle, used especially to fell small
trees and chop wood.

pruning saw
Handsaw with a straight or slightly
curved blade, used to cut relatively
large branches.

pruning shears
Tool resembling large scissors,
used mainly for cutting stems and
small branches.

grafting knife
Small pointed knife, very sharp,
designed to make grafting cuts.

sickle
Tool with a crescent-shaped blade
attached to a short handle, for cutting
grass in areas that are inaccessible to
a lawn mower.

tree pruner
Pruning shears mounted on a long pole
whose blade is activated by a cord, for cutting
hard-to-reach branches.

pruning knife
Small billhook for cutting small branc
or performing various tasks requirin
a light cut.

scythe
Tool with a curved blade connected to a
long handle with two grips, for cutting tall
grass or in an area that is inaccessible to a
lawn mower.

billhook
Tool with a powerful hooked blade,
used especially to cut branches
and undergrowth.

pruning and cutting tools

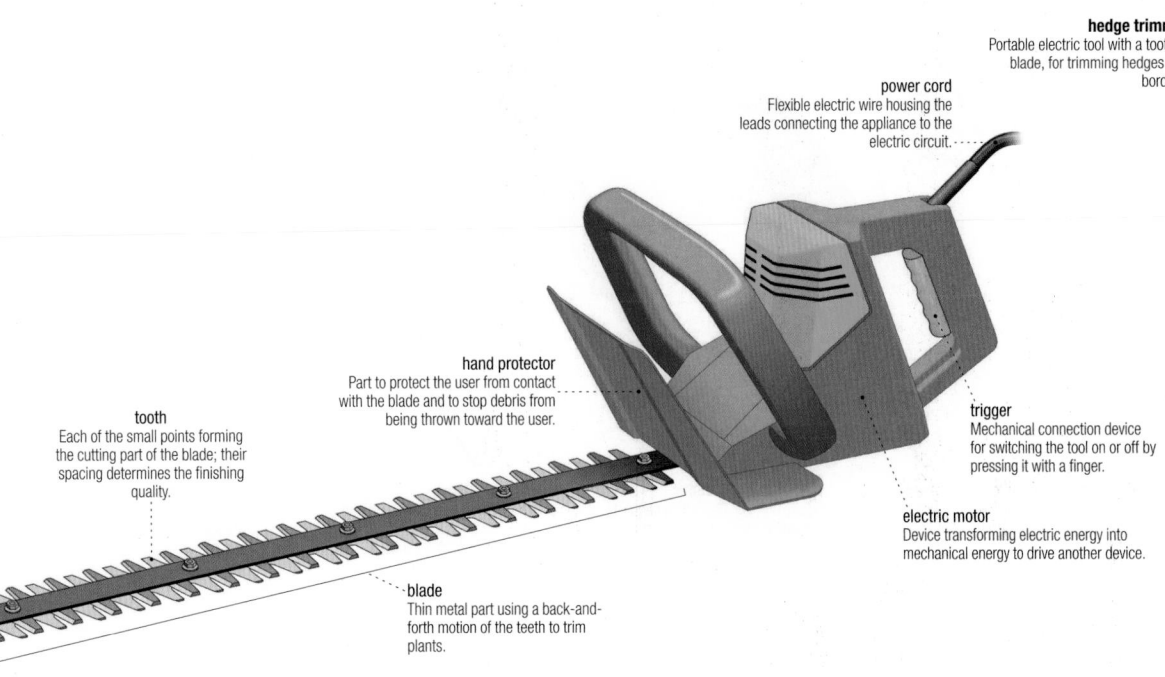

hedge trimmer
Portable electric tool with a toothed blade, for trimming hedges and borders.

power cord
Flexible electric wire housing the leads connecting the appliance to the electric circuit.

hand protector
Part to protect the user from contact with the blade and to stop debris from being thrown toward the user.

tooth
Each of the small points forming the cutting part of the blade; their spacing determines the finishing quality.

trigger
Mechanical connection device for switching the tool on or off by pressing it with a finger.

electric motor
Device transforming electric energy into mechanical energy to drive another device.

blade
Thin metal part using a back-and-forth motion of the teeth to trim plants.

chainsaw
Portable motorized saw with a cutting chain; it is manipulated with two hands to cut tree limbs, fell trees and saw wood.

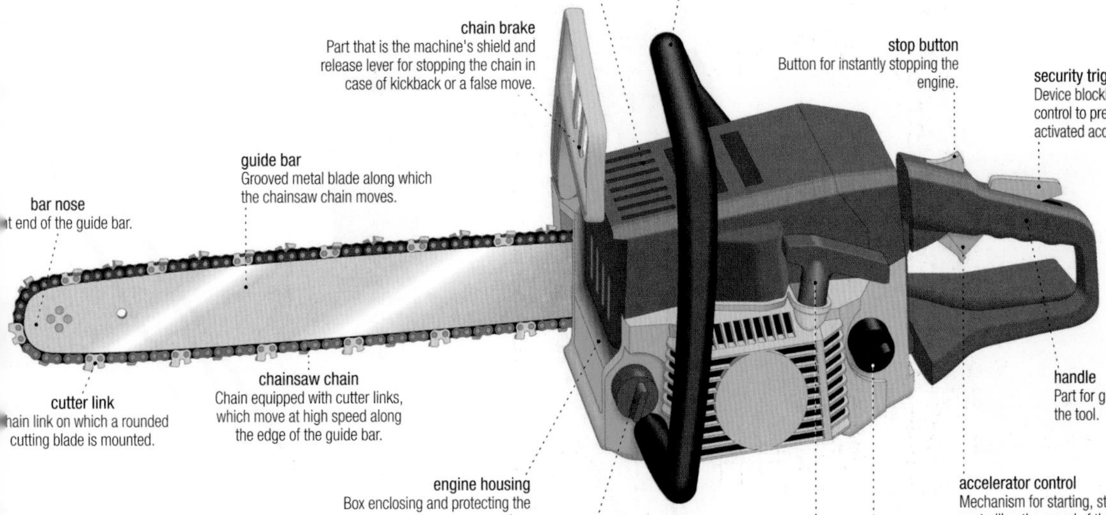

air filter
Device that removes dust from the air entering the engine.

antivibration handle
Auxiliary handle, insulated from the housing by rubber shock absorbers that dampen the vibrations produced by the tool.

chain brake
Part that is the machine's shield and release lever for stopping the chain in case of kickback or a false move.

stop button
Button for instantly stopping the engine.

security trigger
Device blocking the accelerator control to prevent the chain from being activated accidentally.

guide bar
Grooved metal blade along which the chainsaw chain moves.

bar nose
nt end of the guide bar.

cutter link
hain link on which a rounded cutting blade is mounted.

chainsaw chain
Chain equipped with cutter links, which move at high speed along the edge of the guide bar.

handle
Part for gripping and handling the tool.

engine housing
Box enclosing and protecting the engine.

starter handle
Handle connected to a cable that is pulled to start the engine.

accelerator control
Mechanism for starting, stopping and controlling the speed of the chain.

oil pan
Reservoir containing oil for lubricating certain parts of the tool, such as the chain.

fuel tank
Reservoir containing the fuel supplying the engine.

hand tools

Instruments used for working the soil in cramped spaces, such as a flower bed, small clumps, containers and baskets.

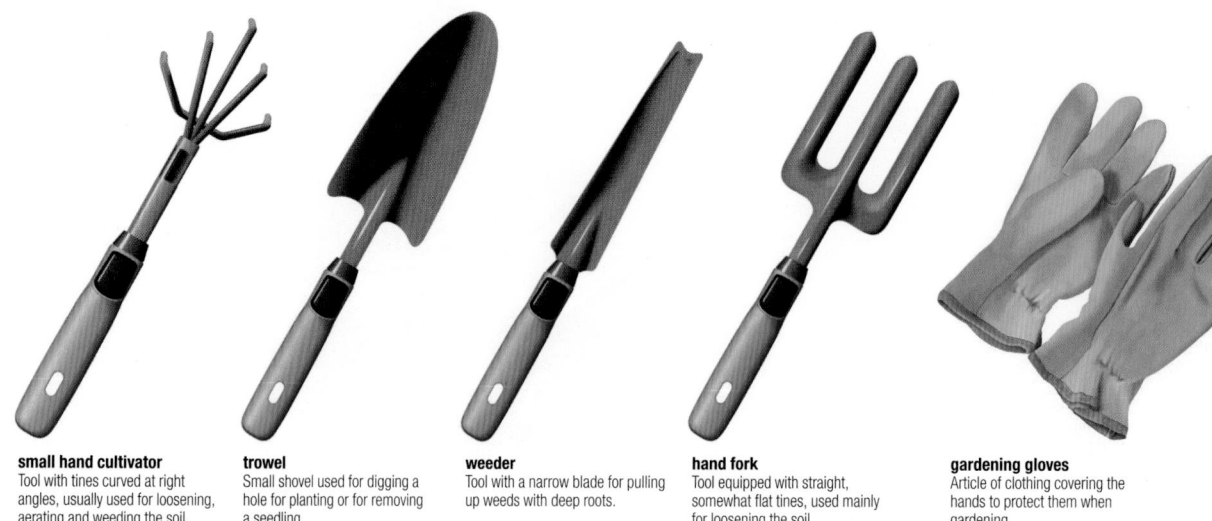

small hand cultivator
Tool with tines curved at right angles, usually used for loosening, aerating and weeding the soil.

trowel
Small shovel used for digging a hole for planting or for removing a seedling.

weeder
Tool with a narrow blade for pulling up weeds with deep roots.

hand fork
Tool equipped with straight, somewhat flat tines, used mainly for loosening the soil.

gardening gloves
Article of clothing covering the hands to protect them when gardening.

seeding and planting tools

st
Stick for training a stem o
supporting a fragile

seeder
Small shovel fitted with a distribution device for sowing seeds without touching them.

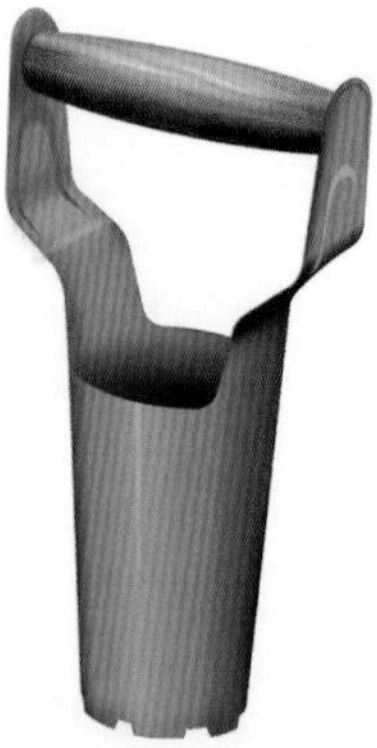

bulb planter
Tool with a cylindrical container for removing a core of soil to create a hole in which plant bulbs or young plants are planted.

spreader
Small handcart with a reservoir and distribution mechanism for evenly spreading seeds or fertilizer on an area.

dibble
Pointed tool for digging a small hole in the ground in which to plant seeds or bulbs.

garden line
Cord stretched between two stakes used as a guide for marking straight fu and edges for a border or a hedge, o demarcating sections of a vegetable ga

lawn care

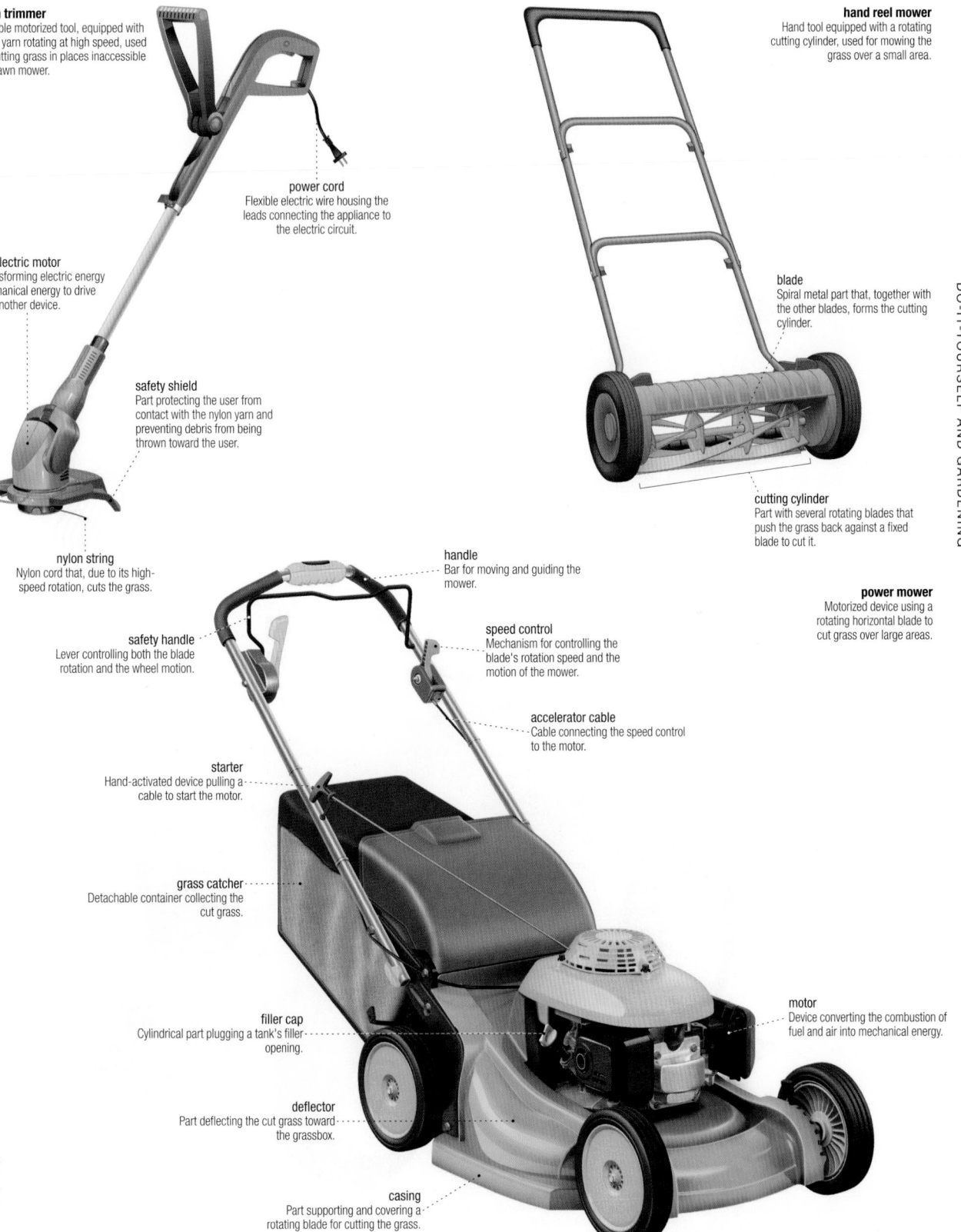

trimmer
ble motorized tool, equipped with
yarn rotating at high speed, used
tting grass in places inaccessible
awn mower.

hand reel mower
Hand tool equipped with a rotating
cutting cylinder, used for mowing the
grass over a small area.

power cord
Flexible electric wire housing the
leads connecting the appliance to
the electric circuit.

lectric motor
sforming electric energy
hanical energy to drive
nother device.

blade
Spiral metal part that, together with
the other blades, forms the cutting
cylinder.

safety shield
Part protecting the user from
contact with the nylon yarn and
preventing debris from being
thrown toward the user.

cutting cylinder
Part with several rotating blades that
push the grass back against a fixed
blade to cut it.

nylon string
Nylon cord that, due to its high-
speed rotation, cuts the grass.

handle
Bar for moving and guiding the
mower.

power mower
Motorized device using a
rotating horizontal blade to
cut grass over large areas.

speed control
Mechanism for controlling the
blade's rotation speed and the
motion of the mower.

safety handle
Lever controlling both the blade
rotation and the wheel motion.

accelerator cable
Cable connecting the speed control
to the motor.

starter
Hand-activated device pulling a
cable to start the motor.

grass catcher
Detachable container collecting the
cut grass.

motor
Device converting the combustion of
fuel and air into mechanical energy.

filler cap
Cylindrical part plugging a tank's filler
opening.

deflector
Part deflecting the cut grass toward
the grassbox.

casing
Part supporting and covering a
rotating blade for cutting the grass.

DO-IT-YOURSELF AND GARDENING

lawn care

roller
Tool consisting of a hollow cylinder, filled with water or sand; it is rolled over the soil in order to tamp it down and even it.

lawn aerator
Roller fitted with points for puncturing the lawn in order to aerate it and facilitate the entry of substances such as water and fertilizers.

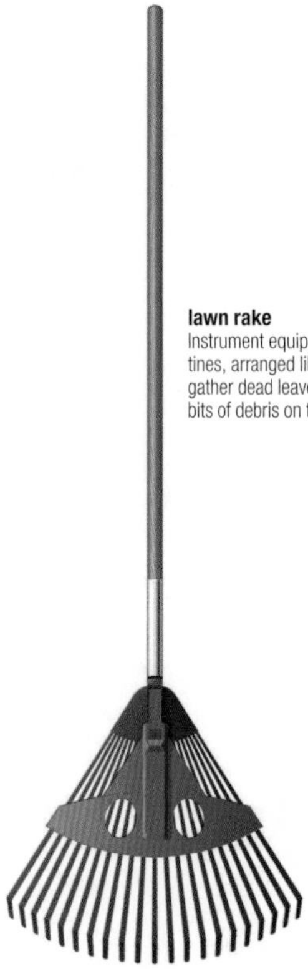

lawn rake
Instrument equipped with flex tines, arranged like a fan, use gather dead leaves, cut grass bits of debris on the lawn.

lawn tractor
Small motorized vehicle upon which a mower deck is fixed, for cutting large expanses of grass.

seat
Part for sitting while operating the vehicle.

ignition key
Part that is inserted into the ignition switch to start or stop the motor.

steering wheel
Circular instrument used by the operator for steering the front wheels.

brake pedal
Lever that the operator presses with the foot to activate the brake system.

mower deck lift lever
Lever for adjusting the mower deck's height.

cruise control lever
Mechanism for selecting the vehicle's speed.

hood
Lidlike part of the body c and protecting the motor.

rear wheel
Circular part rotating around an axle upon which a device rests; in this case, the rear of the vehicle. Its rear wheels are the driving force.

headlight
Lamp on the front of the light up the space in front

forward travel pedal
Lever that is held down to let the vehicle go forward.

reverse travel pedal
Lever that is held down to let the vehicle back up.

deflector
Part projecting the cut grass to the side.

mower deck
Mobile structure supporting and covering one or more rotating blades that cut the grass.

gauge wheel
Small adjustable wheel following the contours of the terrain to give a uniform cut over uneven surfaces.

front wheel
Circular part rotating around an axle upon which a device rests; in this case, the front of the vehicle. Its front wheels guide the lawn tractor.

snow removal tools

Tools used for scooping and moving snow.

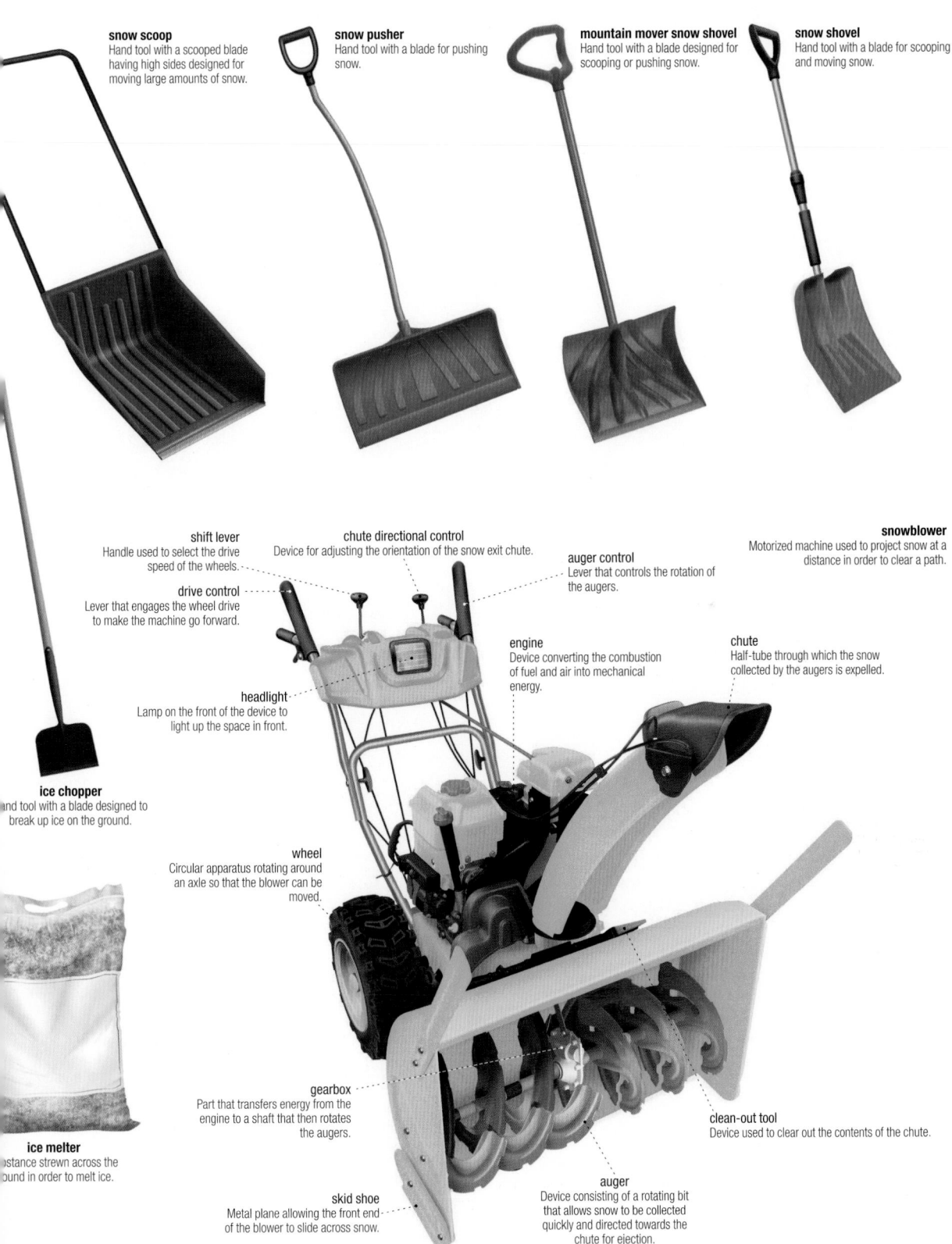

snow scoop
Hand tool with a scooped blade having high sides designed for moving large amounts of snow.

snow pusher
Hand tool with a blade for pushing snow.

mountain mover snow shovel
Hand tool with a blade designed for scooping or pushing snow.

snow shovel
Hand tool with a blade for scooping and moving snow.

DO-IT-YOURSELF AND GARDENING

shift lever
Handle used to select the drive speed of the wheels.

chute directional control
Device for adjusting the orientation of the snow exit chute.

auger control
Lever that controls the rotation of the augers.

snowblower
Motorized machine used to project snow at a distance in order to clear a path.

drive control
Lever that engages the wheel drive to make the machine go forward.

engine
Device converting the combustion of fuel and air into mechanical energy.

chute
Half-tube through which the snow collected by the augers is expelled.

headlight
Lamp on the front of the device to light up the space in front.

ice chopper
Hand tool with a blade designed to break up ice on the ground.

wheel
Circular apparatus rotating around an axle so that the blower can be moved.

gearbox
Part that transfers energy from the engine to a shaft that then rotates the augers.

clean-out tool
Device used to clear out the contents of the chute.

ice melter
Substance strewn across the ground in order to melt ice.

skid shoe
Metal plane allowing the front end of the blower to slide across snow.

auger
Device consisting of a rotating bit that allows snow to be collected quickly and directed towards the chute for ejection.

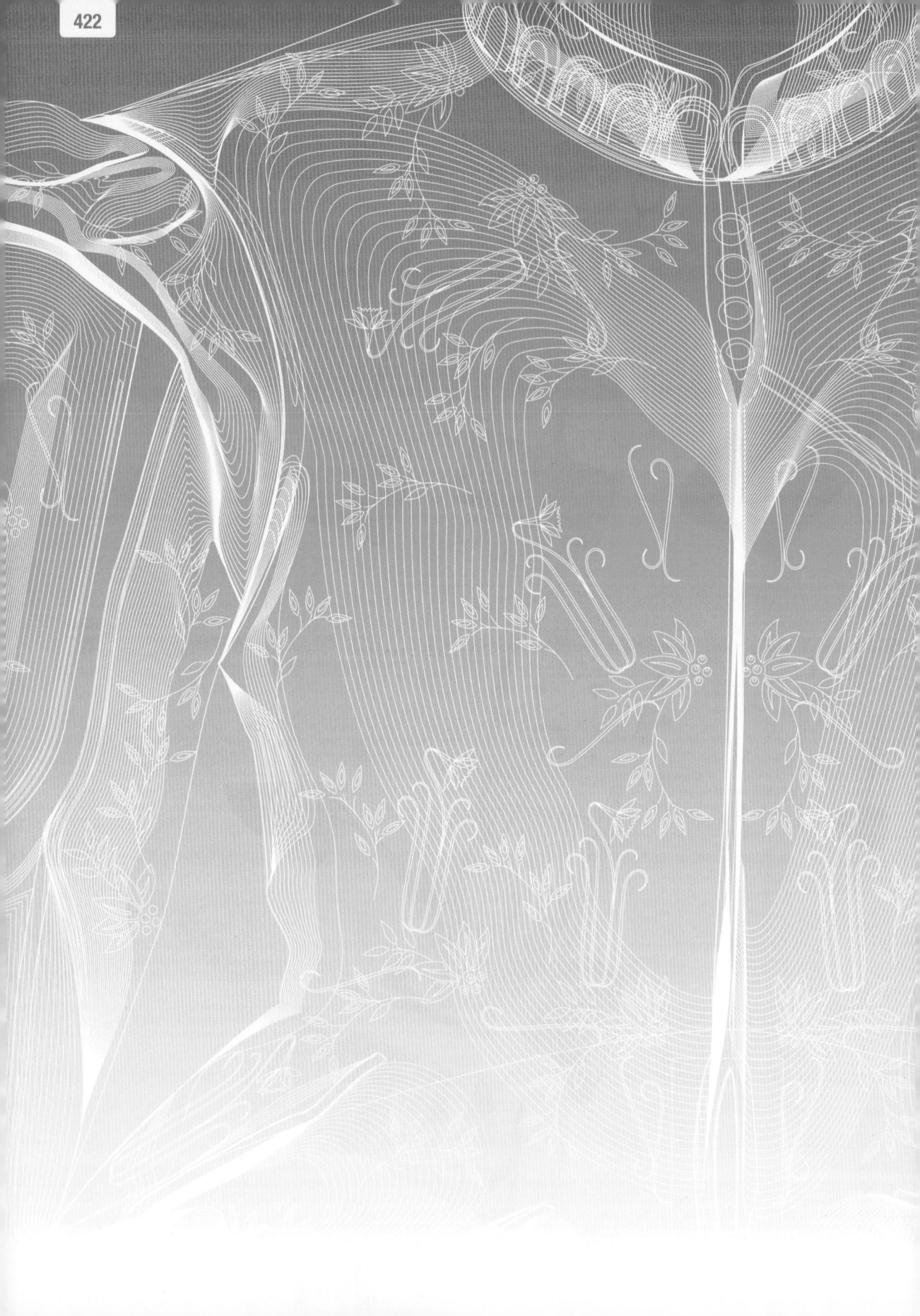

CLOTHING

Any object that covers the body to protect, conceal or adorn it.

fibers

Supple, elongated, threadlike materials used to make textiles.

natural fibers
Fibers of animal or vegetable origin.

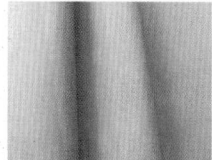

cotton
Fibers from the cotton plant are used to make a soft, comfortable, and easily maintained fabric; the most commonly produced natural fiber in the world.

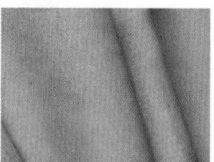

flax
Fibers from the cellulose of the flax plant, which result in a fabric that is light and absorbent, though easily wrinkled.

hemp
Fibers from the cellulose of the h plant. Primarily used in making r

jute
Fibers from the cellulose of the jute plant, which result in a strong and rough fabric often used to make canvas.

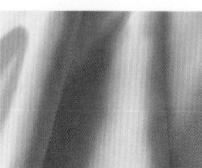

silk
Filament produced by the silkworm as it weaves its cocoon. It results in a fabric that is light, shiny and very soft.

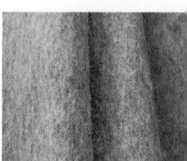

wool
Fiber from the fleece of some animals (goat, sheep, alpaca llama, etc.) that provides good h insulation.

synthetic fibers
Artificially created fibers.

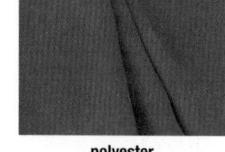

polyester
The most commonly produced synthetic fiber in the world, that results in a strong, comfortable and easily maintained fabric.

viscose
Fiber from which rayon is made.

nylon
Polymer used as a textile fiber. Strong and elastic, it is often used to make stockings, socks or swimsuits.

acrylic fiber
Synthetic fiber produced by polymerization. Results in a soft and shiny fabric.

spandex
Very elastic synthetic fiber, often u in undergarments and sports clotl

woven goods

Soft materials produced by the ordered assembly of woven or knit fibers, used to make items of clothing.

flannel
Lightly fuzzy fabric that is soft to the touch. Often used to make pajamas, nightgowns or bed sheets.

denim
Strong cloth used to make jeans.

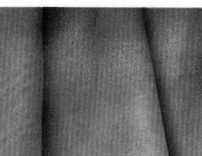

satin
Very glossy and shiny fabric, often used to make undergarments or linings.

serge
Fabric having fine oblique lines, used to make uniforms or suits for men or women.

tulle
Light and transparent mesh fabric. Often used to make specialized costumes (as for ballet dancers) and veils.

velvet
Fabric, very soft to the touch, used to upholster furniture as well as make various items of clothing.

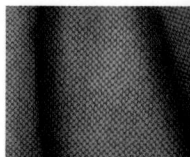

tweed
Fabric usually made of woven wool used to make jackets or suits

CLOTHING

fabric care symbols

Most clothing has labels containing symbols showing the recommended care for the material, based on its specific characteristics.

do not wash

hand wash in lukewarm water

machine wash in lukewarm water at a gentle setting/reduced agitation

machine wash in warm water at a gentle setting/reduced agitation

machine wash in warm water at a normal setting

machine wash in hot water at a normal setting

do not use chlorine bleach

use chlorine bleach as directed

hang to dry

dry flat

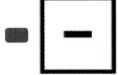 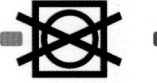

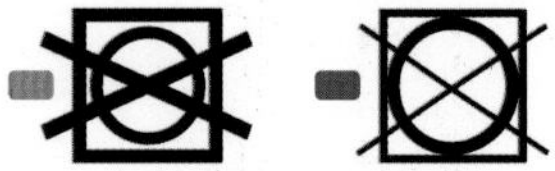

do not tumble dry

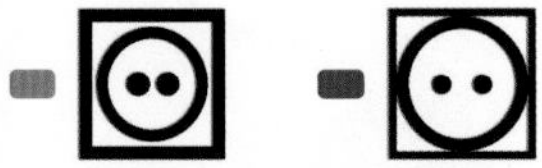

tumble dry at medium temperature

tumble dry at low temperature

drip dry

do not iron

iron at low setting

iron at medium setting

iron at high setting

CLOTHING

 American symbols

European symbols

examples of historical costume

Articles of clothing characteristic of a period, country, condition or occasion.

peplos
In ancient times, a rectangle of
woolen fabric wrapped around the
torso and pinned at the shoulders,
worn by Greek women.

fibula
In ancient times, a pin or metal
fastener used to secure clothing.

fold
Part of the cloth folded over the belt
to make it puff out.

loincloth
Piece of cloth worn around the
loins by Egyptians.

toga
Very long length of woolen fabric that
Romans wrapped around themselves,
draping it over the left shoulder and
arm and leaving the right arm free.

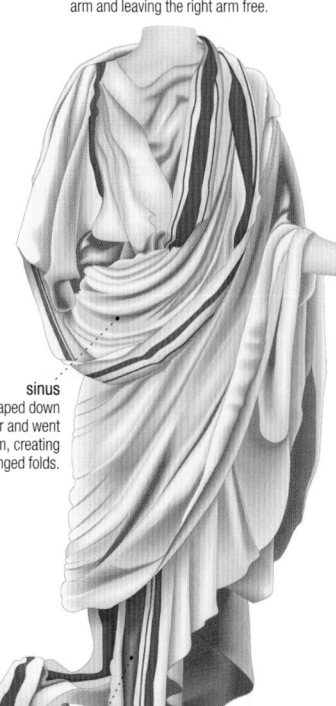

sinus
Part of the toga that draped down
over the left shoulder and went
under the right arm, creating
carefully arranged folds.

purple border
In ancient Rome, the purple border
was worn by magistrates and by
boys until the age of 16.

stola
Long full robe with or without
sleeves and drawn in with a belt; it
was worn by Roman women.

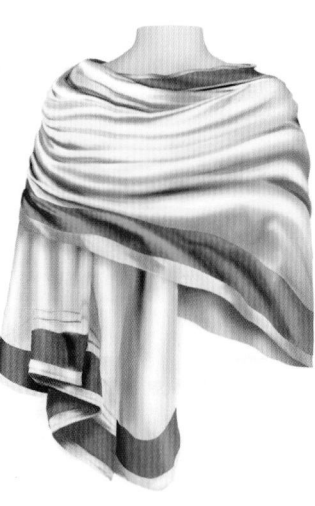

palla
Long rectangular piece of cloth,
folded in half lengthwise and used
as a cloak by Roman women.

chlamys
In ancient times, a rectangle
of woolen fabric pinned on one
shoulder; it was worn by soldiers
next to the skin or over a chiton.

chiton
Tunic worn by Greek men and women i
ancient times, made of two rectangles
linen sewn together to form a tube and
belted at the waist.

examples of historical costume

vertical pocket
Pocket cut along the grain of the fabric.

floating sleeve
Sleeve characterized by a long, sometimes ankle-length panel falling from the elbow.

short sleeve
Half sleeve covering the upper arm and extended by another half sleeve of various shapes.

sleeve
Part of the garment covering the arm; it can be of various shapes and lengths.

fringe
Strip of material with hanging threads used to decorate the border of clothing.

cotehardie
In the 14th century, the cotehardie was a kind of low-cut fitted surcoat with long sleeves left open from the elbow.

farthingale
Bell-shaped petticoat worn in the 16th and 17th centuries, containing rigid hoops that gave a flared shape to the skirt.

dress with crinoline
A 19th-century dress worn over several underskirts, including a full one made of horsehair.

corset
[fit]ting undergarment with stays that [appea]red in the 18th century; women [did] up under their dresses to shape [their w]aists and hold in their stomachs.

underskirt
From the 16th century, the underskirt was a short skirt worn under other skirts; by the late 18th and 19th century, it had become a skirt revealed by an open-fronted dress.

caraco jacket
Close-fitting bodice with sleeves, cut off at the hip and buttoned in front; it appeared in the second half of the 18th century.

ruffle
Funnel-shaped lace cuff with two or three flounces.

stomacher
Decorative triangle worn under the bodice of the dress.

shawl
In fashion since the 19th century, the shawl is a square, rectangular or triangular length of fabric used by women to cover their shoulders.

bustle
Underskirt with a semicircular wire hoop at the back to support the skirt and draw it away from the body.

surcoat
[worn as] a tunic by men and women from the [12th to th]e 15th century; the women's was very [loose wit]h greatly enlarged armholes, which [w]ere often decorated with fur.

dress with panniers
Dress that appeared in the mid-18th century; it was worn over an underskirt with two hoops that made it puff out at the hips.

dress with bustle
Dress that appeared about 1870; it was worn over a bustle; which gave fullness to the back of the skirt.

CLOTHING

examples of historical costume

frock coat costume
Ensemble comprised of breeches, a frock and a waistcoat.

justaucorps
Long garment for men that was close-fitting and slightly flared at the bottom. It was initially worn as a military uniform; after 1670 it became an item of civilian clothing.

frock coat
In the 19th century, a coat with no pockets that was extended by two long panels in the back.

waistcoat
Worn since the end of the 18th century, the waistcoat is tight and sleeveless; the front is buttoned and made of quality material while the back is made of lining.

justaucorps costume
Ensemble comprised of breeches, a justaucorps and a vest.

vest
In the 17th and 18th centuries, the vest was worn under the justaucorps; it hung straight and had two pockets with flaps and tight sleeves.

cape
Very full coat of variable length that covered the body and arms; it had no sleeves or armholes and sometimes had a hood and slits for the arms.

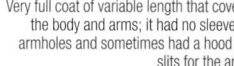

cuff
Reverse side of the sleeve or a strip of material added to the end of a sleeve and folded back.

jacket
Padded and belted male garment worn between the 14th and the 16th centuries, based on the doublet; the belt created folds below the waist and the sleeves widened at the shoulders.

breeches
Tight knee-length pants that appeared in the second half of the 17th century.

breeches
Tight knee-length pants that appeared in the second half of the 17th century.

houppelande
Long full ceremonial garment (man's coat or woman's dress) worn at the end of the 14th century and in the early 15th century.

doublet suit
Ensemble comprised of trunk hose and a doublet.

doublet
Tight padded garment with a belt and sleeves; it was worn by men from the 14th to the 17th century.

wing
Piece of fabric added to the armhole to accentuate the width of the shoulder.

trunk hose
Shorter version of braies and a forerunner of breeches, trunk hose were worn from the 16th to the 17th century; they puffed out and were gathered above the knee.

hanging sleeve
Long sleeve, slashed at the elbow so the arm could extend out of it.

braies
Full pants that were characteristic of Gallic attire; they were pulled in at the waist with a belt and tied at the ankle with straps.

examples of historical costume

gaiter
...er for the top of the shoe and the ...wer part of the leg; it was held in ...ce by an understrap and fastened ... the side with buttons or hooks.

heeled shoe
In the 17th century, the heeled shoe had a large tongue decorated with a bow or a buckle.

clog
Shoe carved from a piece of wood.

tricorne
Men's hat with a brim folded into three points and a relatively flat crown; it was worn in the 17th and 18th centuries.

bicorne
Men's hat with a brim folded into two points; it replaced the tricorne after the French Revolution.

crakow
Shoe characterized by a disproportionately long toe; it was in fashion from the end of the 14th through the 15th century.

collaret
Piece of delicate, pleated or gathered fabric that adorned the neck of a dress; its shape varied greatly from one period to another.

fraise
Stiff pleated collaret worn by men and women from the late 16th century to the beginning of the 17th century.

hennin
In the 15th century, a high cylindrical women's headdress that was covered in expensive fabric; a transparent veil of medium length hung from it.

examples of traditional clothing

Clothing that has characterized different regions for a number of generations.

fez
Skullcap of white or red woolen fabric, usually bearing a tassel; it has long been the traditional Turkish headgear.

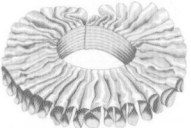

hijab
Scarf worn on the head by Muslim women.

turban
Headgear worn by men in the eastern Mediterranean region and southern Asia and made from a strip of fabric encircling the head.

sarong
Piece of fabric or woven plant fibers that is worn around the waist by certain peoples of South America, Africa and Oceania.

boubou
...rment made from a length ...: folded in two; it is worn by ...African men and women.

caftan
Long full garment, often richly decorated; it is worn by men as ceremonial attire in the eastern Mediterranean region.

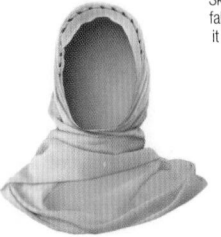

yarmulke
Small round cap covering the top of the head, worn by religious Jews.

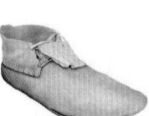

moccasin
Native American shoe with no laces. Flat and very supple, characterized by a flap covering the instep.

kimono
Long-sleeved robe of Japanese origin, worn crossed in front and held closed with a belt.

cheongsam
Chinese gown consisting of one single piece and having a split collar.

sombrero
Wide-brimmed hat worn in some Spanish-speaking countries.

sari
Long strip of fabric traditionally worn by Indian women.

jackets

Sleeved garments that are open at the front and fall to the hips; they are worn over a shirt, vest, sweater, etc. The top part of a suit is called a suit jacket.

double-breasted jacket
Jacket where the front panels overlap when closed; it has a vertical double line of buttons.

collar
Piece sewn onto a garment that finishes or adorns the neck.

peaked lapel
Lapel forming a very small angle where it meets the collar.

lining
Soft fabric cut from the same pattern as the garment inside which it is sewn; it gives body to the garment, embellishes it, hides its seams and makes it warmer.

breast welt pocket
Small decorative pocket to the left of the jacket's lapel where the pocket handkerchief is placed.

double-breasted jacket: back
Jacket where the front panels overlap when closed; it has a vertical double line of buttons.

side back vent
Vertical opening with overlapping edges on each side of the back of the jacket, giving it fullness.

sleeve
Part of the garment covering the arm; it can be of various shapes and lengths.

outside ticket pocket
Small pocket placed at waist level above the jacket's right pocket or sometimes inside the lining on the left side.

patch pocket
Pocket of various shapes and sizes, made of a piece of material sewn onto the garment's outer surface.

flap
Piece of fabric or other material that hangs from the top of a pocket opening to hide it.

vest
Short garment worn over a shirt and under a jacket; it is sleeveless, buttons up the front and has a deep V-neck. The back is made out of lining material.

V-neck
Plunging part of the garment, end the neck and forming a V over the

lining
Soft fabric cut from the same pa the garment inside which it is se gives body to the garment, emb it, hides its seams and makes it warmer.

welt
Narrow strip of material tha attached to the garment or sides and decorates the po opening.

front
Part of the vest that covers the torso.

seam
Decorative set of stitches jo two pieces of a garment, g distinctive line.

single-breasted jacket
Jacket that is neither close-fitting nor flared.

welt pocket
Pocket where the opening is a slit cut into the garment, edged with a welt.

lining
Soft fabric cut from the same pattern as the garment inside which it is sewn; it gives body to the garment, embellishes it, hides its seams and makes it warmer.

adjustable waist tab
Tape used to tighten a garment around the waist by means of a buckle sewn onto the garment or onto another tab.

notch
Angle formed where the collar and the lapel meet.

single-breasted jacket: back
Jacket that is neither close-fitting nor flared.

lapel
Part of the garment turned down over the chest, extending the collar.

pocket handkerchief
Small delicate handkerchief that adorns the upper pocket of a jacket.

front
Part of the jacket covering the front of the torso.

sleeve
Part of the garment covering the arm; it can be of various shapes and lengths.

back
Part of the jacket covering the back of the torso.

flap pocket
Pocket cut into the garment with a flap that can be tucked inside the pocket or worn outside.

center back vent
Vertical opening with overlapping edges at the bottom of the jacket; it extends the center seam at the back, giving the jacket fullness.

CLOTHING

shirt

Garment covering the torso with a collar, a yoke at the back, shirttails and buttons down the front.

parts of a shirt

mples of collars
ar: piece sewn onto a garment
finishes or adorns the neck.

button-down collar
whose points are buttoned to the
shirtfront.

spread collar
ar whose points are spread far
apart.

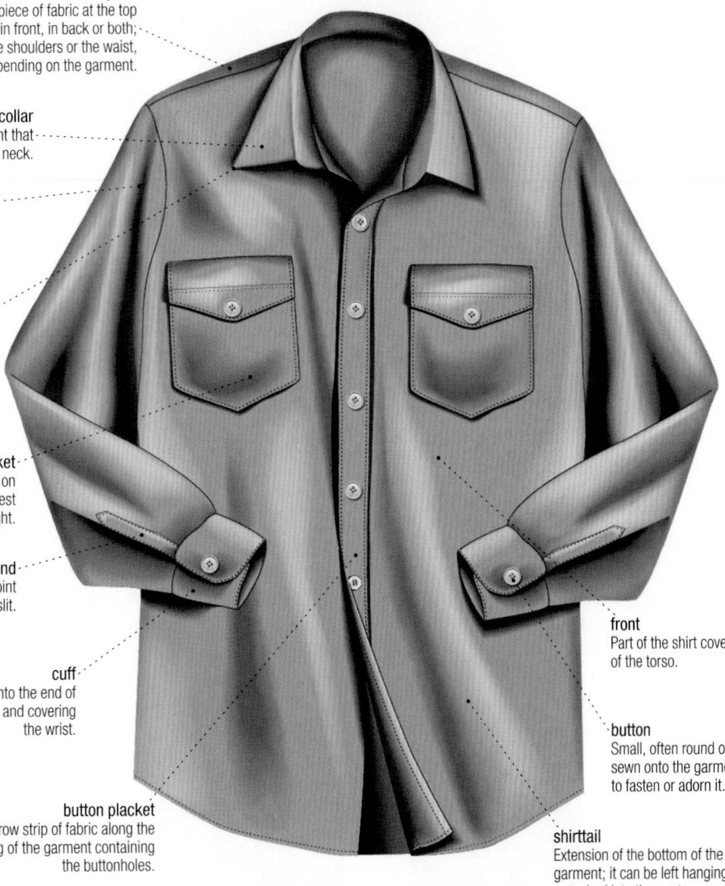

yoke
Variably shaped piece of fabric at the top
of the garment, in front, in back or both;
it begins at the shoulders or the waist,
depending on the garment.

collar
Piece sewn onto a garment that
finishes or adorns the neck.

set-in sleeve
Sleeve cut separately from the
garment and sewn to the armhole.

collar point
Somewhat pointed tip of the collar.

breast pocket
Pocket of various styles usually on
the side of the garment at chest
height.

pointed tab end
Narrow strip of fabric ending in a point
and adorning the sleeve slit.

cuff
Strip of fabric sewn onto the end of
the sleeve tightening it and covering
the wrist.

button placket
Narrow strip of fabric along the
opening of the garment containing
the buttonholes.

front
Part of the shirt covering the front
of the torso.

button
Small, often round object that is
sewn onto the garment and is used
to fasten or adorn it.

shirttail
Extension of the bottom of the
garment; it can be left hanging out
or tucked into the pants.

CLOTHING

accessories
Pieces of fabric used to decorate
a shirt.

ascot tie
Wide necktie with pleats that narrow the part
that goes around the neck; it is knotted loosely
and worn inside the open collar of a shirt.

bow tie
Short necktie consisting of a knot
at the center and a wing on each
side of it.

necktie
Long narrow strip of fabric placed
under the shirt collar and knotted; the
front apron, usually wider than the rear
one, makes the shirt more attractive.

front apron
Wider apron that makes the
shirtfront more attractive.

neck end
Part of the necktie that goes around
the neck, under the collar.

rear apron
Narrower apron that is threaded
through the loop to keep it behind
the front apron.

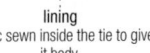

lining
ric sewn inside the tie to give
it body.

keeper
Flat ring behind the front apron that
the rear apron passes through to
hold it in place.

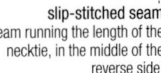

slip-stitched seam
Seam running the length of the
necktie, in the middle of the
reverse side.

pants

Garment for the lower body; it extends from the waist or the hips to the ankles, covering each leg separately.

parts of pants

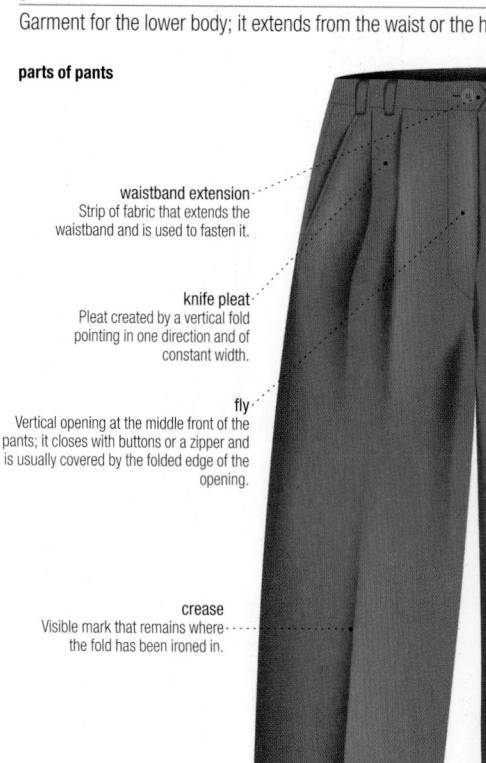

waistband extension
Strip of fabric that extends the waistband and is used to fasten it.

knife pleat
Pleat created by a vertical fold pointing in one direction and of constant width.

fly
Vertical opening at the middle front of the pants; it closes with buttons or a zipper and is usually covered by the folded edge of the opening.

crease
Visible mark that remains where the fold has been ironed in.

cuff
Folded end of the pant leg.

belt loop
Thin vertical strip of material sewn at the waist of pants; a belt passes through it to hold the pants in place.

front top pocket
Front pants pocket that is often curved or diagonal; the opening is cut into the garment or is hidden inside a seam.

waistband
Strip of fabric sewn at the waist of pants forming a hem and holding them in place.

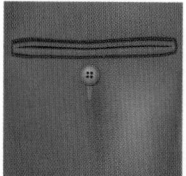

back pocket
Pocket of various kinds in the back of the pants.

suspenders
Narrow straps of adjustable length that are often elasticized; they cross in the back, go over the shoulders and fasten to the pants to keep them in place.

elastic webbing
Narrow strip of stretchable sturdy material.

adjustment slide
Flat ring attached to the elastic strap; it can be moved up or down to adjust the length.

leather end
Usually leather strip used to button the elastic strap to the pants.

button loop
Small slit in a garment through which a button is pushed.

suspender clip
Fastening system made up of two hinged tabs; it can replace the leather end on suspenders.

belt
Strap made of various materials often with a buckle; it is worn around the waist to adjust the fit of a garment, hold it in place or adorn it.

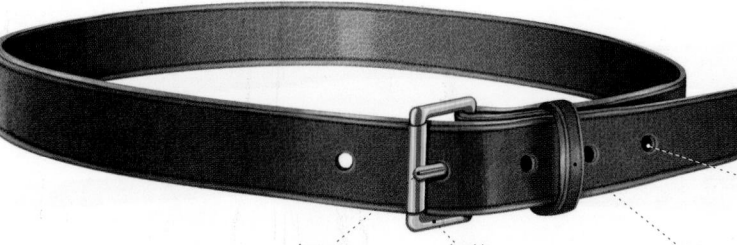

panel
Smooth side of a piece of leather.

tip
End of the belt that passes through the buckle.

punch hole
Perforation in the belt through which the tongue passes.

tongue
Metal tip that pivots on the buckle's axis and fits into a hole, buckling the belt.

buckle
Fastener made up of a ring that secures the two ends of a belt.

belt loop
Flat ring next to the buckle usually made of the same material as the belt; one end of the belt passes through it.

pants

examples of pants
Pants: garment for the lower body, covering each leg separately.

Bermuda shorts
Long shorts ending above the knee.

knickers
Pants with full legs that are gathered below the knee or at the calf.

jeans
nts made of durable, usually blue bric with topstitched seams and ockets that are often reinforced by rivets.

convertible pants
Long pants that can be converted to Bermuda shorts by removing the lower portion attached by a zipper.

shorts
Very short pants covering only the top of the thighs.

sock

Kind of sock ending at calf level.

examples of socks
Sock: knitted garment that covers the foot and part of the leg.

ts of a sock

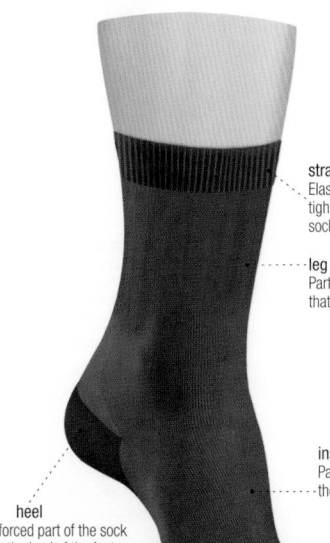

straight-up ribbed top
Elasticized knitted strip that tightens, reinforces and adorns the sock opening.

leg
Part of the sock of varying length that extends above the foot.

instep
Part of the sock that covers the top of the foot.

heel
reinforced part of the sock vers the heel of the foot.

sole
ly reinforced part of the sock at covers the sole of the foot.

toe
Usually reinforced part of the sock that covers the toes of the foot.

executive length
Sock covering the foot and extending to the knee.

ankle length
Sock that covers the foot and extends slightly above the ankle.

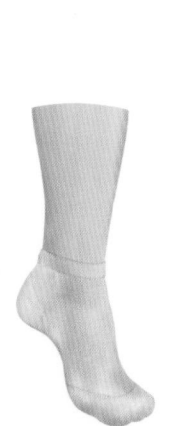

anklet
Light short sock covering only the foot and the ankle.

mid-calf length
Kind of sock ending at calf level.

underwear

Garments worn next to the skin and under other garments.

athletic shirt
Sleeveless tight-fitting undergarment with a very wide neck and armholes.

neckhole
Somewhat low part of the garment that goes around the neck.

armhole
Opening in the garment for the arm or for fitting a sleeve into.

briefs
Short legless undergarment with elastic at the waist and thighs and a fly.

waistband
Strip of elasticized material fitting snugly over the hips to hold the garment in place.

fly
Opening in the front of the briefs.

union suit
Warm undergarment that buttons up the front and combines a long-sleeved undershirt and long drawers.

elasticized leg opening
Opening that is edged with elastic so it fits snugly around the thigh.

crotch
Part of the briefs that goes between the legs.

drawers
Undergarment covering the legs; it has a waistband and is gathered at the ankles with fine ribbing.

bikini briefs
Snug-fitting briefs, low-cut on the hips and high-cut on the thighs.

boxer shorts
Undergarment covering the tops of the thighs and held in place by an elasticized waistband.

coats

Outerwear that is fastened in front; coats are worn over other garments to protect against the cold and inclement weather.

raincoat
Coat, sometimes with a hood, that keeps the rain off because of the kind of material used to make it or because it has been waterproofed.

collar
wn onto the garment that
shes or adorns the neck.

raglan sleeve
ending over the shoulder
hed front and back with a
seam running from under
the armhole to the neck.

notched lapel
orming an angle where it
meets the collar.

tab
w strip of fabric attached
ntally to the sleeve end to
embellish it.

broad welt side pocket
ket; the outer edge of the
opening has a wide welt.

buttonhole
slit in a garment through
which a button is pushed.

side panel
ion of the coat that is left
hanging loose.

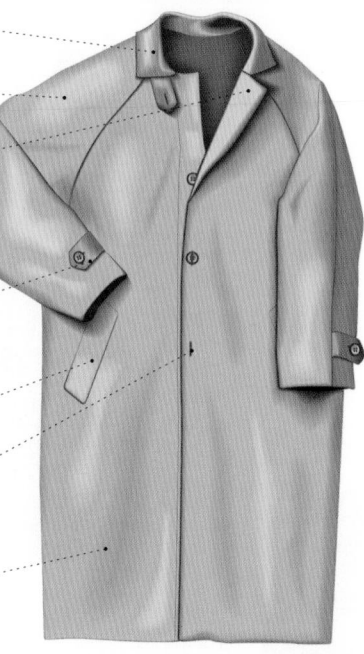

overcoat
Coat ending below the knee and made of heavy fabric, fur or leather.

notched lapel
Lapel forming an angle where it meets the collar.

breast pocket
Pocket of various styles usually on the side of the garment at chest height.

breast dart
Pleat that is narrower at the bottom than at the top; it is sewn into the reverse side of the fabric to reduce fullness around the waist.

flap pocket
Pocket whose opening is covered by a piece of fabric hanging from the top of it.

trench coat
Raincoat characterized by double-breasted buttoning, a belt, gun flaps, a collar with lapels, large pockets and tabs on the sleeves and shoulders.

two-way collar
Collar designed to be worn in
various ways.

gun flap
oose front and back yoke used
s a decorative element and as
otection against wind and rain.

double-breasted buttoning
tening system made up of two
parallel rows of buttons.

belt
ap made of various materials,
with a frame; it is worn around
he waist to adjust the fit of the
ent, hold it in place or adorn it.

belt loop
r ring next to the frame usually
de of the same material as the
elt; one end of the belt passes
through it.

frame
astener made up of a ring that
ecures the two ends of a belt.

epaulet
Decorative tab attached to the shoulder and sometimes buttoned down; it is inspired by the military uniform.

raglan sleeve
Sleeve extending over the shoulder and attached front and back with a slanted seam running from under the armhole to the neck.

sleeve strap loop
Thin strip of material attached vertically to the sleeve; the sleeve strap threads through it to hold it in place.

sleeve strap
Narrow strip of fabric that is sewn horizontally at the bottom of the sleeve to make it less full.

broad welt side pocket
Angled pocket; the outer edge of the opening has a wide welt.

three-quarter coat
Coat ending above the knee and made of quality fabric, fur or leather, with double-breasted buttoning and outside pockets.

coats

parka
Sporty waterproof coat that is often padded or fleece-lined; it has big pockets, a front zipper and sometimes a hood.

snap-fastening tab
Strip of material that borders the front opening of the garment, closing with a row of snap fasteners.

zipper
Closure made up of two lengths of tape edged with teeth that interlock by means of a slide.

sheepskin jacket
Three-quarter coat that crosses over in front and has a belt and patch flap pockets; it is usually made of waterproof fabric, leather or suede, with a lining and a wide collar made of sheepskin.

duffle coat
Hooded casual coat ending at mid-thigh and made of heavy woolen fabric; it is characterized by a yoke and frog closures.

hood
Headgear attached at the garment's neck that can be pulled over the head as protection against cold, rain and snow.

yoke
Variably shaped piece of fabric at the top of the garment, in front, in back or both; it begins at the shoulders or the waist, depending on the garment.

frog
Ornamental loops of braided fabric used to fasten the garment; one serves as the buttonhole and the toggle of the other one passes through it.

patch pocket
Pocket whose opening is covered by a piece of fabric hanging from the top of it.

toggle fastening
Wooden button in the shape of a small log.

jacket
Full jacket ending at the waist, where it is gathered so that it puffs out; it is often made of leather or waterproof material and has cuffed sleeves.

snap fastener
Fastening mechanism made of a socket disk and a ball disk that snap shut when pressed together.

hand-warmer pocket
Pocket in the front of the garment above the waist where the hand can be tucked to protect it against the cold and to rest the arm.

elastic waistband
Strip of elasticized fabric that fits snugly around the waist to hold the garment in place.

windbreaker
Jacket ending below the waist and made of leather or waterproof material.

waistband
Hem at the bottom of the garment that finishes it and encases the drawstring, which adjusts the garment around the hips.

drawstring
Thin string that is threaded inside the waistband and adjusts the windbreaker around the hips.

sweaters

Garments covering the torso and manufactured by hand or by machine from fabric with varying tightness of weave.

V-neck cardigan
Woolen sweater ending at the hips and characterized by front buttons, a V-neck and ribbing at the bottom and wrists.

hanger loop
Small strap attached to the inside of the garment at the neck and used to hang it.

V-neck
Plunging part of the garment encircling the neck and forming a V over the chest.

button
Small, often round object that is sewn onto the garment and is used to fasten or adorn it.

ribbing
Tight elastic knitted strip around the sleeve and the bottom of the garment for tightening, reinforcing and adorning them.

welt pocket
Pocket whose opening is adorned and reinforced by one or two thin strips.

buttoned placket
Narrow strip of fabric edging the opening of a knit shirt and containing several buttonholes.

sweater vest
Sleeveless sweater usually with a wide neck and armholes, intended for wearing over another garment.

knit shirt
Usually short-sleeved sweater that has a pointed turned-down collar; it is often fastened with a placket ending at mid-chest.

crewneck
Sweater with a close-fitting rounded neck.

turtleneck
Sweater with a high close-fitting neck made of ribbing that is folded down; it usually has no fastener.

cardigan
Fine long-sleeved sweater ending at the hips and characterized by front buttoning, a round neck and a ribbed bottom and wrists.

CLOTHING

dresses

Garments made up of a bodice with or without sleeves or a collar and extending into a skirt of variable length.

sheath dress
Unbelted, very tight form-fitting dress.

princess dress
Unbelted dress with a fitted bodice and a full or straight skirt whose cut accentuates the figure.

coat dress
Dress cut like a coat; it fastens all the way up the front and might be lined.

shift dress
Sleeveless dress with no waist, having a relatively high neckline and no collar.

cocktail dress
Short semiformal dress that bares the arms and often the shoulders.

shirtwaist dress
Dress with a bodice that resembles a man's shirt; it usually has a belt and buttons all the way up the front.

drop waist dress
Dress with its waist at hip level.

trapeze dress
Unbelted dress with an increasingly flared skirt that hangs from a tight bodice.

sundress
Very low-cut dress with slim straps, which leave the back and shoulders uncovered.

wraparound dress
Dress that is open from top to bottom; it is fastened by folding one side over the other and holding them in place with a belt.

tunic dress
Two-piece dress made up of a quite long straight skirt and a straight bodice that hangs down over the skirt, sometimes to the knees.

jumper
Sleeveless dress with a very low-cut neckline and armholes; it is worn over a blouse or a sweater.

skirts

Garments held in place by an inner waistband or a belt that goes around the waist; the length of the garment varies.

ruffled skirt
Skirt made up of several horizontal strips of material in superimposed layers; the free edge falls loose, creating folds.

culottes
Garment with a crotch that is hidden by its full folds thus resembling a skirt.

yoke skirt
Skirt with a fitted or shaped piece added on, forming the part from the waist to the hips.

gather skirt
Skirt that is gathered at the waist and falls in wide folds.

pencil skirt
Skirt that is narrow at the waist and fits tightly over the hips and legs.

skort
Wide shorts covered by a flap in the front which makes them resemble a skirt.

straight skirt
Skirt that is narrow at the waist, tight-fitting over the hips and falls straight.

gored skirt
Flared skirt made up of several panels of fabric sewn vertically.

kilt
Pleated wraparound skirt made of tartan; a usually narrow panel crosses over in front and fastens with a pin or a button.

sarong
Beach skirt of variable length and made from a piece of fabric wrapped around the waist.

wraparound skirt
Skirt made up of a single panel crossing over in front or sometimes behind and buttoning on the side.

CLOTHING

tops

Women's garments covering the torso and worn directly over underwear; there are many different varieties made of all kinds of fabric.

body shirt
Tight-fitting blouse in stretchy fabric and ending in a bikini bottom.

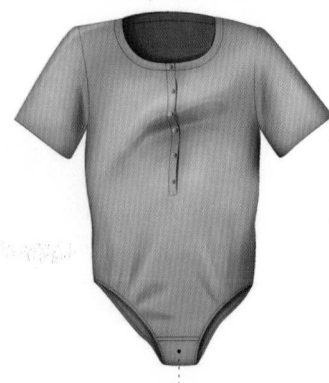

middy
Straight full blouse with a sailor collar and no front opening, ending at the hips.

camisole
A light piece of clothing with thin straps that is often worn alone or under a blouse.

crotch piece
Part of the bikini that goes between the legs; it can sometimes be unfastened so the blouse can be put on over the head.

gather
Small narrow pleat made by drawing thread through the fabric; it is not ironed or sewn down.

yoke
Variably shaped piece of fabric at the top of the garment, in front, in back or both; it begins at the shoulders or the waist, depending on the garment.

classic blouse
Front-buttoning blouse with a collar and long sleeves; it is gathered at the wrists and ends at the hips.

smock
Long unfitted blouse made of soft lightweight material; it is often buttoned in the back and is usually worn over other garments to protect them.

mini shirtdress
Full shirt-blouse ending at mid-thigh and usually worn over a skirt or pants; it has a side slit and rounded shirttails.

tunic
Straight full blouse ending below the waist.

wrapover top
Blouse with two front panels that cross over one another, creating a V-neck; it has ties that fasten at the waist, back or hip.

polo shirt
Usually short-sleeved shirt that has a pointed turned-down collar; it is often fastened with a placket ending at mid-chest.

overblouse
Straight long-sleeved tunic that is often put on over the head; it is gathered by belt or a tie at the waist and hangs over a skirt or pants.

pants

Garment for the lower body, covering each leg separately.

knickers
with full legs that are gathered
below the knee or at the calf.

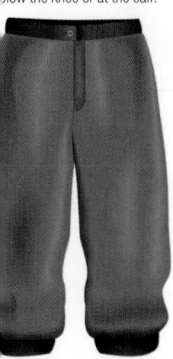

pedal pushers
Tight-fitting pants ending at mid-calf
and having a slit on the outside of
the leg at the knee, which can be
fastened in various ways.

Bermuda shorts
Long shorts ending above the knee.

shorts
Very short pants covering only the
top of the thighs.

ski pants
Generally stretchy pants with legs
that narrow toward the ankle,
ending in an footstrap.

footstrap
Strip of elasticized fabric that
goes under the foot to keep the
pants stretched tight.

jeans
Pants made of durable, usually blue
fabric with topstitched seams and
pockets that are often reinforced
by rivets.

overalls
Pants with shoulder straps and a
piece that covers the chest.

jumpsuit
One-piece garment consisting of
a blouse or shirt with attached
trousers or shorts.

bell bottoms
are tight-fitting to the knee then flare
out and end at the ankle.

cargo pants
Loose-fitting pants with pockets
on the legs.

capri pants
Close-fitting pants that end at
mid-calf.

slim slacks
Pants tailored close to the leg from
hip to ankle.

CLOTHING

jackets, vest and sweaters

Examples of garments covering the chest; they are worn over other garments as protection against the cold or as an accessory.

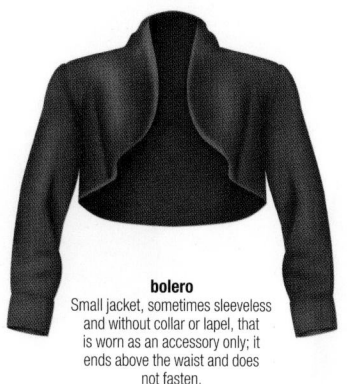

bolero
Small jacket, sometimes sleeveless and without collar or lapel, that is worn as an accessory only; it ends above the waist and does not fasten.

safari jacket
Lightweight long-sleeved shirt-jacket made of plain weave and having a belt and four pockets.

gusset pocket
Patch pocket made fuller by an expandable bottom and sides or by an inverted or round pleat in the middle of the pocket.

spencer
Tight-fitting unbelted jacket ending at the waist; it has long sleeves and often a collar with lapels.

cardigan
Fine long-sleeved sweater ending at the hips and characterized by front buttoning, a round neck and a ribbed bottom and wrists.

crew neck sweater
Sweater with a close-fitting rounded neck.

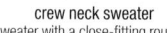

twinset
Outfit made up of a sweater, often crewneck, and a matching cardigan or vest.

pullover
Long-sleeved knit garment usually with a crew neck or V-neck, narrowed around the wrists and waist with ribbed trimming.

vest
Short garment worn over a shirt and under a jacket; it is sleeveless, buttons up the front and has a deep V-neck. The back is made out of lining material.

blazer
Often navy-blue, hip-length jacket characterized by a notched collar, long wide lapels and patch pockets.

coats

Outerwear that is fastened in front and extends at least to the hips; coats are worn over other garments as protection against cold and inclement weather.

topcoat
Coat fitted at the waist and flared at the bottom.

parka
Sporty waterproof coat that is often padded or fleece-lined; it has big pockets, a front zipper and sometimes a hood.

duffle coat
Hooded casual coat ending at mid-thigh and made of heavy woolen fabric; it is characterized by a yoke and frog closures.

hood
Headgear attached at the garment's neck that can be pulled over the head as protection against cold, rain and snow.

zipper
Closure made up of two lengths of tape edged with teeth that interlock by means of a slide.

suit
Outfit made up of a skirt or pants and a long-sleeved jacket made from the same high-quality fabric.

jacket
Garment with sleeves that extends to the hips; it is fastened in front with single- or double-breasted buttoning and sometimes has a belt.

skirt
Garment held in place by an inner waistband or a belt that goes around the waist; the length of the garment varies.

raglan
Somewhat full coat characterized by raglan sleeves and broad welt side pockets.

raglan sleeve
Sleeve extending over the shoulder and attached front and back with a slanted seam running from under the armhole to the neck.

fly front closing
Fastening covered by a placket and consisting of a row of buttons, which are held in place by buttonholes.

broad welt side pocket
Angled pocket; the outer edge of the opening has a wide welt.

jacket
Garment with sleeves that extends to the hips; it is fastened in front with single- or double-breasted buttoning and sometimes has a belt.

pea jacket
Long jacket made of heavy fabric and characterized by double-breasted buttoning, a tailored collar and hand-warmer pockets.

tailored collar
Collar whose fold covers the back of the neck; its lapels form a V where they cross on the chest.

poncho
Cape made from a rectangular piece of material with a hole in the middle for the head to go through.

car coat
Coat loosely based on a man's three-quarter coat but changing more often to reflect the current style; it is shorter than the garment it covers and together they can make an outfit.

hand-warmer pocket
Pocket in the front of the garment above the waist where the hand can be tucked to protect it against the cold and to rest the arm.

mock pocket
Decoration (placket, flap or welt) that simulates a pocket.

overcoat
Long-sleeved article of outerwear made of heavy fabric; it extends to the calf and closes in front with various fastening systems.

pelerine
Coat with a short pelerine.

pelerine
Cape covering the shoulders and chest.

seam pocket
Pocket where the opening is in a side seam of the garment.

cape
Very full coat of variable length that covers the body and arms; it has no sleeves or armholes and sometimes has a hood and slits for the arms.

arm slit
Lateral slit through which the arm can be slipped to give it some freedom of movement.

underwear

Garments worn next to the skin and under other garments.

corselette
Support undergarment combining a
girdle and a bra.

camisole
Short undergarment with an open neck
and shoulder straps; the part covering
the chest can be shaped like a bra.

teddy
Garment combining a camisole and briefs.

bodysuit
Garment combining a bodice and briefs
in a single garment.

panty corselette
Undergarment combining a girdle, a
bra and briefs.

princess seaming
Decorative seam running from the
shoulder or the armhole to the
garment's hem, accentuating the
figure.

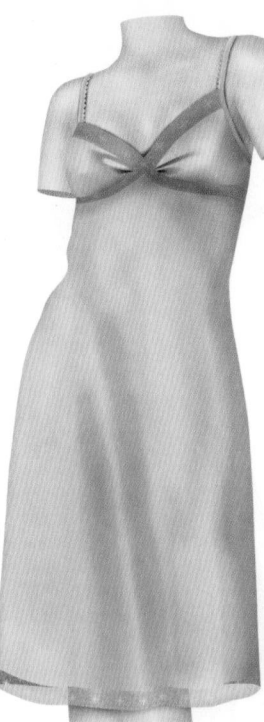

half-slip
Undergarment made up of a
lightweight skirt and an elasticized
waist, substituting for lining.

foundation slip
Undergarment with wide
nonadjustable shoulder straps,
worn under a see-through dress.

slip
Undergarment with narrow adjustable
shoulder straps; the part covering the
chest is usually shaped like a bra.

wasp-waisted corset
Small corset made up of a bra and garter belt, slimming the figure.

underwire
Rigid crescent that edges and reinforces the underside of the cups.

steel
Narrow flexible strip of metal or plastic inserted into a garment to keep it stiff.

bikini
Low-waisted tight-fitting undergarment with high-cut legs.

garter
Elastic strap attached to a girdle, garter belt, etc., with a system for fastening the hose and keeping it taut.

hose
Relatively light knitted women's garment covering the foot and the leg up to the thigh.

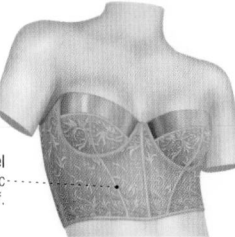

strapless bra
Bra without shoulder straps and with a midriff band that extends to the waist; the cups are preshaped and have underwires and steels.

push-up bra
Bra with cups that leave the upper chest bare and with shoulder straps that sit on the outer edge of the shoulder.

bra
Undergarment made up of cups, shoulder straps and a midriff band, designed to support the chest.

shoulder strap
Narrow strip of fabric that is often adjustable; it goes over the shoulder to connect a garment's front and back.

cup
Main part of the bra that covers and supports the breast.

midriff band
Strip of stretchable fabric connecting the cups; it varies in width and fastens with hooks.

CLOTHING

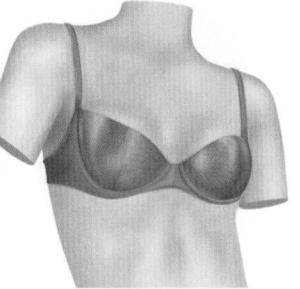

décolleté bra
Very low-cut bra with cups that extend upward toward the shoulder straps.

panel
Foundation piece that flattens the stomach.

girdle
Elasticized undergarment with a stomach panel; it is designed to shape the waist and hips.

briefs
Undergarment that extends fairly low over the hips and is held in place by an elasticized waist.

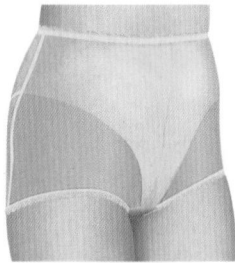

panty girdle
Girdle usually made up of briefs, with or without legs, and removable garters.

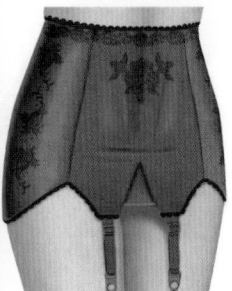

corset
...rdy undergarment with steels and often garters; it is designed to shape the waist and hips.

garter belt
Narrow belt with garters that fastens around the hips.

G-string
Undergarment made up of a piece of fabric covering the pubic area, held up by strings.

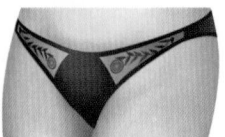

tanga
Undergarment made of a piece of fabric that reveals a portion of the buttocks. It is less revealing than the G-string.

hose

Garments of various stretchy fabrics used to cover the foot and leg; each pair of hose has a different name, depending on its length.

CLOTHING

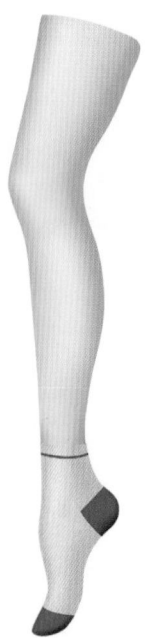

short sock
Light short sock covering only the foot and the ankle.

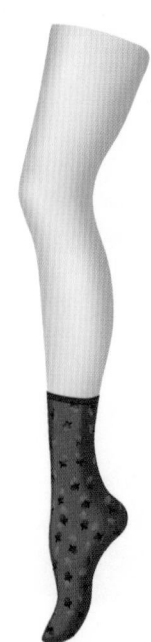

anklet
Sock that covers the foot and extends slightly above the ankle.

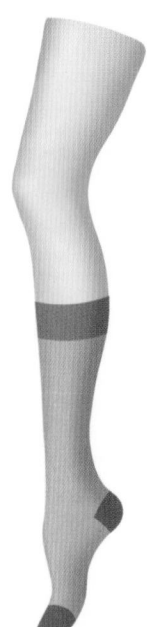

sock
Sock covering the leg to just below the knee.

knee-high sock
Sock covering the foot and extending to the knee.

net stocking
Stocking made of stretchable mesh.

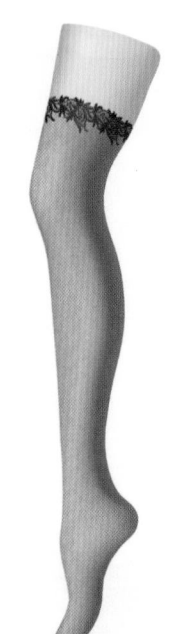

thigh-high stocking
Stocking ending a little above the knee.

stocking
Relatively light knitted women's garment covering the foot and the leg up to the thigh.

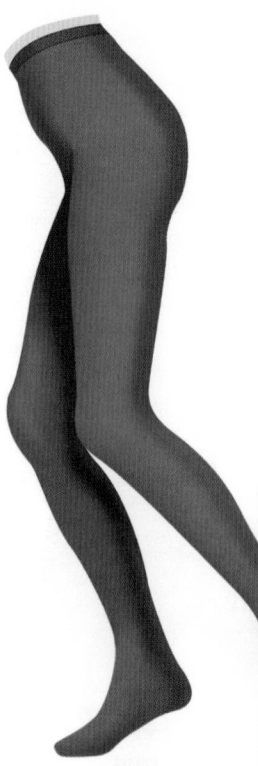

panty hose
Garment made up of two stockings joined by a pair of briefs, sometimes reinforced and held in place by an elasticized waist.

nightclothes

Articles for indoor wear, some of which are worn for sleeping.

bathrobe
Full straight garment with a belt; it is usually made of terry cloth and is worn after a bath or a shower.

nightgown
Long wide full dress, often with shoulder straps, worn next to the skin.

baby doll
Short nightgown that ends at the top of the thighs and is worn with matching briefs.

pajamas
Light full outfit made up of a jacket or tunic and pants with an elasticized or drawstring waist.

negligee
Light elegant women's garment, usually long and décolleté with soft lines; it often comes with a nightgown of the same fabric.

infants' and children's clothing

Garments worn by children from birth to about 12 years of age.

jumpsuit
Low-cut one-piece sleeveless garment with legs and feet.

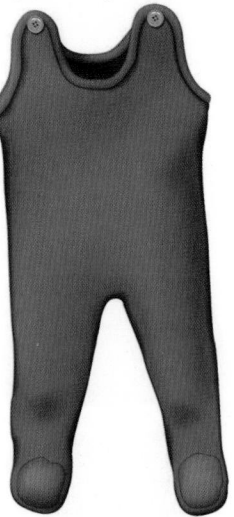

newborn hat
Stretchy headpiece worn by babies to protect their heads from cold.

hood
Part of the garment that is pulled over the head.

false tuck
Strip of material designed to hide a garment's seam or decorate its edge.

bathing wrap
Absorbent piece of fabric with a hood at one corner; it is wrapped around a baby when it comes out of the bath.

bodysuit
One-piece garment for young children, the bottom part of which opens with snaps to facilitate diaper changing.

bootees
Soft-soled pieces of clothing covering the feet.

mittens
Pieces of clothing that cover the hands.

high-back overalls
Pants extended by a front piece covering the chest and another covering the back, connected with shoulder straps.

bunting bag
Hooded coat with a front zipper; it is sewn closed at the bottom and sometimes has no armholes.

adjustable strap
Strip of adjustable fabric that goes over the shoulder to connect a garment's front and back.

bib
Upper part of the overalls, covering the chest from the waist up.

sleepers
Infant nightwear that fastens all the way up the front with snap fasteners.

raglan sleeve
Sleeve extending over the shoulder and attached front and back with a slanted seam running from under the armhole to the neck.

ribbing
Tight elastic knitted strip around the sleeve or the bottom of a garment for tightening, reinforcing and adorning them.

patch pocket
Pocket of various shapes and sizes, made of a piece of material sewn onto the garment's outer surface.

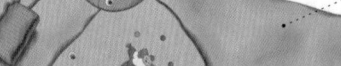

screen print
Pattern printed or sewn on the garment to decorate it.

snap-fastening front
A line of snap fasteners on the front of the garment.

inside-leg snap-fastening
Part along the inner leg of the garment, where snap fasteners make it easier to put the pants on.

top stitching
Stitches on the right side of the fabric used to embellish and reinforce the garment.

inside-leg snap-fastening
Part along the inner leg of the garment, where snap fasteners make it easier to put the pants on.

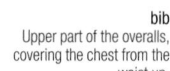

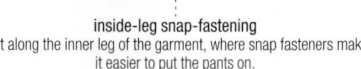

bib
Absorbent piece of fabric tied around a child's neck to protect its clothes from food and saliva.

disposable diaper
Single-use diaper usually with elastic bands around the thighs, that allows the child great liberty of movement.

Velcro closure
Fastening system made of two pieces of material that can be stuck and unstuck multiple times.

anti-leak guard
Elastic used to close the opening of the diaper around the thigh, preventing liquid from escaping.

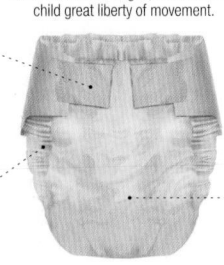

waterproof pants
Material through which liquid cannot pass.

diaper
Absorbent article of clothing used as briefs for babies.

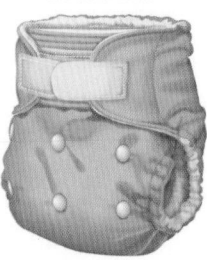

shirt
Long-sleeved baby shirt used as an under- or overgarment, depending on its weight; its characteristic lap shoulders allow the shirt's neck to expand when it is being put on.

sleep sack
Sort of pocket for sleeping in, attached over the shoulders by straps.

rompers
Infant day suit consisting of a short-sleeved blouse or a bib with shoulder straps, which are attached to puffy briefs that fasten at the crotch.

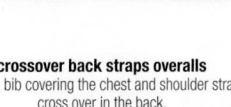

snowsuit
Winter garment consisting of thick overalls and jacket.

crossover back straps overalls
a bib covering the chest and shoulder straps that cross over in the back.

button strap
Narrow strip of fabric that is attached to the garment by buttons and connects the front and back by passing over the shoulder.

bib
Upper part of the overalls, covering the chest from the waist up.

pajamas
Light full outfit made up of a jacket or tunic and pants with an elasticized or drawstring waist.

drawstring hood
Headgear attached at the garment's neck that can be pulled over the head as protection against cold, rain and snow.

snow pants
Thick, waterproof pants that extend up to cover the chest and are held up with suspenders.

sportswear

Clothing worn to engage in a particular sporting activity.

running shoe
Light but sturdy canvas and rubber or leather shoe worn for sports or leisure.

loop
Strip of looped fabric attached to the upper of the shoe to make it easier to insert the foot.

lining
Fabric or leather facing that protects and finishes the inside of the shoe.

nose of the quarter
Part where the quarter extends forward on each side of the shoe.

eyelet
Small metal-rimmed hole through which the lace passes.

counter
Piece used to reinforce the back of the shoe and keep the heel of the foot in place.

tongue
Extension of the vamp that prevents fastening system from rubbing aga foot; it is lifted when the shoe is pull

collar
Strip of fabric or leather along the edge of the lining.

vamp
Part of the shoe that covers the front of the foot.

quarter
Back part of the shoe that surrounds the heel of the foot and extends over the instep to reinforce it.

punch hole
Each of the small holes made shoe to form a decorative pa

stitch
Visible stitching that both embellishes and reinforces the shoe.

heel
Stiff part underneath the shoe that supports the back of the foot.

shoelace
Narrow cord of fabric or leather, flat or round, that is threaded through eyelets or hooks to tighten the shoe.

middle sole
Sole made of various materials, placed over the outsole and cushioning the entire foot.

tag
Metal or plastic sheath that covers each end of a lace to ease it through the eyelets.

stud
Rubber projection molded into the outsole to improve its grip.

outsole
Sturdy piece of rubber o that forms the bottom of and is in contact with the

CLOTHING

T-shirt
Short-sleeved pullover in a T shape, traditionally made of cotton.

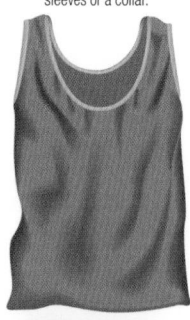

tank top
Short, fairly tight low-cut shirt without sleeves or a collar.

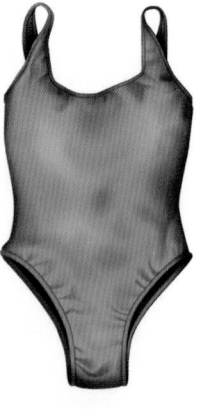

swimsuit
Women's swimming garment that is tight-fitting and usually stretchy; it can be in one piece or consist of briefs and a bikini top.

swimming cap
Headgear used to keep the sw hair in place and protect it from effects of chlorine.

sandal
Light shoe leaving especially the heel uncovered; it often consists only of a sole held on the foot by variously configured straps.

boxer shorts
Briefs covering the top of the thighs; they are gathered by an elasticized waist and have an inner bikini bottom.

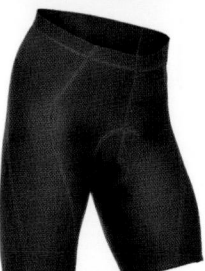

bicycle pants
Skin-tight garment covering the thighs, used mainly for cycling.

brief
Low-waisted briefs with very high-cut legs; they are usually stretchy and tight-fitting and are worn by men for swimming.

hiking boot
Sturdy walking shoe with a thick nonskid sole; it is supported at the ankle and instep by laces threaded through hooks.

sportswear

sweat suit
Outfit made up of a jacket or shirt and pants; it is usually made of jersey fleece and is worn over sports clothes or as casual wear.

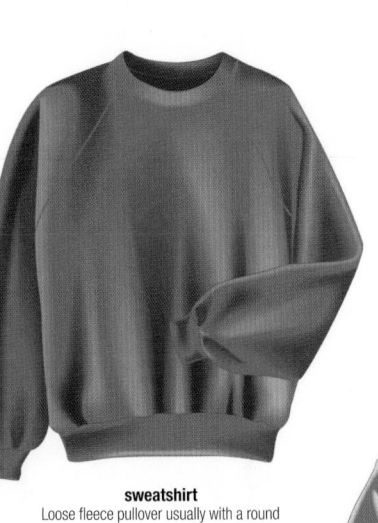

anorak
Waterproof sports jacket with long sleeves, a drawstring hood and waist and gathered wrists.

sweatshirt
Loose fleece pullover usually with a round neck, long sleeves and ribbing at the hips and wrists.

fleece jacket
Sleeved garment made of soft deep-piled woven fabric, closing in the front; it is light and warm, and its thickness depends on the amount of insulation provided.

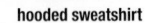

pants
Garment for the lower body; they extend from the waist or the hips to the ankles, covering each leg separately.

sweatpants
Training suit pants with a drawstring waist and ribbed ankles.

hooded sweatshirt
Cotton fleece pullover that is often worn as outerwear; it has ribbing at the wrists and hips, a drawstring hood and a hand-warmer pouch.

pockets

Parts of a garment used to carry things and consisting of a piece of material sewn onto or inside the garment.

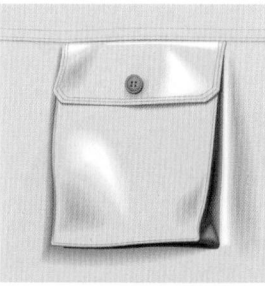

gusset pocket
Patch pocket made fuller by an expandable bottom and sides or by an inverted or round pleat in the middle of the pocket.

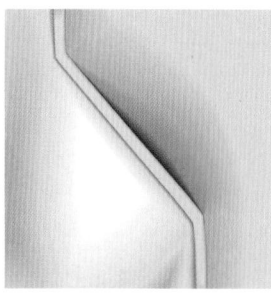

inset pocket
Pocket whose opening contains a decorative seam, giving the garment a distinctive line.

welt pocket
Pocket whose opening is adorned and reinforced by one or two thin strips.

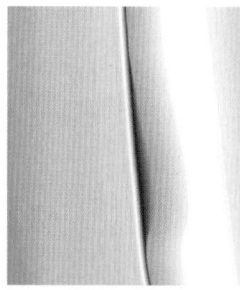

seam pocket
Pocket where the opening is in a side seam of the garment.

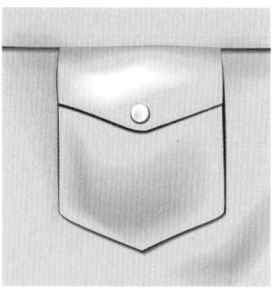

flap pocket
Pocket whose opening is covered by a piece of fabric hanging from the top of it.

broad welt side pocket
Angled pocket; the outer edge of the opening has a wide welt.

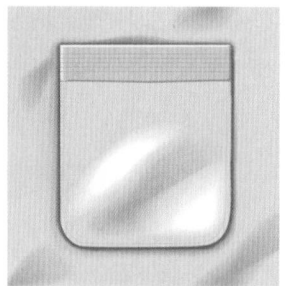

patch pocket
Pocket of various shapes and sizes, made of a piece of material sewn onto the garment's outer surface.

hand-warmer pouch
Patch pocket on the front of a garment; it opens vertically on one or both sides to protect the hands against the cold.

sleeves

Parts of the garment that wholly or partly cover the arms.

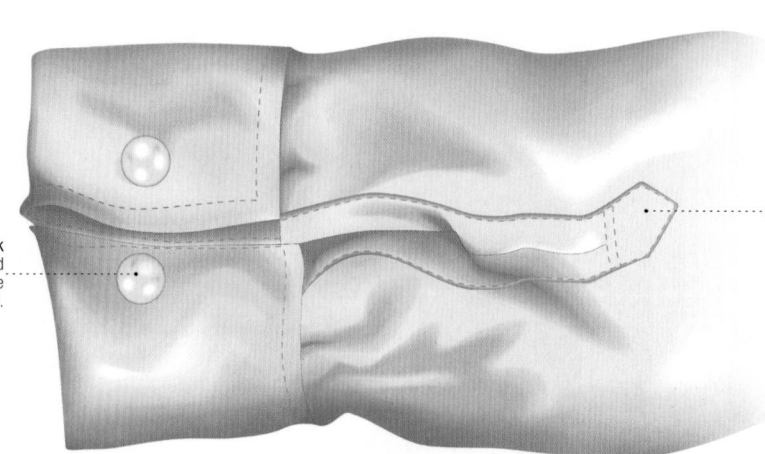

pointed tab end
Narrow strip of fabric ending in a p
and adorning the sleeve slit.

cuff link
Usually metal stud, single or paired with another, for fastening the edges of cuffs.

French cuff
Tight part of a shirt or blouse sleeve made of a wide strip of fabric, which is folded back and fastened edge to edge with cuff links.

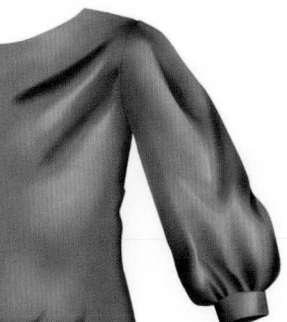

puff sleeve
sleeve that puffs out because
sewn at the armhole and the
the sleeve; it is edged with a
v strip of fabric or elastic.

leg-of-mutton sleeve
Sleeve that is narrow from the wrist to the
elbow and widens from the elbow to the
shoulder, where it is gathered.

bishop sleeve
Long sleeve that puffs out because of pleats
sewn at the bottom and sometimes at the
armhole; it is edged with a narrow strip of
fabric or elastic.

three-quarter sleeve
Sleeve that partially covers the
forearm.

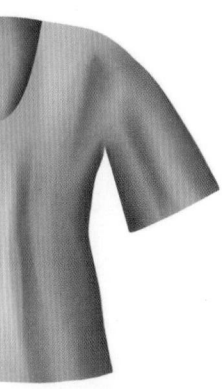

batwing sleeve
th a large armhole that extends
the waist; it narrows gradually
toward the wrist.

cap sleeve
Small sleeve fitting tightly over the
shoulder to fall straight or flare over
the upper arm.

kimono sleeve
Very full sleeve with no seam at the
armhole.

saddle sleeve
Sleeve extending to the neck by a strip
that covers the shoulder.

CLOTHING

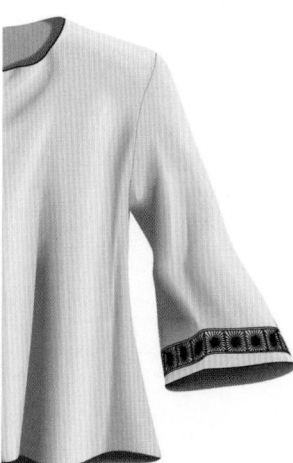

raglan sleeve
extending over the shoulder
ached front and back with a
seam running from under the
armhole to the neck.

shirtsleeve
Moderately full sleeve with a
French cuff; it is slightly pleated
at the bottom and is often
embellished with a pointed tab end.

pagoda sleeve
Sleeve flaring from the elbow to the wrist.

tailored sleeve
Long sleeve made of two pieces
that are cut to follow the shape of
a bent arm.

pleats

Parts of a garment folded over to form a double thickness of material.

knife pleat
Pleat created by a vertical fold pointing in one direction and of constant width.

topstitched pleat
Pleat extending from a series of ornamental stitches on the outside of the fabric.

accordion pleat
Set of thin upright pleats of uniform width along the grain of the fabric.

inverted pleat
Pleat formed by two folds that meet in front and touch on the outside of the fabric, thus forming a hollow in the fabric.

kick pleat
Inverted or flat back pleat a bottom of a straight skirt, pro greater ease of moveme

collars

Pieces sewn onto a garment that finish or adorn the neck.

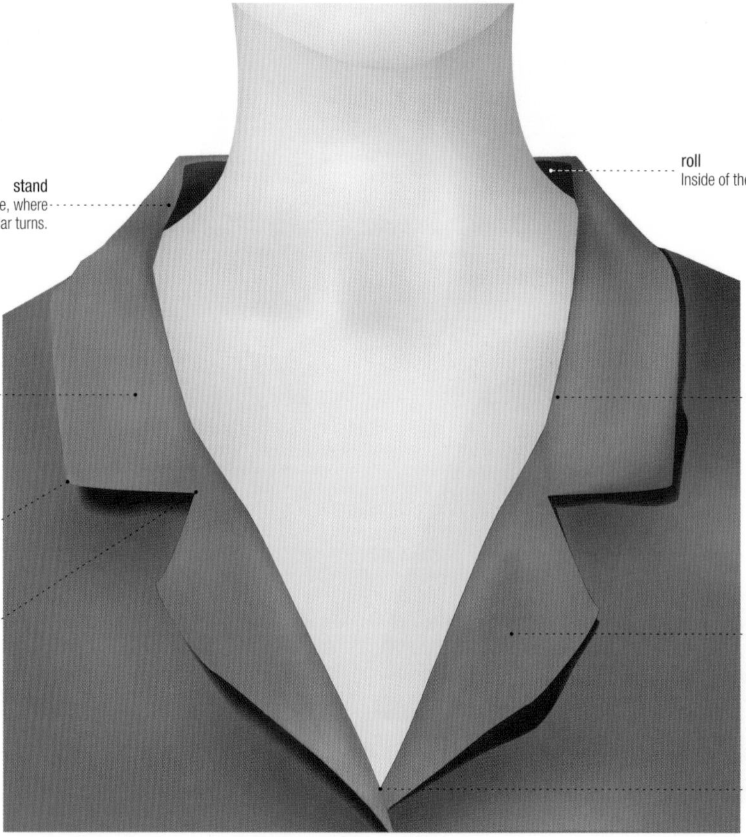

stand
Top edge of the break line, where the collar turns.

roll
Inside of the collar, behind the neck.

fall
Part of the collar that folds back over the garment from the break line.

break line
Line where the collar folds.

collar point
Somewhat pointed tip of the collar.

notch
Angle formed where the collar and the lapel meet.

lapel
Part of a garment turned down over the chest, extending the collar.

leading edge
Folded part of the fabric that runs a the collar.

parts of a collar

CLOTHING

collars

examples of collars
Collar: piece sewn onto a garment
that finishes or adorns the neck.

collaret
Piece of delicate, pleated or gathered fabric
that adorns the neck of a dress; its shape has
varied greatly from one period to another.

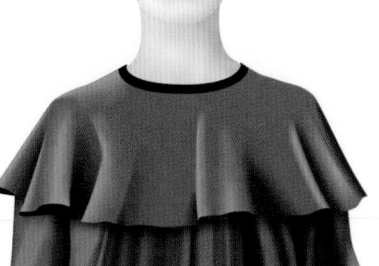

bertha collar
Collar made of a strip of fabric of
variable width and attached to the edge
of a neckline or round neck.

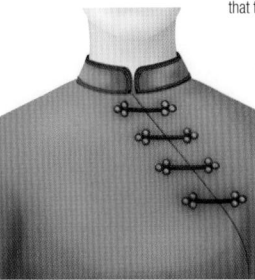

mandarin collar
Stand-up collar with rounded upper
points that come together at the neck,
forming a V.

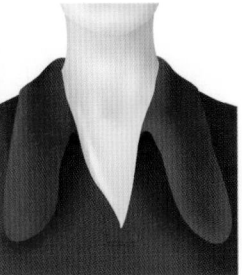

dog-ear collar
...ed-down collar characterized by long, fairly
...de points, which are rounded at the tips.

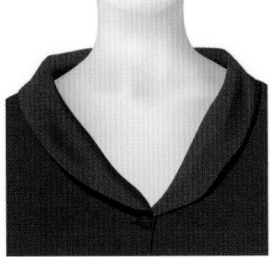

shawl collar
Wide turned-down collar with long rounded
lapels that partially cross in front.

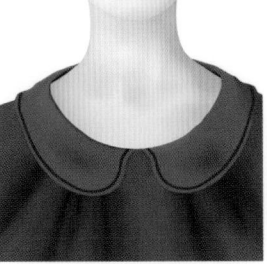

Peter Pan collar
Flat collar of uniform width with
rounded tips; it is sewn onto a fairly
open neck.

shirt collar
Collar with rounded or tapered points
that is sewn onto the neck and turned
down along a fold line, which is higher in
back than in front.

tailored collar
Collar whose fold covers the back
of the neck; its lapels form a V
where they cross on the chest.

bow collar
Collar made of a long strip of soft fabric sewn
onto a round neck; it can be tied in front in
various ways.

jabot
Decoration made up of one or two
pieces of fine soft pleated fabric; it
is attached at the base of the neck
and spreads out over the chest.

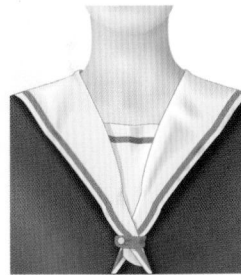

sailor collar
Collar that is square in back and has long lapels
extending over the chest; it is fastened to a V-neck
and, out of modesty, the plunging neckline is often
concealed with a piece of fabric.

turtleneck
High-necked collar that is folded
over; it is usually snug around the
neck and does not fasten.

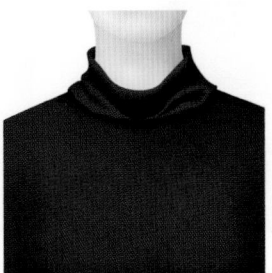

cowl neck
Turtleneck that is large enough to be
draped over the head, making a kind
of hood that frames the face.

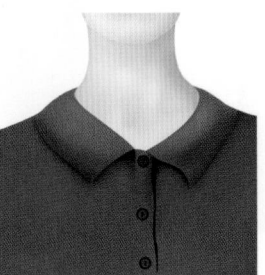

polo collar
Turned-down pointed collar fastened
with a buttoned placket which ends
at mid-chest.

stand-up collar
Collar made of a narrow strip of fabric that
sticks up from a round neck; its edges
meet in front but do not fasten.

necks

Parts of a garment near the wearer's neck.

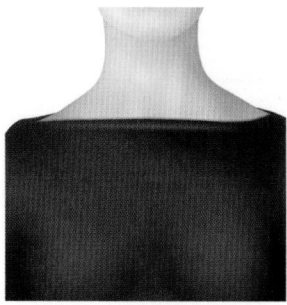

boatneck
Neck tapering to a point on the shoulders.

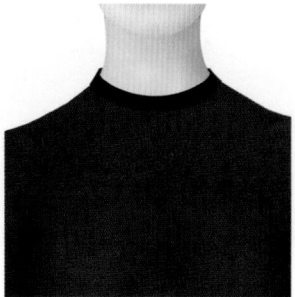

round neck
Rounded neck fitting close to the wearer's neck.

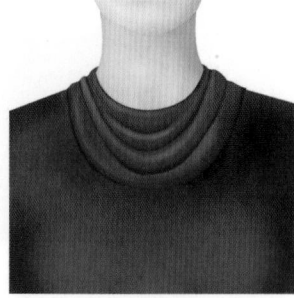

draped neck
Neck with soft pleats that can be arranged in various ways.

necklines

Parts of a garment that reveal the neck and part of the shoulders and chest.

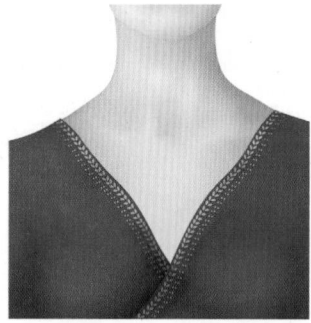

V-shaped neck
Neckline with edges coming together at mid-chest in a V shape.

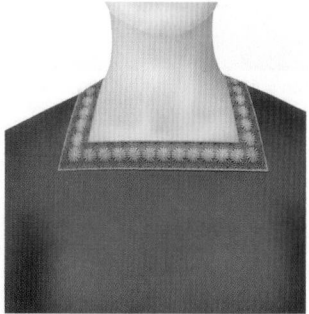

square neck
Neckline with a square neck that reveals the upper part of the chest.

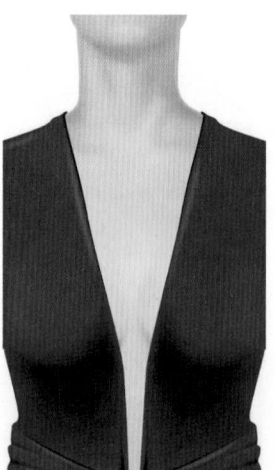

draped neckline
Neckline made up of a series of soft overlapping folds created by the fabric of the bodice.

plunging neckline
Neckline that usually ends in a V and is very low in front or back.

sweetheart neckline
Neckline shaped like the top of a heart.

men's headgear

fedora
Soft hat with a dented crown that is adorned with a wide ribbon; it is made from a single piece and has a brim of uniform width.

bow
Point where the ends of the hatband are tied to trim the hat.

hatband
Wide silk ribbon decorating the base of the crown.

binding
Strip of fabric running along the edge of the hat.

crown
Part of the hat that fits on top of the head.

brim
Part of the hat encircling the base of the crown.

CLOTHING

boater
Stiff straw headgear with a flat brim of uniform width and an oval crown circled with a ribbon; it was worn at the end of the 19th century.

skullcap
Small round cap covering only the top of the head.

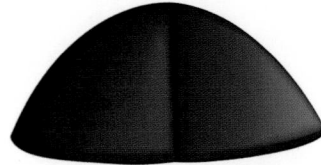

cap
Brimless, somewhat soft headgear that appeared at the end of the 19th century; it has a peak and a flat crown.

garrison cap
Elongated brimless headgear with a soft flexible crown; it is worn over the brow and takes the shape of the head.

top hat
Stiff silk headgear with a high cylindrical crown circled with a ribbon and a narrow brim that is turned up at the sides; it was first worn toward the end of the 18th century.

shapka
Fur hat that is native to Poland; it has ear flaps that can be turned up and tied on top of the head.

hunting cap
Thick soft cap with a peak and ear flaps, which give protection against the cold.

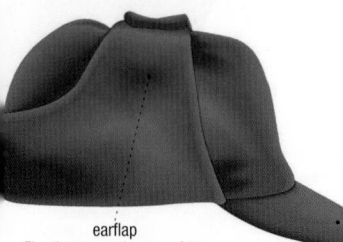

derby
Headgear primarily for men that appeared at the end of the 19th century; it is made of stiff felt with a circular rounded crown and an upturned narrow brim.

panama
Soft headgear from the end of the 19th and the early 20th century; it is made from woven jipijapa leaves and has a dented crown circled with a ribbon.

earflap
Flap that covers the nape of the neck and the ears to keep them warm; it can be turned up and held in place on top of the head.

peak
Part that juts out over the eyes to protect them.

women's headgear

cloche
Hat of the 1920s and '30s with a cylindrical crown and a narrow brim.

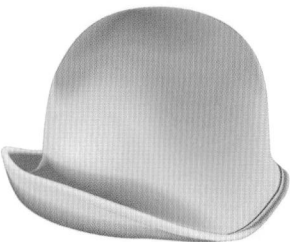

cartwheel hat
Headgear in fashion from the early 20th century, made of straw or light fibers with a large soft brim of uniform width.

pillbox hat
Small low, round or oval toque worn perched on top of the head or pulled down.

toque
Brimless headgear made of fabric or fur, with a cylindrical crown and a flat top that fits snugly on the head.

turban
Headgear made of a long strip of fabric, wound around so that it covers the entire head but leaves the forehead uncovered.

crown
Part of the hat that fits on top of the head.

sailor's hat

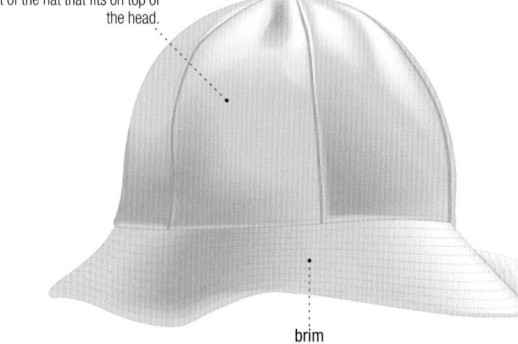

brim
Part of the hat encircling the base of the crown.

southwester
Waterproof headgear with a narrow brim that widens over the nape of the neck to protect it from inclement weather.

unisex headgear

Headgear worn by members of both sexes.

cap
Brimless, somewhat soft headgear that has a peak and a flat crown.

stocking cap
Woolen headgear made from a cylindrical piece that is folded over for double thickness, sewn at one end and decorated with a pompom.

balaclava
Headpiece that covers both head and neck, leaving the face uncovered.

face mask
Headpiece that covers both head and leaving only the eyes uncovered.

beret
Soft brimless headgear with a round flat crown that sometimes puffs out; it fits on the head by means of a simple hemmed rim or a narrow headband.

men's shoes

parts of a shoe

heel grip
...art of the lining that makes it ...r to put the shoe on or holds ...l of the foot inside the shoe, ...pending on the type of shoe.

cuff
...f fabric or leather inside ...running along the edge of the lining.

quarter
...ack part of the shoe that ...unds the heel of the foot ...xtends over the instep to reinforce it.

outside counter
...the quarter that is sewn ...imulated and surrounds the heel of the foot.

heel
...art underneath the shoe ...supports the back of the foot.

top lift
...usually leather or rubber ...affixed under the heel to prevent wear.

nose of the quarter
Part where the quarter extends ...orward on each side of the shoe.

lining
Fabric or leather facing that protects and finishes the inside of the shoe.

tongue
Extension of the vamp that prevents the fastening system from rubbing against the foot; it is lifted when the shoe is put on.

shoelace
Narrow cord of fabric or leather, flat or round, that is threaded through eyelets or hooks to tighten the shoe.

vamp
Part of the shoe that covers the front of the foot.

stitch
Visible stitching that both embellishes and reinforces the shoe.

punch hole
Each of the small holes made in the shoe to form a decorative pattern.

waist
Curved part of the shoe supporting the arch.

tag
Metal or plastic sheath that covers each end of a lace to ease it through the eyelets.

eyelet tab
Piece sewn on to the nose of the quarter to reinforce the shoe; the laces pass through it.

eyelet
Small metal-rimmed hole through which the lace passes.

welt
Thin strip used to join the bottom of the shoe to the part that goes around the foot.

perforated toe cap
Part of the shoe that covers the toes, with perforations forming a more or less conventional decorative pattern.

examples of shoes

outsole
Sturdy piece of rubber or leather that forms the bottom of the shoe and is in contact with the ground.

bootee
Shoe often lined with fur, that covers the ankle.

oxford
Shoe where the top of the nose of the quarter is attached to the vamp, so that only the upper part of the lacing system opens for the foot to slip in.

blucher oxford
Shoe where the noses of the quarter can be spread far apart to make the shoe easier to put on.

cowboy boot
Footwear with a usually pointed toe, rising to the calf, made of leather that is usually decorated in various patterns.

chukka
Ankle-high shoe made of light unlined suede or leather and fastened with laces with two or three sets of eyelets.

rubber
Overshoe made of relatively thin rubber that protects the shoe from mud and water.

work boot
Sturdy shoe, with a thick nonskid sole, that comes up to the ankle and is tied with laces.

CLOTHING

women's shoes

examples of shoes

CLOTHING

T-strap shoe
Heeled shoe derived from the one-bar shoe; the vamp turns into a strap that extends over the instep and ends in a bar.

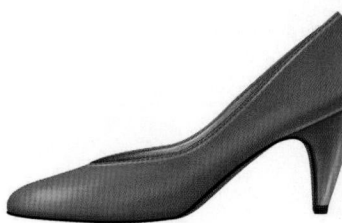

pump
Plain delicate lightweight shoe that leaves the instep uncovered; it has a heel, a thin sole and no fastening system.

strap
Piece running across the top of the shoe in order to keep it on the foot.

one-bar shoe
Heeled shoe characterized by a bar crossing the instep and fastened to the quarter by a buckle or button.

heel
Stiff part underneath the shoe that supports the back of the foot.

sling back shoe
Pump with a rear bar; it can be open at the toe.

thigh boot
Boot that comes up to the thigh, covering most of it.

casual lace-up pump
Comfortable shoe that is suited to walking; it has laces and a sturdy heel.

ankle boot
Tight-fitting laced or buttoned shoe that comes up over the ankle.

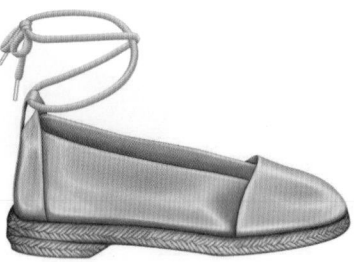

espadrille
Canvas shoe characterized by a woven rope sole; it is sometimes held on the foot by a lace tied around the ankle.

clog
Toeless mule with a thick, generally wooden sole; it is held on the foot by a thick strap.

boot
Shoe that comes up to at least the calf.

ballet flat
Light supple unlined shoe that is tightened by a thin lace and sometimes has a small heel; it leaves the instep uncovered to the base of the toes.

sandal
Light shoe leaving especially the heel uncovered; it often consists only of a sole held on the foot by variously configured straps.

CLOTHING

examples of heels
Heel: stiff part underneath the shoe that supports the back of the foot.

spike heel
Very high heel, tapered at the bottom.

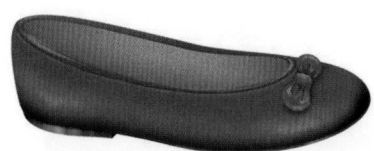

flat heel
Very flat heel made of a thin piece of leather or other material.

wedge heel
High heel that extends under the instep of the shoe.

flared heel
Heel that widens at the bottom.

low heel
Heel of less than two inches.

unisex shoes

Shoes worn by members of both sexes.

mule
Flat, light, usually indoor shoe;
it has a vamp only, leaving the
heel bare.

loafer
Dressy moccasin with a flat heel.

tennis shoe
Flat canvas shoe with a flexible nonskid sole and
a reinforced toe; the sole and toe are both made
of rubber.

moccasin
Flat, very soft slip-on casual shoe with
ridged seams; it is characterized by an
apron sewn onto the vamp, which molds
to the instep.

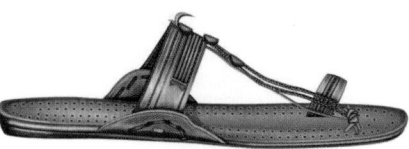

sandal
Shoe with a flat sole that is held on
the foot by thin straps and sometimes
a toe ring.

rain boot
Footwear rising to the calf, made of
waterproof material.

thong
Sandal that is attached to the foot
with nothing more than a Y-shaped
strap, which passes between the
first two toes.

sandal
Flat, light sport shoe with a cutout vamp
that turns into a tongue; a bar passes
through the tongue and fastens at the side
with a buckle.

hiking boot
Sturdy walking shoe with a thick nonskid
sole; it is supported at the ankle and
instep by laces threaded through hooks.

accessories

eshine kit
or case used to store various shoe
products.

shoe polisher
Electric appliance with
interchangeable brushes, used to
polish or shine shoes.

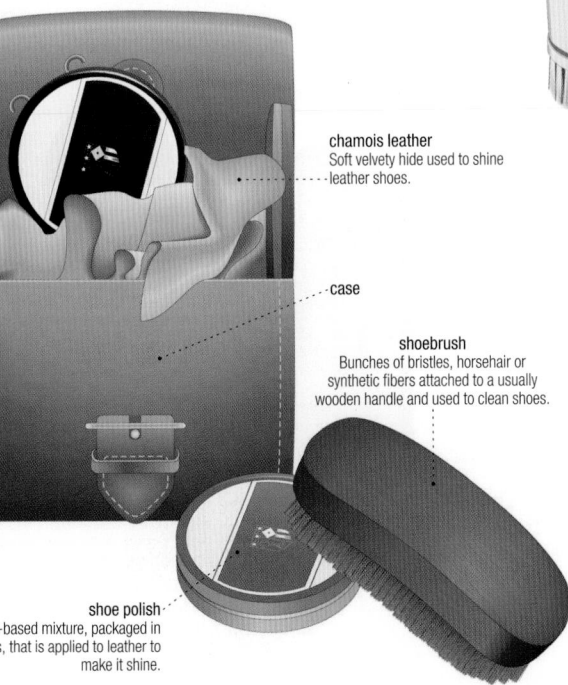

chamois leather
Soft velvety hide used to shine
leather shoes.

case

shoebrush
Bunches of bristles, horsehair or
synthetic fibers attached to a usually
wooden handle and used to clean shoes.

shoe polish
-based mixture, packaged in
, that is applied to leather to
make it shine.

shoehorn
Curved tongue placed at the back
of the shoe to ease it onto the foot.

insole
Removable object placed inside the shoe
to improve its fit, absorb sweat from the
foot or keep it dry.

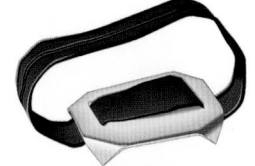

climbing iron
Object with sharp metal spikes that is
attached under the shoe with a strap,
making it possible to walk on hard snow or
ice without slipping.

shoe rack
Device made up of one or several rows
of pouches or hooks, for storing shoes.

shoe tree
Wooden or plastic device that is inserted into
the shoe to restore or maintain its shape.

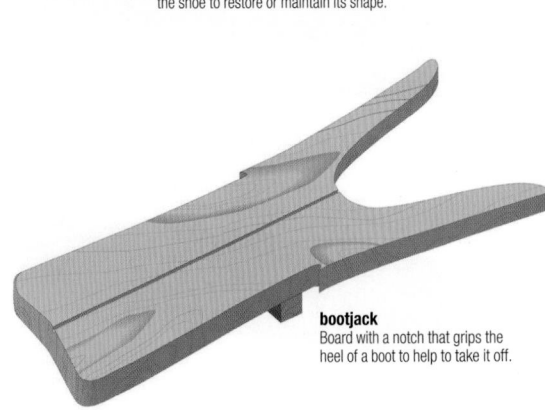

bootjack
Board with a notch that grips the
heel of a boot to help to take it off.

gloves

Items of attire covering the hand to at least the wrist and having finger separations.

men's gloves

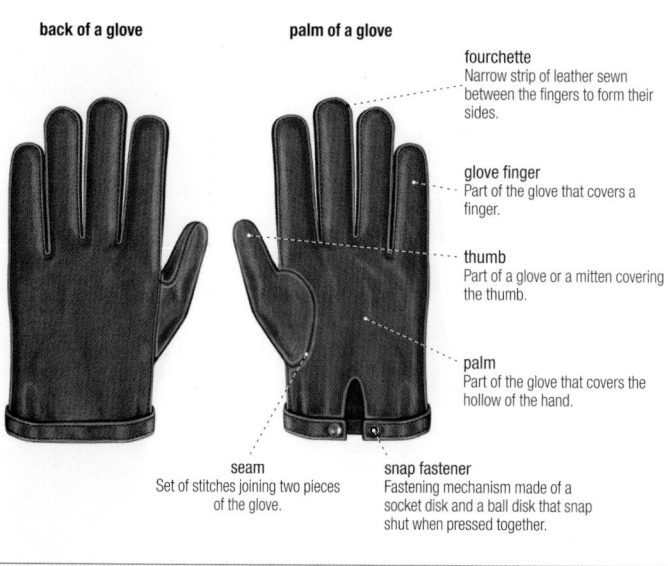

back of a glove

palm of a glove

fourchette
Narrow strip of leather sewn between the fingers to form their sides.

glove finger
Part of the glove that covers a finger.

thumb
Part of a glove or a mitten covering the thumb.

palm
Part of the glove that covers the hollow of the hand.

seam
Set of stitches joining two pieces of the glove.

snap fastener
Fastening mechanism made of a socket disk and a ball disk that snap shut when pressed together.

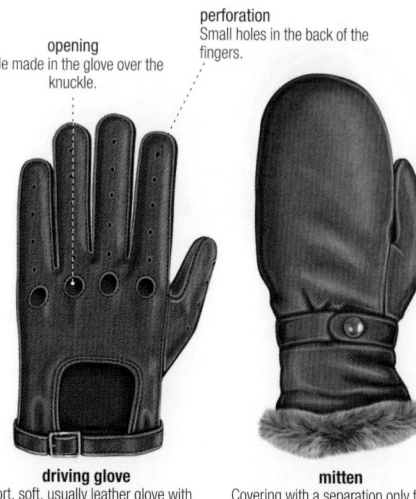

opening
Hole made in the glove over the knuckle.

perforation
Small holes in the back of the fingers.

driving glove
Short, soft, usually leather glove with perforations; it has a vent and other openings that allow the hand to move freely.

mitten
Covering with a separation only for thumb, providing better protection ag the cold while allowing the wearer grasp objects.

women's gloves

gauntlet
Glove to which a somewhat flared cuff is attached at the wrist; it is made of various, often decorative kinds of material.

evening glove
Glove where the gauntlet extends over the elbow.

mitt
Often dressy glove, either long or of medium length; it fits tightly along the arm and covers only the first finger joints.

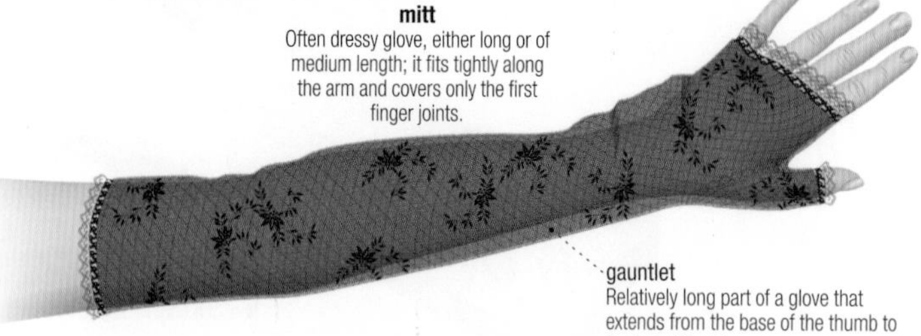

gauntlet
Relatively long part of a glove that extends from the base of the thumb to the top of the glove.

mitten
Covering with a separation only for the thumb, providing better protection against the cold while allowing the wearer to grasp objects.

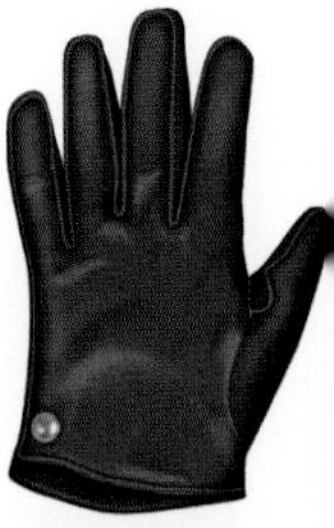

short glove
Glove covering only the hand or extending slightly over the wrist.

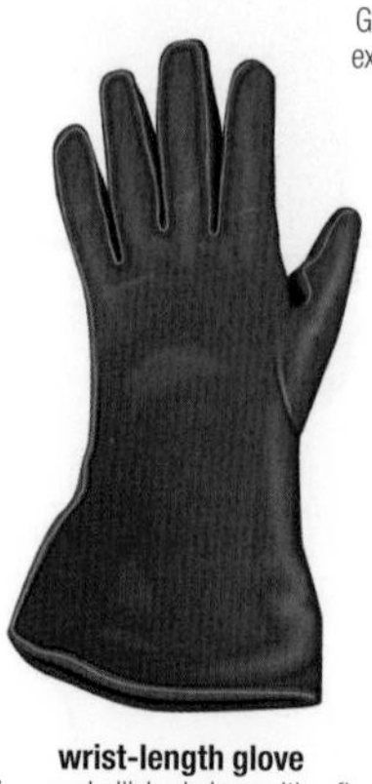

wrist-length glove
Plain unembellished glove with a flared gauntlet covering the wrist.

miscellaneous accessories

scarf
Woven or knit piece of fabric worn around the neck and over the shoulders.

feather
Object covering the bodies of birds, or some light material resembling a bird's feather.

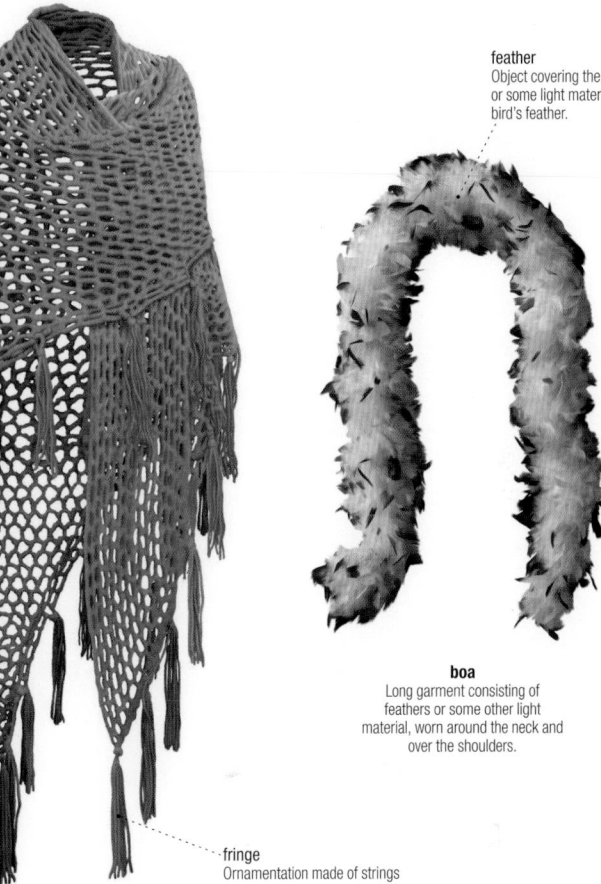

boa
Long garment consisting of feathers or some other light material, worn around the neck and over the shoulders.

fringe
Ornamentation made of strings hanging from a strip of fabric.

shawl
Square, rectangular or triangular piece of fabric, worn around the shoulders by women.

headband
Flexible piece used to keep the ear coverings in place.

ear covering
Lined shell covering the ear.

neck warmer
Tube of fabric worn around the neck in cold weather.

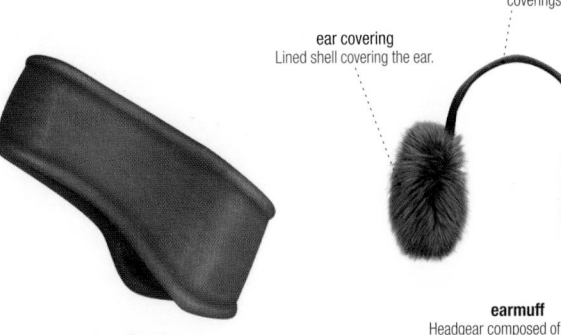

headband
Band of lined fabric worn around the head and covering the ears.

earmuff
Headgear composed of two ear cushions worn to protect the ears from cold.

PERSONAL ACCESSORIES AND ARTICLES

jewelry

Finely crafted articles of adornment that are valued for their materials (gold, silver, gemstones) and workmanship.

earrings
Article of jewelry worn on the earlobe.

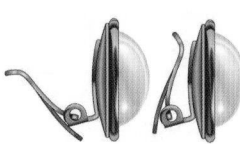

clip earrings
Earrings attached to the earlobe by a spring clip.

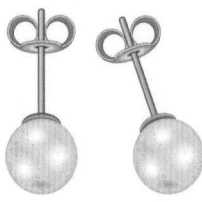

pierced earrings
Earrings with a post, hook or wire that passes through the pierced earlobe; post is capped with a clasp.

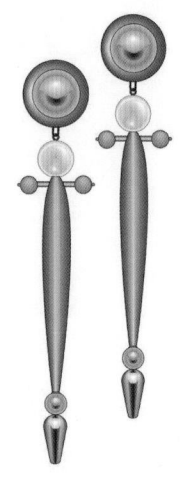

drop earrings
Earrings where the ornamental part hangs down from the ear and varies in shape and length.

screw earrings
Earrings attached to the earlobe by a small screw behind the ear.

hoop earrings
Hoop-shaped earrings with a post that passes through the pierced earlobe and fits into the other end of the ring.

necklaces
Article of jewelry worn around the neck that consists of a band of gold or silver, a circle of set or unset precious stones or pearls strung together.

matinee-length necklace
Necklace that is approximately 20 in long and falls above the chest.

velvet-band choker
Choker consisting of a ribbon to which an ornament is attached.

pendant
Article of jewelry hung from a ch
or a necklace.

rope
Necklace that is over 3 ft long and can be looped several times around the neck and knotted over the chest.

opera-length necklace
Necklace that is approximately 30 in long and falls over the chest.

bib necklace
Necklace consisting of three or more rows.

choker
Necklace that sometimes consists of many rows and is worn high on the neck.

locket
Usually round or oval pendant t
opens to receive a memento o
loved one.

jewelry

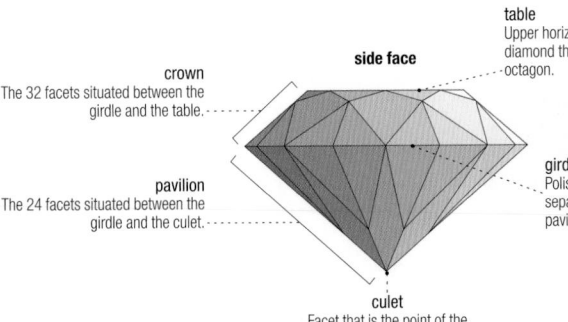

side face

crown
The 32 facets situated between the girdle and the table.

pavilion
The 24 facets situated between the girdle and the culet.

table
Upper horizontal facet of the diamond that has the shape of an octagon.

girdle
Polished or unpolished edge that separates the crown from the pavilion.

culet
Facet that is the point of the pavilion.

brilliant cut facets
The most common cut for a diamond is the brilliant cut; it consists of 58 facets spread over two faces, which are separated by a girdle.

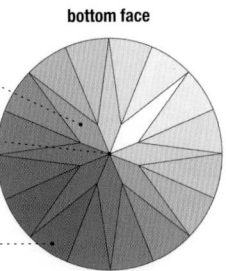

bottom face

pavilion facet (8)
Facet cut on the pavilion side; one point touches the culet and the other the girdle.

culet
Facet that is the point of the pavilion.

lower girdle facet (16)
inted facet cut on the pavilion side; the girdle is its base.

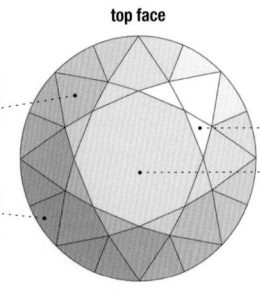

top face

bezel facet (8)
Facet cut on the crown face; the tip touches the table, the point and the girdle.

upper girdle facet (16)
Triangular facet cut on the crown face; the base touches the girdle.

star facet (8)
Triangular facet cut on the crown face; the table is its base.

table
Upper horizontal facet of the diamond that has the shape of an octagon.

cut for gemstones
Cutting a gemstone consists of angling the facets so that the stone's brilliance is intensified.

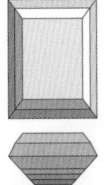

step cut
Cut where the square or rectangular girdle is rounded by parallel rows of rectangular facets; e are more facets on the pavilion side than on the crown side.

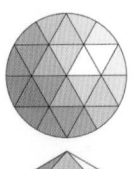

rose cut
Cut with a flat base and a dome made up of triangular facets; the total number of facets is a multiple of three.

table cut
The simplest kind of table cut; the rectangular girdle with sometimes rounded corners is surrounded on each side by a row of facets.

cabochon cut
Unfaceted cut suitable for opaque stones; it has one flat side and one or two convex sides.

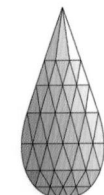

pear-shaped cut
Brilliant full cut with an elongated girdle.

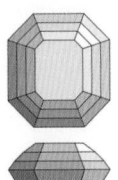

emerald cut
Classic emerald step cut that has a rectangular table with beveled corners and a girdle of the same shape with occasionally beveled corners.

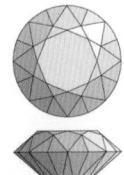

brilliant full cut
Diamond cut with 32 crown facets, 24 pavilion facets, an octagonal table and a culet.

eight cut
Cut often used for smaller diamonds; it has eight crown facets, eight pavilion facets, an octagonal table and a culet.

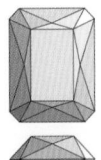
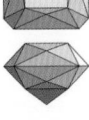

scissors cut
Step cut with triangular facets.

briolette cut
Elongated cut that is completely covered with triangular facets and has neither crown nor pavilion; it is used when stones are to be set in a pendant.

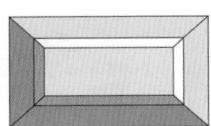

baguette cut
Step cut where the table and girdle are elongated rectangles.

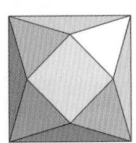

French cut
Cut where the table and the girdle are square and the facets triangular.

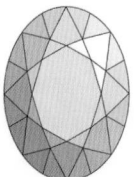

oval cut
Brilliant full cut where the girdle is oval in shape.

navette cut
Brilliant cut with a girdle that is shaped like a spindle with pointed ends.

jewelry

semiprecious stones
Next to precious stones, these stones are the ones whose beauty and durability make them most suitable for jewelry.

amethyst
Stone whose color ranges from pale mauve to deepest purple.

lapis lazuli
Opaque, dark blue stone that is usually speckled; the glittering flecks are proof of its authenticity.

aquamarine
Stone whose color ranges from whitish-pale blue to a deep blue-aqua color.

topaz
Stone with a wide range of colors, including yellowish-orange (the most common), green (the rarest), pink (the most sought-after), blue, brown and colorless.

tourmaline
Usually multicolored stone with a rich array of colors from red to pink and green and on to blue.

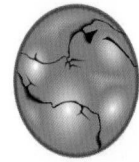

opal
Soft opaque stone that is milky-white or quite dark and gives off rainbowlike reflections.

turquoise
Opaque, light blue stone with tinges of green; it often contains brown, gray or black veins.

garnet
Stone whose color ranges from green to yellow to dark red.

precious stones
The value of these four gemstones is based on their rarity, brilliance and durability.

emerald
Stone whose color varies from greenish-yellow to greenish-blue; an emerald's value is based more on its color than on its purity.

sapphire
This stone can be blue, pink, orange, yellow, green, purple or even colorless; the most sought-after color is purplish-blue.

diamond
The hardest stone is colorless although there are also blue, yellow and pink varieties; it is the most renowned precious stone.

ruby
The rarest of all precious stones is extremely hard; its color varies from a bright pinkish-red to a purplish red, which is the most sought-after color.

rings
Article of jewelry worn on the finger; it might have symbolic significance.

setting
Part of the bezel surrounding and holding the stone.

claw
Small metal hook bent over the stone to hold it in place.

bezel
Single or multiple head of the ring in which the stone is held by claws.

stone
Crafted gem whose beauty, rarity and durability confer a certain value. There are three groups: precious, semiprecious and synthetic.

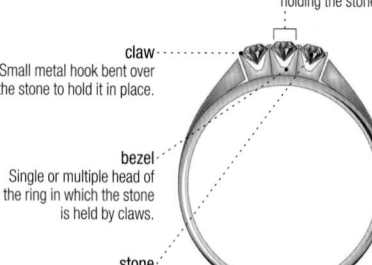

parts of a ring

band ring
Ring of uniform width with no bezel.

class ring
Ring worn by a graduate that is engraved with the school crest and the student's class year; a semiprecious or synthetic stone is sometimes substituted for the crest.

signet ring
Ring with a large flat top that is decorated with initials or coats of a

engagement ring
Ring that is often decorated with a stone and is worn by an engaged woman on her left ring finger.

wedding ring
Ring that is usually a circle of precious metal or two intertwined circles; it is worn by a married person on the left ring finger.

solitaire ring
Ring decorated with a single ge that is usually brilliant cut.

jewelry

bracelets
Flexible article of jewelry worn on the wrist, the arm or sometimes the ankle.

charm bracelet
Bracelet that is made of flattened links and fitted with a clasp.

bangle
Ring-shaped rigid bracelet that slips on over the hand.

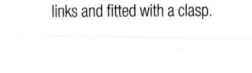

identification bracelet
Charm bracelet with a plate that is usually engraved with a first name.

pins
Article of jewelry used to fasten and adorn a garment.

tie bar
Pincer-shaped article of jewelry clipped halfway up a tie to keep it attached to the shirt.

tiepin
Article of jewelry consisting of a short pointed stem with a head; it is used to hold the two tie aprons together.

collar bar
Article of jewelry consisting of a rod with two capped pins; it is used to hold shirt collar points in place.

stickpin
Article of jewelry consisting of a pointed stem and a decorative head; it is usually worn on women's coat lapels.

brooch
Article of jewelry usually worn by women that consists of a pin with a decorative clasp; it is used to fasten a shawl or collar or adorn a bodice.

charms
Small pieces of costume jewelry attached to a chain or a bracelet.

nameplate
Charm shaped like a small plaque that is usually engraved with a name.

horn
Charm shaped like a horn.

horseshoe
Charm shaped like a horseshoe that is said to bring good luck.

nail care

The means of making the hands and especially the nails more beautiful.

manicure set
Range of instruments used for nail care.

cuticle trimmer
Blade with a concave end that follows the shape of the nail; it is used to trim the strip of skin edging the base of the nail (cuticle).

nail shaper
Beveled blade that is also used to trim the skin edging the nail base.

nail file
Ridged metal blade used to file down and smooth nails.

nail scissors
Scissors with short flat, slightly curved edges that are used to trim fingernails and toenails.

cuticle nippers
Pincers with short convex jaws that are used to trim cuticles.

cuticle pusher
Spatula-shaped instrument used to push back the strip of skin edging the base of the nail.

eyebrow tweezers
Delicate pincers used to pluck out hairs.

case
Usually rigid-sided case that is shaped to fit the articles it is designed to hold.

zipper
Closure made up of two lengths of tape edged with teeth that interlock by means of a slide.

cuticle scissors
Scissors used to trim cuticles; the thin, flat or curved blades are designed to reach the corners of the nails.

strap
Strip of leather or sometimes elasticized material keeping the instruments in place.

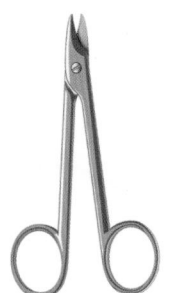

toenail scissors
Scissors with long shanks that are used to trim toenails.

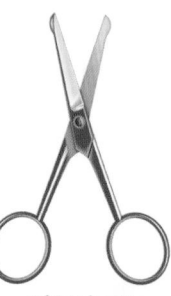

safety scissors
Scissors used to trim nails that are safer to use because of their rounded tips.

nail clippers
Small pincers with curved jaws and often a file that are used to trim nails.

lever
Rod attached to a fulcrum that brings the jaws together when it is pressed down.

nail buffer
Curved instrument used to smooth and polish the surface of the nails.

nail cleaner
Fine-tipped beveled blade used to clean the nail's outer edge.

chamois leather
Soft velvety hide used to polish nails.

jaw
Cutting edges of the nail clippers.

folding nail file
Ridged metal blade used to file down and smooth nails.

nail polish
Product applied to the nails that dries to become a clear or colored coating protecting and adorning the nails.

nail whitener pencil
Pencil that is run under the outer edge of the nail to make it white.

emery boards
Cardboard file with a coarse-grained side used to file down the nail and a finer-grained side to smooth it.

nail polish remover
Product applied to nails to removed nail polish.

makeup

Cosmetics used to beautify the face.

compact
Small flat case housing a container with pressed powder, a powder puff and a mirror.

pressed powder
Creamy powder used to touch up skin tone during the day; it usually comes in a compact.

blusher brush
Slender round-tipped brush with soft flexible bristles; it is smaller than the loose powder brush and is used to pick up and apply powder blusher.

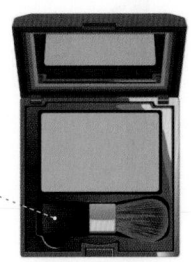

powder blusher
Powdered product applied to the cheekbones and cheeks to accentuate facial lines and emphasize skin tone.

facial makeup
Range of beauty products designed to accentuate the facial features and conceal their imperfections.

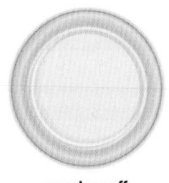

powder puff
Small round, often cotton pad used to apply loose or pressed powder.

liquid foundation
Liquid product applied to the face and neck to even out skin tone.

loose powder brush
Big round-tipped brush with soft flexible bristles; it is used to pick up and apply loose powder.

loose powder
Very fine powder that evens out skin tone, controls oily shine, sets foundation and acts as a base for blusher.

synthetic sponge
Sponge used to spread foundation evenly over the skin.

fan brush
Very flat, very thin brush used to brush away excess loose powder.

eye makeup
Range of beauty products designed to accentuate the eyes and conceal their imperfections.

brow brush and lash comb
The brush is used to smooth the brows and the comb to separate the lashes after mascara has been applied.

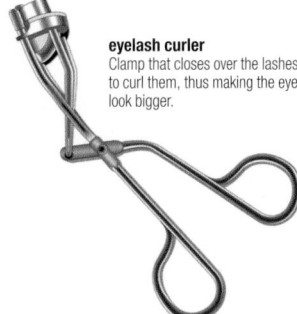

eyelash curler
Clamp that closes over the lashes to curl them, thus making the eyes look bigger.

concealer
Cream applied under the eyes to camouflage dark spots.

eyebrow pencil
Sharp pencil used to enhance eyebrows or change their shape.

liquid eyeliner
Dark liquid product applied at the base of the lashes with a fine-tipped brush to accentuate the eyes.

mascara brush
Small brush used to apply mascara to the lashes.

sponge-tipped applicator
Brush with a sponge at the tip that is used to apply and blend eyeshadow.

liquid mascara
Liquid product applied to the lashes with a brush to lengthen or thicken them or change their color.

cake mascara
Creamy compact product applied to the lashes with a brush to lengthen or thicken them or change their color.

eyeshadow
Product that comes mainly in pressed powder form and is applied to the eyelids to give them color.

makeup

lip makeup
Range of beauty products designed to
redraw the lip line and accentuate the lips.

lip gloss
Oil-based product containing
particles of glitter, applied to the lips
to add color.

lip liner
Pencil used to redraw and enhance the
lip line.

lipstick
Waxy product that comes in stick or
pencil form and is applied to the lips
to give them color.

lip brush
Very delicate brush with short
stiff bristles; it is used to draw the
lip line and apply lipstick inside
that line.

body care

Range of methods promoting physical hygiene and beauty.

cotton swab
Small stick with absorbent cotton
on each end, mainly used to clean
the ears.

stopper
Device inserted into the neck of the
bottle or screwed onto it to close
the bottle.

absorbent cotton
Absorbent white material from which
oils and resinous chemicals have been
removed, used in various ways for
personal hygiene.

bottle
Small container that is often made
of glass.

eau de toilette
Scented concoction that is more
diluted with a water/alcohol mix
than eau de parfum.

makeup remover pad
Small piece of soft material used to
remove makeup.

deodorant
Product applied to the armpits that
eliminates or reduces perspiration
odors.

eau de parfum
Scented concoction added to a water/
alcohol mix; it is more concentrated and
lingers longer than eau de toilette.

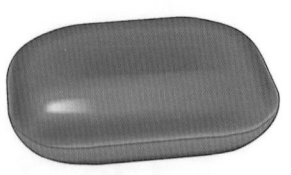

toilet soap
Fragrant fat-based product that is
used for washing the body.

scrub
Cleansing cream containing small
granules used to remove particles
of dead skin.

bath salts
Mineral salts used to perfume and
soften the water in a bath.

moisturizer
Cream used to rehydrate the skin.

hair coloring
Product applied to the hair to
color it.

body care

shampoo
...duct used to wash the hair and the scalp.

hair conditioner
Product applied to the hair after shampooing to strengthen it, improve its appearance and make styling easier.

shower gel
Perfumed water-soluble product used to wash the body.

bubble bath
Product that is poured into the bath under the faucet water; it produces large amounts of foam and scents and colors the bathwater.

lip balm
Oil-based product in a stick or a pencil, applied to the lips to moisturize them.

bath sheet
...ge bath towel used for drying the body after a shower or bath.

bath towel
Usually terry cloth article of bath linen used for drying parts of the body after bathing.

bath brush
Brush with relatively soft, flexible bristles that is used for scrubbing the body during baths or showers.

natural sponge
Particularly soft, flexible, absorbent material that comes from the dried skeleton of a marine animal and is used for bathing.

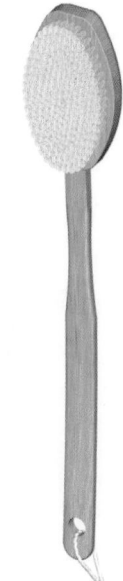

back brush
Bath brush with a handle long enough to scrub all of the back.

washcloth mitt
...th mitt usually made of terry cloth; it fits over ...e hand and is used for washing all or part of the body.

washcloth
Small square towel that is usually made of terry cloth and is used for washing the face.

massage glove
Rough glove used for rubbing the body to exfoliate the skin and stimulate the circulation.

loofah
Particularly soft, flexible, absorbent material that comes from dried plant matter and is used for bathing.

hairdressing

Care and styling of the hair using numerous appliances and accessories.

hairbrushes
Instruments made up of fibers of varying stiffness embedded in a backing; they are used to detangle and style hair.

flat-back brush
Brush with bristles set in a soft rubber backing that is used to detangle wet hair.

round brush
Brush with bristles that completely encircle the backing so that hair can be given a soft wave.

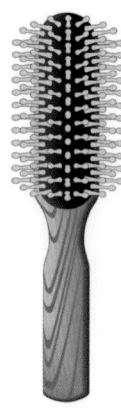

quill brush
Brush with round-tipped bristles set in a concave backing that massages the scalp; it is used for detangling and arranging hair.

vent brush
Brush with very widely spaced bristles set in a perforated backing; it is used during blow-drying to detangle hair and style it for a natural look.

combs
Devices with teeth of varying width and closeness that are used to detangle and style the hair.

Afro pick
Comb with long, widely spaced teeth used for detangling and tidying tightly curled hair without undoing the curls.

teaser comb
Comb whose head has teeth of three different lengths; it is used to brush up the hair to give it more body.

tail comb
Comb with small, closely spaced teeth that is used to arrange the hair.

barber comb
Comb with large, widely spaced teeth for detangling the hair on one side and small, closely spaced teeth used to arrange the hair on the other side.

pitchfork comb
Comb combining a teaser comb and an Afro pick.

rake comb
Comb with broad, widely spaced teeth for detangling hair without damaging it.

hair roller
Instrument around which a lock of hair is wrapped to make it curl.

roller
Cylinder whose length depends on the length of the lock of rolled hair and whose diameter depends on the desired curl size.

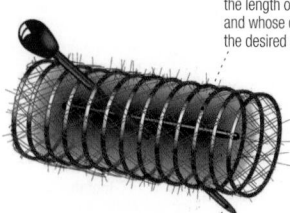

hair roller pin
Pin stuck through the roller to hold the lock of wrapped hair in place.

wave clip
Plastic pin with interlocking teeth used to secure a lock of hair.

hairpin
Bent filament with spread arms that is used to loosely secure a section of hair such as a chignon.

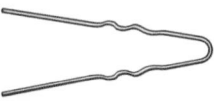

hair clip
Metal pin with elongated jaws that is used during styling to separate out sections of hair not being worked on.

bobby pin
Bent filament with tightly closed arms; it is used to secure a section of hair by holding it firmly in place.

barrette
Bobby pin with a clasp; it is used as adornment or to secure a lock of hair or the whole head of hair.

hairdressing

scissors
Instrument made of two crossed movable branches that are sharpened on the inside edge, used to cut hair.

haircutting scissors
Straight-bladed scissors used to trim hair.

cutting edge
Tapered edge of the blade designed for cutting.

blade
Thin, flat, sharp moving part used to cut hair.

pivot
Hinge pin enabling the blades to open and close.

ringhandle
End of the shank of the scissors where the fingers are placed to move the blades.

blade close stop
Projection on the ring handles that absorbs the impact between them.

shank
Each of the elongated parts that are moved to open and close the blades.

...ched single-edged thinning scissors
...sors that can both trim and thin hair because they have ...aight lower blade and a notched upper blade.

notched double-edged thinning scissors
Scissors with notched blades that thin the hair by cutting individual locks in points.

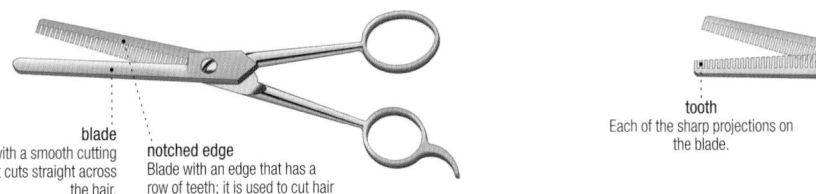

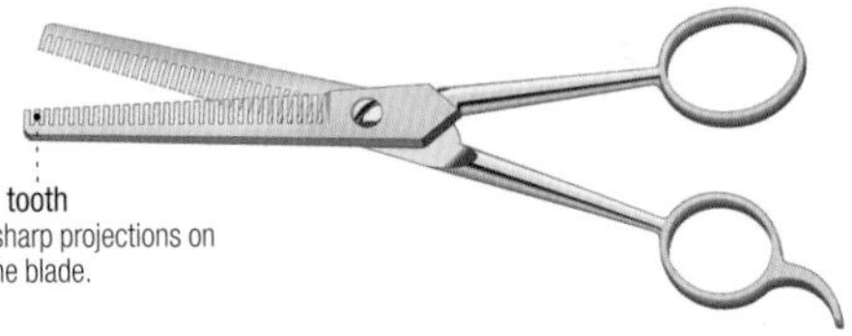

blade
...j part with a smooth cutting ...ge that cuts straight across the hair.

notched edge
Blade with an edge that has a row of teeth; it is used to cut hair in points.

tooth
Each of the sharp projections on the blade.

---

miscellaneous accessories

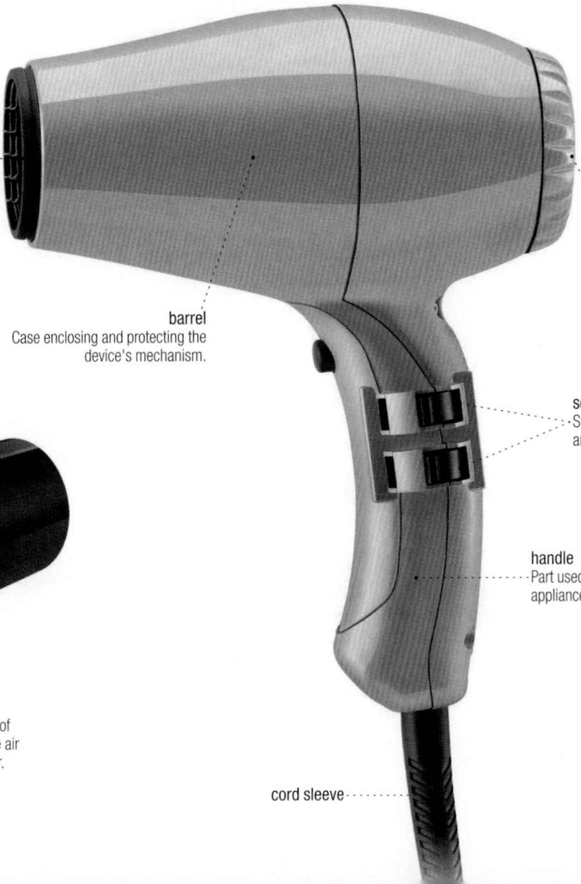

air-outlet grill
Grating through which the hot air is blown; it prevents any contact with the heating element inside.

hair dryer
Electric appliance that blows hot air to dry hair.

air-inlet grill
Grating through which air is drawn in; it prevents hair and other matter from entering the appliance's housing.

barrel
Case enclosing and protecting the device's mechanism.

selector switches
Switches for selecting the temperature and strength of the air jet.

handle
Part used to pick up and handle the appliance.

diffuser
Piece attached to the body of the appliance that directs the air coming from the hair dryer.

cord sleeve

hairdressing

lighted mirror
Mirror with a light fixture and swiveling panels that provide views from different angles.

lighting
Device that emits white light that do[es] not change the color of the hair or sk[in]

side mirror
Mirror that can be swiveled to provide a view of the profile.

dual swivel mirror
Two-sided mirror, one side of which magnified view.

base
Lower part of the mirror that acts as a stand.

on-off switch
Device for turning the lighting on or off.

thinning ra[zor]
Razor whose blade has sharp [teeth] that can cut hair in p[laces]

heated hair roller
Device used to curl the hair with the help of heat.

hair roller
Instrument around which a lock of hair is wrapped to make it curl.

clip
Instrument made of two jointed sections, used to hold the roller in place.

handle
Part used to pick up and handle the appliance.

straightening [iron]
Electric appliance that smoo[ths] and straightens

indicator light
Light showing that the appliance is on.

on-off switch
Button for turning the device on or off.

plate
Heating element that is closed over a lock of curly or wavy hair and drawn along its length to straighten it.

cord sl[eeve]
Protective casing around the [cord] to lessen twisting and p[ulling]

curling iron
Electric appliance used to curl hair.

clamp lever
Piece that is pushed down to open the clamp.

on-off switch
Button for turning the device on or off.

cool tip
End of the barrel that remains cool so that it can be touched with the fingers when handling the appliance.

clamp
Part that closes over and presses down on a lock of hair before it is rolled around the barrel.

power cord
Flexible electric wire housing the leads connecting the appliance to the electric circuit.

barrel
Heated cylinder around which a lock of hair is wrapped.

stand
Piece used to place the appliance on a surface even when the barrel is hot.

handle
Part used to pick up and handle the appliance.

clippers
Electric appliance used to trim a beard [or] very short hair; the adjustable head make[s it] possible to trim to various lengths.

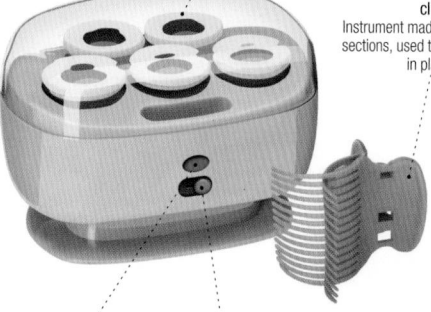

shaving products

Range of appliances and accessories used to cut the beard close to the skin.

shaving cream
oduct applied to the beard before
aving to soften the hairs and help
the blade glide more smoothly.

power cord
Flexible electric wire housing the
leads connecting the appliance to the
electric circuit.

floating head
Base to which the blades are
connected; it pivots as it follows
the facial contours to give a close,
smooth shave.

screen
Grating that protects the skin from contact
with the blades and positions the hair so
that it can be cut more easily.

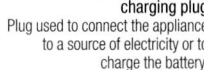

cleaning brush
Brush used for cleaning the blades
and inside the heads.

charge indicator
Signal indicating the amount of
power still available.

charging plug
Plug used to connect the appliance
to a source of electricity or to
charge the battery.

electric razor
Razor with power-activated blades.

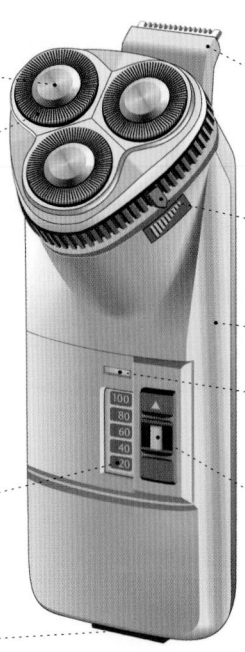

trimmer
Retractable accessory with two
notched blades; it uses a back-
and-forth motion to trim mustaches
and sideburns.

closeness setting
Device that adjusts the height of
the razor heads.

housing
Case enclosing and protecting the
device's mechanism.

charging light
Signal light that indicates when
the razor is recharging or when it
is finished.

on-off switch
Button for turning the device on
or off.

bristle
Part of the shaving brush made of
hog's hair or, more rarely, badger
hair.

shaving brush
ush with long firm bristles that is
ed to apply a thin coat of shaving
lather to the face.

straight razor
Traditional barber's razor that is
made up of a very sharp blade
hinged into a handle.

blade
Long sharp steel surface used for
cutting the beard.

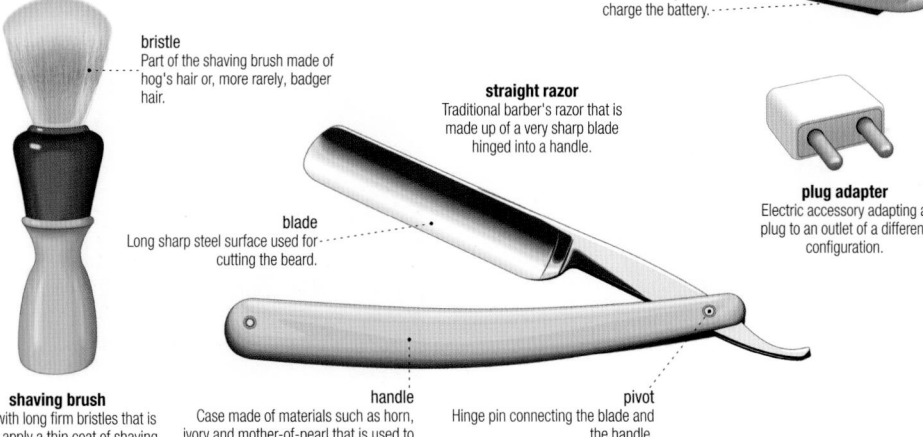

handle
Case made of materials such as horn,
ivory and mother-of-pearl that is used to
manipulate the razor during use and to
store the blade when it is not in use.

pivot
Hinge pin connecting the blade and
the handle.

plug adapter
Electric accessory adapting a
plug to an outlet of a different
configuration.

double-edged blade
Disposable blade with two cutting
edges doubling the blade's useful
life.

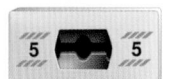

razor blade dispenser
Small metal or plastic box containing
spare blades.

safety razor
Metal hand razor with several stacked blades
which are replaced as needed.

head
End of the razor that holds the
blade in place; the handle is
screwed into it.

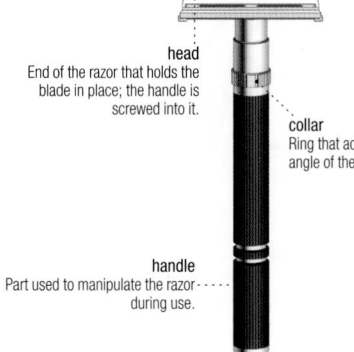

collar
Ring that adjusts the
angle of the blade.

handle
Part used to manipulate the razor
during use.

disposable razor
Plastic razor with one or more
overlapping blades that can be thrown
away after a few shaves.

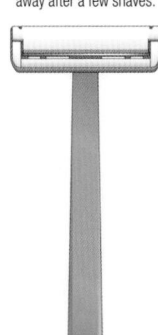

aftershave
on applied to the face after shaving
to soothe and scent the skin.

shaving mug
Container in which the shaving lather is
made before it is applied to the beard.

eyeglasses

Lenses set in frames that are placed in front of the eyes to correct vision or to protect the eyes from the Sun's brilliant rays.

eyeglasses parts

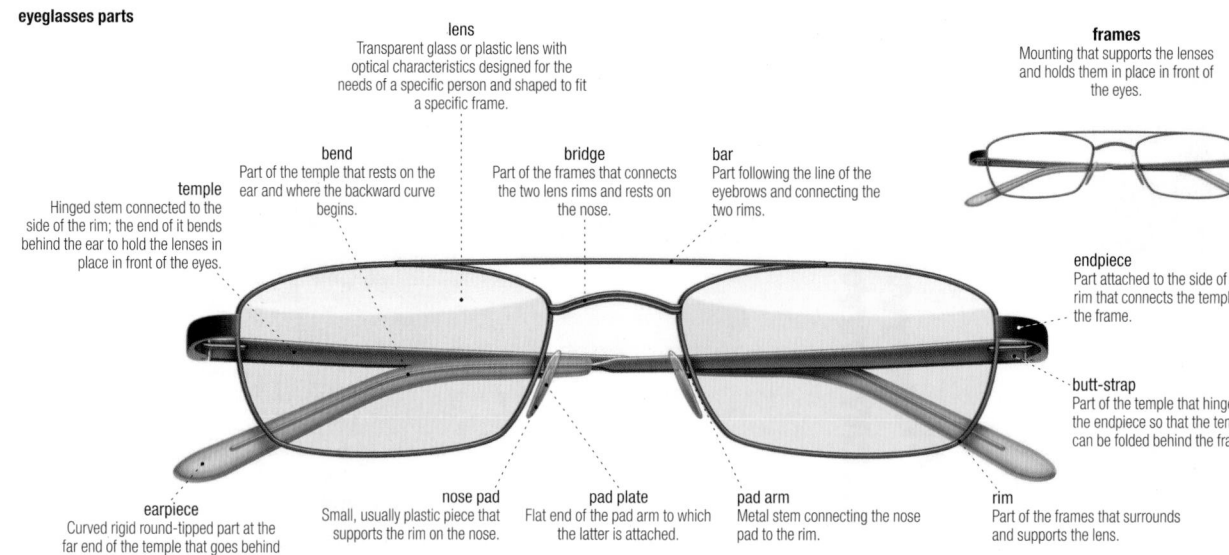

lens
Transparent glass or plastic lens with optical characteristics designed for the needs of a specific person and shaped to fit a specific frame.

frames
Mounting that supports the lenses and holds them in place in front of the eyes.

bend
Part of the temple that rests on the ear and where the backward curve begins.

bridge
Part of the frames that connects the two lens rims and rests on the nose.

bar
Part following the line of the eyebrows and connecting the two rims.

temple
Hinged stem connected to the side of the rim; the end of it bends behind the ear to hold the lenses in place in front of the eyes.

endpiece
Part attached to the side of the rim that connects the temple the frame.

butt-strap
Part of the temple that hinges the endpiece so that the temp can be folded behind the fram

earpiece
Curved rigid round-tipped part at the far end of the temple that goes behind the ear.

nose pad
Small, usually plastic piece that supports the rim on the nose.

pad plate
Flat end of the pad arm to which the latter is attached.

pad arm
Metal stem connecting the nose pad to the rim.

rim
Part of the frames that surrounds and supports the lens.

---

eyeglasses accessories
Objects used with eyeglasses.

clip-on sunglasses
Lenses that can be attached to the frame of the glasses, used to filter sunlight.

lens cleaning cloth
Piece of synthetic fabric used to clean the lenses of glasses.

eyeglasses retainer
Small rope that holds the glasses around the neck.

eyeglasses case
Holder that is shaped to fit glasses and used to carry and protect them.

eyeglasses

PERSONAL ACCESSORIES AND ARTICLES

examples of eyeglasses
The shape of glasses varies depending on the period and their use (e.g., correcting far- or nearsightedness, protecting the eye, magnifying).

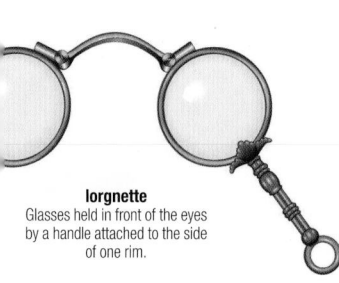

lorgnette
Glasses held in front of the eyes by a handle attached to the side of one rim.

half-glasses
Glasses with half lenses to correct farsightedness; the empty space above them is used to see distances.

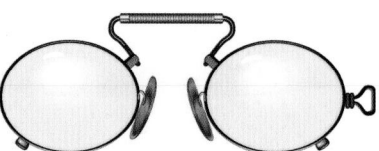

pince-nez
Glasses whose frame has a spring bridge that grips the nose.

opera glasses
optical magnifying instrument held in front of the eyes; it is used for looking at relatively close objects such as at the theater.

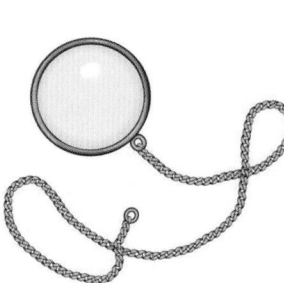

monocle
Single lens held in place under the ridge of the eyebrow.

scissors-glasses
Lorgnette whose lenses fold back over one another and can be slipped into the handle, which also acts as a case.

sunglasses
Glasses with lenses that filter the Sun's glare to protect the eyes.

contact lenses

Transparent visual aid placed over the cornea to correct defective vision.

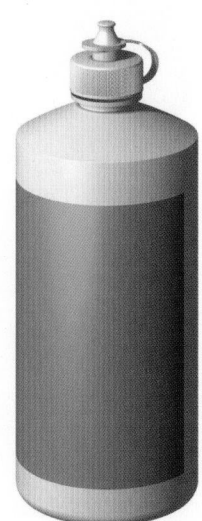

multipurpose solution
Product that cleans, rinses, disinfects and conserves the lenses.

disposable contact lens
Soft lens that lasts from one to 30 days.

soft contact lens
Very thin lens that molds perfectly to the shape of the eye and lasts from one to two years.

hard contact lens
Thicker than the soft contact lens, this lens lasts from two to 10 years.

left side
Place where the lens worn in the left eye is kept.

right side
Place where the lens worn in the right eye is kept.

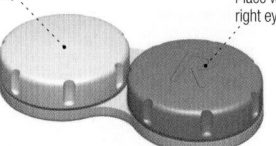
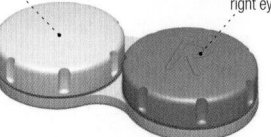

lens case
Container in which the lenses are kept bathed in a multipurpose solution.

lubricant eye drops
Product applied in drops to the eyes to moisten them; the lens does not have to be removed.

dental care

Procedures to care for the mouth and especially the teeth that include brushing, flossing and using mouthwash.

manual toothbrush
Tool used to clean the teeth using a
back and forth motion of the hand.

handle
Part used to pick up and handle
the brush.

bristle
More or less supple filaments that
clean the surface of the teeth.

head
Part of the brush where the bristles are
inserted.

dental floss
Flexible, strong, often waxed strand
is used to clean between the teeth

replacement brush head
Small removable toothbrush
attachment.

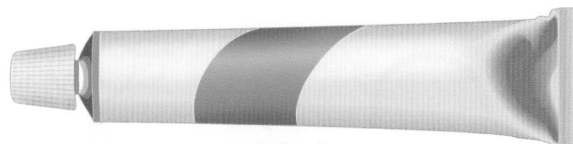

toothpaste
Paste or gel used to clean teeth and gums
by brushing it over the teeth and making
it foam.

shaft
Part through which the motor
transmits movement to the bristles
of the brush head.

dental floss
Flexible, strong, often waxed strand that
is used to clean between the teeth.

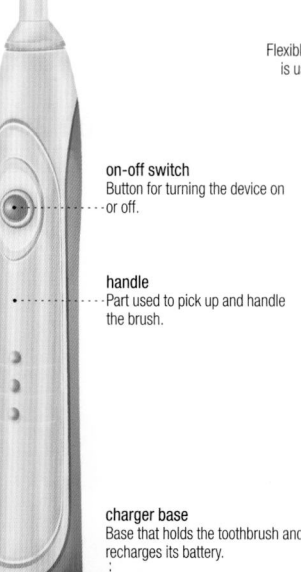

on-off switch
Button for turning the device on
or off.

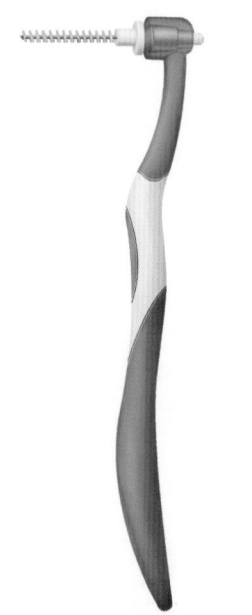

handle
Part used to pick up and handle
the brush.

charger base
Base that holds the toothbrush and
recharges its battery.

dental floss holder
Device upon which dental floss is
stretched to make flossing easier.

interdental brush
Small brush used to clean between
the teeth.

power toothbrush
Electric appliance used for cleaning
teeth with either a rotating or back-
and-forth motion.

mouthwash
Liquid used to gargle, rinse the mouth
freshen the breath.

smoking accessories

Range of objects used for smoking tobacco in pipes, cigars or cigarettes.

...ment consisting of a tobacco ...hat is filled with tobacco and ...n through which the smoke ...aled.

bowl
Lower projecting part of the stummel that is used to hold the pipe.

shank
With the tobacco hole, it forms part of the stummel and acts as a conduit.

cross section of a pipe

peg
Projecting part of the stem that fits into the stummel.

tobacco hole
Part of the pipe that holds the burning tobacco.

air hole
End of the conduit through which smoke passes into the mouth.

..., flat end of the stem that is ...between the teeth.

stem
Part of the pipe that is usually made of hard rubber; it fits into the shank and acts as a conduit.

stummel
Usually wooden part of a pipe that contains the tobacco hole.

filter
Small aluminum tube inserted between the shank and the stem; it is intended to capture some of the smoke's toxic substances.

mortise
Opening made in the stummel that the peg of the stem fits into.

...lighter
...ument containing liquid butane ...etimes mixed with propane that ...ited by a spark produced from ...on.

striker wheel
...all notched wheel that ...produces sparks when ...d against a stone, thus ...gniting the flow of gas.

butane tank
Hollow cylindrical ...mpartment containing liquid butane.

cover
Spring-loaded hood that snaps down to extinguish the flame.

tobacco
Product made from the dried leaves of a nicotine-rich plant; the leaves are treated and made into cigars or cigarettes for smoking.

flame adjustment wheel
Wheel that adjusts the flow of gas escaping from the tank, thus increasing or decreasing the size of the flame.

filler
Inside of a cigar made of two to four different kinds of tobacco leaves, which are cut moderately fine.

wrapper
Thin, very high-grade tobacco leaf used as a casing to wrap around a cigar.

cigar band
Paper ring that encircles the cigar bearing the manufacturer or brand name or a company logo.

cigar
Roll made of pieces of tobacco leaves wrapped in a large high-grade leaf.

tuck
Tip of the cigar that is to be lit; if the tuck is closed, it must be cut off before the cigar can be lit.

bunch
Body of the cigar made up of the cut tobacco leaves and the leaf that is wrapped around them.

head
End of the cigar that is placed in the mouth; it must be clipped before the cigar is lit.

cigarette
Small roll of cut tobacco wrapped in thin paper; it often has a filter at one end and is made for smoking.

paper
Very thin sheet of paper that is wrapped around the tobacco.

filter tip
Tip at the mouth end for capturing some of the smoke's toxic substances.

...chbook
... closed by a flap that contains ... of matches attached to the

cover
Flap that slides under the front flap to close the book.

matchstick
Usually cardboard or wooden body of the match.

head
...e match with a chemical ...ng that lights when struck against another surface.

front flap
Flap under which the matches are attached.

tobacco
Product made from the dried leaves of a nicotine-rich plant; the leaves are treated and made into cigars or cigarettes for smoking.

seam
Line along which the cigarette paper is sealed.

...chbox
...angular or square box with ...ing lid containing loose ...hes.

safety match
Small stem with a head that lights only when struck against a particular surface, thus preventing accidental lighting.

butt
Unburned portion of a cigar or cigarette.

ashtray
Receptacle into which smokers empty their pipe or leave the remains of their cigar or cigarette.

ash
Residue left from burned tobacco.

leather goods

Personal articles made of leather or fake leather.

attaché case
Small plain case with rigid sides that is used to carry documents.

divider
Panel used to keep personal effects separate; it is held by hooks or snap fasteners and contains compartments and pockets.

pocket
Small, soft, flat rectangular pocket that is used to hold similar objects.

hinge
Metal structure consisting of two symmetrical pieces that move on an axis and are used to open and close the case.

lining
Fabric or leather covering that protects and embellishes the inside of the case.

clasp
Metal device such as a clip or fastener that is used to hold an object closed.

expandable file pouch
Set of overlapping pockets used to hold documents.

pen holder
Tubular piece of leather or fabric used to hold pens.

frame
Rectangular metal piece on which the shell is mounted; it supports the hinges, locks and handle.

handle
Part used to pick up and carry the case.

combination lock
Lock that is opened with a combination of numbers.

bottom-fold portfolio
Briefcase with a handle; its sides expand to accommodate more documents or books.

retractable handle
Rigid, flat handle that slides through two openings in the case.

exterior pocket
Flat pocket incorporated with the front of the portfolio and closed with a zipper.

brief
Rectangular bag
compartments that is used to
items such as documents
and b

tab
Small piece with a fastening system that extends a flap or goes over an article's opening to fasten it.

key lock
Lock that opens with a key.

gusset
Piece sewn along the bottom and up the side of a bag to increase its capacity.

checkbook/secretary clutch
Article with compartments of various sizes that is intended to hold identity papers, cards, banknotes, change, a pen and a checkbook.

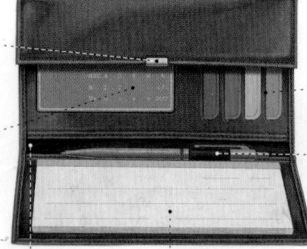
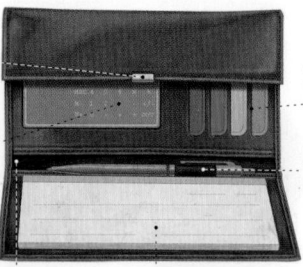

trimming
Metal piece used to reinforce the edge or the corner of certain articles.

calculator
Small self-powered electronic instrument used to automatically make numerical calculations.

card case
Set of adjacent pockets for inserting various cards.

pen holder
Tubular piece of leather or fabric used to hold pens.

hidden pocket
Pocket with a hidden opening.

checkbook
Notebook containing blank checks.

bill compartment
Flat compartment between the back and the inside of a wallet or a card case where banknotes are kept.

card
Article used to hold, organize and p
identity papers and other cards
making them easily vi

windows
Transparent compartm
hold photographs or id

tab
Small piece with a fas
system that extends a
goes over an article's
fasten it.

slot
Narrow elongated opening into which a card is inserted with a part of it projecting so it can be easily recognized.

ID window
A window behind which an identity cards is inserted to protect it and make its front side visible.

wallet
Article with compartments of various
sizes that is designed to hold identity
papers, cards, banknotes and change.

billfold
Case with a number of dividers that
is folded in half and used only for
banknotes.

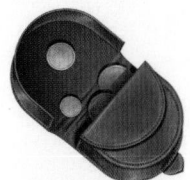

coin purse
Small case of various sizes that
is designed to hold change and is
usually carried in a pocket.

key case
Case accommodating a number
of keys that is designed to protect
a bag or garment from contact
with them.

change purse
Small soft-sided bag with a zipper or
clasp that is used to store change and
sometimes banknotes.

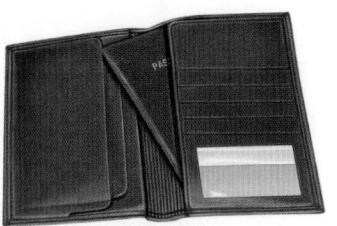

passport case
Case usually separated into several
compartments; one of them is
shaped to hold and protect a
passport.

eyeglasses case
Holder with relatively rigid sides
that is shaped to fit glasses and
used to carry and protect them.

checkbook case
Case that protects a checkbook
from handling and rubbing against
the inside of a pocket or bag.

underarm portfolio
Slim briefcase with only one
compartment.

writing case
Article for holding correspondence
materials such as paper and a pen; it
has a rigid surface for writing.

handbags

Relatively soft and light accessory that contains a pocket and is carried in the hand, under the arm or over the shoulder; it is used to carry various objects.

drawstring bag
Soft-sided cylindrical flat-bottomed bag with a single compartment that might have handles or a shoulder strap.

eyelet
Small metal-rimmed hole through which the drawstring passes.

drawstring
Narrow leather or fabric cord that is flat or round; it is threaded through the eyelets and used to close the bag.

front pocket
Flat compartment affixed to the front of the bag.

handle
Part used to pick up and carry the bag.

flap
Piece sometimes equipped with a fastening system that goes over the opening of an object to close it.

clasp
Metal device such as a clip or fastener that is used to hold an object closed.

lock
Mechanism for an owner to secure an article using a key or a combination.

satchel
Sturdy bag with a handle and shoulder straps; it combines a hand with a brief

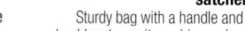

tote bag
Fairly large bag having neither divider nor pocket but with a shoulder strap; it is practical, simple and sturdy.

carrier bag
Large sturdy bag with handles that is used to carry groceries.

box bag
Rigid-sided bag with one or two handles

drawstring bag
Soft cylindrical bag with only one compartment that closes with a drawstring and has a shoulder strap.

messenger bag
Small soft-bodied bag with a shoulder strap, having multiple pockets and compartments.

sea bag
Large, usually leather-bottomed drawstring bag with a shoulder strap attached down the side.

handbags

money belt
Small flat pocket worn under the clothes, used to hide money, passports and other documents.

fanny pack
Small and light bag worn around the waist.

muff bag
Small, light, flat bag with a cord that hangs from the wrist; it is used for carrying very small objects and doubles as a handwarmer.

gusset
Piece sewn along the bottom and up the side of a bag to increase its capacity.

accordion bag
Bag that has soft adjacent pockets with gussets and often zippers; the whole bag is closed with a flap.

shopping bag
Large carrier bag.

men's bag
Small, plain, usually rectangular bag for men with a handle and sometimes a shoulder strap.

duffel bag
Soft, cylindrical bag usually with a zipper along its entire length; it has two symmetrical handles or a shoulder strap.

shoulder strap
Long belt often with a buckle to adjust it; it is used to carry the bag over the shoulder or diagonally across the chest.

buckle
Fastener made up of a ring that secures the two ends of a shoulder strap.

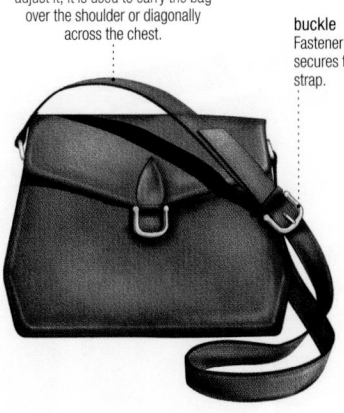

shoulder bag
Bag with an adjustable shoulder strap and a flap or zipper closure.

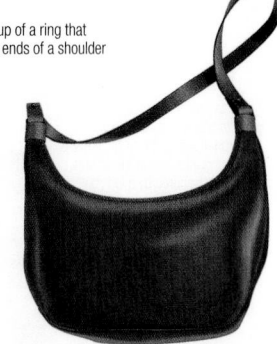

hobo bag
Bag whose bottom consists of a strip that comes up each side as far as the opening and then forms a point where the shoulder strap is attached.

luggage

Articles such as suitcases, boxes and bags that are used to store and protect items packed for a trip.

carry-on bag
Travel bag that can be carried into an airplane cabin because its dimensions do not exceed the limits set by carriers.

handle
Part used to pick up and carry the bag.

shoulder strap
Long belt often with a buckle to adjust it; it is used to carry the bag over the shoulder or diagonally across the chest.

exterior pocket
Flat pocket incorporated with the front of the suitcase and closed with a zipper.

utility case
Multicompartment case designed to hold articles such as toiletries, cosmetics and jewelry.

tote
Light travel bag with soft sides only one compartm

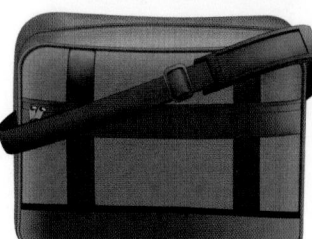

garment bag
Soft-sided carrier that encases and protects clothing; it is hung from a built-in hanger.

identification tag
Small transparent case attached to a suitcase; a label with the owner's name and address is inserted inside it.

handle
Part used to pick up and carry the suitcase.

suitca
Large rectangular piece of h luggage that is often equipped wheels to facilitate transp

frame
Rectangular metal piece on which the shell is mounted; it supports the hinges, locks and handle.

pull strap
Leash attached to the suitcase that is placed over the wrist to pull the suitcase along on its wheels.

zipper
Closure made up of two lengths of tape edged with teeth that interlock by means of a slide.

trim
Parts made of various materials designed to reinforce the bottom of the suitcase.

wheel
Small castor attached to the suitcase so that it can be rolled rather than carried.

trunk
Large rigid sturdy piece of luggage that is used to transport objects.

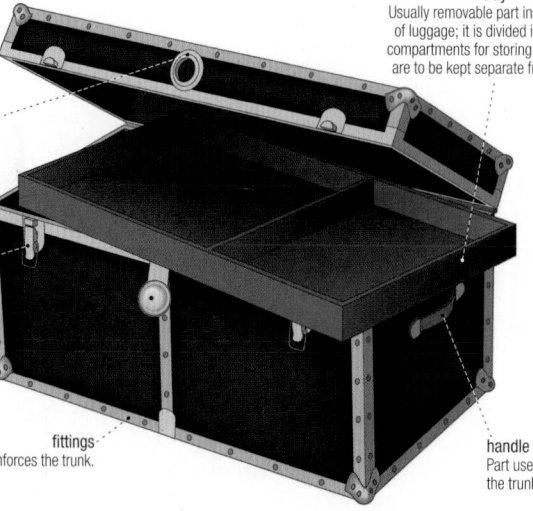

tray
Usually removable part inside a piece of luggage; it is divided into several compartments for storing articles that are to be kept separate from others.

hasp
Fastener that consists of a hinged pin with a lock that is anchored to the inner wall of the trunk; it fits over a ring attached to the lid and is secured by a lock bolt.

latch
Two-part metal accessory that holds the trunk lid closed.

cornerpiece
Metal trim that reinforces the corners of the trunk.

fittings
Metal trim that reinforces the trunk.

handle
Part used to pick up and carry the trunk.

luggage carrier
Wheeled stand that is pulled with a handle; suitcases are placed on it to transport them.

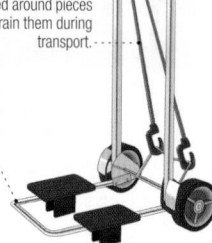

frame
Structure consisting of usually metal pieces forming the framework of an object.

luggage elastic
Sturdy elastic cord with a hook at one end that is wrapped around pieces of luggage to restrain them during transport.

stand
Foldaway part of the luggage carrier on which the suitcases are placed.

luggage

retractable handle
Handle that can be pulled out of the suitcase so it can be pulled or pushed more easily.

ment bag on wheels
ge, flat bag for carrying clothes out folding them.

top carrying handle
Part used to pick up and handle the bag.

backpack
Travel or hiking bag that is worn on the back.

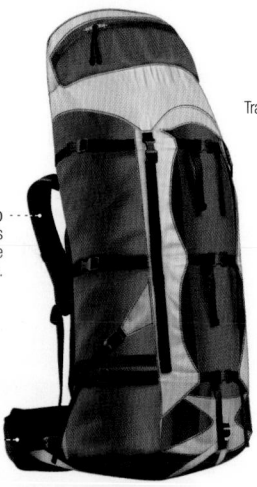

shoulder strap
Fabric band of variable length that goes over the shoulder so the bag can be carried on the back.

hip belt
Fabric strap that fits snugly around the hips and buckles there; it is designed to distribute the bag's weight.

front pocket
Flat compartment located on the front of the bag.

retractable handle
Handle that can be pulled out of the suitcase so it can be pulled or pushed more easily.

upright suitcase
Rectangular suitcase, in a variety of sizes, equipped with wheels and a retractable handle that facilitate transport.

ekender
all rectangular piece of hand luggage that is used short trips.

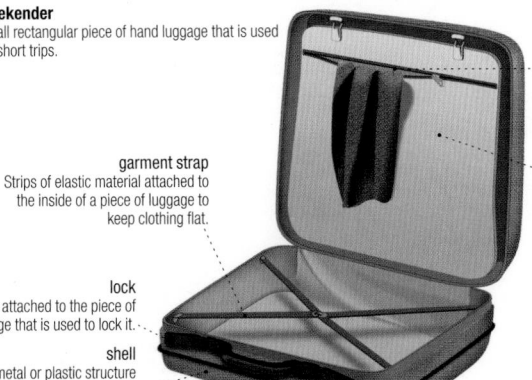

interior pocket
Flat compartment in the internal lining of the suitcase.

garment strap
Strips of elastic material attached to the inside of a piece of luggage to keep clothing flat.

curtain
Panel for keeping papers separate from personal effects; it is held by hooks or snap fasteners and sometimes has a pocket.

lock
attached to the piece of ge that is used to lock it.

shell
netal or plastic structure makes up the suitcase's n pieces; they close one on top of the other.

top computer briefcase
all briefcase with compartments; it carries a op computer and its accessories as well as uments.

computer compartment

document compartment

duffel bag on wheels
Large, soft bag used to transport large objects, clothing and various equipment.

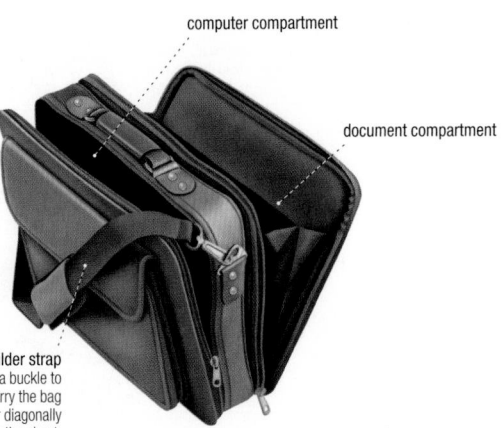

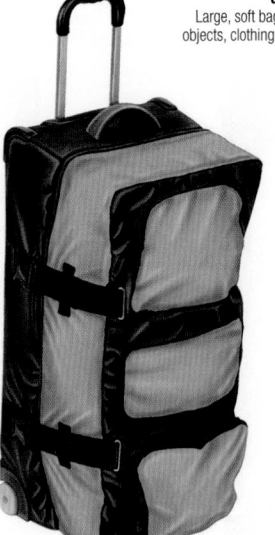

shoulder strap
g belt often with a buckle to ; it is used to carry the bag r the shoulder or diagonally across the chest.

umbrella and stick

The shape, price and materials of these personal articles vary widely according to culture, period and manufacturer.

umbrella
Accessory made up of a handle and fabric stretched over a collapsible metal frame that is used as protection against the rain or sun.

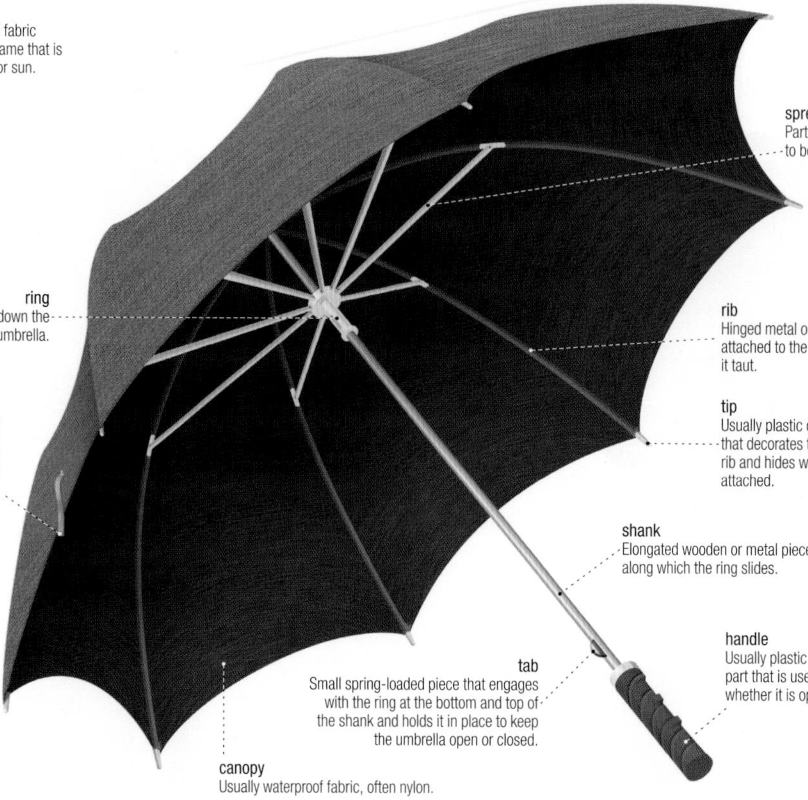

spreader
Part of the frame that is connected to both the ring and a rib.

ring
Piece that slides up and down the shank to open and close the umbrella.

rib
Hinged metal or wooden rod that is attached to the canopy and used to stretch it taut.

tie
Strip of material with a fastener that is wrapped around the closed umbrella to hold the ribs and canopy in place.

tip
Usually plastic or wooden trim that decorates the end of each rib and hides where the canopy is attached.

shank
Elongated wooden or metal piece along which the ring slides.

handle
Usually plastic or sometimes wooden part that is used to hold the umbrella whether it is open or closed.

tab
Small spring-loaded piece that engages with the ring at the bottom and top of the shank and holds it in place to keep the umbrella open or closed.

canopy
Usually waterproof fabric, often nylon.

umbrella stand
Variously shaped accessory or piece of furniture where umbrellas and walking sticks are kept.

telescopic umbrella
Umbrella that can become shorter when closed because it has a collapsible handle and hinged ribs that fold up.

push button
Button that is pushed to activate the umbrella's opening mechanism.

cover
Elongated case that covers the umbrella when it is closed to protect its canopy.

walking stick
Crafted stick used for support when walking.

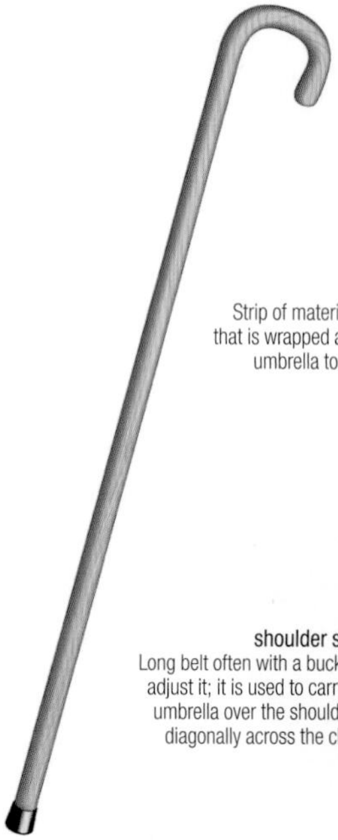

stick umbrella
Umbrella with a handle shaped a walking stick.

ferrule
Usually metal trim covering the tip of an umbrella to decorate it and protect it from contact with the ground.

tie
Strip of material with a fastener that is wrapped around the closed umbrella to hold the ribs and canopy in place.

shoulder strap
Long belt often with a buckle to adjust it; it is used to carry the umbrella over the shoulder or diagonally across the chest.

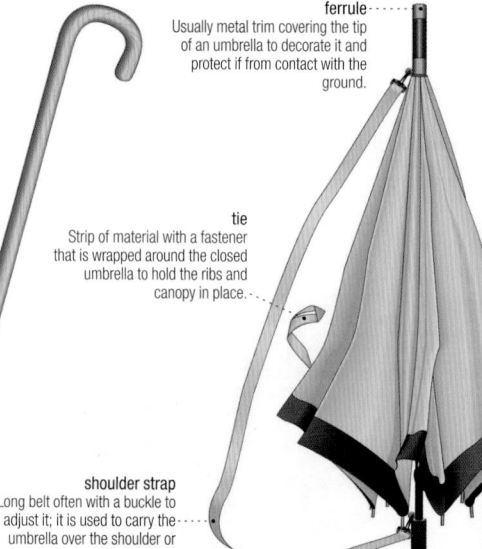

child care items

All the accessories designed and adapted for the transport, feeding and hygiene of young children.

ant car seat
table cushioned seat designed
it a baby, attached to a
cialized base, and fitted with a
ety harness to hold the baby in a
ted position.

carrying handle
Piece used for holding and carrying
the seat.

hood
Small retractable roof to
protect the child from the sun.

cloth baby carrier
Soft harness used for carrying a newborn
against the front of one's body.

wrap baby carrier
Long band of wrapped fabric allowing
an infant to be carried in various ways.

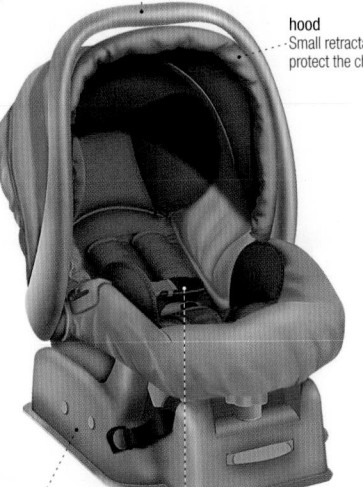

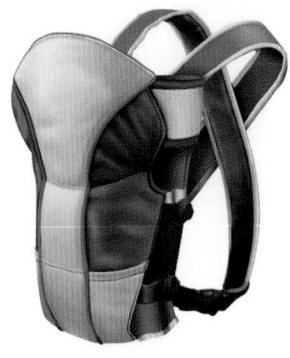
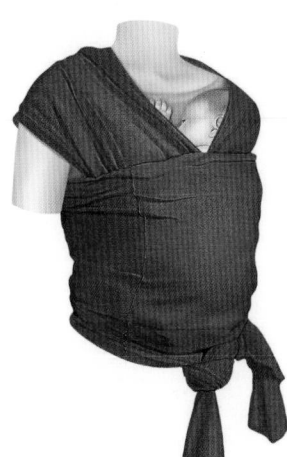

stay-in-car base
Rigid structure attached to the
backseat of the vehicle, on which
the infant car seat is mounted.

harness
Arrangement of straps and buckles
to secure the child in the seat.

stroller
Collapsible carriage designed as a
chair mounted on wheels; it is used
to transport a young child.

ckpack baby carrier
ce of equipment allowing an adult
carry an infant on the back using
oulder straps attached to a seat.

hood
Small retractable roof to protect the
child from the sun.

handle
Piece used for holding and pushing
the stroller.

hood
Small retractable roof to protect the
child from the sun.

headrest
Piece that supports the child's
head.

shoulder strap
nd of variable length that
r the shoulder so the bag
n be carried on the back.

harness
Arrangement of straps and buckles
to secure the child in the seat.

harness
Arrangement of straps and buckles
to secure the child in the seat.

padded hip belt
Fabric strap that fits snugly
round the hips and buckles
there; it is designed to
istribute the baby's weight.

kickstand
Metal structure allowing the baby
carrier to be rested upright on the
ground.

basket
Container for holding
various objects.

child care items

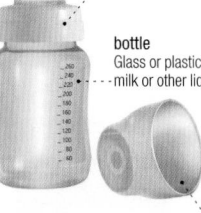

nipple
Piece of rubber or silicone through which the baby can suck the contents of the bottle.

ring
Piece used to attach the nipple to the bottle.

bottle
Glass or plastic container used to serve milk or other liquids.

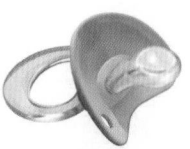

pacifier
Piece of rubber or silicone for the baby to suck on.

baby bottle
Glass or plastic container with a nipple over the opening, for infants to drink from.

cap
Piece covering the nipple and the bottle ring.

portable changing pad
Waterproof cushion on which the baby is placed to have its diaper changed.

pacifier clip
Strap with a clip on one end for attaching a pacifier to the infant's clothing.

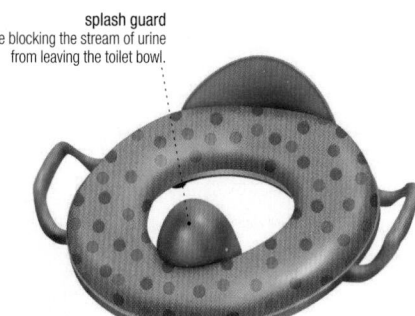

splash guard
Piece blocking the stream of urine from leaving the toilet bowl.

toilet seat reducer
Small seat attached onto the toilet seat to facilitate its use by young children.

diaper bag
Bag designed to carry everything needed to change a baby's diaper.

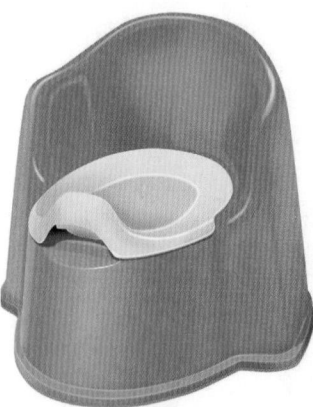

potty-chair
A seat used for toilet training with an opening under which a receptacle is placed.

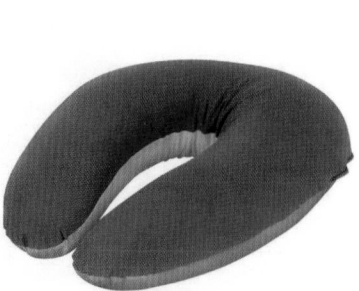

nursing pillow
U-shaped cushion on which the child is rested for ease of nursing.

bassinet
Small portable bed for an infant.

pet care items

All the accessories designed and adapted for the transport, feeding and hygiene of house pets.

muzzle
Assembly of straps used to keep the animal's mouth closed.

leash
Strap made of flexible material attached to the animal's collar and used to restrain it.

two-sided brush
Brush with rigid bristles on one side, and more supple bristles on the other.

nail clipper
Tool for cutting the animal's claws.

tag
Small metal piece attached to a collar, on which information about the animal's identity can be etched.

collar
Strap made of chain or supple material, placed around the animal's neck.

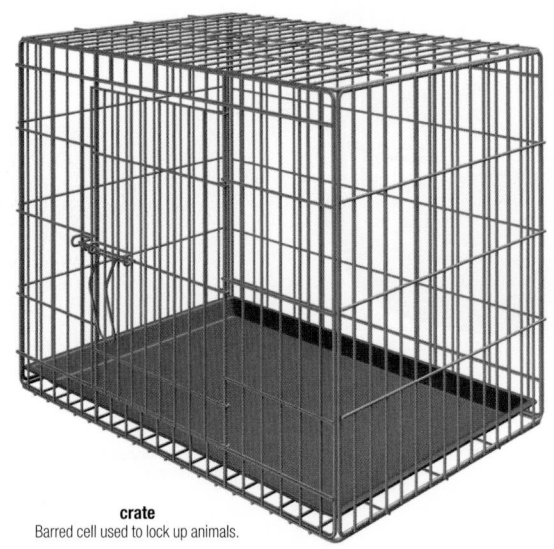

crate
Barred cell used to lock up animals.

pet carrier
Container with bars and a handle, used to transport small animals.

scoop
Tool designed for picking up clumped waste in the litter box.

box
Receptacle for the litter.

litter
Bed of absorbent particles onto which the animal relieves itself.

litter box
Indoor container in which a small animal, usually a cat, relieves itself.

bowl
Container for holding food or water.

bed
Mattress on which the animal can rest.

pet care

birdcage
Piece made up of a metal grill structure mounted on a tray in which the bird lives.

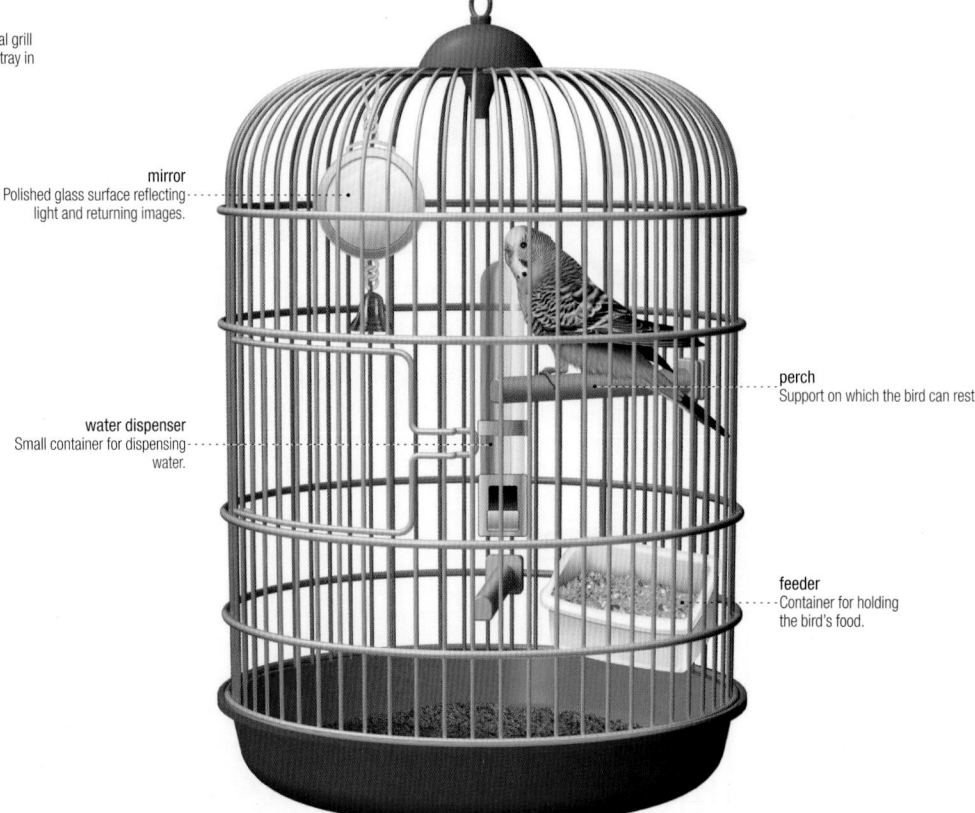

mirror
Polished glass surface reflecting light and returning images.

perch
Support on which the bird can rest.

water dispenser
Small container for dispensing water.

feeder
Container for holding the bird's food.

small animal cage
Piece made up of a metal grill structure mounted on a tray in which a small animal (rat, hamster, mouse, etc.) lives.

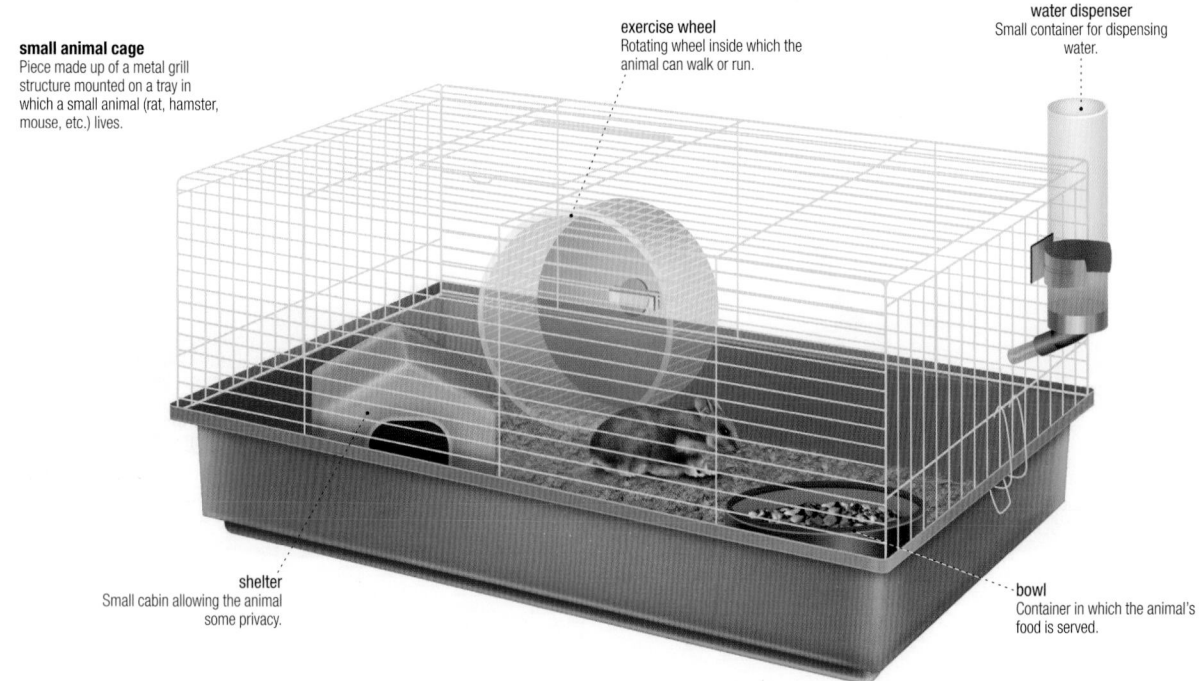

exercise wheel
Rotating wheel inside which the animal can walk or run.

water dispenser
Small container for dispensing water.

shelter
Small cabin allowing the animal some privacy.

bowl
Container in which the animal's food is served.

heating lamp
Apparatus that both lights the
interior of the terrarium and warms
the air.

terrarium
Glass container used to house pet
reptiles.

thermometer/hygrometer
Instrument that allows the
ⁱulation of the temperature and
ⁱdity level inside the terrarium.

water or feeding dish
ⁱainer for holding food or water.

cover
Movable piece that covers the
aquarium.

aquarium
Glass container filled with water, used to
house pet fish.

lighting
Apparatus for providing lighting
inside the aquarium.

thermometer
Instrument that allows the
regulation of the water
temperature.

air pump
Small motor that produces air bubbles in
order to oxygenate the aquarium.

background
Image depicting the ocean floor.

ⁱhnet
ⁱ attached to a frame at the end
ⁱ handle; it is used to take a fish
of the water.

stand
Base on which the aquarium rests.

ARTS AND ARCHITECTURE

pyramid

Construction with a square base and four triangular faces; it served as a tomb for the pharaohs of ancient Egypt, represented here by the pyramid of Khufu.

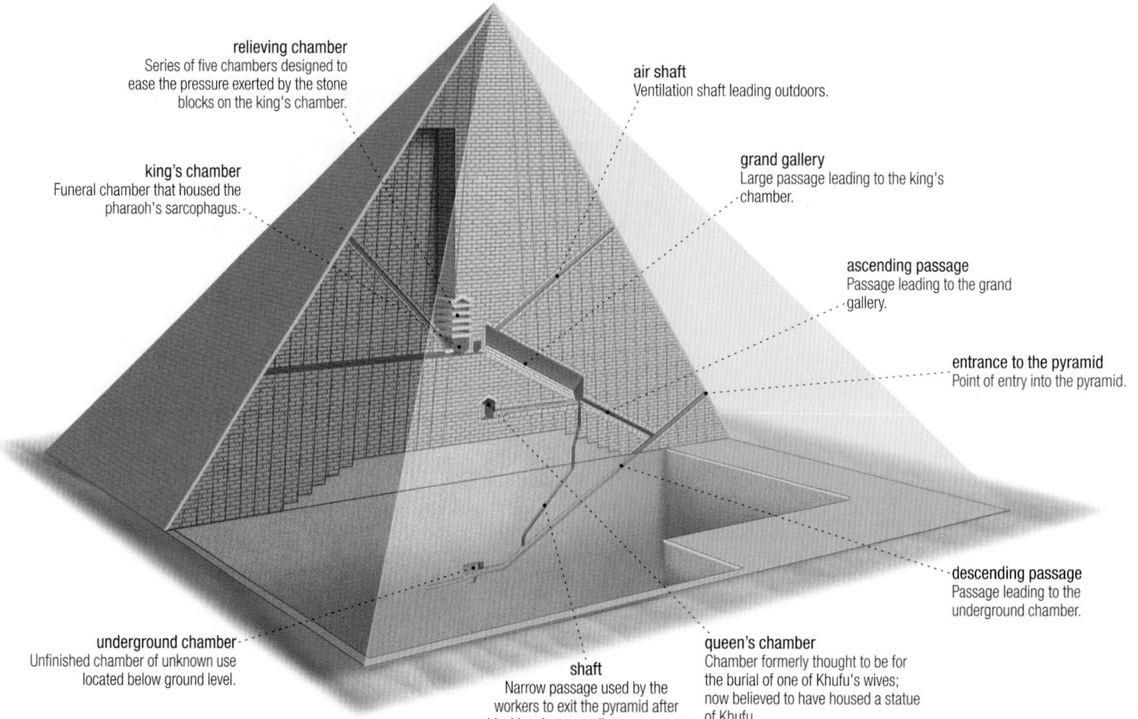

relieving chamber
Series of five chambers designed to ease the pressure exerted by the stone blocks on the king's chamber.

air shaft
Ventilation shaft leading outdoors.

king's chamber
Funeral chamber that housed the pharaoh's sarcophagus.

grand gallery
Large passage leading to the king's chamber.

ascending passage
Passage leading to the grand gallery.

entrance to the pyramid
Point of entry into the pyramid.

descending passage
Passage leading to the underground chamber.

underground chamber
Unfinished chamber of unknown use located below ground level.

shaft
Narrow passage used by the workers to exit the pyramid after blocking the ascending passage at the conclusion of the funeral rites.

queen's chamber
Chamber formerly thought to be for the burial of one of Khufu's wives; now believed to have housed a statue of Khufu.

Greek theater

Open-air structure, often built on a hillside, where theatrical performances were staged during antiquity.

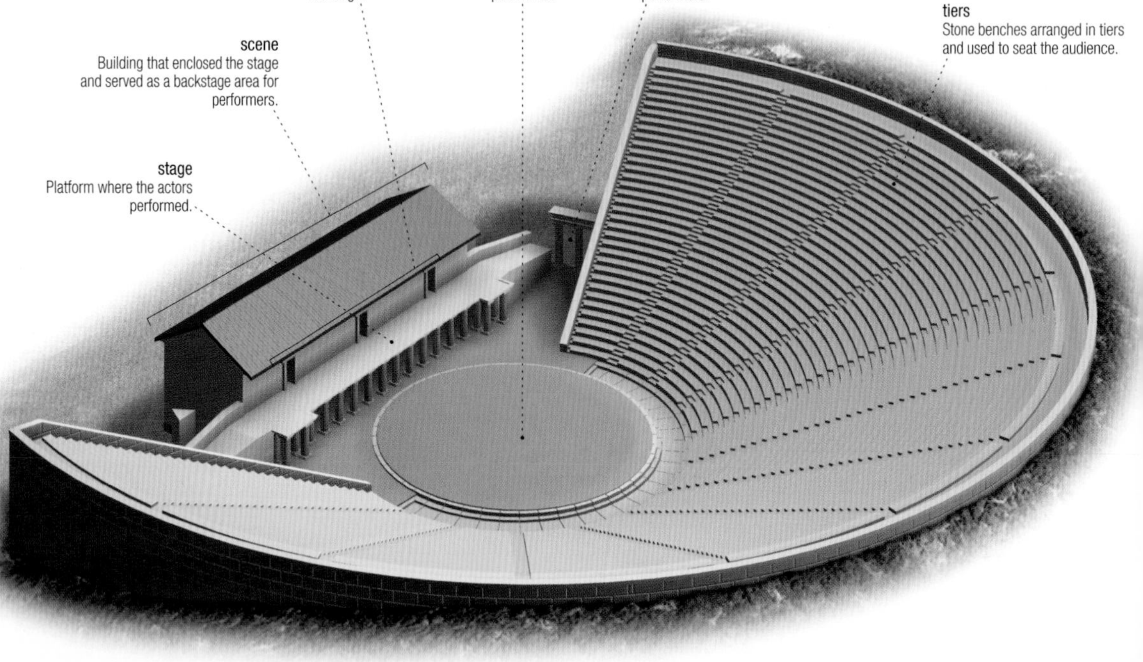

entrances for the actors
Doors used by the actors to go to and from the backstage area and the stage.

orchestra
Space where the chorus performed.

parados
Entrance for the audience and performers.

tiers
Stone benches arranged in tiers and used to seat the audience.

scene
Building that enclosed the stage and served as a backstage area for performers.

stage
Platform where the actors performed.

Greek temple

Building that, in antiquity, was dedicated to a divinity and featured a statue of that divinity.

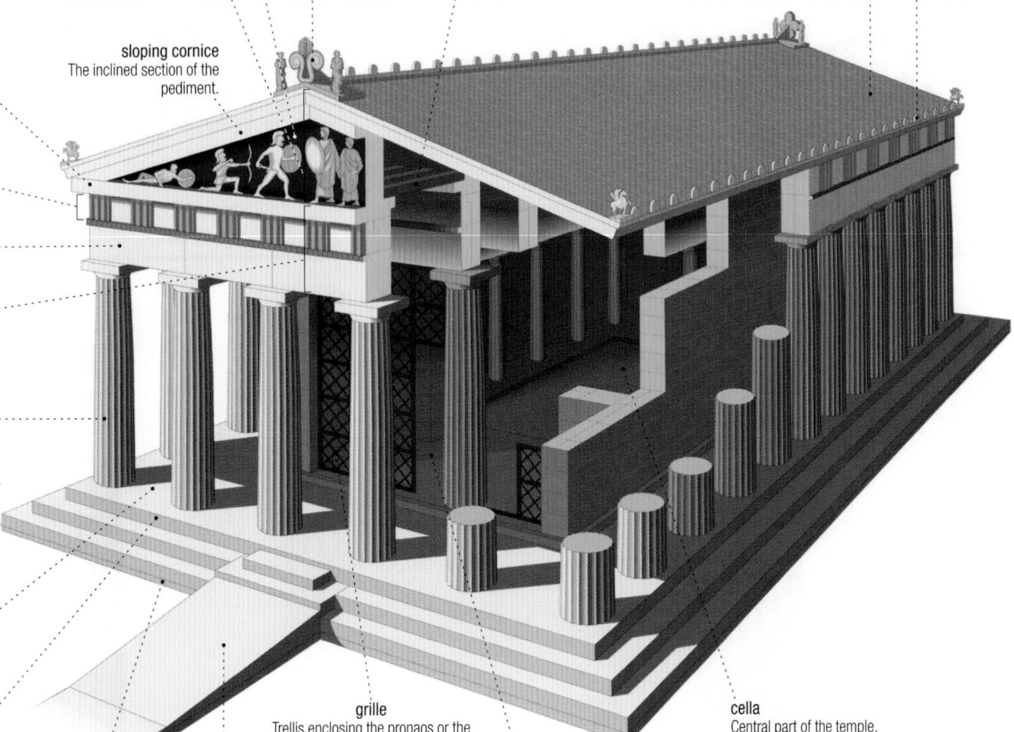

tympanum
Triangular surface between the cornice and the pediment's two sloping cornices.

acroterion
Ornamental feature that rests on a base at the apex and corners of the pediment.

antefix
Ornamental element used to decorate the edges and the peak of the roof.

timber
Framework of beams that supports the roof of the building and provides stability.

tile
Hard surface, usually made of baked molded clay, used as a covering for roofs.

pediment
Triangular section above the entablature.

cornice
Molding projection atop the entablature.

sloping cornice
The inclined section of the pediment.

frieze
...tion of the entablature between ...e cornice and the architrave; its ...oration varies, depending in the architectural style.

architrave
...ower section of the entablature, ...ctly on top of the capitals of the columns.

entablature
Section composed of the architrave, the frieze and the ...rnice; it supports the pediment.

column
...uted circular pillar that supports the entablature.

crepidoma
...upon which the building rests; it is composed of several levels.

peristyle
...olonnade with one or more rows surrounding the temple.

stylobate
...pper section of the crepidoma; it supports the columns.

euthynteria
Base that serves to level the surface on which the temple rests.

ramp
Inclined plane that provides access to the temple.

grille
Trellis enclosing the pronaos or the opisthodomos.

cella
Central part of the temple, designed to house the statue of the divinity.

pronaos
Front section of the temple; it provides access to the cella.

plan of a Greek temple

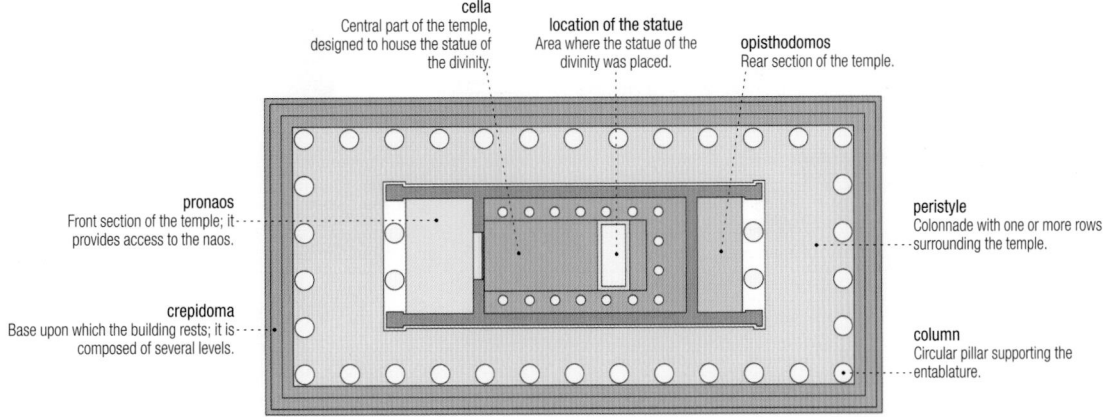

cella
Central part of the temple, designed to house the statue of the divinity.

location of the statue
Area where the statue of the divinity was placed.

opisthodomos
Rear section of the temple.

pronaos
Front section of the temple; it provides access to the naos.

peristyle
Colonnade with one or more rows surrounding the temple.

crepidoma
Base upon which the building rests; it is composed of several levels.

column
Circular pillar supporting the entablature.

architectural styles

The three main architectural styles, or orders, used in ancient Greece are distinguished by the features of their columns and corresponding entablatures.

Doric order
Order characterized by a column with no base, a capital that is not sculpted and a frieze with alternating triglyphs and metopes.

Ionic or[der]
Order characterized by columns w[ith] molded bases, capitals with volu[tes] and a continuously sculpted frie[ze.]

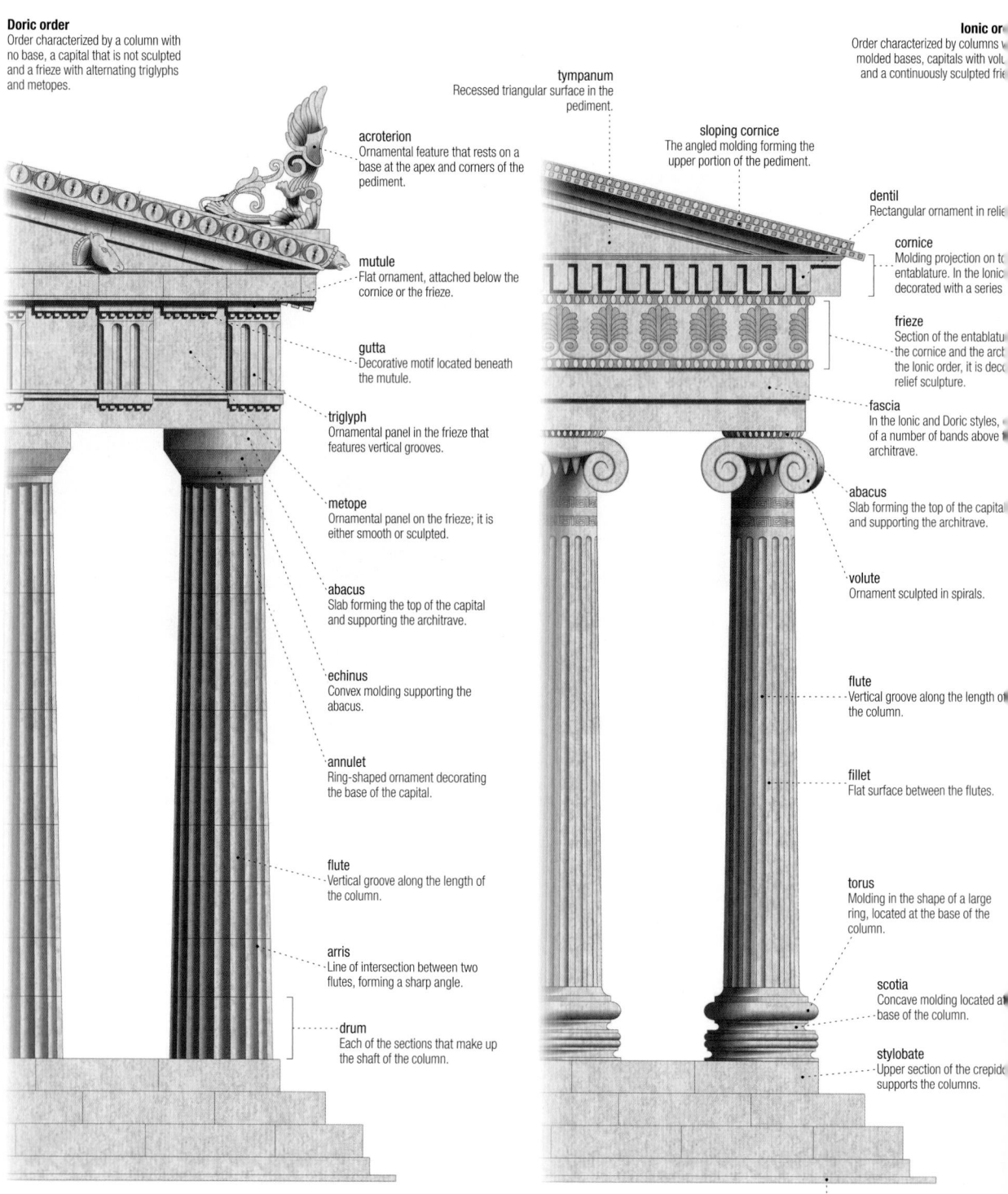

tympanum
Recessed triangular surface in the pediment.

acroterion
Ornamental feature that rests on a base at the apex and corners of the pediment.

mutule
Flat ornament, attached below the cornice or the frieze.

gutta
Decorative motif located beneath the mutule.

triglyph
Ornamental panel in the frieze that features vertical grooves.

metope
Ornamental panel on the frieze; it is either smooth or sculpted.

abacus
Slab forming the top of the capital and supporting the architrave.

echinus
Convex molding supporting the abacus.

annulet
Ring-shaped ornament decorating the base of the capital.

flute
Vertical groove along the length of the column.

arris
Line of intersection between two flutes, forming a sharp angle.

drum
Each of the sections that make up the shaft of the column.

sloping cornice
The angled molding forming the upper portion of the pediment.

dentil
Rectangular ornament in relie[f.]

cornice
Molding projection on t[op] entablature. In the Ionic [it is] decorated with a series [of dentils.]

frieze
Section of the entablatu[re between] the cornice and the arc[hitrave. In] the Ionic order, it is dec[orated with] relief sculpture.

fascia
In the Ionic and Doric styles, [each] of a number of bands above [the] architrave.

abacus
Slab forming the top of the capital and supporting the architrave.

volute
Ornament sculpted in spirals.

flute
Vertical groove along the length of the column.

fillet
Flat surface between the flutes.

torus
Molding in the shape of a large ring, located at the base of the column.

scotia
Concave molding located at the base of the column.

stylobate
Upper section of the crepido[ma that] supports the columns.

euthynteria
Base that serves to level the surface on which the temple rests.

ARTS AND ARCHITECTURE

Corinthian order
Order characterized especially by its capital decorated with acanthus leaves.

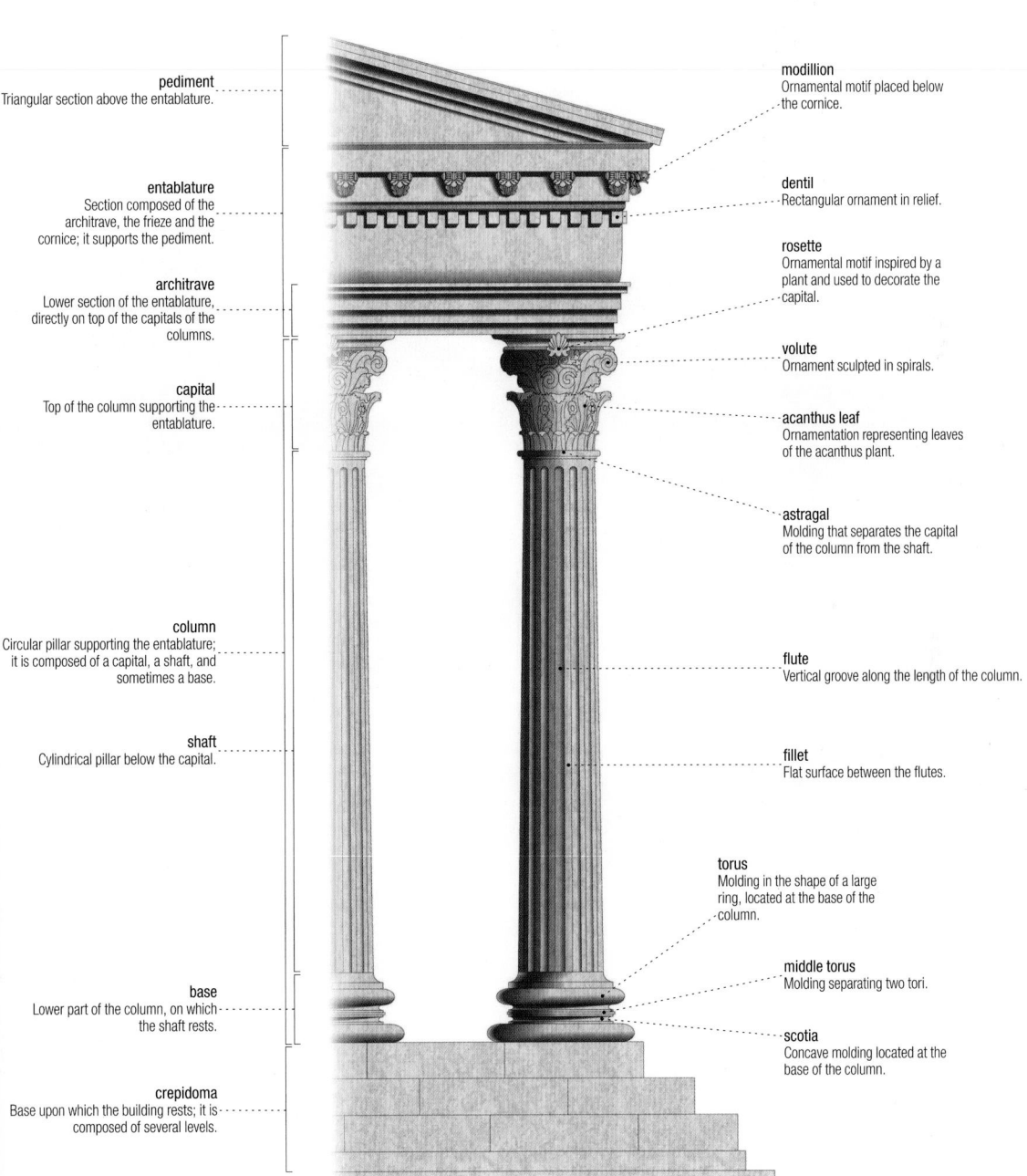

pediment
Triangular section above the entablature.

entablature
Section composed of the architrave, the frieze and the cornice; it supports the pediment.

architrave
Lower section of the entablature, directly on top of the capitals of the columns.

capital
Top of the column supporting the entablature.

column
Circular pillar supporting the entablature; it is composed of a capital, a shaft, and sometimes a base.

shaft
Cylindrical pillar below the capital.

base
Lower part of the column, on which the shaft rests.

crepidoma
Base upon which the building rests; it is composed of several levels.

modillion
Ornamental motif placed below the cornice.

dentil
Rectangular ornament in relief.

rosette
Ornamental motif inspired by a plant and used to decorate the capital.

volute
Ornament sculpted in spirals.

acanthus leaf
Ornamentation representing leaves of the acanthus plant.

astragal
Molding that separates the capital of the column from the shaft.

flute
Vertical groove along the length of the column.

fillet
Flat surface between the flutes.

torus
Molding in the shape of a large ring, located at the base of the column.

middle torus
Molding separating two tori.

scotia
Concave molding located at the base of the column.

ARTS AND ARCHITECTURE

Roman house

For wealthy Romans, family life unfolded in spacious luxurious houses whose rooms were arranged around open-air spaces.

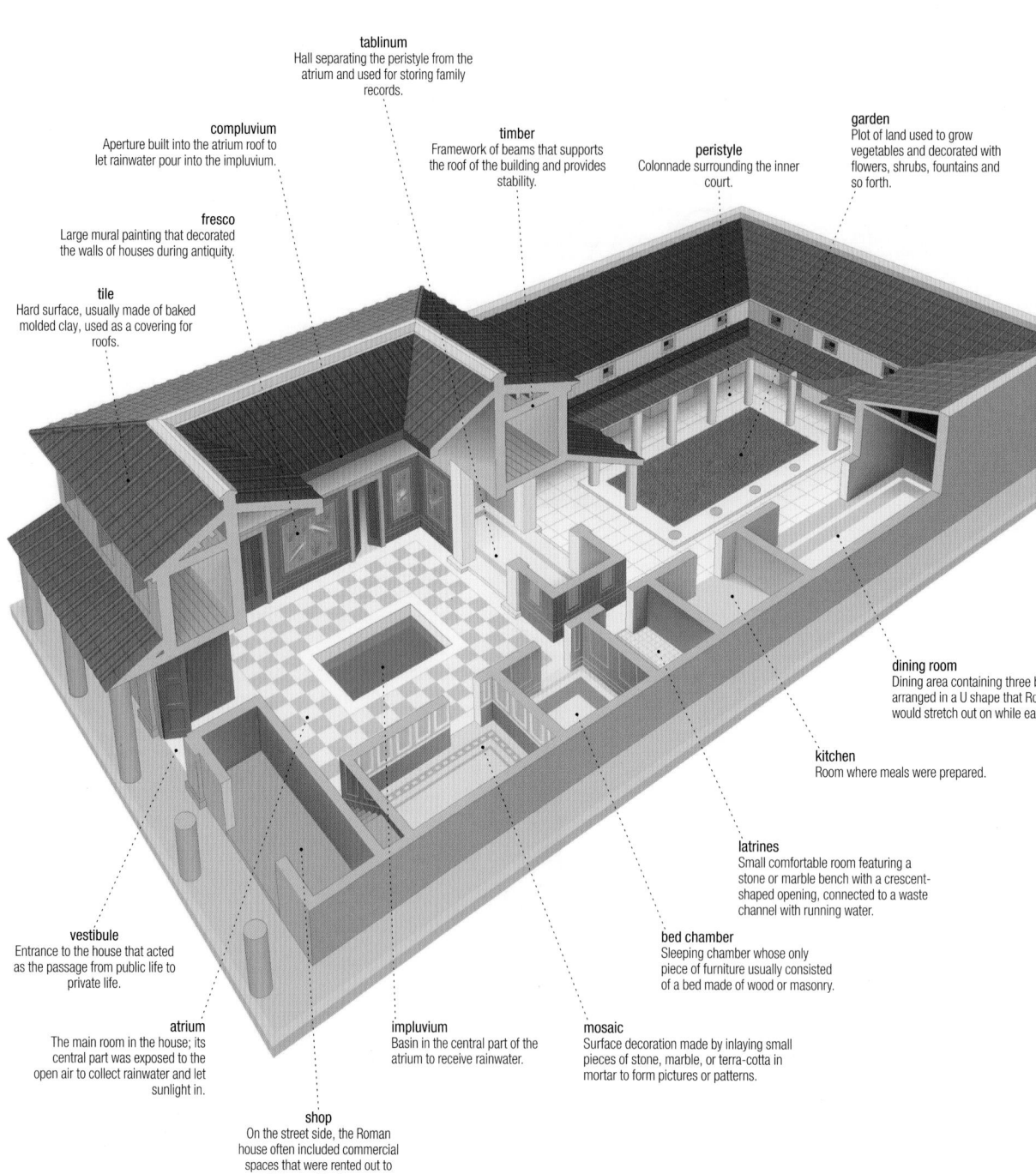

tablinum
Hall separating the peristyle from the atrium and used for storing family records.

compluvium
Aperture built into the atrium roof to let rainwater pour into the impluvium.

timber
Framework of beams that supports the roof of the building and provides stability.

peristyle
Colonnade surrounding the inner court.

garden
Plot of land used to grow vegetables and decorated with flowers, shrubs, fountains and so forth.

fresco
Large mural painting that decorated the walls of houses during antiquity.

tile
Hard surface, usually made of baked molded clay, used as a covering for roofs.

dining room
Dining area containing three bed arranged in a U shape that Roma would stretch out on while eating

kitchen
Room where meals were prepared.

latrines
Small comfortable room featuring a stone or marble bench with a crescent-shaped opening, connected to a waste channel with running water.

bed chamber
Sleeping chamber whose only piece of furniture usually consisted of a bed made of wood or masonry.

vestibule
Entrance to the house that acted as the passage from public life to private life.

atrium
The main room in the house; its central part was exposed to the open air to collect rainwater and let sunlight in.

impluvium
Basin in the central part of the atrium to receive rainwater.

mosaic
Surface decoration made by inlaying small pieces of stone, marble, or terra-cotta in mortar to form pictures or patterns.

shop
On the street side, the Roman house often included commercial spaces that were rented out to artisans and tradesmen.

Roman amphitheater

Oval or round building composed of an arena surrounded by tiers; it was used to stage gladiator fights and other spectacles.

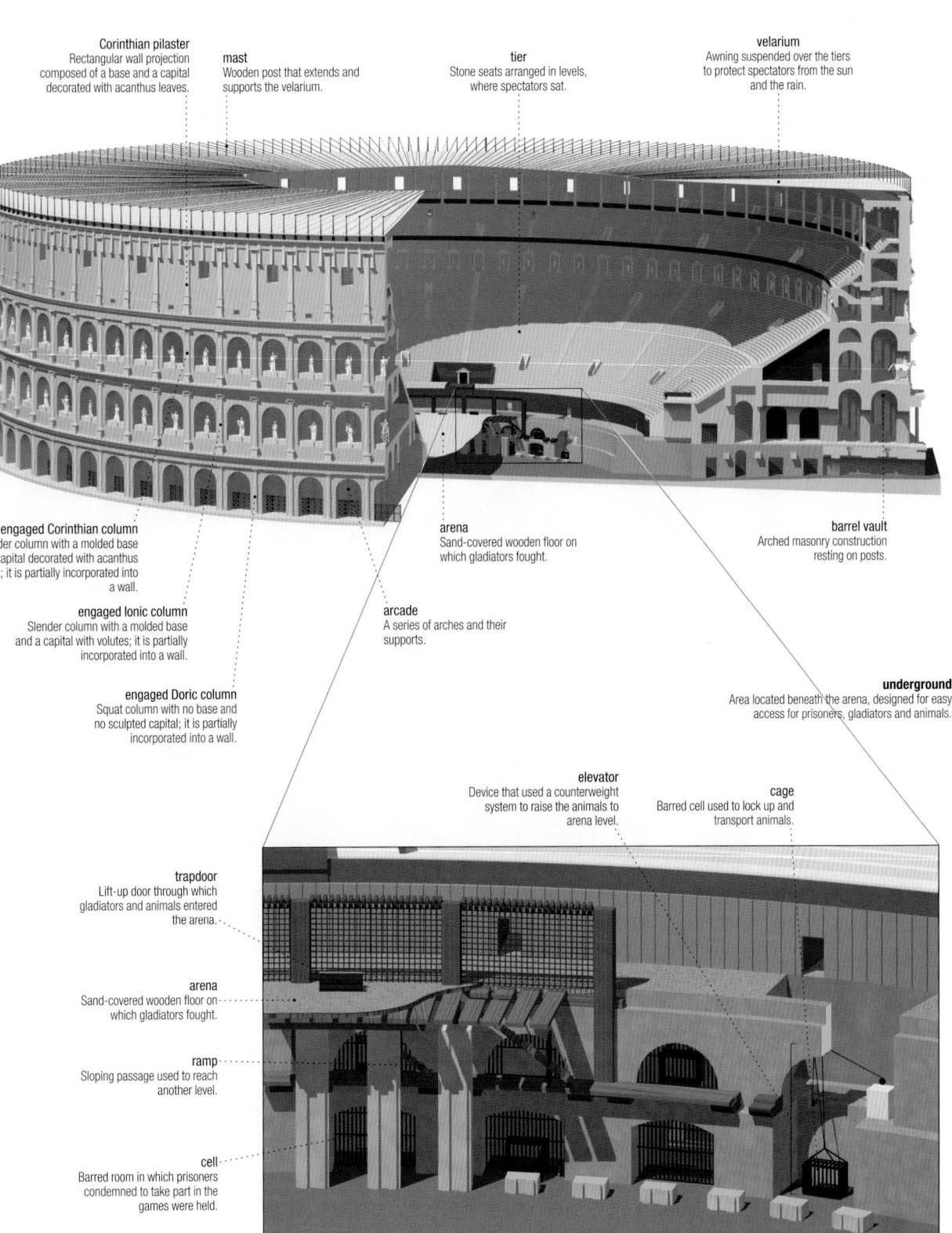

Corinthian pilaster
Rectangular wall projection composed of a base and a capital decorated with acanthus leaves.

mast
Wooden post that extends and supports the velarium.

tier
Stone seats arranged in levels, where spectators sat.

velarium
Awning suspended over the tiers to protect spectators from the sun and the rain.

engaged Corinthian column
...der column with a molded base ...capital decorated with acanthus ...s; it is partially incorporated into a wall.

engaged Ionic column
Slender column with a molded base and a capital with volutes; it is partially incorporated into a wall.

engaged Doric column
Squat column with no base and no sculpted capital; it is partially incorporated into a wall.

arena
Sand-covered wooden floor on which gladiators fought.

arcade
A series of arches and their supports.

barrel vault
Arched masonry construction resting on posts.

underground
Area located beneath the arena, designed for easy access for prisoners, gladiators and animals.

elevator
Device that used a counterweight system to raise the animals to arena level.

cage
Barred cell used to lock up and transport animals.

trapdoor
Lift-up door through which gladiators and animals entered the arena.

arena
Sand-covered wooden floor on which gladiators fought.

ramp
Sloping passage used to reach another level.

cell
Barred room in which prisoners condemned to take part in the games were held.

ARTS AND ARCHITECTURE

castle

Fortified residence of a king or feudal lord, designed to protect against assailants.

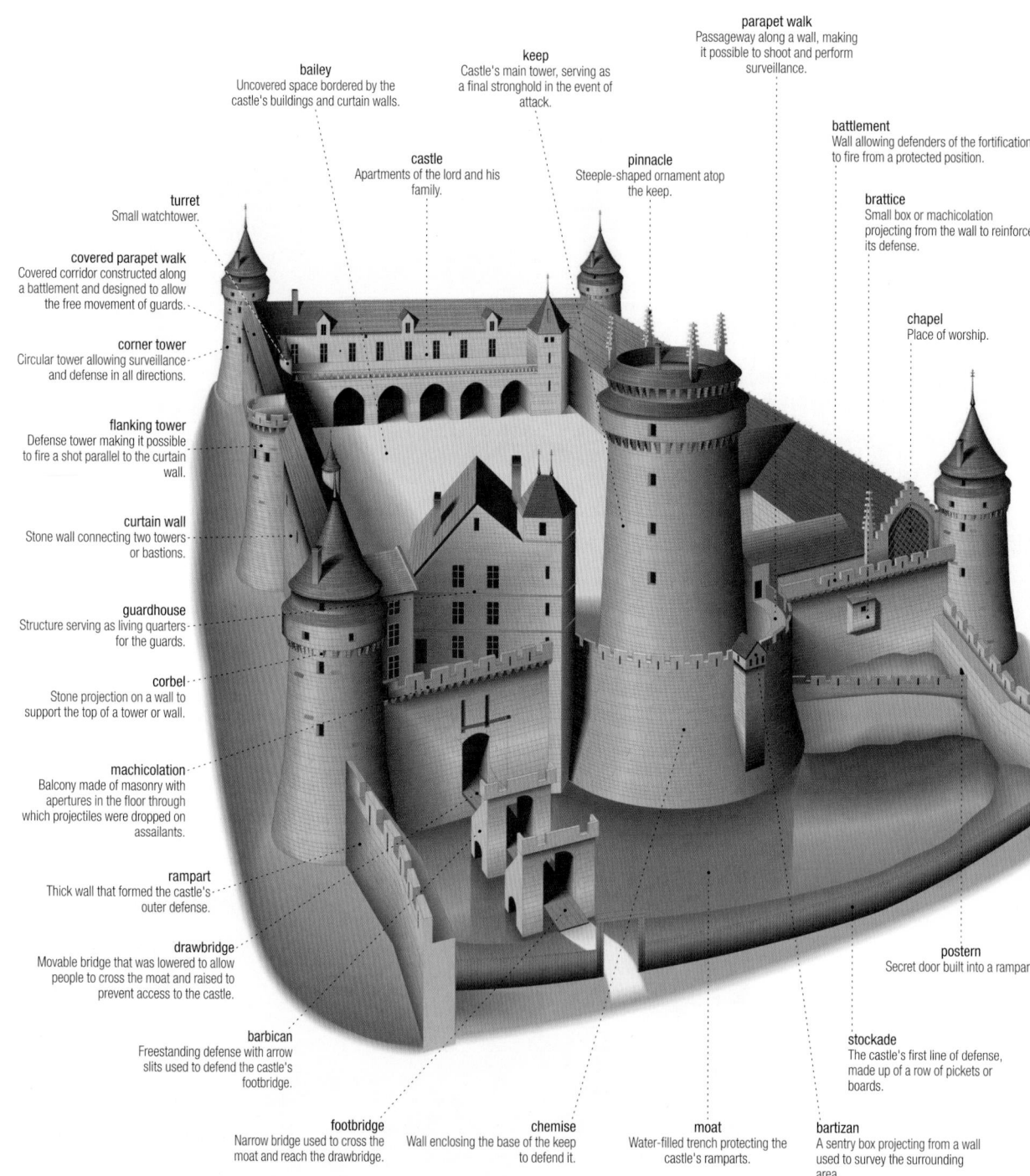

parapet walk
Passageway along a wall, making it possible to shoot and perform surveillance.

bailey
Uncovered space bordered by the castle's buildings and curtain walls.

keep
Castle's main tower, serving as a final stronghold in the event of attack.

battlement
Wall allowing defenders of the fortification to fire from a protected position.

castle
Apartments of the lord and his family.

pinnacle
Steeple-shaped ornament atop the keep.

brattice
Small box or machicolation projecting from the wall to reinforce its defense.

turret
Small watchtower.

covered parapet walk
Covered corridor constructed along a battlement and designed to allow the free movement of guards.

chapel
Place of worship.

corner tower
Circular tower allowing surveillance and defense in all directions.

flanking tower
Defense tower making it possible to fire a shot parallel to the curtain wall.

curtain wall
Stone wall connecting two towers or bastions.

guardhouse
Structure serving as living quarters for the guards.

corbel
Stone projection on a wall to support the top of a tower or wall.

machicolation
Balcony made of masonry with apertures in the floor through which projectiles were dropped on assailants.

rampart
Thick wall that formed the castle's outer defense.

postern
Secret door built into a rampart

drawbridge
Movable bridge that was lowered to allow people to cross the moat and raised to prevent access to the castle.

barbican
Freestanding defense with arrow slits used to defend the castle's footbridge.

stockade
The castle's first line of defense, made up of a row of pickets or boards.

footbridge
Narrow bridge used to cross the moat and reach the drawbridge.

chemise
Wall enclosing the base of the keep to defend it.

moat
Water-filled trench protecting the castle's ramparts.

bartizan
A sentry box projecting from a wall used to survey the surrounding area.

Vauban fortification

Star-shaped military fortification developed by Sébastien de Vauban in the 17th century.

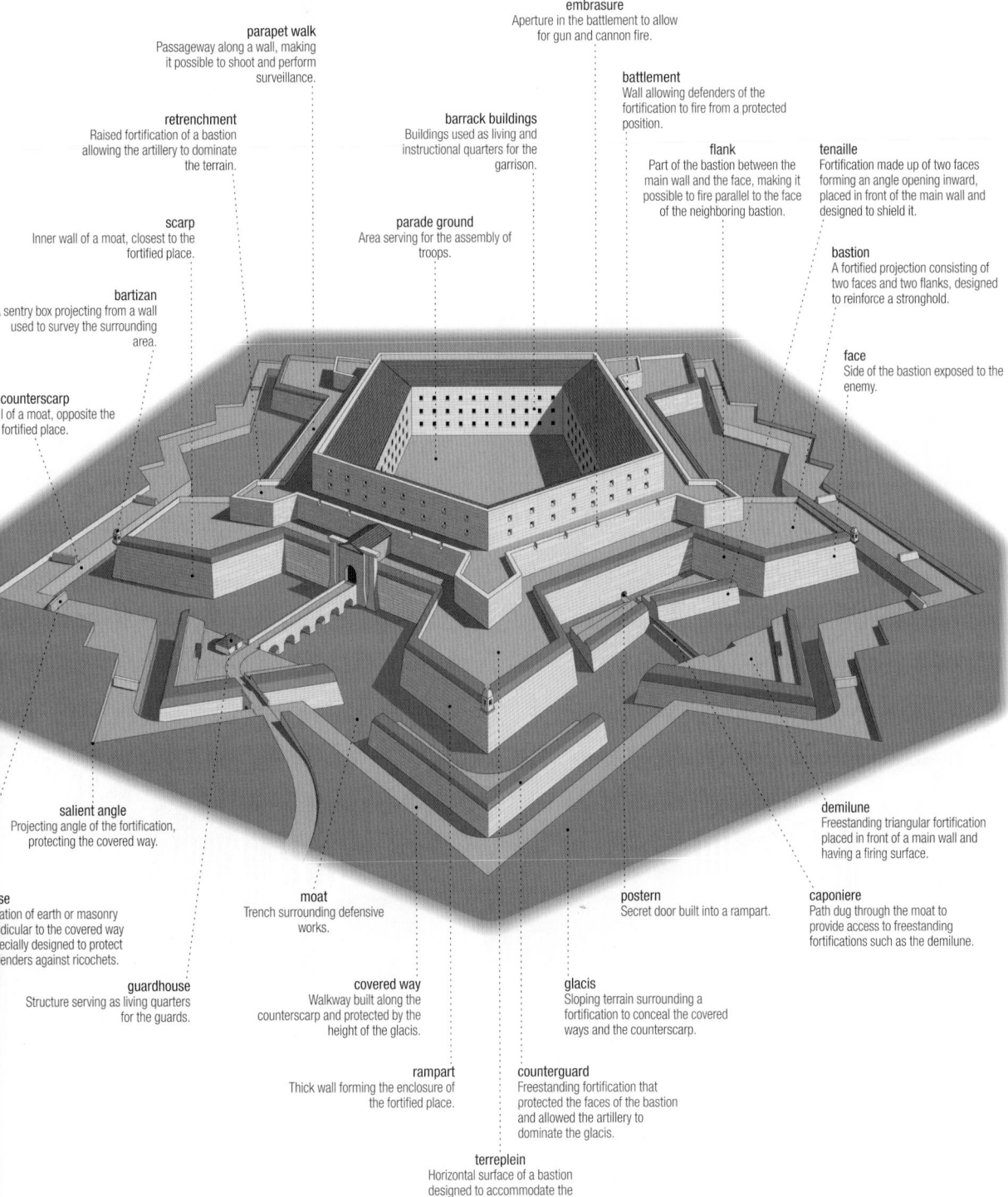

embrasure
Aperture in the battlement to allow for gun and cannon fire.

parapet walk
Passageway along a wall, making it possible to shoot and perform surveillance.

battlement
Wall allowing defenders of the fortification to fire from a protected position.

retrenchment
Raised fortification of a bastion allowing the artillery to dominate the terrain.

barrack buildings
Buildings used as living and instructional quarters for the garrison.

flank
Part of the bastion between the main wall and the face, making it possible to fire parallel to the face of the neighboring bastion.

tenaille
Fortification made up of two faces forming an angle opening inward, placed in front of the main wall and designed to shield it.

scarp
Inner wall of a moat, closest to the fortified place.

parade ground
Area serving for the assembly of troops.

bastion
A fortified projection consisting of two faces and two flanks, designed to reinforce a stronghold.

bartizan
sentry box projecting from a wall used to survey the surrounding area.

face
Side of the bastion exposed to the enemy.

counterscarp
l of a moat, opposite the fortified place.

salient angle
Projecting angle of the fortification, protecting the covered way.

demilune
Freestanding triangular fortification placed in front of a main wall and having a firing surface.

se
ation of earth or masonry
dicular to the covered way
ecially designed to protect
enders against ricochets.

moat
Trench surrounding defensive works.

postern
Secret door built into a rampart.

caponiere
Path dug through the moat to provide access to freestanding fortifications such as the demilune.

guardhouse
Structure serving as living quarters for the guards.

covered way
Walkway built along the counterscarp and protected by the height of the glacis.

glacis
Sloping terrain surrounding a fortification to conceal the covered ways and the counterscarp.

rampart
Thick wall forming the enclosure of the fortified place.

counterguard
Freestanding fortification that protected the faces of the bastion and allowed the artillery to dominate the glacis.

terreplein
Horizontal surface of a bastion designed to accommodate the artillery.

Gothic cathedral

The Gothic style of architecture originated in France, lasted in Europe from the 12th to the early 16th century, and is characterized mainly by pointed arches, ribbed vaults, thin walls, flying buttresses, and large windows.

general view

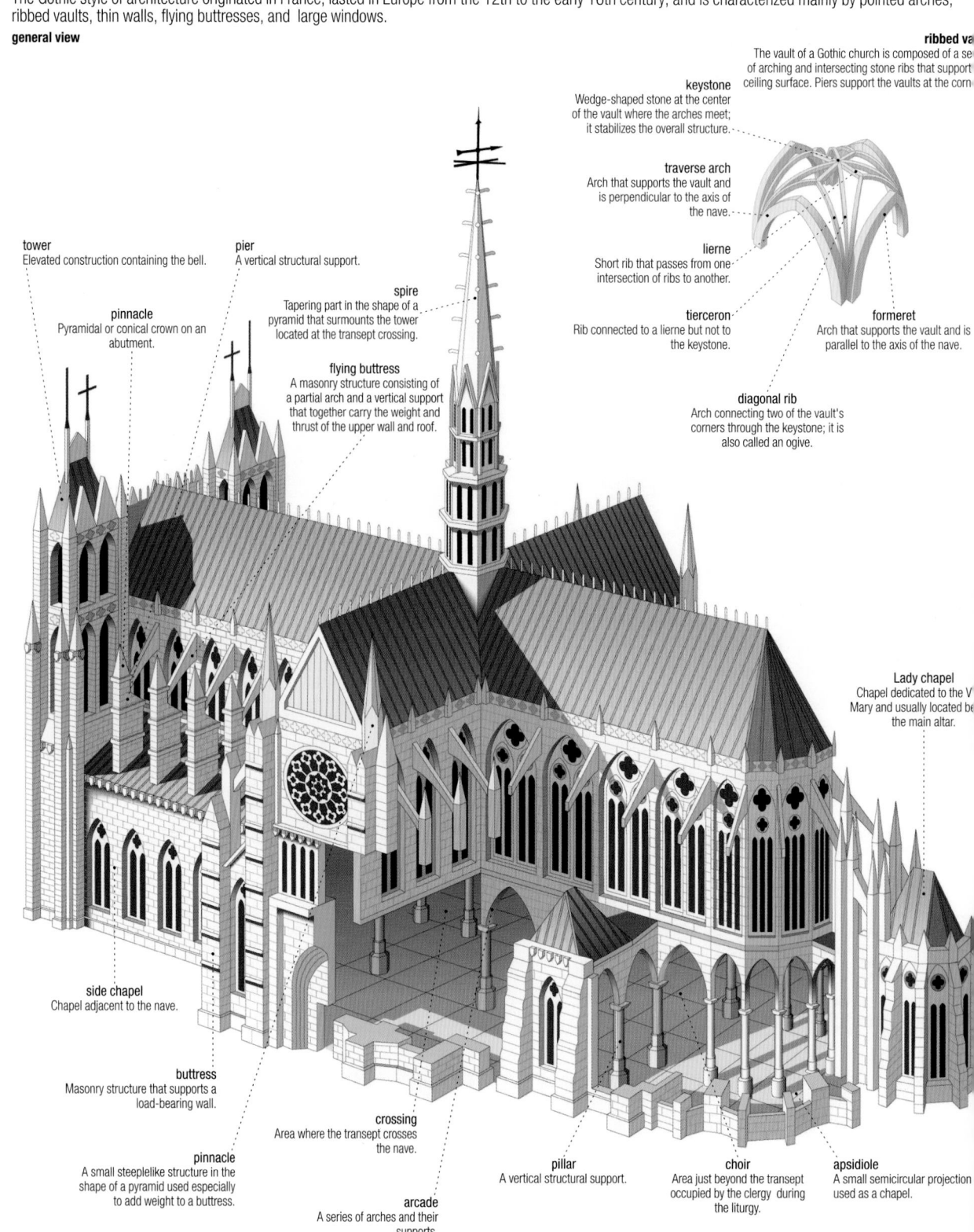

ribbed va[ult]
The vault of a Gothic church is composed of a se[ries] of arching and intersecting stone ribs that support [the] ceiling surface. Piers support the vaults at the corn[ers.]

keystone
Wedge-shaped stone at the center of the vault where the arches meet; it stabilizes the overall structure.

traverse arch
Arch that supports the vault and is perpendicular to the axis of the nave.

lierne
Short rib that passes from one intersection of ribs to another.

tierceron
Rib connected to a lierne but not to the keystone.

formeret
Arch that supports the vault and is parallel to the axis of the nave.

diagonal rib
Arch connecting two of the vault's corners through the keystone; it is also called an ogive.

tower
Elevated construction containing the bell.

pier
A vertical structural support.

spire
Tapering part in the shape of a pyramid that surmounts the tower located at the transept crossing.

pinnacle
Pyramidal or conical crown on an abutment.

flying buttress
A masonry structure consisting of a partial arch and a vertical support that together carry the weight and thrust of the upper wall and roof.

Lady chapel
Chapel dedicated to the V[irgin] Mary and usually located be[hind] the main altar.

side chapel
Chapel adjacent to the nave.

buttress
Masonry structure that supports a load-bearing wall.

crossing
Area where the transept crosses the nave.

pillar
A vertical structural support.

choir
Area just beyond the transept occupied by the clergy during the liturgy.

apsidiole
A small semicircular projection used as a chapel.

pinnacle
A small steeplelike structure in the shape of a pyramid used especially to add weight to a buttress.

arcade
A series of arches and their supports.

Gothic cathedral

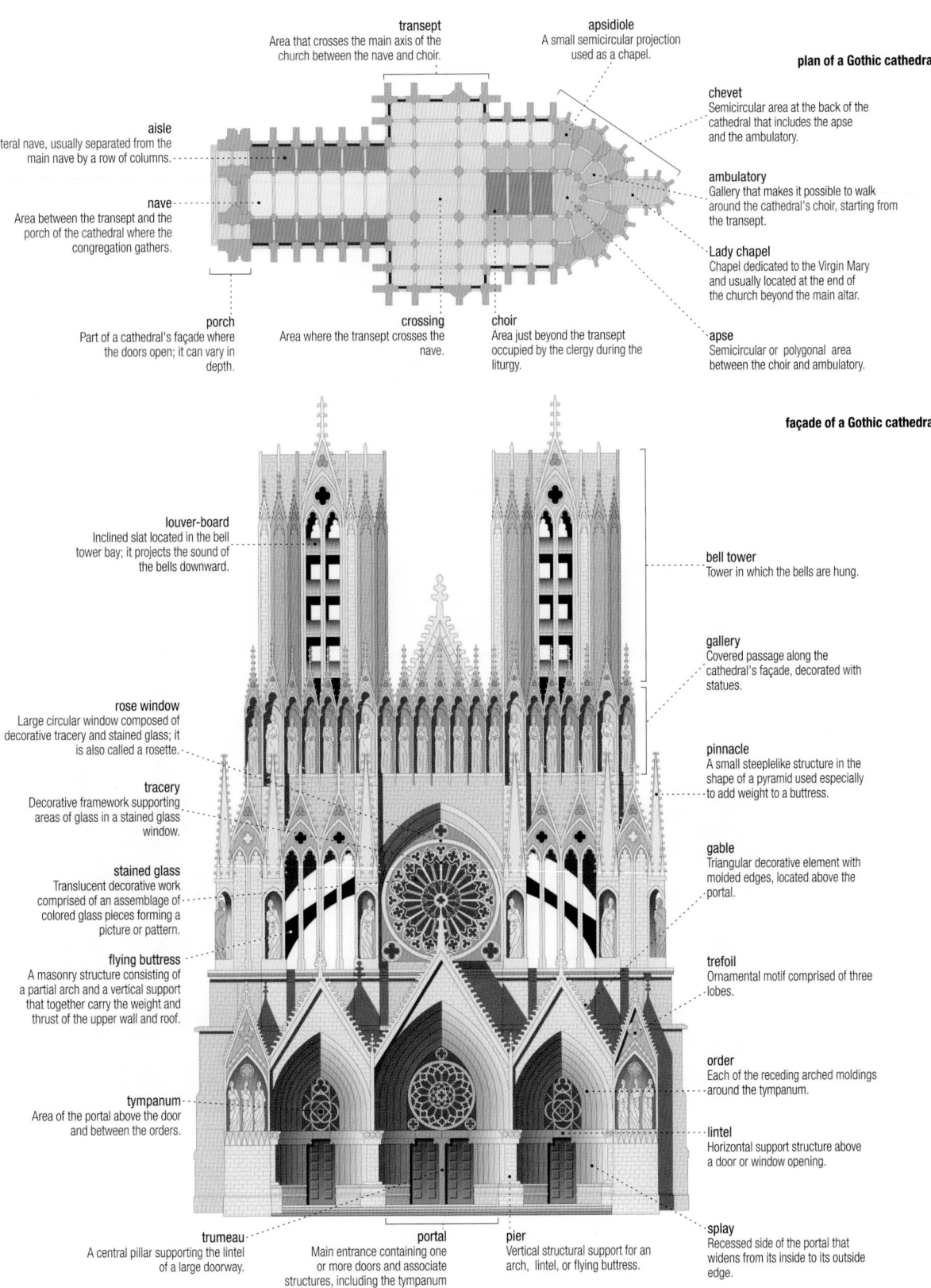

plan of a Gothic cathedral

transept
Area that crosses the main axis of the church between the nave and choir.

apsidiole
A small semicircular projection used as a chapel.

chevet
Semicircular area at the back of the cathedral that includes the apse and the ambulatory.

aisle
Lateral nave, usually separated from the main nave by a row of columns.

ambulatory
Gallery that makes it possible to walk around the cathedral's choir, starting from the transept.

nave
Area between the transept and the porch of the cathedral where the congregation gathers.

Lady chapel
Chapel dedicated to the Virgin Mary and usually located at the end of the church beyond the main altar.

porch
Part of a cathedral's façade where the doors open; it can vary in depth.

crossing
Area where the transept crosses the nave.

choir
Area just beyond the transept occupied by the clergy during the liturgy.

apse
Semicircular or polygonal area between the choir and ambulatory.

façade of a Gothic cathedral

louver-board
Inclined slat located in the bell tower bay; it projects the sound of the bells downward.

bell tower
Tower in which the bells are hung.

gallery
Covered passage along the cathedral's façade, decorated with statues.

rose window
Large circular window composed of decorative tracery and stained glass; it is also called a rosette.

pinnacle
A small steeplelike structure in the shape of a pyramid used especially to add weight to a buttress.

tracery
Decorative framework supporting areas of glass in a stained glass window.

gable
Triangular decorative element with molded edges, located above the portal.

stained glass
Translucent decorative work comprised of an assemblage of colored glass pieces forming a picture or pattern.

trefoil
Ornamental motif comprised of three lobes.

flying buttress
A masonry structure consisting of a partial arch and a vertical support that together carry the weight and thrust of the upper wall and roof.

order
Each of the receding arched moldings around the tympanum.

tympanum
Area of the portal above the door and between the orders.

lintel
Horizontal support structure above a door or window opening.

trumeau
A central pillar supporting the lintel of a large doorway.

portal
Main entrance containing one or more doors and associate structures, including the tympanum and gable.

pier
Vertical structural support for an arch, lintel, or flying buttress.

splay
Recessed side of the portal that widens from its inside to its outside edge.

ARTS AND ARCHITECTURE

Romanesque church

The Romanesque style of architecture lasted in Europe from the mid 11th century to the Gothic period and is characterized mainly by thick walls, rounded arch
barrel vaults, and small windows.

façade of a Romanesque church

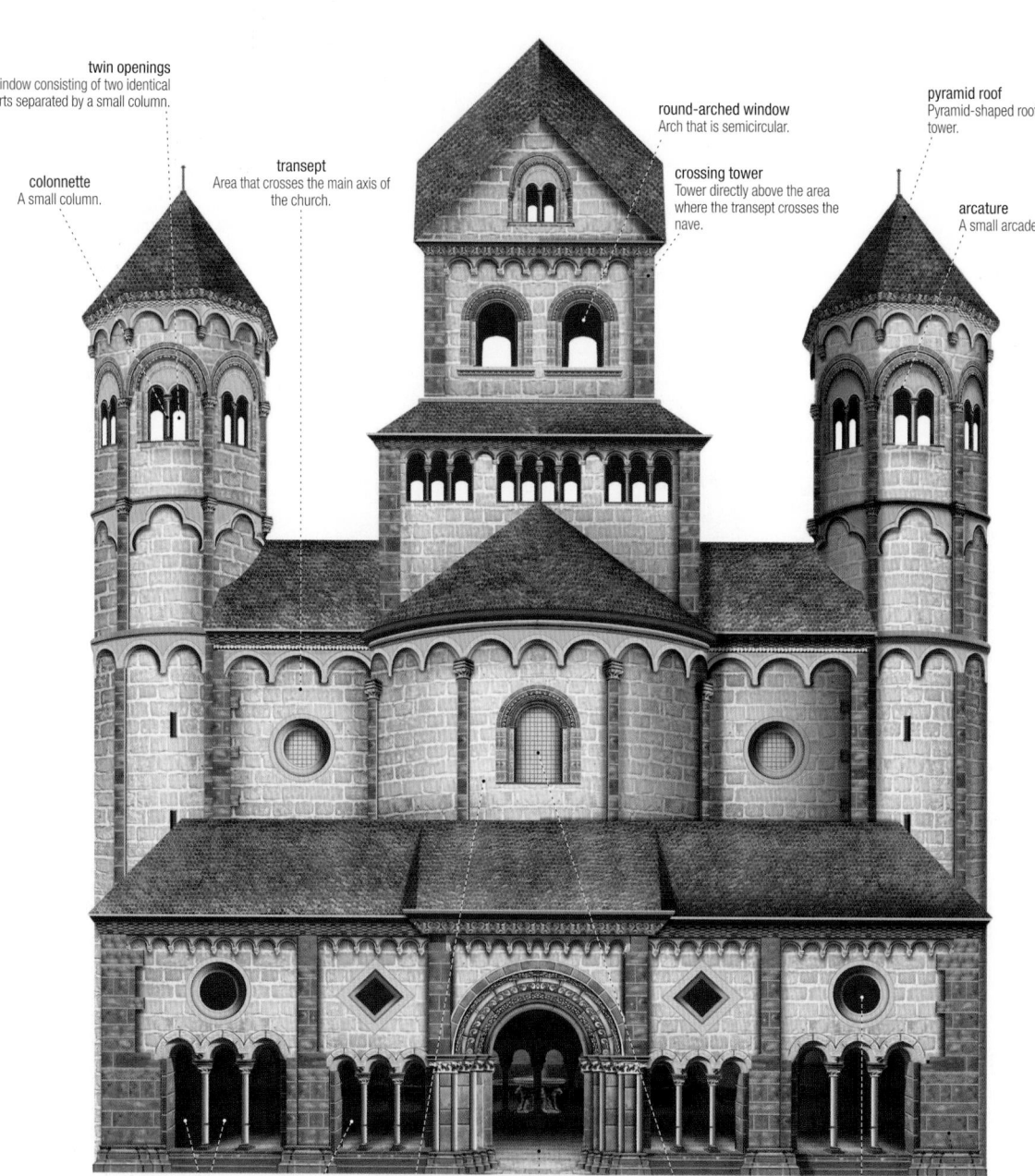

twin openings
Window consisting of two identical parts separated by a small column.

round-arched window
Arch that is semicircular.

pyramid roof
Pyramid-shaped roof at the top tower.

colonnette
A small column.

transept
Area that crosses the main axis of the church.

crossing tower
Tower directly above the area where the transept crosses the nave.

arcature
A small arcade.

arcade
A series of arches with their supports.

apse
Semicircular or polygonal projecting area.

blind arch
Opening under an arch that is closed off by a wall of masonry.

buttress
A projecting structure of r that supports or gives sta wall or building.

atrium
Long open passageway the roof of which is supported by an arcade.

porch
Covered section that juts out at the entrance of the church and leads to a door or open passageway.

oculus
A circular or oval window.

Renaissance villa

The Renaissance style of architecture originated in the early 15th century in Italy and is characterized by the use of elements inspired by the architecture of ancient Greece and Rome, including columns, domes, and rounded arches.

façade of a Renaissance villa

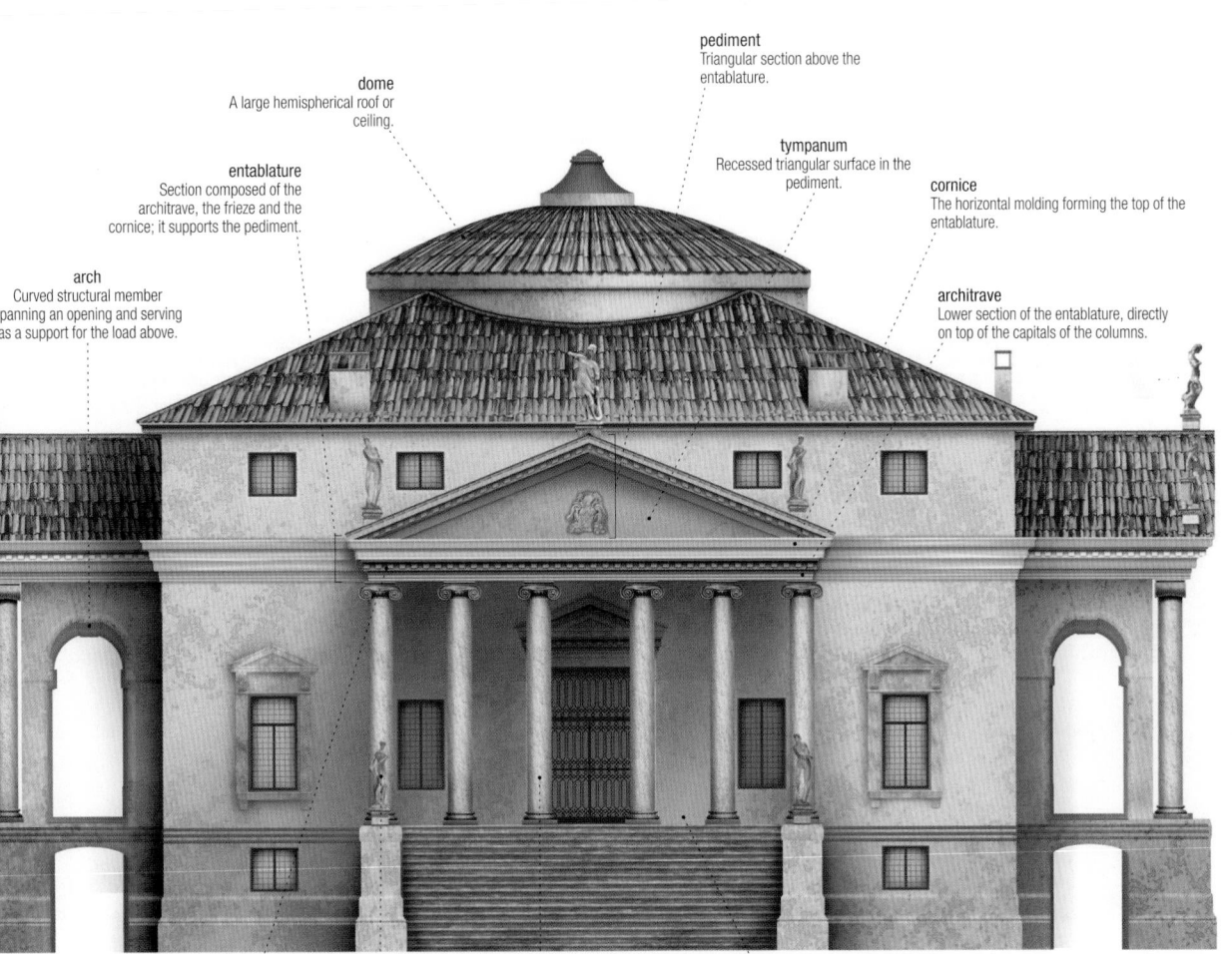

pediment
Triangular section above the entablature.

dome
A large hemispherical roof or ceiling.

tympanum
Recessed triangular surface in the pediment.

entablature
Section composed of the architrave, the frieze and the cornice; it supports the pediment.

cornice
The horizontal molding forming the top of the entablature.

arch
Curved structural member spanning an opening and serving as a support for the load above.

architrave
Lower section of the entablature, directly on top of the capitals of the columns.

frieze
Section of the entablature between the cornice and the architrave; its decoration varies, depending on the architectural style.

sculpture
A three-dimensional work of art.

Ionic column
Slender column with a molded base and a capital with volutes.

portico
Open gallery joined to the main structure, with a roof supported by columns.

ARTS AND ARCHITECTURE

Baroque church

The Baroque style of architecture originated in the late 16th century in Italy and is characterized by complex forms, bold ornamentation, and dramatic effects.

façade of a Baroque church

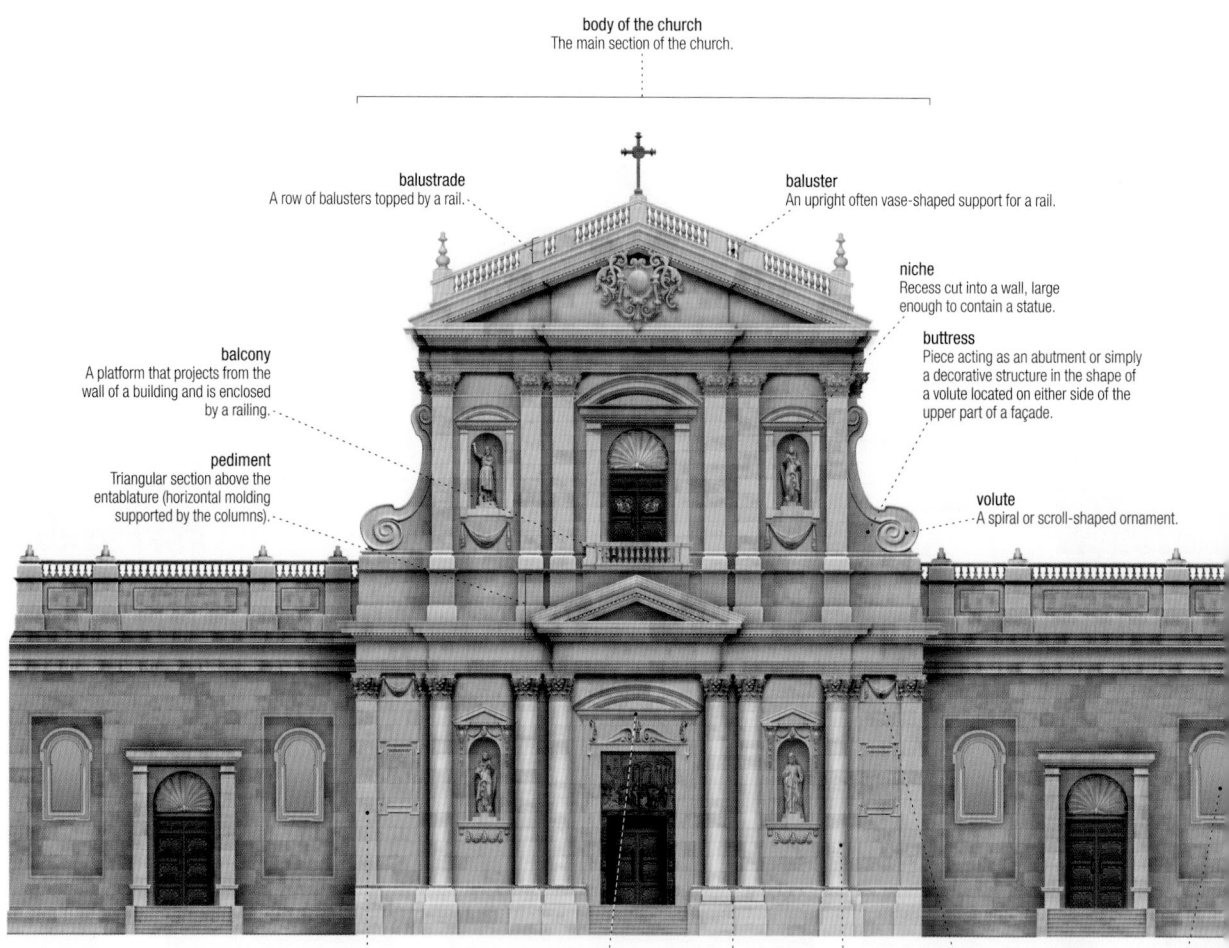

body of the church
The main section of the church.

balustrade
A row of balusters topped by a rail.

baluster
An upright often vase-shaped support for a rail.

niche
Recess cut into a wall, large enough to contain a statue.

balcony
A platform that projects from the wall of a building and is enclosed by a railing.

buttress
Piece acting as an abutment or simply a decorative structure in the shape of a volute located on either side of the upper part of a façade.

pediment
Triangular section above the entablature (horizontal molding supported by the columns).

volute
A spiral or scroll-shaped ornament.

segmental pediment
Variation on the pediment form in which a rounded top replaces the usual triangular shape.

twin columns
Columns of equal diameter grouped into pairs, sometimes placed side by side, but more often spaced apart.

festoon
Carved decoration in the shape of a garland.

rounded arch
Arch that is semicircle

pilaster
A vertical element that is rectangular in shape, is attached to but projects from the wall, and that resembles a column.

engaged column
A column that is attached to a wall.

art deco building

Architectural style of the 1920's and 1930's, characterized especially by bold outlines, geometric and zigzag forms, and streamlined shapes.

façade of an art deco building

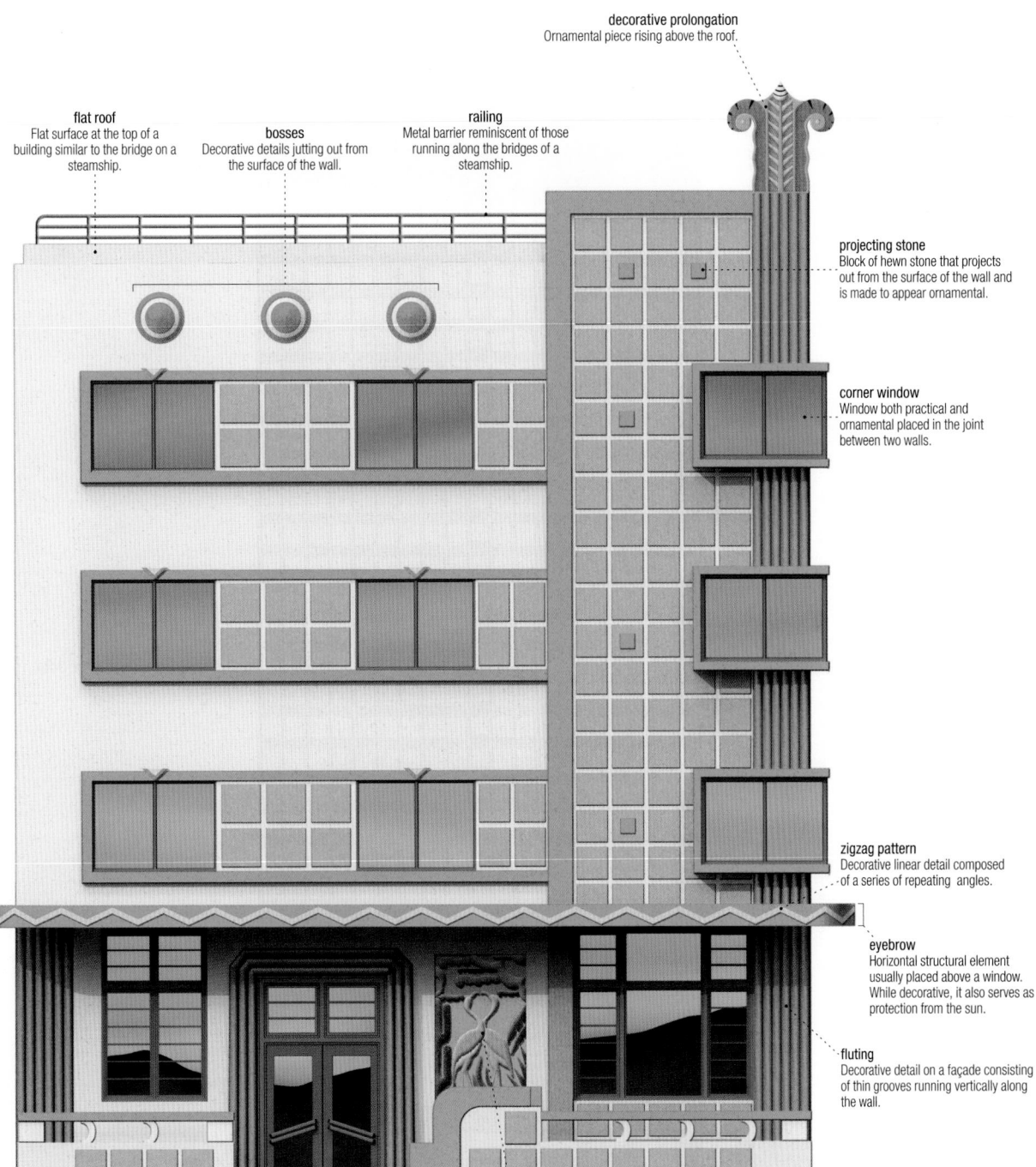

decorative prolongation
Ornamental piece rising above the roof.

flat roof
Flat surface at the top of a building similar to the bridge on a steamship.

bosses
Decorative details jutting out from the surface of the wall.

railing
Metal barrier reminiscent of those running along the bridges of a steamship.

projecting stone
Block of hewn stone that projects out from the surface of the wall and is made to appear ornamental.

corner window
Window both practical and ornamental placed in the joint between two walls.

zigzag pattern
Decorative linear detail composed of a series of repeating angles.

eyebrow
Horizontal structural element usually placed above a window. While decorative, it also serves as protection from the sun.

fluting
Decorative detail on a façade consisting of thin grooves running vertically along the wall.

tropical fauna motif
Decorative detail representing animals from tropical regions.

ARTS AND ARCHITECTURE

international style skyscraper

The International Style of architecture of the 20th century is characterized by the use of modern materials such as steel, glass, and reinforced concrete, the dire expression of structure, and the lack of nonstructural ornament.

façade of an international style skyscraper

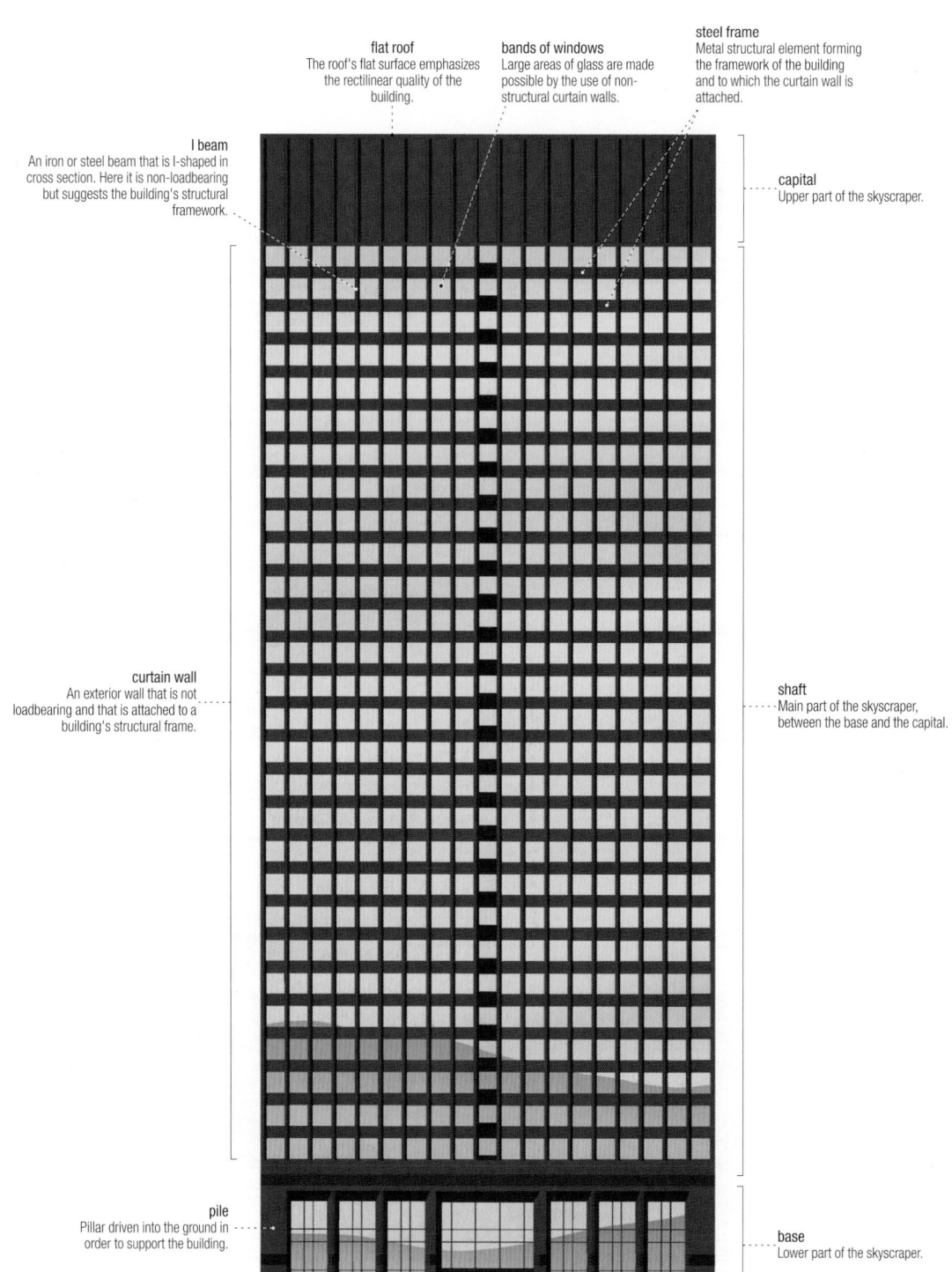

flat roof
The roof's flat surface emphasizes the rectilinear quality of the building.

bands of windows
Large areas of glass are made possible by the use of non-structural curtain walls.

steel frame
Metal structural element forming the framework of the building and to which the curtain wall is attached.

I beam
An iron or steel beam that is I-shaped in cross section. Here it is non-loadbearing but suggests the building's structural framework.

capital
Upper part of the skyscraper.

curtain wall
An exterior wall that is not loadbearing and that is attached to a building's structural frame.

shaft
Main part of the skyscraper, between the base and the capital.

pile
Pillar driven into the ground in order to support the building.

base
Lower part of the skyscraper.

pagoda

A tower in eastern Asia usually with roofs curving upward at the division of each of several stories and used as a temple or memorial.

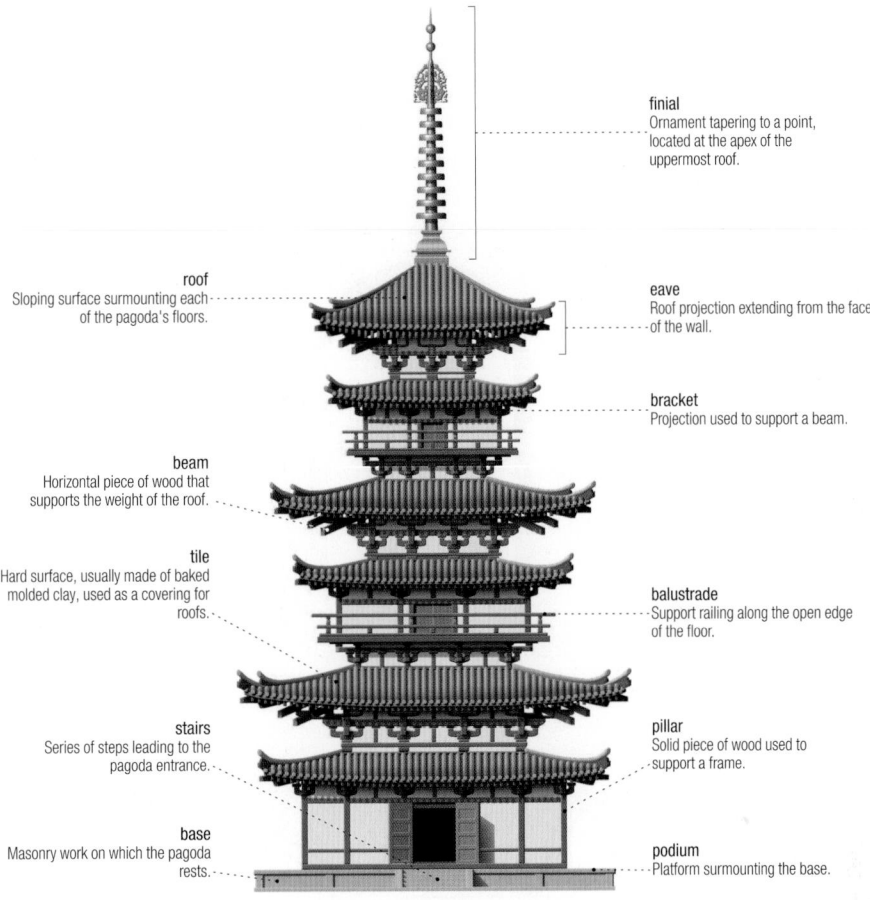

finial
Ornament tapering to a point, located at the apex of the uppermost roof.

roof
Sloping surface surmounting each of the pagoda's floors.

eave
Roof projection extending from the face of the wall.

bracket
Projection used to support a beam.

beam
Horizontal piece of wood that supports the weight of the roof.

tile
Hard surface, usually made of baked molded clay, used as a covering for roofs.

balustrade
Support railing along the open edge of the floor.

stairs
Series of steps leading to the pagoda entrance.

pillar
Solid piece of wood used to support a frame.

base
Masonry work on which the pagoda rests.

podium
Platform surmounting the base.

Aztec temple

Pyramid-shaped religious edifice of pre-Columbian Mexico featuring one or several temples.

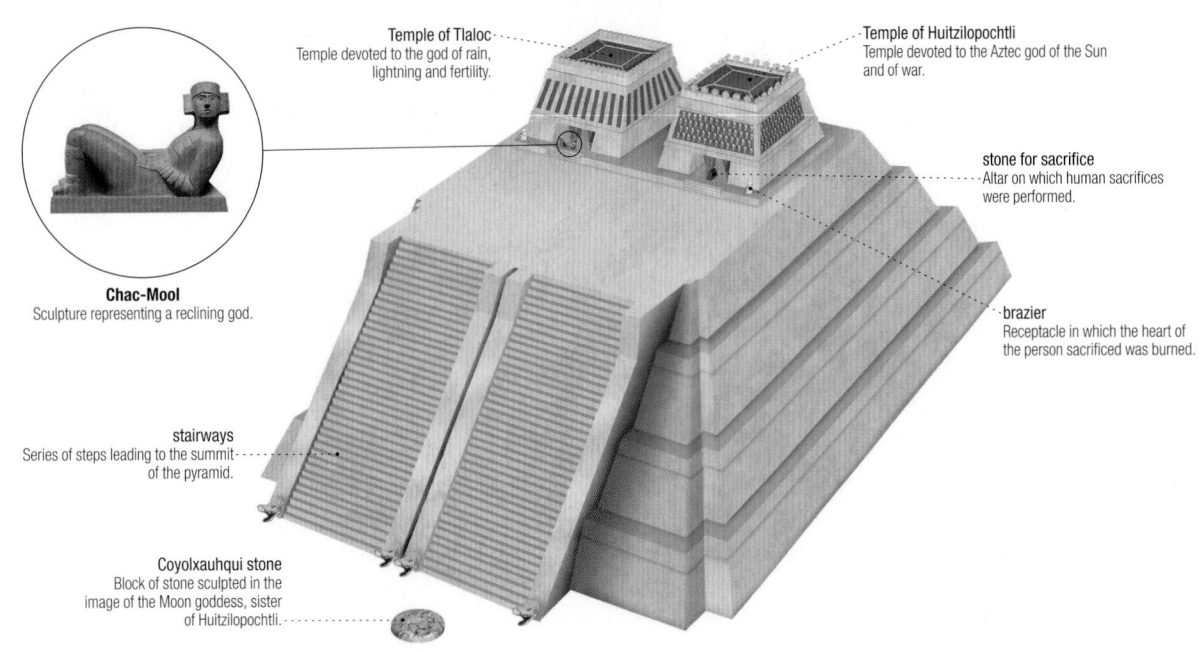

Temple of Tlaloc
Temple devoted to the god of rain, lightning and fertility.

Temple of Huitzilopochtli
Temple devoted to the Aztec god of the Sun and of war.

stone for sacrifice
Altar on which human sacrifices were performed.

Chac-Mool
Sculpture representing a reclining god.

brazier
Receptacle in which the heart of the person sacrificed was burned.

stairways
Series of steps leading to the summit of the pyramid.

Coyolxauhqui stone
Block of stone sculpted in the image of the Moon goddess, sister of Huitzilopochtli.

examples of arches

Arches: curved constructions supported on each side by piers.

semicircular arch
Arch in the form of a semicircle.

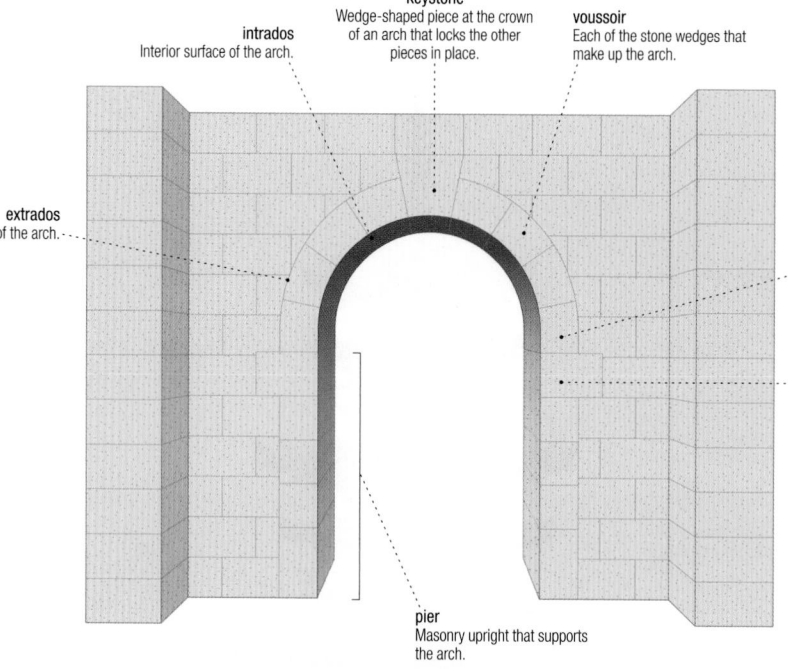

keystone
Wedge-shaped piece at the crown of an arch that locks the other pieces in place.

intrados
Interior surface of the arch.

voussoir
Each of the stone wedges that make up the arch.

extrados
Exterior surface of the arch.

springer
Stone that constitutes the arch's first voussoir and is placed on top of the impost.

impost
Slightly projecting stone that surmounts the pier and supports the springer and the voussoirs.

pier
Masonry upright that supports the arch.

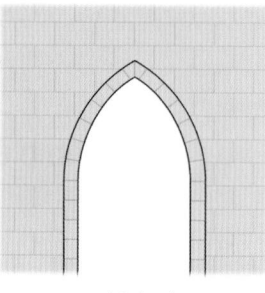

pointed arch
Arch forming an acute angle that is characteristic of Gothic architecture.

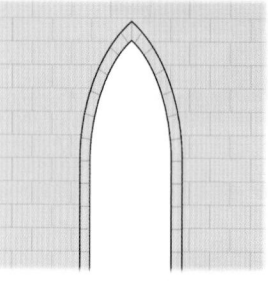

lancet arch
A narrow pointed arch.

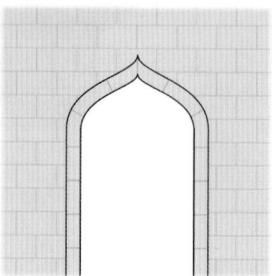

ogee arch
Arch comprised of two symmetrical curves that are alternately convex and concave.

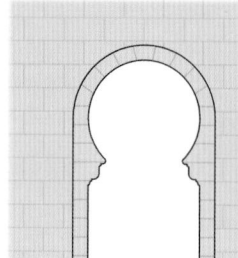

horseshoe arch
Arch whose extremities extend beyond a semicircle; it is characteristic of Arab architecture.

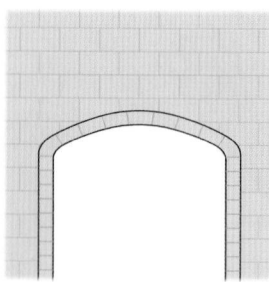

basket handle arch
Arch that is lower than it is wide and forms an ellipse.

stilted arch
Arch that takes the form of a semicircle but is higher than the semicircular arch.

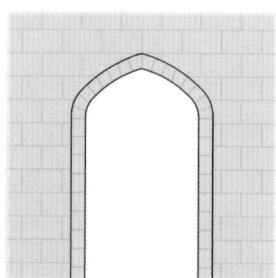

Tudor arch
A low pointed arch that is characteristic of the style that flourished in 16th-century England.

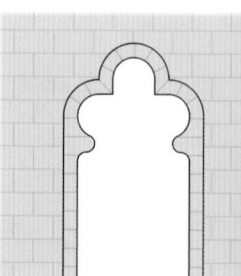

trefoil arch
Arch with three lobes.

examples of doors

Doors: barriers that open and close, usually by swinging or sliding, to permit entry and exit.

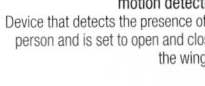

nual revolving door
ting door comprised of three
ur plateglass wings that, when
ed, pivot around a vertical axis
e manner of a turnstile.

canopy
Metal ring forming the upper part
of the enclosure, where the guide
rail for the wings is located.

wing
One of the vertical sections of the
revolving door.

motion detector
Device that detects the presence of a
person and is set to open and close
the wings.

automatic sliding door
Door activated by a motion detector that causes
the wings to slide along a rail.

enclosure
ntermediary space between two
ooms or a room and the outside,
where the door is placed.

push bar
Horizontal part that is pushed to
move the revolving door.

compartment
Part bordered by two wings where one
or more people enter and push the
door to make it rotate.

wing
The part of the door that moves.

strip
Each of the flexible plastic bands
that overlap to close the opening
and move apart to allow a person
though.

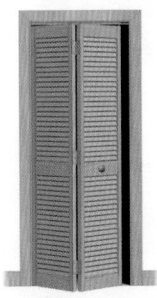

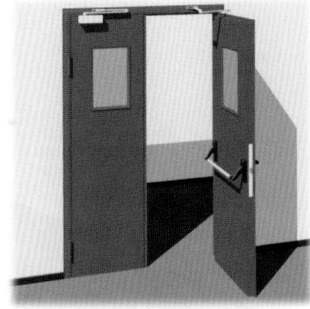

conventional door
Door made up of a panel that
opens and closes by pivoting on
hinges.

folding door
Door composed of hinged panels that
fold together when opened.

strip door
Door comprised of strips of flexible
plastic; it allows easy movement
between two rooms.

fire door
Fireproof door that delays the
spread of flames and smoke during
a fire.

sliding folding door
liding door composed of articulated
nels that fold together when opened.

sliding door
Panel or panels of a door sliding
horizontally along a set of tracks.

sectional garage door
Door composed of articulated horizontal panels
that slide along rails into the roof of the garage.

up and over garage door
Door composed of a single panel that slides
toward the ceiling of the garage.

ARTS AND ARCHITECTURE

examples of roofs

Roof: the covering of a building that rests on the frame and protects it from inclement weather.

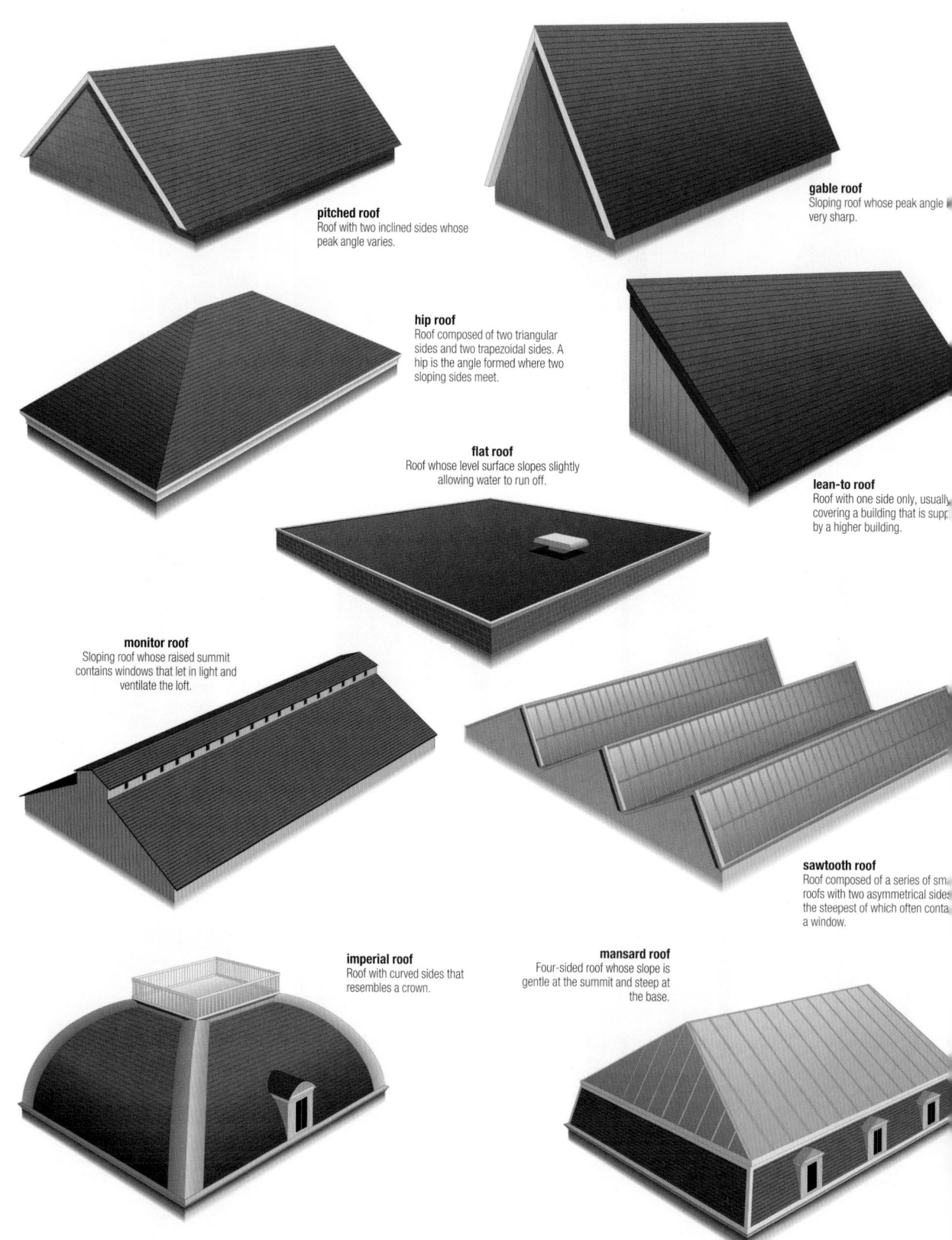

pitched roof
Roof with two inclined sides whose peak angle varies.

gable roof
Sloping roof whose peak angle is very sharp.

hip roof
Roof composed of two triangular sides and two trapezoidal sides. A hip is the angle formed where two sloping sides meet.

flat roof
Roof whose level surface slopes slightly allowing water to run off.

lean-to roof
Roof with one side only, usually covering a building that is supported by a higher building.

monitor roof
Sloping roof whose raised summit contains windows that let in light and ventilate the loft.

sawtooth roof
Roof composed of a series of small roofs with two asymmetrical sides, the steepest of which often contains a window.

imperial roof
Roof with curved sides that resembles a crown.

mansard roof
Four-sided roof whose slope is gentle at the summit and steep at the base.

conical roof
Cone-shaped roof usually
surmounting a turret.

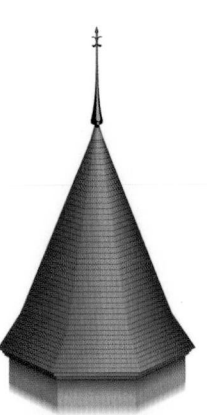

sloped turret
A steep roof made of six sides
meeting at angles.

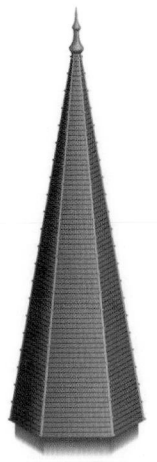

spire roof
Pyramidal or conical roof that usually surmounts
a tower or bell tower.

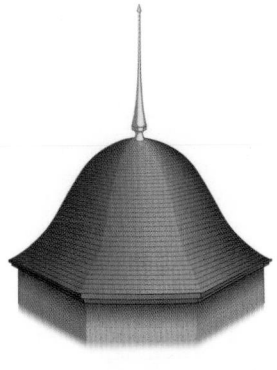

bell roof
Roof covering the hollow semicircular
vault of a building (dome).

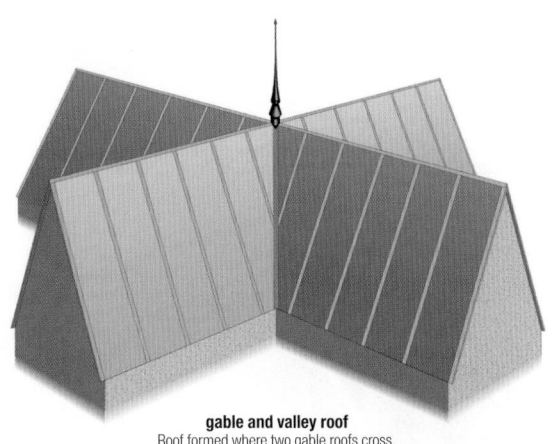
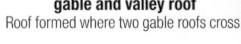

gable and valley roof
Roof formed where two gable roofs cross.

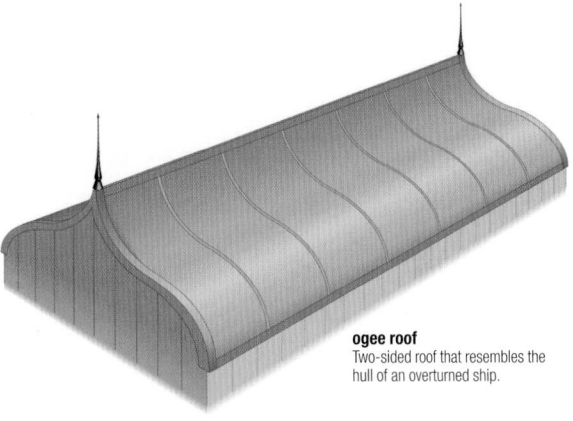

ogee roof
Two-sided roof that resembles the
hull of an overturned ship.

dome roof
Roof covering a large dome that
sometimes rises above the rest of
the roof.

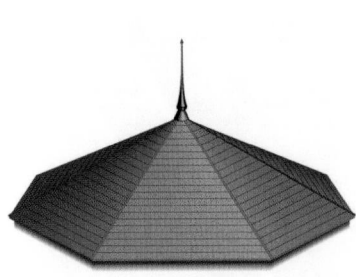

rotunda roof
Roof with several triangular sides on a
polygonal base.

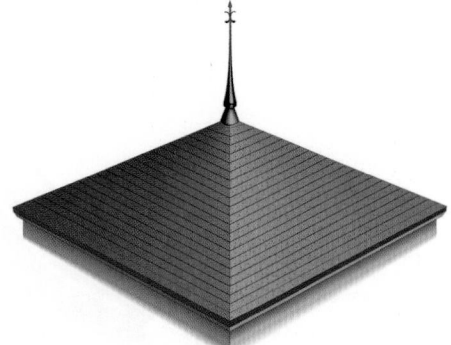

pavilion roof
Roof with four triangular sides that
form a pyramid.

ARTS AND ARCHITECTURE

examples of windows

Window: an opening in the wall of a building that lets in light and air, that usually contains glass, and that is capable of being opened and shut.

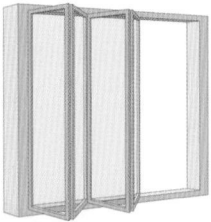

sliding folding window
Sliding window whose sash is composed of a series of articulated panels that fold together when opened.

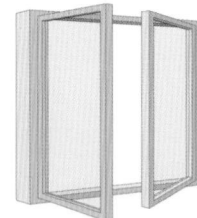

French casement window
Window with two sashes that open in and that are hinged on the side.

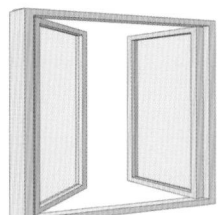

casement window
Window with one or two sashes that open out and are hinged on the side.

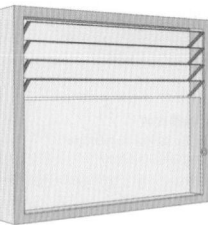

louvered window
Window whose glass louvers rotate along a horizontal axis.

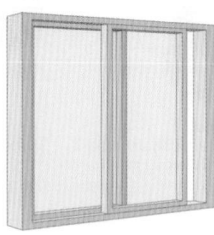

sliding window
Window with one or more sashes that move horizontally along a groove.

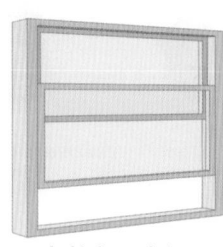

double-hung window
Window with one or more overlapping sashes that slide open vertically.

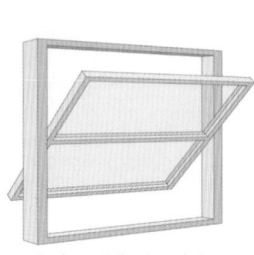

horizontal pivoting window
Window whose sash rotates along a horizontal axis located at its midpoint.

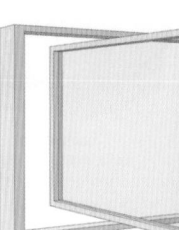

vertical pivoting window
Window whose sash rotates along a vertical axis located at midpoint.

escalator

Moving set of stairs, arranged like an endless belt that ascends or descends continuously to carry people from one level of a building to another.

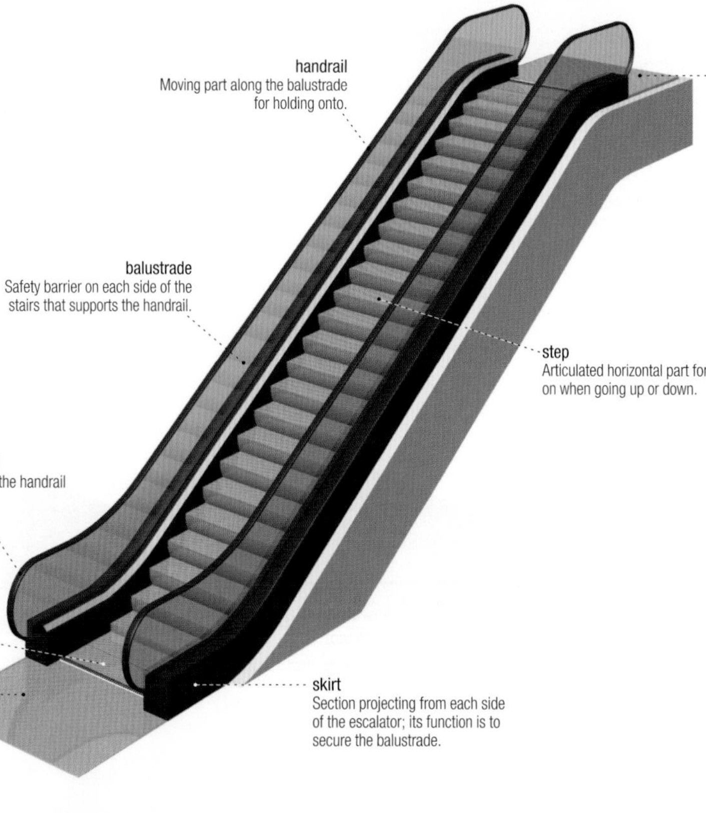

handrail
Moving part along the balustrade for holding onto.

upper landing
Platform located at the head of the escalator.

balustrade
Safety barrier on each side of the stairs that supports the handrail.

step
Articulated horizontal part for standing on when going up or down.

newel
Part around which the handrail runs.

comb
Part with teeth that mesh with the grooves in the step, preventing objects from entering the escalator's internal mechanism.

lower landing
Platform located at the foot of the escalator.

skirt
Section projecting from each side of the escalator; its function is to secure the balustrade.

elevator

Mechanical apparatus used to move people or things to different levels of a building.

elevator mechanism

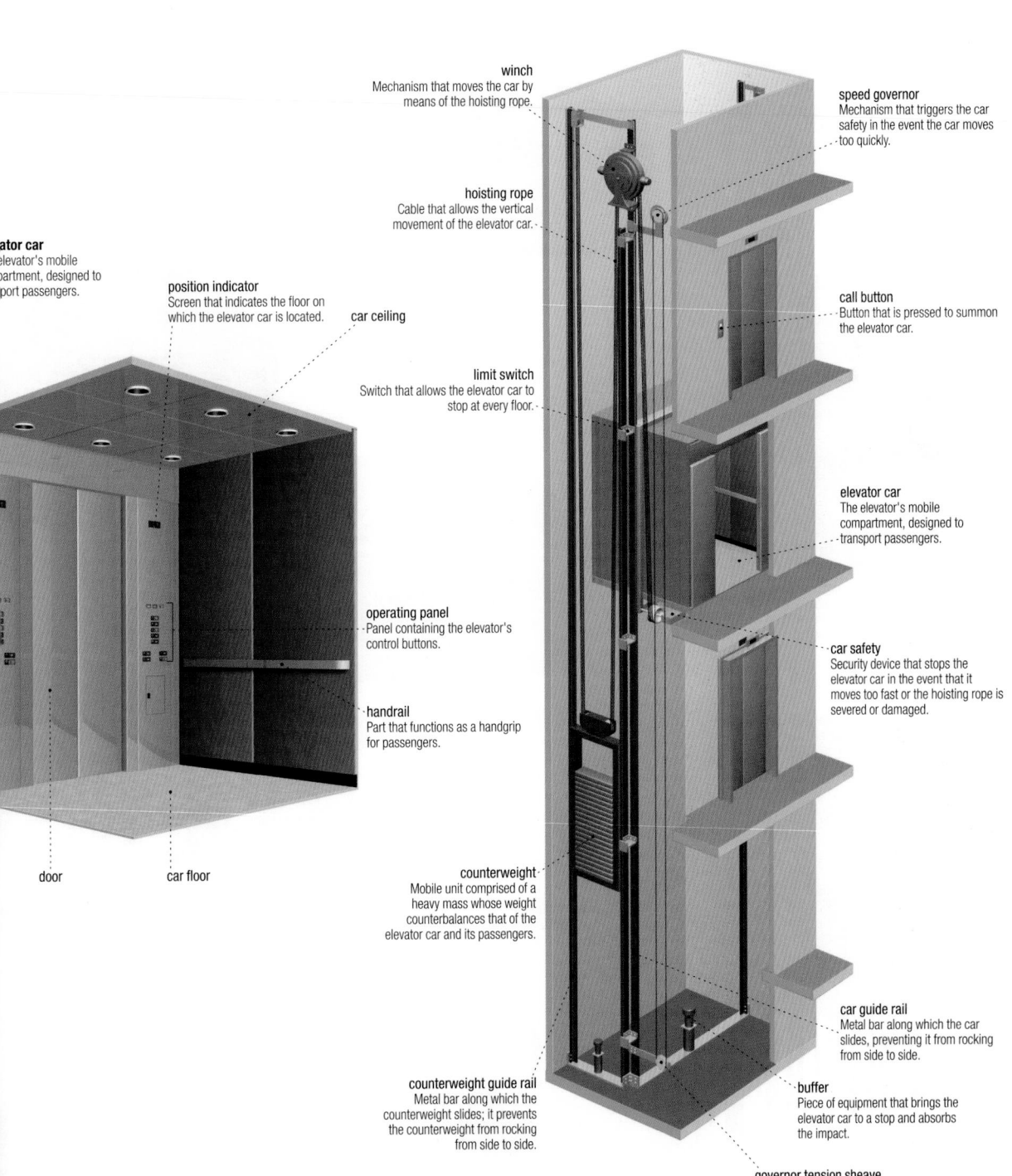

winch
Mechanism that moves the car by means of the hoisting rope.

speed governor
Mechanism that triggers the car safety in the event the car moves too quickly.

hoisting rope
Cable that allows the vertical movement of the elevator car.

elevator car
elevator's mobile compartment, designed to port passengers.

position indicator
Screen that indicates the floor on which the elevator car is located.

car ceiling

call button
Button that is pressed to summon the elevator car.

limit switch
Switch that allows the elevator car to stop at every floor.

elevator car
The elevator's mobile compartment, designed to transport passengers.

operating panel
Panel containing the elevator's control buttons.

car safety
Security device that stops the elevator car in the event that it moves too fast or the hoisting rope is severed or damaged.

handrail
Part that functions as a handgrip for passengers.

door

car floor

counterweight
Mobile unit comprised of a heavy mass whose weight counterbalances that of the elevator car and its passengers.

counterweight guide rail
Metal bar along which the counterweight slides; it prevents the counterweight from rocking from side to side.

car guide rail
Metal bar along which the car slides, preventing it from rocking from side to side.

buffer
Piece of equipment that brings the elevator car to a stop and absorbs the impact.

governor tension sheave
Device that serves to keep the speed governor cable taut.

ARTS AND ARCHITECTURE

traditional houses

The dwellings, current or of former times, that characterize a given culture.

igloo
Dome-shaped Inuit dwelling made of
blocks of snow or ice.

yurt
Portable dwelling of the nomadic
peoples of central and northern
Asia composed of a wooden frame
covered with animal skins or felt.

hut
Rudimentary dwelling made from
tree branches and straw.

hut
Dwelling of African countries, usually
made of straw and clay and covered
with a straw roof.

isba
Dwelling of various countries in
northern Europe, especially Russia,
made of the wood of the fir tree.

wigwam
Round or oval dwelling of Native
Americans in North America made of
poles covered with bark, matting and
skins.

tepee
Conical dwelling of the Native
Americans of the North American
plains, made of poles covered
with skins.

pile dwelling
Dwelling built over water or wet land
and supported by posts.

viga
Heavy beam that transfers the
weight of the roof onto the support
structure.

adobe ho
Dwellings found in Latin Ame
and southwestern U.S. built
sun-dried bricks made fro
mixture of earth and st

ladde
Movable wooden implement with
rungs, for reaching the roof

city houses

Dwelling types found in large urban centers.

two-story house
Single-family dwelling that contains two levels,
the first floor and a second floor.

one-story house
Single-family dwelling that contains only
one level, the first floor.

duplex
Dwelling divided into two separate
living spaces.

town houses
Houses of at least two stories
connected to similar houses by
common walls.

condominiums
Multiple dwellings belonging to separate
owners who share the building's maintenance
costs.

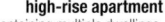

high-rise apartment
Tall building containing multiple dwellings.

museum

Establishment where works of art are stored and exhibited.

general view

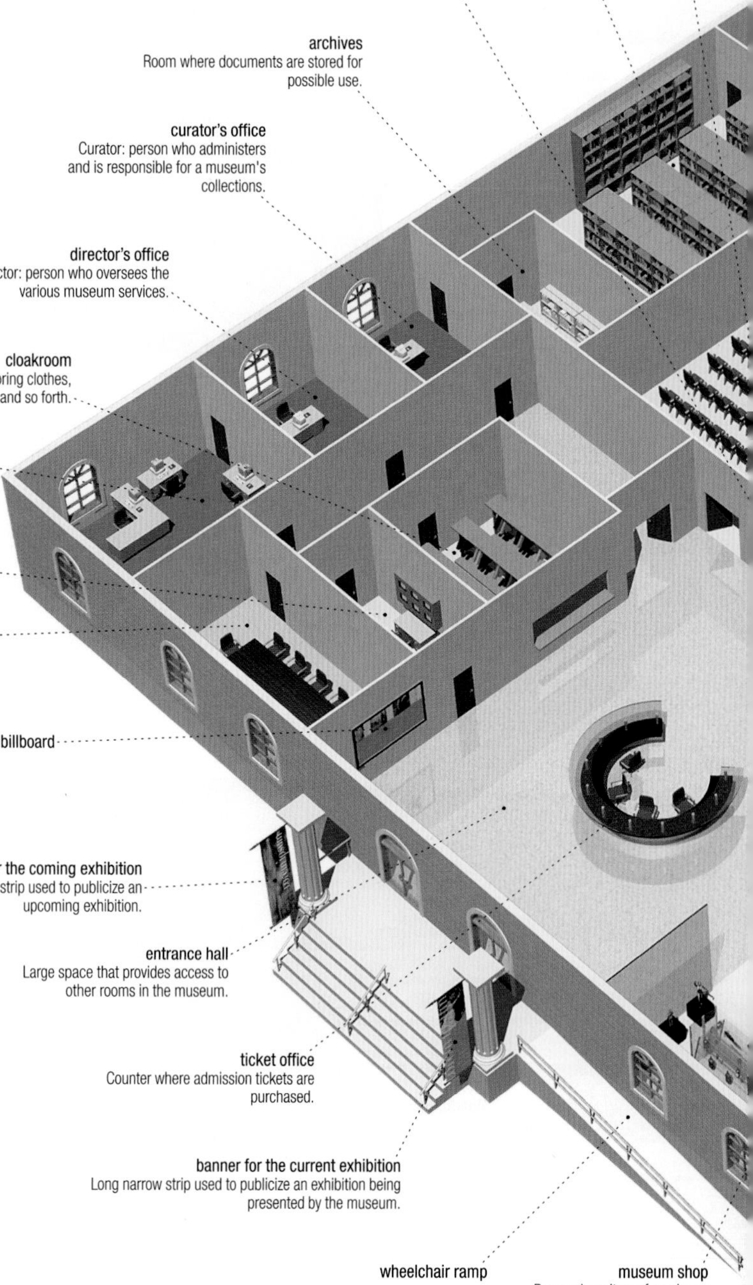

documentation center
Room reserved for museum staff;
it houses technical documentation
related to the museum's activities.

auditorium
Hall designed for the public
attend lectures and audiovisu..
presentations.

ticket clerk

archives
Room where documents are stored for
possible use.

curator's office
Curator: person who administers
and is responsible for a museum's
collections.

director's office
Director: person who oversees the
various museum services.

cloakroom
Space designated for storing clothes,
hats, umbrellas and so forth.

administration
Place where tasks related to the
management of museum services are
carried out.

control center
Room equipped with monitors so staff
members can watch over a museum's
various rooms.

meeting room

exhibition billboard

banner for the coming exhibition
Long narrow strip used to publicize an
upcoming exhibition.

entrance hall
Large space that provides access to
other rooms in the museum.

ticket office
Counter where admission tickets are
purchased.

banner for the current exhibition
Long narrow strip used to publicize an exhibition being
presented by the museum.

wheelchair ramp

museum shop
Room where items for sale are
displayed.

audioguide
Handheld device that allows users to listen, in
their own language, to commentary on the artwork
exhibited.

ARTS AND ARCHITECTURE

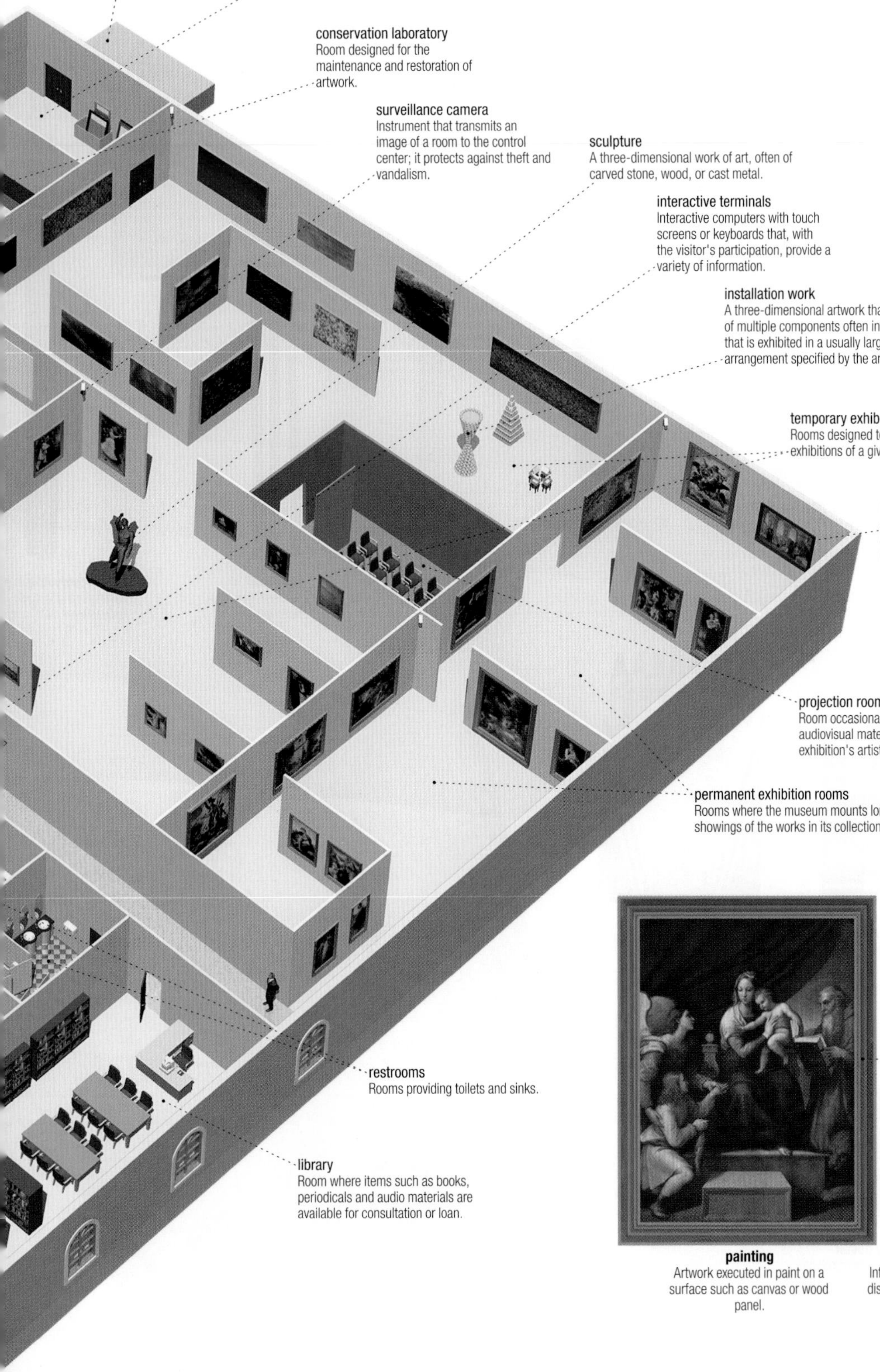

museum

unloading dock
Facility for off-loading crates containing exhibition equipment.

receiving area
Area designed to receive artwork.

conservation laboratory
Room designed for the maintenance and restoration of artwork.

surveillance camera
Instrument that transmits an image of a room to the control center; it protects against theft and vandalism.

sculpture
A three-dimensional work of art, often of carved stone, wood, or cast metal.

interactive terminals
Interactive computers with touch screens or keyboards that, with the visitor's participation, provide a variety of information.

installation work
A three-dimensional artwork that usually consists of multiple components often in mixed media and that is exhibited in a usually large space in an arrangement specified by the artist.

temporary exhibition rooms
Rooms designed to house short-term exhibitions of a given artist or theme.

painting
Artwork executed in paint on a surface such as canvas or wood panel.

projection room
Room occasionally used to present audiovisual materials related to the exhibition's artist or theme.

permanent exhibition rooms
Rooms where the museum mounts long-term showings of the works in its collection.

restrooms
Rooms providing toilets and sinks.

library
Room where items such as books, periodicals and audio materials are available for consultation or loan.

frame
Rigid border that surrounds and protects a painting or engraving and can be hung onto a wall.

painting
Artwork executed in paint on a surface such as canvas or wood panel.

label
Information about an artwork displayed on the wall near the artwork.

ARTS AND ARCHITECTURE

painting and drawing

Arts that use graphics and color to represent or suggest visible or imagined concepts on a surface.

drawing material
Materials, instruments and accessories used to create a drawing.

red ocher pencil
Stick of hematite (iron oxide) used to produce a sketch on paper; the sketch is then transferred to the stone.

Conté crayon
Stick of molded graphite or charcoal mixed with pigment, lamp-black, binding agent, wax or clay, and plasticizer.

paper stump
Small rolled stem of paper, leather or cotton finishing in points and used to spread pencil or pastel on a drawing to produce shading.

marker
Bevel-tipped color felt pen of variable size.

felt-tip pen
Pen whose felt tip is permeated with ink; it comes in a variety of colors.

ink
Liquid preparation, black or colored, used to write or draw.

charcoal
Stick of charcoal used for sketching; it erases easily.

reservoir-nib pe
Drawing instrument with a containing a small amou

oil pastel
Mixture of pigments, wax and sometimes oily substances in stick form.

wax crayons
Sticks composed of pigment molded with wax.

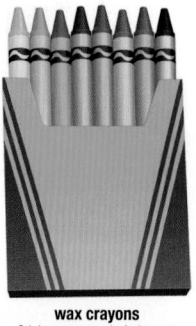

dry pastel
Mixture of pigment powder agglutinated using a gum-based binder, then shaped into sticks and dried.

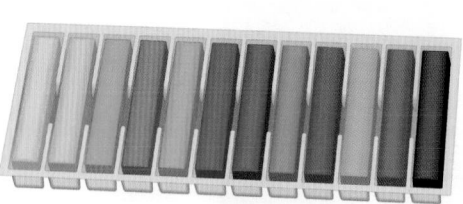

colored pencils
Wood-covered pencils containing sticks of pastel made from pigments, clay and gum.

painting and drawing

ette with dipper
featuring a thumb hole and a dipper; painter uses it to set out colors and hem.

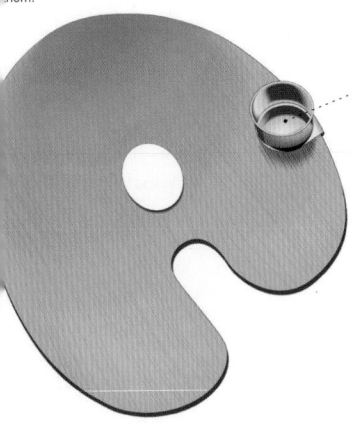

dipper
Small metal receptacle fastened to the palette; it contains the oil and essences used to dilute color.

painting material
Materials, instruments and accessories used to create a painting.

oil/acrylic paint
Oil-based or acrylic pigment that comes in a tube; the artist uses oil or essences to dilute it and prepare it for application.

watercolor/gouache tube
Tube containing watercolor or gouache in paste form.

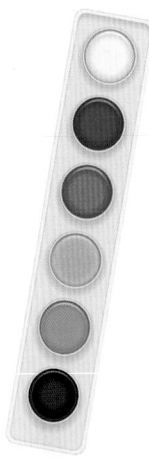

watercolor/gouache cakes
Small watercolor or gouache disks inserted into cells to prevent the colors from mixing.

ette with hollows
featuring a thumb hole and hollows re the paint is placed before it is mixed.

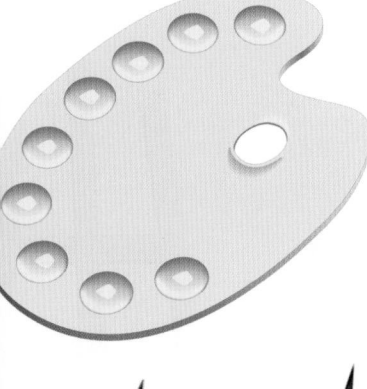

palette knife
Instrument with a flat flexible blade used to mix colors, spread them on a canvas or scrape down the palette.

fan brush
Brush used to achieve color gradations by blending colors that have already been applied to a canvas.

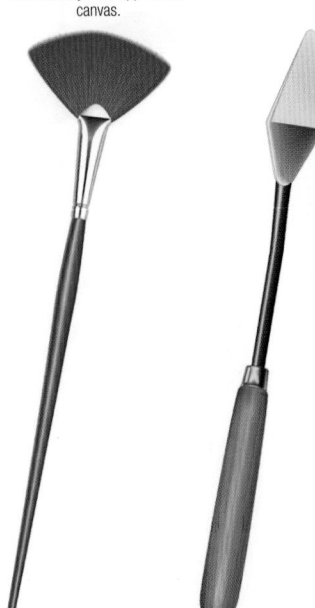

brush
ral or synthetic bristles ed to a handle, used for ng paint, varnish or stain on a base.

sumi-e brush
Brush made from natural bristles affixed to a bamboo handle and used for drawing with black ink.

flat brush
Brush made from natural or synthetic bristles affixed to a handle and used mostly for oil painting on large surfaces.

painting knife
Instrument with a trowel-shaped blade used to mix colors and to spread them on and remove them from the canvas.

painting and drawing

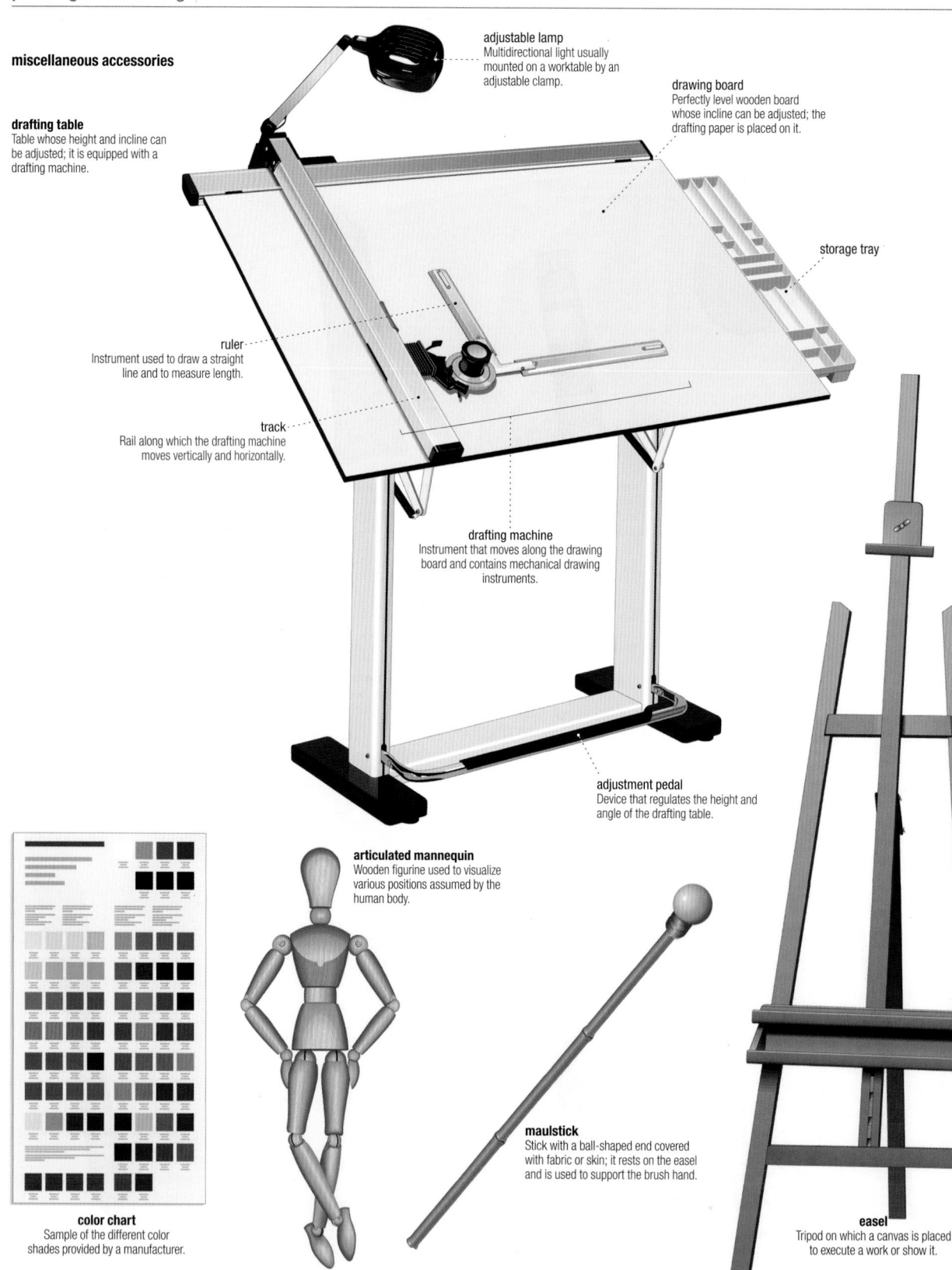

miscellaneous accessories

adjustable lamp
Multidirectional light usually mounted on a worktable by an adjustable clamp.

drawing board
Perfectly level wooden board whose incline can be adjusted; the drafting paper is placed on it.

drafting table
Table whose height and incline can be adjusted; it is equipped with a drafting machine.

storage tray

ruler
Instrument used to draw a straight line and to measure length.

track
Rail along which the drafting machine moves vertically and horizontally.

drafting machine
Instrument that moves along the drawing board and contains mechanical drawing instruments.

adjustment pedal
Device that regulates the height and angle of the drafting table.

articulated mannequin
Wooden figurine used to visualize various positions assumed by the human body.

maulstick
Stick with a ball-shaped end covered with fabric or skin; it rests on the easel and is used to support the brush hand.

color chart
Sample of the different color shades provided by a manufacturer.

easel
Tripod on which a canvas is placed to execute a work or show it.

painting and drawing

airbrush
Instrument that atomizes paint or ink and sprays it onto a surface by means of compressed air pressure.

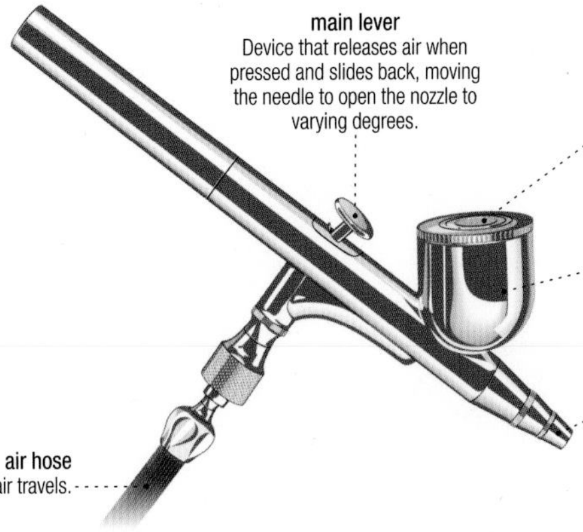

main lever
Device that releases air when pressed and slides back, moving the needle to open the nozzle to varying degrees.

cap

fluid cup
Receptacle that holds the paint, a certain amount of which is drawn in with the air, depending on the position of the needle.

crown
The nozzle cap.

air hose
Flexible tube along which the air travels.

section of an airbrush

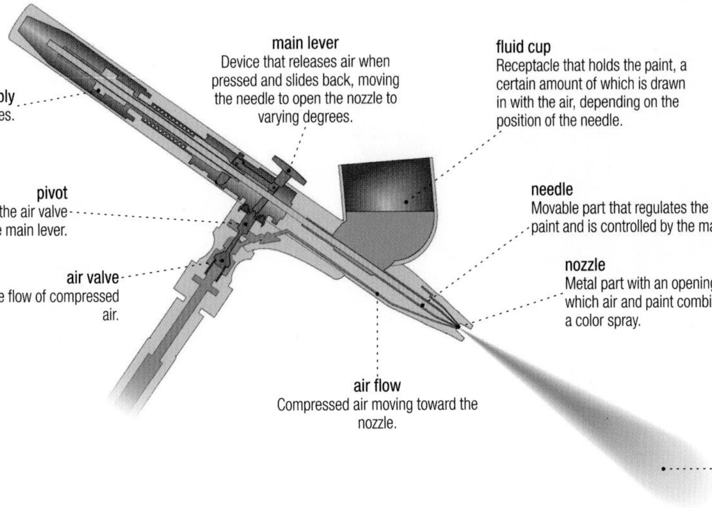

needle assembly
Device in which the needle moves.

main lever
Device that releases air when pressed and slides back, moving the needle to open the nozzle to varying degrees.

fluid cup
Receptacle that holds the paint, a certain amount of which is drawn in with the air, depending on the position of the needle.

pivot
Component that opens the air valve and is controlled by the main lever.

needle
Movable part that regulates the flow of paint and is controlled by the main lever.

air valve
Valve that controls the flow of compressed air.

nozzle
Metal part with an opening through which air and paint combine to create a color spray.

air flow
Compressed air moving toward the nozzle.

color spray
Pulverized paint.

utility liquids
Utility liquids are used to prepare a color or protect a work of art.

turpentine
An essential oil obtained by the distillation of natural resins and used mostly as an oil paint thinner.

fixative
Transparent solution in liquid or aerosol form applied to protect a drawing in charcoal, chalk, pastel or pencil.

varnish
Preparation with no pigment; when applied to a surface, it forms a protective film.

linseed oil
Oil made from linseeds; it acts as a binding agent so that pigment adheres to a surface.

ARTS AND ARCHITECTURE

painting and drawing

ARTS AND ARCHITECTURE

color wheel
Representation of the color spectrum on a circle.

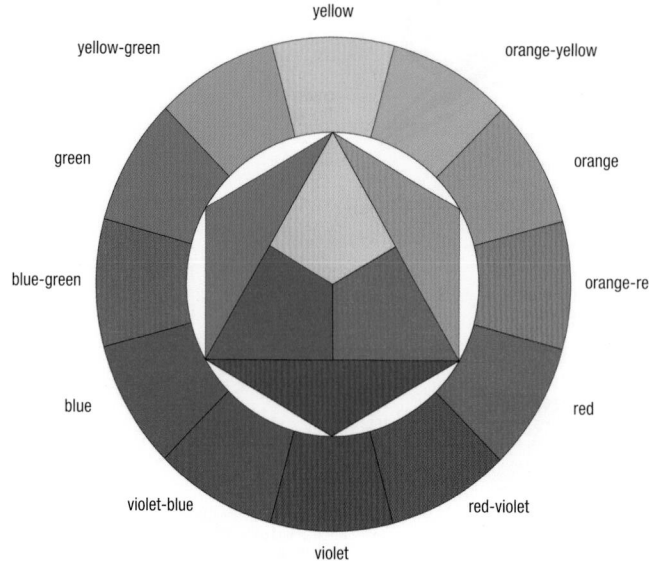

yellow

yellow-green

orange-yellow

green

orange

blue-green

orange-red

blue

red

violet-blue

red-violet

violet

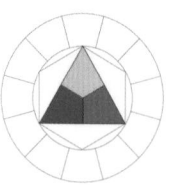

primary colors
Colors that cannot be obtained by mixing other colors.

secondary c
Colors obtained by m
proportions of two pri

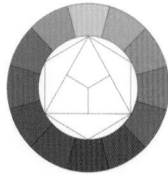

tertiary colors
Colors obtained by mixing equal proportions of a primary color and a secondary color.

major techniques
The processes used to execute drawings and paintings.

gouache
Mixture of roughly ground pigment and chalk agglutinated with a water-soluble binder; when it is diluted, an opaque effect is created.

watercolor
Mixture of pigment powder agglutinated with a water-soluble binder; when it is diluted, a transparent effect is created.

oil painting
Technique used to achieve an opaque, transparent, matte or brilliant finish, depending on the composition of the paint.

charcoal drawing
Sketching technique that can create tones ranging from the darkest blacks to the lightest grays.

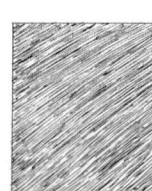

ink drawing
Technique usually involvin
use of a pen to create fin
precise lines.

wax crayon drawing
Technique used mostly by children to create a precise line and a brilliant color effect.

colored pencil drawing
Technique for combining precise lines with color, and then applying layers of color to achieve new shades.

oil pastel drawing
Technique that provides a bold stroke similar to that of an oil painting.

dry pastel drawing
Technique whose powdery line creates a velvety effect.

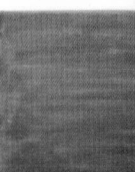

felt-tip pen drawin
Technique for producing p
lines and gradations of c

painting and drawing

panel
Wooden board that serves as a
rigid surface for a painting.

canvas
Piece of fabric covered with a
primer and set on a stretcher;
it serves as the surface for the
painting.

cardboard
Somewhat rigid sheet made of
several layers of paper pulp; its
function is to support a drawing or
painting.

paper
Vegetable substance reduced to
paste, rolled and then dried into thin
sheets that serve as a surface for a
drawing, painting or engraving.

main supports
Surfaces on which paintings, drawings and
engravings are created.

painting: examples of styles
There have been many styles or movements in
painting, characterized by certain pictorial techniques
or particular aesthetic principles.

Baroque
Style in which warm and bright colors
are preferred, and free rein is given to
emotionalism and exuberance. Movement is
generally very important in this style.

classicism
Style characterized by the goal of realistic
representation in form and composition.
Subjects are generally noble and often inspired
by mythology or Antiquity.

ARTS AND ARCHITECTURE

painting and drawing

painting: examples of styles

Impressionism
Style in which artists represent their
impressions rather than the reality of
landscapes, by playing with colors and the
transformation of the exterior nature.

Expressionism
Style presenting deformed and stylized
representations of reality with the goal of
provoking an emotional response. Aggressive
colors are often used.

Cubism
Style in which objects are
deconstructed into colors and
simple geometrical shapes.

abstract art
Style representing only shapes and
colors rather than objects from the
real world.

naive art
Style characterized by the use of bright
colors and mistaken perspective effects.

realism
Style in which artists attempt to objectively
represent scenes of everyday life.

wood carving

Art that consists of carving a piece of wood to represent or suggest an object.

steps

Phases in the development of a wood sculpture.

drawing
Step that involves drawing the piece to be carved on a wooden block.

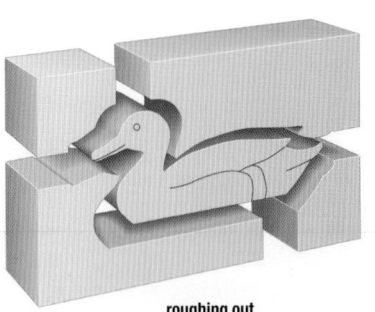

roughing out
Step that involves bringing out the basic contours of a piece.

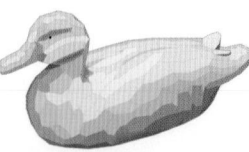

carving
Step that involves shaping and refining the piece.

finishing
Step that involves fine-tuning the details and polishing the surface of a piece until no evidence remains of the tools used.

examples of carving tools

Instruments used in sculpture to cut and file wood.

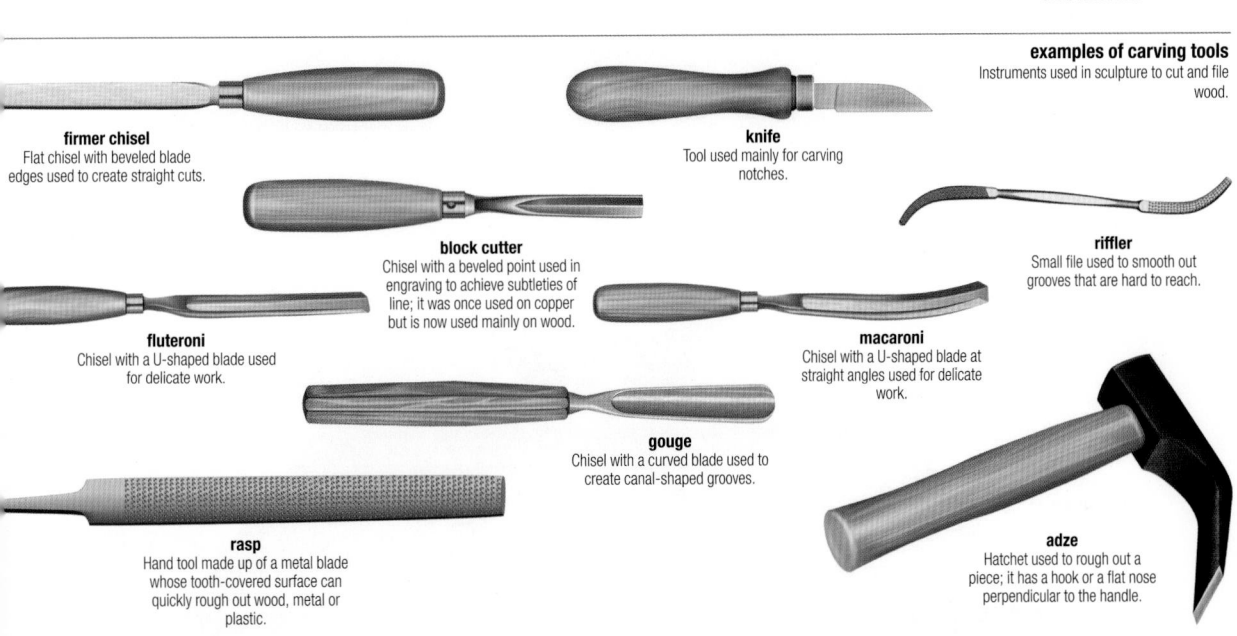

firmer chisel
Flat chisel with beveled blade edges used to create straight cuts.

knife
Tool used mainly for carving notches.

block cutter
Chisel with a beveled point used in engraving to achieve subtleties of line; it was once used on copper but is now used mainly on wood.

riffler
Small file used to smooth out grooves that are hard to reach.

fluteroni
Chisel with a U-shaped blade used for delicate work.

macaroni
Chisel with a U-shaped blade at straight angles used for delicate work.

gouge
Chisel with a curved blade used to create canal-shaped grooves.

rasp
Hand tool made up of a metal blade whose tooth-covered surface can quickly rough out wood, metal or plastic.

adze
Hatchet used to rough out a piece; it has a hook or a flat nose perpendicular to the handle.

major types of blades

blade: the sharp part of a sculptor's chisel.

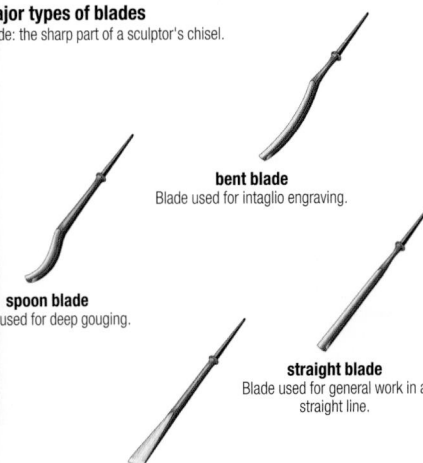

bent blade
Blade used for intaglio engraving.

spoon blade
used for deep gouging.

straight blade
Blade used for general work in a straight line.

blade with two beveled edges
Blade used to execute rectilinear cuts.

carving accessories

carver's bench screw
Threaded instrument used to secure a piece of wood to a stand.

stand
Small stool on which the sculptor places and secures the piece to be worked on.

punch and pattern
The punch, a metal rod, is struck to carve motifs into a slab of wood.

mallet
Hammer used to strike the heel of a sharp tool to force it into the wood.

printing

Reproduction of characters or illustrations by transferring a model to a surface, usually paper, most often using ink.

relief printing
Process that consists of printing an image from a raised figure covered with a film of ink; the image is transferred to a surface by means of pressure.

paper · · · · · · · · · printed image

inked surface · · · · · · · · · raised figure

intaglio printing
Process that consists of printing an image from an incised figure filled with ink; the image is transferred to a surface by means of pressure.

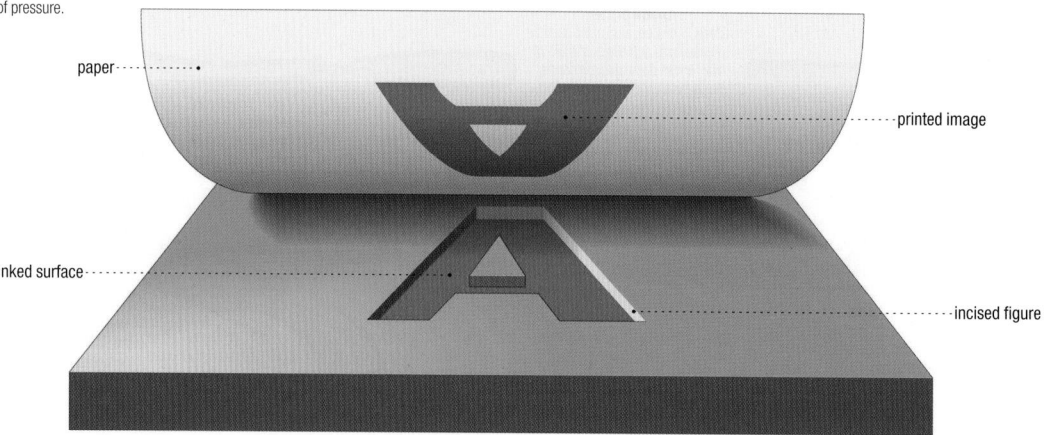

paper · · · · · · · · · printed image

inked surface · · · · · · · · · incised figure

lithographic printing
Process that consists of printing an image from a figure on the same plane as the nonprinted parts, which are protected from the ink by dampening.

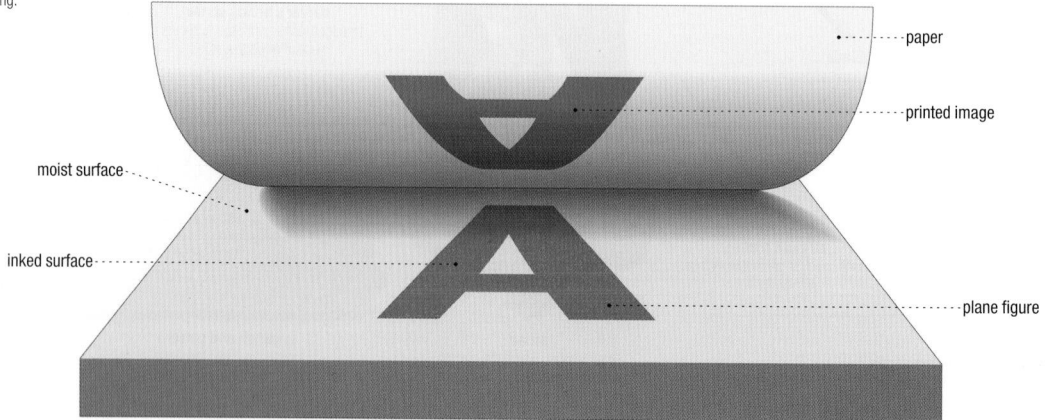

paper

printed image

moist surface · · · · · · · · ·

inked surface · · · · · · · · · plane figure

relief printing process

Technique that consists of creating a raised figure on a piece of wood.

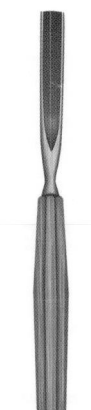

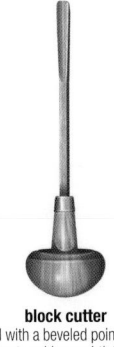

equipment
Collective term for the materials, instruments and tools used for engraving and printing.

block cutter
Chisel with a beveled point used in engraving to achieve subtleties of line; it was once used on copper but is now used mainly on wood.

mallet
...mmer used to strike the heel of ...sharp tool to drive it into wood.

U-shaped gouge
Sharp U-shaped chisel used to remove areas to create large blank spaces.

V-shaped gouge
Sharp V-shaped chisel used to dig deep angular grooves and to remove areas to create smaller blank spaces.

chisel
Sharp tool with a flat beveled blade used for engraving wood in the grain direction; it removes areas to create blank space around the figure and smoothes out the background.

knife
Tool used for engraving in the grain direction of the wood; it brings out the figure by means of incisions.

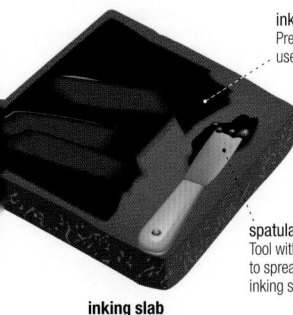

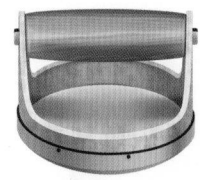

ink
Preparation in black or in color used for printing.

ink
Preparation in black or in color used for printing.

brayer
Instrument used to spread ink on a raised figure.

baren
Instrument that exerts pressure on the back of the paper to help the ink adhere.

spatula
Tool with a flat flexible blade used to spread ink or scrape down the inking slab.

inking slab
Plate on which the ink is spread so it will be evenly distributed on the brayer.

ARTS AND ARCHITECTURE

proof press
Fixed-bed printing press with a cylinder that is moved along an engraved and inked board covered with a sheet of paper.

gripper
Each of the metal pieces mounted on a strip that holds the paper in position under the cylinder.

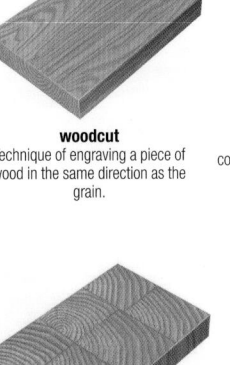
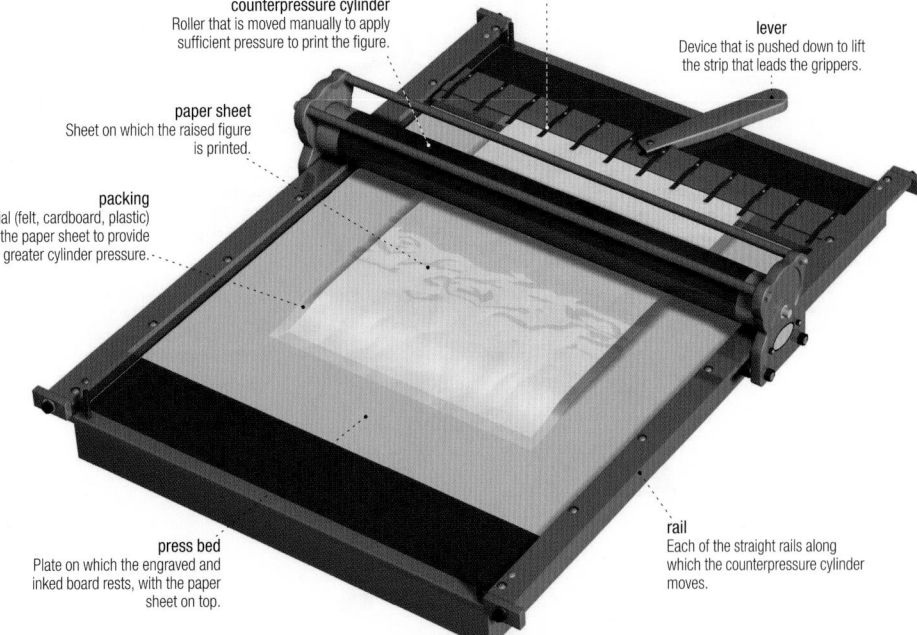

counterpressure cylinder
Roller that is moved manually to apply sufficient pressure to print the figure.

lever
Device that is pushed down to lift the strip that leads the grippers.

paper sheet
Sheet on which the raised figure is printed.

woodcut
Technique of engraving a piece of wood in the same direction as the grain.

packing
Material (felt, cardboard, plastic) covering the paper sheet to provide greater cylinder pressure.

wood engraving
...hnique of engraving a piece of wood against the grain.

press bed
Plate on which the engraved and inked board rests, with the paper sheet on top.

rail
Each of the straight rails along which the counterpressure cylinder moves.

intaglio printing process

Technique that consists of drawing a figure by engraving its lines into a surface, usually a copper plate.

equipment

Collective term for the materials, instruments and tools used for engraving and printing.

brush
Natural or synthetic bristles attached to a handle, used for spreading paint, varnish or stain on a base.

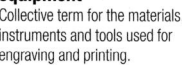

rocking tool
Tool with a thick rounded beveled steel blade; the row of vertical grooves on its sides gives the copper surface a uniform grain.

roulette
Instrument with a steel wheel containing several rows of regular asperities and used to create coarse-grained lines.

etching point
Steel rod used to engrave a figure in copper by biting into the plate or the varnish covering it.

burnisher
Instrument used to refine the cuts and remove irregularities from the metal.

copper plate
Copper is the metal most often used in engraving because it is strong, is malleable enough for engraving and reacts to chemicals.

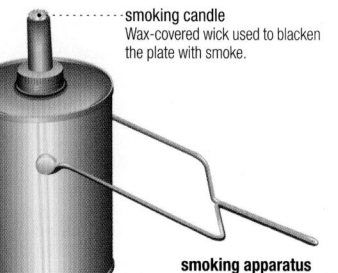

smoking candle
Wax-covered wick used to blacken the plate with smoke.

smoking apparatus
Instrument used to blacken the varnish and the plate with smoke; this makes the figure more visible during the engraving process.

hand vise
Instrument used to hold and handle the plate while smoking it.

scraper
Tool with a pointed triangular blade used to remove burrs, thin strips of copper left on the edge of the groove made by the drypoint.

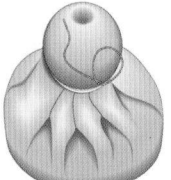
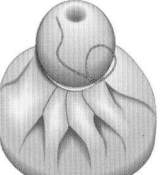

dabber
Instrument made up of a handle placed in a cotton wad and wrapped in silk; it is used to spread varnish on the plate.

tarlatan
Muslin used to wipe excess ink from the surface of the plate.

etching press

Apparatus with two cylinders; to print, an engraved and inked plate and a sheet of paper are pressed between them.

pressure screw
Part that controls cylinder pressure.

felt
Thick piece of fabric placed beneath the paper before it is put under the press; the felt cushions and distributes the pressure.

press bed
Plate that moves between the two cylinders, supporting the engraved board and the paper.

top cylinder
Roller located above the press bed; together with the bottom cylinder, it exerts the pressure required to achieve a good impression of the figure.

bottom cylinder
Roller located beneath the press bed; together with the top cylinder, it exerts the pressure required to achieve a good impression of the figure.

flywheel
Lever that controls the press cylinders.

oilstone
Stone used to sharpen tools.

varnish roller
Instrument used to spread varnish on the surface and prevent ink from adhering to it; it ensures that only the figure is inked.

lithography

Technique of printing from a plane surface using grease to draw a figure on damp limestone; the grease retains ink, the water repels it.

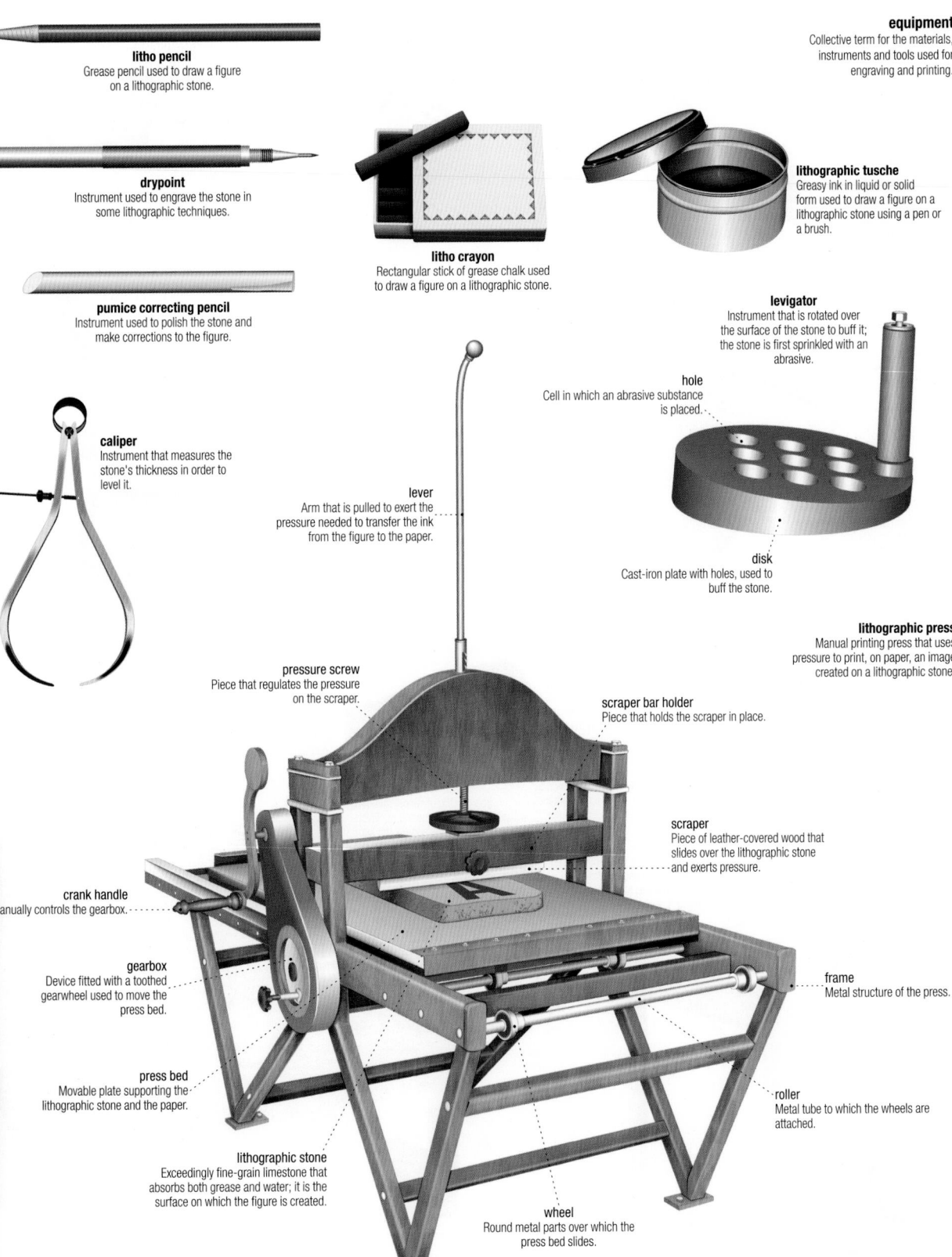

litho pencil
Grease pencil used to draw a figure on a lithographic stone.

drypoint
Instrument used to engrave the stone in some lithographic techniques.

pumice correcting pencil
Instrument used to polish the stone and make corrections to the figure.

litho crayon
Rectangular stick of grease chalk used to draw a figure on a lithographic stone.

equipment
Collective term for the materials, instruments and tools used for engraving and printing.

lithographic tusche
Greasy ink in liquid or solid form used to draw a figure on a lithographic stone using a pen or a brush.

levigator
Instrument that is rotated over the surface of the stone to buff it; the stone is first sprinkled with an abrasive.

hole
Cell in which an abrasive substance is placed.

disk
Cast-iron plate with holes, used to buff the stone.

caliper
Instrument that measures the stone's thickness in order to level it.

lever
Arm that is pulled to exert the pressure needed to transfer the ink from the figure to the paper.

pressure screw
Piece that regulates the pressure on the scraper.

scraper bar holder
Piece that holds the scraper in place.

lithographic press
Manual printing press that uses pressure to print, on paper, an image created on a lithographic stone.

scraper
Piece of leather-covered wood that slides over the lithographic stone and exerts pressure.

crank handle
Manually controls the gearbox.

gearbox
Device fitted with a toothed gearwheel used to move the press bed.

press bed
Movable plate supporting the lithographic stone and the paper.

frame
Metal structure of the press.

roller
Metal tube to which the wheels are attached.

lithographic stone
Exceedingly fine-grain limestone that absorbs both grease and water; it is the surface on which the figure is created.

wheel
Round metal parts over which the press bed slides.

screen printing

Printing technique consisting of transferring an image by ink transfer through a fabric screen onto various media (paper, fabric, glass, etc.). This technique is related to stenciling.

equipment
All materials, instruments and devices used in screen printing.

photo emulsion
Semi-liquid mixture that reacts to light, used together with the sensitizer. Once hardened, it prevents the ink from passing through the screen around the printing zone.

screen printing ink
Thick liquid mixture applied to the printing area, which must first be washed in order to remove all traces of emulsion.

sensitizer
Chemical compound that renders the photosensitive emulsion even more sensitive to light.

stencil
Black design reproduced on a transparency, placed on the glass of the exposure table between the light and the screen. The emulsion remains supple in the areas where the light is blocked by the stencil.

squeegee
Tool with a rubber blade used to press ink through the fabric screen onto the printing area, which has not been exposed to light, thanks to the stencil.

textile printi
Device that allows fabric, generall to be printed with a design of mult. The screens rotate around o attach

design
Image, reproduced on the stencil, that is then transferred onto the screen and printed on the medium.

silk screen frame
Each frame must be attached using precise markers so that the ink is printed in the desired place. One color only is applied to each fabric screen.

silk screen frame
Basic tool of the printing process. It is made of durable material that is reusable and easy to clean.

screen holder
Strong stem that is lowered against the positioning piece which has been adjusted to ensure the right amount of space between the screen and the medium being printed on.

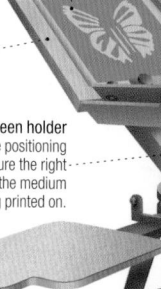

fabric screen mesh
Thin and porous fabric to which the emulsion is applied. At the end of the printing process, the ink is spread onto it and passes through the cloth only in the printing zone.

removable pallet
Adhesive panel on which the fabric is placed, or around which a T-shirt can be placed. They are removable and come in different sizes to accommodate various sizes of fabric.

aluminum frame
Rigid structure to which the fabric screen is attached.

scoop coater
Small, long container used to apply emulsion to both sides of the screen. The mixture must then dry for several hours in the dark.

vacuum printing table
Device for printing a design on a light medium (paper, card stock, etc.), keeping it in place using a vacuum system.

pivoting tray
Rotating table allowing the screens to be moved in order to print the different colors of the design, one after another, on the medium, which stays in a fixed spot.

exposure ta
Exposure device allowing transfer of the design or screen. Under the effect of light, the emulsion hardens, ex in the areas blocked by the ste

silk screen frame
The frame is attached to the hinges and lowered onto the printing surface. The ink is then pressed onto the design which is then transferred onto the paper or cardstock after the ink passes through the holes in the fabric.

rubber lid
Board made of supple material that is stretched onto a rigid frame, which is closed over the screen and kept in place by a vacuum system.

vacuum table
Flat rigid surface perforated with small holes used with the aid of a vacuum to keep the medium against the base during printing and prevent it from sticking to the screen.

transparent working surface
Flat surface through which light can pass.

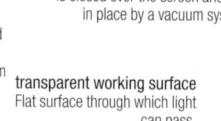

fluorescent lamp
Tube in which the electric current produces ultraviolet radiation converted into visible light by a layer of a fluorescent substance.

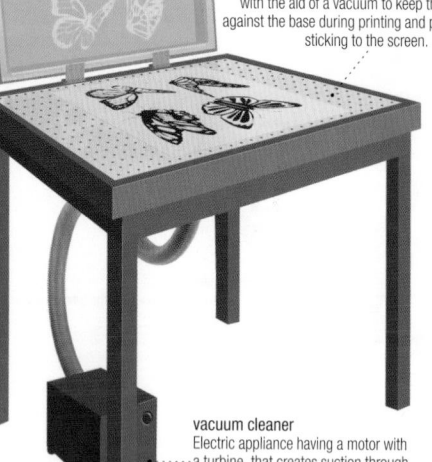

vacuum cleaner
Electric appliance having a motor with a turbine, that creates suction through each small hole of the table by means of an attached hose.

vacuum cleaner
Electric appliance having a motor with a turbine, that creates suction inside the lid by means of an attached hose.

fine bookbinding

Collective term for the manual operations required to bind the sheets of a book together and add an attractive solid cover.

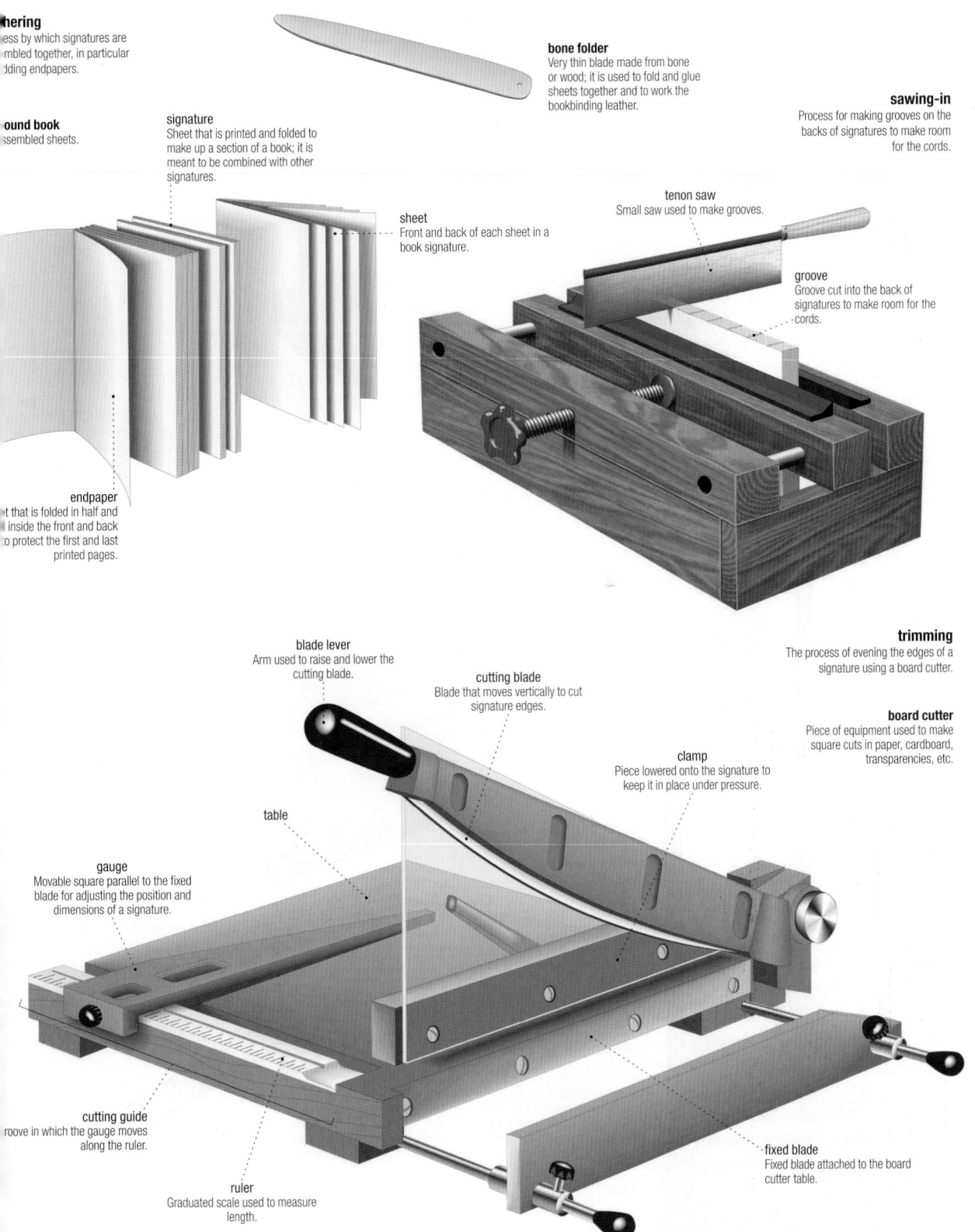

hering
ess by which signatures are
mbled together, in particular
dding endpapers.

bone folder
Very thin blade made from bone
or wood; it is used to fold and glue
sheets together and to work the
bookbinding leather.

sawing-in
Process for making grooves on the
backs of signatures to make room
for the cords.

ound book
ssembled sheets.

signature
Sheet that is printed and folded to
make up a section of a book; it is
meant to be combined with other
signatures.

sheet
Front and back of each sheet in a
book signature.

tenon saw
Small saw used to make grooves.

groove
Groove cut into the back of
signatures to make room for the
cords.

endpaper
t that is folded in half and
l inside the front and back
o protect the first and last
printed pages.

trimming
The process of evening the edges of a
signature using a board cutter.

board cutter
Piece of equipment used to make
square cuts in paper, cardboard,
transparencies, etc.

blade lever
Arm used to raise and lower the
cutting blade.

cutting blade
Blade that moves vertically to cut
signature edges.

clamp
Piece lowered onto the signature to
keep it in place under pressure.

table

gauge
Movable square parallel to the fixed
blade for adjusting the position and
dimensions of a signature.

cutting guide
roove in which the gauge moves
along the ruler.

ruler
Graduated scale used to measure
length.

fixed blade
Fixed blade attached to the board
cutter table.

fine bookbinding

sewing
Process for binding the signatures of a book together using cords.

sewing frame
Wooden frame used to sew together the signatures of a book.

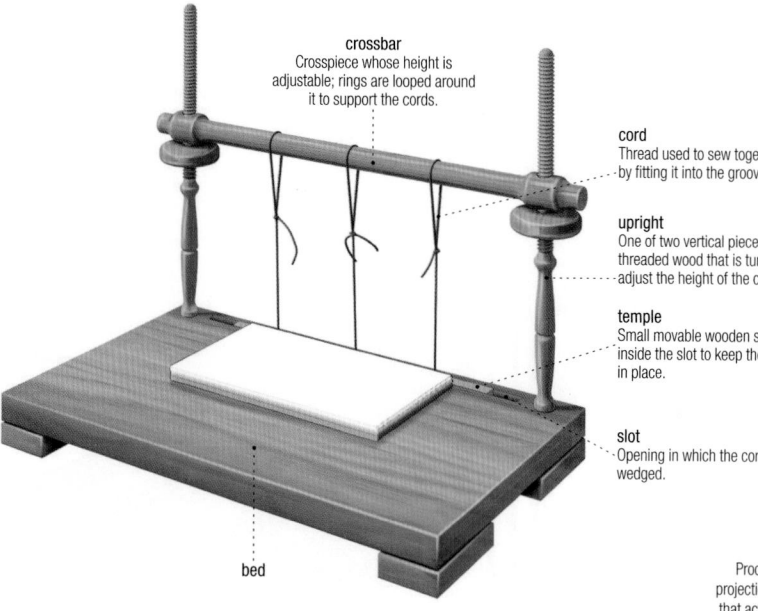

crossbar
Crosspiece whose height is adjustable; rings are looped around it to support the cords.

cord
Thread used to sew together signatures by fitting it into the grooves.

upright
One of two vertical pieces of threaded wood that is turned to adjust the height of the crossbar.

temple
Small movable wooden slat placed inside the slot to keep the cords in place.

slot
Opening in which the cords are wedged.

bed

pressing
Process for exerting pressure on a book being bound in order to flatten the signatures and make them more compact.

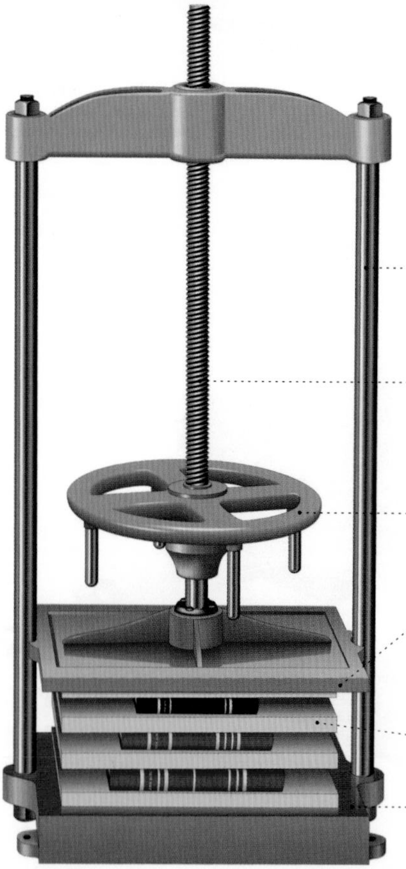

back◀
Process for creating joints, the pa...
projections running the length of the b...
that act as hinges between the spine...
the boa...

standing press
Hand-operated machine for pressing books during the binding process.

backing p▶
Press used to flatten a book so...
the joints can be m...

spine of the book
Part that makes up the back of a book's signatures.

backing board
Metal edge of the press; the back of the signature is placed along this edge and hammered to create joints.

upright
Cylindrical pillar used as a supportive structure.

central screw

handwheel
Wheel-shaped part that pivots around a central screw to move the platen.

platen
Heavy adjustable plate used to exert pressure on one or more books.

pressing board
Small board made of wood or stiff board and used to separate books, protect them and prevent warping.

base

backing hamr▶
Tool used to flatten the back of signatures to...
the spine a fan sha...

claw
The tapered end of the hammer, used to flatten the backs of signatures.

face
Slightly rounded surface used to strike the back of the signature and push it against the backing boards.

handle

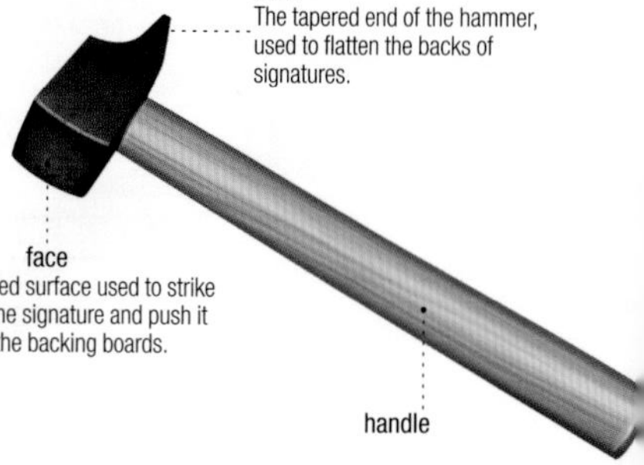

ARTS AND ARCHITECTURE

fine bookbinding

covering
Process of applying a covering material (skin, fabric, paper) to the boards and spine of a book.

bookbinding leather
Animal leather (e.g., goat or calf) used in bookbinding to cover a book.

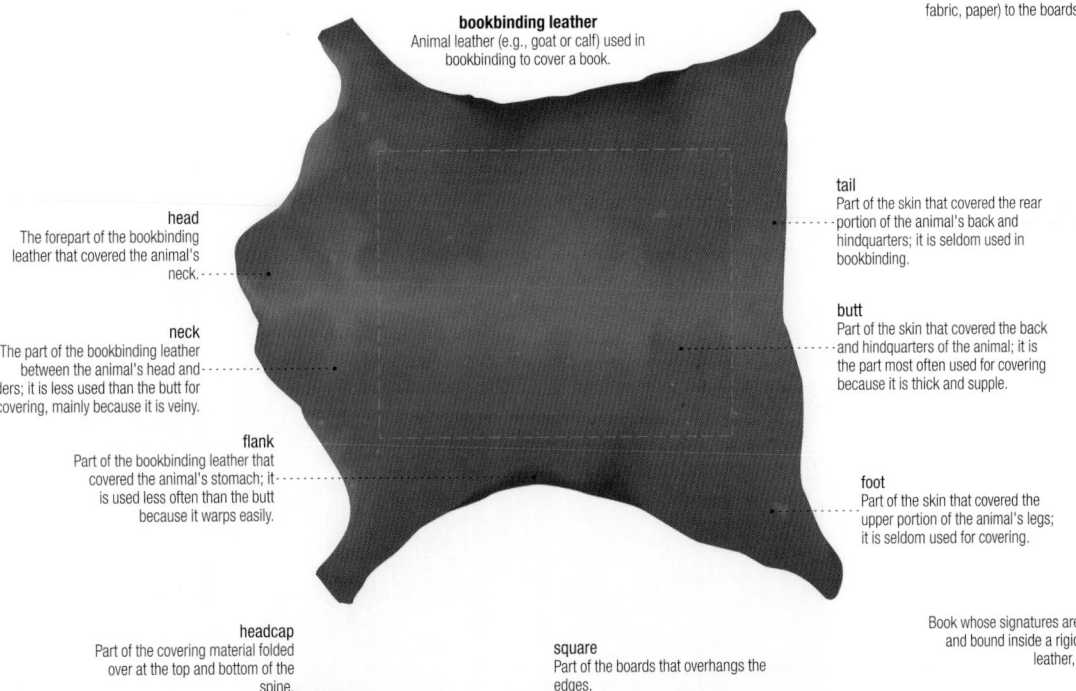

head
The forepart of the bookbinding leather that covered the animal's neck.

neck
The part of the bookbinding leather between the animal's head and shoulders; it is less used than the butt for covering, mainly because it is veiny.

flank
Part of the bookbinding leather that covered the animal's stomach; it is used less often than the butt because it warps easily.

tail
Part of the skin that covered the rear portion of the animal's back and hindquarters; it is seldom used in bookbinding.

butt
Part of the skin that covered the back and hindquarters of the animal; it is the part most often used for covering because it is thick and supple.

foot
Part of the skin that covered the upper portion of the animal's legs; it is seldom used for covering.

bound book
Book whose signatures are sewn together and bound inside a rigid cover made of leather, fabric or paper.

headcap
Part of the covering material folded over at the top and bottom of the spine.

headband
Decorative embroidery that reinforces the book at the top and bottom of the spine.

square
Part of the boards that overhangs the edges.

joint
The hinge of the cover between the spine and boards of a binding.

spine
Part of the binding that connects the boards and is opposite the fore edge.

raised band
Horizontal projection on the spine of the binding; it is molded to a strip of leather or board.

front board
Board that makes up the front of the cover.

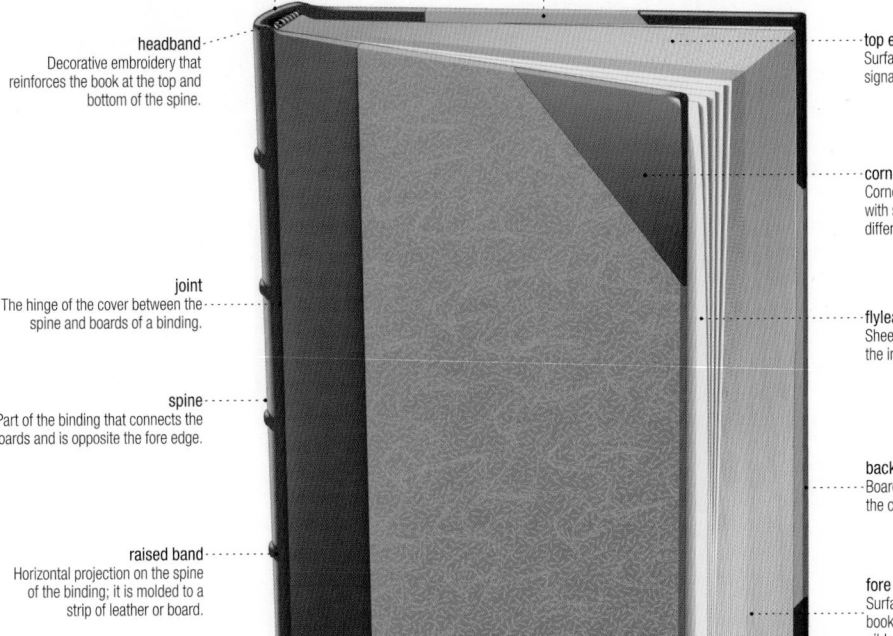

top edge
Surface forming the top side of a book's signatures; it is occasionally gilded.

corner
Corner angle of a board covered with skin or fabric whose color differs from that of the board.

flyleaf
Sheet of endpaper that is not glued to the inside of the board.

back board
Board constituting the rear face of the cover.

fore edge
Surface forming the open side of a book's signatures; it is occasionally gilded.

tail edge
Surface forming the bottom side of a book's signatures; it is occasionally gilded.

theater

Establishment built to present plays, shows, dance performances, concerts and so forth.

general view

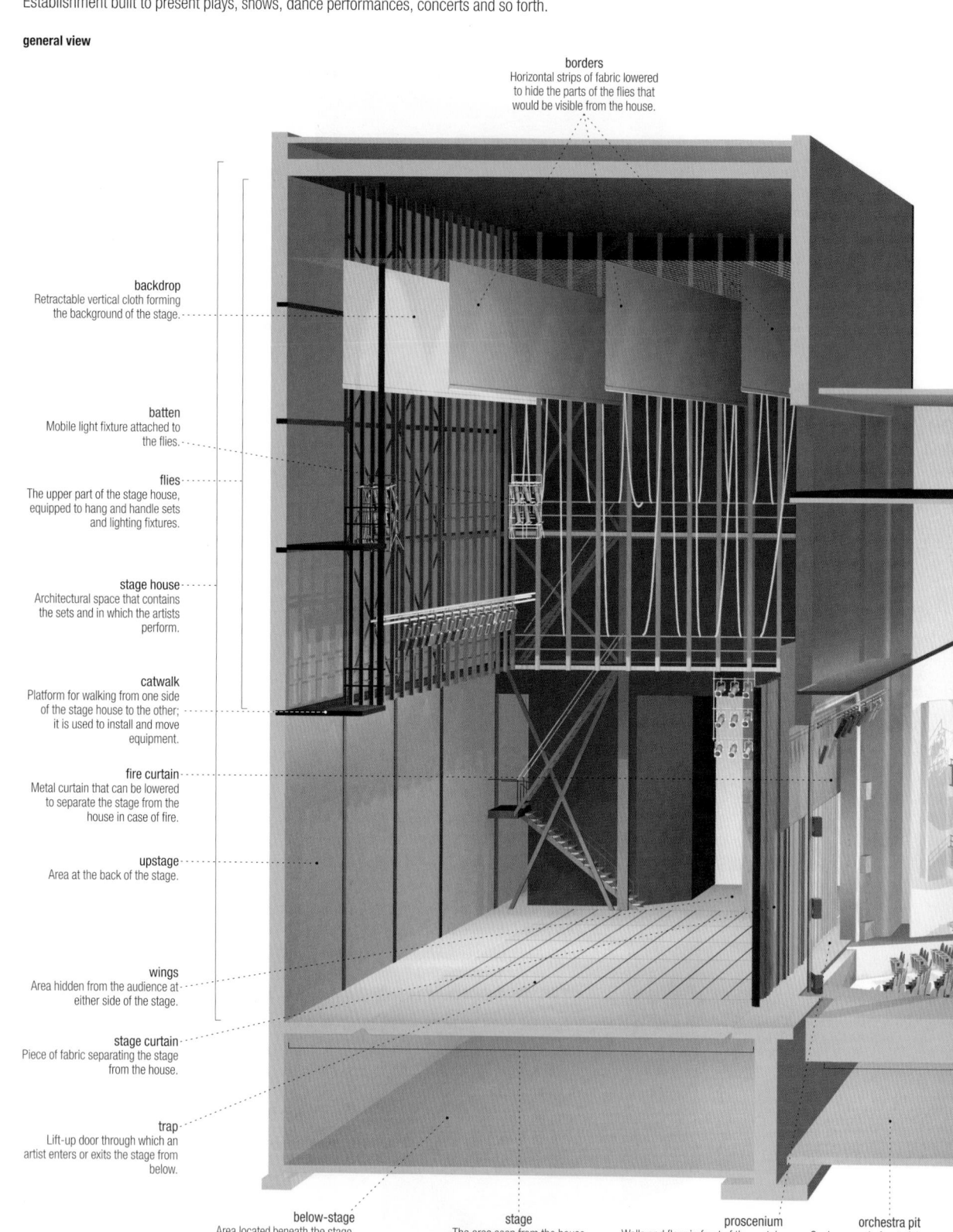

borders
Horizontal strips of fabric lowered to hide the parts of the flies that would be visible from the house.

backdrop
Retractable vertical cloth forming the background of the stage.

batten
Mobile light fixture attached to the flies.

flies
The upper part of the stage house, equipped to hang and handle sets and lighting fixtures.

stage house
Architectural space that contains the sets and in which the artists perform.

catwalk
Platform for walking from one side of the stage house to the other; it is used to install and move equipment.

fire curtain
Metal curtain that can be lowered to separate the stage from the house in case of fire.

upstage
Area at the back of the stage.

wings
Area hidden from the audience at either side of the stage.

stage curtain
Piece of fabric separating the stage from the house.

trap
Lift-up door through which an artist enters or exits the stage from below.

below-stage
Area located beneath the stage.

stage
The area seen from the house where the artists perform.

proscenium
Walls and floor in front of the curtain that frame the stage scene.

orchestra pit
Sunken area in front of the stage for an orchestra or band.

ARTS AND ARCHITECTURE

ARTS AND ARCHITECTURE

stage
The area seen from the house where the artists perform.

lights
Row of projectors set up above the proscenium.

spotlights
Lighting devices that project a concentrated beam of high-intensity light.

border
Horizontal strip of fabric used to hide the parts of the flies that would be visible from the house.

stage curtain
Piece of fabric separating the stage from the house.

acoustic ceiling
Ceiling made of materials that help to project the sound into the house.

upstage
Area at the back of the stage.

control room
Room equipped to control sound, lighting and projection.

prompt side
The left side of the stage as seen by the audience.

opposite prompt side
The right side of the stage as seen by the audience.

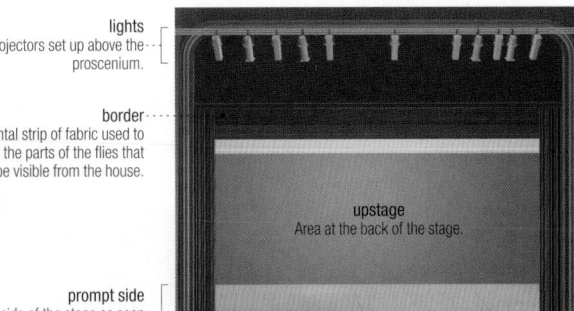

bar
Area where alcoholic drinks are sold.

orchestra
First level of the house

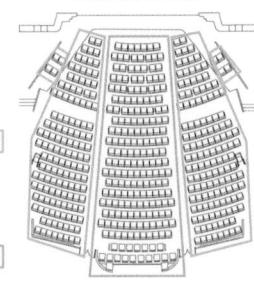

side

center

box
Small partitioned area that seats several people.

mezzanine
Level above the orchestra.

row
Series of seats the same distance from the stage.

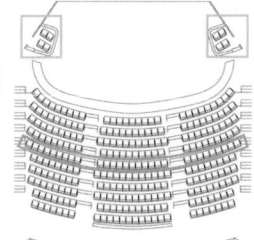

foyers
Anterooms where the audience mingles before the performance and at the intermission.

stairs
Series of steps for moving between floors or levels.

house
art of the theater where the audience sits.

balcony
Level above the mezzanine.

dressing room
Room that the artists use to change costumes, apply makeup and style their hair.

seat
Armchair used to watch a performance.

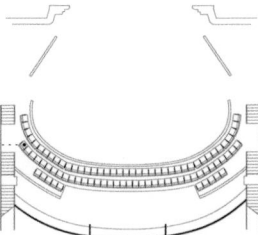

movie set

Sets, materials and personnel needed to shoot a movie or a television program.

general view

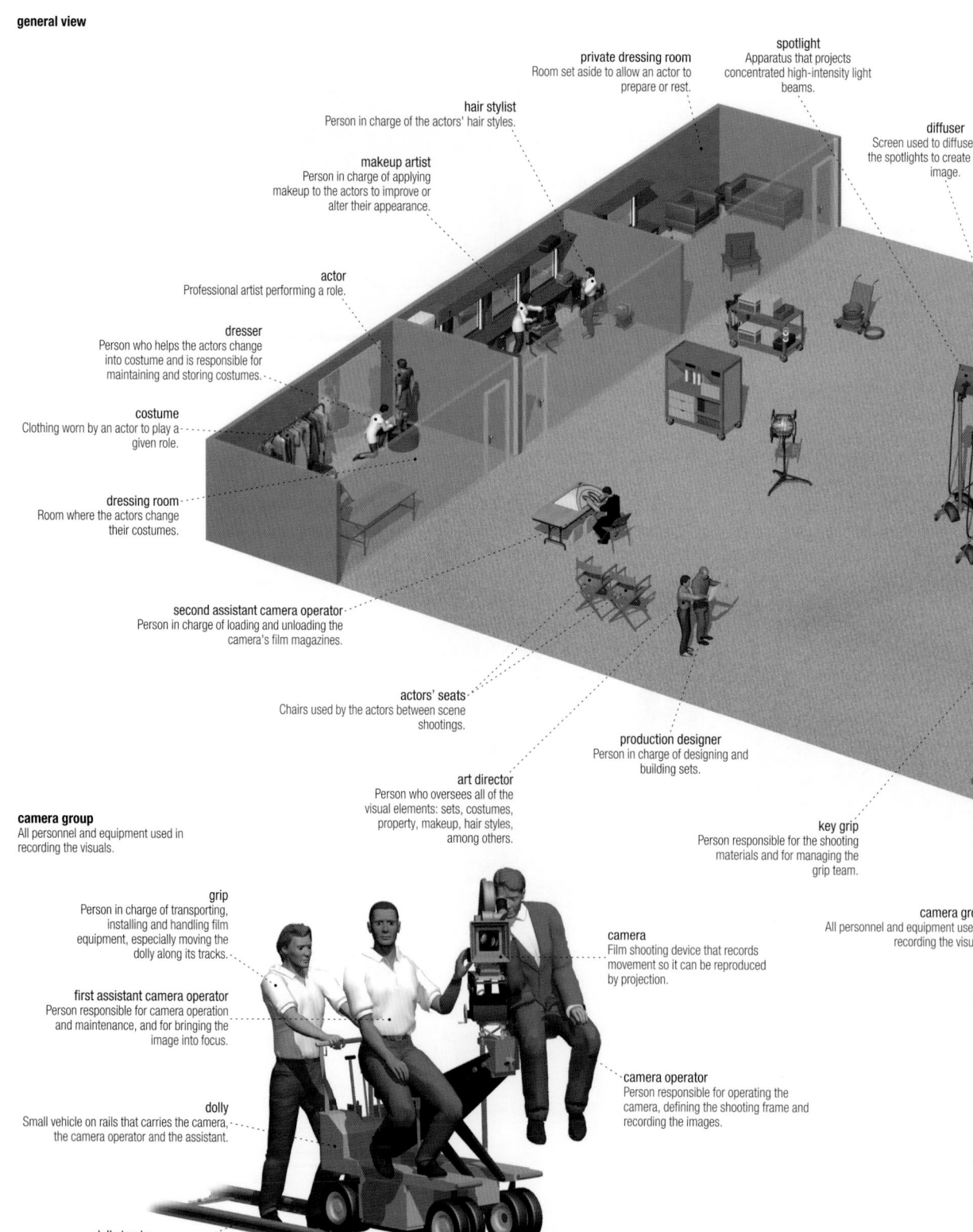

private dressing room
Room set aside to allow an actor to prepare or rest.

spotlight
Apparatus that projects concentrated high-intensity light beams.

hair stylist
Person in charge of the actors' hair styles.

diffuser
Screen used to diffuse l the spotlights to create th image.

makeup artist
Person in charge of applying makeup to the actors to improve or alter their appearance.

actor
Professional artist performing a role.

dresser
Person who helps the actors change into costume and is responsible for maintaining and storing costumes.

costume
Clothing worn by an actor to play a given role.

dressing room
Room where the actors change their costumes.

second assistant camera operator
Person in charge of loading and unloading the camera's film magazines.

actors' seats
Chairs used by the actors between scene shootings.

production designer
Person in charge of designing and building sets.

art director
Person who oversees all of the visual elements: sets, costumes, property, makeup, hair styles, among others.

key grip
Person responsible for the shooting materials and for managing the grip team.

camera group
All personnel and equipment used in recording the visuals.

camera grou
All personnel and equipment used recording the visua

grip
Person in charge of transporting, installing and handling film equipment, especially moving the dolly along its tracks.

camera
Film shooting device that records movement so it can be reproduced by projection.

first assistant camera operator
Person responsible for camera operation and maintenance, and for bringing the image into focus.

camera operator
Person responsible for operating the camera, defining the shooting frame and recording the images.

dolly
Small vehicle on rails that carries the camera, the camera operator and the assistant.

dolly tracks
Rails that guide the dolly when the camera is moving to follow the action.

movie set

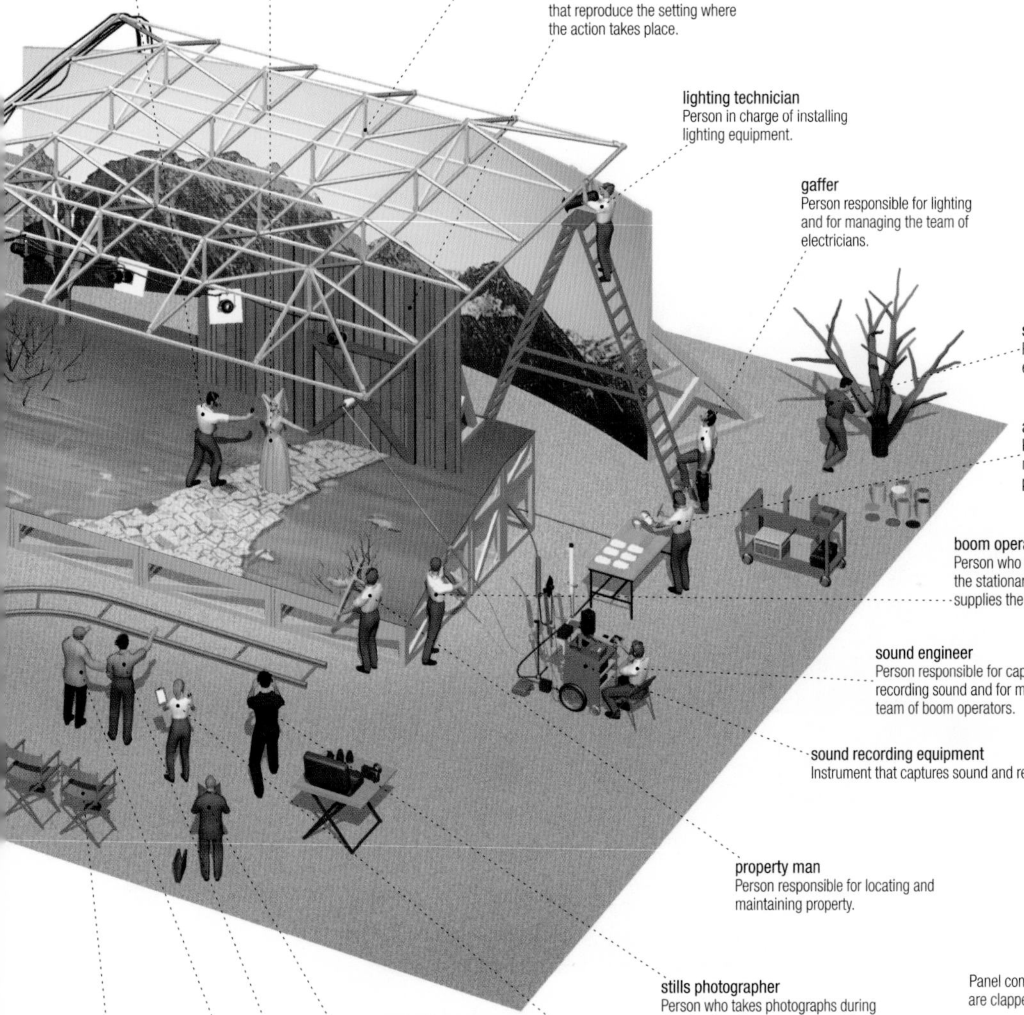

director of photography
Person responsible for the technical and artistic quality of the image.

lighting grid
Grid used to hold the spotlights.

actress
Female actor performing a role.

set
Collective term for the elements that reproduce the setting where the action takes place.

lighting technician
Person in charge of installing lighting equipment.

gaffer
Person responsible for lighting and for managing the team of electricians.

set dresser
Person in charge of arranging set elements.

assistant property man
Person who assists the property man to research and maintain property.

boom operator
Person who handles the boom, installs the stationary microphones and supplies the sound film.

sound engineer
Person responsible for capturing and recording sound and for managing the team of boom operators.

sound recording equipment
Instrument that captures sound and records it on film.

property man
Person responsible for locating and maintaining property.

stills photographer
Person who takes photographs during the shooting; these may be used for reference purposes from one shot to the next or as promotional material.

continuity person
Person who records all the technical and artistic details during shooting to ensure continuity.

producer
Person in charge of the financing and administration of a film or television program.

director's seat
Chair reserved for the director.

assistant director
Director's main assistant, in charge of preparing the shoot and ensuring that everything is done in accordance with the director's instructions.

director
Person in charge of the technical and artistic direction while a movie or a television program is being shot.

ctor's control monitors
lay screen for checking the quality of the frame.

clapper/slate
Panel consisting of two small boards that are clapped together to signal the start of shooting.

time code
Device that indicates the hour, minute, second and number of the frame; it is used to mark the sequence for editing purposes.

ARTS AND ARCHITECTURE

movie theater

Establishment with auditoriums used for projecting films.

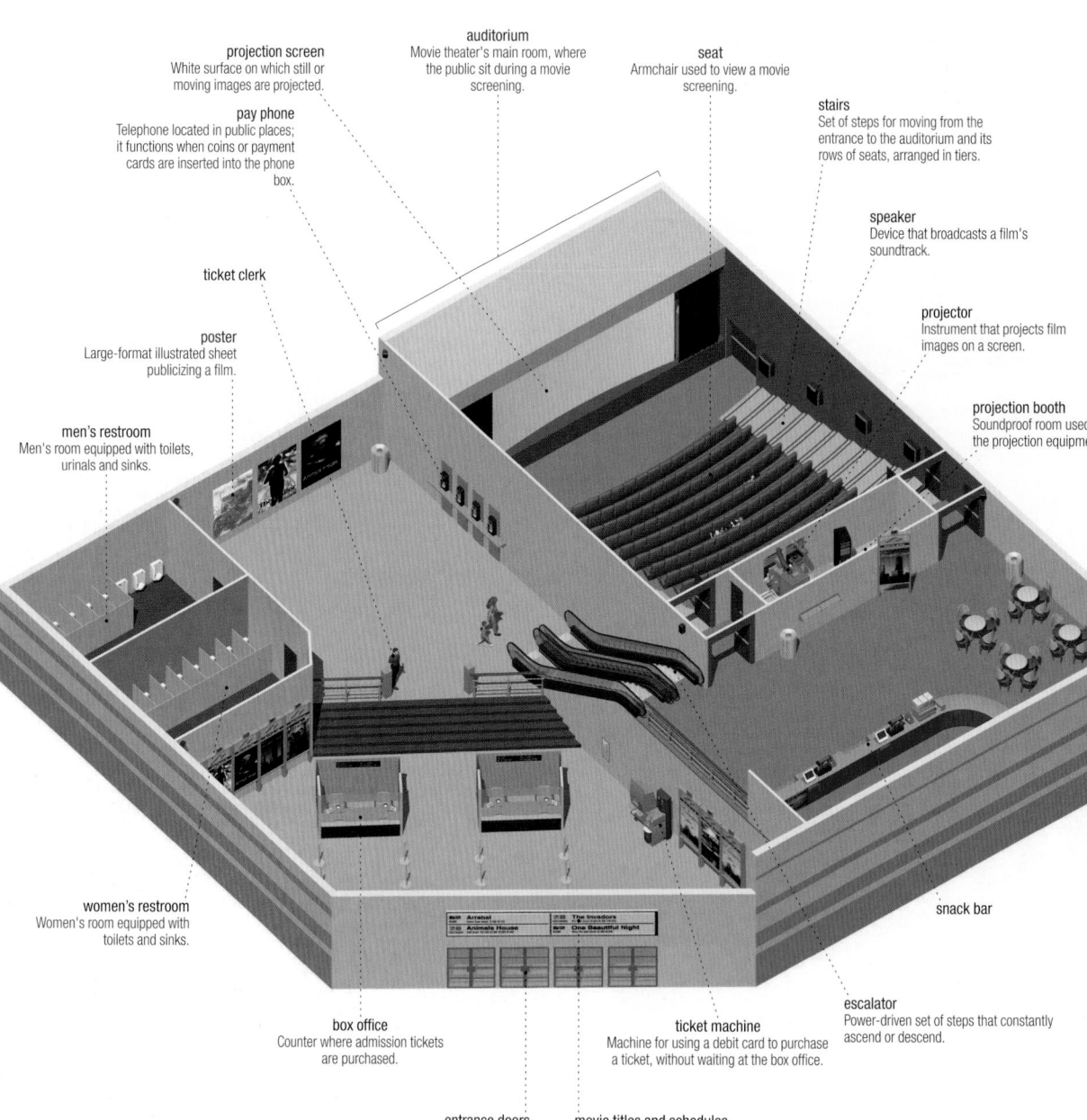

projection screen
White surface on which still or moving images are projected.

auditorium
Movie theater's main room, where the public sit during a movie screening.

seat
Armchair used to view a movie screening.

stairs
Set of steps for moving from the entrance to the auditorium and its rows of seats, arranged in tiers.

pay phone
Telephone located in public places; it functions when coins or payment cards are inserted into the phone box.

speaker
Device that broadcasts a film's soundtrack.

ticket clerk

projector
Instrument that projects film images on a screen.

poster
Large-format illustrated sheet publicizing a film.

projection booth
Soundproof room used to the projection equipment.

men's restroom
Men's room equipped with toilets, urinals and sinks.

women's restroom
Women's room equipped with toilets and sinks.

snack bar

escalator
Power-driven set of steps that constantly ascend or descend.

box office
Counter where admission tickets are purchased.

ticket machine
Machine for using a debit card to purchase a ticket, without waiting at the box office.

entrance doors

movie titles and schedules

symphony orchestra

Large orchestra of strings, woodwinds, brass and percussion led by a conductor.

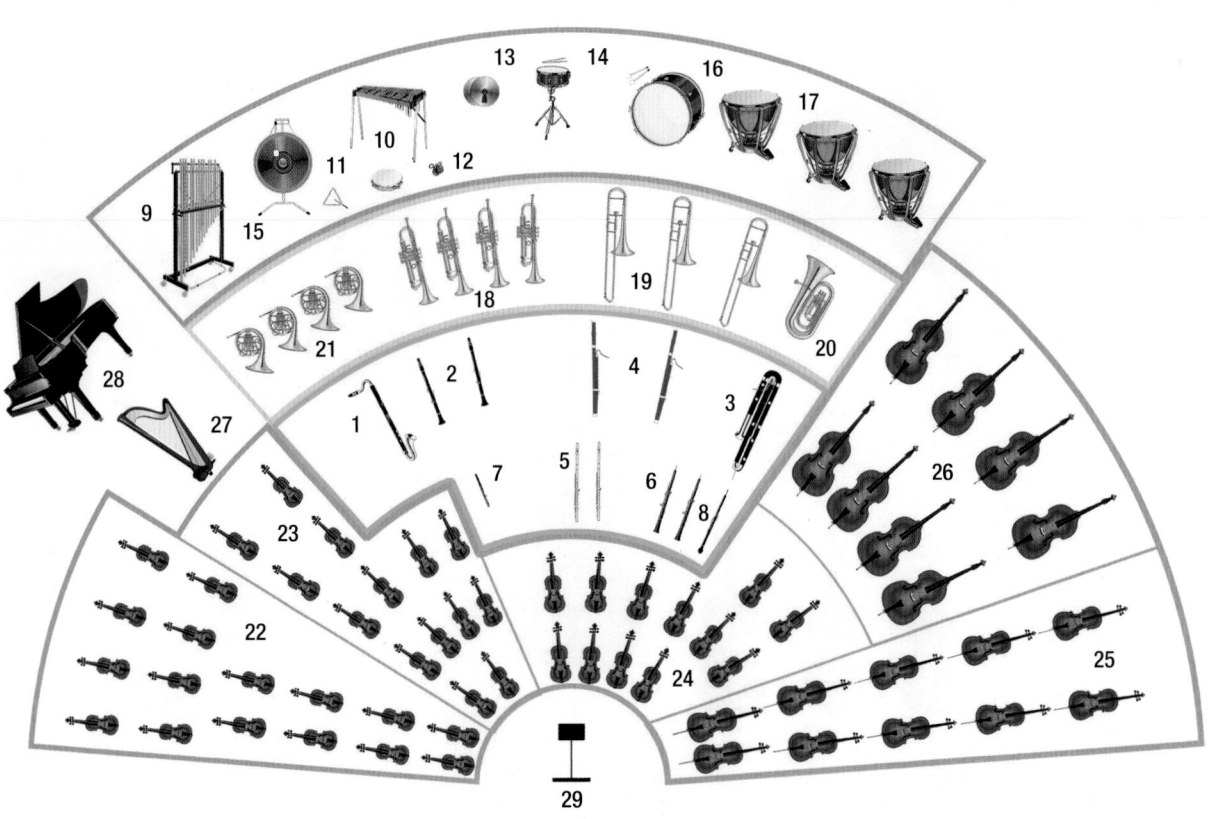

nd family
wind instruments originally
m wood.

clarinet
et with an upturned bell; its
is one octave lower than the
ry clarinet.

ets
-reed instruments whose
rical tube contains holes
closed by keys) and ends in
d bell.

abassoon
e-reed instrument with a very
ube that folds back on itself
and has a range an octave
the bassoon.

ons
e-reed instruments with
ed mouthpiece fitted to a
wooden tube that folds back
elf.

ments with a side mouthpiece
tube containing holes, some
ch are closed by keys.

s
e-reed instruments
sting of a conical tube with
(some closed by keys) and a
y flared bell.

piccolo
7 Small transverse flute whose range
is an octave higher than the regular
transverse flute.

English horn
8 Alto oboe with a pear-shaped bell.

percussion instruments
Group of instruments that are sounded
by striking, shaking or scraping.

tubular bells
9 Series of tuned metal tubes hung
vertically in order of size; small
hammers are used to strike the
tops of the tubes.

xylophone
10 Instrument consisting of tuned
wooden bars placed on top of
resonators arranged in chromatic
order in two rows; the bars are
struck with mallets.

triangle
11 Metal bar bent to form a triangle
open at one corner that is struck
with a metal rod.

castanets
12 Instrument composed of two shell-
shaped pieces of wood held in one
hand and struck together using
the fingers.

cymbals
13 Instrument consisting of two metal
disks that are struck together.

snare drum
14 Drum with snares stretched across
the lower head that produce a
rattling sound when the drum is
struck.

gong
15 Large metal disk with a raised
central portion that is struck using
a mallet.

bass drum
16 Large unpitched drum set on its
side on a frame.

timpani
17 Set of tuned single-headed drums
with bodies consisting of a large
copper bowl.

harp
27 Plucked stringed instrument
consisting of strings of various
lengths attached to a triangular
frame.

brass family
Group of metal wind instruments sounded
by the buzzing of the player's lips.

trumpets
18 Valved instruments consisting
of a coiled cylindrical tube and a
flared bell.

trombones
19 Instruments consisting of a mostly
cylindrical tube with two turns that
is usually played by sliding a length
of tubing to lengthen or shorten it.

tuba
20 Valved instrument whose tonal
range is the lowest in the brass
family; it consists of a coiled
conical tube and an upturned bell.

French horns
21 Valved instruments consisting of
a coiled conical tube and a flared
bell.

piano
28 Stringed instrument whose strings
are struck by hammers controlled
by the keys on a keyboard.

string family
Group of stringed instruments
played with a bow.

first violins
22 Group of violins that typically play
the more prominent parts.

second violins
23 Group of violins that typically play
the less prominent parts.

violas
24 Four-stringed instruments slightly
larger than the violin and tuned a
fifth lower.

cellos
25 Large four-stringed instruments
that are held between the legs
when played and have a range an
octave lower than the viola.

double basses
26 Very large four- or five-stringed
instruments that are played upright
and have a range an octave lower
than the cello.

conductor's podium
29 Small dais that the conductor
stands on to direct the musicians
as they play.

examples of instrumental groups

Groups of instruments and musicians smaller than an orchestra.

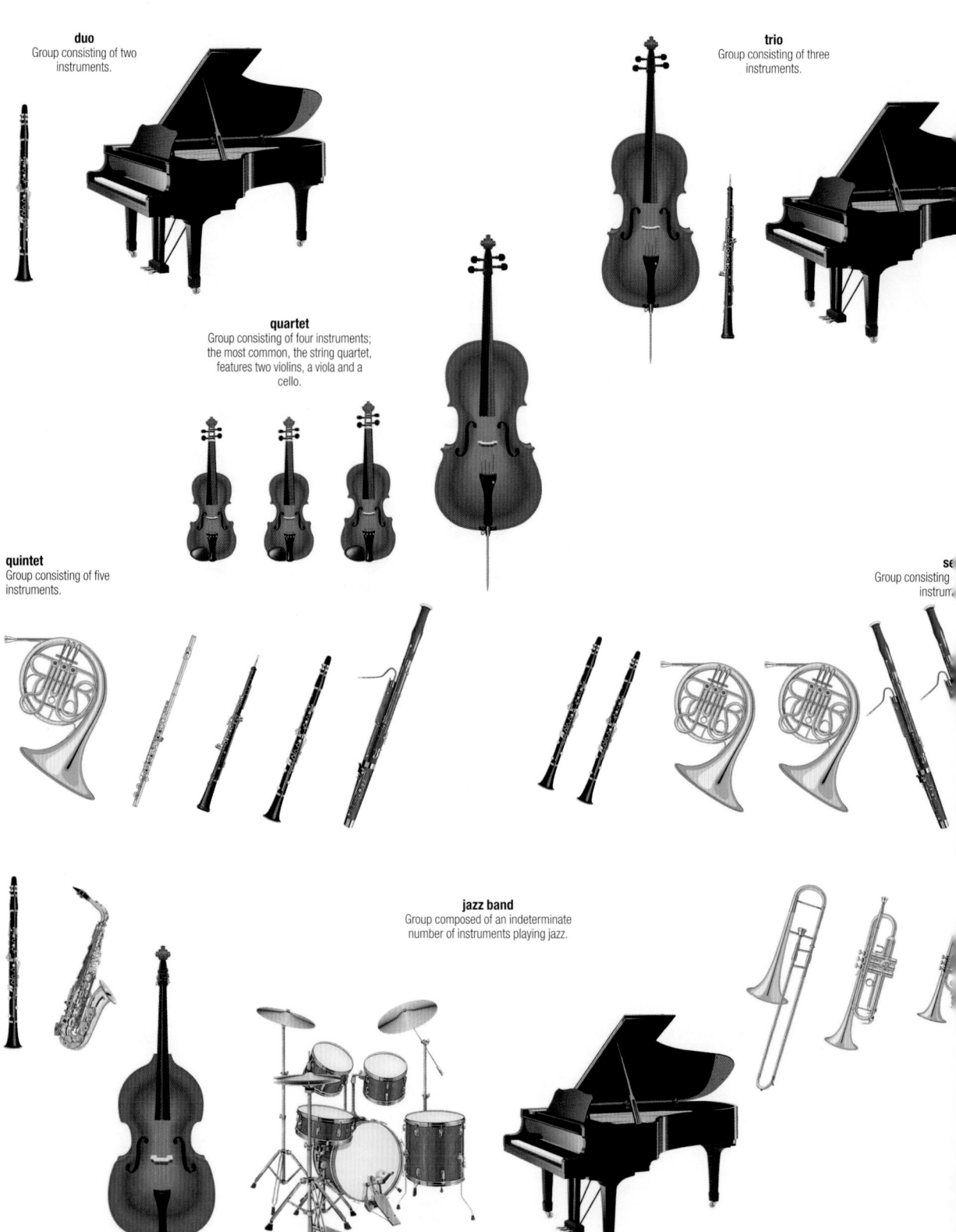

duo
Group consisting of two instruments.

trio
Group consisting of three instruments.

quartet
Group consisting of four instruments; the most common, the string quartet, features two violins, a viola and a cello.

quintet
Group consisting of five instruments.

se
Group consisting
instrum

jazz band
Group composed of an indeterminate number of instruments playing jazz.

stringed instruments

Instruments whose sound is produced by the vibration of plucked or bowed strings amplified by a sound box.

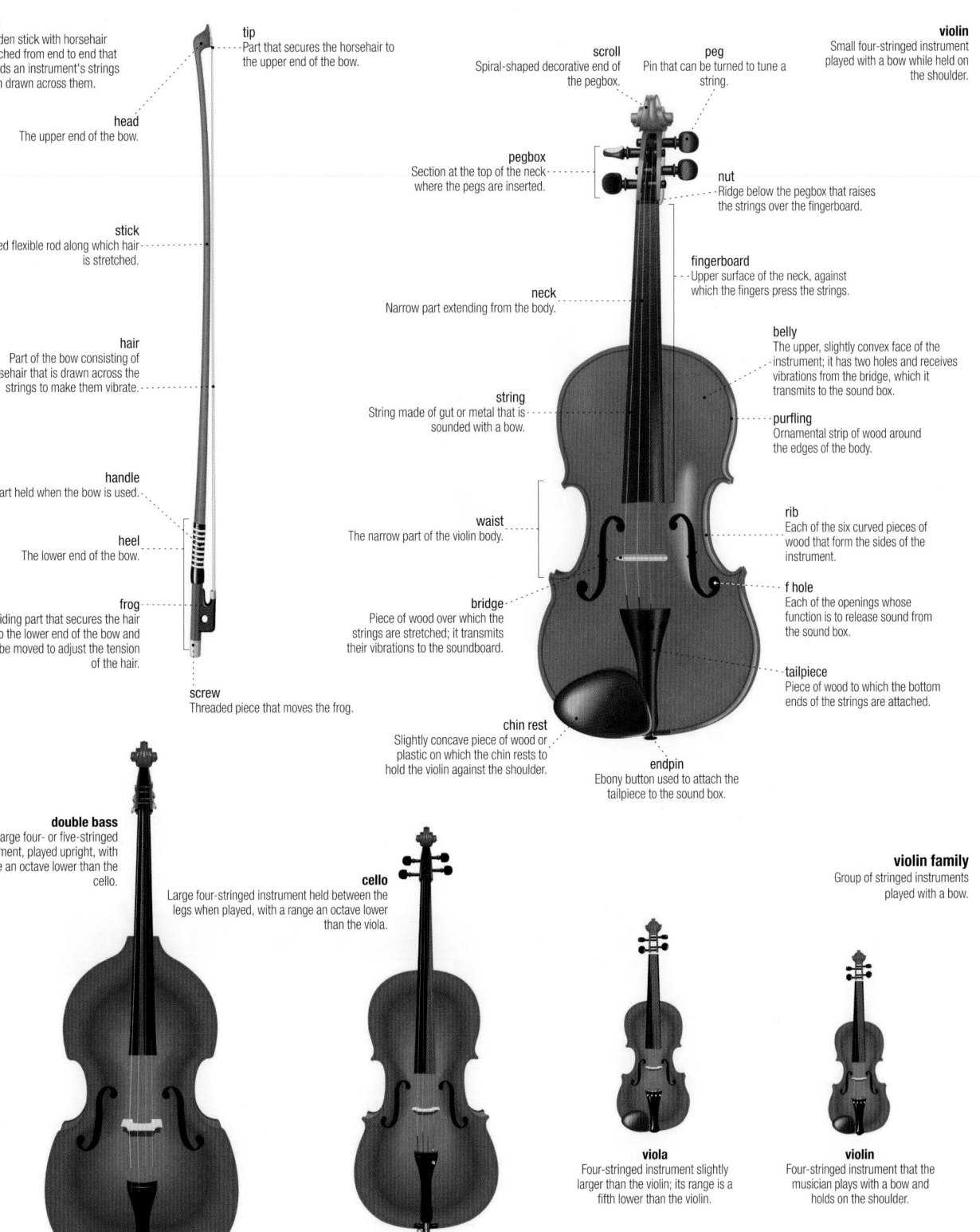

tip
Part that secures the horsehair to the upper end of the bow.

den stick with horsehair
ched from end to end that
ds an instrument's strings
drawn across them.

head
The upper end of the bow.

stick
ed flexible rod along which hair is stretched.

hair
Part of the bow consisting of sehair that is drawn across the strings to make them vibrate.

handle
art held when the bow is used.

heel
The lower end of the bow.

frog
ding part that secures the hair
the lower end of the bow and
be moved to adjust the tension of the hair.

screw
Threaded piece that moves the frog.

scroll
Spiral-shaped decorative end of the pegbox.

peg
Pin that can be turned to tune a string.

pegbox
Section at the top of the neck where the pegs are inserted.

nut
Ridge below the pegbox that raises the strings over the fingerboard.

neck
Narrow part extending from the body.

fingerboard
Upper surface of the neck, against which the fingers press the strings.

string
String made of gut or metal that is sounded with a bow.

belly
The upper, slightly convex face of the instrument; it has two holes and receives vibrations from the bridge, which it transmits to the sound box.

purfling
Ornamental strip of wood around the edges of the body.

waist
The narrow part of the violin body.

rib
Each of the six curved pieces of wood that form the sides of the instrument.

bridge
Piece of wood over which the strings are stretched; it transmits their vibrations to the soundboard.

f hole
Each of the openings whose function is to release sound from the sound box.

tailpiece
Piece of wood to which the bottom ends of the strings are attached.

chin rest
Slightly concave piece of wood or plastic on which the chin rests to hold the violin against the shoulder.

endpin
Ebony button used to attach the tailpiece to the sound box.

violin
Small four-stringed instrument played with a bow while held on the shoulder.

double bass
arge four- or five-stringed
ment, played upright, with
e an octave lower than the cello.

cello
Large four-stringed instrument held between the legs when played, with a range an octave lower than the viola.

viola
Four-stringed instrument slightly larger than the violin; its range is a fifth lower than the violin.

violin
Four-stringed instrument that the musician plays with a bow and holds on the shoulder.

violin family
Group of stringed instruments played with a bow.

ARTS AND ARCHITECTURE

stringed instruments

harp
Plucked stringed instrument consisting of strings of various lengths attached to a triangular frame.

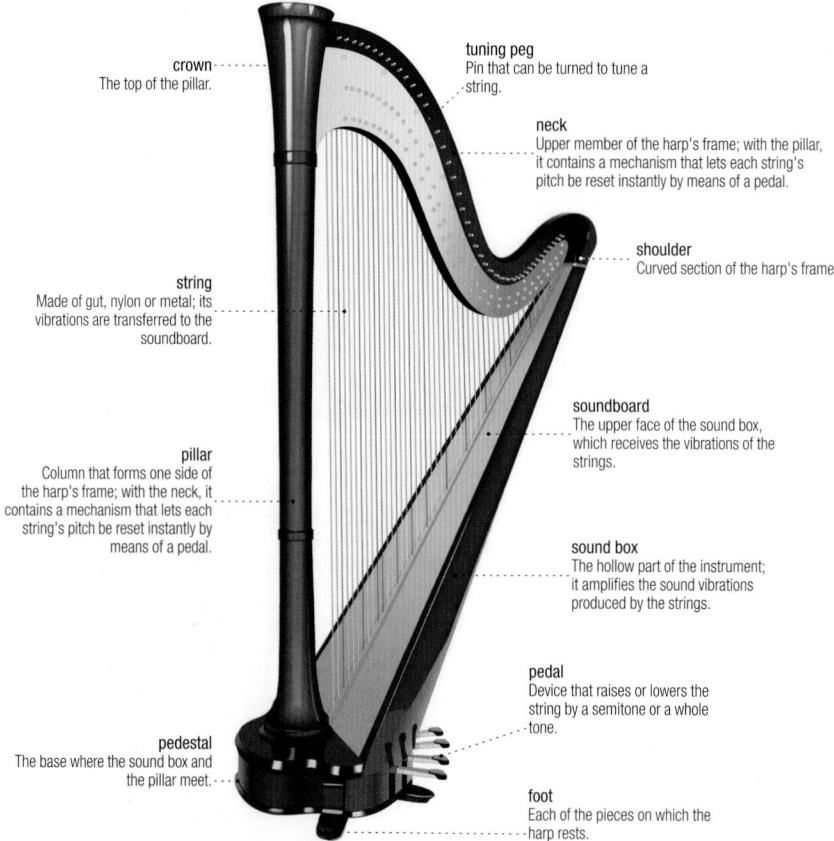

crown
The top of the pillar.

tuning peg
Pin that can be turned to tune a string.

neck
Upper member of the harp's frame; with the pillar, it contains a mechanism that lets each string's pitch be reset instantly by means of a pedal.

shoulder
Curved section of the harp's frame.

string
Made of gut, nylon or metal; its vibrations are transferred to the soundboard.

soundboard
The upper face of the sound box, which receives the vibrations of the strings.

pillar
Column that forms one side of the harp's frame; with the neck, it contains a mechanism that lets each string's pitch be reset instantly by means of a pedal.

sound box
The hollow part of the instrument; it amplifies the sound vibrations produced by the strings.

pedal
Device that raises or lowers the string by a semitone or a whole tone.

pedestal
The base where the sound box and the pillar meet.

foot
Each of the pieces on which the harp rests.

acoustic guitar
Plucked stringed instrument with a flat body and a long fretted neck.

soundboard
The upper face of the instrument; it receives the vibrations from the bridge and transmits them to the sound box.

body
The hollow part of the instrument; it amplifies the sound vibrations produced by the strings.

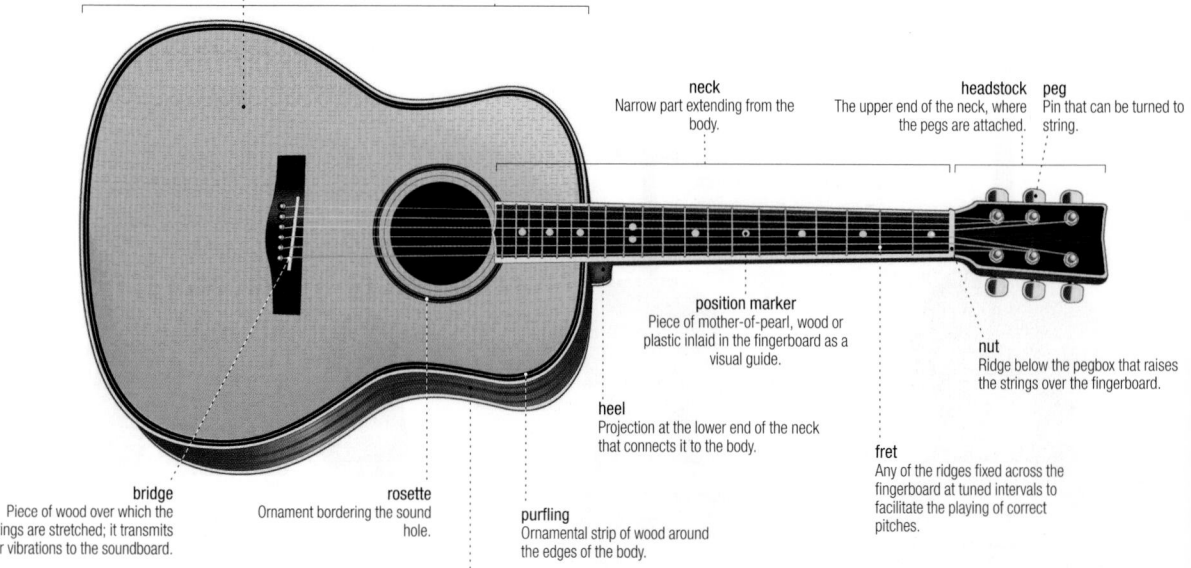

neck
Narrow part extending from the body.

headstock
The upper end of the neck, where the pegs are attached.

peg
Pin that can be turned to string.

position marker
Piece of mother-of-pearl, wood or plastic inlaid in the fingerboard as a visual guide.

nut
Ridge below the pegbox that raises the strings over the fingerboard.

heel
Projection at the lower end of the neck that connects it to the body.

fret
Any of the ridges fixed across the fingerboard at tuned intervals to facilitate the playing of correct pitches.

bridge
Piece of wood over which the strings are stretched; it transmits their vibrations to the soundboard.

rosette
Ornament bordering the sound hole.

purfling
Ornamental strip of wood around the edges of the body.

rib
Each of the thin pieces of wood that form the sides of the instrument.

stringed instruments

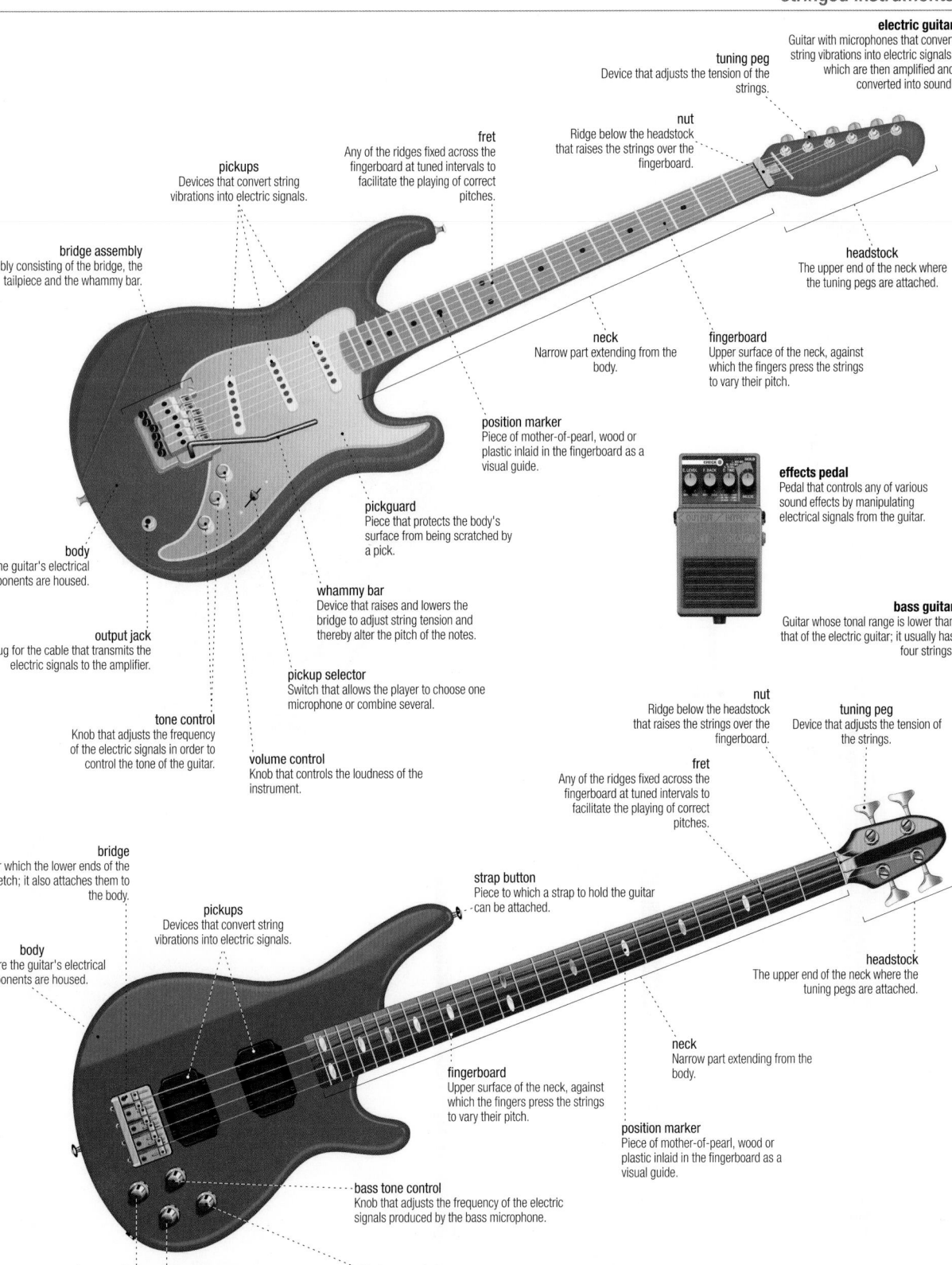

electric guitar
Guitar with microphones that convert string vibrations into electric signals, which are then amplified and converted into sound.

tuning peg
Device that adjusts the tension of the strings.

nut
Ridge below the headstock that raises the strings over the fingerboard.

fret
Any of the ridges fixed across the fingerboard at tuned intervals to facilitate the playing of correct pitches.

pickups
Devices that convert string vibrations into electric signals.

headstock
The upper end of the neck where the tuning pegs are attached.

bridge assembly
embly consisting of the bridge, the tailpiece and the whammy bar.

neck
Narrow part extending from the body.

fingerboard
Upper surface of the neck, against which the fingers press the strings to vary their pitch.

position marker
Piece of mother-of-pearl, wood or plastic inlaid in the fingerboard as a visual guide.

effects pedal
Pedal that controls any of various sound effects by manipulating electrical signals from the guitar.

pickguard
Piece that protects the body's surface from being scratched by a pick.

body
e the guitar's electrical mponents are housed.

output jack
Plug for the cable that transmits the electric signals to the amplifier.

whammy bar
Device that raises and lowers the bridge to adjust string tension and thereby alter the pitch of the notes.

bass guitar
Guitar whose tonal range is lower than that of the electric guitar; it usually has four strings.

pickup selector
Switch that allows the player to choose one microphone or combine several.

tone control
Knob that adjusts the frequency of the electric signals in order to control the tone of the guitar.

volume control
Knob that controls the loudness of the instrument.

nut
Ridge below the headstock that raises the strings over the fingerboard.

tuning peg
Device that adjusts the tension of the strings.

fret
Any of the ridges fixed across the fingerboard at tuned intervals to facilitate the playing of correct pitches.

bridge
ver which the lower ends of the stretch; it also attaches them to the body.

strap button
Piece to which a strap to hold the guitar can be attached.

pickups
Devices that convert string vibrations into electric signals.

headstock
The upper end of the neck where the tuning pegs are attached.

body
here the guitar's electrical mponents are housed.

neck
Narrow part extending from the body.

fingerboard
Upper surface of the neck, against which the fingers press the strings to vary their pitch.

position marker
Piece of mother-of-pearl, wood or plastic inlaid in the fingerboard as a visual guide.

bass tone control
Knob that adjusts the frequency of the electric signals produced by the bass microphone.

volume control
o that controls the loudness of the instrument.

balancer
Knob for adjusting the balance of the two pickups.

treble tone control
Knob that adjusts the frequency of the electric signals produced by the treble microphone.

wind instruments

Collective term for instruments that produce sound by blowing, which causes the air column inside the tube to vibrate; a reed or the lips are used to play them.

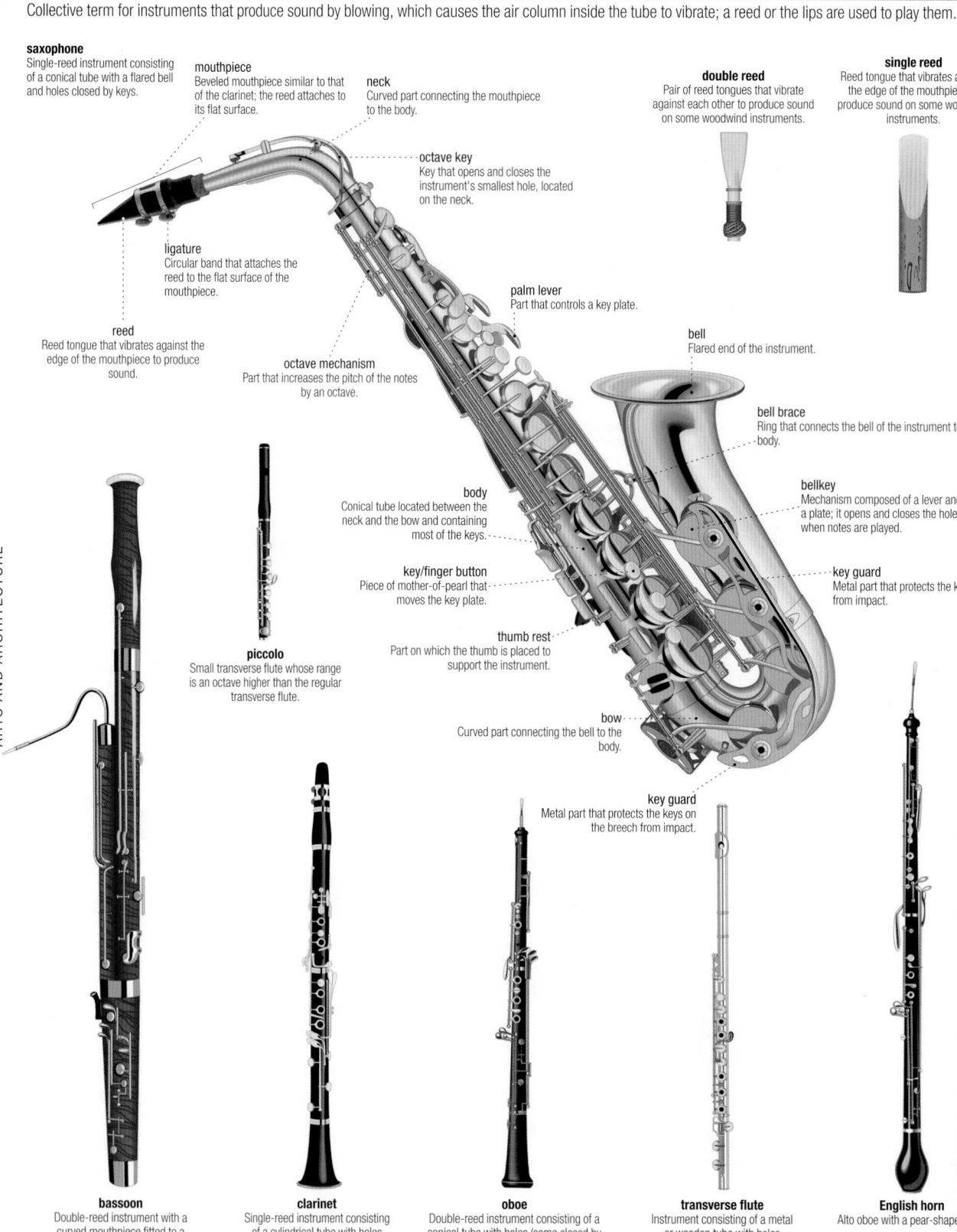

saxophone
Single-reed instrument consisting of a conical tube with a flared bell and holes closed by keys.

mouthpiece
Beveled mouthpiece similar to that of the clarinet; the reed attaches to its flat surface.

neck
Curved part connecting the mouthpiece to the body.

octave key
Key that opens and closes the instrument's smallest hole, located on the neck.

ligature
Circular band that attaches the reed to the flat surface of the mouthpiece.

palm lever
Part that controls a key plate.

reed
Reed tongue that vibrates against the edge of the mouthpiece to produce sound.

octave mechanism
Part that increases the pitch of the notes by an octave.

double reed
Pair of reed tongues that vibrate against each other to produce sound on some woodwind instruments.

single reed
Reed tongue that vibrates a the edge of the mouthpie produce sound on some wo instruments.

bell
Flared end of the instrument.

bell brace
Ring that connects the bell of the instrument t body.

bellkey
Mechanism composed of a lever an a plate; it opens and closes the hole when notes are played.

body
Conical tube located between the neck and the bow and containing most of the keys.

key guard
Metal part that protects the k from impact.

piccolo
Small transverse flute whose range is an octave higher than the regular transverse flute.

key/finger button
Piece of mother-of-pearl that moves the key plate.

thumb rest
Part on which the thumb is placed to support the instrument.

bow
Curved part connecting the bell to the body.

key guard
Metal part that protects the keys on the breech from impact.

bassoon
Double-reed instrument with a curved mouthpiece fitted to a long wooden tube that folds back on itself.

clarinet
Single-reed instrument consisting of a cylindrical tube with holes (some closed by keys) and a flared bell.

oboe
Double-reed instrument consisting of a conical tube with holes (some closed by keys) and a slightly flared bell.

transverse flute
Instrument consisting of a metal or wooden tube with holes (some closed by keys) and a side mouthpiece; it is held horizontally.

English horn
Alto oboe with a pear-shape

wind instruments

finger button
Part that is pressed to control the valves; it is often inlaid with mother-of-pearl.

little finger hook
Part used to support the little finger of the right hand.

bell
Flared end of the instrument.

trumpet
Valved instrument consisting of a coiled cylindrical tube and a flared bell.

mouthpiece receiver
ne end of the tube into which the mouthpiece is inserted.

leadpipe
Part of the tube between the mouthpiece receiver and the tuning slide.

ring
Part that lengthens the third valve slide to tune certain notes while playing.

mouthpiece
shaped part where the aced to blow into the and modulate its sound.

first valve slide
Curved tube that, when the first valve is pressed down, lowers the note by one tone.

tuning slide
Adjustable part that tunes the instrument.

third valve slide
Curved tube that, when the third valve is pressed, lowers notes by three semitones.

water key
Key that drains the moisture that builds up inside the instrument.

thumb hook
Part in which the thumb is inserted to lengthen the first valve slide and tune certain notes while playing.

valve
Device that produces different notes by lengthening the air column inside the tube and releasing the slides.

mute
Device that is inserted into the bell to muffle the sound.

valve casing
Cylindrical tube holding a valve.

second valve slide
Curved tube that, when the second valve is pressed down, lowers the note by a semitone.

French horn
Valved instrument consisting of a coiled conical tube and a flared bell.

cornet
Valved instrument consisting of a coiled, partly conical tube somewhat shorter than a trumpet's.

bugle
Instrument with a conical tube and no valves or keys; it is used mainly for military calls.

tuba
Valved instrument whose tonal range is the lowest in the brass family; it consists of a coiled conical tube and an upturned bell.

euphonium
Valved instrument with a coiled conical tube and a large bell whose range is an octave lower than the trumpet.

trombone
Instrument with a mostly cylindrical tube with two turns; its register is lower than that of the trumpet.

keyboard instruments

Instruments with a series of keys that are pressed to strike or pluck strings and thereby produce sound.

upright piano
A stringed instrument whose strings are struck by hammers controlled by the keys on a keyboard; its soundboard and strings are arranged vertically.

muffler felt
Strip of felt that comes between the strings and the hammer heads when the muffler pedal is pressed; it lowers the volume of sound.

pressure bar
Metal bar under which the strings pass, marking the top of the section of vibrating strings.

pin block
Part in which the tuning pins are anchored.

hammer rail
Felt-covered piece where the hammer shank rests when it falls back.

hammer
Piece of wood with a felt-covered end (head) that strikes one or more strings causing them to vibrate.

tuning pin
Piece of wood or metal where the end of the string is attached; it adjusts string tension to obtain the exact tone.

key
White or black lever pressed by the fingers to trigger a mechanism that causes the hammer to strike one or several strings.

cabinet
Wooden box that encloses the inner workings of the piano and protects them.

keybed
Part of the piano projecting from the case; it supports the keyboard.

fire curtain
Piece of wood over which the strings in the treble range are stretched; it transmits their vibrations to the soundboard.

pedal rod
Piece of wood that connects the pedal to the mechanism.

strings
Metal wires stretched between two fixed points; the hammers strike them, causing them to vibrate and produce sound.

keyboard
Series of piano keys (52 white and 36 black).

soundboard
Flat surface that amplifies the string vibrations transmitted by the bridges.

soft pedal
In the upright piano, it brings the hammers closer to the strings to reduce their impact; in a grand piano, it reduces the number of strings struck for each note.

metal frame
Metal body that supports the tension of the strings.

muffler pedal
In an upright piano, it lowers the muffler felt; in a grand piano, it prolongs the notes (sostenuto pedal).

bass bridge
Piece of wood over which the bass strings are stretched; it transmits their vibrations to the soundboard.

damper pedal
Pedal that raises the dampers to prolong any notes struck after the pedal is pressed.

hitch pin
Piece attached to the metal frame; the lower end of the string attaches to it.

keyboard instruments

string
The strings are: single and made of copper for the bass, double and made of steel for the mid-range, and triple and made of finer steel for the treble range.

damper
Piece of felt-covered wood that rests on the string or strings to stop them from vibrating after the key is released.

damper spring rail
Felt-covered piece where the damper stem rests after leaving the string, allowing the string to vibrate.

hammer butt
Piece that is pushed by the jack, directing the hammer toward the string or strings.

damper lever
Stem with a spring that brings the damper back against the string when a key is released.

jack
able stem that transmits the movement of the action lever to the hammer butt and allows the mer to fall back as soon as it strikes the string or strings.

regulating button
Part that pulls the jack back before the hammer strikes the string or strings.

jack spring
Spring that allows the jack to return to its position under the hammer butt once the key is released.

hammer felt
Felt-covered hammer head that strikes the string or strings and causes them to vibrate.

hammer
Piece of wood with a felt-covered end (head) that strikes one or more strings causing them to vibrate.

hammer rail
Felt-covered piece where the hammer shank rests when it falls back.

hammer shank
Stem to which the hammer is attached.

back check
Metal stem whose felt-covered wooden head cushions the return of the catcher and prevents the hammer from bouncing back.

catcher
Piece that holds the hammer halfway back so that a more rapid succession of notes can be played.

bridle tape
Piece of leather that connects the catcher to a metal stem attached to the action lever; it pulls the hammer back when the key is released.

upright piano action
Mechanism that enables a piano's keys to produce sound from its strings.

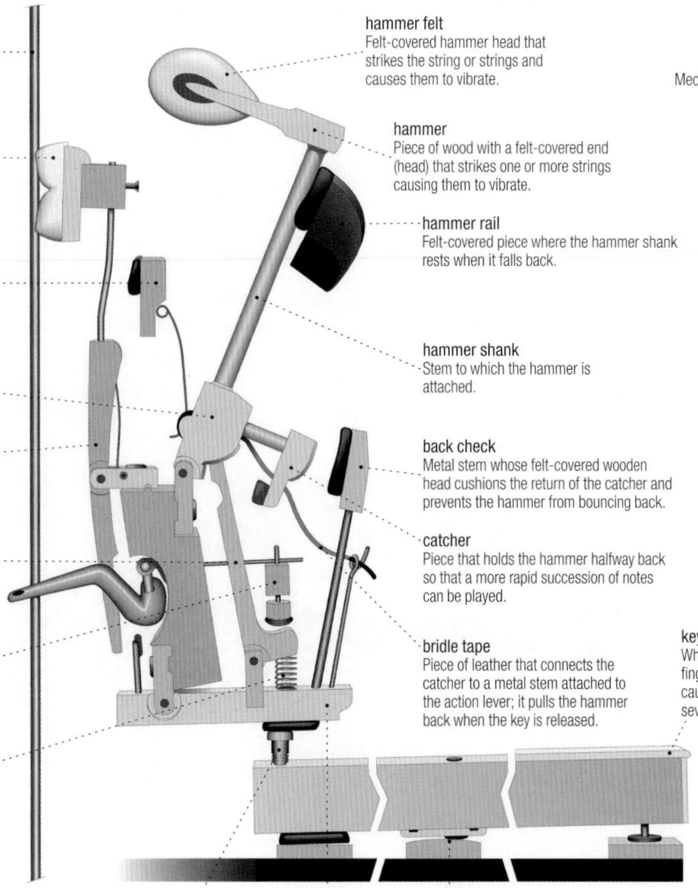

key
White or black lever pressed by the fingers to trigger a mechanism that causes the hammer to strike one or several strings.

capstan screw
Screw that controls and transmits the key movement to the action lever.

wippen
Movable piece that transmits movement to the jack.

balance rail
Piece on which the key balances.

ARTS AND ARCHITECTURE

examples of keyboard instruments

baby grand
Grand piano measuring around 5.5 ft.

cert grand
whose mechanism is horizontal, allowing ianist to better control the sound; it varies in rom 8 to 9 ft.

parlor grand
Grand piano measuring from 6 to 7 ft.

harpsichord
Plucked string instrument with one or two keyboards.

keyboard instruments

organ console
Upright case housing the organ's manuals, pedalboard and controlling mechanisms.

music stand
Inclined board where the organist places music.

draw stop
Knob that can be pulled to activate a row of pipes.

swell organ manual
Keyboard that controls a series of pi enclosed in a wooden box (swell box louvers can be opened by a swell pe increase the volume.

coupler-tilt tablet
Plate that controls the mechanism joining two or more manuals.

great organ manual
Keyboard that controls a series of the brightest and loudest pipes.

manuals
Keyboards, each of which controls a unique set of pipes.

choir organ manual
Keyboard intended principally for accompanying the choir.

thumb piston
Button that activates a combination of stops set in advance.

crescendo pedal
Pedal that can be gradually pressed sound an increasing number of stop

toe piston
Large button controlled by the feet that usually activates a combination of stops set in advance.

pedal key
Lever that is pressed by the foot to sound a bass note.

swell pedals
Pedals that open and close the louvers of the swell box to control the volume of sound from the pipes housed there.

pedalboard
Series of keys that the organist operates by foot.

reed pipe
Pipe in which sound is produced by the vibration of a tongue on the open face of a pipe.

flue
Pipe that sounds when pressu air strikes the edge of a na horizontal opening in its

tuning wire
Metal stem that adjusts the length of the shallot's vibrating part to tune the pipe.

body
Upper part of the pipe; it controls the volume of vibrating air and acts as a resonator.

resonator
Resonant vessel that amplifies the vibrations of the shallot.

block
Movable part inserted into the foot of the pipe; its lower end holds the shallot.

wedge
Piece of wood that attaches the tongue to the upper end of the pipe.

mouth
Horizontal aperture whose edge the air strikes to produce sound.

upper lip
Flat part of the pipe that brea the air exiting the flue, causi column in the body to vibrate

tongue
Small sheet of flexible metal that vibrates on the open face of the shallot; the amplitude of the vibrations determines the pitch of the note.

flue
Narrow slit through which air from the foot passes after hitting the languid.

languid
Metal plate that channels the the flue and mouth.

shallot
Hollow pipe with one open face, on which the tongue vibrates.

lower lip
Flat portion of the foot; it forces air onto the languid.

boot
Lower part of the pipe.

boot
Lower part of the pipe.

foot hole
Opening through which air from the blower enters the pipe.

foot hole
Opening through which air from the blower enters the pipe.

keyboard instruments

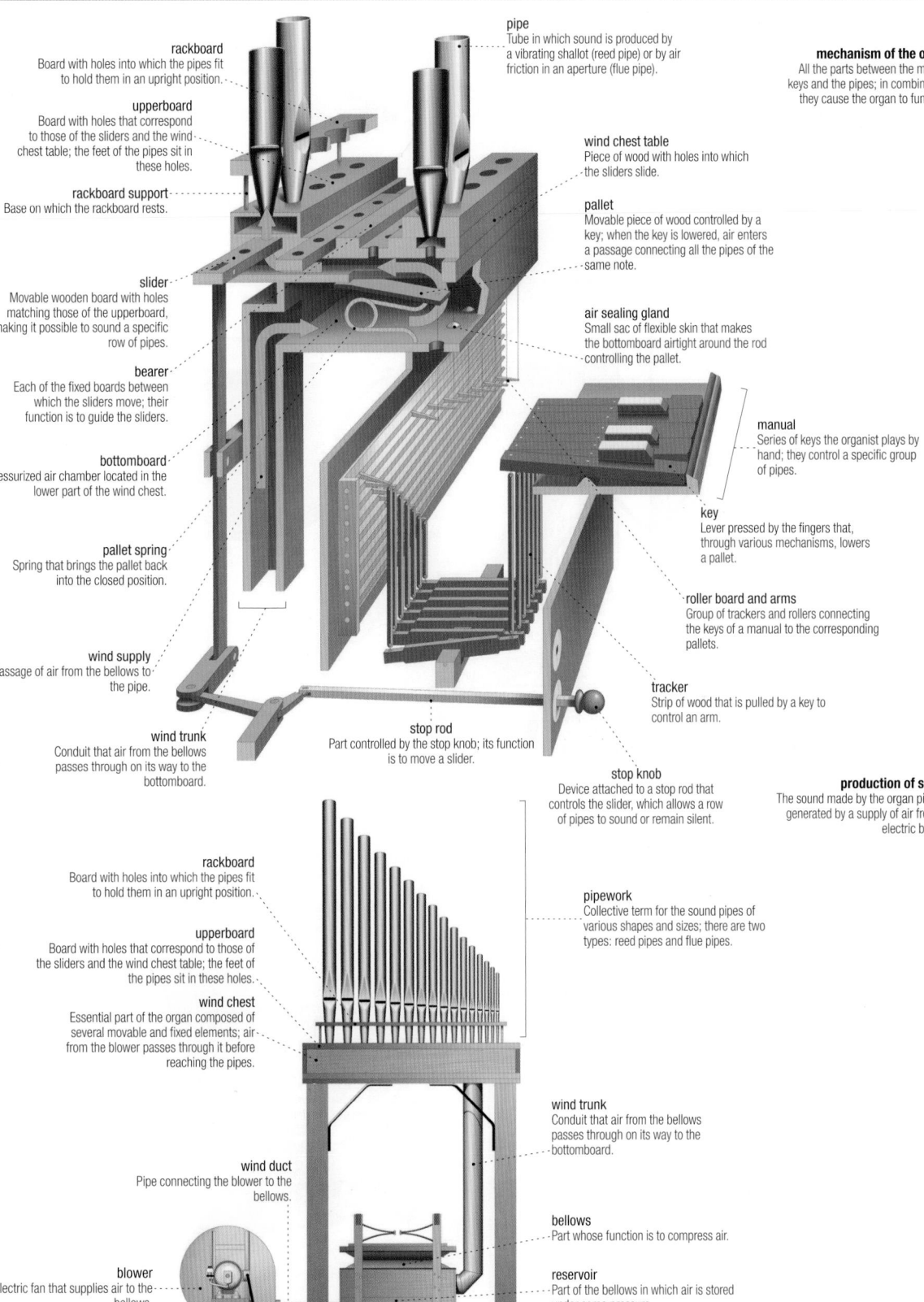

rackboard
Board with holes into which the pipes fit to hold them in an upright position.

upperboard
Board with holes that correspond to those of the sliders and the wind chest table; the feet of the pipes sit in these holes.

rackboard support
Base on which the rackboard rests.

slider
Movable wooden board with holes matching those of the upperboard, making it possible to sound a specific row of pipes.

bearer
Each of the fixed boards between which the sliders move; their function is to guide the sliders.

bottomboard
Pressurized air chamber located in the lower part of the wind chest.

pallet spring
Spring that brings the pallet back into the closed position.

wind supply
Passage of air from the bellows to the pipe.

wind trunk
Conduit that air from the bellows passes through on its way to the bottomboard.

pipe
Tube in which sound is produced by a vibrating shallot (reed pipe) or by air friction in an aperture (flue pipe).

wind chest table
Piece of wood with holes into which the sliders slide.

pallet
Movable piece of wood controlled by a key; when the key is lowered, air enters a passage connecting all the pipes of the same note.

air sealing gland
Small sac of flexible skin that makes the bottomboard airtight around the rod controlling the pallet.

manual
Series of keys the organist plays by hand; they control a specific group of pipes.

key
Lever pressed by the fingers that, through various mechanisms, lowers a pallet.

roller board and arms
Group of trackers and rollers connecting the keys of a manual to the corresponding pallets.

tracker
Strip of wood that is pulled by a key to control an arm.

stop rod
Part controlled by the stop knob; its function is to move a slider.

stop knob
Device attached to a stop rod that controls the slider, which allows a row of pipes to sound or remain silent.

mechanism of the organ
All the parts between the manual keys and the pipes; in combination, they cause the organ to function.

production of sound
The sound made by the organ pipes is generated by a supply of air from an electric blower.

rackboard
Board with holes into which the pipes fit to hold them in an upright position.

upperboard
Board with holes that correspond to those of the sliders and the wind chest table; the feet of the pipes sit in these holes.

wind chest
Essential part of the organ composed of several movable and fixed elements; air from the blower passes through it before reaching the pipes.

wind duct
Pipe connecting the blower to the bellows.

blower
Electric fan that supplies air to the bellows.

pipework
Collective term for the sound pipes of various shapes and sizes; there are two types: reed pipes and flue pipes.

wind trunk
Conduit that air from the bellows passes through on its way to the bottomboard.

bellows
Part whose function is to compress air.

reservoir
Part of the bellows in which air is stored under some pressure.

percussion instruments

Group of instruments that are sounded by striking, shaking or scraping.

drum kit
All the percussion instruments played by a single musician, the drummer.

tom-toms
Pair of drums struck with a mallet or a drumstick.

suspended cymbal
Single cymbal mounted on a stand and played with a mallet, a drumstick or a wire brush.

hi-hat cymbal
Pair of cymbals mounted horizontally and clashed by means of a pedal mechanism.

batter head
Stretched membrane on a snare drum that is struck with a drumstick or a wire brush.

snare drum
Drum with snares stretched across the bottom head that produce a rattling sound when the drum is struck.

tripod stand
Solid base with three feet.

mallet
Metal rod whose end (made of f cork, skin, etc.) is used to strike membrane of the bass drum.

floor tom
Large double-headed drum that mounted upright on three legs.

spur
Retractable metal rod attached to the bottom of a bass drum to stabilize it.

footplate
Device that controls the mallet u to strike the membrane.

leg
Part that supports the drum; its rubber end prevents the drum fr sliding along the floor.

stand
Part on which the bass drum and the pedal rest.

bass drum
Large drum mounted on its side that is struck with a pedal-controlled mallet.

tension screw
Part that adjusts the tension of the membrane.

kettledr
Tuned single-headed drum whose b consists of a large copper b

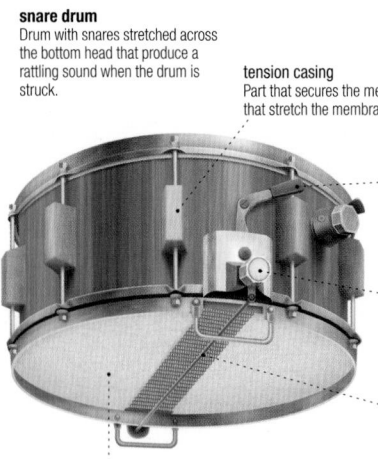

snare drum
Drum with snares stretched across the bottom head that produce a rattling sound when the drum is struck.

tension casing
Part that secures the metal hoops that stretch the membranes.

tension rod
Device that moves the snare closer to or farther from the snare head.

snare strainer
Knob that adjusts snare tension and tone.

snare
Metal wires that vibrate on the snare head when the batter head is struck, producing a rattling sound.

snare head
Membrane over which the snare is stretched.

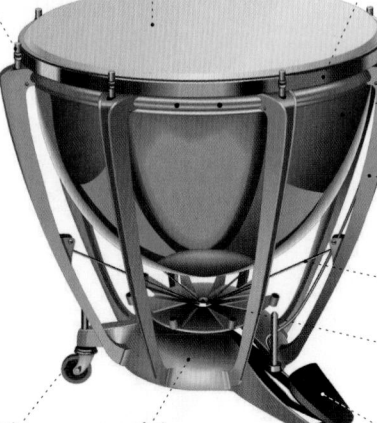

tuning bolt
Metal part connected to the tension rod; by adjusting the tension of the batter head, it changes the drum's pitch.

head
Membrane that is struck with a mallet.

metal counterhoop
Metal hoop that stretches the membrane over the shell to control the tone of the instrument.

tuning gauge
Mechanism used to adjust the d rapidly.

kettle
Large copper bowl that function as a sound box.

strut
Metal frame with several branch it supports the kettle.

tension rod
Metal rod connecting the crown the tie rods.

crown
Plate raised and lowered with th pedal to adjust the position of th tie rods.

caster

foot
The base of the kettledrum.

pedal
Device connected to the crown adjusts the tension of the mem change the tuning of the instrum

percussion instruments

sleigh bells
of hollow metal pieces with a -moving steel ball inside; they e tied to a ribbon and shaken.

set of bells
Series of small bells attached to a ribbon and used as accompaniment.

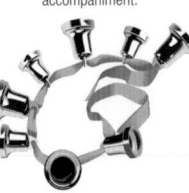

sistrum
Instrument consisting of a frame with crossbars and attached metal disks that strike together when the instrument is shaken.

castanets
Instrument composed of two shell-shaped pieces of wood held in one hand and struck together using the fingers.

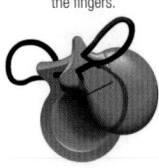

cymbals
Instrument consisting of two metal disks that are struck together.

tambourine
Instrument consisting of a wooden hoop covered with a membrane and fitted with jingles; it can be struck, brushed or shaken.

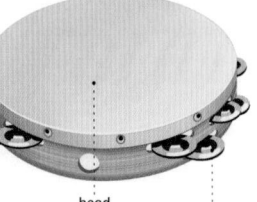

triangle
Metal bar bent to form a triangle open at one corner that is struck with a metal rod.

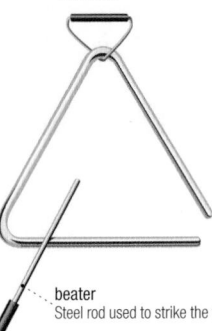

bongos
Pair of small connected drums that are played with the hands.

head
Membrane struck with the palm or the thumb.

jingle
Pair of small metal disks that strike together when the tambourine is shaken.

beater
Steel rod used to strike the triangle.

wire brush
Implement consisting of a handle with a fan of fine steel wires that are brushed across a cymbal or snare drum.

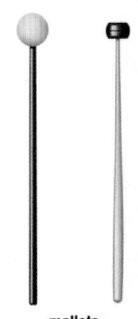

tubular bells
Series of tuned metal tubes hung vertically in order of size; small hammers are used to strike the tops of the tubes.

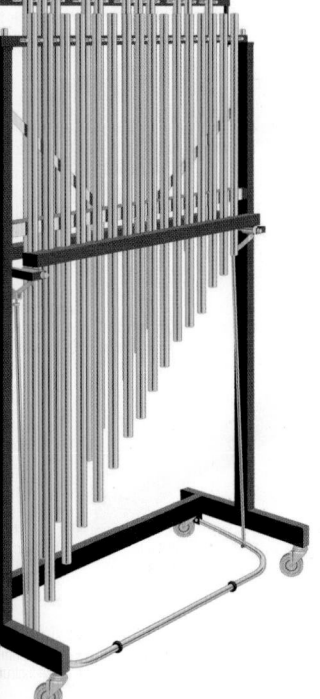

gong
Large metal disk with a raised central portion that is struck using a mallet.

xylophone
Instrument consisting of a set of tuned wooden bars placed on top of resonators arranged in chromatic order in two rows; the bars are struck with mallets.

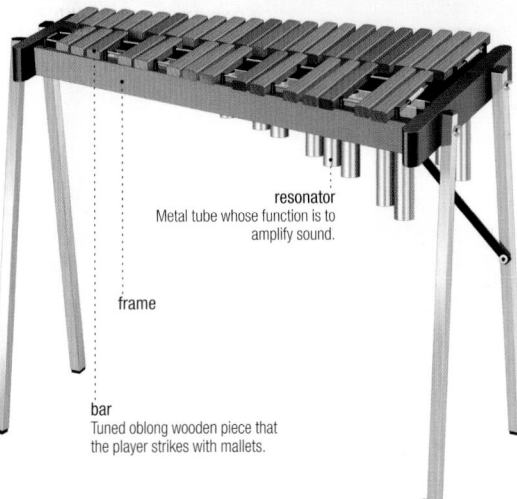

resonator
Metal tube whose function is to amplify sound.

frame

bar
Tuned oblong wooden piece that the player strikes with mallets.

drumsticks
Sticks of wood with olive-shaped heads used to strike a percussion instrument.

mallets
Metal or wooden rods whose end (made of felt, skin, rubber, etc.) is used to strike an instrument.

ARTS AND ARCHITECTURE

electronic music

Music produced by electronic instruments, which are designed to imitate, convert or produce sounds based on electric signals and digital data.

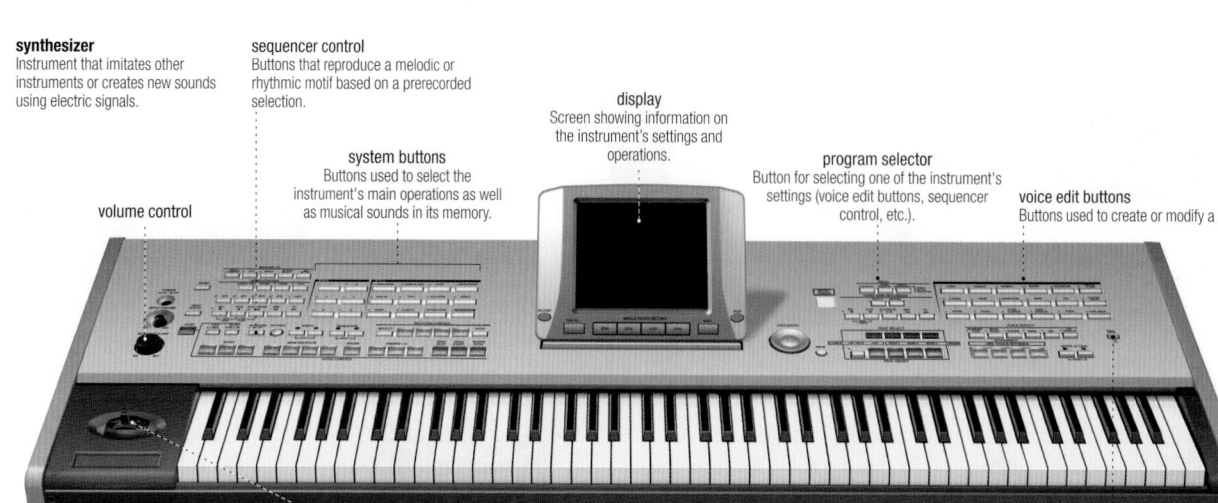

synthesizer
Instrument that imitates other instruments or creates new sounds using electric signals.

sequencer control
Buttons that reproduce a melodic or rhythmic motif based on a prerecorded selection.

display
Screen showing information on the instrument's settings and operations.

system buttons
Buttons used to select the instrument's main operations as well as musical sounds in its memory.

program selector
Button for selecting one of the instrument's settings (voice edit buttons, sequencer control, etc.).

voice edit buttons
Buttons used to create or modify a sou...

volume control

CD/DVD-ROM drive
Playback device using a laser beam to read the data recorded on a compact disc (CD) or digital video disc (DVD).

pitch and modulation switch
Switch that allows the vibration frequency or the quality of a sound to be changed.

keyboard
Series of keys pressed to play a melody using the timbres available on the instrument.

USB port
Connector for attaching a USB device to the... synthesizer.

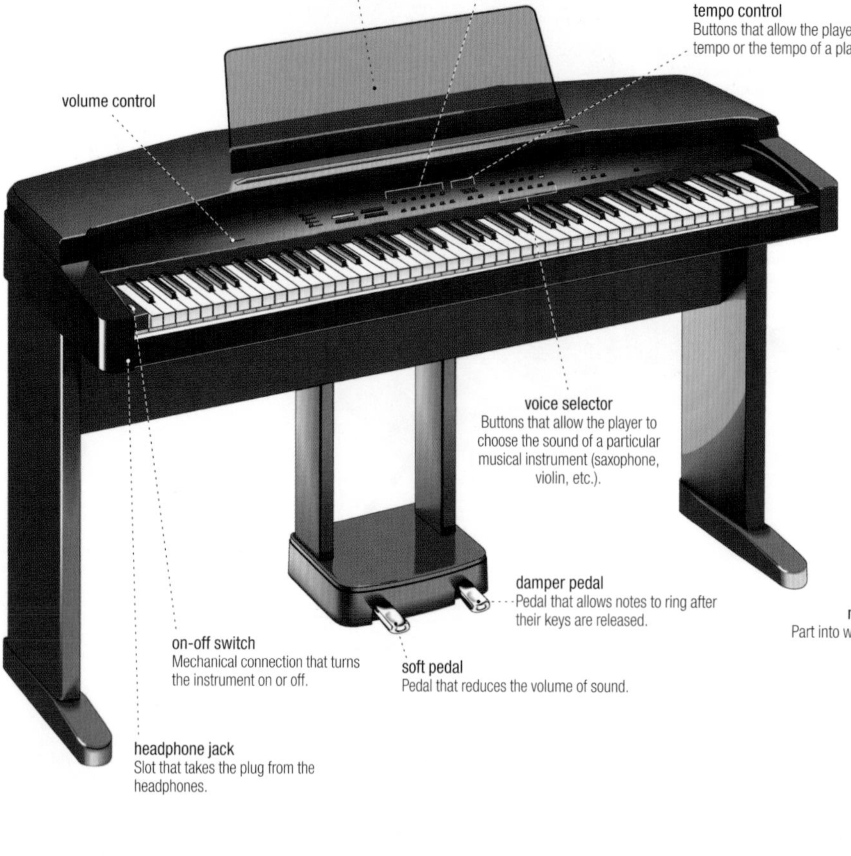

digital piano
Piano designed to reproduce the sound of an acoustic piano and other instruments by converting key strokes into digital data.

music stand
Inclined frame for displaying sheet music.

rhythm selector
Buttons that allow the player to choose an accompanying percussion rhythm (disco, rock, samba, etc.).

tempo control
Buttons that allow the player to vary the metronome tempo or the tempo of a playback recording.

volume control

electronic drum p
Instrument that is struck with drumsticks at diffe... places to produce various percussive sounds... emitting an electric signal that is converted into ... d...

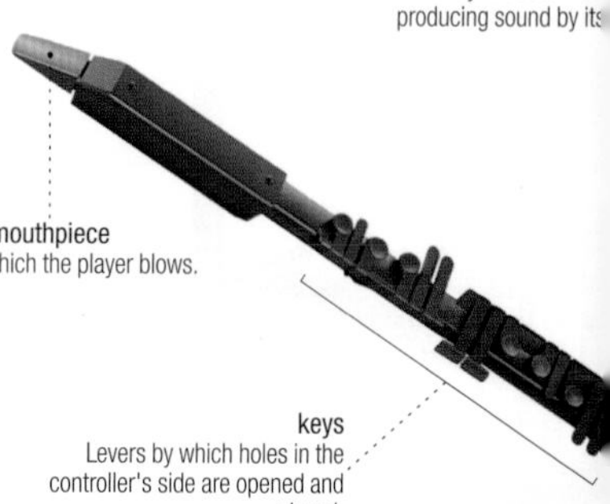

voice selector
Buttons that allow the player to choose the sound of a particular musical instrument (saxophone, violin, etc.).

wind contro
Wind instrument that controls a synthesizer wit... producing sound by its...

damper pedal
Pedal that allows notes to ring after their keys are released.

mouthpiece
Part into which the player blows.

on-off switch
Mechanical connection that turns the instrument on or off.

soft pedal
Pedal that reduces the volume of sound.

headphone jack
Slot that takes the plug from the headphones.

keys
Levers by which holes in the controller's side are opened and closed.

electronic music

accessories and mixing devices
Tools for storing, producing and combining electronic sounds.

drum machine
Instrument that reproduces sounds of percussion on a loop.

amplifier
Device that increases the strength of the audio signal produced by an instrument.

input jack
Receiving piece allowing a musical instrument to be connected to the amplifier.

headphone jack
Slot that takes the plug from the headphones.

sequencer
Component used to record, read and change MIDI data, the digital data used to create electronic music.

speaker
Integrated device used to generate sound.

expander
Synthesizer used to produce sounds based on digital data transmitted by a keyboard, a sequencer or a computer.

musical instrument digital interface (MIDI) cable
Cable connecting two MIDI instruments; the MIDI interface is used to transfer digital data and electric signals.

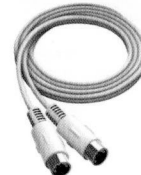

turntable
...nic device that can be used to play and ...the sounds recorded on a vinyl record.

tone arm
Elongated movable part that holds the stylus cartridge and moves it along the surface of the record.

sampler
Component that digitizes and stores sounds based on recordings of various acoustic sources, and reconverts them into sound signals.

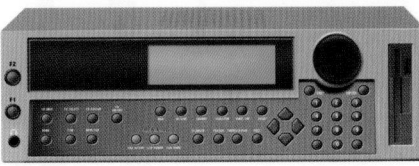

pitch fader
Device used to select the turntable speed (45 or 33 1/3 revolutions per minute).

platter
...ting part on which the record rests when played.

pitch slider
Cursor that slides along a vertical track and controls the speed and tempo of a piece, from a very slow to very fast rhythm.

miniature joystick
Small handle used as a mouse, used among other things to load a list of songs including titles and durations, without leaving the other commands on the console.

DJ console
Housing containing two transmission channels allowing one to work with two pieces of music simultaneously, using precision controls arranged symmetrically on either side.

scratch/jog wheel
Small wheel that can be turned in imitation of the back-and-forth hand movement one would use on a vinyl disc, in order to give the track a unique rhythm.

cue point button
...utton that skips the track back to the ...t cue point inserted and saved in the memory.

headphone jack
Slot that takes the plug from the headphones.

play/pause button
Button used to start or temporarily stop playback.

volume control
Button that controls the loudness of the instrument.

microphone jack
Female connector piece into which the jack (male piece) of the microphone is inserted, enabling the DJ to talk to the audience over the music.

pre-listening button
Control allowing the DJ to prepare the next track without interrupting the music playing for the audience.

volume control
Button that controls the loudness of the instrument.

crossfader
Cursor that slides along a horizontal track allowing the DJ to gradually fade out of one channel's track and into the track on the second channel.

traditional musical instruments

Collective term for the instruments, current or ancient, that characterize a culture, era or style of music.

accordion
Wind instrument composed of keyboards and a manual bellows used to cause the reeds to vibrate and produce sound.

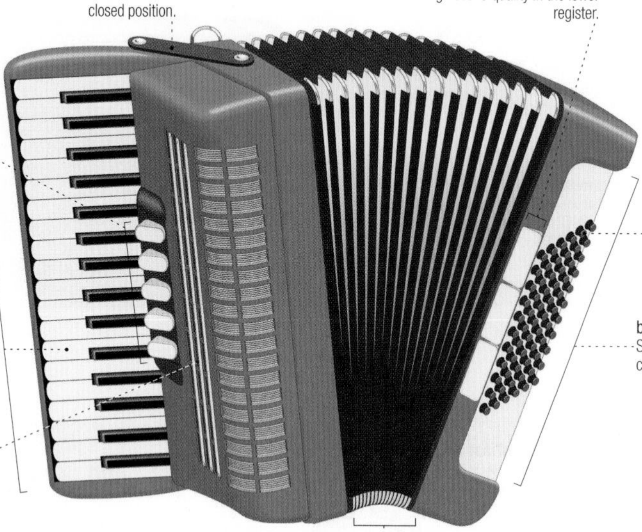

bellows strap
Piece that locks the bellows in a closed position.

bass switches
Switches that change sound quality in the lower register.

harmonica
Instrument composed of small slots with free reeds recessed in a frame, which the player causes to vibrate by exhaling and inhaling.

treble switches
Switches that change sound quality in the higher register.

treble keyboard
Keys used to play the melody.

key
White or black lever pressed to allow air from the bellows to pass, causing the reeds to vibrate and produce sound.

grille
Part through which air and sound pass.

bass button
Button that allows air from the bellows to enter, causing the bass keyboard reeds to vibrate.

bass keyboard
Set of buttons that play individual bass notes or chords.

bagpipes
Instrument with a windbag that is filled by the player's breath and squeezed under the arm to force air through a melody pipe and one or more drone pipes.

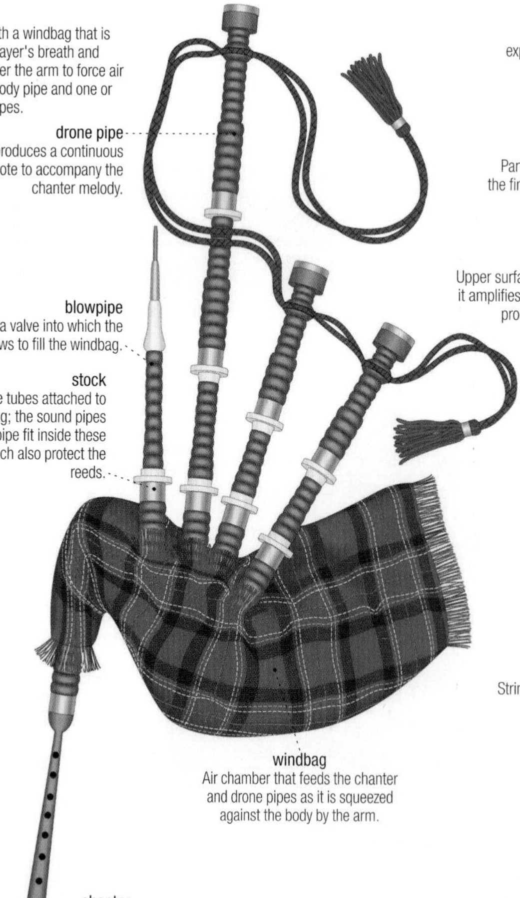

drone pipe
Tube that produces a continuous bass note to accompany the chanter melody.

blowpipe
Tube with a valve into which the player blows to fill the windbag.

stock
Each of the tubes attached to the windbag; the sound pipes and blow pipe fit inside these tubes, which also protect the reeds.

windbag
Air chamber that feeds the chanter and drone pipes as it is squeezed against the body by the arm.

chanter
Tube with finger holes, used to play the melody.

bellows
Apparatus that contracts and expands to control air pressure and cause the reeds to vibrate.

zither
Flat stringed instrument with no neck, associated with the music of Austria and Germany.

fingerboard
Part of the instrument against which the fingers press the strings to change their pitch.

soundboard
Upper surface of the sound box; it amplifies the sound vibrations produced by the strings.

open strings
Strings with fixed pitches, plucked with the fingers of the right hand.

melody strings
Strings that are plucked with a pick attached to the right thumb to create the melody.

didgeri
Wind instrument of Austra aborigines consisting of a wooden tube that produces a d and high harmonies whe player sings in

ba
Stringed instrument of Afr origin with a long fretted neck a tambourine-like b

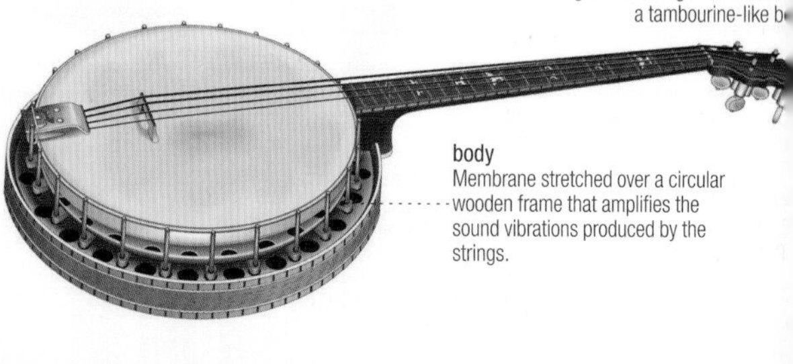

body
Membrane stretched over a circular wooden frame that amplifies the sound vibrations produced by the strings.

traditional musical instruments

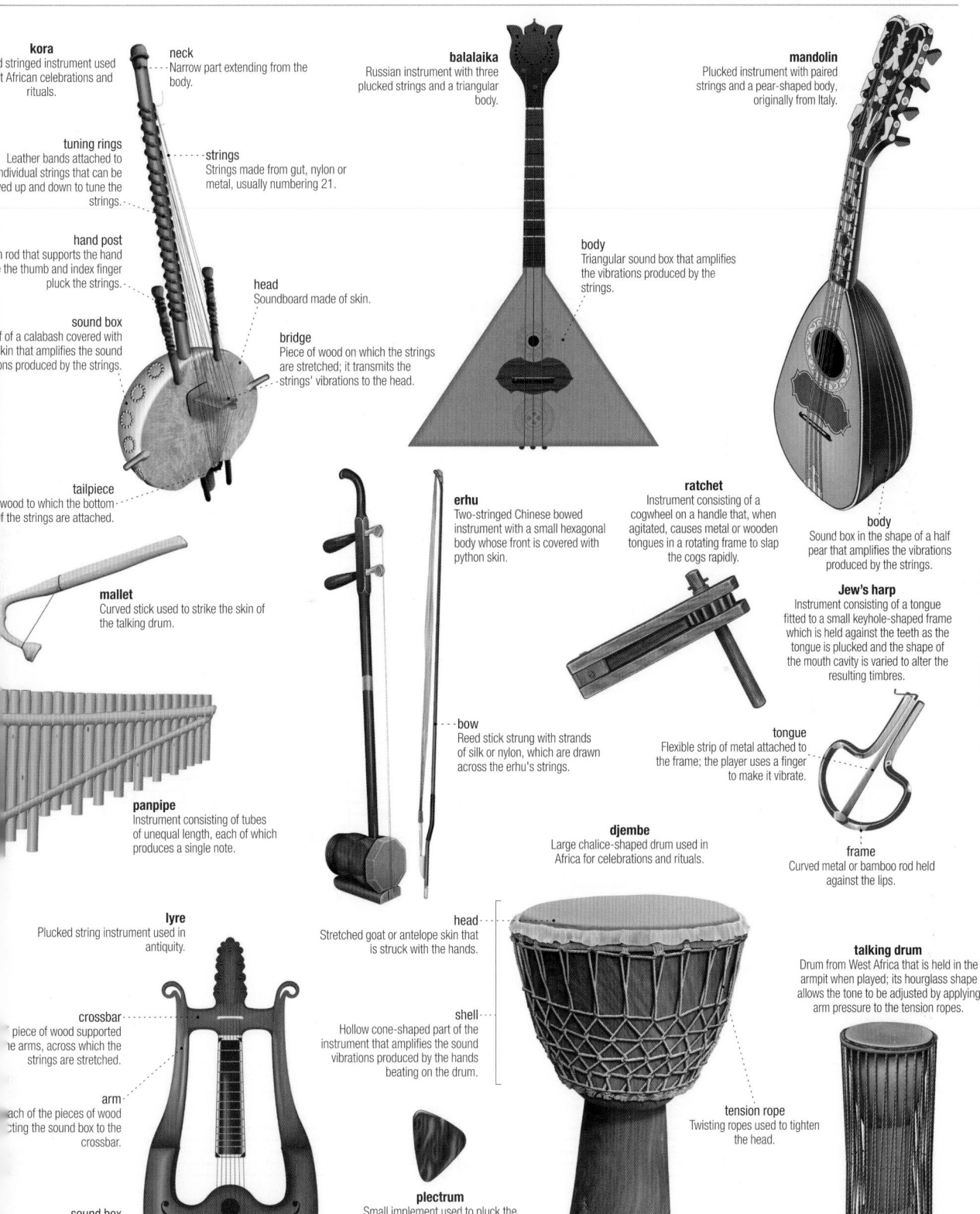

kora
ed stringed instrument used
est African celebrations and
rituals.

neck
Narrow part extending from the
body.

tuning rings
Leather bands attached to
individual strings that can be
ved up and down to tune the
strings.

strings
Strings made from gut, nylon or
metal, usually numbering 21.

hand post
en rod that supports the hand
e the thumb and index finger
pluck the strings.

head
Soundboard made of skin.

sound box
lf of a calabash covered with
skin that amplifies the sound
ons produced by the strings.

bridge
Piece of wood on which the strings
are stretched; it transmits the
strings' vibrations to the head.

tailpiece
wood to which the bottom
f the strings are attached.

mallet
Curved stick used to strike the skin of
the talking drum.

panpipe
Instrument consisting of tubes
of unequal length, each of which
produces a single note.

balalaika
Russian instrument with three
plucked strings and a triangular
body.

body
Triangular sound box that amplifies
the vibrations produced by the
strings.

erhu
Two-stringed Chinese bowed
instrument with a small hexagonal
body whose front is covered with
python skin.

bow
Reed stick strung with strands
of silk or nylon, which are drawn
across the erhu's strings.

ratchet
Instrument consisting of a
cogwheel on a handle that, when
agitated, causes metal or wooden
tongues in a rotating frame to slap
the cogs rapidly.

mandolin
Plucked instrument with paired
strings and a pear-shaped body,
originally from Italy.

body
Sound box in the shape of a half
pear that amplifies the vibrations
produced by the strings.

Jew's harp
Instrument consisting of a tongue
fitted to a small keyhole-shaped
frame which is held against the teeth as the
tongue is plucked and the shape of
the mouth cavity is varied to alter the
resulting timbres.

tongue
Flexible strip of metal attached to
the frame; the player uses a finger
to make it vibrate.

frame
Curved metal or bamboo rod held
against the lips.

djembe
Large chalice-shaped drum used in
Africa for celebrations and rituals.

lyre
Plucked string instrument used in
antiquity.

head
Stretched goat or antelope skin that
is struck with the hands.

crossbar
piece of wood supported
e arms, across which the
strings are stretched.

shell
Hollow cone-shaped part of the
instrument that amplifies the sound
vibrations produced by the hands
beating on the drum.

arm
ach of the pieces of wood
cting the sound box to the
crossbar.

talking drum
Drum from West Africa that is held in the
armpit when played; its hourglass shape
allows the tone to be adjusted by applying
arm pressure to the tension ropes.

tension rope
Twisting ropes used to tighten
the head.

sound box
w body of the instrument,
h amplifies the vibrations
produced by the strings.

plectrum
Small implement used to pluck the
strings on certain instruments; also
called a pick.

musical notation

Symbols written on the staff that represent musical pitches and durations.

staff

A series of five lines and four spaces on which music is written and read: the lower notes are written on the bottom, the higher notes on the top, and the music proceeds from left to right.

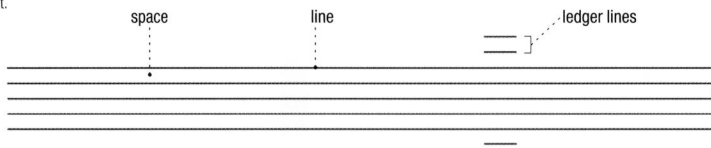

space   line   ledger lines

clefs

Signs placed at the beginning of the staff to indicate the pitches represented by the staff's lines and spaces.

treble clef
Clef indicating that the second line of the staff corresponds to the note G above middle C; it is used to write notes in the middle and treble registers.

bass clef
Clef indicating that the fourth line of the staff corresponds to the note F below middle C; it is used to write notes in the middle and bass registers.

alto clef
Clef indicating that the middle line corresponds to the note middle C; it is used principally for the viola.

time signatures

Numbers or symbols that indicate the meter of a composition.

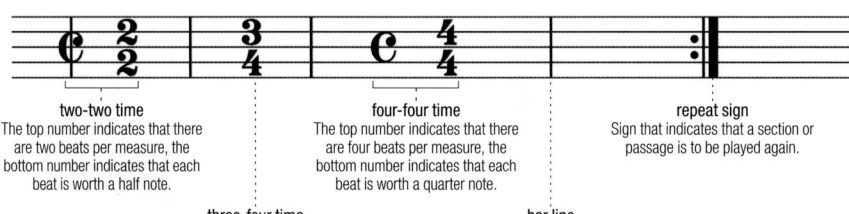

two-two time
The top number indicates that there are two beats per measure, the bottom number indicates that each beat is worth a half note.

three-four time
The top number indicates that there are three beats per measure, the bottom number indicates that each beat is worth a quarter note.

four-four time
The top number indicates that there are four beats per measure, the bottom number indicates that each beat is worth a quarter note.

bar line
Vertical line that marks the end of one measure and the beginning of the next.

repeat sign
Sign that indicates that a section or passage is to be played again.

intervals

Distances in pitch between two successive notes (melodic interval) or simultaneous notes (harmonic interval).

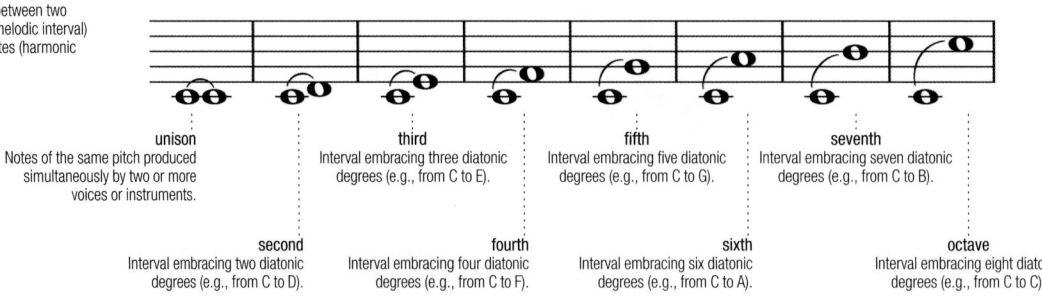

unison
Notes of the same pitch produced simultaneously by two or more voices or instruments.

second
Interval embracing two diatonic degrees (e.g., from C to D).

third
Interval embracing three diatonic degrees (e.g., from C to E).

fourth
Interval embracing four diatonic degrees (e.g., from C to F).

fifth
Interval embracing five diatonic degrees (e.g., from C to G).

sixth
Interval embracing six diatonic degrees (e.g., from C to A).

seventh
Interval embracing seven diatonic degrees (e.g., from C to B).

octave
Interval embracing eight diatonic degrees (e.g., from C to C).

C major scale

Scale based on C and consisting of whole tones except for semitones between E and F and between B and C.

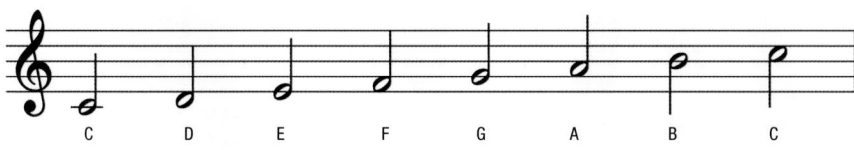

C   D   E   F   G   A   B   C

musical notation

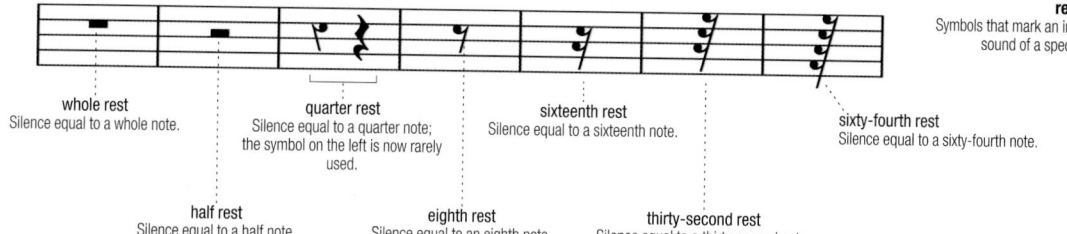

rest symbols
Symbols that mark an interruption of sound of a specific duration.

whole rest
Silence equal to a whole note.

quarter rest
Silence equal to a quarter note; the symbol on the left is now rarely used.

sixteenth rest
Silence equal to a sixteenth note.

sixty-fourth rest
Silence equal to a sixty-fourth note.

half rest
Silence equal to a half note.

eighth rest
Silence equal to an eighth note.

thirty-second rest
Silence equal to a thirty-second note.

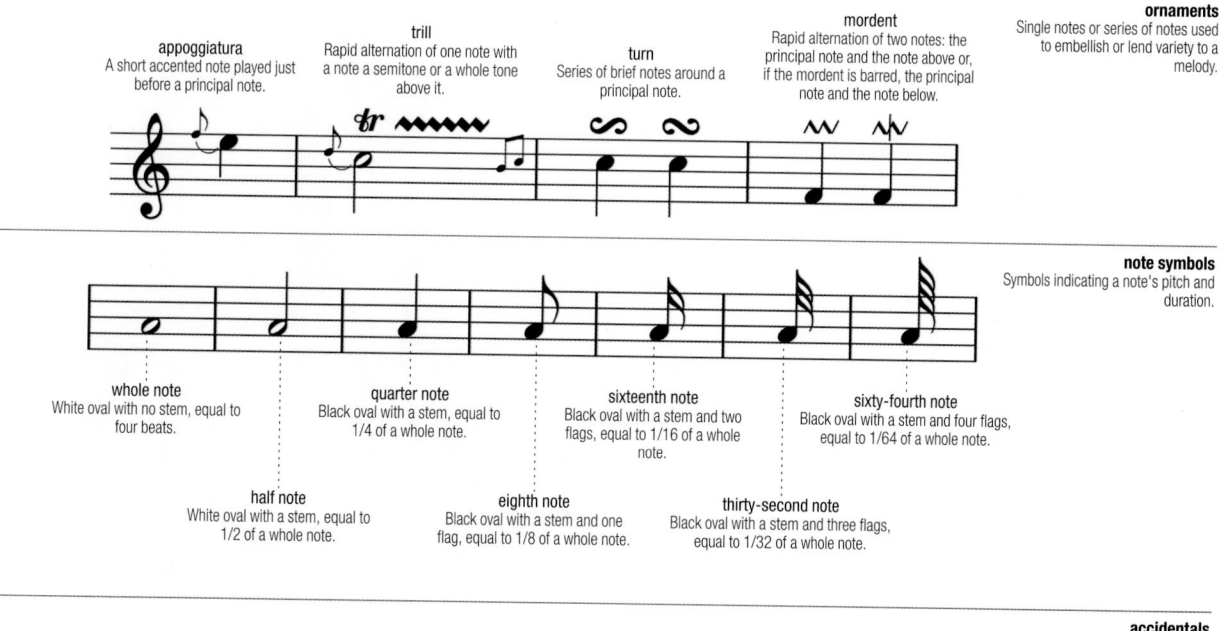

ornaments
Single notes or series of notes used to embellish or lend variety to a melody.

appoggiatura
A short accented note played just before a principal note.

trill
Rapid alternation of one note with a note a semitone or a whole tone above it.

turn
Series of brief notes around a principal note.

mordent
Rapid alternation of two notes: the principal note and the note above or, if the mordent is barred, the principal note and the note below.

note symbols
Symbols indicating a note's pitch and duration.

whole note
White oval with no stem, equal to four beats.

quarter note
Black oval with a stem, equal to 1/4 of a whole note.

sixteenth note
Black oval with a stem and two flags, equal to 1/16 of a whole note.

sixty-fourth note
Black oval with a stem and four flags, equal to 1/64 of a whole note.

half note
White oval with a stem, equal to 1/2 of a whole note.

eighth note
Black oval with a stem and one flag, equal to 1/8 of a whole note.

thirty-second note
Black oval with a stem and three flags, equal to 1/32 of a whole note.

accidentals
Signs used to change the pitch of a note.

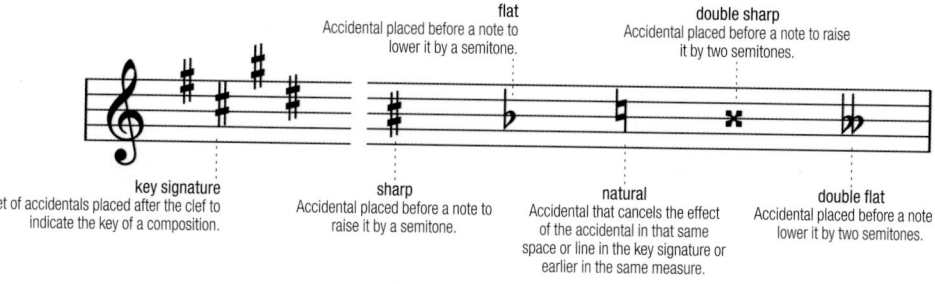

flat
Accidental placed before a note to lower it by a semitone.

double sharp
Accidental placed before a note to raise it by two semitones.

key signature
Set of accidentals placed after the clef to indicate the key of a composition.

sharp
Accidental placed before a note to raise it by a semitone.

natural
Accidental that cancels the effect of the accidental in that same space or line in the key signature or earlier in the same measure.

double flat
Accidental placed before a note to lower it by two semitones.

other signs
Signs that indicate how a note or series of notes should be played.

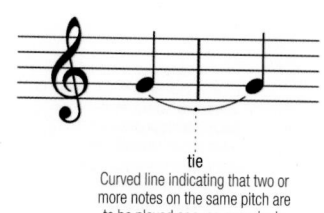

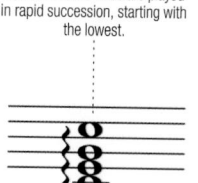

chord
Three or more notes played simultaneously.

tie
Curved line indicating that two or more notes on the same pitch are to be played or sung as a single lengthened note.

accent mark
Sign indicating that a note should be played louder.

arpeggio
A chord whose notes are played in rapid succession, starting with the lowest.

fermata
Sign indicating that the note, chord, or rest under it can be prolonged as long as desired.

musical accessories

Ancillary tools used by musicians.

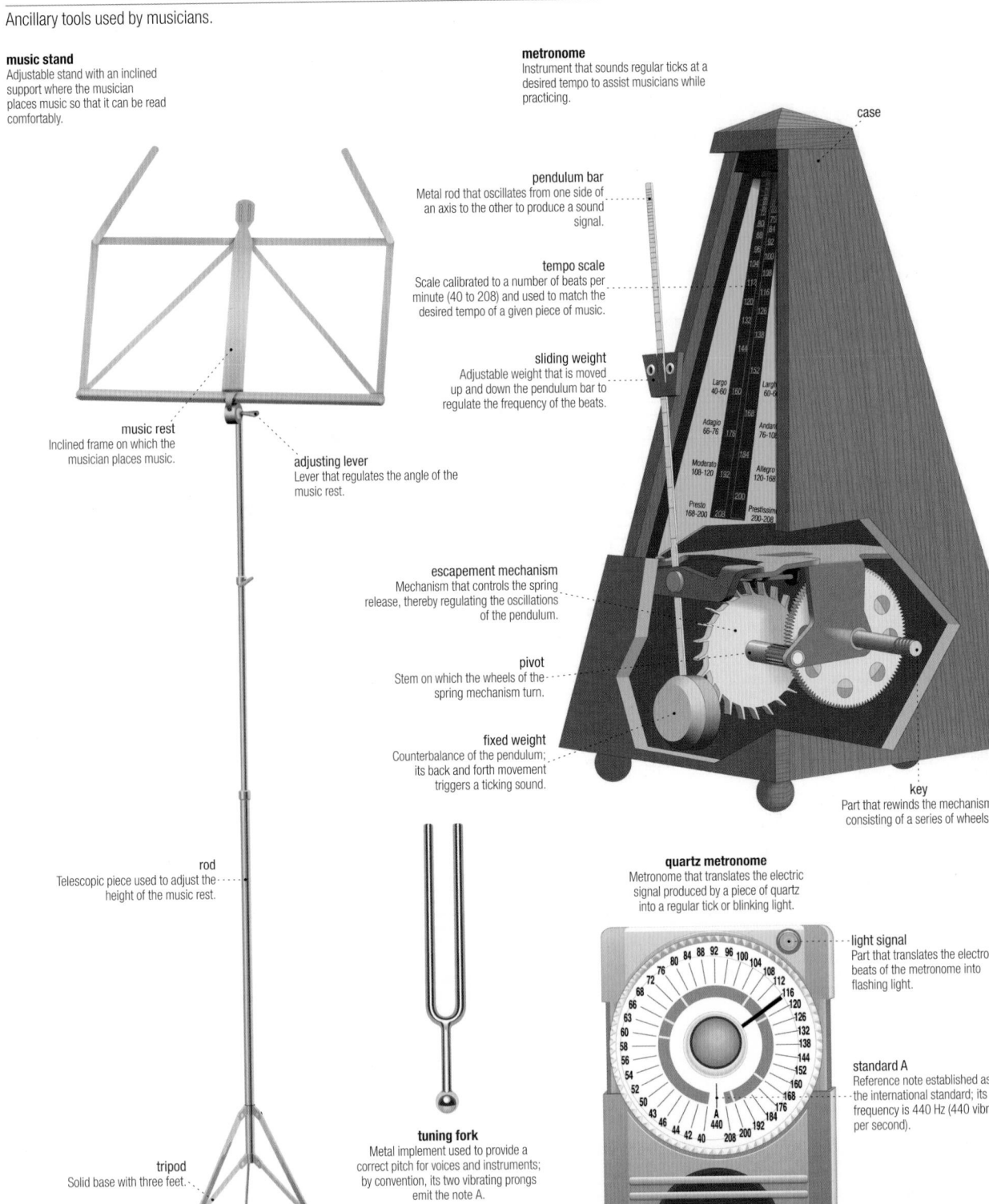

music stand
Adjustable stand with an inclined support where the musician places music so that it can be read comfortably.

metronome
Instrument that sounds regular ticks at a desired tempo to assist musicians while practicing.

case

pendulum bar
Metal rod that oscillates from one side of an axis to the other to produce a sound signal.

tempo scale
Scale calibrated to a number of beats per minute (40 to 208) and used to match the desired tempo of a given piece of music.

sliding weight
Adjustable weight that is moved up and down the pendulum bar to regulate the frequency of the beats.

Largo
40-60

Largh
60-6

Adagio
66-78

Andan
76-10

Moderato
108-120

Allegro
120-168

Presto
168-200

Prestissimo
200-208

music rest
Inclined frame on which the musician places music.

adjusting lever
Lever that regulates the angle of the music rest.

escapement mechanism
Mechanism that controls the spring release, thereby regulating the oscillations of the pendulum.

pivot
Stem on which the wheels of the spring mechanism turn.

fixed weight
Counterbalance of the pendulum; its back and forth movement triggers a ticking sound.

key
Part that rewinds the mechanism, consisting of a series of wheels.

rod
Telescopic piece used to adjust the height of the music rest.

quartz metronome
Metronome that translates the electric signal produced by a piece of quartz into a regular tick or blinking light.

80 84 88 92 96 100 104
76
72 108
68 112
66 116
63 126
60 132
58 138
56 144
54 152
52 160
50 168
A
440
43 176
46 184
44 192
40 208 200

light signal
Part that translates the electronic beats of the metronome into flashing light.

standard A
Reference note established as the international standard; its frequency is 440 Hz (440 vibratic per second).

tuning fork
Metal implement used to provide a correct pitch for voices and instruments; by convention, its two vibrating prongs emit the note A.

tripod
Solid base with three feet.

speaker
Device that translates the metronome's electric signal into

embroidery

Art of stitching designs on fabric, usually using a needle and thread.

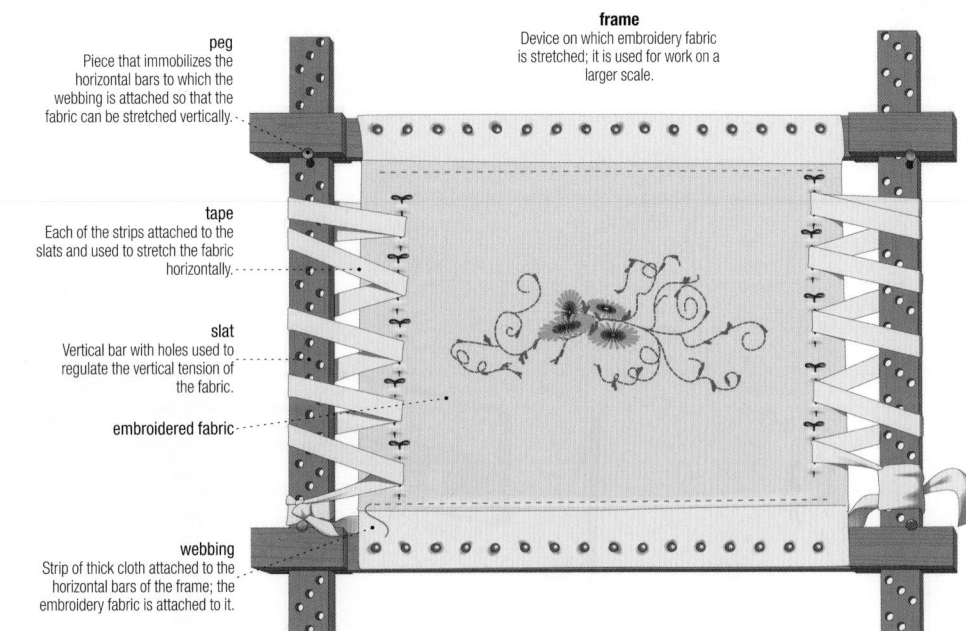

frame
Device on which embroidery fabric is stretched; it is used for work on a larger scale.

peg
Piece that immobilizes the horizontal bars to which the webbing is attached so that the fabric can be stretched vertically.

hoop
Frame consisting of two hoops; one fits inside the other and the fabric is stretched between them. The hoop is used for detail work.

tape
Each of the strips attached to the slats and used to stretch the fabric horizontally.

slat
Vertical bar with holes used to regulate the vertical tension of the fabric.

embroidered fabric

webbing
Strip of thick cloth attached to the horizontal bars of the frame; the embroidery fabric is attached to it.

stitch patterns
There are more than 100 embroidery stitches, grouped into various categories.

cross stitches
es made up of a succession of straight stitches that meet and then change direction.

chevron stitch
tch consisting of diagonal ght stitches that meet at the and bottom of two parallel rows.

herringbone stitch
ch composed of intersecting nal straight stitches following two parallel lines.

couched stitches
Stitches used to fill in and give relief to a design.

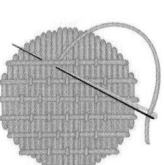

Oriental couching stitch
Vertical stitches are crossed with horizontal lines held together by isolated stitches staggered from one row to the next.

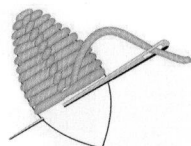

Romanian couching stitch
A stitch forms the base of the embroidery over the entire width of the line, and an angled or vertical stitch covers the center.

loop stitches
Stitches forming an open or closed loop.

chain stitch
Stitch created by forming closed loops that are repeated like the links in a chain.

feather stitch
Stitch created by forming successive open loops, linked or unlinked.

flat stitches
Stitches usually used to fill in a design.

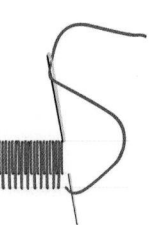

long and short stitch
Stitch consisting of overlapping rows of long and short stitches to cover a surface.

fishbone stitch
Oblique stitch alternately arranged on the left and right of an imaginary axis.

knot stitches
Stitches created by winding the thread around the needle.

bullion stitch
Stitch created by rolling the thread several times around the needle and reinserting the needle a little farther on to create a line of thread.

French knot stitch
Stitch created by rolling the thread two or three times around the needle and reinserting it very close to the original point of insertion to create a cluster.

sewing

Process of joining two items using a needle and a thread.

sewing machine
Machine used to assemble two pieces of fabric by means of a series of stitches made with a needle and thread.

arm
Part that connects the head to the column; it houses part of the needle's drive mechanism.

spool pin
Pivot used to attach the upper spool of thread.

thread guide
Part used to direct the thread.

bobbin winder
Pin on which the bobbin is placed to load it; the spool pin thread is transferred to the bobbin winder.

thread take-up lever
Lever that the upper thread goes through before it is threaded through the needle; it regulates tension.

stitch width selector
Mechanism used to set the stitch width.

handwheel
Dial used to raise and lower needle manually.

pressure dial
Mechanism used to set the pressure of the hinged presser foot on the fabric.

needle position selector
Part that selects the needle pos center or right).

stitch length regulator
Dial used to set the length of the the numbers indicate the length millimeters.

stitch selector
Wheel used to select a stitch pattern.

head
Vertical section that completes the needle's drive mechanism; the presser foot extends from it.

reverse stitch button
Switch that reverses the s direction.

needle
Metal stem that passes the thread through the fabric to form a stitch.

column
Vertical section that supp arm and houses part of th drive mechanism.

flat-bed
Surface over which the pieces of fabric move.

power/light switch
Button that turns the machine and t light on and off.

hinged presser foot
Articulated end of the presser foot; it consists of two branches between which the needle passes.

bobbin
Spool on which the lower thread is wound.

needle plate
Metal plate with an opening that the needle passes through and two slits from which the feed dogs for the fabric protrude.

slide plate
Plate that slides open, providing access to the lower stitching components.

tension dial
Parts that control the tension of the upper thread.

foot con
Mechanism operated by fo controls the sewing machi electric m

ARTS AND ARCHITECTURE

bobbin case
Case placed under the needle plate; the bobbin fits inside it.

bobbin
Spool on which the lower thread is wound.

speed controller
Pedal that regulates the speed of the machine's electric motor; the greater the pressure on it, the greater the speed.

connecting terminal
Part that connects the speed controller to the sewing machine.

latch lever
Mechanism that the bobbin fits into and that regulates lower thread tension.

hook
Fixed lower component containing the latch lever.

sewing

sion block
s that control the tension of the
er thread.

tension spring
g that keeps the upper thread
etween the tension disks.

thread guide
Part that leads the thread toward
the tension disk.

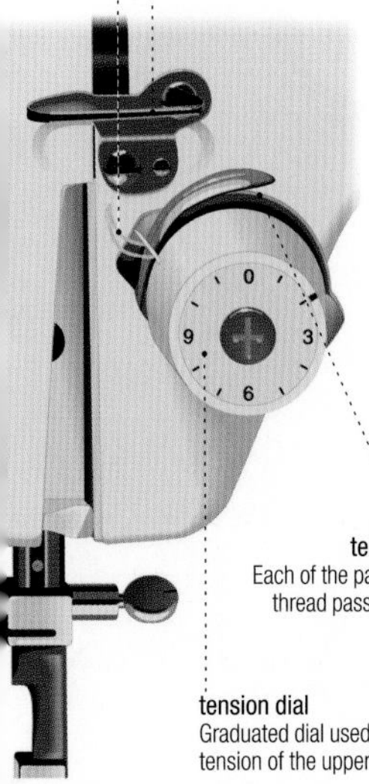

needle
Metal stem that passes the thread
through the fabric to form a stitch.

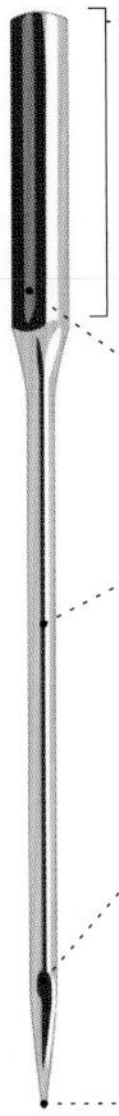

shank
Upper end of the needle that fits
into the needle clamp.

groove
Narrow channel in the needle for
guiding the thread.

blade
Part of the needle between the
shank and the eye.

eye
Hole at the bottom of the needle
that the thread passes through.

point
Lower end of the needle, used to
pierce the fabric.

tension disk
Each of the parts between which the
thread passes during threading.

tension dial
Graduated dial used to regulate the
tension of the upper thread.

needle bar
Cylindrical rod that supports the needle
clamp at its lower end and produces the
up-and-down movement of the needle.

thread guide
Part that guides the thread toward
the eye of the needle.

needle clamp
Part in which the needle shank is
inserted.

thread trimmer
Slit in which the threads are
inserted to cut them after sewing.

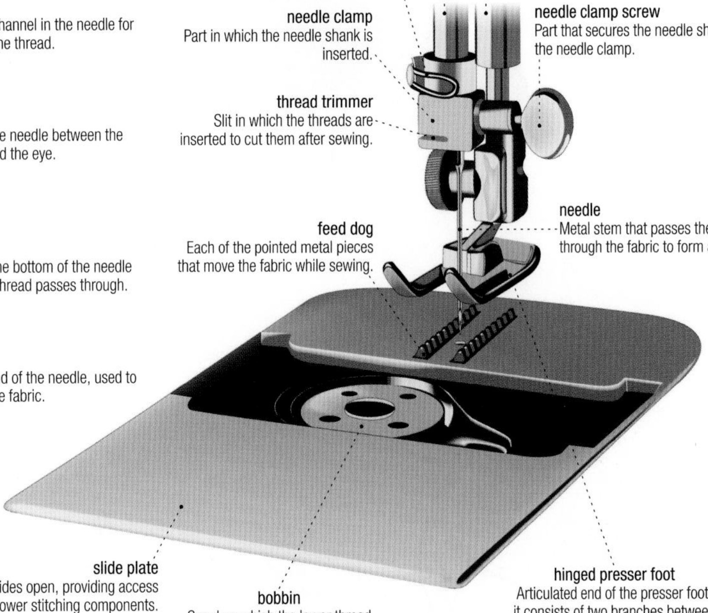

feed dog
Each of the pointed metal pieces
that move the fabric while sewing.

presser foot
Part of the sewing machine that keeps the
fabric flat against the feed dogs during
sewing.

presser bar
Cylindrical rod that ends in the presser foot.

needle clamp screw
Part that secures the needle shank to
the needle clamp.

needle
Metal stem that passes the thread
through the fabric to form a stitch.

slide plate
Plate that slides open, providing access
to the lower stitching components.

bobbin
Spool on which the lower thread
is wound.

hinged presser foot
Articulated end of the presser foot;
it consists of two branches between
which the needle passes.

fasteners
Accessories used to open or close
a garment.

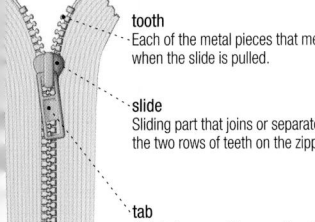

per
sure made up of two lengths of
e edged with teeth that interlock by
ans of a slide.

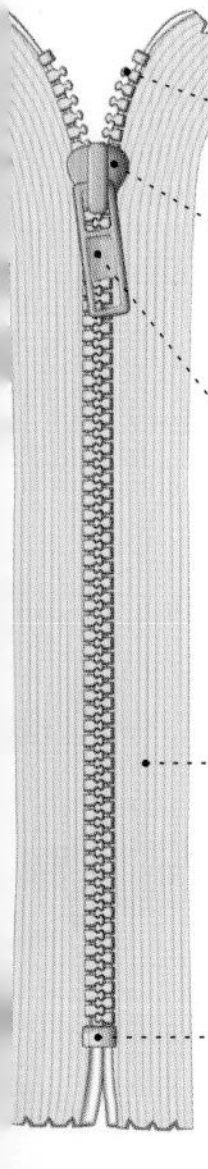

tooth
Each of the metal pieces that mesh
when the slide is pulled.

slide
Sliding part that joins or separates
the two rows of teeth on the zipper.

tab
Metal piece used to move the slide.

tape
Strip of fabric to which the teeth
are attached; it is sewed to each
side of the fabric's seam.

stop
Metal piece that stops the slide at the
lower end of the zipper.

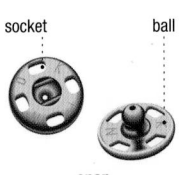

socket   ball

snap
Fastening mechanism made of a
socket disk and a ball disk that snap
shut when pressed together.

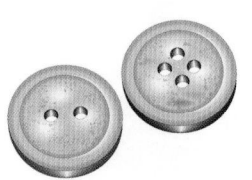

sew-through buttons
Buttons with two or four holes that
the thread passes through to sew
them to a piece of fabric.

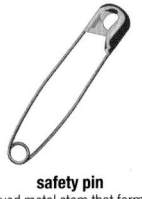

safety pin
Curved metal stem that forms a
spring; the pointed extremity of
its flexible arm is kept in place by
a hook.

shank button
Button with a metal ring that the
thread passes through to sew it to
a piece of fabric.

hook and eyes
Fasteners formed of a metal hook
inserted into a round eye or a
straight eye.

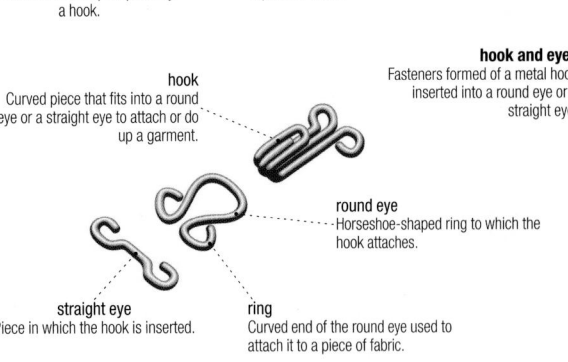

hook
Curved piece that fits into a round
eye or a straight eye to attach or do
up a garment.

straight eye
Piece in which the hook is inserted.

ring
Curved end of the round eye used to
attach it to a piece of fabric.

round eye
Horseshoe-shaped ring to which the
hook attaches.

sewing

sewing accessories

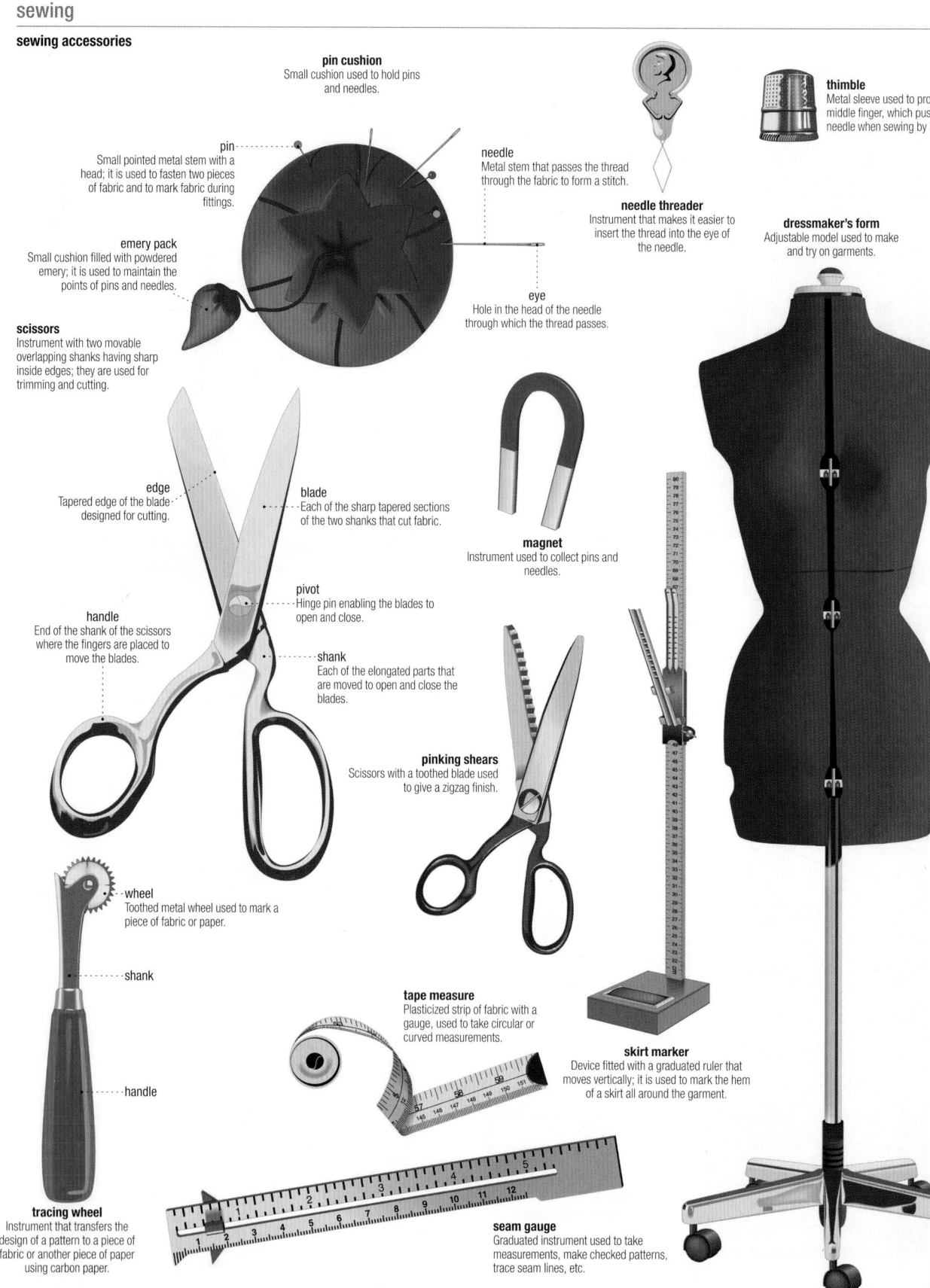

pin cushion
Small cushion used to hold pins and needles.

thimble
Metal sleeve used to prote...
middle finger, which push...
needle when sewing by h...

pin
Small pointed metal stem with a head; it is used to fasten two pieces of fabric and to mark fabric during fittings.

needle
Metal stem that passes the thread through the fabric to form a stitch.

needle threader
Instrument that makes it easier to insert the thread into the eye of the needle.

dressmaker's form
Adjustable model used to make and try on garments.

emery pack
Small cushion filled with powdered emery; it is used to maintain the points of pins and needles.

eye
Hole in the head of the needle through which the thread passes.

scissors
Instrument with two movable overlapping shanks having sharp inside edges; they are used for trimming and cutting.

edge
Tapered edge of the blade designed for cutting.

blade
Each of the sharp tapered sections of the two shanks that cut fabric.

magnet
Instrument used to collect pins and needles.

pivot
Hinge pin enabling the blades to open and close.

handle
End of the shank of the scissors where the fingers are placed to move the blades.

shank
Each of the elongated parts that are moved to open and close the blades.

pinking shears
Scissors with a toothed blade used to give a zigzag finish.

wheel
Toothed metal wheel used to mark a piece of fabric or paper.

shank

handle

tape measure
Plasticized strip of fabric with a gauge, used to take circular or curved measurements.

skirt marker
Device fitted with a graduated ruler that moves vertically; it is used to mark the hem of a skirt all around the garment.

tracing wheel
Instrument that transfers the design of a pattern to a piece of fabric or another piece of paper using carbon paper.

seam gauge
Graduated instrument used to take measurements, make checked patterns, trace seam lines, etc.

sewing

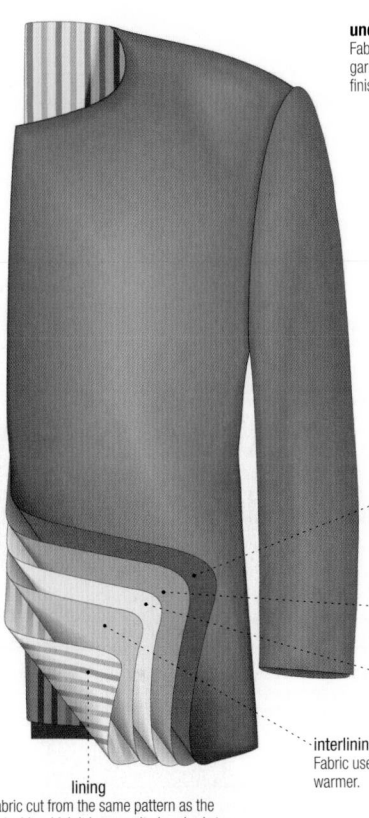

underlying fabrics
Fabrics used to hold the shape of a garment and give it a professional finish.

garment fabric
Principal material used for the garment; it covers the underlying fabrics.

underlining
Fabric used to hold the shape of the garment and make it more opaque.

interfacing
Tear-resistant fabric used to hold the shape of the garment and give it body.

interlining
Fabric used to make a garment warmer.

lining
Fabric cut from the same pattern as the inside which it is sewn; it gives body to ...nent, embellishes it, hides its seams and makes it warmer.

fabric structure
The way the threads of the material are put together during weaving.

bias
Direction of a fabric; it is diagonal to the crosswise grain and the lengthwise grain.

selvage
The finished border of a piece of fabric, woven more tightly than the piece it borders and parallel to the lengthwise grain.

crosswise grain
The threads that are passed through the lengthwise grain from one selvage to another; it is the width of the fabric.

lengthwise grain
Evenly spaced parallel threads arranged lengthwise along the fabric.

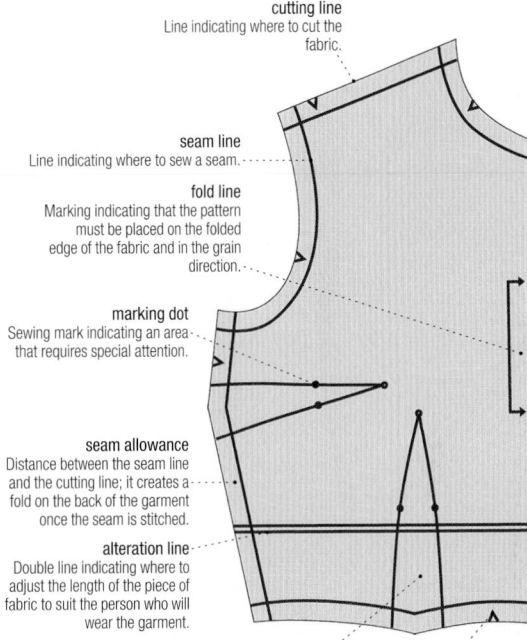

pattern
Paper template used to cut the various pieces of a garment.

cutting line
Line indicating where to cut the fabric.

seam line
Line indicating where to sew a seam.

fold line
Marking indicating that the pattern must be placed on the folded edge of the fabric and in the grain direction.

marking dot
Sewing mark indicating an area that requires special attention.

seam allowance
Distance between the seam line and the cutting line; it creates a fold on the back of the garment once the seam is stitched.

alteration line
Double line indicating where to adjust the length of the piece of fabric to suit the person who will wear the garment.

dart
Symbol indicating the position and width of the fold on the inside of the fabric that makes the garment snugger.

notch
Marking used to precisely match pieces that go together.

zipper line
Line indicating where to position the zipper.

lengthwise grain
Line with arrows indicating how to position the pattern on the fabric so that it lies in the direction of the warp threads.

hemline
Line indicating where to fold the fabric to create the bottom of a garment.

knitting

Creating fabric by using needles to form interlacing stitches.

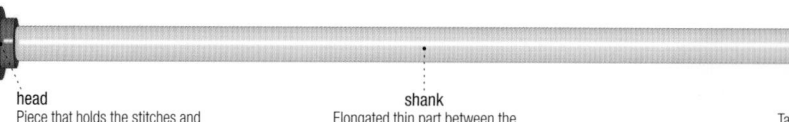

knitting needle
Rigid cylindrical rod used in pairs to knit a piece of fabric.

head
Piece that holds the stitches and prevents them from sliding off the shank.

shank
Elongated thin part between the head and the point; its length and diameter vary, depending on the desired stitch.

poir
Tapered end allowing the needle to b easily inserted in the stitche

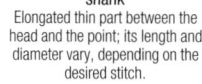

hook
The curved extremity used to catch the thread.

flat part
Flat section used to handle the crochet hook.

crochet h
Instrument used to recover a stitch, create trim and ce seams,

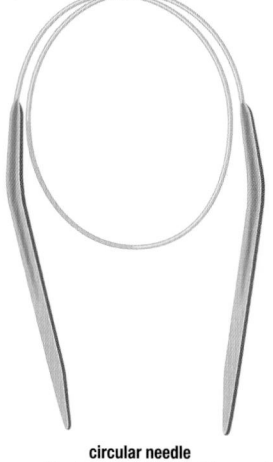

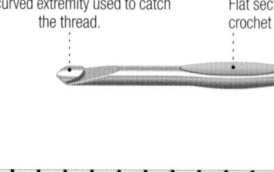

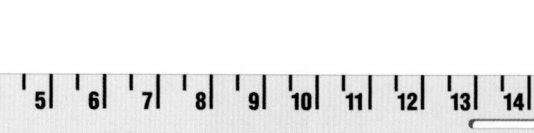

circular needle
Needle used for circular knitting, for seamless pieces or flat pieces with a great number of stitches.

cast-on stitches
Loops that form the starting point of a piece of fabric.

knitting gauge
Instrument used to measure the diameter of needles and to take measurements of a work in progress.

stitch patterns
Arrangement of groups of stitches in one or several rows; they are worked until they form a regularly repeated design or feature.

swatch
Square sample used to calculate the number of stitches and rows on a 2 in² surface so that a consistent pattern can be established.

stockinette stitch
Stitch obtained by alternating a plain row with a purl row.

garter stitch
Stitch obtained by a succession of plain stitches on all the rows.

moss stitch
Stitch obtained by alternating a plain stitch with a purl stitch on one row, and then reversing the order on the next.

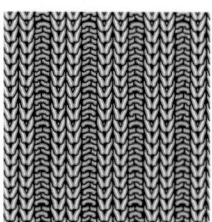

rib stitch
Stitch obtained by alternating plain and purl stitches and by repeating the same order on the following rows.

basket stitch
Stitch obtained by alternating squares composed of plain stitches with squares composed of purl stitches.

cable stitch
Stitch obtained by reversing the st on a row to form an overlap.

knitting

knitting machine
Machine used to knit fabrics mechanically.

carriage handle
Part used to hold and move the main carriage.

tension dial
Graduated dial used to program the size of the stitch.

row number display
Screen indicating the number of the next knitting row.

needle bed and carriages
Metal piece with grooves in which the needles are inserted; the carriages slide over it to create a knit.

row counter
Part that indicates the number of rows knitted.

stitch pattern memory
Keys to place the stitch patterns in memory.

accessory box
Space designed to house the needles, the needle pushers, the attachments and so forth.

main carriage
Device used to drag the arm, determine stitch size and type, etc.

needle bed groove
Grooves where the shanks of the needles appear so they can be moved manually or by using the main carriage.

slide bar
piece with grooves on which ain carriage slides; it guides the main carriage.

variation keys
Keys used to change the shape of a stitch pattern.

correction key
Key that is pressed to undo knitting.

pattern start key
Key used to repeat a pattern starting with the first row.

color display
Screen that posts a number corresponding to a color.

needle bed
etal piece with grooves that the edles fit into; it forms a row that ects the chosen stitch pattern.

rail
Straight part along which the main carriage moves.

lace carriage
Device used for knitting lace.

arm
Device pushed over the needles to move them forward or backward, depending on the chosen stitch pattern.

carriage control dial
Button used to choose a type of stitch, select the needles and lift the main carriage from the needle bed.

arm nut
Button connecting the main carriage to the arm.

stitch control buttons
Buttons used to select a type of stitch (e.g., moss stitch, stocking stitch, garter stitch).

weaving pattern brush
Brush used to clean the needles.

yarn feeder
Part in which the thread is inserted.

weaving pattern lever
Switch that is raised to put the machine in knitting mode.

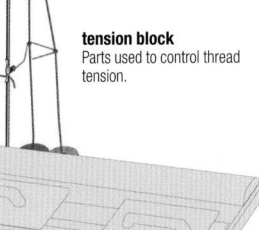

tension block
Parts used to control thread tension.

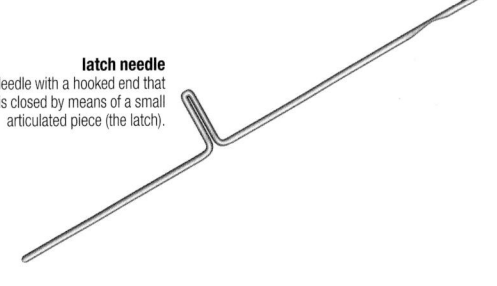

latch needle
Needle with a hooked end that is closed by means of a small articulated piece (the latch).

ARTS AND ARCHITECTURE

weaving

Threads (warp and weft) interlaced at right angles to form cloth.

low-warp loom

Loom on which the warp threads are
arranged horizontally.

general view

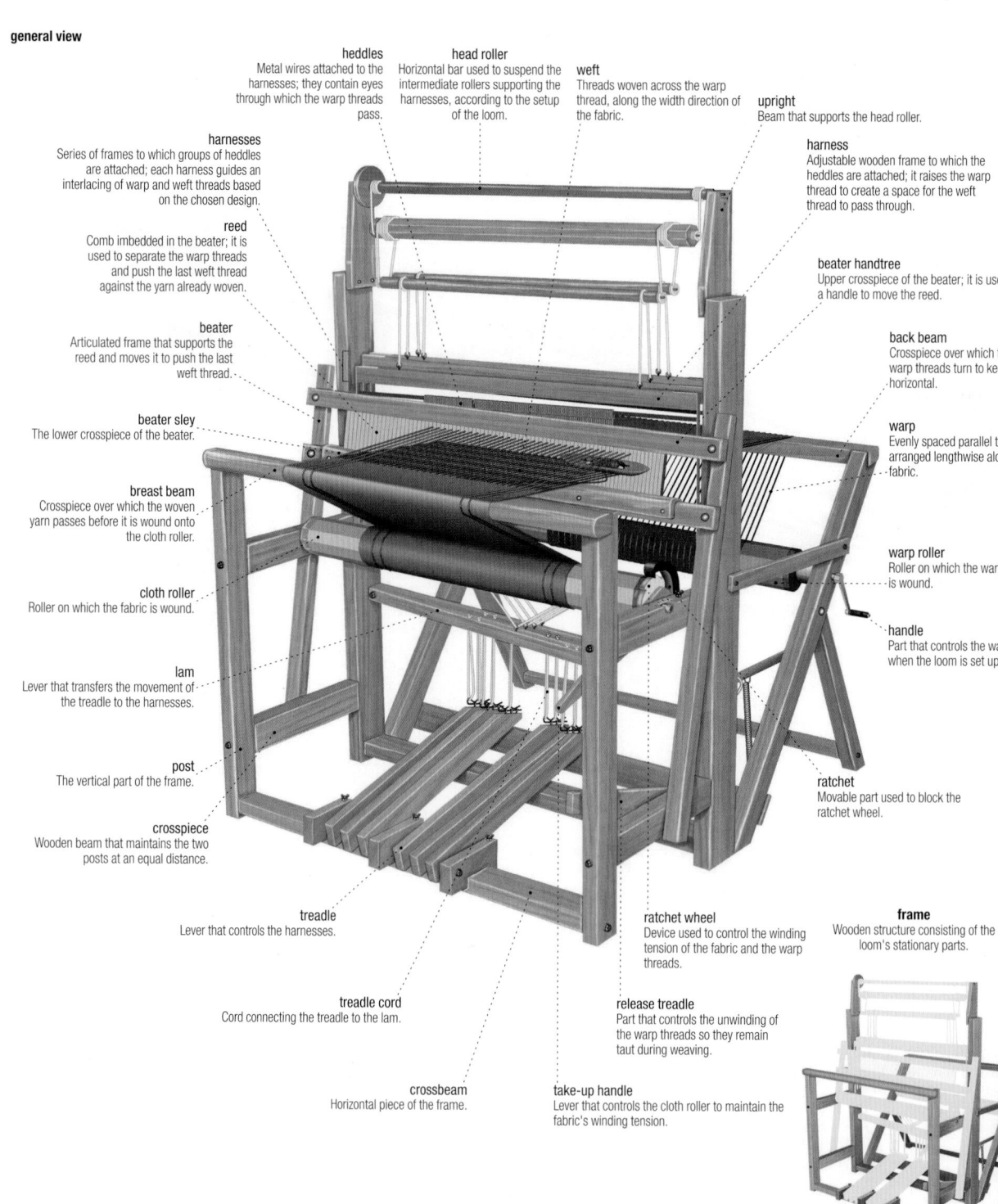

heddles
Metal wires attached to the
harnesses; they contain eyes
through which the warp threads
pass.

head roller
Horizontal bar used to suspend the
intermediate rollers supporting the
harnesses, according to the setup
of the loom.

weft
Threads woven across the warp
thread, along the width direction of
the fabric.

upright
Beam that supports the head roller.

harnesses
Series of frames to which groups of heddles
are attached; each harness guides an
interlacing of warp and weft threads based
on the chosen design.

harness
Adjustable wooden frame to which the
heddles are attached; it raises the warp
thread to create a space for the weft
thread to pass through.

reed
Comb imbedded in the beater; it is
used to separate the warp threads
and push the last weft thread
against the yarn already woven.

beater handtree
Upper crosspiece of the beater; it is use
a handle to move the reed.

beater
Articulated frame that supports the
reed and moves it to push the last
weft thread.

back beam
Crosspiece over which th
warp threads turn to kee
horizontal.

beater sley
The lower crosspiece of the beater.

warp
Evenly spaced parallel th
arranged lengthwise alo
fabric.

breast beam
Crosspiece over which the woven
yarn passes before it is wound onto
the cloth roller.

warp roller
Roller on which the warp
is wound.

cloth roller
Roller on which the fabric is wound.

handle
Part that controls the wa
when the loom is set up.

lam
Lever that transfers the movement of
the treadle to the harnesses.

ratchet
Movable part used to block the
ratchet wheel.

post
The vertical part of the frame.

crosspiece
Wooden beam that maintains the two
posts at an equal distance.

treadle
Lever that controls the harnesses.

ratchet wheel
Device used to control the winding
tension of the fabric and the warp
threads.

frame
Wooden structure consisting of the
loom's stationary parts.

treadle cord
Cord connecting the treadle to the lam.

release treadle
Part that controls the unwinding of
the warp threads so they remain
taut during weaving.

crossbeam
Horizontal piece of the frame.

take-up handle
Lever that controls the cloth roller to maintain the
fabric's winding tension.

weaving

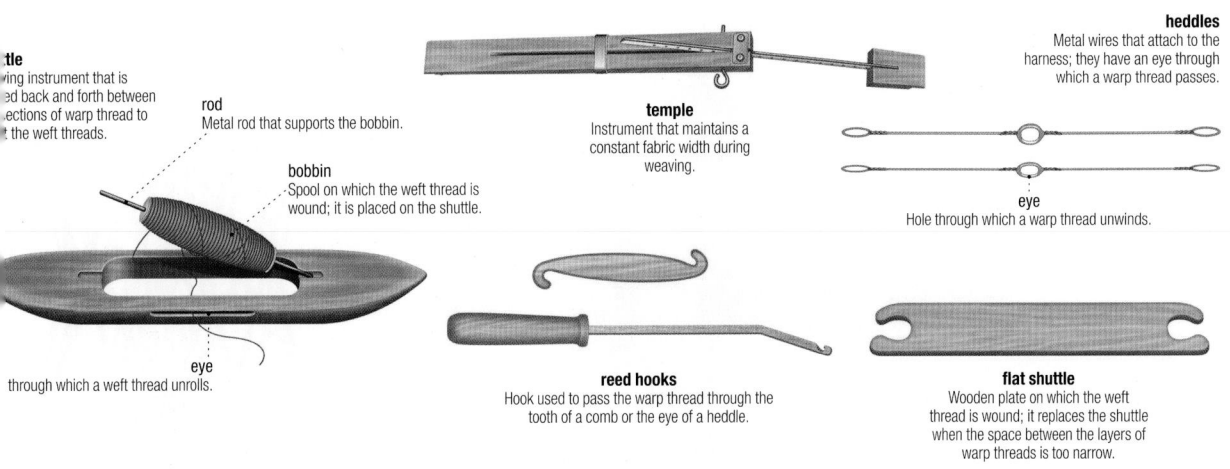

shuttle
Weaving instrument that is passed back and forth between sections of warp thread to insert the weft threads.

rod
Metal rod that supports the bobbin.

bobbin
Spool on which the weft thread is wound; it is placed on the shuttle.

eye
through which a weft thread unrolls.

temple
Instrument that maintains a constant fabric width during weaving.

reed hooks
Hook used to pass the warp thread through the tooth of a comb or the eye of a heddle.

heddles
Metal wires that attach to the harness; they have an eye through which a warp thread passes.

eye
Hole through which a warp thread unwinds.

flat shuttle
Wooden plate on which the weft thread is wound; it replaces the shuttle when the space between the layers of warp threads is too narrow.

high warp loom
Loom on which the warp threads are arranged vertically.

general view

tapestry bobbin
High-warp tapestry instrument used as a shuttle to introduce the weft between the warp threads.

comb
Instrument used to push the weft thread against the yarn already woven.

upright
Vertical section of the frame.

warp
Evenly spaced parallel threads arranged lengthwise along the fabric.

shed stick
Piece of wood that separates the warp based on the weaving pattern specified.

heddle rod
Piece of wood to which the heddles are attached.

vertical frame
Wooden structure consisting of the loom's stationary parts.

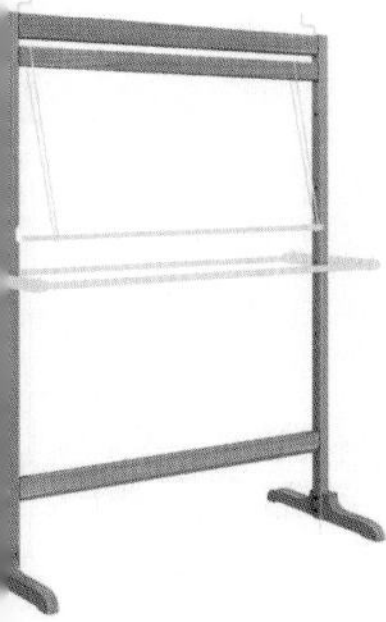

heddles
Small wires with an eye through which the warp thread passes.

tapestry bobbin
High-warp tapestry instrument used as a shuttle to introduce the weft between the warp threads.

weft
Threads woven across the warp thread, along the width direction of the fabric.

crossbar
Horizontal section of the frame.

lease rod
Thin strip of wood passed alternately under and over warp threads to separate the threads.

support
The base on which the loom rests.

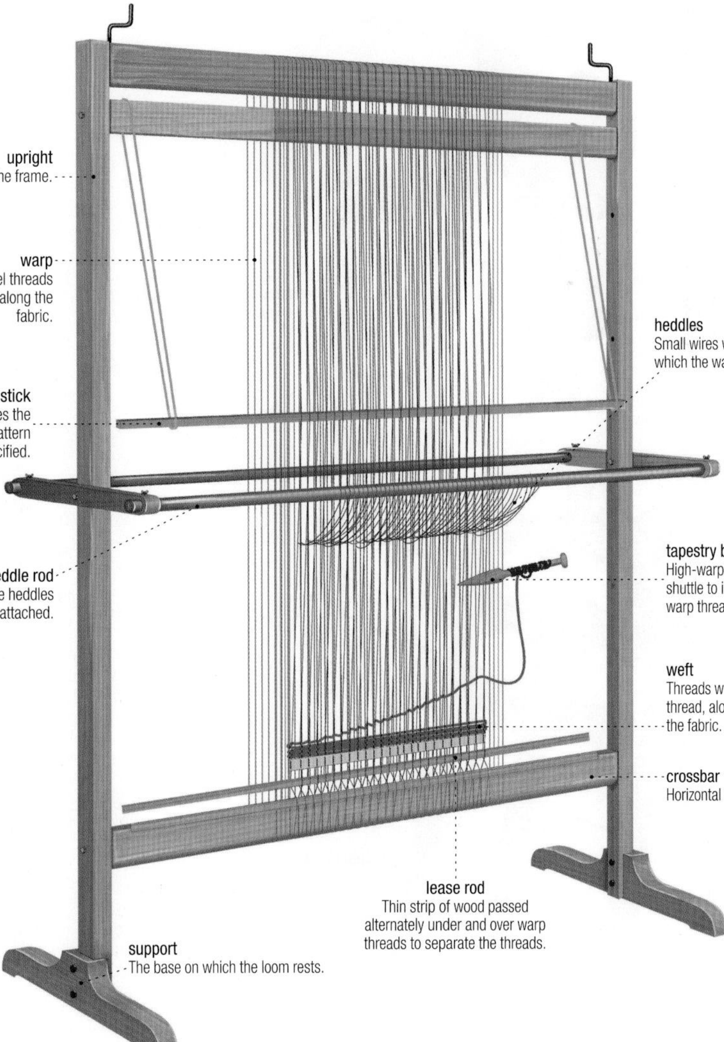

weaving

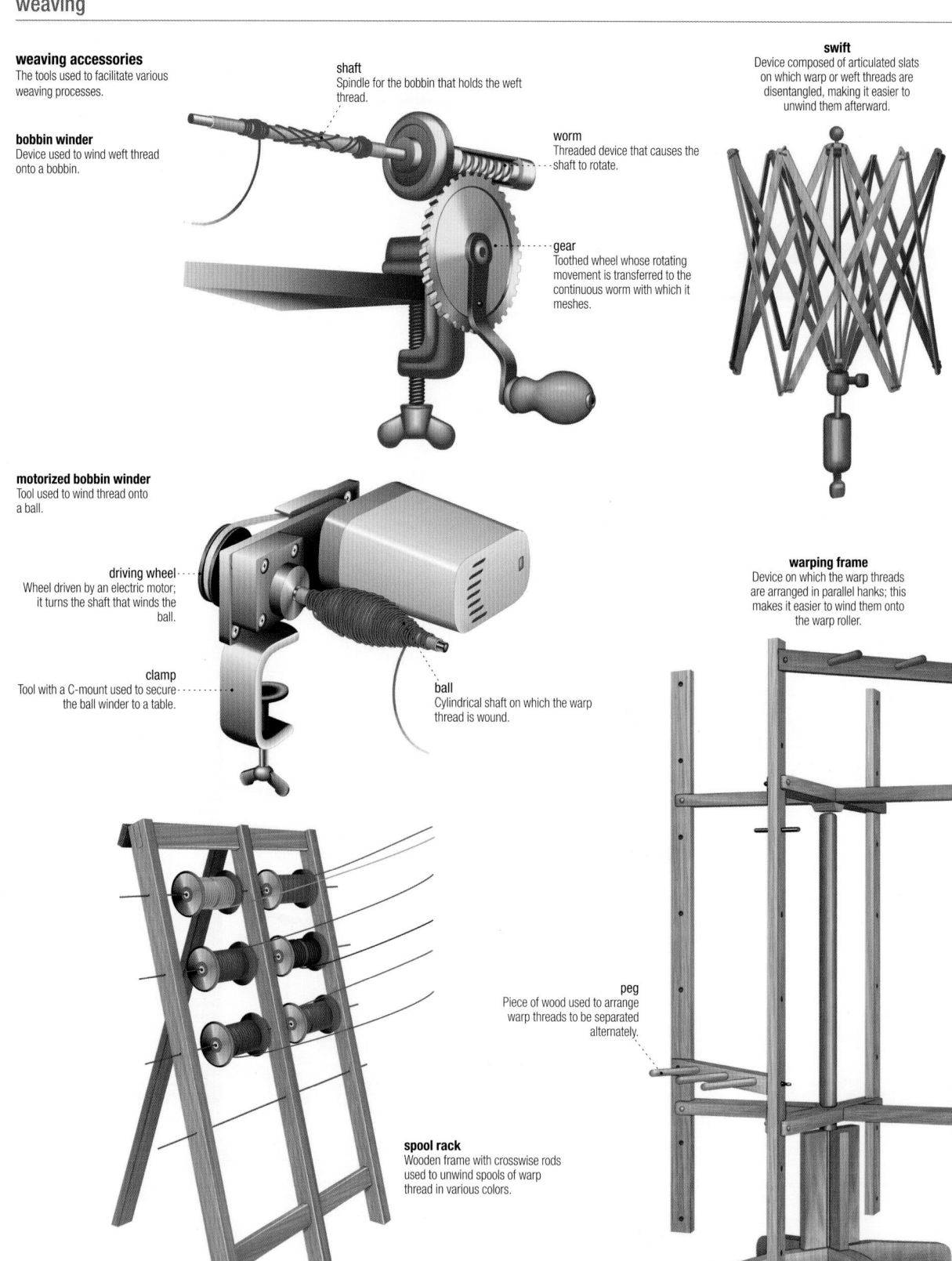

weaving accessories
The tools used to facilitate various weaving processes.

bobbin winder
Device used to wind weft thread onto a bobbin.

shaft
Spindle for the bobbin that holds the weft thread.

worm
Threaded device that causes the shaft to rotate.

gear
Toothed wheel whose rotating movement is transferred to the continuous worm with which it meshes.

swift
Device composed of articulated slats on which warp or weft threads are disentangled, making it easier to unwind them afterward.

motorized bobbin winder
Tool used to wind thread onto a ball.

driving wheel
Wheel driven by an electric motor; it turns the shaft that winds the ball.

clamp
Tool with a C-mount used to secure the ball winder to a table.

ball
Cylindrical shaft on which the warp thread is wound.

warping frame
Device on which the warp threads are arranged in parallel hanks; this makes it easier to wind them onto the warp roller.

peg
Piece of wood used to arrange warp threads to be separated alternately.

spool rack
Wooden frame with crosswise rods used to unwind spools of warp thread in various colors.

weaving

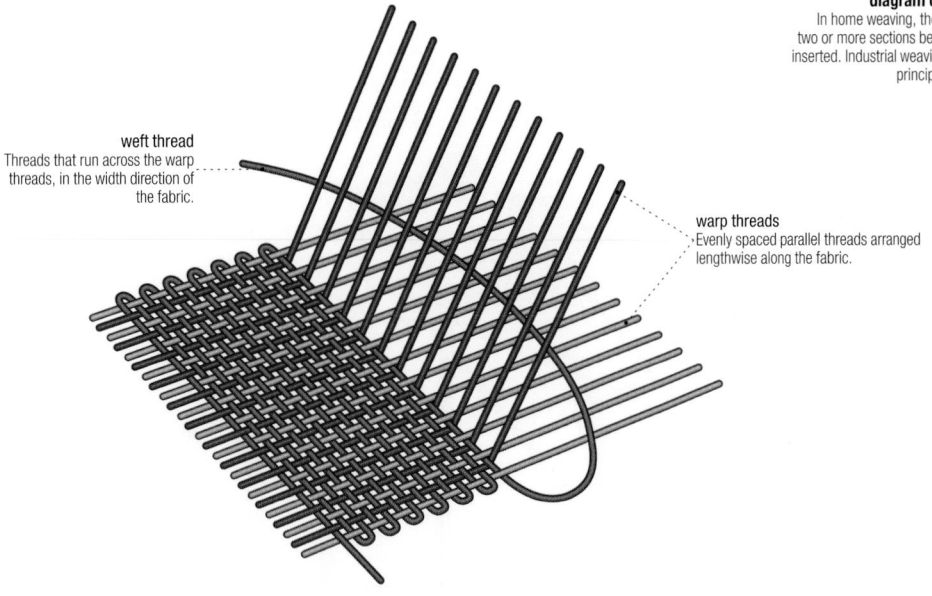

diagram of weaving principle
In home weaving, the warp is separated into two or more sections between which the weft is inserted. Industrial weaving is based on a similar principle but is more complex.

weft thread
Threads that run across the warp threads, in the width direction of the fabric.

warp threads
Evenly spaced parallel threads arranged lengthwise along the fabric.

basic weaves
The principal types of weave.

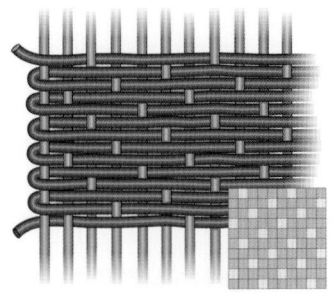

satin weave
Widely spaced weave forming a smooth surface; here, the weft thread passes over four warp threads and then under one.

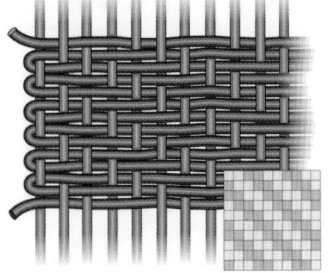

twill weave
Mesh forming oblique lines in the fabric; here, the weft thread passes over and then under two warp threads, and is staggered by one thread per row.

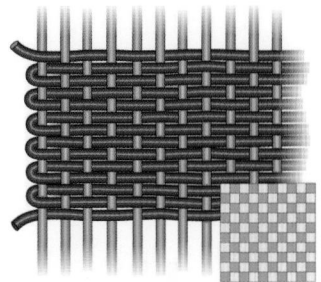

plain weave
Mesh forming a check pattern in the fabric; the weft thread passes over and under a warp thread, and is staggered by one thread per row.

other techniques

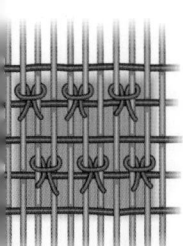

knot
Woolen yarn wound around two warp threads; its ends form the piles on a carpet.

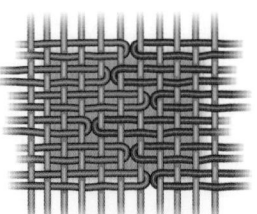

hatching
Technique used to mix colors: a weft thread enters a different color zone, interlocks with a warp thread and comes back to the original color zone.

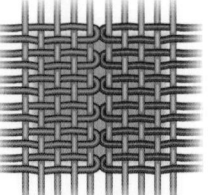

slit
The space where the thread colors change; weft threads and warp threads interlock and then return to their respective zones.

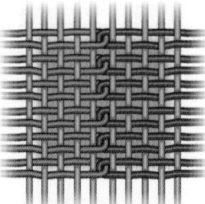

interlock
Section where the colors change; two weft threads of a different color interlock and then return to their respective zones.

pottery

Art of creating objects from clay, which is shaped by hand and hardened in a kiln.

throwing
Process of using a potter's wheel to shape clay by hand to create an object.

ball of clay
Fine-grained material that is soft and plastic when moist; it contains silica and aluminum usually along with other minerals.

potter's wheel
Apparatus used to rotate a ball of clay so that it can be formed into an object using the hands and special tools; a nonmotorized version (kick wheel) is powered by the feet.

bat
Disk placed on the wheel head so that the pieces created can be easily removed.

wheel head
Turning plate controlled by the flywheel; the work in progress is placed on it.

seat

shaft
Metal rod that connects the flywheel to the wheel head, transferring the rotation movement.

footrest

flywheel
Large plate controlling the rotation of the wheel head; it is turned and stopped by the feet.

pottery tools

stilt
Stand on which an object is placed during firing to evenly distribute the heat around it and prevent the glazed surface from fusing to the kiln.

wooden modeling tools
Tools used especially to smooth, shape and decorate clay.

clay cutter
Tool used to cut blocks of clay and remove finished pieces from the turning wheel.

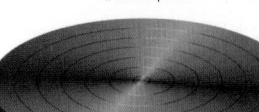

needle tool
Tool used to pierce clay to trim an uneven top edge or carve designs on the surface. It is also used to score a piece of clay to be attached to another piece of clay.

banding wheel
Hand-controlled turning plate used for processes that do not require continuous rotation speed, in particular for decorating a thrown piece.

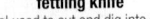

fettling knife
Tool used to cut and dig into clay.

ribs
Wooden, metal or plastic tool used to smooth and shape the surface of an object during throwing.

trimming tool
Tool used especially to remove excess clay from a still-damp, thrown piece.

pyrometric cone
Small ceramic pyramid with a known melting point; it is used to determine the temperature of the firing chamber.

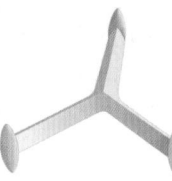

pottery

slab building
...cess by which clay is flattened ...ith a roller, cut into slabs and ...oined together and shaped by ...d to create objects without the use of a potter's wheel.

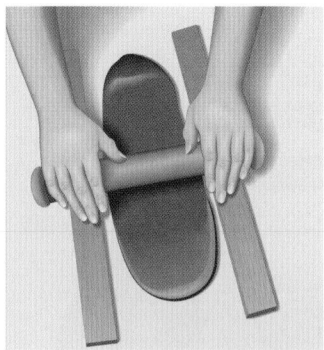

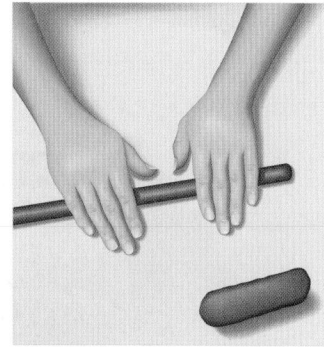

coiling
Process by which long rolls of clay are stacked and joined together and shaped by hand to create objects without the use of a potter's wheel.

firing
Process by which clay is hardened by heating.

electric kiln
Apparatus that uses electricity to produce heat; it is used for firing clay.

lid
Plate that closes the firing chamber.

refractory brick
Brick that can withstand very high temperatures without deforming.

lid brace
Arm used to keep the lid open.

heating element
Electric unit that heats up when current passes through it, releasing heat required to harden the clay.

damper
Hole through which vapor from the wet clay escapes during firing.

manual/automatic mode
Button used to select the manual or automatic mode.

timer
Device used to control the length of time the kiln is heated.

electrical inlet
Device used to draw and control the electric current.

hinge
Articulated fastener that raises and lowers the lid.

firing chamber
Compartment lined with refractory bricks in which the pieces are placed for firing.

temperature control knob
Knob used to select the firing temperature.

indicator light
Light indicating when the desired temperature has been reached.

connecting cable
Flexible cord containing conductors; it connects the apparatus to the electric circuit.

bobbin lace

Openwork fabric created by interlacing thread on bobbins, using a pillow to secure the model to be reproduced.

pillow
Frame used for making lace.

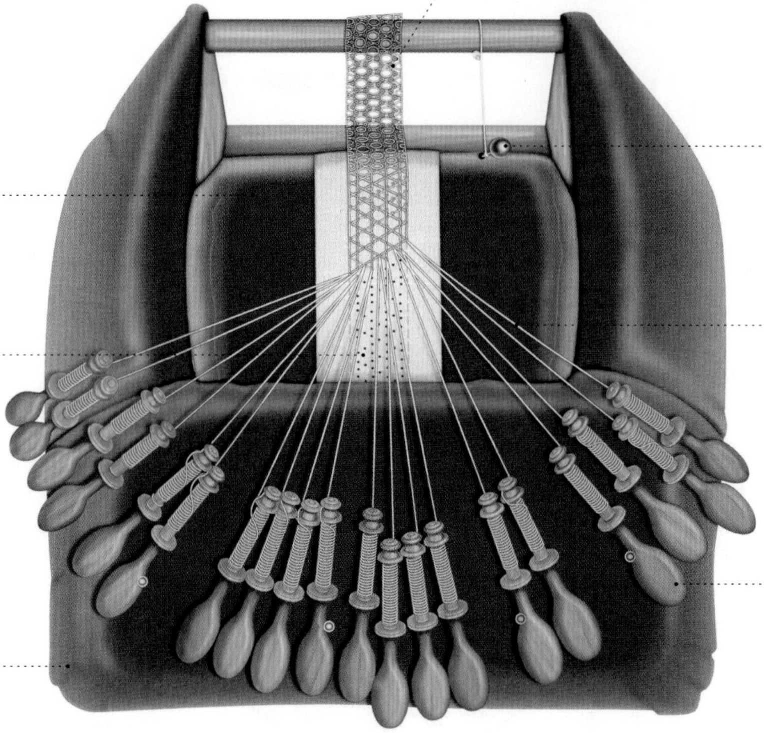

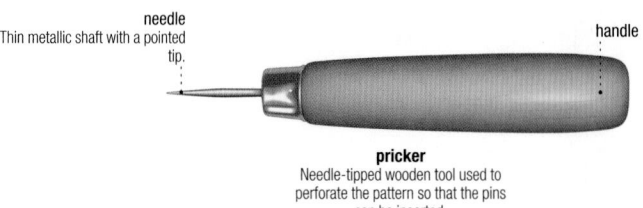

lace
Openwork fabric created by interlacing thread.

stop
Knob that prevents the cylinder from rotating.

revolving cylinder
Movable part that secures the pattern.

thread
Thin strand of textile matter out of which lace is made.

pattern
Design transferred to a board by perforating it with holes; pins are inserted in the holes to create the pattern.

bobbin
Wooden tool on which thread is wo to make lace.

pillow
Stuffed piece used to spread out the bobbins.

needle
Thin metallic shaft with a pointed tip.

handle

pricker
Needle-tipped wooden tool used to perforate the pattern so that the pins can be inserted.

head
The end of the bobbin where the thread is tied into a stop knot.

spool
Shank on which the thread is wound.

handle
Piece of wood held between two fingers to handle the bobbin.

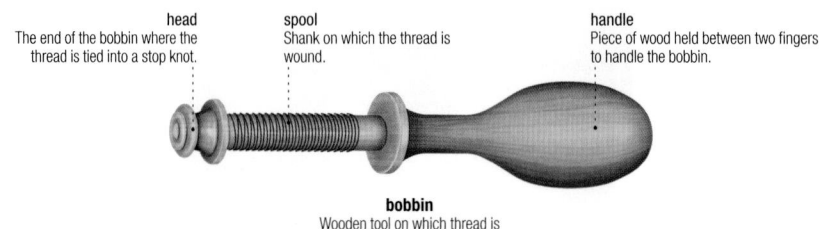

bobbin
Wooden tool on which thread is wound to make lace.

stained glass

Technique for assembling pieces of glass for ornamentation. The oldest technique uses lead and glass together.

solder
Metal rod (lead and tin), that is heated and liquefied and used to join the intersections of the lead came.

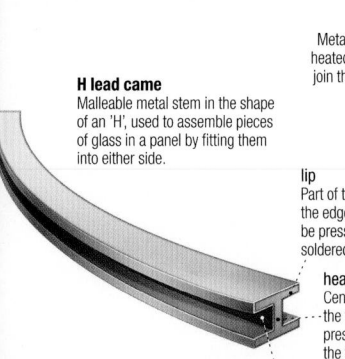

H lead came
Malleable metal stem in the shape of an 'H', used to assemble pieces of glass in a panel by fitting them into either side.

lip
Part of the came that covers the edge of the glass and must be pressed down before being soldered.

U lead came
Malleable metal stem in the shape of an 'U', used in some cases to surround the outside edge of a stained-glass project.

stained glass
Colored glass that is cut into various shapes which are joined using lead came and solder.

heart
Central vertical section of the came separating the two pieces of glass, the edges of which are pressed up against it. Its height corresponds to the thickness of the glass.

channel
Trough of the came into which the piece of glass is inserted.

soldering iron
Tool with a metal point that is heated and used to attach the lead cames where they intersect.

tip
Detachable end of the soldering iron, used to heat the solder to liquefy it before use.

sponge
Spongy material kept moist and used to regularly clean the tip of the soldering iron in order to prevent corrosion induced by tin residue.

sponge
Spongy material used to keep the grinder bit moist by absorbing liquid contained in the reservoir.

diamond grinder
Electric tool for polishing the edges of a piece of glass. This refining step comes after the small glass fragments have been removed using pliers.

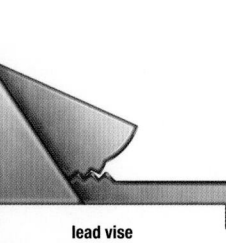

lead vise
Tool into which one end of a came is placed while the other end is grasped in the runner in order to stretch it.

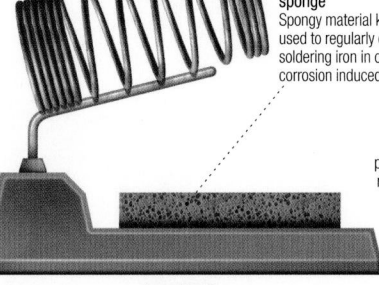

iron stand
Iron piece on which the hot soldering iron can be safely rested.

splash guard
Piece blocking flying glass particles produced by grinding. It is nevertheless recommended to wear safety goggles.

diamond grinder bit
Abrasive cylinder that polishes glass as it spins.

glass cutter
Tool with a hard metal roller for cutting the glass. The pieces on either side of the cut are then detached using pliers.

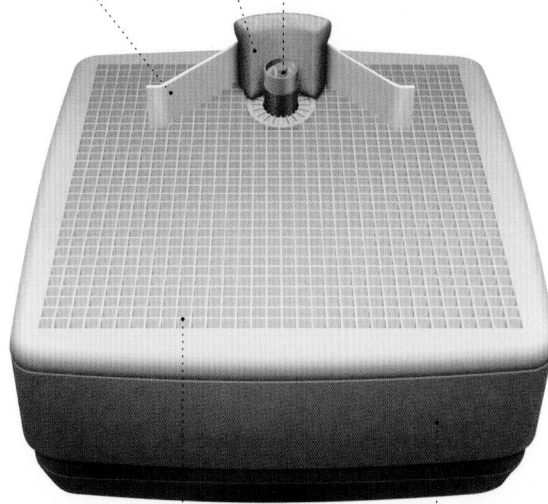

lead knife
Knife with a curved blade used to manipulate and cut the lead came. Is also used as a hammer.

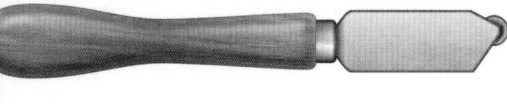

runner
Tool used to stretch the came. An adjusting knob is used to set it to the width of the stem.

work surface
Grid which is pierced with holes that let through glass dust and shards that turn into paste in contact with water.

removable reservoir
Container that can be removed during cleaning and to be refilled with water, to which coolant is added.

COMMUNICATIONS

All the auditory and visual signals humans use to transmit messages, either directly or through channels and equipment.

major language families

Language families are grouped by their related phonetics, grammars and lexicons, or by a shared history.

geographic distribution

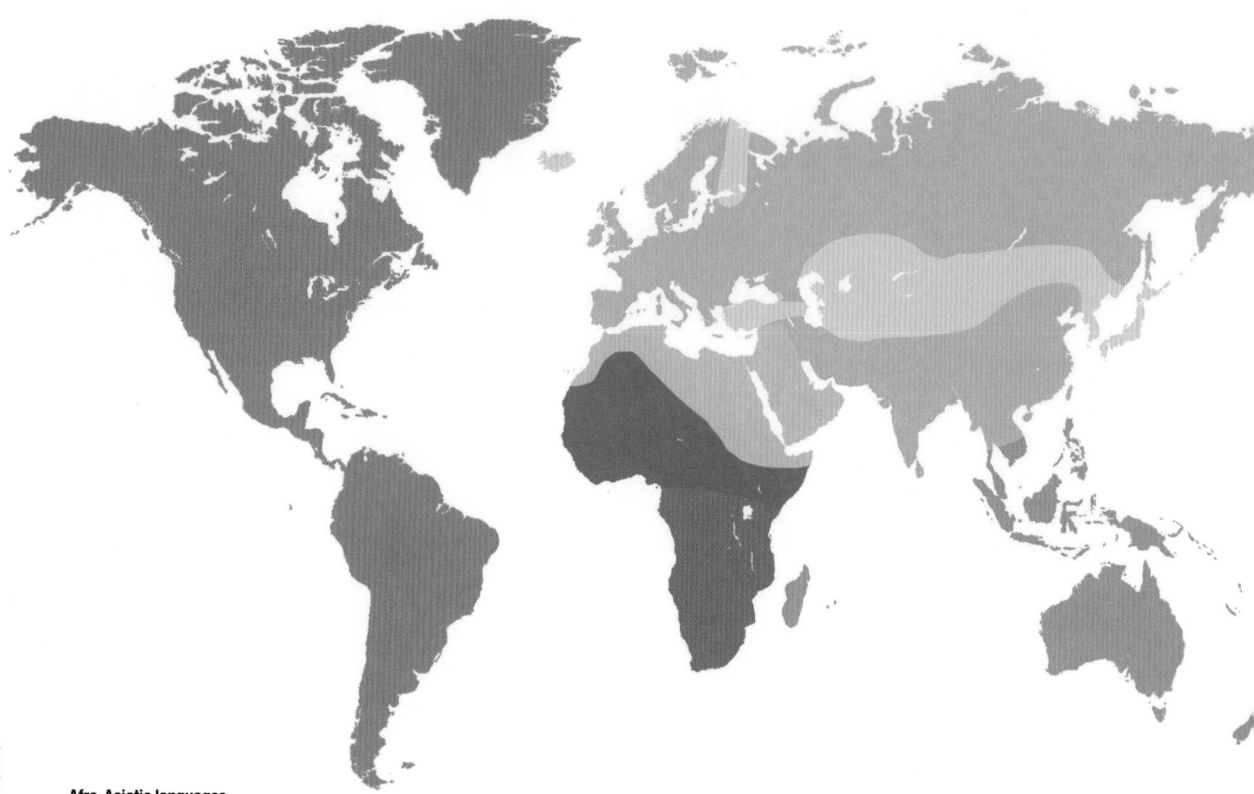

Afro-Asiatic languages
Family of some 120 living languages and several dead languages that are associated with major civilizations (Egyptian, Babylonian, Phoenician).

Arabic
Language of the Koran as well as the Afro-Asiatic language spoken by the greatest number of individuals; it is concentrated mainly in North Africa and the Middle East.

Hebrew
One of the official languages of the State of Israel; it is associated with the Jewish faith and people.

Aramaic
Spoken throughout the Middle East since antiquity; it continues to be spoken in some regions of Turkey, Syria and Iraq.

Amharic
Language spoken mainly in Ethiopia, where it has the status of official language.

Berber
Language of the Berber people of North Africa and spoken mainly in Morocco and Algeria.

Hausa
One of the most widespread languages in western Africa; it is spoken mainly in Niger and Nigeria.

Central African languages
Grouping of some 900 languages that are spoken mostly in central and western Africa.

Fulani
Language spoken in west Africa, especially in Senegal, Guinea, Nigeria and Cameroon.

Wolof
Language spoken in the western part of Africa, including in Senegal and Gambia.

Bambara
Language spoken in Mali and in some neighboring countries, including in Senegal, Guinea and Ivory Coast.

Yoruba
Language spoken mainly in Nigeria, Benin and Togo.

Bantu languages
Family of over 500 languages spoken in the southern half of the African continent.

Swahili
Bantu language spoken by the greatest number of individuals as a second language; it is concentrated mostly in eastern Africa.

Kirundi
Official language of Burundi; it is very similar to Kinyarwanda.

Kinyarwanda
Language spoken mainly in Rwanda.

Lingala
Language spoken mainly as a second language in Congo and the Democratic Republic of the Congo.

Zulu
Language spoken by some people in South Africa and in several neighboring countries such as Swaziland and Mozambique.

Southeast Asian languages
Grouping of languages spoken in Southeast Asia; they are spoken by abo one-quarter of the world's population.

Chinese
Family of languages belonging to the s writing system using ideograms; it incl Mandarin, the most widely spoken lang in the world.

Thai
Official language of Thailand; it is also spoken in certain regions of Laos and Myanmar.

Vietnamese
Language spoken mainly in Vietnam; it usually written using a modified versior the Latin alphabet called "quoc ngu".

Burmese
Language spoken mainly in Myanmar (formerly Burma), where it enjoys the st of official language.

Tibetan
Language spoken in Tibet and certain regions of Nepal and Bhutan; the writte alphabet originated in India.

major language families

Indo-European languages

Group of languages (there are more than 200) sharing a common ancestral language as deduced by a historical comparison of the grammars of the present-day languages. Latin and ancient Greek are Indo-European.

Romance languages
All the European languages derived from Latin; some have spread throughout the world.

French
Language of France and some neighboring countries that spread with the arrival of the French or Belgians to North America, Africa and Asia.

Spanish
Language of Spain that was introduced by the Spanish to most of the Americas (18 countries) and one African country (Equatorial Guinea).

Catalan
Official language of Catalonia, Valencia and Andorra; it is also spoken in the south of France.

Portuguese
Language of Portugal; it spread with the arrival of the Portuguese to Brazil, Africa and Asia.

Italian
National language of Italy and one canton of Switzerland (Tessin).

Romanian
National language of Romania.

Ural-Altaic languages
Grouping of some 100 languages spoken in central and eastern Asia, the Middle East and northern and central Europe.

Japanese
Language spoken throughout the Japanese archipelago; it is written using ideograms or syllabic characters.

Korean
Language spoken mainly in Korea; its lexicon includes many words of Chinese origin.

Mongolian
Official language of Mongolia; it is also spoken by some communities in China and Russia.

Turkish
Official language of Turkey; it is written using the Latin alphabet.

Hungarian
Language spoken in Hungary.

Finnish
With Swedish, one of the national languages of Finland.

Germanic languages
All the languages derived from an early Indo-European dialect, which has since disappeared, as deduced from similarities observed among the languages.

English
Language of England that spread with the British Empire to North America, India, Asia, Oceania and eastern and southern Africa.

German
National language of Germany, Austria and the greatest part of Switzerland.

Dutch
Language spoken mainly in the Netherlands and by the Flemish community in Belgium.

Danish
Scandinavian language spoken mainly in Denmark.

Swedish
Scandinavian language spoken mainly in Sweden and Finland.

Norwegian
Scandinavian language spoken mainly in Norway.

Icelandic
National language of Iceland; it is characterized by its great stability since the Middle Ages.

Yiddish
Language of the Ashkenazi Jews of Europe; it is a product of the fusion of Hebrew with elements of Germanic and Slavic languages.

Malayo-Polynesian languages
Family grouping some 850 languages that are spread over a vast area, including Madagascar, parts of Southeast Asia and the Pacific.

Indonesian
National language of Indonesia; it is closely related to Malay.

Tagalog
Language spoken mainly in the Philippines, where it has the status of an official language.

Malagasy
Language spoken mainly in Madagascar, but also in Comoros and Réunion.

Samoan
Language spoken in the Samoan archipelago of Polynesia in the central Pacific.

Celtic languages
Widely spoken in western Europe throughout antiquity, these languages declined progressively and are found today in only a few regions.

Breton
Language spoken in the west of Brittany (France).

Welsh
One of the official languages of Wales (United Kingdom).

Scottish Gaelic
Language closely related to Irish that is spoken mostly in Scotland (United Kingdom).

Irish
One of the official languages of the Republic of Ireland; it is also spoken in Northern Ireland (United Kingdom).

isolated languages
Some modern Indo-European languages cannot be classified into any subgroup.

Greek
The national language of Greece is directly descended from ancient Greek; its origin can be traced back several centuries before the Common Era.

Albanian
Language spoken mainly in Albania and in some neighboring regions.

Armenian
Very old language that is spoken in the Caucasus region, mainly in Armenia.

Tahitian
Language spoken in French Polynesia.

Hawaiian
Language spoken mainly in Hawaii (United States).

Maori
One of the official languages of New Zealand.

Slavic languages
Group of languages concentrated in Eastern Europe and Russia; they derive from a common extinct Slavic language.

Czech
National language of the Czech Republic that is closely related to Slovak.

Slovak
National language of Slovakia; both Slovak and Czech use the Latin alphabet.

Polish
National language of Poland; it is fairly close to Czech and Slovak.

Russian
National language of Russia that is also widely spoken in the former USSR; Russian is written with the Cyrillic alphabet.

Ukrainian
Language related to Russian that is spoken mainly in Ukraine and in several neighboring states.

Bulgarian
National language of Bulgaria that is written with the Cyrillic alphabet; it is related to Slovene and Serbo-Croatian.

Slovene
Language spoken mainly in Slovenia and written with the Latin alphabet.

Serbian and Croatian
Serbians and Montenegrins use the Cyrillic alphabet while Croatians and Bosnians use the Latin alphabet.

Oceanian languages
All the languages spoken in Oceania; they usually have few ties among themselves or with other language families.

Melanesian languages
Languages spoken in Melanesia, a group of archipelagos in the South Pacific that includes mainly New Guinea, Vanuatu, the Fiji Islands and New Caledonia.

Papuan languages
There are over 800 Papuan languages and dialects; they are spoken mainly on the island of New Guinea.

Australian aboriginal languages
There are a few hundred languages associated with the indigenous peoples of Australia; many are barely spoken today or have disappeared completely.

Indo-Iranian languages
Spoken in Asia and the Middle East, they number the largest group of speakers among all Indo-European language groups.

Persian
Language spoken mainly in Iran and Afghanistan; it is written using the Arabic alphabet.

Urdu
Language spoken mainly in Pakistan and Northern India; it is very similar to Hindi but is written using the Arabic alphabet.

Hindi
Indian language spoken by the largest number of individuals; it is written using the Devanagari alphabet, which is common to several languages derived from Sanskrit.

Amerindian languages
Several hundred languages are associated with the indigenous peoples of the Americas; several are barely spoken today or have disappeared completely.

Inuktitut
Language of the Inuit who live in Alaska, the Canadian North and Greenland.

Cree
Algonquian language associated with the Cree, the largest Amerindian community in Canada, who live in the area between Alberta and Labrador.

Innu
Algonquian language associated with the Montagnais, who live in Eastern Canada, mostly in Quebec (North Shore of the St. Lawrence) and in Labrador.

Navajo
Native language spoken by the Navajo people of the Southwestern United States (Arizona, New Mexico).

Nahuatl
Language of the Aztec Empire that is still widely spoken today in certain regions of central Mexico.

Mayan
Family of languages of the Maya Empire that is spoken in certain regions of southern Mexico, especially the Yucatan Peninsula.

Quechua
Language of the Inca Empire and the language spoken today by the largest number of Amerindians in countries such as Peru, Ecuador and Bolivia.

Aymara
Language spoken mainly in Bolivia and Peru.

Guarani
Language accorded official status in Paraguay; it is also spoken in certain regions of Argentina and Bolivia.

writing

All conventional graphic characters used to represent thoughts and ideas on various media (paper, digital screen, etc.).

traditional writing instruments
Tools and media used in the past or in certain areas for many generations to create written documents.

quill
Large feather with a hollow stalk (calamus) that is sharpened to a point and dipped in ink to write; it was used in the Middle Ages through the early 1800s.

Roman metal pen
Metal writing instrument devised by the Romans in ancient times; it is the ancestor of the modern metal pen, which appeared in the 19th century.

lead pencil
Pencil made of lead with a decorative end; it was first used in the Middle Ages and was later replaced by the graphite lead pencil.

cane pen
Instrument that was used from antiquity through the Middle Ages to write on papyrus and parchment; it remains the traditional instrument of Arabic calligraphy.

stylus
Pointed instrument used by the ancient Greeks to etch wax tablets; the flattened end was used to erase etching.

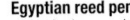

writing brush
Natural or synthetic bristles set into a handle and dipped in ink to write; it has been used for Chinese calligraphy for 4,000 years.

Egyptian reed pen
Small reed that is sharpened to a point and used to draw hieroglyphics on clay tablets or to write in ink on papyrus.

papyrus
Thin paper made from the Cyperus papyrus plant; used in ancient Egypt as the chief writing material.

wax tablet
Wooden surface with raised edges onto which a layer of wax is poured; used since ancient times for writing and erasing characters using a stylus.

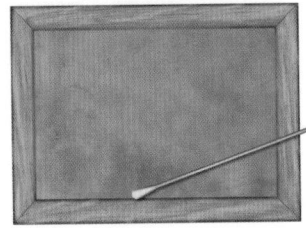

rice paper
Slightly translucent writing paper traditionally made from the rice plant; used for centuries in China, Japan, and Korea.

modern writing instruments
Tools and media currently used to create written documents.

clip
Curved metal bar that attaches the ballpoint pen to a pocket.

cartridge
Small reservoir containing ink and ending in a point.

joint

ballpoint pen
Instrument invented at the beginning of the 20th century; the writing tip holds a small rotating ball.

point
Tip that contains the ball bearing used to deposit ink from the cartridge onto the writing surface.

spring
Elastic metal part that compresses to push the refill out and relaxes to retract it.

thrust device
Protruding part that locks the thrust tube in a forward or retracted position.

thrust tube
Part that is activated by the push button; it pushes out or retracts the writing tip when pressure is applied.

push button
Button controlling the me that advances and retract cartridge.

section of the point

ball bearing
Small metal ball in the point of the pen; when turned, it deposits ink from the cartridge onto the writing surface.

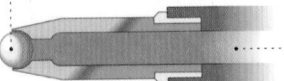

ink
Black or colored liquid used for writing.

refill
Cartridge that is inserted into the body of a ballpoint pen to refill the ink.

writing

fountain pen
Instrument with a metal nib that is attached to a body containing an ink reservoir, usually in the form of a cartridge.

cap
Screw end that covers the nib when the pen is not in use.

nib
Curved writing point fitted with a device to supply ink.

barrel
Part that supports the nib and contains the reservoir that supplies the ink.

air hole
Opening through which air enters the pen to maintain atmospheric pressure.

marker
Felt-tipped color felt pen of variable size.

pencil
Writing instrument made up of a casing of soft wood around a graphite lead; it can be sharpened easily.

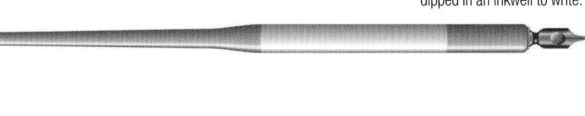

mechanical pencil
Instrument that is made up of a slender tube containing one piece of lead; pressing the push button moves the lead forward.

steel pen
Curved point mounted on a handle; it is dipped in an inkwell to write.

highlighter
Colored marker with transparent ink used to mark important portions of a text.

paper
Flat, thin surface made from plant fibers; usually whitish in color.

COMMUNICATIONS

examples of writing systems
Writing systems: codified set of symbols and characters used by a community to communicate through writing.

abcd

Latin characters
Writing system derived from an alphabet of Roman origin. Used to write most European and Western languages.

اب ت ث

Arabic script
Writing system used to write Arabic and adapted for other languages (such as Persian). Characters are read from right to left.

אבגד

Hebrew characters
Writing system used for Hebrew and Yiddish. Characters are read from right to left.

Cyrillic characters
Writing system used for many Slavic languages (as Russian) and for some non-Slavic languages influenced by Russian.

汉字

Chinese characters
Writing system of the Chinese language made up of graphic symbols for words or ideas.

αβγδ

Greek characters
One of the oldest writing systems, used mainly for the Greek language. Its letters are also used as scientific and mathematical symbols.

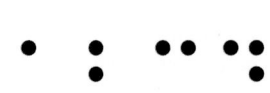

braille
Writing system composed of raised dots on a flat surface, read by visually impaired people using their fingers.

typography

General term for the graphic representation of characters printed on a material or surface, with or without the use of letterpress.

characters of a font
Characters of type that make up the various fonts and are divided into two main types of characters: serif and sans serif.

sans serif type
Type in which the characters lack serifs and generally have strokes of uniform thickness.

abcdefghijklmnopqrstuvwxyz   0123456789

letters   numerals

serif type
Type in which the characters have serifs, short lines extending from the ends of their strokes.

abcdefghijklmnopqrstuvwxyz   0123456

shape of characters
In printing, uppercase characters, small capitals and lowercase characters can be straight (roman) or slanted (italic).

ABCDEF
uppercase
Capital letter used mostly at the beginning of a sentence and for proper names.

ABCDEF
small capital
Capital letter that is the same height as a lowercase letter and is used mainly to write symbols.

abcdef
lowercase
Smaller version of a letter that is generally used for most text wherever a capital letter is not required.

abcdef
italic
Type style with characters slan to the right; it is used mostly identify titles, quotations an foreign words.

weight
Relative thickness of the strokes of a character; the medium and bold weights are the most commonly used.

a
light

a
semi-bold

a
extra-bold

extra-light

a
medium

a
bold

a
black

set width
Relative width of a character.

a
condensed

a
narrow

a
normal

a
wide

a
extended

leading
Vertical space separating two lines of characters; its precise value is proportional to the size of the characters.

Lorem ipsum dolor sit amet, consectetuer adipiscing elit, sed
simple spacing

Lorem ipsum dolor sit amet, consectetuer adipiscing elit, sed
1.5 spacing

Lorem ipsum dolor sit amet, consectetuer adipiscing elit, sed
double spacing

position of a charac
With the exception of superiors inferiors, the characters of a text are us aligned along a horizontal base

H_2SO_4
inferior
Small character placed below the baseline and to the right of another character; it is used mostly in chemical and mathematical formulas.

superior
Small character placed above the right or left of another cha it is sometimes used in abbrev and also to mark footnote

symbols

Conventional characters representing a thing or a concept.

diacritic symbols
Symbols added to a letter; they usually change its pronunciation.

grave accent

acute accent

cedilla

umlaut

circumflex accent

tilde

miscellaneous symbols
Symbols are standardized marks used to refer concisely to a thing, a being or a concept.

registered trademark
certifying that the preceding word has ...n legally registered as a trademark.

copyright
Symbol at the beginning of a work attesting to the author's legal rights to that work; it is used to prevent plagiarism or reproduction without authorization.

ampersand
Symbol representing the word "and"; it is often used in company names.

at sign
Symbol used to introduce the domain name in an email address.

asterisk

punctuation marks
All the standardized marks used to divide a text in order to make it more legible.

dash

hyphen

period

semicolon

comma

ellipses points

colon

apostrophe
Symbol used to indicate the ...ossessive, substitute for letters ...nd numerals that are omitted, or sometimes form a plural word.

braces

parentheses

square brackets

slash

exclamation point

question mark

single quotation marks
Marks used in pairs to indicate a concept or word of special significance or to enclose a quotation within a quotation.

quotation marks
Marks shaped like inverted or regular commas and used in pairs especially to enclose quoted material.

guillemet
Marks used as quotation marks in French writing.

COMMUNICATIONS

postal service network

Infrastructure with which the national postal service delivers the mail entrusted to it.

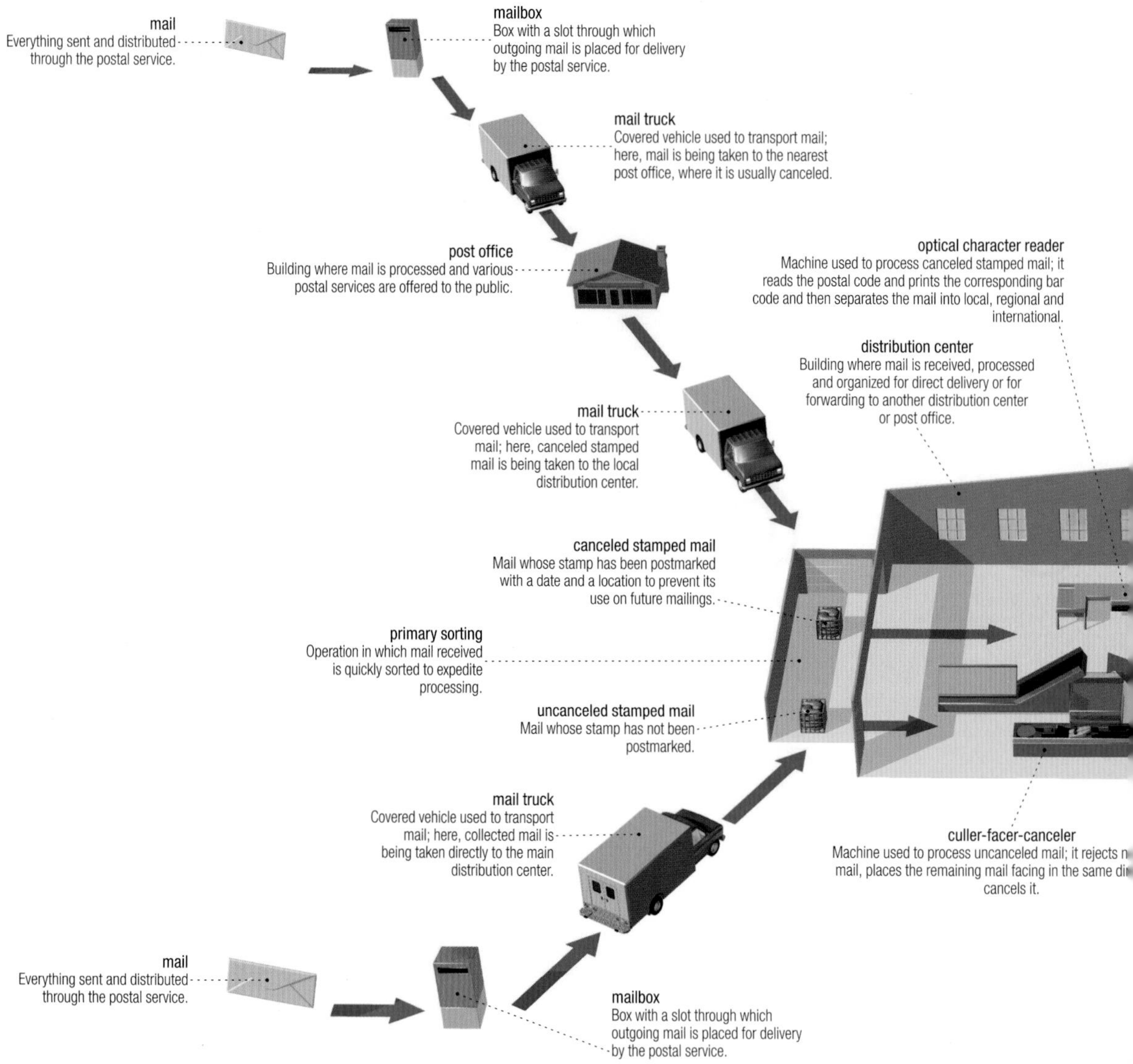
mail
Everything sent and distributed through the postal service.
mailbox
Box with a slot through which outgoing mail is placed for delivery by the postal service.
mail truck
Covered vehicle used to transport mail; here, mail is being taken to the nearest post office, where it is usually canceled.
post office
Building where mail is processed and various postal services are offered to the public.
optical character reader
Machine used to process canceled stamped mail; it reads the postal code and prints the corresponding bar code and then separates the mail into local, regional and international.
distribution center
Building where mail is received, processed and organized for direct delivery or for forwarding to another distribution center or post office.
mail truck
Covered vehicle used to transport mail; here, canceled stamped mail is being taken to the local distribution center.
canceled stamped mail
Mail whose stamp has been postmarked with a date and a location to prevent its use on future mailings.
primary sorting
Operation in which mail received is quickly sorted to expedite processing.
uncanceled stamped mail
Mail whose stamp has not been postmarked.
mail truck
Covered vehicle used to transport mail; here, collected mail is being taken directly to the main distribution center.
culler-facer-canceler
Machine used to process uncanceled mail; it rejects n
mail, places the remaining mail facing in the same di
cancels it.
mail
Everything sent and distributed through the postal service.
mailbox
Box with a slot through which outgoing mail is placed for delivery by the postal service.

COMMUNICATIONS

mail
Everything sent and distributed through the postal service.

.50 EURO

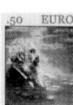

postage stamp
Small adhesive label of varying denominations that is issued by a postal service and used to indicate postage paid.

B Thompson
bracostrasse 35
3052 ES Rotterdam
Netherlands
Phillip Schuman
2002 Euro avenue
Montreal, Canada
H0H 1H1

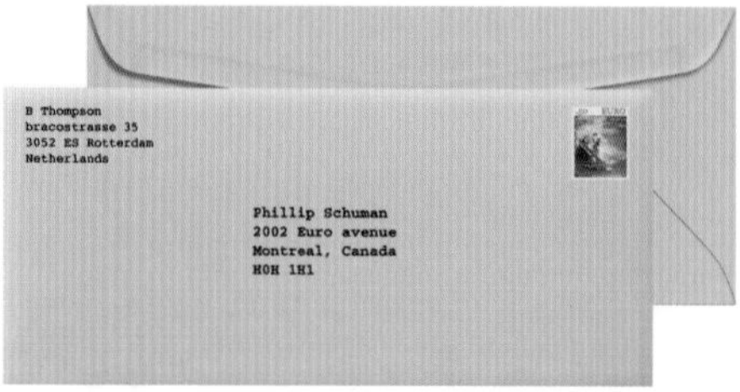

letter
Written message that is inserted into an envelope and addressed to a recipient.

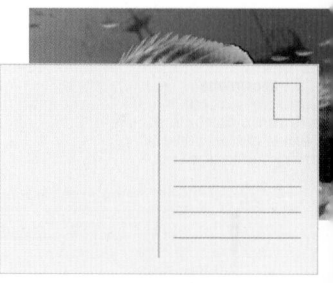

postcard
Photograph or illustration that is printed on flexible cardbo
and has space on the back to write a message and an
address.

postal service network

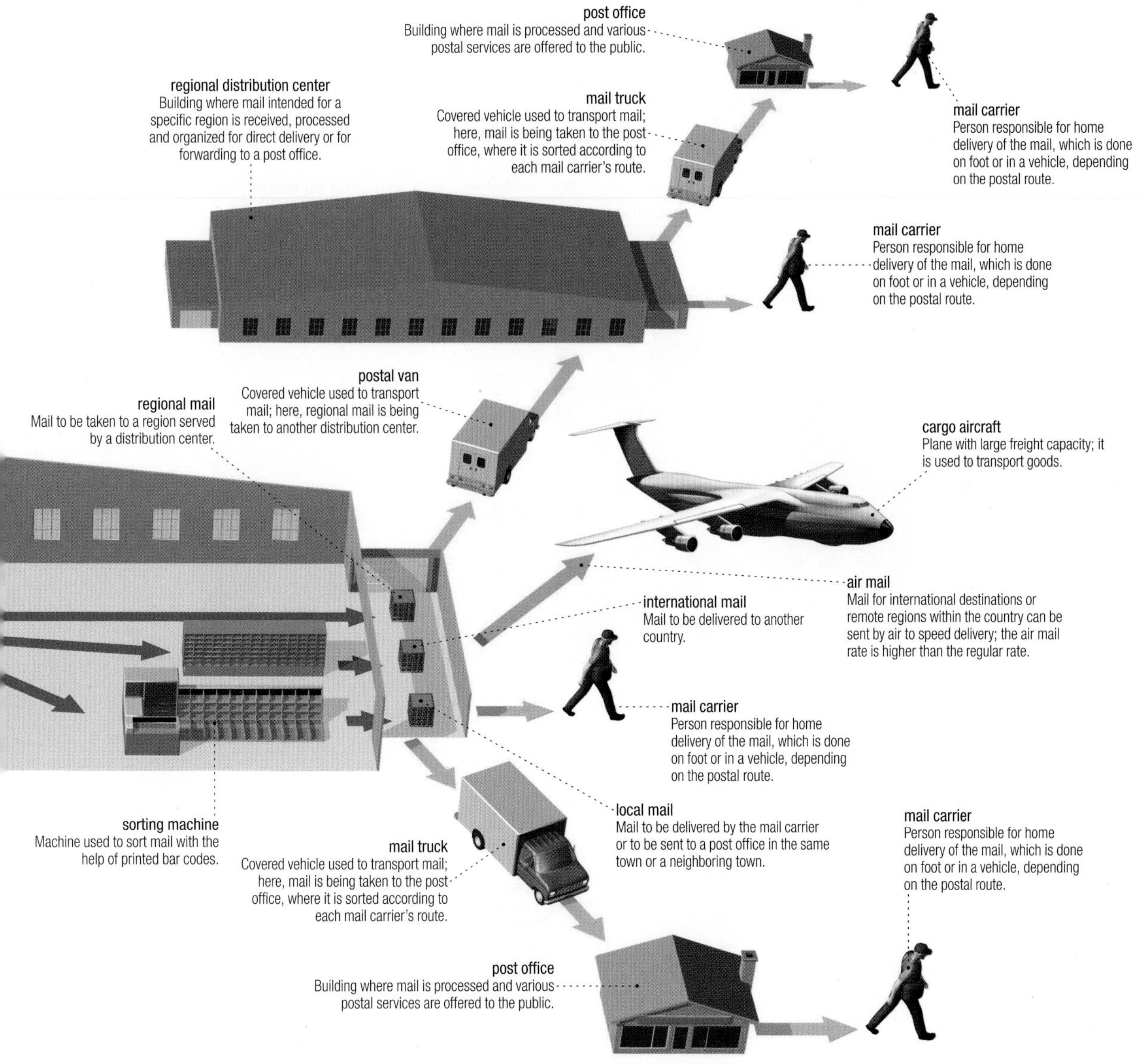
post office
Building where mail is processed and various postal services are offered to the public.
regional distribution center
Building where mail intended for a specific region is received, processed and organized for direct delivery or for forwarding to a post office.
mail truck
Covered vehicle used to transport mail; here, mail is being taken to the post office, where it is sorted according to each mail carrier's route.
mail carrier
Person responsible for home delivery of the mail, which is done on foot or in a vehicle, depending on the postal route.
mail carrier
Person responsible for home delivery of the mail, which is done on foot or in a vehicle, depending on the postal route.
regional mail
Mail to be taken to a region served by a distribution center.
postal van
Covered vehicle used to transport mail; here, regional mail is being taken to another distribution center.
cargo aircraft
Plane with large freight capacity; it is used to transport goods.
international mail
Mail to be delivered to another country.
air mail
Mail for international destinations or remote regions within the country can be sent by air to speed delivery; the air mail rate is higher than the regular rate.
mail carrier
Person responsible for home delivery of the mail, which is done on foot or in a vehicle, depending on the postal route.
sorting machine
Machine used to sort mail with the help of printed bar codes.
mail truck
Covered vehicle used to transport mail; here, mail is being taken to the post office, where it is sorted according to each mail carrier's route.
local mail
Mail to be delivered by the mail carrier or to be sent to a post office in the same town or a neighboring town.
mail carrier
Person responsible for home delivery of the mail, which is done on foot or in a vehicle, depending on the postal route.
post office
Building where mail is processed and various postal services are offered to the public.

COMMUNICATIONS

mail

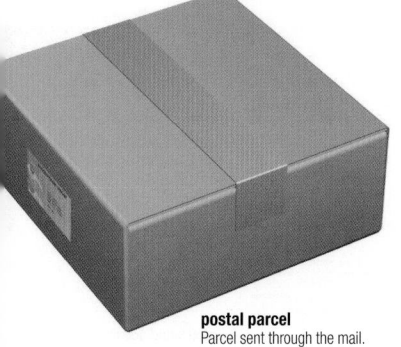

postal parcel
Parcel sent through the mail.

1002002
(BULK)
Phillip Schuman
2002 Euro avenue
Montreal, Canada

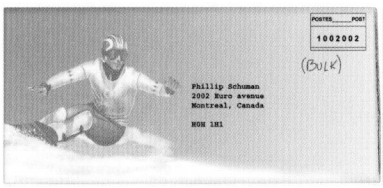

bulk mail
Mail consisting of a large number of letters mailed at the same time by the same sender, usually at a reduced postage rate.

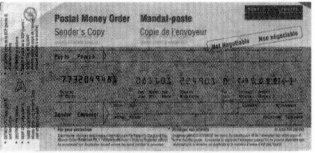

Postal Money Order
Mandat-poste
Sender's Copy
Copie de l'envoyeur

postal money order
A certificate issued by the postal service by which a sender is able to pay a specified sum to a recipient at another location.

newspaper

Usually daily publication whose main purpose is to report and comment on the latest news of society, politics, the arts, sports and other areas of interest.

layout
Arrangement of different elements constituting a newspaper page.

heading
Upper portion of the front page; it usually features the nameplate, the volume number and the date.

section
All the pages of a newspaper that are devoted to one subject such as the arts, the economy, sports, tourism or finance.

article
Stand-alone text forming a whole; it usually presents information, explanation or commentary.

literary supplement
Separate publication dealing with books and authors that is inserted into a newspaper on a regular basis or from time to time.

tabloid
Publication whose format is about half the size of a regular newspaper and contains news in a condensed form.

color supplement
Separate publication that is inserted into a newspaper regularly or from time to time; it is printed in color and often on glossy paper.

columns
Articles published regularly that present information on a given subject.

cartoon
Humorous or satirical drawing; it is usually accompanied by a caption and comments on a news event.

editorial
In-depth article that reflects the collective viewpoint of a newspaper's editorial board.

lead
Short text at the beginning of an article that introduces it or summarizes its contents.

letters to the editor
Part of the newspaper where readers' opinions on topics of general interest are published.

rule
Line of varying thickness used to separate columns, articles and different graphic elements.

Op-Ed article
Article appearing next to or on the page opposite to the editorial and expressing an individual's point of view.

advertisement
Message paid for by an advertiser to inform readers about a business, product or service.

front page
First page of the newspaper.

magazine
A section of the newspaper that resembles a magazine; it is usually abundantly illustrated and deals with subjects for a mass audience.

index
Brief summary of the contents of a newspaper, usually in the form of a table of contents.

subhead
Secondary title that separates and introduces the various parts of an article.

column
The vertical sections of a page; they are separated by white space or a rule.

masthead
Space that usually contains information about the newspaper such as its address, main contributors and subscription information.

obituaries
Listing of death notices and anniversaries of deaths, cards of thanks and remembrances.

nameplate
Title of the newspaper presented in a specific graphic style.

banner
Large headline appearing immediately below the heading and running across multiple columns.

front picture

caption
Short explanatory text accompanying a photograph, image or illustration.

kicker
Short text appearing above the headline that puts the article in context or highlights certain key points.

headline
Word or group of words in large print that introduces an article.

deck
Short block of text positioned under a headline and summarizing the article that follows.

news items
Accounts of various events with no central unifying theme such as accidents, natural disasters and crimes.

shorts
Short untitled informative texts.

column
Regularly published article that presents the comments of one author (reporter or personality) on a chosen subject.

television program schedule

restaurant review
Article in which a reporter gives a personal evaluation of a restaurant.

photo credit line
Mandatory mention of the name of the photographer and the individual holding the rights to the photograph used to illustrate an article or a publication.

classified advertisements
Short ads that are placed by individuals and grouped into categories according to the goods or services offered or sought.

film cameras

Devices composed mainly of a dark chamber and an optic system used to record an image on light-sensitive film.

disposable camera
Small lightweight easy-to-use camera containing a film; it is designed to be used only once.

medium-format SLR (6 X 6)
Midsize camera with interchangeable lenses; it produces 6 cm x 6 cm images on a roll of film.

rangefinder
Photographic device where the viewfinder, independent from the lens, is equipped with a distance gauge (rangefinder) used to focus the camera.

single-lens reflex (SLR) camera
Camera whose interchangeable lens is used to both view and shoot through a slanted mirror that flips up (reflex).

Polaroid® camera
Camera that develops photos without the need for a photo lab. After a photo is taken, the exposed film is ejected from the camera and develops automatically in a few minutes.

view camera
Large camera composed of two telescopic blocks connected to an expansible bellows, which allows the perspective and focus to be checked and adjusted as needed.

films

Thin, flexible, transparent media covered with light-sensitive materials that enable images to be imprinted in a film camera.

film pack
mall rigid box containing a certain number of eet films, which are dispensed successively as the camera operates; they are used in Polaroid® cameras.

roll film
Band of film with a number of exposures; it is rolled on a spool and used in midsize cameras.

cartridge film
Small lightproof container that holds a roll of film with a number of exposures, which is loaded into a camera.

transparency slide
Positive photographic picture (with the same brightness as the original) that is mounted on a transparent backing and usually projected on a screen.

COMMUNICATIONS

film reflex camera

Reflex device in which the image is recorded on light-sensitive film.

front view

exposure adjustment knob
Knob that can deliberately underexpose or overexpose a film when the camera is in automatic exposure mode.

accessory shoe
Device for attaching an accessory to the camera (usually an external flash).

hot-shoe contact
Conduction unit that links the camera's electronic circuitry to the accessory mounted on the accessory shoe.

control panel
Liquid crystal display that shows the camera's various settings.

film advance mode
Control button used to advance the film in the camera body (frame by frame or continuously).

command control dial
Dial used to adjust the various parameters of a mode.

exposure mode
Button for choosing an automatic, semiautomatic or manual setting to control the amount of light that comes in contact with the film.

on-off switch
Button for turning the device on or off.

multiple exposure mode
Control button that blocks the film from advancing to create multiple exposures (several images superimposed on the frame).

shutter release button
Button that controls the exposure through control of the focal plane shutter opening.

film speed
Control button that sets the film's sensitivity to light as expressed by the ISO or ASA number; the higher the number, the more sensitive the film.

self-timer indicator
Light that shows the self-timer is on to delay release of the shutter; this allows the photographer to be in the photo.

remote control terminal
Device that is attached to the camera with a cable so that it can be operated from a distance.

camera body
Rigid sturdy box that contains the camera's mechanism and shields the film from light.

depth-of-field preview button
Button that closes the diaphragm so that the relative various depths can be seen through the viewfinder.

lens release button
Button for removing the lens from the camera body.

focus mode selector
Button that allows the user to choose between an automatic or manual focus to ensure a clear image.

lens
Optical system made up of a set of lenses fixed on a mount; it allows a clear image to be produced on film.

digital non-reflex cameras

Devices composed mainly of a dark chamber and an optic system used to record an image on light-sensitive film.

ultracompact camera
Very small camera, usually completely automatic.

compact camera
Small, easy-to-use camera.

digital reflex camera

Reflex camera that contains a sensor and a microprocessor; it records and stores images in digital form on a memory card.

back view

viewfinder
Device for viewing the scene to be photographed, framing it and adjusting its clarity.

menu button
Button that displays menus on the picture monitor, from which the camera's settings are chosen.

shutter release button
Button that controls the exposure through control of the focal plane shutter opening.

settings display button
Button for displaying the camera's settings on the screen.

mode dial
Dial used to adjust various settings on the camera.

on-off switch
Button for turning the device on or off.

enlarge button
Button used to enlarge a particular image.

strap eyelet
Small ring that holds a strap to help carry the camera.

cover
Part covering the memory card slot.

video and digital terminals
Devices for attaching a camera to a television or a computer.

four-way selector
Button for selecting from the various menus or scrolling through the recorded images.

display
Screen used to view textual information (menus, options), on the images or video clips.

memory card
Removable rigid card; it is a storage medium for photographs taken with a digital camera.

remote control terminal
Device that is attached to the camera by a cable so that it can be operated from a distance.

eject button
Button that pushes a memory card out of the camera.

multi-image jump button
Button for skipping one or several images while viewing recorded images.

display button
Button used to display the recorded photos.

erase button
Button that erases a recorded image from memory.

image review button
Button that displays recorded images.

main functions

image-recording quality
Function enabling the user to control the format and resolution of images.

sensitivity
Button used to select the degree of sensitivity to light of the sensor, expressed according to the ISO or ASA standard.

shutter speed
Number indicating the interval of time during which the sensor should be exposed to light, generally measured in fractions of a second.

metering mode
Method of measuring the intensity of the light hitting and reflected by a subject in order to determine the exposure required.

aperture
Number indicating the aperture of the diaphragm, measured as an f-stop number (the higher the f-stop number, the smaller the aperture).

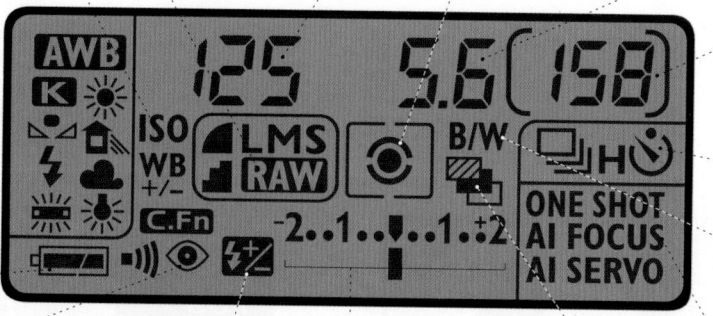

frames remaining/timer
Display of the number of frames remaining or the time before the taking of a photograph set with the timer.

white balance
Correction of colors to compensate for ambient light (daylight, fluorescent or tungsten lighting, etc.).

frame advance mode
Function that enables the user to choose between frame-by-frame mode (one photograph at a time) and burst mode (several consecutive photographs).

black-and-white
Function enabling an image to be recorded using only white, black, and shades of gray.

battery level
Indicator that displays the level of energy in the batteries that supply power to the camera.

red-eye reduction
Mechanism that reduces the red-eye effect by producing a small flash before the main flash goes off.

flash exposure compensation
Mechanism that deliberately reduces or increases the intensity of the flash.

exposure correction
Number representing the modification made to the exposure data when the user wishes to deliberately underexpose or overexpose the subject.

bracketing
Procedure consisting of photographing a single subject several times while varying the exposure index or the white balance.

autofocus
Automatic focusing function that ensures a sharp image.

digital reflex camera

framing
The photographer first frames the scene to be captured using the viewfinder.

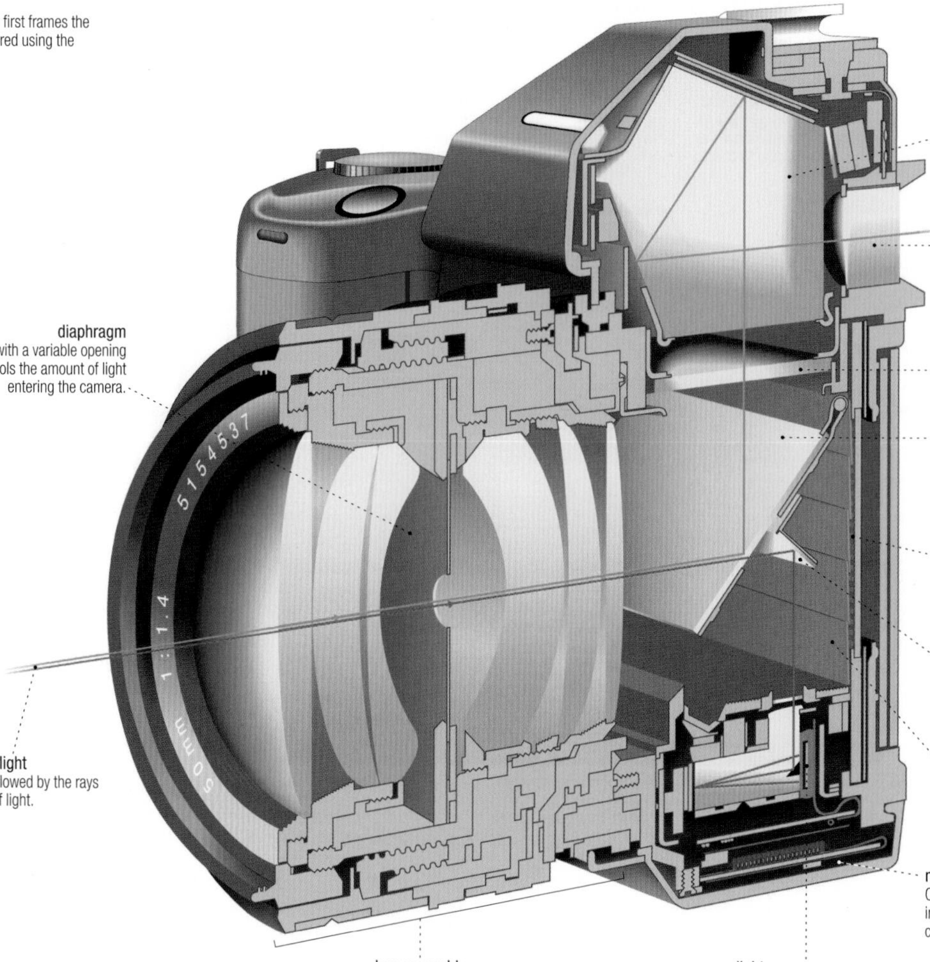

pentaprism
Five-sided block of glass that light beams to the eyepiece; t rights the inverted image form the focusing screen.

viewing lens
Optical disk or system of through which the eye se image produced by the le

diaphragm
Device with a variable opening that controls the amount of light entering the camera.

focusing screen
Ground glass plate on which the image caught by the lens formed; at this point, it is inver from right to left.

reflex mirror
Mirror that redirects light towa the focusing screen.

image sensor
Electronic device that transfor light into analog electric signa storage on a digital medium.

secondary mirror
Mirror that directs part of the light entering the lens through the center of the reflex mirror toward the light sensor.

light
Trajectory followed by the rays of light.

focal plane shutter
Opaque device that opens for a predetermined length of time ba the shutter speed chosen; it allo to come in contact with the sens

memory card slot
Covered slot in which a memory c inserted to record images taken w camera.

lens assembly
Optical system made up of a set of lenses fixed on a mount; it allows a clear image to be produced on sensor.

light sensor
Sensor that measures the light intensity; it is used to determine the correct exposure (shutter speed and diaphragm opening).

memory cards

Removable rigid cards; they are a storage medium for photographs taken with a digital camera.

Memory Stick
Flash memory card in a rectangular-shape case. It was developed in 2000.

xD-Picture card
Very-small-format flash memory card, designed in 2002.

Secure Digital card
Small-format flash memory card that includes a copyright-protection mechanism. It was developed in 2000.

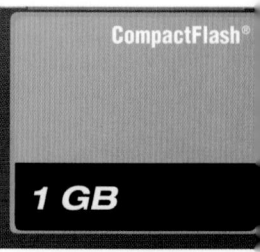

compact flash card
Rigid card used as a storage medium to reco photos taken with digital cameras.

digital reflex camera

photography
Once the shot has been framed the photographer presses the shutter to take the shot which allows the image to be captured by the sensor.

shutter release button
Button that controls the exposure through control of the focal plane shutter opening.

reflex mirror
Mirror that redirects light toward the focusing screen; when the photo is taken, it retracts so that light reaches the sensor.

image sensor
Electronic device that transforms light into analog electric signals for storage on a digital medium.

light
Trajectory followed by the rays of light.

processor
Electronic device that records and stores images in a digital format on a memory card.

adapter ring
Device used to attach a lens to a camera.

memory card slot
Covered slot in which a memory card is inserted to record images taken with the camera.

batteries

Devices that convert chemical energy into electrical energy to supply power to another device.

battery
Device that converts chemical energy into electrical energy to supply power to another device.

battery pack
Device that stores chemical energy during charging and converts it into electrical energy.

button cell
Device that converts chemical energy into electrical energy to supply power to another device.

photographic accessories

Add-on devices that improve or change the way a camera operates.

waterproof case
Rigid container designed to protect a camera from water or bad weather. It is used, among other things, for underwater photography.

cable shutter release
Flexible cable with a trigger that activates the shutter at close range thereby reducing the possibility of moving the camera.

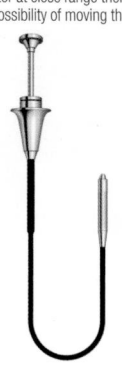

electronic flash
Device with a lamp that produces a brief and intense flash of light; it is used to compensate for inadequate lighting.

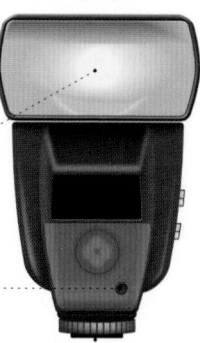

flashtube
Part that concentrates and channels light from the lamp toward the subject to be photographed.

photoelectric cell
Detector that measures the intensity of ambient light and controls the amount of light emitted by the flash.

mounting foot
Device used to mount the flash onto the accessory shoe.

tripod
Adjustable support to which a camera is attached to keep it stable, level and in focus.

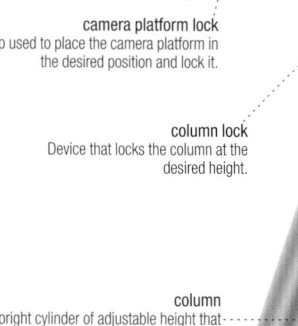

camera platform
Platform that supports the plate and the camera mounted on it.

camera screw
Screw used to attach the plate to the base of the camera.

plate
Detachable plate mounted on the camera platform so that the camera can be attached and removed quickly.

quick release system
Device used to attach the plate to the camera platform and to detach it.

panoramic head
Device atop the column that allows the camera mounted on the platform to pivot horizontally and vertically.

side-tilt lock
Grip that tilts the camera platform downward and locks it in the desired position.

camera platform lock
Grip used to place the camera platform in the desired position and lock it.

horizontal motion lock
Grip that pivots the camera platform from left to right and locks it in the desired position.

column lock
Device that locks the column at the desired height.

column crank
Grip that adjusts the height of the column.

camera bag
Bag with compartments designed to hold and protect a camera and its accessories.

column
Upright cylinder of adjustable height that supports the panoramic head.

collet
Ring that locks the sliding components of the telescoping leg once the desired height is reached.

telescoping leg
Each of the rods used to stabilize the tripod; they are made up of sliding components, which adjust the height.

digital photo frame
Electronic device with a screen for displaying digital photos.

exposure meter
Device with light-sensitive cells that measures the intensity of the light striking or reflected by the subject to determine the correct exposure for a photo.

integrating sphere
Translucent half globe used to measure the intensity of the light striking the subject to be photographed (incident light).

light-reading scale
Graduated scale showing the intensity of the light striking or reflected by the subject.

indicator needle
Thin metal bar that shows the brightness measured by light-sensitive cells on the exposure meter.

aperture scale
Graduated scale that shows the diaphragm's opening measured in f-stops (a high f-stop indicates a small opening).

exposure correction scale
Graduated scale that shows changes made to exposure data when deliberately underexposing or overexposing a scene.

cine scale
Graduated scale that shows the speed at which a motion picture film unwinds; it is expressed in frames per second.

exposure-time scale
Graduated scale that shows the length of time a sensitive surface should be exposed to light, which is determined by the shutter speed.

calculator dial
Rotating dial that adjusts the film speed.

film speed scale
Graded scale indicating the degree of the film's sensitivity to light or the sensitivity of the sensor expressed according to the ISO or ASA standard.

exposure value scale
Graduated scale that shows the amount of light to which the sensitive surface should be exposed.

digital exposure meter
Exposure meter that uses a viewfinder to measure the brightness of precise spots on the scene to be photographed.

integrating sphere
Translucent half globe used to measure the intensity of the light striking the subject to be photographed (incident light).

display
Display area for viewing text data.

average button
Button that determines the correct exposure based on the average brightness of a scene.

lens
Optical system made up of a set of lenses fixed on a mount; it allows a clear image to be produced on sensor.

jog wheel
Wheel for selecting settings or operations.

memory button
Button that displays data stored in memory.

film speed buttons
Button used to select the degree of the sensitivity to light of the film or sensor, expressed according to the ISO or ASA standard.

on-off button
Button used to turn the device on or off.

memory clear button
Button that erases data stored in memory.

mode set button
Button used to choose various settings or options.

flash synchronization port
A port used to link the exposure meter to a flash to synchronize the light produced by the flash with the shutter speed.

lenses

Lenses are characterized by their focal length (between the optical center and the film or sensor), aperture (ratio between the diameter of the lens and the foca length) and angle of view (width of the captured image).

standard lens
Lens that produces an image close to that seen by the human eye.

lens
Transparent optical disks through which ambient light enters; the disks correct each other to improve the quality of the image.

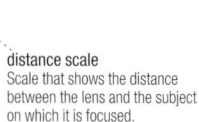

focus setting ring
Setting ring that sharpens the image of a subject.

depth-of-field scale
Scale that shows the zone of sharpest focus around the subject; this is a function of the diaphragm's opening and the distance between the lens and the subject.

lens aperture scale
Graduated scale that controls the diaphragm's opening; it is measured in f-stops and a high f-stop indicates a small opening.

distance scale
Scale that shows the distance between the lens and the subject on which it is focused.

bayonet mount
Device for attaching the lens to the camera body by fitting lugs located on the lens into grooves on the camera and turning.

zoom lens
Lens with a variable focal length so that the visual field can be changed without changing the lens.

lens accessories
All the parts that can be attached to a lens to change its focal length or alter the image projected on the film or sensor.

lens cap
Part that covers and protects the lens when it is not in use.

lens hood
Cone-shaped device that reduces the effect of intense ambient light to improve the image's contrast.

color filter
Colored glass used to alter the characteristics of the light reaching the film or sensor.

close-up lens
Optical disk that changes the focal length of the lens so that very near subjects can be photographed.

polarizing filter
Glass used to reduce reflections from nonmetallic surfaces such as water, glass and asphalt.

objective lens
Optical system made up of a set of lenses fixed on a mount; it allows a clear image to be produced on film or sensor.

tele-converter
Component inserted between the camera and the lens to increase its focal length; this enlarges the image of a distant subject.

telephoto lens
Lens with a long focal length that enlarges the image of a distant subject but reduces the visual field and the depth of field.

macro lens
Lens designed mainly for close-up shots of small objects.

wide-angle lens
Lens with a short focal leng covers a larger visual field t regular lens and provides sig depth of field.

semi-fisheye lens
Lens with a short focal length that covers a wide visual field; it emphasizes the effect of perspective.

fisheye lens
Lens with a very short focal length that covers a visual field of at least a 180°; it creates circular images.

digital photo management

Digital photos can be retouched, stored on various media, or reproduced on paper using a printer.

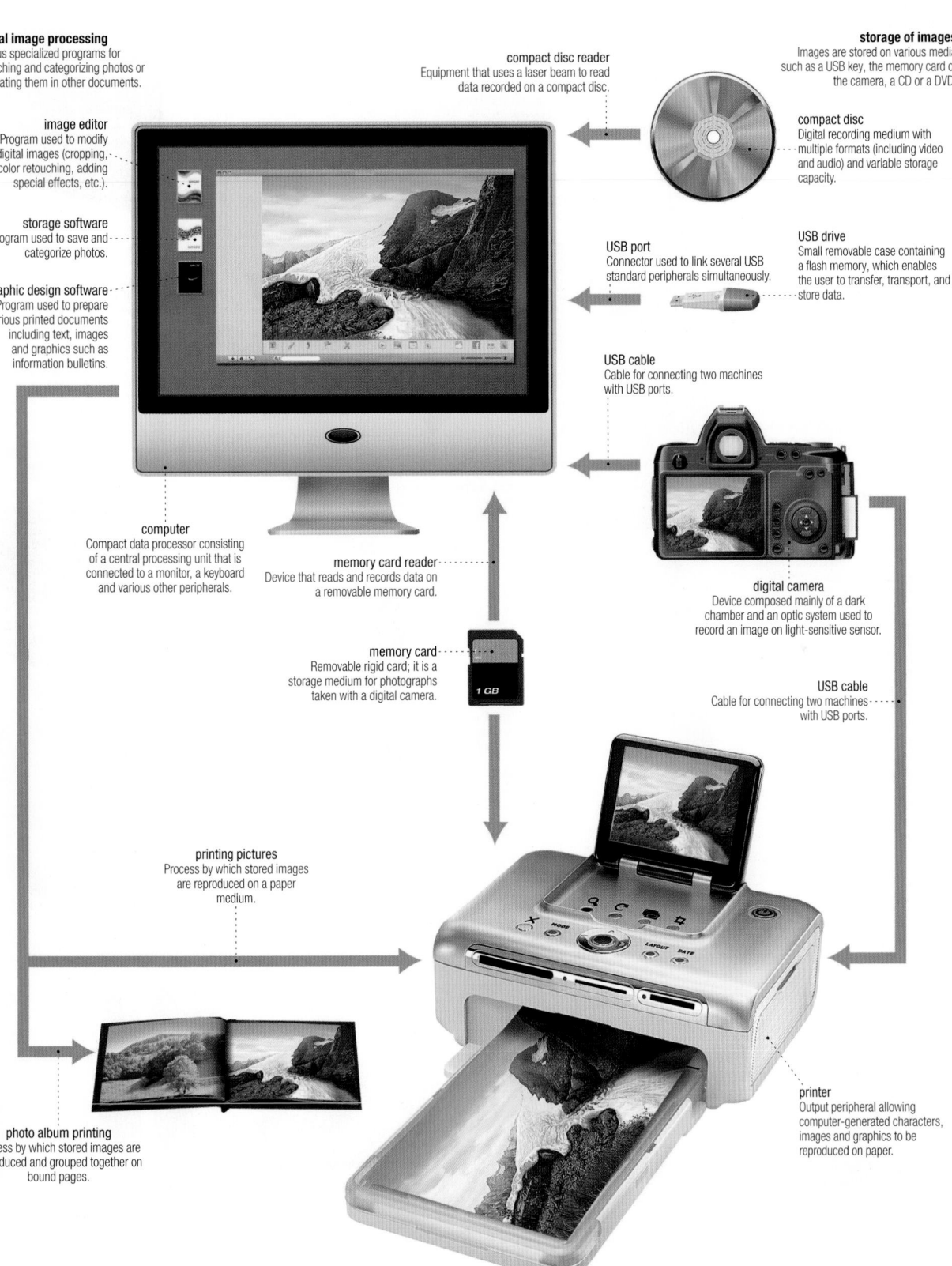

ital image processing
ous specialized programs for
uching and categorizing photos or
rating them in other documents.

image editor
Program used to modify
digital images (cropping,
color retouching, adding
special effects, etc.).

storage software
rogram used to save and
categorize photos.

aphic design software
Program used to prepare
arious printed documents
including text, images
and graphics such as
information bulletins.

compact disc reader
Equipment that uses a laser beam to read
data recorded on a compact disc.

storage of images
Images are stored on various media
such as a USB key, the memory card of
the camera, a CD or a DVD.

compact disc
Digital recording medium with
multiple formats (including video
and audio) and variable storage
capacity.

USB port
Connector used to link several USB
standard peripherals simultaneously.

USB drive
Small removable case containing
a flash memory, which enables
the user to transfer, transport, and
store data.

USB cable
Cable for connecting two machines
with USB ports.

computer
Compact data processor consisting
of a central processing unit that is
connected to a monitor, a keyboard
and various other peripherals.

memory card reader
Device that reads and records data on
a removable memory card.

digital camera
Device composed mainly of a dark
chamber and an optic system used to
record an image on light-sensitive sensor.

memory card
Removable rigid card; it is a
storage medium for photographs
taken with a digital camera.

USB cable
Cable for connecting two machines
with USB ports.

printing pictures
Process by which stored images
are reproduced on a paper
medium.

photo album printing
ess by which stored images are
oduced and grouped together on
bound pages.

printer
Output peripheral allowing
computer-generated characters,
images and graphics to be
reproduced on paper.

COMMUNICATIONS

film processing

Several steps are necessary to reproduce the images from silver gelatin film onto paper.

darkroom equipment
Material required to process film and to print photographs in a darkened room.

timer
Device with a phosphorescent dial that measures the required time for each film processing operation.

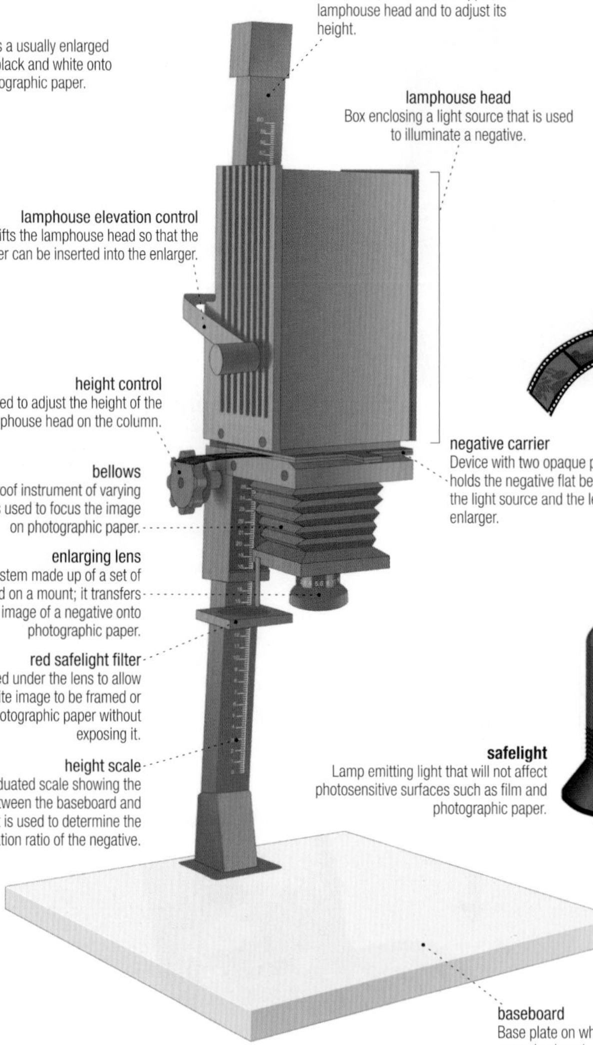

column
Serrated bar mounted on the baseboard; it is used to support the lamphouse head and to adjust its height.

enlarger
Device that projects a usually enlarged negative image in black and white onto light-sensitive photographic paper.

lamphouse head
Box enclosing a light source that is used to illuminate a negative.

negative carrier
Device with two opaque plates that holds the negative flat between the light source and the lens of the enlarger.

lamphouse elevation control
Device that lifts the lamphouse head so that the negative holder can be inserted into the enlarger.

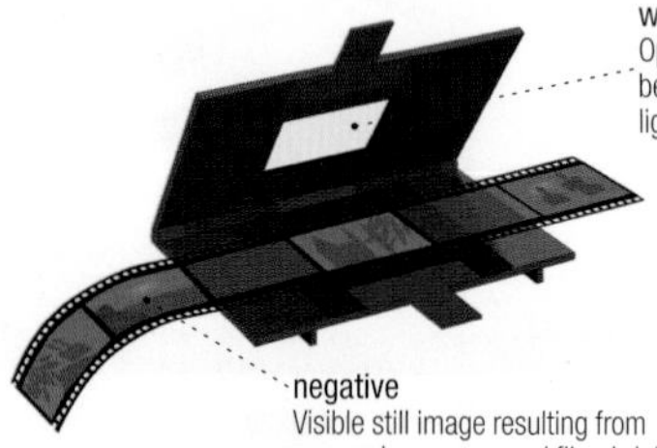

window
Opening that frames the image to be enlarged and stops parasitic light from reaching the baseboard.

developing t
Lightproof container used du the various stages of processin exposed film to obtain a nega

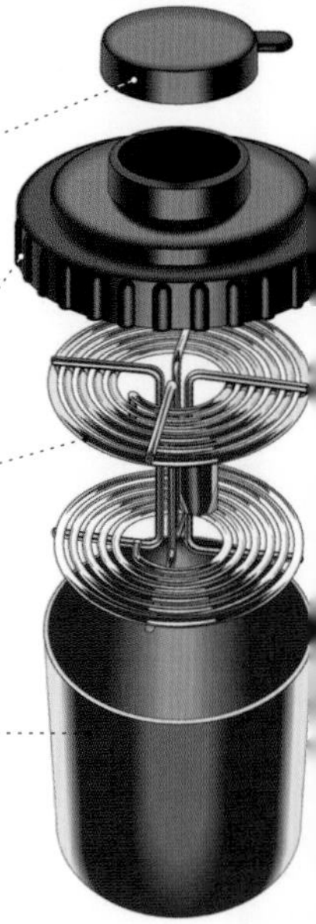

height control
Device used to adjust the height of the lamphouse head on the column.

negative
Visible still image resulting from processing an exposed film; bright areas on the original subject appear dark on the negative.

negative carrier
Device with two opaque plates that holds the negative flat between the light source and the lens of the enlarger.

cap
Removable watertight cover allowing film processing products to be mixed in a tank.

bellows
Lightproof instrument of varying length; it is used to focus the image on photographic paper.

lid
Lightproof tank cover with an opening through which film processing products are added and removed.

enlarging lens
Optical system made up of a set of lenses fixed on a mount; it transfers an enlarged image of a negative onto photographic paper.

red safelight filter
Colored filter placed under the lens to allow the black and white image to be framed or focused onto photographic paper without exposing it.

reel
Holder on which the film is wound; it prevents the film from sticking together and ensures uniform distribution of the processing products.

height scale
Graduated scale showing the distance between the baseboard and the lens; it is used to determine the magnification ratio of the negative.

safelight
Lamp emitting light that will not affect photosensitive surfaces such as film and photographic paper.

tank
Container used to hold the reel and the products required (developer, stop bath, fixer) for each of the processing steps.

baseboard
Base plate on which a photographic paper is placed.

developing baths
Trays used for the various steps in processing exposed photographic paper to obtain a proof in black and white.

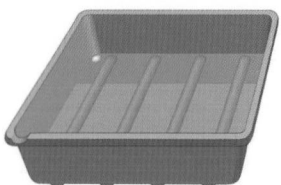

developer bath
Tray containing a chemical that acts on light-exposed photographic paper to reveal an image.

stop bath
Tray containing a chemical that stops the action of the developer.

fixing bath
Tray containing a chemical that fixes the revealed image by making the photographic paper insensitive to light.

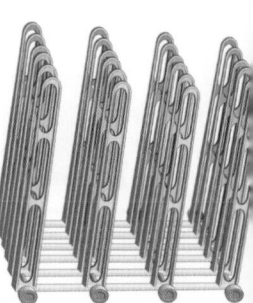

print drying rack
Frame that holds prints once they have passed through the washer so that the water evaporates.

transparency viewing

Transparency: photographic picture that is mounted on a transparent medium and usually projected on a screen.

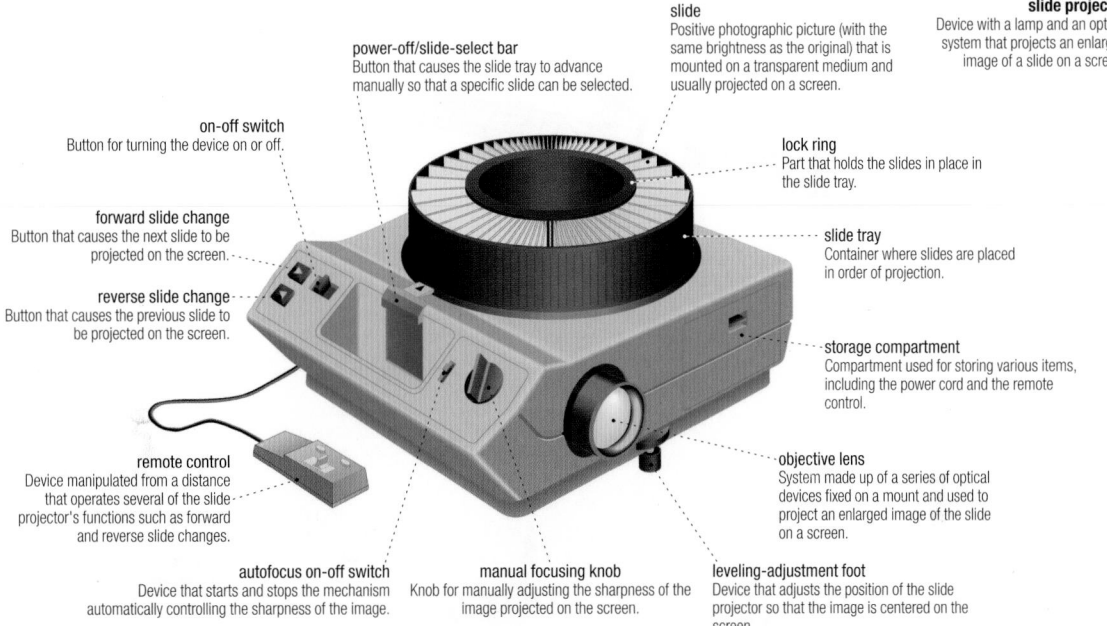

power-off/slide-select bar
Button that causes the slide tray to advance manually so that a specific slide can be selected.

slide
Positive photographic picture (with the same brightness as the original) that is mounted on a transparent medium and usually projected on a screen.

slide projector
Device with a lamp and an optical system that projects an enlarged image of a slide on a screen.

on-off switch
Button for turning the device on or off.

lock ring
Part that holds the slides in place in the slide tray.

forward slide change
Button that causes the next slide to be projected on the screen.

slide tray
Container where slides are placed in order of projection.

reverse slide change
Button that causes the previous slide to be projected on the screen.

storage compartment
Compartment used for storing various items, including the power cord and the remote control.

remote control
Device manipulated from a distance that operates several of the slide projector's functions such as forward and reverse slide changes.

objective lens
System made up of a series of optical devices fixed on a mount and used to project an enlarged image of the slide on a screen.

autofocus on-off switch
Device that starts and stops the mechanism automatically controlling the sharpness of the image.

manual focusing knob
Knob for manually adjusting the sharpness of the image projected on the screen.

leveling-adjustment foot
Device that adjusts the position of the slide projector so that the image is centered on the screen.

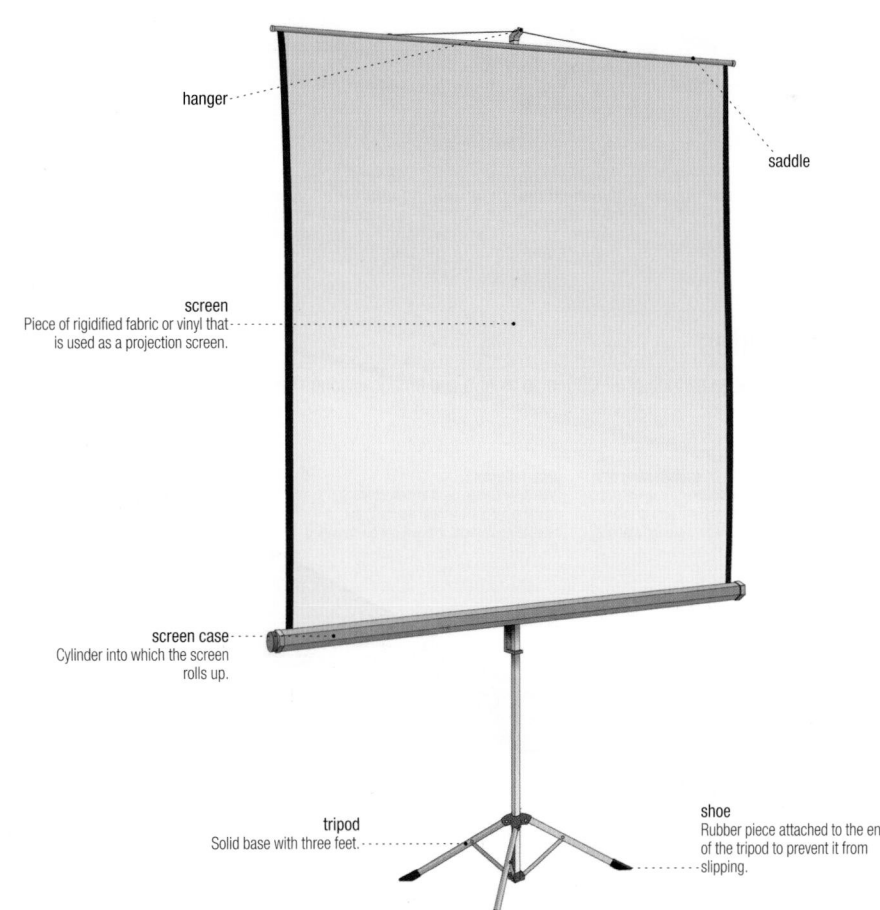

projection screen
White surface on which still or moving images are projected.

hanger

saddle

screen
Piece of rigidified fabric or vinyl that is used as a projection screen.

screen case
Cylinder into which the screen rolls up.

tripod
Solid base with three feet.

shoe
Rubber piece attached to the ends of the tripod to prevent it from slipping.

broadcast satellite communication

Transmission of television signals (pictures and sound) to the general public by means of radio waves relayed by satellite.

broadcasting system
All equipment necessary to broadcast television signals.

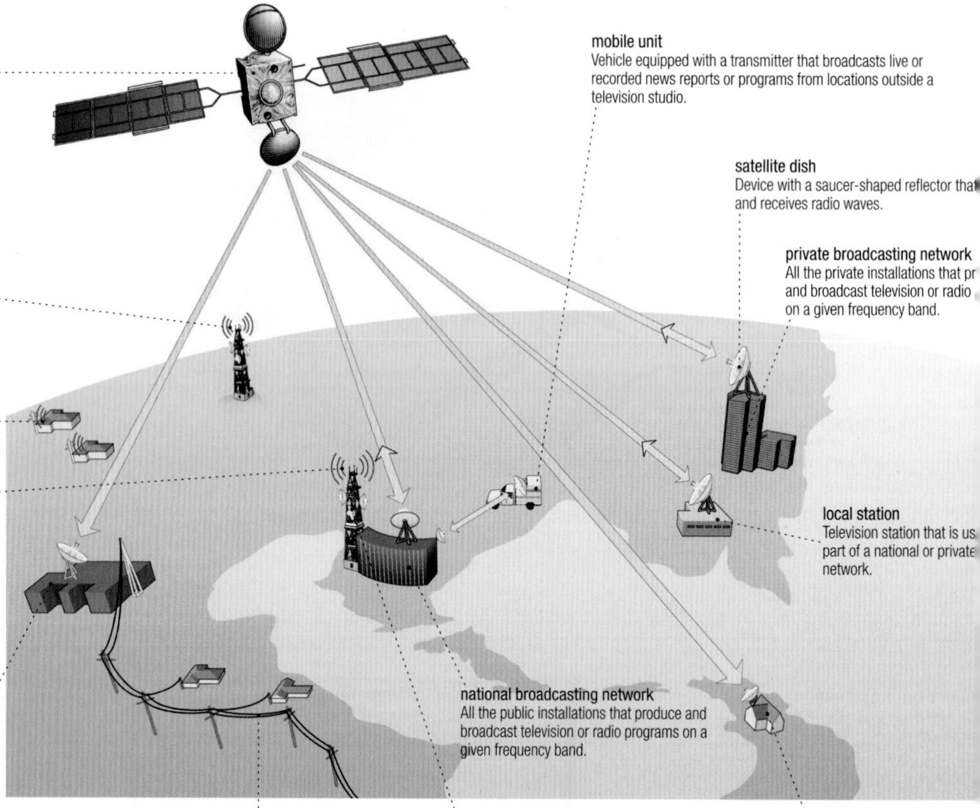

satellite
Space vehicle placed in geostationary orbit at an altitude of 22,000 mi to transmit sound and visual signals in the form of radio waves.

mobile unit
Vehicle equipped with a transmitter that broadcasts live or recorded news reports or programs from locations outside a television studio.

satellite dish
Device with a saucer-shaped reflector that and receives radio waves.

private broadcasting network
All the private installations that pr and broadcast television or radio on a given frequency band.

relay station
Facility receiving and amplifying signals from a transmitting tower and relaying them to another receiver.

home antenna
Small receiving antenna used by a subscriber to capture radio waves emitted by a transmitting tower or relay station.

radio wave transmission
Hertzian waves, also called radio waves, are low-frequency electromagnetic waves; the full spectrum of radio waves is divided into bands for specific uses such as radio and TV. Each band is in turn divided into channels.

local station
Television station that is us part of a national or private network.

national broadcasting network
All the public installations that produce and broadcast television or radio programs on a given frequency band.

cable distributor
Company specializing in the transmission of television signals to customers through a cable network.

distribution by aerial cable network
Signals can be relayed to the customer through a network of suspended cables.

transmitting tower
Facility used to transmit radio waves to a receiver so that television programs can be broadcast locally.

direct home reception
Radio waves are emitted by a satellite and captured directly by the subscriber's satellite dish.

telecommunication satellites

Space vehicles placed into geostationary orbit at an altitude of 22,000 mi to receive and broadcast long-distance signals in the form of radio waves.

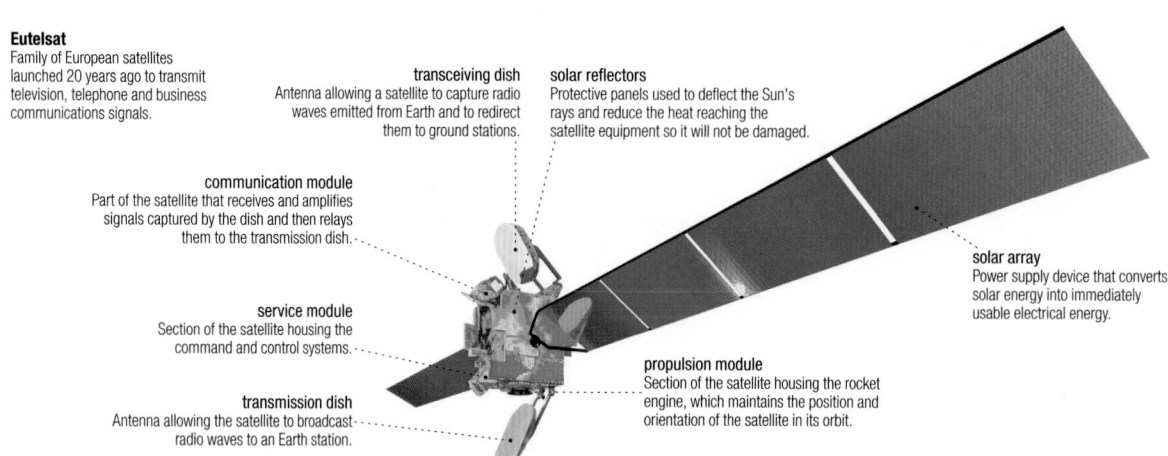

Eutelsat
Family of European satellites launched 20 years ago to transmit television, telephone and business communications signals.

transceiving dish
Antenna allowing a satellite to capture radio waves emitted from Earth and to redirect them to ground stations.

solar reflectors
Protective panels used to deflect the Sun's rays and reduce the heat reaching the satellite equipment so it will not be damaged.

communication module
Part of the satellite that receives and amplifies signals captured by the dish and then relays them to the transmission dish.

solar array
Power supply device that converts solar energy into immediately usable electrical energy.

service module
Section of the satellite housing the command and control systems.

propulsion module
Section of the satellite housing the rocket engine, which maintains the position and orientation of the satellite in its orbit.

transmission dish
Antenna allowing the satellite to broadcast radio waves to an Earth station.

telecommunications by satellite

Transmission of data such as images, sound and computer data using radio waves relayed by satellites.

telecommunications system
All equipment necessary for the transmission of data.

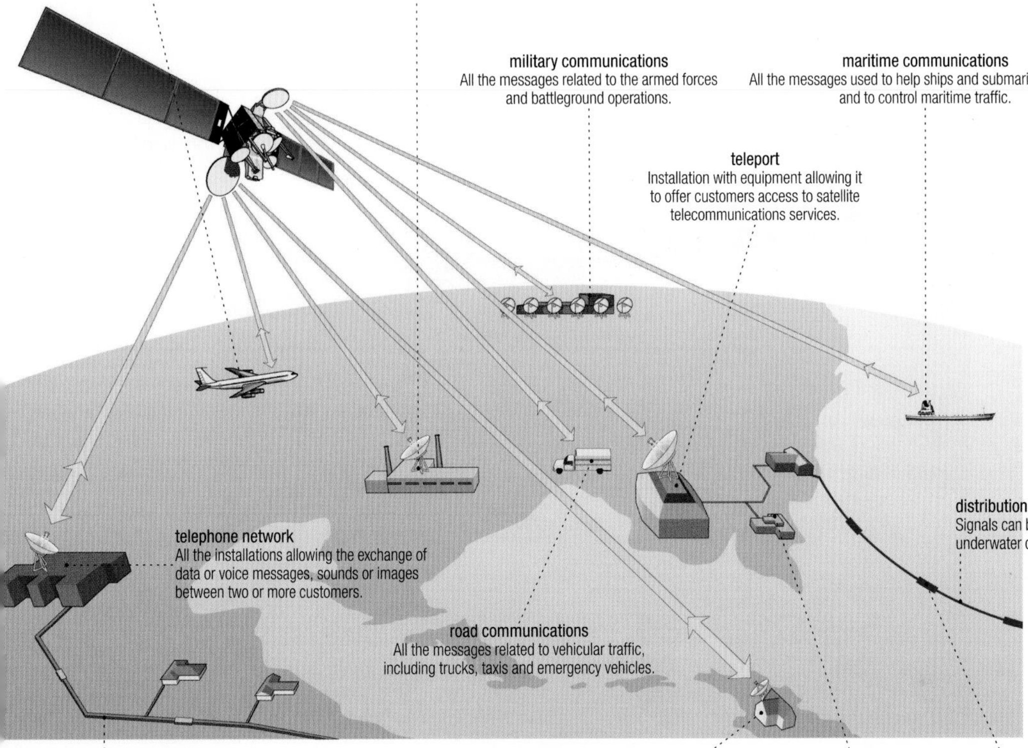

air communications
All the messages used to help aircraft navigate and to control air traffic.

industrial communications
All the messages exchanged by companies involved in the production of goods and services.

military communications
All the messages related to the armed forces and battleground operations.

maritime communications
All the messages used to help ships and submarines navigate and to control maritime traffic.

teleport
Installation with equipment allowing it to offer customers access to satellite telecommunications services.

telephone network
All the installations allowing the exchange of data or voice messages, sounds or images between two or more customers.

road communications
All the messages related to vehicular traffic, including trucks, taxis and emergency vehicles.

distribution by submarine cable
Signals can be relayed through a network of underwater cables.

...ution by underground cable network
...als can be relayed through a network of underground cables.

personal communications
All the messages exchanged between individuals.

consumer

repeater
Device running the length of a cable that receives, amplifies and resends signals to transmit them over long distances.

telecommunication satellites

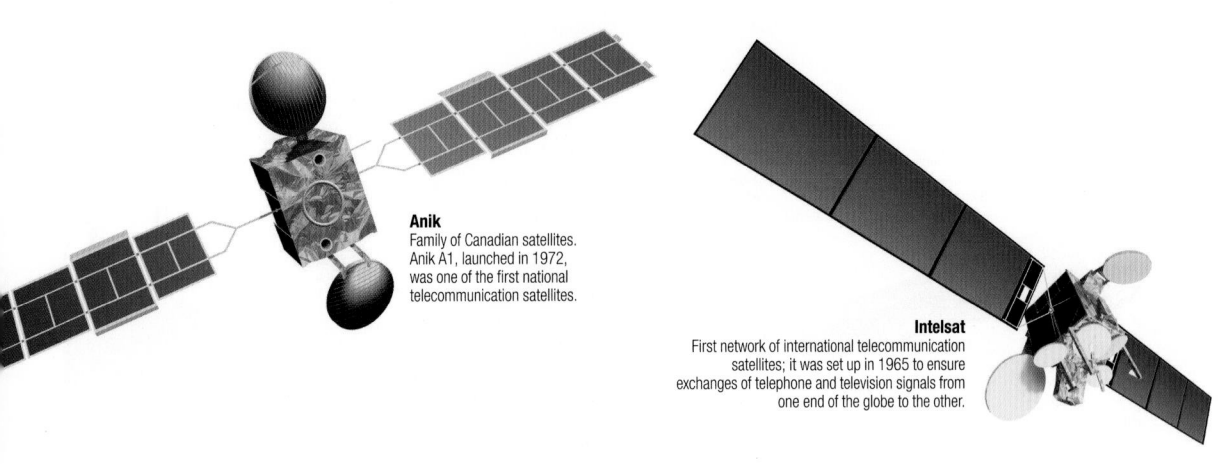

Anik
Family of Canadian satellites. Anik A1, launched in 1972, was one of the first national telecommunication satellites.

Intelsat
First network of international telecommunication satellites; it was set up in 1965 to ensure exchanges of telephone and television signals from one end of the globe to the other.

studio and control room

Area with two rooms separated by a glass window where audio programs are produced, recorded or broadcast.

intercom
Telephone connected to a loudspeaker to which headphones may be connected. It allows communication between the control room and the host in the studio.

acoustic window
Three-layered glass pane used to soundproof each of the control rooms.

timer
Device used to measure intervals of time in minutes, seconds and fractions of a second. It allows the host to see the time remaining in an interview, a program, etc.

monitor loudspeaker
Device that reproduces the audio portion of an on-air program to monitor its sound quality.

volume unit meters
Instruments measuring the relative intensity of the various sounds being broadcast or recorded.

microphone
Device that converts electric pulses into broadcast or recorded sounds.

production clock
Clock used to time a program.

on-air warning light
Light indicating that a program is being broadcast.

headphones
Listening device allowing the host and chroniclers to receive information from the director without interrupting the program.

workstation
Computer equipment with a mul production dashboard used to di manage the audiovisual content (news reports, music, advertiser

host
The person who conducts interviews with the guests provides a link between different segments of the show and, together with the director, ensures that the schedule is followed.

patch rack
Cabinet containing a device used cables to various pieces of equip

chronicler
Person who regularly reports on a topic (current events, literature, sports, etc.) during a program.

turntable
Device using an arm fitted with a stylus cartridge to play back sounds from a record.

timer
Device used by the director and assistant director in order to mark the time allocated for an interview, a program, etc. The time appears on the host's timer screen.

equipment racks
Cabinet in which audio visual equipment and documents are stored.

assistant director
The person who assists the director in all tasks and can replaced the director if necessary.

director
Person who coordinates the production meeting and manages the broadcast controlling technical direction and quality control of a program.

potentiometer
Instrument with a cursor that slides along a straight track allowing the technician to control the sound level.

audio console
Console made up of all the devices used to control, adjust and mix sound.

production intercom
Short distance telephone device allowing the director to transmit information to the host at any time during a show.

microphones and accessories

Microphone: device that converts sounds into electric pulses for broadcasting or recording.

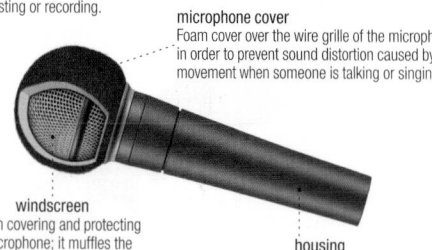

dynamic microphone
Device with a moving coil traveling in a magnetic field that converts sounds into electric pulses for broadcasting or recording.

microphone cover
Foam cover over the wire grille of the microphone in order to prevent sound distortion caused by air movement when someone is talking or singing.

windscreen
Screen covering and protecting a microphone; it muffles the speaker's breathing and the sound of the wind.

housing

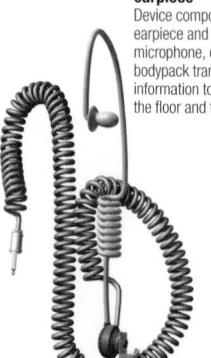

earpiece
Device composed of a small earpiece and a miniature microphone, connected to the bodypack transmitter. It allows information to be shared between the floor and the control room.

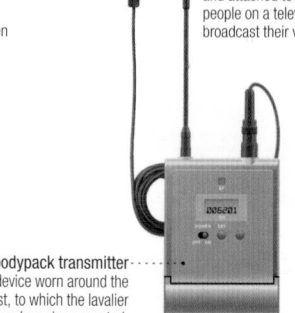

lavalier microphone
Miniature microphone connected to a portable and attached to the cloth people on a television st broadcast their voices.

bodypack transmitter
Small device worn around the waist, to which the lavalier microphone is connected.

program production

All equipment and installations used in the creation, recording, and broadcasting of television programs.

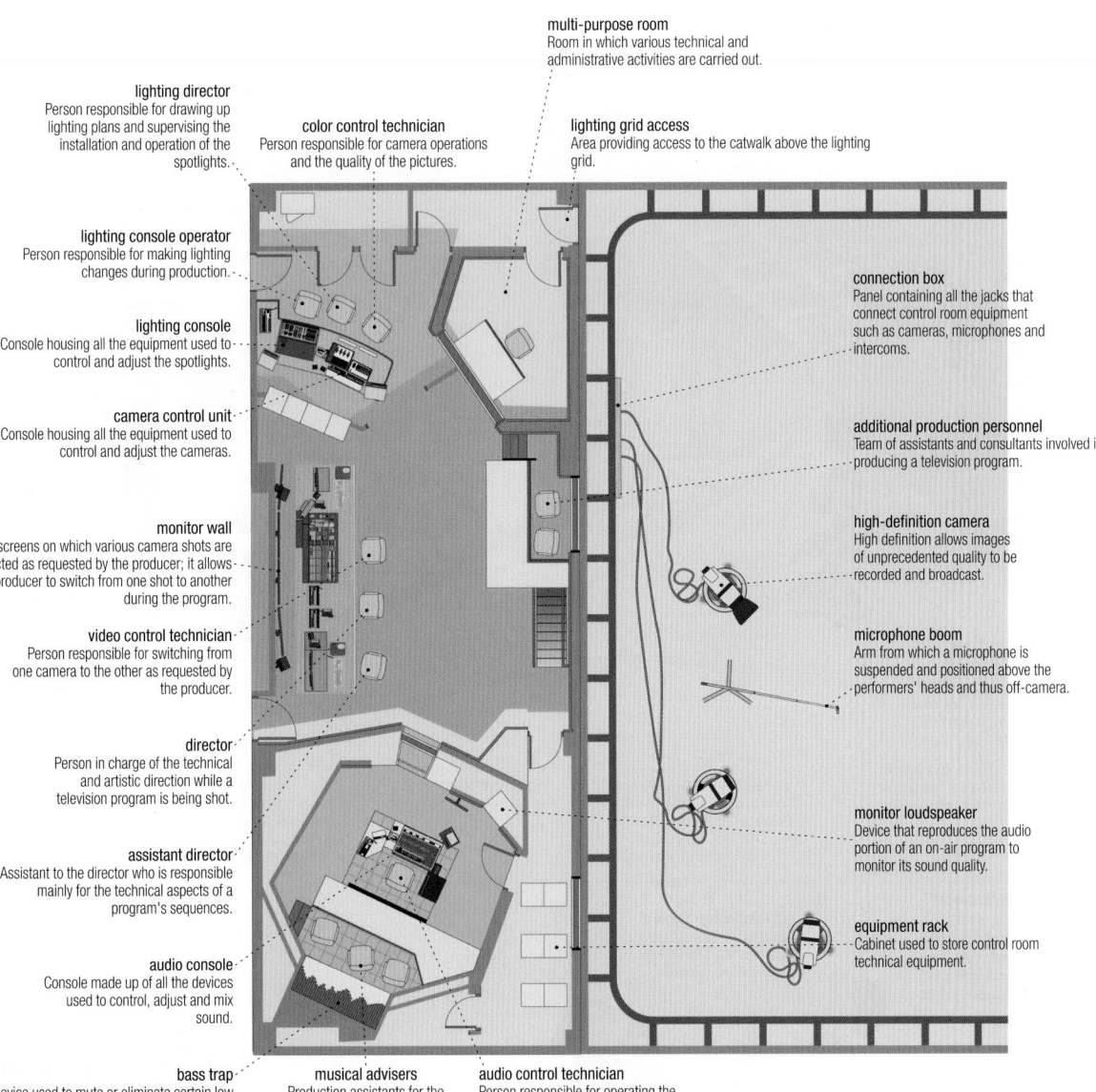

studio set and control rooms
A television studio is made up of a studio floor and three control rooms which contain various consoles for monitoring, recording and transmitting.

multi-purpose room
Room in which various technical and administrative activities are carried out.

lighting director
Person responsible for drawing up lighting plans and supervising the installation and operation of the spotlights.

color control technician
Person responsible for camera operations and the quality of the pictures.

lighting grid access
Area providing access to the catwalk above the lighting grid.

lighting console operator
Person responsible for making lighting changes during production.

connection box
Panel containing all the jacks that connect control room equipment such as cameras, microphones and intercoms.

lighting console
Console housing all the equipment used to control and adjust the spotlights.

additional production personnel
Team of assistants and consultants involved in producing a television program.

camera control unit
Console housing all the equipment used to control and adjust the cameras.

high-definition camera
High definition allows images of unprecedented quality to be recorded and broadcast.

monitor wall
Set of screens on which various camera shots are projected as requested by the producer; it allows the producer to switch from one shot to another during the program.

microphone boom
Arm from which a microphone is suspended and positioned above the performers' heads and thus off-camera.

video control technician
Person responsible for switching from one camera to the other as requested by the producer.

director
Person in charge of the technical and artistic direction while a television program is being shot.

monitor loudspeaker
Device that reproduces the audio portion of an on-air program to monitor its sound quality.

assistant director
Assistant to the director who is responsible mainly for the technical aspects of a program's sequences.

equipment rack
Cabinet used to store control room technical equipment.

audio console
Console made up of all the devices used to control, adjust and mix sound.

bass trap
Device used to mute or eliminate certain low audio frequencies in a room.

musical advisers
Production assistants for the musical portion of a program.

audio control technician
Person responsible for operating the audio console.

COMMUNICATIONS

audio control room
Room with the control and monitoring equipment required for sound recording.

production control room
Area equipped to select and compose pictures to be broadcast or recorded; it is also used to coordinate activities in other control rooms and the studio.

lighting/camera control area
Room equipped to control camera shots and lighting.

studio set
Room designed for recording television program sounds and images; it might be soundproof or not.

program production

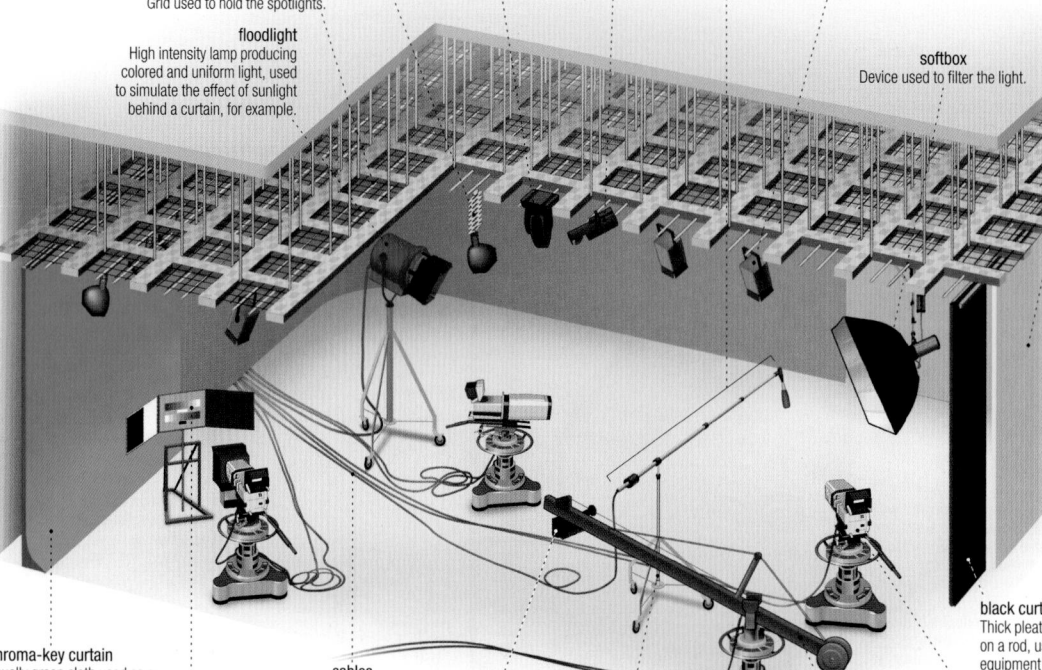

studio set
Room designed for recording television program sounds and images; it might be soundproof or not.

pantograph
Extendable and adjustable frame on which floodlights are hung.

moving light
Light controlled from the lighting desk, the functioning of which (position, color, and shape of the light beam) can be programmed in advance or controlled live.

microphone boom
Arm from which a microphone is suspended and positioned above the performers' heads and thus off-camera.

fixed spotlight
Light attached to a metal ring from which it hangs, providing an motionless beam of light.

moving mirror projector
Light with an attached pivoting mirror to alter the light beam, the position of which is controlled from the lighting desk.

cyclorama
Fixed or removable backdr the set of a program; it is produce various visual

lighting grid
Grid used to hold the spotlights.

floodlight
High intensity lamp producing colored and uniform light, used to simulate the effect of sunlight behind a curtain, for example.

softbox
Device used to filter the light.

chroma-key curtain
Bright, usually green cloth used as a background, to create the illusion in the editing room that two separately-filmed objects are part of the same image.

cables

black curtain
Thick pleated curtain that glide on a rod, used to hide technica equipment or to allow the pass of stagehands during a progra

high-definition camera
High definition allows images unprecedented quality to be re and broadcast.

test pattern
Image used to calibrate and adjust various camera settings.

camera with wide-angle lens
Camera to which is attached a lens that allows a framing wider than the scene to be shot, even if objects or people are at close range.

microphone boom tripod
Very stable three-sided support on wheels.

camera crane
Mobile and articulated device that allows rapid camera movements, and high-angle shots without the camera man having to climb onto a platform.

cameras and accessories

Thanks to film innovation, a large variety of cameras (traditional models, shoulder-mounted, wide-angle, etc.) and accessories (cranes, dollies, etc) can be found on the production floor.

high-definition camera
High definition allows images of unprecedented quality to be recorded and broadcast.

teleprompter
Screen with scrolling text so that the announcer can read without looking away from the camera.

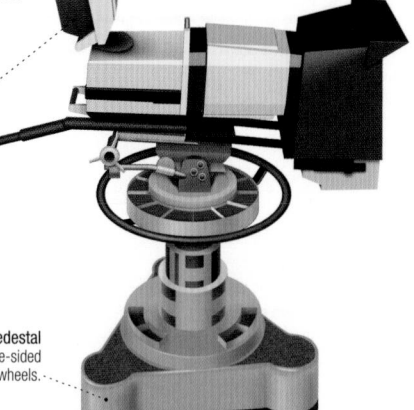

camera viewfinder
Device for viewing the scene to be filmed in order to frame it and bring it into focus.

camera pedestal
Very stable three-sided support on wheels.

scrolling text
Text displayed in an unbroken stream on the teleprompter. Once text has been read it disappears at the top and the following text appears from beneath.

program production

production control room
Area equipped to select and compose pictures to be broadcast or recorded; it is also used to coordinate activities in other control rooms and the studio.

monitor loudspeaker
Device that reproduces the audio portion of an on-air program to monitor its sound quality.

program monitor
Screen showing an image before it is broadcast or recorded, in order to control quality.

production clock
Clock used to time a program.

preview monitor
Screen that allows one to test-run a visual effect before broadcasting or recording it.

monitor wall
screens on which various era shots are projected as uested by the producer; it ws the producer to switch ne shot to another during the program.

intercom microphone
Microphone used by the r, production assistant or cian to transmit directions members in other control rooms or in the studio.

intercom
Telephone connected to a loudspeaker to which hones may be connected. communication between ntrol room and the host in the studio.

special effects monitor
Screen used to view digital special effects generated by a computer.

production desk
All technical equipment in the production control room.

digital console
Equipment used to compose, transmit and save images, and to insert various transition effects between them.

camera monitors
Screens showing the images captured by the floor cameras or coming from various other sources (VCR, film reel, etc.).

switcher console
All the technical equipment (digital console, computers, etc.) used by the video control technician to manage the sound and image quality.

COMMUNICATIONS

cameras and accessories

Steadicam
Portable piece of equipment allowing to operator to carry a camera fixed on a base that ensures steady and high-quality shots.

shoulder mount camcorder
Camera device allowing the cameraman to move about easily, used to film hosts and actors up close.

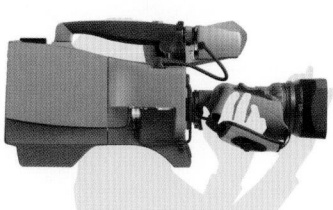

program production

mobile production truck
Vehicle equipped with a transmitter that
broadcasts live or recorded news reports or
programs from locations outside a television
studio.

microwave antenna
Device sending electromagnetic
waves of a slightly higher frequency
than radio waves; it is used to carry
video signals.

audio control room
Room with the control and monitoring
equipment required for sound recording.

production control room
Area equipped to select and compose pictures
to be broadcast or recorded; it is also used to
coordinate the activities of other control rooms
and filming locations.

video control room
Room equipped to control and adjust
camera shots.

monitor loudspeaker
Device that reproduces the audio
portion of an on-air program to
monitor its sound quality.

monitor wall
Set of screens on which various camera shots are
projected as requested by the producer; it allows
the producer to switch from one shot to another
during the program.

color control technician
Person responsible for camera operations and
the quality of the pictures.

equipment rack
Cabinet where the mobile unit's
technical equipment is stored.

preview monitor
Screen that allows one to test-run a
visual effect before broadcasting or
recording it.

camera control unit
Console housing all the equipment used to
control and adjust the cameras.

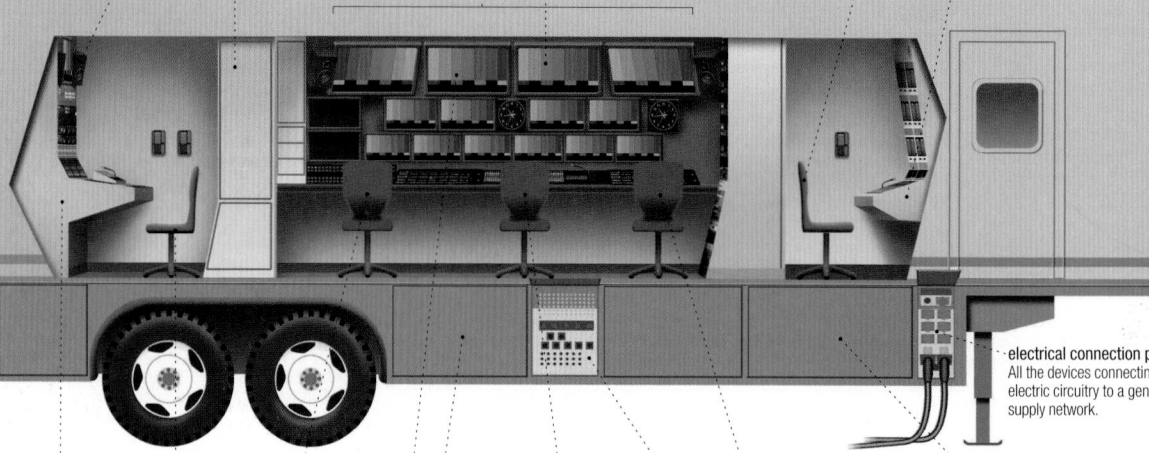

electrical connection panel
All the devices connecting a mobile
electric circuitry to a generator or ele
supply network.

audio console
Console made up of all the
devices used to control, adjust
and mix sound.

director
Person in charge of the technical
and artistic direction while a
television program is being shot.

video control technician
Person responsible for switching from one
camera to the other as requested by the
producer.

technical director
Person responsible for all technical
elements of a production, including
sound and picture quality.

equipment compartment
Compartment used to store equipment requi
produce a program such as cameras and bat

video connection panel
All the devices connecting camera cables to the
control room equipment.

audio control technician
Person responsible for operating
the audio console.

program monitor
Screen showing an image before it
is broadcast or recorded, in order
to control quality.

cable reels compartment
Compartment used to store camera and
lighting cables.

television reception

All equipment used in reproducing the audiovisual elements of programs broadcast by a television station, or recorded on cassette or disk.

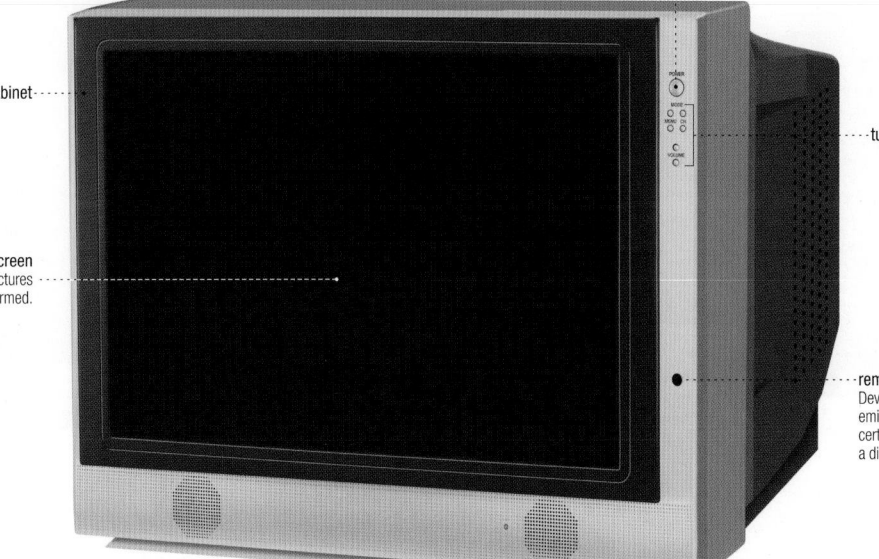

analog television
All techniques, equipment and installations used in broadcasting television programs as analog signals.

on-off button
Mechanical connection that turns the device on or off.

cathode-ray tube television
Receiving device that generates the sound and picture elements of programs broadcast by a television station or recorded on cassette or disc.

cabinet

tuning controls

screen
...ace on which TV pictures are formed.

remote control sensor
Device that receives infrared signals emitted by a remote control so that certain functions can be operated from a distance.

electron gun
Device that emits electron beams toward the screen; there are beams for each of the primary colors, red, green and blue.

grid
Electrode with openings, which allow electrons to pass through; it helps regulate the intensity of the beams directed toward the screen.

...re tube
...y glass tube in which video ...s are converted into electron ...s to produce pictures on the ...

funnel
Flared rear portion of the picture tube.

red beam
Electron beam hitting the sensitive parts of the screen that are designed to emit red light.

magnetic field
Zone exhibiting the properties of a magnet; it controls the direction of the electron beams so that the entire screen is covered.

color selection filter
Perforated metal plate that directs each electron beam toward the sensitive parts of the screen corresponding to its color.

electron gun
Device that emits electron beams toward the screen; there are beams for each of the primary colors, red, green and blue.

green beam
Electron beam hitting the sensitive parts of the screen that are designed to emit green light.

blue beam
Electron beam hitting the sensitive parts of the screen that are designed to emit blue light.

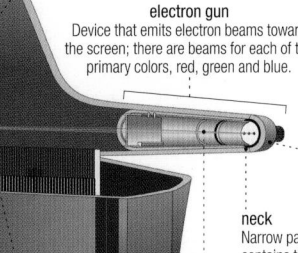

base
Terminal end of the picture tube that connects to outside circuits.

neck
Narrow part of the picture tube that contains the electron gun.

digital-to-analog converter box
Device that transforms digital signals into analog signals readable by a reception device.

protective window
...nt portion of the picture tube that covers the screen.

screen
Surface on which pictures are formed; it is covered with sensitive dots, which emit red, green or blue light when hit by electrons.

electron beam
All the negatively charged particles traveling in the same direction; their intensity varies with the video signal received.

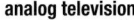

television reception

digital television
All techniques, equipment and installations used in broadcasting television programs as digital signals.

liquid crystal display (LCD) television
Television set with a flat, thin screen that reproduces images by reflecting light onto liquid crystals.

plasma tele
Television set with a flat, thin screen that repro images using light emitted by a mixture of

screen
Surface on which TV pictures are formed.

speaker
Integrated device used to generate sound.

tuning controls

on-off button
Mechanical connection that turns the device on or off.

digital video recorder/receiver
Device that decodes digital television signals transmitted by a satellite or by cable and directs them to a television set. It also allows the user to record television programs.

instant replay button
Button used to review recently broadcast scenes.

fast rewind button
Button used to quickly move backwards through the recording.

stop button
Button that stops the disc or the recording.

fast-forward button
Button used to advance quickly through the recording.

return to live programming button
Button used to return to the program being broadcast.

on-off button
Mechanical connection that turns the device on or off.

display
Screen showing information on the instrument's settings and operations.

record button
Button that starts recording of a program.

function buttons
Buttons controlling various settings of the device.

remote controll
Device that operates functions of the receiver, start, stop and program s from a distance

input device switching button
Button used to switch from the television to a DVD.

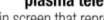

dish antenna
Device with a dish reflector that receives radio signals from a telecommunication satellite.

portable DVD p
Easily portable device that uses a laser be read images and sound recorded on a DVD (versatile

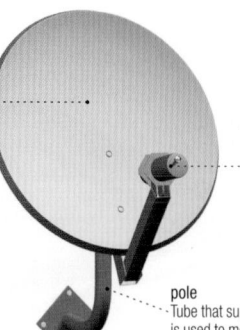

dish
Surface that collects waves and causes them to converge toward the feedhorn.

feedhorn
Device that receives, amplifies and converts waves into signals that can be used by a receiver such as a digital receiver.

pole
Tube that supports the antenna and is used to mount it.

television reception

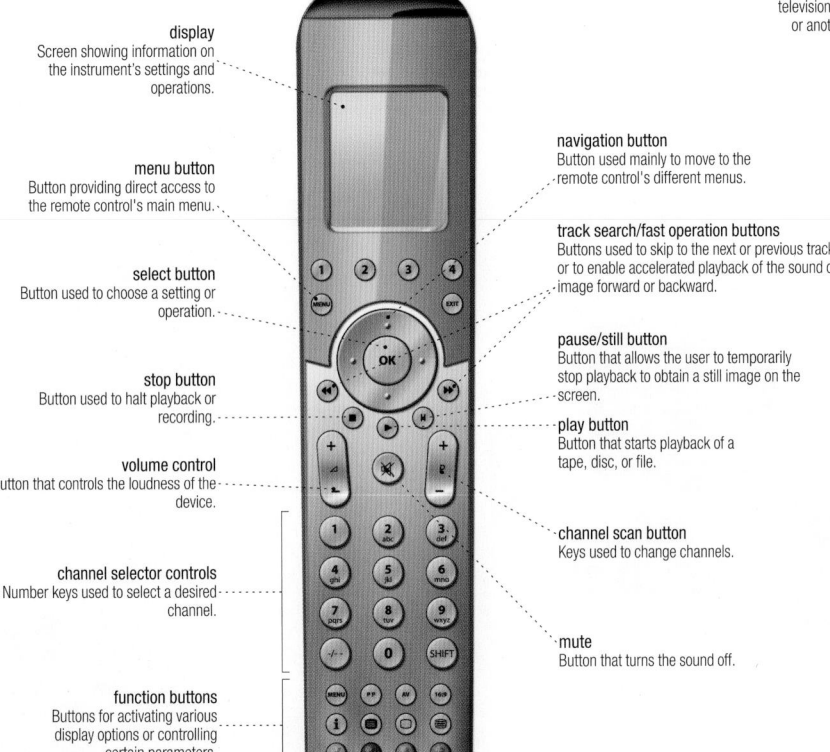

remote control
Device that controls some functions of a television set, tape recorder, DVD player, or another electronic appliance from a distance.

display
Screen showing information on the instrument's settings and operations.

menu button
Button providing direct access to the remote control's main menu.

select button
Button used to choose a setting or operation.

stop button
Button used to halt playback or recording.

volume control
Button that controls the loudness of the device.

channel selector controls
Number keys used to select a desired channel.

function buttons
Buttons for activating various display options or controlling certain parameters.

navigation button
Button used mainly to move to the remote control's different menus.

track search/fast operation buttons
Buttons used to skip to the next or previous track or to enable accelerated playback of the sound or image forward or backward.

pause/still button
Button that allows the user to temporarily stop playback to obtain a still image on the screen.

play button
Button that starts playback of a tape, disc, or file.

channel scan button
Keys used to change channels.

mute
Button that turns the sound off.

on-off button
Mechanical connection that turns the device on or off.

COMMUNICATIONS

videocassette
...d case containing a magnetic ...on which sounds and images ...be recorded.

recording tape
Flexible tape whose surface is covered with a magnetic substance; it is used as a recording medium.

reel
Cylindrical part used to wind ...d unwind the magnetic tape.

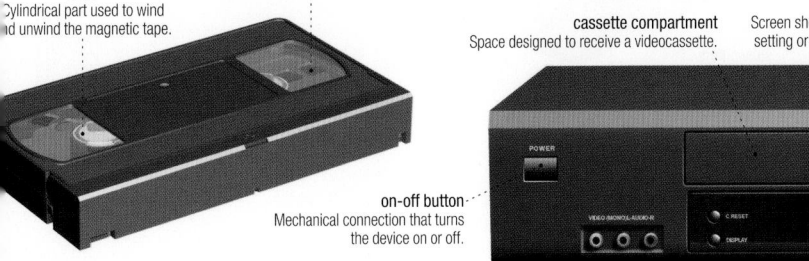

cassette compartment
Space designed to receive a videocassette.

display
Screen showing instructions for setting or operating the player.

videocassette recorder (VCR)
Device for playing back or recording audio and video signals on the magnetic tape of a videocassette.

on-off button
Mechanical connection that turns the device on or off.

...tal video disc
...tal recording medium available in various ...ats, including video, audio and multimedia; it ...greater storage capacity than a compact disc.

on-off button
Mechanical connection that turns the device on or off.

display
Screen showing instructions for setting or operating the player.

record button
Button that starts recording of a program.

DVD recorder
Device that uses a laser beam to record and play back data recorded on a DVD video.

play button
Button that starts playback of a DVD.

stop button
Button that stops the disc or the recording.

channel select buttons
Number keys used to select a desired channel.

disc tray
Part in which a disc is inserted to be played back.

disc tray control

pause/still button
Key that stops a disc momentarily during playback to produce a still image on the screen.

track search/fast operation buttons
Keys used to move to the next or previous scene, or to reverse or fast-forward the playback of a disc.

television reception

home theater
Audiovisual equipment package for home use; it recreates the sound and visual effects found in movie theaters.

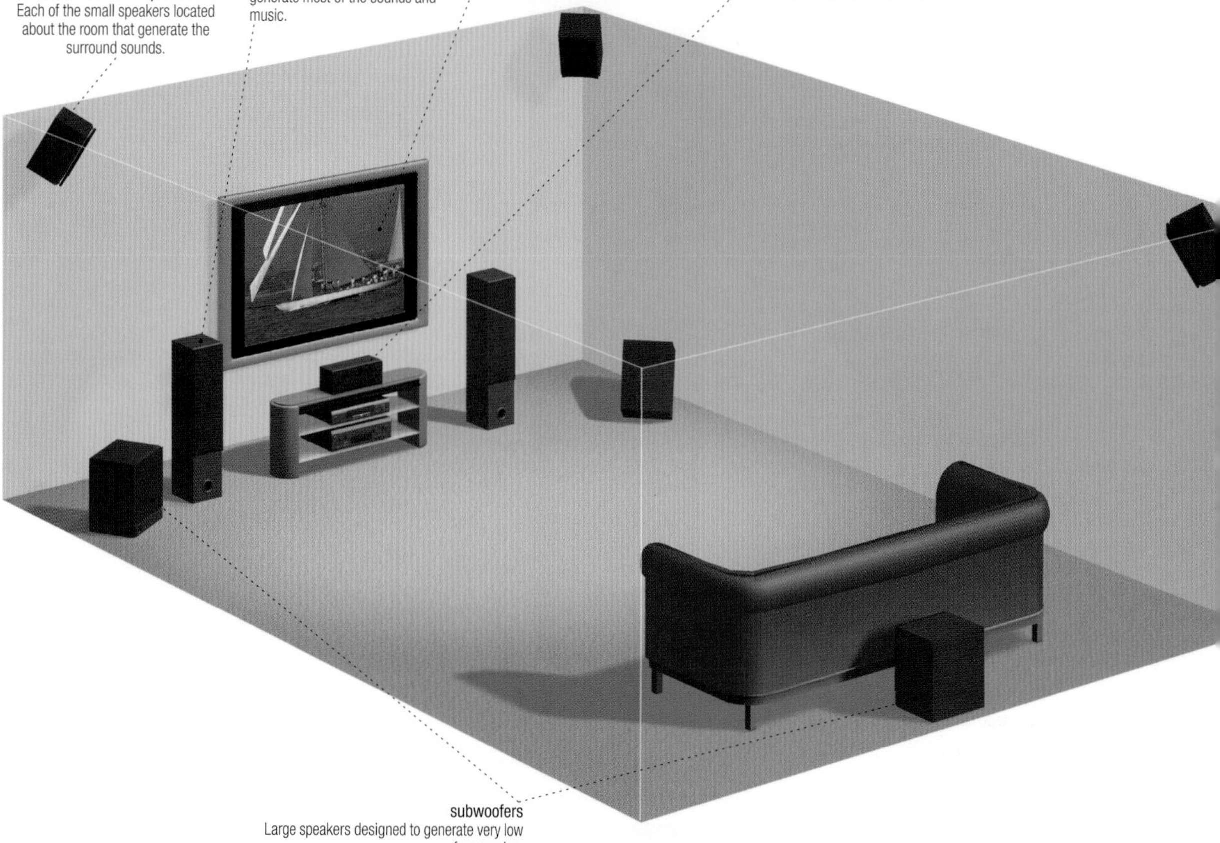

wide-screen television
Television set with a screen having a length-to-height ratio that is identical to a movie theater format.

main speaker
Each of the two speakers located at the sides of a television set that generate most of the sounds and music.

center speaker
Speaker located between the two main speakers that generates dialogue and certain sound effects.

surround-sound speaker
Each of the small speakers located about the room that generate the surround sounds.

subwoofers
Large speakers designed to generate very low frequencies.

COMMUNICATIONS

camcorders

Portable video cameras that record sound and images on various media.

DVD camcorder
Portable video camera that records sounds and images in digital format directly on a digital video disc (DVD).

hard disk drive camcorder
Portable video camera that records sounds and images in digital format on an internal hard disk.

miniDV cassette
Digital videocassette onto which images and sounds are recorded.

electronic viewfinder
Small video monitor for viewing the scene to be filmed in order to frame it and bring it into focus.

zoom button
Button used to adjust the zoom to obtain a distant or close-up view of the subject being filmed.

miniDV camcorder: front view
Portable video camera that records sounds and images in digital format on a miniDV cassette.

recording mode
Button used to select a recording medium (cassette or memory card).

photoshot button
Button used to record a still image on a memory card.

zoom lens
Lens for changing the visual field so that a close-up or distant shot of the subject can be obtained without moving the camcorder.

power/function switch
Button used to turn the camcorder on or off and to select the operating mode including camera, playback and battery recharge.

lamp
Device that produces a light beam used to light the subject being filmed.

hand strap
Adjustable strap for carrying the camcorder

microphone
Device that converts electric pulses into broadcast or recorded sounds.

terminal cover
Cover that protects the camcorder's input and output jacks (microphone, audio-video, DV).

videotape operation controls
Buttons that control viewing of recorded images; they include playback, stop, pause, fast-forward and rewind.

focus button
Button used to focus the image automatically or manually.

miniDV camcorder: rear view

nightshot button
Button for activating the mode that allows filming in the dark.

display
Screen used to view textual information (menus, options), on the images or video clips.

eyepiece
Optical disk or system of disks through which the eye sees the image produced by the lens.

recording start/stop button
Button used to start and stop the recording of pictures and sounds.

rechargeable battery pack
Device that stores chemical energy while charging, then converts it to electric energy.

card slot
Covered slot in which a memory card is inserted to record still images taken with the camcorder.

speaker
Integrated device used to generate sound.

backlighting button
Button used to improve contrast on the screen in order to improve its readability.

widescreen/data code button
Button used to start recording in widescreen format or to insert various data (date, time, etc.) onto the filmed image.

menu button
Button used to display menus for changing settings and accessing the camcorder's options.

elements of a sound reproducing system

All equipment and accessories used in sound reproduction.

amplifier with tuner

Device combining the functions of a tuner (receiving radio signals)
and an amplifier (increasing the strength of a sound signal).

standby/on button
Button used to stop or start the device, or
to put it on sleep mode (waiting state that
reduces energy consumption during periods
of inactivity).

input select buttons
Buttons that select the source of
signals in the device including tuner,
cassette deck, CD or DVD player,
digital audio player.

display
Screen showing instructions for
setting or operating the amplifier.

control select buttons
Buttons used to select vari
settings for sound reprod

input selector
Button used to select the device
that will reproduce the sounds or
images.

headphone jack
Slot that takes the plug from the
headphones.

listening mode buttons
Buttons used to select the sound
reproduction mode, including
monophonic, stereophonic and
ambiophonic.

visual mode buttons
Buttons controlling various image
settings when the receiver is
connected to a television set.

master volume dial
Button that controls the loudness of
the instrument.

ampli-tuner: back view

RS connector
Jack used to connect an external
device that uses the RS interface.

AM and FM antenna terminals
Jacks that connect the AM and FM receiving antennas to the
amplifier with tuner.

HDMI connector
Jack used to connect an
external device that uses the
HDMI interface.

coaxial digital audio input
Connection socket into which a digital
coaxial cable is plugged.

audio/video source inputs/outputs
Coupling jacks that transfer audio and video
signals between the amplifier with tuner and the
various playback and recording devices.

plug
Unit designed to connec
cord to an electrica

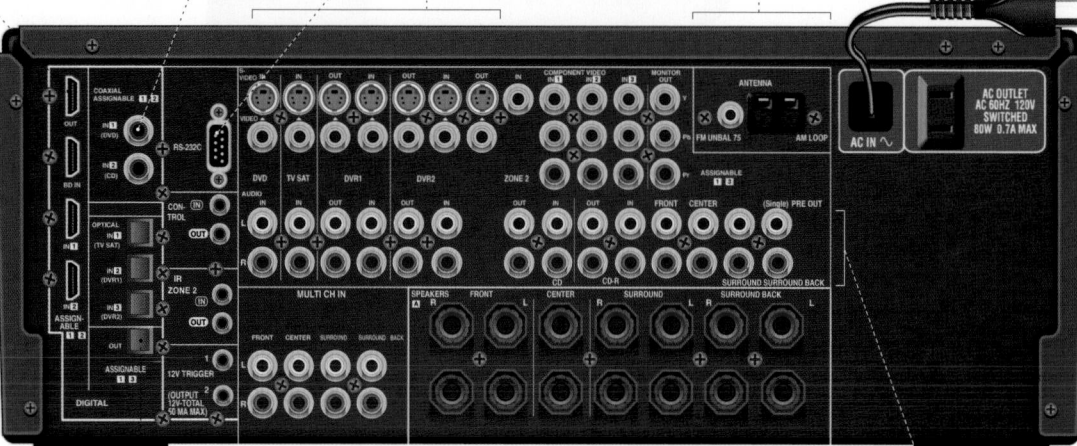

optical digital audio output/input
Connection socket for a receiver or amplifier using an optical
digital audio cable.

multichannel audio inputs
Coupling jacks that transfer audio
signals between the amplifier with
tuner and the various playback
devices.

speaker terminals
Jacks that connect the speakers to the amplifier
with tuner.

multichannel outputs
Connection sockets used in ren
sounds.

elements of a sound reproducing system

compact disc
...l recording medium with
...le formats (including video
...udio) and variable storage
...ity.

technical identification band
Surface on which the disc's identification code is engraved.

compact disc reading
During playback of a compact disc, a sensor analyzes laser beam variations reflected by the disc's surface to re-create the original sound signal.

objective lens
Optical system made up of a set of lenses attached to a mount; it focuses the laser beam onto the section to be played.

asperity
Each of the small protuberances of varying length that encode data on the disc's surface.

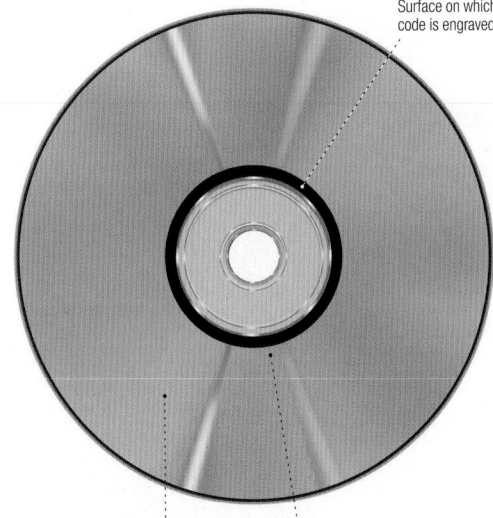

pressed area
Surface that contains the ...ecording; it is coded on a spiral groove pressed into the disc.

reading start
The track on the pressed surface is made up of a series of pits and asperities; a laser beam reads the groove from the inside out.

laser beam
Highly concentrated light beam that scans the surface of a disc; the pits and asperities determine how the light beam is reflected.

aluminum layer
The surface of the disc is covered with a thin layer of aluminum, which reflects the laser beam toward the sensor.

resin surface
Transparent film that covers and protects the aluminum layer.

shuffle play button
Button used to play back tracks in random order chosen by the device.

compact disc player
Device using a laser beam to play back sounds recorded on a compact disc (CD).

on-off button
...chanical connection that turns the device on or off.

direct disc access buttons
Buttons used to play back one of the discs inserted in the player.

repeat button
Button allowing repeated playback of one or several tracks.

track search/fast operation buttons
Buttons used to skip to the next or previous track or to accelerate playback forward or backward.

stop button
Button used to stop playback of a disc.

pause button
Button used to stop playback of a disc temporarily.

play button
Button used to start playback of a disc.

disc skip
Button used to skip to the next disc.

headphone jack
Socket for a headphone plug.

disc compartment
Compartment that contains the tray into which discs are inserted for playback.

display
Screen displaying device settings or operations executed.

disc compartment control
Button that opens and closes the disc tray.

COMMUNICATIONS

elements of a sound reproducing system

cassette
Rigid case containing a recording tape on which sounds can be recorded.

take-up reel
Cylindrical part on which the recording tape winds.

housing

recording tape
Flexible tape whose surface is covered with a magnetic substance; it is used recording medium.

guide roller
Spool that guides the recording tape.

playing window
Opening allowing the recording tape to advance in front of the playback head of the cassette tape deck.

tape guide
Part that holds and guides the recording tape in front of the playing window.

cassette tape deck
Device used to play back and record sounds on a recording tape cassette.

play button
Key used to play back a tape.

tape counter
Device showing the length of a recorded segment on a tape.

fast-forward button
Control key used to fast-forward a tape.

eject button
Key activating the mechanism to eject a cassette from the cassette holder.

counter reset button
Key used to reset a tape counter to zero.

tape selector
The buttons used to indicate clearly the type of recording tape (normal, chrome or metal).

peak level meter
Device showing the intensity of the sound being played back or recorded.

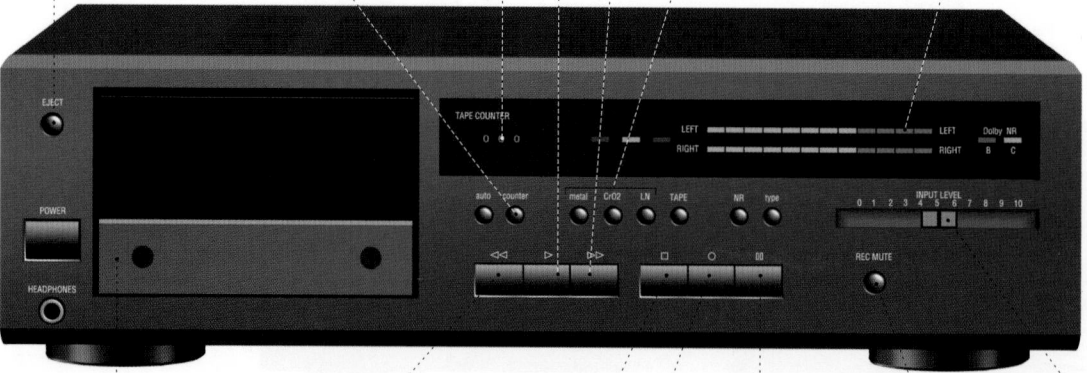

cassette holder
Compartment receiving the cassette for playback.

rewind button
Control key used to rewind a tape.

stop button
Key used to interrupt the playback, recording, rewinding or fast-forwarding of a tape.

record muting button
Key used to record a blank section at the start of a track or between two tracks.

record button
Key used to activate the sound recording mechanism on a tape deck.

pause button
Key used to temporarily stop the playback or recording of a tape.

recording level control
Device used to change the intensity of the recorded sound signals.

elements of a sound reproducing system

record
Usually vinyl, circular medium on which sounds are recorded.

spiral-in groove
Part of the locked groove that marks the beginning of the record.

spiral
Blank part of the locked groove that separates two bands.

tail-out groove
Part of the locked groove that marks the end of the last band.

locked groove
Spiral groove etched into the surface of a record; the stylus cartridge of a record player travels along the groove from the outside in.

center hole
Circular opening for inserting the record on the center of the turntable.

label
Marking affixed to the center of the record that provides information about its contents.

band
Part of the locked groove that contains a recording; the sides of the groove are marked by hills and valleys, which cause the stylus to vibrate.

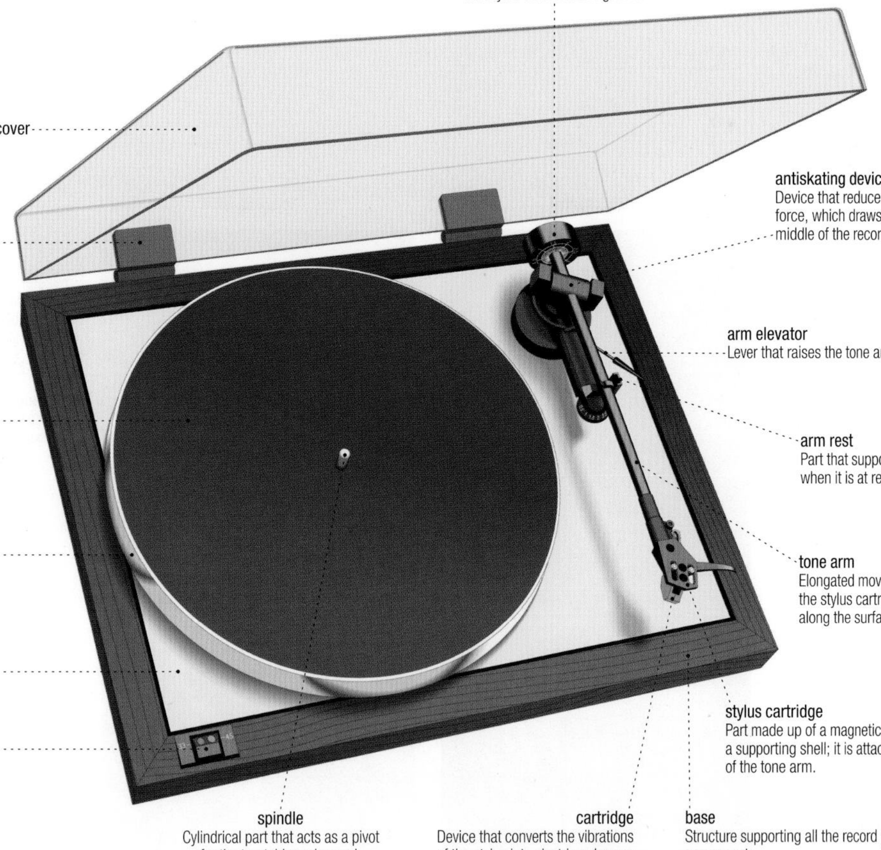

counterweight
Part that regulates the pressure of the stylus on the record groove.

turntable
Device using an arm fitted with a stylus cartridge to play back sounds from a record.

dust cover

antiskating device
Device that reduces the effect of centripetal force, which draws the toner arm toward the middle of the record.

hinge

arm elevator
Lever that raises the tone arm.

rubber mat
Antiskid and antiscratch turntable cover that is usually made of felt or rubber.

arm rest
Part that supports the tone arm when it is at rest.

turntable
Rotating part on which the record rests when played.

tone arm
Elongated movable part that holds the stylus cartridge and moves it along the surface of the record.

base plate
Plate that supports the turntable; it usually attached to the base by a springy suspension.

stylus cartridge
Part made up of a magnetic cartridge and a supporting shell; it is attached to the end of the tone arm.

speed selector
Device used to select the turntable speed (45 or 33 1/3 revolutions per minute).

spindle
Cylindrical part that acts as a pivot for the turntable and record.

cartridge
Device that converts the vibrations of the stylus into electric pulses as it travels along the locked groove.

base
Structure supporting all the record player components.

COMMUNICATIONS

elements of a sound reproducing system

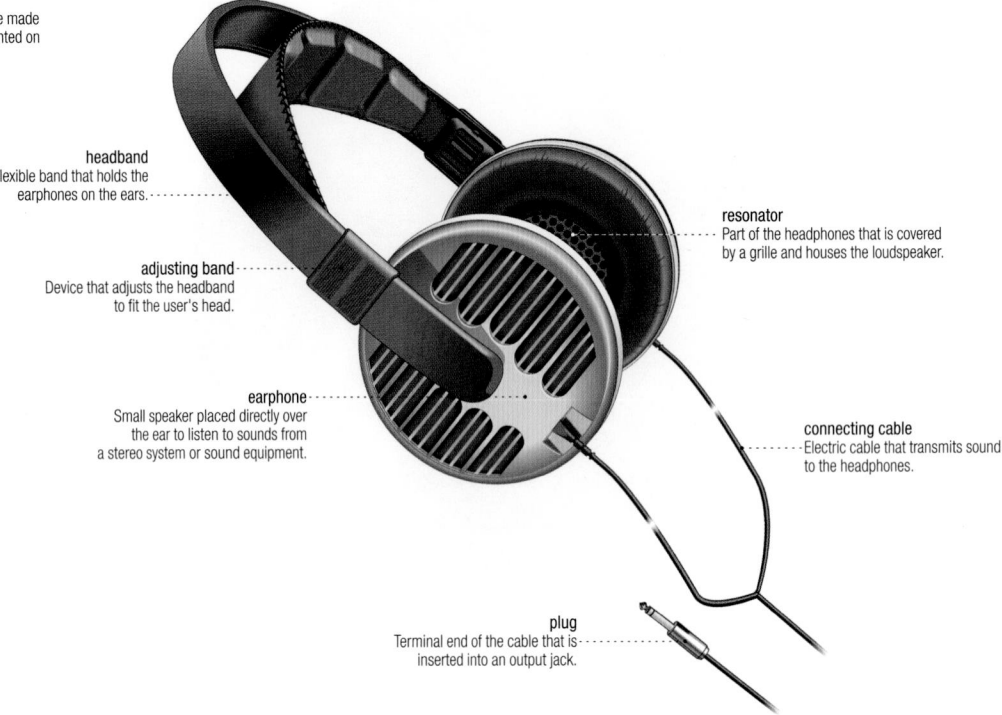

headphones
Sound reproduction device made up of two earphones mounted on a headband.

headband
Flexible band that holds the earphones on the ears.

adjusting band
Device that adjusts the headband to fit the user's head.

earphone
Small speaker placed directly over the ear to listen to sounds from a stereo system or sound equipment.

resonator
Part of the headphones that is covered by a grille and houses the loudspeaker.

connecting cable
Electric cable that transmits sound to the headphones.

plug
Terminal end of the cable that is inserted into an output jack.

loudspeakers
Case enclosing one or several speakers which convert electrical pulses into sound waves.

right channel

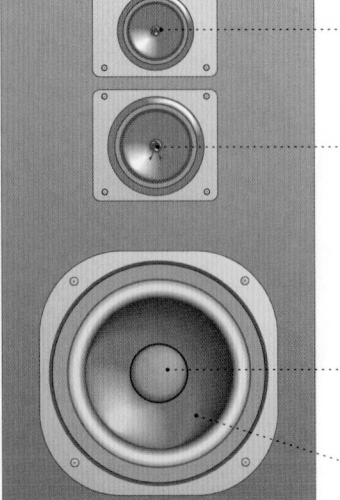

left channel

tweeter
Loudspeaker designed to reproduce the high frequencies of the sound signal.

midrange
Loudspeaker designed to reproduce the middle frequencies of the sound signal.

speaker cover
Thin grille made of fabric or metal that covers and protects the speakers.

woofer
Loudspeaker designed to reproduce the low frequencies of the sound signal.

diaphragm
Cone-shaped flexible part that vibrates to create sound waves in the air.

mini stereo sound system

Sound reproduction system with miniaturized components (including amplifier, tuner, speakers and compact disc player).

portable digital audio player dock
Base into which a digital audio player is inserted in order to transmit stored tracks to the stereo.

amplifier with tuner
Device combining the functions of a tuner (receiving radio signals) and an amplifier (increasing the strength of a sound signal).

loudspeaker
Case enclosing one or several speakers, which convert electric pulses into sound waves by means of an amplifier.

USB port
Connector used to link a standard USB peripheral.

compact disc player
Equipment that uses a laser beam to read data recorded on a compact disc.

portable sound systems

Small self-contained sound reproduction equipment that can be carried easily from one place to another.

ck radio
able radio with a built-in alarm clock
se wake-up mechanism is a buzzer or
dio station setting.

telescoping antenna
FM receiving antenna made up of sections that extend upward.

portable radio
Equipment used to receive signals transmitted by radio stations.

handle

on-off switch
Mechanical connection that turns the device on or off.

station display
Screen displaying the radio broadcasting frequency of the station being received, as well as other information.

bass tone control
Button used to adjust the relative level of low-frequency sounds.

frequency selectors
Buttons used to select an AM or FM band.

treble tone control
Button used to adjust the relative level of high-frequency sounds.

display
n showing instructions for
g or operating the player.

earbuds
Very small speakers placed directly in the ear to hear sounds from the portable audio player.

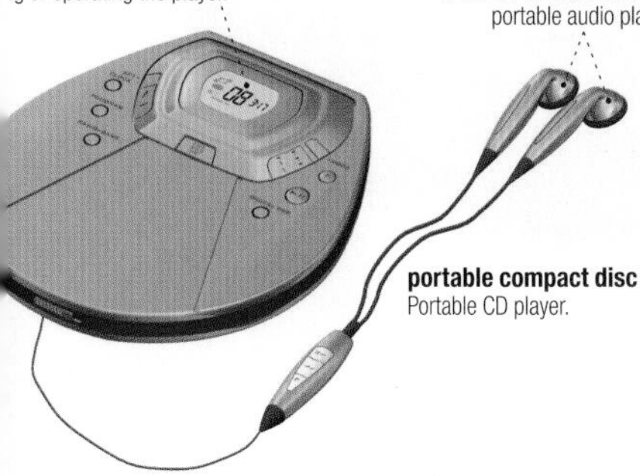

tuning control
Button used to select a broadcast frequency.

volume control
Button that controls the loudness of the radio.

preset station selector
Button used to tune into a station held in memory.

portable compact disc player
Portable CD player.

portable sound systems

portable digital audio player
Portable player for digital music files.

number buttons
Numbered buttons used to enter a station number directly or to recall a station kept in memory.

display
Screen showing information on the instrument's settings and operations.

satellite radio receiver
Device that receives signals from radio stations broadcast to a large territory via satellite.

cable

plug
Tip of the cord, equipped with a pin which is inserted into the earphone jack on the portable player.

display
Display area for viewing text data (menus, options, playlists), images, or videos.

memory button
Button used to record information related to the current program (artist name, track title, etc.).

menu button
Button used to display main menus for selection of settings or operations.

previous/rewind button
Button used to return to the previous track or accelerate playback backward.

next/fast-forward button
Button used to skip to the next track or accelerate playback forward.

preset button
Button used to keep a st memory.

select button
Button used to choose a setting or operation.

play/pause button
Button used to start or temporarily stop playback.

menu button
Button used to access the device's different options.

category buttons
Buttons used to navigate betwe different thematic groups of stations (rock, jazz, classical, sports, etc.).

earbuds
Very small speakers placed directly in the ears to hear sounds from the portable audio player.

display button
Button used to select the items displayed on the screen (artist name, track title, duration, etc.).

tuning control
Control used to choose a station or scroll through menus displayed on the screen.

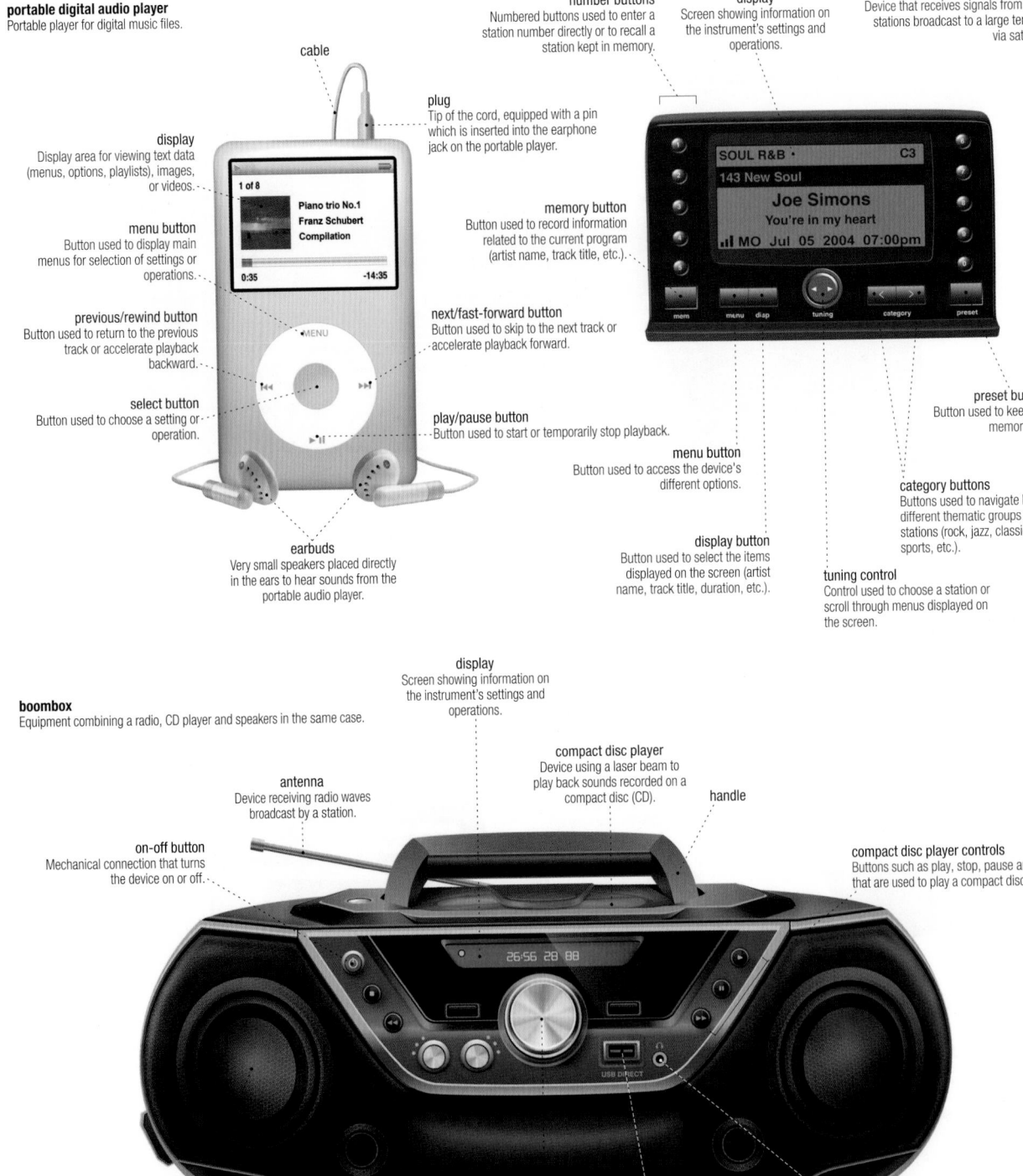

display
Screen showing information on the instrument's settings and operations.

boombox
Equipment combining a radio, CD player and speakers in the same case.

compact disc player
Device using a laser beam to play back sounds recorded on a compact disc (CD).

handle

antenna
Device receiving radio waves broadcast by a station.

on-off button
Mechanical connection that turns the device on or off.

compact disc player controls
Buttons such as play, stop, pause and tra that are used to play a compact disc (CD)

speaker
Integrated device used to generate sound.

headphone jack
Slot that takes the plug from the headphones.

tuning control
Button used to select a broadcast frequency.

USB port
Connector used to link a standard USB peripheral.

Display text: 1 of 8 · Piano trio No.1 · Franz Schubert · Compilation · 0:35 · -14:35 · MENU

Satellite receiver display: SOUL R&B · C3 · 143 New Soul · Joe Simons · You're in my heart · MO Jul 05 2004 07:00pm · mem · menu · disp · tuning · category · preset

Boombox display: 26:56 28 88 · USB DIRECT

walkie-talkie

Portable two-way radio used to relay the human voice over short distances.

display
Screen showing instructions for setting or operating the walkie-talkie.

antenna
Device that emits and receives radio waves.

volume control
Button that controls the loudness of the walkie-talkie.

on-off button
Mechanical connection that turns the device on or off.

scroll button
Button that adjusts the speaker volume and changes equipment settings.

light button
Button that illuminates the display to make the data more legible in poor lighting conditions.

call button
Button that signals the desire to communicate with another user.

menu button
Button that displays the menus so that settings and operations can be selected.

microphone
Device that converts electric pulses into broadcast or recorded sounds.

monitor button
Button used to check if a broadcast or receiving channel is free before transmitting.

lock button
Button that deactivates the menu and scroll buttons to prevent equipment settings from being changed accidentally.

speaker
Integrated device used to generate sound.

push-to-talk switch
When this button is pressed, voice messages can be sent from one extension to another; when it is released, messages can be received.

numeric pager

Portable device that receives digital messages (usually the telephone number of the caller).

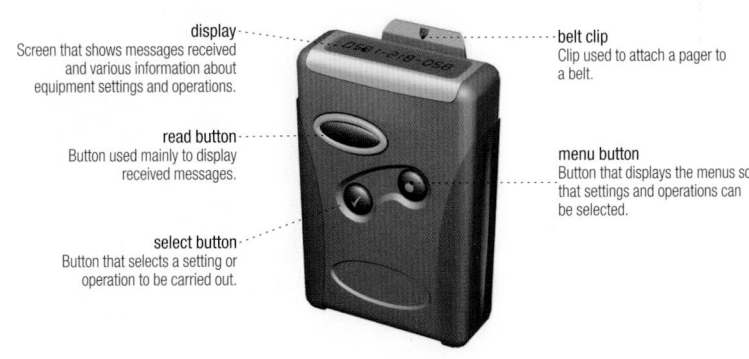

display
Screen that shows messages received and various information about equipment settings and operations.

belt clip
Clip used to attach a pager to a belt.

read button
Button used mainly to display received messages.

menu button
Button that displays the menus so that settings and operations can be selected.

select button
Button that selects a setting or operation to be carried out.

CB radio

Two-way radio often installed in a vehicle; it transmits the human voice over reserved frequencies on a public band.

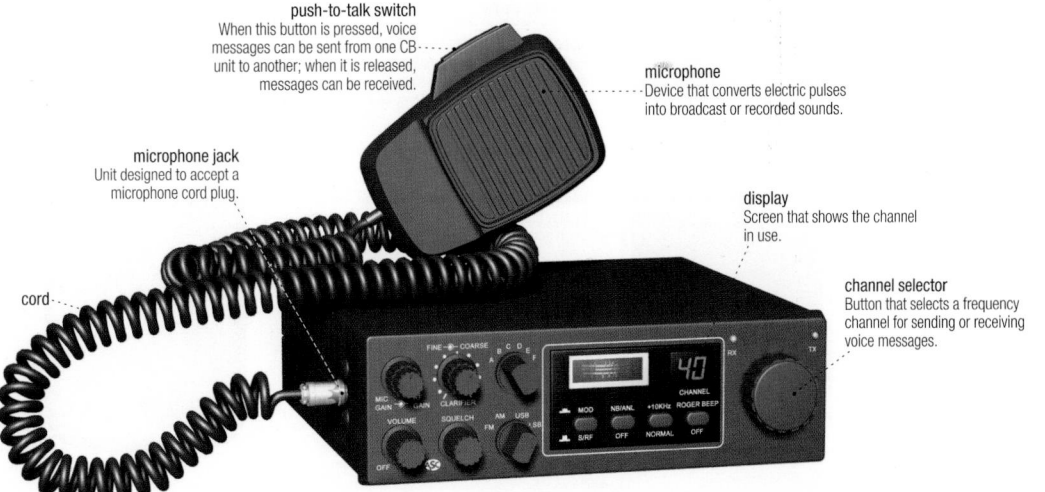

push-to-talk switch
When this button is pressed, voice messages can be sent from one CB unit to another; when it is released, messages can be received.

microphone
Device that converts electric pulses into broadcast or recorded sounds.

microphone jack
Unit designed to accept a microphone cord plug.

display
Screen that shows the channel in use.

cord

channel selector
Button that selects a frequency channel for sending or receiving voice messages.

cellular telephone

Small telephone that transmits voice or text messages via radio waves.

cellular telephone: internal view
Small telephone that transmits voice or text messages via radio waves.

receiver
Small voice reproduction speaker that is placed over the ear.

cellular telephone: external view

portable earpho[ne]
Accessory allowing hands-free opera[tion] of a cellular telepho[ne]

display
Screen used to view textual information (menus, options), on the images or video clips.

menu key
Button providing direct access to the phone's main menu.

antenna
Device that emits and receives radio waves.

earloop
Device used to hold the earpie[ce] on the ear.

navigation key
Button used mainly to scroll through the phone's menus and directories.

soft key
Button used for a user-defined function.

display
Screen showing information on the instrument's settings and operations.

answer/end key
Button used to make or answer a call.

talk key
Button used to make or answer a call.

camera key
Button providing access to the functions of the phone's integrated camera.

alphanumeric keypad
Keys corresponding to letters, numbers and symbols that are used to dial a number, compose a message or access functions.

earpiece
Small voice reproduction spea[ker] that is placed over the ear.

end/power key
Button used to end a phone call and to turn the phone's power on or off.

camera lens
Lens that enables images to be projected onto the sensor of the integrated camera.

microphone
Device that converts electric pulses into broadcast or recorded sounds.

docking station
Base into which the mobile phone is inserted to recharge its battery or synchronize its data with a computer.

battery charger
Device allowing the accumulation of electric current in a battery.

receiver
Small voice reproduction speaker that is placed directly over the ear.

keyboard smartpho[ne]
Device integrating the communica[tion] functions of a mobile phone with management and data process[ing] functions of a personal digital assista[nt].

sliding keyboard
Piece composed of a group of keys corresponding to letters, numbers, a[nd] symbols, that can be slid back behi[nd] the device.

on-off button
Mechanical connection that turns the device on or off.

connector
Linking device used to connect the telephone to the docking station.

USB connector
Linking device used to connect the docking station to the USB port of another device.

touch screen
Display that is sensitive to the touch and the motion of a finger.

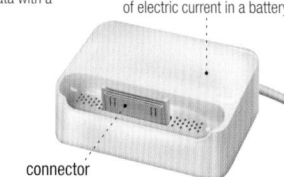

touch screen smartphone: front view
Device integrating the communication functions of a mobile phone with the management and data processing functions of a personal digital assistant.

receiver
Small voice reproduction speaker that is placed directly over the ear.

touch screen smartphone: back vie[w]

on-off button
Mechanical connection that turns the device on or off.

sleep/wake key
Button for starting up or shutting down the device also used to put it on sleep mode (waiting state that reduces energy consumption during periods of inactivity).

speaker
Integrated device used to g[ive] sound.

volume key
Button that controls the loudness of the instrument.

touch screen
Display that is sensitive to the touch and the motion of a finger.

camera lens
Optical system made up o[f] lenses fixed on a mount; it [allows] a clear image to be produc[ed on a] sensor.

application icon
Graphic representation that will start up an application when activated.

menu key
Button providing direct access to the phone's main menu.

talk key
Button used to make or answer a call.

end call key
Button used to end a phone call.

microphone
Device that converts electric s[ignals] into broadcast or recorded s[ounds]

examples of telephones

The shape and function of telephones is constantly evolving; today's phones relay computer data as well as voice communication.

display
Screen that shows various information such as phone settings, text messages, dialed numbers and a caller's name and number.

memory telephone set
Device used to transmit voice across distances over a telephone network. It has buttons used to dial a number, and access functions or preprogrammed numbers.

receiver
Small voice reproduction speaker that is placed over the ear.

handset
Movable part of the telephone made up of the receiver and the transmitter.

on-off light

receiver volume control

transmitter
Device that converts electric pulses into broadcast or recorded sounds.

display setting
Button used to change the display parameters.

ringing volume control
Button that controls the loudness of the ringing.

handset cord

push buttons
Keys corresponding to letters, numbers and symbols that are used to dial a number or access functions.

memory button
Button that automatically dials a telephone number held in memory.

function selectors
Control buttons that operate various equipment functions such as last-number redial, call hold and link.

telephone index
List of frequently used names and telephone numbers.

automatic dialer index
List of names and telephone numbers corresponding to the memory buttons.

cordless telephone network
Network made up of one or more secondary telephones linked by radio waves to a main telephone connected to the outside telephone network.

cordless telephone
Device featuring a handset with antenna that is linked by radio waves to a base.

handset
Movable part of the telephone made up of the receiver and the transmitter.

antenna
Device that emits and receives radio waves.

main telephone
Base unit connected to the telephone network.

secondary telephone
Device connected to the main telephone by radio waves.

base
Used to recharge the battery of the cordless telephone.

examples of telephones

Internet mobile phone
Device used to make telephone calls over the Internet.

display
Screen used to view textual information (menus, options), on the images or video clips.

talk key
Buttons used to signal other users that one wants to communicate with them, or to answer a call.

navigation key
Button used mainly to scroll through the phone's menus and directories.

receiver
Small voice reproduction speaker that is placed directly over the ear.

end/power key
Button used to end a phone call and to turn the phone's power on or off.

alphanumeric keypad
Keys corresponding to letters, numbers and symbols that are used to dial a number, compose a message or access functions.

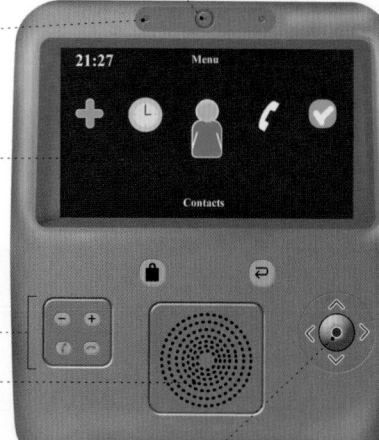

microphone
Device that converts electric pulses into broadcast or recorded sounds.

videoph
Telephone that can transmit v and images over a digital netw

webcam
Miniature digital camera used to transmit video images in real-time or for videoconferencing over the Internet.

touch screen
Display that is sensitive to the touch and the motion of a finger.

call keys
Buttons used to signal other users that one wants to communicate with them, to answer, or to end a call.

speaker
Integrated device used to generate sound.

selection and navigation key
Button used mainly to scroll through the phone's menus and directories or to choose a setting or operation.

pay phone
Telephone located in public places; it functions when coins or payment cards are inserted into the phone box.

coin slot
Slot for inserting coins into a telephone to pay for a call.

volume control
Button that controls the loudness of the phone.

display
Screen that shows a variety of information such as dialed number and prepaid card balance.

next call
Button used to make another telephone call without hanging up the handset.

language display button

push buttons
Keys corresponding to letters, numbers and symbols that are used to dial a number or access functions.

card reader
Device used to read a payment card (credit card, calling card or prepaid card).

handset
Movable part of the telephone made up of the receiver and the transmitter.

armored cord

coin return bucket
Small chamber for retrieving coins.

push-button telepho
Device with alphanumeric keys to a number or access functions; it gradually replaced the dial pho

call director telepho
Device that redirects calls within organization's internal telepho netwo

examples of telephones

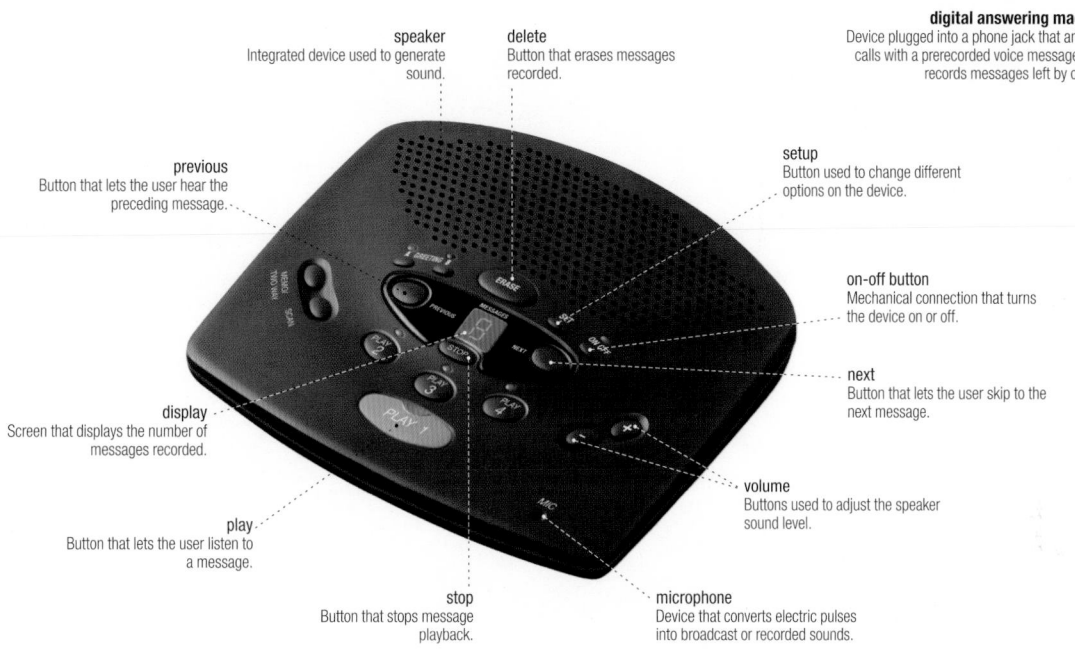

speaker
Integrated device used to generate sound.

delete
Button that erases messages recorded.

digital answering machine
Device plugged into a phone jack that answers calls with a prerecorded voice message, then records messages left by callers.

previous
Button that lets the user hear the preceding message.

setup
Button used to change different options on the device.

on-off button
Mechanical connection that turns the device on or off.

next
Button that lets the user skip to the next message.

display
Screen that displays the number of messages recorded.

play
Button that lets the user listen to a message.

volume
Buttons used to adjust the speaker sound level.

stop
Button that stops message playback.

microphone
Device that converts electric pulses into broadcast or recorded sounds.

facsimile (fax) machine
Equipment used to send written documents over a telephone network.

automatic document feeder
Tray into which outgoing faxes are inserted; it converts graphic data into electric pulses for transmission.

display
Screen showing information on the instrument's settings and operations.

numeric keypad
Keys corresponding to letters, numbers and symbols that are used to dial a number or access functions.

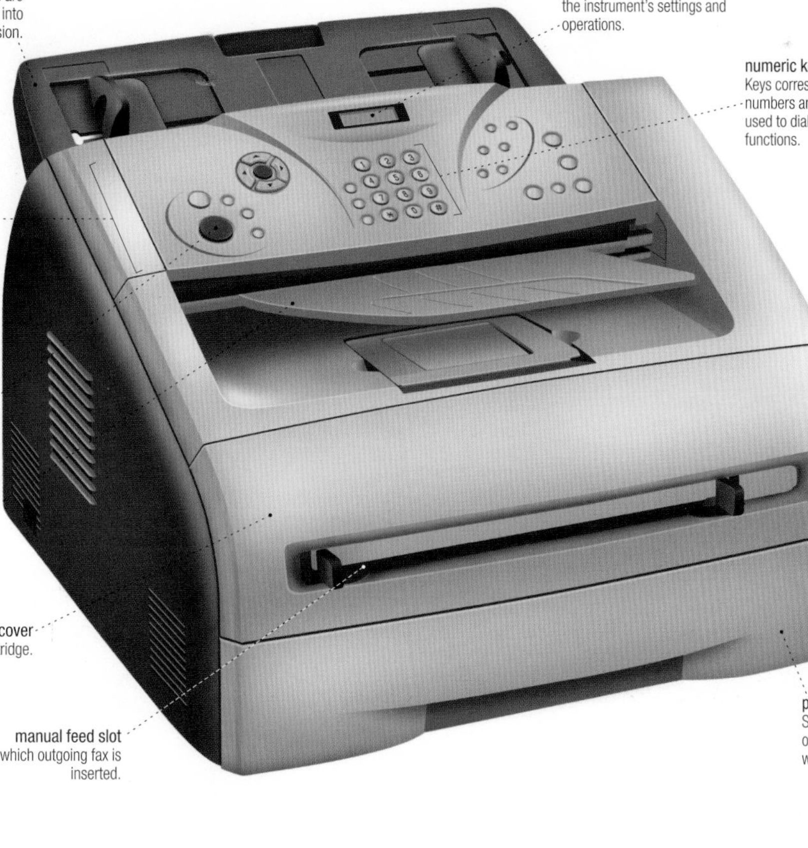

control keys
The buttons used to carry out various operations such as automatic dialing, batch transmission and store-and-forward transmission.

start key
Button used to activate selected commands.

document output tray
Tray in which incoming faxes are collected.

front cover
Piece covering the ink cartridge.

manual feed slot
Slot into which outgoing fax is inserted.

paper tray
Small tray containing blank sheets of paper that are loaded one by one when printing received documents.

COMMUNICATIONS

OFFICE AUTOMATION

The electronic, computer and telecommunications technologies that are applied to office work.

all-in-one computer

Computer with all its main components integrated inside one casing.

front view

display
Screen for visually representing graphic or textual data provided by a computer.

enclosure
Rectangular casing housing the main components of the computer: display, central processing unit, ports and certain accessories.

tapered pedestal
Part supporting the screen.

side view

back v

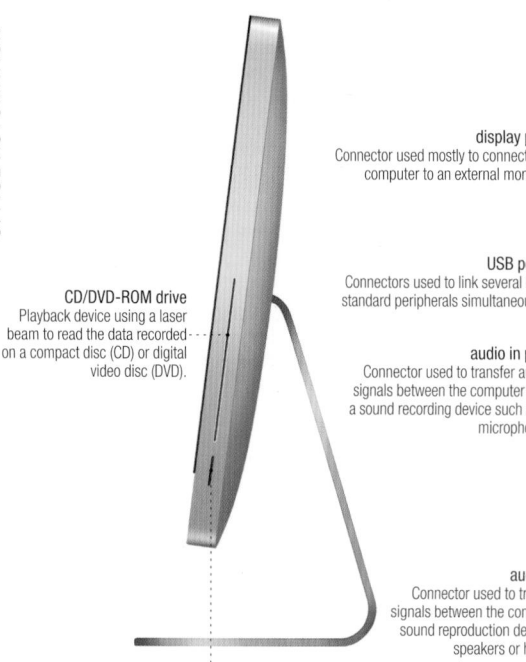

display port
Connector used mostly to connect the computer to an external monitor.

USB ports
Connectors used to link several USB standard peripherals simultaneously.

audio in port
Connector used to transfer audio signals between the computer and a sound recording device such as a microphone.

CD/DVD-ROM drive
Playback device using a laser beam to read the data recorded on a compact disc (CD) or digital video disc (DVD).

audio out port
Connector used to transfer audio signals between the computer and a sound reproduction device such as speakers or headphones.

memory card reader
Device that reads and records data on a memory card.

FireWire port
High-performance connector that conforms to the FireWire standard; it is used to link high-speed peripherals (camcorder, digital camera).

Ethernet port
Connector conforming to the Ethernet protocol; it is used to connect a computer to a local area network or another computer for file sharing.

power cable connector
Recessed area containing metal prongs which are plugged into a cable to connect the computer to a power source.

power button
Button for turning the de or off.

tower case computer

Computer whose main components are assembled in a tower casing separate from the screen.

monitor
Screen for visually representing graphic or textual data provided by a computer.

control buttons
Buttons used to modify the screen settings (brightness, contrast, etc.).

on-off button
Button for turning the device on or off.

indicator light
Signal light indicating that the device is on.

tower case: back view

tower case: front view
Tower case: Enclosure housing the main components of the computer.

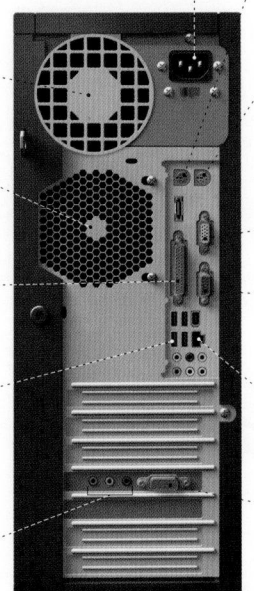

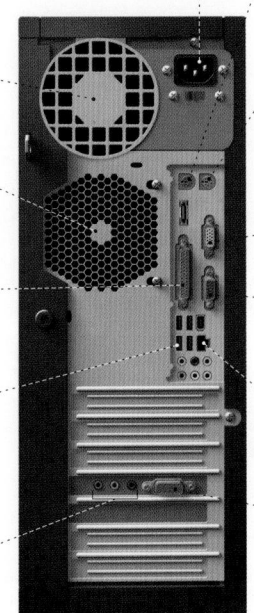

power cable connector
Recessed area containing metal prongs which are plugged into a cable to connect the computer to a power source.

keyboard port
Round connector that links the computer to the keyboard.

CD/DVD-ROM drive
Playback device using a laser beam to read the data recorded on a compact disc (CD) or digital video disc (DVD).

mouse port
Round connector that links the computer to the mouse.

CD/DVD-ROM eject button
Button used to open the CD/DVD-ROM drive to retrieve the inserted disc.

power supply fan
Device blowing air to cool the internal components of the power supply unit.

bay filler panel
Standard-sized panel covering an unused compartment through which electronic hardware can be added.

case fan
Device blowing air to cool the internal components of the tower case.

memory card reader
Device that reads and records data on a memory card.

serial port
Connector used to attach a computer to various peripherals such as an external modem; it is slower than a parallel port as it exchanges only one bit at a time.

reset button
Button used to reboot the computer in the event the system freezes.

parallel port
Connector used mainly to attach the computer to a printer; it is faster than a serial port as it exchanges data in eight-bit groups.

video port
Connector used to attach the computer monitor to the video board; the latter is inserted in the tower case and controls the display of texts and graphics.

power button
Button for turning the device on or off.

USB port
Connector used to link several USB standard peripherals simultaneously; it is faster than serial and parallel ports.

network port
Connector that attaches the computer to a network.

USB port
Connector used to link to a USB standard peripheral; it is faster than serial and parallel ports.

audio jack
Connection device that attaches the computer to a variety of sound recording or reproduction equipment such as a microphone and loudspeakers.

game/MIDI port
Connector that attaches the computer to a game device (e.g., a joystick) or a digital musical instrument.

laptop computer

Small stand-alone microcomputer with a screen and integrated keyboard; it is powered by an internal battery.

front view

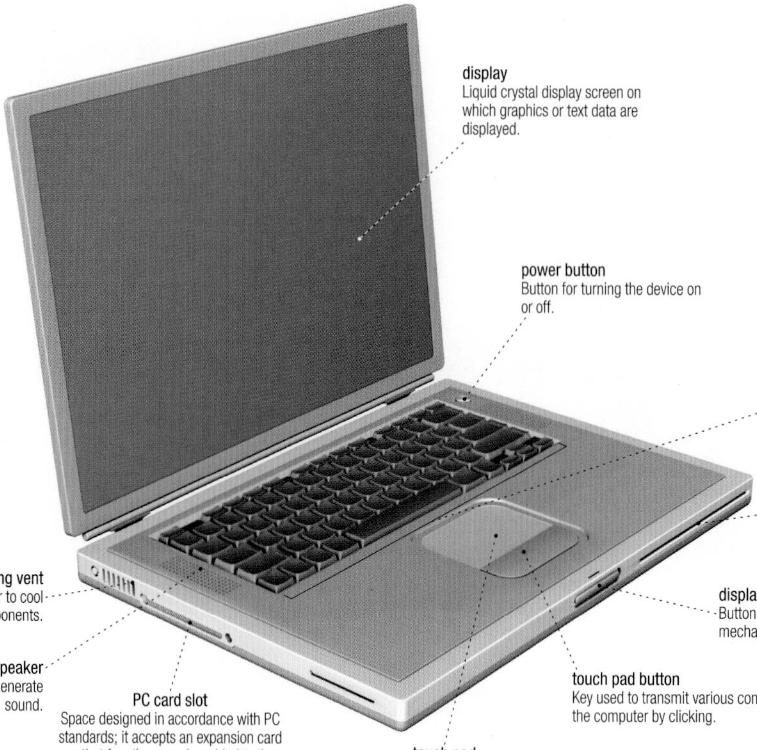

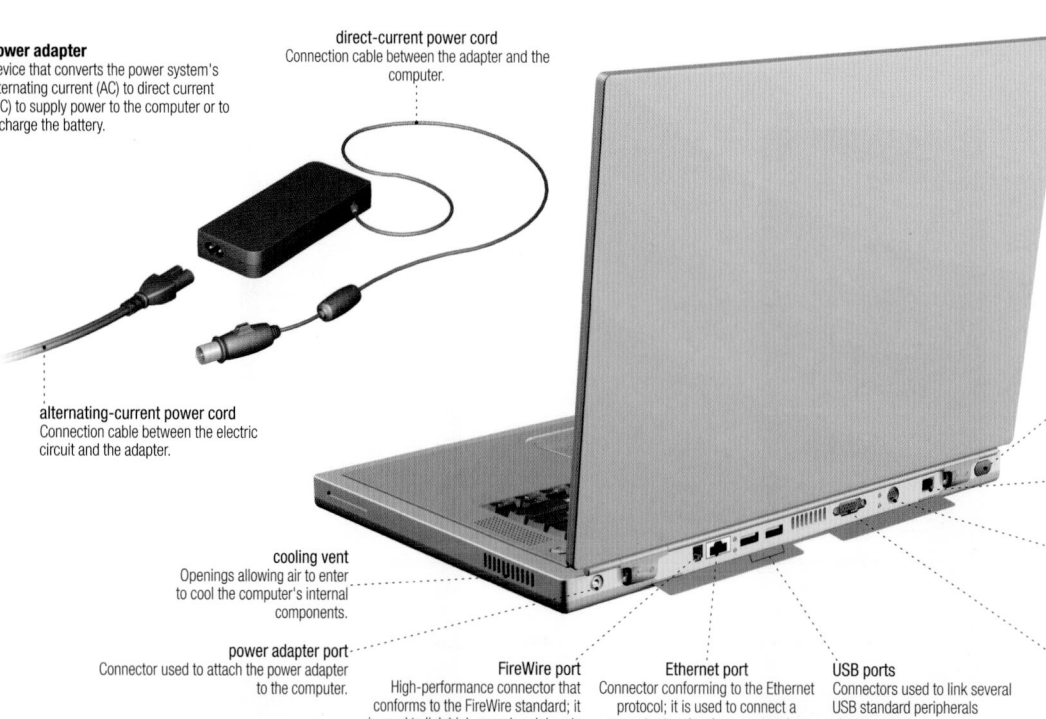

display
Liquid crystal display screen on which graphics or text data are displayed.

power button
Button for turning the device on or off.

keyboard
Keys corresponding to letters, numbers symbols and functions that are used to generate characters or control operations.

CD/DVD-ROM drive
Playback device using a laser b read the data recorded on a co disc (CD) or digital video disc (D

cooling vent
Openings allowing air to enter to cool the computer's internal components.

display release button
Button that frees the screen from the locking mechanism allowing it to be opened.

speaker
Integrated device used to generate sound.

touch pad button
Key used to transmit various commands to the computer by clicking.

PC card slot
Space designed in accordance with PC standards; it accepts an expansion card so that functions can be added to the computer (network card, memory card).

touch pad
Surface that is sensitive to finger motion; it is used to direct the movements of the cursor on the screen.

back v

direct-current power cord
Connection cable between the adapter and the computer.

power adapter
Device that converts the power system's alternating current (AC) to direct current (DC) to supply power to the computer or to recharge the battery.

infrared port
Device that uses infrared s exchange data with a devic a similar port (a network a transmitter-receiver, comp printer).

internal modem port
Connector used to attach modem (a two-way digital changing device) to a telep

alternating-current power cord
Connection cable between the electric circuit and the adapter.

S-Video output
Connector that links a com video output peripheral (te video projector, VCR).

cooling vent
Openings allowing air to enter to cool the computer's internal components.

power adapter port
Connector used to attach the power adapter to the computer.

FireWire port
High-performance connector that conforms to the FireWire standard; it is used to link high-speed peripherals (camcorder, digital camera).

Ethernet port
Connector conforming to the Ethernet protocol; it is used to connect a computer to a local area network or another computer for file sharing.

USB ports
Connectors used to link several USB standard peripherals simultaneously.

video port
Connector used mostly to the computer to an externa monitor.

network devices

Electronic devices allowing computers to exchange data.

wireless network interface card
Expansion card with an integrated antenna; it links a computer to a network access point transceiver via radio waves.

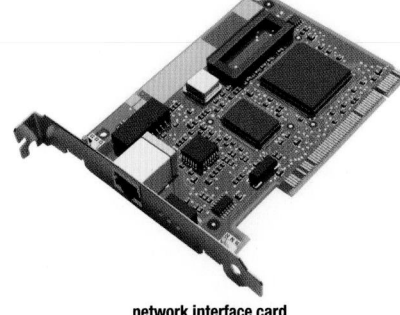

network interface card
Expansion card that connects a computer to a computer network.

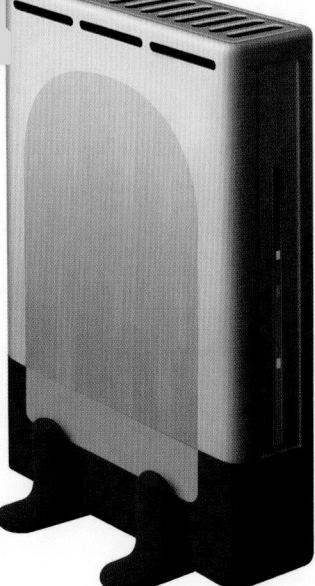

network access point transceiver
Device that links a computer network linked by cable and a computer fitted with a wireless network interface card.

Internet stick
Device with a USB connector that can provide a computer or a mobile phone with Internet access.

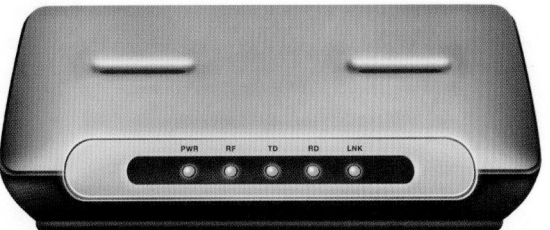

PWR   RF   TD   RD   LNK

modem
Device that converts digital signals into analog signals so that computers can communicate with each other over telephone lines.

OFFICE AUTOMATION

connecting cables

Wires covered in protective sheaths and usually insulated that allow information to be transferred between two computers or devices.

coaxial cable
that holds two insulated concentric ors; it transmits signals in the form of tric pulses without loss of quality.

twisted-pair cable
Cable that contains one or several pairs of twin wires twisted around one another; it transmits signals in the form of electric pulses.

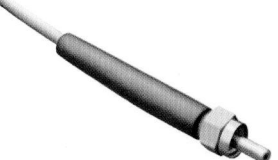

fiber-optic cable
Cable that holds thin glass filaments or optical fibers that transmit signals in the form of light pulses at high speed.

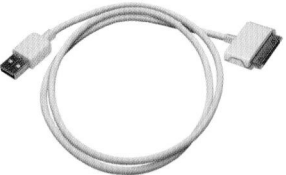

USB cable
Conductor cable used to link one device to another with a USB port.

input devices

Electronic devices used to transmit data and commands to a computer.

keyboard and pictograms

The keyboard contains a group of keys that correspond to characters and functions; the latter are represented by pictograms.

function keys
Keys that control various programmed operations; they vary depending on the software used.

Internet keys
Keys that control the main operations of an Internet browser (previous page, next page, stop, search, start).

e-mail key
Key used to launch e-mail soft automatically.

escape
Cancellation of a current operation or exit from a given situation.

escape key
Key used to cancel a current operation or to exit a given situation.

tabulation key
Key that moves the cursor to the field or tab stop following or preceding it.

tabulation left
Movement of the cursor to the field or tab stop preceding it.

capitals lock key
Key that activates or deactivates the continuous keying of capital letters.

tabulation right
Movement of the cursor to the field or tab stop following it.

shift key
Key used to produce a capital letter or the second character assigned to the key.

capitals lock
Activation or deactivation of the continuous keying of capital letters.

control key
Key that is used in combination with another key to execute a command on the keyboard without having to scroll down the menu.

start key
Key activating the Start menu (found only on Windows® operating systems).

alternate: level 3 select
To generate a third character or a third function assigned to a key, the user depresses the alternate key followed by the desired character or function key.

alternate key
Key that is used in combination with another key to produce a character or to execute the function assigned to it.

shift: level 2 select
To generate a second character or second function assigned to a key, the user depresses the shift key followed by the desired character or function key.

detachable palm rest
Solid or soft accessory attached to the bottom of the keyboard; it is used for resting the wrists while typing.

space bar
Key that inserts a blank space between two words or characters.

control: group select
Symbol assigned to the control key that allows a command to be executed on the keyboard without having to scroll down the menu.

alphanumeric keypad
Keys corresponding to letters, numbers, symbols and functions that are used to generate characters or control operations.

control
Other symbol assigned to the control key.

control
Other symbol assigned to the control key.

alternate
Other symbol assigned to the alternate key.

space
Insertion of a blank space between two words or characters.

nonbreaking space
Insertion of a space to keep two characters or a series of consecutive characters together on the same line.

cursor left
Movement of the cursor one to the left.

input devices

print screen/system request key
Key used to print a copy of the data displayed on the screen or, along with other keys, to unlock the system.

backspace key
ed to delete the character immediately to the left of the cursor.

indicator lights
Signal lights indicating activation of the capitals lock, numeric lock and scroll lock functions.

scrolling lock key
Key used to activate or deactivate scroll mode; this allows the contents of a window to be moved horizontally and vertically using the arrow keys.

pause/break key
Key used to pause or stop the current operation.

insert key
Key that activates or deactivates the overwrite mode; this allows existing characters to be replaced by new characters during data entry.

home key
Key that moves the cursor to the beginning of a line or a document.

numeric lock key
Key that activates or deactivates the numeric keypad.

page up key
Key used to display the preceding page screen.

page down key
Key that displays the next page screen.

enter key
Key used to confirm the execution of a command or, in the case of data entry, to move the cursor to the beginning of the next line.

end key
Key that moves the cursor to the end of a line or a document.

numeric keypad
Keys corresponding to numbers, mathematical operators and functions that are placed in a specific order to speed up numeric data entry.

delete key
Key used to delete a selected item or the character immediately to the right of the cursor.

cursor movement keys
Keys used to move the cursor around the screen.

enter key
Key used to confirm the execution of a command or, in the case of data entry, to move the cursor to the beginning of the next line.

backspace
Other symbol assigned to the backspace key; it deletes the character immediately to the left of the cursor.

print screen
Printing of a copy of the data displayed on the screen.

cursor right
ovement of the cursor one space to the right.

cursor up
Movement of the cursor one space up.

cursor down
Movement of the cursor one space down.

return
Movement of the cursor to the beginning of the next line; the return key also has a validation function (to confirm the execution of a command).

pause
Momentary pause of the current operation.

break
Halting of the current operation.

numeric lock
Activation or deactivation of the numeric keypad.

scrolling
Activation or deactivation of the scroll mode; this allows the contents of a window to be moved horizontally and vertically using the arrow keys.

insert
Activation or deactivation of the overwrite mode; this allows existing characters to be replaced by new characters during data entry.

delete
Deletion of a selected object or character immediately to the right of the cursor.

home
Movement of the cursor to the beginning of a line or document.

end
Movement of the cursor to the end of a line or document.

page up
Display of the preceding page screen.

page down
Display of the next page screen.

OFFICE AUTOMATION

input devices

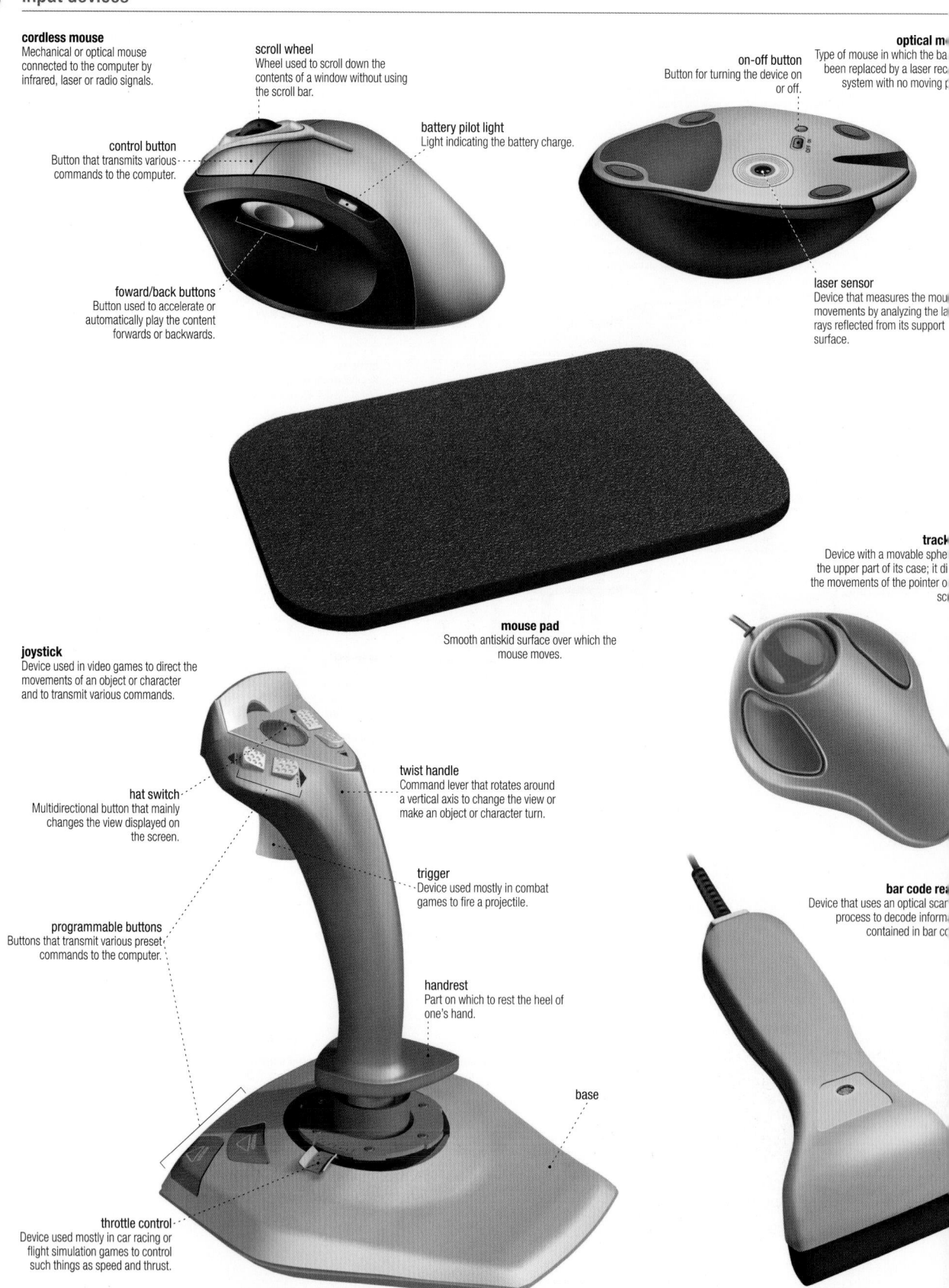

cordless mouse
Mechanical or optical mouse connected to the computer by infrared, laser or radio signals.

scroll wheel
Wheel used to scroll down the contents of a window without using the scroll bar.

on-off button
Button for turning the device on or off.

optical m
Type of mouse in which the ba been replaced by a laser rec system with no moving p

control button
Button that transmits various commands to the computer.

battery pilot light
Light indicating the battery charge.

laser sensor
Device that measures the mou movements by analyzing the la rays reflected from its support surface.

foward/back buttons
Button used to accelerate or automatically play the content forwards or backwards.

mouse pad
Smooth antiskid surface over which the mouse moves.

track
Device with a movable sphe the upper part of its case; it di the movements of the pointer o scr

joystick
Device used in video games to direct the movements of an object or character and to transmit various commands.

twist handle
Command lever that rotates around a vertical axis to change the view or make an object or character turn.

hat switch
Multidirectional button that mainly changes the view displayed on the screen.

trigger
Device used mostly in combat games to fire a projectile.

bar code rea
Device that uses an optical scan process to decode inform contained in bar co

programmable buttons
Buttons that transmit various preset commands to the computer.

handrest
Part on which to rest the heel of one's hand.

base

throttle control
Device used mostly in car racing or flight simulation games to control such things as speed and thrust.

input devices

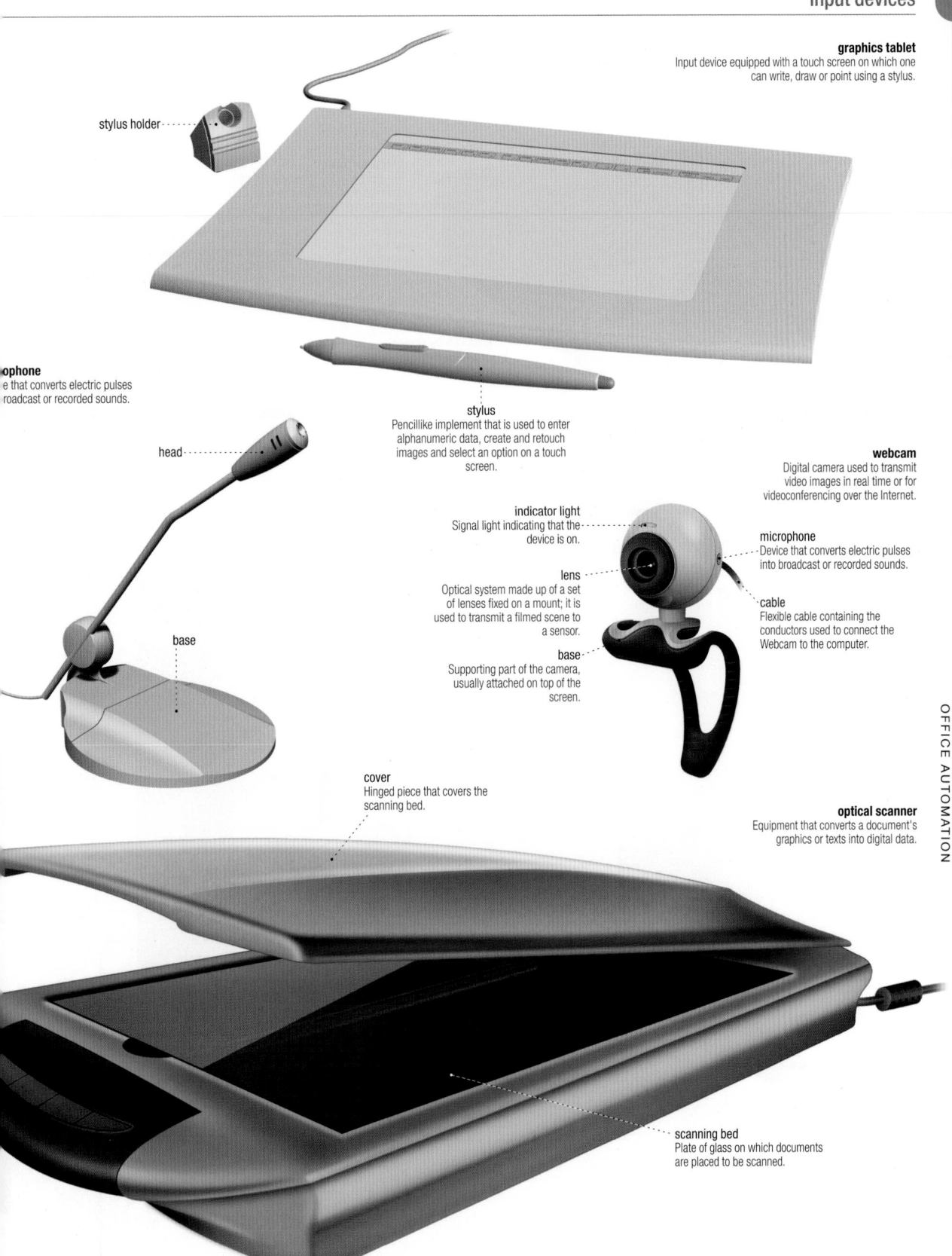

graphics tablet
Input device equipped with a touch screen on which one can write, draw or point using a stylus.

stylus holder

ophone
e that converts electric pulses
roadcast or recorded sounds.

stylus
Pencillike implement that is used to enter alphanumeric data, create and retouch images and select an option on a touch screen.

head

base

indicator light
Signal light indicating that the device is on.

lens
Optical system made up of a set of lenses fixed on a mount; it is used to transmit a filmed scene to a sensor.

base
Supporting part of the camera, usually attached on top of the screen.

webcam
Digital camera used to transmit video images in real time or for videoconferencing over the Internet.

microphone
Device that converts electric pulses into broadcast or recorded sounds.

cable
Flexible cable containing the conductors used to connect the Webcam to the computer.

cover
Hinged piece that covers the scanning bed.

optical scanner
Equipment that converts a document's graphics or texts into digital data.

scanning bed
Plate of glass on which documents are placed to be scanned.

OFFICE AUTOMATION

output devices

Electronic devices used to view or print the results of data processing done on a computer.

projector
Device that projects electronic images on a screen from sources such as computers, DVD players, camcorders and VCRs.

control panel
Panel housing the projector's operating buttons.

on-off switch
Button for turning the device on or off.

dot matrix pr
Printer with a movable printhead, wh made up of a set of small pins that stri ink ribbon to

connector panel
The jacks used to connect the projector to various video equipment such as DVD players, camcorders and VCRs.

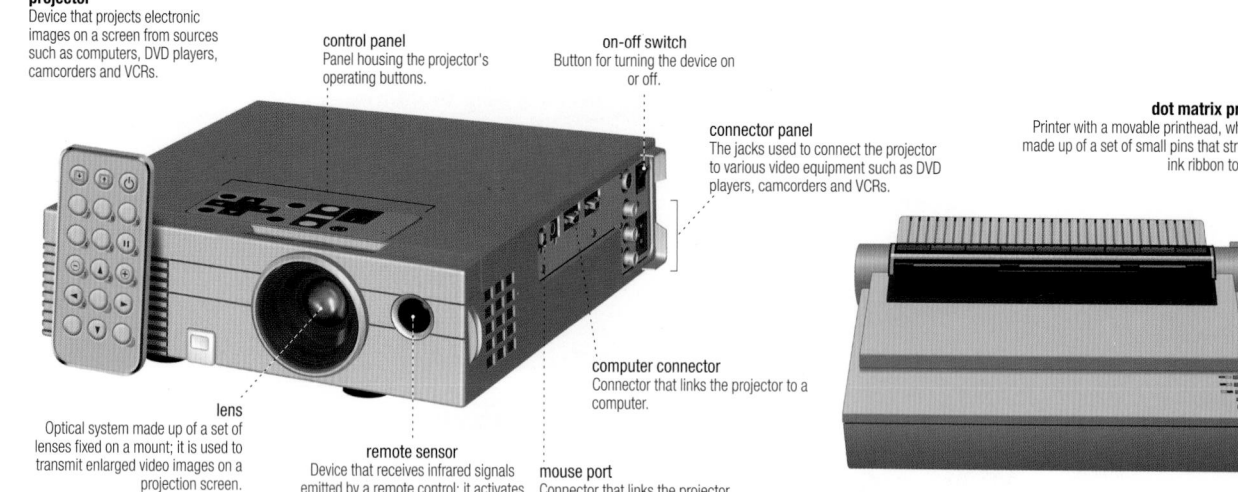

computer connector
Connector that links the projector to a computer.

lens
Optical system made up of a set of lenses fixed on a mount; it is used to transmit enlarged video images on a projection screen.

remote sensor
Device that receives infrared signals emitted by a remote control; it activates certain projector functions from a distance.

mouse port
Connector that links the projector to a mouse used to control the device.

plotter
Printer for printing documents (plans, diagrams, technical drawings) on large sheets of paper.

ink cartridge
Removable container filled with liquid ink, to be installed in an inkjet printer.

toner cartridge
Removable container filled with fine particles of dry ink; it is designed for a laser printer.

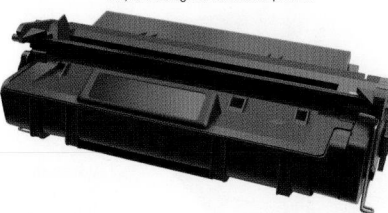

laser printer
Printer in which powdered ink in a cartridge is projected onto a rotating cylinder by laser beam and then fixed onto the paper using heated rollers.

output tray
y that collects paper as it exits the printer.

front panel
Rigid plate covering the printer's ink cartridge.

control panel
Panel containing the printer function buttons.

cooling vents
gs allowing air to enter to cool printer's internal components.

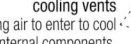

paper guide
Movable device used to adjust the position of the paper sideways.

input tray
Small drawer that contains blank sheets of standard-sized sheets of paper to be fed one at a time during printing.

OFFICE AUTOMATION

display
Screen for visually representing graphic or textual data.

cover
Moving piece that covers the platen glass.

input paper tray
Part that contains blank sheets of paper to be fed one at a time during printing.

combination printer and scanner
Device that combines the functions of a printer with the ability to create digital images of printed documents.

operation panel
Panel containing the printer function buttons.

platen glass
Glass plate on which is placed the sheet to be copied.

memory card slot
evice that reads and records data on a memory card.

USB port
Connector used to link several USB standard peripherals simultaneously.

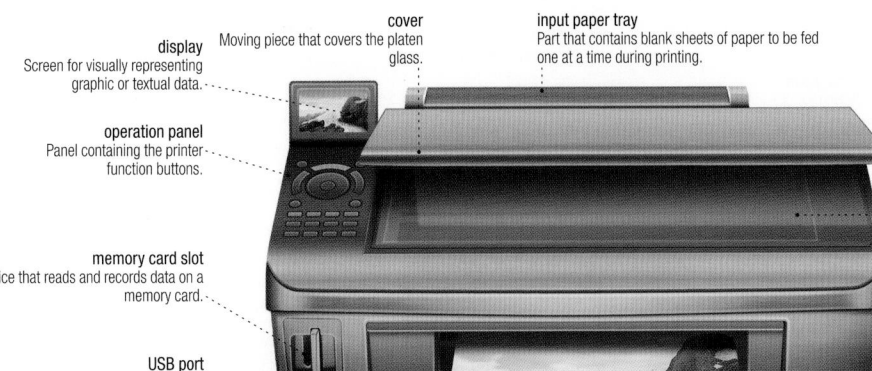

output tray
Tray that collects paper as it exits the printer.

data storage devices

Electronic devices used to record or save data on a magnetic or optical medium.

external hard drive
Independent device connected by a cable to a computer, that reads and saves data on a hard drive located inside its casing.

USB port
Connector used to link several USB standard peripherals simultaneously.

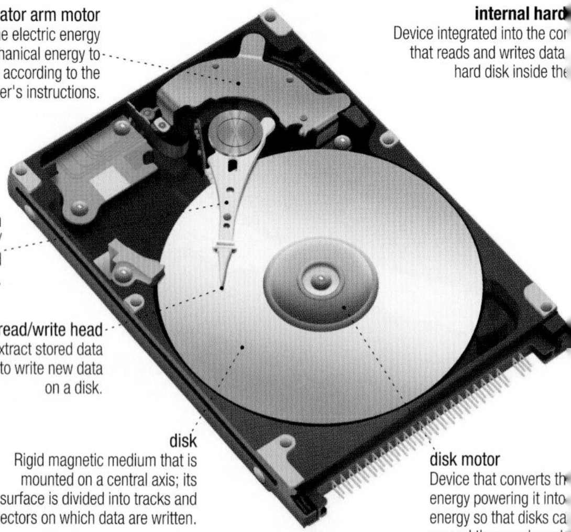

actuator arm motor
Device that converts the electric energy powering it into mechanical energy to move the actuator arm according to the computer's instructions.

internal hard
Device integrated into the co... that reads and writes data hard disk inside the

actuator arm
Movable arm bearing the read/ write head; it moves the head across the surface of the disk.

read/write head
Device used to extract stored data from a disk or to write new data on a disk.

DVD burner
Device used to record data on a writable or rewritable optical disc by means of laser engraving

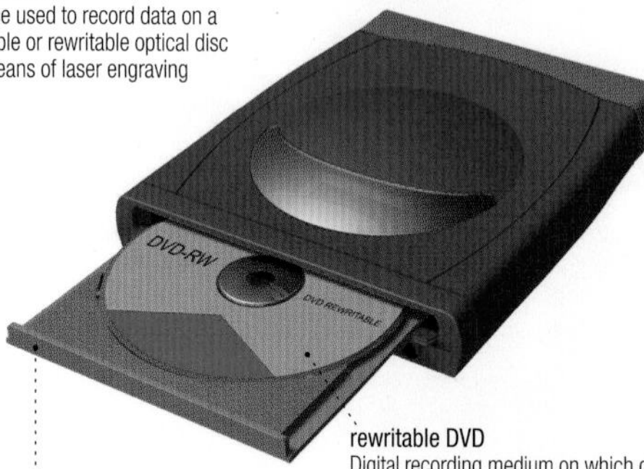

disk
Rigid magnetic medium that is mounted on a central axis; its surface is divided into tracks and sectors on which data are written.

disk motor
Device that converts th... energy powering it into energy so that disks ca... several thousand revol... minute.

memory card reader
Independent device, linked to a computer via a cable or a USB connector, that reads and records data on a memory card.

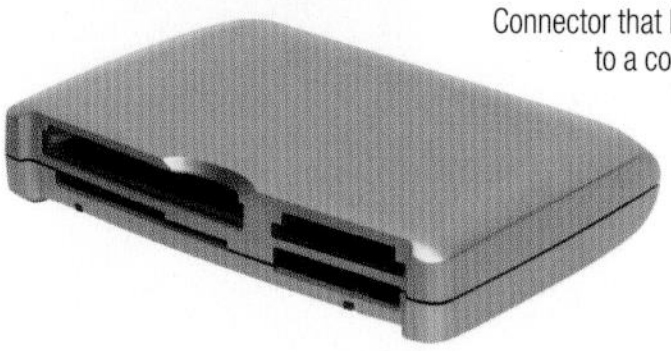

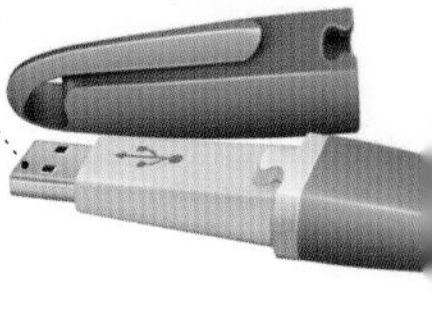

USB connector
Connector that links the flash drive to a computer's USB port.

USB flash drive
Small removable case containing a... memory, which enables the user to... transport, and store data.

rewritable DVD
Digital recording medium on which data can be engraved and erased several times.

disc tray
Part in which a disc is inserted to be played back.

protection devices

Devices used to protect computer equipment from any surge in the electrical supply.

uninterruptible power supply (UPS): back view

uninterruptible power supply (UPS): front view
UPS: device used to regulate the power supply to the computer and its peripherals by limiting the effects of cuts, surges or dips in the electric circuit voltage.

power
Device containing plugs used... several devices to the electrical through a single electrical wa... also containing a surge pro...

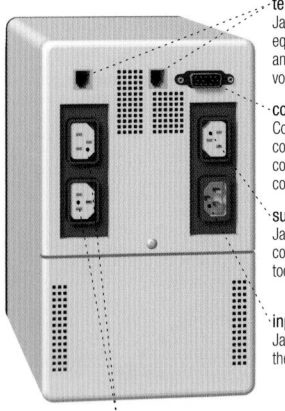

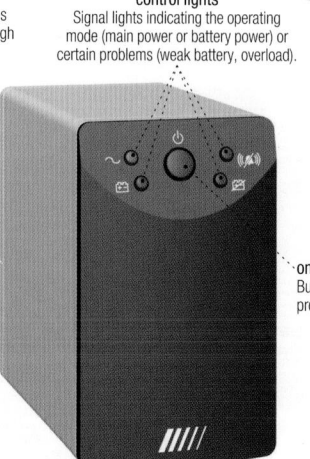

telephone surge protection jacks
Jacks designed to protect communications equipment (such as telephones, fax machines and modems) from damage caused by too high voltage.

computer interface port
Connector attaching the UPS to the computer; software can then turn the computer off before the battery runs out completely.

surge protection receptacle
Jack designed to protect equipment connected to it from damage caused by too high voltage.

input receptacle
Jack used to connect the UPS to the electric grid.

battery backup/surge protection receptacles
Antisurge sockets attached to a battery so that equipment connected to them has electric power in the event of a power outage.

control lights
Signal lights indicating the operating mode (main power or battery power) or certain problems (weak battery, overload).

on/off/test button
Button that turns on the UPS and begins the procedure of checking the status of the battery.

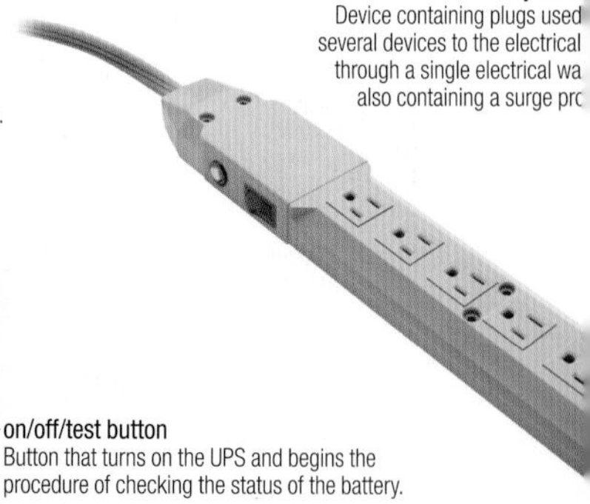

miscellaneous computer tools

Electric devices used in managing and displaying various digital data (text, images, sound, video).

interactive whiteboard
Device consisting of a large touch screen onto which are projected (using a video projector) images displayed on the screen of a computer.

projector
Device that projects electronic images from a computer on a screen.

touch screen
Display that is sensitive to the touch and the motion of a finger.

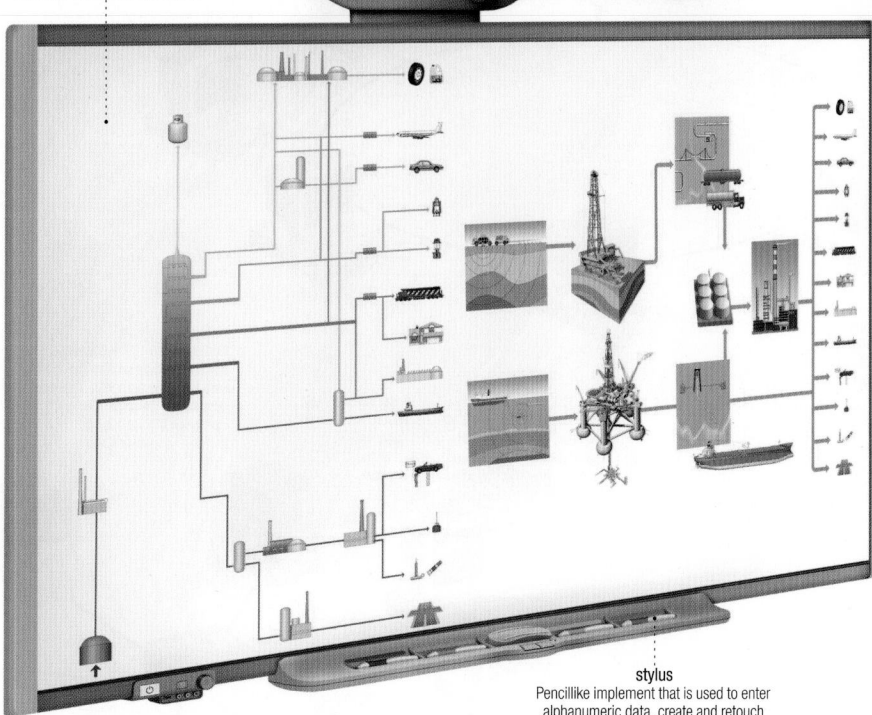

stylus
Pencillike implement that is used to enter alphanumeric data, create and retouch images and select an option on a touch screen.

OFFICE AUTOMATION

et computer
ll portable computer used mainly personal management tasks, eation (games) and information ks, various applications).

sleep/wake button
Button for starting up or shutting down the device also used to put it on sleep mode (waiting state that reduces energy consumption during periods of inactivity).

digital book reader
Small portable computer in the shape of a book; it is used to download, store and read electronic books.

mute button
Button that turns the sound off.

volume buttons
Buttons that controls the loudness of the device.

touch screen
Display that is sensitive to the touch and the motion of a finger.

touch screen
Display that is sensitive to the touch and the motion of a finger.

home button
Button used to return to the main menu of the tablet.

function buttons
Buttons controlling diverse functions (next page, preceding page, go back, etc.).

examples of networks

Networks are classified mainly by size (local area or wide area network) and topography (including ring, bus and star).

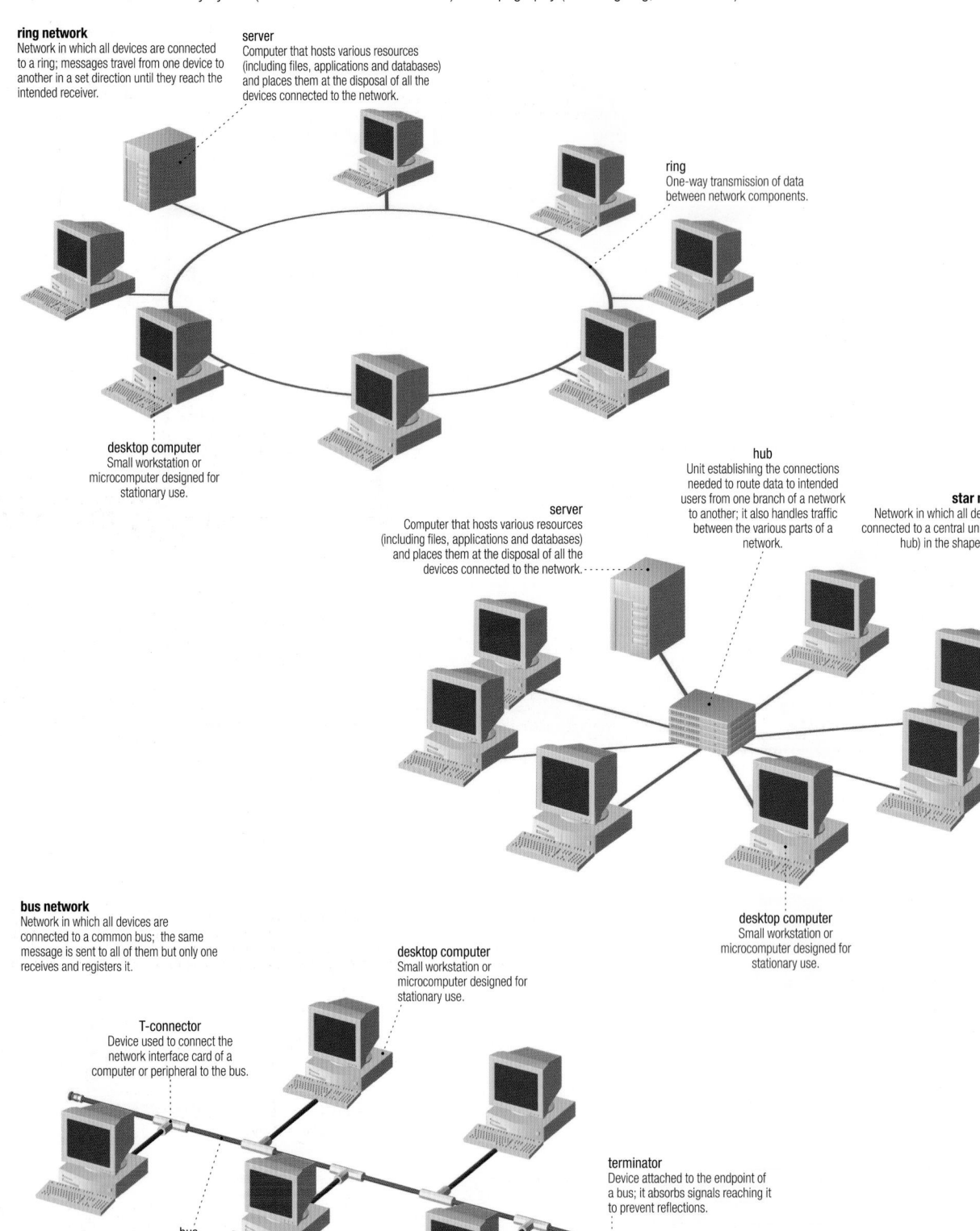

ring network
Network in which all devices are connected to a ring; messages travel from one device to another in a set direction until they reach the intended receiver.

server
Computer that hosts various resources (including files, applications and databases) and places them at the disposal of all the devices connected to the network.

ring
One-way transmission of data between network components.

desktop computer
Small workstation or microcomputer designed for stationary use.

hub
Unit establishing the connections needed to route data to intended users from one branch of a network to another; it also handles traffic between the various parts of a network.

server
Computer that hosts various resources (including files, applications and databases) and places them at the disposal of all the devices connected to the network.

star netw
Network in which all devices connected to a central unit (he hub) in the shape of a

desktop computer
Small workstation or microcomputer designed for stationary use.

bus network
Network in which all devices are connected to a common bus; the same message is sent to all of them but only one receives and registers it.

desktop computer
Small workstation or microcomputer designed for stationary use.

T-connector
Device used to connect the network interface card of a computer or peripheral to the bus.

terminator
Device attached to the endpoint of a bus; it absorbs signals reaching it to prevent reflections.

bus
Linear cable ensuring two-way transmission of data between network components.

OFFICE AUTOMATION

examples of networks

wide area network
Private or public network spanning a large area (a region or country); it usually brings together several local area networks.

hub
Unit establishing the connections needed to route data to intended users from one branch of a network to another; it also handles traffic between the various parts of a network.

desktop computer
Small workstation or microcomputer designed for stationary use.

server
Computer that hosts various resources (including files, applications and databases) and places them at the disposal of all the devices connected to the network.

uninterruptible power supply (UPS)
Device used to regulate the power supply to the computer and its peripherals by limiting the effects of cuts, surges or dips in the electric circuit voltage.

routers
Interconnecting devices ensuring transmission of data between two or more networks by determining the best path for them.

telephone/cable/satellite line
Linking of off-site devices by telephone network, cable network or telecommunications satellite.

laptop computer
Small stand-alone microcomputer with a screen and integrated keyboard; it is powered by an internal battery.

file server
Server hosting a set of data files that are at the disposal of all computers connected to the network.

dedicated line
Telephone or cable communications link reserved for one use or for a specific user.

firewall
evice controlling data that circulate ween a public network (such as the) and a private network; it prevents unauthorized access to the latter.

switch
Unit establishing the connections needed to route data to intended users from one branch of a network to another; it also handles traffic between the various parts of a network.

modem
Device that converts digital signals into analog signals so that computers can communicate with each other over telephone lines.

Internet
work consisting of thousands c and private networks of izes; it is linked by a set of communications protocols.

gateway
Interconnecting device linking different networks.

backbone
Main artery of a network characterized by a high throughput; it transmits data between secondary networks.

printer
Output peripheral allowing computer-generated characters, images and graphics to be reproduced on paper.

hub
Unit that receives all messages by the devices connected to it redistributes them to all users.

bridge
Interconnecting device linking similar networks.

backup storage unit
Storage peripheral used to copy data onto a removable medium to facilitate retrieval in the event of loss.

Internet

Global network consisting of thousands of public and private networks of varying sizes; it is linked by a set of standard communications protocols.

uniform resource locator (URL)
All the data allowing access to a resource hosted by an Internet server (e.g., a Web page).

communication protocol
Part of the URL address specifying the language used to exchange data. The HTTP protocol, which allows the transfer of Web pages, is the best known.

domain name
Part of the URL address specifically designating the host. It must be registered with a domain name registrar.

file format
Group of letters specifying the way in which file data is encoded. For example, Web documents are generally written in HTML format.

http://www.un.org/aboutun/index.html

double slash

second-level domain
Part of the domain name that designates the server name.

file
Part of the URL address specifying the name of the unit of data (file) corresponding to the chosen resource.

server
Part of the URL address identifying the type of server. The best known is the Web server (www), which, as its name implies, hosts Web sites.

top-level domain
Part of the domain name that designates the country of origin or the category of organization (including government agency, commercial business and educational institution).

directory
Part of the URL address showing where the resource is located on the server.

browser
Software used to search and consult Internet sites.

uniform resource locator (URL)
All the data allowing access to a resource hosted by an Internet server (e.g., a Web page).

microwave relay station
Facility that receives and amplifies signals transmitted in the form of microwaves and relays them to another receiver.

submarine line
Linking of off-site devices by underwater cable.

telephone or cable line
Linking of two off-site devices by cable within a telephone network.

hyperlinks
Elements of a Web page (words, images or icons) that, when activated, allow direct access to another linked page.

desktop computer
Small workstation or microcomputer designed for stationary use.

browser
Software used to search and consult Internet sites.

e-mail software
Software used to format, send and receive messages over the Internet.

Internet service provider
Company that is permanently connected to the Internet; it provides individuals and organizations with access to various Internet services.

dedicated lin
Telephone or cab communications link res one use or for a speci

Internet user
Person using the Internet.

modem
Device that converts digital signals into analog signals so that computers can communicate with each other over telephone lines.

ac
Communication provides subscribers connection to

server
Computer that hosts various resources (including files, applications and databases) and places them at the disposal of all the devices connected to the network.

Internet uses

A number of user types use Internet tools and resources to communicate, find information and entertainment, make purchases and manage funds.

health organization
The Internet fosters exchanges between researchers, health professionals and patients.

educational institution
he Internet provides teachers, researchers and udents with countless opportunities to research and exchange information.

government organization
The Internet has made it easy for government departments and agencies to communicate with other organizations and with the citizens they serve.

cultural organization
The Internet allows the public to learn about programs offered by cultural organizations in a city or region.

enterprise
The Internet facilitates exchanges between employees within the same company and between the company and its customers and suppliers.

home user
Anyone can access the Internet from home through an Internet service provider (ISP).

industry
The Internet allows a manufacturer to communicate with its suppliers, customers and regulatory bodies.

commercial concern
A company that specializes in product marketing can use the Internet to contact suppliers and customers.

ecommunication satellite
ellite designed and placed into geostationary it to ensure long-range reception and nsmission of signals in the form of radio ves.

tellite earth station
cility that transmits radio waves to a satellite and receives io waves from a satellite.

uter
erconnecting device that transmits a between two or more networks by ermining the best path for them.

server
Computer that hosts various resources (including files, applications and databases) and places them at the disposal of all the devices connected to the network.

e-mail
Service by which messages are exchanged between users of a computer network.

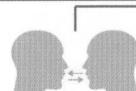

chat room
Activity allowing two or more Internet users to converse in writing in real time.

newsgroup
Service enabling a group of people to discuss various subjects live or on a time-delay basis.

blog
Web site in the form of a personal journal in which a person shares opinions or impressions in notes or short articles.

database
Group of data related to the same topic that is arranged in order and available for direct consultation by several users.

information spreading
Transmission of information about an organization, an event, a product or a topic, usually by creating or updating a Web site.

search
Locating information on a given topic in the hope of finding something useful; it is usually done with the help of a search engine.

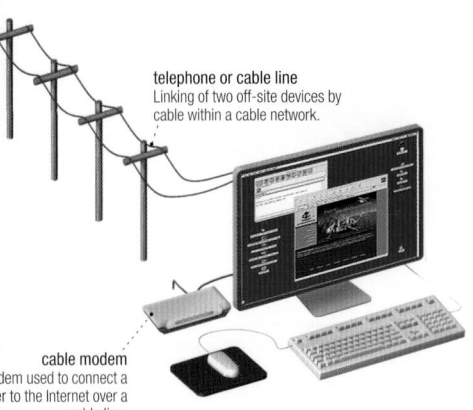

telephone or cable line
Linking of two off-site devices by cable within a cable network.

cable modem
dem used to connect a er to the Internet over a cable line.

online game
Video game accessible over the Internet; users can play solo or with multiple players at a distance.

e-commerce
Sale or promotion of products and services over the Internet.

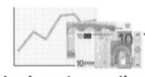

business transactions
Operations involving financing and funds management (e.g., arranging a loan or transferring funds) over the Internet.

videotelephony
Transmission of voices and images through a computerized network.

telephony
Transmission of voices through a computerized network.

podcasting
Service for automatic downloading of audio or video files for transfer to a portable digital audio player to be listened to later.

office organization

Typical arrangement of the rooms in an organization.

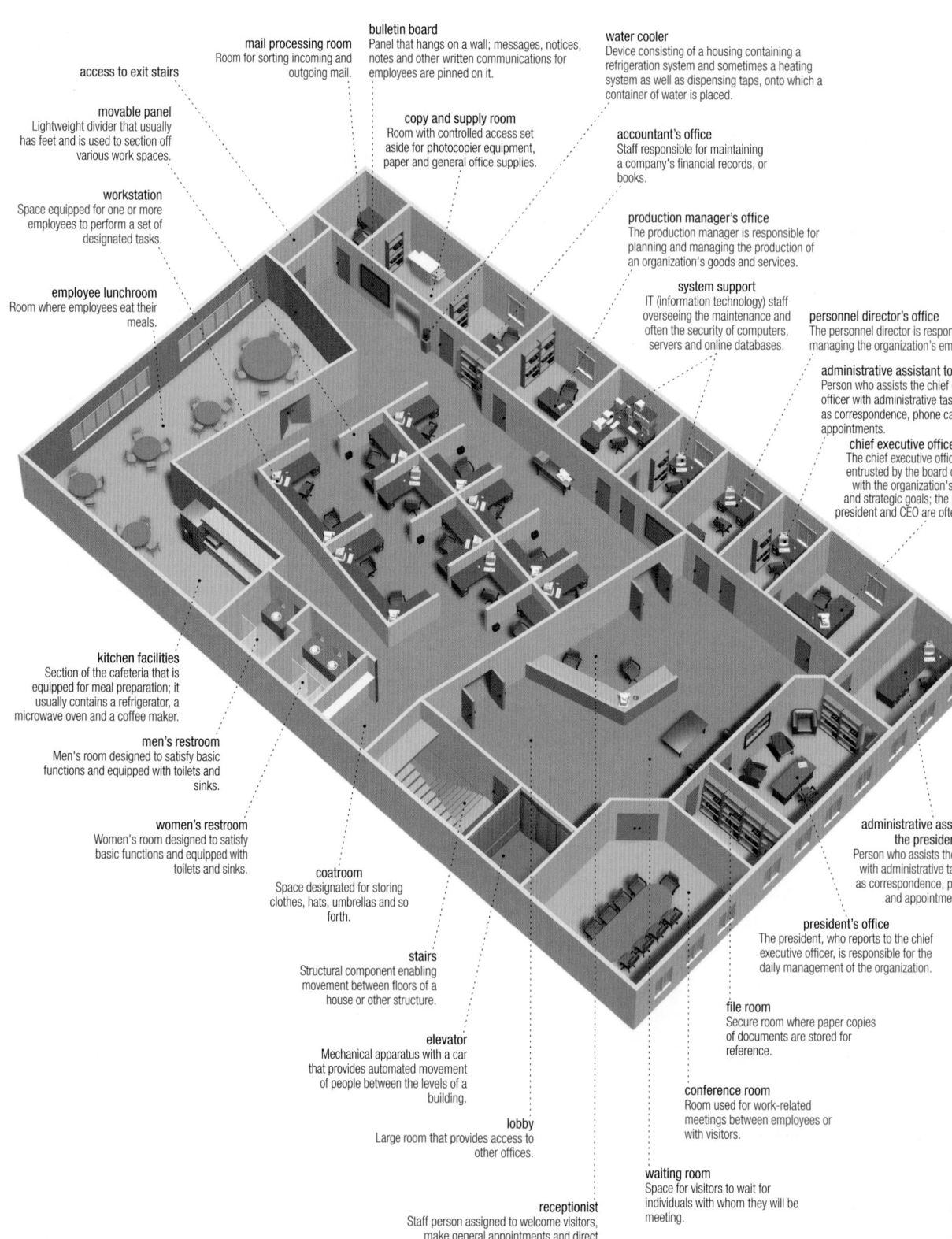

mail processing room
Room for sorting incoming and outgoing mail.

access to exit stairs

movable panel
Lightweight divider that usually has feet and is used to section off various work spaces.

workstation
Space equipped for one or more employees to perform a set of designated tasks.

employee lunchroom
Room where employees eat their meals.

bulletin board
Panel that hangs on a wall; messages, notices, notes and other written communications for employees are pinned on it.

copy and supply room
Room with controlled access set aside for photocopier equipment, paper and general office supplies.

water cooler
Device consisting of a housing containing a refrigeration system and sometimes a heating system as well as dispensing taps, onto which a container of water is placed.

accountant's office
Staff responsible for maintaining a company's financial records, or books.

production manager's office
The production manager is responsible for planning and managing the production of an organization's goods and services.

system support
IT (information technology) staff overseeing the maintenance and often the security of computers, servers and online databases.

personnel director's office
The personnel director is respons[...] managing the organization's emp[...]

administrative assistant to t[...]
Person who assists the chief e[...] officer with administrative task[...] as correspondence, phone cal[...] appointments.

chief executive officer
The chief executive office[...] entrusted by the board o[...] with the organization's [...] and strategic goals; the p[...] president and CEO are ofte[...]

kitchen facilities
Section of the cafeteria that is equipped for meal preparation; it usually contains a refrigerator, a microwave oven and a coffee maker.

men's restroom
Men's room designed to satisfy basic functions and equipped with toilets and sinks.

women's restroom
Women's room designed to satisfy basic functions and equipped with toilets and sinks.

coatroom
Space designated for storing clothes, hats, umbrellas and so forth.

stairs
Structural component enabling movement between floors of a house or other structure.

elevator
Mechanical apparatus with a car that provides automated movement of people between the levels of a building.

lobby
Large room that provides access to other offices.

administrative assi[...] the presiden[...]
Person who assists the [...] with administrative tas[...] as correspondence, ph[...] and appointmen[...]

president's office
The president, who reports to the chief executive officer, is responsible for the daily management of the organization.

file room
Secure room where paper copies of documents are stored for reference.

conference room
Room used for work-related meetings between employees or with visitors.

waiting room
Space for visitors to wait for individuals with whom they will be meeting.

receptionist
Staff person assigned to welcome visitors, make general appointments and direct phone calls.

office furniture

All the furniture in an office; it is intended mainly for filing, storage and carrying out work tasks.

filing furniture
Piece of furniture used to file documents by category or in a given order.

lateral filing cabinet
Compartmentalized piece of furniture with flipper doors; it is used to hold hanging files.

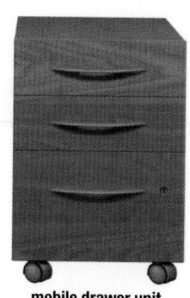

mobile drawer unit
Small piece of furniture on casters or legs; it contains drawers and is usually placed under a desk or table.

mobile filing unit
Small piece of furniture on casters; it is used to hold hanging files.

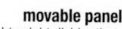

coat hooks
Hook or set of hooks attached to a wall and used to hang such items as clothing, hats and umbrellas.

movable panel
Lightweight divider that usually has feet and is used to section off various work spaces.

storage furniture
Furniture serving to archive, support or protect various objects.

display cabinet
Cabinet with usually folding, slanted shelves; it is used to display and stack books, magazines and brochures.

stationery cabinet
Large two-door cabinet with shelves; it is used to store office supplies and items used daily.

coat tree
pole on legs that has hooks ang such items as clothing, hats and umbrellas.

denza
low office furniture with vers or compartments to store us objects.

coat rack
Structure on legs or casters that is fitted with a rod to hang clothing.

locker
Large two-door cabinet fitted with a bar to hang clothing and a shelf to stack various items.

office furniture

work furniture
Furniture designed to facilitate office work, from writing to working at a computer or typewriter.

return
Auxiliary desktop that is used especially to hold a typewriter or computer.

c...
Piece of furniture wit... perpendicular work sur... equipped with one or more st... dra...

desk mat
Accessory on which paper is placed for writing; it protects the desktop.

typist's chair
Padded chair on casters; the back can be tilted and adjusted for height.

swivel-tilter armchair
Armchair designed to swivel horizontally around an axis and to tilt forward and back.

computer d...
Piece of work furniture desi... to hold the main compon... of a computer (casing, sc... keyboard, ...

printer table
Table designed to hold a printer and its accessories.

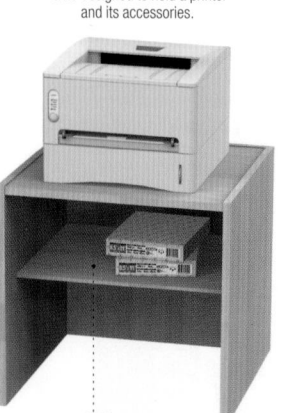

pull-out keyboard shelf
Small retractable shelf on which the keyboard and mouse are placed.

central unit platform
Small rolling shelf on which the casing of the computer is kept.

executive d...
Desk with a large desktop ... space and two built-in file dra...

footrest
Adjustable piece used for resting the feet on under the work desk.

shelf
Horizontal space on which various accessories can be stored (extra paper, for example).

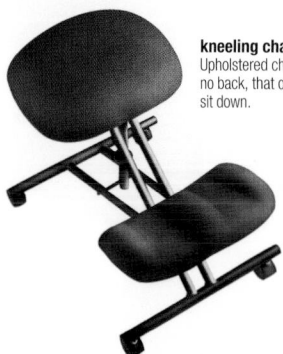

kneeling chair
Upholstered chair on wheels, with no back, that one kneels on to sit down.

photocopier

Equipment fitted with a photographic device, which reproduces written texts and images.

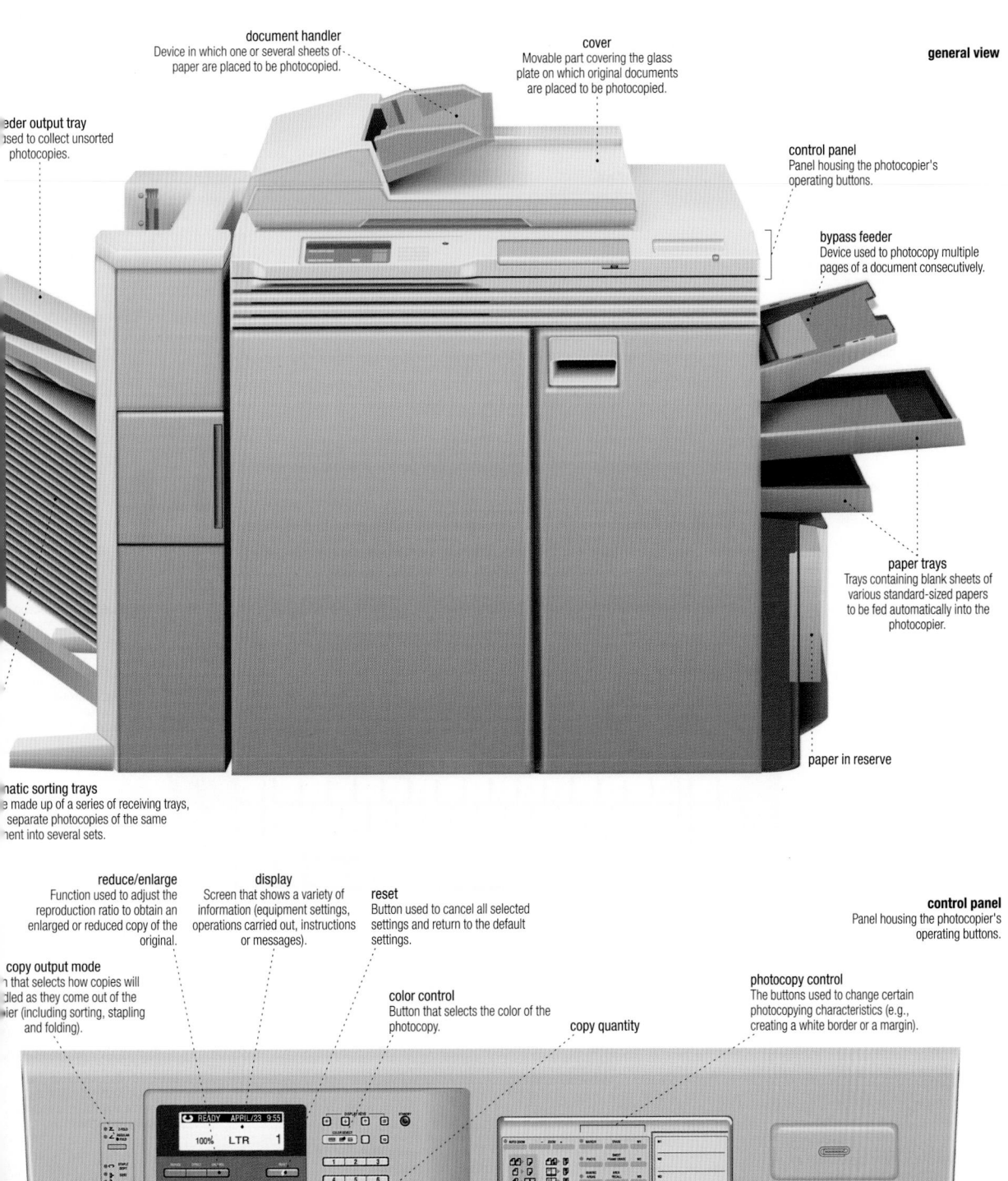

general view

document handler
Device in which one or several sheets of paper are placed to be photocopied.

cover
Movable part covering the glass plate on which original documents are placed to be photocopied.

control panel
Panel housing the photocopier's operating buttons.

bypass feeder
Device used to photocopy multiple pages of a document consecutively.

...eder output tray
...used to collect unsorted photocopies.

paper trays
Trays containing blank sheets of various standard-sized papers to be fed automatically into the photocopier.

paper in reserve

...matic sorting trays
...e made up of a series of receiving trays, ...separate photocopies of the same ...ent into several sets.

reduce/enlarge
Function used to adjust the reproduction ratio to obtain an enlarged or reduced copy of the original.

display
Screen that shows a variety of information (equipment settings, operations carried out, instructions or messages).

reset
Button used to cancel all selected settings and return to the default settings.

control panel
Panel housing the photocopier's operating buttons.

...copy output mode
...n that selects how copies will ...dled as they come out of the ...ier (including sorting, stapling and folding).

color control
Button that selects the color of the photocopy.

copy quantity

photocopy control
The buttons used to change certain photocopying characteristics (e.g., creating a white border or a margin).

...contrast control
...ion that adjusts the degree of ...ness (density) of a photocopy automatically or manually.

start
Button used to begin making one or several photocopies based on the selected settings.

stop
Button used to stop making photocopies or to cancel the number of copies shown on the display screen.

two-sided copies
Button that chooses between one-sided printing (front only) and two-sided printing (front and back).

original overlay
Function that combines two original documents into one photocopy.

office supplies

Equipment, instruments and accessories needed to carry out office tasks.

electronic typewriter
Equipment with a keyboard that is used to produce typewritten documents; it has certain word processing functions and an integrated memory.

top plate
Tipping cover under which the ink cartridge usually lies.

paper support
Folding part used to keep the paper in a vertical position.

paper bail release lever
Device used to raise and lower the paper bail.

printing unit
Movable device with raised characters, which strike an inked ribbon to print on paper.

paper bail
Part that holds the paper against the platen.

paper release lever
Device that releases the pressure of the platen on the paper so that the paper can be cleared or moved.

pitch scale
Graduated scale that shows the different spacing available; it is measured in number of characters per unit of length.

platen
Rubber roller over which paper passes during printing.

variable spacer
Thumb wheel that controls th of the platen so the paper can up or down.

margin release
Key used to print characters outside the margin limits.

tabulator
Key that moves the printing unit or cursor to the next tab stop.

indent
Key used to move the left margin temporarily to indent a line or paragraph.

character correction
Key used to erase the ch next to the printing unit o

half indexing
Key used to automaticall paper up and down.

decimal tab
Key that aligns numbers columns at a preset decimal tab stop.

margin control
Key used to set the left a margins.

EXEGI MONUMENTUM AERE PERENNIUS

centering
Key used to center a text automatically between two margins or two tab stops.

tab setting
Key used to insert or remove a standard or decimal tab stop.

text display
Liquid crystal display that shows keyed-in text as well as information about the machine's settings and operations carried out.

set
Key used to confirm the execution of a command or the choice of a setting.

spelling corrector
Key used to activate or deactivate the automatic spell checking of text being keyed in.

code
Key that is used with another key to execute various programmed commands.

relocation
Key used to automatically reposition the printing unit or cursor at the last keystroke position before making a correction.

text
Key used to store texts in memory and to call them up later to make changes or to print them.

shift lock key
Key that activates or deactivates the continuous keying of capital letters.

shift key
Key used to produce a capital letter or the second character assigned to the key.

space bar
Key that inserts a blank space between two words or characters.

return key
Key that moves the printing unit or cursor to the beginning of the next line.

mode
Key that is used with another key to choose a setting (character pitch, line spacing, ribbon type).

word correction
Key used to erase the word immediately to the left of the printing unit or cursor.

OFFICE AUTOMATION

office supplies

for calculating

add to memory
Key used to save the displayed number in memory.

case
Envelope for carrying and protecting the calculator.

solar cell
Device that converts sunlight into electric current to power a pocket calculator.

pocket calculator
Small self-powered calculator used to perform simple mathematical operations.

memory recall/memory clear key
used to display or erase the data saved in the memory.

clear entry key
Key used to erase the last number entered.

display
Screen that shows the last number entered or the result of operations carried out.

DUAL POWER

power on/clear key
Button for turning the calculator on or off, and also resetting it to zero.

subtract from memory
Key used to erase the displayed number from memory.

square root key
Key used to derive the square root of a number; this is the number that is multiplied by itself to give the basic number.

number key
Key used to enter a number.

percent key
Key used to obtain the decimal form of a displayed number by dividing it by 100; it is used mainly to calculate percentages.

subtraction key
Key used to calculate the difference between two numbers.

division key
Key used to calculate the quotient of two numbers.

decimal key
Key used to insert a decimal symbol to separate the whole and fraction parts of a number.

change sign key
Key used to change the plus or minus sign of the displayed number.

multiplication key
Key used to calculate the product of two numbers.

equals key
Key used to display the results of operations carried out.

addition key
Key used to add two numbers.

ting calculator
e calculator with an integrated
r; it is used mainly in business
administration.

graphing calculator
Calculator designed to perform specific scientific and technical mathematical operations, and to convert data into graphs.

OFFICE AUTOMATION

backlight screen
Screen lit from behind in order to improve the contrast of the display.

printer
Device that makes a hard copy of data transmitted by the calculator.

access to the second level of operations
Key used to select a second function controlled by a key.

cursor movement keys
Keys used to move the cursor around the screen.

display
Screen showing the problem to be solved and its solution, or the graph corresponding to the data entered.

ecimal point selector switch
evice used to adjust the number
ecimals making up the fraction
of a number.

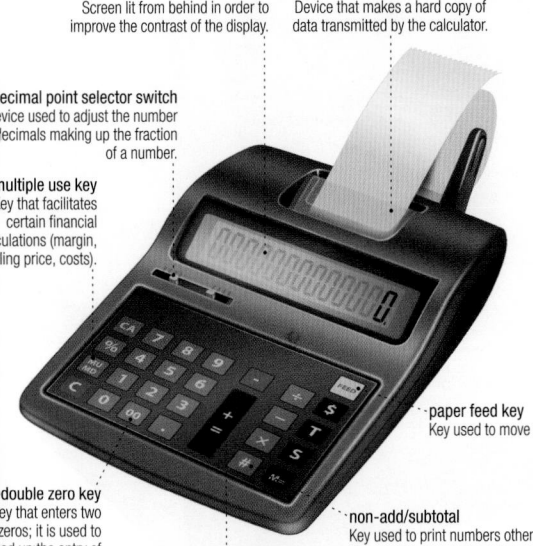

editing keys
Button used to modify values or expressions.

graphing keys
Buttons used to convert the displayed coordinates into graphs.

nultiple use key
ey that facilitates
certain financial
culations (margin,
ling price, costs).

scientific calculator keys
Specialized calculations include square root, trigonometry and logarithms.

advanced function keys
Buttons used to access menus of specialized functions (adding applications, financial calculations, etc.).

paper feed key
Key used to move the paper forward.

basic operations
Basic calculations include adding, subtracting, multiplying and dividing.

double zero key
ey that enters two
zeros; it is used to
ed up the entry of
large numbers.

non-add/subtotal
Key used to print numbers other than calculations (codes, dates) or to obtain the results of an operations subset.

add/equals key
Key used to display the results of operations carried out; on some calculators, it can also be used to do repeated calculations.

USB cable
Conductor cable used to link two devices with USB ports.

first level of operations
All the operations directly controlled by the scientific calculator keys.

second level of operations
All the supplementary functions listed above the keys and accessible using the access to the second level of operations.

office supplies

for time management and notetaking

tear-off calendar
Pad of tear-off sheets printed with the day and date; it is used to jot down appointments and things to do.

calendar pad
Sheets of paper printed with the day and date and on a ring base; it is used to jot down appointments and things to do.

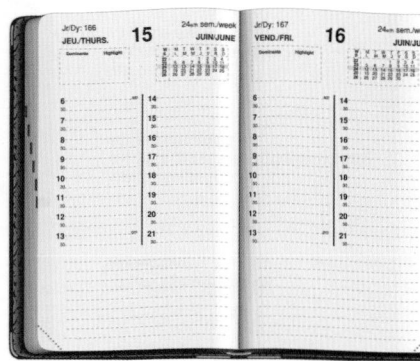

appointment book
Notebook that is printed with the day and date; it is used to jot down appointments and things to do.

dater
Device consisting of movable strips embossed with a series of digits and letters; it is used to print the date.

display
Liquid crystal display showing a variety of information (including date, hour and settings).

time c
Device used to print the arrival and depa times of employees on time c

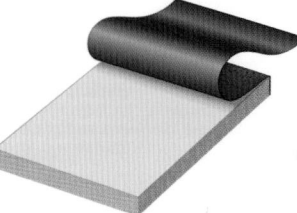

memo pad
Set of tear-off sheets of paper used mainly for taking notes.

sticky note
Small piece of paper with a sticky strip on the back for temporary attachment to a surface.

time card
Card on which an empl and departure times a that worked time can calculated

spiral binder
Notebook made up of a set of punched sheets of paper bound together with a spiral wire of metal or plastic.

clipboard
Rigid board fitted with a spring clip under which sheets of paper are placed mainly to take notes.

...dded envelope
...elope that is lined with bubble wrap to protect
contents from humidity and impact damage.

self-sealing flap
Flap coated with an adhesive
substance; it seals an envelope
on contact.

letter opener
Small knife used to open envelopes
and cut sheets of paper.

numbering machine
Device consisting of movable strips
embossed with a series of digits; it is
used to print numbers.

letter scale
Scale used to weigh a letter or
parcel.

...no book
...ral-bound sheets of lined paper;
...se books were originally used by
...nographers to take dictation.

air bubbles
Small air pockets that form a
protective cushion around the
contents of an envelope.

fingertip
Rubber sheath to cover the finger; it is used
mainly to turn pages more easily or to sort
papers or banknotes more quickly.

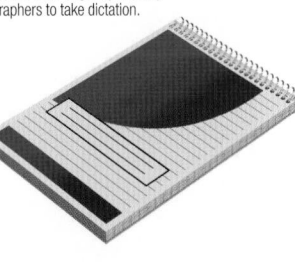

...gnature book
...gister made up of sheets of blotting
...per; documents that require a
...nager's signature are placed in it.

moistener
Device used to moisten postage
stamps and labels.

stamp rack
Rack used to hold such items
as rubber stamps for dating and
numbering.

stamp pad
Ink-saturated pad on which a
rubber stamp is moistened prior to
stamping.

rubber stamp
Device consisting of an embossed
rubber strip that is inked to print a
stamp on an object or document.

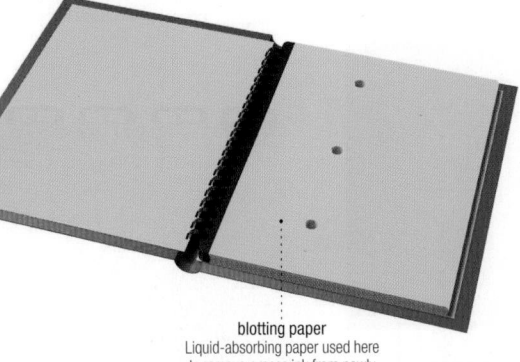

blotting paper
Liquid-absorbing paper used here
to remove excess ink from newly
signed documents.

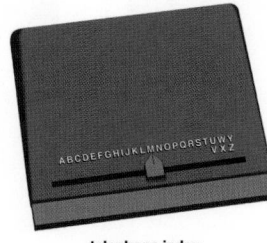

telephone index
Book in which frequently used names,
addresses and telephone numbers are
written and stored in alphabetical order.

rotary file
Device with a set of files that rotate
on a spindle for easy consultation.

...stage meter
...achine used to print a postage
...eter stamp on an envelope or label
...lieu of using a postage stamp.

postmarking module
Unit housing the machine's control buttons;
it is used to set the prepaid postage meter
with the correct amount of postage.

desk tray
Container that usually has several
compartments; it is used to handle
incoming and outgoing mail.

feed deck
Device on which envelopes are
placed to be stamped with a
postage meter.

base

office supplies

for filing

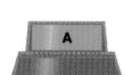

window tab
Tab with an opening to hold an identification label.

self-adhesive labels
Small pieces of paper used to identify objects; they are coated on one side with an adhesive that sticks without wetting.

tab
Piece of metal or plastic that is attached to a file guide, folder or file so it can be quickly retrieved. Also called a flag.

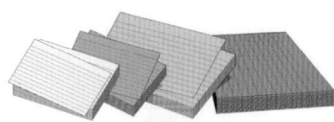

index cards
Heavyweight sheets of paper of varying sizes that are used to record information on a given topic.

sheet protector
Transparent plastic envelope in which documents are kept to protect them.

fastener binder
Binder with a flexible rod fitted with two sliding rings; it is used to hold and file punched sheets of paper.

dividers
Heavyweight sheets of paper with side tabs; they are used to separate groups of pages inside a binder.

folder
Rigid cardboard that is folded in half; documents on the same topic are placed in it.

spring binder
Binder in which sheets of paper are held in place by the pressure of springs.

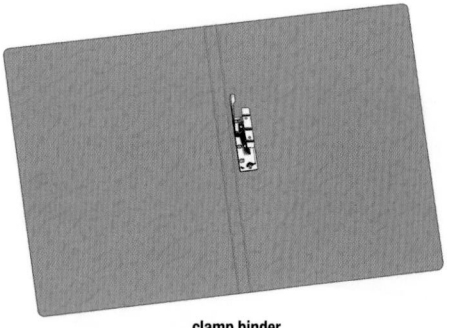

clamp binder
Binder fitted with a spring clip; it is used to hold and file sheets of paper.

hanging file
Folder fitted with metal hangers that is hung in a filing cabinet drawer.

file guides
Heavyweight sheets of paper with a tab at the top; they are used to separate groups of documents or folders in a filing cabinet drawer.

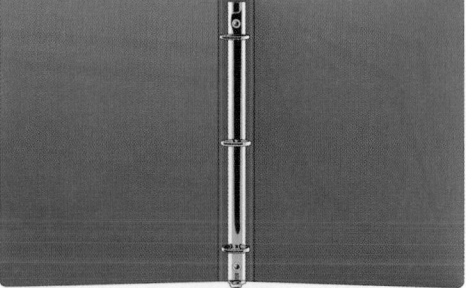

ring binder
Hardcover binder fitted with rings; it is used to hold and file punched sheets of paper.

document folder
Folder with pockets used to hold information documents; they are often handed out to meeting participants or journalists.

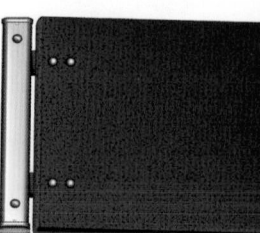

post binder
Binder with two rods that fit into a hinge; it is used to hold and file punched sheets of paper.

archboard
Rigid board fitted with two arched metal clips on which punched sheets are placed.

art and photo envelope
Plastic pocket with an airtight closing system, used to store documents in when transporting them.

index card drawer
Small built-in drawer designed for storage and filing of index cards.

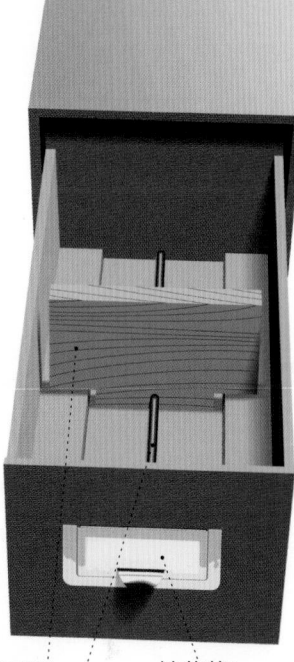

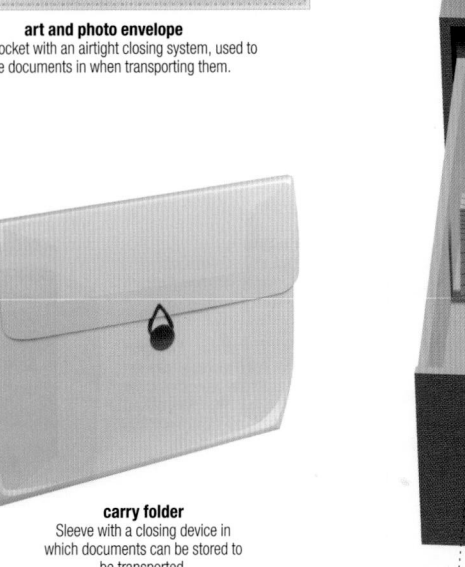

index card cabinet
Small file drawer designed to hold and store index cards in a set order.

carry folder
Sleeve with a closing device in which documents can be stored to be transported.

compressor
Movable panel that holds index cards in an upright position.

label holder
Part with an opening to hold an identification label.

metal rail
Cylindrical rod along which the compressor moves.

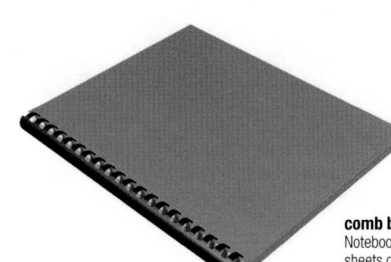

comb binding
Notebook made up of a set of punched sheets of paper that are bound together with a toothed plastic strip.

expanding file
Usually expandable file with compartments; it is used to store documents by subject.

filing box
Small open cardboard box that is mainly used to hold magazines, catalogs and brochures.

label maker
Device used to print characters on a self-adhesive strip.

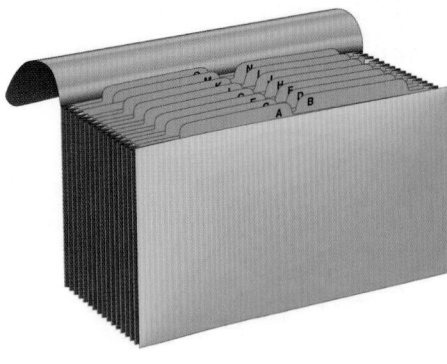

OFFICE AUTOMATION

office supplies

miscellaneous articles

tape guide
Device used as a visual guide to apply the adhesive tape to a specific area.

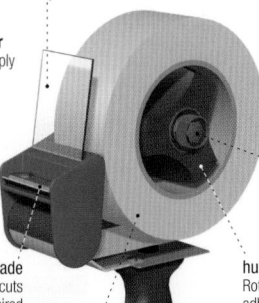

box sealing tape dispenser
Device that is used to unroll, apply and cut a roll of adhesive tape using one hand.

tension adjusting screw
Screw that adjusts the speed at which the tape unrolls.

cutting blade
Thin flat metal piece that cuts the adhesive tape to the desired length.

hub
Rotating piece on which the roll of adhesive tape is mounted.

tape
Strip of plastic with one side covered in an adhesive substance.

handle

paper clips
Small clips made from a piece of bent metal wire; they are used to hold a few sheets of paper or index cards.

thumbtacks and pushpins
Small tacks with short pointy ends; they are easily pushed in with the finger and are used to attach sheets of paper, cardboard or posters to a surface.

pencil sharpener
Portable device used to sharpen pencils by rotating them in a cone-shaped chamber fitted with a blade.

electric pencil sharpener
Desk tool used to sharpen pencils an automatic rotating bla

receptacle for shavings
Container where the pencil shavings are collected.

leads tube
Small container filled with refill leads for mechanical pencils.

paper fasteners
Small clips made of two bars, which spread open to hold sheets of paper or cardboard.

paper clip holder
Small box containing paper clips, which are released one by one through a magnetic opening.

magnet
Material that produces a magnetic field; it attracts paper clips to the top and holds them in place around the opening.

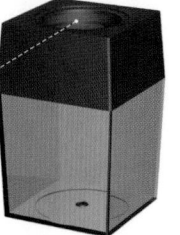

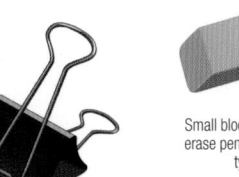

eraser
Small block of rubber used t erase pencil marks and some types of ink.

correction pen
Pen containing a liquid substance allowing one to mask printed or handwritten characters in order to write over them.

clip
Device with two articulated arms that are pressed together to hold such items as sheets of paper and index cards.

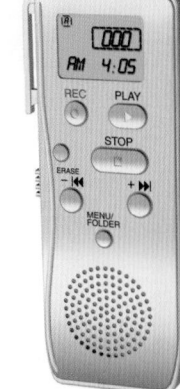

glue stick
Tube that contains a small stick of solid adhesive matter to be applied to a surface.

tape dispenser
Holder that eases the unrolling and cutting of a roll of adhesive tape.

staple remover
Device used to remove staples from sheets of paper.

digital voice recorder
Portable device used to reco voice messages in digital for

pencil sharpener
Office device with a rotating blade that is controlled by a crank; it is used to sharpen pencils.

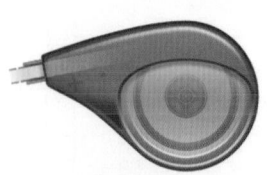

correction tape
Adhesive tape that covers up printed or written characters so that corrections can be made.

spindle file
Holder fitted with a pointy rod on which notes and bills are stacked.

staples
Pieces of metal wire for loading in a stapler; they are used to fasten sheets of paper together.

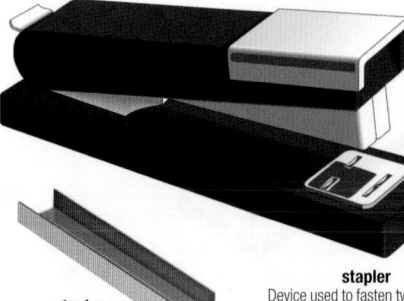

stapler
Device used to fasten two sheets of paper together staples.

head projector
e that projects the enlarged image
ocument printed on a transparency
screen located behind the user.

projection head
Movable part that contains the lens
and mirror; a focusing ring changes its
position to give a clear image on the
screen.

account book
Book with columns in which the
financial data of an organization (such
as sales, purchases, receipts and
expenditures) are recorded.

optical lens
Transparent optical disk that
tures the light from the optical
stage and makes it converge
toward the mirror.

mirror
Polished glass surface that directs
light from the lens toward the
projection screen.

optical stage
ss plate that is lit by an internal
the document to be projected
is placed on it.

cutting head
Unit with an opening where paper
enters; it is fitted with a cutting device
to destroy documents.

wastebasket
Basket that collects shredded
documents.

wastebasket
Basket in which unneeded
documents are discarded.

etin board
d that hangs on a wall; messages, notices,
s and other written communications are
ed on it.

paper shredder
Device that reduces paper documents to illegible
fragments.

bookends
Items designed to hold binders or
books tightly against one other.

lightbox
Screen that is illuminated from
behind and used to examine
items such as negatives, slides,
transparencies and drawings.

posting surface

paper punch
Device used to punch holes in
sheets of paper.

slotted box
Box with flaps that is formed from a
single piece of sturdy cardboard; it
is used to collect various items for
storage or shipping.

flap
Articulated piece that folds over the
opening of the box to close it.

er cutter
e of equipment used to make
re cuts in paper, cardboard,
sparencies, etc.

hand hole

OFFICE AUTOMATION

TRANSPORT AND MACHINERY

road system

Network of thoroughfares providing for the flow of traffic.

cross section of a road
Road: thoroughfare connecting two geographical points, usually urban centers.

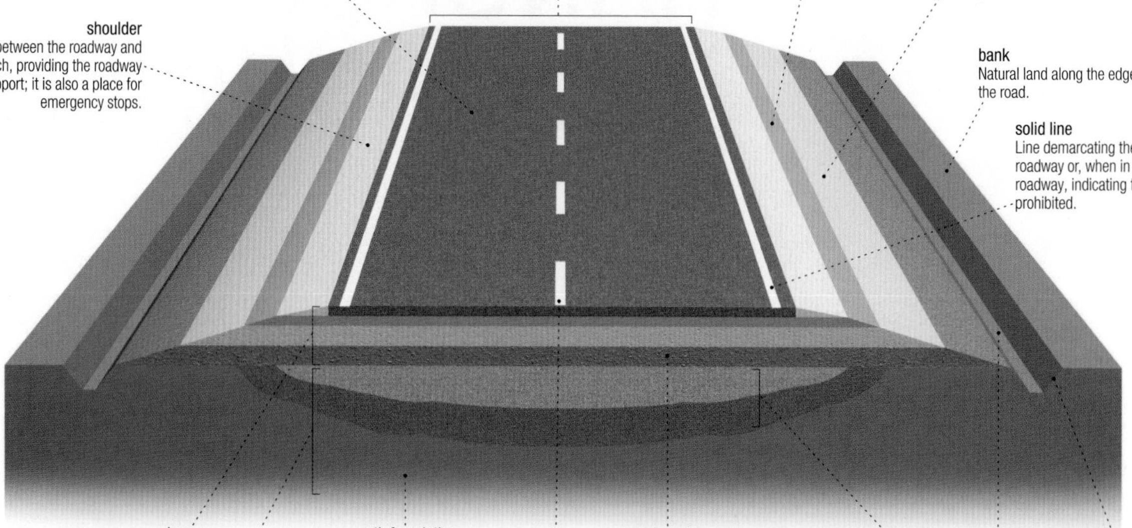

surface course
Roadway's driving surface; it is smooth, impermeable and provides a good grip for vehicles.

roadway
Surface upon which vehicles drive.

base course
Top foundation layer, made up of fine compacted material; the driving surface lies on it.

subbase
Base of a roadway, made up of coarse compacted gravel, making the roadway solid and stable.

shoulder
Area between the roadway and the ditch, providing the roadway lateral support; it is also a place for emergency stops.

bank
Natural land along the edge of the road.

solid line
Line demarcating the edg roadway or, when in the c roadway, indicating that p prohibited.

base
Series of layers above the embankment reducing stress exerted by the traffic and preventing the bed from deforming.

earth foundation
Part of the ground that was not excavated during the road's construction.

subgrade
Layer supporting the base course and the subbase and providing drainage.

embankment
Layers of material used to build up or level the route the road is to take.

slope
Steeply sloped ground bet ditch and the bank and b the ditch and the shou

bed
Composed of the embankment and the earth foundation; the base rests on it.

broken line
Line demarcating the two lanes of the roadway and showing that passing is permitted.

ditch
Ditch parallel to the roadway; surface water drains into it.

examples of interchanges
Interchange: structure linking roads or freeways so they do not intersect.

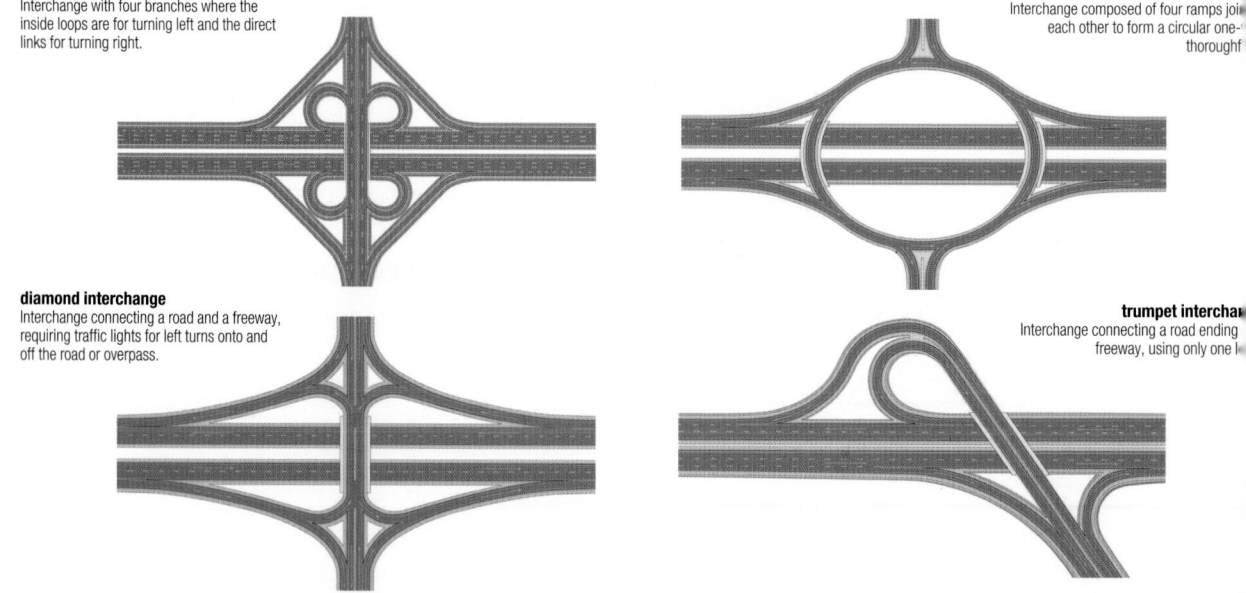

cloverleaf
Interchange with four branches where the inside loops are for turning left and the direct links for turning right.

traffic cir
Interchange composed of four ramps joi each other to form a circular one- thoroughf

diamond interchange
Interchange connecting a road and a freeway, requiring traffic lights for left turns onto and off the road or overpass.

trumpet interchan
Interchange connecting a road ending freeway, using only one l

road system

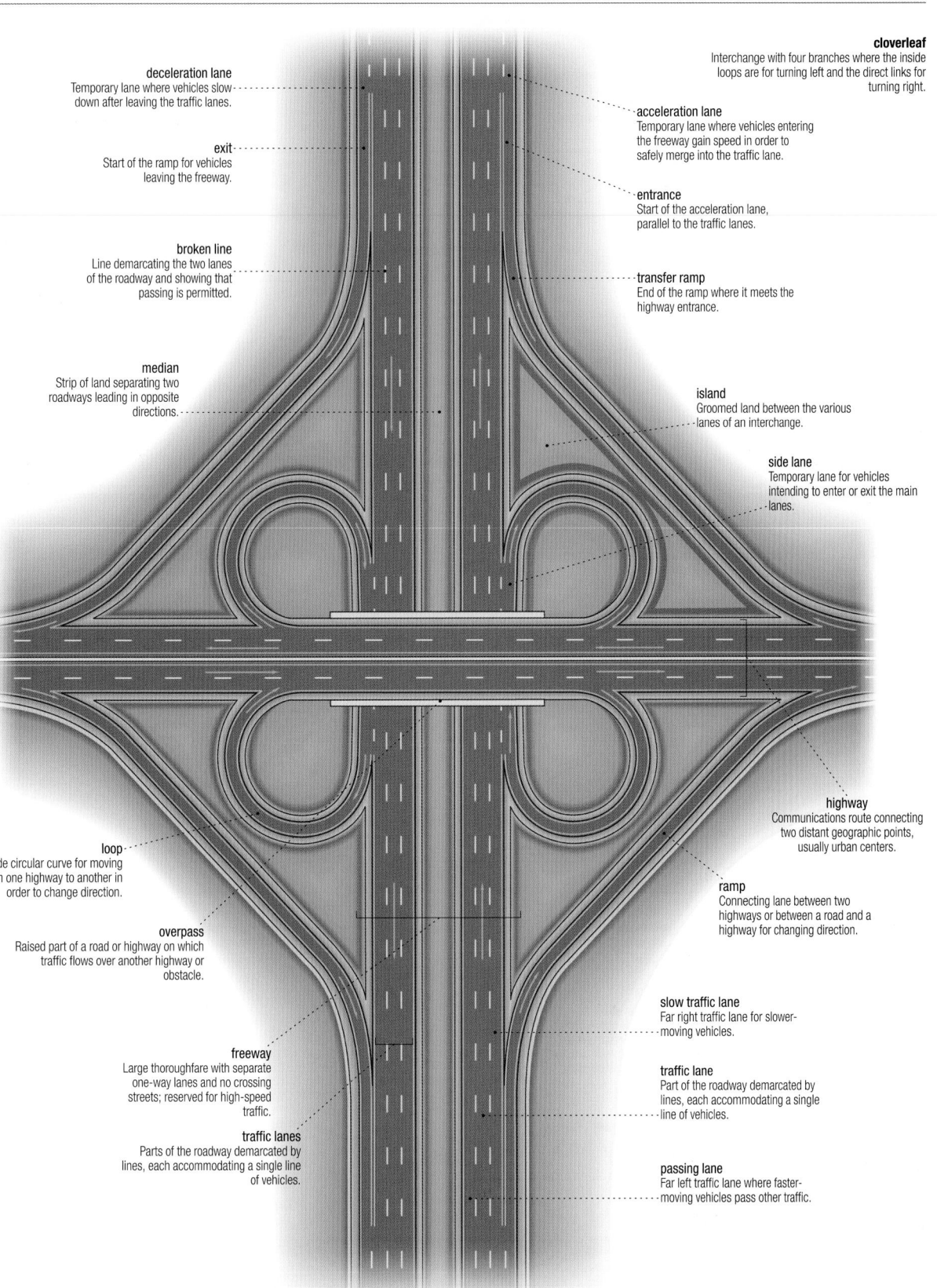

cloverleaf
Interchange with four branches where the inside loops are for turning left and the direct links for turning right.

deceleration lane
Temporary lane where vehicles slow down after leaving the traffic lanes.

acceleration lane
Temporary lane where vehicles entering the freeway gain speed in order to safely merge into the traffic lane.

exit
Start of the ramp for vehicles leaving the freeway.

entrance
Start of the acceleration lane, parallel to the traffic lanes.

broken line
Line demarcating the two lanes of the roadway and showing that passing is permitted.

transfer ramp
End of the ramp where it meets the highway entrance.

median
Strip of land separating two roadways leading in opposite directions.

island
Groomed land between the various lanes of an interchange.

side lane
Temporary lane for vehicles intending to enter or exit the main lanes.

highway
Communications route connecting two distant geographic points, usually urban centers.

loop
Wide circular curve for moving from one highway to another in order to change direction.

ramp
Connecting lane between two highways or between a road and a highway for changing direction.

overpass
Raised part of a road or highway on which traffic flows over another highway or obstacle.

slow traffic lane
Far right traffic lane for slower-moving vehicles.

traffic lane
Part of the roadway demarcated by lines, each accommodating a single line of vehicles.

freeway
Large thoroughfare with separate one-way lanes and no crossing streets; reserved for high-speed traffic.

traffic lanes
Parts of the roadway demarcated by lines, each accommodating a single line of vehicles.

passing lane
Far left traffic lane where faster-moving vehicles pass other traffic.

TRANSPORT AND MACHINERY

TRANSPORT AND MACHINERY

fixed bridges

Structures enabling traffic to clear an obstacle, such as a river, gorge or highway.

beam bridge
Bridge whose deck is composed of one or several beams, which are supported by piers across the open space.

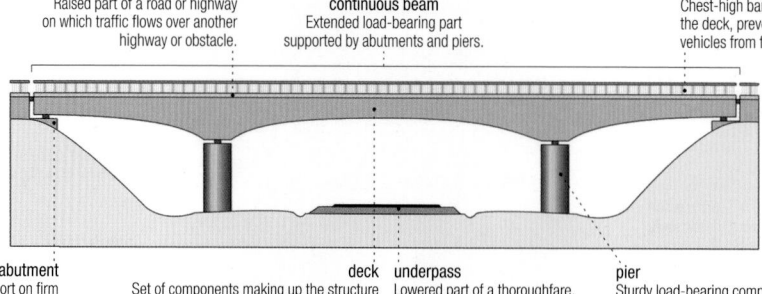

overpass
Raised part of a road or highway on which traffic flows over another highway or obstacle.

continuous beam
Extended load-bearing part supported by abutments and piers.

parapet
Chest-high barrier on each side of the deck, preventing people and vehicles from falling off.

abutment
A pier's point of support on firm ground.

deck
Set of components making up the structure that carries the bridge's traffic lanes.

underpass
Lowered part of a thoroughfare, enabling traffic to flow under another roadway or obstacle.

pier
Sturdy load-bearing component placed at intervals to support the bridge's beams.

examples of beam bridges
Depending on the length of the roadway above the obstacle, the bridge could comprise one or more beams.

viaduct
A long high bridge composed of several beams that crosses a valley.

multiple-span beam bridge
Bridge whose deck is composed of several juxtaposed beams, each one supported at each end.

simple-span beam bridge
Bridge whose deck is composed of only one continuous beam.

suspension bridge
Bridge whose long deck is suspended from load-bearing cables, which are supported by the towers and anchored in the ground at both ends of the bridge.

deck
Set of components making up the structure that carries the bridge's traffic lanes.

suspension cable
Very strong, flexible component made of steel wires; it bears the weight of the deck.

suspender
Cable or metal rod connecting the suspension cable to the deck, supporting it.

tower
Elevated structure made of metal or reinforced concrete; it supports the cables.

approach ramp
Lane for accessing the bridge.

abutment
Solid concrete construction whose mass counterbalances the weight of the suspended roadway.

anchorage block
Concrete structure on each side of the abutment; it is buried deep in the ground and the end of the suspension cable is attached to it.

tower foundation
Solid concrete base that is anchored in the ground.

center span
Section of the deck entirely suspended between the towers.

side span
Section of the span between the tower and the abutment.

cantilever bridge
Bridge whose two main spans extend toward each other and support a short suspended span, which bears less load.

cantilever span
Span with a complex framework on each side of a central pillar; one end of the span rests on the ground and the other supports a suspended span.

suspended span
Short center span resting on the ends of the two cantilever spans.

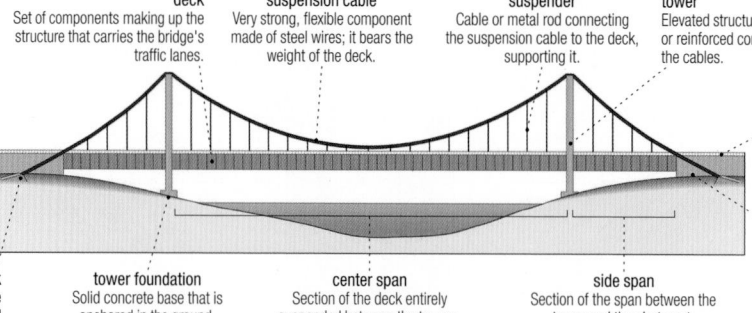

fixed bridges

trussed arch
Arched girder consisting of two chords joined by a triangulated network of struts.

arch
Metal bow-shaped structure supporting the deck, whose load it transfers to the abutments.

upper chord
Upper lengthwise steel girder forming the metal arch.

arch bridge
Bridge whose deck is supported by suspenders attached to an arch, which exerts diagonal thrust against the lateral supports.

portal frame
Part of the deck's frame over firm ground, lying on columns.

pier
Solid concrete construction acting as counterweight to the thrust of the arch against the abutment.

column
Sturdy component forming a vertical support.

thrust
Point at which the arch is supported by the abutment.

abutment
Base of the pier; it supports the arch's weight and thrust.

lower chord
Lower lengthwise steel girder forming the metal arch.

deck
Set of components making up the structure that carries the bridge's traffic lanes.

examples of arch bridges
Among arch bridges, the position of the deck in relation to the arch varies.

deck arch bridge
Bridge whose deck is located above the arch upon which it rests.

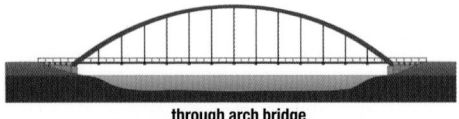

through arch bridge
Bridge whose deck is located below the arch from which it is suspended.

portal bridge
Bridge resting on diagonal beams that are embedded in the deck.

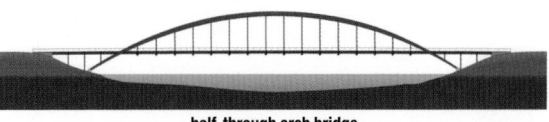

half-through arch bridge
Bridge whose deck is located within the arch from which it is suspended in the middle, and on which it rests, at each end.

examples of arches
The concept of the arch varies in relation to the way it absorbs and transfers the roadway's weight to its support points.

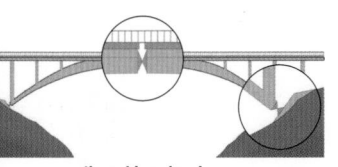

three-hinged arch
Arch with three hinge joints: one at each end and one at the center.

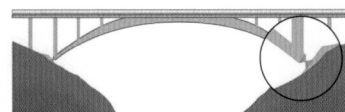

two-hinged arch
Arch whose ends rest on an abutment attached by a hinge joint.

fixed arch
Nonarticulated arch, embedded in each of its supports.

cable-stayed bridges
Bridges whose deck is supported at several points by stays and rests on one or more towers.

cable stay anchorage
Apparatus by which one end of the stay is attached to the tower and the other to the end of the deck.

stays
Usually metal cables connected at one end to the top of the tower, and supported by the deck at the other end.

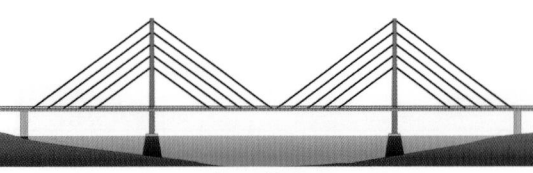

fan cable stays
Bridge for which the distance between the anchorage points of the stays on the tower is less than the distance between the anchorage points on the deck.

harp cable stays
Bridge whose stays are parallel.

movable bridges

Bridges whose decks move to free up the transportation channel they cross, or that are built temporarily while awaiting a permanent structure.

swing bridge
Bridge whose deck pivots around a vertical axle.

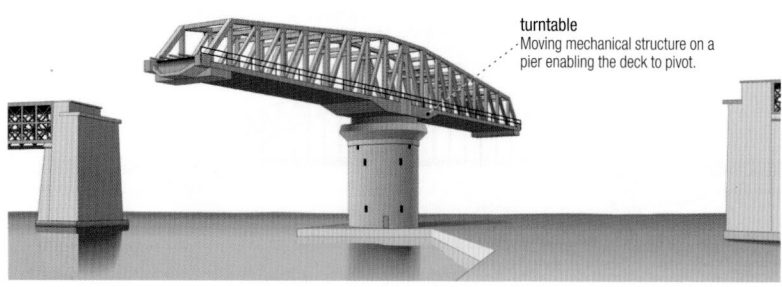

turntable
Moving mechanical structure on a pier enabling the deck to pivot.

manrope
Chest-high barrier on each side of the deck, preventing people and vehicles from falling off.

pontoon
Floating caisson filled with air and supporting the deck.

counterweight
Concrete or cast-iron mass, balancing the weight of the deck and facilitating its movement.

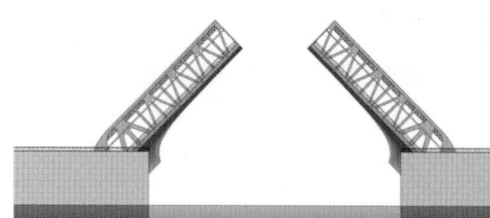

single-leaf bascule bridge
Drawbridge whose deck is raised by means of a counterweight mechanism.

floating bridge
Bridge whose deck rests on pontoons that can be taken apart to open the bridge.

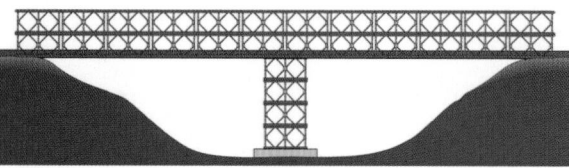

Bailey bridge
Steel bridge, often temporary, whose standardized truss components make it easy to assemble quickly.

double-leaf bascule bridge
Drawbridge whose deck is composed of two spans joining each other at the middle of the bridge and pivoting around a vertical axle at each abutment.

guiding tower
Pylon equipped with pulleys and cables for hoisting the deck.

trolley
Part of the bridge moved by a motor; it glides along rails installed under the deck.

lift span
Deck suspended at each end by cables hoisting it up along the guiding towers.

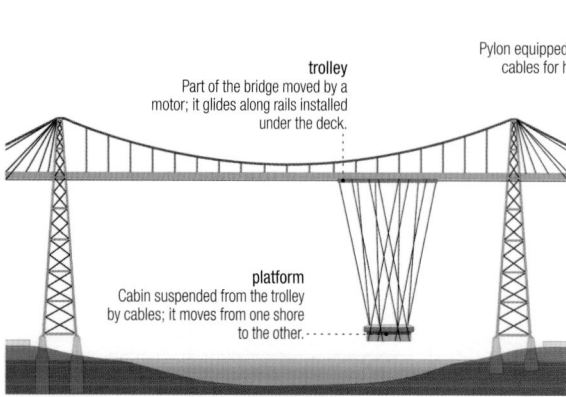

platform
Cabin suspended from the trolley by cables; it moves from one shore to the other.

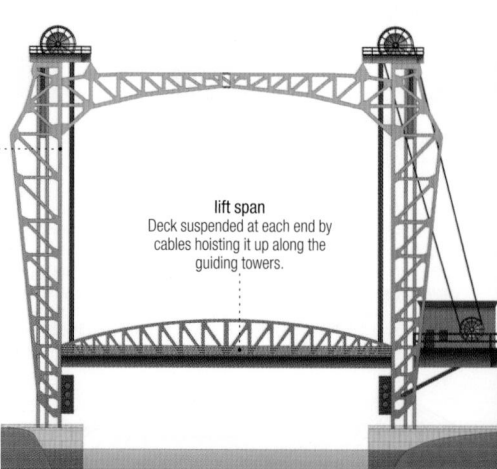

transporter bridge
Bridge with a very high deck from which a moving platform is suspended to transport pedestrians and vehicles.

lift bridge
Bridge whose deck is raised by a system of cables.

road tunnel

Underground passage for a road under an obstacle, such as a river or a hill.

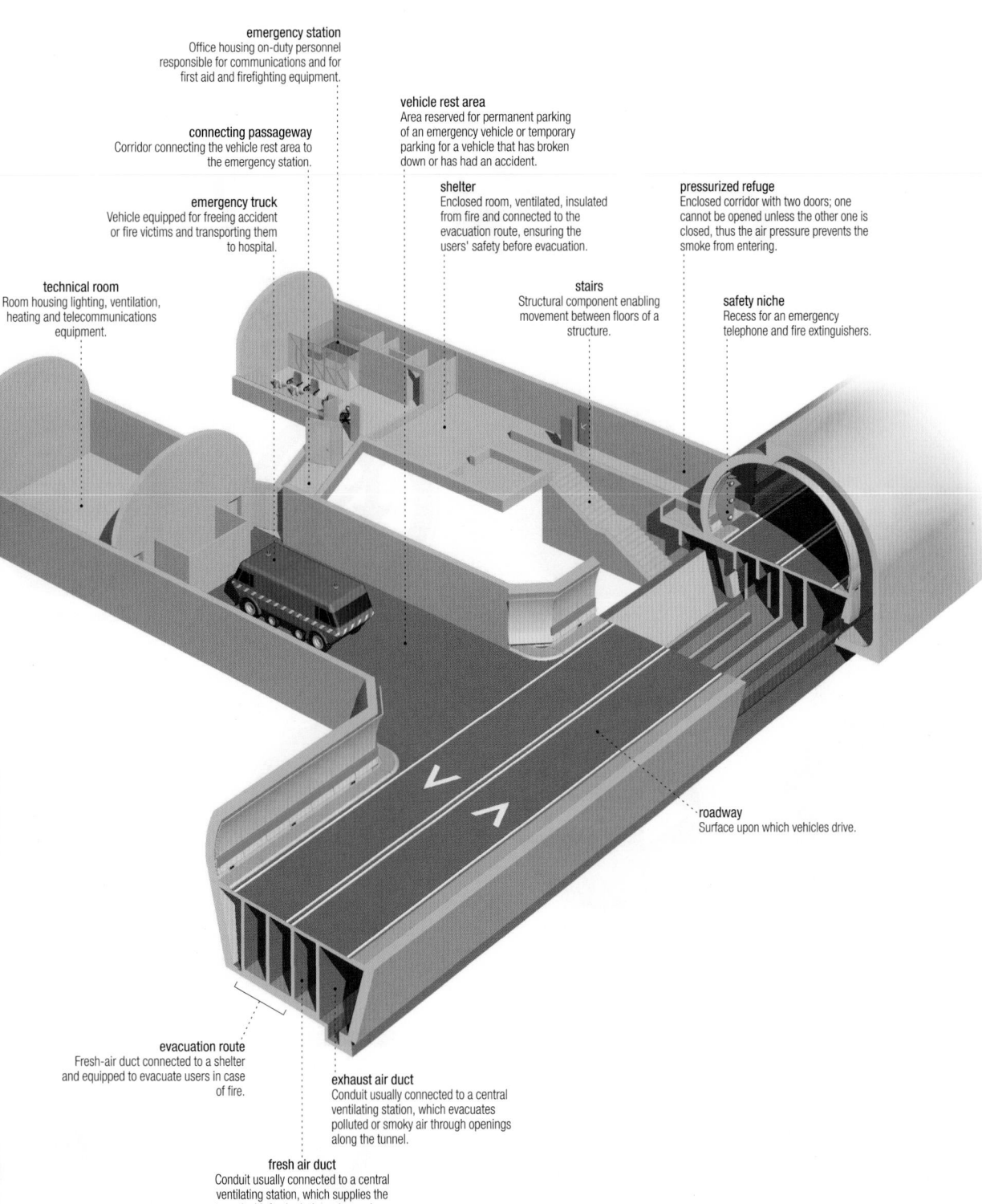

emergency station
Office housing on-duty personnel responsible for communications and for first aid and firefighting equipment.

vehicle rest area
Area reserved for permanent parking of an emergency vehicle or temporary parking for a vehicle that has broken down or has had an accident.

connecting passageway
Corridor connecting the vehicle rest area to the emergency station.

shelter
Enclosed room, ventilated, insulated from fire and connected to the evacuation route, ensuring the users' safety before evacuation.

pressurized refuge
Enclosed corridor with two doors; one cannot be opened unless the other one is closed, thus the air pressure prevents the smoke from entering.

emergency truck
Vehicle equipped for freeing accident or fire victims and transporting them to hospital.

technical room
Room housing lighting, ventilation, heating and telecommunications equipment.

stairs
Structural component enabling movement between floors of a structure.

safety niche
Recess for an emergency telephone and fire extinguishers.

roadway
Surface upon which vehicles drive.

evacuation route
Fresh-air duct connected to a shelter and equipped to evacuate users in case of fire.

exhaust air duct
Conduit usually connected to a central ventilating station, which evacuates polluted or smoky air through openings along the tunnel.

fresh air duct
Conduit usually connected to a central ventilating station, which supplies the tunnel with fresh air through openings at the side of the roadway.

TRANSPORT AND MACHINERY

road signs

Objects such as signs, traffic lights and road markings, aimed at ensuring the safety of the road's users and increasing traffic-flow efficiency.

major international road signs
Main signs used by countries complying with the Vienna International Convention, which provides some international uniformity to road signs.

right bend

double bend

roadway narrows

stop at intersection

no entry

no U-turn

passing prohibited

direction to be followed

direction to be followed

direction to be followed

directions to be followed

one-way traffic

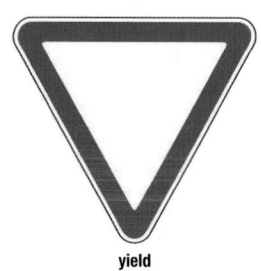
two-way traffic

yield

priority intersection

falling rocks

overhead clearance

signal ahead

school zone

pedestrian crossing

roadwork ahead

slippery road

railroad crossing

deer crossing

steep hill

bumps

closed to pedestrians

closed to bicycles

closed to motorcycles

closed to trucks

TRANSPORT AND MACHINERY

road signs

major North American road signs

Main signs used in Canada and the United States, inspired more or less by the signs endorsed by the Vienna International Convention of 1968.

stop at intersection

no entry

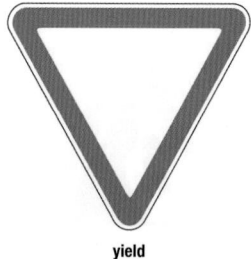

yield

closed to motorcycles

closed to pedestrians

closed to bicycles

closed to trucks

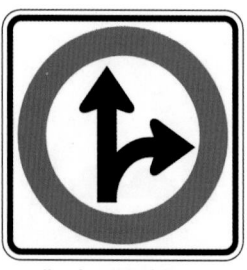

directions to be followed

direction to be followed

direction to be followed

direction to be followed

no U-turn

passing prohibited

one-way traffic

two-way traffic

double bend

merging traffic

right curve

roadway narrows

slippery road

deer crossing

roadwork ahead

bumps

steep hill

falling rocks

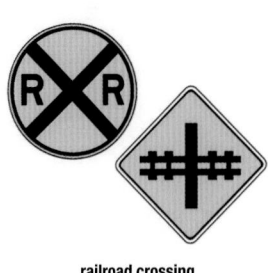

railroad crossing

overhead clearance

signal ahead

school zone

pedestrian crossing

TRANSPORT AND MACHINERY

service station

general view

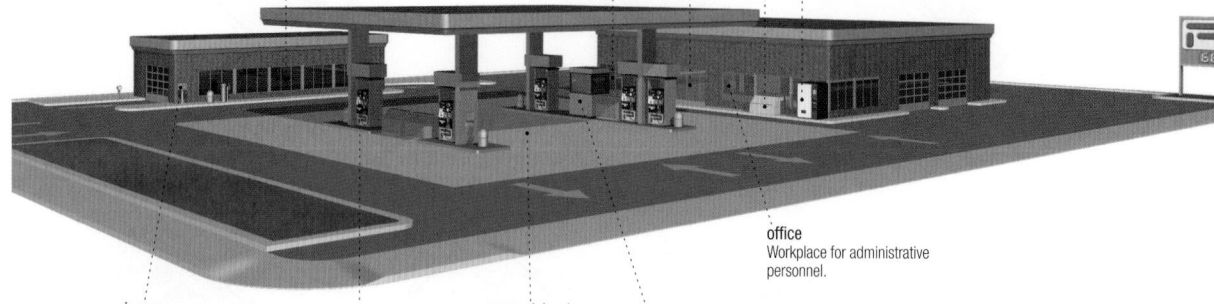

service bay
Workshop where engines and their related systems are maintained and repaired.

ice dispenser
Refrigerated box containing bags of ice for self-service.

car wash
Station where vehicles are automatically washed.

maintenance
Workshop where the necessary checks and adjustments are made to vehicles.

vending machine
Automated machine serving soft drinks; it is activated by the insertion of coins into a slot.

office
Workplace for administrative personnel.

air pump
Machine connected to a compressor, used for inflating tires to their required air pressure.

pump island
Space where the gasoline pumps are installed.

kiosk
Hut where customers can quickly settle their fuel bills.

gasoline pump
Machine with a pump for refilling vehicles with fuel.

gasoline pump
Machine with a pump for refilling vehicles with fuel.

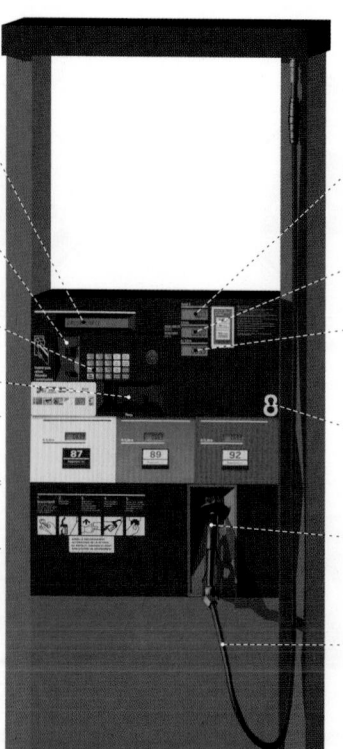

display
Surface displaying instructions for customers paying by card.

card reader slot
The card is inserted into the device, which verifies the customer's personal identification number (PIN) before the transaction can begin.

alphanumeric keyboard
Set of buttons for entering numbers, letters and other kinds of information.

slip presenter
Slot through which the user is given the payment receipt for the card payment.

type of fuel
Choice of available fuels (such as diesel and gasoline) and the price of each per volume unit (liter or gallon).

operating instructions
Set of instructions explaining the steps to follow to use the gasoline pump.

total sale display
Screen displaying the total price, corresponding to the volume of fuel pumped.

volume display
Screen displaying, in gallons or liters, the volume of fuel pumped.

price per gallon/liter
Screen displaying the price per volume unit (liter or gallon) of the fuel chosen.

pump number

pump nozzle
Gun-shaped spout at the end of the gasoline pump hose and used to pour fuel into the vehicle's tank.

gasoline pump hose
Flexible pipe connected to the pump, maintaining fuel flow.

automobile

Motor vehicle with four wheels, developed for transporting a small number of people and small loads.

examples of cars
Styles vary from manufacturer to manufacturer and from year to year but there is little variation in the basic model.

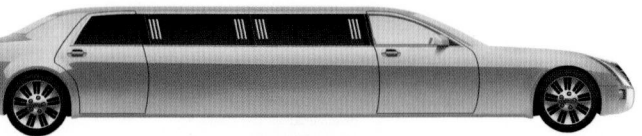

limousine
Spacious deluxe sedan with four or more doors; the passenger area is separated from the chauffeur's.

micro compact car
Very small automobile with two seats and integrated cargo area, designed to be driven and parked in large cities.

convertible
Automobile with two or four doors and a soft or hard retractable roof.

sports car
Automobile with an aerodynamic look with two doors, a small trunk separate from the passenger compartment and, sometimes, narrow rear seats.

two-door sedan
Automobile with two doors, a trunk separate from the passenger compartment and four seats.

minivan
Automobile with three rows of seats; the last row can be folded down to enlarge the cargo area.

hatchback
Automobile with two doors and a lift gate, folding front seats granting access to the rear seats, and a cargo area integrated with the passenger compartment.

four-door sedan
Automobile with four doors and a trunk separate from the passenger compartment.

station wagon
Automobile with four doors, a large cargo area integrated with the passenger compartment and folding rear seats for enlarging the cargo area.

crossover vehicle
Car that combines the characteristics of different categories of vehicle (sedan, van, family, sport utility).

four-door hatchback
Car having four doors and a hatchback as well as back seats that can usually be folded down to gain access to the trunk, which is integrated into the interior.

pickup truck
Automobile used for transporting materials that has an uncovered bed closed off by a gate.

sport-utility vehicle (SUV)
Car designed to drive on all types of road, or over rocky terrain, having a spacious interior and a large amount of storage space.

off-road vehicle
Automobile designed to be driven on any kind of roadway or on rugged terrain.

TRANSPORT AND MACHINERY

automobile

body
Automobile structure designed to house and protect the mechanical components, the passengers and cargo.

windshield
Glass and plastic pane protecting the occupants from inclement weather while providing good visibility.

outside mirror
Mirror fixed to the outside of the passenger compartment enabling the driver to see behind and along the sides of the vehicle without turning around.

windshield wiper
Rubber squeegee, usually mounted in a pair; it is activated by a motor and cleans the windshield.

cowl
Transverse component of the body between the hood and the windshield allowing air into the passenger compartment.

washer nozzle
Device squirting liquid on the windshield in order to clean it.

hood
Lidlike part of the body covering and protecting the engine.

grille
Plastic or metal grating in front of the vehicle protecting the radiator and serving as decoration.

bumper molding
Metal or plastic trim embellishing the front and rear bumpers.

headlight
Lamp on the front of the vehicle to light up the space in front.

front fascia
Component on the exterior of the body below the bumpers reducing air resistance.

fender
Component of the body forming a streamlined and aerodynamic casing around the wheels.

TRANSPORT AND MACHINERY

automobile

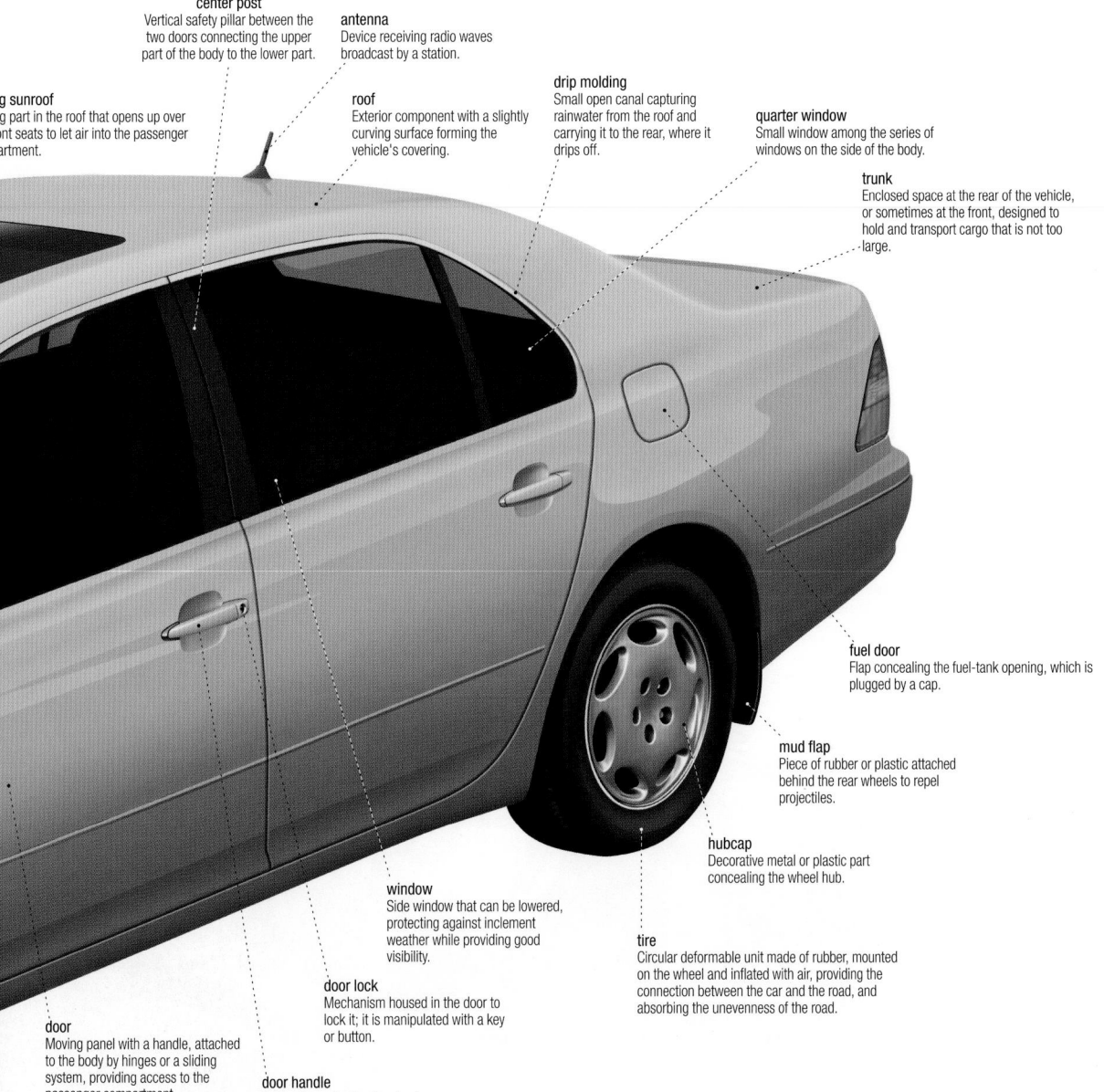

center post
Vertical safety pillar between the two doors connecting the upper part of the body to the lower part.

antenna
Device receiving radio waves broadcast by a station.

drip molding
Small open canal capturing rainwater from the roof and carrying it to the rear, where it drips off.

quarter window
Small window among the series of windows on the side of the body.

g sunroof
g part in the roof that opens up over nt seats to let air into the passenger artment.

roof
Exterior component with a slightly curving surface forming the vehicle's covering.

trunk
Enclosed space at the rear of the vehicle, or sometimes at the front, designed to hold and transport cargo that is not too large.

fuel door
Flap concealing the fuel-tank opening, which is plugged by a cap.

mud flap
Piece of rubber or plastic attached behind the rear wheels to repel projectiles.

hubcap
Decorative metal or plastic part concealing the wheel hub.

window
Side window that can be lowered, protecting against inclement weather while providing good visibility.

tire
Circular deformable unit made of rubber, mounted on the wheel and inflated with air, providing the connection between the car and the road, and absorbing the unevenness of the road.

door lock
Mechanism housed in the door to lock it; it is manipulated with a key or button.

door
Moving panel with a handle, attached to the body by hinges or a sliding system, providing access to the passenger compartment.

door handle
Device for activating the door's opening mechanism.

dy side molding
al or plastic part attached along the rs to protect them against light impact.

automobile

automobile systems: main parts
A vehicle is composed of basic mechanical parts and devices making up its systems; each of them fulfills a specific function.

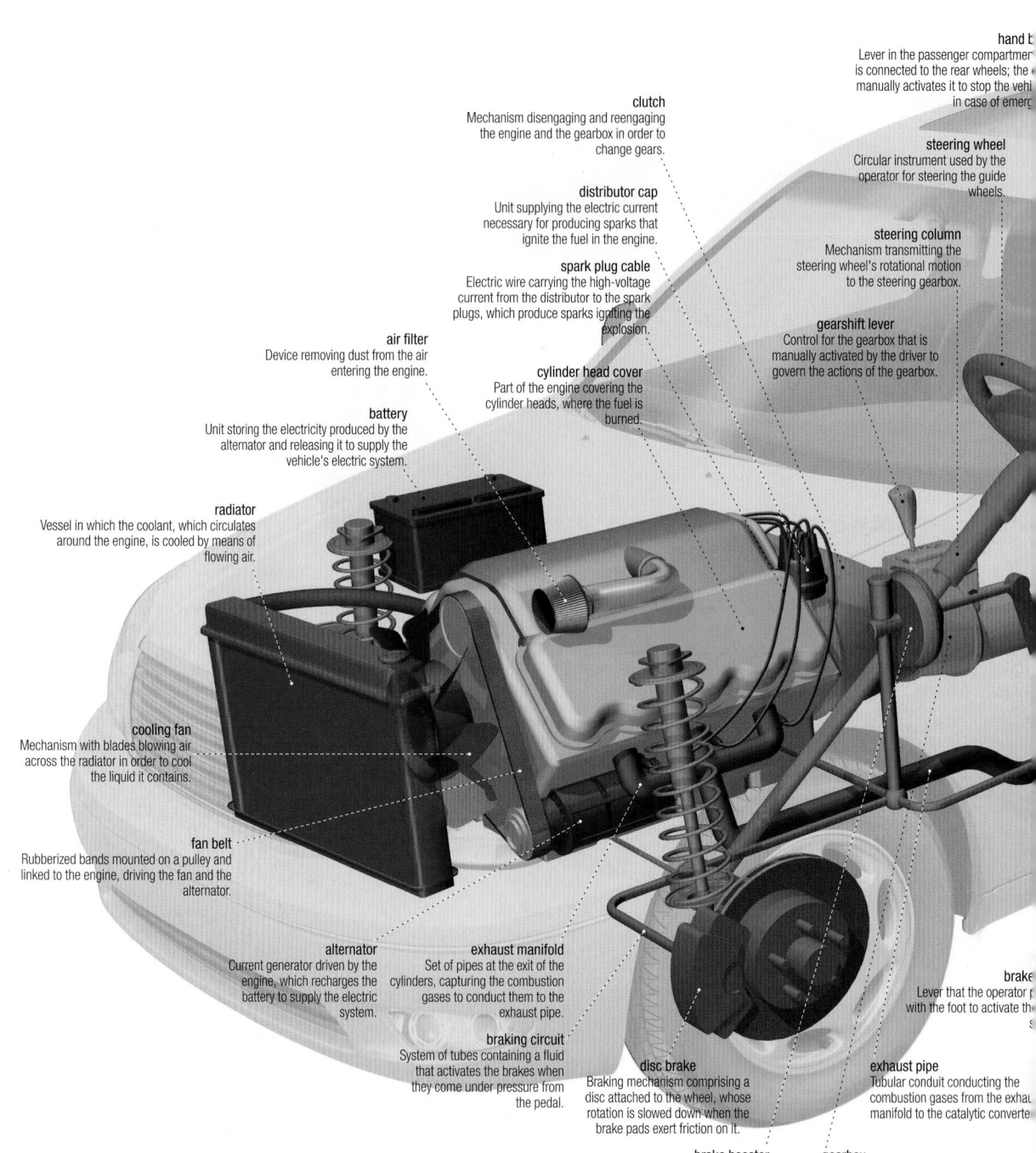

hand b...
Lever in the passenger compartmer... is connected to the rear wheels; the ... manually activates it to stop the vehi... in case of emerg...

clutch
Mechanism disengaging and reengaging the engine and the gearbox in order to change gears.

steering wheel
Circular instrument used by the operator for steering the guide wheels.

distributor cap
Unit supplying the electric current necessary for producing sparks that ignite the fuel in the engine.

steering column
Mechanism transmitting the steering wheel's rotational motion to the steering gearbox.

spark plug cable
Electric wire carrying the high-voltage current from the distributor to the spark plugs, which produce sparks igniting the explosion.

gearshift lever
Control for the gearbox that is manually activated by the driver to govern the actions of the gearbox.

air filter
Device removing dust from the air entering the engine.

cylinder head cover
Part of the engine covering the cylinder heads, where the fuel is burned.

battery
Unit storing the electricity produced by the alternator and releasing it to supply the vehicle's electric system.

radiator
Vessel in which the coolant, which circulates around the engine, is cooled by means of flowing air.

cooling fan
Mechanism with blades blowing air across the radiator in order to cool the liquid it contains.

fan belt
Rubberized bands mounted on a pulley and linked to the engine, driving the fan and the alternator.

alternator
Current generator driven by the engine, which recharges the battery to supply the electric system.

exhaust manifold
Set of pipes at the exit of the cylinders, capturing the combustion gases to conduct them to the exhaust pipe.

brake...
Lever that the operator p... with the foot to activate th... s...

braking circuit
System of tubes containing a fluid that activates the brakes when they come under pressure from the pedal.

disc brake
Braking mechanism comprising a disc attached to the wheel, whose rotation is slowed down when the brake pads exert friction on it.

exhaust pipe
Tubular conduit conducting the combustion gases from the exhau... manifold to the catalytic converte...

brake booster
Mechanism amplifying the force exerted by the driver on the brake pedal.

gearbox
Unit changing the ratio between the rotation speed of the engine and that of the wheels in the forward gears, or reversing the rotation in the reverse gear.

automobile

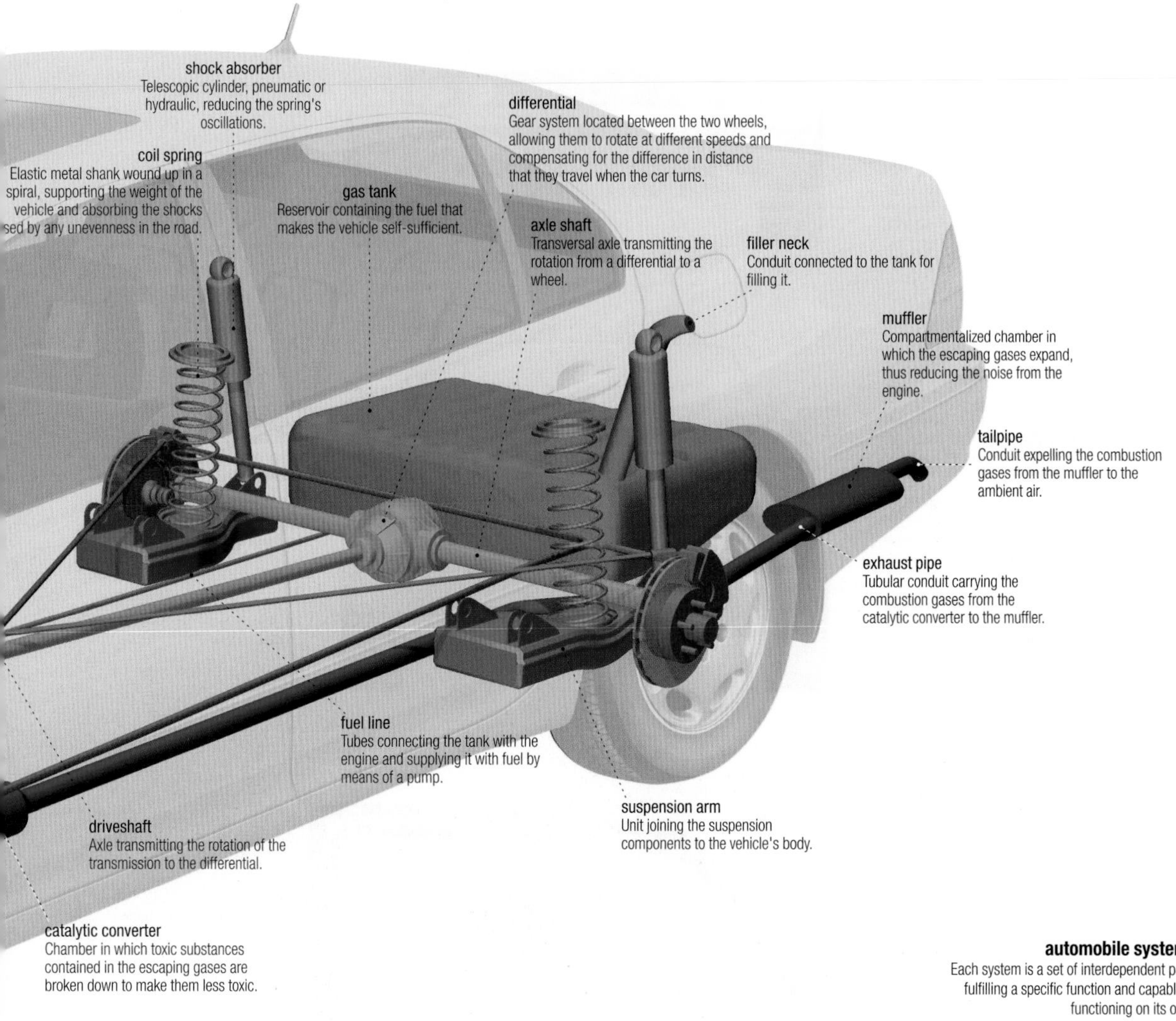

shock absorber
Telescopic cylinder, pneumatic or hydraulic, reducing the spring's oscillations.

coil spring
Elastic metal shank wound up in a spiral, supporting the weight of the vehicle and absorbing the shocks ...sed by any unevenness in the road.

gas tank
Reservoir containing the fuel that makes the vehicle self-sufficient.

differential
Gear system located between the two wheels, allowing them to rotate at different speeds and compensating for the difference in distance that they travel when the car turns.

axle shaft
Transversal axle transmitting the rotation from a differential to a wheel.

filler neck
Conduit connected to the tank for filling it.

muffler
Compartmentalized chamber in which the escaping gases expand, thus reducing the noise from the engine.

tailpipe
Conduit expelling the combustion gases from the muffler to the ambient air.

exhaust pipe
Tubular conduit carrying the combustion gases from the catalytic converter to the muffler.

fuel line
Tubes connecting the tank with the engine and supplying it with fuel by means of a pump.

suspension arm
Unit joining the suspension components to the vehicle's body.

driveshaft
Axle transmitting the rotation of the transmission to the differential.

catalytic converter
Chamber in which toxic substances contained in the escaping gases are broken down to make them less toxic.

automobile systems
Each system is a set of interdependent parts fulfilling a specific function and capable of functioning on its own.

transmission system
Set of components transmitting the motion produced by the motor to the wheels.

steering system
Set of components that direct the front wheels to guide the vehicle as it moves.

suspension system
Set of components that joins the wheels to the vehicle's body while reducing shocks caused by the road's unevenness and improving the hold on the road.

electrical system
Set of components supplying the necessary current for starting the vehicle and operating its electric accessories.

gasoline engine
Engine in which a mixture of air and gasoline is compressed and ignited to produce an explosion whose energy is converted into mechanical energy.

braking system
Set of components that reduce the vehicle's speed, eventually to a halt, and keep it in place while parked.

fuel supply system
Set of components supplying the fuel to the engine.

exhaust system
Set of components designed to expel the engine's burned gases into the ambient air.

cooling system
Set of components that prevents the temperature of the engine from rising excessively.

TRANSPORT AND MACHINERY

automobile

headlights
Set of regulation luminous devices placed on the front of a vehicle for illuminating and signaling.

high beam
Lamp illuminating the road over a long distance (100 yards), used outside urban areas.

low beam
Lamp illuminating the road at short distances (30 yards), used instead of high beam to avoid blinding drivers coming in the opposite direction.

fog light
Lamp whose light rays are directed toward the roadway and illuminate the road shoulder, by which the driver navigates in the event of fog.

turn signal
Device emitting an intermittent light, signaling a change of the vehicle's direction or a temporary hazard to other vehicles.

side marker light
Colored light demarcating the width of the vehicle.

taillights
Set of regulation lighting devices placed at the rear of a vehicle and used for signaling.

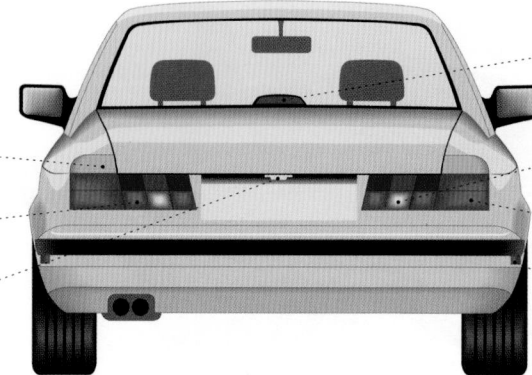

turn signal
Device emitting an intermittent light, signaling a change of the vehicle's direction or a temporary hazard to other vehicles.

brake light
Light that goes on automatically when the driver steps on the brake pedal in order to warn the vehicles following it.

license plate light
Lighting device for a vehicle's license plate, making it visible in darkness.

center high-mounted stop light
Light that goes on automatically when the driver steps on the brake pedal in order to warn the vehicles following it.

back-up light
White lamp that turns on automatically to warn motorists and pedestrians when the driver puts the car in reverse.

taillight
Lamp turning on automatically when the front lights are lit, making the vehicle visible for up to 150 yards.

side marker light
Colored light demarcating the width of the vehicle.

door
Moving panel with a handle, attached to the body by hinges or a sliding system, providing access to the passenger compartment.

interior door handle
Mechanism for opening the door from the inside of the vehicle.

assist grip
Handle allowing the passenger to pull the door inward in order to close it.

outside mirror control
Lever for adjusting the position of the outside mirror from the inside.

window crank handle
Handily placed lever that turns to activate the mechanism raising and lowering the window.

hinge
Articulating mechanism supporting the door and enabling it to pivot while it is being opened and closed.

accessory pocket
Open compartment fitted into the bottom of the door, for storing small objects.

window
Side window that can be lowered; it protects against inclement weather while ensuring good visibility.

interior door lock button
Visible end of the rod activating the lock; it is lifted or lowered to unlock and lock the door.

armrest
Support fixed to the door, for resting the arm.

lock
Mechanism housed in the door to lock it; it is manipulated with a key or button.

trim panel
Component covered with fabric, plastic or leather, upholstering the inside of the door.

inner door shell
The door's metal structure, serving to absorb impacts; it also encloses the locking mechanisms and, when it is lowered, the window.

automobile

bucket seat: front view

bucket seat: upholstered and adjustable seat that envelopes the occupant's body, keeping it in place during turns and providing greater comfort.

shoulder belt
Strap crossing in front of the passenger's thorax, from the shoulder to the hip.

sliding rail
Metal part along which the seat moves forward and backward.

sliding lever
Handle for moving the seat toward or away from the dashboard, in relation to needed legroom.

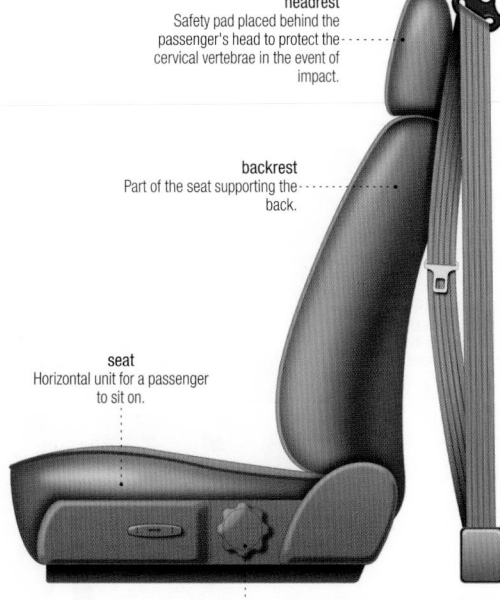

headrest
Safety pad placed behind the passenger's head to protect the cervical vertebrae in the event of impact.

backrest
Part of the seat supporting the back.

seat
Horizontal unit for a passenger to sit on.

adjustment knob
The seat's regulating mechanism, for changing the angle of the backrest to an almost horizontal position.

seat belt
Safety device fitted with sliding straps, keeping the passenger in the seat in the event of an accident.

armrest
Folding support in the middle of the rear seat, for resting the forearm.

rear seat
Bench containing several spaces installed in the rear of the passenger compartment and occupying its full width.

webbing
Center belt in the rear seat, strapping in the passenger's pelvis and restraining only the lower part of the body in the event of impact.

buckle
Clasp keeping the seat belt around the passenger and released by pressing with the finger.

bench seat
Horizontal unit for sitting on, providing up to three spaces.

automobile

dashboard
Component in the passenger compartment that contains the instrument panel, the manual controls, storage and other accessories.

rearview mirror
Mirror mounted on the windshield, positioned by the driver so that the vehicles following behind can be seen in it.

vanity mirror
Small mirror on the inside of the sun visor.

wiper switch
Electric mechanism for switching on the windshield wipers, controlling their speed and activating the windshield washer fluid.

onboard computer
Computer integrated into the vehicle; it provides information about the vehicle's main components and helps the driver with tasks related to driving.

sun visor
Movable panel that the passenger can lower over the upper part of the windshield or of the side window to prevent being blinded by the Sun.

cruise control
Mechanism enabling the driver to maintain a cruising speed for the vehicle.

ignition switch
Switch activated by a contact key allowing a current from the battery to flow to the starter.

horn
Device emitting a loud sound that the driver can use to attract the attention of a pedestrian or other user of the road.

vent
Opening, usually covered by an adjustable grille, allowing warm or cold air into the passenger compartment.

glove compartment
Small storage space fitted with locking door.

climate control
Mechanism operating the heating or air-conditioning system and controlling its intensity.

steering wheel
Circular instrument used by the driver for steering the guide wheels.

audio system
Sound-reproduction device with a tuner and a cassette or CD player.

clutch pedal
Pedal pushed to change gears.

gearshift lever
Control for the gearbox that is manually activated by the driver to change gears.

headlight/turn signal
Lever having several positions that control the turn signals and the low and high beams.

parking brake lever
Lever connected to the rear-wheel brakes that the driver activates manually to stop the vehicle, or in case of emergency.

center console
Component located between the front seats and containing certain accessories and control devices, especially the parking brake and gearshift levers.

brake pedal
Lever that the driver presses with the foot to activate the brake system.

gas pedal
Unit controlled by the foot to increase, maintain or decrease the vehicle's speed.

air bag restraint system
Automatic safety device containing air bags that, in the event of impact, instantly come between the occupants and the dashboard.

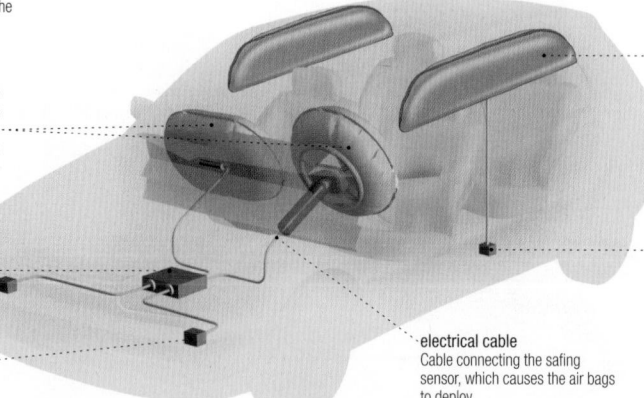

side curtain air bag
Flexible envelope, encased above the doors, that inflates with pressurized gas when it receives a signal from the crash sensor.

front air bags
Flexible envelopes encased in the dashboard, the steering wheel or the doors, which inflate with pressurized gas when receiving the signal from the safing sensor.

side crash sensor
Device located on the side of the vehicle that, in the event of a collision, transmits the signal it receives.

safing sensor
Device that receives the signal from the primary sensor and deploys the air bags. It has safeguards against deploying accidentally.

electrical cable
Cable connecting the safing sensor, which causes the air bags to deploy.

primary crash sensor
Device located at the front of the vehicle, which, in the event of collision, transmits the pulse it receives to the safing sensor.

automobile

instrument panel
Set of dials and warning lights within the driver's view that report on the vehicle's functioning.

seat-belt warning light
Warning light showing that one or more seat belts are not buckled or are not buckled correctly.

alternator warning light
Warning light showing that the battery needs recharging.

odometer
Mechanism measuring, in kilometers or miles, the total distance traveled by the vehicle since it left the factory.

trip odometer
Mechanism measuring partial distances traveled by the vehicle in kilometers or miles; it can be reset to zero.

door open warning light
Warning light showing that one or more doors, the tail gate or trunk are open or ajar.

speedometer
Dial showing the speed at which the vehicle is moving, in kilometers or miles per hour.

fuel indicator
Dial whose needle is connected to a float in the gas tank; it shows the level of fuel still available.

tachometer
Dial showing the engine's rotation speed in revolutions per minute.

warning lights
Small lights that go on and off to indicate whether the vehicle's various systems are functioning properly.

low fuel warning light
Warning light showing that the gas tank is almost empty.

turn signal indicator
Intermittent light, often accompanied by a sound, showing that a turn signal is in use.

high beam indicator light
Light showing that the high beams are on.

oil warning light
Warning light showing that the engine's oil level is lower than the minimum required.

temperature indicator
Dial showing the temperature of the engine's coolant.

windshield wiper
Rubber squeegee, usually mounted in a pair; it is activated by a motor and cleans the windshield.

windshield wiper blade
Metal part supporting the wiper through the actions of two small connecting rods.

articulation
Assembly enabling the blade to pivot on the end of the arm so that it adapts to the curvature of the windshield.

wiper
Thin rubber blade wiping the water and dust from the windshield.

wiper arm
Metal rod with a to-and-fro motion that exerts a uniform pressure on the blade attached to it.

tension spring
Spring causing the arm to exert pressure on the blade.

fluted shaft
Part driven by an electric motor, whose rotating motion it converts alternating motion through two connecting rods.

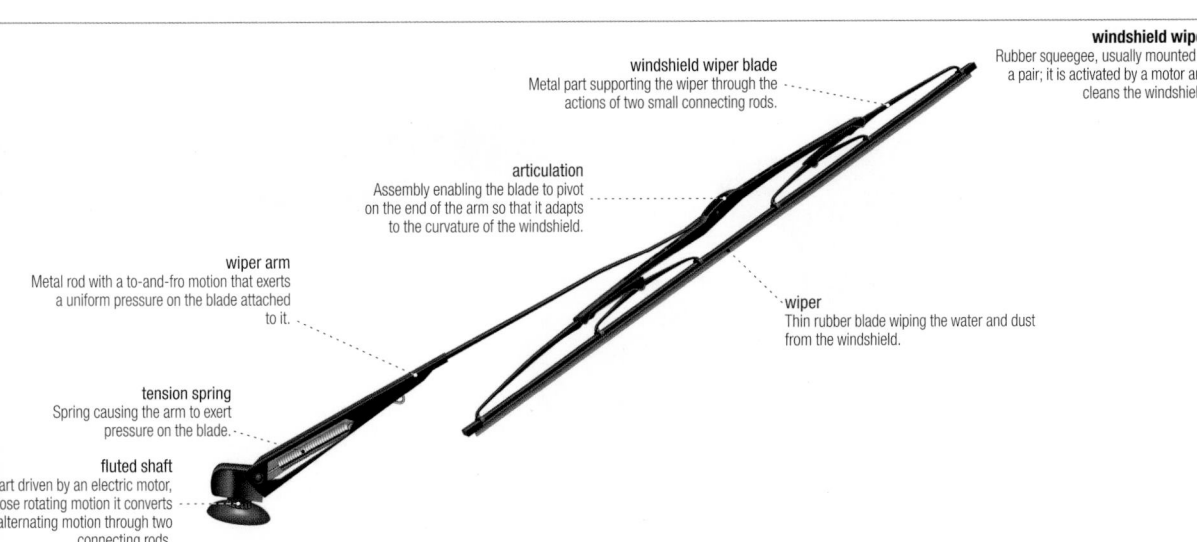

TRANSPORT AND MACHINERY

electric automobile

Car propelled by an electric motor whose energy is provided by a battery.

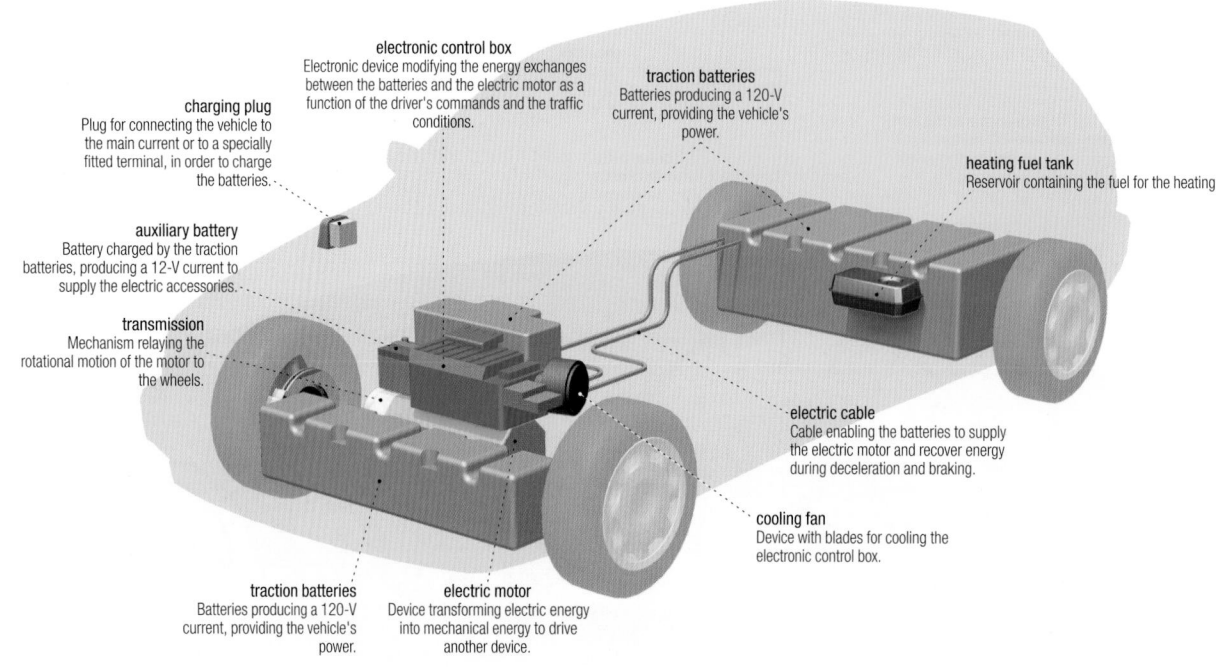

electronic control box
Electronic device modifying the energy exchanges between the batteries and the electric motor as a function of the driver's commands and the traffic conditions.

charging plug
Plug for connecting the vehicle to the main current or to a specially fitted terminal, in order to charge the batteries.

traction batteries
Batteries producing a 120-V current, providing the vehicle's power.

heating fuel tank
Reservoir containing the fuel for the heating sy

auxiliary battery
Battery charged by the traction batteries, producing a 12-V current to supply the electric accessories.

transmission
Mechanism relaying the rotational motion of the motor to the wheels.

electric cable
Cable enabling the batteries to supply the electric motor and recover energy during deceleration and braking.

cooling fan
Device with blades for cooling the electronic control box.

traction batteries
Batteries producing a 120-V current, providing the vehicle's power.

electric motor
Device transforming electric energy into mechanical energy to drive another device.

hybrid automobile

Car powered by an internal combustion engine and an electric motor, reducing gasoline consumption and polluting emissions.

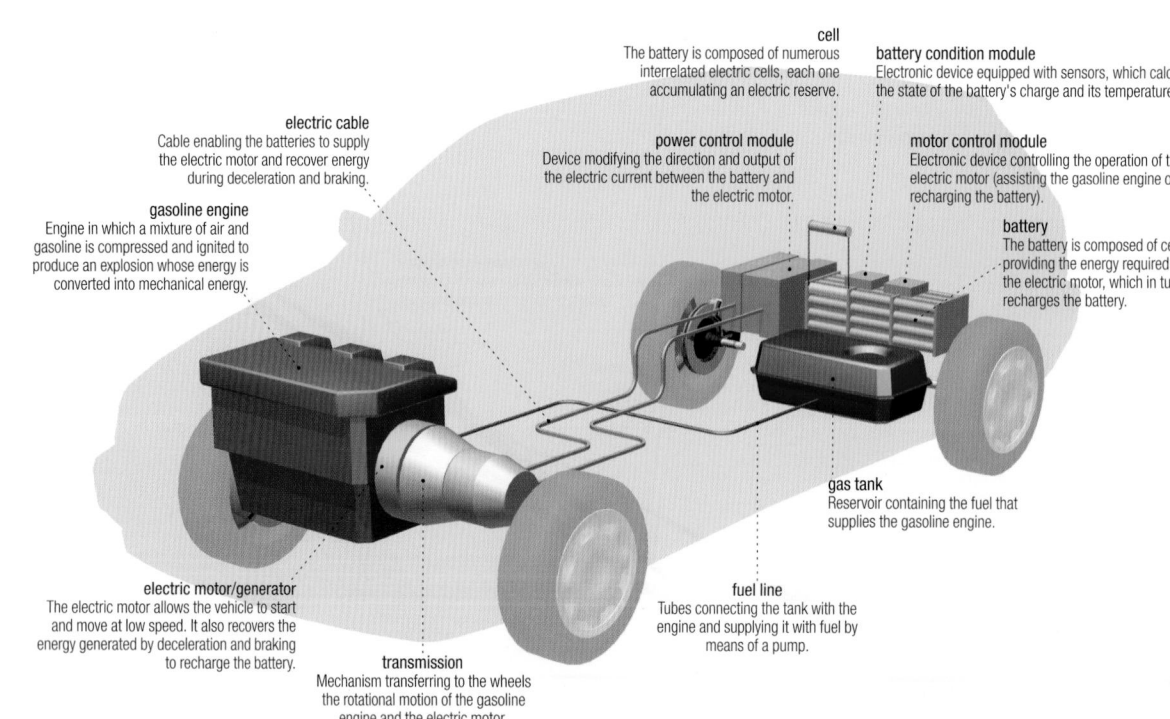

cell
The battery is composed of numerous interrelated electric cells, each one accumulating an electric reserve.

battery condition module
Electronic device equipped with sensors, which calcu the state of the battery's charge and its temperature.

electric cable
Cable enabling the batteries to supply the electric motor and recover energy during deceleration and braking.

power control module
Device modifying the direction and output of the electric current between the battery and the electric motor.

motor control module
Electronic device controlling the operation of the electric motor (assisting the gasoline engine or recharging the battery).

gasoline engine
Engine in which a mixture of air and gasoline is compressed and ignited to produce an explosion whose energy is converted into mechanical energy.

battery
The battery is composed of cell providing the energy required by the electric motor, which in turn recharges the battery.

gas tank
Reservoir containing the fuel that supplies the gasoline engine.

electric motor/generator
The electric motor allows the vehicle to start and move at low speed. It also recovers the energy generated by deceleration and braking to recharge the battery.

transmission
Mechanism transferring to the wheels the rotational motion of the gasoline engine and the electric motor.

fuel line
Tubes connecting the tank with the engine and supplying it with fuel by means of a pump.

brakes

Units slowing down or stopping the rotation of the vehicle's wheels.

caliper
Viselike part comprising a piston, which straddles the brake disc and supports the brake pads.

disc brake
Braking mechanism with a disc attached to the wheel, whose rotation is slowed down when the brake pads exert friction on it.

brake line
Tube carrying the brake fluid, which becomes pressurized when the driver steps on the brake pedal.

piston
Part put into motion by hydraulic pressure, which pushes the brake pads to squeeze the disc.

disc
Round plate interlocked with the wheel whose rotation slows down as it is braked by the friction of the brake pads.

brake pad
Metal plate that is held by the caliper; it is covered with a heat-resistant material that rubs against the disc to slow down its rotation.

anchor pin
Axle serving as an anchoring point for the brake shoe, enabling it to move when acted upon by the piston.

brake shoe
Crescent-shaped part interlocked with an anchor pin; it is fitted with a lining, which moves against the interior surface of the drum to slow its rotation.

drum brake
Braking mechanism comprising a drum interlocked with the wheel; the brake shoes rub against the drum to slow down the wheel's rotation.

return spring
Spring returning the brake shoe to its initial position once the pressure on the brake pedal has ceased.

wheel cylinder
Mechanism with a cylinder and two pistons that converts the hydraulic pressure in the master cylinder to mechanical force that is applied to the brake shoes.

piston
Part that slides in the cylinder under hydraulic pressure and pushes the brake shoe against the drum.

backing plate
Fixed part serving as a mount for the brake shoes, cylinder and anchor pin.

lug
Part for assembling and interlocking the drum and the wheel.

brake lining
Band of material attached to the brake shoe; heat resistant, it increases the frictional force on the drum.

drum
Part interlocked with the wheel so that the wheel slows its rotation when the brake shoes rub against the inside of the drum.

antilock braking system (ABS)
Electronic device controlling the hydraulic pressure in the braking circuit, to prevent the wheels from locking.

brake fluid reservoir
Reservoir supplying the master cylinder with the fluid that transmits pressure to the brakes after the driver presses the brake pedal.

brake booster
Mechanism amplifying the force exerted by the driver on the brake pedal.

electronic control unit
...ce that, as a result of signals received from the ...heel speed sensor, controls the brake pressure ...odulator to give the optimal hydraulic pressure.

master cylinder
Mechanism composed of a cylinder and pistons that converts the mechanical force of the brake pedal into hydraulic pressure that is transmitted to the brakes.

brake pedal
Lever that the driver presses with the foot to activate the brake system.

sensor wiring circuit
Set of electric wires transmitting the signals from the sensor to the electronic control unit.

pump and motor assembly
Pump driven by an electric motor, circulating the brake fluid from the accumulator to the master cylinder.

accumulator
Device temporarily holding the hydraulic brake fluid while the modulator lowers the pressure.

wheel speed sensor
Device sensing the rotation speed of a wheel and transmitting that information to the control unit.

disc brake
Braking mechanism with a disc attached to the wheel, whose rotation is slowed down when the brake pads exert friction on it.

braking circuit
System of tubes containing a fluid that activates the brakes when they come under pressure from the pedal.

brake pressure modulator
Hydraulic unit fitted with electric valves that, depending on the signals received from the electronic control unit, adjusts the pressure in each wheel cylinder.

types of engines

Engines: machines that convert the combustion of an air/fuel mixture into mechanical energy.

turbo-compressor engine

Engine equipped with a device combining a turbine with a compressor, which increases the amount of air entering the engine to increase its efficiency.

exhaust gas admission
The flow of the exhaust gas is conducted directly from the combustion chamber to the turbo compressor to drive the turbine.

intake manifold
After cooling, the air is again conducted to the combustion chamber, which takes in more air.

warm-air outlet
When compressed, the temperature of the air increases greatly, which can make it less effective.

exhaust manifold
Set of pipes at the exit of the cylinders; it captures the exhaust gases and conducts t to the turbo-compressor.

exhaust valve
Part that opens to allow the burned gases to escape.

charge air cooler
The heat exchanger cools the compressed air before it enters the cylinders.

combustion chamber
Part of the cylinder in which the pressurized air/fuel mixture is ignited and burned.

piston
Metal moving part in the cylinder and attached to the connecting rod; it compresses the air/fuel mixture, then receives the thrust from the burned gases.

driven compressor wheel
Part integrated with the driving turbine wheel; it spins very quickly as it draws in air and compresses it.

exhaust pipe
Tubular conduit conducting the exhaust gases from the turbo-compressor to the muffler.

driving turbine wheel
Part converting the energy from the exhaust gases into rotational energy to activate the compressor.

four-stroke-cycle engine

Combustion engine whose cycle (intake, compression, combustion, exhaust) requires two up-and-down movements of the piston.

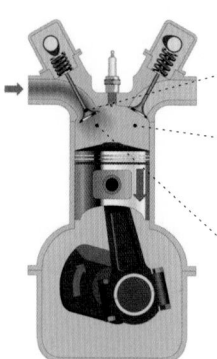

intake valve
Part that opens to let the air/fuel mixture into the cylinder.

cylinder
Chamber closed by two valves; in it, the piston moves and the air/fuel mixture is burned.

air/fuel mixture
Mixture prepared in the carburetor, containing an amount of fuel proportional to the amount of air entering.

intake
Phase during which the exhaust valve opens and the piston comes down and draws the air/fuel mixture into the combustion chamber.

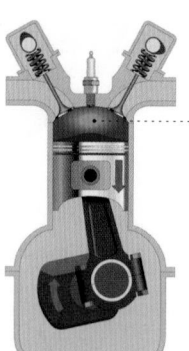

explosion
Ignition of the air/fuel mixture produces a major energy release that pushes the piston downward.

combustion
Phase during which the expansion of the combustion gases pushes the piston downward, driving the rotation of the crankshaft.

exhaust valve
Part that opens to allow the burned gases to escape.

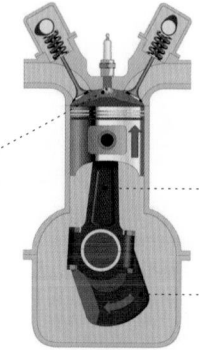

spark
Spark produced when an electric current arcs between the two electrodes of a spark plug and ignites the air/fuel mixture.

connecting rod
Articulated shank powered by the gas explosion; it transmits the thrust from the piston to the crankshaft.

crankshaft
Shaft consisting of a series of cranks, which convert the alternate rectilinear motion of the piston/connecting rod assembly into a continuous circular motion.

compression
Phase during which the piston goes up to compress the air/fuel mixture. At the height of the compression, the spark plug produces a spark.

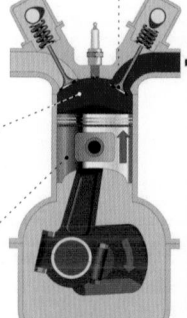

burned gases
Mixture of gases (carbon monoxide, nitrogen oxide and unburned hydrocarbons) filling the combustion chamber after the explosion.

piston
Metal moving part in the cylinder and attached to the connecting rod; it compresses the air/fuel mixture, then receives the thrust from the burned gases.

exhaust
Phase during which the exhaust valve opens and the piston moves back up to expel the burned gases.

types of engines

two-stroke-cycle engine cycle

Two-stroke engine: combustion engine whose cycle (intake, compression, combustion and exhaust) requires one up-and-down movement of the piston.

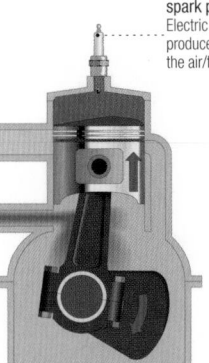
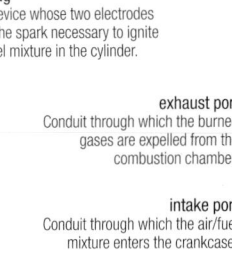
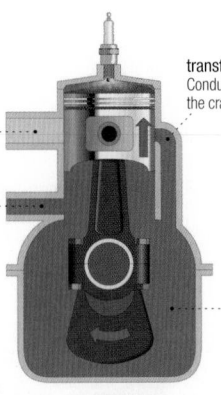

spark plug
Electric device whose two electrodes produce the spark necessary to ignite the air/fuel mixture in the cylinder.

exhaust port
Conduit through which the burned gases are expelled from the combustion chamber.

intake port
Conduit through which the air/fuel mixture enters the crankcase.

transfer port
Conduit conducting the air/fuel mixture from the crankcase to the cylinder.

crankcase
Sealed enclosure where the air/fuel mixture enters and the piston/connecting rod moves.

compression/intake
...nning of the first stroke during which the ...n moves up, drawing the air/fuel mixture ...o the crankcase and compressing the mixture in the cylinder.

combustion
End of the first stroke during which a spark ignites the air/fuel mixture.

exhaust/scavenging
Second stroke during which the piston is pushed back by the expansion of the burned gases, which are then expelled and replaced by the mixture coming from the crankcase.

rotary engine cycle

Rotary engine: combustion engine in which the combustion chamber is divided by a rotor into three turning parts of unequal volume.

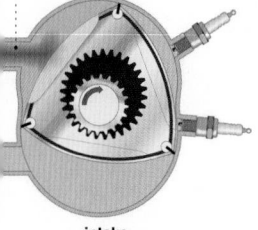
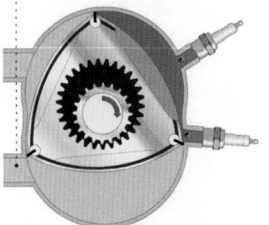
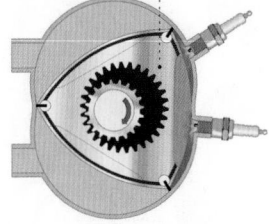
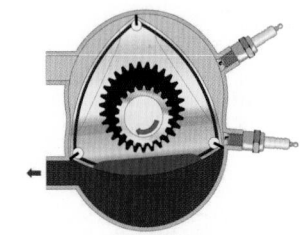

intake manifold
Passages through which the air/fuel mixture enters the cylinder.

exhaust manifold
Pipe through which the burned gases are expelled from the cylinder.

rotor
Triangular piston turning eccentrically around an axle and transmitting a rotational motion directly to the crankshaft.

intake
...he air/fuel mixture enters the cylinder ...rough the intake manifold; the rotor's ...notion forces it into the next chamber.

compression
The rotor's rotation reduces the volume in the chamber and compresses the mixture.

power
When the compression level is reached, the spark plugs produce sparks that ignite the air/fuel mixture.

exhaust
In the passage before the exhaust manifold, the burned gases are expelled by the rotor.

diesel engine cycle

Diesel engine: combustion engine in which the compressed air becomes sufficiently hot to ignite the injected fuel.

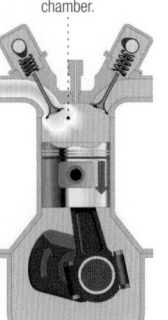
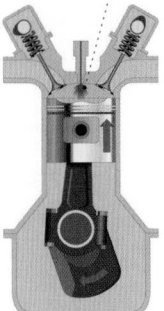
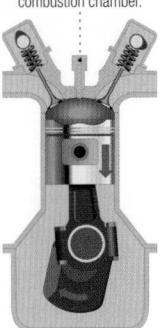
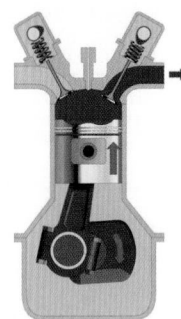

air
Air enters the combustion chamber.

injection/combustion
Fuel ignites immediately when it is injected into the hot air at very high pressure.

fuel injector
Device spraying the fuel into the combustion chamber.

intake
...se during which the exhaust valve ...ens and the piston comes down ...draws the air/fuel mixture into the combustion chamber.

compression
Stroke during which the piston rises, compressing the air, which becomes heated under the pressure.

power
Stroke during which the expansion of the burning gases pushes the piston downward.

exhaust
Phase during which the piston moves up and forces the burned gases toward the exhaust valve.

types of engines

interior of a gasoline engine
Gasoline engine: engine in which a mixture of air and gasoline is compressed and ignited to produce an explosion whose energy is converted into mechanical energy.

camshaft
Axle driven by a belt, a chain or gears connected to the crankshaft, controlling the opening and closing of the valves.

inlet valve
Part that opens to let the air/fuel mixture into the cylinder.

fuel injector
Device spraying the fuel into the combustion chamber.

distributor cap
Unit supplying the electric current necessary for producing sparks that ignite the fuel in the engine.

timing belt
Strap connecting the crankshaft to the camshaft.

valve spring
Spring that brings the valve back into the closed position.

intake manifold
Passages through which the air/ fuel mixture enters the cylinder.

rocker arm
Lever, activated by the camshaft, that drives the inlet and exhaust valves to open them.

piston skirt
Side surface of a piston guiding it along the inside of the cylinder.

cylinder head cover
Part of the engine covering the cylinder heads, where the fuel is burned.

combustion chamber
Part of the cylinder in which the pressurized air/fuel mixture is ignited and burned.

vacuum diaphragm
Device connected to the dis cap specifying the precise n ignition must be produced re the engine's rotation speed.

piston ring
Circular ring mounted on the piston providing a seal between it and the cylinder.

spark plug cable
Electric wire carrying the high-v current from the distributor to th plugs, which produce sparks ig explosion.

connecting rod
Articulated shank powered by the gas explosion; it transmits the thrust from the piston to the crankshaft.

spark plug
Electric device whose tw produce the spark neces the air/fuel mixture in the

alternator
Current generator driven by the engine, which recharges the battery to supply the electric system.

exhaust manifold
Set of pipes at the exit o capturing the combustio conduct them to the exh

cooling fan
Mechanism with blades blowing air across the radiator in order to cool the liquid it contains.

flywheel
Disk connected to the crar which uses the kinetic ene produced at combustion to the crankshaft rotation du rest of the cycle.

pulley
Part attached to a shaft, whose rotational movement it transmits by means of a belt.

exhaust valve
Part that opens to allow the burned gases to escape.

fan belt
Rubberized bands mounted on a pulley and linked to the engine, driving the fan and the alternator.

engine block
Main engine casing, which encloses the cylinders.

crankshaft
Shaft consisting of a series of cranks, which convert the alternate rectilinear motion of the piston/connecting-rod assembly into a continuous circular motion.

oil pan
Container closing the bottom of the engine block; it is the reservoir for the oil that lubricates the engine's moving parts.

piston
Metal moving part in the cylinder and attached to the connecting rod; it compresses the air/fuel mixture, then receives the thrust from the burned gases.

oil pan gasket
Packing providing the seal between the oil pan and the engine block.

oil drain plug
Plug closing the hole at the bottom of the oil pan through which used oil is removed.

air conditioner compressor
Component of the air-conditioning system circulating coolant, which cools the air in the passenger compartment when it is hot outside.

radiator

Vessel in which the coolant, which circulates around the engine, is cooled by means of flowing air.

filler cap
plugging the radiator's filling opening and
regulating the pressure in the cooling system.

grille
Grating on the radiator's front side,
protecting it from impact.

cooling fan
Mechanism with blades blowing air
across the radiator in order to cool
the liquid it contains.

temperature sensor
Device immersed in the coolant that
switches on the fan when the coolant
reaches a predetermined temperature.

electric fan motor
Device transforming electric energy
into mechanical energy to drive the
cooling fan.

lower radiator hose
Rubber hose connecting the cooling-circuit
components to each other.

spark plug

Electric device whose two electrodes produce the spark necessary to ignite the air/gasoline mixture in the cylinder.

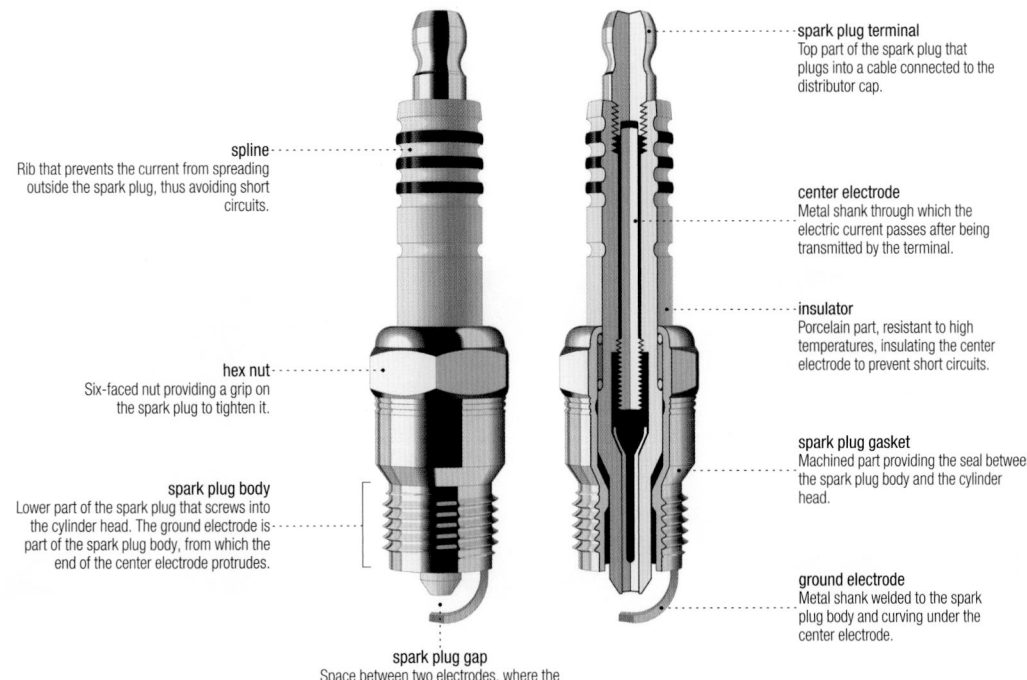

spline
Rib that prevents the current from spreading
outside the spark plug, thus avoiding short
circuits.

spark plug terminal
Top part of the spark plug that
plugs into a cable connected to the
distributor cap.

center electrode
Metal shank through which the
electric current passes after being
transmitted by the terminal.

insulator
Porcelain part, resistant to high
temperatures, insulating the center
electrode to prevent short circuits.

hex nut
Six-faced nut providing a grip on
the spark plug to tighten it.

spark plug gasket
Machined part providing the seal between
the spark plug body and the cylinder
head.

spark plug body
Lower part of the spark plug that screws into
the cylinder head. The ground electrode is
part of the spark plug body, from which the
end of the center electrode protrudes.

ground electrode
Metal shank welded to the spark
plug body and curving under the
center electrode.

spark plug gap
Space between two electrodes, where the
spark is created.

TRANSPORT AND MACHINERY

tire

Circular deformable unit made of rubber, mounted on the wheel and inflated with air, providing the connection between the car and the road, and absorbing the unevenness of the road.

parts of a tire

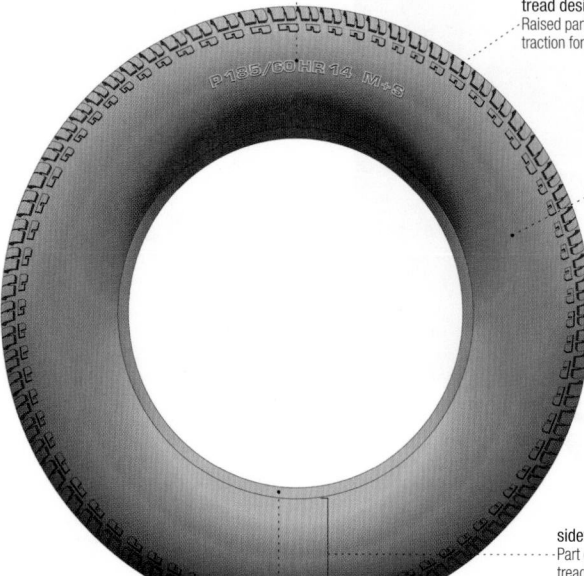

technical specifications
Alphanumeric code molded onto the side of the tire, showing its characteristics.

tread design
Raised part of the tire tread that improves traction for various usage conditions.

curb guard
Round protrusion of the rubber wall, protecting it from side impact and wear.

sidewall
Part of the tire located between the tread and the bead.

bead
Part of the tire that encloses a rigid steel wire that keeps the tire on the rim and makes it watertight.

disk
A part of the rim that is fixed at its center on the wheel's axle.

wheel
Circular unit turning around an axle; it supports the weight of the vehicle and transmits the thrust, steering and braking action.

rim
Metal circle constituting the wheel's circumference and on which the tire is mounted.

examples of tires
Depending on the intended conditions and uses, tire construction (e.g., type of rubber, tread design, width) varies widely.

performance tire
Wide tire that withstands particularly high temperatures and offers superior performance in holding the road and handling turns.

all-season tire
Tire designed for driving on roads that are dry, wet or slightly snow-covered.

winter tire
Tire characterized by ridges providing a good grip on snow- and ice-covered roads.

touring tire
Tire designed for driving on dry or wet roads, but not recommended for snow or ice.

studded tire
Tire whose tread is fitted with studs, which provide a good grip on icy roads.

tire

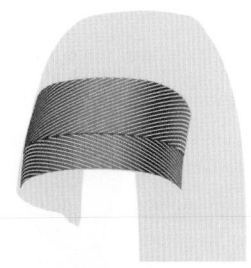

bias-ply tire
Tire with plies whose cords cross each other and are diagonal to the direction of the tread.

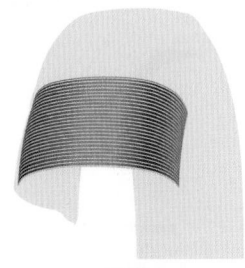

radial tire
Tire with plies whose cords are perpendicular to the direction of the tread.

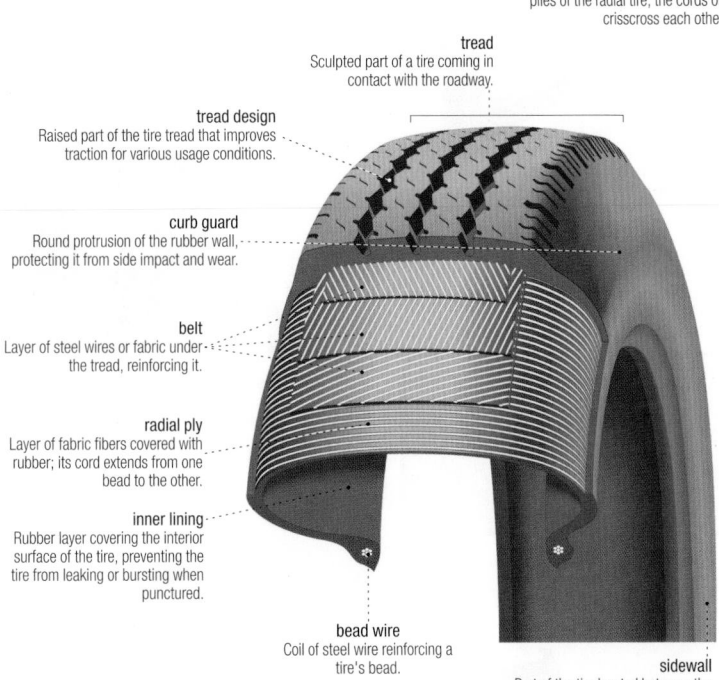

steel belted radial tire
Hybrid tire with additional belts laid on top of the plies of the radial tire; the cords of these belts crisscross each other diagonally.

tread
Sculpted part of a tire coming in contact with the roadway.

tread design
Raised part of the tire tread that improves traction for various usage conditions.

curb guard
Round protrusion of the rubber wall, protecting it from side impact and wear.

belt
Layer of steel wires or fabric under the tread, reinforcing it.

radial ply
Layer of fabric fibers covered with rubber; its cord extends from one bead to the other.

inner lining
Rubber layer covering the interior surface of the tire, preventing the tire from leaking or bursting when punctured.

bead wire
Coil of steel wire reinforcing a tire's bead.

sidewall
Part of the tire located between the tread and the bead.

battery

Unit storing the electricity produced by the alternator and releasing it to supply the vehicle's electric system.

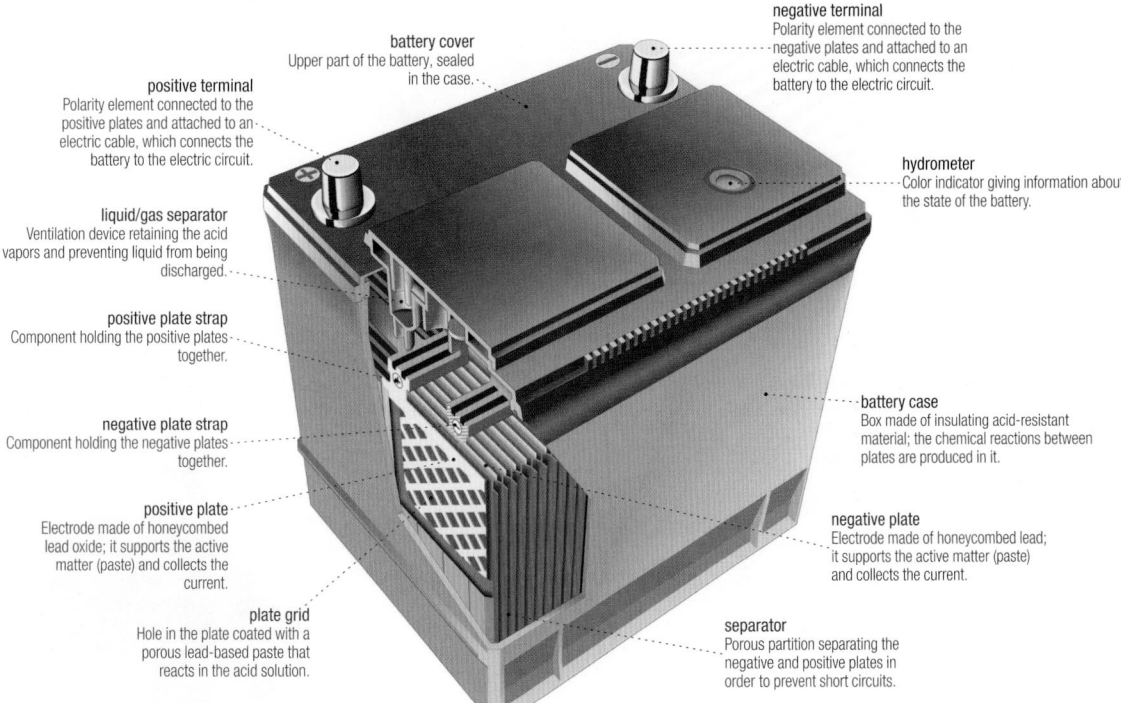

battery cover
Upper part of the battery, sealed in the case.

negative terminal
Polarity element connected to the negative plates and attached to an electric cable, which connects the battery to the electric circuit.

positive terminal
Polarity element connected to the positive plates and attached to an electric cable, which connects the battery to the electric circuit.

hydrometer
Color indicator giving information about the state of the battery.

liquid/gas separator
Ventilation device retaining the acid vapors and preventing liquid from being discharged.

positive plate strap
Component holding the positive plates together.

negative plate strap
Component holding the negative plates together.

positive plate
Electrode made of honeycombed lead oxide; it supports the active matter (paste) and collects the current.

plate grid
Hole in the plate coated with a porous lead-based paste that reacts in the acid solution.

battery case
Box made of insulating acid-resistant material; the chemical reactions between plates are produced in it.

negative plate
Electrode made of honeycombed lead; it supports the active matter (paste) and collects the current.

separator
Porous partition separating the negative and positive plates in order to prevent short circuits.

TRANSPORT AND MACHINERY

accessories

Secondary components of a vehicle, used for its maintenance, safety and such.

hitch ball
Device for hooking up a trailer or caravan to a vehicle.

ball mount
Part attached under the rear of the vehicle, with a hitch ball on one end; the trailer's or caravan's hitch articulates with it.

jumper cables
Cables fitted with alligator clips for connecting an emergency battery to a discharged one.

cable
Insulated conductive wires that transmit the electric current and are covered by a protective sheath.

black clamp
A black clamp is fitted on the negative terminal of the emergency battery; the other is attached to a metal part of the other car.

floor mat
Fabric or rubber covering placed under the passengers' feet in order to protect the floor of the vehicle.

sun visor
Screen placed inside the windshield of a parked vehicle to protect the passenger compartment from the sun.

red clamp
A red clamp is fitted on the positive terminal of both batteries.

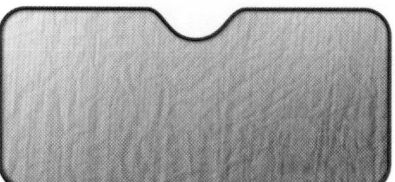

four-way lug wrench
Wrench for tightening and loosening the wheel nuts; it is made up of two crossed rods with each end having a different size.

snow brush with scraper
Small broom with one end for removing snow from the vehicle and the other for scraping ice off the windows.

ski rack
Support placed on the vehicle's roof, for mounting and transporting skis.

bike carrier
Support placed on the roof rear of the vehicle, on whic more bicycles can be mou transported.

roller shade
Shade with a roller containing a spring that causes the shade cloth to roll up; it is usually placed on a side window.

roof rack
Support mounted on the roof; baggage is stowed on it using straps.

jack
Mechanism activated by a handle, for raising the vehicle.

child car seat
Chair adapted to the size of a child; it is equipped with a safety harness for keeping the child seated and attached to the rear seat by the seat belt.

car cover
Flexible casing for covering and protecting the vehicle from the sun, dust and inclement weather.

handle
Lever comprising two right-angle bends, for activating the jack mechanism to raise and lower it.

head support
Component that holds the child's head.

harness
Series of straps and buckles that hold the child in the seat.

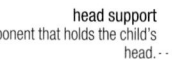

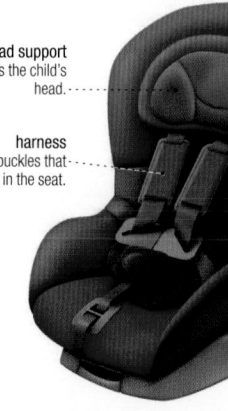

campers

Motorized or towed vehicle fitted out as a dwelling.

trailer
Camper fitted out as a dwelling, usually pulled by an automobile.

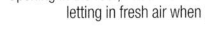

roof vent
Opening in the roof, fitted with a cover, for letting in fresh air when parked.

side vent
Grille on the side of the body, for letting in fresh air.

body
Rigid metal frame comprising the body of the camper.

sun visor
Device protecting against the sun.

propane gas cylinder
Tank containing a gas reserve for supplying the camper's stove and heating system.

awning channel
Track where the edge of an awning is inserted so it can be spread on the side of the camper.

grab handle
Vertical handle, placed at shoulder height near the door, that one holds to step up into the camper.

hydraulic jack
Mechanism composed of a cylinder and a piston and activated by hydraulic pressure; it allows the landing gear to be deployed by turning a crank.

outlet
Device connected to the main current by an electric cord, which transmits the electric current to the appliances in the camper.

landing gear
The towing hitch's telescopic support, which props up the camper when it is parked.

storage compartment
artment for storing bulky objects, usually ssible from the inside and the outside of the camper.

towing hitch
Device placed at the end of the tow bar, securing the camper to the hitch ball of the vehicle towing it.

tow bar
Metal piece attached to the camper's chassis; it comprises a towing hitch and enables the camper to be connected to the towing vehicle.

retractable step
Folding apparatus attached to the door sill, for stepping up into or down from the camper.

door
Opening comprising a leaf pivoting on hinge pins, for entering and exiting the camper.

tow safety chain
Part of an antitheft device attached to the towing hitch, which stops anyone from hitching or unhitching the camper.

lighting cable
Electric wire for connecting the camper's lighting and signaling system to that of the vehicle towing it.

roof
Rigid part enclosing the top of the body and protecting the sections when they are folded up.

screen door
Door fitted with a wire cloth that lets air and light pass through while protecting against mosquitoes.

canopy
Canvas awning supported by a framework; it protects an outdoor space from the rain and sun.

tent trailer
Camper with a collapsible section that is opened up when at rest and folded up again before moving, to lessen wind resistance.

window
Flexible canvas opening, letting in air and light, supported by a framework when it is opened out.

bunk
Area for sleeping, supported by a frame when opened out.

body
Rigid metal frame comprising the body of the camper.

spare tire
Supplementary wheel for replacing a wheel whose tire is punctured.

stabilizer jack
Retractable support placed under the camper to keep it steady when parked.

luggage rack
Support mounted on the roof; baggage is stowed on it using straps.

air conditioner
Device cooling and ventilating the camper's interior air when it is hot outside.

motor home
Motorized vehicle outfitted as a dwelling.

ladder
Device composed of steps and stiles, for accessing the vehicle's roof.

TRANSPORT AND MACHINERY

bus

Motorized vehicle for city or intercity transportation of passengers who are standing or seated.

school bus
Motorized vehicle for transporting schoolchildren and equipped with specialized safety devices.

rearview mirror
Mirror fixed to the outside of the passenger compartment enabling the driver to see behind and along the sides of the vehicle without turning around.

blind spot mirror
Exterior convex mirror providing a wider field of vision than a conventional mirror.

flashing lights
Flashing red lights at the front and rear of the bus that the driver activates at each stop to signal other vehicles to stop.

crossover mirror
Convex mirror allowing the driver to see front of the bus.

crossing arm
Pivoting rod deployed at each stop so that the schoolchildren stay in the driver's field of vision while passing in front of the bus.

coach
Motorized vehicle for intercity transportation of seated passengers over medium and long distances.

engine air intake
Opening through which outside air enters the vehicle's engine.

door

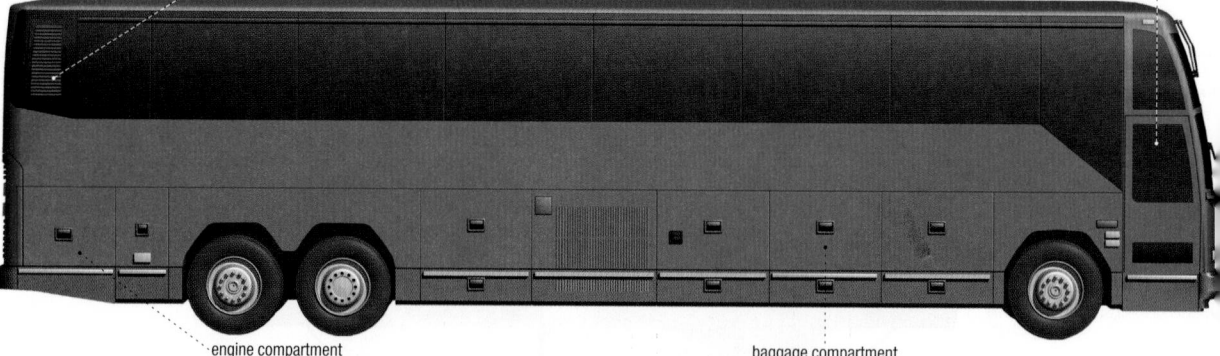

engine compartment
Housing for the engine under the vehicle's chassis, accessible by a door.

baggage compartment
Large compartment beneath the vehicle's floor, fitted with side doors, in which passengers' baggage is deposited.

city bus
Motorized vehicle for city transportation of passengers who are standing or seated.

air intake
Opening in the roof, fitted with a cover, for letting fresh air into the bus.

route sign
Screen usually on the front, rear and right side of the vehicle, displaying the number of the bus's route.

double-leaf door
Wide door divided into two movable parts, which double back to each side to allow several people to pass through at once.

bus

double-decker bus
Bus equipped with two levels connected by stairs.

upper deck
Upper floor of the bus.

route sign
Screen usually on the front, rear and right side of the vehicle, displaying the number of the bus's route.

West Coast mirror
Mirror fixed to the outside of the passenger compartment enabling the driver to see behind and along the sides of the vehicle without turning around.

lift door

handrail
Support rail equipped with a belt restraining the wheelchair when the platform is being raised and lowered.

wheelchair lift
lifting device deployed so that a wheelchair can be raised into and lowered from a bus or van.

platform
Horizontal part moving up and down for the wheelchair; it rests on the ground in the lower position and forms the doorsill in the upper position.

entrance door

specialized transportation bus
Motorized vehicle designed to provide urban and long-distance transportation services for passengers who use wheelchairs.

blind spot mirror
Exterior convex mirror providing a wider field of vision than a conventional mirror.

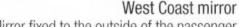

articulated bus
Bus with two aligned compartments, connected by an articulated joint.

articulated joint
Part connecting the rigid sections by a waterproof bellows and a turning platform shared by the two sections.

rear rigid section

front rigid section

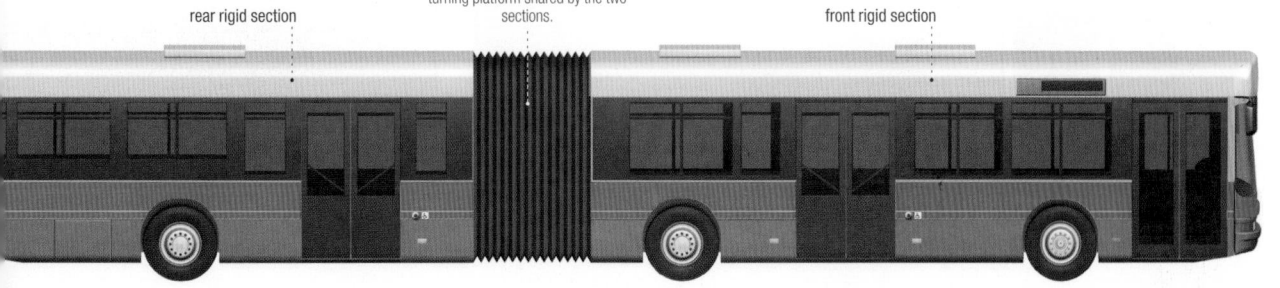

TRANSPORT AND MACHINERY

trucking

Transportation of cargo by truck.

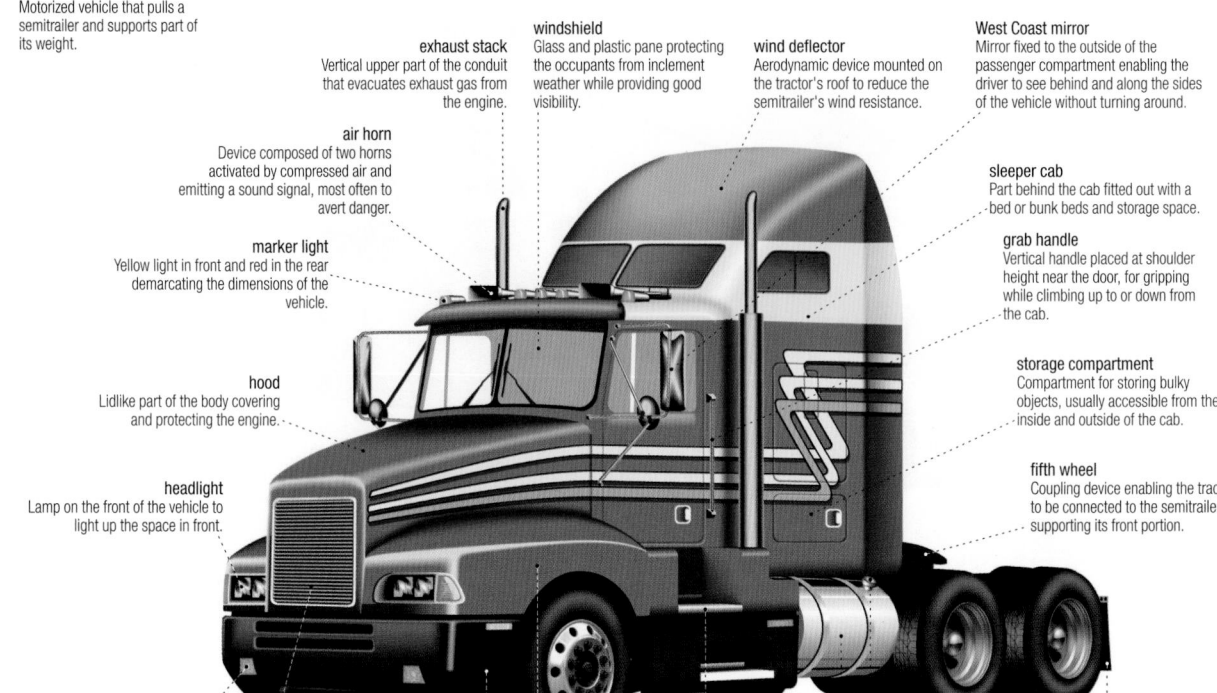

truck tractor
Motorized vehicle that pulls a semitrailer and supports part of its weight.

exhaust stack
Vertical upper part of the conduit that evacuates exhaust gas from the engine.

windshield
Glass and plastic pane protecting the occupants from inclement weather while providing good visibility.

wind deflector
Aerodynamic device mounted on the tractor's roof to reduce the semitrailer's wind resistance.

West Coast mirror
Mirror fixed to the outside of the passenger compartment enabling the driver to see behind and along the sides of the vehicle without turning around.

air horn
Device composed of two horns activated by compressed air and emitting a sound signal, most often to avert danger.

sleeper cab
Part behind the cab fitted out with a bed or bunk beds and storage space.

grab handle
Vertical handle placed at shoulder height near the door, for gripping while climbing up to or down from the cab.

marker light
Yellow light in front and red in the rear demarcating the dimensions of the vehicle.

storage compartment
Compartment for storing bulky objects, usually accessible from the inside and outside of the cab.

hood
Lidlike part of the body covering and protecting the engine.

fifth wheel
Coupling device enabling the tractor to be connected to the semitrailer and supporting its front portion.

headlight
Lamp on the front of the vehicle to light up the space in front.

fog light
Lamp whose light rays are directed toward the roadway and illuminate the road shoulder, by which the driver navigates in the event of fog.

step
Tread or set of treads built into the body for climbing up to or down from the cab.

mud flap
Piece of rubber or plastic attached behind the rear wheels to repel projectiles.

radiator grille
Plastic or metal grating in front of the vehicle; it protects the vehicle's radiator and serves as decoration.

bumper
Malleable element partially absorbing shocks, thus protecting the body and the engine parts from damage.

wheel
Circular unit turning around an axle; it supports the weight of the vehicle and transmits the thrust, steering and braking actions.

tire
Circular deformable unit made of rubber, mounted on the wheel and inflated with air, providing the connection between the truck tractor and the road and absorbing the unevenness of the road.

fender
Part of the body covering the wheel.

fuel tank
Reservoir containing the diesel fuel that makes the vehicle self-sufficient.

filler cap
Part screwed into the fuel filler neck to close it.

tandem tractor trailer
Set of vehicles comprising a tractor, a semitrailer and a trailer.

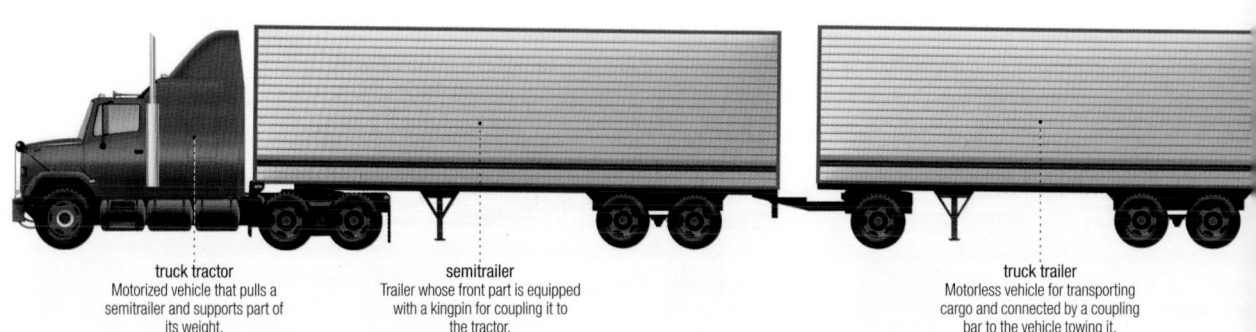

truck tractor
Motorized vehicle that pulls a semitrailer and supports part of its weight.

semitrailer
Trailer whose front part is equipped with a kingpin for coupling it to the tractor.

truck trailer
Motorless vehicle for transporting cargo and connected by a coupling bar to the vehicle towing it.

trucking

refrigerated semitrailer
Semitrailer equipped with a refrigeration unit and an insulated compartment for transporting perishable goods.

marker light
Yellow light in front and red in the rear demarcating the dimensions of the vehicle.

frontwall

refrigeration unit
Device using compression to lower the temperature inside the semitrailer to a predetermined level.

vent door
Grille through which the air cools the refrigerant.

battery box
Compartment containing the battery supplying the electric energy required to operate the refrigeration unit.

Partlow chart
Device monitoring the temperature in the semitrailer.

sidewall

electrical connection
Electric wire connecting the semitrailer's lighting and signaling system with that of the tractor.

reflector
Device reflecting light back toward its source so that other drivers can see the semitrailer.

landing gear
Telescopic support keeping the semitrailer level when uncoupled.

kingpin
Axle of attachment housed in the tractor's fifth wheel; it allows the semitrailer and the tractor to articulate.

mud flap
of rubber or plastic attached
the rear wheels to repel
projectiles.

side rail
Thick piece along the length of the chassis frame, reinforcing it.

sand shoe
Part attached to the foot of the landing gear to increase stability.

auxiliary tank
Reservoir containing the fuel used to operate the refrigeration unit.

landing gear crank
Bent lever activating the elevating cylinder to deploy the landing gear.

flatbed semitrailer
Semitrailer composed of a platform around which detachable side panels can be placed.

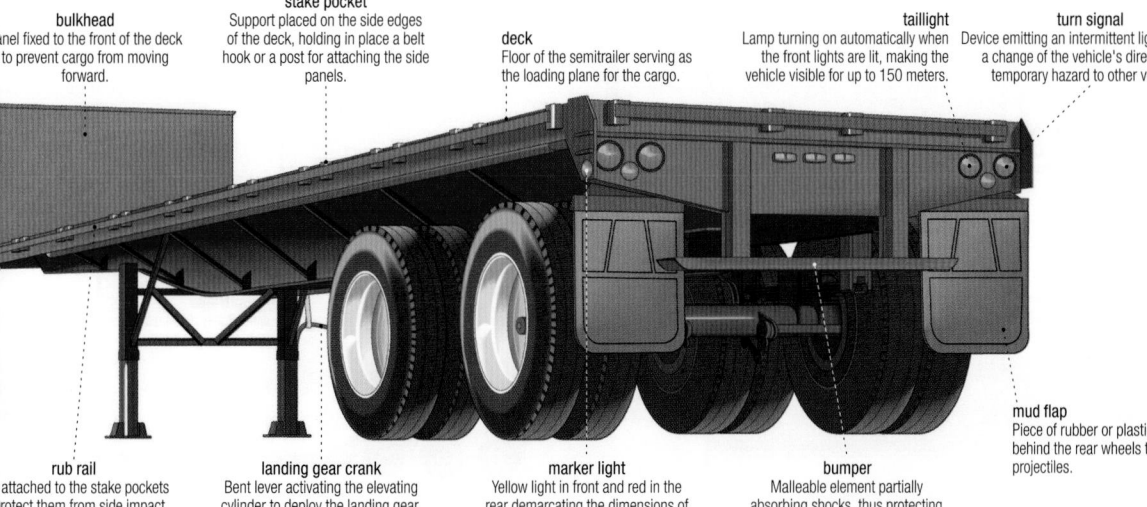

bulkhead
nel fixed to the front of the deck
to prevent cargo from moving
forward.

stake pocket
Support placed on the side edges of the deck, holding in place a belt hook or a post for attaching the side panels.

deck
Floor of the semitrailer serving as the loading plane for the cargo.

taillight
Lamp turning on automatically when the front lights are lit, making the vehicle visible for up to 150 meters.

turn signal
Device emitting an intermittent light, signaling a change of the vehicle's direction or a temporary hazard to other vehicles.

rub rail
attached to the stake pockets
rotect them from side impact.

landing gear crank
Bent lever activating the elevating cylinder to deploy the landing gear.

marker light
Yellow light in front and red in the rear demarcating the dimensions of the vehicle.

bumper
Malleable element partially absorbing shocks, thus protecting the body from damage.

mud flap
Piece of rubber or plastic attached behind the rear wheels to repel projectiles.

TRANSPORT AND MACHINERY

trucking

examples of semitrailers

Semitrailers: trailers whose front portion is equipped with a kingpin for coupling them to a tractor.

automobile transport semitrailer
Semitrailer equipped with several sloped platforms for transporting vehicles.

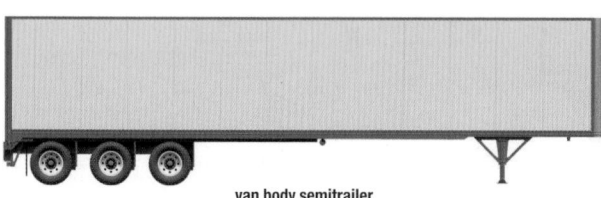

van body semitrailer
Semitrailer comprising a closed box, rigid or made of thick fabric (tarpaulin and sliding curtains).

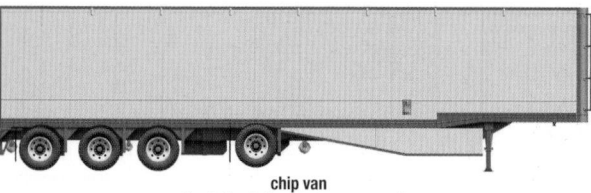

chip van
Semitrailer designed to transport wood in chip form.

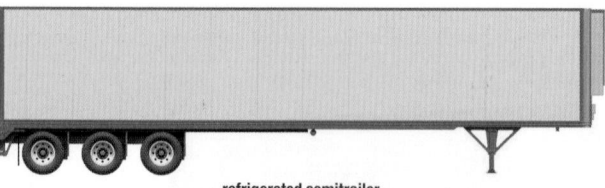

refrigerated semitrailer
Semitrailer equipped with a refrigeration unit and an insulated compartment for transporting perishable goods.

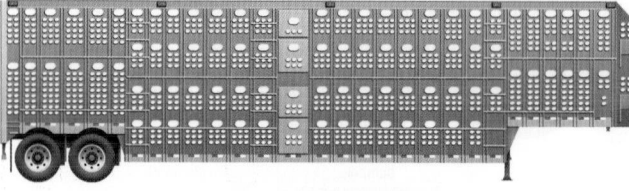

possum-belly body semitrailer
Semitrailer designed to transport livestock; it is composed of several perforated compartments.

tank body
Closed tank divided into several compartments of various sizes.

tank trailer
Semitrailer for transporting bulk products in liquid, powder or gas form.

dump body
Open or closed container; when raised by the elevation cylinder, it discharges its bulk material.

dump semitrailer
Semitrailer equipped with a dump body for transporting in bulk.

twist lock
Locking mechanism housed in the middle part of the trailer used to secure the container.

container semitrailer
Semitrailer composed of only a chassis; containers of standard sizes are loaded on it to transport cargo.

log semitrailer
Semitrailer with folding side posts for transporting tree trunks.

double drop lowbed semitrailer
Semitrailer for transporting heavy machinery.

TRANSPORT AND MACHINERY

trucking

examples of trucks
Trucks: motorized vehicles for transporting cargo and providing maintenance and safety.

loading hopper
reservoir that takes the [...] and then feeds it to the packer body.

packer body
Bin equipped with a hydraulic system that compresses household garbage.

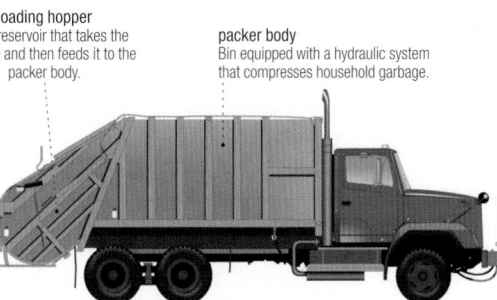

garbage truck
Dump truck for collecting household garbage.

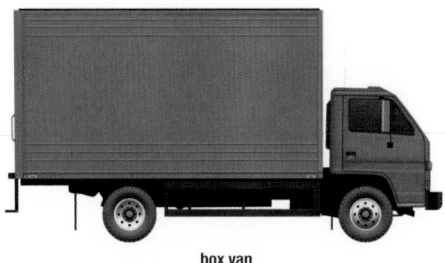

box van
Truck whose box is rigid and closed.

dump body
[o]pen or closed container; when [rai]sed by the elevation cylinder it discharges its bulk material.

dump truck
Truck equipped with a dump body; it is used for bulk transport.

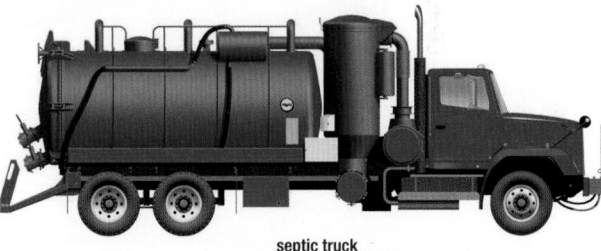

septic truck
Truck equipped with a tank, a pump and a long pipe, for emptying septic tanks and other pipes.

cement truck
Truck equipped with a rotating tub, for transporting fresh cement, which it pours out down a chute.

tank body
Closed tank divided into several compartments of various sizes.

tank truck
Truck for transporting bulk products in liquid, powder or gas form.

tow truck
Truck for towing vehicles that have broken down.

cable
Resistant cord whose length is varied to handle load.

boom
Thick sturdy metal beam, which the elevating cylinder raises.

hook
Part that is detached from the towing device while the vehicle's front wheels are placed in position, then reattached to raise it.

elevating cylinder
Hydraulic device consisting of a telescopic arm, for lifting a heavy load.

towing device
Lifting device where the front wheels of the towed vehicle are placed.

detachable body truck
Truck for transporting containers, which it loads and unloads using a mechanical arm.

winch controls
Control mechanisms for the electric motor, which powers the spool's rotation.

winch
Mechanism with a steel cable rolled around a spool, for pulling and raising heavy loads, such as a vehicle that has broken down.

motorcycle

Two-wheeled motorized vehicle whose engine cylinder is larger than 125 cubic centimeters.

side view

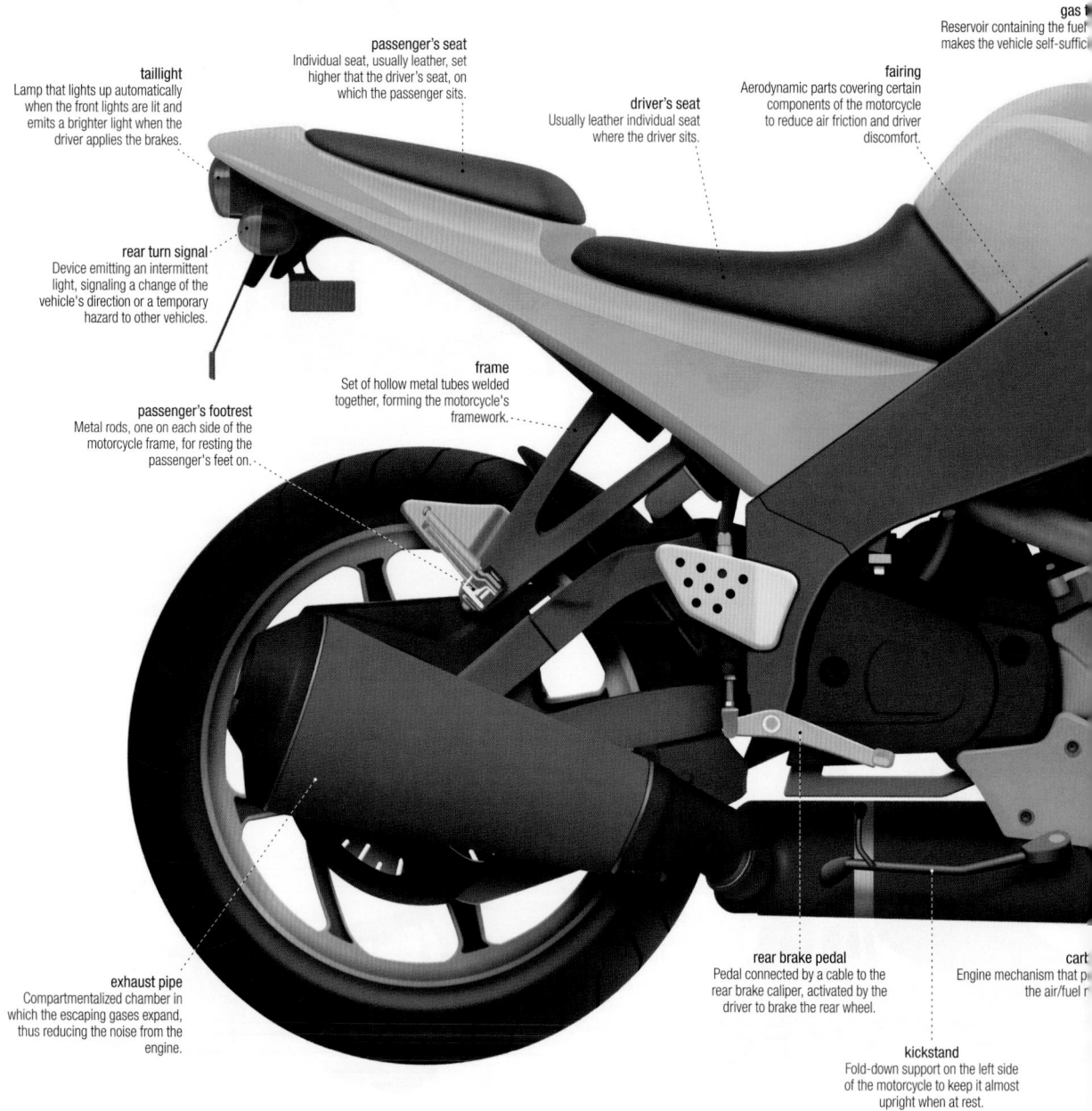

gas t
Reservoir containing the fuel
makes the vehicle self-suffici

taillight
Lamp that lights up automatically
when the front lights are lit and
emits a brighter light when the
driver applies the brakes.

passenger's seat
Individual seat, usually leather, set
higher that the driver's seat, on
which the passenger sits.

driver's seat
Usually leather individual seat
where the driver sits.

fairing
Aerodynamic parts covering certain
components of the motorcycle
to reduce air friction and driver
discomfort.

rear turn signal
Device emitting an intermittent
light, signaling a change of the
vehicle's direction or a temporary
hazard to other vehicles.

frame
Set of hollow metal tubes welded
together, forming the motorcycle's
framework.

passenger's footrest
Metal rods, one on each side of the
motorcycle frame, for resting the
passenger's feet on.

exhaust pipe
Compartmentalized chamber in
which the escaping gases expand,
thus reducing the noise from the
engine.

rear brake pedal
Pedal connected by a cable to the
rear brake caliper, activated by the
driver to brake the rear wheel.

cart
Engine mechanism that p
the air/fuel r

kickstand
Fold-down support on the left side
of the motorcycle to keep it almost
upright when at rest.

motorcycle

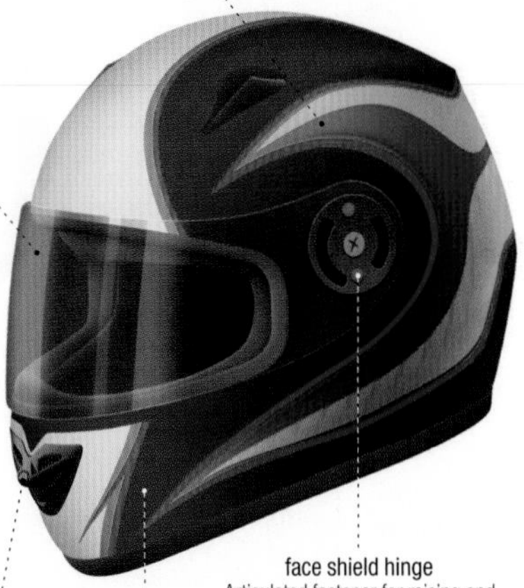

shell
Exterior surface made of durable materials (thermoplastic or composite materials) that absorb shocks.

full-face motorcycle helmet
Hard-surfaced headgear that protects the driver's head, face and neck in the event of a collision.

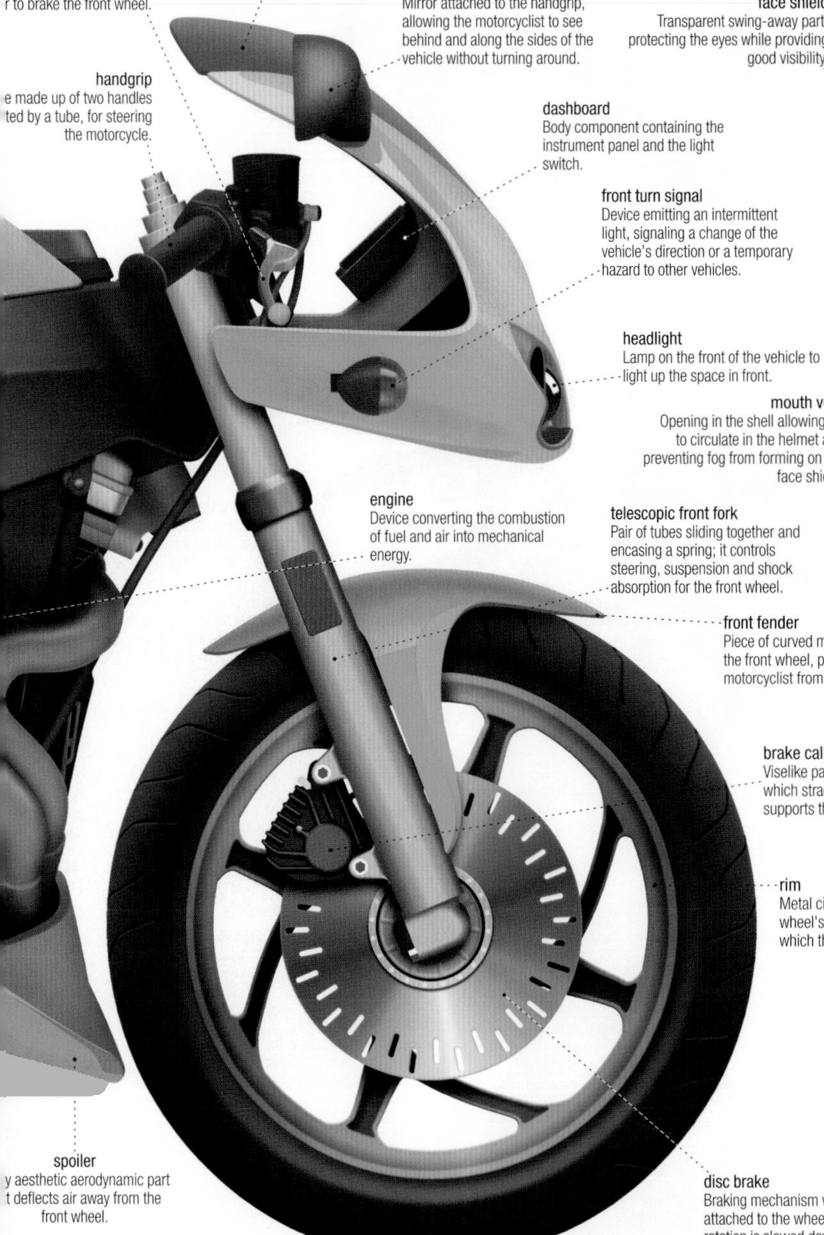

windshield
Glass and plastic pane in front, protecting the motorcyclist from the wind and inclement weather.

front brake lever
connected by a cable to the caliper, activated by the r to brake the front wheel.

mirror
Mirror attached to the handgrip, allowing the motorcyclist to see behind and along the sides of the vehicle without turning around.

face shield
Transparent swing-away part, protecting the eyes while providing good visibility.

handgrip
e made up of two handles ted by a tube, for steering the motorcycle.

dashboard
Body component containing the instrument panel and the light switch.

front turn signal
Device emitting an intermittent light, signaling a change of the vehicle's direction or a temporary hazard to other vehicles.

headlight
Lamp on the front of the vehicle to light up the space in front.

face shield hinge
Articulated fastener for raising and lowering the face shield.

mouth vent
Opening in the shell allowing air to circulate in the helmet and preventing fog from forming on the face shield.

chin bar
Part of the shell protecting the motorcyclist's chin.

engine
Device converting the combustion of fuel and air into mechanical energy.

telescopic front fork
Pair of tubes sliding together and encasing a spring; it controls steering, suspension and shock absorption for the front wheel.

front fender
Piece of curved metal covering the front wheel, protecting the motorcyclist from being splashed.

brake caliper
Viselike part composed of a piston, which straddles the brake disc and supports the brake pads.

rim
Metal circle constituting the wheel's circumference and on which the tire is mounted.

spoiler
y aesthetic aerodynamic part t deflects air away from the front wheel.

disc brake
Braking mechanism with a disc attached to the wheel, whose rotation is slowed down when the brake pads exert friction on it.

TRANSPORT AND MACHINERY

motorcycle

dashboard
Body component containing the instrument panel and the ignition switch.

oil warning light
Light showing that the oil pressure in the engine's lubrication system is below the minimum necessary.

high beam indicator light
Light showing that the high beams are on.

turn signal indicator
Intermittent light, often accompanied by a sound, showing that a turn signal is in use.

neutral indicator
Light showing that none of the gears is engaged; that is, the engine's rotation is not being transmitted to the wheels.

low fuel warning light
Warning light showing that the gas tank is almost empty.

speedometer
Dial showing the speed at which the vehicle is moving, in kilometers or miles per hour.

tachometer
Dial showing the engine's rotation speed in revolutions per minute.

ignition switch
Switch activated by a contact key allowing a current from the battery to flow to the starter.

view from above

mirror
Mirror attached to the handgrip, allowing the motorcyclist to see behind and along the sides of the vehicle without turning around.

headlight
Lamp on the front of the vehicle to light up the space in front.

front turn signal
Device emitting an intermittent light, signaling a change of the vehicle's direction or a temporary hazard to other vehicles.

clutch lever
Lever for disengaging then engaging the engine and the gearbox, allowing the gears to be changed.

front brake lever
Lever connected by a cable to the front brake caliper, activated by the driver to brake the front wheel.

dip switch
Button for switching between low and high beam.

twist grip throttle
Acceleration handle that the driver turns to increase or reduce the amount of air/fuel mixture entering the engine and hence its running speed.

horn
Device emitting a loud sound that the driver can use to attract the attention of a pedestrian or other user of the road.

emergency switch
Device for cutting the engine in case of emergency.

gas tank cap
Part screwed into the fuel filler neck to close it.

starter button
Switch engaging the starter, which engages the engine.

gearshift lever
Pedal located under the motorcyclist's left foot, for changing the ratio between the motor's speed of rotation and that of the wheels.

clutch housing
Rigid covering protecting the clutch mechanism.

driver's footrest
Metal rods, one on each side of the motorcycle frame, for resting the driver's feet on.

rear brake pedal
Pedal connected by a cable to the rear brake caliper, activated by the driver to brake the rear wheel.

passenger's footrest
Metal rods, one on each side of the motorcycle frame, for resting the passenger's feet on.

rear turn signal
Device emitting an intermittent light, signaling a change of the vehicle's direction or a temporary hazard to other vehicles.

exhaust pipe
Compartmentalized chamber in which the escaping gases expand, thus reducing the noise from the engine.

taillight
Lamp that lights up automatically when the front lights are lit and emits a brighter light when the driver applies the brakes.

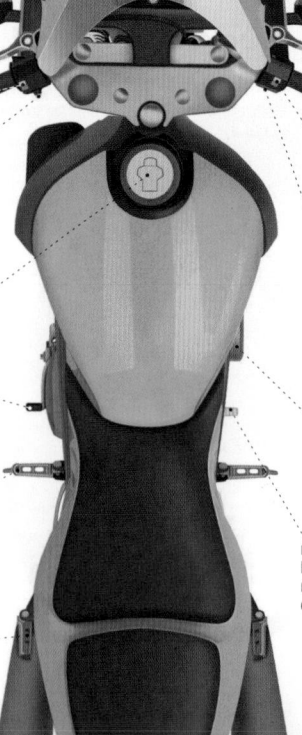

motorcycle

r scooter
rized vehicle with two small
ls, embellished with fairing,
cterized by an open frame
flat floor.

seat
Usually leather seat where the
driver sits.

luggage rack
t the rear of the vehicle,
ng a trunk or for lashing
n luggage using straps.

mirror
Mirror attached to the handgrip,
allowing the motorcyclist to see
behind and along the sides of the
vehicle without turning around.

apron
Aerodynamic component in sheet
metal or plastic, trimming the
steering column and protecting the
driver from the wind and inclement
weather.

floorboard
Wide flat surface for resting the
feet on.

seat
Usually leather seat where the
driver sits.

examples of motorcycles

off-road motorcycle
Motorcycle designed for traveling over
rough terrain, with features such as a
raised engine, extended suspension,
elevated muffler and tires with studs.

telescopic front fork
Pair of sliding tubes enclosing
a spring; it controls steering,
suspension and shock absorption
on the front wheel.

knobby tread tire
Tire whose tread is fitted with
blocks of rubber, providing better
traction on rough terrain.

touring motorcycle
Motorcycle providing comfort for
the driver and the passenger, with
features such as wide fairing,
extended handgrips and footrests for
stretching the legs.

ed
le designed like a bicycle,
quipped with an engine
e cylinder is no larger than
ubic centimeters.

carrier
at the rear of the vehicle,
ing a trunk or for lashing
n luggage using straps.

kickstand
Fold-down support on the right
side of the moped to keep it almost
upright when at rest.

antenna
Device receiving radio waves
broadcast by a station.

backrest
Part supporting the back.

top box
Usually rigid and waterproof
compartment, behind the
passenger seat, for stowing light
objects.

saddlebag
Usually rigid and waterproof
luggage, attached to each side of
the passenger seat.

windshield
Glass and plastic pane in front,
protecting the motorcyclist from the
wind and inclement weather.

passenger's seat
Individual seat, usually leather, set higher
that the driver's seat, on which the
passenger sits.

driver's seat
Usually leather individual seat where
the driver sits.

4x4 all-terrain vehicle

Four-wheeled all-terrain vehicle (ATV) for traversing most kinds of terrain, equipped with a motorcycle engine.

rear cargo rack
Support at the rear of the vehicle,
for attaching a trunk or for lashing
down luggage using straps.

seat
Usually leather seat where the
driver sits.

gas tank
Reservoir containing the fuel that
makes the vehicle self-sufficient.

handgrip
Extension of the handlebars used
for steering the ATV.

rear fender
Piece of curved metal covering
the rear wheel, for protecting the
motorcyclist from being splashed.

muffler
Compartmentalized chamber in which
the escaping gases expand, thus
reducing the noise from the engine.

bumper
Malleable component partly
absorbing impact in the event of a
front-on collision.

front shock absorber
Cylindrical mechanism attached to
the front wheel and coupled with a
spring; it absorbs shocks caused
by unevenness in the road.

gearshift lever
Pedal located under the driver's
foot, for changing the ratio between
the motor's speed of rotation and
that of the wheels.

TRANSPORT AND MACHINERY

bicycle

Frame vehicle steered by the front wheel and propelled by the rear wheel, which in turn is driven, via a chain, by a pedal mechanism.

parts of a bicycle

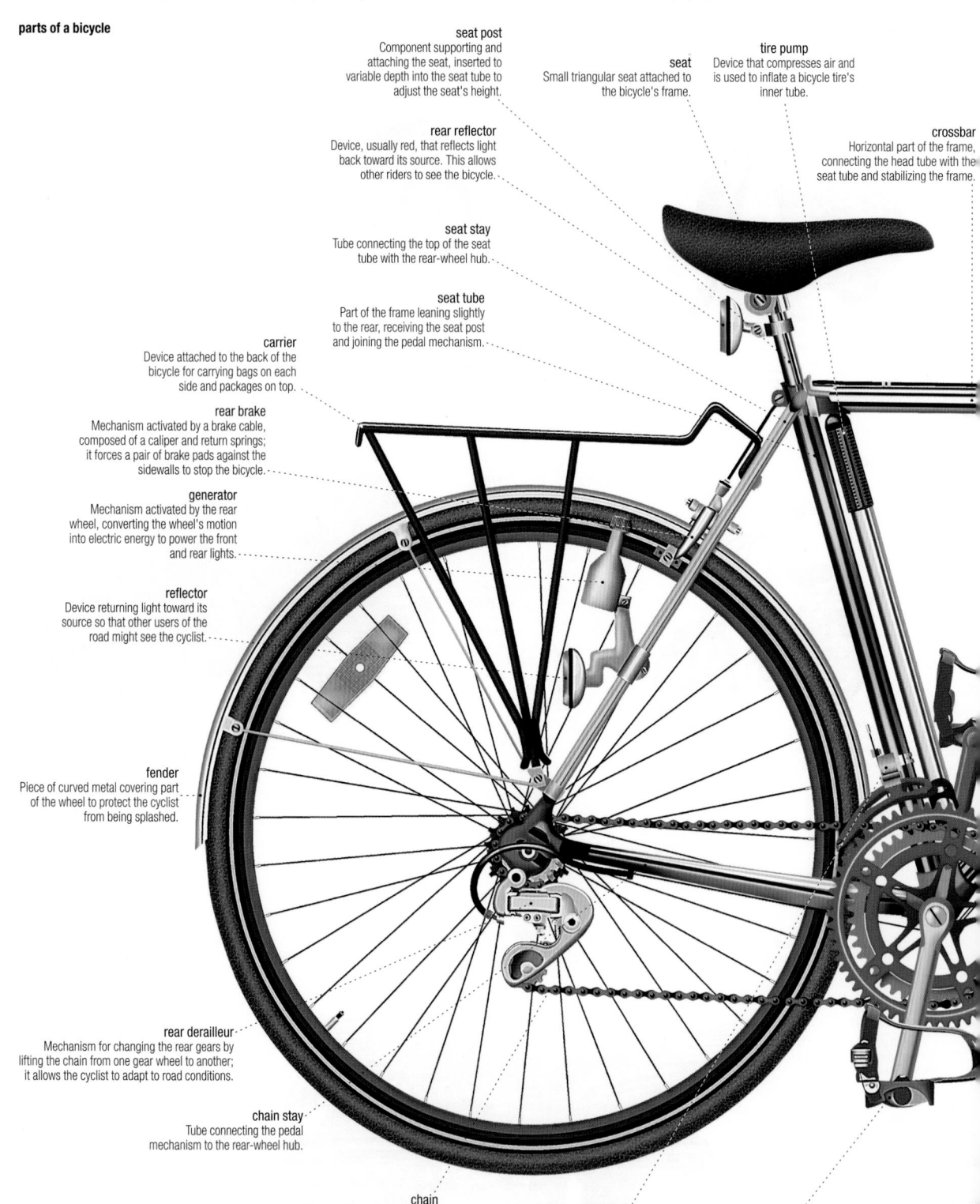

seat post
Component supporting and attaching the seat, inserted to variable depth into the seat tube to adjust the seat's height.

seat
Small triangular seat attached to the bicycle's frame.

tire pump
Device that compresses air and is used to inflate a bicycle tire's inner tube.

crossbar
Horizontal part of the frame, connecting the head tube with the seat tube and stabilizing the frame.

rear reflector
Device, usually red, that reflects light back toward its source. This allows other riders to see the bicycle.

seat stay
Tube connecting the top of the seat tube with the rear-wheel hub.

seat tube
Part of the frame leaning slightly to the rear, receiving the seat post and joining the pedal mechanism.

carrier
Device attached to the back of the bicycle for carrying bags on each side and packages on top.

rear brake
Mechanism activated by a brake cable, composed of a caliper and return springs; it forces a pair of brake pads against the sidewalls to stop the bicycle.

generator
Mechanism activated by the rear wheel, converting the wheel's motion into electric energy to power the front and rear lights.

reflector
Device returning light toward its source so that other users of the road might see the cyclist.

fender
Piece of curved metal covering part of the wheel to protect the cyclist from being splashed.

rear derailleur
Mechanism for changing the rear gears by lifting the chain from one gear wheel to another; it allows the cyclist to adapt to road conditions.

chain stay
Tube connecting the pedal mechanism to the rear-wheel hub.

chain
Set of metal links meshing with the sprockets on the chain wheel and gear wheel to transmit the pedaling motion to the rear wheel.

front derailleur
Mechanism for changing the front gears by lifting the chain from one chain wheel to another; it allows the cyclist to adapt to road conditions.

pedal
Part attached to a crank that the cyclist rotates to provide the bicycle's power.

toe c
Metal device attached to the peda that covers the front of the fee keeping the feet in the prop position and increasing pedali pow

bicycle

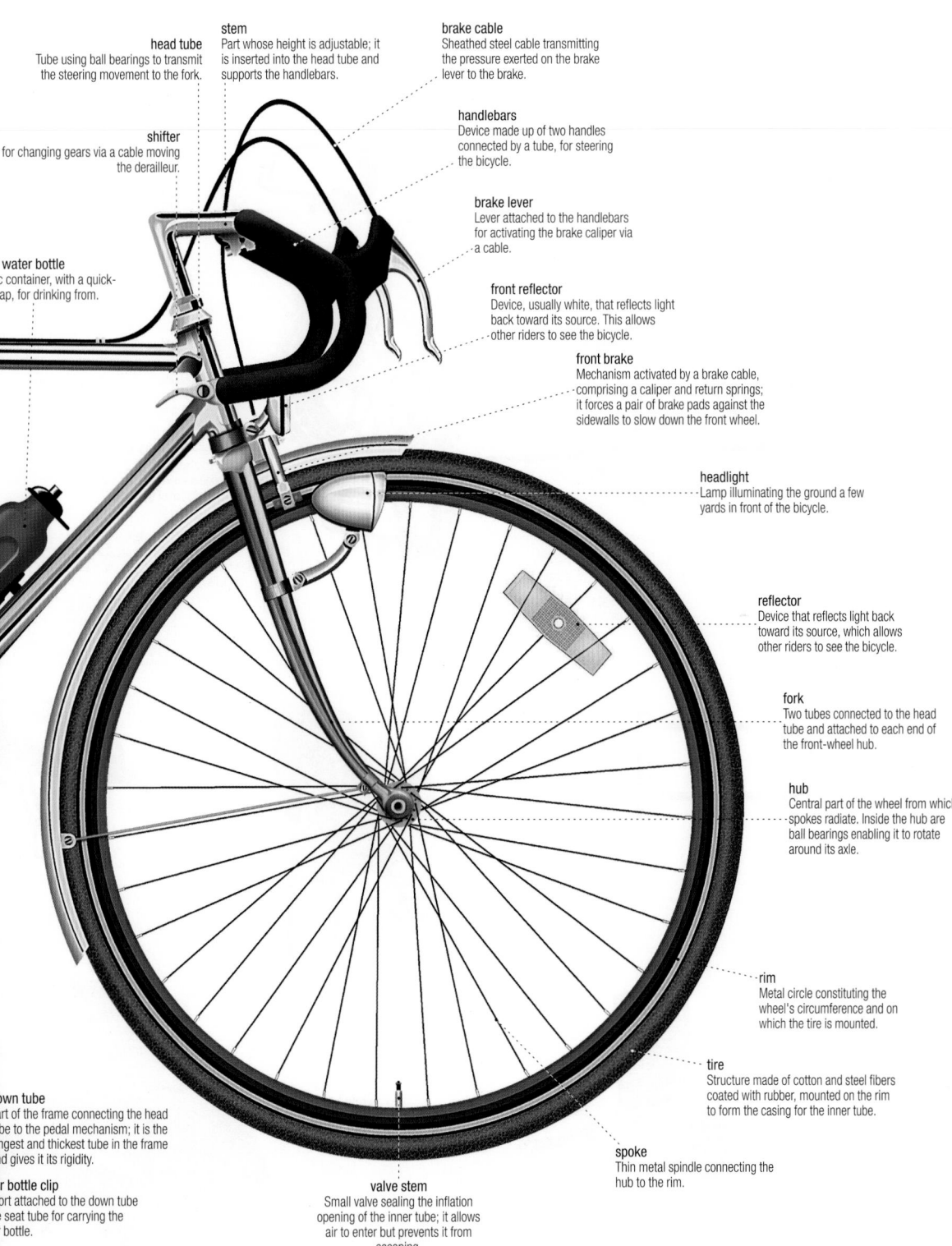

head tube
Tube using ball bearings to transmit the steering movement to the fork.

stem
Part whose height is adjustable; it is inserted into the head tube and supports the handlebars.

brake cable
Sheathed steel cable transmitting the pressure exerted on the brake lever to the brake.

shifter
for changing gears via a cable moving the derailleur.

handlebars
Device made up of two handles connected by a tube, for steering the bicycle.

brake lever
Lever attached to the handlebars for activating the brake caliper via a cable.

water bottle
 container, with a quick-ap, for drinking from.

front reflector
Device, usually white, that reflects light back toward its source. This allows other riders to see the bicycle.

front brake
Mechanism activated by a brake cable, comprising a caliper and return springs; it forces a pair of brake pads against the sidewalls to slow down the front wheel.

headlight
Lamp illuminating the ground a few yards in front of the bicycle.

reflector
Device that reflects light back toward its source, which allows other riders to see the bicycle.

fork
Two tubes connected to the head tube and attached to each end of the front-wheel hub.

hub
Central part of the wheel from which spokes radiate. Inside the hub are ball bearings enabling it to rotate around its axle.

rim
Metal circle constituting the wheel's circumference and on which the tire is mounted.

tire
Structure made of cotton and steel fibers coated with rubber, mounted on the rim to form the casing for the inner tube.

own tube
art of the frame connecting the head be to the pedal mechanism; it is the ngest and thickest tube in the frame nd gives it its rigidity.

r bottle clip
ort attached to the down tube e seat tube for carrying the bottle.

valve stem
Small valve sealing the inflation opening of the inner tube; it allows air to enter but prevents it from escaping.

spoke
Thin metal spindle connecting the hub to the rim.

TRANSPORT AND MACHINERY

bicycle

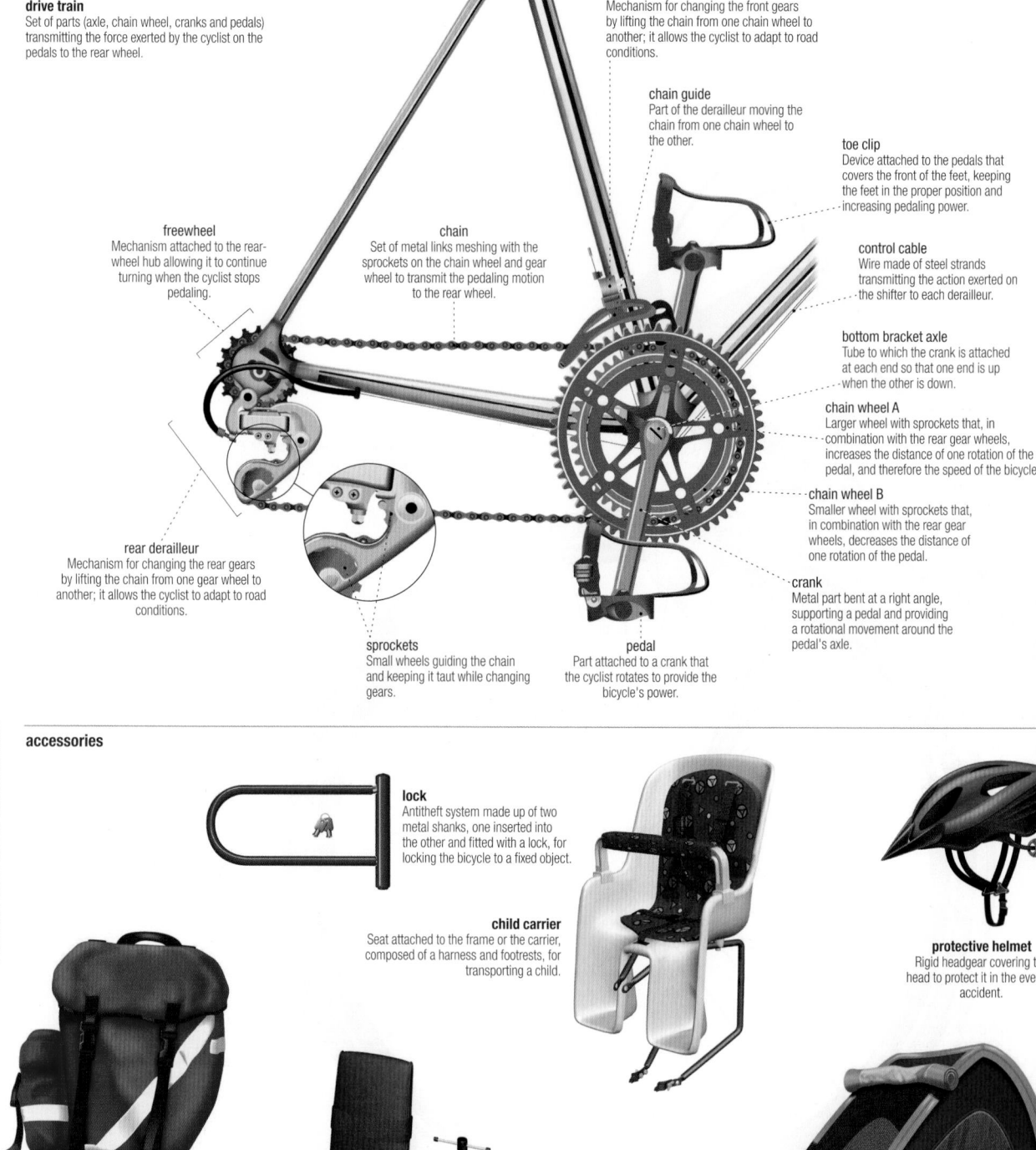

drive train
Set of parts (axle, chain wheel, cranks and pedals) transmitting the force exerted by the cyclist on the pedals to the rear wheel.

front derailleur
Mechanism for changing the front gears by lifting the chain from one chain wheel to another; it allows the cyclist to adapt to road conditions.

chain guide
Part of the derailleur moving the chain from one chain wheel to the other.

toe clip
Device attached to the pedals that covers the front of the feet, keeping the feet in the proper position and increasing pedaling power.

freewheel
Mechanism attached to the rear-wheel hub allowing it to continue turning when the cyclist stops pedaling.

chain
Set of metal links meshing with the sprockets on the chain wheel and gear wheel to transmit the pedaling motion to the rear wheel.

control cable
Wire made of steel strands transmitting the action exerted on the shifter to each derailleur.

bottom bracket axle
Tube to which the crank is attached at each end so that one end is up when the other is down.

chain wheel A
Larger wheel with sprockets that, in combination with the rear gear wheels, increases the distance of one rotation of the pedal, and therefore the speed of the bicycle.

chain wheel B
Smaller wheel with sprockets that, in combination with the rear gear wheels, decreases the distance of one rotation of the pedal.

rear derailleur
Mechanism for changing the rear gears by lifting the chain from one gear wheel to another; it allows the cyclist to adapt to road conditions.

crank
Metal part bent at a right angle, supporting a pedal and providing a rotational movement around the pedal's axle.

sprockets
Small wheels guiding the chain and keeping it taut while changing gears.

pedal
Part attached to a crank that the cyclist rotates to provide the bicycle's power.

accessories

lock
Antitheft system made up of two metal shanks, one inserted into the other and fitted with a lock, for locking the bicycle to a fixed object.

child carrier
Seat attached to the frame or the carrier, composed of a harness and footrests, for transporting a child.

protective helmet
Rigid headgear covering th head to protect it in the even accident.

bicycle bag
Bag that can be attached to the handlebars or the carrier.

child bike trailer
Motorless vehicle hitched to a bicycle, designed to carry one or two children.

tool kit
Set of tools for simple repairs and adjustments, such as fixing a flat tire, replacing spokes or adjusting brakes.

examples of bicycles

trailer bike
Child's bicycle with one wheel; the frame is an extended hitch that fits onto an adult bicycle.

child's tricycle
Very stable three-wheeled vehicle with pedals driving either the front wheel or the rear wheels, for the use of young children.

training wheel
small wheel attached to the rear of the bicycle to improve stability; used to teach young children to ride.

child's bicycle
Bicycle adapted to a child's size, sometimes outfitted with training wheels.

BMX bike
Strong small bicycle, for acrobatics and competitions on bumpy tracks.

road bicycle
Bicycle with narrow tires, lightweight frame and handlebars that position the cyclist for optimum aerodynamics, designed for road racing.

mountain bike
Bicycle with large wheels with treads with studs, a strong frame, numerous gears and powerful brakes, for navigating all kinds of terrain.

bicycle

examples of bicycles

rear basket
Container attached to the rear of the tricycle used to transport various objects.

adult tricycle
Very stable three-wheeled vehicle with pedals driving either the front wheel or the rear wheels.

recumbent bicycle
Bicycle with a slightly reclined seat that supports the back, allowing the rider's legs to pedal horizontally.

city bicycle
Bicycle designed for comfort and safety while taking short trips on city streets.

battery
Batteries that supply the energy required to run the electric motor.

electric bicycle
Bicycle outfitted with an electric motor that assists the rider.

touring bicycle
Intermediate bicycle between a road bicycle and a city bicycle, designed for traveling long distances in comfort.

tandem bicycle
Bicycle with two places; both cyclists pedal simultaneously but only the person in front steers.

TRANSPORT AND MACHINERY

railroad station

Covered building for the public where trains and passengers arrive and depart.

passenger station
Covered building for the public where trains and passengers arrive and depart.

station platform
Area alongside the tracks, for passengers to embark and disembark the train, or for loading and unloading cargo from the cars.

commuter train
Local train running frequently each day between an urban center and its suburbs or neighboring cities.

main lines
Tracks for trains traveling long distances.

suburban commuter railroad
Railroad connecting an urban center to its suburbs and neighboring cities.

siding
Side track not used for railroad traffic but for shunting, marshaling or loading and unloading.

bumper
Buffer placed at the end of a track stopping the train from running off the end of the track.

grade crossing
Intersection of a railroad and a road, with or without warning lights.

platform shelter
Roof protecting passengers waiting on the platform from inclement weather.

footbridge
Elevated walkway for passengers to cross over a set of tracks.

semaphore
Light for relaying information such as the speed of trains and the distance between them.

parking
Area for parking vehicles.

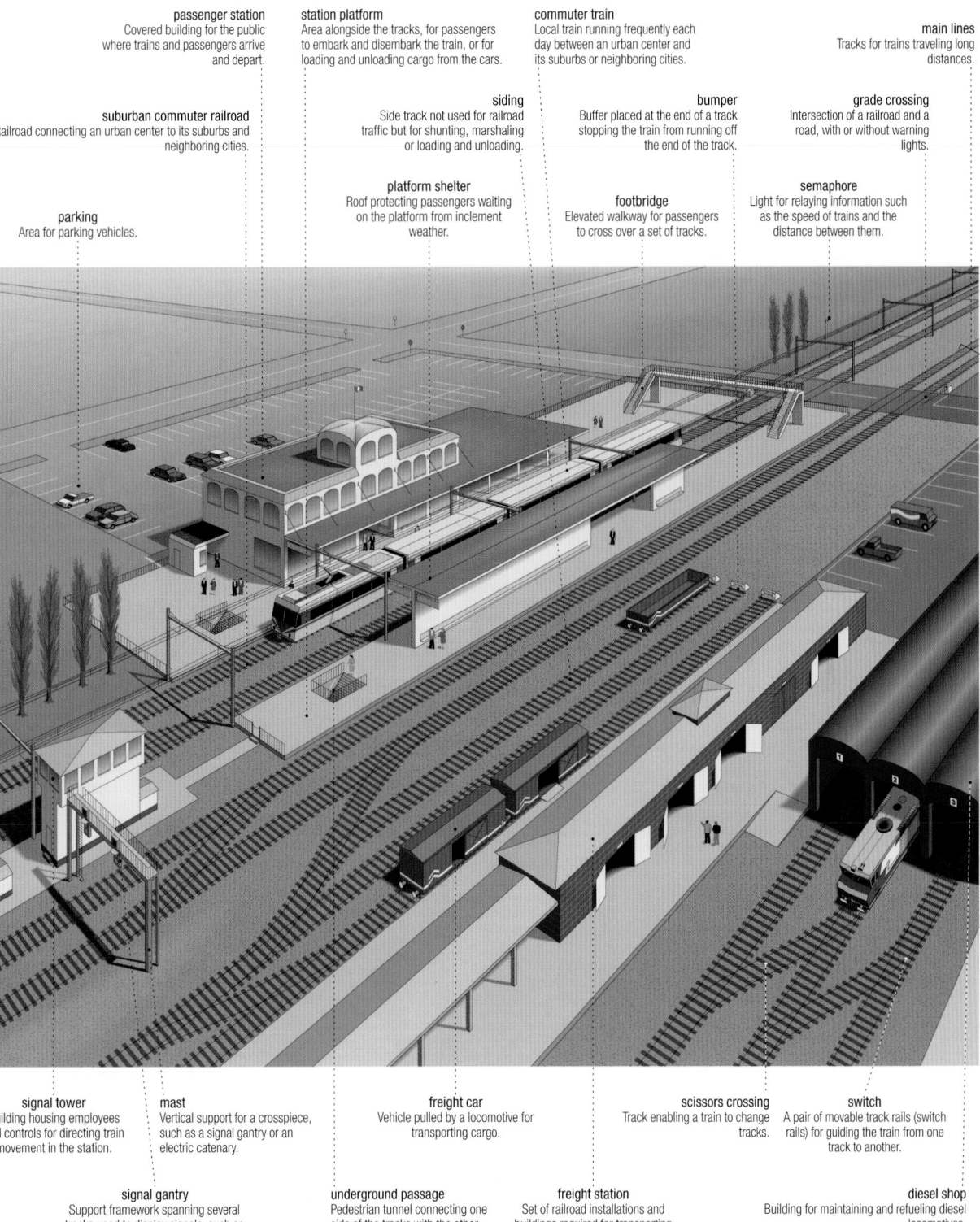

signal tower
Building housing employees and controls for directing train movement in the station.

mast
Vertical support for a crosspiece, such as a signal gantry or an electric catenary.

freight car
Vehicle pulled by a locomotive for transporting cargo.

scissors crossing
Track enabling a train to change tracks.

switch
A pair of movable track rails (switch rails) for guiding the train from one track to another.

signal gantry
Support framework spanning several tracks used to display signals, such as tricolor lights and speed-limit panels.

underground passage
Pedestrian tunnel connecting one side of the tracks with the other.

freight station
Set of railroad installations and buildings required for transporting cargo.

diesel shop
Building for maintaining and refueling diesel locomotives.

TRANSPORT AND MACHINERY

passenger station

Covered building for the public where trains and passengers arrive and depart.

office
Workplace of the employees managing the station.

indicator board
Panel showing the destination and the configuration of the train, such as type and numbering of cars.

baggage cart
Four-wheeled handcart available to passengers for transporting baggage inside the station.

baggage lock
Metal compartments for keeping lugga temporarily for a small f

glassed roof
Large glassed surface forming the walls and roof.

metal structure
Set of metal components comprising the skeleton of a building and supporting its roof; here, the roof is made of glass.

platform number

passenger train
Set of cars coupled together and pulled along tracks by a locomotive.

concourse
Large space for passengers and the public at large housing the various services of the station, such as ticket sales, information counter and shops.

platform edge
Zone along the edge of the platform, usually demarcated by a safety line.

ticket collecte
Person checking that pa tickets correspond destinations.

baggage room
Counter where passengers leave their baggage to be taken to the train's baggage car, if it has one.

passenger platform
Area alongside the tracks for passengers to embark and disembark trains.

departure time indicator

railroad track
A pair of parallel rails laid end to end and on which trains run.

parcel office
Courier-service window for sending envelopes and packages to be dispatched by train.

destination
Name of the last station where the train stops at the end of its route.

schedules
Grid showing the departure and arrival times of the trains, their number and their destination or point of departure.

platform entrance
Area leading to the platforms, sometimes reserved for passengers who have valid tickets.

types of passenger cars

Cars: vehicles with various layouts that are pulled by locomotives, for transporting and providing services to passengers.

coach car
Car with two rows of benches or seats for transporting passengers in the seated position.

luggage rack
Space at the entrance of the car for stowing large pieces of luggage.

adjustable seat
Seat whose back can be changed from a sitting position to a reclining position.

center aisle
Walkway between the two rows of benches or seats, for going from one end of the car to the other.

vestibule
Entrance compartment of the car.

vestibule door
Sometimes sliding door on the threshold plate at the top of the steps, providing access to the car.

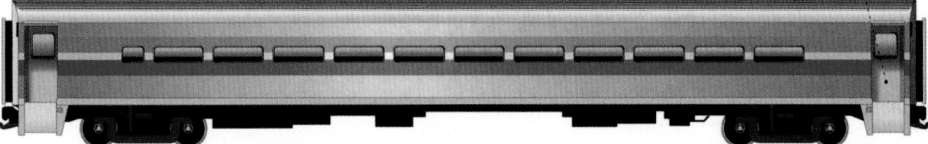

sleeping car
Car with compartments laid out as small bedrooms.

berth
Sometimes folding bench located in a compartment, for sleeping.

restroom
Compartment equipped with a toilet and a sink.

linen
Storage for linens needed for the trip, such as towels and sheets.

sleeping compartment
Compartment laid out with berths.

wheelchair
Place with special fittings designed for wheelchairs.

corridor connection
Device where two cars articulate together; passengers and personnel can pass through to get from one car to the next.

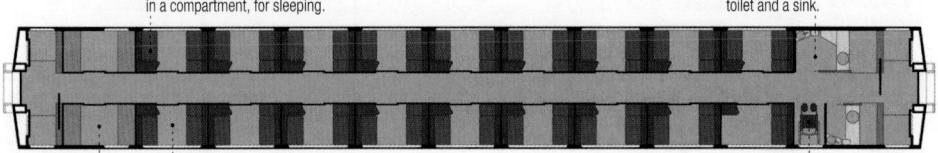

dining car
Car laid out for serving meals.

dining section
Part of the car where passengers can eat or drink.

steward's desk
Table for laying out the dishes used for the various courses and food that is ready to serve.

storage space
Place where employees keep materials for providing service during the trip.

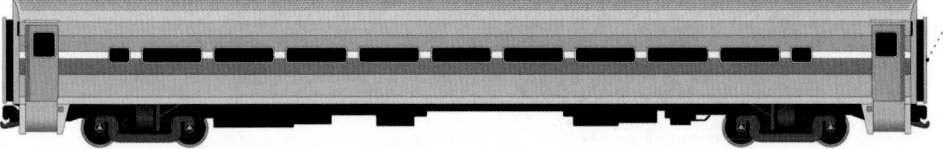

panoramic window
Large window offering an unobstructed view of the passing countryside.

kitchen
Room where meals are prepared.

crew's locker
Compartment at the entrance where personnel can stow their coats and other personal effects.

grab handle
Vertical handle at shoulder height next to the door for gripping when climbing up to or down from the car.

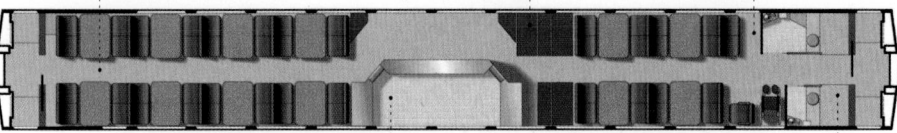

TRANSPORT AND MACHINERY

diesel-electric locomotive

Vehicle with a diesel engine turning a generator that in turn powers the electric traction motors.

cross section of a locomotive

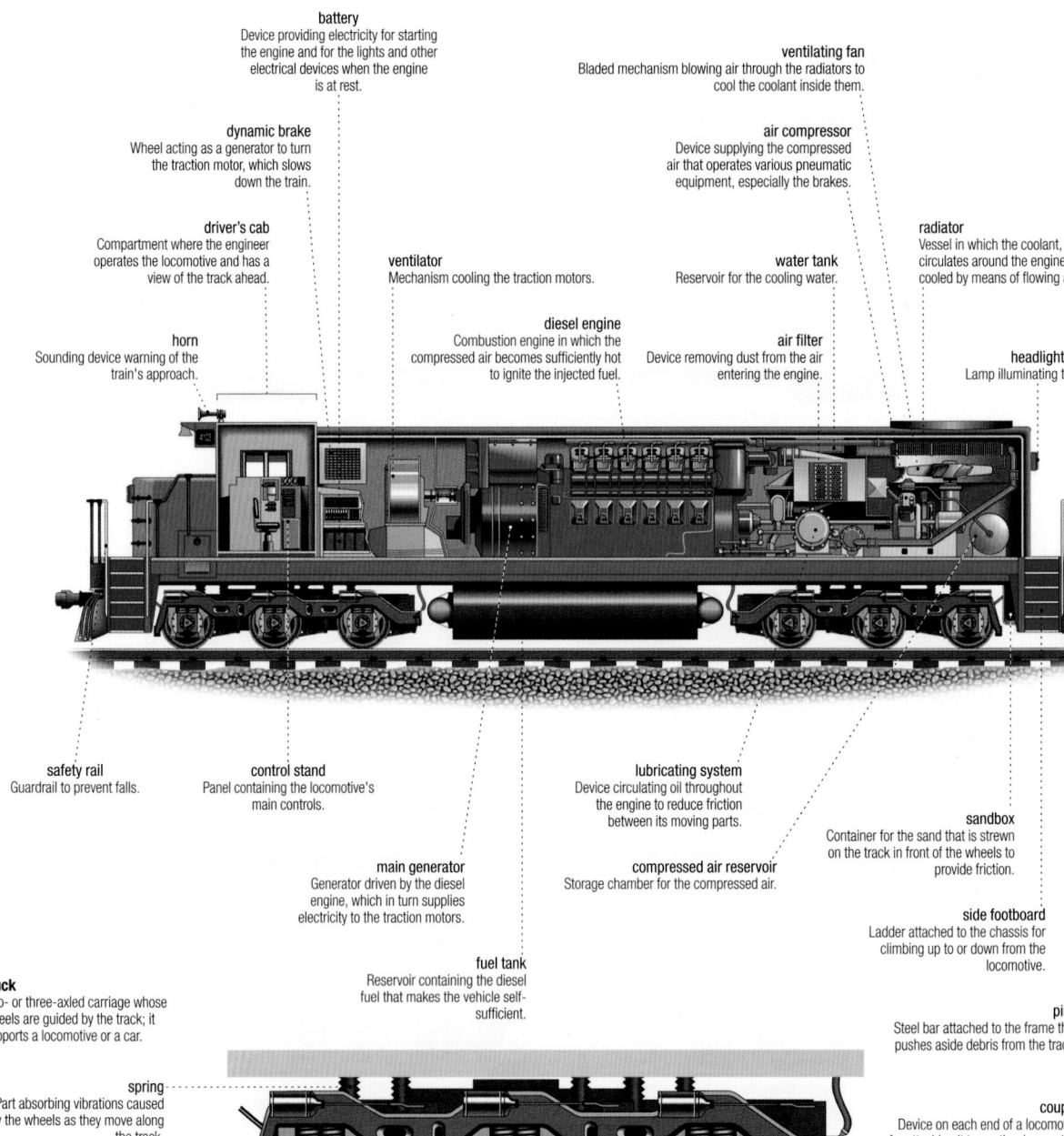

battery
Device providing electricity for starting the engine and for the lights and other electrical devices when the engine is at rest.

ventilating fan
Bladed mechanism blowing air through the radiators to cool the coolant inside them.

dynamic brake
Wheel acting as a generator to turn the traction motor, which slows down the train.

air compressor
Device supplying the compressed air that operates various pneumatic equipment, especially the brakes.

driver's cab
Compartment where the engineer operates the locomotive and has a view of the track ahead.

ventilator
Mechanism cooling the traction motors.

water tank
Reservoir for the cooling water.

radiator
Vessel in which the coolant, whi circulates around the engine, is cooled by means of flowing air.

horn
Sounding device warning of the train's approach.

diesel engine
Combustion engine in which the compressed air becomes sufficiently hot to ignite the injected fuel.

air filter
Device removing dust from the air entering the engine.

headlight
Lamp illuminating the t

safety rail
Guardrail to prevent falls.

control stand
Panel containing the locomotive's main controls.

lubricating system
Device circulating oil throughout the engine to reduce friction between its moving parts.

sandbox
Container for the sand that is strewn on the track in front of the wheels to provide friction.

main generator
Generator driven by the diesel engine, which in turn supplies electricity to the traction motors.

compressed air reservoir
Storage chamber for the compressed air.

side footboard
Ladder attached to the chassis for climbing up to or down from the locomotive.

truck
Two- or three-axled carriage whose wheels are guided by the track; it supports a locomotive or a car.

fuel tank
Reservoir containing the diesel fuel that makes the vehicle self-sufficient.

pilot
Steel bar attached to the frame that pushes aside debris from the track.

spring
Part absorbing vibrations caused by the wheels as they move along the track.

coupler
Device on each end of a locomotive for attaching it to another locomotive

axle
Transversal part under a vehicle passing through the hubs of the wheels, which support it.

journal box
Part connecting the axle to the truck frame.

truck frame
Framework supporting the axles, suspension, brakes and traction motors.

high-speed train

High-speed passenger train (between 135 and 190 mph) powered by electricity, with a power car at each end and a limited number of cars in between.

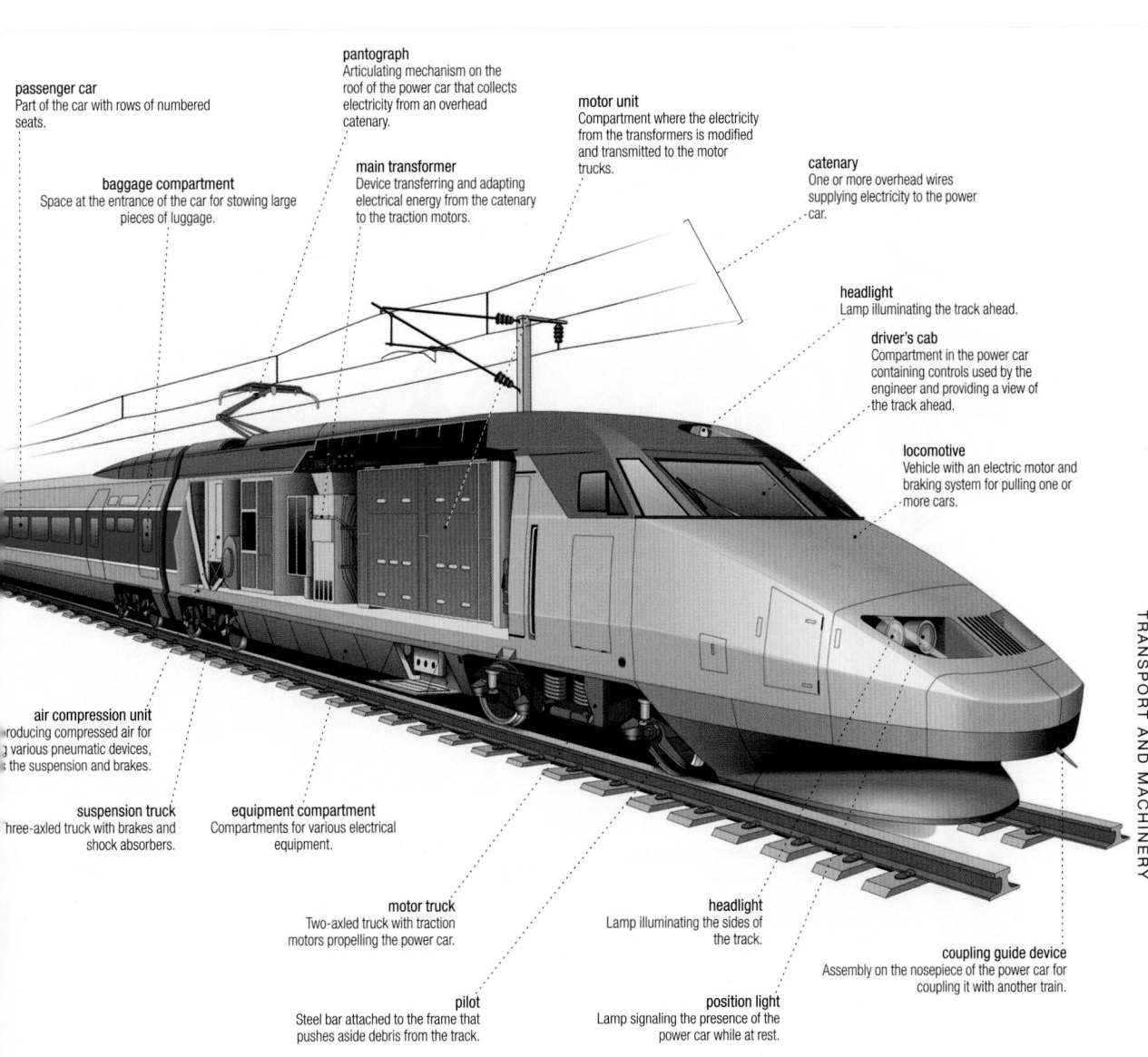

passenger car
Part of the car with rows of numbered seats.

baggage compartment
Space at the entrance of the car for stowing large pieces of luggage.

pantograph
Articulating mechanism on the roof of the power car that collects electricity from an overhead catenary.

main transformer
Device transferring and adapting electrical energy from the catenary to the traction motors.

motor unit
Compartment where the electricity from the transformers is modified and transmitted to the motor trucks.

catenary
One or more overhead wires supplying electricity to the power car.

headlight
Lamp illuminating the track ahead.

driver's cab
Compartment in the power car containing controls used by the engineer and providing a view of the track ahead.

locomotive
Vehicle with an electric motor and braking system for pulling one or more cars.

air compression unit
producing compressed air for various pneumatic devices, the suspension and brakes.

suspension truck
Three-axled truck with brakes and shock absorbers.

equipment compartment
Compartments for various electrical equipment.

motor truck
Two-axled truck with traction motors propelling the power car.

headlight
Lamp illuminating the sides of the track.

coupling guide device
Assembly on the nosepiece of the power car for coupling it with another train.

pilot
Steel bar attached to the frame that pushes aside debris from the track.

position light
Lamp signaling the presence of the power car while at rest.

yard

Set of tracks where freight trains are reconfigured to contain cargo cars with the same destination and then dispatched.

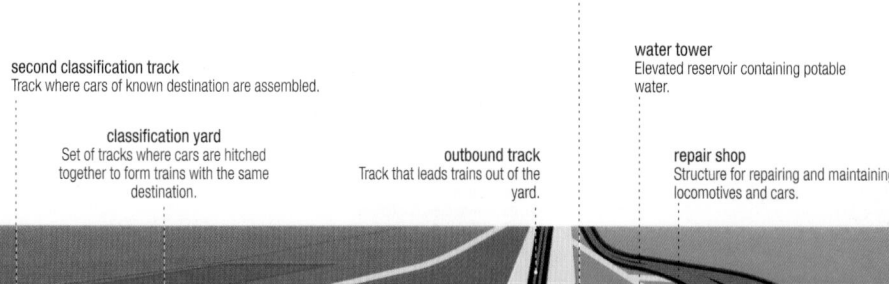

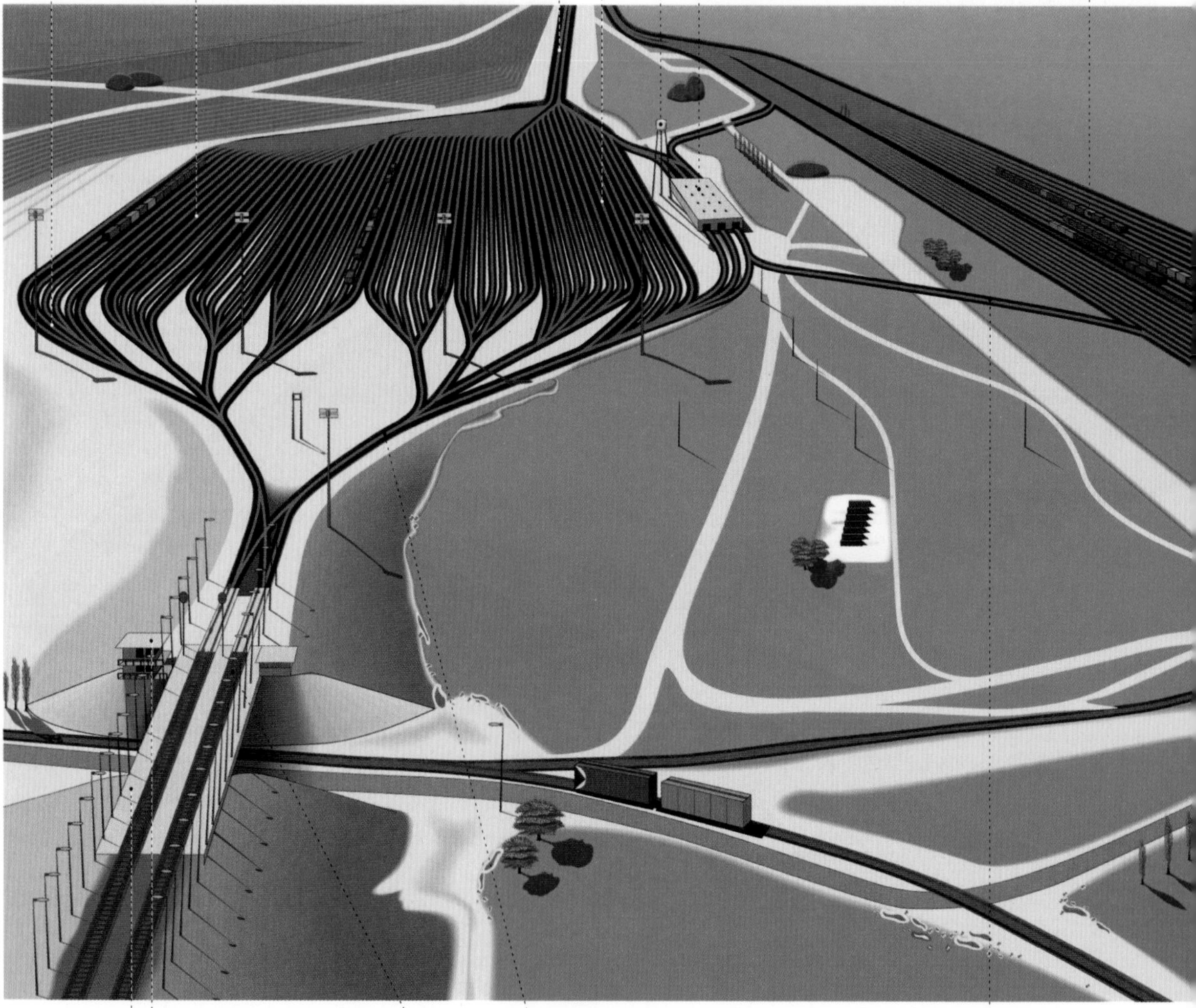

car cleaning yard
Set of tracks where cars are cleansed of any cargo residue before going back into circulation.

second classification track
Track where cars of known destination are assembled.

water tower
Elevated reservoir containing potable water.

receiving yard
Set of tracks where arriving trains park and are unhitched from their locomotives.

classification yard
Set of tracks where cars are hitched together to form trains with the same destination.

outbound track
Track that leads trains out of the yard.

repair shop
Structure for repairing and maintaining locomotives and cars.

hump office
Office where train formations are programmed and car shunting is controlled.

first classification track
Track where cars for the second classification track are switched.

locomotive track
Track that leads locomotives to the shop for maintenance.

hump
Sloped part of the track where cars are pushed up a hill (hump) by a locomotive.

hump lead
Track where cars are released to coast onto other tracks for switching onto outbound trains.

freight car

Vehicle pulled by a locomotive for transporting cargo.

boxcar
Car covered with a waterproof casing and having sliding side doors, for transporting cargo that must be protected from the weather and theft.

horizontal end handhold
Crossbar for holding onto when moving from one side of the car to the other while coupling.

hand brake wheel
el for manually activating the brake.

corner cap
Metal part reinforcing and protecting the edges of the car.

routing cardboard
Placard for a label listing the car's contents.

placard board
Placard for a label warning of dangerous material.

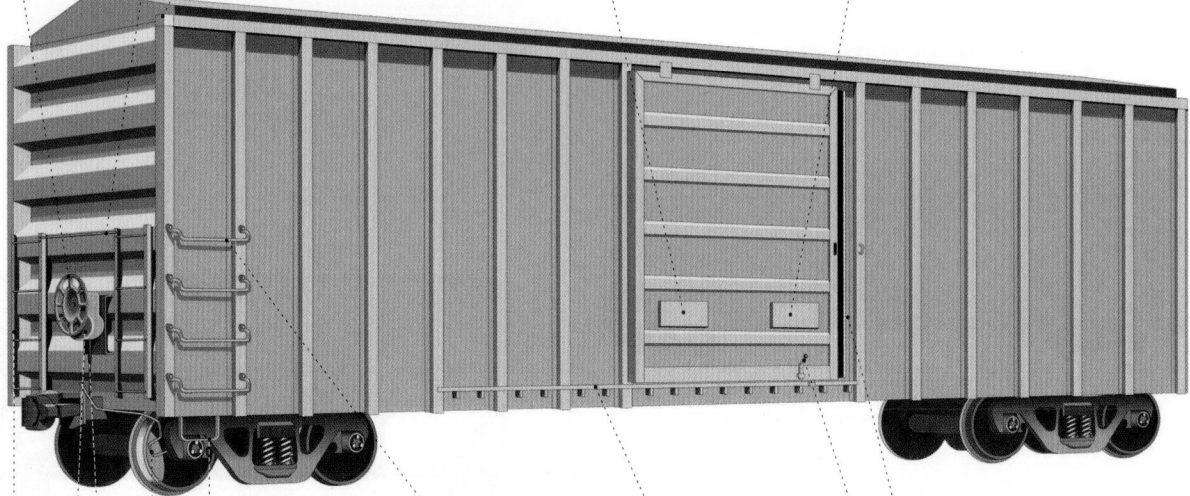

sill step
U-shaped support situated under the car's frame for reaching the ladder.

side ladder
Ladder on the side of the car for accessing the end ladder.

sliding channel
Groove guiding and supporting the door as it slides open and shut.

door stop
Part stopping the door when it is closed.

telescoping uncoupling rod
Rod ending in a bent handle for uncoupling the cars.

locking lever
Bar that locks the door and prevents it from sliding.

hand brake winding lever
Vertical metal shaft, with one end connected by a chain to the hand brake wheel and the wheel house, for setting the hand brake.

hand brake gear housing
Part covering a chain transmitting the wheel's turning movement to the hand brake winding lever.

automatic coupler
Device on each end of a locomotive or car for attaching it to another locomotive or car.

end ladder
Ladder for climbing up and down the car to carry out certain tasks, such as uncoupling the cars and setting the hand brake.

coupler knuckle pin
Part around which the coupler knuckle pivots to open and uncouple.

coupler knuckle
Articulated component that interlocks with the corresponding part on another car or locomotive.

freight car

examples of freight cars

The shape of the cars varies depending on the type of cargo being transported.

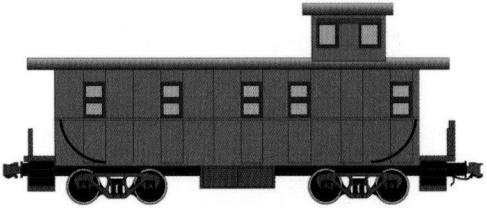

caboose
Car that was formerly at the end of a train; it housed personnel, provisions and tools.

tank car
Car with a sealed reservoir for carrying liquids and gases.

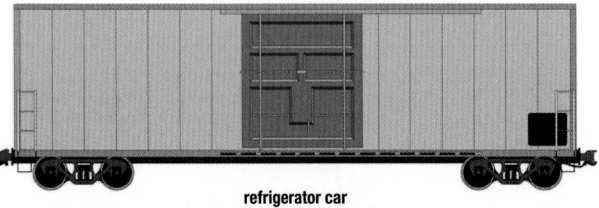

refrigerator car
Closed-box insulated car with a refrigeration unit for carrying perishable foodstuffs.

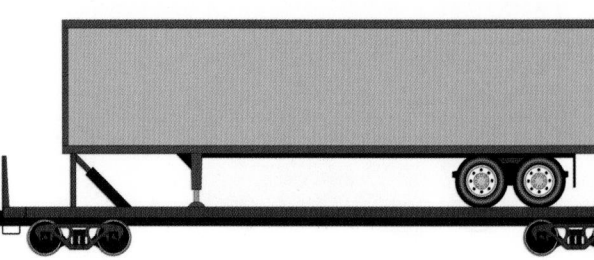

intermodal car
Flat car for carrying semitrailers.

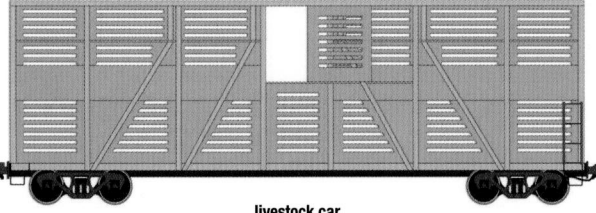

livestock car
Car with slatted sides for carrying livestock; it sometimes has two decks.

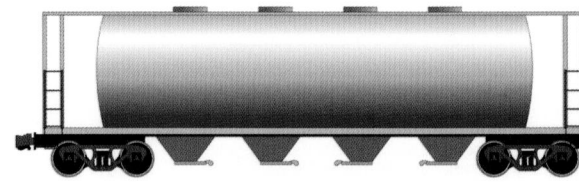

hopper car
Car for carrying bulk cargo; it has dump doors on the bottom for unloading the cargo.

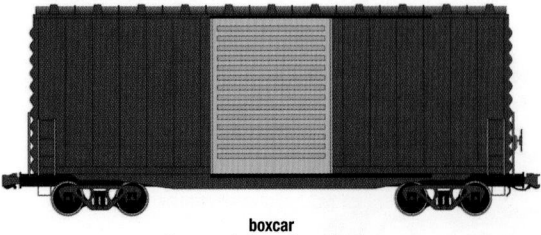

boxcar
Car covered with a waterproof casing and having sliding side doors, for transporting cargo that must be protected from the weather and theft.

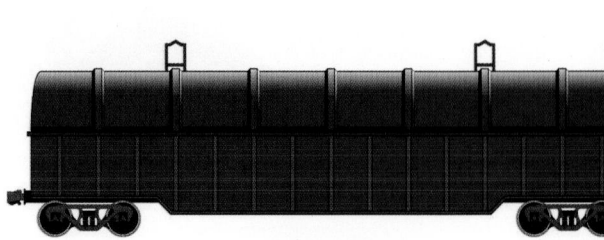

covered gondola car
Gondola with of a retractable metal roof for carrying bulk cargo.

TRANSPORT AND MACHINERY

freight car

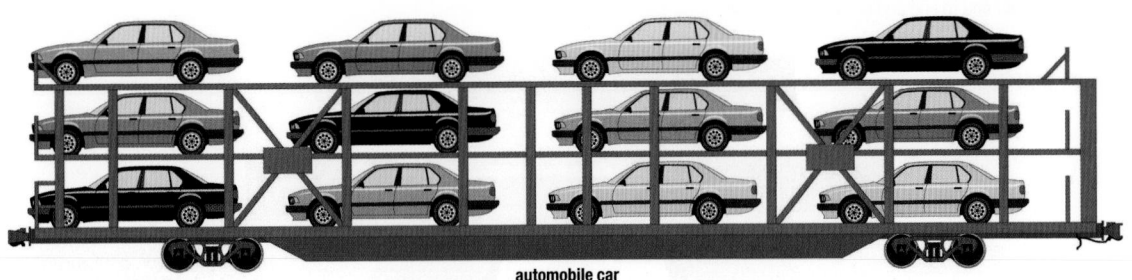

automobile car
Multilevel car for carrying vehicles, which are strapped down.

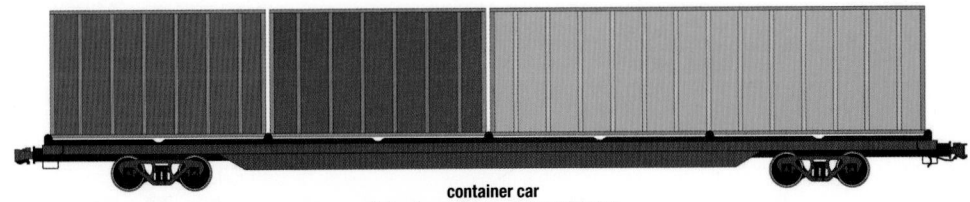

container car
Flatcar for carrying standard-size shipping boxes.

depressed-center flatcar
Car with two extra trucks and a lowered deck for carrying heavy equipment.

gondola car
Open-top car for carrying heavy bulk material, such as scrap metal and construction material.

bulkhead flatcar
Flat car with sturdy plates at each end for carrying loose cargo (usually logs).

hopper ore car
Usually open-top hopper car of limited capacity for carrying minerals.

flatcar
Car with a simple wooden deck for carrying large objects, such as pipes, logs and heavy machinery.

wood chip car
Open-top gondola car with a large compartment for carrying wood chips.

TRANSPORT AND MACHINERY

railroad track

A pair of parallel rails laid end to end and on which trains run.

rail joint
Fasteners joining the ends of rails.

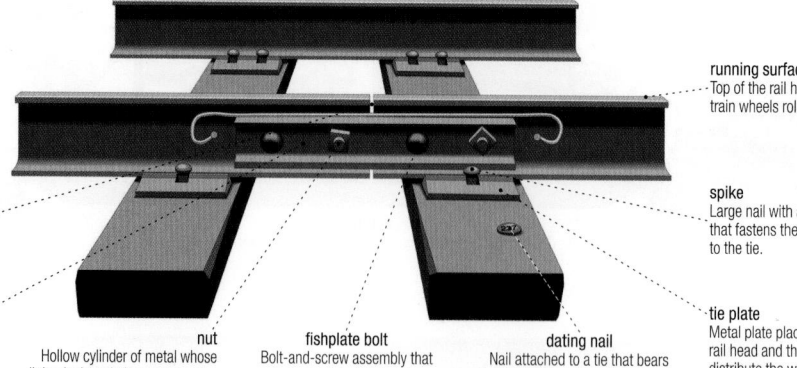

running surface
Top of the rail head on which the train wheels roll.

expansion space
Space left between two joining rails to absorb expansion due to heat.

spike
Large nail with a hooked head that fastens the base of the rail to the tie.

fishplate
Long steel plate that is fitted into the two sides of the rail webs to join them end to end.

nut
Hollow cylinder of metal whose lining is threaded to screw onto a corresponding bolt.

fishplate bolt
Bolt-and-screw assembly that fastens a fishplate to rails.

dating nail
Nail attached to a tie that bears the two last numbers of the year in which the tie was laid.

tie plate
Metal plate placed between the rail head and the tie that helps to distribute the weight of the train on the tie.

remote-controlled switch
Device operated from a distance for opening and closing a pair of movable track rails (switch points) to guide a train from one track to another.

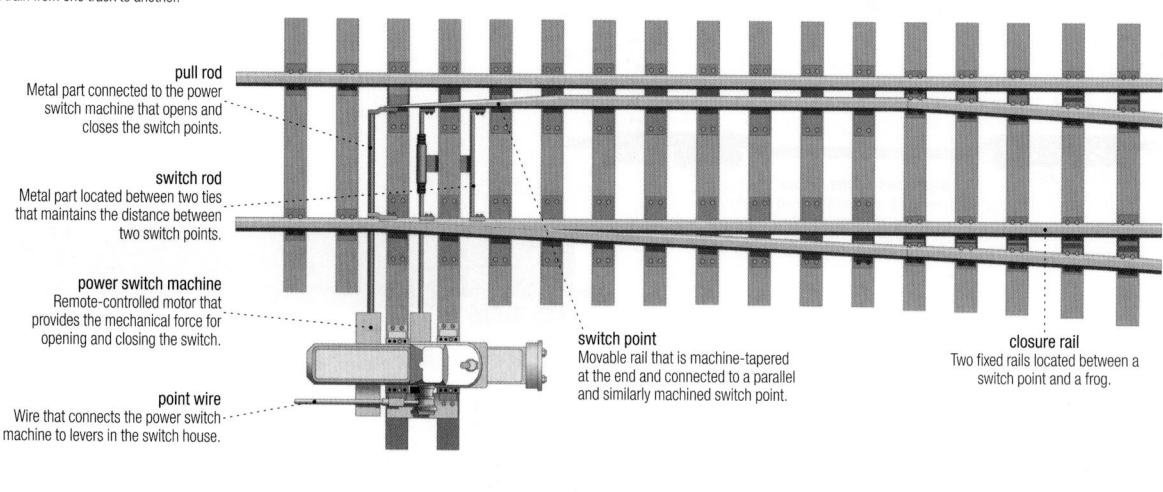

pull rod
Metal part connected to the power switch machine that opens and closes the switch points.

switch rod
Metal part located between two ties that maintains the distance between two switch points.

power switch machine
Remote-controlled motor that provides the mechanical force for opening and closing the switch.

point wire
Wire that connects the power switch machine to levers in the switch house.

switch point
Movable rail that is machine-tapered at the end and connected to a parallel and similarly machined switch point.

closure rail
Two fixed rails located between a switch point and a frog.

manually operated switch
Device operated by hand for opening and closing a pair of movable track rails (switch points) to guide a train from one track to another.

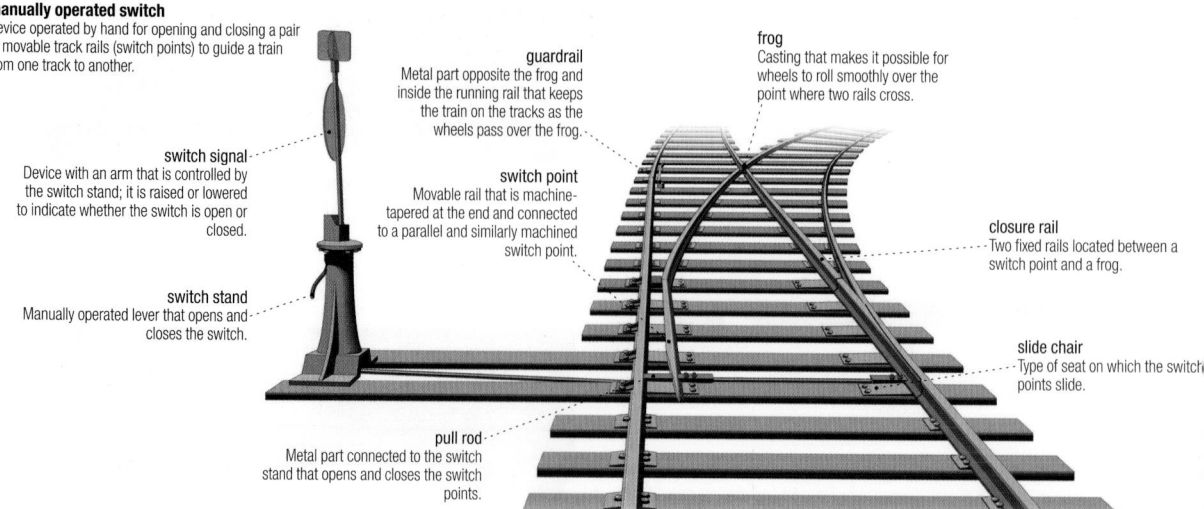

guardrail
Metal part opposite the frog and inside the running rail that keeps the train on the tracks as the wheels pass over the frog.

frog
Casting that makes it possible for wheels to roll smoothly over the point where two rails cross.

switch signal
Device with an arm that is controlled by the switch stand; it is raised or lowered to indicate whether the switch is open or closed.

switch point
Movable rail that is machine-tapered at the end and connected to a parallel and similarly machined switch point.

closure rail
Two fixed rails located between a switch point and a frog.

switch stand
Manually operated lever that opens and closes the switch.

slide chair
Type of seat on which the switch points slide.

pull rod
Metal part connected to the switch stand that opens and closes the switch points.

railroad track

ad track foundation
on which railroad track lies.

cross section of a rail

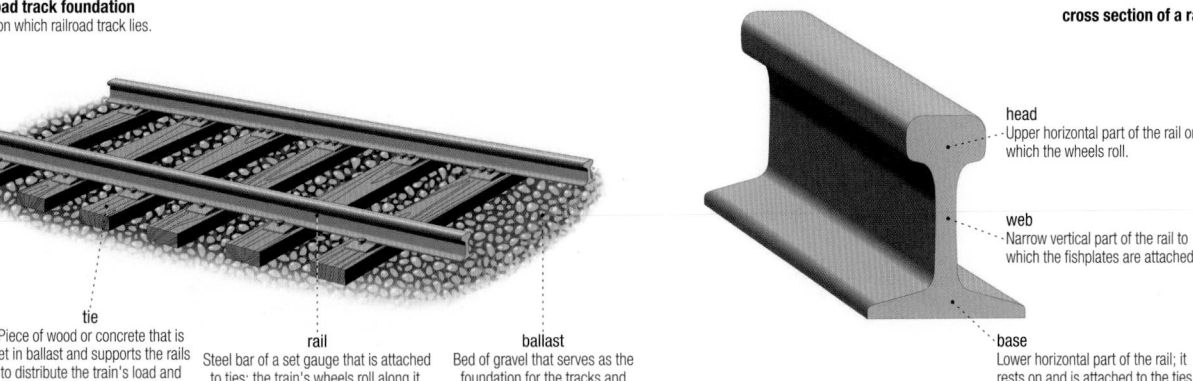

head
Upper horizontal part of the rail on which the wheels roll.

web
Narrow vertical part of the rail to which the fishplates are attached.

base
Lower horizontal part of the rail; it rests on and is attached to the ties.

tie
Piece of wood or concrete that is set in ballast and supports the rails to distribute the train's load and keep the rails parallel.

rail
Steel bar of a set gauge that is attached to ties; the train's wheels roll along it.

ballast
Bed of gravel that serves as the foundation for the tracks and provides drainage.

crossing gate

Intersection of a railroad and a road, with or without warning lights.

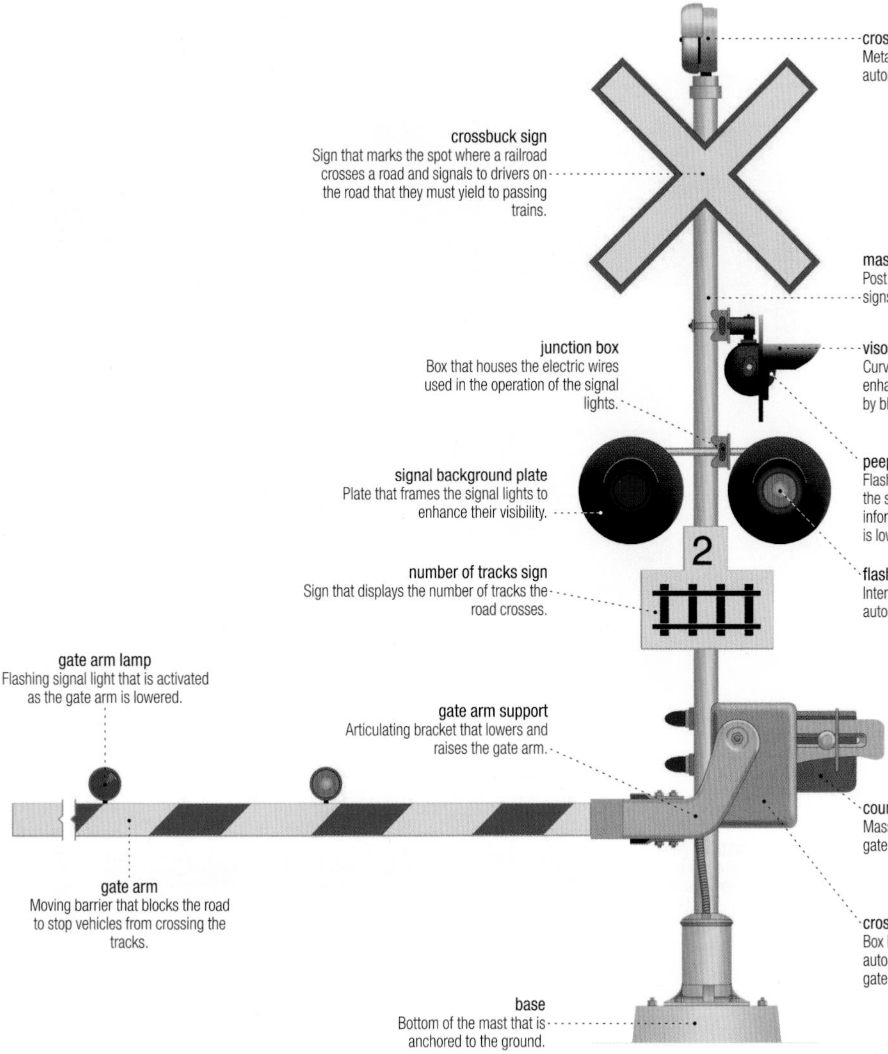

crossing bell
Metal sounding device that rings automatically as a train approaches.

crossbuck sign
Sign that marks the spot where a railroad crosses a road and signals to drivers on the road that they must yield to passing trains.

mast
Post that supports the crossing signs and signal lights.

junction box
Box that houses the electric wires used in the operation of the signal lights.

visor
Curved sheet of metal that enhances a signal light's visibility by blocking sunlight.

signal background plate
Plate that frames the signal lights to enhance their visibility.

peep hole
Flashing signal light that is activated at the same time as the flashing lights to inform the engineer that the gate arm is lowered.

number of tracks sign
Sign that displays the number of tracks the road crosses.

flashing light
Intermittent signal light that is activated automatically as the train approaches.

gate arm lamp
Flashing signal light that is activated as the gate arm is lowered.

gate arm support
Articulating bracket that lowers and raises the gate arm.

counterweight
Mass that provides balance to the gate arm to facilitate its movement.

gate arm
Moving barrier that blocks the road to stop vehicles from crossing the tracks.

crossing gate mechanism
Box housing the mechanism that automatically lowers and raises the gate arm.

base
Bottom of the mast that is anchored to the ground.

subway

Electrified urban railroad built mainly underground for transporting passengers at frequent intervals.

subway station
Structure and facilities that provide passengers access to the subway.

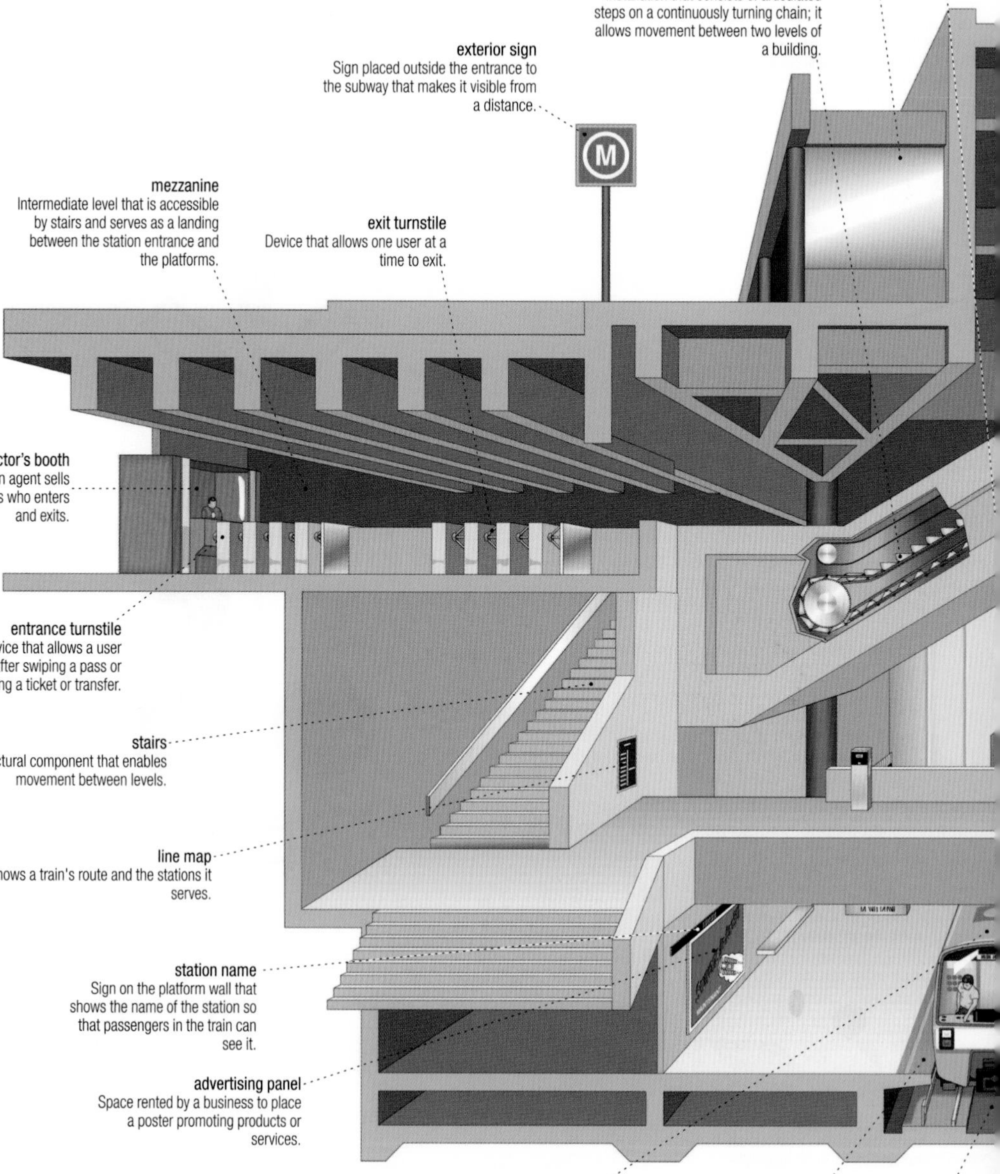

tunnel
Underground passageway through which the subway train travels between stations.

station entrance
Small structure built on a public thoroughfare that provides access to the subway station.

escalator
Installation that consists of articulated steps on a continuously turning chain; it allows movement between two levels of a building.

exterior sign
Sign placed outside the entrance to the subway that makes it visible from a distance.

mezzanine
Intermediate level that is accessible by stairs and serves as a landing between the station entrance and the platforms.

exit turnstile
Device that allows one user at a time to exit.

ticket collector's booth
Kiosk protected by glass where an agent sells tickets and passes, and controls who enters and exits.

entrance turnstile
Automatic device that allows a user to enter after swiping a pass or inserting a ticket or transfer.

stairs
Structural component that enables movement between levels.

line map
Chart that shows a train's route and the stations it serves.

station name
Sign on the platform wall that shows the name of the station so that passengers in the train can see it.

advertising panel
Space rented by a business to place a poster promoting products or services.

subway train
Set of cars that is pulled by a motor car and carries passengers.

platform edge
Zone along the edge of the platform, usually demarcated by a safety line.

track
Course that consists of electrified rails on which

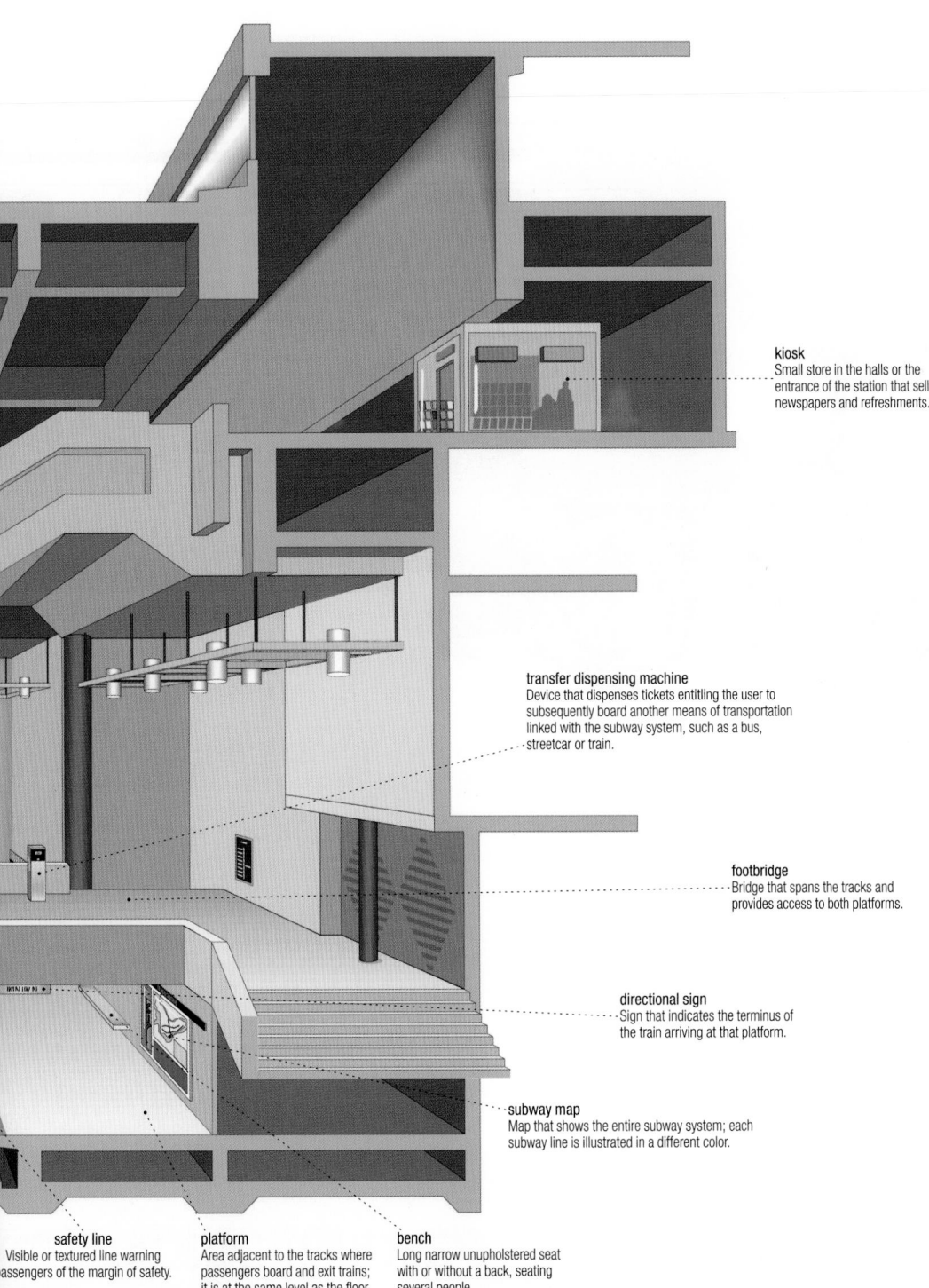

kiosk
Small store in the halls or the
entrance of the station that sells
newspapers and refreshments.

transfer dispensing machine
Device that dispenses tickets entitling the user to
subsequently board another means of transportation
linked with the subway system, such as a bus,
streetcar or train.

footbridge
Bridge that spans the tracks and
provides access to both platforms.

directional sign
Sign that indicates the terminus of
the train arriving at that platform.

subway map
Map that shows the entire subway system; each
subway line is illustrated in a different color.

safety line
Visible or textured line warning
passengers of the margin of safety.

platform
Area adjacent to the tracks where
passengers board and exit trains;
it is at the same level as the floor
of the trains.

bench
Long narrow unupholstered seat
with or without a back, seating
several people.

TRANSPORT AND MACHINERY

subway

passenger car
Vehicle that rolls along subway tracks
and transports passengers.

communication set
Loudspeaker phone used for
talking to the train driver.

emergency brake
Device that stops the train; it
is available to users in case of
emergency.

side door
Sliding door that opens onto the station
platforms for passengers to enter
and exit.

ventilator
Grille that circulates fresh air
throughout the car.

side handrail
Handle on the wall next to the door
for passengers to hold onto while
the train is in motion.

light
Fixtures for illuminatin
of the car.

inflated guiding tire
Tire mounted at right angles to the
carrying tire; it rolls against the guiding
bar to guide the truck.

inflated carrying tire
Nitrogen-filled tire that supports and
conveys the car.

suspension
Assembly that dissipates the
vibrations occurring as the wheels
roll along the tracks.

window
Opening containing thick glass that
does not open.

advertising sign
Poster on a space rented by a business
that promotes products or services.

handrail
Floor-to-ceiling pole in the middle
of the aisle for passengers to hold
onto while the train is in motion.

subway map
Map that shows the entire subway system; each
subway line is illustrated in a different color.

single seat
Seat for one passenger.

heating vent
Grating through which warm air is
forced to heat the car interior.

subway train
Set of cars that is pulled by a motor
car and carries passengers.

doub
Bench with space
pass

motor car
Vehicle with an electric motor and
braking system for pulling one or
more cars.

truck
Carriage whose motorized wheels
pull the subway car.

trailer car
Freewheeling car pulled by a
motor car.

motor car
Vehicle with an electric motor and
braking system for pulling one or
more cars.

subway

truck and track
The most up-to-date subway trucks ride on tires, which provide fast acceleration and little noise or vibration.

steel safety wheel
Auxiliary regular train wheel that comes in contact with the running rail in the event the tire deflates and during switching.

inflated carrying tire
Nitrogen-filled tire that supports and conveys the car.

sliding block
Shoe taking the current from the guiding and current bar.

inflated guiding tire
Tire mounted at right angles to the carrying tire; it rolls against the guiding bar to guide the truck.

guiding and current bar
al bar against which the guiding tire rolls; it also supplies the traction current.

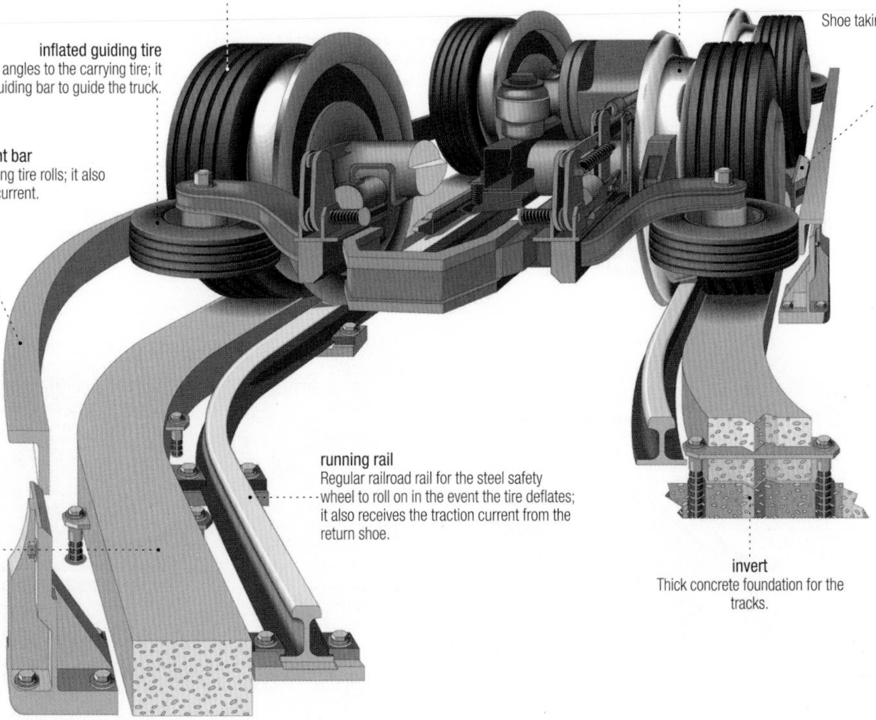

running rail
Regular railroad rail for the steel safety wheel to roll on in the event the tire deflates; it also receives the traction current from the return shoe.

runway
oncrete track that is fixed
ert on which the tires roll.

invert
Thick concrete foundation for the tracks.

streetcar

Electrically powered vehicle for transporting people; it rolls on tracks embedded in city streets and on the edge of roadways.

pantograph
Articulating mechanism on the roof of the streetcar that collects electricity from an overhead catenary.

catenary
One or more overhead wires supplying electricity to the streetcar.

route sign
that is usually placed on the
ear and side of the streetcar
to show its route number.

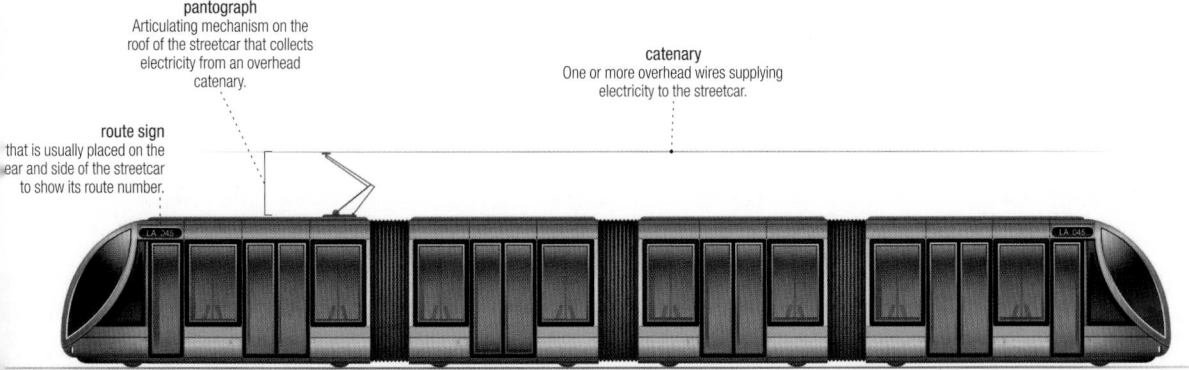

harbor

Site for refueling and repairing ships, loading and unloading cargo and embarking and disembarking passengers.

canal lock
Structure with a lock chamber that can be filled with water or emptied to raise or lower a ship from one water level to another.

dry dock
Dock where water is pumped out so that a ship's hull can be repaired, cleaned or painted.

dock crane
Crane that rolls along rails the length of the wharf and uses a moving arm to load and unload cargo in forms such as container, bulk and break bulk.

gate
Waterproof device that closes a dock.

container-loading bridge
Cantilevered gantry crane along the quay for loading and unloading containers.

transit shed
Warehouse located near the wharf for temporarily storing cargo.

bulk terminal
Area with installations and equipment to store, sort and handle bulk items, such as ore and coal.

wharf
Structure for docking ships so that passengers can embark and disembark and cargo can be loaded and unloaded.

cold shed
Insulated refrigerated structure for storing perishable foodstuffs.

lighthouse
Tower with a powerful lamp at the top for guiding ships.

passenger terminal
Structures and facilities where passengers embark and disembark ships.

oil terminal
Area with installations and equipment to store petroleum products and load them into tankers.

tanker
Ship with large reservoirs for transporting liquid petroleum products.

ferryboat
Shuttle boat for carrying vehicles with their cargo and passengers.

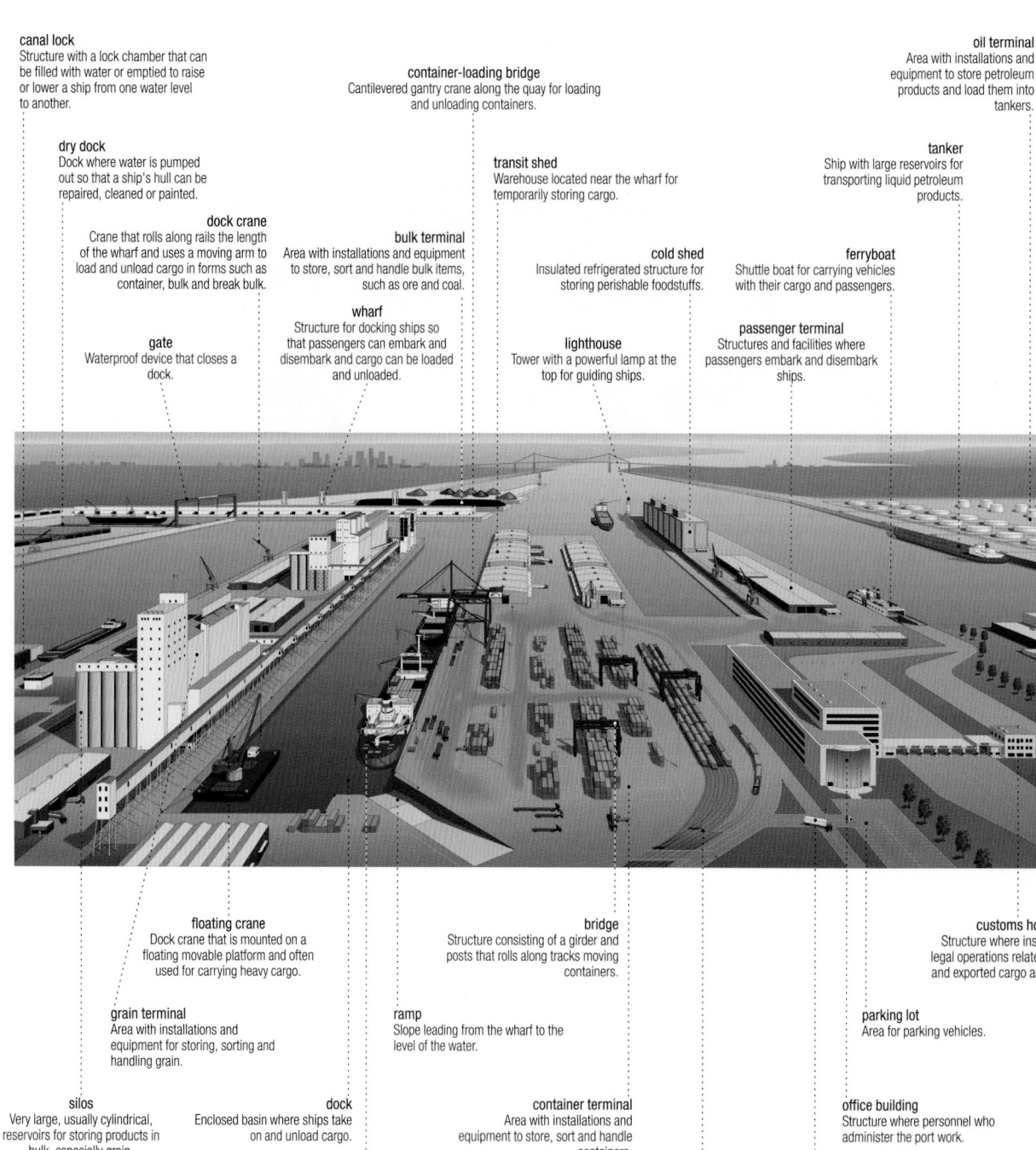

floating crane
Dock crane that is mounted on a floating movable platform and often used for carrying heavy cargo.

grain terminal
Area with installations and equipment for storing, sorting and handling grain.

silos
Very large, usually cylindrical, reservoirs for storing products in bulk, especially grain.

dock
Enclosed basin where ships take on and unload cargo.

container ship
Ship that is designed for transporting cargo in containers in its hold and on its deck.

bridge
Structure consisting of a girder and posts that rolls along tracks moving containers.

ramp
Slope leading from the wharf to the level of the water.

container terminal
Area with installations and equipment to store, sort and handle containers.

terminal railway
Railroad tracks leading onto a wharf for transshipping containers from a ship to a car or vice versa.

customs house
Structure where inspec[...] legal operations related to [...] and exported cargo are ca[...]

parking lot
Area for parking vehicles.

office building
Structure where personnel who administer the port work.

road transport
Transportation of cargo by truck on public roads.

canal lock

Structure with a lock chamber that can be filled with water or emptied to raise or lower a ship from one water level to another.

parts of a canal lock

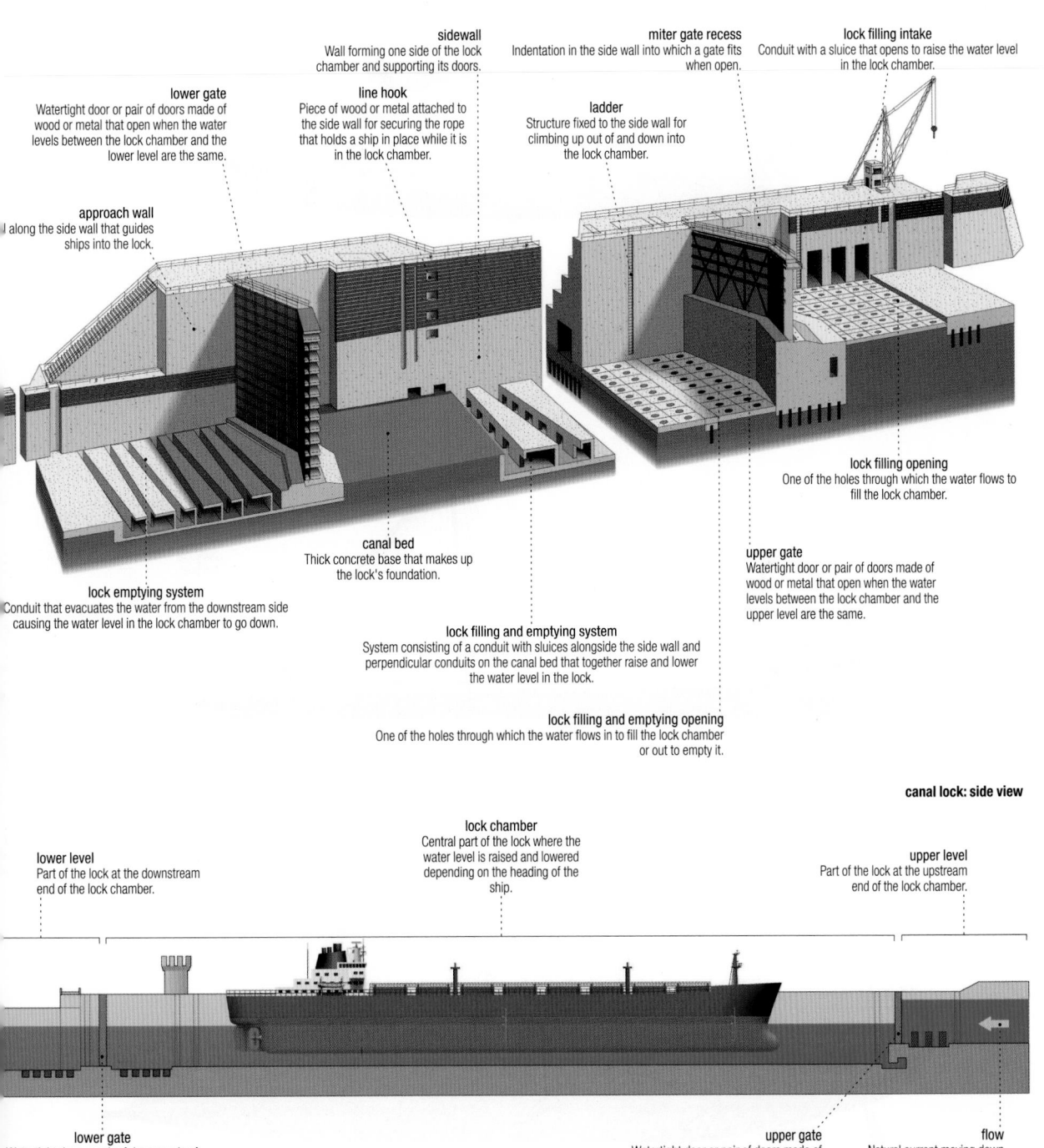

sidewall
Wall forming one side of the lock chamber and supporting its doors.

miter gate recess
Indentation in the side wall into which a gate fits when open.

lock filling intake
Conduit with a sluice that opens to raise the water level in the lock chamber.

lower gate
Watertight door or pair of doors made of wood or metal that open when the water levels between the lock chamber and the lower level are the same.

line hook
Piece of wood or metal attached to the side wall for securing the rope that holds a ship in place while it is in the lock chamber.

ladder
Structure fixed to the side wall for climbing up out of and down into the lock chamber.

approach wall
Wall along the side wall that guides ships into the lock.

lock filling opening
One of the holes through which the water flows to fill the lock chamber.

canal bed
Thick concrete base that makes up the lock's foundation.

upper gate
Watertight door or pair of doors made of wood or metal that open when the water levels between the lock chamber and the upper level are the same.

lock emptying system
Conduit that evacuates the water from the downstream side causing the water level in the lock chamber to go down.

lock filling and emptying system
System consisting of a conduit with sluices alongside the side wall and perpendicular conduits on the canal bed that together raise and lower the water level in the lock.

lock filling and emptying opening
One of the holes through which the water flows in to fill the lock chamber or out to empty it.

canal lock: side view

lower level
Part of the lock at the downstream end of the lock chamber.

lock chamber
Central part of the lock where the water level is raised and lowered depending on the heading of the ship.

upper level
Part of the lock at the upstream end of the lock chamber.

lower gate
Watertight door or pair of doors made of wood or metal that open when the water levels between the lock chamber and the lower level are the same.

upper gate
Watertight door or pair of doors made of wood or metal that open when the water levels between the lock chamber and the upper level are the same.

flow
Natural current moving down the grade from upstream to downstream.

TRANSPORT AND MACHINERY

ancient ships

Over the course of history, navigation has played a key role in discovering new lands and in developing trade between peoples.

longship
Sailing ship used by the Vikings during the Middle Ages; it had square sails, oars and a prow and stern that were usually sculpted.

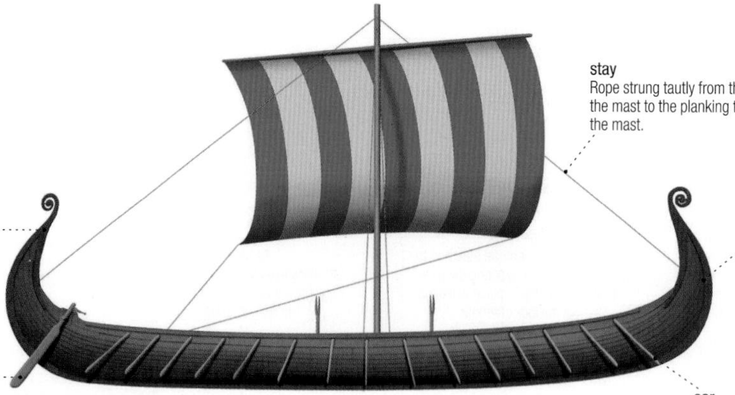

stay
Rope strung tautly from the top of the mast to the planking to stabilize the mast.

stern
Rear end of a ship.

stempost
Main timber reinforcing the prow.

steering oar
Oar at the back of the ship acting as rudder.

oar
Long piece of wood that is broad and flat at one end; it is mounted on the boat and pulled by one or more people to propel the boat.

galley
Warship with a sail and oars that was used from ancient times until the 18th century.

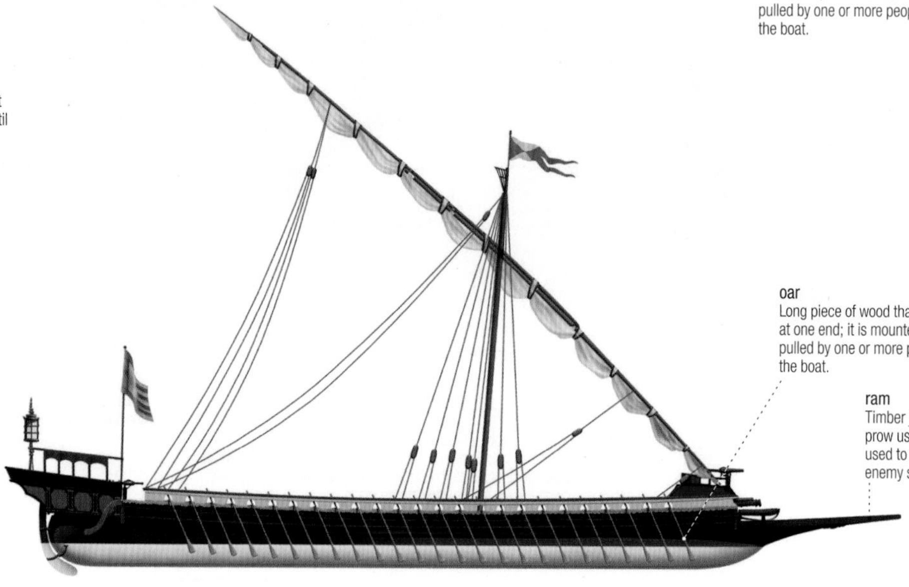

oar
Long piece of wood that is broad and flat at one end; it is mounted on the boat and pulled by one or more people to propel the boat.

ram
Timber jutting out in front of t[ ] prow usually at water level; it used to punch holes in the hu[ ] enemy ships.

trireme
Warship used by the Romans with a ram, a sail and three vertical rows of oars.

figurehead
Sculpted timber on the prow of a[ ] ship in ancient times that depicte[ ] a human, a god or a mythical creature.

steering oar
Oar at the back of the ship acting as rudder.

oar
Long piece of wood that is broad and flat at one end; it is mounted on the boat and pulled by one or more people to propel the boat.

ram
Timber jutting out in front of the prow usually at water level; it was used to punch holes in the hulls of enemy ships.

ancient ships

side-wheeler
Ship used in the 19th century that was propelled by steam, which turned two paddle wheels.

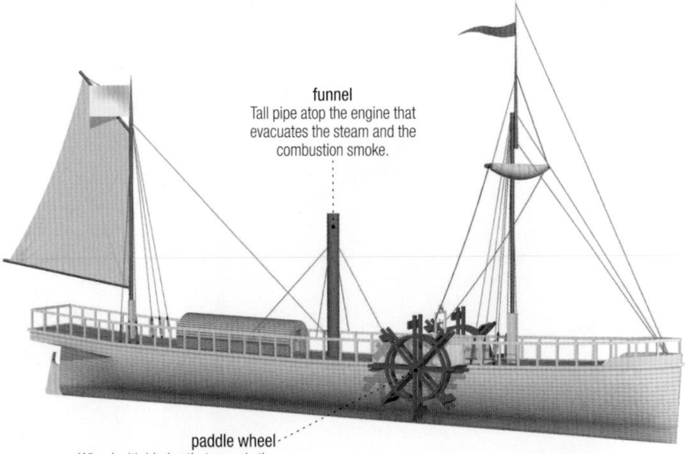

funnel
Tall pipe atop the engine that evacuates the steam and the combustion smoke.

paddle wheel
Wheel with blades that propels the boat; it is driven by a steam engine.

galleon
Large warship with sails that was used by the Spanish in the 17th and 18th centuries for trading with the colonies.

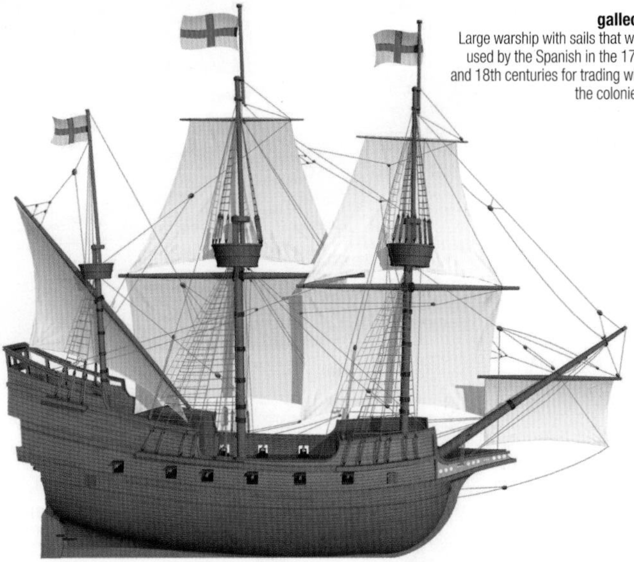

avel
ship with three or four masts; as used especially in the 15th 16th centuries for exploration.

traditional ships

oats characteristic of various parts of the world for a number of generations; they are used as a means of transportation, for fishing, commerce and exploration.

out canoe
t boat used in Africa and Oceania is made from one piece of wood is propelled by a paddle or a sail.

outrigger boom
Wooden pole connecting the outrigger to the hull.

hull
Part of the boat's structure that forms a watertight vessel.

outrigger canoe
Dugout canoe that is stabilized by one or two outriggers.

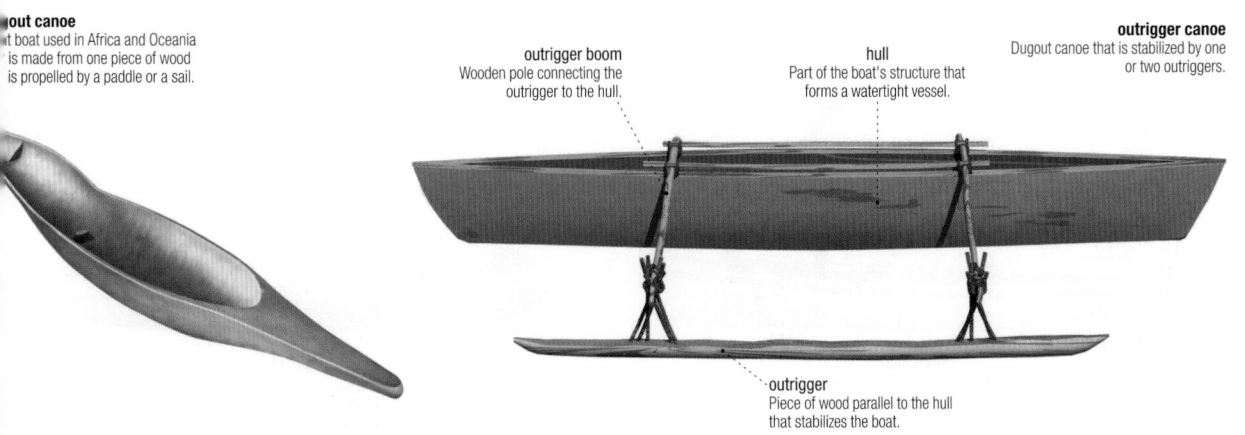

outrigger
Piece of wood parallel to the hull that stabilizes the boat.

TRANSPORT AND MACHINERY

traditional ships

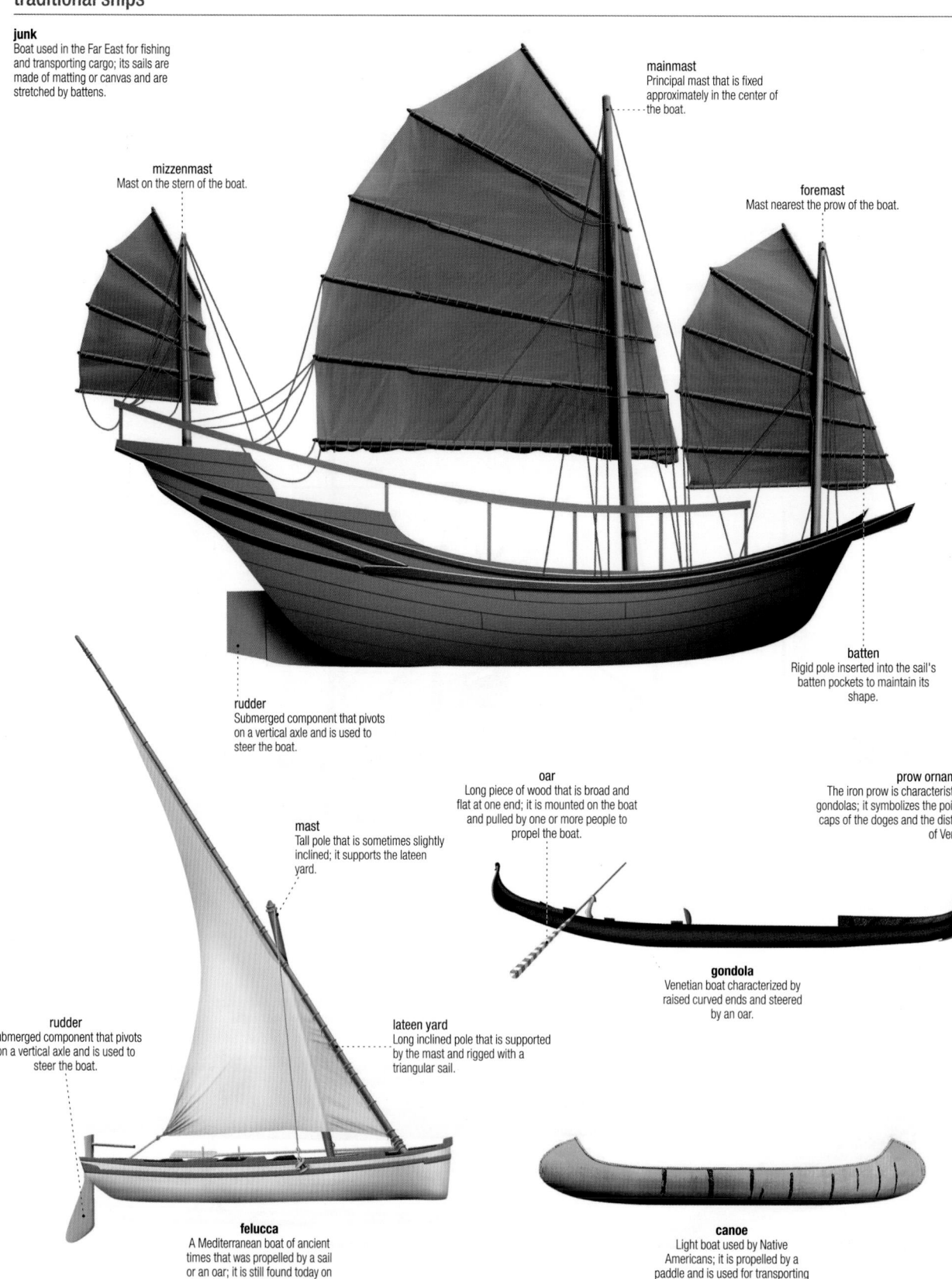

junk
Boat used in the Far East for fishing and transporting cargo; its sails are made of matting or canvas and are stretched by battens.

mainmast
Principal mast that is fixed approximately in the center of the boat.

mizzenmast
Mast on the stern of the boat.

foremast
Mast nearest the prow of the boat.

batten
Rigid pole inserted into the sail's batten pockets to maintain its shape.

rudder
Submerged component that pivots on a vertical axle and is used to steer the boat.

oar
Long piece of wood that is broad and flat at one end; it is mounted on the boat and pulled by one or more people to propel the boat.

prow orname
The iron prow is characteristic gondolas; it symbolizes the pointe caps of the doges and the distric of Venic

mast
Tall pole that is sometimes slightly inclined; it supports the lateen yard.

gondola
Venetian boat characterized by raised curved ends and steered by an oar.

rudder
Submerged component that pivots on a vertical axle and is used to steer the boat.

lateen yard
Long inclined pole that is supported by the mast and rigged with a triangular sail.

felucca
A Mediterranean boat of ancient times that was propelled by a sail or an oar; it is still found today on the Nile.

canoe
Light boat used by Native Americans; it is propelled by a paddle and is used for transporting people and cargo.

examples of sails

ils: sections of durable fabric that are sewn together and mounted on a mast; they create a surface that causes a boat to move when the wind blows against it.

Bermuda sail
Triangular sail that is also called a Marconi sail; its longest side is attached directly to a tall mast and its base is attached to a pole called a boom.

gaff sail
Trapezoidal sail that is rigged entirely aft of the mast; its top edge is supported by a diagonal yard called a gaff.

lug sail
Trapezoidal sail that hangs from a yard; it is attached to the mast one-third of the way from its end.

lateen sail
Triangular sail supported by a long tilted yard called a lateen yard; it is attached to the mast in its middle.

square sail
Trapezoidal sail that hangs from a yard; it is attached to the mast in its middle.

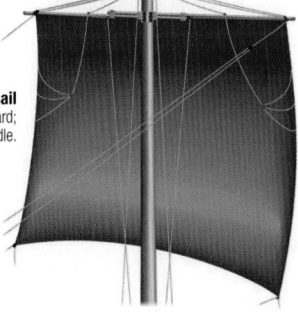

spritsail
Trapezoidal sail that is rigged entirely aft of the mast and is supported by a long, diagonal yard, called a sprit; it articulates at the bottom of the mast.

examples of rigs

Rigs: various combinations of sails that distinguish one sailboat from another.

yawl
Fishing boat with a tall mast and one gaff or Bermuda sail; it has two jibs and a small mast aft of the tiller.

ketch
Two-masted pleasure sailboat; it has a mainmast and a mizzenmast fore of the tiller, which distinguishes it from the cutter.

schooner
Two-masted ship with a foremast and a mainmast; it has gaff sails and topsails and sometimes a staysail.

whale boat
Fishing boat propelled mainly by oars but sometimes fitted with one or two lug sails and a jib.

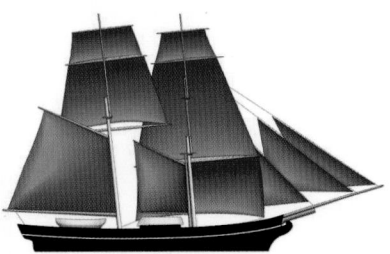

brigantine
Two-masted ship that is lighter than the brig and rigged differently.

brig
Two-masted ship with a foremast and a mainmast and square sails; a spanker can be added to the mainmast and three jibs to a bowsprit.

four-masted bark

Sailboat with four masts and square sails except for the jiggermast, which carries a gaff sail.

upper section of mizzenmast

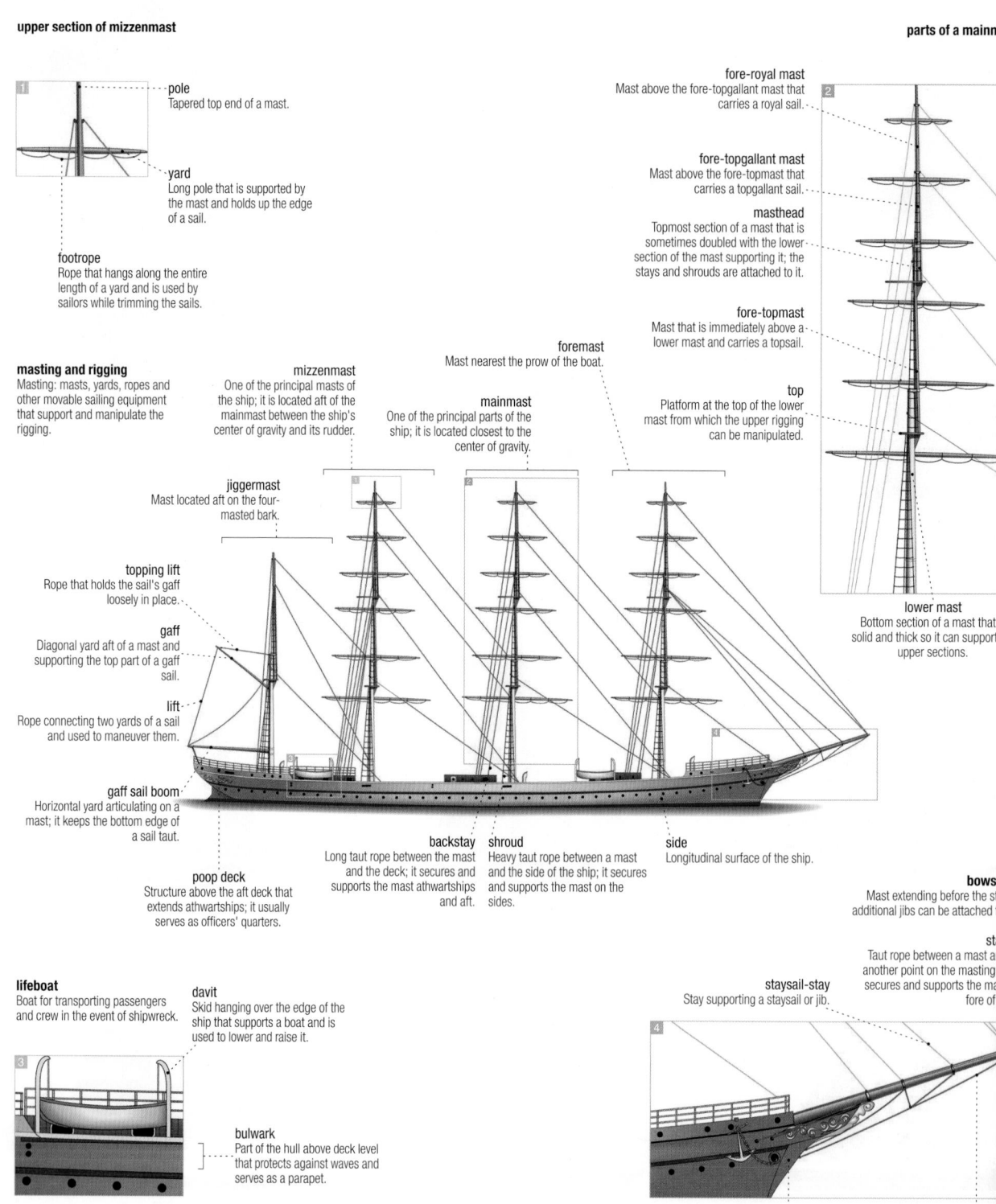

pole
Tapered top end of a mast.

yard
Long pole that is supported by the mast and holds up the edge of a sail.

footrope
Rope that hangs along the entire length of a yard and is used by sailors while trimming the sails.

fore-royal mast
Mast above the fore-topgallant mast that carries a royal sail.

fore-topgallant mast
Mast above the fore-topmast that carries a topgallant sail.

masthead
Topmost section of a mast that is sometimes doubled with the lower section of the mast supporting it; the stays and shrouds are attached to it.

fore-topmast
Mast that is immediately above a lower mast and carries a topsail.

top
Platform at the top of the lower mast from which the upper rigging can be manipulated.

masting and rigging
Masting: masts, yards, ropes and other movable sailing equipment that support and manipulate the rigging.

mizzenmast
One of the principal masts of the ship; it is located aft of the mainmast between the ship's center of gravity and its rudder.

foremast
Mast nearest the prow of the boat.

mainmast
One of the principal parts of the ship; it is located closest to the center of gravity.

jiggermast
Mast located aft on the four-masted bark.

topping lift
Rope that holds the sail's gaff loosely in place.

gaff
Diagonal yard aft of a mast and supporting the top part of a gaff sail.

lift
Rope connecting two yards of a sail and used to maneuver them.

gaff sail boom
Horizontal yard articulating on a mast; it keeps the bottom edge of a sail taut.

lower mast
Bottom section of a mast that solid and thick so it can support upper sections.

poop deck
Structure above the aft deck that extends athwartships; it usually serves as officers' quarters.

backstay
Long taut rope between the mast and the deck; it secures and supports the mast athwartships and aft.

shroud
Heavy taut rope between a mast and the side of the ship; it secures and supports the mast on the sides.

side
Longitudinal surface of the ship.

bowsp
Mast extending before the st additional jibs can be attached t

sta
Taut rope between a mast an another point on the masting; secures and supports the ma fore of

lifeboat
Boat for transporting passengers and crew in the event of shipwreck.

davit
Skid hanging over the edge of the ship that supports a boat and is used to lower and raise it.

staysail-stay
Stay supporting a staysail or jib.

bulwark
Part of the hull above deck level that protects against waves and serves as a parapet.

stem
Main timber reinforcing the prow.

bobstay
Rope counterbalancing the tension caused by the stays and the staysail-stays on the bowsprit.

four-masted bark

sails
A sailboat's sails that are rigged on the bowsprit, the foremast, the main masts, the jiggermast and between these masts.

mizzen royal staysail
Triangular sail rigged on the stay supporting the aft fore-royal mast.

mizzen topgallant staysail
Triangular sail on the stay supporting the aft fore-topgallant mast.

main royal sail
Small square sail above the topgallant sail at the top of the mainmast.

mizzen topmast staysail
Triangular sail on the stay supporting the aft fore-topmast.

main upper topgallant sail
Square sail under the main royal sail.

jigger topgallant staysail
Highest triangular sail among the sails rigged between the mizzenmast and the jiggermast.

main lower topgallant sail
Square sail between the main upper topgallant sail and the main upper topsail.

fore royal sail
Small square sail at the top of the foremast above the fore topgallant sail.

jigger topmast staysail
Triangular sail below the jigger topgallant staysail.

main upper topsail
Square sail between the main lower topgallant sail and the main lower topsail.

upper fore topgallant sail
Square sail below the fore royal sail.

mizzen royal brace
...at causes the yard supporting the royal sail to pivot around the mizzenmast.

lower fore topgallant sail
Square sail between the upper fore topgallant sail and the upper fore topsail.

gaff topsail
...ail above a gaff sail and between the gaff and the top of the mast.

upper fore topsail
Square sail between the lower fore topgallant sail and the lower fore topsail.

spanker
...ail for the mizzenmast.

flying jib
Very light triangular staysail that is foremost on the bowsprit.

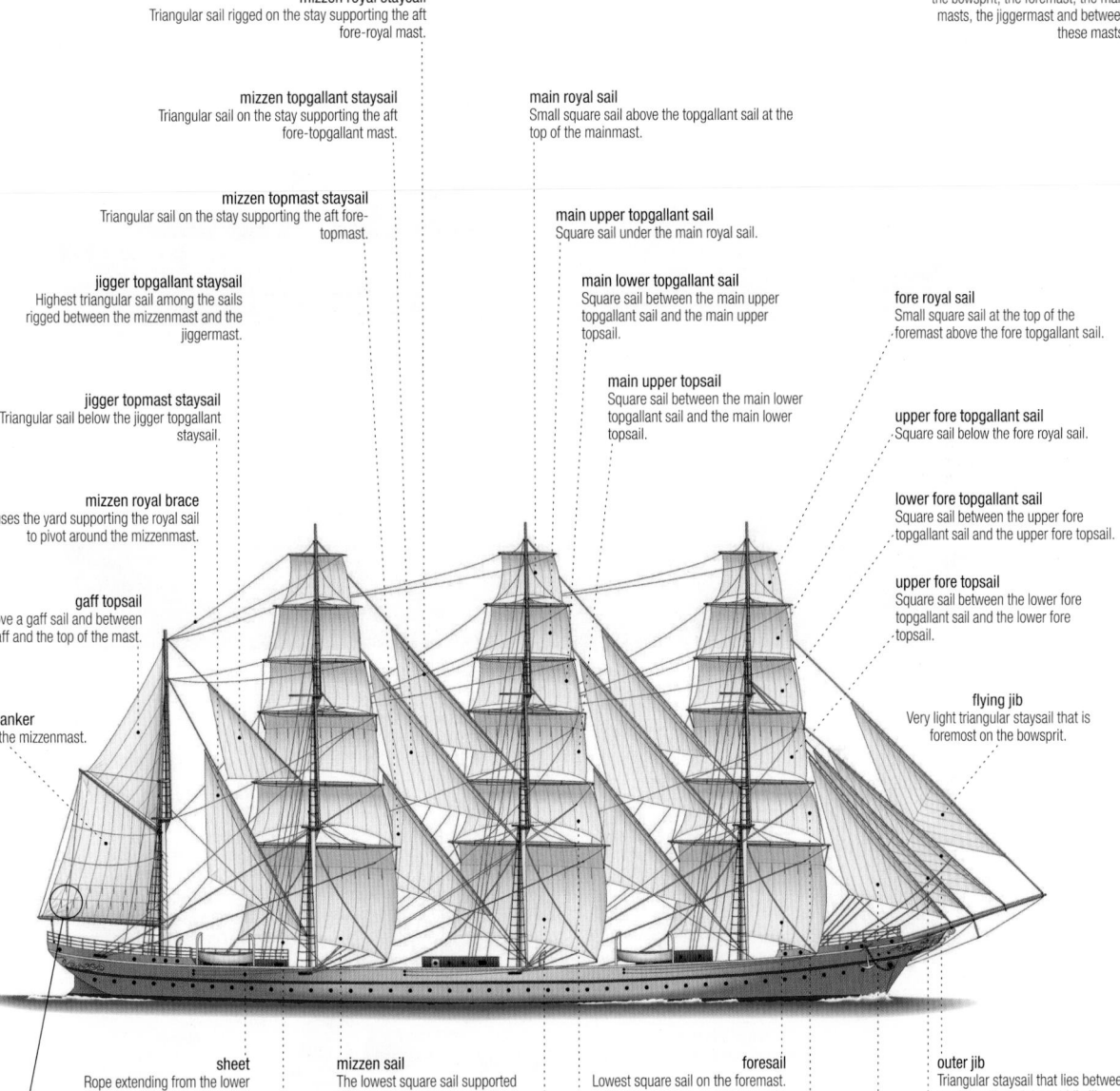

sheet
Rope extending from the lower corner of a sail for trimming it with respect to the wind direction.

mizzen sail
The lowest square sail supported by the mizzenmast.

foresail
Lowest square sail on the foremast.

outer jib
Triangular staysail that lies between the flying jib and the middle jib.

halyard
Rope for hoisting a sail or a yard.

main sail
Lowest square sail on the mainmast.

main lower topsail
Square sail above the main sail.

middle jib
Triangular staysail that lies between the outer jib and the inner jib.

lower fore topsail
Square sail above the foresail.

inner jib
Very heavy triangular staysail that lies farthest aft on the bowsprit.

reef band
Reinforced horizontal strip of canvas; a part of the sail can be gathered and tied to it to reduce the sail's wind surface.

reef point
One of several short ropes attached along the reef band on both sides of the sail for tying up the reefed sail.

examples of boats and ships

Boats and ships: floating structures for underwater exploration and transporting passengers and cargo across water.

drill ship
Ship for drilling for oil in deep water (half mile or more); it is more mobile but less stable than a drilling rig.

derrick
Metal structure erected over an oil well; tools for drilling through rock are raised and lowered through it.

bulk carrier
Ship for transporting raw dry materials, such as grain, coal and ore.

radar
Detection device that emits radio waves and receives their echo; it is used to avoid collisions and to navigate when visibility is reduced.

container ship
Ship that is designed for transporting cargo in containers in its hold and on its deck.

stack
Tall pipe atop the engine that evacuates the steam and the combustion smoke.

chart room
Office in which charts and other navigation documents are kept.

radio antenna
Metal conductor that emits and receives radio waves for communications.

bridge
Covered glassed-in platform from which officers and crew navigate the vessel.

crew quarters
Compartments for housing crew members.

lifeboat
Boat used for evacuating people from the ship in case of emergency.

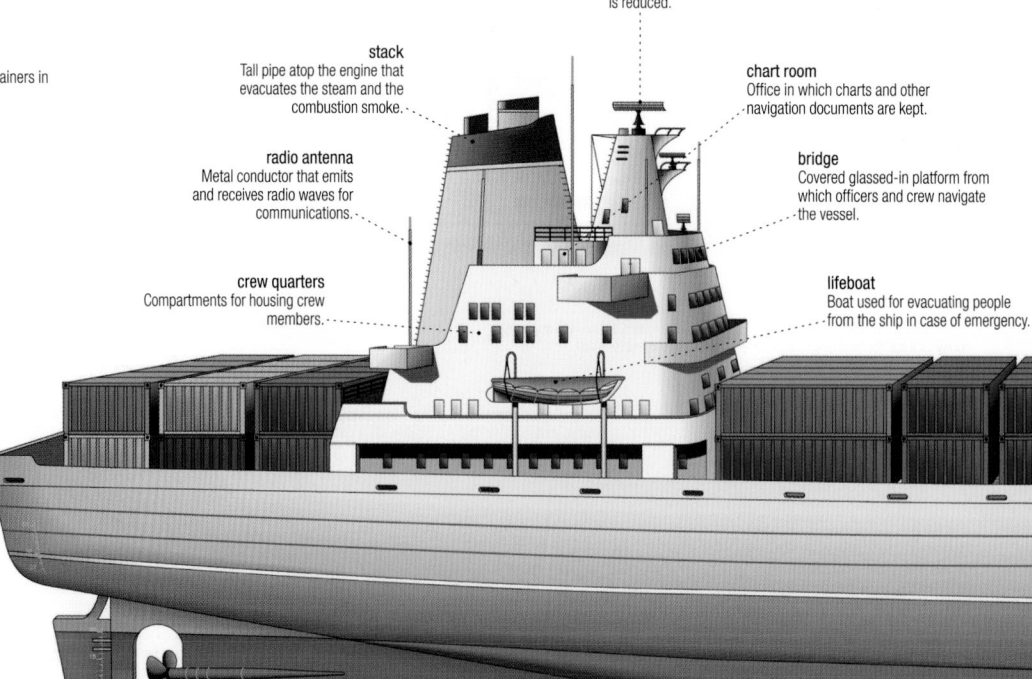

examples of boats and ships

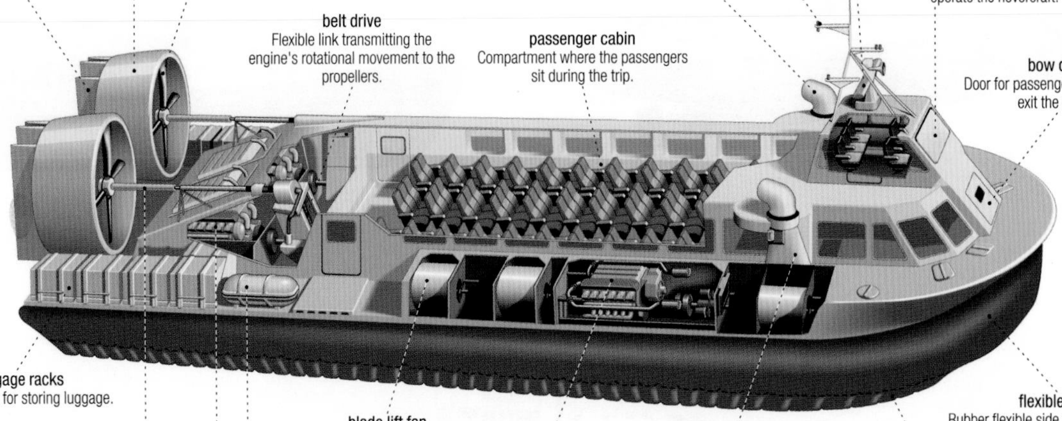

propeller duct
Metal part that surrounds the propeller and increases its power by concentrating its air intake.

dynamics propeller
Device that is made up of blades integrated with a shaft; it pushes air behind the hovercraft thus causing a forward movement.

rudder
...ting part behind the propeller ...st for steering the hovercraft.

radar
Detection device that emits radio waves and receives their echo; it is used to avoid collisions and to navigate when visibility is reduced.

navigation light
Lamp that is visible from afar to signal the hovercraft's presence.

hovercraft
Propeller vehicle that moves above water (or land) by gliding on a cushion of air it creates by blowing downward.

air intake
Intake opening for the fan.

control deck
Compartment from which the pilots operate the hovercraft.

belt drive
Flexible link transmitting the engine's rotational movement to the propellers.

passenger cabin
Compartment where the passengers sit during the trip.

bow door
Door for passengers to enter and exit the cabin.

baggage racks
...partment for storing luggage.

driveshaft
Part transmitting the engine's rotational movement to the propellers.

life raft
Inflatable boat that transports passengers and crew in case of emergency.

blade lift fan
Device blowing air downward under the hovercraft to keep it levitated.

lift-fan air inlet
Duct through which air enters, which is then blown downward under the hovercraft by the blade lift fan.

diesel lift engine
Power source using the combustion of an air/fuel mixture to drive the blade lift fan.

flexible skirt
Rubber flexible side that surrounds the edge of the hull to trap the air blown down by the lift fan; this increases pressure, which in turn causes lift.

skirt finger
Flexible and pliable extension to the skirt that adapts to the surface of the water.

diesel propulsion engine
Power source using the combustion of an air/fuel mixture to drive the propellers.

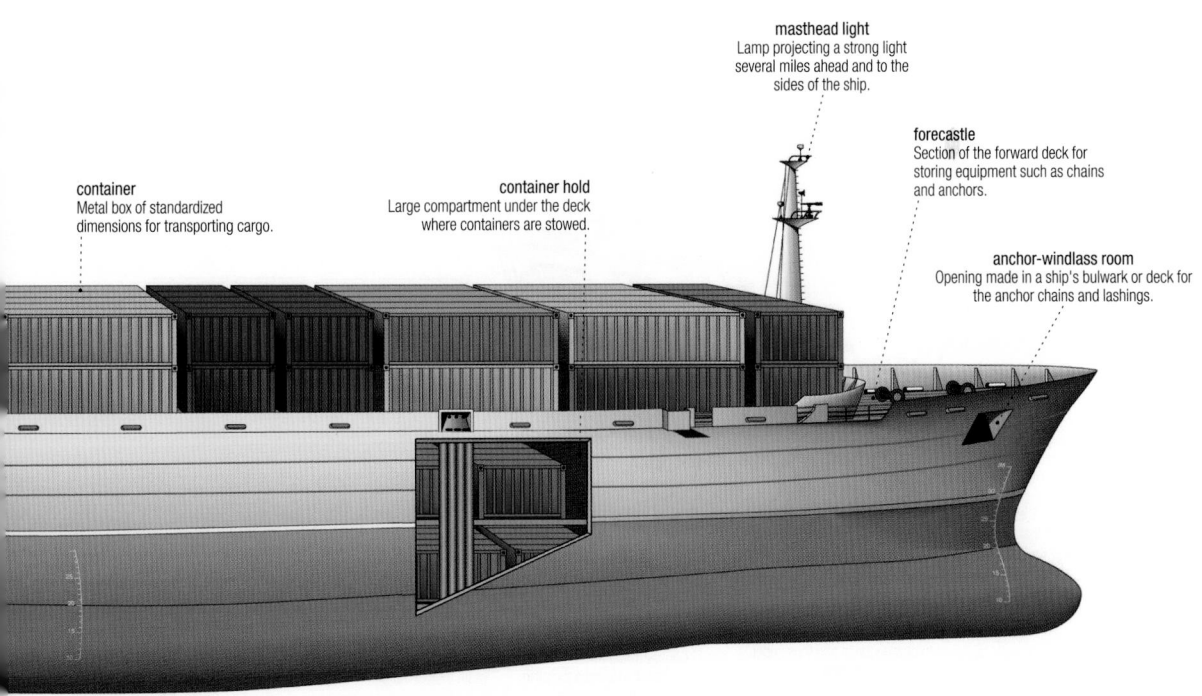

masthead light
Lamp projecting a strong light several miles ahead and to the sides of the ship.

forecastle
Section of the forward deck for storing equipment such as chains and anchors.

container
Metal box of standardized dimensions for transporting cargo.

container hold
Large compartment under the deck where containers are stowed.

anchor-windlass room
Opening made in a ship's bulwark or deck for the anchor chains and lashings.

examples of boats and ships

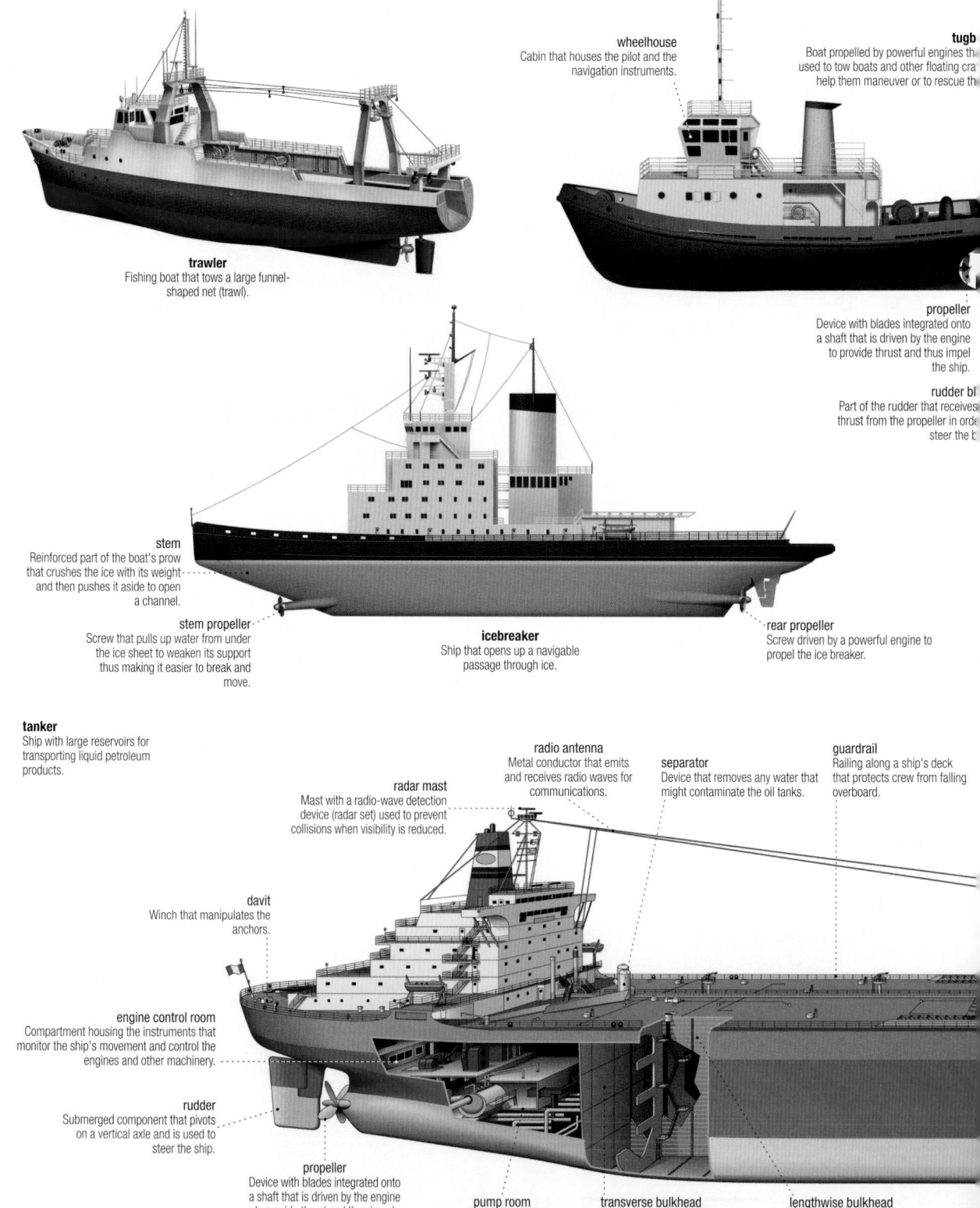

trawler
Fishing boat that tows a large funnel-shaped net (trawl).

wheelhouse
Cabin that houses the pilot and the navigation instruments.

tugb
Boat propelled by powerful engines tha used to tow boats and other floating cra help them maneuver or to rescue th

propeller
Device with blades integrated onto a shaft that is driven by the engine to provide thrust and thus impel the ship.

rudder bl
Part of the rudder that receives thrust from the propeller in orde steer the b

stem
Reinforced part of the boat's prow that crushes the ice with its weight and then pushes it aside to open a channel.

stem propeller
Screw that pulls up water from under the ice sheet to weaken its support thus making it easier to break and move.

icebreaker
Ship that opens up a navigable passage through ice.

rear propeller
Screw driven by a powerful engine to propel the ice breaker.

tanker
Ship with large reservoirs for transporting liquid petroleum products.

radio antenna
Metal conductor that emits and receives radio waves for communications.

separator
Device that removes any water that might contaminate the oil tanks.

guardrail
Railing along a ship's deck that protects crew from falling overboard.

radar mast
Mast with a radio-wave detection device (radar set) used to prevent collisions when visibility is reduced.

davit
Winch that manipulates the anchors.

engine control room
Compartment housing the instruments that monitor the ship's movement and control the engines and other machinery.

rudder
Submerged component that pivots on a vertical axle and is used to steer the ship.

propeller
Device with blades integrated onto a shaft that is driven by the engine to provide thrust and thus impel the ship.

pump room
Compartment housing the machinery that pumps the oil in and out of the tanks.

transverse bulkhead
Wall that divides the hold across the width thus demarcating the tanks.

lengthwise bulkhead
Wall that divides the hold along the length demarcate the tanks.

examples of boats and ships

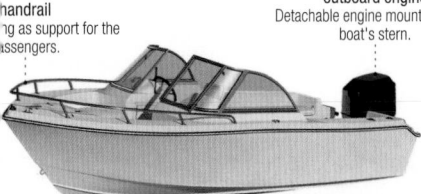

rboat
ure boat with an outboard engine
uising and waterskiing on inland
ways.

handrail
g as support for the
assengers.

outboard engine
Detachable engine mounted on the
boat's stern.

sundeck
Part of the deck for relaxation; it is
surrounded by a handrail.

cabin cruiser
Pleasure boat of various sizes and
speeds with a cabin fit to live in;
it can navigate the sea and inland
waterways.

houseboat
Motorized pleasure boat for
navigating inland waterways; it is
characterized by a long deck and a
cabin fit to live in.

pilothouse
Compartment from which the pilot
operates the boat.

fore and aft passage
Passageway on the deck that
connects the bow and the stern.

wheelhouse
houses the pilot and the
navigation instruments.

self-propelled barge
Large flat-bottomed vessel used
to transport cargo on rivers and
canals.

cargo hold
Spacious compartment where
cargo is stored.

loading arm
Device that facilitates the loading
and unloading of cargo from the
barge.

with pulleys that is mounted
t for handling loads.

foremast
Mast located near the bow of the
deck that supports the navigation
lights.

air relief valve
Device that allows air to escape as oil fills
the tanks to displace it.

derrick mast
Short thick mast that supports the
derrick.

tank
Watertight reservoir; the hold
is divided into several tanks to
prevent sloshing.

tank hatch cover
Watertight door that provides
access to a tank.

bitt
Metal cylindrical fittings attached
to the deck for fastening mooring
ropes and tow lines.

foam monitor
Pressurized mechanism that produces
foam for extinguishing fires.

main deck
Flat top that seals the hull and
protects the cargo; it provides
space for crew to circulate and for
auxiliary equipment.

mooring winch
Motorized spool around which a
mooring cable is wound.

sover cargo deck line
pipe that runs transversally and is
to fill and empty the tanks.

wall side
Vertical part of the hull below the
water line.

web frame
Metal reinforcement that spans the
hull transversally.

center keelson
Metal girder that runs along the
ship's longitudinal axis to reinforce
the bottom of the hull.

bulbous bow
Bulge in the bottom part of the
stem that reduces the hull's water
resistance.

TRANSPORT AND MACHINERY

examples of boats and ships

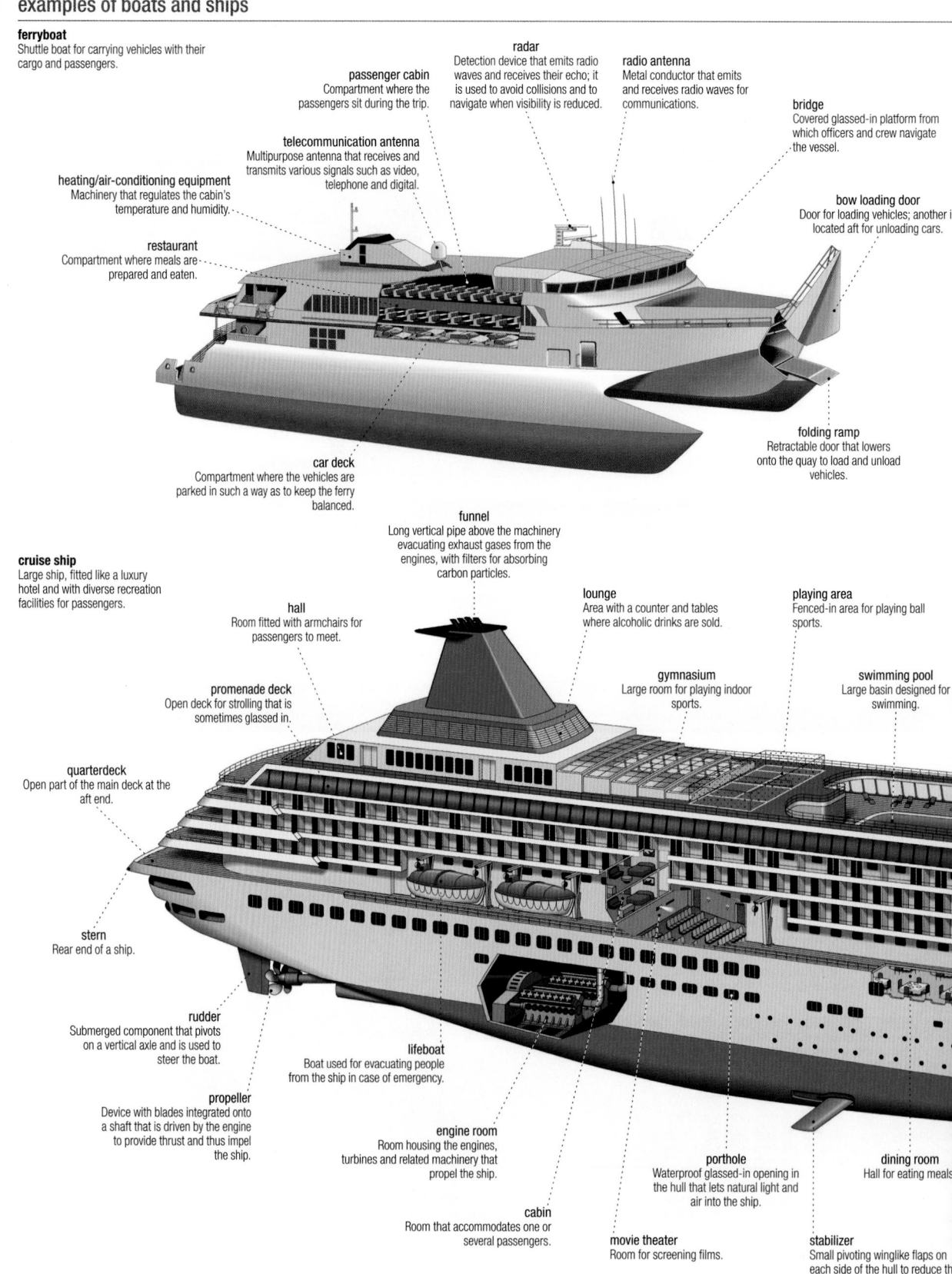

ferryboat
Shuttle boat for carrying vehicles with their cargo and passengers.

passenger cabin
Compartment where the passengers sit during the trip.

radar
Detection device that emits radio waves and receives their echo; it is used to avoid collisions and to navigate when visibility is reduced.

radio antenna
Metal conductor that emits and receives radio waves for communications.

telecommunication antenna
Multipurpose antenna that receives and transmits various signals such as video, telephone and digital.

bridge
Covered glassed-in platform from which officers and crew navigate the vessel.

heating/air-conditioning equipment
Machinery that regulates the cabin's temperature and humidity.

bow loading door
Door for loading vehicles; another is located aft for unloading cars.

restaurant
Compartment where meals are prepared and eaten.

folding ramp
Retractable door that lowers onto the quay to load and unload vehicles.

car deck
Compartment where the vehicles are parked in such a way as to keep the ferry balanced.

funnel
Long vertical pipe above the machinery evacuating exhaust gases from the engines, with filters for absorbing carbon particles.

cruise ship
Large ship, fitted like a luxury hotel and with diverse recreation facilities for passengers.

hall
Room fitted with armchairs for passengers to meet.

lounge
Area with a counter and tables where alcoholic drinks are sold.

playing area
Fenced-in area for playing ball sports.

promenade deck
Open deck for strolling that is sometimes glassed in.

gymnasium
Large room for playing indoor sports.

swimming pool
Large basin designed for swimming.

quarterdeck
Open part of the main deck at the aft end.

stern
Rear end of a ship.

rudder
Submerged component that pivots on a vertical axle and is used to steer the boat.

lifeboat
Boat used for evacuating people from the ship in case of emergency.

propeller
Device with blades integrated onto a shaft that is driven by the engine to provide thrust and thus impel the ship.

engine room
Room housing the engines, turbines and related machinery that propel the ship.

porthole
Waterproof glassed-in opening in the hull that lets natural light and air into the ship.

dining room
Hall for eating meals

cabin
Room that accommodates one or several passengers.

movie theater
Room for screening films.

stabilizer
Small pivoting winglike flaps on each side of the hull to reduce the rolling motion.

examples of boats and ships

hydrofoil
Fast boat with foils, which lift and support the hull above water when cruising speed is reached.

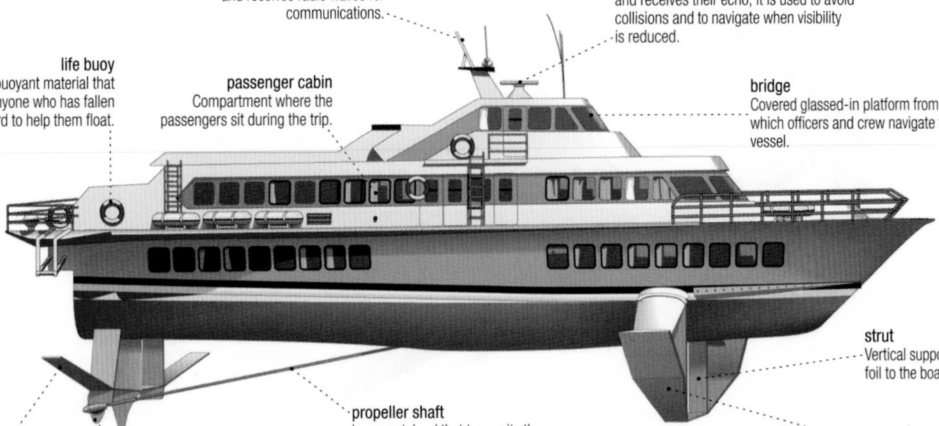

radio antenna
Metal conductor that emits and receives radio waves for communications.

radar
Detection device that emits radio waves and receives their echo; it is used to avoid collisions and to navigate when visibility is reduced.

life buoy
Ring made of buoyant material that is thrown to anyone who has fallen overboard to help them float.

passenger cabin
Compartment where the passengers sit during the trip.

bridge
Covered glassed-in platform from which officers and crew navigate the vessel.

strut
Vertical support that connects each foil to the boat's hull.

rear foil
Wing on each side of the stern.

propeller
Device with blades integrated onto a shaft that is driven by the engine to provide thrust and thus impel the ship.

propeller shaft
Long metal rod that transmits the motor's rotational movement to the propeller.

front foil
Wing on each side of the prow.

surface-piercing foils
Parts that lift the boat when cruising speed has been reached; they also stabilize the boat.

communication antenna
purpose antenna that receives and mits various signals such as video, hone and digital.

radio antenna
Metal conductor that emits and receives radio waves for communications.

sundeck
Usually the highest and sunniest deck with a pool and lounge chairs.

radar
Detection device that emits radio waves and receives their echo; it is used to avoid collisions and to navigate when visibility is reduced.

open-air terrace
Outdoor platform that is formed from the roof of the deck below and is protected by a guardrail.

bridge
Covered glassed-in platform from which officers and crew navigate the vessel.

forecastle
Open foremost part of the main deck.

port side
Left side of the ship when looking forward.

bow
Foremost part of the ship.

anchor-windlass room
Opening in the hull for the ship's anchor chains and towropes.

bulbous bow
Bulge in the bottom part of the stem that reduces the hull's water resistance.

ballroom
rge hall with a dance floor for holding dances and balls.

captain's quarters
Lodgings for the captain located aft of the bridge on the starboard side.

bow thruster
Propeller on each side of the stem bulb for maneuvering the ship to port or starboard at slow speeds.

starboard side
Right side of the ship when looking forward.

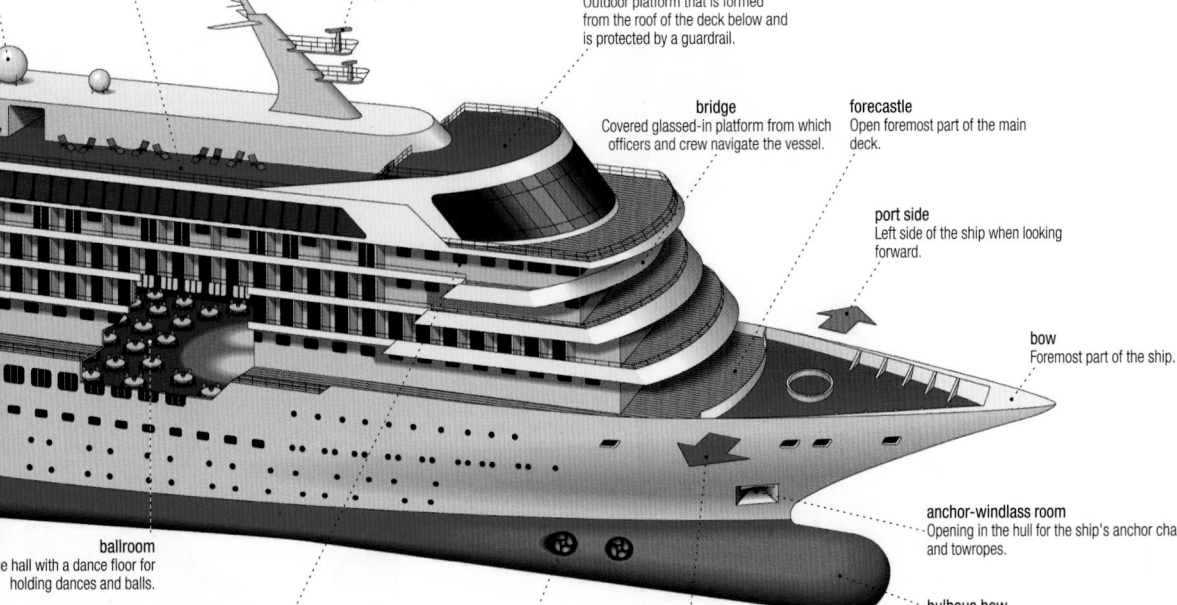

anchor

Usually steel part that is attached to a chain or cable; it hooks onto the bottom of a body of water to keep the boat from moving.

parts of an anchor
The traditional anchor is made up of a shank with a stock at one end and two arms ending in palms at the other end.

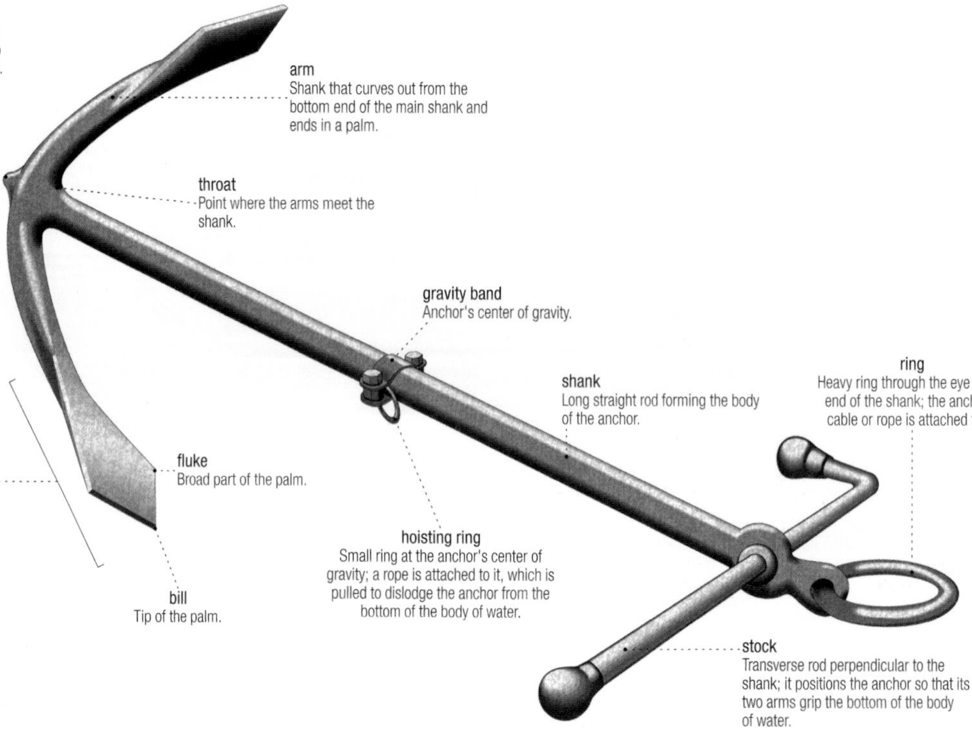

arm
Shank that curves out from the bottom end of the main shank and ends in a palm.

crown
Point at the end of the shank.

throat
Point where the arms meet the shank.

gravity band
Anchor's center of gravity.

shank
Long straight rod forming the body of the anchor.

ring
Heavy ring through the eye at the end of the shank; the anchor's cable or rope is attached to it.

palm
Flat pointed part at the end of the arm; it sinks into the ground beneath the water to grip it.

fluke
Broad part of the palm.

hoisting ring
Small ring at the anchor's center of gravity; a rope is attached to it, which is pulled to dislodge the anchor from the bottom of the body of water.

bill
Tip of the palm.

stock
Transverse rod perpendicular to the shank; it positions the anchor so that its two arms grip the bottom of the body of water.

examples of anchors
The weight and the shape of the arms of anchors are designed to hook onto various bottoms (such as firm, loose or reedy).

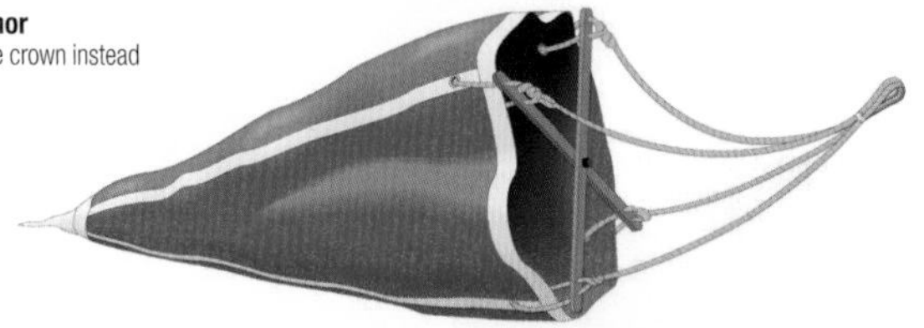

sea anchor
Solid cone-shaped canvas sack that is dragged behind a boat to counter heaving and strong winds.

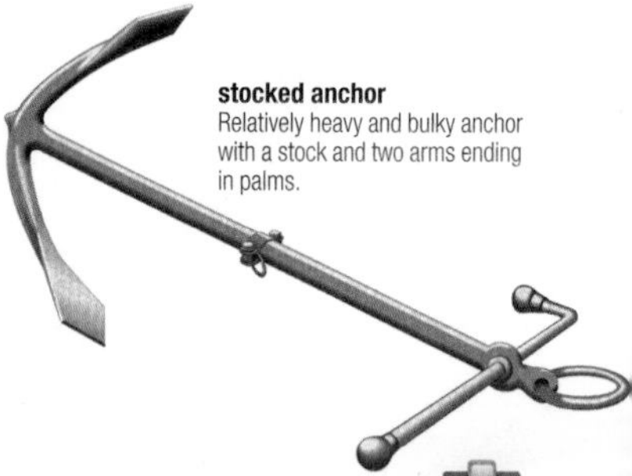

stocked anchor
Relatively heavy and bulky anchor with a stock and two arms ending in palms.

mushroom anchor
Anchor with a large crown instead of arms.

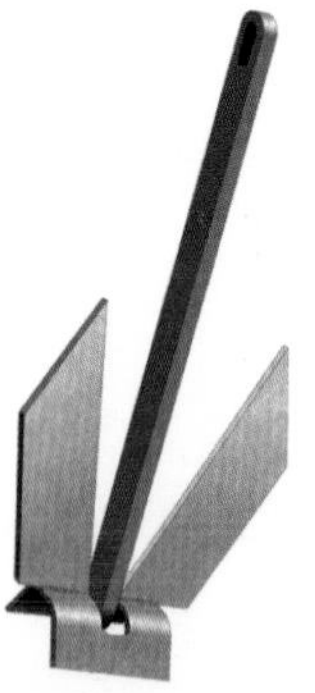

stockless anchor
Relatively light anchor with a pair of pivoting palms that fold along the shank.

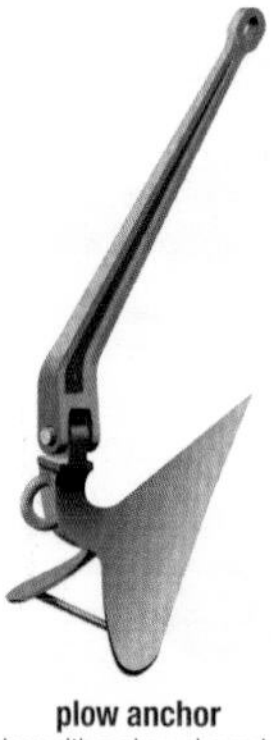

plow anchor
Anchor with a plow-shaped arm that pivots on the shank and hooks onto most bottoms.

grapnel
Small anchor with four, sometimes folding, cruciform arms.

screw anchor
Spiral-shaped anchor inserted into the seabed or bank in the manner of a screw.

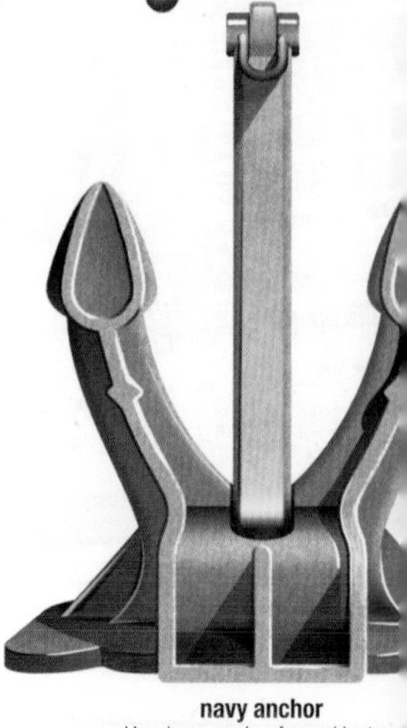

navy anchor
Very large anchor formed by two arms attached to a shank. Used by large vessels.

life-saving equipment

Instruments and equipment for signaling a boat's presence and for saving people from drowning.

life raft
Inflatable boat where passengers can take refuge in case of emergency.

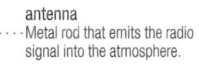

antenna
Metal rod that emits the radio signal into the atmosphere.

canopy
Covering that automatically deploys to protect against wind, rain and spray.

strobe
Lamp that produces an intense light from a gas, which glows between two electrodes.

distress beacon
Device that automatically transmits a radio distress signal giving its precise position.

boarding ladder
Nylon straps that form steps for climbing into the life raft.

buoyancy tube
Inflatable tube that serves as a hull to make the raft float.

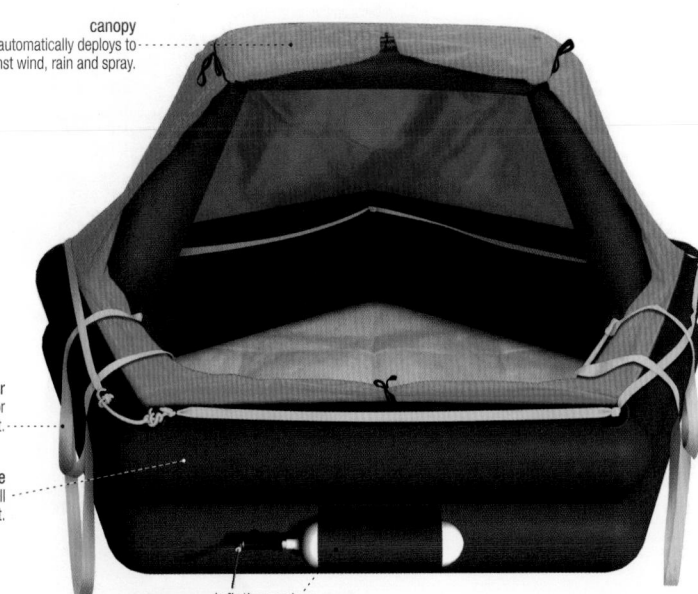

trumpet
Bell mouth that amplifies the sound emitted by a diaphragm when compressed air passes over it.

inflation system
Device containing pressurized air that automatically inflates the buoyancy tubes when the life raft is launched.

life buoy
Ring made of buoyant material that is thrown to anyone who has fallen overboard to help them float.

canister
Small container of compressed air.

foghorn
Instrument that makes a regulation sound when visibility is reduced to indicate the presence of a boat.

ring
Rigid buoyant circle that a person in the water slips under the arms.

rope
Nylon rope that can be caught with the boat hook to hoist a person out of the water.

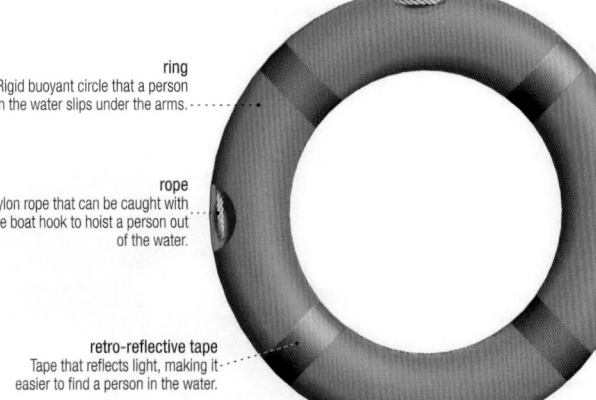

retro-reflective tape
Tape that reflects light, making it easier to find a person in the water.

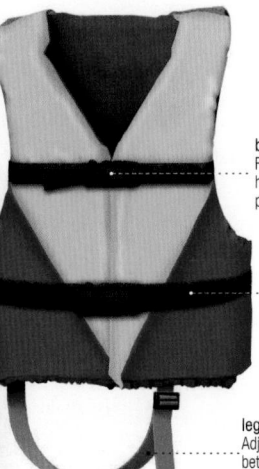

buckle
Fastener with two elements that hook together and unfasten when pressed.

belt
Nylon strap that adjusts to the wearer's size to keep the life jacket in place.

handle
Elongated part for handling the hook and reaching distant objects.

hook
Curved end for hooking a rope or fishing an object out of the water.

leg strap
Adjustable nylon belt that goes between the legs to prevent the life jacket from riding up.

life jacket
Buoyant vest filled with air or plastic foam that is used to keep a person afloat.

boat hook
Usually telescopic pole with a tip and a hook; it is used to maneuver a boat alongside quays, to hook an object and to fathom the bottom.

navigation devices

Examples of instruments that are used on a ship to determine its position and to chart and stay a course.

sextant
Optical instrument for measuring the angle between a heavenly body and the horizon to determine the ship's position.

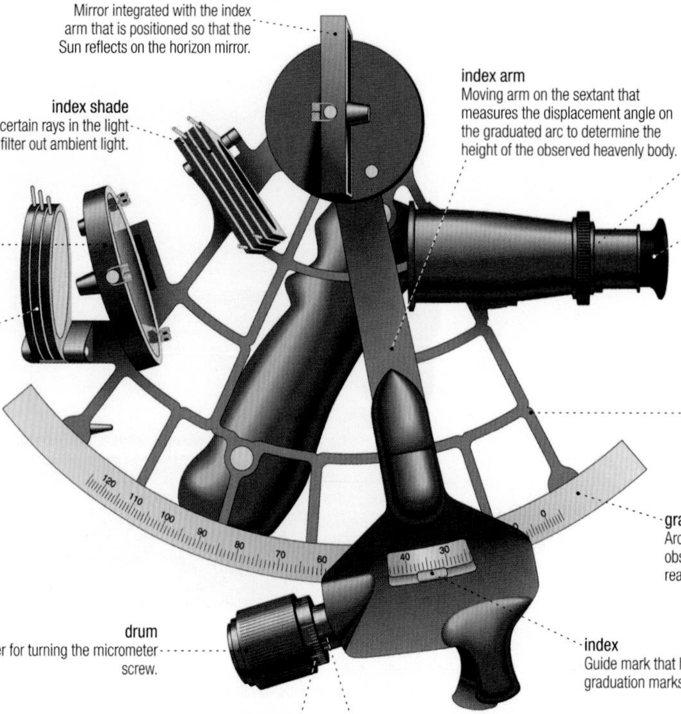

index mirror
Mirror integrated with the index arm that is positioned so that the Sun reflects on the horizon mirror.

index arm
Moving arm on the sextant that measures the displacement angle on the graduated arc to determine the height of the observed heavenly body.

index shade
Colored glass that blocks certain rays in the light spectrum to filter out ambient light.

telescope
Optical instrument that magnifies an observed object.

lens hood
Device attached to the telescope's eyepiece that shields the eye from light coming from the source and from strong ambient light.

horizon mirror
Fixed mirror in front of the telescope; it is aimed at the horizon and the image of the Sun is projected on it.

horizon shade
Colored glass that blocks certain rays in the light spectrum to filter out ambient light.

frame
Support for the various components of the sextant.

graduated arc
Arc graduated in degrees; the observed angle measurement is read from it.

drum
Cylinder for turning the micrometer screw.

index
Guide mark that helps to read the graduation marks on the arc.

micrometer screw
Screw with a head graduated in minutes that is turned to set the index arm precisely.

vernier scale
Small graduated rule that slides along the ruler and is used to read very precise measurements.

liquid compass
Instrument with magnets that floats on a liquid; it indicates magnetic north.

sliding cover
Retractable cover that protects the glass dome from scratches when not in use.

glass dome
Transparent nondistorting hemispherical cover for the bowl containing the liquid.

compass card
Rotating disk graduated from 0° to 360° and integrated with two magnets; it shows the cardinal points and the points in between.

pivot
Axle around which the compass card rotates.

bowl
Watertight case containing the magnetic elements, which float in a liquid (oil or alcohol) to reduce oscillations.

navigation devices

marine VHF radio
Device using very high frequency
radio waves for voice transmission.

handset
Component of the marine radio that
includes the microphone and main
communications buttons.

channel selection buttons
Buttons that select a frequency channel for
sending or receiving voice messages.

microphone
Device that converts electric pulses into
broadcast sounds.

watch button
Button that automatically changes radio
frequency to a predetermined setting in
order to receive any emergency broadcasts.

push-to-talk button
Button that, when held in, transmits
the user's voice.

speaker
Integrated device used to generate
sound.

display
Screen on which text data is
displayed.

distress button
Button that issues a distress call in
an emergency.

ar
e that reads reflected sound waves in water,
ly for measuring the depth of the water
ath a boat.

satellite navigation system
Device that uses radio signals transmitted
by a network of satellites to plot a boat's
position and course on a chart.

display
Screen on which graphics or text
data are displayed.

display
Liquid crystal display screen on which
graphics or text data are displayed.

GPS receiver-antenna
External antenna and GPS receiver that
receive radio waves from satellites to
calculate the boat's position.

bracket
Support fixed onto a surface that
holds the display.

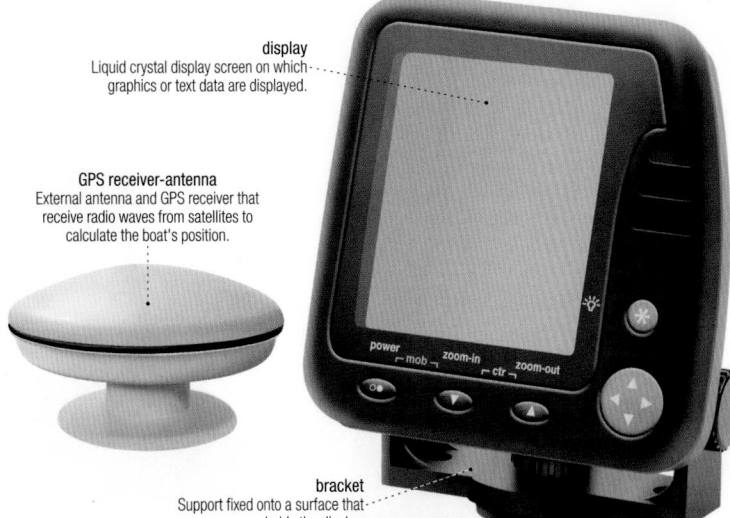

TRANSPORT AND MACHINERY

maritime signals

Beacons and devices located on the sea, coasts and waterways that emit light, sound and radio waves to aid navigation.

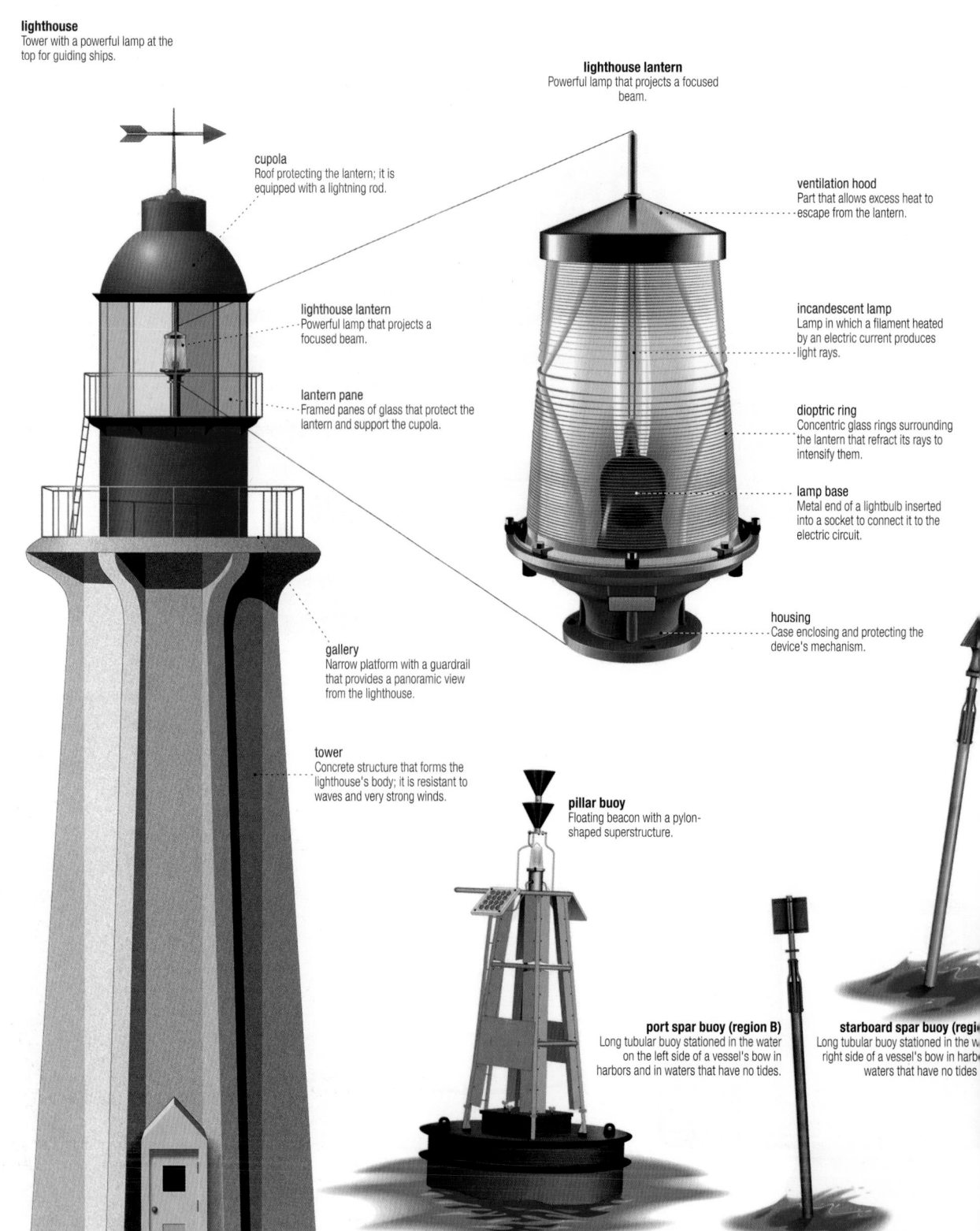

lighthouse
Tower with a powerful lamp at the top for guiding ships.

lighthouse lantern
Powerful lamp that projects a focused beam.

cupola
Roof protecting the lantern; it is equipped with a lightning rod.

ventilation hood
Part that allows excess heat to escape from the lantern.

lighthouse lantern
Powerful lamp that projects a focused beam.

incandescent lamp
Lamp in which a filament heated by an electric current produces light rays.

lantern pane
Framed panes of glass that protect the lantern and support the cupola.

dioptric ring
Concentric glass rings surrounding the lantern that refract its rays to intensify them.

lamp base
Metal end of a lightbulb inserted into a socket to connect it to the electric circuit.

gallery
Narrow platform with a guardrail that provides a panoramic view from the lighthouse.

housing
Case enclosing and protecting the device's mechanism.

tower
Concrete structure that forms the lighthouse's body; it is resistant to waves and very strong winds.

pillar buoy
Floating beacon with a pylon-shaped superstructure.

port spar buoy (region B)
Long tubular buoy stationed in the water on the left side of a vessel's bow in harbors and in waters that have no tides.

starboard spar buoy (regi
Long tubular buoy stationed in the w right side of a vessel's bow in harbo waters that have no tides

maritime signals

al buoy
ng beacon with a cone-
d superstructure.

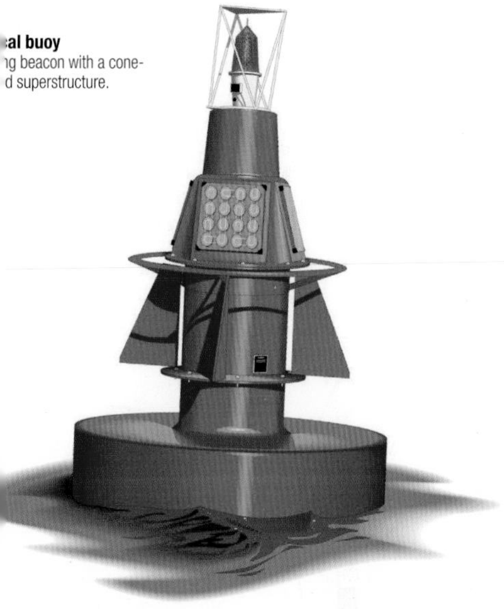

high focal plane buoy
Floating beacon whose light is
especially high above the surface
of the water.

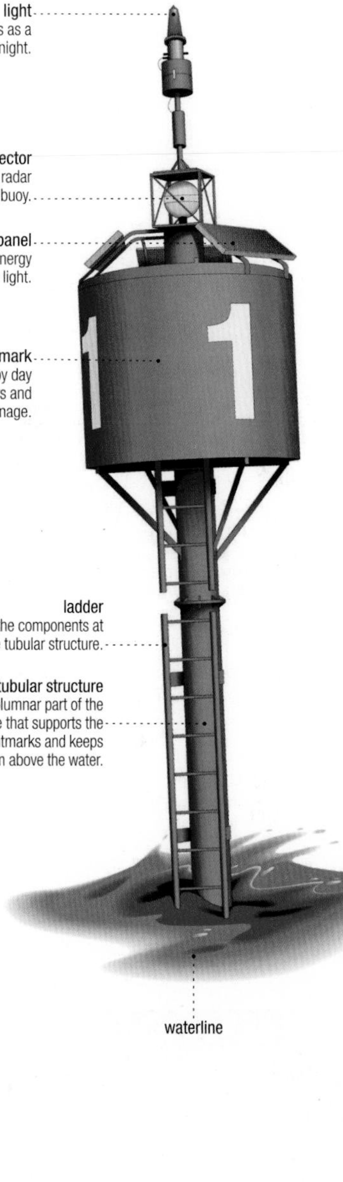

light
Light beam that serves as a
navigation aid at night.

radar reflector
Metal part that reflects ships' radar
signals so they can locate the buoy.

photovoltaic panel
Device that converts solar energy
into electricity to power the light.

daymark
Navigation aid that is visible by day
only; it displays various colors and
signage.

ladder
For accessing the components at
the top of the tubular structure.

tubular structure
Columnar part of the
superstructure that supports the
day- and nightmarks and keeps
them above the water.

waterline

drical buoy
ng beacon with a cylindrical
structure.

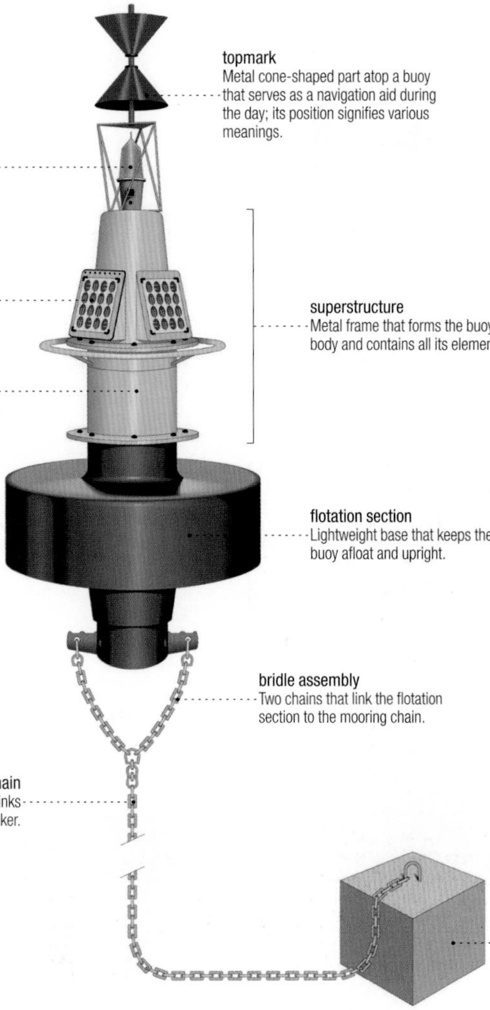

topmark
Metal cone-shaped part atop a buoy
that serves as a navigation aid during
the day; its position signifies various
meanings.

light
Light beam that serves as a
navigation aid at night.

photovoltaic panel
vice that converts solar energy
 electricity to power the light.

superstructure
Metal frame that forms the buoy's
body and contains all its elements.

daymark
gation aid that is visible by day
it displays various colors and
signage.

flotation section
Lightweight base that keeps the
buoy afloat and upright.

bridle assembly
Two chains that link the flotation
section to the mooring chain.

mooring chain
Long, very sturdy chain that links
the buoy to the sinker.

sinker
Heavy object often made of
concrete; it rests on the bottom
of the waterway to keep the buoy
in place.

maritime buoyage system

Buoys, beacons and lights located along coasts and waterways to guide ships and boats.

cardinal marks
Buoys of standardized colors, topmarks
and lights whose placement alone or in
a pattern corresponds to the divisions of
a compass.

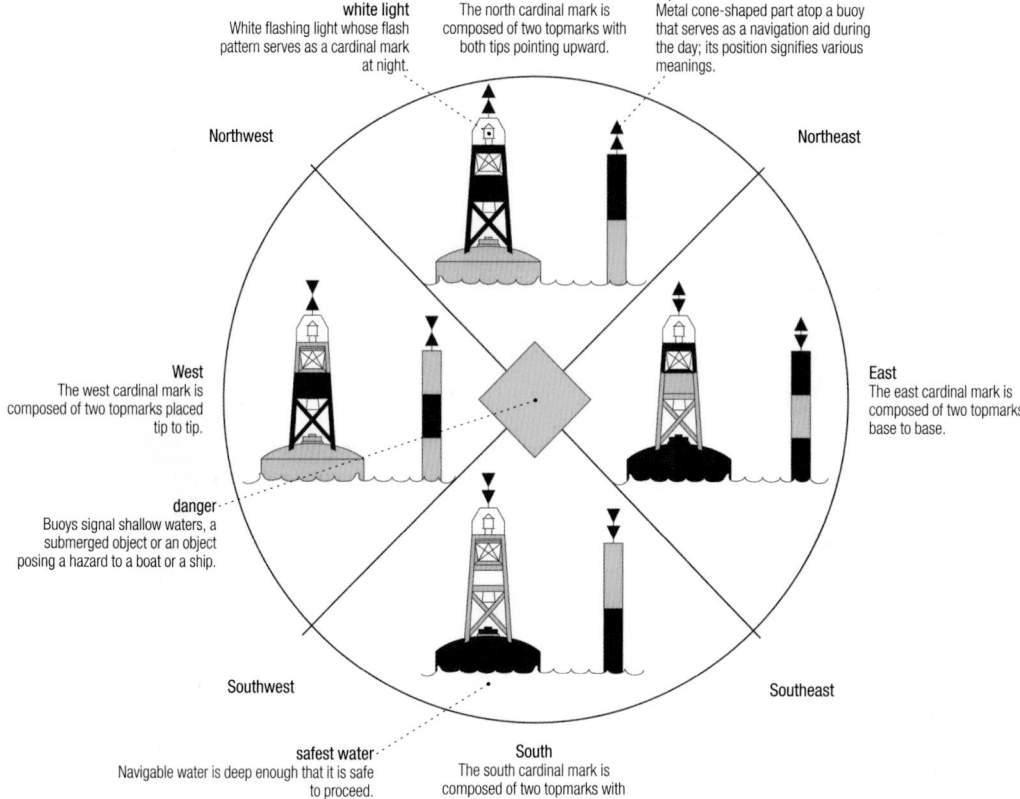

white light
White flashing light whose flash
pattern serves as a cardinal mark
at night.

North
The north cardinal mark is
composed of two topmarks with
both tips pointing upward.

topmark
Metal cone-shaped part atop a buoy
that serves as a navigation aid during
the day; its position signifies various
meanings.

Northwest

Northeast

West
The west cardinal mark is
composed of two topmarks placed
tip to tip.

East
The east cardinal mark is
composed of two topmarks placed
base to base.

danger
Buoys signal shallow waters, a
submerged object or an object
posing a hazard to a boat or a ship.

safest water
Navigable water is deep enough that it is safe
to proceed.

Southwest

South
The south cardinal mark is
composed of two topmarks with
both tips pointing downward.

Southeast

buoyage regions
The color of the buoys that indicate starboard
and port is the opposite in various parts of
the world.

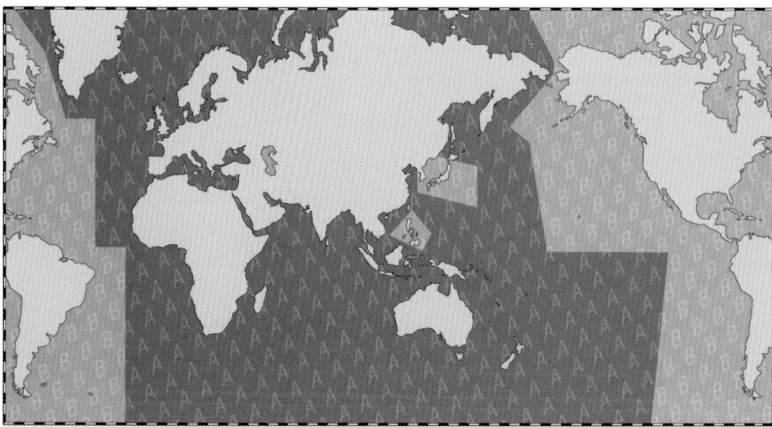

port side
Left side of the ship when looking
forward.

starboard side
Right side of the ship wl
forward.

region A
Region A includes Europe, Africa and most
of Asia and Oceania; starboard buoys are
green, while port side buoys are red.

region B
Region B includes the Ame
Japan, Korea and the Philip
starboard buoys are red, wł
side buoys are red.

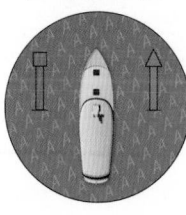

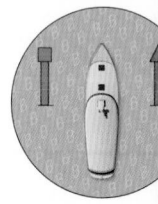

maritime buoyage system

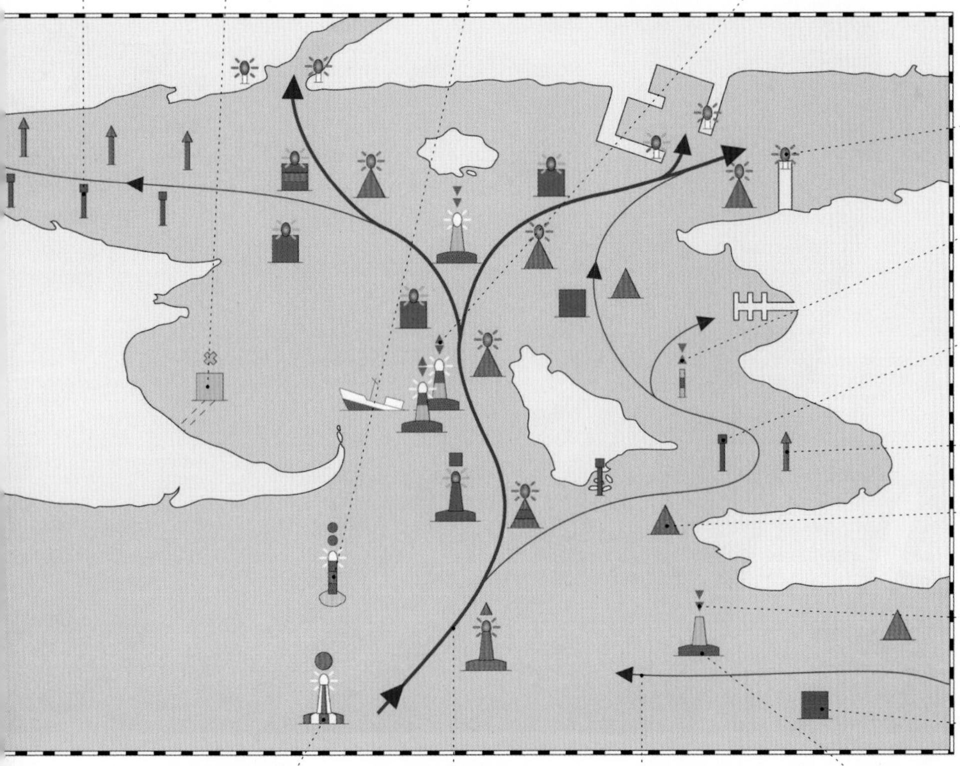

rhythm of marks by night
Lights that shine at night; their color and the frequency of their flashing signal various meanings, including the source of the light.

light
The light's color and brightness vary during the period as a function of the type of light.

darkness
No light.

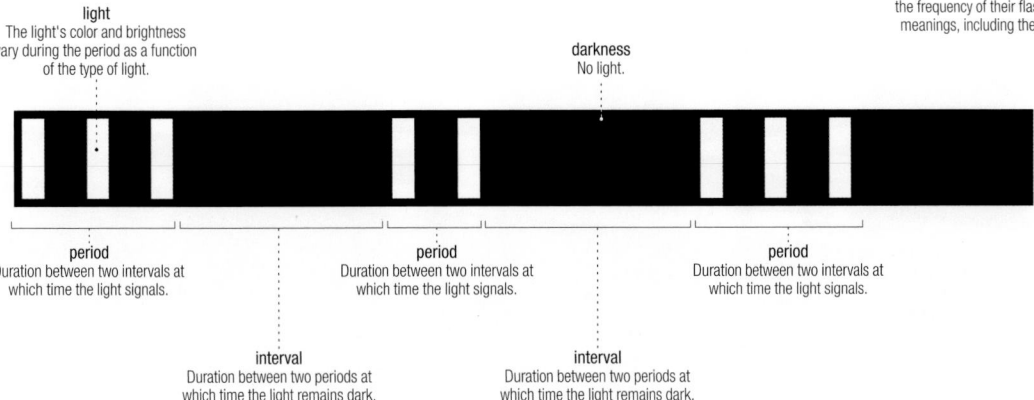

period
Duration between two intervals at which time the light signals.

period
Duration between two intervals at which time the light signals.

period
Duration between two intervals at which time the light signals.

interval
Duration between two periods at which time the light remains dark.

interval
Duration between two periods at which time the light remains dark.

seamarks (region B)
System B combines lateral and cardinal marks. It is the opposite of system A, in which starboard marks are red and port marks are green.

special mark
Buoy marking an area that is regulated for a specific use (such as military exercises or fishing) or contains submerged obstacles (such as cables or pipelines).

isolated danger mark
Buoy marking an isolated danger zone beyond which the waters are navigable.

East cardinal mark
Buoy with two base-to-base topmarks that is placed to the east of a danger zone.

spar buoy
tubular buoy used in harbors and n waters that have no tides.

light
Light beam that serves as a navigation aid at night.

West cardinal mark
Buoy with two point-to-point topmarks that is placed to the west of a danger zone.

port side
Mark the ship must keep on the left side of its prow as it navigates a channel.

starboard side
Mark the ship must keep on the right side of its prow as it navigates a channel.

conical buoy
Floating beacon with a cone-shaped superstructure.

South cardinal mark
Buoy with two topmarks pointing downward that is placed to the south of a danger zone.

lateral mark
Red or green buoy that indicates the port or starboard limits of the channel.

safe water mark
Buoy signaling that the water is navigable.

preferred channel
Navigation lane with beacons; it is the shortest and safest way to a harbor or for navigating near a coast or through a waterway.

secondary channel
Navigation lane with beacons that is longer or more difficult than the preferred channel.

pillar buoy
Floating beacon with a pylon-shaped superstructure.

TRANSPORT AND MACHINERY

airport

Location that contains all the technical and commercial facilities needed to support air traffic.

exterior view

high-speed exit taxiway
Lane linking the landing runway with a taxiway that is used by aircraft after landing to free up the runway.

control tower cab
Glassed-in office where the air traffic controllers coordinate aircraft movement such as takeoff, landing and flight.

control tower
Structure supporting the control tower cab, which provides a wide view of the runways and terminals.

access road
Part of the network of roads s the airport.

bypass taxiway
Branch for right turns.

taxiway
Lane used by aircraft for entering and exiting the apron.

apron
Lane used by aircraft for entering or exiting the maneuvering area.

service road
Lane reserved for airport service vehicles.

maneuvering area
Area crossed by an aircraft to or exit a parking spot.

airport

taxiway
...e used by aircraft for entering ...r exiting a takeoff or landing runway.

passenger terminal
Structure through which passengers pass before or after their flight to pick up or leave their baggage and to go through customs.

maintenance hangar
Structure where aircraft are maintained and repaired.

parking area
Area where aircraft park between flights for maintenance or overhaul.

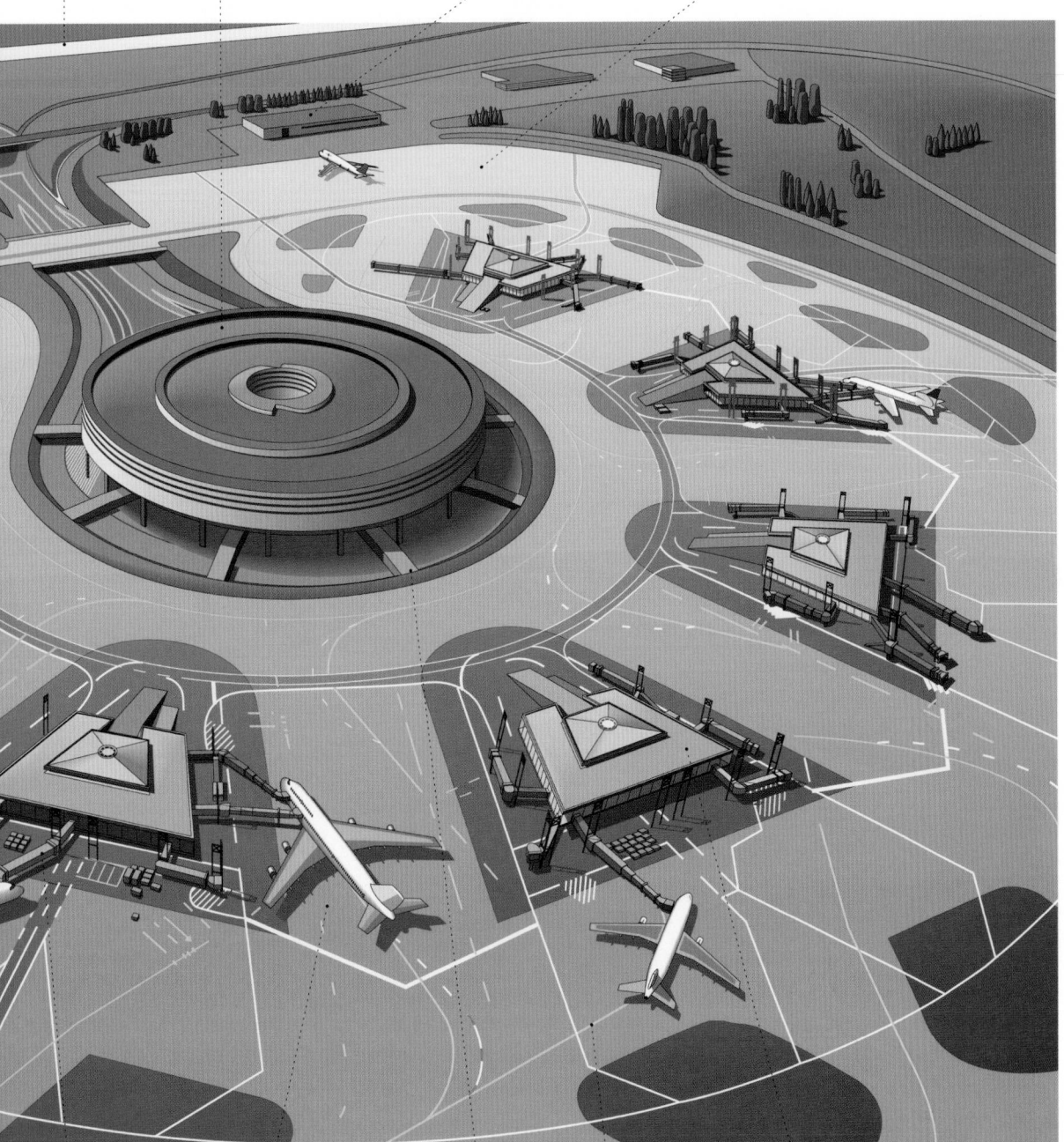

jet bridge
Mobile corridor connecting the passenger loading area with the aircraft.

service area
Area around an aircraft that is reserved for service vehicles and ground crew attending to arriving or departing aircraft.

boarding walkway
Underground corridor linking the main terminal with passenger gates.

taxiway line
Yellow line painted on the ground that shows aircraft the route to follow on the apron or the maneuvering area.

satellite terminal
Pavilion for passengers to reach aircraft that is linked by an underground corridor or by vehicles with the main terminal.

airport

passenger terminal
Structure through which passengers pass before or after their flight to pick up or leave their baggage and to go through customs.

self-service check-in kiosk
Automatic teller that allows passengers to print their own boarding pass and luggage tags.

ticket counter
Desk where an airline or travel agent sells tickets for flights.

information counter
Desk where information can be obtained about flights and ground transportation.

baggage claim area
Area where the baggage conveyor belt emerges for passengers to pick up their luggage.

automatic door
Door automatically opening and closing for people to go through.

hotel reservation desk
Counter where a hotel room can be reserved.

baggage check-in counter
Desk where an employee checks weighs passengers' baggage and boarding passes.

lobby
Large entrance hall of the terminal for passengers and the people accompanying them.

parking
Area for parking vehicles.

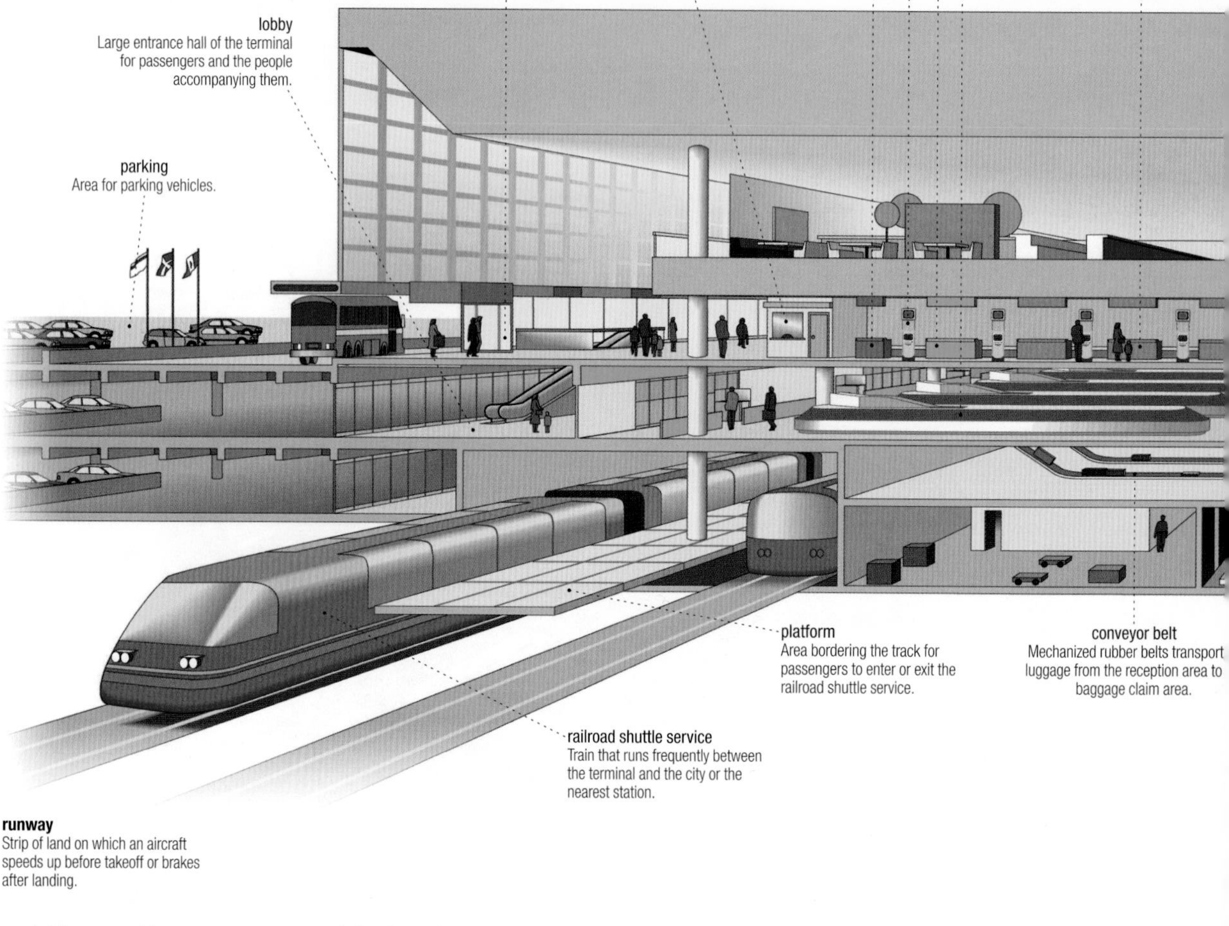

platform
Area bordering the track for passengers to enter or exit the railroad shuttle service.

conveyor belt
Mechanized rubber belts transport luggage from the reception area to baggage claim area.

railroad shuttle service
Train that runs frequently between the terminal and the city or the nearest station.

runway
Strip of land on which an aircraft speeds up before takeoff or brakes after landing.

holding area marking
Line that shows an aircraft where to wait for clearance from the control tower before entering the runway for takeoff.

runway designation marking
Number that, when multiplied by 10, shows the runway's position in relation to magnetic north.

runway center line markings
Wide broken white line that shows the center of the runway.

runway side stripe markings
Wide solid white line that marks the edges of the runway.

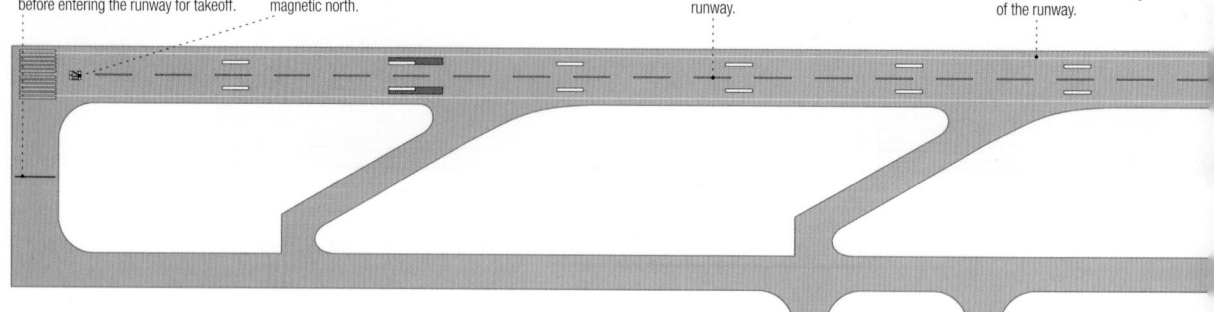

airport

urity check
datory checkpoint for passengers before boarding
re their identification and luggage are inspected.

duty-free shop
Store located near the boarding
room where tax-free goods are sold
(e.g., perfume, alcohol, leather
goods).

freight dispatching
Room where luggage and cargo
are inspected, sorted and loaded
onto carts transporting them to
the aircraft.

observation deck
Mezzanine that is open to the
public and overlooks the departure
and arrival area and the runways.

flight information board
Panel listing and updating all the airport's
arrivals and departures as well as the flight
departure gate numbers.

passport control
Booth where passengers show their
passports before entering or leaving
the boarding room.

waiting area
Area where passengers wait before
boarding.

passenger transfer vehicle
Vertically adjustable vehicle with a cabin for
transporting passengers between the aircraft and
the terminal.

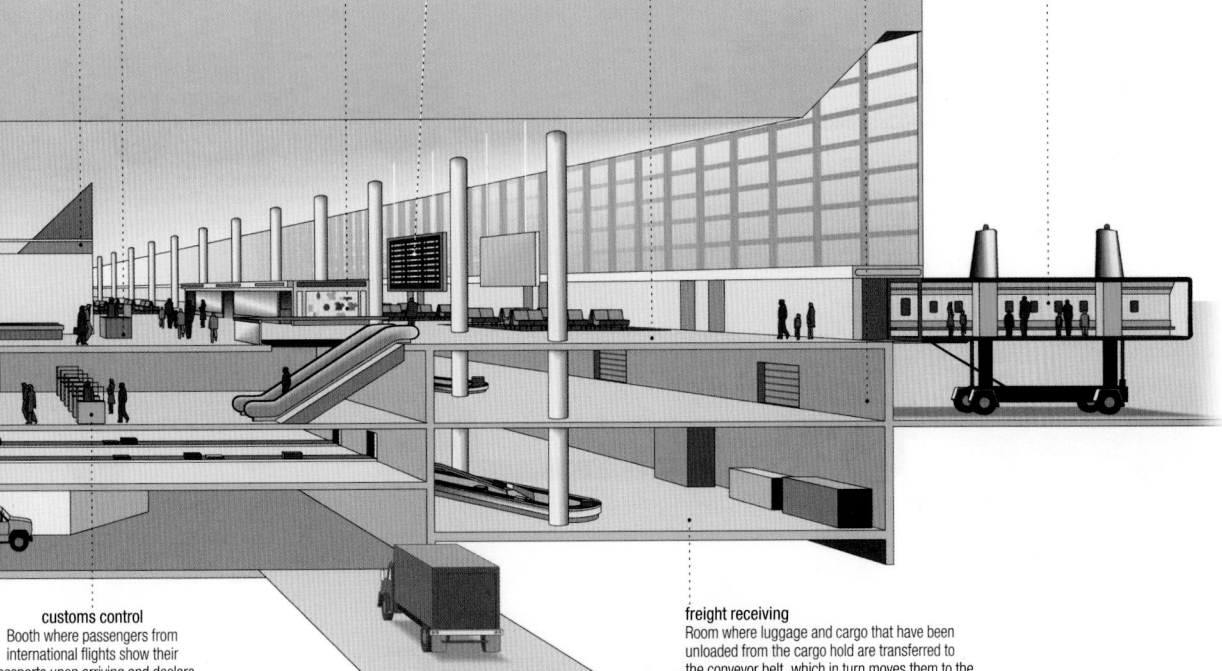

customs control
Booth where passengers from
international flights show their
passports upon arriving and declare
any imported merchandise.

freight receiving
Room where luggage and cargo that have been
unloaded from the cargo hold are transferred to
the conveyor belt, which in turn moves them to the
baggage claim area.

exit taxiway
Lane connecting the runway with
a taxiway so that incoming aircraft
can exit the runway as soon as
possible after landing.

runway touchdown zone marking
Pair of lines painted at each end of the runway that shows
where aircraft should touch down on the runway.

runway threshold markings
Longitudinal lines painted at each end of the
runway to show its limits.

fixed distance marking
Lines painted at regular intervals so
that pilots can gauge distances on the
runway.

airport

airport ground equipment
Equipment and materials for preparing an aircraft for its next flight; this includes cleaning, performing checks, refueling and boarding.

tow bar
Device that connects the tow tractor to the aircraft's front landing gear.

tow tractor
Very heavy vehicle that pulls or pushes an aircraft onto the maneuvering area or the parking area.

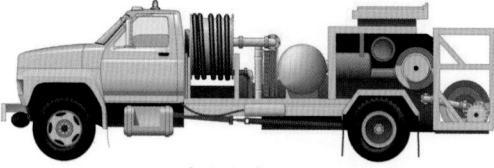

air start unit
Vehicle that is equipped with an air compressor driven by a gas turbine; it pumps air into the aircraft's jet engines to start them.

jet refueler
Truck that pumps fuel from underground tanks into the aircraft's tanks.

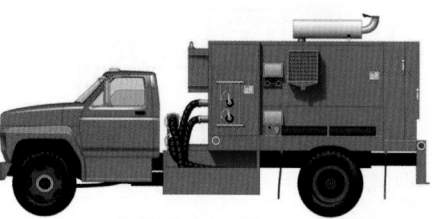

electrical power unit
Vehicle that is equipped with a transformer to provide electricity to the aircraft when its auxiliary generator set is at rest.

ground air conditioner
Truck that contains a device for treating the aircraft's interior air (ventilation and cooling or heating) when the aircraft is at rest.

aircraft maintenance truck
Vehicle that is used by technical maintenance crew when servicing an aircraft.

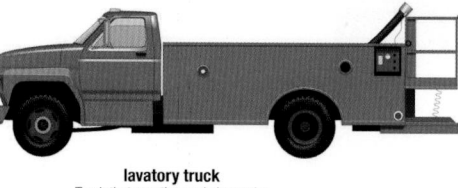

lavatory truck
Truck that empties and cleans the aircraft's toilets.

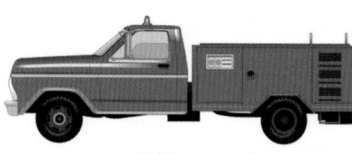

potable water truck
Truck that fills the aircraft's water tanks with drinking water.

wheel chock
Object that is placed against the landing gear's wheels to keep the aircraft stationary when on the ground.

boom truck
Vehicle that is equipped with a bucket at the end of an articulating pivoting arm; technicians stand in it to work on aircraft.

airport

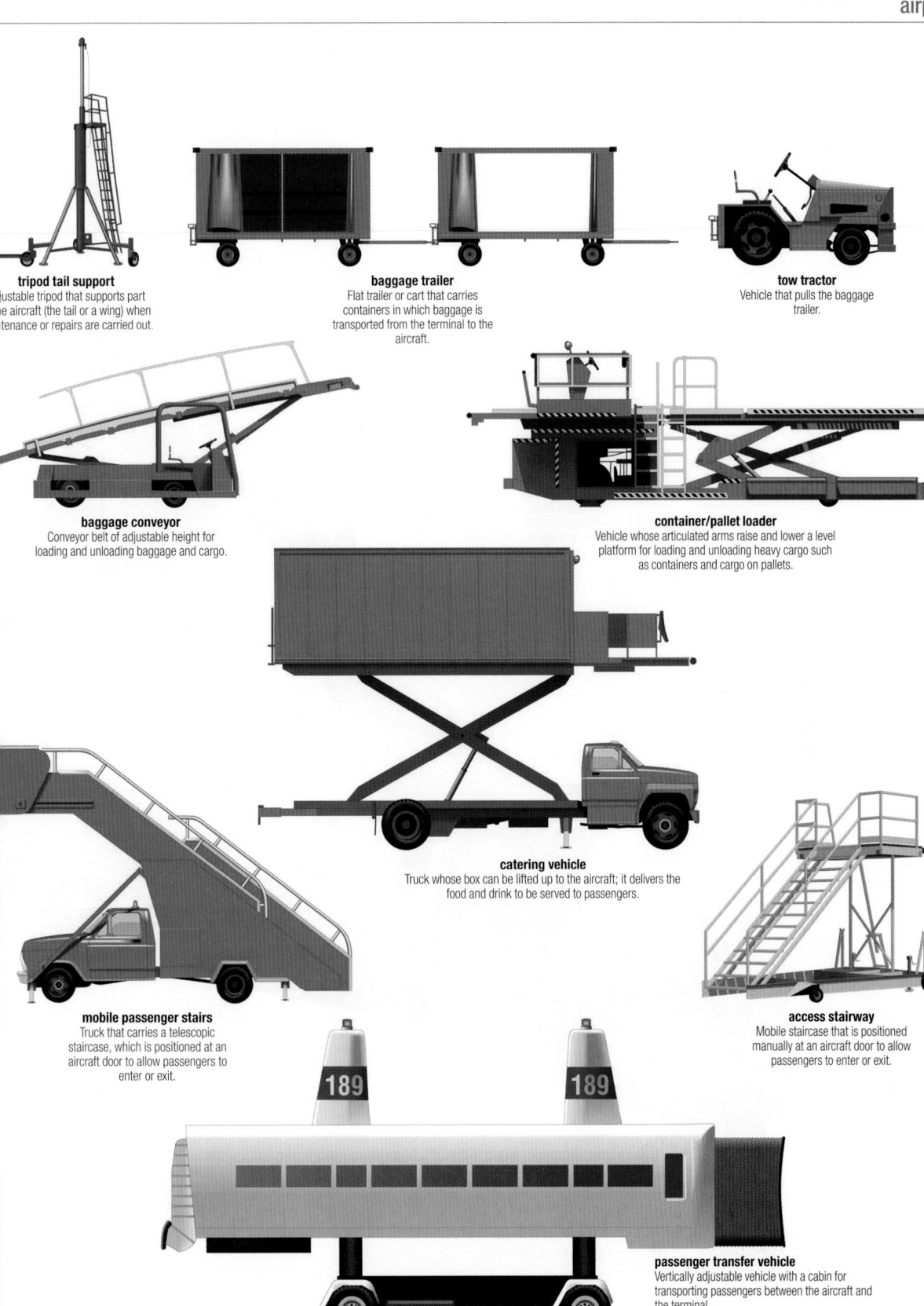

tripod tail support
djustable tripod that supports part
e aircraft (the tail or a wing) when
tenance or repairs are carried out.

baggage trailer
Flat trailer or cart that carries
containers in which baggage is
transported from the terminal to the
aircraft.

tow tractor
Vehicle that pulls the baggage
trailer.

baggage conveyor
Conveyor belt of adjustable height for
loading and unloading baggage and cargo.

container/pallet loader
Vehicle whose articulated arms raise and lower a level
platform for loading and unloading heavy cargo such
as containers and cargo on pallets.

catering vehicle
Truck whose box can be lifted up to the aircraft; it delivers the
food and drink to be served to passengers.

mobile passenger stairs
Truck that carries a telescopic
staircase, which is positioned at an
aircraft door to allow passengers to
enter or exit.

access stairway
Mobile staircase that is positioned
manually at an aircraft door to allow
passengers to enter or exit.

passenger transfer vehicle
Vertically adjustable vehicle with a cabin for
transporting passengers between the aircraft and
the terminal.

long-range jet

Aircraft that transports passengers and cargo traveling long distances at high altitudes (between 30,000 and 40,000 ft).

general view

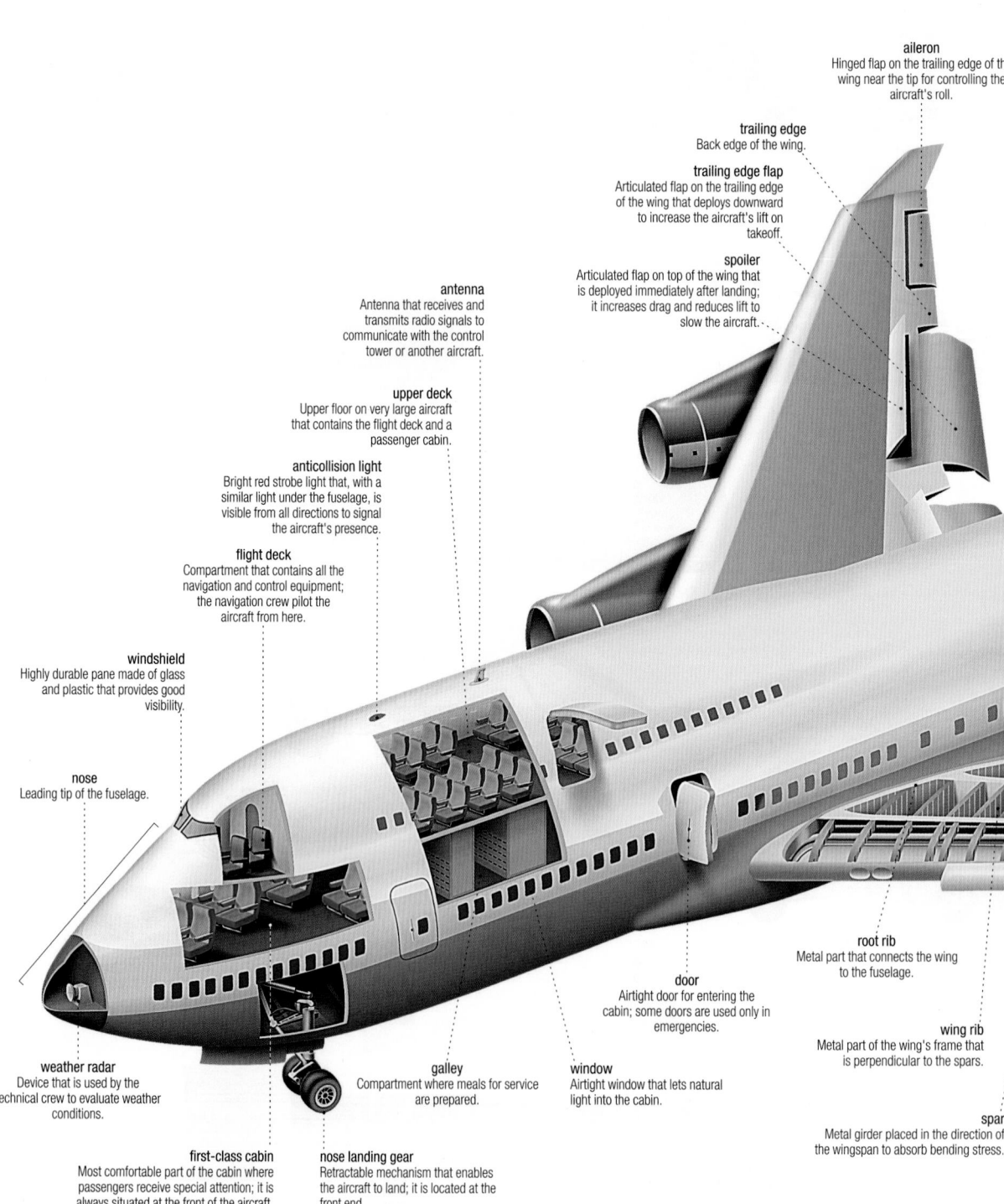

aileron
Hinged flap on the trailing edge of the wing near the tip for controlling the aircraft's roll.

trailing edge
Back edge of the wing.

trailing edge flap
Articulated flap on the trailing edge of the wing that deploys downward to increase the aircraft's lift on takeoff.

spoiler
Articulated flap on top of the wing that is deployed immediately after landing; it increases drag and reduces lift to slow the aircraft.

antenna
Antenna that receives and transmits radio signals to communicate with the control tower or another aircraft.

upper deck
Upper floor on very large aircraft that contains the flight deck and a passenger cabin.

anticollision light
Bright red strobe light that, with a similar light under the fuselage, is visible from all directions to signal the aircraft's presence.

flight deck
Compartment that contains all the navigation and control equipment; the navigation crew pilot the aircraft from here.

windshield
Highly durable pane made of glass and plastic that provides good visibility.

nose
Leading tip of the fuselage.

weather radar
Device that is used by the technical crew to evaluate weather conditions.

first-class cabin
Most comfortable part of the cabin where passengers receive special attention; it is always situated at the front of the aircraft.

nose landing gear
Retractable mechanism that enables the aircraft to land; it is located at the front end.

galley
Compartment where meals for service are prepared.

window
Airtight window that lets natural light into the cabin.

door
Airtight door for entering the cabin; some doors are used only in emergencies.

root rib
Metal part that connects the wing to the fuselage.

wing rib
Metal part of the wing's frame that is perpendicular to the spars.

spar
Metal girder placed in the direction of the wingspan to absorb bending stress.

long-range jet

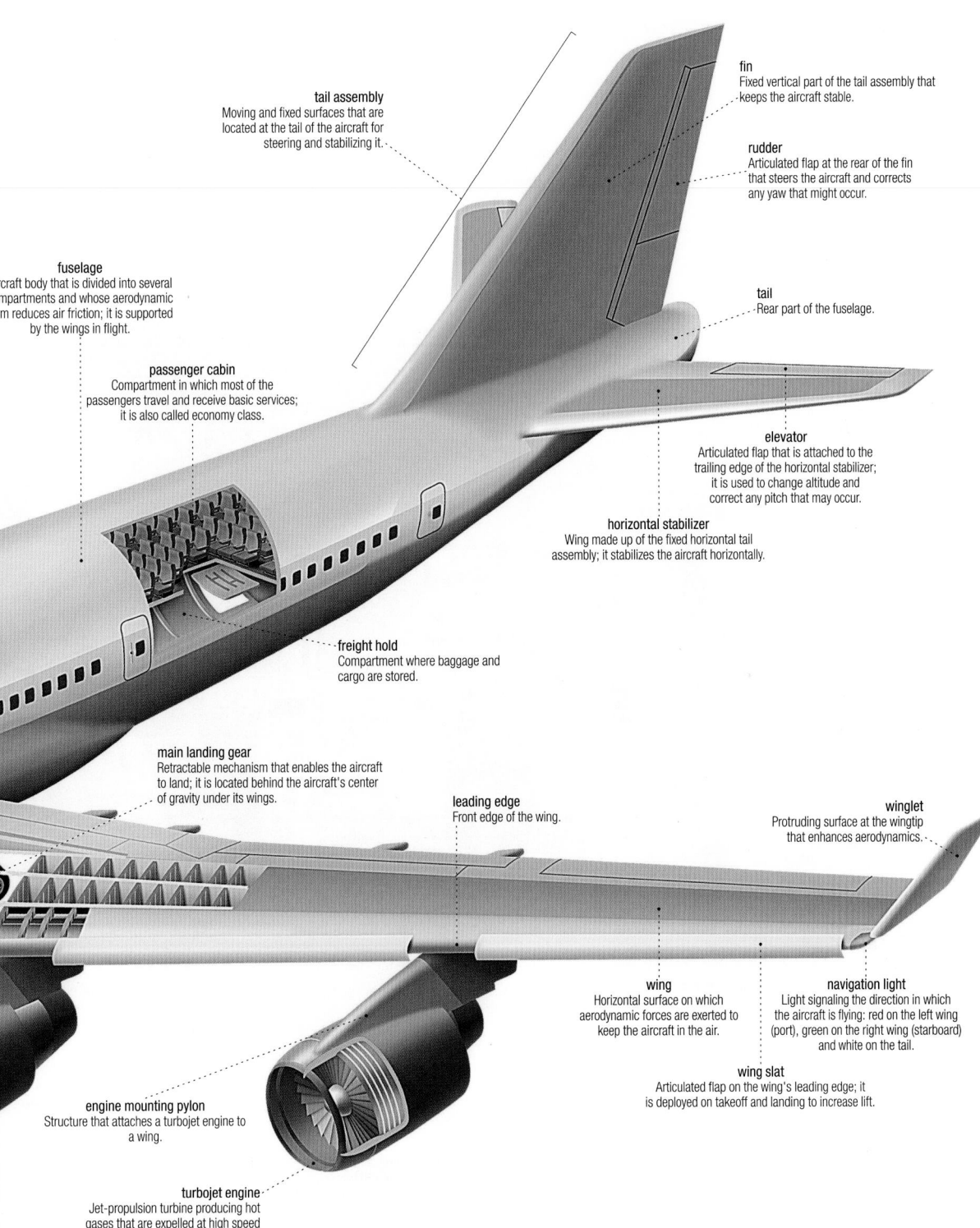

tail assembly
Moving and fixed surfaces that are located at the tail of the aircraft for steering and stabilizing it.

fin
Fixed vertical part of the tail assembly that keeps the aircraft stable.

rudder
Articulated flap at the rear of the fin that steers the aircraft and corrects any yaw that might occur.

fuselage
Aircraft body that is divided into several compartments and whose aerodynamic form reduces air friction; it is supported by the wings in flight.

tail
Rear part of the fuselage.

passenger cabin
Compartment in which most of the passengers travel and receive basic services; it is also called economy class.

elevator
Articulated flap that is attached to the trailing edge of the horizontal stabilizer; it is used to change altitude and correct any pitch that may occur.

horizontal stabilizer
Wing made up of the fixed horizontal tail assembly; it stabilizes the aircraft horizontally.

freight hold
Compartment where baggage and cargo are stored.

main landing gear
Retractable mechanism that enables the aircraft to land; it is located behind the aircraft's center of gravity under its wings.

leading edge
Front edge of the wing.

winglet
Protruding surface at the wingtip that enhances aerodynamics.

wing
Horizontal surface on which aerodynamic forces are exerted to keep the aircraft in the air.

navigation light
Light signaling the direction in which the aircraft is flying: red on the left wing (port), green on the right wing (starboard) and white on the tail.

wing slat
Articulated flap on the wing's leading edge; it is deployed on takeoff and landing to increase lift.

engine mounting pylon
Structure that attaches a turbojet engine to a wing.

turbojet engine
Jet-propulsion turbine producing hot gases that are expelled at high speed to provide the thrust necessary to propel the aircraft.

TRANSPORT AND MACHINERY

long-range jet

flight deck
Compartment that contains navigation equipment and controls and from which the crew pilots the aircraft.

autopilot controls
Device that enables the aircraft to be piloted and kept on course automatically.

spea
Integrated device that re audible messages such as ala to the p.

engine and crew alarm display
Screen that controls the engines and displays alarm signals in the event of system failure.

landing gear lever
Control for lowering and raising the landing gear.

lighting
Device that diffuses light over a shelf on which the pilots place navigation charts.

standby attitude indicator
Screen that shows the aircraft's position in relation to the horizon; it is used in the event the flight display fails.

windshield
Highly durable pane made of glass and plastic that provides good visibility.

overhead switch panel
Panel made up of the switches that cut the hydraulic, electric and fuel circuits.

standby airspeed indicator
Instrument that shows the aircraft's speed; it is used in the event the flight display fails.

standby altimeter
Instrument that shows the vertical distance between the aircraft and the ground; it is used in the event the flight display fails.

navigation display
Screen that shows the aircraft's position and flight plan and weather conditions.

primary flight display
Screen that shows the main parameters necessary for piloting (aircraft's position in relation to the horizon, altitude and course).

control column
Steering component that causes an aircraft to bank to the left or to the right and to ascend or descend.

control wheel
Lever that activates the control column from back to front and from side to side.

speedbrake lever
Command stick that releases the wing flaps to brake the aircraft immediately after landing.

systems display
Screen that controls various systems, such as air pressure and the electric and hydraulic circuits.

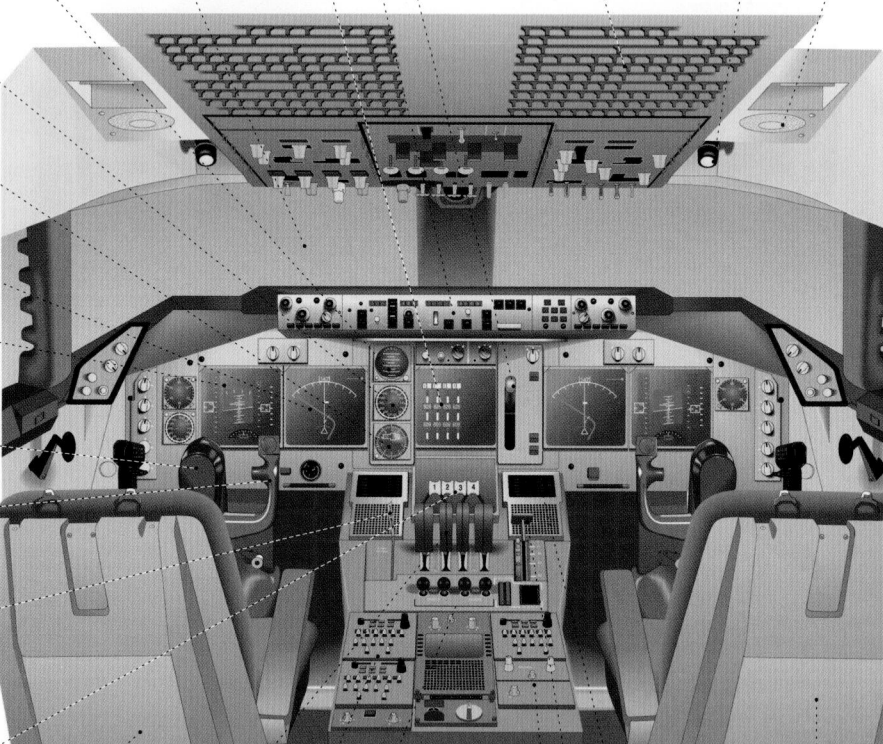

captain's seat
Left seat occupied by the pilot, who is in charge of the flight and the crew.

first officer's seat
Right seat occupied by the cop who is second in comman

throttles
Control levers for the engines; they regulate speed and thrust.

transponder
Instruments that, with the autopilot, control the engine power and guide the aircraft on course.

communication panels
Panel for selecting radio frequencies on which pilots can send or receive.

control console
Component located between the two seats that contains part of the instrumentation.

flap lever
Control stick that activates the wing slats and the trailing edge flaps.

engine fuel valves
Knobs for opening and shutting the fuel supply to the engines.

air data computer
Computer that calculates the flight parameters (speed, altitude, etc.).

long-range jet

inner stators
Set of fixed blades that corrects the airflow that is deflected as it passes through the blades of the axial compressor.

outer stators
Set of fixed blades that corrects the airflow that is deflected as it passes through the fan.

fan
Blower sucking air into the turbofan engine.

turbine-compressor shaft
Axle transmitting the turbine's rotational movement to the compressors.

pipe diffuser
Conduit with several exit orifices that connects the centrifugal compressor to the combustion chamber; its purpose is to direct the flow and slow down the airflow to increase its pressure.

annular combustion chamber
Enclosure consisting of two concentric hydraulic cylinders that surrounds the turbine-compressor shaft and where combustion occurs.

bypass duct
Channel that conducts some of the air sucked in by the fan, which contributes to the engine's thrust.

turbofan engine
Jet engine with a fan and two airflows; one airflow passes through the combustion chamber and the other bypasses it.

exhaust guide vanes
Protruding parts directing the exhaust gases straight out.

cone
Located on the tip of the fan that creates an aerodynamic flow into the fan blades.

exhaust duct
Opening through which the exhaust gases are evacuated; the duct is usually cone-shaped in order to narrow the gas flow, thus increasing thrust.

axial compressor
Engine component in which air is highly compressed by a set of small fan blades to increase the engine's output and reduce fuel consumption.

centrifugal compressor
Engine components that use centrifugal force to compress air and expel it at very high speed to the combustion chamber by the pipe diffuser.

power turbine
Turbine that is driven by the gases expelled by the combustion chamber; it drives the axial compressor and the fan. It is independent of the compressor turbine.

mounting point
Part where the engine is mounted on the aircraft.

fuel control
Device measuring the amount of fuel injected into the combustion chamber.

ignition box
Device that produces the electric pulses supplying the system that sets off combustion.

accessory gearbox
Mechanism that drives various accessories such as the alternator and the hydraulic, fuel and oil pumps.

compressor turbine
Turbine that is activated by the gas produced in the combustion chamber; it drives the centrifugal compressor and the accessories.

operation cycle

TRANSPORT AND MACHINERY

air intake
Phase during which the fan pulls air into the turbofan engine.

compression
Phase during which some of the air flowing through the engine is compressed before it enters the combustion chamber.

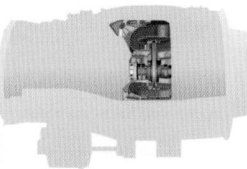

combustion
Phase during which the compressed air enters the combustion chamber, where it is mixed with fuel and ignited.

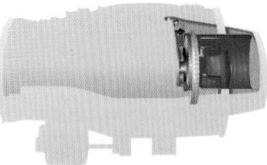

exhaust
Phase during which the air expands and produces a thrust that activates the turbines and propels the turbofan engine.

examples of airplanes

Ever since the first airplane, Éole, in 1890, the shape of aircraft has evolved constantly as new aerodynamic discoveries were made and engine power increase▪

floatplane
Airplane designed to take off from and land on water.

three-blade propeller
Propulsion device with three blades that are arranged around an axle and driven by a motor.

high wing
Wing mounted on top of the fuselage.

bipla▪
Airplane with two superimpo▪ and parallel sets of wir▪

upper wing

float
Watertight structure attached under the fuselage that enables the seaplane to float and move on water.

wings
Surfaces upon which aerodynamic forces are exerted to cause the airplane to fly.

lower wing

light aircraft
Airplane that usually has a single engine and cruises between 90 and 150 mph; it is used for recreation and traveling short distances.

wing strut
Rigid or flexible component that braces an airplane's wing and connects the wing to the fuselage or connects the two wings on a biplane.

high-frequency antenna cable
Wire enabling radio communication for the aircraft.

business aircr▪
Airplane with a limited number▪ seats; it is usually used by head▪ corporations for business tr▪

two-blade propeller
Propulsion device with two blades that are arranged around an axle and driven by a motor.

canopy
Glassed covering over the cockpit.

vertical take-off and landing (VTOL) aircraft
Airplane that can move vertically in order to take off from and land on short runways; it is usually used in combat.

winglet
Protruding surface at the wingtip that enhances aerodynamics.

swiveling nozzle
Duct that can be pointed downward to increase the engine's vertical thrust during vertical landing and takeoff.

amphibious firefighting aircr▪
Airplane with large water tanks; used to fight forest fi▪

three-blade propeller
Propulsion device with three blades that are arranged around an axle and driven by a motor.

water-tank area
Area with a hatch that scoops up water from the surface of a body of water to fill its tanks so that it can dump the water in flight.

float
Watertight structure that p▪ the airplane from tipping ▪ fills its tanks.

examples of airplanes

lth aircraft
aft that cannot be detected
dar because of the radar-
rbing facets covering its
age.

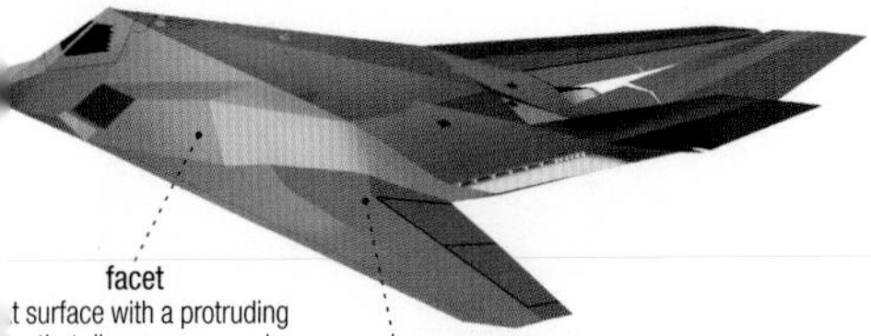

facet
t surface with a protruding
ge that disperses any radar
es hitting it and makes them
undetectable.

radar-absorbent material
Material that absorbs radar waves before they strike
any metal part of the aircraft in order to muffle the
sound of the echo.

rotodome
Domelike rotating structure that
houses radar antennae.

radar aircraft
Surveillance aircraft for locating
and identifying aircraft in flight.

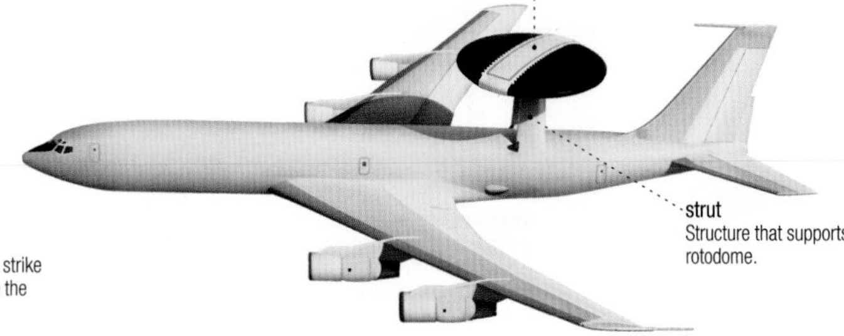

strut
Structure that supports the
rotodome.

erjumbo
ane that can transport a large
oer of passengers (more than

variable ejector nozzle
Duct whose mouth widens as the
plane climbs, thus enabling the
engines to increase output.

supersonic liner
Passenger aircraft whose cruising speed
(1,500 mph) is faster than the speed of
sound (761 mph). The Concorde was the
best known commercial aircraft of this type.

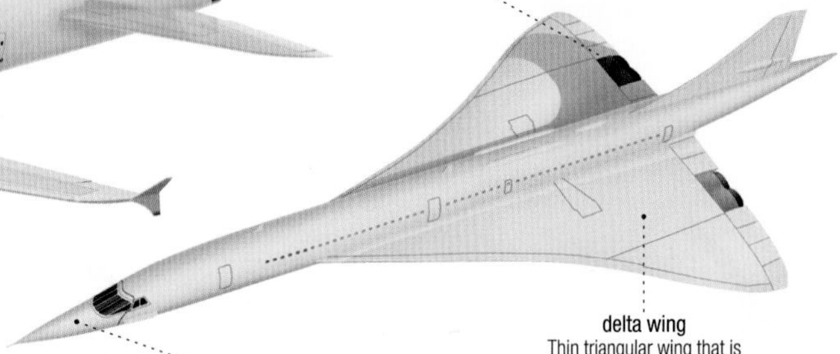

droop nose
Articulated nose that is lowered on
takeoff and landing to provide the
pilot with better visibility.

delta wing
Thin triangular wing that is
especially aerodynamic.

go aircraft
e with large freight capacity; it
ed to transport goods.

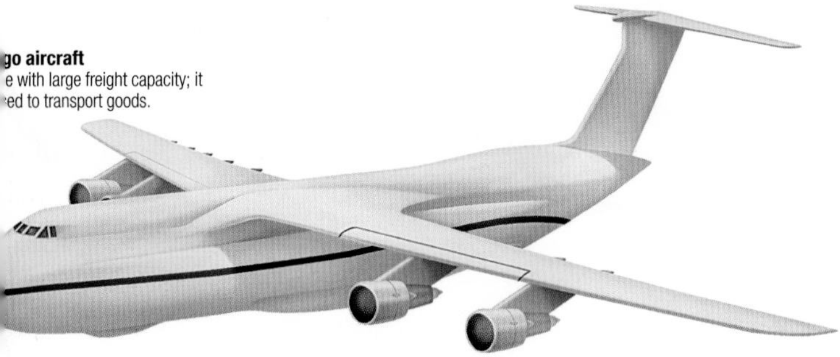

examples of tail shapes

Moving and fixed surfaces that are located at the tail of the aircraft for steering and stabilizing it.

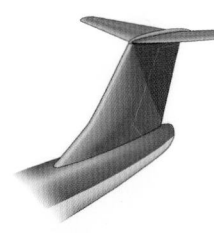

T-tail unit
unit made up of two horizontal
ponents attached at the top of
a vertical component.

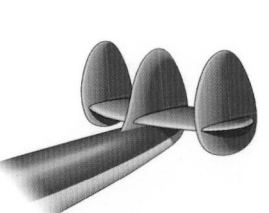

triple tail unit
Tail unit made up of three vertical
components attached to a horizontal
component.

fuselage mounted tail unit
Tail unit made up of two horizontal components
attached to the tail.

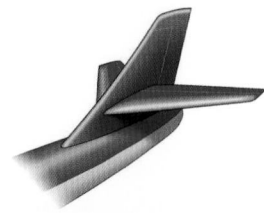

cruciform tail unit
Tail unit made up of two horizontal components attached
halfway up a vertical component.

examples of wing shapes

From one era to the next and depending on the type of aircraft, the shape and position of the wings in relation to the fuselage has varied.

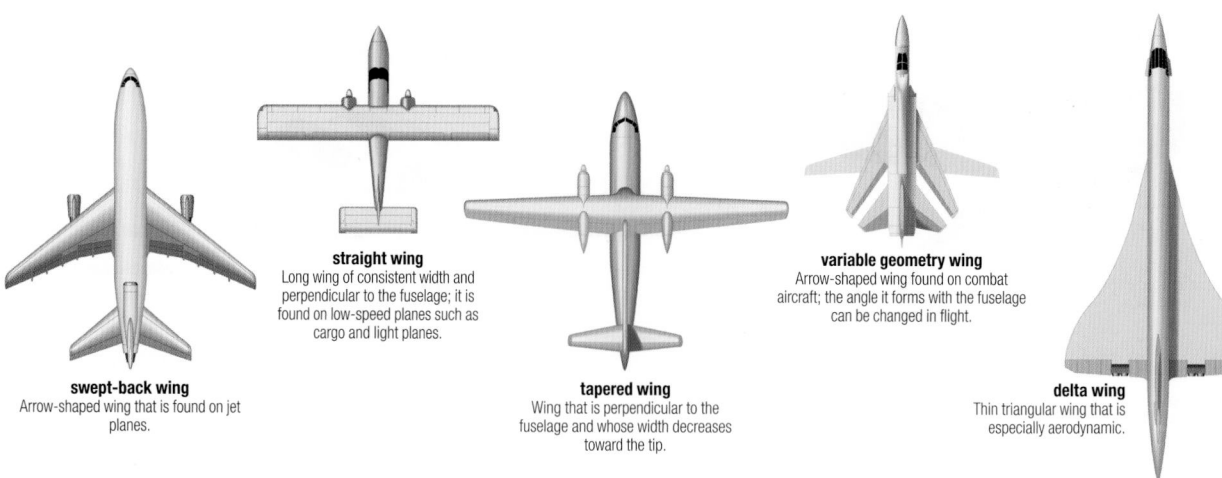

straight wing
Long wing of consistent width and perpendicular to the fuselage; it is found on low-speed planes such as cargo and light planes.

variable geometry wing
Arrow-shaped wing found on combat aircraft; the angle it forms with the fuselage can be changed in flight.

swept-back wing
Arrow-shaped wing that is found on jet planes.

tapered wing
Wing that is perpendicular to the fuselage and whose width decreases toward the tip.

delta wing
Thin triangular wing that is especially aerodynamic.

movements of an airplane

Changes exerted on an aircraft in flight that affect its behavior; a pilot must know how to correct them.

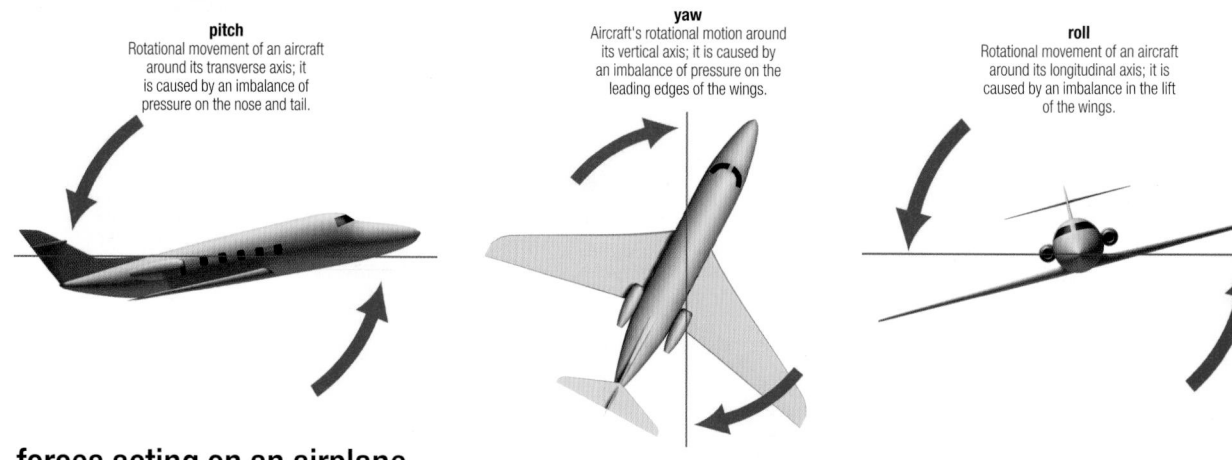

pitch
Rotational movement of an aircraft around its transverse axis; it is caused by an imbalance of pressure on the nose and tail.

yaw
Aircraft's rotational motion around its vertical axis; it is caused by an imbalance of pressure on the leading edges of the wings.

roll
Rotational movement of an aircraft around its longitudinal axis; it is caused by an imbalance in the lift of the wings.

forces acting on an airplane

Physical phenomena that affect the movement of an aircraft in flight.

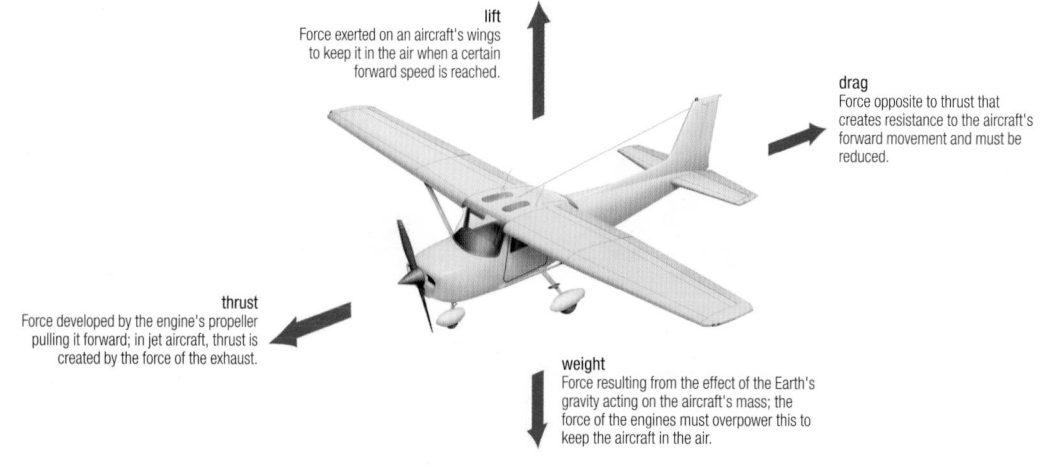

lift
Force exerted on an aircraft's wings to keep it in the air when a certain forward speed is reached.

drag
Force opposite to thrust that creates resistance to the aircraft's forward movement and must be reduced.

thrust
Force developed by the engine's propeller pulling it forward; in jet aircraft, thrust is created by the force of the exhaust.

weight
Force resulting from the effect of the Earth's gravity acting on the aircraft's mass; the force of the engines must overpower this to keep the aircraft in the air.

helicopter

Aircraft whose lift agent is a rotor on a vertical axle.

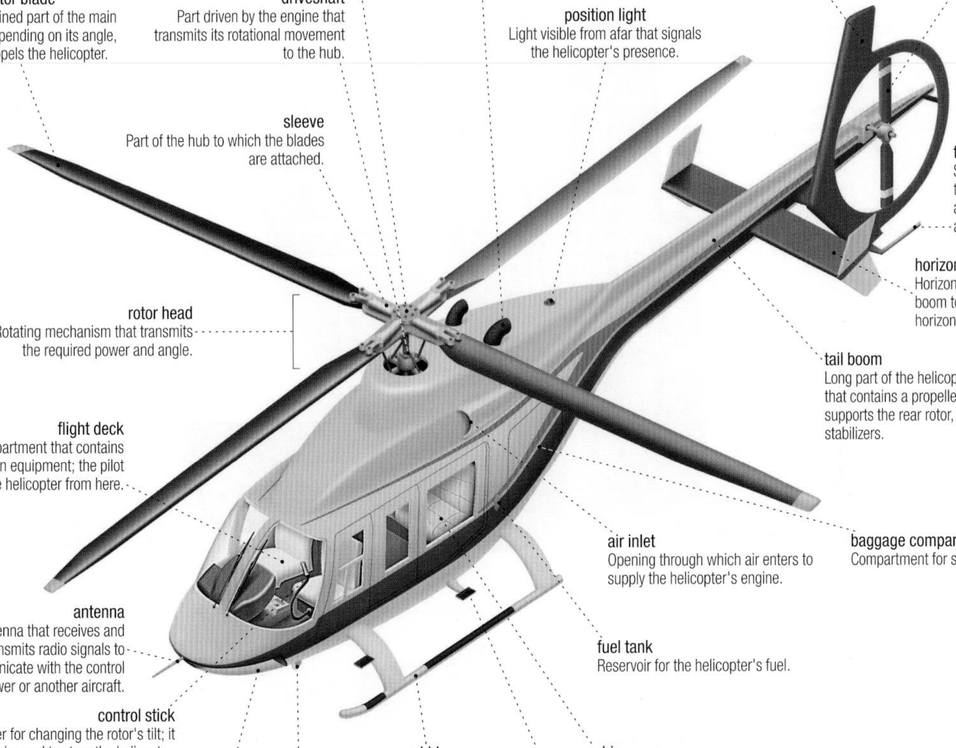

rotor hub
Center part of the rotor head that connects the driveshaft to the blades.

exhaust pipe
Opening through which the exhaust gases are evacuated.

fin
Fixed vertical part mounted on the tail boom to keep the helicopter flying straight.

anti-torque tail rotor
Rotor on a horizontal axle that prevents the helicopter from spinning due to the effect of the main rotor.

rotor blade
g streamlined part of the main or that, depending on its angle, ts and propels the helicopter.

driveshaft
Part driven by the engine that transmits its rotational movement to the hub.

position light
Light visible from afar that signals the helicopter's presence.

sleeve
Part of the hub to which the blades are attached.

tail skid
Support attached to the tail end of the boom that protects it and the anti-torque tail rotor in the event of a landing with the nose up.

horizontal stabilizer
Horizontal wing mounted on the tail boom to stabilize the helicopter's horizontal movement.

rotor head
Rotating mechanism that transmits the required power and angle.

tail boom
Long part of the helicopter's frame that contains a propeller shaft and supports the rear rotor, fin and stabilizers.

flight deck
Compartment that contains navigation equipment; the pilot erates the helicopter from here.

air inlet
Opening through which air enters to supply the helicopter's engine.

baggage compartment
Compartment for storing luggage.

antenna
Antenna that receives and transmits radio signals to communicate with the control tower or another aircraft.

fuel tank
Reservoir for the helicopter's fuel.

control stick
Lever for changing the rotor's tilt; it is used to steer the helicopter.

skid
Tube on which the helicopter lands and rests.

cabin
Compartment where the passengers ride.

landing window
Window by the pilot's feet for seeing the ground when landing.

landing light
Spotlight that is aimed at the ground for landing at night.

boarding step
Step attached to the fuselage for boarding the helicopter.

examples of helicopters

Because they can take off and land vertically, helicopters are more effective than airplanes in certain situations.

tactical transport helicopter
military helicopter for transporting troops, all combat vehicles and various objects.

helitanker
Helicopter with a water tank that is used to fight forest fires.

ambulance helicopter
Helicopter for transporting the sick and injured and providing medical assistance.

helitank
Tank filled with water by a long pipe hanging underneath; it uses a hatch to empty the water in flight.

typical devices

Machines and equipment used to move and stack goods in a store or warehouse.

forklift
Motorized cart for lifting and moving pallets to stack them or load them onto a truck.

mast
Post along which the carriage slides using a hydraulic system.

crosshead
Upper pulley of the hydraulic cylinder around which the chain turns to manipulate the carriage.

lifting chain
Chain that lifts and lowers the carriage along the masts.

hydraulic system
Device using pressurized fluid to operate the carriage.

carriage
Component that supports the fork arms and slides along the masts.

fork arm
Part at a right angle that is attached to the carriage and, with its twin, makes up the fork.

fork
Instrument made up of two arms that is inserted into a pallet's entry to lift it.

overhead guard
Metal framework that protects the operator and the cab against falling goods.

mast operating lever
Lever controlled by the operator to move the carriage along the masts.

engine compartment
Electric motor or combustion engine that supplies the power to propel the truck and operate the fork.

frame
Forklift truck's metal structure.

pallets
Usually wooden platform for loads; forklift and hydraulic pallet trucks can slip their forks underneath them in order to handle goods.

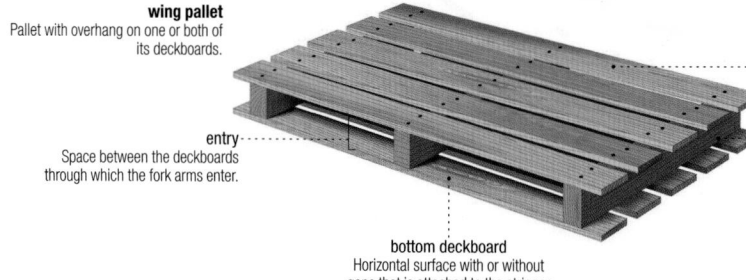

wing pallet
Pallet with overhang on one or both of its deckboards.

entry
Space between the deckboards through which the fork arms enter.

top deckboard
Flat horizontal surface with or without gaps between the planks; the goods rest on it.

stringer
Part supporting the deckboards and providing the gap for the fork arms to fit through.

bottom deckboard
Horizontal surface with or without gaps that is attached to the stringer and rests on the ground.

double-decked pa[llet]
Pallet with an upper and lo[wer] deckboard that is someti[mes] revers[...]

box pallet
Pallet with three or four sides; it is used to handle bulk merchandise.

side
Wall with or without gaps between the planks that slides back or can be removed; it keeps the goods in place and can withstand loads stacked on top.

pallet
Part of the box pallet supporting the load; it supports the box pallet on the ground and provides the place where the forks enter.

block
Supporting part underneath the deckboard that is wide enough to allow the fork arms to enter.

half-side
Half wall that is sometimes detachable; it facilitates the loading and unloading of the contents of the pallet.

single-decked pa[llet]
Pallet with one deckbo[ard]

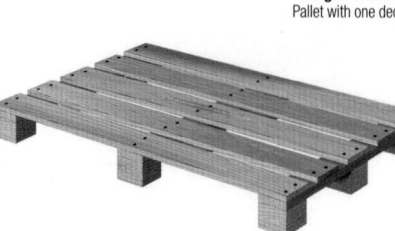

typical devices

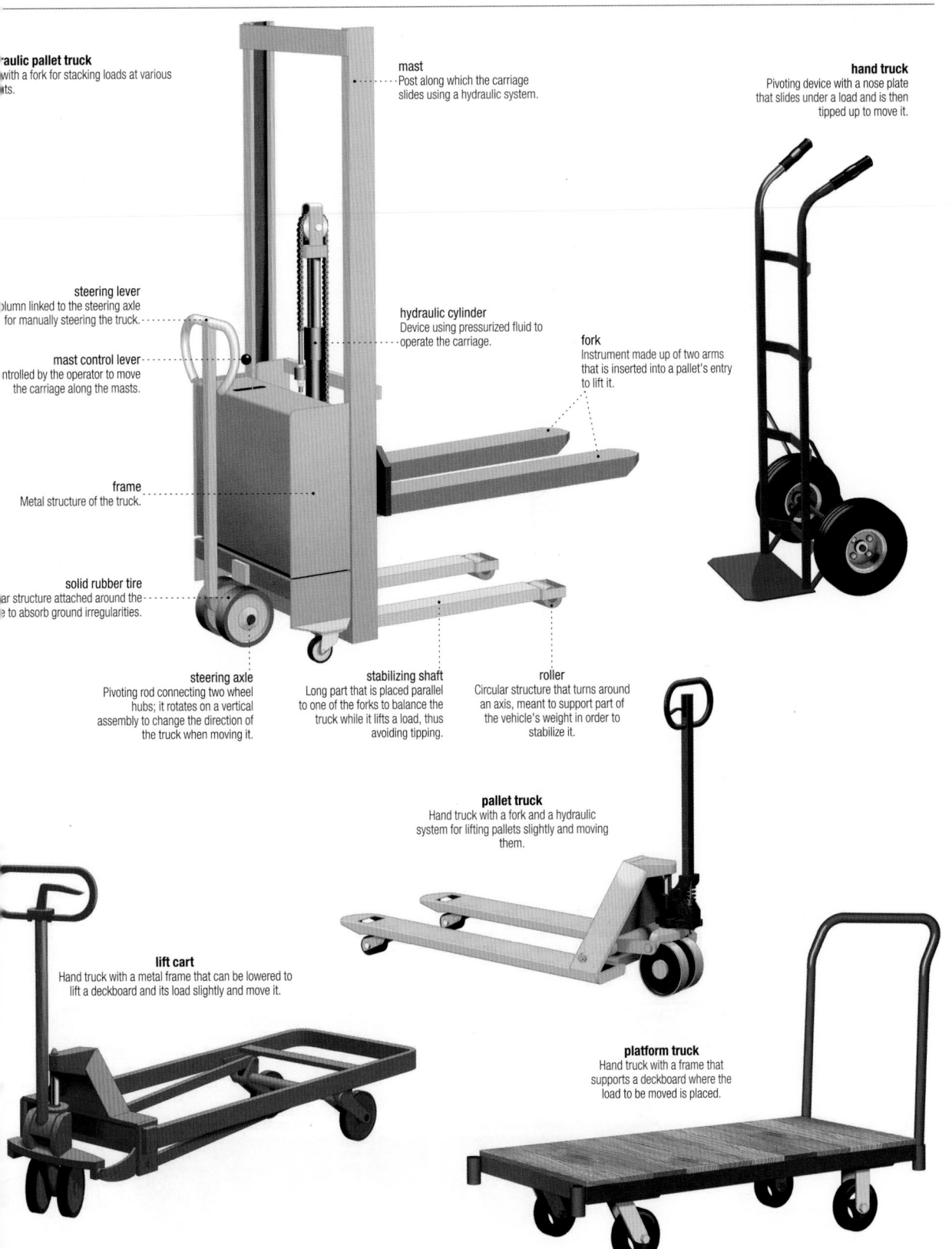

...raulic pallet truck
...with a fork for stacking loads at various
...ts.

mast
Post along which the carriage
slides using a hydraulic system.

hand truck
Pivoting device with a nose plate
that slides under a load and is then
tipped up to move it.

steering lever
...olumn linked to the steering axle
for manually steering the truck.

hydraulic cylinder
Device using pressurized fluid to
operate the carriage.

mast control lever
...ntrolled by the operator to move
the carriage along the masts.

fork
Instrument made up of two arms
that is inserted into a pallet's entry
to lift it.

frame
Metal structure of the truck.

solid rubber tire
...ar structure attached around the
... to absorb ground irregularities.

steering axle
Pivoting rod connecting two wheel
hubs; it rotates on a vertical
assembly to change the direction of
the truck when moving it.

stabilizing shaft
Long part that is placed parallel
to one of the forks to balance the
truck while it lifts a load, thus
avoiding tipping.

roller
Circular structure that turns around
an axis, meant to support part of
the vehicle's weight in order to
stabilize it.

pallet truck
Hand truck with a fork and a hydraulic
system for lifting pallets slightly and moving
them.

lift cart
Hand truck with a metal frame that can be lowered to
lift a deckboard and its load slightly and move it.

platform truck
Hand truck with a frame that
supports a deckboard where the
load to be moved is placed.

TRANSPORT AND MACHINERY

cranes

Examples of lifting devices for picking up and moving very heavy loads.

tower crane
Crane used on construction sites with a usually horizontal jib mounted on top of a tower.

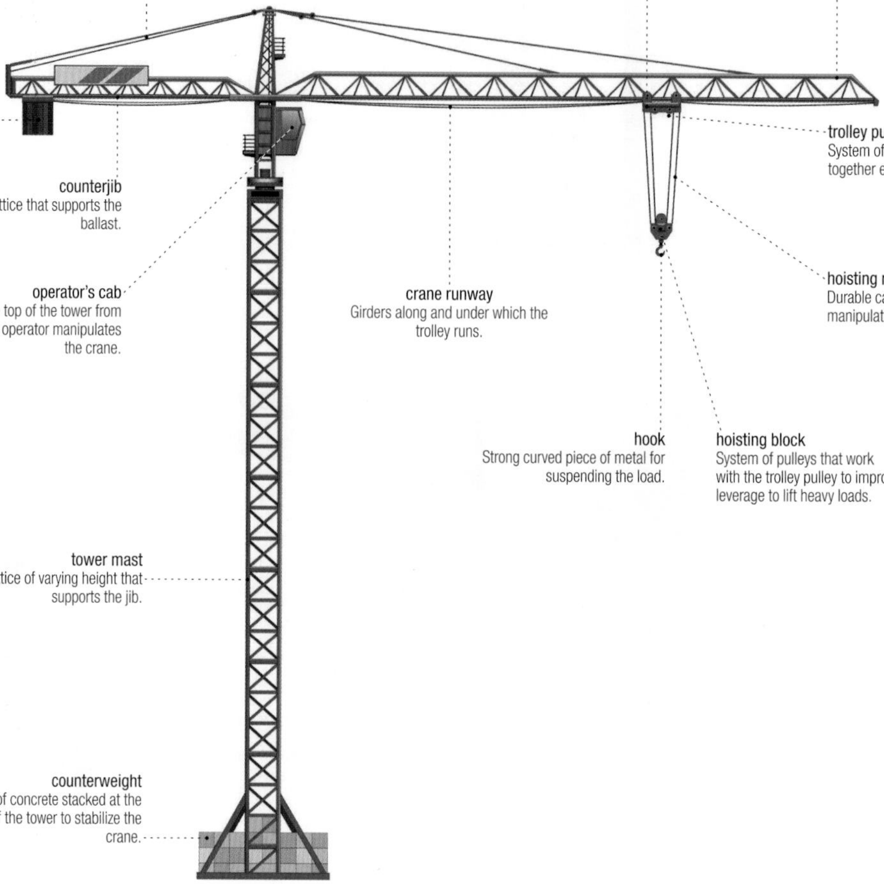

jib tie
Metal cable that distributes the tension.

trolley
Vehicle running along and under the jib; the hoisting rope is suspended from it.

jib
Metal lattice that pivots on the tower and lifts and extends the hoisting system.

counterjib ballast
Concrete mass attached to the counterjib to balance the weight of the jib and its load.

trolley pulley
System of several pulleys together enhance leverage.

counterjib
Metal lattice that supports the ballast.

operator's cab
Cab at the top of the tower from which the operator manipulates the crane.

crane runway
Girders along and under which the trolley runs.

hoisting rope
Durable cable of variable manipulating loads.

hook
Strong curved piece of metal for suspending the load.

hoisting block
System of pulleys that work with the trolley pulley to improve leverage to lift heavy loads.

tower mast
Metal lattice of varying height that supports the jib.

counterweight
Blocks of concrete stacked at the base of the tower to stabilize the crane.

truck crane
Mobile telescopic crane that is mounted on the chassis of a straight truck.

telescopic boom
Boom whose parts slide one inside the other so that its height can be adjusted and it can be stored compactly for transportation.

elevating cylinder
Hydraulic device that consists of a telescopic arm for raising and lowering the boom.

operator's cab
Cab attached to the chassis from which the operator manipulates the crane.

outrigger
Retractable component that braces the truck against the forces of its load when stationary.

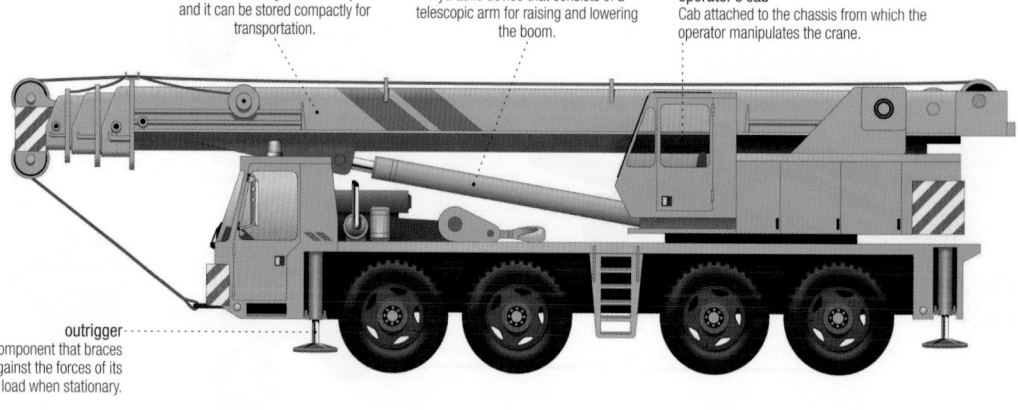

gantry crane
Lifting device with posts and cantilevered girders that move along rails or on tires to handle containers.

hoisting system
Device moving along the jib that uses cables, winches and pulleys to lift and move containers.

jib
Horizontal component overhanging the crane that extends the hoisting system as far out as possible.

containers
Metal boxes of standardized size for transporting cargo.

tower
Post that supports the crane.

running track
Rail along which the crane moves.

container

Metal box of standardized size for transporting cargo.

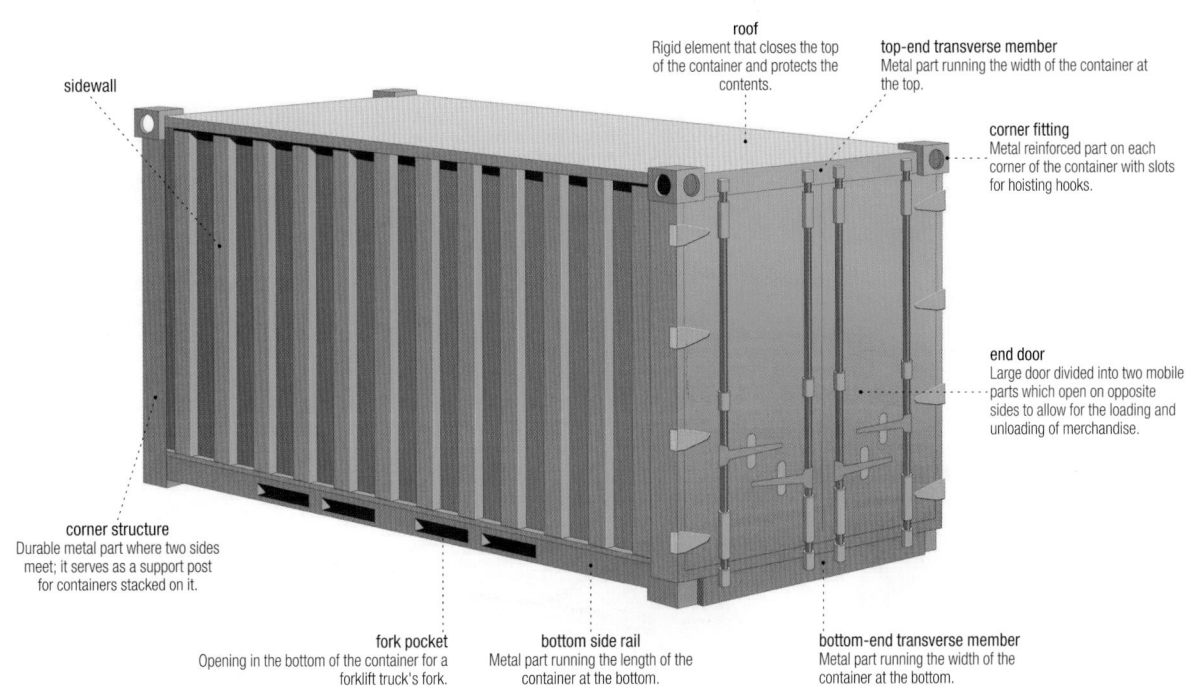

roof
Rigid element that closes the top of the container and protects the contents.

top-end transverse member
Metal part running the width of the container at the top.

sidewall

corner fitting
Metal reinforced part on each corner of the container with slots for hoisting hooks.

end door
Large door divided into two mobile parts which open on opposite sides to allow for the loading and unloading of merchandise.

corner structure
Durable metal part where two sides meet; it serves as a support post for containers stacked on it.

fork pocket
Opening in the bottom of the container for a forklift truck's fork.

bottom side rail
Metal part running the length of the container at the bottom.

bottom-end transverse member
Metal part running the width of the container at the bottom.

bulldozer

Excavation machine for pushing materials; it is made up of a crawler tractor, a blade and often a ripper.

general view

diesel engine compartment
Combustion engine in which the compressed air becomes sufficiently hot to ignite the injected fuel.

air filter
Device that removes dust from the air entering the engine.

cab
Compartment from which the operator controls the bulldozer.

exhaust pipe stack
Conduit through which the combustion gases are expelled into the ambient air.

ripper cylinder
Hydraulic device with a telescopic arm that manipulates the ripper.

blade lift cylinder
Hydraulic device with a telescopic arm for raising and lowering the blade.

blade
Concave metal equipment for moving earth by pushing it along the ground; it is held up by two articulated arms and caused to swivel by hydraulic cylinders.

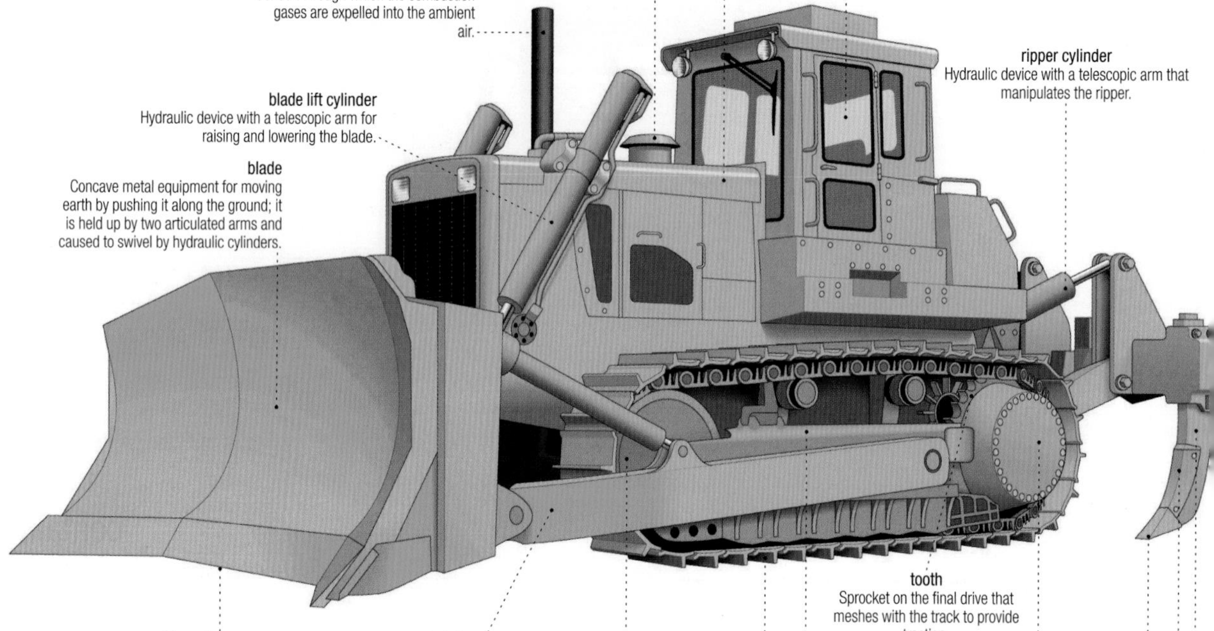

tooth
Sprocket on the final drive that meshes with the track to provide traction.

cutting edge
Bottom sharp part of the blade that scrapes the ground; it is replaced when worn out.

push frame
Lengthwise part articulating with the roller frame and the blade.

track idler
Wheel connected to the final drive by the roller frame; it keeps the track taut and aligned.

final drive
Motor wheel with teeth that drives the track.

track
Chain made up of articulated shoes that rolls between the wheels and the ground; it allows the bulldozer to move over rough terrain.

ripper tip tooth
Part attached to the end of the tooth that breaks into hard ground; it is replaced when worn out.

track roller frame
Lengthwise part forming the track's chassis; the final drive and the track idler are attached to it.

shank protector
Part attached on the inner side of a tooth to brace the tooth; it is replaced when worn out.

ripper shank
Part of the ripper that digs into the ground to break it up.

main parts

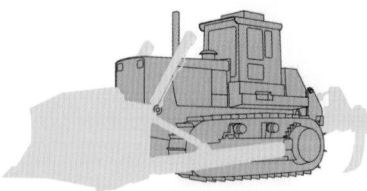

crawler tractor
Machine that can move along rough ground by means of two tracks; it is equipped with a blade and a ripper.

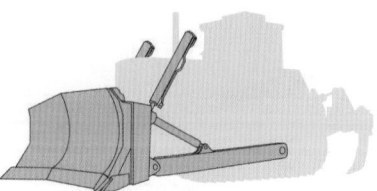

blade
Concave metal equipment for moving earth by pushing it along the ground; it is held up by two articulated arms and caused to swivel by hydraulic cylinders.

ripper
Equipment for breaking up hard earth; it is made up of a frame fitted with one to three teeth and is mounted on the back of a bulldozer.

backhoe loader

Excavation machine made up of a wheel tractor, a backhoe and a front-end loader.

general view

▪▪er arm
▪▪lating part of the backhoe that moves
▪▪ucket toward and away from the
▪▪▪r.

boom
Oscillating part of the backhoe that
moves the dipper arm and thus the
bucket up and down.

dipper arm cylinder
Hydraulic device consisting of a telescopic
arm that controls the movement of the
dipper arm.

backward bucket
Bucket for digging into the ground; it is
loaded by dragging it toward the tractor.

cab
Compartment from which the operator
controls the wheel loader.

bucket cylinder
Hydraulic device composed of a telescopic
arm that controls the movement of the
bucket lever.

bucket lever
Part impelled by the bucket hydraulic
cylinder that allows the bucket to swivel on
a horizontal axis.

backhoe controls
Set of levers for manipulating the backhoe.

bucket
Deep scoop that can be raised
and tipped.

bucket cylinder
Hydraulic device consisting of a
telescopic arm that controls the back-
and-forth motion of the bucket.

boom cylinder
▪raulic device consisting of a telescopic arm
that controls the movement of the boom.

diesel engine compartment
Combustion engine in which the compressed air
becomes sufficiently hot to ignite the injected
fuel.

lift arm
Lever that connects the loader to the
tractor; it raises and lowers the loader.

bucket hinge pin
Set of parts that causes the backhoe to move around
a vertical axle to swivel the bucket from side to side.

lift arm cylinder
Hydraulic telescopic device that raises and
lowers the lift arm.

cutting edge
Protrusions along the rim of the bucket
that cut into the material to be moved.

main parts

front-end loader
Equipment for lifting objects or material to be
moved or loaded; it consists of a bucket and
a lift arm impelled by hydraulic cylinders.

wheel tractor
Machine whose chassis can be
articulated; it is equipped with a
backhoe and a loader.

backhoe
Equipment for digging into the ground and
moving rubble; it consists of a bucket, an arm
and a boom impelled by hydraulic cylinders.

scraper

Machine that uses a blade to scrape the ground or roadbed and store the rubble in a bowl for disposal.

gooseneck
Arch serving as a coupling between the bowl and the tractor.

steering cylinder
One of two hydraulic cylinders on each side of the gooseneck that articulates with the bowl behind the tractor.

elevator
Belt fitted with chains and vanes that pulverizes the excavated material and chucks it into the bowl; in reverse gear it empties the bowl.

tractor engine compartment
Part of the machine made up of a powerful diesel engine and a cab from which to drive and operate it.

draft tube
Transverse tube welded to the gooseneck; it supports the two draft arms and uses hydraulic cylinders to lower and raise the bowl.

bowl
Open container in the front with a cutting edge; it is loaded and unloaded while in operation and removed for transport.

cutting edge
Usually toothed blade that is mounted on the front of the bowl; it scrapes off the top layer of a roadway or other surface.

draft arm
One of two shafts on each side that is supported by the draft tube; the bowl is raised and lowered between them.

power shovel

Machine made up of a pivot cab with a bucket attached for moving various types of material.

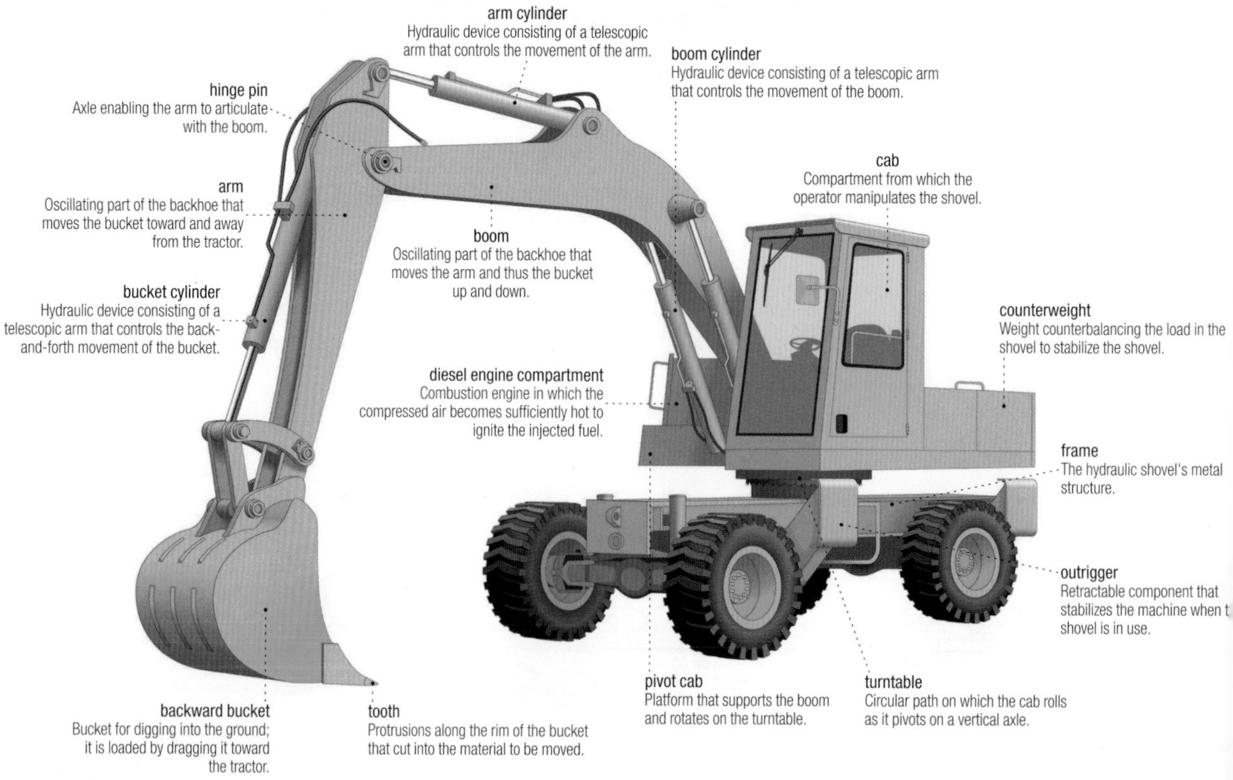

arm cylinder
Hydraulic device consisting of a telescopic arm that controls the movement of the arm.

boom cylinder
Hydraulic device consisting of a telescopic arm that controls the movement of the boom.

hinge pin
Axle enabling the arm to articulate with the boom.

cab
Compartment from which the operator manipulates the shovel.

arm
Oscillating part of the backhoe that moves the bucket toward and away from the tractor.

boom
Oscillating part of the backhoe that moves the arm and thus the bucket up and down.

counterweight
Weight counterbalancing the load in the shovel to stabilize the shovel.

bucket cylinder
Hydraulic device consisting of a telescopic arm that controls the back-and-forth movement of the bucket.

diesel engine compartment
Combustion engine in which the compressed air becomes sufficiently hot to ignite the injected fuel.

frame
The hydraulic shovel's metal structure.

outrigger
Retractable component that stabilizes the machine when the shovel is in use.

backward bucket
Bucket for digging into the ground; it is loaded by dragging it toward the tractor.

tooth
Protrusions along the rim of the bucket that cut into the material to be moved.

pivot cab
Platform that supports the boom and rotates on the turntable.

turntable
Circular path on which the cab rolls as it pivots on a vertical axle.

grader

Machine with a swiveling blade situated between two wheel shafts for leveling the ground or clearing debris off a roadway.

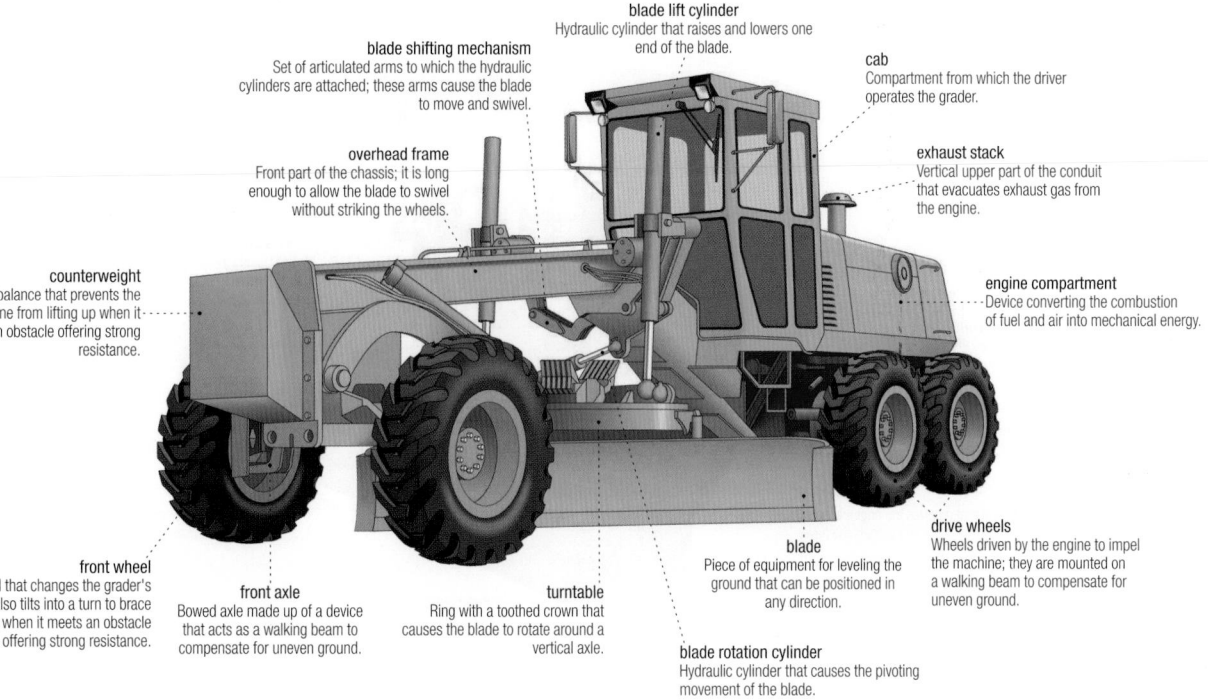

blade lift cylinder
Hydraulic cylinder that raises and lowers one end of the blade.

blade shifting mechanism
Set of articulated arms to which the hydraulic cylinders are attached; these arms cause the blade to move and swivel.

cab
Compartment from which the driver operates the grader.

overhead frame
Front part of the chassis; it is long enough to allow the blade to swivel without striking the wheels.

exhaust stack
Vertical upper part of the conduit that evacuates exhaust gas from the engine.

counterweight
Counterbalance that prevents the machine from lifting up when it meets an obstacle offering strong resistance.

engine compartment
Device converting the combustion of fuel and air into mechanical energy.

front wheel
Wheel that changes the grader's direction; it also tilts into a turn to brace the thing when it meets an obstacle offering strong resistance.

front axle
Bowed axle made up of a device that acts as a walking beam to compensate for uneven ground.

turntable
Ring with a toothed crown that causes the blade to rotate around a vertical axle.

blade
Piece of equipment for leveling the ground that can be positioned in any direction.

drive wheels
Wheels driven by the engine to impel the machine; they are mounted on a walking beam to compensate for uneven ground.

blade rotation cylinder
Hydraulic cylinder that causes the pivoting movement of the blade.

dump truck

Truck equipped with a dump body; it is used for bulk transport.

canopy
Metal surface that protects the cab from falling material during loading.

rib
Crosspiece welded to the outside walls of the dump body to reinforce it.

cab
Compartment from which the driver operates the truck.

dump body
Open or closed container; when raised by the elevation cylinder, it discharges its bulk material.

diesel engine compartment
Combustion engine in which the compressed air becomes sufficiently hot to ignite the injected fuel.

ladder
Device composed of treads and side rails that provides access to the cab.

frame
Metal structure of the dump truck.

asphalt paver

Vehicle used in the construction of roads that spreads bituminous coatings such as asphalt.

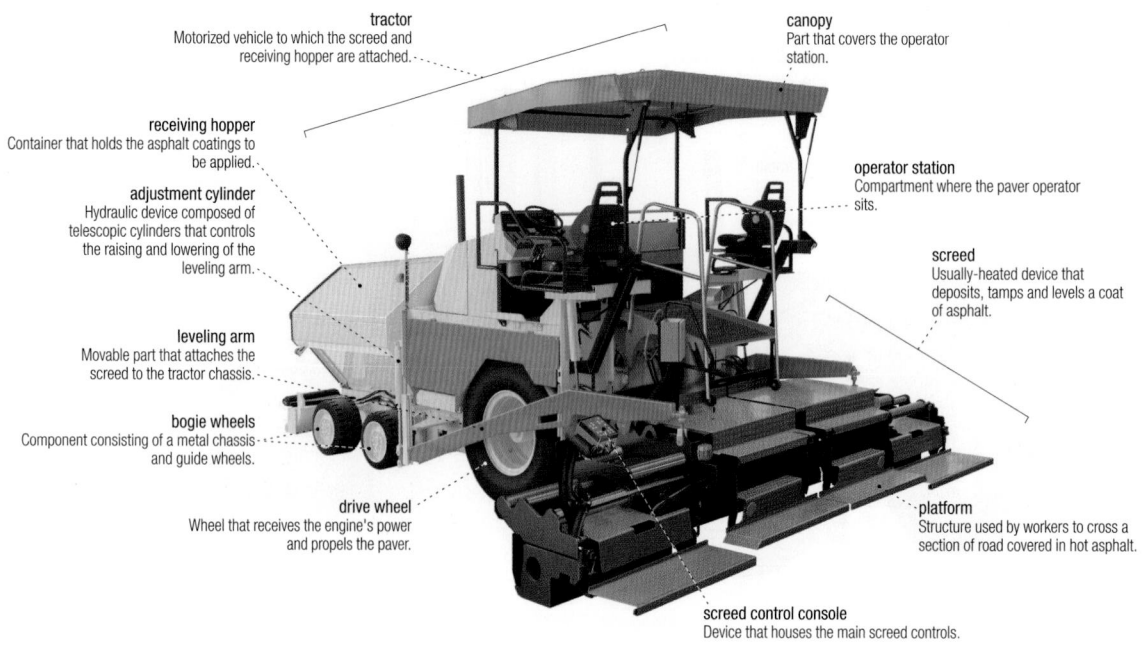

tractor
Motorized vehicle to which the screed and receiving hopper are attached.

canopy
Part that covers the operator station.

receiving hopper
Container that holds the asphalt coatings to be applied.

operator station
Compartment where the paver operator sits.

adjustment cylinder
Hydraulic device composed of telescopic cylinders that controls the raising and lowering of the leveling arm.

screed
Usually-heated device that deposits, tamps and levels a coat of asphalt.

leveling arm
Movable part that attaches the screed to the tractor chassis.

bogie wheels
Component consisting of a metal chassis and guide wheels.

drive wheel
Wheel that receives the engine's power and propels the paver.

platform
Structure used by workers to cross a section of road covered in hot asphalt.

screed control console
Device that houses the main screed controls.

road roller

Vehicle with cylindrical metal rollers; used in the compaction of earthen or asphalted surfaces.

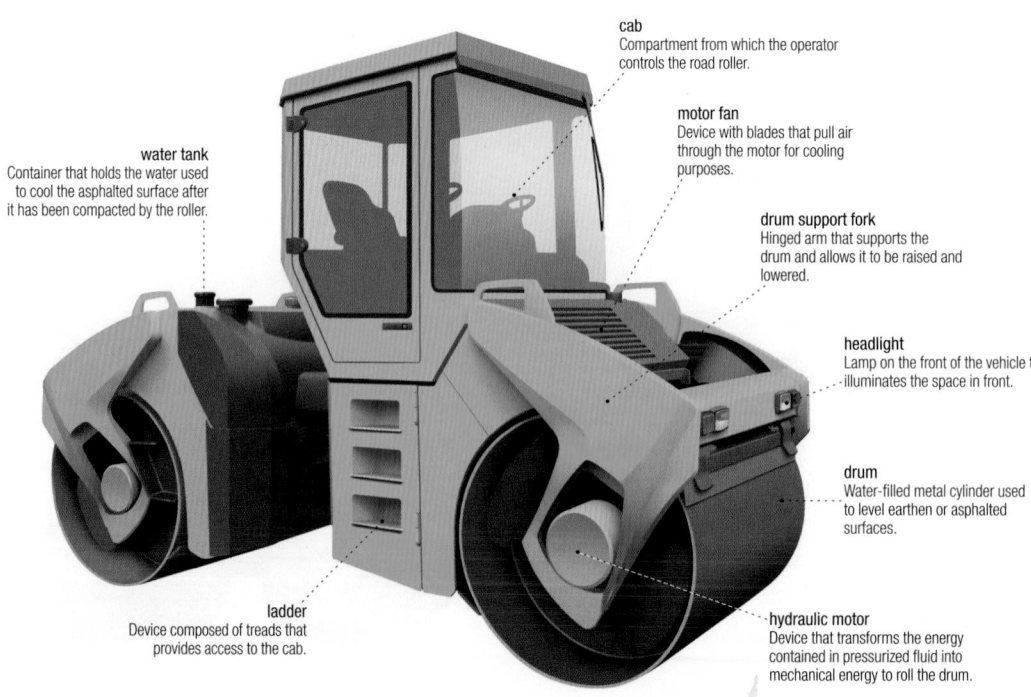

cab
Compartment from which the operator controls the road roller.

motor fan
Device with blades that pull air through the motor for cooling purposes.

water tank
Container that holds the water used to cool the asphalted surface after it has been compacted by the roller.

drum support fork
Hinged arm that supports the drum and allows it to be raised and lowered.

headlight
Lamp on the front of the vehicle that illuminates the space in front.

drum
Water-filled metal cylinder used to level earthen or asphalted surfaces.

ladder
Device composed of treads that provides access to the cab.

hydraulic motor
Device that transforms the energy contained in pressurized fluid into mechanical energy to roll the drum.

snowblower

Vehicle with a mechanism that draws up snow from the road and projects it some distance or into a dump truck.

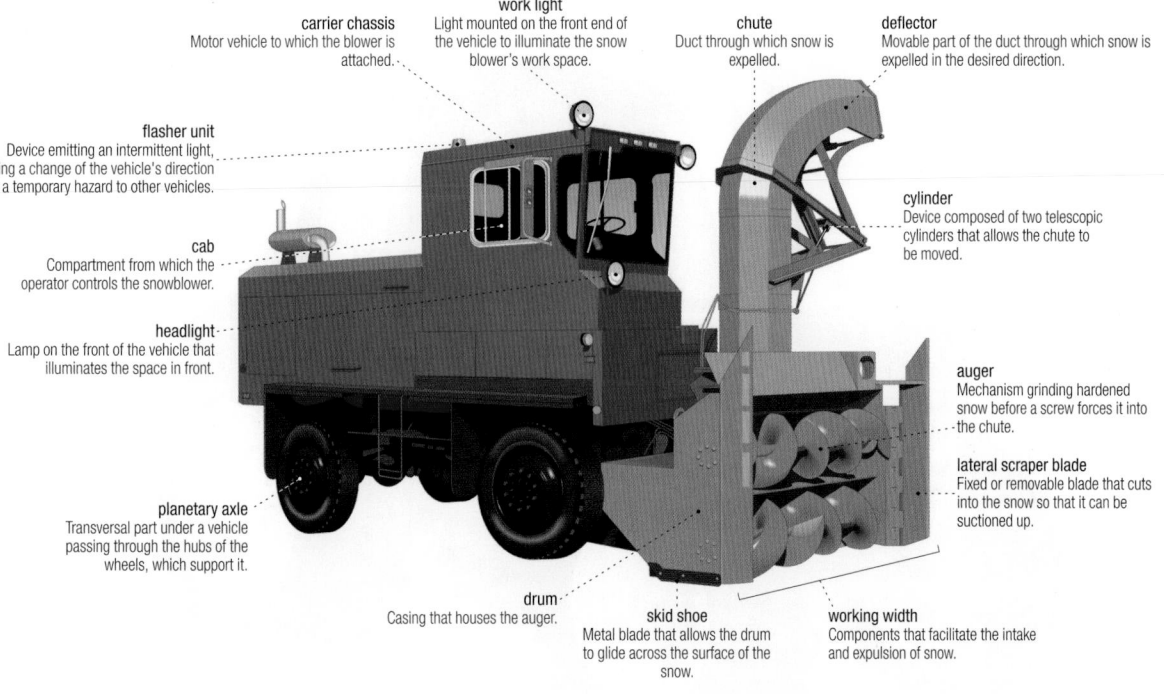

work light
Light mounted on the front end of the vehicle to illuminate the snow blower's work space.

carrier chassis
Motor vehicle to which the blower is attached.

chute
Duct through which snow is expelled.

deflector
Movable part of the duct through which snow is expelled in the desired direction.

flasher unit
Device emitting an intermittent light, ...ling a change of the vehicle's direction r a temporary hazard to other vehicles.

cylinder
Device composed of two telescopic cylinders that allows the chute to be moved.

cab
Compartment from which the operator controls the snowblower.

headlight
Lamp on the front of the vehicle that illuminates the space in front.

auger
Mechanism grinding hardened snow before a screw forces it into the chute.

lateral scraper blade
Fixed or removable blade that cuts into the snow so that it can be suctioned up.

planetary axle
Transversal part under a vehicle passing through the hubs of the wheels, which support it.

drum
Casing that houses the auger.

skid shoe
Metal blade that allows the drum to glide across the surface of the snow.

working width
Components that facilitate the intake and expulsion of snow.

street sweeper

Vehicle for cleaning city streets, equipped with a collection body, rotating brushes, a vacuum cleaner and a watering device.

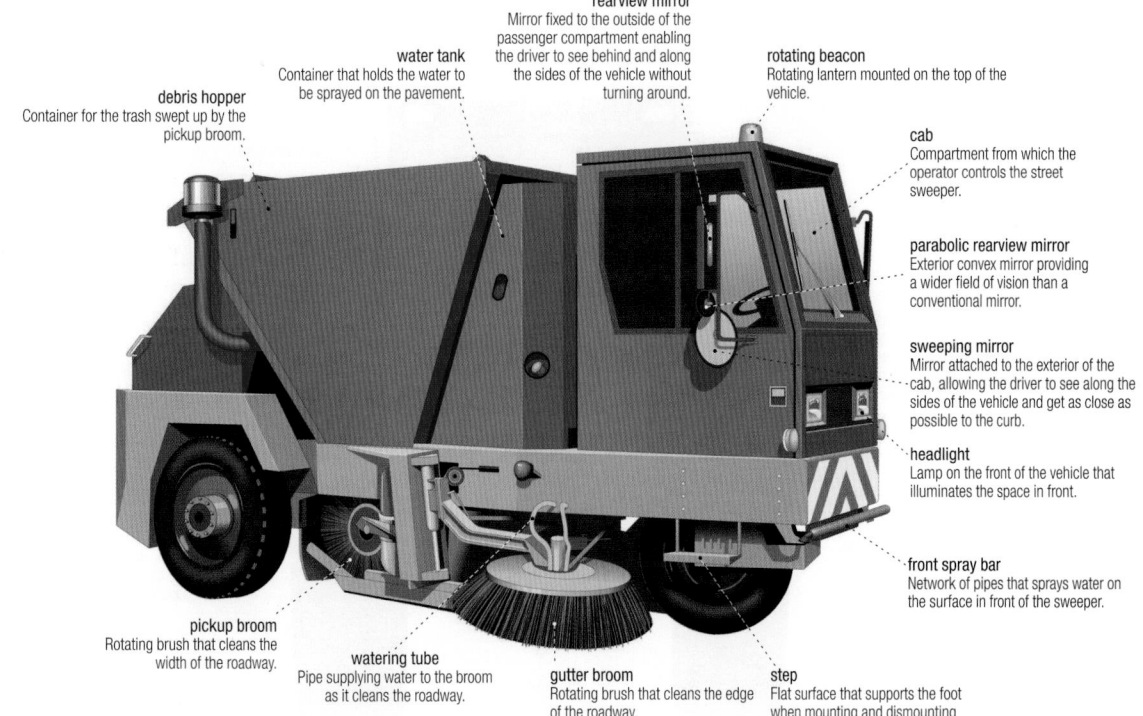

rearview mirror
Mirror fixed to the outside of the passenger compartment enabling the driver to see behind and along the sides of the vehicle without turning around.

water tank
Container that holds the water to be sprayed on the pavement.

rotating beacon
Rotating lantern mounted on the top of the vehicle.

debris hopper
Container for the trash swept up by the pickup broom.

cab
Compartment from which the operator controls the street sweeper.

parabolic rearview mirror
Exterior convex mirror providing a wider field of vision than a conventional mirror.

sweeping mirror
Mirror attached to the exterior of the cab, allowing the driver to see along the sides of the vehicle and get as close as possible to the curb.

headlight
Lamp on the front of the vehicle that illuminates the space in front.

front spray bar
Network of pipes that sprays water on the surface in front of the sweeper.

pickup broom
Rotating brush that cleans the width of the roadway.

watering tube
Pipe supplying water to the broom as it cleans the roadway.

gutter broom
Rotating brush that cleans the edge of the roadway.

step
Flat surface that supports the foot when mounting and dismounting the cab.

tractor

Motorized machine used for operating farm equipment and tools.

front view

exhaust stack
Vertical upper part of the conduit
that evacuates exhaust gas from
the engine.

cab
Compartment from which the
operator drives the truck and
operates the tools or agricultural
machinery.

headlight
Lamp on the front of the vehicle that
illuminates the space in front.

counterweight
Mass that balances and stabilizes the tool
hitched to the tractor.

engine compartment
Device converting the combustion of
fuel and air into mechanical energy.

front wheel
Wheel that changes the tractor's
direction; it is usually smaller than the
rear wheel.

step
Tread or set of treads built into the
body for climbing up to or down
from the cab.

steering wheel
Circular instrument used by the operator fo
steering the guide wheels.

fender
Part of the body that covers part of
the wheel and serves as a shield
from flying mud.

rim
Metal circle constituting the w
circumference and upon whic
tire is mounted.

tread bar
Raised part of the tire tread
improves traction for variou
conditions.

driving wheel
Wheel that receives the engine's power
and propels the tractor.

rear view

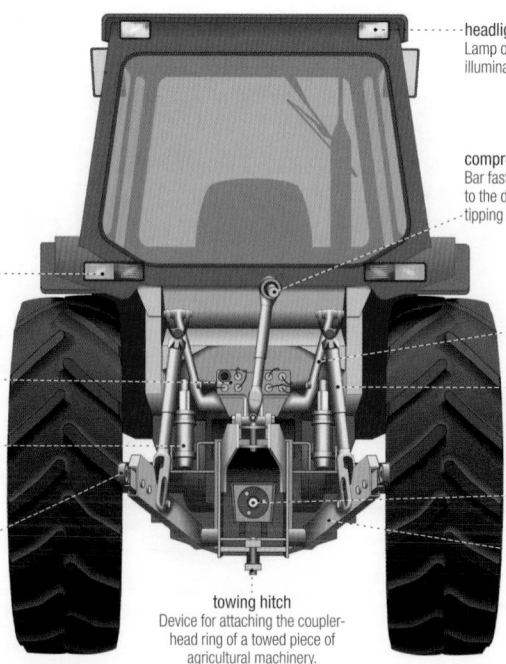

taillight
Lamp that illuminates automatically when
the front lights are on and shines more
brightly when the operator steps on the
brake pedal.

hydraulic coupler
Device for attaching the hydraulic
hoses so that power can be
transmitted to the attached tool.

hydraulic cylinder
Hydraulically powered device made
up of a cylinder and a piston, which
drive the draft link.

coupler head
Linking device between the tool and
the draft link.

towing hitch
Device for attaching the coupler-
head ring of a towed piece of
agricultural machinery.

headlight
Lamp on the rear of the vehicle that
illuminates the work area.

compression link
Bar fastened to a tool that is coupled
to the draft link to prevent it from
tipping up or down.

rock shaft lift arm
Part controlled by the hydraulic cylinder that rai
and lowers a tool by means of the lifting link an
the draft link.

lifting link
Part adjustable to several positions that
connects the draft link to the rock shaft
lift arm.

power take-off
Mechanism consisting of a grooved shaft
that uses the engine's power or the tractor's
movement to drive a tool or equipment being
towed.

draft link
Bar with a coupler head for towing.

agricultural machinery

Mechanized devices used in farming.

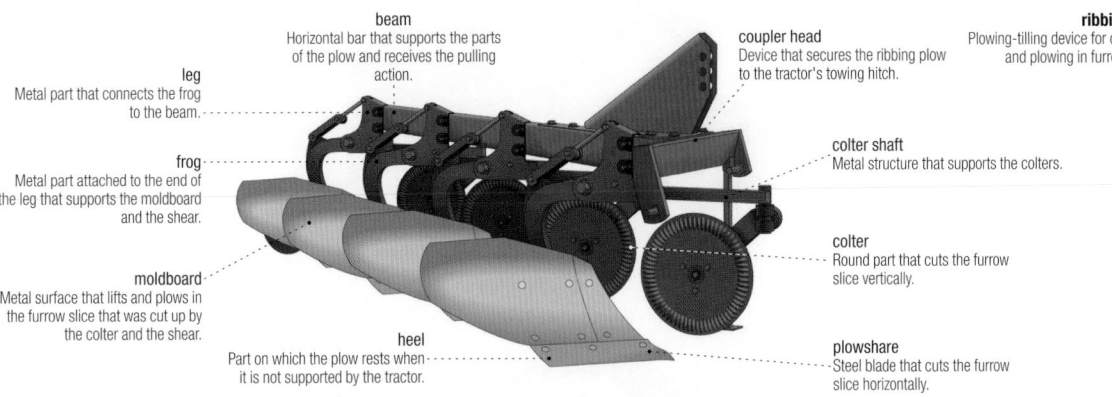

beam
Horizontal bar that supports the parts of the plow and receives the pulling action.

leg
Metal part that connects the frog to the beam.

frog
Metal part attached to the end of the leg that supports the moldboard and the shear.

moldboard
Metal surface that lifts and plows in the furrow slice that was cut up by the colter and the shear.

heel
Part on which the plow rests when it is not supported by the tractor.

coupler head
Device that secures the ribbing plow to the tractor's towing hitch.

ribbing plow
Plowing-tilling device for cutting up and plowing in furrow slices.

colter shaft
Metal structure that supports the colters.

colter
Round part that cuts the furrow slice vertically.

plowshare
Steel blade that cuts the furrow slice horizontally.

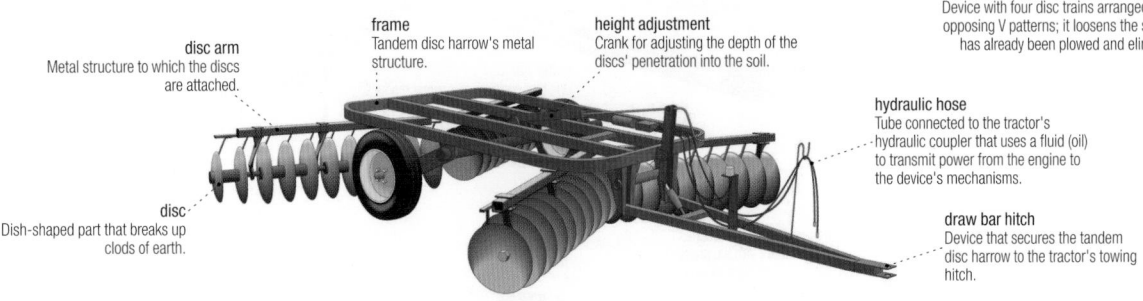

tandem disc harrow
Device with four disc trains arranged in two opposing V patterns; it loosens the soil that has already been plowed and eliminates weeds.

disc arm
Metal structure to which the discs are attached.

frame
Tandem disc harrow's metal structure.

height adjustment
Crank for adjusting the depth of the discs' penetration into the soil.

hydraulic hose
Tube connected to the tractor's hydraulic coupler that uses a fluid (oil) to transmit power from the engine to the device's mechanisms.

disc
Dish-shaped part that breaks up clods of earth.

draw bar hitch
Device that secures the tandem disc harrow to the tractor's towing hitch.

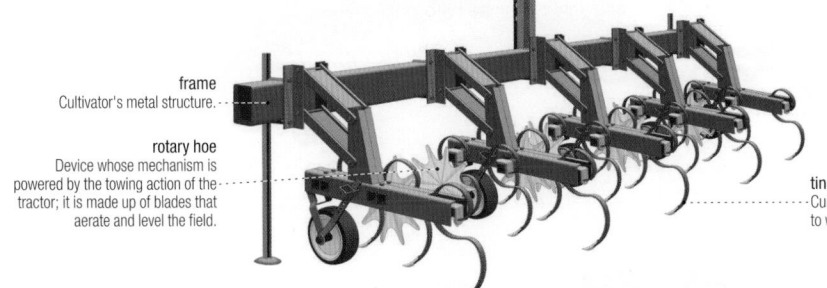

cultivator
Device with tines for working the top layer of the soil; it usually completes the plowing operation.

frame
Cultivator's metal structure.

rotary hoe
Device whose mechanism is powered by the towing action of the tractor; it is made up of blades that aerate and level the field.

tine
Curved prong that digs into the soil to work it by moving it sideways.

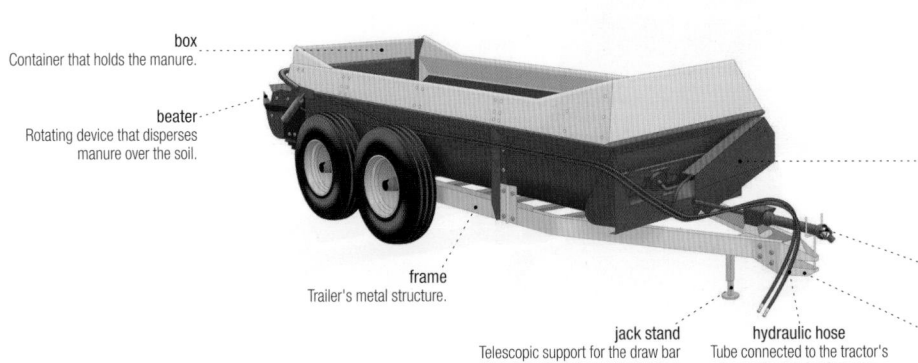

manure spreader
Device for scattering a mixture of litter and fermented animal waste over the soil to fertilize it.

box
Container that holds the manure.

beater
Rotating device that disperses manure over the soil.

chain drive
Belt that transmits the rotational movement of the power take-off shaft to the moving floor of the trailer to bring the manure back to the beater.

power take-off shaft
Device that hitches the machine's shaft to the tractor's power train to transmit the necessary power to operate it.

frame
Trailer's metal structure.

jack stand
Telescopic support for the draw bar hitch that supports the trailer when stationary.

hydraulic hose
Tube connected to the tractor's hydraulic coupler that uses a fluid (oil) to transmit power from the engine to the device's mechanisms.

draw bar hitch
Device that secures the manure spreader to the tractor's towing hitch.

TRANSPORT AND MACHINERY

agricultural machinery

rake
Device for turning over hay.

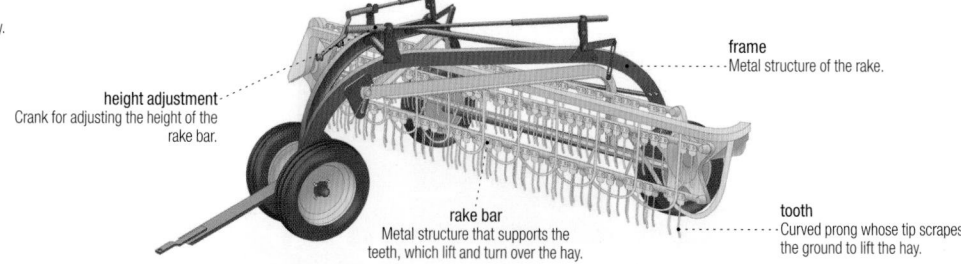

frame
Metal structure of the rake.

height adjustment
Crank for adjusting the height of the rake bar.

rake bar
Metal structure that supports the teeth, which lift and turn over the hay.

tooth
Curved prong whose tip scrapes the ground to lift the hay.

flail mower
Device that cuts the forage stalks as it moves and prepares them for the next harvesting phase (drying on the field and collection).

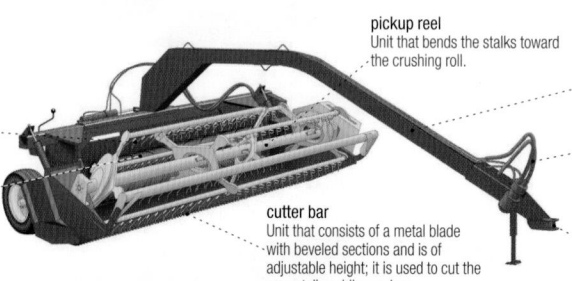

pickup reel
Unit that bends the stalks toward the crushing roll.

tow bar
Metal part with a draw bar hitch head that secures the flail mower to a tractor.

tooth
Curved tip for picking up the cut stalks.

hydraulic hose
Tube connected to the tractor's hydraulic coupler that uses a fluid (oil) to transmit power from the engine to the device's mechanisms.

crushing roll
One of two cylinders that crush and bend the stalks as they are fed between them; the crop is then deposited in a row on the ground.

cutter bar
Unit that consists of a metal blade with beveled sections and is of adjustable height; it is used to cut the crop stalks while moving.

draw bar hitch head
Device that secures the flail mower to the tractor's towing hitch.

hay baler
Device that harvests the forage and compresses it into bales.

plungerhead
Mechanical device that pushes the hay or straw into the press chamber by squeezing it forcibly.

press chamber
Device that shapes the bales of hay or straw.

binder
Device that ties the bales of hay or straw using string or wire.

tow bar
Metal part consisting of a towing hitch that connects the hay baler to the tractor.

power take-off shaft
Device that hitches the machine's shaft to the tractor's power train to transmit the necessary power to operate it.

draw bar hitch head
Device that secures the hay baler to the tractor's towing hitch.

pickup cylinder
Rotating unit that picks up the cut grass (such as straw or forage) to convey it to the plungerhead.

forage harvester
Device that harvests herbage (such as alfalfa, clover and corn) for feeding livestock.

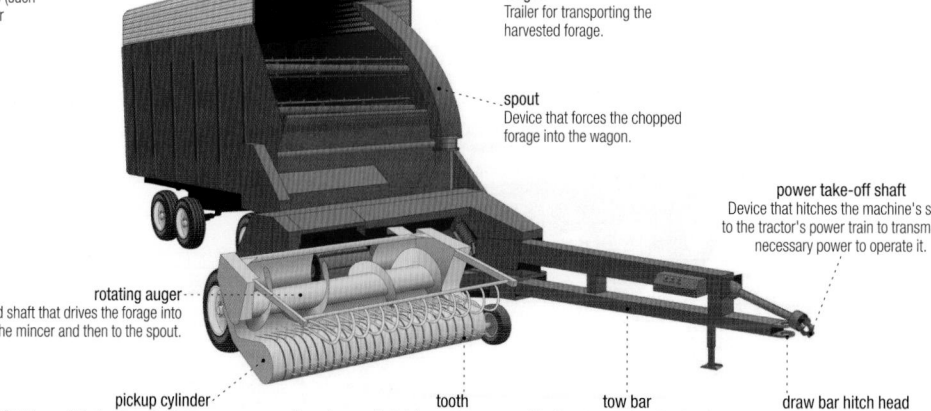

wagon
Trailer for transporting the harvested forage.

spout
Device that forces the chopped forage into the wagon.

power take-off shaft
Device that hitches the machine's shaft to the tractor's power train to transmit the necessary power to operate it.

rotating auger
Threaded shaft that drives the forage into the mincer and then to the spout.

pickup cylinder
Rotating unit that gathers the forage, which is then chopped and blown into the wagon.

tooth
Curved prong that picks up the forage from the ground.

tow bar
Metal part consisting of a draw bar hitch head that connects the forage harvester to the tractor.

draw bar hitch head
Device that secures the forage harvester to the tractor's towing hitch.

agricultural machinery

drill
ing tool that spreads and plows
s into the soil following straight
(furrows).

grain tube
Tube through which the seeds flow from
the bottom of the hopper to be dropped
into the furrow.

hopper
Container that is usually shaped like
an inverted pyramid; it holds the seeds
to be sown.

chain drive
Distribution unit that regulates the
flow of seeds into the grain tube.

colter
Round part that cuts the furrow slice
vertically.

covering disk
One of a pair of circular parts that
work together to close up the furrow.

press wheel
Wheel that tamps the earth to plow
the seeds down to a certain depth.

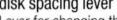

disk spacing lever
Lever for changing the distance between the sowing
lines.

ensiling tube
Duct through which the forage is
blown into the silo.

forage blower
Farm machine that forces the
harvested forage (e.g., grass, wheat
and corn) into the silo.

maneuvering bar
Rod for adjusting the blower to the
desired position.

fan tube
Duct through which the forage is
blown toward the ensiling tube.

fan
Machine that produces airflow
to force the forage through the
ensiling tube and onto the silo.

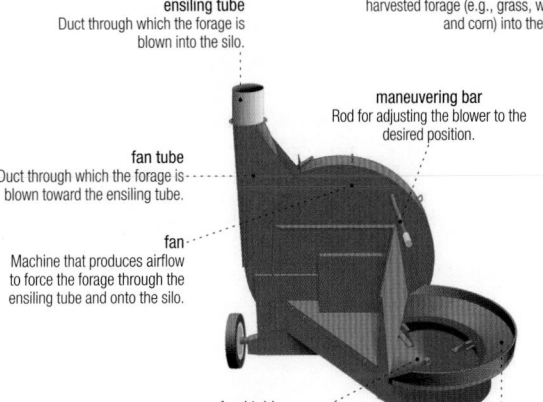

feed table
Rotating plate that moves the forage
into the fan.

hopper
Container that holds harvested
forage coming from a trailer, truck
or ensiling trailer.

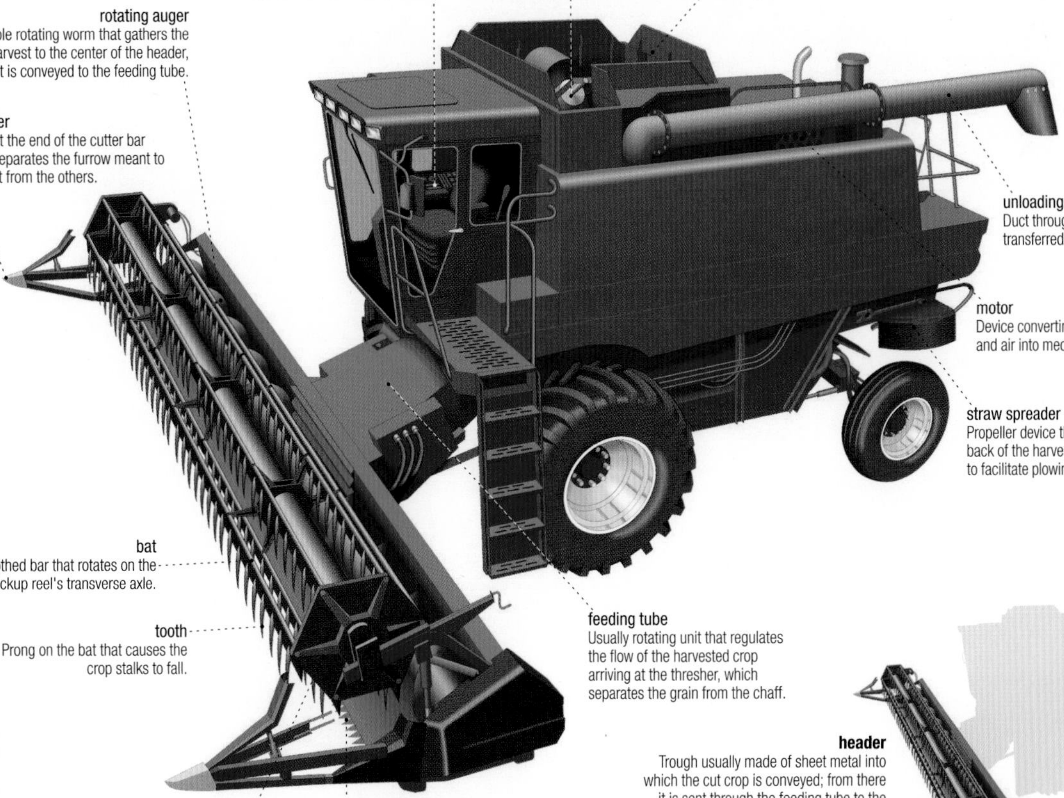

combine harvester
Vehicle that harvests seed crops,
usually grain; it cuts, threshes and
separates the seeds from the chaff.

cab
Compartment from which the driver
operates the combine harvester.

grain elevator
Mechanism that conveys the
harvested grain to the tank.

grain tank
Container that temporarily stores
harvested grain.

rotating auger
ble rotating worm that gathers the
arvest to the center of the header,
it is conveyed to the feeding tube.

er
at the end of the cutter bar
separates the furrow meant to
t from the others.

unloading tube
Duct through which the grain is
transferred from the tank to a trailer.

motor
Device converting the combustion of fuel
and air into mechanical energy.

straw spreader
Propeller device that spreads hay from the
back of the harvester the width of the cut
to facilitate plowing the hay under the soil.

bat
othed bar that rotates on the
ickup reel's transverse axle.

tooth
Prong on the bat that causes the
crop stalks to fall.

feeding tube
Usually rotating unit that regulates
the flow of the harvested crop
arriving at the thresher, which
separates the grain from the chaff.

header
Trough usually made of sheet metal into
which the cut crop is conveyed; from there
it is sent through the feeding tube to the
thresher.

pickup reel
Rotating unit underneath the cutter
bar that draws the stalks into the
rotating auger.

cutter bar
Unit that consists of a metal blade
with beveled sections and is of
adjustable height; it is used to cut the
crop stalks while moving.

TRANSPORT AND MACHINERY

ENERGY

The power to perform work, produced from natural phenomena (e.g., the Sun and the wind) or raw materials (e.g., coal and petroleum).

production of electricity from geothermal energy

Hot water contained in the ground near a volcano, geyser or other thermal source is piped to the surface by drilling to extract steam and produce electricity.

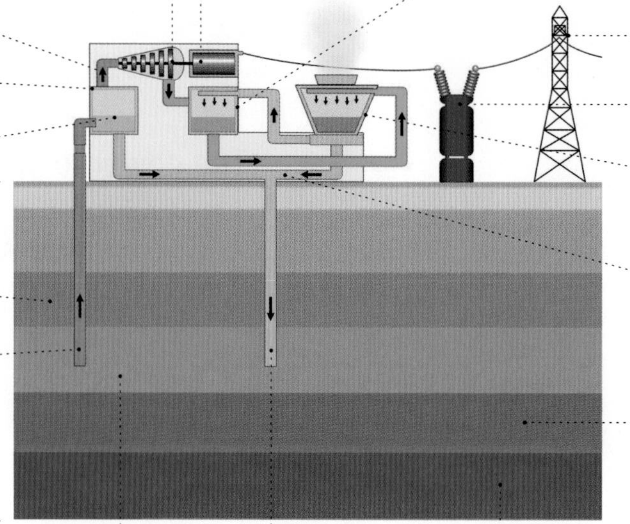

turbine
Steam-powered machine whose wheel transmits mechanical energy to the generator and causes it to rotate.

generator
Turbine-powered rotating machine that converts mechanical energy into electric energy and directs it toward a transmission network.

condenser
Circuit that cools the steam from the turbine and condenses it into water.

steam
Gaseous state of water; steam pressure operates the turbine.

high-tension electricity transmission
Using high-voltage lines to transmit electric[ity] long distances reduces the strength of the [current] and, as a result, energy losses.

exchange zone
Device that separates water from steam, which it recovers to operate the turbine; the water is reinjected into the aquifer.

voltage increase
At the outlet end of the power plant, the transformer increases the voltage; this reduces energy losses during transmission over long distances.

water-steam mix
Hot water extracted from the aquifer; as it rises to the surface, it is partially turned into steam.

cooling tower
Device that cools the condenser's hot water on contact with the air; some of the water evaporates and the rest is reinjected into the condenser and the aquifer.

upper confining bed
Layer of impermeable rock that covers the confined aquifer.

water
Liquid made up of hydrogen and oxygen that becomes steam at 212°F; the water transfers Earth's internal heat.

production well
Borehole dug into the ground to allow the hot water contained in the aquifer to be pumped to produce electricity.

lower confining bed
Layer of impermeable rock that transmits heat from the magma chamber to the aquifer.

geothermal field
Area of Earth's crust where a pocket of hot confined water is close enough to the surface to be exploited.

confined aquifer
Layer of porous sedimentary rock between two impermeable layers where water accumulates at an average temperature of 400°F.

injection well
Borehole that is drilled into the ground to return water to the aquifer, where it is reheated after its heat has been extracted.

magma chamber
Pocket of magma (molten rock emerging from Earth's crust) that constitutes a heat source; it transmits its thermal energy to water.

geothermal house

Dwelling with a heating or cooling system that relies on geothermal energy.

independent geothermal heating
System that uses heat trapped in the ground to heat a house.

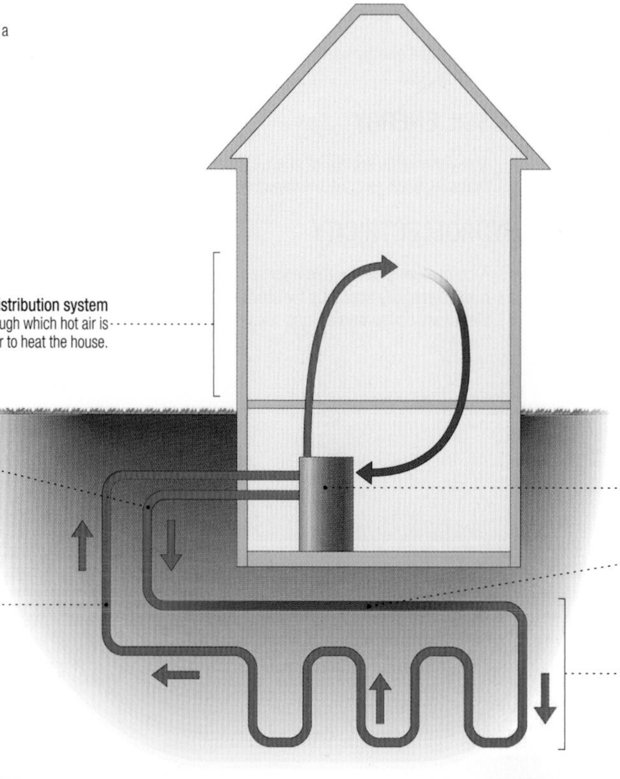

interior distribution system
Network of ducts through which hot air is propelled in order to heat the house.

cold coolant
Coolant: fluid that circulates in the underground loop. The pump extracts heat from the coolant and redirects it back to the underground loop.

heat pump
Heat exchange device between the house and the underground loop.

hot coolant
Coolant: fluid that circulates in the underground loop. Flowing hot coolant absorbs heat held in the ground and transmits it to the heat pump.

transfer of heat to coolant

underground loop
Underground pipelines through which coolant liquid flows.

ENERGY

coal mine

The underground or open-pit facilities that are set up around a coal deposit in order to extract it.

conveyor
rials-handling device that
of a conveyor belt (sturdy
on rollers) that is used to
rt coal extracted from the
mine.

dump
hat is made up of residue
from mining operations.

trench
gthwise excavation that is
de down to the top of the
re layer in order to extract
its coal.

roof
ologic stratum that covers
he ore seam; it is of more
nt formation than the ore.

strip mine
Type of mining that is used especially
for large shallow deposits; coal or ore
is extracted by digging a trench in the
ground surface.

mechanical shovel
Earthmover that consists of a
movable cab with an articulated arm
fitted with a bucket (scoop); it is used
for digging and handling loads.

bucket wheel excavator
Earthmover that consists of a wheel
fitted with buckets (scoops); it is
used to dig into rock to extract
materials, which are then dumped
onto a conveyor.

overburden
Part of the ground that covers the
ore beds; it is removed to reach
the deposit.

face
Part of the quarry that is being
excavated and from which ore is
progressively extracted.

bulldozer
Excavation machine for pushing
materials; it is made up of a crawler
tractor, a blade and often a ripper.

belt loader
Movable materials-handling device that
is fitted with an inclined conveyor belt; it
is used mainly to raise loads.

bench
One of the levels of a quarry
that are arranged like steps of a
staircase and from which coal or
ore is extracted.

ground surface
The land that covers the deposit.

open-pit mine
Type of mining that is used for shallow
deposits; coal or ore is extracted by
digging a succession of benches from the
surface of the ground downward.

face
ertical surface created by
niting a deposit to extract
its ore.

haulage road
bad leading to the quarry;
is used to haul coal to the
treatment plant.

overburden
Part of the ground that covers the
ore beds; it is removed to reach
the deposit.

bench height
Vertical distance between the
horizontal planes of two benches.

ramp
Roadway between two benches; it is
inclined so that motorized vehicles can
remove the ore extracted from the various
levels.

crater
Depression that forms the bottom
of the quarry; it is a result of the
extraction of deposits.

coal ore
Solid fossil fuel that is black and
contains a large amount of carbon.

ENERGY

coal mine

jackleg drill
Percussive tool that is powered by compressed air; it is used to bore holes into hard rock. The air leg makes the job easier for the drill operator.

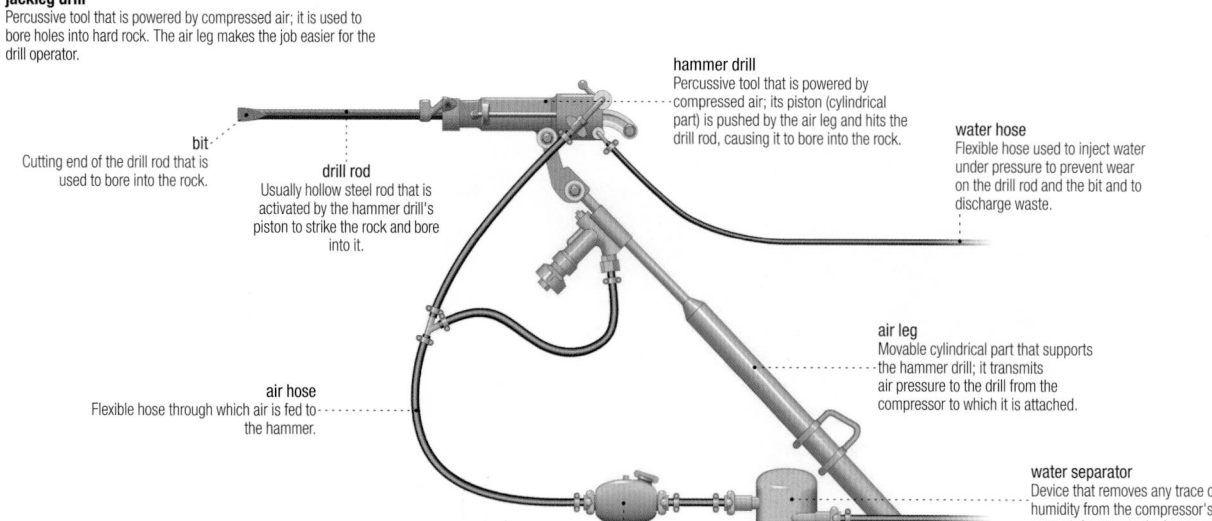

hammer drill
Percussive tool that is powered by compressed air; its piston (cylindrical part) is pushed by the air leg and hits the drill rod, causing it to bore into the rock.

water hose
Flexible hose used to inject water under pressure to prevent wear on the drill rod and the bit and to discharge waste.

bit
Cutting end of the drill rod that is used to bore into the rock.

drill rod
Usually hollow steel rod that is activated by the hammer drill's piston to strike the rock and bore into it.

air leg
Movable cylindrical part that supports the hammer drill; it transmits air pressure to the drill from the compressor to which it is attached.

air hose
Flexible hose through which air is fed to the hammer.

water separator
Device that removes any trace of humidity from the compressor's a prevent damage to the hammer.

oiler
Device that allows oil to enter the hammer to prevent wear of its moving parts.

maintenance shop
Work area where machinery is maintained and repaired.

pithead
The surface facilities needed for underground mining (including extraction machinery, storage areas and offices).

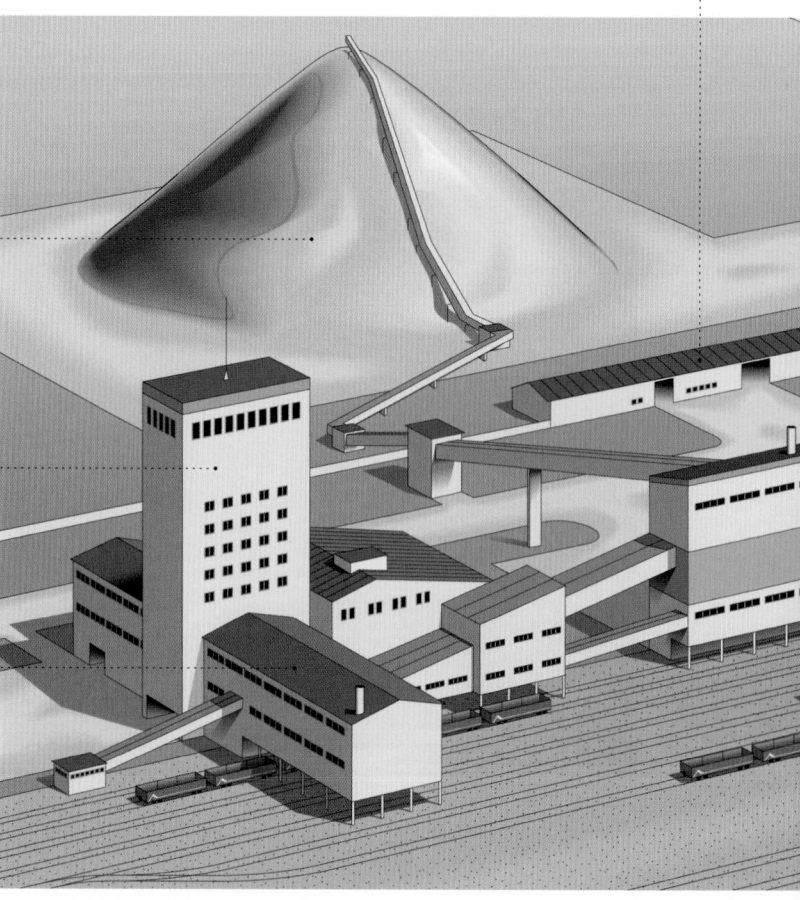

dump
Pile that is made up of residue from mining operations.

main fan
Device that ensures air exchange in the mine; air is drawn through one shaft and exits through another.

loading bunker
Reservoir where processed coal is stored before being loaded onto freight cars to be transported by rail to the power plant.

coal mine

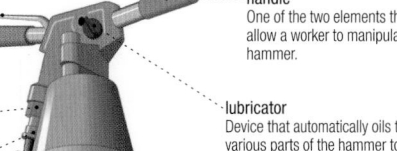

jackhammer
Percussive tool that is powered by compressed air; with the help of a piston, it activates a tool, which breaks through very hard matter such as rock and concrete.

control lever
Grip used to operate the hammer; the lever opens the throttle valve so that air can enter the hammer.

handle
One of the two elements that allow a worker to manipulate the hammer.

throttle valve
Movable part that is opened by the control lever to let compressed air into the hammer.

lubricator
Device that automatically oils the various parts of the hammer to prevent wear.

flexible hose connection
Fastening device with a metal part that accepts the flexible hose so that compressed air can enter the hammer.

silencer
Device that lessens the noise caused when air exits the hammer.

flexible hose
Flexible hose through which compressed air from the compressor it is attached to enters the hammer.

exhaust port
Opening through which compressed air is expelled from the pneumatic hammer.

chuck
Part of the hammer to which the tool is fastened.

retainer
Device that holds the tool in place in the chuck.

tool
Cylindrical rod that is set in motion by compressed air pressure from the hammer; it is used to break hard surfaces.

frame
ing at the top of the shaft that ects the aboveground facilities ding ventilation fans and s) to the underground areas mined.

miners' changing room
Area with sanitary facilities (showers, toilets) where miners can go mainly to change their clothes.

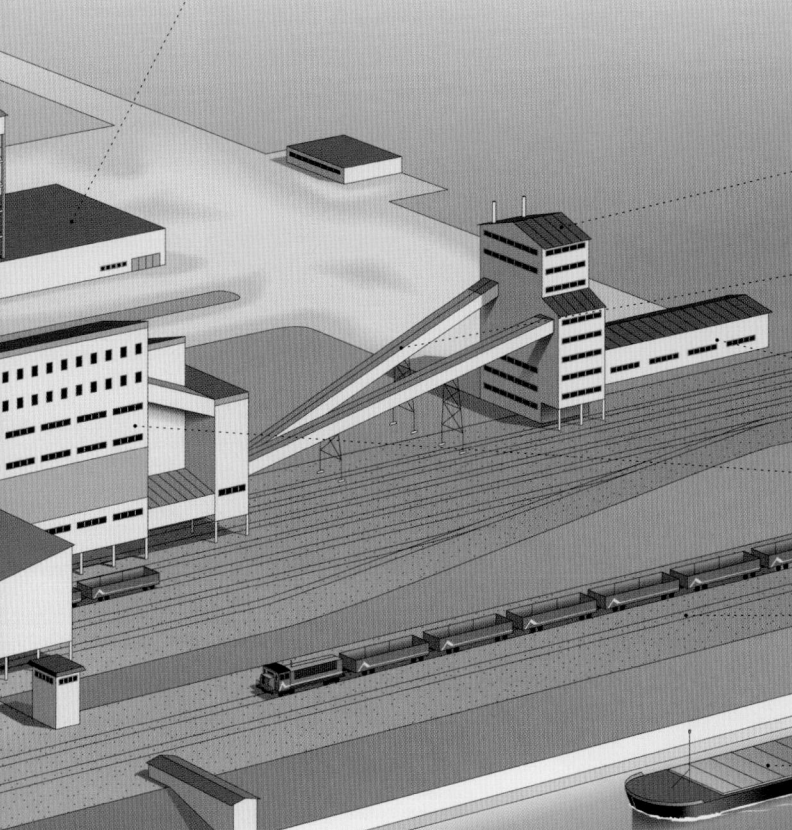

winding tower
Building that houses the shaft's hoisting equipment (including motors and hoisting cables); it provides communication between the surface and the mine galleries.

conveyor
Materials-handling device that consists of a conveyor belt (sturdy belt on rollers); it is used to carry coal to the treatment plant.

hoist room
Area that houses the hoist (cylinder) on which the hoisting cables are wound; it controls movement of the elevators and skip hoists in the shaft.

treatment plant
Place where all processing activities (including crushing and washing) are carried out to prepare the coal for market.

railroad track
The tracks formed of two parallel rails on which trains travel to transport coal.

maritime transport
Means of transport that uses barges to transport coal over water.

ENERGY

coal mine

underground mine
Property in which excavations are
carried out to extract deeply embedded
(between 30 and 11,500 ft) coal for
industrial mining.

headframe
Opening at the top of the shaft that
connects the aboveground facilities
(including ventilation fans and hoists)
to the underground areas being mined.

vertical shaft
Shaft that is dug perpendicular to
the surface; it serves various levels
and is used mainly to transport
personnel, equipment and ore.

elevator
Power lift fitted with a cab that transports
coal or miners between the various levels.

chute
Vertical or inclined passageway
through which ore, equipment,
personnel and air move from one
level of the mine to the other.

cross cut
Horizontal passageway that cuts
through the ore bed perpendicularly;
it provides communication between
the passageways and helps to
ventilate the mine.

manway
Passageway allowing workers to
move around in the mine.

drift
Passageway dug horizontally along
the grade line of the ore seam; it can
also be dug into the ore vertically.

face
The exposed surface that extends
laterally into the rock as coal is
extracted.

winding tower
Building that houses the shaft's hoisting
equipment (including motors and hoisting
cables); it provides communication between
the surface and the mine galleries.

winding shaft
Shaft that is dug vertically into the
ground; coal is removed from the
through it using hoisting machine

pillar
Mass of ore that is left unmined
regular intervals in an excavation
(chamber); it provides stability for
upper layers.

room
Cavity that remains after the ore
extracted; pillars support its roof

level
The horizontal passageways that
branch off from the shaft at the
same depth; they are usually at
regular intervals.

top road
Horizontal passageway that serv
the highest level of a panel.

deck
Extraction layer between two lev
mining is usually done in stages
descending order.

skip
Elevator consisting of a skip buc
that is activated by a hoist; it is
used to bring coal and people to
the surface.

ore pass
Inclined route that takes coal to
level; coal that falls on the mine
usually crushed before being bro
to the surface.

panel
Unit of rock that is being mined;
is contained between vertical an
horizontal planes and is demarc
by various passageways.

landing
Landing located around a shaft
each level; coal is collected here
before being moved to the surfa

sump
Bottom of the shaft in which wa
runoff accumulates inside the
mine before being pumped to th
surface.

bottom road
Horizontal passageway that serves
the base of a panel.

winze
Vertical or inclined passageway
that connects two levels; it is dug
downward from inside the mine
and not from the surface.

thermal energy

Energy that is produced by turning water into steam through the burning of fuel (e.g., petroleum and coal) or through nuclear reaction.

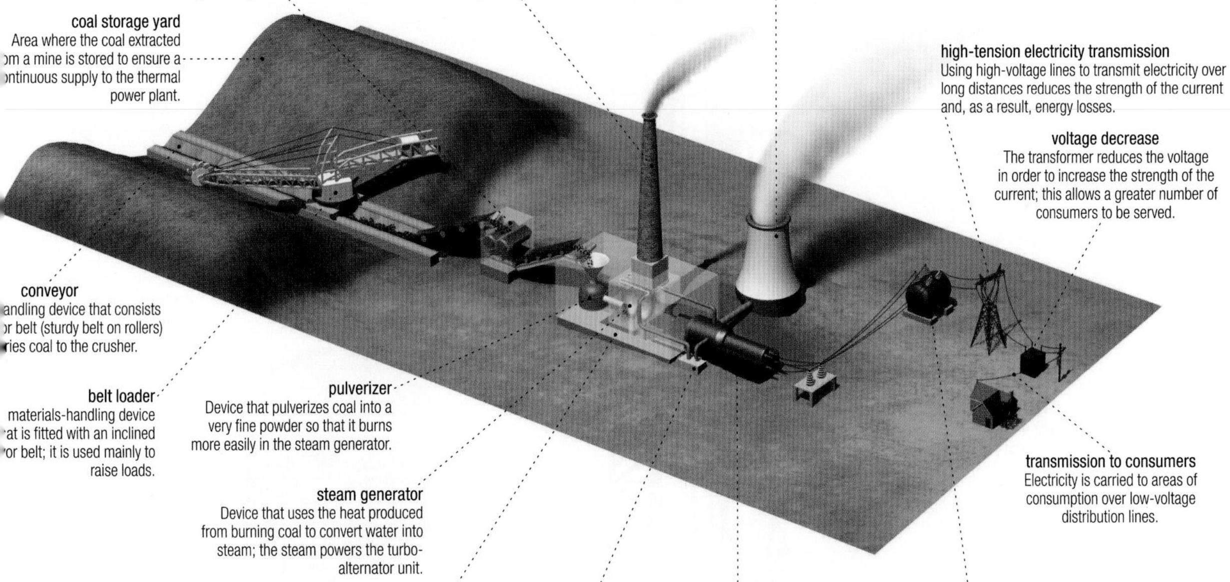

crusher
Device that pulverizes the coal carried by the conveyor belt into relatively fine fragments.

stack
Pipe through which gases produced by burning coal are discharged; these gases are first partially cleaned to reduce pollution.

cooling tower
Device that cools the heated water in the condenser through contact with the air; a small amount of water evaporates and the rest is reinjected into the condenser.

production of electricity from thermal energy
The heat that is given off by burning combustible fuels in the thermal power plant converts water into steam; the steam turns a turbo-alternator unit to produce electricity.

coal storage yard
Area where the coal extracted from a mine is stored to ensure a continuous supply to the thermal power plant.

high-tension electricity transmission
Using high-voltage lines to transmit electricity over long distances reduces the strength of the current and, as a result, energy losses.

voltage decrease
The transformer reduces the voltage in order to increase the strength of the current; this allows a greater number of consumers to be served.

conveyor
handling device that consists or belt (sturdy belt on rollers) ries coal to the crusher.

belt loader
materials-handling device at is fitted with an inclined or belt; it is used mainly to raise loads.

pulverizer
Device that pulverizes coal into a very fine powder so that it burns more easily in the steam generator.

steam generator
Device that uses the heat produced from burning coal to convert water into steam; the steam powers the turbo-alternator unit.

coal-fired thermal power plant
Plant that produces electricity from thermal energy by burning coal.

condenser
Circuit that cools the steam from the turbine and condenses it into water, which is reintroduced into the steam generator.

turbo-alternator unit
Device with a turbine that transmits the water's mechanical energy to the alternator's rotor to make it turn to produce electricity.

voltage increase
At the outlet end of the power plant, the transformer increases the voltage; this reduces energy losses during transmission over long distances.

transmission to consumers
Electricity is carried to areas of consumption over low-voltage distribution lines.

oil

mmable, relatively viscous oily liquid that is used as an energy source; it is made up of various hydrocarbons resulting from the decomposition of plant life over millions of years.

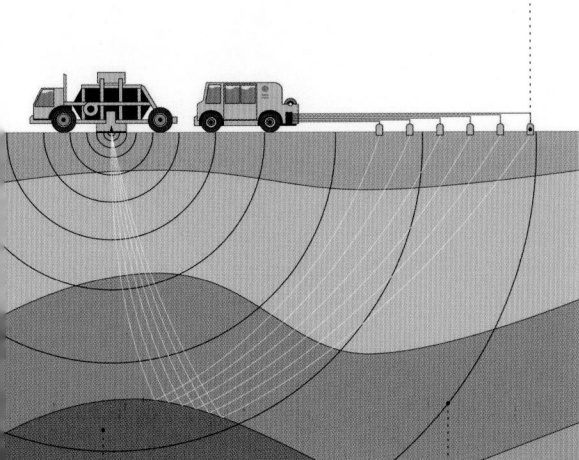

ace prospecting
rching for potential oil deposits udying the structure of the oil using a seismograph.

seismographic recording
A recording made using an apparatus called a seismograph; its analysis of shock wave echoes detects the presence of rock layers that might contain pockets of petroleum or gas.

petroleum trap
Assemblage of porous rocks that contain recoverable oil reserves, which are produced from marine or land deposits.

shock wave
The shock wave spreads and sends back an echo, which varies with the density and depth of the layers of subsoil; with this information, the composition of the subsoil can be determined.

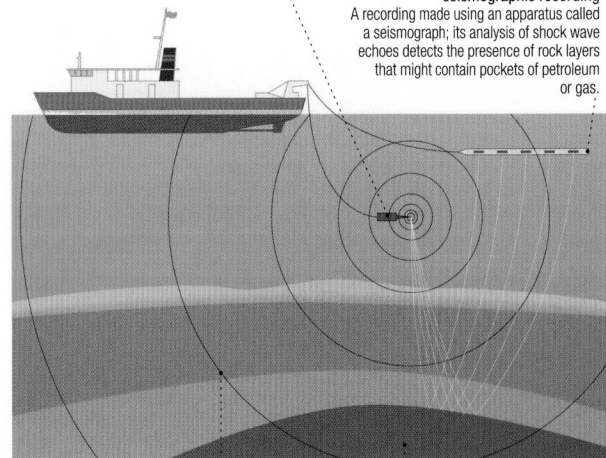

blasting charge
Quantity of explosives (substances capable of discharging high-temperature gases over a very short time period) that produce shock waves when detonated.

offshore prospecting
Vibrations from an exploding charge in the sea are used to locate oil deposits; prospecting offshore is more difficult than on land.

seismographic recording
A recording made using an apparatus called a seismograph; its analysis of shock wave echoes detects the presence of rock layers that might contain pockets of petroleum or gas.

shock wave
The shock wave spreads and sends back an echo, which varies with the density and depth of the layers of subsoil; with this information, the composition of the subsoil can be determined.

petroleum trap
Assemblage of porous rocks that contain recoverable oil reserves, which are produced from marine or land deposits.

ENERGY

oil

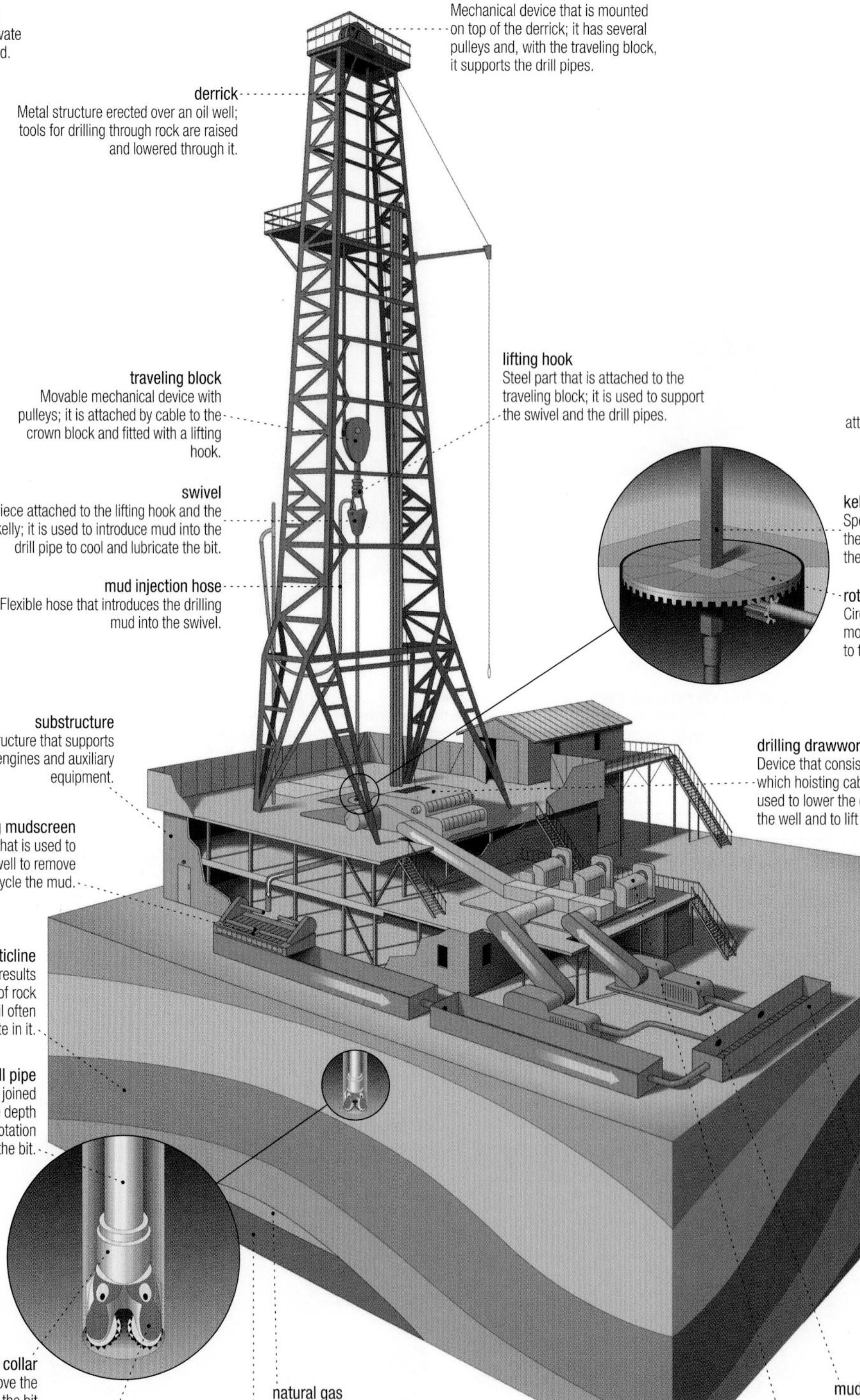

drilling rig
All the drilling machinery and devices that are used to excavate and extract oil from the ground.

crown block
Mechanical device that is mounted on top of the derrick; it has several pulleys and, with the traveling block, it supports the drill pipes.

derrick
Metal structure erected over an oil well; tools for drilling through rock are raised and lowered through it.

traveling block
Movable mechanical device with pulleys; it is attached by cable to the crown block and fitted with a lifting hook.

lifting hook
Steel part that is attached to the traveling block; it is used to support the swivel and the drill pipes.

rotary syst
Drilling device in which a kel attached to a rotary table; with the of powerful motors, it transmits rotative movement to the ke

swivel
Piece attached to the lifting hook and the kelly; it is used to introduce mud into the drill pipe to cool and lubricate the bit.

kelly
Special square rod that is screwed t the top of the drill pipes and driven the rotary table.

mud injection hose
Flexible hose that introduces the drilling mud into the swivel.

rotary table
Circular table that is moved by powe motors; it transmits its rotative mov to the drill pipes by means of the ke

substructure
Metal infrastructure that supports the derrick, engines and auxiliary equipment.

drilling drawworks
Device that consists of a cylinder on which hoisting cables are wound; it is used to lower the drill pipes and bit into the well and to lift them out.

vibrating mudscreen
Perforated vibrating tray that is used to filter mud as it exits the well to remove debris and recycle the mud.

anticline
Geologic stratum that results from the convex folding of rock formations; large pools of oil often accumulate in it.

drill pipe
Hollow steel rods that are joined together according to the depth of the excavation; their rotation activates the bit.

mud pit
Basin that contains mud (a m water, clay and chemical pro mainly to cool and lubricate t remove debris.

drill collar
Heavy steel tube immediately above the bit that applies a certain weight to the bit to help it cut into the rock.

mud pump
Device that circulates the mud in the drilling rig.

bit
Rotating drill bit with toothed steel or diamond wheels; it bores into rock to break it up and drill a hole.

natural gas
Mixture of gaseous hydrocarbons (mainly methane) that are found in underground deposits, which sometimes also contain crude oil; it is used mainly as a fuel.

oil
Flammable, relatively viscous oily liquid that is used as an energy source; it is made up of various hydrocarbons resulting from the decomposition of plant life over millions of year.

impervious rock
Layer of impermeable rock that covers and protects the oil deposit; it prevents hydrocarbons from migrating into other rocks.

engine
Device converting the combustion of fuel ar into mechanical energy.

ENERGY

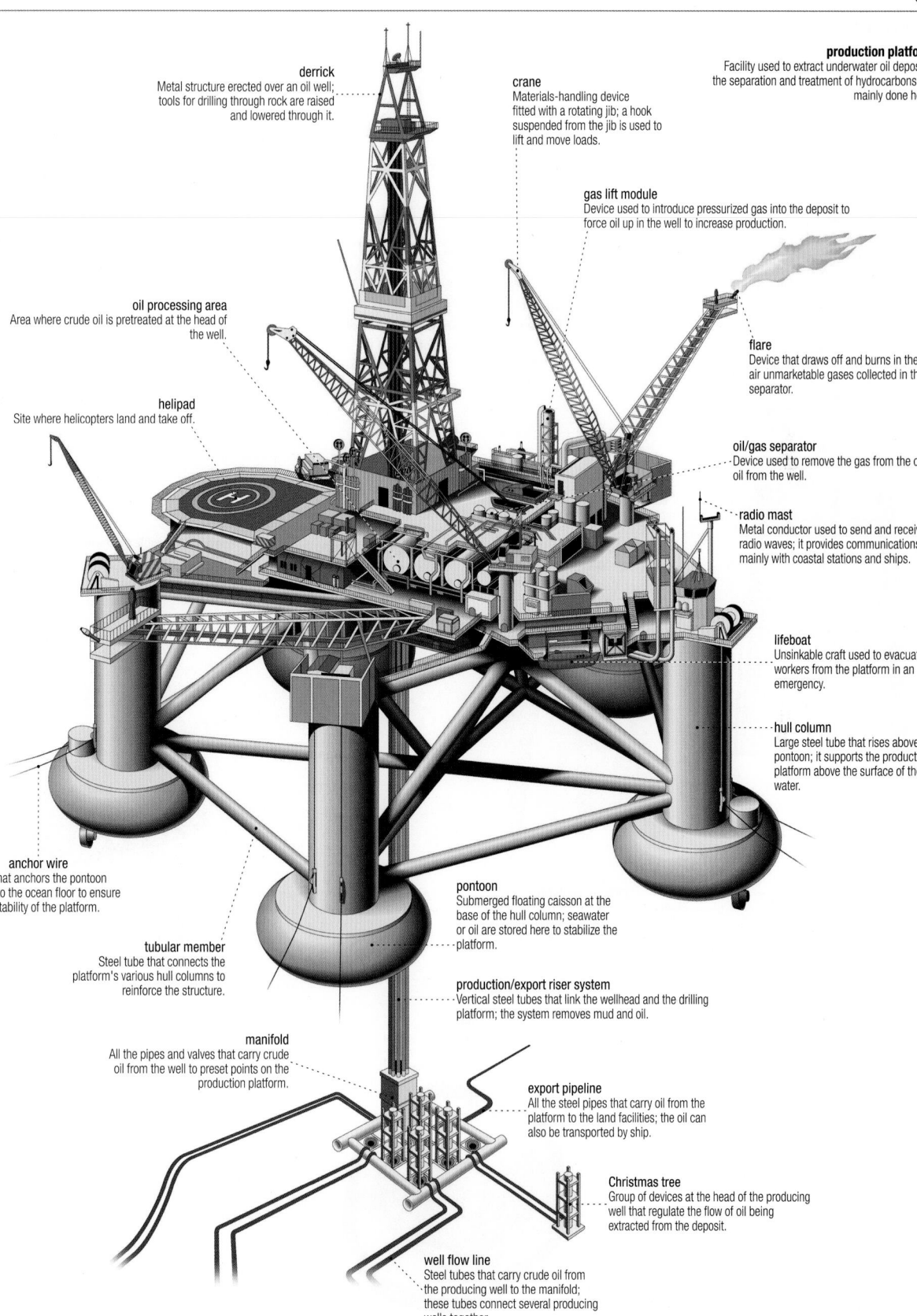

derrick
Metal structure erected over an oil well;
tools for drilling through rock are raised
and lowered through it.

crane
Materials-handling device
fitted with a rotating jib; a hook
suspended from the jib is used to
lift and move loads.

production platform
Facility used to extract underwater oil deposits;
the separation and treatment of hydrocarbons are
mainly done here.

gas lift module
Device used to introduce pressurized gas into the deposit to
force oil up in the well to increase production.

oil processing area
Area where crude oil is pretreated at the head of
the well.

flare
Device that draws off and burns in the
air unmarketable gases collected in the
separator.

helipad
Site where helicopters land and take off.

oil/gas separator
Device used to remove the gas from the crude
oil from the well.

radio mast
Metal conductor used to send and receive
radio waves; it provides communications
mainly with coastal stations and ships.

lifeboat
Unsinkable craft used to evacuate
workers from the platform in an
emergency.

hull column
Large steel tube that rises above the
pontoon; it supports the production
platform above the surface of the
water.

anchor wire
Wire that anchors the pontoon
surely to the ocean floor to ensure
the stability of the platform.

tubular member
Steel tube that connects the
platform's various hull columns to
reinforce the structure.

pontoon
Submerged floating caisson at the
base of the hull column; seawater
or oil are stored here to stabilize the
platform.

production/export riser system
Vertical steel tubes that link the wellhead and the drilling
platform; the system removes mud and oil.

manifold
All the pipes and valves that carry crude
oil from the well to preset points on the
production platform.

export pipeline
All the steel pipes that carry oil from the
platform to the land facilities; the oil can
also be transported by ship.

Christmas tree
Group of devices at the head of the producing
well that regulate the flow of oil being
extracted from the deposit.

well flow line
Steel tubes that carry crude oil from
the producing well to the manifold;
these tubes connect several producing
wells together.

ENERGY

oil

offshore drilling

There are various types of underwater oil drilling installations; the one used depends on the location of the deposit and the depth of the water.

drill ship
Ship for drilling for oil in deep water (3,300 ft and more); it is more mobile but less stable than a semisubmersible or jack-up platform.

fixed platform
Structure that is mainly used at moderate depths (up to 1,300 ft); it rests on the seabed on pillars buried deep in the sea floor.

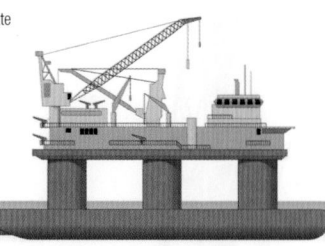

emergency support vessel
Floating structure equipped with specialized equipment; it is used for rescue operations on drilling rigs.

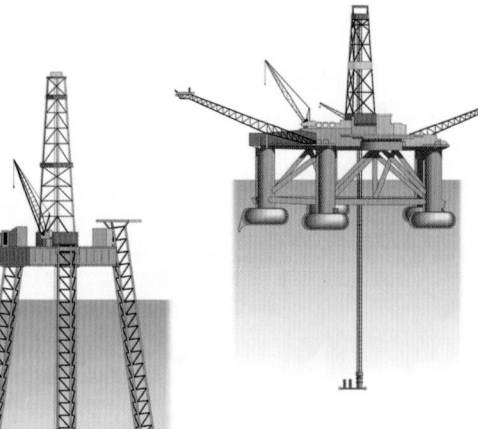

semisubmersible platform
Movable structure that is anchored to the seabed and used at depths of 350 to 1,650 ft; it is mounted on pontoons submerged at about 100 ft to provide stability.

jack-up platform
Movable structure that is used in shallow water (between 65 and 330 ft); it is raised above sea level on retractable pillars resting on the ocean floor.

pier
Structure that extends into the sea from a land-based installation; it is used for land drilling extending offshore (about 10 ft deep).

oil extraction from oil sands

Activity undertaken to extract hydrocarbons from deposits of oil sands. Bitumen can be extracted from an open pit mine or underground techniques, which involve injecting steam into a well.

oil sand
Mineral composed of a grain of sand coated with a layer of water and a layer of bitumen.

water
Liquid made up of hydrogen and oxygen that becomes steam at 212°F or 100°C.

sand
Small fragment of rock or mineral.

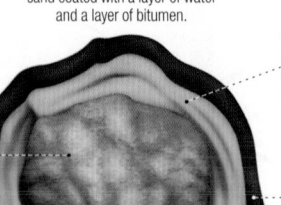

bitumen
Semi-solid form of raw petroleum.

ENERGY

oil

open-pit mining
Extraction technique that involves excavating the ground to
extract exploitable oil sands.

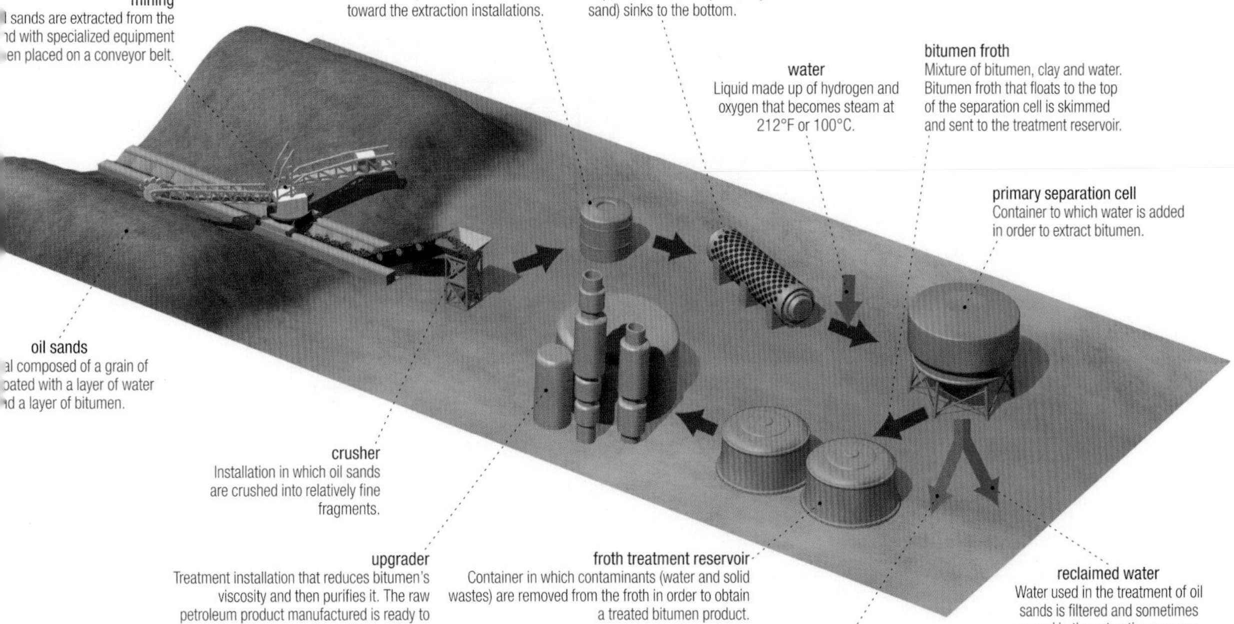

rotary breaker
Container in which the oil sand
mixture decants: bitumen froth rises
to the top, while sediment (rock, clay,
sand) sinks to the bottom.

surge bin
Container into which water is added to
oil sands in order to facilitate their transit
toward the extraction installations.

mining
l sands are extracted from the
d with specialized equipment
en placed on a conveyor belt.

water
Liquid made up of hydrogen and
oxygen that becomes steam at
212°F or 100°C.

bitumen froth
Mixture of bitumen, clay and water.
Bitumen froth that floats to the top
of the separation cell is skimmed
and sent to the treatment reservoir.

primary separation cell
Container to which water is added
in order to extract bitumen.

oil sands
al composed of a grain of
pated with a layer of water
d a layer of bitumen.

crusher
Installation in which oil sands
are crushed into relatively fine
fragments.

upgrader
Treatment installation that reduces bitumen's
viscosity and then purifies it. The raw
petroleum product manufactured is ready to
be sent to a refinery.

froth treatment reservoir
Container in which contaminants (water and solid
wastes) are removed from the froth in order to obtain
a treated bitumen product.

reclaimed water
Water used in the treatment of oil
sands is filtered and sometimes
reused in the extraction process.

sand
Small fragments of rock or mineral
extracted from the bitumen froth
at various stages of the extraction
process.

cyclic steam injection
Extraction technique that involves injecting steam into a
well in order to heat the bitumen, which is then pumped
toward the surface.

am-assisted gravity drainage
action technique that involves injecting steam into a well in order
eat the bitumen, which then flows toward a second well.

soak phase
Second step in the extraction
process, during which bitumen
is heated in order to reduce its
viscosity.

pumping
Third step of the extraction
process, during which heated
bitumen is pumped toward the
surface.

steam injection
First step in the extraction process,
during which steam is introduced
into the well.

injection well
Cavity bored into the ground that
allows for steam to be introduced
into the oil sand deposit.

well
Cavity bored into the ground
through which steam is introduced
into the oil sands deposit and
bitumen is pumped to the surface.

production well
Cavity bored into the ground that
ws for the collection of bitumen
and its transit to the surface.

surface installations
Facilities and equipment required
to exploit, treat and store
hydrocarbons.

reservoir
Porous rock formations that contain
exploitable petroleum reserves in
the form of oil sands.

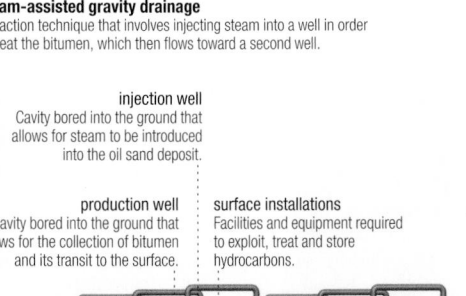

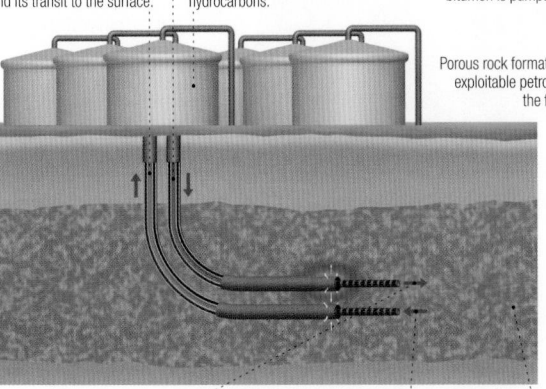

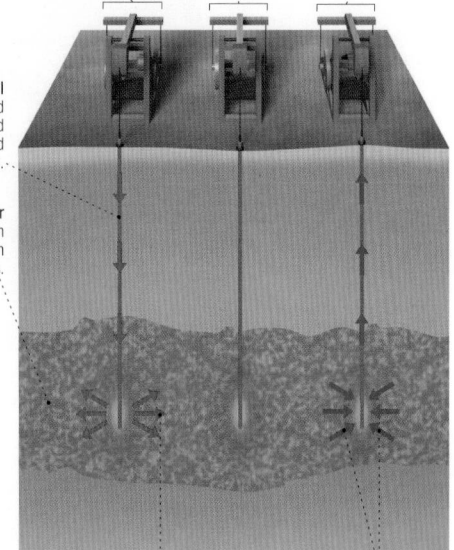

steam
Gaseous state of water. Injected
steam heats the bitumen, which
reduces its viscosity.

oil
Natural mineral oil consisting of
a mix of hydrocarbons. Heated
oil is pulled by gravity toward the
production well.

reservoir
Porous rock formations that contain
exploitable petroleum reserves in
the form of oil sands.

steam
Gaseous state of water. Injected
steam heats the bitumen, which
reduces its viscosity.

heated oil and water

ENERGY

oil

Christmas tree
Group of devices at the head of the producing well that regulate the flow of oil being extracted from the deposit.

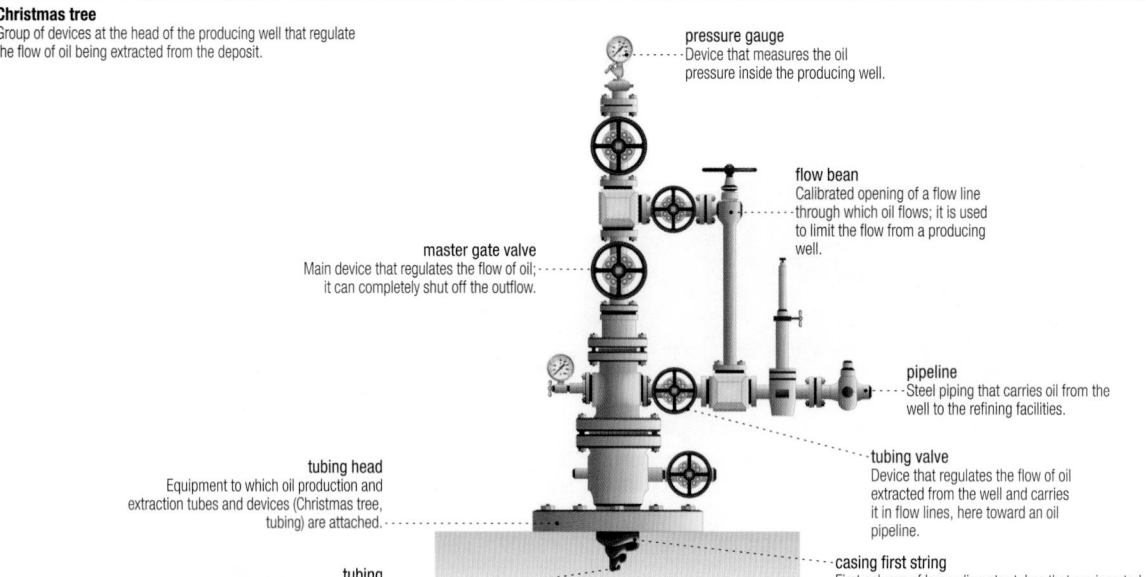

pressure gauge
Device that measures the oil pressure inside the producing well.

flow bean
Calibrated opening of a flow line through which oil flows; it is used to limit the flow from a producing well.

master gate valve
Main device that regulates the flow of oil; it can completely shut off the outflow.

pipeline
Steel piping that carries oil from the well to the refining facilities.

tubing head
Equipment to which oil production and extraction tubes and devices (Christmas tree, tubing) are attached.

tubing valve
Device that regulates the flow of oil extracted from the well and carries it in flow lines, here toward an oil pipeline.

tubing
Last column of small steel tubes to be inserted in the well; they are used to bring oil to the surface.

casing first string
First column of large-diameter tubes that are inserted into the producing well mainly to strengthen its walls.

crude oil pipeline
Continuous underground, aboveground or underwater oil pipeline that can be thousands of kilometers long (the Trans-Siberian pipeline is 3,800 mi long).

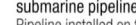

offshore well
Hole dug in the sea floor to extract oil deposits; equipment such as the Christmas tree rests on the seabed.

production platform
Facility used to extract underwater oil deposits; the separation and treatment of hydrocarbons are mainly done here.

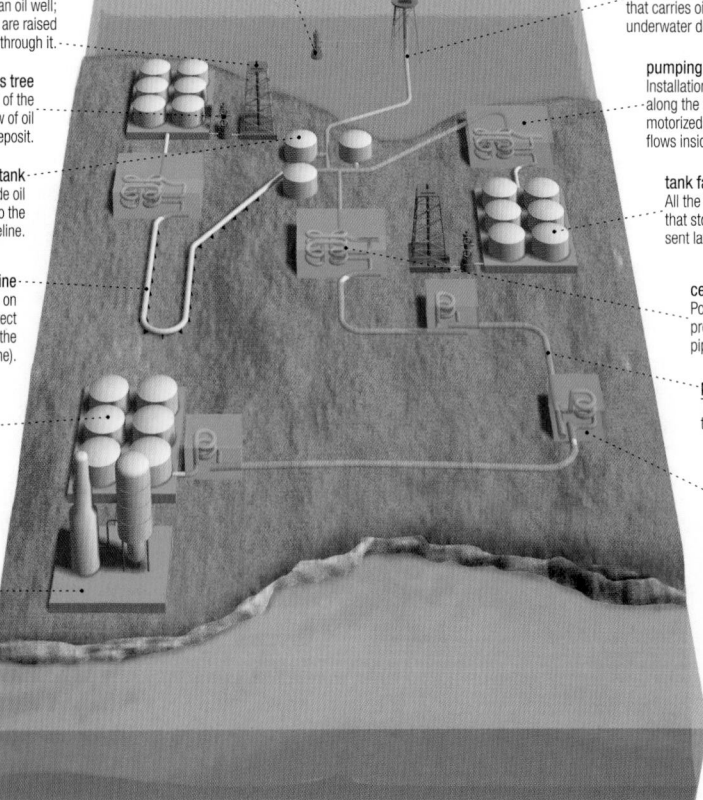

derrick
Metal structure erected over an oil well; tools for drilling through rock are raised and lowered through it.

Christmas tree
Group of devices at the head of the producing well that regulate the flow of oil being extracted from the deposit.

buffer tank
Large container that stores crude oil temporarily before it is pumped back into the pipeline.

aboveground pipeline
Oil pipeline that rests on aboveground supports to protect it from frozen ground (e.g., the Alaska pipeline).

terminal
Facility located at the end of the pipeline that includes equipment such as tanks and pumps; it receives the crude oil before it is refined.

refinery
Plant in which crude oil is refined (separated and scrubbed) to obtain a broad range of finished products (including motor fuel and oils).

submarine pipeline
Pipeline installed on the seabed that carries oil extracted from an underwater deposit to shore.

pumping station
Installation located at regular intervals along the pipeline that is fitted with motorized pumps; it ensures that the oil flows inside the pipeline.

tank farm
All the facilities (such as tanks and pumps) that store large quantities of crude oil to be sent later to the refinery.

central pumping station
Powerful pumping station that maintains the pressure required to move the oil along the pipeline to the next pumping station.

pipeline
The steel piping that carries oil from one treatment facility to another.

intermediate booster station
Booster station that reinforces the action central station and maintains the flow pipeline network.

oil

tanks
Large covered cylindrical containers that are usually made of steel; liquid or gaseous oil products are stored here between the time they are refined and sold.

spray nozzle
Device that sprays water onto the roof of the tank to cool it when the temperature rises.

breather valve
Movable part that regulates the internal pressure of the tank; pressure fluctuates during emptying and filling and with the temperature.

manhole
Round opening in the tank that is covered with a plate; workers can pass through it.

fixed-roof tank
Fixed roof that keeps the tank sealed tightly; it is used to store heavy products such as diesel fuel, kerosene and asphalt.

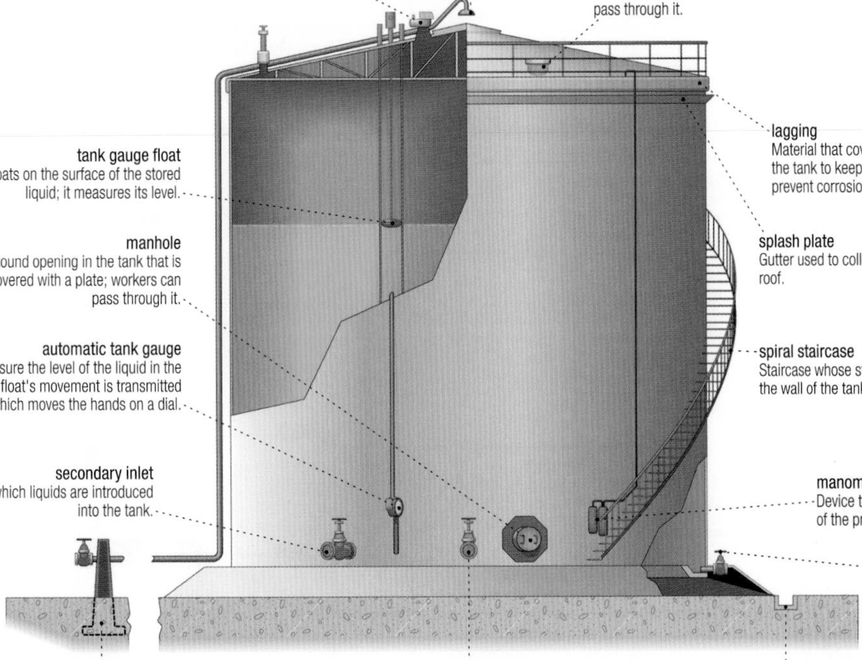

tank gauge float
Element that floats on the surface of the stored liquid; it measures its level.

lagging
Material that covers the wall of the tank to keep it watertight and prevent corrosion.

manhole
Round opening in the tank that is covered with a plate; workers can pass through it.

splash plate
Gutter used to collect water draining from the roof.

automatic tank gauge
Device used to measure the level of the liquid in the tank; the tank gauge float's movement is transmitted to a magnet, which moves the hands on a dial.

spiral staircase
Staircase whose stairs wind around the wall of the tank to the roof.

secondary inlet
Small pipe through which liquids are introduced into the tank.

manometer
Device that measures the pressure of the product inside the tank.

drain valve
Device for emptying the liquid from the tank.

bund wall
Cement wall around the tank that protects the environment in the event of accidental leakage.

main inlet
Large pipe through which liquids are introduced into the tank.

concrete drain
Small concrete trench used to drain off the product in the event of a spill or when the tank is emptied.

floating-roof tank
Tank whose floating roof rests directly on the surface of the liquid to minimize the evaporation of hydrocarbons; it is used to store the most volatile products.

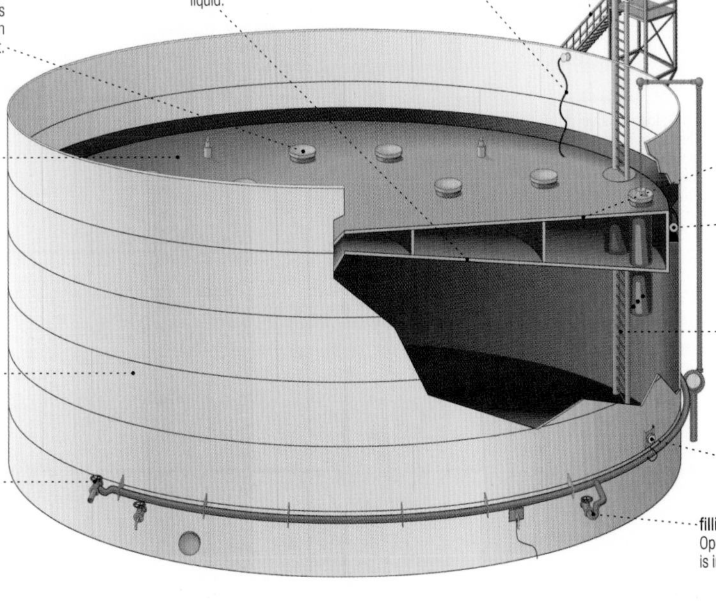

ground
Wire that connects the tank and its contents to the ground to prevent static electricity from accumulating and avoid the risk of fire.

bottom deck
Lower part of the roof; it rests directly on the surface of the stored liquid.

stairs
Structural element giving access to the roof of the tank.

manhole
Round opening in the tank that is covered with a plate; workers can pass through it.

top deck
Upper part of the roof; the space between the top and bottom decks is used to contain evaporated hydrocarbons.

floating roof
Metal cover that rests on the surface of the stored liquid; it fluctuates with the level of the fluid and slides vertically inside the shell.

sealing ring
Part that fills the space between the roof and the shell to prevent any hydrocarbons from evaporating and polluting the atmosphere.

ladder
Movable device that consists of rungs (crossbars); it is used to climb up and down.

shell
Vertical cylindrical wall of the tank.

thermometer
Device that sets and controls the temperature of the product inside the tank.

drain valve
Device for emptying the liquid from the tank.

filling inlet
Operation by which a liquid product is introduced into the tank.

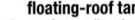

ENERGY

oil

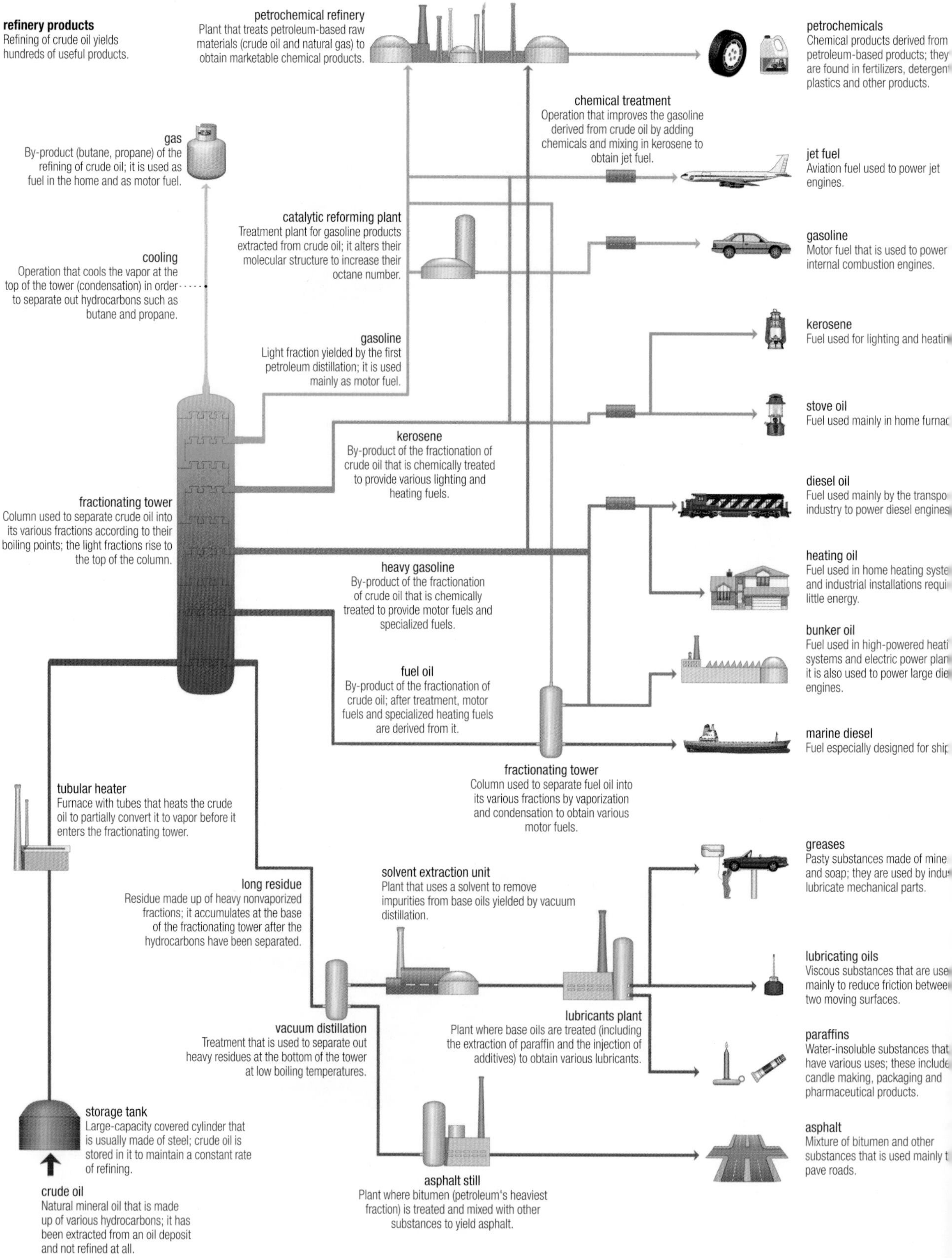

refinery products
Refining of crude oil yields
hundreds of useful products.

petrochemical refinery
Plant that treats petroleum-based raw
materials (crude oil and natural gas) to
obtain marketable chemical products.

petrochemicals
Chemical products derived from
petroleum-based products; they
are found in fertilizers, detergent
plastics and other products.

chemical treatment
Operation that improves the gasoline
derived from crude oil by adding
chemicals and mixing in kerosene to
obtain jet fuel.

jet fuel
Aviation fuel used to power jet
engines.

gas
By-product (butane, propane) of the
refining of crude oil; it is used as
fuel in the home and as motor fuel.

catalytic reforming plant
Treatment plant for gasoline products
extracted from crude oil; it alters their
molecular structure to increase their
octane number.

gasoline
Motor fuel that is used to power
internal combustion engines.

cooling
Operation that cools the vapor at the
top of the tower (condensation) in order
to separate out hydrocarbons such as
butane and propane.

gasoline
Light fraction yielded by the first
petroleum distillation; it is used
mainly as motor fuel.

kerosene
Fuel used for lighting and heating

stove oil
Fuel used mainly in home furnac

kerosene
By-product of the fractionation of
crude oil that is chemically treated
to provide various lighting and
heating fuels.

diesel oil
Fuel used mainly by the transpo
industry to power diesel engines

fractionating tower
Column used to separate crude oil into
its various fractions according to their
boiling points; the light fractions rise to
the top of the column.

heavy gasoline
By-product of the fractionation
of crude oil that is chemically
treated to provide motor fuels and
specialized fuels.

heating oil
Fuel used in home heating syste
and industrial installations requi
little energy.

bunker oil
Fuel used in high-powered heati
systems and electric power plan
it is also used to power large die
engines.

fuel oil
By-product of the fractionation of
crude oil; after treatment, motor
fuels and specialized heating fuels
are derived from it.

marine diesel
Fuel especially designed for ship

fractionating tower
Column used to separate fuel oil into
its various fractions by vaporization
and condensation to obtain various
motor fuels.

tubular heater
Furnace with tubes that heats the crude
oil to partially convert it to vapor before it
enters the fractionating tower.

greases
Pasty substances made of mine
and soap; they are used by indu
lubricate mechanical parts.

long residue
Residue made up of heavy nonvaporized
fractions; it accumulates at the base
of the fractionating tower after the
hydrocarbons have been separated.

solvent extraction unit
Plant that uses a solvent to remove
impurities from base oils yielded by vacuum
distillation.

lubricating oils
Viscous substances that are use
mainly to reduce friction betwee
two moving surfaces.

vacuum distillation
Treatment that is used to separate out
heavy residues at the bottom of the tower
at low boiling temperatures.

lubricants plant
Plant where base oils are treated (including
the extraction of paraffin and the injection of
additives) to obtain various lubricants.

paraffins
Water-insoluble substances that
have various uses; these include
candle making, packaging and
pharmaceutical products.

storage tank
Large-capacity covered cylinder that
is usually made of steel; crude oil is
stored in it to maintain a constant rate
of refining.

asphalt still
Plant where bitumen (petroleum's heaviest
fraction) is treated and mixed with other
substances to yield asphalt.

asphalt
Mixture of bitumen and other
substances that is used mainly t
pave roads.

crude oil
Natural mineral oil that is made
up of various hydrocarbons; it has
been extracted from an oil deposit
and not refined at all.

ENERGY

natural gas

Mixture of gaseous hydrocarbons (mainly methane) that are found in underground deposits, which sometimes also contain crude oil; it is used mainly as a fuel.

pressure regulator
Device that allows for the lowering and maintenance of constant pressure on gas that enters a building.

natural gas pipeline system
Interconnected pipeline network that allows for the distribution of natural gas.

gas meter
Instrument that measures a building's gas consumption.

shutoff valve
Device that allows for the total interruption of gas service in the event of a leak.

dial
Device that indicates the quantity of gas consumed.

mercaptan injection
Installation in which mercaptan (or thiol), which smells strongly of rotten eggs, is added to the gas. Mercaptan makes gas leaks immediately detectable.

processing plant
Installation that allows for the removal of impurities (mostly sulfur) contained in natural gas.

regulating station
Installation usually situated at the network's entry into a neighborhood, in which the pipeline gas is depressurized for a second time so that it can be distributed to customers.

delivery station
Installation usually situated on the outskirts of a city, in which the pipeline's gas is depressurized.

derrick
al structure erected over gas well; tools for drilling ough rock are raised and lowered through it.

domestic consumer

well
vity bored into the or the exploitation ural gas deposits.

oil
ble, relatively viscous oily that is used as an energy e; it is made up of various arbons resulting from the mposition of plant life over millions of year.

natural gas
Mixture of gaseous hydrocarbons (mainly methane) that are found in underground deposits, which sometimes also contain crude oil; it is used mainly as a fuel.

compressor station
Installation situated at regular intervals along a gas pipeline designed to maintain gas pressure and a constant rate of flow in the pipes.

compressor
Device that compresses gas in order to turn it into a liquid for relatively long storage. In liquid form, the gas occupies 600 times less space.

liquefaction, storage and regasification plant
Installation in which gas can be compressed into a liquid for storage and later reconverted to gas for transportation.

gas pipeline
Underground, underwater or elevated steel pipeline that allows for natural gas to travel long distances.

underground storage
Natural gas can be stored in liquid form in an airtight chamber in the rock.

outdoor storage tank
Large cylindrical container in which natural gas is stored in gaseous or liquid form.

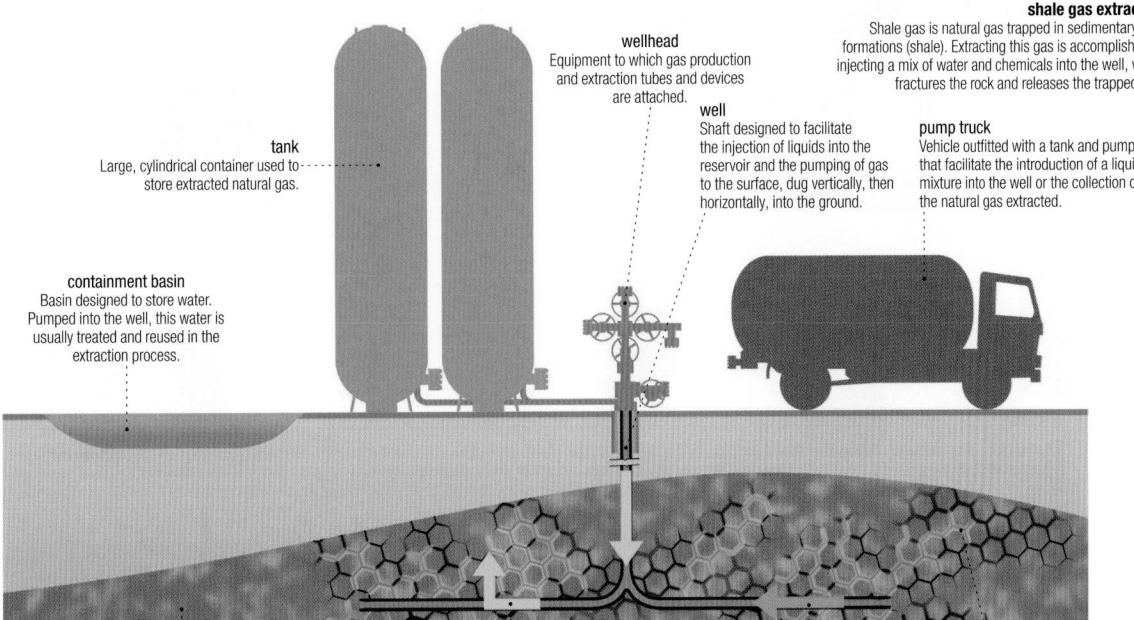

shale gas extraction
Shale gas is natural gas trapped in sedimentary rock formations (shale). Extracting this gas is accomplished by injecting a mix of water and chemicals into the well, which fractures the rock and releases the trapped gas.

wellhead
Equipment to which gas production and extraction tubes and devices are attached.

well
Shaft designed to facilitate the injection of liquids into the reservoir and the pumping of gas to the surface, dug vertically, then horizontally, into the ground.

pump truck
Vehicle outfitted with a tank and pump that facilitate the introduction of a liquid mixture into the well or the collection of the natural gas extracted.

tank
Large, cylindrical container used to store extracted natural gas.

containment basin
Basin designed to store water. Pumped into the well, this water is usually treated and reused in the extraction process.

shale
Foliated sedimentary rock. This rock may contain organic matter, which breaks down into hydrocarbons as it decays.

water, sand and chemicals

natural gas and waste
Fracturing releases the natural gas trapped in the shale. This can then be pumped to the surface.

fracturing
Technique that breaks up shale by injecting a high-pressure mix of sand, water and chemicals into the well.

ENERGY

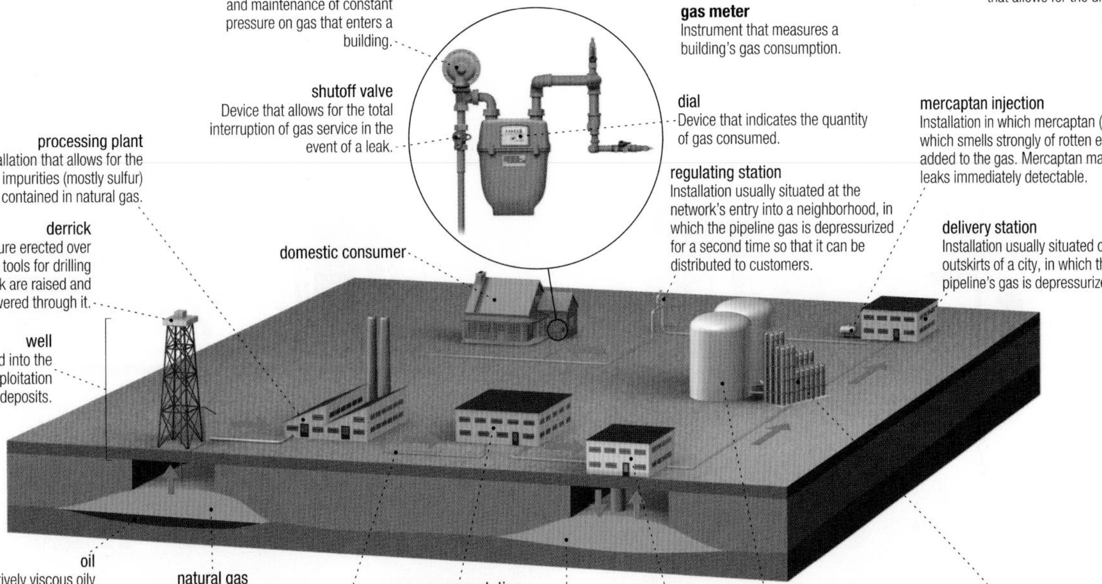

alternative fuel

Non-fossil fuels helpful in the overall reduction of air pollution caused by motor vehicles.

biodiesel production
Biodiesel fuel, made from animal fat or vegetable oil, is produced by a chemical process known as transesterification.

vegetable oil
Fatty substance of plant origin. Oil extracted from crops like canola or soy can be used to make biodiesel fuels.

animal fat
Fatty substance of animal origin.

recycled frying oil
Liquid fat previously used to cook food.

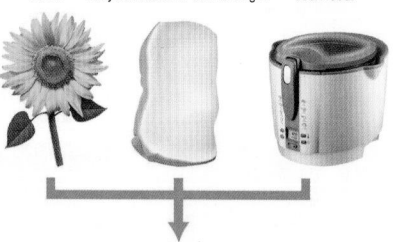

transesterification
Chemical process by which unprocessed oil, mixed with alcohol and a catalyst, separates into two substances: glycerin and biodiesel.

pretreatment
Processes undertaken to remove impurities from raw materials.

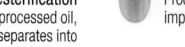

methanol
Methyl alcohol

catalyst
Substance used to speed up a chemical reaction.

treatment
Process by which impurities are removed from biodiesel.

settling
Process by which glycerin is separated from the biodiesel.

water and methanol rectification

biodiesel
Renewable and biodegradable fuel made from animal fat or vegetable oil.

glycerin
Colorless, viscous triol, used mainly in cosmetics. A common ingredient in soaps and creams.

bioethanol production
Bioethanol is produced by fermenting the sugars contained in various type of plants.

sugar plants
Sucrose-producing crops such as sugar cane or sugar beets.

cereals
Starch-producing crops such as corn, wheat, barley, sorghum and potato.

cellulosic biomass
Substance consisting of cellulose-containing plant matter such as wood, straw grasses and the non-food byproducts of edible crops

pretreatment
Raw materials are dried, then ground or shredded. With cereal starch is then converted into glucose through a process known as saccharification.

hydrolysis
Process by which complex sugar (cellulose) are turned into simple sugars (glucose). Hydrolysis is the technique generally used when converting cellulosic biomass.

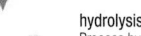

fermentation
Process by which alcohol-based sugars are converted using yeast. This yields a highly diluted form of ethanol, which requires further processing.

distillation
Process which separates ethanol from water by boiling. Since ethanol boils at a lower temperature than water, it evaporates before the water in the mixture begins to boil.

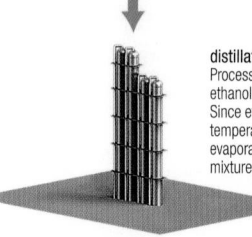

ethanol fuel
Fuel made by fermenting the sugars contained in various plant

hydroelectric complex

The reservoir structures and installations that use water power to produce electricity.

exterior view

crest of spillway
Cement crest over which the reservoir's overflow discharges when the spillway gates are opened.

spillway gate
Movable vertical panel; it is opened to allow the reservoir's overflow to pass through.

spillway
Channel that discharges excess water from the reservoir during flooding to avoid submerging the dam.

top of dam
Upper part of the dam; it rises above the water level of the reservoir by several yards.

penstock
Channel that carries water under pressure to the power plant's turbines.

reservoir
Basin formed by the construction of a dam; it holds back a very large volume of water so that the flow rate can be controlled.

headbay
Part of the reservoir immediately in front of the dam where the current originates.

gantry crane
Hoisting device in the form of a bridge; it moves along rails.

diversion tunnel
Underground conduit that diverts water during construction.

afterbay
Area of the watercourse where water is discharged after passing through the turbines.

control room
Area that contains the various control and monitoring devices required for the production of electricity.

spillway chute
Inclined surface along which discharged water flows out.

power plant
Plant that uses an energy source, here water, and converts it into electricity.

bushing
Device that allows the conductor to pass through the wall of the transformer and separates it from the latter.

training wall
hat separates the spillway es; it is used to direct the water flow.

log chute
Structure that allows floating wood to travel from upstream to downstream of the dam.

machine hall
Area that houses the generator units used to produce electricity.

dam
Barrier built across a watercourse in order to build up a supply of water for use as an energy source.

ENERGY

hydroelectric complex

cross section of a hydroelectric power plant
Hydroelectric power plant: plant that produces electricity
from energy generated by flowing water.

circuit breaker
Mechanism automatically cutting
off the power supply in the event
of overload.

gate
Movable vertical panel that
controls the volume of water in the
penstock.

transformer
Device used to alter the electric voltage;
voltage is increased as the current leaves
the power plant so that it can be carried
over long distances.

bushing
Device that allows the conductor to pass
through the wall of the transformer and
separates it from the latter.

gantry crane
Hoisting device in the form of a
bridge; it moves along rails.

busbar
Large aluminum conductor that
transmits electric current from the
alternator to the transformer.

lightning arrester
Device that protects the electric facilities from
power surges caused by lightning.

traveling crane
Hoisting device that travels along
aboveground parallel rails; it is used to lift
and carry heavy loads.

machine hall
Area that houses the generator units
used to produce electricity.

access gallery
Underground passageway
provides access to variou
the dam so that it can be
and maintained.

gantry crane
Hoisting device in the form
bridge; it moves along rai

scroll case
Duct shaped like a spiral
that is used to distribute v
uniformly around the turb
make it turn smoothly.

afterbay
Area of the watercourse v
water is discharged after
through the turbines.

gate
Movable vertical panel tha
the discharge of water to
tailrace.

water intake
Structure that directs water from the
headbay to the penstock to power
the plant.

draft tube
Conduit at the base of the turbine
that increases the runner's output
by reducing the pressure of the
water as it exits.

generator unit
Device with a turbine that transmits
the water's mechanical energy to
the generator's rotor to make it turn
to produce electricity.

tailrace
Channel that discharges water
toward the afterbay in order to
return it to the watercourse.

screen
Assembly of bars placed in front
of the water intake to hold back
anything that could hinder the
operation of the turbine.

penstock
Channel that carries water under
pressure to the power plant's
turbines.

reservoir
Basin formed by the construction of
a dam; it holds a very large volume
of water so that the flow rate can
be controlled.

hydroelectric complex

rotor
Movable part of the generator that is made up of electromagnets; its rotation induces an electric current in the stator.

exciter
Device that supplies electric current to the rotor's electromagnets.

stator
Stationary part of the generator that consists of a coil of copper conductors, which collects the electric current produced by the rotor.

generator unit
Device with a turbine that transmits the water's mechanical energy to the generator's rotor to make it turn to produce electricity.

thrust bearing
Unit that bears the thrust of the turbine and the weight of the rotating parts of the generator unit.

generator
Machine that consists of a rotor and a stator; it produces an electric current.

gate operating ring
Movable device that controls the opening and closing of the wicket gates.

shaft
Cylindrical part that communicates the movement of the turbine's runner to the generator's rotor.

turbine headcover
Structure that covers the upper part of the turbine's runner.

runner blade
Stationary curved plate on the turbine's runner; it receives the thrust of the water to turn the runner.

spiral case
Duct shaped like a spiral staircase that is used to distribute water uniformly around the turbine to make it turn smoothly.

stay vane blade
Fixed panel that receives pressurized water from the spiral case and directs it over the wicket gates.

wicket gate
Movable panel that regulates the flow of water entering the turbine to ensure a constant rotational speed of the runner.

stay ring
Set of two rings linked together by the stay vanes.

runner
Movable part of the turbine that transmits the movement of the water to the shaft to which it is attached to turn the rotor.

bottom ring
Circular part under the wicket gates that holds them in place.

draft tube
Conduit at the base of the turbine that increases the runner's output by reducing the pressure of the water as it exits.

draft tube liner
Covering that is usually made of steel; it protects the draft tube from erosion.

hydraulic turbine
Machine whose runner is powered by water; it transmits mechanical energy to the rotor to make it turn.

runners
Movable parts of the turbine that transmit the movement of the water to the shaft to which they are attached to turn the rotor.

Pelton runner
Type of runner that is suited to high water sources (usually over 1,000 ft) and low flow rates.

bucket
Small bucket that is attached to the turbine's runner; water enters it to turn the wheel.

coupling bolt
Element made up of a nut and a bolt that attaches the runner to the shaft plate to transmit its movement to the runner.

Francis runner
Most common type of runner that is suited to average heights of water (usually between 100 and 1,000 ft).

plan runner
Type of runner that is suited to low heights of water (usually between and 200 ft) and variable flow rates.

hub
Part of the runner that holds the shaft; the runner blades are attached to it.

runner blade
Movable part that is fixed to the hub of the runner; it turns through the action of water power on it.

hub cover
Cover for the lower cone-shaped part of the hub.

bucket ring
Disk housing all the turbine buckets that activates the runner.

blade
Stationary curved plate on the turbine's runner; it receives the thrust of the water to turn the runner.

ring
Circular part that supports the wicket gates.

hydroelectric complex

types of power plants
Hydroelectric power plants can be supplied by flowing water or water contained in an artificial reservoir.

run-of-the-river power plant
Plant built directly over the waterway from which power is derived. Power output depends on the water's flow rate.

floodgate
Movable vertical panel that controls the discharge of water.

dam
Retaining structure built across a waterway in order to convert its flow into a source of energy.

spillway
Channel that discharges exces during flooding to avoid subm the dam.

power plant
Plant that uses an energy source, here water, and converts it into electricity.

transformer
Device used to alter the electric voltage; voltage is increased as the current leaves the power plant so that it can be carried over long distances.

powerline
Using high-voltage lines to transmit electricity over long distances reduces the strength of the current and, as a result, energy losses.

power station with reservoir
Plant supplied by an artificial reservoir created by the construction of a dam.

reservoir
Basin formed by the construction of a dam; it holds back a very large volume of water so that the flow rate can be controlled.

gravity dam
Barrier built across a watercourse in order to build up a supply of water for use as an energy source.

steps in production of electricity

In a hydroelectric power plant, water is turned into electricity, which is carried to consumers along a transportation and distribution network.

energy transmission at the generator voltage
Electric power produced by the generator is transmitted to a transformer at the power plant outlet.

voltage increase
outlet end of the power plant, the transformer eases the voltage; this reduces energy losses during transmission over long distances.

energy integration to the transmission network
The electricity produced is integrated into the network.

voltage decrease
Before integrating the electricity into the distribution network, the voltage is progressively decreased to 240 V.

d of water
dam raises the water level to e a vertical drop along the th of the penstock.

high-tension electricity transmission
Using high-voltage lines to transmit electricity over long distances reduces the strength of the current and, as a result, energy losses.

transmission to consumers
The electricity is carried to areas of consumption by low-voltage distribution lines.

pply of water
d in a basin created by am, which holds back a e volume of water.

production of electricity by the generator
The generator produces electricity through the movement of the rotor in the stator.

water under pressure
ater takes on energy as it down the penstock and is with force to the turbine.

transmission of the rotative movement to the rotor
The movement of the turbine is transmitted to the rotor by the shaft.

transformation of mechanical work into electricity
The generator converts water power into electricity.

rotation of the turbine
Flowing water applies pressure to the turbine's blades to make it turn.

turbined water draining
After passing through the turbine, the water rejoins the watercourse.

ENERGY

examples of dams

There are masonry dams, concrete dams and embankment dams; the choice depends on criteria such as the nature of the ground, the shape of the valley and the materials available.

buttress dam

Used mainly in wide valleys, it consists of an impermeable wall, which is shored up by a series of buttresses to transmit the thrust of the water to the foundation.

cross section of a buttress

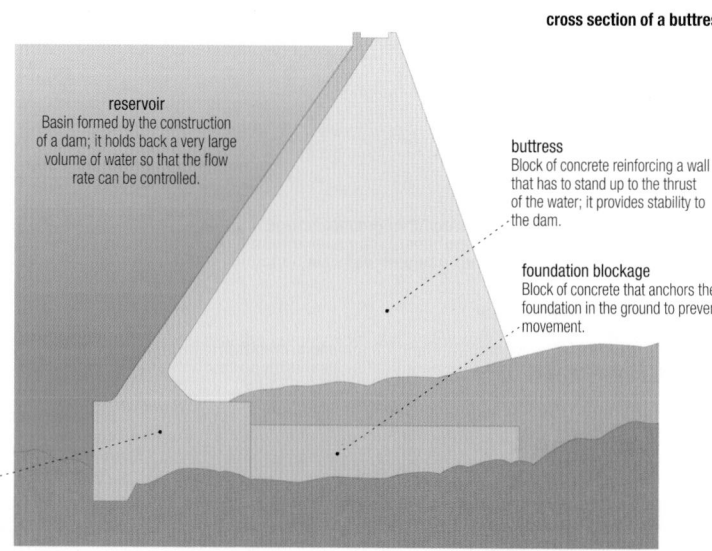

reservoir
Basin formed by the construction of a dam; it holds back a very large volume of water so that the flow rate can be controlled.

buttress
Block of concrete reinforcing a wall that has to stand up to the thrust of the water; it provides stability to the dam.

foundation blockage
Block of concrete that anchors the foundation in the ground to prevent movement.

foundation
Concrete structure that supports the weight of the dam and transmits it to the ground to provide stability to the dam.

embankment dam

Formed of mounds of earth or rocks, it is used mainly when the subsoil does not allow for construction of a concrete dam.

cross section of an embankment dam

top of dam
Upper part of the dam; it rises above the water level of the reservoir by several yards.

berm
Horizontal ledge that stabilizes the upstream or downstream shoulder.

downstream shoulder
Soil embankment that, together with the upstream shoulder, provides stability to the structure.

drainage layer
Layer of permeable materials that is inserted into large-scale dams to collect infiltrated water.

drainage blanket
Layer of permeable materials ◄ foundation of the dam; it colle◄ infiltrated water and prevents ◄ of the base of the dam.

wave wall
Small wall located at the top of the upstream shoulder that protects the dam against waves.

clay core
Central portion of the dam that is usually made of compact clay to make it watertight.

downstream to◄
Area where the downstrea◄ and the foundation of the d◄

reservoir
Basin formed by the construction of a dam; it holds back a very large volume of water so that the flow rate can be controlled.

pitching
Layer of rock or concrete blocks that covers the upstream shoulder to prevent erosion.

upstream toe
Area where the upstream shoulder and the foundation of the dam meet.

upstream blanket
Impermeable layer that consists of compact clay; it rests on the bottom of the dam to prevent infiltration.

upstream shoulder
Soil embankment located on the reservoir side; its mass provides stability to the dam.

cutoff trench
Area of the foundation of the dam that is connected to the core; it contains impermeable materials to limit leakage and infiltration under the dam.

sand
Granular material that is inserted between the core and the shoulder; it filters particles carried by the water flow to prevent erosion.

foundation of dam
Natural terrain (such as rock, san◄ or clay) on which the dam is built

ENERGY

examples of dams

cross section of an arch dam

ENERGY

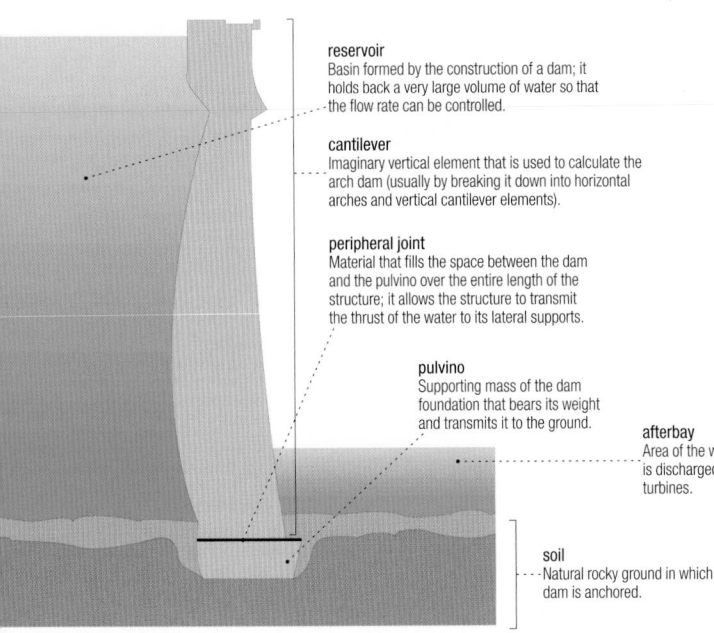

arch dam
Its curvature allows most of the water's thrust to be transmitted to the usually narrow valley slopes supporting it.

reservoir
Basin formed by the construction of a dam; it holds back a very large volume of water so that the flow rate can be controlled.

cantilever
Imaginary vertical element that is used to calculate the arch dam (usually by breaking it down into horizontal arches and vertical cantilever elements).

peripheral joint
Material that fills the space between the dam and the pulvino over the entire length of the structure; it allows the structure to transmit the thrust of the water to its lateral supports.

pulvino
Supporting mass of the dam foundation that bears its weight and transmits it to the ground.

afterbay
Area of the watercourse where water is discharged after passing through the turbines.

soil
Natural rocky ground in which the dam is anchored.

cross section of a gravity dam.

gravity dam
Its huge mass resists the thrust of the water to prevent it from overturning or sliding; this type of dam is usually used to hold back large volumes of water.

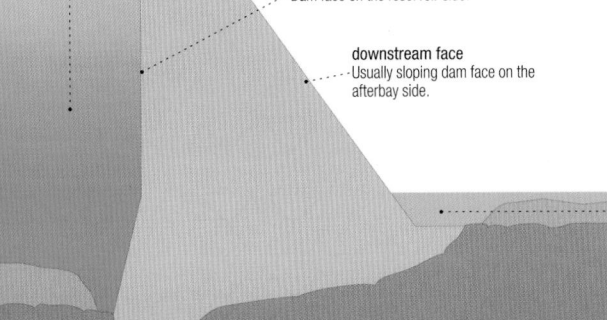

reservoir
Basin formed by the construction of a dam; it holds back a very large volume of water so that the flow rate can be controlled.

top of dam
Upper part of the dam that usually contains a roadway.

upstream face
Dam face on the reservoir side.

downstream face
Usually sloping dam face on the afterbay side.

afterbay
Area of the watercourse where water is discharged after passing through the turbines.

cutoff trench
Watertight structure that extends the foundations of the dam into the ground; it limits leakage and infiltration under the dam.

electricity transmission

Electricity is carried by overhead and underground lines; due to high cost, underground lines are used mainly in cities.

examples of towers

Tower: metal structure that holds the electric wires above the ground.

waist-type tower
Four-legged pylon well suited for uneven terrain.

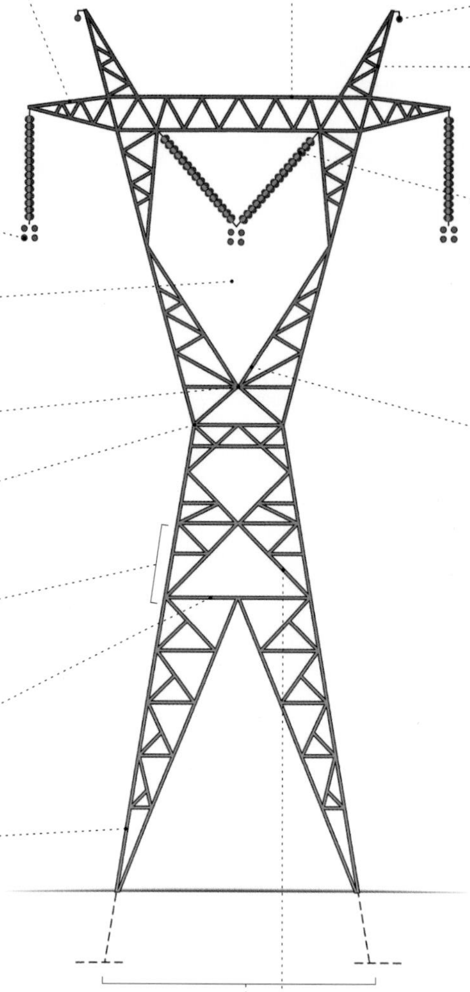

crossarm
Horizontal element that protrudes on each side of the pylon; it supports the bundles by means of suspension insulator strings.

beam gantry
Horizontal element of the pylon top; it supports the bundles inside the pylon window.

overhead ground wire
Conductor that is connected to the ground and attached above the bundles of the overhead lines to protect them from lightning.

ground-wire peak
Projection atop the pylon that supports the overhead ground wire.

bundle
Conductor cables that are kept a constant distance apart by spacers; they are used to transport current.

suspension insulator string
Insulators that are assembled in a vertical or oblique chain; the overhead line conductors hang from it.

pylon window
Space bounded by the inner side of the arms of the K-frame and the beam gantry.

pylon top
Upper portion of the pylon where the insulator strings and bundles are attached.

node
Point at which several legs and bars come together.

K-frame
Part of the pylon that rests on the waist; it has two branches that end at the beam gantry.

waist
Demarcation bar between the pylon top and body that is held tightly between them.

panel
Part of the pylon between two horizontal members.

pylon body
Part of the pylon support between the top and the foot.

horizontal member
Horizontal bar that connects the main legs to strengthen them.

main leg
One of the two tower legs of the pylon body; it supports mainly vertical weights.

pylon foot
Lower part of the pylon that is usually underground; the legs are anchored to it.

base width
Space between the foundation axes of the main legs.

diagonal
Diagonal bar that connects two main legs or a horizontal member and a main leg.

double-circuit configuration tower
Four-legged pylon that takes up minimal ground space.

tubular steel pole
Smallest type of tower, consistin of a single-shaft, vertical pylon. Used mostly in urban environments.

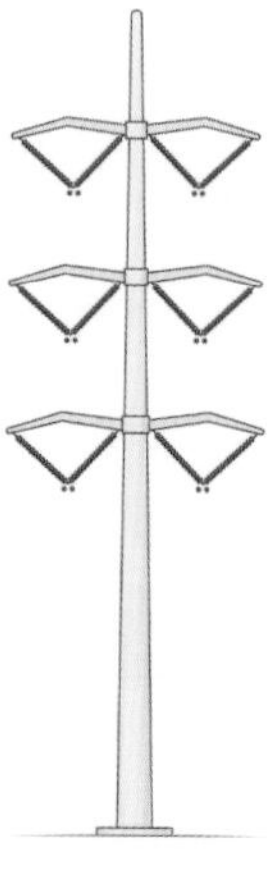

ENERGY

electricity transmission

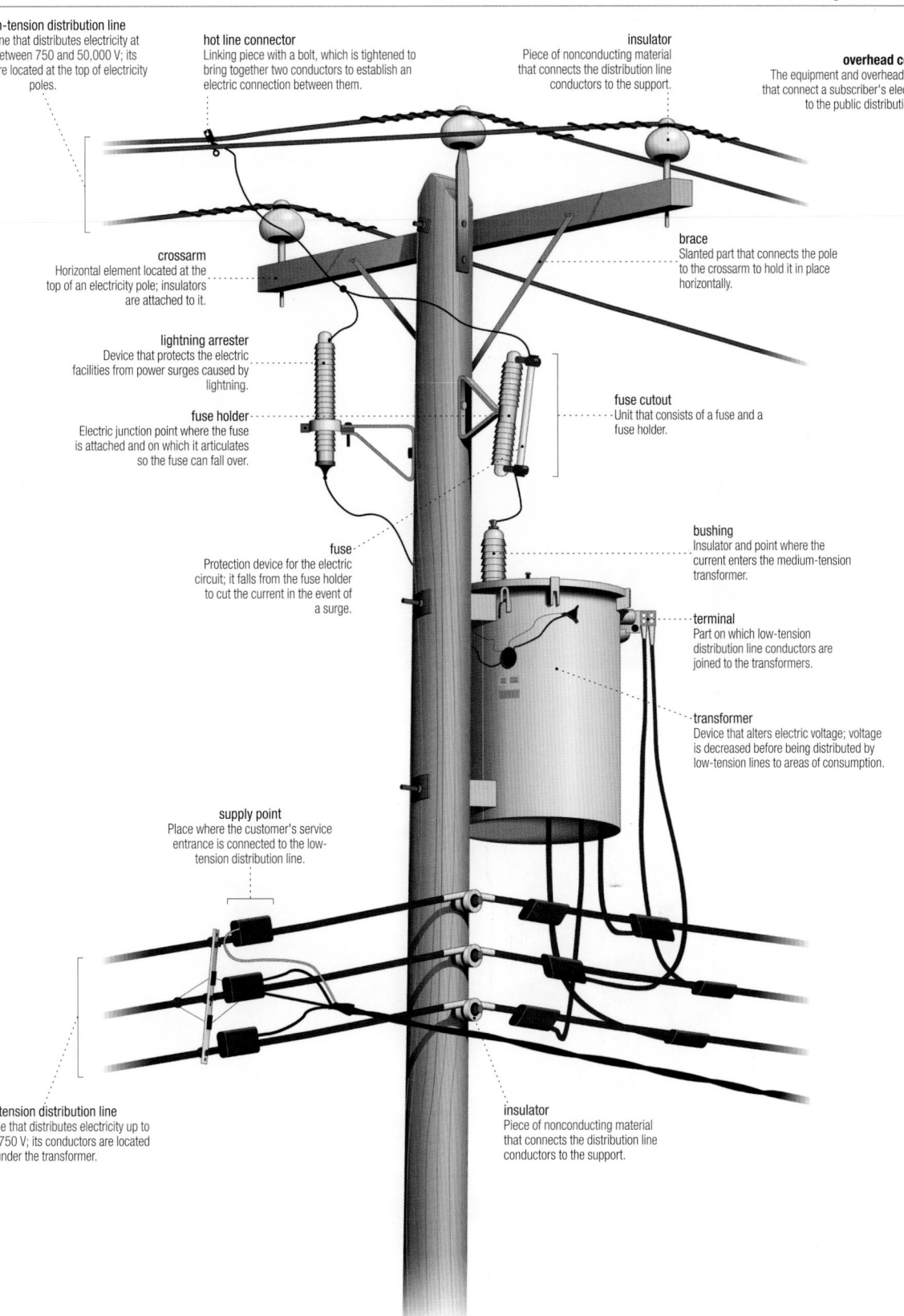

um-tension distribution line
d line that distributes electricity at
e between 750 and 50,000 V; its
s are located at the top of electricity
poles.

hot line connector
Linking piece with a bolt, which is tightened to
bring together two conductors to establish an
electric connection between them.

insulator
Piece of nonconducting material
that connects the distribution line
conductors to the support.

overhead connection
The equipment and overhead conductors
that connect a subscriber's electric system
to the public distribution network.

crossarm
Horizontal element located at the
top of an electricity pole; insulators
are attached to it.

brace
Slanted part that connects the pole
to the crossarm to hold it in place
horizontally.

lightning arrester
Device that protects the electric
facilities from power surges caused by
lightning.

fuse holder
Electric junction point where the fuse
is attached and on which it articulates
so the fuse can fall over.

fuse cutout
Unit that consists of a fuse and a
fuse holder.

bushing
Insulator and point where the
current enters the medium-tension
transformer.

fuse
Protection device for the electric
circuit; it falls from the fuse holder
to cut the current in the event of
a surge.

terminal
Part on which low-tension
distribution line conductors are
joined to the transformers.

transformer
Device that alters electric voltage; voltage
is decreased before being distributed by
low-tension lines to areas of consumption.

supply point
Place where the customer's service
entrance is connected to the low-
tension distribution line.

w-tension distribution line
d line that distributes electricity up to
of 750 V; its conductors are located
under the transformer.

insulator
Piece of nonconducting material
that connects the distribution line
conductors to the support.

ENERGY

tidal power plant

Plant that harnesses tidal power (the motion of the rising and falling tides) to produce electric power.

exterior view

inactive dike
Part of the dam made up mainly of
rocky material; it is built between
the plant and the operating dam to
separate the basin from the sea.

operating dam
Structure with gates that control the
basin level in relation to the level
of the sea.

bank
Strip of land bordering the sea.

floodgate
Movable vertical panel that controls
the rate of flow of the water
between the sea and the basin.

sea
Vast body of saltwater at some
distance inland; it is not as deep as
an ocean.

power plant
Part of the dam housing bulb units
that are powered by the rise and
fall of the sea to produce electricity.

lock
Structure with doors and gates that is
built between the sea and the basin;
it allows boats to pass from one level
to the other.

administrative building
Construction containing the offices of the
personnel managing the facilities.

substation
The devices (such as transformers and
changeover switches) that increase the
voltage of the electricity and carry it to
the network.

basin
Area in which water is stored at
tide; the basin empties out thro
penstocks at low tide.

cross section of a tidal power plant

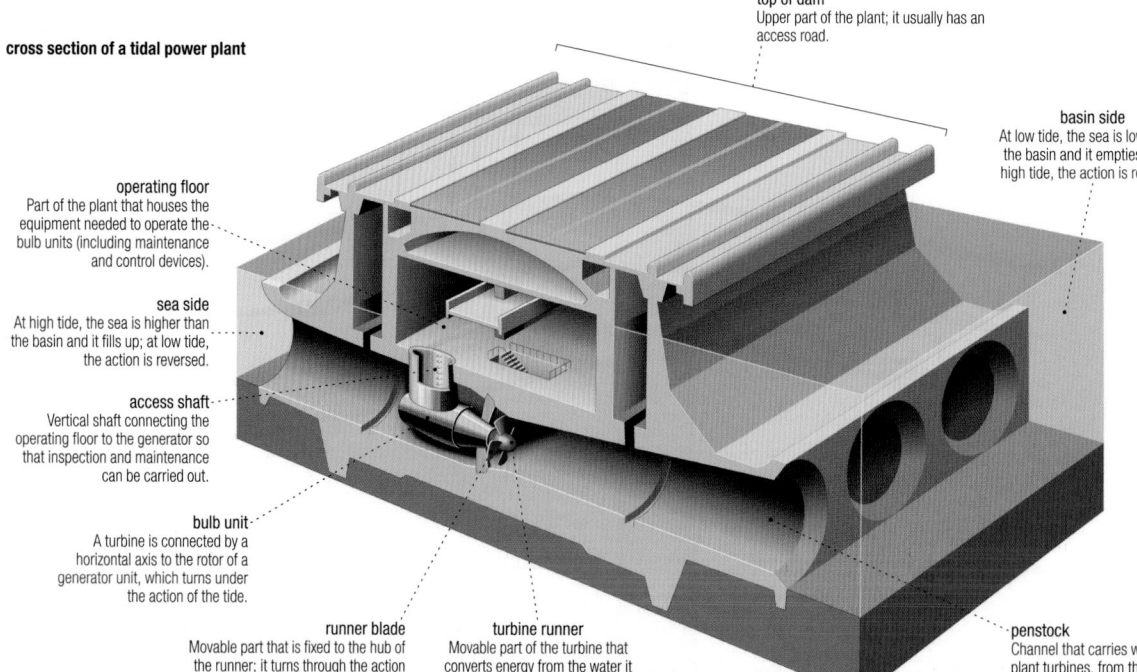

top of dam
Upper part of the plant; it usually has an
access road.

basin side
At low tide, the sea is lower than
the basin and it empties out; at
high tide, the action is reversed.

operating floor
Part of the plant that houses the
equipment needed to operate the
bulb units (including maintenance
and control devices).

sea side
At high tide, the sea is higher than
the basin and it fills up; at low tide,
the action is reversed.

access shaft
Vertical shaft connecting the
operating floor to the generator so
that inspection and maintenance
can be carried out.

bulb unit
A turbine is connected by a
horizontal axis to the rotor of a
generator unit, which turns under
the action of the tide.

runner blade
Movable part that is fixed to the hub of
the runner; it turns through the action
of water power on it.

turbine runner
Movable part of the turbine that
converts energy from the water it
receives into mechanical energy, which
is transmitted to the generator's rotor.

penstock
Channel that carries water to the
plant turbines, from the sea to the
basin or from the basin to the sea.

ENERGY

production of electricity from nuclear energy

A nuclear fission chain reaction is started and controlled inside the reactor to produce electricity.

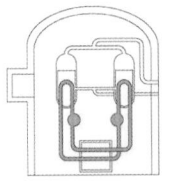

coolant
Liquid or gas (including heavy water and carbon dioxide) that circulates inside the reactor; it harnesses and transports the heat released during fission of the fuel.

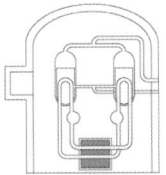

moderator
Substance (ordinary water, heavy water, graphite) that slows the fast-moving neutrons emitted during fission to increase the probability of new collisions.

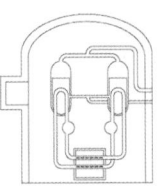

fuel
Matter placed in the core of the reactor that contains heavy atoms (uranium, plutonium); energy is extracted from it by fission.

heat production
Step during which the heat produced by atomic fission transforms water (held in a generator) into steam.

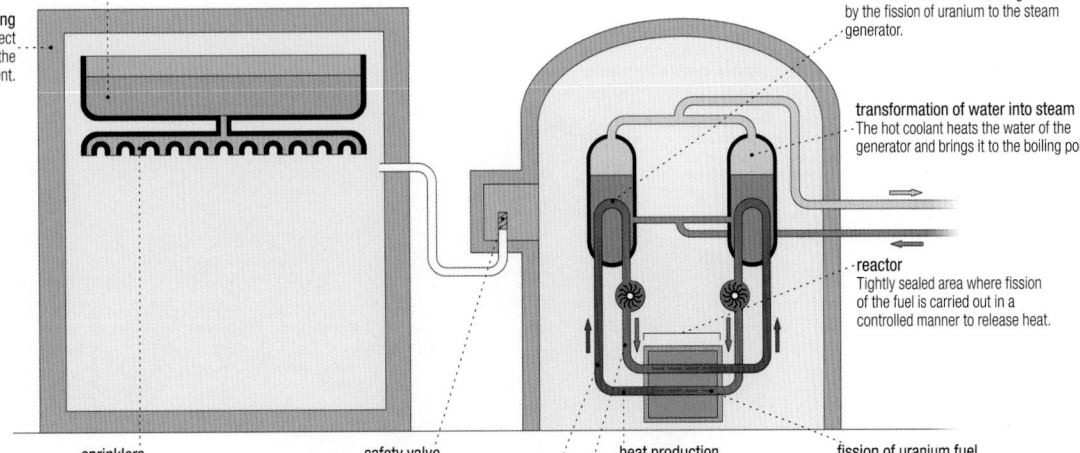

transfer of heat to water
The coolant releases the heat given off by the fission of uranium to the steam generator.

transformation of water into steam
The hot coolant heats the water of the generator and brings it to the boiling point.

reactor
Tightly sealed area where fission of the fuel is carried out in a controlled manner to release heat.

dousing water tank
[th]at contains water to cool the radioactive [...] the reactor in the event of an accident; this prevents a rise in pressure.

[c]ontainment building
[b]uilding used to collect [radio]active steam from the [...]e event of an accident.

sprinklers
Devices that release water to condense radioactive steam.

safety valve
Device that lowers the pressure inside the reactor by discharging the radioactive steam to the containment building.

heat production
The fission of atoms releases intense heat (between 575°F and 925°F), which is transmitted to the coolant.

fission of uranium fuel
The nuclei of the atoms break up; this frees neutrons and releases energy in the form of heat.

hot coolant
The coolant extracts heat from the fuel and carries it toward the steam generator.

cold coolant
After releasing its heat to the steam generator, the cold coolant returns to the reactor.

electricity production
Step during which the rotation of a steam turbine generates electricity.

turbine driven by steam pressure
Steam from the steam generator turns the turbine runner, which is connected to the generator.

generator driven by turbine shaft
The rotational movement of the turbine is transmitted to the generator's rotor.

production of electricity by the generator
The generator produces electricity through the movement of the rotor in the stator.

electricity transmission
Using high-voltage lines to transmit electricity over long distances reduces the strength of the current and, as a result, energy losses.

voltage increase
At the outlet end of the power plant, the transformer increases the voltage; this reduces energy losses during transmission over long distances.

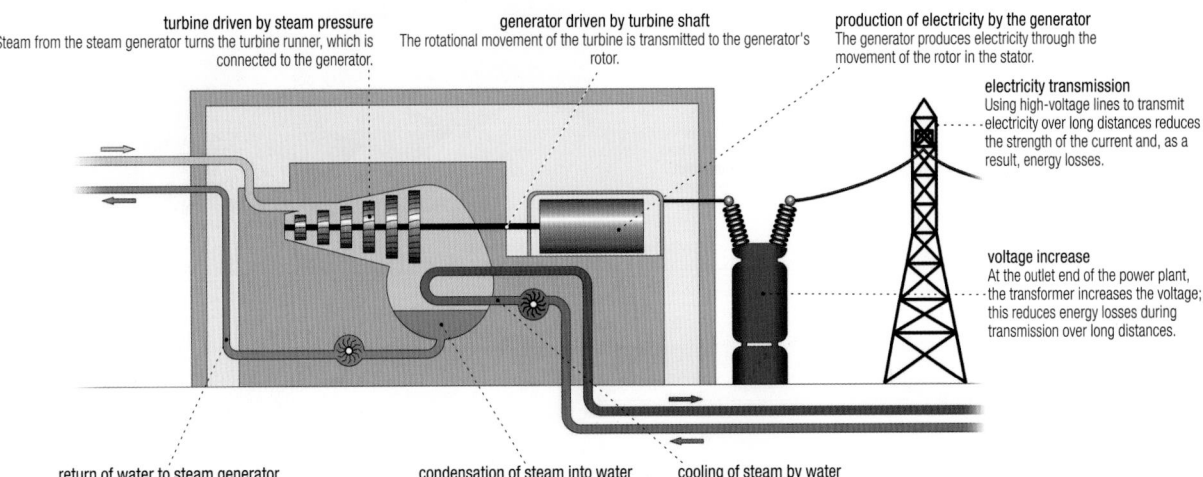

return of water to steam generator
[Aft]er passing through the turbine, water produced by the condensation of the steam returns to the steam generator.

condensation of steam into water
At the turbine outlet, the steam cools and condenses into water.

cooling of steam by water
Cooling of the steam from the turbine is done with river or lake water.

ENERGY

nuclear generating station

Plant that produces electricity from thermal energy generated by the fission of fuel atoms in a reactor.

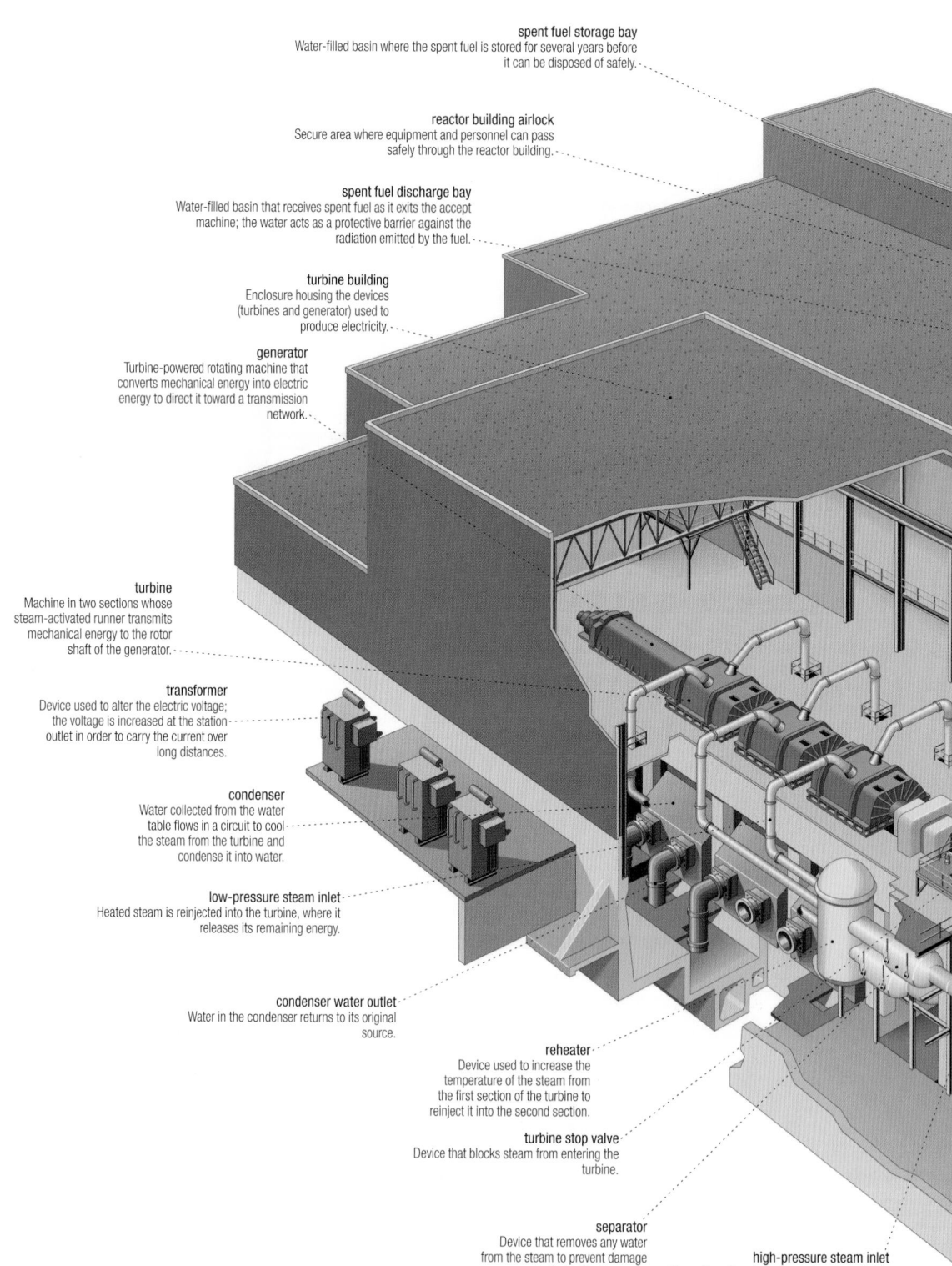

spent fuel storage bay
Water-filled basin where the spent fuel is stored for several years before it can be disposed of safely.

reactor building airlock
Secure area where equipment and personnel can pass safely through the reactor building.

spent fuel discharge bay
Water-filled basin that receives spent fuel as it exits the accept machine; the water acts as a protective barrier against the radiation emitted by the fuel.

turbine building
Enclosure housing the devices (turbines and generator) used to produce electricity.

generator
Turbine-powered rotating machine that converts mechanical energy into electric energy to direct it toward a transmission network.

turbine
Machine in two sections whose steam-activated runner transmits mechanical energy to the rotor shaft of the generator.

transformer
Device used to alter the electric voltage; the voltage is increased at the station outlet in order to carry the current over long distances.

condenser
Water collected from the water table flows in a circuit to cool the steam from the turbine and condense it into water.

low-pressure steam inlet
Heated steam is reinjected into the turbine, where it releases its remaining energy.

condenser water outlet
Water in the condenser returns to its original source.

reheater
Device used to increase the temperature of the steam from the first section of the turbine to reinject it into the second section.

turbine stop valve
Device that blocks steam from entering the turbine.

separator
Device that removes any water from the steam to prevent damage to the turbine's runner.

high-pressure steam inlet
Steam from the steam generators is carried to the first section of the turbine; here, it cools down and loses some of its energy.

ENERGY

nuclear generating station

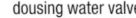

dousing water valve
Device that releases water from the dousing water tank in the reactor building to condense the radioactive steam.

deuterium oxide upgrading
In power stations where heavy water is used as a moderator, a filter holds back steam (deuterium oxide) at the mouth of the stack.

reactor building
Concrete structure surrounding the reactor vessel; it is a protective barrier against radioactivity.

dousing water tank
Vat that contains water to cool the radioactive steam in the reactor in the event of an accident; this prevents a rise in pressure.

steam generator room cooler
Cooling system that controls the temperature of the room housing the generators.

steam generator
Apparatus that turns water into steam, which in turn activates the turbine.

heat transport pump
Apparatus that circulates the coolant fluid between the reactor and the steam generator.

feeder header
Large-diameter pipe that collects the coolant fluid at the reactor inlet and outlet.

reactor
Tightly sealed area where fission of the fuel is carried out in a controlled manner to release heat.

containment wall
Safety wall that separates the reactor from the rest of the building.

fueling machine
Remote-controlled cylinder used to load and unload the reactor.

control room
Area that houses the personnel and equipment used to operate and monitor the power station.

steam release pipes
All the pipes used to carry steam to the separator outlet.

main steam header
Device that collects and disperses steam from the steam generators.

main steam pipes
All the pipes used to carry steam to the steam generator outlet.

condenser cooling water inlet
Channel through which water from a watercourse is pumped into the condenser.

condenser backwash outlet
Channel through which condensed water from the steam in the turbine returns to the water table.

condenser backwash inlet
Inlet channel for the water needed for the condensation circuit of the steam in the turbine.

condenser cooling water outlet
Channel through which the water from the condenser returns to the watercourse from which it came.

ENERGY

fuel handling sequence

Uranium is made into pellets, which are pressed into fuel bundles to be used in the reactor and then stored in cooling bays.

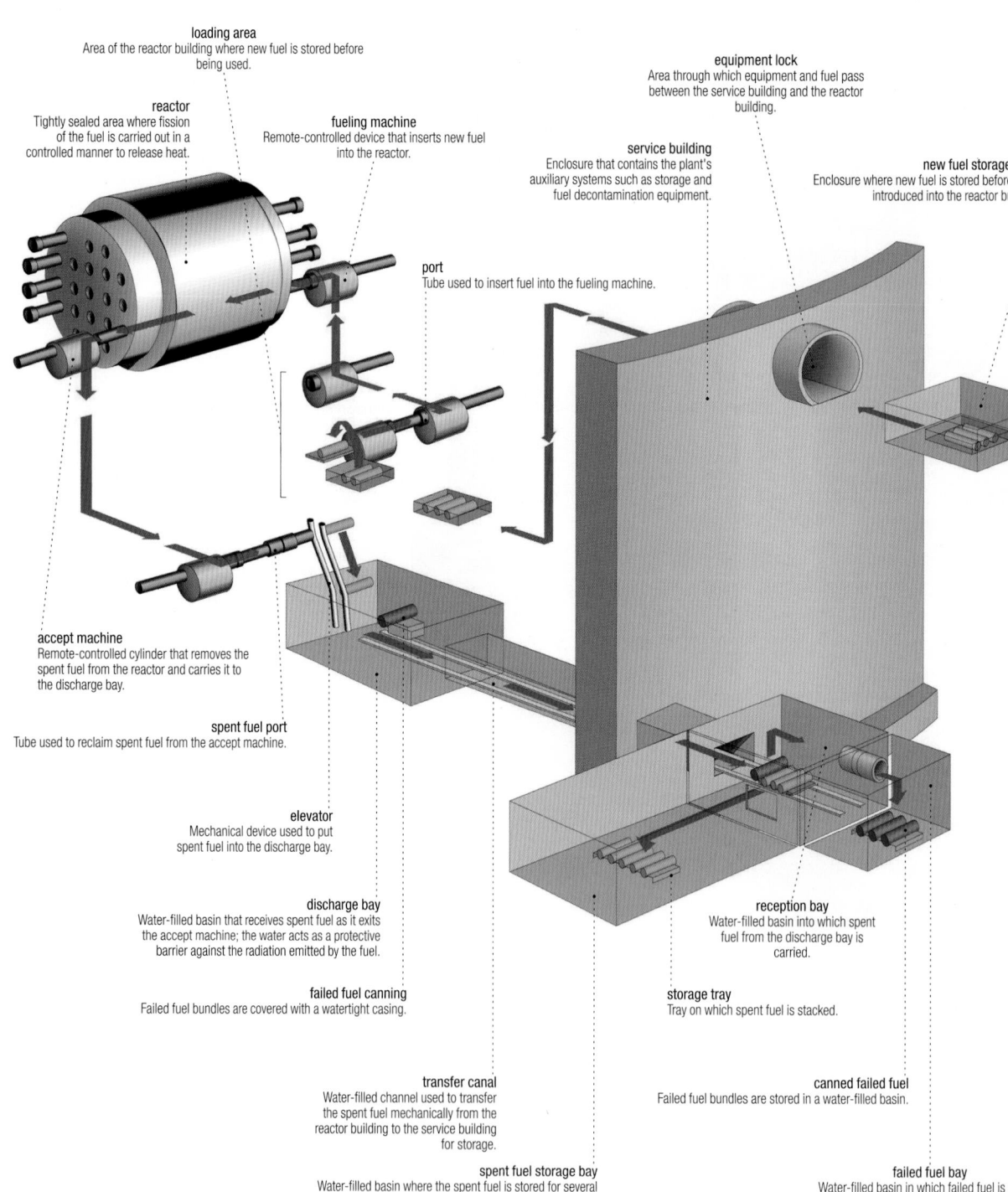

loading area
Area of the reactor building where new fuel is stored before being used.

equipment lock
Area through which equipment and fuel pass between the service building and the reactor building.

reactor
Tightly sealed area where fission of the fuel is carried out in a controlled manner to release heat.

fueling machine
Remote-controlled device that inserts new fuel into the reactor.

service building
Enclosure that contains the plant's auxiliary systems such as storage and fuel decontamination equipment.

new fuel storage ▮
Enclosure where new fuel is stored before ▮ introduced into the reactor buil

port
Tube used to insert fuel into the fueling machine.

accept machine
Remote-controlled cylinder that removes the spent fuel from the reactor and carries it to the discharge bay.

spent fuel port
Tube used to reclaim spent fuel from the accept machine.

elevator
Mechanical device used to put spent fuel into the discharge bay.

discharge bay
Water-filled basin that receives spent fuel as it exits the accept machine; the water acts as a protective barrier against the radiation emitted by the fuel.

reception bay
Water-filled basin into which spent fuel from the discharge bay is carried.

failed fuel canning
Failed fuel bundles are covered with a watertight casing.

storage tray
Tray on which spent fuel is stacked.

transfer canal
Water-filled channel used to transfer the spent fuel mechanically from the reactor building to the service building for storage.

canned failed fuel
Failed fuel bundles are stored in a water-filled basin.

spent fuel storage bay
Water-filled basin where the spent fuel is stored for several years before it can be disposed of safely.

failed fuel bay
Water-filled basin in which failed fuel is st

fuel bundle

Fuel pencils that are grouped in parallel for introduction into the reactor.

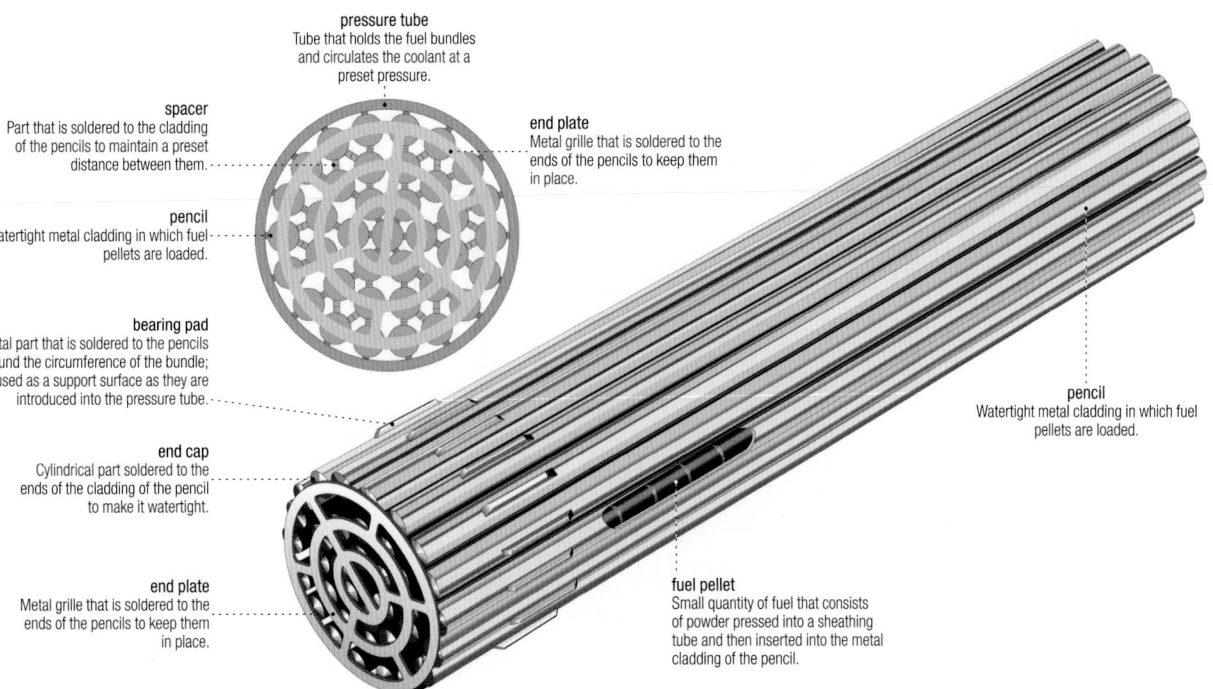

pressure tube
Tube that holds the fuel bundles and circulates the coolant at a preset pressure.

spacer
Part that is soldered to the cladding of the pencils to maintain a preset distance between them.

end plate
Metal grille that is soldered to the ends of the pencils to keep them in place.

pencil
Watertight metal cladding in which fuel pellets are loaded.

bearing pad
Metal part that is soldered to the pencils around the circumference of the bundle; used as a support surface as they are introduced into the pressure tube.

pencil
Watertight metal cladding in which fuel pellets are loaded.

end cap
Cylindrical part soldered to the ends of the cladding of the pencil to make it watertight.

end plate
Metal grille that is soldered to the ends of the pencils to keep them in place.

fuel pellet
Small quantity of fuel that consists of powder pressed into a sheathing tube and then inserted into the metal cladding of the pencil.

nuclear reactor

Tightly sealed area where fission of the fuel is carried out in a controlled manner to release heat.

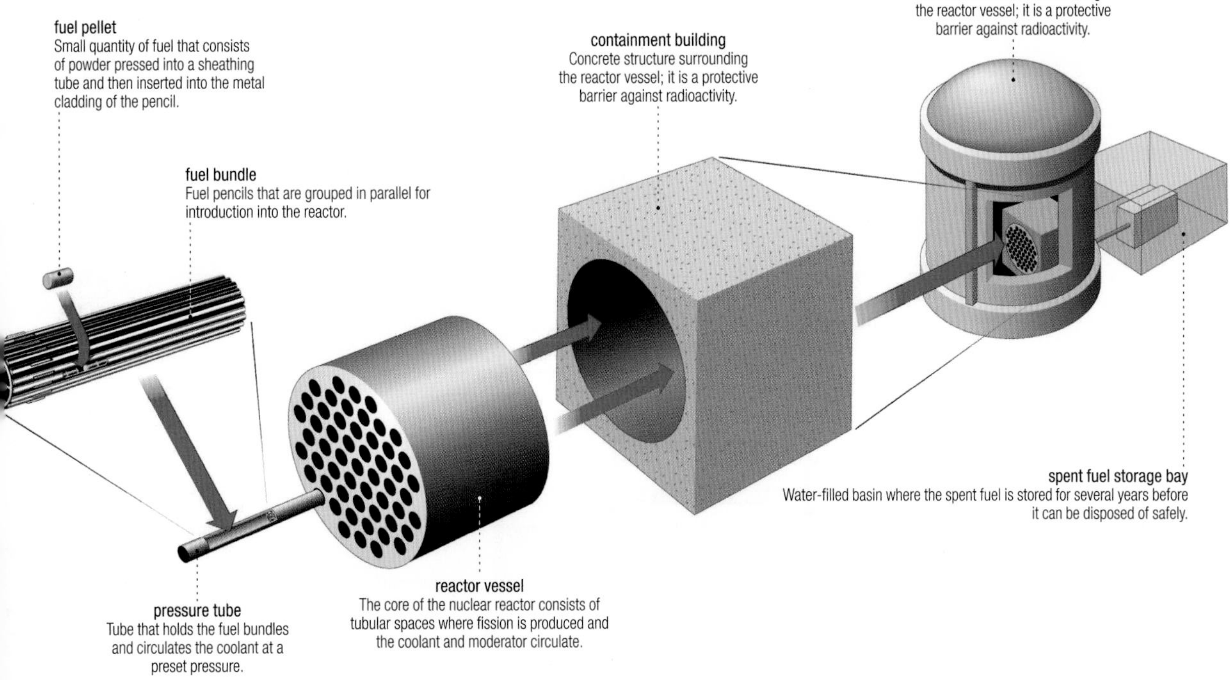

fuel pellet
Small quantity of fuel that consists of powder pressed into a sheathing tube and then inserted into the metal cladding of the pencil.

fuel bundle
Fuel pencils that are grouped in parallel for introduction into the reactor.

containment building
Concrete structure surrounding the reactor vessel; it is a protective barrier against radioactivity.

reactor building
Concrete structure surrounding the reactor vessel; it is a protective barrier against radioactivity.

spent fuel storage bay
Water-filled basin where the spent fuel is stored for several years before it can be disposed of safely.

pressure tube
Tube that holds the fuel bundles and circulates the coolant at a preset pressure.

reactor vessel
The core of the nuclear reactor consists of tubular spaces where fission is produced and the coolant and moderator circulate.

ENERGY

types of reactors

Nuclear reactors are classified according to fuel, moderator and coolant types.

carbon dioxide reactor
Developed for the most part in Great Britain and France, it was replaced by the pressurized water reactor, which performs better and is less expensive.

fueling machine
Remote-controlled device that inserts new fuel into the reactor.

concrete shielding
Concrete structure that holds back radioactive products in the event of an accident.

carbon dioxide gas coolant
Carbon dioxide that recovers the heat from the reactor core and transfers it to the heat exchanger.

control rod
Tube that contains a neutron-absorbing material (boron, cadmium) that is introduced into the reactor core to control its power.

reactor core
Center section of the nuclear reactor where fission reactions take place.

heat exchanger
Tubing system that is submerged in the hot carbon dioxide; here, water is turned into steam to power the turbine.

steam outlet
Water that has been vaporized in the carbon dioxide is carried to the turbine to produce electricity.

blower
Device that circulates carbon dioxide in the reactor core.

feedwater
Piping carries water from the condenser to the heat exchanger, where it is turned into steam.

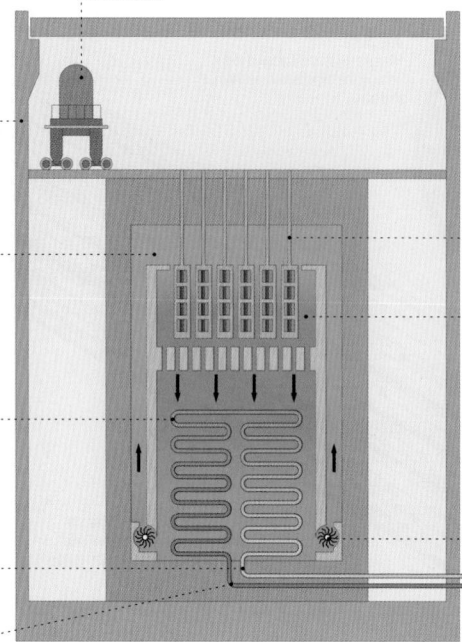

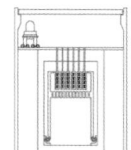

fuel: natural uranium
Natural uranium: fuel extracted from consists of a mixture of three uranium (uranium-234, -235 and -238

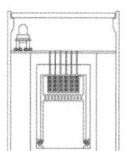

moderator: graphite
Moderator: medium that slows speed of the neutrons to mainta continuous chain reaction.

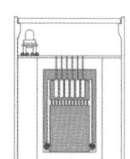

coolant: carbon dioxide
Carbon dioxide: gas that is heavier t and is produced by burning graph

heavy-water reactor
The advantage of this type of reactor is that it does not require fuel enrichment; it is used mainly in Canada, Argentina and India.

pump
Apparatus that circulates the coolant fluid between the reactor and the steam generator.

pressurizer
Device that keeps the coolant water at a preset temperature to prevent it from boiling.

concrete shielding
Concrete structure that holds back radioactive products in the event of an accident.

control rod
Tube that contains a neutron-absorbing material (boron, cadmium) that is introduced into the reactor core to control its power.

pressurized heavy water
Heavy water that is heated in the reactor core is kept under pressure to prevent it from boiling.

fuel
Matter that is placed in the reactor core; it contains heavy atoms (uranium, plutonium) from which power is extracted by fission.

fueling machine
Remote-controlled device that inserts new fuel into the reactor.

moderator tank
Steel tank that contains cold heavy water from the moderator.

safety tank
Tank where cold heavy water from the moderator flows to stop fission reactions in the event of an emergency.

steam generator
Device that uses heat from the coolant to turn water into steam to activate the turbine.

steam outlet
Steam from the generator is carried to the turbine and generator to produce electricity.

feedwater
Piping carries water from the condenser to the steam generator, where it is turned into steam.

cold heavy water
A pumping system ensures that heavy water around the moderator tank circulates, cools and is purified.

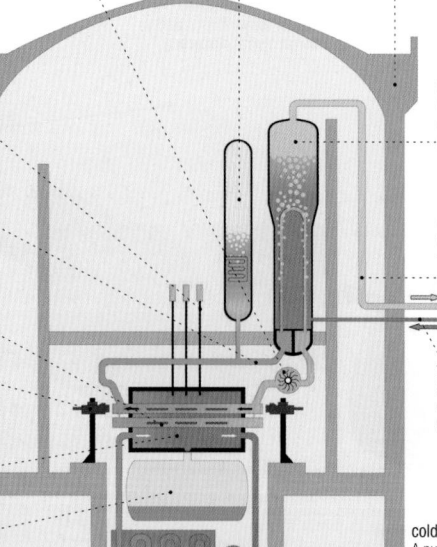

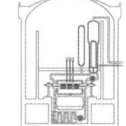

fuel: natural uranium
Natural uranium: fuel extracted from consists of a mixture of three uranium (uranium-234, -235 and -238

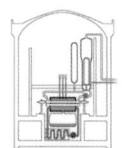

moderator: heavy water
Heavy water: water consisting of h hydrogen (deuterium) and oxygen; slow down neutrons.

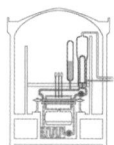

coolant: pressurized heavy w
Heavy water is kept at a set pressure to from boiling.

types of reactors

ENERGY

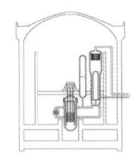

fuel: enriched uranium
iched uranium: uranium produced by
ating natural uranium to increase the
ty of fissionable isotopes (uranium-253)
contained in it.

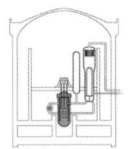

moderator: natural water
Natural water: water found in its
natural state.

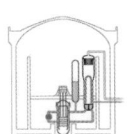

coolant: pressurized water
urized water: natural water kept under a
set pressure to prevent it from boiling.

pressurized water reactor
The most common type of reactor in the world; water from
the coolant is kept under heavy pressure to prevent it from
vaporizing.

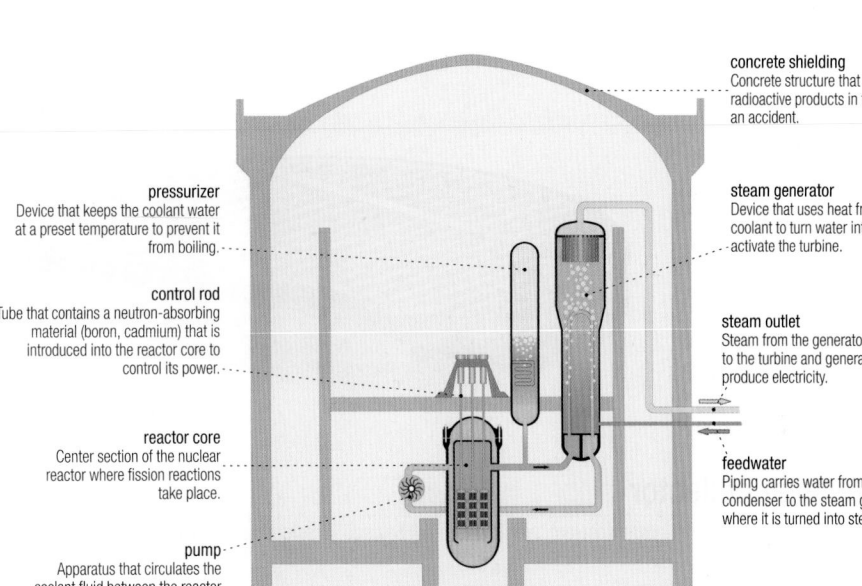

pressurizer
Device that keeps the coolant water
at a preset temperature to prevent it
from boiling.

control rod
Tube that contains a neutron-absorbing
material (boron, cadmium) that is
introduced into the reactor core to
control its power.

reactor core
Center section of the nuclear
reactor where fission reactions
take place.

pump
Apparatus that circulates the
coolant fluid between the reactor
and the steam generator.

concrete shielding
Concrete structure that holds back
radioactive products in the event of
an accident.

steam generator
Device that uses heat from the
coolant to turn water into steam to
activate the turbine.

steam outlet
Steam from the generator is carried
to the turbine and generator to
produce electricity.

feedwater
Piping carries water from the
condenser to the steam generator,
where it is turned into steam.

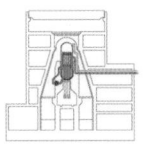

fuel: enriched uranium
iched uranium: uranium produced by
ating natural uranium to increase the
ity of fissionable isotopes (uranium-253)
contained in it.

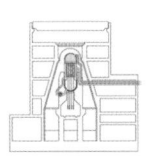

moderator: natural water
atural water: water found in its natural
state.

coolant: boiling water
ater: natural water that boils and vaporizes
ntact with the heat released by the fuel.

boiling water reactor
In this second most common reactor, boiling occurs directly
in the reactor core; it is used mainly in the United States,
Sweden and Japan.

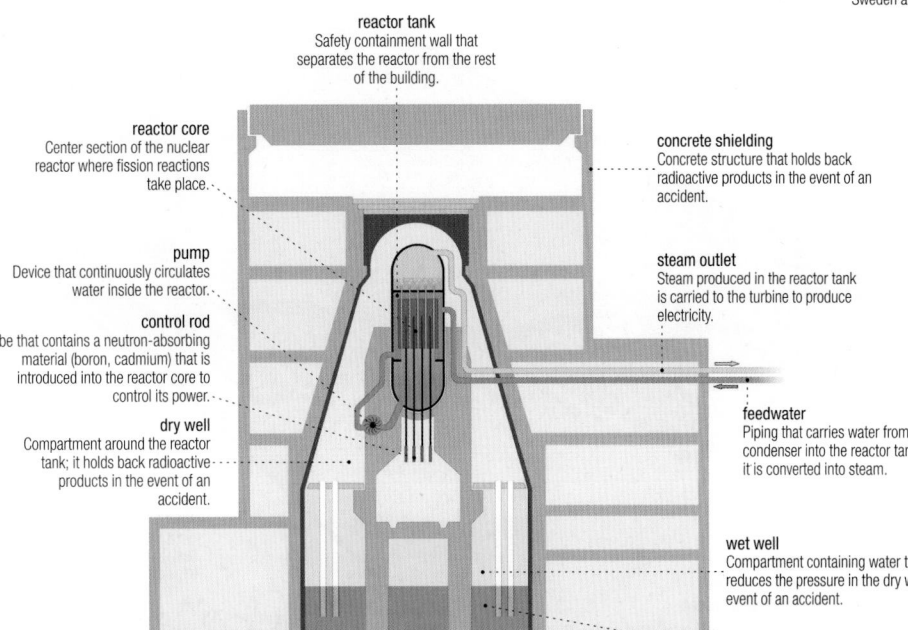

reactor tank
Safety containment wall that
separates the reactor from the rest
of the building.

reactor core
Center section of the nuclear
reactor where fission reactions
take place.

pump
Device that continuously circulates
water inside the reactor.

control rod
Tube that contains a neutron-absorbing
material (boron, cadmium) that is
introduced into the reactor core to
control its power.

dry well
Compartment around the reactor
tank; it holds back radioactive
products in the event of an
accident.

concrete shielding
Concrete structure that holds back
radioactive products in the event of an
accident.

steam outlet
Steam produced in the reactor tank
is carried to the turbine to produce
electricity.

feedwater
Piping that carries water from the
condenser into the reactor tank, where
it is converted into steam.

wet well
Compartment containing water that
reduces the pressure in the dry well in the
event of an accident.

condensation pool
Water-filled basin that is used to lower the
pressure in the reactor tank in the event of an
accident.

solar cell

Device used to convert solar energy directly into electric energy (photovoltaic effect).

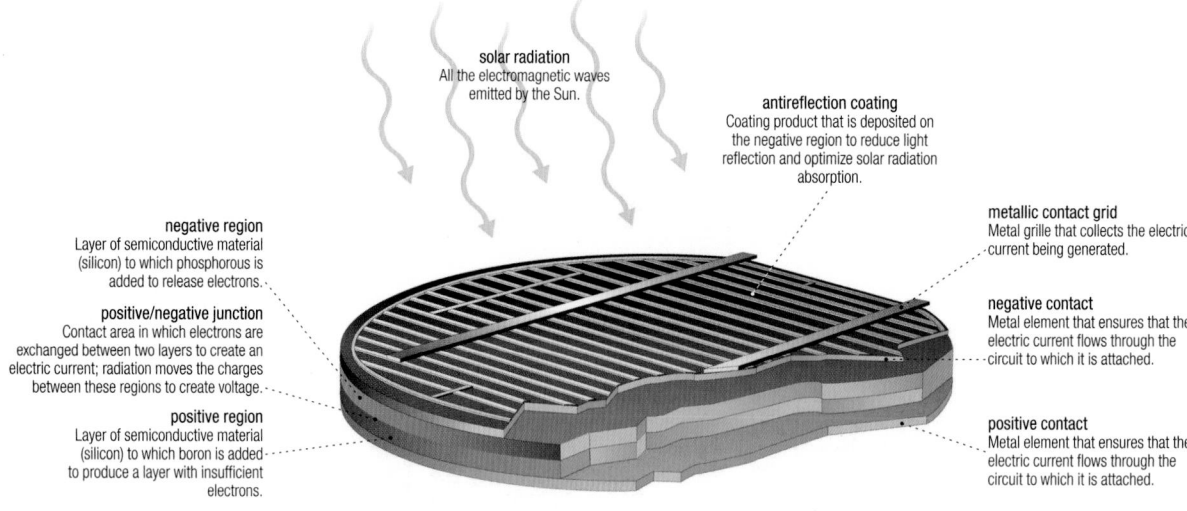

solar radiation
All the electromagnetic waves emitted by the Sun.

antireflection coating
Coating product that is deposited on the negative region to reduce light reflection and optimize solar radiation absorption.

metallic contact grid
Metal grille that collects the electric current being generated.

negative region
Layer of semiconductive material (silicon) to which phosphorous is added to release electrons.

positive/negative junction
Contact area in which electrons are exchanged between two layers to create an electric current; radiation moves the charges between these regions to create voltage.

positive region
Layer of semiconductive material (silicon) to which boron is added to produce a layer with insufficient electrons.

negative contact
Metal element that ensures that the electric current flows through the circuit to which it is attached.

positive contact
Metal element that ensures that the electric current flows through the circuit to which it is attached.

flat-plate solar collector

Device that collects solar radiation and heats a coolant, which in turn will be used in residential settings to heat water or the home.

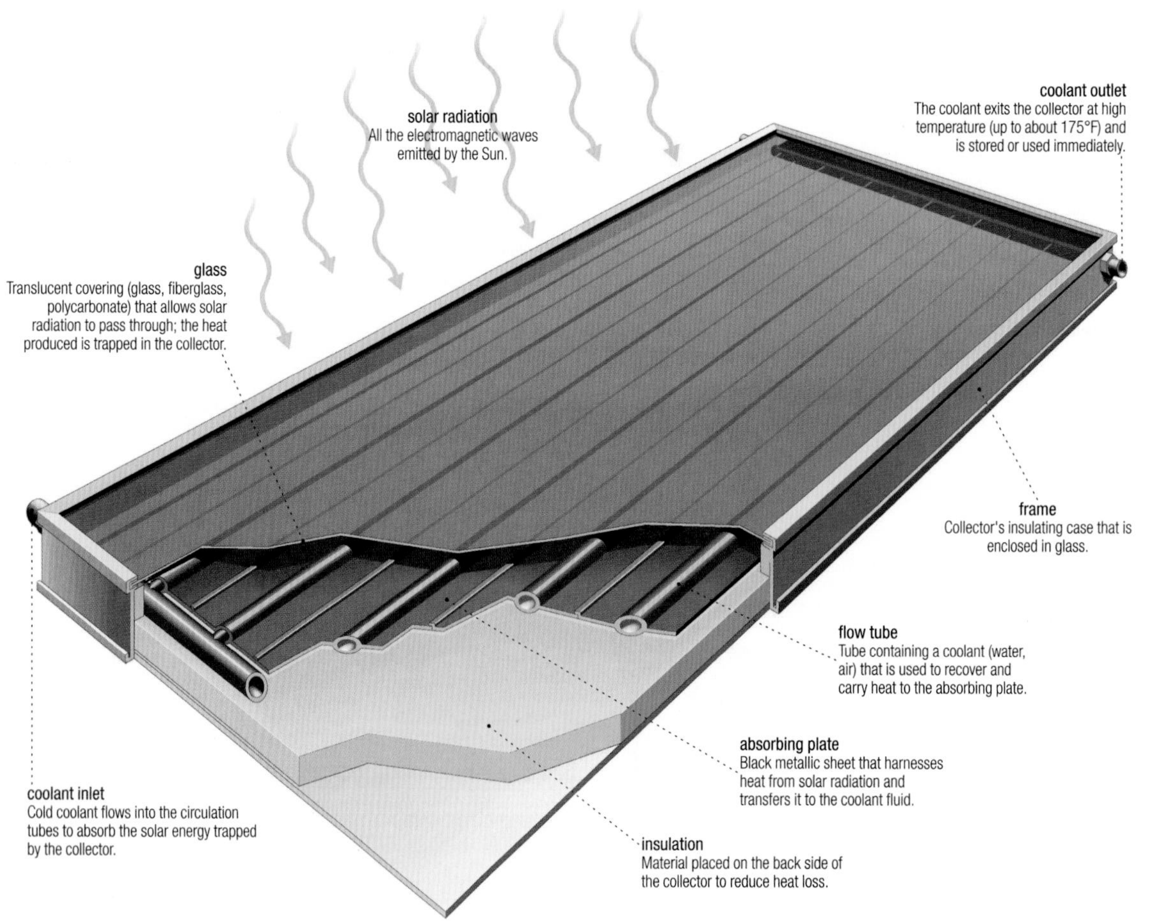

solar radiation
All the electromagnetic waves emitted by the Sun.

coolant outlet
The coolant exits the collector at high temperature (up to about 175°F) and is stored or used immediately.

glass
Translucent covering (glass, fiberglass, polycarbonate) that allows solar radiation to pass through; the heat produced is trapped in the collector.

frame
Collector's insulating case that is enclosed in glass.

flow tube
Tube containing a coolant (water, air) that is used to recover and carry heat to the absorbing plate.

coolant inlet
Cold coolant flows into the circulation tubes to absorb the solar energy trapped by the collector.

absorbing plate
Black metallic sheet that harnesses heat from solar radiation and transfers it to the coolant fluid.

insulation
Material placed on the back side of the collector to reduce heat loss.

solar cell system

Unit that is usually made up of 36 solar cells, each of which produces a voltage of 0.5 V; it is used to power low-voltage devices.

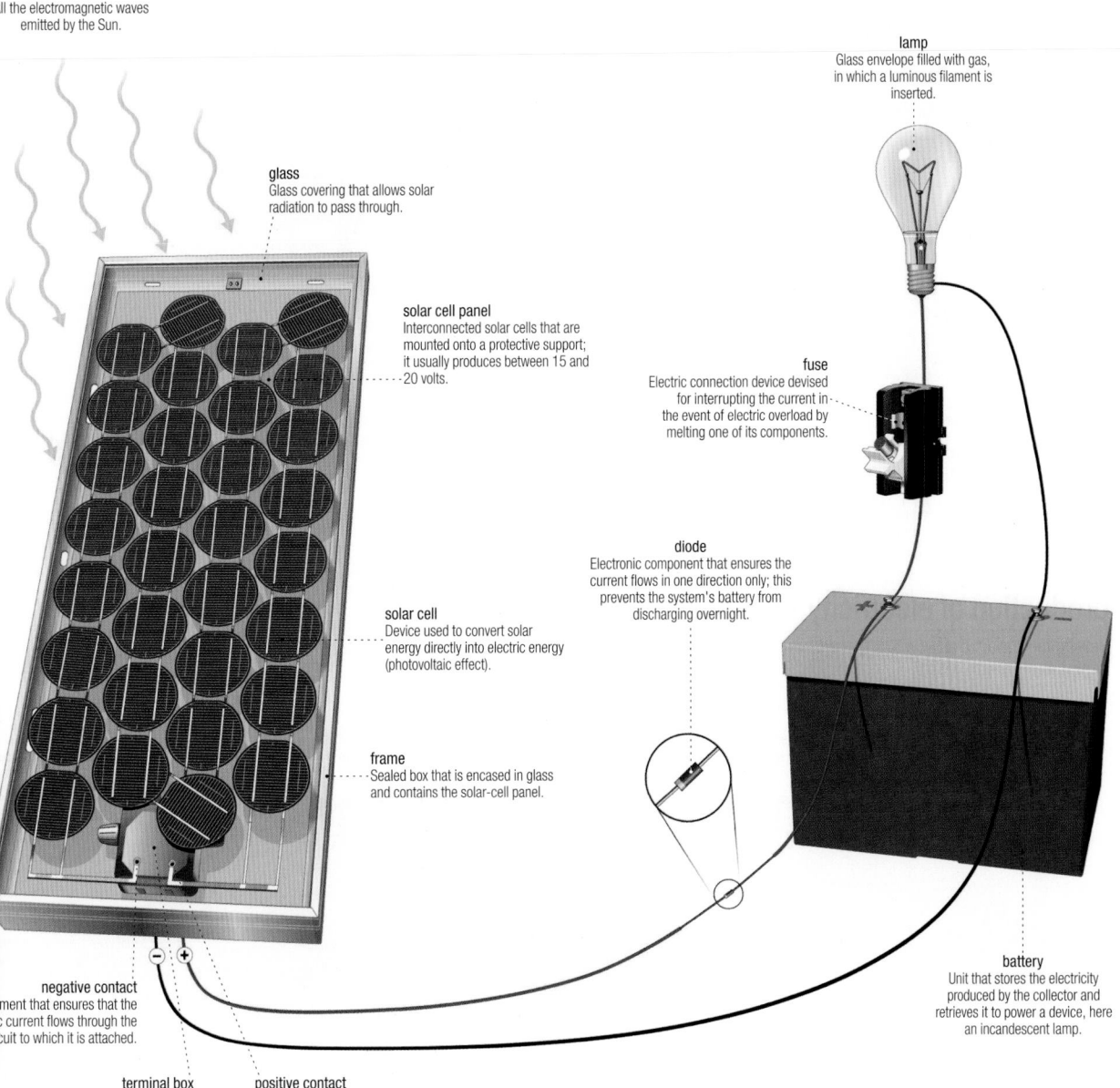

solar radiation
All the electromagnetic waves emitted by the Sun.

lamp
Glass envelope filled with gas, in which a luminous filament is inserted.

glass
Glass covering that allows solar radiation to pass through.

solar cell panel
Interconnected solar cells that are mounted onto a protective support; it usually produces between 15 and 20 volts.

fuse
Electric connection device devised for interrupting the current in the event of electric overload by melting one of its components.

diode
Electronic component that ensures the current flows in one direction only; this prevents the system's battery from discharging overnight.

solar cell
Device used to convert solar energy directly into electric energy (photovoltaic effect).

frame
Sealed box that is encased in glass and contains the solar-cell panel.

negative contact
ment that ensures that the current flows through the uit to which it is attached.

terminal box
Box in which the electric cables powering the battery are connected to the collector's positive and negative contacts.

positive contact
Metal element that ensures that the electric current flows through the circuit to which it is attached.

battery
Unit that stores the electricity produced by the collector and retrieves it to power a device, here an incandescent lamp.

ENERGY

solar furnace

Plant that concentrates solar radiation to reach very high temperatures (over 5,400°F) as part of a research effort to develop experimental materials (including astronautic materials and ceramics).

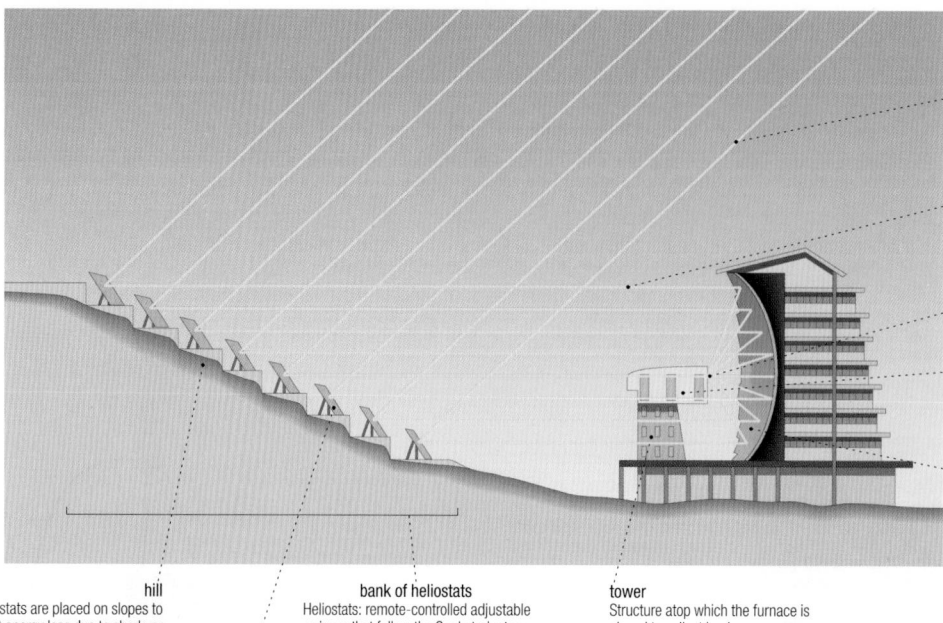

solar radiation
All the electromagnetic waves emitted by the Sun.

reflected solar ray
Solar rays that reach the helios are sent to the parabolic mirror.

target area
Point where solar rays reflected the parabolic mirror converge.

furnace
Reaching temperatures of over 5,400°F, it is mainly used to process and develop materials.

parabolic mirror
Curved mirror that concentrate Sun's rays toward one point in furnace (the target area).

hill
Heliostats are placed on slopes to prevent energy loss due to shade or the interception of reflected rays by neighboring mirrors.

bank of heliostats
Heliostats: remote-controlled adjustable mirrors that follow the Sun's trajectory and concentrate solar radiation toward the boiler at the top of the tower.

tower
Structure atop which the furnace is placed to collect luminous energy; it usually reaches a height of 65 ft.

reflecting surface
Polished metallized glass that receives solar radiation and direct it to the parabolic mirror.

production of electricity from solar energy

Heating the coolant directly with solar rays turns water into steam, which then turns the turbo-alternator to produce electricity.

solar radiation
The Sun emits waves in the form of luminous radiation (41% visible light, 52% infrared light and 7% ultraviolet light).

reflected solar ray
Solar rays trapped by heliostats are sent to the boiler.

coolant
Fluid (e.g., a mixture of melted salts) that traps the heat from concentrated solar radiation and carries it to the turbine.

boiler
Enclosure in which the concentrated heat from the Sun's rays raises the temperature of the coolant.

tower
Structure atop which the boiler sits and collects luminous energy; it can reach 325 ft. in height.

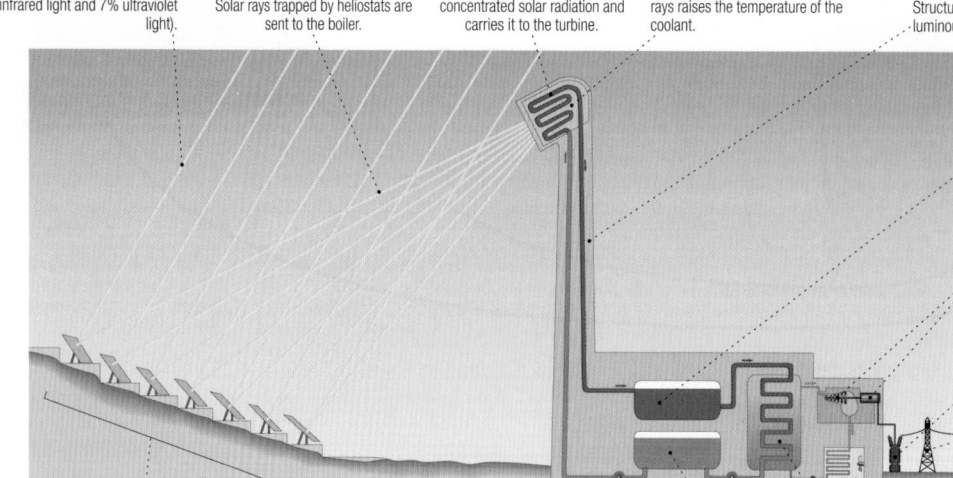

hot coolant
The coolant extracts heat from the boiler and carries it to the steam generator and turbine.

turbo-alternator
Device that uses steam to convert mechanical force generated by the rotation of the turbine into electric.

transformer
Device used to alter the electric voltage; the voltage is increased a the plant outlet in order to carry the current over long distances.

electricity transmission network
Electricity is carried over vast dista a network of cables that extends f power plant to consumers.

condenser
Circuit that cools the steam from the turbine and condenses it into water, which is reintroduced into the steam generator.

bank of heliostats
Heliostats: remote-controlled adjustable mirrors that follow the Sun's trajectory and concentrate solar radiation toward the boiler at the top of the tower.

pump
Device that ensures that the cold coolant liquid flows to the boiler.

cold coolant
After releasing its heat to the steam generator, the cold coolant returns to the boiler.

steam generator
Device that uses heat to convert water into steam to activate the turbo-alternator.

solar house

Solar energy can be used to heat and supply hot water to a home.

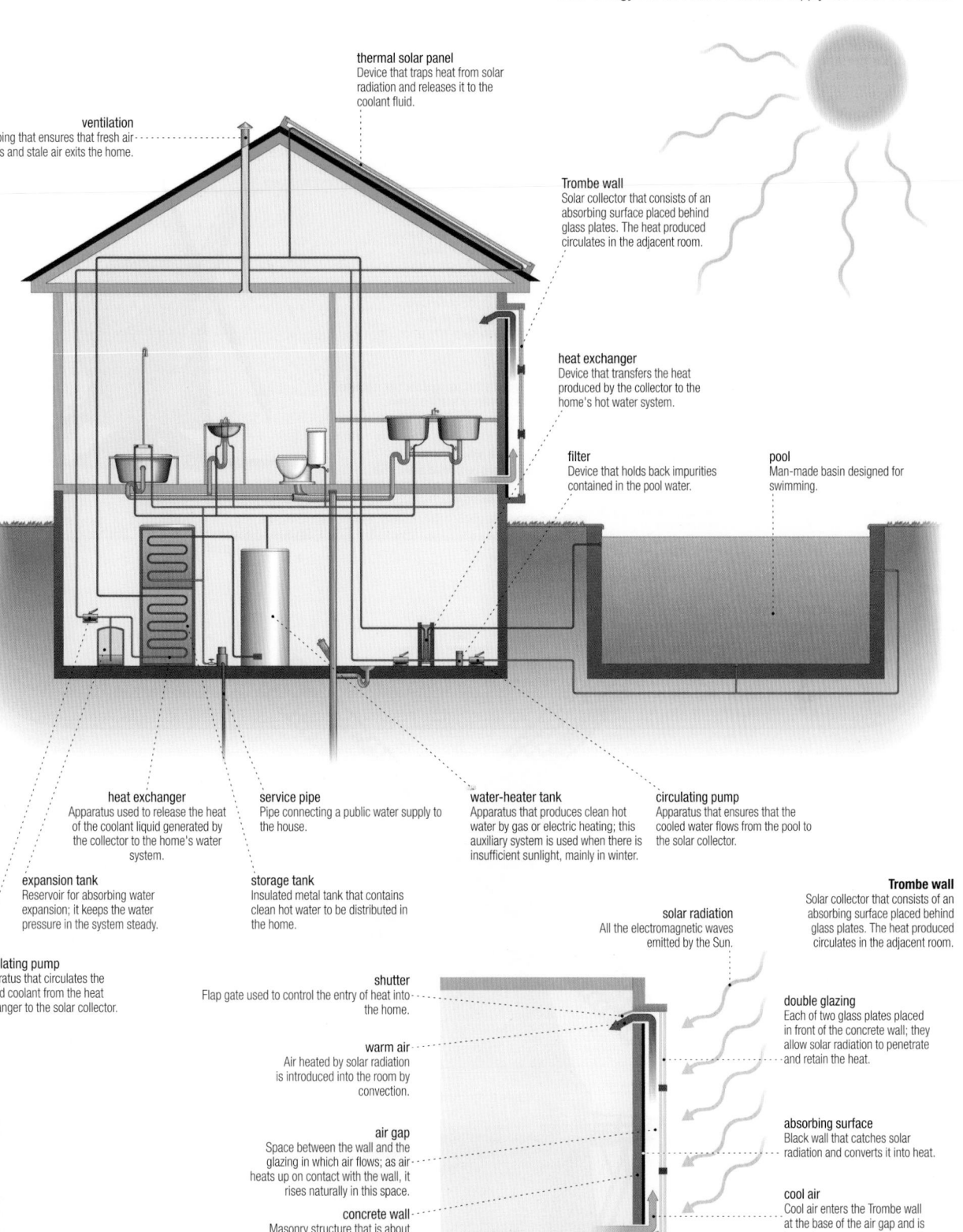

thermal solar panel
Device that traps heat from solar radiation and releases it to the coolant fluid.

ventilation
...ping that ensures that fresh air ...rs and stale air exits the home.

Trombe wall
Solar collector that consists of an absorbing surface placed behind glass plates. The heat produced circulates in the adjacent room.

heat exchanger
Device that transfers the heat produced by the collector to the home's hot water system.

filter
Device that holds back impurities contained in the pool water.

pool
Man-made basin designed for swimming.

heat exchanger
Apparatus used to release the heat of the coolant liquid generated by the collector to the home's water system.

service pipe
Pipe connecting a public water supply to the house.

water-heater tank
Apparatus that produces clean hot water by gas or electric heating; this auxiliary system is used when there is insufficient sunlight, mainly in winter.

circulating pump
Apparatus that ensures that the cooled water flows from the pool to the solar collector.

expansion tank
Reservoir for absorbing water expansion; it keeps the water pressure in the system steady.

storage tank
Insulated metal tank that contains clean hot water to be distributed in the home.

solar radiation
All the electromagnetic waves emitted by the Sun.

Trombe wall
Solar collector that consists of an absorbing surface placed behind glass plates. The heat produced circulates in the adjacent room.

...ulating pump
...aratus that circulates the ...ed coolant from the heat ...anger to the solar collector.

shutter
Flap gate used to control the entry of heat into the home.

warm air
Air heated by solar radiation is introduced into the room by convection.

air gap
Space between the wall and the glazing in which air flows; as air heats up on contact with the wall, it rises naturally in this space.

concrete wall
Masonry structure that is about 15 in thick; it has a black surface to absorb heat from the Sun to heat the air.

double glazing
Each of two glass plates placed in front of the concrete wall; they allow solar radiation to penetrate and retain the heat.

absorbing surface
Black wall that catches solar radiation and converts it into heat.

cool air
Cool air enters the Trombe wall at the base of the air gap and is heated on contact with the wall.

ENERGY

windmills

Machines that convert wind energy into mechanical energy; they were used in the past to mill grain and pump water.

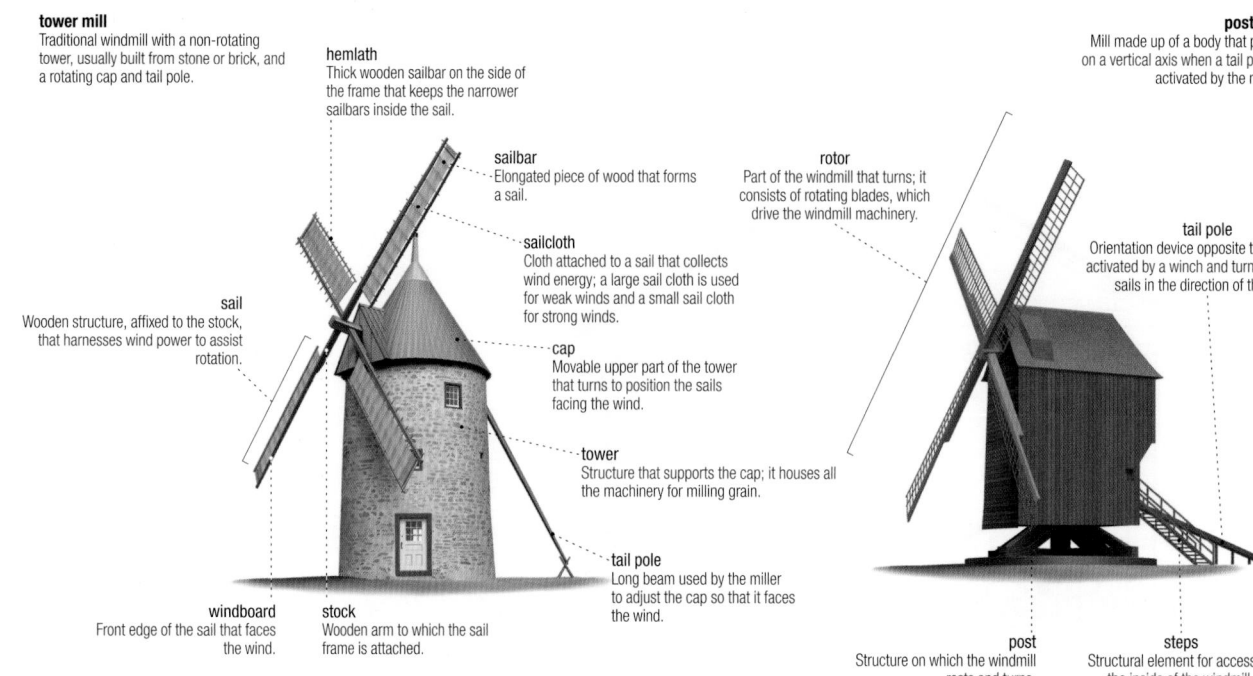

tower mill
Traditional windmill with a non-rotating tower, usually built from stone or brick, and a rotating cap and tail pole.

post m
Mill made up of a body that pi
on a vertical axis when a tail p
activated by the m

hemlath
Thick wooden sailbar on the side of the frame that keeps the narrower sailbars inside the sail.

sailbar
Elongated piece of wood that forms a sail.

rotor
Part of the windmill that turns; it consists of rotating blades, which drive the windmill machinery.

tail pole
Orientation device opposite th
activated by a winch and turns
sails in the direction of th

sailcloth
Cloth attached to a sail that collects wind energy; a large sail cloth is used for weak winds and a small sail cloth for strong winds.

sail
Wooden structure, affixed to the stock, that harnesses wind power to assist rotation.

cap
Movable upper part of the tower that turns to position the sails facing the wind.

tower
Structure that supports the cap; it houses all the machinery for milling grain.

tail pole
Long beam used by the miller to adjust the cap so that it faces the wind.

windboard
Front edge of the sail that faces the wind.

stock
Wooden arm to which the sail frame is attached.

post
Structure on which the windmill rests and turns.

steps
Structural element for accessi
the inside of the windmill.

smock mill
Windmill with a hexagonal or octagonal wooden tower, cap and fantail (to facilite the cap's rotation).

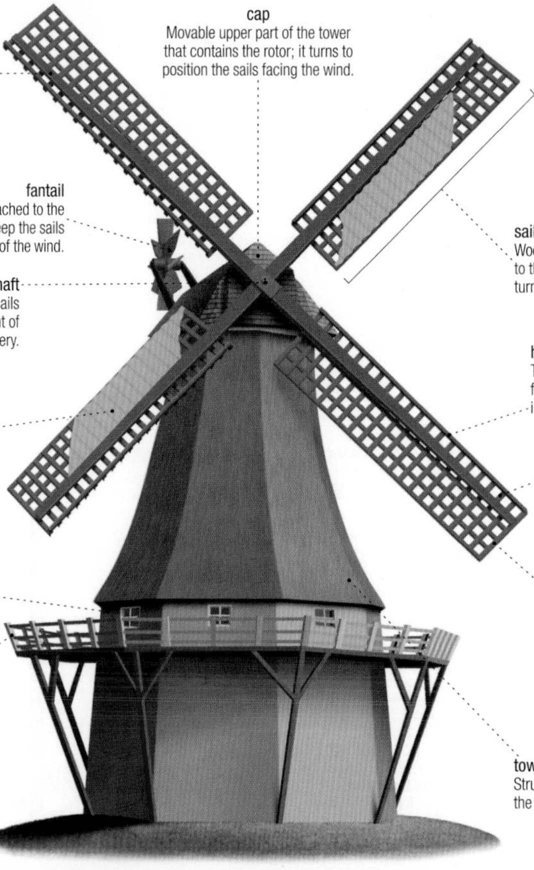

cap
Movable upper part of the tower that contains the rotor; it turns to position the sails facing the wind.

stock
Wooden arm to which the sail frame is attached.

fantail
Orientation device that is attached to the cap, allowing it to rotate to keep the sails in the direction of the wind.

windshaft
Cylindrical part on which the sails turn; it transmits the movement of the rotor to the windmill machinery.

sail
Wooden structure that is attached to the stock; the force of the wind turns it to drive the rotor.

sailcloth
Cloth attached to a sail that collects wind energy; a large sail cloth is used for weak winds and a small sail cloth for strong winds.

hemlath
Thick wooden sailbar on the side of the frame that keeps the narrower sailbars inside the sail.

sailbar
Elongated piece of wood that forms a sail.

uplong
A wooden bar that supports and strengthens the sailbars.

floor
Level for accessing the inside of the mill; grain is usually stored at its base.

gallery
Passageway used to move around the mill floor.

tower
Structure that supports the cap; it houses all the machinery for milling grain.

ENERGY

wind turbines and electricity production

Wind turbine: machine that harnesses energy from the wind and converts it into mechanical energy to activate the alternator.

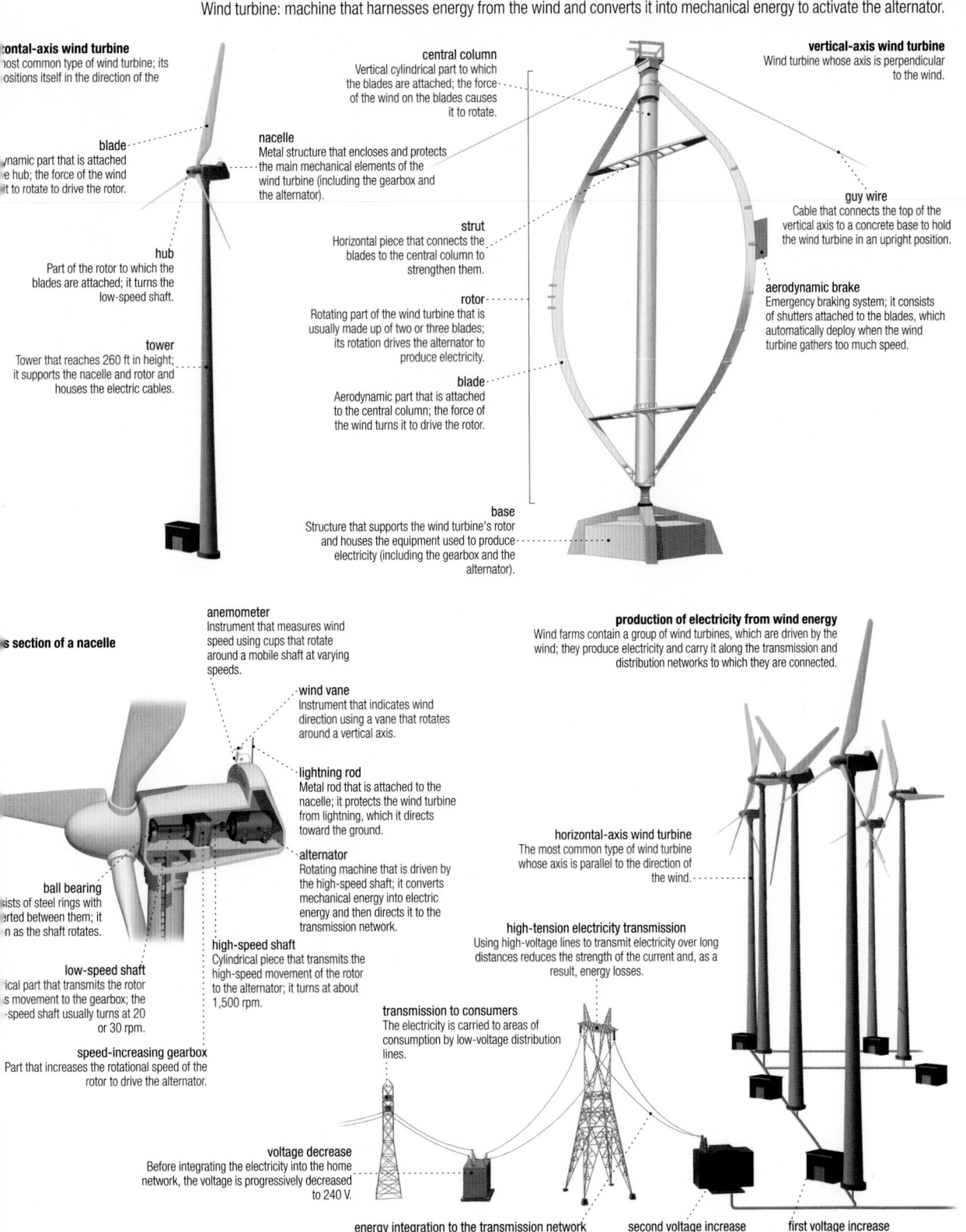

ontal-axis wind turbine
most common type of wind turbine; its
ositions itself in the direction of the

central column
Vertical cylindrical part to which
the blades are attached; the force
of the wind on the blades causes
it to rotate.

vertical-axis wind turbine
Wind turbine whose axis is perpendicular
to the wind.

blade
ynamic part that is attached
e hub; the force of the wind
it to rotate to drive the rotor.

nacelle
Metal structure that encloses and protects
the main mechanical elements of the
wind turbine (including the gearbox and
the alternator).

guy wire
Cable that connects the top of the
vertical axis to a concrete base to hold
the wind turbine in an upright position.

hub
Part of the rotor to which the
blades are attached; it turns the
low-speed shaft.

strut
Horizontal piece that connects the
blades to the central column to
strengthen them.

aerodynamic brake
Emergency braking system; it consists
of shutters attached to the blades, which
automatically deploy when the wind
turbine gathers too much speed.

rotor
Rotating part of the wind turbine that is
usually made up of two or three blades;
its rotation drives the alternator to
produce electricity.

tower
Tower that reaches 260 ft in height;
it supports the nacelle and rotor and
houses the electric cables.

blade
Aerodynamic part that is attached
to the central column; the force of
the wind turns it to drive the rotor.

base
Structure that supports the wind turbine's rotor
and houses the equipment used to produce
electricity (including the gearbox and the
alternator).

anemometer
Instrument that measures wind
speed using cups that rotate
around a mobile shaft at varying
speeds.

s section of a nacelle

production of electricity from wind energy
Wind farms contain a group of wind turbines, which are driven by the
wind; they produce electricity and carry it along the transmission and
distribution networks to which they are connected.

wind vane
Instrument that indicates wind
direction using a vane that rotates
around a vertical axis.

lightning rod
Metal rod that is attached to the
nacelle; it protects the wind turbine
from lightning, which it directs
toward the ground.

horizontal-axis wind turbine
The most common type of wind turbine
whose axis is parallel to the direction of
the wind.

alternator
Rotating machine that is driven by
the high-speed shaft; it converts
mechanical energy into electric
energy and then directs it to the
transmission network.

ball bearing
sists of steel rings with
erted between them; it
n as the shaft rotates.

high-tension electricity transmission
Using high-voltage lines to transmit electricity over long
distances reduces the strength of the current and, as a
result, energy losses.

high-speed shaft
Cylindrical piece that transmits the
high-speed movement of the rotor
to the alternator; it turns at about
1,500 rpm.

low-speed shaft
ical part that transmits the rotor
s movement to the gearbox; the
-speed shaft usually turns at 20
or 30 rpm.

transmission to consumers
The electricity is carried to areas of
consumption by low-voltage distribution
lines.

speed-increasing gearbox
Part that increases the rotational speed of the
rotor to drive the alternator.

voltage decrease
Before integrating the electricity into the home
network, the voltage is progressively decreased
to 240 V.

energy integration to the transmission network
The electricity produced is integrated into the network.

second voltage increase

first voltage increase
Increase in voltage: transformers carry
high-voltage electricity produced by the
alternator to reduce loss during transport.

ENERGY

SCIENCE

A body of knowledge, often formulated as laws and theories, based on the collection of data through observation and experiment.

matter

Any substance that has mass, is composed of atoms and occupies space.

atom
Fundamental unit of matter having unique chemical properties; it is composed of a nucleus and an electron cloud. One type of atom is distinguished from another by the number of protons in its nucleus.

nucleus
Central part of the atom whose electric charge is positive; it is composed of protons and neutrons, around which electrons move.

d quark
The d quark (down) is one of six types of quarks (constituent particles of protons and neutrons); it has a negative electric charge.

neutron
Constituent particle of an atom's nucleus whose electric charge is neutral; it is composed of one u quark and two d quarks.

u quark
The u quark (up) is one of six types of quarks (constituent particles of the protons and neutrons); it has a positive electric charge.

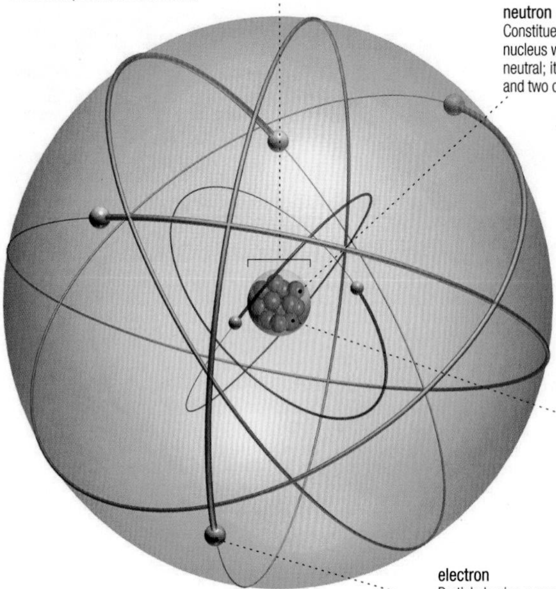

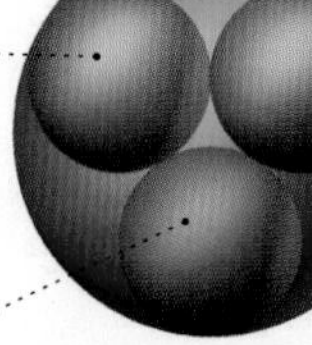

neutron
Constituent particle of an atom's nucleus whose electric charge is neutral; it is composed of one u quark and two d quarks.

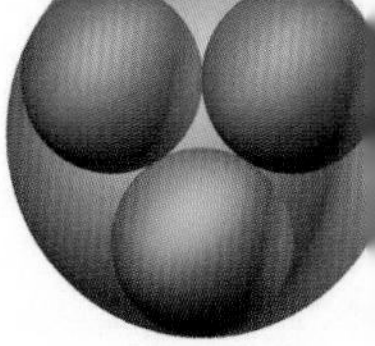

proton
Constituent particle of an atom's nucleus whose electric charge positive; it is composed of two u q and one d quark.

proton
Constituent particle of an atom's nucleus whose electric charge is positive; it is composed of two u quarks and one d quark.

mole
Matter composed of atoms that consti the smallest unit of a pure body that exist in a free state (e.g., water and ca diox.

atoms
Almost all matter in the universe is composed of approximately 100 types of atoms.

electron
Particle having a negative electric charge that moves around the nucleus of the atom.

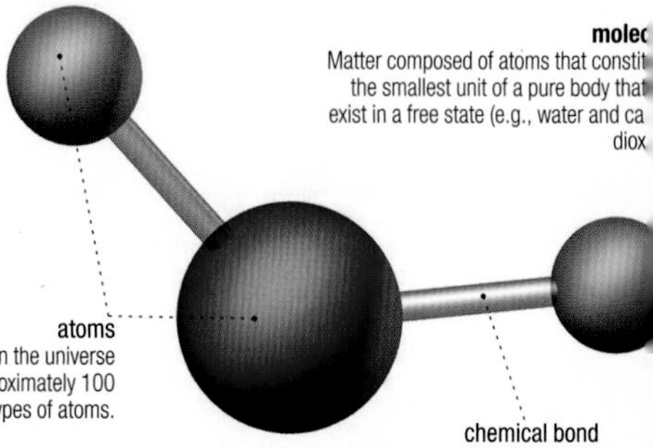

chemical bond
Force that unites two atoms throu sharing of a common electron (co bond) or the transfer of electrons bond) to form a molecule.

states of matter
Matter exists in three fundamental states (solid, liquid and gaseous), which depend on the temperature and pressure to which the matter is subjected.

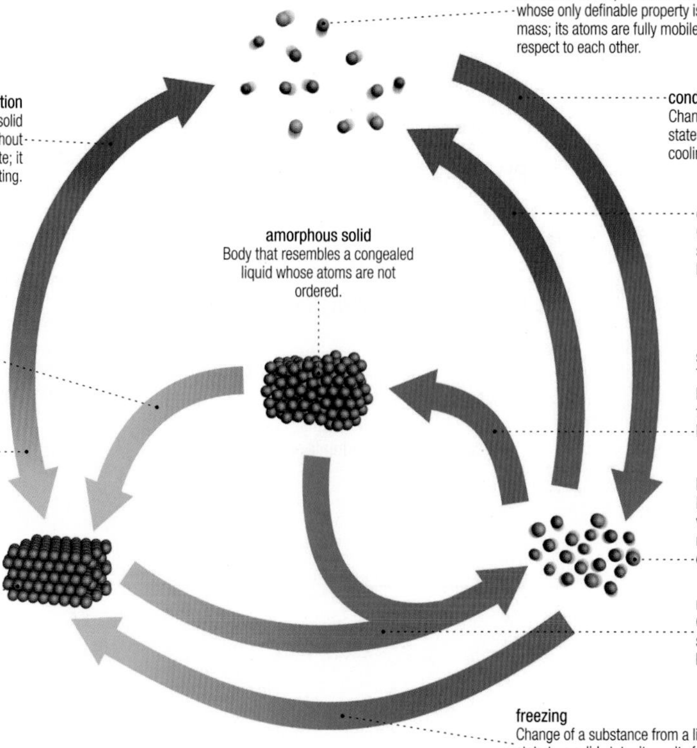

gas
Malleable and expandable matter whose only definable property is mass; its atoms are fully mobile with respect to each other.

sublimation
Change of a substance from a solid state directly to a gaseous state without passing through the liquid state; it results from heating.

condensation
Change of a substance from a gaseous state to a liquid state; it results from cooling.

evaporation
Change of a substance from a liquid state to a gaseous state; it results from heating.

crystallization
Change of a substance from an amorphous state to a crystallized state; it results from cooling, which causes the atoms to become ordered.

amorphous solid
Body that resembles a congealed liquid whose atoms are not ordered.

supercooling
The process of cooling a liquid below the point at which it normally freezes (solidifies); its atoms become unstable.

condensation
Change of a substance from a gaseous state to a solid state; it results from cooling.

liquid
Matter having a definite mass and volume but no shape; its atoms are relatively mobile in relation to each other.

solid
Rigid body possessing mass, volume and a definite form; its atoms are linked to each other and are almost completely at rest.

melting
Change of a substance from a solid state to a liquid state; it results from heating.

freezing
Change of a substance from a liquid state to a solid state; it results from cooling.

matter

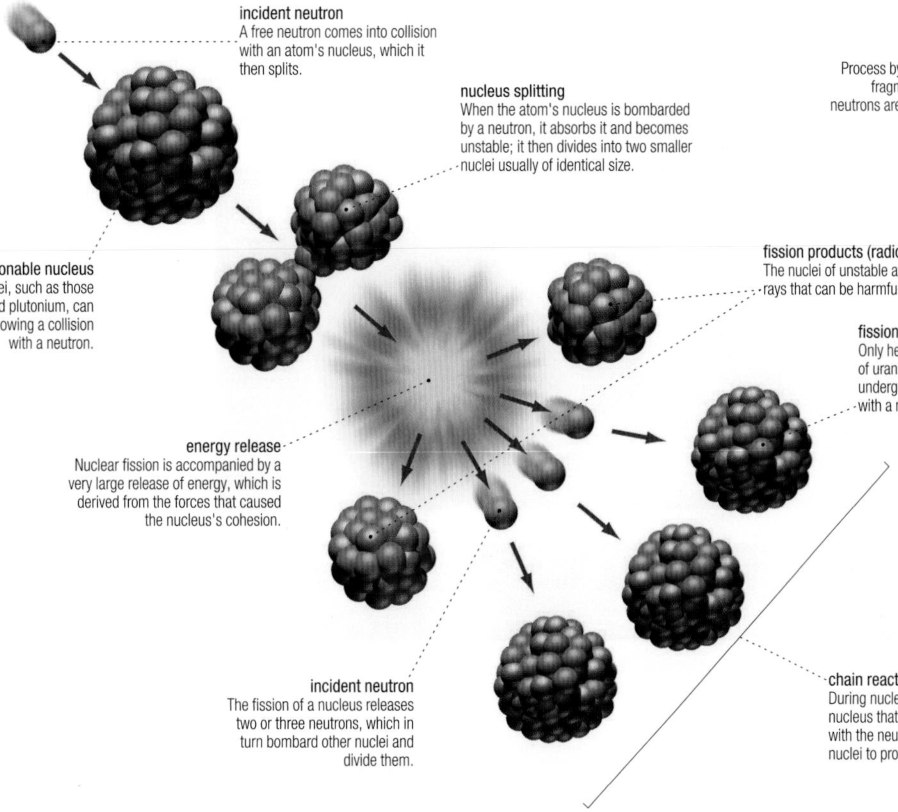

incident neutron
A free neutron comes into collision with an atom's nucleus, which it then splits.

nucleus splitting
When the atom's nucleus is bombarded by a neutron, it absorbs it and becomes unstable; it then divides into two smaller nuclei usually of identical size.

nuclear fission
Process by which the atoms' nuclei become fragmented (e.g., in a nuclear reactor); neutrons are released and energy is produced in the form of heat.

fissionable nucleus
Only heavy nuclei, such as those of uranium and plutonium, can undergo fission following a collision with a neutron.

fission products (radioactive nuclei)
The nuclei of unstable atoms produced by fission emit rays that can be harmful to living organisms.

fissionable nucleus
Only heavy nuclei, such as those of uranium and plutonium, can undergo fission following a collision with a neutron.

energy release
Nuclear fission is accompanied by a very large release of energy, which is derived from the forces that caused the nucleus's cohesion.

incident neutron
The fission of a nucleus releases two or three neutrons, which in turn bombard other nuclei and divide them.

chain reaction
During nuclear fission, parts of the atom's nucleus that have been broken off by collision with the neutron will in turn bombard other nuclei to produce more fission.

heat transfer
Heat transfer within or between matter occurs in three ways: conduction, convection and radiation.

convection
Heat transfer in a fluid that is caused by a variation in temperature resulting from the movement of molecules. Here, the heated water expands, rises and releases its heat to the surrounding air.

vapor
Gaseous state of water above its boiling point (water boils and is converted to vapor at 212°F or 100°C at sea level).

liquid
Matter having a definite mass and volume but no shape; its atoms are relatively mobile in relation to each other.

radiation
Heat transfer in the form of electromagnetic waves emitted by a heated body (solid, liquid or gas).

convection current
Movement of fluid caused by a difference in density, which transfers heat. The heated water rises and is replaced by the cooler water from the surface.

solid
Rigid body possessing mass, volume and a definite form; its atoms are linked to each other and are almost completely at rest.

conduction
Heat transfer in a body (usually a solid) or between two bodies in contact; the molecules vibrate but no matter leaves its place in the solid.

flame
Incandescent gas resulting from the combustion of a mixture of gas and air; it produces heat and light.

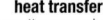
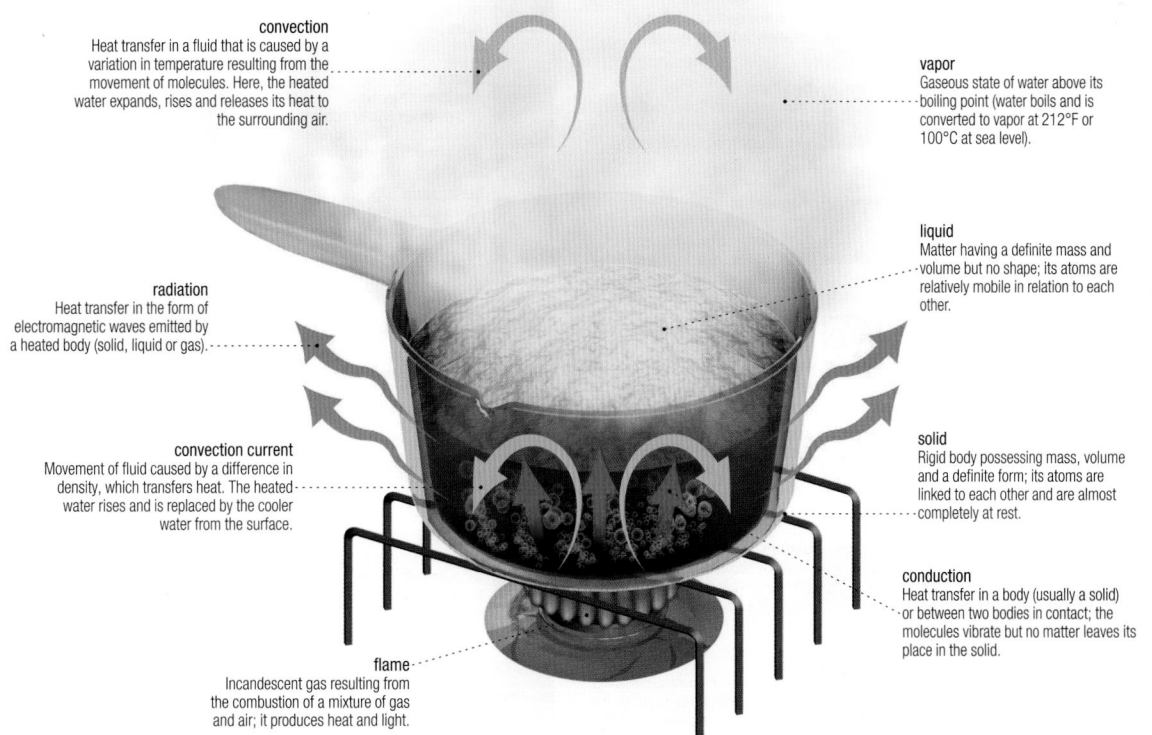

SCIENCE

chemical elements

There are more than 110 chemical elements, most of which are naturally present in the universe. The others are created artificially in the laboratory.

periodic table of elements

Table created by Dmitry Mendeleyev in 1869 that classifies the known chemical elements. The elements are classified in order of their atomic weight and arranged into groups having similar properties.

atomic number
Number that indicates the order of a chemical element in the table of elements and corresponds to the number of protons contained in its nucleus.

symbol
The name of each chemical element is represented by one or two letters, the first of which is in uppercase (e.g., O for oxygen, Cl for chlorine).

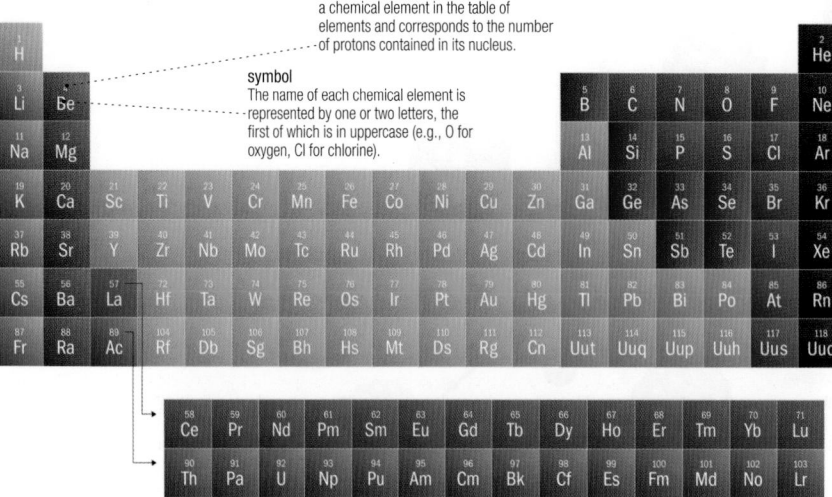

other metals

These elements are not part of any other c of metal; they are sometimes called posttra metals.

aluminum
Light metal that is used espec aeronautics, cars, buildings, e cables, kitchen utensils and pa

gallium
Rare metal that is used especi in high-temperature thermome electroluminescent diodes and television screens (the color g

indium
Very rare metal that is used es race car engines and electroni and as a coating for glass.

tin
Metal that is used especially a anticorrosive for copper and st a component in the preparatio welding and toothpaste.

thallium
Metal that is used especially in infrared detectors and some k of glass.

lead
Heavy toxic metal that is used corrosion, as a protection agai and in accumulator batteries, glass.

bismuth
Relatively rare metal that is us especially in alloys and cosme in medicine to treat gastric ulc diarrhea.

polonium
Very rare radioactive metal tha fuel in nuclear reactors; it emi that is much more powerful th uranium.

ununtrium
Synthetic radioactive element, created in a laboratory in 2004 made by fusing atoms of bism and zinc.

ununquadium
Synthetic radioactive element observed in a laboratory in 19 Though classified a metal, the element displays properties of noble gas.

ununpentium
Synthetic radioactive element, created in a laboratory in 2004 made by fusing atoms of calci and americium.

ununhexium
Synthetic radioactive element, created in a laboratory in 2000 made by fusing atoms of calci and curium.

hydrogen
This gas is the most abundant element in the universe and makes up part of the composition of water. It is used especially in petrochemistry and rocket fuel.

alkali metals
Generally soft and silvery and very good conductors of heat and electricity; they are very reactive with nonmetals and break down in water.

lithium
The lightest of all the metals is used especially in alloys for the aerospace industry and in household batteries; its salts are used in medicine.

sodium
Metal that is used especially in streetlights, kitchen salt (sodium chloride) and the manufacture of glass and cosmetic products.

potassium
Very reactive light metal that is used especially in fertilizer and matches; its salts are used in medicine.

rubidium
Metal similar to potassium but much rarer that is used in the manufacture of photoelectric cells and special kinds of glass and lasers.

cesium
Rare metal that is used especially in photoelectric cells, atomic clocks, infrared lamps and treating certain cancers.

francium
The heaviest of the alkali metals is very rare and radioactive and has a very short half-life (about 22 minutes).

alkaline earth metals
Generally silvery and malleable and good conductors of heat and electricity; they react easily with nonmetals and water.

beryllium
Uncommon metal that is used especially in alloys for the aerospace industry and as a moderator in nuclear reactors.

magnesium
Metal necessary for the growth and metabolism of most living organisms; it is also a component of aluminum alloys.

calcium
Metal that is one of the most essential elements in bones and teeth; it is also a component of cement, plaster and some alloys.

strontium
Relatively rare metal that is used especially in pyrotechnics (fireworks), the manufacture of magnets and medicine.

barium
Relatively abundant metal that is used especially in lubricants, pyrotechnics (fireworks), paint and radiology.

radium
Extremely radioactive metal present in very low quantities in uranium ore; it is used mainly in medicine to treat cancer.

semimetals (metalloids)
Nonmetallic elements that are lusterless and solid; they possess a certain amount of electric and thermal conductivity.

boron
Semimetal that is used especially as a neutron absorber in nuclear reactors, as a rocket fuel and in detergents.

silicon
Most common element on the planet after oxygen; it is used mostly in the manufacture of electronic devices because of its semiconductor properties.

germanium
Rare semimetal that is used especially in the manufacture of electronic devices and in optical equipment (camera and microscope lenses).

arsenic
Toxic semimetal that is used especially in the manufacture of semiconductors and in very low doses as a therapeutic agent.

selenium
Semimetal that is usually used in photoelectric cells and semiconductors; it is an indispensable trace element for organisms.

antimony
Toxic semimetal that is used in several alloys (mostly with lead) and especially in making metal for printing type and semiconductors.

tellurium
Rare semimetal that is used especially in the manufacture of detonators, electric resistors, rubber, ceramics and glass.

chemical elements

...nsition metals

...ally less reactive than alkali metals and ...aline earth metals but very good electric ... thermal conductors. Many of these metals ...m vital alloys.

scandium `21 Sc`
Rare and very light metal that is employed in aerospace construction because of its high fusion point (about 2,700°F or 1,500°C).

titanium `22 Ti`
Metal that is used in several alloys employed in the manufacture of precision items and as a coating for light aerospace parts.

vanadium `23 V`
Metal that is used mainly in alloys, to which it provides highly anticorrosive properties.

chromium `24 Cr`
Bright metal that is used as an anticorrosive coating and in the manufacture of hard and resistant alloys; it gives emeralds and rubies their color.

manganese `25 Mn`
Hard metal that is used mainly in the manufacture of specialty steels and household batteries; it is also an indispensable trace element for humans.

iron `26 Fe`
The most used metal in the world due to its variety of alloys (steel, cast iron); it helps move oxygen through the body.

cobalt `27 Co`
Strong metal that is used in alloys (cutting tools, magnets) and in radiotherapy; it also yields a blue pigment.

nickel `28 Ni`
Hard metal that resists corrosion; it is used in the manufacture of coins and cutlery, and as a protective coating for other metals (iron, copper).

copper `29 Cu`
Reddish-brown metal that is a very good conductor of heat and electricity; it is used mainly in the manufacture of electric wire and alloys (brass, bronze).

zinc `30 Zn`
Relatively abundant metal that is resistant to corrosion; it is used especially in the manufacture of alloys, tires, paint, ointments and perfume.

yttrium `39 Y`
Rare metal used in the manufacture of alloys, electronic components, lasers, television screens and in nuclear reactors.

zirconium `40 Zr`
Metal that is used in alloys for the nuclear industry (protective sheathing, fuel rods) and in jewelry (imitation diamonds).

niobium `41 Nb`
Rare metal that is used especially in alloys for jet aircraft, missiles, nuclear reactors, cutting tools, and pacemakers.

molybdenum `42 Mo`
Hard metal that is used in alloys (aircraft, missiles, nuclear reactors), electric lights and electronic tubes.

technetium `43 Tc`
Radioactive metal (first element to have been produced artificially) that makes steel corrosion-free and is used in medical imaging.

ruthenium `44 Ru`
Rare metal that hardens platinum and palladium; it is used in the manufacture of electric contacts, spark plugs and jewelry.

rhodium `45 Rh`
Rare metal that resists corrosion and hardens platinum and palladium; it is used especially in catalytic converters and jewelry.

palladium `46 Pd`
Rare and precious metal that is used especially in dentistry (dental prostheses), jewelry (white gold) and in catalytic converters.

silver `47 Ag`
Precious metal that is the best conductor of heat and electricity; it is used especially in the manufacture of mirrors, jewelry and coins.

cadmium `48 Cd`
Metal that is used especially as a protective covering for steel, in rechargeable batteries and in nuclear reactors (control rods).

hafnium `72 Hf`
Rare metal that is used in the control rods of nuclear reactors, filaments for incandescent lamps and jet engines.

tantalum `73 Ta`
Somewhat rare metal that is highly resistant to heat; it is used especially in nuclear reactors, missiles and capacitors.

tungsten `74 W`
Metal that is resistant to very high heat; it is used in filaments for incandescent lamps and cutting tools.

rhenium `75 Re`
Rare metal that is resistant to wear and corrosion; it is used especially in pen tips and incandescent filaments for ovens.

osmium `76 Os`
Rare metal often alloyed with iridium and platinum; it is used in pen tips, bearings, compass needles and jewelry.

iridium `77 Ir`
Rare metal that is often alloyed with platinum; it is used especially in electric contacts and jewelry.

platinum `78 Pt`
Very rare metal used especially as a catalyst in chemistry (petrochemicals, vitamins), in jewelry and in precision equipment.

gold `79 Au`
Precious metal (nuggets, flakes) that is used as currency (ingots) and in jewelry, dentistry and electronics.

mercury `80 Hg`
Rare poisonous metal that is liquid at room temperature and that is used in measuring instruments (thermometers, barometers) and in the electricity industry.

rutherfordium `104 Rf`
Artificial radioactive element that was first produced in laboratories in the 1960s; it has applications only in scientific research.

dubnium `105 Db`
Artificial radioactive element that was first produced in laboratories in the 1960s.

seaborgium `106 Sg`
Artificial radioactive element that was first produced in laboratories in 1974; it is made by fusing atoms of californium and oxygen.

bohrium `107 Bh`
Artificial radioactive element that was first produced in laboratories in 1976; it is made by fusing atoms of bismuth and chromium.

hassium `108 Hs`
Artificial radioactive element that was first produced in laboratories in 1984; it is made by fusing atoms of lead and iron.

meitnerium `109 Mt`
Artificial radioactive element that was first produced in laboratories in 1982; it is made by fusing atoms of bismuth and iron.

darmstadtium `110 Ds`
Artificial radioactive element that was first produced in laboratories in 1994; it is made by fusing atoms of nickel and lead.

roentgenium `111 Rg`
Artificial radioactive element that was first produced in laboratories in 1994; it is made by fusing atoms of bismuth and nickel.

copernicium `112 Cn`
Artificial radioactive element that was first produced in laboratories in 1996; it is made by fusing atoms of lead and zinc.

...nmetals

...nmetallic elements that are lusterless and ...malleable; they are mostly gases and ...ids and are usually poor conductors of heat ...d electricity.

carbon `6 C`
Element common in its pure state (diamond, graphite) or found in combination (air, coal, petroleum); it is present in animal and plant tissue.

nitrogen `7 N`
Gas that constitutes about 78% of the Earth's atmosphere, present in all animal and vegetable tissue (proteins), and in fertilizer, ammonia and explosives.

oxygen `8 O`
Gas that is the most abundant element on Earth and that comprises about 20% of the atmosphere; it is used to breathe and in the manufacture of steel.

fluorine `9 F`
Gas that is used especially for enriching uranium and manufacturing antistick coatings; it is present in bones and teeth.

phosphorus `15 P`
Solid used especially in fertilizer (phosphates), matches and pyrotechnics (fireworks); it is also necessary for human beings.

sulfur `16 S`
Solid that is quite common in nature; it is used in car batteries, fertilizer, paint, explosives, pharmaceuticals and rubber.

chlorine `17 Cl`
Abundant toxic gas that is used to whiten fabric and paper, disinfect water and manufacture various other products (solvents).

bromine `35 Br`
Very toxic liquid that is used mainly to manufacture tear gas, dyes and disinfectants and in photography and medications.

iodine `53 I`
Solid that is used especially in medicine as an antiseptic and to treat hyperthyroidism, in photography and dyes; it is also essential for the human body.

astatine `85 At`
Radioactive element that is extremely rare in nature; it is used in medicine to study the thyroid gland and to detect cancerous tumors.

ununseptium `117 Uus`
Synthetic radioactive element, created in a laboratory in 2010; it is made by fusing atoms of calcium and berkelium.

chemical elements

noble gases

Family of chemical elements also called inert, as they are weakly reactive.

2 He — **helium**
The lightest of the noble gases is noncombustible and abundant in the stars; it is used especially in inflating aerostats (such as balloons and airships).

10 Ne — **neon**
Noble gas that is used mainly in lighting (billboards, television tubes and fog lamps), but also as a liquid coolant.

18 Ar — **argon**
Most abundant of the noble gases; it is used especially in incandescent lamps and in welding (protective gas).

36 Kr — **krypton**
Noble gas that is used in some incandescent lamps and in photography.

54 Xe — **xenon**
Rarest gas in the atmosphere; it is used mainly in discharge lamps, flash bulbs and lasers.

86 Rn — **radon**
Highly radioactive noble gas that is used mainly in medicine (destroying cancerous tumors) and in predicting earthquakes.

118 Uuo — **ununoctium**
Synthetic radioactive element, created in a laboratory in 2002, made by fusing atoms of calcium and californium.

lanthanides (rare earth)

Very reactive elements found in the lanthanide series (monazite, xenotime); some are relatively abundant in the Earth's crust.

57 La — **lanthanum**
Metal that reacts with water to yield hydrogen; it is used especially in flint alloys and optical glass.

58 Ce — **cerium**
The most common metal of the lanthanide group and the main constituent of flint alloys (misch metal).

59 Pr — **praseodymium**
Metal that is used especially in protective lenses, colorants for glass, flint alloys (misch metal) and permanent magnets.

60 Nd — **neodymium**
One of the most reactive of rare metals; it is used mainly to manufacture lasers, eyeglasses and permanent-magnet alloys.

61 Pm — **promethium**
Radioactive metal that is used mainly in specialized batteries and luminescent coatings for watches, and as a source of X-rays in medicine.

62 Sm — **samarium**
Rare radioactive metal that is used especially in optical glass, lasers, nuclear reactors (absorbing neutrons) and permanent magnets.

63 Eu — **europium**
The most reactive metal of the lanthanide group; it is used especially in television screens (the color orange) and nuclear reactors (absorbing neutrons).

64 Gd — **gadolinium**
Metal that is often alloyed with chromed steel; it is used especially in the manufacture of permanent magnets, magnetic heads and electronic components.

65 Tb — **terbium**
Rare metal that is used especially in lasers and semiconductors.

66 Dy — **dysprosium**
Very rare metal that is used especially in permanent magnets, lasers and nuclear reactors (absorbing neutrons).

67 Ho — **holmium**
Very rare metal with limited applications; it is used in lasers and for coloring glass.

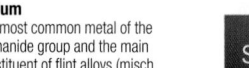

68 Er — **erbium**
Metal that is used mainly in some alloys (especially with vanadium), lasers and infrared-absorbing glass, and as a colorant for glass and enamel.

69 Tm — **thulium**
The rarest of the lanthanide grou it is used as a source of X-rays in portable radiology equipment an the manufacture of ferrites (mag ceramics).

70 Yb — **ytterbium**
Metal that is used in the manufa of stainless steel, in lasers and a a source of radiation in portable radiology equipment.

71 Lu — **lutetium**
Very rare metal that is difficult to it has no real industrial applicatio can be used as a catalyst (crackir hydrogenation).

actinides

Radioactive elements that are abundant in nature (elements 89 to 92) or made artificially (elements 93 to 103). Most of them have no industrial applications.

89 Ac — **actinium**
Metal that is present in small quantities in uranium ore; it is used mainly as a source of neutrons in nuclear reactors.

90 Th — **thorium**
Natural metal that is used especially in alloys, photoelectric cells and uranium production.

91 Pa — **protactinium**
Very rare metal that is present in uranium ore; it has few applications outside of scientific research.

92 U — **uranium**
Naturally abundant metal that is used mainly as fuel in nuclear reactors as well as in nuclear weapons.

93 Np — **neptunium**
Rare metal that is produced from uranium; it is used in neutron-detection instruments.

94 Pu — **plutonium**
Metal that is produced from uranium; it is used especially as fuel in nuclear reactors as well as in nuclear weapons.

95 Am — **americium**
Metal that is produced from plutonium; it is used mainly in smoke detectors and in radiology.

96 Cm — **curium**
Metal that is produced in small amounts from plutonium; it is used especially in thermoelectric generators for spacecraft propulsion.

97 Bk — **berkelium**
Metal that is produced in small amounts from americium; it is used for scientific research only.

98 Cf — **californium**
Metal produced from curium that is used especially in the treatment of cancer and in some measuring instruments such as humidistats.

99 Es — **einsteinium**
Metal that was discovered in 1952 among the debris of the first thermonuclear explosion in the Pacific; it is used for scientific research only.

100 Fm — **fermium**
Metal that was discovered at the same time as einsteinium; it is used for scientific research only.

101 Md — **mendelevium**
Metal that is produced from einsteinium; it is named in honor of the chemist Mendeleyev (who classified the elements).

102 No — **nobelium**
Metal that is produced from curium; it is named in honor of Alfred Nobel (inventor of dynamit and founder of the Nobel Prize).

103 Lr — **lawrencium**
Metal that is produced from californium; it is used for scientifi research only.

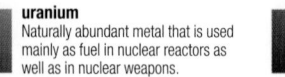

laboratory equipment

These materials are highly varied: measurement instruments, various containers, heat sources, experimentation materials and mounting hardware.

rod
Long metal part to which various laboratory devices can be clamped.

holder
Part with a screw for attaching a clamp onto the stand's rod.

graduated cylinder
Graduated tube with a spout that is used especially for measuring small amounts of liquid with precision.

straight stopcock burette
Long graduated tube for measuring liquids with high precision; it is fitted with a valve for manually regulating the flow.

serological pipette
Fine tube that is open at both ends; it is used to transfer very precise quantities of liquids from one container to another.

clamp/holder
Part attached to the stand's rod by a holder and having tongs that clamp onto the laboratory equipment to hold it in place.

base
Heavy metal pedestal supporting the rod.

stand
nit consisting of a base and a d; it supports various laboratory paratuses such as burettes and flasks.

petri dish
Flat transparent box for culturing microorganisms; it has a cover to protect them from contamination.

test tube
Cylindrical tube used to conduct various chemical experiments on small quantities (normally, it is not filled above one-third).

gas burner
Device that is fueled by gas to produce a flame for heating chemical products.

bottle
ner of various sizes and and usually with a straight k for holding liquids.

wash bottle
Flexible container that is squeezed lightly to squirt a liquid; it is used especially for cleaning equipment (test tubes, pipettes).

round-bottom flask
Spherical container used mainly for boiling liquids.

beaker
Graduated container with a spout; it is used to create reactions (precipitation, electrolysis) and to measure approximate amounts of liquid.

Erlenmeyer flask
Graduated cone-shaped container that is used very frequently in laboratories; it can have a stopper and is used especially for mixing and measuring liquids.

SCIENCE

gearing systems

Mechanisms consisting of toothed parts that mesh to transmit the rotational motion of the shafts they are a part of.

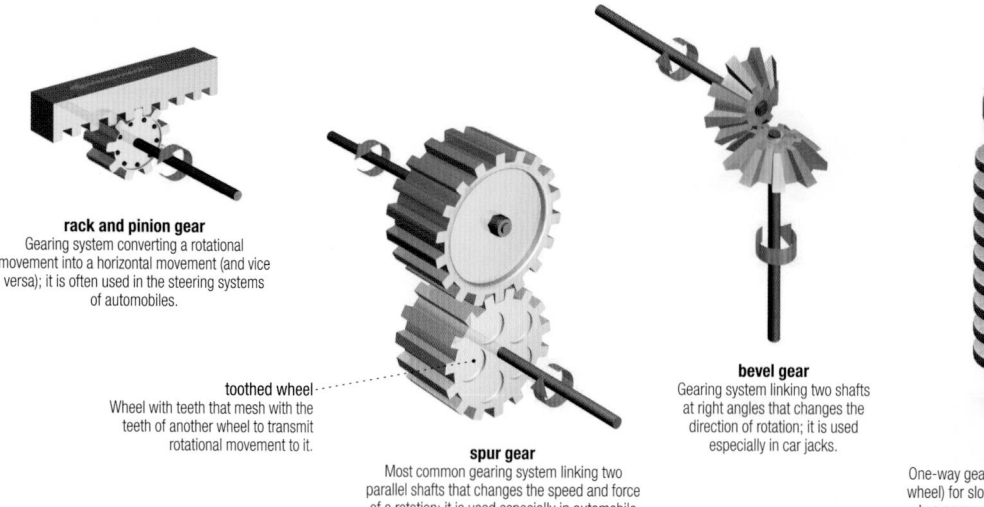
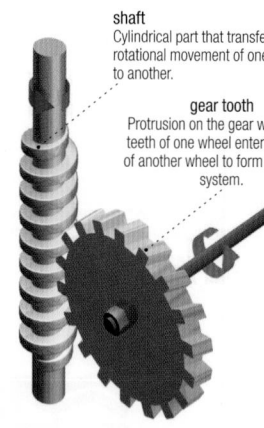

shaft
Cylindrical part that transfer rotational movement of one to another.

gear tooth
Protrusion on the gear w teeth of one wheel enter of another wheel to form system.

rack and pinion gear
Gearing system converting a rotational movement into a horizontal movement (and vice versa); it is often used in the steering systems of automobiles.

toothed wheel
Wheel with teeth that mesh with the teeth of another wheel to transmit rotational movement to it.

spur gear
Most common gearing system linking two parallel shafts that changes the speed and force of a rotation; it is used especially in automobile transmissions.

bevel gear
Gearing system linking two shafts at right angles that changes the direction of rotation; it is used especially in car jacks.

worm gear
One-way gearing system (only the screw can drive the wheel) for slowing down the speed of rotation between two perpendicular axles; it is used especially in the automobile industry.

double pulley system

System consisting of two pulleys with a rope running around them to lift a load. Using two or more pulleys reduces the amount of effort needed.

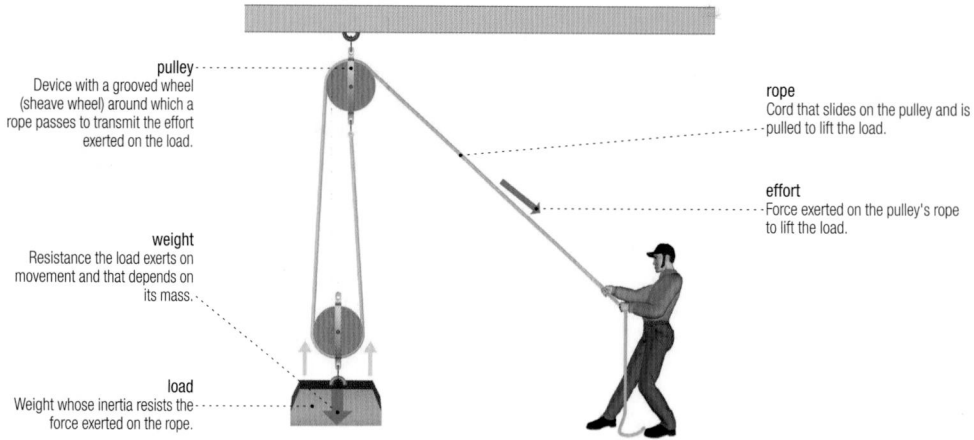

pulley
Device with a grooved wheel (sheave wheel) around which a rope passes to transmit the effort exerted on the load.

rope
Cord that slides on the pulley and is pulled to lift the load.

effort
Force exerted on the pulley's rope to lift the load.

weight
Resistance the load exerts on movement and that depends on its mass.

load
Weight whose inertia resists the force exerted on the rope.

lever

System consisting of a bar pivoting on a fulcrum to lift a load. The amount of effort required is related to the position of the pivot and the length of the bar.

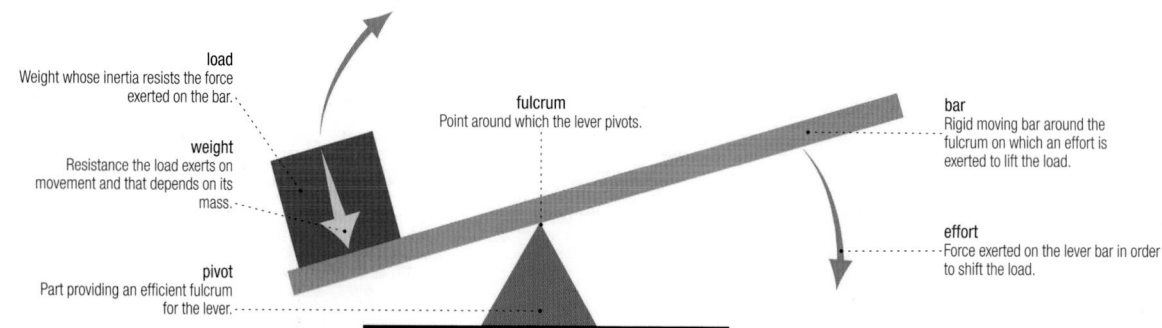

load
Weight whose inertia resists the force exerted on the bar.

fulcrum
Point around which the lever pivots.

bar
Rigid moving bar around the fulcrum on which an effort is exerted to lift the load.

weight
Resistance the load exerts on movement and that depends on its mass.

effort
Force exerted on the lever bar in order to shift the load.

pivot
Part providing an efficient fulcrum for the lever.

SCIENCE

magnetism

...ction exerted by magnets and magnetic fields and phenomena. Magnetism can be characterized by the forces of attraction and repulsion between two masses.

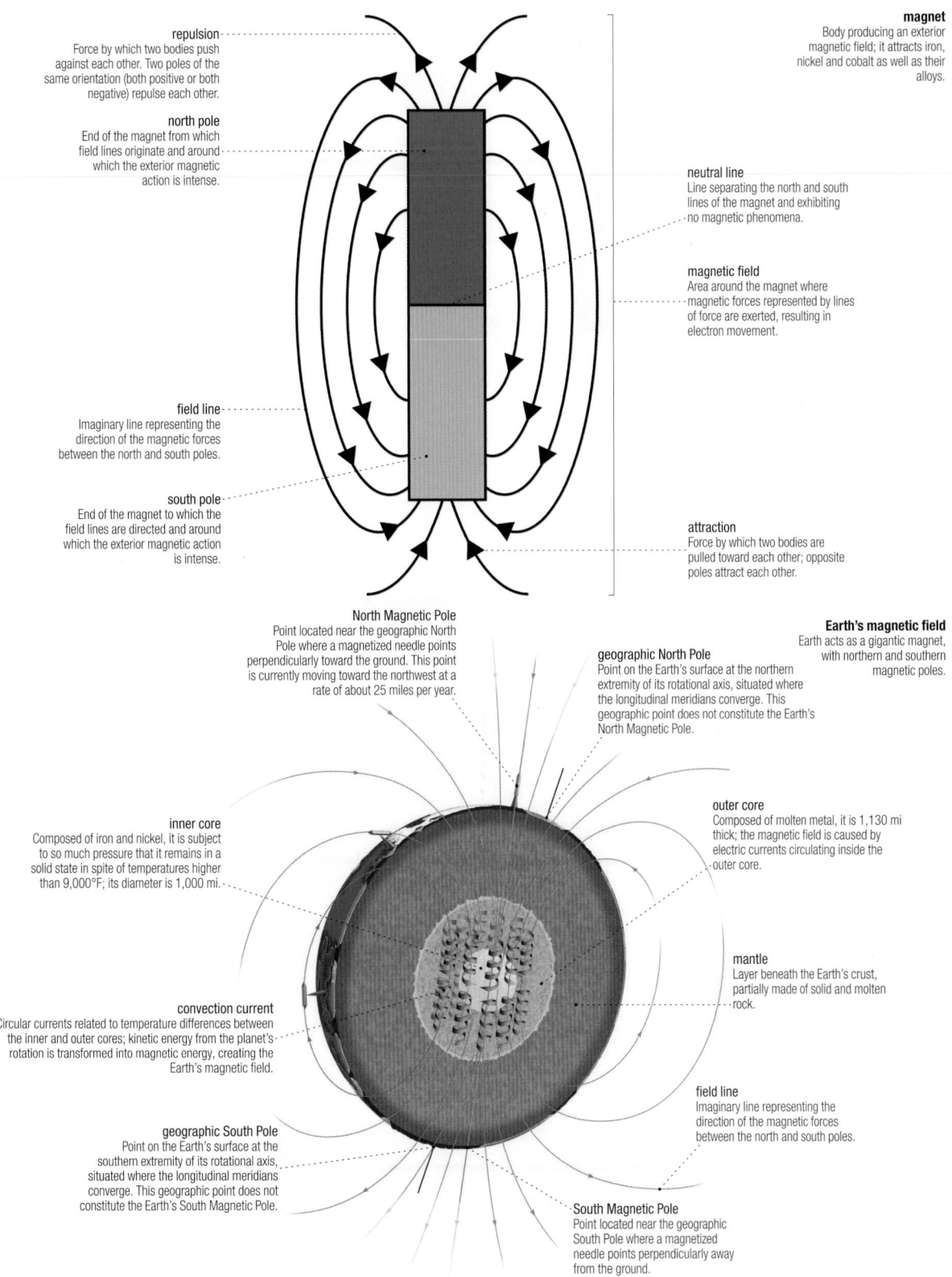

magnet
Body producing an exterior magnetic field; it attracts iron, nickel and cobalt as well as their alloys.

repulsion
Force by which two bodies push against each other. Two poles of the same orientation (both positive or both negative) repulse each other.

north pole
End of the magnet from which field lines originate and around which the exterior magnetic action is intense.

neutral line
Line separating the north and south lines of the magnet and exhibiting no magnetic phenomena.

magnetic field
Area around the magnet where magnetic forces represented by lines of force are exerted, resulting in electron movement.

field line
Imaginary line representing the direction of the magnetic forces between the north and south poles.

south pole
End of the magnet to which the field lines are directed and around which the exterior magnetic action is intense.

attraction
Force by which two bodies are pulled toward each other; opposite poles attract each other.

North Magnetic Pole
Point located near the geographic North Pole where a magnetized needle points perpendicularly toward the ground. This point is currently moving toward the northwest at a rate of about 25 miles per year.

geographic North Pole
Point on the Earth's surface at the northern extremity of its rotational axis, situated where the longitudinal meridians converge. This geographic point does not constitute the Earth's North Magnetic Pole.

Earth's magnetic field
Earth acts as a gigantic magnet, with northern and southern magnetic poles.

inner core
Composed of iron and nickel, it is subject to so much pressure that it remains in a solid state in spite of temperatures higher than 9,000°F; its diameter is 1,000 mi.

outer core
Composed of molten metal, it is 1,130 mi thick; the magnetic field is caused by electric currents circulating inside the outer core.

mantle
Layer beneath the Earth's crust, partially made of solid and molten rock.

convection current
Circular currents related to temperature differences between the inner and outer cores; kinetic energy from the planet's rotation is transformed into magnetic energy, creating the Earth's magnetic field.

field line
Imaginary line representing the direction of the magnetic forces between the north and south poles.

geographic South Pole
Point on the Earth's surface at the southern extremity of its rotational axis, situated where the longitudinal meridians converge. This geographic point does not constitute the Earth's South Magnetic Pole.

South Magnetic Pole
Point located near the geographic South Pole where a magnetized needle points perpendicularly away from the ground.

SCIENCE

electrical circuit

Interlinked series of electric conductors.

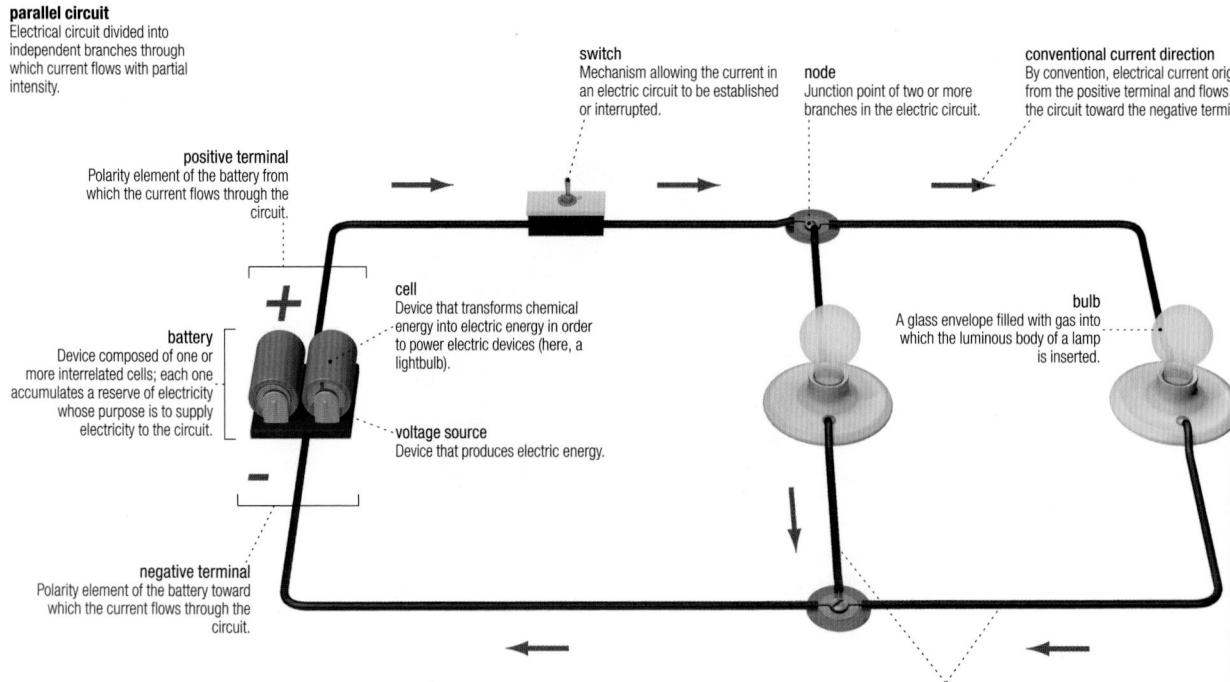

series circuit
Electrical circuit along which all points receive the same intensity of current.

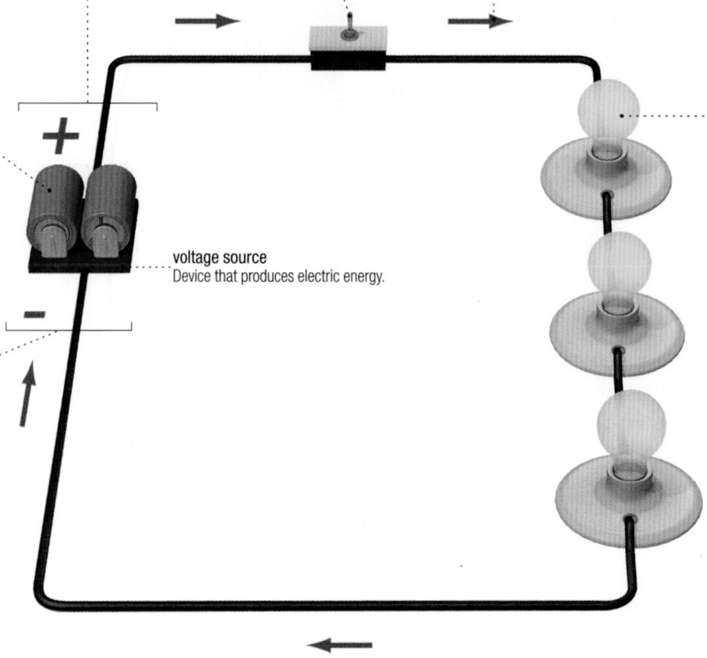

positive terminal
Polarity element of the battery from which the current flows through the circuit.

switch
Mechanism allowing the current in an electric circuit to be established or interrupted.

conventional current direction
By convention, electrical current originates from the positive terminal and flows through the circuit toward the negative terminal.

cell
Device that transforms chemical energy into electric energy in order to power electric devices (here, a lightbulb).

bulb
A glass envelope filled with gas i which the luminous body of a lar is inserted.

battery
Device composed of one or more interrelated cells; each one accumulates a reserve of electricity whose purpose is to supply electricity to the circuit.

voltage source
Device that produces electric energy.

negative terminal
Polarity element of the battery toward which the current flows through the circuit.

parallel circuit
Electrical circuit divided into independent branches through which current flows with partial intensity.

switch
Mechanism allowing the current in an electric circuit to be established or interrupted.

node
Junction point of two or more branches in the electric circuit.

conventional current direction
By convention, electrical current orig from the positive terminal and flows the circuit toward the negative termi

positive terminal
Polarity element of the battery from which the current flows through the circuit.

cell
Device that transforms chemical energy into electric energy in order to power electric devices (here, a lightbulb).

bulb
A glass envelope filled with gas into which the luminous body of a lamp is inserted.

battery
Device composed of one or more interrelated cells; each one accumulates a reserve of electricity whose purpose is to supply electricity to the circuit.

voltage source
Device that produces electric energy.

negative terminal
Polarity element of the battery toward which the current flows through the circuit.

branches
Parts of the circuit between two consecutive nodes; they constitute independent electric circuits.

generators

Devices that convert mechanical energy (here, a shaft's rotational motion) into electric energy by moving a coil inside a magnet (electromagnetic induction).

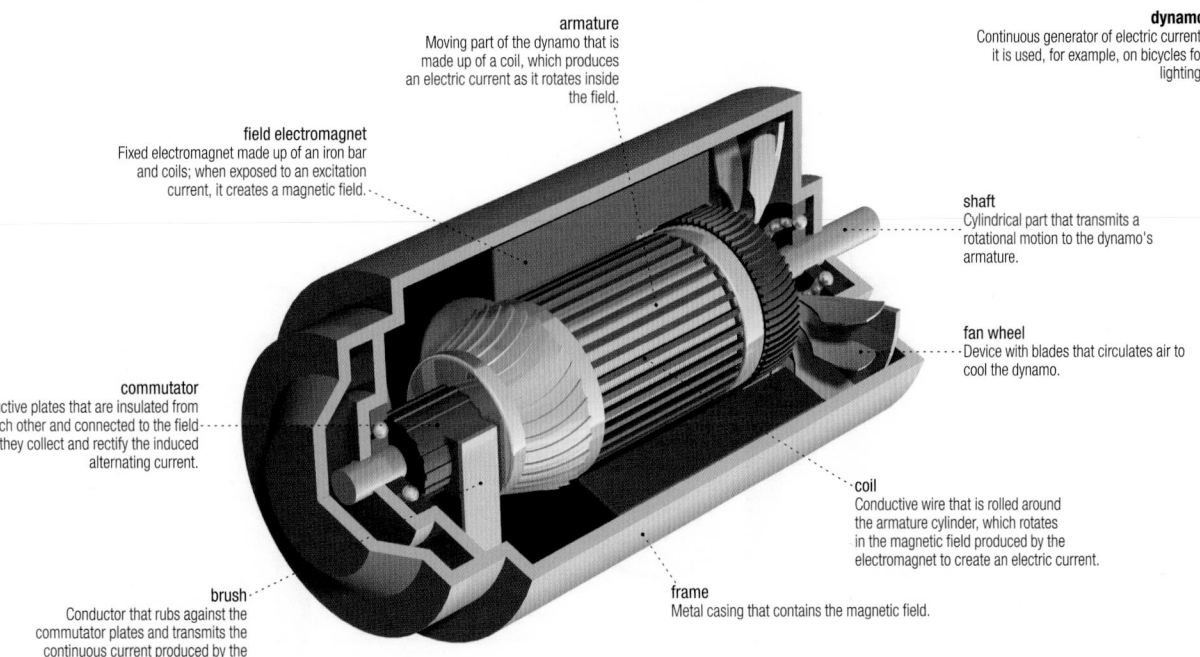

armature
Moving part of the dynamo that is made up of a coil, which produces an electric current as it rotates inside the field.

dynamo
Continuous generator of electric current; it is used, for example, on bicycles for lighting.

field electromagnet
Fixed electromagnet made up of an iron bar and coils; when exposed to an excitation current, it creates a magnetic field.

shaft
Cylindrical part that transmits a rotational motion to the dynamo's armature.

fan wheel
Device with blades that circulates air to cool the dynamo.

commutator
Conductive plates that are insulated from each other and connected to the field coil; they collect and rectify the induced alternating current.

coil
Conductive wire that is rolled around the armature cylinder, which rotates in the magnetic field produced by the electromagnet to create an electric current.

brush
Conductor that rubs against the commutator plates and transmits the continuous current produced by the dynamo to an exterior circuit.

frame
Metal casing that contains the magnetic field.

alternator
Generator of alternating current that is used especially in the automobile industry (powering electrical devices) and in power plants.

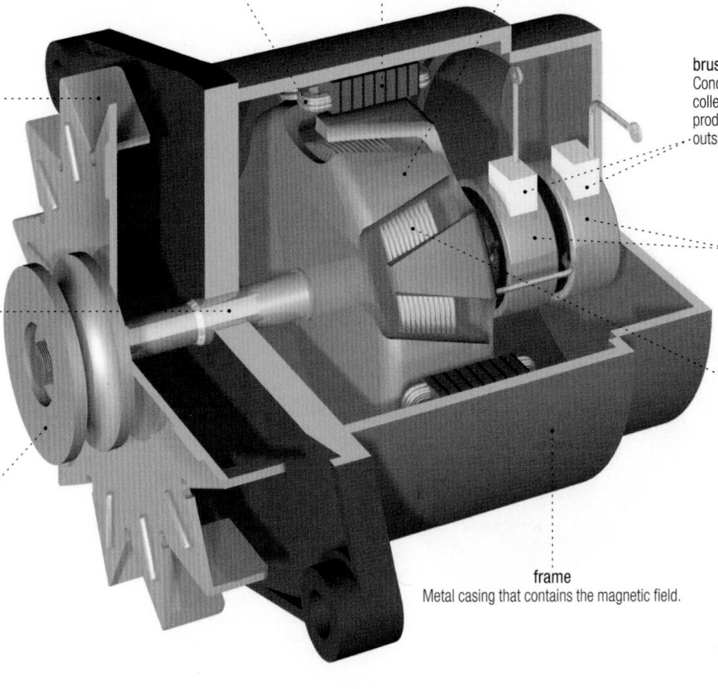

armature core
Fixed cylinder with a winding; the rotor turns within it to produce the electric current.

armature winding
Conductive wire on the armature; the rotor moves in front of it to produce an alternating current.

claw-pole rotor
Moving cylindrical part made up of a field winding between two pole shoes; it creates the rotating magnetic field required to operate the alternator.

fan wheel
Device with blades that circulates air to cool the alternator.

brushes
Conductive parts that rub against the collector rings and transmit the current produced by the alternator to an outside circuit.

shaft
Rod that is rotated by the pulley, which in turn causes the claw-pole rotor to rotate.

collector rings
Insulated conductor collars that are connected to the coil of the field; they gather the induced alternating electric current.

field winding
Conductive wire on the cylinder rotor; when exposed to an excitation current, it creates a magnetic field.

drive pulley
Mechanical unit integrated with the shaft; it is rotated by a belt that is connected to an engine.

frame
Metal casing that contains the magnetic field.

dry cells

Devices that transform chemical energy into electric energy (direct current); they usually cannot be recharged and the electrolyte is fixed in place.

carbon-zinc cell
Battery that produces 1.5 V (also called Leclanché); its use is very widespread (pocket calculators, portable radios, alarm clocks).

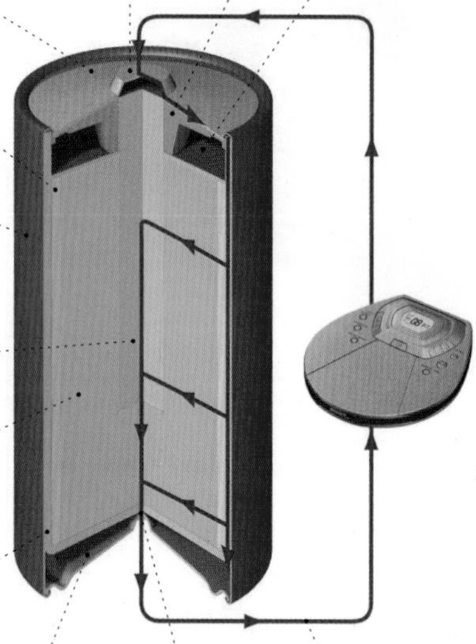

alkaline manganese-zinc ◀
High-performance battery that produces 1 and has a longer life span than the carbon-cell; it is used in devices such as flashligh portable CD players and camera flash u▮

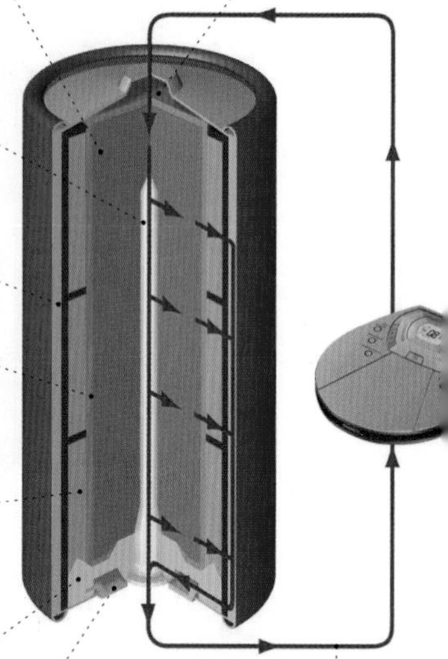

positive terminal
Polarity element of the battery toward which the electrons flow.

sealing plug
Material that seals the battery.

top cap
Upper metal cover; the positive terminal is located at its center.

washer
Disk that compresses the depolarizing mix.

zinc-electrolyte mix (anode)
Substance that is made up of zinc and electrolyte (potassium hydroxide); it constitutes the positive electrode (anode).

sealing material
Material (nylon) that seals the battery.

electrolytic separator
Porous paper combined with a chemical paste (ammonium chloride) that separates the two electrodes; this allows electrons to pass, thus conducting electricity.

electron collector
Zinc rod that is connected to the bottom cap; it collects the electrons from the anode that are attracted to the cathode.

jacket
Battery's protective plastic casing.

carbon rod (cathode)
Carbon rod set in the depolarizing mix; it constitutes the battery's negative electrode (cathode) collecting the electrons returning from the circuit.

steel casing
Covering that protects the battery.

separator
Porous paper combined with a chemical paste (potassium hydroxide) that separates the two electrodes; this allows electrons to pass, thus conducting electricity.

depolarizing mix
Mixture of carbon and manganese dioxide that augments conductivity by acting as a barrier to polarization.

manganese mix (cathode)
Substance made up of manganese dioxide and carbon; it constitutes the negative electrode (cathode).

zinc can (anode)
Zinc receptacle that constitutes the battery's positive electrode (anode).

sealing plug
Material that seals the battery.

bottom cap
Lower metal cover; the negative terminal is located at its center.

negative terminal
Polarity element of the battery from which the electrons flow.

direction of electron flow
When a chemical reaction occurs, the electrons move from the negative terminal toward the positive terminal, thus creating an electric current.

bottom cap
Lower metal cover; the negative terminal is located at its center.

direction of electron flow
When a chemical reaction occurs, the move from the negative terminal tow positive terminal, thus creating an e current.

electronics

The scientific study of the behavior of the electron and its applications, such as computers, medicine and automation.

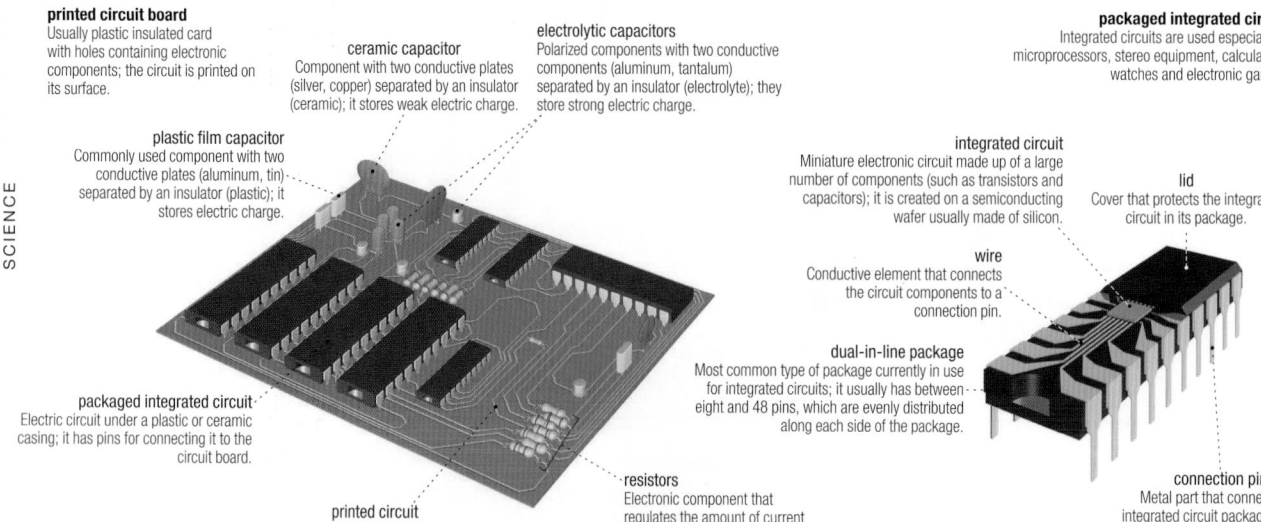

printed circuit board
Usually plastic insulated card with holes containing electronic components; the circuit is printed on its surface.

ceramic capacitor
Component with two conductive plates (silver, copper) separated by an insulator (ceramic); it stores weak electric charge.

electrolytic capacitors
Polarized components with two conductive components (aluminum, tantalum) separated by an insulator (electrolyte); they store strong electric charge.

packaged integrated circ▮
Integrated circuits are used especiall microprocessors, stereo equipment, calculate watches and electronic gam▮

plastic film capacitor
Commonly used component with two conductive plates (aluminum, tin) separated by an insulator (plastic); it stores electric charge.

integrated circuit
Miniature electronic circuit made up of a large number of components (such as transistors and capacitors); it is created on a semiconducting wafer usually made of silicon.

lid
Cover that protects the integrat▮ circuit in its package.

wire
Conductive element that connects the circuit components to a connection pin.

dual-in-line package
Most common type of package currently in use for integrated circuits; it usually has between eight and 48 pins, which are evenly distributed along each side of the package.

packaged integrated circuit
Electric circuit under a plastic or ceramic casing; it has pins for connecting it to the circuit board.

printed circuit
All of the conductive metal bands on an insulated base (card), which connect a circuit's components and allow a current to flow through it.

resistors
Electronic component that regulates the amount of current flowing in a circuit.

connection pin
Metal part that connec▮ integrated circuit package▮ metal bands of the printed▮ which it is soldere▮

electromagnetic spectrum

Electromagnetic waves that are classified in ascending order of energy (frequency); they propagate at the speed of light (300,000 km/s).

microwaves
Short electromagnetic waves; their many applications include radar detection and microwave ovens.

ultraviolet radiation
Electromagnetic waves used especially to tan skin and in microscopy, medicine and lighting (fluorescent tubes).

radio waves
Very long electromagnetic waves (over 1 meter or 3 feet) having low frequency; they are used to transmit information (television, radio).

infrared radiation
Electromagnetic waves emitted by warm objects; their many uses include heating, medicine, aerial photography and weaponry.

X-rays
Electromagnetic waves used especially in radiology; frequent exposure can be harmful.

gamma rays
Electromagnetic waves of very high frequency that are emitted by radioactive bodies; they are the most radiant and harmful rays and are used especially in treating cancer.

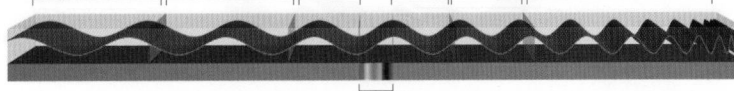

visible light
Electromagnetic radiation that is perceived by the human eye and ranges from red to violet.

wave

Oscillation caused by a disturbance; as it propagates through a medium (mechanical waves) or a vacuum (electromagnetic waves), it carries energy.

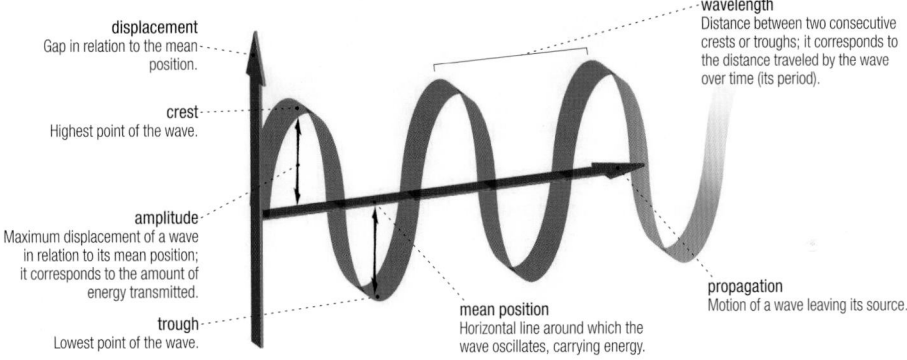

wavelength
Distance between two consecutive crests or troughs; it corresponds to the distance traveled by the wave over time (its period).

displacement
Gap in relation to the mean position.

crest
Highest point of the wave.

amplitude
Maximum displacement of a wave in relation to its mean position; it corresponds to the amount of energy transmitted.

trough
Lowest point of the wave.

mean position
Horizontal line around which the wave oscillates, carrying energy.

propagation
Motion of a wave leaving its source.

color synthesis

Technique of generating color by combining light rays or subtracting them to obtain a colored image.

additive color synthesis
superimposition of primary ors (blue, green and red) is used ecially in electronic screens evision, computer, video) to obtain rmediate tints.

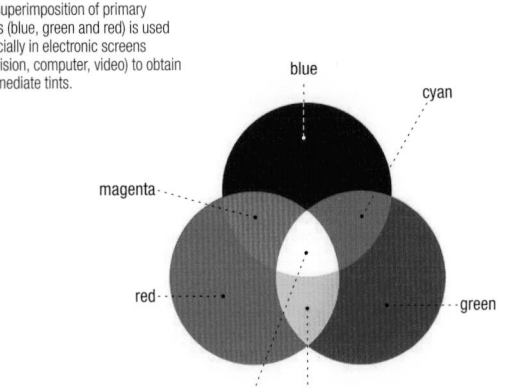

blue
cyan
magenta
red
green
white
yellow

subtractive color synthesis
The absorption of certain light rays (blue, green, red) by colored filters (yellow, magenta, cyan) is used in industries such as photography, film production and printing to obtain intermediate tints.

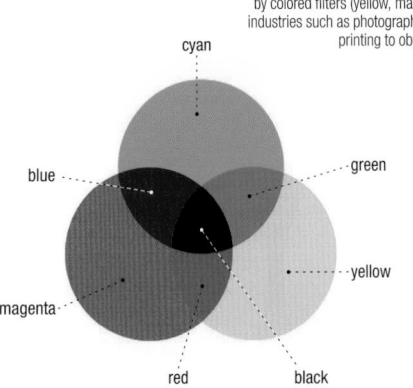

cyan
blue
green
magenta
yellow
red
black

light waves trajectory

Light waves traveling through space can be distorted as they encounter different surfaces and cross through different media.

light reflection
Change of light ray direction resulting from contact with an obstruction.

incident ray
Ray of light traveling toward a reflecting surface.

reflected ray
Ray of light travelling away from the reflective surface after contact.

reflecting surface
Surface capable of reversing the direction of the rays of light that hit it.

light refraction
Distortion of light as it passes from one medium to another.

incident ray
Ray of light traveling toward a refracting surface.

refracting surface
Surface separating two transparent media that refract light differently.

refracted ray
Ray of light diverted by its contact with a different medium.

lenses

Transparent pieces of material (usually glass) that cause light rays to converge or diverge to form a sharp image and are used in eyeglasses, microscopes, telescopes and cameras.

converging lenses
Thicker in the center than on the edges; they cause parallel light rays emanating from an object to converge onto the same point.

convex lens
Lens with one side bulging outward; the greater the bulge, the more the light rays converge.

biconvex lens
Lens with both faces bulging outward.

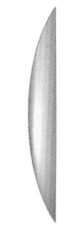

plano-convex lens
Lens with one flat side and one convex side (bulging outward).

positive menisc
Lens where the concave si inward) is less pronounce convex side (bulging ou

diverging lenses
Thicker on the edges than in the center; they cause parallel light rays emanating from an object to diverge.

concave lens
Lens with one side curving inward; the greater the curvature, the more the light rays diverge.

biconcave lens
Lens with both sides curving inward.

plano-concave lens
Lens with one flat side and one concave side (curving inward).

negative menisc
Lens where the con side (curving inward) i pronounced than the cor (bulging outward

mirror

Polished glass surface that reflects the surrounding light.

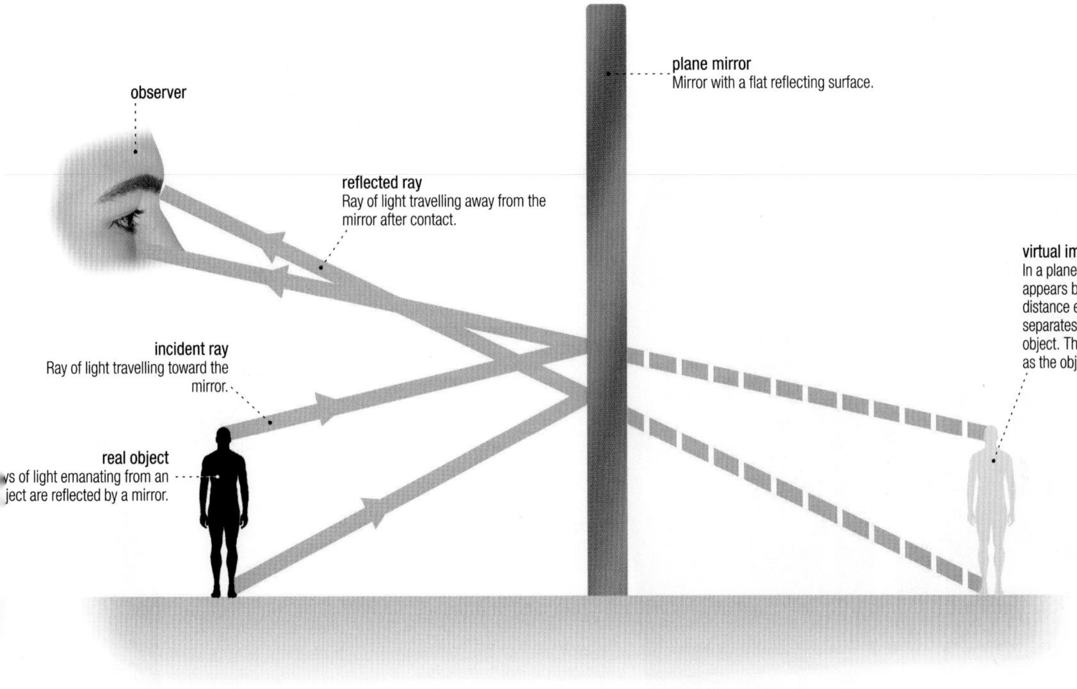

plane mirror
Mirror with a flat reflecting surface.

observer

reflected ray
Ray of light travelling away from the mirror after contact.

virtual image
In a plane mirror, the image appears behind the mirror, at a distance equivalent to that which separates the mirror from the object. The image is the same size as the object, but reversed.

incident ray
Ray of light travelling toward the mirror.

real object
ys of light emanating from an ject are reflected by a mirror.

optical devices

Instruments that use the properties of light reflection for a variety of applications such as observing distant objects, enlarging nearby objects, etc.

pulsed ruby laser
Device that produces a thin and very intense colored light beam; its various applications include fiber optics, manufacturing and surgery.

fully reflecting mirror
Reflects all the light energy toward the partially reflecting mirror. The reflection between the mirrors intensifies the light to form a highly concentrated beam.

flash tube
Lamp that acts as an energy source by emitting a flash of white light, which excites the ruby atoms and causes them to emit photons.

photon
Energy particle emitted by the ruby cylinder's atoms as they are excited by flashes in the tube.

partially reflecting mirror
Its partial transparency allows light beams to escape.

laser beam
powerful monochrome that is emitted by the device.

cooling cylinder
Casing in which water generally circulates to cool the ruby cylinder, which becomes very hot as it produces the beam.

ruby cylinder
Ruby bar (crystallized alumina that contains chromium atoms). It has mirrors at each end, which form the amplification medium to produce the laser beam.

reflecting cylinder
Laser's metal casing whose inside is polished so that it reflects the light toward the ruby cylinder.

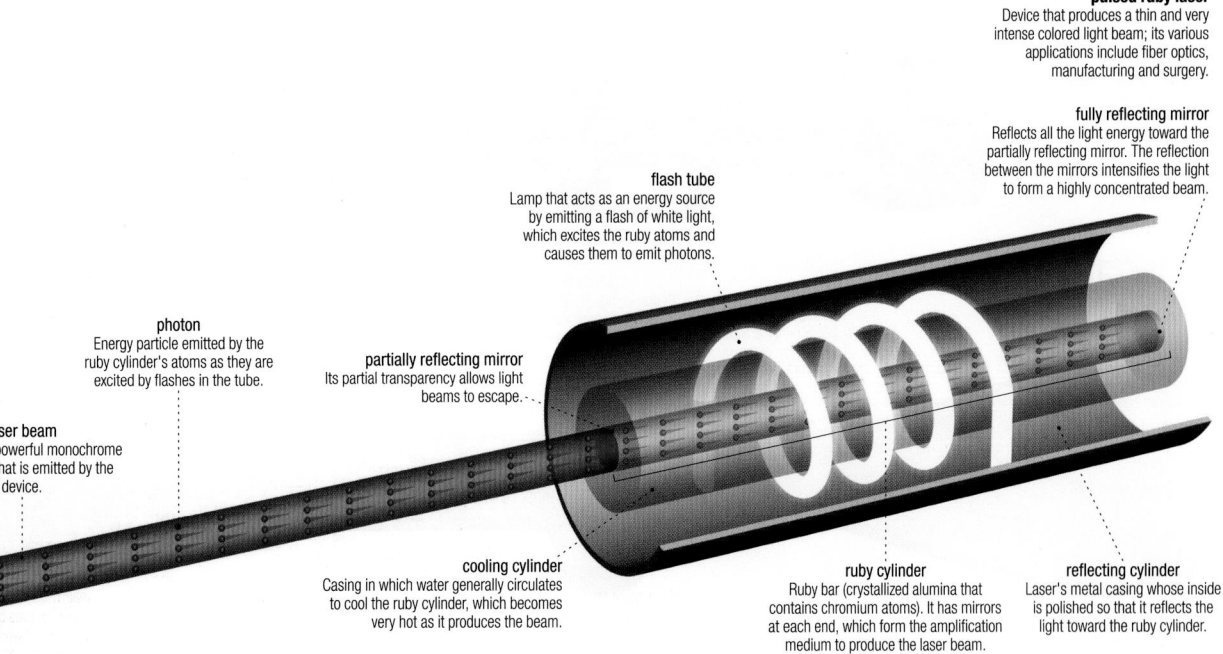

SCIENCE

optical devices

prism binoculars
Optical instrument made up of two identical telescopes, one for each eye; it magnifies both near and distant objects.

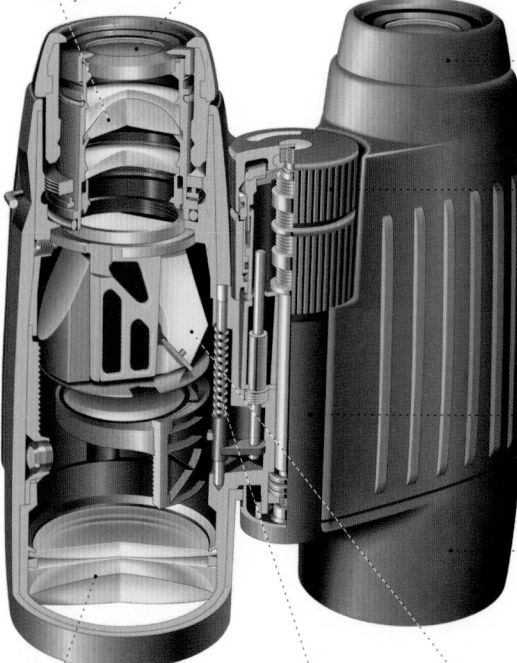

lens system
Optical system made up of a set of lenses through which light passes to transmit a magnified image of an object to the eye.

eyepiece
Optical disk or system of disks through which the eye sees the image produced by the lens.

focusing ring
Ring on each eyepiece for manually correcting for the difference between the user's eyes.

central focusing wheel
Focusing ring for both the objective lenses; it is used to manually adjust the sharpness of the image.

bridge
Part of the frame joining the two telescopes.

body
Cylindrical body of the binoculars that houses the optical system and through which the light rays pass.

objective lens
Lens that captures the light from the observed object and causes it to converge to form a magnified inverted image.

hinge
Mechanism for adjusting the distance between the eyepieces to the user's eyes.

Porro prism
Dual-prism system (blocks of glass at right angles) found in most binoculars; it diverts the light rays toward the eyepiece to correct the inverted image formed in the objective lens.

magnifying glass
Converging lens that magnifies the image of an object.

telescopic sight
Optical instrument mounted on a rifle or a measuring device to increase accuracy.

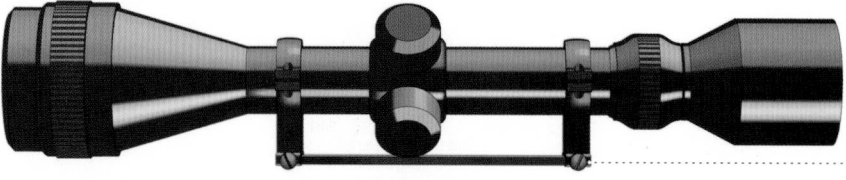

dovetail
Device for mounting the te[l] sight onto a device or firea[rm]

cross section of a telescopic sight

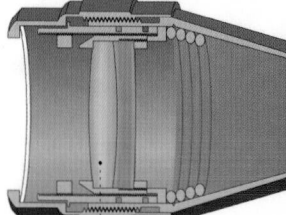

winding adjustment
Button for positioning the sight horizontally to offset any divergence of the target from the reticle.

elevation adjustment
Button for positioning the sight vertically to offset any divergence of the target from the reticle.

erecting lenses
Lens system that returns the inverted image formed on the objective lens.

field lens
Lens placed between the objectiv[e] and the eyepiece to widen the fie[ld] of vision.

objective lens
Lens that captures the light from the observed object and causes it to converge to form a magnified inverted image.

main scope tube
Cylindrical body of the telescopic sight that houses the optical system and through which the light travels.

turret cap
Part covering and protecting an adjustment button.

reticle
Optical system made up of two fine crossed wires to create a precise point as a sighting reference.

eyepiece
Optical disk or system of disks through which the eye sees the image produced by the lens.

optical devices

microscopes

Optical instruments that consist of a system of lenses designed for observing organisms that are very small or invisible to the naked eye by magnifying their images.

monocular microscope
Microscope with a single eyepiece.

eyepiece
System of lenses that acts as a magnifier; the eye looks through it to see an enlarged image of the image produced by the objective.

revolving nosepiece
Rotating plate to which objectives of different powers are fixed to allow them to be used in succession during a study.

drawtube
Cylindrical tube that houses the microscope's eyepiece; it is often made up of two converging lenses.

stage clip
Springlike metal blade that keeps the glass slide on the stage.

coarse adjustment knob
Medium-precision focusing device for adjusting the distance between the objective and the object under study.

objective
System that captures the light from the observed object and makes it converge to form an enlarged inverted image.

fine adjustment knob
High-precision focusing device for adjusting the distance between the objective and the object under study.

glass slide
Fine glass plate on which the object to be studied is placed.

arm
Vertical part of the microscope that supports the components (drawtube, stage) and contains the focusing mechanisms.

stage
Metal plate with an opening in the middle; the glass slide and the components keeping it in place are placed on it.

condenser
Optical system that is usually made up of two lenses, which concentrate the light reflected by the mirror onto the object under study.

base
Support that stabilizes the microscope.

mirror
Polished glass surface that reflects the surrounding light onto the object under study to illuminate it.

binocular microscope
Microscope comprising two eyepieces; it allows both eyes to be used during observation, providing a degree of depth to the image and preventing eyestrain.

drawtube
One of two cylindrical tubes that house the eyepieces; it is often made up of two converging lenses.

body tube
Metal casing that houses the microscope's two eyepieces and through which light rays pass.

eyepiece
System of lenses that acts as a magnifier; the eye looks through it to see an enlarged image of the image produced by the objective.

revolving nosepiece
Rotating plate to which objectives of different powers are fixed to allow them to be used in succession during a study.

limb top
Upper part of the arm that supports the revolving nosepiece.

arm
Vertical part of the microscope that supports the components (drawtube, stage) and contains the focusing mechanisms.

objective
System that captures the light from the observed object and makes it converge to form an enlarged inverted image.

mechanical stage
Adjustable part with two guiding screws that moves an object from right to left and from front to back on the stage.

stage clip
Springlike metal blade that keeps the glass slide on the stage.

stage
Metal plate with an opening in the middle; the glass slide and the components keeping it in place are placed on it.

glass slide
Fine glass plate on which the object to be studied is placed.

fine adjustment knob
High-precision focusing device for adjusting the distance between the objective and the object under study.

condenser adjustment knob
Screw that centers the condenser's light beam in the field of vision by moving it along a horizontal plane.

coarse adjustment knob
Medium-precision focusing device for adjusting the distance between the objective and the object under study.

field lens adjustment
Device with a variable-diameter opening that adjusts the amount of light illuminating the object.

mechanical stage control
Device for raising and lowering the mechanical stage.

base
Support that stabilizes the microscope.

lamp
Electric device that produces a light beam to illuminate the object under study.

condenser
Optical system that usually has two lenses to concentrate the light emitted from the lamp onto the object under study.

condenser height adjustment
Screw for raising and lowering the condenser.

SCIENCE

optical devices

microscopes

cross section of an electron microscope

Electron microscope: device that uses an electron beam (as opposed to light) to provide magnification that is markedly superior to that of an optical microscope.

electron gun
Device that usually consists of a tungsten filament that is heated to produce an intense electron beam, which illuminates the specimen.

electron beam
Set of negatively charged particles that propagate toward the specimen.

electron beam positioning
Control that positions the electron beam along the optical axis so that it reaches the specimen.

vacuum manifold
Conduit connected to a pump that creates enough of a vacuum in the microscope that it can function.

beam diameter reduction
The two lenses of the condenser cause the divergent electron beam emitted by the gun to converge.

condenser
System of magnetic lenses (electromagnets producing a magnetic field when excited by an electric current) that concentrates the beam onto the specimen under study.

focusing lenses
System of magnetic lenses (electromagnets) that concentrate the electron beam on one spot on the specimen.

aperture changer
Device that adjusts the diaphragm opening in order to change the diameter of the beam.

aperture diaphragm
Device with an opening whose diameter can be changed to narrow or widen the diameter of the electron beam.

visual transmission
The electron beam explores the surface of the specimen, which in turn emits electrons to form a point-by-point image on the screen.

stage
Adjustable metal plate (stage) on which the specimen is mounted in order to study it.

vacuum chamber
Part of the microscope in which pressure can be reduced so that the electrons can move.

electron microscope elements

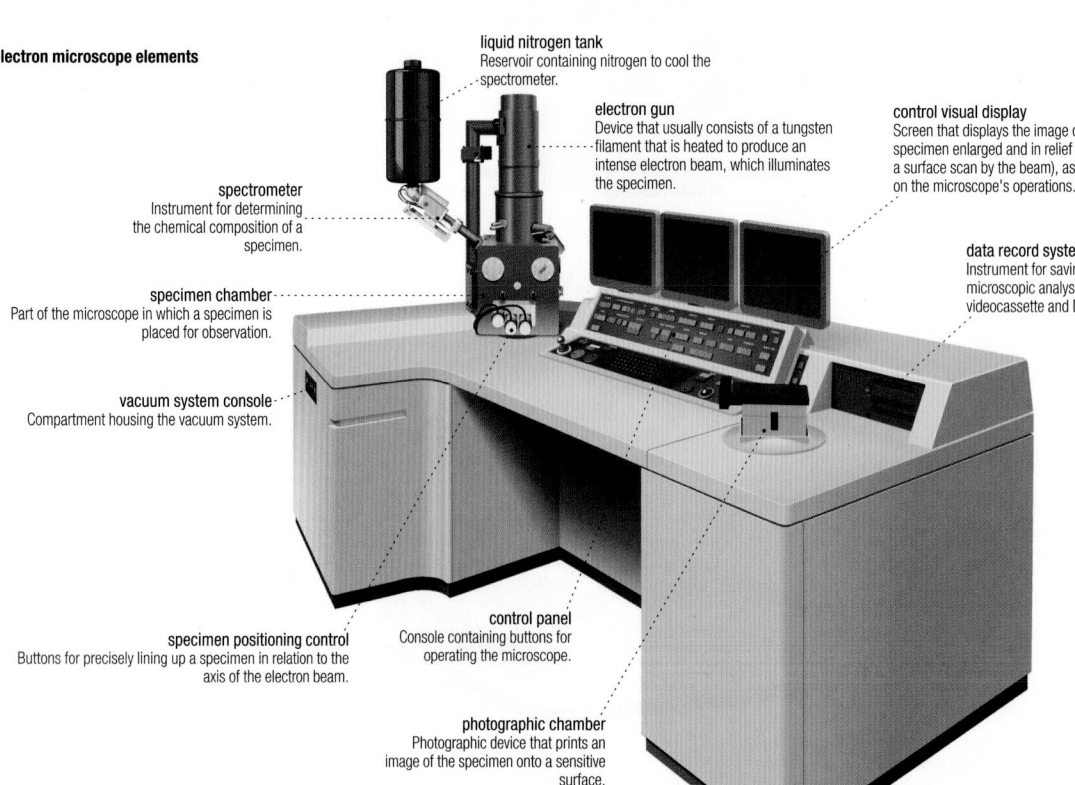

liquid nitrogen tank
Reservoir containing nitrogen to cool the spectrometer.

electron gun
Device that usually consists of a tungsten filament that is heated to produce an intense electron beam, which illuminates the specimen.

control visual display
Screen that displays the image of the specimen enlarged and in relief (as a result of a surface scan by the beam), as well as data on the microscope's operations.

spectrometer
Instrument for determining the chemical composition of a specimen.

data record system
Instrument for saving data pertaining to the microscopic analysis onto media such as videocassette and DVD.

specimen chamber
Part of the microscope in which a specimen is placed for observation.

vacuum system console
Compartment housing the vacuum system.

specimen positioning control
Buttons for precisely lining up a specimen in relation to the axis of the electron beam.

control panel
Console containing buttons for operating the microscope.

photographic chamber
Photographic device that prints an image of the specimen onto a sensitive surface.

SCIENCE

measure of temperature

Temperature: physical quantity corresponding to the level of heat or cold, which is measured by means of a thermometer.

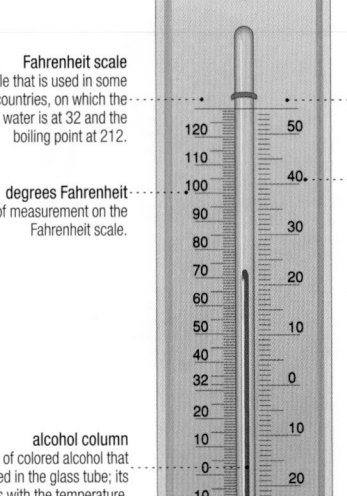

hol thermometer
ment for measuring temperature by
s of alcohol contained in a graduated

Fahrenheit scale
e scale that is used in some
king countries, on which the
int of water is at 32 and the
boiling point at 212.

degrees Fahrenheit
nits of measurement on the
Fahrenheit scale.

alcohol column
antity of colored alcohol that
ntained in the glass tube; its
varies with the temperature.

alcohol bulb
reservoir containing colored
ohol (methanol, ethanol) that
nd rises in the capillary tube
as the temperature rises.

Celsius scale
Temperature scale that is based on a
graduation from 0 (freezing point of
water) to 100 (boiling point of water); it
was formerly called the centigrade scale.

degrees Celsius
Units of measurement on the
Celsius scale.

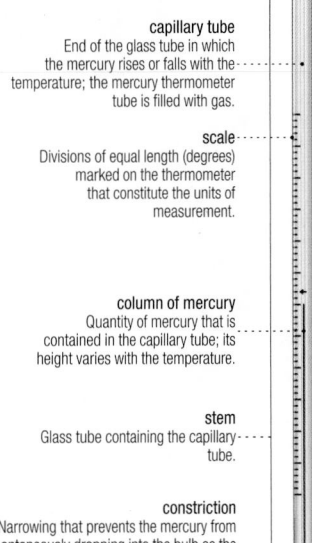

expansion chamber
Space that is taken up by the gas in the
capillary tube; it is pushed back as the
mercury rises into it.

clinical thermometer
Thermometer used to take the
temperature of the human body; it
is graduated from 94°F to 108°F.

capillary tube
End of the glass tube in which
the mercury rises or falls with the
temperature; the mercury thermometer
tube is filled with gas.

scale
Divisions of equal length (degrees)
marked on the thermometer
that constitute the units of
measurement.

column of mercury
Quantity of mercury that is
contained in the capillary tube; its
height varies with the temperature.

stem
Glass tube containing the capillary
tube.

constriction
Narrowing that prevents the mercury from
spontaneously dropping into the bulb as the
temperature lowers (the thermometer must
be shaken to make it go down).

mercury bulb
Glass reservoir containing mercury
(a liquid metal) that expands and
rises in the capillary tube as the
temperature rises.

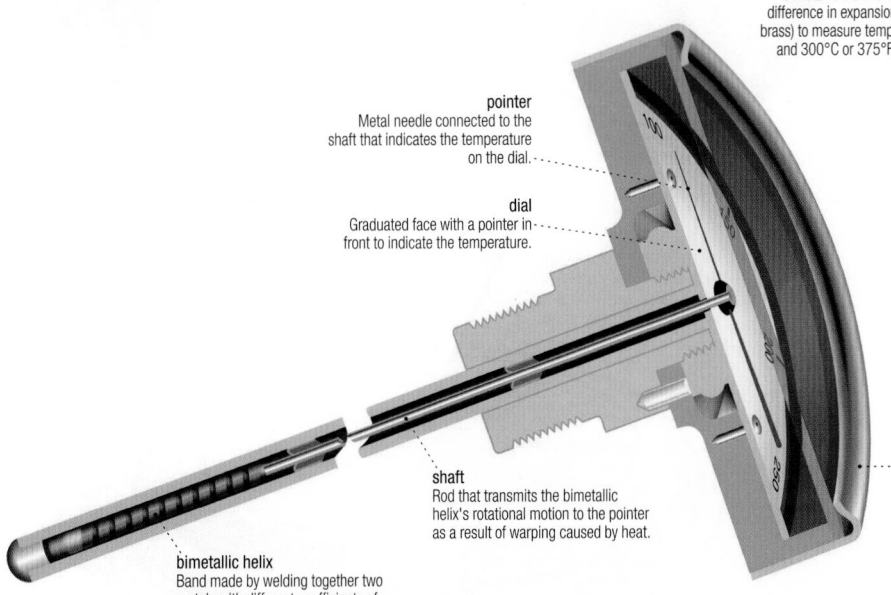

cross section of a bimetallic thermometer
Bimetallic thermometer: thermometer that uses the
difference in expansion of two metals (usually iron and
brass) to measure temperatures between 30°C or 86°F
and 300°C or 375°F; it is used especially in industry
and in kitchen thermometers.

pointer
Metal needle connected to the
shaft that indicates the temperature
on the dial.

dial
Graduated face with a pointer in
front to indicate the temperature.

shaft
Rod that transmits the bimetallic
helix's rotational motion to the pointer
as a result of warping caused by heat.

bimetallic helix
Band made by welding together two
metals with different coefficients of
expansion; it curls as the temperature
changes.

case
Outer covering that encloses and
protects the device's mechanism.

SCIENCE

measure of time

Time: physical quantity corresponding to a phenomenon or an event that is measured with devices such as watches and stopwatches.

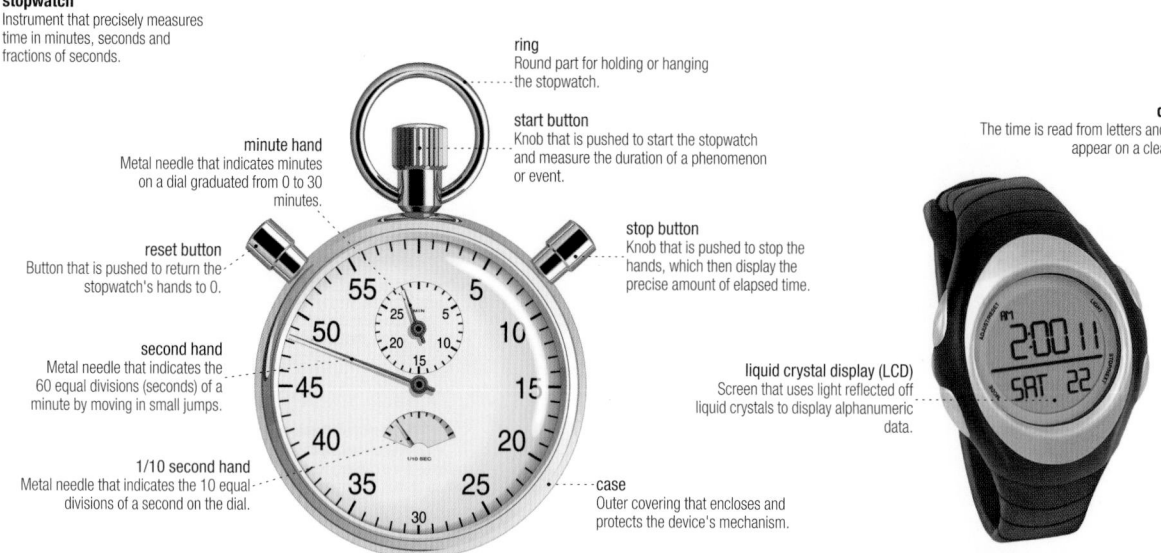

stopwatch
Instrument that precisely measures time in minutes, seconds and fractions of seconds.

ring
Round part for holding or hanging the stopwatch.

start button
Knob that is pushed to start the stopwatch and measure the duration of a phenomenon or event.

minute hand
Metal needle that indicates minutes on a dial graduated from 0 to 30 minutes.

stop button
Knob that is pushed to stop the hands, which then display the precise amount of elapsed time.

reset button
Button that is pushed to return the stopwatch's hands to 0.

second hand
Metal needle that indicates the 60 equal divisions (seconds) of a minute by moving in small jumps.

liquid crystal display (LCD)
Screen that uses light reflected off liquid crystals to display alphanumeric data.

1/10 second hand
Metal needle that indicates the 10 equal divisions of a second on the dial.

case
Outer covering that encloses and protects the device's mechanism.

digital wa
The time is read from letters and numbers appear on a clear backgro

mechanical watch
Set of geared wheels that reduce the force transmitted by a spiral spring to cause the watch's hands to rotate.

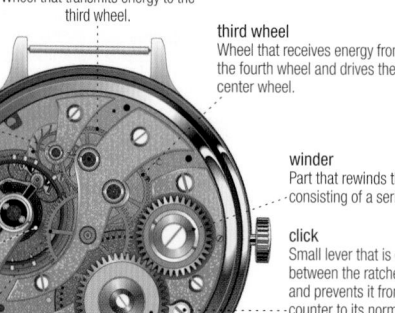

fourth wheel
Wheel that transmits energy to the third wheel.

third wheel
Wheel that receives energy from the fourth wheel and drives the center wheel.

dial
Graduated face over which the hands move to indicate the time.

jewel
Very hard stone (formerly a ruby, today a rock crystal) that resists wear; the rotation axle of a wheel rests on it.

winder
Part that rewinds the mechanism, consisting of a series of wheels.

escape wheel
Last wheel of the gear train with special teeth that causes the watch to operate regularly and continuously; it controls the movement of the other wheels.

click
Small lever that is engaged between the ratchet-wheel teeth and prevents it from rotating counter to its normal direction.

hairspring
Flat spiral spring that causes the wheels of a watch to move over a certain period of time.

center wheel
Wheel that is connected to the hands and causes them to rotate on the dial.

ratchet wheel
Toothed wheel having only one direction of rotation; it is kept in place by the click.

analog wa
The time is displayed by hands, w move around the

crown
Knob with sprockets t connected to the winder; to manually wind the wa set its time.

strap
Leather, fabric, plastic or metal bracelet with a clasp; it is used to hold a watch on the wrist.

sundial
Vertical or horizontal face with divisions that correspond to the hours of the day, which are indicated by the shadow of a gnomon cast by the Sun.

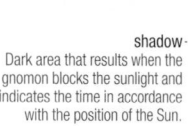

gnomon
Part aligned with the Earth's axis; its shadow indicates the time as it moves over the sundial.

shadow
Dark area that results when the gnomon blocks the sunlight and indicates the time in accordance with the position of the Sun.

dial
Face marked with numbers over which shadows are cast by the gnomon to indicate the approximate time of day.

measure of time

grandfather clock
Clock with a pendulum that
is operated by weights and
housed in a tall (usually over
2 m high) straight body, which
stands upright on the floor.

body
Usually wooden box that
houses and protects the clock's
mechanism.

Moon dial
Face divided into 29 1/2 days that is
represented by a moon whose movement
indicates the phases of the Moon: first quarter,
full moon, last quarter, new moon.

hour hand
Metal needle that points at the
24 hours of a day on the dial.

minute hand
Metal needle that points at the
60 minutes of an hour on the dial.

dial
Graduated face over which the
hands move to indicate the time.

weight
Heavy body that hangs from the
main wheel; its descent provides
the necessary energy for the
clock's mechanism.

pendulum
Unit whose regular swinging
motion controls the workings of the
clock's mechanism.

chain
Series of interlaced rings to which
weights are attached.

plinth
Base that supports the clock and
makes it stable.

weight-driven clock mechanism
This clock is operated by weights that, under gravity,
drive the hands of the clock in their rotational movement
by means of a gear train.

pinion
Small wheel with teeth that is
mounted on a shaft and transmits
the rotational movement of one
wheel to another.

pallet
Anchor-shaped part that frees and
constrains the escape wheel's teeth to
maintain the pendulum's back-and-
forth movement.

escape wheel
Last wheel of the gear train with special
teeth that causes the clock to operate
regularly and continuously and controls
the movement of the other wheels.

suspension spring
Small rigid plate from which the
pendulum hangs.

spindle
Cylindrical part that transfers the
rotational movement of one part
to another.

fork
Part that is operated by the escape
wheel to cause the pendulum's
movement.

center wheel
Wheel that is connected to the
hands and causes them to rotate
on the dial.

third wheel
Wheel that receives energy from
the center wheel and drives the
escape wheel.

click
Small lever that is engaged
between the ratchet-wheel teeth
and prevents it from rotating
counter to its normal direction.

minute hand
Metal needle that points at the
60 minutes of an hour on the dial.

hour hand
Metal needle that points at the
24 hours of a day on the dial.

pendulum rod
Rigid bar to which the pendulum
bob is attached.

winding mechanism
Device that raises the weights to
start anew the cycle of the clock's
mechanism.

pendulum bob
Weight attached to the end of the
pendulum rod.

main wheel
First wheel in the gear train that
transmits the driving force of the
weights to the other wheels to
turn them.

ratchet wheel
Toothed wheel having only one
direction of rotation; it is kept in
place by the click.

weight
Heavy body that hangs from the
main wheel; its descent provides
the necessary energy for the
clock's mechanism.

drum
Cylinder around which the weights'
cord or chain winds when the clock
is rewound.

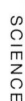

measure of weight

Mass: physical quantity that characterizes an amount of matter (mass) that is measured by means of a scale.

beam balance
Compares the mass of a body with that of another body of known mass (weight); when two pans hanging from a bar (beam) are in balance, the two weights are equal.

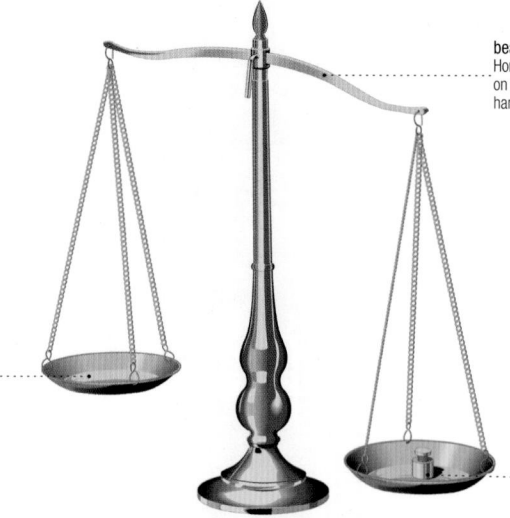

beam
Horizontal metal bar that balances on a vertical axis and has pans hanging from each end.

pan
Flat rigid support that holds either the body to be weighed or the weights.

weight
Piece of metal, such as copper or iron, of known mass that is placed on a pan to balance the scale and thereby assess the corresponding mass of a body.

unequal-arm balance
Scale used for weighing loads that has a beam with arms of different lengths; the shorter arm supports the pan and the longer arm supports the weights that slide to attain a balance.

sliding weight
Sliding part that is moved along the beams until a balance between the two masses is attained.

notch
Groove in which a sliding weight catches so that a precise reading on the graduated scale can be taken.

rear beam
Rigid metal bar along which the sliding weight slides to provide a relatively precise reading of the mass.

vernier
Small graduated dial that slides along the beams and provides a very precise reading of the mass.

pan hook
Curved part from which the pan is hung by means of rods.

magnetic damping system
Device made up of magnets that reduce the beams' oscillations when the weights are moved to provide a quick reading of the mass.

front beam
Rigid metal bar along which the sliding weight slides to provide a very precise reading of the mass.

graduated scale
The divisions of equal length marked on the scale's beam that constitute the units of measurement.

pan
Flat rigid stand on which the body to be weighed is placed.

base
Support that provides stability to the scale.

Roberval's balance
Scale that operates on the same principle as the beam balance; the pans are stabilized by a shank and rest on the beam.

pointer
Metal needle that indicates the point of equilibrium on the dial when the beam is level.

dial
Graduated surface with a pointer in front that indicates the point of equilibrium for the two pans.

weight
Piece of metal, such as copper or iron, of known mass that is placed on a pan to balance the scale and thereby assess the corresponding mass of a body.

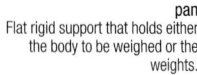

pan
Flat rigid support that holds either the body to be weighed or the weights.

beam
Horizontal metal bar that balances on a vertical axis and supports a pan on each end.

base
Support that provides stability to the scale.

SCIENCE

measure of weight

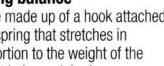

ng balance
e made up of a hook attached
spring that stretches in
ortion to the weight of the
t being weighed.

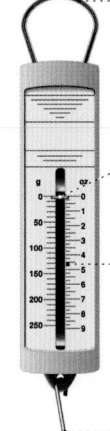

ring
Round part for holding or hanging
the spring balance.

pointer
Pointer connected to the spring
that moves along a graduated scale
to indicate the weight of the body
being weighed.

graduated scale
The divisions of equal length
that are marked on the spring
balance and constitute the units of
measurement.

hook
Curved part on which the body to
be weighed is hung.

electronic scale
Commercial scale that weighs and
calculates the price of a quantity
of merchandise and displays these
elements.

weight
Display that shows the weight of
the item.

unit price
Display that shows the unit price of
an item.

display
Each of the three screens that
show various numeric information
(e.g., weight, unit price and total
price).

total
Display that shows the price of
each weighed article and, at the
end of the transaction, the total
price of all purchases.

platform
Flat rigid surface on which the
items to be weighed are placed.

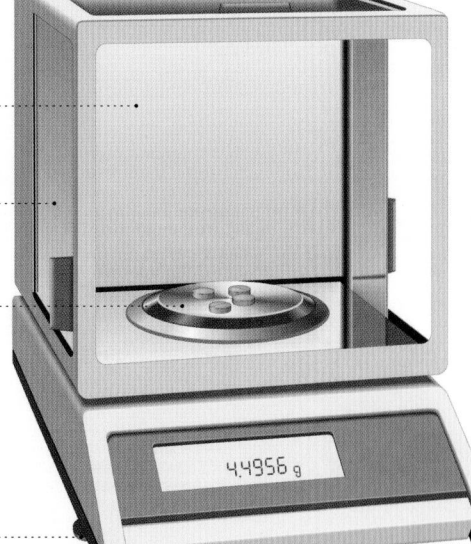

function keys
Set of keys that perform various
operations (e.g., data entry,
calculations and printing receipts).

product code
Code assigned to a product that
can be selected by pressing a
pre-set key.

numeric keyboard
Set of keys with numbers and
symbols that are used especially
to enter the unit prices or codes
of items.

printout
Paper on which various data are
printed (e.g., the weight, quantity
and price of the items weighed).

hroom scale
e used for weighing a person;
s a spring mechanism that
presses in proportion to the
ht.

display
Screen that indicates the weight in
numbers.

weighting platform
Flat base that a person stands
upon to be weighed.

analytical balance
Used especially in the laboratory
for taking very precise weight
measurements.

glass case
Glass box that protects the pan from
air currents and dust that might
cause a false reading of the weight.

door access
Sliding doors that provide easy
access to the inside of the glass
case.

pan
Flat rigid support on which the
specimen is placed.

leveling screw
Screw for adjusting the level of the
balance's base.

SCIENCE

measure of distance

Distance: interval separating two points in space.

pedometer
Device that counts the number of steps taken by a walker or runner to measure the distance traveled.

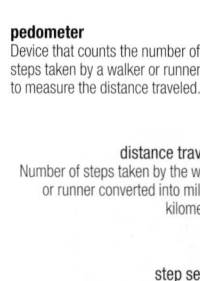

reset button
Key used to reset the counter to 0.

distance traveled
Number of steps taken by the walker or runner converted into miles or kilometers.

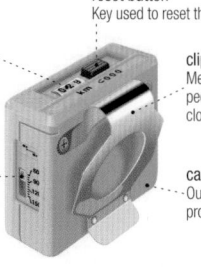

clip
Metal fastener for attaching the pedometer to a belt or article of clothing.

step setting
Button for adjusting the average length of a step in the walk or run.

case
Outer covering that encloses and protects the device's mechanism.

measuring wh
Device that measures ground dista based on the number of revolut made by its wh

pistol grip
Part shaped like a pistol grip so the wrist remains straight while holding the device.

measure wheel
Circular instrument rotating aroun axle so that the device can be mov

laser rangefinder
Device that uses a reflected laser beam to measure the distance between the operator and the object observed.

laser beam emitter
Projection source for a laser beam used to measure distance.

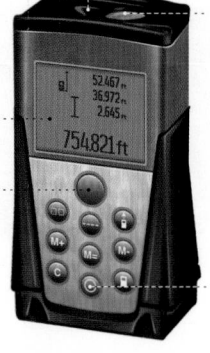

sensor
Lens that captures the laser beam reflected back by the targeted object.

display
Screen that provides data on the rangefinder's calibration or the calculations performed.

52.467 m
36.972 m
2.645 m

754.821 ft

measuring button
Button pushed to start measuring process.

on-off button
Mechanical connection that turns the device on or off.

stand
Retractable support rod that holds the device upright, at a slight incline, while not in motion.

counter
Component that measures distance of a journey based on the number of revolutions made by the wheel.

measure of thickness

Thickness: dimension corresponding to the distance between two surfaces of the same body.

vernier caliper
Precision instrument for measuring the thickness and diameter of mechanical parts.

clamping screws
Screws that lock the vernier and the clamping block in their final positions in order to preserve the measurement obtained.

clamping block
Part that chocks the vernier against the part to be measured.

vernier
Small graduated rule that slides along the ruler and is used to read very precise measurements.

ruler
Graduated instrument ending in a fixed jaw that measures the thickness or diameter of an object.

fixed jaw
Tapered part at the end of the ruler that supports the object to be measured; the object is place between the two jaws, which are gently tightened.

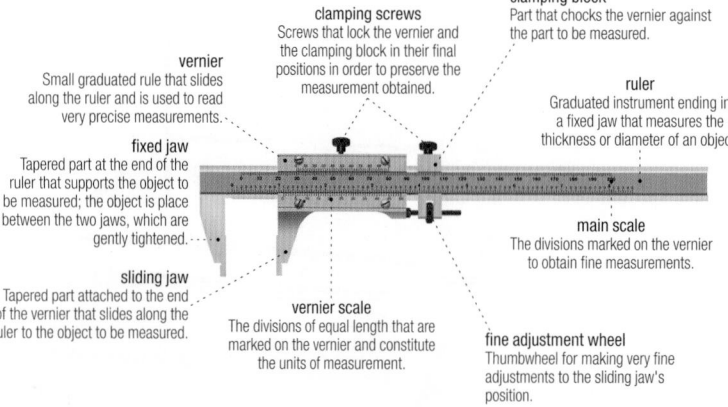

main scale
The divisions marked on the vernier to obtain fine measurements.

sliding jaw
Tapered part attached to the end of the vernier that slides along the ruler to the object to be measured.

vernier scale
The divisions of equal length that are marked on the vernier and constitute the units of measurement.

fine adjustment wheel
Thumbwheel for making very fine adjustments to the sliding jaw's position.

frame
Horseshoe-shaped part that supports the anvil and a graduated device from which the measurement is read.

micrometer cal
Instrument that measures thickness or the diameter of relat small parts; it produces finer res than a vernier cal

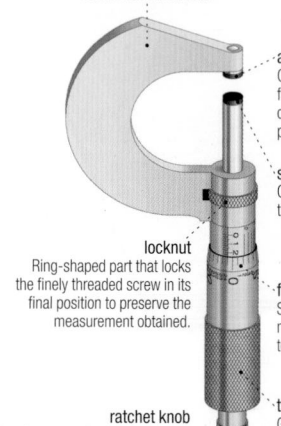

anvil
Cylindrical part that is attached frame of the micrometer to supp object to be measured; the obje placed between the anvil and th

spindle
Cylindrical end of the finely threaded screw.

locknut
Ring-shaped part that locks the finely threaded screw in its final position to preserve the measurement obtained.

finely threaded screw
Screw driven by the ratchet kno moves the spindle against the o to be measured.

thimble
Graduated cylindrical part that i activated by the finely threaded and measures the thickness wit precision.

ratchet knob
Part that stops the finely threaded screw when the pressure on the object being measured is sufficient.

measure of length

Length: the longer dimension of an object as opposed to its width.

ruler
Instrument for measuring length.

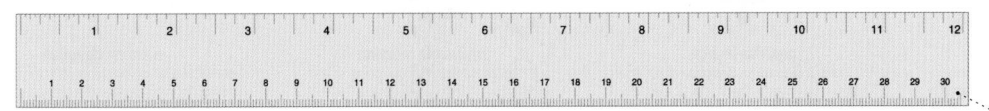

scale
The divisions of equal length that are marked on the ruler and constitute the units of measurement.

measure of angles

Angle: figure formed by two intersecting lines or planes; it is measured in degrees.

theodolite
Sighting instrument that is used especially in astronomy, geodesy and navigation for measuring horizontal and vertical angles.

optical sight
Device with an eyepiece that precisely aims the telescope at the target whose angles are to be measured.

alidade
Part of the theodolite that rotates on a vertical axle to measure angles by means of the telescope.

telescope
Optical instrument composed of several lenses; it can be adjusted in the horizontal and vertical planes and is used to observe distant objects.

adjustment for vertical-circle image
Knob that adjusts the sharpness of the image of the vertical circle (graduated from 0° to 360°) in order to read the angles on the vertical axis.

illumination mirror
Adjustable polished glass surface that reflects light onto the circles so that the angles can be read.

micrometer screw
Knob that adjusts the micrometer to give a very precise reading of the circles' measurements.

adjustment for horizontal-circle image
Knob that adjusts the sharpness of the image of the horizontal circle (graduated from 0° to 360°) in order to read the angles on the horizontal axis.

alidade level
Transparent tube that contains liquid and an air bubble; it serves as a guide for aligning the alidade with the vertical axis.

horizontal clamp
Knob that locks the alidade to prevent it from rotating.

leveling head level
Transparent tube that contains liquid and an air bubble; it serves as a guide for aligning the leveling head with the horizontal plane.

leveling screw
Screw that adjusts the theodolite's leveling head level on the horizontal plane.

leveling head
Platform serving as a support for the theodolite.

base plate
Plate to which the leveling head is attached by means of three leveling screws.

leveling head locking knob
Knob that locks the alidade to the leveling head.

bevel square
Instrument whose movable arms are used for measuring or for marking an angle.

protractor
Graduated semicircular instrument for measuring and drawing angles.

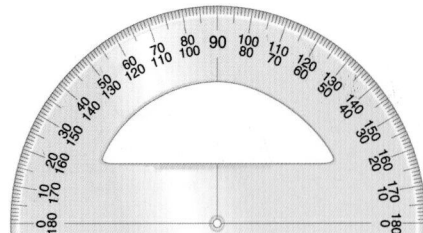

SCIENCE

chemistry

Science that studies the constitution of substances and their interaction; chemical symbols offer an easier way of writing down the names of the elements, formulas and chemical reactions.

negative charge
Symbol that indicates a surplus of electrons in an atom, which means the atom has a negative electric charge. The chlorine atom, for example, forms a negative ion that is denoted as Cl⁻.

positive charge
Symbol that indicates a loss of electrons in an atom, which means the atom has a positive electric charge. The sodium atom, for example, forms a positive ion that is denoted as Na⁺.

reversible reaction
Chemical reaction that can occur in both directions; the products obtained (direct reaction) react between themselves to change back into the original reactants (inverse reaction).

reaction direction
A chemical reaction corresponds to the conversion of reactants in products and is obtained by the reaction of one of the reactants. The arrow indicates the direction in which this irreversible reaction occurs.

compound representation
Compound: substance made of two or more chemical elements.

chemical formula
Written convention that describes the number and type of atoms that constitute a chemical compound.

water
Compound formed by two atoms of hydrogen and one atom of oxygen.

common name
Name by which a compound is known.

biology

The scientific study of living organisms (humans, animals and plants) from the point of view of their structure and how they function and reproduce.

female
Symbol denoting that a being has female reproductive organs.

Rhesus factor negative
Individuals not carrying the Rh molecule (antigen) are Rh negative; the Rh factor plays an important role in pregnancy (the parents' factors must be compatible).

birth
Symbol placed before a date denoting a person's year of birth.

male
Symbol denoting that a being has male reproductive organs.

Rhesus factor positive
Individuals are Rh positive when their red blood cells carry an Rh molecule (antigen); the Rh factor is positive in about 85% of the population.

death
Symbol placed before a date denoting a person's year of death.

International System of Units (SI)

Decimal system established by the 11th General Conference on Weights and Measures (GCWM) in 1960 and used by many countries.

measurement of frequency	measurement of electric potential difference	measurement of electric charge	measurement of energy
## Hz	## V	## C	## J
hertz	**volt**	**coulomb**	**joule**
...ency of a periodic phenomenon whose period is 1 second.	Difference in potential between two points of a conductor carrying a constant current of 1 ampere when the power between these points is 1 watt.	Amount of electricity carried in 1 second by a current of 1 ampere.	Amount of energy released by the force of 1 newton acting through a distance of 1 meter.

measurement of power	measurement of force	measurement of electric resistance	measurement of electric current
## W	## N	## Ω	## A
watt	**newton**	**ohm**	**ampere**
...ergy transfer of 1 joule during 1 second.	Force required to impart an acceleration of 1 m/s^2 to a body having a mass of 1 kg.	Electrical resistance between two points of a conductor carrying a current of 1 ampere when the difference in potential between them is 1 volt.	Constant current of 1 joule per second in a conductor.

measurement of length	measurement of mass	measurement of Celsius temperature	measurement of thermodynamic temperature
## m	## kg	## °C	## K
meter	**kilogram**	**degree Celsius**	**kelvin**
...istance traveled by light in a ...cuum in 1/299,792,458 of a second.	Mass of a platinum prototype that was accepted as the international reference in 1889; it is stored at the International Bureau of Weights and Measures.	1/100 of the difference between the freezing point of water (0°C) and its boiling point (100°C) at standard atmospheric pressure.	Zero kelvin (absolute zero) is equal to minus 273.16°C.

measurement of amount of substance	measurement of radioactivity	measurement of pressure	measurement of luminous intensity
## mol	## Bq	## Pa	## cd
mole	**becquerel**	**pascal**	**candela**
Quantity of matter equal to the number of atoms in 0.012 kg of carbon 12.	Radioactivity of a substance in which one atom disintegrates per second.	Uniform pressure exerted on a flat surface of 1 m^2 with a force of 1 newton.	Unit of light intensity equivalent to a radiant intensity of 1/683 watts per steradian (solid angle).

SCIENCE

Roman numerals

Uppercase letters that represented numbers in ancient Rome; they are still seen today in uses such as clock and watch dials and pagination.

one
Letter whose value is 1 unit.

five
Letter whose value is 5 units.

ten
Letter whose value is 10 units.

fifty
Letter whose value is 50 units.

one hundred
Letter whose value is 100 units.

five hundred
Letter whose value is 500 units.

one thousand
Letter whose value is 1,000 un

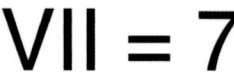

addition
The value of a letter placed to the right of another letter of greater or equal value is added to the value of the letter on the left.

subtraction
The value of a letter placed to the left of a letter of greater value is subtracted from the value of the letter on the right.

$$MCMXLVII = 1947$$

synthesis
Complex numbers are calculated by adding together the value of the letters from right to left, while subtracting the value of those letters that are inferior in value to the one that precedes them.

geometry

Mathematical discipline that studies the relations between points, straight lines, curves, surfaces and volumes.

degree
Symbol placed in superscript after a number to denote the opening of an angle or the length of an arc, or in front of an uppercase letter to identify a scale of measurement.

minute
Symbol placed in superscript after a number that denotes degrees in sixtieths of a measure.

second
Symbol placed in superscript after a number that denotes degrees in sixtieths of a minute.

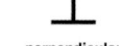

pi
Constant that represents the ratio of a circle's circumference to its diameter; its value is approximately 3.1416.

perpendicular
Symbol denoting that a straight meets another at a right angl

is parallel to
Symbol denoting that two straight lines remain at a constant distance from one another.

is not parallel to
Symbol denoting that two straight lines do not remain at a constant distance from one other.

right angle
Angle formed by two lines or two perpendicular planes that measures 90°.

obtuse angle
Angle between 90° and 180°.

acute angle
Angle that is smaller than a ri angle (less than 90°).

mathematics

The science that uses deductive reasoning to study the properties of abstract entities such as numbers, space and functions and the relations between them.

minus/negative
…n denoting that a number is to …subtracted from another; the result is a difference.

plus/positive
Sign denoting that a number is to be added to another; the result is a sum.

multiplied by
Sign denoting that a number is to be multiplied by another; the result is a product.

divided by
Sign denoting a number (dividend) is to be divided by another (divisor); the result is a quotient.

equals
Sign denoting the result of an operation.

is not equal to
…n denoting that the result of an …ration does not have the same …ue as the figure to the right of the symbol.

is approximately equal to
Sign denoting that the result of an operation is close to the value of the figure to the right of the symbol.

is equivalent to
Sign denoting that the value on the left is the same magnitude as the one on the right.

is identical with
Binary sign denoting that the result of the operation noted on the left has the same value as the operation noted on the right.

is not identical with
Binary sign denoting that the result of the operation noted on the left does not have the same value as the operation noted on the right.

plus or minus
…n denoting that the positive and …ative values of the number that …ws bracket a range of values.

is less than or equal to
Sign denoting that the result of an operation is equal to or of smaller magnitude than the number that follows.

is less than
Sign denoting that the value on the left is of smaller magnitude than the number that follows.

is greater than or equal to
Sign denoting that the result of an operation is equal to or of greater magnitude than the number that follows.

is greater than
Sign denoting that the value on the left is of greater magnitude than the number that follows.

empty set
…n denoting that a set contains no elements.

union of two sets
Binary sign denoting that a set is composed of the sum of the elements of two sets.

intersection of two sets
Binary sign denoting that two sets M and N have elements in common.

is included in/is a subset of
Binary sign denoting that a set A on the left is part of the set B on the right.

percent
Sign denoting that the number preceding it is a fraction of 100.

is an element of
…inary sign denoting that the …ment on the left is included in the set on the right.

is not an element of
Binary sign denoting that the element on the left is not included in the set on the right.

sum
Sign indicating that several values are to be added together (their sum).

square root of
Sign denoting that, when a number is multiplied by itself, the result is the number that appears below the bar.

fraction
Sign denoting that the number on the left of the slash (numerator) is one part of the number on the right of the slash (denominator).

infinity
Symbol denoting that a value has no upper limit.

integral
Result of the integral calculation used especially to determine an area and to resolve a differential equation.

factorial
Product of all positive whole numbers less than and equal to a given number. For example, the factorial of 4 is: 4! = 1x2x3x4 = 24.

graphic representations

Conventional symbols or figures that seek to depict phenomena or facts.

angles
Figures formed by two intersecting lines or planes; they are measured in degrees.

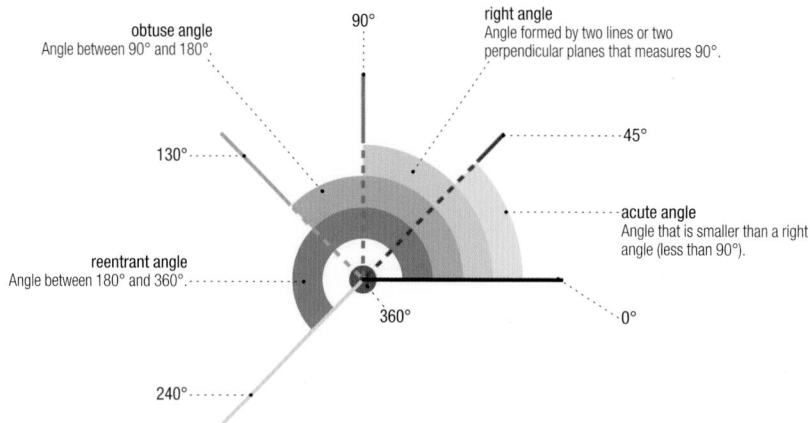

obtuse angle
Angle between 90° and 180°.

90°

right angle
Angle formed by two lines or two perpendicular planes that measures 90°.

130°

45°

acute angle
Angle that is smaller than a right angle (less than 90°).

reentrant angle
Angle between 180° and 360°.

360°

0°

240°

circle
Closed plane curve; all its points are the same distance from a fixed point (center).

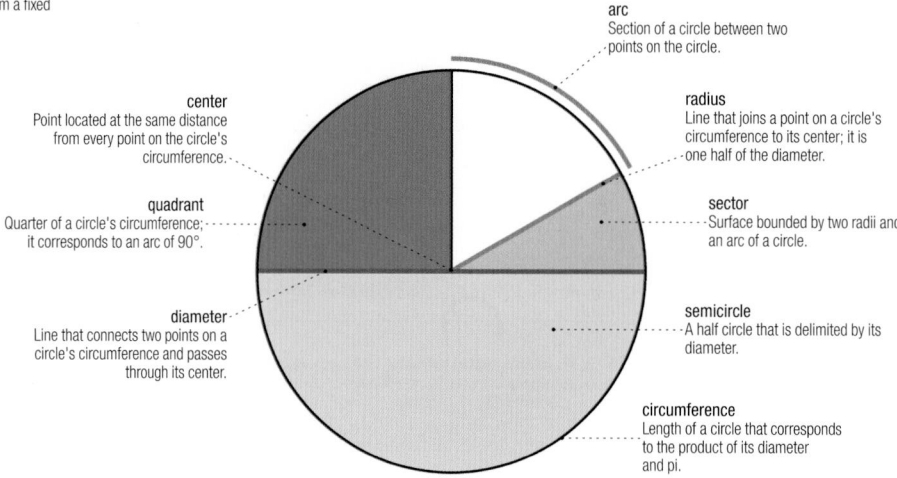

arc
Section of a circle between two points on the circle.

center
Point located at the same distance from every point on the circle's circumference.

radius
Line that joins a point on a circle's circumference to its center; it is one half of the diameter.

quadrant
Quarter of a circle's circumference; it corresponds to an arc of 90°.

sector
Surface bounded by two radii and an arc of a circle.

diameter
Line that connects two points on a circle's circumference and passes through its center.

semicircle
A half circle that is delimited by its diameter.

circumference
Length of a circle that corresponds to the product of its diameter and pi.

statistics
Mathematical discipline that studies and calculates probabilities, generally through the collection and analysis of data.

line chart
Chart used to depict the evolution of data over a period of time, using a line formed by joining the points of data.

histogram
Chart composed of consecutive columns whose height is proportional to the quantity represented.

y-axis
Vertical axis on a chart. On a line chart, it usually indicates data variation.

pie chart
Chart used to depict proportionality in a set of data, using a circle divided into sectors.

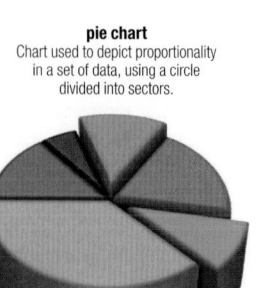

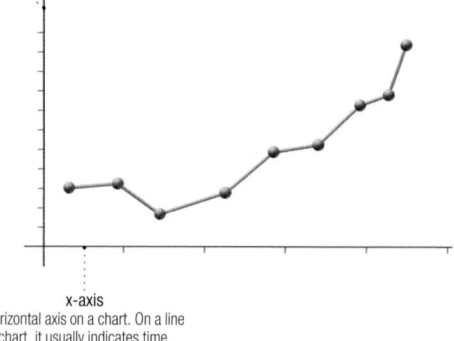

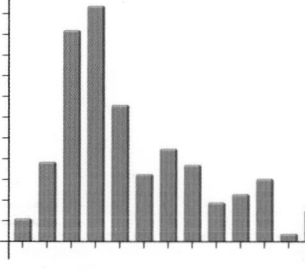

x-axis
Horizontal axis on a chart. On a line chart, it usually indicates time.

graphic representations

polygons
Geometric plane figures with several sides and a number of equal angles.

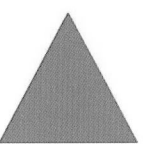

triangle
ee-sided polygon; triangles are alene (no side is equal to any) isosceles (two sides equal) or equilateral (all sides equal).

square
Equilateral rectangle with four right angles.

rectangle
Quadrilateral whose opposite sides are equal in length; the sides meet at right angles.

rhombus
Equilateral parallelogram.

trapezoid
Quadrilateral with two sides (bases) that are parallel. It is isosceles when it has two sides that are equal and not parallel, and rectangle when two of its sides form a right angle.

parallelogram
ezoid whose opposite sides are el and of equal length; the sides do not meet at right angles.

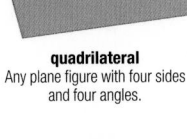

quadrilateral
Any plane figure with four sides and four angles.

regular pentagon
Polygon with five (penta = five) sides and equal angles.

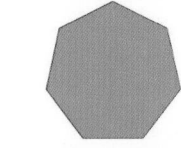

regular hexagon
Polygon with six (hexa = six) sides and equal angles.

regular heptagon
Polygon with seven (hepta = seven) sides and equal angles.

regular octagon
lygon with eight (octo = eight) sides and equal angles.

regular nonagon
Polygon with nine (nona = nine) sides and equal angles.

regular decagon
Polygon with 10 (deca = ten) sides and equal angles.

regular hendecagon
Polygon with 11 (hendeca = eleven) sides and equal angles.

regular dodecagon
Polygon with 12 (dodeca = twelve) sides and equal angles.

solids
Geometric shapes in three dimensions that are delimited by surfaces.

helix
ume or solid of spiral shape that turns at a constant angle.

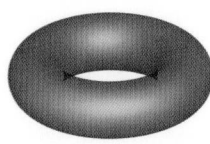

torus
Volume or solid generated by the rotation of a circle at an equal distance from its center of rotation.

hemisphere
Half sphere cut along its diameter.

sphere
Volume with all the points on its surface the same distance from its center; the solid thus delimited is a round ball.

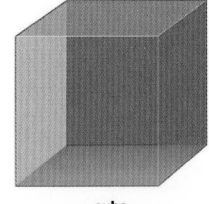

cube
Volume or solid with six square sides of equal area and six equal edges; it has eight vertices.

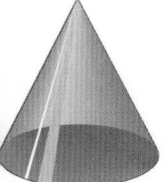

cone
lume or solid generated by the tion of a straight line (generatrix) g a circular line (directrix) from a fixed point (vertex).

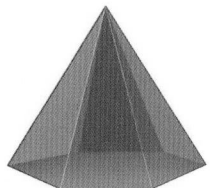

pyramid
Volume or solid generated by straight lines (edges) connecting the angles of a polygon (base) to the vertex and whose sides form triangles.

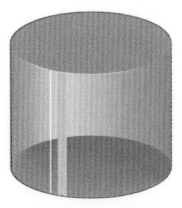

cylinder
Volume or solid generated by the rotation of a straight line (generatrix) moving along a curved line (directrix).

parallelepiped
Volume or solid with six sides (parallelograms) that are parallel in pairs.

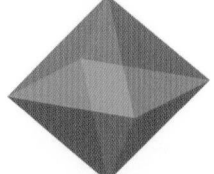

regular octahedron
Volume or solid with eight triangular sides of equal area; it has six vertices and 12 edges.

SCIENCE

SOCIETY

Collective environment inhabited by human beings and characterized by institutions, culture, a concern for the common good and collective security.

metropolitan area

Vast urban concentration consisting of a city and its suburbs.

main components

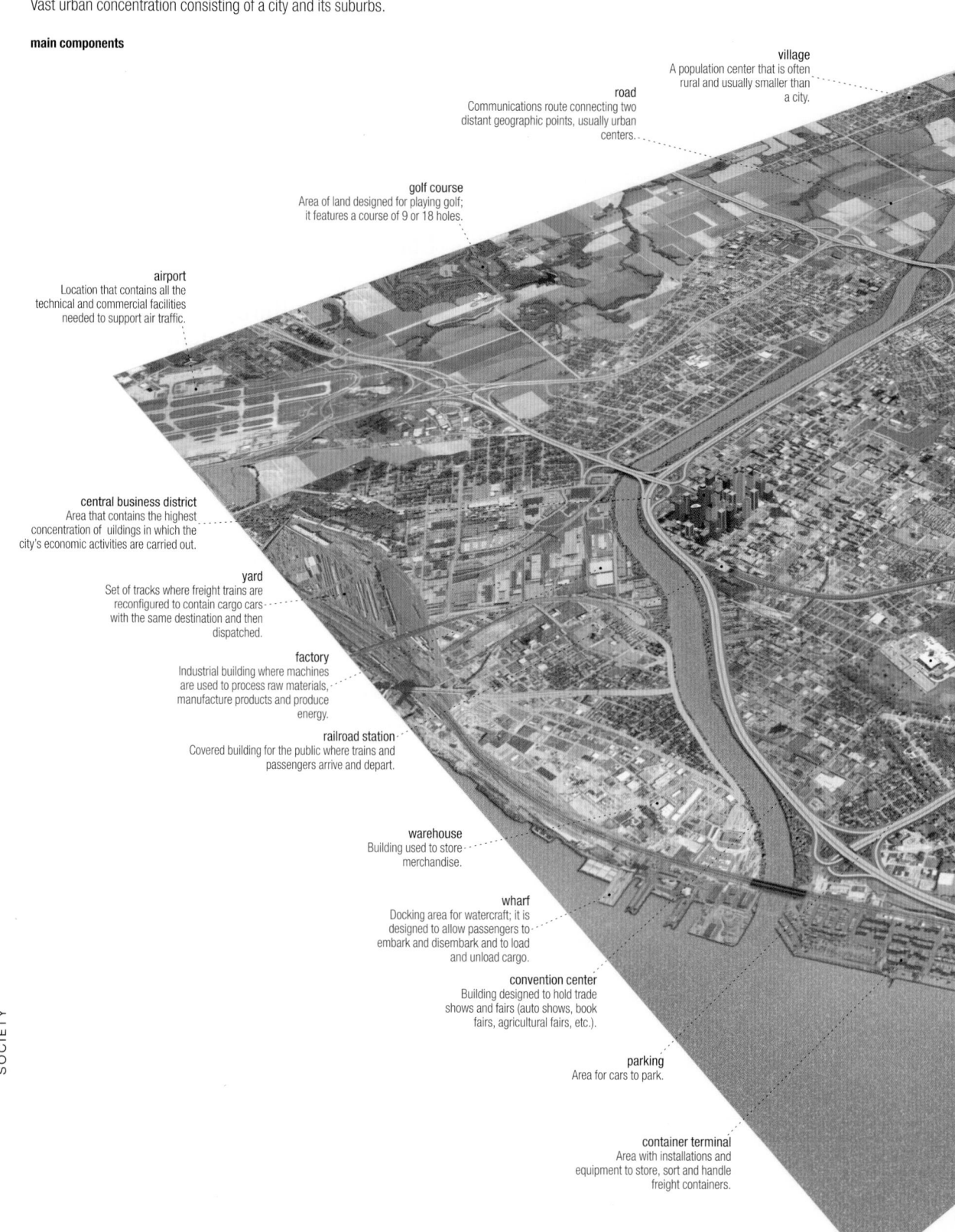

village
A population center that is often rural and usually smaller than a city.

road
Communications route connecting two distant geographic points, usually urban centers.

golf course
Area of land designed for playing golf; it features a course of 9 or 18 holes.

airport
Location that contains all the technical and commercial facilities needed to support air traffic.

central business district
Area that contains the highest concentration of uildings in which the city's economic activities are carried out.

yard
Set of tracks where freight trains are reconfigured to contain cargo cars with the same destination and then dispatched.

factory
Industrial building where machines are used to process raw materials, manufacture products and produce energy.

railroad station
Covered building for the public where trains and passengers arrive and depart.

warehouse
Building used to store merchandise.

wharf
Docking area for watercraft; it is designed to allow passengers to embark and disembark and to load and unload cargo.

convention center
Building designed to hold trade shows and fairs (auto shows, book fairs, agricultural fairs, etc.).

parking
Area for cars to park.

container terminal
Area with installations and equipment to store, sort and handle freight containers.

metropolitan area

railroad track
A pair of parallel rails laid end to end and on which trains run.

beltway
High-speed road that circles the downtown area, making it possible to divert traffic away from downtown or connect two outlying communities.

freeway
Large thoroughfare with separate one-way lanes and no crossing streets; reserved for high-speed traffic.

landfill
Site designated for waste disposal.

main zones

interchange
Construction connecting several roads or highways that meet without crossing.

residential district
Zone reserved almost exclusively for housing.

suburb
A smaller community within commuting distance of a city.

country
Land and housing outside a developed area.

commercial zone
Zone reserved almost exclusively for business.

stadium
Large building that is covered or uncovered and surrounded by grandstands; it contains a field used for athletic events.

shopping mall
Covered space that houses retail stores, one or more megastores and various services such as banks and restaurants.

downtown
Central district of a city where the main cultural, economic and commercial activities are carried out.

refinery
Plant where substances such as sugar and oil are processed.

industrial area
Zone reserved almost exclusively for industry.

sports complex
Installations (buildings, playing fields, etc.) that are used for participating in sports.

port
Area designed for shipping activities.

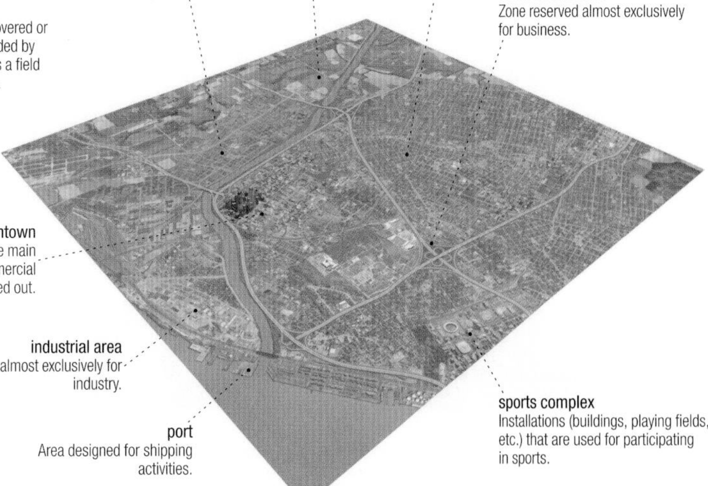

downtown

Central district of a city where the main cultural, economic and commercial activities are carried out.

general view

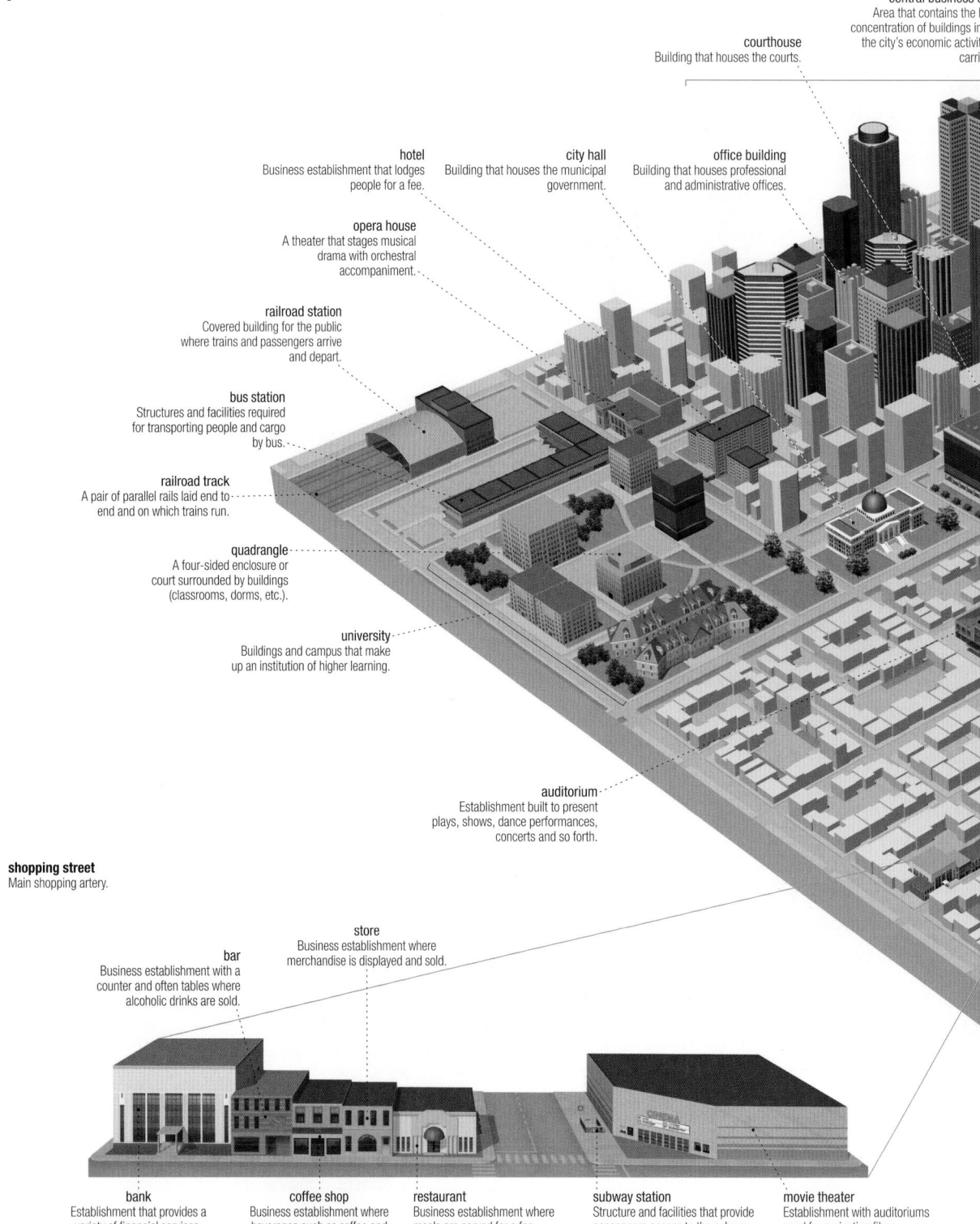

central business distr
Area that contains the highe
concentration of buildings in wh
the city's economic activities a
carried o

courthouse
Building that houses the courts.

hotel
Business establishment that lodges
people for a fee.

city hall
Building that houses the municipal
government.

office building
Building that houses professional
and administrative offices.

opera house
A theater that stages musical
drama with orchestral
accompaniment.

railroad station
Covered building for the public
where trains and passengers arrive
and depart.

bus station
Structures and facilities required
for transporting people and cargo
by bus.

railroad track
A pair of parallel rails laid end to
end and on which trains run.

quadrangle
A four-sided enclosure or
court surrounded by buildings
(classrooms, dorms, etc.).

university
Buildings and campus that make
up an institution of higher learning.

auditorium
Establishment built to present
plays, shows, dance performances,
concerts and so forth.

shopping street
Main shopping artery.

store
Business establishment where
merchandise is displayed and sold.

bar
Business establishment with a
counter and often tables where
alcoholic drinks are sold.

bank
Establishment that provides a
variety of financial services.

coffee shop
Business establishment where
beverages such as coffee and
sometimes light meals are served
for a fee.

restaurant
Business establishment where
meals are served for a fee.

subway station
Structure and facilities that provide
passengers access to the subway.

movie theater
Establishment with auditoriums
used for projecting films.

SOCIETY

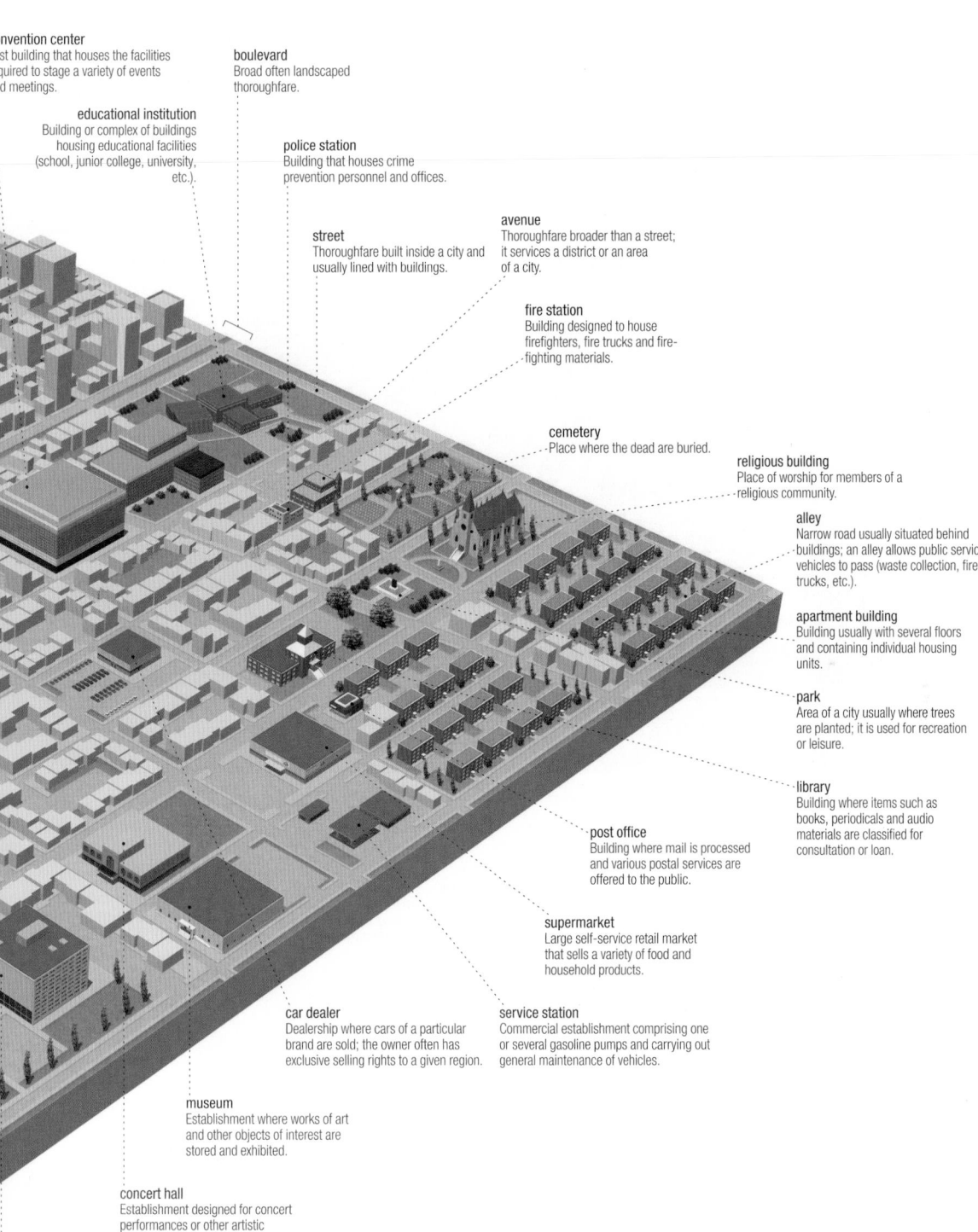

convention center
Vast building that houses the facilities required to stage a variety of events and meetings.

boulevard
Broad often landscaped thoroughfare.

educational institution
Building or complex of buildings housing educational facilities (school, junior college, university, etc.).

police station
Building that houses crime prevention personnel and offices.

street
Thoroughfare built inside a city and usually lined with buildings.

avenue
Thoroughfare broader than a street; it services a district or an area of a city.

fire station
Building designed to house firefighters, fire trucks and fire-fighting materials.

cemetery
Place where the dead are buried.

religious building
Place of worship for members of a religious community.

alley
Narrow road usually situated behind buildings; an alley allows public service vehicles to pass (waste collection, fire trucks, etc.).

apartment building
Building usually with several floors and containing individual housing units.

park
Area of a city usually where trees are planted; it is used for recreation or leisure.

library
Building where items such as books, periodicals and audio materials are classified for consultation or loan.

post office
Building where mail is processed and various postal services are offered to the public.

supermarket
Large self-service retail market that sells a variety of food and household products.

car dealer
Dealership where cars of a particular brand are sold; the owner often has exclusive selling rights to a given region.

service station
Commercial establishment comprising one or several gasoline pumps and carrying out general maintenance of vehicles.

museum
Establishment where works of art and other objects of interest are stored and exhibited.

concert hall
Establishment designed for concert performances or other artistic events.

hospital
Establishment where the sick are given medical and surgical care and where babies are born.

SOCIETY

street

Thoroughfare built inside a city and usually lined with buildings.

section of a street
Depiction of a network of cables and piping systems buried beneath a roadway.

street light
Automated device used to illuminate a public thoroughfare.

median strip
A strip separating traffic lanes that go in opposite directions; also called a center divider.

roadway
Surface upon which vehicles drive.

traffic lights
Automated lighting device that controls traffic at some intersections.

fire hydrant
A pipe connected to a water main; firefighters attach their hoses to it to obtain water for fighting fires.

sidewalk
Pedestrian walkway bordering a street.

curb
Masonry construction bordering roadway and built above it to con water flow.

pedestrian crossing
Lane that is reserved for pedestr indicated by stripes painted on th at intersections.

manhole
Hole with a removable cover for accessing the water mains.

bus stop
Area where buses stop to let passengers on and off.

storm drain
Conduit connecting a building's downspout to the sewer.

barrier
Movable fence placed across the roadway, sidewalk or elsewhere to redirect traffic.

bus shelter
Covered shelter for public transit users.

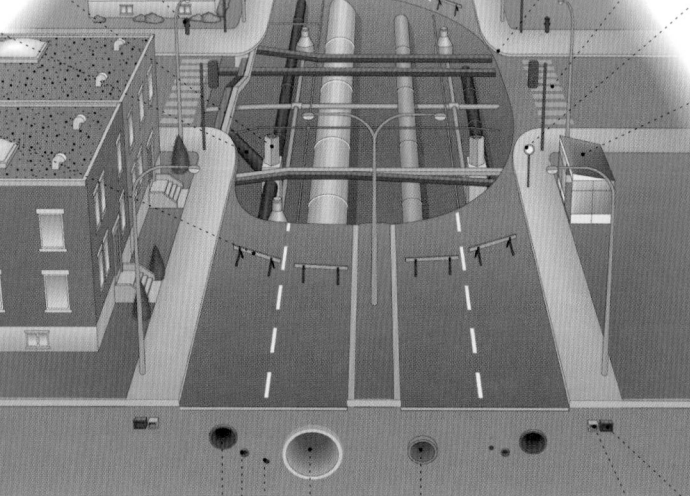

sewer
Pipe that collects wastewater and runoff and conveys them to the main sewer.

service main
Extremely high-flow pipe linked to smaller distribution pipes with far smaller volumes of flow.

electrical cable
Cable linking an electrical power s to its users.

main sewer
Large-diameter pipe that collects wastewater and sewer runoff and conveys them to a treatment plant.

telephone cable
Cable linking a telephone exchange to its users.

traffic lights
Automated lighting device that controls traffic at some intersections.

red light
The red traffic light means "stop".

yellow light
The yellow traffic light means to slow down and prepare to stop at an intersection.

green light
The green traffic light means "go".

gas main
Pipe that conveys gas to buildings and houses.

water main
Pipe that conveys drinking water to buildings and residences.

pedestrian light
Automated lighting device that controls pedestrian traffic at some intersections.

pedestrian call button
Manual control used to obtain a green light.

office building

Building that houses professional and administrative offices.

general view

panoramic window
Large window set into a wall; it provides a wide view of the surrounding area.

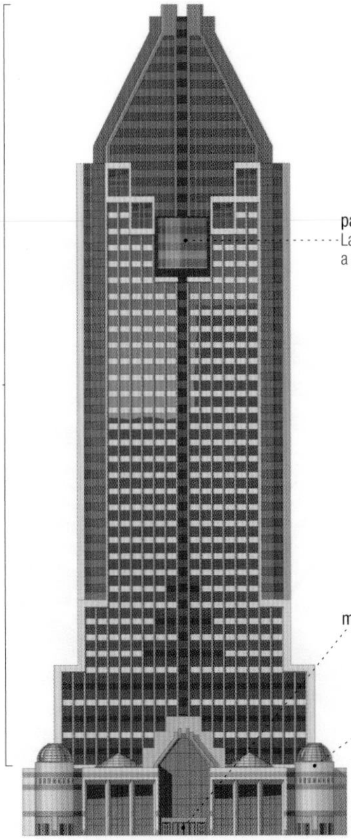

office tower
Tall building that houses offices.

main entrance

rotunda
Circular building often topped with a dome.

podium
Broad spacious section of a building made up of one or more floors and located at the base of a building; the tower rises above it.

podium and basement

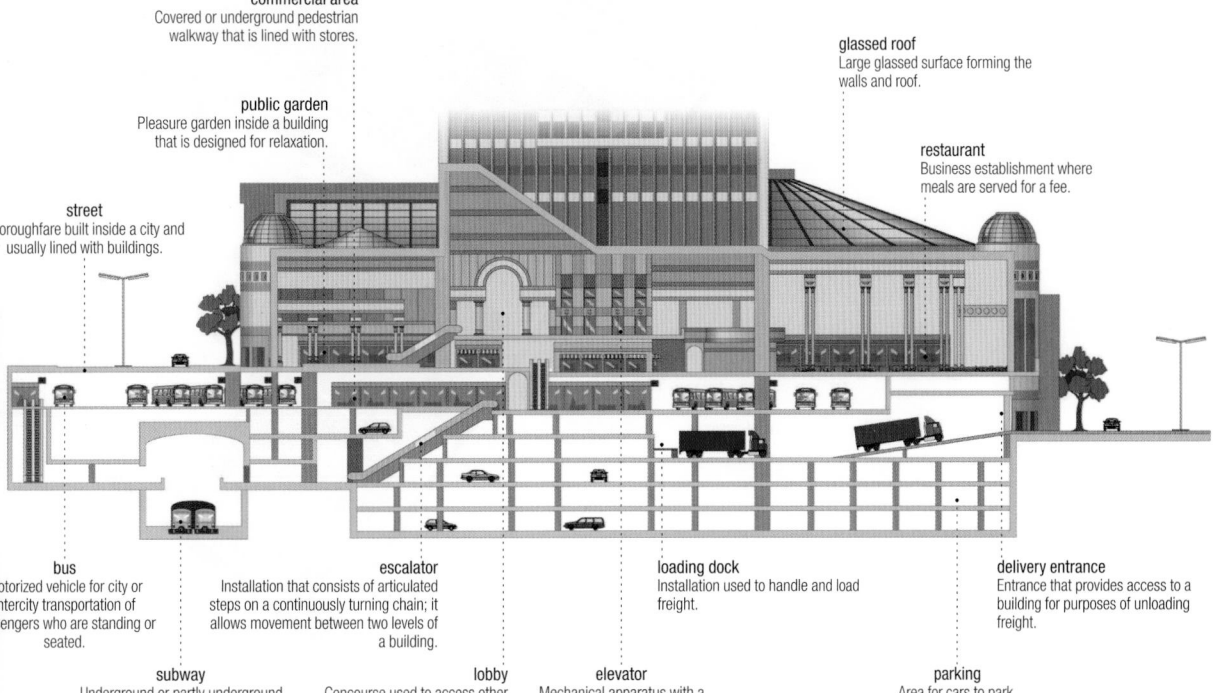

commercial area
Covered or underground pedestrian walkway that is lined with stores.

glassed roof
Large glassed surface forming the walls and roof.

public garden
Pleasure garden inside a building that is designed for relaxation.

restaurant
Business establishment where meals are served for a fee.

street
Thoroughfare built inside a city and usually lined with buildings.

bus
Motorized vehicle for city or intercity transportation of passengers who are standing or seated.

escalator
Installation that consists of articulated steps on a continuously turning chain; it allows movement between two levels of a building.

loading dock
Installation used to handle and load freight.

delivery entrance
Entrance that provides access to a building for purposes of unloading freight.

subway
Underground or partly underground train that runs on electric tracks and serves a city's districts.

lobby
Concourse used to access other rooms as well as stairs and elevators.

elevator
Mechanical apparatus with a car that provides automated movement of people between the levels of a building.

parking
Area for cars to park.

SOCIETY

shopping mall

Covered space that houses retail stores, one or more megastores and various services such as banks and restaurants.

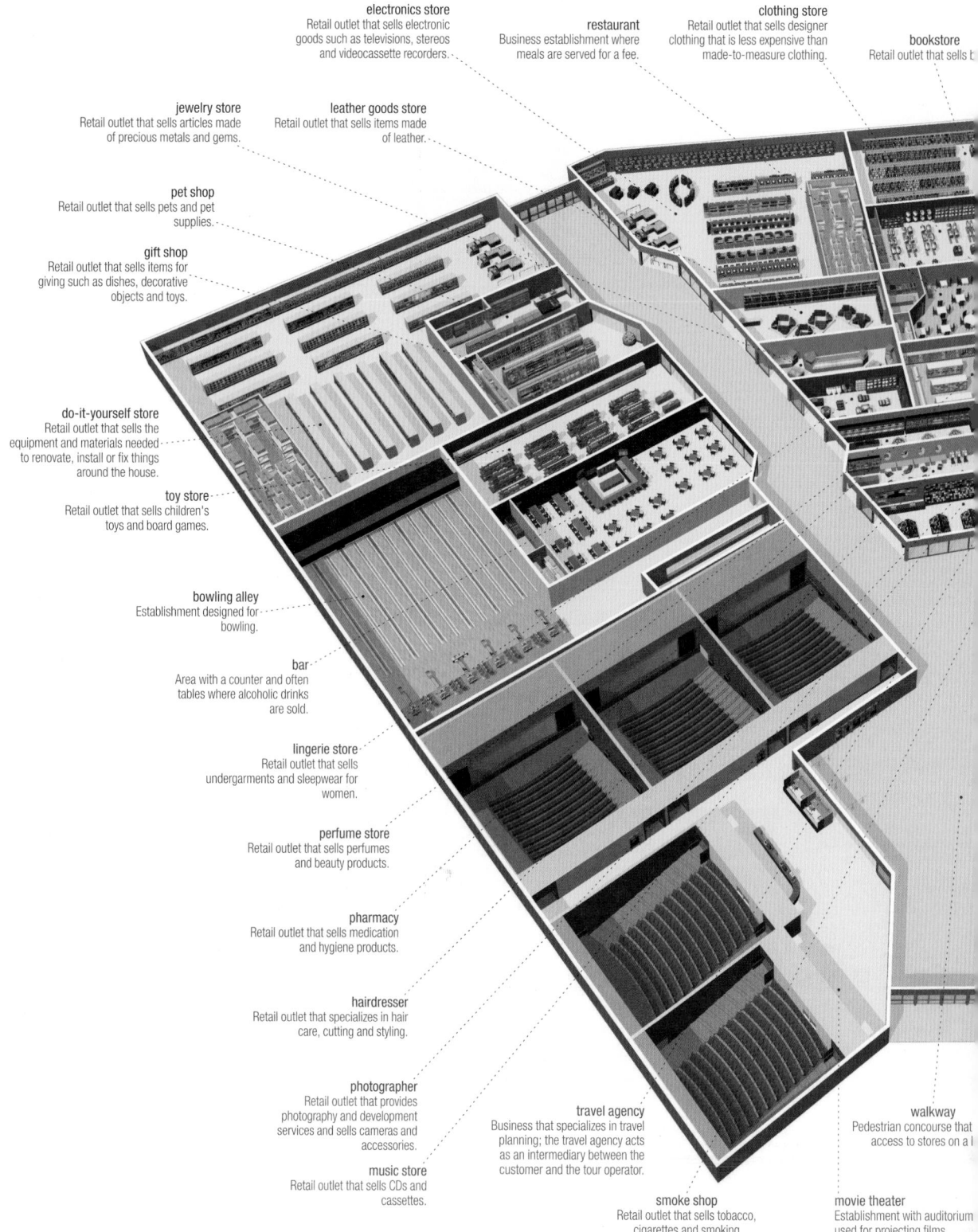

electronics store
Retail outlet that sells electronic goods such as televisions, stereos and videocassette recorders.

restaurant
Business establishment where meals are served for a fee.

clothing store
Retail outlet that sells designer clothing that is less expensive than made-to-measure clothing.

bookstore
Retail outlet that sells b

jewelry store
Retail outlet that sells articles made of precious metals and gems.

leather goods store
Retail outlet that sells items made of leather.

pet shop
Retail outlet that sells pets and pet supplies.

gift shop
Retail outlet that sells items for giving such as dishes, decorative objects and toys.

do-it-yourself store
Retail outlet that sells the equipment and materials needed to renovate, install or fix things around the house.

toy store
Retail outlet that sells children's toys and board games.

bowling alley
Establishment designed for bowling.

bar
Area with a counter and often tables where alcoholic drinks are sold.

lingerie store
Retail outlet that sells undergarments and sleepwear for women.

perfume store
Retail outlet that sells perfumes and beauty products.

pharmacy
Retail outlet that sells medication and hygiene products.

hairdresser
Retail outlet that specializes in hair care, cutting and styling.

photographer
Retail outlet that provides photography and development services and sells cameras and accessories.

music store
Retail outlet that sells CDs and cassettes.

travel agency
Business that specializes in travel planning; the travel agency acts as an intermediary between the customer and the tour operator.

smoke shop
Retail outlet that sells tobacco, cigarettes and smoking accessories.

walkway
Pedestrian concourse that access to stores on a l

movie theater
Establishment with auditorium used for projecting films.

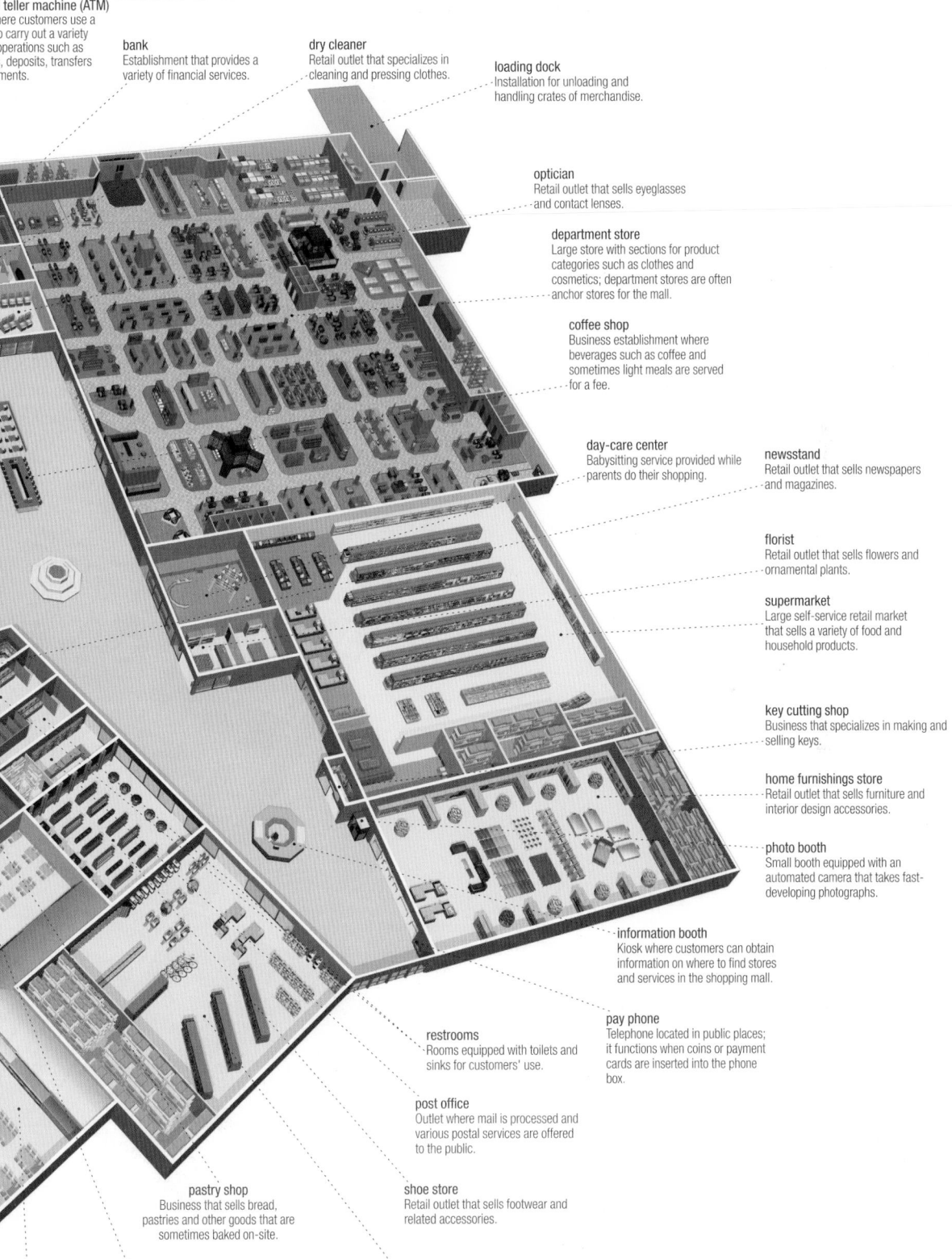

ed teller machine (ATM)
where customers use a
to carry out a variety
ls, deposits, transfers
ayments.

bank
Establishment that provides a
variety of financial services.

dry cleaner
Retail outlet that specializes in
cleaning and pressing clothes.

loading dock
Installation for unloading and
handling crates of merchandise.

optician
Retail outlet that sells eyeglasses
and contact lenses.

department store
Large store with sections for product
categories such as clothes and
cosmetics; department stores are often
anchor stores for the mall.

coffee shop
Business establishment where
beverages such as coffee and
sometimes light meals are served
for a fee.

day-care center
Babysitting service provided while
parents do their shopping.

newsstand
Retail outlet that sells newspapers
and magazines.

florist
Retail outlet that sells flowers and
ornamental plants.

supermarket
Large self-service retail market
that sells a variety of food and
household products.

key cutting shop
Business that specializes in making and
selling keys.

home furnishings store
Retail outlet that sells furniture and
interior design accessories.

photo booth
Small booth equipped with an
automated camera that takes fast-
developing photographs.

information booth
Kiosk where customers can obtain
information on where to find stores
and services in the shopping mall.

pay phone
Telephone located in public places;
it functions when coins or payment
cards are inserted into the phone
box.

restrooms
Rooms equipped with toilets and
sinks for customers' use.

post office
Outlet where mail is processed and
various postal services are offered
to the public.

pastry shop
Business that sells bread,
pastries and other goods that are
sometimes baked on-site.

shoe store
Retail outlet that sells footwear and
related accessories.

food court
f the mall where fast-food
ants serve inexpensive
idly prepared food.

bench
Long narrow unupholstered seat
with or without a back, seating
several people.

sporting goods store
Retail outlet that sells sports articles
such as sportswear, equipment and
accessories.

SOCIETY

department store

Large store with sections (departments) for various product categories such as clothes, stationery and cosmetics.

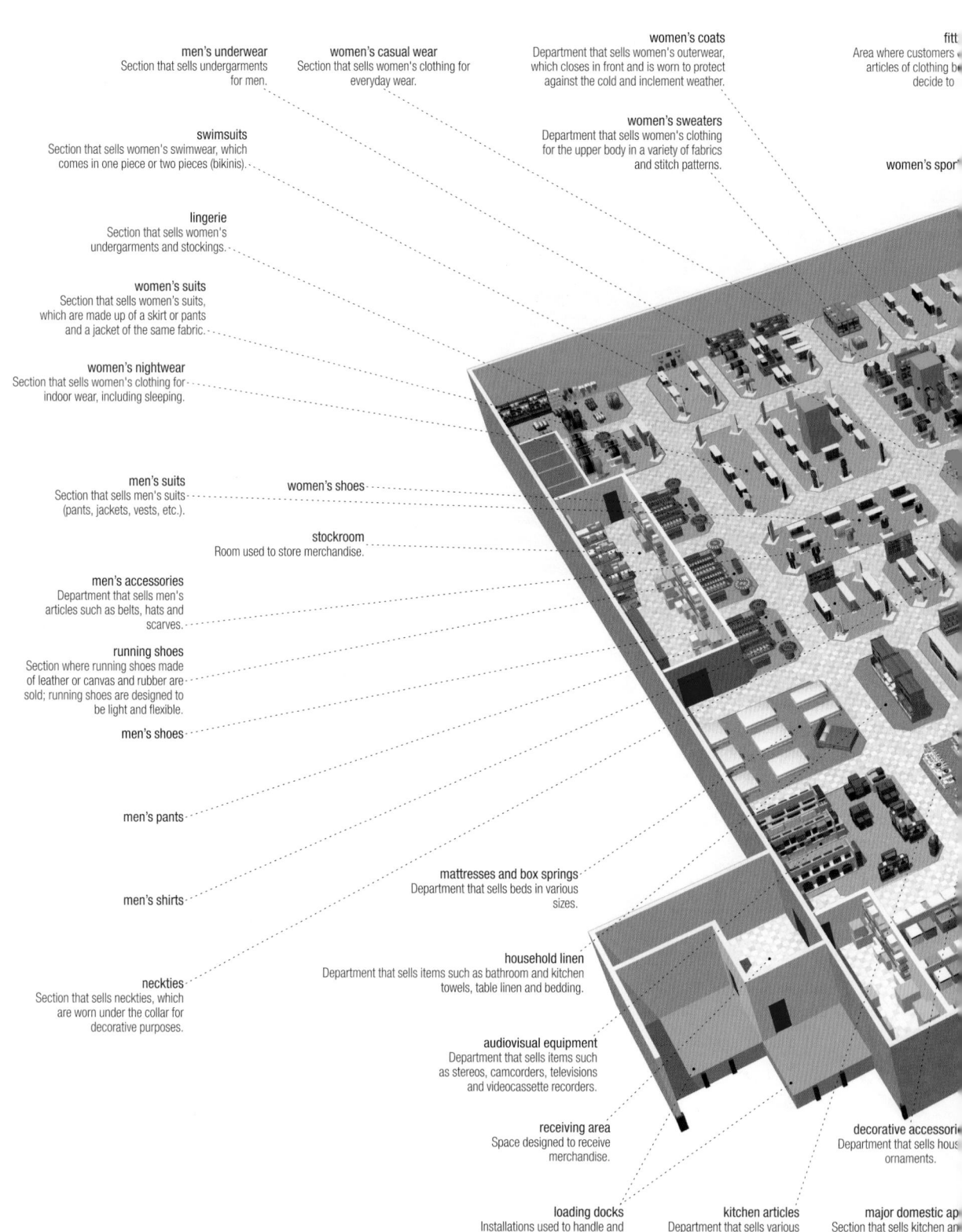

men's underwear
Section that sells undergarments for men.

women's casual wear
Section that sells women's clothing for everyday wear.

women's coats
Department that sells women's outerwear, which closes in front and is worn to protect against the cold and inclement weather.

fitt
Area where customers •
articles of clothing b•
decide to

swimsuits
Section that sells women's swimwear, which comes in one piece or two pieces (bikinis).

women's sweaters
Department that sells women's clothing for the upper body in a variety of fabrics and stitch patterns.

women's spor

lingerie
Section that sells women's undergarments and stockings.

women's suits
Section that sells women's suits, which are made up of a skirt or pants and a jacket of the same fabric.

women's nightwear
Section that sells women's clothing for indoor wear, including sleeping.

men's suits
Section that sells men's suits (pants, jackets, vests, etc.).

women's shoes

stockroom
Room used to store merchandise.

men's accessories
Department that sells men's articles such as belts, hats and scarves.

running shoes
Section where running shoes made of leather or canvas and rubber are sold; running shoes are designed to be light and flexible.

men's shoes

men's pants

men's shirts

mattresses and box springs
Department that sells beds in various sizes.

household linen
Department that sells items such as bathroom and kitchen towels, table linen and bedding.

neckties
Section that sells neckties, which are worn under the collar for decorative purposes.

audiovisual equipment
Department that sells items such as stereos, camcorders, televisions and videocassette recorders.

receiving area
Space designed to receive merchandise.

decorative accessori•
Department that sells hous•
ornaments.

loading docks
Installations used to handle and unload crates and pallets of merchandise.

kitchen articles
Department that sells various utensils, articles for baking, cookware, etc.

major domestic ap•
Section that sells kitchen an•
appliances such as refr•
stoves, dishwashers,
machines ar•

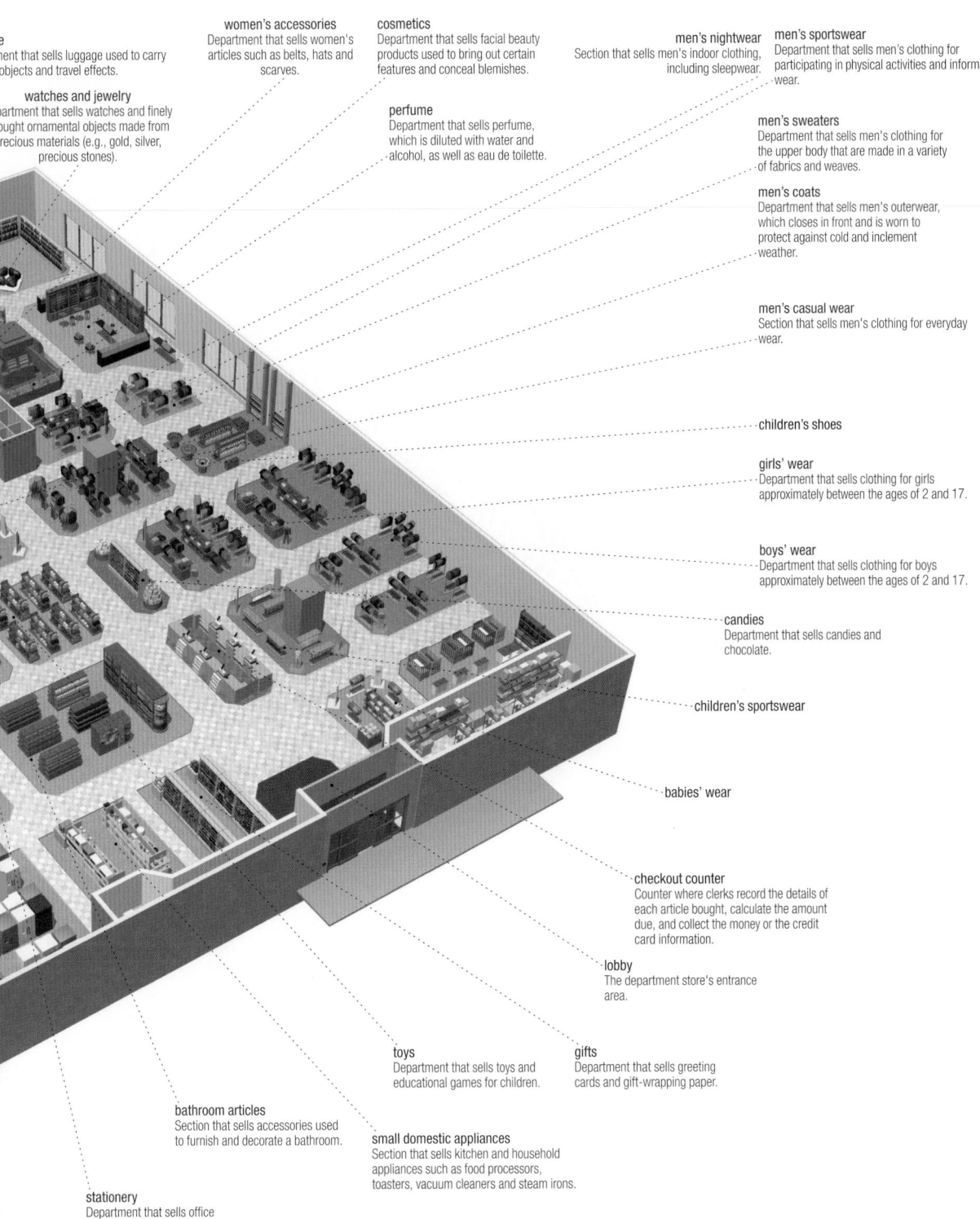

ge
ment that sells luggage used to carry
objects and travel effects.

watches and jewelry
epartment that sells watches and finely
rought ornamental objects made from
precious materials (e.g., gold, silver,
precious stones).

women's accessories
Department that sells women's
articles such as belts, hats and
scarves.

cosmetics
Department that sells facial beauty
products used to bring out certain
features and conceal blemishes.

perfume
Department that sells perfume,
which is diluted with water and
alcohol, as well as eau de toilette.

men's nightwear
Section that sells men's indoor clothing,
including sleepwear.

men's sportswear
Department that sells men's clothing for
participating in physical activities and informal
wear.

men's sweaters
Department that sells men's clothing for
the upper body that are made in a variety
of fabrics and weaves.

men's coats
Department that sells men's outerwear,
which closes in front and is worn to
protect against cold and inclement
weather.

men's casual wear
Section that sells men's clothing for everyday
wear.

children's shoes

girls' wear
Department that sells clothing for girls
approximately between the ages of 2 and 17.

boys' wear
Department that sells clothing for boys
approximately between the ages of 2 and 17.

candies
Department that sells candies and
chocolate.

children's sportswear

babies' wear

checkout counter
Counter where clerks record the details of
each article bought, calculate the amount
due, and collect the money or the credit
card information.

lobby
The department store's entrance
area.

toys
Department that sells toys and
educational games for children.

gifts
Department that sells greeting
cards and gift-wrapping paper.

bathroom articles
Section that sells accessories used
to furnish and decorate a bathroom.

small domestic appliances
Section that sells kitchen and household
appliances such as food processors,
toasters, vacuum cleaners and steam irons.

stationery
Department that sells office
supplies.

dinnerware, glassware and silverware
Section that sells articles used to serve food and drinks.

SOCIETY

convention center

Vast building that houses the facilities required to stage a variety of events and meetings.

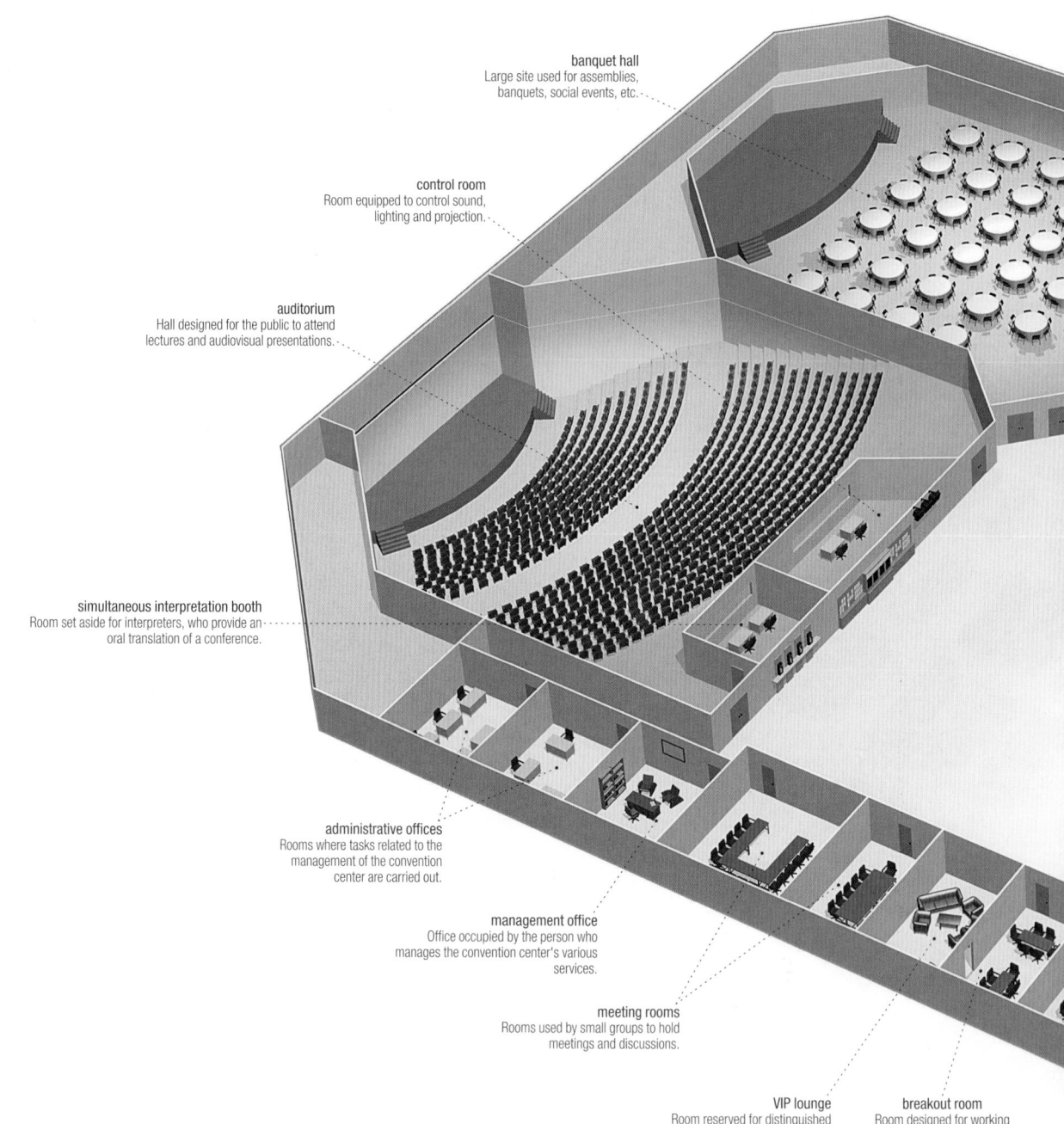

banquet hall
Large site used for assemblies, banquets, social events, etc.

control room
Room equipped to control sound, lighting and projection.

auditorium
Hall designed for the public to attend lectures and audiovisual presentations.

simultaneous interpretation booth
Room set aside for interpreters, who provide an oral translation of a conference.

administrative offices
Rooms where tasks related to the management of the convention center are carried out.

management office
Office occupied by the person who manages the convention center's various services.

meeting rooms
Rooms used by small groups to hold meetings and discussions.

VIP lounge
Room reserved for distinguished guests.

breakout room
Room designed for working sessions involving small groups.

conference room
Room that is big enough to hold a relatively large number of people.

convention center

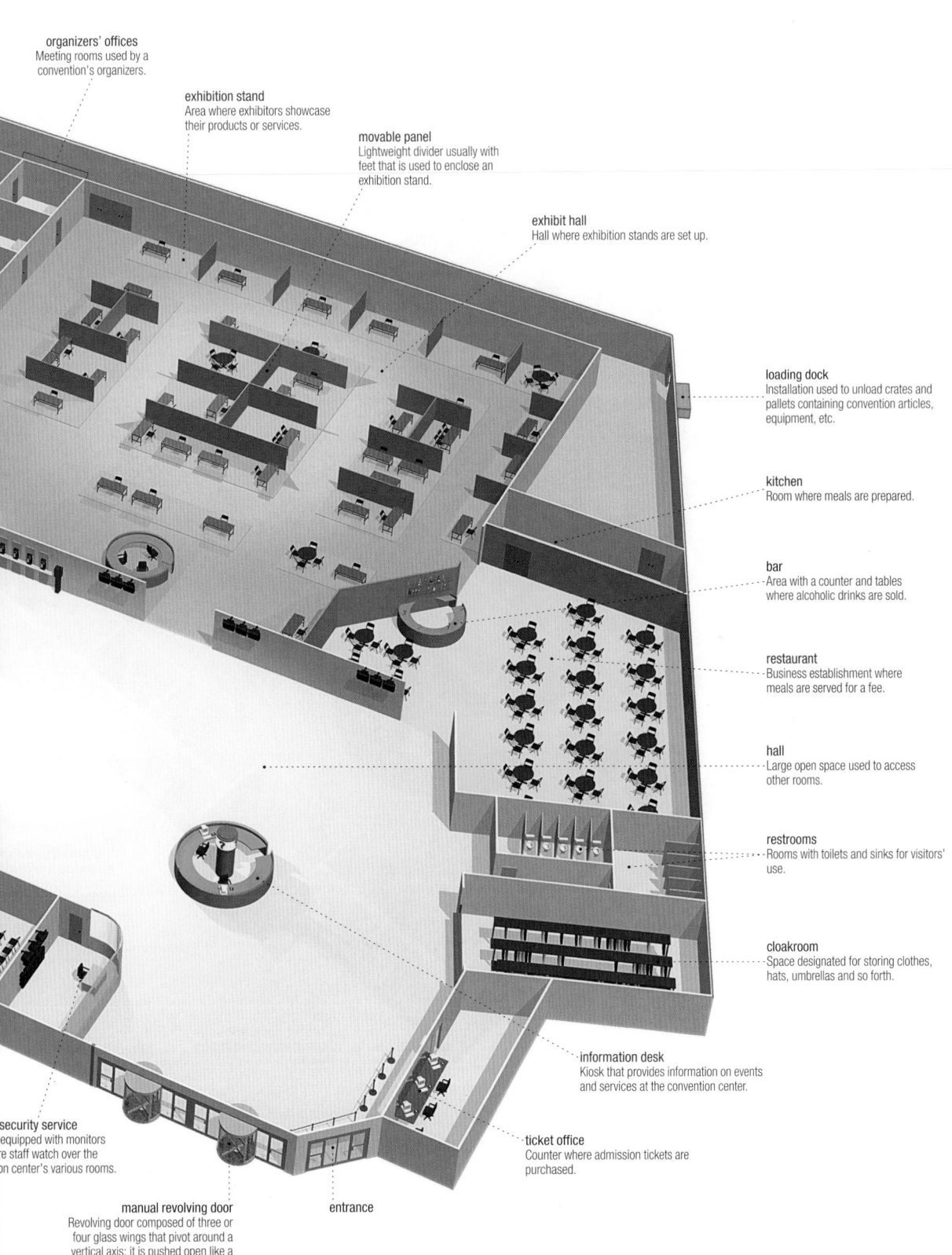

organizers' offices
Meeting rooms used by a convention's organizers.

exhibition stand
Area where exhibitors showcase their products or services.

movable panel
Lightweight divider usually with feet that is used to enclose an exhibition stand.

exhibit hall
Hall where exhibition stands are set up.

loading dock
Installation used to unload crates and pallets containing convention articles, equipment, etc.

kitchen
Room where meals are prepared.

bar
Area with a counter and tables where alcoholic drinks are sold.

restaurant
Business establishment where meals are served for a fee.

hall
Large open space used to access other rooms.

restrooms
Rooms with toilets and sinks for visitors' use.

cloakroom
Space designated for storing clothes, hats, umbrellas and so forth.

information desk
Kiosk that provides information on events and services at the convention center.

security service
equipped with monitors re staff watch over the on center's various rooms.

ticket office
Counter where admission tickets are purchased.

manual revolving door
Revolving door composed of three or four glass wings that pivot around a vertical axis; it is pushed open like a turnstile.

entrance

hotel

Business establishment that lodges people for a fee.

reception level
The ground floor of the hotel.

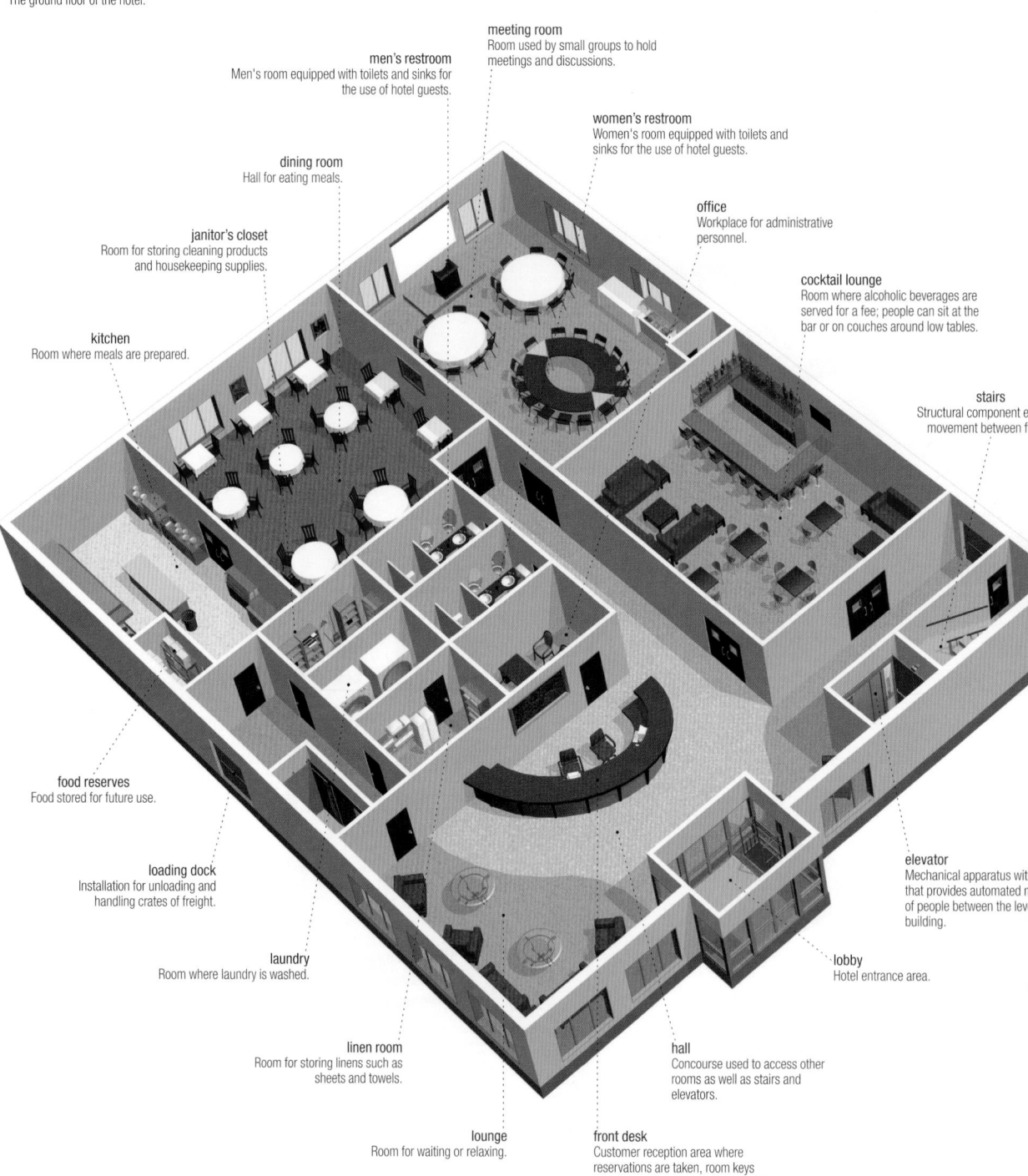

meeting room
Room used by small groups to hold meetings and discussions.

men's restroom
Men's room equipped with toilets and sinks for the use of hotel guests.

women's restroom
Women's room equipped with toilets and sinks for the use of hotel guests.

dining room
Hall for eating meals.

office
Workplace for administrative personnel.

janitor's closet
Room for storing cleaning products and housekeeping supplies.

cocktail lounge
Room where alcoholic beverages are served for a fee; people can sit at the bar or on couches around low tables.

kitchen
Room where meals are prepared.

stairs
Structural component e movement between fl

food reserves
Food stored for future use.

elevator
Mechanical apparatus with that provides automated m of people between the leve building.

loading dock
Installation for unloading and handling crates of freight.

lobby
Hotel entrance area.

laundry
Room where laundry is washed.

linen room
Room for storing linens such as sheets and towels.

hall
Concourse used to access other rooms as well as stairs and elevators.

lounge
Room for waiting or relaxing.

front desk
Customer reception area where reservations are taken, room keys are given out and hotel bills are paid.

hotel

hotel rooms
Rooms designed to lodge people.

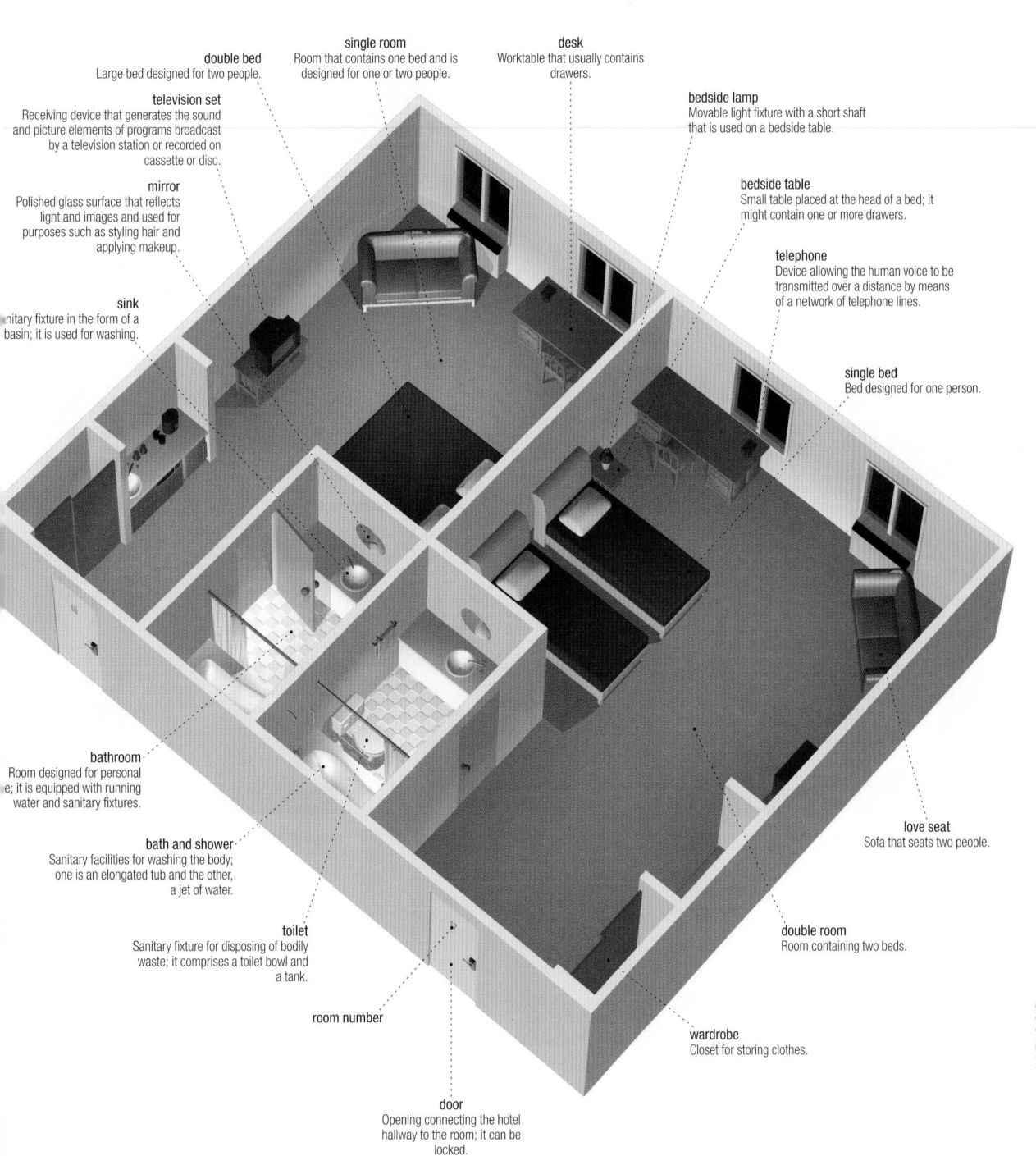

single room
Room that contains one bed and is designed for one or two people.

double bed
Large bed designed for two people.

desk
Worktable that usually contains drawers.

bedside lamp
Movable light fixture with a short shaft that is used on a bedside table.

television set
Receiving device that generates the sound and picture elements of programs broadcast by a television station or recorded on cassette or disc.

bedside table
Small table placed at the head of a bed; it might contain one or more drawers.

mirror
Polished glass surface that reflects light and images and used for purposes such as styling hair and applying makeup.

telephone
Device allowing the human voice to be transmitted over a distance by means of a network of telephone lines.

sink
Sanitary fixture in the form of a basin; it is used for washing.

single bed
Bed designed for one person.

bathroom
Room designed for personal [...]e; it is equipped with running water and sanitary fixtures.

love seat
Sofa that seats two people.

bath and shower
Sanitary facilities for washing the body; one is an elongated tub and the other, a jet of water.

toilet
Sanitary fixture for disposing of bodily waste; it comprises a toilet bowl and a tank.

double room
Room containing two beds.

room number

wardrobe
Closet for storing clothes.

door
Opening connecting the hotel hallway to the room; it can be locked.

SOCIETY

common symbols

Pictograms used in public areas or along thoroughfares to advertise services or warn of prohibitions.

men's restroom
Men's room equipped with toilets and sinks.

women's restroom
Women's room equipped with toilets and sinks.

wheelchair access

no wheelchair access

picnic area

picnics prohibited

camping (tent)

camping prohibited

coffee shop

restaurant

service station

camping (trailer)

camping (trailer and tent)

police

hospital

first aid

pharmacy

fire extinguisher

common symbols

escalator

stairs

elevator

dogs prohibited

car rental

baggage lockers

lodging

no smoking

bus stop

airport

post office

taxi transportation

telephone

information

information

lost and found articles

currency exchange

SOCIETY

bank branch

Establishment that provides a variety of financial services.

automated teller machine (ATM)
Machine where customers use a debit card to carry out a variety of banking operations such as withdrawals, deposits, transfers and bill payments.

operation keys
Keys for using an on-screen menu to choose from items such as accounts, withdrawals, deposits and account balances.

deposit slot
Cash and check deposits and bill payments are enclosed in an envelope and inserted into this slot.

display
Screen featuring various menus and indicating the steps to follow to complete a transaction.

card reader slot
The card is inserted into the device, which verifies the customer's personal identification number (PIN) before the transaction can begin.

transaction record slot
Receipt or record of a transaction that is printed after the transaction is complete.

waiting area
Space reserved for customers waiting for an appointment in a specific department.

professional training office
Room reserved for providing training employees.

insurance services
Offices where customers consult bank staff about insurance services for automobiles, travel, homes, etc.

brochure rack
Rack used to display brochures and flyers containing information on services offered by the bank.

financial services
Offices where bank staff meet with customers to discuss financial services such as mortgages and investments.

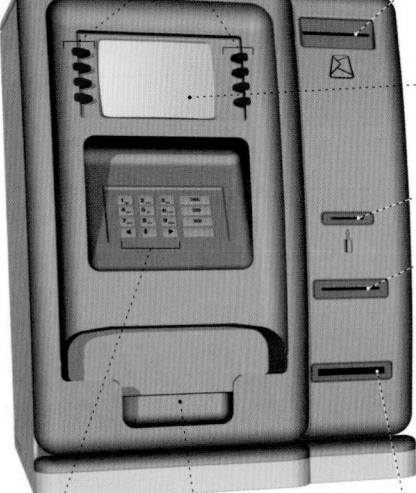

alphanumeric keyboard
Series of keys corresponding to letters and numbers that the customer uses to enter personal data such as a personal identification number and a transaction amount.

cash dispenser
The machine is equipped with an optical device that calculates the number of banknotes to be issued.

passbook update slot
Customers can print out their account balances before or after a transaction.

conference room
Room that is big enough to hold a relatively large number of people.

photocopier
Machine for reprography.

information desk
Kiosk where customers can obtain information about banking services.

loan services
Offices where bank staff meet with customers who are applying for a loan.

reception desk
Area where customers are met.

meeting room
Room used by small groups to hold meetings and discussions.

security grille
Sliding or folding bars that isolate the bank's automatic teller machines when the bank is closed.

lot
The bank's entrance a

bank branch

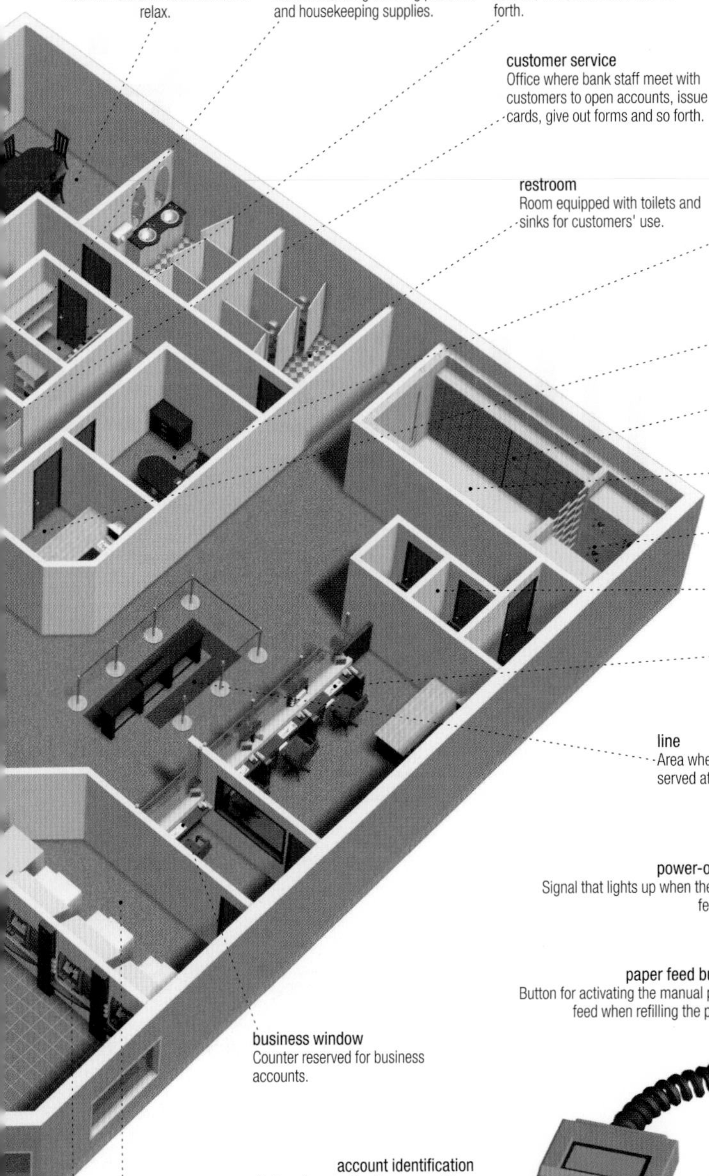

staff lounge
Room where staff eat meals and relax.

janitor's closet
Room for storing cleaning products and housekeeping supplies.

cloakroom
Space designated for storing clothes, hats, umbrellas and so forth.

customer service
Office where bank staff meet with customers to open accounts, issue debit cards, give out forms and so forth.

restroom
Room equipped with toilets and sinks for customers' use.

manager's office

secretary's office

safe deposit box
Compartment rented by customers to store valuable objects and documents in a safe place.

vault
Reinforced fireproof room containing the bank safe and the customers' safe deposit boxes; access to it is tightly controlled.

safe
Reinforced fireproof safe used to hold the bank's cash supply and negotiable documents.

coupon booth
Small closed cubicle used by a customer to open a safe deposit box.

window
Counter where bank tellers serve customers.

line
Area where customers wait to be served at a wicket.

power-on/paper-detect light
Signal that lights up when the machine is on and blinks when the paper feed is complete.

electronic payment terminal
Apparatus by which shoppers can use a debit or credit card to pay for their purchases.

paper feed button
Button for activating the manual paper feed when refilling the paper.

transaction receipt
Receipt or record of a transaction that is printed after the transaction is complete.

display
Screen featuring various menus and indicating the steps to follow to complete a transaction.

operation keys
Keys for selecting from a menu (e.g., debit card, credit card).

business window
Counter reserved for business accounts.

account identification
Buttons for selecting the account from which to make a payment.

card reader slot
The card is inserted into the device, which verifies the customer's personal identification number (PIN) before the transaction can begin.

cash supply
Room where bank staff replenish the automatic teller machines and collect deposits and bills.

programmable function keys
Keys that program the machine to execute specific functions.

automated teller machine (ATM)
Machine where customers use a debit card to carry out a variety of banking operations such as withdrawals, deposits, transfers and bill payments.

night deposit box
Wicket used by business customers outside of banking hours.

personal identification number (PIN) pad
Small keypad connected to an electronic payment terminal; it is used to enter a personal identification number when making a payment.

confirmation key
Button for authorizing the transaction.

alphanumeric keyboard
A series of keys corresponding to letters, numbers and symbols that the customer uses to enter a purchase amount, a PIN, etc.

SOCIETY

examples of currency abbreviations

Currency abbreviation: abbreviation assigned to the currency of a country or group of countries; its reference value is guaranteed by a competent authority, usually a central bank.

cent
A subdivision of certain currencies, including the dollar, the rupee and the shilling.

euro
The euro is the common currency of the countries that belong to the European Union; it was introduced in January 2002.

peso
The peso is the currency of Argentina, Chile, Colombia, Cuba, the Dominican Republic, Mexico, the Philippines, and Uruguay; however, this symbol is used only in the Philippines. Other countries using the peso use the dollar sign as its symbol.

pound
The pound is used in the United Kingdom, Egypt and Lebanon, among other countries; it is the oldest currency in Europe.

dollar
Decimal monetary unit used in certain countries where English is spoken, including Canada, the U.S., Australia and New Zealand.

rupees
The rupee is the currency of India, Nepal, Pakistan, Sri Lanka, Mauritius and the Seychelles; it is a descendant of the silver rupee, which was first used in the 16th century.

new shekel
The new shekel is the currency of Israel; it replaced the old shekel in 1985.

yen
The yen is the currency of Japan; the word means "round" or "circle" in Japanese.

yuan
The yuan is the currency of Chil

money and modes of payment

All the legal instruments of payment issued by a bank.

coin: obverse
The coin is currency in the form of embossed metal; specific coins are characterized by their value, appearance, weight and diameter.

edge
Surface forming the thickness of a coin; it can be smooth, grooved or engraved.

date
The year a coin was issued.

denomination
A coin's value is indicated on the reverse.

coin: reverse

rim
Slightly raised ring marking the edge of a coin.

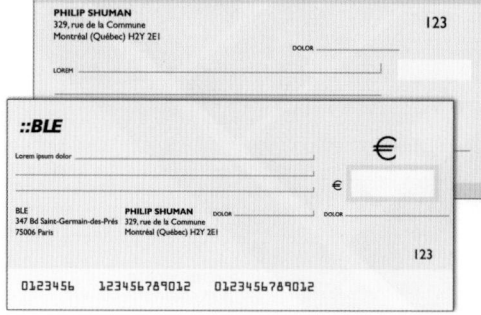

check
Written document by which the owner of the funds authorizes the bank to pay a third party a specific sum from the owner's account.

traveler's check
Check for a specific amount that is issued by a bank and used by travelers in lieu of cash.

money and modes of payment

initials of the issuing bank

security thread
...re to prevent counterfeiting; a dark line that is visible in ...smitted light is inserted into the paper.

hologram foil strip
A feature to prevent counterfeiting; the image on the strip changes when the banknote is tilted.

portrait
Portrait of a famous person such as a prime minister, president, king or queen that appears on a banknote.

banknote: front
A banknote is paper currency issued by a country's central bank or by an economic community.

serial number
Each banknote is identified by a unique combination of numbers and letters.

watermark
A feature to prevent counterfeiting; an image that is visible in transmitted light is incorporated into the paper.

color shifting ink
A feature to prevent counterfeiting; a special ink is used that changes color when viewed from various angles.

official signature
Banknotes are signed by people such as the central bank's governor (Canada) or president (EU) or the Secretary of the Treasury (U.S.).

serial number
Each banknote is identified by a unique combination of numbers and letters.

banknote: back

motto
Saying or maxim that symbolizes a country or expresses an idea or a common experience.

name of the currency

denomination
The value of a banknote is indicated on the front and back.

debit card
A card like a credit card that allows the holder to make electronic payments and to use an automatic teller machine for making withdrawals.

magnetic stripe
Band containing the information required to use a credit card.

cardholder's signature

chip
Microchip that communicates with a terminal with or without contact.

card number

credit card
Card issued by a bank that allows the holder to make a purchase without having to pay immediately.

card number
The card holder's identification number, which validates the person's signature.

cardholder's name
Name of the credit card holder.

expiration date
Date (month and year) beyond which the card is no longer valid.

SOCIETY

court

Place where trials are held before a judge and sometimes a jury to determine if a person accused of a crime is guilty or innocent.

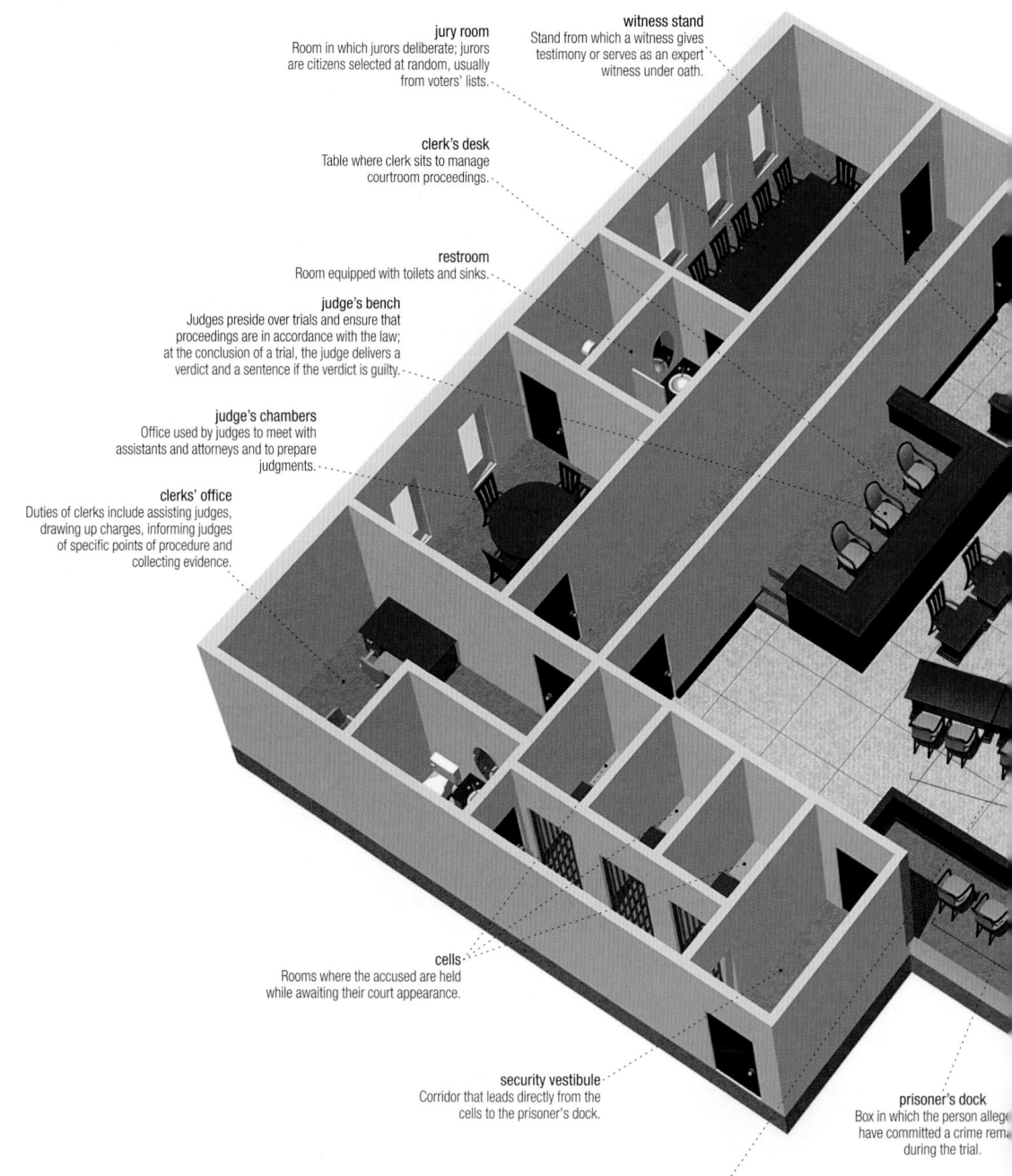

jury room
Room in which jurors deliberate; jurors are citizens selected at random, usually from voters' lists.

witness stand
Stand from which a witness gives testimony or serves as an expert witness under oath.

clerk's desk
Table where clerk sits to manage courtroom proceedings.

restroom
Room equipped with toilets and sinks.

judge's bench
Judges preside over trials and ensure that proceedings are in accordance with the law; at the conclusion of a trial, the judge delivers a verdict and a sentence if the verdict is guilty.

judge's chambers
Office used by judges to meet with assistants and attorneys and to prepare judgments.

clerks' office
Duties of clerks include assisting judges, drawing up charges, informing judges of specific points of procedure and collecting evidence.

cells
Rooms where the accused are held while awaiting their court appearance.

security vestibule
Corridor that leads directly from the cells to the prisoner's dock.

prisoner's dock
Box in which the person allege have committed a crime rema during the trial.

defense counsel's table
Defense attorneys advise and represent the accused and attempt to prove the person's innocence.

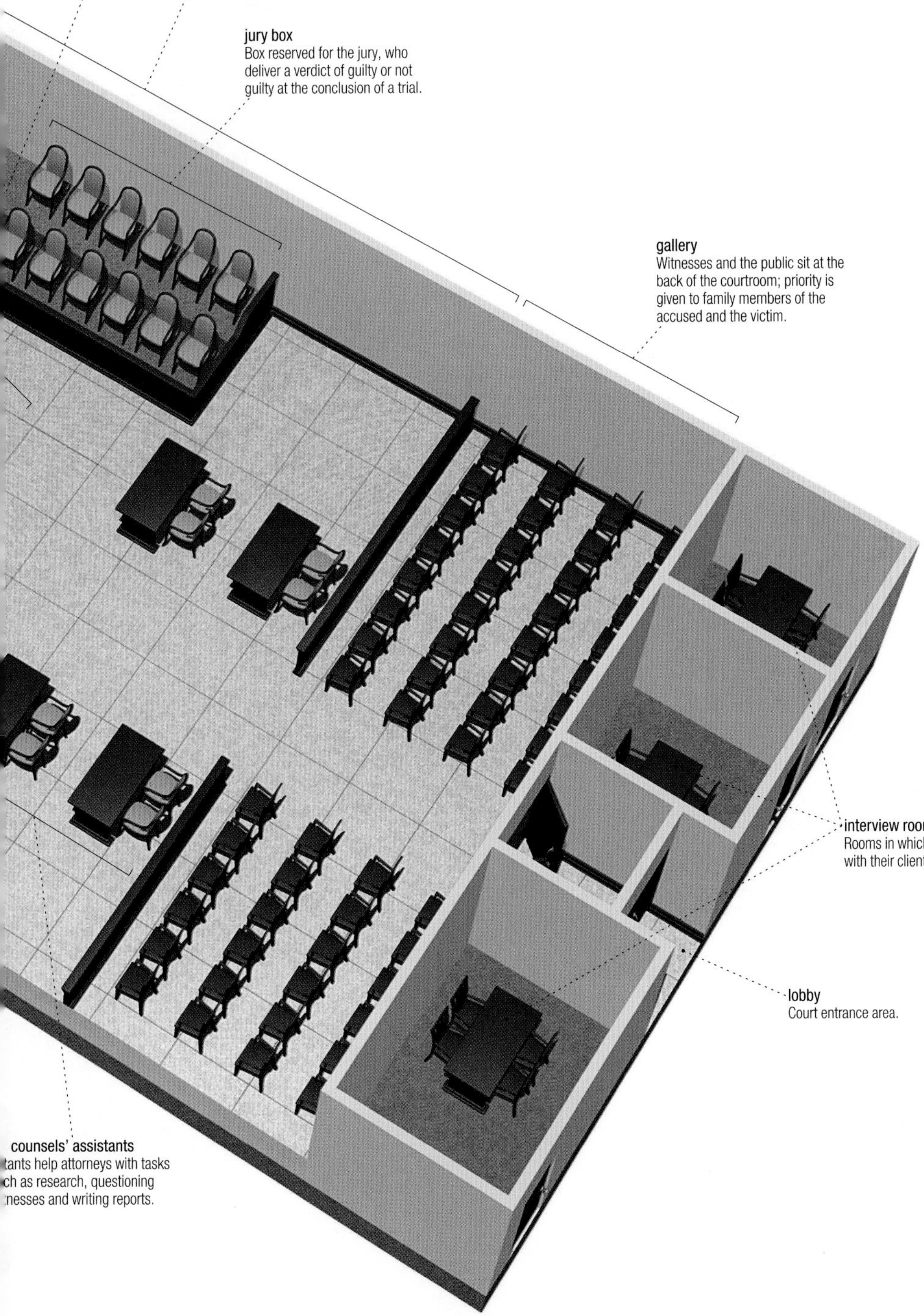

court

prosecution's table
Prosecuting attorneys ensure that laws are enforced on behalf of society; they attempt to prove that the accused is guilty.

courtroom
Area of the court reserved for the main players in a trial, including the judge, jury, accused and attorneys.

jury box
Box reserved for the jury, who deliver a verdict of guilty or not guilty at the conclusion of a trial.

gallery
Witnesses and the public sit at the back of the courtroom; priority is given to family members of the accused and the victim.

interview rooms
Rooms in which attorneys consult with their clients.

lobby
Court entrance area.

counsels' assistants
ants help attorneys with tasks ch as research, questioning nesses and writing reports.

prison

Place of detention designed to hold people awaiting trial and people already serving sentences.

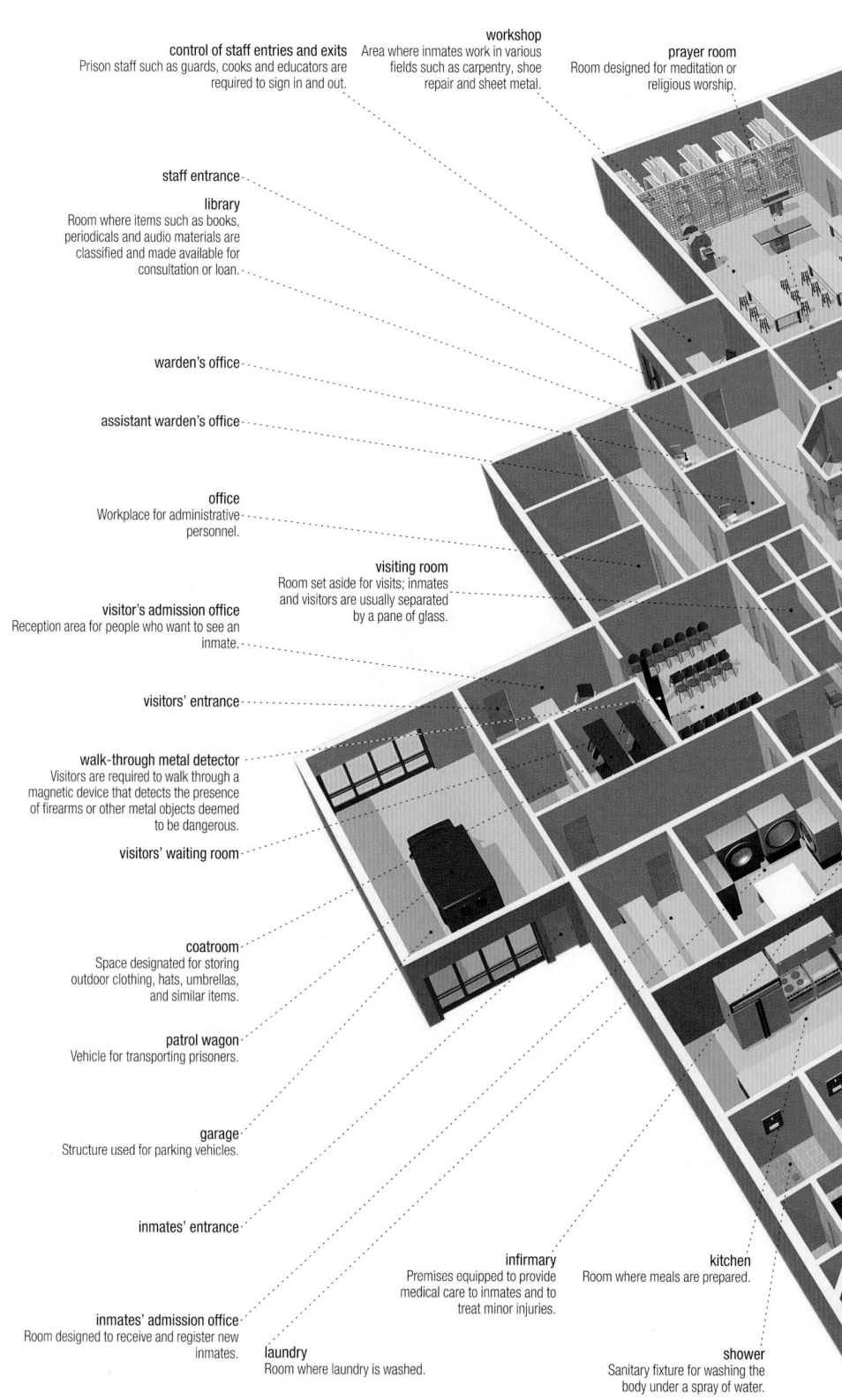

control of staff entries and exits
Prison staff such as guards, cooks and educators are required to sign in and out.

workshop
Area where inmates work in various fields such as carpentry, shoe repair and sheet metal.

prayer room
Room designed for meditation or religious worship.

staff entrance

library
Room where items such as books, periodicals and audio materials are classified and made available for consultation or loan.

warden's office

assistant warden's office

office
Workplace for administrative personnel.

visiting room
Room set aside for visits; inmates and visitors are usually separated by a pane of glass.

visitor's admission office
Reception area for people who want to see an inmate.

visitors' entrance

walk-through metal detector
Visitors are required to walk through a magnetic device that detects the presence of firearms or other metal objects deemed to be dangerous.

visitors' waiting room

coatroom
Space designated for storing outdoor clothing, hats, umbrellas, and similar items.

patrol wagon
Vehicle for transporting prisoners.

garage
Structure used for parking vehicles.

inmates' entrance

infirmary
Premises equipped to provide medical care to inmates and to treat minor injuries.

kitchen
Room where meals are prepared.

inmates' admission office
Room designed to receive and register new inmates.

laundry
Room where laundry is washed.

shower
Sanitary fixture for washing the body under a spray of water.

prison

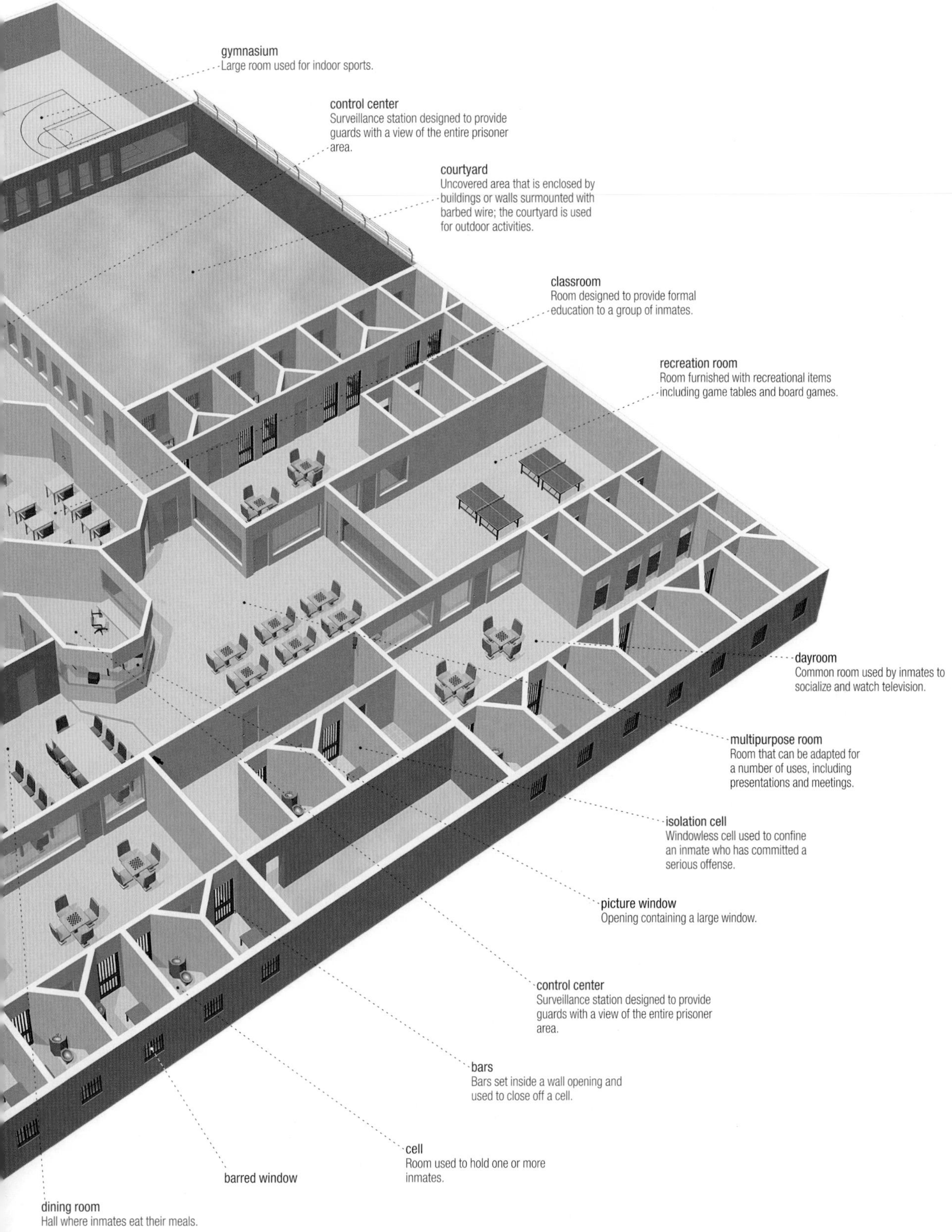

gymnasium
Large room used for indoor sports.

control center
Surveillance station designed to provide guards with a view of the entire prisoner area.

courtyard
Uncovered area that is enclosed by buildings or walls surmounted with barbed wire; the courtyard is used for outdoor activities.

classroom
Room designed to provide formal education to a group of inmates.

recreation room
Room furnished with recreational items including game tables and board games.

dayroom
Common room used by inmates to socialize and watch television.

multipurpose room
Room that can be adapted for a number of uses, including presentations and meetings.

isolation cell
Windowless cell used to confine an inmate who has committed a serious offense.

picture window
Opening containing a large window.

control center
Surveillance station designed to provide guards with a view of the entire prisoner area.

bars
Bars set inside a wall opening and used to close off a cell.

cell
Room used to hold one or more inmates.

barred window

dining room
Hall where inmates eat their meals.

library

Place where items such as books, periodicals and audio materials are classified and made available for consultation or loan.

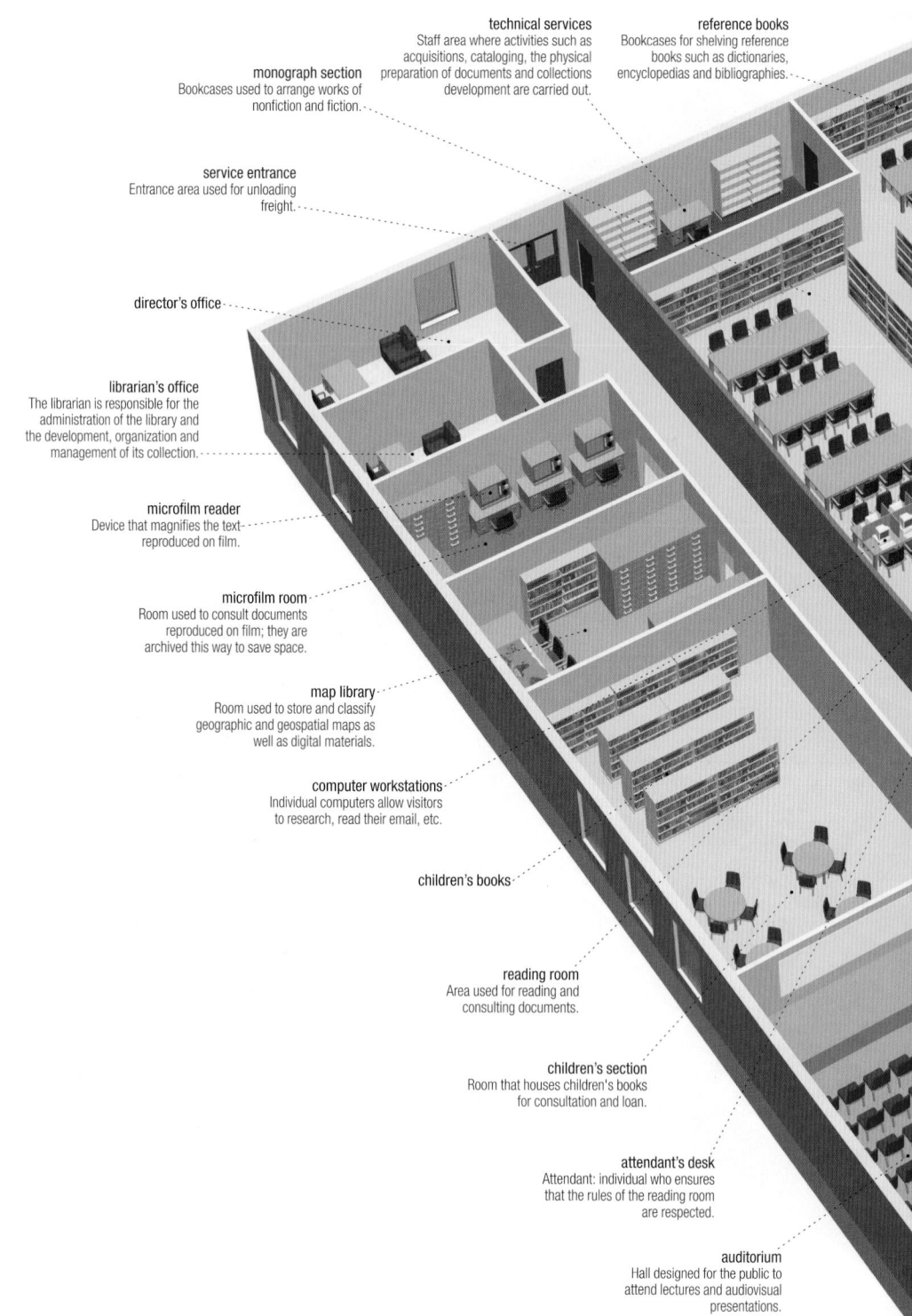

technical services
Staff area where activities such as acquisitions, cataloging, the physical preparation of documents and collections development are carried out.

reference books
Bookcases for shelving reference books such as dictionaries, encyclopedias and bibliographies.

monograph section
Bookcases used to arrange works of nonfiction and fiction.

service entrance
Entrance area used for unloading freight.

director's office

librarian's office
The librarian is responsible for the administration of the library and the development, organization and management of its collection.

microfilm reader
Device that magnifies the text reproduced on film.

microfilm room
Room used to consult documents reproduced on film; they are archived this way to save space.

map library
Room used to store and classify geographic and geospatial maps as well as digital materials.

computer workstations
Individual computers allow visitors to research, read their email, etc.

children's books

reading room
Area used for reading and consulting documents.

children's section
Room that houses children's books for consultation and loan.

attendant's desk
Attendant: individual who ensures that the rules of the reading room are respected.

auditorium
Hall designed for the public to attend lectures and audiovisual presentations.

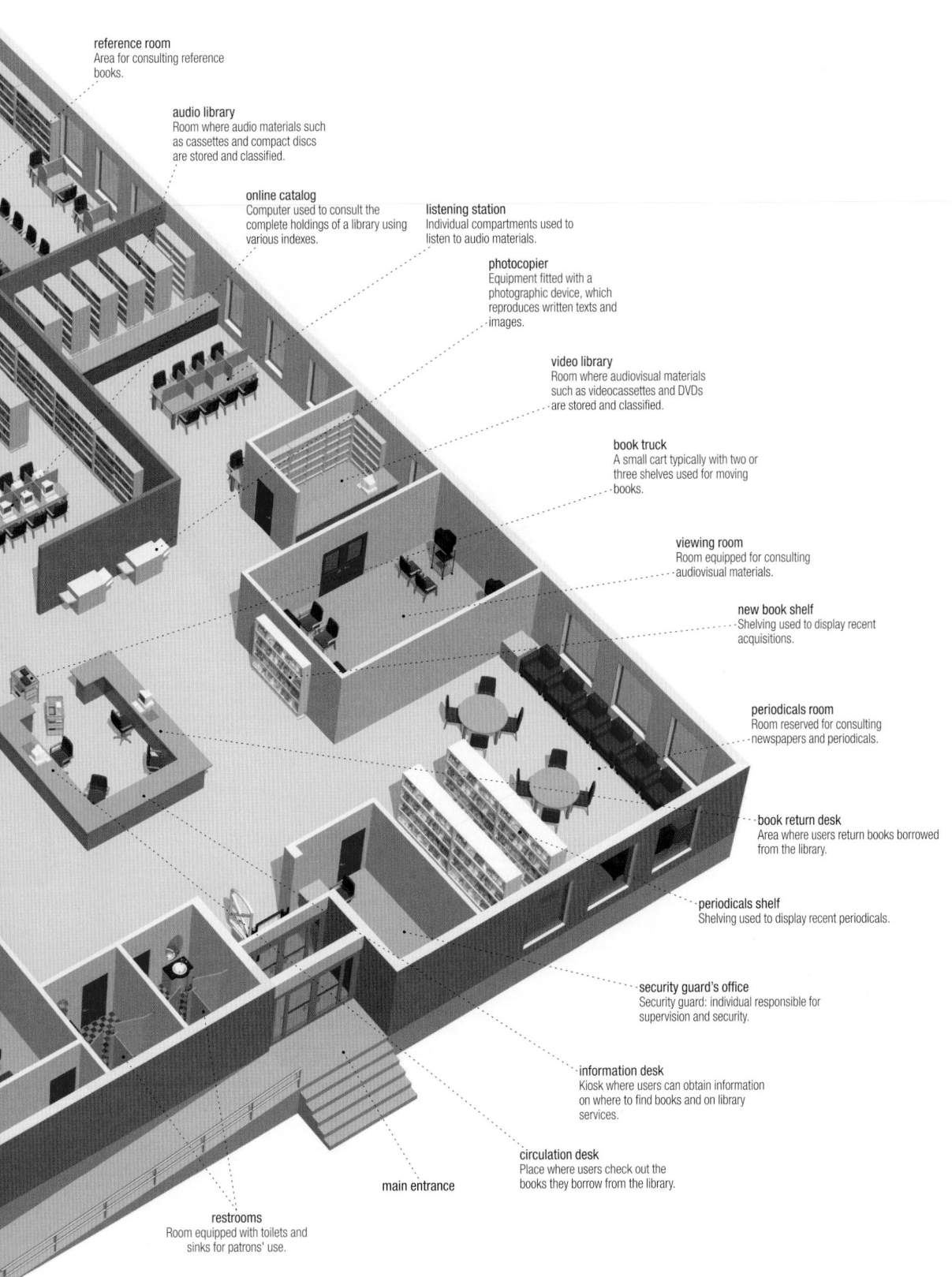

reference room
Area for consulting reference books.

audio library
Room where audio materials such as cassettes and compact discs are stored and classified.

online catalog
Computer used to consult the complete holdings of a library using various indexes.

listening station
Individual compartments used to listen to audio materials.

photocopier
Equipment fitted with a photographic device, which reproduces written texts and images.

video library
Room where audiovisual materials such as videocassettes and DVDs are stored and classified.

book truck
A small cart typically with two or three shelves used for moving books.

viewing room
Room equipped for consulting audiovisual materials.

new book shelf
Shelving used to display recent acquisitions.

periodicals room
Room reserved for consulting newspapers and periodicals.

book return desk
Area where users return books borrowed from the library.

periodicals shelf
Shelving used to display recent periodicals.

security guard's office
Security guard: individual responsible for supervision and security.

information desk
Kiosk where users can obtain information on where to find books and on library services.

circulation desk
Place where users check out the books they borrow from the library.

main entrance

restrooms
Room equipped with toilets and sinks for patrons' use.

school

Teaching institution: the term "school" usually refers to an elementary, middle or high school.

general view

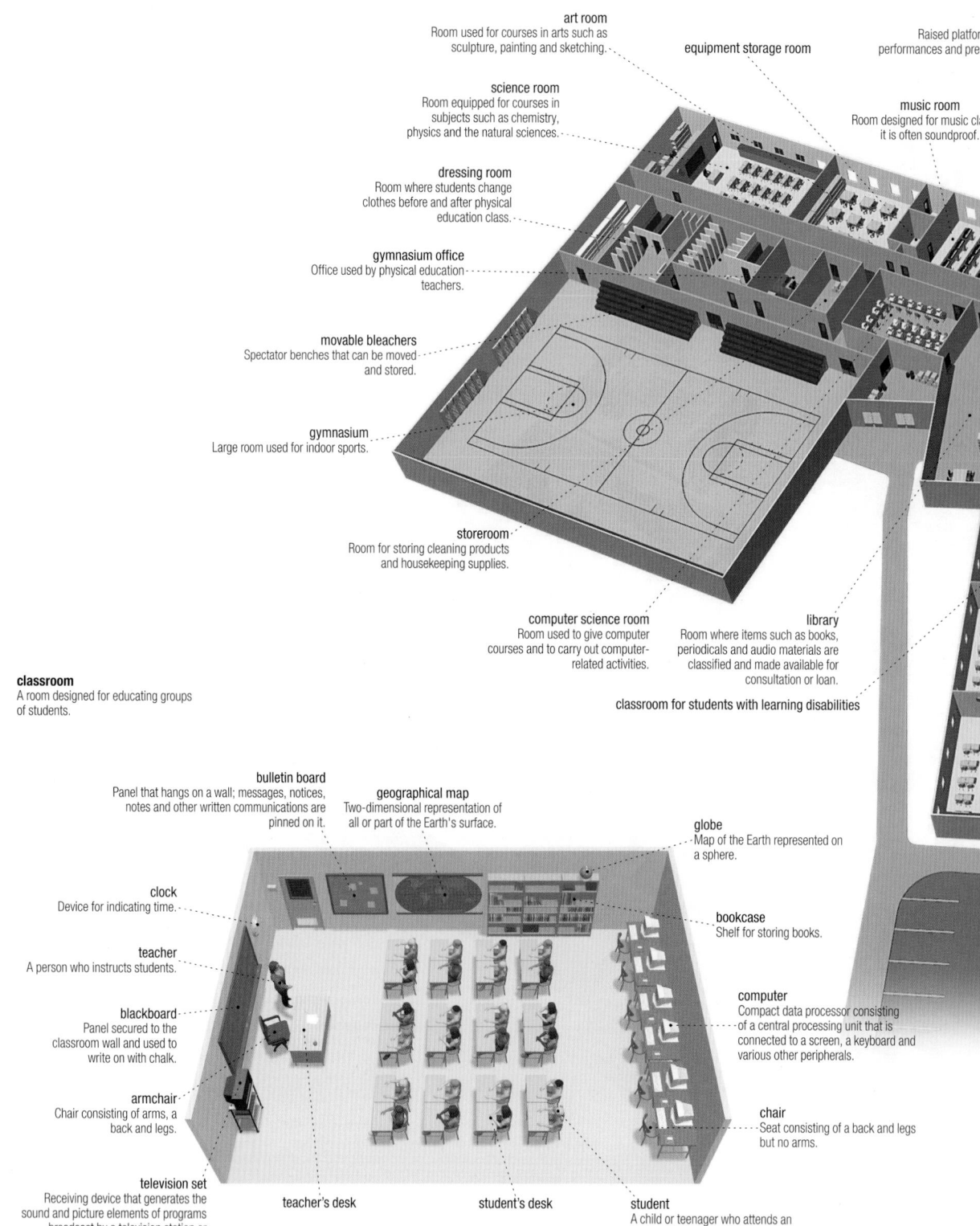

art room
Room used for courses in arts such as sculpture, painting and sketching.

equipment storage room

Raised platform u
performances and presen

science room
Room equipped for courses in subjects such as chemistry, physics and the natural sciences.

music room
Room designed for music classe
it is often soundproof.

dressing room
Room where students change clothes before and after physical education class.

gymnasium office
Office used by physical education teachers.

movable bleachers
Spectator benches that can be moved and stored.

gymnasium
Large room used for indoor sports.

storeroom
Room for storing cleaning products and housekeeping supplies.

computer science room
Room used to give computer courses and to carry out computer-related activities.

library
Room where items such as books, periodicals and audio materials are classified and made available for consultation or loan.

classroom for students with learning disabilities

classroom
A room designed for educating groups of students.

bulletin board
Panel that hangs on a wall; messages, notices, notes and other written communications are pinned on it.

geographical map
Two-dimensional representation of all or part of the Earth's surface.

globe
Map of the Earth represented on a sphere.

clock
Device for indicating time.

bookcase
Shelf for storing books.

teacher
A person who instructs students.

computer
Compact data processor consisting of a central processing unit that is connected to a screen, a keyboard and various other peripherals.

blackboard
Panel secured to the classroom wall and used to write on with chalk.

armchair
Chair consisting of arms, a back and legs.

chair
Seat consisting of a back and legs but no arms.

television set
Receiving device that generates the sound and picture elements of programs broadcast by a television station or recorded on cassette or disc.

teacher's desk

student's desk

student
A child or teenager who attends an elementary, middle or high school.

eteria
e where students eat their
als.

students' lockers
Lockers with a shelf where
students store clothes and school
materials.

kitchen
Room where meals are prepared.

main entrance

supervisor's office
Office used by an individual in
charge of discipline at the school.

restrooms
Room equipped with toilets and
sinks for patrons' use.

courtyard
Uncovered space bordered by
buildings or fences and used for
outdoor activities.

classroom
A room designed for educating
groups of students.

students' lounge
Room used by students as a
meeting or lounge area.

teachers' lounge
Room used by teachers as a
meeting or lounge area.

administrative office
Work area for administrative
personnel.

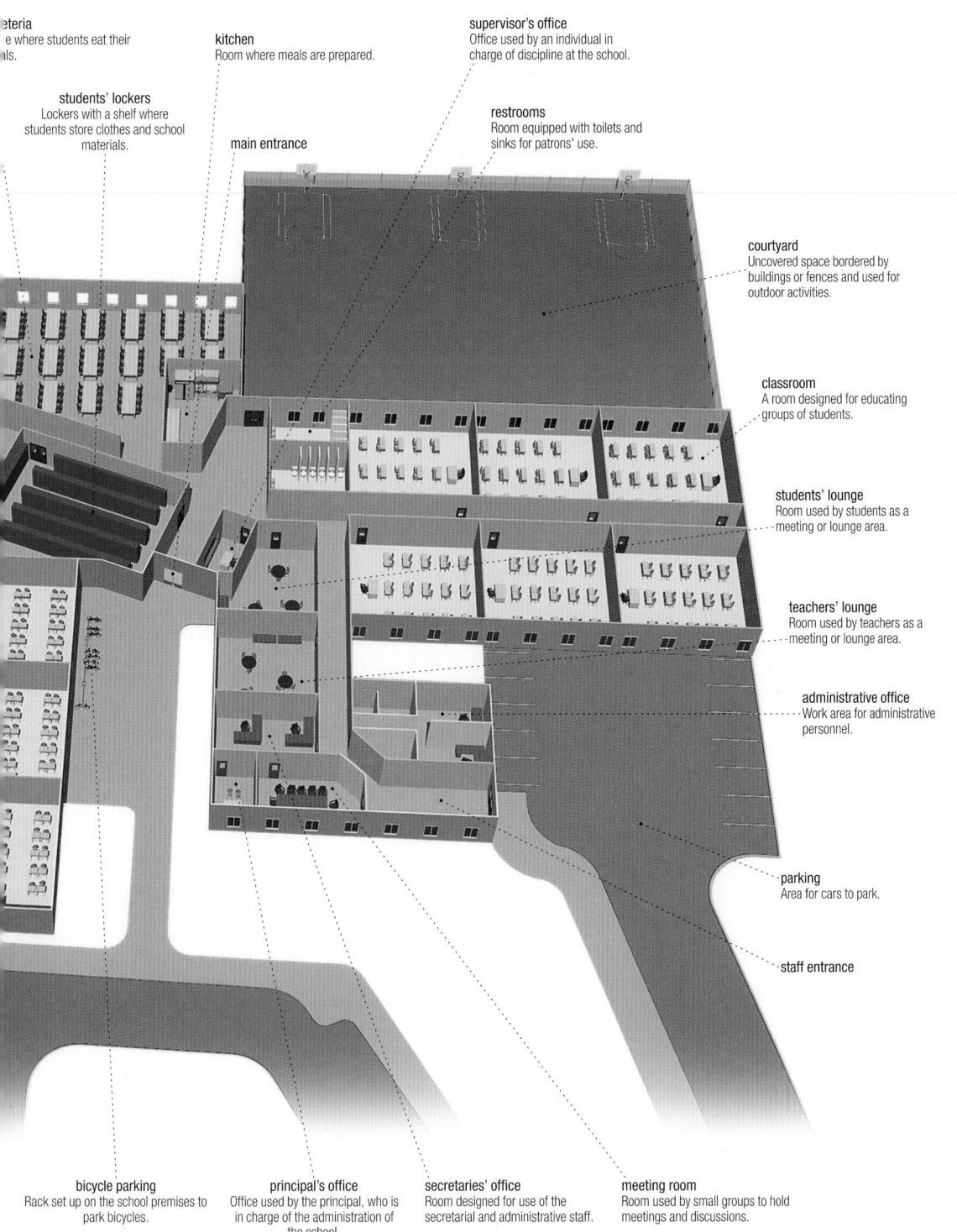

parking
Area for cars to park.

staff entrance

bicycle parking
Rack set up on the school premises to
park bicycles.

principal's office
Office used by the principal, who is
in charge of the administration of
the school.

secretaries' office
Room designed for use of the
secretarial and administrative staff.

meeting room
Room used by small groups to hold
meetings and discussions.

chronology of religions

Religions have usually been initiated by a prophet or an event; they have overlapped and influenced one another throughout the course of history.

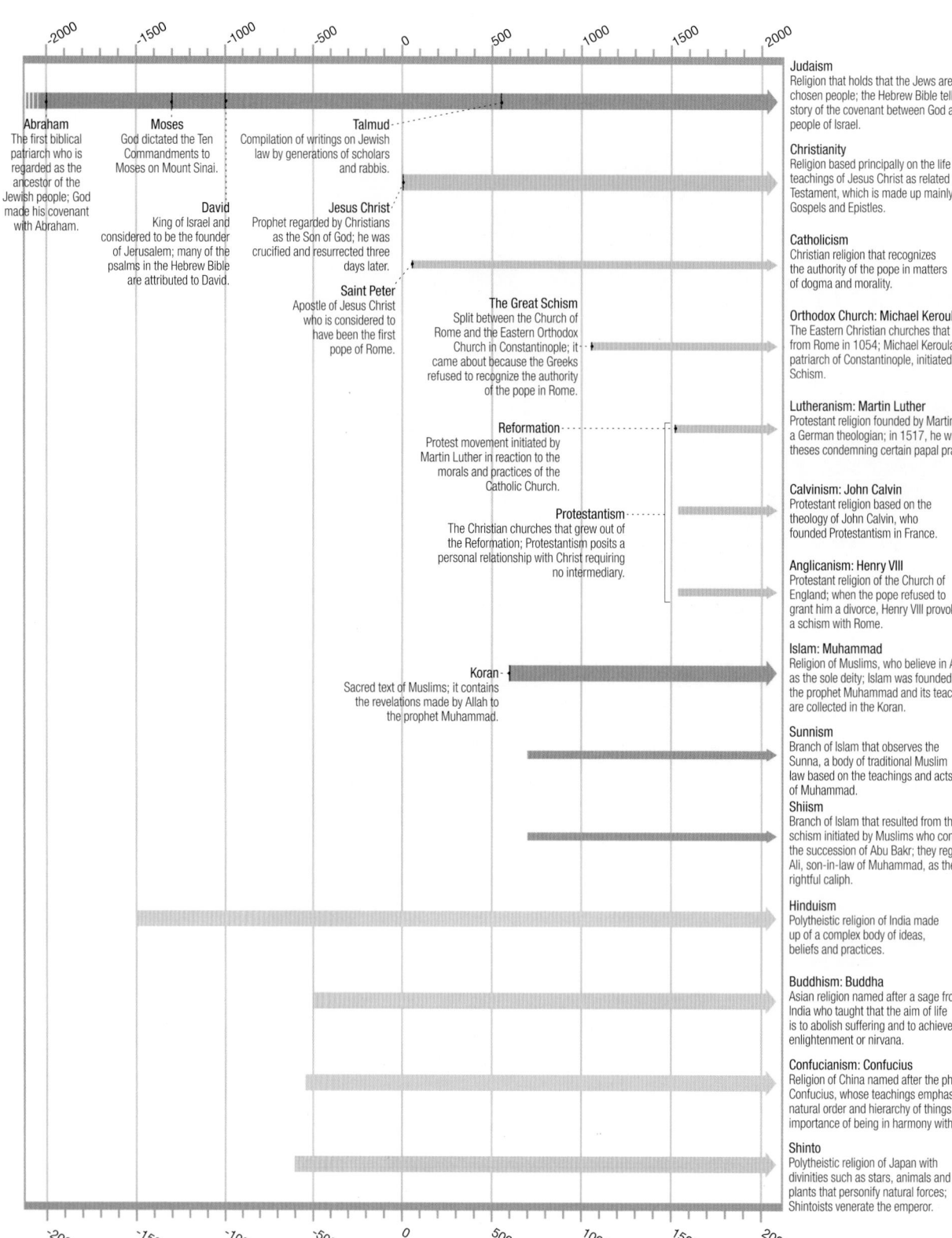

Abraham
The first biblical patriarch who is regarded as the ancestor of the Jewish people; God made his covenant with Abraham.

Moses
God dictated the Ten Commandments to Moses on Mount Sinai.

David
King of Israel and considered to be the founder of Jerusalem; many of the psalms in the Hebrew Bible are attributed to David.

Talmud
Compilation of writings on Jewish law by generations of scholars and rabbis.

Jesus Christ
Prophet regarded by Christians as the Son of God; he was crucified and resurrected three days later.

Saint Peter
Apostle of Jesus Christ who is considered to have been the first pope of Rome.

The Great Schism
Split between the Church of Rome and the Eastern Orthodox Church in Constantinople; it came about because the Greeks refused to recognize the authority of the pope in Rome.

Reformation
Protest movement initiated by Martin Luther in reaction to the morals and practices of the Catholic Church.

Protestantism
The Christian churches that grew out of the Reformation; Protestantism posits a personal relationship with Christ requiring no intermediary.

Koran
Sacred text of Muslims; it contains the revelations made by Allah to the prophet Muhammad.

Judaism
Religion that holds that the Jews are God's chosen people; the Hebrew Bible tells the story of the covenant between God and people of Israel.

Christianity
Religion based principally on the life and teachings of Jesus Christ as related in the Testament, which is made up mainly of Gospels and Epistles.

Catholicism
Christian religion that recognizes the authority of the pope in matters of dogma and morality.

Orthodox Church: Michael Keroularios
The Eastern Christian churches that separated from Rome in 1054; Michael Keroularios, patriarch of Constantinople, initiated the Schism.

Lutheranism: Martin Luther
Protestant religion founded by Martin Luther, a German theologian; in 1517, he wrote theses condemning certain papal practices.

Calvinism: John Calvin
Protestant religion based on the theology of John Calvin, who founded Protestantism in France.

Anglicanism: Henry VIII
Protestant religion of the Church of England; when the pope refused to grant him a divorce, Henry VIII provoked a schism with Rome.

Islam: Muhammad
Religion of Muslims, who believe in Allah as the sole deity; Islam was founded by the prophet Muhammad and its teachings are collected in the Koran.

Sunnism
Branch of Islam that observes the Sunna, a body of traditional Muslim law based on the teachings and acts of Muhammad.

Shiism
Branch of Islam that resulted from the schism initiated by Muslims who contest the succession of Abu Bakr; they regard Ali, son-in-law of Muhammad, as the rightful caliph.

Hinduism
Polytheistic religion of India made up of a complex body of ideas, beliefs and practices.

Buddhism: Buddha
Asian religion named after a sage from India who taught that the aim of life is to abolish suffering and to achieve enlightenment or nirvana.

Confucianism: Confucius
Religion of China named after the philosopher Confucius, whose teachings emphasize natural order and hierarchy of things and importance of being in harmony with nature.

Shinto
Polytheistic religion of Japan with divinities such as stars, animals and plants that personify natural forces; Shintoists venerate the emperor.

church

Place of Christian worship.

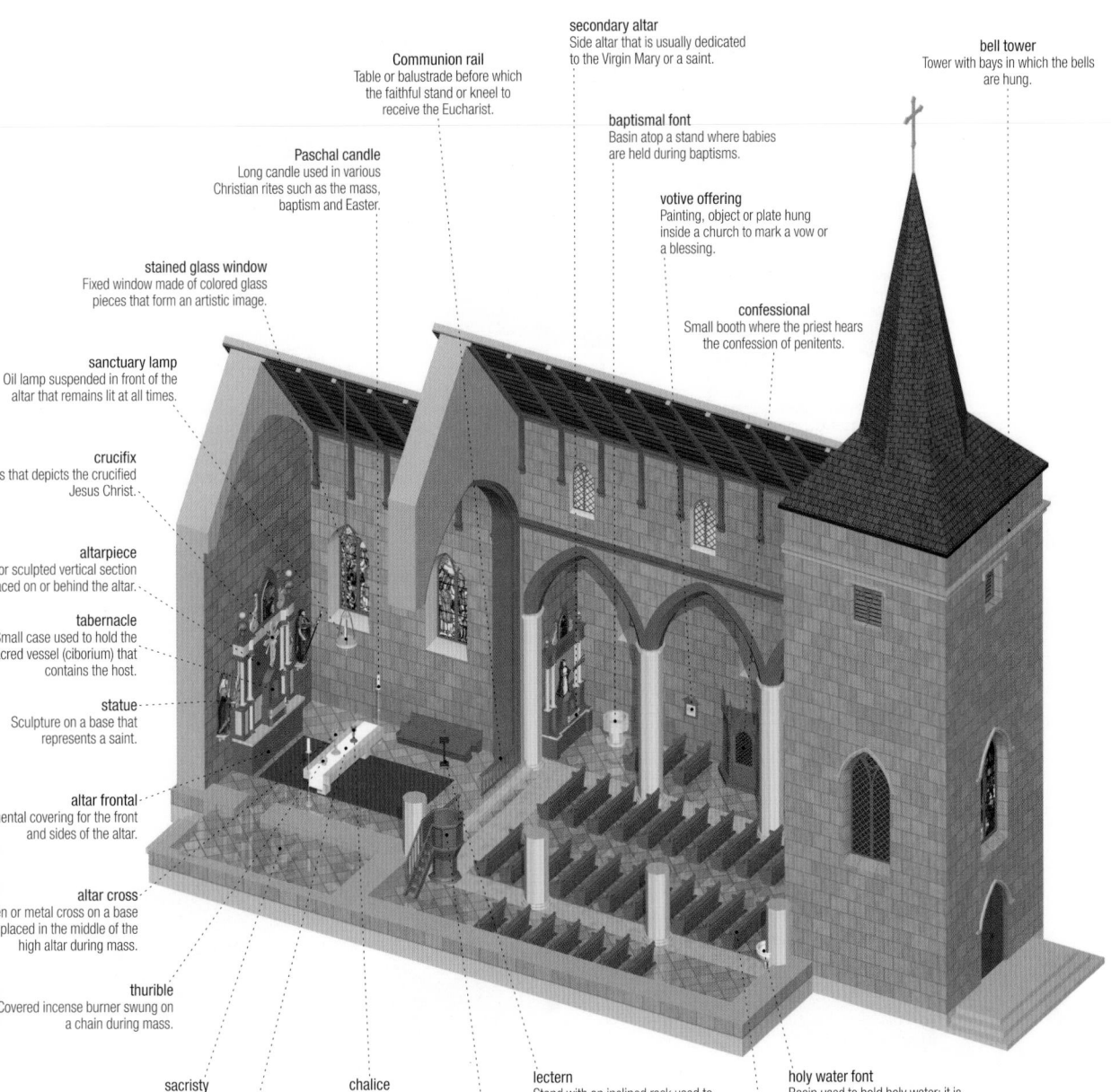

secondary altar
Side altar that is usually dedicated to the Virgin Mary or a saint.

Communion rail
Table or balustrade before which the faithful stand or kneel to receive the Eucharist.

bell tower
Tower with bays in which the bells are hung.

baptismal font
Basin atop a stand where babies are held during baptisms.

Paschal candle
Long candle used in various Christian rites such as the mass, baptism and Easter.

votive offering
Painting, object or plate hung inside a church to mark a vow or a blessing.

stained glass window
Fixed window made of colored glass pieces that form an artistic image.

confessional
Small booth where the priest hears the confession of penitents.

sanctuary lamp
Oil lamp suspended in front of the altar that remains lit at all times.

crucifix
s that depicts the crucified Jesus Christ.

altarpiece
or sculpted vertical section aced on or behind the altar.

tabernacle
Small case used to hold the acred vessel (ciborium) that contains the host.

statue
Sculpture on a base that represents a saint.

altar frontal
hental covering for the front and sides of the altar.

altar cross
en or metal cross on a base placed in the middle of the high altar during mass.

thurible
Covered incense burner swung on a chain during mass.

sacristy
Area where sacred vessels and sacerdotal vestments are kept.

chalice
Cup in which the wine is consecrated during celebration of the mass.

lectern
Stand with an inclined rack used to hold books such as hymnals and the Bible.

holy water font
Basin used to hold holy water; it is located near the entrance so that the faithful can cross themselves on entering.

high altar
The main altar in a church located near the back of the choir (apse).

pulpit
Raised platform used to address the congregation.

pew
Long narrow seat for several people.

synagogue

Place of worship in the Jewish religion.

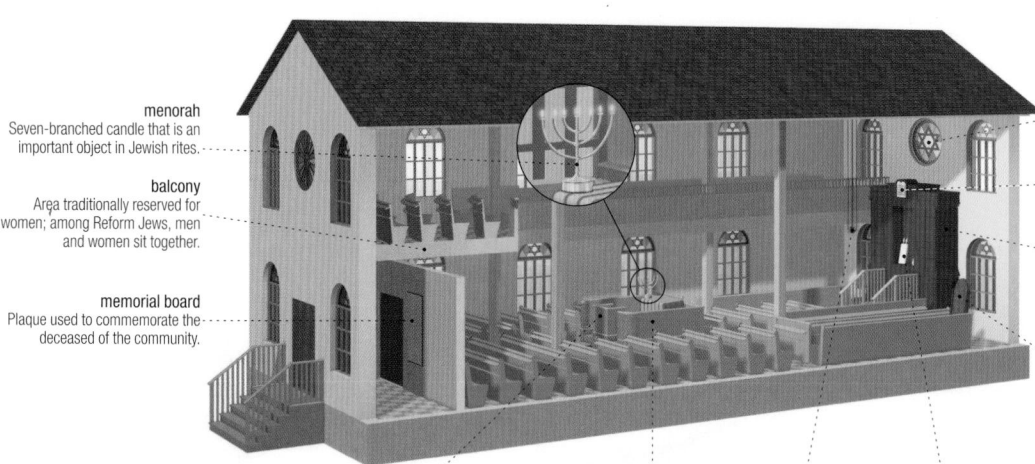

menorah
Seven-branched candle that is an important object in Jewish rites.

balcony
Area traditionally reserved for women; among Reform Jews, men and women sit together.

memorial board
Plaque used to commemorate the deceased of the community.

Star of David
Emblem of Judaism that is ma[...] of two overlapping triangles fo[...] six-pointed star; it was the sea[...] Solomon, son of David.

Ten Commandments
The precepts transmitted by G[...] Moses; they form the basis of Jewish faith.

ark
Cabinet used to store the scro[...] the Torah.

rabbi's or cantor's seat
Armchair used by the commun[...] religious leader who leads the service.

pulpit
Raised platform on which the Torah scrolls are placed for public reading.

bimah
Platform from which a rabbi conducts services.

ner tamid (eternal light)
Suspended lamp that is lit at all times; it is in memory of God's eternal presence and the eternal flame of the Temple in Jerusalem.

Torah scrolls
Rolls of parchment on which the Pentateuch (the first five books of the Hebrew bible) is written in hand.

mosque

Place of worship in the Islamic religion.

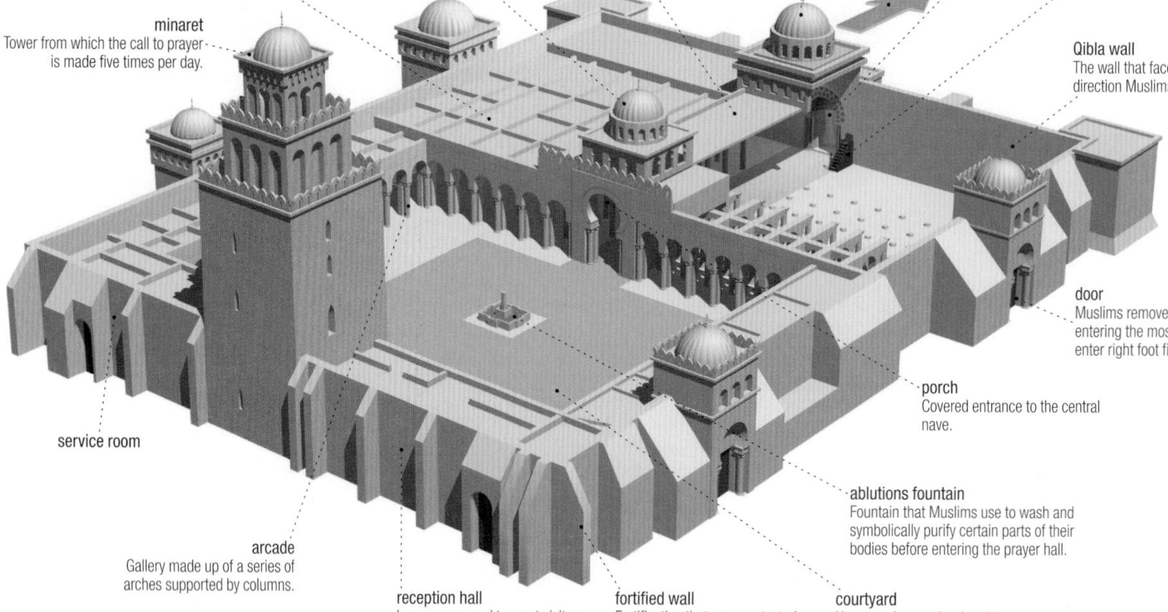

porch dome
Decorative dome atop the porch.

central nave
The mosque's principal nave; it adjoins the Mihrab.

Mihrab dome
Dome over the back of the central nave near the Mihrab.

direction of Mecca
Mecca: the religious capital of Islam is located in Saudi Arabia; Muslim prayers are always performed facing Mecca.

Mihrab
Empty niche in the Qibla wall indicating the direction of Mecca[...]

Minbar
A pulpit at the head of a stair[...] the Prophet and the first calip[...] preached from the Minbar bu[...] imams preach from one of the[...] as a sign of respect.

prayer hall
Area made up of several naves and covered with rugs; Muslims remove their shoes to pray.

minaret
Tower from which the call to prayer is made five times per day.

Qibla wall
The wall that faces Mecca, direction Muslims face to p[...]

door
Muslims remove their shoe[...] entering the mosque and a[...] enter right foot first.

service room

porch
Covered entrance to the central nave.

ablutions fountain
Fountain that Muslims use to wash and symbolically purify certain parts of their bodies before entering the prayer hall.

arcade
Gallery made up of a series of arches supported by columns.

reception hall
Large room used to greet visitors.

fortified wall
Fortification that once protected inhabitants seeking refuge inside the mosque during conflicts.

courtyard
Uncovered space bordered by the shady arcades; the ablutions fountain is located in the center of it.

heraldry

The study of heraldic emblems and devices used to distinguish communities and families.

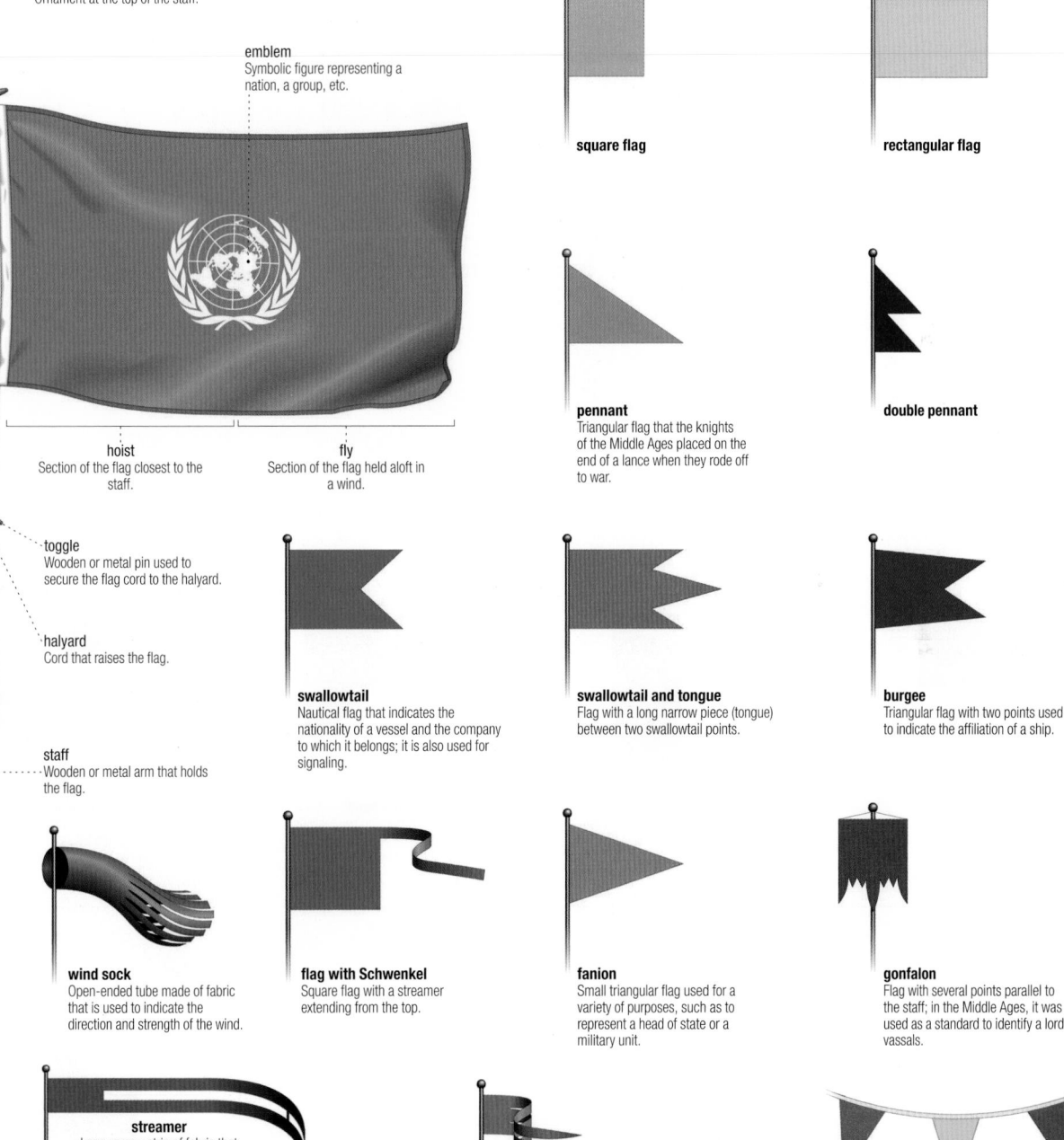

rts of a flag
: strip of fabric attached to a
ff and bearing the emblem of a
ntry or group.

finial
Ornament at the top of the staff.

emblem
Symbolic figure representing a nation, a group, etc.

hoist
Section of the flag closest to the staff.

fly
Section of the flag held aloft in a wind.

toggle
Wooden or metal pin used to secure the flag cord to the halyard.

halyard
Cord that raises the flag.

staff
Wooden or metal arm that holds the flag.

base

flag shapes

square flag

rectangular flag

pennant
Triangular flag that the knights of the Middle Ages placed on the end of a lance when they rode off to war.

double pennant

swallowtail
Nautical flag that indicates the nationality of a vessel and the company to which it belongs; it is also used for signaling.

swallowtail and tongue
Flag with a long narrow piece (tongue) between two swallowtail points.

burgee
Triangular flag with two points used to indicate the affiliation of a ship.

wind sock
Open-ended tube made of fabric that is used to indicate the direction and strength of the wind.

flag with Schwenkel
Square flag with a streamer extending from the top.

fanion
Small triangular flag used for a variety of purposes, such as to represent a head of state or a military unit.

gonfalon
Flag with several points parallel to the staff; in the Middle Ages, it was used as a standard to identify a lord's vassals.

streamer
Long narrow strip of fabric that usually bears a motto.

oriflamme
Pageantry banner with several points.

bunting
Row of flags in various colors used as a party ornament.

SOCIETY

heraldry

shield divisions
Shield: panel that is divided into nine sections and bears armorial figures.

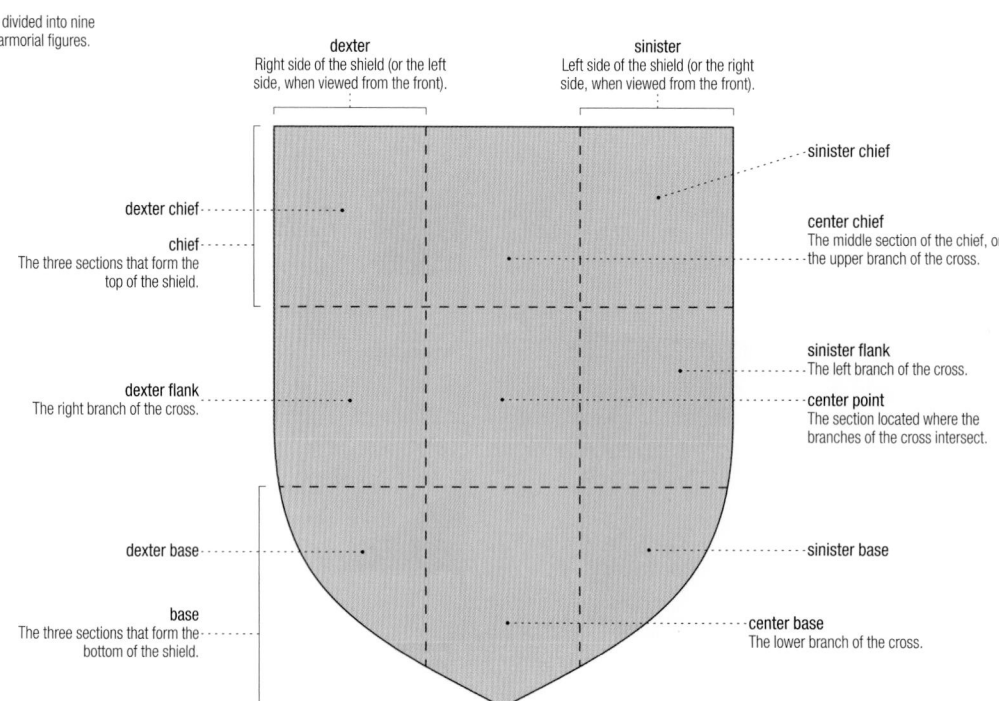

dexter
Right side of the shield (or the left side, when viewed from the front).

sinister
Left side of the shield (or the right side, when viewed from the front).

dexter chief

chief
The three sections that form the top of the shield.

sinister chief

center chief
The middle section of the chief, or the upper branch of the cross.

dexter flank
The right branch of the cross.

sinister flank
The left branch of the cross.

center point
The section located where the branches of the cross intersect.

dexter base

sinister base

base
The three sections that form the bottom of the shield.

center base
The lower branch of the cross.

examples of partitions
Partitions: divisions made by lines on the shield to form an even number of sections.

per fess
Shield divided into two sections by a horizontal line in the center.

party
Shield divided into two sections by a vertical line in the center.

per bend
Shield divided into two sections by a diagonal line from the dexter chief to the sinister base.

quarterly
Shield divided into two sections: on top, the left side of a per fess and on the bottom, the right side of a party.

examples of ordinaries
Ordinaries: divisions made by lines on the shield to form an odd number of sections.

chief
Figure covering the top third of the shield.

chevron
Figure shaped like an inverted V; its diagonal lines start in the dexter base and the sinister base and meet in the center chief.

pale
Figure covering the vertical branch of the cross.

cross
Figure covering the center horizontal and vertical sections of the shield.

heraldry

examples of metals

Metals: yellow represents or (gold) and white represents argent (silver).

examples of furs

Furs: combinations of colors, including metallic colors that represent fur.

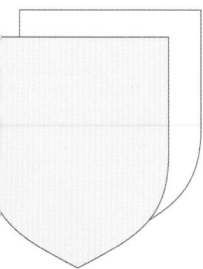

argent
color yellow or silver; when the ld is black and white, argent is esignated by a white surface.

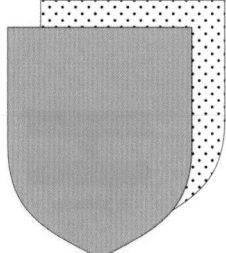

or
The color gold; when the shield is black and white, or is designated by a dotted surface.

ermine
Fur represented by a silver field containing sable-colored markings.

vair
Fur represented by silver and azure bells that meet where they come to a point.

examples of charges

Charge: figure represented on the shield.

lion passant
The lion is the animal most often epicted in heraldry and symbolizes ength and courage; the lion passant is a walking lion.

fleur-de-lis
Heraldic figure often represented on old coats of arms of France and Quebec.

eagle
The eagle is the bird most often depicted in heraldry and symbolizes power; when the tips of the wings point downward, they are said to be conjoined in lure.

crescent
Crescent-shaped figure with points (horns) that usually point to the chief of the shield.

mullet
Five-pointed star whose top point is directed toward the center chief.

examples of colors

Colors: colors other than metallic.

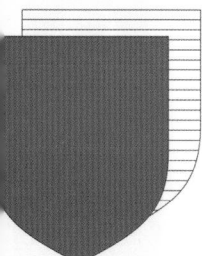

azure
hade of blue; when the shield s black and white, azure is esignated by horizontal lines.

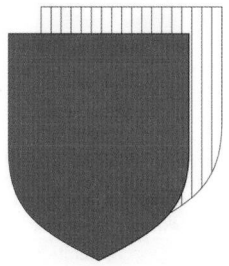

gules
The color red; when the shield is black and white, gules is designated by vertical lines.

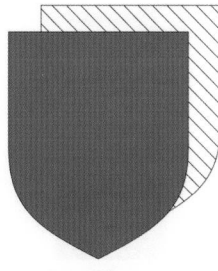

vert
The color green; when the shield is black and white, vert is designated by diagonal lines from left to right.

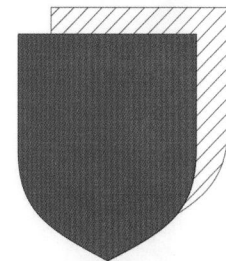

purpure
The color violet; when the shield is black and white, purpure is designated by diagonal lines from right to left.

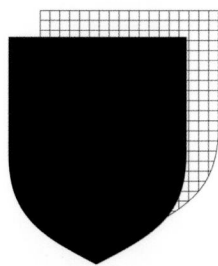

sable
The color black; when the shield is black and white, sable is designated by a cross-hatched or black surface.

UN members flags

Flag: emblem depicted on a piece of fabric attached to a staff or printed on a document or an escutcheon. The flags illustrated here are those of UN member countries.

Americas

1
Canada

2
United States of America

3
Mexico

4
Honduras

5
Guatemala

6
Belize

7
El Salvador

8
Nicaragua

9
Costa Rica

10
Panama

11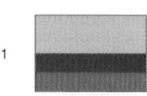
Colombia

12
Venezuela

13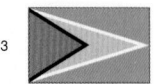
Guyana

14
Suriname

15
Ecuador

16
Peru

17
Brazil

18
Bolivia

19
Paraguay

20
Chile

21
Argentina

22
Uruguay

Caribbean Islands

23
Bahamas

24
Cuba

25
Jamaica

26
Haiti

27
Saint Kitts and Nevis

28
Antigua and Barbuda

29
Dominica

30
Saint Lucia

UN members flags

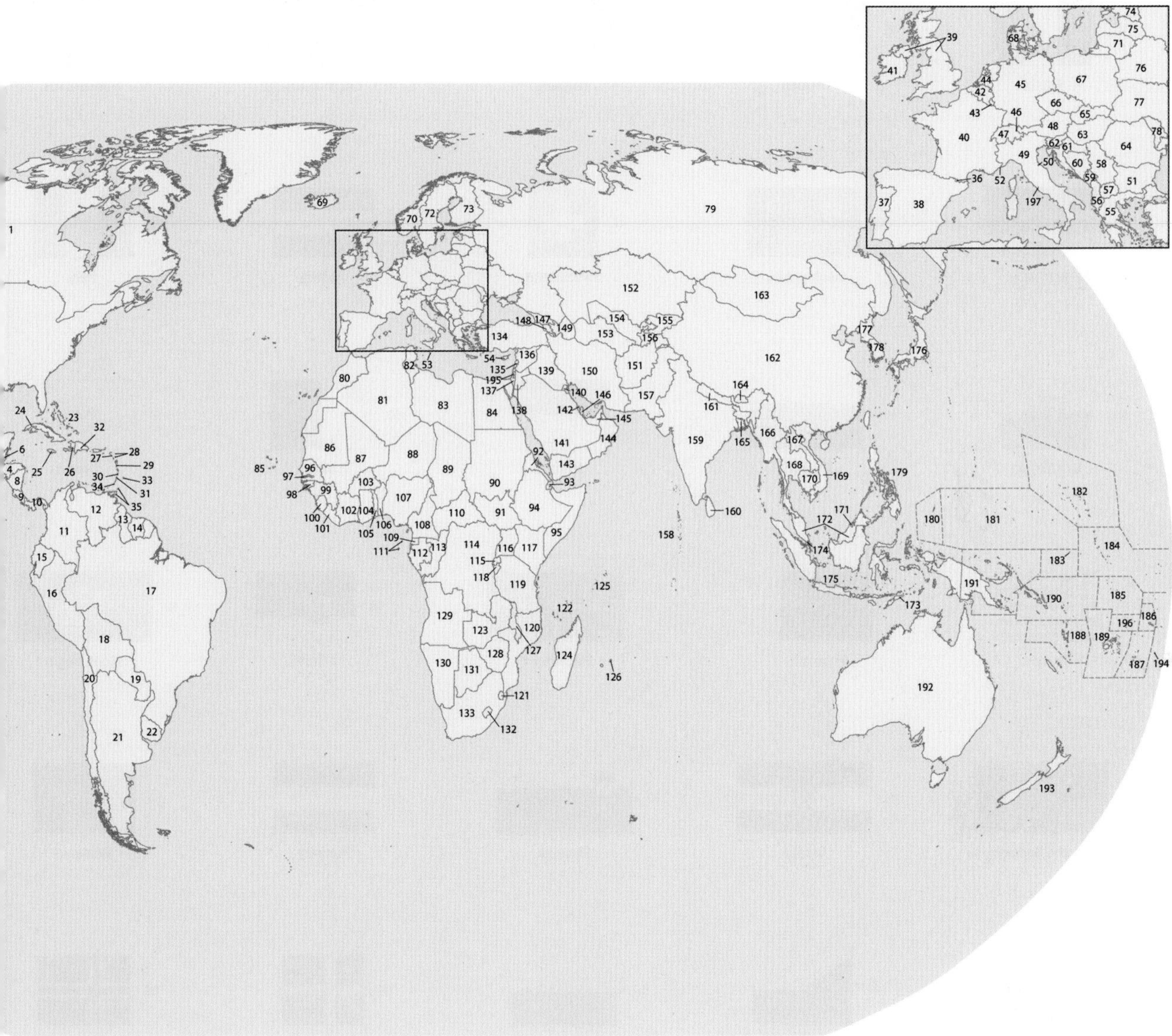

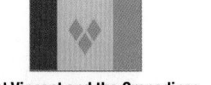

nt Vincent and the Grenadines

32

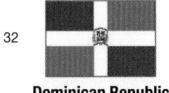

Dominican Republic

33

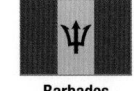

Barbados

34

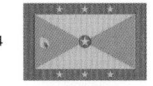

Grenada

35

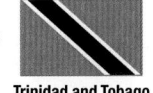

Trinidad and Tobago

Europe

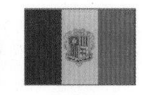

Andorra

37

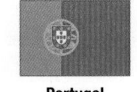

Portugal

38

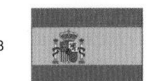

Spain

39

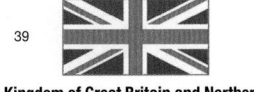

United Kingdom of Great Britain and Northern Ireland

UN members flags

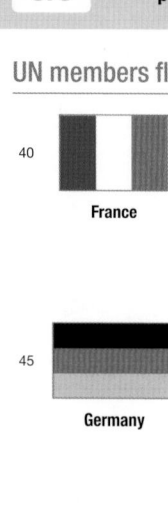
40 France

41 Ireland

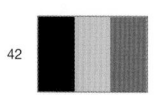
42 Belgium

43 Luxembourg

44 Netherlands

45 Germany

46 Liechtenstein

47 Switzerland

48 Austria

49 Italy

50 San Marino

51 Bulgaria

52 Monaco

53 Malta

54 Cyprus

55 Greece

56 Albania

57 Macedonia

58 Serbia

59 Montenegro

60 Bosnia and Herzegovina

61 Croatia

62 Slovenia

63 Hungary

64 Romania

65 Slovakia

66 Czech Republic

67 Poland

68 Denmark

69 Iceland

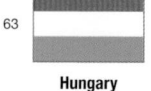
70 Norway

71 Lithuania

72 Sweden

73 Finland

74 Estonia

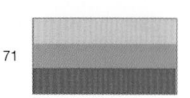
75 Latvia

76 Belarus

77 Ukraine

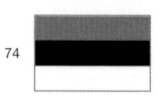
78 Moldova

79 Russia

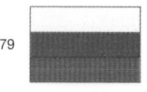

UN members flags

Africa

| Morocco | 81  Algeria | 82  Tunisia | 83 Libya |

Egypt | 85 Cape Verde | 86 Mauritania | 87 Mali | 88 Niger

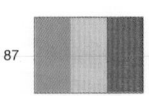

Chad | 90 Sudan | 91 Republic of South Sudan | 92 Eritrea | 93 Djibouti

Ethiopia | 95 Somalia | 96 Senegal | 97 Gambia | 98 Guinea-Bissau

99 Guinea | 100 Sierra Leone | 101 Liberia | 102 Ivory Coast (Côte d'Ivoire) | 103 Burkina Faso

04 Ghana | 105 Togo | 106 Benin | 107 Nigeria | 108 Cameroon

09 Equatorial Guinea | 110 Central African Republic | 111 Sao Tome and Principe | 112 Gabon | 113 Republic of the Congo

14 ocratic Republic of the Congo | 115 Rwanda | 116 Uganda | 117 Kenya | 118 Burundi

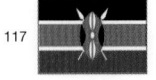

SOCIETY

UN members flags

119 **Tanzania**	120 **Mozambique**	121 **Swaziland**	122 **Comoros**	123 **Zambia**
124 **Madagascar**	125 **Seychelles**	126 **Mauritius**	127 **Malawi**	128 **Zimbabwe**
129 **Angola**	130 **Namibia**	131 **Botswana**	132 **Lesotho**	133 **South Africa**

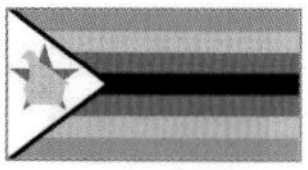

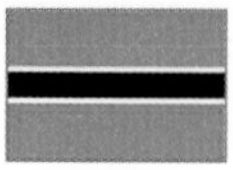

Asia

134 **Turkey**	135 **Lebanon**	136 **Syria**	137 **Israel**	138 **Jordan**
139 **Iraq**	140 **Kuwait**	141 **Saudi Arabia**	142 **Bahrain**	143 **Yemen**
144 **Oman**	145 **United Arab Emirates**	146 **Qatar**	147 **Georgia**	148 **Armenia**
149 **Azerbaijan**	150 **Iran**	151 **Afghanistan**	152 **Kazakhstan**	153 **Turkmenistan**

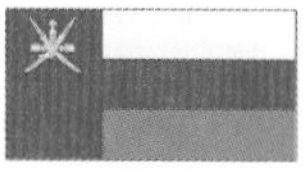

Uzbekistan 154

Kyrgyzstan 155

Tajikistan 156

Pakistan 157

Maldives 158

UN members flags

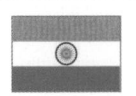
India

160

Sri Lanka

161

Nepal

162

China

163

Mongolia

Bhutan

165

Bangladesh

166

Myanmar

167

Laos

168

Thailand

Vietnam

170

Cambodia

171

Brunei

172

Malaysia

173

East Timor

Singapore

175

Indonesia

176
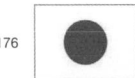
Japan

177

North Korea

178

South Korea

Oceania

Philippines

180

Palau

181

Micronesia

Marshall Islands

183

Nauru

184

Kiribati

185

Tuvalu

Samoa

187

Tonga

188

Vanuatu

189

Fiji

Solomon Islands

191

Papua New Guinea

192

Australia

193

New Zealand

SOCIETY

UN observers flags

Flag: emblem depicted on a piece of fabric attached to a staff or printed on a document or an escutcheon. The flags shown are those of states that are not members of the UN, but are nonetheless recognized by the organization.

194

Cook Islands

195

Palestine

196

Niue

197

Vatican City State

international organizations flags

Flag: emblem depicted on a piece of fabric attached to a staff or printed on a document or an escutcheon. The flags shown here are those of organizations that bring together governmental or private groups from various countries.

United Nations (UN)
International organization set up in 1945 with 193 current members. The UN's main goal is to maintain peace and security and to promote human rights.

United Nations Educational, Scientific and Cultural Organization (UNESCO)
Specialized UN agency set up in 1945. UNESCO is best known for its World Heritage program, which lists the most important cultural and natural sites on the planet.

International Olympic Committee (IOC)
Organization founded in 1894 by Pierre de Coubertin. The IOC leads the international Olympic movement and controls various sporting federations.

European Union (EU)
Association of 27 independent states that have granted some measure of competency to shared institutions.

Commonwealth
Organization of 54 countries, mostly former British colonies or protectorates.

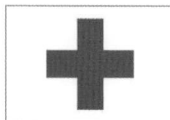

Red Cross
Consortium of humanitarian organizations dating back to 1863 whose main goal is to provide assistance in areas devastated by war or natural disaster.

Red Crescent
Consortium of humanitarian organizations dating back to 1863 whose main goal is to provide assistance in areas devastated by war or natural disaster.

North Atlantic Treaty Organization (NATO)
Political and military alliance for peace and security, founded in 1949. Currently, NATO consists of 28 member states from Europe and North America.

International Organisation of La Francophonie
Organization of 75 member states and governments that use the French language.

Sovereign Military Order of Malta
Catholic religious community dedicated to humanitarian aid, officially founded in 1961. The organization is a descendant of the Order of Saint John of Jerusalem, created around 1080 to provide medical care for pilgrims in the Holy Lands.

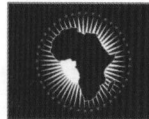

African Union
Institution created in 2002 that seeks to promote democracy and development in Africa.

League of Arab States (Arab League)
Organization founded in 1945 consisting of 22 Arab-speaking member states, mostly from North Africa and the Middle East.

Organisation of Islamic Cooperation
Institution set up in 1969 consisting of 57 member states whose populations are Muslim, at least in part.

weapons in the Stone Age

Weapons used mainly for hunting during the prehistoric Paleolithic and Neolithic periods.

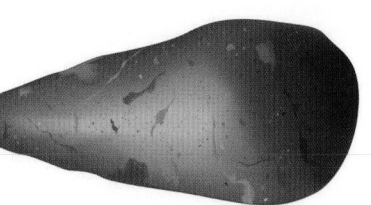

polished stone hand axe
Crudely worked stone attached to a shaft.

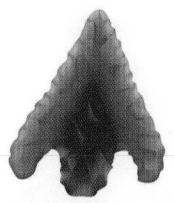

flint arrowhead
Wedge-shaped piercing tip attached to
the end of an arrow; it is made from flint (a
quartz rock) that is chipped to produce a
sharp point and edges.

flint knife
Piece of flint carved in the shape of
a blade and mounted on a shaft.

weapons in the age of the Romans

Weapons used during the period of antiquity dominated by the Roman Empire (1st century BC to AD 476).

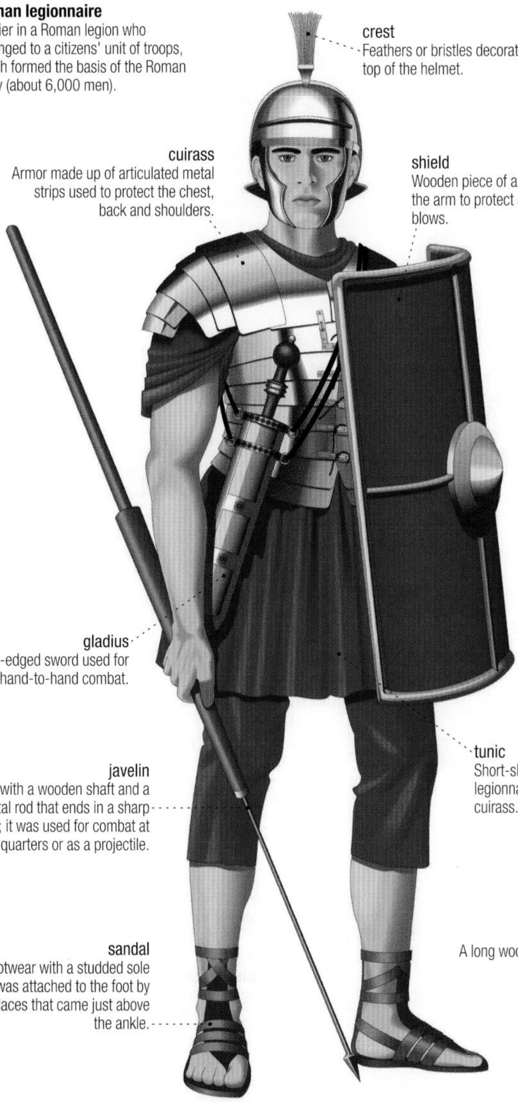

man legionnaire
...dier in a Roman legion who
...nged to a citizens' unit of troops,
...ch formed the basis of the Roman
...y (about 6,000 men).

crest
Feathers or bristles decorating the
top of the helmet.

cuirass
Armor made up of articulated metal
strips used to protect the chest,
back and shoulders.

shield
Wooden piece of armor carried on
the arm to protect against enemy
blows.

Gallic warrior
The Gallic warrior belonged to a
clan governed by a chieftain; his
armor was rudimentary and he often
fought bare-chested.

helmet
Protective metal headpiece.

shield
Wooden piece of armor carried on
the arm to protect against enemy
blows.

breeches
Full pants that were characteristic
of Gallic attire; they were pulled in
at the waist with a belt and tied at
the ankle with straps.

gladius
...e-edged sword used for
...hand-to-hand combat.

tunic
Short-sleeved garment that
legionnaires wore under the
cuirass.

javelin
...with a wooden shaft and a
...etal rod that ends in a sharp
...); it was used for combat at
...quarters or as a projectile.

sandal
...otwear with a studded sole
...was attached to the foot by
...laces that came just above
the ankle.

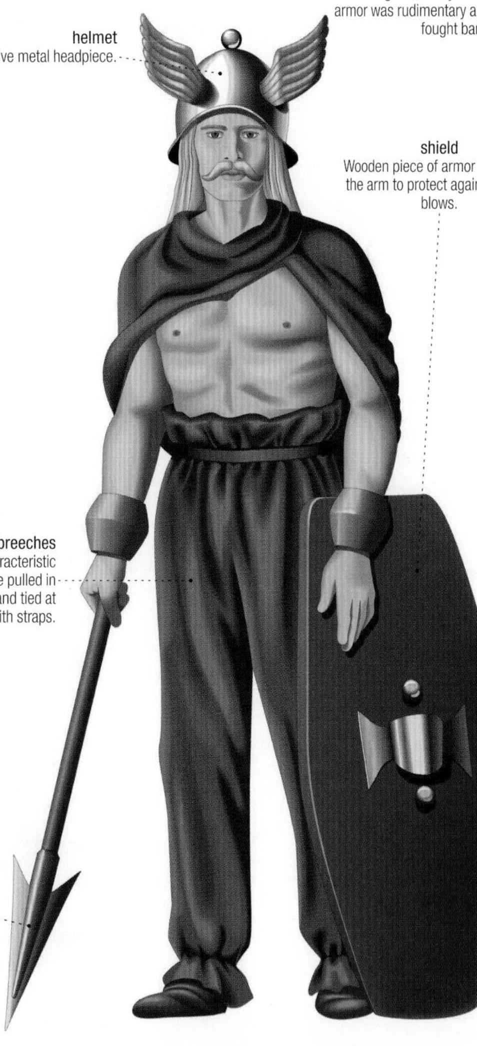

spear
A long wooden pole with a pointed
steel head.

SOCIETY

armor

Assemblage of molded and articulated metal pieces worn as protection during the Middle Ages.

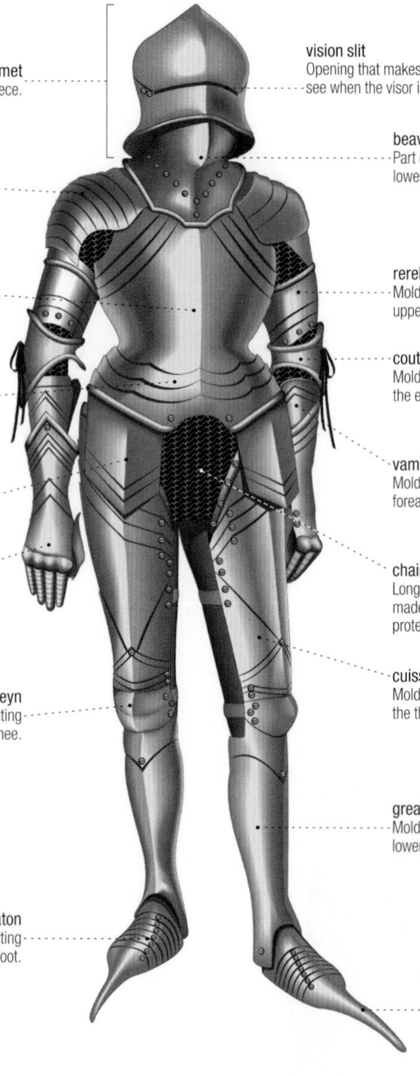

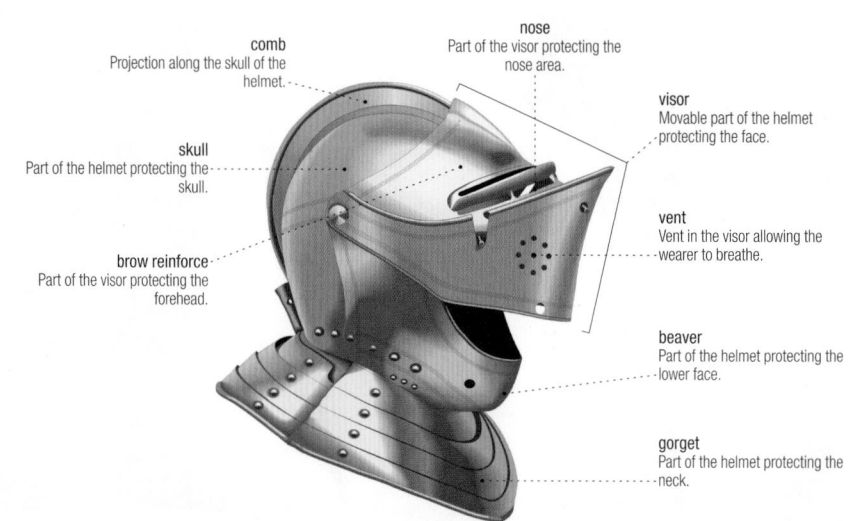

helmet
Protective metal headpiece.

vision slit
Opening that makes it possible to see when the visor is down.

pauldron
Molded metal piece protecting the shoulder.

beaver
Part of the helmet protecting the lower face.

breastplate
Molded metal piece protecting the chest.

rerebrace
Molded metal piece protecting the upper arm.

skirt
Molded metal piece protecting the stomach and upper hip.

couter
Molded metal piece protecting the elbow.

tasset
Molded metal piece protecting the upper thigh.

vambrace
Molded metal piece protecting the forearm.

gauntlet
Molded metal piece protecting the hand.

chain mail
Long shirt with sleeves and a hood made up of metal links worn to protect the chest and the head.

cuisse
Molded metal piece protecting the thigh.

poleyn
Molded metal piece protecting the knee.

greave
Molded metal piece protecting the lower leg.

sabaton
Molded metal piece protecting the foot.

poulaine
Elongated metal point forming the end of the sabaton.

helmet
Protective metal headpiece.

comb
Projection along the skull of the helmet.

nose
Part of the visor protecting the nose area.

skull
Part of the helmet protecting the skull.

visor
Movable part of the helmet protecting the face.

brow reinforce
Part of the visor protecting the forehead.

vent
Vent in the visor allowing the wearer to breathe.

beaver
Part of the helmet protecting the lower face.

gorget
Part of the helmet protecting the neck.

bows and crossbow

Weapons for hunting and war employing a bowstring which is pulled to fire a projectile such as an arrow or bolt.

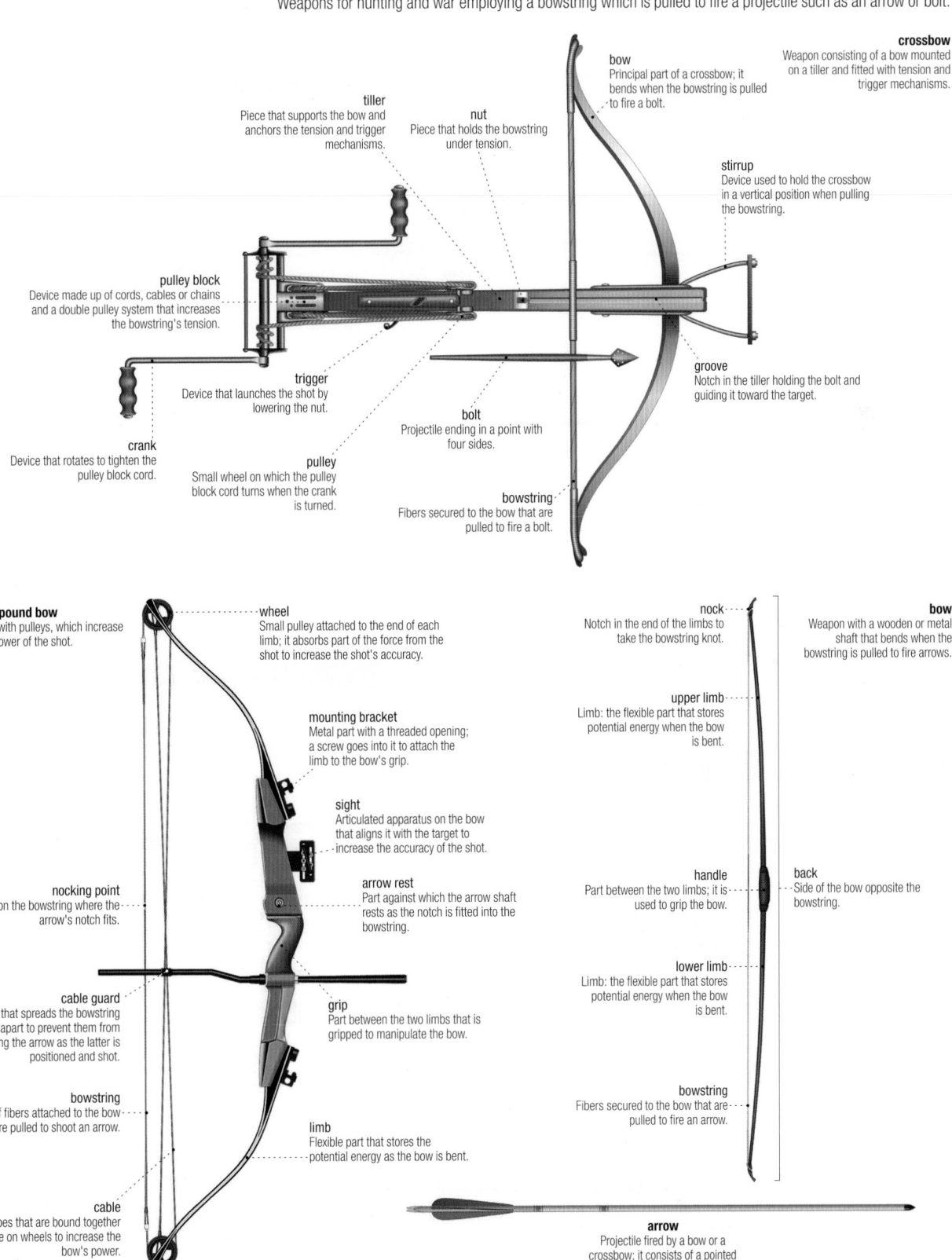

crossbow
Weapon consisting of a bow mounted on a tiller and fitted with tension and trigger mechanisms.

bow
Principal part of a crossbow; it bends when the bowstring is pulled to fire a bolt.

tiller
Piece that supports the bow and anchors the tension and trigger mechanisms.

nut
Piece that holds the bowstring under tension.

stirrup
Device used to hold the crossbow in a vertical position when pulling the bowstring.

pulley block
Device made up of cords, cables or chains and a double pulley system that increases the bowstring's tension.

trigger
Device that launches the shot by lowering the nut.

groove
Notch in the tiller holding the bolt and guiding it toward the target.

crank
Device that rotates to tighten the pulley block cord.

bolt
Projectile ending in a point with four sides.

pulley
Small wheel on which the pulley block cord turns when the crank is turned.

bowstring
Fibers secured to the bow that are pulled to fire a bolt.

mpound bow
w with pulleys, which increase power of the shot.

wheel
Small pulley attached to the end of each limb; it absorbs part of the force from the shot to increase the shot's accuracy.

nock
Notch in the end of the limbs to take the bowstring knot.

bow
Weapon with a wooden or metal shaft that bends when the bowstring is pulled to fire arrows.

mounting bracket
Metal part with a threaded opening; a screw goes into it to attach the limb to the bow's grip.

upper limb
Limb: the flexible part that stores potential energy when the bow is bent.

sight
Articulated apparatus on the bow that aligns it with the target to increase the accuracy of the shot.

arrow rest
Part against which the arrow shaft rests as the notch is fitted into the bowstring.

handle
Part between the two limbs; it is used to grip the bow.

back
Side of the bow opposite the bowstring.

nocking point
k on the bowstring where the arrow's notch fits.

lower limb
Limb: the flexible part that stores potential energy when the bow is bent.

cable guard
rt that spreads the bowstring es apart to prevent them from hing the arrow as the latter is positioned and shot.

grip
Part between the two limbs that is gripped to manipulate the bow.

bowstring
of fibers attached to the bow are pulled to shoot an arrow.

limb
Flexible part that stores the potential energy as the bow is bent.

bowstring
Fibers secured to the bow that are pulled to fire an arrow.

cable
opes that are bound together ide on wheels to increase the bow's power.

arrow
Projectile fired by a bow or a crossbow; it consists of a pointed shaft notched at one end with fletching for stability in flight.

thrusting and cutting weapons

Weapons with steel blades of various lengths designed to pierce or cut.

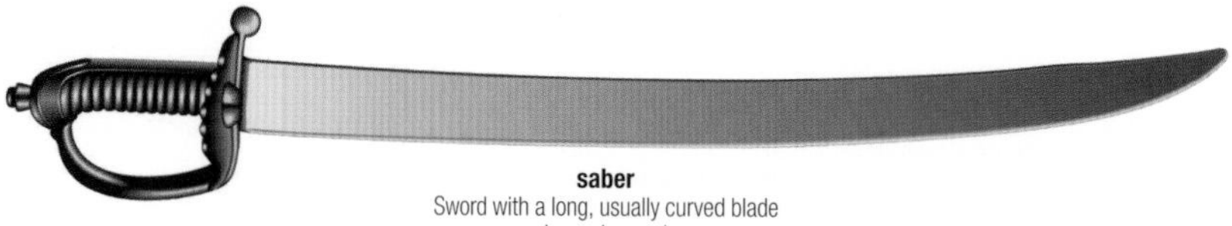

saber
Sword with a long, usually curved blade
and one sharp edge.

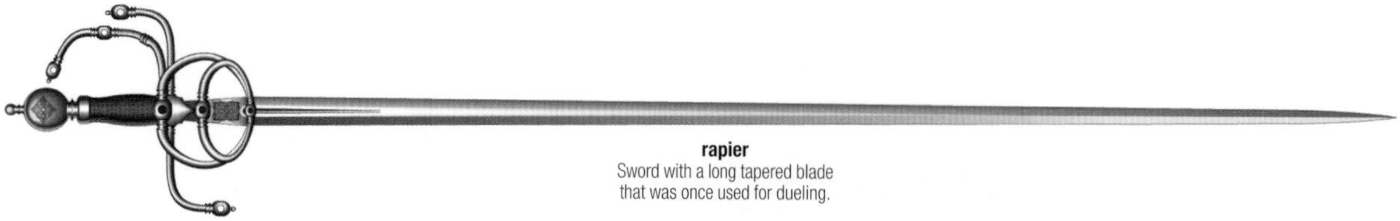

rapier
Sword with a long tapered blade
that was once used for dueling.

broadsword
Long heavy double-edged sword
held with two hands and used mainly
during the Middle Ages.

stiletto
Small sword with a tapered pointed
blade small enough to slip between
the links of chain mail.

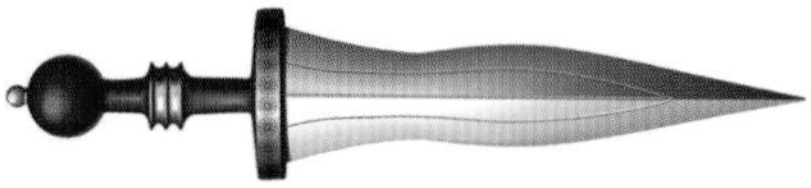

dagger
A stabbing knife usually carried as a
secondary weapon.

poniard
A dagger-like weapon with a usually
slender blade of triangular or square
cross section.

machete
Large single-edged knife of tropical
countries sometimes used as a weapon but
mainly used as a tool for clearing paths and
cutting crops such as sugarcane.

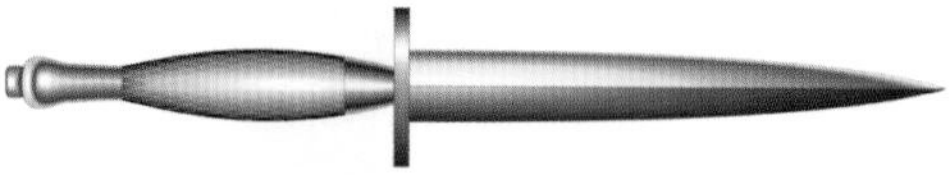

commando knife
Double-edged knife initially designed for
commandos for close combat.

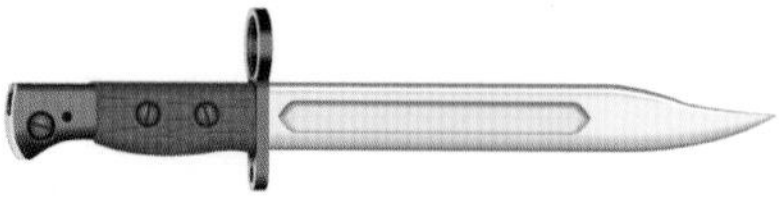

hilted bayonet
Weapon with a complete handle
that could be attached to a gun
barrel by means of a metal ring.

plug bayonet
Weapon with a tapered handle inserted
into the barrel of a gun; when in place,
the gun could not be fired or loaded.

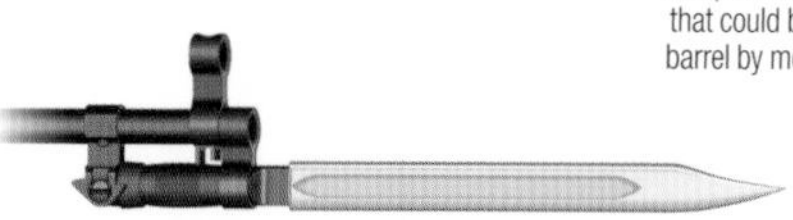

integral bayonet
Weapon permanently attached to a gun; it folded
back or slid along the barrel.

socket bayonet
Weapon with a bayonet ring on the gun
barrel; when in place, the gun could
still be fired and loaded.

hunting arms

Firearms used to kill wild animals.

breech
Part of the rifle at the rear of the barrel.

telescopic sight
Telescope mounted on a rifle to increase accuracy in aiming.

barrel
Tubular part that guides the trajectory of the projectile.

rifle (rifled bore)
Portable firearm that shoots a single bullet: the grooved inside of the barrel imparts a spinning motion to the bullet that increases the accuracy of its trajectory.

hammer
Part that strikes the firing pin, which in turn strikes the cartridge primer causing the powder charge to explode.

rear sight
Articulated graduated aiming device attached to the back of the barrel; the rear sight is lined up with the front sight when aiming.

front sight
Metal aiming device attached to the front of the barrel.

...bber or plastic covering
...to the end of the stock to
...and protect it.

muzzle
Opening through which the bullet leaves the barrel.

stock
Part that rests against the shoulder for support.

lever
Device that ejects spent cases and permits new cartridges to be loaded.

trigger guard
Metal piece covering and protecting the trigger.

trigger
Device that is pressed to fire the weapon.

shotgun (smooth bore)
Portable firearm with a barrel lacking inside grooves, designed to shoot a number of pellets at a time.

pistol grip
Part used to grasp the firearm with the trigger hand.

hammer
Part that triggers the shot by striking the firing pin, which in turn strikes the cartridge primer causing the powder charge to explode.

ventilated rib
Strip with air holes for cooling the barrel of the shotgun.

front sight
Metal aiming device attached to the front of the barrel.

...bber or plastic covering
...to the end of the stock to
...and protect it.

breech
Part of the rifle at the rear of the barrel.

forearm
Frame made of wood on which the barrel is fitted.

barrel
Tubular part that guides the trajectory of the projectile.

trigger guard
Metal piece covering and protecting the trigger.

trigger
Device that is pressed to fire the weapon.

muzzle
Opening through which the projectiles leave the barrel.

stock
...om part of the gun that is
...ed to hold and aim it.

...rtridge (rifle)
...ce of ammunition made up of a
...gle projectile (bullet), an explosive
...arge (propellant) and a primer, all
...cked inside a case.

nose
Tip of the bullet; the nose determines how the bullet will penetrate the target upon impact.

crimping
Ridged edges of the case that are used to close the cartridge and keep the pellets inside.

cartridge (shotgun)
Piece of ammunition made up of multiple projectiles (pellets), an explosive charge and a primer, all packed inside a case.

bullet
Rifle projectile; it separates from its case as it is driven in a straight line by an explosion.

core
...ntral part of the bullet; it is made of lead.

jacket
Metal coating that protects the bullet as it moves along the barrel of the firearm.

pellets
Small round shotgun projectiles that are sprayed out under pressure from the wad; they are made of lead, copper or nickel.

plastic case
Plastic cover containing the explosive charge and the pellets.

case
...ylindrical cover that contains the cartridge's explosive charge and projectile.

wad
Piece of felt or plastic that separates the pellets from the charge; when moved by the explosion, it drives the pellets forward at high speed.

propellant
...xplosive substance used to drive the projectile.

base
Metal-covered part of the case that contains the primer and charge.

primer
Metal part filled with a shock-...ensitive explosive that ignites the propellant.

cup
Metal base of the case that contains the primer.

primer
Cap filled with a shock-sensitive explosive that ignites the charge.

charge
Explosive substance used to drive the projectile.

SOCIETY

handguns

Short-barreled, light firearms held with one hand.

pistol
Short light handgun that is held in one hand; it is loaded with a magazine inside the butt.

hammer
Part that strikes the firing pin, which in turn strikes the cartridge primer causing the powder charge to explode.

rear sight
Notched projection that is lined up visually with the front sight when taking aim.

barrel
Tubular part that guides the trajectory of the bullet.

front sight
Metal aiming device attached to the front of the barrel.

slide
Movable part used to load the firing chamber; it recoils when a shot is fi and pushes a new cartridge into the chamber of the barrel.

magazine
Device that slides into the butt of the pistol; it contains cartridges, which are automatically fed into the barrel of the pistol.

trigger guard
Metal piece covering and protecting the trigger.

trigger
Device that is pressed to fire the weapon.

cartridge
Ammunition consisting of a projec (ball or lead), an explosive char (gunpowder) and a primer collect inside a casing.

magazine base
The bottom of the magazine.

magazine catch
Device that joins the magazine to the butt.

butt
The bottom part of the gun that is used to hold and aim it.

revolver
Pistol with a rotary magazine, which usually contains six cartridge chambers.

cylinder
Rotary magazine that contains the cartridges.

front sight
Metal aiming device attached to the front of the barrel.

muzzle
Opening through which the bullet leaves the barrel.

hammer
Part that strikes the firing pin, which in turn strikes the cartridge primer causing the powder charge to explode.

barrel
Tubular part that guides the trajectory of the bullet.

butt
The bottom part of the gun that is used to hold and aim it.

trigger guard
Metal piece covering and protecting the trigger.

trigger
Device that is pressed to fire the weapon.

electroshock weapon
Weapon devised to paralyze the target by firing two stun probes that deliver a powerful electric shock.

replaceable cartridge
Ammunition pack that holds the stun probes.

trigger
Device that is pressed to release the stun probes.

historical firearms

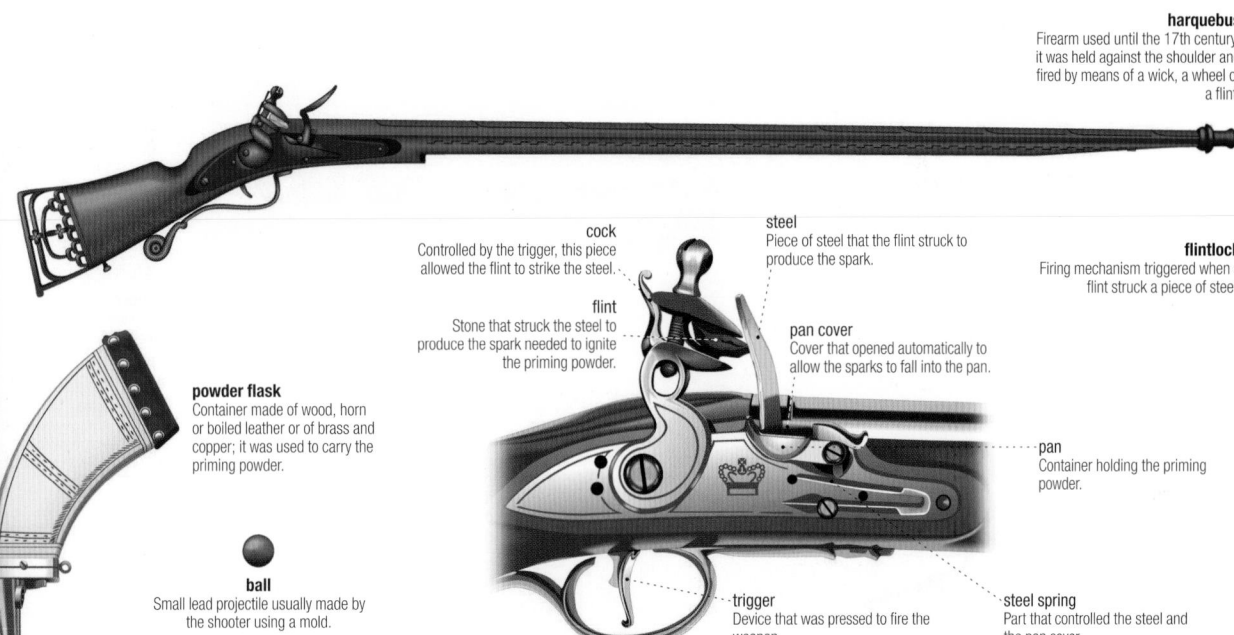

harquebus
Firearm used until the 17th century; it was held against the shoulder and fired by means of a wick, a wheel or a flint.

cock
Controlled by the trigger, this piece allowed the flint to strike the steel.

steel
Piece of steel that the flint struck to produce the spark.

flintlock
Firing mechanism triggered when a flint struck a piece of steel.

flint
Stone that struck the steel to produce the spark needed to ignite the priming powder.

pan cover
Cover that opened automatically to allow the sparks to fall into the pan.

powder flask
Container made of wood, horn or boiled leather or of brass and copper; it was used to carry the priming powder.

pan
Container holding the priming powder.

ball
Small lead projectile usually made by the shooter using a mold.

trigger
Device that was pressed to fire the weapon.

steel spring
Part that controlled the steel and the pan cover.

historical cannon and mortar

Stationary firearms designed for direct fire (cannon) or high-angle fire (mortar).

projectiles
Hard heavy objects launched by cannons and mortars.

firing accessories
Instruments used to load a cannon or mortar.

solid shot
Hard spherical projectile that was loaded into cannons; they were first made of stone, then of cast iron from the 16th century.

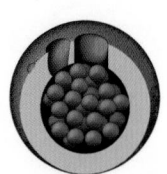

hollow shot
Spherical projectile filled with gunpowder and grapeshot that exploded on impact.

grapeshot
Projectile composed of lead or iron balls that dispersed on exiting the cannon.

bar shot
Projectile made up of solid shot at opposite ends of a steel bar or a chain; it was used to destroy a ship's masting.

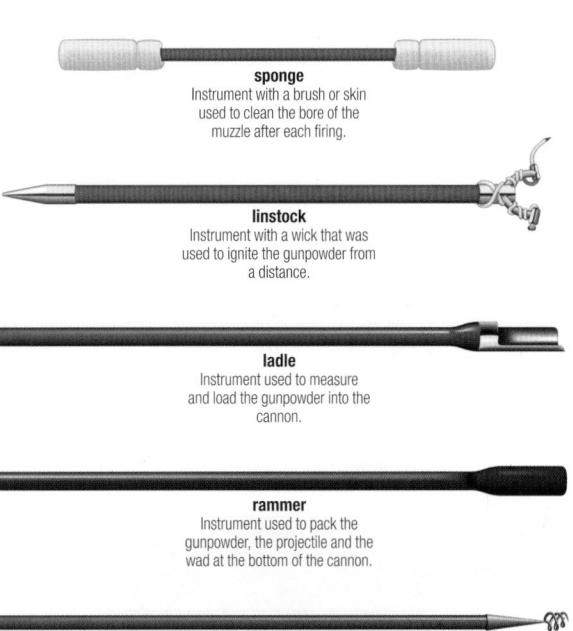

sponge
Instrument with a brush or skin used to clean the bore of the muzzle after each firing.

linstock
Instrument with a wick that was used to ignite the gunpowder from a distance.

ladle
Instrument used to measure and load the gunpowder into the cannon.

rammer
Instrument used to pack the gunpowder, the projectile and the wad at the bottom of the cannon.

worm
Instrument used to remove wad debris while leaving the powder in place.

historical cannon and mortar

cross section of a muzzle-loading cannon

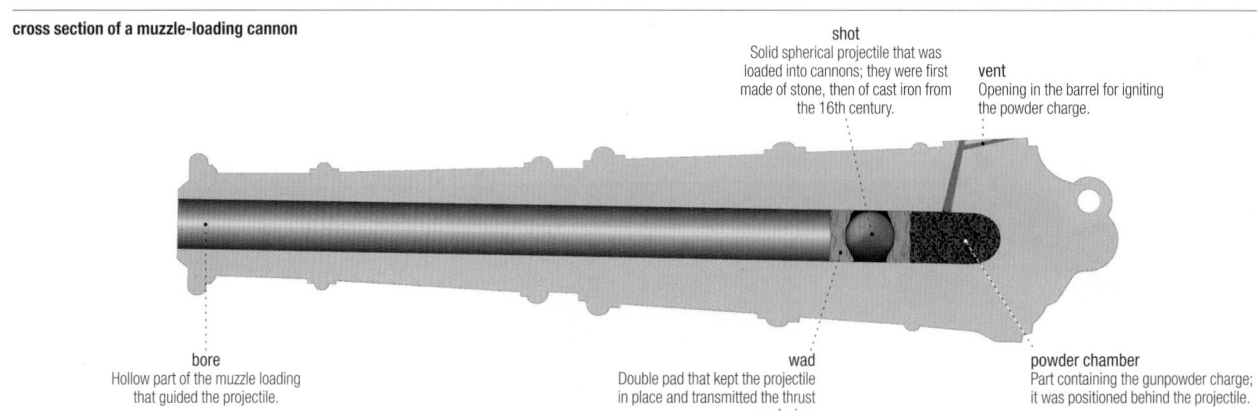

shot
Solid spherical projectile that was loaded into cannons; they were first made of stone, then of cast iron from the 16th century.

vent
Opening in the barrel for igniting the powder charge.

bore
Hollow part of the muzzle loading that guided the projectile.

wad
Double pad that kept the projectile in place and transmitted the thrust explosion.

powder chamber
Part containing the gunpowder charge; it was positioned behind the projectile.

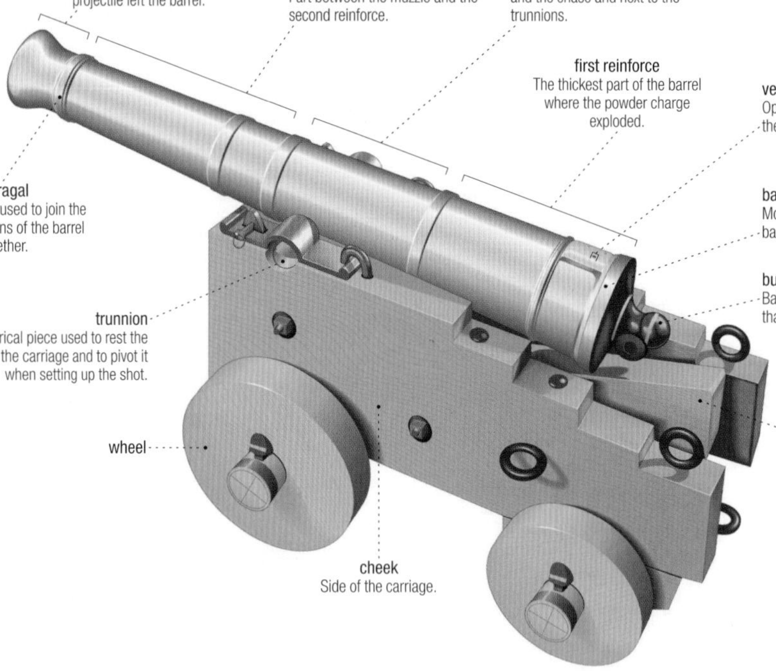

muzzle-loading cannon
The muzzle characterized all nonportable firearms such as cannon and mortar.

muzzle
Opening through which the projectile left the barrel.

chase
Part between the muzzle and the second reinforce.

second reinforce
Part between the first reinforce and the chase and next to the trunnions.

first reinforce
The thickest part of the barrel where the powder charge exploded.

vent
Opening in the barrel for igniting the powder charge.

astragal
The moldings used to join the various sections of the barrel together.

base ring
Molding around the back end of the barrel.

button
Ball at the back end of the barrel that was used to lift the cannon.

trunnion
Cylindrical piece used to rest the barrel on the carriage and to pivot it when setting up the shot.

wedge
Device used to adjust and secure the barrel in a specific firing position.

wheel

cheek
Side of the carriage.

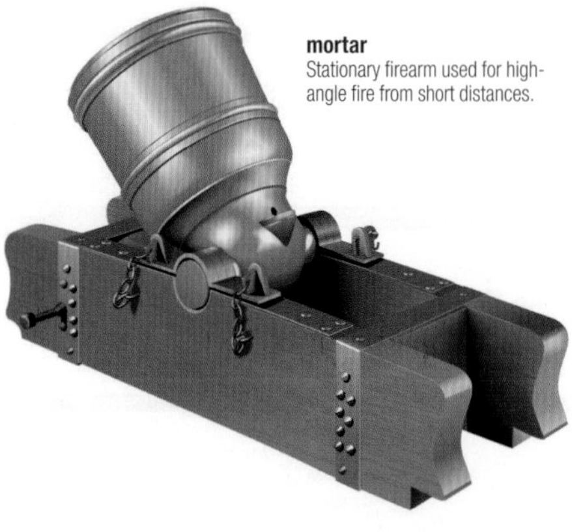

mortar
Stationary firearm used for high-angle fire from short distances.

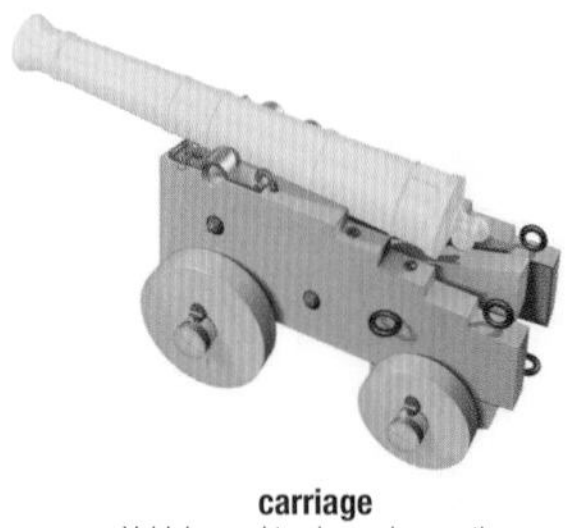

carriage
Vehicle used to aim and move the cannon.

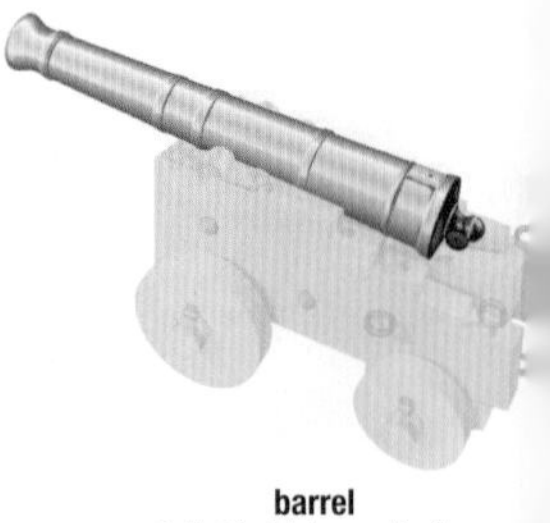

barrel
Cylindrical tube used to fire projectiles.

assault weapons

Automatic or semiautomatic weapons designed for military use by individual soldiers.

submachine gun
Shoulder-held automatic assault weapon that fires handgun cartridges in bursts.

front sight
Metal aiming device attached to the front of the barrel.

rear sight
Aiming device attached to the back of the barrel; the rear sight is lined up with the front sight when aiming.

barrel
Tubular part that guides the trajectory of the projectile.

pistol grip
Part for holding the weapon; its shape is similar to that of a pistol butt.

trigger
Device that is pressed to fire the weapon.

trigger guard
Metal piece covering and protecting the trigger.

magazine
Part containing the cartridges, which are automatically fed into the gun barrel.

assault rifle
Portable assault weapon designed for both automatic and semiautomatic fire.

rear sight
Aiming device attached to the back of the barrel; the rear sight is lined up with the front sight when aiming.

ejection port
Hole from which the empty shell casings are ejected.

barrel
Tubular part that guides the trajectory of the projectile.

front sight housing
Device that protects the front sight from impact.

handguard
Piece that protects the shooter's hand from the heat of the barrel.

pistol grip
Part for holding the weapon; its shape is similar to that of a pistol butt.

trigger
Device that is pressed to fire the weapon.

magazine
Part containing the cartridges, which are automatically fed into the gun barrel.

light machine gun
Light long-range assault weapon designed for both automatic and semiautomatic fire; its barrel is supported by a bipod.

rear sight
Aiming device attached to the back of the barrel; the rear sight is lined up with the front sight when aiming.

carrying handle
Handle for carrying the weapon.

front sight housing
Device that protects the front sight from impact.

flash hider
Muzzle attachment designed to cool the gases and reduce muzzle flash.

cover
Part that opens to access the weapon's breech.

barrel jacket
Perforated or water-filled metal tube around the barrel; during firing, the tube fills with water to cool down the barrel.

barrel
Tubular part that guides the trajectory of the projectile.

gas cylinder
Gases released by the exploding cartridge enter this cylinder and automatically push the cartridge up into the weapon's breech.

trigger
Device that is pressed to fire the weapon.

butt
Back part of the weapon that is held against the shoulder.

pistol grip
Part for holding and aiming the weapon; its shape is similar to that of a pistol butt.

bipod
Support with two legs used to stabilize the weapon when firing.

movable weapons

Mobile, high-caliber weaponry.

modern howitzer
Direct-fire piece of artillery that fires shells with relatively high trajectories; its size is between that of a cannon and a mortar.

breechblock operating lever assembly
Lever that opens and closes the breechblock to load and unload the howitzer.

recuperator cylinder
Hydraulic cylinder used to bring the barrel back into firing position.

recuperator cylinder front he
Part that is removed to check and rep recuperator cylinder's hydraulic fl

breechblock
Sturdy block mechanism at the end of the barrel for withstanding the backward thrust of the firing explosion.

elevating arc
Device with an arc-shaped cogwheel that is used to adjust the height of the shot.

recoil sleigh
Double ring on the end of the cradle that allows the barrel to recoil when the charge explodes.

sliding breech
Metal casing that houses the breechblock.

firing shaft
Metal rod that transfers the thrust of the firing lanyard to the trigger when the howitzer is fired.

barrel
Tubular part that gu trajectory of the pr

towing eye
Ring used to attach the howitzer to a towing vehicle.

drawbar
Metal rod used to tow the howitzer and move the spades.

cradle
Piece on which the barrel rests.

locking ring
Piece that locks the barrel assembly and the recoil system

carriage
Mounting for the barrel that sits on top of the trail; its function is to aim and move the barrel.

trail
Support for the carriage; it is used to point the howitzer toward the target.

equilibrator
Mechanism for balancing the barrel as it is raised or lowered.

elevating handwheel
Mechanism used to regulate the mortar's angle of fire.

float
Metal plate that supports the trail during firing and prevents the spades from sinking too deeply into the ground.

lifting handle
Handle used to lift the trail to move the howitzer.

spade
Spade-shaped prong that is used to anchor the weapon to the ground in firing position.

firing lanyard
Cord that is pulled to fire a shell.

muzzle
Opening through which the projectile leaves the tube.

modern mortar
Portable muzzle-loaded infantry weapon used to discharge high-angle fire at short ranges.

sight
Device used to set the line of fire.

elevating handle
Mechanism used to regulate the mortar's angle of fire.

traversing handle
Device used to adjust the direction of the mortar.

tube
Cylinder that guides the trajectory of the projectile.

bipod
Two-legged support that stabilizes the weapon during firing.

base plate
Part designed to prevent the tube from sinking into the ground from the impact of recoil.

movable weapons

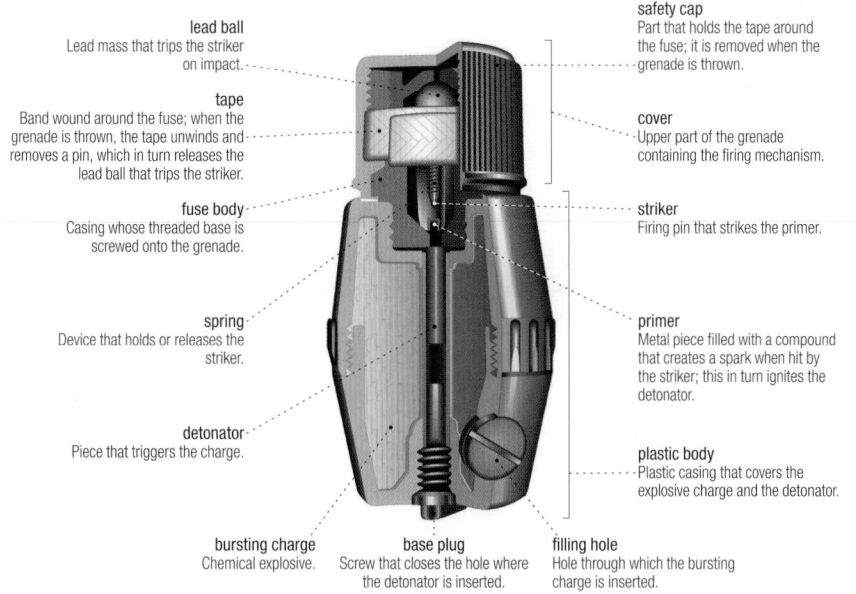

hand grenade
Light explosive missile thrown by hand.

lead ball
Lead mass that trips the striker on impact.

tape
Band wound around the fuse; when the grenade is thrown, the tape unwinds and removes a pin, which in turn releases the lead ball that trips the striker.

fuse body
Casing whose threaded base is screwed onto the grenade.

spring
Device that holds or releases the striker.

detonator
Piece that triggers the charge.

safety cap
Part that holds the tape around the fuse; it is removed when the grenade is thrown.

cover
Upper part of the grenade containing the firing mechanism.

striker
Firing pin that strikes the primer.

primer
Metal piece filled with a compound that creates a spark when hit by the striker; this in turn ignites the detonator.

plastic body
Plastic casing that covers the explosive charge and the detonator.

bursting charge
Chemical explosive.

base plug
Screw that closes the hole where the detonator is inserted.

filling hole
Hole through which the bursting charge is inserted.

bazooka
Portable weapon that launches antitank rockets.

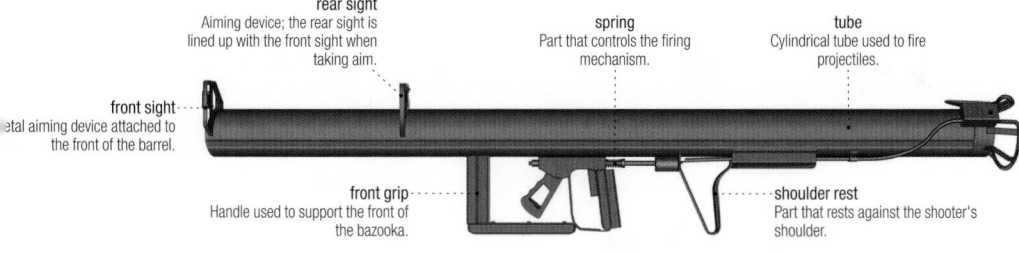

rear sight
Aiming device; the rear sight is lined up with the front sight when taking aim.

front sight
Metal aiming device attached to the front of the barrel.

spring
Part that controls the firing mechanism.

tube
Cylindrical tube used to fire projectiles.

front grip
Handle used to support the front of the bazooka.

shoulder rest
Part that rests against the shooter's shoulder.

recoilless rifle
Portable weapon that functions by balancing thrust; to prevent recoil, a gas jet is ejected in the opposite direction from the projectile.

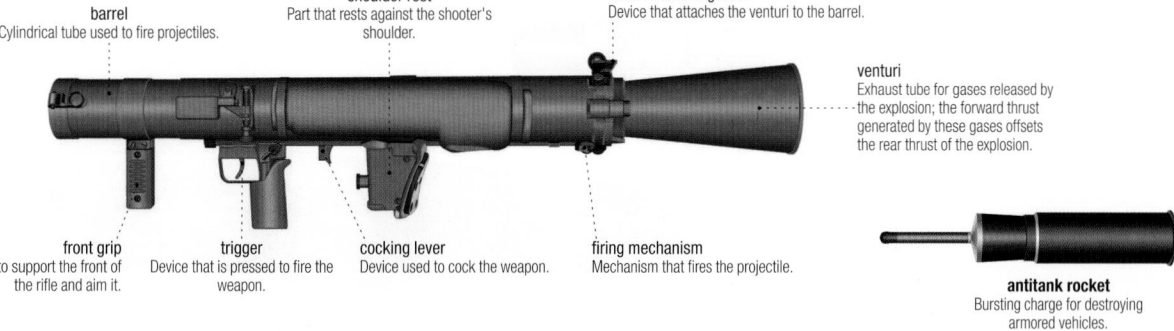

barrel
Cylindrical tube used to fire projectiles.

shoulder rest
Part that rests against the shooter's shoulder.

venturi fastening lever
Device that attaches the venturi to the barrel.

venturi
Exhaust tube for gases released by the explosion; the forward thrust generated by these gases offsets the rear thrust of the explosion.

front grip
Used to support the front of the rifle and aim it.

trigger
Device that is pressed to fire the weapon.

cocking lever
Device used to cock the weapon.

firing mechanism
Mechanism that fires the projectile.

antitank rocket
Bursting charge for destroying armored vehicles.

SOCIETY

missiles

Self-propelled projectiles that carry a destructive payload.

structure of a missile

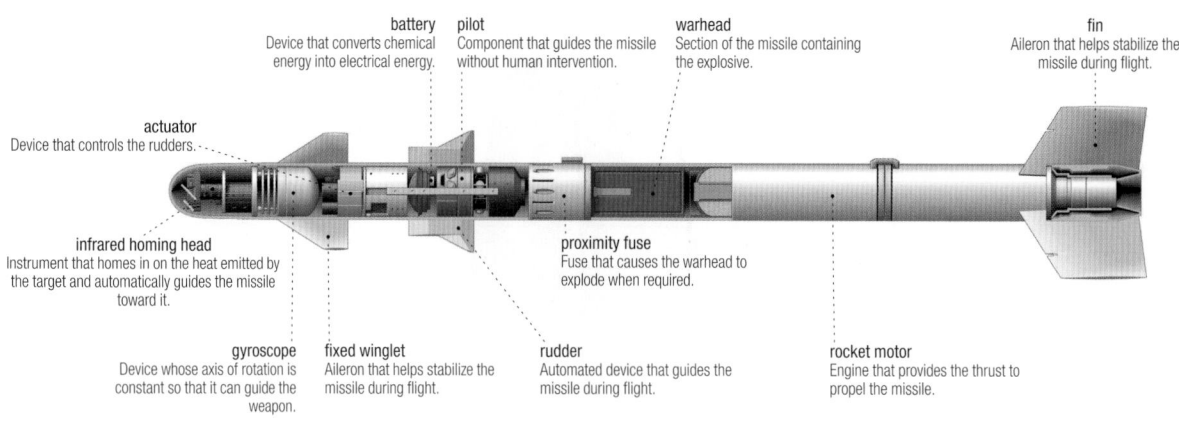

battery
Device that converts chemical energy into electrical energy.

pilot
Component that guides the missile without human intervention.

warhead
Section of the missile containing the explosive.

fin
Aileron that helps stabilize the missile during flight.

actuator
Device that controls the rudders.

infrared homing head
Instrument that homes in on the heat emitted by the target and automatically guides the missile toward it.

proximity fuse
Fuse that causes the warhead to explode when required.

gyroscope
Device whose axis of rotation is constant so that it can guide the weapon.

fixed winglet
Aileron that helps stabilize the missile during flight.

rudder
Automated device that guides the missile during flight.

rocket motor
Engine that provides the thrust to propel the missile.

major types of missiles
Missiles are classified according to the launch point and the nature of the target.

antitank missile
Missile designed to destroy tanks and armored vehicles.

air-to-air missile
Missile fired from a helicopter or other aircraft; its target is an aircraft or another missile.

surface-to-air missile
Missile fired from a launcher or a ground vehicle; its target is an aircraft or another missile.

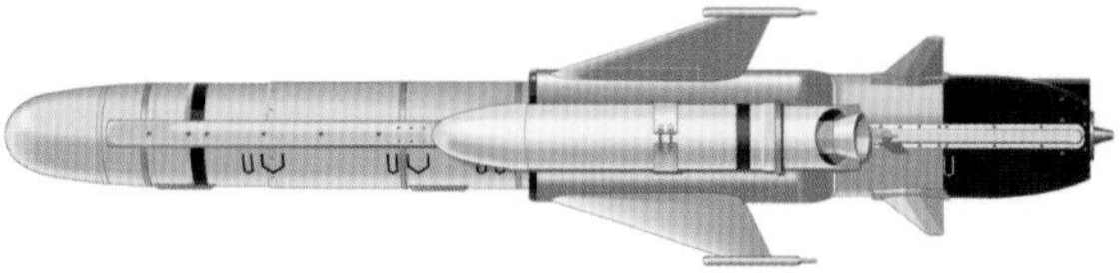

antiship missile
Missile designed to destroy ships.

antiradar missile
Missile designed to destroy radar systems.

surface-to-subsurface missile
Missile designed to destroy submarines.

air-to-surface missile
Missile fired at a ground target from a helicopter or other aircraft.

tank

Armed and armored vehicle mounted on tracks.

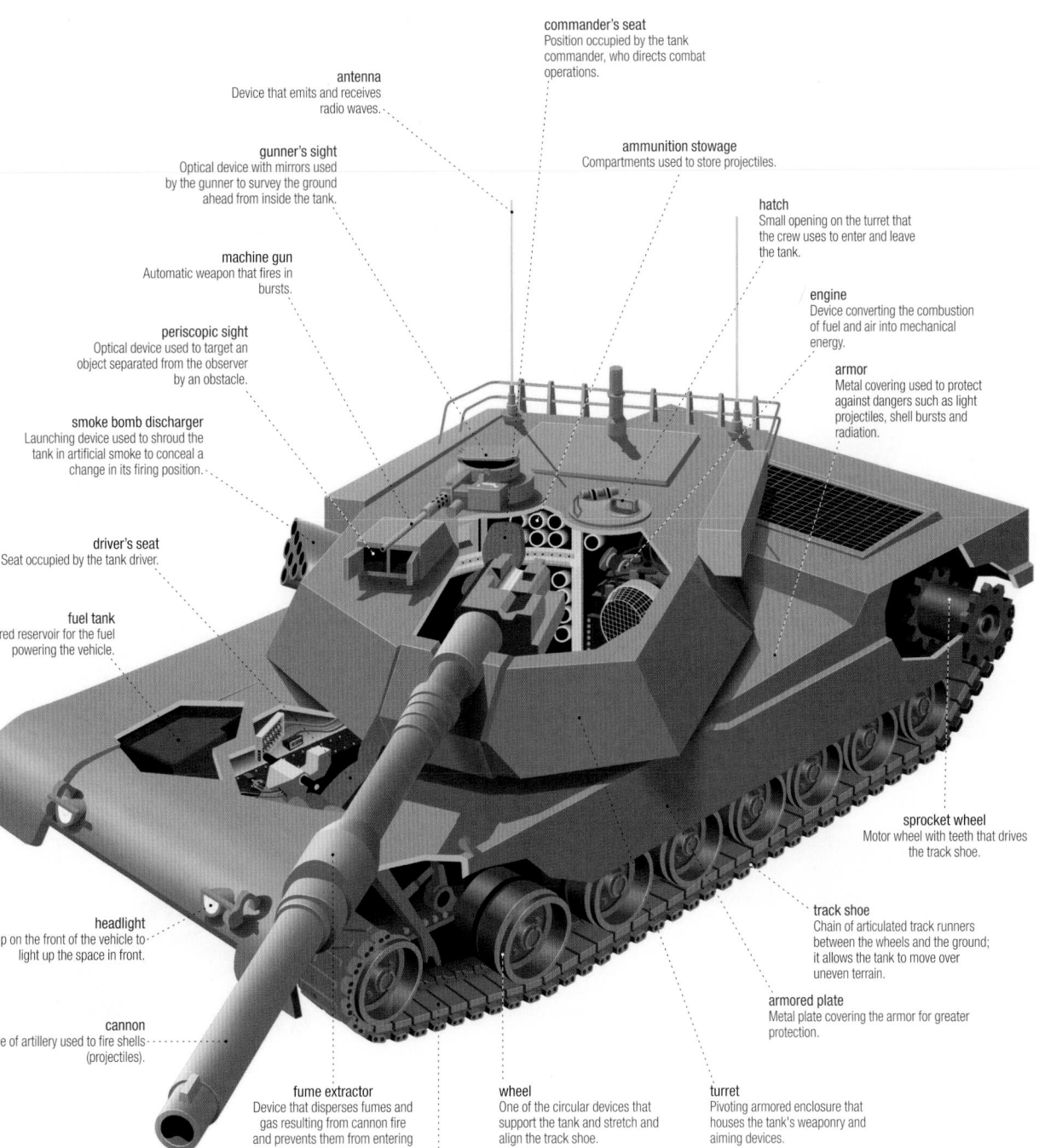

commander's seat
Position occupied by the tank commander, who directs combat operations.

antenna
Device that emits and receives radio waves.

ammunition stowage
Compartments used to store projectiles.

gunner's sight
Optical device with mirrors used by the gunner to survey the ground ahead from inside the tank.

hatch
Small opening on the turret that the crew uses to enter and leave the tank.

machine gun
Automatic weapon that fires in bursts.

engine
Device converting the combustion of fuel and air into mechanical energy.

periscopic sight
Optical device used to target an object separated from the observer by an obstacle.

armor
Metal covering used to protect against dangers such as light projectiles, shell bursts and radiation.

smoke bomb discharger
Launching device used to shroud the tank in artificial smoke to conceal a change in its firing position.

driver's seat
Seat occupied by the tank driver.

fuel tank
mored reservoir for the fuel powering the vehicle.

sprocket wheel
Motor wheel with teeth that drives the track shoe.

track shoe
Chain of articulated track runners between the wheels and the ground; it allows the tank to move over uneven terrain.

headlight
amp on the front of the vehicle to light up the space in front.

armored plate
Metal plate covering the armor for greater protection.

cannon
Piece of artillery used to fire shells (projectiles).

fume extractor
Device that disperses fumes and gas resulting from cannon fire and prevents them from entering the tank.

wheel
One of the circular devices that support the tank and stretch and align the track shoe.

turret
Pivoting armored enclosure that houses the tank's weaponry and aiming devices.

track link
One of a series of articulated pieces that forms the track shoe.

SOCIETY

combat aircraft
Military aircraft used for attack purposes.

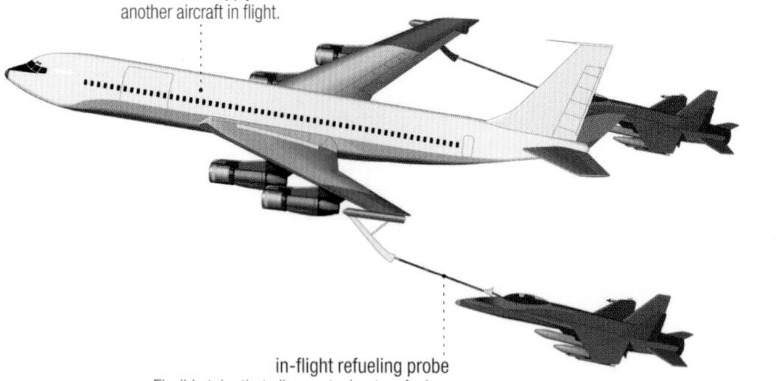

SOCIETY

in-flight refueli
Action of refueling a plane from a tanker in flig

radar antenna
Antenna designed to detect objects by emitting radio waves and capturing the echo they reflect.

rudder
Mobile part of the tail assembly that is used to balance the yaw (lateral movement) of an aircraft.

tanker
Aircraft used to supply fuel to another aircraft in flight.

parachute
Device that opens from the tail of the aircraft to reduce speed on landing.

fin
Fixed vertical part of the tail assembly that keeps the aircraft stable.

exhaust nozzle
Conduit through which hot gases from the turbojet engine are released.

in-flight refueling probe
Flexible tube that allows a tanker to refuel an aircraft in flight.

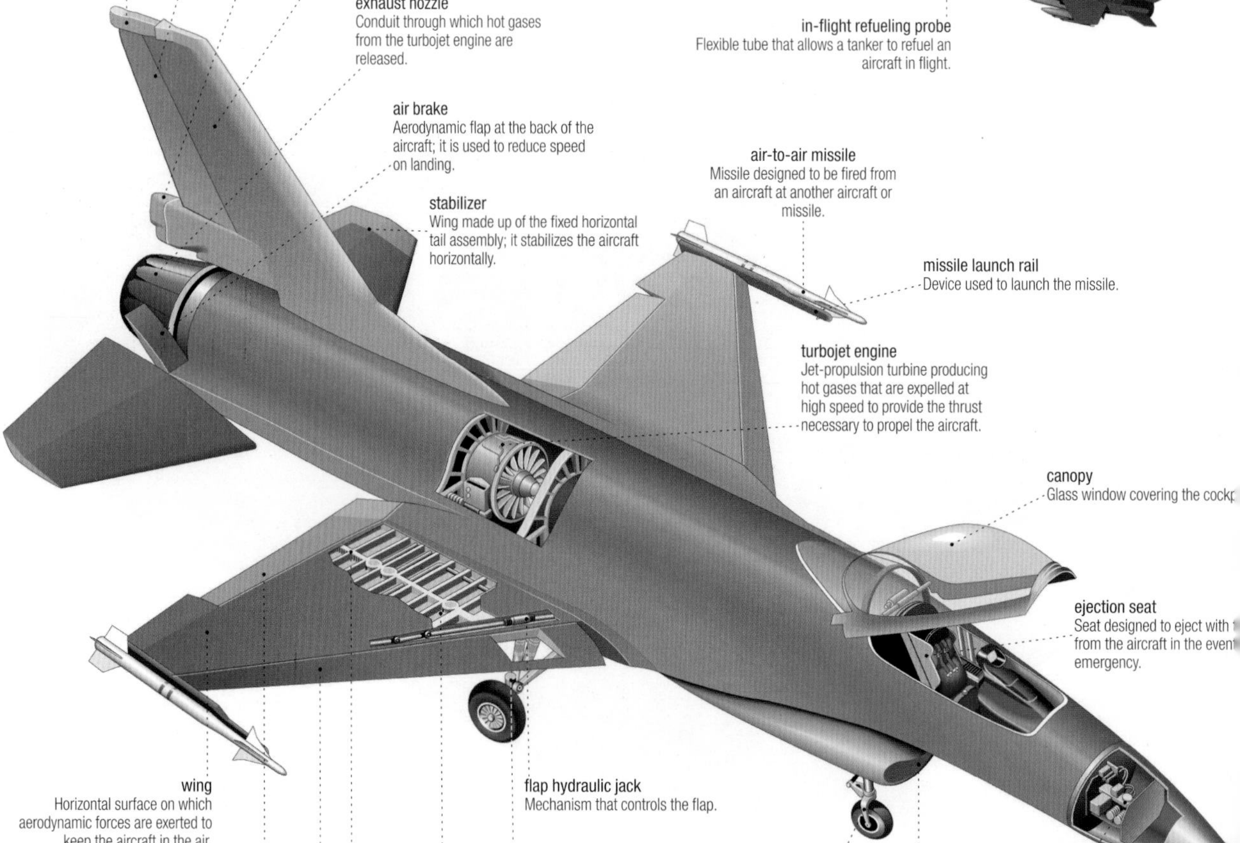

air brake
Aerodynamic flap at the back of the aircraft; it is used to reduce speed on landing.

air-to-air missile
Missile designed to be fired from an aircraft at another aircraft or missile.

stabilizer
Wing made up of the fixed horizontal tail assembly; it stabilizes the aircraft horizontally.

missile launch rail
Device used to launch the missile.

turbojet engine
Jet-propulsion turbine producing hot gases that are expelled at high speed to provide the thrust necessary to propel the aircraft.

canopy
Glass window covering the cockp

ejection seat
Seat designed to eject with from the aircraft in the even emergency.

wing
Horizontal surface on which aerodynamic forces are exerted to keep the aircraft in the air.

flap hydraulic jack
Mechanism that controls the flap.

trailing edge flap
Articulated flap on the trailing edge of the wing that deploys downward to increase the aircraft's lift on takeoff.

main landing gear
Retractable mechanism that enables the aircraft to land; it is located behind the aircraft's center of gravity under its wings.

radar unit
Device that uses radio waves to detect objects such as other aircraft.

leading edge flap
Articulated panel on the front of the wing.

fuel tank
Reservoir containing the fuel that allows the aircraft to fly.

front landing gear
Retractable mechanism that enables the aircraft to land; it is located at the front end.

motor air inlet
Part that supplies the turbojet with the air required for combustion.

wing box
Metal substructure of the wings; the trailing and leading edge flaps are connected to it.

radome
Rigid casing that radio waves can pass through; it protects the radar system.

warships

Ships outfitted with the equipment and weaponry required to attack a target or defend itself from hostility.

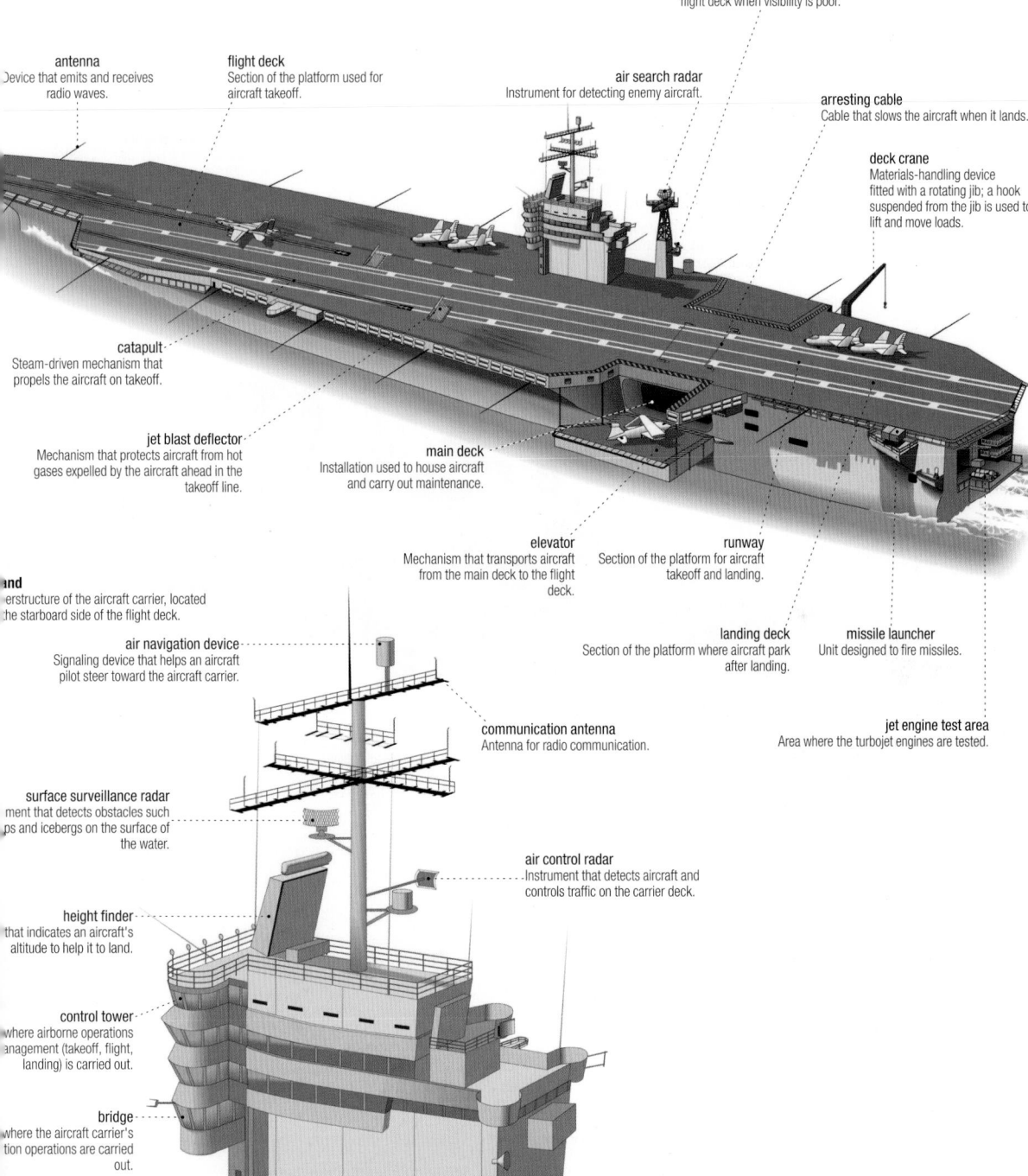

aircraft carrier
Warship designed to carry combat aircraft and provide a flight deck for takeoff and landing.

landing radar
Instrument that directs pilots to the flight deck when visibility is poor.

antenna
Device that emits and receives radio waves.

flight deck
Section of the platform used for aircraft takeoff.

air search radar
Instrument for detecting enemy aircraft.

arresting cable
Cable that slows the aircraft when it lands.

deck crane
Materials-handling device fitted with a rotating jib; a hook suspended from the jib is used to lift and move loads.

catapult
Steam-driven mechanism that propels the aircraft on takeoff.

jet blast deflector
Mechanism that protects aircraft from hot gases expelled by the aircraft ahead in the takeoff line.

main deck
Installation used to house aircraft and carry out maintenance.

elevator
Mechanism that transports aircraft from the main deck to the flight deck.

runway
Section of the platform for aircraft takeoff and landing.

and
erstructure of the aircraft carrier, located the starboard side of the flight deck.

landing deck
Section of the platform where aircraft park after landing.

missile launcher
Unit designed to fire missiles.

air navigation device
Signaling device that helps an aircraft pilot steer toward the aircraft carrier.

communication antenna
Antenna for radio communication.

jet engine test area
Area where the turbojet engines are tested.

surface surveillance radar
ment that detects obstacles such ps and icebergs on the surface of the water.

air control radar
Instrument that detects aircraft and controls traffic on the carrier deck.

height finder
that indicates an aircraft's altitude to help it to land.

control tower
where airborne operations anagement (takeoff, flight, landing) is carried out.

bridge
where the aircraft carrier's tion operations are carried out.

warships

frigate
Warship used for antiaircraft,
antisubmarine and antiship operations.

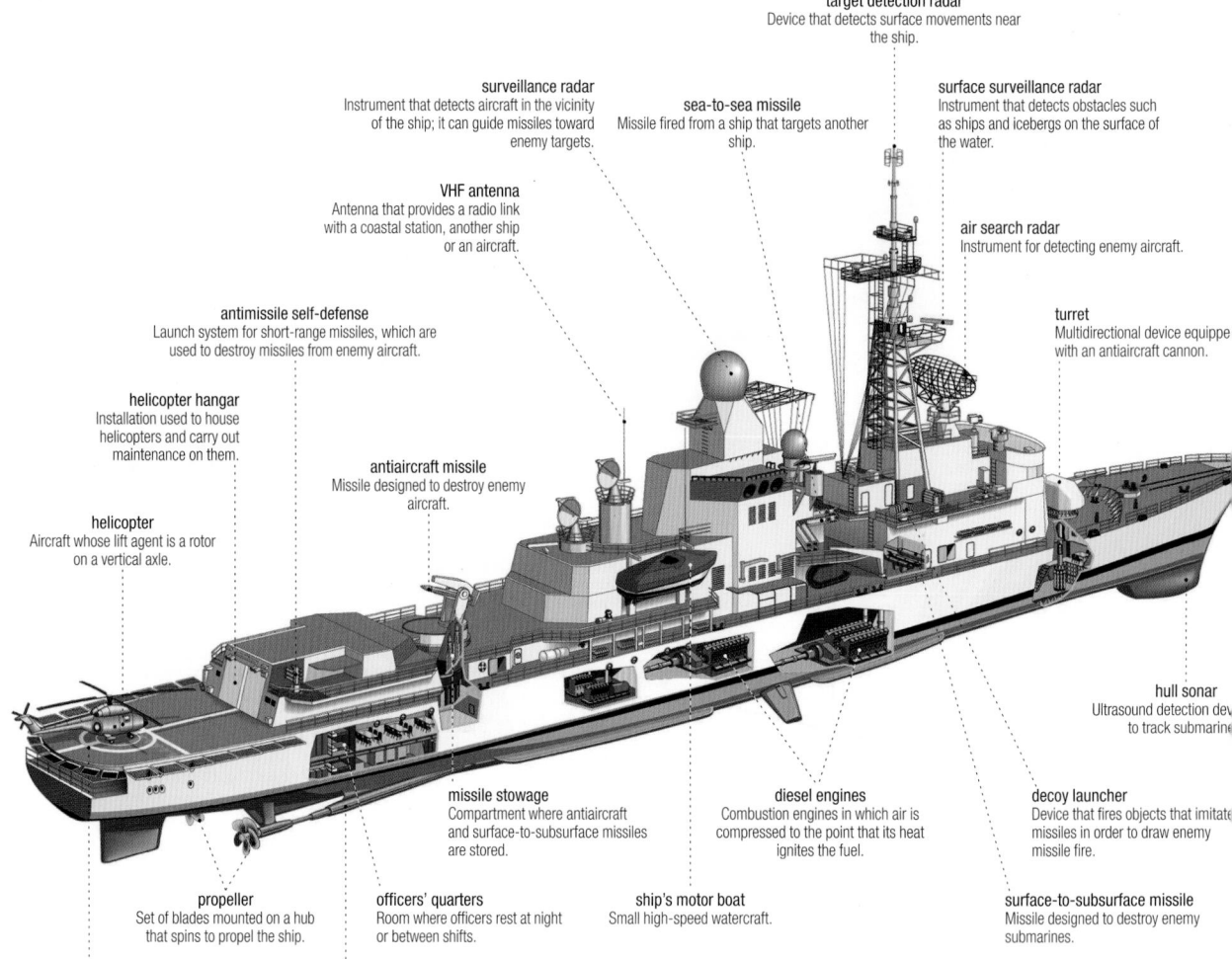

target detection radar
Device that detects surface movements near
the ship.

surveillance radar
Instrument that detects aircraft in the vicinity
of the ship; it can guide missiles toward
enemy targets.

sea-to-sea missile
Missile fired from a ship that targets another
ship.

surface surveillance radar
Instrument that detects obstacles such
as ships and icebergs on the surface of
the water.

VHF antenna
Antenna that provides a radio link
with a coastal station, another ship
or an aircraft.

air search radar
Instrument for detecting enemy aircraft.

antimissile self-defense
Launch system for short-range missiles, which are
used to destroy missiles from enemy aircraft.

turret
Multidirectional device equippe
with an antiaircraft cannon.

helicopter hangar
Installation used to house
helicopters and carry out
maintenance on them.

antiaircraft missile
Missile designed to destroy enemy
aircraft.

helicopter
Aircraft whose lift agent is a rotor
on a vertical axle.

hull sonar
Ultrasound detection dev
to track submarine

missile stowage
Compartment where antiaircraft
and surface-to-subsurface missiles
are stored.

diesel engines
Combustion engines in which air is
compressed to the point that its heat
ignites the fuel.

decoy launcher
Device that fires objects that imitate
missiles in order to draw enemy
missile fire.

propeller
Set of blades mounted on a hub
that spins to propel the ship.

officers' quarters
Room where officers rest at night
or between shifts.

ship's motor boat
Small high-speed watercraft.

surface-to-subsurface missile
Missile designed to destroy enemy
submarines.

shaft
Device driven by a diesel engine;
it transfers rotary movement to the
propeller.

helicopter flight deck
Area designed for helicopter takeoff and landing.

nuclear submarine
Underwater warship that operates on nuclear energy; it can remain underwater for months without surfacing.

eller
f blades mounted on a hub that
to propel the ship.

airlock
Hatch that serves as a passage between the outside and the aft area of the submarine.

upper rudder
Blade that can be turned remotely by the helmsman to steer the submarine.

propulsion machinery control room
Command station for the engine room.

conning tower
Superstructure from which the periscopes and antennas emerge.

emergency electric motor
Motor that replaces the main motor in the event of a breakdown.

turbo-alternator
Device that uses steam to convert the mechanical force generated by the rotation of the turbine into electricity.

steam generator
Device in which water is converted into steam using heat from the cooling system; it powers the turbo-alternator.

sail plane
Adjustable fin at the front of the submarine; it is used for diving and surfacing.

torpedo room
Room that houses the torpedoes and firing tubes.

main electric motor
Engine that drives the propeller; the turbo-alternator supplies it with electricity.

reactor
Device in which nuclear fission is produced; this releases the heat required to evaporate the water in the steam generator.

engine room
Room that houses the electric motors.

electricity production room
Room where the instruments that produce electricity are housed.

nuclear boiler room
Room that houses the reactor.

torpedo
Self-propelled weapon containing an explosive charge that is designed to attack enemy ships and submarines.

firing tube
Chamber that houses the torpedoes for firing.

ving plane
djustable rudder at the stern that
lows the submarine to dive and
rface.

attack periscope
Device used to examine the surface of the water; its discreet head allows the submarine to approach an enemy without being noticed.

radar antenna
Antenna designed to detect objects by emitting radio waves and capturing the echo they reflect.

radio antenna
Antenna transmitting and receiving radio waves for communications.

conning tower
Superstructure from which the periscopes and antennas emerge.

multipurpose antenna
Device that transmits and receives radio waves on an extremely broad range of frequencies.

navigation periscope
Device used to examine the surface of the water; its wide head provides a broad field of vision.

officers' quarters
Room where officers rest at night or between shifts.

operation control room
Room in which submarine combat operations and navigation maneuvers are coordinated.

computer room
Room in which radar, sonar and other data transmitted to the submarine are processed.

kitchen
Room where meals are prepared.

dining room
Hall for eating meals.

fire prevention

The means and instruments used to prevent and fight fires.

fire station
Building designed to house firefighters, fire trucks and firefighting materials.

documentation center
Room used to store documentation such as security documents related to buildings in a specific area, maps and municipal emergency plans.

officers' dormitory
Room where officers rest at night or between firefighting operations.

administrative office
Workplace for administrative personnel.

fire prevention education officer's office
Fire prevention education officer: person responsible visiting buildings in a specific area and ensuring that prevention measures are applied.

firefighters' dormitory
Room furnished with several beds where firefighters rest at night or between firefighting operations.

chief's office
Work area reserved for the fire chief.

meeting roo
Room used by fire personnel to hold m and discussion

officers' toilets and showers

firefighters' toilets and showers

turnouts
Garment made of water- and fire-resistant fabric that protects the firefighter against flames, water and steam.

locker room
Room in which employees store their street clothes.

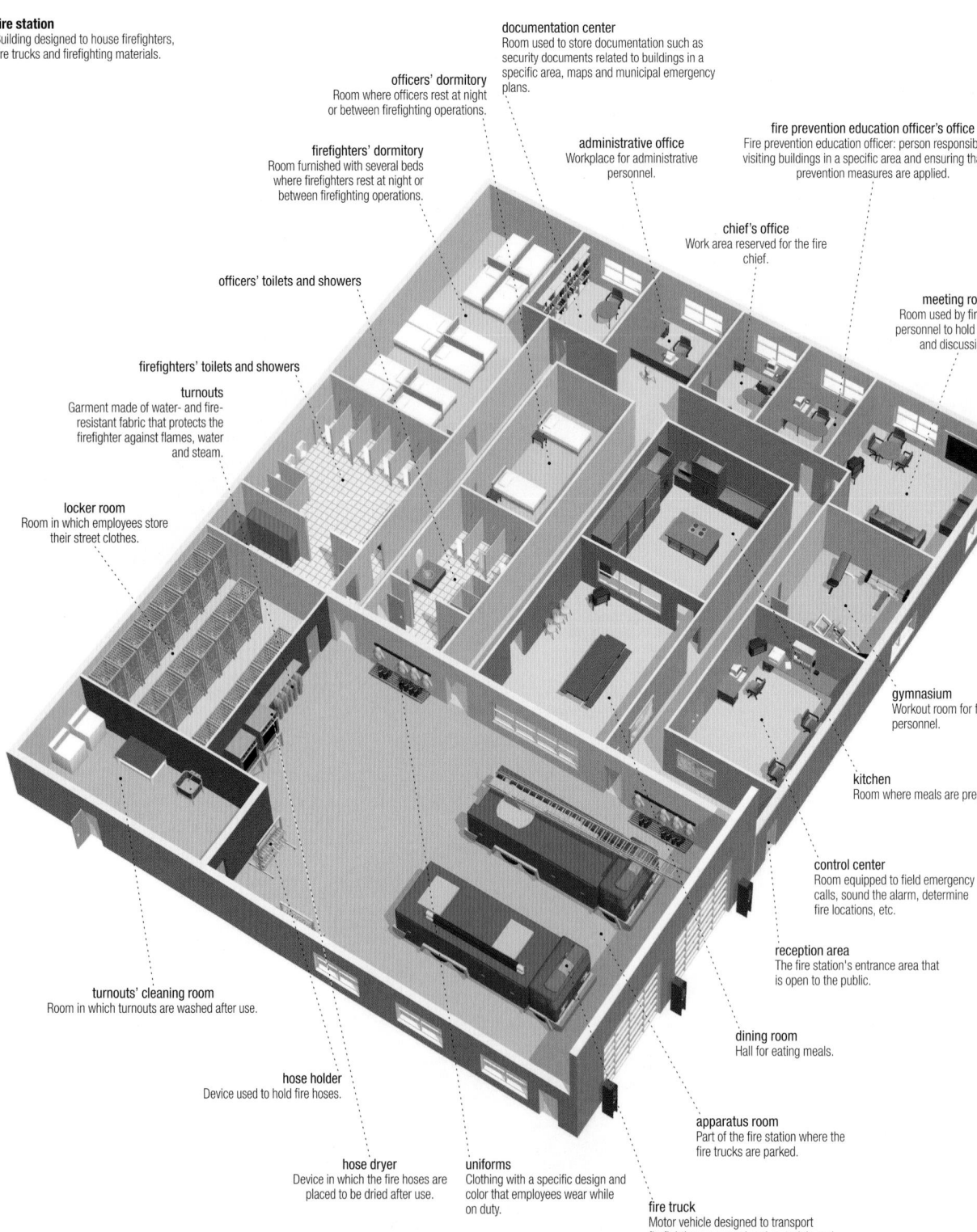

gymnasium
Workout room for fir personnel.

kitchen
Room where meals are prepa

control center
Room equipped to field emergency calls, sound the alarm, determine fire locations, etc.

reception area
The fire station's entrance area that is open to the public.

turnouts' cleaning room
Room in which turnouts are washed after use.

dining room
Hall for eating meals.

hose holder
Device used to hold fire hoses.

apparatus room
Part of the fire station where the fire trucks are parked.

hose dryer
Device in which the fire hoses are placed to be dried after use.

uniforms
Clothing with a specific design and color that employees wear while on duty.

fire truck
Motor vehicle designed to transport firefighting personnel and materials and to supply water to the fire hose nozzles.

nd lamp
nting device that is worn by the
fighter while on duty.

spotlight
Apparatus that projects
concentrated high-intensity light
beams.

strap
Band of leather or fabric secured to
the spotlight; it can be held or worn
as a shoulder strap.

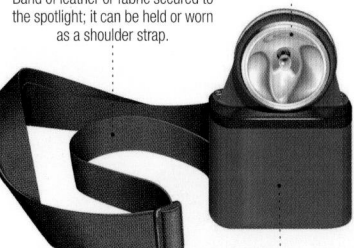

battery
Device that converts chemical
energy into electrical energy.

e helmet
adpiece designed to protect the head
m impact, flames and water.

firefighter
Person responsible for fighting
fires, intervening in natural
disasters and undertaking rescue
operations.

fire helmet
Headpiece designed to protect the head from
impact, flames and water.

compressed-air cylinder
Container filled with compressed air that
allows the firefighter to breathe when the
air is smoky or strongly contaminated.

full face mask
Mask that covers the entire face;
it protects the respiratory tract and
the eyes.

self-contained breathing apparatus
Device that protects against inhaling toxic
gas, smoke, dust, etc.

air-supply tube
Conduit that funnels air from the
cylinder to the mask.

pressure demand regulator
Device that reduces air pressure from the
cylinder and regulates the flow of air to the
mask.

man down alarm
Device that emits a strong signal so that
a firefighter can be located in a blaze; it is
activated by the firefighter or after a period
of immobility.

turnouts
Garment made of water- and fire-
resistant fabric that protects the
firefighter against flames, water and
steam.

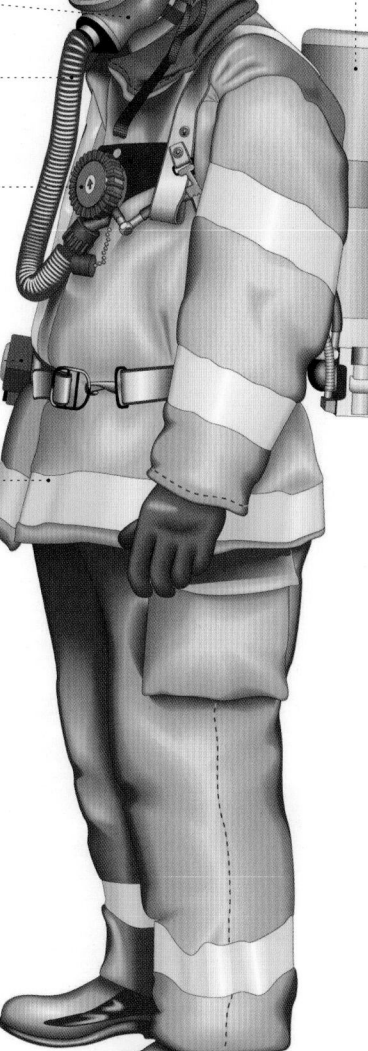

reflective stripe
Strip that reflects light so that it is
easier to locate the firefighter when
visibility is reduced.

face shield
Adjustable visor that protects the
upper face area.

chin strap
Strap that fastens the helmet to the head.

neck guard
Fireproof fabric that protects the
nape of the neck and the ears.

chin guard
Fireproof fabric that protects the
lower face area.

rubber boot
Water-resistant fireproof boot that
protects the foot from burns and
other injury.

fire prevention

fire trucks

Motor vehicles designed to transport firefighting personnel and materials and to supply water to the fire hose nozzles.

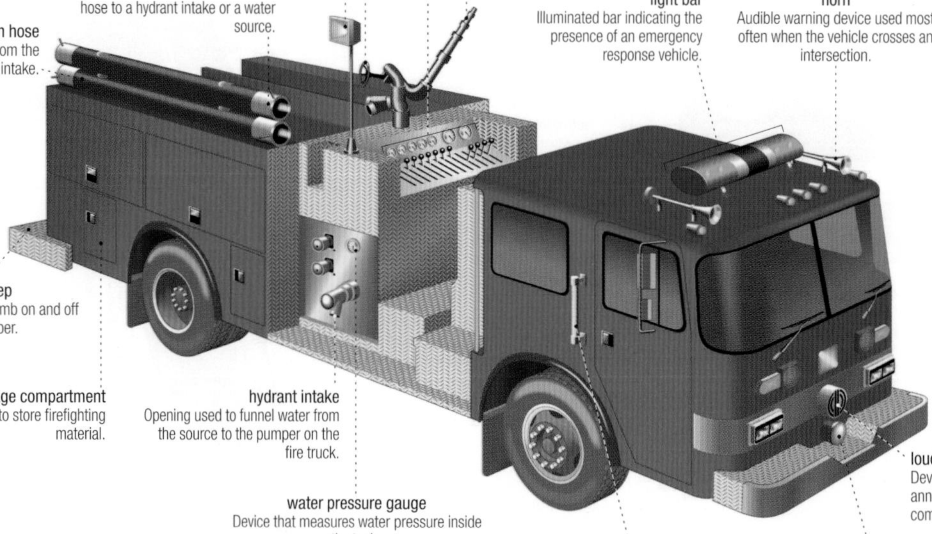

control wheel
Device used to operate the deluge gun.

control panel
Panel with a set of controls, which are used to operate the equipment.

pumper

Motor vehicle with a water tank and a pump to funnel pressurized water to the fire hose nozzles.

spotlight
Device that emits a concentrated high-intensity light beam; it can be fully rotated.

deluge gun
Pump that delivers a strong jet of water.

fitting
Device that connects the suction hose to a hydrant intake or a water source.

light bar
Illuminated bar indicating the presence of an emergency response vehicle.

horn
Audible warning device used most often when the vehicle crosses an intersection.

suction hose
Tube that carries water from the source to a hydrant intake.

rear step
Platform used to climb on and off the pumper.

storage compartment
Compartment used to store firefighting material.

hydrant intake
Opening used to funnel water from the source to the pumper on the fire truck.

loudspeaker
Device used to issue public announcements or transmi communications.

water pressure gauge
Device that measures water pressure inside the tank.

grab handle
Vertical handle placed at shoulder level close to the door; it is used to climb into and out of the vehicle.

hydrant intake
Opening used to funnel water from the source to the pumper on the fire truck.

ladder truck

Motor vehicle equipped with a tower ladder, which is used to fight a fire from above and access the upper reaches of a building from the outside.

telescopic boom
Extensible device that raises the sliding ladders of the tower ladder to the desired height.

Mars light
Revolving light on the roof of the moving vehicle; it is used when an operation is in progress.

ladder pipe noz
Device mounted on the end of t telescopic boom; it forms and direct water jet onto a fire or onto the upp reaches of a buildir

elevating cylinder
Device that raises the tower ladder and keeps it stable.

turntable mounting
Pivoting device that supports and positions the tower ladder.

tower ladder
Set of extension ladders for changing the height of the tower ladder.

top ladder
Sliding ladder that makes up the highest part of the tower ladder.

spotlight
Device that emits a concentrated high-intensity light beam; it can be fully rotated.

storage compartment
Compartment used to store firefighting material.

outrigger
Device that stabilizes the vehicle when the ladders are deployed.

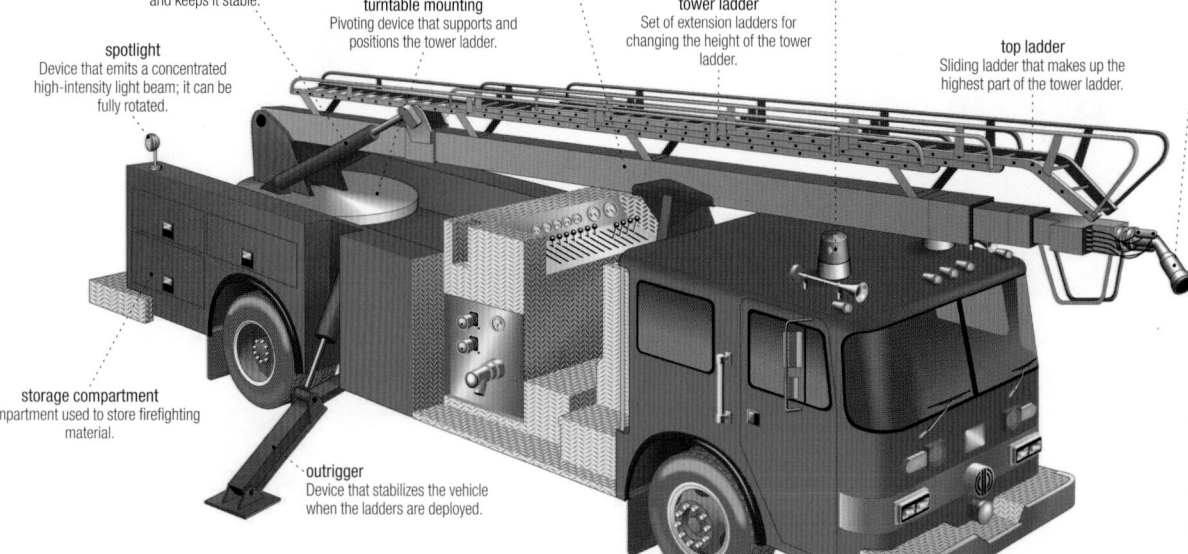

SOCIETY

fire prevention

fire hydrant
A pipe connected to a water main; firefighters attach their hoses to it to supply their trucks.

cover
Part of the detector that shields the smoke detection mechanism.

base
Part of the detector that is attached to a surface; the cover screws into the base.

test button
Device that is pressed to determine whether the sound signal is functioning.

indicator light
Light indicating that the detector is in alarm mode.

smoke or heat detector
Device that emits a powerful alarm signal when it detects smoke or heat.

firefighting material

pin
Security device that is pulled to operate the trigger.

trigger
Device that is pressed to spray the fire area.

nozzle
Device that is connected to the end of a fire hose; it forms and directs a jet of water.

hose
Flexible conduit that is maneuvered to aim the nozzle at the fire.

ladder and hose strap
Band that secures a hose to a ladder or other stationary object.

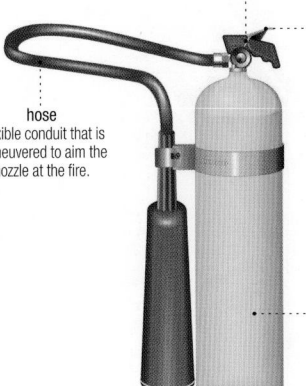

tank
Metal container that is filled with pressurized liquid, powder or gas; it is replenished periodically.

portable fire extinguisher
Portable device used to extinguish a fire using liquid, powder or gas released under pressure.

dividing breeching
Y-shaped device used to connect two hoses to a water outlet.

fire hydrant wrench
Tool with a square opening nut used to manipulate the fire hydrant opening.

fire hose
Flexible hose that carries water from the pressurized water source to the nozzle or a fire apparatus.

percussion bar
Tool with a deer foot that is used to force open locks, padlocks, etc.

ax
Tool with a sharp blade and a pick attached to the end of a handle; it is used to create openings by forcing open doors and windows.

pike pole
Tool with a hook and a pike attached to a long handle; it is used for operations such as piercing walls and ceilings and carrying out underwater searches.

roof ladder
Straight ladder with one end having fixed or detachable hooks to keep the ladder in place on a structure.

crime prevention

The means used to prevent occurrences such as violence, delinquency and acts of aggression.

police station
Building that houses crime
prevention personnel and offices.

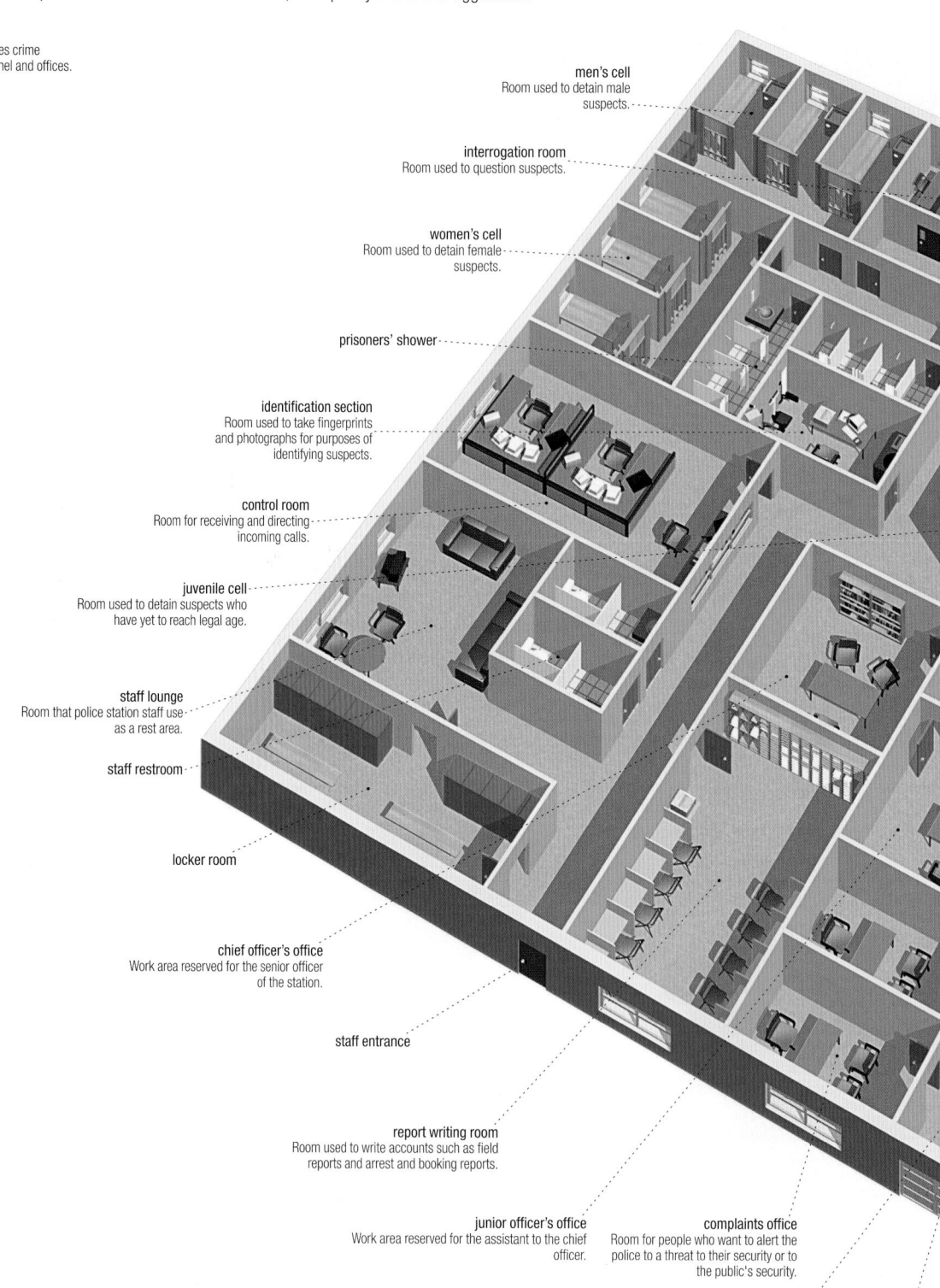

men's cell
Room used to detain male
suspects.

interrogation room
Room used to question suspects.

women's cell
Room used to detain female
suspects.

prisoners' shower

identification section
Room used to take fingerprints
and photographs for purposes of
identifying suspects.

control room
Room for receiving and directing
incoming calls.

juvenile cell
Room used to detain suspects who
have yet to reach legal age.

staff lounge
Room that police station staff use
as a rest area.

staff restroom

locker room

chief officer's office
Work area reserved for the senior officer
of the station.

staff entrance

report writing room
Room used to write accounts such as field
reports and arrest and booking reports.

junior officer's office
Work area reserved for the assistant to the chief
officer.

complaints office
Room for people who want to alert the
police to a threat to their security or to
the public's security.

waiting room
Area where citizens wait to see a
police officer.

main entrance

crime prevention

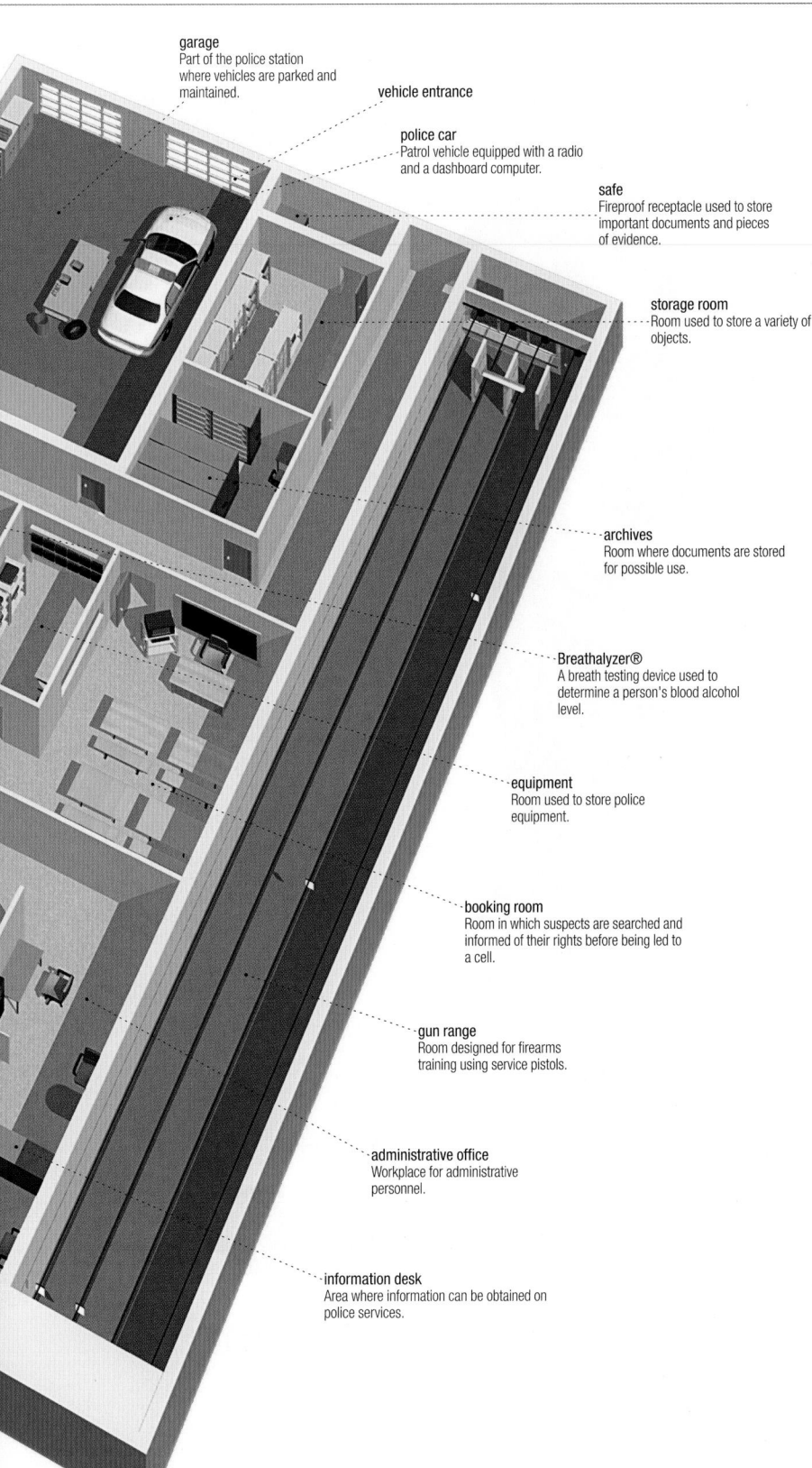

garage
Part of the police station where vehicles are parked and maintained.

vehicle entrance

police car
Patrol vehicle equipped with a radio and a dashboard computer.

safe
Fireproof receptacle used to store important documents and pieces of evidence.

storage room
Room used to store a variety of objects.

archives
Room where documents are stored for possible use.

Breathalyzer®
A breath testing device used to determine a person's blood alcohol level.

equipment
Room used to store police equipment.

booking room
Room in which suspects are searched and informed of their rights before being led to a cell.

gun range
Room designed for firearms training using service pistols.

administrative office
Workplace for administrative personnel.

information desk
Area where information can be obtained on police services.

crime prevention

police officer
Uniformed person responsible for maintaining law and order.

cap
Brimless, somewhat soft headgear that has a peak and a flat crown.

badge
Symbol indicating the force an officer belongs to as well as the officer's identification number.

shoulder strap
Decorative tab attached to the shoulder and sometimes buttoned down; it is inspired by the military uniform.

rank insignia
Symbol indicating a police officer's rank.

name tag
A strip of plastic or metal showing a police officer's name.

uniform
Garment of a specific color and style that is worn by police officers on duty.

duty belt
Belt that the police officer wears to carry equipment.

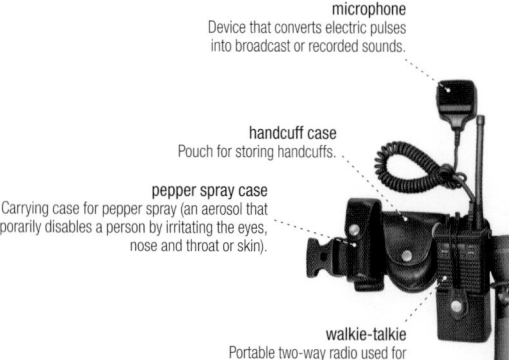

microphone
Device that converts electric pulses into broadcast or recorded sounds.

latex glove case
Pouch for carrying gloves worn to pick up pieces of evidence or contaminated objects such as used syringes.

handcuff case
Pouch for storing handcuffs.

pistol
Short lightweight handgun that is loaded from the butt.

pepper spray case
Carrying case for pepper spray (an aerosol that temporarily disables a person by irritating the eyes, nose and throat or skin).

ammunition pouch
Pouch for storing ammunition clips for the pistol.

walkie-talkie
Portable two-way radio used for communication between police officers.

holster
Case used to carry and protect a pistol.

flashlight
Battery-operated portable lighting device; it consists of a small high-intensity light enclosed in a cylindrical case.

baton holder
Ring used to hold a baton.

expandable baton
Extensible blunt instrument made of steel.

crime prevention

police car: dashboard equipment
The dashboard's main console is outfitted
with equipment used by patrol officers.

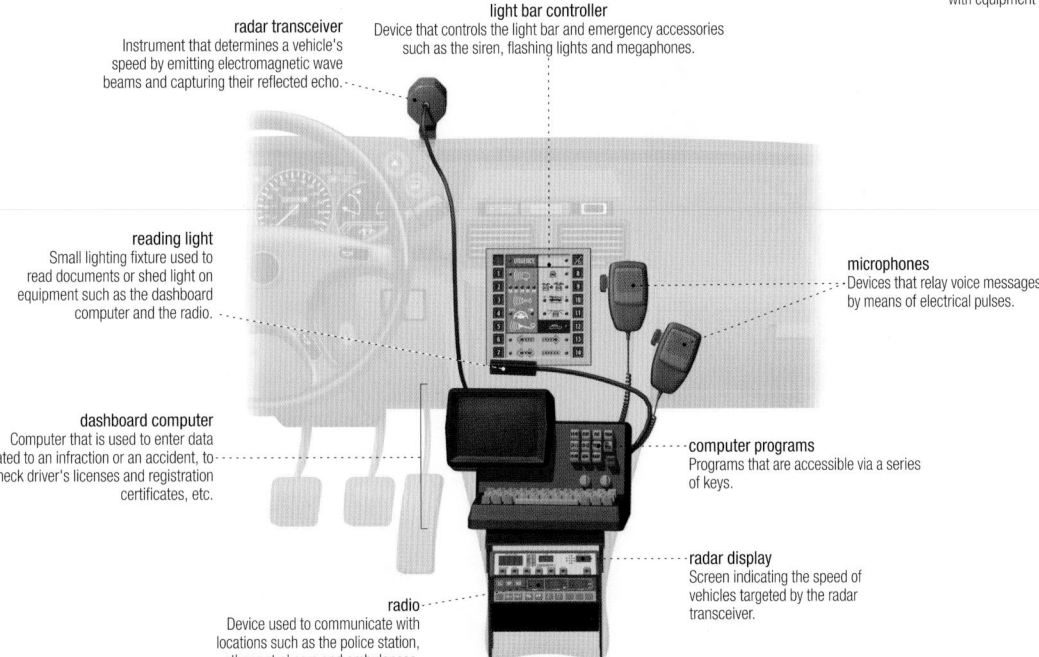

radar transceiver
Instrument that determines a vehicle's
speed by emitting electromagnetic wave
beams and capturing their reflected echo.

light bar controller
Device that controls the light bar and emergency accessories
such as the siren, flashing lights and megaphones.

microphones
Devices that relay voice messages
by means of electrical pulses.

reading light
Small lighting fixture used to
read documents or shed light on
equipment such as the dashboard
computer and the radio.

dashboard computer
Computer that is used to enter data
related to an infraction or an accident, to
check driver's licenses and registration
certificates, etc.

computer programs
Programs that are accessible via a series
of keys.

radar display
Screen indicating the speed of
vehicles targeted by the radar
transceiver.

radio
Device used to communicate with
locations such as the police station,
other patrol cars and ambulances.

police car
Patrol vehicle equipped with a radio
and a dashboard computer.

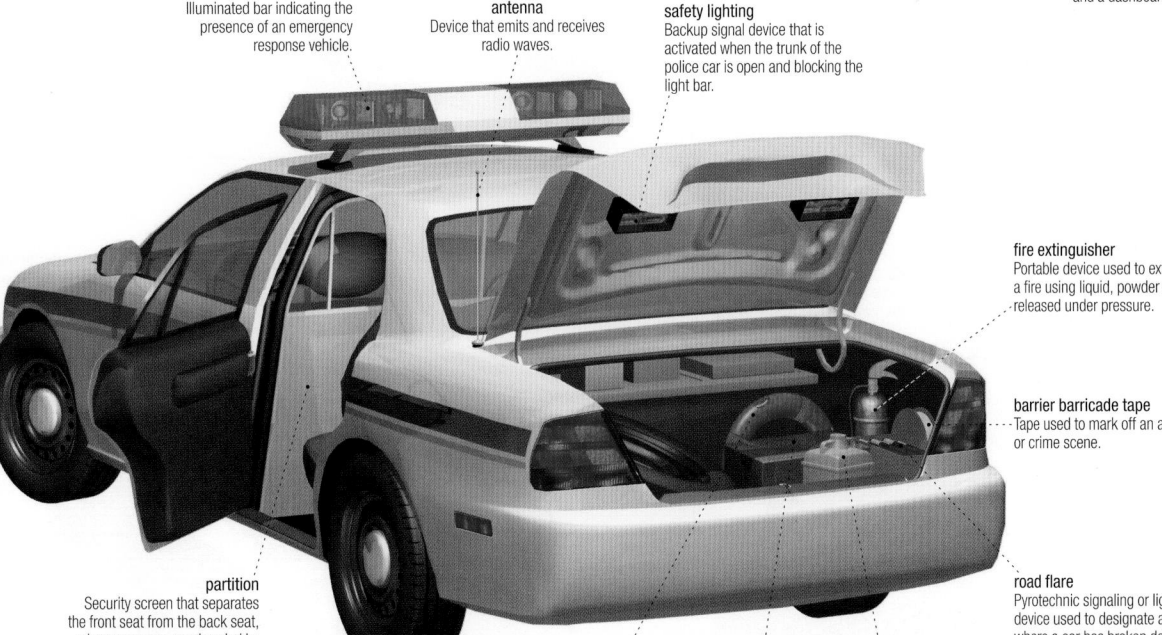

light bar
Illuminated bar indicating the
presence of an emergency
response vehicle.

antenna
Device that emits and receives
radio waves.

safety lighting
Backup signal device that is
activated when the trunk of the
police car is open and blocking the
light bar.

fire extinguisher
Portable device used to extinguish
a fire using liquid, powder or gas
released under pressure.

barrier barricade tape
Tape used to mark off an accident
or crime scene.

partition
Security screen that separates
the front seat from the back seat,
where persons apprehended by
police are placed.

road flare
Pyrotechnic signaling or lighting
device used to designate an area
where a car has broken down or an
accident has occurred.

life buoy
Ring made of buoyant material that
is thrown into the water to help a
person in distress keep afloat.

first aid kit
Box that contains the materials
required to administer first aid,
including bandages, medication
and instruments.

used syringe box
Container used to collect syringes left
behind by drug users.

SOCIETY

ear protection

Devices that deaden workplace noise and noise caused by power tools.

safety earmuffs
Pair of rigid shells that are connected by a headband and contain soft foam cushions.

headband
Flexible piece that keeps the earmuffs in place.

earplu
Device with plugs that are secur to the entrance of the audito canal by a headbar

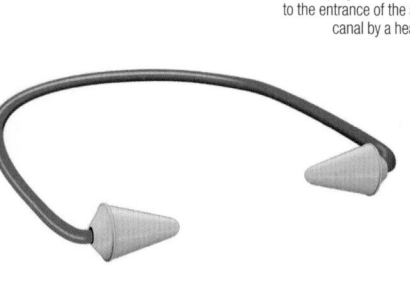

foam cushion
Soft material that fits around the ears to make the headband more comfortable.

eye protection

Eyewear that protects the eyes from impact, flying objects and heat.

safety glasses
Glasses that consist of plastic lenses attached to a frame with temples; they come with or without side protection.

safety goggl
Watertight glasses with a one-pie frame that provide front and side e protectio

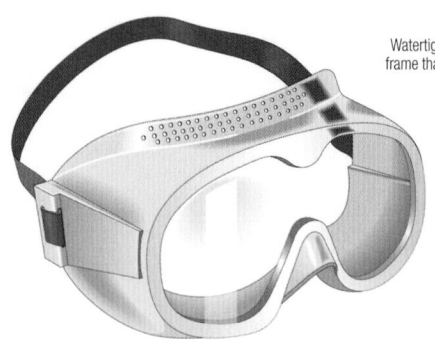

head protection

Safety helmet that protects against falling objects and impact.

hard hat: front view
Hard hat: hard headgear that protects the head.

rib
Ridge that reinforces the top of the helmet.

suspension band
Belt on the inner top of the helmet that is made of resistant fabric to cushion the impact of blows to the head.

headband
Band that surrounds the base of the skull to keep the helmet in place.

hard hat: interior vie
Hard hat: hard headgear that protects the hea

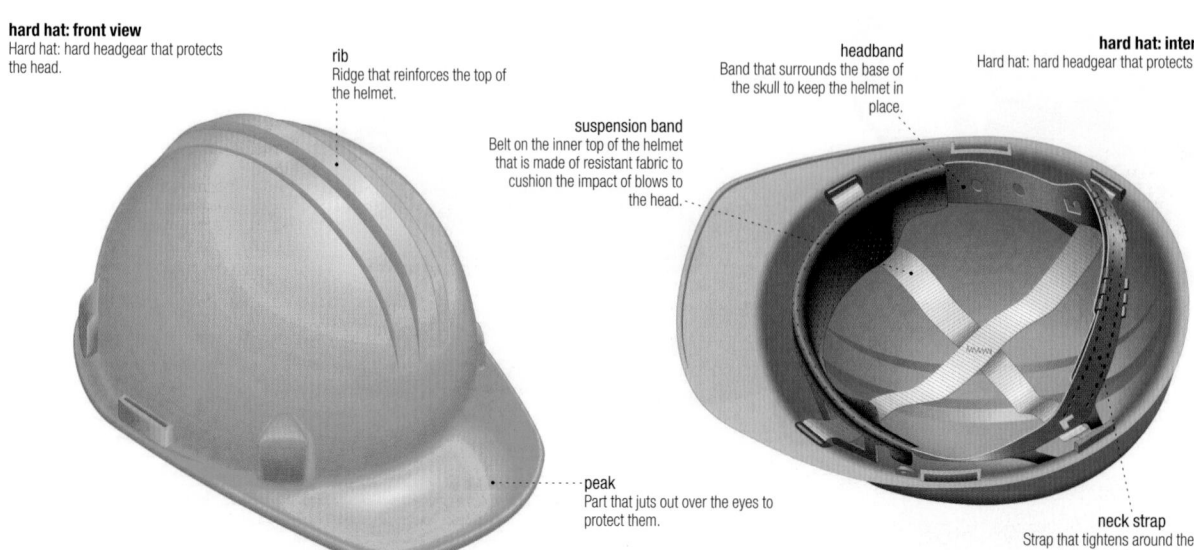

peak
Part that juts out over the eyes to protect them.

neck strap
Strap that tightens around the nape to keep the helmet in place.

respiratory system protection

Mask used to protect the respiratory tract from elements such as polluted air, dust, smoke and volatile chemicals.

full-mask respirator
Mask that filters out contaminated air; it covers the entire facial area to protect the nose, mouth and eyes.

facepiece
Part of the mask that adheres to the face and prevents ambient air from entering.

visor
Transparent part of the mask that allows the user to see.

cartridge
Device that filters out contaminated air by absorbing harmful substances.

head harness
Straps that attach at the back of the head to secure the mask to the face.

inhalation valve
Device that allows air to enter the mask and prevents exhaled air from exiting through the air intake.

filter cover
Device that protects the cartridge filter.

exhalation valve
Device that allows air to be expelled from the mask.

disposable respirator
Disposable mask that covers and protects the nose and mouth from dust and other particulate matter.

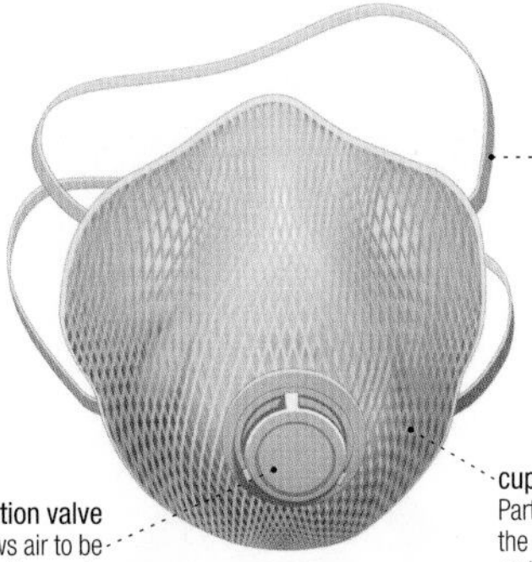

headband
Elastic band that secures the mask to the bottom of the face.

exhalation valve
Device that allows air to be expelled from the mask.

cup gasket
Part of the mask that adheres to the bottom of the face and prevents ambient air from entering.

foot protection

Shoes and accessories worn to protect the feet from dangers such as falling objects, intense heat and sharp tools.

safety boot
Highly durable boot with an insulated nonslip sole and a reinforced toe; it comes up over the ankles.

toe guard
Accessory worn over a shoe to protect the end of the foot.

reinforced toe
Metal shell between the top of the boot and its lining; it protects the toes.

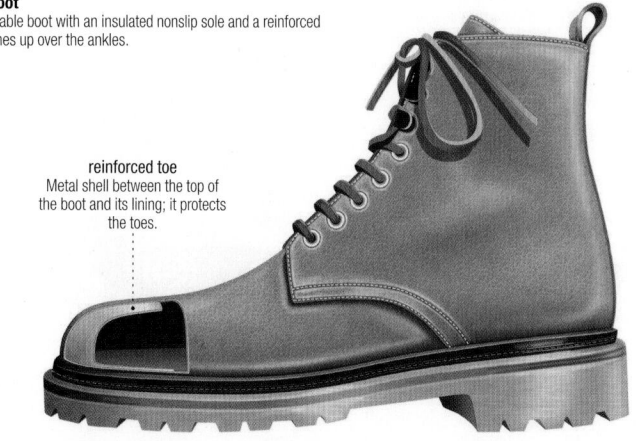

safety symbols

The pictograms used to warn of danger or indicate that safety equipment is mandatory.

dangerous materials

Pictogram warning of materials that pose a health or environmental risk because of their properties or reactions.

corrosive
Pictogram warning of materials that can damage living tissue or other bodies such as metal.

high voltage
Pictogram warning of the danger of electric shock or burns.

explosive
Pictogram warning of materials that explode by chemical reaction.

flammable
Pictogram warning of flammable materials.

radioactive
Pictogram warning of radioactive materials.

poison
Pictogram warning of materials harmful to an organism when inhaled, ingested or absorbed by the skin.

protection

Pictogram warning that protective equipment is mandatory on certain parts of the body.

eye protection
Pictogram warning that safety glasses are mandatory.

ear protection
Pictogram warning that equipment that reduces noise perception is mandatory.

head protection
Pictogram warning that safety helmets are mandatory.

hand protection
Pictogram warning that protective gloves are mandatory.

foot protection
Pictogram warning that protective footwear or accessories are mandatory.

respiratory system protection
Pictogram warning that respirators are mandatory.

ambulance

Vehicle designed to transport the sick and injured to the hospital and equipped to administer first aid.

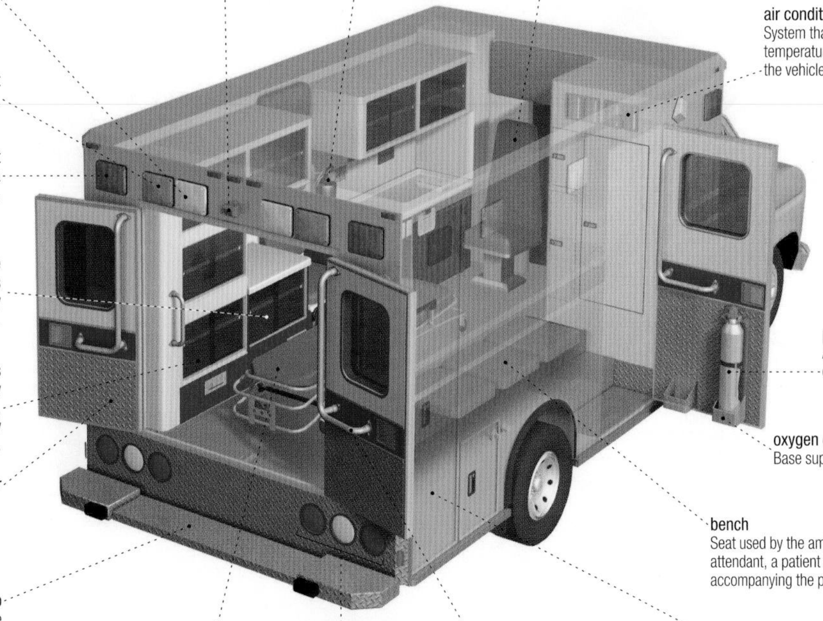

scene light
Spotlight that provides illumination at the scene of an emergency.

camera
Device that allows the driver to see behind the vehicle.

aspirator
Device using suction to remove fluids or solid matter from the body.

ambulance attendant's seat

air conditioning system
System that regulates the temperature and purifies the air inside the vehicle.

halogen light
High-intensity emergency light.

strobe light
Emergency light that emits a succession of brief flashes.

drug storage
Cabinet for storing the medications (painkillers, insulin) used frequently or needed quickly.

first aid supplies
Cabinet for storing emergency response materials (bandages, latex gloves, syringes) used by ambulance attendants.

rear door

rear step
Platform at the back of the ambulance that is used to climb in and out.

stretcher
Folding bed on wheels that is used to transport the sick and the injured.

taillights
Set of regulation lighting devices placed at the rear of a vehicle and used for signaling.

handle

portable oxygen cylinder
An easy-to-carry tank filled with compressed oxygen.

oxygen cylinder bracket
Base supporting the oxygen cylinder.

bench
Seat used by the ambulance attendant, a patient or a person accompanying the patient.

backboard storage
Backboard: device used to restrict movement of a patient suspected of having a spinal injury.

medical equipment

The combination of devices, equipment and supplies used for first aid, transportation of the sick and injured or medical tests.

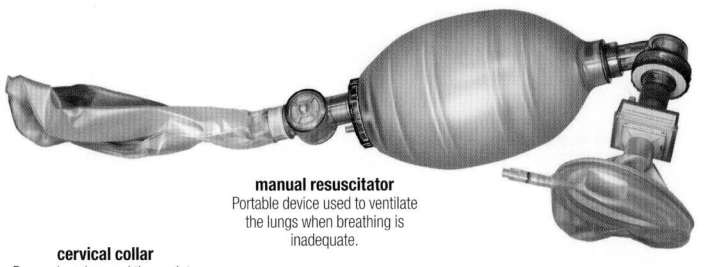

manual resuscitator
Portable device used to ventilate the lungs when breathing is inadequate.

oxygen mask
Device placed over the nose and mouth to help breathing by means of a steady flow of oxygen.

oropharyngeal airway
Hollow tube placed over the tongue that curves down into the opening of the pharynx (oropharynx); it keeps the mouth and throat clear and prevents the tongue from blocking the airway.

cervical collar
Brace placed around the neck to restrict movement of the cervical spine.

aspirator
Device using suction to remove fluids or solid matter from the body.

defibrillator
Device that releases a brief but powerful electric charge to restore normal heart rhythm after cardiac arrest.

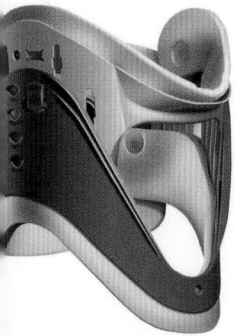

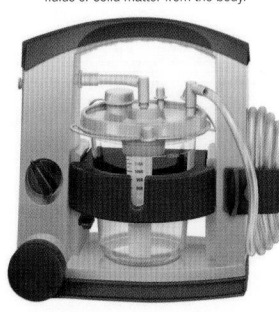

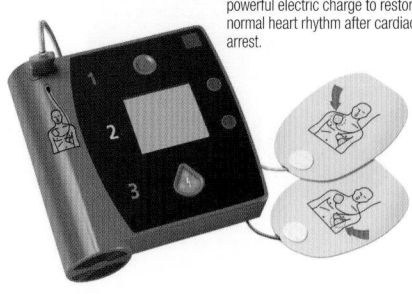

medical equipment

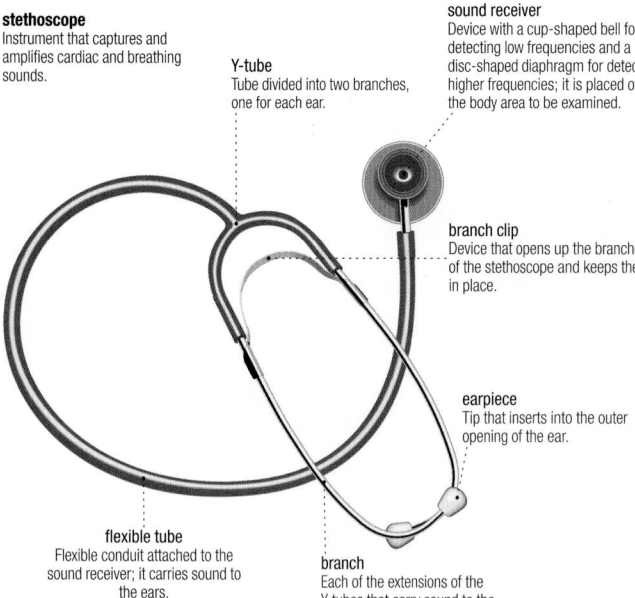

stethoscope
Instrument that captures and amplifies cardiac and breathing sounds.

Y-tube
Tube divided into two branches, one for each ear.

sound receiver
Device with a cup-shaped bell for detecting low frequencies and a disc-shaped diaphragm for detecting higher frequencies; it is placed over the body area to be examined.

branch clip
Device that opens up the branches of the stethoscope and keeps them in place.

earpiece
Tip that inserts into the outer opening of the ear.

flexible tube
Flexible conduit attached to the sound receiver; it carries sound to the ears.

branch
Each of the extensions of the Y-tubes that carry sound to the ears.

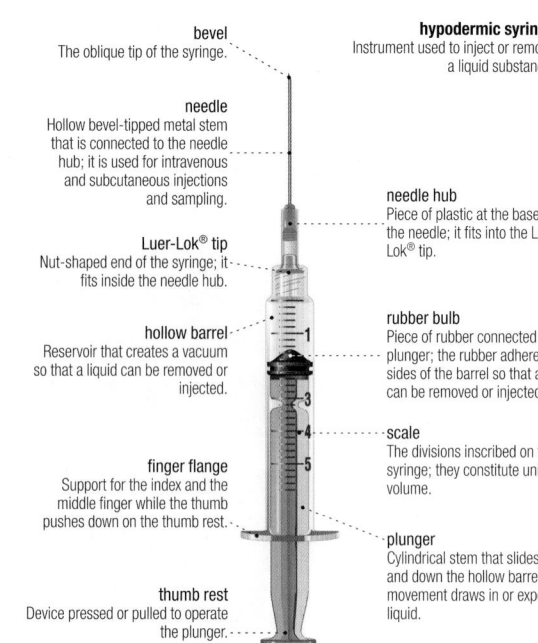

bevel
The oblique tip of the syringe.

needle
Hollow bevel-tipped metal stem that is connected to the needle hub; it is used for intravenous and subcutaneous injections and sampling.

Luer-Lok® tip
Nut-shaped end of the syringe; it fits inside the needle hub.

hollow barrel
Reservoir that creates a vacuum so that a liquid can be removed or injected.

finger flange
Support for the index and the middle finger while the thumb pushes down on the thumb rest.

thumb rest
Device pressed or pulled to operate the plunger.

hypodermic syringe
Instrument used to inject or remove a liquid substance.

needle hub
Piece of plastic at the base of the needle; it fits into the Luer-Lok® tip.

rubber bulb
Piece of rubber connected to the plunger; the rubber adheres to the sides of the barrel so that air can be removed or injected.

scale
The divisions inscribed on the syringe; they constitute units of volume.

plunger
Cylindrical stem that slides up and down the hollow barrel; its movement draws in or expels liquid.

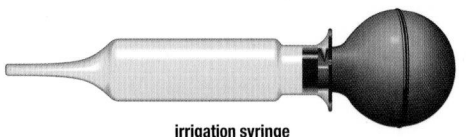

irrigation syringe
Syringe used to cleanse a body part or opening by flushing with a saline or medicated solution.

blood collection assembly
Devices that facilitate the collection of a blood sample so that it can be tested in a laboratory.

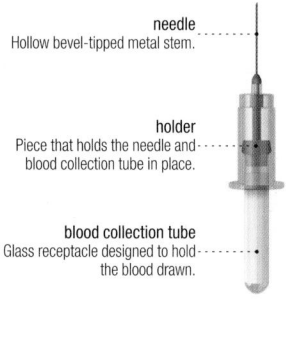

needle
Hollow bevel-tipped metal stem.

holder
Piece that holds the needle and blood collection tube in place.

blood collection tube
Glass receptacle designed to hold the blood drawn.

venom extractor
Device that uses suction on a part of a limb or the body to extract toxins from an insect sting or snakebite.

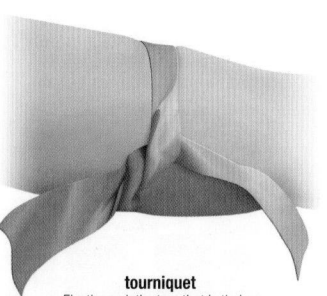

tourniquet
Elastic or cloth strap that is tied or twisted tight around a limb; used to stop the flow of blood from a serious wound or restrict the flow when taking a blood sample.

lancing device
Small instrument used to procure a drop of blood from the tip of a finger.

medical equipment

blood pressure monitor
Device composed of a pneumatic cuff and a pressure gauge; it is used to measure systolic (heart contraction) and diastolic (heart relaxation) pressure in the blood vessels.

air tube
Flexible conduit linking the cuff to the pressure gauge.

pneumatic cuff
Device that wraps around the arm and squeezes the brachial artery when inflated; blood pressure is measured when the air is slowly let out of the cuff.

latex glove
Thin rubber glove worn by medical personnel to prevent infection or contagion.

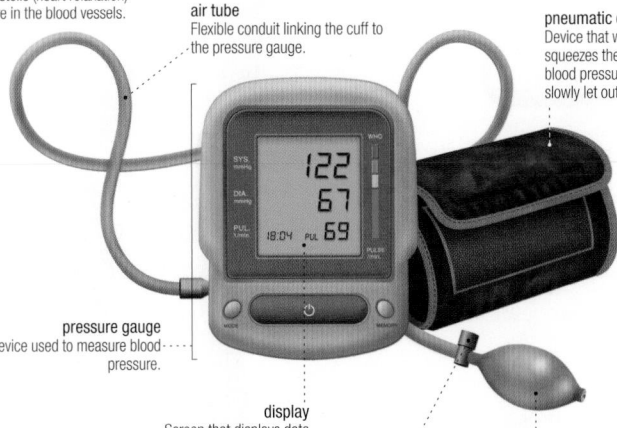

pressure gauge
Device used to measure blood pressure.

display
Screen that displays data concerning the tests being conducted (blood pressure, pulse).

air-pressure pump
Small pump used to inflate the cuff.

pressure control valve
Valve used to expel air from the cuff to reduce pressure.

surgical mask
Mask made of flexible fabric that covers the mouth and nose to impede transmission of germs and bacteria that cause infection.

ambulance stretcher
Folding bed on wheels that is used to transport the sick and the injured.

pole stretcher
Cloth-covered wooden or metal frame used to transport the sick and the injured.

swing-down side rail
Metal bar attached to the frame that moves up or down and locks in place; it is used to protect the patient from falls.

restraint straps
Strips of fabric attached to the frame that help keep the patient on the stretcher.

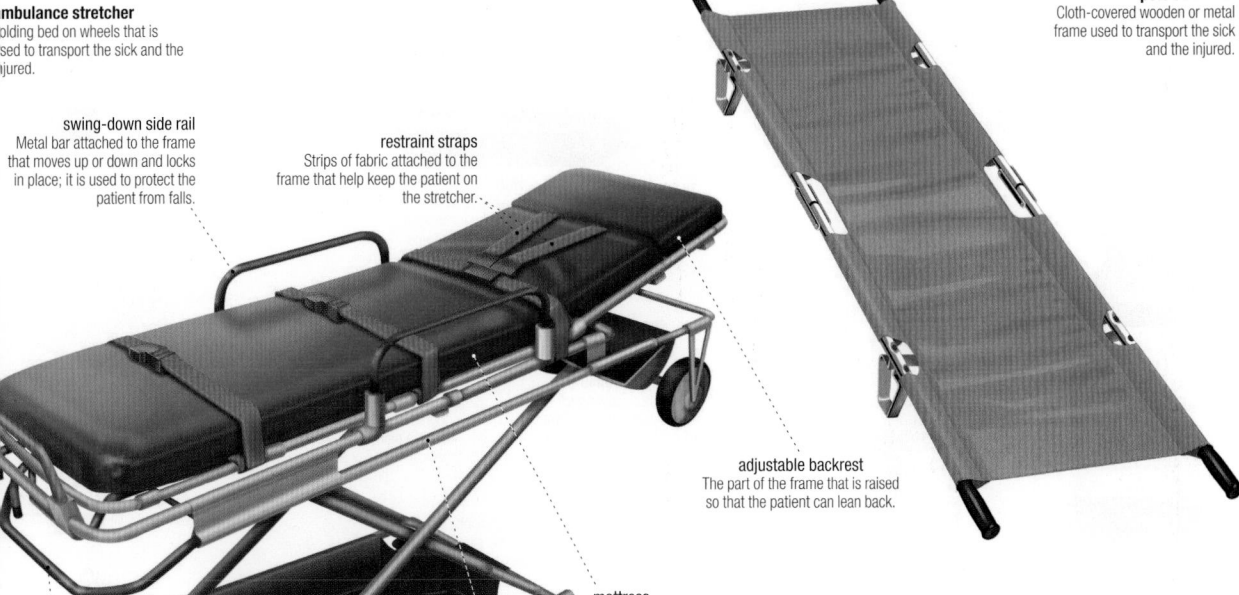

adjustable backrest
The part of the frame that is raised so that the patient can lean back.

mattress
Large padded cushion on which the patient lies.

transport handle
Metal bar that is fixed in place; allows the stretcher to be held when lifted or moved.

frame
Metal structure that supports the mattress above its feet.

locking wheels
Small wheels that can be locked in place allow the stretcher to be moved with ease.

medical equipment

thermometers

Instruments that measure body temperature; depending on the type, the tip is inserted into the mouth, rectum, opening of the ear or under the armpit.

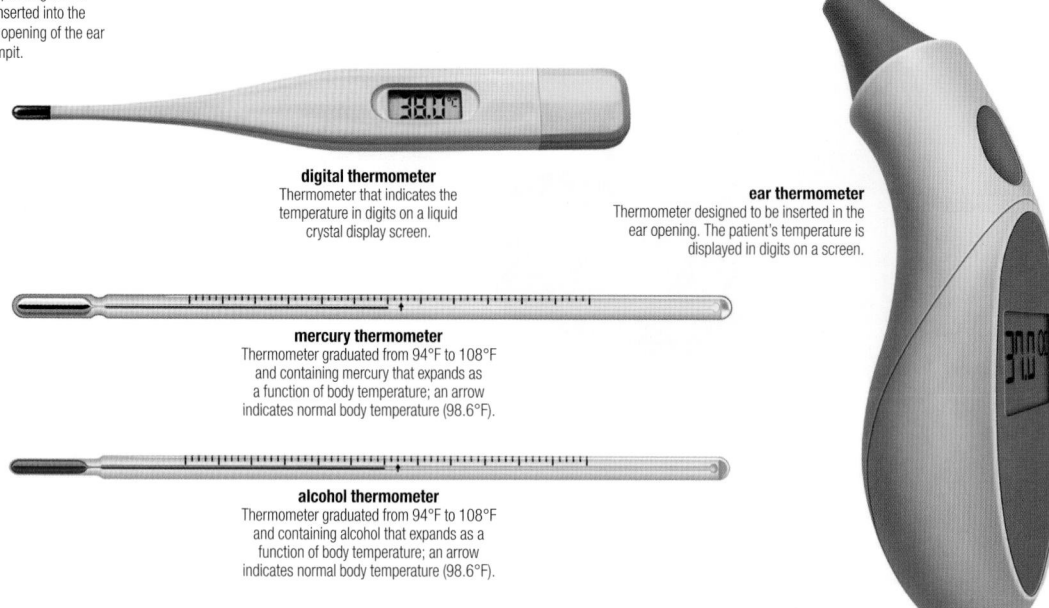

digital thermometer
Thermometer that indicates the temperature in digits on a liquid crystal display screen.

ear thermometer
Thermometer designed to be inserted in the ear opening. The patient's temperature is displayed in digits on a screen.

mercury thermometer
Thermometer graduated from 94°F to 108°F and containing mercury that expands as a function of body temperature; an arrow indicates normal body temperature (98.6°F).

alcohol thermometer
Thermometer graduated from 94°F to 108°F and containing alcohol that expands as a function of body temperature; an arrow indicates normal body temperature (98.6°F).

forms of medications

The various forms of medications that are commercially available.

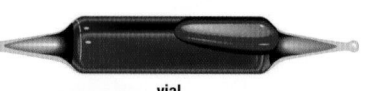

vial
Bulging glass tube sealed at its ends; it contains a specific dose of medication or a pharmaceutical product in liquid form.

hard gelatin capsule
Rigid water-soluble shell composed of gelatin having two halves that fit together; it is filled with a medication or a pharmaceutical product.

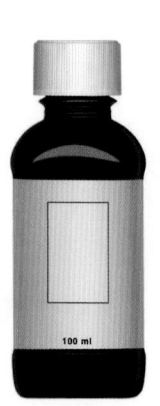

soft gelatin capsule
Flexible water-soluble shell composed of gelatin and filled with a liquid dose of medication or a pharmaceutical product.

tablet
Pill made of compressed inert ingredients such as starch or cellulose that contains a dose of medication or a pharmaceutical product.

transdermal patch
Adhesive patch applied to the skin that releases a medication or pharmaceutical product gradually.

syrup
Usually flavored solution containing a medication or pharmaceutical product to be taken orally.

nasal spray
Device used to spray a mist of medication up the nasal passages.

mouthpiece
Part of the metered dose inhaler that is inserted into the mouth to direct the medicated aerosol into the lungs.

cap
Piece that covers the mouthpiece when the metered dose inhaler is not in use.

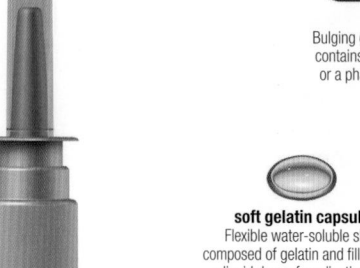

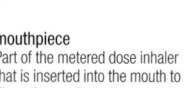

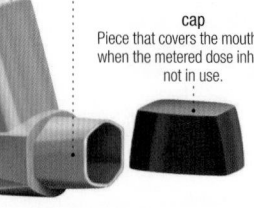

auto-injector
Syringe used to deliver one pre-measured dose of medication (such as epinephrine for a severe allergic reaction).

metered dose inhaler
Device that releases a specific dose of medication in aerosol form into the respiratory tract; it is used mainly to treat lung conditions such as asthma and bronchitis.

suppository
Solid dose of medication to be inserted in the rectum.

ointment
Thick unguent containing a medication or pharmaceutical product to be applied directly to the skin.

first aid kit

Box that contains the materials required to administer first aid, including bandages, medication and instruments.

cotton swabs
Sticks whose ends are covered with cotton wadding; they are used to apply medication and clean wounds.

triangular bandage
Triangular piece of fabric used as an arm sling.

splints
Small strips of wood, metal or plastic used to restrict movement of a fracture, sprain or dislocation.

aspirin
Tablet used to treat pain, fever and inflammation.

iodine
Antiseptic used to clean and disinfect skin or wounds.

adhesive bandages
Adhesive strips with a piece of gauze for dressing wounds.

adhesive tape
Sticky tape used to fasten bandages, compresses and other materials to a wound.

sterile pads
Pieces of sterilized gauze that are folded into several layers and used to dress wounds.

absorbent cotton
Absorbent white cotton containing no fatty or resinous substances; it is used to clean wounds.

gauze roller bandages
Roll of extremely light cotton fabric used to make compresses, pressure bandages or dress wounds.

hydrogen peroxide
Antiseptic used to clean skin or minor wounds.

first aid manual
Booklet describing how to treat common injuries and illnesses.

elastic support bandage
Stretchable fabric that is rolled around a limb, joint, or other body part to provide support, reduce swelling or secure a bandage or splint.

antiseptic
Substance used on skin to kill germs and bacteria that can cause infection.

scissors
Instrument with two movable overlapping shanks having sharp inside edges; they are used for trimming and cutting.

tweezers
Instrument used to remove fragments of a foreign body (usually splinters) accidentally introduced under the skin.

sterile pad
Piece of sterilized gauze that is folded into several layers and used to dress wounds.

adhesive bandage
Adhesive strip with a piece of gauze for dressing wounds.

gauze roller bandage
Roll of extremely light cotton fabric used to make compresses, pressure bandages or dress wounds.

cotton swabs
Stick whose ends are covered with cotton wadding; it is used to apply medication and clean wounds.

triangular bandage
Triangular piece of fabric used as an arm sling.

splint
Small strip of wood, metal or plastic used to restrict movement of a fracture, sprain or dislocation.

absorbent cotton
Absorbent white cotton containing no fatty or resinous substances; it is used to clean wounds.

walking aids

Weight-bearing devices used to help a person move about.

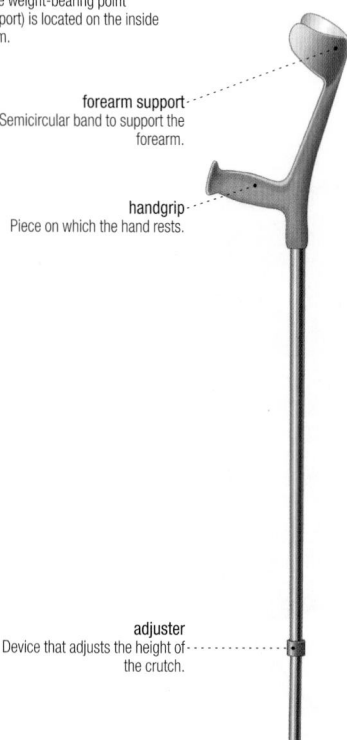

forearm crutch
Crutch whose weight-bearing point (forearm support) is located on the inside of the forearm.

forearm support
Semicircular band to support the forearm.

handgrip
Piece on which the hand rests.

adjuster
Device that adjusts the height of the crutch.

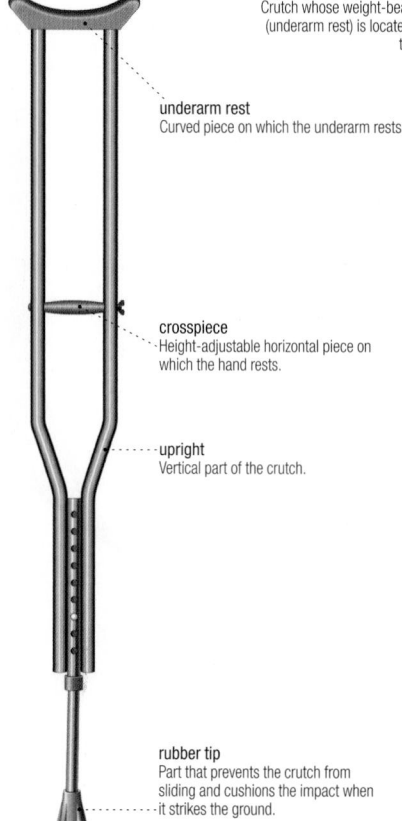

underarm crutch
Crutch whose weight-bearing point (underarm rest) is located beneath the armpit.

underarm rest
Curved piece on which the underarm rests.

crosspiece
Height-adjustable horizontal piece on which the hand rests.

upright
Vertical part of the crutch.

rubber tip
Part that prevents the crutch from sliding and cushions the impact when it strikes the ground.

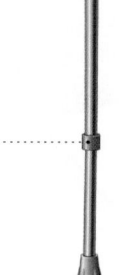

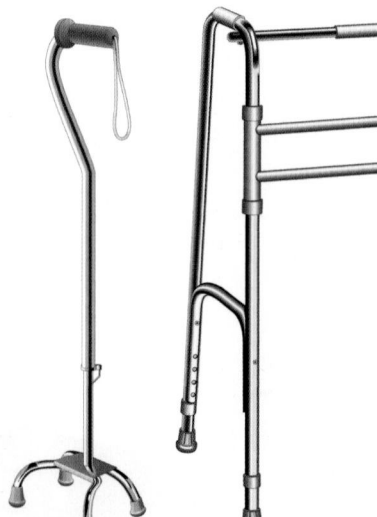

crook cane
Cane with a curved handle.

Fritz cane
Cane with a slightly curved handle.

offset cane
Adjustable cane with a handle designed to offer additional support.

quad cane
Offset cane with a four-legged base.

walker
Support that slides or is lifted to help people who are too weak or unstable to walk unaided.

moving aids

Devices that feature seats on wheels, motorized or manually operated, that give persons with impaired mobility a way to get around.

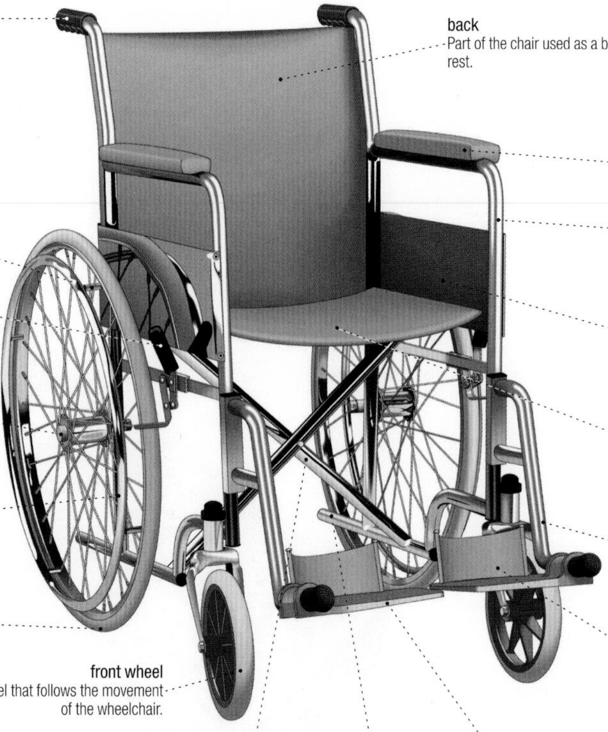

handle
Handle used to push the wheelchair.

back
Part of the chair used as a back rest.

wheelchair
Chair with arms and a back that is mounted on wheels; it enables a person who has difficulty walking to move about.

armrest
Side part supporting the arm.

spacer
The pieces that separate the push rim from the wheel.

arm
Part of the structure that supports the wheelchair's front mechanism.

brake
Handle that slows down the wheelchair or restricts its movement by blocking the wheel.

clothing guard
Part of the wheelchair that separates the seat from the movement of the wheels.

hub
Central part of the wheel from which spokes radiate. Inside the hub are ball bearings enabling it to rotate around its axle.

seat
Level part of the armchair for sitting upon.

push rim
Circular piece that a person pushes to propel and maneuver the wheelchair.

hanger bracket
Pivoting piece that supports the footrest; it is adjustable and removable.

large wheel
Circular piece connected to the hub; its rubber tires provide rolling comfort.

heel loop
Part of the footrest that prevents the feet from sliding back.

front wheel
Wheel that follows the movement of the wheelchair.

cross brace
Folding crosspiece connecting and stabilizing the two sides of the wheelchair.

tipping lever
Piece that the person pushing the wheelchair presses down on with the foot to lift the front of the wheelchair.

footrest
Removable piece on which the feet rest.

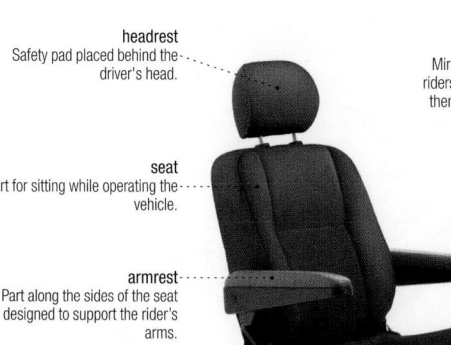

four-wheel scooter
Small, four-wheeled motor vehicle designed to give those who have difficulty walking a way to get around.

headrest
Safety pad placed behind the driver's head.

mirror
Mirrored surface placed so that riders can see behind or alongside themselves without turning their heads.

console
Panel where the scooter's control instruments are located.

seat
Part for sitting while operating the vehicle.

handle
Part composed of two handles joined by a stem that allows the rider to steer the scooter.

turn signal
Device emitting an intermittent light, signaling a change of the vehicle's direction.

armrest
Part along the sides of the seat designed to support the rider's arms.

battery box
Casing designed to hold the battery that charges the scooter's electric motor.

headlight
Lamp on the front of the vehicle to light up the space in front.

front bumper
Malleable element partially absorbing shocks, thus protecting the body from damage.

wheel
Round attachment that revolves around an axle, giving the scooter the ability to move forward and in reverse.

floor
Wide flat surface for resting the feet on.

hospital

Facility where the sick and the injured are given medical and surgical care, where babies are delivered, and where medical research and teaching may be conducted.

emergency room
Department that receives the sick and the injured and treats those who require immediate care.

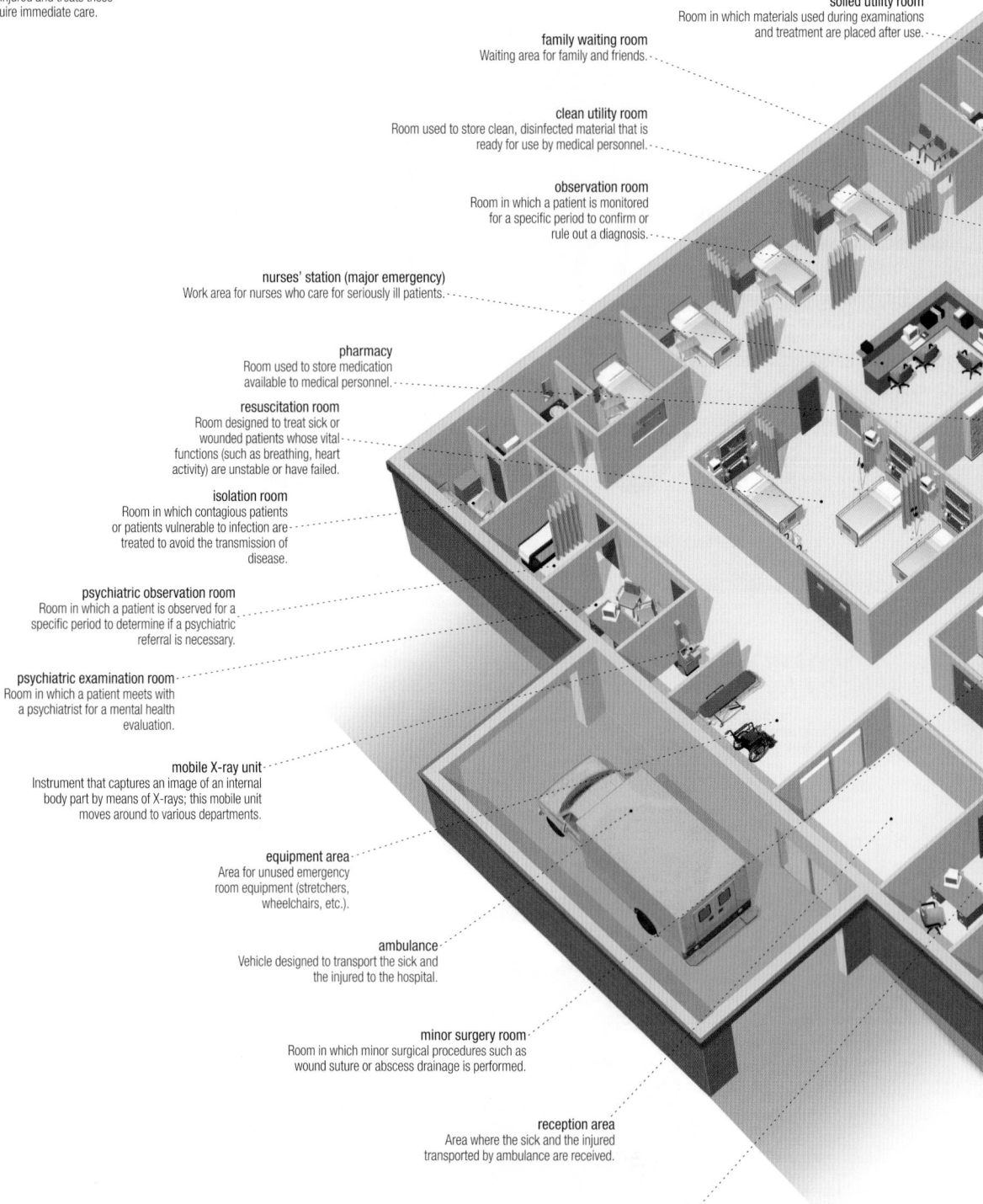

soiled utility room
Room in which materials used during examinations and treatment are placed after use.

family waiting room
Waiting area for family and friends.

clean utility room
Room used to store clean, disinfected material that is ready for use by medical personnel.

observation room
Room in which a patient is monitored for a specific period to confirm or rule out a diagnosis.

nurses' station (major emergency)
Work area for nurses who care for seriously ill patients.

pharmacy
Room used to store medication available to medical personnel.

resuscitation room
Room designed to treat sick or wounded patients whose vital functions (such as breathing, heart activity) are unstable or have failed.

isolation room
Room in which contagious patients or patients vulnerable to infection are treated to avoid the transmission of disease.

psychiatric observation room
Room in which a patient is observed for a specific period to determine if a psychiatric referral is necessary.

psychiatric examination room
Room in which a patient meets with a psychiatrist for a mental health evaluation.

mobile X-ray unit
Instrument that captures an image of an internal body part by means of X-rays; this mobile unit moves around to various departments.

equipment area
Area for unused emergency room equipment (stretchers, wheelchairs, etc.).

ambulance
Vehicle designed to transport the sick and the injured to the hospital.

minor surgery room
Room in which minor surgical procedures such as wound suture or abscess drainage is performed.

reception area
Area where the sick and the injured transported by ambulance are received.

emergency physician's office
Emergency physician: doctor who specializes in treating emergency room patients.

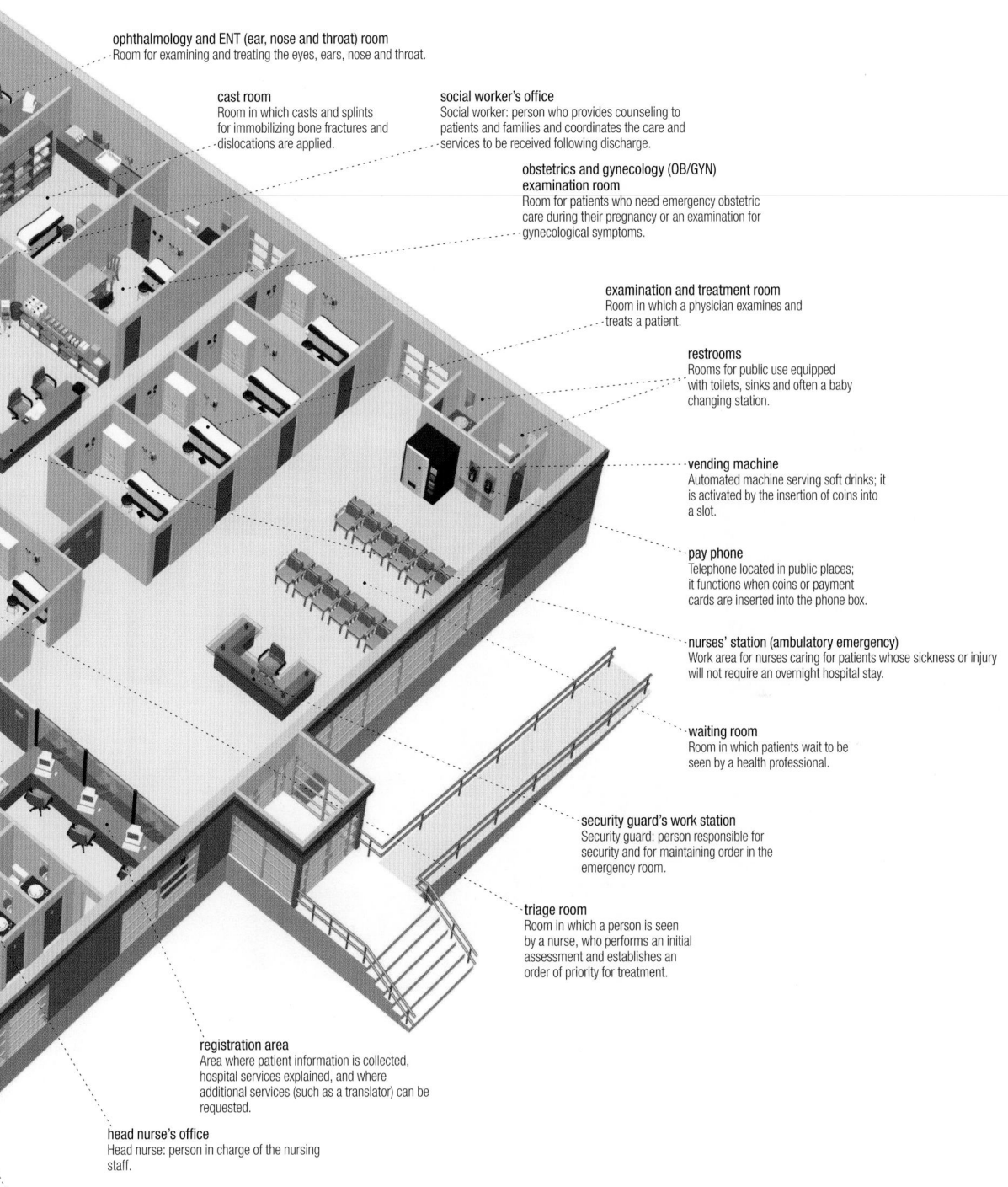

ophthalmology and ENT (ear, nose and throat) room
Room for examining and treating the eyes, ears, nose and throat.

cast room
Room in which casts and splints for immobilizing bone fractures and dislocations are applied.

social worker's office
Social worker: person who provides counseling to patients and families and coordinates the care and services to be received following discharge.

obstetrics and gynecology (OB/GYN) examination room
Room for patients who need emergency obstetric care during their pregnancy or an examination for gynecological symptoms.

examination and treatment room
Room in which a physician examines and treats a patient.

restrooms
Rooms for public use equipped with toilets, sinks and often a baby changing station.

vending machine
Automated machine serving soft drinks; it is activated by the insertion of coins into a slot.

pay phone
Telephone located in public places; it functions when coins or payment cards are inserted into the phone box.

nurses' station (ambulatory emergency)
Work area for nurses caring for patients whose sickness or injury will not require an overnight hospital stay.

waiting room
Room in which patients wait to be seen by a health professional.

security guard's work station
Security guard: person responsible for security and for maintaining order in the emergency room.

triage room
Room in which a person is seen by a nurse, who performs an initial assessment and establishes an order of priority for treatment.

registration area
Area where patient information is collected, hospital services explained, and where additional services (such as a translator) can be requested.

head nurse's office
Head nurse: person in charge of the nursing staff.

staff lounge
Room used by staff as a rest area.

hospital

patient room
Room for patients whose care requires them
to stay overnight or longer in a hospital; it can
be private (one bed), semiprivate (two beds)
or common (more than two beds).

intravenous stand
Long metal rod with a hook that is supported by a base
with wheels; it is used to suspend a bag containing a
solution that is slowly and continuously injected into the
patient's vein.

bedside lamp
Adjustable light fixture secured to
the wall at the head of the bed.

oxygen outlet
Device that supplies oxygen to a patient's
room.

physician
Holder of a degree in medicine, the
physician establishes the diagnosis
and prescribes treatment and
medication.

resident
Medical school graduate receiving
advanced training in a medical
specialty before becoming fully
licensed to practice medicine.

bedside table
Small table placed at the head of a bed; it
might contain one or more drawers.

patient
Person who undergoes treatment,
a medical examination or a surgical
procedure.

shower
Sanitary fixture for washing the body
under a spray of water.

overbed table
Table with wheels and a tray that
slides over the bed.

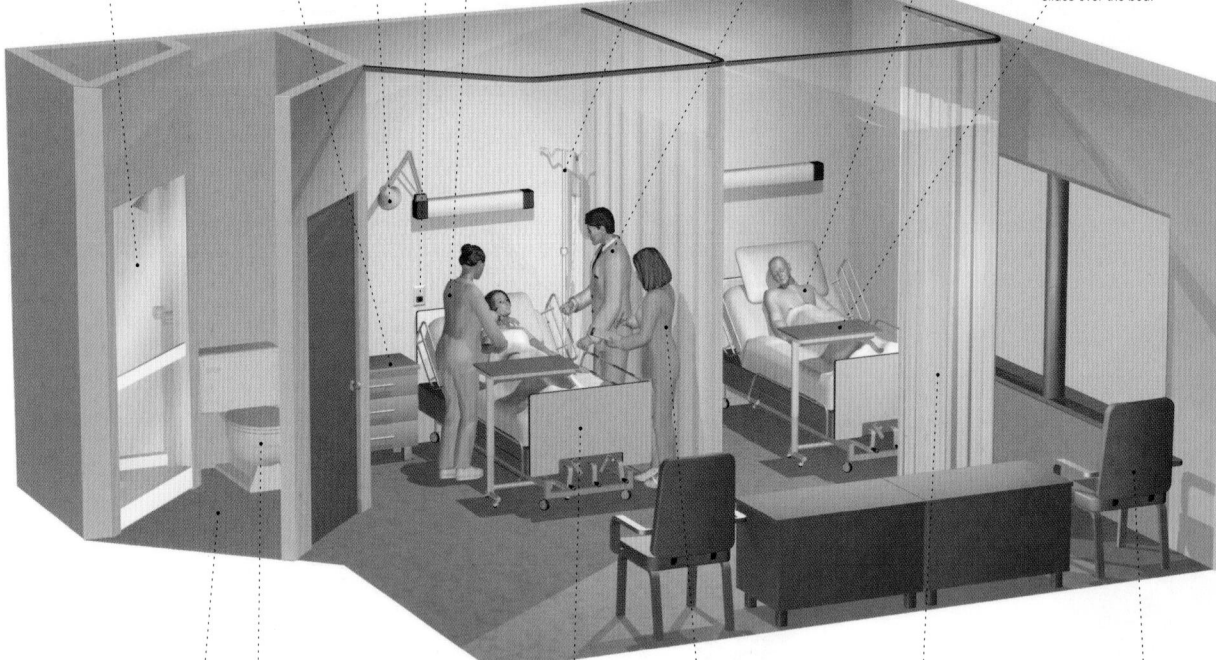

bathroom
Room designed for personal
hygiene; it is equipped with running
water and sanitary fixtures.

hospital bed
Bed with an adjustable base,
wheels and side rails (movable bars
used to protect patients from falls).

nurse
Holder of a degree in nursing, the
nurse treats patients under the
direction of the physician.

privacy curtain
Curtain used to separate one
patient's area from another's or to
provide privacy.

patient's chair
Chair for a patient or visitor.

toilet
Plumbing fixture used to receive bodily
waste; it has a bowl and a flusher.

hospital

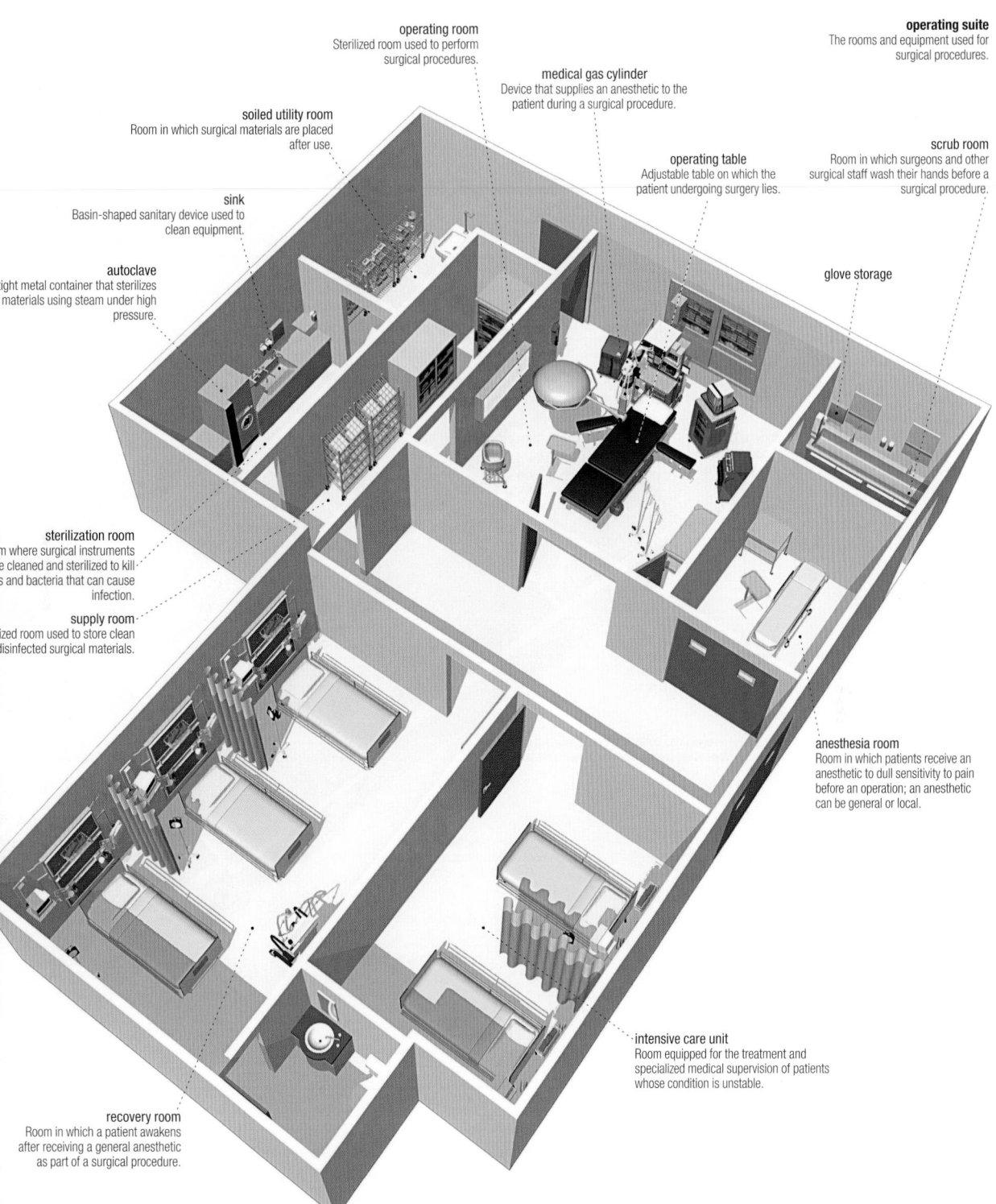

operating room
Sterilized room used to perform surgical procedures.

operating suite
The rooms and equipment used for surgical procedures.

medical gas cylinder
Device that supplies an anesthetic to the patient during a surgical procedure.

soiled utility room
Room in which surgical materials are placed after use.

operating table
Adjustable table on which the patient undergoing surgery lies.

scrub room
Room in which surgeons and other surgical staff wash their hands before a surgical procedure.

sink
Basin-shaped sanitary device used to clean equipment.

glove storage

autoclave
tight metal container that sterilizes materials using steam under high pressure.

sterilization room
m where surgical instruments e cleaned and sterilized to kill s and bacteria that can cause infection.

supply room
ized room used to store clean disinfected surgical materials.

anesthesia room
Room in which patients receive an anesthetic to dull sensitivity to pain before an operation; an anesthetic can be general or local.

intensive care unit
Room equipped for the treatment and specialized medical supervision of patients whose condition is unstable.

recovery room
Room in which a patient awakens after receiving a general anesthetic as part of a surgical procedure.

hospital

ambulatory care unit
Center offering surgical and medical services to patients whose care will not require an overnight hospital stay.

observation room
Room where a patient is kept under surveillance for a specific period following a surgical procedure.

operating room
Room used to perform minor surgical procedures.

surgeon's scrub sink
Plumbing fixture used by surgeons to disinfect their hands before minor surgery.

sterilization room
Room where instruments are cleaned and sterilized to kill germs and bacteria that can cause infection.

undressing booth
Area where a patient puts on a hospital gown.

treatment room
Room in which a physician treats a patient.

pathology laboratory
Room with the equipment required to analyze samples.

nurses' lounge

specimen collection room
Room in which a nurse collects blood and urine samples for analysis.

specimen collection center waiting room
Area where persons wait to have samples taken.

medical records
Room where patient records are stored for future consultation.

reception area
Room designed to receive people.

main entrance

main waiting room
Area used by patients waiting for consultation.

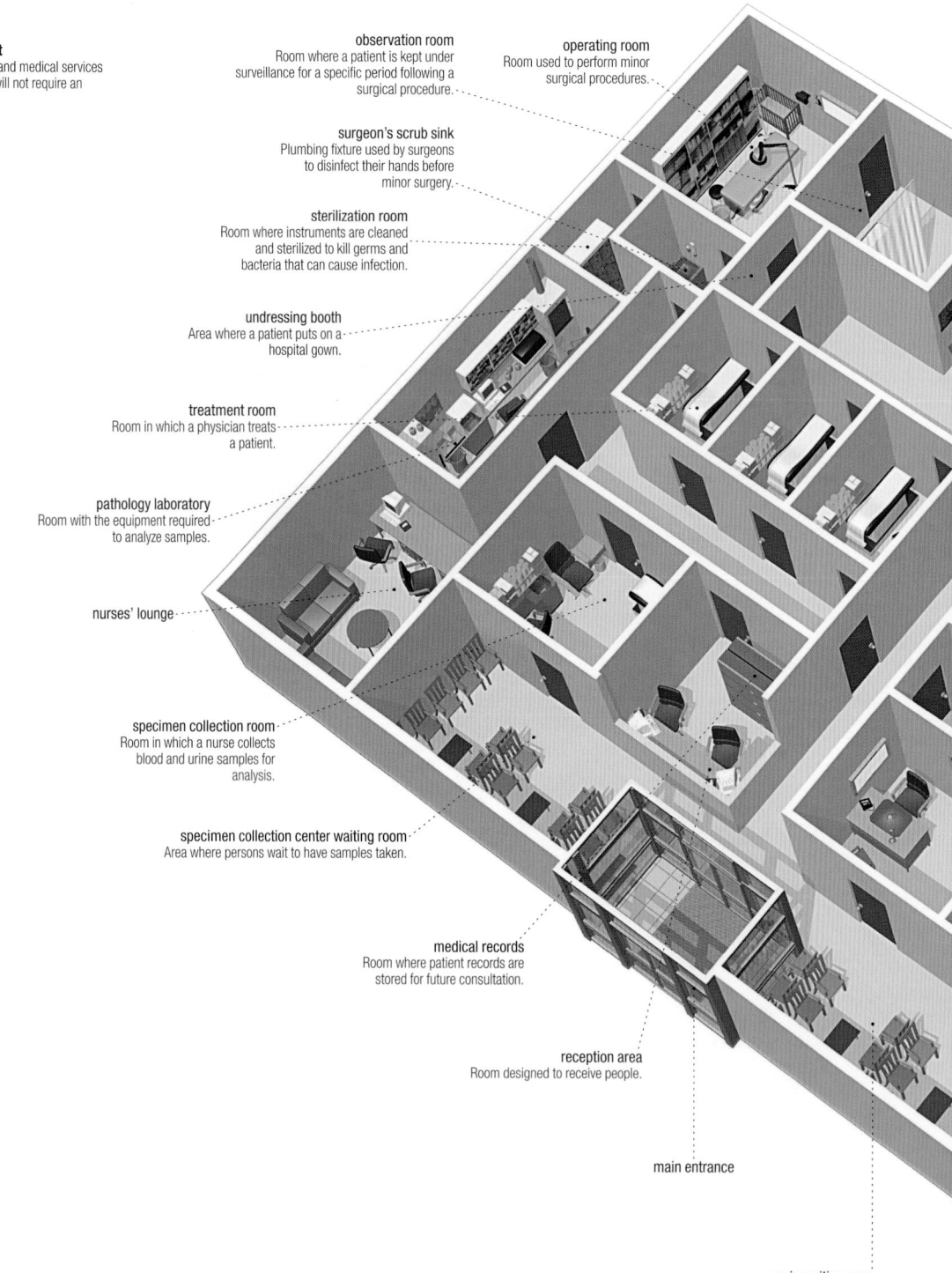

hospital

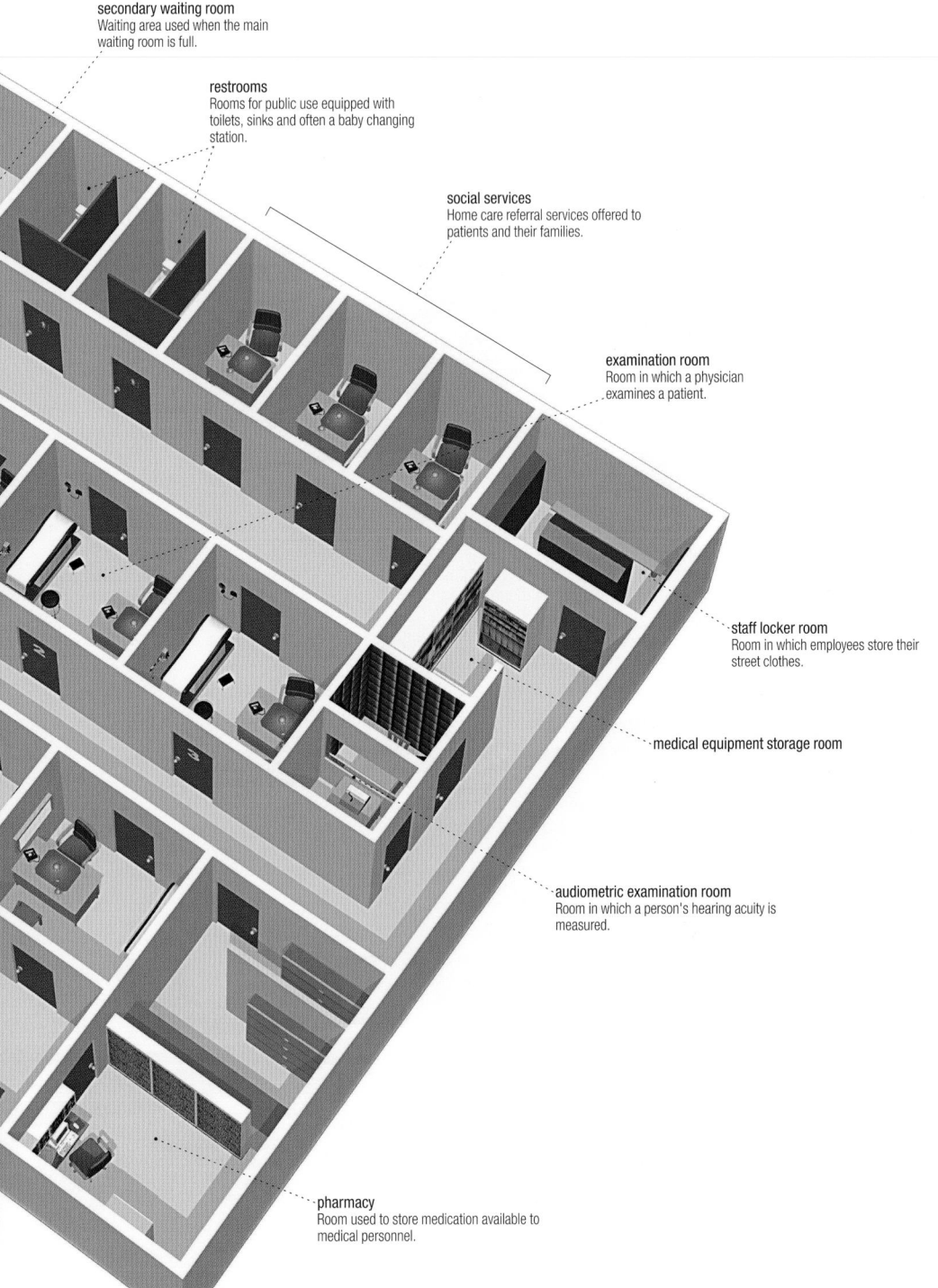

secondary waiting room
Waiting area used when the main waiting room is full.

restrooms
Rooms for public use equipped with toilets, sinks and often a baby changing station.

social services
Home care referral services offered to patients and their families.

examination room
Room in which a physician examines a patient.

staff locker room
Room in which employees store their street clothes.

medical equipment storage room

audiometric examination room
Room in which a person's hearing acuity is measured.

pharmacy
Room used to store medication available to medical personnel.

medical examinations

Evaluation of a person's physical health through the use of various tools.

X-ray

Imaging technique that uses radiographic waves (X-rays) to create a two-dimensional image of the inside of the body.

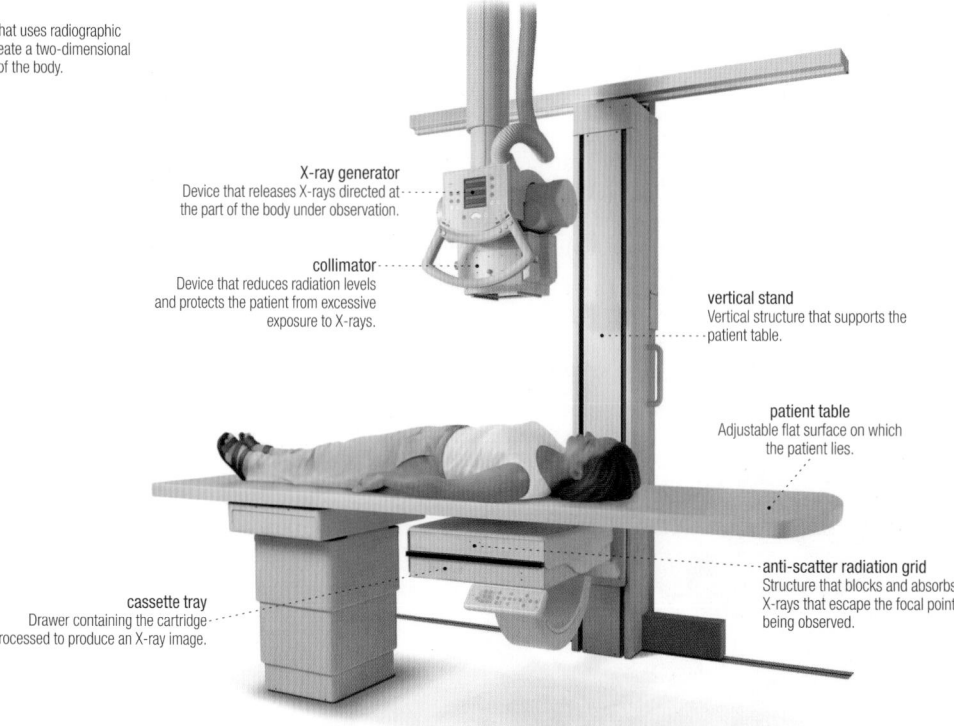

X-ray generator
Device that releases X-rays directed at the part of the body under observation.

collimator
Device that reduces radiation levels and protects the patient from excessive exposure to X-rays.

vertical stand
Vertical structure that supports the patient table.

patient table
Adjustable flat surface on which the patient lies.

anti-scatter radiation grid
Structure that blocks and absorbs X-rays that escape the focal point being observed.

cassette tray
Drawer containing the cartridge processed to produce an X-ray image.

magnetic resonance imaging (MRI)

Medical imaging technique that produces two- and three-dimensional images of internal organs by harnessing the magnetic properties of the body's hydrogen atoms.

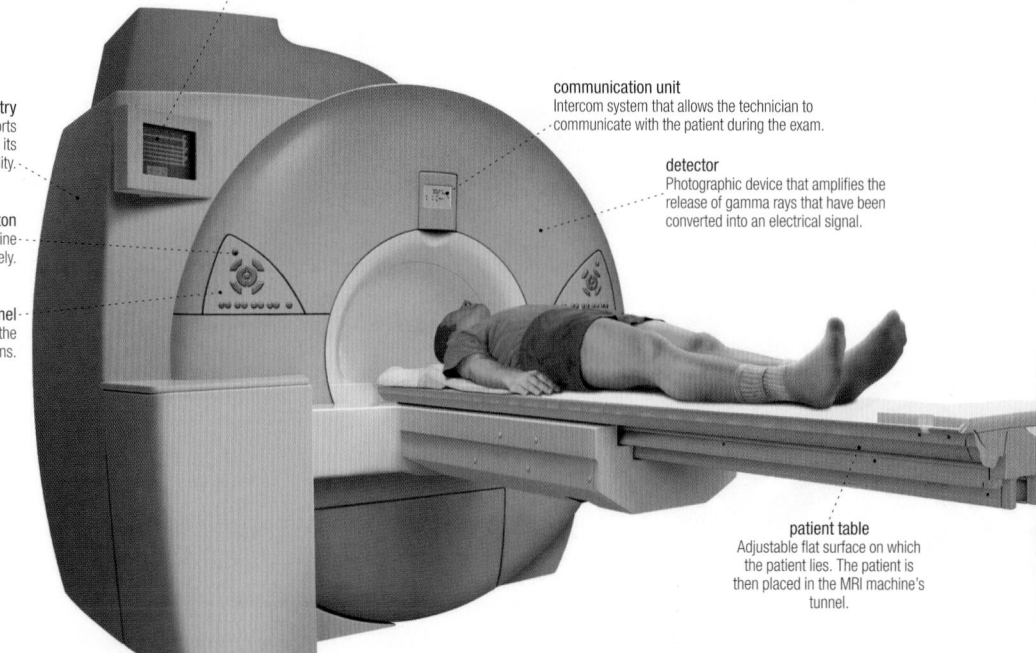

display
Screen that provides data on the machine's settings and the images obtained during the procedure.

gantry
Vertical structure that supports the detector and facilitates its adjustability.

communication unit
Intercom system that allows the technician to communicate with the patient during the exam.

detector
Photographic device that amplifies the release of gamma rays that have been converted into an electrical signal.

emergency stop button
Button that stops the machine immediately.

control panel
Panel of buttons that control the machine's functions.

patient table
Adjustable flat surface on which the patient lies. The patient is then placed in the MRI machine's tunnel.

medical examinations

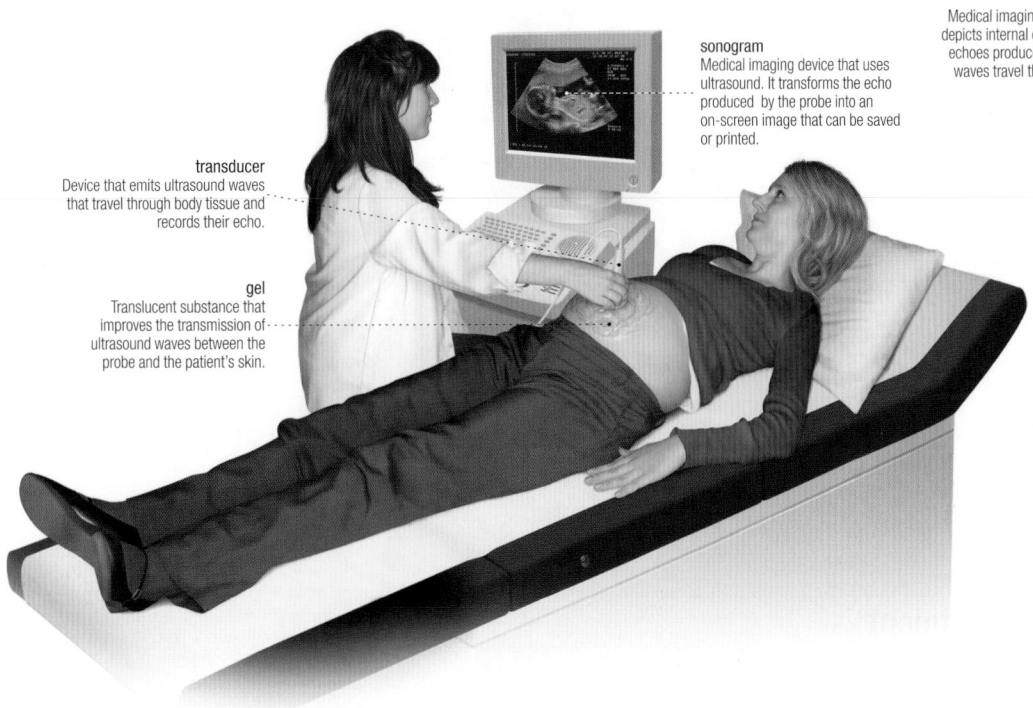

ultrasound
Medical imaging technique that depicts internal organs using the echoes produced as ultrasound waves travel through the body.

sonogram
Medical imaging device that uses ultrasound. It transforms the echo produced by the probe into an on-screen image that can be saved or printed.

transducer
Device that emits ultrasound waves that travel through body tissue and records their echo.

gel
Translucent substance that improves the transmission of ultrasound waves between the probe and the patient's skin.

stress test
Test that measures the heart's electrical activity during periods of physical exertion.

electrocardiogram
Chart that interprets the heart's electrical activity; the line should visually represent a regular series of spikes that rise and fall with the patient's heartbeat.

electrode
Skin patch affixed to the patient's chest and midsection that monitors the heart's electrical activity as it beats.

patient cable
Cable that links the electrode to the electrocardiogram machine.

blood pressure monitor
Device composed of a pneumatic cuff attached to the arm and a pressure gauge; it is used to measure systolic (heart contraction) and diastolic (heart relaxation) pressure in the blood vessels.

keyboard
Keys corresponding to letters, numbers, symbols and functions that are used to generate characters or control operations.

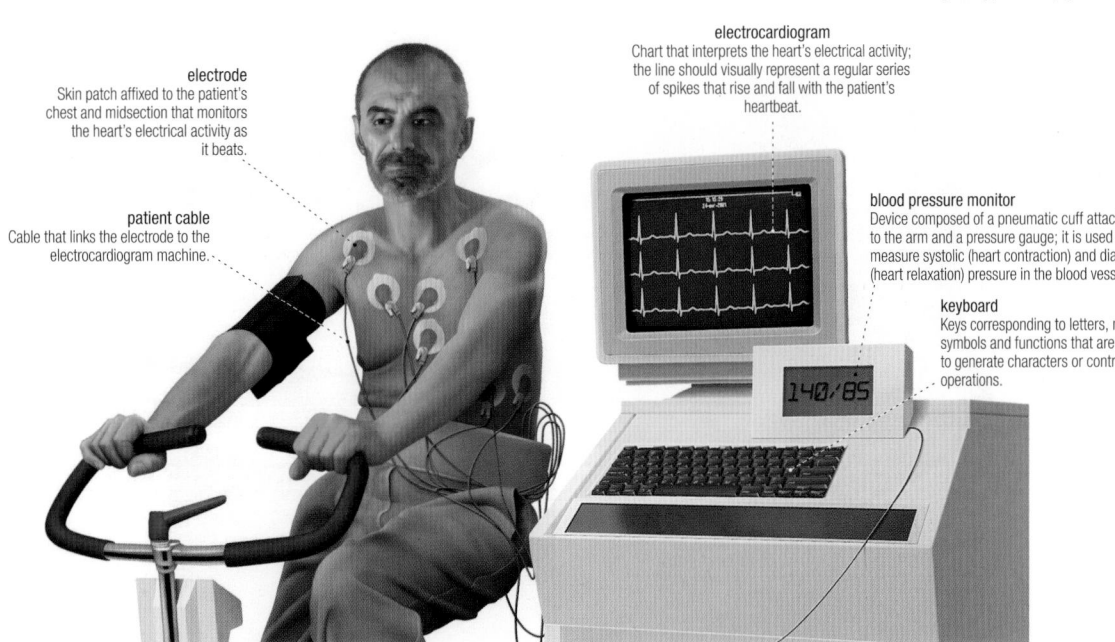

SOCIETY

medical examinations

endoscopy
Examination of the inside of
an organ or cavity using an
endoscope.

flexible tube
Cable that transmits images from
the lens to the eyepiece.

endoscope
Device consisting of an eyepiece, a flexible
tube and a lens with a self-contained
lighting system that is introduced via body
cavity (mouth, nose, anus, vagina).

eyepiece
Optical disk or system of disks
through which the eye sees the
image produced by the lens.

lens
Optical system made up of a set of
lenses fixed on a mount; it allows a
clear image to be produced.

medical treatment

Procedure that seeks to improve a person's physical health.

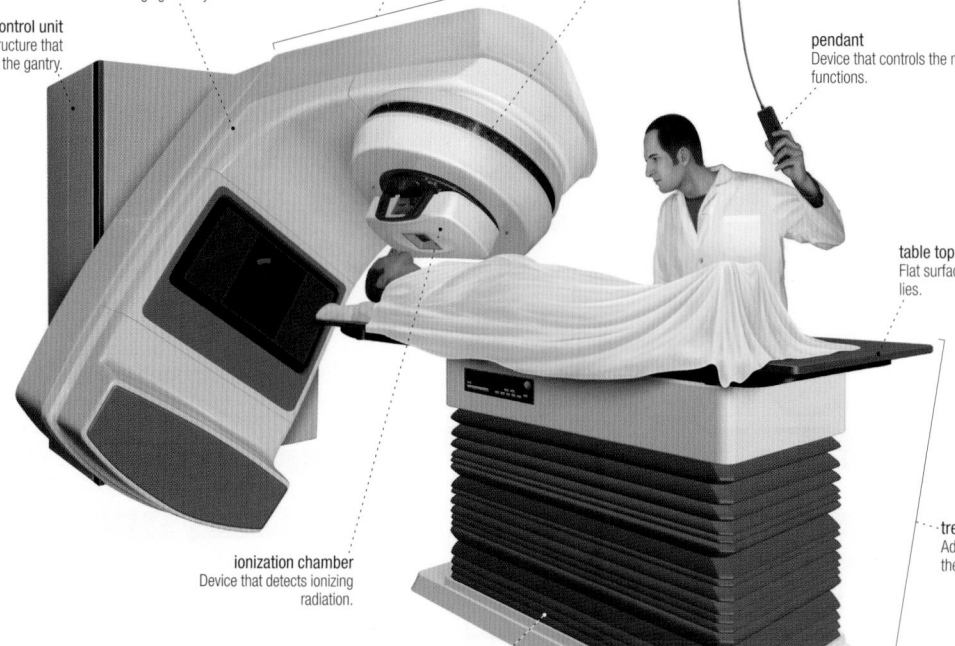

radiotherapy
Cancer treatment that administers
ionizing radiation in order to
damage the patient's DNA, killing
cancer cells in the process.

gantry
Movable structure that supports the
machine's diagnostic arm. Radiation
is focused on part of the body where
the tumor is located in order to avoid
damaging healthy tissue.

electron accelerator
Device that generates beams of
photons or high-energy electrons.

multileaf collimator
Device that reduces radiation
levels and protects the patient from
excessive exposure.

control unit
Fixed vertical structure that
supports the gantry.

pendant
Device that controls the machine's
functions.

table top
Flat surface on which the patient
lies.

ionization chamber
Device that detects ionizing
radiation.

treatment table
Adjustable flat surface on
the patient lies.

adjustable supporting frame
Base structure that allows the table
top to be raised and lowered.

pacemaker
Electronic implant that emits an electrical impulse in order to maintain a regular cardiac rhythm in patients with heart damage.

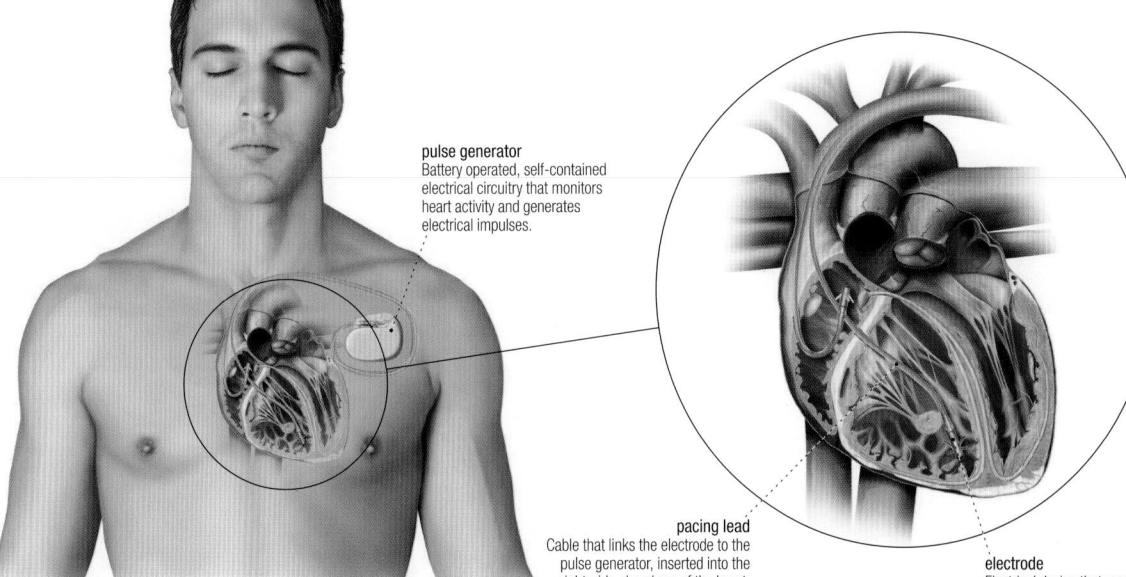

pulse generator
Battery operated, self-contained electrical circuitry that monitors heart activity and generates electrical impulses.

pacing lead
Cable that links the electrode to the pulse generator, inserted into the right-side chambers of the heart.

electrode
Electrical device that monitors and controls cardiac rhythm, transmitting regular electrical impulses emitted by the pulse generator to the heart tissue.

dialysis
Blood purification technique that consists of removing, filtering and re-introducing clean blood into the patient's bloodstream. Blood is filtered by an artificial membrane located outside the body.

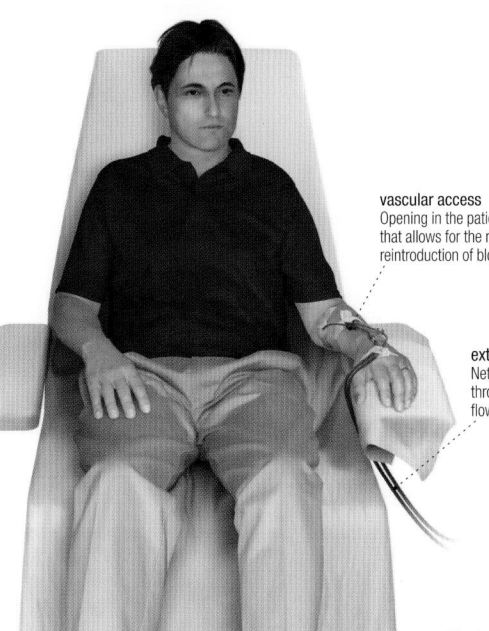

vascular access
Opening in the patient's vein that allows for the removal and reintroduction of blood.

extracorporeal circuit tubing
Network of catheters and tubes through which the patient's blood flows.

clean blood
Toxins and excess water are removed from the blood, which is then re-introduced into the patient's bloodstream.

fresh dialysate
Liquid capable of absorbing blood impurities that is pumped into the dialyzer.

dialyzer
Medical device designed to purify a patient's blood.

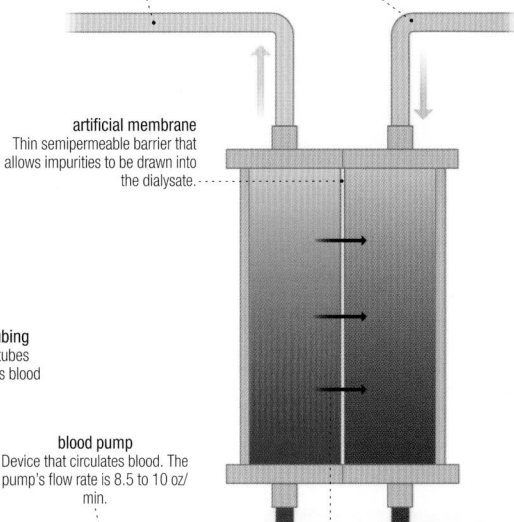

artificial membrane
Thin semipermeable barrier that allows impurities to be drawn into the dialysate.

blood pump
Device that circulates blood. The pump's flow rate is 8.5 to 10 oz/min.

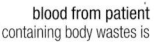

blood from patient
Blood containing body wastes is pumped into the dialyzer.

used dialysate
Blood impurities are washed away in the dialysate.

blood waste
Blood impurities are drawn through the artificial membrane and absorbed into the dialysate.

family relationships

The relationships between the various generations of a family, including their spouses.

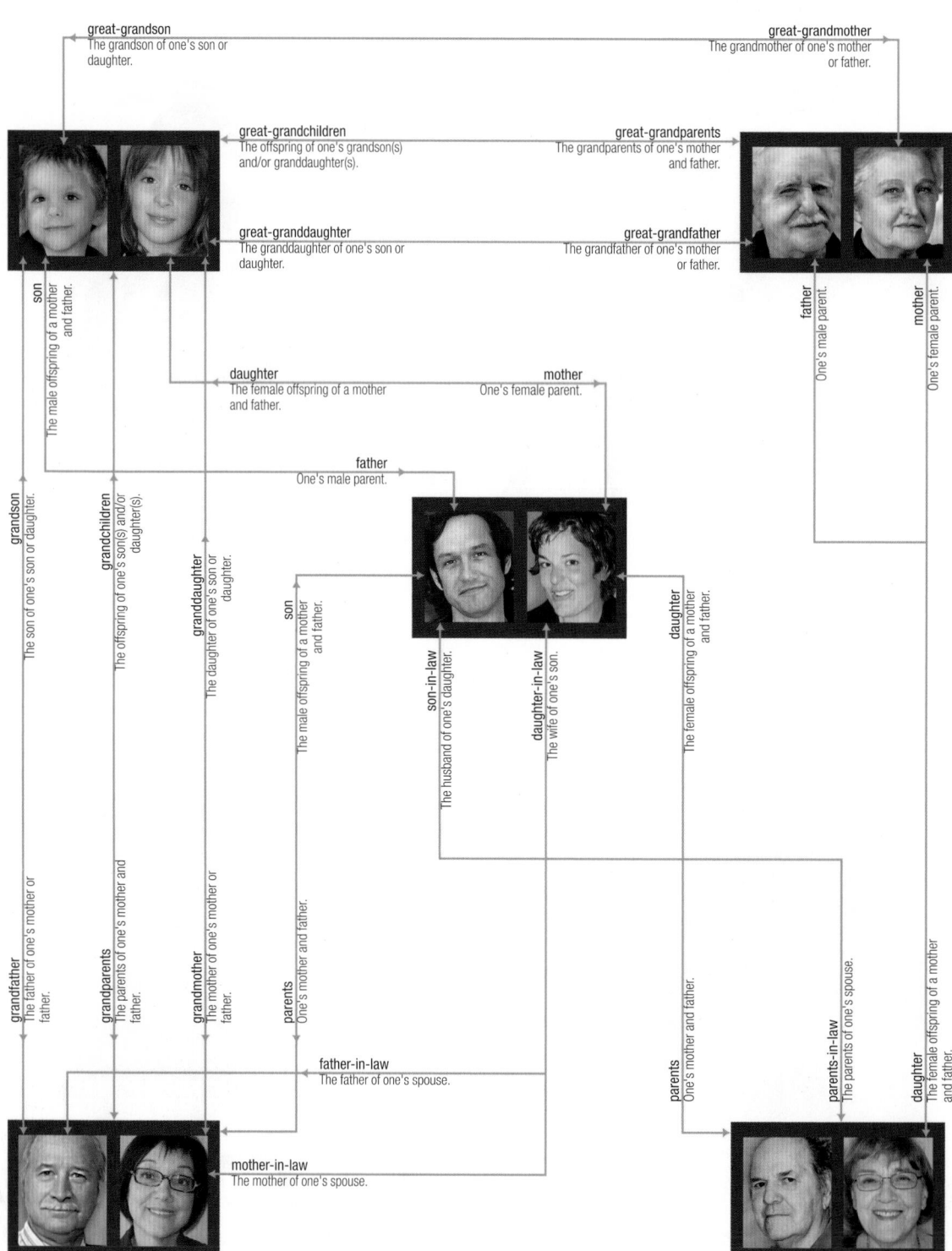

great-grandson
The grandson of one's son or daughter.

great-grandmother
The grandmother of one's mother or father.

great-grandchildren
The offspring of one's grandson(s) and/or granddaughter(s).

great-grandparents
The grandparents of one's mother and father.

great-granddaughter
The granddaughter of one's son or daughter.

great-grandfather
The grandfather of one's mother or father.

son
The male offspring of a mother and father.

father
One's male parent.

mother
One's female parent.

daughter
The female offspring of a mother and father.

mother
One's female parent.

father
One's male parent.

grandson
The son of one's son or daughter.

grandchildren
The offspring of one's son(s) and/or daughter(s).

granddaughter
The daughter of one's son or daughter.

son
The male offspring of a mother and father.

son-in-law
The husband of one's daughter.

daughter-in-law
The wife of one's son.

daughter
The female offspring of a mother and father.

grandfather
The father of one's mother or father.

grandparents
The parents of one's mother and father.

grandmother
The mother of one's mother or father.

parents
One's mother and father.

parents
One's mother and father.

parents-in-law
The parents of one's spouse.

daughter
The female offspring of a mother and father.

father-in-law
The father of one's spouse.

mother-in-law
The mother of one's spouse.

family relationships

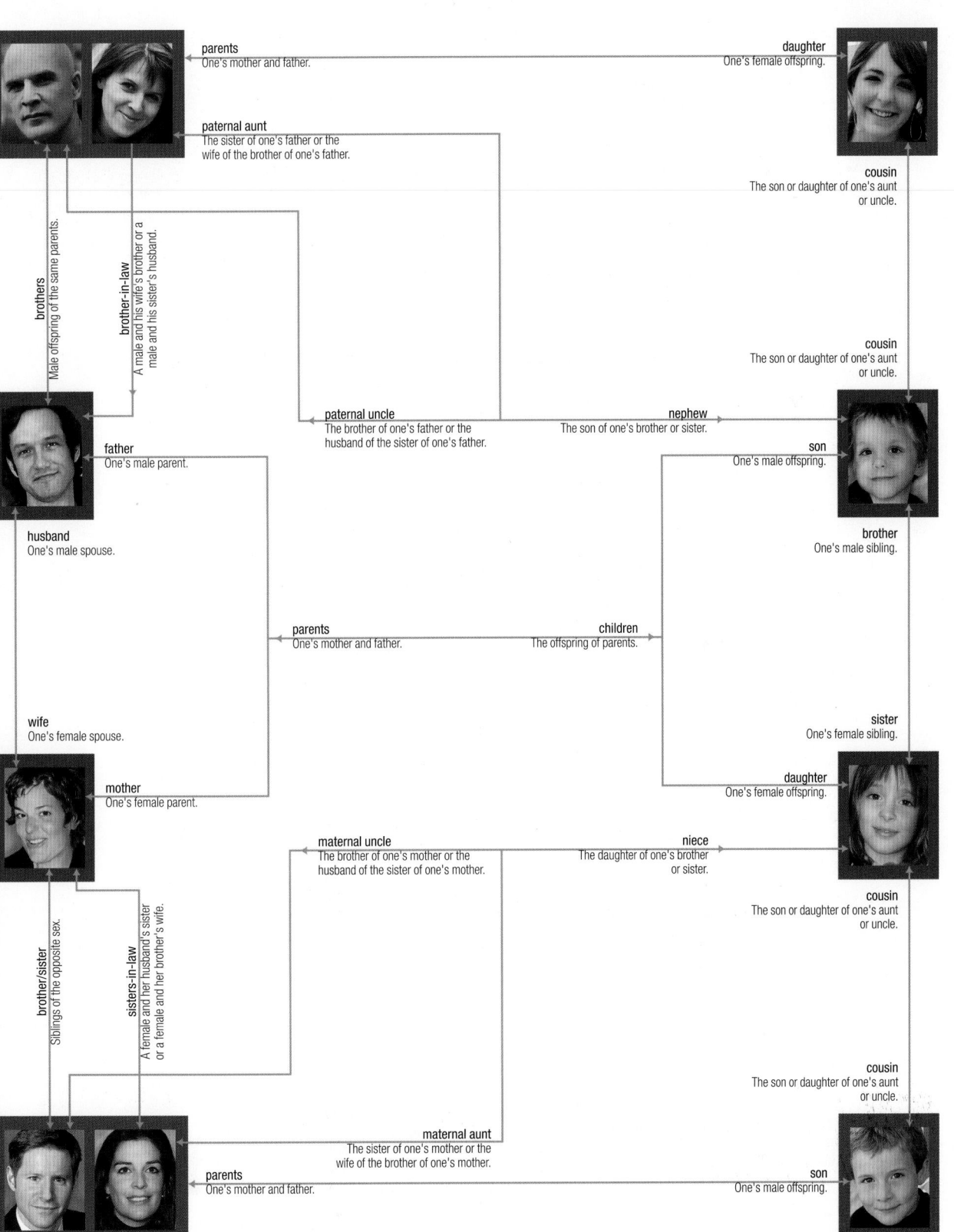

parents
One's mother and father.

daughter
One's female offspring.

paternal aunt
The sister of one's father or the
wife of the brother of one's father.

cousin
The son or daughter of one's aunt
or uncle.

brothers
Male offspring of the same parents.

brother-in-law
A male and his wife's brother or a
male and his sister's husband.

cousin
The son or daughter of one's aunt
or uncle.

paternal uncle
The brother of one's father or the
husband of the sister of one's father.

nephew
The son of one's brother or sister.

son
One's male offspring.

father
One's male parent.

husband
One's male spouse.

brother
One's male sibling.

parents
One's mother and father.

children
The offspring of parents.

wife
One's female spouse.

sister
One's female sibling.

mother
One's female parent.

daughter
One's female offspring.

maternal uncle
The brother of one's mother or the
husband of the sister of one's mother.

niece
The daughter of one's brother
or sister.

cousin
The son or daughter of one's aunt
or uncle.

brother/sister
Siblings of the opposite sex.

sisters-in-law
A female and her husband's sister
or a female and her brother's wife.

cousin
The son or daughter of one's aunt
or uncle.

maternal aunt
The sister of one's mother or the
wife of the brother of one's mother.

parents
One's mother and father.

son
One's male offspring.

SOCIETY

SPORTS AND GAMES

Activities practiced for recreational purposes (fun, relaxation, health) and often taking the form of competitions sanctioned by official bodies.

sports complex

Installations (buildings, playing fields, etc.) that are used for participating in sports.

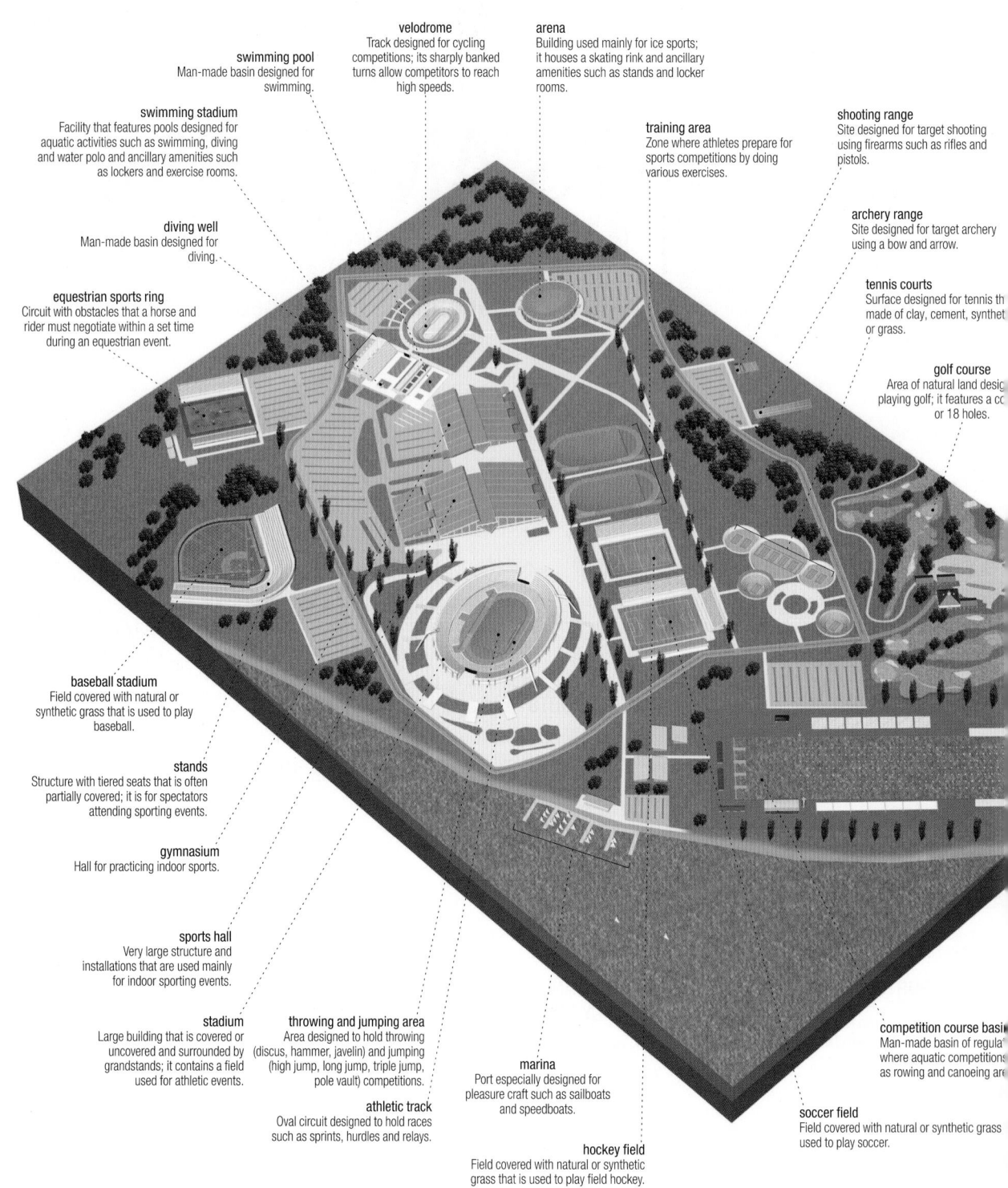

velodrome
Track designed for cycling competitions; its sharply banked turns allow competitors to reach high speeds.

arena
Building used mainly for ice sports; it houses a skating rink and ancillary amenities such as stands and locker rooms.

swimming pool
Man-made basin designed for swimming.

swimming stadium
Facility that features pools designed for aquatic activities such as swimming, diving and water polo and ancillary amenities such as lockers and exercise rooms.

training area
Zone where athletes prepare for sports competitions by doing various exercises.

shooting range
Site designed for target shooting using firearms such as rifles and pistols.

diving well
Man-made basin designed for diving.

archery range
Site designed for target archery using a bow and arrow.

equestrian sports ring
Circuit with obstacles that a horse and rider must negotiate within a set time during an equestrian event.

tennis courts
Surface designed for tennis th made of clay, cement, synthet or grass.

golf course
Area of natural land desig playing golf; it features a co or 18 holes.

baseball stadium
Field covered with natural or synthetic grass that is used to play baseball.

stands
Structure with tiered seats that is often partially covered; it is for spectators attending sporting events.

gymnasium
Hall for practicing indoor sports.

sports hall
Very large structure and installations that are used mainly for indoor sporting events.

stadium
Large building that is covered or uncovered and surrounded by grandstands; it contains a field used for athletic events.

throwing and jumping area
Area designed to hold throwing (discus, hammer, javelin) and jumping (high jump, long jump, triple jump, pole vault) competitions.

marina
Port especially designed for pleasure craft such as sailboats and speedboats.

competition course basi
Man-made basin of regula where aquatic competitions as rowing and canoeing are

athletic track
Oval circuit designed to hold races such as sprints, hurdles and relays.

soccer field
Field covered with natural or synthetic grass used to play soccer.

hockey field
Field covered with natural or synthetic grass that is used to play field hockey.

scoreboard

Display surface posting information related to a sporting event in progress (time, standings, results, etc.).

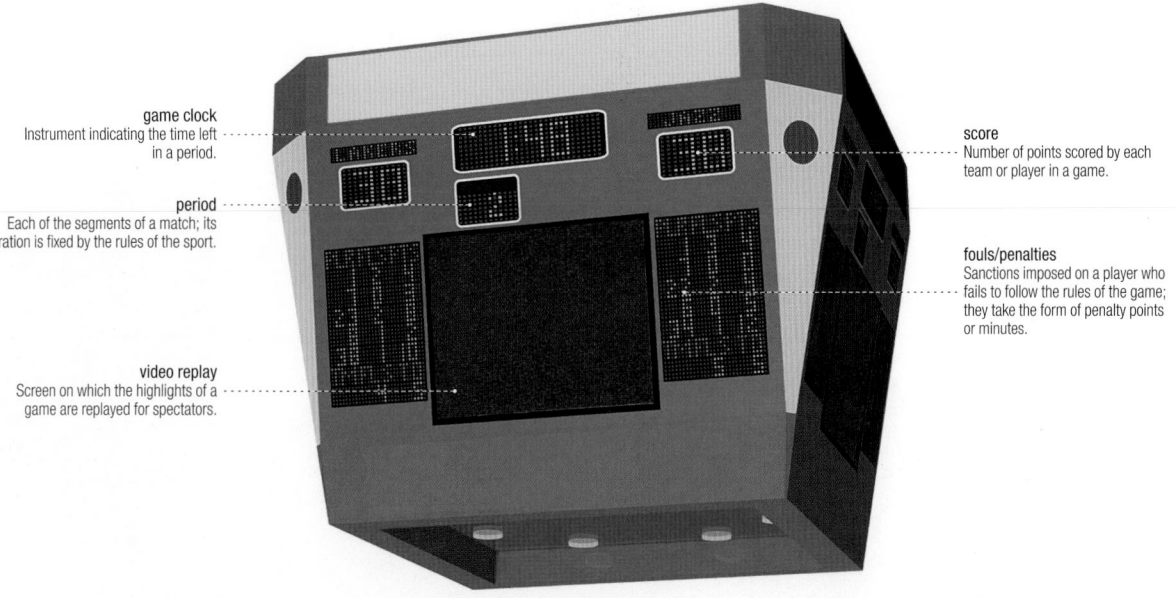

game clock
Instrument indicating the time left in a period.

period
Each of the segments of a match; its duration is fixed by the rules of the sport.

video replay
Screen on which the highlights of a game are replayed for spectators.

score
Number of points scored by each team or player in a game.

fouls/penalties
Sanctions imposed on a player who fails to follow the rules of the game; they take the form of penalty points or minutes.

competition

Sporting event in which several players or teams play against each other; it might be a championship, a cup, a tournament or a rally.

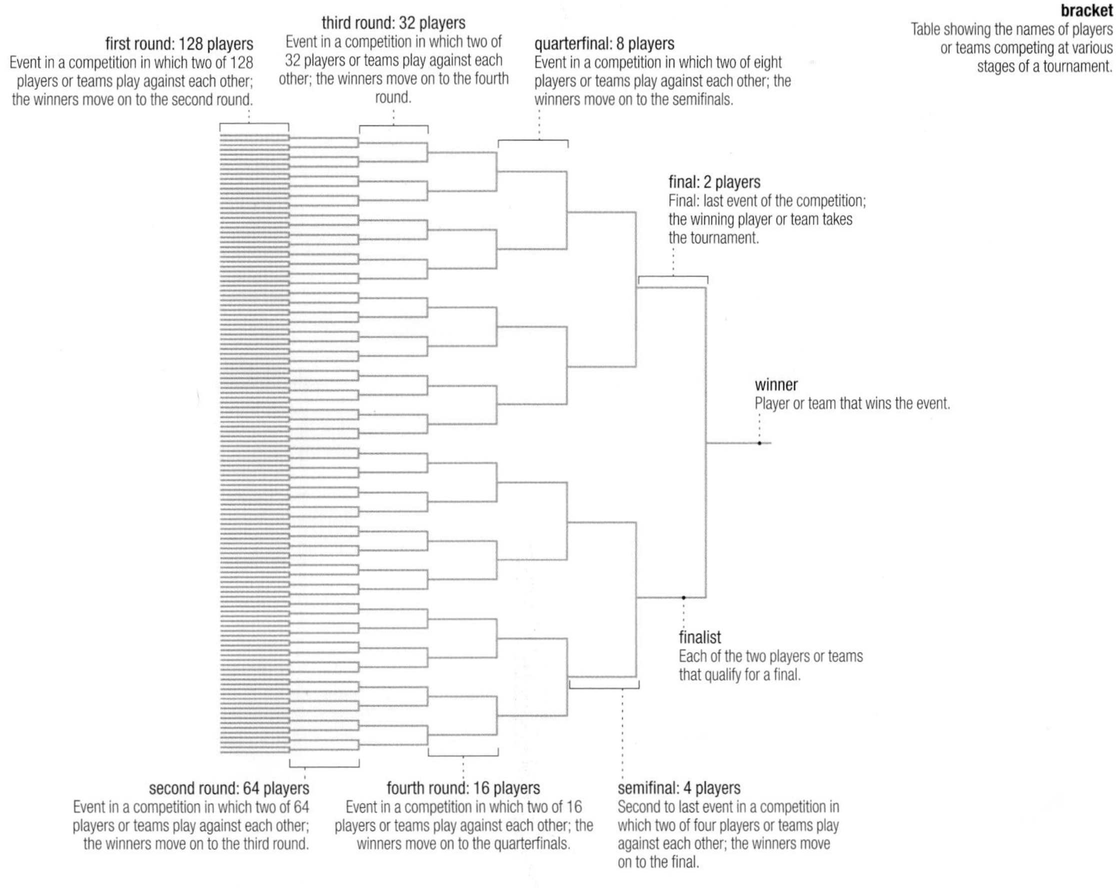

bracket
Table showing the names of players or teams competing at various stages of a tournament.

first round: 128 players
Event in a competition in which two of 128 players or teams play against each other; the winners move on to the second round.

third round: 32 players
Event in a competition in which two of 32 players or teams play against each other; the winners move on to the fourth round.

quarterfinal: 8 players
Event in a competition in which two of eight players or teams play against each other; the winners move on to the semifinals.

final: 2 players
Final: last event of the competition; the winning player or team takes the tournament.

winner
Player or team that wins the event.

finalist
Each of the two players or teams that qualify for a final.

second round: 64 players
Event in a competition in which two of 64 players or teams play against each other; the winners move on to the third round.

fourth round: 16 players
Event in a competition in which two of 16 players or teams play against each other; the winners move on to the quarterfinals.

semifinal: 4 players
Second to last event in a competition in which two of four players or teams play against each other; the winners move on to the final.

track and field

Field designed for participating in track and field and for staging competitions; it is often surrounded by grandstands for seating spectators.

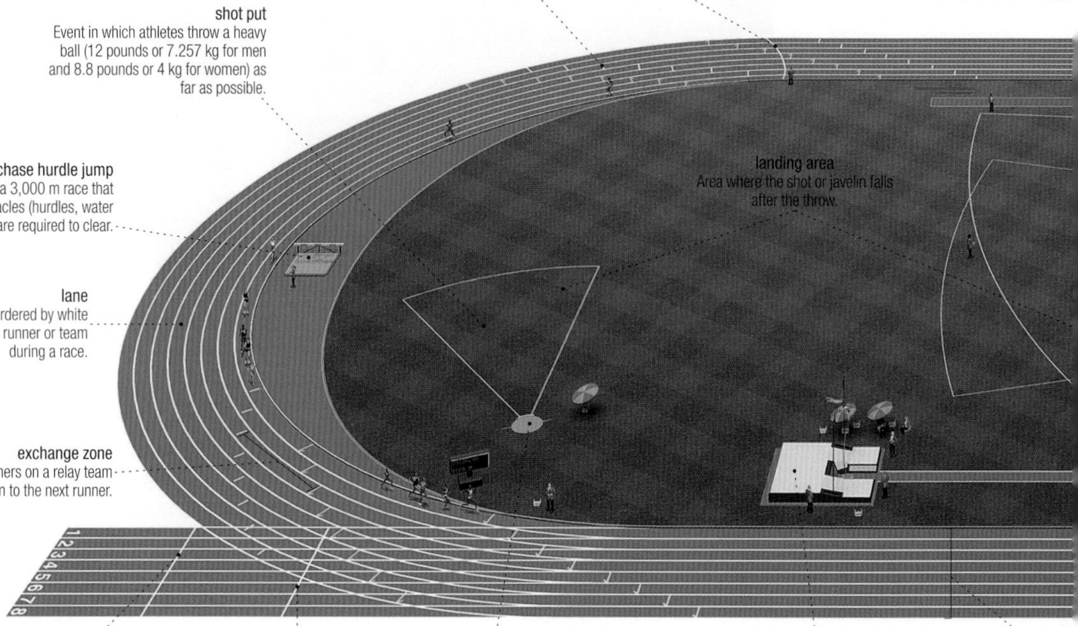

long jump and triple jur
Track and field events that require jumping
far as possible from a given point (long jur
or beginning with a running start followed
a hop, a stride and a jur

200 m starting line

5,000 m starting line

shot put
Event in which athletes throw a heavy
ball (12 pounds or 7.257 kg for men
and 8.8 pounds or 4 kg for women) as
far as possible.

landing area
Area where the shot or javelin falls
after the throw.

steeplechase hurdle jump
Track event held on a 3,000 m race that
includes artificial obstacles (hurdles, water
jumps), which the runners are required to clear.

lane
Long narrow strip bordered by white
lines and reserved for a runner or team
during a race.

exchange zone
Area in which the runners on a relay team
pass the baton to the next runner.

110 m hurdles starting line

100 m and 100 m hurdles starting line

throwing circle
Area where the athlete winds up
to throw the shot; the thrower may
not leave this area before the shot
touches the ground.

pole vault
Athletic event in which a pole is
used to vault over the highest
possible crossbar.

track
Oval circuit designed to
such as sprints, hurdles

track equipment
All the regulation equipment used for
sporting events, including timekeeping
systems, starting pistols, cameras and
hurdles.

starting pistol
Firearm used by a judge to signal
the start of a race by firing blanks
into the air.

baton
Small, very light wooden or metal
stick that is passed from one
runner to the next during a relay
race.

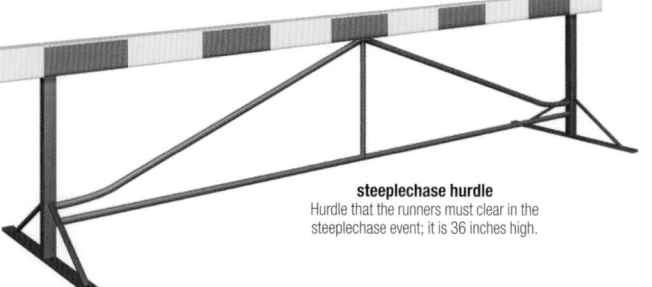

steeplechase hurdle
Hurdle that the runners must clear in the
steeplechase event; it is 36 inches high.

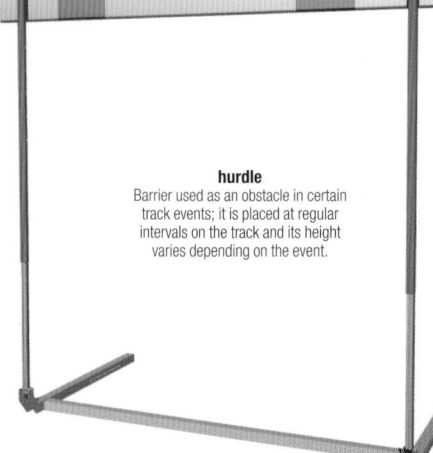

hurdle
Barrier used as an obstacle in certain
track events; it is placed at regular
intervals on the track and its height
varies depending on the event.

discus and hammer throw
Disciplines in which athletes attempt to throw a discus (2 kg for men and 1 kg for women) or hammer (16 lbs or 7.257 kg for men and 4 kg for women) as far as possible.

1,500 m starting line

safety cage
Wire fence bordering the throwing circle; it protects the spectators, competitors and officials in the event of a missed throw.

throwing circle
Area where the athlete winds up to throw the discus or hammer; the athlete may not leave this area before the object touches the ground.

scoreboard
Display surface posting information related to a sporting event in progress (time, standings, results, etc.).

approach
Track that the athlete uses to build up momentum before a javelin throw.

javelin throw
Discipline in which athletes attempt to throw a javelin (800 g for men and 600 g for women) as far as possible.

high jump
Athletic event that requires jumping as high as possible to clear a horizontal bar, relying solely on leg thrust.

finish line
Line marking the end of a race.

800 m starting line

10,000 m and 4 x 400 m relay starting line

400 m, 400 m hurdles, 4 x 100 m relay starting line

shirt
Supple, relatively tight-fitting garment covering the athlete's upper body.

number
Numbered piece of square paper or fabric that athletes wear on their backs or chests for easy identification.

runner: starting block
Starting block: device made up of two adjustable pedals that allow sprinters to give themselves momentum during a start.

shorts
Short and light pants.

pedal
Piece where the athlete places the feet; its angle can be adjusted.

track shoe
Shoe with a spiked sole that provides good traction during a race.

starting line
Line marking the start of the race.

notch
Each of the grooves used to secure the pedals.

lane line
White band bordering the lanes on the track.

anchor
Piece that secures the starting block to the track.

rack
Metal bar with notches that is used to adjust the position of the starting blocks.

spike
Metal piece attached to the front part of the sole to avoid slipping on the track and achieve better thrust.

block
Piece on which runners place their feet to give themselves momentum at the start of a race.

base
Piece that supports the pedal.

SPORTS AND GAMES

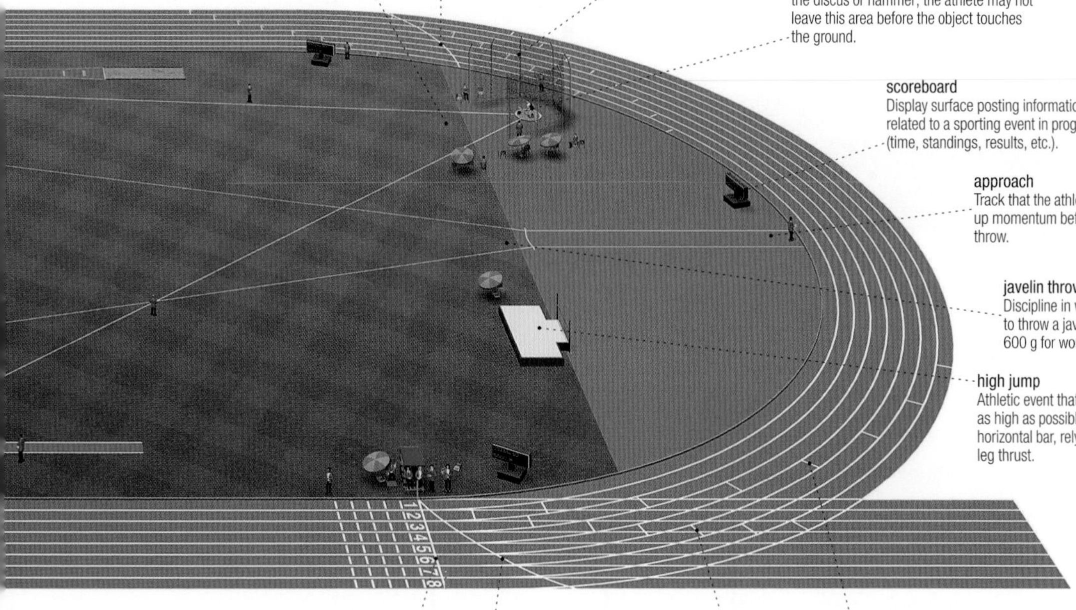

jumping

The four jumping events are the high jump, long jump, triple jump and pole vault.

high jump
Athletic event that requires jumping as high as possible to clear a horizontal bar, relying solely on leg thrust.

upright
Vertical post of adjustable height supporting the high jump crossbar.

crossbar
Long horizontal bar that the athlete must clear without knocking it over; it rests on mounts attached to two uprights.

landing area
Padded area where the athlete lands after a jump.

pole vault
Athletic event in which a pole is used to vault over the highest possible crossbar.

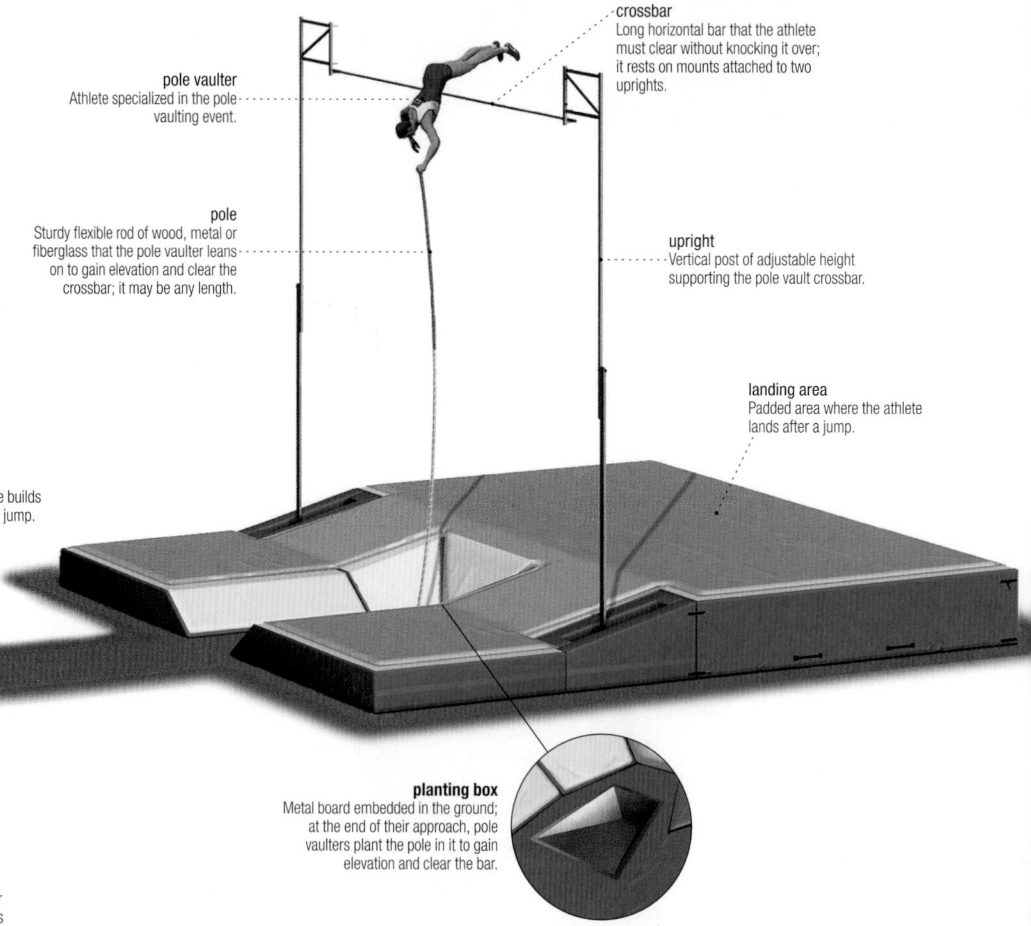

crossbar
Long horizontal bar that the athlete must clear without knocking it over; it rests on mounts attached to two uprights.

pole vaulter
Athlete specialized in the pole vaulting event.

pole
Sturdy flexible rod of wood, metal or fiberglass that the pole vaulter leans on to gain elevation and clear the crossbar; it may be any length.

upright
Vertical post of adjustable height supporting the pole vault crossbar.

landing area
Padded area where the athlete lands after a jump.

approach
Track on which the athlete builds up the speed required to jump.

planting box
Metal board embedded in the ground; at the end of their approach, pole vaulters plant the pole in it to gain elevation and clear the bar.

pole
Sturdy flexible rod of wood, metal or fiberglass that the pole vaulter leans on to gain elevation and clear the crossbar; it may be any length.

tip
Piece of rubber attached to the lower extremity of the pole to prevent it from slipping inside the planting box.

jumping

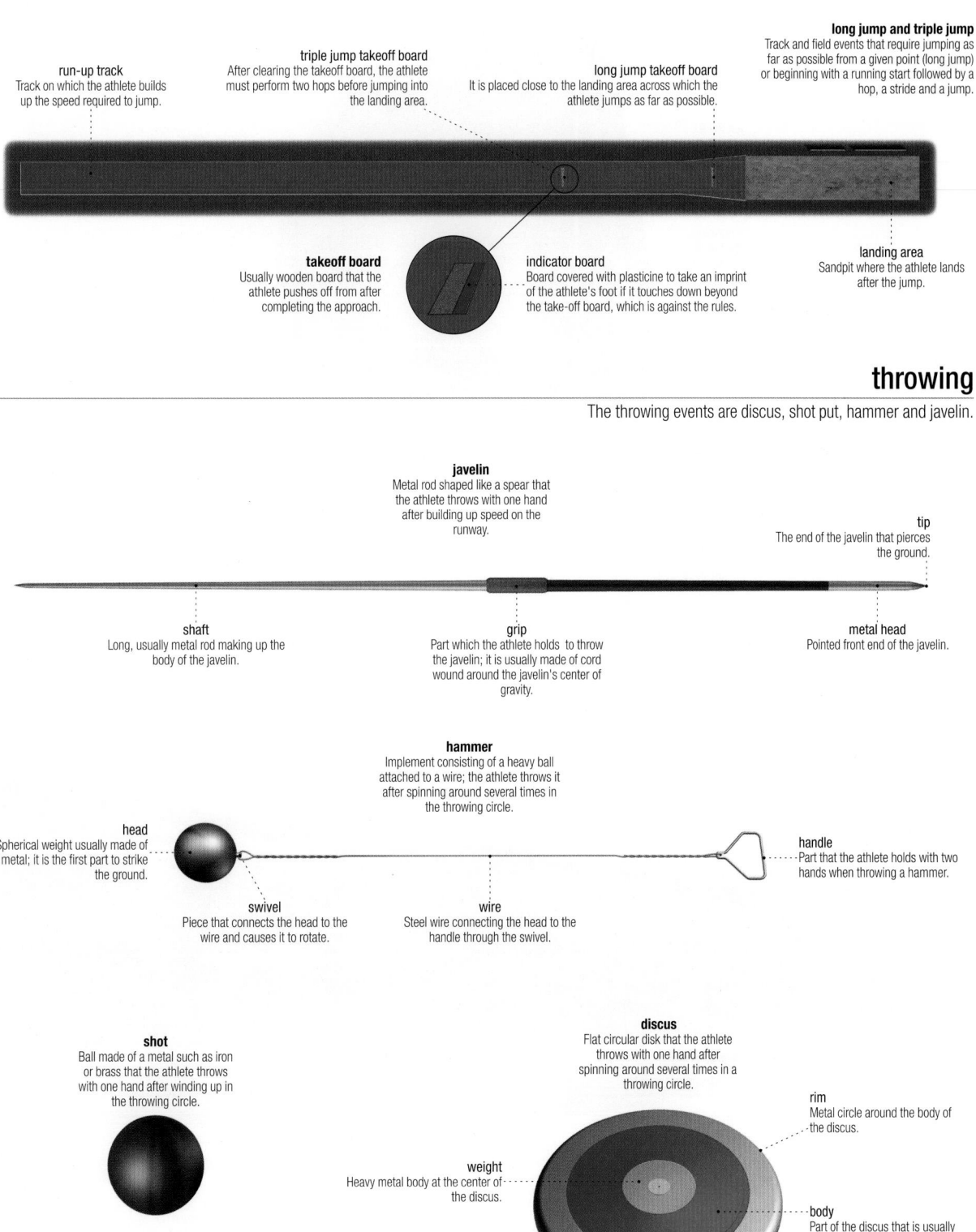

run-up track
Track on which the athlete builds up the speed required to jump.

triple jump takeoff board
After clearing the takeoff board, the athlete must perform two hops before jumping into the landing area.

long jump takeoff board
It is placed close to the landing area across which the athlete jumps as far as possible.

long jump and triple jump
Track and field events that require jumping as far as possible from a given point (long jump) or beginning with a running start followed by a hop, a stride and a jump.

takeoff board
Usually wooden board that the athlete pushes off from after completing the approach.

indicator board
Board covered with plasticine to take an imprint of the athlete's foot if it touches down beyond the take-off board, which is against the rules.

landing area
Sandpit where the athlete lands after the jump.

throwing

The throwing events are discus, shot put, hammer and javelin.

javelin
Metal rod shaped like a spear that the athlete throws with one hand after building up speed on the runway.

tip
The end of the javelin that pierces the ground.

shaft
Long, usually metal rod making up the body of the javelin.

grip
Part which the athlete holds to throw the javelin; it is usually made of cord wound around the javelin's center of gravity.

metal head
Pointed front end of the javelin.

hammer
Implement consisting of a heavy ball attached to a wire; the athlete throws it after spinning around several times in the throwing circle.

head
Spherical weight usually made of metal; it is the first part to strike the ground.

handle
Part that the athlete holds with two hands when throwing a hammer.

swivel
Piece that connects the head to the wire and causes it to rotate.

wire
Steel wire connecting the head to the handle through the swivel.

shot
Ball made of a metal such as iron or brass that the athlete throws with one hand after winding up in the throwing circle.

discus
Flat circular disk that the athlete throws with one hand after spinning around several times in a throwing circle.

rim
Metal circle around the body of the discus.

weight
Heavy metal body at the center of the discus.

body
Part of the discus that is usually made of wood or plastic.

baseball

Sport with two opposing teams of nine players who attempt to score runs by hitting a ball with a bat and running from one base to the next until they reach home plate.

player positions
The team playing the field has nine players who try to prevent the opposing team from reaching bases and scoring points.

left fielder
Position that covers left field.

center fielder
Position in center field; covering the greatest area, this player anticipates where the ball will be hit and coordinates the positions of the outfielders.

shortstop
Position between second and third base; this player's role is to catch a ball hit in that direction and relay it to a teammate, depending on the game situation.

right fielder
Position that covers right field; if a fielder catches the ball before it touches the ground, the batter is retired.

third baseman
Position near third base; this player needs a powerful arm to throw the ball directly to first base when the situation calls for it.

second baseman
Position near second base. This player, like all other infielders, retires an opponent by tagging the runner, ball in hand, before the runner reaches base.

catcher
Position behind home plate; this player catches the ball thrown by the pitcher and indicates the type of pitch to throw to retire the batter.

pitcher
Position opposite home plate; this player throws the ball to the opposing batter, using various pitches to try to prevent the batter from obtaining a hit.

first baseman
Position near first base that takes part in most defensive plays; the batter is retired if the first baseman, ball in hand, touches the base before the batter.

baseball field
Surface on which a baseball game is played; it is in the shape of a quarter circle and is covered with dirt and natural or synthetic grass.

on-deck circle
Area reserved for the next batter; players on the team batting remain at bat until three outs have been recorded.

third base
Cushion attached to the ground that the player tries to reach after touching second base; if the player reaches home plate without being retired, one run is scored.

foul line
Two straight lines bordering the playing field; they run from home plate to the outfield fence.

backstop
Chain-link barrier located behind home plate; it prevents the ball from reaching the spectators.

dugout
Partially closed area for the coaches, manager, substitute players and the team at bat.

coaches' box
Each of two areas reserved for base coaches who use signals to communicate strategy to runners and batters.

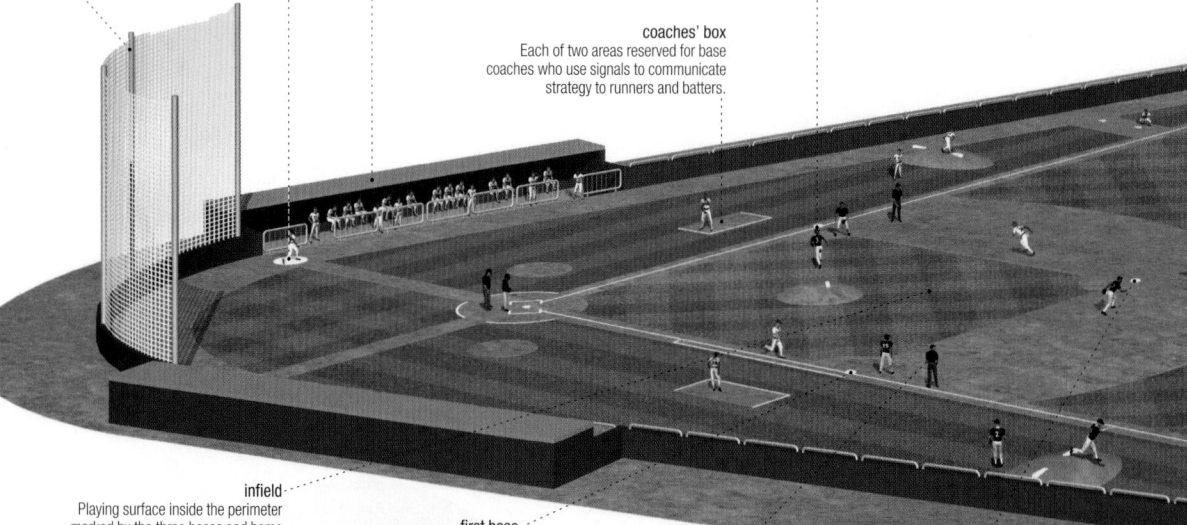

infield
Playing surface inside the perimeter marked by the three bases and home plate; it includes a dirt area bordering the outfield.

first base
Cushion attached to the ground that is the first base the batter reaches after hitting the ball; the player may stop there or move on to other bases.

base umpire
Official who makes calls on runners at the bases.

second base
Cushion attached to the ground that the player tries to reach after touching first base, after the ball has been hit.

bullpen
Warm-up area for reserve pitchers.

home-plate umpire
[Of]ficial who calls balls and strikes, and [si]gnals when the batter has struck out [three strikes) or when a runner is retired at home plate.

batter
Player who takes position to hit the ball; to score a run, the batter must touch three successive bases and then home plate.

pitcher
Position opposite home plate; this player throws the ball to the opposing batter, using various pitches to try to prevent the batter from getting a hit.

pitch
When the batter is in position, the pitcher throws the ball toward home plate; the batter judges the pitch and decides whether or not to try to hit it.

catcher
Position behind home plate; this player catches the ball thrown by the pitcher and indicates the type of pitch to throw to retire the batter.

home plate
Rubber plate that the batter stands beside to face the pitcher; it marks the pitcher's strike zone and the umpire calls balls and strikes in relation to it.

pitcher's mound
Small mound of earth from which the pitcher throws the ball toward the batter; it is 10 inches higher than home plate.

pitcher's rubber
Band of rubber attached to the ground; the pitcher stands on it to throw a pitch.

left field
Section of the outfield behind third base, or to the left of the batter.

outfield fence
Barrier bordering the outfield, which is the playing surface between the two foul lines and beyond the infield.

center field
Section of the outfield behind second base, directly facing the batter.

right field
Section of the outfield behind first base, or to the right of the batter.

foul pole
Each of the vertical posts indicating the end of the foul lines; a ball hit outside the foul lines is called a foul ball.

warning track
Area indicating to the outfielders that the fence is near; a home run is a ball hit over the fence and inside the foul lines.

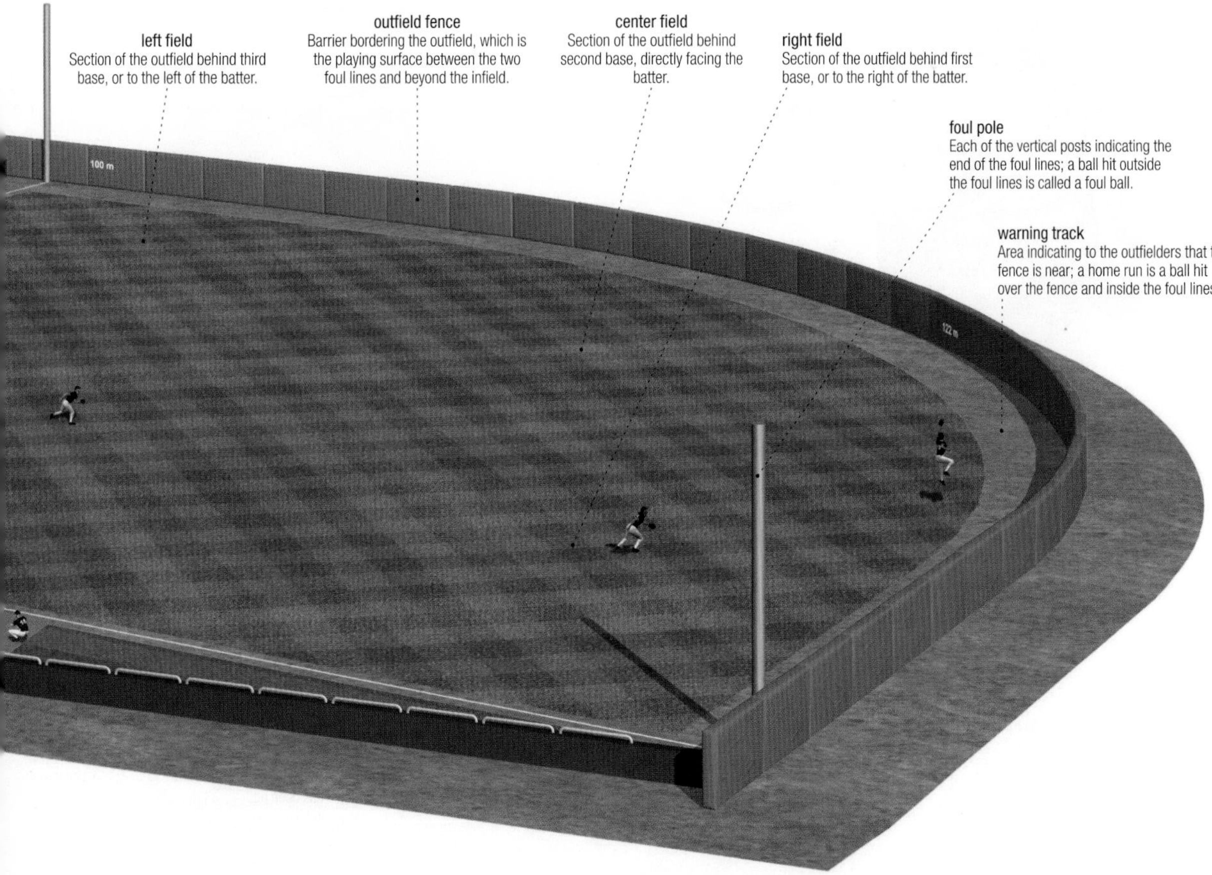

100 m

122 m

baseball

baseball
Hard ball with a circumference of
9 inches; its outer layer is made of
two white pieces of leather sewn
together.

bat
Club made of wood or aluminum
that the batter uses to hit the ball;
its maximum length is 42 in.

batter's helmet
Rigid piece of equipment for
protecting the head from the ball's
impact; it has side protection for
the ears and temples.

batt
Player who takes position to hit t
ball; the batter grasps the hand
of the b

catcher
Position behind home plate; this player catches
the ball thrown by the pitcher. The catcher
wears equipment that protects against the ball,
which can travel over 100 mph.

mask
Cage that protects the catcher's
head and face.

chest protector
Heavily padded vest that protects
the catcher's chest.

frame
Intersecting bars attached to the front of
the mask; it protects the catcher's eyes
and face while providing good visibility.

throat protector
Hard piece attached to the mask;
it protects the catcher's neck and
throat.

batting glove
Piece of leather covering the hand and
wrist; it is designed to give the batter a
good grip on the bat.

jersey
Flexible garment covering the
upper body; it features the team
emblem and the player's name
and number.

undershirt
Relatively tight-fitting stretchy
garment with short or long sleeve
that players wear under the team
shirt.

pants
Flexible stretchy garment covering
the lower body from the waist to
the shins or ankles.

catcher's glove
Glove with a heavily padded inside
surface to cushion the impact of
catching the ball.

stirrup sock
Colored sock whose lower
extremity is an elastic that passes
beneath the foot; it is usually worn
over a white sock.

spikes
Footwear whose sole contains small
spikes to provide good traction.

toe guard
Piece of equipment made of hard
molded plastic that protects the toes.

shin guard
Piece of equipment made of
hard molded plastic that protects
the leg.

knee pad
Piece of equipment made of hard
molded plastic that protects the
knee.

ankle guard
Piece of equipment made of hard molded
plastic that protects the ankle and shin
from impact when the ball ricochets off
the bat.

baseball

baseball bat
Club made of wood or aluminum that the batter uses to hit the ball; its maximum length is 42 in.

knob
Circular piece on the end of the handle; it prevents the hand from slipping off the bat.

handle
The narrowest part of the bat that the player grasps; it is sometimes covered with antislip material.

crest
Symbol representing the brand of the bat or its manufacturer.

barrel
The widest part of the bat and the part that strikes the ball; it must not exceed 2.75 in in diameter.

ection of a baseball
aseball has a cork core, which is apped in layers of rubber, wound with rn and covered with leather.

cork ball
mall sphere of cork that forms the central part of the ball.

yarn ball
Yarn wound around the center of the ball.

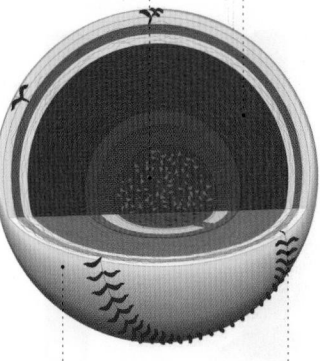

cover
Outer layer of the ball made up of two white pieces of leather joined by stitching.

stitches
The sewing that joins the two parts of the cover; it traditionally uses red thread.

web
Part of the glove between the thumb and the index finger; it forms a small pocket in which the ball is caught.

fielder's glove
Large leather glove for catching baseballs; design varies depending on the player's position.

strap
The intersecting leather straps that make up the web.

thumb
Part of the glove covering the thumb.

finger
Part of the glove that covers each of the fingers.

palm
Part of the glove that covers the hollow of the hand.

heel
The bottom part of the glove.

lace
Narrow cord passed through the eyelets to join or tighten the parts of the glove.

softball

Sport akin to baseball but played on a smaller field; it differs from baseball in that the pitcher throws the ball underhand and not overhand.

softball glove
Leather glove for catching softballs, longer and wider than a baseball fielder's glove.

softball bat
Club made usually of aluminum that the batter uses to hit the ball; it is often somewhat longer and lighter than a baseball bat.

softball
Hard ball with a circumference of 12 inches; it is manufactured in the same way as a baseball.

SPORTS AND GAMES

cricket

Sport with two opposing teams of 11 players who attempt to score points by hitting a ball with a bat and running between two wickets; teams alternate between offense (at the bat) and defense (in the field).

batsman
Player who takes position to hit the ball; like all cricketers, this player wears the traditional white or cream white.

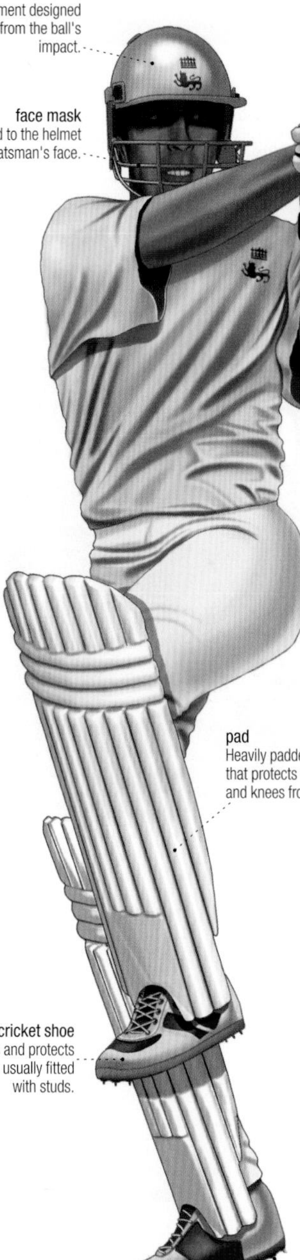

bat
Piece formed of a flat section connected to a rubber-covered handle that the batsman uses to hit the ball; its maximum length is 38 inches.

cricket ba
Hard ball with a circumference 9 inches; it is made with a co core, which is wound with threa and covered with leathe

leather skin
Outside layer of the ball made of pieces of red leather joined by stitching.

helmet
Hard piece of equipment designed to protect the head from the ball's impact.

face mask
Wire mask attached to the helmet to protect the batsman's face.

seam
Sewing that joins the leather cover; it traditionally uses white thread.

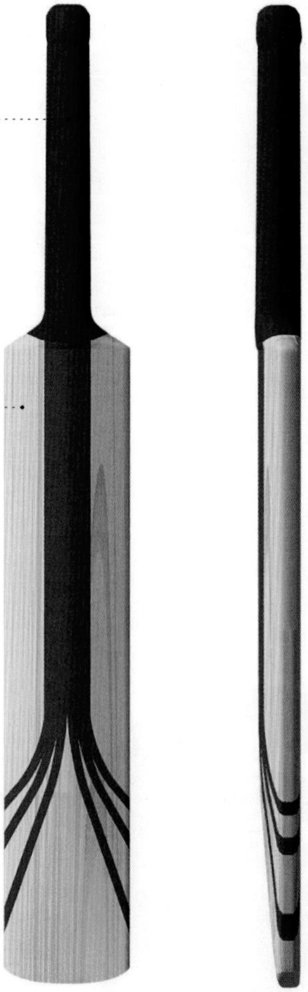

glove
Padded piece of equipment covering the hand and wrist; it is shaped around the fingers and is flexible enough to provide a good grip on the bat.

ba
Piece formed of a flat section connecte to a rubber-covered handle tha the batsman uses to hit the ball; i maximum length is 38 inche

handle
Part used to hold and manipulate the bat.

willow
Flat surface that the batsman uses to hit the ball; it is made of willow wood and its maximum length is 4.75 inches.

pad
Heavily padded piece of equipment that protects the batsman's legs and knees from the ball's impact.

cricket shoe
Shoe that supports and protects the ankle; its sole is usually fitted with studs.

stud
Each of the small spikes attached to the sole to provide traction when batting or running.

front view

side view

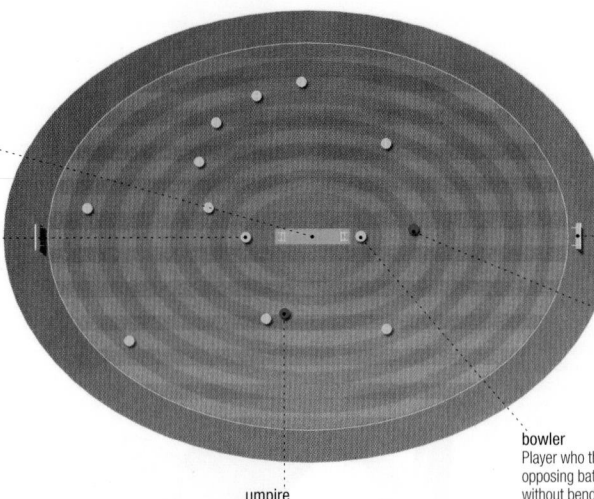

player positions
The team in the field, or the defending team, must catch the ball hit by the batsman and throw it toward one of the wickets to topple it.

pitch
Rectangular surface in midfield where the bowler and the batsman face each other; it contains two wickets that are about 20 m apart.

wicketkeeper
Player positioned behind the batting wicket; the only defensive player who wears gloves, the wicketkeeper tries to catch balls missed by the batsman.

screen
Rectangular surface behind each wicket; it minimizes distraction so that the batsman can follow the movement of the ball.

umpire
Official responsible for applying the rules of delivery; this umpire is positioned behind the bowler's wicket.

bowler
Player who throws the ball toward the opposing batsman. He projects the ball without bending the elbow, generally after a run of a few meters.

umpire
Official who enforces the rules; positioned to the side of the batsman's wicket, this umpire signals when a batsman is retired or when there is an infraction.

wicket
Piece made up of stumps with detachable bails; the wicket is considered toppled when at least one of the bails falls.

bail
The two horizontal pieces balanced on top of the stumps; they fall over when the ball strikes the wicket.

stump
The three vertical pieces that make up the wicket; the space between the stumps is smaller than the diameter of the ball.

pitch
Rectangular surface in midfield where the bowler and the batsman face each other; it contains two wickets that are 20 m apart.

wicketkeeper
Player positioned behind the batting wicket; the only defensive player who wears gloves, the wicketkeeper tries to catch balls missed by the batsman.

batsman
Player who takes position to hit the ball and protect the wicket; each time the player runs between the two wickets before the ball arrives, one point is scored.

bowling crease
Line perpendicular to the return crease; the wicket is embedded in the center of it.

popping crease
Line drawn 4 feet from the wicket; at the end of a run, the batsman is safe after touching the ground behind this line with the bat or a part of the body.

bowler
Player who throws the ball toward the opposing batsman standing in front of the wicket. If the bowler topples the wicket, the batsman is retired.

delivery
Thrown at speeds reaching 100 mph, the ball usually bounces once before reaching the batsman.

return crease
The two lines on each side of wicket that demarcate the space in which the ball must be thrown or hit.

umpire
Official responsible for applying the rules of delivery; this umpire is positioned behind the bowler's wicket.

wicket
Piece made up of stumps with detachable bails; a defender can retire a batsman by toppling the wicket before the batsman completes the run between wickets.

field hockey

Sport with two opposing teams of 11 players who attempt to score in the opponent's goal by hitting a ball with a stick.

goalkeeper
Player whose role is to prevent the ball from entering the goal; the goalkeeper may touch the ball with any part of the body but cannot hold it with the hands.

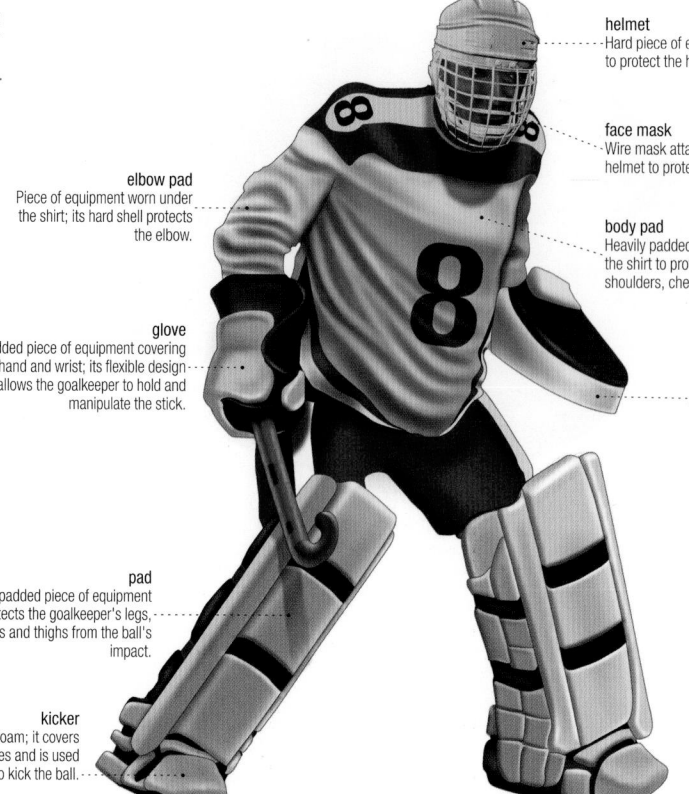

helmet
Hard piece of equipment designed to protect the head.

face mask
Wire mask attached to the front of the helmet to protect the goalkeeper's face.

elbow pad
Piece of equipment worn under the shirt; its hard shell protects the elbow.

body pad
Heavily padded vest worn under the shirt to protect the goalkeeper's shoulders, chest and back.

glove
Padded piece of equipment covering the hand and wrist; its flexible design allows the goalkeeper to hold and manipulate the stick.

blocking glove
Rigid foam glove that is worn on the free hand; the goalkeeper uses its flat side to block the ball.

pad
Heavily padded piece of equipment that protects the goalkeeper's legs, knees and thighs from the ball's impact.

kicker
Piece made of rigid foam; it covers the goalkeeper's shoes and is used to kick the ball.

stick
Wooden or composite stick with a rounded side and a flat side, which is used to manipulate the ball.

goal
Cage made up of a net mounted on a frame; a goal is scored each time a team hits the ball into the opposing goal from inside the striking circle.

coach
The team's leader; the coach plots strategy and decides who plays in different situations.

hockey ball
Hard plastic ball with a circumference of 9 in; its traditionally white surface is usually grooved.

handle
Part for holding and manipulating the stick.

tape
Rubber or plastic tape wound around the handle to prevent the hands from slipping.

goal line
Line marking the ends of the playing field; the ball must cross this line for the goal to count as a point.

striking circle
Semicircle located in front of the goal; a goal can only be scored when the attacker hits the ball inside the opponent's striking circle.

toe
Curved end of the stick used to stop, manipulate and hit the ball.

5.5 yd line
Line where the attacker puts the ball back into play if the defenders push it behind their own goal line.

sideline
Line marking the sides of the playing field; when the ball crosses this line, the opposing team puts it back into play at the same place.

25 yd line
Line used to position the players w the ball is put back into play; positi depends on whether the ball went play between the 25 yd lines or bet one of them and the goal line

hockey player
A field hockey player is allowed to touch the ball only with the stick.

jersey
Flexible garment covering the upper body; it features the team emblem and the player's name and number.

stick
Wooden or composite stick with a rounded side and a flat side, which is used to manipulate and shoot the ball.

shorts
Very short pants covering only the top of the thighs; women field hockey players usually wear a pleated skirt.

shin guard
Piece of equipment made up of a hard plastic molding that protects the player's legs.

shoe
Footwear that protects and supports the ankle; flexible plastic studs are attached to its sole to provide good traction.

cials
viduals in charge of keeping e, recording player substitutions filling out the score sheet.

right wing
Offensive position to the right of the center forward and near the sideline; this player's main role is to thwart opponents and score goals.

right inside forward
Position to the right of the center forward; a true playmaker, this player receives passes from the defenders or halfs and creates offensive chances.

center half
Key position behind the backs in the center of the field; this player receives the ball and passes it in any direction.

right half
Position to the right of the center half; this player tries to take the ball from the opponent and move it up to the wings or forwards.

right back
Defensive position behind the halfs on the right side of the field; this player attempts to prevent the opponent from creating scoring chances.

players' bench
Area reserved for substitute players and coaches; a team can have up to 16 players but only 11 play at once.

hockey field
Surface covered with natural or synthetic grass (60 yd x 100 yd) on which a field hockey game is played; a game is made up of two 35-minute periods.

goalkeeper
Player whose role is to prevent the ball from entering the goal; the goalkeeper may touch the ball with any part of the body but cannot hold it with the hands.

corner flag
Small post with a flag on top; it marks the intersection of the goal line and the sideline.

referee
One of two officials responsible for applying the rules; this individual penalizes players who commit infractions and awards penalty shots.

left back
Defensive position behind the halfs on the left side of the field; this player's role is to prevent the opponent from obtaining scoring chances.

left wing
Offensive position to the left of the center forward and near the sideline; this player's main role is to thwart opponents and score goals.

left half
Position to the left of the center half; this player's main role is to take the ball from the opponent and move it up to the wings or forwards.

center line
dividing the field into two zones, r each team; face-offs are held s line at the start of a period and after a goal is scored.

left inside forward
Position to the left of the center forward; a true playmaker, this player receives passes from defenders or halfs and generates offensive chances.

center forward
Offensive position that covers the center of the field; this player tries to score goals by getting within the striking circle.

soccer

Sport with two opposing teams of 11 players who attempt to score in the opponent's goal by kicking or knocking the ball in with any part of the body except the arms and hands.

soccer player
A soccer player is allowed to touch the ball with any part of the body except the arms and hands.

jersey
Flexible garment covering the upper body; it features the team emblem and the player's name and number.

goalkeeper's gloves
Gloves that cover and protect the goalkeeper's hands and wrists and improve the grip on the ball.

shorts
Short and light pants.

interchangeable stud
Removable cleat that attaches to the sole. To ensure that shoes are appropriate for the playing field, studs are available in a variety of sizes.

soccer shoe
Shoe made of leather, soft rubber or plastic; studs are att. to its sole to provide good traction.

shin guard
Piece of equipment made up of a hard plastic molding; it protects the soccer player's legs.

sock
Garment worn over the foot and up to the knee; it completely covers the shin guard.

soccer ball
Inflated ball made of leather or synthetic material; its circumference varies between 27 and 27.5 in.

soccer field
Rectangular surface covered with natural or synthetic grass on which a soccer match is played; a game has two 45-minute halves.

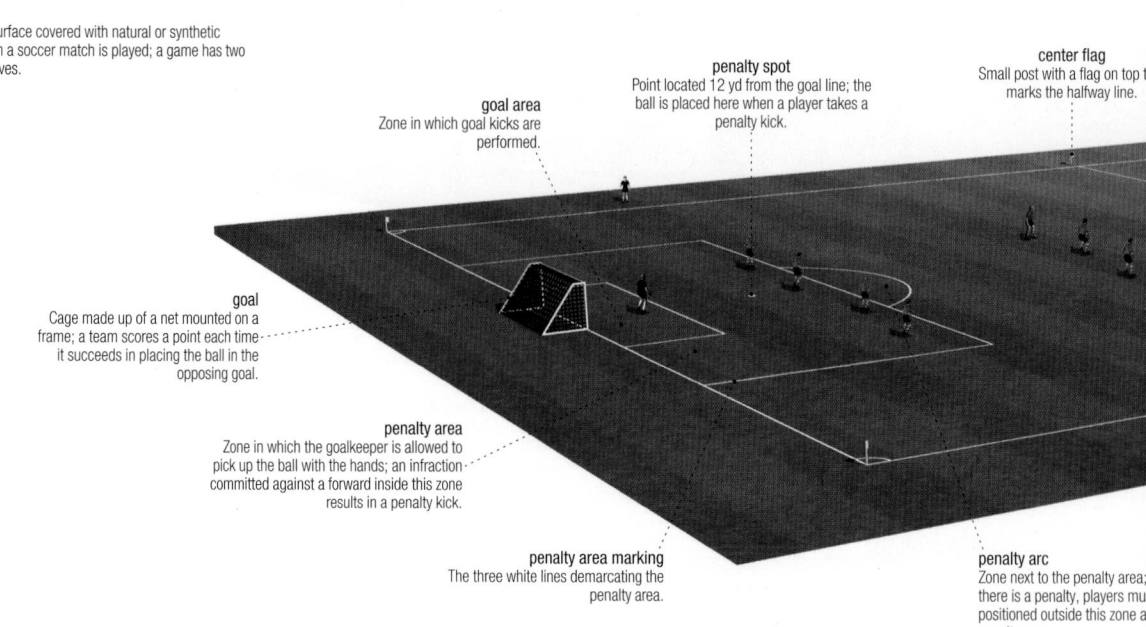

goal area
Zone in which goal kicks are performed.

penalty spot
Point located 12 yd from the goal line; the ball is placed here when a player takes a penalty kick.

center flag
Small post with a flag on top tha marks the halfway line.

goal
Cage made up of a net mounted on a frame; a team scores a point each time it succeeds in placing the ball in the opposing goal.

penalty area
Zone in which the goalkeeper is allowed to pick up the ball with the hands; an infraction committed against a forward inside this zone results in a penalty kick.

penalty area marking
The three white lines demarcating the penalty area.

penalty arc
Zone next to the penalty area; w there is a penalty, players must positioned outside this zone and penalty area.

left back
Defensive position that covers the left side of the field; this player's main role is to slow or stop an opponent's progress toward the goal.

left midfielder
Center position that plays on the left side of the field; this player uses playmaking skills to pass the ball to the forwards.

defensive midfielder
Center position; this player tries to take the ball from the opponent before that player reaches the defenders and quickly mount a counterattack.

player positions
Various tactical schemes are used in soccer; among the best known is the 4-4-2, a formation with four defenders, four midfielders and two forwards.

sweeper
...sition that stays back, anticipates defensive mistakes by teammates and makes up for them; this player is not required to closely mark an opposing player.

forward
Offensive position usually placed behind the striker; this player uses speed to make crisp accurate passes.

goalkeeper
Position whose role is to prevent the ball from entering the goal; this is the only player allowed to touch the ball with the hands.

striker
Offensive position whose main role is to score goals; this player plays a forward position in the opposing team's zone.

stopper
Position that stays back, marks an opposing forward and prevents that player from being in a scoring position.

right back
Defensive position that covers the right side of the field; this player's role is to impede an opponent's progress toward the goal.

right midfielder
Center position that plays on the right side of the field; this player uses playmaking skills to pass the ball to the forwards.

defensive midfielder
Center position; this player tries to take the ball from the opponent before that player reaches the defenders and quickly mount a counterattack.

referee
Official responsible for applying the rules; this individual keeps time, signals penalties, issues warnings (yellow card) and ejects players (red card).

corner flag
Small post with a flag on top; it marks the intersection of the goal line and the touch line.

center spot
Point in the middle of the halfway line where the ball is placed before a kickoff at the start of a half or after a goal has been scored.

corner arc
Zone where the ball is placed when there is a corner kick, which is awarded when a defender puts the ball behind the goal line.

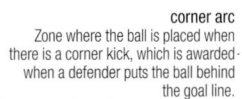

linesman
Official who signals offsides and penalties not seen by the referee or when the ball is out of play.

touch line
Line along the sides of the playing field; when the ball crosses this line, it is put back into play at the same place.

halfway line
Line dividing the field into two zones, one for each team; the teams switch zones at halftime.

center circle
Circle drawn at midfield; during kickoffs, only the players on the team with ball possession are allowed into this circle.

substitutes' bench
Area reserved for coaches, technical staff and substitute players; a team cannot make more than three substitutions per game.

soccer

techniques

Players must master a variety of skills that allow them to retrieve the ball, make passes to team members or shoot for the goal.

free kick

Technique of sending the ball directly toward the opposing team's goal; awarded after a player penalty.

penalty kick

Free kick taken from the penalty spot. Awarded after a defense penalty in the penalty area.

dribbling

A feint of the feet that allows a player to maintain control of the ball and get past an opponent.

heading

Technique that allows a player to retake the ball in midair and redirect it.

tackling

Maneuver in which a player tries to kick the ball away from the opposing team's striker, often by sliding on the grass. The tackle cannot involve contact with the opposing team's player.

lacrosse

Sport in which two ten-player teams use crosses to propel the ball into the opposing team's goal.

lacrosse field

Rectangular surface (110 yd x 60 yd), covered with natural or artificial grass, on which lacrosse is played. A match is divided into four 25-minute quarters.

restraining line

Line that delimits the attack or defensive area.

endline

Line that delimits the boundaries of play at each end of the field. If a ball travels beyond the endline, it gets returned to team of the player who was closest to the ball when it went out of bounds.

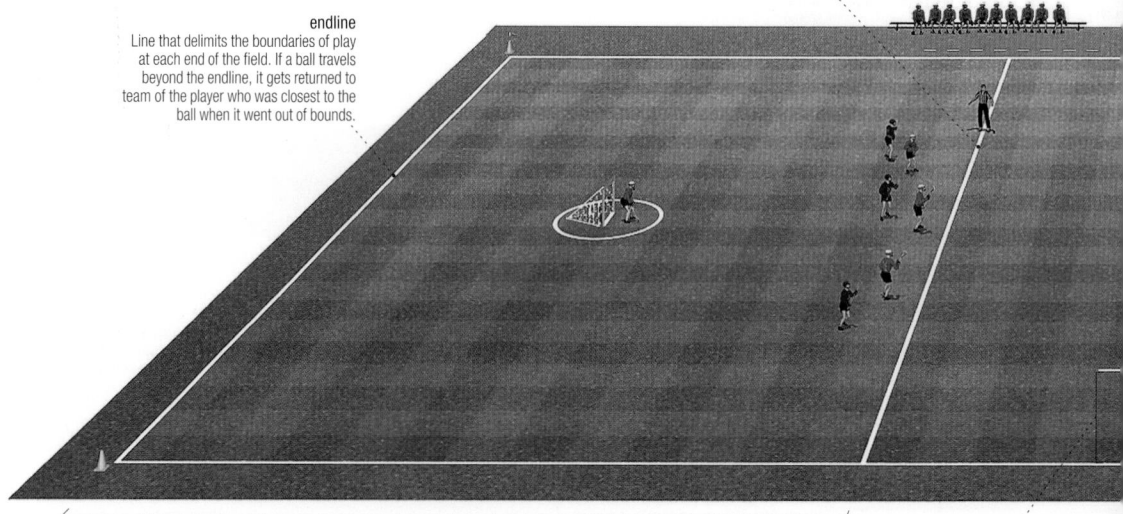

attack/defensive area

Play area between the endline and restraining line, containing your team's goal (your team's defensive area) or the opposing team's goal (your team's attack area).

wing area

Area in which a wing player must operate in a face-off.

echniques
layers must master a variety of kills that allow them to retrieve he ball, make passes to team members or shoot for the goal.

face-off
Each quarter begins after the umpire sounds his whistle and the ball has been placed in front of two opposing players who attempt to capture it with their crosses.

lacrosse ball
Hard white (or orange) rubber ball, with a circumference of approximately 8 in and weighing about 5 oz.

head
Part of the cross made up of the sidewall and pocket.

crosse
Wooden, aluminum or plastic stick with a pocket at the end for catching, carrying and throwing the ball.

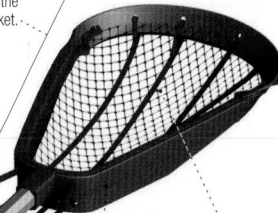

handle
Part that facilitates holding and handling the cross. Offensive players' crosses are shorter than those carried by defensive players.

pocket
Netting made of leather, linen or nylon designed to catch and throw the ball.

sidewall
Rigid frame for the pocket. The goalkeeper's cross has a wider sidewall than other players' sticks.

scooping
Technique in which the player scoops a ball up from the ground using the crosse's pocket.

passing
Technique permitting the player to throw the ball in his crosse's pocket to another team member.

helmet
Hard piece of equipment designed to protect the head.

fficials
eople responsible for seeing hat matches are properly played scorer, timekeeper, players' bench fficials).

goal
Cage formed of netting mounted on a metal frame; a team scores a goal each time it lodges the ball inside the opposing goal.

midfield line
Line dividing the field into two zones, one for each team, at the center of which teams face off at the beginning of each period or after a goal.

umpire
Official responsible for ensuring that regulations are adhered to. The umpire resolves disputed plays and sees that the game unfolds without incident.

sideline
Line that delimits the boundaries of play along the sides of the field.

crease
Circular area surrounding the goal. The goalkeeper is the only player allowed in the crease.

rugby

Sport with two opposing teams of 15 players that attempt to score points by carrying the ball into the in goal or kicking it between the uprights.

player positions
A team is made up of seven backs and eight forwards; organized into three rows, the forwards take part in scrums and line-outs.

right center
Back positioned near the right wing; an excellent passer, this player challenges opposing centers and breaks down the defense.

fullback
Position in front of the goal; this player is the last line of defense for an opponent attempting to score a try.

left center
Back position near the left wing; an excellent passer, this player challenges opposing centers and breaks down the defense.

stand-off half
Position that acts as a link between the scrum half and the backs; an excellent strategist, this player directs the team's offense.

scrum half
Position that acts as a link between the forwards and the backs; this player recovers the ball in a scrum and mounts the team's attack.

right wing
Back positioned on the right of the field; this player uses speed and agility to thwart opponents and score points.

left wing
Back who covers the left side of the field; this player uses speed and agility to thwart opponents and score points.

flank forward
Third-row position to the right of the no. 8 forward; this player uses power and speed to play offensive and defensive roles.

no. 8 forward
Third-row position between the two flank forwards; when play is in progress, this player relays the ball from the forwards to the halfs.

third row
Group made up of the no. 8 forward and the two flank forwards; it is the last line of players in a scrum.

flank forward
Third-row position to the left of the no. 8 forward; this player combines power with speed to play offensive and defensive roles.

second row
Group made up of two forwards; one of its roles is to support the first row in a scrum.

lock forward
Second-row position on the left side of the field; this player's main role is to recover the ball during line-outs, rucks and mauls.

first row
Group made up of the hooker and the two props; the first rows meet in the scrum and try to prevent the opponent from moving the ball forward.

loose head prop
Forward positioned left of the hooker; in a scrum, this player supports the hooker and pushes the opponent to gain field advantage.

tight head prop
Forward position to the right of the hooker; in a scrum, this player supports the hooker and pushes the opponent forward to gain field advantage.

lock forward
Second-row position on the right of the field; one of this player's roles is to recover the ball during line-outs, rucks and mauls.

hooker
Position between the two props; this player attempts to gain possession of the ball in a scrum and to kick it back to teammates.

10 m line
Line parallel to the halfway line and 10 m from it; it marks the minimum distance the ball must travel during the kickoff.

rugby field
Rectangular surface covered with natural or synthetic grass on which a rugby game is played; a game consists of two 40-minute periods.

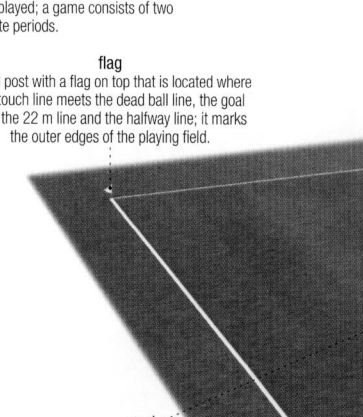

flag
Small post with a flag on top that is located where the touch line meets the dead ball line, the goal line, the 22 m line and the halfway line; it marks the outer edges of the playing field.

goal line
Line marking the start of the in-goal zone.

goal
Frame consisting of two uprights and a crossbar; a team scores points by kicking the ball between the uprights.

dead ball line
Line marking the end of the in-goal zone.

22 m line
Line parallel to the goal line and 22 m from it; it is where the ball is put back into play after a kickoff.

rugby player
An individual who plays rugby; some players are allowed to wear protective equipment such as shin guards and shoulder pads made from flexible material.

jersey
Flexible garment covering the upper body; it features the team emblem and the player's name and number.

rugby ball
Inflatable egg-shaped ball made of leather or synthetic material; meant to be manipulated with the hands or the feet, it is carried, passed laterally and kicked.

shorts
Very short pants covering only the top of the thighs.

sock
Garment worn over the foot and up to the knee.

ruck
Play when the ball is on the ground and the players on both teams pile on top of it to gain possession of it.

cleated shoe
Shoe whose sole contains small spikes to provide good traction.

referee
Official responsible for applying the rules; this individual keeps track of time, signals infractions and can expel a player from a game.

15 m line
Line parallel to the touch line and 15 m from it; a player is not allowed to stand behind this line during a line-out.

in goal
Zone in which a try is scored; worth five points, a try is scored when the player grounds the ball in the opposing in goal.

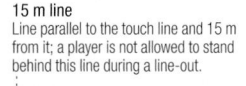

5 m line
Line parallel to the touch line and 5 m from it; it marks the position of the first player in a line-out formation.

touch judge
Official whose role includes signaling when the ball leaves the field of play and when a field goal is scored (the ball passes between the goals posts and over the crossbar).

halfway line
Line separating the field into two sides, one for each team; the kickoff is held on the halfway line.

touch line
Line along the sides of the playing field; when the ball crosses this line, it is thrown back into play by a line-out.

football

Sport with two opposing teams of 11 players who attempt to score points by moving the ball into the end zone or kicking it between the goalposts.

scrimmage: defense
The defense tries to prevent the opponent's movement toward the end zone by stopping runs and passes.

right defensive end
Position to the right of the right defensive tackle; this player pressures the quarterback and tries to stop outside runs.

right cornerback
Position at the far right of the main defensive line; this player is very fast and covers the opposing team's wide receiver.

right outside linebacker
Position near or behind the main defensive line on the right side of the field; agile and versatile, this player is effective against running and passing plays.

right defensive tackle
Position to the right of the middle linebacker; powerful and tough, this player is especially effective at stopping running plays.

free safety
Position behind the main defensive line on the right side of the field; this player is used mostly for the ability to cover passes.

left defensive tackle
Position to the left of the middle linebacker; powerful and tough, this player is especially effective at stopping running plays.

middle linebacker
Position behind the main defensive line; this player combines speed and size especially to stop running plays in the center of the field.

left outside linebacker
Position near or behind the main defensive line on the left side of the field; agile and versatile, this player is effective against passing and running plays.

left defensive end
Position on the outside of the left defensive tackle; this player pressures the quarterback and tries to stop the outside run.

American football field
Rectangular surface (53.3 x 120 yards) covered with natural or synthetic grass on which a football game is played; a game consists of four 15-minute quarters.

neutral zone
Gap the equivalent of one ball length, it separates the offense and defense on the line of scrimmage and cannot be crossed before the snap.

left cornerback
Position at the far left of the main defensive line; this player is very fast and usually covers the opposing team's wide receiver.

strong safety
Position behind the main defensive line on the left side of the field; an excellent tackler, this player is often relied on to stop running plays.

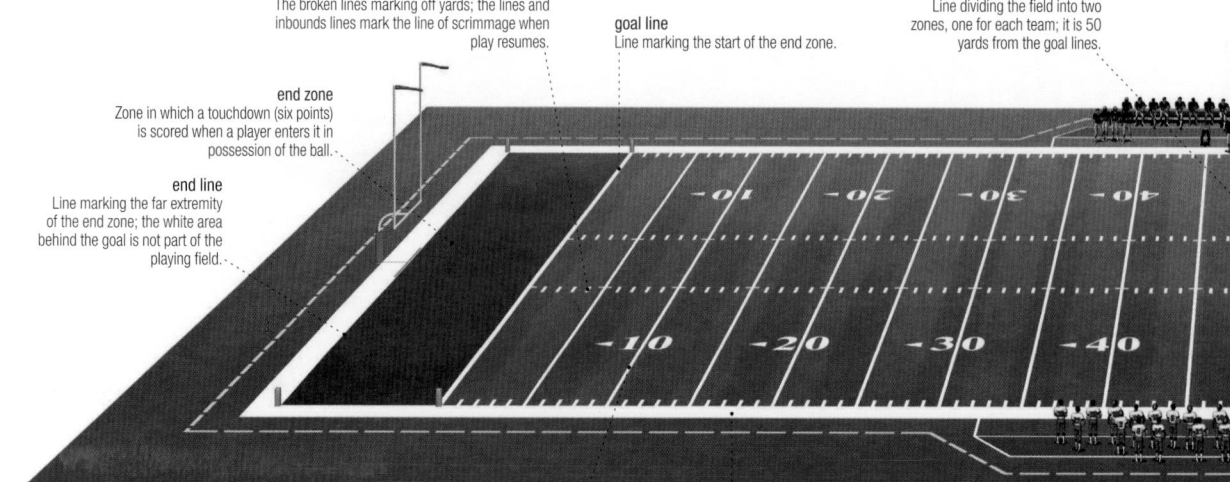

inbounds line
The broken lines marking off yards; the lines and inbounds lines mark the line of scrimmage when play resumes.

goal line
Line marking the start of the end zone.

fifty-yard line
Line dividing the field into two zones, one for each team; it is 50 yards from the goal lines.

end zone
Zone in which a touchdown (six points) is scored when a player enters it in possession of the ball.

end line
Line marking the far extremity of the end zone; the white area behind the goal is not part of the playing field.

yard line
The solid lines at five-yard intervals that mark the distance from the goal line; at the start of a game, the ball is kicked off from the thirty-yard line.

sideline
Line demarcating the sides of the playing field; the play is whistled dead when the ball or a player in possession of the ball crosses it.

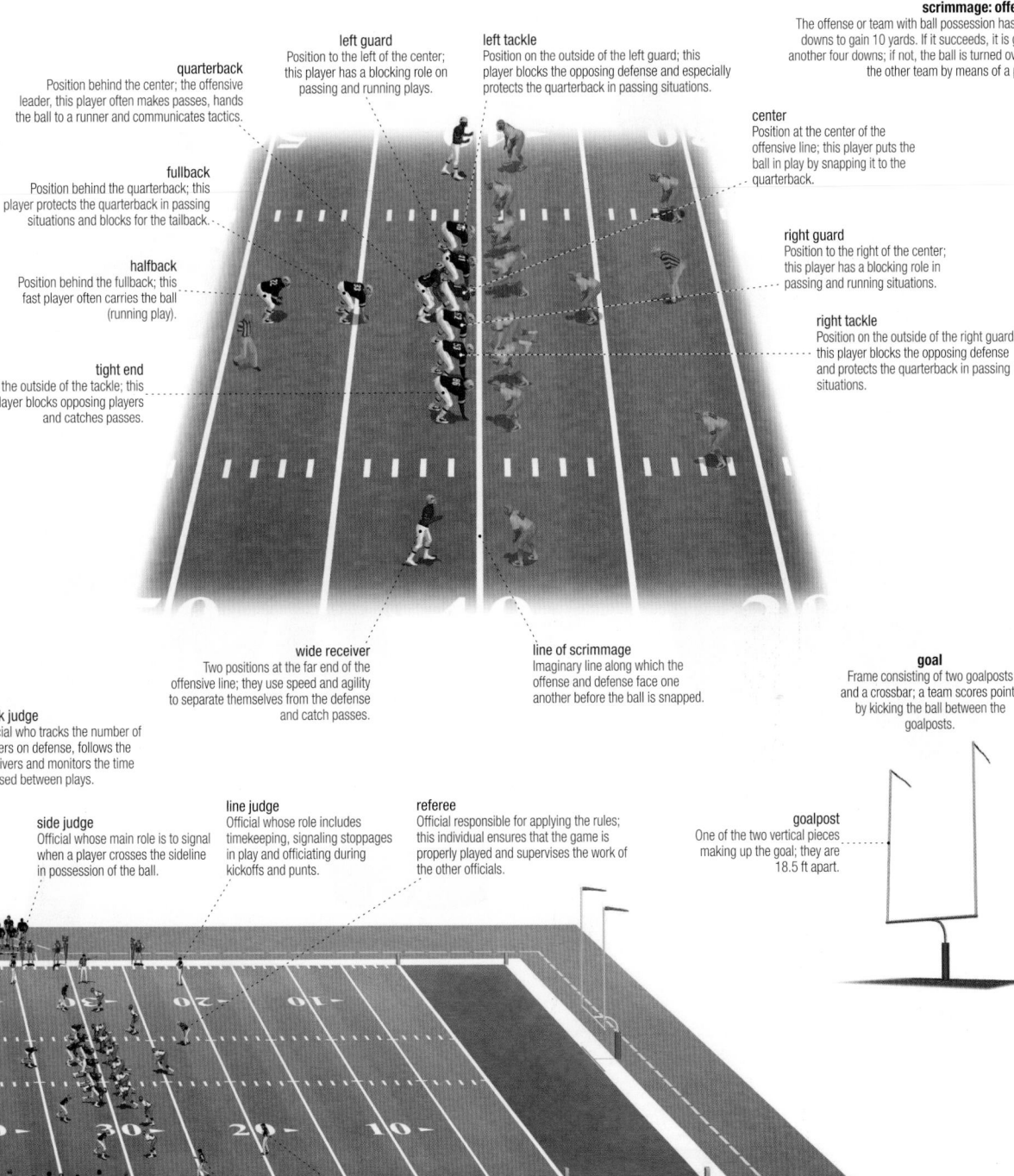

scrimmage: offense
The offense or team with ball possession has four downs to gain 10 yards. If it succeeds, it is given another four downs; if not, the ball is turned over to the other team by means of a punt.

quarterback
Position behind the center; the offensive leader, this player often makes passes, hands the ball to a runner and communicates tactics.

left guard
Position to the left of the center; this player has a blocking role on passing and running plays.

left tackle
Position on the outside of the left guard; this player blocks the opposing defense and especially protects the quarterback in passing situations.

center
Position at the center of the offensive line; this player puts the ball in play by snapping it to the quarterback.

fullback
Position behind the quarterback; this player protects the quarterback in passing situations and blocks for the tailback.

right guard
Position to the right of the center; this player has a blocking role in passing and running situations.

halfback
Position behind the fullback; this fast player often carries the ball (running play).

right tackle
Position on the outside of the right guard; this player blocks the opposing defense and protects the quarterback in passing situations.

tight end
n on the outside of the tackle; this tile player blocks opposing players and catches passes.

wide receiver
Two positions at the far end of the offensive line; they use speed and agility to separate themselves from the defense and catch passes.

line of scrimmage
Imaginary line along which the offense and defense face one another before the ball is snapped.

goal
Frame consisting of two goalposts and a crossbar; a team scores points by kicking the ball between the goalposts.

back judge
Official who tracks the number of players on defense, follows the receivers and monitors the time elapsed between plays.

goalpost
One of the two vertical pieces making up the goal; they are 18.5 ft apart.

side judge
Official whose main role is to signal when a player crosses the sideline in possession of the ball.

line judge
Official whose role includes timekeeping, signaling stoppages in play and officiating during kickoffs and punts.

referee
Official responsible for applying the rules; this individual ensures that the game is properly played and supervises the work of the other officials.

players' bench
Area for substitute players and coaches; a team's players are divided into three units: offense, defense and special teams.

umpire
Official in charge of checking player equipment and signaling infractions near the line of scrimmage.

head linesman
Official who signals stoppages in play and indicates exactly where to position the ball after it leaves the field of play.

football

football player
Football players' protective equipment varies depending on the player's role and position on the field.

helmet
Rigid piece of equipment designed to protect the head; it is lined with absorbent materials such as foam and air pockets.

chin strap
Strap that fastens the helmet to the head.

face mask
Metal cage attached to the helmet; it protects the football player's face.

player's number
Number identifying the player; ranges of numbers are used to designate positions.

jersey
Flexible garment covering the upper body; it features the team emblem and the player's name and number.

wristband
Band of fabric that the quarterback wears around the wrist; it features a small window in which a note card is inserted.

pants
Light stretchy garment covering the lower body from the waist to the knees; it has pockets for holding protective pieces.

arm guard
Padded piece of equipment that protects the player's arms.

thigh pad
Padded piece of equipment that protects the thighs; it usually fits into a pocket inside the pants.

knee pad
Padded piece of equipment designed to protect the knee; it usually fits into a pocket inside the pants.

sock
Garment worn over the foot and up to the knee.

cleats
Footwear whose sole contains small spikes to provide good traction.

protective equipment
Because of the violent contact and frequency of falls, football players wear heavy protective equipment.

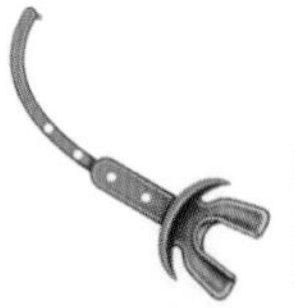

mouth guard
Device that protects the football player's teeth; it fits between the cheeks and the teeth.

neck pad
Padded piece of equipment that protects the player's neck.

shoulder pad
Piece of equipment that consists of rigid molded plastic designed to protect the shoulder.

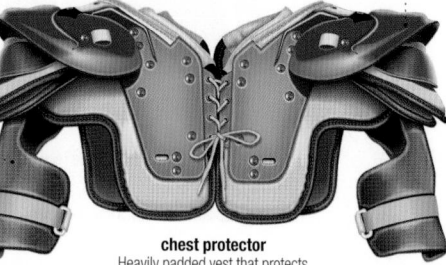

chest protector
Heavily padded vest that protects the football player's chest and back.

rib pad
Rigid jacket designed to protect the rib cage.

elbow pad
Padded piece of equipment designed to protect the elbow.

lumbar pad
Part of the hip pad that covers the coccyx.

football
Inflatable oval leather ball that is smaller than a rugby ball; it has laces that provide a grip on the ball.

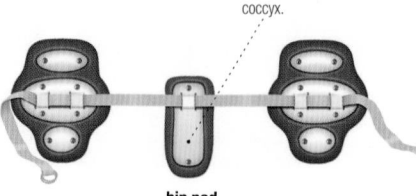

hip pad
Piece of equipment consisting of three rigid molds designed to protect the hips and coccyx.

forearm pad
Padded piece of equipment designed to protect the forearm.

protective cup
Piece of equipment that consists of rigid molded plastic designed to cover a player's genital organs.

Canadian football

Similar to American football, it has two opposing teams of 12 players; the main difference is that there are only three downs to gain 10 yards.

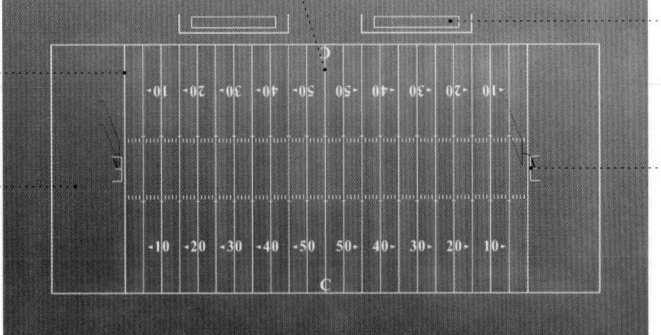

center line
Line dividing the field into two zones, one for each team; it is 55 yards from the goal lines.

Canadian football field
Rectangular surface covered with natural or synthetic grass; it is longer (150 yards) and wider (65 yards) than an American football field.

goal line
Line marking the start of the end zone; the goalposts are located on this line.

players' bench
Area for substitute players and coaches; a team's players are divided into three units: offense, defense and special teams.

end zone
Zone in which a touchdown (six points) is scored when a player enters it in possession of the ball.

goal
Frame consisting of two goalposts and a crossbar; a team scores points by kicking the ball between the goalposts.

netball

Sport played mainly by women with two opposing teams of seven players; teams score points by throwing a ball into the opponent's basket.

goal shooter
Position always in the goal third or goal circle; this player's role is to break away from the goalkeeper, catch passes and shoot on goal.

goalkeeper
osition that defends the team's goal third; this player's role is to prevent the opposing shooter from gaining possession of the ball.

goal circle
rcular zone in front of the goal; ots can only be taken from this nd only by a goal attack or goal shooter.

wing attack
Position that covers the center and goal thirds (except the goal circle); this player uses speed and agility to pass the ball to the shooter or the goal attack.

umpire
One of two officials responsible for applying the rules; this individual's role includes signaling infractions and when the ball leaves the court.

goal
Structure made up of a basket and its supporting goalpost; a team scores each time it puts the ball into the opposing team's basket.

ring
Circular piece on which the netting is mounted; it is 15 in in diameter.

goal defense
Position that moves in the center and defense thirds (including the goal circle); one of this player's roles is to defend against the goal attack.

netball court
Hard rectangular surface (50 ft x 100 ft) on which a netball game is played; a game consists of four 15-minute periods.

goalpost
Vertical post 10 ft high that supports the basket; it is attached to the floor in the middle of the back line.

goal third
Area between the back line and the center third; defenders and the goalkeeper are not allowed to enter their team's goal third.

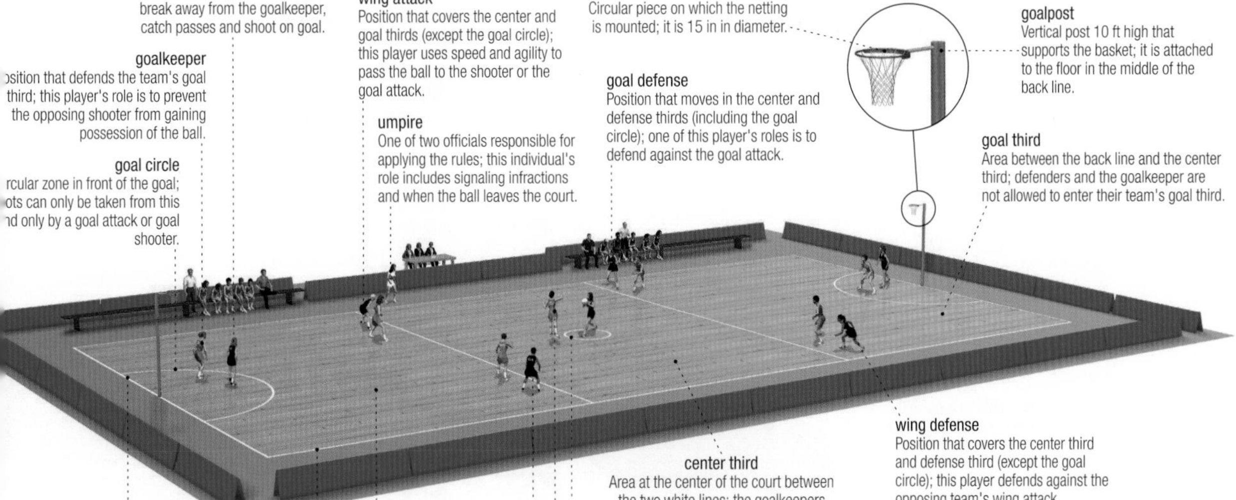

wing defense
Position that covers the center third and defense third (except the goal circle); this player defends against the opposing team's wing attack.

back line
Line marking the ends of the court; when the ball crosses this line, one team puts it back into play at the same place.

sideline
Line along the sides of the playing field; when the ball crosses this line, it is put back into play at the same place.

defense third
Area between the back line and the center third; attacks and the shooter are not allowed to enter their team's defense third.

center third
Area at the center of the court between the two white lines; the goalkeepers and goal shooters are not allowed to enter this area.

central circle
Circular zone in the center of the court; at the start of a game and after a goal, the center on one of the teams puts the ball into play from this point.

center
Position that covers the entire court except the goal circles; this player is the link between the team's offense and defense thirds.

goal attack
Position that covers the center third and goal third (including the goal circle); this player is one of two allowed to shoot on goal.

netball
Inflated ball usually made of leather and with a diameter of 8.5 in; players are not allowed to carry the ball or hold on to it for more than three seconds.

basketball

Sport with two opposing teams of five players who score points by throwing a ball into the opposing team's basket.

basketball player
Member of a basketball team; a player moves the ball forward by dribbling, which is bouncing the ball with one hand.

basketball
Inflated orange ball made up of eight pieces of leather or synthetic material; it has a circumference of 30 in.

player's number
The number identifying a player; they are worn on the front and back of the shirt.

jersey
Flexible garment covering the upper body; it features the team emblem and the player's name and number.

shorts
Short pants covering the top of the thighs.

shoe
Antiskid sneaker that protects the foot and provides ankle support.

basketball court
Hard rectangular surface on which a basketball game is played; games are usually divided into two halves or four quarters.

score
Official who records points and fouls committed by the players.

timekeeper
Official who keeps time; this individual stops the clock when play stops and starts it again when play resumes.

shot clock operator
Official who keeps track of a team's possession time (maximum 30 seconds before a shot is made).

referee
Official responsible for applying the rules and calling fouls.

referee
Official responsible for applying the rules; this individual throws jump balls and calls fouls.

sideline
Line along the sides of the court; when the ball crosses this line, it is put back into play at the same place.

semicircle
Semicircular zone where the player takes position to make a free throw, which is worth one point.

restraining circle
Circle around the center circle; players not taking part in the jump ball must be outside this circle.

midcourt line
Line dividing the court into two halves, one for each team; the team with ball possession has 10 seconds to carry it into the opposing team's zone.

center cir
Circle at center court used fo jump ball at the start of the game jump ball is when the ball is tos into the air by the referee and opponents jump up and attemp tap the ball toward a teamma

shooting guard
Position that assists the point guard; an excellent shooter, this player usually takes shots from areas far away from the basket.

point guard
Position that directs the attack; this player is highly skilled at controlling and passing the ball.

player positions
Five players per team are on the court; they all play both offense and defense.

center
Position that defends the basket from close in and collects rebounds; this player is often the tallest on the team.

power forward
Position that performs the same tasks as the center, generally played in front of the basket; this player is very active and mobile.

small forward
Position that covers the side of the court; this player has offensive (shooting, passing) and defensive abilities.

backboard
Rigid board attached to the back of the basket; it is usually made of transparent material so that spectators behind the basket can follow the action.

backstop
Structure made up of a basket and its support; a team scores each time it puts the ball into the opposing team's basket.

rim
Circular orange piece on which the net is mounted; it is 18 in in diameter and 10 ft above floor level.

coach
The team's leader; the coach plots strategy and decides who plays in different situations.

net
Flexible netting attached to the rim; it slows the ball when it passes through the basket.

basket
Structure made up of a net mounted on a rim; a basket is worth one, two or three points, depending on where the shot was taken from.

assistant coach
Person who assists the coach and can replace the coach if needed.

trainer
Individual who treats injured players.

backboard support
Oblique piece that supports the backboard and the basket.

padded upright
Vertical piece covered with protective padding; it holds the backboard support.

padded base
Base covered with protective padding; it supports and stabilizes the backstop.

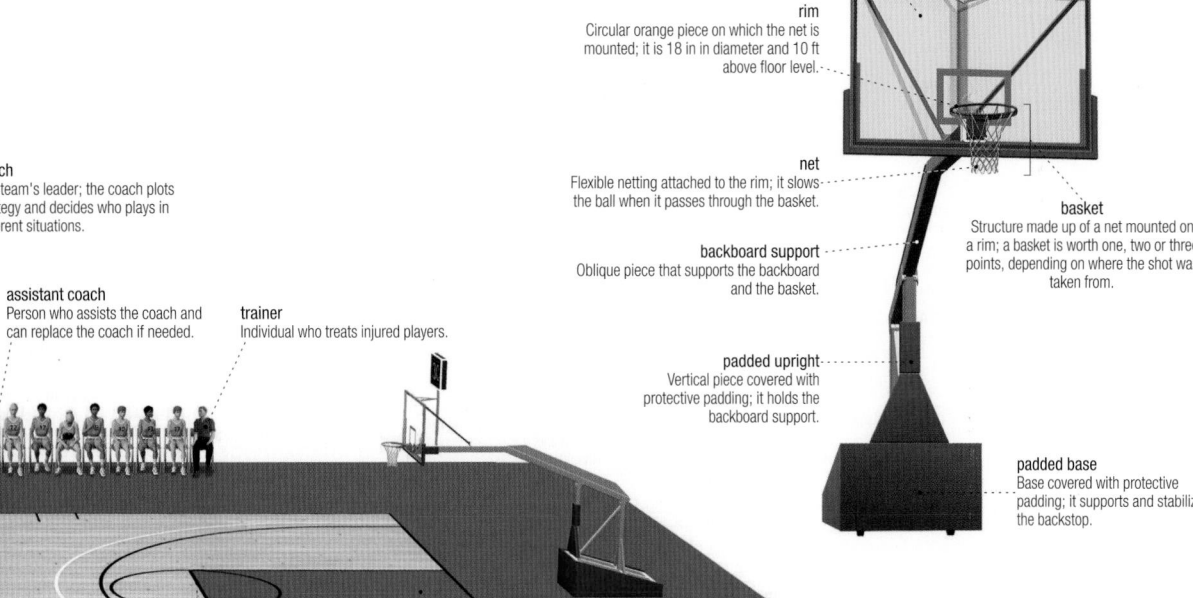

end line
Line marking the ends of the court; when the ball crosses this line, one team puts it back into play at the same place.

three-point line
...urved line located at a distance of ...ft to 23.75 ft from the front of the ...ket. A basket shot from beyond this line is worth three points.

free throw line
Line parallel to the end line; the shooter stands behind it for a free throw (shot awarded after a foul).

free throw lane
An area between the end line and the free throw line; an offensive player is not allowed to stay in it for more than three seconds.

volleyball

Sport with two opposing teams of six players who try to ground the ball in the opposing zone by hitting it over the net with their hands.

volleyball court
Hard rectangular surface (30 ft x 60 ft) on which a volleyball game is played; the first team to win three sets wins the game.

umpire
Official who signals net faults or faults committed on the attack line and advises the referee when required.

left attacker
Position to the left of the attack zone; this player's main role is making attack hits to score points.

end line
Line demarcating the ends of the court; the right back takes position behind this line to deliver a serve.

libero
Position specialized in receiving serve this player only plays back while othe teammates change positions during course of a game.

left back
Position on the left side of the back zone; this player's main role is making digs on short balls.

white tape
Strip of tape with a cable passing through it; it is attached to posts to suspend the net.

free zone
Area at least 6.5 ft wide surrounding the court.

scorer
Official who fills in the score sheet, calls stoppages in play and supervises player rotations.

antenna
Flexible rods at each end of the net; they mark off the net area and the ball must stay inside them to remain in play.

linesman
One of four officials who use a to signal a dead ball, service contact with the antennas,

players' bench
Area for substitute players and coaches; a team can have 12 players, six of whom are on the court during play.

back zone
Area between the attack line and the end line; it is usually occupied by the backs.

sideline
Line that demarcates the sides of the play area; a rally ends when the ball falls outside the sideline.

post
Upright used to stretch the net using white tape; the top of the net is just over 2 m above floor level.

referee
Official responsible for applying the rules; this individual follows the ga from a raised platform set up at or end of the net.

center back
Position in the back zone; this player's main role is to recover long balls and blocked balls.

vertical side band
Vertical strip of white canvas at the ends of the net.

attack line
Line 10 ft from the net; the backs must make attack hits from behind this line.

net
Open-meshed divider stretched across the middle of the court; players must hit the ball over it.

right back
Position on the right side of the back zone; this player's main role is making digs on short balls.

right attacker
Position to the right of the attack zone; this player's main role is making attack hits to score points.

center attacker
Position that covers the center of the attack zone; this player's main role is to counter the opponent's attacks.

attack zone
Area between the net and the attack line; it is usually occupied by the attackers.

volleyball
Inflated ball covered with soft leathe and with a circumference of about 26 in; it must always be hit and cann be held or thrown.

techniques
Players must master various techniques to dig up the ball, pass it and make attack hits.

dig
Technique used to play a long ball; the player lunges forward to hit the ball with one or two hands.

bump
Technique of extending the arms, joining the hands and striking the ball with the forearms; it is usually used to receive serves.

serve
Technique for putting the ball in play; a player usually serves the ball with one hand held above the head.

volleyball

beach volleyball court
Rectangular surface covered with sand on which a
volleyball game is played; the first team to win two sets
wins the match.

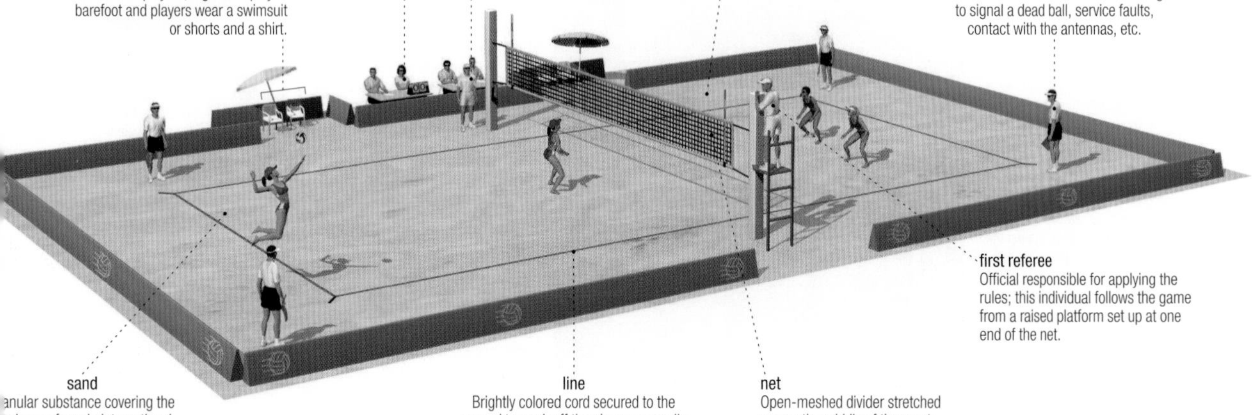

scorer
Official who holds the scorecard
and signals stoppages in play.

second referee
Official who signals net faults or faults
committed on the attack line and advises
the first referee when required.

free zone
Area at least 10 ft wide
surrounding the court.

line judge
One of four officials who use a red flag
to signal a dead ball, service faults,
contact with the antennas, etc.

players' chairs
Rest area for players; a game is played
barefoot and players wear a swimsuit
or shorts and a shirt.

first referee
Official responsible for applying the
rules; this individual follows the game
from a raised platform set up at one
end of the net.

sand
anular substance covering the
aying surface; in international
mpetitions, it must be at least
16 in deep.

line
Brightly colored cord secured to the
ground to mark off the play area; a rally
ends when the ball falls outside the lines
of play.

net
Open-meshed divider stretched
across the middle of the court;
players must hit the ball over it.

beach volleyball
Ball with the same dimensions as a volleyball;
it is heavier and contains less air mainly to
counter the wind.

techniques

set
Pass executed with the fingertips, using
a pushing motion with the arms; the set
marks the transition between receiving
and attacking.

spike
Offensive play that consists of
striking the ball with the palm from
above the level of the net.

block
Defensive play in which one or more front
court players extend their arms and try
to intercept the ball at the point where it
crosses the net.

SPORTS AND GAMES

team handball

Sport with two opposing teams of seven players who try to score points by throwing the ball into the opposing team's net.

player positions

Each team is allowed seven players on the court; players are not allowed to take more than three steps with the ball or to hold it for more than three seconds.

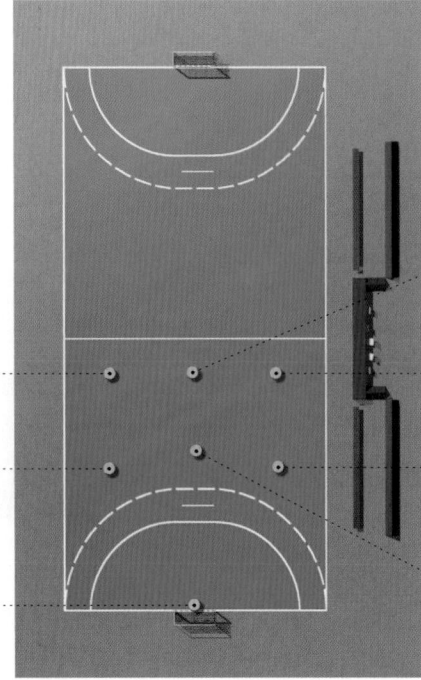

center forward
Position in the center court area between the wingers; this player tries to slip through the defense and create holes in it.

handball
Inflated ball usually covered with leather; it has a circumference of 21 in (women) to 24 in (men) and can be thrown, hit with the fist or dribbled.

left winger
Position that covers the left side of the court; using speed and agility, this player is often at the sideline stretching the defense and creating scoring chances.

right winger
Position that covers the right side of the court; using speed and agility, this player is often at the sideline stretching the defense and creating scoring chances.

left back
Position behind the wingers on the left side of the court; an excellent shooter, this player also defends against the opponent's line player or back.

right back
Position behind the wingers on the right side of the field; an excellent shooter, this player also defends against an opposing line player or back.

center back
Position in the center court area between the backs; this player is the team's offensive leader.

goalkeeper
Position whose role is to prevent the ball from entering the net; this player is the only one allowed to touch the ball with the feet.

handball court

Hard rectangular surface (20 m x 40 m) on which a handball game is played; a game is made up of two 30-minute periods with a 10-minute break between them.

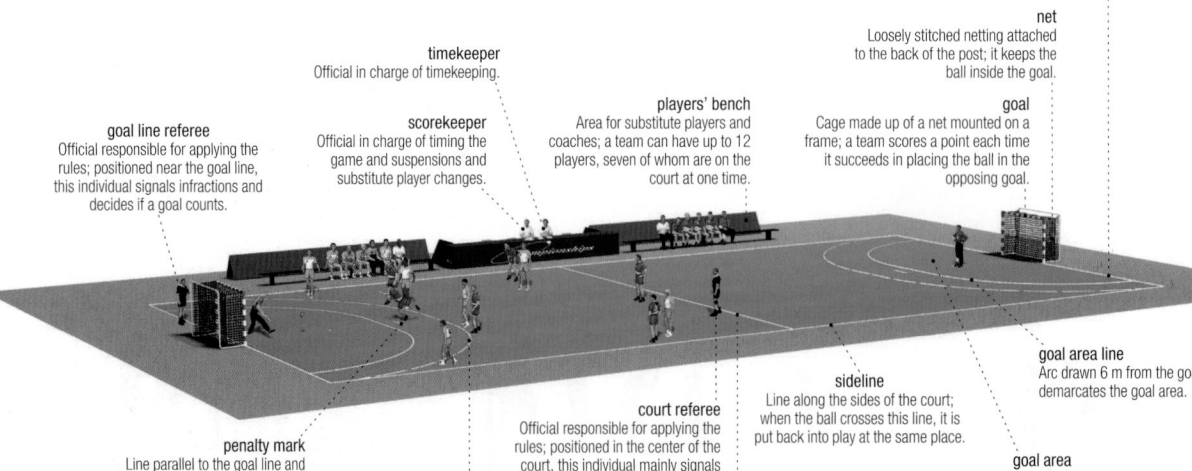

goal line
Line at the ends of the court that demarcates the play area; a goal is scored when the ball crosses this line.

net
Loosely stitched netting attached to the back of the post; it keeps the ball inside the goal.

timekeeper
Official in charge of timekeeping.

players' bench
Area for substitute players and coaches; a team can have up to 12 players, seven of whom are on the court at one time.

goal
Cage made up of a net mounted on a frame; a team scores a point each time it succeeds in placing the ball in the opposing goal.

goal line referee
Official responsible for applying the rules; positioned near the goal line, this individual signals infractions and decides if a goal counts.

scorekeeper
Official in charge of timing the game and suspensions and substitute player changes.

goal area line
Arc drawn 6 m from the goal; it demarcates the goal area.

sideline
Line along the sides of the court; when the ball crosses this line, it is put back into play at the same place.

court referee
Official responsible for applying the rules; positioned in the center of the court, this individual mainly signals player infractions.

goal area
Semicircular zone reserved for the goalkeeper; a player with ball possession may jump above this area when taking a shot.

penalty mark
Line parallel to the goal line and 7 m from it; a 7 m free throw (a shot awarded after a penalty) is taken from behind this line.

free throw line
Arc drawn 9 m from the goal; during a 7 m free throw, all players except the shooter must be outside the zone demarcated by this line.

center line
Line dividing the court into two zones, one for each team; throw-offs are held on this line at the start of a period and after a goal.

table tennis

Sport with two or four opposing players with paddles; they hit a ball onto opposite sides of a net dividing a table in half.

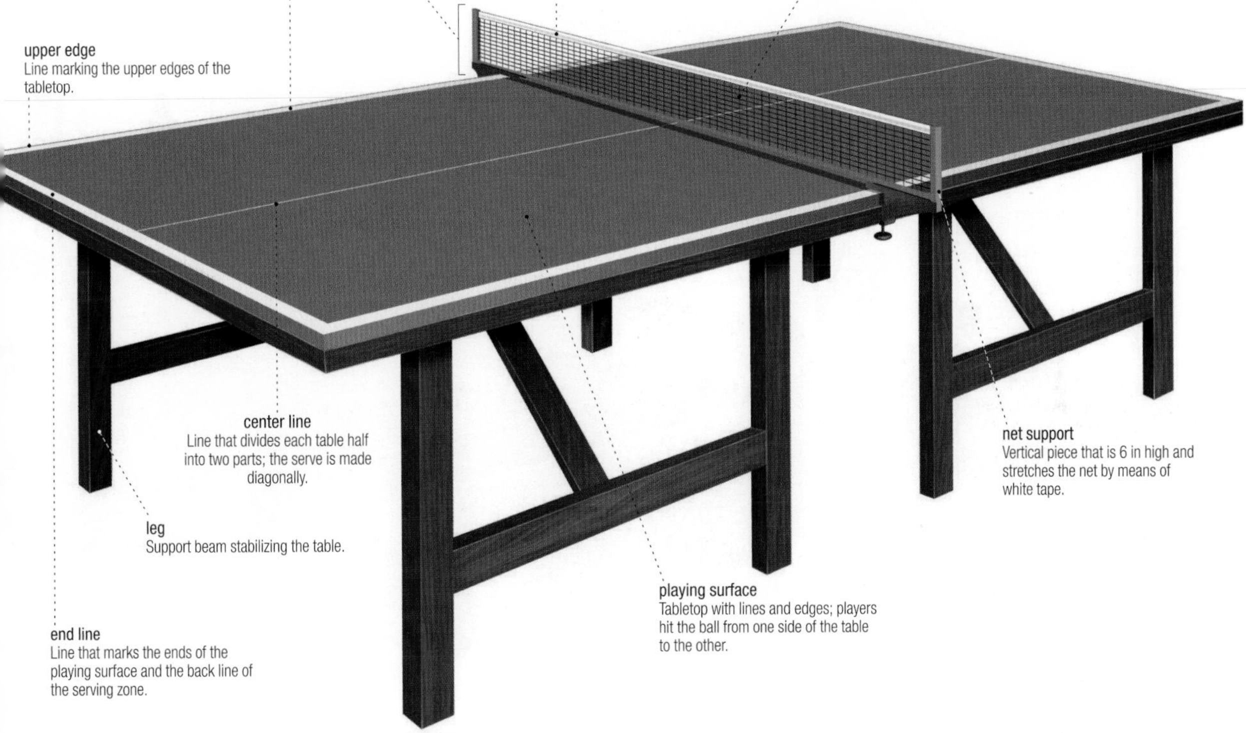

sideline
Line marking the sides of the playing surface.

net
Open-meshed divider across the middle of the table; players must hit the ball over it.

white tape
Strip of material with a cord passing through it; the cord is attached to the net supports to suspend the net.

mesh
The tiny squares make up the net; they are formed of interlaced threads.

tennis table
Rectangular wooden table (9 ft x 5 ft) that is 2.5 ft above the ground; it is divided in half by a net.

upper edge
Line marking the upper edges of the tabletop.

center line
Line that divides each table half into two parts; the serve is made diagonally.

leg
Support beam stabilizing the table.

end line
Line that marks the ends of the playing surface and the back line of the serving zone.

net support
Vertical piece that is 6 in high and stretches the net by means of white tape.

playing surface
Tabletop with lines and edges; players hit the ball from one side of the table to the other.

table tennis paddle
Paddle used to strike the ball; paddles come in a variety of shapes, sizes and weights.

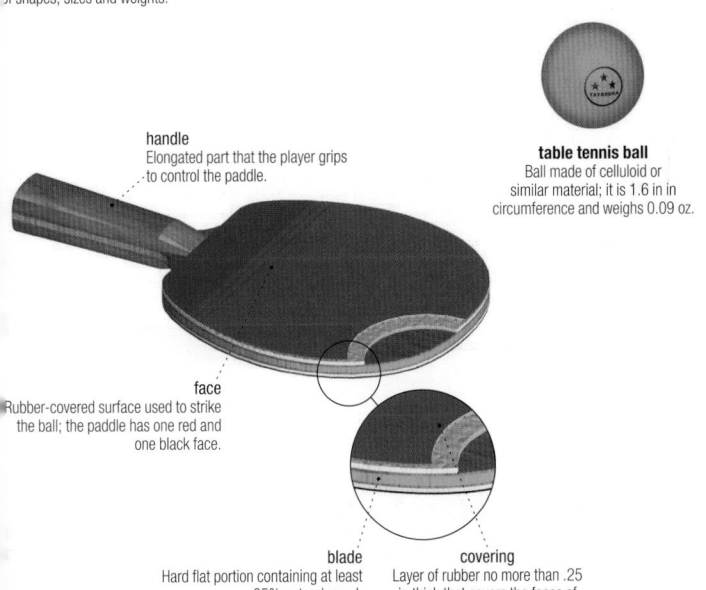

handle
Elongated part that the player grips to control the paddle.

table tennis ball
Ball made of celluloid or similar material; it is 1.6 in in circumference and weighs 0.09 oz.

face
Rubber-covered surface used to strike the ball; the paddle has one red and one black face.

blade
Hard flat portion containing at least 85% natural wood.

covering
Layer of rubber no more than .25 in thick that covers the faces of the blade.

types of grip
There are two principal paddle grips.

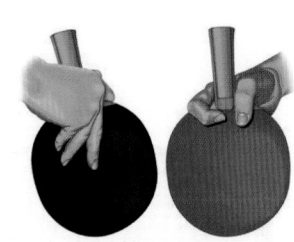

penholder grip
Grip that is suited to offensive play although it weakens the backhand: the table tennis player uses only one paddle face.

shake-hands grip
The most common grip; both paddle faces can be used and the player can hit forehand and backhand.

badminton

Sport with two or four opposing players that is similar to tennis; players use rackets to hit a shuttlecock onto opposite sides of a net that divides a court in half.

badminton court
Synthetic or hardwood surface that is designed to provide good traction; badminton is usually played indoors.

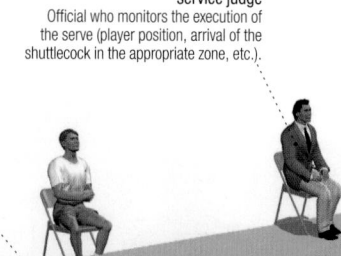

service judge
Official who monitors the execution of the serve (player position, arrival of the shuttlecock in the appropriate zone, etc.).

center line
Line dividing each court half into two sides; the center line separates the left and right service zones.

linesman
One of 10 officials who ensure that the shuttlecock remains inside the lines of play and inform the umpire when a fault is committed.

back boundary line
Line that marks the ends of the playing area and, in singles play, the service zone.

long service line
Line that marks the back of the service zone for doubles matches.

server
Player who puts the shuttlecock into play; the server and receiver stand diagonally opposite each other.

badminton racket
The racket used to strike the shuttlecock is lighter (about 3 oz) and narrower than a tennis racket; its head is about 9 in long and 11 in wide.

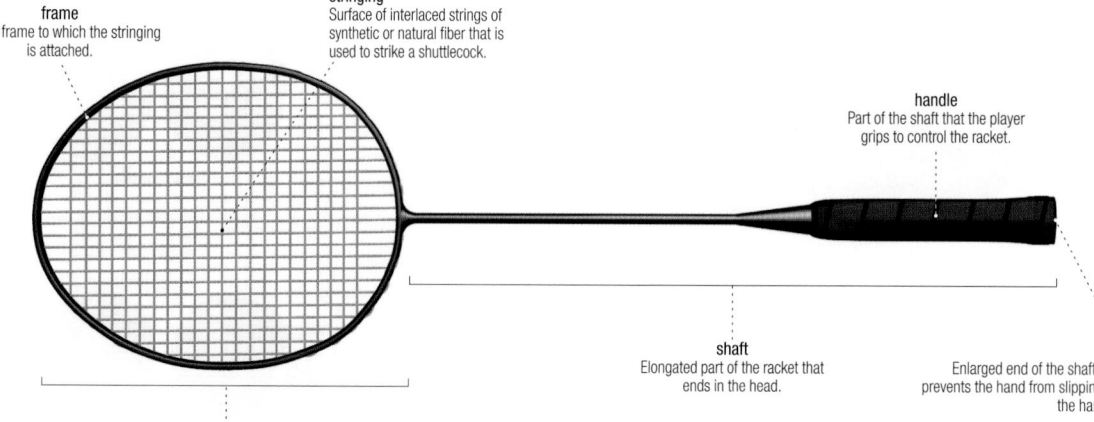

frame
Racket frame to which the stringing is attached.

stringing
Surface of interlaced strings of synthetic or natural fiber that is used to strike a shuttlecock.

handle
Part of the shaft that the player grips to control the racket.

shaft
Elongated part of the racket that ends in the head.

butt
Enlarged end of the shaft that prevents the hand from slipping off the handle.

head
Oval part of the racket, including the frame and the stringing.

white tape
Strip of tape with a cord passing through it; it is attached to posts to suspend the net.

receiver
Player who receives the shuttlecock put into play by the server.

net
Open-meshed divider stretched across the middle of the court at a height of 5 ft; players must hit the shuttlecock over it.

post
Vertical bar used to stretch the net by means of white tape.

umpire
Official responsible for applying the rules; the umpire ensures that the match runs smoothly and rules on contentious points.

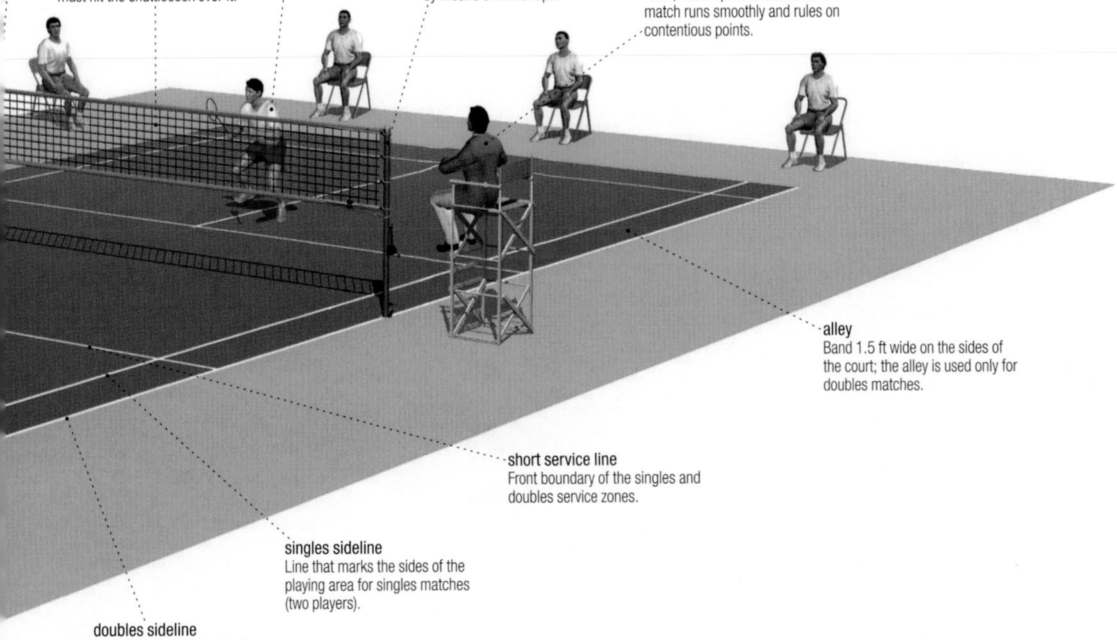

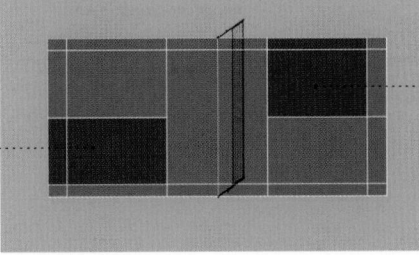

alley
Band 1.5 ft wide on the sides of the court; the alley is used only for doubles matches.

short service line
Front boundary of the singles and doubles service zones.

singles sideline
Line that marks the sides of the playing area for singles matches (two players).

doubles sideline
Line that marks the sides of the playing area for doubles matches (two teams of two players).

service zones
Zones where the server and receiver must remain for a serve; once the serve is delivered, players can move all over the court.

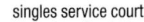

singles service court
Service zone used by a player for singles matches; the singles playing area measures 44 ft x 17 ft.

doubles service court
Service zone used by a player for doubles matches; the doubles playing area measures 44 ft x 20 ft.

synthetic shuttlecock
Small plastic cone that is sturdier than the feathered shuttlecock and is usually used for training; it weighs about 0.2 oz, the same as the feathered shuttlecock.

feathered shuttlecock
Small piece of cork with 14 to 16 feathers; it is used in competitions.

feather crown
Feathers or synthetic materials attached to the shuttlecock tip to stabilize it and make it aerodynamic.

cork tip
The rounded base of the shuttlecock; it can also be made of synthetic materials.

racquetball

Indoor sport with two or four opposing players with rackets; the players rally a bouncing ball using all surfaces of the court.

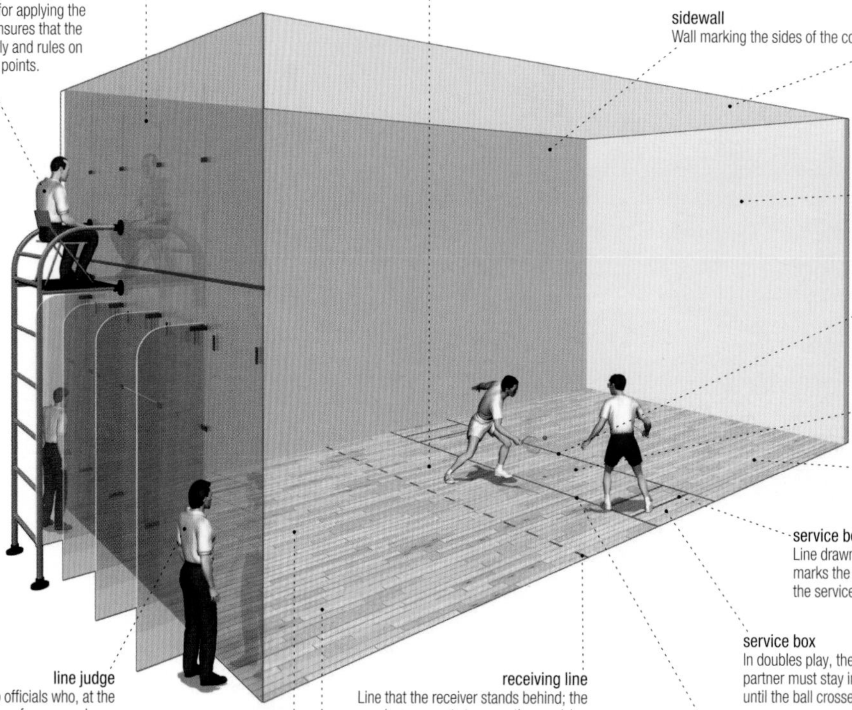

racquetball court
Enclosed space whose surfaces make up the playing area; it is 40 ft long, 20 ft wide and 20 ft high.

center court
Part of the court behind the short line and between the sidewalls; it is a strategic zone that players attempt to control.

back wall
Wall marking the back of the court behind the players.

referee
Official responsible for applying the rules; the referee ensures that the match runs smoothly and rules on contentious points.

sidewall
Wall marking the sides of the court.

ceiling
Horizontal surface making up the upper part of the court; the ceiling is part of the playing area.

front wall
Wall facing the players; the service is made onto it.

service line
Line marking the front of the service zone.

service zone
Zone where a player stands to serve; the ball must bounce once in this zone before it is served.

frontcourt
Area between the front wall and the short line.

service box line
Line drawn 18 in from the sidewall that marks the service box at both ends of the service zone.

service box
In doubles play, the server's partner must stay inside this area until the ball crosses the short line.

short line
Line dividing the court in half; the serve must cross the short line after bouncing off the front wall.

line judge
The two officials who, at the request of the referee or a player, confirm or reverse the referee's decision.

receiving line
Line that the receiver stands behind; the receiver may not step over the receiving line until the serve crosses it.

backcourt
Zone between the short line and the back wall.

floor
Horizontal surface that is usually made of wooden slats; the ball may only bounce once on it.

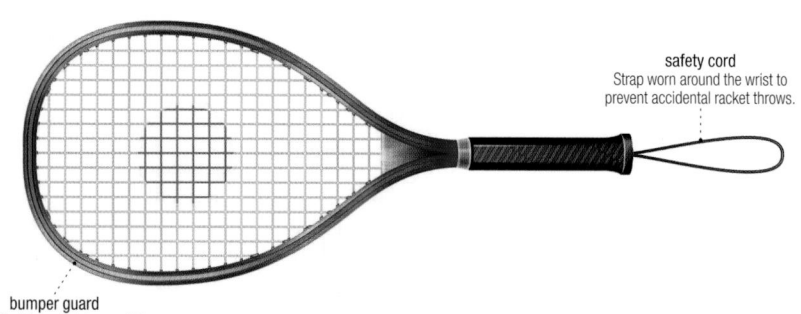

racquetball racket
Racket that is used to strike the ball; it has a short shaft, an elongated head and its maximum length is 22 in.

safety cord
Strap worn around the wrist to prevent accidental racket throws.

racquetball
Rubber ball that is filled with compressed air and weighs 1.4 oz; official balls bear the initials I.R.F. (International Racquetball Federation).

bumper guard
Strip of flexible material around the racket frame to protect it.

protective goggles
Mandatory glasses designed to prevent eye injuries.

squash

Sport similar to racquetball; its court size and equipment are different and the ceiling is excluded from the playing area.

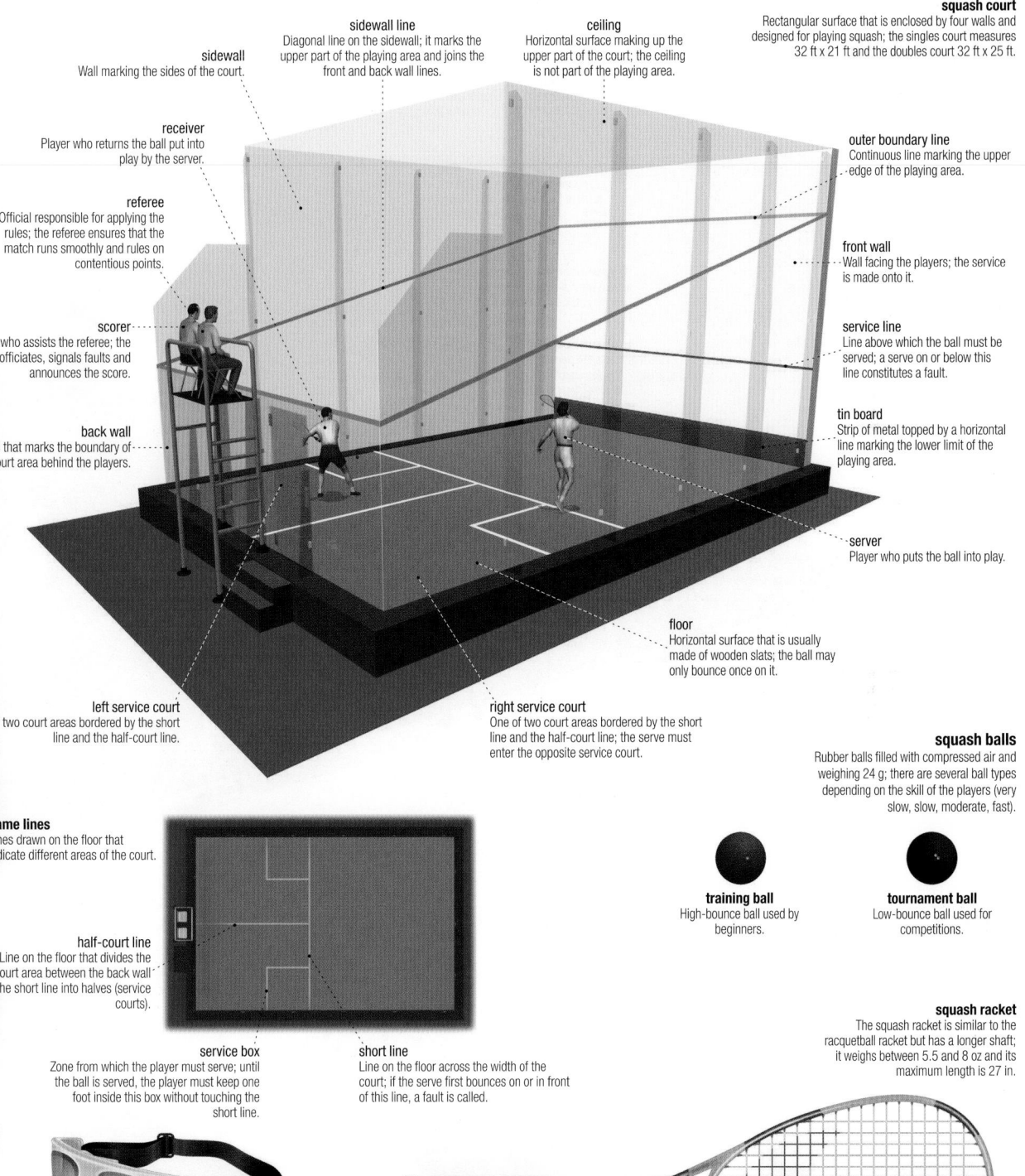

sidewall line
Diagonal line on the sidewall; it marks the upper part of the playing area and joins the front and back wall lines.

ceiling
Horizontal surface making up the upper part of the court; the ceiling is not part of the playing area.

squash court
Rectangular surface that is enclosed by four walls and designed for playing squash; the singles court measures 32 ft x 21 ft and the doubles court 32 ft x 25 ft.

sidewall
Wall marking the sides of the court.

receiver
Player who returns the ball put into play by the server.

referee
Official responsible for applying the rules; the referee ensures that the match runs smoothly and rules on contentious points.

scorer
who assists the referee; the officiates, signals faults and announces the score.

back wall
that marks the boundary of ourt area behind the players.

outer boundary line
Continuous line marking the upper edge of the playing area.

front wall
Wall facing the players; the service is made onto it.

service line
Line above which the ball must be served; a serve on or below this line constitutes a fault.

tin board
Strip of metal topped by a horizontal line marking the lower limit of the playing area.

server
Player who puts the ball into play.

floor
Horizontal surface that is usually made of wooden slats; the ball may only bounce once on it.

left service court
f two court areas bordered by the short line and the half-court line.

right service court
One of two court areas bordered by the short line and the half-court line; the serve must enter the opposite service court.

squash balls
Rubber balls filled with compressed air and weighing 24 g; there are several ball types depending on the skill of the players (very slow, slow, moderate, fast).

training ball
High-bounce ball used by beginners.

tournament ball
Low-bounce ball used for competitions.

ame lines
nes drawn on the floor that dicate different areas of the court.

half-court line
Line on the floor that divides the court area between the back wall the short line into halves (service courts).

service box
Zone from which the player must serve; until the ball is served, the player must keep one foot inside this box without touching the short line.

short line
Line on the floor across the width of the court; if the serve first bounces on or in front of this line, a fault is called.

squash racket
The squash racket is similar to the racquetball racket but has a longer shaft; it weighs between 5.5 and 8 oz and its maximum length is 27 in.

protective goggles
Glasses designed to prevent eye injuries; the risk of injury in squash is low but real, and goggles are recommended.

tennis

Sport with two or four opposing players with rackets who hit a ball onto opposite sides of a net dividing a court in half.

tennis court
Rectangular surface (78 ft x 27 ft for singles, 78 ft x 36 ft for doubles) designed for playing tennis; it is divided in half by a net.

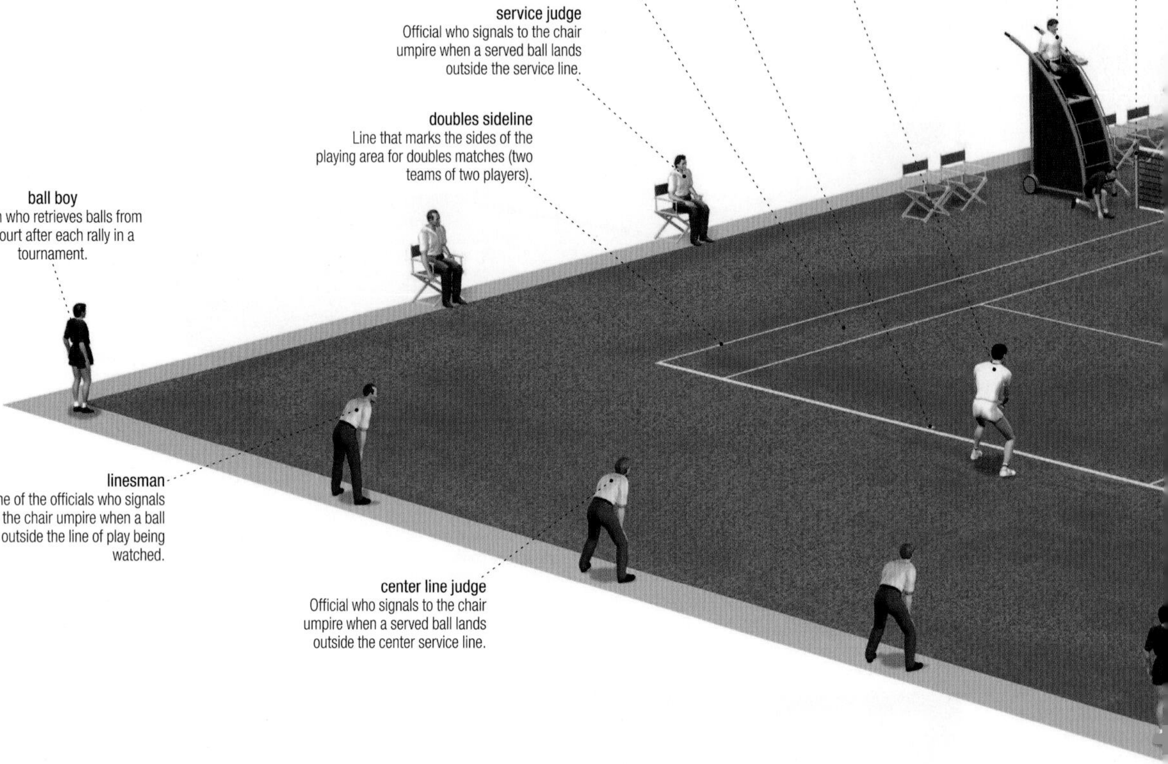

center mark
Broken line marking the middle of the baseline; players use the center mark to take position for serving or receiving.

receiver
Player who returns the ball put into play by the server.

net post
Vertical pole that stretches the net band; it keeps the net at a regulation height (3.5 ft) at the posts.

alley
Band that is 4.5 ft wide on the sides of the court; the alley is used only for doubles matches.

chair umpire
Official responsible for applying the rules; the umpire ensures that the match runs smoothly and rules on contentious points.

service judge
Official who signals to the chair umpire when a served ball lands outside the service line.

doubles sideline
Line that marks the sides of the playing area for doubles matches (two teams of two players).

ball boy
Person who retrieves balls from the court after each rally in a tournament.

linesman
One of the officials who signals to the chair umpire when a ball lands outside the line of play being watched.

center line judge
Official who signals to the chair umpire when a served ball lands outside the center service line.

strokes

With the exception of the serve, all tennis strokes are backhands or forehands; for a right-handed player, strokes on the right are forehands and strokes on the left are backhands.

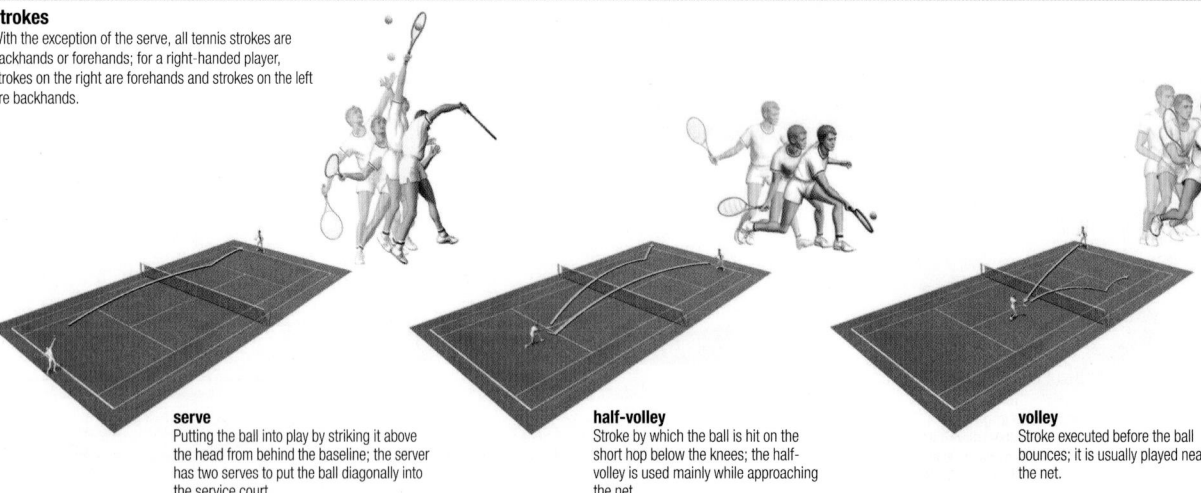

serve
Putting the ball into play by striking it above the head from behind the baseline; the server has two serves to put the ball diagonally into the service court.

half-volley
Stroke by which the ball is hit on the short hop below the knees; the half-volley is used mainly while approaching the net.

volley
Stroke executed before the ball bounces; it is usually played near the net.

tennis

foot fault judge
Official responsible for signaling foot faults, which occur when the server steps on the line in the process of serving (the server can step on the line anytime after that).

right service court
Zone in which the serve must bounce; it is diagonally opposite the server.

center strap
Strip of fabric connected to the ground in the center of the net; it keeps the net at regulation height (3 ft) at its center.

net band
Strip of fabric with a cable passing through it; it is attached to poles to suspend the net.

server
Player who puts the ball into play; the server and receiver must stand in diagonally opposite zones.

left service court
Zone in which the serve must bounce; it is diagonally opposite the server.

service line
Line on each side of the net and parallel to it at a distance of 21 ft; it marks the back boundary of the service courts.

baseline
Line marking the end of the court; the server stands behind the baseline.

singles sideline
Line that marks the side of the playing area for singles matches (two players).

net judge
Official who signals to the chair umpire when a served ball touches the top of the net; the net judge also regulates net height before and during a match.

forecourt
Zone between the net and the service line.

net
Open-meshed divider stretched across the middle of the court; players must hit the ball over it.

center service line
Line dividing each forecourt in half.

backcourt
Zone between the service line and the baseline.

strokes

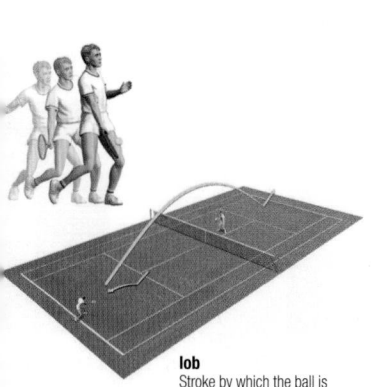

lob
Stroke by which the ball is sent high into the air over the opponent's head when this player is in the forecourt.

drop shot
Short shot by which the ball falls just behind the net with almost no bounce.

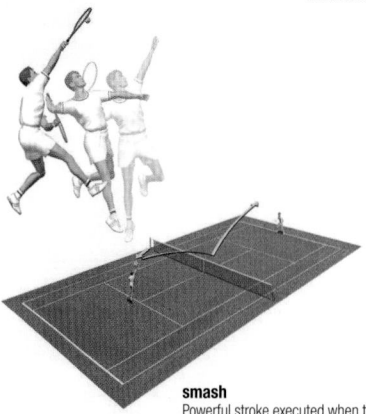

smash
Powerful stroke executed when the ball is over the head; usually played after a lob, the smash is meant to bounce out of the opponent's reach.

SPORTS AND GAMES

tennis

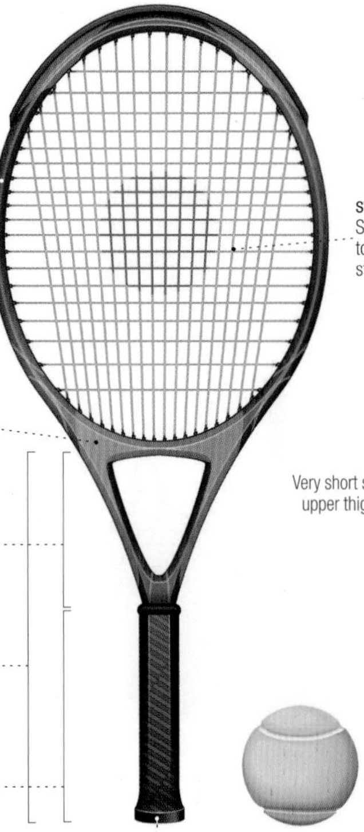

tennis racket
Racket with an oval head that is used to strike the ball; its maximum length is 29 in.

frame
Racket frame to which the stringing is attached.

head
Oval part of the racket, including the frame and the stringing.

shoulder
Base of the racket head joining it to the throat.

throat
Part joining the handle to the racket head.

shaft
Elongated part of the racket that ends in the head.

handle
Part that the player grips to control the racket.

butt
Enlarged end of the shaft that prevents the hand from slipping off the handle.

polo shirt
Usually short-sleeved sweater that has a pointed turned-down collar; it is often fastened with a placket ending at mid-chest.

stringing
Synthetic or natural cords strung together to form a surface used to strike the ball.

tennis playe
Female competitors play i tournament matches of three sets male competitors play in tournamen matches of three or five sets

skirt
Very short skirt covering only the upper thighs; women wear it to play tennis.

wristband
Strip of fabric worn around the wrist; it absorbs sweat from the forehead and face.

tennis ball
Rubber ball that weighs about 2 oz and is filled with compressed air; it is covered with felt to make it more adherent.

sock
Article of clothing that covers the foot and ankle.

tennis shoe
A lightweight usually low-cut sneaker.

scoreboard
Board that posts details on the match in progress; a match is divided into sets, games and points.

previous sets

set
Series of games; a tennis match consists of three or five sets (two or three winning sets).

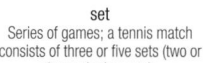

players

points
Points that make up a game: 15 (1st po 30 (2nd point), 40 (3rd point), game (4th point); the player who wins four points (c consecutive points in the event of a tie s 40-40, called deuce) wins the game.

game
Series of four points; the player who wins six games takes the set if this player holds a two-game lead.

playing surfaces
Tennis is played on various indoor and outdoor surfaces; playing strategies are adapted to the court surface.

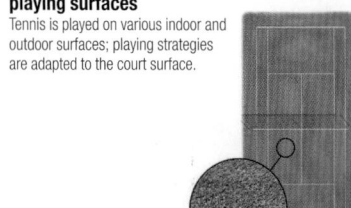

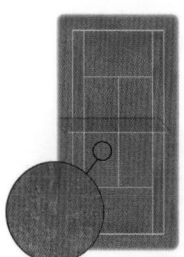

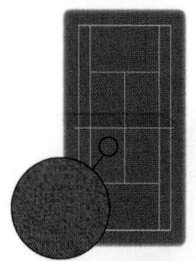

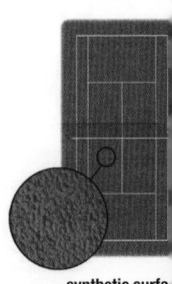

grass
Extremely fast playing surface that favors a serve-and-volley game; grass surfaces are increasingly rare due to high maintenance costs.

clay
Slow and comfortable surface given to long rallies; clay courts require regular but low-cost maintenance.

hard surface
Surface given to fast bounces; hard surfaces quickly wear out shoes and balls.

synthetic surfa
Soft elastic surface tha excellent bounce and red risk of injury.

gymnastics

Sports discipline practiced on the ground and with apparatuses such as rings, bars and beams.

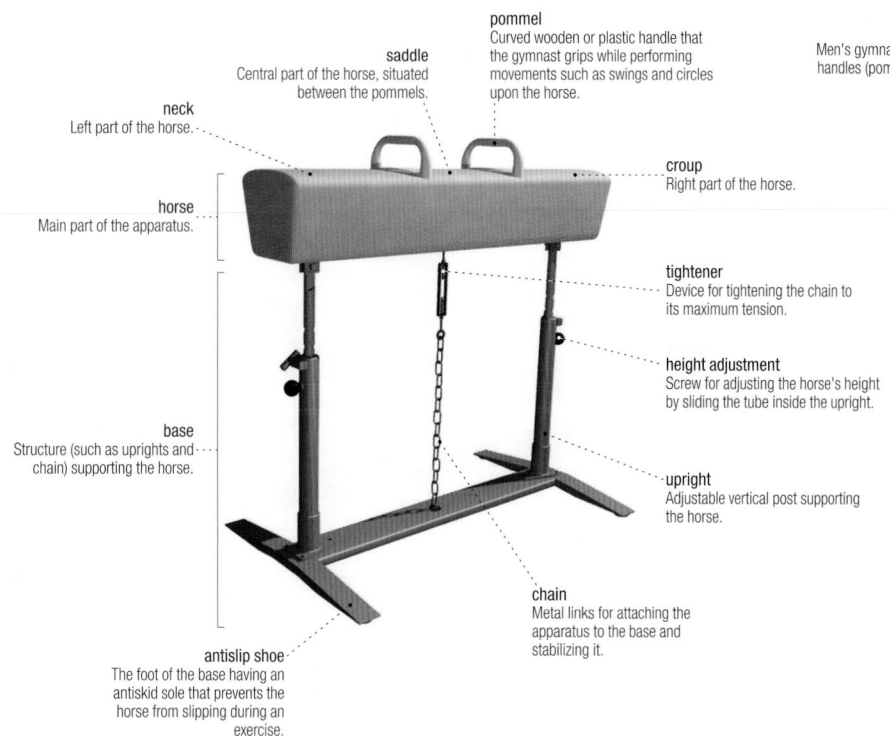

pommel
Curved wooden or plastic handle that the gymnast grips while performing movements such as swings and circles upon the horse.

pommel horse
Men's gymnastics apparatus with two handles (pommels), around which the gymnast maneuvers.

saddle
Central part of the horse, situated between the pommels.

neck
Left part of the horse.

croup
Right part of the horse.

horse
Main part of the apparatus.

tightener
Device for tightening the chain to its maximum tension.

height adjustment
Screw for adjusting the horse's height by sliding the tube inside the upright.

base
Structure (such as uprights and chain) supporting the horse.

upright
Adjustable vertical post supporting the horse.

chain
Metal links for attaching the apparatus to the base and stabilizing it.

antislip shoe
The foot of the base having an antiskid sole that prevents the horse from slipping during an exercise.

balance beam
Women's gymnastics apparatus made up of a long horizontal bar, on which the gymnast performs static and dynamic balance exercises.

height adjustment
Crank for raising and lowering the uprights to adjust the beam's height.

beam
Rectangular wooden or steel bar; it is 16 ft long, 6 in wide, 4 ft above the floor and covered with a nonskid surface.

upright
Adjustable post supporting the beam.

vault
Men's and women's gymnastics apparatus that is similar to a pommel horse; after a run, the gymnast supports the body on it with both hands to make a jump.

springboard
Board with springs to give it elasticity so that the gymnast can gain momentum before performing certain exercises such as vaulting.

gymnastics

event platform
Platform that contains the
necessary material and
apparatuses to hold gymnastics
competitions.

overall standings scoreboard
Board on which the performances and the
gymnasts' marks are posted.

balance beam
Women's gymnastics apparatus made
up of a long horizontal bar, on which the
gymnast performs static and dynamic
balance exercises.

floor exercise a
40 ft² pad on which the gymnast perfo
exercises on the fl

uneven parallel bars
Women's gymnastics apparatus made
up of two horizontal bars of different
heights for performing various acrobatic
exercises.

pommel horse
Men's gymnastics apparatus with
two handles (pommels), around
which the gymnast maneuvers.

line judge
Official who ensures that the
gymnasts on the floor stay within
the floor exercise area.

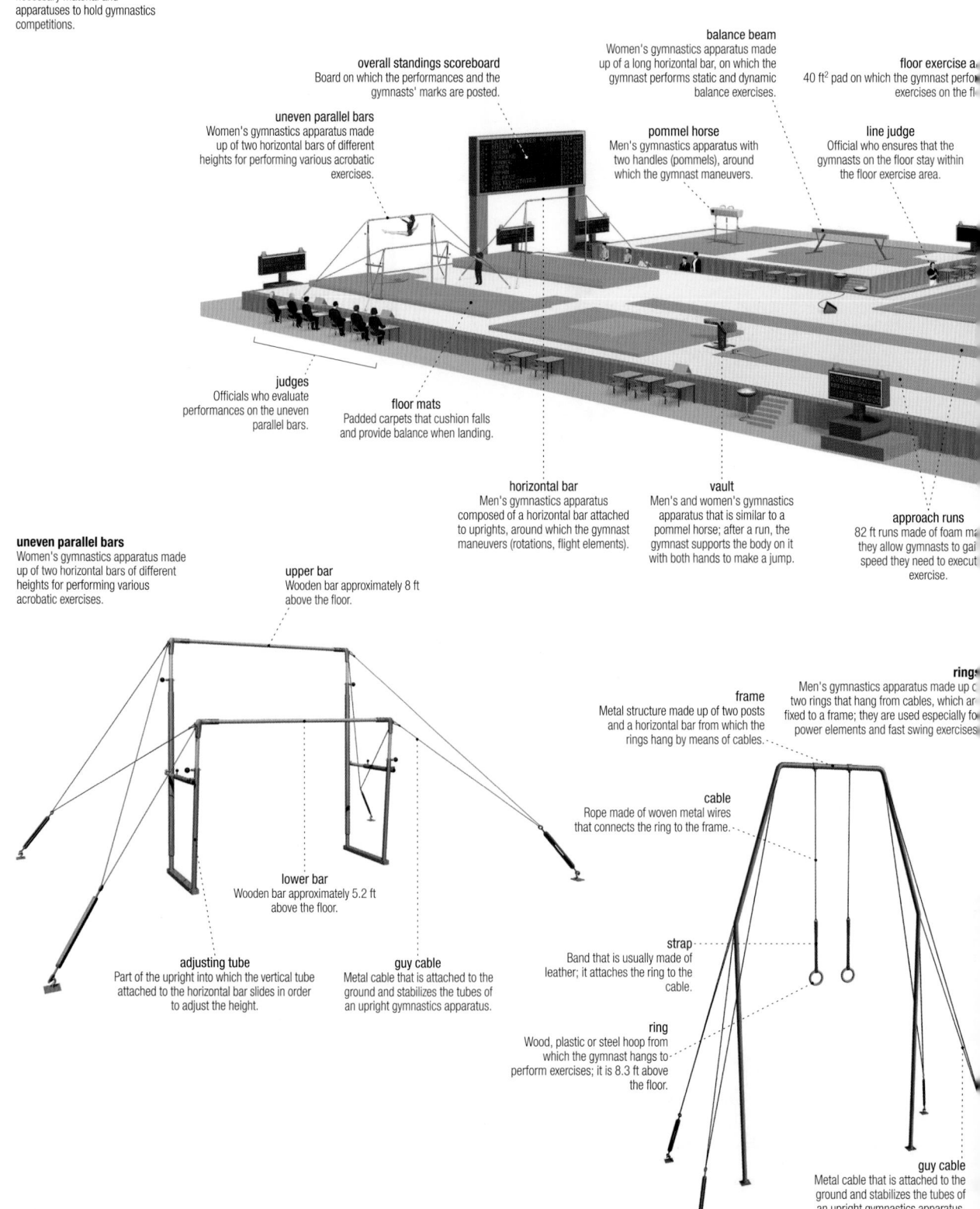

judges
Officials who evaluate
performances on the uneven
parallel bars.

floor mats
Padded carpets that cushion falls
and provide balance when landing.

horizontal bar
Men's gymnastics apparatus
composed of a horizontal bar attached
to uprights, around which the gymnast
maneuvers (rotations, flight elements).

vault
Men's and women's gymnastics
apparatus that is similar to a
pommel horse; after a run, the
gymnast supports the body on it
with both hands to make a jump.

approach runs
82 ft runs made of foam ma
they allow gymnasts to gai
speed they need to execut
exercise.

uneven parallel bars
Women's gymnastics apparatus made
up of two horizontal bars of different
heights for performing various
acrobatic exercises.

upper bar
Wooden bar approximately 8 ft
above the floor.

rings
Men's gymnastics apparatus made up o
two rings that hang from cables, which ar
fixed to a frame; they are used especially fo
power elements and fast swing exercises

frame
Metal structure made up of two posts
and a horizontal bar from which the
rings hang by means of cables.

cable
Rope made of woven metal wires
that connects the ring to the frame.

lower bar
Wooden bar approximately 5.2 ft
above the floor.

adjusting tube
Part of the upright into which the vertical tube
attached to the horizontal bar slides in order
to adjust the height.

guy cable
Metal cable that is attached to the
ground and stabilizes the tubes of
an upright gymnastics apparatus.

strap
Band that is usually made of
leather; it attaches the ring to the
cable.

ring
Wood, plastic or steel hoop from
which the gymnast hangs to
perform exercises; it is 8.3 ft above
the floor.

guy cable
Metal cable that is attached to the
ground and stabilizes the tubes of
an upright gymnastics apparatus.

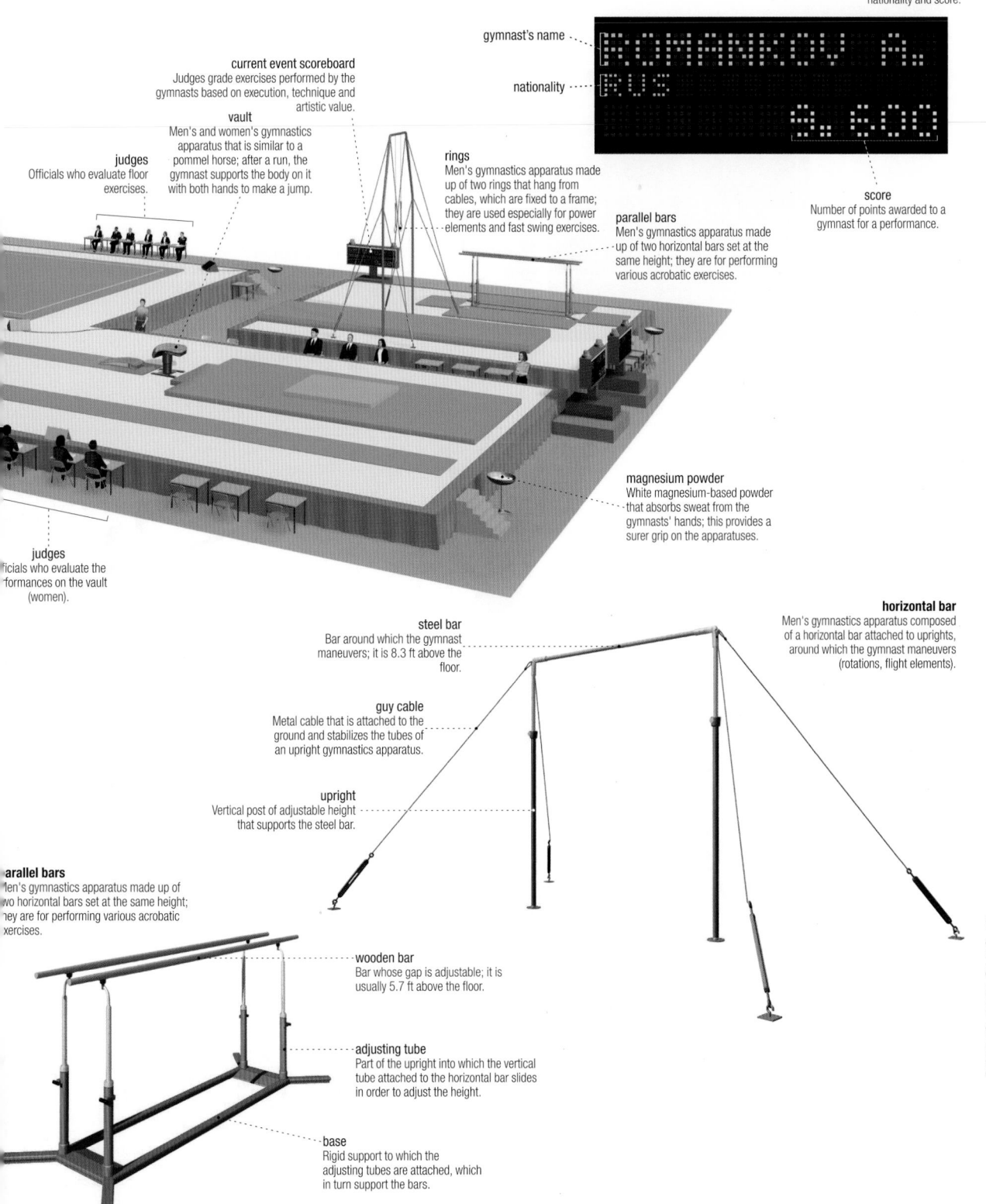

scoreboard
Board that displays information about a sports competition in progress such as gymnast's name, nationality and score.

gymnast's name
nationality

ROMANKOV A.
RUS
9.600

score
Number of points awarded to a gymnast for a performance.

current event scoreboard
Judges grade exercises performed by the gymnasts based on execution, technique and artistic value.

vault
Men's and women's gymnastics apparatus that is similar to a pommel horse; after a run, the gymnast supports the body on it with both hands to make a jump.

judges
Officials who evaluate floor exercises.

rings
Men's gymnastics apparatus made up of two rings that hang from cables, which are fixed to a frame; they are used especially for power elements and fast swing exercises.

parallel bars
Men's gymnastics apparatus made up of two horizontal bars set at the same height; they are for performing various acrobatic exercises.

magnesium powder
White magnesium-based powder that absorbs sweat from the gymnasts' hands; this provides a surer grip on the apparatuses.

judges
ficials who evaluate the formances on the vault (women).

steel bar
Bar around which the gymnast maneuvers; it is 8.3 ft above the floor.

horizontal bar
Men's gymnastics apparatus composed of a horizontal bar attached to uprights, around which the gymnast maneuvers (rotations, flight elements).

guy cable
Metal cable that is attached to the ground and stabilizes the tubes of an upright gymnastics apparatus.

upright
Vertical post of adjustable height that supports the steel bar.

arallel bars
Men's gymnastics apparatus made up of wo horizontal bars set at the same height; hey are for performing various acrobatic xercises.

wooden bar
Bar whose gap is adjustable; it is usually 5.7 ft above the floor.

adjusting tube
Part of the upright into which the vertical tube attached to the horizontal bar slides in order to adjust the height.

base
Rigid support to which the adjusting tubes are attached, which in turn support the bars.

SPORTS AND GAMES

rhythmic gymnastics

Combining gymnastics with dance, this women's discipline requires suppleness, strength and dexterity for manipulating the apparatuses.

exercise area
40 ft² pad on which the gymnast performs.

superior jury
Group composed of the chair of the joint technical committee and two assistants. This group oversees the competition and the work performed by the judges.

assistant judge
Official who lowers scores for penalties, such as when a gymnast fails to stay within the floor exercise area.

artistic value judges
Officials (4) who evaluate the composition of the exercise: choreography, rhythm, harmony and originality.

difficulty judges
Officials (4) who evaluate the difficulty of the exercise: movements executed and specific handling of the apparatuses.

execution judges
Officials (4) who evaluate the execution quality of the exercise: technical faults, apparatus mastery, coordination and expressiveness.

apparatus
Rhythmic gymnastics is practiced using five accessories (apparatuses), which for the most part are made of synthetic material.

clubs
Apparatuses that are manipulated in a choreography made up of rotations, throwing and asymmetrical movements.

rope
Apparatus whose length is proportional to the gymnast's height; it is used mainly for jumping.

ribbon
Band that the gymnast must keep constantly moving by forming very precise figures, such as serpentines, spirals and circles.

ball
Sphere that the gymnast manipulates to bring out suppleness and corporal expression, as well as the contrast between power for throwing and gentleness for catching.

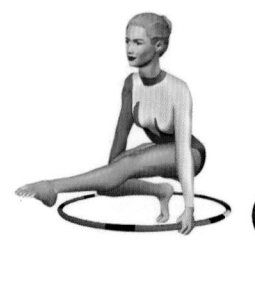

hoop
Rigid apparatus used in a wide variety of manipulations, such as rotations, throwing, rolls and passing through.

trampoline

Field which consists of performing jumps and figures on an apparatus made up of a bed stretched by springs.

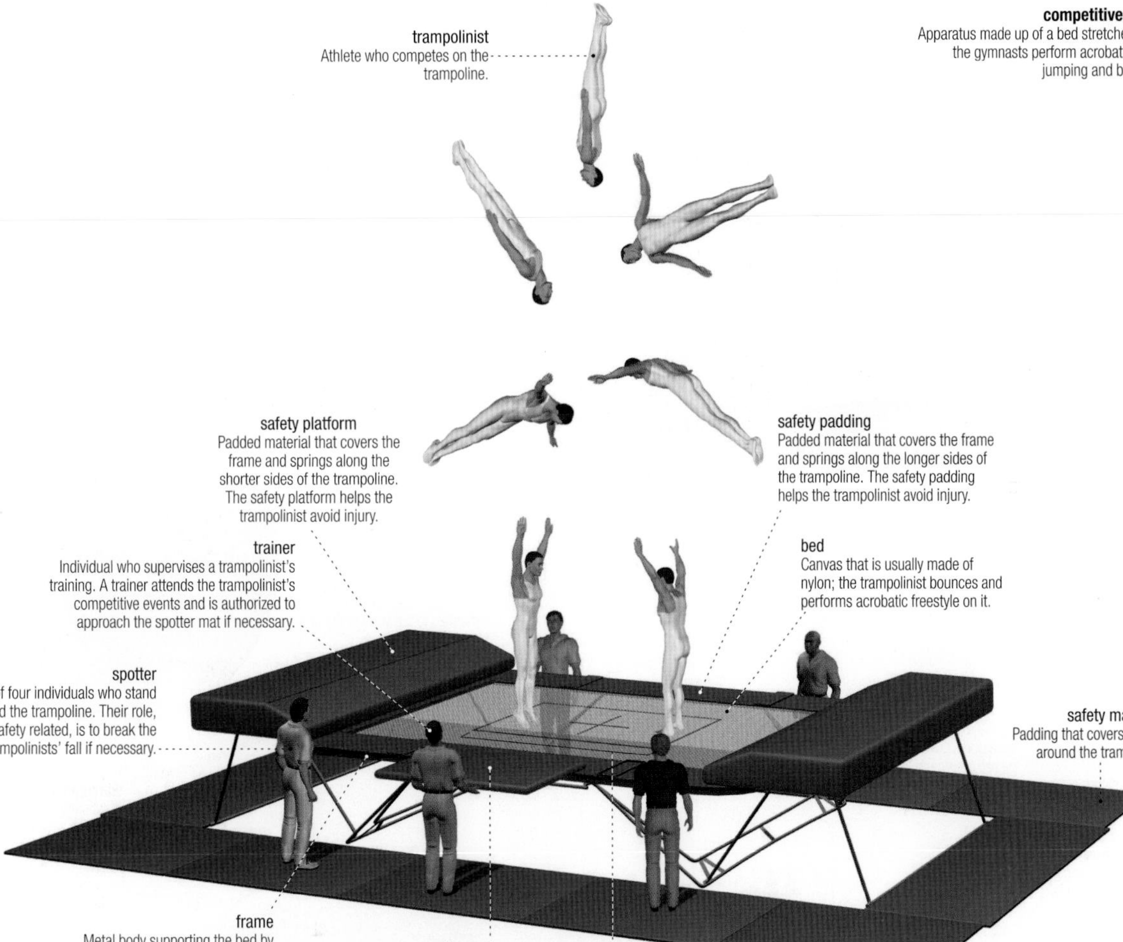

trampolinist
Athlete who competes on the trampoline.

competitive trampoline
Apparatus made up of a bed stretched by springs; the gymnasts perform acrobatic freestyle by jumping and bouncing on it.

safety platform
Padded material that covers the frame and springs along the shorter sides of the trampoline. The safety platform helps the trampolinist avoid injury.

safety padding
Padded material that covers the frame and springs along the longer sides of the trampoline. The safety padding helps the trampolinist avoid injury.

trainer
Individual who supervises a trampolinist's training. A trainer attends the trampolinist's competitive events and is authorized to approach the spotter mat if necessary.

bed
Canvas that is usually made of nylon; the trampolinist bounces and performs acrobatic freestyle on it.

spotter
One of four individuals who stand around the trampoline. Their role, safety related, is to break the trampolinists' fall if necessary.

safety mat
Padding that covers the ground around the trampoline.

frame
Metal body supporting the bed by means of springs.

spotter mat
Backup padding that the trainer can place beneath the trampoline in order to break a fall. It is also used to stop a trampolinist's rebound from the bed.

jumping zone
Area demarcated by red lines drawn around the center of the bed, within which jumps and figures are performed.

leisure trampoline
Apparatus made up of a bed stretched by springs on which one performs jumps.

safety net
Soft weave designed to prevent falls that surrounds the trampoline.

upper support pole
Pole that supports the safety net.

jumping mat
Canvas usually stretched by springs on which one performs jumps.

frame pad
Padded material that covers the frame and springs along the sides of the trampoline.

leg
Metal structure supporting the trampoline frame.

water polo

Sport played in a pool with two teams of seven opposing players who attempt to score points at the opposite goal using a ball.

water polo player
Member of a water polo team; during a game, the player must always stay in the water, never touch the bottom and not hold on to the sides of the pool.

cap
Flexible cap with ear protectors on which the player's number is written; each team wears a cap of a distinct color.

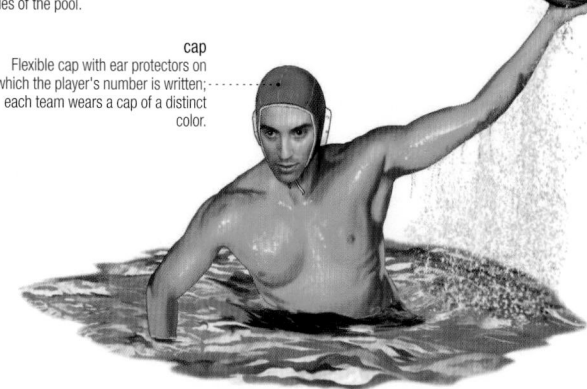

water polo ball
Waterproof sphere that is filled with air and is usually yellow; the players (except for the goalkeeper) may not hold the ball with both hands.

goa
Cage made up of a net mounted on a frame; a team scores a point each time it succeeds in placing the ball in the opposing goal

crossbar
Horizontal part connecting the two posts; the bar and the posts are made of plastic, metal or wood.

net
Loosely stitched netting attached to the back of the posts; it keeps the ball inside the goal.

floater
Float that keeps the goal above the surface of the water; the goal is also held in place by cables attached to the sides of the pool.

post
Two vertical supports for the goal; they are located 10 ft from each other.

water polo pool
Pool in which a water polo game takes place; a game has four periods of seven minutes each divided by breaks of two minutes each.

timekeepers
Officials in charge of the game's time, exclusions, continuous possession of the ball (maximum 35 seconds before taking a shot) and so on.

secretaries
Officials who write up the game's report (such as goals scored, fouls and exclusions) and signal the return of temporarily excluded players.

team bench
Space where substitute players and team officials sit; a team has 13 players but only seven are in the water at the same time.

goal judge
Official whose main function is to decide on the validity of goals and to report balls gone behind the goal line (corners).

goal line
Line that the ball must pass to score a goal; the players line up along it before a period begins.

2 m line

5 m line

referee
Official who is in charge of enforcing the rules; this individual supervises the game and signals violations by blowing a whistle.

half-distance line
Mark dividing the pool into two zones, one per team; the teams change zones after two periods of play.

goalkeeper
Player whose role is to prevent the ball from entering the goal; the goalkeeper wears a red cap.

excluded players re-entry area
Space where players who commit an exclusion foul serve a 20-second penalty.

coach
The team's leader; the coach strategy and decides who play different situations.

swimming

Sport consisting of swimming a defined distance (which varies depending on the four recognized stroke categories) as quickly as possible.

types of strokes
Four basic categories are recognized by the International Amateur Swimming Federation (FINA): the breaststroke, the butterfly, the backstroke and freestyle.

starting dive
Dive enabling the swimmer to thrust the body into the water; the swimmer pushes off with the legs, extends the body and enters the water head first.

breathing in
Action of drawing air into the lungs; to breathe in, the swimmer turns the head slightly, without lifting it.

front crawl stroke
Stroke executed in a prone position with alternating overarm strokes and a flutter kick; the usual stroke used in freestyle races.

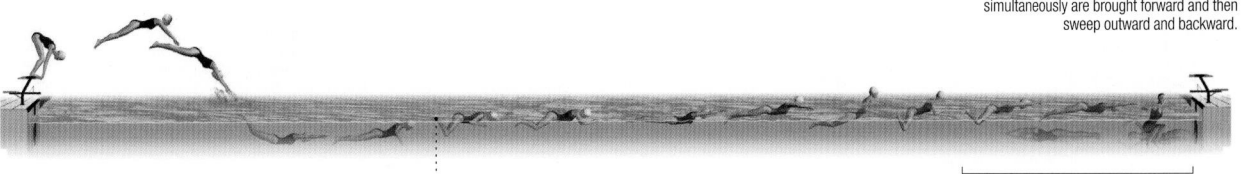

crawl kick
Movement in which the outstretched legs alternate in beating up and down.

breathing out
Expulsion of air; the swimmer breathes out when the face is underwater.

flip turn
Movement for making a turn: the swimmer curls downward, pivots, then pushes from the wall with the feet.

turning wall
Wall that the swimmer must touch before turning around; during the turn, the athlete pushes from the wall with the feet.

breaststroke
Stroke in which the arms and legs simultaneously are brought forward and then sweep outward and backward.

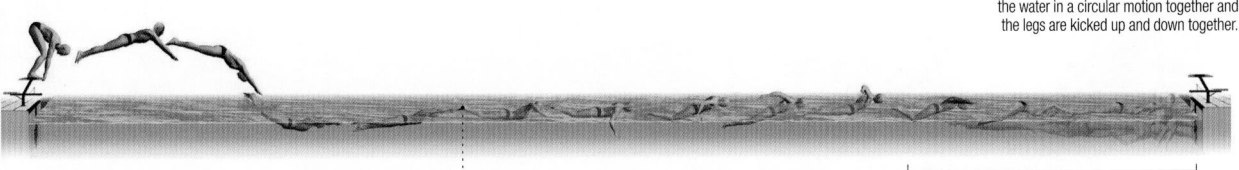

breaststroke kick
Movement in which the swimmer bends the legs and then stretches them simultaneously toward the outside.

breaststroke turn
Movement for making a half turn; the swimmer touches the wall with both hands, pivots, then pushes from the wall with the feet.

butterfly stroke
Stroke in which the arms are brought out of the water in a circular motion together and the legs are kicked up and down together.

butterfly kick
Vertical simultaneous movement of the legs that completes an undulation started by the upper body; the legs always stay together.

butterfly turn
Movement for making a half turn; the swimmer touches the wall with both hands, pivots, then pushes from the wall with the feet.

backstroke
Stroke executed on the back and consisting of an alternating circular arm pull and a flutter kick.

backstroke start
Movement by which the swimmer starts from within the pool; at the signal, the swimmer lets go of the starting grip and then pushes from the wall with the feet.

flip turn
Movement for making a turn; the swimmer arrives in the dorsal position, pivots, then pushes from the wall with the feet.

swimming

starting block
Metal elevated structure from which the swimmer dives into the pool to start a race.

swimsuit
Almost always stretchy, skintight clothing that is worn for swimming; the materials used are designed to provide optimum hydrodynamics.

cap
Headgear that reduces water resistance, keeps the swimmer's hair in place and protects it against the effects of chlorine.

platform
Rigid board with a nonskid surface that is attached to the top of the starting block; the swimmer takes position and, at the starter's signal, dives into the pool.

swimming goggles
Goggles that protect the eyes from irritating substances and provide good visibility in the water.

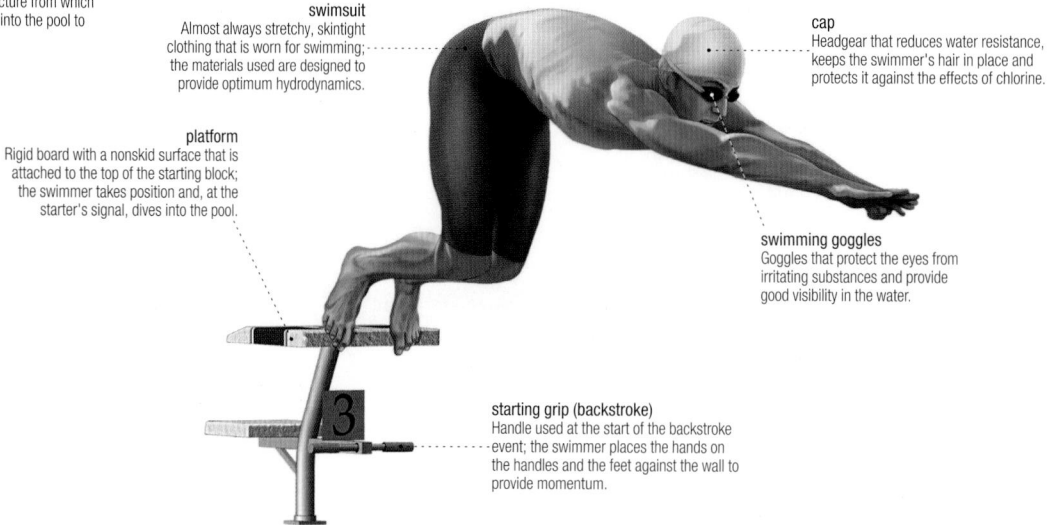

starting grip (backstroke)
Handle used at the start of the backstroke event; the swimmer places the hands on the handles and the feet against the wall to provide momentum.

referee
Official who enforces the rules and oversees the progress of the competition; the referee ratifies the judges' decisions and resolves any disputes that may arise.

starter
Official who gives the start signal; false starts lead to the disqualification of the swimmer in error.

stroke judge
Each of the four officials checking the acceptability of the swimmers' movements, depending on the stroke category.

false start rope
Rope that is 50 ft from the wall; it is dropped into the water in the event of a false start to inform the swimmers that they must resume their starting positions.

finish wall
Wall that the swimmer must touch to end a race; it is also the wall for turning around during events longer than 100 m in an Olympic-sized pool.

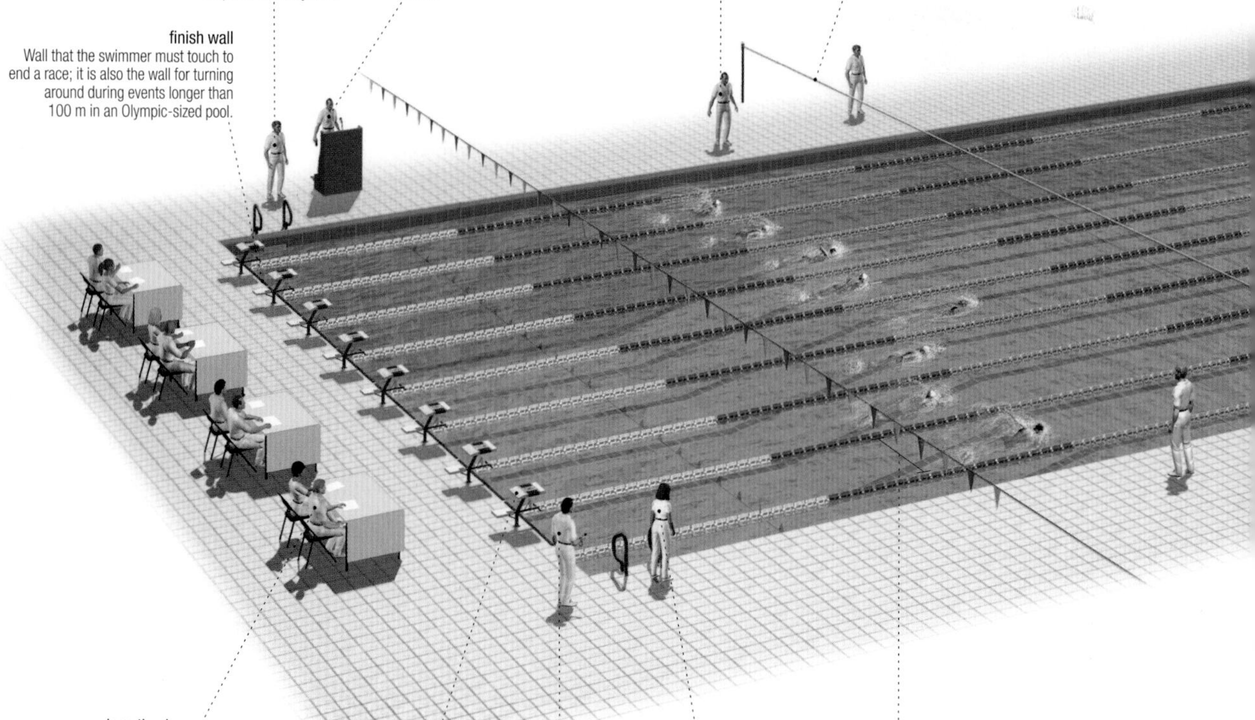

lane timekeeper
Official who manually registers the finish time of the competitor swimming in an assigned lane.

lane
The strips, numbered from 1 to 8, that are reserved for swimmers during a race; swimmers must stay in the same lane throughout the event.

starting block
Metal elevated structure from which the swimmer dives into the pool to start a race.

chief timekeeper
Official who collects the times registered by the lane timekeepers; these data are used in the event the electronic timer fails.

placing judge
Official who confirms the times registered by the electronic timer after checking with the timekeepers.

scoreboard
Posting surface displaying various data regarding the event in progress.

event
Type of competition in progress; it is based on the distance to swim and the category of stroke.

lane
Number of the lane assigned to each athlete.

timer
Time elapsed since the beginning of the race.

swimmer's country

swimmer's name

order of finish
Classification of contestants at the end of the race in ascending order of finish times.

swim times
Total duration of a contestant's race; it is measured in hundredths of a second.

backstroke turn indicator
...e with pennants that is strung 16 ft from the finish ...turning walls; backstroke swimmers use it to judge distance.

sidewall
...all forming the side of the pool; there ... at least 20 in between the side wall and the outside lane ropes.

turning wall
Wall that the swimmer must touch before turning around; during the turn, the athlete pushes from the wall with the feet.

turning judges
Officials checking the validity of the turns; in the 800 m and 1500 m events, they inform the swimmers of how many lengths they have left to do.

competitive course
The events, for singles and teams, take place in a pool that is 25 m or 50 m (Olympic-sized pool) long.

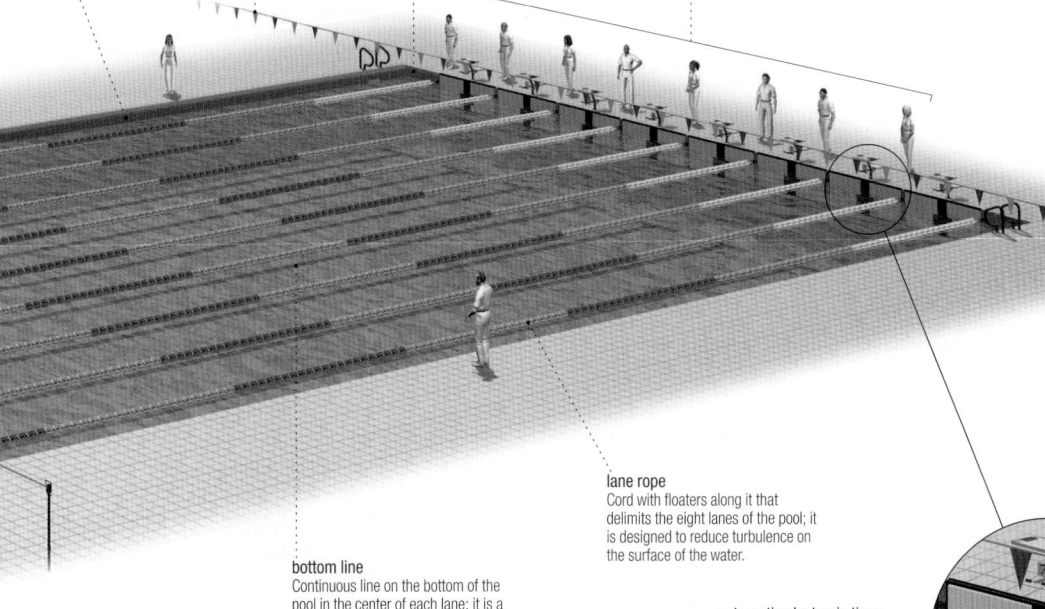

lane rope
Cord with floaters along it that delimits the eight lanes of the pool; it is designed to reduce turbulence on the surface of the water.

bottom line
Continuous line on the bottom of the pool in the center of each lane; it is a visual guide for the swimmer.

automatic electronic timer
Apparatus for automatically registering the swimmer's finish time; it is activated at the start and stops when the swimmer comes into contact with the wall.

diving

Sport consisting of executing simple to complex dives into the water from a platform or a springboard.

starting positions

Dives are started with or without run-up walks and in one of the positions recognized by the International Amateur Swimming Federation (FINA).

reverse dive
Dive started facing the water; the athlete then performs one or more backward spins.

inward dive
Dive started with the back turned toward the water; the diver then performs one or more forward spins.

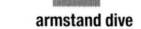

backward dive
Dive started with the back turned toward the water; the competitor then executes one or more backward spins.

forward dive
Dive started facing the water and followed by one or more forward spins.

armstand dive
Started on the hands for five seconds; this type of dive is done from a platform.

flight positions

Position of the body between the start and the entry; it must match one of the three positions authorized by FINA.

tuck position
Position in which the body is bent at the knees and hips with the knees and the feet together; the hands hold the legs.

straight position
Position in which the body remains perfectly straight and the arms are free (above the head or along the body).

pike position
Position in which the body is bent hips and the legs are outstretched arms are free.

diving installations

Equipment (such as springboards, platforms and tower) for diving; during a competition, the divers execute several dives and the points they earn are cumulative.

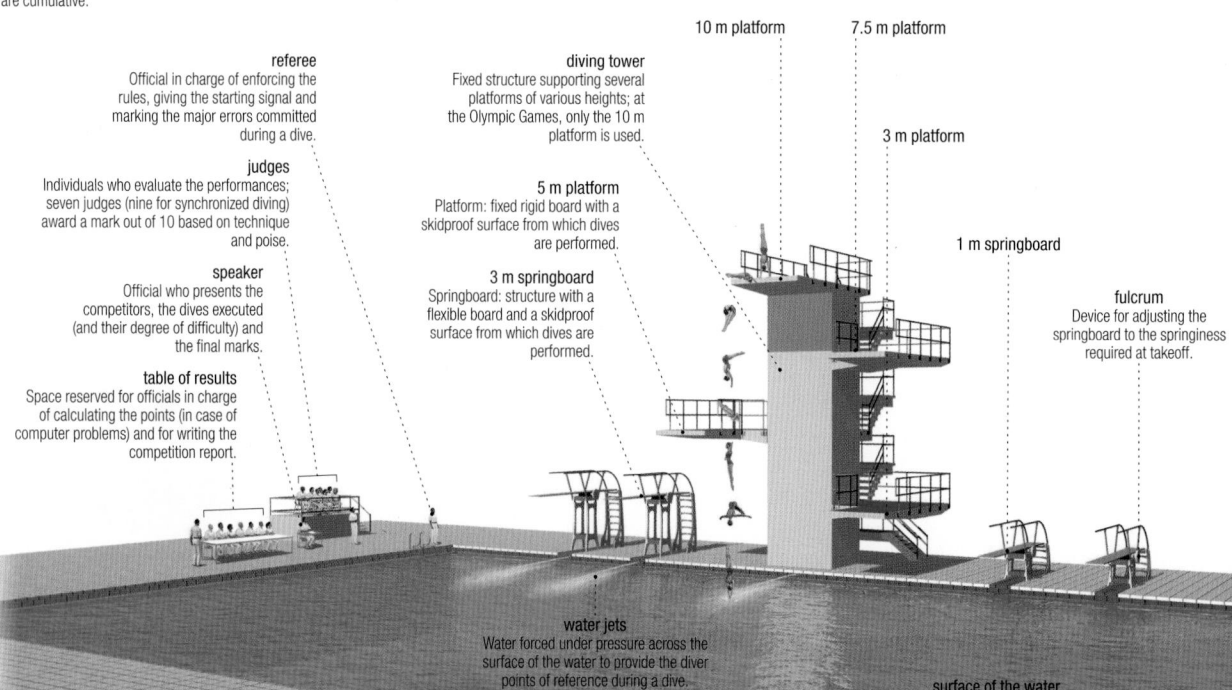

referee
Official in charge of enforcing the rules, giving the starting signal and marking the major errors committed during a dive.

judges
Individuals who evaluate the performances; seven judges (nine for synchronized diving) award a mark out of 10 based on technique and poise.

speaker
Official who presents the competitors, the dives executed (and their degree of difficulty) and the final marks.

table of results
Space reserved for officials in charge of calculating the points (in case of computer problems) and for writing the competition report.

diving tower
Fixed structure supporting several platforms of various heights; at the Olympic Games, only the 10 m platform is used.

5 m platform
Platform: fixed rigid board with a skidproof surface from which dives are performed.

3 m springboard
Springboard: structure with a flexible board and a skidproof surface from which dives are performed.

10 m platform

7.5 m platform

3 m platform

1 m springboard

fulcrum
Device for adjusting the springboard to the springiness required at takeoff.

water jets
Water forced under pressure across the surface of the water to provide the diver points of reference during a dive.

surface of the water

diving

examples of dives

There are some 90 different dives that are distinguished by their start position, their form in flight and the figure presented (somersault, twist).

entries

The diver enters the water in the vertical position, head or feet first, while attempting to produce the least amount of splashing possible.

feet-first entry

head-first entry

synchronized diving

Dive performed simultaneously by two athletes forming a team; the positions are the same as for individual events and must be executed simultaneously.

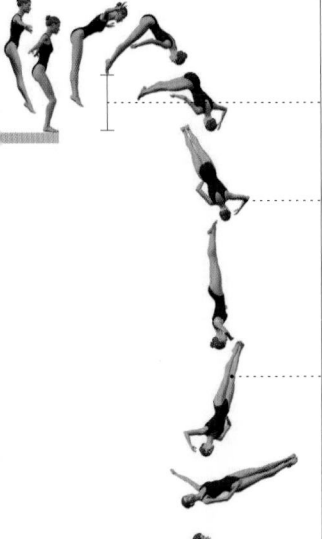

height of the dive
Elevation attained during takeoff; it must be sufficient enough for the diver to complete the series of planned movements.

arm position
Depending on the type of dive, the arms may be stretched along the body, toward the feet, over the head or by the sides.

leg position
While in flight, the feet must be together and the toes extended, regardless of the type of dive.

flight
Part of the dive between the start and the entry; whatever the type of dive chosen, the diver must demonstrate suppleness, elegance and fluidity.

entry
Final part of the dive, the moment when the diver enters the water.

forward somersault with a twist
Dive started with a run-up walk in the forward position; the diver then executes a forward body spin and enters the water feet first.

reverse dive with a twist
Dive started in reverse position; the athlete then executes a body spin and enters the water head first.

forward three-and-a-half somersault tuck
Dive started in the forward position; during flight, three and one-half rotations are executed in a tucked position and the water is entered head first.

sailing

Sport navigation practiced on a sailboat. There are several classes of sailboats and various types of competitions such as regattas and transoceanic races.

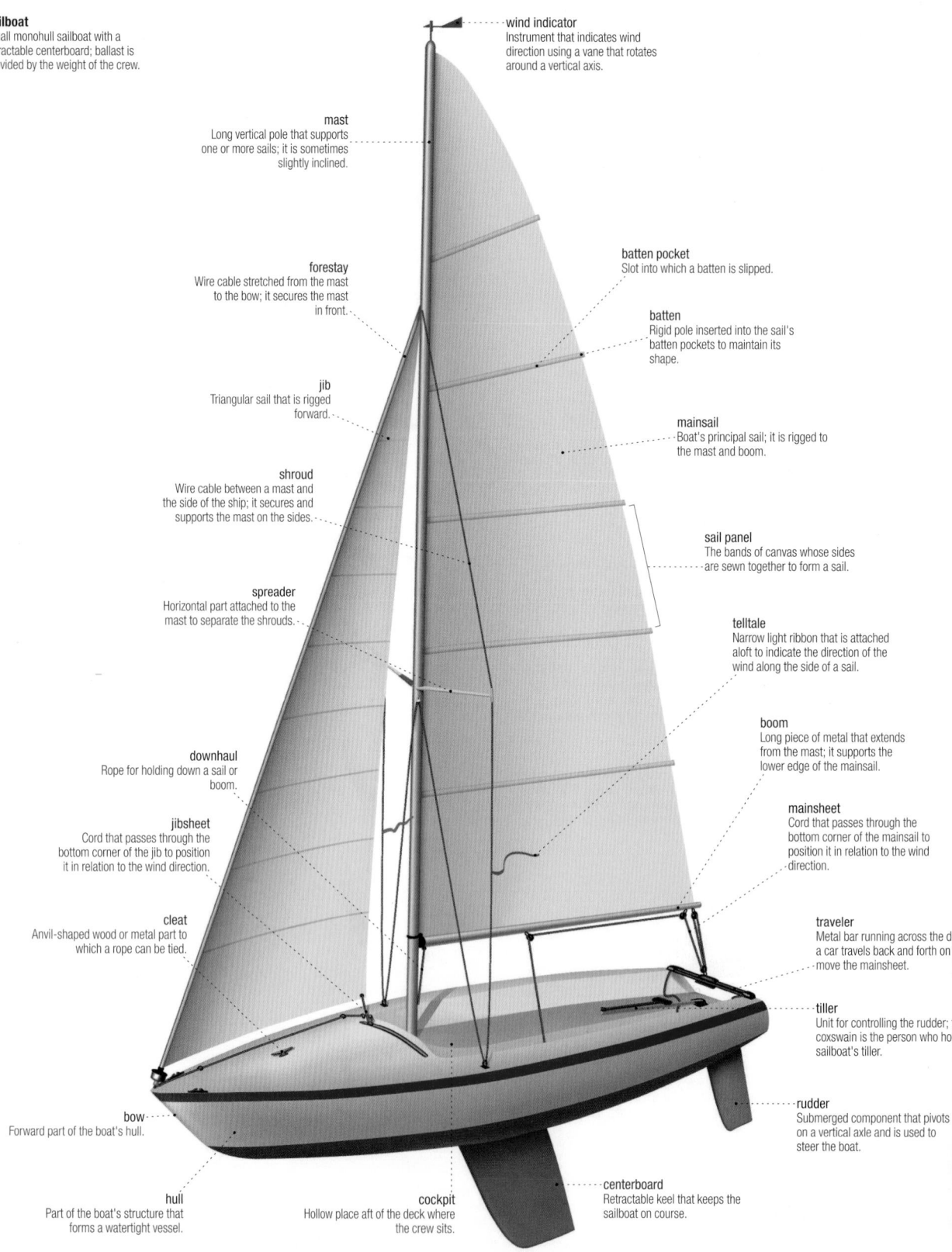

sailboat
Small monohull sailboat with a retractable centerboard; ballast is provided by the weight of the crew.

wind indicator
Instrument that indicates wind direction using a vane that rotates around a vertical axis.

mast
Long vertical pole that supports one or more sails; it is sometimes slightly inclined.

batten pocket
Slot into which a batten is slipped.

forestay
Wire cable stretched from the mast to the bow; it secures the mast in front.

batten
Rigid pole inserted into the sail's batten pockets to maintain its shape.

jib
Triangular sail that is rigged forward.

mainsail
Boat's principal sail; it is rigged to the mast and boom.

shroud
Wire cable between a mast and the side of the ship; it secures and supports the mast on the sides.

sail panel
The bands of canvas whose sides are sewn together to form a sail.

spreader
Horizontal part attached to the mast to separate the shrouds.

telltale
Narrow light ribbon that is attached aloft to indicate the direction of the wind along the side of a sail.

boom
Long piece of metal that extends from the mast; it supports the lower edge of the mainsail.

downhaul
Rope for holding down a sail or boom.

mainsheet
Cord that passes through the bottom corner of the mainsail to position it in relation to the wind direction.

jibsheet
Cord that passes through the bottom corner of the jib to position it in relation to the wind direction.

cleat
Anvil-shaped wood or metal part to which a rope can be tied.

traveler
Metal bar running across the de a car travels back and forth on move the mainsheet.

tiller
Unit for controlling the rudder; t coxswain is the person who hol sailboat's tiller.

bow
Forward part of the boat's hull.

rudder
Submerged component that pivots on a vertical axle and is used to steer the boat.

hull
Part of the boat's structure that forms a watertight vessel.

cockpit
Hollow place aft of the deck where the crew sits.

centerboard
Retractable keel that keeps the sailboat on course.

sailing

multihulls
Sailboats made out of two or three parallel hulls joined together; the hulls are long, narrow and lightweight so that high speeds can be attained.

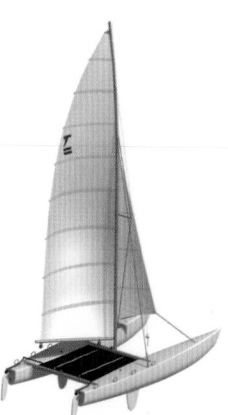

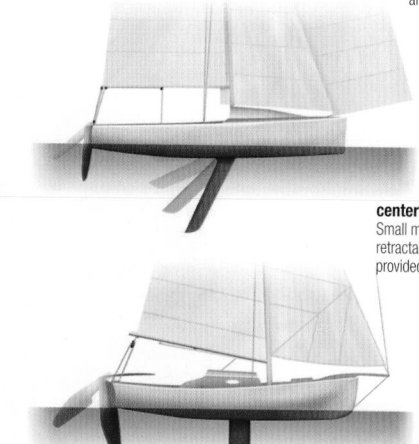

centerboard boat
Small monohull sailboat with a retractable centerboard; ballast is provided by the weight of the crew.

catamaran
Sailboat with two identical hulls that are connected by a rigid structure, which supports a cabin or a deck.

trimaran
Sailboat consisting of a central hull stabilized by two smaller hulls on each side (floaters); the hulls are joined by two rigid link arms.

keel boat
Small monohull sailboat with a fixed and weighted skeg (keel) to keep the boat stable and prevent it from capsizing in the wind.

upperworks
Small equipment and accessories on a boat's deck especially for rigging, adjusting and handling the sails.

snap shackle
Metal ring that closes automatically with a spring; it is used to attach various elements such as sheets and sails.

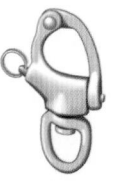

hank
Hook that is kept closed by a piston mechanism and set on a shank, which rotates on a ring; it prevents the ropes that are attached to it from twisting.

shackle
U-shaped part that closes with a threaded shank; it is used especially for joining two chains or for attaching ropes.

fairlead
Open part that is used to guide mooring ropes.

cleat
Anvil-shaped wood or metal part to which a rope can be tied.

turnbuckle
Instrument for adjusting the tension of a rope; it is made up of a hollow cylindrical body with a threaded shank screwed onto each end.

clam cleat
Device made up of two jaws with springs for locking a rope; after the rope is pulled, it stays in place.

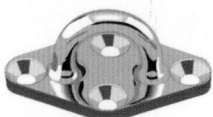

sheet lead
Ringed part through which a sheet passes to change its direction; it must be perfectly smooth to prevent wear on the rope.

winch
Small crank for heaving a rope tight; it usually has a ratchet preventing it from rotating in the counter direction.

traveler
Metal bar running across the deck; a car travels back and forth on it to move the mainsheet.

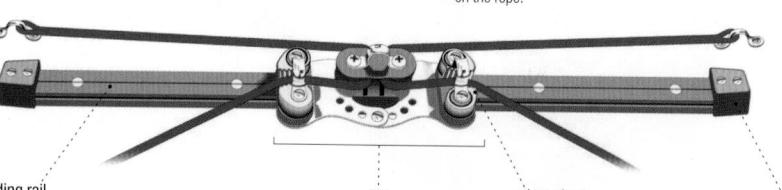

sliding rail
Straight rail along which the car moves.

car
Moving device that is connected to the mainsheet; the movement of the car quickly changes the sail position in relation to the wind.

clam cleat
Device made up of two jaws with springs for locking a rope; after the rope is pulled, it stays in place.

end stop
Part for locking the sideways movement of the car.

sailing

points of sailing
Courses of a sailboat relative to the direction of the wind; the sailboat navigates portside or starboardside, depending on which side the wind is coming from.

wind
Displacement of air caused by variations in pressure between two regions of the atmosphere.

on the wind
Points of sailing in between a headwind and a close reach that are used especially when tacking; the sails are near the boat's center line.

on the wind
Points of sailing in between a headwind and a close reach that are used especially when tacking; the sails are near the boat's center line.

reaching
Points of sailing in between a full and by and a running; the sails swing farther and farther from the boat's center line.

reaching
Points of sailing in between a full and by and a running; the sails swing farther and farther from the boat's center line.

full and by
Point of sailing of a sailboat going against the wind at an angle of about 60°.

on the wind
Point of sailing of a sailboat sailing against the wind at an angle of about 45°.

close reach
Point of sailing in which the sailboat comes up against the wind at an angle of about 70°.

beam reach
Point of sailing in between a wind abeam and a broad reach; the sailboat navigates by following the wind at an angle of about 135°.

in irons
Point of sailing in which the sailboat is pointing directly into the wind and thus unable to make headway; a sailboat cannot sail directly into the wind.

close hauled
Point of sailing in which the boat sails as close to the wind as possible, usually at an angle of about 45°; close hauled is the limit of sailing against the wind.

wind abeam
Point of sailing of a sailboat traveling at right angles to the wind.

broad reach
Fastest point of sailing, in between a beam reach and a down wind; the angle between the boat and the eye (axis) of the wind is wide.

running
Point of sailing of a boat going in the same direction as the wind.

sailing course
Olympic events take place on a triangular course whose length varies depending on variables such as the characteristics of the water and the wind direction.

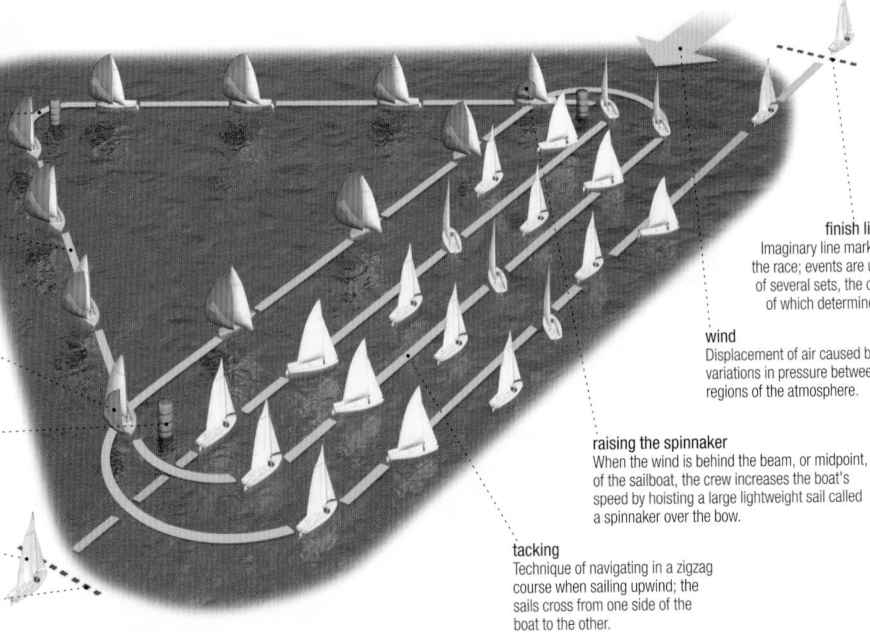

jibe
Technique for changing the sailboat's course when the wind is coming from the rear by letting the sails cross from one side of the boat to the other.

second leg at reach
The sailboat first navigates the reach with the wind on the starboard side until the third buoy (first leg at reach), then sails a second straight line to the reach with the wind on the port side.

lowering the spinnaker
The crew lowers the spinnaker when the sailboat turns into the wind, after the second leg at reach.

buoy
Floating object that marks out the race. An Olympic-type race has three buoys that are arranged in a triangle; they are rounded in a specific order.

start into a headwind
The race begins facing upwind; sailboats must then tack until the second buoy, which is located straight ahead.

starting line
Imaginary line marking the beginning of the race; when the starting signal is given, all the sailboats must be behind this line.

finish line
Imaginary line marking the end of the race; events are usually made up of several sets, the combined result of which determines the winner.

wind
Displacement of air caused by variations in pressure between two regions of the atmosphere.

raising the spinnaker
When the wind is behind the beam, or midpoint, of the sailboat, the crew increases the boat's speed by hoisting a large lightweight sail called a spinnaker over the bow.

tacking
Technique of navigating in a zigzag course when sailing upwind; the sails cross from one side of the boat to the other.

sailboard

Floating board with a sail; it is used in windsurfing, a sport consisting of gliding on water.

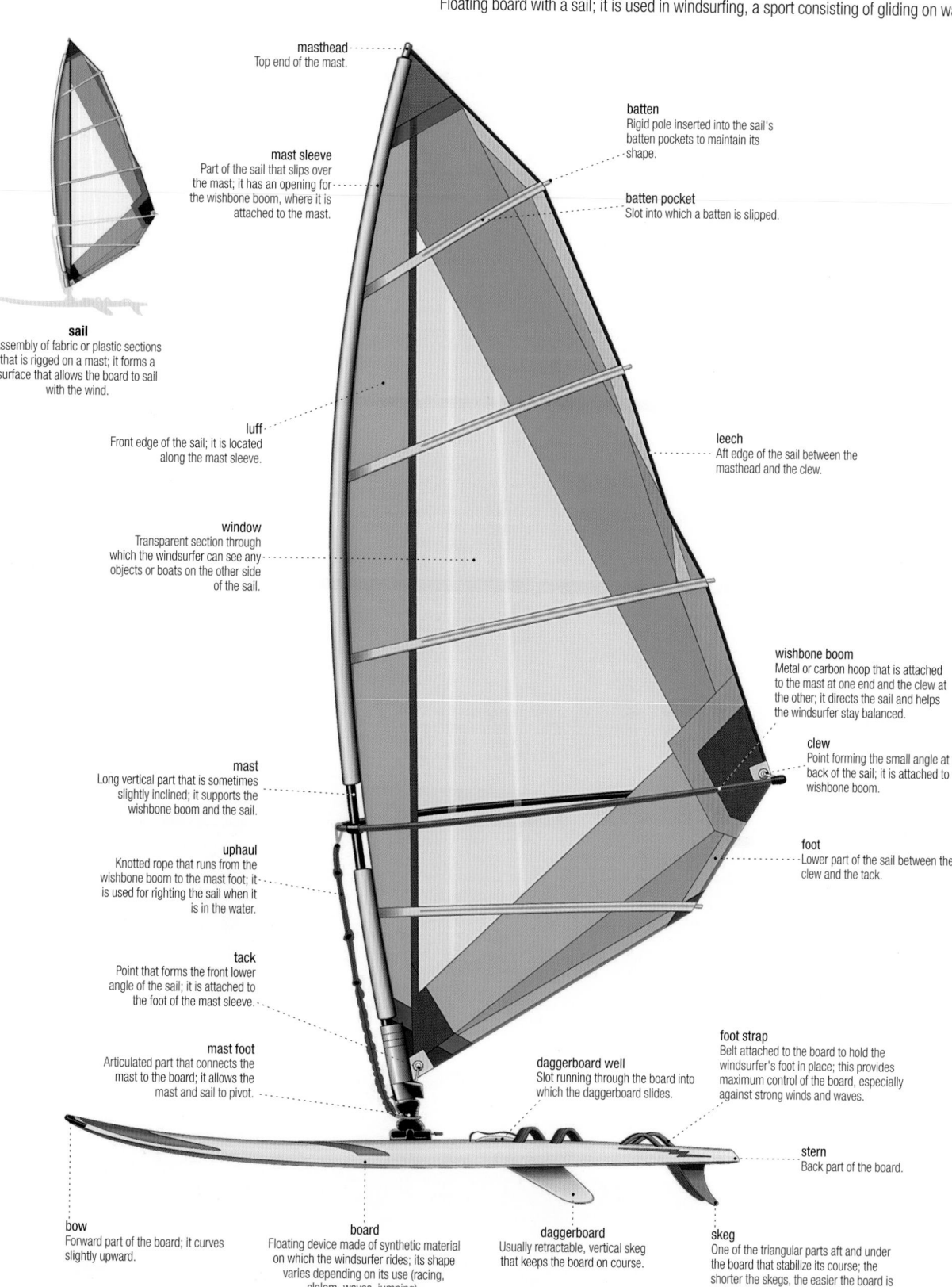

masthead
Top end of the mast.

batten
Rigid pole inserted into the sail's batten pockets to maintain its shape.

mast sleeve
Part of the sail that slips over the mast; it has an opening for the wishbone boom, where it is attached to the mast.

batten pocket
Slot into which a batten is slipped.

sail
Assembly of fabric or plastic sections that is rigged on a mast; it forms a surface that allows the board to sail with the wind.

luff
Front edge of the sail; it is located along the mast sleeve.

leech
Aft edge of the sail between the masthead and the clew.

window
Transparent section through which the windsurfer can see any objects or boats on the other side of the sail.

wishbone boom
Metal or carbon hoop that is attached to the mast at one end and the clew at the other; it directs the sail and helps the windsurfer stay balanced.

clew
Point forming the small angle at the back of the sail; it is attached to the wishbone boom.

mast
Long vertical part that is sometimes slightly inclined; it supports the wishbone boom and the sail.

foot
Lower part of the sail between the clew and the tack.

uphaul
Knotted rope that runs from the wishbone boom to the mast foot; it is used for righting the sail when it is in the water.

tack
Point that forms the front lower angle of the sail; it is attached to the foot of the mast sleeve.

foot strap
Belt attached to the board to hold the windsurfer's foot in place; this provides maximum control of the board, especially against strong winds and waves.

mast foot
Articulated part that connects the mast to the board; it allows the mast and sail to pivot.

daggerboard well
Slot running through the board into which the daggerboard slides.

stern
Back part of the board.

bow
Forward part of the board; it curves slightly upward.

board
Floating device made of synthetic material on which the windsurfer rides; its shape varies depending on its use (racing, slalom, waves, jumping).

daggerboard
Usually retractable, vertical skeg that keeps the board on course.

skeg
One of the triangular parts aft and under the board that stabilize its course; the shorter the skegs, the easier the board is to handle.

rowing and sculling

Sport consisting of a speed race in a straight line over a maximum distance of 2000 m; races take place on calm water in boats designed for the purpose.

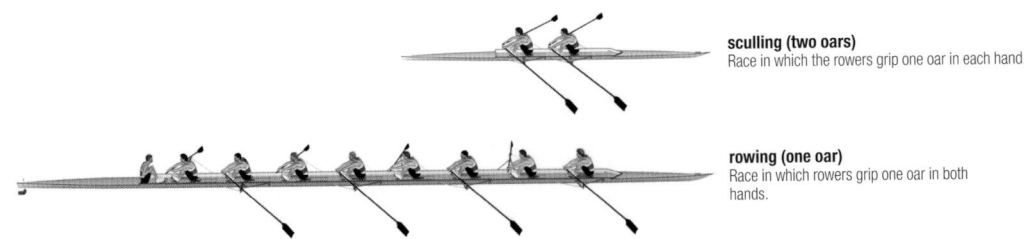

sculling (two oars)
Race in which the rowers grip one oar in each hand.

rowing (one oar)
Race in which rowers grip one oar in both hands.

types of oars

Oar: instrument that is made up of a slightly curved blade, which is connected to a long shaft; it propels the boat.

sculling oar

Short oar that is manipulated with one arm; it is used in tandem with a second oar to propel a sculling boat.

grip
End of the oar that is gripped by the rower.

rubber sheath
Plastic or rubber casing that covers and protects the shaft; the collar is mounted on it.

blade
Larger end of the oar that is thrust into the water to propel the boat; it is often asymmetrical in order to maximize its hold in the water.

shaft
Elongated part that is usually made of wood or carbon; the blade is attached to it.

collar
Ring that is mounted on the rubber sheath and rests on the oarlock to prevent the oar from slipping; it can be moved to change its leverage effect.

blade
Larger end of the oar that is thru the water to propel the boat; it is asymmetrical in order to maxim hold in the water.

sweep oar

Oar that is manipulated with both arms and is used to propel a sweep boat; it is longer than a sculling oar and has a larger blade.

parts of a boat

Boat: long and tapered lightweight vessel that is propelled by one to eight rowers; their oars are supported by an outrigger.

rudder cable
Cable used by the coxswain to direct the rudder; in a coxless boat, the cable may be connected to a rower's foot stretcher.

coxswain's seat
Part on which the coxswain sits facing the rest of the team; the coxswain steers the boat and gives the rowers instructions and the strokes per minute to follow.

foot stretcher
Part attached to the bottom of the boat; it supports the rowers' feet to provide the best draw.

sliding sea
Part on which the rower sit it slides along rails to increas movement range and efficienc

rudder
Submerged component that pivots on a vertical axle and is used to steer the boat.

rowing and sculling basin

Usually man-made body of water where rowing and canoe-kayak races are held; ideally, it is in the lee of the wind and without a current.

starting zone
The first 110 yd of the course inside which a race may be invalidated due to technical difficulties.

course buoys
Floating white units in the center of the course that demarcate the six to eight lanes of the basin.

course umpire
Official who follows the competitors during the race on board a boat; the course umpire may disqualify a boat straying from its lane.

start buoys
Floating yellow or orange units in the first 275 yd of the course that demarcate the six to eight lanes of the basin.

aligner
Official who checks that all boats are lined up at the start line.

starter
Official who summons the competitors and gives the starting signal; the starter also decides if there is a false start.

starting jetty
Floating platform on which an official stands; the role of this individual is to keep the boats immobile and in line before the start.

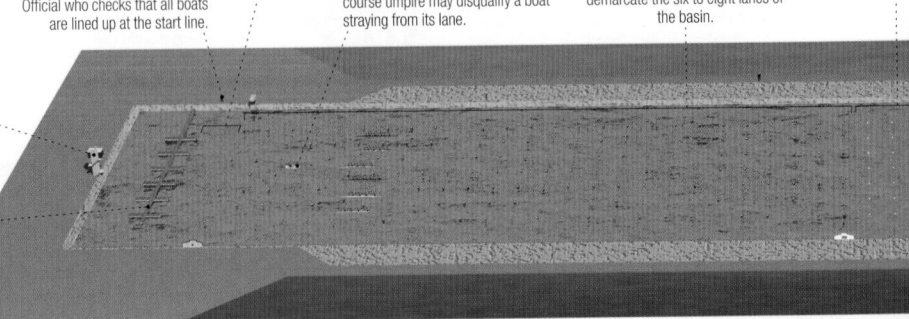

rowing and sculling

sculling boats

Boats in which the rowers have two oars and there are one, two, four and sometimes eight rowers; a sculling boat is rarely guided by a coxswain.

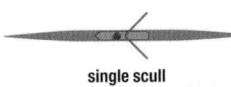

single scull
Sculling boat for one rower; it is the smallest and lightest of the rowboats.

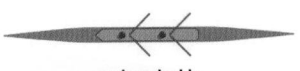

coxless double
Sculling boat for two rowers; like the single scull, it is rudderless and is steered by applying unequal force against the oars.

sweep boats

Boats in which the rowers have one oar and there are two, four or eight rowers; a sweep boat might be guided by a coxswain.

coxswain
Person who steers the boat and gives the rowers instructions and the strokes per minute to follow.

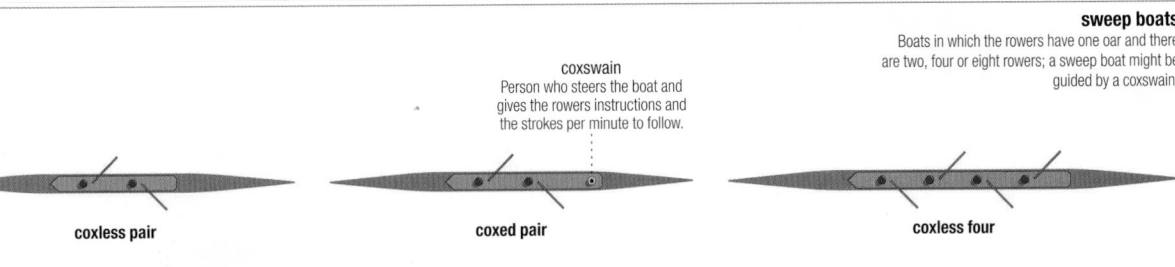

coxless pair

coxed pair

coxless four

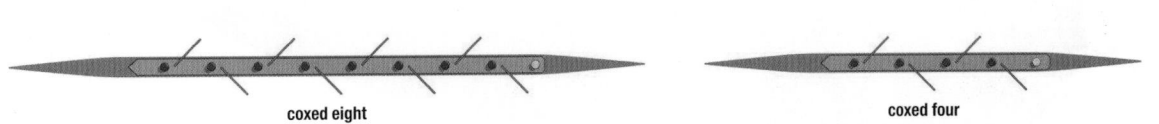

coxed eight

coxed four

outrigger
Metal adjustable structure that supports the oar within the rower's reach.

bow ball
Rubber or plastic globe forward on the hull; it is the deciding factor in a photo finish and serves as protection in the event of collision.

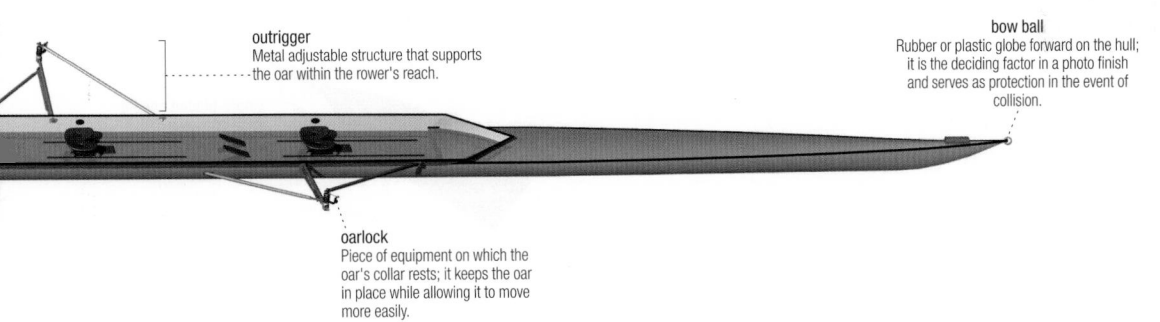

oarlock
Piece of equipment on which the oar's collar rests; it keeps the oar in place while allowing it to move more easily.

finish buoys
Floating yellow or orange units that demarcate the six to eight lanes of the basin for the last 275 yd of the course.

finish line judge
Official who validates the boats' placement and the race time.

finish line
Line marking the end of a race that is demarcated by two red flags atop buoys; a crew ends the race when the forward part of the boat crosses it.

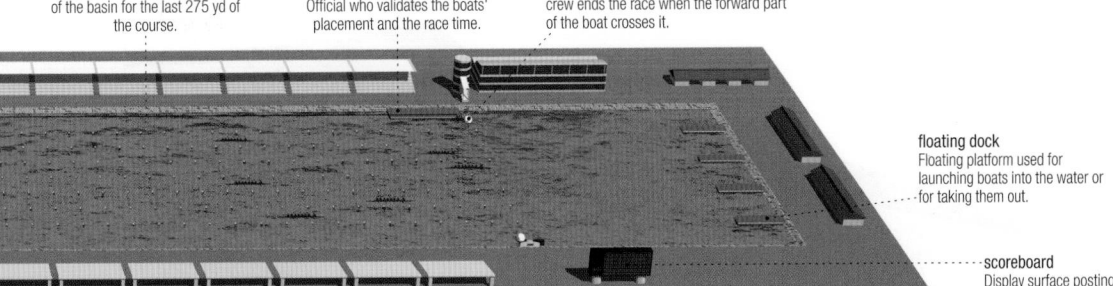

floating dock
Floating platform used for launching boats into the water or for taking them out.

scoreboard
Display surface posting information related to a sporting event in progress (time, standings, results, etc.).

canoe

Sport or leisure activity that involves rowing a canoe on a body of water.

whitewater canoe
Enclosed boat with one or two seats, propelled by a kneeling rower with a single-bladed paddle. Designed to navigate a waterway's rapids.

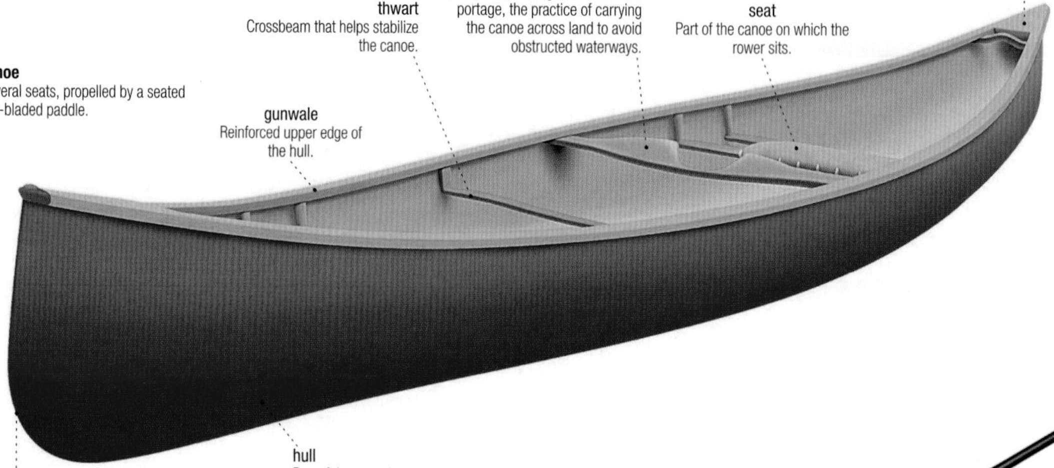

end deck
Covered front and back ends of the canoe that improve the hull's stiffness.

carrying yoke
Crossbeam situated in the middle of the canoe designed to facilitate portage, the practice of carrying the canoe across land to avoid obstructed waterways.

thwart
Crossbeam that helps stabilize the canoe.

seat
Part of the canoe on which the rower sits.

recreational canoe
Open boat with several seats, propelled by a seated rower with a single-bladed paddle.

gunwale
Reinforced upper edge of the hull.

hull
Part of the canoe's structure that forms a watertight vessel.

forestem
Forward part of the canoe hull.

single-bladed paddle
Instrument made up of a flat oar blade attached to a handle for propelling and steering a canoe.

canoe-kayak: flatwater racing

Sport consisting of a speed race in a straight line; races take place on calm water in canoes or kayaks with one or more places.

C1 canoe
Open pointed boat that is propelled with a single-bladed paddle in a kneeling position; the V-shaped hull is somewhat unstable but gives maximum glide.

deck
Enclosed area fore and aft; it reinforces the canoe's hull and prevents water from entering the cockpit.

forestem
Somewhat pointed forward part of the canoe hull.

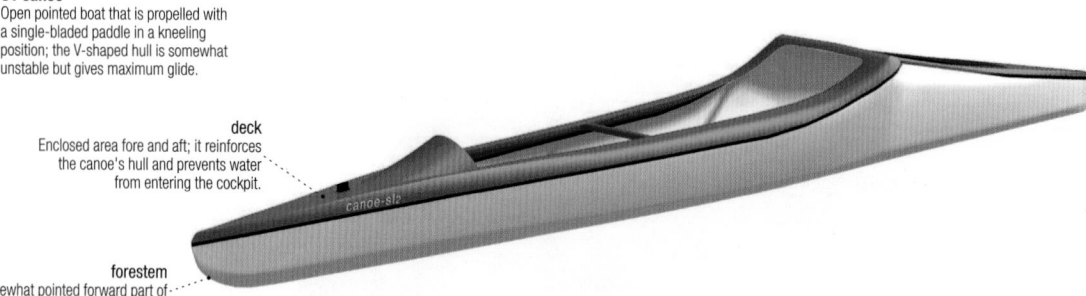

kayak

Sport or leisure activity that involves rowing a kayak on a body of water.

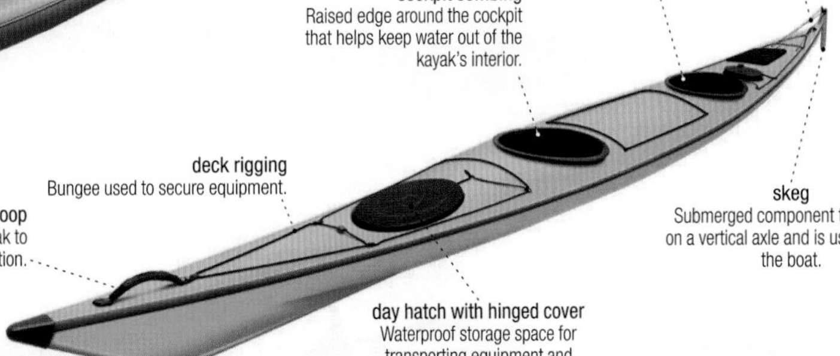

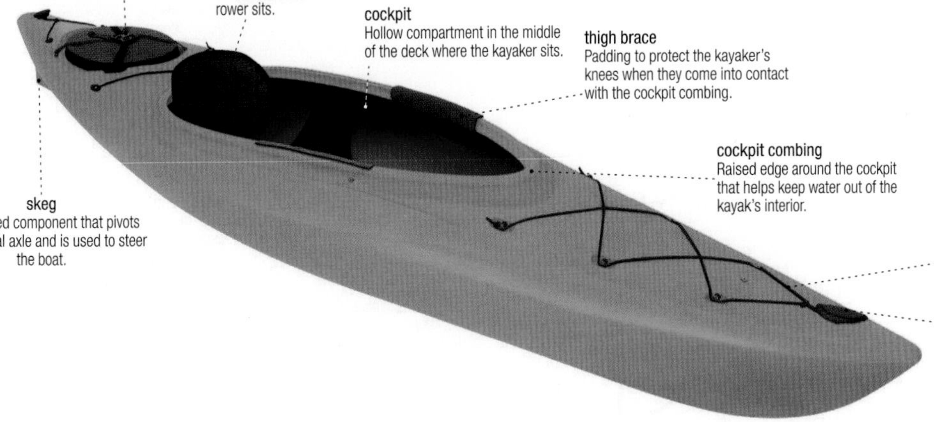

double-bladed paddle
...nent with two curved oar blades that
...attached to a handle; it propels and
...the kayak by paddling on alternating
sides of the boat.

whitewater kayak
Long and narrow enclosed boat, propelled by
a seated rower with a double-bladed paddle.
Designed to navigate a waterway's rapids.

two-paddler sea kayak
Long and sturdy enclosed boat with two
seats, propelled by seated rowers with
double-bladed paddles. Designed to
navigate coastal seawaters.

spray skirt
Flexible waterproof part that is
attached around the opening; it fits
snugly around the kayaker's waist to
prevent water from entering the boat.

cockpit
Hollow compartment in the middle
of the deck where the kayaker sits.

rudder halyard
Rudder cordage that facilitates
steering.

cockpit combing
Raised edge around the cockpit
that helps keep water out of the
kayak's interior.

deck rigging
Bungee used to secure equipment.

grab loop
Component that allows the kayak to
be held, facilitating transportation.

skeg
Submerged component that pivots
on a vertical axle and is used to steer
the boat.

day hatch with hinged cover
Waterproof storage space for
transporting equipment and
personal belongings.

...ay hatch with hinged cover
Waterproof storage space for
transporting equipment and
personal belongings.

seat
Part of the kayak on which the
rower sits.

cockpit
Hollow compartment in the middle
of the deck where the kayaker sits.

thigh brace
Padding to protect the kayaker's
knees when they come into contact
with the cockpit combing.

one-paddler recreational kayak
Enclosed single-seat boat with a rounded
hull to ensure stability and maneuverability,
propelled by a seated rower with a double-
bladed paddle. Designed for use in still
waters.

cockpit combing
Raised edge around the cockpit
that helps keep water out of the
kayak's interior.

skeg
...bmerged component that pivots
...a vertical axle and is used to steer
the boat.

deck rigging
Bungee used to secure equipment.

grab loop
Component that allows the kayak to
be held, facilitating transportation.

canoe-kayak: flatwater racing

seat
Position taken for paddling; once
seated, the kayaker can control the
rudder with a bar by using the feet.

K1 kayak
Closed tapered boat that is propelled
with a double-bladed paddle in a
seated position; it has a rudder to
facilitate steering.

tapered end
Tapered end of the kayak; the
V-shaped hull is very unstable but
can glide very quickly.

rudder
Submerged device with a rotating
flat surface that is integrated with
a vertical axle and used to steer
the kayak.

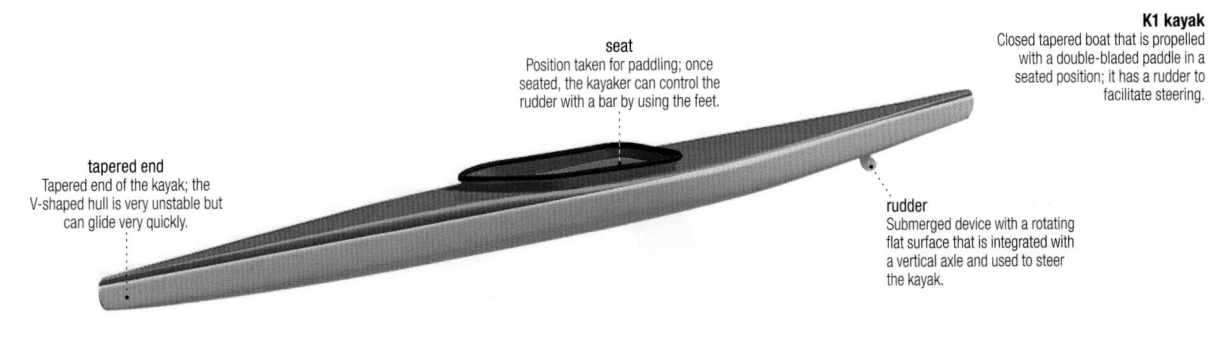

waterskiing

Sport in which the skier is towed by a motorboat and glides on the surface of the water on one or two skis, or a board; there are a number of disciplines, including jumping, slalom and figures.

examples of skis

Water skiing can be done on two skis (twin skis and jump skis), on one ski (figures and slalom) or on a board.

tip
Front end of the ski; it curves upward to prevent catching on the surface of the water.

twin skis
Very stable skis with broad tips that have various uses; one of the skis has a second binding so that it can be used as a slalom ski.

binding
Device that keeps the foot in place on the ski; it is usually made of natural or synthetic rubber and releases the foot easily in the event of a fall.

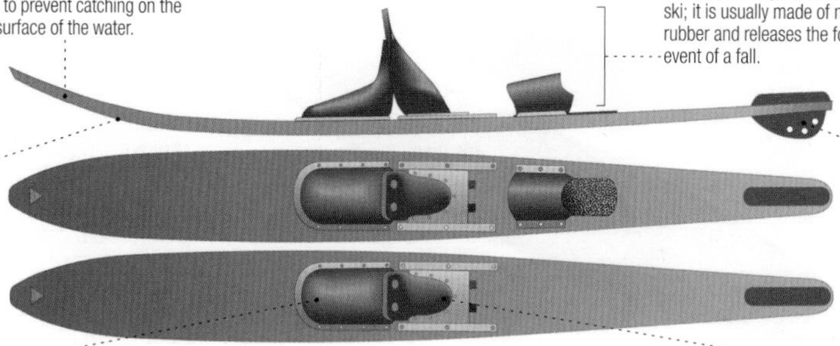

bottom
Carefully polished part forming the underside of the ski; it has different shapes (flat, concave or tunnel) depending on the desired effect.

fin
Skeg at the rear underside of the ski that provides directional stability.

toepiece
Front part of the binding; it covers the foot and part of the ankle.

heelpiece
Back part of the binding that covers the heel and the bottom of the leg; it reduces sideways motion.

slalom ski
Single ski with two bindings and a tapered rounded tail; it has a long fin to provide stability during tight turns.

jump skis
Very sturdy skis that are longer and wider than other types of skis; they provide the stability necessary for performing jumps from a jump ramp.

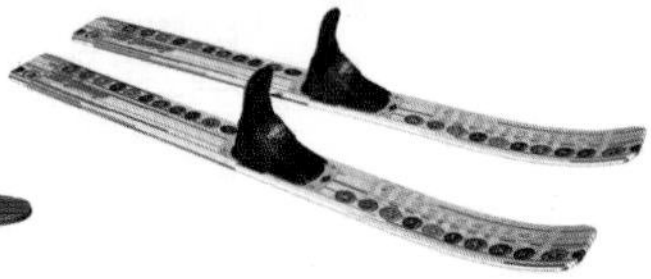

wakeboard
Board with transversally positioned bindings; used for slalom, jumps or acrobatic figures.

trick ski
Single ski that is wider and shorter than a twin ski and has two bindings and no fin; it is very maneuverable and is used to perform acrobatic figures.

back binding
Device that keeps the back foot in place on the ski; it is often identical to the front binding but can also be a simple toe strap.

front binding
Device that keeps the front foot in place on the ski; it is usually shaped like a boot and made of natural or synthetic rubber.

tail
Rear end of the ski.

examples of handles

Regular and slalom handles that the skier grips to be towed by the boat; they vary in shape depending on the type of skiing performed.

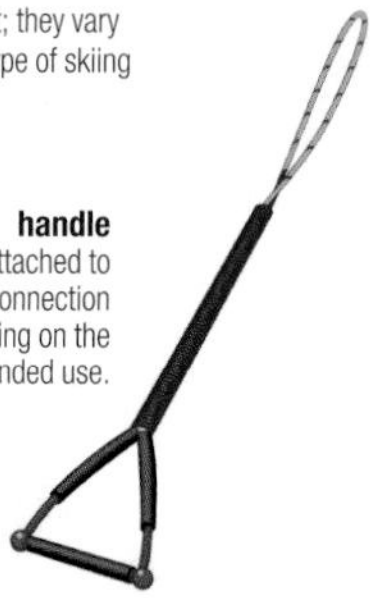

slalom handle
Rigid bar whose ends are attached to a tow line by a long flexible V-shaped connection.

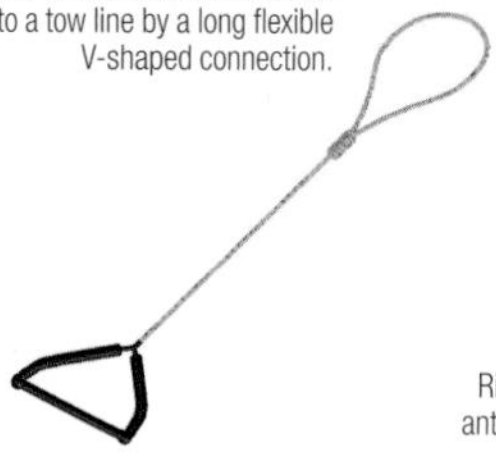

trick handle
Long rigid handle with a toe strap; it is used mainly for acrobatic tricks.

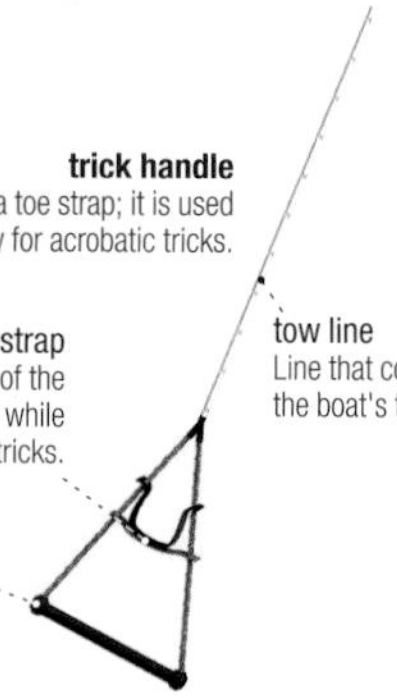

handle
Rigid bar whose ends are attached to a tow line by a V-shaped connection of varying flexibility depending on the intended use.

toe strap
Foot strap for holding one of the skier's feet; it provides traction while performing tricks.

tow line
Line that connects the handle the boat's towing cable.

tow bar
Rigid handle that is covered with antiskid material; the skier grips it while being towed.

surfing

Sport consisting of riding the front side of a breaking wave on a surfboard.

surfer
Person who engages in surfing while standing on a surfboard.

leash
Strap that secures the wakeboarder's ankle to the board.

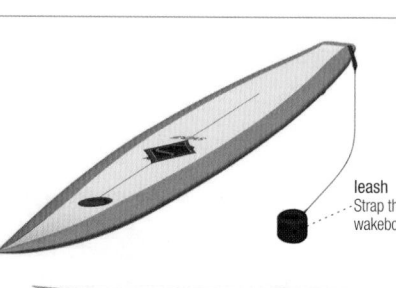

boot
Synthetic rubber shoe that is used for surfing in cold water or for protecting the feet from coral and rocks.

surfboard
Floating board made of synthetic material; its length and shape vary depending on the intended use.

skeg
Triangular part at the rear underside of the board that provides directional stability

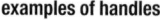
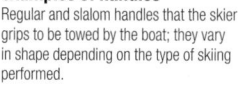

scuba diving

Sport consisting of descending underwater and swimming around with a portable supply of air.

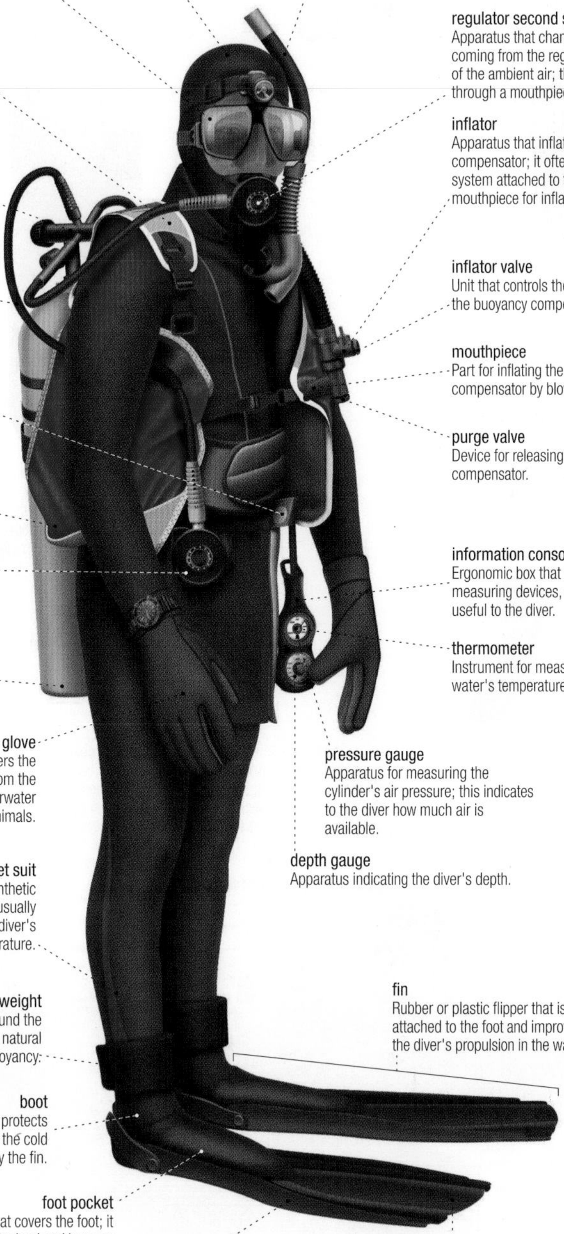

mask
Watertight part that is made up of glass surrounded by a rubber skirt; it covers the nose and eyes and provides good visibility underwater.

hood
Synthetic rubber cap that covers the head and neck to protect them against the cold.

snorkel
Rigid or flexible tube that enables the diver to breathe from just under the surface without lifting the head out of the water; it provides a comfortable and efficient position for swimming.

scuba diver
Person who engages in scuba diving; the diver wears diving gear and carries equipment that makes it possible to stay underwater for as long as the air supply lasts.

harness
Piece of equipment with straps and suspenders; the diver uses it to carry one or more cylinders of compressed air on the back.

regulator second stage
Apparatus that changes the pressure of the air coming from the regulator first stage to the pressure of the ambient air; the diver breathes this air in through a mouthpiece.

regulator first stage
Apparatus attached to the cylinder valve that lowers the air pressure coming from the cylinder to an intermediate value (medium pressure).

inflator
Apparatus that inflates the buoyancy compensator; it often includes a mechanical system attached to the regulator as well as a mouthpiece for inflating it manually.

air hose
Flexible tube that connects the regulator first stage to the emergency regulator.

inflator valve
Unit that controls the amount of air entering the buoyancy compensator.

weight belt
Fabric sash worn around the waist; it contains a variable number of weights to compensate for the diver's natural flotation.

mouthpiece
Part for inflating the buoyancy compensator by blowing.

buoyancy compensator
Float device whose volume of air can be increased or decreased at will to stabilize the diver underwater; it can be used to return to the surface and to keep afloat without effort.

purge valve
Device for releasing air from the buoyancy compensator.

emergency regulator
Regulator second stage that is connected by a hose to the regulator first stage; it is used to supply air to a diver in difficulty.

information console
Ergonomic box that houses various measuring devices, which are useful to the diver.

compressed-air cylinder
Device containing air of diminished volume due to pressure; it stores air that can be used by the diver underwater.

thermometer
Instrument for measuring the water's temperature.

knife
Instrument made up of a handle and a cutting blade; it is often serrated for cutting rope, algae and other objects blocking the way.

diving glove
Piece of synthetic rubber that covers the hand and wrist to protect them from the cold and from being hurt by underwater objects, plants and animals.

pressure gauge
Apparatus for measuring the cylinder's air pressure; this indicates to the diver how much air is available.

wet suit
Insulating outfit made out of synthetic rubber; a small amount of water is usually allowed to seep in and assume the diver's body temperature.

depth gauge
Apparatus indicating the diver's depth.

sheath
Usually hard casing that covers and protects a knife.

ankle weight
Weighted band worn around the ankle to offset the diver's natural buoyancy.

fin
Rubber or plastic flipper that is attached to the foot and improves the diver's propulsion in the water.

boot
Synthetic rubber boot that protects the foot and ankle from the cold and from being rubbed by the fin.

foot pocket
Part of the fin that covers the foot; it can be open at the heel and have an adjustable strap or be entirely closed.

rail
Side reinforcement of the fin; it makes the blade stiffer and improves the fin's efficiency.

blade
Thrusting part of the fin that is an extension of the foot pocket; its length and stiffness determine its thrusting power.

strap
Flexible strong belt that attaches the sheath to the diver (usually around the upper leg).

speargun
Weapon that uses pressurized air to launch an arrow at a fish or other marine animal underwater; the arrow is attached to the gun by a rope.

boxing

Sport in which two opponents wearing gloves fight each other with their fists (English boxing) or with their fists and feet (savate or French boxing) following a code of rules.

boxer
Athlete who engages in boxing; boxers are classified into weight categories.

headgear
Rigid piece of equipment that protects the head especially during training and in Olympic boxing.

boxing glove
Padded covering for the hand and wrist to dampen the impact of punching.

boxing trunks
Shorts coming down to mid-thigh.

punching bag
Leather or canvas bag that is filled with sand and weighs about 65 lb; the boxer trains by hitting it powerfully.

speed ball
Inflated leather bag that the boxer hits when training; it helps develop speed and punching coordination.

ring
Square podium that is surrounded by stretched ropes and measures from 18 to 22 ft on the inside of the ropes; the boxing bout takes place on it.

boxer
Athlete who practices boxing; boxers are classified into weight categories.

referee
Official who enforces the rules and directs the fight in the ring; after the bout, this individual collects and checks the judges' scores.

timekeeper
Official who controls the number of breaks and rounds and their duration by ringing a gong or bell, except in the case of a knockout.

rope
Grouping of threads forming a cable 1 to 2 in thick that stretches between posts to delimit the ring.

turnbuckle
Metal part that is covered with padded matting and stretches the ropes around the ring.

corner pad
Padded layer covering the posts to prevent injuries.

ring post
Pole located at the four corners of the ring that supports and stretches the ropes.

trainer
Person who supervises the boxer's training and is present during contests to coach the boxer on strategy.

second
Person who assists a boxer and ministers to him between rounds.

corner stool
Corner seat on which the boxer sits during breaks.

corner
Angle formed by the intersection the ropes; the red and blue corne are reserved for the boxers, the other two are neutral.

ring step
Structural component for acc the ring.

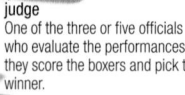

judge
One of the three or five officials who evaluate the performances; they score the boxers and pick the winner.

physician
Person who treats the boxers in the event of injury; a doctor's presence is mandatory and this individual may end a fight in the event of serious injury.

apron
Part of the ring that is outside the ropes; the floor of the ring is about 3 ft high and must extend beyond the ropes by at least 18 in.

canvas
Covering for breaking falls that is made of flexible material and is about .5 in thick; a canvas is stretched on it.

ringside
Area surrounding the ring.

boxing

boxing equipment
Boxers use several types of protective gear to lessen the impact of their opponent's blows.

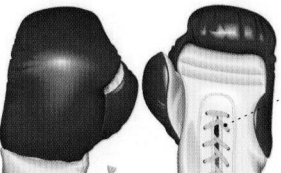

boxing gloves
Padded coverings for the hand and wrist to dampen the impact of punching.

lace
Narrow cord that passes through the glove's eyelets to tighten it around the hand and wrist.

handwrap
Band of soft fabric (gauze) that is wrapped around the hand underneath the glove; it protects the hand against fractures and supports the wrist.

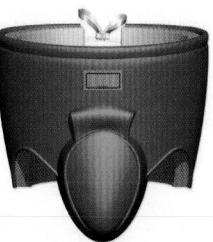

protective cup
Molded plastic equipment that protects an athlete's genitals.

mouthpiece
Protective device for the boxer's teeth that is placed between the cheeks and teeth during a fight.

wrestling

Sport in which two opponents fight bare-handed and seek to pin each other to the floor using various holds.

starting positions
The wrestlers start the bout standing on opposite sides of the white circle; this circle is in the middle of the central wrestling area and is 3.2 ft in diameter.

crouching position (freestyle wrestling)
Freestyle wrestling allows the wrestler to use the entire body; this provides for a larger variety of holds than in Greco-Roman wrestling.

standing position (Greco-Roman wrestling)
In Greco-Roman wrestling, it is forbidden to seize the opponent below the hips and to use one's legs for a hold or to defend oneself.

wrestler
Athlete who engages in wrestling; wrestlers are classified into weight categories.

singlet
Tight-fitting one-piece outfit.

wrestling shoe
Flexible leather boot that covers the ankle; it has no heel and no metal parts.

protection area
Area that is 5 ft wide and surrounds the passivity zone; it provides safety if the wrestler is thrown out of the wrestling area.

wrestling area
Mat with an area of 40 ft² for a wrestling match; a bout has two 3-minute periods with a break of 30 seconds.

wrestler
Athlete who practices wrestling; wrestlers are classified into weight categories.

referee
Official in charge of enforcing the rules who directs the fight on the mat and wears red and blue sleeves to indicate points.

central wrestling area
Circle inside the passivity zone that is 23 ft in diameter; the bout takes place within it.

judge
Official who assigns the points for the technical action as instructed by the referee or the mat chairperson and registers them on the scoreboard.

passivity zone
Red band that is 3.2 ft wide; it delimits and is part of the wrestling surface (30 ft in diameter).

mat chairperson
Official who coordinates the work of the referee and the judge; in the event of disagreement, he settles it. He may also interrupt the bout.

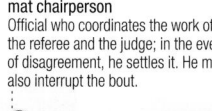

judo

Sport of Japanese origin that is practiced with bare hands and consists of unbalancing the opponent with holds; Judo means "the gentle way".

mat
Surface that measures 46 ft x 52 ft and is used for practicing judo; it is made up of smaller mat squares (tatamis).

contestant
One of two athletes (here, judokas) who confront each other in a bout; contestants are classified into weight categories.

scorers and timekeepers
The scorers show the results on the scoreboards and the timekeepers monitor the time during the bout.

scoreboard
Board that displays various data about the contest taking place (such as points and penalties); there are two scoreboards, one manual and one electronic, in each contest area.

medical team
Physicians tend to the judo the event of injury; their pres mandatory and they may end in the event of serious inj

safety area
Surface that is 10 ft wide and surrounds the danger area; it provides safety if the contestant if thrown out of the contest area.

contest area
Area on which the bout takes place; it includes the danger area, measures 26 x 33 ft and has lines to indicate the positions of the judokas at the start and end of the bout.

referee
Official who enforces the rules and directs the bout on the mat; this individual is assisted by the two judges.

danger area
Red band that is 3.2 ft wide delimits and is part of the co area.

judge
One of the two officials who assist the referee; they check especially that the holds are allowable and take place within the bounds of the contest area.

judogi
Clothing worn when practicing judo that is made of cotton or a similar fabric; one judoka wears a white judogi while the other wears a blue one.

jacket
Clothing with wide sleeves that covers the chest and part of the hips; women wear a white bodysuit or jerkin under the jacket.

examples of holds and throws
There are more than 40 holds in judo: floor grips (strangles, locks, holdings) and standing throws (shoulders, arms, hips, legs).

belt
Band of fabric about 10 ft long that is wrapped twice around the waist and whose color indicates the judoka's level.

trousers
Garment for the lower body; it extends from the waist or the hips to the ankles, covering each leg separately.

holding
The assailant uses pressure on the shoulders to pin the opponent to the floor.

stomach throw
The assailant pulls the opponent forward and puts a foot on the his stomach, causing the opponent to be thrown over the assailant's shoulder.

sweeping hip throw
The assailant pushes the opponent's leg, causing the opponent's torso to rotate and flip over the assailant's hip.

major outer reaping throw
Using the right leg, the assailant sweeps up the opponent's left leg from behind, causing the opponent to fall backward.

major inner reaping thro
Using the right leg, the assailant sweeps up the opponent's right leg from the front, causing the opponent to fall backwar

naked strangle
From behind, the assailant's arm puts pressure on the opponent's neck, constricting breathing or cutting off the flow of blood and oxygen to the brain.

arm lock
To force submission, the assailant exerts pressure on the opponent's elbow joint against its natural bending direction.

one-arm shoulder thro
Placing the forearms under the opponent's armpits, the assailant lifts th opponent over his back, propelling the opponent forwar

karate

Self-defense sport of Japanese origin that is practiced with bare hands; the blows, which are usually given with the hands and the feet, must stop before reaching the opponent's body.

karateka
Athlete who engages in karate; some, but not all, organizations classify karatekas by weight.

karate-gi
Clothing worn when practicing karate; it includes a jacket and pants that are usually made of cotton.

contest area
Mat with an area of 26 ft^2 on which the bout takes place; it is surrounded by a safety surface.

referee's line
Mark designating the regulation position of the referee during the bout.

obi
Long wide belt that is tied around the waist to close the jacket; its color indicates the contestant's level.

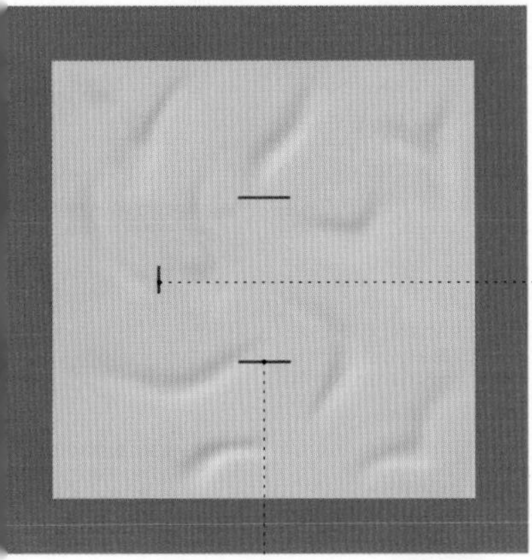

competitors' line
Mark designating the karatekas' position at the start of the bout and after any interruption.

competition area
Surface for practicing karate; bouts last a maximum of three minutes.

arbitration committee
Group of upper-level officials who especially supervise the bout as it unfolds and check that the referee and the judges perform their duties correctly.

corner judge
One of the four officials who assist the referee, give their opinions especially about the referee's decisions and judge the actions of the karatekas.

scorekeeper
Official who tracks the karatekas' points and penalties.

timekeeper
Official who monitors the duration of the bout.

referee
Official who enforces the rules, directs the bout on the mat, awards the points and gives out warnings and penalties.

karateka
Athlete who practices karate; some, but not all, organizations classify karatekas by weight.

SPORTS AND GAMES

taekwondo

Self-defense sport of Korean origin practiced with bare hands; contestants score points based on their ability to strike target zones on their opponent's body during a bout.

competition area
Surface designed for taekwondo. Bouts are divided into three rounds of three minutes each.

dobok
Clothing worn when practicing taekwondo, consisting of a long, loose jacket and pair of pants, usually made of cotton.

timekeeper
Official who monitors the duration of the bout.

recorder
Official who registers the contestants' points and penalties, as indicated by the judges.

medical team
Physicians tend to the contestants in the event of injury; their presence is mandatory and they may end a bout in the event of serious injury.

contestant
One of two athletes who confront each other in a bout; contestants are classified into weight categories.

corner judge
One of three officials who scores contestant performance.

contest area
Square floor mat with 26.25-ft sides on which a bout takes place.

center referee
Official who enforces the rules and directs the bout on the mat; this individual is assisted by the three judges.

alert area
Floor surface surrounding the contest area, designed to protect contestants who fall out of bounds.

boundary line
Line that delimits the boundaries of the contest area.

taekwondo equipment
Due to the roughness of the moves and the frequency of takedowns, combatants must wear heavy protection.

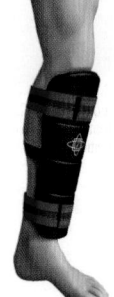

head guard
Hard piece of equipment designed to protect the head.

forearm guard
Padded piece of equipment designed to protect the forearm.

male groin protector
Piece of equipment that consists of rigid molded plastic designed to cover a contestant's genital organs.

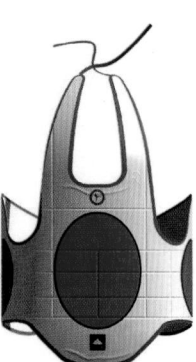

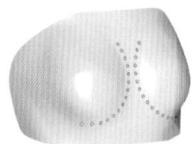
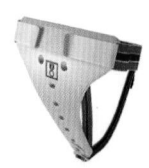

chest protector
Heavily padded vest that protects the contestant's chest.

belt
Band of fabric that is wrapped around the waist and whose color indicates the contestant's level.

breast guard
Rigid piece of equipment designed to protect a female contestant's breasts.

shin guard
Piece of equipment that consists of hard molded plastic to protect the contestant's legs.

female groin protector
Stiff, plastic piece of equipment designed to protect a female contestant's groin area.

techniques
Contestants must be able to attack their opponents and defend themselves while on the ground or in the air. Most strikes are delivered by foot.

front kick
The attacker prepares to perform a kick to the ribs; relaxed movement and rotation of the hips make for maximum force. The defender begins to jump away.

stance
A state of readiness allowing the contestant to deliver or deflect a strike. Rapid movement helps reduce the surface area that can be struck by an opponent.

extension
By jumping, the defender moves out of striking range.

block
Move used to deflect a kick. An effective dodge can reduce the force of an attack by almost 75%.

flying side kick
The defender attempts a flying side kick. The force of this move is greatest when leg is extended.

kendo

Sport of Japanese origin that is a form of fencing; the opponents wear protection and fight with a bamboo saber.

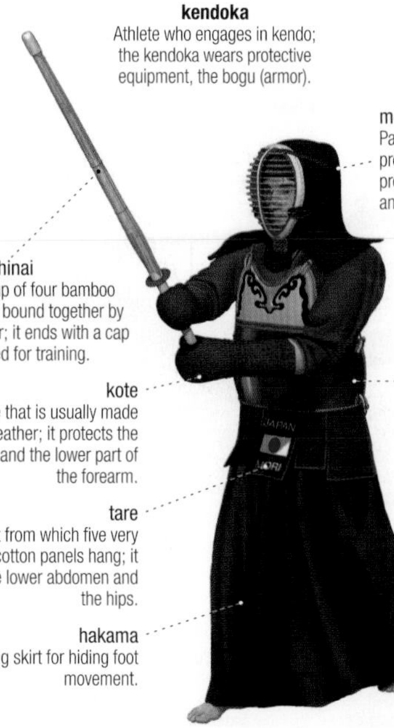

kendoka
Athlete who engages in kendo; the kendoka wears protective equipment, the bogu (armor).

men
Padded helmet with a steel grate that protects the head and face; it also provides protection for the shoulders and throat.

shinai
made up of four bamboo that are bound together by leather; it ends with a cap d is used for training.

kote
k glove that is usually made n and leather; it protects the e wrist and the lower part of the forearm.

do
Breastplate that is usually made from bamboo blades covered with leather; it protects the front and sides of the torso.

tare
ick belt from which five very thick cotton panels hang; it ects the lower abdomen and the hips.

hakama
Long skirt for hiding foot movement.

kote-uchi
Strike to the wrist, moving vertically down along the central axis of the body.

men-uchi
Strike to the forehead. The force of the movement begins in the left ankle, thrusting the attacker's body forward.

do-uchi
Strike delivered to the right side at a 45° angle. The symbolic goal is to cut one's opponent in two.

tsuki-uchi
Strike to the throat. The strike is made with the tip of the shinai in a lunging movement with the entire body.

techniques
An attack is performed simultaneously with the body, the shinai and a shout (kiai). When striking, the attacker shouts the name of the body part targeted.

chief referee
Official who enforces the rules, directs the bout and awards the points and penalties to the contestants.

scorekeepers
One of two officials who register the contestants' points and penalties, as given by the referee.

competition area
Smooth wooden floor on which the kendo bout takes place; a bout usually lasts five minutes.

assistant referee
One of two officials who assist the chief referee and are involved in scoring the contestants, using flags.

timekeeper
Official who monitors the duration of the bout.

danger zone
hat is 5 ft wide and delimits the contest area.

competitors' line
Mark that designates the competitors' positions at the start of the bout.

center
Cross that indicates the center of the contest area.

sumo

Japanese wrestling that is linked to Shintoism; it is practiced by very large corpulent wrestlers who try to make the opponent touch the ground or throw him out of the contest area.

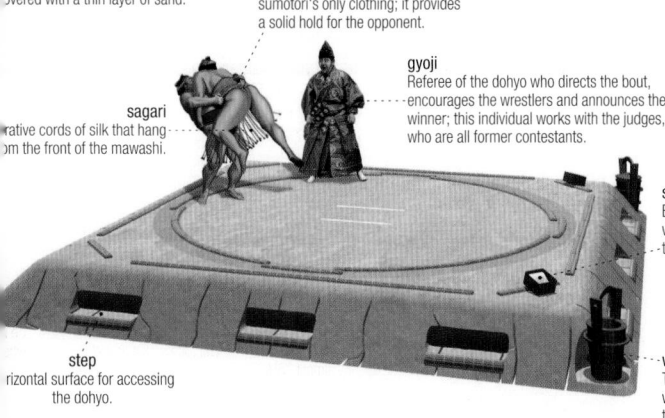

ohyo
ound combat area that is 15 ft in ameter; it consists of packed clay overed with a thin layer of sand.

mawashi
Silk belt about 33 ft long that is the sumotori's only clothing; it provides a solid hold for the opponent.

sagari
rative cords of silk that hang om the front of the mawashi.

gyoji
Referee of the dohyo who directs the bout, encourages the wrestlers and announces the winner; this individual works with the judges, who are all former contestants.

salt
Before the start of the bout, the wrestlers toss a handful of salt on the dohyo, a Shinto purification rite.

step
rizontal surface for accessing the dohyo.

water
The wrestlers rinse their mouths with purifying water before starting the bout.

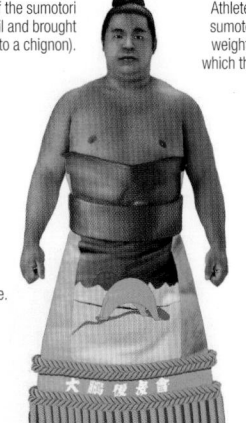

mage
Traditional hairstyle of the sumotori (hair slicked with oil and brought forward into a chignon).

sumotori
Athlete who engages in sumo; sumotoris are not classified by weight but into levels, through which they ascend by winning a series of victories.

kung fu

One of several types of sport of Chinese origin practiced with or without weapons; it is similar to karate but requires more legwork.

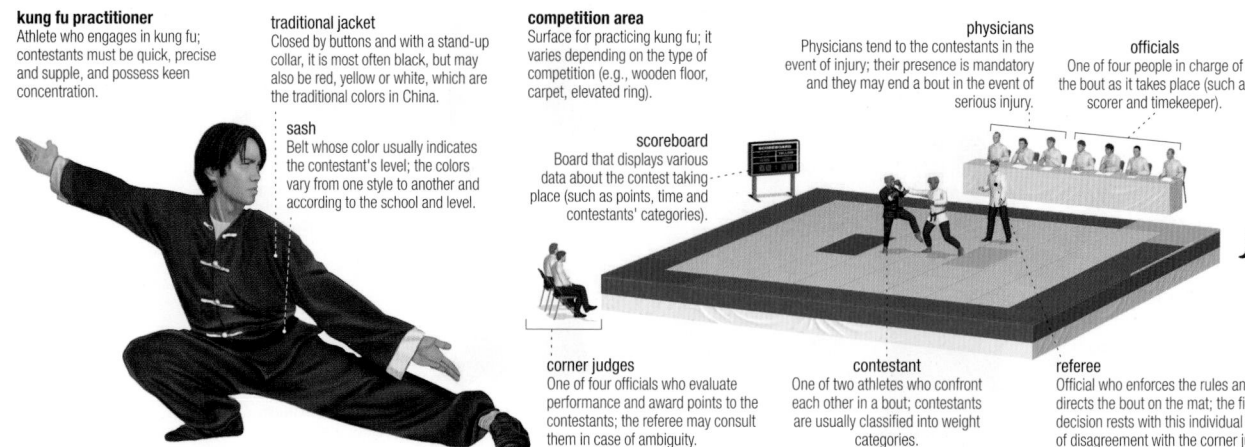

kung fu practitioner
Athlete who engages in kung fu; contestants must be quick, precise and supple, and possess keen concentration.

traditional jacket
Closed by buttons and with a stand-up collar, it is most often black, but may also be red, yellow or white, which are the traditional colors in China.

sash
Belt whose color usually indicates the contestant's level; the colors vary from one style to another and according to the school and level.

competition area
Surface for practicing kung fu; it varies depending on the type of competition (e.g., wooden floor, carpet, elevated ring).

scoreboard
Board that displays various data about the contest taking place (such as points, time and contestants' categories).

physicians
Physicians tend to the contestants in the event of injury; their presence is mandatory and they may end a bout in the event of serious injury.

officials
One of four people in charge of the bout as it takes place (such as scorer and timekeeper).

corner judges
One of four officials who evaluate performance and award points to the contestants; the referee may consult them in case of ambiguity.

contestant
One of two athletes who confront each other in a bout; contestants are usually classified into weight categories.

referee
Official who enforces the rules and directs the bout on the mat; the fir decision rests with this individual i of disagreement with the corner ju

jujitsu

Sport of Japanese origin based on throws, holds and blows to vital points of the body; it gave rise to judo.

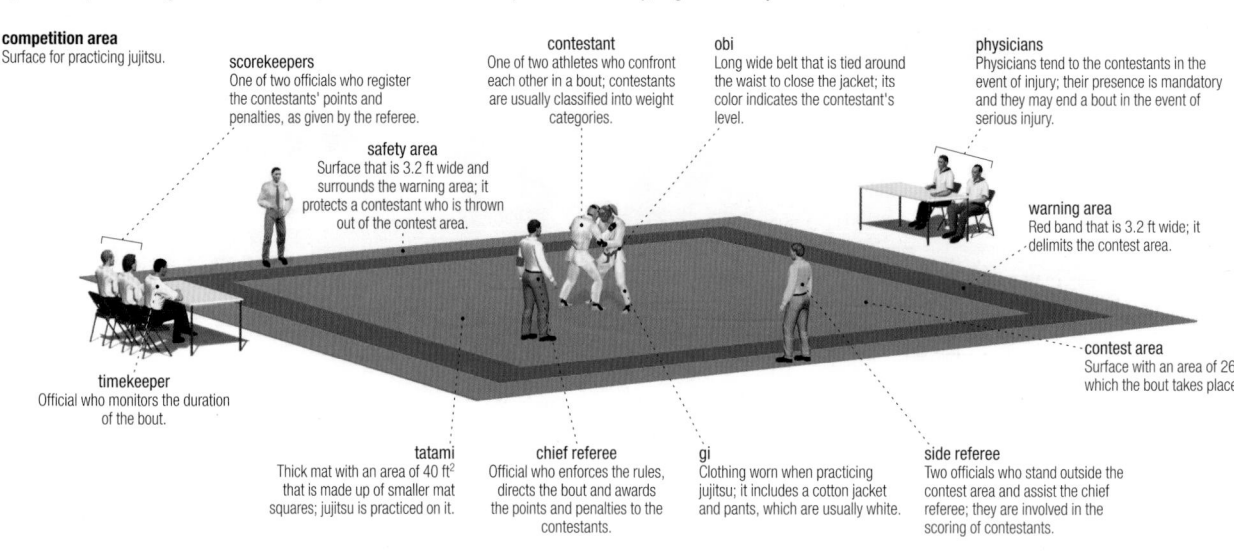

competition area
Surface for practicing jujitsu.

scorekeepers
One of two officials who register the contestants' points and penalties, as given by the referee.

contestant
One of two athletes who confront each other in a bout; contestants are usually classified into weight categories.

obi
Long wide belt that is tied around the waist to close the jacket; its color indicates the contestant's level.

physicians
Physicians tend to the contestants in the event of injury; their presence is mandatory and they may end a bout in the event of serious injury.

safety area
Surface that is 3.2 ft wide and surrounds the warning area; it protects a contestant who is thrown out of the contest area.

warning area
Red band that is 3.2 ft wide; it delimits the contest area.

timekeeper
Official who monitors the duration of the bout.

contest area
Surface with an area of 26 which the bout takes place

tatami
Thick mat with an area of 40 ft² that is made up of smaller mat squares; jujitsu is practiced on it.

chief referee
Official who enforces the rules, directs the bout and awards the points and penalties to the contestants.

gi
Clothing worn when practicing jujitsu; it includes a cotton jacket and pants, which are usually white.

side referee
Two officials who stand outside the contest area and assist the chief referee; they are involved in the scoring of contestants.

aikido

Defensive sport of Japanese origin that consists of neutralizing an armed or unarmed opponent by means of dodging, throwing and holding, using bare hands.

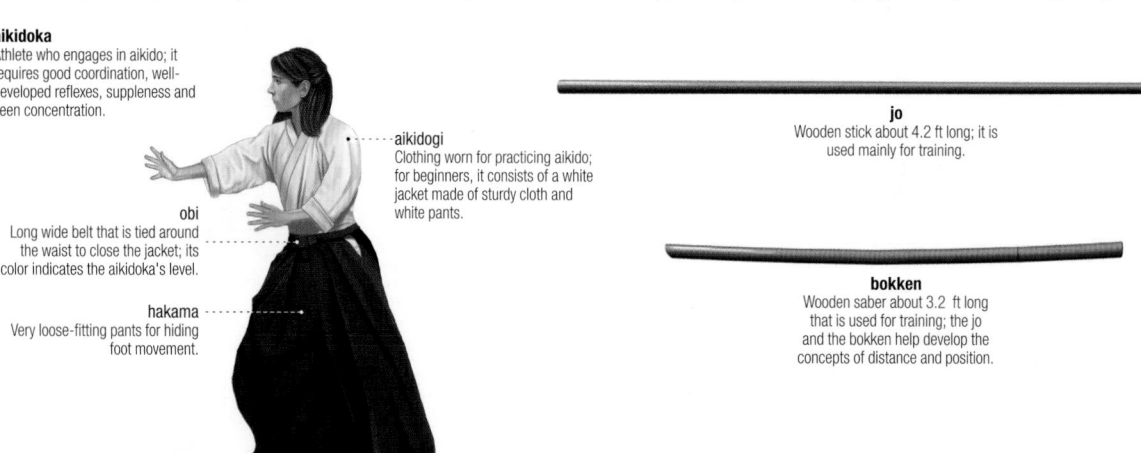

aikidoka
Athlete who engages in aikido; it requires good coordination, well-developed reflexes, suppleness and keen concentration.

obi
Long wide belt that is tied around the waist to close the jacket; its color indicates the aikidoka's level.

aikidogi
Clothing worn for practicing aikido; for beginners, it consists of a white jacket made of sturdy cloth and white pants.

hakama
Very loose-fitting pants for hiding foot movement.

jo
Wooden stick about 4.2 ft long; it is used mainly for training.

bokken
Wooden saber about 3.2 ft long that is used for training; the jo and the bokken help develop the concepts of distance and position.

fencing

Sport with two opponents who attempt to touch each other with weapons (épée, foil or saber) on a specific part of the body.

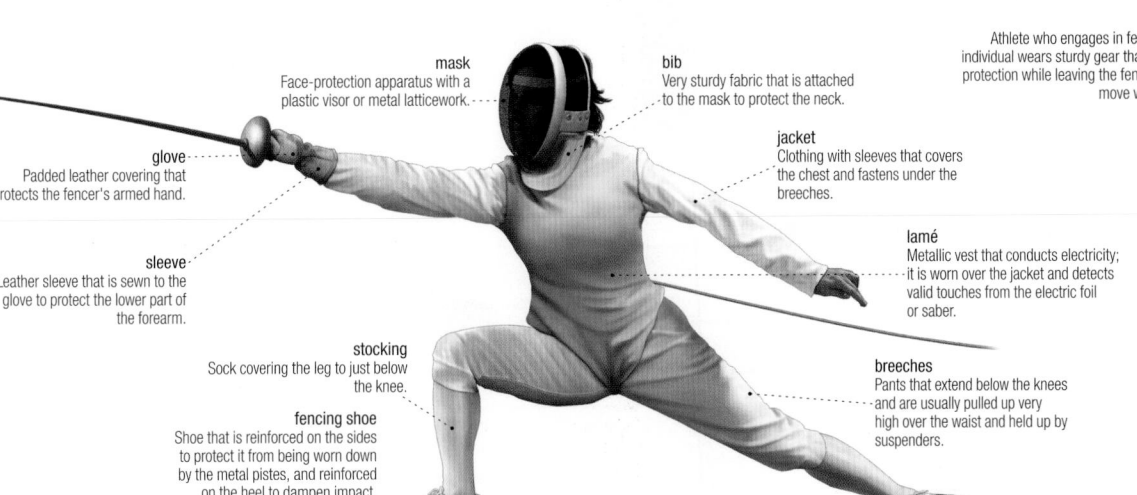

fencer
Athlete who engages in fencing; this individual wears sturdy gear that provides protection while leaving the fencer free to move with agility.

mask
Face-protection apparatus with a plastic visor or metal latticework.

bib
Very sturdy fabric that is attached to the mask to protect the neck.

jacket
Clothing with sleeves that covers the chest and fastens under the breeches.

glove
Padded leather covering that protects the fencer's armed hand.

lamé
Metallic vest that conducts electricity; it is worn over the jacket and detects valid touches from the electric foil or saber.

sleeve
Leather sleeve that is sewn to the glove to protect the lower part of the forearm.

stocking
Sock covering the leg to just below the knee.

breeches
Pants that extend below the knees and are usually pulled up very high over the waist and held up by suspenders.

fencing shoe
Shoe that is reinforced on the sides to protect it from being worn down by the metal pistes, and reinforced on the heel to dampen impact.

target areas

Depending on the weapon used, the fencer may touch different parts of an opponent's body to score points.

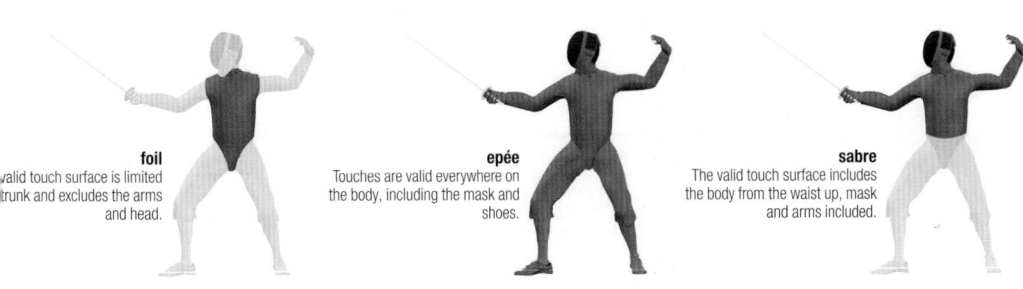

foil
valid touch surface is limited trunk and excludes the arms and head.

epée
Touches are valid everywhere on the body, including the mask and shoes.

sabre
The valid touch surface includes the body from the waist up, mask and arms included.

fencing piste

Area on which the match takes place; it is 46 ft long and between 5 and 6.5 ft wide.

timekeeper
Official who monitors the duration of the match; a single match is made up of three manches (sets) of three minutes, with a one-minute break between each manche.

electric foil
Its end contains an electric button that senses hits; a hit is registered only when the pressure on the tip of the blade is greater than 1.1 lb (maximum weight of the foil).

foil warning line
Line 3.2 ft from the rear limit line warning the foilist that the end of the piste is near.

scoring light
Light that switches on to signal valid hits (red and green lights) and nonvalid hits (white lights).

electrical scoring apparatus
Electrical apparatus for registering the fencers' hits by means of a body wire.

reel
Device that keeps the body wire under constant tension by following the forward and backward movements of the fencer.

judge
Each of the officials who assist the president; they stand beside the piste and especially check the validity of the hits.

on-guard line
Line 6.5 ft from the center line; the fencer must stay behind it to start and when resuming combat after a valid hit.

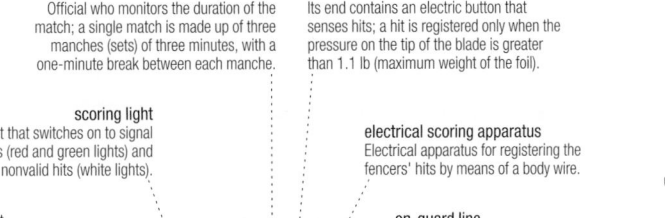

body wire
Insulated electric wire that runs through the fencer's equipment and connects the weapon to the electrical scoring apparatus by means of the reel.

rear limit line
Line 23 ft from the center line that indicates that the fencer is outside the piste; when a fencer passes this line, a hit is awarded to the opponent.

scorer
Official who registers the fencers' hits and penalties.

president
Official who enforces the rules and is especially in charge of conducting the match and controlling the scoring apparatus.

saber and épée warning line
Line 6.5 ft from the rear limit line to warn the épéeist and the sabreur that they are near the end of the piste.

center line
Line that divides the piste into two equal parts, one for each fencer.

fencing

positions
Way of holding the weapon to wield or parry a hit, depending on the direction of the tip (button); the positions are the opposite for right-handed people.

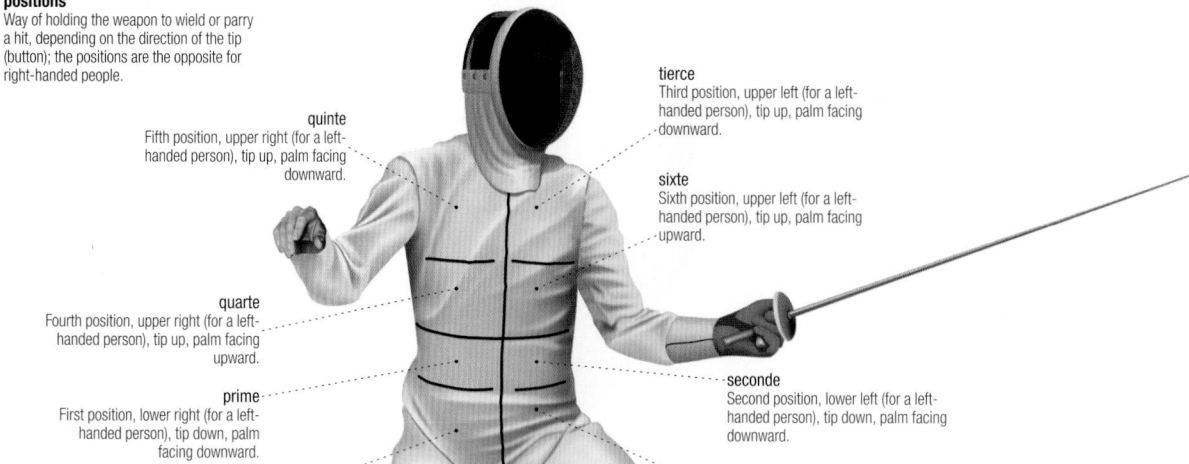

quinte
Fifth position, upper right (for a left-handed person), tip up, palm facing downward.

tierce
Third position, upper left (for a left-handed person), tip up, palm facing downward.

sixte
Sixth position, upper left (for a left-handed person), tip up, palm facing upward.

quarte
Fourth position, upper right (for a left-handed person), tip up, palm facing upward.

prime
First position, lower right (for a left-handed person), tip down, palm facing downward.

septime
Seventh position, lower right (for a left-handed person), tip down, palm facing upward.

seconde
Second position, lower left (for a left-handed person), tip down, palm facing downward.

octave
Eighth position, lower left (for a left-handed person), tip down, palm facing upward.

---

fencing weapons
In the Olympic Games, the foil, the épée and the saber are used by both men and women.

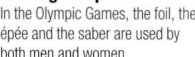

foil
Lightweight thrusting weapon (maximum weight of 1.1 lb) with a flexible blade whose cross section is square or rectangular.

épée
Thrusting weapon with a tapered blade whose cross section is a triangle; it is more rigid and heavier than a foil, weighing up to 1.7 lb.

saber
Thrusting, cutting and slicing weapon whose blade is usually curved and sharp on one side only; its maximum weight is 1.1 lb, the same as that of the foil.

parts of the weapon
Weapons can be thrusting (touch made with the tip of the blade), cutting (with the blade) or slicing (with the back edge).

pommel
Metal knob at the end of the handle to balance the weapon.

hilt
Part of the weapon to which the blade is attached.

blade
Hitting part of the weapon; measuring about 3 feet, it is made of flexible metal and is thin and tapered.

button
Bulbous end of the blade; with electric weapons, the button triggers the switch of the electric apparatus when it makes a valid touch.

grip
Wood, metal or plastic part for holding and wielding the weapon.

guard
Metal rounded part that protects the armed hand during a match.

forte
Thickest part of the blade, near the guard.

medium
Part of the blade between the forte and the foible.

foible
Thinnest part of the blade, up to its end.

weightlifting

Sport that consists of lifting the heaviest load possible (barbell) over the head using two types of lifts (clean and jerk; snatch).

barbell
Gym equipment made up of disks of various weights attached in equal weights to each end of a long bar, which is lifted with two hands.

weightlifter
An athlete who practices weightlifting.

wristband
Band of fabric that is 4 in wide or less and is worn around the wrist to support it when lifting.

weightlifting belt
Girdle that is 5 in wide or less and supports the dorsal and abdominal muscles during lifting.

sleeveless jersey
Tight top that covers the torso while leaving the shoulders free; a T-shirt may be worn under the jersey.

trunks
Tight shorts that end above the knees.

knee wrap
Band of fabric 1 ft wide or less that is worn around the knee to support it when lifting.

weightlifting shoe
Shoe with an antiskid sole and raised heel that stabilizes the foot during lifting.

strap
Adjustable band for tightening the shoe around the foot.

clean and jerk
Type of lift that is executed in two stages; the bar is first raised to shoulder level (clean) and then quickly raised over the head (jerk), using the leg muscles.

snatch
Type of lift that is more difficult than the clean and jerk; it consists of raising the load over the head as high as possible in a continuous quick movement.

competition area
Weightlifting competitions are held on an elevated platform. Weightlifters announce their starting lift, which they then must complete successfully within three attempts.

platform
Slip-resistant platform on which the weightlifter competes.

weightlifter
An athlete who practices weightlifting. Weightlifters are divided into weight divisions.

magnesium powder
White magnesium-based powder that absorbs sweat from the hands; this provides a surer grip on the bar.

scoreboard
Board that displays data during the competition, such as the athlete's name and nationality, and the amount of weight being lifted.

loaders
Individuals responsible for changing the weights on the barbell.

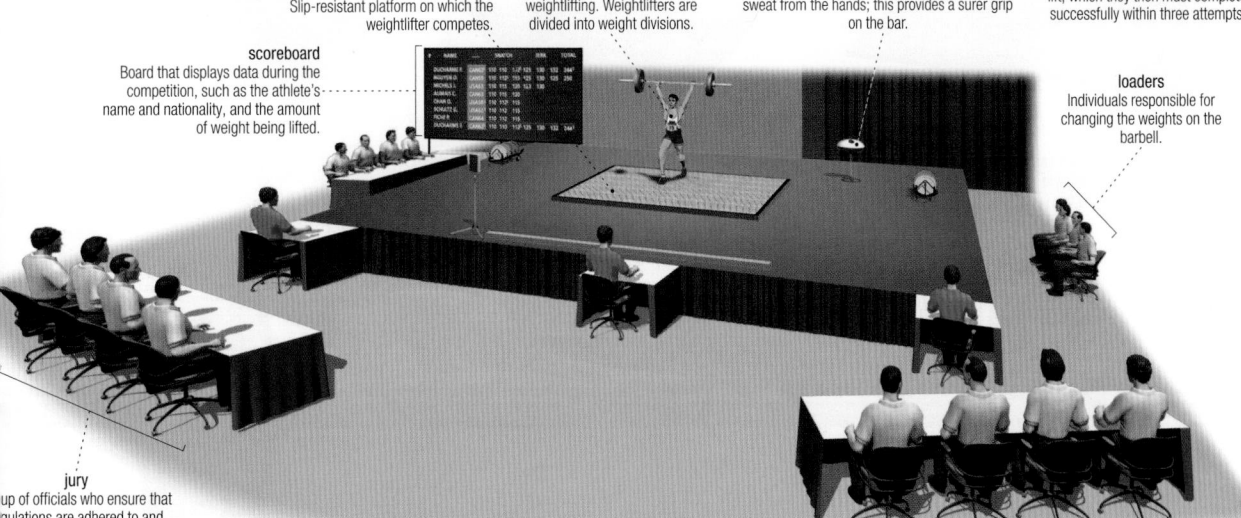

jury
up of officials who ensure that gulations are adhered to and rvise the judges. They have the ority to void a judge's decision concerning lift attempts.

SPORTS AND GAMES

fitness equipment

Material and apparatuses for carrying out exercises aimed at maintaining the physique and increasing muscular strength, flexibility and endurance.

dumbbell
Gym equipment that consists of two equal weights attached to each end of a short bar, which is lifted with one hand to develop mainly the arm muscles.

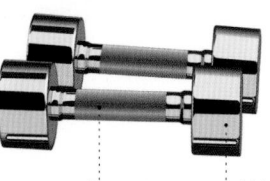

handgrips
Apparatus with two handles connected by a spring; it is gripped with the hand to strengthen mainly the hand, wrist and forearm muscles.

ankle/wrist weight
Wide flexible band of preset mass that is worn around the wrist or ankle to increase resistance during exercise.

jump rope
Cord with handles that is repeatedly swung over the head then jumped over; the athlete jumps once per cycle to strengthen mainly the leg and buttock muscles.

bar
Metal shaft that connects two weights; the athlete grips it to manipulate the weights.

weight
Round metal mass of various weights and sizes that is attached to each end of the bar.

chest expander
Apparatus with springs connected to two handles; it is stretched with the hands to develop the muscles in the upper torso and the arms.

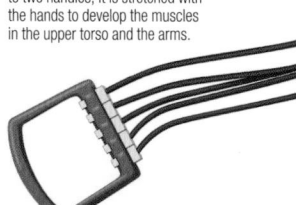

twist bar
Bar consisting of a tension spring and two grips; the athlete bends it to strengthen the upper part of the body (such as the arms and shoulders).

tension spring
Metal elastic part that bends from the force the athlete exerts on its ends; it then returns to its original shape.

grip
Part by which the athlete holds twist bar.

exercise ball
Air-filled rubber (natural or synthetic) ball, used to perform conditioning exercises to improve flexibility, balance and strength in certain muscle groups.

exercise mat
Small mat used for floor exercises, such as sit-ups, or to practice yoga, etc.

aerobics step
Small bench mainly used to facilitate a variety of aerobic movements.

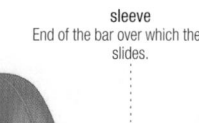

barbell
Gym equipment made up of cast-iron disks of various weights attached in equal weights to each end of a long bar, which is lifted with two hands.

disk
Cylindrical mass covered with rubber that is attached to the bar; the disks vary in weight from 0.5 to 55 lb.

collar
Metal part that is clamped around the bar on both sides of the disk to keep it in place.

sleeve
End of the bar over which the collar slides.

bar
Metal pole linking two disks that the athlete grips to raise the barbell; it has ridges to provide a solid grip.

fitness equipment

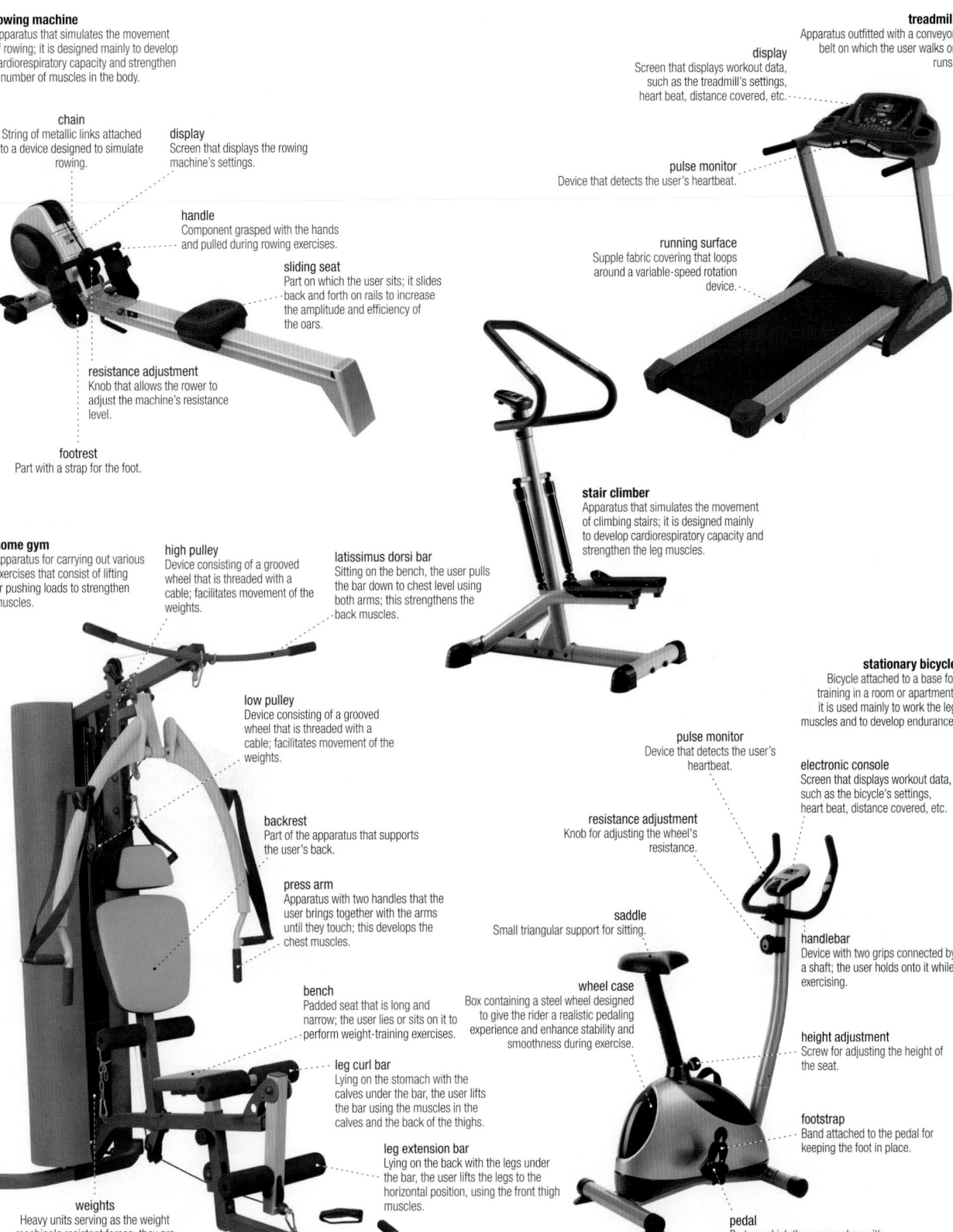

rowing machine
Apparatus that simulates the movement of rowing; it is designed mainly to develop cardiorespiratory capacity and strengthen a number of muscles in the body.

chain
String of metallic links attached to a device designed to simulate rowing.

display
Screen that displays the rowing machine's settings.

handle
Component grasped with the hands and pulled during rowing exercises.

sliding seat
Part on which the user sits; it slides back and forth on rails to increase the amplitude and efficiency of the oars.

resistance adjustment
Knob that allows the rower to adjust the machine's resistance level.

footrest
Part with a strap for the foot.

treadmill
Apparatus outfitted with a conveyor belt on which the user walks or runs.

display
Screen that displays workout data, such as the treadmill's settings, heart beat, distance covered, etc.

pulse monitor
Device that detects the user's heartbeat.

running surface
Supple fabric covering that loops around a variable-speed rotation device.

stair climber
Apparatus that simulates the movement of climbing stairs; it is designed mainly to develop cardiorespiratory capacity and strengthen the leg muscles.

home gym
Apparatus for carrying out various exercises that consist of lifting or pushing loads to strengthen muscles.

high pulley
Device consisting of a grooved wheel that is threaded with a cable; facilitates movement of the weights.

latissimus dorsi bar
Sitting on the bench, the user pulls the bar down to chest level using both arms; this strengthens the back muscles.

low pulley
Device consisting of a grooved wheel that is threaded with a cable; facilitates movement of the weights.

backrest
Part of the apparatus that supports the user's back.

press arm
Apparatus with two handles that the user brings together with the arms until they touch; this develops the chest muscles.

bench
Padded seat that is long and narrow; the user lies or sits on it to perform weight-training exercises.

leg curl bar
Lying on the stomach with the calves under the bar, the user lifts the bar using the muscles in the calves and the back of the thighs.

leg extension bar
Lying on the back with the legs under the bar, the user lifts the legs to the horizontal position, using the front thigh muscles.

weights
Heavy units serving as the weight machine's resistant forces; they are regulated by adjusting the height of the weights to be lifted.

stationary bicycle
Bicycle attached to a base for training in a room or apartment; it is used mainly to work the leg muscles and to develop endurance.

pulse monitor
Device that detects the user's heartbeat.

electronic console
Screen that displays workout data, such as the bicycle's settings, heart beat, distance covered, etc.

resistance adjustment
Knob for adjusting the wheel's resistance.

saddle
Small triangular support for sitting.

wheel case
Box containing a steel wheel designed to give the rider a realistic pedaling experience and enhance stability and smoothness during exercise.

handlebar
Device with two grips connected by a shaft; the user holds onto it while exercising.

height adjustment
Screw for adjusting the height of the seat.

footstrap
Band attached to the pedal for keeping the foot in place.

pedal
Part on which the user pushes with the foot to make the flywheel spin.

SPORTS AND GAMES

show jumping

Competition during which a horse and its rider clear a series of different obstacles on a set course as quickly as possible.

obstacles
Elements that the horse and rider must clear during a competition; a penalty is given when the animal upsets one of the movable components of an obstacle.

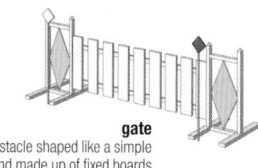

gate
Obstacle shaped like a simple fence and made up of fixed boards laid side by side.

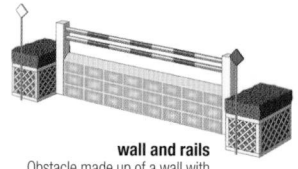

wall and rails
Obstacle made up of a wall with one or two movable bars on top.

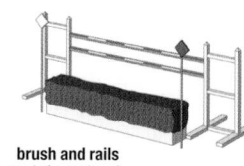

brush and rails
Obstacle composed of a section of brush topped by one or two rails.

post and plank
Obstacle composed of wide movable boards (planks) that are laid one on top of another; planks are less stable than bars.

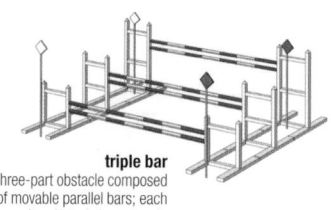

triple bar
Three-part obstacle composed of movable parallel bars; each successive obstacle increases in height.

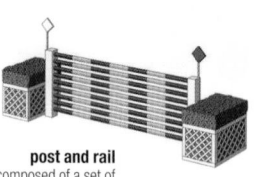

post and rail
Obstacle composed of a set of movable bars that are laid one on top of another.

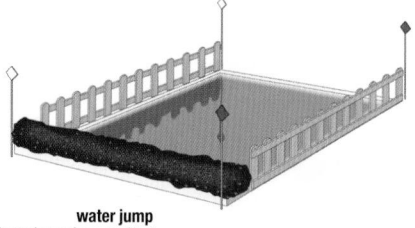

water jump
Obstacle made up of a water-filled ditch with a hedge in front; the horse commits a fault if it touches the water or the lath marking the end of the river.

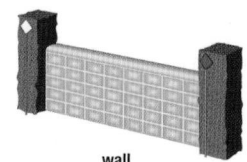

wall
Obstacle composed of a set of usually wooden, stacking blocks; the top of the wall is rounded to prevent the horses from being hurt.

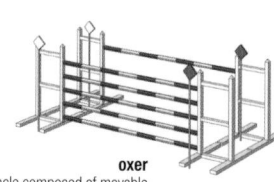

oxer
Two-part obstacle composed of movable parallel bars; there are two designs, one of identical heights (square oxer) and one of different heights (jumping oxer).

competition ring
Closed terrain marked with 12 to 15 obstacles that the horse and rider must clear in a set order while committing the fewest faults possible.

obstacle steward
Person in charge of righting the upset obstacles.

wall
Obstacle composed of a set of usually wooden, stacking blocks; the top of the wall is rounded to prevent the horses from being hurt.

post and plank
Obstacle composed of wide movable boards (planks) that are laid one on top of another; planks are less stable than bars.

combination
Set of two or more obstacles that are grouped together and count as a single obstacle; each of its obstacles must be cleared separately.

veterinarians
Doctors who treat animals; they examine the horses before the competition and may intervene in the event of injury.

course

finish

start

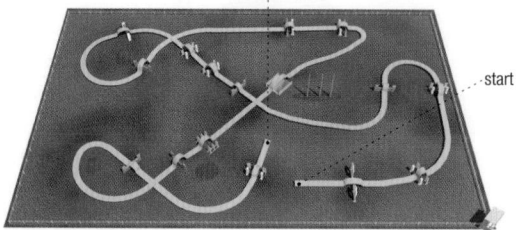

show jumping

riding cap
Reinforced hat that is traditionally covered with black velvet; it protects the rider's head against impact.

jodhpurs
Usually light-colored long pants that are very tight over the knees and legs and are kept stretched by foot straps.

rider
Person riding a horse; during a jump, the rider leans toward the horse's neck with the feet supported by the stirrups.

riding jacket
The rider's long dark-colored jacket; it is usually worn over a white shirt and a white tie.

saddle
Somewhat curved unit that is made mostly of leather; it is set on the horse's back for the rider to sit on.

riding glove
Covering for the hand and wrist that takes the shape of the fingers; it provides a good grip on the reins and protects the hands from chafing.

saddle pad
Padded part that is placed under the saddle to protect the horse's back from chafing; it also protects the saddle from the horse's sweat.

riding crop
Thin flexible stick that the rider uses to spur on the horse.

stirrup iron
Metal ring that hangs from each side of the saddle to support the rider's feet.

breastplate
Strap around the horse's chest that prevents the saddle from sliding back.

shin boot
Equipment placed around the cannon of the horse's leg to protect it from injury.

girth
Strap around the horse's belly that keeps the saddle on its back.

coronet boot
Usually rubber item of equipment that covers the horse's hoof to prevent injury.

water jump
Obstacle made up of a water-filled ditch with a hedge in front; the horse commits a fault if it touches the water or the lath marking the end of the river.

course steward
Official in charge of enforcing the rules and of the layout of the course; during the competition, the steward also controls who enters and exits the track.

oxer
Two-part obstacle composed of movable parallel bars; there are two designs, one of identical heights (square oxer) and one of different heights (jumping oxer).

first aid team
Medical staff who are ready to act in the event of injury to a rider.

jury
Jump judges (usually four) who calculate the competitors' penalties based on the course and the marking system chosen.

double
Obstacle composed of two single components that are very close together; the horse must clear it in a single jump.

riding

Sport or recreation that consists of riding a horse; specialized equipment is necessary for steering and controlling the horse.

double bridle

Head harness that enables the rider to steer a horse by using one or two bits in the horse's mouth, which are connected to the reins.

crownpiece
Strap that runs over the horse's head behind the ears; it keeps the snaffle and cheek straps in place.

browband
Strap that runs around the front of the horse's head; it prevents the bridle from sliding backward.

snaffle strap
Strap that runs along the horse's cheek and connects the crownpiece to the snaffle bit; it keeps the bit in the desired place in the horse's mouth.

cheek strap
Strap that runs along the horse's cheek and connects the crownpiece to the curb bit; it keeps the bit in the desired place in the horse's mouth.

throat latch
Strap that runs under the horse's throat to prevent the bridle from sliding forward; it must be loose enough to allow the horse to breathe freely.

noseband
Part of the bridle that runs around the head above the nostrils; it prevents the horse from opening its mouth and losing the bit.

snaffle rein
Strap that the rider holds to control the snaffle bit and thus steer the horse.

curb bit
Bit composed of a mouth and two side bars; it lowers the horse's nose.

curb rein
Strap that the rider holds to control the curb bit and thus steer the horse.

snaffle bit
Bit composed of a mouth and two side rings; it lifts the horse's head.

curb chain
Metal chain that hangs from the cheek rings and passes under the horse's jaw to secure the bit.

snaffle bits

Bits composed of a mouth and two side rings; they lift the horse's head and are used only in combination with a curb bit.

snaffle bit parts

jointed mouthpiece
Part composed of two articulated bars that is placed in the horse's mouth; it is controlled by the reins to steer the animal.

full cheek snaffle bit with toggles
Bit whose mouth has toggles, which make the horse relax its jaws.

rein ring
Round part attached to the end of the mouth; the snaffle rein is attached to it.

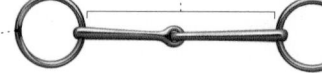

full cheek snaffle bit
Mouth with two side bars preventing the rings from entering the horse's mouth, while relaying clear signals through the reins.

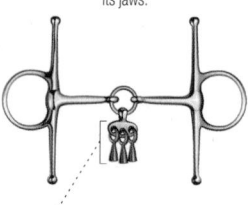

rubber snaffle bit
Bit made up of a straight mouth, which is covered with rubber; it is softer than steel and reduces the pressure of the bit on the horse's mouth.

egg butt snaffle bit
Bit composed of two fixed oval rings; it is designed to prevent injury to the corners of the horse's mouth.

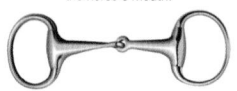

toggles
Metal chains that hang from the middle of the mouth; the horse tends to play with these parts, which makes it relax its jaws.

curb bits

Bits composed of a mouth and two side bars; they lower the horse's nose and are used in conjunction with a snaffle bit.

curb bit parts

sliding cheek bit
Bit whose mouth slides up and down the cheeks; this action is gentler to the horse but provides slightly less control.

port
Curvature of the mouth that is designed to reduce the pressure exerted by the bit on the horse's tongue.

military bit
Bit that can be used alone; it combines the characteristics of snaffle and curb bits.

cheek ring
Round part forming the end of the upper cheek; the curb chain and the cheek strap are attached to it.

curb hook
Part that connects the curb chain to the cheek ring.

purchase
Upper part of the bar that holds the mouth.

lip strap ring
Round part for attaching a false curb chain (strap preventing the horse from seizing the arms of the bit's mouth with its mouth).

jointed mouth Pelham bit
Curb bit whose mouth is composed of two articulated parts; it is gentler to the horse than a straight mouth bit.

curb chain
Metal chain that hangs from the cheek rings and passes under the horse's jaw to secure the bit.

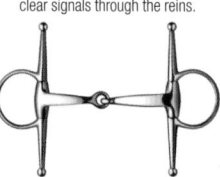

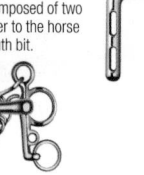

mouthpiece
Metal bar that is placed in the horse's mouth; it is controlled by the reins to steer the animal.

rein ring
Round part that is attached to the end of the lower cheek; the curb rein is attached to it.

shank
Lower part of the bar that holds the mouth; it is usually longer than the upper cheek.

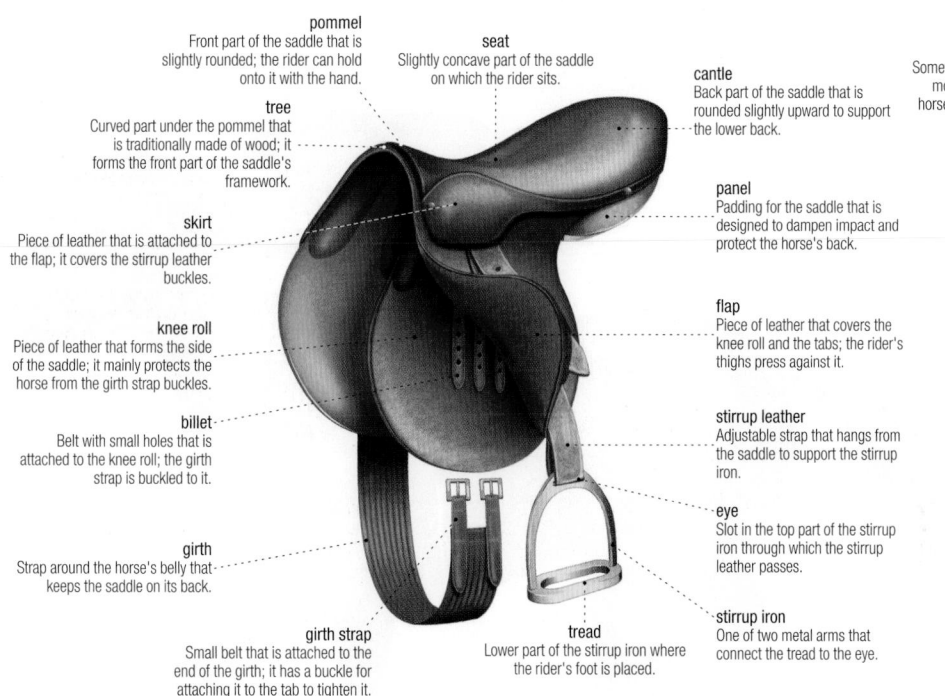

pommel
Front part of the saddle that is slightly rounded; the rider can hold onto it with the hand.

seat
Slightly concave part of the saddle on which the rider sits.

cantle
Back part of the saddle that is rounded slightly upward to support the lower back.

English saddle
Somewhat curved unit that is made mostly of leather; it is set on the horse's back for the rider to sit on.

tree
Curved part under the pommel that is traditionally made of wood; it forms the front part of the saddle's framework.

panel
Padding for the saddle that is designed to dampen impact and protect the horse's back.

skirt
Piece of leather that is attached to the flap; it covers the stirrup leather buckles.

flap
Piece of leather that covers the knee roll and the tabs; the rider's thighs press against it.

knee roll
Piece of leather that forms the side of the saddle; it mainly protects the horse from the girth strap buckles.

stirrup leather
Adjustable strap that hangs from the saddle to support the stirrup iron.

billet
Belt with small holes that is attached to the knee roll; the girth strap is buckled to it.

eye
Slot in the top part of the stirrup iron through which the stirrup leather passes.

girth
Strap around the horse's belly that keeps the saddle on its back.

stirrup iron
One of two metal arms that connect the tread to the eye.

girth strap
Small belt that is attached to the end of the girth; it has a buckle for attaching it to the tab to tighten it.

tread
Lower part of the stirrup iron where the rider's foot is placed.

dressage

Discipline in which a rider takes a horse through a series of freestyle or school figures, called tests, on a ring especially designed for the purpose.

show ring
Flat rectangular grounds where the competitors perform their tests; each routine must be executed in precise time, sometimes to music.

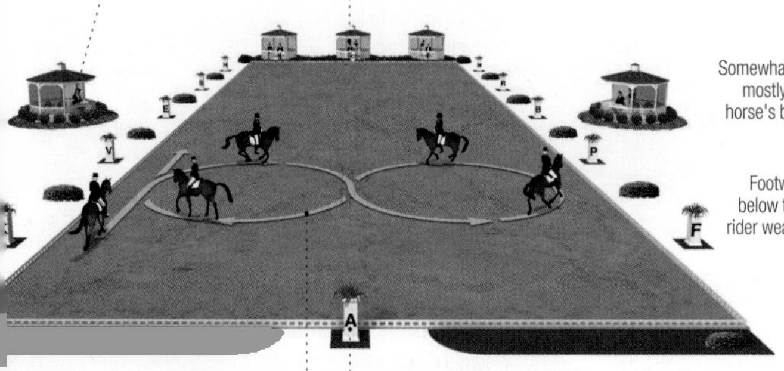

rider
Person who rides a horse; during dressage competitions, the rider's attire and the horse's harness are strictly regulated.

jacket
Long-sleeved coat that is closed in front and often has tails; it is dark in color and is worn over a white shirt and a white tie.

judge
Person in charge of evaluating the performances; five judges (including president) are positioned around the ring and score each figure out of 10.

judge
Person in charge of evaluating the performances; five judges (including a president) are positioned around the ring and score each figure out of 10.

glove
Covering for the hand and wrist that takes the shape of the fingers; white gloves are mandatory in dressage competitions.

saddle
Somewhat curved unit that is made mostly of leather; it is set on the horse's back for the rider to sit on.

boot
Footwear that comes up to just below the knee; in dressage, the rider wears black boots over white pants.

stirrup iron
Metal ring that hangs from each side of the saddle to support the rider's feet.

figure
Set of codified movements recognized by the International Federation for Equestrian Events; a high-level test consists of up to 35 figures to execute from memory.

marker letter
One of several signs placed around the ring at regular intervals; they act as reference points for the rider during the execution of the figures.

girth
Strap around the horse's belly that keeps the saddle on its back.

horse racing

Racetrack-run speed race between horses mounted by jockeys or hitched to sulkies.

mounted racing
Speed race on a track where jockeys ride horses, usually at a gallop.

riding cap
Hard piece of equipment designed to protect the head.

shadow roll
Part that blocks the horse's of the ground; this prevents horse from mistaking shadow obstacles to jump over.

jockey
Person who rides a racehorse; a jockey rides with very short stirrups and the body hunched over the horse's neck.

saddle
Slightly curved part that is usually made of leather; it is laid on the horse's back for the jockey to sit on.

rein
Strap that the jockey holds to control the bit to steer the horse.

saddlecloth
Padded piece of cloth underneath the saddle that protects the horse's back from chafing and protects the saddle from the horse's sweat.

riding crop
Thin flexible stick that the rider uses to spur on the horse.

girth
Strap around the horse's belly that keeps the saddle on its back.

racetrack
Place that is designed for horse races; it is made up of an oval track (flat or with obstacles) and stands.

length post
Markers that are placed at regular intervals along the track so that jockeys can assess the distance still to cover.

judges' stand
Space reserved for the track judges who establish the horses' order of arrival at the finish line, using the video footage if necessary.

far turn
Last turn; the homestretch begins at the exit from it.

tote board
Display board that shows the various data on the race (such as class and betting information); it sometimes has a giant screen.

backstretch
Straight part on the side opposite the stands.

stable
Building where the horses are boarded and cared for.

grandstand
Space reserved for spectators.

homestretch
Straight line between the far turn and the finish line; it constitutes the last sprint before the end of the race.

clubhouse
Building that houses various services such as bar, restaurant, glassed-in stands and betting booths.

starting gate
Mobile, compartmentalized barrier behind which the horses line up before the start; at a signal, all the compartment gates open at the same time.

paddock
Area where the horses and their jockeys are presented to the public before a race.

finish line
Line that marks the end of a race; a video camera helps identify the winner when the horses are bunched very close together.

clubhouse turn
First turn after the start and near the clubhouse; the jockeys try to position their horses on the inside track to reduce the distance to cover.

horse racing

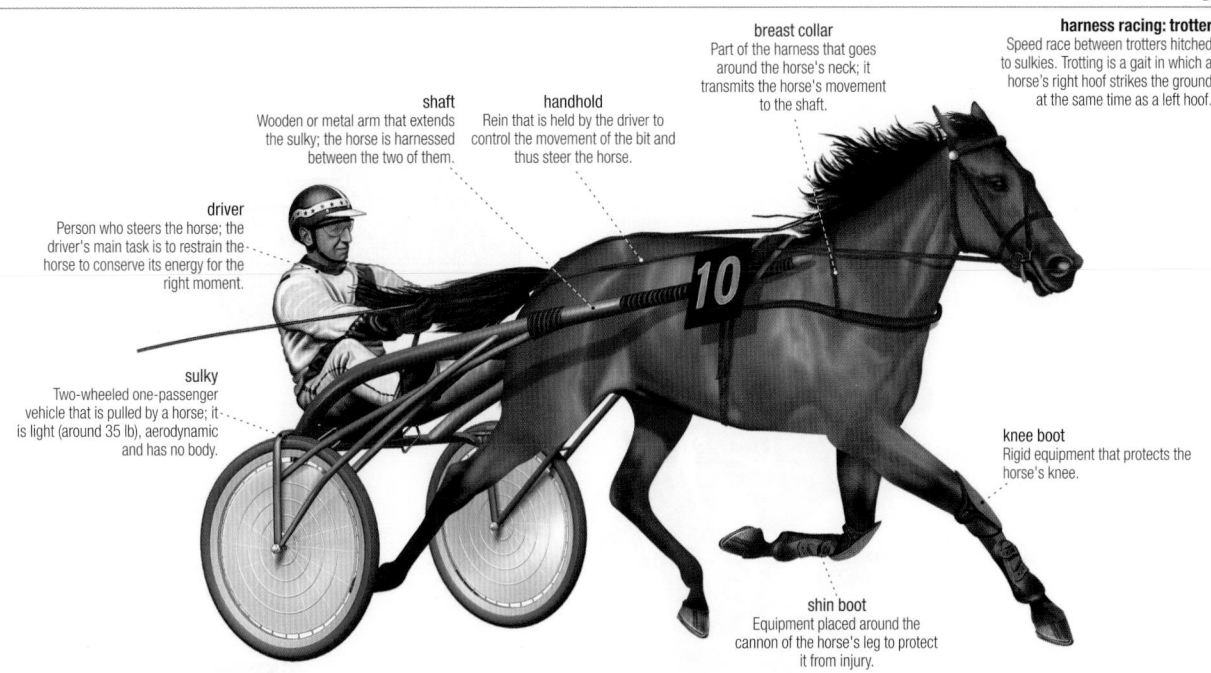

harness racing: trotter
Speed race between trotters hitched to sulkies. Trotting is a gait in which a horse's right hoof strikes the ground at the same time as a left hoof.

breast collar
Part of the harness that goes around the horse's neck; it transmits the horse's movement to the shaft.

shaft
Wooden or metal arm that extends the sulky; the horse is harnessed between the two of them.

handhold
Rein that is held by the driver to control the movement of the bit and thus steer the horse.

driver
Person who steers the horse; the driver's main task is to restrain the horse to conserve its energy for the right moment.

sulky
Two-wheeled one-passenger vehicle that is pulled by a horse; it is light (around 35 lb), aerodynamic and has no body.

knee boot
Rigid equipment that protects the horse's knee.

shin boot
Equipment placed around the cannon of the horse's leg to protect it from injury.

folding wing
...rt of the starting gate that folds ...ward as the vehicle leaves the ...arting line to let the horses by.

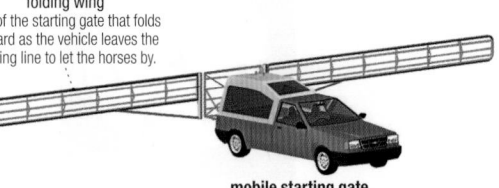

mobile starting gate
Vehicle with two folding wings; it is used to start the race by getting the horses running.

harness racing: pacer
Speed race between pacers hitched to sulkies. Pacing is a gait in which the horse alternates between using its right-side and left-side hooves to propel itself forward.

back pad
Padded part set on the horse's back; the back strap goes over it.

overcheck
Strap that connects the bridle to the back pad; it lifts the horse's head so it maintains the pace.

head number
Numbered plate that is attached to the horse's head for identification by the public and the judges.

back strap
Reinforced strap that is attached to the back pad; it is fitted with girths that can be attached to the shafts.

blinker
Rigid part that is attached to the cheek strap; it reduces the horse's lateral vision.

head pole
Stick attached along the horse's head; it prevents the horse from turning its head during turns.

hobble hanger
One of four straps that support the hobble.

breast collar
Part of the harness that goes around the horse's neck; it transmits the horse's movement to the shaft.

driver
...rson who steers the horse; the ...er's main task is to restrain the ...e to conserve its energy for the right moment.

shaft
Wooden or metal arm that extends the sulky; the horse is harnessed between the two of them.

shaft holder
Strap that attaches the shaft to the horse's harness.

knee boot suspender
Strap that goes around the horse's wither; it keeps its knee boot in place.

seat
...art on which the driver sits to steer the sulky.

knee boot
Rigid equipment that protects the horse's knee.

spoked wheel
Round unit that is held by fine metal rods radiating from an axle; it allows the sulky to move.

shin boot
Equipment placed around the cannon of the horse's leg to protect it from injury.

surcingle
Strap that goes under the horse's belly; it keeps the back pad and shaft holder in place.

hobble
Set of straps on each side of the horse that connect the forelegs and hind legs; they help the horse maintain the pace.

bell boot
Usually rubber item of equipment that covers the horse's hoof to prevent injury.

polo

Sport with two opposing teams of four riders who play on a level field; they try to score points through the opponents' goal by hitting a ball along the ground with a mallet.

rider and horse
The players ride horses whose manes are shaved and tails plaited to avoid catching; the players also change horses at every chukker (period).

head
Usually cigar-shaped piece of hardwood; the player strikes the ball with it.

shaft
Long part of the mallet that is usually made of bamboo and has a fixed head at the end; it can be rigid or flexible, depending on the player's preference.

mallet
Part consisting of a shaft and a head that is used by the player to hit the ball along the ground; it must be held in the right hand.

helmet
Rigid piece of equipment that protects the rider's head; it usually has a protective grille.

ELLERSTINA	
ADOLFO CAMBIASOH	10
MARIANO AGUERRE	9
GONZALO PIERES	10
CARLOS GRACIDA	10
	39

team name

player handicap
Index of skill assigned to each player on a scale from -2 to 10; a player with a handicap of 4 may play in international matches.

team handicap
Sum of the handicaps of all the players on the team; the team with the lowest handicap begins a match with a head start in goals.

handicaps board
Panel that displays the handicaps of the players and the teams.

saddle
Somewhat curved unit that is made mostly of leather; it is set on the horse's back for the rider to sit on.

knee pad
Hard leather piece of equipment that protects the rider's knee.

polo pony
Small horse that is bred and schooled for polo; calm and docile, it can start, stop and change directions very quickly.

noseband
Part of the bridle that runs around the head above the nostrils; it prevents the horse from opening its mouth and losing the bit.

bit
Device that is inserted in the horse's mouth; the rider steers the horse using the reins, which in turn move the bit in the horse's mouth.

martingale
Strap that is connected to the noseband to prevent the horse from throwing its head back; this prevents blows to its head during abrupt stops.

shin boot
Equipment placed around the cannon of the horse's leg to protect it from injury.

bell boot
Usually rubber item of equipment that covers the horse's hoof to prevent injury.

polo ball
White sphere of wood or plastic with a diameter of 3 to 3.5 in.

time clock
Apparatus that measures time, for managing a chukker's duration.

polo field
Grass-covered surface where a polo match is played; a game usually takes place over six 7-minute chukkers (periods), interrupted by breaks of 3 to 5 minutes.

player 1
Forward position whose chief purpose is to score goals; this player's horse must be quick and agile.

player 2
Forward position whose chief purpose is to drive the ball into the opponent's territory; this player's horse must be intrepid and energetic.

60 yd line

tower
Building that houses the scorekeeper, the announcer and a third umpire, who is in charge of settling any dispute that may arise on the field.

mounted umpire
Playing-field official (there are two umpires) who is in charge of applying the rules; they perform the throw-ins and give penalties for fouls.

sideline
Line that is often bordered by planks to delimit the playing zone on each side of the field; the players have the right to cross it or to bounce the ball off it.

goalpost
Pole marking one end of the goal; a team scores a point when the ball is shot between the posts of the opponents' goal.

player 4
Position that provides rear defense; this player can hit a ball very far and rides a horse that is husky, tough and fast.

center T mark
T-shaped mark at the center of the field; at the start of a chukker and after a goal, the players line up on each side of it for the throw-in.

goal judge
Official placed behind the goal who waves a flag when a goal is scored; the goal judge may also assist the umpires when incidents occur near the goal.

30 yd line

40 yd line
Line from which a free hit may be made; depending on the seriousness of the foul, the free hit is made from the 30 yd, 40 yd or 60 yd line.

player 3
Player who is the pivot between the attack and the defense; this player is usually team captain, has a high handicap and is an excellent strategist.

archery

Sport that consists of using a bow to shoot an arrow as close as possible to the middle of a target set a fixed distance away.

arrow
Projectile fired by a bow or a crossbow; it consists of a shaft, a point and a heel with a notch and fletching.

shaft
Long rod that makes up the body of the arrow; it is made of carbon fiber or an alloy of aluminum and carbon.

fletching
Feather or synthetic material attached to the base of the arrow to stabilize it during flight.

point
Pointed metal end of the arrow; depending on the power of the bow used, points of different weights are used.

nock
Slot into which the bowstring fits to keep the arrow in place while shooting it.

compound bow
Bow with a system of cables and wheels that increases its shooting power; it requires less effort for the archer to draw back the bowstring.

cable
Assembly of steel wires that runs around the wheels to increase the bow's power.

mounting bracket
Metal part with a threaded opening; a screw goes into it to attach the limb to the bow's grip.

nocking point
Mark on the bowstring where the arrow's nock fits.

arrow rest
Part against which the arrow shaft rests as the nock in fitted into the bowstring.

grip
Part between the two limbs that is gripped to manipulate the bow.

cable guard
Part that spreads the bowstring cables apart to prevent them from touching the arrow as the latter is nocked and shot.

bowstring
Fibers secured to a bow that were stretched to fire an arrow.

archer
Person who practices archery.

sight
culated apparatus on the bow that aligns it with the target to ease the accuracy of the shot.

bare bow
Bow made up of a piece of wood and a string that are joined without screws; it is usually very powerful but is less accurate than a compound bow.

stabilizer
Weight that is attached to the bow by a shaft to stabilize the bow during and after shooting; it dampens the vibrations caused by the bowstring as the arrow is released.

arm guard
Piece of leather or plastic that protects the forearm from friction from the bowstring.

accessory pouch

quiver
Case that is carried on the back or the hip; the arrows are stored in it during the shoot.

limb
Flexible part that stores the potential energy as the bow is stretched.

wheel
Small pulley attached to the ends of the limbs; it absorbs part of the force from the shot and it increases the shot's accuracy.

target
Surface of varying diameter at which the archer shoots; it is divided into concentric circles corresponding to point zones.

bull's-eye
Circle 4.8 in in diameter in the middle of the target; it is 4.3 ft from the ground and worth 10 points. The value of the other circles decreases toward the edge of the target.

chest protector
Piece of leather or plastic that protects the chest from the friction of the bowstring and flattens the clothing to the body so it does not interfere with the shot.

finger tab
Piece of leather or plastic that protects the archer's fingers from the friction of the bowstring.

shooting range
Outdoor rectangular area that is 110 m long and set up for archery; it is surrounded by an exclusion zone for the protection of the spectators.

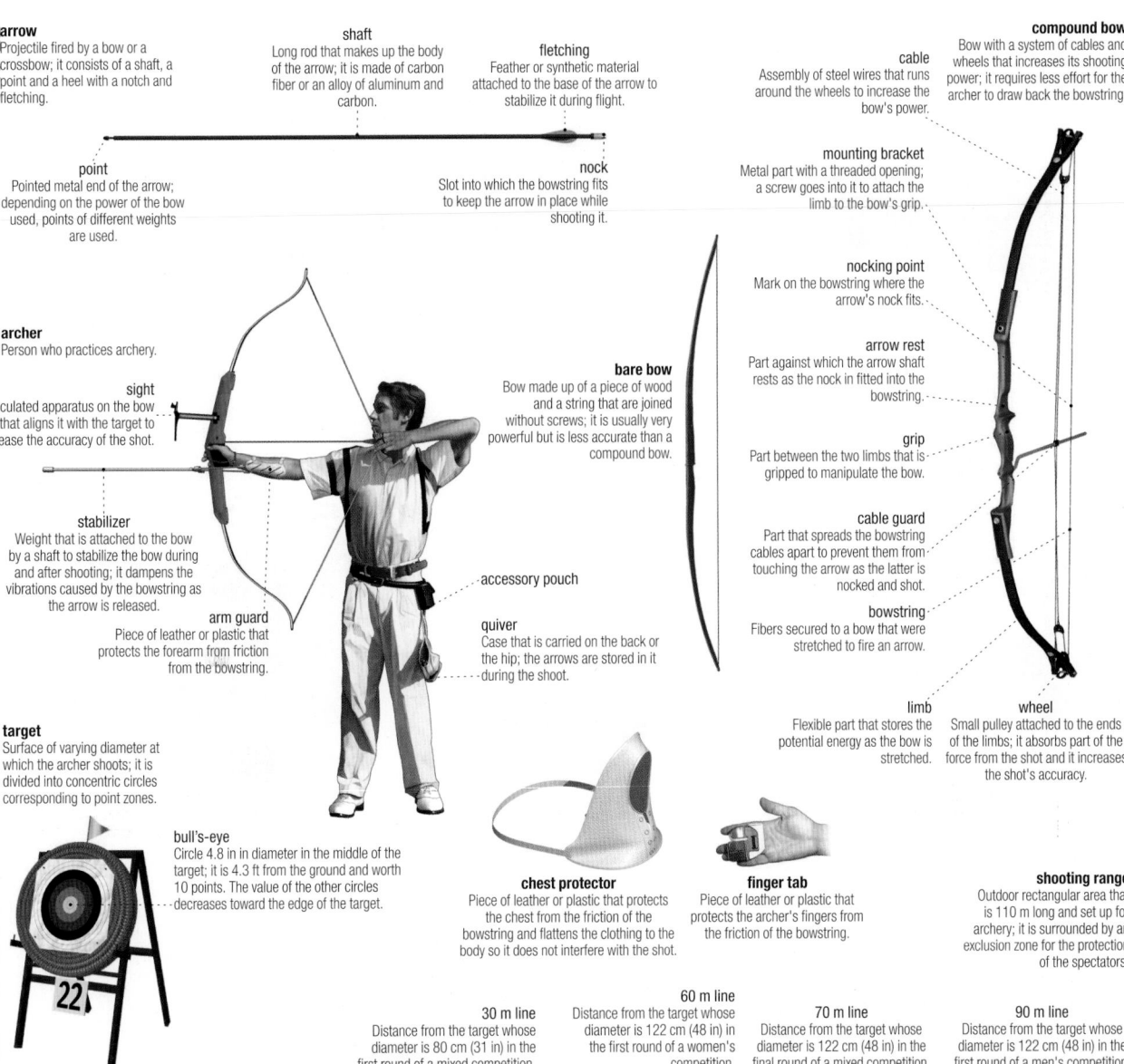

30 m line
Distance from the target whose diameter is 80 cm (31 in) in the first round of a mixed competition.

60 m line
Distance from the target whose diameter is 122 cm (48 in) in the first round of a women's competition.

70 m line
Distance from the target whose diameter is 122 cm (48 in) in the final round of a mixed competition.

90 m line
Distance from the target whose diameter is 122 cm (48 in) in the first round of a men's competition.

signal lights
Lamps accompanied by sounds that mark the progress of the competition (such as the positioning of the archers on the shooting line and the end of the shoot).

judge
Official who checks various elements, such as the shooting distances, the size of the targets, equipment compliance and the archer's position, and ensures that the time is respected.

50 m line
Distance from the target whose diameter is 80 cm (31 in) in the first round of a mixed competition.

director of shooting
Official whose responsibilities include monitoring the competition's progress, settling any disputes that may arise and monitoring the shooting time with sound signals.

scorers
Officials who are in charge of registering the points obtained by the archers.

shooting line
Line at which the archer stands to shoot with one foot placed on each side of it.

telescope
Optical instrument whose use is authorized for making out the precise spots where the arrows hit the target.

shotgun shooting

Sport that consists of shooting at a moving target using a shotgun; the gun is loaded with cartridges to destroy the target in flight.

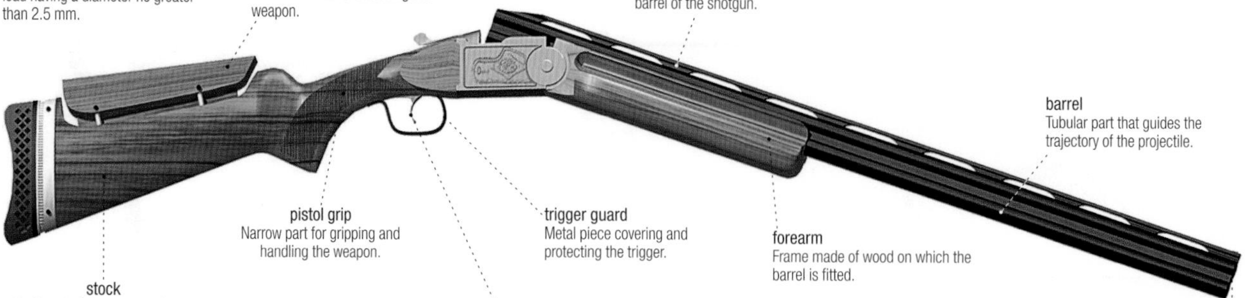

shotgun
Shoulder weapon made up of a long barrel attached to a frame; it uses cartridges loaded with 24 g of lead having a diameter no greater than 2.5 mm.

cheek piece
Movable and adjustable part against which the shooter can rest his cheek when shouldering the weapon.

ventilated rib
Strip with air holes for cooling the barrel of the shotgun.

barrel
Tubular part that guides the trajectory of the projectile.

pistol grip
Narrow part for gripping and handling the weapon.

trigger guard
Metal piece covering and protecting the trigger.

forearm
Frame made of wood on which the barrel is fitted.

stock
Back part of the weapon that is held against the shoulder.

trigger
Device that is pressed to fire the weapon.

muzzle
Opening through which the projectile leaves the barrel.

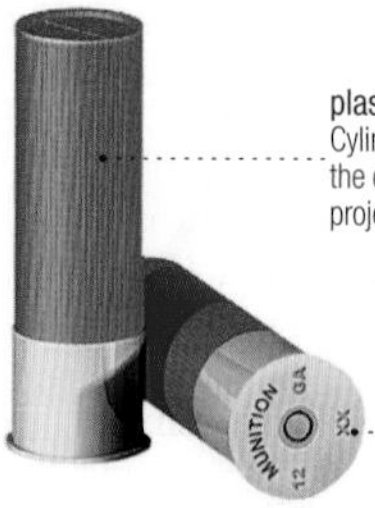

plastic case
Cylindrical cover that contains the cartridge's gunpowder and projectile.

base
Metal base of the case that contains the primer.

cartridges
Ammunition consisting of a projectile (ball or lead), an explosive charge (gunpowder) and a primer collected inside a casing.

clay pigeon
Clay disk that weighs 3.5 oz and is 4.25 in in diameter; it serves as the shooting target.

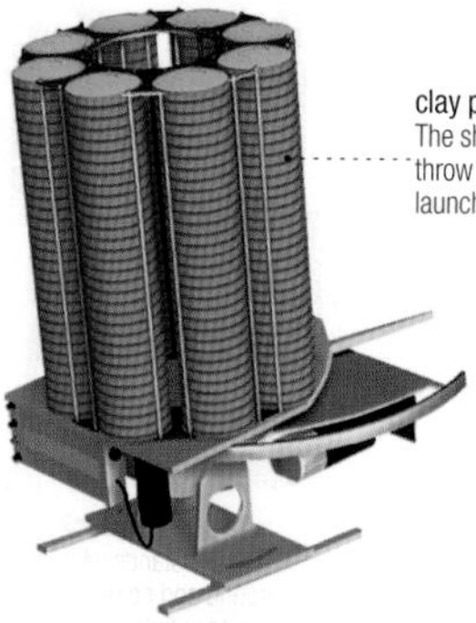

clay pigeon
The shooter shouts the order to throw a clay pigeon, which mu[...] launched within three seconds[...]

trap
Apparatus that is controlled manually or automatically; it propels clay pigeons at varying speeds, heights and directions.

shooting range
Area that faces the targets, which includes the shooting stations.

chief range officer
Official who is in charge of calling the shooters to their positions; this individual also verifies the compliance of the equipment and the shooting positions.

shooting station
Area where the competitors stand to shoot at the targets.

trench
Ditch that is about 6.5 ft deep where the trap machines are stationed; it is 16 yds from the shooting station.

scorer
Official who marks the shooters' results on score sheets and on the scoreboard.

shooter
Person who practices shotgun shooting or participates in a competition.

chief referee
Official who is in charge of all technical and logistical aspects of the competition.

assistant referee
Official who checks whether or not the target has been hit; if it was not hit, the assistant referee reports this fact immediately.

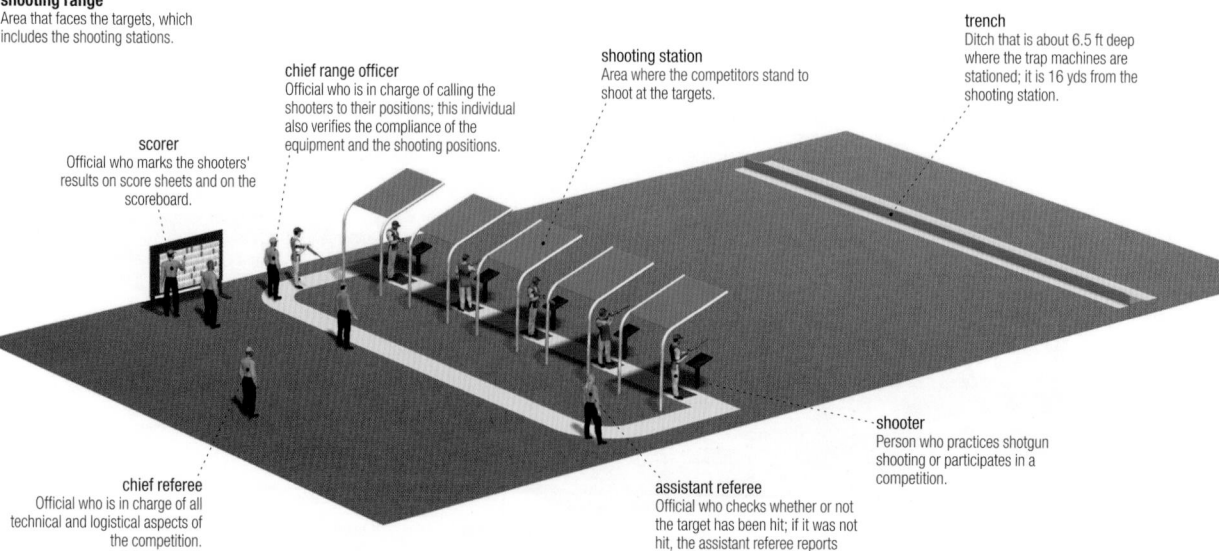

rifle shooting

Sport that consists of using a rifle to shoot projectiles at a target a given distance away; the goal is to hit the target's center.

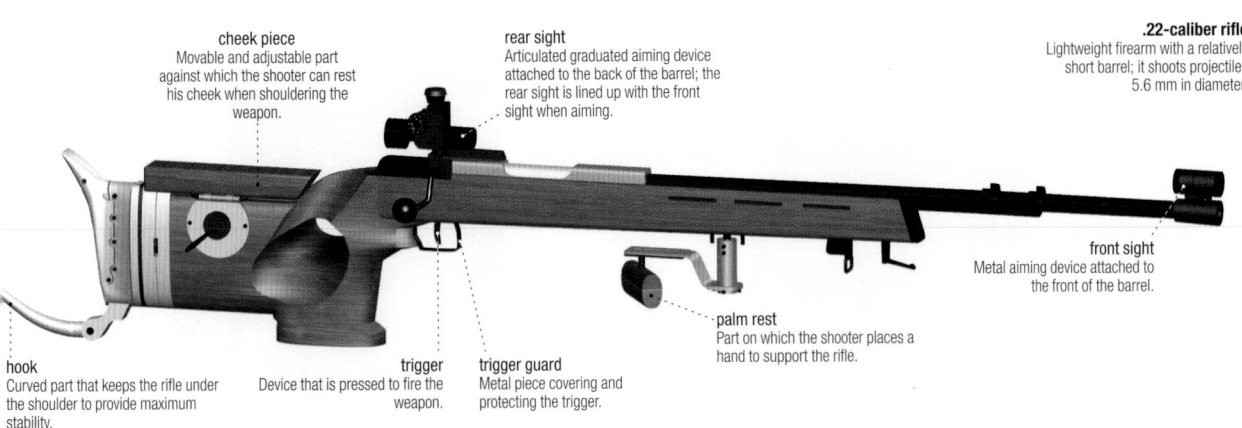

cheek piece
Movable and adjustable part against which the shooter can rest his cheek when shouldering the weapon.

rear sight
Articulated graduated aiming device attached to the back of the barrel; the rear sight is lined up with the front sight when aiming.

.22-caliber rifle
Lightweight firearm with a relatively short barrel; it shoots projectiles 5.6 mm in diameter.

front sight
Metal aiming device attached to the front of the barrel.

palm rest
Part on which the shooter places a hand to support the rifle.

hook
Curved part that keeps the rifle under the shoulder to provide maximum stability.

trigger
Device that is pressed to fire the weapon.

trigger guard
Metal piece covering and protecting the trigger.

shooting positions

For the 5.6 mm (.22-caliber rifle) weapons and the 4.5 mm air rifle, the disciplines vary according to distance, number of shots and the position.

cartridges
Ammunition consisting of a projectile (ball or lead), an explosive charge (gunpowder) and a primer collected inside a casing.

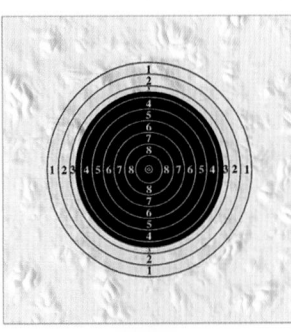

target
Surface 6.1 in in diameter that is marked by the bullets; it is divided into concentric circles corresponding to point zones.

kneeling position
e points of contact with the ground
e allowed: left foot, right knee and
of the right foot (for a right-handed
son); the rifle must be held in two
nds, against the aiming shoulder.

standing position
The shooter stands with two feet on the ground and no other support; the rifle is held in both hands, against the shoulder and along the aiming cheek.

prone position
Lying on the stomach, the shooter holds the weapon with two hands and one shoulder; the cheek can be held against the stock but the forearm cannot touch the ground.

pistol shooting

Sport that consists of using a pistol to shoot projectiles at a target a given distance away; the goal is to hit the target's center.

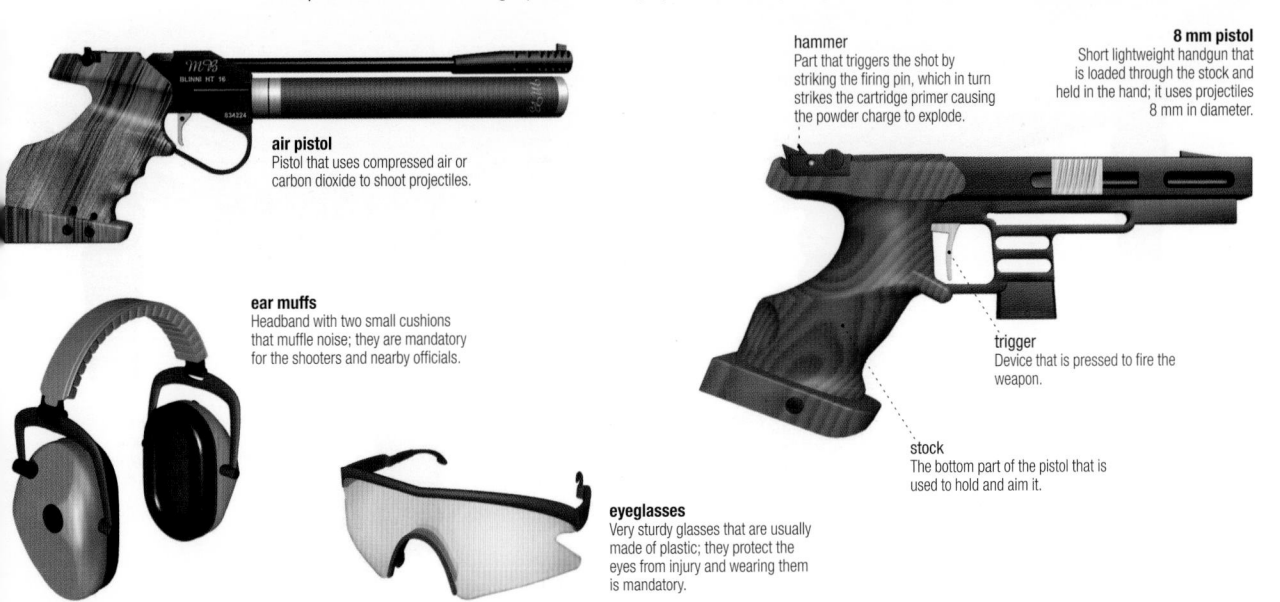

hammer
Part that triggers the shot by striking the firing pin, which in turn strikes the cartridge primer causing the powder charge to explode.

8 mm pistol
Short lightweight handgun that is loaded through the stock and held in the hand; it uses projectiles 8 mm in diameter.

air pistol
Pistol that uses compressed air or carbon dioxide to shoot projectiles.

ear muffs
Headband with two small cushions that muffle noise; they are mandatory for the shooters and nearby officials.

trigger
Device that is pressed to fire the weapon.

stock
The bottom part of the pistol that is used to hold and aim it.

eyeglasses
Very sturdy glasses that are usually made of plastic; they protect the eyes from injury and wearing them is mandatory.

billiards

Games that are played on a special table; they use a cue to hit a cue ball either against two balls or to drive another into a pocket.

carom billiards
Game that is played on a pocketless table with three balls (one red and two white); players hit their own white balls to hit the other balls.

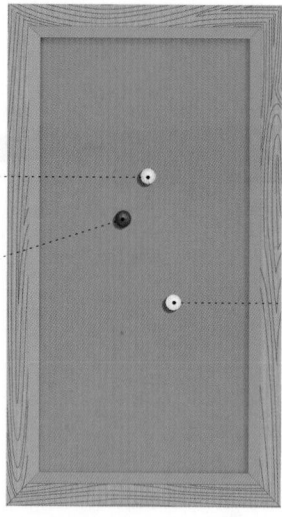

cue ball
White ball that the player hits with the cue to hit the red ball and the opponent's ball; it is the only ball that may be hit with the cue.

red ball
Ball the player must touch to score a carom.

object balls
Balls that the player must drive into the pockets often in a set order; at the start of the game, they are arranged in a triangle.

white object ball
Ball the player must hit to score a carom (move in which the player's ball hits the two other balls); it is also the opponent's cue ball.

cue ball
White ball the player hits with the cue to hit the other balls and pocket them; it is the only ball that may be hit with the cue.

pool
Also known as American billiards, it is played on a table with six pockets using 15 object balls and a white ball; the goal is to drive the balls into the pockets in a set order.

pocket
One of the six holes into which the player must drive the balls.

billiards table
Surface on which the balls roll; it is supported by legs, has a rectangular top and is horizontal and level.

D
Semicircle whose center is on and in the middle of the balk line; the game starts from here.

balk line spot
Spot in the middle of the balk line that marks the position of the brown ball in snooker (there are two other spots at the intersections of the balk line and the "D").

balk area
Zone bordered by the balk line and the head cushion, including the "D"; this zone is used only in English billiards.

bottom pocket
Corner pocket located at the head cushion and next to the balk area.

center spot
Spot that marks the position of the blue ball in snooker; it is located halfway between the center pockets and the head and foot cushions.

baize
Felt fabric that covers the playing surface and the inner side of the rails.

head cushion
Rubber padding that covers the inner side of the rail next to the balk area; the balls bounce against it.

pyramid spot
Spot that marks the position of the pink ball in snooker; it is halfway between the center spot and the foot cushion on the table's longitudinal center line.

top pocket
Corner pocket located at the foot cushion and opposite the balk area.

balk line
Line marked across the width of the table 29 in from the head cushion; it serves as a benchmark for snooker at the start of the game.

hook
Curved part positioned along the tables that holds the cues and the rack.

billiard spot
Spot that marks the position of the black ball in snooker; it is about 13 in from the foot cushion on the table's longitudinal center line.

side pocket
Side pocket in the middle of the table's side rail.

rail
Table frame to which the rubber is attached and covered with felt; it delimits the playing surface.

foot cushion
Rubber padding that covers the inner side of the rail opposite the balk area; the balls bounce against it.

billiards

snooker
Billiards that is played on a table with six pockets and uses 22 balls (15 red, six of various colors and one white); the goal is to alternately pocket the red balls and the colored balls.

English billiards
Billiards played in the United Kingdom on a table with six pockets using three balls (one red and two white); the goal is to pocket the balls or use one ball to hit the other two.

cue ball
White ball the player hits with the cue to hit the other balls and pocket them; it is the only ball that may be hit with the cue.

cue ball
White ball that belongs to one of the players; it is put into play from the "D".

white object ball
White ball that belongs to the other player; it is also the ball that the first player must hit or pocket.

yellow ball
Ball that is worth two points; it is placed to the right of the "D", in relation to the head cushion.

green ball
Ball that is worth three points; it is placed to the left of the "D", with respect to the head cushion.

brown ball
Ball that is worth four points; it is placed on the balk line spot.

blue ball
Ball that is worth five points; it is placed on the center spot.

pink ball
Ball that is worth six points; it is placed on the pyramid spot.

red ball
Ball that the player must hit or pocket; at the start of the game, it is placed on the billiard spot.

red balls
Balls that are worth one point each. At the start of the game, they are arranged in a triangle behind the pink ball; as long as the player has not pocketed all the red balls, the colored balls are placed back on the table in their original spots.

black ball
Ball that is worth seven points; it is placed on the billiard spot.

rack
Triangular piece of wood or plastic for lining up the balls on the table at the start of a game.

chalk
Small cube of chalky powder that is rubbed onto the tip of the cue to improve contact with the cue ball.

cue
Long wooden stick that the player holds to hit the cue ball; the player chooses the cue's diameter, length and weight (no more than 25 oz).

joint
Cylindrical part for joining the shaft with the butt of a collapsible cue.

ferrule
Piece of hard plastic at the front end of the cue to support the tip.

tip
Round piece of leather or felt on the end of the cue for hitting the cue ball; it is also the only component that can touch a ball.

shaft
Tapered part of the cue on which the player places the fingers to line up the shot.

butt
Wide part of the cue; players choose the diameter that best fits their hands.

bridge
Stick with a toothed head for shooting with the cue when the cue ball is out of the player's reach.

notch
Space between the teeth on which the cue's shaft is placed.

shaft
Long part of the bridge; the endpiece is attached to it.

endpiece
Piece of toothed metal to support and guide the cue.

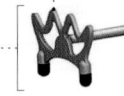

lawn bowling

Ball sport of British origin in which two opposing players or teams play on a green; balls (bowls) are thrown as close as possible to a target (jack).

bowling technique
The thrower takes three steps to wind up, unlike pétanque where the thrower keeps the feet together.

bowls
They are made of wood, rubber or other material and are not perfectly spherical (diameter of about 4.75 to 5.75 in, weight up to 3.5 lb).

jack
Small ball that is made of wood or lignite and is 2.5 in in diameter; it is the lawn bowling target and the point of reference for scoring.

forward swing
The player bends slightly forward and places the arm behind the body to gain momentum for the throw.

delivery
The player bends the knees to accelerate the motion before releasing the bowl.

follow-through
The player swings the arm forward toward the jack after throwing the bowl.

green
Surface of natural or synthetic grass that is bordered by a ditch and a bank; the lawn bowling green is divided into several parallel playing surfaces.

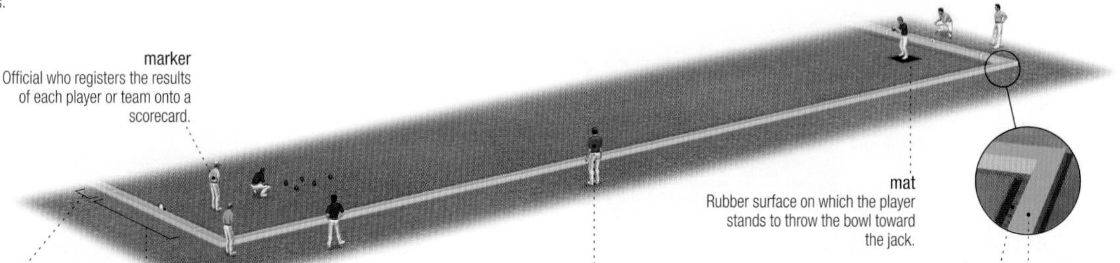

marker
Official who registers the results of each player or team onto a scorecard.

mat
Rubber surface on which the player stands to throw the bowl toward the jack.

dead bowl area
Zone outside the limits of the rink where bowls are considered out of bounds.

rink
Area 18 to 21 ft wide x 40 to 42 yd long that is laid out for playing lawn bowling.

umpire
Official who is in charge of enforcing the rules; the umpire can expel a player or team from the competition it they refuse to comply with a decision.

ditch
Small culvert that surrounds the green; a bowl falling into the ditch is considered out of bounds.

bank
Small wall that surrounds the to delimit the playing field; it no higher than 9 in.

pétanque

Ball sport that originated in the south of France in which two opposing players or teams throw balls (bowls) as close as possible to a target (jack).

pétanque playing field
Area laid out for playing pétanque; matches can be played on a lawn, earth or sand. For international competitions, the field measures 13 ft x 49 ft.

referee
Official who is in charge of enforcing the rules; the referee ensures that the equipment and installation are in compliance.

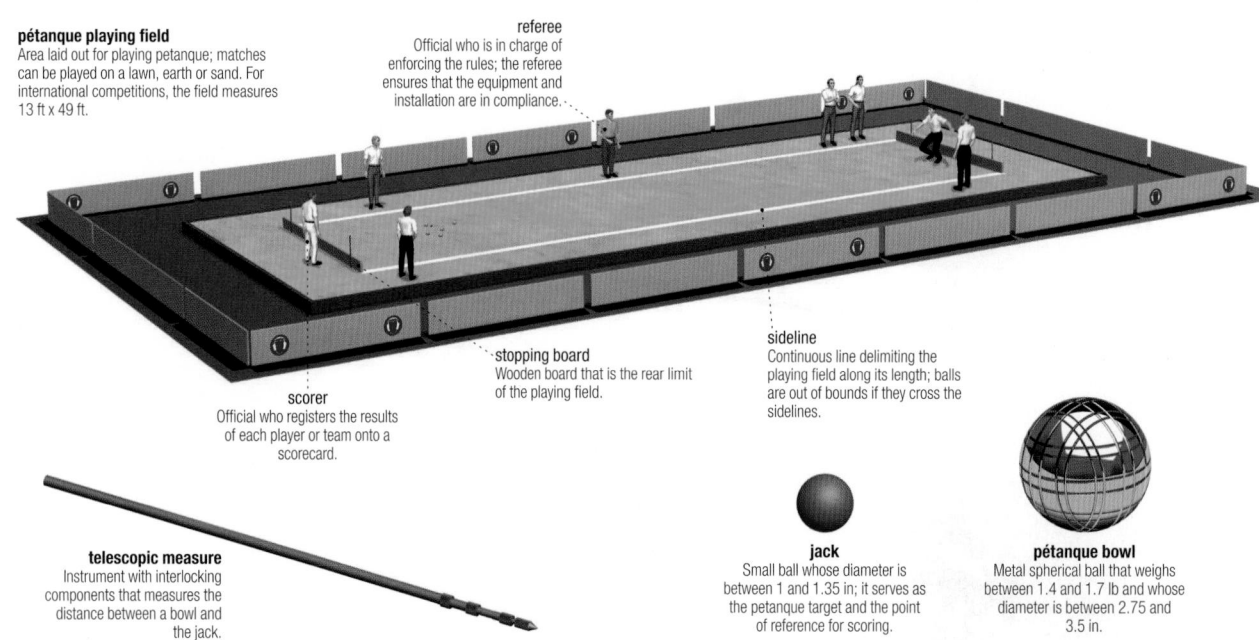

scorer
Official who registers the results of each player or team onto a scorecard.

stopping board
Wooden board that is the rear limit of the playing field.

sideline
Continuous line delimiting the playing field along its length; balls are out of bounds if they cross the sidelines.

telescopic measure
Instrument with interlocking components that measures the distance between a bowl and the jack.

jack
Small ball whose diameter is between 1 and 1.35 in; it serves as the petanque target and the point of reference for scoring.

pétanque bowl
Metal spherical ball that weighs between 1.4 and 1.7 lb and whose diameter is between 2.75 and 3.5 in.

bowling

Game of U.S. origin that consists of rolling a ball down a lane to knock down pins standing at the end.

examples of pins

Their shapes are specific to each variety of the game.

American duckpin
One of 10 pins that is lightweight and 9.4 in high; the game is played almost exclusively in the United States.

tenpin
Pin that weighs 3.5 to 3.7 lb and measures 15 in high; this is the most widespread type of bowling in the world.

candlepin
Cylindrical pin that is about 16 in high; this game with 10 pins is played in some provinces of Canada and states of the United States.

fivepin
Lightweight pin that is about 12 in high and has a rubber band around it; this five-pin game is very popular in Canada.

Canadian duckpin
Similar to American duckpin, it has a rubber band around it to make it heavier; this 10-pin game is very widespread in Canada.

---

bowling shoe
For a right-handed person, the left sole is made of leather (for sliding) and the right sole of rubber (for stopping).

bowling ball
Large ball that the player rolls to hit the pins.

headpin
Also called the kingpin, it makes up the point of the triangle formed by the pins.

setup
Set of 10 pins arranged in an equilateral triangle at the end of each lane of the alley.

pin
Piece of wood that is covered with plastic; it is stood on end on the floor and the player knocks it over with a ball.

pocket
Tactical zone where the player rolls the ball to try to hit all the pins with one ball (strike).

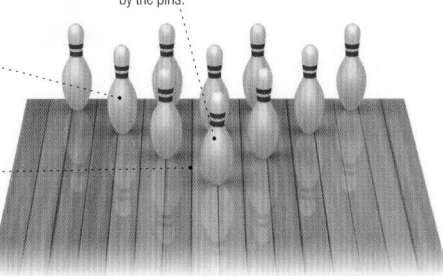

ball return
Mechanical device (track) between the lanes that returns the balls the players threw toward the setup.

score console
Panel that displays the data of the game in progress (such as points for each frame for each player, total for previous games and the results for each team).

ball
Spherical object that is rolled using the hand to knock down the pins. Made in a range of weights, it has three holes for gripping with the fingers.

bowler
Player who practices bowling; the first world championships for women took place in 1963.

keyboard
Set of keys for registering points scored (number of pins knocked over) for each frame and for the game total.

ball stand
Rack that holds the bowling balls that are not in use.

setup
Set of 10 pins arranged in an equilateral triangle at the end of each lane of the alley.

bowling alley
Set of lanes that are made of wood or synthetic material and are laid out for bowling.

bowler
Player who practices bowling; the first world championships for men took place in 1954.

pit
Area at the end of the lane; the hit pins fall into it.

gutter
Ditch on both sides of the alley's lanes; a ball that falls into it is out of play.

approach
Lane on which the player makes the forward swing (usually three normal steps and one sliding) before rolling the ball.

foul line
Line behind which the player must stay when rolling the ball down the lane at delivery; crossing this line is a foul.

golf

Sport whose objective is to complete a set course by hitting a ball with a club; the player who uses the least number of strokes is the winner.

golf course

Area of land set up for playing golf, usually with 18 holes.

hole
One of the separate parts of a golf course that includes its own tee and green.

clubhouse
Structure located usually near the first and last holes that provides various services to golfers (such as a bar, restaurant and lockers).

practice green
Separate green that is used to practice putting.

sand bunker
Area along the fairway or near the green that is filled with sand.

green
Smooth area of very short grass around the hole into which the ball must be played; the golfer uses a putter to roll the ball into the hole.

cart path
Lane for golf carts to follow along the course.

fairway
Area of short grass that lies between the tee and the green.

pond
Small shallow body of water that can be natural or man-made.

trees
Wooded part of the golf course.

rough
Area of long grass located along the edge of the fairway and near the green.

teeing ground
Flat area of short grass from which the player tees off to start play on each hole; a hole will often include more than one tee so that it can played at different lengths by players of different skill levels.

water hazard
Natural or man-made body of water (such as a lake, pond or river) that constitutes an obstacle for the golfer.

holes

Parts of a golf course that each include their own tee and green; in principle, each hole is played in an estimated number of strokes, its par.

par 3 hole
The player tries to reach the green on the tee shot and then make two putts.

par 4 hole
The player tries to reach the green on the second stroke and then make two putts. If a par 4 hole is completed in 3 strokes, it's a birdie.

tee shot
First stroke that is hit to start play on a hole; the ball is usually placed on a tee.

approach shot
Stroke made from the fairway to the green.

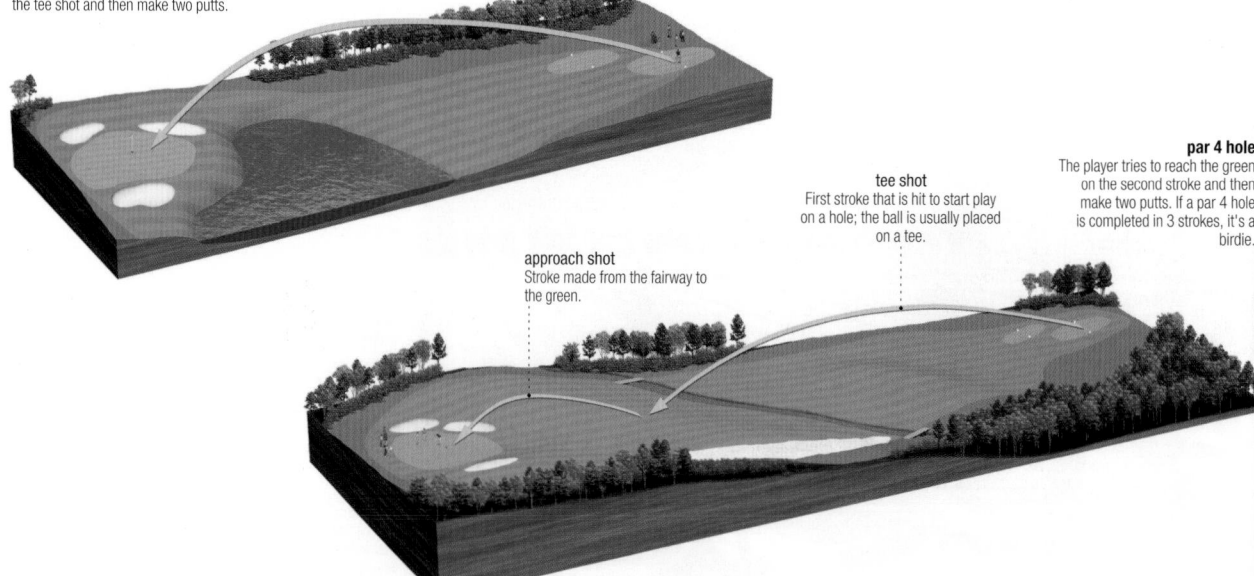

golf

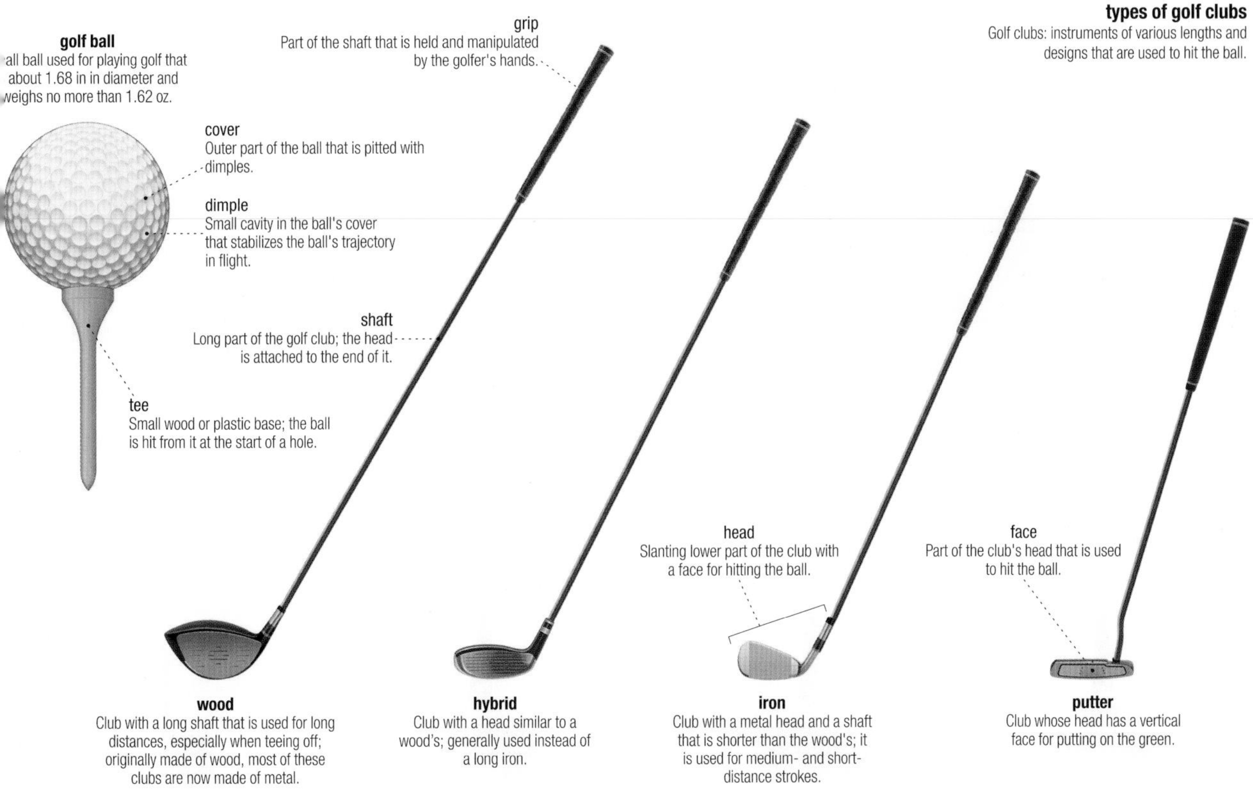

golf ball
...all ball used for playing golf that ...about 1.68 in in diameter and ...weighs no more than 1.62 oz.

cover
Outer part of the ball that is pitted with dimples.

dimple
Small cavity in the ball's cover that stabilizes the ball's trajectory in flight.

tee
Small wood or plastic base; the ball is hit from it at the start of a hole.

grip
Part of the shaft that is held and manipulated by the golfer's hands.

shaft
Long part of the golf club; the head is attached to the end of it.

head
Slanting lower part of the club with a face for hitting the ball.

face
Part of the club's head that is used to hit the ball.

types of golf clubs
Golf clubs: instruments of various lengths and designs that are used to hit the ball.

wood
Club with a long shaft that is used for long distances, especially when teeing off; originally made of wood, most of these clubs are now made of metal.

hybrid
Club with a head similar to a wood's; generally used instead of a long iron.

iron
Club with a metal head and a shaft that is shorter than the wood's; it is used for medium- and short-distance strokes.

putter
Club whose head has a vertical face for putting on the green.

holes

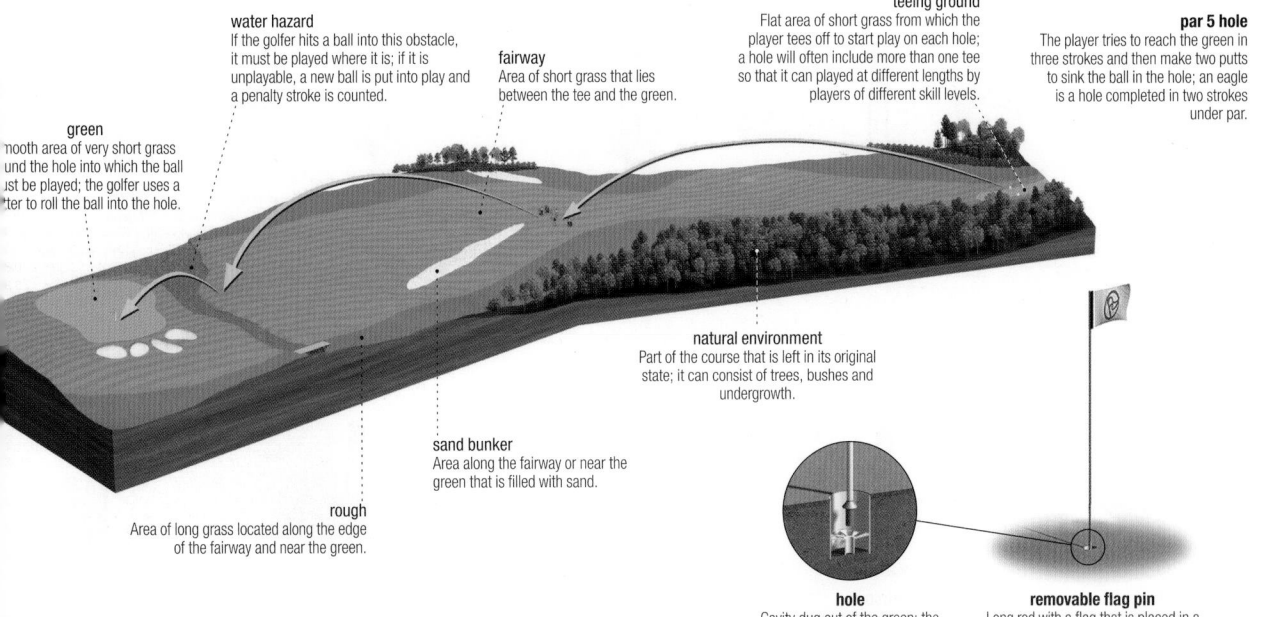

water hazard
If the golfer hits a ball into this obstacle, it must be played where it is; if it is unplayable, a new ball is put into play and a penalty stroke is counted.

fairway
Area of short grass that lies between the tee and the green.

teeing ground
Flat area of short grass from which the player tees off to start play on each hole; a hole will often include more than one tee so that it can played at different lengths by players of different skill levels.

par 5 hole
The player tries to reach the green in three strokes and then make two putts to sink the ball in the hole; an eagle is a hole completed in two strokes under par.

green
...mooth area of very short grass ...und the hole into which the ball ...ust be played; the golfer uses a ...ter to roll the ball into the hole.

natural environment
Part of the course that is left in its original state; it can consist of trees, bushes and undergrowth.

sand bunker
Area along the fairway or near the green that is filled with sand.

rough
Area of long grass located along the edge of the fairway and near the green.

hole
Cavity dug out of the green; the player must roll the ball into it to complete a hole.

removable flag pin
Long rod with a flag that is placed in a hole to mark the hole's location so that it can be seen from far away.

golf

wood
The woods are usually numbered from 1 to 7, according to the inclination of their faces and the ranges of their strokes.

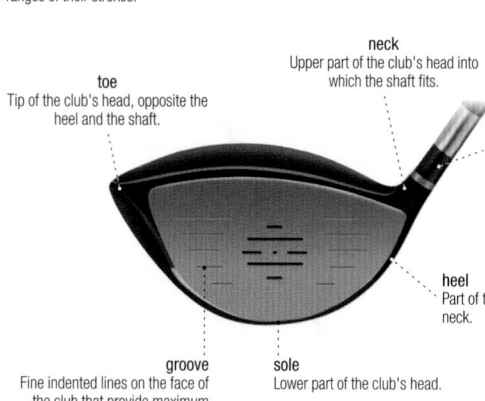

toe
Tip of the club's head, opposite the heel and the shaft.

neck
Upper part of the club's head into which the shaft fits.

ferrule
Ringlike part at the joint of a club's shaft and head that holds them securely together.

heel
Part of the club's head under the neck.

groove
Fine indented lines on the face of the club that provide maximum control of the ball.

sole
Lower part of the club's head.

iro
Club used to hit the ball on the fairwa or green. Irons are numbered from to 9, according to the length of the shafts and their range; the angle of th sole increases in inclination to crea curved trajectories of varying height

ferrule
Ringlike part at the joint of a club's shaft and head that holds them securely together.

neck
Upper part of the club's head into which the shaft fits.

toe
Tip of the club's head, opposite the heel and the shaft.

groove
Fine indented lines on the face of the club that provide maximum control of the ball.

sole
Lower part of the club's head.

heel
Part of the club's head under the neck.

driver
Wood with a very long range that is the longest of the golf clubs; it is used especially for tee shots. The inclination angle of its face varies from 8° to 10°.

3-wood
Wood whose range is between 210 and 240 yds; the inclination angle of its face is about 15°.

5-wood
Wood whose range is between 200 and 220 yds; the inclination angle of its face is about 18°.

putter
Club whose head has a vertical face for putting on the green.

3-iron
Long iron whose range is between 180 and 205 yds; the inclination angle of its face varies from 20° to 22°.

4-iron
Long iron whose range is between 175 and 200 yd; the inclination angle of its face varies from 22° to 24°.

5-iron
Medium iron whose range is between 165 and 195 yds; the inclination angle of its face varies from 26° to 28°.

6-iron
Medium iron whose range is between 155 and 180 yds; the inclination angle of its face varies from 30° to 32°.

7-iron
Medium iron whose range is between 140 and 170 yds; the inclination angle of its face varies from 34° to 36°.

8-iron
Short iron whose range is between 135 and 155 yds; the inclination angle of its face varies from 38° to 40°.

9-iron
Short iron whose range is between 130 and 145 yds; the inclination angle of its face varies from 42° to 44°.

pitching wedge
Short iron used mainly for approach strokes on the fairway, at about 110 yds from the hole; the inclination angle of its face varies from 47° to 52°.

sand wedge
Short iron used mainly for hitting the ball out of sand bunkers; the inclination angle of its face varies from 54° to 58°.

lob wedge
Short iron used for playing high ar precise strokes near the green (less 55 yds); the inclination angle of its f varies from 60° to 64°.

golf

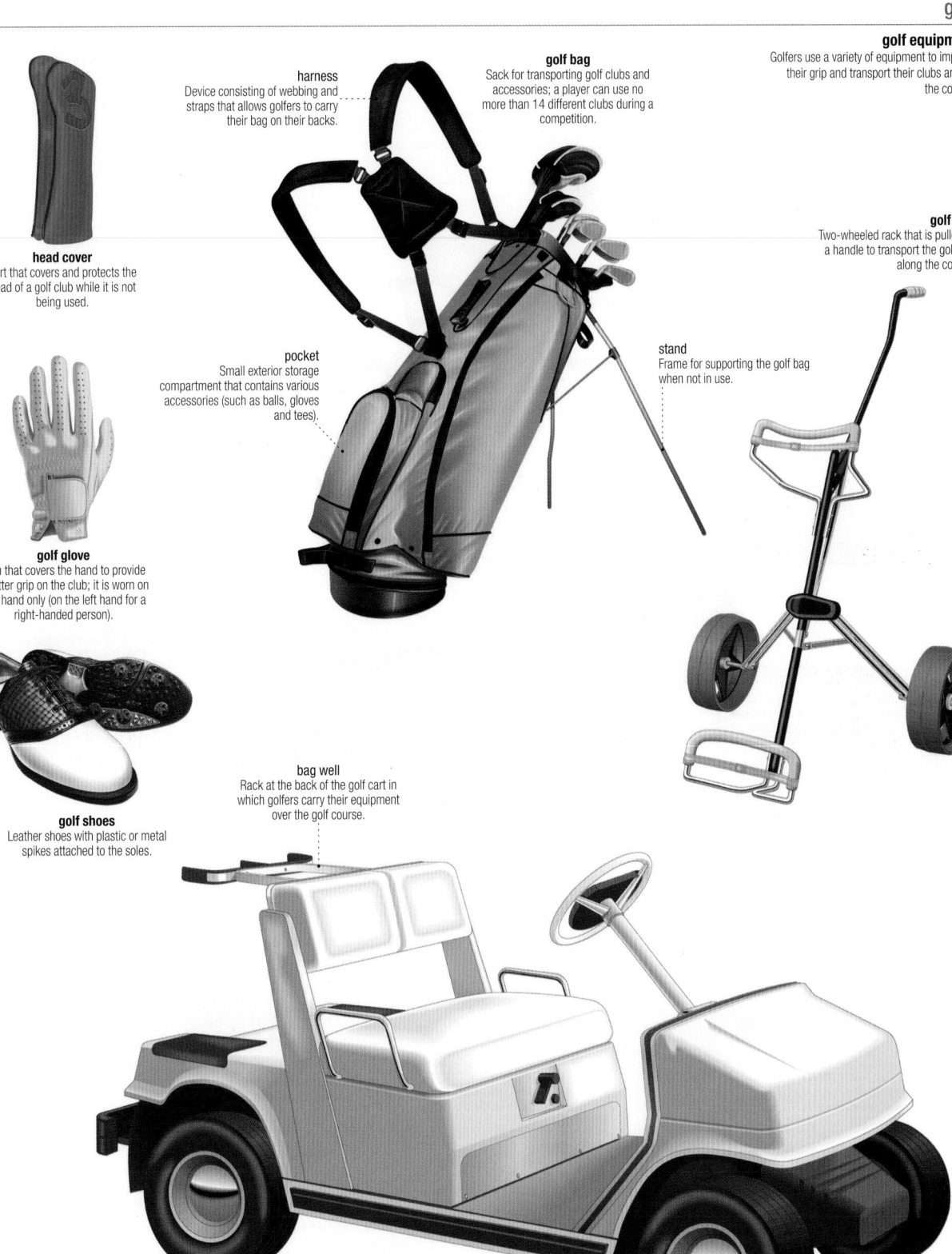

golf equipment
Golfers use a variety of equipment to improve their grip and transport their clubs around the course.

harness
Device consisting of webbing and straps that allows golfers to carry their bag on their backs.

golf bag
Sack for transporting golf clubs and accessories; a player can use no more than 14 different clubs during a competition.

head cover
Part that covers and protects the head of a golf club while it is not being used.

golf cart
Two-wheeled rack that is pulled by a handle to transport the golf bag along the course.

pocket
Small exterior storage compartment that contains various accessories (such as balls, gloves and tees).

stand
Frame for supporting the golf bag when not in use.

golf glove
Item that covers the hand to provide a better grip on the club; it is worn on one hand only (on the left hand for a right-handed person).

golf shoes
Leather shoes with plastic or metal spikes attached to the soles.

bag well
Rack at the back of the golf cart in which golfers carry their equipment over the golf course.

electric golf cart
Small motorized vehicle that is used by golfers to move from one hole to another along the golf course.

road racing

Sport that consists of racing a bicycle on a road for one day or in stages.

road-racing bicycle and cyclist
Road-racing bicycle: bicycle that is designed for speed; it has narrow tires, a lightweight frame and handlebars conducive to an aerodynamic position for the cyclist.

helmet
Hard piece of equipment designed to protect the head.

jersey
Stretchy tight clothing that covers the top of the athlete's body.

shorts
Tight clothing that covers the athlete's thighs to prevent them from rubbing against the seat.

glove
Leather item that reduces vibration and protects the hand against impact.

frame
Bicycle structure made of aluminum or carbon fiber; it is rigid, lightweight and very sturdy.

brake lever and shifter
The brake handle activates the brake caliper to which it is connected by a cable; the shifter is used to change the position of the chain.

tire
Structure made of cotton and steel fibers coated with rubber, mounted on the rim to form the casing for the inner tube.

brake
Mechanism composed of two brake pads that is activated by a brake cable; the pads are driven by a caliper and return springs to squeeze the wheel rim and slow down the wheel.

derailleur
Mechanism for changing the rear gears by lifting the chain from one gear wheel to another; it allows the cyclist to adapt to road conditions.

fork
Two tubes connected to the head tube and attached to each end of the front-wheel hub.

wheel
Disk that turns around an axle at its center and enables the bicycle to move; its weight and shape influence the bike's performance.

shoe
Shoe with notches in the sole that fit into a corresponding part on the pedal to keep the foot secure on the pedal.

pedal
Part attached to a crank that the cyclist rotates to provide the bicycle's power.

chain wheel
Wheel with teeth that, in combination with the rear sprockets, increases or decreases the distance traveled by a turn of the pedal crank.

road-racing competition
Event that consists of riding a bicycle a given distance on a road as quickly as possible.

motorcycle-mounted camera
Motorcycle used by the cameraman who records the race for broadcast.

leading motorcycle
Motorcycle traveling in front of the first rider; its rider announces the cyclists coming up and checks that the way is clear.

peloton
Compact grouping of cyclists; depending on the race, there can be 150 or more athletes.

following car
Vehicle in which a team's coach, mechanics and trainers ride.

race director
Person who is in charge of organizing the race and monitors its progress from a car.

leading bunch
Compact grouping of cyclists at the front of the race.

mountain biking

Sport that consists of performing acrobatic exercises or racing offtrack (on a rough or steep course) on a bicycle.

cross-country bicycle and cyclist
Cross-country bicycle: relatively small, sturdy bicycle designed for performing acrobatics and competing in competitions on rough terrain.

protective goggles
One-piece watertight eyewear that protects the eyes from flying mud, stones and insects.

downhill bicycle and cyclist
Downhill bicycle: small, very sturdy bicycle for racing on rough ground with steep hills and strewn with obstacles.

goggles
Eyewear with plastic lenses fitted in a frame with arms; it protects the eyes from flying mud, stones and insects.

back suspension
Device that dampens vibrations from the wheels; this increases the bicycle's stability and its grip on the trail.

chin strap
Part of the helmet that protects the cyclist's chin.

front fork
Fork whose air/oil or elastomer suspension provides a controlled ride over rough terrain.

pedal with wide platform
Wide pedal providing good footing.

raised handlebar
Grip whose elevated position makes the bicycle easier to steer when going downhill.

clipless pedal
Pedal with a safety system so that the foot can be attached or detached quickly.

hydraulic disc brake
Brake with jaws that squeeze a disc to slow down the wheel; the braking power is produced by hydraulic pressure.

track cycling

Sport that consists of riding a bicycle on a closed track; the two types of track cycling events are speed and endurance.

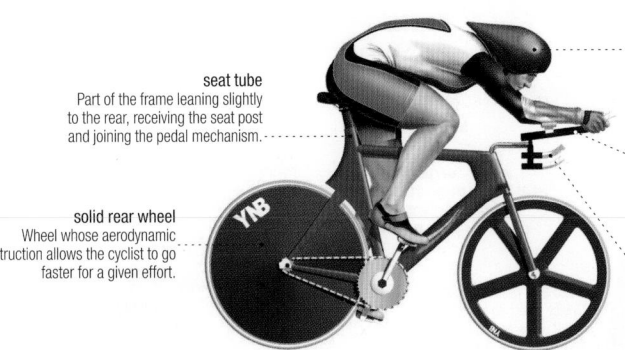

seat tube
Part of the frame leaning slightly to the rear, receiving the seat post and joining the pedal mechanism.

solid rear wheel
Wheel whose aerodynamic construction allows the cyclist to go faster for a given effort.

helmet
Rigid piece of protective equipment for the head that is streamlined for maximum aerodynamics.

handlebar
Grip that extends forward so that the cyclist can ride in an aerodynamic position.

handlebar grip
Each of the two low-mounted handle grips that allow the rider to start in the dance position (standing on the pedals).

pursuit bicycle and racer
Pursuit bicycle: bicycle with limited equipment, that is, no brakes, no derailleur (no gears) and no freewheel.

velodrome
Inclined oval course that is 250 m long (short track) or 333.33 m or 400 m long (long tracks) and whose width varies from 7 to 9 m.

pursuit line
Line indicating the start and finish point for the pursuit events.

jury platform
Place where the 10 judges stand by to monitor the progress of the race and give the results.

blue band
Strip where a racer gains speed before entering the track (sprint) and leaves it at the end of an event or to recover (American track).

finish line
Point that marks the end of all events (such as time trial and sprint), except the pursuit.

competitors' compound
Rest and assistance area for athletes between races where the coaches, mechanics and trainers stand by.

sprinters' line
Line that separates two lanes during a race or sprint.

200 m line
Point from which the racers are timed in the sprint event.

straightaway
Route that varies in length depending on the overall length of the track and is graded from 4° to 13°.

BMX

Sport that consists of performing freestyle acrobatics using a small, one-speed bicycle.

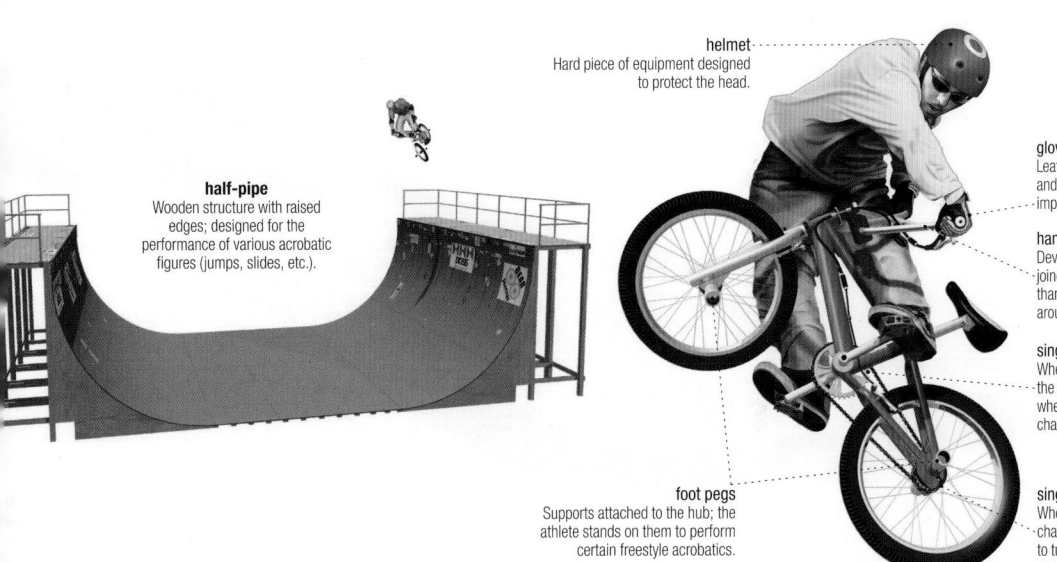

helmet
Hard piece of equipment designed to protect the head.

half-pipe
Wooden structure with raised edges; designed for the performance of various acrobatic figures (jumps, slides, etc.).

BMX bicycle and cyclist
BMX bicycle: small, single-gear bicycle for performing acrobatic figures.

glove
Leather item that reduces vibration and protects the hand against impact.

handlebar
Device consisting of two handles joined by a bar that can turn 360° thanks to a ring system that rotates around its axis.

single chain wheel
Wheel with teeth that is connected to the sprocket by a chain enabling the wheel to turn; the wheel has only one chain wheel as there is only one gear.

single sprocket
Wheel with teeth that is connected to the chain wheel by a chain enabling the wheel to turn; the bicycle has only one sprocket as there is only one gear.

foot pegs
Supports attached to the hub; the athlete stands on them to perform certain freestyle acrobatics.

SPORTS AND GAMES

auto racing

Speed event in which competitors driving race cars must make a predetermined number of laps around a track.

driver
Athlete who drives in a car race.

balaclava
Cap made of fireproof material that covers the head and neck and leaves the face uncovered.

undergarment
Clothing made of fireproof material that is worn under the suit; the undergarment and the driving suit must cover the neck, wrists and ankles.

earplugs/earbuds
Small plugs placed directly in the ears to dampen the noise from the engines and to allow radio communications between the driver and the team.

head and neck support (HANS) system
Device attached to the driver's crash helmet, consisting of a stiff collar and shoulder anchors, that protects a driver's head and neck in a collision.

wet-weather tire
Molded tire used on a wet track evacuate a large quantity of water 185 mph, it evacuates more than gallons of water per second.

checkered flag
Black-and-white checkered flag that signals the end of a race or trial session.

gloves
Item made of fireproof material that covers the hands and wrists; the gloves must fit tightly over the wrists and cover the sleeves of the suit.

dry-weather tire
Grooved tire providing a good gri on a dry track.

crash helmet
Hard piece of equipment designed to protect the head.

flame-resistant driving suit
Molded one-piece outfit that is made of fireproof material; it protects the driver from serious burns for several seconds.

starting grid
Position of the cars at the start of the race according to the time obtained during qualifications; the grid is made up of two cars per line in staggered formation.

shoe
Fire-resistant shoe that covers the entire foot and ankle.

pole position
First position at the starting grid that is obtained by the driver who earned the best time during the qualification session.

track
Closed course of a car race alternating between straight lines and more or less tight curves.

pits
Spaces reserved for each team where the drivers stop during the race to refuel and change their tires.

Formula 1 circuit
Driving surface of various lengths for race cars; the driver completes as many laps as necessary to accumulate 190 mi during a Grand Prix.

starting line
Line that marks the beginning of the race; when the starting signal is given, all the cars must be behind this line.

chicane
Succession of small tight curves designed to break up a straight fast portion of a circuit; it forces drivers to slow down.

gravel bed
Clear space located especially at curves where a car can slow down in case of a skid or spin.

pit lane
Lane that cars take to get to the pits; it has a speed limit.

curb
Concrete structure at the beginning and end of curves; it provides a visual landmark and delimits the track.

tire barrier
Security device for absorbing impact in case of collision or if cars leave the track.

auto racing

spoiler
Part using air pressure to increase the load on the rear and front wheels to improve the tires' grip on the track.

roll structure
Structure composed of metal loops to protect the driver if the car rolls over.

camera
Exposure apparatus for following a driver's vehicle during an event; each car is equipped with at least one camera.

cockpit
Part of the body where the driver sits that houses the equipment necessary for driving the car.

radio antenna
Device that emits and receives radio waves for communications between the driver and the team during the event.

examples of racing cars
Racing cars have a variety of characteristics that suit the type of track on which they compete (closed circuit, road circuit, etc.), as well as the type of race (speed or endurance) they are designed for.

Formula 1 car
Single-seater for racing on a closed circuit that can reach speeds of 225 mph; formula 1 is very popular in Europe.

Pitot tube
Measuring device for calculating the actual speed of the car by taking into account the influence of the wind.

side fairings
Malleable structure that absorbs the impact from a collision; the side fairings house especially radiators and electronic components.

steering wheel
Unit enabling the driver to steer the turning wheels; a veritable dashboard, it is equipped with several controls such as the clutch and gear shifter.

Indy car
...dier and faster than a formula ...a straight line, it is designed to ...ace on an oval or road circuit.

stock car
A racing car that conforms externally to a commercial car model and is raced usually on oval paved tracks.

Formula 3000 car
Single-seater that is less powerful than a formula 1 car but similar to it; formula 3000 is considered a school for formula 1.

sport prototype car
Powerful single-seater race car, usually designed for endurance competitions.

rally car
Two-seater touring car for racing long distances on the road, in several stages and within a given time.

pit stop
Stop that lasts a few seconds; it is taken by drivers during a race to refuel, change tires and make necessary mechanical adjustments.

starter mechanic
Mechanic who uses a starter to make the car run again if the engine stalls after refueling.

compressed-air tank
Reservoir containing compressed air for the pneumatic drills.

chief mechanic
Person who directs the mechanics; using a sign called a lollipop, this individual lets the driver know when the car can leave again.

jack
Mechanism activated by a handle, for raising the vehicle.

mechanic
Person in charge of changing the tires. One mechanic loosens the center lug nut, a second one takes the tire off and a third one puts the new tire on.

pneumatic drill
Instrument for tightening and loosening the center lug nut for each wheel.

motorcycling

Competitions involving motorcycles.

Grand Prix motorcycle and rider
Speed grand prix: streamlined motorcycle designed to race on a usually flat, closed road circuit; it can reach speeds of 200 mph.

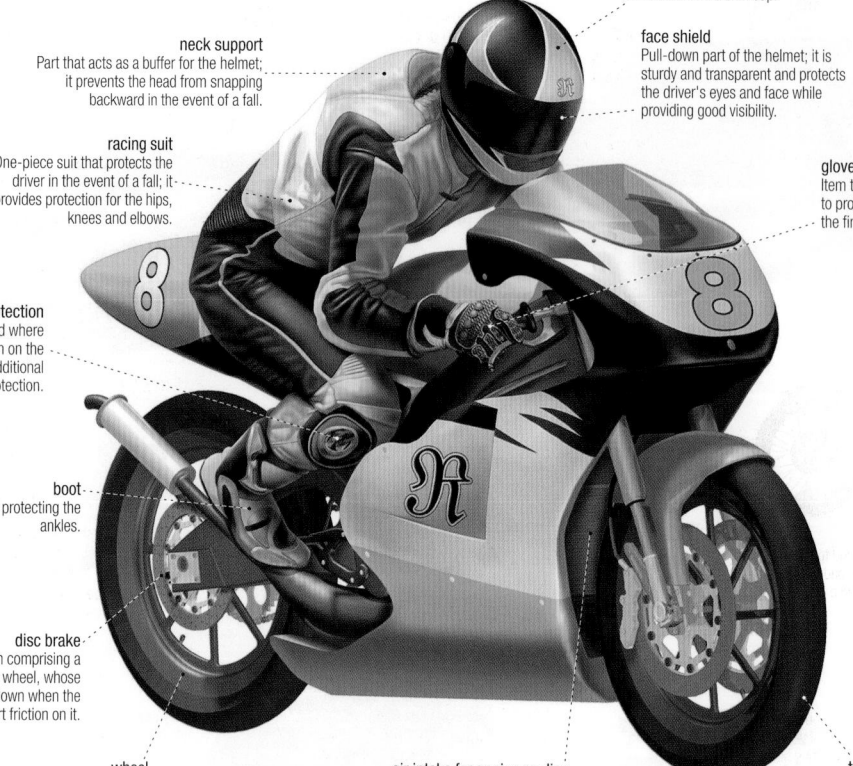

full-face helmet
Rigid piece of equipment that protects the head; it is equipped with a visor and a chin cup.

face shield
Pull-down part of the helmet; it is sturdy and transparent and protects the driver's eyes and face while providing good visibility.

neck support
Part that acts as a buffer for the helmet; it prevents the head from snapping backward in the event of a fall.

racing suit
One-piece suit that protects the driver in the event of a fall; it provides protection for the hips, knees and elbows.

glove
Item that covers the hand and wrist to protect them; it is reinforced at the fingers.

rub protection
Hard plastic part attached where the suit rubs the most often on the track in order to provide additional protection.

boot
High leather boot protecting the ankles.

disc brake
Braking mechanism comprising a disc attached to the wheel, whose rotation is slowed down when the brake pads exert friction on it.

wheel
Circular unit turning around an axle; it supports the weight of the vehicle and transmits the thrust, steering and braking actions.

air intake for engine cooling
Opening for letting the outside air in to cool the engine.

tire
Circular deformable unit made of rubber mounted on the wheel and inflated with air, providing the connection between motorcycle and the road, absorbing the unevenness of the road.

Grand Prix circuit
Racecourse typically between 2 and 6 mi long that is specially built or consists of closed-off public roads.

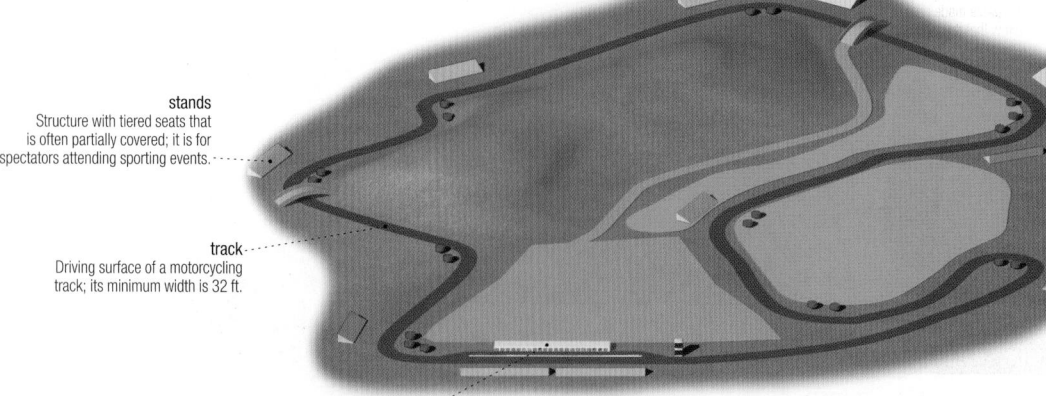

stands
Structure with tiered seats that is often partially covered; it is for spectators attending sporting events.

track
Driving surface of a motorcycling track; its minimum width is 32 ft.

pits
Spaces reserved for each team where the drivers stop during the race to refuel and change their tires.

motorcycling

trial motorcycle
Light motorcycle that is agile and easy to handle; it is designed for all-terrain obstacle races. The goal is to clear the obstacles while keeping both feet off the ground at all times.

rally motorcycle
All-terrain motorcycle designed to travel long distances on the road, in several stages and within a limited time.

motocross and supercross motorcycle and rider
Slim lightweight motorcycle for racing on a closed rough circuit with uneven ground, bumps and hillocks.

protective suit
Clothing consisting of a top and pants that protect the driver in the event of a fall; extra padding (such as for the elbows, knees and back) is optional.

glove
Item that covers the hand and wrist in order to protect them; it is made of synthetic material and is padded inside and out.

pants
Garment for the lower body; it extends from the waist or the hips to the ankles, covering each leg separately.

helmet
Hard piece of equipment designed to protect the head.

protective goggles
Equipment that protects the eyes; it is covered with several layers of plastic, which the driver peels off when they become dirty.

hand protector
Rigid part in front of the handlebar to protect the hand in the event of impact.

number plate
Rectangular plate on the front and sides of the motorcycle; it carries a number to identify the driver.

fork
Sliding tube that encloses a spring; it forms the steering, suspension and shock-absorbing mechanisms of the front wheel.

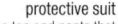
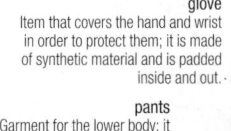

nubby tire
Tire whose tread is fitted with blocks of rubber, providing better traction on rough terrain.

boot
High leather boot protecting the ankles.

protective plate
Metal part under the motorcycle that protects it from shocks and prevents damage from striking obstacles.

multiple jumps
Series of several bumps that the racer clears in a single jump, as opposed to clearing each jump separately.

bridge
Humped structure that constitutes an obstacle for the racers.

triple jump
Obstacle made up of three bumps in a row that the racer must clear in one jump; the motorcycle must land on the far incline of the third bump.

obstacles
Elements, such as bumps, spines and bridges, that the racers must clear during an event.

bump
Rounded protrusion on the circuit that constitutes an obstacle for the racers.

spine
High bump enabling the racers to perform spectacular jumps.

motocross circuit
Sometimes covered, man-made track that is composed of earth or a mixture of sand and clay; it is strewn with obstacles and bumps to incite jumps.

start area
The starting line must be wide enough to accommodate the racers lined up abreast; each one needs a breadth of 3.3 ft.

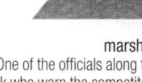

marshall
One of the officials along the [tra]ck who warn the competitors [of] potential danger by means of yellow flags.

markers
Long ribbons on the sides of the track that delimit a safety zone for the racers and spectators.

riders
Racers participating in a motorcycling event.

straw bales
Protective barriers placed at the curves to absorb impact in the event a racer skids out.

starting gate
Transversal device that serves as the motorcycles' starting point; it folds up or down so that the racers can push off.

personal watercraft

Motorized boat that moves quickly on water (about 65 mph); it is propelled by a turbine that sucks in water in front of it and shoots it out behind.

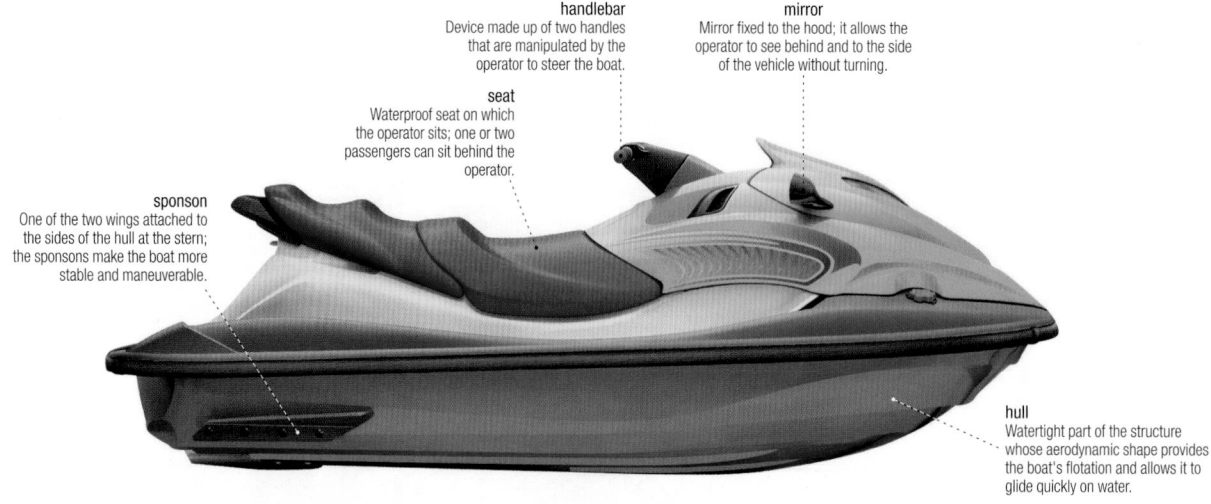

handlebar
Device made up of two handles that are manipulated by the operator to steer the boat.

mirror
Mirror fixed to the hood; it allows the operator to see behind and to the side of the vehicle without turning.

seat
Waterproof seat on which the operator sits; one or two passengers can sit behind the operator.

sponson
One of the two wings attached to the sides of the hull at the stern; the sponsons make the boat more stable and maneuverable.

hull
Watertight part of the structure whose aerodynamic shape provides the boat's flotation and allows it to glide quickly on water.

snowmobile

Motorized vehicle with a track and skis for moving rapidly on snow; some snowmobiles reach speeds of 125 mph.

seat
Seat, usually made of leather, on which the operator sits; a passenger can sit behind the operator.

brake handle
Lever the operator activates to slow down or stop the snowmobile.

handlebar
Device made up of two handles that the operator manipulates to steer the snowmobile.

windshield
Resistant glass and plastic panel that protects the operator from the wind and inclement weather.

backrest
Part supporting the passenger's lower back.

headlight
Lamp on the front of the vehicle to light up the space in front.

luggage rack
Structure attached to the rear of the snowmobile for transporting baggage.

cab
Lidlike part of the body that covers and protects the engine.

rear bumper
Malleable component attached to the rear of the snowmobile to dampen impact in the event of collision; it also acts as a handle for moving the snowmobile.

air scoop
Opening for letting the outside air in to cool the engine.

snow guard
Rubber or plastic part attached to the rear of the track that protects against flying snow.

sprocket
Wheel with teeth, which make successive contact with the track teeth to transmit its motion and propel the snowmobile.

track
Belt into which the sprockets mesh; it provides the snowmobile's traction.

footboard
Step used to board the snowmobile.

reflector
Device that reflects light back to its source to make the snowmobile visible at night.

body
Snowmobile structure that houses and protects the mechanical components.

idler wheel
Wheel that keeps the track taut.

shock absorber
Cylindrical device that is attached to the ski and coupled with a spring; it absorbs shocks caused by unevenness on the snow.

ski
Relatively wide blade that is attached to the front of the snowmobile and allows it to glide on snow; the skis are steered by the handlebars.

curling

Sport with two opposing teams of four players who slide stones over an ice surface in the direction of a target.

curling brush
Brush that is rubbed over the ice in front of a moving stone to alter its trajectory or improve its sliding.

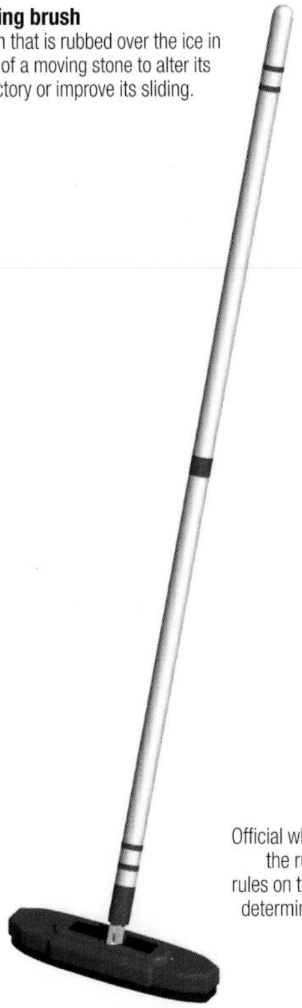

curling stone
Circular piece of polished granite; in the course of an end, each team takes turns to throw eight stones of the same color.

electronic handle
Handle used to manipulate the stone, equipped with an electronic device that indicates if the stone is released before it reaches the hog line.

curling sheet
Ice surface on which a match is played; when an end is complete, the next end starts from the opposite end of the sheet.

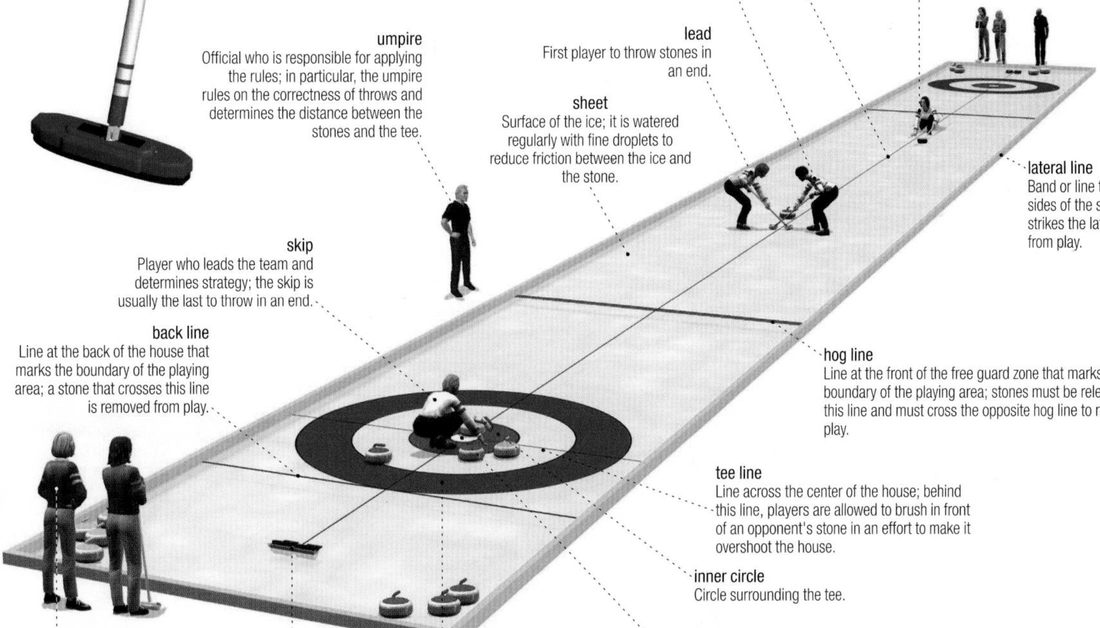

center line
Line that divides the sheet in half; the stone is thrown and released relatively close to this line.

vice skip
Player who assists the skip in devising playing tactics; the vice-skip usually throws third in an end.

second
Second player to throw stones in an end.

umpire
Official who is responsible for applying the rules; in particular, the umpire rules on the correctness of throws and determines the distance between the stones and the tee.

lead
First player to throw stones in an end.

sheet
Surface of the ice; it is watered regularly with fine droplets to reduce friction between the ice and the stone.

lateral line
Band or line that delimits the sides of the sheet; a stone that strikes the lateral line is removed from play.

skip
Player who leads the team and determines strategy; the skip is usually the last to throw in an end.

back line
Line at the back of the house that marks the boundary of the playing area; a stone that crosses this line is removed from play.

hog line
Line at the front of the free guard zone that marks the boundary of the playing area; stones must be released before this line and must cross the opposite hog line to remain in play.

tee line
Line across the center of the house; behind this line, players are allowed to brush in front of an opponent's stone in an effort to make it overshoot the house.

inner circle
Circle surrounding the tee.

curler
ing player who throws two s in each of the 10 ends that make up a match.

hack
Rubber foothold at each end of the sheet that the thrower uses to push off.

outer circle
Circle forming the outer limit of the house.

tee
Circle forming the center of the house; once all the stones are thrown, the team with the stone closest to the tee wins the end.

playing areas

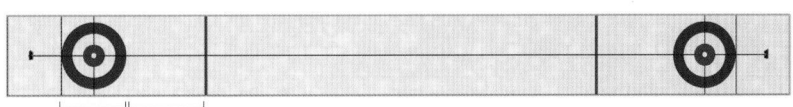

house
Series of concentric circles forming the scoring zone; a point is scored for each stone that lies closer to the tee than the opposing team's stones.

free guard zone
Area between the house and the hog line; leads may not remove the opposing team's stones from play.

ice hockey

Sport that is played on an ice rink with two opposing teams of six players; goals are scored by using a stick to put a puck in the opposing net.

ice hockey player
Member of an ice hockey team; players wear a variety of protective equipment to prevent injury caused by falls or body checks.

visor
Transparent piece of equipment secured to the front of the helmet to protect the eyes and upper face.

helmet
Hard piece of equipment designed to protect the head.

team's emblem
Logo representing the team that is printed on the front of the jersey.

player's number
Number that identifies the hockey player; numbers typically range from 1 to 99 and are sewn onto the back and the sleeves of the jersey.

glove
Padded covering for the hand and wrist that takes the shape of the fingers; it must be flexible enough to provide a good grip on the stick.

pants
Padded clothing attached around the waist by a belt or suspenders; they protect the pelvis, buttocks and thighs.

stocking
Stretchy piece of fabric that covers the leg and thigh; it is worn over the pads to keep the muscles warm.

skate
Reinforced boot equipped with a blade for gliding over ice.

blade
Narrow metal blade that is attached to the skate boot; its curved ends help the player to turn.

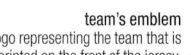

rink
Ice surface on which a hockey game is played; a game consists of three 20-minute periods with two 15-minute intermissions.

face-off spot
Each of the spots where a referee or linesman drops the puck to put it in play.

right defense
Position to the right of the center and behind the wing; this player tries to prevent the opponent from approaching the goal.

left defense
Position to the left of the center and behind the wing; this player tries to prevent the opponent from approaching the goal.

goal line
Red line that the puck must cross for a goal to be scored; the red line also marks the icing line.

glass protector
Reinforced glass panel that is mounted on top of the boards to protect spectators from high shots and players' sticks.

players' bench
Bench used by the coaches and by inactive players; each team has about 20 players but only six are on the ice at the same time.

rink corner
The four rounded corners of the rink where body checks are often thrown.

goal judge
Off-ice official who is positioned at the end of the rink behind the goal; the goal judge turns on a red light when the puck crosses the goal line.

goalkeeper
Player whose role is to prevent the puck from entering the goal; the goalkeeper usually plays the entire game.

boards
Wooden or fiberglass boards that surround the rink and delimit the playing area.

face-off circle
Circle around a face-off spot; two players line up on each side of this spot for a face-off while the other players remain outside the circle.

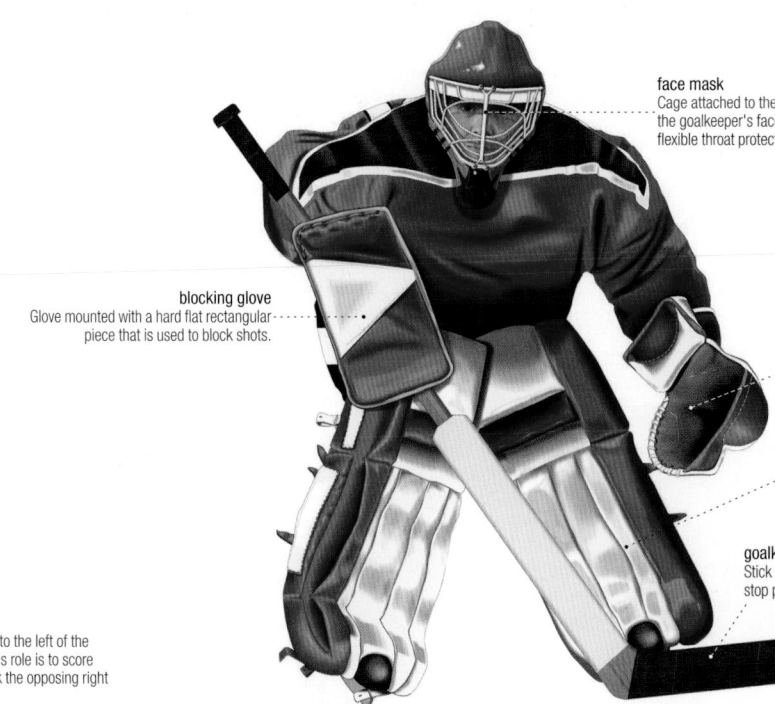

goalkeeper
Player whose role is to prevent the puck from entering the goal; the goalkeeper, who faces shots reaching speeds of 95 mph, wears heavy protective equipment.

face mask
Cage attached to the helmet to protect the goalkeeper's face and head; a flexible throat protector is attached to it.

blocking glove
Glove mounted with a hard flat rectangular piece that is used to block shots.

catching glove
Basket-shaped glove that is closed by pinching the hand; the goalkeeper uses it to catch and immobilize the puck.

goalkeeper's pad
Heavily padded piece of equipment that protects the goalkeeper's legs, knees and thighs from the impact of shots.

goalkeeper's stick
Stick featuring a large lower half and blade so that the goalkeeper can stop pucks more easily.

goal crease
Semicircle reserved for the goalkeeper; the referee disallows a goal if a player interferes with the goalkeeper inside the goal crease.

ft wing
ffensive position to the left of the enter; this player's role is to score als and to check the opposing right ing.

referee
Official who is responsible for applying the rules; the referee, who wears a red armband, officiates and drops the puck for face-offs at the start of a period.

assistant coach
Person who assists the coach; there are usually two assistant coaches behind the bench, one in charge of the offense and the other in charge of the defense.

blue line
Two lines that divide the rink into three equal parts; an offside is called when a player crosses the opposing blue line before the puck.

goal
Cage formed of netting mounted on a metal frame; a team scores a goal each time it lodges the puck inside the opposing goal.

coach
The team's leader; the coach plots strategy and decides who plays in different situations.

neutral zone
Area between the two blue lines where player changes are made and where various offensive and defensive strategies are initiated.

linesman
One of two officials who signal offsides and icings; they do most of the face-offs and also signal infractions to the referee.

goal lights
The red light signals a goal while the green light, which is connected to the official time clock, signals a stoppage in play or the end of a period.

center face-off circle
Circle in the middle of the rink; face-offs are held in the center circle at the start of a period and after a goal.

center
Player who usually takes the face-offs; a key player on a team, the center plays an offensive and a defensive role.

right wing
Offensive position to the right of the center; this player's role is to score goals and to check the opposing left wing.

officials' bench
Bench reserved for some of the off-ice officials (timekeeper and penalty keeper, scorer, announcer).

center line
Line that divides the rink into two zones, one for each team; teams change zones after each period.

penalty box
Bench reserved for penalized players; penalties vary between two and 10 minutes, depending on the seriousness of the infraction.

penalty box official
Official who is responsible for maintaining order on the penalty bench.

ice hockey

ice hockey equipment
Players wear substantial protective gear designed to prevent injury from falls, blows and shots.

goalkeeper's stick
Stick featuring a large lower half and blade so that the goalkeeper can stop pucks more easily.

player's stick
Long wooden or synthetic stick that consists of a blade set at an angle to a shaft.

 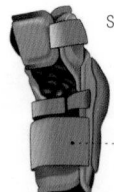

cuff
Elastic band that covers the upper part of the forearm; it fastens the elbow pad in place.

butt end
Upper end of the shaft; it is usually covered with rubber tape to prevent the hand from slipping off the stick.

neck guard
Nylon neck guard that is worn under the shoulder pads to protect the hockey player's neck and throat.

elbow pads
Piece of equipment that consists of a hard shell to protect the elbow; it also covers part of the arm and the forearm.

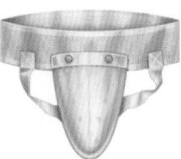

throat protector
Hard part secured to the goalkeeper's mask that covers the throat and the neck; it rises and falls with the goalkeeper's movements.

shaft

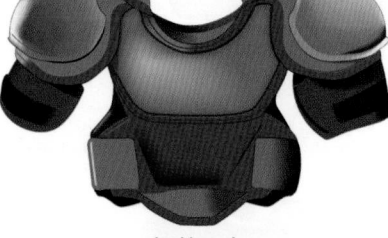

shoulder pads
Padded vest with two hard shells designed to protect the shoulders; they cover the chest and upper back but provide less coverage than the goalkeeper's chest pad.

protective cup
Piece of equipment that consists of rigid molded plastic designed to cover a player's genital organs.

heel
Back end of the blade.

puck
Black disk that is made of hard rubber; the puck is refrigerated before a game to improve its sliding action and reduce bouncing.

blade
Lower part of the stick that is used to stop, pass and shoot the puck; it is curved to ease puck handling.

arm pad
Part of the goalkeeper's chest pad that covers the arm.

knee pad
Part of the pads that covers the knees.

goalkeeper's chest pad
Heavily padded vest that protects the goalkeeper's shoulders, chest, stomach, back and arms.

player's skate
Reinforced boot equipped with a blade for gliding over ice.

tendon guard
Rigid part that covers the lower leg.

toe box
Hard shell that forms the end of the boot; it protects the toes from shots and slashes.

boot
Sturdy flexible boot with a lace; it protects and supports the foot and ankle and is made of leather or synthetic materials.

goalkeeper's skate
Skate that is reinforced on the sides and equipped with a long low straight blade; it is designed to improve the goalkeeper's balance.

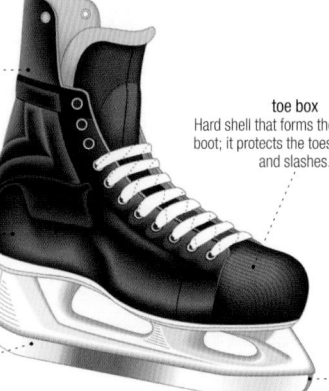

shin guards
Pieces of equipment that consist of hard molded plastic to protect the hockey player's legs and knees.

blade
Narrow metal blade that is attached to the skate boot; its curved ends help the player to turn.

point
Front tip of the blade.

figure skating

Sport that consists of executing jumps, spins and figures while skating to music; it includes singles skating, pairs skating and ice dancing.

lining
Padded layer of fabric or leather that covers and protects the inside of the boot.

hook
Small piece of curved metal used to attach the lace.

backstay
Reinforcement at the back of the boot.

tongue
Piece that extends from the boot and prevents the foot from rubbing against the lace; it is lifted to slip the foot into the boot.

figure skate
Reinforced boot with a blade that makes it possible to glide over the ice; figure skating is hard on the ankles so the skate provides maximum ankle support.

lace
Narrow cord of fabric or leather, flat or round, that is threaded through eyelets or hooks to tighten the boot.

boot
Sturdy flexible boot with a lace; it protects and supports the foot and ankle and is made of leather or synthetic materials.

eyelet
Small metal-rimmed hole through which the lace passes.

dance blade
Blade whose heel is shorter and whose toe picks are less pronounced to facilitate the execution of complex movements and to prevent the toe picks from catching.

heel
Stiff part underneath the boot that supports the back of the foot.

sole
Sturdy plastic or wooden sole that forms the bottom of the boot; the blade screws into the sole.

free skating blade
Blade with toe picks that facilitate the execution of jumps and spins; its curvature is more pronounced than that of the dance blade.

stanchion
Vertical part that extends up from the blade to secure it to the sole.

edge
Part of the blade that bites into the ice; the blade has two edges (inside and outside), which are separated by a groove.

blade
Narrow tapering strip of metal that is attached to the sole; the lower part is made of hardened steel to keep the edges sharp.

toe pick
Small teeth at the front end of the blade; they serve as the pivot point during spins and also make it possible to take off and land during jumps.

examples of jumps

Jump: movement by which the skater leaves the ice and spins in the air before landing.

axel
Jump of one and a half rotations with takeoff from the forward edge; invented by the Norwegian Axel Paulsen in 1882, it is considered the most difficult jump.

salchow
Single-rotation jump with takeoff from the back inside edge; the Swede Ulrich Salchow created it in 1909.

toe loop
Single-rotation toe jump with takeoff and landing on the same foot; it is considered the easiest of the toe jumps.

flip
Single-rotation toe jump with takeoff from the back inside edge and landing on the opposite foot; the flip is in fact a toe salchow.

lutz
Single-rotation toe jump with takeoff from the back outside edge and landing on the opposite foot; the Austrian Alois Lutz invented it in 1913.

referee
Official who is responsible for the eligibility of officials, skaters and the judging panel and the allowability of controversial decisions.

assistant referee
Individual who assists the referee and is authorized to replace him or her if necessary.

technical delegates
Official who ensures that technical installations are in compliance with the standards of the International Skating Union (ISU).

judges
Officials who are responsible for evaluating performances; during international competitions, nine judges are chosen at random from the nations represented.

rink
Ice surface on which skaters execute their programs; program duration varies depending on the event (between 2 min. 40 sec. and 4 min. 30 sec.).

timekeeper
Person who monitors the length of performances to ensure that skaters respect the allotted time.

technical specialist
Official who identifies the technical elements performed by the skater and their level of difficulty. The information is then transmitted to the judges.

pair
Team formed of a man and a woman; like singles skaters, pairs take part in two events: the technical program and the free program.

technical controller
Official who supervises the work of the technical specialist. He or she can immediately correct any error observed.

coaches
Individuals who oversee the training and preparation of skaters for competitions; coaches provide final advice prior to performances.

speed skating

Race on ice between individuals or teams held on a long or short track.

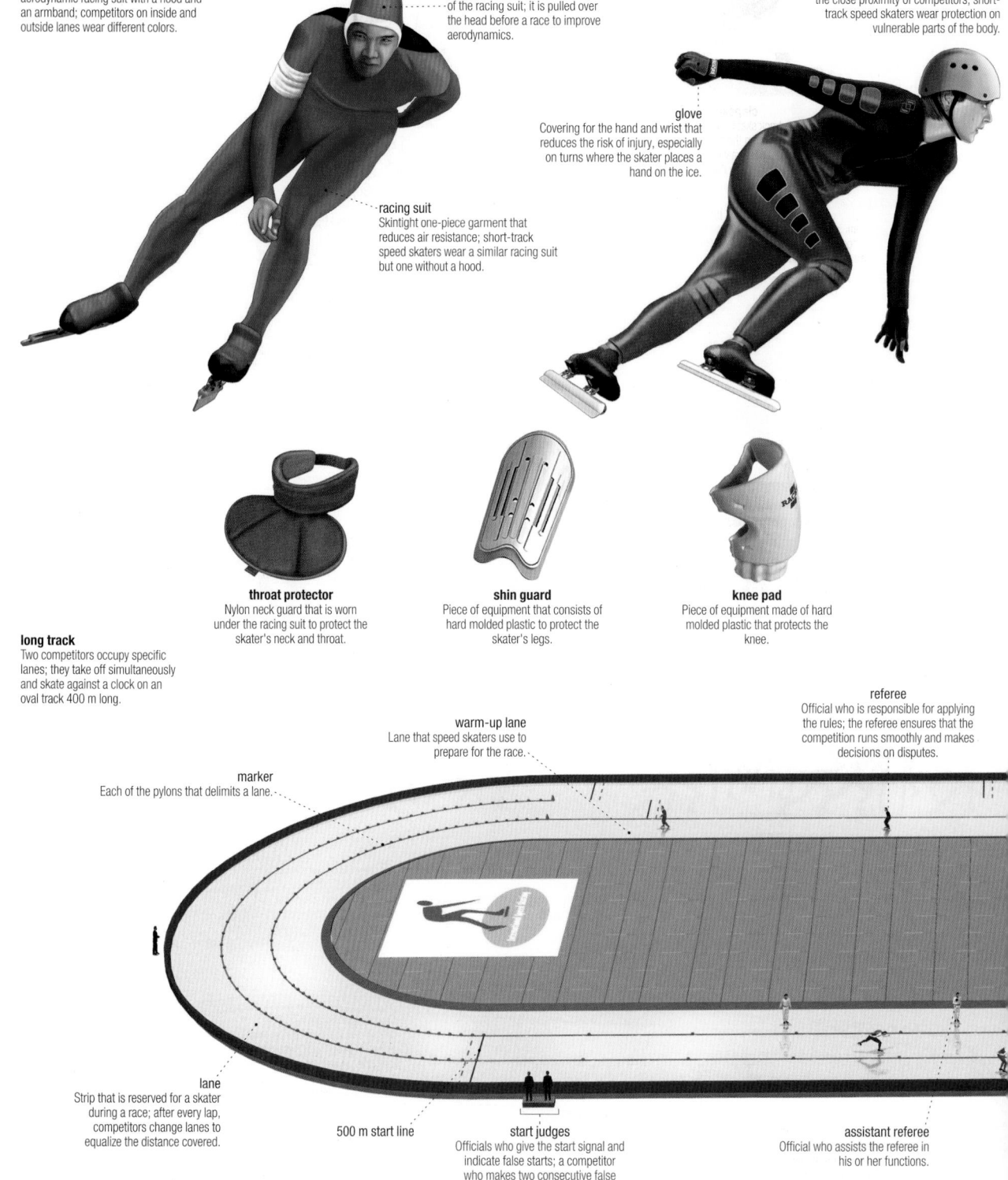

skater (long track)
The long-track speed skater wears an aerodynamic racing suit with a hood and an armband; competitors on inside and outside lanes wear different colors.

hood
Headgear attached to the neck of the racing suit; it is pulled over the head before a race to improve aerodynamics.

skater (short track)
Because of the high risk of falling and the close proximity of competitors, short-track speed skaters wear protection on vulnerable parts of the body.

glove
Covering for the hand and wrist that reduces the risk of injury, especially on turns where the skater places a hand on the ice.

racing suit
Skintight one-piece garment that reduces air resistance; short-track speed skaters wear a similar racing suit but one without a hood.

throat protector
Nylon neck guard that is worn under the racing suit to protect the skater's neck and throat.

shin guard
Piece of equipment that consists of hard molded plastic to protect the skater's legs.

knee pad
Piece of equipment made of hard molded plastic that protects the knee.

long track
Two competitors occupy specific lanes; they take off simultaneously and skate against a clock on an oval track 400 m long.

referee
Official who is responsible for applying the rules; the referee ensures that the competition runs smoothly and makes decisions on disputes.

warm-up lane
Lane that speed skaters use to prepare for the race.

marker
Each of the pylons that delimits a lane.

lane
Strip that is reserved for a skater during a race; after every lap, competitors change lanes to equalize the distance covered.

500 m start line

start judges
Officials who give the start signal and indicate false starts; a competitor who makes two consecutive false starts is disqualified.

assistant referee
Official who assists the referee in his or her functions.

speed skating

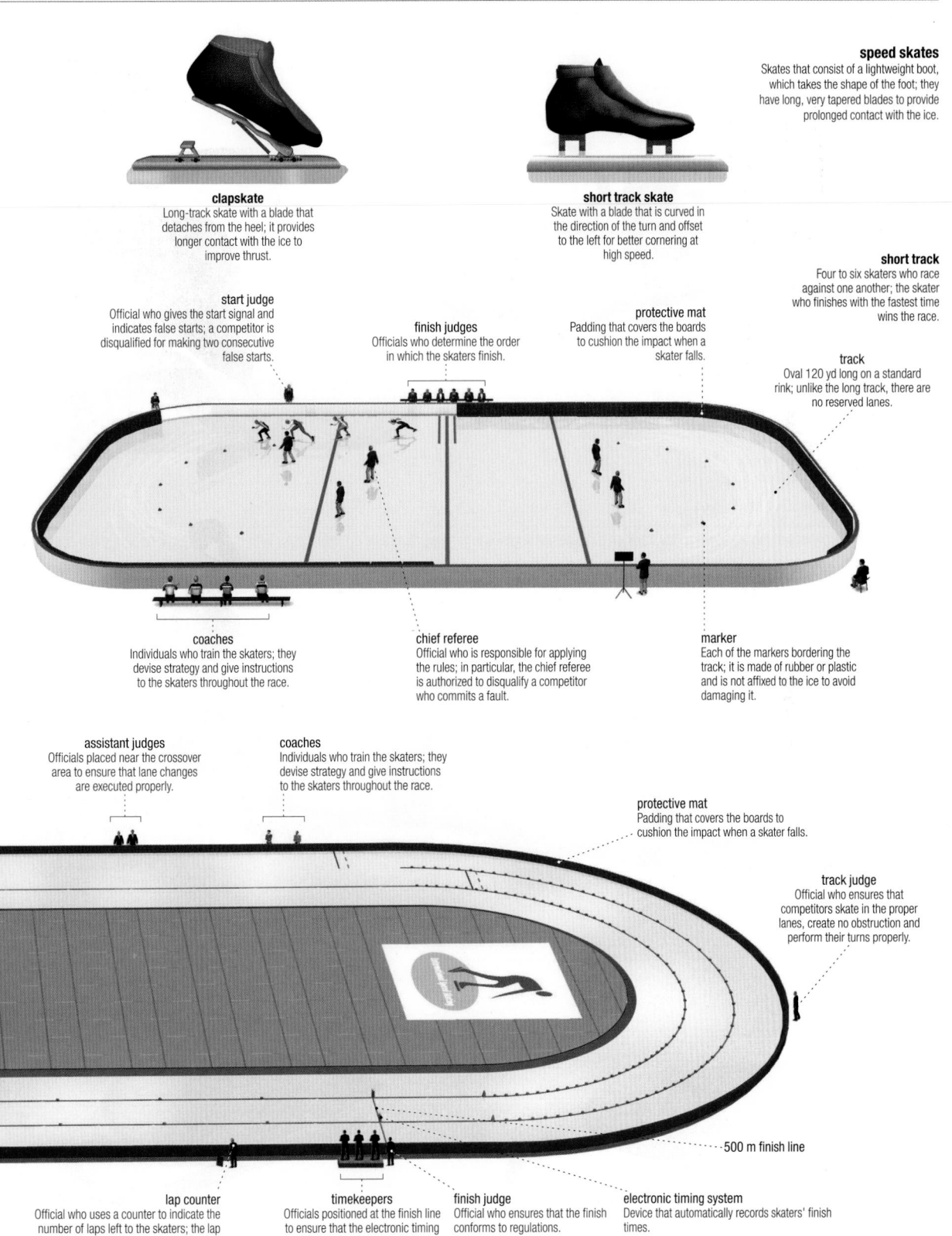

speed skates
Skates that consist of a lightweight boot, which takes the shape of the foot; they have long, very tapered blades to provide prolonged contact with the ice.

clapskate
Long-track skate with a blade that detaches from the heel; it provides longer contact with the ice to improve thrust.

short track skate
Skate with a blade that is curved in the direction of the turn and offset to the left for better cornering at high speed.

short track
Four to six skaters who race against one another; the skater who finishes with the fastest time wins the race.

start judge
Official who gives the start signal and indicates false starts; a competitor is disqualified for making two consecutive false starts.

finish judges
Officials who determine the order in which the skaters finish.

protective mat
Padding that covers the boards to cushion the impact when a skater falls.

track
Oval 120 yd long on a standard rink; unlike the long track, there are no reserved lanes.

coaches
Individuals who train the skaters; they devise strategy and give instructions to the skaters throughout the race.

chief referee
Official who is responsible for applying the rules; in particular, the chief referee is authorized to disqualify a competitor who commits a fault.

marker
Each of the markers bordering the track; it is made of rubber or plastic and is not affixed to the ice to avoid damaging it.

assistant judges
Officials placed near the crossover area to ensure that lane changes are executed properly.

coaches
Individuals who train the skaters; they devise strategy and give instructions to the skaters throughout the race.

protective mat
Padding that covers the boards to cushion the impact when a skater falls.

track judge
Official who ensures that competitors skate in the proper lanes, create no obstruction and perform their turns properly.

500 m finish line

lap counter
Official who uses a counter to indicate the number of laps left to the skaters; the lap counter also rings a bell at the start of the last lap.

timekeepers
Officials positioned at the finish line to ensure that the electronic timing system functions properly; they keep time manually if necessary.

finish judge
Official who ensures that the finish conforms to regulations.

electronic timing system
Device that automatically records skaters' finish times.

SPORTS AND GAMES

bobsled

Sport that consists of racing down an icy track on a two- or four-person bobsled; bobsleds reach speeds of over 85 mph.

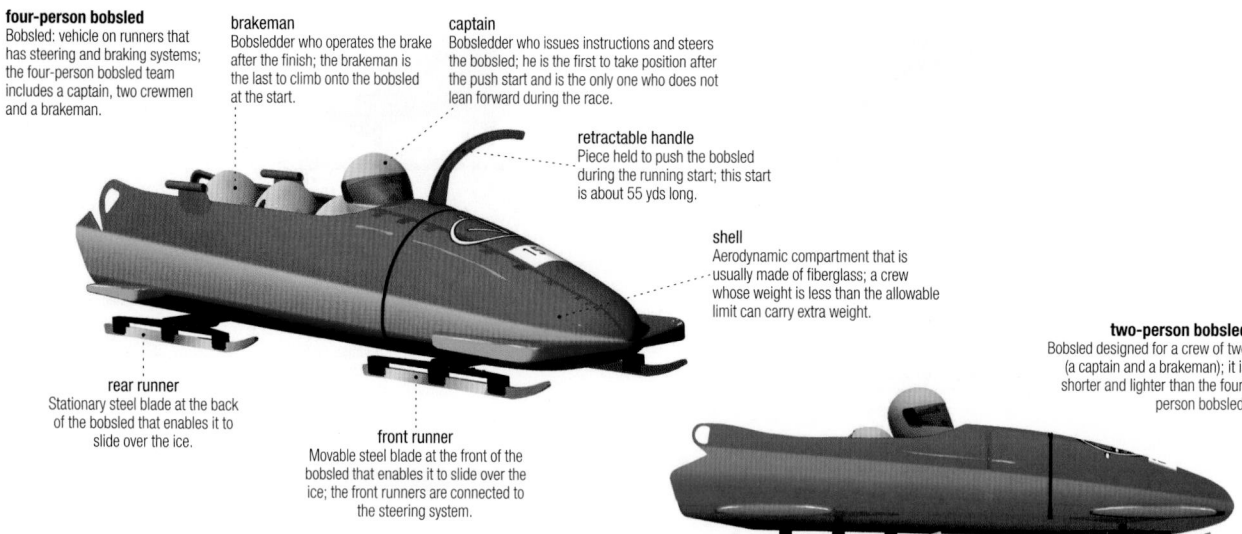

four-person bobsled
Bobsled: vehicle on runners that has steering and braking systems; the four-person bobsled team includes a captain, two crewmen and a brakeman.

brakeman
Bobsledder who operates the brake after the finish; the brakeman is the last to climb onto the bobsled at the start.

captain
Bobsledder who issues instructions and steers the bobsled; he is the first to take position after the push start and is the only one who does not lean forward during the race.

retractable handle
Piece held to push the bobsled during the running start; this start is about 55 yds long.

shell
Aerodynamic compartment that is usually made of fiberglass; a crew whose weight is less than the allowable limit can carry extra weight.

two-person bobsled
Bobsled designed for a crew of two (a captain and a brakeman); it is shorter and lighter than the four-person bobsled.

rear runner
Stationary steel blade at the back of the bobsled that enables it to slide over the ice.

front runner
Movable steel blade at the front of the bobsled that enables it to slide over the ice; the front runners are connected to the steering system.

luge

Speed sport that consists of racing down an icy track on a singles or doubles luge; luge racers lie on their backs with their feet forward and reach speeds of 90 mph.

luge racer
Athlete who engages in the sport of luge; the luge racer starts a race in a seated position, then uses the runners to generate momentum and the hands to accelerate before lying down.

sled
Wooden fiberglass or plastic platform with a backless seat; luge racers lie on their backs.

one-piece suit
Skintight one-piece garment that reduces air resistance; a luge racer can carry extra weight underneath the suit to reach the maximum allowable weight.

crash helmet
Hard piece of equipment designed to protect the head.

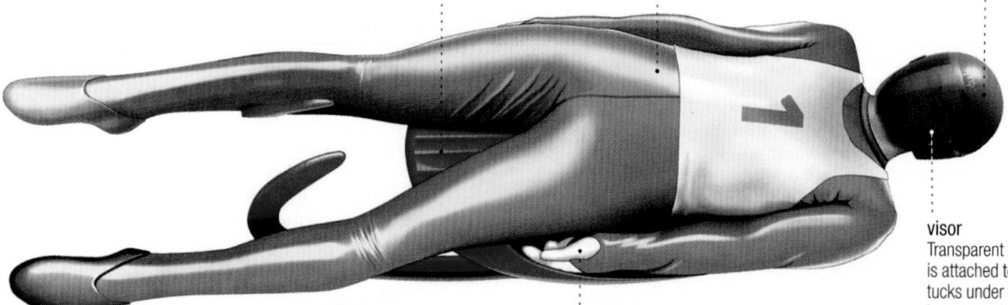

visor
Transparent or tinted piece of equipment that is attached to the front of the helmet and tucks under the chin to reduce air resistance; it protects the eyes and the face.

glove
Covering for the hand and wrist; the fingertips contain studs for greater manual traction at the start.

singles luge
Luge designed for a single racer; it is shorter and lighter that the doubles luge.

doubles luge
Luge designed for two racers; the luge racer on top (the heavier of the two to improve aerodynamics) is held in place by a strap.

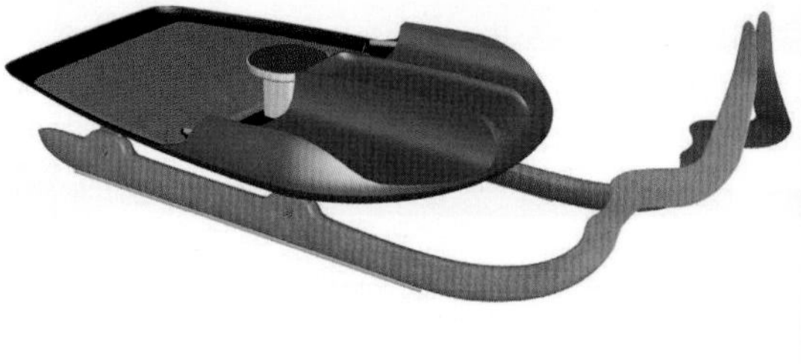

runner
Piece or wood or fiberglass that is attached to the bottom of the sled; the luge racer steers by applying foot pressure to the front of the runners.

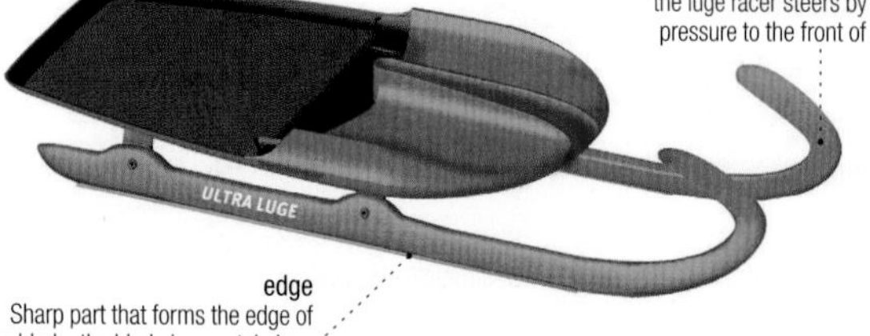

ULTRA LUGE

edge
Sharp part that forms the edge of the blade; the blade is a metal piece placed under the runner so that the luge can slide over the ice.

skeleton

Sport that consists of racing down an icy track on a skeleton, which can reach speeds of 85 mph; sledders lie head forward on their stomachs.

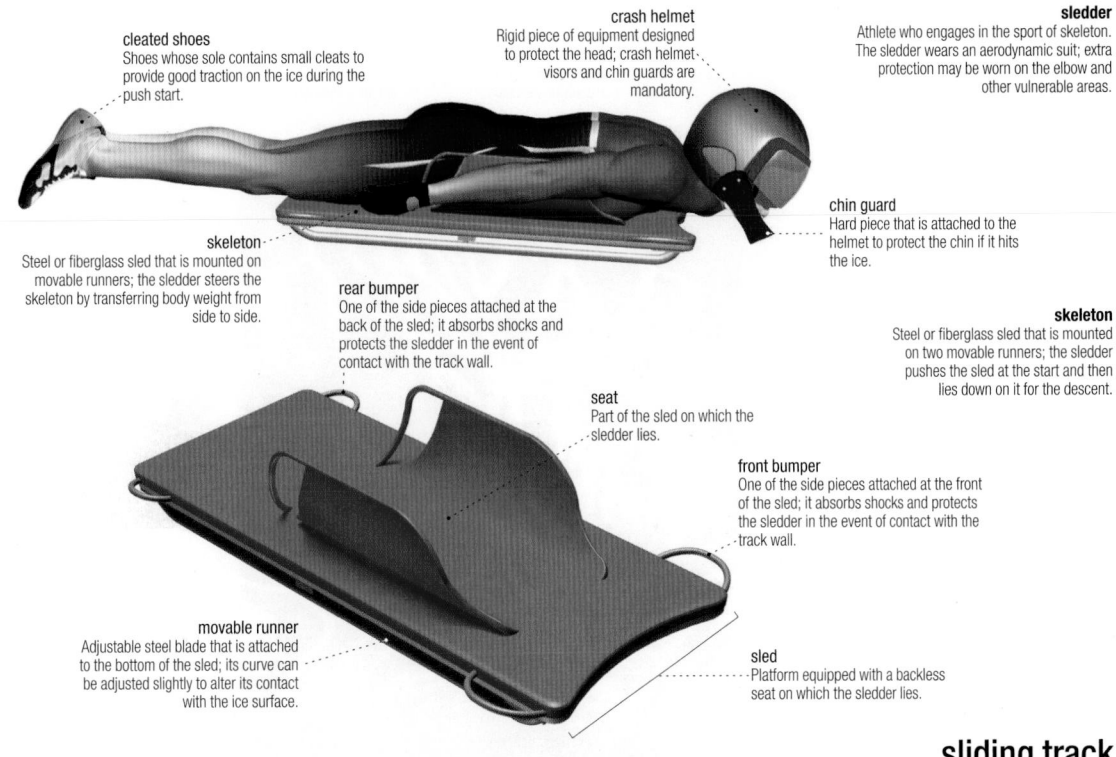

cleated shoes
Shoes whose sole contains small cleats to provide good traction on the ice during the push start.

crash helmet
Rigid piece of equipment designed to protect the head; crash helmet visors and chin guards are mandatory.

sledder
Athlete who engages in the sport of skeleton. The sledder wears an aerodynamic suit; extra protection may be worn on the elbow and other vulnerable areas.

skeleton
Steel or fiberglass sled that is mounted on movable runners; the sledder steers the skeleton by transferring body weight from side to side.

chin guard
Hard piece that is attached to the helmet to protect the chin if it hits the ice.

rear bumper
One of the side pieces attached at the back of the sled; it absorbs shocks and protects the sledder in the event of contact with the track wall.

skeleton
Steel or fiberglass sled that is mounted on two movable runners; the sledder pushes the sled at the start and then lies down on it for the descent.

seat
Part of the sled on which the sledder lies.

front bumper
One of the side pieces attached at the front of the sled; it absorbs shocks and protects the sledder in the event of contact with the track wall.

movable runner
Adjustable steel blade that is attached to the bottom of the sled; its curve can be adjusted slightly to alter its contact with the ice surface.

sled
Platform equipped with a backless seat on which the sledder lies.

sliding track

Concrete structure that is covered with an artificial sheet of ice; bobsled, luge and skeleton races are held on it.

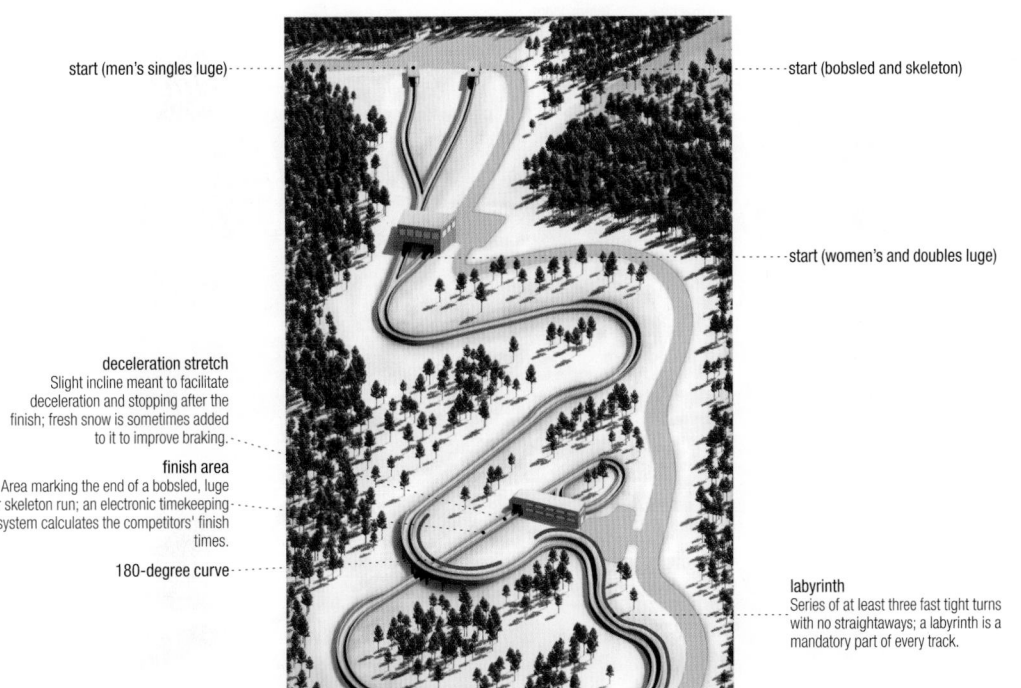

start (men's singles luge)

start (bobsled and skeleton)

start (women's and doubles luge)

deceleration stretch
Slight incline meant to facilitate deceleration and stopping after the finish; fresh snow is sometimes added to it to improve braking.

finish area
Area marking the end of a bobsled, luge or skeleton run; an electronic timekeeping system calculates the competitors' finish times.

180-degree curve

labyrinth
Series of at least three fast tight turns with no straightaways; a labyrinth is a mandatory part of every track.

ski resort

Resort area with the facilities required for skiing and snowboarding; it also lodges skiers and snowboarders.

general view

gondola
Mechanical lift made up of a series of closed cabins that are suspended from a single cable; skis and snowboards are hung outside the cabin.

ski lift arrival area

summit lodge

summit
Highest point on the mountain; it marks the starting point of most alpine ski trails.

intermediate slope
Relatively steep slope geared to intermediate skiers and snowboarders who know the basics of their sport.

easy slope
Wide gentle and well-cleared slope for skiing and snowboarding beginners.

chairlift
Mechanical lift that is suspended from a single cable; it is made up of a series of seats for two to eight skiers or snowboarders who wear their equipment while going up and down.

ski area
Network of trails that makes up a ski resort; they can be built on one or more slopes, on one mountain or on adjacent mountains.

expert slope
Extremely difficult slope geared to expert skiers and snowboarders; these slopes are usually very steep and include moguls and tight turns.

alpine ski trail
Slope groomed for alpine skiing or snowboarding; a sign indicates the level of difficulty by means of a color-coded system.

difficult slope
Steep slope geared to experienced skiers and snowboarders.

patrol and first aid station
Building reserved for the ski patrol; it houses equipment for administering first aid to injured or sick skiers.

main lodge
Building that brings together various services such as restaurants, bars, boutiques and day care.

lodging
The businesses, buildings and dwellings that make it possible to enjoy a relatively long-term stay at a ski resort.

snow-grooming machine
A tracked vehicle used to prepare trails; it packs fresh snow, evens out bumps and replaces snow on uncovered areas.

skiers' lodge
Multipurpose building providing a variety of services such as cafeteria, lockers, rental and repair shop and ski school.

chairlift departure area

view of the base of the mountain

ski school
Business that offers skiing or snowboarding lessons to individuals or groups of all levels.

T-bar
Mechanical lift that consists of a series of inverted T-shaped bars that hold two people; as the T-bar pulls them, their skis or snowboards slide along the ground.

cross-country ski trail
Trail groomed for cross-country skiing; a sign indicates the level of difficulty by means of a color-coded system.

gondolas departure area

condominium
Group of lodgings belonging to separate owners who share the building's maintenance costs.

ice rink
Ice surface designed for skating.

mountain lodge
Small, usually wooden dwelling built on the side of a mountain; it sometimes provides direct access to the ski area.

hotel
Business establishment that lodges people for a fee.

information desk
Kiosk that provides information on a ski resort's facilities, events and services.

village
Place in which lodging and ski resort services are concentrated.

parking
Area for cars to park.

snowboarding

Sport that consists of sliding over a snow-covered surface on a board fitted with foot bindings; the snowboard is steered by bending the knees.

snowboarder
Person who engages in snowboarding; the competitive snowboarder usually specializes in one particular discipline.

helmet
Rigid piece of equipment that is designed to protect the head; helmets are mandatory for racing.

goggles
Equipment that protects the eyes against the sun and the elements; the filtered lenses optimize depth perception.

glove
Covering for the hand and wrist that protects them against the cold and snow in the event of a fall.

shin guard
Piece of equipment made of hard molded plastic that protects the snowboarder's legs.

hard boot
Boot used for alpine events; it provides firm support and makes it possible to immediately transfer body movement to the board.

coveralls
Skintight one-piece garment that reduces air resistance.

snowboard
Board with foot bindings that is designed for sliding over snow-covered surfaces.

flexible boot
flexible boot that is designed for freestyle and all-terrain snowboarding; it allows the snowboarder to perform a broad range of movements and figures.

freestyle snowboard
Wide flexible snowboard used for figures; the nose and tail are identical so that the snowboarder can take off and land in both directions.

plate binding
Binding used with hard boots; it has a metal toeplate that keeps the boot firmly in place to provide maximum stability.

alpine snowboard
Long narrow rigid snowboard that is designed to reach high speeds.

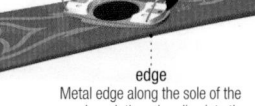

soft binding
Binding used with flexible boots; the soft binding has straps to secure the foot and padded ankle supports.

tail
Back end of the snowboard; unlike the tail of the freestyle snowboard, the alpine snowboard tail is not designed for going backward.

edge
Metal edge along the sole of the snowboard; the edge digs into the snow and makes turning possible.

nose
Front end of the snowboard; its slightly upturned curve cuts through the snow and helps to avoid catching an edge.

competition site (half-pipe)
The half-pipe event is set to music and consists of executing acrobatic figures by sliding from one side of a track with banked edges (half-pipe) to the other.

judges' stand
Stand reserved for the five judges who evaluate specific criteria such as maneuvers with and without rotation, jump height and overall impression.

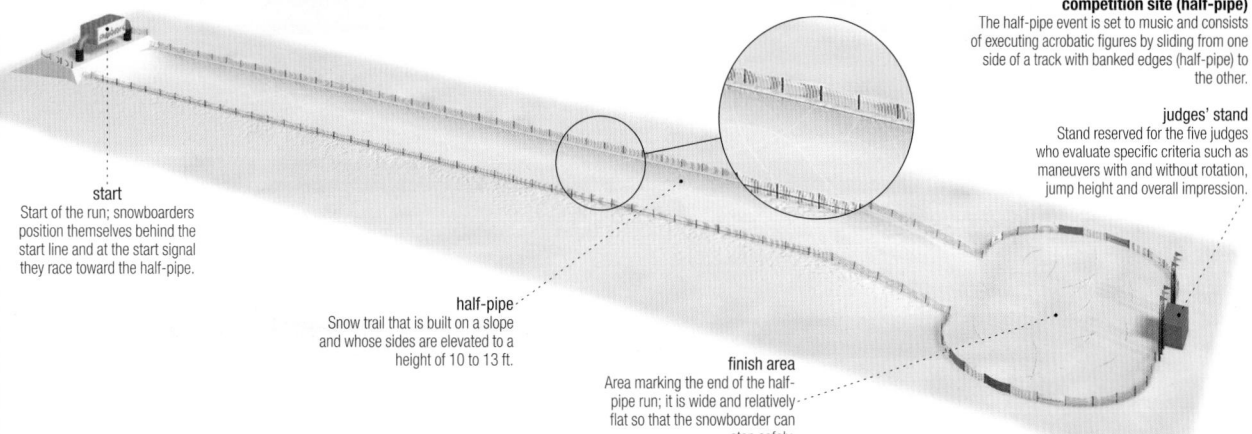

start
Start of the run; snowboarders position themselves behind the start line and at the start signal they race toward the half-pipe.

half-pipe
Snow trail that is built on a slope and whose sides are elevated to a height of 10 to 13 ft.

finish area
Area marking the end of the half-pipe run; it is wide and relatively flat so that the snowboarder can stop safely.

alpine skiing

Sport that consists of racing on alpine skis down a snow-covered slope with a medium or steep drop.

alpine skier
Person who engages in alpine skiing; competitive alpine skiers specialize in one or more of four events.

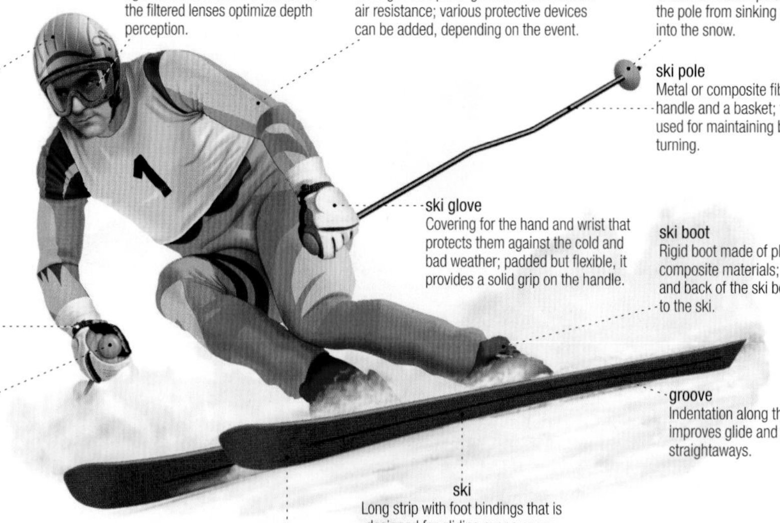

ski goggles
Equipment that protects the eyes against the sun and the elements; the filtered lenses optimize depth perception.

ski suit
Skintight one-piece garment that reduces air resistance; various protective devices can be added, depending on the event.

basket
Circular piece attached to the bottom of the ski pole; it prevents the pole from sinking too deeply into the snow.

helmet
Rigid piece of equipment that is designed to protect the head; helmets are mandatory for racing.

ski pole
Metal or composite fiber rod with a handle and a basket; the ski pole is used for maintaining balance and for turning.

ski glove
Covering for the hand and wrist that protects them against the cold and bad weather; padded but flexible, it provides a solid grip on the handle.

ski boot
Rigid boot made of plastic or composite materials; the front and back of the ski boot attach to the ski.

wrist strap
Strap that is attached to the handle and worn around the wrist to prevent the skier from losing a pole when sticking it into the ground.

handle

groove
Indentation along the bottom that improves glide and stability on straightaways.

alpine ski
Long strip with foot bindings that is designed for gliding over a snow-covered surface; it is usually made of composite fibers.

ski
Long strip with foot bindings that is designed for gliding over a snow-covered surface; it is usually made of composite fibers.

bottom
Carefully polished piece that forms the bottom of the ski; a wax suited to snow conditions is applied to the bottom to obtain the best possible glide.

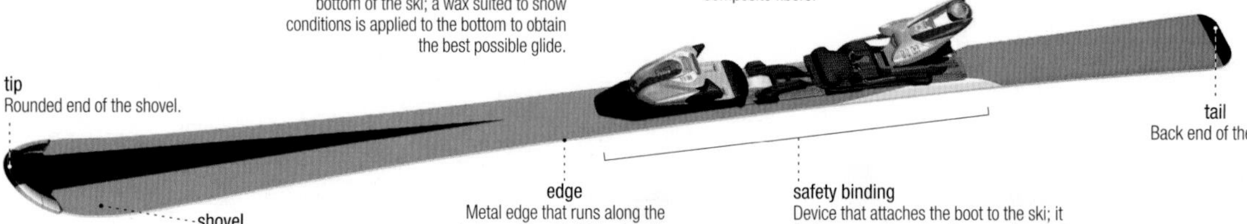

tip
Rounded end of the shovel.

tail
Back end of the ski.

shovel
Front end of the ski; its upward curve cuts through snow and helps to avoid catching an edge.

edge
Metal edge that runs along the bottom of the ski; it bites into the snow and makes turning possible.

safety binding
Device that attaches the boot to the ski; it features an automatic release system that frees the boot when too much pressure is exerted on it.

examples of skis
Skis are adapted to the requirements of each event; their performance on snow depends on their length, width and design.

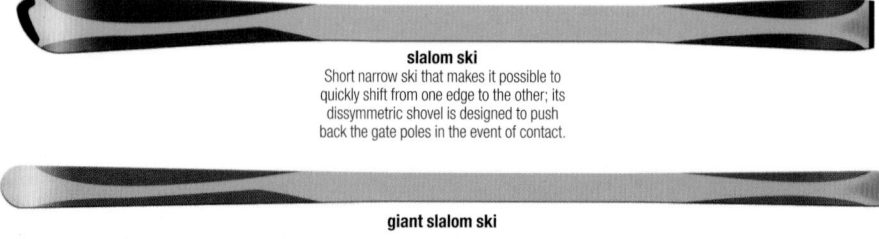

skiboard
Very short ski for performing jumps and other acrobatics.

slalom ski
Short narrow ski that makes it possible to quickly shift from one edge to the other; its dissymmetric shovel is designed to push back the gate poles in the event of contact.

giant slalom ski

downhill and super-G ski
Long rigid ski that provides a high level of stability and excellent glide; it is designed for straightaways and for speed.

technical events

During each event, skiers take turns attempting to complete the descent as fast as possible while following the established course.

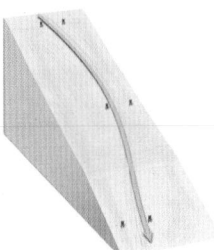

downhill
Speed event held on a steep course with long straightaways and wide fast turns; downhill skiers reach speeds of over 75 mph.

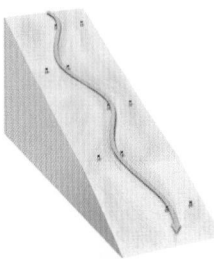

super giant (super-G) slalom
Event that combines the speed of downhill with the technique of giant slalom; the super-G course is shorter than the downhill course and has more gates.

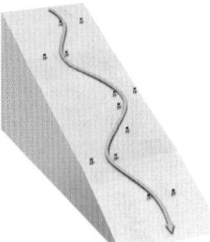

giant slalom
Technical event whose course has fewer gates and longer curves than the special slalom course.

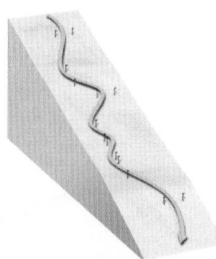

special slalom
Technical event whose course includes numerous sharp turns; the skier must graze the gate poles to keep the best trajectory.

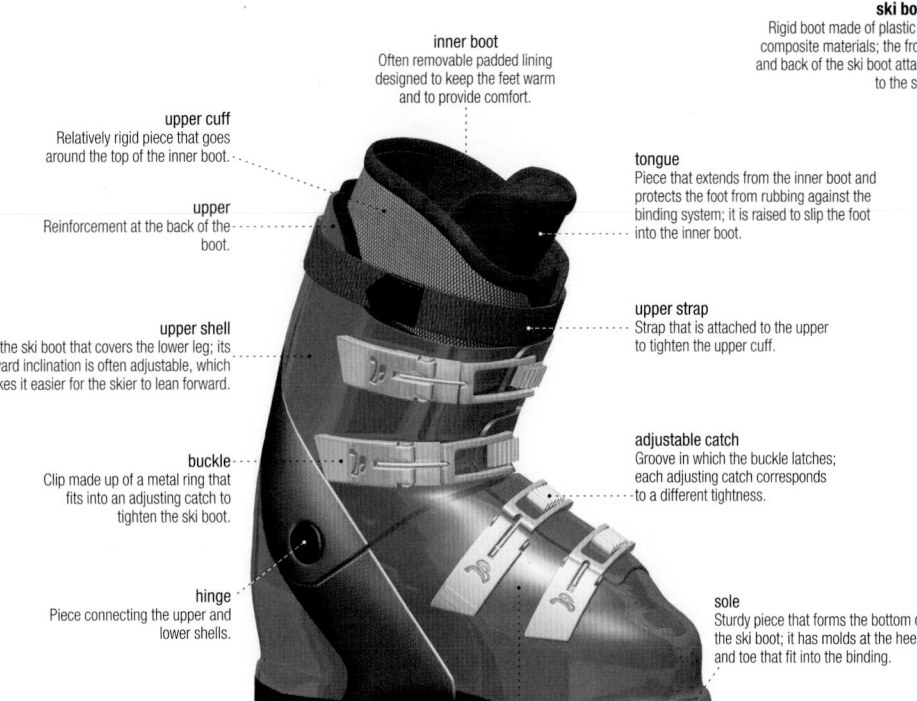

inner boot
Often removable padded lining designed to keep the feet warm and to provide comfort.

ski boot
Rigid boot made of plastic or composite materials; the front and back of the ski boot attach to the ski.

upper cuff
Relatively rigid piece that goes around the top of the inner boot.

tongue
Piece that extends from the inner boot and protects the foot from rubbing against the binding system; it is raised to slip the foot into the inner boot.

upper
Reinforcement at the back of the boot.

upper strap
Strap that is attached to the upper to tighten the upper cuff.

upper shell
Part of the ski boot that covers the lower leg; its forward inclination is often adjustable, which makes it easier for the skier to lean forward.

adjustable catch
Groove in which the buckle latches; each adjusting catch corresponds to a different tightness.

buckle
Clip made up of a metal ring that fits into an adjusting catch to tighten the ski boot.

sole
Sturdy piece that forms the bottom of the ski boot; it has molds at the heel and toe that fit into the binding.

hinge
Piece connecting the upper and lower shells.

lower shell
Part of the ski boot that covers the foot and the ankle.

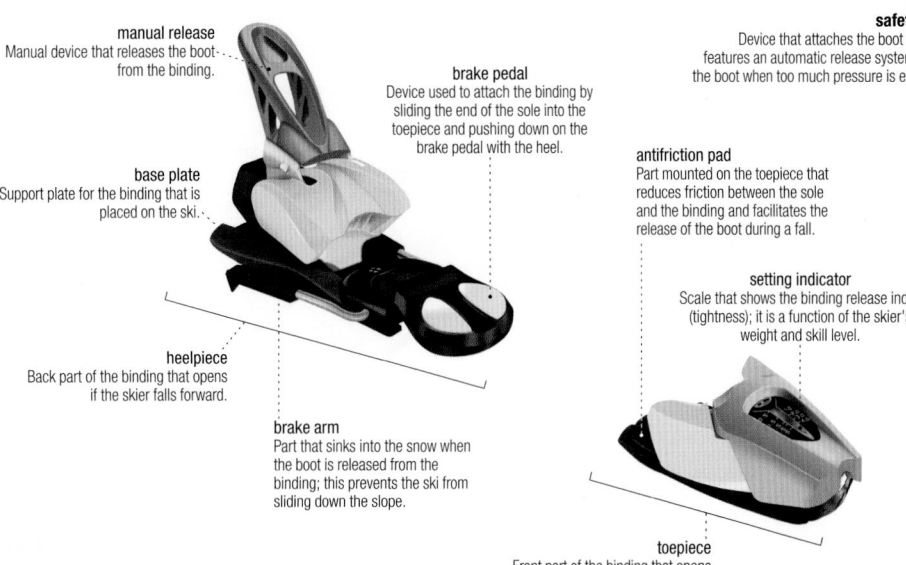

manual release
Manual device that releases the boot from the binding.

brake pedal
Device used to attach the binding by sliding the end of the sole into the toepiece and pushing down on the brake pedal with the heel.

safety binding
Device that attaches the boot to the ski; it features an automatic release system that frees the boot when too much pressure is exerted on it.

base plate
Support plate for the binding that is placed on the ski.

antifriction pad
Part mounted on the toepiece that reduces friction between the sole and the binding and facilitates the release of the boot during a fall.

setting indicator
Scale that shows the binding release index (tightness); it is a function of the skier's weight and skill level.

heelpiece
Back part of the binding that opens if the skier falls forward.

brake arm
Part that sinks into the snow when the boot is released from the binding; this prevents the ski from sliding down the slope.

toepiece
Front part of the binding that opens at the side if the skier's leg twists.

SPORTS AND GAMES

freestyle skiing

Sport that consists of performing various figures and tricks on skis; it includes three events: moguls, aerial skiing and acroski (ballet).

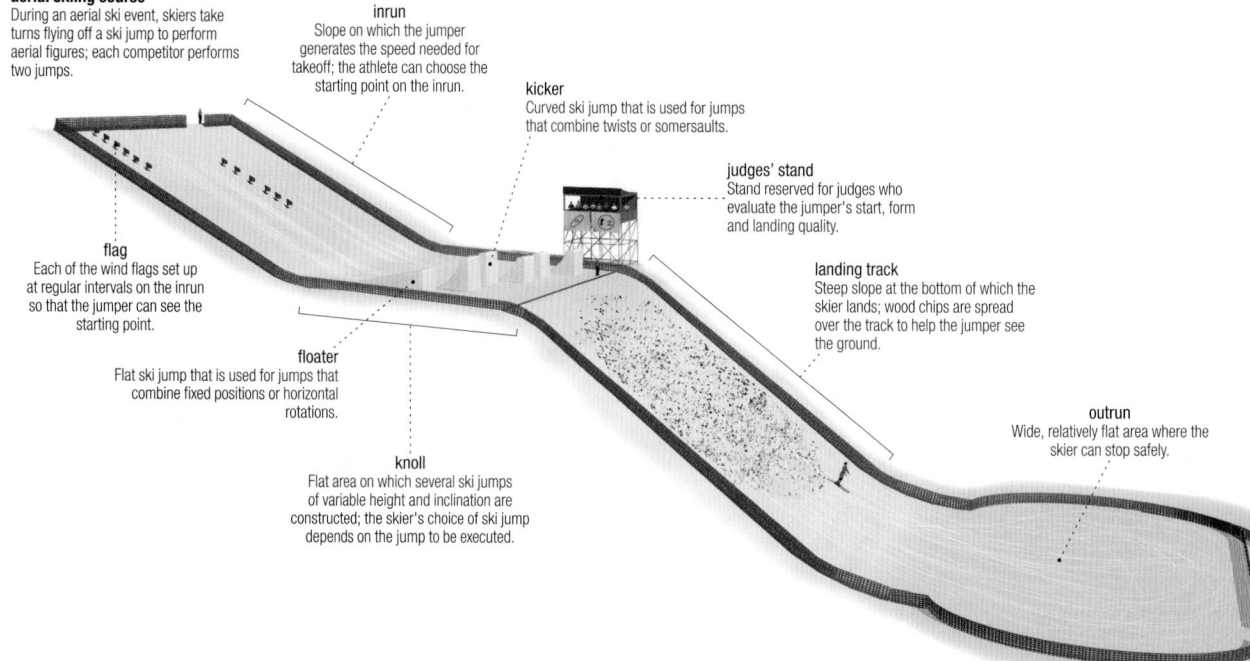

moguls course
Steep straight course with bumps that the skier uses to turn; two jumps are integrated into the run.

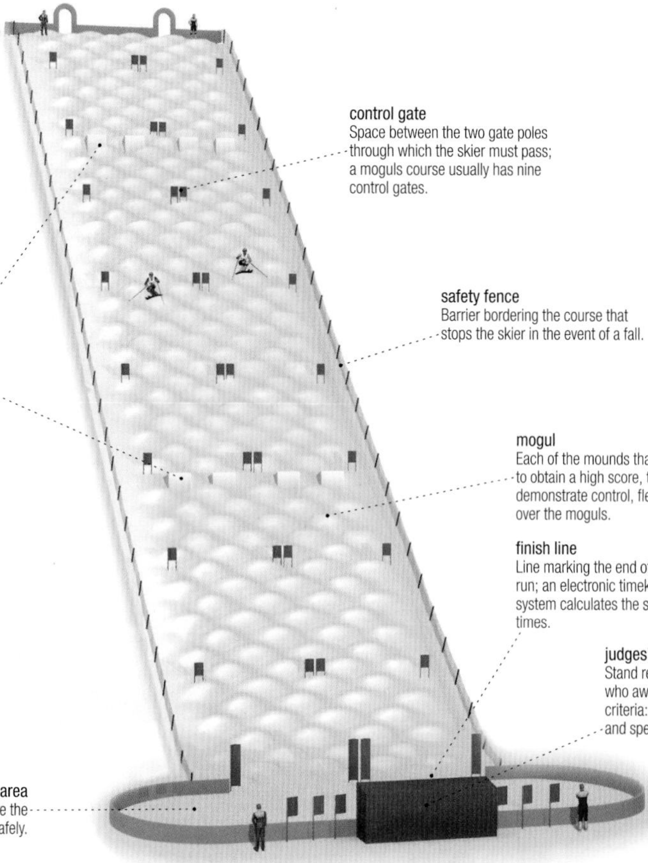

control gate
Space between the two gate poles through which the skier must pass; a moguls course usually has nine control gates.

kickers
Accumulations of snow designed to allow the skier to execute a jump; only straight jumps are allowed in a moguls competition.

safety fence
Barrier bordering the course that stops the skier in the event of a fall.

mogul
Each of the mounds that dot the course; to obtain a high score, the skier must demonstrate control, flexibility and speed over the moguls.

finish line
Line marking the end of a moguls run; an electronic timekeeping system calculates the skiers' finish times.

judges' stand
Stand reserved for the judges who award marks based on three criteria: turn quality, jump quality and speed.

stopping area
Wide, relatively flat area where the skier can stop safely.

aerial skiing course
During an aerial ski event, skiers take turns flying off a ski jump to perform aerial figures; each competitor performs two jumps.

inrun
Slope on which the jumper generates the speed needed for takeoff; the athlete can choose the starting point on the inrun.

kicker
Curved ski jump that is used for jumps that combine twists or somersaults.

judges' stand
Stand reserved for judges who evaluate the jumper's start, form and landing quality.

flag
Each of the wind flags set up at regular intervals on the inrun so that the jumper can see the starting point.

landing track
Steep slope at the bottom of which the skier lands; wood chips are spread over the track to help the jumper see the ground.

floater
Flat ski jump that is used for jumps that combine fixed positions or horizontal rotations.

knoll
Flat area on which several ski jumps of variable height and inclination are constructed; the skier's choice of ski jump depends on the jump to be executed.

outrun
Wide, relatively flat area where the skier can stop safely.

ski jumping

Sport that consists of covering the greatest possible distance in the air after jumping off a ski jump; the jumper's style is marked by judges.

jumping technique
The jump lasts five to eight seconds and volves four stages, each of which requires a specific technique.

inrun
The ski jumper descends the inrun in a tuck position, reaching speeds of over 50 mph.

takeoff
On reaching the end of the take-off table, the ski jumper quickly straightens up and stretches forward to obtain maximum lift.

flight
The ski jumper leans forward to improve aerodynamics and places the skis in a V position to promote lift and prolong flight.

landing
The landing is made in telemark position, with one leg placed slightly ahead of the other; this distributes landing impact throughout the entire body.

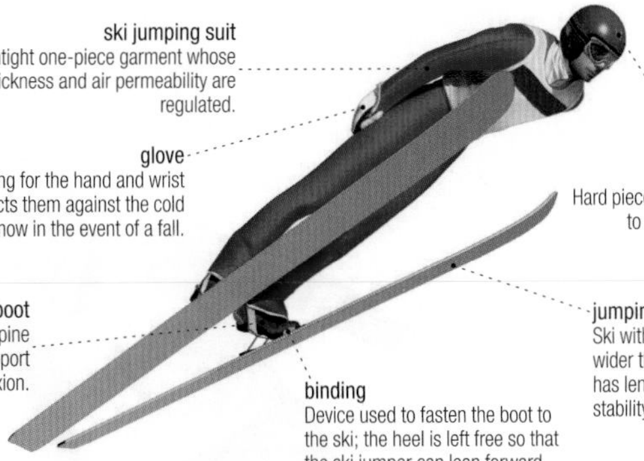

ski jumping suit
Skintight one-piece garment whose thickness and air permeability are regulated.

glove
Covering for the hand and wrist that protects them against the cold and snow in the event of a fall.

ski jumping boot
Boot that is more flexible than an alpine ski boot; it provides good ankle support while allowing forward flexion.

ski jump
Extremely steep artificial track that is covered with snow; Olympic events are held on a large ski jump (120 m) and on a normal ski jump (90 m).

takeoff table
Flat surface at the bottom of the ski jump that slopes at an angle of about 10°; the skier takes off from it.

landing slope
Upper part of the landing area; the ski jumper should fly over it during a jump but it does provide a safe landing area in the event of a short jump.

norm point
Point marking the start of the finish area.

landing area
Steep slope in the middle of which the ski jumpers land; it is divided into several sections.

critical point
Point that marks the length of an ideal jump; points are deducted when the landing is short of or added when the ski jumper lands beyond the critical point.

jury point
Mark indicating the maximum distance that jumpers can safely stay in the air.

ski jumper
Athlete who engages in ski jumping; the ski jumper takes part in individual (large jump, normal jump) and team (large jump) events.

helmet
Hard piece of equipment designed to protect the head.

jumping ski
Ski without edges that is longer and wider than an alpine ski; its bottom has lengthwise grooves that provide stability in a straight line.

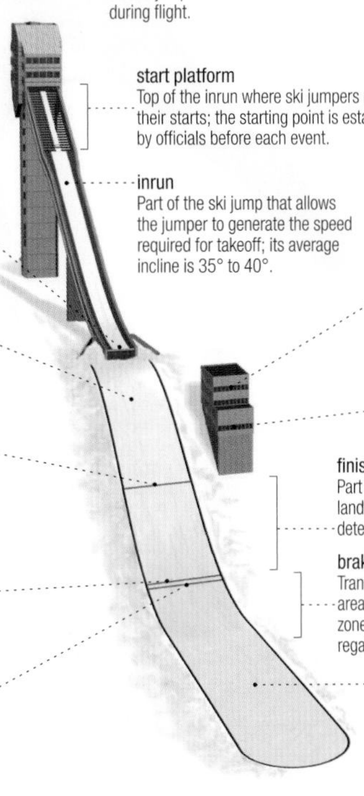

binding
Device used to fasten the boot to the ski; the heel is left free so that the ski jumper can lean forward during flight.

start platform
Top of the inrun where ski jumpers make their starts; the starting point is established by officials before each event.

inrun
Part of the ski jump that allows the jumper to generate the speed required for takeoff; its average incline is 35° to 40°.

ski jumping track
During a ski jumping event, each competitor executes two jumps and points are awarded for style and distance.

coaches' stand
Stand from which coaches observe the jumps executed by the athletes.

judges' stand
Stand reserved for judges; five style judges specifically evaluate take-off precision and control, flight position and landing quality.

finish area
Part of the landing area where ski jumpers land; distance markers allow officials to determine the length of each jump.

braking zone
Transition zone between the finish area and the outrun; the braking zone is the area where the ski jumper regains balance and decelerates.

outrun
Wide, relatively flat area where the skier can stop safely.

speed skiing

Sport that consists of skiing down an extremely steep straight slope to reach the highest possible speed.

speed track
Extremely steep and perfectly even slope that speed skiers take turns descending; the skier who posts the highest speed wins the event.

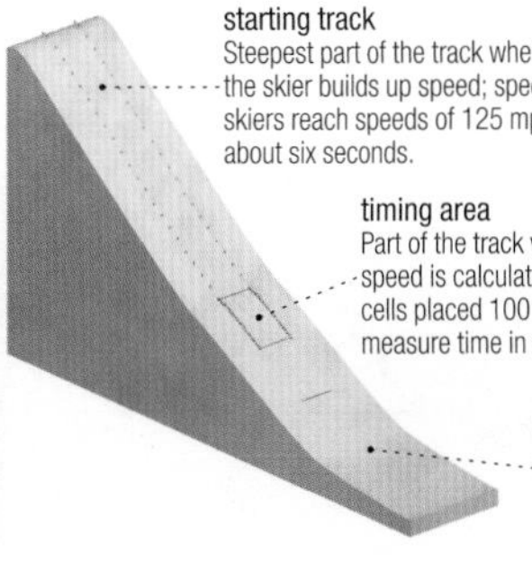

starting track
Steepest part of the track where the skier builds up speed; speed skiers reach speeds of 125 mph in about six seconds.

timing area
Part of the track where the speed skier's speed is calculated; two photoelectric cells placed 100 m (about 330 ft) apart measure time in milliseconds.

deceleration and braking zone
Zone where the speed skier slows down and stops; to achieve this, the speed skier straightens up and performs two wide turns.

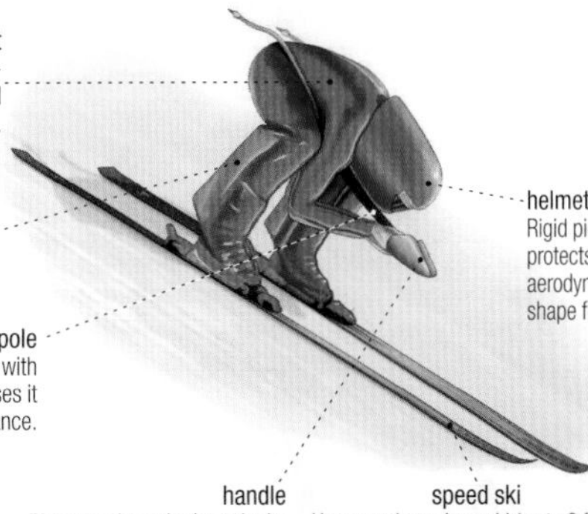

speed skiing suit
Skintight one-piece garment made of plastic-coated synthetic fibers to ensure optimal aerodynamics.

fairing
Piece of compressed foam that is slipped under the suit to improve air flow without causing air turbulence around the leg.

pole
Metal or composite fiber rod with a handle; the speed skier uses it for balance.

handle
Piece used to grip the pole; its streamlined shape ensures better air flow; the handle does not have a wrist strap.

speed skier
Athlete who engages in speed skiing; high-level speed skiers reach speeds of more than 150 mph.

helmet
Rigid piece of equipment that protects the head; it also improves aerodynamics with its streamlined shape fitted to the skier's head.

speed ski
Heavy and very long ski (up to 8 ft) with a thick bottom; its edges are not very sharp to prevent them from catching at high speed and causing crashes.

SPORTS AND GAMES

cross-country skiing

Sport that consists of skiing over snow-covered surfaces on gently sloping terrain using a variety of techniques (skating step, diagonal step).

cross-country skier
Person who engages in cross-country skiing; the competitive skier takes part in various individual (classic, freestyle, pursuit, sprint) and team (relay) events.

turtleneck
Knit fabric top with a high collar formed of ribbing that folds over around the neck; it has no closing mechanism.

ski hat
Headgear made of a tubular piece of fabric folded back to form a double layer; its top is sewn and sometimes features a pom-pom.

waxing kit
Kit that contains a number of waxes suited to a variety of snow conditions and the accessories used to apply or remove them.

cork
Piece of cork used to spread an even layer of wax onto the bottom.

pole grip

pole shaft

ski pole
Metal or composite fiber rod with a handle and a basket; the ski pole is used for maintaining balance and thrusting.

basket
Circular piece attached to the bottom of the ski pole; it prevents the pole from sinking too deeply into the snow.

ski suit
Skintight garment that reduces air resistance; it is lightweight and allows heat generated by the skier to be released.

wax
Substance applied to the bottom of the skis; waxes include glide wax, which reduces friction on snow, and kick wax, which improves traction.

scraper
Blade used to remove kick wax or smooth the ski bottom after applying glide wax.

wrist strap
Strap that is attached to the pole grip and worn around the wrist to prevent the skier from losing a pole when sticking it into the ground.

glove
Covering for the hand and wrist that protects them against cold and against chafing by the pole handle; it is thinner than an alpine ski glove.

cross-country ski
Long strip designed to glide over a snow-covered surface; light and narrow, it has a relatively pronounced camber between the shovel and the tail.

cross-country skiing boot
Lightweight flexible boot that provides good ankle mobility; the skating step requires a more rigid boot than the traditional boot.

binding
Device that fixes the boot toe to the ski, leaving the heel free.

shovel
Front end of the ski; its upward curve cuts through snow and helps to avoid catching an edge.

cross-country ski
Long strip designed to glide over a snow-covered surface; light and narrow, it has a relatively pronounced camber between the shovel and the tail.

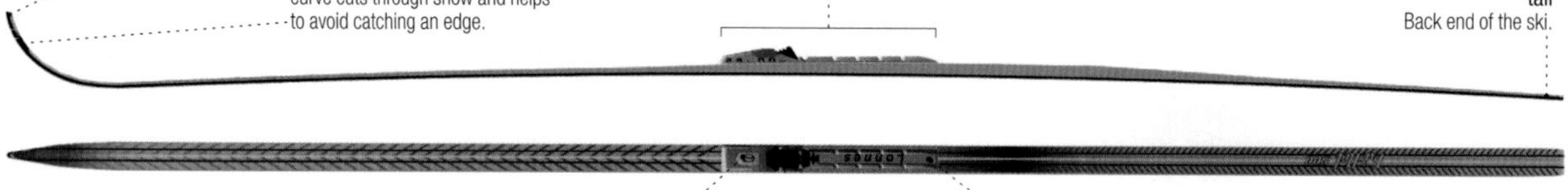

ski tip
Rounded end of the shovel.

shovel
Front end of the ski; its upward curve cuts through snow and helps to avoid catching an edge.

toe binding
Binding with a mechanism that locks only the front of the boot.

tail
Back end of the ski.

skating step
Technique that allows the cross-country skier to drive forward by pushing to the side like a skater; it is faster than the diagonal step.

toepiece
Mechanism used to block the front end of the boot.

heelplate
Back part of the binding; it has notches that fit into the sole of the boot to prevent the foot from twisting to the side.

diagonal step
Classic cross-country skiing technique; the skis remain parallel except in sharp turns or steep climbs.

skating kick
Side kick executed by leaning on the inside of one ski while keeping the body weight on the other ski.

gliding phase
Transition phase between two pushes; the skier returns the take-off leg to its initial position while moving the support ski forward.

pushing phase
Thrusting movement that begins by quickly pushing the take-off leg backwards; the skier alternates this movement from one leg to the other.

gliding phase
Transition phase between two pushes; the skier returns the take-off leg to its initial position while moving the support ski forward.

pushing phase
Rapid repetition of the pushing pha increases the skier's speed.

biathlon

Sport that combines cross-country ski racing with a precision shooting competition; the biathlon includes individual and team events (relays).

shooting positions
An event includes several shooting sessions that alternate between prone and standing positions; the biathlete shoots between breaths to stabilize the rifle.

prone position

standing position

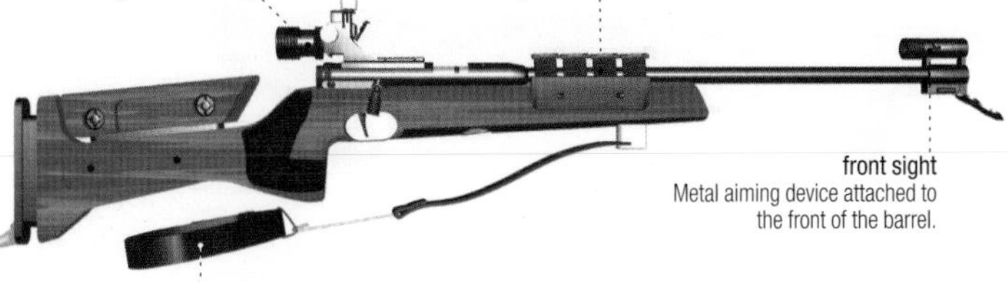

rear sight
Articulated graduated aiming device attached to the back of the barrel; the rear sight is lined up with the front sight when aiming.

magazine
Part containing the cartridges, which are automatically fed into the gun barrel.

biathlon rifle
Lightweight rifle with a relatively short barrel; biathletes use a .22-caliber rifle that is loaded manually or with a magazine.

front sight
Metal aiming device attached to the front of the barrel.

shooting slip
Strap used to stabilize the rifle when shooting from a prone position.

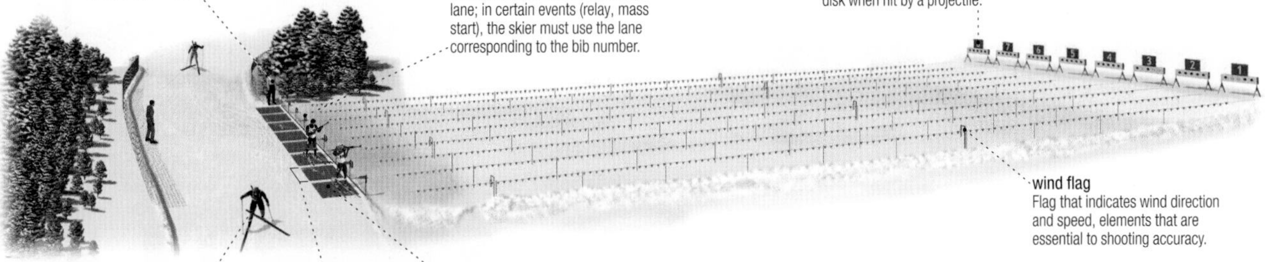

referee
Person who ensures that the rules are observed and the shooting phase runs smoothly.

lane number
Number that identifies a shooting lane; in certain events (relay, mass start), the skier must use the lane corresponding to the bib number.

target
Circular object that forms the target in the shooting competition; the targets are black but are covered with a white disk when hit by a projectile.

shooting range
Area designed for shooting competitions; the athlete has a limited number of cartridges to hit a specific number of targets placed side by side.

wind flag
Flag that indicates wind direction and speed, elements that are essential to shooting accuracy.

biathlete
Athlete who practices the biathlon; during the skiing portion, the biathlete shoulders the rifle using a harness.

shooting place
Area where the biathlete sets up to shoot; each missed target entails a penalty (time added or an extra loop on skis).

nonslip mat
Mat placed in front of each lane to prevent the skis from sliding during the shot.

snowshoeing

Leisure activity that involves walking in the snow, wearing large soles, available in a variety of shapes, that are fitted to one's shoes.

elliptical snowshoe
Snowshoe with rounded ends and no tail; it is made of synthetic materials and is easy to maneuver in wooded areas.

aluminum frame
The frame of the snowshoe varies in length and width, depending on the expected use; lightweight and sturdy, the frame allows the snowshoer to glide over the snow.

crampon system
Metal points that are placed under the harness to improve traction on hard snow and ice.

traditional snowshoe
Wooden snowshoe with a long tail; it is especially suited to walking in a straight line in open areas.

tip
Rounded, slightly raised front end of the snowshoe.

body
Central part of the snowshoe that supports the snowshoer's foot.

frame
The outline of the snowshoe is traditionally made of wood.

deck
Piece of synthetic fabric that is attached to the frame; it bears the snowshoer's weight and prevents sinking into the snow.

lacing
The interlaced leather straps that are stretched across the frame; it bears the snowshoer's weight and prevents sinking into the snow.

toe hole
Opening that allows the foot to move forward; this provides a natural walking motion and improves traction.

tail
The elongated part at the back of the snowshoe; it acts as a rudder to facilitate walking in a straight line.

front crossbar
Crossbar in front of the harness that strengthens the frame; the lacing is attached to it.

back crossbar
Crossbar behind the harness that strengthens the frame; the lacing is attached to it.

harness
Device that attaches the boot to the snowshoe but allows the foot to pivot freely.

master cord
Part of the lacing that supports the harness and on which the foot pivots when walking.

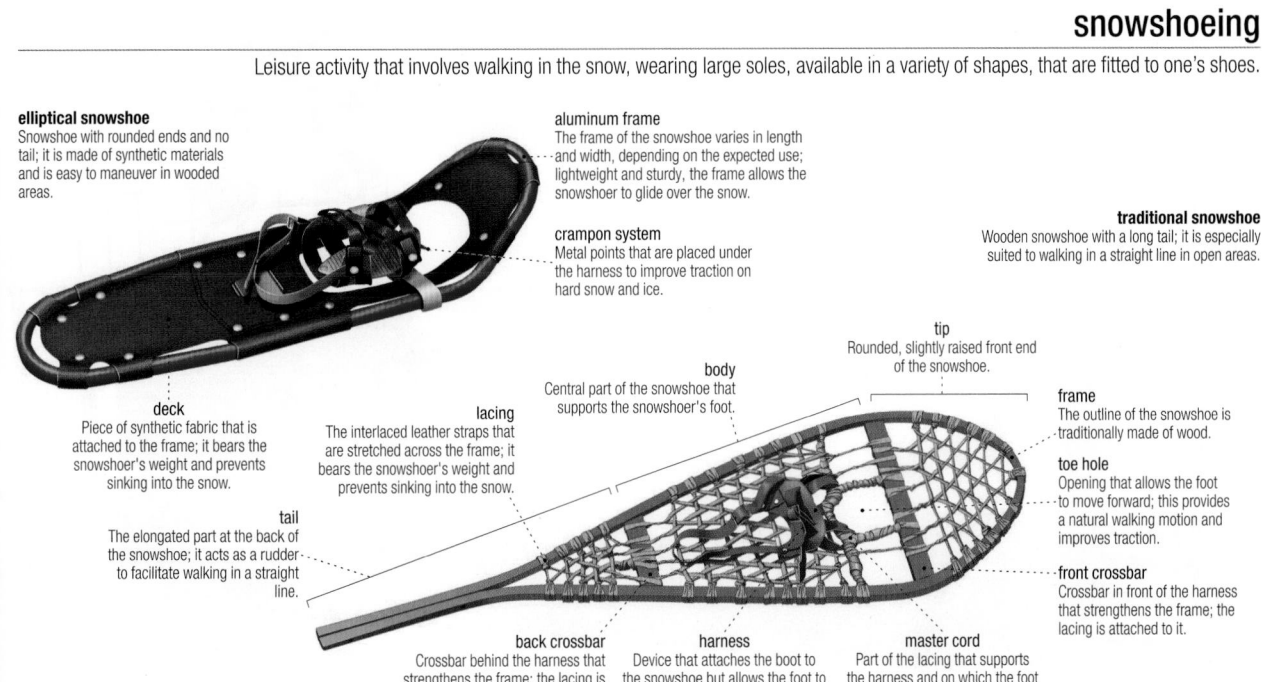

skateboarding

Sport that involves descents, turns and tricks on a specially designed or improvised surface; the skateboarder uses a board mounted on small wheels.

inferior view

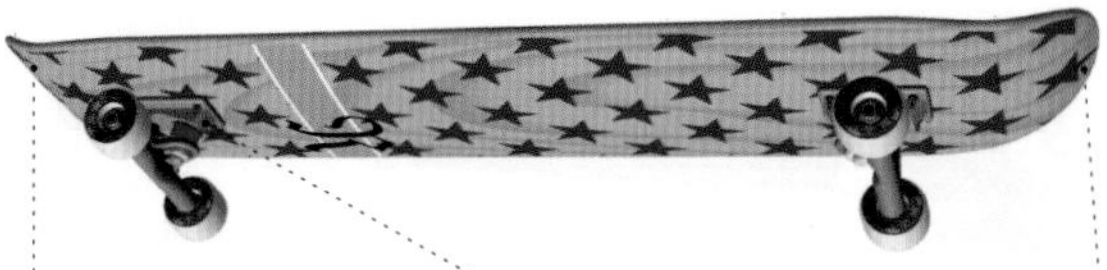

skateboarder
Athlete who engages in skateboarding; because of the risk of injury from falling, the athlete usually wears several pieces of protective equipment.

knee pad
Piece of equipment made of hard molded plastic that protects the knee.

tail
Rear end of the board.

truck
Device that connects the wheels to the board; it enables the wheels to change direction.

nose
Front end of the board.

elbow pad
Piece of equipment with a hard outer shell that is used to protect the elbow.

superior view

grip tape
Rough surface attached to the board that helps the skater's shoes adhere to it.

helmet
Hard piece of equipment designed to protect the head.

wheel
Small round object that turns on an axis so the board can move backward or forward; its diameter and durability vary with the activity.

coping
Metal rail at the platform's edge; skateboarding tricks include sliding along it and balancing on it with one hand or the board.

half-pipe
Wooden structure with raised edges; designed for the performance of various acrobatic figures (jumps, slides, etc.).

guardrail
Metal handrail attached to the platform.

platform
Flat level surface at the top of the ramp; it can be more than 10 ft above the ground.

coping
Metal rail at the platform's edge; skateboarding tricks include sliding along it and balancing on it with one hand or the board.

vertical section
Level section at the end of the ramp; it is used by the skateboarder to gain sufficient height for doing tricks in the air.

flat
Flat level surface between the two curved sections of the ramp.

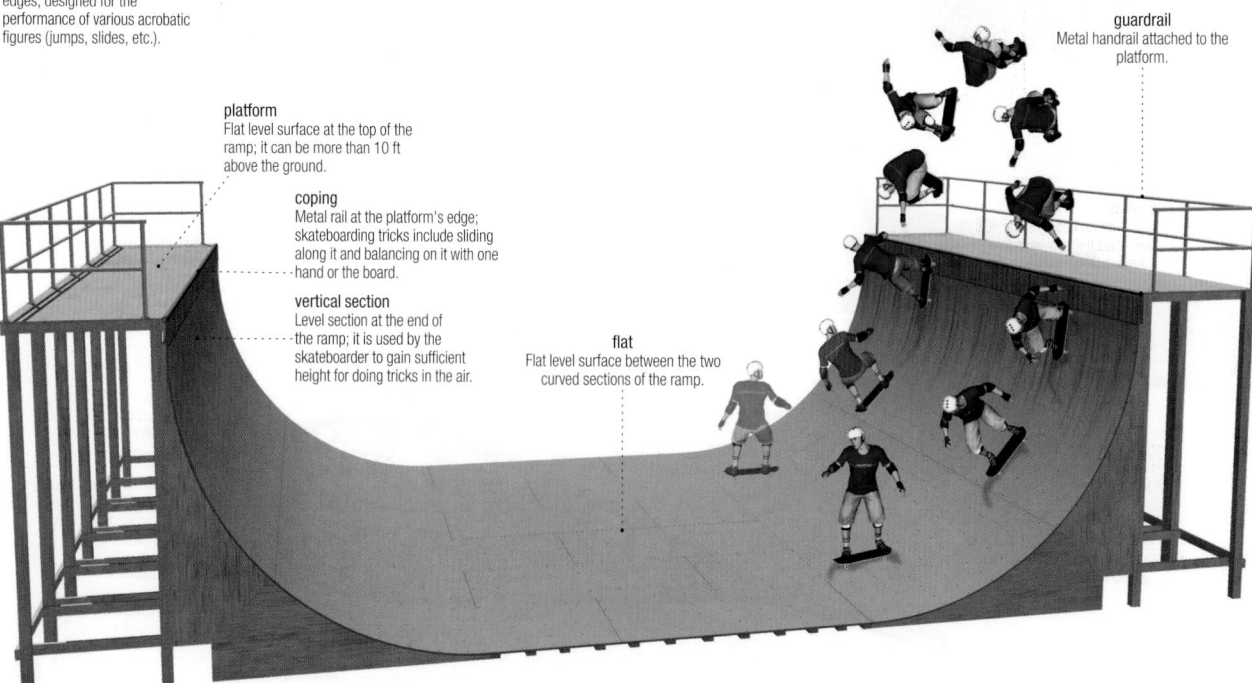

in-line skating

Range of activities that use skates fitted with small wheels: hockey, sprints, acrobatics on ramps or specially designed tracks, etc.

acrobatic skate
Skate with a plastic boot that is designed to provide maximum support and protect against impact when the skater is doing tricks.

inner boot
Cushioned, often removable lining that is designed for greater comfort inside the boot.

upper shell
Part of the boot that covers the lower part of the leg; it is usually hinged at the ankle.

skater
Athlete who engages in in-line skating; because of the risk of injury from falling, the athlete usually wears several pieces of protective equipment.

helmet
Hard piece of equipment designed to protect the head.

frame
Device that is attached to the sole of the boot to support the wheels.

wheel
Round object that turns on an axis so the skate can move backward or forward.

elbow pad
Padded piece of equipment designed to protect the elbow.

knee pad
Piece of equipment made of hard molded plastic that protects the knee.

in-line speed skate
Skate with a light low-cut soft boot that is often molded to the foot; it has five wheels to provide greater contact with the ground.

wrist guard
Piece of equipment with a hard plastic structure that protects the hand and the wrist.

in-line skate
Reinforced boot with four wheels placed in a straight line; it is used to move around on a hard, relatively smooth surface.

in-line hockey skate
Skate that is similar to an ice hockey skate; it is made up of a semisoft leather or nylon boot with reinforced side panels.

hybrid boot
Shoe that protects and supports the foot and ankle. Depending on the type of skating, a hybrid boot can be flexible, semi-stiff, or stiff (shell).

hook and loop fastener
Strap of Velcro that fastens the boot over the ankle.

lacing closure
Lacing tied to secure the boot on the foot.

frame
Device that connects the wheels to the boot.

heel brake
Rubber pad at the back of the skate that enables the skater to slow down or stop.

wheel
Round object that turns on an axis so the skate can move backward or forward.

bearings
Wheel's rotational axis that connects it to the frame.

parachuting

Range of sporting activities that all include opening a parachute in the air after jumping from an airplane.

sky diving
Sport that consists of jumping out of an airplane, falling freely for a certain period while performing various maneuvers and then opening a parachute.

reserve parachute
Extra parachute used in the event the main one malfunctions; an automatic activation device deploys it when a predetermined safe altitude is reached.

main parachute
The parachute deployed by the sky diver when in the air; if a problem arises, the reserve parachute can be deployed.

boot
Reinforced shoe used for sky diving that provides good ankle support for the landing.

helmet
Hard-shelled piece of equipment that protects the head against impact and the cold.

goggles
Equipment that protects the eyes against cold and wind and provides good visibility during the jump.

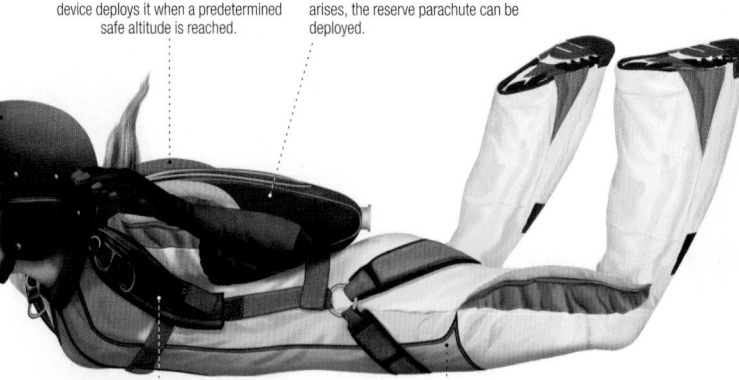

harness
Arrangement of straps that connects the sky diver to the suspension lines of the main and reserve canopies; it is stowed in a pack before departure.

one-piece coverall
Overalls designed to protect the sky diver against cold and reduce the danger of snagging on equipment.

altimeter
Device that indicates the sky diver's altitude to help with the decision of when to open the parachute.

canopy
Structure made of fabric cells that, when filled with air, forms a rectangular surface with the aerodynamic properties of an airplane wing.

parachute
Equipment consisting of a canopy that is connected to a harness by suspension lines; it is deployed at a given altitude to slow a sky diver's descent.

stabilizer
Fabric triangle attached to the sides of the canopy; it is used primarily to stabilize the parachute.

pilot chute
Small parachute that deploys the canopy; to open the parachute, the sky diver opens the pilot chute, which pulls the canopy out of the pack.

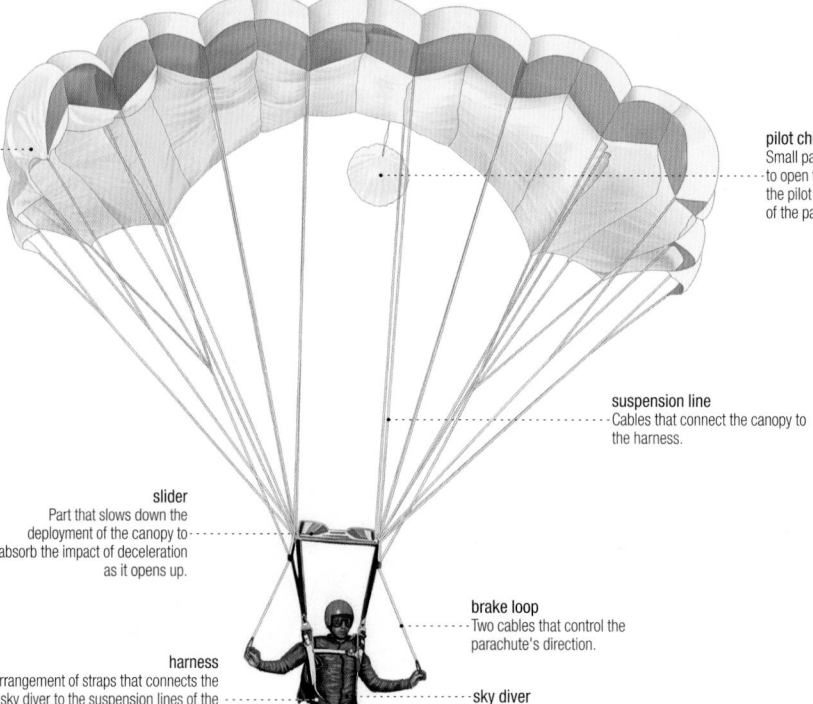

suspension line
Cables that connect the canopy to the harness.

slider
Part that slows down the deployment of the canopy to absorb the impact of deceleration as it opens up.

brake loop
Two cables that control the parachute's direction.

harness
Arrangement of straps that connects the sky diver to the suspension lines of the main and reserve canopies; it is stowed in a pack before departure.

sky diver
Person who jumps with a parachute; this individual might compete in free fall or canopy maneuvers, landing accuracy or other kinds of events.

hang gliding

Sport where a pilot strapped to a hang glider or a paraglider launches from a mountain slope, gains altitude and remains aloft for some distance.

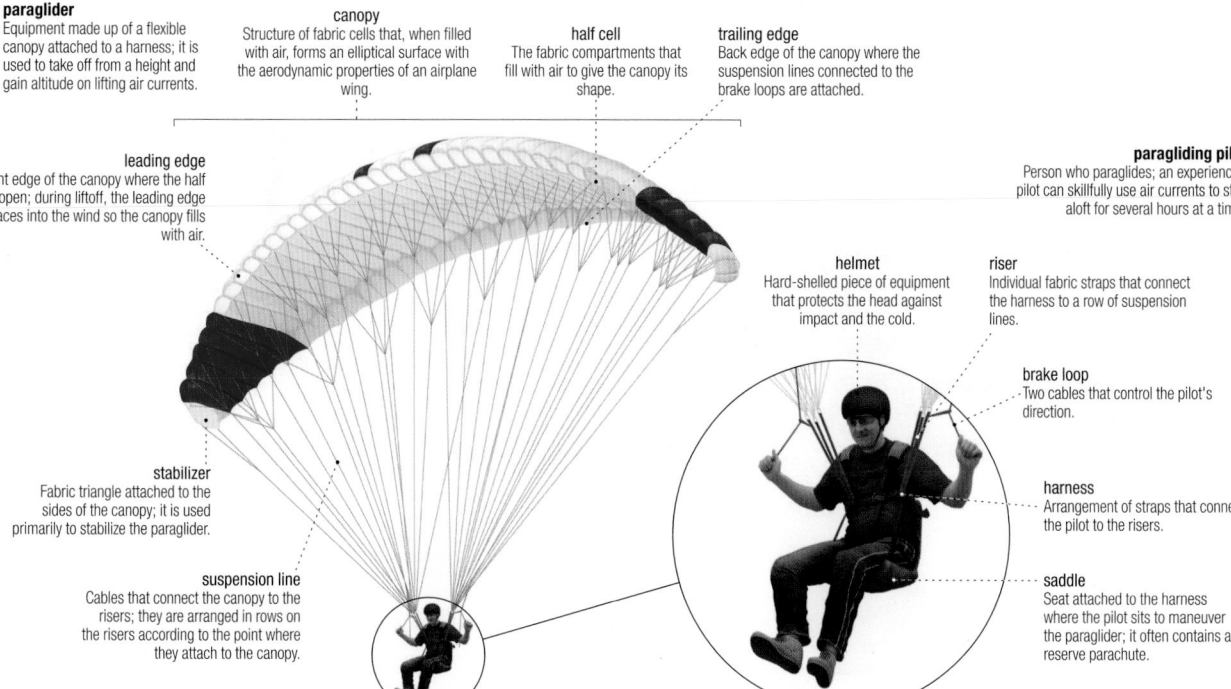

paraglider
Equipment made up of a flexible canopy attached to a harness; it is used to take off from a height and gain altitude on lifting air currents.

canopy
Structure of fabric cells that, when filled with air, forms an elliptical surface with the aerodynamic properties of an airplane wing.

half cell
The fabric compartments that fill with air to give the canopy its shape.

trailing edge
Back edge of the canopy where the suspension lines connected to the brake loops are attached.

leading edge
Front edge of the canopy where the half is open; during liftoff, the leading edge faces into the wind so the canopy fills with air.

paragliding pilot
Person who paraglides; an experienced pilot can skillfully use air currents to stay aloft for several hours at a time.

helmet
Hard-shelled piece of equipment that protects the head against impact and the cold.

riser
Individual fabric straps that connect the harness to a row of suspension lines.

brake loop
Two cables that control the pilot's direction.

harness
Arrangement of straps that connect the pilot to the risers.

stabilizer
Fabric triangle attached to the sides of the canopy; it is used primarily to stabilize the paraglider.

saddle
Seat attached to the harness where the pilot sits to maneuver the paraglider; it often contains a reserve parachute.

suspension line
Cables that connect the canopy to the risers; they are arranged in rows on the risers according to the point where they attach to the canopy.

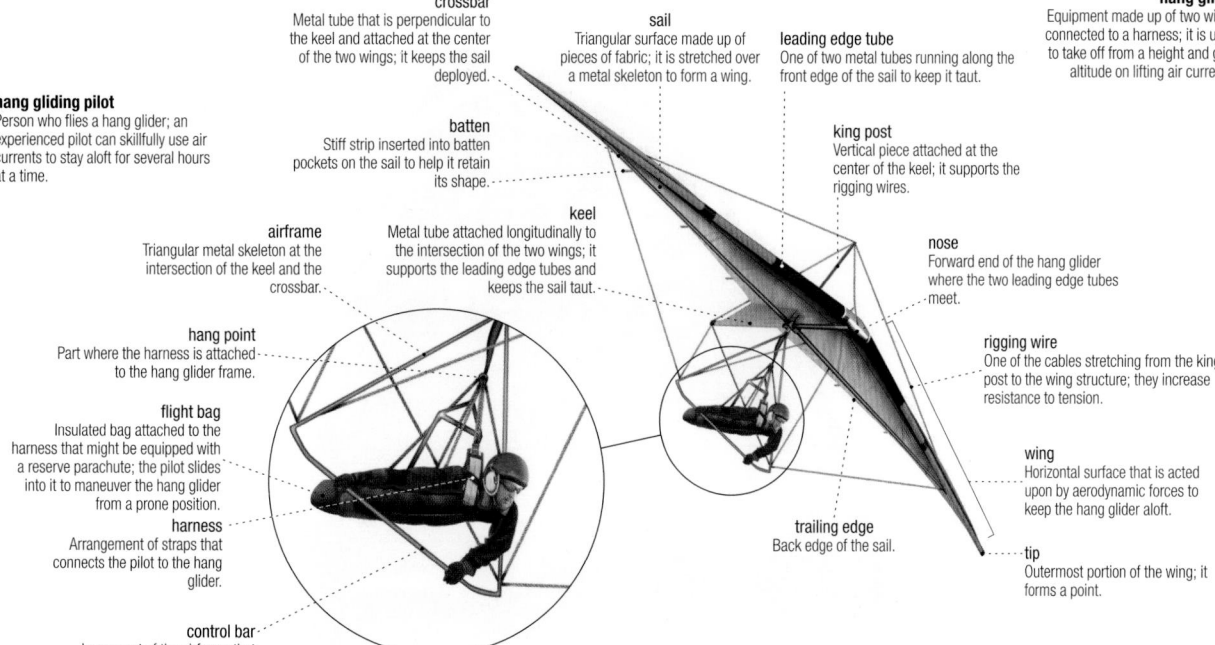

crossbar
Metal tube that is perpendicular to the keel and attached at the center of the two wings; it keeps the sail deployed.

sail
Triangular surface made up of pieces of fabric; it is stretched over a metal skeleton to form a wing.

leading edge tube
One of two metal tubes running along the front edge of the sail to keep it taut.

hang glider
Equipment made up of two wings connected to a harness; it is used to take off from a height and gain altitude on lifting air currents.

hang gliding pilot
Person who flies a hang glider; an experienced pilot can skillfully use air currents to stay aloft for several hours at a time.

batten
Stiff strip inserted into batten pockets on the sail to help it retain its shape.

king post
Vertical piece attached at the center of the keel; it supports the rigging wires.

airframe
Triangular metal skeleton at the intersection of the keel and the crossbar.

keel
Metal tube attached longitudinally to the intersection of the two wings; it supports the leading edge tubes and keeps the sail taut.

nose
Forward end of the hang glider where the two leading edge tubes meet.

hang point
Part where the harness is attached to the hang glider frame.

rigging wire
One of the cables stretching from the king post to the wing structure; they increase resistance to tension.

flight bag
Insulated bag attached to the harness that might be equipped with a reserve parachute; the pilot slides into it to maneuver the hang glider from a prone position.

wing
Horizontal surface that is acted upon by aerodynamic forces to keep the hang glider aloft.

harness
Arrangement of straps that connects the pilot to the hang glider.

trailing edge
Back edge of the sail.

tip
Outermost portion of the wing; it forms a point.

control bar
Lower part of the airframe that enables the pilot to maneuver the hang glider.

SPORTS AND GAMES

glider

Small engineless aircraft that is launched by a tow plane and stays aloft on air currents.

general view

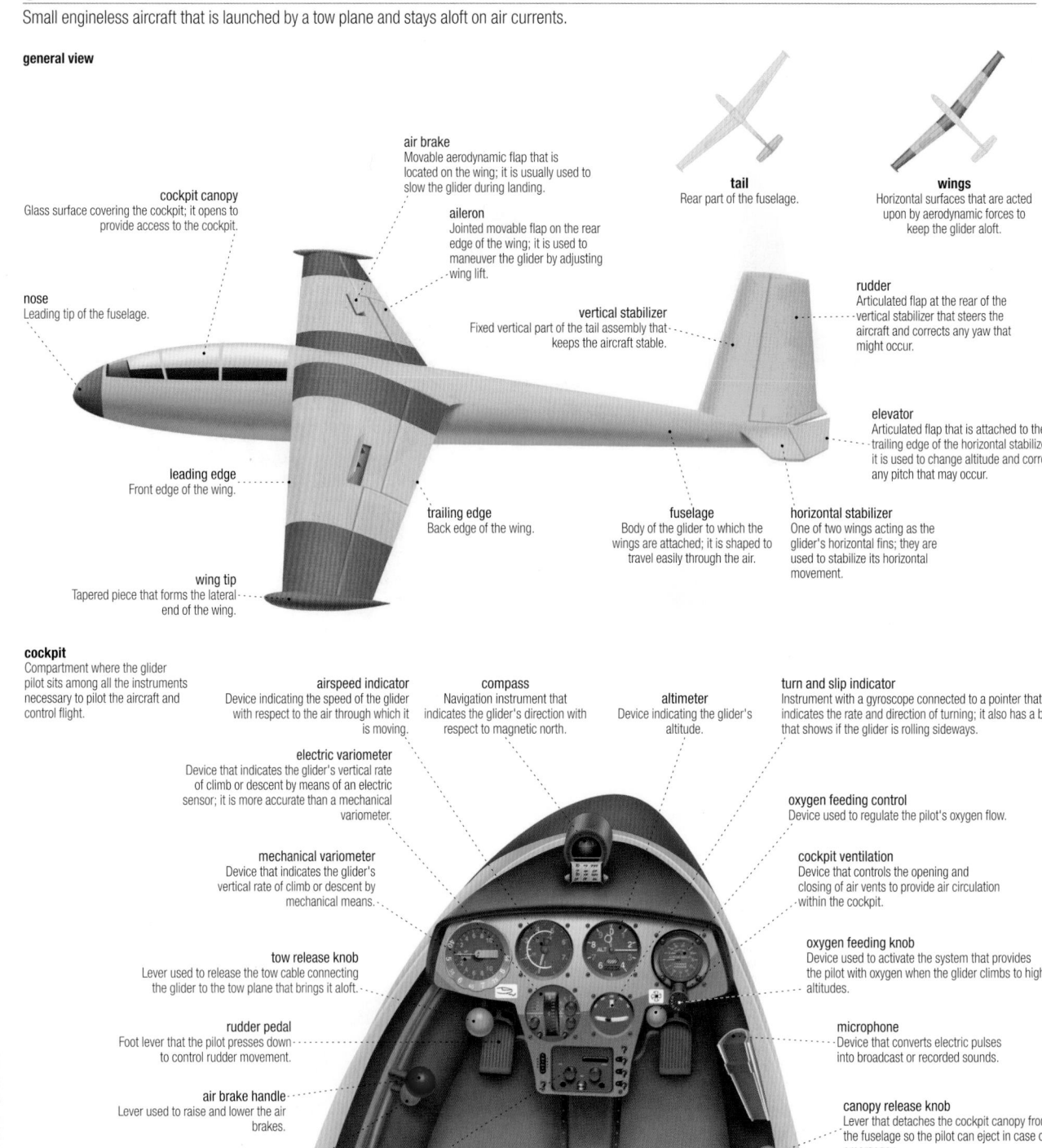

air brake
Movable aerodynamic flap that is located on the wing; it is usually used to slow the glider during landing.

aileron
Jointed movable flap on the rear edge of the wing; it is used to maneuver the glider by adjusting wing lift.

cockpit canopy
Glass surface covering the cockpit; it opens to provide access to the cockpit.

vertical stabilizer
Fixed vertical part of the tail assembly that keeps the aircraft stable.

nose
Leading tip of the fuselage.

tail
Rear part of the fuselage.

wings
Horizontal surfaces that are acted upon by aerodynamic forces to keep the glider aloft.

rudder
Articulated flap at the rear of the vertical stabilizer that steers the aircraft and corrects any yaw that might occur.

elevator
Articulated flap that is attached to the trailing edge of the horizontal stabilizer; it is used to change altitude and correct any pitch that may occur.

leading edge
Front edge of the wing.

trailing edge
Back edge of the wing.

fuselage
Body of the glider to which the wings are attached; it is shaped to travel easily through the air.

horizontal stabilizer
One of two wings acting as the glider's horizontal fins; they are used to stabilize its horizontal movement.

wing tip
Tapered piece that forms the lateral end of the wing.

cockpit
Compartment where the glider pilot sits among all the instruments necessary to pilot the aircraft and control flight.

airspeed indicator
Device indicating the speed of the glider with respect to the air through which it is moving.

compass
Navigation instrument that indicates the glider's direction with respect to magnetic north.

altimeter
Device indicating the glider's altitude.

turn and slip indicator
Instrument with a gyroscope connected to a pointer that indicates the rate and direction of turning; it also has a ball that shows if the glider is rolling sideways.

electric variometer
Device that indicates the glider's vertical rate of climb or descent by means of an electric sensor; it is more accurate than a mechanical variometer.

oxygen feeding control
Device used to regulate the pilot's oxygen flow.

cockpit ventilation
Device that controls the opening and closing of air vents to provide air circulation within the cockpit.

mechanical variometer
Device that indicates the glider's vertical rate of climb or descent by mechanical means.

oxygen feeding knob
Device used to activate the system that provides the pilot with oxygen when the glider climbs to high altitudes.

tow release knob
Lever used to release the tow cable connecting the glider to the tow plane that brings it aloft.

microphone
Device that converts electric pulses into broadcast or recorded sounds.

rudder pedal
Foot lever that the pilot presses down to control rudder movement.

air brake handle
Lever used to raise and lower the air brakes.

canopy release knob
Lever that detaches the cockpit canopy from the fuselage so the pilot can eject in case of emergency.

turn and slip knob
Lever that maintains the position of the control stick to reduce pilot fatigue.

control stick
Lever used to control the ailerons and the elevator.

radio
Apparatus that sends and receives signals to communicate with another glider or with a ground station.

seat
Place where the pilot sits to maneuver the glider; the pilot is strapped into the seat and wears a mandatory reserve parachute.

ballooning

Sport of traveling in a balloon carried along by the wind; flights take place at dawn and dusk, when winds are light and the air is stable.

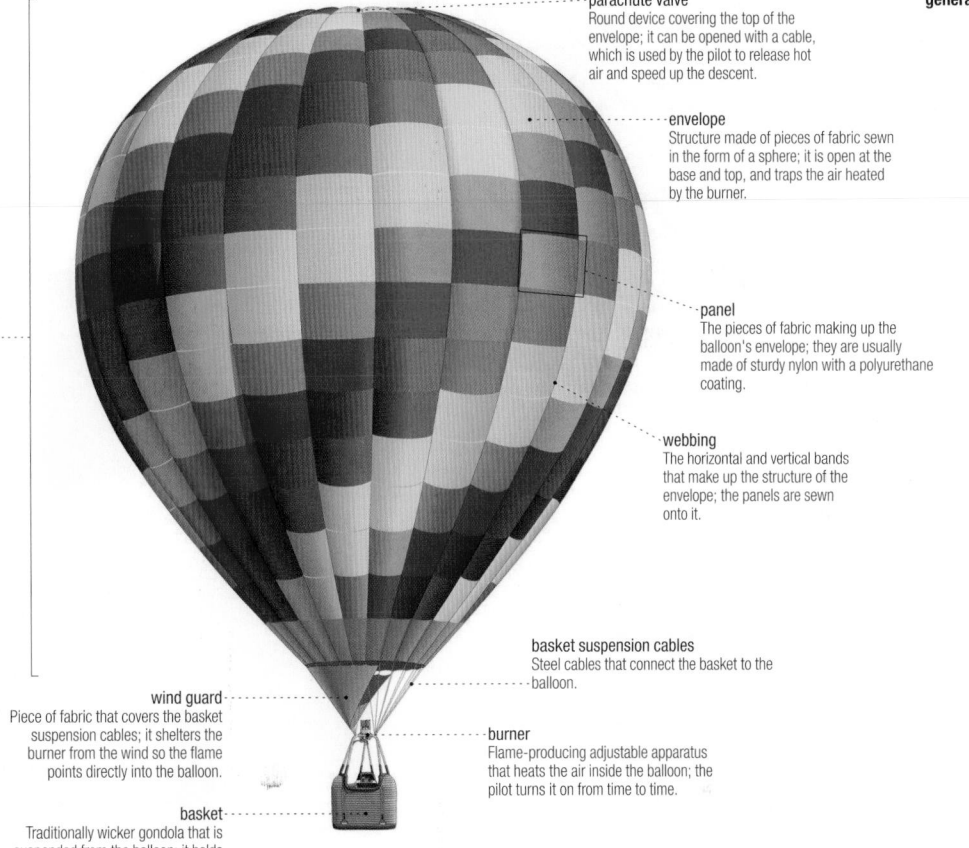

general view

parachute valve
Round device covering the top of the envelope; it can be opened with a cable, which is used by the pilot to release hot air and speed up the descent.

envelope
Structure made of pieces of fabric sewn in the form of a sphere; it is open at the base and top, and traps the air heated by the burner.

balloon
Fabric bag filled with hot air that is lighter than the surrounding air; this causes the apparatus to rise and float in the atmosphere.

panel
The pieces of fabric making up the balloon's envelope; they are usually made of sturdy nylon with a polyurethane coating.

webbing
The horizontal and vertical bands that make up the structure of the envelope; the panels are sewn onto it.

basket suspension cables
Steel cables that connect the basket to the balloon.

wind guard
Piece of fabric that covers the basket suspension cables; it shelters the burner from the wind so the flame points directly into the balloon.

burner
Flame-producing adjustable apparatus that heats the air inside the balloon; the pilot turns it on from time to time.

basket
Traditionally wicker gondola that is suspended from the balloon; it holds passengers, fuel cylinders and flight instruments.

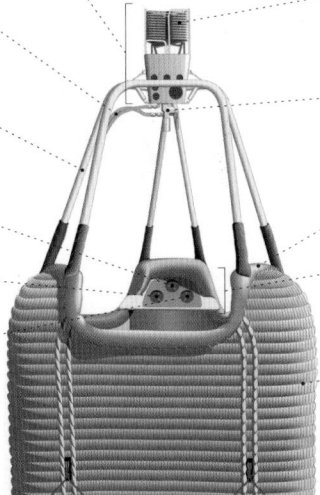

burner
Flame-producing adjustable apparatus that heats the air inside the balloon; the pilot turns it on from time to time.

heating coil
Tubing in which liquid fuel from the cylinders is heated; the fuel emerges as a gas and is then lit by a pilot flame.

basket
Traditionally wicker gondola that is suspended from the balloon; it holds passengers, fuel cylinders and flight instruments.

fuel lines
Flexible hoses that connect the fuel cylinders to the burner.

load support
Rigid framework that supports the burner; the basket suspension cables are attached to it.

blast valve
Part that opens so fuel can enter the burner.

padding
Leather or foam trimming around the basket's upper rim that improves passenger comfort.

variometer
Device that indicates the balloon's vertical rate of climb or descent.

flight instruments
Devices by which the pilot navigates and controls the flight; they include an altimeter, variometer, thermometer, compass and GPS.

altimeter
Device that indicates the balloon's altitude.

thermometer
Instrument that measures the temperature of the ambient air or of the hot air inside the envelope.

wicker basket
Very sturdy yet pliant gondola that can absorb the impact of landing.

basket handle
One of the parts used to hold and move the basket; they are also used as a means of anchoring the basket to the ground where necessary.

hardwood base
Wooden floor that supports the passengers and any equipment carried in the basket.

SPORTS AND GAMES

mountaineering

Sport that involves climbing a mountain, natural rock face or artificial climbing structure.

rock climber
Person who climbs natural rock faces or artificial climbing structures.

rock
Steep rock face ascended by rock climbers.

quickdraw
Piece of safety equipment that consists of a runner used to keep the rope away from the rock face so it can slide freely and is not worn away by rubbing.

belay rope
Rope that secures the climber in the event of a fall to ensure a safe climb up the rock face.

climbing shoe
Soft shoe with an adherent sole.

roped party
Group of climbers who are connected to one another by one or more ropes during an ascent.

leader
The most experienced climber who climbs at the head of the roped party and marks out the climbing route.

artificial climbing structure
Fixed or movable indoor or outdoor surface used by climbers as a rock face to practice their sport as a leisure or competitive activity.

belay beam
Piece at the top of an artificial climbing structure that supports the belay ropes.

runner
Piece of equipment made up of two carabiners connected together by a nylon loop of variable length.

seat harness
Accessory connected to the rope that consists of a number of straps to support the climber's thighs and pelvis.

route judge
Person who ensures safety and observes the climbers' maneuvers.

jury president
Person who supervises all competition activities and presides over any disputes.

timekeeper
Person who ensures that the route is climbed within the set time frame.

belayer
Person who protects the rock climbers from falling and ensure they do not swap information during an event.

---

mountaineering equipment
Complete range of accessories used in mountaineering.

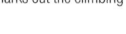

latch
Part over which the gate closes.

gate
Moving metal part that opens inward and has a spring-loaded closure.

screw sleeve
Device that locks the gate into a closed position.

locking carabiner
Metal ring with a gate that, once closed, can be locked with a screw sleeve; this makes it safer than the D carabiner.

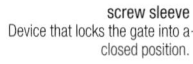

D carabiner
Metal ring that opens and closes with a spring-loaded gate; it is used for attaching rope to a piton, a chock, etc.

rope
Thin cable with a braided center core that makes it stretchy and strong and a woven sheath that surrounds and protects the core.

expansion bolt
Piton that is driven into a hole previously made in the rock.

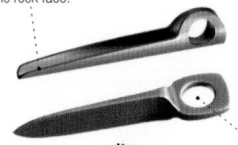

blade
Part that is driven into the crack in the rock face.

piton
Metal spike with a blade that is driven into a crack in the rock face; it ends in an eye to which a belay rope can be attached with a carabiner.

eye
Hole that is large enough for a carabiner to snap on so that a rope can be attached to the piton.

descender
Metal accessory through which a rope slides that is used to protect the rope and the climber's hands; it acts as a brake during rappel descents.

chock
Metal device that is inserted into a crack in the rock face and held in place by tension; it is extended by a steel cable to which a carabiner can snap on.

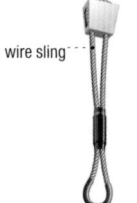

wire sling

seat harness
Accessory connected to the belay rope that consists of a number of straps to support the climber's thighs and pelvis.

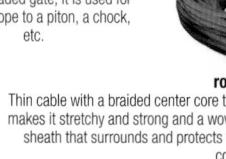

mountaineering

mountaineer
Person who climbs mountains.

handholds
Projection over which the hand is placed or hollow into which the fingers are inserted in order to advance.

foothold
Projection on which the foot is placed or hollow into which it is inserted in order to advance.

helmet lamp
Lamp that is attached to the helmet so that the mountaineer's hands remain free.

helmet
Solid piece of equipment to protect the head from falling rocks or impacts with rock or ice.

pinch
Hold that is squeezed between the thumb and fingers.

edging
Hold that consists of placing the foot's inside edge on a projection and turning the heel toward the rock face.

parka
Waterproof sports jacket with long sleeves, a drawstring hood and waist and gathered wrists.

hood
Headgear that covers the head and neck with an opening for the face.

knapsack
Travel or hiking bag that is worn on the back and is used to transport clothing, camping equipment, etc.

rope
Thin cable with a braided center core that makes it stretchy and strong and a woven sheath that surrounds and protects the core.

crimp
Closed hold with the fingertips on the rock face and the thumb pushed against the index finger.

mountaineering shovel
Instrument used to dig and remove snow.

mitten
Covering with a separation only for the thumb, providing better protection against the cold while allowing the wearer to grasp objects.

piton-carrier
Metal ring on which pitons are hung.

climbing harness
Accessory connected to the belay rope that consists of a number of straps; it supports the mountaineer's thighs and pelvis, back and sometimes shoulders.

carabiner
Metal ring that opens and closes with a spring-loaded gate and that might be equipped with a locking device; it is used to attach rope to a piton, a chock, etc.

chock
Metal device that is inserted into a crack in the rock face and held in place by tension; it is extended by a steel cable to which a carabiner can snap on.

open hand
Open hold with the fingers outstretched and the palm gripping the rock.

hammer ax
Hammer that doubles as an ice ax; it is used to drive in pitons, cut footholds, break ice on the rock face, etc.

ice piton
Metal spike with a blade that is driven into ice or hard-packed snow; it ends in an eye to which a belay rope can be attached using a carabiner.

ice ax
Small ax used by the mountaineer for cutting footholds, judging snow depth, gaining a firm grip in ice or hard-packed snow, etc.

pants
Waterproof pants that usually extend below the knee.

ice screw
Threaded metal tube that is screwed into ice or hard-packed snow to help with belaying and advancing.

gaiter
Piece of sturdy waterproof fabric that covers the leg.

mountaineering boot
Sturdy shoe with spikes that is used to advance over snow or ice.

crampon
Each of the front spikes; they are tilted at a 45° angle.

spike
Pointed object that provides balance and prevents slipping when the mountaineer is moving over snow or ice.

mountaineering equipment

ice ax
Small ax used by the mountaineer for cutting footholds, judging snow depth, gaining a firm grip in ice or hard-packed snow, etc.

head
semicircular part that contains the pick and the adze.

adze
sharp-edged part that is used to cut footholds.

pick
Part that is driven into ice or hard-packed snow in order to advance.

shaft
Long wooden or metal part used to hold and handle the ice ax.

spike
Sharp-tipped end of the shaft; it is used to cut footholds and to gain a firm grip in ice or hard-packed snow.

leash
Strap that attaches the ice ax to the wrist.

hammer ax
Hammer that doubles as an ice ax; it is used to drive in pitons, cut footholds, break ice on the rock face, etc.

hammerhead
Flat surface used by the mountaineer to strike pitons.

pick
Part that is driven into ice or hard-packed snow in order to advance.

tubular ice screw
Threaded metal tube that is screwed into ice or hard-packed snow to help with belaying and advancing.

ring
Metal loop into which carabiners are inserted.

camping

Recreational activity that consists of sleeping in a portable shelter such as a tent or trailer and traveling with equipment designed for outdoor living.

examples of tents

Tents: portable waterproof soft-sided shelters that are stretched taut over a frame and temporarily pitched outdoors.

two-person tent
Tent that can accommodate two people.

line tightener
Device used to stretch a guy line taut.

guy line
Cable used to stretch the tent frame taut and hold it firmly in place on the ground.

pole
Flexible tubing that forms an arch to support the tent.

integrated groundsheet
Waterproof material sewn into the bottom of the tent; it protects the interior from ground dampness and runoff.

peg
Small post that is driven into the ground to hold the tent in place.

rainfly
Piece of waterproof material that covers the inner tent; it protects it from rain and provides an extra layer of insulation.

family tent
Spacious tent with two or three rooms that can accommodate about four people.

rainfly
Piece of waterproof material that covers the inner tent; it protects it from rain and provides an extra layer of insulation.

screen window
Opening that lets air and light and keeps mosquitoes out.

stake loop
One of the fabric circles attached to the tent's outer edge; stakes are driven through the loops to anchor the tent to the ground.

wall
Side part of the tent that is reinforced.

guy line
Cable used to stretch the tent frame taut and hold it firmly in place on the ground.

bedroom
Part of the tent that serves as a sleeping area.

living room
Part of the tent that serves as a common living area.

pole
Flexible tubing that forms an arch to support the tent.

ridge tent
Spacious tent with sufficient interior capacity to accommodate a number of people or group activities.

wall tent
Very spacious, rectangular tent that often has a number of interior dividers; it accommodates a number of people.

camping

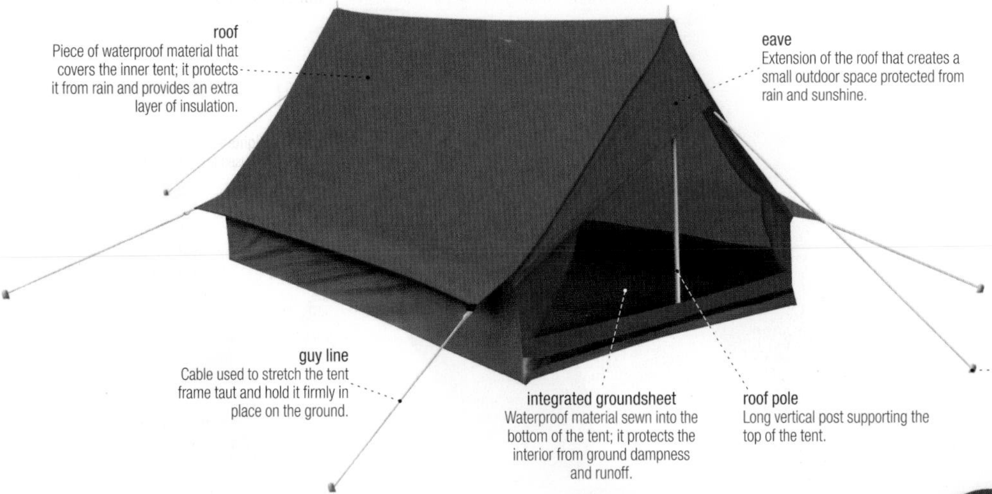

roof
Piece of waterproof material that covers the inner tent; it protects it from rain and provides an extra layer of insulation.

eave
Extension of the roof that creates a small outdoor space protected from rain and sunshine.

pup tent
Tent where the material is stretched taut on both sides of a summit rod, which is supported by two poles.

guy line
Cable used to stretch the tent frame taut and hold it firmly in place on the ground.

integrated groundsheet
Waterproof material sewn into the bottom of the tent; it protects the interior from ground dampness and runoff.

roof pole
Long vertical post supporting the top of the tent.

peg
Small post that is driven into the ground to hold the tent in place.

one-person tent
Small low-roofed tent with enough room to accommodate one person.

dome tent
Hemispheric tent whose shape is framed by curved poles rather than stakes and guy lines, and which can thus be moved easily.

pop-up tent
Round tent with a framework that deploys automatically.

lantern
Safe portable light source that can be used both inside and outside a tent.

globe
Translucent or transparent heat-resistant covering that protects the light source and diffuses its light.

pump
Device that increases the air pressure inside the tank so the fuel vaporizes.

burner frame
Aluminum housing protecting the burner.

pressure regulator
Device that controls the pressure of the vaporized fuel and adjusts the light's brightness.

leakproof cap
Stopper for the fuel refill opening; it is threaded to prevent leakage.

tank
Canister containing the liquid fuel and air that supply the burner.

propane or butane accessories
Complete range of portable appliances that run on liquid or gas fuel and are used to light, cook or heat.

heater
Appliance with a heating element to generate heat and a reflector to radiate it.

double-burner camp stove
Two-burner appliance used to cook and reheat food.

single-burner camp stove
Single-burner appliance used to cook and reheat food.

burner
Combustion device for an air-gas mixture.

wire support
Metal grill used as a base to support cooking utensils.

control valve
Device that switches the fuel intake on and off and adjusts its volume of flow.

tank
Canister containing the pressurized fuel that supplies the burners.

SPORTS AND GAMES

camping

sleeping bags
Insulated fabric coverings that close with a zipper and are used to stay warm when sleeping outdoors.

rectangular bag
Sleeping bag that is spacious enough to give the body room to move.

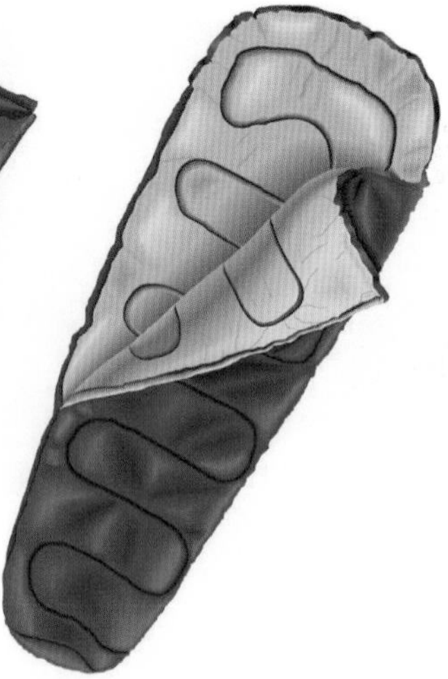

backpack bivy
Sleeping bag with a hood that forms a tent over the head and upper body.

semi-mummy bag
Sleeping bag with a less spacious design to better retain body heat.

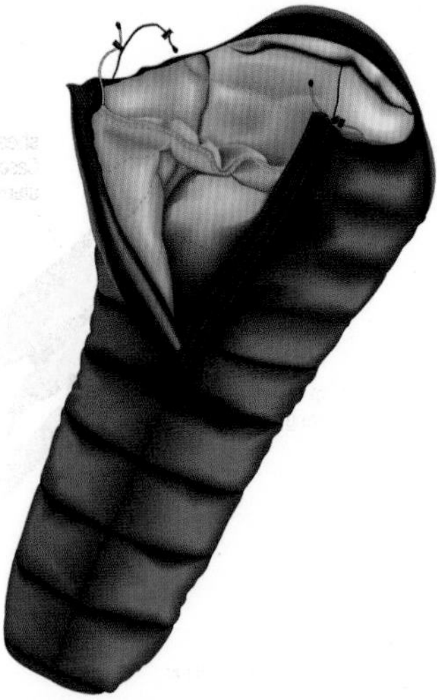

mummy bag
Sleeping bag shaped like the body; it has a part that covers the head and neck with an opening for the face.

bed and mattress
Accessories that a person lies down on to sleep or rest.

folding cot
Portable bed made of fabric that is stretched over a collapsible frame.

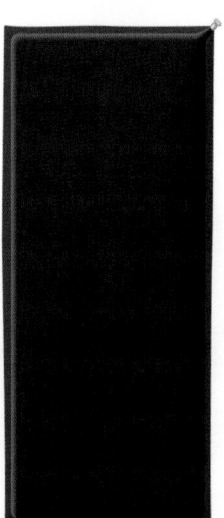

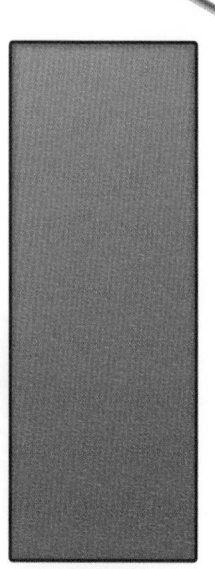

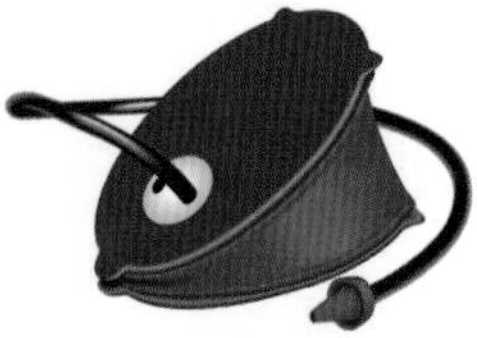

inflator-deflator
Device used to inflate and deflate air mattresses.

inflator
Device used to inflate air mattresses.

air mattress
Rubber or plastic bag that is filled with air; it usually has a pillow.

self-inflating mattress
Rubber, plastic or nylon bag that inflates with air by itself, without the need of an inflator.

foam pad
Long thin cushion made of soft material.

camping

cutlery set
Range of compact table utensils (knife, fork and spoon) used by the camper to eat.

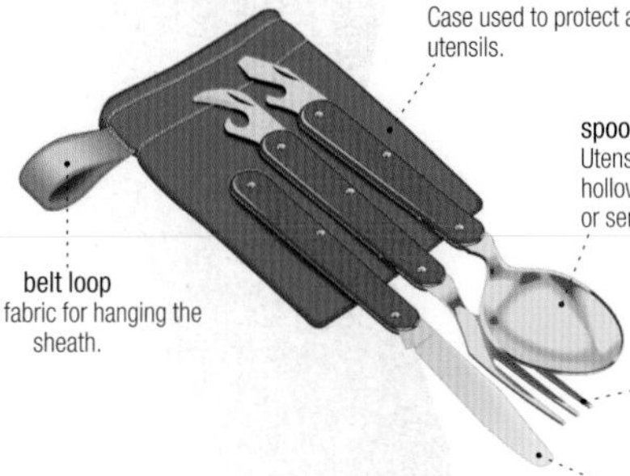

sheath
Case used to protect and carry the utensils.

spoon
Utensil consisting of a handle and a hollow part that is used to eat liquid or semisolid foods.

belt loop
Strip of fabric for hanging the sheath.

fork
Utensil with tines used to spear food and carry it to the mouth.

knife
Utensil consisting of a handle and a sharp blade used to cut food into bite-sized pieces.

coffee pot
Container used to brew coffee.

cooking set
Stackable set of dishes, utensils and containers that are used to cook outdoors.

cup
Container used to consume liquids or semisolid foods.

handle
Part used to hold and move the frying pan.

frying pan
Utensil used to fry, sauté or brown food.

saucepan
Stockpot with somewhat high sides, used to cook food in a liquid.

plate
Large piece of flat or shallow dinnerware, usually containing individual portions of solid food.

---

camping equipment
Range of accessories used when camping to store food, cut wood, etc.

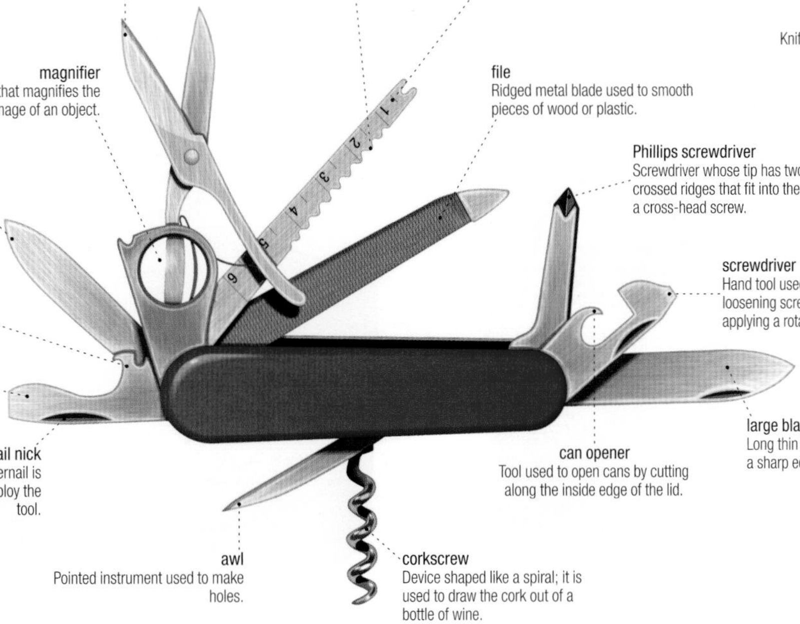

scissors
Instrument with two movable overlapping shanks having sharp inside edges; they are used for trimming and cutting.

fish scaler
Jagged blade used to scale fish.

ruler
Instrument for measuring length.

multipurpose knife
Knife with a large assortment of blades and instruments.

magnifier
Converging lens that magnifies the image of an object.

file
Ridged metal blade used to smooth pieces of wood or plastic.

pen blade
Small thin piece of metal with a sharp edge used as a secondary knife for more delicate tasks.

Phillips screwdriver
Screwdriver whose tip has two crossed ridges that fit into the head of a cross-head screw.

screwdriver
Hand tool used for tightening or loosening screws and bolts by applying a rotating motion.

bottle opener
Instrument used to remove caps from bottles.

screwdriver
Hand tool used for tightening or loosening screws and bolts by applying a rotating motion.

large blade
Long thin solid piece of metal with a sharp edge that is the main knife.

nail nick
Part where the fingernail is inserted; it is used to deploy the tool.

can opener
Tool used to open cans by cutting along the inside edge of the lid.

awl
Pointed instrument used to make holes.

corkscrew
Device shaped like a spiral; it is used to draw the cork out of a bottle of wine.

camping

camping equipment

backpack
Travel or hiking bag that is worn on the back and is used to transport clothing, camping equipment, etc.

top flap
Piece of fabric that folds over the opening of the backpack.

shoulder strap
Fabric band of variable length that goes over the shoulder so the bag can be carried on the back.

tightening buckle
Device used to adjust the length of the strap.

side compression strap
Fabric band that reduces the size of the bag and keeps the contents in place.

front compression strap
Fabric band connected to the top flap strap and used to fasten the backpack.

waist belt
Fabric strap that fits snugly around the hips and buckles there; it is designed to distribute the bag's weight.

strap loop
Buckle through which the strap passes.

filter
Device that purifies water by neutralizing bacteria or removing impurities.

water purifier
Container outfitted with a filtration system designed to make water drinkable.

sport bottle
Container designed to carry liquids.

hurricane lamp
Portable lantern with a glass globe and metal frame to protect the flame from wind and impact.

thermos bottle
Container with a vacuum between the inner and insulated outer walls; it is designed to maintain its contents at a desired temperature.

bottle
Container used to hold liquids or semisolid foods.

stopper
Part used to close the neck of the bottle.

cup
Cap used as a container to consume liquid or semisolid foods.

canteen
Portable container used to store liquids.

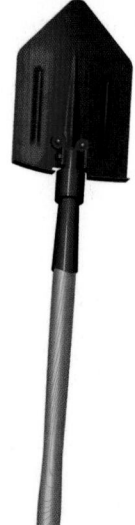

folding shovel
Tool with a collapsible handle; it is used as a shovel or a pickax.

water carrier
Container with a spigot that is used to store drinking water when camping.

cooler
Thermally insulated chest that is used to keep food cold with ice cubes or blocks of ice.

camping

headlamp
Lamp held on the head by an adjustable strap, leaving the user's hands free.

knife
Tool consisting of a sharp blade and a handle; it is used to cut items such as rope and fishing line.

sheath
Casing to cover the knife blade when it is not in use.

folding saw
Collapsible tool with folding, serrated blade used to saw wood.

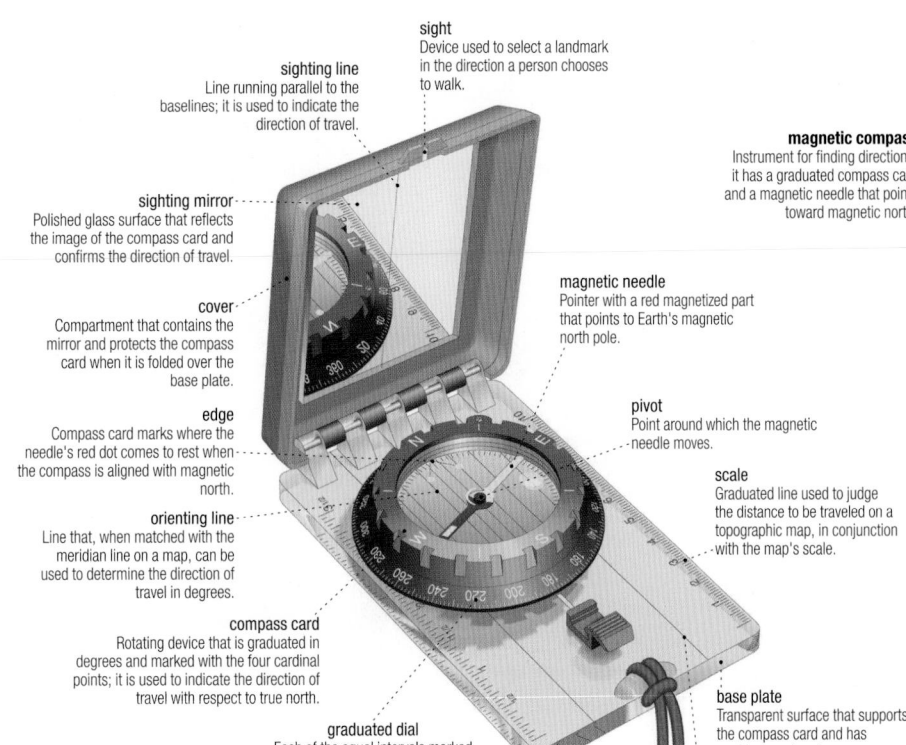

sight
Device used to select a landmark in the direction a person chooses to walk.

sighting line
Line running parallel to the baselines; it is used to indicate the direction of travel.

magnetic compass
Instrument for finding directions; it has a graduated compass card and a magnetic needle that points toward magnetic north.

sighting mirror
Polished glass surface that reflects the image of the compass card and confirms the direction of travel.

magnetic needle
Pointer with a red magnetized part that points to Earth's magnetic north pole.

cover
Compartment that contains the mirror and protects the compass card when it is folded over the base plate.

pivot
Point around which the magnetic needle moves.

edge
Compass card marks where the needle's red dot comes to rest when the compass is aligned with magnetic north.

scale
Graduated line used to judge the distance to be traveled on a topographic map, in conjunction with the map's scale.

orienting line
Line that, when matched with the meridian line on a map, can be used to determine the direction of travel in degrees.

compass card
Rotating device that is graduated in degrees and marked with the four cardinal points; it is used to indicate the direction of travel with respect to true north.

base plate
Transparent surface that supports the compass card and has markings and scales.

graduated dial
Each of the equal intervals marked on the dial that indicate the angle in degrees of the points on the compass card.

direction-of-travel arrows
Line marked on the base plate that is placed on top of a topographic map; it shows the direction of the place toward which the person wishes to travel.

hatchet
Small ax used to cut wood.

leather sheath
Casing to cover the head of the hatchet when it is not in use.

folding armchair
Light seat that folds up for easy transportation and storage.

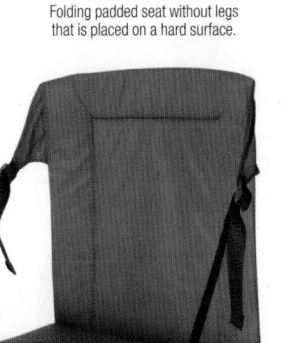

stadium seat cushion
Folding padded seat without legs that is placed on a hard surface.

folding grill
Hinged metal utensil to cook food over a campfire.

SPORTS AND GAMES

knots

Intertwining of two ropes or of one rope back on itself; they are used to tie two ropes together or one rope to an object.

square knot
Knot used to join two ropes of equal diameter firmly together.

overhand knot
Basic all-purpose knot tied by simply looping the rope back on itself.

running bowline
Knot pulled tight around an object to hold it in place.

sheet bend
Knot used to join together two ropes of different diameters.

double sheet bend
Knot with the same function as the sheet bend but the second loop makes the knot stronger and more secure.

granny knot
Knot used to tie two ropes together; it is used only when they will need to be untied easily.

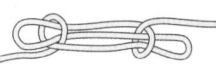

sheepshank
Knot used to temporarily shorten a rope.

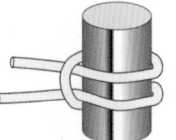

cow hitch
Knot used to join a rope to a ring, mast, yard, etc.

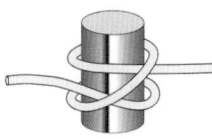

clove hitch
Knot used to join a rope to a stationary object or to another rope.

fisherman's knot
Knot used to tie together two ropes of equal diameter or two ends of fishing line.

heaving line knot
Knot used to add weight to the end of a rope so it can be thrown.

figure-eight knot
Any knot used to increase the diameter of a rope end.

common whipping
Winding a cord around a rope end to prevent its strands from unraveling.

bowline
Knot used to create a loop at the end of a rope that cannot slip and in which a person can sit to be raised or lowered.

bowline on a bight
Knot with the same function as the bowline but with two ropes to make the loop; one forms the seat and the other goes around the waist.

short splice
Splice: joining two ropes by interweaving their strands.

forming
To create a splice, the strands of each rope are first unraveled and then interwoven.

completion
To complete a splice, the strand ends of each rope are tucked into the other one.

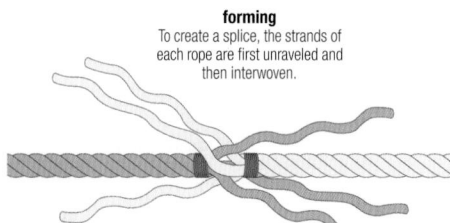

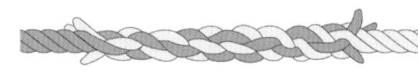

cable
Flexible, very strong cord made of twisted or braided ropes.

twisted rope
Strand of rope that is twisted with others to make a cable.

braided rope
Cable made by braiding strands together.

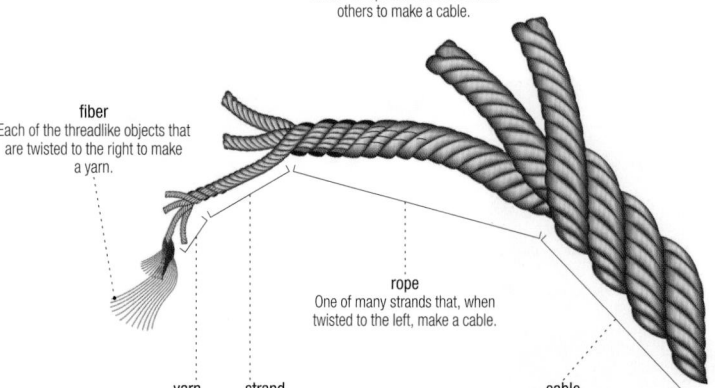

fiber
Each of the threadlike objects that are twisted to the right to make a yarn.

rope
One of many strands that, when twisted to the left, make a cable.

yarn
Each of the threads made of fibers that are twisted to the left to make a strand.

strand
One of many strands of yarn that, when twisted to the right, make a twisted rope.

cable
Flexible, very strong cord made of twisted ropes.

core
Mass of braided threads that give the rope its strength.

sheath
Casing made of interwoven threads that protects the core and makes it resistant to rubbing.

fishing

Outdoor leisure activity consisting of trying to catch fish with a fishing rod.

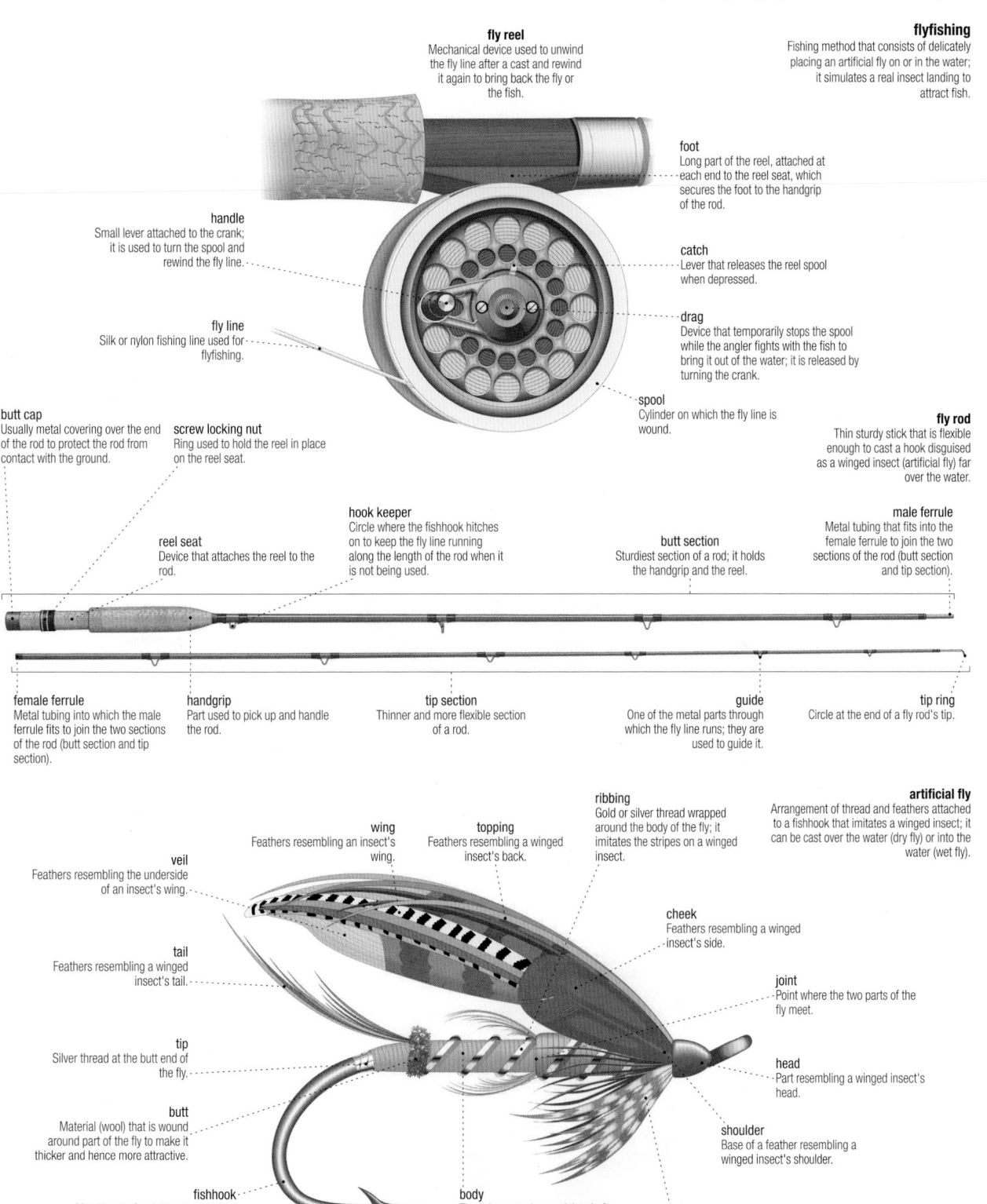

fly reel
Mechanical device used to unwind the fly line after a cast and rewind it again to bring back the fly or the fish.

flyfishing
Fishing method that consists of delicately placing an artificial fly on or in the water; it simulates a real insect landing to attract fish.

foot
Long part of the reel, attached at each end to the reel seat, which secures the foot to the handgrip of the rod.

handle
Small lever attached to the crank; it is used to turn the spool and rewind the fly line.

catch
Lever that releases the reel spool when depressed.

drag
Device that temporarily stops the spool while the angler fights with the fish to bring it out of the water; it is released by turning the crank.

fly line
Silk or nylon fishing line used for flyfishing.

spool
Cylinder on which the fly line is wound.

fly rod
Thin sturdy stick that is flexible enough to cast a hook disguised as a winged insect (artificial fly) far over the water.

butt cap
Usually metal covering over the end of the rod to protect the rod from contact with the ground.

screw locking nut
Ring used to hold the reel in place on the reel seat.

hook keeper
Circle where the fishhook hitches on to keep the fly line running along the length of the rod when it is not being used.

butt section
Sturdiest section of a rod; it holds the handgrip and the reel.

male ferrule
Metal tubing that fits into the female ferrule to join the two sections of the rod (butt section and tip section).

reel seat
Device that attaches the reel to the rod.

female ferrule
Metal tubing into which the male ferrule fits to join the two sections of the rod (butt section and tip section).

handgrip
Part used to pick up and handle the rod.

tip section
Thinner and more flexible section of a rod.

guide
One of the metal parts through which the fly line runs; they are used to guide it.

tip ring
Circle at the end of a fly rod's tip.

ribbing
Gold or silver thread wrapped around the body of the fly; it imitates the stripes on a winged insect.

artificial fly
Arrangement of thread and feathers attached to a fishhook that imitates a winged insect; it can be cast over the water (dry fly) or into the water (wet fly).

veil
Feathers resembling the underside of an insect's wing.

wing
Feathers resembling an insect's wing.

topping
Feathers resembling a winged insect's back.

cheek
Feathers resembling a winged insect's side.

tail
Feathers resembling a winged insect's tail.

joint
Point where the two parts of the fly meet.

tip
Silver thread at the butt end of the fly.

head
Part resembling a winged insect's head.

butt
Material (wool) that is wound around part of the fly to make it thicker and hence more attractive.

shoulder
Base of a feather resembling a winged insect's shoulder.

fishhook
Metal hook of variable size attached to the end of float tackle and baited with a natural or artificial lure intended to catch a fish.

body
Thread wrapped around the shaft of a fishhook to resemble a winged insect's body.

hackle
Rooster feathers used to imitate a winged insect's feet and neck.

SPORTS AND GAMES

fishing

casting
Fishing that consists of letting a hook drop and sink into the water and reeling it back in to simulate the movement of a small fish.

spinning rod
Stick whose length and sturdiness varies with the kind of fishing being done; it is used to cast a hook carried along by a weight, sinker or spinner far over the water.

screw locking nut
Ring used to hold the reel in place on the reel seat.

reel seat
Device that attaches the reel to the rod.

male ferrule
Metal tubing that fits into the female ferrule to join the two sections of the rod (butt section and tip section).

female ferrule
Metal tubing into which the male ferrule fits to join the two sections of the rod (butt section and tip section).

butt grip
Part used to pick up and handle the rod.

butt guide
Large-diameter circle used to guide the slack line.

tip ring
Circle at the end of a spinning rod's tip.

open-face spinning reel
Reel from which the line unwinds as it comes off the upper sides of the spool, which does not rotate but remains in place.

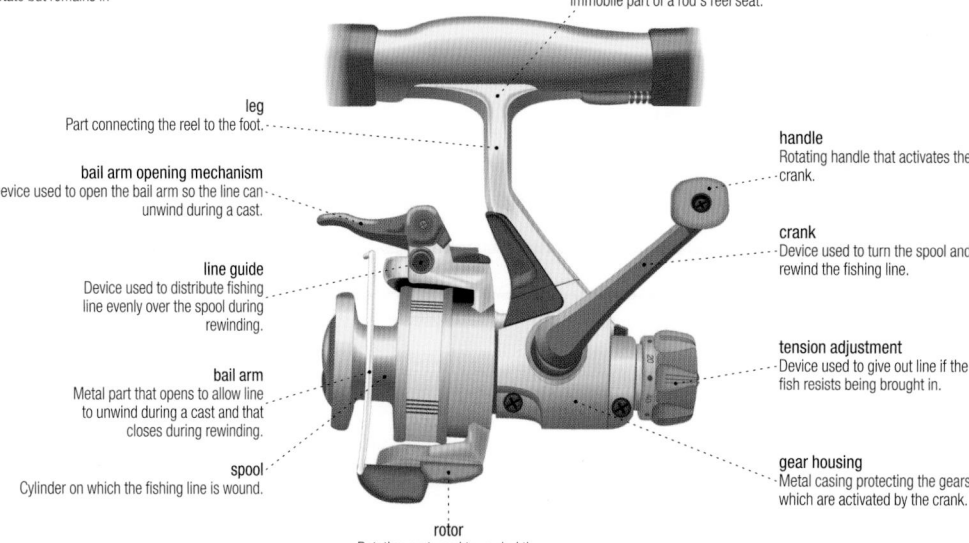

foot
Immobile part of a rod's reel seat.

leg
Part connecting the reel to the foot.

handle
Rotating handle that activates the crank.

bail arm opening mechanism
Device used to open the bail arm so the line can unwind during a cast.

crank
Device used to turn the spool and rewind the fishing line.

line guide
Device used to distribute fishing line evenly over the spool during rewinding.

tension adjustment
Device used to give out line if the fish resists being brought in.

bail arm
Metal part that opens to allow line to unwind during a cast and that closes during rewinding.

spool
Cylinder on which the fishing line is wound.

gear housing
Metal casing protecting the gears, which are activated by the crank.

rotor
Rotating part used to rewind the fishing line.

baitcasting reel
Reel from which the line unwinds due to the rotation of the spool on its axis.

spool-release mechanism
Mechanism that releases the brake so the spool can once again turn freely.

star drag wheel
Star-pointed wheel that stops the fishing line from unwinding when the hooked fish pulls on the line.

spool
Cylinder on which the fishing line is wound.

spool axle
Metal rod around which the fishing line is wound.

crank
Device used to turn the spool and rewind the fishing line.

stand
Long part of the reel, attached at each end to the reel seat, which secures the reel to the handgrip of the rod.

SPORTS AND GAMES

fishing

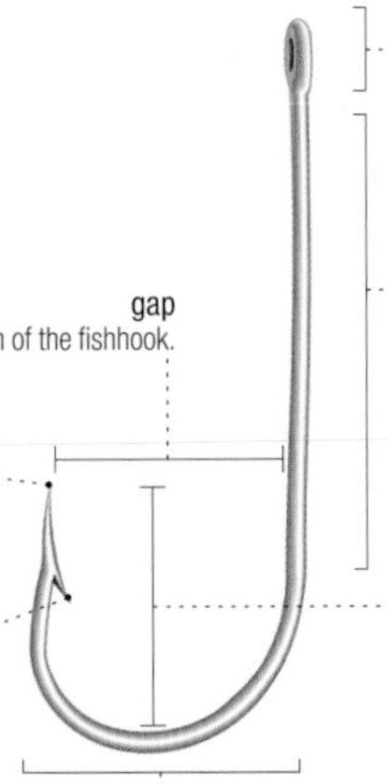

fishhook
Metal hook of variable size attached to the end of float tackle and baited with a natural or artificial lure intended to catch a fish.

eye
Hole through which the fishing line passes so the fishhook can be attached to the line or to float tackle.

shank
Straight part between the bend and the eye of the fishhook.

gap
Width of the fishhook.

point
Pointed end of the fishhook that catches on the fish's mouth.

barb
Reverse projection that prevents the fishhook from falling out of the fish's mouth.

throat
Depth of the fishhook.

bend
Rounded end of the fishhook.

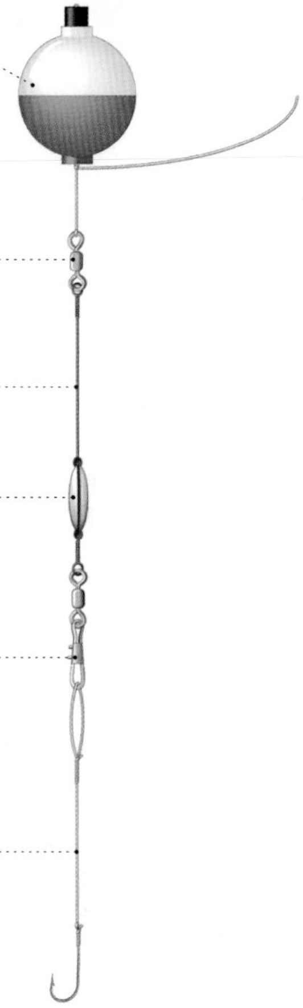

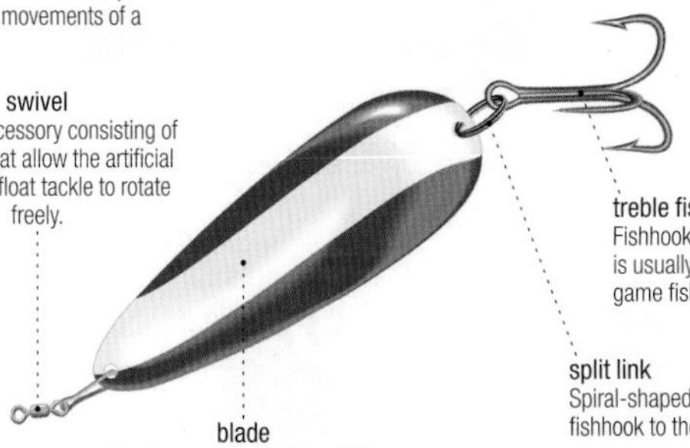

spinner
Artificial metal lure whose shape and color imitate the movements of a small fish.

swivel
Rotating accessory consisting of two eyes that allow the artificial lure or the float tackle to rotate freely.

treble fishhook
Fishhook with three points that is usually used to catch large game fish.

split link
Spiral-shaped ring connecting the fishhook to the blade.

blade
Rotating metal object to which the swivel and the fishhook are attached.

float tackle
Range of accessories at the end of the fishing line and ending with the fishhook; the length of the leader depends on the kind of fish being caught.

bobber
Light object filled with air that keeps the bait at a certain depth below water level and signals a bite by its movement.

swivel
Rotating accessory consisting of two eyes that allow the artificial lure or the float tackle to rotate freely.

leader
Length of steel wire between the fishing line and the fishhook that prevents the line from being cut by predatory fish such as pike.

sinker
Small lead object used to weight the line during the cast and to carry the fishhook underwater.

snap link
Metal ring that opens and closes with a spring-loaded gate; it is used to connect the snelled fishhook to a swivel.

snelled fishhook
Ready-tied fishhook attached to float tackle at the end of the fishing line.

fishing clothing and accessories

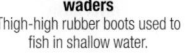

waders
Thigh-high rubber boots used to fish in shallow water.

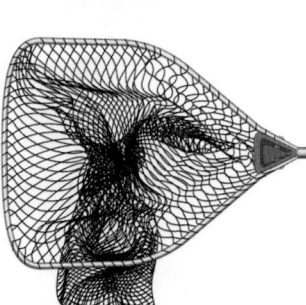

tackle box
Compartmentalized box used to store and carry bait and fishing equipment.

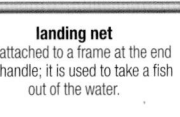

creel
Basket used to store and carry the catch.

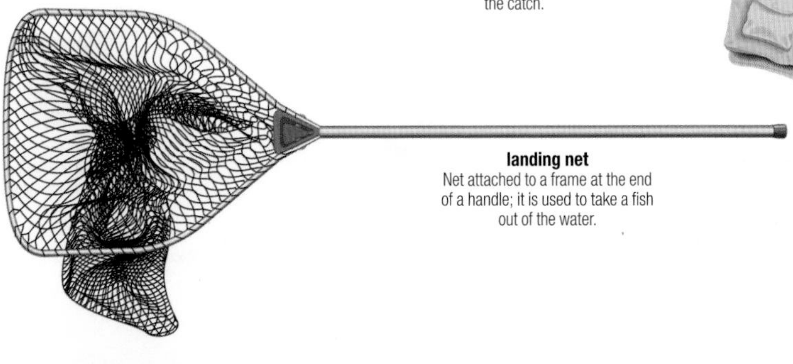

landing net
Net attached to a frame at the end of a handle; it is used to take a fish out of the water.

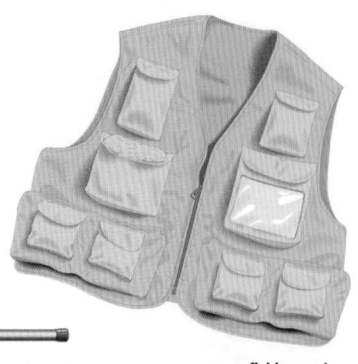

fishing vest
Sleeveless jacket with many pockets for carrying small objects (license, sinkers, etc.).

SPORTS AND GAMES

dice and dominoes

Cubes (dice) or pieces divided into two ends (dominoes) with numbers indicated by pips or figures.

ordinary die
Small cube marked on each side with one to six pips; it is used in various games (backgammon, Monopoly®, Yahtzee®, etc.).

poker die
Small cube marked on each side with card symbols; it is used to play poker dice, a game similar to poker, which is played with five dice.

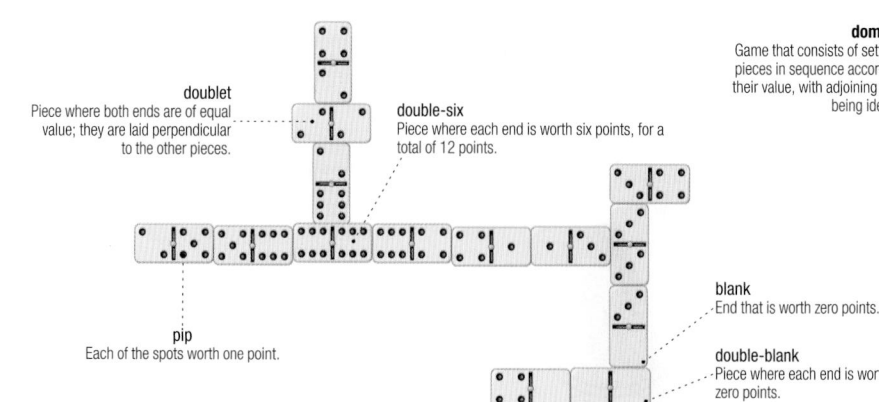

doublet
Piece where both ends are of equal value; they are laid perpendicular to the other pieces.

double-six
Piece where each end is worth six points, for a total of 12 points.

dominoes
Game that consists of setting up pieces in sequence according to their value, with adjoining pieces being identical.

blank
End that is worth zero points.

double-blank
Piece where each end is worth zero points.

pip
Each of the spots worth one point.

playing cards

Rectangular pieces of cardboard used to play various games; they have figures, signs and numbers on one side and are divided into four suits.

suits
Sign that indicates one of the four groups of cards in a deck.

hearts
Suit that uses a red heart as its symbol.

diamonds
Suit that uses a red diamond as its symbol.

clubs
Suit that uses a stylized black clover as its symbol.

spades
Suit that uses a stylized black spearhead as its symbol.

court and special cards
The four figures represent ranking members of medieval society.

joker
Card depicting a court jester; in most games, its value is the cardholder's choice.

ace
Card with a single sign that usually has the highest value in the suit.

king
Figure depicting a king that usually has the second-highest value in the suit.

queen
Figure depicting a queen that usually has the third-highest value in the suit.

jack
Figure depicting an equerry that usually has the fourth-highest value in the suit.

standard poker hands
Combinations of a maximum of five cards in poker, shown here in ascending order of value.

high card
Highest-value single card, when no combinations are possible.

one pair
Two cards of equal value.

two pairs
Contains two pairs.

three of a kind
Three cards of equal value.

straight
Five consecutive cards of mixed suits.

flush
Five nonconsecutive cards of the same suit.

full house
Three of a kind with a pair.

four of a kind
Four cards of equal value.

straight flush
Five consecutive cards of the same suit.

royal flush
Five consecutive cards of the same suit from the 10 to the ace.

board games

Complete range of games that use a playing surface on which game pieces (tokens, dice, counters, etc.) are placed.

backgammon
Game of strategy in which two players move checkers around a board; players try to collect and bear them off while preventing the opponent's checkers from moving.

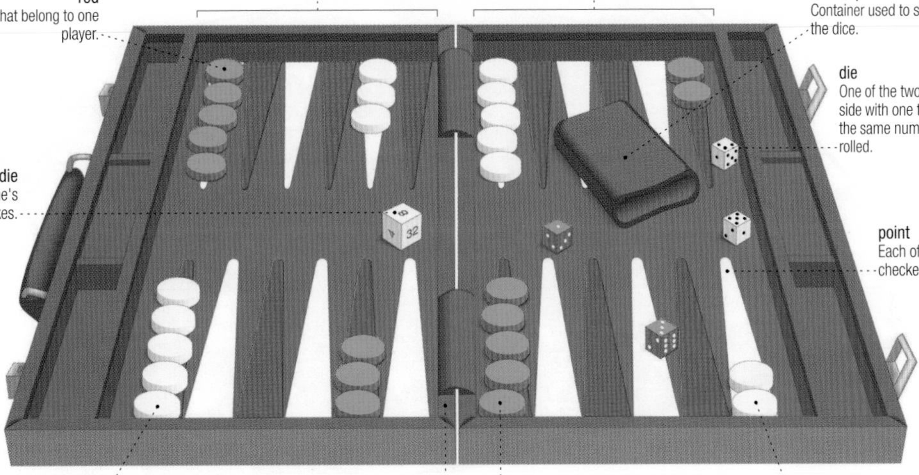

outer table
Area with 12 points that the checkers must move across to reach the inner table; opponents move in opposite directions.

inner table
Table that a player's checkers must enter before they can be borne off; the player who first bears off all his or her checkers wins the game.

red
Red checkers that belong to one player.

dice cup
Container used to shake and throw the dice.

die
One of the two small cubes marked on each side with one to six pips; the checker moves the same number of points as the number rolled.

doubling die
Die used to increase the game's stakes.

point
Each of the spaces on which the checkers are placed.

white
White checkers that belong to one player.

bar
Line that divides the board's inner and outer tables; the checkers hit by the opposing player are placed on it.

checkers
Each of the counters used to play; the checkers are moved from one point to the next based on the number of pips shown on the dice.

runner
One of two checkers belonging to a player placed at the start of the game on the opponent's inner table; it must leave that position before any other checkers of the same color can be moved.

die
Small cube whose sides are marked with between one and six dots. Each number represents the number of squares a playing piece can be moved.

ludo
Game of chance in which players try to move their four playing pieces toward the center of the board as quickly as possible.

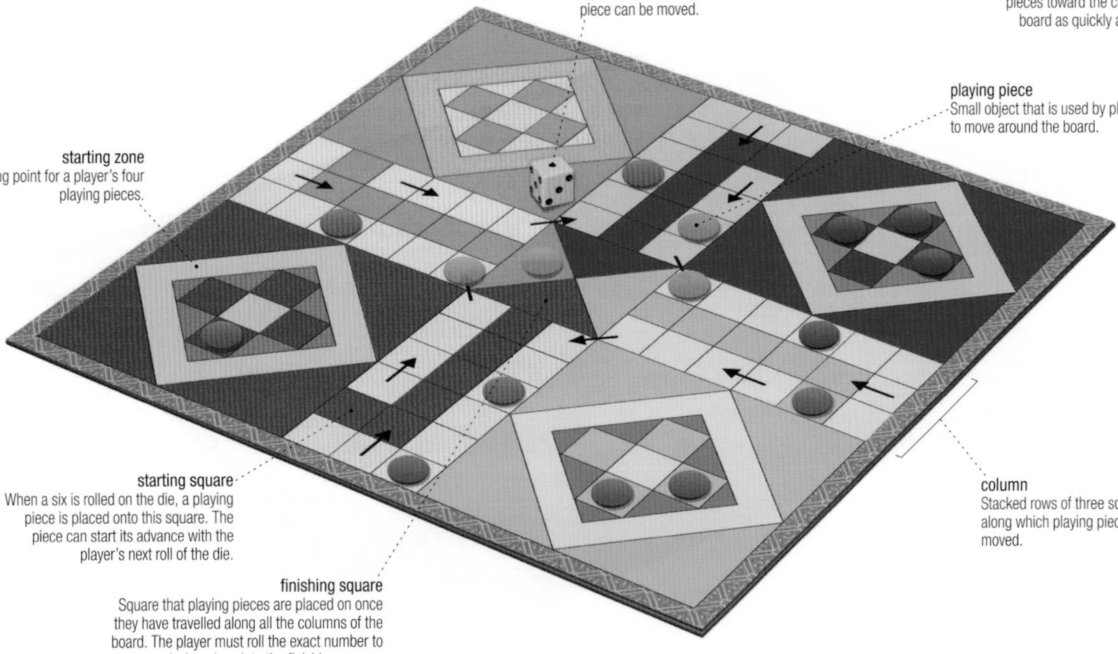

playing piece
Small object that is used by players to move around the board.

starting zone
Starting point for a player's four playing pieces.

starting square
When a six is rolled on the die, a playing piece is placed onto this square. The piece can start its advance with the player's next roll of the die.

finishing square
Square that playing pieces are placed on once they have travelled along all the columns of the board. The player must roll the exact number to move a playing piece into the finishing square.

column
Stacked rows of three squares along which playing pieces are moved.

board games

snakes and ladders

Game of chance in which the goal is to reach the last space on the board by using the ladders and avoiding the snakes.

die
One of the two small cubes marked on each side with one to six pips.

playing piece
Small object that is used by players to move around the board.

finish
Last square on the board. The first player to reach the finish wins the game.

snake
When a token lands on the head of a snake, it must be moved down to the snake's tail.

ladder
When a token lands at the foot of a ladder, it is moved directly to the top of the ladder.

game board
Playing surface that is divided into spaces around which playing pieces move.

square
One of the game board's 100 spaces on which playing pieces are placed.

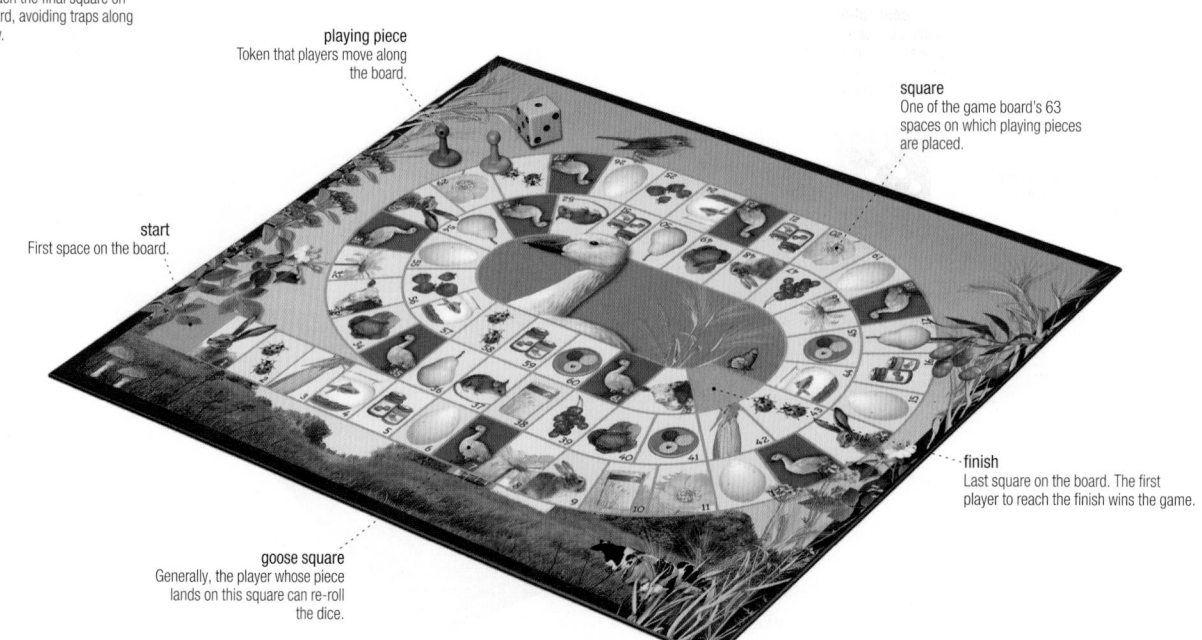

game of the goose

Game of chance in which the goal is to reach the final square on the board, avoiding traps along the way.

playing piece
Token that players move along the board.

square
One of the game board's 63 spaces on which playing pieces are placed.

start
First space on the board.

finish
Last square on the board. The first player to reach the finish wins the game.

goose square
Generally, the player whose piece lands on this square can re-roll the dice.

board games

chess pieces
At the beginning of the game, each player has 16 pieces with different moves and value: a king, a queen, two rooks, two bishops, two knights and eight pawns.

pawn
Piece that can advance one square at a time except at the beginning of the game, when it can advance one or two squares; it captures opposing pieces diagonally.

rook
Piece that can move backward or forward vertically in a column or side to side horizontally in a row for as many squares as the player chooses.

bishop
Piece that can move backward or forward diagonally for as many squares as the player chooses.

knight
Piece that can move in an L-shape of two squares in one row or column and one square in a perpendicular row or column; the knight is the only piece that can jump over any other piece.

king
The most important piece in the game; it can move backward or forward in all directions one square at a time.

queen
The most powerful attack piece; it can move backward or forward in all directions for as many squares as the player chooses.

chess
Game where two players move pieces around a board in order to "checkmate" the opponent (i.e., attack the king in such a manner that no escape is possible).

queen's side
Each of the pieces in columns *a* to *d* on the board.

king's side
Each of the pieces in columns *e* to *h* on the board.

chessboard
Board divided into 64 black and white squares; the corner square on each player's left must be black.

white square
Light-colored square; when the game begins, the white queen is on a square of her own color.

black square
Dark-colored square; when the game begins, the black queen is on a square of her own color.

chess notation
Means of using letters and numbers to identify the chessboard squares; it is used to situate pieces, transcribe games, follow moves, etc.

Black
Pieces belonging to one of the two players.

White
Pieces belonging to one of the two players; White starts the game.

types of movements
Each piece moves in a specific way: diagonally, vertically, horizontally or in a L-shape.

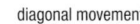
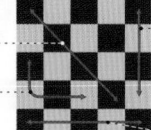

diagonal movement
Forward or backward movement along an oblique line.

L-shaped movement
L-shaped movement; moving one square forward or backward and then two squares laterally, or two squares forward or backward and then one square laterally.

vertical movement
Moving forward or backward along a column.

horizontal movement
Moving to the right or left along a row.

major motions
The various movements are made by placing stones on a liberty, which is an empty, adjacent horizontal or vertical intersection.

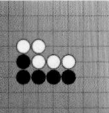

connection
When a stone occupies a liberty belonging to a stone of the same color, the two stones are connected; a chain is made up of two or more connected stones.

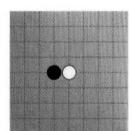

contact
Point where two stones occupying adjacent intersections meet.

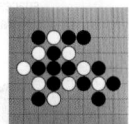

capture
When a stone or chain of stones is completely surrounded by the opponent's stones, it is captured and removed from the board.

board
Grid made of 19 horizontal and vertical lines; the stones are placed where the lines intersect. The Japanese name for the board is "goban."

go
Japanese name for a strategic game that originated in China; players take turns placing stones on the intersections of a board to surround his or her opponent and control the most territory.

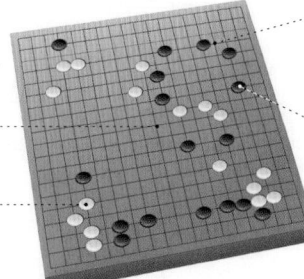

handicap spot
Each of the nine points on the board where stones belonging to the weaker player are placed when the players are of unequal strength.

center
Central intersection on the board.

black stone
One player's token; in the game of go, there are 181 black stones and the player with these stones moves first.

white stone
One player's token; in the game of go, there are 180 white stones.

checkers
Game that consists of capturing all the opposing counters by jumping over them, provided that the square behind each one is free.

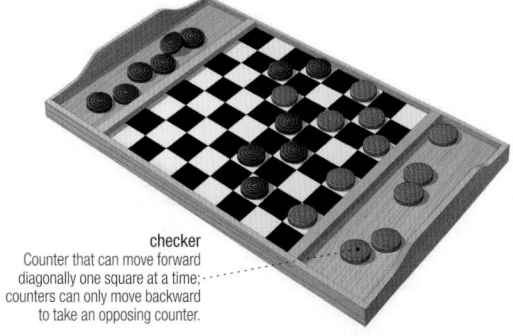

checkerboard
Board divided into black and white squares.

checker
Counter that can move forward diagonally one square at a time; counters can only move backward to take an opposing counter.

jigsaw puzzle

Puzzle that consists of a picture divided into irregularly shaped pieces that must be put back together.

piece
Each of the fragments that fit together to create a picture.

picture
Image put back together by assembling the pieces.

board
Flexible surface on which the puzzle pieces are laid out; it can be rolled up while the puzzle is still unfinished.

mah-jongg

Game for four players that originated in China; players score points by creating combinations of four sets of tiles (run, three-of-a-kind or square) and one pair.

square
Four-sided structure of tiles divided into four cardinal points; each player is a wind from one of those points.

East
Player who is the East wind and who starts the game; this player's points are automatically doubled.

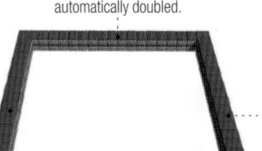

South
Player who is the South wind.

North
Player who is the North wind.

West
Player who is the West wind.

wall
Each player draws 36 tiles to build a wall that is 18 tiles long and two tiles high; the four walls are joined together to form a square.

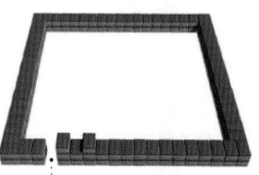

breaking the wall
Opening in the wall that determines the place from which the tiles will be drawn.

suit tiles
Mah-jongg has 108 suit tiles: four matching sets of each of the nine circles, nine characters and nine bamboos.

circles
Each of the tiles depicting an ascending number of circles.

characters
Each of the tiles depicting an ideogram, which represents numbers one through nine.

bamboos
Each of the tiles depicting bamboo shoots, with the first tile showing a bird.

honor tiles
Mah-jongg has 28 honor tiles that are worth twice the points; there are four identical sets of four winds and four identical sets of three dragons.

winds
Each of the tiles representing the East, South, West and North winds.

dragons
Each of the tiles depicting a red, green or white dragon.

bonus tiles
Mah-jongg has eight bonus tiles that are also known as Supreme Honor tiles; they are not used in making combinations but they add points.

flower tiles
Each of the four tiles depicting flowers.

season tiles
Each of the four tiles depicting the seasons.

video games

Interactive computer programs that perform display-based games (action, strategy, simulation, role-playing, etc.) in which the player controls activity through the use of peripheral devices.

video entertainment system
Group of units (game console and visual display) that allows a person to control the action in a game displayed on a screen by means of a controller.

display
Surface on which the images appear.

game console
Personal computer used to play video games; it is directed by a controller and plugs directly into the television.

eject button
Button that allows a player to retrieve a disc from the game console.

action buttons
Buttons used to perform various operations (grasp an object, jump, shoot, etc.).

cover
Part that covers the location of memory-card readers.

joysticks
Analog devices that replace the directional buttons.

CD/DVD player
Device that uses a laser beam to read data written on a compact disc, game disc or DVD.

reset button
Button used to reboot the game console in the event the system freezes.

directional buttons
Buttons that are used to control the movement of objects or characters and enter various commands.

controller
Game peripheral with buttons and joysticks that control movement, enter commands and perform operations.

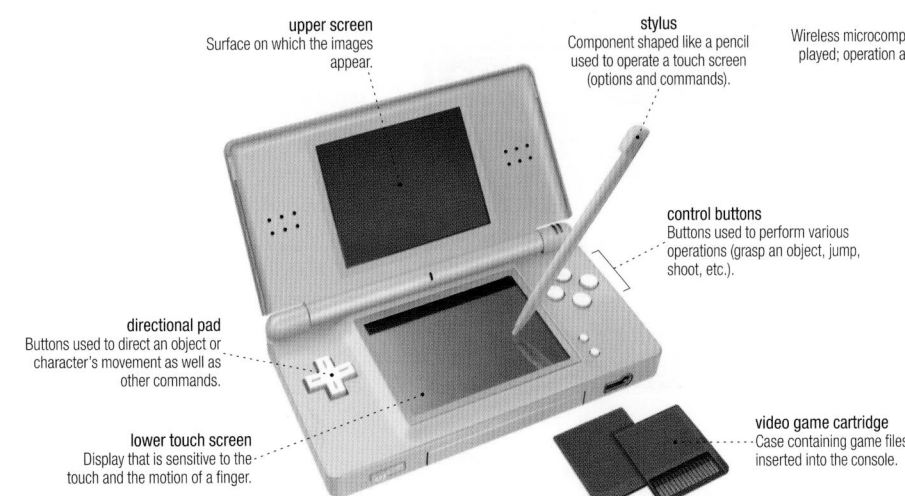

upper screen
Surface on which the images appear.

stylus
Component shaped like a pencil used to operate a touch screen (options and commands).

portable game console
Wireless microcomputer on which video games are played; operation and commands are activated by buttons or a stylus.

control buttons
Buttons used to perform various operations (grasp an object, jump, shoot, etc.).

directional pad
Buttons used to direct an object or character's movement as well as other commands.

lower touch screen
Display that is sensitive to the touch and the motion of a finger.

video game cartridge
Case containing game files; inserted into the console.

roulette

Gambling game that involves dropping a small ball into a revolving wheel; the aim is to bet on the winning number or color.

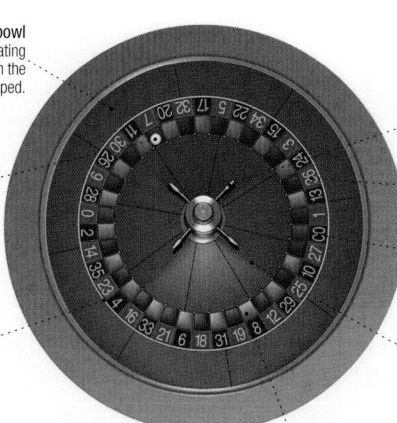

roulette wheel
Piece of equipment used to determine the winning number and color.

stationary bowl
Basin inside which the rotating wheel turns and into which the ivory ball is dropped.

ivory ball
Small ball that the croupier drops into the stationary bowl; it rolls around the rotating wheel and stops in one of the compartments to determine the winning number and color.

fret
Each of the metal edges separating the compartments.

cross handle
Grip shaped like a cross that is used by the croupier to rotate the wheel.

number
Each of the red or black numbers 1 through 36, including a green zero and double zero.

double zero
Number added to the American roulette wheel.

rotating wheel
Wheel with 38 numbered compartments that turns inside a stationary bowl.

compartment
Each of the hollow slots in front of a number where the ball can land to determine the winning number and color.

French roulette wheel
Piece of equipment used to determine the winning number and color; the French roulette wheel has no double zero compartment.

American roulette table
Surface with designated betting spaces on which players place chips to represent their bets.

single zero
If the zero comes up, any chips that players bet on red, black, even, odd, high or low are imprisoned.

main section
Grid on which the numbered betting spaces are printed.

low (1 to 18)
The chip is placed on this square to bet on numbers 1 through 18; if one of those numbers comes up, the bet wins the original stake.

dozen (1 to 12)
The chip is placed on this square to bet on numbers 1 through 12; if one of those numbers comes up, the bet wins twice the original stake.

even
The chip is placed on this square to bet on the even numbers; if one of those numbers comes up, the bet wins the original stake.

red
The chip is placed on this square to bet on the red numbers; if one of those numbers comes up, the bet wins the original stake.

dozen (13 to 24)
The chip is placed on this square to bet on numbers 13 through 24; if one of those numbers comes up, the bet wins twice the original stake.

black
The chip is placed on this square to bet on the black numbers; if one of those numbers comes up, the bet wins the original stake.

en prison
Area where the chip is placed when the bet is imprisoned; it is either released or lost on the following turn.

odd
The chip is placed on this square to bet on the odd numbers; if one of those numbers comes up, the bet wins the original stake.

high (19 to 36)
The chip is placed on this square to bet on numbers 19 through 36; if one of those numbers comes up, the bet wins the original stake.

dozen (25 to 36)
The chip is placed on this square to bet on numbers 25 through 36; if one of those numbers comes up, the bet wins twice the original stake.

double zero
Number added to the American betting layout; the chip is placed in the center of the square and if that number comes up, the bet wins back 35 times the original stake.

five-number bet
The chip is placed in the upper left hand corner of square 1; if 00, 0, 1, 2 or 3 comes up, the bet wins back six times the original stake.

square bet
The chip is placed at the intersection of four numbers; if one of those numbers comes up, the bet wins back eight times the original stake.

split bet
The chip is placed on a line dividing two numbers; if one of those two numbers comes up, the bet wins back 17 times the original stake.

line
The chip is placed on the line dividing the final two squares in two adjacent rows; if one of those six numbers comes up, the bet wins back five times the original stake.

straight bet
The chip is placed squarely in the center of any number; if that number comes up, the bet wins back 35 times the original stake.

street bet
The chip is placed on the outside edge of a row; if one of the three numbers in the row comes up, the bet wins 11 times the original stake.

two columns split bet
The chip is placed on one of the two lines between the three lower squares; if one of the numbers in those two columns comes up, the bet wins half the original stake.

column
Each of the three vertical rows of 12 numbers.

French roulette table
The French layout has all 36 numbers (even and odd, red and black, high and low) but only one zero.

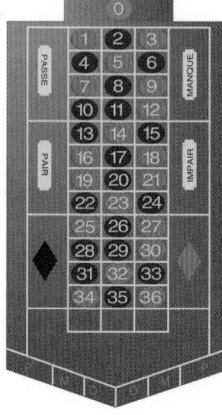

darts

Game of skill in which darts are thrown, three in succession, at a dartboard to accumulate a specific number of points (either 301 or 501).

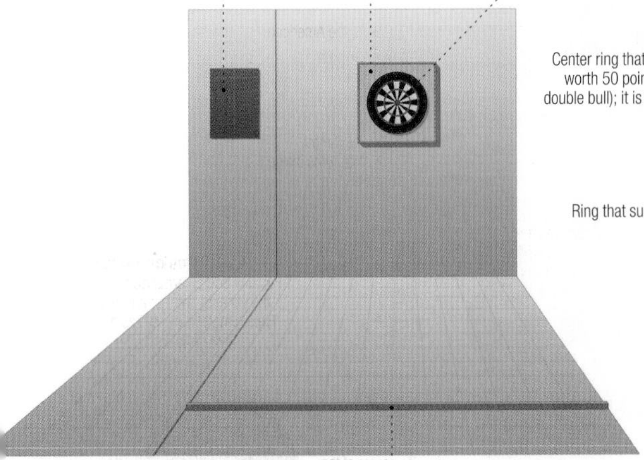

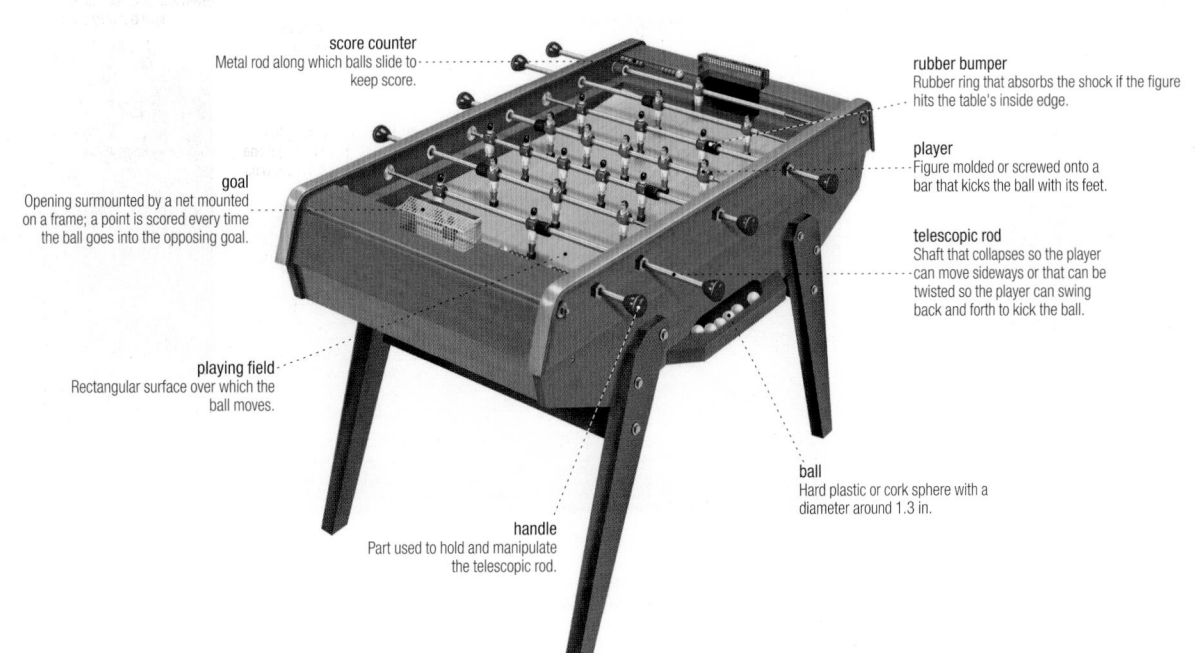

playing area
Zone marked off with lines that is set up for playing darts.

dartboard
Round object measuring 13 in in diameter that is divided into areas ranging in value from one to 20 points; it is used as a target for dart throwing.

segment score number
Number of points a dartboard segment is worth.

double ring
Ring that surrounds a zone where the segment points are doubled.

scoreboard
Board used to record the players' scores.

protective surround
Covering that protects the wall from being hit by darts.

dartboard
Round object measuring 13 in in diameter that is divided into areas ranging in value from one to 20 points; it is used as a target for dart throwing.

bull's-eye
Center ring that surrounds a zone worth 50 points (also called the double bull); it is set at about 5.5 ft above the floor.

outer bull
Ring that surrounds a zone worth 25 points.

triple ring
Ring that surrounds a zone where the segment points are tripled.

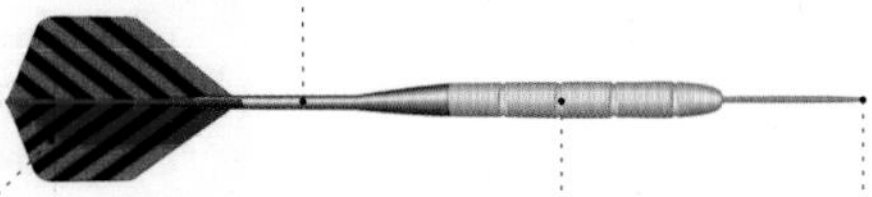

shaft
Metal stem that is used to grip the dart to throw it.

dart
Small metal-tipped missile that is thrown by hand at a dartboard.

oche
Line that is 7.75 ft from the target; the player stands behind it to throw the dart.

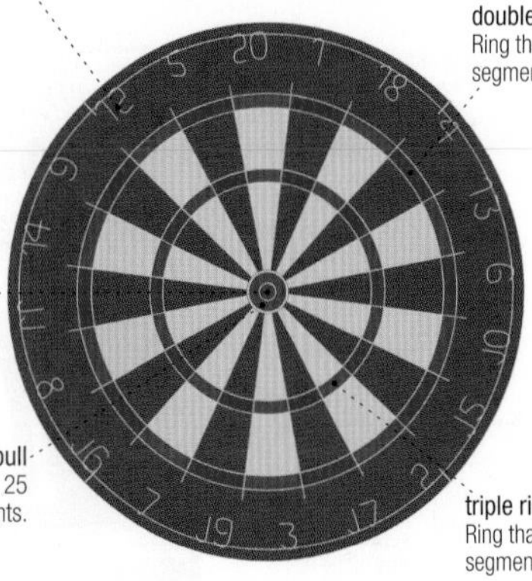

flight
Feathers or synthetic material attached to the back end of the dart to provide stability during flight.

barrel
Wider part of the dart whose type is determined by its weight distribution (smooth, ringed or knurled design).

point
Metal pointed front end of the dart that sticks in the dartboard.

soccer table

Table soccer game with figures mounted on telescopic rods.

score counter
Metal rod along which balls slide to keep score.

rubber bumper
Rubber ring that absorbs the shock if the figure hits the table's inside edge.

player
Figure molded or screwed onto a bar that kicks the ball with its feet.

goal
Opening surmounted by a net mounted on a frame; a point is scored every time the ball goes into the opposing goal.

telescopic rod
Shaft that collapses so the player can move sideways or that can be twisted so the player can swing back and forth to kick the ball.

playing field
Rectangular surface over which the ball moves.

ball
Hard plastic or cork sphere with a diameter around 1.3 in.

handle
Part used to hold and manipulate the telescopic rod.

slot machine

Electronic or mechanical gambling machine that is operated by inserting a coin into a slot in order to obtain a sequence of winning symbols.

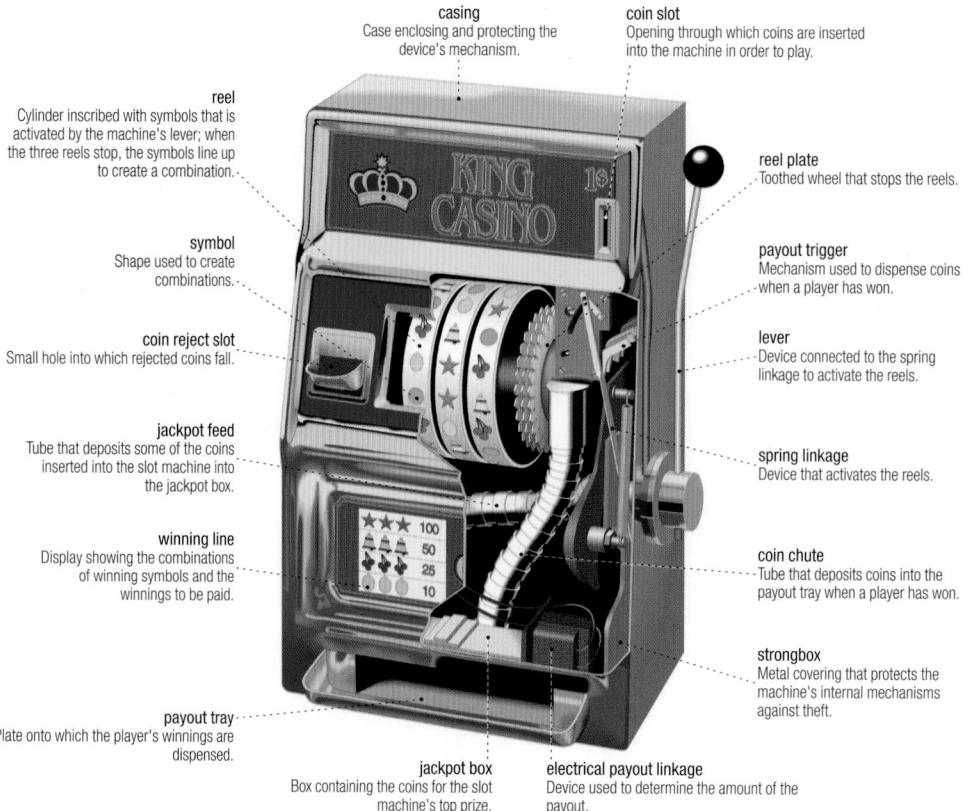

casing
Case enclosing and protecting the device's mechanism.

coin slot
Opening through which coins are inserted into the machine in order to play.

reel
Cylinder inscribed with symbols that is activated by the machine's lever; when the three reels stop, the symbols line up to create a combination.

reel plate
Toothed wheel that stops the reels.

symbol
Shape used to create combinations.

payout trigger
Mechanism used to dispense coins when a player has won.

coin reject slot
Small hole into which rejected coins fall.

lever
Device connected to the spring linkage to activate the reels.

jackpot feed
Tube that deposits some of the coins inserted into the slot machine into the jackpot box.

spring linkage
Device that activates the reels.

winning line
Display showing the combinations of winning symbols and the winnings to be paid.

coin chute
Tube that deposits coins into the payout tray when a player has won.

strongbox
Metal covering that protects the machine's internal mechanisms against theft.

payout tray
Plate onto which the player's winnings are dispensed.

jackpot box
Box containing the coins for the slot machine's top prize.

electrical payout linkage
Device used to determine the amount of the payout.

Ultimate

Game or sport practiced with a flat, circular implement that is thrown between players.

disc
Flat, circular implement thrown by players singlehandedly, generating a spin.

playing field
Ultimate: Sport between two seven-person teams who score points by reaching their opponent's end zone through a series of successive passes of a flying disc.

playing field proper
Area of play in between end zones.

end zone
One point is awarded when a player on the offensive team catches the disc in the opposing team's end zone.

brick mark
Point located 20 yd from the end zone; point from where the game is restarted in certain situations.

perimeter line
Line delimiting the area of play along the sides of the field.

pinball machine

Arcade game in which the goal is to obtain points by directing a metallic ball around the game surface using the machine's flippers.

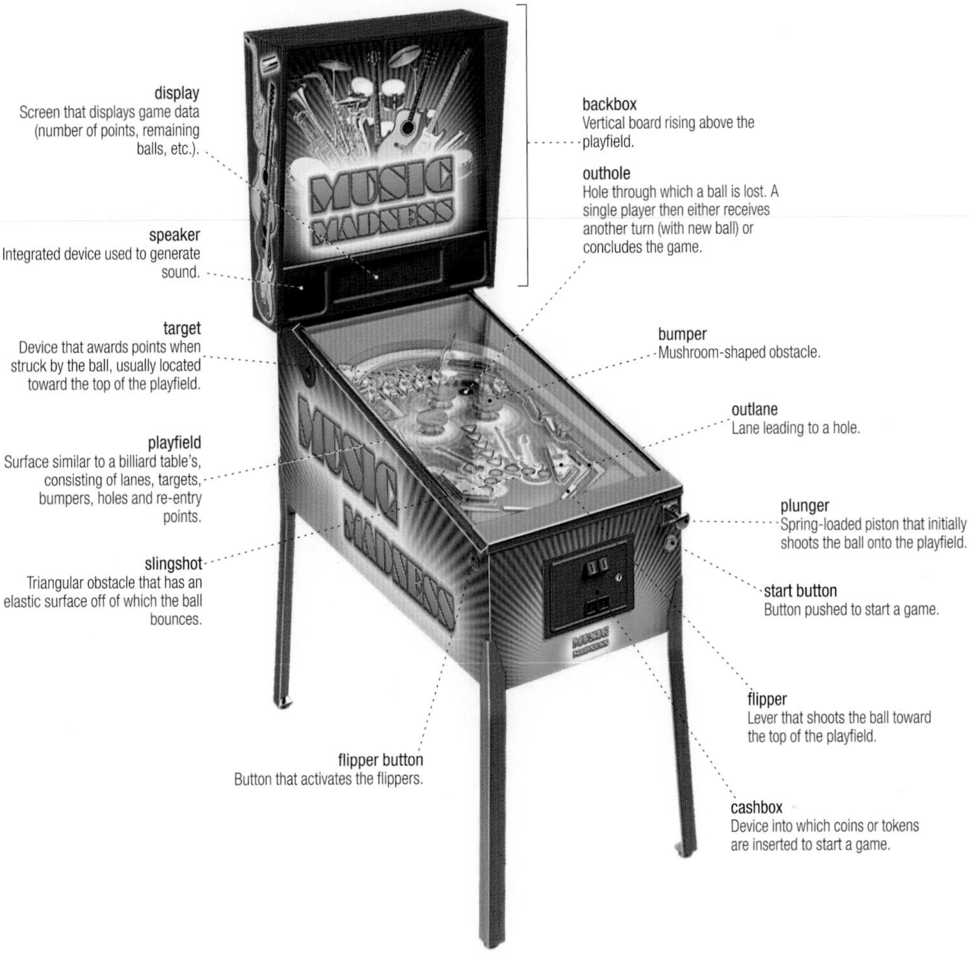

display
Screen that displays game data (number of points, remaining balls, etc.).

speaker
Integrated device used to generate sound.

target
Device that awards points when struck by the ball, usually located toward the top of the playfield.

playfield
Surface similar to a billiard table's, consisting of lanes, targets, bumpers, holes and re-entry points.

slingshot
Triangular obstacle that has an elastic surface off of which the ball bounces.

backbox
Vertical board rising above the playfield.

outhole
Hole through which a ball is lost. A single player then either receives another turn (with new ball) or concludes the game.

bumper
Mushroom-shaped obstacle.

outlane
Lane leading to a hole.

plunger
Spring-loaded piston that initially shoots the ball onto the playfield.

start button
Button pushed to start a game.

flipper
Lever that shoots the ball toward the top of the playfield.

flipper button
Button that activates the flippers.

cashbox
Device into which coins or tokens are inserted to start a game.

kite

Object made of fabric stretched across a light frame; held aloft by pulling flying lines against the wind.

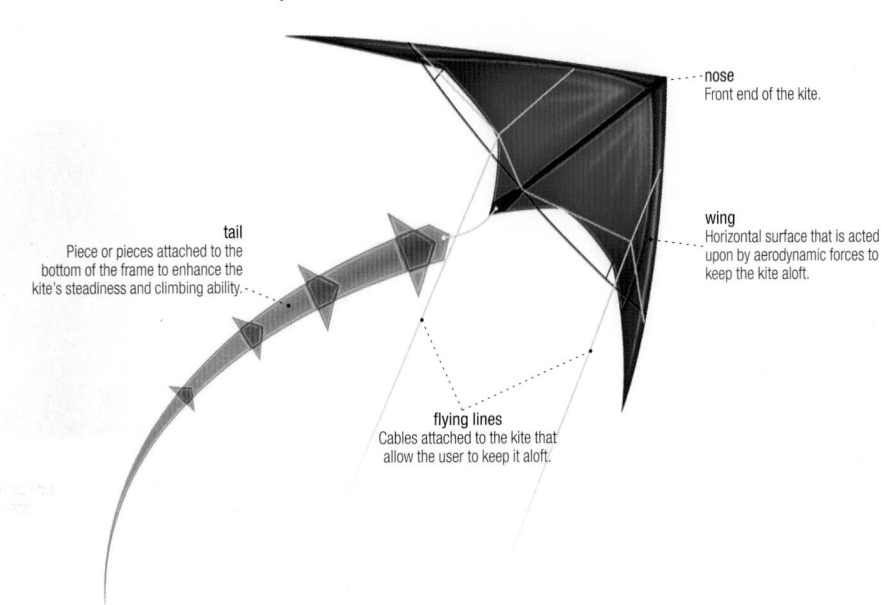

nose
Front end of the kite.

tail
Piece or pieces attached to the bottom of the frame to enhance the kite's steadiness and climbing ability.

wing
Horizontal surface that is acted upon by aerodynamic forces to keep the kite aloft.

flying lines
Cables attached to the kite that allow the user to keep it aloft.

INDEX

Index

INDEX